P9-BHX-381

THE
CAMBRIDGE BIBLIOGRAPHY
OF
ENGLISH LITERATURE

IN FOUR VOLUMES

VOLUME I

THE
CAMBRIDGE BIBLIOGRAPHY
OF
ENGLISH LITERATURE

Edited by

F. W. BATESON

VOLUME I
600–1660

CAMBRIDGE
AT THE UNIVERSITY PRESS
1969

PUBLISHED BY
THE SYNDICS OF THE CAMBRIDGE UNIVERSITY PRESS
Bentley House, 200 Euston Road, London N.W.1
American Branch: 32 East 57th Street, New York, N. Y. 10022

Standard Book Number : 521 04499 5

First published 1940
Reprinted 1955   1966   1969

CAMROSE LUTHERAN COLLEGE
LIBRARY

2011
B 28 | 15,676
1940
V. 1

First Printed in Great Britain at the
University Press, Cambridge
Reprinted by photolithography in Great Britain
by Bookprint Limited, Crawley, Sussex

PREFACE

THIS BIBLIOGRAPHY (*C.B.E.L.*) is a descendant—though not such a direct descendant as was originally contemplated—of *The Cambridge History of English Literature* (*C.H.E.L.*), edited by A. W. WARD and A. R. WALLER, 1907–1916. To each of the chapters of the *C.H.E.L.* there was appended a bibliography; and while the usefulness of the text has been but little impaired by the passage of time, the bibliographies have become in varying degrees out-of-date and misleading. The *C.B.E.L.* is at once a recognition of that fact and an endeavour to rectify it by supplying a modern equivalent of the *C.H.E.L.* bibliographies—a modern equivalent, not a modern edition. The old bibliographies were not intended to stand by themselves. Each of them was simply a supplement to its own chapter and each had the disadvantage that its compilation was a law to itself. A few of the lists have been revised and incorporated here, but for the most part the *C.B.E.L.* is a distinct entity with its own arrangement, scope and style, and its own army of contributors.

SCOPE OF THE WORK. A work of reference is a machine for answering questions. What are the questions which the *C.B.E.L.* has been constructed to answer? The *C.B.E.L.* sets out to record, as far as possible in chronological order, the authors, titles and editions, with relevant critical matter, of all the writings in book-form (whether in English or Latin) that can still be said to possess some literary interest, by natives of what is now the British Empire, up to the year 1900.[1] It does not include, therefore, except occasionally and in special circumstances, (1) notes of the contents of books, (2) bibliographical descriptions of the editions, (3) short pamphlets, contributions to periodicals or miscellanies, or (after 1500) manuscripts, (4) the literature of the United States.[2]

GENERAL ARRANGEMENT. The only practical alternative to the chronological scheme that has been adopted would have been a catalogue of English writers or writings in alphabetical order. But alphabetical juxtapositions are completely artificial. (Daborne follows Cynewulf, not because there is a subterranean connection between Anglo-Saxon poetry and the Jacobean drama, but because D follows C.) It has seemed preferable to retain by a chronological arrangement

---

[1] The *terminus ad quem* is of writers, not of books. The test has been whether a writer could be said to be 'established' by 1900.

[2] Omissions (3) and (4) only apply to original writings. No limitations of form, nationality or date have been imposed on the critical and expository sections.

the order of fact—i.e. that sequence of styles and forms, Brunetière's *l'évolution des genres*, which remains the basis of literary history. The *C.B.E.L.* is thus something more than a catalogue. It is, in addition, a short-hand history of English literature. Used with discretion, some of the sections will tell the diligent enquirer more about their subject-matter than does the ordinary text-book. In a few places, where nothing seemed to be gained by a chronological arrangement and there were possibilities of confusion, an alphabetical order has been used. And an alphabetical index of subjects, writers' names and anonymous works will be found in Volume IV.

SUBDIVISIONS. The *Bibliography* has been divided into five chronological compartments: (1) the Anglo-Saxon period (A.D. 600–1100); (2) the Middle English period (1100–1500); (3) the Renaissance to the Restoration (1500–1660); (4) the Restoration to the Romantic Revival (1660–1800); (5) the Nineteenth Century (1800–1900). In addition, a preliminary 'General Introduction' covers a number of subjects that could not be conveniently divided up among the five periods. Within the periods the subdivision has been by *form* (Poetry, Drama, Fiction, etc.), and an 'Introduction' has been prefixed in order to provide a background (intellectual, social and political) to the purely literary history of each period. The advantages of the scheme both in flexibility and comprehensiveness have out-weighed the nuisance of the occasional inevitable overlappings. A writer who was born in one period and died in the next, or who wrote poems and plays, or novels and essays, will normally be found with all his works in one section of one period only. Cross-references make his apologies elsewhere.

DEGREE OF DETAIL. The different forms and subjects have been treated in varying degrees of detail. This is a bibliography of English literature, and writers who were primarily literary artists—that is to say, the poets, dramatists, novelists, essayists and critics—have been allowed more elbow-room than all but the very greatest historians, theologians, philosophers, scholars or scientists. More-over, with the exception of the newspapers and magazines (which have been recorded more fully than in any previous publication), it has only been possible to list representative specimens of the enormous mass of ephemeral literature—political and controversial pamphlets, anonymous and pseudonymous squibs, mock-biographies, *et hoc genus omne*—that has been issued since the invention of printing. Nevertheless, it may be claimed that no type of printed book, from the chapbook to the scientific treatise, from the collection

of hymns to the gift-book, from the schoolboy's 'crib' to the treatise
on whist, has been altogether neglected. The most important writers
have had all their books recorded, and in some but not all cases their
contributions to magazines as well, followed by a generous selection
from the available biographical and critical literature about them.
Minor poets, dramatists, novelists and essayists have generally been
allotted respectively a complete list of their poems, plays, novels or
collections of essays together with some, in the case of the less prolific
all, of their other writings. The historians receive almost equally
generous treatment. On the other hand, at any rate after 1660, in
such bypaths of literature as letter-writing, sport, oratory, travel,
law, science and scholarship it has usually been thought sufficient to
list the principal works of the more eminent writers only.

STYLE OF ENTRIES. The titles recorded are intended to re-
produce the wording and spelling of the title-pages of the first
editions. Some attempt has been made to keep the original punctuation and capitalisation of the older and more important books, but
it is often impossible to translate the facts of a title-page without
an elaborate system of symbols, and the stops and capitals of most
modern and some older works have been unblushingly normalised.
The first few words of the original titles have always been kept, but
the later parts of the longer titles have often been abbreviated
without the conventional dots. The number of volumes, if more than
one, and the place of publication, if other than London, are always
recorded, though not necessarily in the style of the original editions,
and the dates of publication have been similarly modernised. The
date of the first edition is usually followed by (1) dates of the extant
editions and translations up to 50 years from the first—a period long
enough to cover authors' revisions and to indicate the immediate
success of a work—and (2) details of the more important or convenient modern editions and reprints.[1] Changes of title and revisions

---

[1] A semi-colon usually divides one edition from the next, but commas have been
used when two or more editions share the same number of volumes or the same place
of publication (other than London). Dates of editions are always given in full in order
to avoid confusion. Thus, whereas 'A History of England. 4 vols. 1729–40' would
simply mean that the fourth volume of the first edition was dated 1740, the entry
'A History of England. 4 vols. 1729, 1740' would mean that the second edition (of
1740) was, like the first (of 1729), in four volumes. The dates are generally those of the
title-pages and are therefore not all New Style, but a title-page date in both Old and
New Styles is only recorded in New Style. The number of an edition is only noted when
a break in the series makes it probable that a further edition has still to be located;
e.g. 'Theseus. 1716; 1718 (3rd edn)'. Publishers' re-issues masquerading as new
éditions behind a fresh date or title are recorded where noted, but are not treated as
editions. The location of unique copies has been sporadically attempted, especially
after 1640 when the Short Title Catalogue is no longer available, but a reliable register
is not at present practicable.

of the text are noted briefly, but not mere typographical 'curiosities.

CRITICAL MATTER. The lists of secondary books and articles under such headings as 'Biography and Criticism' or 'Modern Studies' are necessarily selective. It is realised, however, that they are likely to prove one of the most useful features of the work and every effort has been made not to exclude any important piece of criticism or exposition.[1] Biographical matter has received less consideration, purely biographical sources often being omitted when available in the *D.N.B.*, and the *D.N.B.* itself has usually been taken for granted. A key to the abbreviations used for the more familiar journals and series will be found on p. xl.

ACKNOWLEDGMENTS. The *C.B.E.L.* has gathered to itself a multitude of friends and assiduous helpers in the course of its compilation. The names of the contributors, to whom my debt and the *Bibliography's* is greatest, are recorded on p. xxxix. They have had much to put up with from an editor who was determined to impose a degree of order and uniformity upon the chaos of English literature. How much, and with what patience and courtesy his exactions have been borne, only that editor knows. I also owe a great deal to Mr Arundell Esdaile of the British Museum and Mr S. C. Roberts of the University Press, who laid the all-important foundations on which I have built. Nor must the gallant army of proof-readers be forgotten. Mr L. F. Powell, with characteristic generosity, has read all the proofs and has made many valuable suggestions. Mr F. J. Norton of the Cambridge University Library, who read the proofs of Volume I, Dr G. B. Harrison, who read the 1500–1660 sections, Professor R. S. Crane of Chicago, who besides reading the 1660–1800 sections has been a guide and friend throughout, and Professors W. D. Templeman, C. F. Harrold and F. E. Faverty, who have kindly taken parts of the Nineteenth Century under their wings, have all been of the very greatest help. I have also to thank Mr Edmund Blunden, Dr R. W. Chapman, Professor B. I. Evans, the Hon. R. E. Gathorne-Hardy, Mr J. Isaacs, Dr A. K. McIlwraith, Professor G. H. Nettleton, Mr J. M. Osborn, Mr Michael Sadleir,

---

[1] Although it has occasionally been possible to include more recent items, the earlier sections of Volume I are only complete to the end of 1935 and the later sections to 1936. Similarly Volume II is only complete to the end of 1937 and Volume III to the end of 1938. Delays entailed by the war and by the preparation of the Index have been aggravated, I am afraid, by the editor's stubborn insistence on checking and revising the great majority of the sections himself.

Dr Charles Singer, Professor J. W. Spargo, Professor J. R. Sutherland and Dr F. T. Wood for much valuable advice and incidental assistance. To my wife, who came to my rescue on the Index, I owe a more intimate debt.

As to the future, the *Annual Bibliography of English Literature*, edited under the auspices of the Modern Humanities Research Association and now published by the University Press, will provide most valuable material for supplements to the *C.B.E.L.* to be issued at suitable intervals.

Lastly, it need scarcely be added that in a work of this kind the margin of error is exceptionally wide. With the help of authors, critics, collectors, librarians, booksellers and others it is confidently hoped that mistakes and omissions in this first issue of the *C.B.E.L.* will be gradually repaired.

F. W. BATESON

CONTENTS

GENERAL INTRODUCTION

I. BIBLIOGRAPHIES

II. HISTORIES AND ANTHOLOGIES

III. PROSODY AND PROSE RHYTHM

IV. LANGUAGE

B. *Dictionaries:*

C. *Syntax:*

D. *Vocabulary, Word-Formation, etc.:*

E. *Old English Phonology and Grammar:*

F. *Middle English Phonology and Grammar:*

G. *Modern English Phonology:*

H. *Place and Personal Names:*

THE ANGLO-SAXON PERIOD (TO 1100)

I. OLD ENGLISH LITERATURE

II. WRITINGS IN LATIN

THE MIDDLE ENGLISH PERIOD (1100–1500)

1. INTRODUCTION

I. BIBLIOGRAPHIES, SURVEYS, ANTHOLOGIES AND DICTIONARIES

II. THE POLITICAL BACKGROUND

III. THE SOCIAL BACKGROUND

IV. EDUCATION

2. MIDDLE ENGLISH LITERATURE

I. THE MIDDLE ENGLISH ROMANCES

III. Geoffrey Chaucer

G. 'Canterbury Tales':

3. THE FIFTEENTH CENTURY

I. THE ENGLISH CHAUCERIANS

II. MIDDLE SCOTS WRITERS

III. BOOK PRODUCTION AND DISTRIBUTION

IV. EDUCATION

V. THE SOCIAL BACKGROUND

VI. THE POLITICAL BACKGROUND

2. THE POETRY

I. GENERAL INTRODUCTION

II. THE TUDOR POETS

III. The Elizabethan Sonneteers

IV. Minor Tudor Verse

V. The Jacobean and Caroline Poets

II. THEATRES AND ACTORS

III. THE PURITAN ATTACK UPON THE STAGE

IV. THE MORALITIES

V. THE EARLY COMEDIES

VI. THE EARLY TRAGEDIES

VII. The Later Elizabethan Dramatists

VIII. The Minor Elizabethan Drama, 1580–1603

IX. William Shakespeare

CONTENTS

'As You Like It' . . . . *page* 564
'Twelfth Night' 564
'Hamlet' 565
'The Merry Wives of Windsor' 568
'Troilus and Cressida' 568
'All's Well That Ends Well' 569
'Measure for Measure' 569
'Othello' 570
'King Lear' 571
'Macbeth' 572
'Antony and Cleopatra' 572
'Coriolanus' 573
'Timon of Athens' 573
'Cymbeline' 573
'The Winter's Tale' 574
'The Tempest' 574
'Henry the Eighth' 575
'Sir Thomas More' 576
'Edward the Third' 577
'Pericles' 578
'The Two Noble Kinsmen' 578
Other Plays that have been ascribed to Shakespeare . . . 579

C. *The Poems:*

'Venus and Adonis' 580
'Lucrece' 580
'The Passionate Pilgrim' 581
'The Phoenix and Turtle' 581
'The Sonnets' 581
'A Lover's Complaint' 583

IV. THE CRITICISM OF SHAKESPEARE:

A. *Technical Criticism:*

(1) Sources and Influences:
(*a*) Collections of Shakespeare's Sources, (*b*) Modern Studies 583
(2) Transmission of the Text, Chronology, Authenticity, and
Related Problems 585
(3) Textual Criticism 587
(4) Language, Vocabulary, Style and Prosody 588

B. *Aesthetic Criticism:*

(1) Anthologies of Shakespearian Criticism 590
(2) The History of Shakespearian Criticism 591
(3) The Principal Critics to 1800 591
(4) The Nineteenth and Twentieth Centuries:
(*a*) Discussions of the Trends in Shakespearian Criticism, (*b*) General
Criticism, (*c*) Special Studies 594

C. *Shakespeare's Influence:*

(1) Shakespearian Adaptations and Shakespeare's Literary
Influence in England 598

4. RELIGIOUS PROSE: CONTROVERSIAL AND DEVOTIONAL

5. POPULAR AND MISCELLANEOUS PROSE

6. HISTORY, PHILOSOPHY, SCIENCE AND
OTHER FORMS OF LEARNING

7. SCOTTISH LITERATURE

LIST OF CONTRIBUTORS
TO VOLUME I

H. G. A.	H. G. ALDIS	M. McK.	MISS M. McKISACK
J. W. A.	J. W. ADAMSON	A. F. S. P.	A. F. S. PEARSON
E. B.	E. BENSLY	F. J. P.	F. J. POWICKE
E. Bl.	E. BLUNDEN	G. P.	G. PARSLOE
F. S. B.	F. S. BOAS	G. B. P.	G. B. PARKS
F. W. B.	F. W. BAXTER	G. R. P.	G. R. POTTER
H. J. B.	H. J. BYROM	H. G. P.	H. G. POLLARD
J. E. B.	J. E. BUTT	A. W. R.	A. W. REED
P. H. B.	P. HUME BROWN	C. F. R.	MISS C. F. RICHARDSON
T. H. B.	T. H. BANKS	F. J. E. R.	F. J. E. RABY
W. P. B.	W. P. BARRETT	H. E. R.	H. E. ROLLINS
A. M. C.	A. M. CLARK	S. R.	MISS SYBIL ROSENFELD
C. H. C.	C. H. CONLEY	W. L. R.	W. L. RENWICK
H. C.	H. CRAIG	D. H. S.	D. H. STEVENS
J. W. C.	J. W. CUNLIFFE	F. S.	F. SIDGWICK
W. C.	W. CREIZENACH	F. E. S.	F. E. SCHELLING
D. C. D.	D. C. DOUGLAS	G. G. S.	G. GREGORY SMITH
G. D.	G. DAVIES	H. S.	H. SELLERS
A. E.	A. ESDAILE	H. A. C. S.	H. A. C. STURGESS
U. M. E.-F.	MISS U. M. ELLIS-FERMOR	J. S.	J. SPARROW
A. F.	A. FEUILLERAT	J. G. S.	MISS J. G. SCOTT
W. F.	W. FALCONER	M. A. S.	M. A. SHAABER
A. H.	A. HARBAGE	M. S. S.	MISS M. S. SERJEANTSON
D. H.	D. HAMER	P. S.	P. SIMPSON
F. H.	MISS F. HALSEY	W. R. S.	W. R. SORLEY
F. E. H.	F. E. HUTCHINSON	E. N. S. T.	E. N. S. THOMSON
H. H.	H. HIGGS	G. T.	G. TILLOTSON
J. W. H.	J. W. HEBEL	J. A. K. T.	J. A. K. THOMPSON
E. I.	MRS E. ISAACS	N. R. T.	N. R. TEMPEST
G. L. K.	G. L. KEYNES	A. W.	MISS A. WALKER
S. V. K.	S. V. KEELING	A. M. W.	A. M. WILLIAMS
A. M. C. L.	A. M. C. LATHAM	B. W.	MISS BEATRICE WHITE
F. L. L.	F. L. LUCAS	F. W.	FOSTER WATSON
S. V. L.	S. V. LARKEY	F. P. W.	F. P. WILSON
G. M.	MISS G. MURPHY	G. W.	G. WATERHOUSE
H. F. M.	H. F. MOULE	J. D. W.	J. DOVER WILSON
H. M. M.	H. M. MARGOLIOUTH	J. E. W.	J. E. WELLS
L. C. M.	L. C. MARTIN	R. A. W.	R. A. WILSON
A. K. McI.	A. K. McILWRAITH	T. A. W.	T. A. WALKER

REVISIONS AND SPECIAL CONTRIBUTIONS

O. BARFIELD
H. S. BENNETT
MISS M. COATE
D. C. COLLINS

MRS J. E. HESELTINE
A. K. HAMILTON JENKIN
B. L. MANNING

The compiler's initials will be found at the end of each main section. In sections for which more than one contributor is responsible, each subsection has been initialled. The sections taken over from the *C.H.E.L.* and revised by another hand are signed with the initials both of the original compiler and the reviser, e.g. A.B.C., *rev.* X.Y.Z. Other revisions are indicated in foot-notes. The uninitialled sections have been contributed by the Editor.

KEY TO ABBREVIATIONS USED

AJPhil.	American Journal of Philology.
Ang.	Anglia.
Ang. Anz.	Anglia Anzeiger.
Ang. Bbl.	Beiblatt zur Anglia.
Archiv	(Herrig's) Archiv für das Studium der neueren Sprachen
BBA.	Bonner Beiträge zur Anglistik.
CHEL.	Cambridge History of English Literature.
DNB.	Dictionary of National Biography.
E. and S.	(English Association's) Essays and Studies.
EETS.	Early English Text Society.
EHR.	English Historical Review.
E. Studien	Englische Studien.
E. Studies	English Studies.
GM.	Gentleman's Magazine.
JEGP.	Journal of English and Germanic Philology.
MLN.	Modern Language Notes.
MLR.	Modern Language Review.
MP.	Modern Philology.
N. & Q.	Notes and Queries.
PG.	Paul's Grundriss der germanischen Philologie.
PQ.	Philological Quarterly.
QF.	Quellen und Forschungen.
RDM.	Revue des deux Mondes.
RES.	Review of English Studies.
SEP.	Studien zur englischen Philologie.
Sh. Jb.	Shakespeare Jahrbuch.
STS.	Scottish Text Society.
Stud. Phil.	Studies in Philology.
TLS.	(London) Times Literary Supplement.
WB.	Wiener Beiträge zur englischen Philologie.
ZDA.	Zeitschrift für deutsches Alterthum.

Italicized abbreviations, e.g. *Billings, Hammond, TFT.*, are each restricted to particular sections, to the beginnings of which reference should be made for their explanation.

GENERAL INTRODUCTION

GENERAL INTRODUCTION

I. BIBLIOGRAPHIES

General Lists and Sources: Bibliographical Sources; Journals; Current Lists of New Books and Articles; General Sources; General Library Catalogues.

Specialized Lists: Catalogues of Manuscripts; Catalogues of Particular Periods; Scottish, Welsh and Irish Books; English Universities and Provinces; Religious Bodies.

(1) LISTS OF BIBLIOGRAPHICAL SOURCES

Courtney, W. P. A Register of National Bibliography. 3 vols. 1905–12.

Northup, C. S. A Register of the Bibliographies of the English Language and Literature. New Haven, 1925.

Esdaile, A. The Sources of English Literature. (Sandars Lectures.) Cambridge, 1928.

Cross, T. P. A List of Books and Articles designed to serve as an Introduction to the Bibliography and Methods of English Literary History. Chicago, 1932 (6th rev. edn). [First pbd 1919.]

(2) JOURNALS, ETC.

Anglia. Halle, 1877–. [With Beiblatt (reviews and notices only), Halle, 1891–.]

Archiv für das Studium der neueren Sprachen [= Herrig's Archiv]. [Various places], 1846–.

ELH, A Journal of English Literary History. Baltimore, 1934–.

Englische Studien. Leipzig, 1877–.

English Studies. Amsterdam, 1919–.

Essays and Studies. English Ass. 1910–. [Annual.]

Jahrbuch für romanische und englische Sprache und Litteratur. Berlin, 1859–76.

The Journal of Germanic Philology. Bloomington, 1897–1902. [Continued as The Journal of English and Germanic Philology. Bloomington (later Urbana), 1903–.]

The Library. 1899–1919. [Incorporated from 1920 with the Transactions of the Bibliographical Society.]

The Modern Language Review. Cambridge, 1905–.

Modern Language Notes. Baltimore, 1886–.

Modern Philology. Chicago, 1903–.

Notes and Queries. 1849–.

Oxford Bibliographical Society: Proceedings and Papers. Oxford, 1923–.

Philological Quarterly. Iowa City, 1922–.

The Publications of the Modern Language Association of America. New York, 1886–.

The Review of English Studies. 1925–.

La Revue anglo-américaine. Paris, 1923–.

Revue de la Littérature comparée. Paris, 1921–.

Studies in Philology. Chapel Hill, 1904–.

The Times Literary Supplement. 1902–.

Transactions of the Bibliographical Society. 1893–. [Incorporating The Library from 1920.]

(3) CURRENT LISTS OF NEW ENGLISH BOOKS IN GENERAL

The English Catalogue of Books. (1835–.) 1864–. [With a retrospective volume (1801–36) by R. A. Peddie and Q. Waddington, 1914. The English Catalogue amalgamated The London Catalogue (1700–) in 1773, and a rival, The British Catalogue (1837–52), in 1853. Now annual, with a quinquennial cumulation. Based on the lists in the (weekly) Publishers' Circular, 1837–. Arranged by authors and titles.]

Whitaker's Cumulative Booklist. 1924–. [Classified, with index. Based on the (weekly) Publisher and Bookseller.]

The Times Literary Supplement. 1902–.

The British Museum. List of Accessions. 1881–. [Monthly, formerly fortnightly. The English titles form the first section of each part.]

The United States Catalog. Books in Print. New York, 1900–.

(4) CURRENT LISTS OF ENGLISH STUDIES

Annual Bibliography of English Language and Literature (1920–). Mod. Humanities Research Ass. Cambridge, 1921–.

English Association Bulletin. 1907–. [Three times a year.]

The Year's Work in English Studies. English Ass. 1921–. [A critical survey of new books and articles; includes a section of 'Bibliographica.']

The Review of English Studies. 1925–. [Includes quarterly lists of articles in periodicals.]

(5) GENERAL SOURCES

Stephen, Sir Leslie, and Lee, Sir Sidney. The Dictionary of National Biography. [With Supplements.] London, Oxford, 1885–.

Watt, Robert. Bibliotheca Britannica; or
a General Index to British and Foreign
Literature. 4 vols. Edinburgh, 1824.

Lowndes, W. T. The Bibliographer's Manual
of English Literature. 4 vols. 1834; rev.
H. G. Bohn, 11 vols. 1858–64.

Allibone, S. A. A Critical Dictionary of
English Literature and British and Ameri-
can Authors. [With Supplement by J. F.
Kirk.] 5 vols. Philadelphia, 1859–91.

Quaritch, B. General Catalogue of Books.
17 vols. 1887–97.

De Ricci, S. The Book-Collector's Guide.
Philadelphia, 1921.

—— English Collectors of Books and MSS
(1530–1930) and their Marks of Ownership. (Sandars Lectures.) Cambridge, 1930.

A List of Books quoted in the Oxford English
Dictionary. [Appended to Supplement,
1933.]

Livingston, L. S. Auction Prices of Books.
4 vols. New York, 1905. [The material
of the next two, to 1904, in a single alphabet
of authors.]

Book Prices Current. 1888–. [Annual. Indexes (1887–1916), 3 vols. 1901–20.]

American Book-prices Current. New York,
1895–. [Annual. Index (1916–22), 1925.]

Karslake, F. Book Auction Records. 1903–.
[Annual. Indexes(1902–23), 2 vols.1924–8.]

British Museum. List of Catalogues of English
Book Sales, 1676–1900. 1915.

(6) GENERAL LIBRARY CATALOGUES

British Museum. Catalogue of Printed Books.
1881–1905. [With the Supplement, including all books in the library at the end of
1900. Periodical accession parts have been
published since.] [New edn], 1931–.

—— Subject Index of Modern Works added to
the Library (1881–). 1902–. [Commenced
unofficially by G. K. Fortescue, and often
known by his name.]

Bodleian Library, Oxford. Catalogus librorum
impressorum. 4 vols. Oxford, 1843–51.
[Does not cover the Douce collection, of
which a separate catalogue was pbd in 1840.]

National Library of Scotland (formerly Advocates'). Catalogue of the Printed Books in
the Library of the Faculty of Advocates.
6 vols.andSupplement,Edinburgh,1867–79.

Dublin, Trinity College. Catalogus librorum
impressorum. 9 vols. Dublin, 1864–87.

Corser, T. Collectanea Anglo-poetica: or a
Bibliographical and Descriptive Catalogue
of a Portion of a Collection of Early English
Poetry. Chetham Soc. 11 vols. Manchester,
1860–83. [Corser's Sale Catalogues, 1868–
76, add to these.]

Crawford, Earls of. Bibliotheca Lindesiana:
the Catalogue of the Printed Books Preserved at Haigh Hall, Wigan. 8 vols.
1910–3. [The main catalogue occupies vols.
I–IV. Vols. V, VI, VIII are devoted to proclamations, and vol. VII to philately.]

Douce, F. Catalogue of the Printed Books
and Manuscripts bequeathed by Francis
Douce to the Bodleian Library. Oxford,
1840.

Heber, Richard. A Catalogue of Heber's
Collection of Early English Poetry. Ed.
J. P. Collier, [1834].

—— Bibliotheca Heberiana. [1834–6.] [The
auction sale catalogues.]

[Hoe, R.] A Catalogue of Books by English
Authors who lived before the Year 1700.
5 vols. New York, 1903–5.

—— A Catalogue of Books in English later
than 1700. New York, 1905. [Hoe's Sale
Catalogue, 1912, adds to these.]

Cole, G. W. Huntington Library. Check Lists.
New York, 1919–20.

[Ellis, F. S.] The Huth Library. A Catalogue.
5 vols. 1880.

[Wise, T. J.] The Ashley Library: a Catalogue
of Printed Books, Manuscripts and Autograph Letters collected by T. J. Wise.
10 vols. 1922–30. [The poetical and prose
works of the English poets since 1600.]

The Britwell Handlist, or Short-Title Catalogue of the Principal Volumes to the Year
1800 formerly in the Library of Britwell
Court. 2 vols. 1933.

(7) CATALOGUES OF MANUSCRIPTS

[See also p. 6 below under Middle English.]

(a) General

[A corpus of handlists of Western MSS is
projected by Mr Seymour de Ricci, beginning
with his Census of Medieval and Renaissance
Manuscrips in the United States and Canada,
vol. I, New York, 1935.]

Bernard, E. Catalogi Librorum MSS Angliae
et Hiberniae, cum Indice [by H. Wanley].
Oxford, 1697.

Wanley, H. Antiquae Literaturae Septentrionalis Liber alter, seu Librorum vett.
Septentrionalium in Angliae Bibliothecis,
necnon multorum alibi Catalogus. Oxford,
1705. [Vol.IIIof theThesaurus of G.Hickes.]

Brown, Carleton. A Register of Middle
English Religious and Didactic Verse.
2 vols. Bibliog. Soc. 1916–20.

Singer, D. W. Catalogue of Latin and Vernacular Manuscripts in Great Britain and
Ireland dating from before theXVI Century.
1928–.

BIBLIOGRAPHIES

5

(b) British Museum

Catalogues of the various collections:

Additional and Egerton. 1836–.
Arundel and Burney. 1834–40. [Index, 1840.]
Cotton. 1802.
Hargrave. 1818.
Harleian. 4 vols. 1808–12.
Lansdowne. 1819.
Old Royal and King's. 4 vols. 1921.
Sloane, Birch, etc. 1782. [Index to Sloane, 1904.]
Stowe. 1895–6.
Catalogue of Romances. By H. L. D. Ward and J. A. Herbert. 3 vols. 1883–1910.

(c) Oxford

(i) Bodleian

Catalogus codicum manuscriptorum Bibliothecae Bodleianae. 1845–. [The parts containing English MSS are: ii, Catalogus Codicum Laudianorum, ed. H. O. Coxe, 1858–85; iv, Codices T. Tanneri, ed. A. Hackman, 1859; v (fasc. 1–5), Codices R. Rawlinson (A—D), ed. W. D. Macray, 1862–1900; ix, Codices a K. Digby anno 1654 donati, ed. W. D. Macray, 1883; x, A Descriptive, Analytical, and Critical Catalogue of the MSS bequeathed unto the University of Oxford by E. Ashmole, ed. W. H. Black, 1845; Index (by W. D. Macray), 1886.]
A Summary Catalogue of Western Manuscripts which have not hitherto been catalogued in the Quarto Series. Ed. F. Madan (and H. H. E. Craster), Oxford, 1895–.

(ii) Colleges

Catalogus Codicum manuscriptorum qui in Collegiis Aulisque Oxonii adservantur. Ed. H. O. Coxe, 2 vols. Oxford, 1852.
Catalogus Codicum manuscriptorum qui in Bibliotheca Aedis Christi apud Oxonienses adservantur. Ed. G. W. Kitchin, Oxford, 1867.

(d) Cambridge University, Colleges, etc.

Catalogue of MSS in the Library of the University of Cambridge. 6 vols. Cambridge, 1856–67.
[Catalogues of Western MSS in the University and College Libraries of Cambridge. Ed. M. R. James], Cambridge, 1895–1925:
Christ's College. 1905.
Clare College. 1905.
Corpus Christi College. 2 vols. 1909–12.
Emmanuel College. 1904.
Fitzwilliam Museum. 1895.
—— (McClean Collection.) 1912.

Gonville and Caius College. 3 vols. 1907–14.
Jesus College. 1895.
King's College. 1895.
Magdalene College. 1909.
—— Bibliotheca Pepysiana. 1923. (Mediaeval MSS Cat. pt iii.)
Pembroke College. 1905.
Peterhouse. 1899.
Queens' College. 1905.
Sidney Sussex College. 1895.
St Catharine's College. 1925.
St John's College. 1913.
Trinity College. 4 vols. 1900–4.
Trinity Hall. 1907.

(e) Aberdeen University

A Catalogue of the Medieval Manuscripts. Ed. M. R. James, Cambridge, 1932.

(f) Edinburgh University

A Descriptive Catalogue of Western Manuscripts. Ed. Catherine Borland, Edinburgh, 1916.
Handlist of the Mediaeval Manuscripts. Ed. M. R. James, Cambridge Antiquarian Soc. 1912.

(g) Glasgow University

Catalogue of MSS in the Library of the Hunterian Museum. Glasgow, 1908.

(h) Lambeth Palace

Catalogue of the Archiepiscopal Manuscripts. [Ed. H. J. Todd], 1812.
Descriptive Catalogue of the Manuscripts. Ed. M. R. James and C. Jenkins, 5 pts, Cambridge, 1930–3.

(i) Manchester, John Rylands Library

Hand-List of the Collection of English Manuscripts. Ed. M. Tyson, Manchester, 1929. [See also the general catalogue of the library, by E. Gordon Duff, 1899.]

(j) Other Collections

Hoe, R. Catalogue of Manuscripts. New York, 1909.
Morgan, J. Pierpont. Catalogue of Manuscripts from the Library of William Morris. Ed. M. R. James, New York, 1906.
Phillipps, Sir T. Catalogus Librorum manuscriptorum in Bibliotheca D. Thomae Phillipps. 3 pts, 1837–[67].
—— Sale Catalogues. 1886, 1889, 1895 ('Bibliotheca Phillippica').

Canterbury Cathedral. Catalogue of the Books, both Manuscript and Printed. 1802.

The Ancient Libraries of Canterbury and Dover. The Catalogue of the Libraries of Christ Church Priory and St Augustine's Abbey at Canterbury and of St Augustine's Priory at Dover. Ed. M. R. James, Cambridge, 1903.

College of Arms. Catalogue of the Arundel Manuscripts. Ed. W. H. Black, 1829.

Dublin. Catalogue of the Manuscripts in the Library of Trinity College. Ed. T. K. Abbott, 1900.

Durham Cathedral. Codicum Manuscriptorum Catalogus. Ed. T. Rud, 1825.

Gray's Inn. Catalogue of Ancient Manuscripts. 1869.

Lincoln's Inn. Catalogue of Manuscripts. Ed. J. Hunter, 1838.

Lincoln Cathedral. Catalogue of the Books and Manuscripts. Ed. S. F. Apthorp, 1859.

National Library of Wales. Catalogue of Manuscripts. Aberystwyth, 1921–.

Worcester Cathedral. Catalogue of Manuscripts. Ed. J. K. Floyer and S. G. Hamilton, 1906.

(8) PERIODS

[Reference should also be made to the sections below devoted to particular periods and authors.]

(a) Old English

[See above: (7) Catalogues of Manuscripts.]

(b) Middle English

Wells, J. E. A Manual of the Writings in Middle English, 1050–1400. New Haven, 1916. [Supplements, 1919, 1923, 1926, 1929, 1932, 1935.]

Gross, C. The Sources and Literature of English History to 1485. 1915 (rev. edn).

Kingsford, C. L. English Historical Literature in the Fifteenth Century. Oxford, 1913.

Leland, J. Commentarii de Scriptoribus Britannicis. Ed. A. Hall, Oxford, 1709.

Bale, John. Illustrium majoris Britanniae Scriptorum Summarium. Ipswich, 1548; Basle, 1557–9.

(c) Modern English

(i) 1475–1500

Duff, E. Gordon. Fifteenth Century English Books. Bibliog. Soc. 1917.

—— William Caxton. Caxton Club, Chicago, 1905.

Blades, W. Biography and Typography of William Caxton. 1877. [Rev. from the author's The Life and Typography of William Caxton, 1861–3.]

de Ricci, S. A Census of Caxtons. Bibliog. Soc. 1909.

Gesamtkatalog des Wiegendruckes. Leipzig, 1925–. [Includes all English incunabula.]

(ii) 1475–1640

Pollard, A. W. and Redgrave, G. R. A Short-Title Catalogue of Books printed in England, Scotland and Ireland, and of English Books printed abroad, 1475–1640. Bibliog. Soc. 1926. [A second volume of indexes, etc., is in preparation. This work incorporates the substance of the existing catalogues of English books to 1640; but fuller accounts of the material are found in special lists, of which a few follow.]

Ames, J. Typographical Antiquities from 1471 [sic] to 1600, augmented by W. Herbert. 3 vols. 1785–90. [Ames's original edn appeared in 1749; an enlarged new edn was commenced by T. F. Dibdin (vols. I–IV, 1810–9).]

Maunsell, A. The First [and The Seconde] Part of the Catalogue of English Printed Books. 1595. [Pt 1, Divinity; pt 2, Sciences.]

British Museum. Catalogue of Books in the Library of the British Museum printed in England, Scotland and Ireland, and of Books in English printed abroad, to 1640. Ed. George Bullen, 3 vols. 1884.

Cambridge University Library. Early English Printed Books in the Library, 1475–1640. Ed. C. E. Sayle, 4 vols. Cambridge, 1900–7.

John Rylands Library, Manchester. Catalogue of Books in the John Rylands Library printed in England, Scotland and Ireland, and of Books in English printed abroad to 1640. Ed. E. Gordon Duff, Manchester, 1895. [Supersedes Dibdin's Bibliotheca Spenceriana for the Althorp books.]

New York Public Library. Check-list of Early English Printing, 1475–1640, in the Library. Ed. D. C. Haskell, New York, 1925.

Collier, J. P. A Bibliographical and Critical Account of the Rarest Books in the English Language. 2 vols. 1865. [Incorporates the catalogue of the Bridgwater Library.]

Brydges, Sir S. E. Censura Literaria. 10 vols. 1805–9, 1815.

—— The British Bibliographer. 4 vols. 1810–4. [In collaboration with J. Haslewood.]

—— Restituta. 4 vols. 1814–6.

Cambridge, Trinity College. Catalogue of English Books before 1601. Ed. R. Sinker, Cambridge, 1885.

Oxford, Magdalen College. List of Books Printed before 1641, of which the Bodleian Library has no Copy. Ed. G. R. Driver, Oxford Bibliog. Soc. 1929. [Intended as the first instalment of a catalogue of early ptd books in the various libraries in the University of Oxford.]

Oxford, Wadham College. A Short Catalogue of Books printed in England and English Books printed abroad before 1641. Ed. H. A. Wheeler, 1929.

Lambeth Palace. An Index of English Books printed before 1600. Ed. S. R. Maitland, 1845.

Society of Antiquaries. Catalogue of a Collection of Printed Broadsides. Ed. R. Lemon, 1866.

Pepys Library (Magdalene College, Cambridge). Catalogue. Pt III. (English books printed to 1558.) Ed. E. Gordon Duff, 1914.

(iii) 1475–1700

Stationers, The Company of. A Transcript of the Registers of the Company, 1554–1640. Ed. E. Arber, 5 vols. 1875–94.

—— A Transcript of the Registers of the Worshipful Company, from 1640 to 1708. Ed. G. E. Briscoe Eyre, transcribed by H. R. Plomer, 3 vols. Roxburghe Club, 1913–4.

The Term Catalogues, 1668–1709, with a Number for Easter Term, 1711. Ed. E. Arber, 3 vols. 1903–6

[There were other lesser trade lists, which may be found listed by W. Eames in A. Growoll, Three Centuries of English Book-trade Bibliography, New York, 1903.]

British Museum. Catalogue of the Pamphlets, Books, Newspapers and Manuscripts relating to the Civil War, the Commonwealth, and Restoration. Collected by G. Thomason, 1640–1661. Ed. G. K. Fortescue, 2 vols. 1908.

Hazlitt, W. C. Handbook to the Popular, Poetical and Dramatic Literature of Great Britain, from the Invention of Printing to the Restoration. 1867. [Continued as Bibliographical Collections and Notes (1474–1700), 6 vols. 1876–1903; General Index, by G. J. Gray, 1893.]

Quaritch, B. Catalogue of Books in English History and Literature (1483–1700). 1922.

Davies, G. A Bibliography of British History. Stuart Period, 1603–1714. Royal Hist. Soc. 1928.

Abbott, W. C. A Bibliography of Oliver Cromwell. Cambridge, U.S.A. 1929.

Read, C. Bibliography of British History. Tudor Period, 1485–1603. Oxford, 1933.

(iv) 18th Century

Texas, University of. Catalogue of the Library of the late John Henry Wrenn. Ed. H. B. Wrenn and T. J. Wise, Austin, 1920. [Especially rich in the Augustan period, and including the library of G. A. Aitken.]

Williams, J. B. Guide to the Printed Materials for English Social and Economic History, 1750–1850. 2 vols. New York, 1926.

[This period is largely covered by R. Watt, Bibliotheca Britannica, 1824, but is otherwise very little served by bibliographers: it is, however, rich in the bibliographies of single authors.]

(v) 19th–20th Century

[See above, (3) Current Lists of New English Books in General.]

(9) SCOTTISH BOOKS

National Library of Scotland (Advocates' Library). Catalogue of the Printed Books. 7 vols. Edinburgh, 1867–79.

Aberdeen University. Catalogue of the Library. 3 vols. Aberdeen, 1873–4. [With supplements: King's College (1875–87), 1887; Marischal College (1874–96), 1897.]

Edinburgh University. Catalogue of the Printed Books in the Library. 3 vols. Edinburgh, 1918–23.

Glasgow University. Catalogus impressorum Librorum in Bibliotheca Universitatis Glasguensis. [With 2 supplements.] Glasgow, 1791–1836.

St Andrews University. Catalogus Librorum. 1826.

—— Catalogue of Books added (1867–8 to 1900). St Andrews, 1869–1902. [Continued by the Library Bulletin.]

Signet Library. Catalogue of the Printed Books. 2 pts and 2 supplements. Edinburgh, 1871–91. [Continued by annual supplements.]

Aldis, H. G. A List of Books printed in Scotland before 1700, including those printed forth of the Realm for Scottish Booksellers. Edinburgh Bibliog. Soc. 1904.

Johnstone, J. F. K. and Robertson, A. W. Bibliographia Aberdonensis. 2 vols. Third Spalding Club, Aberdeen, 1929–30.

Dickson, R. and Edmond J. P. Annals of Scottish Printing from 1507 to the Beginning of the Seventeenth Century. Cambridge, 1890.

Edinburgh Bibliographical Society Publications. Edinburgh, 1896–.

(10) WELSH BOOKS

Rowlands, W. Cambrian Bibliography; from 1546 to the End of the Eighteenth Century. Ed. D. S. Evans, Llanidloes, 1869.

National Library of Wales. Bibliotheca Celtica: a Register of Publications relating to Wales and the Celtic Peoples and Languages (1909–). Aberystwyth, 1910–.

Jones, J. I. History of Printing and Printers in Wales to 1810 (1823). Cardiff, 1925.

(11) IRISH BOOKS

Dublin, Trinity College. Catalogus Librorum impressorum. Dublin, 1864–87.

Cambridge University. Catalogue of the Bradshaw Collection of Irish Books. Ed. C. Sayle, 3 vols. Cambridge, 1916.

Dix, E. R. McC. Catalogue of Early Dublin-printed Books, 1601–1700. Dublin, 1898–1912. [The same author has produced numerous lists surveying provincial Irish printing.]

(12) THE ENGLISH UNIVERSITIES AND PROVINCES

Gross, C. A Bibliography of British Municipal History. Cambridge, U.S.A. 1897.

Humphreys, A. L. A Handbook to County Bibliography. 1917.

Buckinghamshire.

Gough, Henry. Bibliotheca Buckinghamiensis. Aylesbury, 1890.

Cambridge.

Bowes, R. Catalogue of Books printed at or relating to the University, Town and County of Cambridge, 1521–1893. (Index by E. Worman.) 2 pts, Cambridge, 1894.

Cooper, C. H. and T. Athenae Cantabrigienses, 1500–1611. 3 vols. 1858–1913.

Roberts, S. C. A History of the Cambridge University Press, 1521–1921. Cambridge, 1921. [With a bibliography, 1521–1790.]

University Library, Cambridge. Catalogue of the Clark Collection of Books and Papers relating to the University, Town and County of Cambridge. Ed. A. T. Bartholomew, Cambridge, 1912.

Venn, J. and J. A. Alumni Cantabrigienses (–1900). Pt 1 (–1751). 4 vols. 1922–7. [Only incidentally and indirectly bibliographical.]

Walker, T. A. A Peterhouse Bibliography. Cambridge, 1924.

Cheshire.

Cooke, J. H. Bibliotheca Cestriensis. Warrington, 1904.

Cornwall.

Boase, G. C. and Courtney, W. P. Bibliotheca Cornubiensis. 3 vols. 1874–82.

Devonshire.

Brushfield, T. N. The Literature of Devonshire to 1640. 1893 (priv. ptd).

Davidson, J. Bibliotheca Devoniensis. Exeter, 1852. [Supplements, 1862.]

Dredge, J. T. Devon Booksellers and Printers in the Seventeenth and Eighteenth Centuries. 3 pts, Plymouth, 1885–7.

Dorsetshire.

Mayo, C. H. Bibliotheca Dorsetiensis. 1885.

Gloucestershire.

Austin, R. Catalogue of the Gloucestershire Collection. Gloucester Public Library. Gloucester, 1928.

Hyett, F. A. and Bazeley, W. The Bibliographer's Manual of Gloucestershire Literature. 5 vols. Gloucester, 1895–1915.

Matthews, E. R. N. Bristol Bibliography. Bristol, 1916.

Hampshire.

Gilbert, H. M. and Godwin, G. N. Bibliotheca Hamtoniensis. Southampton, 1891.

Kent.

Smith, J. R. Bibliotheca Cantiana. 1837.

Lancashire.

Fishwick, H. The Lancashire Library. 1875.

Liverpool Prints and Documents. Liverpool Public Library. Liverpool, 1908.

Sparke, A. [A bibliography in preparation.]

Leicestershire, see *Staffordshire, etc.*

Lincolnshire.

Corns, A. R. Bibliotheca Lincolniensis. Lincoln Public Library. Lincoln, 1904.

Norfolk.

Quinton, J. Bibliotheca Norfolciensis. Norwich, 1896. [Catalogue of the Norfolk collection of J. J. Colman.]

Northamptonshire.

Taylor, John. Bibliotheca Northamtoniensis. Northampton, [1869?].

Northumberland.

Local Catalogue of Material concerning Newcastle and Northumberland. Newcastle-on-Tyne Public Library. Newcastle-on-Tyne, 1932.

Welford, R. Early Newcastle Typography. Archaeologia Aeliana. Newcastle, 1906.

Nottinghamshire.

Creswell, S. F. Collections towards the History of Printing in Nottinghamshire. 1863.

Oxford.

Madan, F. A Chart of Oxford Printing. 1909.

—— Oxford Books. Vols. I–III ('1468'–1680), Oxford, 1895–1931.

Somerset.

Green, E. Bibliotheca Somersetensis. 3 vols. Taunton, 1902.

Staffordshire, Suffolk, Warwickshire, Worcestershire, and Leicestershire.

Bloom, J. H. English Tracts, Pamphlets and Printed Sheets. Vol. I, Suffolk (–1680); vol. II, Leicestershire, Staffordshire, Warwickshire, Worcestershire (–1680). 1922–3. [No more pbd.]

Staffordshire.

Simms, R. Bibliotheca Staffordiensis. Lichfield, 1894.

Worcestershire.

Bibliography of Worcestershire. 4 pts, Oxford, 1898–.

Yorkshire.

Boyne, William. Yorkshire Library. 1869.
Davies, R. A Memoir of the York Press. 1868.

(13) RELIGIOUS BODIES

Catholics.

Gillow, Joseph. A Bibliographical Dictionary of the English Catholics. 5 vols. 1885–1902.
De Backer, A. and A. Bibliothèque de la Compagnie de Jésus. Bibliographie. Rev. C. Sommervogel, 10 vols. Brussels, 1890–1912.
Sommervogel, C. Dictionnaire des Ouvrages anonymes et pseudonymes publiés par les Religieux de la Société de Jésus. Paris, 1884.

Society of Friends.

Smith, Joseph. A Descriptive Catalogue of Friends' Books. 2 vols. 1867–93.
—— Bibliotheca Antiquakeriana. 1873.

Congregationalists.

Dexter, H. M. Congregationalism of the Last Three Centuries as seen in its Literature. 1880.

Baptists.

Whitley, W. T. Baptist Bibliography. 2 vols. 1916–22. A. E.

II. HISTORIES AND ANTHOLOGIES

General Histories: English Literature; Scottish Literature; the Literary Kinds (Poetry, Prose, Drama); Reference-Books.
Anthologies: Verse; Prose; Plays.

[A brief selection confined, unless otherwise stated, to surveys and anthologies of the *whole* of English literature. For works of more limited scope the various periods and types should be consulted.]

(1) GENERAL HISTORIES OF ENGLISH LITERATURE

Bale, John. Illustrium majoris Britanniae Scriptorum, hoc est Angliae, Cambriae, ac Scotiae Summarium. Ipswich, 1548; Basle, 1557–9 (enlarged).
—— Index Britanniae Scriptorum. Ed. R. L. Poole and Mary Bateson, Oxford, 1902.
Leland, John. Commentarii de Scriptoribus Britannicis. Ed. Anthony Hall, 2 vols. Oxford, 1709.
Pits, John. Relationum historicarum de Rebus Anglicis. Tom. I. Ed. William Bishop, Paris, 1619.
Tanner, Thomas. Bibliotheca Britannico-Hibernica. Ed. D. Wilkins, 1748.
Berkenhout, John. Biographia Literaria; or, a Biographical History of Literature. 1777. [Only completed to 16th cent.]
Hallam, Henry. Introduction to the Literature of Europe, in the Fifteenth, Sixteenth, and Seventeenth Centuries. 4 vols. 1837–9.
Wright, Thomas. Biographia Britannica Literaria. 2 vols. Royal Soc. Lit. 1842–6. [Only completed to Anglo-Norman period.]
Arnold, Thomas. A Manual of English Literature. 1862.
Taine, H. Histoire de la Littérature anglaise. 4 vols. Paris, 1863–4; tr. Eng. 2 vols. Edinburgh, 1871.
Morley, Henry. A First Sketch of English Literature. 1873; 1892 (rev. edn).
—— English Writers: an Attempt towards a History of English Literature. 11 vols. 1887–95. [To Shakespeare.]
ten Brink, B. Geschichte der englischen Literatur. 2 vols. Berlin, 1877–93 (vol. I rev. A. Brandl, 1899); tr. Eng. 3 vols. 1883–96. [To Renaissance.]
Engel, Eduard. Geschichte der englischen Literatur. Leipzig, 1883; tr. Eng. 1902.
Koerting, G. Grundriss der Geschichte der englischen Litteratur. Münster, 1887, 1910 (5th rev. edn).
Jusserand, J. J. Histoire littéraire du Peuple anglais. 2 vols. Paris, 1894–1904; tr. Eng. 3 vols. 1895–1909. [To Civil War.]
Handbooks of English Literature. Ed. John Hales, 10 pts, 1895–1903. [Age of Alfred, Age of Chaucer, Transition Age, by F. J. Snell; Age of Shakespeare, 2 vols., by J. W. Allan and T. Seccombe; Age of Milton, by J. B. Masterman; Age of Dryden, by R. Garnett; Age of Pope, by J. Dennis; Age of Johnson, by T. Seccombe; Age of Wordsworth, by C. H. Herford; Age of Tennyson, by H. Walker.]

Wülcker, R. Geschichte der englischen Litteratur. 2 vols. Leipzig, 1896, 1906–7.

Gosse, Sir Edmund. A Short History of Modern English Literature. 1897.

Periods of European Literature. Ed. George Saintsbury, 12 vols, Edinburgh 1897–1908. [Dark Ages, by W. P. Ker; Flourishing of Romance, by G. Saintsbury; Fourteenth Century, by F. J. Snell; Transition Period, by G. Gregory Smith; Earlier Renaissance, by G. Saintsbury; Later Renaissance, by David Hannay; First Half of Seventeenth Century, by H. J. C. Grierson; Augustan Ages, by O. Elton; Mid-Eighteenth Century, by J. H. Millar; Romantic Revolt, by C. E. Vaughan; Romantic Triumph, by T. S. Omond; Later Nineteenth Century, by G. Saintsbury.]

Saintsbury, George. A Short History of English Literature. 1898.

Garnett, Richard and Gosse, Sir Edmund. English Literature: an Illustrated Record. 4 vols. 1903.

Seccombe, T. and Nicoll, Sir W. R. History of English Literature. 2 vols. 1906.

The Cambridge History of English Literature. Ed. Sir A. W. Ward and A. R. Waller, 14 vols. Cambridge, 1907–16 (re-issued 1932 without bibliographies). [Vol. xv, Index, 1927.]

Schroeer, M. M. A. Grundzüge und Haupttypen der englischen Literaturgeschichte. 2 pts, Berlin, 1911–4, 1922–7 (rev.).

Buchan, John, Newbolt, Sir Henry, and Baker, Ernest. A History of English Literature. 1923.

Legouis, Émile and Cazamian, Louis. Histoire de la Littérature anglaise. Paris, 1924; tr. Eng. 2 vols. 1926–7.

Groom, B. A Literary History of England. 1929.

Legouis, Émile. A Short History of English Literature. Tr. Eng. Oxford, 1934.

(2) General Histories of Scottish Literature

Dempster, Thomas. Historia Ecclesiastica Gentis Scotorum, sive de Scriptoribus Scotis. 1627; ed. David Irving, Bannatyne Club, 1829.

Campbell, Alexander. Introduction to the History of Poetry in Scotland. Edinburgh, 1798–9.

Sibbald, J. Chronicle of Scottish Poetry. 4 vols. Edinburgh, 1802.

Irving, David. The Lives of the Scotish Poets. 2 vols. Edinburgh, 1804.

—— The History of Scotish Poetry. Ed. J. A. Carlyle, Edinburgh, 1861.

Irving, David. Lives of Scotish Writers. 2 vols. Edinburgh, 1839.

Ross, J. M. Scottish History and Literature to the Reformation. Glasgow, 1884.

Veitch, J. The Feeling for Nature in Scottish Poetry. 2 vols. Edinburgh, 1887.

—— History and Poetry of the Scottish Border. 2 vols. Edinburgh, 1893.

Walker, H. Three Centuries of Scottish Literature. 2 vols. Glasgow, 1893.

Henderson, T. F. Scottish Vernacular Literature. 1898.

Millar, J. H. A Literary History of Scotland. 1903.

Mackenzie, A. M. An Historical Survey of Scottish Literature to 1714. 1933.

(3) Histories of the Literary Kinds

The Types of English Literature. Ed. W. A. Neilson, 5 vols. Boston, 1907–16. [Popular Ballad, by F. B. Gummere; Literature of Roguery, by F. W. Chandler; Tragedy, by A. H. Thorndike; Lyric, by F. E. Schelling; Saints' Legends, by G. H. Gerould.]

The Channels of English Literature. Ed. Oliphant Smeaton, 8 vols. 1912–25. [Essay and Essayists, Satire and Satirists, by H. Walker; Epic, by W. M. Dixon; Lyric, by Ernest Rhys; Philosophy, by J. Seth; Novel, by G. Saintsbury; Drama, by F. E. Schelling; Biography, by W. Dunn.]

Hogarth Lectures on Literature. Ed. G. Rylands and L. Woolf, 1927–. [English Biography, by H. Nicolson; The Structure of the Novel, by E. Muir; Phases of English Poetry, by H. Read; The Whirligig of Taste, by E. E. Kellett; Nature in English Literature, by E. Blunden; Notes on English Verse Satire, by H. Wolfe; Politics and Literature, by G. D. H. Cole; The Course of English Classicism, by S. Vines; Some Religious Elements in English Literature, by Rose Macaulay.]

(a) Poetry

Phillips, Edward. Theatrum Poetarum, or a Complete Collection of the Poets. 1674; ed. Sir S. E. Brydges, 1800.

Winstanley, William. Lives of the Most Famous English Poets. 1687.

Jacob, Giles. Lives of the English Poets. 1720.

Cibber, Theophilus. An Account of the Lives of the Poets of Great Britain and Ireland. 5 vols. 1753. [Compiled by R. Shiels.]

Warton, Thomas. The History of English Poetry. 3 vols. 1774–81; ed. W. C. Hazlitt, 4 vols. 1871. [12th–16th cents.]

Johnson, Samuel. The Lives of the Most Eminent English Poets. 4 vols. 1781; ed. G. B. Hill. 3 vols. Oxford, 1905.

The English Poets. Ed. T. H. Ward, 5 vols. 1880–1918. [Introductions.]

Courthope, W. J. A History of English Poetry. 6 vols. 1895–1910.

Gayley, C. M. and Young, C. C. The Principles and Progress of English Poetry. New York, 1904.

Saintsbury, G. A History of English Prosody. 3 vols. 1906–10.

Greg, W. W. Pastoral Poetry and Pastoral Drama. 1906.

Previté-Orton, C. W. Political Satire in English Poetry. Cambridge, 1910.

Dixon, W. M. English Epic and Heroic Poetry. 1912.

Reed, E. B. English Lyrical Poetry from its Origins to the Present Time. New Haven, 1912.

Crosland, T. W. H. The English Sonnet. 1917.

Kitchin, George. A Survey of Burlesque and Parody in English. Edinburgh, 1931.

Elton, O. The English Muse. 1933.

(b) Prose

(i) The Novel

Dunlop, John. The History of Fiction. 3 vols. Edinburgh, 1814; rev. H. Wilson, 2 vols. 1888.

Scott, Sir Walter. The Lives of the Novelists. 2 vols. Paris, 1825.

Masson, David. British Novelists and their Styles. Cambridge, 1859.

Raleigh, Sir Walter. The English Novel. 1894. [To 1800.]

Cross, W. L. The Development of the English Novel. New York, 1899.

Baker, E. A. The History of the English Novel. 6 vols. 1924–.

Prothero, R. E. (Baron Ernle). The Light Reading of our Ancestors. [1927.] [To Scott.]

Lovett, R. M. and Hughes, H. S. The History of the Novel in England. Boston, 1932.

(ii) Other Forms of Prose

Gray, W. The Origin and Progress of English Prose Literature. 1835.

Minto, William. A Manual of English Prose Literature. 1872.

Earle, John. English Prose. 1890.

Saintsbury, George. A History of Criticism and Literary Taste in Europe. 3 vols. 1900–4.

—— A History of English Criticism. 1911.

Burr, A. D. The Autobiography. Boston, 1909.

Merrill, E. The Dialogue in English Literature. New Haven, 1911.

Darton, F. J. H. Children's Books in England. Cambridge, 1932.

(c) Drama

Langbaine G. An Account of the English Dramatic Poets. 1691; rev. C. Gildon, 1699 (as The Lives of the Poets). [A dictionary.]

[Baker, D. E.] The Companion to the Play-House. 2 vols. 1764; rev. I. Reed, 2 vols. 1782 (as Biographia Dramatica); rev. S. Jones, 4 vols. 1812 (as Biographia Dramatica). [A dictionary.]

Ward, Sir A. W. A History of English Dramatic Literature to the Death of Queen Anne. 2 vols. 1875; 3 vols. 1899 (rev. edn).

Collier, J. P. The History of English Dramatic Poetry. 3 vols. 1879. [To the Restoration.]

Creizenach, W. Geschichte des neueren Dramas. 5 vols. Halle, 1895–1916, 1911 (rev. edn).

Greg, W. W. Pastoral Poetry and Pastoral Drama. 1906.

Matthews, Brander. The Development of the Drama. 1914.

Archer, William. The Old Drama and the New. 1923.

Nicoll, Allardyce. British Drama. 1925.

Thorndike, A. H. English Comedy. New York, 1929.

(4) REFERENCE-BOOKS

(a) General

[A number of general works of reference are included among the Bibliographies in the preceding section. These have not generally been repeated here. A much fuller list, not restricted to English literature, is provided by T. P. Cross, A List of Books and Articles designed to serve as an Introduction to the Bibliography and Methods of English Literary History, Chicago, 1932 (6th rev. edn).]

Watt, Robert. Bibliotheca Britannica; or a General Index to British and Foreign Literature. 4 vols. Edinburgh, 1824. [Includes critical comments.]

Chambers, Robert. Cyclopaedia of English Literature. 2 vols. Edinburgh, 1843–4; rev. R. Carruthers, 4 vols. 1857–60. [Entirely re-written, ed. D. Patrick, 3 vols. 1901–3.]

Allibone, S. A. A Critical Dictionary of English Literature and British and American Authors. 3 vols. Philadelphia, 1859–71. Supplement by J. F. Kirk, 2 vols. Philadelphia, 1892. [Quotes contemporary reviews.]

Halkett, S. and Laing, J. A Dictionary of the Anonymous and Pseudonymous Literature of Great Britain. 1882–8; rev. J. Kennedy, W. A. Smith and A. F. Johnson, 7 vols. Edinburgh 1926–34.

Adams, W. D. Dictionary of English Litera-
ture. A Comprehensive Guide to English
Authors and their Works. 1884.
Ryland, F. Chronological Outlines of English
Literature. 1890; 1914 (rev.).
Sharp, R. F. A Dictionary of English Authors.
1897; 1904 (rev.).
Moulton, C. W. The Library of Literary
Criticism of English and American Authors.
8 vols. Buffalo, 1901–5. [Excerpted criti-
cisms, mainly of the 19th century, arranged
to form a history of English literature.]
Stonehill, C. A. and H. W., and Block, A.
Anonyma and Pseudonyma. 4 vols. 1926–7.
Harvey, Sir P. The Oxford Companion to
English Literature. Oxford, 1932.
Ghosh, J. C. and Withycombe, E. G. Annals
of English Literature, 1475–1925. Oxford,
1935.

(b) Special

Carpenter, F. I. An Outline- Guide to the
Study of English Lyric Poetry. Chicago,
1897.
Gayley, C. M. and Scott, F. N. An Intro-
duction to the Methods and Materials of
Literary Criticism. The Bases in Aesthetics
and Poetics. Boston, 1899.
Gayley, C. M. and Kurtz, B. P. Methods and
Materials of Literary Criticism. Lyric, Epic
and Allied Forms of Poetry. Boston, 1920.
Esdaile, A. List of English Tales and Prose
Romances printed before 1740. Bibliog.
Soc. 1912.
Baker, E. A. and Packman, J. A Guide to the
Best Fiction, English and American, in-
cluding Translations from Foreign Lan-
guages. 1932 (rev.).
Lowe, R. W. A Bibliographical Account of
English Theatrical Literature. 1888.
Bates, K. L. and Godfrey, L. B. English
Drama. A Working Basis. Wellesley, 1896.
Adams, W. D. A Dictionary of the Drama.
Vol. I (A–G; all pbd), 1904.
Clarence, R. 'The Stage' Cyclopaedia. A
Bibliography of [English] Plays. 1909.
[Muddiman, J. G.] Tercentenary Handlist of
English and Welsh Newspapers, Magazines
and Reviews. 1920.
Kennedy, A. G. A Bibliography of Writings
on the English Language. Cambridge,
U.S.A. 1927.

(5) ANTHOLOGIES

[The principal general collections of reprints,
such as the Harleian Miscellany, Arber's
Garner, and the publications, transactions and
miscellanies of various learned societies, are
listed pp. 317–9 below.]

(a) Verse

Johnson, Samuel. The Works of the English
Poets. 68 vols. 1779–81; 75 vols. 1790
(enlarged edn).
[Ellis, George.] Specimens of the Early
English Poets. 1790; 3 vols. 1801 (enlarged
edn). [Supplemented by R. Southey
Specimens of the Later English Poets
3 vols. 1807.]
Anderson, Robert. The Works of the British
Poets. 14 vols. Edinburgh, 1792–1807.
Chalmers, Alexander. The Works of the
English Poets. 21 vols. 1810. [Incorporates
and expands Johnson's collection.]
Campbell, Thomas. Specimens of the British
Poets. 7 vols. 1819; rev. Peter Cunningham
1841.
Aikin, John. Select Works of the British
Poets. 1824. [Supplemented by R. Southey
Select Works of the British Poets from
Chaucer to Jonson, [1831].]
Palgrave, F. T. The Golden Treasury. 1861
1891 (rev. edn).
—— The Treasury of Sacred Song. Oxford
1889.
Locker-Lampson, F. Lyra Elegantiarum, a
Collection of Social and Occasional Verse
1867; ed. C. Kernahan, 1891.
Hunt, Leigh, and Lee, S. A. The Book of the
Sonnet. 2 vols. 1867.
Trench, R. C. A Household Book of English
Poetry. 1868.
Hales, J. W. Longer English Poems. 1872.
Ward, T. H. The English Poets. 5 vols. 1880-
1918.
Main, D. M. A Treasury of English Sonnets
1880.
Gosse, Sir Edmund. English Odes. 1881.
Caine, Sir T. Hall. Sonnets of Three Centuries
1882.
Arber, Edward. British Anthologies. 10 vols
1899–1901. [From a Dunbar Anthology to
a Cowper Anthology.]
Quiller-Couch, Sir A. T. The Oxford Book o
English Verse. 1900.
—— English Sonnets. 1910.
Lloyd, M. Elegies Ancient and Modern
Trenton, 1903.
Hadow, G. E. and W. H. The Oxford Treasury
of English Literature. 3 vols. 1906–8.
Nicholson, D. H. S. and Lee, A. H. E. The
Oxford Book of English Mystical Verse. 1916
Williams, Charles. The New Book of English
Verse. 1936.

(b) Prose

Chalmers, Alexander. The British Essayists
45 vols. 1802–3.
Scoones, W. E. Four Centuries of English
Letters. 1880.

Saintsbury, George. Specimens of English Prose Style. 1885.

Craik, Henry. English Prose. 5 vols. 1893–6.

Hopkins, A. B. and Hughes, H. S. The English Novel before the Nineteenth Century. Boston, 1915.

Peacock, W. English Prose. 5 vols. 1921–2.

Ponsonby, Arthur. English Diaries. 1923.

—— More English Diaries. 1927.

Murphy, G. A Cabinet of Characters. 1925.

Quiller-Couch, Sir A. T. The Oxford Book of English Prose. 1925.

Read, H. and Dobrée, B. The London Book of English Prose. 1931.

Smith, Logan P. A Treasury of English Aphorisms. 1931.

(c) Plays

[Dodsley, R.] A Select Collection of Old Plays. 12 vols. 1744; ed. W. C. Hazlitt, 15 vols. 1874–6. [To Restoration.]

Bell's British Theatre. 34 vols. 1791–7. [Pbd by John Bell.]

Inchbald, Elizabeth. The British Theatre. 25 vols. 1808.

[Scott, Sir Walter.] Ancient British Drama. 3 vols. 1810. [To Restoration.]

—— Modern British Drama. 5 vols. 1811. [Restoration to 1800.]

D[aniel], G. Cumberland's British Theatre. 48 vols. 1829.

Gayley, C. M. Representative English Comedies. 3 vols. New York, 1903. [To 1642.]

Tatlock, J. S. P. and Martin, R. G. Representative English Plays. New York, 1916, 1923.

III. PROSODY AND PROSE RHYTHM

Prosody: Before Chaucer (Books; Articles); Chaucer and After (Books; Articles).

Prose Rhythm: Books; Articles.

(1) PROSODY BEFORE CHAUCER

(a) Books

Conybeare, J. J. The Metre of Anglo-Saxon Poetry. [In Illustrations of Anglo-Saxon Poetry, 1826.]

Mone, F. J. Hymni Latini Medii Aevi. 3 vols. 1853–5.

Schubert, H. De Anglo-Saxonum Arte Metrica. Berlin, 1870.

Vetter, T. Zum Muspilli und zur germanischen Alliterationspoesie. Vienna, 1872.

Rieger, M. Zur Rhythmik des germanischen Alliterationsverses. Die alt- und angelsächsische Verskunst. Zeitschrift für deutsche Philologie, VII, 1876, and Halle, 1876.

Schipper, J. M. Altenglische Metrik. [Vol. I of Englische Metrik, Bonn, 1881–8.]

—— Grundriss der englischen Metrik. Vienna, 1895. [An abridgment of Englische Metrik; tr. Eng. (as A History of English Versification), Oxford, 1910.]

Frucht, P. Metrisches und Sprachliches zu Cynewulfs Elene, Juliana, und Crist. Greifswald, 1887.

Cremer, M. Metrische und sprachliche Untersuchung der altenglischen Gedichte Andreas, Guthlac, Phoenix [Elene, Juliana, Crist]. Bonn, 1888.

Bright, J. W. Anglo-Saxon Versification. [Appendix II of An Anglo-Saxon Reader, New York, 1891.]

Fuhr, K. Die Metrik des westgermanischen Alliterationsverses. Marburg, 1892.

ten Brink, B. Altenglische Literatur. [In PG. vol. II¹, 1893.]

Lawrence, J. Chapters on Alliterative Verse. 1893.

Sievers, E. Altgermanische Metrik. Halle, 1893.

—— Angelsächsische Grammatik. Halle, 1898.

—— Altgermanische Metrik. [In PG. vol. II², 1905.]

Kaluza, M. Der altenglische Vers: eine metrische Untersuchung. 2 vols. Berlin, 1894.

—— Englische Metrik in historischer Entwicklung dargestellt. Berlin, 1909. [Tr. Eng. A. C. Dunstan as A Short History of English Versification, 1911.]

Tamson, G. J. Word-Stress in English. Halle, 1898.

Huguenin, J. Secondary Stress in Anglo-Saxon [determined by metrical criteria]. Baltimore, 1901.

Deutschbein, M. Zur Entwicklung des englischen Alliterationsverses. Halle, 1902.

Ker, W. P. The Dark Ages. Edinburgh, 1904.

McNary, S. J. Studies in Layamon's Verse. Baltimore, 1904.

Pilch, L. Umwandlung des altenglischen Alliterationsverses in den mittelenglischen Reimvers. Königsberg, 1904.

Setzler, E. B. On Anglo-Saxon Versification from the Standpoint of Modern English Versification. Baltimore, 1904.

Luick, K. Englische Metrik. [In PG. vol. II², 1905.]

Bohlen, A. Zusammengehörige Wortgruppen, getrennt durch Cäsur oder Versschluss, in der angelsächsischen Epik. Berlin, 1908.

Krauel, H. Der Haken- und Langzeilenstil im Beowulf. Göttingen, 1908.

Tschischwitz, B. Die Metrik der angelsächsischen Psalmenübersetzung. Breslau, 1908.

Boer, R. C. Die altenglische Heldendichtung. Halle, 1912.

—— Studiën over de Metrik van het Alliteratievers. Amsterdam, 1916.

Classen, E. On Vowel Alliteration in the Old Germanic Languages. Manchester, 1913.

Sedgefield, W. J. Beowulf. Manchester, 1913.

—— Anglo-Saxon Verse-Book. Manchester, 1922.

Schumacher, K. Studien über den Stabreim in der mittelenglischen Alliterationsdichtung. Bonner Studien zur englischen Philologie, XI, 1914.

Brink, A. Stab und Wort im Gawain. SEP. LIX, 1920.

Finsterbusch, F. Der Versbau der mittelenglischen Dichtungen Sir Perceval of Galles und Sir Degravant. Vienna, 1920.

Leonard, W. E. The Scansion of Middle English Alliterative Verse. Madison, 1920.

Neuner, E. Über ein- und dreihebige Verse in der altenglischen alliterierenden Poesie. Berlin, 1920.

Huchon, R. Histoire de la Langue anglaise. Vol. I, Paris, 1923.

Klaeber, F. Beowulf and the Finnsburg Fragment. 1923.

Heusler, A. Deutsche Versgeschichte mit Einschluss des altenglischen und altnordischen Stabreimverses. [In PG. vol. VIII[1], 1925.]

Reichardt, K. Studien zu den Skalden des 9. und 10. Jahrhunderts. Leipzig, 1928.

Oakden, J. P. Alliterative Poetry in Middle English. 2 pts, Manchester, 1930–5.

Andrew, S. O. The Old English Alliterative Measure. Croydon, 1931.

(b) *Articles in Periodicals and Journals of Learned Societies*

Horn, C. R. Zur Metrik des Heliand. PBB. V, 1877.

Schipper, J. M. Zur Zweihebungstheorie der alliterierenden Halbzeile. E. Studien, V, 1882.

—— Metrische Randglossen. E. Studien, IX, 1886, x, 1887.

Trautmann, M. Zur alt- und mittelenglischen Verslehre. Ang. Anz. V, 1882.

—— Metrische Antglossen. Ang. Anz. VIII, 1885.

—— Zur Kenntnis des altgermanischen Verses, vornehmlich des Altenglischen. Ang. Bbl. V, 1894.

—— Die neuste Beowulfausgabe und die altenglische Verslehre. BBA. XVII, 1905

—— Der Heliand, eine Übersetzung aus dem Altenglischen. BBA. XVII, 1905.

Trautmann, M. Zum altenglischen Versbau. E. Studien, XLIV, 1912.

—— Sprache und Versbau der altenglischen Rätsel. Ang. XXXVIII, 1914.

Menthel, E. Zur Geschichte des otfridischen Verses im Englischen. Ang. Anz. VIII, 1885, x, 1887.

Sievers, E. Zur Rhythmik des germanischen Alliterationsverses. PBB. x, 1885. [Two pts, Beowulf in first.]

—— Zur Rhythmik [etc.]. Pt III. Der angelsächsische Schwellvers. PBB. XII, 1887.

—— Die Entstehung des deutschen Reimverses. PBB. XIII, 1887.

Gummere, F. B. The Translation of Beowulf and the Relations of Ancient and Modern English Verse. AJ. Phil. VII, 1886.

Luick, K. Über den Versbau des angelsächsischen Gedichtes Judith. PBB. XI, 1886.

—— Zur Theorie der Entstehung der Schwellverse. PBB. XIII, 1887.

—— Die englische Stabreimzeile im 14., 15., und 16. Jahrhundert. Ang. XI, 1889. [Two pts.]

—— Zur Metrik der mittelenglischen reimendalliterierenden Dichtung. Ang. XII, 1889.

—— Zur altenglischen und altsächsischen Metrik. PBB. xv, 1891.

—— Zur mittelenglischen Verslehre. Ang. XXXVIII, 1914. [Two pts.]

Kauffmann, F. Die sogenannten Schwellverse der alt- und angelsächsischen Dichtung. PBB. xv. 1890.

Foster, G. Judith. Studies in Metre, Language and Style. QF. LXXI, 1892.

Heath, H. F. The Old English Alliterative Line. Trans. Philolog. Soc. pt II, 1893.

Bradshaw, M. The Versification of the Old English Poem Phoenix. AJ. Phil. xv, 1894.

Brenner, O. Zur Verteilung der Reimstabe in der alliterierenden Langzeile. PBB. XIX, 1894.

Kaluza, M. Die Schwellverse in der altenglischen Dichtung. E. Studien, XXI, 1895.

—— Zur Betonungs- und Verslehre des Altenglischen. [In Festschrift Oskar Schade, Königsberg, 1896.]

Fischer, R. [Review of F. Graz, Die Metrik der Cädmonischen Dichtungen.] Anzeiger für deutsches Altertum, XXIII, 1897.

Tamson, G. J. Word-Stress in English. SEP. III. 1898.

Bright, J. W. Proper Names in Old English Verse. PMLA. XIV, 1899.

Emerson, O. F. Transverse Alliteration in Teutonic Poetry. JEGP. III, 1900.

—— Imperfect Lines in the Pearl and the Rimed Parts of Sir Gawain and the Green Knight. MP. XIX. 1921.

Mennicken, F. Versbau und Sprache in Huchowns Morte Arthure. BBA. v, 1900.

Clark, J. Early Alliterative Verse. Proc. Royal Philosophical Soc. Glasgow, 1902.

Krämer, E. Untersuchungen zu den altenglischen Metren des Boetius. BBA. VIII, 1902.

Sokoll, E. Zur Technik des altgermanischen Alliterationsverses. Beiträge zur neueren Philologie, 1902.

Morgan, P. Q. Zur Lehre von der Alliteration in der westgermanischen Dichtung. PBB. XXXIII, 1907. [Beowulf in ch. I.]

Schmitz, T. Die Sechstakter in der altenglischen Dichtung. Ang. XXXIII, 1910. [Two pts.]

Bülbring, K. D. Untersuchungen zur mittelenglischen Metrik. [In Festschrift für Lorenz Morsbach, SEP. L, 1913].

Fijn van Draat, P. The Cursus in Old English Poetry. Ang. XXXVIII, 1914.

Heusler, A. Stabreim. Hoops Reallexikon, vol. IV, 1918.

—— Deutsche Versgeschichte mit Einschluss des altenglischen und altnordischen Stabreimverses. I. [In PG. vol. VIII³, 1925.]

Rankin, J. W. Rhythm and Rime before the Norman Conquest. PMLA. XXXVI. 1921.

Liebermann, F. Reim neben Alliteration in Anglolatein um 680. Archiv, CXLI, 1921.

Huttenbrenner, F. Probe eines metrischen Wörterbuchs für das Altenglische (Phönix). E. Studien, LVI, 1922.

Routh, J. Anglo-Saxon Meter. MP. XXI, 1924.

Greg, W. W. The Five Types in Anglo-Saxon Verse. MLR. XX, 1925.

Stewart, G. R. The Meter of Piers Plowman. PMLA. XLII, 1927.

Holthausen, F. Metrisches. Ang. Bbl. XXXIX, 1928.

Scripture, E. W. Die Grundgesetze des altenglischen Stabreimverses. Ang. LII, 1928.

—— Der Versrhythmus in King Horn. Ang. LII, 1928.

—— Experimentelle Untersuchungen über die Metrik in Beowulf. Archiv für die gesamte Psychologie, LXVI, 1928.

Day, M. Strophic Division in Middle English Alliterative Verse. E. Studien, LXVI, 1931.

(2) MODERN ENGLISH PROSODY
(From Chaucer onwards)

[Many of the early texts are reprinted in Arber's English Reprints, 1868, and in Elizabethan Critical Essays, ed. G. Gregory Smith, 2 vols. Oxford, 1904.]

(a) Books

Ascham, Roger. The Scholemaster. 1570. [Contains refs. to metre.]

Gascoigne, George. Certayne Notes of Instruction in English Verse. 1575.

Lodge, Thomas. A Defence of Poetry, Music, and Stage Plays. 1579. [Rptd Shakespeare Soc. 1853, and in Works, ed. Sir E. Gosse, Glasgow, 1872–82.]

Harvey, Gabriel, and Spenser, Edmund. Three Letters. 1580.

—— —— Two Letters. 1580. [All rptd in Oxford Spenser.]

Stanyhurst, Richard. Aeneid. Leyden, 1582. [Preface Too the Reader refers to quantitative metre.]

James VI of Scotland. Essays of a Prentice. Edinburgh, 1584. [Contains one on metre.]

Webbe, William. A Discourse of English Poetry. 1586.

[Puttenham, George.] The Art of English Poesie. 1588.

Nash, Thomas. [Preface to Robert Greene's Menaphon.] [1589?]

—— Strange news of the intercepting certain letters. 1592. [Rptd in Works, ed. A. B. Grosart, 6 vols. 1883–5.]

Harvey, Gabriel. Four Letters. 1592.

—— Letter Book. [First pbd Camden Soc. 1884, also by A. B. Grosart in Works of Harvey, 3 vols. 1884–5.]

Sidney, Sir Philip. Apologie for Poetrie. 1595.

Campion, Thomas. Observations on the Art of English Poetry. 1602.

Daniel, Samuel. A Defence of Rhyme. [1603?–1607.]

Beaumont, Sir John. To his late Majesty James I Concerning the true form of English Poetry. [1629?] [Rptd in Chalmers' Poets, vol. VI, 1810.]

Jonson, Ben. An English Grammar. 1640. [Contains only a brief ref. to metre.]

—— Conversations with Drummond of Hawthornden. Ed. R. F. Patterson, 1923. [Contains only occasional refs. to metre.]

D., J. [Introduction to Joshua Poole's English Parnassus 'being a short Institution of English Poesy,' 1657.]

Dryden, John. [Essays and Prefaces contain occasional refs. to metre. Rptd in Essays of John Dryden, ed. W. P. Ker, 2 vols. Oxford, 1900.]

Woodford, Samuel. Paraphrase of the Psalms. 1667. [Preface.]

—— Paraphrase of the Canticles. 1679. [Preface.]

Milton, John. Paradise Lost. 1668. [Note on the verse.]

Bysshe, Edward. The Art of English Poetry. 3 pts, 1702. [Enlarged and altered in subsequent edns.]

Coward, William. Licentia Poetica Discuss'd. 1709.

Watts, Isaac. Horae Lyricae. 1709. [Refs. to metre in Preface.]

Brightland, John. English Grammar. 1711.

Swift, J. Proposal for correcting the English tongue. 1712.

Gildon, Charles. The Complete Art of Poetry. 2 vols. 1718. [Refs. to metre in vol. i.]

—— The Laws of Poetry Explained and Illustrated. 1721.

Theobald, L. [Note to edition of Shakespeare, 1733.]

An Introduction of the Ancient Greek and Latin Measures into British Poetry. 1737.

Pemberton, Henry. Observations on Poetry, especially the Epic. 1738.

[Benson, William.] Letters concerning poetical translations, and Virgil's and Milton's Arts of Verse. 1739.

Manwaring, Edward. Of Harmony and Numbers, in Latin and English Prose, and in English Poetry. 1744.

Say, Samuel. Critical Essays. [In Poems, 1745.]

Mason, John. The Power of Numbers and the Principle of Harmony in Poetic Compositions. 1749. [Rev. and rpbd with a paper on prose rhythm as Two Essays on the Power of Numbers, 1761.]

Fortescue, James. Pomeroy Hill. With other Poems. 1754. [Contains a preface on Prosody.]

Johnson, Samuel. Grammar. [In The Dictionary, 1755. Contains a section on Prosody.]

—— The Rambler. Nos. 86, 88, 90, 94, 139, 140, 1751.

—— The Lives of the Poets. 4 vols. 1781. [Contains a few refs. to prosody.]

Beauties of Poetry displayed. 2 vols. 1757. [Prosody in preface.]

Gray, Thomas. Fragments for the History of Poetry, 1760. [In Works, ed. Sir E. Gosse, 4 vols. 1884.]

—— Observations on English Metre, 1760. 1814.

Foster, J. An Essay on the Different Nature of Accent and Quantity. Eton, 1762.

Home, Henry (Lord Kames). Elements of Criticism. 3 vols. Edinburgh, 1762.

Newbery, J. The Art of Poetry on a New Plan. 2 vols. 1762. [Contains occasional brief refs. to prosody.]

Webb, Daniel. Remarks on the Beauties of Poetry. 1762.

—— Observations on the Correspondence between Poetry and Music. 1769.

Brown, J. A Dissertation on Poetry and Music. 1763.

Shenstone, W. Essays. [In Works, 3 vols. 1764–9.]

Rice, J. An Introduction to the Art of Reading with Propriety and Elegance. 1765.

Hawkins, Sir J. History of Music. 5 vols. 1771.

Burnett, James (Lord Monboddo). The Origin and Progress of Language. 6 vols. 1773–92. [Refs. to prosody in vol. ii.]

Herries, J. The Elements of Speech. 1773.

Kenrick, W. Rhetorical Grammar. [Prefixed to A New Dictionary of the English Language, 1773. Contains a section on prosody.]

Tucker, Abraham. Vocal Sounds, by Edward Search, Esq. 1773.

Mitford, William. Essay on the Harmony of Language. 1774. [Rptd with alterations and addns as An Inquiry into the Principles of Harmony in Language, 1804.]

Warton, Thomas. History of English Poetry. 3 vols. 1774–81.

Sheridan, Thomas. The Art of Reading. Dublin, 1775. [Contains principles stated in Dissertation and Lectures on Elocution, 1762; and in Prosodical Grammar in Dictionary, 2 vols. 1780.]

Steele, Joshua. Prosodia Rationalis. 1775. [Incomplete. Complete edn, 1779.]

Tyrwhitt, Thomas. An Essay on the Language and Versification of Chaucer. [In The Canterbury Tales of Chaucer, vol. iv, 1775.]

Beattie, James. An Essay on Poetry and Music as they affect the Mind. [In Essays, Edinburgh, 1776.]

Blair, Hugh. Lectures on Rhetoric and Belles Lettres. 2 vols. 1783. [Contains refs. to harmony in language.]

Nares, Robert. Elements of Orthoepy. 1784.

Bayly, Anselm. The Alliance of Musick, Poetry, and Oratory. 1789.

Walker, J. Principles of English Pronunciation. [Prefixed to A Critical Pronouncing Dictionary, 1791.]

—— Key to the Classical Pronunciation of Proper Names. 1798.

Sayers, F. English Metre. [In Disquisitions, 1793. Omitted from later edns. Rptd in Poetical Works, 1830.]

Murray, Lindley. English Grammar. 1795. [Contains a section on prosody.]

Smith, Adam. Of the affinity between certain English and Italian verses. [In Essays on Philosophical Subjects, 1795.]

Fogg, P. W. Dissertations Grammatical and Philological. [In Elementa Anglicana, vol. ii (nos. xi and xii on prosody and versification), Stockport, 1796.]

[Horsley, Samuel.] On the Prosodies of the Greek and Latin Languages. 1796.

[Warner, J.] Metronariston. 1797.

Robertson, J. An Essay on the Nature of the English Verse. 1799.

Roe, R. B. The Elements of English Metre. 1801.

—— The Principles of Rhythm both in Speech and Music; Especially as Exhibited in the Mechanism of English Verse. Dublin, 1823.

Knight, R. P. Analytical Enquiry into the Principles of Taste. 1805.

Odell, J. An Essay on the Elements, Accents and Prosody, of the English Language. 1806.

Gregory, G. Letters on Literature, Taste, and Composition. 2 vols. 1808.

Carey, J. Practical English Prosody and Versification. 1809; 1816 (new and improved edn).

Thelwall, J. Selections for a Course of Instructions on the Rhythmus and Utterance of the English Language. 1812. [Introductory Essay on the study of English Rhythmus.]

Coleridge, S. T. [Preface to] Christabel. 1816. [Other refs. to metre in Biographia Literaria, 1817; Lectures on Shakespeare, 1818; Table-Talk, 1835.]

Chapman, J. The Music, or Melody and Rhythmus, of Language. Edinburgh, 1818.

—— The Original Rhythmical Grammar of the English Language. Edinburgh, 1821. [Based on Steele's Prosodia Rationalis.]

Tillbrook, S. Historical and Critical Remarks upon the Modern Hexametrists and upon Mr. Southey's Vision of Judgment. Cambridge, 1822.

Brown, Goold. The Institutes of English Grammar. New York, 1827 (3rd edn). [Contains a section on prosody.]

Crowe, W. A Treatise on English Versification. 1827.

Rush, J. The Philosophy of the Human Voice. Philadelphia, 1827.

Barber, J. A Grammar of Elocution. New Haven, 1830.

Forde, W. The True Spirit of Milton's Versification. 1831.

Gardiner, W. The Music of Nature. 1832.

[Blundell, J.] Hexametrical Experiments. 1838. [Contains full notes and introductions.]

Guest, Edwin. History of English Rhythms. 2 vols. 1838; ed. with corrections and notes W. W. Skeat, 1882.

Horne, R. H. The Poems of Geoffrey Chaucer modernized. 1841. [Introduction on verse.]

Latham, R. G. The English Language. 1841. [Pt v, On the Prosody of the English Language. Enlarged in later edns, 1855, etc.]

O'Brien, W. The Ancient Rhythmical Art Recovered. Dublin, 1843.

Vandenhoff, G. The Art of Elocution. 1846. [Enlargement of A Plain System of Elocution, New York, 1844.]

Humphrey, Asa. The English Prosody: with Rules deduced from the Genius of our Language, and the Examples of the Poets. Boston, 1847.

Everett, E. A System of English Versification. New York, 1848.

Brown, G. The Grammar of English Grammars. Boston, 1850. [Pt 4 on prosody.]

Dallas, E. S. Poetics: an Essay on Poetry. 1852. [Refs. to prosody in bk iii, pt ii, ch. 2.]

Evans, R. W. A Treatise on Versification, Ancient and Modern. 1852.

Spiers, A. A. Study of English Poetry. 1855.

Masson, D. Essays on English Poets. Cambridge, 1856. [Contains refs. to versification. A survey of Milton's versification is to be found in Milton's Works, ed. D. Masson, 3 vols. 1882.]

Bathurst, C. Remarks on the Differences in Shakespeare's Versification in Different Periods of his Life. 1857.

Freeman-Mitford, J. T. F. (Earl of Redesdale). Thoughts on Prosody. Oxford, 1859.

—— Further Thoughts on Prosody. Oxford, 1859.

Marsh, G. P. Lectures on the English Language. New York, 1860.

Angus, J. Handbook of the English Tongue. 1862.

Arnold, T. A Manual of English Literature, Historical and Critical. With an Appendix on English Metres. 1862.

Abbott, E. A. A Shakespearian Grammar. 1869; 1870 (rev. edn).

Brewer, R. F. A Manual of English Prosody. 1869. [Rptd with addns as Orthometry, 1893.]

Hood, Tom (the younger). The Rules of Rhyme; a Guide to English Versification. 1869.

—— Practical Guide to English Versification. To which are added Bysshe's Rules for making English Verse, etc. 1877.

Wadham, E. English Versification. 1869.

Sylvester, J. J. The Laws of Verse. 1870.

Abbott, E. A. and Seeley, J. R. English Lessons for English People. 1871.

Earle, J. The Philology of the English Tongue. Oxford, 1871. [Ch. xii Of Prosody.]

Ellis, Robinson. Translation of Catullus in the Original Metres. 1871. [Preface.]

Sweet, Henry. History of English Sounds. 1874. [Rptd from Trans. Philolog. Soc. 1873–4. Enlarged edn, Oxford, 1884.]

2

Conway, Gilbert. A Treatise on Versification. 1878.

Gurney, E. The Power of Sound. 1880.

—— Tertium Quid. 2 vols. 1887. [Refs. to prosody in vol. ii.]

Lanier, Sidney. The Science of English Verse. Boston, 1880.

Ruskin, J. Elements of English Prosody. Orpington, Kent, 1880.

Hodgson, S. H. English Verse. [In Outcast Essays, 1881.]

Schipper, J. M. Englische Metrik. 3 vols. (vol. i and vol. ii, pts 1 and 2), Bonn, 1881–8.

—— Grundriss der englischen Metrik. Vienna, 1895; tr. Eng. Oxford, 1910. [An abridgment of the Englische Metrik.]

Browne, G. H. Notes on Shakspere's Versification. Boston, 1884.

Witcomb, C. On the Structure of English Verse. 1884.

Calverley, C. S. On Metrical Translation. [In Literary Remains, 1885.]

Gummere, F. B. Handbook of Poetics. Boston, 1885.

—— The Beginnings of Poetry. New York, 1901.

Mayor, J. B. Chapters on English Metre. Cambridge, 1886.

—— A Handbook of Modern English Metre. Cambridge, 1903.

Raymond, G. L. Poetry as a Representative Art. New York, 1886.

—— Rhythm and Harmony in Poetry and Music. New York, 1895.

Bridges, Robert. Milton's Prosody. [In Clarendon Press Milton, Oxford, 1887. Several times enlarged and pbd separately, 1889, etc. Pbd with W. J. Stone, On the Use of Classical Metres in English, Oxford, 1901.]

[Blake, J. W.] Accent and Rhythm explained by the Law of Monopressures. Edinburgh, 1888.

Davidson, J. W. The Poetry of the Future. New York, 1888.

Mead, W. E. The Versification of Pope in its Relation to the Seventeenth Century. Leipzig, 1889.

Bateson, H. D. English Rhythms. 1891.

—— An Introduction to the Study of English Rhythms. Manchester, 1904.

Parsons, J. C. English Versification for the Use of Students. Boston, 1891.

Corson, H. A Primer of English Verse. Boston, 1892.

Skeat, W. W. The Complete Works of Geoffrey Chaucer. 6 vols. Oxford, 1894. [Versification in vol. vi.]

Courthope, W. J. History of English Poetry. 6 vols. 1895–1910. [Contains scattered remarks on versification.]

Symonds, J. A. Blank Verse. 1895. [Appeared first in Fortnightly Rev. Dec. 1874.]

Beatty, A. Browning's Verse-Form: its Organic Character. New York, 1897.

Omond, T. S. English Verse-Structure. Edinburgh, 1897.

—— English Hexameters. Edinburgh, 1897.

—— English Metrists. Pt i, Tunbridge Wells, 1903.

—— A Study of Metre. 1903.

—— Metrical Rhythm. Tunbridge Wells, 1905.

—— English Metrists in the Eighteenth and Nineteenth Centuries. Oxford, 1907. [Pt ii of English Metrists. Rptd with pt i and other addns in one vol. Oxford, 1921.]

Robertson, J. M. New Essays Towards a Critical Method. 1897. [Contains an appendix on Accent, Quantity and Feet.]

Lewis, C. M. The Foreign Sources of Modern English Versification. New York, 1898.

—— The Principles of English Verse. New York, 1906.

Gayley, C. M. and Scott, F. N. An Introduction to the Methods and Materials of Literary Criticism. Boston, 1899. [Prosody in ch. vii.]

Gayley, C. M. and Young, C. C. The Principles and Progress of English Poetry. New York, 1904.

Stone, W. J. On the Use of Classical Metres in English. Oxford, 1899. [Rpbd with R. Bridges, Milton's Prosody, Oxford, 1901.]

van Dam, B. A. P. and Stoffel, C. W. Shakespeare, Prosody and Text. Leyden, 1900.

—— —— Chapters on English Printing, Prosody, and Pronunciation (1550–1700). Heidelberg, 1902.

Harford, F. K. A Note on the Scansion of the Pentameter. Oxford, 1900.

Brown, G. D. Syllabification and Accent in the Paradise Lost. Baltimore, 1901.

Dabney, J. P. The Musical Basis of Verse. New York, 1901.

Archer, W. Poets of the Younger Generation. 1902.

Liddell, M. H. An Introduction to the Scientific Study of English Poetry. New York, 1902.

—— A Brief Abstract of a New English Prosody. Lafayette, Indiana, 1914.

Miller, C. W. E. The Relation of the Rhythm of Poetry to that of the Spoken Language. Baltimore, 1902.

Scripture, E. W. The Elements of Experimental Phonetics. New York, 1902.

—— Grundzüge der englischen Verswissenschaft. Marburg, 1929.

ten Brink, B. The Language and Metre of Chaucer. 1902. [Tr. M. Bentinck Smith

PROSODY AND PROSE RHYTHM

Alden, R. M. English Verse. New York, 1903.
—— An Introduction to Poetry. New York, 1909.

Victory, L. H. Essay on Elementary Metres. [In Imaginations in the Dust, vol. ii, 1903.]

Miller, R. D. Secondary Accent in Modern English Verse (Chaucer to Dryden). Baltimore, 1904.

More, P. E. The Science of English Verse. [In Shelburne Essays, First Series, Boston, 1904.]

Northcroft, G. J. H. How to write Verse: being Studies in the Principles and Practice of the Art of English Verse-structure. 1904.

Schmidt, F. Short English Prosody for Use in Schools. Leipzig, 1904.

Thomson, W. The Basis of English Rhythm. Glasgow, 1904.
—— The Rôle of Number in the Rhythm of Ancient and Modern Languages. 1907.
—— Rhythm and Scansion. 1911.
—— Scansion and Rhythm. 1913.
—— The Laws of Speech-Rhythm. 1914.
—— The Rhythm of Speech. Glasgow, 1923.

Tolman, A. H. The Views about Hamlet and other Essays. Boston, 1904.

Rudmose-Brown, T. B. Étude comparée de la Versification française et de la Versification anglaise. Grenoble, 1905.

Melton, W. F. The Rhetoric of John Donne's Verse. Baltimore, 1906.

Saintsbury, G. A History of English Prosody 3 vols. 1906–10.
—— The Cambridge History of English Literature. 14 vols. 1907–16. [The Prosody of Old and Middle English, vol. i, ch. 18; Prosody from Chaucer to Spenser, vol. iii, ch. 13; The Prosody of the Seventeenth Century, vol. viii, ch. 9; The Prosody of the Eighteenth Century, vol. xi, ch. 11; The Prosody of the Nineteenth Century, vol. xiii, ch. 7.]
—— Historical Manual of English Prosody. 1910.

Brown, W. Time in English Verse Rhythm. New York, 1908.

Verrier, Paul. Essai sur les Principes de la Métrique anglaise. 3 vols. Paris, 1909–10.
—— Questions de Métrique anglaise. Paris, 1912.

Woodraw, H. A Quantitative Study of Rhythm. New York, 1909.

Bright, J. W. and Miller, R. D. The Elements of English Versification. Boston, 1910.

Morton, E. P. The Technique of English non-dramatic Blank Verse. Chicago, 1910.

Hall, W. W. English Poesy: an Induction. 1911.

Kaluza, M. A Short History of English Versification. Tr. A. C. Dunstan, 1911.

Matthews, Brander. A Study of Versification. Boston, 1911.

MacDonagh, T. Thomas Campion and the Art of English Poetry. Dublin, 1913.

Cowl, R. P. The Theory of Poetry in England. 1914.

Datta, Roby. Prosody and Rhetoric. Calcutta, 1915.

Odling, W. The Technic of Versification. Oxford, 1916.

Lamborn, E. A. G. The Rudiments of Criticism. Oxford, 1916.

Lowell, Amy. Tendencies in Modern American Poetry. Boston, 1917.
—— Poetry and Poets. Boston, 1930. [Remarks on the cadences of free verse are also to be found in the prefaces to some of her works.]

Andrews, C. E. The Writing and Reading of Verse. New York, 1918.

Crapsey, A. A Study in English Metrics. New York, 1918.

Hopkins, G. M. The Poems of Gerard Manley Hopkins, now first published. Ed. (with notes) Robert Bridges, 1918. [See Preface and Notes.]

Jacob, C. F. The Foundations and Nature of Verse. New York, 1918.

Snell, A. L. F. Pause; a Study of its Nature and its Rhythmical Function in Verse, especially Blank Verse. Ann Arbor, 1918.

Bayfield, M. A. The Measures of the Poets: a new System of English Prosody. Cambridge, 1919.
—— A Study of Shakespeare's Versification. Cambridge, 1920.

Lowes, J. L. Convention and Revolt in Poetry. Boston, 1919. [Ch. 6, Rhyme, Metre and Vers Libre.]

Beschorner, F. Verbale Reime bei Chaucer. SEP. lx, 1920.

Jones, L. Free Verse and its Propaganda. 1920. [Rptd from The Sewanee Rev. of July and September.]

Perry, Bliss. A Study of Poetry. Boston, 1920.

Pyre, J. F. A. The Formation of Tennyson's Style: a Study, primarily of the Versification of the Early Poems. Madison, 1921.
—— A Short Introduction to English Versification. New York, 1929.

Baum, P. F. The Principles of English Versification. Cambridge, U.S.A. 1922.

Graves, Robert. On English Poetry. 1922.

Murry, J. M. The Problem of Style. 1922.

Stewart, G. R. Modern Metrical Technique as Illustrated by Ballad Meter (1700–1920). New York, 1922.
—— The Technique of English Verse. New York, 1930.

2-2

Strunk, W. English Metres. Cornell Co-operative Soc., Ithaca, 1922.

Abercrombie, Lascelles. Principles of English Prosody. Pt i. The Elements. 1923.

—— Poetry: its Music and Meaning. Oxford, 1932.

Smith, Egerton. The Principles of English Metre. Oxford, 1923.

Damon, S. Foster. William Blake, his Philosophy and Symbols. Boston, 1924.

Grew, Sidney. A Book of English Prosody. 1924.

Arnell, C. J. The Art and Practice of Versification. Exeter, 1925.

Morris, A. R. The Orchestration of the Metrical Line: an Analytical Study of Rhythmical Form. Boston, 1925.

Scott, J. H. Rhythmic Verse. Iowa City, 1925.

Sonnenschein, E. A. What is Rhythm? Oxford, 1925.

Felkin, F. W. The Craft of the Poet: an Outline of English Verse Composition. 1926.

Monroe, H. Poets and their Art. New York, 1926. [Contains a section on Poetic Rhythms.]

Untermeyer, L. The Forms of Poetry; a Pocket Dictionary of Verse. New York, 1926.

Lindsay, J. The Metric of William Blake. [In Poetical Sketches by William Blake, 1927.]

Rickert, E. New Methods for the Study of Literature. Chicago, 1927.

Spindler, R. Englische Metrik in ihren Grundzügen an Hand ausgewählter Textproben dargestellt. Munich, 1927.

Andersen, J. C. The Laws of Verse. Cambridge, 1928.

Hatcher, H. H. The Versification of Robert Browning. Columbus, 1928.

Young, Sir G. An English Prosody on Inductive Lines. Cambridge, 1928.

Chapin, E. and Thomas, R. A New Approach to Poetry. Chicago, 1929.

Richards, I. A. Practical Criticism. 1929.

Taig, Thomas. Rhythm and Metre. Cardiff, 1929.

Wilson, K. M. The Real Rhythm in English Poetry. Aberdeen, 1929.

Hamer, E. The Metres of English Poetry. 1930.

Lahey, G. F. Gerard Manley Hopkins. Oxford, 1930. [Prosody in ch. vi.]

Hickson, E. C. The Versification of Thomas Hardy. Philadelphia, 1931.

Johnson, Burges. New Rhyming Dictionary and Poets' Handbook. 1931. [Gives examples of metres and stanzas.]

Lanz, H. The Physical Basis of Rime. An Essay on the Aesthetics of Sound. Palo Alto, 1931.

Lewis, R. B. Creative Poetry. Palo Alto, 1931.

Timberlake, P. W. The Feminine Ending in English Blank Verse. Menasha, Wisconsin, 1931.

Smith, Chard P. Pattern and Variation in Poetry. New York, 1932.

Propst, L. An Analytical Study of Shelley's Versification. Iowa City, 1933.

Stephens, W. H. Elements of English Verse as a Science and an Art. A New Approach to Poetry. 1933.

Barkas, P. A Critique of Modern English Prosody (1880–1930). SEP. LXXXII, 1934.

Maynard, T. The Connection between the Ballade, Chaucer's Modification of it, Rime Royal and the Spenserian Stanza. Washington, 1934.

Richter, W. Der Hiatus im englischen Klassizismus (Milton, Dryden, Pope). Schramberg, 1934.

Swann, R. and Sidgwick, F. The Making of Verse. 1934.

Leathes, Sir S. Rhythm in English Poetry. 1935.

Schramm, W. L. Approaches to a Science of English Verse. Iowa City, 1935.

(b) Articles in Periodicals

[Goldsmith, O. ?] Essay on Versification. British Mag. Jan. 1763. [Rptd in Works as No. 18 of Miscellaneous Essays.]

Young, W. On Rhythmical Measures. Trans. Royal Soc. Edinburgh, ii, pt ii, 1786.

Herbert, W. An Enquiry into the Principles of Harmony in Language. By W. Mitford. Edinburgh Rev. vi, 1805.

Bryant, W. C. On the Use of Trisyllabic Feet in Iambic Verse. North American Rev. ix, 1819. [Rptd with addns in Works, vol. i, New York, 1884.]

A Vision of Judgment by Robert Southey, Esq. Edinburgh Rev. xxxv, 1821.

Wilson, J. Noctes Ambrosianae. No. 39. Blackwood's Mag. xxiv, 1828.

An Essay on Accent and Quantity. By John Foster. Second Edition 1763. Eclectic Rev., N.S., iii, 1838.

Felton, C. C. Ballads and other Poems. By Henry Wadsworth Longfellow. North American Rev. lv, 1842.

M.-C. Homer's Iliad. Westminster Rev. xliii, 1845.

Oxenford, J. The Practice of Writing English in Classical Metres. Classical Museum, iii, 1846.

Malden, H. On Greek and English Versification. Proc. Philolog. Soc. iii, 1847.

Poe, E. A. The Rationale of Verse. Southern Literary Messenger, xiv, 1848. [2 papers.]

Whelpley, J. D. The Art of measuring Verses. American Rev. 1848.

Patmore, Coventry. English Metrical Critics. North British Rev. XXVII, 1857. [Rptd with slight changes as Essay on English Metrical Law in Amelia, 1878.]

Barham, T. F. On Metrical Time, or the Rhythm of Verse, Ancient and Modern. Trans. Philolog. Soc. 1860–1.

Spedding, J. Arnold on Translating Homer. Fraser's Mag. LXIII, 1861. [Rptd with addns in Reviews and Discussions, 1879.]

Cayley, C. B. Remarks and Experiments on English Hexameters. Trans. Philolog. Soc. 1862–3.

Lindner, F. The Alliteration in Chaucer's Canterbury Tales. [In Essays on Chaucer, his Words and Works, ed. F. J. Furnivall, Chaucer Soc., ser. 2, 1868–74.]

Monro, C. J. Latin Metres in English. Journ. Philology, IV, 1872.

Ellis, A. J. On the Physical Constituents of Accent and Emphasis. Trans. Philolog. Soc. 1873–4.

Mayor, J. B. Dr Guest and Dr Abbott on English Metre. Trans. Philolog. Soc. 1873–4.
—— English Metre. Together with Mr A. J. Ellis's Remarks on Prof. Mayor's Two Papers on Rhythm, an Appendix by J. B. Mayor, and Additional Observations by A. J. Ellis. Trans. Philolog. Soc. 1875–6.
—— English Metre. Trans. Philolog. Soc. 1877.
—— A Classification of Shelley's Metres. Shelley Soc. 1888.

Sweet, H. The History of English Sounds. Trans. Philolog. Soc. 1873–4.

Jenkin, F. Papers on Metre. Saturday Rev. Feb.–March, 1883. [Rptd in Memoir by R. L. Stevenson, Edinburgh, 1887.]

Goodell, T. D. Quantity in English Verse. Trans. American Philolog. Ass. XVI, 1885.

Stevenson, R. L. On some Technical Elements of Style in Literature. Contemporary Rev. XLVII, 1885. [Rptd in Essays in the Art of Writing, 1905.]

Price, T. R. The Construction and Types of Shakespeare's Verse as seen in Othello. [In Papers of the New York Shakespeare Soc. 1888.]

Browne, W. H. Certain Considerations touching the Structure of English Verse. MLN. IV, 1889.

Humphreys, M. W. On the Equivalence of Rhythmical Bars and Metrical Feet. Trans. American Philolog. Ass. XXIII, 1892.

Bateson, H. D. The Rhythm of Coleridge's Christabel. Manchester Quart. XIII, 1894. [Rptd separately with addns, Manchester, 1904.]

Bolton, T. L. Rhythm. American Journ. Psychology, VI, 1894.

Larminie, W. The Development of English Metres. Contemporary Rev. LXVI, 1894.

Skeat, W. W. On the Scansion of English Poetry. Trans. Philolog. Soc. 1895–8.

Omond, T. S. English Prosody. GM. Feb. 1898.
—— Arnold and Homer. E. & S. III, 1912.
—— Some Thoughts about Verse. English Ass. Lecture, 1923.

Omond, T. S., Thomas, W. and Williams, R. A. Notes. MLR. V, 1910.

Alden, R. M. The Time Element in English Verse. MLN. XIV, 1899.
—— The Mental Side of Metrical Form. MLR. IX, 1914.

Hurst, A. S. and McKay, J. Experiments on Time Relations of Poetical Metres. University of Toronto Stud. Psychology, ser. 3, 1899.

Ker, W. P. Analogies between English and Spanish Verse. Trans. Philolog. Soc. 1899.
—— De Superbia Carminum. MLR. XIII, 1918.

Morton, E. P. A Method of teaching Metrics. MLN. XV, 1900.
—— The Spenserian Stanza before 1700. MP. IV, 1907.
—— The Spenserian Stanza in the Eighteenth Century. MP. X, 1913.

Bright, J. W. Concerning Grammatical Ictus in English Verse. [In An English Miscellany presented to Dr Furnivall, Oxford, 1901.]
—— Rhythmic Elements in English. University of Texas Bulletin, 1 Jan. 1917.

Squire, C. R. A Genetic Study of Rhythm. American Journ. Psychology, XII, 1901.

Triplett, N. and Sanford, E. C. Studies of Rhythm and Meter. American Journ. Psychology, XII, 1901.

Wallin, J. E. W. Researches on the Rhythm of Speech. Studies from the Yale Psychological Laboratory, VII, 1901.

McKerrow, R. B. The Use of so-called Classical Metres in Elizabethan Verse. Mod. Lang. Quart. IV, 1901, V, 1902.

Smith, M. Bentinck. Some Remarks on Chapter III of ten Brink's 'Chaucers Sprache und Verskunst.' Mod. Lang. Quart. V, 1902.

van Dam, B. A. P. Robert Bridges, Milton's Prosody and William Johnson Stone, Classical Metres in English Verse. E. Studien, XXXII, 1903.

van Dyke, H. Some Remarks on the Study of English Verse. Atlantic Monthly, XCII, 1903.

Newman, E. Articles on the Rationale of English Verse-Rhythm. Weekly Critical Rev. 3, 10, 17, 24 Sept., Paris, 1903.

Scott, F. N. The Most Fundamental Differentia of Poetry and Prose. PMLA. XIX, 1904.
—— The Genesis of Speech. PMLA. XXIII, 1908.

Bourne, G. Rhythm and Rhyme. Macmillan's Mag. June, 1906.

Keary, C. F. Some Thoughts on the Technique of Poetry. Fortnightly Rev. LXXX, 1906.

Thomas, W. Milton's Heroic Line viewed from an Historical Standpoint. MLR. II, 1907, III, 1908.

Andersen, J. C. Metre. Trans. New Zealand Inst. 1908.

—— A Natural Classification of English Poetry. Trans. New Zealand Inst. 1909.

—— Classification of Verse. Trans. New Zealand Inst. 1910.

—— The Verse-Unit. Trans. New Zealand Inst. 1911.

Bridges, R. A Letter to a Musician on English Prosody. Musical Antiquary, I, 1909.

—— Humdrum and Harum-Scarum, a Lecture on Free Verse. London Mercury, VII; North American Rev. CCXVI, 1922. [Rptd in Collected Essays, Papers, etc., of Robert Bridges, Oxford, 1928.]

English Prosody. Edinburgh Rev. CCXIII, 1911.

English Prosody. Quart. Rev. CCXV, 1911.

Rudmose-Brown, T. B. Verrier's Essai sur les Principes de la Métrique Anglaise. MLR. VI, 1911.

—— English and French Metric. MLR. VIII, 1913.

—— English and French Metric. MLR. X, 1915.

Brown, W. Temporal and Accentual Rhythm. University of California Psychological Rev. XVIII, 1911.

Robertson, J. M. Form in Poetry. English Rev. VIII, 1911.

—— The Evolution of English Blank Verse. Criterion, Feb. 1924.

Verrier, Paul. English Metric. MLR. VII, 1912.

—— English and French Metric. MLR. IX, 1914.

Hardie, W. R. What is Metre, and how should it be Taught? Proc. Classical Ass. Scotland, 1913.

Bayfield, M. A. Our Traditional Prosody and an Alternative. MLR. XIII, 1918.

Lowell, Amy. The Rhythms of Free Verse. Dial, 17 Jan. 1918.

—— Some Musical Analogies in Modern Poetry. Musical Quart. VI, 1920.

Patterson, W. M. New Verse and New Prose. North American Rev. CCVII, 1918.

Saintsbury, G. Some Recent Studies in English Prosody. Proc. British Academy, 1919–20.

Creek, H. L. Rising and Falling Rhythms in English Verse. PMLA. XXXV, 1920.

Hickey, E. The Making of English Blank Verse. Nineteenth Century, LXXXVIII, 1920.

Snell, A. L. F. An Objective Study of Syllabic Quantity in English Verse. PMLA. XXXIV, 1920.

van Doorn, W. Vers Libre in Theory and Practice. E. Studies, III, 1921.

Sapir, E. The Musical Foundations of Verse. JEGP. XX, 1921.

Williams, R. C. Metrical Form of the Epic, as discussed by Sixteenth-Century Critics. MLN. XXXVI, 1921.

Inge, W. R. Classical Metres in English Poetry. [In Trans. Royal Soc. Lit., Essays by Divers Hands, ed. W. R. Inge, 1922.]

Jones, L. A Principle of Prosody. Freeman, 26 April 1922.

Lotspeitch, C. M. Poetry, Prose and Rhythm. PMLA. XXXVII, 1922.

—— The Metrical Element of Pope's Illustrative Couplets. JEGP. XXVI, 1927.

Nethercot, A. H. The Reputation of John Donne as Metrist. Sewanee Rev. XXX, 1922.

Russell, C. E. Principles of Prosody. Freeman, 5 July 1922. [See Reply by L. Jones, Freeman, 30 Aug. 1922.]

Strachey, J. St Loe. The Vicissitudes of Blank Verse. London Mercury, VI, 1922. [See correspondence by T. S. Omond and others.]

Croll, M. W. Music and Metrics: a Reconsideration. Stud. Phil. XX, 1923.

Hall, W. C. Rhythm. Manchester Quart. L, 1924.

—— Blank Verse. Manchester Quart. LI, 1925.

Hills, E. C. Meter in Anglo-American Free Verse. University of California Chronicle, July 1924.

Hollowell, B. M. Elizabethan Hexametrists. PQ. III, 1924.

Shipley, J. T. Spenserian Prosody: the Couplet Forms. Stud. Phil. XXI, 1924.

Sonnenschein, E. A. What is Blank Verse? Contemporary Rev. CXXVI, 1924.

Hammond, E. P. The Nine-syllabled Pentameter Line in some post-Chaucerian Manuscripts. MP. XXIII, 1925.

Monroe, H. A Word about Prosody. Poetry, XXVII, 1925.

Moore, T. Sturge. A Canon for English Verse. TLS. 1 Oct.–3 Dec. 1925. [See also correspondence by various authors including A. Y. Campbell, E. A. Sonnenschein, T. M. Crump, J. P. Postgate, T. S. Moore, W. D. Sargeaunt, and E. A. Bather.]

Routh, J. English Iambic Meter. PMLA. XL, 1925.

Stewart, G. R. The Iambic-Trochaic Theory in relation to Musical Notation of Verse. JEGP. XXIV, 1925.

—— The Meter of the Popular Ballad. PMLA. XL, 1925.

Welch, C. Some Experimental Work in Speech-Rhythm. Quart. Journ. Speech, XI, 1925.

Fort, M. D. The Metres of the Brome and Chester Abraham and Isaac Plays. PMLA. xli, 1926.

MacColl, D. S. Metre. Saturday Rev. 6, 13 Feb. 1926. [See also E. A. Sonnenschein, *ibid.* 6 March 1926.]

Pope, E. F. The Critical Background of the Spenserian Stanza. MP. xxiv, 1926.

Whitmore, C. E. A Proposed Compromise in Metrics. PMLA. xli, 1926.

Abbott, A. Rhythm in Poetry. Teachers College Record, xxviii, 1927.

Banks, T. H. Miltonic Rhythm. PMLA. xlii, 1927.

Dukes, A. Forms of Dramatic Verse. Theatre Arts Monthly, xi, 1927.

Jacob, C. F. Rhythm in Prose and Poetry. Quart. Journ. Speech, xiii, 1927.

Scripture, E. W. The Choriambus in English Verse. PMLA. xliii, 1928.

Boas, C. The Metre of The Testament of Beauty. London Mercury, xxii, 1930.

Wyld, H. C. Observations on Pope's Versification. MLR. xxv, 1930.

Fairclough, H. R. The Influence of Virgil upon the Forms of English Verse. Classical Journ. xxvi, 1930.

Thieme, H. P. Rhythm. [In Mélanges Baldensperger, vol. ii, Paris, 1930.]

Trevelyan, R. C. Classical and English Verse-Structure. E. & S. xvi, 1931.

Woody, L. Masefield's Use of Dipodic Meter. PQ. x, 1931.

Oliphant, E. H. C. Sonnet Structure: an Analysis. PQ. xi, 1932.

Buchanan, V. Versification. English Journ. xxii, 1933.

Creel, W. How to Hear Time Values in Verse. English Journ. xxii, 1933.

Jespersen, O. Notes on Metre. [In Linguistica, Copenhagen, 1933.]

Eichler, A. Taktumstellung und schwebende Betonung. Archiv, clxv, 1934.

Schramm, W. L. Time and Intensity in English Tetrameter Verse. PQ. xiii, 1934.

Willcock, G. D. Passing Pitefull Hexameters. A Study in Quantity and Accent in English Renaissance Verse. MLR. xxix, 1934.

Wallerstein, R. C. The Development of the Rhetoric and Metre of the Heroic Couplet, especially in 1625–1645. PMLA. l, 1935.

(3) PROSE RHYTHM

[Included in this list are some general studies of the *cursus*.]

(a) *Books*

Melmoth, W. The letters of Sir Thomas Fitzosborne on Several Subjects. 1742. [Letter XIV to Orontes. Concerning the neglect of oratorical numbers.]

Mason, J. The Power and Harmony of Prosaic Numbers. 1749. [Rev. and rptd with a paper on prosody as Two Essays on the Power of Numbers, 1761.]

Rockinger, L. Briefsteller und Formelbücher des elften bis vierzehnten Jahrhunderts. Quellen und Erörterungen zur bayerischen und deutschen Geschichte, ix, Munich, 1863.

Valois, N. De Arte scribendi Epistolas apud Gallicos medii Aevi Scriptores Rhetoresve. Paris, 1880.

Graf, E. Rhythmus und Metrum. Zur Synonymik. Marburg, 1891.

Havet, Louis. La Prose métrique de Symmaque et les Origines métriques du Cursus. Paris, 1892.

Marbe, K. Über den Rhythmus der Prosa. Giessen, 1904.

Zielinski, Theodor. Das Clauselgesetz in Ciceros Reden. Pt 1. Philologus, supplementary vol. ix, 1904.

—— Das Ausleben des Clauselgesetzes in der römischen Kunstprosa. Leipzig, 1906.

—— Der constructive Rhythmus in Ciceros Reden. Pt 2. Philologus, supplementary vol. xiii, 1914.

Blass, Friedrich. Die Rhythmen der asianischen und römischen Kunstprosa. Leipzig, 1905.

Jordan, H. Rhythmische Prosa in der altchristlichen lateinischen Literatur. Leipzig, 1905.

Meyer, W. Gesammelte Abhandlungen zur mittellateinischen Rhythmik. Berlin, 1905.

Laurand, L. Études sur le Style des Discours de Cicéron. Paris, 1907.

Lipsky, Abram. Rhythm as a Distinguishing Characteristic of Prose Style. New York, 1907.

Western, A. On Sentence-Rhythm and Word-Order in Modern English. Christiania, 1908.

Clark, A. C. Fontes Prosae Numerosae. Oxford, 1909.

—— The Cursus in Mediaeval and Vulgar Latin. Oxford, 1910.

—— Prose-Rhythm in English. Oxford, 1913.

Fijn van Draat, P. Rhythm in English Prose. Heidelberg, 1910.

Landry, E. La Théorie du Rhythme et le Rhythme du Français déclamé. Paris. 1911.

Saintsbury, G. A History of English Prose Rhythm. 1912.

Gropp, F. Zur Ästhetik und statistischen Beschreibung des Prosarhythmus. Würzburg, 1915.

Patterson, W. M. The Rhythm of Prose. New York, 1917.

de Groot, A. W. A Handbook of Antique Prose-Rhythm. Hague, 1918.

de Groot, A. W. De Numero oratorio latino. Groningen, 1919.

—— Der antike Prosarhythmus. Zugleich Fortsetzung des Handbook of Antique Prose-Rhythm. Groningen, 1921.

Parrish, W. M. The Rhythm of Oratorical Prose. [In Studies in Rhetoric and Public Speaking, in honor of James Albert Winans, ed. A. M. Drummond, New York, 1925.]

Scott, J. H. Rhythmic Prose. Iowa City, 1925.

Scott, J. H. and Chandler, Z. E. Phrasal Patterns in English Prose. New York, 1932.

Ipsen, G. and Karg. F. Schallanalytische Versuche. Heidelberg, 1928.

Read, H. English Prose Style. 1928.

Griffith, Helen. Time Patterns in Prose. Princeton, 1929.

Novotný, F. État actuel des Études sur le Rhythme de la Prose Latine. Lemberg, 1929.

Williams, W. E. Plain Prose. New York, 1929.

Tempest, N. R. The Rhythm of English Prose. Cambridge, 1930.

(b) Articles in Periodicals and Journals of Learned Societies

Valois, N. Étude sur le Rhythme des Bulles pontificales. Bibliothèque de l'École des Chartes, XLII, Paris, 1881.

Vacandard, E. Le Cursus dans la Liturgie de l'Office Divin. Revue des Questions historiques, LXXVIII, 1904.

Clark, A. C. Zielinski's Clauselgesetz. Classical Rev. XIX, 1905.

Scott, F. N. The Scansion of Prose-Rhythm. PMLA. XX, 1905.

—— The Accentual Structure of Isolable English Phrases. PMLA. XXXIII, 1918.

Zielinski, Theodor. Der Rhythmus der römischen Kunstprosa und seine psychologische Grundlagen. Archiv für die gesammte Psychologie, VII, 1906.

Shelly, J. Rhythmical Prose in Latin and English. Church Quart. Rev. April 1912.

Elton, O. English Prose Numbers. E. & S. IV, 1913. [Rptd in A Sheaf of Papers, Liverpool, 1922.]

MacColl, D. S. Rhythm in English Verse, Prose and Speech. E. & S. V, 1914.

Fijn van Draat, P. Voluptas Aurium. E. Studien, XLVIII, 1915.

—— The Place of the Adverb. A Study in Rhythm. Neophilologus, VI, 1920.

Foster, F. M. K. Cadence in English Prose. JEGP. XVI, 1917.

Croll, M. W. The Cadence of English Oratorical Prose. Stud. Phil. XVI, 1919.

Routh, J. Prose-Rhythms. PMLA. XXXVIII, 1923.

Gerould, G. H. Abbot Aelfric's Rhythmic Prose. MP. XXII, 1925.

Tempest, N. R. Rhythm in the Prose of Sir Thomas Browne. RES. III, 1927.

N. R. T.

IV. LANGUAGE

General Works: Bibliographies; Histories of English; Dictionaries and Glossaries.

Syntax: General; Old English; Middle English; Modern English.

Vocabulary and Word-Formation: General; Old, Middle and Modern English; Loan-Words.

Phonology and Grammar: Old English (Textbooks, Dialects, Illustrative texts); Middle English; Modern English.

Place and Personal Names: Place Names (General, Special districts); Personal Names.

A. GENERAL WORKS

(1) BIBLIOGRAPHIES

Lange, P. and Petri, A. Übersicht über die im Jahre 1891 [–1906] auf dem Gebiete der englischen Philologie erschienenen Bücher, Schriften und Aufsätze. Beigabe zur Anglia, 1894–1909.

Wells, J. E. A Manual of the Writings in Middle English, 1050–1400. New Haven, 1918. [Six supplements, 1919–35.]

Kennedy, A. G. A Bibliography of Writings on the English Language. Cambridge, U.S.A. 1927.

Tucker, L. L. and Benham, A. R. A Bibliography of Fifteenth Century Literature. Seattle, 1928.

Heusinkveld, A. H. and Bashe, E. J. A Bibliographical Guide to Old English. Iowa City, 1931.

(2) HISTORIES OF THE LANGUAGE, HISTORICAL GRAMMARS, ETC.

Morris, R. Historical Outlines of English Accidence. 1872; rev. L. Kellner and H. Bradley, 1895.

Sweet, H. History of English Sounds. Oxford, 1888.

—— A New English Grammar, Logical and Historical. 2 pts, Oxford, 1892–9.

—— Short Historical English Grammar. Oxford, 1892.

Kluge, F. Geschichte der englischen Sprache. [In PG. vol. I², pp. 926–49, 989–1070, Strasburg, 1891; 2nd edn, 1896–1901.]

Emerson, O. F. The History of the English Language. New York, 1894.

Kaluza, M. Historische Grammatik der englischen Sprache. 2 vols. Berlin, 1900–1, 1906–7.

Bradley H. The Making of English. 1904.

—— Changes in the Language to the Days of Chaucer. [In CHEL. vol. I, ch. xix, pp. 379–406.]

Jesperson, O. Growth and Structure of the English Language. Leipzig, 1905, 1919.

Wyld, H. C. Historical Study of the Mother Tongue. 1906.

—— The Growth of English. 1907; 1910.

—— A Short History of English. 1913; 1927 (rev. edn).

Luick, K. Historische Grammatik der englischen Sprache. Pts I–IX, Leipzig, 1914–29.

Classen, E. Outlines of the History of the English Language. 1919.

Thomas, P. G. An Introduction to the History of the English Language. 1920.

Huchon, R. Histoire de la Langue anglaise. Vol. I (450–1066), Paris, 1923. Vol. II (1066–1475), Paris, 1930.

Horn, W. Die englische Sprachwissenschaft. [In Streitberg Festgabe, Leipzig, 1924, pp. 512–84.]

McKnight, G. H. and Emsley, B. Modern English in the Making. New York, 1928.

Baugh, A.C. History of the English Language. New York, 1935.

(3) MONOGRAPHS, ETC., ON SPECIAL POINTS, DEALING WITH MORE THAN ONE PERIOD

Luick, K. Quantitätsveränderungen im Laufe der englischen Sprachentwicklung. Ang. xx, 1898.

Wyld, H. C. Contributions to the History of the Guttural Sounds in English. Trans. Philolog. Soc. 1899–1902.

Horn, W. Beiträge zur Geschichte der englischen Gutturallaute. Berlin, 1901.

Ekwall, E. Zur Geschichte der stimmhaften interdentalen Spirans im Englischen. Lund, 1906.

Hackmann, W. G. Kürzung langer Tonvokale vor einfachen auslautenden Konsonanten in einsilbigen Wörtern im Alt-, Mittel- und Neuenglischen. SEP. x, 1908.

Roedler, E. Die Ausbreitung des s-Plurals im Englischen. Ang. XL, 1915–6.

Gevenich, O. Die englische Palatalisierung von k > č im Lichte der englischen Ortsnamen. SEP. LVII, 1918.

Holmqvist, E. On the History of the English Present Inflections, particularly -th and -s. Heidelberg, 1921.

B. DICTIONARIES
(1) GENERAL

A New English Dictionary on Historical Principles. Ed. Sir J.A.H. Murray, H. Bradley, Sir W. A. Craigie, C. T. Onions, Oxford, 1884–1928. [Corrected re-issue, with Introduction, Supplement and Bibliography, 13 vols. 1933.]

Holthausen, F. Etymologisches Wörterbuch der englischen Sprache. Leipzig, 1927 (2nd and rev. edn).

Craigie, Sir W. A. A Dictionary of the Older Scottish Tongue. Chicago, 1931–.

Wyld, H. C. The Universal Dictionary of the English Language. 1932.

Little, W., Fowler, H. W. and Coulson, J. The Shorter Oxford Dictionary. Ed. C. T. Onions, 2 vols. Oxford, 1933.

Webster's Dictionary. Ed. W. A. Neilson, Springfield, 1934 (2nd edn).

[See also M. M. Mathews, A Survey of English Dictionaries, Oxford, 1933.]

(2) OLD ENGLISH
(a) General

Grein, C. W. M. Sprachschatz der angelsächsischen Dichter. 2 vols. Cassel, 1861–4; ed. F. Holthausen and J. Köhler, Heidelberg, 1912–4.

Bosworth, J. An Anglo-Saxon Dictionary. Ed. T. N. Toller, 4 pts, Oxford, 1882–98. [Supplements, 1908, 1920.]

Hall, J. R. Clark. A Concise Anglo-Saxon Dictionary. Cambridge, 1895, 1916, 1931 (rev.).

Sweet, H. A Student's Dictionary of Anglo-Saxon. Oxford, 1897.

Napier, A. S. Contributions to Old English Lexicography. Trans. Philolog. Soc. 1906.

Holthausen, F. Altenglisches etymologisches Wörterbuch. Heidelberg, 1934.

(b) Glossaries, etc., of Individual Texts
[In alphabetical order of texts.]

Wyatt, A. J. and Johnson, H. H. A Glossary to Aelfric's Homilies. 1890.

Holder, A. Beowulf. Wortschatz mit sämtlichen Stellennachweisen. 12 pts, Germanischen Bücherschatz, 1896.

Cook, A. S. A Concordance to Beowulf. Halle, 1911.

Braasch, T. Vollständiges Wörterbuch zur sog. Caedmonschen Genesis. Anglistische Forschungen, LXXVI, 1933.

Simons, R. Cynewulf's Wortschatz. BBA. III, 1899.

Lindelöf, U. Wörterbuch zur Interlinearglosse des Rituale Ecclesiae Dunelmensis. BBA. IX. 1901.

Cook, A. S. A Glossary of the Old North-umbrian Gospels. Halle, 1894.

Schulte, E. Glossar zu Farman's Anteil an der Rushworth-Glosse (R^1). Bonn, 1904.

Lindelöf, U. Glossar zur altnorthumbrischen Evangelien-übersetzung in der Rushworth-Handschrift. Helsingfors, 1897.

Förster, M. Lexicalisches zum Vercelli-Codex cxvii. [In Morsbach Festschrift, Halle, 1913, pp. 148 ff.]

Zeuner, R. Wortschatz des sogenannten Kentischen Psalters [MS Vesp. A i]. A–cunnan. 2 pts, Gera, 1891–1910.

Wyld, H. C. and Thomas, P. G. A Glossary of the Mercian Hymns in MS Vespasian A i. Otia Merseiana, iv, 1904.

Grimm, C. Glossar zum Vespasian-Psalter und den Hymnen. Anglistische Forsch-ungen, xviii, 1906.

Harris, M. A. Glossary of the West Saxon Gospels. Boston, 1899.

Dodd, L. H. A Glossary of Wulfstan's Homi-lies. New York, 1908.

(3) MIDDLE ENGLISH

(a) General, and Individual Texts

Mayhew, A. L. and Skeat, W. W. A Concise Middle-English Dictionary. Oxford, 1888.

Stratmann, F. H. A Middle-English Dictionary. Ed. H. Bradley, Oxford, 1891.

Skeat, W. W. Glossarial Index to the Works of Geoffrey Chaucer. Oxford, 1899.

Tolkien, J. R. R. A Middle English Vocabu-lary. Oxford, 1922. [Glossary to K. Sisam, Fourteenth Century Verse and Prose.]

A Middle English Dictionary. Madison. [In preparation.]

(b) Glossaries, etc., compiled during Middle English Period

Anglo-Saxon and Old English Vocabularies. (11th to 15th cent.) Ed. T. Wright, rev. R. P. Wülcker, 2 vols. 1884.

Promptorium Parvulorum. English-Latin, 1440. Ed. E. L. Mayhew, EETS. Ex. Ser. 1908.

Catholicon Anglicum. English-Latin, 1483. Ed. S. J. Herrtage, Camden Soc. 1882.

(4) ENGLISH SINCE CHAUCER

Schmidt, A. Shakespeare-Lexicon. 3rd edn, rev. G. Sarrazin, Berlin, 1902.

Onions, C. T. A Shakespeare Glossary. Ox-ford, 1911.

Skeat, W. W. A Glossary of Tudor and Stuart Words. Ed. A. L. Mayhew, Oxford, 1914.

Kellner, L. Shakespeare-Wörterbuch. Leip-zig, 1922.

A Dictionary of Early Modern English. Madison. [In preparation.]

C. SYNTAX

(1) GENERAL

(a) General Works

Kellner, L. Historical Outlines of English Syntax. 1892.

Sweet, H. New English Grammar, Logical and Historical. Pt ii, Syntax. Oxford, 1899.

Einenkel, E. Geschichte der englischen Sprache: Syntax. [In PG. vol. i, pp. 1071-1151, 2nd edn, Strasburg, 1901; 3rd edn 1916.]

Onions, C. T. Advanced English Syntax. 1904.

Boedtker, A. T. Critical Contributions to Early English Syntax. 2 sers. Christiania, 1908–10.

(b) Monographs, etc., on Special Points, dealing with more than One Period

Jespersen, O. Studier over engelske Kasus. Copenhagen, 1891.

Einenkel, E. Das englische Indefinitum. Ang. xxvi; 1903, xxvii, 1904. [Also Halle, 1903–4.]

—— Die englische verbal Negation. Ang. xxxv, 1911–2.

—— Zur Geschichte des englischen Gerun-diums. Ang. xxxvii, 1913, xxxviii, 1914.

Curme, G. O. A History of the English Relative Constructions. JEGP. xi, 1912.

Kreickemeier, H. Die Wortstellung im Nebensatz des Englischen. Giessen, 1915.

Steadman, J. M. The Origin of the Historical Present in English. Stud. Phil. xiv, 1917.

Aronstein, P. Die periphrastische Form im Englischen. Ang. xlii, 1918–9.

Small, G. W. The Comparison of Inequality. Baltimore, 1924.

—— The Germanic Case of Comparison with a Special Study of English. Linguistic Soc. of America, 1929.

(2) OLD ENGLISH

(a) General

Chase, F. A Bibliographical Guide to Old English Syntax. Leipzig, 1896.

(b) Special Points

Lüttgens, C. Über Bedeutung und Gebrauch der Hülfsverben im frühen Altenglischen. Wismar, 1888.

Callaway, M. The Absolute Participle in Anglo-Saxon. Baltimore, 1889.

Callaway, M. Appositive Participle in Anglo-Saxon. PMLA. XVI, 1901.

—— The Infinitive in Anglo-Saxon. Washington, 1913.

—— The Temporal Subjunctive in Old English. Austin, 1931.

—— The Consecutive Subjunctive in Old English. Mod. Lang. Ass. of America, 1933.

Smith, C. A. The Order of Words in Anglo-Saxon. Baltimore, 1893.

Henshaw, A. The Syntax of the Indicative and Subjunctive Moods in the Anglo-Saxon Gospels. Leipzig, 1894.

Gorell, J. H. Indirect Discourse in Anglo-Saxon. Baltimore, 1895.

Barnouw, A. Textkritische Untersuchungen nach dem Gebrauch des bestimmten Artikels und des schwachen Adjektivs in der altenglischen Poesie. Leyden, 1902.

Shearin, H. The Expression of Purpose in Old English Prose. New York, 1903.

Shipley, G. The Genitive Case in Anglo-Saxon Poetry. Baltimore, 1903.

Henk, O. Die Frage in der altenglischen Dichtung. Kiel, 1904.

Adams, A. The Syntax of the Temporal Clause in Old English Prose. New York, 1907.

Benham, A. The Clause of Result in Old English Prose. Ang. XXXI, 1908.

Püttmann, A. Die Syntax der sogenannten progressiv Form im Alt- und Frühmittelenglischen. Ang. XXXI, 1908.

Riggert, G. Der syntaktische Gebrauch des Infinitivs in der altenglischen Poesie. Kiel, 1909.

Burnham, J. Concessive Constructions in Old English Prose. New York, 1911.

Sorg, W. Zur Syntax und Stilistik des Pronominalgebrauches in der älteren angelsächsischen Dichtung. Breslau, 1912.

Nadler, H. Studien zum attributiven Genitiv des Angelsächsischen. Berlin, 1916.

Hübener, G. Zur Erklärung der Wortstellungsentwicklung im Angelsächsischen. Ang. XXXIX, 1916.

Frary, L. G. Studies in the Syntax of the Old English Passive. Baltimore, 1930.

Glunz, H. Die Verwendung des Konjunktivs im Altenglischen. Leipzig, 1930.

Andrew, S. O. Some Principles of Old English Word-Order. Medium Aevum, III, 1934.

Behre, F. The Subjunctive in Old English Poetry. Gothenburg, 1934.

Süsskand, P. Geschichte des unbestimmten Artikels in Alt- und Frühmittelenglischen. SEP. LXXXV, 1935.

(c) Individual Authors and Texts

Wohlfahrt, T. Die Syntax des Verbums in Ælfric's Übersetzung des Heptateuch und des Buches Hiob. Munich, 1886.

Schrader, B. Studien zur Aelfricschen Syntax. Jena, 1887.

Kühn, P. T. Die Syntax des Verbums in Aelfrics Heiligenleben. Leipzig, 1889.

Ropers, K. Zur Syntax und Stilistik des Pronominalgebrauchs bei Aelfric. Kiel, 1918.

Bock, K. Die Syntax der Pronomina und Numeralia in König Alfred's Orosius. Göttingen, 1887.

Hüllweck, A. Über den Gebrauch des Artikels in den Werken Alfred's des Grossen. Dessau, 1887.

Haarstrick, A. Untersuchungen über die Präpositionen bei Alfred dem Grossen. Kiel, 1890.

Lehmann, A. Der syntaktische Gebrauch des Genitivs in Ælfred's Orosius. Leipzig, 1891.

Wülfing, E. Die Syntax in den Werken Alfreds des Grossen. 3 vols. Bonn, 1894–1901.

Rauert, M. Die Negation in den Werken Alfreds. Kiel, 1910.

Holtbür, F. Der syntaktische Gebrauch des Genitivs in Andreas, Guthlac, Phoenix, dem heiligen Kreuz und der Höllenfahrt. Ang. VI, 1883.

Reussner, H. Untersuchungen über die Syntax in dem angelsächsischen Gedicht vom heiligen Andreas. Leipzig, 1889.

Kube, E. Die Wortstellung in der Sachsenchronik. Jena, 1886. [Parker MS.]

Robertson, W. A. Tempus und Modus in der altenglischen Chronik. Marburg, 1906.

Lange, F. Darstellung der syntaktischen Erscheinungen im angelsächsischen Gedichte von Byrhtnoþ's Tod. Rostock, 1906.

Nader, E. Dativ und Instrumental im Beowulf. Vienna, 1883.

—— Tempus und Modus im Beowulf. Ang. X, 1887–8, XI, 1888–9.

Köhler, K. Der syntaktische Gebrauch des Infinitivs und Particips im Beowulf. Münster, 1886.

Schücking, L. L. Die Grundzüge der Satzverknüpfung im Beowulf. Pt I, Halle, 1904.

Ries, J. Die Wortstellung im Beowulf. Halle, 1907.

Schuchardt, R. Die Negation im Beowulf. Berlin, 1910.

Flamme, J. Syntax der Blickling Homilien. Bonn, 1884.

Hofer, O. Der syntaktische Gebrauch des Dativs und Instrumentals in den Cædmon beigelegten Dichtungen. Ang. VII, 1884.

Meyer, E. Darstellung der syntaktischen Erscheinungen in dem angelsächsischen Gedicht Crist und Satan. Rostock, 1898.

Schürmann, A. Darstellung der Syntax in Cynewulf's Elene. Münster, 1884.

Conradi, B. Darstellung der Syntax in Cynewulf's Gedicht Juliana. Leipzig, 1886.

Prollius, M. Über den syntaktischen Gebrauch des Conjunktivs in den Cynewulfschen Dichtungen Elene, Juliana und Crist. Marburg, 1888.

Rose, A. Darstellung der Syntax in Cynewulf's Crist. Leipzig, 1890.

Kopas, W. Die Grundzüge der Satzverknüpfung in Cynewulf's Schriften. Breslau, 1900.

Dethloff, R. Darstellung der Syntax im angelsächsischen Gedicht Daniel. Rostock, 1907.

Kempf, E. Darstellung der Syntax in der sogenannten Caedmonschen Exodus. Leipzig, 1888.

Seyfarth, H. Der syntaktische Gebrauch des Verbums in dem Caedmon beigelegten angelsächsischen Gedicht von der Genesis. Leipzig, 1891.

Halfter, O. Die Satzverknüpfung in der älteren Genesis. Kiel, 1915.

Furkert, M. Der syntaktische Gebrauch des Verbums in dem angelsächsischen Gedichte vom Heiligen Guthlac. Leipzig, 1889.

Foster, T. Judith. Studies in Metre, Language and Style. Strasburg, 1892.

Oldenburg, K. Untersuchungen über die Syntax in dem altenglischen Gedicht Judith. Rostock, 1907.

Bale, C. The Syntax of the Genitive Case in the Lindisfarne Gospels. Iowa City, 1907.

Callaway, M. Studies in the Syntax of the Lindisfarne Gospels. Stud. Phil. v. 1918.

Ahrens, J. Darstellung der Syntax im angelsächsischen Gedicht Phoenix. Rostock, 1904.

Madert, A. Die Sprache der altenglischen Rätsel des Exeterbuches. Marburg, 1900.

Schneider, R. Satzbau und Wortschatz der altenglischen Rätsel des Exeterbuches. Breslau, 1913.

Tilley, M. P. Zur Syntax Waerferths. Leipzig, 1903.

Timner, B. J. Studies in Bishop Waerferth's Translation of the Dialogues of Gregory the Great. Groningen, 1934.

Fraatz, P. Darstellung der syntaktischen Erscheinungen in den angelsächsischen Waldere-Bruchstücken. Rostock, 1908.

Jacobsen, R. Darstellung der syntaktischen Erscheinungen im angelsächsischen Gedicht vom Wanderer. Rostock, 1901.

Daniels, A. Kasus Syntax zu den Predigten Wulfstans. Leiden, 1904.

Mohrbutter, A. Darstellung der Syntax in den vier echten Predigten Wulfstans. Münster, 1885.

(3) MIDDLE ENGLISH

(a) General

Einenkel, E. Streifzüge durch die mittelenglische Syntax. Münster, 1887.

Nilsson, E. E. The Syntax of the Homilies and Homiletic Treatises of the XII and XIII Centuries edited by R. Morris. Lund, 1900.

Dubislav, G. Studien zur mittelenglischen Syntax. Ang. XL, 1915, XLIV, 1921, XLVI 1922.

(b) Special Points

Einenkel, E. Das persönliche Pronomen im Mittelenglischen. Neuphilologisches Centralblatt, III, 1889, pp. 5–14, 48–54, 82–6, 105–11.

—— Der Infinitiv im Mittelenglischen. Ang. XII, 1891.

Wichers, P. Über die Bildung der zusammengesetzten Zeiten der Vergangenheit im Frühmittelenglischen. Kiel, 1889.

Bearder, J. W. Über den Gebrauch der Präpositionen in der altschottischen Poesie. Halle, 1894.

Böhme, W. Die Temporalsätze in der Übergangszeit vom Angelsächsischen zum Altenglischen. Halle, 1903.

van der Gaaf, W. The Transition from the Impersonal to the Personal Construction in Middle English. Heidelberg, 1904.

Swane, W. Studien zur Casussyntax des Frühmittelenglischen. Kiel, 1904.

Rossman, B. Zum Gebrauch der Modi und Modalverbe in Adverbialsätzen im Frühmittelenglischen. Kiel, 1909.

Janus, R. Der syntaktische Gebrauch des Numerus im Frühmittelenglischen. Kiel, 1913.

Sanders, H. Der syntaktische Gebrauch des Infinitivs im Frühmittelenglischen. Kiel, 1915.

Zilling, O. Das Hilfsverb do im Mittelenglischen. Giessen, 1921.

Gebhardt, L. Das unausgedrückte Subjekt im Mittelenglischen. Giessen, 1922.

(c) Individual Authors and Texts

[In alphabetical order.]

Koziol, H. Grundzüge der Syntax der mittelenglischen Stabreimdichtungen. Wiener Beiträge, LVIII, 1932.

Dahlstedt, A. The Word-Order of the Ancren Riwle. Sundsvall, 1903.

Dieth, E. Flexivisches und Syntaktisches über das Pronomen in der Ancren Riwle. Zürich, 1919.

Kolkwitz, M. Das Satzgefüge in Barbour's Bruce und Henry's Wallace. Halle, 1893.

Schrader, A. Das altenglische Relativpronomen mit besonderer Berücksichtigung der Sprache Chaucers. Kiel, 1880.

Graef, A. Das Perfectum bei Chaucer. Kiel, 1888.

—— Die präsentischen Tempora bei Chaucer. Ang. XII, 1889.

—— Das Futurum bei Chaucer. Flensburg, 1893.

Kent, C. W. On the Use of the Negative by Chaucer. PMLA. V. 1890.

Wilson, L. R. Chaucer's Relative Constructions. Stud. Phil. I, 1906.

Kenyon, J. S. Syntax of the Infinitive in Chaucer. Chaucer Soc. 1909.

Eitle, H. Die Satzverknüpfung bei Chaucer. Heidelberg, 1914.

—— Die Unterordnung der Sätze bei Chaucer. Heidelberg, 1914.

Heuer, H. Studien zur syntaktischen und stilistischen Funktion des Adverbs bei Chaucer und im Rosenroman. Anglistische Forschungen, LXXV, 1932.

Eichhorn, E. Das Partizipium bei Gower im Vergleich mit Chaucer's Gebrauch. Kiel, 1912.

Wolff, A. K. Zur Syntax des Verbums im altenglischen Lay of Havelok the Dane. Leipzig, 1909.

Azzalino, W. Die Wortstellung im King Horn. Halle, 1915.

Funke, O. Kasus-Syntax bei Orm und Laȝamon. Munich, 1907.

Lichtsinn, P. Der syntaktische Gebrauch des Infinitivs in Laȝamon's Brut. Kiel, 1913.

Courmont, A. Studies in Lydgate's Syntax in the Temple of Glass. Paris, 1912.

Hüttmann, E. Das Partizipium präsentis bei Lydgate im Vergleich mit Chaucer's Gebrauch. Kiel, 1914.

Juhl, H. Der syntaktische Gebrauch des Infinitivs bei John Lydgate. Kiel, 1921.

Buchtenkirch, E. Der syntaktische Gebrauch des Infinitivs in Occleve's De Regimine Principum. Jena, 1889.

Weyel, F. Der syntaktische Gebrauch des Infinitivs im Ormulum. Meiderich, 1896.

Zenke, W. Synthesis und Analysis des Verbums im Ormmulum. Halle, 1910.

Laeseke, B. Ein Beitrag zur Stellung des Verbums in Ormulum. Kiel, 1917.

Weinmann, P. Über den Gebrauch des Artikels im Ormmulum. Kiel, 1920.

Ebisch, F. W. Zur Syntax des Verbums im altenglischen Gedicht Eule und Nachtigall. Leipzig, 1905.

Breier, W. Synthesis und Analysis des Konjunktivs im Owl and Nightingale. SEP. L, 1913.

Zickner, B. Syntax und Stil in Reginald Pecock's Repressor. Greifswald, 1900.

Rothstein, E. Die Wortstellung in der Peterborough Chronicle. Halle, 1922.

Wandschneider, W. Zur Syntax des Verbs in Langley's Vision. Kiel, 1887.

Henningsen, H. Über die Wortstellung in den Prosaschriften Richard Rolles of Hampole. Erlangen, 1911.

Pitschel, E. H. Zur Syntax des mittelenglischen Gedichtes William of Palerne. Marburg, 1890.

Smith, H. Syntax der Wycliffe-Purveyschen Übersetzung. Ang. XXX, 1907.

Thamm, W. Das Relativpronomen in der Bibelübersetzung Wyclifs und Purveys. Berlin, 1908.

(4) Modern English

(a) General

Franz, W. Zur Syntax des älteren Neuenglisch. E. Studien, XVII, 1892, XVIII, 1893, XX, 1895.

Jespersen, O. A Modern English Grammar on Historical Principles. I, Sounds and Spellings; II, Syntax. Heidelberg, 1909–31.

—— The Essentials of English Grammar. 1933.

Poutsma, H. A. A Grammar of Late Modern English. 5 vols. Groningen, 1914–26.

Kruisinga, E. A. A Handbook of Present-Day English. Pt 2 (English Accidence and Syntax), 3 vols. Groningen, 1931–2 (5th and rev. edn).

Kurath, H. and Curme, G. O. A Grammar of the English Language. Vol. III (Syntax) by G. O. Curme. Boston, 1931.

(b) Special Points

Kellner, L. Zur Syntax des englischen Verbums, mit besonderer Berücksichtigung Shakespeare's. Vienna, 1885.

Ross, C. H. The Absolute Participle in Middle and Modern English. PMLA. VIII, 1893.

Spies, H. Studien zur Geschichte des englischen Pronomens im XV und XVI Jahrhundert. (Flexionslehre und Syntax.) SEP. I, 1897.

Knecht, J. Die Kongruenz zwischen Subjekt und Prädikat und die 3. Person pluralis praesentis auf -s im Elisabethanischen Englisch. Anglistische Forschungen, XXXIII, 1911.

Fries, C. C. The Rules of Common School Grammars [1586–1825]. PMLA. XLII, 1927.
Trnka, B. On the Syntax of the English Verb from Caxton to Dryden. Prague, 1930.

(c) Individual Authors
[In alphabetical order.]

Rohs, A. Syntaktische Untersuchungen zu Bacon's Essays. Marburg, 1889.
Klausmann, G. Formenlehre und Syntax des Verbums in der Froissart-Übersetzung von Lord Berners. Greifswald, 1919.
de Reul, P. The Language of Caxton's Reynard the Fox. Ghent, 1901.
Kellner, L. Caxton's Syntax and Style. EETS. Ex. Ser. 1890.
Baldwin, C. The Inflections and Syntax of the Morte d'Arthur of Sir Thomas Malory. Boston, 1894.
Dekker, A. Some Facts concerning the Syntax of Malory's Morte Darthur. Amsterdam, 1932.
Harz, H. Die Umschreibung mit *do* in Shakespeare's Prosa. Neue anglistischen Arbeiten, II, 1918.
[See also Kellner, 1885, p. 29 above.]

D. VOCABULARY, WORD-FORMATION, ETC.

(1) GENERAL
(a) General Works
A New English Dictionary. [See p. 25 above.]
Skeat, W. W. Principles of English Etymology. Ser. 1, Oxford, 1887, 1892.
—— Notes on English Etymology. Oxford, 1901.
Greenough, J. B. and Kittredge, G. L. Words and their Ways in English Speech. New York, 1901.
Smith, Logan P. The English Language. 1912.
—— Words and Idioms in the English Language. 1925.
McKnight, G. H. English Words and their Background. New York, 1923.
Aronstein, P. Englische Wortkunde. Leipzig, 1925.
Barfield, O. History in English Words. 1926.
Weekley, E. Words Ancient and Modern. 2 sers. 1926–7.
—— Words and Names. 1932.
—— Something about Words. 1935.
Groom, B. A Short History of English Words. 1934.

[Some of the General Histories given under A (1) contain chapters on Vocabulary.]

(b) Special Points
Fijn van Draat, P. The Loss of the Prefix *ge-* in the English Verb. E. Studien, XXXI, 1902, XXXII, 1903, XXXVI, 1906.
Hemken, E. Das Aussterben alter Substantiva im Verlaufe der englischen Sprachgeschichte. Kiel, 1906.
Oberdörffer, W. Aussterben altenglischer Adjectiva und ihr Ersatz im Verlaufe der englischen Sprachgeschichte. Kiel, 1908.
Offe, J. R. W. Aussterben alter Verba und ihr Ersatz im Verlaufe der englischen Sprachgeschichte. Kiel, 1908.
Efvergren, C. Names of Places in a Transferred Sense in English. Lund, 1909.
Rotzoll, E. Das Aussterben alt- und mittelenglischer Deminutivbildungen im Neuenglischen. Heidelberg, 1909.
Weick, F. Das Aussterben des Präfixes *ge-* im Englischen. Darmstadt, 1911.
Teichert, J. F. Über das Aussterben alter Wörter im Verlaufe der englischen Sprachgeschichte. Erlangen, 1912.
Bengtsson, E. Studies on Passive Nouns with a Concrete Sense in English. Lund, 1927.
Schreuder, H. Pejorative Sense Development in English. Groningen, 1929.
Jaeschke, K. Beiträge zur Frage des Wortschwundes im Englischen. Breslau, 1931.
Stern, G. Meaning and Change of Meaning. With Special Reference to the English Language. Gotenburg, 1932.

(2) OLD ENGLISH
(a) General
Bode, W. Die Kenningar in der angelsächsischen Dichtung. Strasburg, 1886.
Stevenson, W. H. Some Old English Words omitted or imperfectly explained in Dictionaries. Trans. Philolog. Soc. 1895.
Swaen, A. E. H. Contributions to Anglo-Saxon Lexicography. E. Studien, XXVI, XXXII, XXXIII, XXXV, XXXVII, XXXVIII, XL, XLIII, XLIX, LIII, LIV, 1899–1920.
Jordan, R. Eigentümlichkeit des anglischen Wortschatzes. Anglistische Forschungen, XVII, 1906.
Förster, M. Beiträge zur altenglischen Wortkunde aus ungedruckten volkskundlichen Texten. E. Studien, XXXIX, 1908.
Rankin, J. W. A Study of the Kennings in Anglo-Saxon Poetry. JEGP. VIII, 1909, IX, 1910.
Schlutter, O. B. Weitere Beiträge zur altenglischen Wortforschung. Ang. XXXVII, XXXVIII, XXXIX, XL, XLII, XLIII, XLIV, XLV, XLVI, 1913–22.
Schücking, L. L. Untersuchungen zur Bedeutungslehre der angelsächsischen Dichtersprache. Germanische Bibliothek, pt ii, vol. XI, 1915.

Keiser, A. The Influence of Christianity on the Vocabulary of Old English Poetry. Urbana, 1919.

Grundy, G. B. On the Meanings of certain Terms in the Anglo-Saxon Charters. E. & S. VIII, 1922.

Wyld, H. C. Diction and Imagery in Anglo-Saxon Poetry. E. & S. XI, 1925.

(b) Special Points

(i) Word-formation

Harrison, T. P. The Separable Prefixes in Anglo-Saxon. Baltimore, 1892.

Thiele, O. Die konsonantischen Suffixe der Abstrakta des Altenglischen. Darmstadt, 1902.

Krackov, O. Die Nominalcomposita als Kunstmittel im altenglischen Epos. Berlin, 1903.

Schön, E. Die Bildung des Adjektivs im Altenglischen. Kiel, 1905.

Schuldt, C. Die Bildung der schwachen Verba im Altenglischen. Kiel, 1905.

Nicolai, O. Die Bildung des Adverbs im Altenglischen. Kiel, 1907.

Both, M. Die konsonantischen Suffixe altenglischer Konkreta und Kollektiva. Kiel, 1909.

Kärre, K. Nomina Agentis in Old English. Upsala, 1915.

(ii) Special Classes of Words

Hoops, J. Über die altenglischen Pflanzennamen. Freiburg, 1889.

Whitman, C. H. The Birds of Old English Literature. JEGP. II, 1898.

—— The Old English Mammal Names. JEGP. VI, 1906.

—— The Old English Animal Names. Ang. XXX, 1907.

Jordan, R. Die altenglischen Säugetiernamen. Heidelberg, 1902.

Willms, J. E. Gebrauch der Farbenbezeichnungen in der Poesie Altenglands. Münster, 1902.

Ströbe, L. L. Die altenglischen Kleidernamen. Leipzig, 1904.

Cortelyou, J. Die altenglischen Namen der Insekten, Spinnen- und Krustentiere. Heidelberg, 1906.

Keller, M. L. The Anglo-Saxon Weapon Names. Anglistische Forschungen, XV, 1906.

Garrett, R. M. Precious Stones in Old English Literature. Leipzig, 1908.

Klump, W. Die altenglischen Handwerkernamen. Anglistische Forschungen, XXIV, 1908.

Schnepper, H. Die Namen der Schiffe und Schiffsteile. Kiel, 1908.

Fehr, B. Sprache des Handels in Altengland. St Gallen, 1909.

Graf, L. Landwirtschaftliches im altenglischen Wortschatze. Breslau, 1909.

Jacobs, H. Die Namen der profanen Wohn- und Wirtschaftsgebäude und Gebäudeteile im Altenglischen. Kiel, 1911.

Thoene, F. Die Namen der menschlichen Körperteile bei den Angelsachsen. Kiel, 1912.

Hansen, A. Angelsächsische Schmucksachen und ihre Bezeichnungen. Kiel, 1913.

Matzerath, J. Die altenglischen Namen der Geldwerte, Masse und Gewichte. Bonn, 1913.

Wolf, A. Die altenglischen Fischnamen. Breslau, 1919.

Jente, R. Die mythologischen Ausdrücke im altenglischen Wortschatz. Anglistische Forschungen, LVI, 1921.

Szogs, A. Die Ausdrücke für 'Arbeit' und 'Beruf' in Altenglischen. Anglistische Forschungen, LXXIII, 1931.

Mincoff, M. K. Die Bedeutungsentwicklung der angelsächsischen Ausdrücke für 'Kraft' und 'Macht.' Palaestra, CLXXXVIII, 1933.

Weman, B. Old English Semantic Analysis and Theory with Special Reference to Verbs denoting Locomotion. Lund, 1933.

Bäck, H. The Synonyms for 'child,' 'boy,' 'girl' in Old English. An Etymological-Semasiological Investigation. Lund, 1934.

(c) Vocabulary of Individual Authors and Texts

[In alphabetical order.]

Meissner, P. Studien zum Wortschatz Aelfrics. Archiv, CLXVI, 1934–5.

Schemann, K. Die Synonyma im Beowulfsliede. Münster, 1882.

Banning, A. Die epischen Formeln in Bēowulf. Marburg, 1886.

Sonnefeld, G. Stilistisches und Wortschatz im Beowulf. Strasburg, 1893.

Kistenmacher, R. Die wörtlichen Wiederholungen im Beowulf. Greifswald, 1898.

Scheinert, M. Die Adjektiva im Beowulfepos als Darstellungsmittel. PBB. XXX, 1905.

Ziegler, H. Der poetische Sprachgebrauch in den sogenannten Cædmonschen Dichtungen. Münster, 1883.

Jansen, G. Beiträge zur Synonymik und Poetik der Dichtungen Cynewulf's. Münster, 1883.

Simons, R. Cynewulf's Wortschatz. BBA. III, 1899.

Geisel, I. Sprache und Wortschatz der altenglischen Guthlac-Übersetzung. (Prose.) Basle, 1915.

Hüttenbrenner, F. Probe eines metrischen Wörterbuch für das Altenglische. (Phoenix.) E. Studien, LVI, 1922.

Schlutter, O. B. Zum Wortschatz des Regius und Eadwine Psalters. E. Studien, XXXVIII, 1907.

Herzfeld, G. Die Räthsel des Exeterbuches. Berlin, 1890.

Schneider, R. Satzbau und Wortschatz der altenglischen Rätsel des Exeterbuches. Breslau, 1913.

Förster, M. Lexikalisches zum Vercelli-Codex. SEP. L, 1913.

(3) MIDDLE ENGLISH

(a) General

Hein, J. Über die bildliche Verneinung in der mittelenglischen Poesie. Ang. XV, 1892–3.

Mendenhall, J. C. Aureate Terms; a Study in the Literary Diction of the 15th Century. Philadelphia, 1917.

(b) Special Points

(i) Word-formation

Höge, O. Die Deminutivbildungen im Mittelenglischen. Heidelberg, 1906.

Booker, J. M. The French 'Inchoative' Suffix -ss and the French -ir Conjugation in Middle English. Stud. Phil. IX, 1912.

Jessen, T. Über die Bildung des Adverbs im Mittelenglischen. Kiel, 1922.

(ii) Special Classes of Words

Earle, J. English Plant-names from the 10th to the 15th Century. Oxford, 1880.

Voltmer, B. Die mittelenglische Terminologie der ritterlichen Verwandtschafts- und Standesverhältnisse nach den höfischen Epen und Romanzen des 13. und 14. Jahrhunderts. Kiel, 1911.

Döll, H. Mittelenglische Kleidernamen im Spiegel literarischer Denkmäler des 14. Jahrhunderts. Giessen, 1932.

Krebs, K. Der Bedeutungswandel von mittelenglischem "clerk" und damit zusammenhängende Probleme. Bonner Studien, XXI, 1933.

Steinki, J. Die Entwicklung der englischen Relativ-pronomina in spätmittelenglischer und frühneuenglischer Zeit. Ohlau, 1933.

Fettig, A. Die Gradadverbien im Mittelenglischen. Anglistische Forschungen, LXXIX, 1934.

(c) Individual Authors and Texts

[In alphabetical order.]

Zeise, R. Wortschatz der Ancren Riwle. Jena, 1823.

Wallenberg, J. K. The Vocabulary of Dan Michel's Ayenbite of Inwyt. Upsala 1923.

Kennedy, A. G. On the Substantivation of Adjectives in Chaucer. Lincoln, Nebraska 1905.

von Gross, E. Bildung des Adverbs bei Chaucer. Berlin, 1921.

Barth, C. Der Wortschatz des Cursor Mundi. Königsberg, 1903.

Tiete, G. Zu Gower's Confessio Amantis: Lexicalisches. Breslau, 1889.

Tatlock, J. S. P. Epic Formulas, especially in Laʒamon. PMLA. XXXVIII, 1923.

Wülfing, J. E. Das Bild und die bildliche Verneinung im Laud-Troy-Book. Ang. XXVII, 1904, XXVIII, 1905.

Fife, R. H. Der Wortschatz des englischen Maundeville nach der Version des Cotton-Ms. Titus C. XVI. Leipzig, 1902.

Dobson, M. The Vocabulary of the A-Text of Piers the Plowman. Ang. XXXIII, 1910.

Schneider, J. P. The Prose Style of Richard Rolle of Hampole. Baltimore, 1906.

Kullnick, M. Studien über den Wortschatz in Sir Gawayne. Berlin, 1902.

Schmittbetz, K. Das Adjektiv in Sir Gawayn and the Grene Knyʒt. Ang. XXXII, 1909.

[Further studies will also generally be found below under the respective writers or works.]

(4) MODERN ENGLISH

(a) General

Gerloff, W. Über die Veränderungen im Wortgebrauch in den englischen Bibelübersetzungen der Hexapla (1388–1611). Berlin, 1902.

Reuning, K. Das Altertümliche im Wortschatz der Spenser Nachahmungen. Strasburg, 1912.

Platt, J. The Development of English Colloquial Idiom during the Eighteenth Century. RES. II, 1926.

Funke, O. Englische Sprachphilosophie im späteren 18. Jahrhundert. Berne, 1934.

(b) Special Points

(i) Word-formation

Gerber, E. Die Substantivierung des Adjektivs im 15. und 16. Jahrhundert. Göttingen, 1895.

(ii) Special Classes of Words

Fehr, B. Beiträge zur Sprache des Handels in England im 16. und 17. Jahrhundert. E. Studien, XLII, 1910.

Matthews, W. London Slang at the Beginning of the XVIII Century. N. & Q. 15, 22, 29 June 1935.

(c) Individual Authors and Texts

[In alphabetical order.]

Fromm, C. Über den verbalen Wortschatz in Sir Thomas Malory's Roman Le Morte Darthur. Marburg, 1914.

Vogt, R. Das Adjektiv bei Christopher Marlowe. Berlin, 1908.

Lockwood, L. E. Lexicon to the English Poetical Works of John Milton. 1907.

Ekwall, E. Shakespeare's Vocabulary, its Etymological Elements. Lundström, 1908.

Franz, W. Die Wortbildung bei Shakespeare. E. Studien, xxxv, 1905.

Morsbach, L. Shakespeare und der Euphuismus. Göttingen, 1908.

Draper, J. W. The Glosses to Spenser's Shepheardes Calendar. JEGP. xviii, 1919.

Padelford, F. M. and Maxwell, W. C. Compound Words in Spenser's Poetry. JEGP. xxv, 1926.

(5) Loan-Words

(a) General

Pogatscher, A. Zur Lautlehre der griechischen, lateinischen und romanischen Lehnwörter im Altenglischen. QF. lxiv, 1888.

Skeat, W. W. Principles of English Etymology. Second Series. The Foreign Element. Oxford, 1891.

MacGillivray, H. S. The Influence of Christianity on the Vocabulary of Old English. Halle, 1902.

erjeantson, M. S. A History of Foreign Words in English. 1935.

(b) Celtic

Schlutter, O. B. Altenglische Entlehnung aus dem Keltischen. Ang. xxxvi, 1912.

Förster, M. Keltisches Wortgut im Englischen. Halle, 1921.

—— Englisch-Keltisches. E. Studien, lvi, 1922.

(c) Dutch

Toll, J. M. Niederländisches Lehngut im Mittelenglischen. SEP. lxix, 1925.

Bense, J. F. A Dictionary of the Low-Dutch Element in the English Vocabulary. Hague, 1926–.

Logeman, H. Low-Dutch Elements in English. Neophilologus, xvi, 1930.

Clark, G. N. The Dutch Influence on the English Vocabulary. SPE. Tract, 1935.

(d) French

Behrens, D. Französische Elemente im Englischen. [In PG. vol. i^2, pp. 950–88, Strasburg, 1896.]

Sykes, F. H. French Elements in Middle English. Oxford, 1899.

Vising, J. Franska Spraket in England. Gotenburg, 1902.

Hoevelmann, K. Zum Konsonantismus der altfranzösischen Lehnwörter in der mittelenglischen Dichtung des 14. und 15. Jahrhunderts. Kiel, 1903.

Remus, H. Die kirchlichen und speziellwissenschaftlichen romanischen Lehnworte Chaucers. SEP. xiv, 1906.

Faltenbacher, H. Die romanischen, speziell französischen und lateinischen Lehnwörter bei Caxton. Munich, 1907.

Mettig, R. Das französische Element im Alt- und Mittelenglischen. E. Studien, xli, 1909–10.

Reismüller, G. Romanische Lehnwörter bei Lydgate. Leipzig, 1911.

Noejd, R. The Vocalism of Romanic Words in Chaucer. Upsala, 1919.

Funke, O. Zur Wortgeschichte der französischen Elemente im Englischen. E. Studien, lv, 1921.

Luick, K. Über die Betonung der französischen Lehnwörter im Mittelenglischen. Germanisch-romanische Monatsschrift, ix, 1921.

Kroll, A. Die französischen Lehn- und Fremdwörter in der englischen Sprache der Restaurationszeit. Breslau, 1933.

Feist, R. Studien zur Rezeption des französischen Wortschatzes im Mittelenglischen. Leipzig, 1934.

(e) Latin

Dellit, O. Über lateinische Elemente im Mittelenglischen. Marburg, 1905.

Luick, K. Zu den lateinischen Lehnwörtern im Altenglischen. Archiv, cxxvi, 1911.

Funke, O. Die gelehrten lateinischen Lehn- und Fremdwörter in der altenglischen Literatur. Halle, 1914.

(f) Scandinavian

Brate, E. Nordische Lehnwörter im Ormulum. Halle, 1884.

Sarrazin, G. Altnordisches im Beowulfliede. PBB. xi, 1886.

Wall, A. A Contribution towards the Study of the Scandinavian Element in the English Dialects. Ang. xx, 1897–8.

Björkman, E. Scandinavian Loan-Words in Middle English. 2 vols. SEP. vii, xi, 1900.

(g) Other Languages

Taylor, Walt. Arabic Words in English. SPE. Tract, 1933.

3

Carr, C. T. The German Influence on the English Vocabulary. SPE. Tract, 1934.
Praz, M. The Italian Element in English. E. & S. xv, 1929.
Dayrush, A. A. Persian Words in English. SPE. Tract, 1934. [Includes R. C. Goffin, Some Notes on Indian English.]

E. OLD ENGLISH PHONOLOGY AND GRAMMAR

(1) TEXT-BOOKS, MONOGRAPHS, ETC.

(a) General

Sievers, E. Angelsächsische Grammatik. Halle, 1882, 1898.
—— An Old English Grammar. Tr. A. S. Cook, Boston, 1885, 1903.
Bright, J. W. An Outline of Anglo-Saxon Grammar. 1895; 1901.
Dieter, F. Laut- und Formenlehre der altgermanischen Dialekte: Altenglisch. Leipzig, 1898–1900. [Pt i, chs. 4, 10; pt ii, chs. 16, 22.]
Bülbring, K. D. Altenglisches Elementarbuch. (Lautlehre.) Heidelberg, 1902.
Wright, J. and E. M. An Old English Grammar. Oxford, 1908, 1925.
Wardale, E. E. An Old English Grammar. 1922; 1926.

(b) (i) Special Points

Lichtenheld, A. Das schwache Adjektiv im Angelsächsischen. ZDA. xvi, 1873.
Lindelöf, U. Über die Verbreitung des sogenannten u- (o-) Umlauts in der starken Verbalflexion des Altenglischen. Archiv, LXXXIX, 1892.
Pogatscher, A. Über die Chronologie des altenglischen i-Umlauts. PBB. xviii, 1894.
Bülbring, K. D. Altenglischen Palatalumlaut vor ht, hs, hþ. Ang. Bbl. x, 1899.
Sievers, E. Zum angelsächsischen Vokalismus. Leipzig, 1900.
Wyld, H. C. West Germanic a in Old English. Otia Merseiana, iv, 1904.
Weyhe, H. Zur Synkope nach kurzer Tonsilbe im Altenglischen. PBB. xxx, 1905, xxxi, 1906.
Richter, C. Chronologische Studien zur angelsächsischen Literatur auf Grund sprachlichmetrischer Kriterien. SEP. xxxiii, 1910.
Kügler, H. Ie und seine Parallelformen im Angelsächsischen. Berlin, 1916.
Borowski, B. Zum Nebenakzent beim altenglischen Nominalkompositum. Halle, 1921.
—— Lautdubletten im Altenglischen. Halle, 1924.
Weber, G. Suffixvocal nach kurzer Tonsilbe von r, n, m im Angelsächsischen. Palaestra, CLVI, Leipzig, 1927.

Flasdieck, H. M. Miszellen zur altenglischer Grammatik: I. Zur relativen Chronologie des Velarumlauts im Westmittelland. Ang. XLI, 1930.
—— Untersuchungen über die germanischen schwachen Verben III. Klasse. Ang. LIX 1935; Halle, 1935.
Gericke, B. and Greul, W. Das Personalpronomen der 3. Person in spätangelsächsischen und frühmittelenglischen Texten Ein Beitrag zur altenglischen Dialektgeographie. Palaestra, CXCIII, 1934.
Förster, M. Zur i-Epenthese im Altenglischen Ang. LIX, 1935.

(ii) Special Periods

Dieter, F. Über Sprache und Mundart de ältesten englischen Denkmäler. Göttingen 1885.
Chadwick, H. M. Studies in Old English Trans. Cambridge Philolog. Soc. iv, 1899.
Weightman, J. The Language and Dialect o the later Old English Poetry. Liverpool 1907.
Schlemilch, W. Beiträge zur Sprache spätaltenglischer Denkmäler. Halle, 1914.

(c) O.E. Dialects

Cosijn, P. J. Altwestsächsische Grammatik 2 vols. Hague, 1883–8.
Lindelöf, U. Beiträge zur Kenntnis des Altnorthumbrischen. Helsingfors, 1893.
Wolff, R. Untersuchung der Laute in der kentischen Urkunden. Heidelberg, 1893.
Wyatt, A. J. An Elementary Old English Grammar (Early West Saxon). Cambridge 1897.
Weightman, J. Vowel-levelling in Early Kentish and the Use of the Symbol ę in Old English Charters. E. Studien, xxxv 1905.
Bryan, W. F. Studies in the Dialects of the Kentish Charters of the Old English Period Menasha, Wisconsin, 1915.

(d) O.E. Texts

[In alphabetical order.]

Braunschweiger, M. Flexion des Verbums in Ælfric's Grammar. Marburg, 1890.
Brühl, C. Die Flexion des Verbums in Ælfric' Heptateuch und Buch Hiob. Marburg,1892
Brüll, H. Die altenglische Lateingrammatik des Ælfric. Berlin, 1904.
Wilkes, J. Lautlehre zu Ælfric's Heptateuch und Buch Hiob. BBA. xxi, 1905.
Schüller, O. Lautlehre von Ælfric's 'Lives o Saints'. Bonn, 1908.
Glaeser, K. Lautlehre der Aelfricschen Homilien in der Hs. Cotton Vespasianus D xiv. Leipzig, 1916.

Göhler, T. Lautlehre der altenglischen Hexameron-Homilie des Abtes Aelfric. Weida, 1933.
[See also Cosijn, 1883–8, p. 34 above.]
Hulme, W. H. Die Sprache der altenglischen Bearbeitung der Soliloquien Augustin's. Freiburg, 1894.
Deutschbein, M. Dialektisches in der angelsächsischen Übersetzung von Bedas Kirchengeschichte. PBB. XXVI, 1901.
Krawutschke, A. Die Sprache der Boethius-Uebersetzung des K. Alfred. Berlin, 1902.
Eger, O. Dialektisches in den Flexionsverhältnissen der angelsächsischen Bedaübersetzung. Leipzig, 1910.
Bauer, H. Über die Sprache und Mundart der altenglischen Dichtungen Andreas, Guðlac, Phoenix, Hl. Kreuz und Höllenfahrt Christi. Marburg, 1890.
Cosijn, P. J. De oudste westsaksische Chroniek [Parker MS]. Taalkundige Bijdragen, II, Haarlem, 1879.
Flohrschütz, A. Die Sprache der Handschrift D der angelsächsischen Annalen im MS. Cotton Tib. B. IV. Jena, 1909.
Märkisch, R. Die altenglische Bearbeitung der Erzählung von Apollonius von Tyrus. Palaestra, VI, 1899.
Hermanns, W. Lautlehre und dialektische Untersuchung der altenglischen Interlinearversion der Benediktinerregel. Bonn, 1906.
Rohr, G. Die Sprache der altenglischen Prosabearbeitungen der Benediktiner Regel. Bonn, 1912.
Davidson, C. The Phonology of the Stressed Vowels in Beowulf. PMLA. VII, 1892.
Thomas, P. G. Dialect in Beowulf. MLR. I, 1905–6.
Morsbach, L. Zur Datierung des Beowulfepos. Göttingen, 1906.
Hardy, A. K. Die Sprache der Blickling Homilien. Leipzig, 1899.
Groschopp, C. Das angelsächsische Gedicht Crist und Satan. Ang. VI, 1883.
Leiding, H. Die Sprache der Cynewulfschen Dichtungen Crist, Juliana und Elene. Göttingen, 1888.
Lindelöf, U. Die Sprache des Rituals von Durham. Helsingfors, 1890.
Benno, H. Die Sprache der altenglischen Glosse zu Eadwines Canterbury Psalter. Würzburg, 1903.
Hein, B. Sprache von Eadwine Psalter. Würzburg, 1903.
Williams, O. T. The Dialect of the Text of the Northumbrian Genealogies. MLR. IV, 1909.
Kamp, A. Die Sprache der altenglischen Genesis. Münster, 1913.

Kolkwitz, M. Zum Erfurter Glossar. Ang. XVII, 1894–5.
Chadwick, H. M. Studies in Old English. Cambridge, 1899.
Sauer, P. R. Zur Sprache des Leidener Glossars cod. Voss. lat. 4o, 69. Munich, 1917.
Lefèvre, P. Das altenglische Gedicht vom heiligen Guthlac. Ang. VI, 1883.
Boll, P. Die Sprache der altenglischen Glossen in MS Harley 3376. Bonn, 1904.
Brenner, E. Die Glosse des altenglischen Juniuspsalters. Anglistische Forschungen, XXIII, 1908.
Williams, I. F. The Significance of the Symbol ꞓ in the Kentish Glosses. Otia Merseiana, IV, 1904.
—— Grammatical Investigation of the Old Kentish Glosses. BBA. XIX, 1906.
Müller, R. Über die Namen des Liber Vitae. Palaestra, IX, 1901.
Lea, E. M. The Language of the Northumbrian Gloss to the Gospel of St. Mark. Ang. XVI, 1893–4.
Füchsel, H. Die Sprache der northumbrischen Interlinearversion zum Johannes-Evangelium. Ang. XXIV, 1901.
Foley, E. H. The Language of the Northumbrian Gloss to Matthew. New York, 1903.
Kellum, M. D. The Language of the Northumbrian Gloss to St. Luke. New York, 1906.
Carpenter, H. C. A. Die Deklination in der northumbrischen Evangelienübersetzung der Lindisfarner Handschrift. Bonn, 1910.
Kolbe, Th. Die Konjugation der Lindisfarner Evangelien. Bonn, 1912.
Madert, A. Die Sprache der altenglischen Rätsel des Exeterbuches. Marburg, 1900.
Trautmann, M. Sprache und Versbau der altenglischen Rätsel. Ang. XXXVIII, 1914.
Zupitza, J. Mercisches aus der Hs. Royal 2 A 20 im Britischen Museum. ZDA. XXXIII, 1889.
Otten, G. The Language of the Rushworth Gloss to the Gospel of St. Matthew. Leipzig, 1890.
Brown, E. M. Die Sprache der Rushworth-Glossen zum Evangelium Matthäus. 2 pts, Göttingen, 1891–2.
Lindeloef, U. Die südnorthumbrische Mundart des zehnten Jahrhunderts. BBA. X, 1901.
Zeuner, R. Die Sprache des Kentischen Psalters (Vespasian A 1). Halle, 1881.
Bülbring, K. D. E and æ in the Vespasian Psalter. [In Furnivall Miscellany, Oxford, 1901.]
Hecht, H. Die Sprache der altenglischen Dialoge Gregors. Berlin, 1900.

3-2

Trilsbach, G. Die Lautlehre der spätwest-
sächsischen Evangelien. Bonn, 1905.
Dunkhase, H. Die Sprache der Wulfstanschen
Homilien. Jena, 1906.

(2) OLD ENGLISH TEXTS

(a) Readers

Zupitza, J. Altenglisches Übungsbuch.
Vienna, 1874, 1882 (as Alt- und mittel-
englisches Übungsbuch); ed. J. Schipper,
Vienna, 1897; ed. A. Eichler, 1922.
Sweet, H. An Anglo-Saxon Reader in Prose
and Verse. Oxford, 1876, 1894, 1922.
—— The Oldest English Texts. EETS. 1885.
(OET.)
—— A Second Anglo-Saxon Reader, Archaic
and Dialectal. Oxford, 1887.
—— First Steps in Anglo-Saxon. Oxford,
1897.
Kluge, F. Angelsächsisches Lesebuch. Halle,
1888, 1915.
MacLean, G. E. The Old and Middle English
Reader. New York, 1893.
Harmer, F. E. Select English Historical
Documents of the Ninth and Tenth Cen-
turies. Cambridge, 1914.
Wyatt, A. J. An Anglo-Saxon Reader. Cam-
bridge, 1919.
—— The Threshold of Anglo-Saxon. Cam-
bridge, 1926.
Sedgefield, W. J. An Anglo-Saxon Verse
Book. Manchester, 1922.
—— An Anglo-Saxon Prose Book. Manches-
ter, 1928.
Krapp, G. P. and Kennedy, A. P. Anglo-
Saxon Reader. New York, 1929.
Flom, G. T. Introductory Old English Gram-
mar and Reader. Boston, 1930.

(b) Texts illustrating O.E. Dialects *

[OET. = Oldest English Texts,
ed. H. Sweet, EETS.]

West Saxon

Early Charters. 778, etc. OET.
King Alfred's Cura Pastoralis. Hatton MS 20;
Cott. MS Tib. B xi. c. 900. Ed. H. Sweet,
2 vols. EETS. 1871–2.
K. Alfred's Orosius. Lauderdale MS. c. 900.
Ed. H. Sweet, EETS. 1883.
Parker MS of Anglo-Saxon Chronicle, to 891.
Corpus Christi College Cambridge MS 173
(Parker MS). Ed. C. Plummer (in Two Anglo-
Saxon Chronicles, 2 vols. Oxford, 1889–92).
Ælfric's Heptateuch. Laud MS E 19. c. 1000.
Ed. C. W. M. Grein (in Bibliothek der
angelsächsischen Prosa, vol. III, 1898).

Ælfric's Lives of the Saints. Cott. MS Julius
E vii. c. 1000. Ed. W. W. Skeat, EETS.
4 vols. 1881–1900.
Ælfric's Grammar and Glossary. St John's
College Oxford MS. c. 1000. Ed. J. Zupitza,
Berlin, 1880.
Ælfric's Homilies. Cambridge MS. c. 1000.
Ed. B. Thorpe (in Homilies of the Anglo-
Saxon Church, 2 vols. 1844–6).
Late West Saxon Gospels. Corpus Christi
College Cambridge MS. c. 1000. Ed. W. W.
Skeat (in Gospels in Anglo-Saxon, 1871–87).

Saxon Patois

Harleian Gloss. Harl. MS 3376. 10th cent.
[In Wright-Wülcker, Anglo-Saxon and Old
English Vocabularies, vol. I, 1884.]
Blickling Homilies. Blickling MS. Dated 971.
Ed. R. Morris, 2 pts, EETS. 1880.

Kentish

Early Charters. 679, etc. OET.
Bede Glosses. Cott. MS Tib. C ii. c. 900.
OET.
Kentish Glosses. Cott. MS Vesp. D vi. 10th
cent. [In Sweet, Second Anglo-Saxon
Reader.]
Kentish Hymn. Cott. MS Vesp. D vi. 10th
cent. [In Kluge, Angelsächsisches Lese-
buch.]
Kentish Psalm. Cott. MS Vesp. D vi. 10th
cent. [In Sweet, Anglo-Saxon Reader.]

Mercian

Epinal Glossary. Epinal MS 17. c. 700.
OET.
Corpus Glossary. Corpus Christi College
Cambridge MS cxliv. c. 750. OET.
Early Charters. 736, etc. OET.
Vespasian Psalter. Cott. MS Vesp. A i.
c. 800–850. OET.
Rushworth (1). Gospel of St. Matthew. (Inter-
linear.) Rushworth MS 950–1000. Ed.
W. W. Skeat (in Gospels in Anglo-Saxon,
1871–87).
Royal Glosses. Royal MS 2 A 20. c. 1000.
ZDA. xxxiii, 1889.

Northumbrian

Ruthwell Cross Inscription. 8th cent. (?).
OET.
English Names in Bede's Historia Ecclesias-
tica. Moore MS, Public Lib. Cambridge.
c. 737. OET.
Cædmon's Hymn. Moore MS of Bede. c. 737.
OET.
Personal Names in Liber Vitae. Cott. MS
Dom. A vii. c. 800. OET.

---

* The classification in this section and in the sections on Middle and Modern English owes much to
the bibliographies in H. C. Wyld, Short History of English, 1927.

Northumbrian Genealogies. Cott. MS Vesp. B VI. Early 9th cent. OET.

Leiden Riddle. Leiden University Lib. MS Voss 106. 9th cent. OET.

Bede's Death-song. St. Gall MS 254. 9th cent. OET.

Durham Ritual (interlinear gloss of c. 950; Northern Northumbr.). Durham Cathedral Lib. MS A IV, 19. Surtees Soc. 1841. [See also Trans. Philolog. Soc. 1877–9.]

Lindisfarne Gospels (Durham Book). Interlinear gloss of c. 950; Northern Northumbrian. Cott. MS Nero D IV. Ed. W. W. Skeat (in Gospels in Anglo-Saxon, 1871–87).

Rushworth (2). Gospels of St. Mark, St. Luke and St. John (interlinear; Southern Northumbrian). Rushworth MS 950–1000. Ed. W. W. Skeat (in Gospels in Anglo-Saxon, 1871–87).

F. MIDDLE ENGLISH PHONOLOGY AND GRAMMAR

(1) TEXT-BOOKS, MONOGRAPHS, ETC.

(a) General

Morsbach, L. Mittelenglische Grammatik. Pt I, Halle, 1896.

Jordan, R. Die mittelenglischen Mundarten. Germanisch-romanische Monatsschrift, II, 1910.

—— Handbuch der mittelenglischen Grammatik. Pt I, Lautlehre. Heidelberg, 1925.

Wright, J. and E. M. An Elementary Middle English Grammar. 1923; 1928 (rev.).

Jordan, R. Handbuch der mittelenglischen Grammatik. Heidelberg, 1934.

(b) Special Points

Maack, R. Die Flexion des englischen Substantivs von 1100 bis etwa 1250. Strasburg, 1888.

Luick, K. Untersuchungen zur englischen Lautgeschichte. Strasburg, 1896. [i, u in open syllables.]

—— Über die Entwickelung von altenglischen u-, i- und die Dehnung in offener Silbe überhaupt. Archiv, CII, CIII, 1899.

—— Studien zur englischen Lautgeschichte. Vienna, 1903. [Shortening of long vowels.]

Heuser, W. Die mittelenglische Entwicklung von ŭ in offener Silbe. E. Studien, XXVII, 1899–1900.

Pogatscher, A. Die englische ǣ/ē-Grenze. Ang. XXIII, 1900–1.

Diehn, O. Die Pronomina im Frühmittelenglischen. Heidelberg, 1901.

Wyld, H. C. The History of Old English Fronted (Palatalized) Initial ȝ in the Middle and Modern English Dialects. Otia Merseiana, II, 1901.

Wyld, H. C. Treatment of Old English ȳ in the Dialects of the Midland and S.E. Counties in Middle English. E. Studien, XLVII, 1913.

—— Old English ȳ in the Dialects of the South and S.W. Counties in Middle English. E. Studien, XLVII, 1914.

Knapp, O. Die Ausbreitung des flektierten Genitivs auf -s im Mittelenglischen. E. Studien, XXXI, 1902.

Vogel, E. Zur Flexion des englischen Verbums im XI. und XII. Jahrhundert. Jena, 1902.

Bülbring, K. D. Die Schreibung eo im Ormulum. BBA. XVII, 1905.

Cornelius, H. Die altenglische Diphthongierung durch Palatale im Spiegel der mittelenglischen Dialekte. SEP. XXX, 1907.

Eilers, F. Die Dehnungen vor dehnenden Konsonantenverbindungen im Mittelenglischen. Halle, 1907.

Mařik, J. W-Schwund im Mittel- und Frühneuenglischen. Vienna, 1911.

Gabrielson, A. The Influence of W- in Old English as seen in the Middle English Dialects. Gotenburg, 1912.

Ekwall, E. Ortsnamenforschung ein Hilfsmittel für das englische Sprachgeschichte. Germanisch-romanische Monatsschrift, V, 1913. [Old English ā, ȳ in Lancs.]

—— Contributions to the History of Old English Dialects. Lund, 1917. [æ before l + cons. and i-mutation of this group.]

Ritter, O. Zur englischen ǣ/ē Grenze. Ang. XXXVII, 1913.

Brandl, A. Zur Geographie der altenglischen Dialekte. Berlin, 1915. [Old English ǣ, ȳ.]

Bryan, W. F. The Midland Present Plural Indicative ending -e(n). MP. XVIII, 1921.

Lindkvist, H. On the Origin and History of the English Pronoun she. Ang. XLIV, 1921.

Marquardt, P. Das starke Participium Praeteriti im Mittelenglischen. Berlin, 1922.

Serjeantson, M. S. The Dialectal Distribution of certain Phonological Features in Middle English. E. Studies, IV, 1922. [æ + l + cons.; ĕa–i; ĕo; ȳ.]

—— The Development of Old English ēag, ēah in Middle English. JEGP. XXVI, 1927.

Taylor, A. B. On the History of Old English ēa, ēo in Middle Kentish. MLR. XIX, 1924.

Mackenzie, B. A. A Special Dialectal Development of O.E. ēa. E. Studien, LXI, 1927.

Malone, K. When did Middle English begin? [In Curme Studies, Baltimore, 1930.]

Langenfelt, G. Select Studies in Colloquial English of the Late Middle Ages. Lund, 1933.

(c) M.E. Dialects

General

Menner, R. J. and Patch, H. R. A Bibliography of Middle English Dialects. Stud. Phil. xx, 1923.

Moore, S., Meech, S. B. and Whitehall, H. Middle English Dialect Characteristics and Dialect Boundaries. Michigan Essays and Stud. xiii, 1935.

London

Lekebusch, J. Die Londoner Urkundensprache von 1430–1500. Halle, 1906.

Doelle, E. Zur Sprache Londons vor Chaucer. Halle, 1913.

Heuser, W. Alt-London. Osnabrück, 1914.

Mackenzie, B. A. Contributions to the History of the Dialect of London in the Middle English Period. Oxford, 1928.

East Midland

Wyld, H. C. South-Eastern and South-East Midland Dialects in Middle English. E. & S. vi, 1920.

West Midland

Hulbert, J. R. The 'West Midland' of the Romances. MP. xix, 1921.

Menner, R. J. Sir Gawain and the Green Knight and the West Midland Dialect. PMLA. xxxvii, 1922.

—— Four Notes on the West Midland Dialect. MLN. xli, 1926.

Serjeantson, M. S. The Dialects of the West Midlands in Middle English. RES. iii, 1927.

Northern English

Baumann, I. Die Sprache der Urkunden aus Yorkshire. Anglistische Forschungen, xi, 1902.

Hanssen, H. Die Geschichte der starken Zeitwörter im Nordenglischen. Kiel, 1906.

Heuser, W. Die ältesten Denkmäler und die Dialekte des Nordenglischen. Ang. xxxi, 1908.

Vikar, A. Contributions to the History of the Durham Dialects. Malmö, 1922.

Orton, H. The Medial Development of M.E. ŏ (tense), FR. ü (= [ȳ]) and M.E. eu (O.E. ēow) in the Dialects of the North of England. E. Studien, lxiii, 1929.

Peitz, A. Der Einfluss des nördlichen Dialektes im Mittelenglischen auf die entstehende Hochsprache. Bonner Studien, xx, 1933.

Scottish

Reeves, W. P. A Study in the Language of Scottish Prose before 1600. Baltimore, 1893.

Ackermann, A. Die Sprache der ältesten schottischen Urkunden. Göttingen, 1897.

Gregory Smith, G. Specimens of Middle Scots. Edinburgh, 1902. [Introduction.]

Knopff, P. Darstellung der Ablautsverhältnisse in der schottischen Schriftsprache. Berne, 1904.

Southern

Bülbring, K. D. Geschichte des Ablauts der starken Zeitwörter innerhalb des Südenglischen. QF. lxiii, 1889.

South-Eastern and Kentish

Konrath, M. Zur Laut- und Flexionslehre des Mittelkentischen. Archiv, lxxxviii, lxxxix, 1892.

Danker, O. Die Laut- und Flexionslehre der mittelkentischen Denkmäler. Strasburg, 1897.

Heuser, W. Zum kentischen Dialekt im Mittelenglischen. Ang. xvii, 1894–5.

Wyld, H. C. The Surrey Dialect in the xiiith Century. E. Studies, iii, 1921.

[See also Wyld, 1920, under East Midland above.]

(d) M.E. Texts

[In alphabetical order.]

Langer, F. Zur Sprache des Abingdon Chartulars. Berlin, 1904.

Fick, W. Zum mittelenglischen Gedicht von der Perle; Eine Lautuntersuchung. Kiel, 1885.

Knigge, F. Die Sprache des Dichters von Sir Gawayne und der sogenannten Early English Alliterative Poems. Marburg, 1885.

Mühe, T. Über den in MS Cotton Titus D xviii enthaltenen Text der Ancren Riwle. Göttingen, 1902.

Williams, I. Language of Cleopatra MS. of Ancren Riwle. Arg. xxviii, 1905.

Ostermann, H. Lautlehre des germanischen Wortschatzes in der von Morton herausgegebenen Handschrift der Ancren Riwle. BBA. xix, 1905.

Heuser, W. Die Ancren Riwle. Ang. xxx, 1907.

Dieth, E. Flexivisches und syntaktisches über das Pronomen in der Ancren Riwle. Zürich, 1919.

Rasmussen, J. K. Die Sprache John Audelays. Bonn, 1914.

Morris, R. Ayenbite of Inwyt. EETS. 1866.

Jensen, H. Die Verbalflexion im Aȝenbite of Inwit. Kiel, 1908.

Dölle, R. Graphische und lautliche Untersuchung von Aȝenbite of Inwit. Bonn, 1912.

Henschel, F. H. Darstellung der Flexions-lehre in Barbour's Bruce. Leipzig, 1886.

Mühleisen, F. W. Untersuchungen von Barbour's Bruce. Bonn, 1913.

Williams, O. T. On O.E. *a*, *ā* and *æ* in the Rimes of Barbour's Brus and in Modern Scotch Dialects. Trans. Philolog. Soc. 1911–15.

Tachauer, J. Die Laute und Flexionen der 'Winteney-Version' der Regula S. Benedicti. Würzburg, 1900.

Kock, E. A. Rule of St. Benet: Northern Versions. EETS. 1902.

Hagel, F. Zur Sprache der mittelenglischen Prosaversion der Benediktiner Regel. Ang. XLIII, 1920.

Hallbäck, E. S. The Language of the Middle English Bestiary. Lund, 1905.

Hoofe, A. Lautuntersuchungen zu Osbern Bokenam's Legenden. E. Studien, VIII, 1885.

Perrin, L. P. Über Thomas Castleford's Chronik. Boston, 1890.

ten Brink, B. Chaucers Sprache und Verskunst. Leipzig, 1884; rev. F. Kluge, Leipzig, 1899, 1920; tr. Eng. 1901.

Frieshammer, J. Die sprachliche Form der Chaucerschen Prosa. SEP. XLII, 1910.

Wild, F. Die sprachlichen Eigentümlichkeiten der wichtigeren Chaucer-Handschriften und die Sprache Chaucers. Vienna, 1915.

Bihl, J. Die Wirkungen des Rhythmus in der Sprache von Chaucer und Gower. Anglistische Forschungen, I, 1916.

Langhans, V. Der Reimvokal *e* bei Chaucer. Ang. XLIV, 1921.

Curtis, F. J. The Middle Scotch Romance of Clariodus. Ang. XVII, 1894–5.

Williams, R. A. Die Vokale der Tonsilben im Codex Wintoniensis. Ang. XXV, 1902.

Napier, A. S. Compassio Mariae. [In History of Holy Rood Tree, EETS. 1904.]

Hupe, H. Cursor Mundi. EETS. 1893.

Strandberg, O. Rime-Vowels of Cursor Mundi. Upsala, 1919.

Baildon, H. B. On the Rimes in the Authentic Poems of Wm. Dunbar. Freiburg, 1899.

Hilmer, H. Die Sprache von Genesis und Exodus. Sondershausen, 1876.

Fahrenberg, F. Zur Sprache der Confessio Amantis. Archiv, LXXXIX, 1892.

Schultz, E. Die Sprache der English Guilds. Jena, 1891.

Moeller, W. Dialekt und Stil des mittelenglischen Guy of Warwick in der Fassung der Auchinleckhandschrift. Königsberg, 1917.

Schlüter, A. Über die Sprache und Metrik der mittelenglischen weltlichen und geistlichen Lieder des XIII. Jahrhunderts. Göttingen, 1910. [Poems of Harl. MS 2253.]

Hohmann, L. Über Sprache und Stil des altenglischen Lai Havelok þe Dane. Marburg, 1886.

Schmidt, F. Zur Heimatbestimmung des Havelok. Göttingen, 1900.

Napier, A. S. Jacob and Josep. Oxford, 1916.

Kirschten, W. Überlieferung und Sprache der Romanze The Lyfe of Ipomadon. Marburg, 1885.

Wolderich, W. Über Sprache und Heimat einiger Gedichte des Jesus und Cotton MS. Halle, 1909.

Stodte, H. Über die Sprache und Heimat der Katherine-Gruppe. Göttingen, 1896.

Reimann, M. Die Sprache der mittelkentischen Evangelien. Berlin, 1883.

Heuser, W. Die Kildare-Gedichte. BBA. XIV, 1904.

Hall, J. King Horn. Oxford, 1901.

Stadlmann, A. Die Sprache der mittelenglischen Predigtsammlung in der Hs. Lambeth 487. Vienna, 1921.

Lucht, P. B. Lautlehre der älteren Laʒamon-Handschrift. Weimar, 1905.

Luhmann, A. Die Überlieferung von Laʒamon's Brut. Halle, 1905.

Lange, H. Das Zeitwort in den beiden Handschriften von Laʒamon's Brut. Strasburg, 1906.

Kühl, O. Der Vokalismus der Laʒamon-Handschrift B. Halle, 1913.

Kramer, M. Sprache und Heimat des sogenannten Ludus Coventriae. Halle, 1892.

Hingst, H. Sprache John Lydgate's aus seinen Reimen. Greifswald, 1908.

Weber, O. Language of the Metrical Homilies. Berne, 1902.

Hall, J. The Poems of Lawrence Minot. Oxford, 1914.

Seyferth, P. Sprache und Metrik des mittelenglischen strophischen Gedichtes 'Le Morte Arthur.' Berliner Beiträge zur germanischen und romanischen Philologie, VIII, 1895.

Mennicken, F. Versbau und Sprache in Huchown's Morte Arthure. BBA. V, 1900.

Wetzlar, A. Sprache sowie Glossar der nordenglischen Homiliensammlung des Edinburger Royal College of Physicians. Freiburg, 1907.

Vollmer, E. Sprache und Reime des Londoners Hoccleve. Ang. XXI, 1898–9.

Napier, A. S. Notes on the Orthography of the Ormulum. EETS. 1893.

Lambertz, P. Die Sprache des Ormulum nach der lautlichen Seite untersucht. Marburg, 1904.

Zenke, W. Synthesis und Analysis des Verbums im Orrmulum. Halle, 1910.

Björkman, E. Orrms Doppelkonsonanten. Ang. xxxvii, 1913.

Flasdieck, H. M. Die sprachliche Einheit des Ormmulums. Ang. xlvii, 1923.

Breier, W. Eule und Nachtigall. SEP. xxxix, 1910.

Wells, J. E. Accidence in Owl and Nightingale. Ang. xxxiii, 1910.

Struever, C. Die mittelenglische Übersetzung des Palladius. Göttingen, 1887.

Hoffmann, A. Laut- und Formenlehre in Reginald Pecocks Repressor. Greifswald, 1900.

Schmidt, Fr. Studies in the Language of Pecock. Upsala, 1900.

Hitchcock, E. V. Pecock: Folewer. EETS. 1924.

Behm, O. P. Language of the Later Part of the Peterborough Chronicle. Upsala, 1884.

Meyer, H. Zur Sprache der jüngeren Teile der Chronik von Peterborough. Freiburg, 1889.

Teichmann, E. Die Verbalflexion in William Langland's Buche von Peter dem Pflüger. Aix, 1887.

Chambers, R. W. The Authorship of Piers Plowman. MLR. v. 1910.

—— The Three Texts of Piers Plowman and their Grammatical Forms. MLR. xiv, 1919.

Skeat, W. W. The Proverbs of Alfred. Oxford, 1907.

Borgström, E. The Proverbs of Alfred. Lund, 1908.

Hirst, T. O. Phonology of the London MS. of the Earliest Complete English Prose Psalter. Bonn, 1907.

Serjeantson, M. S. The Dialect of the Earliest Complete English Prose Psalter. E. Studies, vi, 1924.

Wende, E. Überlieferung und Sprache des mittelenglischen Psalters. Breslau, 1884. [Surtees.]

Bertram, A. Essay on the Dialect, Language and Metre of Ratis Raving. Sondershausen, 1896.

Ostermann, L. Untersuchungen zu Ratis Raving. BBA. xii, 1902.

Tonndorf, M. Rauf Coilyar. Halle, 1893.

Hellmers, G. H. Über die Sprache Robert Mannyngs of Brunne. Göttingen, 1885.

Boerner, O. Reimuntersuchung über die Qualität der betonten langen E-Vokale bei Robert of Brunne. Halle, 1903.

—— Die Sprache Robert Mannyng's of Brunne. Göttingen, 1904.

Pabst, F. Die Sprache der mittelenglischen Reimchronik des Robert von Gloucester. 1. Lautlehre. Berlin, 1889.

—— Die Flexionsverhältnisse bei Robert von Gloucester. Ang. xiii, 1891.

Ullmann, J. Studien zu Richard Rolle von Hampole. E. Studien, vii, 1884.

Napier, A. S. On the Language of the History of the Rood-tree. EETS. 1894.

Heuser, W. Die mittelenglischen Legenden von St. Editha und St. Etheldreda. Erlangen, 1887.

Fischer, R. Zur Sprache und Autorschaft der mittelenglischen Legenden St. Editha und St. Etheldreda. Ang. xi, 1888–9.

Williams, I. F. The Language of Sawles Warde. Ang. xxix, 1906.

Mohr, F. Sprachliche Untersuchungen zu den mittelenglischen Legenden aus Gloucestershire. Bonn, 1889.

Brown, B. D. A Study of the Middle English Poem known as the Southern Passion. Oxford, 1926.

Pfeffer, R. Die Sprache des Polychronicons John Trevisas. Bonn, 1912. [Tiberius MS.]

Krüger, A. L. Sprache und Dialekt der mittelenglischen Homilien in der Handschrift B 14.52 Trinity College, Cambridge. Göttingen, 1885.

Strauss, O. Die Sprache der mittelenglischen Predigtsammlung in der Handschrift Trinity College, Cambridge B 14.52. Vienna, 1916.

Schmidt, G. Über die Sprache und Heimat der Vices und Virtues. Leipzig, 1899.

Philippsen, M. Die Deklination in den Vices und Virtues. Göttingen, 1911.

Meyerhoff, E. Die Verbalflexion in den Vices und Virtues. Kiel, 1913.

Neufeldt, E. Zur Sprache des Urkundenbuches von Westminster. Rostock, 1917. [Cott. MS Faust. A iii.]

Schüddekopf, W. A. Sprache und Dialekt des mittelenglischen Gedichtes William of Palerne. Göttingen, 1886.

Gasner, E. Über Wycliffes Sprache. Göttingen, 1891.

—— Beiträge zum Entwickelungsgang der neuenglischen Schriftsprache auf Grund der neuenglischen Bibelversion wie sie auf Wyclif und Purvey zurückgehen sollen. Nuremberg, 1891.

Skeat, W. W. On the Dialect of Wycliffe's Bible. Trans. Philolog. Soc. 1895.

Hudnall, R. H. A Presentation of the Grammatical Inflections in Andrew of Wyntoun's Orygynale Cronykil of Scotland. Leipzig, 1898.

Kamann, H. Über Quellen und Sprache der York Plays. Leipzig, 1887.

(2) MIDDLE ENGLISH TEXTS

(a) Readers, etc.

Mätzner, E. Altenglische Sprachproben. Pt I, Berlin, 1867.

Morris, R. and Skeat, W. W. Specimens of Early English. Pt I, 1150–1300; pt II, 1298–1393. Oxford, 1882–72; 1898–4 (rev. edn).

Sweet, H. First Middle English Primer. Oxford, 1884.

Emerson, O. F. Middle English Reader. New York, 1905, 1915 (rev. edn).

Brandl, A. and Zippel, O. Mittelenglische Sprach- und Literaturproben. Berlin, 1917.

Hall, J. Selections from Early Middle English. 2 vols. Oxford, 1920.

Sisam, K. Fourteenth Century Verse and Prose. [Glossary by J. R. R. Tolkien.] Oxford, 1921.

Brown, Carleton. Religious Lyrics of the XIVth Century. Oxford, 1924.

—— English Lyrics of the Thirteenth Century. Oxford, 1932.

[For a somewhat fuller list of M.E. readers see p. 114 below.]

(b) Texts illustrating M.E. Dialects

London

1. *Essex and City of London.*

Vices and Virtues. Stowe MS 240. *c.* 1200. Ed. F. Holthausen, EETS. 1888.

Arthour and Merlin. Auchinleck MS. 1330–40. Ed. W. D. B. Turnbull, Abbotsford Club, 1838.

Seven Sages of Rome. Auchinleck MS. 1330–40. Ed. H. Weber (in Metrical Romances, 3 vols. 1810).

Lyfe of Alisaunder. Laud Misc. MS I 74. *c.* 1400. Ed. H. Weber (in Metrical Romances, 3 vols. 1810).

2. *Middlesex and Western London, including Texts influenced by City Dialect.*

Lambeth Homilies. Lambeth MS 487. *c.* 1200. Ed. R. Morris, EETS. 1868.

Trinity Homilies. Trinity College Cambridge MS B 14.52. Early 13th cent. Ed. R. Morris, EETS. 1873.

Westminster Cartulary. Cott. MS Faust. A III. Early 13th cent. Ed. E. A. Neufeldt (in Sprache des Urkundenbuches von Westminster, Berlin, 1907).

Proclamation of Henry III. 1258. Ed. O. F. Emerson (in Middle English Reader, New York, 1905).

Adam Davy's Five Dreams about Edward II. Laud MS 622. *c.* 1400. Ed. F. J. Furnivall, EETS. 1878.

London Charters and Documents: (i) 1384–1450 (see L. Morsbach, Englische Schriftsprache, 1888); (ii) 1430–1500 (see J. Lekebusch, Londoner Urkundensprache, 1906).

History of St. Bartholomew's Church. Cott. MS Vesp. B IX. *c.* 1400. Ed. Sir N. Moore, EETS. 1923.

3. *Later London.*

A Book of London English, 1384–1425. Ed. R. W. Chambers and H. Daunt, Oxford, 1931.

Chaucer's Works. 15th cent. MSS. Ed. W. W. Skeat, 6 vols. Oxford, 1894.

Gower's English Works. 14th and 15th cent. MSS. Ed. G. C. Macaulay, 4 vols. Oxford, 1899–1902.

Travels of Sir John Mandeville. Cott. MS Titus C XVI. *c.* 1410–20. Ed. J. O. Halliwell [-Phillipps], 1866.

Hoccleve's Works. 15th cent. Ed. F. J. Furnivall and Sir I. Gollancz, 2 pts, EETS. Ex. Ser. 1892-7.

Lydgate's Works. 15th cent. Ed. J. Schick, H. Bergen and H. N. MacCracken, 6 vols. EETS. Ex. Ser. 1891–1935.

South-Eastern

Kentish Sermons. Laud MS 471. 1200–50. Ed. R. Morris, EETS. 1872.

Vespasian Homilies. Cott. MS Vesp. A 22. 1200–50. Ed. R. Morris, EETS. 1868.

Aȝenbite of Inwyt. Arundel MS 57. 1340. Ed. R. Morris, EETS. 1868.

William of Shoreham's Poems. BM. Add. MS 17376. *c.* 1350. Ed. M. Konrath, EETS. Ex. Ser. 1902.

Southern

Winteney Version of Rule of St Benedict. Cott. MS Claud. D III. Early 13th cent. Ed. A. Schroeer, Halle, 1888.

Owl and Nightingale. Cott. MS Calig. A IX. 1200–50. Ed. J. E. Wells, 1907.

Chertsey Cartulary. Cott. MS Vitell. A XIII. *c.* 1260–80. Ed. J. M. Kemble (in Codex Diplomaticus, 1839).

Usages of Winchester. MS in Guildhall, Winchester. 14th cent. Ed. T. and L. T. Smith, EETS. 1870.

Sir Firumbras. Ashmole MS 33. *c.* 1380–1400. Ed. S. J. Herrtage, EETS. Ex. Ser. 1879.

St Editha and St Etheldreda. Cott. MS Faust. B III. *c.* 1420. Ed. F. Holthausen, 1883.

Central Midlands

Earliest Complete English Prose Psalter. BM. Add. MS 17376. 1340–50. Ed. K. D. Bülbring, EETS. 1891.
English Addresses in Knighton's Chronicon. 1381. Ed. J. R. Lumby, 2 vols. Rolls. Ser. 1889–95.
Parlement of the Thre Ages. BM. Add. MS 31042. 15th cent. Ed. Sir I. Gollancz, 1915.
Wynnere and Wastoure. BM. Add. MS 31042. 15th cent. Ed. Sir I. Gollancz, 1920.
Coventry Leet Book. 15th cent. Ed. M. D. Harris, 4 pts, EETS. 1907–13.

East Midland

1. *South-East Midland*

Floris and Blauncheflur. Cott. MS Vitell. D III. 1250–1300. Egerton MS 2862. 1390–1400. Ed. E. Hausknecht (in Sammlung englischer Denkmäler, Berlin, 1885).
Osbern Bokenam's Lives of Saints. Arundel MS 327. 1447. Ed. C. Horstmann, 1883.
Octovian. Cott. MS Calig. A II. 15th cent. Ed. H. Weber (in Metrical Romances, 3 vols. 1810).

2. *North-East Midland.*

Peterborough Chronicle. Laud Misc. MS 636, last hand (annals of 1132–54). *c.* 1154. Ed. C. Plummer (in Two Anglo-Saxon Chronicles, Oxford, 1889–92).
Ormulum. Bodl. MS Junius 1. *c.* 1200. Ed. R. Holt, 2 vols. Oxford, 1878.
Bestiary. Arundel MS 292. Late 13th cent. Ed. R. Morris, EETS. 1872.
Genesis and Exodus. Corpus Christi College Cambridge MS 444. *c.* 1300. Ed. R. Morris, EETS. 1865.
Lay of Havelok. Laud Misc. MS 108. *c.* 1300–20. Ed. W. W. Skeat, Oxford, 1902.
Works of Robert Mannyng of Brunne. 14th cent. Rimed Story. Ed. T. Hearne, Oxford, 1725; ed. F. J. Furnivall, Rolls. Ser. 1889. Handlyng Synne. Ed. F. J. Furnivall, 2 pts, EETS. 1901–3.
Norfolk Guilds. *c.* 1389. Ed. T. and L. T. Smith, EETS. 1870.
Emare. Cott. MS Calig. A II. 15th cent. Ed. E. Rickert, EETS. Ex. Ser. 1906.

West Midland

1. *South-West Midland.*

Laʒamon's Brut. (B.) Cott. MS Otho C XIII. *c.* 1250. Ed. Sir F. Madden, 1847.

South English Legendary. Laud MS 108. *c.* 1280–90. Ed. C. Horstmann, EETS. 1887.
Legends of Ashmole MS 43. *c.* 1300.
Legends of Harl. MS 2277. *c.* 1300.
Robert of Gloucester's Chronicle. Earliest MS, Cott. Calig. A XI. 1320–30. Ed. W. A. Wright, 2 vols. Rolls. Ser. 1887.
(?) William of Palerne. King's College Cambridge MS 13. *c.* 1350. Ed. W. W. Skeat, EETS. Ex. Ser. 1867.
Trevisa. Translation of Higden's Polychronicon. St John's College Cambridge MS H 1. *c.* 1400. Ed. C. Babington and J. R. Lumby, 4 vols. Rolls Ser. 1865–86.

2. *Central West Midland.*

Laʒamon's Brut. (A.) Cott. MS Calig. A IX. *c.* 1205. Ed. Sir F. Madden, 1847.
Katherine Group (Legends of St Katherine, St Marherete, St Juliana). Royal MS A XXVII. *c.* 1230. Ed. T. O. Cockayne, E. Brock and E. Einenkel, 3 vols. EETS. 1866–84.
Sawles Warde. Royal MS 17 A XXVII. *c.* 1230. Ed. R. Morris, EETS. 1868.
Ancren Riwle. Cott. MS Titus D XVIII. 1230–50. Ed. J. Morton, Camden Soc. 1853.
English Poems of Harl. MS 2253. *c.* 1310. Ed. K. Boeddeker (in Altenglische Dichtungen, 1878).
Poems of William Herebert. Phillipps MS 8336. 14th cent. Ed. Carleton Brown (in Religious Lyrics of 14th Century, Oxford, 1924).
Short Metrical Chronicle. Royal MS 12 C XII. *c.* 1340. Ed. J. Ritson (in Metrical Romances, 1802, 1884 (rev. edn)).
Texts of Vernon MS. 1370–80.

3. *North-West Midland.*

Compassio Mariae. Bodl. MS Tanner 169*. *c.* 1250. Ed. A. S. Napier, EETS. 1894.
Sir Gawayne and the Grene Knight. Cott MS Nero A x. *c.* 1400. Ed. R. Morris, EETS. 1864, 1912; ed. J. R. Tolkien and E. V. Gordon, Oxford, 1925.
Early English Alliterative Poems: Pearl, Cleanness and Patience. Cott. MS Nero A x. *c.* 1400. Ed. R. Morris, EETS. 1864.
Romances of Ireland MS. 15th cent. (*a*) Awntyrs off Arthure; (*b*) The Avowynge of King Arthur; (*c*) Sir Amadace. Ed. J. Robson (as Three Early English Metrical Romances, Camden Soc. 1842).
St Erkenwald. Harl. MS 2250. 15th cent. Ed. Sir I. Gollancz, 1922.
Poems of John Audelay. *c.* 1426. Ed. J. O. Halliwell [-Phillipps], Percy Soc. 1844.

Works of John Mirk. 15th cent. Ed. F. Peacock and H. Erbe, 2 vols. EETS. and EETS. Ex. Ser. 1868–1909.

Alexander and Dindimus. Bodl. MS 264. c. 1450. Ed. W. W. Skeat, EETS. Ex. Ser. 1878.

Gest Historiale of the Destruction of Troy. Hunterian Museum MS, Glasgow. c. 1450. Ed. D. Donaldson and G. A. Panton, 2 pts, EETS. 1869–74.

Lay Folk's Mass-Book. Gonville and Caius College Cambridge MS 84. c. 1450. Ed. T. F. Simmons, EETS. 1879.

Boke of Curtasye. Sloane MS 1986. c. 1460. Ed. F. J. Furnivall, EETS. 1868.

Liber Cure Cocorum. Sloane MS 1986. c. 1460. Trans. Philolog. Soc. 1864.

Alisaunder. Bodley Greaves MS 60. 16th cent. Ed. W. W. Skeat, EETS. Ex. Ser. 1867.

Northern

Northern Homily Cycle. Royal College of Physicians Edinburgh MS. Early 14th cent. Ed. J. Small (in English Metrical Homilies, Edinburgh, 1862).

Works of Richard Rolle of Hampole. 14th cent. Ed. R. Morris, 1863; ed. C. Horstmann (in Yorkshire Writers, 1895–6).

Surtees Psalter. Cott. MS Vesp. D VII. c. 1350. Surtees Soc. 1843–7.

Sir Percyvelle of Galles. Thornton MS. 1350–1400. Ed. J. O. Halliwell [-Phillipps], Thornton Romances, Camden Soc. 1844.

Cursor Mundi. Cott. MS Vesp. A III (c. 1400), etc. Ed. R. Morris and H. Hupe, 6 pts, EETS. 1874–93.

Laurence Minot. Cott. MS Galba E IX. Early 15th cent. Ed. J. Hall, Oxford, 1915.

Northern Prose Version of Rule of St. Benedict. Lansdowne MS 378. Early 15th cent. Ed. E. A. Kock and H. Murray, EETS. 1902–11.

Scottish

Andrew of Wyntoun's Orygynale Cronykil. c. 1430. Ed. F. J. Andrews, 4 vols. STS. 1902–9.

Lancelot of the Laik. University Lib. Cambridge MS Kk I 5. 15th cent. Ed. W. W. Skeat, EETS. 1865.

Ratis Raving. University Lib. Cambridge MS Kk I 5. 15th cent. Ed. J. R. Lumby, EETS. 1870.

Barbour's Bruce. St John's College Cambridge MS G 23 (1487); Nat. Lib. Scotland MS (1489). Ed. W. W. Skeat, 4 pts, EETS. Ex. Ser. 1870–89; ed. W. M. Mackenzie, 1909.

Taill of Rauf Coilȝear. (Orig. c. 1475–1500.) Printed text of 1572. Ed. S. J. Herrtage, EETS. Ex. Ser. 1882.

G. MODERN ENGLISH PHONOLOGY

(1) TEXT-BOOKS

(a) General

(i) Modern

Ellis, A. J. On Early English Pronunciation. 5 vols. EETS. 1867–89.

Morsbach, L. Über den Ursprung der neuenglischen Schriftsprache. Heilbronn, 1888.

Luick, K. Beiträge zur englischen Grammatik. Ang. XIV, 1891, XVI, 1893–4, XX, 1897–8, XXIX, 1906, XXX, 1907, XLV, 1921.

Rudolf, E. Die englische Orthographie von Caxton bis Shakespeare. Marburg, 1904.

Diehl, L. Englische Schreibung und Aussprache im Zeitalter Shakespeares. Ang. XXIX, 1906. [Also Giessen, 1906.]

Horn, W. Historische neuenglische Grammatik. I. Lautlehre. Strasburg, 1908.

Zachrisson, R. E. The Pronunciation of English Vowels, 1400–1700. Gotenburg, 1913.

—— A Contribution to the History of the Early New English Pronunciation. E. Studien, LII, 1918.

—— English Pronunciation at Shakespeare's Time, as taught by William Bullokar. Upsala, 1927.

Wyld, H. C. History of Modern Colloquial English. 1920.

—— Studies in English Rhymes from Surrey to Pope. 1923.

Flasdieck, H. M. Forschungen zur Frühzeit der neuenglischen Schriftsprache. SEP. LXV, 1922.

Wright, J. and E. M. Elementary Historical New English Grammar. 1924.

(ii) Contemporary

1. *Seventeenth and Eighteenth Century Writers.*

Viëtor, W. Aussprache des Englischen nach englisch-deutschen Grammatiken vor 1750. Marburg, 1886.

Holthausen, F. Die englische Aussprache bis zum Jahre 1750 nach dänischen und schwedischen Zeugnissen. Göteborgs Högskolas Årsskrift, 2 pts, 1895–6.

Spira, T. Englische Lautentwicklung nach französischen Grammatikerzeugnissen. QF. CXV, 1912.

Kökeritz, H. English Pronunciation as described in Shorthand Systems of the 17th and 18th Centuries. Studia Neophilologica, VII, 1935.

2. *Individual Grammarians.*

Palsgrave, J. Lesclaircissement de la langue francoise. 1530; ed. F. Genin, Paris, 1852.

Du Wes, G. An Introductorie. 1532; ed. F. Genin (in edn of Palsgrave, above), Paris, 1852.

Salesbury, W. Account of English Pronunciation. 1547. [In A. J. Ellis, On Early English Pronunciation (see above), pp. 768–87.]

—— Account of Welsh Pronunciation. 1567. [In A. J. Ellis, Early English Pronunciation, pp. 743–68.]

Smith, Sir Thomas. De Recta et Emendata Linguae Anglicae Scriptione Dialogus. 1568; ed. O. Deibel, Halle, 1913.

Hart, J. An Orthographie. 1569. [See O. Jespersen, John Hart's Pronunciation of English (1569–70), Heidelberg, 1907.]

Bellot, J. Le Maistre d'Escole Anglois. 1580; ed. T. Spira, Halle, 1912.

Bullokar, W. Booke at large for the amendment of Orthographie for English Speech. 1580; ed. M. Plessow, Palaestra, LII, 1906.

Mulcaster, R. The Elementarie. 1582; ed. E. T. Campagnac, Oxford, 1925.

Coote, E. The English School-maister. 1596. [See E. Horn, Coote's Bemerkungen über englische Aussprache, Ang. XXVIII, 1905.]

Gill, A. Logonomia Anglica. 1619; ed. O. Jiriczek, QF. XC, 1903.

Mason, G. Grammaire Angloise. 1622; 1633; ed. R. Brotanek, Halle, 1905.

Butler, C. English Grammar. 1634; ed. A. Eichler, Halle, 1910.

Daines, S. Orthoepia Anglicana. 1640; ed. M. Roesler and R. Brotanek, Halle, 1908.

Hodges, R. The English Primrose. 1644; ed. H. Kauter, Heidelberg, 1930.

Wallis, J. Grammatica Linguae Anglicanae. 1653. [See L. Morel, De Johannis Wallisii grammatica linguae Anglicanae, Paris, 1895.]

Cooper, C. Grammatica Linguae Anglicanae. 1685; ed. J. D. Jones, Halle, 1912.

Jones, J. Practical Phonography. 1701; ed. E. Ekwall, Halle, 1907.

Lediard, T. Grammatica Anglicana Critica. 1725. [In A. J. Ellis, Early English Pronunciation, pp. 1040 ff.]

Bertram, C. The Royal English-Danish Grammar. Copenhagen, 1753.

Elphinston, J. The Principles of the English Language. 1765. [See E. Müller, Englische Lautlehre nach James Elphinston (1765, 1787, 1796), Heidelberg, 1914.]

Nares, R. Elements of Orthoepy. 1784. [See W. Bendix, Englische Lautlehre nach Nares, Darmstadt, 1921.]

Walker, J. Rhetorical Grammar. 1801 (2nd edn).

Bachelor, T. Orthoepical Analysis of the English Language. 1809.

(b) Special Points and Periods

Luick, K. Untersuchungen zur englischen Lautgeschichte. Strasburg, 1896.

—— Der Ursprung der neuenglischen ai- und au-Diphthonge. E. Studien, XXVII, 1899, XXIX, 1901.

—— Studien zur englischen Lautgeschichte. Vienna, 1903.

—— Über die neuenglische Vokalverschiebung. E. Studien, XLV, 1912.

—— Über Vokalverkürzung in abgeleiteten und zusammengesetzten Wörtern. E. Studien, LIV, 1920.

—— Gab es im Frühneuenglischen einen ü-Laut? Ang. XLV, 1921.

Spies, H. Studien zur Geschichte des englischen Pronomens im XV. und XVI. Jahrhundert. SEP. I, 1897.

Blach, S. Die Schriftsprache in der Londoner Paulsschule zu Anfang des XVI. Jahrhunderts. Halberstadt, 1905.

Horn, W. Untersuchungen zur neuenglischen Lautgeschichte. QF. XCVIII, 1905.

Price, H. T. History of Ablaut in the Strong Verbs from Caxton to the end of the Elizabethan Period. Bonn, 1910.

Horn, J. Das englische Verbum nach den Zeugnissen von Grammatikern des 17. und 18. Jahrhunderts. Darmstadt, 1911.

Eckhardt, E. Die neuenglische Verkürzung langer Tonsilbenvokale in abgeleiteten und zusammengesetzten Wörtern. E. Studien, L, 1916–7.

—— Die Quantität einfacher Tonvokale in offener Silbe bei zwei- oder dreisilbigen Wörtern französischer Herkunft in heutigen Englisch. Ang. LX, 1936.

Tietjens, E. Englische Zahlwörter des 15. und 16. Jahrhunderts. Greifswald, 1922.

Weiss, A. Die Mundart im englischen Drama von 1642–1800. Giessen, 1924.

Kihlbom, A. A Contribution to the Study of Fifteenth-Century English. Upsala, 1926.

Mackie, W. S. On the Independent Development of the Middle English Vowels in Early New English. MLR. XXIV, 1929.

Zachrisson, R. E. The Early English Loan-Words in Welsh and the Chronology of the English Sound-Shift. [In Klaeber Studies, Minneapolis, 1929.]

Cardim, L. Portuguese-English Grammarians and Eighteenth-Century Spoken English. Porto, 1930.

Morsbach, L. Probleme der neuenglischen Schriftsprache in ihrer Frühzeit. [In Jespersen Miscellany, Copenhagen, 1930.]

Flasdieck, H. M. Studien zur schriftsprachlichen Entwicklung der neuenglischen Velarvokale in Verbindung mit R. Ang. LVI, 1932; Halle, 1932.

Reinhold, C. A. Neuenglisch *ou* [*ow*] und seine Geschichte. Palaestra, CLXXXIX, 1934.

Matthews, W. Sailors' Pronunciation in the Second Half of the Seventeenth Century. Ang. LIX, 1935.

(c) *Dialects*

Ellis, A. J. On Early English Pronunciation. 5 vols. EETS. 1867–89.

Murray, Sir J. A. H. The Dialect of the Southern Counties of Scotland. 1873.

Halliwell[-Phillips], J. O. A Dictionary of Archaic and Provincial Words. 1878 (9th edn).

Wright, J. A Grammar of the Dialect of Windhill in the West Riding. 1892.

—— The English Dialect Dictionary. Oxford, 6 vols. 1896–1905.

—— The English Dialect Grammar. Oxford, 1905.

Wall, A. A Contribution towards the Study of the Scandinavian Elements in the English Dialects. Ang. xx, 1897.

Grüning, B. Schwund und Zusatz von Konsonanten in den neuenglischen Dialekten. Strasburg, 1904.

Hargreaves, A. Grammar of the Dialect of Adlington. Anglistische Forschungen, XIII, 1904.

Kruisinga, E. A Grammar of the Dialect of West Somerset. Bonner Beiträge, XVIII, 1905.

Franzmeyer, F. Studien über den Konsonantismus und Vokalismus der neuenglischen Dialekte. Strasburg, 1906.

Hirst, T. O. A Grammar of the Dialect of Kendal (Westmorland). Heidelberg, 1906.

Mutschmann, H. A Phonology of the North-Eastern Scotch Dialect. Bonn, 1909.

Binzel, A. Die Mundart von Suffolk in frühneuenglischer Zeit. Darmstadt, 1912.

Sixtus, J. Der Sprachgebrauch des Dialekt-Schriftstellers Frank Robinson zu Bowness in Westmoreland. Palaestra, CXVI, 1912.

Brilioth, B. A Grammar of the Dialect of Lorton (Cumberland). Oxford, 1913.

Grant, W. The Pronunciation of English in Scotland. Cambridge, 1914.

Klein, W. Der Dialekt von Stokesley in Yorkshire. Berlin, 1914.

Cowling, G. H. The Dialect of Hackness (North-East Yorkshire). Cambridge, 1915.

Wilson, Sir James. Lowland Scotch. Oxford, 1915.

Albrecht, T. Der Sprachgebrauch des Dialektdichters Charles E. Benham zu Colchester. Palaestra, CXI, 1916.

Baumann, I. Die Sprache der Urkunden aus Yorkshire im 15. Jahrhundert. Heidelberg, 1922.

Vikar, A. Contribution to the History of the Durham Dialects. Malmö, 1922.

Gepp, E. An Essex Dialect Dictionary. 1923 (2nd edn).

Watson, G. The Roxburghshire Word-Book. Cambridge, 1923.

Brandl, A. Englische Dialekte. Berlin, 1927.

—— Lebendige Sprache: Beobachtungen an Lautplatten englischer Dialektsätze. Sitz. der Preuss. Akad. der Wiss. Berlin, 1928, pp. 72–81.

Reaney, P. H. A Grammar of the Dialect of Penrith. Manchester, 1927.

Kökeritz, H. The Phonology of the Suffolk Dialect. Upsala, 1932.

Dieth, E. A Grammar of the Buchan Dialect (Aberdeenshire). Vol. I, Cambridge, 1933.

Ehrmann, L. and Scherer, H. Die Dialekte von Norfolk und von Lanarkshire (Glasgow). Palaestra, CLXXXV, 1933.

Orton, H. The Phonology of a South Durham Dialect. 1933.

(d) *Texts and Authors*

[In alphabetical order.]

Wille, J. Die Orthographie in Roger Ascham's Toxophilus und Scholemaster. Marburg, 1889.

Meech, S. B. Nicholas Bishop, an Exemplar of the Oxford Dialect of the Fifteenth Century. PMLA. XLIX, 1934.

Prins, A. A. The Booke of the Common Prayer, 1549. An Inquiry into its Language. Amsterdam, 1933.

Harder, B. Die Reime von Butlers Hudibras. Königsberg, 1900.

Gabrielson, A. Edward Bysshe's Dictionary of Rhymes (1702) as a Source of Information on Early Modern English Pronunciation. Upsala, 1930.

Dibelius, W. John Capgrave und die englische Schriftsprache. Ang. XXIII, 1900–1, XXIV, 1901.

Roemstedt, H. Die englische Schriftsprache bei Caxton. Göttingen, 1891.

Süssbier, K. Die Sprache der Cely-Papers. Berlin, 1905.

Swearingen, G. F. Die englische Schriftsprache bei Coverdale. Weimar, 1904.

Gerken, H. Die Sprache des Bischofs Douglas von Dunkeld. Strasburg, 1898.

Larue, J. L. Das Pronomen in den Werken des schottischen Bischofs Gavin Douglas. Strasburg, 1908.

Dierberger, J. John Drydens Reime. Freiburg, 1895.

Segelhorst, W. Die Sprache des English Register of Godstowe Nunnery (c. 1450). Marburg, 1908.

Fuhr, K. Lautuntersuchungen zu Stephen Hawes 'Pastime of Pleasure.' Marburg, 1891.

Schau, K. Sprache und Grammatik der Dramen Marlowes. Leipzig, 1901.

Grünzinger, M. Die neuenglische Schriftsprache in den Werken des Sir Thomas More. Freiburg, 1909.

Delcourt, J. Essai sur la Langue de Sir Thomas More d'après ses Œuvres anglaises. Paris, 1914.

Blume, R. Die Sprache der Paston Letters. Bremen, 1882.

Neumann, G. Die Orthographie der Paston Letters von 1422–61. SEP. VII, 1904.

Mead, W. H. The Versification of Pope. 1889.

McLean, L. M. The Riming-system of Alexander Pope. PMLA. VI, 1891.

Abbott, E. A. Shakespearian Grammar. 1869; 1870 (rev. edn).

Lummert, A. Die Orthographie der ersten Folio-Ausgabe der Shakespere'schen Dramen. Halle, 1883.

Franz, W. Shakespeare-Grammatik. Leipzig, 1900, 1924.

—— Orthographie, Lautgebung und Wortbildung in den Werken Shakespeares. Heidelberg, 1905.

Viëtor, W. Shakespeare Pronunciation. Marburg, 1906.

Zachrisson, R. E. Shakespeares Uttal. Studier i modern Sprakvetenskap, Upsala, 1914.

Kaffenberger, E. Englische Lautlehre nach Thomas Sheridan's 'Dictionary of the English Language' (1780). Beiträge Englands und Nordamerikas, III, 1926.

Whitehall, H. A Short Study of the Vowels in the Language of the Shuttleworth Accounts (1582–1621). PQ. X, XI, 1931–2.

Schoeneberg, G. Die Sprache John Skeltons in seinen kleineren Werken. Marburg, 1888.

Düring, H. Über die Pronomina bei Spenser. Halle, 1891.

Bauermeister, K. Zur Sprache Spenser's auf Grund der Reime der Faerie Queene. Freiburg, 1896.

Boehm, K. Spensers Verbalflexion. Berlin, 1909.

Hoelper, F. Die englische Schriftsprache in Tottel's Miscellany. Strasburg, 1894.

Sopp, W. Orthographie und Aussprache der ersten neuenglischen Bibelübersetzung des William Tyndale. Ang. XII, 1889.

Wyld, H. C. Spoken English of the Early Eighteenth Century. Mod. Lang. Teaching, XI, 1915. [Wentworth Papers.]

(2) DOCUMENTS ILLUSTRATING THE DEVELOPMENT OF ENGLISH SINCE THE TIME OF CHAUCER

(a) Books of Extracts

Skeat, W. W. Specimens of English Literature from 1394–1579. Oxford, 1871, 1892.

Flügel, E. Neuenglisches Lesebuch. I. Die Zeit Heinrichs VIII. Halle, 1895.

Davis, C. English Pronunciation from the Fifteenth Century to the Eighteenth. 1934.

(b) Texts illustrating the Development of Early Modern English

Fifty Earliest English Wills. 1387–1454. Ed. F. J. Furnivall, EETS. 1882.

Original Letters Illustrative of British History [15th and 16th cents.]. Ed. Sir H. Ellis, 3 sers. 1824–46.

Capgrave's Chronicle. 15th cent. Ed. F. C. Hingeston, Rolls Ser. 1858.

Palladius on Husbondrie. c. 1420. MS at Colchester. Ed. B. Lodge, EETS. 1872.

The Paston Letters. 1424–1506. Ed. J. Gairdner, 4 vols. 1896.

Letters and Papers of John Shillingford, Mayor of Exeter. 1447–50. Ed. S. A. Moore, Camden Soc. 1871.

Rewle of Sustris Menouressess. Bodleian MS 585. c. 1450. Ed. R. W. Chambers and W. W. Seton, EETS. 1914.

English Register of Godstow Nunnery. Rawlinson MS B 408. 1450. Ed. A. Clark 3 pts, EETS. 1905–11.

Lincoln Diocesan Documents. 1450–1544. Ed. A. Clark, EETS. 1914.

Register of Oseney Abbey. P.R.O. King's Remembrancer, Misc. Books 26. 1460. EETS. 1907.

Booke of Quintessence. Sloane MS 73. 1460–70. Ed. F. J. Furnivall, EETS 1866.

Bury Wills and Inventories. 1463–1569. Camden Soc. 1850.

Short English Chronicle. 1464. Camden Soc. 1880.

Ordinances of Exeter Tailors' Gild. Ordinances of Worcester. 1466–7. Ed. T. and L. T. Smith, EETS. 1870.

Chronicle of William Gregory. c. 1467. Camden Soc. 1876.

Cely Papers. 1473–88. Camden Soc. 1900.

Letters and Papers of the Verney Family 1478–1639. Camden Soc. 1853.

Monk of Evesham. 1482. Ed. E. Arber, 1869.

Knaresborough Wills. 1512, etc. 2 vols. Surtees Soc. 1902–5.

Lord Berners' Translation of Froissart. 1520. Ed. W. P. Ker, 6 vols. 1901–3.

Rede me and be not wrothe. 1528. Ed. E. Arber, 1871.

Ascham. Toxophilus. 1545. Ed. E. Arber, 1868.

Latimer. Seven Sermons. 1549. Ed. E. Arber, 1869.

Diary of Henry Machyn. 1550–3. Camden Soc. 1847.

Darrell-Hungerford Letters. 1560, etc. [In H. Hall, Society in the Elizabethan Age, 1887.]

Ascham. The Scholemaster. 1570. Ed. E. Arber, 1870.

Gabriel Harvey's Letter Book. 1573–80. Ed. E. J. L. Scott, Camden Soc. 1884.

Alleyne Papers. 1580–1661. Ed. J. P. Collier, Shakespeare Soc. 1843.

Queen Elizabeth's Letters to James VI. 1582–1602. Camden Soc. 1849.

Queen Elizabeth's Englishings. 1593. Ed. C. Pemberton, EETS. 1899.

Memoirs of Edward Alleyne. 1593–1626. Shakespeare Soc. 1843.

Letters of Lady Brilliana Harley. 1625–43. Camden Soc. 1853.

Correspondence of Dr. Basire. 1634–75. Ed. W. N. Darnell, 1831.

Memoirs of the Verney Family. 1639–96. Ed. Lady Verney, 1894.

The Wentworth Papers. 1705–39. Ed. J. J. Cartwright, 1883.

H. PLACE AND PERSONAL NAMES

(1) PLACE-NAMES

(a) General and Special Points

Binz, G. Zeugnisse zur germanischen Sage in England. PBB. xx, 1895.

Jellinghaus, H. Englische und niederdeutsche Ortsnamen. Ang. xx, 1897–8.

Middendorf, H. H. B. Altenglisches Flurnamenbuch. Halle, 1902.

Stolze, M. Zur Lautlehre der altenglischen Ortsnamen im Domesday Book. Berlin, 1902.

Zachrisson, R. E. A Contribution to the Study of Anglo-Norman Influence on English Place-Names. Lund, 1909.

—— The French Definite Article in English Place-Names. Ang. xxxiv, 1911.

—— English Place-Names in -ing of Scandinavian Origin. Upsala, 1924.

—— English Place-Names and River-Names containing the Primitive Germanic Roots *vis, *vask. Upsala, 1926.

—— Five Years of English Place-Name Study (1922–7). A Critical Survey. E. Studien, LXII, 1927.

—— Romans, Kelts and Saxons in Ancient Britain. Upsala, 1927.

Zachrisson, R. E. English Place-Name Puzzles. A Methodical Investigation into the Question of Personal Names or Descriptive Words in English Place-Names. Upsala, 1933.

—— English Place-Names in the Light of the Terminal Theory. Upsala, 1934.

Bradley, H. English Place-Names. E. & S. I, 1910.

McClure, E. British Place-Names in their Historical Setting. 1910.

Alexander, H. The Particle -ing in Place-Names. E. & S. II, 1911.

Lindkvist, H. Middle English Place-Names of Scandinavian Origin. Upsala, 1912.

Cornelius, H. Die englischen Ortsnamen auf -wick, -wich. SEP. L, 1913.

Ekwall, E. Die Ortsnamenforschung ein Hilfsmittel für das Studium der englischen Sprachgeschichte. Germanisch-romanische Monatsschrift, v, 1913.

—— Scandinavians and Celts in the North West of England. Lunds Universitets Årsskrift, N.S. xIV, 1918.

—— English Place-Names in -ing. Lund, 1923.

—— An Old English Sound Change and some English Forest Names. Ang. Bbl. xxxvI, 1925.

—— Ablaut in Flussnamen. Ang. Bbl. xxxvI, 1925.

—— English River Names. Oxford, 1928.

—— Studies on English Place and Personal Names. Lund, 1931.

Mawer, A. Some Unconsidered Elements in English Place-Names. E. & S. IV, 1913.

—— Animal and Personal Names in Old English Place-Names. MLR. xIV, 1919.

—— Problems of Place-Name Study. Cambridge, 1929.

—— The Scandinavian Settlements in England as reflected in English Place-Names. Acta Philologica Scandinavica, VII, 1932.

Moorman, F. W. English Place-Names and Teutonic Sagas. E. & S. v, 1914.

Walker, B. Interchange and Substitution of Second Elements in Place-Names. E. Studien, LI, 1917–8.

Ritter, O. Vermischte Beiträge zur englischen Sprachgeschichte. Halle, 1922.

English Place-Name Society. Introduction to Survey of English Place-Names. Vol. I: I, W. J. Sedgefield: Methods of Place-Name Study; II, E. Ekwall: The Celtic Element; III, F. M. Stenton: The English Element; IV, E. Ekwall: The Scandinavian Element; v, R. E. Zachrisson: The French Element; vI, J. Tait: The Feudal Element; vII, H. C. Wyld: Place-Names and English Linguistic Studies; vIII, S. J. Crawford: Place-Names and Archaeology; IX, F. M. Stenton: Personal Names in English Place-Names, Cambridge, 1924.

Anglica: Untersuchungen zůr englischen Philologie, Alois Brandl überreicht. Leipzig, 1925.

Karlström, S. Old English Compound Place-Names in -ing. Upsala, 1927.

Magoun, F. P. Place Names in the Parker Chronicle. Harvard Stud. XVIII, 1935.

(b) *Special Districts*
[In alphabetical order.]

Ekwall, E. The Concise Oxford Dictionary of English Place-Names. Oxford, 1936.

English Place-Name Society. Vol. III. The Place-Names of Bedfordshire and Huntingdonshire. Cambridge, 1926.

Skeat, W. W. Place-Names of Berkshire. Oxford, 1911.

Stenton, F. M. Place-Names of Berkshire. Reading, 1911.

English Place-Name Society. Vol. II. The Place-Names of Buckinghamshire. Cambridge, 1925.

Skeat, W. W. Place-Names of Cambridgeshire. Cambridge, 1911.

Sedgefield, W. J. The Place-Names of Cumberland and Westmorland. 1915.

Walker, B. Place-Names of Derbyshire. Journ. Derbyshire Archaeological and Natural Hist. Soc. XXXVI, 1914–5.

Blomé, K. B. The Place-Names of North Devonshire. Upsala, 1929.

English Place-Name Society. Vols. VIII, IX. The Place-Names of Devon. Cambridge, 1931–2.

Fägersten, A. The Place-Names of Dorset. Upsala, 1933.

Mawer, A. The Place-Names of Northumberland and Durham. Cambridge, 1920.

English Place-Name Society. Vol. XII. The Place-Names of Essex. Cambridge, 1935.

Baddeley, W. St Clair. Place-Names of Gloucestershire. 1914.

Baddeley, W. St Clair. Place-Names of Herefordshire. Trans. Bristol and Gloucester Archaeological Soc. XXXIX, 1913.

Bannister, A. T. Place-Names of Herefordshire. Cambridge, 1913.

Skeat, W. W. Place-Names of Hertfordshire. Hertford, 1904.

Skeat, W.W. Place-Names of Huntingdonshire. Proc. Cambridge Antiquarian Soc. X, 1904.

Wallenberg, J. K. Kentish Place-Names in Kentish Charters before the Conquest. Upsala, 1932.

Wyld, H. C. and Hirst, T. O. The Place-Names of Lancashire. 1911.

Ritter, O. Über einige Ortsnamen aus Lancashire. E. Studien, LIV, 1920.

Ekwall, E. The Place-Names of Lancashire. Manchester, 1921.

Gover, J. E. B. Place-Names of Middlesex. 1922.

English Place-Name Society. Vol. X. The Place-Names of Northamptonshire. Cambridge, 1933.

Mawer, A. Early Northumbrian History in the Light of Place-Names. Archaeologia Aeliana, XVIII, 1921.

Mutschmann, H. The Place-Names of Nottinghamshire. Cambridge, 1913.

Alexander, H. The Place-Names of Oxfordshire. Oxford, 1912.

Ritter, O. Zu einigen Ortsnamen aus Oxfordshire. E. Studien, LVI, 1922.

Bowcock, A. B. Place-Names of Shropshire. Shrewsbury, 1923.

Duignan, W. H. Notes on Staffordshire Place-Names. Oxford, 1912.

Skeat, W. W. Place-Names of Suffolk. Cambridge, 1913.

Hopwood, D. The Place Names of the County of Surrey including London in Surrey. Capetown, 1927.

English Place-Name Society. Vol. XI. The Place-Names of Surrey. Cambridge, 1934.

Roberts, R. G. Place-Names of Sussex. Cambridge, 1914.

English Place-Name Society. Vol. VI. The Place-Names of Sussex. 2 pts, Cambridge, 1929–30.

Duignan, W. H. Warwickshire Place-Names. Oxford, 1912.

Ekblom, E. Place-Names of Wiltshire. Upsala, 1917.

English Place-Name Society. Vol. IV. The Place-Names of Worcestershire. Cambridge, 1927.

Moorman, F. W. West Riding Place-Names. Thoresby Soc., Leeds, 1910.

Goodall, A. Place-Names of S.W. Yorkshire. Cambridge, 1913, 1914 (rev. edn).

—— The Scandinavian Element in Yorkshire Place-Names. Trans. Yorkshire Dialect Soc. III (17), 1915.

Zachrisson, R. E. Some Yorkshire Place-Names. MLR. XXI, 1926.

English Place-Name Society. Vol. V. The Place-Names of the North Riding of Yorkshire. Cambridge, 1928.

(2) PERSONAL NAMES

Bardsley, C. W. Our English Surnames. 1873; 1897.

Searle, W. G. Onomasticon Anglo-Saxonicum. A List of Anglo-Saxon Proper Names from the Time of Beda to that of King John. Cambridge, 1897.

Koehler, T. Die altenglischen Namen in Baedas Historia Ecclesiastica und auf den altnorthumbrischen Münzen. Berlin, 1908.

Koepke, J. Altnordische Personennamen bei den Angelsachsen. Berlin, 1909.

Bjoerkman, E. Nordische Personennamen in England in alt- und frühmittelenglischer Zeit. SEP. xxxvii, 1910.

—— Studien über die Eigennamen im Beowulf. SEP. lviii, 1920.

Forssner, T. Continental-Germanic Personal Names in England in Old and Middle English Times. Upsala, 1916.

Zachrisson, R. E. Notes on Early English Personal Names. Studier i modern Språkvetenskap, Upsala, 1917.

Hackenberg, E. Die Stammtafeln der angelsächsischen Königsreiche. Berlin, 1918.

Redin, M. Studies of Uncompounded Personal Names in Old English. Upsala, 1919.

Metzger, F. Angelsächsische. Völker- und Ländernamen. Berlin, 1921.

Förster, M. Proben eines Eigennamen-Wörterbuches. Germanisch-romanische Monatsschrift, xi, 1923.

Böhler, M. Die altenglischen Frauennamen. Berlin, 1930.

Dickins, B. English Names and Old English Heathenism. E. & S. xix, 1934.

Meier, A. Die alttestamentliche Namengebung in England. Leipzig, 1934.

Fransson, G. Middle English Surnames of Occupation, 1100–1350. With an Excursus on Toponymical Surnames. Lund, 1935.

M. S. S.

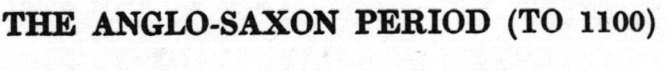

THE ANGLO-SAXON PERIOD (TO 1100)

THE ANGLO-SAXON PERIOD (TO 1100)

I. OLD ENGLISH LITERATURE

General Works: Bibliographies, Histories, Anthologies, Ancillary Studies.

Poetry: General Studies and Anthologies; Beowulf and Finnsburg; Minor Heroic Poems; Elegiac Poems; Riddles; Caedmon School; Cynewulf School; Minor Religious, Didactic and Gnomic Poems; Historical Poems; Miscellaneous Poems.

Prose: General Studies and Anthologies; Alfredian Prose; Chronicles; Aelfric, Wulfstan, Homilies, Saints' Legends and Other Religious and Didactic Prose; Gospels and Psalters; Laws and Charters; Science and Medicine.

A. GENERAL WORKS

(1) BIBLIOGRAPHIES

Wülcker, R. Grundriss zur Geschichte der angelsächsischen Litteratur. Leipzig, 1885.

Koerting, Gustav. Grundriss der Geschichte der englischen Litteratur. Münster, 1887, 1910 (5th edn).

Edwardes, Marian. A Summary of the Literature of Modern Europe from the Origins to 1400. 1907.

Ayres, H. M. A Bibliographical Sketch of Anglo-Saxon Literature. New York, 1910.

Kennedy, A. G. A Bibliography of Writings on the English Language. Cambridge, U.S.A. 1927.

Schütt, J. H. A Guide to English Studies: the Study of Old and Middle English Literature. E. Studies, IX, 1927.

Heusinkveld, A. H. and Bashe, E. J. A Bibliographical Guide to Old English. Iowa City, 1931.

[See also bibliographies in Chambers' Introduction to Beowulf (1920), and Klaeber's edn of Beowulf (1922).]

(2) HISTORIES OF OLD ENGLISH LITERATURE

(a) General

Twisden, R. Historiae anglicanae Scriptores. 1652.

Wharton, H. Anglia Sacra. 2 vols. 1692.

Hickes, G. Linguarum Veterum Septentrionalium Thesaurus Grammatico-Criticus et Archaeologicus. Vol. I, pt i, Institutiones Grammaticae Anglo-Saxonicae et Moeso-Gothicae. Pt ii, Institutiones Franco-Theotiscae. Vol. II, pt i, Grammaticae Islandicae Rudimenta. Pt ii, De Literaturae Septentrionalis Utilitate, sive de Linguarum Veterum Septentrionalium usu Dissertatio Epistolaris, cum Numismatibus Saxonicis. Vol. III. Antiquae Literaturae Septentrionalis Liber alter seu Humphredi Wanleii Librorum Veterum Septentrionalium Catalogus. Oxford, 1703–5.

Wright, T. Biographia Britannica Literaria. Vol. I, 1842.

Behnsch, O. Geschichte der englischen Sprache und Literatur von den ältesten Zeiten bis zur Einführung der Buchdruckerkunst. Breslau, 1853.

Taine, H. Histoire de la Littérature anglaise. Paris, 1863–4, 1881 (5th edn).

Morley, H. English Writers. Vol. I, 1864; 1891 (3rd edn).

Ebert, A. Allgemeine Geschichte der Literatur des Mittelalters im Abendlande. 3 vols. Leipzig, 1874–87, 1889 (new edn of vol. I)

ten Brink, B. Geschichte der englischen Literatur. Vol. I, Berlin, 1877; ed. A. Brandl, Strasburg, 1899; tr. Eng. 1883.

Azarias, Brother. The Development of English Literature: Old English Period. New York, 1879, 1890 (3rd edn).

Grein, C. W. M. Übersicht der angelsächsischen Litteratur. [In Kurzgefasste angelsächsische Grammatik, Kassel, 1880.]

Earle, J. Anglo-Saxon Literature. 1884.

Wülcker, R. Grundriss zur Geschichte der angelsächsischen Litteratur. Leipzig, 1885.

—— Geschichte der englischen Litteratur von den Anfängen bis zur Gegenwart. Leipzig, 1896, 1907.

Koerting, G. Grundriss der Geschichte der englischen Literatur. Münster, 1887, 1905 (4th edn).

Brooke, Stopford A. History of Early English Literature to the Accession of King Alfred. 2 vols. 1892.

—— English Literature from the Beginning to the Norman Conquest. 1898.

Koegel, R. Geschichte der deutschen Literatur. Vol. I, pt i, Strasburg, 1894.

Jusserand, J. J. Histoire littéraire du Peuple anglais. Vol. I, Paris, 1894, 1896.

Griffin, W. H. A Handbook of English Literature. 1897.

Ker, W. P. Epic and Romance. 1897.

—— The Dark Ages. 1904.

Cambridge History of English Literature. Vol. I, Cambridge, 1907.

Dale, E. National Life and Character in the Mirror of Early English Literature. Cambridge, 1907.

Brandl, A. Geschichte der altenglischen Literatur. Strasburg, 1908. [Rptd from PG.².]

Snell, F. J. The Age of Alfred (664–1154). 1912.

Benham, A. R. English Literature from Widsith to the Death of Chaucer. New Haven, 1916.

Huchon, R. Histoire de la Langue anglaise. Vol. I (450–1066), Paris, 1923.

Legouis, E. and Cazamian, L. Histoire de la Littérature anglaise. Paris, 1924; tr. Eng. 2 vols. 1926–7.

Thomas, P. G. English Literature before Chaucer. 1924.

Routh, H. V. God, Man, and Epic Poetry. Vol. II (Medieval), Cambridge, 1927.

Schroeer, M. M. A. Grundzüge und Haupttypen der englischen Literaturgeschichte. Pt I (Sammlung Göschen), 1927 (3rd edn).

Wardale, E. E. Chapters in Old English Literature. 1935.

(b) Monographs, etc.

Hunt, T. W. Ethical Teachings in Old English Literature. New York, 1892.

Stevens, W. O. The Cross in the Life and Literature of the Anglo-Saxons. New Haven, 1904.

Pfändler, W. Die Vergnügungen der Angelsachsen. Ang. XXIX, 1906.

Mosher, J. A. The Exemplum in Early Religious and Didactic Literature of England. New York, 1911.

Brotanek, R. Texte und Untersuchungen zur altenglischen Literatur- und Kirchengeschichte. Halle, 1913.

Jente, R. Die mythologische Ausdrücke im altenglischen Wortschatz. Anglistische Forschungen, LVI, 1921.

Kirtlan, E. J. The Relation of Sin and Fate in Anglo-Saxon Literature. London Quart. Rev. XXIII, 1922.

Chambers, R. W. The Lost Literature of Medieval England. Library, VI, 1925.

Neusprachliche Studien. Festgabe Karl Luick zu seinem 60. Geburtstage. Marburg, 1925.

Phillpotts, B. S. Wyrd and Providence in Anglo-Saxon Thought. E. & S. XIII, 1927.

Faverty, F. E. Legends of Joseph in Old and Middle English. PMLA. XLIII, 1928.

Ricci, A. The Anglo-Saxon Eleventh-Century Crisis. RES. V, 1929.

Wilson, R. M. Lost Literature in Old and Middle English. Leeds Stud. no. 2, 1933.

(3) ANTHOLOGIES

(a) In Old English

Thorpe, B. Analecta Anglo-Saxonica. 1834; 1846.

Leo, H. Altsächsische und angelsächsische Sprachproben. Halle, 1838.

Wright, T. and Halliwell [-Phillipps], J. O. Reliquiae Antiquae. 2 vols. 1841–3.

Ebeling, F. W. Angelsächsisches Lesebuch. Leipzig, 1847.

Klipstein, L. F. Analecta Anglo-Saxonica. 2 vols. New York, 1849.

Ettmüller, E. Engla and Seaxna Scopas and Boceras. Quedlinburg, 1850.

Rieger, M. Alt- und angelsächsisches Lesebuch. Giessen, 1861.

Zupitza, J. Altenglisches Übungsbuch. Vienna, 1874; 2nd edn, with title Alt- und mittelenglisches Übungsbuch, 1882; rev. J. Schipper, 1897; rev. A. Eichler, 1922.

Sweet, H. An Anglo-Saxon Reader. Oxford, 1876; rev. C. T. Onions, 1922.

—— The Oldest English Texts. EETS. 1885.

—— A Second Anglo-Saxon Reader: Archaic and Dialectal. Oxford, 1887.

Kluge, F. Angelsächsisches Lesebuch. Halle, 1888, 1915.

Bright, J. W. An Anglo-Saxon Reader. New York, 1891; rev. J. R. Hulbert, 1935.

MacLean, G. E. The Old and Middle English Reader on the Basis of Prof. Julius Zupitza's Alt- und mittelenglisches Übungsbuch. New York, 1893, 1922.

Wyatt, A. J. An Anglo-Saxon Reader. Cambridge, 1919.

—— The Threshold of Anglo-Saxon. Cambridge, 1926.

Sedgefield, W. J. An Anglo-Saxon Verse Book. Manchester, 1922.

—— An Anglo-Saxon Prose Book. Manchester, 1928.

(b) In translation

Sampson, G. The Cambridge Book of Prose and Verse: From the Beginnings to the Cycles of Romance. Cambridge, 1924.

(4) ANCILLARY STUDIES

(a) The Germanic Background

Grimm, W. Die deutsche Heldensage. Göttingen, 1829, 1889 (3rd edn).

Grimm, J. Deutsche Mythologie. Göttingen, 1835, 1875 (4th edn); tr. Eng. J. S. Stallybrass, 1883.
—— Über das Verbrennen der Leichen. [In Kleinere Schriften, vol. II, Berlin, 1865.]
Mone, F. J. Untersuchungen zur Geschichte der teutschen Heldensage. Quedlinburg, 1836.
Zeuss, J. C. Die Deutschen und die Nachbarstämme. Munich, 1837.
Simrock, F. Deutsche Mythologie. Bonn, 1853.
Müllenhoff, K. Zeugnisse und Excurse zur deutschen Heldensage. ZDA. XII, 1860.
—— Deutsche Altertumskunde. Berlin, 1870; rev. M. Roediger, 1890.
Müller, W. Mythologie der deutschen Heldensage. Heilbronn, 1886.
Bradley, H. The Goths. 1888.
Rydberg, V. Teutonic Mythology. Tr. Eng. B. Anderson, 1889.
Gummere, F. B. Germanic Origins: A Study in Primitive Culture. New York, 1892.
Sijmons, B. Heldensage. [In PG. vol. III, Strasburg, 1893.]
Jónsson, F. Den oldnorske og oldislandske Litteraturs Historie. 3 vols. Copenhagen, 1893–1902.
Jiriczek, O. L. Die deutsche Heldensage. (Sammlung Göschen.) Leipzig, 1894; tr. Eng. M. Bentinck Smith, 1902 (as Northern Hero Legends).
—— Deutsche Heldensagen. Vol. I, Strasburg, 1898.
Binz, G. Zeugnisse zur germanischen Sage in England. PBB. XX, 1895.
Golther, W. Handbuch der germanischen Mythologie. Leipzig, 1895.
Kluge, F. Zeugnisse zur germanischen Sage in England. E. Studien, XXI, 1895.
Schauffler, T. Zeugnisse zur Germania des Tacitus aus der altnordischen und angelsächsischen Dichtung. Vol. I, Ulm, 1898.
Heyne, M. Fünf Bücher deutscher Hausaltertümer. 3 vols. Leipzig, 1899–1903.
Mogk, E. Deutsche Mythologie. [In PG.², Strasburg, 1900.]
John, Ivor B. Popular Studies in Mythology, Romance and Folklore. Vol. XI, 1901.
Schrader, O. Reallexikon der indogermanischen Altertumskunde. Vol. I, Strasburg, 1901, 1917.
Herrmann, Paul. Erläuterungen zu den neun ersten Büchern des Saxo Grammaticus. 2 pts, Leipzig, 1901–22.
Chantepie de la Saussaye, P. D. The Religion of the Teutons. 4 vols. Boston, 1902.
Kauffmann, F. Northern Mythology. Tr. Eng. M. Steele Smith, 1903.
—— Deutsche Altertumskunde. Vol. I, Munich, 1913.

Heusler, A. Lied und Epos in germanischer Sagendichtung. Dortmund, 1905.
—— Geschichtliches und Mythisches in der germanischen Heldensage. Sitzungsber. d. kgl. preuss. Akad. d. Wissensch. XXXVII, 1909.
—— Die altgermanische Dichtung. Berlin, 1923.
Groenbech, Vilhelm. Vor Folkeæt i Oldtiden. 4 vols. Copenhagen, 1909–12.
Meyer, R. M. Altgermanische Religionsgeschichte. Leipzig, 1910.
Clarke, M. G. Sidelights on Teutonic History during the Migration Period. Cambridge, 1911.
Hoops, J. Reallexikon der germanischen Altertumskunde. Strasburg, 1911–.
Maurus, P. Die Wielandsage in der Literatur. Munich, 1911.
Schoenfeld, M. Wörterbuch der altgermanischen Personen- und Völkernamen. Heidelberg, 1911.
Chadwick, H. M. The Heroic Age. Cambridge, 1912.
Widsith. Ed. R. W. Chambers, Cambridge, 1912.
von der Leyen, F. Die deutschen Heldensagen. Munich, 1912, 1923.
Moorman, F. W. English Place-Names and Teutonic Sagas. E. & S. V, 1914.
Neckel, G. Adel und Gefolgschaft. Ein Beitrag zur germanischen Altertumskunde. PBB. XLI, 1916.
Flom, G. T. Alliteration and Variation in Old Germanic Name-giving. MLN. XXXII, 1917.
Jente, R. Die mythologischen Ausdrücke im altenglischen Wortschatz. Heidelberg, 1921.
Wolters, F. and Petersen, C. Die Heldensagen der germanischen Frühzeit. Breslau, 1921.
Larsen, H. Wudga: a Study in the Theodoric Legends. PQ. I, 1922.
Krappe, A. H. The Legend of Roderick, Last of the Visigothic Kings, and the Ermanarich Cycle. Heidelberg, 1923.
—— Études de Mythologie et de Folklore germaniques. Paris, 1929.
Malone, K. The Literary History of Hamlet. I. The Early Tradition. Anglistische Forschungen, LIX, 1923.
Major, A. F. Ship Burials in Scandinavian Lands and the Beliefs that Underlie them. Folk-Lore, XXV, 1924.
Singer, S. Stil und Weltanschauung der altgermanischen Poesie. [In Festschrift für Oskar Walzel, Wildpark-Potsdam, 1924.]
Wadstein, E. Norden och Västeuropa i gammal Tid. Stockholm, 1925.
Philippson, E. Germanisches Heidentum bei den Angelsachsen. Leipzig, 1929.

Schütte, G. Our Forefathers. Tr. Eng. 2 vols. Cambridge, 1929–33.
Jordans, W. Der germanische Volksglaube von den Toten und Dämonen im Berg. Die Spuren in England. Bonner Studien, XVII, 1933.

(b) Archaeology and History

Turner, Sharon. History of the Anglo-Saxons. 3 vols. 1799–1805; 1836 (6th edn).
Lingard, G. The Antiquities of the Anglo-Saxon Church. 1810.
Lappenberg, J. M. Geschichte von England. Vol. I, Hamburg, 1834; tr. Eng. B. Thorpe, 1845; rev. E. C. Otté, 2 vols. 1883.
Maurer, K. Über das Wesen des ältesten Adels der deutschen Stämme: Die Angelsachsen. Munich, 1846.
Kemble, J. M. The Saxons in England. 1849; rev. W. de G. Birch, 1876.
Worsaae, J. An Account of the Danes and Norwegians in England, Scotland and Ireland. 1852.
Haigh, D. H. The Conquest of Britain by the Saxons. 1861.
Wright, T. The Celt, the Roman and the Saxon, 1861.
—— A History of English Culture. 1871.
Freeman, E. A. A Short History of the Norman Conquest of England. Vol. I, 1867.
Haddan, A. W. and Stubbs, W. Councils and Ecclesiastical Documents relating to Great Britain and Ireland. Vol. III, Oxford, 1869–78.
Memorials of St Dunstan. Ed. W. Stubbs, Rolls Ser. 1874.
Steenstrup, J. C. H. R. Normannerne. 4 vols. Copenhagen, 1876–82. [Vol. III, Viking Kingdoms in the British Isles; vol. IV, Danish Institutions in England.]
Mullinger, J. B. Schools of Charles the Great and the Restoration of Education in the Ninth Century. 1877.
Bright, J. W. Chapters of Early English Church History. Oxford, 1878; 1897 (3rd edn).
Raine, J. The Historians of the Church of York. Rolls Ser. 1879.
Green, J. R. The Making of England, 1881.
—— The Conquest of England. 1883.
Müller, Sophus. Die Tierornamentik im Norden. Hamburg, 1881.
Guest, E. Origines Celticae, and other Contributions to the History of Britain. 2 vols. 1883.
Seebohm, F. The English Village Community. 1883.
Poole, R. L. Illustrations of the History of Medieval Thought. 1884; 1920 (rev. edn).
—— The Beginning of the Year in the Anglo-Saxon Chronicle. EHR. XVI, 1901.

Poole, R. L. St Wilfred and the See of Ripon. EHR. XXXIV, 1919.
Streatfield, G. S. Lincolnshire and the Danes. 1884.
Simcox, W. H. Alfred's Year of Battles. EHR. I, 1886.
—— The House of Ethelwulf. EHR. II, 1887.
Keary, C. F. A Catalogue of English Coins in the British Museum. Anglo-Saxon Series. 2 vols. 1887.
—— The Vikings in Western Christendom. 1891.
Malden, E. H. The West-Saxon Conquest of Surrey. EHR. III, 1888.
Du Chaillu, P. B. The Viking Age. 2 vols. 1889.
Liebermann, F. Die Heiligen Englands. Angelsächsisch und lateinisch herausgegeben. Hanover, 1889.
—— The National Assembly in the Anglo-Saxon Period. Halle, 1913.
—— Vorstufen zur staatlichen Einheit Britanniens bis 1066. E. Studien, LX, 1925.
Little, A. G. Gesiths and Thegns. EHR. IV, 1889.
Elton, C. Origins of English History. 1890.
Round, J. H. Gafol. EHR. V, 1890.
—— Military Tenure before the Conquest. EHR. XII, 1897.
—— The Officers of Edward the Confessor. EHR. XIX, 1904.
Taranger, A. Den Angelsaksiske Kirkes Indflydelse paa den norske. Norske Historiske Forening, Christiania, 1890.
Fischer, A. Aberglaube unter den Angelsachsen. Meiningen, 1891.
Stevenson, W. H. Old English Charters to St Denis. EHR. VI, 1891.
—— Notes on Old English Historical Geography. EHR. XI, 1896.
—— Burh—geat—setl. EHR. XII, 1897.
—— The Date of the Death of King Alfred. EHR. XIII, 1898.
—— The Great Commendation to King Edgar [973]. EHR. XIII, 1898.
—— The Beginnings of Wessex. EHR. XIV, 1899.
—— Dr Guest and the English Conquest of South Britain. EHR. XVII, 1902.
—— A Latin Poem addressed to King Athelstan. EHR. XXVI, 1911.
Wells, B. W. Eddi's Life of Wilfred. EHR. VI, 1891.
Gregory Smith, I. Christian Monasticism from the Fourth to the Ninth Centuries. 1892.
Holmes, T. S. The Conversion of Wessex. EHR. VII, 1892.
West, A. F. Alcuin and the Rise of the Christian Schools. 1892.

Tupper, F. History and Texts of the Benedictine Reform of the 10th Century. MLN. VIII, 1893.

Vinogradoff, P. Folkland. EHR. VIII, 1893.

—— Hide and sulung. EHR. XIX, 1904.

—— The Growth of the Manor. 1905.

—— English Society in the Eleventh Century. Oxford, 1908.

Maitland, F. W. Domesday Book and Beyond. Cambridge, 1897.

Howorth, H. H. The Beginnings of Wessex. EHR. XIII, 1898.

Miles, G. The Bishops of Lindisfarne, Hexham, Chester-le-Street and Durham, A.D. 635–1020. 1898.

Ramsay, J. H. The Foundations of England. 2 vols. 1898.

Taylor, C. S. The Origin of the Mercian Shires. Trans. Bristol and Gloucester Archaeological Soc. XXI, 1898.

Traill, H. D. Social England. Vol. I, 1898.

Collingwood, W. G. Early Sculptured Crosses. Kendal, 1899.

—— Scandinavian Britain. 1908.

—— Some Early Yorkshire Crosses. Trans. Thoresby Soc. XXII, 1914.

—— Angles, Danes and Norsemen in the District of Huddersfield. Huddersfield, 1921.

—— Northumbrian Crosses of the Pre-Norman Age. 1927.

Hunt, W. The History of the English Church from its Foundation to the Norman Conquest. 1899.

Roeder, F. Die Familie bei den Angelsachsen. SEP. IV, 1899.

Searle, W. G. Anglo-Saxon Bishops, Kings and Nobles. Cambridge, 1899.

Adams, G. B. Anglo-Saxon Feudalism. American Hist. Rev. VII, 1901.

Chadwick, H. M. Early Inscriptions in the North of England. Trans. Yorkshire Dialect Soc. 1901.

—— Origin of the English Nation. Cambridge, 1907.

—— The Heroic Age. Cambridge, 1912.

Graham, R. Intellectual Influence of English Monasticism between the 10th and 12th Centuries. Trans. Royal Hist. Soc. XVII, 1903.

Brown, G. Baldwin. The Arts in Early England. 6 vols. 1903–30.

—— The Arts and Crafts of our Teutonic Forefathers. Edinburgh, 1911.

Larson, L. M. The King's Household in England before the Norman Conquest. Madison, 1904.

—— The Political Policies of Cnut as King of England. American Hist. Rev. XV, 1910.

—— Canute the Great. 1912.

Salin, B. Die altgermanische Tierornamentik. Stockholm, 1904.

Davis, H. W. C. Cumberland before the Norman Conquest. EHR. XX, 1905.

Stenton, F. M. Godmundeslaech. EHR. XX, 1905.

—— Æthelwerd's Account of the Last Years of King Alfred's Reign. EHR. XXIV, 1909.

—— Types of Manorial Structure in the Northern Danelaw. Oxford, 1910.

—— The Danes at Thorney Island in 893. EHR. XXVII, 1912.

—— The Supremacy of the Mercian Kings. EHR. XXXIII, 1918.

—— The Danes in England. History, V, 1920.

—— Documents Illustrative of the Social and Economic History of the Danelaw. Oxford, 1920.

Hodgkin, T. Political History of England to 1066. 1906.

Godsal, P. T. The Storming of London, and the Thames Valley Campaign. 1908.

—— The Conquests of Ceawlin: the Second Bretwalda. 1924.

Ehrismann, G. Religionsgeschichtliche Beiträge zum germanischen Frühchristentum. PBB. XXXV, 1909.

Clapham, J. H. The Horsing of the Danes. EHR. XXV, 1910.

McClure, E. British Place-Names in their Historical Setting. 1910.

Oman, C. England before the Norman Conquest. 1910.

Brownbill, J. The Tribal Hidage. EHR. XXVII, 1912.

Cam, H. M. Local Government in Francia and England (768–1034). 1912.

Bartels, A. Rechtsaltertümer in der angelsächsischen Dichtung. Kiel, 1913.

Major, A. F. The Early Wars of Wessex. 1913.

Mawer, A. The Scandinavian Kingdom of Northumbria. [In Essays presented to William Ridgeway, Cambridge, 1913.]

—— The Vikings. Cambridge, 1913.

—— The Vikings. History, IX, 1924.

Lees, B. M. Alfred the Great. New York, 1915.

Morris, W. A. The Office of Sheriff in the Anglo-Saxon Period. EHR. XXXI, 1916.

Neckel, G. Adel und Gefolgschaft. PBB. XLI, 1916.

Beaven, M. L. R. The Regnal Dates of Alfred, Edward the Elder and Athelstan. EHR. XXXII, 1917.

—— The Beginning of the Year in the Alfredian Chronicle. EHR. XXXIII, 1918.

—— King Eadmund I and the Danes of York. EHR. XXXIII, 1918.

Howorth, H. H. The Golden Age of the Early English Church. 3 vols. 1917.

Keim, H. W. Aeþelwold und die Mönchreform in England. Ang. XLI, 1917.

Ekwall, E. Scandinavians and Celts in the North-West of England. Lund, 1918.

—— How Long did the Scandinavian Language survive in England? [In Jespersen Miscellany, Copenhagen, 1930.]

Grundy, G. B. The Saxon Battlefields of Wiltshire. Archaeological Journ. LXXV, 1918.

Hackenberg, E. Die Stammtafeln der angelsächsischen Königreiche. Berlin, 1918.

Robinson, J. A. St Oswald and the Church of Worcester. British Academy Supplementary Papers, V, 1919.

—— Saxon Bishops of Wells. British Academy Supplementary Papers, VI, 1920.

—— The Times of St Dunstan. Oxford, 1923.

Treiter, M. Die Urkundendatierung in angelsächsischer Zeit. Berlin, 1920.

Bugge, S. The Norse Settlements in the British Islands. Trans. Royal Hist. Soc. IV, 1921.

Wheeler, G. H. The Genealogy of the Early West Saxon Kings. EHR. XXXVI, 1921.

Cambridge Medieval History. Vol. III, Cambridge, 1922.

Fox, C. Anglo-Saxon Monumental Sculpture in the Cambridge District. Trans. Cambridge Antiquarian Soc. XVII, 1922.

Hepple, R. B. The Monastery School at Jarrow. History, VII, 1922.

Lennard, R. V. The Northmen in English History. Quart. Rev. CCXXXIX, 1923.

—— The Character of the Anglo-Saxon Conquests. History, XVIII, 1933.

Smith, R. A. Early Anglo-Saxon Weights. Antiquaries Journ. III, 1923.

—— Guide to Anglo-Saxon Antiquities in the British Museum. 1923.

Steenstrup, J. Études sur les Temps des Vikings. Copenhagen, 1923.

Broensted, J. Early English Ornament. Tr. Eng. A. F. Major, 1924.

Leeds, E. Thurlow. The Archaeology of the Anglo-Saxon Settlement. Oxford, 1925.

—— The West Saxon Invasion and the Icknield Way. History, X, 1925.

—— The Early Saxon Penetration of the Upper Thames Area. Antiquaries Journ. XIII, 1933.

Chambers, R. W. England before the Norman Conquest. 1926.

Åberg, Nils. The Anglo-Saxons in England. Cambridge, 1927.

Cook, A. S. Bishop Cuthwini of Leicester (680–91), Amateur of Illustrated Manuscripts. Speculum, II, 1927.

Hübener, G. England und die Gesittungsgrundlage der europäischen Frühgeschichte. Frankfort, 1931.

Crawford, S. J. Anglo-Saxon Influence on Western Christendom, 600–800. Oxford, 1933.

Jolliffe, J. E. A. Pre-Feudal England: the Jutes. 1933.

Lamb, J. W. Saint Wulstan, Prelate and Patriot. 1933.

Henel, H. Studien zum altenglischen Computus. Leipzig, 1934.

—— Altenglischer Mönchsaberglaube. E. Studien, LXIX, 1935.

Grube, F. W. Meat Foods of the Anglo-Saxons. JEGP. XXXIV, 1935.

Hodgkin, R. H. History of the Anglo-Saxons. 2 vols. Oxford, 1935.

(c) Palaeography

(i) Latin Script

Wattenbach, W. Anleitung zur lateinischen Palaeographie. Leipzig, 1886 (4th edn).

—— Das Schriftwesen im Mittelalter. Leipzig, 1896 (3rd edn).

Thompson, E. Maunde. Handbook of Greek and Latin Palaeography. 1894 (2nd edn).

—— The History of English Handwriting, A.D. 700–1400. Trans. Bibliog. Soc. V, 1901.

—— Introduction to Greek and Latin Palaeography. 1912.

Arndt, W. Lateinische Schrift. Rev. H. Bloch. [In PG. vol. I², 1901.]

Keller, W. Angelsächsische Palaeographie. Palaestra, XLIII, 1906. [Also in Hoops, Reallexikon.]

Lindsay, W. M. Early Irish Minuscule Script. 1910.

Crawford, S. J. The Worcester Marks and Glosses of the Old English MSS. in the Bodleian. Ang. LII, 1928.

Facsimiles of National MSS. of England. (Ordnance Survey.) Ed. W. B. Sanders, 4 pts, Southampton, 1867–71.

Westwood, J. O. Facsimiles of the Miniatures and Ornaments of Anglo-Saxon and Irish MSS. 1868.

Facsimiles of Ancient Charters in the British Museum. Ed. E. A. Bond, 4 pts, 1873–8.

Facsimiles of MSS. and Inscriptions. Ed. E. A. Bond, E. M. Thompson, G. F. Warner, Palaeographical Soc. 1873–94.

Facsimiles of Anglo-Saxon Manuscripts. (Ordnance Survey.) Ed. W. B. Sanders, Southampton, 1878–84.

Facsimiles of Biblical MSS. in the British Museum. Ed. F. G. Kenyon, 1900.

Facsimiles of Ancient MSS. Ed. E. M. Thompson, G. F. Warner, F. G. Kenyon, New Palaeographical Soc. 1903–.

Millar, E. G. English Illuminated MSS. from the Tenth to the Thirteenth Century. Paris, 1926.

—— Lindisfarne Gospels. [See Gospels, p. 95 below.]

REF
Z
2011
B28
15,676
CAMROSE LUTHERAN COLLEGE
LIBRARY

(ii) Runic Script

1. *General.*

Grimm, W. Über deutsche Runen. Göttingen, 1821.

—— Zur Literatur der Runen. Wiener Jahrbuch der Literatur, XLIII, 1828.

Liljegren, J. G. Run-Lära. Stockholm, 1832.

Kemble, J. M. On Anglo-Saxon Runes. Archaeologia, XXVIII, 1840.

Liliencron, R. V. and Müllenhoff, K. Zur Runenlehre. Kiel, 1852.

Kirchhoff, A. Das gothische Runenalphabet. Berlin, 1854 (2nd edn).

Zacher, J. Das gotische Alphabet Vulfilas und das Runenalphabet. Leipzig, 1855.

Stephens, G. The Old Northern Runic Monuments. 4 vols. Copenhagen, 1866–84.

—— Handbook of the Old Northern Runic Monuments. 1884.

—— The Runes, whence came they? 1894.

Arnamagnæanske Haandskrift, no. 28, Codex Runicus, in facsimile. Ed. Kommissionen for det Arnamagnæanske Legat, Copenhagen, 1877.

Thorsen, P. G. Om Runernes Brug til Skrift udenfor det Monumentale. Copenhagen, 1877.

Olsen, B. M. Runerne i den oldislandske Literatur. Copenhagen, 1883.

Burg, F. Die älteren nordischen Runeninschriften. Berlin, 1885.

Wimmer, L. F. A. Die Runenschrift. Tr. Eng. F. Holthausen, Berlin, 1887 (2nd edn).

Henning, R. Die deutschen Runendenkmäler. Strasburg, 1889.

Sievers, E. Runen und Runeninschriften. [In PG. vol. I², 1891.]

Bugge, S. Norges Indskrifter med de öldre Runer. Christiania, 1891–1903.

Viëtor, W. Die northumbrischen Runensteine. Marburg, 1895.

Hempl, G. The Collingham Runic Inscription. MLN, XII, 1896.

—— The Origin of the Runes. JEGP. II, 1899.

—— The Runes and the Germanic Shift. JEGP. IV, 1902.

Barnouw, A. J. Die Runenstelle der Himmelfahrt. Archiv, CVII, 1902.

von Friesen, O. Om runskriftens Härkomst. Språkvetenskapliga Sällskapets i Uppsala Förhandl, Upsala, 1904–6. [Also in Hoops, Reallexikon.]

Gering, H. Neuere Schriften zur Runenkunde. Zeitschrift für deutsche Philologie, XXXVIII, 1905.

Kermode, P. M. C. Manx Crosses. 1907.

Paues, A. C. Runes and Manuscripts. CHEL. vol. I, 1907.

Neckel, G. Zur Einführung in die Runenforschung. Germanisch-romanische Monatsschrift, I, 1909.

Feist, S. Die religionsgeschichtliche Bedeutung der ältesten Runeninschriften. JEGP. XXI, 1922.

Cahen, M. L'Écriture runique chez les Germains. Scientia, 1923.

—— Origine et Développement de l'Écriture runique. Mémoires de la Société linguistique, XXIII, 1923.

Mackensen, C. J. S. Om Runene og Runenornes Upvindeke. Norsk Tidsskrift for Sprogvidenskap, I, 1928.

Dickins, B. The Runic Inscription of Maeshowe. Kirkwall, 1931.

Wrenn, C. L. Late Old English Rune-Names. Medium Aevum, I, 1932.

Arutz, H. Runenkunde. Halle, 1935.

[See also Trautmann, 1899, Tupper, 1912, under Cynewulf: General, pp. 75–6 below.]

2. *Ruthwell and Bewcastle Crosses.*

Nicholson, W. [Letter written in 1685.] [In Camden's Britannia, ed. E. Gibson, 1695.]

Hickes, G. Ruthwell Cross. [In Thesaurus, vol. I, pt iii, Plate 4, Oxford, 1703.]

Gordon, A. Itinerarium septentrionale. 1726. [P. 160, Plates 57, 58.]

Smith, G. Bewcastle Cross. GM. XII, 1742. [Pp. 132, 318, 368, 529.]

de Cardonell, A. Vetusta Monumenta. Trans. Soc. Antiquaries, II, 1789. [Plates 54, 55.]

Hutchinson, W. The History of the County of Cumberland. 2 vols. Carlisle, 1794.

Howard, H. Bewcastle Cross. Archaeologia, XIV, 1801.

Lysons, D. L. and S. Magna Britannia. Vol. IV, 1806–22.

Duncan, H. Archaeologia Scotica. Trans. Soc. Antiquaries of Scotland, IV, Edinburgh, 1833. [Plate 13.]

Kemble, J. Ruthwell Cross. Archaeologia, XXVIII, 1840. [See Additional Observations on the Runic Obelisk at Ruthwell, Archaeologia, XXX, 1843; P. A. Munch, Norsk Literaturtidende, I–IV, Christiania, 1845.]

Maughan, J. The Maiden Way. Archaeological Journ. XI, 1854.

—— Memoir on the Roman Station and Runic Cross at Bewcastle. 1857.

Haigh, D. H. Bewcastle. Archaeologia Aeliana, I, 1857.

Wilson, D. Prehistoric Annals of Scotland. Vol. II, Cambridge, 1863, pp. 319–29 (2nd edn).

Dietrich, F. Disputatio de Cruce Ruthwellensi. Marburg, 1865.

Stuart, J. Sculptured Stones of Scotland. 2 vols. Spalding Club, Aberdeen, 1867.

Anderson, J. Scotland in Early Christian Times. Ser. 2, Edinburgh, 1881.

[MacFarlan, J.] The Ruthwell Cross. Edinburgh, 1885.

Sweet, H. The Oldest English Texts. EETS. 1885, pp. 124 ff.

Viëtor, W. Beiträge zur Textkritik der northumbrischen Runensteine. Marburg, 1894. [See also Viëtor, 1895, under Runic Script: General, above.]

Cook, A. S. Notes on the Ruthwell Cross. PMLA. xvii, 1902.

—— The Bewcastle Cross. MLN. xviii, 1903.

—— The Date of the Ruthwell and Bewcastle Crosses. Trans. Connecticut Academy, xvii, 1912.

—— Some Accounts of the Bewcastle Cross between the Years 1607 and 1861. New Haven, 1914.

Anderson, J. and Allen, J. R. The Early Christian Monuments of Scotland. Edinburgh, 1903.

Zupitza, J. Verse vom Kreuze zu Ruthwell. [In Alt- und mittelenglisches Übungsbuch, 1904 (7th edn).]

Lethaby, O. Is Ruthwell Cross an Anglo-Celtic Work? Archaeological Journ. lxx, 1913.

Forbes, M. D. and Dickins, B. The Ruthwell and Bewcastle Crosses. MLR. x, 1915.

Browne, G. F. The Ancient Cross Shafts at Bewcastle and Ruthwell. Cambridge, 1916.

Brandl, A. Zur Zeitbestimmung des Kreuzes von Ruthwell. Archiv, cxxxvi, 1917.

Reeves, W. P. The Date of the Bewcastle Cross. MLN. xxxv, 1920.

Webster, A. B. The Ruthwell and Bewcastle Crosses. [In G. Baldwin Brown's The Arts in Early England, vol. v, 1921.]

Ross, A. S. C. The Linguistic Evidence for the Date of the 'Ruthwell Cross.' MLR. xxviii, 1933.

3. *Franks Casket.*

Franks, A. W. Memoir on the Casket. Archaeological Journ. xvi, 1859.

Hofmann, K. Über die Clairmonter Runen. Sitzungsber. d. kgl. bayer. Akad. d. Wissensch. 1871, pp. 665 ff.

Sweet, H. Garsecg. E. Studien, ii, 1879.

Grein, C. W. M. and Wülcker, R. Bibliothek der angelsächsischen Poesie. Vol. i, Hamburg, 1883.

Gering, H. Zum Clermonter Runenkästchen. Zeitschrift für deutsche Philologie, xxxiii, 1900.

Wadstein, E. The Clermont Runic Casket. Upsala, 1900. [With five plates.]

Napier, A. S. The Franks Casket. [In An English Miscellany presented to Dr Furnivall, Oxford, 1901, pp. 362–81, with six facsimiles.]

Viëtor, W. Das angelsächsische Runenkästchen aus Auzon bei Clermont-Ferrand. Marburg, 1901. [With five plates.]

Hempl, G. The Variant Runes on the Franks Casket. Boston, 1902.

von Grienberger, [T.] Zu den Inschriften des Clermonter Runenkästchens. Ang. xxvii, 1904. [See Zeitschrift für deutsche Philologie, xxxiii, 1904.]

Holthausen, F. Zum Clermonter Runenkästchen. Ang. Bbl. xvi, 1905.

Smith, R. A. Guide to the Anglo-Saxon Antiquities in the British Museum. 1928.

Brown, G. Baldwin. The Arts in Early England. Vol. vi, 1930.

Clark, E. G. The Right Side of the Franks Casket. PMLA. xlv, 1930.

Souers, P. W. Harvard Stud. xvi, 1934, pp. 163 ff., xviii, 1935, pp. 199 ff.

B. POETRY

(1) GENERAL WORKS ON OLD ENGLISH POETRY

(a) *General*

Conybeare, J. J. Illustrations of Anglo-Saxon Poetry. 1826.

Longfellow, H. W. Poets and Poetry of Europe. 1838.

Sweet, H. Sketch of the History of Anglo-Saxon Poetry. [In T. Warton's History of English Poetry, vol. ii, 1871.]

Hammerich, F. Älteste christliche Epik der Angelsachsen, Deutschen und Nordländer. Übersetzung von A. Michelsen. Gütersloh, 1874.

Guest, E. History of English Rhythms. 1838; ed. W. W. Skeat, 1882.

Merbod, R. Aesthetische Studien zur angelsächsischen Poesie. Breslau, 1883.

Lithgow, A. D. Anglo-Saxon Alliterative Poetry. Trans. Royal Soc. Lit. xv, 1893.

Courthope, W. J. History of English Poetry. Vol. i, 1895.

Barnouw, A. J. Schriftuurlijke Poëzie der Angelsaken. Hague, 1907; tr. Eng. Louise Dudley, 1914 (as Anglo-Saxon Christian Poetry).

Chadwick, H. M. Early National Poetry. CHEL. vol. i, 1907.

Hart, W. M. Ballad and Epic. Harvard Stud. xi, 1907.

Smithson, G. A. The Old English Christian Epic. Berkeley, 1911.

Sarrazin, G. Von Kädmon bis Kynewulf. Berlin, 1913.

Iecht, H. and Schücking, L. L. Die englische Literatur im Mittelalter. Vol. I, Die angelsächsische und frühmittelenglische Dichtung. Wildpark-Potsdam, 1927.

(b) *Monographs, etc.*

Iaigh, D. H. The Anglo-Saxon Sagas; an Examination of their Value as Aids to History. 1861.

Sievers, E. Collationen angelsächsischer Gedichte. [Genesis, Exodus, Daniel, Christ and Satan.] ZDA. xv, 1863.

Grein, C. W. M. Zur Textkritik der angelsächsischen Dichter. Germania, x, 1865.

Lichtenheld, A. Das schwache Adjektiv im Angelsächsischen. ZDA. xvi, 1873.

Heinzel, R. Über den Stil der altgermanischen Poesie. QF. x, 1875.

Schultze, M. Altheidnisches in der angelsächsischen Poesie, speciell im Beowulfsliede. Berlin, 1877.

Gummere, F. B. The Anglo-Saxon Metaphor. Freiburg, 1881.

—— Translation of Old English Verse. MLN. xxv, 1910. [See G. C. Child, MLN. xxv, 1910.]

Merbach, H. Das Meer in der Dichtung der Angelsachsen. Breslau, 1884.

Bode, W. Die Kenningar in der angelsächsischen Dichtung. Darmstadt, 1886.

Tolman, A. H. The Style of Anglo-Saxon Poetry. Trans. Mod. Lang. Ass. of America, III, 1887.

Kail, J. Über die Parallelstellen in der angelsächsischen Poesie. Ang. xII, 1889.

Garnett, J. M. The Translation of Anglo-Saxon Poetry. PMLA. vi, 1891.

—— Recent Translations of Old English Poetry. PMLA. xviii, 1903.

Abbey, C. J. Religious Thought in Old English Verse. 1892.

Sarrazin, G. Parallelstellen in altenglischer Dichtung. Ang. xiv, 1892.

—— Zur Chronologie und Verfasserfrage altenglischer Dichtungen. E. Studien, xxxviii, 1907.

Wülcker, R. Die Entstehung der christlichen Dichtung bei den Angelsachsen. Berichte über d. Verhandl. d. kgl. sächs. Gesellsch. d. Wissensch., Phil.-hist. Kl. II, Leipzig, 1893.

Holthausen, F. Beiträge zur Erklärung und Textkritik altenglischer Dichtungen. Indogermanische Forschungen, iv, 1894.

—— Kleinere altenglische Dichtungen. Ang. xli, 1917. [A few fragments from various MSS, and a note on the Franks Casket.]

—— Zu altenglischen Gedichten. Ang. Bbl. xxxii, 1921.

—— Studien zur altenglischen Dichtung. Ang. xlvi, 1922.

Holthausen, F. Zu altenglischen Dichtungen. Ang. Bbl. xxxiv, 1923.

Mead, W. E. Color in Old English Poetry. PMLA. xiv, 1899.

Myers, I. T. A Study in Epic Development. New Haven, 1901.

Otto, E. Typische Schilderungen von Lebewesen, Gegenständlichen und Vorgängen im weltlichen Epos der Angelsachsen. Berlin, 1901.

Heusler, A. Der Dialog in der altgermanischen erzählenden Dichtung. ZDA. xlvi, 1902.

Abbetmayer, C. Old English Poetical Motives derived from the Doctrine of Sin. New York, 1903.

Panzer, F. Das altdeutsche Volksepos. Halle, 1903.

Grüters, O. Über einige Beziehungen zwischen altsächsischer und altenglischer Dichtung. BBA. xvii, 1905.

Hanscom, E. D. The Feeling for Nature in Old English Poetry. JEGP. v, 1905.

Skemp, A. R. Transformation of Scriptural Story, Motive and Conception in Anglo-Saxon Poetry. MP. iv, 1906.

Brandl, A. Zur Gotensage bei den Angelsachsen. Archiv, cxx, 1908.

Grau, G. Quellen und Verwandtschaften der älteren germanischen Darstellungen des jüngsten Gerichtes. SEP. xxxi, 1908.

Olrik, A. Epische Gesetze der Volksdichtung. ZDA. li, 1909–10.

Rankin, J. W. A Study of the Kennings in Anglo-Saxon Poetry. JEGP. viii, 1909, ix, 1910.

—— Rhythm and Rime before the Norman Conquest. PMLA. xxxvi, 1921.

Richter, C. Chronologische Studien zur angelsächsischen Literatur auf Grund sprachlichmetrischer Kriterien. Halle, 1910.

Bartels, A. Rechtsaltertümer in der angelsächsischen Dichtung. Kiel, 1913.

Webster, A. B. Translation from Old into Modern English. E. & S. v, 1914.

Schücking, L. L. Untersuchungen zur Bedeutungslehre der angelsächsischen Dichtersprache. Heidelberg, 1915.

Keiser, A. The Influence of Christianity on Old English Poetry. Urbana, 1918.

Kock, E. A. Jubilee Jaunts and Jottings. 250 Contributions to the Interpretation and Prosody of Old West Teutonic Alliterative Poetry. Lunds Univ. Årsskrift, N.S. i, xiv, 1918.

—— Interpretations and Emendations of Early English Texts, ix, x. Ang. xlvi, 1922.

—— Plain Points and Puzzles. Sixty Notes on Old English Poetry. Lunds Univ. Årsskrift, N.S. i, xvii, 1922.

—— Interpretations and Emendations of Early English Texts. Ang. xlvii, 1923.

Imelmann, R. Forschungen zur altenglischen Poesie. Berlin, 1920.

Sedgefield, W. J. Suggested Emendations in Old English Poetical Texts. MLR. xvi, 1921.

Pons, E. Odoacre dans la Poésie anglo-saxonne. Revue Germanique, July 1922.

—— Le Thème et le Sentiment de la Nature dans la Poésie anglo-saxonne. Strasburg, 1925.

Singer, S. Stil und Weltanschauung der altgermanischen Poesie. [In Festschrift für Oskar Walzel, Wildpark-Potsdam, 1924.]

Wyld, H. C. Diction and Imagery in Anglo-Saxon Poetry. E. & S. xi, 1925.

Emerson, O. F. Originality in Old English Poetry. RES. ii, 1926.

Kissack, R. A. The Sea in Anglo-Saxon and Middle English Poetry. Washington University Stud. xiii, 1926.

Klaeber, F. Weitere Randglossen zu Texterklärungen. Ang. Bbl. xxxviii, 1927.

van der Merwe Scholtz, H. The Kenning in Anglo-Saxon and Old Norse Poetry. Utrecht, 1927.

Buckhurst, H. Terms and Phrases for the Sea in Old English Poetry. [In Klaeber Studies, Minneapolis, 1929.]

Ricci, A. The Chronology of Anglo-Saxon Poetry. RES. v, 1929.

Baum, P. F. The Character of Anglo-Saxon Verse. MP. xxviii, 1930.

Bartlett, A. C. The Larger Rhetorical Patterns in Anglo-Saxon Poetry. New York, 1935.

(2) ANTHOLOGIES
(a) In Old English

Conybeare, J. J. Illustrations of Anglo-Saxon Poetry. 1826.

Grein, C. W. M. Bibliothek der angelsächsischen Poesie. Göttingen, 1857–8.

Wülcker, R. Bibliothek der angelsächsischen Poesie. 3 vols. Hamburg, 1881–98. [Revision of Grein.]

—— Kleinere angelsächsische Dichtungen. Halle, 1882.

Moeller, H. Das altenglische Volksepos in der ursprünglichen strophischen Form. Kiel, 1883.

Sedgefield, W. J. Beowulf. Together with Widsith, Waldere, Deor. Manchester, 1913 (2nd edn).

Runic and Heroic Poems of the Old Teutonic Peoples. Ed. and tr. Bruce Dickins, Cambridge, 1915.

Schücking, L. L. Kleines angelsächsisches Dichterbuch. Lyrik und Heldenepos. Cöthen, 1919.

Anglo-Saxon and Norse Poems. Ed. and tr. N. Kershaw, Cambridge, 1922.

Sedgefield, W. J. An Anglo-Saxon Verse Book. Manchester, 1922.

(b) In translation

Grein, C. W. M. Dichtungen der Angelsachsen stabreimend übersetzt. Göttingen, 1857–9.

Cook, A. S. and Tinker, C. B. Select Translations from Old English Poetry. Boston, 1902, 1926 (rev. edn).

Spaeth, J. D. Old English Poetry: Translations into Alliterative Verse with Introduction and Notes. Princeton, 1922. [See also Dickins, 1915 and Kershaw, 1922, above.]

Gordon, R. K. Anglo-Saxon Poetry. 1927 (Everyman's Lib.)

(3) CHIEF MS SOURCES OF POETRY
(a) Beowulf MS: Cotton, Vitellius A xv

Holder, A. Beowulf. Vol. i. Abdruck der Handschrift. Freiburg, 1881, 1895 (3rd edn)

Wülcker, R. Beowulf: Text nach der Handschrift. Bibliothek der angelsächsischen Poesie, vol. i, 1881–3.

Zupitza, J. Beowulf. Autotypes of the Unique Cotton MS. Vitellius A xv; with Transliteration and Notes. EETS. 1882.

Sisam, K. The Beowulf Manuscript. MLR. xi 1916.

Förster, M. Die Beowulf-Handschrift. Berichte d. sächs. Akad. d. Wissensch. lxxi, Leipzig, 1919.

Rypins, S. I. The Beowulf Codex. MP. xvii 1920.

(b) The Exeter Book

Conybeare, J. J. Account of a Saxon MS. preserved in the Cathedral Library at Exeter Archaeologia, xvii, 1814.

Chambers, R. British Museum Transcripts of the Exeter Book, BM. Add. 9067. 1831–2

Thorpe, B. Codex Exoniensis. Soc. Antiquaries, 1842. [With trn.]

Schipper, J. Collation der Exeter-Handschrift. Germania, xix, 1874.

Warren, F. E. The Leofric Missal, xix–xxvi Oxford, 1883.

Gollancz, Sir I. The Exeter Book. EETS. 1895 [With trn.]

The Exeter Book of Old English Poetry. With Introductory Chapters by R. W. Chambers, M. Förster and R. Flower, and Collotype Facsimile. Bradford, 1933.

Mackie, W. S. (ed.). The Exeter Book. Part ii. Poems ix–xxxii. EETS. 1934.

(c) MS Bodley, Junius xi

Ellis, Sir H. and Palgrave, F. Account of an Illuminated MS. of Cædmon's Paraphrase Archaeologia, xxiv, 1833.

The Cædmon MS. of Anglo-Saxon Biblical Poetry. Junius xi, in the Bodleian Library. Introd. facs. Sir Israel Gollancz, Oxford, 1927.
The Junius Manuscript. Ed. G. P. Krapp, New York, 1930.

(d) The Vercelli Book

Kemble, J. M. The Poetry of the Codex Vercellensis: Ælfric Soc.: The Legend of St Andrew, 1843; The Fates of the Twelve Apostles, 1846. [See also Quart. Rev. lxxv, 1845.]
Wülcker, R. Über das Vercellibuch. Ang. v, 1882.
—— Die angelsächsische Handschrift zu Vercelli, in Lichtdruck getreu nachgebildet. Leipzig, 1894.
Cook, A. S. Cardinal Guala and the Vercelli Book. University of California Lib. Bulletin, x, 1888.
—— Supplementary Note to 'Cardinal Guala and the Vercelli Book.' MLN. iv, 1889.
Krapp, G. P. The First Transcript of the Vercelli Book. MLN. xvii, 1902.
The Vercelli Book. Ed. G. P. Krapp, New York, 1932.

(4) Beowulf and Finnsburg

[The Beowulf MS is Cotton, Vitellius A xv. The MS of The Fight at Finnsburg has been lost; a transcript was given by George Hickes in his Thesaurus, vol. i (see History of Old English Literature: General, p. 53).]

(a) Editions

Thorkelin, G. J. De Danorum Rebus gestis Seculis III et IV. Poëma Danicum Dialecto Anglo-Saxonica. Copenhagen, 1815.
Grundtvig, N. F. S. [Finnsburg.] Bjowulfs Drape, pp. xl-xlv. [See Grundtvig, 1820, under Translations, p. 64.]
—— Beowulfes Beorh eller Bjovulfs-Drapen. Copenhagen, 1861.
Conybeare, J. J. [Finnsburg.] Illustrations, pp. 175-82. [See Conybeare, 1826, under Anthologies, p. 62 above.]
Kemble, J. M. Beowulf, the Traveller's Song, and the Battle of Finnesburh. 1833; 1835.
Schaldemose, F. Beo-Wulf og Scopes Widsið, to angelsaxiske Digte med Oversættelse og oplysende Anmærkninger. Copenhagen, 1847, 1851.
Klipstein, L. F. [Finnsburg.] Analecta. [See Klipstein, 1849, under Anthologies, p. 54 above],
Ettmüller, L. [Finnsburg.] Engla and Seaxna Scopas. [See Ettmüller, 1850, under Anthologies, p. 54 above.]

Ettmüller, L. Carmen de Beóvulfi, Gautarum Regis, Rebus praeclare gestis atque Interitu, quale fuerit antequam in Manus Interpolatoris, Monachi Vestsaxonici, incideret. Zürich, 1875.
Thorpe, B. The Anglo-Saxon Poems of Beowulf, the Scop or Gleeman's Tale, and Finnesburg, with a Literal Translation. 1855.
Grein, C. W. M. Beóvulf, Ueberfall in Finnsburg. [In Bibliothek der angelsächsischen Poesie, vol. i, Göttingen, 1857.]
—— Beovulf, nebst den Fragmenten Finnsburg und Valdere. Cassel, 1867.
Heyne, M. Beovulf, mit ausführlichem Glossar. Paderborn, 1863; rev. A. Socin, 1888; rev. L. L. Schücking, 1908, 1918 (12th edn).
Arnold, T. Beowulf, with a Translation, Notes and Appendix. 1876.
Wülcker, R. Das Beowulfslied. [In Bibliothek der angelsächsischen Poesie, vol. i, Hanover, 1881-3.]
—— [Finnsburg.] Kleinere angelsächsische Dichtungen. [See Wülcker, 1882, under Anthologies, p. 62 above.]
Harrison, J. A. and Sharp, R. Beowulf. Boston, 1883, 1894 (4th edn).
Moeller, H. Das altenglische Volksepos in der ursprünglichen strophischen Form. Kiel, 1883.
Holder, A. Beowulf. Berichtigter Text und Wörterbuch. Freiburg, 1884, 1899.
Wyatt, A. J. Beowulf, edited with Textual Footnotes, Index of Proper Names, and Glossary. Cambridge, 1894, 1898. [See also Chambers, 1914.]
Trautmann, M. [Finnsburg.] Finn und Hildebrand. BBA. vii, 1903.
—— Das Beowulflied. Das Finn-Bruchstück und die Waldhere-Bruchstücke. Bearbeiteter Text und deutsche Übersetzung. BBA. xvi, 1904.
Holthausen, F. Beowulf nebst dem Finnsburg-Bruchstück. Pt i, Texte; pt ii, Einleitung, Glossar und Anmerkungen. Heidelberg, 1905-6, 1912-3 (3rd edn), 1929 (rev.).
Sedgefield, W. J. Beowulf, with Introduction. Manchester, 1910, 1913, 1935 (rev.).
—— [Finnsburg.] [In Anglo-Saxon Verse Book, Manchester, 1922.]
Chambers, R. W. Beowulf with the Finnsburg Fragment. Ed. A. J. Wyatt. New edn, rev. Cambridge, 1914.
Dickins, Bruce. [Finnsburg.] Runic and Heroic Poems of the Old Teutonic Peoples. 1915. [See Anthologies, p. 62 above.]
Mackie, W. S. [Finnsburg.] JEGP. xvi, 1917.
Klaeber, F. Beowulf, and the Fight at Finnsburg. Boston, 1922, 1928.

(b) Translations

Turner, Sharon. History of the Anglo-Saxons. 1805. [Pp. 398–408. See also 3rd edn, vol. III, 1820.]

Grundtvig, N. F. S. Bjowulfs Drape. Copenhagen, 1820.

Kemble, J. M. A Translation of Beowulf, with Glossary, Preface and Notes. 1837.

Ettmüller, L. Beowulf, stabreimend übersetzt, mit Einleitung und Anmerkungen. Zürich, 1840.

Thorpe, B. [See Editions, 1855, p. 63 above.]

Grein, C. W. M. Dichtungen der Angelsachsen. [See Anthologies in Translation, 1857, p. 62 above.]

Uhland, L. Finnsburg. Germania, II, 1857.

Heyne, M. Beowulf übersetzt. Paderborn, 1863, 1915 (3rd edn).

Botkine, L. Beowulf en français. Havre, 1877.

Garnett, J. M. Beowulf, and the Fight at Finnsburg, translated. Boston, 1882, 1900 (4th edn).

Earle, J. The Deeds of Beowulf. Oxford, 1892.

Hall, J. L. Beowulf translated. Boston, 1892.

Morris, W. and Wyatt, A. J. The Tale of Beowulf. Kelmscott Press, 1895; 1898.

Hall, J. R. Clark. Beowulf and the Fight at Finnsburg. A Translation into Modern English Prose. 1901; 1911.

—— Beowulf: a Metrical Translation. Cambridge, 1914.

Tinker, C. B. Beowulf translated out of the Old English. New York, 1902.

—— The Translations of Beowulf: A Critical Bibliography. New Haven, 1903.

Child, C. G. Beowulf and the Finnesburh Fragment translated. Boston, 1904.

Vogt, P. Beowulf. Halle, 1905.

Gering, H. Beowulf nebst dem Finnsburg-Bruchstück übersetzt. Heidelberg, 1906, 1914.

Gummere, F. B. The Oldest English Epic. Beowulf, Finnsburg, Waldere, Deor, and the German Hildebrand, translated in the Original Metre. New York, 1909.

Kirtlan, E. J. The Story of Beowulf. 1913.

Dickins, Bruce. Finnsburg. [In Runic and Heroic Poems, Cambridge, 1915.]

Leonard, W. E. Beowulf, a New Verse Translation. New York, 1923.

Chambers, R. W. [Finnsburg.] [In G. Sampson's Cambridge Book of Prose and Verse, Cambridge, 1924.]

Strong, Archibald. Beowulf translated into Modern English Rhyming Verse; with a Foreword on Beowulf and the Heroic Age by R. W. Chambers. 1925.

Crawford, D. H. Beowulf translated into English Verse, with an Introduction, Notes and Appendices. 1926.

Wyld, H. C. Experiments in Translating Beowulf. [In Klaeber Miscellany, Minneapolis, 1929.]

[See also Trautmann, 1903–4, under Editions, p. 63 above.]

(c) Critical Studies

Mone, F. J. Zur Kritik des Gedichts von Beowulf. [In Untersuchungen zur Geschichte der teutschen Heldensage, Quedlinburg, 1836.] ·

Leo, H. Bëówulf, nach seinem Inhalte, und nach seinen historischen und mythologischen Beziehungen betrachtet. Halle, 1839.

Müllenhoff, K. Sceáf und seine Nachkommen ZDA. VII, 1849.

—— Der Mythus von Beówulf. ZDA. VII, 1849

—— Die innere Geschichte des Beovulfs ZDA. XIV, 1869.

—— Beovulf. Berlin, 1889.

Brynjulfsson, G. Oldengelsk og Oldnordisk Antikuarisk Tidsskrift, Copenhagen, 1852.

Bouterwek, K. W. Das Beowulflied. Germania, I, 1856.

—— Zur Kritik des Beowulfliedes. ZDA. XI 1859.

Rieger, M. Ingaevonen, Istaevonen, Hermionen. ZDA. XI, 1859.

—— Zum Beowulf. Zeitschrift für deutsche Philologie, III, 1871.

—— Zum Kampf in Finnsburg. ZDA. XLVIII 1905–6.

Grein, C. W. M. Die historischen Verhältnisse des Beowulfliedes. Jahrbuch für romanische und englische Litteratur, IV, 1862.]

Holtzmann, A. [Review of Heyne's trn of Finnsburg.] Germania, VIII, 1863.

Koehler, A. Germanische Altertümer im Beóvulf. Germania, XIII, 1868.

Bugge, S. Spredte Iagttagelser vedkommende de oldengelske Digte om Beówulf og Waldere. Tidsskrift for Philologi og Pædagogik, VIII, 1868–9.

—— Zum Beowulf. Zeitschrift für deutsche Philologie, IV, 1873.

—— Studien über das Beowulfepos. PBB. XII, 1887.

Dederich, H. Historische und geographische Studien zum angelsächsischen Beóvulfliede Cologne, 1877.

Schultze, M. Altheidnisches in der angelsächsischen Poesie, speciell im Beowulfsliede. Berlin, 1877.

Suchier, H. Ueber die Sage von Offa und Ðryðo. PBB. IV, 1877.

Müller, N. Die Mythen im Beówulf. Leipzig 1878.

Gering, H. Der Beówulf und die isländische Grettissaga. Ang. III, 1880.

Roenning, F. Beovulfs-kvadet; en literærhistorisk Undersøgelse. Copenhagen, 1883

Sievers, E. Zum Beowulf. PBB. ix, 1883.
—— Die Heimat des Beowulfdichters. PBB. xi, 1886.
—— Altnordisches im Beowulf? PBB. xii, 1886.
—— Zur Texterklärung des Beowulf. Ang. xiv, 1892.
—— Beowulf und Saxo. Berichte d. kgl. Gesellsch. d. Wissensch. xlvii, 1895.
—— Zum Beowulf. PBB. xxix, 1904.
—— Gegenbemerkungen zum Beowulf. PBB. xxxvi, 1910.
Krüger, T. Über Ursprung und Entwickelung des Beowulfliedes. Archiv, lxxi, 1884.
—— Zum Beowulfliede. Bromberg, 1884.
Gummere, F. B. The Translation of Beowulf, and the Relations of Ancient and Modern English Verse. AJ. Phil. vii, 1886.
Lehmann, H. Über die Waffen im angelsächsischen Beowulfliede. Germania, xxxi, 1886.
Sarrazin, G. Die Beowulfsage in Dänemark. Beowa und Böthvar. Beowulf und Kynewulf. Ang. ix, 1886.
—— Der Schauplatz des ersten Beowulfliedes und die Heimat des Dichters. PBB. xi, 1886.
—— Altnordisches im Beowulfliede. PBB. xi, 1886.
—— Beowulf-Studien. Berlin, 1888.
—— Neue Beowulf-Studien. E. Studien, xxiii, 1896.
—— Die Hirschhalle. Der Balder-Kultus in Lethra. Ang. xix, 1897.
—— Rolf Krake und sein Vetter im Beowulfliede. E. Studien, xxiv, 1897.
—— Neue Beowulf-Studien. E. Studien, xxxv, 1905.
—— Neue Beowulf-Studien. E. Studien, xlii, 1910.
Schilling, H. Notes on the Finnsaga. MLN. i, 1886.
—— The Finnsburg-Fragment and the Finn-Episode. MLN. ii, 1887.
Skeat, W. W. On the Signification of the Monster Grendel with a Discussion of ll. 2076–2100. Journ. Philology, xv, 1886.
ten Brink, B. Beowulf. Untersuchungen. QF. lxii, 1888.
Laistner, L. Das Rätsel der Sphinx. Berlin, 1889.
Lüning, O. Die Natur in der altgermanischen und mittelhochdeutschen Epik. Zürich, 1889.
Miller, T. The Position of Grendel's Arm in Heorot. Ang. xii, 1889.
Jellinek, M. H. Zum Finnsburgfragment. PBB. xv, 1891.
Bugge, S. and Olrik, A. Røveren ved Gråsten og Beowulf. Dania, i, 1891.

Schroeer, A. Zur Texterklärung des Beowulf. Ang. xiii, 1891.
Cosijn, P. J. Aanteekeningen op den Beowulf. Leyden, 1891–2.
Elton, O. The First Nine Books of the Danish History of Saxo Grammaticus. 1894. [Trn.]
Bright, J. W. Notes on the Beowulf. MLN. x, 1895.
Kluge, F. Der Beowulf und die Hrolfs Saga Kraka. E. Studien, xxii, 1895–6.
Blackburn, F. A. The Christian Coloring in the Beowulf. PMLA. xii, 1897.
Henning, R. Sceaf und die westsächsische Stammtafel. ZDA. xli, 1897.
Arnold, T. Notes on Beowulf. 1898.
Cook, A. S. An Irish Parallel to the Beowulf Story. Archiv, ciii, 1899.
—— The Possible Begetter of the Old English Beowulf and Widsith. Trans. Connecticut Academy of Arts and Sciences, xxv, 1922.
—— Theodebert of Austrasia. JEGP. xxii, 1923.
—— Aldhelm and the Source of Beowulf 2523. MLN. xl, 1925.
—— Beowulfian and Odyssean Voyages. Trans. Connecticut Academy of Arts and Sciences, xxviii, 1926.
—— The Beowulfian 'Maðelode.' JEGP. xxv, 1926.
—— Greek Parallels to certain Features of the Beowulf. PQ. v, 1026.
—— Hellenic and Beowulfian Shields and Spears. MLN. xli, 1926.
Trautmann, M. Berichtigungen, Vermutungen und Erklärungen zum Beowulf. BBA. ii, 1899.
—— Finn und Hildebrand. BBA. vii, 1903, xvii, 1905.
Holthausen, F. Finnsburg. PBB. x, 1000.
—— Beiträge zur Erklärung des altenglischen Epos. 1. Zum Beowulf. Zeitschrift für deutsche Philologie, xxxvii, 1905.
—— Zum Finnsburg-Fragment. Zeitschrift für deutsche Philologie, xxxvii, 1905.
—— Zur Datierung des Beowulf. Ang. Bbl. xviii, 1907.
Klaeber, F. A few Beowulf Notes. MLN. xvi, 1901.
—— Beowulf's Character. MLN. xvii, 1902.
—— Zum Beowulf. Archiv, cviii, 1902.
—— Bemerkungen zum Beowulf. Archiv, cxv, 1905.
—— Notizen zur Texterklärung des Beowulf. Ang. xxviii, 1905.
—— Studies in the Textual Interpretation of Beowulf. MP. iii, 1905–6.
—— Notizen zum Beowulf. Ang. xxix, 1906.
—— Minor Notes on the Beowulf. JEGP. vi, 1907.
—— Zum Beowulf. E. Studien, xxxix, 1908.

Klaeber, F. Zum Finnsburg Kampfe. E. Studien, xxxix, 1908.
—— Textual Notes on Beowulf. JEGP. viii, 1909.
—— Die ältere Genesis und der Beowulf. E. Studien, xlii, 1910.
—— Aeneis und Beowulf. Archiv, cxxvi, 1911.
—— Die christlichen Elemente im Beowulf. Ang. xxxv, xxxvi, 1911–2.
—— Observations on the Finn Episode. JEGP. xiv, 1915.
—— Concerning the relation between Exodus and Beowulf. MLN. xxxiii, 1918.
—— Concerning the Functions of Old English geweorðan. JEGP. xviii, 1919.
—— Textual Notes on Beowulf. MLN. xxxiv, 1919.
—— Der Held Beowulf in deutscher Sagenüberlieferung. Ang. xlvi, 1922.
—— Beowulfiana. Ang. i, 1926.
—— Attila's and Beowulf's Funeral. PMLA. xlii, 1927.
Barnouw, A. J. Textkritische Untersuchungen nach dem Gebrauch des bestimmten Artikels und des schwachen Adjektivs in der altenglischen Poesie. Leyden, 1902.
Boer, R. C. Die Béowulfsage. Arkiv för nordisk Filologi, xix, 1902.
—— Finnsage und Nibelungensage. ZDA. xlvii, 1903–4.
—— Die altenglische Heldendichtung. 1. Beowulf. Halle, 1912.
—— Studier over Skjoldungedigtningen. Aarbøger for Nordisk Oldkyndighed og Historie, iii, pt xii, 1922.
Brandl, A. Ueber den gegenwärtigen Stand der Beowulf-Forschung. Archiv, cviii, 1902.
—— Die Urstammtafel der Westsachsen und das Beowulf-Epos. Archiv, cxxxvii, 1918.
Olrik, A. Danmarks Heltedigtning. 1. Rolf Krake og den ældre Skjoldungrække. Copenhagen, 1903.
—— Danmarks Heltedigtning. 2. Starkad den gamle og den yngre Skjoldungrække. Copenhagen, 1910.
—— The Heroic Legends of Denmark translated, and revised in Collaboration with the Author by L. M. Hollander. New York, 1919.
—— Nogle Grundsætninger for Sagnforskning. Copenhagen, 1921.
Stjerna, K. Hjälmar och Svärd i Beovulf. [In Studier tillägnade O. Montelius, Stockholm, 1903.]
—— Vendel och Vendelkråka. Arkiv för nordisk Filologi, xxi, 1904.
—— Arkeologiska Anteckningar till Beovulf. Kungl. Vitterhets Akademiens Månadsblad, 1907 (for 1903–5).
—— Essays on Questions connected with the Old English Poem of Beowulf. Tr. and ed. J. R. Clark Hall, Coventry, 1912.

Abbott, W. C. Hrothulf. MLN. xix, 1904. [See also F. Klaeber, MLN. xx, 1905.]
Kock, E. A. Beowulf. Ang. xxvii, 1904.
—— Interpretations and Emendations o Early English Texts. iv. Beowulf. Ang xlii, 1918.
Rickert, E. The Old English Offa-Saga. MP ii, 1904.
Schücking, L. L. Die Grundzüge der Satzverknüpfung im Beowulf. Pt i. SEP. xv 1904.
—— Beowulfs Rückkehr. SEP. xxi, 1905.
—— Das angelsächsische Totenklagelied. E Studien, xxxix, 1908.
—— Wann entstand der Beowulf? Glossen Zweifel und Fragen. PBB. xlii, 1917.
—— Wiðergyld (Beowulf, 2051). E. Studien liii, 1920.
—— Die Beowulfdatierung. Eine Replik PBB. xlvii, 1923.
—— Heldenstolz und Würde im Angelsächsischen. Abh. der sächs. Akad. der Wiss Phil.-hist. Kl. xlii, no. 5, Leipzig, 1933.
Routh, J. E. Two Studies on the Ballad Theory of the Beowulf: 1. The Origin o the Grendel Legend; 2. Irrelevant Episode and Parentheses as Features of Anglo Saxon Poetic Style. Baltimore, 1905.
Scheinert, M. Die Adjektiva im Beowulfepos als Darstellungsmittel. PBB. xxx, 1905.
Heusler, A. Zur Skiöldungendichtung. ZDA xlviii, 1905–6.
Emerson, O. F. Legends of Cain, especially in Old and Middle English. PMLA. xxi 1906.
—— Grendel's Motive in Attacking Heorot MLR. xvi, 1921.
—— The Punctuation of Beowulf and Literary Interpretation. MP. xxiii, 1926.
Morsbach, L. Zur Datierung des Beowulfepos Nachrichten d. kgl. Gesellsch. d. Wissensch zu Göttingen, Phil.-hist. Kl. 1906.
Ries, J. Die Wortstellung im Beowulf. Halle 1907.
Schück, H. Folknamnet Geatas i den fornengelska Dikten Beowulf. Upsala 1907.
—— Studier i Beowulfsagen. Upsala, 1909.
Bjoerkman, E. Über den Namen der Jüten E. Studien, xxxix, 1908.
—— Beowulf och Sveriges Historia. Nordisk Tidsskrift, vii, 1917.
—— Zu altenglisch EOte, Yte, usw., dänischen Jyder, 'Jüten.' Ang. Bbl. xxviii 1917.
—— Bēow, Bēaw und Bēowulf. E. Studien lii, 1918.
—— Scedeland, Scedenig. Namn och Bygd vi, 1918.
—— Bedwig in den westsächsischen Genealogien. Ang. Bbl. xxx, 1919.

Bjoerkman, E. Zu einigen Namen im Bēowulf: Breca, Brondingas, Wealhþēo(w). Ang. Bbl. xxx, 1919.

—— Hæðcyn und Hakon. E. Studien, LIV, 1920.

—— Studien über die Eigennamen im Beowulf. SEP. LVIII, 1920.

Weyhe, H. König Ongentheow's Fall. E. Studien, XXXIX, 1908.

Child, G. C. Gummere's 'Oldest English Epic.' MLN. XXIV, 1909.

Deutschbein, M. Die sagenhistorischen und literarischen Grundlagen des Beowulfepos. Germanisch-romanische Monatsschrift, I, 1909.

—— Beowulf der Gautenkönig. [In Morsbach Festschrift, pp. 291–7, Halle, 1913.]

Lawrence, W. W. Some disputed Questions in Beowulf-criticism. PMLA. XXIV, 1909.

—— The Haunted Mere in Beowulf. PMLA. XXVII, 1912.

—— The Breca Episode in Beowulf. [In Anniversary Papers to G. L. Kittredge, Boston, 1913.]

—— Beowulf and the Tragedy of Finnsburg. PMLA. XXX, 1915.

—— The Dragon and his Lair in Beowulf. PMLA. XXXIII, 1918.

—— Beowulf and Epic Tradition. Cambridge, U.S.A. 1928.

Bradley, H. Beowulf. Ency. Brit. vol. III, 1910.

—— The Numbered Sections in Old English Poetical MSS. Proc. British Academy, VII, 1915.

Panzer, F. Studien zur germanischen Sagengeschichte. 1. Beowulf. Munich, 1910.

Sedgefield, W. J. Notes on Beowulf. MLR. V, 1910.

Smithson, G. A. The Old English Christian Epic in Comparison with the Beowulf. Berkeley, 1910.

von Grienberger, T. Bemerkungen zum Beowulf. PBB. XXXVI, 1910.

Blackburn, F. A. A Note on Beowulf. MP. IX, 1911.

Liebermann, F. Grendel als Personenname. Archiv, CXXVI, 1911.

—— Ort und Zeit der Beowulfdichtung. Nachrichten d. kgl. Gesellsch. d. Wissensch. zu Göttingen, Phil.-hist. Kl. 1920.

Heusler, A. [Articles in Hoops' Reallexikon, 1911–9.]

Chambers, R. W. Six Thirteenth Century Drawings illustrating the Story of Offa and of Thryth (Ðriða) from MS. Cotton, Nero D I. 1912 (priv. ptd).

—— The 'Shifted Leaf' in Beowulf. MLR. X, 1915.

—— Beowulf: An Introduction to the Study of the Poem with a Discussion of the Stories of Offa and Finn. Cambridge, 1921, 1932 (enlarged).

Chambers, R. W. Beowulf and the Heroic Age. [In Strong's trn, 1925.]

—— Beowulf's Fight with Grendel, and its Scandinavian Parallels. E. Studies, XI, 1929.

Meyer, W. Beiträge zur Geschichte der Eroberung Englands durch die Angelsachsen. Halle, 1912.

Schütte, G. The Geats of Beowulf. JEGP. XI, 1912.

—— Vor Folkegruppe Godtjod. Copenhagen, 1926.

Stefanovič, S. Ein Beitrag zur angelsächsischen Offa-sage. Ang. XXXV, 1912.

Belden, H. M. Onela the Scylfing and Ali th Bold. MLN. XXVIII, 1913.

Nerman, B. Vilka Konungar ligga i Uppsala Högar? Upsala, 1913.

—— Ottar Vendelkråka och Ottarshögen i Vendel. Upplands Fornminnesförenings Tidskrift, VII, 1917.

—— Ynglingasagan i arkeologisk Belysning. Fornvännen, pp. 226–61, 1917.

Thomas, P. G. Beowulf and Daniel A. MLR. VIII, 1913.

von Sydow, C. W. Irisches in Beowulf. Verhandlungen der 52. Versammlung deutscher Philologen in Marburg, 1913.

—— Grendel i anglosaxiska Ortnamen. Namn och Bygd, II, 1914.

—— Beowulf och Bjarke. Studier i Nordisk Filologi, XIV, 1923.

—— Beowulfskalden och nordisk Tradition. Lund, 1923.

—— Scyld Scefing. Namn och Bygd, XII, 1924.

Moorman, F. W. English Place-Names and Teutonic Sagas. E. & S. V, 1914.

Olson, O. L. Beowulf and the Feast of Bricriu. MP. XI, 1914.

—— The Relation of the Hrólfs Saga Kraka and the Bjarkarímur to Beowulf. Chicago, 1916.

Kier, C. Beowulf, et Bidrag til Nordens Oldhistorie. Copenhagen, 1915.

Green, A. The Opening of the Episode of Finn in Beowulf. PMLA. XXXI, 1916.

Pizzo, Enrico. Zur Frage der ästhetischen Einheit des Beowulf. Ang. XXXIX, 1916.

Aurner, N. S. An Analysis of the Interpretations of the Finnsburg Documents. Iowa City, 1917.

—— Hengest. A Study in Early English Hero Legend. Iowa City, 1921.

Ayres, H. M. The Tragedy of Hengest in Beowulf. JEGP. XVI, 1917.

Mead, G. W. Wiðerʒyld of Beowulf 2051. MLN. XXXII, 1917.

Rooth, E. G. T. Der Name Grendel in der Beowulfsage. Ang. Bbl. XXVIII, 1917.

Hackenberg, E. Die Stammtafeln der angelsächsischen Königreiche. Berlin, 1918.

Hubbard, F. G. The Plundering of the Hoard in Beowulf. Madison, 1918.

Leonard, W. E. Beowulf and the Nibelungen Couplet. Madison, 1918.

Brown, Carleton. Beowulf 1080–1106. MLN. xxxiv, 1919.

Förster, M. Die Beowulf-Handschrift. Leipzig, 1919.

Hoops, J. Das Verhüllen des Haupts bei Toten, ein angelsächsisch-nordischer Brauch. E. Studien, LIV, 1920.

—— Beowulfstudien. Anglistische Forschungen, LXXIV, 1932.

—— Kommentar zum Beowulf. Heidelberg, 1932.

Imelmann, R. Forschungen zur altenglischen Poesie. Vols. IX–XIII. Berlin, 1920.

La Cour, V. Lejrestudier. Danske Studier, 1920.

Noreen, A. Yngve, Inge, Inglinge [Ingwine]. Namn och Bygd, VIII, 1920.

Schreiner, K. Die Sage von Hengest und Horsa. Entwicklung und Nachleben bei den Dichtern und Geschichtschreibern Englands. Berlin, 1921.

Rypins, S. I. A Contribution to the Study of the Beowulf Codex. PMLA. xxxvi, 1921.

Herman, Paul. Die Heldensagen des Saxo Grammaticus. [Pt II of Erläuterungen zu den neun ersten Büchern der dänischen Geschichte des Saxo Grammaticus, Leipzig, 1922.]

Mackie, W. S. The Fight at Finnsburg. MLR. XVII, 1922.

Matter, H. Englische Gründungssagen. Anglistische Forschungen, LVIII, 1922.

Patzig, H. Zur Episode von Đryð in Beowulf. Ang. XLVI, 1922.

—— Zum Beowulf-Text. Ang. XLVII, 1922.

Keller, W. [Review of Förster's Die Beowulf-Handschrift.] Ang. Bbl. xxxiv, 1923.

Malone, K. The Literary History of Hamlet. 1. The Early Tradition. Heidelberg, 1923.

—— King Alfred's 'Geats.' MLR. xx, 1925.

—— The Finn Episode in Beowulf. JEGP. xxv, 1926.

—— Hrethric. PMLA. XLII, 1927.

Williams, R. A. The Finn Episode in Beowulf. Cambridge, 1924.

Briggs, W. D. On Kemp Malone's Literary History of Hamlet, 1. JEGP. xxiv, 1925.

Craigie, W. A. Interpolations and Omissions in Anglo-Saxon Poetic Texts. Philologica, II, 1925.

Wadstein, E. Norden och Västeuropa i gammal Tid. Stockholm, 1925.

Crawford, S. J. Ealu-scerwen (ll. 767–9). MLR. xxi, 1926.

Hübener, G. Beowulf und die Psychologie der Standesentwicklung. Germanisch-romanische Monatsschrift, xiv, 1926.

Hübener, G. Beowulf and Germanic Exorcism. RES. xi, 1935.

Stroemholm, D. Försök över Beowulfdikten och Ynglingasagan. Edda, xxv, 1926.

Magoun, F. P. The Burning of Heorot: an Illustrative Note. MLN. XLII, 1927.

Wessén, E. De nordiska Folkstammarna i Beowulf. Kungl. Vitterhets Hist. och Antik. Akad. Handlingar, Stockholm, 1927.

—— Nordiska Namnstudier. Uppsala Univ. Årsskrift, 1927.

Haber, T. B. A Comparative Study of the Beowulf and the Aeneid. Princeton, 1931.

Olivero, F. Introduzione al Beowulf. Turin, 1934.

Berendsohn, W. A. Zur Vorgeschichte des Beowulf. Copenhagen, 1935.

Girvan, R. Beowulf and the Seventh Century. 1935.

Herben, S. J. Heorot. PMLA. L, 1935.

(5) MINOR HEROIC POEMS

(a) *Deor*

MS. Exeter Book, fol. 100.

Editions.

Malone, K. Deor. 1933.

[Also in the following:
Conybeare, Illustrations, 1826 (with trn).
Grimm, Die deutsche Heldensage, 1828.
Thorpe, Codex Exoniensis, 1842 (with trn).
Klipstein, Analecta, 1849.
Ettmüller, Scopas, 1850.
Grein, Bibliothek der angelsächsischen Poesie, 1857.
Rieger, Lesebuch, 1861.
Wülcker, Kleinere angelsächsische Dichtungen, 1882.
—— Bibliothek der angelsächsischen Poesie, vol. I, 1881–3.
Sedgefield, Beowulf, 2nd edn, 1913.
—— Anglo-Saxon Verse Book, 1922.
Dickins, Runic and Heroic Poems, 1915 (with trn).
Wyatt, Anglo-Saxon Reader, 1919.
Schücking, Kleines angelsächsisches Dichterbuch, 1919.]

Translations.
Haigh, D. H. Atlantic Monthly, LXVII, 1891.
Burton, R. The Oldest English Lyric. Poet-Lore, v, 1893.
Gummere, F. B. The Oldest English Epic. 1909. [Pp. 185 ff.]

Criticism.
Müllenhoff, K. Sängernamen. ZDA. VII, 1849.
—— Deor's Klage. ZDA. XI, XII, 1859.
Tupper, J. W. Deor's Complaint. MLN. x, 1895.
—— Deor. MP. IX, 1911.

Tupper, J. W. The Third Strophe of Deor. Ang. xxxvii, 1913.

Bugge, S. The Norse Lay of Wayland and its Relation to English Tradition. Sagabook of Viking Club, ii, 1900.

Maurus, P. Die Wielandsage in der Literatur. Munich, 1902.

Klaeber, F. Zu Deors Klage, 15 ff. Ang. Bbl. xvii, 1906.

—— The First Line of Deor. Ang. Bbl. xxxii, 1921.

Stefanovič, S. Zu Deor, v. 14–17. Ang. xxxiii, 1910. [See also Ang. xxxvi, 1913.]

Lawrence, W. W. The Song of Deor. MP. ix, 1911.

von Grienberger, T. Déor. Ang. xlv, 1921.

(b) Waldere

MS. Two leaves in the Royal Library at Copenhagen, MS 167 b.

Editions.

Stephens, G. Two Leaves of King Waldere's Lay. Copenhagen, 1860. [With trn.]

Dietrich, F. and Müllenhoff, K. Waldere. ZDA. xii, 1860–5.

Weinhold, K. [In Scheffel and Holder's Waltharius, Stuttgart, 1874, pp. 168 ff.]

Holthausen, F. Die altenglischen Waldere-Bruchstücke. Mit vier Autotypen. Gotenburg, 1899.

Norman, F. Waldere. 1934.

[Also in the following:

Rieger, Lesebuch, 1861.

Grein, Beovulf, 1867.

Wülcker, Bibliothek der angelsächsischen Poesie, vol. i, 1881–3.

—— Kleinere angelsächsische Dichtungen, 1882.

Moeller, Das altenglische Volksepos, 1883.

Heinzel (see below), 1889.

Trautmann (see below), 1900.

Kluge, Lesebuch, 1902.

Holthausen, Beowulf, 3rd edn, 1912–3.

Sedgefield, Beowulf, 2nd edn, 1913.

—— Anglo-Saxon Verse Book, 1922.

Dickins, Runic and Heroic Poems, 1915 (with trn).

Wyatt, Anglo-Saxon Reader, 1919.]

[Translations also in:

Gummere, Oldest English Epic, 1909.

Clarke, Sidelights, 1911.]

Criticism.

Bugge, S. Spredte Iagttagelser. [See Beowulf, 1868–9, p. 64, above.]

Koelbing, E. Die Waldere-Fragmente. E. Studien, v, 1882.

Dieter, F. Die Walderefragmente und die ursprüngliche Gestalt der Walthersage. Ang. x, 1888, xi, 1889.

Heinzel, R. Über die Walthersage. Vienna, 1889.

Kelle, J. Geschichte der deutschen Literatur. Berlin, 1892. [Vol. i, pp. 218–26.]

Learned, M. D. The Saga of Walther of Aquitaine. PMLA. iv, 1892.

Cosijn, P. J. De Waldere-Fragmenten. Verslagen en Mededeelingen d. Akad. van Wetenschappen; Afd. Letterkunde, ser. 3, pt xii, p. 1, 1895.

Althof, H. Über einige Stellen im Waltharius und die angelsächsischen Waldere-Fragmente. Weimar, 1899.

—— Waltharii Poesis. Leipzig, 1899–1905.

—— Das Waltharilied. Leipzig, 1902.

—— Über einige Namen im Waltharius. Zeitschrift für deutsche Philologie, xxxiv, 1902.

Symons, B. [In PG. vol. iii², 1900.]

Trautmann, M. Zur Berichtigung der Waldere-Bruchstücke. BBA. v, 1900.

—— Zum zweiten Waldhere-Bruchstück. BBA. xi, 1901.

Boer, R. C. Untersuchungen über die Hildesage. Zeitschrift für deutsche Philologie, xl, 1907–8.

Eckerth, W. Das Waltherlied. Halle, 1909 (2nd edn).

Droege, K. Nibelungenlied und Waltharius. ZDA. lii, 1909–10.

Simons, L. Waltharius en de Walthersage. Leuvensche Bijdragen, xi, 1913–4.

Leitzmann, A. Walther und Hiltgunt bei den Angelsachsen. Halle, 1917.

Krappe, A. H. The Legend of Walther and Hildegund. JEGP. xxii, 1923.

Schücking, L. L. Waldere und Waltharius. E. Studien, lx, 1925.

Wolff, L. Zu den Waldere-Bruchstücken. ZDA. lxii, 1925.

Klaeber, F. Zu den Waldere-Bruchstücken. Ang. li, 1927.

(c) Widsið

MS. Exeter Book, fols. 84 b–87 a.

Editions.

Kemble, J. M. Traveller's Song. [In The Anglo-Saxon Poems of Beowulf, etc., 1833.]

Ettmüller, L. Scôpes vidsidh. Sängers Weitfahrt. Ædhelstans Sieg bei Brunanburg. Angelsächsisch und deutsch. Zürich, 1839. [See also Schaldemose, 1847, under Beowulf, p. 63 above.]

Chambers, R. W. Widsith: a Study in Old English Heroic Legend. Cambridge, 1912 (with trn).

Malone, K. Widsith. 1935.

[Also in the following:
Conybeare, Illustrations, 1826.
Guest, History of English Rhythms, 1838
(with trn).
Leo, Sprachproben, 1838 (with trn).
Ebeling, Lesebuch, 1847.
Klipstein, Analecta, 1849.
Ettmüller, Scopas, 1850.
Thorpe, Beowulf, 1855.
Rieger, Lesebuch, 1861.
Wülcker, Bibliothek der angelsächsischen
Poesie, vol. I, 1881-3.
—— Kleinere angelsächsische Dichtungen,
1882.
Moeller, Altenglisches Volksepos, 1883.
Kluge, Lesebuch, 1897 (2nd edn).
Sedgefield, Beowulf, 1910.
—— Anglo-Saxon Verse Book, 1922.]
Translations.
Gummere, F. B. Widsith, a Translation.
MLN. IV, 1889. [See also Gummere, Oldest
English Epic, 1909.]
Schütte, G. [Tr. into Danish.] [In Oldsagn
om Godtjod, Copenhagen, 1907.]
Criticism.
Lappenberg, J. M. [Review of Leo's Sprach-
proben.] Jahrbuch für wissenschaftliche
Kritik, II, 1838.
Müllenhoff, K. Die deutschen Völker in Nord-
und Ostsee in ältester Zeit. Nordal-
bingische Studien, I, 1844.
—— Zur Kritik des angelsächsischen Volks-
epos. 2. Widsith. ZDA. XI, 1859.
Maurer, K. Islands und Norwegens Verkehr
mit dem Süden. Zeitschrift für deutsche
Philologie, II, 1870.
Schipper, J. Zum Codex Exoniensis. Ger-
mania, XIX, 1874.
Lawrence, W. W. Structure and Interpreta-
tion of Widsith. MP. IV, 1906.
Siebs, O. Wídsíð. [In Festschrift für Wilhelm
Viëtor, Marburg, 1910.]
Anscombe, A. Widsith. Ang. XXXIV, 1911.
Jiriczek, O. Seafola in Widsith. E. Studien,
LIV, 1920.
Sievers, E. Zum Widsith. Texte und For-
schungen zur englischen Kulturgeschichte,
[In Festgabe für F. Liebermann, Halle,
1921.]
von Grienberger, T. Widsíð. Ang. XLVI, 1922.
Malone, K. The 'Widsith' and the 'Hervarar-
saga.' PMLA. XL, 1925.
Much, R. Widsith. Beiträge zu einem Com-
mentar. ZDA. LXII, 1925.
Klaeber, F. Widsíð. Ang. Bbl. XXXVIII, 1926.

(6) ELEGIAC POEMS

(a) General

Sieper, E. Die altenglische Elegie. Strasburg,
1915.

Ricci, H. L'Elegia pagana Anglosassone.
Florence, 1923.

(b) The Wanderer

MS. Exeter Book, fols. 76 b-78 a.
Editions.
[Thorpe, Codex Exoniensis, 1842 (with trn).
Klipstein, Analecta, 1849.
Ettmüller, Scopas, 1850.
Rieger, Lesebuch, 1861.
Sweet, Anglo-Saxon Reader, 1876.
Wülcker, Kleinere angelsächsische Dichtungen,
1882.
—— Bibliothek der angelsächsischen Poesie,
vol. I, 1881-3.
Bright, Anglo-Saxon Reader, 1893.
Schücking, Kleines angelsächsisches Dich-
terbuch, 1919.
Wyatt, Anglo-Saxon Reader, 1919.
Kershaw, Anglo-Saxon and Norse Poems,
1922 (with trn).
Sedgefield, Anglo-Saxon Verse Book, 1922.]
Translations.
Hickey, E. H. The Wanderer. Academy,
14 May 1881.
Sims, W. R. The Wanderer. MLN. v, 1899.
Criticism.
Rieger, M. Über Cynewulf v. Zeitschrift für
deutsche Philologie, I, 1869.
Ferrell, C. Old Germanic Life in the Anglo-
Saxon Wanderer and Seafarer. MLN. IX,
1894.
Bright, J. W. The Wanderer, 78-84. MLN.
XIII, 1898.
Lawrence, W. W. The Wanderer and the Sea-
farer. JEGP. IV, 1902.
Boer, R. C. The Wanderer. Zeitschrift für
deutsche Philologie, XXXV, 1902-3.
Imelmann, R. Wanderer und Seafarer im
Rahmen der altenglischen Odoakerdichtung.
Berlin, 1908.
Hempel, H. Untersuchungen zum Wanderer.
Halle, 1915.
Ashdown, M. The Wanderer, ll. 41-43. MLR.
XXII, 1927.

(c) The Seafarer

MS. Exeter Book, fols. 81 b-83 a.
Editions.
[Thorpe, Codex Exoniensis, 1842 (with trn).
Ettmüller, Scopas, 1850.
Grein, Bibliothek der angelsächsischen Poesie,
1857.
Sweet, Anglo-Saxon Reader, 1876.
Wülcker, Kleinere angelsächsische Dichtungen,
1882.
—— Bibliothek der angelsächsischen Poesie,
vol. I, 1881-3.
Schücking, Kleines angelsächsisches Dichter-
buch. 1919.

Kershaw, Anglo-Saxon and Norse Poems, 1922 (with trn).
Sedgefield, Anglo-Saxon Verse Book, 1922.]

Translation.
Merry, G. R. Academy, 8 Feb. 1890.

Criticism.
Rieger, M. Der Seefahrer als Dialog herge-stellt. Zeitschrift für deutsche Philologie, I, 1869.
Kluge, F. Der Seefahrer. E. Studien, VI, 1882, VIII, 1883.
Hoenncher, E. Zur Dialogeinteilung im See-fahrer. Ang. IX, 1886.
Boer, R. C. Seafarer. Zeitschrift für deutsche Philologie, XXXV, 1902–3.
Holthausen, F. Zur altenglischen Literatur: Seefahrer. Ang. Bbl. XIX, 1908.
—— Seefahrer, 68–71. Ang.Bbl.XXXVIII,1927.
Sisam, K. The Seafarer, ll. 72 ff. E. Studien, XLVI, 1913.
Daunt, M. The Seafarer, ll. 97–102. MLR. XI, 1916.
—— Some Difficulties of the Seafarer re-considered. MLR. XIII, 1918.
[See also Ferrell, 1894, Lawrence, 1902, and Imelmann, 1908, under Wanderer, above.]

(d) The Husband's Message

MS. Exeter Book, fol. 123 a, b.

Editions.
Blackburn, F. A. The Husband's Message, and the accompanying Riddles of the Exeter Book. JEGP. III, 1901. [With trn.]

[Also in the following:
Thorpe, Codex Exoniensis, 1842 (with trn).
Klipstein, Analecta, 1849.
Ettmüller, Scopas, 1850.
Grein, Bibliothek der angelsächsischen Poesie, 1857.
Wülcker,KleinereangelsächsischeDichtungen, 1882.
—— Bibliothek der angelsächsischen Poesie, vol. I, 1881–3.
Schücking, Kleines angelsächsisches Dichter-buch, 1919.
Wyatt, Anglo-Saxon Reader, 1919.
Kershaw, Anglo-Saxon and Norse Poems, 1922 (with trn).
Sedgefield, Anglo-Saxon Verse Book, 1922.]

Criticism.
Hicketier, F. Klage der Frau, Botschaft des Gemahls, und Ruine. Ang. XI, 1889.
Trautmann, M. Zur Botschaft des Gemahls. Ang. XVI, 1894.
Holthausen, F. Zur Botschaft des Gemahls. Ang. Bbl. XXXIV, 1923.
[See also Imelmann, 1907, under Wolf and Eadwacer, below.]

(e) The Wife's Complaint

MS. Exeter Book, fol. 115 a, b.

Editions.
[Conybeare, Illustrations, 1826 (with trn).
Thorpe, Codex Exoniensis, 1842 (with trn).
Klipstein, Analecta, 1849.
Ettmüller, Scopas, 1850.
Grein, Bibliothek der angelsächsischen Poesie, 1857.
Wülcker,KleinereangelsächsischeDichtungen, 1882.
—— Bibliothek der angelsächsischen Poesie, vol. I, 1881–3,
Schücking, Kleines angelsächsisches Dichter-buch, 1919.
Kershaw, Anglo-Saxon and Norse Poems, 1922 (with trn).
Sedgefield, Anglo-Saxon Verse Book, 1922.]

Criticism.
Roeder, F. Die Familie bei den Angelsachsen. SEP. IV, 1899.
Rickert, E. The Wife's Complaint. MP. II, 1905. [See W. W. Lawrence, MP. v, 1908.]
Stefanovič, S. Das angelsächsische Gedicht Die Klage der Frau. Ang. XXXII, 1909.
[See also Hicketier, 1889, under Husband's Message, above.]

(f) The Ruin

MS. Exeter Book, fols. 123 b–124 b,

Editions.
Leo, H. Carmen Anglosaxonicum in Codice Exoniensi servatum quod vulgo inscribitur Ruinæ. Halle, 1865.
Earle, J. An Ancient Saxon Poem of a City in Ruins, supposed to be Bath. Bath, 1872. [With trn.]

[Also in the following:
Conybeare, Illustrations, 1826.
Thorpe, Codex Exoniensis, 1842.
Klipstein, Analecta, 1849.
Ettmüller, Scopas, 1850.
Grein, Bibliothek der angelsächsischen Poesie, 1857.
Wülcker,KleinereangelsächsischeDichtungen, 1882.
—— Bibliothek der angelsächsischen Poesie, vol. I, 1881–3.
Schücking, Kleines angelsächsisches Dichter-buch, 1919.
Kershaw, Anglo-Saxon and Norse Poems, 1922.]

Criticism.
Wülcker, R. Ruine. Ang. II, 1879.
Earle, J. The Ruined City. Academy, 12 July 1884.
[See also Hicketier, 1889, under Husband's Message, above.]

(g) *Wolf and Eadwacer*

MS. Exeter Book, fol. 100 b.

Editions. [See under Riddles. See also Sedge-field, Anglo-Saxon Verse Book, 1922.]

Criticism.

Bradley, H. The First Riddle of the Exeter Book. Academy, 24 March 1888. [Rptd in Collected Papers, 1928.]

Gollancz, Sir I. Reports of Societies. Philological. Academy, 23 Dec. 1893.

—— Wulf and Eadwacer. An Anglo-Saxon Monodrama in Five Acts. Athenaeum, 23 Dec. 1893.

Holthausen, F. Klage um Wulf. Ang. xv, 1893.

Lawrence, W. W. The First Riddle of Cynewulf. PMLA. xvii, 1902.

Imelmann, R. Die altenglische Odoaker-Dichtung. Berlin, 1907.

Trautmann, M. Das sogenannte Erste Rätsel. Ang. xxxvi, 1912.

Budjuhn, G. Leodum is minum—ein altenglischer Dialog. Ang. xl, 1916.

Patzig, H. Zum ersten Rätsel des Exeterbuches. Archiv, cxlv, 1923.

(7) RIDDLES

MS. Exeter Book, fols. 101 a–115 a, 122 b–123 a, 124 b–130 b.

Editions.

Thorpe, B. Codex Exoniensis. 1842. [Pp. 380–441, 470–2, 479–500 (with trn).]

Grein, C. W. M. Bibliothek der angelsächsischen Poesie. Vol. ii, Göttingen, 1858.

Wülcker, R. Bibliothek der angelsächsischen Poesie. Vol. iii, Hanover, 1897–8.

Tupper, F. The Riddles of the Exeter Book. 1910.

Wyatt, A. J. Old English Riddles. Boston, 1912.

Trautmann, M. Die altenglischen Rätsel. Heidelberg, 1915.

Translations.

Grein, C. W. M. Dichtungen der Angelsachsen. Vol. ii, Göttingen, 1863.

Brooke, Stopford A. Early English Literature. 1892. [Selection.]

Criticism.

Dietrich, F. Die Rätsel des Exeterbuches. ZDA. xi, 1859, xii, 1860.

Müller, E. Die Rätsel des Exeterbuches. Cöthen, 1861.

Grein, C. W. M. Zu den Rätseln des Exeterbuches. Germania, x, 1865.

Ebert, A. Die Rätsel-Poesie der Angelsachsen. Berichte über d. Verhandl. d. kgl. sächs. Gesellsch. d. Wissensch., Phil.-hist. Kl. xxix, Leipzig, 1877.

Prehn, A. Komposition und Quellen der Rätsel des Exeterbuches. Neuphilologische Studien, no. 3, Paderborn, 1883.

Trautmann, M. Cynewulf und die Rätsel. Ang. Anz. vi, 1883.

—— Zum 89. (95.) Rätsel. Ang. Anz. vii, 1884.

—— Die Auflösungen der altenglischen Rätsel. Ang. Bbl. v, 1894.

—— Zu den altenglischen Rätseln. Ang. xvii, 1895.

—— Alte und neue Antworten auf altenglische Rätsel. BBA. xix, 1905.

—— Zum Streit um die altenglischen Rätsel. Ang. xxxvi, 1912.

—— Das Geschlecht in den altenglischen Rätseln. Ang. Bbl. xxv, 1914.

—— Die Quellen der altenglischen Rätsel. Sprache und Versbau der altenglischen Rätsel. Zeit, Heimat und Verfasser der altenglischen Rätsel. Ang. xxxviii, 1914.

—— Zu den Lösungen der Rätsel des Exeterbuches. Ang. Bbl. xxv, 1914.

—— Zu meiner Ausgabe der altenglischen Rätsel. Ang. xlii, 1918.

Hicketier, F. Fünf Rätsel des Exeterbuches. Ang. x, 1888.

Nuck, R. Zu Trautmanns Deutung des ersten und neunundachtzigsten Rätsels. Ang. x, 1888.

Herzfeld, G. Die Rätsel des Exeterbuches und ihr Verfasser. Acta Germanica, ii, pt i, Berlin, 1890.

Cook, A. S. Recent Opinion concerning the Riddles of the Exeter Book. MLN. vii, 1892.

Walz, J. A. Notes on the Anglo-Saxon Riddles. Harvard Stud. v, 1896.

Madert, A. Die Sprache der altenglischen Rätsel des Exeterbuches und die Cynewulffrage. Marburg, 1900.

Blackburn, F. A. The Husband's Message and the Accompanying Riddles of the Exeter Book. JEGP. iii, 1901.

Erlemann, E. Zu den altenglischen Rätseln. Archiv, cxi, 1903.

—— Zum 90. angelsächsischen Rätsel. Archiv, cxv, 1905.

Tupper, F. The Holme Riddles. (Harl. MS 1960.) PMLA. xvii, 1903.

—— The Comparative Study of Riddles; Originals and Analogues of the Exeter Book Riddles. MLN. xviii, 1903.

—— Solutions of the Exeter Book Riddles. MLN. xxi, 1906.

Holthausen, F. Zur altenglischen Literatur. 11. Rätsel. Ang. Bbl. xvi, 1905.

—— Zur Textkritik altenglischer Dichtungen. E. Studien, xxxvi, 1906.

—— Zu den altenglischen Rätseln. Ang. xxxv, 1912; Ang. Bbl. xxx, 1912.

Holthausen, F. Nochmals die altenglischen Rätsel. Ang. xxxviii, 1914.
—— Zu den altenglischen Rätseln. E.Studien, li, 1917.
Liebermann, F. Das angelsächsische Rätsel, 56: 'Galgen' als Waffenständer. Archiv, cxiv, 1905.
Sonke, E. Zu dem 25. Rätsel des Exeterbuches. E. Studien, xxxvii, 1907.
Schlutter, O. B. Das Leidener Rätsel. Ang. xxxii, 1909. [See also J. H. Kern, Ang. xxxiii, 1910.]
Bradley, H. Two Riddles of the Exeter Book. [5, 90.] MLR. vi, 1911.
Wood, G. A. The Anglo-Saxon Riddles. Aberystwyth Stud. i, 1912, ii, 1914.
von Ehrhardt-Siebold, E. Die lateinischen Rätsel der Angelsachsen. Heidelberg, 1925.

(8) Cædmon School

(a) General

Editions.
Cædmonis Monachi Paraphrasis Poetica Genesios Anglo-Saxonice conscripta, et nunc primum edita a Francisco Junio, F. F. Amstelodami, apud Christophorum Gunradi, Typis et Sumptibus Editoris. 1655.
Thorpe, B. Cædmon's Metrical Paraphrase of Parts of the Holy Scriptures, in Anglo-Saxon. Soc. Antiquaries, 1832. [With trn.]
Bouterwek, K. W. Cædmons des Angelsachsen biblische Dichtungen. 2 vols. Vol. i, Gütersloh, 1851; vol. ii, Elberfeld, 1854.
Grein, C. W. M. Bibliothek der angelsächsischen Poesie. 1857.
Wülcker, R. Bibliothek der angelsächsischen Poesie. Vol. ii, 1888–94.
[See also Gollancz's edn of Facsimile under Chief MS Sources of Poetry, p. 63 above.]

Translations.
Bosanquet, W. H. F. The Fall of Man or Paradise Lost of Cædmon. 1860.
Kennedy, C. W. The Cædmon Poems. 1916.

Criticism.
Bouterwek, K. W. De Cedmone Poeta Anglo-Saxonum vetustissimo brevis Dissertatio. Elberfeld, 1845.
—— Über Caedmon, den ältesten Dichter, und desselben metrische Paraphrase der heiligen Schrift. Elberfeld, 1845.
Dietrich, F. Zu Cædmon. Textverbesserungen. ZDA. x, 1858.
Sandras, S. G. De Carminibus Anglo-Saxonicis Cædmoni adjudicatis Disquisitio. Paris, 1859.

Goetzinger, E. Über die Dichtungen des Angelsachsen Cædmon und deren Verfasser. Göttingen, 1860.
Balg, H. Der Dichter Cædmon und seine Werke. Bonn, 1882.
Sievers, E. Zu Codex Junius xi. PBB. x, 1885.
Stoddard, F. H. The Cædmon Poems in MS Junius xi. Ang. x, 1888.
Lawrence, J. On Codex Junius xi. Ang. xii, 1889.
Wülcker, R. Der Name Cædmon. Ang. Bbl. ii, 1891.
Graz, F. Die Metrik der sogenannten Cædmonschen Dichtungen, mit Berücksichtigung der Verfasserfrage. Weimar, 1894.
Crawford, S. J. The Cædmon Poems. Ang. xlix, 1926.
Klaeber, F. Analogues of the Story of Cædmon. MLN. xlii, 1927.
Clubb, M. D. The Second Book of the Cædmonian MS. MLN. xlii, 1928.

(b) Cædmon's Hymn

MS. Cambridge University Lib. Kk.5.16, fol. 128 b. [Photolithographed by the Palaeographical Soc.: Facsimiles of Ancient MSS, pt ix, plate 140. See Palaeography, p. 58 above.]

Editions.
Smith, A. H. Three Northumbrian Poems: Caedmon's Hymn; Bede's Death Song; The Leiden Riddle. 1933.
[Also in the following:
Wanley's Catalogus, 1705 (= vol. iii of Hickes, Thesaurus.)
Conybeare, Illustrations, 1826.
Bouterwek, Cædmon, 1851–4.
Stephens, Runic Monuments, vol. ii, 1866–84.
Zupitza, Alt- und mittelenglisches Übungsbuch, 1874.
Sweet, Anglo-Saxon Reader, 1876.
—— Oldest English Texts, 1885.
MacLean, Old English and Middle English Reader, 1894.
Sedgefield, Anglo-Saxon Verse Book, 1922.]

Criticism.
Wülcker, R. Cædmon's Hymnus. PBB. iii, 1876
Zupitza, J. Cædmon's Hymnus. ZDA. xxii, 1878.
Schroeer, A. Über den Hymnus Cædmon's. Archiv, cxv, 1905.
Wüst, P. Zwei neue Handschriften von Cædmons Hymnus. ZDA. xlviii, 1906.
Frampton, M. G. Cædmon's Hymn. MP. xxii, 1924.
Cook, A. S. King Oswy and Cædmon's Hymn. Speculum, ii, 1927.

(c) Genesis

MS. Bodley, Junius XI.

Editions.

[For complete edns see under Cædmon School: General, p. 73 above. Extracts in many anthologies.]

Klaeber, F. The Later Genesis and other Old English and Old Saxon Texts relating to the Fall of Man. Heidelberg, 1913, 1931 (with supplement).

Holthausen, F. Die ältere Genesis. Heidelberg, 1914.

Translations.

Greverus, J. P. E. Cædmon's Schöpfung und Abfall der bösen Engel. Oldenburg, 1852.

Mason, L. Genesis A translated from the Old English. New Haven, 1915.

Criticism.

Windisch, W. O. E. Der Heliand und seine Quellen. Leipzig, 1868.

Sievers, E. Der Heliand und die angelsächsische Genesis. Halle, 1875. [See also Ang. v, 1882.]

—— Caedmon und Genesis. [In Brittanica, Leipzig, 1929.]

Wülcker, R. Cædmon und Milton. Ang. IV, 1881.

—— Die Bedeutung einer neuen Entdeckung für die angelsächsische Literaturgeschichte. Berichte über d. Verhandl. d. kgl. sächs. Gesellsch. d. Wissensch., Phil.-hist. Kl. Lepzig, 1888, pp. 209–18.

Ebert, A. Zur angelsächsischen Genesis und Exodus. Ang. v, 1882.

Hoenncher, E. Studien zur angelsächsischen Genesis. Ang. VII, 1884, VIII, 1885.

Stoddard, F. H. Accent Collation of Cædmon's Genesis B. MLN. II, 1887.

Heinze, A. Zur altenglischen Genesis. Berlin, 1889.

Merrill, K. and M'Clumpha, C. F. Parallelisms of the Anglo-Saxon Genesis. MLN. v, 1890.

Ferrell, C. C. Teutonic Antiquities in the Anglo-Saxon Genesis. Leipzig, 1893.

Zangemeister, R. and Braune, W. Bruchstücke der altsächsischen Bibeldichtung aus der Bibliothek Palatina. Heidelberg, 1894.

Gallée, J. H. Altsächsische Sprachdenkmäler. Leyden, 1895.

Vetter, F. Die neuentdeckte deutsche Bibeldichtung des 9. Jahrhunderts. Mit dem Text und der Übersetzung der neuaufgefundenen vatikanischen Bruchstücke. Basle, 1895.

Graz, F. Beiträge zur Textkritik der sogenannten Caedmonschen Genesis. Königsberg. [Rptd from Festschrift zu O. Schades 70. Geburtstag, 1896.]

Jovy, H. Untersuchungen zur altenglischen Genesisdichtung. BBA. v, 1899.

Behagel, O. Der Heliand und die angelsächsische Genesis. Giessen, 1902; Halle, 1910.

Holthausen, F. Zur altsächsischen und jüngeren altenglischen Genesis. Ang. Bbl XIII, 1902.

Grüters, O. Über einige Beziehungen zwischen altsächsischer und altenglischer Dichtung. BBA. XVII, 1905.

Emerson, O. F. Legends of Cain, especially in Old and Middle English. PMLA. XXI 1906.

—— Notes on Old English: Genesis, l. 1147 MLR. XIV, 1919.

von Gajšek, S. Milton und Caedmon. Vienna 1911.

Gerould, G. H. The Transmission of Genesis B MLN. XXVI, 1911.

Moore, S. The Old English Genesis, ll. 1145 1446–8. MLR. VI, 1911.

Klaeber, F. Notizen zur jüngeren Genesis Ang. XXXVII, 1913.

—— Zur jüngeren Genesis. Ang. XLIX, 1926.

Bradley, H. The 'Cædmonian' Genesis. E & S. VI, 1920.

McKillop, A. D. Illustrative Notes on Genesis B. JEGP. XX, 1921.

Crawford, S. J. A Latin Parallel for Part o the Later Genesis. Ang. XLVIII, 1924.

Bruckner, W. Die altsächsische Genesis und der Heliand, das Werk eines Dichters Berlin, 1930.

(d) Exodus

MS. Bodley, Junius XI.

[Facsimile included in Skeat's Twelve Facsimiles of Old English MSS, Oxford, 1892.]

Editions.

Hunt, T. W. Cædmon's Exodus and Daniel. Boston, 1889 (3rd edn).

Blackburn, F. A. Exodus and Daniel. Boston 1907.

Sedgefield, W. J. An Anglo-Saxon Verse Book Manchester, 1922.

Translation.

Johnson, W. S. Translation of the Old English Exodus. JEGP. v, 1903.

Criticism.

Strobl, J. Zur sogenannten Cædmonschen Exodus. Germania, XX, 1875.

Groth, E. Komposition der altenglischen Exodus. Göttingen, 1883.

Rau, Max. Germanische Altertümer in der angelsächsischen Exodus. Leipzig, 1890.

Mürkens, G. Untersuchungen über das altenglische Exoduslied. BBA. II, 1899.

Bright, J. W. Notes on the Caedmonian Exodus. MLN. xvii, 1902.
—— The Relation of the Cædmonian Exodus to the Liturgy. MLN. xxvii, 1912.
Holthausen, F. Zur Quellenkunde der altenglischen Exodus. Archiv, cxv, 1905.
Moore, S. Sources of the Old English Exodus. MP. ix, 1911.
Napier, A. S. The Old English Exodus, ll. 63–134. MLR. vi, 1911.
[See also Ebert, 1882, under Genesis above and Klaeber, 1918, under Beowulf, p. 66.]

(e) Daniel

MS. Bodley, Junius xi.

Editions.
[See edns of Cædmonian Poems, and also Hunt and Blackburn under Exodus, above.]

Criticism.
Hofer, O. Über die Entstehung des angelsächsischen Gedichtes Daniel. Ang. xii, 1889.
Steiner, G. Über die Interpolation im angelsächsischen Gedichte Daniel. Leipzig, 1889.
Napier, A. S. Zu Daniel 266–7. Archiv, xcviii, 1897. [See also H. Bradley, Archiv, xcix, 1898.]
Fulton, E. The Anglo-Saxon Daniel. MLN. xvi, 1901.
Dethloff, R. Daniel. Rostock, 1907.
Schmidt, W. Die altenglische Dichtung Daniel. Bonn, 1907.
—— Daniel und Azarias. BBA. xxiii, 1907.
Thomas, P. G. Beowulf and Daniel A. MLR. viii, 1913.

(f) Azarias

MS. Exeter Book, fols. 53 a–55 b.

Editions.
Thorpe, Codex Exoniensis, 1842 (with trn).
Grein, Bibliothek der angelsächsischen Poesie, 1857.
Wülcker, Bibliothek der angelsächsischen Poesie, vol. ii, 1888–94.]
[See also under Daniel, above.]

(g) Christ and Satan

MS. Bodley, Junius xi.

Edition.
Clubb, M. D. Christ and Satan, an Old English Poem. New Haven, 1925.
[For other edns and trns see under Cædmonian Poems above.]

Criticism.
Groschopp, F. Das angelsächsische Gedicht Crist und Satan. Ang. vi, 1883.
Kühn, A. Über die angelsächsischen Gedichte von Christ und Satan. Jena, 1883.
Bright, J. W. Jottings on the Cædmonian Christ and Satan. MLN. xviii, 1903.

Frings, T. Christ und Satan. Zeitschrift für deutsche Philologie, xlv, 1913–4.

(9) Cynewulf School

(a) General

[For complete edns of Cynewulfian Poems see Vercelli Book and Exeter Book under Chief MS Sources, p. 53. Extracts in many anthologies. For Bibliography, see Kennedy's trn, and K. Jansen's Cynewulf-Forschung, 1908.]

Translation.
Kennedy, C. W. The Poems of Cynewulf. Translated into English Prose. 1910.

Criticism.
Leo, H. Quae de se ipso Cynevulfus Poeta Anglo-Saxonicus tradiderit. Halle, 1857.
Dietrich, F. Commentatio de Kynewulfi Poetae Aetate. Marburg, 1859.
Rieger, M. Über Cynewulf. Zeitschrift für deutsche Philologie, i, 1869.
Wülcker, R. Über den Dichter Cynewulf. Ang. i, 1878. [See also many later vols.]
—— Cynewulfs Heimat. Ang. xvii, 1895.
D'Ham, O. Der gegenwärtige Stand der Cynewulffrage. Limburg, 1883.
Jansen, G. Beiträge zur Synonymik und Poetik der allgemein als acht anerkannten Dichtungen Cynewulfs. Münster, 1883.
Sarrazin, G. Beowulf und Kynewulf. Ang. ix, 1886.
Cremer, M. Metrische und sprachliche Untersuchung der altenglischen Gedichte Andreas, Guthlac, Phoenix, Elene, Juliana, Crist. Bonn, 1888.
Sievers, E. Zu Cynewulf. Ang. xiii, 1891.
—— Zu Cynewulf. [In Luick Festschrift, Marburg, 1925.]
Mather, F. J. The Cynewulf Question from a Metrical Point of View. MLN. vii, 1892.
Price, M. B. Teutonic Antiquities in the generally acknowledged Cynewulfian Poetry. Leipzig, 1896.
Trautmann, M. Kynewulf der Bischof und Dichter. BBA. i, 1898.
—— Zu Cynewulfs Runenstellen. BBA. ii, 1899.
—— Berichtungen, Erklärungen, und Vermutungen zu Cynewulf's Werken. BBA. xxiii, 1907.
Liebermann, F. Zur Cynewulffrage. Archiv, cv, 1900.
Strunk, W. Notes on Cynewulf. MLN. xvii, 1902.
Brown, C. F. Cynewulf and Alcuin. PMLA. xviii, 1903.
—— The Autobiographical Element in the Cynewulfian Rune Passages. E. Studien, xxxviii, 1907.

Jansen, K. Die Cynewulf-Forschung von ihren Anfängen bis zur Gegenwart. BBA. xxiv, 1908.

von der Warth, J. J. Metrisch-sprachliches und Textkritisches zu Cynewulfs Werken. Bonn, 1908.

Tupper, F. The Philological Legend of Cynewulf. PMLA. xxvi, 1911.

—— The Cynewulfian Runes of the Religious Poems. MLN. xxvii, 1912.

Lindeman, J. M. A Note on Cynewulf. MLN. xxxix, 1924.

Cook, A. S. Cynewulf's Part in our Beowulf. Trans. Connecticut Academy, xxvii, 1925.

Sisam, K. Cynewulf and his Poetry. British Academy Lecture, 1933.

(b) Crist

MS. Exeter Book, fols. 8 a–32 b.

Editions.

Gollancz, Sir I. Cynewulf's Christ. 1892. [With trn.]

Cook, A. S. The Christ of Cynewulf. A Poem in Three Parts: The Advent, the Ascension and the Last Judgment. Boston, 1900.

Translation.

Whitman, C. H. The Christ of Cynewulf. Boston, 1900.

Criticism.

Dietrich, F. Cynewulf's Crist. ZDA. ix, 1853.

Cook, A. S. Cynewulf's Principal Source for the Third Part of Christ. MLN. iv, 1889.

—— Bemerkungen zu Cynewulfs Christ. [In Philologische Studien, Festgabe für E. Sievers, Halle, 1896.]

—— Crist 77, 320, 952. J[E]GP. i, 1897.

—— Alfred's Soliloquies and Cynewulf's Crist. MLN. xvii, 1902.

Trautmann, M. Der sogenannte Crist. Ang. xviii, 1896.

Blackburn, F. A. Is the Christ of Cynewulf a Single Poem? Ang. xix, 1897.

Schwarz, F. Cynewulf's Anteil am Crist. Eine metrische Untersuchung. Königsberg, 1905.

Binz, G. Untersuchungen zum altenglischen sogenannten Christ. [In Festschrift zur 49ten Versammlung deutscher Philologen und Schulmänner, Basle, 1907. Also pbd separately, Leipzig, 1907.]

Gerould, G. H. Studies in the Christ. E. Studien, xli, 1909.

Moore, S. Notes on the Old English Christ. Archiv, cxxxi, 1914.

—— The Source of Christ 416 ff. MLN. xxix, 1914.

—— The Old English Christ. Is it a Unit? JEGP. xiv, 1915.

Burgert, E. The Dependence of Part I of Cynewulf's Christ upon the Antiphonary. Washington, 1921.

Willard, R. Vercelli Homily viii and the Christ. PMLA. xlii, 1927.

Howard, E. J. Cynewulf's Christ, 1665–1693. PMLA. xlv, 1930.

[See also Bourauel, 1901, under Andreas, below.]

(c) Elene

MS. Vercelli Book, fols. 121 a–133 b.

Editions.

[See Grimm, 1840, under Andreas, below.]

Zupitza, J. Cynewulf's Elene. Berlin, 1877, 1899 (4th edn).

Kent, C. W. Elene. Boston, 1889.

Holthausen, F. Cynewulf's Elene. Heidelberg, 1905, 1910.

Cook, A. S. The Old English Elene, Phoenix and Physiologus. New Haven, 1919.

Translations.

Weymouth, R. F. A Literal Translation of Cynewulf's Elene. 1888.

Garnett, J. M. Elene, Judith, Maldon and Brunnanburgh. Boston, 1889.

Menzies, J. Cynewulf's Elene. A Metrical Translation from Zupitza's Edition. Edinburgh, 1894.

Holt, L. H. The Elene of Cynewulf. New Haven, 1904.

Criticism.

Gloede, O. Untersuchung über die Quelle zu Cynewulf's Elene. Rostock, 1885. [See also Ang. ix, 1886.]

Cook, A. S. The Date of the Old English Elene. Ang. xv, 1893.

Swaen, A. E. H. Notes on Cynewulf's Elene. Ang. xvii, 1895.

Holthausen, F. Zur Quelle von Cynewulf Elene. Zeitschrift für deutsche Philologie xxxvii, 1905.

Trautmann, M. Nachträge zur Elene, Andreas und Runenstellen. BBA. xxiii, 1907.

Kern, J. H. Altenglische Varia. 2. Zur Elene. E. Studien, li, 1917.

[See also Kent, 1887, under Andreas, below.]

(d) Juliana

MS. Exeter Book, fols. 65 b–76 a.

Edition.

Strunk, W. Juliana. Boston, 1904.

Translations.

Murch, H. S. Translation of Cynewulf's Juliana. JEGP. v, 1904.

Kennedy, C. W. The Legend of St Juliana.
Translated from the Latin of the Acta
Sanctorum and the Anglo-Saxon of Cyne-
wulf. Princeton, 1906.

Criticism.

Gloede, O. Cynewulf's Juliana und ihre
Quelle. Ang. xi, 1889.

Pearce, W. Concerning Juliana. MLN. vii,
1892.

Backhaus, O. Über die Quelle der mittelenglischen Legende von der heiligen Juliana
und ihr Verhältnis zu Cynewulfs Juliana.
Halle, 1899.

Garnett, J. M. The Latin and the Anglo-Saxon
Juliana. PMLA. xiv, 1899.

(e) *Fates of the Apostles*

MS. Vercelli Book, fols. 52 b–54 a.

Editions.

[See Thorpe, 1836, Krapp, 1906, under
Andreas, below.]

Translation.

Olivero, F. The Fates of the Apostles.
Translation and Critical Commentary. Milan,
1927.

Criticism.

Napier, A. S. The Old English Poem The Fates
of the Apostles. Academy, 8 Sept. 1888.

—— Fata Apostolorum. ZDA. xxxiii, 1889.

Cook, A. S. The Affinities of the Fata Apostolorum. MLN. iv, 1889.

Sarrazin, G. Die Fata Apostolorum und der
Dichter Kynewulf. Ang. xii, 1889.

Brandl, A. Zu Cynewulfs Fata Apostolorum.
Archiv, c, 1898.

Holthausen, F. Zur Quelle der altenglischen
Fata Apostolorum. Archiv, cvi, 1901.

Barnouw, A. J. Die Schicksale der Apostel
doch ein unabhängiges Gedicht. Archiv,
cviii, 1902.

Hamilton, G. L. The Sources of the Fates of
the Apostles and Andreas. MLN. xxxv,
1920.

[See also Trautmann, 1897, and Bourauel,
1901, under Andreas, below.]

(f) *Andreas*

MS. Vercelli Book, fols. 29 b–52 b.

Editions.

Thorpe, B. [Appendix B to a report on
Rymer's Foedera (The Legend of St
Andrew; The Fates of the Twelve Apostles).
Ptd 1836; pbd 1869.]

Grimm, J. Andreas und Elene. Cassel,
1840.

Baskerville, W. M. Andreas. A Legend of
St Andrew. Boston, 1885.

Krapp, G. P. Andreas and the Fates of the
Apostles. Boston, 1906.

Translation.

Root, R. K. Andreas. The Legend of St
Andrew. New Haven, 1899.

[See also Hall, 1902, under Judith, p. 78
below.]

Criticism.

Fritzsche, A. Das angelsächsische Gedicht
Andreas und Cynewulf. Halle, 1879. [Also
Ang. ii, 1879.]

Ramhorst, F. Das altenglische Gedicht vom
heiligen Andreas und der Dichter Cynewulf.
Leipzig, 1885.

Zupitza, J. Zur Frage nach der Quelle von
Cynewulfs Andreas. ZDA. xxx, 1886.

Bright, J. W. Notes on the Andreas. MLN.
ii, 1887.

Kent, C. W. Teutonic Antiquities in Andreas
and Elene. Leipzig, 1887.

Wülcker, R. Der Dichter Cynewulf und das
Andreasgedicht. Berichte d. kgl. sächs.
Gesellsch. d. Wissensch. Leipzig, 1888.

Sarrazin, G. Noch einmal Cynewulfs Andreas.
Ang. Bbl. vi, 1895.

Trautmann, M. Der Andreas doch von Cynewulf. Ang. Bbl. vi, 1895.

—— Wer hat die Schicksale der Apostel
zuerst für den Schluss des Andreas erklärt?
Ang. Bbl. vii, 1897.

Buttenwieser, E. C. Studien über die Verfasserschaft des Andreas. Heidelberg, 1899.

Bourauel, J. Zur Quellen und Verfasserfrage
von Andreas, Crist und Fata. BBA. xi,
1901.

Skeat, W. W. Andreas and Fata Apostolorum.
[In Furnivall Miscellany, Oxford, 1901,
pp. 408–20.]

Krapp, G. P. Notes on the Andreas. MP. ii,
1905.

Cook, A. S. The Authorship of the Old English
Andreas. MLN. xxxiv, 1919.

—— The Old English Andreas and Bishop
Acca of Hexham. Trans. Connecticut
Academy, xxvi, 1924.

—— Bitter Beer-Drinking. MLN. xl, 1925.

Holthausen, F. Andreas. Ang. Bbl. xxxi,
1920.

[See also Trautmann, 1907, under Elene,
and Hamilton, 1920, under Fates of the
Apostles, above.]

(g) *Phoenix*

MS. Exeter Book, fols. 55 b–65 b.

Editions.

Grundtvig, N. F. S. Phenix-Fuglen. Copenhagen, 1840.

Schlotterose, O. Die altenglische Dichtung
Phoenix. BBA. xxv, 1908.

[See also Cook, 1919, under Elene, above.]

Translations.
Stephens, G. Archaeologia, xxx, 1844, pp. 256–322.
Grein, C. W. M. Der Vogel Phönix. Rinteln, 1854.
Sims, W. R. The Happy Land: from the Phoenix. MLN. vii, 1892.
[See also Hall, 1902, under Judith, below.]

Criticism.
Gäbler, H. Über die Autorschaft des angelsächsischen Gedichtes vom Phoenix. Ang. iii, 1880.
Kluge, F. Zum Phoenix. E. Studien, viii, 1885.
Fulton, E. On the Authorship of the Anglo-Saxon Poem Phoenix. MLN. xi, 1896.

(h) Dream of the Rood

MS. Vercelli Book, fols. 104 b–106 a. [For the Ruthwell Cross, see under Runes, pp. 59–60 above.]

Editions.
Pacius, A. Das heilige Kreuz. Gera, 1873. [With trn.]
Cook, A. S. The Dream of the Rood. Oxford, 1905.
Ricci, A. Il Sogno della Croce, riveduto nel Testo, con Versione, Introduzione e Note. Florence, 1926.
Dickins, B. and Ross, A. S. C. The Dream of the Rood. 1934.
Bütow, H. Altenglische Traumgeschicht vom Kreuz. Anglistische Forschungen, lxxviii, 1935.

Translation.
Roy, J. A. The Dream of the Rood. An Old English Poem done into Modern Verse. 1912.

Criticism.
Ebert, A. Der Traum vom heiligen Kreuz. Berichte d. kgl. sächs. Gesellsch. d. Wissensch. Leipzig, 1884.
Brandl, A. Zum angelsächsischen Gedichte Traumgesicht vom Kreuze Christi. Berlin, 1905.

(i) Guðlac

MS. Exeter Book, fols. 33 a–52 b.

Editions.
[See Cynewulf School: General, pp. 75–6, and Chief MS Sources, p. 62.]

Criticism.
Charitius, F. Über die angelsächsischen Gedichte vom heiligen Guthlac. Ang. ii, 1879.
Lefèvre, P. Das altenglische Gedicht vom heiligen Guthlac. Ang. vi, 1883.

Forstmann, H. Das altenglische Gedich Guthlac der Einsiedler und die Guthlac Vita des Felix. BBA. xii, 1902.
Klaeber, F. Guðlac 1252 ff. Ang. Bbl. xv, 1904

(j) Physiologus

MS. Exeter Book: Panther, fols. 95 b–96 b Whale, fols. 96 b–97 b; Partridge, fols. 97 b–98 b.

Edition.
Cook, A. S. The Old English Physiologus. Tex and Prose Translation. With a Verse Translation by J. H. Pitman. New Haven 1922. [Text rptd from Elene, etc. 1919.]

Criticism.
Ebert, A. Der angelsächsische Physiologus Ang. vi, 1883.
Lauchert, F. Geschichte des Physiologus Strasburg, 1890.
Mann, M. F. Zur Bibliographie des Physio logus. Ang. Bbl. x, xii, xiii, 1900–3.
Sokoll, E. Zum angelsächsischen Physiologus Marburg, 1900.

(k) Harrowing of Hell

MS. Exeter Book, fols. 119 b–121 b.

Edition.
Cramer, J. Quelle, Verfasser und Text de altenglischen Gedichtes Christi Höllen fahrt. Ang. xix, 1897.

Criticism.
Kirkland, J. H. A Study of the Harrowing o Hell. 1885.
Barnouw, A. J. Die Runenstelle der Himmel fahrt. Archiv, cvii, 1901.
Holthausen, F. Zur altenglischen Literatur Christi Höllenfahrt. Ang. Bbl. xix, 1908.

(10) MINOR RELIGIOUS, DIDACTIC AND GNOMIC POEMS

(a) Judith

MS. Cotton, Vitellius A xv, fols. 199 a–206 [For the MS see Beowulf MS under Chie MS Sources, p. 62 above.]

Editions.
Nilsson, L. G. Judith. Copenhagen, 1858 [With Swedish trn.]
Cook, A. S. Judith. An Old English Epi Fragment. With Introduction, Translation Glossary, etc. Boston, 1888, 1904 (Belles Lettres Ser.).

[Also, complete or in extracts, in:
Thwaites, Heptateuchus, etc., 1698 (see Ælfric, p. 90 below).
Thorpe, Analecta, 1834.
Leo, Sprachproben, 1838.

Klipstein, Analecta, 1849.
Ettmüller, Scopas, 1850.
Grein, Bibliothek der angelsächsischen Poesie, 1857.
Rieger, Lesebuch, 1861.
Zupitza, Lesebuch, 1874.
Sweet, Anglo-Saxon Reader, 1876.
Wülcker, Bibliothek der angelsächsischen Poesie, vol. II, 1888–94.
Wyatt, Anglo-Saxon Reader, 1919.]

Translations.
[See Garnett, 1889, under Cynewulf: Elene, p. 76 above.]
Hickey, E. H. Judith. Journ. Education, N.S., XI, 1889.
Elton, O. Judith. [ll. 1–121.] [In Furnivall Miscellany, Oxford, 1901.]
Hall, J. L. Judith, Phoenix and other Anglo-Saxon Poems. New York, 1912.

Criticism.
Cook, A. S. Notes on a Northumbrianised Version of Judith. Trans. American Philolog. Ass. XX, 1889.
—— Notes on Judith. JEGP. V, 1903.
Foster, T. Gregory. Judith. Studies in Metre, Language and Style. QF. LXXI, 1892.
Neumann, M. Über das altenglische Gedicht von Judith. Kiel, 1892.
Brincker, F. Germanische Altertümer in dem angelsächsischen Gedicht Judith. Hamburg, 1898.
Smyth, E. The Numbers in the MS. of the Old English Judith. MLN. XX, 1905.

(b) Judgement Poems

MSS. (a) Be Domes Dæge (Hwæt ic ana æt). Corpus Christi College Cambridge CCI.
(b) Last Judgement (Ðæt gelimpan sceal). Exeter Book, fols. 115 b–117 b.

Editions.
Thorpe, Codex Exoniensis, 1842 (a).
Grein, Bibliothek der angelsächsischen Poesie, 1857 (b).
R. Lumby, Be Domes Dæge, etc. EETS. 1876 (a).
Wülcker, Bibliothek der angelsächsischen Poesie, vol. II, 1888–94 (a); vol. III, 1897–8 (b).

Translations.
[See Thorpe and Lumby above.]
Brandl, A. Be Domes Dæge. Ang. IV, 1881.
Doering, G. The Anglo-Saxon Poets on the Judgment Day. Halle, 1890.
Loche, J. J. Be Domes Dæge. Bonn, 1906. [Also BBA. XXII, 1908.]
Grau, G. Quellen und Verwandtschaften der älteren germanischen Darstellungen des jüngsten Gerichts. SEP. XXXI, 1908.

(c) Addresses of Soul to Body

i. Address of the Lost Soul to the Body. MSS. (a) Exeter Book, fols. 98 a–100 a; (b) Vercelli Book, fols. 101 b–103 a.
ii. Address of the Saved Soul to the Body. MS. Vercelli Book, fols. 103 a, b.

Editions.
Conybeare, J. J. Archaeologia, XVII, 1812. [i (a), ll. 1–26 and end. Also in Illustrations, 1826.]
Thorpe, B. [In Appendix to Cooper's Report on Rymer's Foedera, 1836 (i (b), and ii).]
—— Codex Exoniensis. 1842. [i (a).]

[Also in the following:
Ettmüller, Scopas, 1850 (i (a, b)).
Grein, Bibliothek der angelsächsischen Poesie, 1857 (i (a, b); ii).
Wülcker, Bibliothek der angelsächsischen Poesie, vol. II, 1888–94 (i (a, b); ii).]

Criticism.
Rieger, M. Addresses of Soul and Body. Germania, III, 1858.
—— Addresses of Soul and Body. Zeitschrift für deutsche Philologie, I, 1868.
Varnhagen, H. Addresses of Soul and Body. Ang. II, 1879.
Kleinert, G. Über den Streit zwischen Leib und Seele. Halle, 1880.
Atkinson, R. The Passions and the Homilies from the Leabhar Breac. Dublin, 1887.
Kurtz, B. P. Gifer the Worm. An Essay toward the History of an Idea. Berkeley, 1929.
Willard, R. The Address of the Soul to the Body. PMLA. L, 1935.

(d) Menologium

MS. Cotton, Tiberius B I, fols. 112 a–114 b.
Editions.
Fox, S. Menologium seu Calendarium Poeticum. 1830. [With trn.]
Bouterwek, K. W. Calendecwide, i.e. Menologium Ecclesiae Anglo-Saxonicae poeticum. Gütersloh, 1857.
Imelmann, R. Das altenglische Menologium. Berlin, 1902.

[Also in the following:
Hickes, Thesaurus, vol. I, 1703–5.
Ebeling, Lesebuch, 1847.
Grein, Bibliothek der angelsächsischen Poesie, vol. II, 1858.
Earle, Two of the Saxon Chronicles Parallel, 1865 (see Chronicles, p. 88 below).
Wülcker, Bibliothek der angelsächsischen Poesie, vol. II, 1888–94.
Earle and Plummer, Two of the Saxon Chronicles Parallel, 1892 (see Chronicles, p. 89 below).]

Criticism.
Liebermann, F. Zum alten Menologium. Archiv, cx, 1903.

(e) Wonders of Creation

MS. Exeter Book, fols. 92 b–94 a (Wilt þu, fus hæle).

Editions.
[Thorpe, Codex Exoniensis, 1842 (with trn).
Grein, Bibliothek der angelsächsischen Poesie, 1857.
Wülcker, Bibliothek der angelsächsischen Poesie, vol. iii, 1897–8.]
[Abridged trn in Conybeare, Illustrations, 1826.]

(f) Hymns, Prayers, etc.

(i) Bede's Death-song

MS. St Gall 254, Epistola Cuðberti ad Cuðwinum.

Editions.
Epistola Cuoberti. [In Introduction to Wheloc's edn of Bede's Historia Ecclesiastica, 1643; also in Twisden's Historiae anglicanae Scriptores, 1652. Also in later edns of Bede.]
Smith, A. H. Three Northumbrian Poems. 1933.

[The Old English Hymn also in the following:
H. Hattemer, Denkmahle des Mittelalters, vol. ii, St Gallen, 1844.
Ettmüller, Scopas, 1850.
Rieger, Lesebuch, 1861.
Zupitza, Übungsbuch, 1882.
Sweet, Oldest English Texts, EETS. 1885.
—— Second Anglo-Saxon Reader, 1887.
MacLean, Old and Middle English Reader, 1894.
Sedgefield, Anglo-Saxon Verse Book, 1922.]

Criticism.
Brotanek, R. Zur Überlieferung des Sterbegesanges Bedas (mit einem Facsimile). [In Texte und Untersuchungen, Halle, 1913.]
Förster, M. Paläographisches zu Bedas Sterbespruch. Archiv, cxxxv, 1917.

(ii) Metrical Psalms

A. Psalms li–cl. MS. Paris, Bibliothèque Nationale, Fonds latin 8824. [See prose version of Psalms l–lx in same MS, under Psalters, p. 96 below.]
B. Psalm 50. MS. Cotton, Vespasian D vi, fols. 70 a–73 b.
C. Fragments in Benedictine Rule in Bodley, MS Junius 121.

Editions.
Thorpe, B. Libri Psalmorum Versio antiqua Latina cum Paraphrasi Anglo-Saxonica. Oxford, 1835. [A.]

Thorpe, B. [In Appendix B to Cooper' Report on Rymer's Foedera, 1835 (A).]
Krapp, G. P. The Paris Psalter and th Meters of Boethius. New York, 1932.
[Also in the following:
Grein, Bibliothek der angelsächsischen Poesie vol. ii, 1858 (A, B, C).
Wülcker, Bibliothek der angelsächsische Poesie, vol. iii, 1897–8 (A, B, C).]
[B also in Sweet, Anglo-Saxon Reader, 7t edn, 1894; E. Thomson, Godcunde Lar an Ðeowdom, 1849; Bouterwek, Cædmon, 1854.

Criticism.
Dietrich, F. Hycgan und Hopian. ZDA. ix 1853.
Tanger, G. Collation des Psalters. Ang. Anz vi, 1883.
Bartlett, H. The Metrical Division of the Pari Psalter. Baltimore, 1896.
Holthausen, F. Zur altenglischen metrische Psalmenübersetzung. Ang. Bbl. xxxi 1920.
Brüning, E. Die altenglischen metrische Psalmen in ihrem Verhältnis zur latein schen Vorlage. Königsberg, 1921.

(iii) Prayers

A. (Æla drihten leof.) MS. Cotton, Juliu A ii, fol. 136 a.
B. (Æla frea beorhta.) MS. Cotton, Juliu A ii, fol. 136 a.
C. (Æla leohtes leoht.) MS. Cotton, Juliu A ii, fols. 136 a–137 a.
D. (Ahelpe min.) MS. Exeter Book, fols 117 b–119 b.
[A, and B to l. 8, also in Lambeth MS 427 fol. 183 b.]

Editions.
[A, B and C in the following:
Junius, Cædmonis Monachi Paraphrasis Poe tica, 1655.
E. Thomson, Godcunde Lar and Ðeowdom 1849.
Bouterwek, Cædmon, 1849–54.
Grein, Bibliothek der angelsächsischen Poesie vol. ii, 1858.
Wülcker, Bibliothek der angelsächsische Poesie, vol. ii, 1888–94.
Lambeth MS of A and B in H. Logema Anglo-Saxonica Minora, Ang. xi, 1889.
D in:
Thorpe, Codex Exoniensis, 1842.
Grein, Bibliothek der angelsächsischen Poesie vol. ii, 1858.
Wülcker, Bibliothek der angelsächsische Poesie, vol. ii, 1888–94.]

Criticism (on D).
Dietrich, F. Disputatio de Cruce Ruth wellensi. Marburg, 1865.

Rieger, M. Über Cynewulf. Zeitschrift für deutsche Philologie, I, 1868.

(iv) Paternosters

A. ([Halig] fæder, þu þe on heofunum.) MS. Exeter Book, fol. 122 a.

B. (Fæder mancynnes.) MS. Bodley, Junius 121, fol. 45.

C. (Ðu eart ure fæder.) MS. Corpus Christi College Cambridge CCI.

Editions.

[A in:

Thorpe, Codex Exoniensis, 1842.

Grein, Bibliothek der angelsächsischen Poesie, vol. II, 1858.

Wülcker, Bibliothek der angelsächsischen Poesie, vol. II, 1888–94.

B in:

Wanley, Catalogus, 1705.

Thomson, Godcunde Lar and Ðeowdom, 1849.

Ettmüller, Scopas, 1850.

Bouterwek, Cædmon, 1854.

Grein, Bibliothek der angelsächsischen Poesie, vol. I, 1858.

Wülcker, Bibliothek der angelsächsischen Poesie, vol. II, 1888–94.

C in:

Wanley, Catalogus, 1705.

Klipstein, Analecta, 1849.

Ettmüller, Scopas, 1850.

Grein, Bibliothek der angelsächsischen Poesie, vol. II, 1858.

Lumby, Be Domes Dæge, EETS. 1876.

Wülcker, Bibliothek der angelsächsischen Poesie, vol. II, 1888–94.]

(v) Hymns

A. (Wuton wuldrian.) MS. Cotton, Vespasian D VI, fols. 68 b–69 b.

B. (Sy þe wuldor.) MSS. Bodley, Junius 121, fols. 43 b–44 b; Corpus Christi College Cambridge CCI.

C. Durham Hymns. (Interlinear version of Latin hymns.) MS. Durham Cathedral Lib. B iii, 32.

Editions.

[A in:

Wright, Reliquiæ Antiquæ, vol. I, 1841.

F. Dietrich, Anglo-saxonica, Marburg, 1854.

Grein, Bibliothek der angelsächsischen Poesie, vol. II, 1858.

Wülcker, Bibliothek der angelsächsischen Poesie, vol. II, 1888–94.

B in:

Hickes, Thesaurus, 1703–5 (ll. 1–50).

Wanley, Catalogus, 1705.

Thomson, Godcunde Lar and Ðeowdom, 1849.

Klipstein, Analecta, 1849.

Ettmüller, Scopas, 1850.

Bouterwek, Cædmon, 1854.

Grein, Bibliothek der angelsächsischen Poesie, vol. II, 1858.

Lumby, Be Domes Dæge, EETS. 1876.

Wülcker, Bibliothek der angelsächsischen Poesie, vol. II, 1888–94.

C in:

J. Stevenson, The Latin Hymns of the Anglo-Saxon Church, Surtees Soc. 1851.]

(vi) Creed

(Ælmihtig fæder up on rodore.) MS. Bodley, Junius, fols. 46 a–47 a.

Editions.

[Wanley, Catalogus, 1705.

Thomson, Godcunde Lar and Ðeowdom, 1849.

Ettmüller, Scopas, 1850.

Bouterwek, Cædmon, 1854.

Grein, Bibliothek der angelsächsischen Poesie, vol. II, 1858.

Wülcker, Bibliothek der angelsächsischen Poesie, vol. II, 1888–94.

(g) *Didactic Poems*

(i) Gifts of Men (Bi monna cræftum)

MS. Exeter Book, fols. 78 a–80 a (Fela bið on foldum).

Editions.

[Thorpe, Codex Exoniensis, 1842.

Klipstein, Analecta, 1849.

Grein, Bibliothek der angelsächsischen Poesie, vol. I, 1857.

Wülcker, Bibliothek der angelsächsischen Poesie, vol. III, 1897–8.

Sedgefield, Anglo-Saxon Verse Book, 1922.]

Criticism.

Rieger, M. Über Cynewulf. Zeitschrift für deutsche Philologie, I, 1868.

(ii) A Father's Instruction (Fæder Larcwidas)

MS. Exeter Book, fols. 80 a–81 b (Ðus frod fæder freobearn lærde).

Editions.

[Thorpe, Codex Exoniensis, 1842.

Klipstein, Analecta, 1849.

Ettmüller, Scopas, 1850.

Grein, Bibliothek der angelsächsischen Poesie, vol. II, 1858.

Wülcker, Kleinere angelsächsische Dichtungen, 1882.

—— Bibliothek der angelsächsischen Poesie, vol. I, 1881–3.

Sedgefield, Anglo-Saxon Verse Book, 1922.]

Criticism.

Bright, J. W. Notes on Fæder Larcwidas. MLN. x, 1895.

6

(iii) Mind of men (Bi manna mode)

MS. Exeter Book, fols. 83 a–84 b (Hwæt me frod wita).

Editions.
[Thorpe, Codex Exoniensis, 1842.
Ettmüller, Scopas, 1850.
Grein, Bibliothek der angelsächsischen Poesie, vol. I, 1857.
Wülcker, Bibliothek der angelsächsischen Poesie, vol. III, 1897–8.
Sedgefield, Anglo-Saxon Verse Book (ll. 1–50, 'A Bad Character'), 1922.]

(iv) Fates of Men (Be manna wyrdum)

MS. Exeter Book, fols. 87 a–88 b (Ful oft þæt gegongeð).

Editions.
[Thorpe, Codex Exoniensis, 1842.
Klipstein, Analecta, 1849.
Ettmüller, Scopas, 1850.
Grein, Bibliothek der angelsächsischen Poesie, vol. I, 1857.
Wülcker, Bibliothek der angelsächsischen Poesie, vol. III, 1897–8.
Sedgefield, Anglo-Saxon Verse Book, 1922.]

Criticism.
Rieger, M. Über Cynewulf. Zeitschrift für deutsche Philologie, I, 1868.
Bradley, H. Two Corruptions in Old English MSS. Academy, 28 Jan. 1893.

(v) Alms

MS. Exeter Book, fols. 121 b–122 b (Wel bið ðam eorle).

Editions.
[Thorpe, Codex Exoniensis, 1842.
Ettmüller, Scopas, 1850.
Grein, Bibliothek der angelsächsischen Poesie, vol. II, 1858.
Wülcker, Bibliothek der angelsächsischen Poesie, vol. III, 1897–8.]

(vi) Pharaoh

MS. Exeter Book, fol. 122 a (Saga me hwæt þær weorudes).

Editions.
[Thorpe, Codex Exoniensis, 1842.
Grein, Bibliothek der angelsächsischen Poesie, vol. II, 1858.
Wülcker, Bibliothek der angelsächsischen Poesie, vol. III, 1897–8.]

(vii) Maxims

MS. Exeter Book, fols. 122 a, b (Gefeoh nu on ferðe).

Editions.
[Thorpe, Codex Exoniensis, 1842.
Grein, Bibliothek der angelsächsischen Poesie, vol. II, 1858 (Hymnen XI).

Wülcker, Bibliothek der angelsächsische Poesie, vol. II, 1884–94 (Bruchstück eine Lehrdichtes).]

(viii) Falseness of Men (Bi manna lease)

MS. Vercelli Book, fols. 104 a, b.

Editions.
[Thorpe, Appendix B to Cooper's Report o Rymer's Foedera, 1836.
Kemble, Codex Vercelliensis, vol. II, 1856.
Grein, Bibliothek der angelsächsischen Poesie vol. II, 1858.
Wülcker, Bibliothek der angelsächsische Poesie, vol. II, 1888–94.]

(ix) Lar

MS. Corpus Christi College Cambridge cc (Nu lære ic þe).

Editions.
[Lumby, Be Domes Dæge, EETS. 1876.
Wülcker, Bibliothek der angelsächsische Poesie, vol. II, 1888–94 (Ermahnung).]

(x) Call to Prayer

MS. Corpus Christi College Cambridge cc (Ðænne gemiltsaþ þe).

Editions
[Wanley, Catalogus, 1705.
Turner, History of the Anglo-Saxons, 1799 1805.
Lumby, Be Domes Dæge, EETS. 1876.]

(xi) Salomon and Saturn

A. MS. Corpus Christi College Cambridg 422, fols. 1–26 (ll. 1–506).
B. MS. Corpus Christi College Cambridg 41, fols. 196–8 (ll. 1–94).
[See prose version in Cott. MS Vitell. A xv also a fragment of a different prose version in Corpus Christi College Cambridge MS 42 fols. 6–12.]

Editions.
[J. M. Kemble, The Dialogue of Salomon an Saturnus, Ælfric Soc. 1848 (verse and pros versions).
Grein, Bibliothek der angelsächsischen Poesie vol. II, 1858.
Wülcker, Bibliothek der angelsächsischen Poesie, vol. III, 1897–8.

Extracts in:
Conybeare, Illustrations, 1826.
Bouterwek, Cædmon, 1854.
Rieger, Lesebuch, 1861.
Wyatt, Anglo-Saxon Reader, 1919.]

Criticism.
von der Hagen, F. H. Einleitung zur Ausgab des Salomon und Morolf. Deutsche Gedicht des Mittelalters, I. Berlin, 1808. [Se J. Grimm, Heidelberger Jahrbücher, XLV 1908.]

Hofmann, C. Über Jourdain de Blaivies, Apollonius von Tyrus, Salomo und Markulf. Sitzungsber. d. Münchener Akad., Phil.-hist. Kl. 1870.

Schaumberg, W. Untersuchungen über das deutsche Spruchgedicht: Salomo und Morolf. PBB. II, 1876.

Schipper, J. Salomon and Saturn. A Comparison of MS. A with MS. B. Germania, XXII, 1877.

Sweet, H. Collation of the poetical Salomon and Saturn with the MS. Ang. I, 1878.

Vogt, F. Die deutschen Dichtungen von Salomon und Markolf. Vol. I, 1880.

Zupitza, J. Zu Salomon und Saturn. Ang. III, 1880.

MacCallum, M. W. Solomon in Europe, and Anglo-Saxon Jocoseria. [In Studies in Low German and High German, 1884.]

Duff, E. G. Dialogus, or Communing between the Wise King Salomon and Marcolphus. 1892.

Holthausen, F. Zu Salomo und Saturn. Ang. XXIII, 1901.

—— Zu Salomo und Saturn. E. Studien, XXXVII, 1906.

—— Zu Salomo und Saturn. Ang. Bbl. XXI, 1910, XXVII, 1916, XXXI, 1920.

von Vincenti, A. Die altenglischen Dialoge von Salomon und Saturn. Munich, 1904.

(xii) Gnomic Poems
A. MS. Exeter Book, fols. 88 b–90 a (Frige me frodum wordum).

B. MS. Exeter Book, fols. 90 a–91 a (Forst sceal freosan).

C. MS. Exeter Book, fols. 91 a–92 b (Ræd sceal mon secgan).

D. MS. Cotton, Tiberius B I, 113 a, b (Cyning sceal rice).

Editions.

[Hickes, Thesaurus, 1703 (B, C, D).

Conybeare, Illustrations, 1826 (B, D).

Fox, Menologium, 1830 (D).

Thorpe, Codex Exoniensis, 1842 (A, B, C).

Ebeling, Lesebuch, 1847 (D).

Ettmüller, Scopas, 1850 (A, B, C, D).

Grein, Bibliothek der angelsächsischen Poesie, vol. II, 1858 (A, B, C, D).

Rieger, Lesebuch, 1861 (B).

Sweet, Anglo-Saxon Reader, 1876 (D).

Wülcker, Kleinere angelsächsische Dichtungen, 1882 (A, B, C, D).

—— Bibliothek der angelsächsischen Poesie, vol. I, 1881–3 (A, B, C, D).

B. C. Williams, Gnomic Poetry in Anglo-Saxon (A, B, C, D), New York, 1914.

Sedgefield, Anglo-Saxon Verse Book, 1922 (D).]

Criticism.

Rieger, M. Über Cynewulf. Zeitschrift für deutsche Philologie, I, 1868.

Strobl, J. Zur Spruchdichtung bei den Angelsachsen. ZDA. XXXI, 1887.

Müller, H. Über die angelsächsische Versus Gnomici. Jena, 1893.

(xiii) Metra of Boethius
[See Alfred: Boethius, p. 87.]

(11) HISTORICAL POEMS
General
Abegg, D. Zur Entwicklung der historischen Dichtung bei den Angelsachsen. QF. LXXIII, 1894.

(a) Battle of Maldon
MS. Cotton, Otho A XII, burnt in 1731. [Ptd T. Hearne in Johannis Glastoniensis Chronica sive Historia de Rebus Glastoniensibus, 2 vols. Oxford, 1726.]

Editions.

Crow, C. L. Maldon and Brunanburh. Two Old English Songs of Battle. Boston, 1897.

Sedgefield, W. J. The Battle of Maldon and Short Poems from the Saxon Chronicle. Boston, 1904.

Ashdown, M. English and Norse Documents relating to the Reign of Ethelred the Unready. Cambridge, 1930.

[Also in the following:
Thorpe, Analecta, 1834.

Ebeling, Lesebuch, 1847.

Klipstein, Analecta, 1849.

Ettmüller, Scopas, 1850.

Grein, Bibliothek der angelsächsischen Poesie, vol. I, 1857.

Rieger, Lesebuch, 1861.

Sweet, Anglo-Saxon Reader, 1876.

Wülcker, Kleinere angelsächsische Dichtungen, 1882.

—— Bibliothek der angelsächsischen Poesie, vol. I, 1881–3.

Bright, Anglo-Saxon Reader, 1892.

Wyatt, Anglo-Saxon Reader, 1919.

Sedgefield, Anglo-Saxon Verse Book, 1922.]

Translations.

[See Garnett, 1889, under Cynewulf: Crist, p. 76.]

Sims, W. R. The Battle of Maldon. MLN. VII, 1892.

Ker, W. P. [Made 1887. Ptd in R. W. Chambers, England before the Norman Conquest, 1926.]

Criticism.

Zernial, U. Das Lied von Byrhtnoths Fall. Berlin, 1882.

Jespersen, O. Zu Byrhtnoð 212. Nordisk Tidsskrift, ser. 3, I, 1893.

Liebermann, F. Zur Geschichte Byrhtnoths, des Helden von Maldon. Archiv, CI, 1898.

Emerson, O. F. Notes on Old English Maldon. MLR. xiv, 1919.

Klaeber, F. Zu Byrhtnoþ's Tod. E. Studien, lv, 1921.

Laborde, E. D. The Style of The Battle of Maldon. MLR. xix, 1924.

Phillpotts, B. S. The Battle of Maldon: some Danish Affinities. MLR. xxiv, 1929.

(b) Battle of Brunanburh

[In four MSS of the Anglo-Saxon Chronicle:
A. Corpus Christi College Cambridge 173.
B. Cotton, Tiberius A vi.
C. Cotton, Tiberius B i.
D. Cotton, Tiberius B iv.]

Edition.
Sedgefield, W. J. The Battle of Maldon. 1904.

[Also in many anthologies, including:
Hickes, Thesaurus, 1703–5.
Ettmüller, Scopes vidsidh, 1839.
Grein, Bibliothek der angelsächsischen Poesie, vol. i, 1857.
Wülcker, Bibliothek der angelsächsischen Poesie, vol. i, 1881–3.
Bright, Anglo-Saxon Reader, 1892.
Wyatt, Anglo-Saxon Reader, 1919.
Kershaw, Anglo-Saxon and Norse Poems, 1922.
Also in edns of Chronicle.]

Translations.
[Garnett, Elene, etc., 1889. (See Cynewulf, p. 76.) In Thorpe's Anglo-Saxon Chronicle; Warton, History of English Poetry; and by Tennyson.]

Criticism.
Klaeber, F. A Note on the Battle of Brunanburh. [In Anglica (Brandl Festschrift), Leipzig, 1925.]

(c) Other Poems in the Chronicle

A. 941–2. Redemption of the Five Boroughs (Her Eadmund cing). [MSS as Brunanburh.]

B. 959. Reign of Edgar (On his dagum). MSS. Cotton, Tiberius B iv; Bodley, Laud 636.

C. 972–4. (a) Edgar's Coronation (Her Eadgar wæs). MSS. Cotton, Tiberius A vi; Corpus Christi College Cambridge 173. (b) Edgar's Death (Her geendode). MSS. Cotton, Tiberius A vi, Tiberius B i; Corpus Christi College Cambridge 173. [Shorter version of (b) in Cotton, Tiberius B iv; Bodley, Laud 636.]

D. 975. Ælfere (On his dagum). MS. Cotton, Tiberius B iv.

E. 979. Murder of Edward at Corfe (Ne wearð Angelcynne). MS. Bodley, Laud 636.

F. 1011. Capture of Ælfheah (Wæs ða ræpling). MS. Laud 636.

G. 1036. Ælfred the Atheling (Ac Godwine hine þa gelette). MSS. Cotton, Tiberius B i; Tiberius B iv.

H. 1057. Arrival of Edward son of Ironside (Her com Eadward æþeling). MS. Cotton, Tiberius B iv.

I. 1065. Edward the Confessor (Her Eadward kingc). MSS. Cotton, Tiberius B i, Tiberius B iv.

J. 1067. Marriage of Margaret (Cwæð þæt heo hine). MS. Cotton, Tiberius B iv.

K. 1086. William the Conqueror (He rixade ofer Englæland). MS. Bodley, Laud 636.

Editions.
[In edns of Chronicle. A, C, G, I, also in Grein, Bibliothek der angelsächsischen Poesie, 1857, and Wülcker, Bibliothek der angelsächsischen Poesie, vol. i, 1881–3. I in Sedgefield, Anglo-Saxon Verse Book, 1922. A in F. Liebermann, Das Gedicht von König Eadmund I, a. 942, Archiv, cxlviii, 1925.]

Criticism.
Neuendorff. Das Gedicht auf den Tod Eadweards des Martyrers [E]. Archiv, cxxviii, 1912.

Mawer, A. The Redemption of the Five Boroughs [A]. EHR. xxxviii, 1923.

(12) MISCELLANEOUS POEMS

(a) Durham Poem

MS. Cambridge University Lib. H i 27, p. 202 (Simeon of Durham). [Formerly also in Cotton, Vitellius D xx.]

Editions.
[Hickes, Thesaurus, 1703–5 (Cotton).
W. Somner, in R. Twisden's Historiae Anglicanae Scriptores, 1652 (Cambridge University Lib.)
J. Oelrich, Angelsächsische Chrestomathie, Hamburg, 1798.
Wright, Reliquiae Antiquae, vol. i, 1841.
T. Arnold, in Symeonis Monachi opera omnia, vol. i, Rolls Ser. 1882.
Wülcker, Kleinere angelsächsische Dichtungen, 1882.
—— Bibliothek der angelsächsischen Poesie, vol. i, 1881–3.]

Criticism.
Holthausen, F. Gedicht auf Durham. Ang. Bbl. xxxi, 1920.

(b) Franks Casket
[See Palaeography, p. 60.]

(c) Rhyming Poem
MS. Exeter Book, fols. 94 a–95 b.

Editions.
[Conybeare, Illustrations, 1826 (with trn).

Thorpe, Codex Exoniensis, 1842.
—— Analecta, 1846.
Ettmüller, Scopas, 1850.
Grein, Bibliothek der angelsächsischen Poesie, vol. II, 1858.
Kluge, Lesebuch, 1888.
Wülcker, Bibliothek der angelsächsischen Poesie, vol. III, 1897–8.
Schücking, Kleines angelsächsisches Dichterbuch, 1919.
Sedgefield, Anglo-Saxon Verse Book, 1922.
W. S. Mackie, The Old English Rhymed Poem, JEGP. XXI, 1922 (with trn).
F. Holthausen, Das altenglische Reimlied. Neue Ausgabe, E. Studien, XLV, 1931.]
Criticism.
Grein, C. W. M. Das Reimlied des Exerbuches. Germania, x, 1865.
Rieger, M. Über Cynewulf IV. Zeitschrift für deutsche Philologie, I, 1868.
Sievers, E. Zum angelsächsischen Reimlied. PBB. XI, 1886.
Holthausen, F. Zum Reimlied. Ang. Bbl. xx, 1909, XXI, 1910.
—— Das altenglische Reimlied. SEP. L, 1913.
—— Das Reimlied. Ang. Bbl. XXXI, 1920.

(d) Rune-Song

MS. Cotton, Otho B x (burnt in 1731).
Editions.
Hickes, Thesaurus, 1703.
W. Grimm, Über deutsche Runen, pp. 217–25, Göttingen, 1821.
Ettmüller, Scopas, 1850.
Grein, Bibliothek der angelsächsischen Poesie, vol. II, 1858.
Rieger, Lesebuch, 1861.
L. Botkine, La Chanson des Runes, Havre, 1879 (with trn).
Wülcker, Kleinere angelsächsische Dichtungen, 1882.
—— Bibliothek der angelsächsischen Poesie, vol. I, 1881–3.
Dickins, Runic and Heroic Poems, 1915 (with trn).]
Criticism.
Hempl, G. Hickes's Additions to the Runic Poem. MP. I, 1904.
von Grienberger, T. Das angelsächsische Runengedicht. Ang. XLI, 1921.
Klaeber, F. Die Ing-Verse im angelsächsischen Runengedicht. Archiv, CXLIII, 1921.
Keller, W. Zum altenglischen Runengedicht. Ang. LX, 1936.

(e) Brussels Cross Inscription

Logeman, H. L'Inscription anglo-saxonne du Reliquaire dit de la Vraie-Croix du Trésor de l'Église des SS. Michel et Gudule à Bruxelles. Ghent, 1891.

Cook, A. S. The Date of the Old English Inscription on the Brussels Cross. MLR. x, 1915.
[See also Cook, The Date of the Ruthwell and Bewcastle Crosses, under Palaeography, p. 60.]

(f) Charms
[See Science and Medicine, p. 98.]

C. PROSE
(1) GENERAL
Tupper, J. W. Tropes and Figures in Anglo-Saxon Prose. Baltimore, 1897.
Cook, A. S. Biblical Quotations in Old English Prose Writers. 1898.
Klaeber, F. Notes on Old English Prose Texts. MLN. XVIII, 1903.

(2) ANTHOLOGIES
(a) In Old English
Cockayne, O. Narratiunculae Anglice conscriptae. 1861.
—— The Shrine. 13 pts, 1864–9.
Grein, C. W. M. Bibliothek der angelsächsischen Prosa. Cassel, 1872–. [Continued by R. Wülcker and H. Hecht at Leipzig and Hamburg, 13 vols. to 1933.]
Leonhardi, G. Kleinere angelsächsische Denkmäler. 1. Das Læceboc. 2. Die Lacnunga. 3. Der Lorica-Hymnus. 4. Das Lorica-Gebet und die Lorica-Namen. Bibliothek der angelsächsischen Prosa, vol. VI, 1905.
Sedgefield, W. J. An Anglo-Saxon Prose Book. Manchester, 1928.

(b) In Translation
Cook, A. S. and Tinker, C. B. Select Translations from Old English Prose. Boston, 1908.

(3) ALFREDIAN PROSE
King Alfred: General
The Whole Works of Alfred the Great. Ed. J. A. Giles, Jubilee edn, 3 vols. Oxford, 1852–8.
Asser. De Rebus gestis Aelfredi Magni. [Ed. M. Parker, in Thomas of Walsingham, 1574; ed. F. Wise, Oxford, 1722 (from Cott. MS Otho A XII, now burnt); ed. T. D. Hardy, in Monumenta Historiae Britannorum, 1848.]
Spelman, J. Aelfredi Magni Vita. [Pbd in a Latin version by C. Wase, Oxford, 1678. Eng. version, ed. T. Hearne, Oxford, 1709.]
Manning, O. King Alfred's Will. 1788; 1828. [Text and trn.]
von Stolberg, F. L. Leben Alfred des Grossen. Münster, 1815.

Wright, T. Biographia Britannica Literaria. 2 vols. 1842–6.
Pauli, R. König Aelfred. Berlin, 1851; tr. Eng., rev. author, ed. T. Wright, 1852; ed. B. Thorpe, 1853.
Winkelmann, E. Geschichte der Angelsachsen bis zum Tode König Aelfreds. Berlin, 1883.
Freeman, E. A. [Article on Aelfred in DNB. 1885.]
Cooke, J. H. Life of Alfred the Great. 1899.
Alfred the Great. Containing Chapters on his Life and Times. By Mr Frederic Harrison, the Lord Bishop of Bristol, Professor Charles Oman, etc. 1899.
Bowker, A. Alfred the Great. 1899.
Stevenson, W. H. On the Date of the Death of King Alfred. EHR. XLIX, 1899.
—— Asser's Life of Alfred, together with the Annals of St. Neots. Oxford, 1904.
Conybeare, E. Alfred in the Chroniclers. 1900.
Brooke, Stopford A. King Alfred as Educator of his People and Man of Letters. 1901.
Earle, J. The Alfred Jewel. Oxford, 1901.
Harrison, F. The Writings of King Alfred. [In Harvard Addresses, New York, 1901.]
Plummer, C. The Life and Times of Alfred the Great. Oxford, 1902.
Miles, L. Y. King Alfred in Literature. Baltimore, 1902.
Thomas, P. G. Alfred and the Old English Prose of his Reign. CHEL. vol. I, 1907.
Koeppel, E. Zur Chronologie der Übersetzungen des Königs Alfred. Ang. Bbl. XIX, 1908.
Browne, G. F. King Alfred's Books. 1920.
Borenski, L. Der Stil König Alfreds. Leipzig, 1934.

(a) Gregory's Pastoral Care
MSS.
(a) Bodley, Hatton 20.
(b) Cotton, Tiberius B XI.
(c) Bodley, Junius 53.
(d) Cotton, Otho B II.
(e) Three Cambridge MSS, Corpus Christi College, Trinity College, and University Lib.
(f) One leaf at Cassel.
Edition.
Sweet, H. King Alfred's West Saxon Version of Gregory's Pastoral Care. 2 vols. EETS. 1871. [With trn.]
Criticism.
Fleischhauer, W. Über den Gebrauch des Conjunctivs in Alfred's altenglischer Übersetzung von Gregor's Cura Pastoralis. Erlangen, 1885.
Dewitz, A. Untersuchungen über Alfreds des Grossen westsächsische Übersetzung der Cura Pastoralis Gregors. Breslau, 1889.

Wack, G. Über das Verhältnis von König Alfreds Übersetzung der Cura Pastoralis zum Original. Greifswald, 1889.
Kern, J. H. Zur Cura Pastoralis. PBB. XVI, 1892.
—— Zur Cura Pastoralis. Ang. XXXIII, 1910.
Holthausen, F. Die Gedichte in Aelfreds Übersetzung der Cura Pastoralis. Archiv, CVI, 1901.
Mosher, J. A. The Exemplum in the Early Religious and Didactic Literature of England. New York, 1911.
Jost, K. Zu den Handschriften der Cura Pastoralis. Ang. XXXVII, 1913.
Klaeber, F. Zu König Ælfreds Vorrede zu seiner Übersetzung der Cura Pastoralis. Ang. XLVII, 1923.

(b) Bede's Ecclesiastical History
MSS.
(a) Bodley, Tanner 10.
(b) Corpus Christi College Cambridge 41.
(c) Cotton, Otho B XI.
(d) Corpus Christi College Oxford 279.
(e) Cambridge University Lib. Kk 3, 18.
(f) Cotton, Domitian A IX, fol. 100 (see J. Zupitza, ZDA. V, 1886).
Editions.
Wheloc, A. Historiae Ecclesiasticae Gentis Anglorum Libri v. Cambridge, 1643–4.
Smith, J. Historiae ecclesiasticae Gentis Anglorum Libri quinque. Cambridge, 1722.
Miller, T. The Old English Version of Bede's Ecclesiastical History. 4 pts, EETS. 1890–8.
Schipper, J. König Alfred's Übersetzung von Bedas Kirchengeschichte. Bibliothek der angelsächsischen Prosa, vol. IV, 1897–1900.
Criticism.
Stevenson, J. Bede. Historia Ecclesiastica. English Historical Soc. Lecture, 1838.
Wülcker, R. Über die Quellen Layamons. PBB. III, 1876.
Schmidt, A. Untersuchungen über König Alfreds Bedaübersetzung. Berlin, 1889.
Miller, T. Place-Names in the English Bede and the Localization of the MSS. QF. LXXVIII, 1896.
Schipper, J. Gegenwärtiger Stand der Forschung über König Aelfred's Bedaübersetzung. Sitzungsber. d. kgl. Akad. d. Wissensch., Vienna, 1898.
Klaeber, F. An Emendation in the Old English Version of Bede IV 24. J[E]GP. III, 1901.
—— Zur altenglischen Bedaübersetzung. Ang. XXV, 1902, XXVII, 1904.

Hart, J. M. Rhetoric in the Translation of Bede. [In Furnivall Miscellany, Oxford, 1901.]

Fijn van Draat, P. The Authorship of the Old English Bede. A Study in Rhythm. Ang. xxxix, 1916.

Malone, K. King Alfred's 'Geats." MLR. xx, 1925.

Potter, S. On the Relation of the Old English Bede to Werferth's 'Gregory' and to Alfred's Translations. Prague, 1930.

(c) Boethius

MSS.

(a) Cotton, Otho A vi. (With Metra in verse.)

(b) Bodley 180. (With Metra in prose.)

(c) Fragment forming the last leaf of Bodley 86.

(d) Copy of (b) by Junius, collated with (a).

Editions.

Rawlinson, C. An. Manl. Sever. Boethi Consolationis Philosophiae Libri v. Anglo-Saxonice redditi ab Alfredo inclyto Anglo-Saxonum Rege. Oxford, 1698.

Cardale, J. S. King Alfred's Anglo-Saxon Version of Boethius: with an English Translation. 1829.

Fox, S. King Alfred's Anglo-Saxon Version of Boethius with a Literal English Translation. 1864.

Sedgefield, W. J. King Alfred's Old English Version of Boethius de Consolatione Philosophiae. Oxford, 1899.

Krämer, E. Die altenglischen Metra des Boetius. BBA. viii, 1902.

Krapp, G. P. The Paris Psalter and the Meters of Boethius. New York, 1932.

Translation.

Sedgefield, W. J. King Alfred's Version of the Consolations of Boethius. Done into English, with an Introduction. Oxford, 1900.

Criticism.

Hartmann, M. Ist König Alfred der Verfasser der alliterierenden Übertragung der Metra des Boetius? Ang. v, 1882.

Zimmermann, O. Über den Verfasser der altenglischen Metren des Boethius. Greifswald, 1882.

Leicht, A. Ist König Alfred der Verfasser der alliterierenden Metra des Boetius? Ang. vi, 1883. [See also Ang. vii, 1884.]

Napier, A. S. Bruchstück einer altenglischen Boetius-Handschrift (Bodl. MS Junius 86 l). ZDA. xix, 1887.

—— Zum altenglischen Boetius. PBB. xxiv, 1899.

Cossack, H. Über die altenglische metrische Bearbeitungen von Boethius, De Consolatione Philosophiae. Leipzig, 1889.

Stewart, H. F. Boethius: an Essay. Edinburgh, 1891.

Schepss, G. Zu König Alfred's Boethius. Archiv, xciv, 1895.

Förster, M. Zum altenglischen Boethius. Archiv, cvi, 1901.

Klaeber, F. Notes on Old English Prose Texts. I. Boethius. MLN. xviii, 1903.

Fehlauer, F. Die englischen Übersetzungen von Boethius' De Consolatione Philosophiae. I. Die alt- und mittelenglischen Übersetzungen. Berlin, 1909.

Kern, J. H. A Few Notes on the Metra of Boethius in Old English. Neophilologus, viii, 1923.

(d) Orosius

MSS.

(a) Lauderdale-Tollemache. [Helmingham, Suffolk.]

(b) Cotton, Tiberius B i.

(c) Transcript of (b) by Junius.

Editions.

Barrington, D. The Anglo-Saxon Version from the Historian Orosius. Together with an English Translation. 1773.

Bosworth, J. King Alfred's Anglo-Saxon Version of Orosius. 1855–9.

Sweet, H. King Alfred's Orosius. Old English Text and Latin Original. From Lord Tollemache's 9th Century MS. EETS. 1883.

—— Extracts from Alfred's Orosius. Oxford, 1885.

Translations.

Thorpe, B. Orosius. [In Pauli's Life, 1853.]

Hampson, R. T. On the Geography of King Alfred the Great. [In Bosworth's Orosius, 1859.]

Criticism.

Schilling, H. König Aelfred's angelsächsische Bearbeitung der Weltgeschichte des Orosius. Halle, 1886.

Wülfing, J. The Anglo-Saxon Orosius. MLN. ix, 1894.

Markham, C. Alfred as a Geographer. [In Bowker's Alfred the Great, 1899.]

Geidel, H. Alfred der Grosse als Geograph. Munich, 1904.

Logemann, W. S. The mægð that Wulfstan found among the Esthonians. E. Studien, xl, 1909.

Napier, A. S. Two Fragments of Alfred's Orosius. MLR. viii, 1913.

Laborde, E. D. King Alfred's System of Geographical Description in his Version of Orosius. Geographical Journ. lxii, 1923.

Craigie, Sir W. A. The Nationality of King Alfred's Wulfstan. JEGP. xxiv, 1925.

Hübener, G. Alfred und Osteuropa. E. Studien, lx, 1925.

Kirkman, A. Proper Names in the Old English Orosius. MLR. xxv, 1930.

Malone, K. King Alfred's North. A Study in Mediaeval Geography. Speculum, v, 1930.
—— On King Alfred's Geographical Treatise. Speculum, VIII, 1933.

(e) Chronicle
[See Chronicles, below.]

(f) Laws
[See Laws and Charters, p. 96.]

(g) Psalter
[See Gospels, etc, p. 96.]

(h) St Augustine's Soliloquies
MSS.
(a) Cotton, Vitellius A xv.
(b) Copy of (a) by Junius, Bodley, Junius 70.
Editions.
Cockayne, O. The Shrine. 1864–9. ['Blooms.']
Hulme, W. H. 'Blooms.' E. Studien, XVIII, 1893, XIX, 1894.
Hargrove, H. L. King Alfred's Old English Version of St Augustine's Soliloquies. New Haven, 1902–5. [With trn.]
Endter, W. König Alfred der Grosse: Bearbeitung der Soliloquien des Augustinus. Bibliothek der angelsächsischen Prosa, vol. XI, 1922.
Criticism.
Wülcker, R. Über die angelsächsische Bearbeitung der Soliloquien Augustins. PBB. IV, 1877.
Wülfing, J. Zu Alfreds Soliloquien. E. Studien, xx, 1894.
Hubbard, F. G. The Relation of the Blooms of King Alfred to the Anglo-Saxon Translation of Boethius. MLN. IX, 1894.
Cook, A. S. Alfred's Soliloquies and Cynewulf's Christ. MLN. XVII, 1902.
Jost, K. Zur Textkritik der altenglischen Soliloquienbearbeitungen. Ang. Bbl. XXXI, 1920, XXXII, 1921.

(i) Wærferþ's Translation of Gregory's Dialogues
MSS.
(a) Cotton, Otho C I.
(b) Corpus Christi College Cambridge S 10.
(c) Bodley, Hatton 76.
Edition.
Hecht, H. Waerferth von Worcester, Bischof, Übersetzung der Dialoge Gregors. Bibliothek der angelsächsischen Prosa, vol. v, 1901–7.
Criticism.
rebs, H. Die angelsächsische Übersetzung der Dialoge Gregors. Ang. II, III, 1879.

Johnson, H. Gab es zwei von einander unabhängige altenglische Übersetzungen der Dialoge Gregors? Berlin, 1884.
Holthausen, F. Die alliterierende Vorrede zur altenglischen Übersetzung von Gregors Dialogen. Archiv, CV, 1901.
Scherer, G. Zur Geographie and Chronologie des angelsächsischen Wortschatzes, im Anschluss an Bischof Waerferths Übersetzung der 'Dialoge' Gregors. Berlin, 1928.

(j) Martyrology
MSS.
(a) BM. Add. 23211.
(b) Three later MSS.
Editions.
Cockayne, O. The Shrine. 1864–9.
Herzfeld, G. An Old English Martyrology. EETS. 1900.
Criticism.
Liebermann, F. Zum Old English Martyrology. Archiv, CV, 1900.

(4) CHRONICLES
MSS.
A. Corpus Christi College Cambridge 173. (To 1070, Parker.)
B. Cotton, Otho B XI. (A transcript of A. Only three leaves left. Ed. Wheloc in full.)
C. Cotton, Tiberius A VI. (To 977. Identical with D. Canterbury.)
D. Cotton, Tiberius B I. (To 1066, Abingdon.)
E. Cotton, Tiberius B IV. (To 1079, Worcester.)
F. Laud 636. (To 1154, Peterborough.)
G. Cotton, Domitian A VIII. (To 1058. Summary of F. Canterbury.)
H. Cotton, Domitian A IX, fol. 9. (1113–4.)
I. Cotton, Caligula A xv, fols. 132 b ff. (Marginal historical notes to 1130.)
Editions.
Wheloc, A. Historiae Ecclesiasticae Gentis Anglorum, Libri v. 1643–4. [Appendix to Bede.]
Gibson, E. Chronicon Saxonicum. Oxford, 1692. [With Latin trn.]
Ingram, J. The Saxon Chronicle. 1823. [With trn.]
Petrie, Henry. The Anglo-Saxon Chronicle. [Monumenta Historia Britannorum, vol. I, 1848.]
Thorpe, B. The Anglo-Saxon Chronicle 2 vols. Rolls Ser. 1861. [With trn.]
Earle, J. Two of the Anglo-Saxon Chronicles Parallel. Oxford, 1865. [A and F.]
Zupitza, J. Fragment einer englischen Chronik aus den Jahren 1113 und 1114. Ang. I, 1878. [Cott. MS Dom. A IX.]
Liebermann, F. Ungedruckte Anglo-normannische Geschichtsquellen. Strasburg, 1879.

Plummer, C. Two of the Saxon Chronicles Parallel. [A and F.] With Supplementary Extracts from all others. 2 vols. Oxford, 1892–9. [On the basis of Earle.]

Classen, E. and Harmer, F. E. An Anglo-Saxon Chronicle from BM. Cott. MS. Tiberius B iv. Manchester, 1926.

Smith, A. H. The Parker Chronicle. 1935.

Translations.

Gurney, A. A Literal Translation of the Saxon Chronicle. 1819 (priv. ptd).

Giles, J. A. The Venerable Bede's Ecclesiastical History of England. Also the Anglo-Saxon Chronicle. 1847.

——— The Anglo-Saxon Chronicle. Edited from the Translation in Monumenta Historiae Britannorum and Other Versions. 1912. (Bohn.)

Gomme, E. E. C. The Anglo-Saxon Chronicle. 1909.

Ingram, J. Anglo-Saxon Chronicle. 1912. (Everyman's Lib.)

Criticism.

Schmid, R. Die Chronik der Angelsachsen. Leipzig, 1828.

Pauli, R. [Review of Earle's edn.] Göttingischer Gelehrter Anzeiger, xxxvi, 1866.

Grubitz, E. Kritische Untersuchung über die angelsächsischen Annalen bis zum Jahre 893. Göttingen, 1868.

Kern, J. H. Zur angelsächsischen Chronik. PBB. xvi, 1892.

Haworth, H. H. Notes on the Anglo-Saxon Chronicle. EHR. xv, 1900.

Liebermann, F. Zu den angelsächsischen Annalen. Archiv, cvi, 1901.

——— Zu den angelsächsischen Annalen. Archiv, cxlv, 1923.

Bell, A. Cynewulf and Cyneheard in Gaimar. MLR. x, 1915.

Viglione, F. Studio critico-filologico sul' Anglo-Saxon Chronicle. Pavia, 1922.

Robinson, J. A. The Times of St Dunstan. Oxford, 1923.

Mawer, A. Notes and Documents. The Redemption of the Five Boroughs. EHR. xxxviii, 1923.

——— Some Place-Name Identifications in the Anglo-Saxon Chronicles. Leipzig, 1925.

Stenton, F. M. The South-Western Element in the Old English Chronicle. [In Essays presented to T. F. Tout, Manchester, 1925.]

Magoun, F. P. Cynewulf, Cyneheard, and Osric. Ang. lviii, 1933.

Thorogood, A. J. The Anglo-Saxon Chronicle in the Reign of Ecgberht. EHR. xlviii, 1933.

(5) LATER PROSE

(a) *Ælfric*

(i) General

Bale, J. Illustrium Majoris Britanniæ Scriptorum Summarium. Ipswich, 1548.

Cave, W. Scriptores Ecclesiastici. Vol. ii, 1688.

Wharton, H. Anglia Sacra. Vol. i, 1691.

Wilkins, D. Concilia Britannica. Vol. i, 1737.

Migne, J. Patrologia Latina. Vol. cxxxix, Paris, 1853.

Dietrich, E. Abt Aelfrik. Zeitschrift für historische Theologie, xxv, xxvi, Gotha, 1855–6.

Menthel, E. Zur Geschichte des Otfridschen Verses in England. Ang. viii, 1886.

Brandeis, A. Die Alliteration in Aelfric's metrischen Homilien. Vienna, 1897.

White, C. L. Aelfric. A New Study of his Life and Writings. New Haven, 1898.

Gerould, G. H. Abbot Ælfric's Rhythmic Prose. MP. xxii, 1925.

Jost, K. Unechte Ælfrictexte. Ang. li, 1927.

(ii) Lives of Saints

MSS. Cotton, Julius E vii; Cotton, Otho B x and Vitellius D xvii (both injured in the Cottonian fire).

[Single lives or groups of lives in other MSS.]

Editions.

Skeat, W. W. Aelfric's Metrical Lives of Saints, in MS. Cotton, Jul. E vii. 4 pts, EETS. 1881–1900.

Assmann, B. Angelsächsische Homilien und Heiligenleben. Bibliothek der angelsächsischen Prosa, vol. iii, 1889.

Criticism.

Holthaus, E. Ælfric's Heiligenleben. Ang. Anz. vi, 1883.

Zupitza, J. Bemerkungen zu Ælfric's Lives of Saints. [Skeat's edn.] ZDA. xxix, 1885.

Napier, A. S. A Fragment of Ælfric's Lives of Saints. MLN. ii, 1887.

Herzfeld, G. Aelfric's Lives of Saints. E. Studien, xvi, 1891.

Ott, J. H. Über die Quellen der Heiligenleben in 'Ælfric's Lives of Saints.' Halle, 1892.

Gerould, G. H. Ælfric's Lives of St Martin of Tours. JEGP. xxiv, 1925.

Bethurum, D. The Form of Aelfric's Lives of the Saints. Stud. Phil. xxix, 1932.

(iii) Catholic Homilies

MSS.

A. (2 vols. of Homilies.) Cambridge University Lib. (1st group), Corpus Christi College Cambridge 188, and BM. Royal 7 C xii.

B. (Homilies arranged chronologically.) Cotton, Vitellius C v, and Bodley, NE. F 4, 10 and 11.

C. (Including Ælfric's Homilies among others.) Bodley, Junius 22 and 24; Bodley, NE. F 4, 12; Cotton, Vitellius D xvii; Vespasian D xiv; Faustina A ix; Corpus Christi College Cambridge 162, 302, 178; etc.

Editions.

Thorpe, B. Homilies of the Anglo-Saxon Church. 2 vols. Aelfric Soc. 1844–6.

Sweet, H. Selected Homilies of Ælfric. Oxford, 1885.

Assmann, B. Angelsächsische Homilien und Heiligenleben. Bibliothek der angelsächsischen Prosa, vol. iii, 1889.

Sweet, H. Selections from Aelfric's Homilies. Oxford, 1896.

Criticism.

Förster, M. Ueber die Quellen von Aelfrics Homiliae Catholicae. 1. Legenden. Berlin, 1892.

—— Über die Quellen von Ælfric's exegetischen Homiliae Catholicae. Ang. xvi, 1894.

Napier, A. S. Fragments of an Aelfric MS. of the Initio Creatorum. MLN. viii, 1893.

Stephan, A. Eine weitere Quelle von Ælfric's Gregorhomilie. Ang. Bbl. xiv, 1903.

Gerould, G. H. Ælfric's Legend of St Swithin. Ang. xxxiii, 1909.

Brotanek, R. Zwei Homilien des Aelfric [MS Lat. 993 in Bibliothèque Nationale, Paris]. [In Texte und Untersuchungen, Halle, 1913.]

Fehr, B. Über einige Quellen in Ælfric's Homiliae Catholicae. Archiv, cxxx, 1913.

Sisam, K. MSS. Bodley 340 and 342. Aelfric's Catholic Homilies. RES. vii, viii, ix, 1931–3.

Halvarson, N. O. Doctrinal Terms in Aelfric's Homilies. Iowa City, 1932.

(iv) Other Homilies

Sigeferþ Homily (On Chastity). MSS. Vespasian D xiv; Faustina A ix; Vitellius C v; Corpus Christi College Cambridge 302. Ed. B. Assmann, Bibliothek der angelsächsischen Prosa, vol. iii, 1885.

Wulfgeat Homily. MSS. Bodley, Laud Misc. 509, Junius 121 and 23. Ed. Assmann, as above.

Homily on the Birth of the Virgin. MSS. Bodley, Junius 24; Corpus Christi College Cambridge 188 and 303. Ed. Assmann.

Homily for the Birthday of a Confessor. MSS. Corpus Christi College Cambridge 178 and 188; Bodley, Junius 22 and 24; Bodley, NE. F 4, 12; Cotton, Vitellius D xvii (injured). Ed. Assmann.

Homily on John xi. 47–54. MSS. Corpus Christi College Cambridge 162 and 302, Cotton, Faustina A ix. Ed. Assmann.

Homily on John xvi. 16–22. MS. Trinity College Cambridge B 15, 34. Ed. Assmann.

On the Sevenfold Gifts. MSS. (A) Bodley, Junius 99; Corpus Christi College Cambridge 201; (B) Bodley, Junius 23 and 24; Bodley, NE. F 4, 12; Cotton, Tiberius C vi; Trinity College Cambridge. Ed. A. S. Napier, Berlin, 1883 (Wulfstan, Sammlung der ihm zugeschriebenen Homilien). [See also D. Zimmermann, Die beiden Fassungen des dem Abt Ælfric zugeschriebenen angelsächsischen Traktats über die siebenfältigen Gaben des heiligen Geistes, Leipzig 1888.]

(v) Interrogations

MSS. Corpus Christi College Cambridge 162 (2 copies), 178 and 303; Cotton, Julius E vii; Bodley, Junius 23 and 24.

Editions.

Bouterwek, K. W. Interrogationes Sigwulfi Presbyteri. Screadunga, 17–23. Elberfeld, 1858.

MacLean, G. E. Ælfric's Version of Alcuin's Interrogationes Sigewulfi in Genesin. Halle, 1883. [Also Ang. vi, vii, 1883–4.]

Mitchell, F. H. Ælfric's Sigewulfi Interrogationes. Zürich, 1888.

Tessmann, E. A. Aelfrics altenglische Bearbeitung der Interrogationes Sigewulfi presbyteri in Genesin des Alcuin. Berlin, 1892.

(vi) Hexameron

MSS. Cotton, Otho B x; Bodley, Junius 23 and 24; Corpus Christi College Cambridge S 6 and S 7.

Editions.

Norman, H. W. The Anglo-Saxon Version of the Hexameron of St Basil, and Admonitio ad Filium Spiritualem. 1849. [With trn.]

Crawford, S. J. Exameron anglice. Bibliothek der angelsächsischen Prosa, vol. x, 1921. [With trn.]

Criticism.

Emerson, O. F. Notes on Old English. Archiv cxlv, 1923. [I. Aelfric's Hexameron; II Apollonius.]

(vii) Advice to a Spiritual Son

MS. Bodley, Hatton 100. Ed. H. W. Norman (with Hexameron).

(viii) Heptateuch

MSS. Bodley, Laud E 19; Cambridge University Lib.; Cotton, Claudius B iv; Cotton, Otho B x.

Editions.

Thwaites, E. Heptateuchus, Liber Job Evangelium Nicodemi et Judith. Oxford, 1698.

Grein, C. W. M. Älfrik de Vetere et Novo Testamento, Pentateuch, Josua, Buch der Richter und Hiob. Bibliothek der angelsächsischen Prosa, vol. i, 1872.
—— Aelfric's metrischer Auszug aus dem Buch der Richter. Ang. ii, 1879.
Crawford, S. J. The Lincoln Fragment of the Old English Version of the Heptateuch. MLR. xv, 1920.
—— The Old English Heptateuch. MS. Cotton, Claudius B iv. Ælfric's Treatise on the Old and New Testament, and his Preface to Genesis. EETS. 1921.

(ix) Judith

MSS. Corpus Christi College Cambridge 303; Cotton, Otho B x.
Editions.
Assmann, B. Das Buch Judith. Bibliothek der angelsächsischen Prosa, vol. iii, 1885.
—— Abt Aelfric's angelsächsische Homilie über das Buch Judith. Ang. x, 1888.

(x) Esther

MS. 17th cent. copy of MS by William L'Isle in Bodley, Laud 381. Ed. B. Assmann [Abt Aelfric's angelsächsische Bearbeitung des Buches Esther, Halle, 1885). [Also, with addns, in Ang. ix, 1886.]

(xi) Job

MS. 17th cent. copy of MS by William L'Isle in Bodley, Laud 381.
Editions.
Thwaites, Heptateuchus, etc., 1698.
Grein, Bibliothek der angelsächsischen Prosa, vol. i, 1872.
B. Assmann, Abt Ælfric's angelsächsische Bearbeitung des Buches Hiob, Druck mit der Handschrift verglichen, Ang. ix, 1886.]
Criticism.
Förster, M. Ælfric's Job. Ang. xv, 1891.

(xii) De Vetere et Novo Testamento

MS. Bodley, Laud E 19.
Editions.
L'Isle, W. A Saxon Treatise concerning the Old and New Testament. 1623.
Grein, C. W. M. De Vetere et Novo Testamento, Pentateuch, etc. Bibliothek der angelsächsischen Prosa, vol. i, 1872.
Crawford, S. J. The Old English Heptateuch, etc. EETS. 1921.

(xiii) Pastoral Letters

MS.
(a) For Wulfsige: Corpus Christi College Cambridge 190; Bodley, Junius 121.
(b) For Wulfstan: Corpus Christi College Cambridge 190 and 201; Bodley, Junius 121; Bodley, NE. F 4, 12; Cotton, Tiberius A iii.

Editions.
Thorpe, B. Ancient Laws and Institutes of England. 1840.
Fehr, B. Aelfric's Hirtenbriefe in altenglischer und lateinischer Fassung. Bibliothek der angelsächsischen Prosa, vol. ix, 1914.

(xiv) Latin Life of Æthelwold

MS. Bibliothèque Nationale Paris, Lat. 5362. Ed. J. Stevenson (Chronicon Monasterii de Abingdon, Rolls Ser. 1858).

(xv) Excerpts from Æðelwold

MSS. Corpus Christi College Cambridge 178 and 197; Cotton, Titus A iv; Cotton, Faustina A x; Fragment in Cotton, Tiberius A iii.; Wells Fragment.
Editions.
Schroeer, A. Bibliothek der angelsächsischen Prosa. Vol. ii, 1885–8.
Breck, E. Fragment of Ælfric's Translation of Æðelwold's 'De Consuetudine Monachorum' and its Relation to other MSS. Ed. from MS. Cotton, Tiberius A iii. Leipzig, 1887.

(xvi) De Temporibus

MSS. Cotton, Tiberius A iii and B v; Cotton, Titus A xv.
Editions.
Wright, T. Popular Treatises on Science. 1841.
Bouterwek, K. W. Screadunga. Elberfeld, 1858.
Cockayne, O. Leechdoms. Vol. iii, Rolls Ser. 1866.
Criticism.
Reum, A. De Temporibus ein echtes Werk des Abtes Ælfric. Ang. x, 1888.

(xvii) Grammar

MSS. All Souls' College Oxford; Corpus Christi College Cambridge; Durham Cathedral Lib.; Cotton, Faustina; Harleian; Cotton, Julius; St John's College Oxford; Paris; Royal; Sigmaringen; Trinity College Cambridge; Cambridge University Lib.; Worcester Cathedral Lib.
Editions.
Somner, W. Dictionarium Saxonico-Latino-Anglicum. Ælfrici Abbatis Grammatica Latino-saxonica, cum Glossario. Oxford, 1659.
Philipps, T. A Fragment of Ælfric's Anglo-Saxon Grammar, Ælfric's Glossary, etc. 1838. [Worcester MS.]
Zupitza, J. Aelfric's Grammatik und Glossar. Berlin, 1880. [St John's MS.]
Criticism.
Liebermann, F. Aus Aelfric's Grammatik und Glossar. Archiv, xcii, 1894.

Brüll, H. Die altenglische Latein-Grammatik des Ælfric. Berlin, 1900.

(xviii) Glossary

In the following MSS of the Grammar: Corpus Christi College Cambridge; Cotton, Faustina; Harleian; Cotton, Julius; St John's College Oxford; Cambridge University Lib.; Worcester Cathedral Lib.

Editions.

[See Somner, Philipps and Zupitza, under Grammar, above.]

Wright, T. Anglo-Saxon and 'Old English Vocabularies. Rev. R. Wülcker, 2 vols. 1884.

(xix) Colloquium

MSS. Cotton, Tiberius A III; St John's College Oxford.

Editions.

[Leo, Sprachproben, 1835.
Thorpe, Analecta, 1846.
Ebeling, Lesebuch, 1847.
Klipstein, Analecta, 1849.
Wright, Vocabularies, 1884 (see Glossary).]

Criticism.

Zupitza, J. Die ursprüngliche Gestalt von Ælfric's Colloquium. ZDA. XXXI, 1887.

Schroeder, E. Colloquium Aelfrici. ZDA. XLI, 1897.

(b) Wulfstan

MSS. Bodley, Junius 22, 23, 24, 99 and 121; Bodley, NE. F 4, 12; Ashmole 328; Corpus Christi College Cambridge S 9, 13, 14, 18, L 12, and K 2; Trinity College Cambridge; Cotton, Nero A I; Tiberius A III, A XIII, and C VI; Otho B X; Cleopatra B XIII; York Cathedral Lib.; Lambeth 489.

Editions.

Elstob, W. Sermo Lupi Episcopi, Saxonice. Oxford, 1701.

Napier, A. S. Wulfstan's Homilies. Berlin, 1883.

[Sermo Lupi also in: Ebeling, Lesebuch, 1847; Rieger, Lesebuch, 1861; Sweet, Anglo-Saxon Reader, 1876; Wyatt, Anglo-Saxon Reader, 1919.]

Criticism.

Dixon, W. H. Fasti Eboracenses. 1863.

Napier, A. S. Über die Werke des altenglischen Erzbischofs Wulfstan. Weimar, 1882.

Einenkel, E. Der Sermo Lupi ad Anglos ein Gedicht. Ang. VII, 1883.

Kinard, J. P. A Study of Wulfstan's Homilies, their Style and Sources. Baltimore, 1897.

Liebermann, F. Wulfstan und Cnut. Archiv, CIII, 1899.

—— Zu Wulfstans Homilien. Archiv, CLI, 1926.

Priebsch, R. The Chief Sources of some Anglo-Saxon Homilies. Otia Merseiana, I, 1899.

Feiler, E. Das Benediktiner-Offizium, ein altenglisches Brevier aus dem XI. Jahrhundert. Ein Beitrag zur Wulfstanfrage. Anglistische Forschungen, IV, 1900.

Keller, W. Die litterarischen Bestrebungen von Worcester in angelsächsischer Zeit. QF. LXXXIV, 1900.

Becher, C. F. Wulfstans Homilien. Leipzig, 1910.

Fehr, B. Das Benediktiner-Offizium und die Beziehungen zwischen Ælfric und Wulfstan. E. Studien, XLVI, 1913.

Jost, K. Wulfstan und die angelsächsische Chronik. Ang. XLVII, 1923.

[See also Dietrich, 1855, under Aelfric, p. 89.]

(c) Blickling Homilies

MS. At Blickling Hall, Norfolk.

Edition.

Morris, R. The Blickling Homilies, 971 A.D. 3 pts, EETS. 1874–80.

Criticism.

Zupitza, J. Blickling Homilies. Anzeiger für deutsches Altertum, I, 1876.

—— Kritische Beiträge zu den Blickling Homilies und Blickling Glosses. ZDA. XXVI, 1881.

Holthausen, F. Zu den Blickling Homilien. E. Studien, XIV, 1890.

—— Zu den Blickling Homilies. Archiv, CXII, 1894.

Förster, M. Zu den Blickling Homilies. Archiv, XCI, 1893.

—— Zur vierten Blickling Homily. Archiv, CIII, 1899.

Fiedler, H. The Source of the First Blickling Homily. Mod. Lang. Quart. VI, 1904.

Napier, A. S. Notes on the Blickling Homilies MP. I, 1904.

Kern, J. H. Zu den Blickling Homilies E. Studien, LII, 1918.

Willard, R. On Blickling Homily XIII: The Assumption of the Virgin. RES. XII, 1936.

(d) Vercelli Homilies

MS. Vercelli Book, fols. 1 a–29 b, 54 a–101 b, 106 b–120 b.

Editions.

Förster, M. Der Vercelli-Codex C XVII, nebst Abdruck einiger altenglischen Homilien der Handschrift. [In Morsbach Festschrift, SEP. L, 1913.]

—— Die Vercelli-Homilien. Bibliothek der angelsächsischen Prosa, vol. XII, 1932.

[See for criticism Willard, 1927, under Cynewulf: Christ, p. 76.]

(e) *Homily on the Observance of Sunday*

MSS. Corpus Christi College Cambridge
40 and 162. Ed. A. S. Napier (in Furnivall
Miscellany, Oxford, 1901).

(f) *Byrhtferþ's Homilies*

[See edn of his works under Science, p. 97.]

(g) *Cambridge Homilies*

Willard, R. Two Apocrypha in Old English
Homilies. Leipzig, 1935.

(h) *Saints' Legends and Lives*

(i) St Guðlac

MS. Vercelli Book, fols. 133b–135b; Cotton,
Vespasian D xxi, fols. 18–41.

Edition.

Goodwin, C. W. The Anglo-Saxon Version of
the Life of St Guthlac. With a Translation
and Notes. 1848.

Criticism.

Gonser, P. Das angelsächsische Prosa-Leben
des heiligen Guthlac. Anglistische Forschungen, xxvii, 1909.

Kern, J. H. Altenglische Varia. 1. Zum prosa
Guthlac. E. Studien, li, 1917.

(ii) St Swiðun

MS. Fragment at Gloucester. Ed. facs. and
tr. J. Earle, 1861.

(iii) St Neot

MS. Cotton, Vespasian D xiv.

Editions.

Gorham, G. C. History and Antiquities of
Einesbury and St Neot. 1820–4.

Cockayne, O. The Shrine. 1864–9. [With
trn.]

Wülcker, R. Ein angelsächsisches Leben des
Neot. Ang. iii, 1880.

Criticism.

Koelbing, E. Leben des Neot. E. Studien,
vi, 1880.

(iv) St Margaret

MS. Cotton, Tiberius A iii. Ed. O.
Cockayne (in Narratiunculae, 1861).

(v) St Veronica

MSS. Cambridge University Lib.; Corpus
Christi College Cambridge D 5 (fragment);
Cotton, Vespasian D xiv (part).

Editions.

Müller, L. C. Collectanea Anglo-Saxonica,
1835.

Goodwin, C. W. The Anglo-Saxon Legends of
St Andrew and St Veronica. 1851. [With
trn.]

(vi) St Mary of Egypt

[A fragment published by Earle in his edn
of St Swiðun.]

(vii) St Christopher

[A fragment in Cott. MS Vitell. A xv.]

Editions.

Herzfeld, G. Das Cristoforus-Fragment.
E. Studien, xiii, 1891.

Rypins, S. Three Old English Prose Texts.
EETS. 1921.

Criticism.

Einenkel, E. Das altenglische Cristoforus-
Fragment. Ang. xvii, 1895.

(viii) St Chad

MS. Bodley, Junius 24. Ed. A. S. Napier
(Ein altenglisches Leben des heiligen Chad,
1888).

(ix) Legends of the Cross

[See Middle English, p. 173].

(x) Malchus

MS. Cotton, Otho C i. Ed. O. Cockayne
(The Shrine, 1864–9).

(xi) Jamnes and Mambres

Fragment in Cott. MS Tib. B v. Ed.
O. Cockayne (Narratiunculae, 1861).

(i) *Other Religious Prose*

(i) Gospel of Nicodemus

MSS. Cambridge University Lib.; Cotton,
Vitellius A xv.

Editions.

Thwaites, E. Heptateuchus, Liber Job, Evangelium Nicodemi et Judith. Oxford, 1698.

Hulme, W. H. The Old English Version of
the Gospel of Nicodemus. PMLA. xiii,
1898.

—— The Old English Gospel of Nicodemus.
MP. i, 1904.

Crawford, S. J. The Gospel of Nicodemus.
Edinburgh, 1927.

Criticism.

Wülcker, R. Das Evangelium Nicodemi in
der abendländischen Literatur. Paderborn,
1872.

(ii) Benedictine Rule

MSS.

(a) Corpus Christi College Cambridge 178;
Corpus Christi College Oxford; Cotton, Titus
A iv.

(b) Cotton, Tiberius A iii.

Editions.

Schroeer, A. Die angelsächsischen Prosabearbeitungen der Benedictinerregel [Corpus
Christi College Cambridge 178]. Bibliothek
der angelsächsischen Prosa, vol. II, 1885–8.

Logeman, H. The Rule of St Benet. Latin and
Anglo-Saxon Interlinear Version [Tib. A
III]. EETS. 1888.

Criticism.

Logeman, W. S. Interlinear Version of De
Consuetudine Monachorum [Tib. A III].
Ang. XIII, XV, 1891–3.

Tupper, F. History and Texts of the Benedictine Reform of the 10th Century. MLN.
VIII, 1893.

Liebermann, F. Von der angelsächschen
Benedictinerregel. Archiv, CIV, 1900.

—— Aethelwolds Anhang zur Benedictinerregel. Archiv, CVIII, 1902.

Blair, D. O. H. The Rule of St Benedict.
Fort Augustus, 1906.

(iii) Benedictine Office

MSS. Bodley, Junius 121; Corpus Christi
College Cambridge S 18.

Editions.

Letters which passed between Dr. Hickes and
a Popish Priest [with trn by W. Elstob].
1705.

Thomson, E. Godcunde Lar and Ðeowdom.
1849. [With trn.]

Bouterwek, K. W. Cædmon's des Angelsachsen
biblische Dichtungen. Elberfeld, 1854.

(iv) Penitentials

Raith, J. Die altenglische Version des
Halitgar'schen Bussbuches (sog. Poeniten-
tiale Pseudo-Ecgberti). Bibliothek der
angelsächsischen Prosa, vol. XIII, 1933.

Spindler, R. Das altenglische Bussbuch (sog.
Confessionale Pseudo-Ecgberte). Ein Beitrag zur den kirchichen Gesetzen der Angelsachsen. Leipzig, 1934.

(j) Didactic Prose

(i) Distichs of Cato

MSS. Trinity College Cambridge R 9, 17;
Cotton, Julius A II; Cotton, Vespasian D IV.

Editions.

Müller, L. C. Collectanea Anglo-Saxonica.
1835.

Kemble, J. M. The Dialogue of Salomon and
Saturnus. Aelfric Soc. 1848.

Nehab, J. Der altenglische Cato. Berlin,
1879. [See review by G. Schleich, Ang. III,
1879.]

Translation.

Chase, W. J. The Distichs of Cato: A Famous
Medieval Textbook. Translated from the
Latin. Madison, 1922.

(ii) Salomon and Saturn

MS. Cotton, Vitellius A xv. [See the metrical version, under Didactic Poems, p. 82.]

Editions.

[Thorpe, Analecta, 1834.

Ebeling, Lesebuch, 1847.

Kemble, Dialogue of Salomon and Saturnus,
1848, pp. 178–93.

Klipstein, Analecta, 1849.

Ettmüller, Scopas, 1850.]

(k) Eastern Themes

(i) Alexander's Letter to Aristotle

MS. Cotton, Vitellius A xv.

Editions.

Cockayne, O. Alexander to Aristotle
[In Narratiunculae Anglice Conscriptae.
1861.]

Baskervill, W. M. Epistola Alexandri ad
Aristotelem. Ang. IV, 1881.

Rypins, S. Three Old English Prose Texts
MS Cotton, Vitellius A xv. EETS. 1921
[Alexander's Letter, St Christopher
Wonders of the East.]

Criticism.

Holder, A. Collationen zu angelsächsischen
Werken. II. Epistola Alexandri ad Aristotelem. Ang. I, 1878.

Bradley, H. and Sisam, K. Textual Notes or
the Old English Epistola Alexandri. MLR
XIV, 1919.

Rypins, S. The Old English Epistola Alexandri
ad Aristotelem. MLN. XXXVIII, 1923.

(ii) Wonders of the East

MSS. Cotton, Tiberius B v; Cotton
Vitellius A xv. (See Beowulf MS, p. 62.)

Editions.

Knappe, F. Das angelsächsische Prosastück
die Wunder des Ostens. Nach beider
Handschriften. Greifswald, 1906.

Rypins, S. Three Old English Prose Texts
EETS. 1921.

Criticism.

Holder, A. Collationen zu angelsächsischen
Werken. 1. De Rebus in Orientale Mira
bilibus. Ang. I, 1878.

(iii) Apollonius of Tyre

MS. Corpus Christi College Cambridge 201

Editions.

Thorpe, B. Apollonius of Tyre. With a Trans
lation. 1834.

Zupitza, J. Die altenglische Bearbeitung de
Erzählung von Apollonius von Tyrus
Archiv, XCVII, 1896.

Criticism.

Copland, R. Apollonius of Tyre. Printed by Wynkyn de Worde, 1510. Ed. C. J. Ashbee, 1870.

Zupitza, J. Verbesserungen und Erklärungen. 1. Apollonius. Ang. i, 1878.

—— Welcher Text liegt der altenglischen Bearbeitung der Erzählung von Apollonius von Tyrus zu Grunde? Romanische Forschungen, iii, 1886.

Cook, A. S. First Book in Old English. 1894. [Extract.]

Riese, A. Historia Apolloni Regis Tyri. Leipzig, 1893. [Latin Text.]

Smyth, A. H. Shakespeare's Pericles and Apollonius of Tyre. Philadelphia, 1898.

Klebs, E. Die Erzählung von Apollonius aus Tyrus. Berlin, 1899.

Märkisch, R. Die altenglische Bearbeitung der Erzählung von Apollonius von Tyrus. Palaestra, 1899.

Singer, S. Apollonius von Tyrus. Berlin, 1906.

(6) GOSPELS AND PSALTERS

(a) *Gospels*

MSS.

(a) Lindisfarne Gospels (Cotton, Nero D iv).

(b) Rushworth Gospels (Bodley).

(c) Late West-Saxon Gospels (Corpus Christi College Cambridge 140; Cambridge University Lib. Ii 2, 11; Bodley, Hatton 65; Bodley, NE. F 3, 15 (441); Cotton, Otho C i almost entirely burnt); BM. Royal I A xiv).

Editions.

The Gospels of the fower Evangelistes, translated in the olde Saxons tyme out of Latin. [Ed. J. Foxe,] 1571; ed. [from an earlier copy] T. Marshall, Dordrecht, 1665.

Thorpe, B. Tha Halgan Godspel on Englisc. 1842. [Late West Saxon.]

Stevenson, J. and Waring, G. The Lindisfarne and Rushworth Gospels. Surtees Soc. 1854–65.

Bouterwek, K. W. Die vier Evangelien in altnorthumbrischer Sprache. Gütersloh, 1857.

Kemble, W. F. and Hardwick, C. The Gospel according to St Matthew, in Anglo-Saxon and Northumbrian Versions, synoptically arranged. Cambridge, 1858. [Same MSS as Skeat, 1871.]

Bosworth, J. and Waring, G. The Gothic and Anglo-Saxon Gospels, with the Versions of Wyclif and Tyndale. 1865. [Old English text from Corpus Christi College Cambridge MS 140, with some readings from Cambridge University Lib. MS Ii 2, 11.]

Skeat, W. W. The Holy Gospels. Cambridge, 1871–87. [In Anglo-Saxon, Northumbrian and Old Mercian versions, synoptically arranged. From the following MSS: Rushworth, Lindisfarne, Bodley, Hatton 65, and Corpus Christi College Cambridge 140, with readings from Cambridge University Lib. Ii 2, 11, and BM. Royal I A xiv.]

Bright, J. W. The Gospel of St Luke in Anglo-Saxon. Oxford, 1893. [Late West Saxon.]

—— The Gospels of St Matthew, St Mark and St John, in West Saxon. 3 vols. Boston, 1904. (Belles Lettres Ser.)

The Lindisfarne Gospels. Three Plates in Colour and Thirty-six in Monochrome. Introd. E. G. Millar, 1924.

Criticism.

Napier, A. S. Bruchstücke einer altenglischen Evangelien-Handschrift. Archiv, lxxxvii, 1891.

Harris, L. M. Studies in the Anglo-Saxon Version of the Gospels. 1. The Form of the Latin Original and Mistaken Renderings. Baltimore, 1901.

Schulte, E. Untersuchung der Beziehungen der altenglischen Matthäusglosse im Rushworth-MS. zu dem lateinischen Text der Handschrift. Bonn, 1903.

Glunz, H. Die lateinische Vorlage der westsächsischen Evangelienversion. Leipzig, 1928.

Ross, A. S. C. The Errors in the Old English Gloss to the Lindisfarne Gospels. RES. viii, 1932.

Chadwick, D. E., Judge, C. B. and Ross, A. S. C. Collation of an Extract from the Lindisfarne Gospels. Leeds Stud. no. 3, 1934.

(b) *Psalters*

(i) General

Lindeloef, U. Studien zu altenglischen Psalterglossen. BBA. xiii, 1904.

Wildhagen, K. Studien zum Psalterium Romanum in England und zu seinen Glossierungen. [In Morsbach Festschrift, SEP. l, 1913.]

Heinzel, O. Kritische Entstehungsgeschichte des angelsächsischen Interlinearpsalters. Palaestra, 1926.

(ii) Arundel Psalter

MS. BM. Arundel 60. Ed. G. Oess (Der altenglische Arundel-Psalter, Anglistische Forschungen, xxiv, 1910).

(iii) Bosworth Psalter

MS. BM. Add. 37517. Ed. U. Lindeloef (Die altenglischen Glossen im Bosworth-Psalter, Helsingfors, 1909).

(iv) Cambridge Psalter

MS. Cambridge University Lib. Ff 1, 23. Ed. K. Wildhagen (Der Cambridger Psalter, Bibliothek der angelsächsischen Prosa, vol. VII, 1910).

(v) Canterbury Psalter

MS. Trinity College Cambridge R 17, 23. Ed. F. Harsley (Eadwine's Canterbury Psalter, EETS. 1889); ed. facs. M. R. James, 1935.

Wildhagen, K. Über die in Eadwine's Canterbury Psalter enthaltene altenglische Psalter-Interlinearversion. Göttingen, 1903.

—— Zum Eadwine- und Regius-Psalter. E. Studien, XXXIX, 1908.

(vi) Junius Psalter

MS. Bodley, Junius 27. Ed. E. Brenner (Die Interlinear-Glosse der Handschrift Junius 27 der Bodleiana zu Oxford, Anglistische Forschungen, XXIII, 1909).

Brenner, E. Die Glosse des altenglischen Juniuspsalters und ihr Verhältnis zu der des Vespasianpsalters. Heidelberg, 1908.

(vii) Lambeth Psalter

MS. Lambeth 427. Ed. U. Lindeloef (Der Lambeth-Psalter, 2 pts, Helsingfors, 1909–14).

(viii) Paris Psalter

MS. Bibliothèque Nationale Paris, Latin 8824. Ed. B. Thorpe (Libri Psalmorum cum Paraphrasi Anglo-Saxonica, Oxford, 1835); ed. J. W. Bright and R. L. Ramsay (The West-Saxon Psalms, 1908); ed. G. P. Krapp, New York, 1932.

Tanger, G. Collationen des Pariser altenglischen Psalters mit Thorpe's Ausgabe. Ang. Anz. VI, 1883.

Wichmann, J. König Aelfred's angelsächsische Übertragung der Psalmen 1–li exclusive. Ang. XI, 1889.

Bruce, J. D. The Anglo-Saxon Version of the Book of Psalms, commonly known as the Paris Psalter. Baltimore, 1893.

—— Immediate and Ultimate Source of the Rubrics and Introductions to the Psalms in the Paris Psalter. MLN. VIII, 1893.

Wichmann, J. Psalms. PMLA. IX, 1894. [See also J. D. Bruce, PMLA. IX, 1894.]

Grattan, J. H. G. On the Text of the Prose Portion of the Paris Psalter. MLR. IV, 1909.

Förster, M. Die altenglischen Texte in der Pariser Nationalbibliothek. E. Studien, LXII, 1927.

[For the metrical section of this Psalter see under Poetry, p. 80.]

(ix) Royal Psalter

MS. BM. Royal II B v. Ed. F. Roeder (De altenglische Regius-Psalter, SEP. XVIII 1904).

(x) Salisbury Psalter

MS. Salisbury Cathedral Library. Ed. R Wülcker (Aus englischen Bibliotheken, Ang II, 1879).

(xi) Vespasian Psalter

MS. Cotton, Vespasian A I. Ed. H. Swee (Oldest English Texts, EETS. 1885; an Second Anglo-Saxon Reader, Oxford, 1887)

(7) LAWS AND CHARTERS

MSS. [Laws in the following:
(a) Corpus Christi College Cambridge 383.
(b) Corpus Christi College Cambridge 173.
(c) Cotton, Nero A I, and E I.
(d) Harley 55.
(e) Textus Roffensis. Rochester Cathedra Lib.
(f) BM. Burney 277.
(g) Corpus Christi College Cambridge 201.
(h) Cotton, Otho B XI.
(i) Canterbury Cathedral Lib. B 2.
(k) Corpus Christi College Cambridge 265.

Editions of Laws.
Lambarde, W. Ἀρχαιονομία, sive de priscis Anglorum Legibus Libri, Sermone anglico, Vetustate antiquissima. 1568; rev. A. Wheloc, Cambridge, 1644.

Wilkins, D. Leges Anglo-Saxonicae ecclesiasticae et civiles. 1721.

Schmid, R. Die Gesetze der Angelsachsen. 1. Teil, den Text nebst Übersetzung enthaltend. Leipzig, 1832, 1858.

Thorpe, B. Ancient Laws and Institutes of England. 2 vols. 1840.

Cook, A. S. Extracts from the Anglo-Saxon Laws. New York, 1880.

Liebermann, F. Gesetze der Angelsachsen. Halle. I. 1903; II, I, 1906; II, II, 1912; III, 1916. [With trns.]

Attenborough, F. L. The Laws of the Earliest English Kings. Cambridge, 1922. [With trns. See also review by K. Sisam in MLR. XVIII, 1923.]

Robertson, A. J. The Laws of the Kings of England from Edmund to Henry I. Cambridge, 1925. [With trns.]

Criticism.
Johnson, J. A Collection of the Laws and Canons of the Church of England. Oxford, 1850.

Maurer, K. Angelsächsische Rechtsverhältnisse. Munich, 1853–6.

Stubbs, W. Constitutional History of England. 3 vols. Oxford, 1874.

Essays on Anglo-Saxon Law. Ed. H. Adams, Boston, 1876.

Liebermann, F. Gerefa, herausgegeben mit Einleitung. Corpus Christi College Cambridge MS 383, fol. 102. Ang. IX, 1886.

—— Die angelsächsische Verordnung über die Dunsæte. Archiv, CII, 1899.

—— Zum angelsächsischen Krönungseid. Archiv, CIX, 1903.

—— Urkunden im spätesten Westsächsisch. Archiv, CXLIII, 1922.

—— Ist Lambardes Text der Gesetze Æthelstans neuzeitliche Fälschung? Ang. Bbl. XXXV, 1924.

Pollock, F. Anglo-Saxon Law. EHR. VIII, 1893.

—— English Law before the Norman Conquest. [In Bowker's Alfred the Great, 1899. Also in Law Quart. Rev. XIV, 1898.]

Pollock, F. and Maitland, F. W. History of English Law before Edward I. 2 vols. Cambridge, 1895, 1898.

Turk, M. H. The Legal Code of Aelfred the Great. 1893.

Zinkeisen, F. The Anglo-Saxon Courts of Law. Political Science Quart. X, 1895.

Wroblewski, L. Über die altenglischen Gesetze des Königs Knut. Berlin, 1901.

Seebohm, F. Tribal Custom in Anglo-Saxon Law. 1902.

Holdsworth, Sir W. History of English Law. 3 vols. 1903–9 and 1914–5.

Chadwick, H. M. Studies on Anglo-Saxon Institutions. Cambridge, 1905.

Vinogradoff, Sir P. Transfer of Land in Old English Law. Harvard Law Rev. XX, 1907.

—— Romanistische Einflüsse im angelsächsischen Recht, das Buchland. [Mélanges Fitting, vol. II, Montpellier, 1908.]

Davis, H. W. C. The Anglo-Saxon Laws. EHR. XXVIII, 1913.

Sisam, K. The Authenticity of certain Texts in Lambard's Archaionomia. MLR. XX, 1925.

Editions of Charters, etc.

Kemble, J. M. Codex Diplomaticus Aevi Saxonici. 6 vols. English Hist. Soc. 1839, etc.

Thorpe, B. Diplomatarium Anglicum. 1865.

Birch, W. de G. Cartularium Saxonicum. 1885, etc.

—— Index Saxonicus: An Index to all the Names of Persons in the Cartularium Saxonicum. 1899.

Earle, J. A Handbook to the Land Charters and other Saxonic Documents. Oxford, 1888.

Napier, A. S. and Stevenson, W. H. Anecdota Oxoniensia. The Crawford Collection of Early Charters and Documents. Oxford, 1895.

Liebermann, F. Drei northumbrische Urkunden um 1100. Archiv, CXI, 1904.

Stevenson, W. H. Yorkshire Surveys and other Eleventh Century Documents in the York Gospels. EHR. XXVII, 1912.

Pierquin, H. Recueil général des Chartes anglo-saxonnes. Les Saxons en Angleterre (604–1061). Paris, 1913.

Harmer, F. E. Select English Historical Documents of the Ninth and Tenth Centuries. Cambridge, 1914.

Craster, H. H. E. Some Anglo-Saxon Records of the See of Durham. Archaeologia Aeliana, 1925.

Whitelock, D. Anglo-Saxon Wills. Cambridge, 1930.

Förster, M. Die Freilassungsurkunden des Bodmin-Evangeliars. [In Jespersen Miscellany, Copenhagen, 1930.]

(8) SCIENCE AND MEDICINE

(i) Byrhtferþ

Kluge, F. Angelsächsische Excerpte aus Byrhtferth's Handboc oder Enchiridion. Ang. VIII, 1885. [MS Bodley, Ashmole 328.]

Crawford, S. J. Byrhtferth's Manual (A.D. 1011). Pt I, EETS. 1929.

Classen, E. Ueber das Leben und die Schriften Byrhtferðs. Leipzig, 1896.

Forsey, G. F. Byrhtferth's Preface. Speculum, III, 1928.

Crawford, S. J. Byrhtferth of Ramsey and the Anonymous Life of St Oswald. [In Speculum Religionis, 1929.]

Ker, N. R. Two Notes on MS. Ashmole 328. Medium Aevum, IV, 1935.

(ii) Medical Recipes, etc.

Cockayne, O. Leechdoms, Wort-Cunning and Starcraft illustrating the History of Science in this Country before the Norman Conquest. 3 vols. Rolls Ser. 1864–6.

Leonhardi, G. Das Læceboc. Die Lacnunga. [In Kleinere angelsächsische Denkmäler. Bibliothek der angelsächsischen Prosa, vol. VI, 1905.]

Hilbelink, A. J. G. Cotton MS. Vitellius C III of the Herbarium Apuleii. Text and Grammar. Amsterdam, 1930.

Grendon, F. The Anglo-Saxon Charms. New York, 1931.

Wright, T. Popular Treatises on Science in Anglo-Saxon, Anglo-Norman and English. 1841.

7

Payne, J. F. English Medicine in the Anglo-Saxon Times. Oxford, 1904.

Singer, C. Early English Magic and Medicine. British Academy, 1921.

Thorndike, L. History of Magic and Experimental Science. Vol. i, 1923.

Liebermann, F. Angelsächsische Arzneikunde im 12. Jahrhundert fortlebend. Archiv, CXLVII, 1924.

(iii) Charms

Individual Charms in the following MSS: Cotton, Caligula A VII, fols. 171 a–173 a; BM. Harley 585, fols. 160–163, 167, 175–176, 180–181, 185; BM. Royal 12 D XVII, fol. 125; Corpus Christi College Cambridge 41, 202, 216, 226, 350, etc.

[Most of the charms are ed. by Cockayne (Leechdoms, etc., see above, Medical), and by R. Wülcker, Bibliothek der angelsächsischen Poesie, vol. i, 1881–3.]

Zupitza, J. Ein verkannter englischer und zwei bisher ungedruckte lateinische Bienensegen. Ang. i, 1878.

—— Ein Zauberspruch. ZDA. XXXI, 1887.

Hoops, J. Über die altenglischen Pflanzennamen. Freiburg, 1889.

Priebsch, R. An Old English Charm and the 'Wiener Hundesegen.' Academy, May 23, 1896.

Liebermann, F. Eine angelsächsische Fieberbeschwörung. Archiv, CIV, 1900. [See also A. S. Napier, ibid.]

Holthausen, F. Zum Neunkräutersegen. Ang. Bbl. XVI, 1905, XXIX, 1918.

McBryde, D. Anglo-Saxon Charms. MLN. XXI, 1906.

Grendon, F. The Anglo-Saxon Charms. Journ. American Folk-Lore, XXII, 1909.

Skemp, A. R. The Old English Charms. MLR. VI, 1911.

Meissner, R. Die Zunge des grossen Mannes. Ang. XL, 1916.

Holthausen, F. Zu den altenglischen Zaubersprüchen und Segen. Ang. Bbl. XXXI, 1920.

Horn, W. Der altenglische Zauberspruch gegen den Hexenschuss. [In Hoops Festschrift, Heidelberg, 1925.]

Grattan, J. H. G. Three Anglo-Saxon Charms from the 'Lacnunga.' MLR. XXII, 1927.

Bradley, H. The Song of the Nine Magic Herbs. [In Collected Papers, 1928.]

M. S. S.

II. WRITINGS IN LATIN

General Works: Collections of Sources; Literary Histories.

Particular Writers: British Celtic Writers; Early Irish Writers; Early Anglo-Saxon Writers; Later Anglo-Saxon Writers; Later Irish Writers.

A. GENERAL WORKS

(1) PRINCIPAL COLLECTIONS OF SOURCES

Acta Sanctorum. Antwerp, 1643–.

Mabillon, J. Acta Sanctorum ordinis Sancti Benedicti. Paris, 1668–; Venice, 1733–.

Patrologia Latina. Ed. J. P. Migne, Paris, 1844–.

Rees, W. J. Lives of the Cambro-British Saints. Welsh MSS Soc. Llandovery, 1854.

Keil, H. Grammatici Latini. 7 vols. Leipzig, 1857–.

Rerum Britannicarum medii aevi Scriptores (Chronicles and Memorials of Great Britain and Ireland during the Middle Ages). Rolls Ser. 1858–.

Raine, J. The Historians of the Church of York and its Archbishops. 3 vols. Rolls Ser. 1879–94.

Monumenta Germaniae Historica. Poetae Latini Aevi Carolini. 4 vols. Berlin, 1881–1923.

Analecta Hymnica Medii Aevi. Ed. G. M. Dreves, C. Blume and H. M. Bannister, 55 vols. Leipzig, 1886–1922.

Plummer, C. Vitae Sanctorum Hiberniae. 2 vols. Oxford, 1910.

(2) LITERARY HISTORIES, ETC.

Wright, T. Biographia Britannica Literaria (Anglo-Saxon Period). 1842.

Hauréau, B. Les Écoles d'Irlande. [In Singularités historiques et littéraires, Paris, 1861. To be read cautiously.]

Haddan, A. W. and Stubbs, W. Councils and Ecclesiastical Documents relating to Great Britain and Ireland. 4 vols. Oxford, 1869–78.

Warren, F. E. The Liturgy and Ritual of the Celtic Church. Oxford, 1881.

Zimmer, H. Über die Bedeutung des irischen Elements für die mittelalterliche Kultur. Preussische Jahrbücher, LIX, 1887, pp. 28 ff.

Hauck, A. Kirchengeschichte Deutschlands. 5 vols. Leipzig, 1887–1920; 1904 (4th edn of vol. I).

Ebert, A. Allgemeine Geschichte der Literatur des Mittelalters im Abendlande bis zum Beginne des XI. Jahrhunderts. Vols. I and II, Leipzig, 1889 (2nd edn); vol. III, 1887; tr. French, 3 vols. Paris, 1883–9.

Bellesheim, A. Geschichte der katholischen Kirche in Irland. 3 vols. Mainz, 1890–1.

Manitius, M. Geschichte der christlich-lateinischen Poesie bis zur Mitte des VIII. Jahrhunderts. Stuttgart, 1891.

—— Geschichte der lateinischen Literatur des Mittelalters. 3 vols. Munich, 1911–31.

Gross, C. Sources and Literature of English History from the Earliest Times to about 1485. Cambridge, U.S.A. 1897, 1915.

Stephens, W. R. W. and Hunt, W. History of the English Church. Vol. i (597–1066), 1899.

Zimmer, H. The Celtic Church in Britain and Ireland. 1902.

Roger, M. L'Enseignement des Lettres classiques d'Ausone à Alcuin. Paris, 1905.

Esposito, M. The Latin Writers of Mediaeval Ireland. Hermathena, xiv, 1907, pp. 519 ff.; Supplement, ibid. xv, 1908, pp. 353 ff.

Turner, W. Irish Teachers in the Carolingian Revival of Learning. Catholic University Bulletin, Washington, xiii, 1907, pp. 282 ff., 562 ff.

Gougaud, L. Les Chrétientés celtiques. Paris, 1911; tr. Eng. 1932 (enlarged).

—— L'Œuvre des Scotti dans l'Europe continentale. Revue d'Histoire ecclésiastique, ix, 1908, pp. 21 ff., 255 ff.

—— Étude sur les 'Loricae' celtiques et sur les Prières qui s'en rapprochent. Bulletin d'ancienne Littérature et d'Archéologie chrétiennes, i, 1911, pp. 265 ff., ii, 1912, pp. 33 ff., 101 ff.

—— The Achievement and Influence of Irish Monks. Studies, xx, 1931, pp. 195 ff.

—— Les Surnuméraires de l'Émigration scottique (VIᵉ–VIIIᵉ Siècles). Revue Bénédictine, xliii, 1931, pp. 296 ff.

—— Les Scribes monastiques d'Irlande au Travail. Revue d'Histoire ecclésiastique, xxvii, 1931, pp. 293 ff.

The Cambridge Medieval History. 8 vols. Cambridge, 1911–36.

Raby, F. J. E. A History of Christian-Latin Poetry from the Beginnings to the End of the Middle Ages. Oxford, 1927.

Ueberweg, F. Grundriss der Geschichte der Philosophie. Vol. ii, Berlin, 1928. [Die patristische und scholastische Philosophie, ed. B. Geyer.]

Kenney, J. F. The Sources for the Early History of Ireland: an Introduction and Guide. Vol. i, Ecclesiastical, New York, 1929. [Very valuable for some English writers also, e.g. Gildas, Nennius, Aldhelm, Bede.]

Laistner, M. L. W. Thought and Letters in Western Europe A.D. 500 to 900. 1931.

MacNeill, E. Beginnings of Latin Culture in Ireland. Studies, xx, 1931, pp. 39 ff.

Wright, F. A. and Sinclair, T. A. A History of Later Latin Literature. 1931.

Baxter, J. H., Johnson, C. and Willard, J. F. An Index of British and Irish Latin Writers, A.D. 400–1520. Archivum Latinitatis Medii Aevi, vii, 1932, pp. 7 ff.

Crawford, S. J. Anglo-Saxon Influence on Western Christendom. Oxford, 1933.

Ogilvy, J. D. A. Anglo-Saxon Scholarship, 597–780. University of Colorado Stud. xxii, 1935, pp. 327 ff.

—— Books known to Anglo-Latin Writers from Aldhelm to Alcuin (670–804). Cambridge, U.S.A. 1936.

B. BRITISH CELTIC WRITERS

(1) GILDAS (d. c. 570)

(a) Works

De excidio et conquestu Britanniae. Ed. J. Stephenson, English Hist. Soc. 1838 (= Migne, Patrologia Latina, vol. lxix); ed. T. Mommsen (in Chronica Minora, vol. iii, pt i, Monumenta Germaniae Historica, Auct. Antiq. vol. xiii); ed. H. Williams (as Gildas, The Ruin of Britain (text and trn), Hon. Soc. of Cymmrodorion, 1899).

Poems ascribed to Gildas:

Lorica. Analecta Hymnica, vol. li, p. 159; Irish Liber Hymnorum, vol. i, 1898, p. 206; F. J. H. Jenkinson, Hisperica Famina, Cambridge, 1908, p. 52. [Both Mommsen and Wilhelm Meyer doubt whether Gildas is the author; against H. Zimmer, Nennius Vindicatus, Berlin, 1893, pp. 301 ff.]

[Prayer] pro itineris et navigii prosperitate. W. Meyer, Gildae oratio rythmica, Nachrichten d. kgl. Gesellsch. d. Wissensch. zu Göttingen, 1912, pp. 48 ff. [This may well be by Gildas.]

(b) Monographs

de la Borderie, A. La Date de la Naissance de Gildas. Revue Celtique, vi, 1883, pp. 1 ff.

—— L'Historia Britonum attribuée à Nennius et l'Historia Britannica avant Geoffroi de Monmouth. Paris, 1883.

Wade-Evans, A. W. Notes on the Excidium Britanniae. Celtic Rev. i, 1905, pp. 289 ff.

—— The Ruin of Britannia. Celtic Rev. ii, 1905, pp. 46 ff., 126 ff. [Answered by E. W. B. Nicholson, The Ruin of History, ibid. ii, 1906, pp. 369 ff.]

—— The 'Picti' and 'Scotti' in the Excidium Britanniae. Celtic Rev. ix, 1914, pp. 314 ff.

—— The Romani in the Excidium Britanniae. Celtic Rev. ix, 1914, pp. 35 ff.

—— The Saxones in the Excidium Britanniae. Celtic Rev. x, 1915, pp. 215 ff., xi, 1916, pp. 322 ff.

Wade-Evans, A. W. The Scotti and Picti in the Excidium Britanniae. Archaeologia Cambrensis, ser. 6, x, 1910, pp. 449 ff.

—— The Saxones in the Excidium Britanniae. Archaeologia Cambrensis, ser. 6, xi, 1911, pp. 170 ff.

—— Some Insular Sources of the Excidium Britanniae. Y Cymmrodor, xxvii, 1917, pp. 37 ff.

—— Gildas and Modern Professors. Y Cymmrodor, xxxi, 1921, pp. 60 ff.

Fonssagrives, J. S. Gildas de Ruis et la Société bretonne au VIe Siècle. Paris, 1908.

Thurneysen, R. Zum Geburtsjahr des Gildas. Zeitschrift für keltische Philologie, xiv, 1923, pp. 13 ff.

Wheeler, G. H. Gildas de Excidio Britanniae, Chapter 26. EHR. xli, 1926, pp. 497 ff.

Lot, F. De la Valeur historique du De Excidio et Conquestu Britanniae de Gildas. [In Mediæval Studies in Memory of Gertrude S. Loomis, Paris, 1927.]

—— Bretons et Anglais au Ve et VIe Siècles. British Academy Lecture, 1930.

Ernault, E. Sur le Nom breton de Gildas. Revue Celtique, xlviii, 1931, pp. 130 ff.

Burkitt, F. C. The Bible of Gildas. Revue Bénédictine, xlvi, 1934, pp. 206 ff.

(2) Historia Britonum and Nennius

[The problems which this complex of writings presents are summarised in Manitius, Geschichte der lateinischen Literatur des Mittelalters, vol. i, pp. 240 ff.; in Kenney, Sources for the Early History of Ireland, pp. 152 ff.; and in F. Lot, Nennius et l'Historia Britonum, 2 vols. Paris, 1934–6 (includes text). The contents of the collection (the individual members of which are, for the most part, composite in character: see Kenney, p. 154) are, according to one arrangement (BM. Harl. MS 3859), Computus and De sex aetatibus mundi; Historia Britonum (description of Britain; Brutus legend; Irish events; sons of Noah; Roman conquest of Britain; legend of the Christian king Lucius; end of Roman dominion; coming of Saxons; St Germanus; Ambrosius; Vortigern and his descendants); Vita Patricii; Arthur legend; Genealogies of Saxon kings and computus; Annales Cambriae; Welsh genealogies; list of British cities; mirabilia Britanniae.]

(a) Texts

Historia Britonum. Ed. J. Stevenson, English Hist. Soc. 1838; ed. A. Schulz (San-Marte), Berlin, 1844; ed. T. Mommsen, Chronica Minora, vol. iii, Monumenta Germaniae Historica, Auct. Antiq. vol. xiii; ed. F. Lot, Paris, 1934.

(b) Monographs

Zimmer, H. Nennius Vindicatus. Berlin, 1893.

Duchesne, L. Nennius Retractatus. Revue Celtique, xv, 1894, pp. 174 ff.

Howorth, H. Nennius and the Historia Britonum. Archaeologia Cambrensis, ser. 6, xvii, 1917, pp. 87 ff., 321 ff.

Liebermann, F. Nennius the Author of the Historia Brittonum. [In Essays in Mediaeval History presented to T. F. Tout, Manchester, 1925. Regards Nennius as the true compiler of the collection.]

Loth, J. Remarques à l'Historia Britonum dite de Nennius. Revue Celtique, xlix, 1932, pp. 150 ff.

Thurneysen, R. Nochmals Nennius. Zeitschrift für keltische Philologie, xx, 1935, pp. 185 ff.

(3) Hisperica Famina

[A composition in a mysterious speech (Geheimsprache), composed of a mixture of Hebrew, Greek and Vulgar Latin along with words of no known origin. It was probably written in Britain in the 6th cent., and not in Ireland as Jenkinson and others have supposed. This speech has some affinity with that used by Virgilius Maro, the grammarian of Toulouse. His works are edited by H. Huemer, Virgilii Maronis Grammatici Opera, Leipzig, 1886; on him, see D. Tardi, Les Epitomae de Virgile de Toulouse, Paris, 1928, and Huemer, Die Epitomae des Grammaticus Virgilius Maro nach dem Fragmentum Vindobonense 19556, Wiener Sitzungsber. xcix, 1882, pp. 509 ff.; H. Zimmer, Über direkte Handelsverbindungen Westgalliens mit Irland, Berliner Sitzungsber. 1909, thinks (pp. 1031 ff.) that Virgil came to Ireland at the end of the 5th cent., but his arguments lack conviction. It is better to place Virgil at the end of the 6th cent.]

(a) Texts

Ed. A. Mai, Classici Auctores, vol. v, Rome, 1833, pp. 479 ff. (= Migne, Patrologia Latina, vol. xc); ed. J. M. Stowasser, Incerti auctoris Hisperica Famina, Vienna, 1887; ed. F. J. H. Jenkinson, The Hisperica Famina, Cambridge, 1908.

Luxemburg and Paris fragments. F. J. Mone, Die gallische Sprache und ihre Brauchbarkeit, Karlsruhe, 1851 (Institut de Luxembourg, 1896); H. Zimmer, Neue Fragmente von Hisperica Famina, Nachrichten der kgl. Gesellsch. d. Wissensch. zu Göttingen, 1895, pp. 117 ff.; H. Bradshaw, Collected Papers of Henry Bradshaw, Cambridge, 1889, pp. 463 ff.

(b) Monographs

Geyer, P. Die Hisperica Famina. Archiv für lateinische Lexikographie und Grammatik, II, 1885, pp. 255 ff.

Stowasser, J. M. Zu den Hisperica Famina. Archiv für lateinische Lexikographie und Grammatik, III, 1886, pp. 168 ff. [See pp. 546 ff. by R. Thurneysen.]

—— Das Luxemburger Fragment. Wiener Studien, IX, 1887, pp. 309 ff.

—— De quarto quodam Scoticae Latinitatis specimine. Fünfzehnter Jahresbericht über das k. k. Franz-Joseph-Gymnasium in Wien, 1889.

Rhys, J. The Luxembourg Folio. Revue Celtique, I, 1870, pp. 346 ff.

—— The Luxembourg Fragment. Revue Celtique, XIII, 1892, pp. 248 ff.

Zimmer, H. Nennius Vindicatus. Berlin, 1893. [Pp. 291 ff.]

Goetz, G. Über Dunkel- und Geheimsprache im späten und mittelalterlichen Latein. Leipziger Sitzungsber. 1896, pp. 62 ff.

Ellis, R. Notes on MSS. of Catullus and Hisperica Famina. Hermathena, XII, 1902, pp. 22 ff.

—— On the Hisperica Famina. Journ. Philology, XXVIII, 1903, pp. 209 ff.

Polheim, K. Die lateinische Reimprosa. Leipzig, 1925, p. 286. [The Hisperica Famina are not simple rimed prose, but have a structure that suggests verse.]

(4) Pieces Related to Hisperica Famina

(a) Lorica of Gildas. [See p. 99.]
(b) Rubrisca, alphabetical poem (? by Olimbrianus; see verse 78). [Text in Jenkinson, pp. 55 ff.]
(c) Alphabetical hymn, Adelphus adelpha meter. [Text in Jenkinson, pp. 61 ff.; see also R. Thurneysen, Gloses bretonnes, Revue Celtique, XI, 1890, pp. 86 ff.; bibliography in Manitius, Geschichte der lateinischen Literatur des Mittelalters, vol. I, p. 160.]

C. IRISH WRITERS, FIRST PERIOD

(1) Irish Hymns

[For literature concerning individual hymns, see Kenney, Sources for the Early History of Ireland, pp. 250 ff., and pp. 724 ff. for hymns (probably Irish) in Book of Cerne, and other codices.]

Hymnodia Hiberno-Celtica. Ed. C. Blume, Analecta Hymnica, vol. LI, pp. 259 ff. [A corpus of Irish-Celtic Latin hymns, including those in the Liber Hymnorum, Bangor Antiphonary and Book of Cerne.]

The Irish Liber Hymnorum. Ed. J. H. Bernard and R. Atkinson, 2 vols. Henry Bradshaw Soc. 1898.

The Antiphonary of Bangor (with facsimile of MS). Ed. F. E. Warren, 2 vols. Henry Bradshaw Soc. 1893–5. [It is not an Antiphonary, but a collection of hymns, prayers, etc.; date, end of 7th cent.]

(2) Irish Liturgical Books

[See Kenney, pp. 689 ff. for full bibliography and reference to fragments.]

(a) The Bobbio Missal. 3 vols. Henry Bradshaw Soc. 1917–24.
(b) The Stowe Missal. 2 vols. Henry Bradshaw Soc. 1906–15.
(c) The Antiphonary of Bangor. [See above under Irish Hymns.]

(3) St Patrick (d. 463)

Confessio, etc. Ed. N. J. D. White. [In Libri sancti Patricii: the Latin Writings of St Patrick, Proc. Royal Irish Academy, XXV, sect. c, 1905, pp. 201 ff.; also in Libri sancti Patricii, 1918.] [For further bibliography, see Kenney, p. 166.]

Bury, J. B. Life of S. Patrick and his Place in History. 1905.
Meissner, J. L. C. The British Tradition of St Patrick's Life. Proc. Royal Irish Academy, XL, sect. c, 1931–2, pp. 356 ff.
Müller, K. Der heilige Patrick. Nachrichten d. kgl. Gesellsch. d. Wissensch. zu Göttingen, 1931, pp. 62 ff.
Hitchcock, F. H. M. The Confessio and Epistola of Patrick of Ireland and their Literary Affinities in Irenaeus, Cyprian and Orientius. Hermathena, XLVII, 1932, pp. 20 ff.

(4) Columba or Colum-cille (d. 597)

[Among the poems ascribed to him, two have the best claim: (i) Altus prosator. Analecta Hymnica, vol. LI, pp. 275 ff.; Liber Hymnorum, vol. I, 1898, pp. 66 ff.; ed. C. Cuissard, La Prose de S. Columba, Revue Celtique, V, 1881, pp. 205 ff. For MSS and bibliography see Kenney, pp. 263 f. (ii) Noli Pater. Analecta Hymnica, vol. LI, p. 286; Liber Hymnorum, vol. I, 1898, p. 88.]

Menzies, L. St Columba of Iona. 1920.
Anderson, A. O. Early Sources of Scottish History. Vol. I, 1922, pp. 17 ff.
Lindsay, W. M. Columba's Altus and the Abstruse Glossary. Classical Quart. XVII, 1923, pp. 197 f.
Simpson, W. D. The Historical Saint Columba. Aberdeen, 1927 (2nd edn).

(5) COLUMBANUS (d. 615)

(a) Works

Letters and Poems. Migne, Patrologia Latina, vol. LXXX; ed. W. Gundlach, Monumenta Germaniae Historica,Epist. vol. III,pp.182ff. [Four of these are poems, which Gundlach regards as authentic; see Über die Columban-Briefe, Neues Archiv, XIII, 1888, pp. 499 ff.]
  Seebass, O. Über die Handschriften der Sermonen und Briefe Columbas von Luxeuil. Neues Archiv, XVII, 1892, pp. 245 ff. [Answered by Gundlach, Zu den Columbanbriefen. Eine Entgegnung, ibid. pp. 425 ff.]
Sermons or Homilies. Migne, Patrologia Latina, vol. LXXX, cols. 229–60. [Four of these may be by Columbanus. They are nos. 3, 11, 14, 17, and are ed. by O. Seebass in Zeitschrift für Kirchengeschichte, XIV, 1894, pp. 76 ff.]
The Rule of Columbanus and the Penitential. [See Kenney, pp. 197 ff.; and G. Domenici in Rivista Storica Benedettina, XI, 1920, pp. 185 ff.]
[Columbanus may be the author of A boating song, ed. E. Dümmler, Neues Archiv, VI, 1881, pp. 190 f.]

(b) Biographies and Studies

Martin, E. S. Columban. Paris, 1905.
Metlake, G. The Life and Writings of S. Columban. Philadelphia, 1914.
Domenici, G. S. Colombano. La Civiltà cattolica, 1916.
Lugnano, P. S. Colombano, Monaco e Scrittore. Rivista Storica Benedettina, VII, 1916, pp. 5 ff.
Laux, J. J. Der heilige Kolumban. Freiburg, 1919.
Pellizzari, A. S. Colombano e le Lettere. Scuola cattolica, 15 July 1923, pp. 524 ff.
Krusch, B. Zur Mönchsregel Columbans. Neues Archiv, XLVI, 1925, pp. 148 ff.
Morin, G. Le 'Liber S. Columbani in psalmos' et le ms. Ambros. C. 101. inf. Revue Bénédictine, XXXVIII, 1926, pp. 164 ff.

(6) ADAMNAN, ABBOT OF IONA (d. 704)

Vita Sancti Columbae. Ed. W. Reeves, The Life of St Columba, from a MS of the Eighth Century, Edinburgh, 1857 (with notes, etc.; indispensable); ed. W. F. Skene, The Historians of Scotland, vol. VI, Edinburgh, 1874; ed. W. M. Metcalfe, Pinkerton's Lives of the Scottish Saints, vol. I, Paisley, 1889; ed. J. T. Fowler, Adamni Vita S. Columbae, Oxford, 1894. [For MSS see Kenney, pp. 429 ff. On the shorter recension (in Migne, Patrologia Latina, vol. LXXXVIII) see Kenney, p. 431.]

Huyshe, W. The Life of S. Columba. Tr. Eng. 1906.
De locis sanctis. Ed. T. Tobler, Itinera Hierosolymitana, vol. I, Geneva, 1879; ed. P. Geyer, Corpus Scriptorum Ecclesiasticorum Latinum, vol. XXXIX, Vienna, 1898. [This work was used by Bede in his own treatise on the Holy Places. Adamnan got his information from Arculf, a Gallic bishop who was wrecked on his return from Palestine and came to Iona.]
Commentary on Virgil. [Adamnan may be the original compiler of a collection of scholia on the Eclogues and Georgics. For bibliography and discussion see Kenney,pp.286 f.]

(7) MINOR IRISH LATIN WRITERS

(a) Augustine,an Irishman (fl. 655). De mirabilibus sanctae scripturae. Migne, Patrologia Latina, vol. XXXV, cols. 2149 ff. [See L. Gougaud, Christianity in Celtic Lands 1932, p. 266, and W. Reeves, On Augustine, an Irish Writer of the Seventh Century, Proc. Royal Irish Academy, VII, 1861, p. 515, and Kenney, pp. 275 ff.]
(b) Lathcen (d. 661). Abridgement of Gregory's Moralia. [See L. Gougaud, Christianity in Celtic Lands, 1932, p. 267, and Kenney, pp. 278 ff.]
(c) Aileran the Wise (d. 665). (i) Interpretatio mystica progenitorum domini Jesu Christi Migne, Patrologia Latina, vol. LXXX, cols. 327 ff., completed in C. MacDonnell, Proc Royal Irish Academy, VIII, 1857–61, pp 369 ff. (ii) Poem on the Canons of Eusebius. Migne, Patrologia Latina, vol. CI, col 729. [See Kenney, p. 280, and D. de Bruyne Une Poésie inconnue d'Aileran le Sage, Re vue Bénédictine, XXIX, 1911, p. 339 f.]

(8) ANONYMOUS IRISH LATIN WRITINGS

(a) Versus cuiusdam Scotti de Alfabeto. Ed. E. Baehrens, Poetae Latini Minores, vol. v, pp. 375 ff. Leipzig, 1883. [About middle of 7th cent. Riddles on the letters of the alphabet.]
  Müller, L. Versus Scoti cuiusdam de Alphabeto. Rheinisches Museum, XX 1865, pp. 357 ff.
  —— Zu den versus Scoti cuiusdam de Alphabeto. Rheinisches Museum, XXII, 1867, pp. 500 ff.
  Wagner, W. Zu den versus Scoti cuiusdam de Alphabeto. Rheinisches Museum, XXII, 1867, pp. 629 ff.
  Grosse, E. Zu den versus Scoti cuiusdam de Alphabeto. Rheinisches Museum, XXIV, 1869, pp. 614 ff.
  Klein, J. Zu den versus Scoti cuiusdam de Alphabeto. Rheinisches Museum, XXXI, 1876, pp. 465 ff.

Buecheler, F. Coniectanea. Rheinisches Museum, xxxvi, 1881, p. 340.

Manitius, M. Geschichte der christlich-lateinischen Poesie, p. 484; Geschichte der lateinischen Literatur des Mittelalters, vol. i, pp. 190 ff.

b) The Berne Collection of Riddles. Ed. A. Riese, Anthologia Latina, 1869–70, no. 481 (Aenigmata Codicis Bernensis, 611). Schenkl, K. Handschriftliches zur lateinischen Anthologie. Wiener Studien, ii, 1880, pp. 296 ff.

Meyer, W. Anfang und Ursprung der lateinischen und griechischen rythmischen Dichtung. Abhandl. d. bayer. Akad. xvii, 1886, pp. 417 ff. [Text.]

c) Vere novo florebat. Ed. A. Riese, Anthologia Latina, 1869–70, no. 941.

d) Perge carina. Ed. J. B. Pitra, Spicilegium Solesmense, vol. iii, 1855, pp. 399 ff.

e) Rauca sonora Languida voce. Ed. A. Riese, Anthologia Latina, 1869–70, no. 739.

f) Incipit de signis et prodigiis et de quibusdem Hyberniae admirandis. Ed. A. Riese, Anthologia Latina, 1869–70, no. 791 (31 verses); ed. T. Mommsen, Monumenta Germaniae Historica, Auct. Antiq. vol. xiii, pp. 219 ff.

[For literature of the last four poems, see Kenney, pp. 733 f.]

g) De duodecim abusivis saeculi. Ed. W. Hartel, Cypriani Opera, vol. iii, pp. 152 ff., Corpus Scriptorum Ecclesiasticorum Latinorum, vol. iii, Vienna, 1868; ed. S. Hellmann, Pseudo-Cyprianus de XII abusivis saeculi, Texte und Untersuchungen, vol. xxxiv, pt i, Leipzig, 1909. [Anonymous work, *c.* middle of 7th cent., written in S.E. Ireland; it has been attributed to Cyprian, to Augustine and to Isidore, and was very popular.]

D. ANGLO-SAXON WRITERS, FIRST PERIOD

(1) ALDHELM (d. 709)

(a) Works

Opera. Ed. J. A. Giles, Oxford, 1844 (= Migne, Patrologia Latina, vol. lxxxix); ed. R. Ehwald, Monumenta Germaniae Historica, Auct. Antiq. vol. xv, 1919 (critical edn).

(b) Monographs and Studies

Müller, L. Zu Aldhelmus. Rheinisches Museum, xxii, 1867, pp. 150 f.

Manitius, M. Zu Aldhelm und Beda. Wiener Sitzungsber. cxiii, 1886, pp. 532 ff. [On the authors quoted by Aldhelm and Bede.]

Zupitza, J. Eine Conjectur zu Aldhelm. Romanische Forschungen, iii, 1887, p. 280.

Zimmer, H. Keltische Beiträge, I. ZDA. xxxii, 1887, p. 202. [Date of Aldhelm's letter to Ealfrid; before 690.]

Bönhoff, L. Aldhelm von Malmesbury. Dresden, 1894.

Browne, G. F. Aldhelm. 1903.

Mazzoni, D. Aldhelmiana. Studio critico letterario su Aldhelmo di Sherborne. Rome, 1916. [From Rivista Storica Benedettina, 1915.]

Strecker, K. Aldhelms Gedichte in Tegernsee. Archiv, cxliii, 1922, pp. 177 ff.

Cook, A. S. Aldhelm's Legal Studies. JEGP. vii, 1924, pp. 101 ff.

—— Aldhelm and the Source of Beowulf 2523. MLN. xl, 1926, pp. 137 ff.

Pitman, J. H. The Riddles of Aldhelm. New Haven, 1925.

von Ehrhardt-Siebold, E. Aldhelm's Chrismal. Speculum, x, 1935, pp. 276 ff.

(2) AETHELWALD

[Author of some of a group of rhythmical Latin poems which were formerly ascribed to Aldhelm; see Raby, Christian-Latin Poetry, pp. 144 f.]

Poems. [In Ehwald's edn of Aldhelm, pp. 519 ff.; also in P. Jaffé, Monumenta Moguntina, Bibliotheca Rerum Germanicarum, vol. iii, Berlin, 1866, pp. 38 ff.]

Traube, L. Karolingische Dichtungen. Berlin, 1888, pp. 130 ff.

Bradley, H. Some Poems ascribed to Aldhelm. EHR. xv, 1900, pp. 291 f.

(3) FELIX, MONK OF CROYLAND (*fl.* 730)

Life of S. Guthlac. Ed. J. Mabillon, Acta SS. ordinis S. Benedicti, vol. iii, pt i, pp. 263 ff.; Acta SS. April. vol. ii, pp. 38 ff.; ed. R. Gough, The History and Antiquities of Croyland Abbey, 1783, pp. 131 ff.; ed. C. W. Goodwin, 1848 (with Anglo-Saxon version). [See Wright, Biographia Britannica Literaria, vol. i, pp. 246 ff.]

(4) EDDIUS STEPHANUS (*fl.* 711–731)

The Life of Bishop Wilfrid. Ed. B. Colgraves, Cambridge, 1927. [Also ed. W. Levison, Monumenta Germaniae Historica, Script. Rerum Merov. vol. vi, pp. 163 f.; and J. Raine, Historians of the Church of York, vol. i, pp. 1 ff.]

Wells, B. W. Eddi's Life of Wilfrid. EHR. vi, 1891, pp. 535 ff.

(5) TATWINE, ARCHBISHOP OF CANTERBURY
(d. 734)

De octo partibus orationis. MS. Rome codex Palatinus, 1746, fols. 99 ff. Ed. in part A. Wilmanns, Der Katalog der Lorscher Klosterbibliothek aus dem zehnten Jahrhundert, Rheinisches Museum, XXIII, 1868, pp. 398 ff. [See Roger, L'Enseignement des Lettres classiques, p. 338, and n. 1.]
—— Aenigmata. Ed. T. Wright, Anglo-Latin Satirical Poets of the Twelfth Century, Rolls Ser. vol. II, 1872, pp. 525 ff.

(6) EUSEBIUS OR HWAETBERHT (fl. 730)

Aenigmata. Ed. T. Wright, Anecdota Bedae, Lanfranci, et aliorum, Caxton Soc. 1851, pp. 54 ff.
Buecheler, F. Coniectanea. Rheinisches Museum, XXXVI, 1881, pp. 340 ff.

(7) BEDE (d. 735)

Opera. Paris, 1544; Basle, 1563; Cologne, 1612, 1688; ed. J. A. Giles, 12 vols. 1843–4 (= Migne, Patrologia Latina, vols. XC–XCV).
Bedae Opera Historica. Ed. C. Plummer, 2 vols. Oxford, 1896; ed. J. E. King, 2 vols. 1930 (Loeb edn).

(a) Grammatical Works

De metrica arte. Ed. H. Keil, Grammatici Latini, vol. VII, pp. 217 ff.
De schematibus et tropis. Ed. C. Halm, Rhetores Latini Minores, Leipzig, 1863, pp. 607 ff.
De orthographia. Ed. H. Keil, Grammatici Latini, vol. VII, pp. 261 ff.

[See Roger, L'Enseignement des Lettres classiques, pp. 331–2, for Cunabula grammaticae artis Donati (Migne, Patrologia Latina, vol. XC) doubtfully attributed to Bede.]

(b) Scientific Works

De natura rerum. (Giles and Migne.)
De temporibus liber. (Giles and Migne.) [The Chronicle is in Bedae Chronica Minora, ed. T. Mommsen, Monumenta Germaniae Historica, Auct. Antiq. vol. XIII.]
De ratione temporum. (Giles and Migne.) [The Chronicle is in Monumenta Germaniae Historica, Auct. Antiq. vol. XIII. The De ratione Computi (Migne, vol. XC, p. 579) is not by Bede, but is an abstract. See C. T. Fordyce, A Rhythmical Version of Bede's De ratione temporum, Archivum Latinitatis Medii Aevi, 1927, pp. 59 ff.]

(c) Historical Works

Historia Ecclesiastica gentis Anglorum. Strasburg, [c. 1475]; Antwerp, 1550; Cologne, 1601; Cambridge, 1643–4; Paris, 1681; ed. J. Smith, Cambridge, 1722 (valuable); ed. J. Stevenson, 1838; vols. III, IV, ed. J. E. B. Mayor and J. R. Lumby, 3rd edn, Cambridge, 1881; ed. A. Holder, 2nd edn, 1890, Freiburg.
[On MSS see Manitius, Geschichte der lateinischen Literatur des Mittelalters, vol. I, pp. 70 ff.; Plummer, vol. I, pp. lxxx ff.; E. A. Lowe, A New MS Fragment of Bede's Historia Ecclesiastica, EHR. XLI, 1926, pp. 244 ff.; O. Dobiache-Rojdestvensky, Un Manuscrit de Bède à Leningrad, Speculum, III, 1928, pp. 314 ff. For King Alfred's translation of the Historia Ecclesiastica, see pp. 86–7 above.]
   Jones, P. F. A Concordance to the Historia Ecclesiastica of Bede. Cambridge, U.S.A. 1929.
   Poole, R. L. The Chronology of Bede's Historia Ecclesiastica and the Councils of 679–680. [Studies in Chronology and History, Oxford, 1934.]
Vita b. Abbatum Benedicti, Ceolfridi, Eosterwini, Sigfridi atque Hwaetberhti (Plummer.)
Vita Sancti Cudbercti.
   Metrical Life and Prose Life. (Giles and Migne.) [These are based on the anonymous Life, ed. Acta SS., Mart. vol. III pp. 117 ff.]
   Werner, J. Bedas metrische Vita Sancti Cuthberti. Leipzig, 1935.
Vita Sancti Felicis. (Giles and Migne.) [A paraphrase in prose of Paulinus of Nola' verse-life.]
De locis sanctis. Ed. T. Tobler, Itinera Hierosolymitana, vol. I, Geneva, 1879; ed. P. Geyer, Corpus Scriptorum Ecclesiasticorum Latinorum, vol. XXXIX, Vienna, 1898.

(d) Theological Works

Commentaries. (Giles and Migne.)
   Bruyne, A. de. Note sur les MSS et les Éditions du Commentaire de Bède sur les Proverbes. Journ. Theological Stud. XXVIII. 1926–7, pp. 182 ff.
   Morin, G. Notes sur plusieurs Écrits attribués à Bède le Vénérable. Revue Bénédictine, XI, 1894, pp. 289 ff.
   —— Le Pseudo-Bède sur les Psaumes et l'Opus super Psalterium de Maître Manegold de Lautenbach. Revue Bénédictine, XXVIII, 1911, pp. 331 ff.
   Schönbach, A. F. Über einige Evangelienkommentare des Mittelalters. Wiener Sitzungsber. CXLVII, pt iv, 1903.

Lehmann, P. Wert und Echtheit einer Beda abgesprochenen Schrift. Abhandl. d. bayer. Akad. IV, 1919. [The Liber quaestionum.]

Sutcliffe, E. F. Some Footnotes to the Fathers. Biblica, VI, 1925, pp. 205 ff.

—— Quotations in the Venerable Bede's Commentary on St. Mark. Biblica, VII, 1926, pp. 428 ff.

—— The Venerable Bede's Knowledge of Hebrew. Biblica, XVI, 1935, pp. 300 ff.

Wilmart, A. La Collection de Bède le Vénérable sur l'Apôtre. Revue Bénédictine, XXXVIII, 1926, pp. 16 ff.

Laistner, M. L. W. Source-Marks in Bede MSS. Journ. Theological Stud. XXXIV, 1933, pp. 350 ff.

Homilies on the Gospel.

Morin, G. La Liturgie de Naples au temps de S. Grégoire, d'après deux Évangeliaires du VIIᵉ Siècle. Revue Bénédictine, VIII, 1891, pp. 481 ff., 529 ff.

—— Le Recueil primitif des Homélies de Bède sur l'Évangile. Revue Bénédictine, IX, 1892, pp. 316 ff.

Ahrens, E. Das ursprüngliche Homiliar Bedas und sein Einfluss auf Aelfrics Homiliae Catholicae. Münster, 1923.

Martyrology. Act. SS. Mart. vol. II, pp. vi ff.

Quentin, H. Les Martyrologes historiques du Moyen Age. Paris, 1908.

—— 'Bède le Vénérable'. [In F. Cabrol, Dictionnaire d'Archéologie chrétienne, Paris, 1903.]

(e) Poetry

[Bede's Liber Hymnorum is lost (Historia Ecclesiastica, vol. v, p. 24); but some hymns may have survived. Dreves prints sixteen in Analecta Hymnica, vol. L, pp. 96 ff. The text of the hymn to Etheldreda is in Historia Ecclesiastica, IV, 20. Poems in Giles and Migne.]

Lehmann, P. Die Erstveröffentlichung von Bedas Psalmen-Gedichten. Zeitschrift für Kirchengeschichte, XXXIV, 1913, pp. 89 ff.

Meyer, W. Bedae oratio ad Deum. Nachrichten von d. kgl. Gesellsch. d. Wissensch. zu Göttingen, 1912, pp. 228 ff.

—— Poetische Nachlese aus dem sogenannten Book of Cerne in Cambridge und aus der Londoner Codex Regius 29 xx. Nachrichten von d. kgl. Gesellsch. d. Wissensch. zu Göttingen, 1917, pp. 598 ff.

Raby, F. J. E. Christian-Latin Poetry. Oxford, 1927, pp. 145 ff.

(f) Biographies and Studies

Gehle, H. De Baedae venerabilis vita et scriptis. Leyden, 1838.

Werner, K. Beda der Ehrwürdige und seine Zeit. Vienna, 1875.

Mommsen, T. Die Papstbriefe bei Beda. Neues Archiv, XVII, 1892, pp. 387 ff.

Zimmer, H. Zur Orthographie des Namens Beda. Neues Archiv, XXVII, 1902, pp. 211 ff.

Browne, G. F. The Venerable Bede. 1919.

Cook, A. S. Bede and Gregory of Tours. PQ. VI, 1927.

Canter, H. V. The Venerable Bede and the Colosseum. Trans. American Philolog. Ass. LXI, 1930, pp. 150 ff.

Jones, C. W. Bede and Vegetius. Classical Rev. XLVI, 1932, pp. 248 ff.

Davis, R. Bede's Early Reading. Speculum, VIII, 1933, pp. 179 ff.

Laistner, M. L. W. Bede as a Classical and a Patristic Scholar. Trans. Royal Hist. Soc. 1933, pp. 69 ff.

—— The Spanish Archetype of MS. Harley 4980 (Bede's Exposition of Acts). Journ. Theological Stud. XXVII, 1936, pp. 132 ff.

Macdonald, G. Bede and Vegetius. Classical Rev. XLVII, 1933, p. 124.

Raby, F. J. E. Bède le Vénérable. Dictionnaire d'Histoire et de Géographie Ecclésiastiques, vol. VII, 1934.

—— Bede, 735–1935. Laudate, XIII, 1935, pp. 140 ff.

Thompson, A. H. et al. Bede. His Life, Times and Writings, Oxford, 1935. [W. Levison, Bede as Historian, has good bibliography; M. L. W. Laistner, The Library of the Venerable Bede, is valuable.]

[See also the articles on Bede in DNB. (C. Plummer); Wetzer und Weltes Kirchenlexikon, Freiburg, 1903; Hauck's Realencyklopädie für protestantische Theologie, Leipzig, 1896–.]

(8) BIBLES AND PRAYER BOOKS

Chapman, J. Notes on the Early History of the Vulgate Gospels. Oxford, 1908.

Gasquet, F. A. and Bishop, E. The Bosworth Psalter. 1908, pp. 152 f.

The Book of Cerne. Ed. A. B. Kuypers, Cambridge, 1902. [A private prayer book; with strong Irish elements and Irish hymns; see E. Bishop, Liturgica Historica, Oxford, 1918, pp. 192 ff.]

E. ANGLO-SAXON WRITERS, SECOND PERIOD

(1) BONIFACE OR WYNFRITH (d. 755)

(a) Works

De partibus Orationis. Ed. A. Mai, Classici Auctores, vol. VII, Rome, 1835, pp. 475 ff. [See Roger, L'Enseignement des Lettres classiques, pp. 334 ff. and, for additional fragment, W. N. Du Rien, Schedae Vaticanae, Leyden, 1860, p. 141. See also K. Bursian, Die Grammatik des Winfried-Bonifacius, Münchener Sitzungsber. 1873, pp. 457 ff.]

[Treatise] De caesuris. Ed. T. Gaisford, Scriptores latini Rei metricae, Oxford, 1837, pp. 577 ff.; ed. A. Wilmanns, Der Katalog der Lorscher Bibliothek aus dem 10. Jahrhundert, Rheinisches Museum, XXIII, 1868, p. 403 (part). [See also Roger, L'Enseignement des Lettres classiques, pp. 364 ff.]

Letters. Ed. J. A. Giles, 2 vols. 1844 (= Migne, Patrologia Latina, vol. LXXXIX); ed. P. Jaffé, Bibliotheca Rerum Germanicarum, vol. III, 1866 (part); ed. E. Dümmler, Monumenta Germaniae Historica, Epist. vol. III; ed. M. Tangl, Die Briefe des heiligen Bonifatius und Lull, Monumenta Germaniae Historica, Epist. Select. vol. I, Berlin, 1916.

Poems. [Besides the poems included in his Letters, Boniface wrote poetical riddles. The Aenigmata Bonifatii are in E. Dümmler, Monumenta Germaniae Historica, Poet. Lat. Aevi Carol. vol. I, pp. 1 ff.]

(b) Biography and Criticism

Müller, L. Zu den Räthseln des heiligen Bonifacius. Rheinisches Museum, XXII, 1866, pp. 151 f.

Bishop, E. St Boniface and his Correspondence. Proc. Devonshire Ass. VIII, 1876, pp. 497 ff.

Hahn, H. Bonifaz und Lul. Leipzig, 1883.

Kurth, G. S. Boniface. Paris, 1902.

Traube, L. Die älteste Handschrift der Aenigmata Bonifatii. Neues Archiv, XXVII, 1902, pp. 211 ff.

Koch, H. Stellung des heiligen Bonifaz zu Bildung und Wissenschaft. Pastoralbl. f. d. Diözese Ermland, 1905.

Hauck, A. Kirchengeschichte Deutschlands. Vol. I, Leipzig, 1906, pp. 432 ff.

Browne, G. F. Boniface of Crediton. 1910.

James, M. R. S. Boniface's Poem to Nithardus. EHR. XXIX, 1914, p. 94.

Tangl, M. Bonifatiusfragen. Abhandl. d. Berlin. Akad. 1919 (ii).

Laux, J. J. Der heilige Bonifatius. Freiburg, 1922.

Lehmann, P. Die Grammatik aus Aldhelms Kreise. Historische Vierteljahrsschrift, XXVII, 1932, pp. 758 ff.

Fickermann, N. Der Widmungsbrief des hl. Bonifatius. Neues Archiv, L, 1933, pp. 210 ff.

[See also Bibliography on Boniface, Cambridge Medieval History, vol. II, pp. 794 ff.]

(2) AETHELWULF (fl. 802)

Poem on the Abbots and Miracles of the Church of Lindisfarne. Ed. T. Arnold (in Symeonis Monachi Opera, Rolls Ser. vol. I, 1882, pp. 265 ff.); ed. E. Dümmler, Monumenta Germaniae Historica, Poet. Lat.

Aevi Carol. vol. I, pp. 583 ff. [See T. Wright, Biographia Britannica Literaria, vol. I, pp. 370 ff.; L. Traube, Karolingische Dichtungen, Berlin, 1888, pp. 7 ff.]

(3) ALCUIN (d. 804)

(a) Collected Works

Opera. Regensburg, 1777; Migne, Patrologia Latina, vols. C and CI.

(b) Separate Works

Poems. Monumenta Germaniae Historica, Poet. Lat. Aevi Carol. vol. I, pp. 160 ff.

Hymns. Analecta Hymnica, vol. L, pp. 152 ff.

Strecker, K. Drei Rhythmen Alkuins. Neues Archiv, XLIII, 1921, p. 387 ff. [See Monumenta Germaniae Historica, Poet. Lat. Aevi Carol. vol. IV, pp. 904 ff.]

von Winterfeld, P. Wie sah der Codex Blandinus vetustissimus des Horaz aus? Rheinisches Museum, LX, 1905, pp. 31 ff. [To show that Alcuin had not read Horace, and was not the author of Conflictus veris et hiemis.]

Grammar. Migne, Patrologia Latina, vol. CI; ed. E. Putsche, Grammaticae Latinae Auctores Antiqui, Hanover, 1605, p. 2075.

Frees, J. De Alcuini arte grammatica commentatio. Münster, 1886.

De orthographia. Ed. H. Keil, Grammatici Latini, vol. VII, pp. 295 ff.

De rhetorica. Ed. C. Halm, Rhetores Latini Minores, Leipzig, 1863, pp. 525 ff.

De dialectica. Migne, Patrologia Latina, vol. CI.

Disputatio regalis et nobilissimi iuvenis Pippini cum Albino scholastico. Ed. W. Wilmanns, ZDA. XIV, 1867, pp. 531 ff.

Letters. Ed. P. Jaffé, Monumenta Alcuiniana, Bibliotheca Rerum Germanicarum, vol. VI, Berlin, 1873, pp. 132 ff.; ed. E. Dümmler, Monumenta Germaniae Historica, Epist. vol. IV, pp. 18 ff.

[For information as to Alcuin's mathematical and astronomical interests and his Propositiones ad acuendos iuvenes and De saltu lunae ac bissexto, see Manitius, Geschichte der lateinischen Literatur des Mittelalters, vol. I, pp. 285 ff.]

(c) Biographies and Monographs

Monnier, F. Alcuin et Charlemagne. Paris, 1864.

Sickel, T. Alcuinstudien, I. Wiener Sitzungsber. LXXIX, 1875, pp. 461 ff.

Werner, K. Alcuin und sein Jahrhundert. Vienna, 1881.

Dümmler, E. Alchvinstudien. Berliner Sitzungsber. 1891, pp. 49 ff.

Dümmler, E. Zur Lebensgeschichte Alchvins. Neues Archiv, xviii, 1893, pp. 53 ff.

West, A. F. Alcuin. 1893.

Ditscheid, H. Alkuins Leben und Bedeutung für der religiösen Unterricht. Coblenz, 1902.

Gaskoin, C. J. B. Alcuin, his Life and his Work. Cambridge, 1904.

Wilmot-Buxton, E. M. Alcuin. New York, 1922.

Taylor, P. The Construction 'habere with infinitive' in Alcuin as Expression of the Future. Romanic Rev. xv, 1924, pp. 123 ff.

Sanford, E. Alcuin and the Classics. Classical Journ. xx, 1925, pp. 526 ff.

Delius, W. War Alchvin Mönch? Theologische Studien und Kritiken, ciii, 1931, pp. 465 ff.

Ramackers, J. Eine unbekannte Handschrift der Alcuinbriefe. Neues Archiv, l, 1933, pp. 425 ff.

(d) Alcuin and the Liturgy

Bishop, E. Liturgica Historica. Oxford, 1918, pp. 47 ff. [The Gregorian Sacramentary, sent to Charles the Great by Pope Hadrian, was enlarged and edited by Alcuin, who, for this purpose, drew largely on the 'Gelasian' Sacramentary. The resultant Sacramentary is the foundation of the present Roman missal.]

Alfonso, P. Alcuino e il Sacramentario Gregoriano. Rivista liturgica, 1924, pp. 115 ff.

Lietzmann, H. Handschriftliches zu Alkuins Ausgabe und Sakramentarium. Jahrbuch für Liturgiewissenschaft, v, 1925, pp. 68 ff.

Capelle, B. Alcuin et l'Histoire du Symbole de la Messe. Recherches de Théologie ancienne et médiévale, vi, 1934, pp. 249 ff.

[For Alcuin's liturgical writings generally, see under 'Alcuin' in F. Cabrol, Dictionnaire d'Archéologie chrétienne, Paris, 1903.]

(4) ASSER, BISHOP OF SHERBORNE (d. 910)

Life of King Alfred. Ed. W. H. Stevenson, Oxford, 1904.

(5) FRITHEGODE OR FRIDEGODUS (fl. 950)

Life of Wilfrid. Mabillon, Acta SS. vol. iii, i, p. 150 (= Migne, Patrologia Latina, vol. cxxxiii). [A versification of Eddius.] Ed. J. Raine, The Historians of the Church of York, vol. i, pp. 105 ff. [The Vita Audoeni, in Acta SS. Aug. vol. iv, pp. 810 ff. is probably not by Frithegode; see Manitius, Geschichte der lateinischen Literatur des Mittelalters, vol. ii, pp. 501.]

(6) WULFSTAN OF WINCHESTER (fl. 965)

Vita Ethelwoldi. Mabillon, Acta SS. vol. v, pp. 606 (= Migne, Patrologia Latina, vol. cxxxvii).

Vita S. Swithuni. Mabillon, Acta SS. vol. v, pp. 628 (= Migne, Patrologia Latina, vol. cxxxvii). [This is a versification of Lantfred's Life of S. Swithin, which is in Acta SS. Jul. vol. i, pp. 328 ff. Part only is printed; the prologue in Mabillon, Acta SS.; extracts also in Wright, Biographia Britannica Literaria, vol. i, pp. 472 f.; Ebert, Allgemeine Geschichte der Literatur des Mittelalters, vol. iii, pp. 498.]

Hymns. Analecta Hymnica, vol. xlviii, pp. 9 ff., vol. li, pp. 164 ff.

Sequences. Analecta Hymnica, vol. xl, pp. 180 ff., 154 ff., 288 ff., vol. xxxvii, pp. 265 f., 138 f.

Blume, C. Wolstan von Winchester und Vital von Saint-Evroult, Dichter der drei Lobgesänge auf die heiligen Aethelwold, Birin und Swithun. Wiener Sitzungsber. cxlvi, pt iii, 1903.

F. IRISH WRITERS, SECOND PERIOD

(1) JOSEPHUS SCOTTUS (d. after 791; friend of Alcuin)

Poems. Ed. E. Dümmler, Monumenta Germaniae Historica, Poet. Lat. Aevi Carol. vol. i, pp. 150 ff.

(2) DUNGAL (fl. 787, Hibernicus Exul; came from Ireland to S. Denis; friend of Charles the Great)

Letters, including astronomical work addressed to Charles. Ed. E. Dümmler, Monumenta Germaniae Historica, Epist. vol. iv, pp. 570 ff.

Responsa [against Claudius of Turin]. Migne, Patrologia Latina, vol. cv, cols. 453 ff. [Prologue only in Monumenta Germaniae Historica, Epist. vol. iv, pp. 583 ff.]

Poems. Ed. E. Dümmler, Monumenta Germaniae Historica, Poet. Lat. Aevi Carol. vol. i, pp. 395 ff., vol. ii, pp. 664 f.

[On the various Dungals, see L. Traube, Dungali, Abhandl. d. bayer. Akad. xix, 1891, pp. 332 ff.; also L. Gougaud, L'Œuvre des Scotti dans l'Europe continentale, Revue d'Histoire ecclésiastique, ix, 1908, pp. 257 ff. But M. Esposito, The Poems of Colmanus 'Nepos Cracavist'; and Dungalus 'Praecipuus Scottorum,' Journ. Theological Stud. xxxiii, 1932, pp. 113 ff., rejects (p. 125) the identification of Dungal with Hibernicus Exul, whom he prefers to identify with Dicuil. This article also contains an account of Donatus, the Irish bishop of Fiesole (d. 876), whose poems are in Monumenta Germaniae Historica, Poet. Lat. Aevi Carol. vol. III, pp. 691 f. Esposito (p. 129) thinks that Donatus was the author of the poem printed in K. Strecker, Ein neues Dungal? Zeitschrift für romanische Philologie, XLI, 1921, pp. 566 ff. Colmanus was a ninth-century Irishman settled on the continent.]

(3) SMARAGDUS OF ST MIHIEL (*fl.* 800, not improbably Irish; a grammarian)

Expositio libri Comitis [on Epistles and Gospels for Sundays]. Migne, Patrologia Latina, vol. CII, cols. 13 ff.

Via Regia (to Charles). Migne, Patrologia Latina, vol. CII, cols. 933 ff.

Diadema Monachorum. Migne, Patrologia Latina, vol. CII, cols. 593 ff.

Expositio in regula S. Benedicti. Migne, Patrologia Latina, vol. CII, cols. 689 ff. [See E. Bishop, Liturgica Historica, Oxford, 1918, pp. 214 f.]

Liber in partibus Donati. Part in H. Keil, De grammaticis quibusdam latinis infimae Aetatis Commentatio, Erlangen, 1868, pp. 19 ff. [See for other references, Manitius, Geschichte der lateinischen Literatur des Mittelalters, vol. I, p. 467; Kenney, p. 544.]

Poems. Ed. E. Dümmler, Monumenta Germaniae Historica, Poet. Lat. Aevi Carol. vol. I, pp. 604 ff., vol. II, pp. 698.

Laistner, M. L. W. The Date and the Recipient of Smaragdus' Via Regia. Speculum, III, 1928, pp. 392 ff.

(4) DICUIL (d. *c.* 825, grammarian at Carolingian court)

(*a*) *Works*

Astronomical Work (dedicated to Louis the Pious; written in prose and verse). For MSS, see Kenney, p. 546; ed. E. Dümmler, Neues Archiv, IV, 1879, pp. 256 ff. (poems only); ed. K. Strecker, Monumenta Germaniae Historica, Poet. Lat. Aevi Carol. vol. IV, pp. 659 ff.

Esposito, M. An Unpublished Astronomical Treatise by the Irish Monk Dicuil. Proc. Royal Irish Academy, XXVI, sect. c, 1907, pp. 378 ff.

Liber de mensura orbis terrae. Ed. J. A. Letronne, Recherches géographiques et critiques sur le Livre de mensura orbis terrae, Paris, 1814; ed. G. Parthey, Dicuili liber de mensura orbis terrae, Berlin, 1870; some verses from, in E. Dümmler, Monumenta Germaniae Historica, Poet. Lat. Aevi Carol. vol. II, pp. 666 ff. [See bibliography in Kenney, p. 547.]

Poem: De arte grammatica. Ed. H. Keil, Grammatici Latini, vol. III, p. 390; ed. E. Dümmler, Monumenta Germaniae Historica, Poet. Lat. Aevi Carol. vol. II, pp. 667 f.

(*b*) *Monographs*

Esposito, M. Dicuil, an Irish Monk in the 9th Century. Dublin Rev. 1905, pp. 327 ff.

—— An Irish Teacher at the Carolingian Court: Dicuil. Studies, III, 1914, pp. 651 ff.

van der Vyver, A. Dicuil et Micon de Saint-Riquier. Revue Belge de Philologie et d'Histoire, XIV, 1935, pp. 25 ff.

(5) CLEMENS SCOTTUS (*fl.* 826, grammarian at Court of Charles the Great)

Ars grammatica. [For MSS, see Kenney, p. 537.] Ed. (parts) H. Keil, Grammatici Latini, vol. I, pp. xix ff. and De grammaticis quibusdam latinis infimae Aetatis Commentatio, Erlangen, 1868, pp. 9 ff.; ed M. Esposito, Hiberno-Latin MSS. in the Libraries of Switzerland, Proc. Royal Irish Academy, XXX, sect. c, 1912, pp. 8 ff. [See B. Hauréau, Singularités historiques et littéraires, pp. 19 ff., Paris, 1861.]

(6) MALSACHANUS (8th or 9th cent.)

Ars Malsachani. Ed. M. Roger, Traité du Verbe publié d'après le MS. lat. 13026 de la Bibliothèque Nationale, Paris, 1905.

(7) CRUINDMELUS (1st half of 9th cent.; Irishman in Frankish Empire)

Ars metrica. Ed. J. Huemer, Vienna, 1883 [See Kenney, p. 552 and Manitius Geschichte der lateinischen Literatur de Mittelalters, vol. I, pp. 523 ff.]

(8) SEDULIUS SCOTTUS (*fl.* 850, an Irish scholar who settled at Liége)

(*a*) *Works*

Poems. Ed. L. Traube, Monumenta Germaniae Historica, Poet. Lat. Aevi Carol vol. III, pp. 151 ff.; ed. E. Dümmler, Seduli Scoti carmina quadraginta, Halle, 186 (not complete).

Levillain, L. Date et Interprétation d'un Poème de Sedulius Scottus. Moyen Âge VI, 1935, pp. 199 ff.

Hymns. Analecta Hymnica, vol. L, pp. 229 ff

Grammatical: Commentary on Eutyches. Ed H. Hagen, Anecdota Helvetica, Leipzig 1870.

[See M. Roger, Le commentariolum i artem Eutychii de Sedulius Scottus, Revu de Philologie, 1906, pp. 122 f.

Theological Works. [The Collectaneum in omnes beati Pauli epistolas is in Migne, Patrologia Latina, vol. CIII, pp 9 ff.; Collectaneum in Mattheum is not printed; see Kenney, p. 565 and Manitius, Geschichte der lateinischen Literatur des Mittelalters, vol.I,pp. 317 f. On the former,see A. Souter, The Sources of Sedulius Scottus' Collectaneum on the Epistles of St Paul, Journ. Theological Stud. XVIII, 1917, pp. 184 ff. Other theological works are in Migne, Patrologia Latina, vol. CIII.]

iber de rectoribus Christianis. Ed. S. Hellmann, Sedulius Scottus, Munich, 1906.

Tiralla, H. Das augustinische Idealbild der christlichen Obrigkeit als Quelle des Fürstenspiegels des Sedulius Scottus und Hincmar von Reims. Greifswald, 1916.
Martini, G. Un Codice sconosciuto del 'De rectoribus Christianis' di Sedulio Scoto. Bullet. Istit. stor. ital. Arch. Murator. L, 1935.

ollektaneum (a collection of extracts made by Sedulius in the course of his reading; of great importance). [See Kenney, p. 566; Manitius, Geschichte der lateinischen Literatur des Mittelalters, vol. I, pp. 320 ff.; and above all, L. Traube, Die Excerptensammlung der Handschrift C 14 in der Bibliothek des Hospitals Cues, in Abhandl. d. bayer. Akad. XIX, 1891, pp. 364 ff.]

(b) Monographs

Iellmann, S. Sedulius Scottus. Munich, 1906.
irenne, H. Sedulius de Liège. Mémoires couronnés et autres Mémoires publiés par l'Académie royale de Belgique, XXXIII, Sept. 1882.
raube, L. Sedulius Scottus. Abhandl. d. bayer. Akad. XIX, 1891, pp. 338 ff.

(9) JOHANNES SCOTUS ERIGENA (d. 860)

[For full bibliography and MSS, see Kenney, p. 569 ff.; also Ueberweg-Geyer, Grundriss er Geschichte der Philosophie, vol. II, pp. 93 f.]

(a) Collected Works

pera. Migne, Patrologia Latina, vol. CXX.

(b) Individual Works

xcerpta Macrobii, etc. (extracts from Macrobius). Ed. H. Keil, Grammatici Latini, vol. v, pp. 599 ff.

ommentary on Martianus Capella. Extracts in B. Hauréau, Notices et Extraits des MSS, XX, pt ii, Paris, 1862, pp. 1 ff.; M. Manitius, Didaskaleion, vol. I, 1912, pp. 139 ff., vol. II, pp. 43 ff.

Laistner, M. L. W. Martianus Capella and his Ninth Century Commentators. Bulletin of the John Rylands Lib. IX, pt i, 1925, pp. 130 ff.

Narducci, M. Bollettino di Bibliografia e di Storia delle Scienze matematiche e fisiche, XV, 1882, pp. 505 ff.

Commentary on Boethius, Opuscula Sacra. Ed. E. K. Rand, Johannes Scotus, Munich, 1906, pp. 3 ff. [There is also a life of Boethius attributed to John; see Kenney, p. 585; ed. R. Peiper, in De Consolatione, Leipzig, 1871.]

Translation of the Solutiones of Priscianus Lydus. Ed. I. Bywater, Prisciani Lydi quae extant, Berlin, 1886, pp. 41 ff.

Esposito, M. Priscianus Lydus and Johannes Scotus. Classical Rev. XXXII, 1918, pp. 21 ff.

De Praedestinatione. Migne, Patrologia Latina, vol. CXXII, cols. 347 ff.; the dedication is in E. Dümmler, Monumenta Germaniae Historica, Epist. vol. v, pp. 630 f. [Prudentius of Troyes answered this; Migne, op. cit. vol. CXV, cols. 1009 ff.]

Περὶ Φύσεων Μερισμοῦ, de divisione naturae. Migne, Patrologia Latina, vol. CXXII, cols. 439 ff.

Schmitt, A. Zwei noch unbenützte Handschriften des Johannes Scotus Erigena. Bamberg, 1900.
Dräseke, J. Johannes Scotus Erigena und dessen Gewährsmänner in seinem Werke, De divisione Naturae libri v. Studien zur Geschichte der Theologie und der Kirche, IX, pt ii, 1902, pp. 10 ff.
Lehmann, P. Johannes Scotus über die Kategorien. Philologische Wochenschrift, XLI, 1921, pp. 670 ff.

Translation of Works of the Pseudo-Dionysius. Migne, Patrologia Latina, vol. CXXII, cols. 1023 ff.

Grabmann, M. Pseudo-Dionysius Areopagita in lateinischen Übersetzungen des Mittelalters. Festgabe Ehrhard, Bonn, 1922, pp. 181 ff.
Lehmann, P. Zur Kenntnis der Schriften des Dionysius Areopagita im Mittelalter. Revue Bénédictine, XXXV, 1923, pp. 81 ff.

Commentary on the Pseudo-Dionysius. Migne, Patrologia Latina, vol. CXXII, cols. 125 ff.

Translation of the Ambigua of Maximus Confessor. Ed. T. Gale, Appendix to De divisione Naturae, Oxford, 1681; Migne, Patrologia Latina, vol. CXXII, cols. 1193 ff.

Poems. Ed. L. Traube, Monumenta Germaniae Historica, Poet. Lat. Aevi Carol. vol. III, pp. 518 ff.

[For Homily on Prologue to Gospel of S. John, fragments of commentary on that Gospel, and Commentary on Old Testament, see Kenney, pp. 585 ff.]

(c) *Biographies and Monographs*

Hermens, O. Das Leben des Scotus Erigena. Jena, 1868.

Dräseke, J. Zu Johannes Scotus Erigena. Zeitschrift für wissenschaftliche Theologie, XLVI, 1903, pp. 563 ff., XLVII, 1904, pp. 121 ff.

Brilliantoff, A. Zu Maximus Confessor. Zeitschrift für wissenschaftliche Theologie, XLVII, 1904, pp. 250 ff. [Influence of Maximus on John.]

—— Der Einfluss der orientalischen Theologie auf die occidentalische in der Werken des Johannes Scotus Erigena. St Petersburg, 1908.

Rand, E. K. Johannes Scotus. Munich, 1906.

Baldini, P. Scoto Erigena e la Filosofia religiosa nel IX Secolo. Rivista storica critica delle Scienze teologiche, II, 1906, pp. 413 ff.

Jacquin, M. Le Néo-platonisme de Jean Scot. Revue des Sciences philosophiques et théologiques, I, 1907, pp. 674 ff. [See J. Dräseke, Zum Neuplatonismus Erigenas, Zeitschrift für Kirchengeschichte, XXXIII, 1912, pp. 73 ff.]

Esposito, M. Latin Writers of Mediaeval Ireland, Supplement. Hermathena, XV, 1908, pp. 362 f.

Lehmann, P. Zur Kenntnis und Geschichte einiger Joh. Scotus zugeschriebener Werke. Hermes, LII, 1917, pp. 122 ff.

Schneider, A. Die Erkenntnislehre d Johannes Erigena im Rahmen ihrer met physischen und anthropologischen Vorau setzungen. 2 vols. Berlin, 1921–3.

Bett, H. Johannes Scotus Erigena. Cambridge, 1925.

Doerries, H. Zur Geschichte der Mystik.- Erigena und der Neoplatonismus. Tübinge 1925.

Théry, G. Scot Érigène, Traducteur de Deny Archivum Latinitatis Medii Aevi, VI, 193 pp. 185 ff.

—— Scot Érigène, Introducteur de Deny New Scholasticism, V, 1933, pp. 91 ff.

Cappuyns, M. Jean Scot Érigène, sa Vie, sc Œuvre, sa Pensée. Louvain, 1933.

(10) OTHER IRISH WRITINGS

(a) Anonymous commentary on Donatu [See Kenney, p. 553.]

(b) Dunchad's Writings. [See Kenney, p.573

(c) Anonymous poems by Irishmen. E L. Traube, Carmina Scottorum latina graecanica, Monumenta Germaniae Hi torica, Poet. Lat. Aevi Carol. vol. I pp. 685 ff., vol. IV, pp. 1117 ff. [See Kenne pp. 603 f.]

F.J.E.

THE MIDDLE ENGLISH PERIOD
(1100–1500)

1. INTRODUCTION

I. BIBLIOGRAPHIES, SURVEYS, ANTHOLOGIES AND DICTIONARIES

(1) BIBLIOGRAPHIES

(a) General Bibliographies

[See also Brandl, CHEL., Edwardes, Körting, under Histories and Summaries, below.]

Wells, J. E. A Manual of the Writings in Middle English, 1050–1400. New Haven, 1918. Six Supplements, 1919, 1923, 1926, 1929, 1932, 1935. [Bound separately, and Manual and first 3 Supplements bound together. Complete bibliography, and summary of MSS, sources, date, dialect, authorship, etc., with synopsis and criticism to July 1935 for every ptd work.]

—— Fifteenth Century Writings in English. [In preparation.]

Tucker, L .L. and Benham, A. R. A Bibliography of Fifteenth Century Literature. Seattle, 1928.

(b) Catalogues and Collections of Manuscripts

[See also catalogues of the libraries and collections mentioned under individual pieces below.]

Ward, H. L. D. Catalogue of Romances in the Department of MSS of the British Museum. 2 vols. 1883–93. [Vol. III, by J. A. Herbert, 1910.]

Skeat, W. W. Twelve Facsimiles of Old English MSS. Oxford, 1892.

Hammond, E. P. Ashmole 59 and other Shirley MSS. Ang. xxx, 1907.

—— English Verse between Chaucer and Surrey. Durham, North Carolina, 1927.

Greg, W. W. Facsimiles of Twelve Early English MSS in the Library of Trinity College, Cambridge. Oxford, 1913.

Brown, Carleton A. Register of Middle English Religious and Didactic Verse. 2 vols. Bibliog. Soc, 1916–20.

Singer, D. W. Handlist of Scientific MSS in the British Isles before the Sixteenth Century. Library, x, 1919.

—— Catalogue of Latin and Vernacular Manuscripts in Great Britain and Ireland dating from before the XVI Century. 1928–.

List of Rotographs of MSS and Rare Printed Books, Made for the Modern Language Association of America. PMLA. XLIV, 1929, XLIX, 1934.

Union Catalogue of Photo Facsimiles in North American Libraries. Library of Congress. Yardley, Pennsylvania, 1929.

(2) HISTORIES AND SUMMARIES

Warton, Thomas. History of English Poetry. 3 vols. 1774–81; ed. W. C. Hazlitt, 4 vols. 1871.

Ritson, Joseph. Biographia Poetica. 1802. [12th–16th cents.]

ten Brink, B. Geschichte der englischen Literatur. 2 vols. Berlin, 1887–93 (vol. I, rev. A. Brandl, 1899); tr. Eng. 3 vols. 1883–96.

Koerting, G. Grundriss der Geschichte der englischen Litteratur. Münster, 1887; 1910 (5th edn).

Morley, H. English Writers. 11 vols. 1887–1895. [Vols. III–v.]

Brandl, A. Mittelenglische Literatur. Strasburg, 1892, 1909. [Pt 1, vol. II of H. Paul's Grundriss der germanischen Philologie.]

Jusserand, J. J. Histoire littéraire du Peuple anglais. Paris, 1894; tr. Eng. 3 vols. 1895–1909, 1926 (3rd edn). [Vol. I.]

Courthope, W. J. History of English Poetry. 6 vols. 1895–1910. [Vol. I.]

Wülcker, R. Geschichte der englischen Literatur. 2 vols. Leipzig, 1896, 1906–7.

Saintsbury, George. Flourishing of Romance and the Rise of Allegory. Edinburgh, 1897.

—— Short History of English Literature. 1898.

Snell, F. J. Fourteenth Century. 1899.

—— Age of Chaucer. 1901.

—— Age of Transition. 2 vols. 1905.

Pollard, A. W. Middle English Literature. [Chambers's Cyclopaedia of English Literature, vol. I, 1901.]

Ker, W. P. Essays on Medieval Literature. 1905.

—— English Literature, Medieval. 1912.

Schofield, W. H. English Literature from the Norman Conquest to Chaucer. 1906.

Edwardes, Marian. Summary of the Literatures of Modern Europe to 1400. 1907.

Cambridge History of English Literature. Vols. I, II, Cambridge, 1907–8.

Kingsford, C. L. English Historical Literature of the Fifteenth Century. Oxford, 1913.

Baldwin, C. S. Introduction to Medieval English Literature. New York, 1914.

Krapp, G. P. The Rise of English Literary Prose. New York, 1915.

Berdan, J. M. Early Tudor Poetry, 1485–1547. New York, 1920.

Champion, P. H. Histoire poétique du quinzième Siècle. Paris, 1923.

Chaytor, H. J. The Troubadours and England. Cambridge, 1923.

Legouis, E. and Cazamian, L. Histoire de la Littérature anglaise. Paris, 1924; tr. Eng. 2 vols. 1926–7.

Thomas, P. G. English Literature before Chaucer. 1924.

Hecht, H. and Schücking, L. L. Die englische Literatur im Mittelalter. 6 pts, Potsdam, 1927–30.

Schirmer, W. F. Der englische Frühhumanismus: ein Beitrag zur englischen Literaturgeschichte des 15. Jahrhunderts. Leipzig, 1931.

Chambers, R. W. On the Continuity of English Prose from Alfred to More. EETS. 1932.

(3) Collections of Selected Pieces

[See also collections under various section heads below.]

Hartshorne, C. H. Ancient Metrical Tales. 1829.

Mätzner, E. Altenglische Sprachproben. 2 pts, Berlin, 1867–1900.

Morris, R. Specimens of Early English. Oxford, 1867.

Wülcker, R. Altenglische Lesebuch. 2 pts, Halle, 1874–9. [Pt i, 1250–1350; pt ii, 1350–1500.]

Zupitza, J. Altenglisches Übungsbuch. Vienna, 1874; 2nd edn, with title Alt- und mittelenglisches Übungsbuch, 1882; 13th edn, rev. A. Eichler, 1928.

Morris, R. and Skeat, W. W. Specimens of Early English. 3 pts, Oxford, 1882–71, 1885–92 (rev.).

Sweet, H. First Middle English Primer. Oxford, 1884.

—— Second Middle English Primer. Oxford, 1885.

Craik, H. English Prose. 5 vols. 1893–6. [Vol. i.]

MacLean, G. E. Old and Middle English Reader. New York, 1893, 1922.

Pollard, A. W. Fifteenth Century Prose and Verse. Arber's English Garner, 1903.

Kluge, F. Mittelenglisches Lesebuch. Halle, 1904, 1912.

Emerson, O. F. Middle English Reader. New York, 1905, 1915 (rev. edn).

Cook, A. S. Literary Middle English Reader. Boston, 1915.

Brandl, A. and Zippel, P. Mittelenglische Sprach- und Literaturproben. Berlin, 1917, 1927.

Segar, M. G. Some Minor Poems of the Middle Ages. 1917.

Hall, J. Selections from Early Middle English. 2 pts, Oxford, 1920.

Sisam, K. Fourteenth Century Verse and Prose. Oxford, 1921. [Glossary by J. R. R. Tolkien.]

Sampson, G. The Cambridge Book of Prose and Verse. Cambridge, 1924.

Hammond, E. P. English Verse between Chaucer and Surrey. Durham, North Carolina, 1927.

Gerould, G. H. Old English and Medieval Literature. New York, 1929.

Brunner, C. and Hittmair, R. Mittelenglisches Lesebuch für Anfänger. Heidelberg, 1929.

(4) Collections of Modern Renderings

[For modernisations of individual pieces or authors, see under individual items; and see under the several section heads for collections of types.]

Arber, E. The Dunbar Anthology. 1901.

Rickert, E. Early English Romances in Verse. 2 vols. 1908. [Vol. i, Romances of Love; vol. ii, Romances of Friendship.]

Pancoast, H. S. and Spaeth, J. D. Early English Poems. New York, 1911.

Weston, J. L. Romance, Vision, and Satire. Boston, 1912.

—— Chief Middle English Poets. Boston, 1914.

Shackford, M. H. Legends and Satires. Boston, 1913.

Segar, M. G. A Medieval Anthology. 1915.

Neilson, W. A. and Webster, K. G. T. Chief British Poets of the 14th and 15th Centuries. Boston, 1916.

Benham, A. R. English Literature from Widsith to the Death of Chaucer. New Haven, 1916.

(5) Dictionaries, Glossaries

[See also Mätzner, Brandl and Zippel, and Sisam under Collections of Selected Pieces, above.]

Promptorium Parvulorum. The First English-Latin Dictionary. Ed. A. L. Mayhew, EETS. 1908.

Catholicon Anglicum, or English-Latin Word-Book. 1483. Ed. S. J. Herrtage, EETS. 1881; Camden Soc. 1882.

Coleridge, H. Glossarial Index to the Printed English Literature of the 13th Century. 1859; 1863 (as Dictionary of the First and Oldest Words).

Mayhew, A. L. and Skeat, W. W. Concise Dictionary of Middle English. Oxford, 1888.

Stratmann, F. H. Middle English Dictionary. Enlarged and rev. H. Bradley, Oxford, 1891, 1914.

Tatlock, J. S. P. and Kennedy, A. G. Concordance to the Complete Works of Geoffrey Chaucer and to the Romaunt of the Rose. Carnegie Inst. of Washington, 1927.

J. E. W.

II. THE POLITICAL BACKGROUND

(1) ORIGINAL SOURCES

(a) Official Records and Collections of Documents

Bémont, C. Chartes des Libertés anglaises 1100–1305. Paris, 1892.

British Borough Charters. Vol. I, 1042–1216, ed. A. Ballard; vol. II, 1216–1307, ed. A. Ballard and J. Tait, Cambridge, 1913–23.

Borough Customs. Ed. Mary Bateson, 2 vols. Selden Soc. 1904–6.

Calendar of the Charter Rolls. 6 vols. Rolls Ser. 1903–27. [1226–1516.]

Calendar of the Close Rolls. Rolls Ser. 1892–. [1227–1419.]

Calendar of the Patent Rolls. 49 vols. Rolls Ser. 1891–1914. [1232–1485.]

Cartulaire de l'ancienne Estaple de Bruges. Ed. L. Gilliodts van Severen, 4 vols. Société d'Emulation de Bruges, 1904–6. [862–1492.]

Documents Illustrative of English History in the Thirteenth and Fourteenth Centuries. Ed. H. Cole, Record Commission, 1844.

Domesday Book. Ed. A. Farley and Sir H. Ellis, Record Commission, 1783–1816.

Smith, J. T. English Gilds. Ed. L. T. Smith, EETS. 1870.

Foedera, Conventiones, Litterae, etc. Ed. T. Rymer and R. Sanderson, 4 vols. Record Commission, 1816–69. [1101–1654.]

Syllabus of Documents in Rymer's Foedera. Ed. T. D. Hardy, 3 vols. Rolls Ser. 1869–85.

McKechnie, W. S. Magna Carta. Glasgow, 1914 (2nd edn).

Memoranda de Parliamento. Ed. F. W. Maitland, Rolls Ser. 1893. [1305.]

Proceedings and Ordinances of the Privy Council of England. Ed. Sir H. Nicholas, 7 vols, Record Commission, 1834–7. [1386–1542.]

Prynne, W. A Brief Register of Parliamentary Writs. 4 pts, 1659–64.

Rotuli Parliamentorum. 6 vols. 1783; Index, 1832. [1278–1503.]

Statutes of the Realm. Ed. A. Luders et al. 11 vols. Record Commission, 1810–28. [1235–1713.]

Stubbs, W. Select Charters of English Constitutional History. 1913 (rev. H. W. C. Davis).

(b) Chronicles, Letters and Royal Biographies

The Anglo-Saxon Chronicle. Ed. Charles Plummer, 2 vols. Oxford, 1892–9.

Annales Monastici. Ed. H. R. Luard, 5 vols. Rolls Ser. 1864–9. [A.D. 1–1432. Vol. I, Annals of Margam, Tewkesbury and Burton; vol. II, Annals of Winchester and Waverley; vol. III, Annals of Dunstable and Bermondsey; vol. IV, Annals of Oseney and Worcester; Wykes' Chronicle; vol. V, Index and glossary.]

The Anonimalle Chronicle. Ed. V. H. Galbraith, Manchester, 1927. [1333–81.]

Baker, Geoffrey le. Chronicon. Ed. E. M. Thompson, Oxford, 1889. [1303–56.]

Canterbury, Gervase of. Historical Works. Ed. W. Stubbs, 2 vols. Rolls Ser. 1879–80. [1100–1328.]

Capgrave, John. The Chronicle of England. Ed. F. C. Hingeston, Rolls Ser. 1858. [Creation to 1417.]

Cely Papers (1475–88). Ed. H. E. Malden, Royal Hist. Soc. 1900.

Chandos, The Herald of. Life of the Black Prince. Ed. M. K. Pope and E. C. Lodge, Oxford, 1910.

Chronica Monasterii Sancti Albani. Ed. H. T. Riley, 12 vols. Rolls Ser. 1863–76. [793–1488.] [Walsingham's Historia Anglicana, Ypodigma Neustriae, and Gesta Abbatum; Rishanger; two anonymous chronicles; Trokelowe; Blaneford; Opus Chronicorum; Annales Ricardi II et Henrici IV; Amundesham's annals; an anonymous chronicle; Registra Abbatum.]

Chronicles and Memorials of the Reign of Richard I. Ed. W. Stubbs, 2 vols. Rolls Ser. 1864–5. [Vol. I, Itinerarium Peregrinorum et Gesta Regis Ricardi, 1187–99; vol. II, Epistolae Cantuarienses.]

Chronicles of London. Ed. C. L. Kingsford, Oxford, 1905. [Three English Chronicles, 1189–1432; 1415–43; 1440–1516.]

Chronicles of the Mayors and Sheriffs of London. Tr. H. T. Riley, 1863. [1188–1274.]

Chronicles of the Reigns of Edward I and Edward II. Ed. W. Stubbs, 2 vols. Rolls Ser. 1882–3. [Vol. I, Annales Londonienses and Annales Paulini; vol. II, Commendatio lamentabilis Edwardi I, Gesta Edwardi de Carnarvon, Vita Edwardi II, and More's Vita et Mors Edwardi II.]

Chronicles of the Reigns of Stephen, Henry II and Richard I. Ed. R. Howlett, 4 vols. Rolls Ser. 1884–9. [Vols. I and II, William of Newburgh and the Draco Normannicus; vol. III, Gesta Stephani; Chronicle of Richard of Hexham; Aelred of Rievaulx' Relatio de Standardo; Jordan Fantosme, and Richard of Devizes; vol. IV, Robert of Torigni.]

Chronicles of the White Rose of York. Ed. J. A. Giles, 1845.

Chronicon Angliae. Ed. E. M. Thompson, Rolls Ser. 1874. [1328–88.]

Chronicon Angliae, temporibus Ricardi II, Henrici IV, Henrici V, et Henrici VI. Ed. J. A. Giles, 1848.

Clarke, M. V. and Galbraith, V. H. The Deposition of Richard II. Manchester, 1930. [A Chronicle of Dieulacres Abbey.]

Cotton, Bartholomew. Historia Anglicana. Ed. H. R. Luard, Rolls Ser. 1859. [A.D. 449–1298.]

Diceto, Ralph de. Opera Historica. Ed. W. Stubbs, 2 vols. Rolls Ser. 1876. [Creation to 1240.]

Durham, Simeon of. Opera omnia. Ed. T. Arnold, 2 vols. Rolls Ser 1882–5. [635–1154.]

Eulogium Historiarum. Ed. F. S. Haydon, 3 vols. Rolls Ser. 1858–63. [Creation to 1413.]

Fabyan, Robert. The New Chronicles of England and France. Ed. Sir H. Ellis, 1811. [From Brutus to 1485.]

Flores Historiarum. Ed. H. R. Luard, 3 vols. Rolls Ser. 1890. [Creation to 1326.]

Froissart, Jean. Chroniques. Ed. Kervyn de Lettenhove, 25 vols. Brussels, 1867–77. [1307–1400.]

Giraldus Cambrensis. Opera. Vols. I–IV, ed. J. S. Brewer; vols. V–VII, J. F. Dimock; vol. VIII, G. F. Warner. 8 vols. Rolls Ser. 1861–91.

Hall's Chronicle. Ed. Sir H. Ellis, 1809. [1399–1547.]

Hemingburgh, Walter of. Chronicon de Gestis Regum Angliae. Ed. H. C. Hamilton, 2 vols. English Hist. Soc. 1848–9. [1048–1346.]

Henrici Quinti Angliae Regis Gesta. Ed. B. Williams, English Hist. Soc. 1850.

Higden, Ranulf. Polychronicon. Vols. I–II, ed. Churchill Babington; vols. III–IX, ed. J. R. Lumby, 9 vols. Rolls Ser. 1865–86. [Creation to 1394.]

Historia Vitae et Regni Ricardi II, a Monacho quodam de Evesham consignata. Ed. T. Hearne, Oxford, 1729. [1377–1402.]

Historical Collections of a Citizen of London in the Fifteenth Century. Ed. James Gairdner, Camden Soc. 1876. [Page's poem on the siege of Rouen; Lydgate's verses on the kings of England; Gregory's Chronicle.]

Journal d'un Bourgeois de Paris, 1405–49. Ed. A. Tuetey, Société de l'Histoire de Paris, 1881.

Knighton, Henry. Chronicon. Ed. J. R. Lumby, 2 vols. Rolls Ser. 1889–95. [959–1395.]

Malmesbury, William of. De Gestis Regum Angliae Libri quinque (449–1127); Historiae novellae Libri tres (1125–42). Ed. W. Stubbs, 2 vols. Rolls Ser. 1887–9.

Materials for the History of Thomas Becket. Ed. J. C. Robertson, 7 vols. Rolls Ser. 1875–85.

Memorials of Henry V. Ed. C. A. Cole, Rolls Ser. 1858.

More, Sir Thomas. History of King Richard III. Ed. J. R. Lumby, Cambridge, 1883.

Murimuth, Adam. Continuatio Chronicarum. Ed. E. M. Thompson, Rolls Ser. 1889. [1303–47.]

Ordericus Vitalis. Historia Ecclesiastica. Ed. A. le Prévost, 5 vols. Société de l'Histoire de France, Paris, 1838–55. [A.D. 1–1141.]

Paris, Matthew. Chronica majora. Ed. H. R. Luard, 7 vols. Rolls Ser. 1872–83. [Creation to 1259.]

—— Historia Anglorum. Ed. F. Madden, 3 vols. Rolls Ser. 1866–9. [1067–1253.]

The Paston Letters. Ed. J. Gairdner, 6 vols. 1904.

The Stonor Letters and Papers. Ed. C. L. Kingsford, 2 vols. 1919. [1290–1483.]

Supplementary Stonor Letters and Papers Ed. C. L. Kingsford, Camden Misc. vol XIII, 1924. [1314–1487.]

Three Fifteenth Century Chronicles. Ed. J. Gairdner, Camden Soc. 1880. [A Short English Chronicle; Historical memoranda; Brief notes; a brief Latin Chronicle, 1429–71.]

Usk, Adam of. Chronicon. Ed. E. M. Thompson, Royal Soc. Lit. 1904 (2nd edn). [1377–1421.]

Vergil, Polydore. Anglicae Historiae Libri xxvii. Leyden, 1651. [Earliest times to 1538.]

Wendover, Roger of. Flores Historiarum Ed. H. O. Coxe, 4 vols and appendix, English Hist. Soc. 1841–44. [Creation to 1235.]

Worcester, Florence of. Chronicon ex Chronicis. Ed. B. Thorpe, 2 vols. English Hist Soc. 1848–9. [A.D. 450–1295.]

(c) *Opera and Miscellaneous Treatises*

Bracton, Henry of. De Legibus et Consuetudinibus Angliae. Ed. G. E. Woodbine 2 vols. New Haven, 1915–22.

Bracton's Note Book. Ed. F. W. Maitland 3 vols. 1887.

THE POLITICAL BACKGROUND 117

Dialogus de Scaccario. Ed. A. Hughes,
C. G. Crump, and C. Johnson, Oxford, 1902.
[Trn in E. F. Henderson, Select Historical
Documents of the Middle Ages, 1892, pp.
20–134.]
Fortescue, Sir John. Works. Ed. Thomas,
Lord Clermont, 2 vols. 1869.
—— The Governance of England. Ed.
C. Plummer, Oxford, 1885.
Glanvill, Ranulf de. Tractatus de Legibus et
Consuetudinibus Regni Angliae. 1780.
Gascoigne, Thomas. Loci e Libro Veritatum.
Ed. J. E. T. Rogers, Oxford, 1881.
Henley, Walter of. On Husbandry. Ed.
E. Lamond, Royal Hist. Soc. 1890.
Ioannis Saresberiensis Policratici Libri viii.
Ed. C. C. J. Webb, 2 vols. Oxford, 1909.
The Libelle of Englyshe Polycye. Ed. Sir G.
Warner, Oxford, 1926.
Map, Walter. De Nugis Curialium. Ed.
M. R. James, 1914. [Tr. M. R. James, 1923.]
Modus tenendi Parliamentum. Ed. T. D.
Hardy, Record Commission, 1846.
Pecock, Reginald. The Repressor of overmuch
Blaming of the Clergy. Ed. Churchill
Babington, 2 vols, Rolls Ser. 1860.
Wyclif, John. Select English Works. Ed.
T. Arnold, 3 vols. Oxford, 1869–71.
—— English Works, hitherto Unprinted. Ed.
F. D. Matthew, EETS. 1880.
—— Latin Works. 32 vols. Wyclif Soc.
1883–1913.

(2) MODERN WRITERS

(a) *General History and Biography*

Barnard, F. P. Edward IV's French Expedi-
tion of 1475. Oxford, 1925.
Bémont, C. Simon de Montfort. Paris, 1884.
The Cambridge Medieval History. Ed. J. R.
Tanner, C. W. Previté-Orton and Z. N.
Brooke, 1911–. [Vol. v, Contest of Empire
and Papacy, c. 1050–1200; vol. vi, Victory
of the Papacy, c. 1200–1300; vol. vii,
Decline of Empire and Papacy.]
Christie, Mabel. Henry VI. 1922.
Davies, J. C. The Baronial Opposition to
Edward II. Cambridge, 1918.
Davis, H. W. C. The Anarchy of Stephen's
Reign. EHR. xviii, 1903.
Déprez, E. Les Préliminaires de la Guerre de
Cent Ans. Paris, 1902.
Eyton, R. W. Court, Household and Itinerary
of Henry II. 1878.
Freeman, E. A. History of the Norman
Conquest. 6 vols. Oxford, 1867–79.
—— The Reign of William Rufus and the
Accession of Henry I. 2 vols. Oxford,
1882.
Gairdner, J. The Houses of Lancaster and
York. 1886 (6th edn).

Gairdner, J. Life and Reign of Richard III.
Cambridge, 1898 (3rd edn).
Hughes, Dorothy. The Early Years of Edward
III. 1915.
The Political History of England. Ed. W.
Hunt and R. L. Poole, 12 vols. 1905–.
[Vol. ii, 1066–1216, by G. B. Adams; vol.
iii, 1216–1377, by T. F. Tout; vol. iv, 1377–
1485, by Sir C. W. C. Oman.]
Jenks, E. Edward Plantagenet. 1902.
Kingsford, C. L. Henry V. New York,
1901.
Longman, W. The Life and Times of Edward
III. 2 vols. 1869.
Morris, J. E. The Welsh Wars of Edward I.
Oxford, 1901.
Norgate, Kate. England under the Angevin
Kings. 2 vols. 1887.
—— John Lackland. 1902.
—— The Minority of Henry III. 1912.
Oman, Sir C. W. C. Warwick the Kingmaker.
1891.
—— A History of the Art of War. 2 vols.
1924 (2nd edn).
A History of England in Seven Volumes.
Ed. Sir C. W. C. Oman, 1904–. [Vol. ii, Eng-
land under the Normans and Angevins, by
H. W. C. Davis; vol. iii, England in the
Later Middle Ages, by K. H. Vickers.]
Owen, L. V. D. The Connection between
England and Burgundy during the First
Half of the Fifteenth Century. Oxford,
1909.
Powicke, F. M. The Loss of Normandy.
Manchester, 1913. [1189–1204.]
Prothero, G. W. The Life of Simon de Mont-
fort. 1877.
Ramsay, J. H. The Foundations of England.
2 vols. 1898. [55 B.C.–A.D. 1154.]
—— The Angevin Empire. 1903. [1154–
1216.]
—— The Dawn of the Constitution. 1908.
[1216–1307.]
—— The Genesis of Lancaster. Oxford, 1913.
[1307–99.]
—— Lancaster and York. 2 vols. Oxford,
1892. [1399–1485.]
Round, J. H. Geoffrey de Mandeville. 1892.
Salzman, L. F. Henry II. 1914.
Scofield, Cora L. The Life and Reign of
Edward IV. 2 vols. 1923.
Smith, S. Armitage. John of Gaunt. 1904.
Stenton, F. M. William the Conqueror. New
York, 1908.
Stubbs, W. Historical Introductions to the
Rolls Series. 1902.
Trevelyan, G. M. A History of England.
1928 (6th edn).
Tout, T. F. Edward I. 1903.
—— The Place of the Reign of Edward II in
English History. Manchester, 1914.

Vickers, K. H. Humphrey, Duke of Gloucester. 1907.

Wallon, H. Richard II. 2 vols. Paris, 1864.

Wylie, J. H. History of England under Henry IV. 4 vols. 1884–98.

—— The Reign of Henry V. 3 vols. 1914–29.

(b) Constitutional and Legal History

Adams, G. B. The Origin of the English Constitution. New York, 1912.

—— Councils and Courts in Anglo-Norman England. New Haven, 1926.

Baldwin, J. F. The King's Council in England during the Middle Ages. Oxford, 1913.

Bolland, W. C. A Manual of Year Book Studies. Cambridge, 1925.

Dowell, Stephen. A History of Taxation and Taxes in England. 4 vols. 1888 (2nd edn).

Harcourt, L. W. V. His Grace the Steward and Trial of Peers. 1907.

Holdsworth, Sir W. S. A History of English Law. 9 vols. 1927 (4th edn).

McIlwain, C. H. The High Court of Parliament. New Haven, 1910.

Magna Carta Commemoration Essays. Ed. H. E. Malden, 1917.

Maitland, F. W. The Constitutional History of England. Cambridge, 1908.

Morris, W. A. The Early English County Court. Berkeley, 1926.

Neale, J. E. The Commons' Privilege of Free Speech in Parliament. [In Tudor Studies ed. R. W. Seton-Watson, 1924.]

Pasquet, D. An Essay on the Origins of the House of Commons. Cambridge, 1925.

Petit-Dutaillis, C. La Monarchie féodale en France et en Angleterre, Xe–XIIIe Siècle. Paris, 1933.

Petit-Dutaillis, C. and Lefebvre, G. Studies and Notes Supplementary to Stubbs' Constitutional History. 3 vols. Manchester, 1911–29.

Pike, L. O. A Constitutional History of the House of Lords. 1894.

Plucknett, T. F. T. The Place of the Council in the Fifteenth Century. Trans. Royal Hist. Soc., ser. 4, I, 1918.

—— Statutes and their Interpretation in the First Half of the Fourteenth Century. Cambridge, 1922.

—— The Lancastrian Constitution. [In Tudor Studies ed. R. W. Seton-Watson, 1924.]

Pollock, Sir F. and Maitland, F. W. The History of English Law before the Time of Edward 1. 2 vols. Cambridge, 1923 (3rd edn).

Poole, R. L. The Exchequer in the Twelfth Century. Oxford, 1912.

Pollard, A. F. The Evolution of Parliament. 1926 (2nd edn).

Porrit, E. A. The Unreformed House of Commons. 2 vols. Cambridge, 1903.

Rezneck, S. The Early History of the Parliamentary Declaration of Treason. EHR XLII, 1927.

Richardson, H. G. The Origins of Parliament Trans. Royal Hist. Soc., ser. 4, XI, 1928.

Stenton, F. M. The First Century of English Feudalism, 1066–1166. Oxford, 1932.

Stubbs, W. The Constitutional History of England. 3 vols. Oxford, 1880. [To 1485.

Tout, T. F. Chapters in the Administrative History of Medieval England. 5 vols. Manchester, 1920–30.

Vinogradoff, Sir P. Roman Law in Medieval Europe. 1909.

White, A. B. The Making of the English Constitution, 447–1485. New York, 1908.

Wilkinson, B. The Chancery under Edward III. Manchester, 1929.

(c) Social and Economic History

[See also, for a more detailed bibliography, the section on The Social Background, pp. 119–24 below.]

Bateson, Mary. Medieval England. 1903.

Boissonade, P. Life and Work in Medieval Europe. Tr. Eileen Power, 1927.

Cam, H. M. The Hundred and the Hundred Rolls. 1930.

Christie, Mabel. The Evolution of the English Farm. 1927.

Colby, C. W. The Growth of Oligarchy in English Towns. EHR. v, 1890.

Coulton, G. G. Chaucer and his England. 1927 (4th edn).

Haward, W. I. Economic Aspects of the Wars of the Roses in East Anglia. EHR. XLI, 1926.

Haward, W. I. and Duncan, H. M. Village Life in the Fifteenth Century. 1928.

Jacob, E. F. Studies in the Period of Baronial Reform and Rebellion, 1258–67. Oxford, 1925.

Kriehn, G. The English Rising in 1450. Strasburg, 1892.

Law, Alice. The English Nouveaux-Riches in the Fourteenth Century. Trans. Royal Hist. Soc., N.S. IX, 1895.

Leach, A. F. The Schools of Medieval England. 1915.

Morris, W. A. The Frankpledge System. New York, 1910.

Oman, Sir C. W. C. The Great Revolt of 1381. Oxford, 1906.

Putnam, B. H. The Justices of Labourers in the Fourteenth Century. EHR. XXI, 1906.

—— The Enforcement of the Statutes of Labourers, 1349–59. New York, 1908.

Redstone, V. B. The Social Condition of England during the Wars of the Roses. Trans. Royal Hist. Soc., N.S. xvi, 1902.

Unwin, G. Finance and Trade under Edward III. Manchester, 1918.

(d) Ecclesiastical History and Political Philosophy

Allen, J. Inquiry into the Rise and Growth of the Royal Prerogative in England. 1849.

Brooke, Z. N. The English Church and the Papacy, 1066–1200. Cambridge, 1931.

Capes, W. W. The English Church in the Fourteenth and Fifteenth Centuries. 1900.

Carlyle, R. W. and Carlyle, A. J. A History of Medieval Political Theory in the West. 5 vols. 1903–28.

Church, R. W. St Anselm. 1888.

Coulton, G. G. Five Centuries of Religion. Cambridge, 1929 (2nd edn).

Deeley, Ann. Papal Provision and Royal Rights of Patronage in the Early Fourteenth Century. EHR. xliii, 1928.

Figgis, J. N. The Theory of the Divine Right of Kings. Cambridge, 1896.

Foligno, C. Latin Thought during the Middle Ages. Oxford, 1929.

Gairdner, J. Lollardy and the Reformation in England. 4 vols. 1908–13.

Gasquet, F. A. Parish Life in Medieval England. 1909 (2nd edn).

—— English Monastic Life. 1910 (4th edn).

Graham, Rose. St Gilbert of Sempringham and the Gilbertines. 1901.

—— English Ecclesiastical Studies. 1929.

Jessop, A. The Coming of the Friars. 1890 (4th edn).

Lechler, G. V. John Wiclif and his English Precursors. 1884.

Little, A. G. The Franciscan School at Oxford. Archivum Franciscanum Historicum, xix, Quaracchi, 1926.

Loserth, J. Huss und Wiclif. Munich, 1925.

Macdonald, A. J. Lanfranc. 1926.

Maitland, F. W. Roman Canon Law in the Church of England. 1898.

Owst, G. R. Preaching in Medieval England. Cambridge, 1926.

Palmer, R. L. English Monasteries in the Middle Ages. 1930.

Poole, R. L. Wycliffe and Movements for Reform. 1889.

—— Illustrations of the History of Medieval Thought and Learning. 1920 (2nd edn).

Power, E. Medieval English Nunneries. Cambridge, 1922.

Powicke, F. M. Stephen Langton. Oxford, 1928.

Rashdall, H. The Universities of the Middle Ages. 2 vols. Oxford, 1895.

Richardson, H. G. The Parish Clergy of the Thirteenth and Fourteenth Centuries. Trans. Royal Hist. Soc., ser. 3, vi, 1912.

Snape, R. H. English Monastic Finances in the Later Middle Ages. Cambridge, 1926.

Stephens, W. R. W. The English Church, 1066–1272. 1901.

Stevenson, F. S. Robert Grosseteste. 1899.

Wood-Legh, K. L. Studies in Church Life in England under Edward III. Cambridge, 1934.

Workman, H. B. John Wyclif; a Study of the English Medieval Church. 2 vols. Oxford, 1926.

M. McK.

III. THE SOCIAL BACKGROUND

(1) Original Sources

(a) General

[The chronicles, valuable as they are for social history, are not included in this list since they will be found above, pp. 115–6.]

Anglia Sacra. Ed. Henry Wharton, 2 vols. 1691. [Contains many valuable texts, some of which are still unavailable elsewhere.]

Borough Customs. Ed. Mary Bateson, 2 vols. Selden Soc. 1904–6.

Bracton, Henry de. Bracton's Note Book. Ed. F. W. Maitland, 3 vols. 1887.

—— De Legibus et Consuetudinibus Angliae. Ed. G. E. Woodbine, 2 vols. New Haven, 1915–22.

British Borough Charters, 1042–1216. Ed. A. Ballard, Cambridge, 1913.

British Borough Charters, 1216–1307. Ed. J. Tait and A. Ballard, Cambridge, 1923.

Calendar of Charter Rolls. Public Record Office, 1903–12.

Calendar of Documents preserved in France illustrative of the History of Great Britain and Ireland. Ed. J. H. Round, P.R.O. 1899. [Vol. i, 918–1206.]

The Cely Papers, 1475–1488. Ed. H. S. Malden, Royal Hist. Soc. 1900.

A Common Place Book of the Fifteenth Century. Ed. L. T. Smith, 1886.

Dialogus de Scaccario. Ed. A. Hughes, C. G. Crump, and C. Johnson, Oxford, 1902.

Documents and Accounts in Manners and Household Expenses in England. Ed. B. Botfield, Roxburghe Club, 1841.

Domesday Book. Ed. Sir H. Ellis, 2 vols. (with 3 supplementary vols.), Record Commission, 1783. [A facs. text was issued by the Ordnance Survey Office (Southampton, 1861–4) and trns of the sections relevant to the various counties are included in the Victoria County History.]

English Gilds. The Original Ordinances of more than One Hundred English Gilds. Ed. J. T. and L. T. Smith, EETS. 1870.

Fasciculi Zizaniorum magistri Iohannis Wyclif cum tritico ascribed to Thomas Netter of Walden. Ed. W. W. Shirley, Rolls Ser. 1858.

Fees, Book of, commonly called the Testa de Nevill. Ed. H. C. Maxwell Lyte, P.R.O. 1920, etc.

Feudal Aids. 6 vols. P.R.O. 1899–1920.

Formulare Anglicanum. Ed. T. Madox, 1702. [A valuable collection of charters which illustrate many features of English feudal society.]

Fortescue, Sir John. The Governance of England. Ed. C. Plummer, Oxford, 1885. [Written in the third quarter of the 15th cent.]

Gascoigne, Thomas. Loci e Libro Veritatum. Ed. J. E. T. Rogers, Oxford, 1881. [This contains passages from Gascoigne's theological dictionary which bear upon the social conditions of the 15th cent.]

Glanvill, Ranulf de. Tractatus de legibus et consuetudinibus regni Angliae. 1554. [Written in the last quarter of the 12th cent.]

Household Books of John duke of Norfolk and Thomas earl of Surrey, 1481–1490. Ed. J. P. Collier, Roxburghe Club, 1844.

Manners and Household Expenses of England in the Thirteenth and Fourteenth Centuries. Ed. T. H. Turner, Roxburghe Club, 1841.

Map, Walter. De Nugis Curialium. Ed. M. R. James, Oxford, 1914.

Monasticon Anglicanum. Ed. Sir W. Dugdale, 3 vols. 1655–73; rev. with 2 add. vols. J. Stevens, 1722–3; rev. J. Cley, H. Ellis and B. Bulkeley, 6 vols. in 8, 1817–30 and 1846. [Contains a very large number of charters for the whole medieval period and a mass of material of the greatest possible value.]

The Paston Letters, 1422–1509. Ed. with Notes and Introduction J. Gairdner, 6 vols. 1904.

Pecock, R. The Repressor of overmuch Blaming of the Clergy. Ed. C. Babington, Rolls Ser. 1860.

Placita Anglo Normannica: Law Cases from William I to Richard I preserved in Historical Records. Ed. M. M. Bigelow, Boston, 1879.

Placita de Quo Warranto Edward I–Edward III. Ed. W. Illingworth, Record Commission, 1818.

Placitorum Abbrevatio, Richard I–Edward II. Record Commission, 1811.

The Plumpton Correspondence. Ed. T. Stapleton, Camden Soc. 1839. [Written in 15th cent.]

The Political Songs of England. Ed. T. Wright, Camden Soc. 1839.

Political Poems and Songs relating to English History. Ed. T. Wright, Rolls Ser. 1859.

Red Book of the Exchequer. Ed. H. Hall 3 vols. Rolls Ser. 1896. [This includes bu does not supersede Liber Niger Scaccarii ed. T. Hearne, 2 vols. Oxford, 1728.]

Rotuli Hundredorum temp. Hen. III e Edw. I. Record Commission, 2 vols. 1812–8 [Contains a mass of tenurial and manoria information.]

Select Cases concerning the Law Merchant Ed. H. Hall, Selden Soc. 1908.

Select Cases from the Coroners' Rolls, 1265–1413. Ed. C. Gross, Selden Soc. 1896.

Select Cases in Chancery, 1364–1471. Ed W. P. Baildon, Selden Soc. 1896.

Select Cases before the King's Council. Ed Selden Soc. 1918.

Select Charters illustrative of English Con stitutional History. Ed. W. Stubbs, Oxford 1913 (9th edn).

Select Pleas in Manorial and Seignorial Courts Ed. F. W. Maitland, Selden Soc. 1889 [With a valuable introduction.]

Select Pleas of the Crown. Ed. F. W. Mait land, Selden Soc. 1888. [With a valuabl introduction.]

Statutes of the Realm. Record Commission 1810–22.

Testa de Nevill. [See Fees, Book of.]

Walter of Henley. Walter of Henley's Hus bandry. Ed. E. Lamond, Royal Hist Soc. 1890. [Deals with the management o rural estates; written in the 13th cent.]

Wardrobe Accounts. Liber Quotidianus con trarotularis Garderobae A.D. 1299–1300. Soc Antiquaries, 1787. [Deals with the roya administration.]

William of Malmesbury. Vita Wulfstani. Ed R. R. Darlington, Royal Hist. Soc. 1928.

Year Books. Selden Soc. 1903–.

(b) Local

[The most valuable sources for Englisl social history in the Middle Ages are com prised in local records. These often possess a wide general importance. In particular the cartularies and registers of religious house contain a mass of material of the utmos general value.]

Abingdon. Chronicon Monasterii de Abing don. Ed. J. Stevenson, 2 vols. Rolls Ser 1858.

Battle. Custumals of Battle Abbey, 1283–1312. Ed. S. R. Scargill-Bird, Camden Soc 1887.

Bath. Two Chartularies of the Priory of St Peter at Bath. Ed. W. Hunt, Somerset Record Soc. 1893.

Beverley Town Documents. Ed. A. F. Leach, Selden Soc. 1900.

The Boldon Buke, a Survey of the Possessions of the See of Durham made by Bishop Hugh Pudsey in 1183. Ed. W. Greenwell, Surtees Soc. 1852. [A trn and a commentary is to be found in the Victoria County History of Durham.]

Bristol. The Little Red Book of Bristol. Ed. F. B. Bickley, Bristol, 1900.

Bury St Edmunds. Memorials of St Edmund's Abbey. Ed. T. Arnold, 3 vols. Rolls Ser. 1890–6.

—— Pinchbeck Register. Ed. Lord Francis Hervey, Oxford, 1925.

—— Feudal Documents from the Abbey. Ed. D. C. Douglas, 1931. (British Academy Records of Social and Economic History, vol. VIII.)

Canterbury. The Register of St Augustine's Abbey. Ed. G. J. Turner and H. E. Salter, 1915. (British Academy Records of Social and Economic History, vols. II and III.) [See also under Fleet.]

Colchester. Cartularium monasterii S. Iohannis Baptiste de Colcestria. Ed. S. A. Moore, 2 vols. Roxburghe Club, 1897.

Coventry. The Coventry Leet Book: Records of the City Court Leet, 1420 1555. Ed. M. D. Harris, EETS. 1907–9.

Crabhouse. The Register of Crabhouse Nunnery. Ed. Mary Bateson, Trans. Norfolk and Norwich Archaeological Soc. XI, 1892.

Danelaw. Documents illustrative of the Social and Economic History of the Danelaw. Ed. F. M. Stenton, 1920. (British Academy Records of Social and Economic History, vol. v.) [With an important general introduction.]

Durham. Feodarium prioratus Dunelmensis. Ed. W. Greenwell, Surtees Soc. 1872.

—— Registrum Palatinum Dunelmense. Ed. T. D. Hardy, 3 vols. Rolls Ser. 1873–8.

Ely. Inquisitio comitatus Cantabrigiensis. Subjicitur Inquisitio Eliensis. Ed. N.E.S.A. Hamilton, Royal Soc. Lit. 1876. [Important for Domesday criticism.]

Eynsham. The Eynsham Cartulary. Ed. H. E. Salter, Oxford Hist. Soc. 1907–8.

Fleet. A Terrier of Fleet. Ed. H. Neilson, 1920. (British Academy Records of Social and Economic History, vol. IV.) [This vol. also contains An Eleventh Century Inquisition of S. Augustine's, Canterbury, ed. A. Ballard.]

Gilbertine Houses. Transcripts of Charters relating to Gilbertine Houses. Ed. F. M. Stenton, Lincoln Record Soc. 1922. [With a valuable general introduction.]

Gloucester. Historia et Cartularium Monasterii S. Petri Gloucestrie. Ed. W. Hart, 3 vols. 1863–7.

Guisborough. Cartularium Prioratus de Gysburne. Ed. W. Brown, 2 vols. Surtees Soc. 1889–94.

Hexham. The Priory of Hexham: its Title Deeds, Black Book, etc. Ed. J. Raine, Surtees Soc. 1865.

Leicester. Records of the Borough of Leicester. Ed. Mary Bateson, Cambridge, 1899.

Lincolnshire. The Lincolnshire Domesday and the Lindsey Survey. Ed. C. W. Foster and T. Longley, Lincoln Record Soc. 1924.

London. Domesday of St Paul's of the Year 1222. Ed. W. H. Hale, Camden Soc. 1858.

—— Memorials of London and London Life: a Series of Extracts from the Archives of the City of London, 1276–1419. Tr. and ed. H. T. Riley, 1868.

—— Munimenta Gildhallae Londoniensis. Liber Albus. Liber Custumarium et Liber Horn. Ed. H. T. Riley, 3 vols. Rolls Ser. 1859–62.

Malmesbury. Registrum Malmesburiensis. Ed. J. S. Brewer, 2 vols. Rolls Ser. 1879–80.

Manchester. Mauncestre: Chapters from the Early History of the Barony or Manor and the Borough of Manchester. Ed. J. Harland, 3 vols. Chetham Soc. 1861–2.

Newminster. Chartularium Abbathiae de Novo Monasterio Ordinis Cisterciensis. Ed. J. T. Fowler, Surtees Soc. 1878.

Northamptonshire. Northamptonshire Geld Roll. Ed. Sir H. Ellis (in Introduction to Domesday, vol. I, 1873).

Norwich. Leet Jurisdiction in the City of Norwich during the Thirteenth and Fourteenth Centuries. Ed. W. Hudson, Selden Soc. 1892.

Nottingham. Records of the Borough of Nottingham. Ed. W. H. Stevenson, 5 vols. 1882–1900.

—— Royal Charters granted to the Burgesses of Nottingham. Ed. W. H. Stevenson, 1890.

Oxford. Facsimiles of Early Charters in Oxford Muniment Rooms. Ed. H. E. Salter, Oxford, 1930.

—— Cartulary of the Monastery of St Frideswide at Oxford. Ed. S. R. Wigram, 2 vols. Oxford Hist. Soc. 1895–6.

Peterborough. Chronicon Petroburgense. Ed. T. Stapleton, Camden Soc. 1849.

Pickering. Honor and Forest of Pickering. Ed. R. B. Turton, 4 vols. North Riding Record Soc. 1894–7.

Ramsey. Cartularium Monasterii de Rameseia. Ed. W. H. Hart, 3 vols. Rolls Ser. 1884–93.

Richmond (Yorks). Registrum Honoris de Richmond. Ed. R. Gale, 1722.

Rievaulx. Cartularium Abbathiae de Rievalle. Ed. J. C. Atkinson, Surtees Soc. 1889.

Rochester. Textus Roffensis. Ed. T. Hearne, Oxford, 1720.

—— Registrum Roffense. Ed. J. Thorpe (the elder), 1769.

St Albans. Gesta Abbatium Monasterii S. Albani a Thoma Walsingham. Ed. H. T. Riley, 3 vols. 1867–9.

Salisbury. Vetus Registrum Sarisberiense. Ed. W. H. R. Jones, 2 vols. Rolls Ser. 1883–4.

Whalley. The Coucher Book or Chartulary of Whalley Abbey. Ed. W. A. Hulton, 4 vols. Chetham Soc. 1847–9.

Winchester. Liber Vitae: Register of New Minster and Hyde Abbey Winchester. Ed. W. de G. Birch, Hampshire Record Soc. 1892.

—— Liber Monasterii de Hyda. Ed. E. Edwards, Rolls Ser. 1866.

Winchcombe. Landboc sive Registrum Monasterii beatae Mariae Virginis et Sancti Cenhelmi de Winchelcumba. Ed. D. Royce, Exeter, 1892.

Worcester. Registrum Prioratus beatae Mariae Wigorniensis. Ed. W. H. Hale, Camden Soc. 1865.

—— Hemingi Chartularium Ecclesiae Wigorniensis. Ed. T. Hearne, 2 vols. Oxford, 1723.

Yorkshire. Yorkshire Charters. Ed. W. Farrer, 3 vols. Edinburgh, 1914–6.

(2) SECONDARY WORKS

(a) General and Miscellaneous

[The standard general histories will not be found in this list since they are included above, pp. 117–8. Some supplementary studies will also be found in the section on Social and Economic History above, p. 118.]

Abram, A. Social England in the Fifteenth Century. 1909.

—— English Life and Manners in the Later Middle Ages. 1913.

Ashley, W. J. An Introduction to English Economic History and Theory. 2 vols. 1888–93.

Ault, W. O. Private Jurisdiction in England. New Haven, 1923.

Ballard, A. The Domesday Inquest. 1906.

Belloc, H. The Old Road. 1904.

—— The Stane Street. 1913.

Brand, J. Observations on Popular Antiquities chiefly illustrating the Origin of our Vulgar Customs. Rev. Sir H. Ellis, 2 vols. 1813.

Calthorpe, D. C. English Costume. 4 vols. 1906.

Cambridge Medieval History. Cambridge, 1911–. [Special articles passim.]

Carlyle, T. Past and Present. 1843, etc.

Chadwick, D. Social Life in the Days of Piers Plowman. Cambridge, 1922.

Chambers, Sir E. K. The Mediaeval Stage. 2 vols. Oxford, 1903.

Clapham, A. W. English Romanesque Architecture after the Conquest. Oxford, 1934.

Coulton, G. G. Five Centuries of Religion. Cambridge. 1923–.

—— Life in the Middle Ages. 4 vols. 1928–30.

—— Social Life in England from the Conquest to the Reformation. Cambridge, 1918.

Creighton, C. A History of Epidemics in England. 2 vols. Cambridge, 1891–4.

The Legacy of the Middle Ages. Ed. G. C. Crump and E. F. Jacob, Oxford, 1926.

Cunningham, W. The Growth of English Industry and Commerce. 2 vols. Cambridge, 1890–2.

Denton, W. England in the Fifteenth Century. 1888.

Douglas, D. C. The Age of the Normans. 1925.

Dugdale, W. Origines Juridiciales. 1680 (3rd edn).

Eckenstein, L. Woman under Monasticism, A.D. 500–1500. Cambridge, 1896.

Fairholt, F. W. Costume in England. 2 vols. 1885.

Furnivall, F. J. Early English Meals and Manners. EETS. 1868.

Gasquet, F. A. English Monastic Life. 1904.

—— The Black Death. 1908.

—— Parish Life in Mediaeval England. 1906.

Goldschmidt, S. Geschichte der Juden in England bis zu ihrer Verbannung. Pt I: XI. und XII. Jahrhundert. Berlin, 1886.

Gomme, G. L. Handbook of Folk-Lore. Folk-Lore Soc. 1887.

Gras, N. S. B. The Early English Customs System. Cambridge, U.S.A. 1918.

Green, J. R. History of the English People. 8 vols. 1905–8.

Hall, H. Court Life under the Plantagenets. 1890.

Hazeltine, H. D. Die Geschichte des englischen Pfandrechts. Breslau, 1907.

Holdsworth, Sir W. S. History of English Law. 1903, etc.

Huizinga, J. The Waning of the Middle Ages. 1924.

Jessop, A. Studies of a Recluse. 1895.

Jusserand, J. J. Histoire littéraire du Peuple Anglais. 2 vols. Paris, 1894–1906.

Jusserand, J. J. Les Anglais au Moyen Âge: la Vie nomade et les Routes d'Angleterre au XIVe Siècle. Paris, 1884; tr. Eng. 1920.

Kelly, F. M. and Schwabe, R. A Short History of Costume and Armour. 1931.

Kingsford, C. L. Prejudice and Promise in Fifteenth Century England. Oxford, 1925.

Knoop, D. and Jones, G. P. The Mediaeval Mason. Manchester, 1933.

Liebermann, F. Über Pseudo-Cnuts Constitutiones de foresta. Halle, 1894. [The best account of forest history to 1217.]

Lipson, E. An Introduction to the Economic History of England. Vol. I, 1915.

Little, A. G. Studies in English Franciscan History. Manchester, 1917.

Madox, T. Baronia Anglica. 1736; 1841.

Manning, B. L. The People's Faith in the Time of Wyclif. Cambridge, 1919.

Mead, W. E. The English Mediaeval Feast. Boston, 1931.

Morris, W. A. The Early English County Court. Berkeley, 1926.

—— The Mediaeval English Sheriff to 1300. Manchester, 1927.

Neilson, G. Trial by Combat. 1890.

Owst, G. R. Preaching in Mediaeval England. Cambridge, 1926.

—— Literature and Pulpit in Medieval England. Cambridge, 1933.

Petit-Dutaillis, C. Studies Supplementary to Stubbs' Constitutional History. 3 vols. Manchester, 1908–29.

Pike, L. O. A History of Crime in England. 2 vols. 1873–6.

Planché, J. R. A Cyclopaedia of Costume. 2 vols. 1876–9.

Pollard, A. F. The Evolution of Parliament. 1920.

Pollock, Sir F. and Maitland, F. W. The History of English Law. 2 vols. Cambridge, 1898.

Poole, R. L. Wycliffe and Movements for Reform. 1889.

Prynne, W. A Short Demurrer to the Jewes long discontinued Remitters into England. 2 pts, 1665–6. [Of considerable general value for the history of the Jews in England.]

Round, J. H. Feudal England. 1895.

—— The Commune of London and Other Studies. 1899.

Ruding, R. Annals of the Coinage of Great Britain. 3 vols. 1817–9.

Salzman, L. F. English Life in the Middle Ages. 1926.

Saunders, O. E. A History of English Art in the Middle Ages. Oxford, 1932.

Strutt, J. Horda Angelcynnan: a Complete View of the Manners, Customs, Arms, Habits, etc., of the Inhabitants of England. 3 vols. 1774–6.

Strutt, J. Gliggamena Angel-leod: Sports and Pastimes of the People of England. 1801.

Stubbs, W. Constitutional History of England. 3 vols. Oxford, 1886, etc.

—— Seventeen Lectures on Mediaeval and Modern History. Oxford, 1886.

—— Historical Introductions to the Rolls Series. 1902.

—— Lectures on Early English History. 1906.

Swartout, R. E. The Monastic Craftsman. Cambridge, 1932.

Tait, J. Mediaeval Manchester and the Beginnings of Lancashire. Manchester, 1904.

Thayer, J. B. A Preliminary Treatise on Evidence at the Common Law. Pt I, Development of Trial by Jury. Boston, 1898.

Tout, T. F. Chapters in the Administrative History of Mediaeval England. 6 vols. Manchester, 1920–34.

Social England. Ed. H. D. Traill and J. S. Mann, 6 vols. 1901–4.

Trevelyan, G. M. England in the Age of Wycliffe. 1899.

Turner, C. J. R. A History of Vagrants and Vagrancy. 1887.

Victoria History of the Counties of England. 1900–.

Wright, T. A History of Domestic Manners and Sentiments in England. 1862.

(b) Agriculture, the Manor and the Peasantry

Coulton, G. G. The Medieval Village. Cambridge, 1925.

Curtler, W. H. R. A Short History of English Agriculture. Oxford, 1909.

Douglas, D. C. Social Structure of Medieval East Anglia. Oxford, 1927.

Gray, H. L. English Field Systems. Cambridge, U.S.A. 1915.

Hone, N. J. The Manor and Manorial Records. 1906.

Levett, A. E. The Black Death on the Estates of the See of Winchester. Oxford, 1916.

Maitland, F. W. Domesday Book and Beyond. Cambridge, 1898.

Meitzen, A. Siedelung und Agrarwesen der West Germanen und Ostgermanen der Kelten, Romer, Finnen und Slawen. 3 vols. and atlas, Berlin, 1895. [Vol. II, pp. 97–140, deals with England.]

Nasse, E. Über die mittelalterliche Feldgemeinschaft und die Einhebungen des 16. Jahrhunderts in England. Bonn, 1869; tr. Eng. 1871.

Page, W. T. The End of Villainage in England. New York, 1900.

Petit Dutaillis, C. Les Prédications populaires. Les Lollards et le Soulèvement des Travailleurs anglais en 1381. [In Études d'Histoire du Moyen Âge dédiées à Gabriel Monod, Paris, 1896.]

Powell, E. The Rising in East Anglia in 1381. Cambridge, 1896.

Reville, A. Le Soulèvement des Travailleurs d'Angleterre en 1381. Société de l'École des Chartes, Mémoires et Documents, vol. ii, Paris, 1898.

Rogers, J. E. T. A History of Agriculture and Prices in England, 1259–1793. 7 vols. Oxford, 1866–1902.

—— Six Centuries of Work and Wages. 2 vols. Oxford, 1884.

Schmidt, K. Jus Primae Noctis. Freiburg, 1881.

Seebohm, F. English Village Community. 1883, etc.

Somner, W. A Treatise on Gavelkind. 1660; 1726.

Stenton, F. M. Types of Manorial Structure in the Northern Danelaw. Oxford, 1910.

Trenholme, N. M. The Right of Sanctuary in England. Columbia, Mo. 1903.

Trevelyan, G. M. and Powell, E. The Peasant's Rising and the Lollards. 1899.

Vinogradoff, Sir P. Villainage in England. Oxford, 1892.

—— English Society in the Eleventh Century. Oxford, 1908.

—— Growth of the Manor. 1911.

(c) The Towns and Town Life

Ballard, A. The English Borough in the Twelfth Century. Cambridge, 1914.

Green, A. S. Town Life in the Fifteenth Century. 2 vols. 1894.

Gross, C. The Gild Merchant. Oxford, 1890.

Knoll, K. London im Mittelalter. Vienna, 1932.

Madox, T. Firma Burgi. 1726.

Maitland, F. W. Township and Borough. Cambridge, 1898.

von Ochenkowski, W. Englands wirthschaftliche Entwickelung im Ausgang des Mittelalters. Jena, 1879.

Salzman, L. F. English Industry of the Middle Ages. 1913, 1923.

Stow, J. Survey of London. Ed. C. L. Kingsford, Oxford, 1909.

D. C. D.

IV. EDUCATION

[This section should be used in conjunction with the parallel, and considerably fuller section for the 1500–1660 period, pp. 364–80 below, which it partly overlaps.]

(1) ORIGINAL AUTHORITIES

(a) Manuscripts

[Many documents (mainly legal) referring to the early history of Oxford and Cambridge are to be found in the treasuries or muniment rooms of the several colleges, and in the registries of the two universities.

Thomas Baker (1656–1740), sometime Fellow of St John's, a laborious and accurate antiquary, left extensive writings, which are preserved in the Harleian collection in the BM. and in the Cambridge University Lib. In the antiquarian collections made by William Cole (1714–1782), vicar of Milton, Cambridgeshire, and bequeathed by him to the BM. is much useful material extracted by him from original sources (Index by G. J. Gray, Cambridge, 1912). For Oxford there exist the MS collections of Robert Hare (Privilegia Memorabilia) and of Bryan Twyne.]

(b) Printed Books

(i) Oxford

Corpus Statutorum Universitatis Oxoniensis Oxford, 1768. [With Appendix.]

Statutes of the Colleges of Oxford, with the Royal Patents of Foundation, Injunctions of Visitors, etc. 3 vols. 1853.

Collectanea. Ed. C. R. L. Fletcher and M. Burrows, 2 sers. Oxford Hist. Soc. 1885.

Salter, H. E. Mediaeval Archives of the University of Oxford. 2 vols. Oxford 1920–1.

Statuta antiqua Universitatis Oxoniensis Ed. S. Gibson, Oxford, 1931.

(ii) Cambridge

Statuta Academiae Cantabrigiensis. Cambridge, 1785.

Documents relating to the University and Colleges of Cambridge. 3 vols. 1852.

Tanner, J. R. The Historical Register of the University of Cambridge. Cambridge, 1917.

(iii) Scottish Universities

Report of Commissioners to visit the Universities of Scotland. 4 vols. 1831; Evidence 1837. [Appendices of documents.]

Early Records of the University of St Andrews. Ed. J. M. Anderson, Edinburgh 1926.

(2) Modern Authorities

(i) General

Denifle, H. Die Entstehung der Universitäten des Mittelalters bis 1400. Berlin, 1885.

Laurie, S. S. The Rise and Early Constitution of Universities. 1886.

Rashdall, H. The Universities of Europe in the Middle Ages. 2 vols. Oxford, 1895, 1936 (rev.). [The history of Oxford and Cambridge is dealt with in vol. II, pt 2.]

Sandys, Sir J. E. English Scholars of Paris and Franciscans of Oxford. CHEL. vol. I, 1907.

Haskins, C. H. Mediaeval Universities. The Rise of Universities. New York, 1923.

(ii) Oxford

Hobhouse, Edmund. Sketch of the Life of Walter de Merton. Oxford, 1859.

Clark, A. The Colleges of Oxford: their History and Traditions. 1891.

Little, A. G. The Grey Friars in Oxford. Oxford, 1892.

Mallet, C. E. A History of the University of Oxford. 3 vols. 1924–7.

(iii) Cambridge

[The Trans. of the Cambridge Antiquarian Soc. contain many valuable documents and articles connected with the early history of the University.]

Willis, R. and Clark, J. W. The Architectural History of the University of Cambridge. 4 vols. Cambridge, 1886.

Leathes, S. M. Grace Book A (1454–1488). Cambridge, 1897.

Bateson, Mary. Grace Book B (1488–1511). 2 vols. Cambridge, 1903–5.

Searle, W. G. Grace Book Γ. (1511–1542) Cambridge, 1908.

Venn, J. Early Collegiate Life. Cambridge. 1913.

(iv) Scottish Universities

Lyon, C. J. History of St Andrews, Episcopal, Monastic, Academic and Civil. 2 vols. Edinburgh, 1843.

Innes, C. Sketches of Early Scottish History. Edinburgh, 1861.

Anderson, J. M. The University of St Andrews. Cupar, 1878; Supplement, 1883.

Rait, R. S. The Universities of Aberdeen. Aberdeen, 1895.

Herkless, J. and Hannay, R. K. The College of St Leonard. Edinburgh, 1905.

Coissac, J. B. Les Universités d'Écosse (1410–1560). Paris, 1915.

Forbes, F. A. The Founding of a Northern University. 1920.

(v) Public Schools

Creasy, E. S. Some Account of the Foundation of Eton College. 1848.

Knight, S. The Life of Dr John Colet, Founder of St Paul's School. Oxford, 1823.

Seebohm, F. The Oxford Reformers. 1887.

[The account of St Paul's School must be supplemented by the documents ptd by A. F. Leach in Archaeologia, LXXII, 1910.]

Lowth, R. Life of William of Wykeham. 1759.

Walcott, M. E. C. William of Wykeham and his Colleges. 1852.

Moberley, G. H. Life of William of Wykeham. Winchester, 1887.

Leach. A. F. Early Education in Worcester, 685–1770. Worcestershire Hist. Soc. 1913.

William Fitz-Stephen; London Schools in the Twelfth Century. [Norman London, Hist. Ass. leaflets, 93, 94, 1934.]

(vi) Some Textbooks

Aelfric Abbas. Excerptiones de Prisciano minore vel majore. ('Aelfric's Grammar.') Sententiam Latini Sermonis (with Aelfric Bata: 'Aelfric's Colloquy'). [See J. Zupitza, Aelfrics Grammatik und Glossar, Berlin, 1880; T. Wright and R. Wülcker, Anglo-Saxon and Old English Vocabularies, 2 vols. 1884.]

Anwykyll, J. Compendium totius Grammatices. Oxford, 1483; Antwerp, 1489.

Chase, W. J. The Distichs of Cato. Madison, 1922.

—— The Ars Minor of Donatus. Madison, 1926.

Isidore of Seville, Etymologiarum Libri xx. Oxford, 1911.

Keil, H. Grammatici Latini. 7 vols. and Supplement, Leipzig, 1855–80.

Martianus Capella. Libri Novem Martiani Capellae. Ed. C. F. Hermann, Marburg, 1835. [See P. R. Cole, Ausonius, Capella and the Theodosian Code, New York, 1909 (contains analyses of Capella).]

Orosius, Paulus. Adversus Paganos Historiarum Libri VII. Leyden, 1738.

Promptorium Parvulorum sive Clericorum [c. 1411]. Ed. A. Way, Camden Soc. 1843–65.

Paetow, L. J. The Arts Course at Medieval Universities. Champaign, Illinois, 1910.

Reichling, D. Das Doctrinale des Alexander de Villa-Dei. Monumenta Germaniae Paedagogica, vol. XII, Berlin, 1893.

Sandys, Sir J. E. A History of Classical Scholarship. 3 vols. Cambridge, 1903–8.

(vii) General and Miscellaneous Studies

Adamson, J. W. A Short History of Education. Cambridge, 1919, 1930 (rev.).
—— Education. [In Mediaeval Contributions to Modern Civilisation, 1921.]
—— Education. [In The Legacy of the Middle Ages, Oxford, 1926.]
Alcuin. Monumenta Alcuiniana. [In Bibliotheca Rerum Germanicarum, vol. vi, Berlin, 1873.]
Gaskoin, C. J. B., Alcuin, his Life and Work. Cambridge, 1904.
Browne, G. F. Alcuin of York. 1908.
Aldhelmi Opera. Ed. R. Ewald, Berlin, 1913–9. [See Epistulae, pp. 475–503.]
Browne, G. F. Aldhelm, his Life and Times. 1903.
Alfred the Great. Gregory's Pastoral Care: Alfred's West Saxon Version. EETS. 1871.
Brooke, S. A. King Alfred as Educator of his People. 1901.
Plummer, C. Life and Times of Alfred the Great. Oxford, 1902.
Bacon, Roger. Compendium Studii Philosophiae. 1859.
Bateson, Mary. Mediaeval England. 1903.
Bede. Epistula ad Ecgbertum Episcopum. [In Baedae Opera Historica, ed. C. Plummer, vol. i, Oxford, 1896. Tr. Eng. in Biographical Writings and Letters of Venerable Bede. By J. A. Giles, 1845.]
Berlière, U. Les Écoles abbatiales au Moyen Âge. Revue Bénédictine, vi, 1894, pp. 499–511.
—— Les Collèges Bénédictins aux Universités du Moyen Âge. Revue Bénédictine, x, 1898, pp. 145–58.
—— Ecoles claustrales au Moyen Âge. Bulletin de la Classe des Lettres et des Sciences morales et politiques de l'Académie royale de Belgique, 1921, pp. 550–72.
Coulton, G. G. Religious Education before the Reformation. 1906. [Rptd in Medieval Studies, 1913.]
—— Monastic Schools in the Middle Ages. 1913. [Rptd in Medieval Studies, 1913.]
—— Social Life in Britain: Conquest to Reformation. Cambridge, 1918.
Crawford, S. J. The Anglo-Saxon Influence in Western Christendom. Oxford, 1933.
Creighton, M. The Early Renaissance in England. Cambridge, 1895.
Deanesly, M. The Lollard Bible. Cambridge, 1920.
—— Mediaeval Schools to c. 1300. Cambridge Medieval History, vol. v, 1929.
Gasquet, F. A. The Eve of the Reformation. 1919.
Graham, Rose. The Intellectual Influence of English Monasticism between the Tenth

and Twelfth Centuries. Trans. Royal Hist Soc. xvii, 1903.
Hepple, R. B. Mediaeval Education in England. Hist. Ass. leaflet, 1932.
James, M. R. Two Ancient English Scholars (Aldhelm and William of Malmesbury) Glasgow, 1931.
—— The Christian Renaissance. Cambridge Modern History, vol. i, 1902.
Jebb, R. C. Humanism in Education. 1899.
—— The Classical Renaissance. Cambridge Modern History, vol. i, 1902.
Jenkinson, Hilary. The Teaching and Practice of Handwriting in England. History, xi 1926.
Jessopp, A. The Coming of the Friars. 1889
Jourdain, C. Excursions historiques et philosophiques à travers le Moyen Âge. Paris 1888.
Laistner, M. L. W. Thought and Letters in Western Europe, A.D. 500–900. 1931.
Leach, A. F. Some Results of Research in the History of Education in England. Proc British Academy, vi, 1915.
Little, A. G. The Educational Organisation of the Friars in Medieval England. Trans Royal Hist. Soc. viii, 1894.
—— Studies in English Franciscan History Manchester, 1917.
Maitland, S. R. The Dark Ages. 1845.
Maître, L. Les Écoles épiscopales et monastiques en Occident avant les Universités (768–1180). Paris, 1886–1924 (rev. edn).
Parmentier, J. Histoire de l'Éducation en Angleterre. Paris, 1896.
Parry, A. W. Education in England in the Middle Ages. 1920.
Paues, A. C. Runes and Manuscripts. CHEL vol. i, 1907.
Poole, R. L. Illustrations of the History of Mediaeval Thought. 1884; 1920 (rev.).
—— The Exchequer in the Twelfth Century. Oxford, 1912. [Abacus and Algorism.]
Rait, R. S. Life in the Medieval University Cambridge, 1912.
—— Learning and Education. [In Mediaeval England, Oxford, 1924.]
Roger, M. L'Enseignement des Lettres classiques d'Ausone à Alcuin. Paris, 1905.
Schirmer, W. F. Der englische Frühhumanismus. Leipzig, 1931.
Schmid, K. A. Geschichte der Erziehung Ed. G. Schmid, vol. ii, Stuttgart, 1892.
Stubbs, W. Literature and Learning at the Court of Henry II. [In Seventeen Lectures on the Study of Mediaeval History, Oxford, 1886.]
Thorndike, L. Science and Thought in the Fifteenth Century. New York, 1929.
Vickers, K. H. Humphrey Duke of Gloucester. 1907.

Walker, T. A. English and Scottish Education; Universities and Public Schools to the Time of Colet. CHEL. vol. II, 1908.

Woodward, W. H. Desiderius Erasmus concerning the Aim and Method of Education. Cambridge, 1904.

—— Studies in Education during the Age of the Renaissance. Cambridge, 1906.

(viii) Knightly and Courtly Education

Berners, Dame Juliana (?). The Boke of St Albans. [See TLS. 9 Aug. 1928, p. 573.]

La Curne de Ste-Palaye. Mémoires sur l'Ancienne Chevalerie. 3 vols. Paris, 1781.

Furnivall, F. J. Education in Early England. EETS. 1867.

—— Manners and Meals in Olden Time. EETS. 1868. [A miscellany including The Babees Book, two Bokes of Nurture, Bokes of Kervynge, Curtasye, Schoole of Vertue, etc.]

Mills, C. The History of Chivalry. 2 vols. 1825-6.

Wright, T. Feudal Manuals of English History compiled for the use of the Feudal Gentry and Nobility. 1872.

De Principis Institutione. [The treatises with this or an equivalent title are numerous; they relate to moral and political, rather than to intellectual education. Recent studies on the topic: L. K. Born, Speculum, III, 1928; A. F. Arrowood, Speculum, x, 1935.]

(ix) Education of Girls

Gardiner, Dorothy. English Girlhood at School. Oxford, 1929.

La Tour-Landry. The Book of the Knight (1371). EETS. 1906. [A sixteenth century English trn.]

Power, Eileen. Mediaeval English Nunneries, 1275–1535. Cambridge, 1922. [Ch. vi and Appendix B.]

T. A. W., *rev.* G. R. P. and J. W. A.

2. MIDDLE ENGLISH LITERATURE

I. THE MIDDLE ENGLISH ROMANCES

General Works: Bibliographies and Summaries, General Treatments, Special Studies, Collected Editions, Modern Renderings.

The Cyclic Romances: Arthurian Romances (General studies, Studies of particular phases and heroes, Arthurian romances in English), Charlemagne Romances, Romances of Alexander, Romances of Troy, Romances of Thebes, Romances of Godfrey of Bouillon.

The Non-Cyclic Romances: Romances of English Heroes, Breton Lais, Miscellaneous Romances.

I. THE ROMANCES IN GENERAL

(a) *Bibliographies and Summaries*

Billings, A. H. Guide to the Middle English Metrical Romances (English and Germanic Legends, Cycles of Charlemagne and Arthur). New York, 1901. [Synopses, summary of criticism, bibliographies.] (*Billings*.)

Esdaile, A. List of English Tales and Prose Romances printed before 1740. Bibliog. Soc. 1912.

Wells, J. E. Manual of the Writings in Middle English. New Haven, 1916. [With 6 Supplements, 1919, 1923, 1926, 1929, 1932, 1935. Treats all romances to 1500; gives for each the facts on MSS, authorship, date and dialect, with a synopsis of the story, a summary of criticism, and a full bibliography to July 1935.] (*Wells*.)

Hibbard, L. A. Medieval Romance in England. A Study of the Sources and Analyses of the Non-Cyclic Metrical Romances. New York, 1924. [Versions, MSS, origins, bibliographies—especially good for foreign versions.] (*Hibbard*.)

Thompson, Stith. Motif-Index of Folk-Literature. A Classification of Narrative Elements in Folk-Tales, Ballads, Myths, Fables, Mediaeval Romances, Exempla, Fabliaux, Jest-Books and Local Legends. Bloomington, 1932–

(b) *General Treatments*

Morley, H. English Writers. 11 vols. 1887–95. [See vol. III, pp. 120, 251, 264, 375.]

Ward, H. L. D. and Herbert, J. A. Catalogue of Romances in the Department of Manuscripts of the British Museum. 3 vols. 1883–1910. (*Ward*.)

ten Brink, B. Early English Literature. 3 vols. 1883–96. [See vol. I, pp. 119, 164, 180, 225, 234, 253, 327, 336.] (*ten Brink*.)

Saintsbury, G. The Flourishing of Romance. Edinburgh, 1897.

Ker, W. P. Epic and Romance. 1897; 1908.

Schofield, W. H. English Literature from the Norman Conquest to Chaucer. 1906. [See pp. 145, 476.] (*Schofield*.)

Cambridge History of English Literature. Cambridge, 1907. [Vol. I, chs. xii, xiii, with bibliography.]

Edwardes, M. Summary of the Literatures of Modern Europe. 1907. [See for English p. 94; for French, pp. 150, 167.]

Lawrence, W. W. Medieval Story. New York, 1911.

Spence, L. Dictionary of Medieval Romance and Romance Writers. 1913. [Synopses, notes on writers, works and personages.]

Leach, H. G. Angevin Britain and Scandinavia. Cambridge, U.S.A. 1921.

Baker, E. A. The History of the English Novel. Vol. I (The Age of Romance), 1924. [General bibliographies, table of topics.]

Barrow, S. F. Medieval Society Romances. New York, 1924.

Taylor, A. B. An Introduction to Medieval Romance. 1930.

(c) *Special Studies*

Söchtig, P. Zur Technik altenglischer Spielmannsepen. Leipzig, 1903.

Grossmann, W. Frühmittelenglische Zeugnisse über Minstrels. Brandenburg, 1906.

Kahle, R. Der Klerus im mittelenglischen Versroman. Strasburg, 1906.

Deutschbein, M. Studien zur Sagengeschichte Englands. Cöthen, 1906.

Geissler, O. Religion und Aberglaube in den mittelenglischen Versromanzen. Halle, 1908.

Ker, W. P. Romance. Oxford, 1909; 1913.

Hübner, W. Die Frage in einigen mittelenglischen Versromanen. Kiel, 1910.

Voltmer, B. Die mittelenglische Terminologie der ritterlichen Verwandtschafts- und Standesverhältnisse. Kiel, 1911.

Creek, H. Character in the 'Matter of England' Romances. JEGP. x, 1911, pp. 429, 585. Urbana, 1911.

Vitter, E. Das bürgerliche Leben im mittelenglischen Versroman. Kiel, 1912.

Borchers, K. H. Die Jagd in den mittelenglischen Romanzen. Kiel, 1912.

Peters, F. Die englischen Angriffswaffen zur Zeit der Einführung der Feuerwaffen (1300–1350.) Anglistische Forschungen, xxxviii, 1913.

Lausterer, P. Der syntaktische Gebrauch des Artikels in den älteren mittelenglischen Romanzen. Kiel, 1914.

Curry, W. C. Medieval Ideal of Personal Beauty in Metrical Romances. Baltimore, 1916.

Villson, E. Middle English Legends of Visits to the Under-world, and their Relations to Metrical Romances. Chicago, 1917.

Veston, J. L. Mystery Survivals in Medieval Romance. Quest, Jan. 1920.

Prothero, R. E. (Baron Ernle). Light Reading of our Ancestors. 1921.

Ashdown, M. Single Combat in English and Scandinavian Tradition and Romance. MLR. xvii, 1922, p. 113.

Griffin, N. E. Definition of Romance. PMLA. xxxviii, 1922, p. 50.

Funke, O. Die Fügung 'ginnen' mit dem Infinitiv in Mittelenglischen. E. Studien, lvi, 1922, p. 1.

McKeehan, I. P. Some Relationships between the Legends of British Saints and the Medieval Romances. University of Chicago Abstracts of Theses, Humanistic Ser. ii, 1923–4, p. 381.

Brunner, K. Romanzen und Volksballaden. Palaestra, cxlviii, 1925, p. 75.

Holthausen, F. Zur Textkritik mittelenglischen Romanzen. [In Luick Festgabe, Marburg, 1925.]

Patch, H. R. Chaucer and Medieval Romance. [In Essays in Memory of B. Wendell, Cambridge, U.S.A. 1926.]

Cristensen, P. A. Beginnings and Endings of the Middle English Metrical Romances. Stanford University Abstracts of Dissertations, ii, 1927, p. 105.

Harris, A. E. Heroine of the Middle English Romances. Western Reserve University Stud. ii, no. iii, 1928, p. 4.

Everett, D. A Characterization of the English Medieval Romances. E. & S. xv, 1929, p. 98.

Loops, R. Der Begriff 'Romance' in der mittelenglischen und frühneuenglischen Literatur. Anglistische Forschungen, lxviii, 1929.

Oakden, J. P. Alliterative Poetry in Middle English. 2 pts, Manchester, 1930–5.

Cagleson, H. Costume in the Middle English Metrical Romances. PMLA. xlvii, 1932, p. 339.

Koziol, H. Grundzüge der Syntax der mittelenglischen Stabreimdichtungen. Wiener Beiträge, lviii, 1932.

—— Zur Frage der Verfasserschaft einiger mittelenglischer Stabreimdichtungen. E. Studien, lxvii, 1932, p. 165.

Trounce, A. McI. The English Tail-Rhyme Romances. Medium Aevum, i, 1932, pp. 87, 168, ii, 1933, pp. 34, 189, iii, 1934, p. 30.

Lippmann, K. Das ritterliche Persönlichkeitsideal in der mittelenglischen Literatur des 13. und 14. Jahrhunderts. Leipzig, 1933.

Reinhard, R. The Survival of Geis in Mediaeval Romance. Halle, 1933.

Tuve, R. Seasons and Months. Studies in a Tradition of Middle English Poetry. Paris, 1933.

Whiting, B. J. Proverbs in certain Middle English Romances in relation to their French Sources. Harvard Stud. xv, 1933, p. 75.

(d) Collected Editions

Ritson, J. Ancient Engleish Metrical Romanceës. 3 vols. 1802.

Weber, H. Metrical Romances of the XIII, XIV, and XV Centuries. 3 vols. Edinburgh, 1810.

Utterson, R. Select Pieces of Early Popular Poetry. 2 vols. 1817. [From black-letter prints.]

Laing, D. Select Remains of the Ancient Popular Poetry of Scotland. 1822; 1885 (rev. J. Small).

—— Early Metrical Tales. 1826; 1889.

—— Early Popular Poetry of Scotland and the Northern Border. Rev. W. C. Hazlitt, 1895. [An amalgamation of the preceding items.]

Thoms, W. J. Collection of Early Prose Romances. 3 vols. 1828–7; 1907 (rev. H. Morley et al.).

Hartshorne, C. H. Ancient Metrical Tales. 1829.

Madden, Sir F. Sir Gawayne. Bannatyne Club, 1839.

Robson, J. Three Early English Metrical Romances. Camden Soc. 1842.

Halliwell[-Phillipps], J. O. Thornton Romances. Camden Soc. 1844.

Hazlitt, W. C. Remains of the Early Popular Poetry of England. 4 vols. 1864–6.

Hales, J. W. and Furnivall, F. J. Percy Folio Manuscript. 4 vols. 1867–9.

McKnight, G. H. Middle English Humorous Tales in Verse. Boston, 1913.

French, W. E. and Hale, C. B. Middle English Metrical Romances. New York, 1930.

9

(e) *Collections of Abstracts or Modern Renderings*

Ellis, G. Specimens of Early English Metrical Romances. 3 vols. 1805; 1848 (rev. J. O. Halliwell[-Phillipps]).

Ashton, J. Romances of Chivalry. 1890.

Weston, J. L. Sir Cleges. Sir Libeaus Desconus. 1902.

—— Romance Vision, and Satire. Boston, 1912.

—— Chief Middle English Poets. Boston, 1914.

Darton, F. J. H. Wonder Book of Old Romance. New York, 1907.

Rickert, E. Early English Romances in Verse. 2 vols. 1908. [Vol. I, Romances of Love; vol. II, Romances of Friendship.]

Hibbard, L. A. Three Middle English Romances. New York, 1911.

II. The Cyclic Romances

A. ARTHURIAN ROMANCES

(1) The Legends in General

[For bibliographies and summaries see *Wells*, pp. 27, 766, 953, 1003, 1050, 1101, 1167, 1205, 1259, 1296, 1344, 1383; *Billings*, p. 85; J. D. Bruce, Evolution of Arthurian Romance to 1300, Göttingen, 1923; Sir E. K. Chambers, Arthur of Britain, 1927, p. 283; G. Gröber, Grundriss der romanischen Philologie, vol. II[1], Strasburg, 1902, pp. 288, 363, 469, 495, 551, 585, 996, 1195, and Register, p. 1254; G. Paris, Littérature française au Moyen-âge, Paris, 1890, sects. 53 ff.; Ency. Brit. under 'Arthur,' 'Lancelot,' 'Tristram,' 'Merlin,' 'Perceval,' 'Holy Grail,' 'Gawain'; J. L. Weston, King Arthur and his Knights, 1905; W. P. Ker, CHEL. vol. I, pp. 243, 461; and J. Parry, A Bibliography of Critical Arthurian Literature, 1922–1929, New York, 1931. For general treatment see Histoire littéraire de la France, vol. XXX, p. 1; Romania, X, 1882, p. 464; *ten Brink*, vol. I, pp. 134, 140, 164, 171, 187; *Schofield*, pp. 159, 475. See also under individual sections and items below.]

Ritson, J. Life of King Arthur. 1825.

Paris, P. Romans de la Table Ronde. 5 vols. Paris, 1868–77.

Malory's Morte Darthur. Ed. H. O. Sommer, 3 vols. 1889–91. [Vol. III.]

Rhys, J. Arthurian Legend. Oxford, 1891.

Puetz, F. R. Zur Geschichte der Entwicklung der Arthursage. Bonn, 1892.

Hoeppner, A. B. Arthur's Gestalt in der Literatur Englands. Leipzig, 1892.

MacCallum, M. W. Tennyson's Idylls and Arthurian Story. Glasgow, 1894.

Wülcker, R. P. Die Arthursage in der englischen Literatur. Leipzig, 1895.

Ker, W. P. Epic and Romance. 1897; 1908 [Ch. v.]

Newell, W. W. King Arthur and the Table Round. Boston, 1897.

—— Arthurian Notes. MLN. XVII, 1902, p. 277; PMLA. XX, 1905, p. 622.

Saintsbury, G. The Flourishing of Romance. Edinburgh, 1897.

Nutt, A. Celtic and Medieval Romance. 1899.

Weston, J. L. King Arthur and his Knights, a Survey. 1899; 1905 (rev. edn).

Briggs, W. D. King Arthur in Cornwal. JEGP. III, 1900, p. 342.

Brown, A. C. L. Round Table before Wace. Harvard Stud. VII, 1900.

Dickinson, W. H. King Arthur in Cornwal. New York, 1900.

Lot, F. Nouvelles Études. Romania, I, 1901.

Kittredge, G. L. Arthur and Gorlagon. Harvard Stud. VIII, 1903, p. 149.

Paton, L. A. Fairy Mythology of the Arthurian Romances. Radcliffe Monographs, XIII, 1903.

Mott, L. F. Round Table. PMLA. XX, 1905, p. 231.

Fletcher, R. H. Arthurian Material in the Chronicles. Harvard Stud. X, 1906.

Maynadier, G. H. Arthur of the English Poets. Boston, 1907.

Sommer, H. O. Vulgate Version of the Arthurian Romances. 8 vols. Washington, 1908–11.

Jones, W. L. King Arthur in History and Legend. Cambridge, 1911

Lawrence, W. W. Medieval Story. New York, 1911.

Loth, J. Contributions à l'Étude des Romans de la Table Ronde. Paris, 1912.

Leach, H. G. Angevin Britain and Scandinavia. Cambridge, U.S.A. 1921. [Pp. 135, 227, bibliography, p. 400.]

Bruce, J. D. Evolution of Arthurian Romance to 1300. 2 vols. Göttingen, 1923–4.

Malone, K. Historicity of Arthur. JEGP. XXIII, 1924, p. 463.

—— Artorius. MP. XXII, 1924–5, p. 367.

Plesner, K. F. Engelsk Arthur-Digtning. Studier fra Sprog- og Oldtidsforskning. Copenhagen, 1925.

Ven-ten Bensel, E. F. W. M. van der, Character of Arthur in English Literature. Amsterdam, 1925.

Singer, S. Die Artussage. Berne 1926.

Chambers, Sir E. K. Arthur of Britain. 1927 [See its bibliography.]

Faral, E. La Légende Arthurienne; Études et Documents. Paris, 1929.

Cross, T. P. and Nitze, W. A. Lancelot and Guenevere. A Study of the Origins of Courtly Love. Chicago, 1930.

Lewis, C. B. Classical Mythology and Arthurian Romance. Oxford, 1932.

(2) Particular Phases and Heroes

(a) Merlin and the Youth of Arthur

[*Wells*, pp. 38, 768, 797, 1004, 1050, 1102, 297, 1385; *Billings*, p. 114; *Ward*, vol. I, p. 207, 278, 371, 384; G. Paris, Littérature française au Moyen-âge, Paris, 1890, sect. 54 nd bibliography, sects. 54, 60, 57–63.]

Mead, W. E. Outlines of the Legend of Merlin. EETS. 1899.

Lot, F. Études sur Merlin. Paris, 1900.

Taylor, R. Political Prophecy in England. New York, 1911. [Chs. i–iii.]

Schulz, A. (San-Marte). Die Sagen von Merlin. Halle, 1854.

Paris, G. and Ulrich, J. Huth Merlin. Société des anciens Textes français, 1886.

Ward, H. L. D. Merlin Silvester. Romania, XXII, 1888, p. 504.

Rhys, J. Arthurian Legend. Oxford, 1891.

Sommer, H. O. Le Roman de Merlin. 1904.

Weston, J. L. Legend of Merlin. Folk-Lore, XVII, pt ii, 1906, p. 30.

Maynadier, G. H. Arthur of the English Poets. Boston, 1907. [Chs. iii, vi.]

Bond, R. W. MLR. XI, 1916, p. 347. [Review of Taylor.]

Bruce, J. D. Evolution of Arthurian Romance to 1300. 2 vols. Göttingen, 1923–4.

Paton, L. A. Prophécies de Merlin. 2 vols. New York, 1926–7.

Chambers, Sir E. K. Arthur of Britain. 1927. [Ch. ii and bibliography.]

(b) Lancelot, and the Death of Arthur

[*Wells*, pp. 45, 769, 1004, 1102, 1298, 1385; *Billings*, p. 192; G. Gröber, Grundriss, as under Legends in General, above p. 130; G. Paris, Littérature française au Moyen-âge, Paris, 1890, sects. 60–2; Histoire littéraire de la France, vol. xxx; Ency. Brit. under Lancelot'; *Ward*, vol. I, p. 345.]

Paris, P. Romans de la Table Ronde. 8 vols. Paris, 1868–77. [Vol. III.]

Paris, G. Romania, x, 1881, p. 465, XII, 1883, p. 459, XVI, 1887, p. 100.

Malory's Morte Darthur. Ed. H. O. Sommer, vol. III, 1891. [P. 176.]

Rhys, J. Arthurian Legend. Oxford, 1891. [Pp. 127, 145, *passim*.]

Weston, J. L. Legend of Sir Lancelot du Lac. 1901.

—— Three Days' Tournament. 1902.

—— King Arthur and his Knights. 1899; 1905. [P. 38.]

Maynadier, G. H. Arthur of the English Poets. Boston, 1907. [P. 87.]

French Vulgate Lancelot. Ed. H. O. Sommer. [Vols. III, IV, v of Vulgate Version of the Arthurian Romances, Washington, 1910–2.]

Bruce, J. D. Development of the Mort Arthur Theme. Romanic Rev. IV, 1913, p. 403. [See its notes for bibliography.]

—— Composition of Prose Lancelot. Romanic Rev. IX, 1918, pp. 241, 353, x, 1919, pp. 48, 97.

—— Evolution of Arthurian Romance to 1300. 2 vols. Göttingen, 1923–4.

Lot, F. Étude sur le Lancelot en Prose. Paris, 1916.

App, A. J. Lancelot in English Literature. Washington, 1929.

(c) Gawain

[*Wells*, pp. 51, 769, 953, 1004, 1050, 1102, 1168, 1206, 1260, 1298, 1344, 1385; G. Gröber, Grundriss, as above; Histoire littéraire de la France, vols. xxx, xxxIII; Romania, xxxIII, 1904, p. 333.]

Rhys, J. Arthurian Legend. Oxford, 1891.

Weston, J. L. Legend of Sir Gawain. 1897; 1900. [See its bibliography.]

—— Wife of Bath's Tale. Folk-Lore, xII, 1901, p. 373.

—— Sir Gawain and the Grail Castle. 1903.

—— Legend of Sir Perceval. 2 vols. 1906–9. [Vol. I, p. 282 (on English romances).]

—— 'Gawain'. Ency. Brit.

Maynadier, G. H. Wife of Bath's Tale. 1901.

—— Arthur of the English Poets. Boston, 1907.

Bruce, J. D. Evolution of Arthurian Romance to 1300. 2 vols. Göttingen, 1923–4.

Ray, B. K. Character of Gawain. Dacca University Bulletin, XI, 1926.

(d) Perceval

[*Wells*, pp. 71, 772, 955, 1005, 1103, 1168, 1207, 1298, 1386; *Billings*, p. 134; Ency. Brit.; G. Paris, Littérature française au Moyen-âge, Paris, 1890, sects. 59, 60. See also under Holy Grail below.]

Hertz, W. Die Sage vom Parzival und dem Gral. Breslau, 1882.

—— Die Sage vom Parzival. Stuttgart, 1884.

Nutt, A. Studies on the Legend of the Holy Grail. 1888.

Golther, W. Chrestien's Conte del Graal in seinem Verhältniss zum englischen Sir Perceval. Sitzungsber. d. Münch. Akad., Phil.-Hist. Kl. II, 1890, p. 203.

Golther, W. Ursprung und Entwicklung der Sage vom Parzival. Bayreuther Blätter, vii, 1891.
—— Parzival und der Gral in der Dichtung des Mittelalters. Stuttgart, 1925.
Harper, G. M. Legend of the Holy Grail. PMLA. viii, 1893, p. 77.
Newell, W. W. Legend of the Holy Grail. Cambridge, U.S.A. 1902.
Weston, J. L. Legend of Sir Perceval. 2 vols. 1906–9. [See its bibliography.]
Maynadier, G. H. Arthur of the English Poets. Boston, 1907. [P. 107.]
Strucks, C. Der junge Parzival. Münster, 1910.
Woods, G. B. Reclassification of the Perceval Romances. PMLA. xxvii, 1912, p. 524.
Bruce, J. D. Evolution of Arthurian Romance to 1300. 2 vols. Göttingen, 1923–4.

(e) The Holy Grail

[Wells, pp. 74, 773, 1005, 1103, 1207, 1299, 1387; Histoire littéraire de la France, vol. xxx; G. Gröber, Grundriss, vol. ii¹, Strasburg, 1902, pp. 502, 724, 996, 1195; Ency. Brit. See also under Perceval, above]

Birch-Hirschfeld, A. Die Sage vom Gral. Leipzig, 1877.
Nutt, A. Studies on the Legend of the Holy Grail. 1888.
—— Legends of the Holy Grail. 1902.
Harper, G. M. Legend of the Holy Grail. PMLA. viii, 1893, p. 77.
Wechssler, E. Die Sage vom Heiligen Gral. Halle, 1898. [See its bibliography.]
Kempe, D. Legend of the Holy Grail. EETS. Ex. Ser. 1905.
Maynadier, G. H. Arthur of the English Poets. Boston, 1907. [P. 106.]
Peebles, R. The Legend of Longinus. Bryn Mawr, 1911.
Weston, J. L. Quest of the Holy Grail. 1913. [General survey of theories.]
—— From Ritual to Romance. Cambridge, 1920.
Rosenberg, A. Longinus in England. Berlin, 1917.
Nitze, W. Chronology of Grail Romances. MP. xvii, 1919–20, pp. 151, 605; Manly Anniversary Studies, Chicago, 1923.
Bruce, J. D. Evolution of Arthurian Romance to 1300. 2 vols. Göttingen, 1923–4.
Golther, W. Parzival und der Gral in der Dichtung. Stuttgart, 1925.
Jaffray, R. King Arthur and the Holy Grail. 1928.

(f) Tristram

[Wells, pp. 78, 774, 1005, 1103, 1207, 1299, 1387; Histoire littéraire de la France, vol. xix,

p. 687; Romania, xv, 1886, p. 481, xvi, 1887 p. 288, xvii, 1888, p. 603, xviii, 1889, pp. 322 510; P. de Julleville, Histoire de la Langue e de la Littérature françaises, vol. i, Paris, 1896 p. 259 and bibliography, p. 340; G. Paris Littérature française au Moyen-âge, Paris 1890, sect. 56; Ency. Brit.; G. Gröber, Grund riss, vol. ii¹, Strasburg, 1902, pp. 470, 489 490, 492, 499, 593, 726, 999, 1006.]

Michel, F. Tristan: Recueil de ce qui reste de Poèmes relatifs à ses Aventures. 3 vols 1835–9.
Golther, W. Die Sage von Tristan un Isolde. Munich, 1887. [Origin and develop ment.]
—— Tristan und Isolde in den Dichtunge des Mittelalters und der neuen Zeit. Leip zig, 1907.
—— Zeitschrift für romanische Philologie xii, 1888, p. 348; Zeitschrift für franzö sische Sprache und Literatur, xxii, 1900 p. 1.
Paris, G. Poèmes et Légendes du Moyen Âge Paris, 1900. [P. 113.]
Bossert, A. La Légende chevaleresque d Tristan et Iseult. Paris, 1902.
Maynadier, G. H. Arthur of the Englis Poets. Boston, 1907. [P. 153.]
Bruce, J. D. Evolution of Arthurian Romanc to 1300. 2 vols. Göttingen, 1923–4.
Kelemina, J. Geschichte der Tristansage Vienna, 1923.
Ranke, F. Tristan und Isold. Munich, 1925

(3) The Early Chronicle Treatments

(a) Nennius

[Wells, pp. 30, 767, 1004, 1297, 1384; DNB. Ency. Brit.; J. D. Bruce, Evolution o Arthurian Romance, Göttingen, 1923 (index) Chambers, as below. See also p. 100 above]

Historia Britonum. Ed. T. Mommsen, Monu menta Germaniae Historica, vol. xiii, Berlin 1898, p. 111; tr. J. A. Giles (in Six Ol English Chronicles, 1848, 1901).

Studies.
de la Borderie, A. L'Histoire Britonum Paris, 1883. [Summary of earlier criticism
Zimmer, H. Nennius Vindicatus. Berlin 1893.
Zimmer, H. and Mommsen, T. Neues Archi d. Gesells. für ältere deutsche Geschicht kunde, xix, 1894, pp. 283, 436.
Thurneysen, R. Zeitschrift für deutsch Philologie, xxviii, 1896, p. 80.
Feuerhard, P. Geoffrey of Monmouth un das Alte Testament. Halle, 1915.
Chambers, Sir E. K. Arthur of Britain. 1927 [Index.]

(b) Geoffrey of Monmouth

[*Wells*, pp. 30, 767, 1004, 1101, 1167, 1205, 1260, 1297, 1344, 1384; Chambers, as below; Griscom, as below. See also p. 285 below.]

Historia Regum Britanniae. Ed. A. Schulz (San-Marte), Halle, 1853; ed. A. Griscom, New York, 1929; tr. J. A. Giles (in Six Old English Chronicles,1848,1901); tr. S.Evans, 1904 (Everyman's Lib.).

Vita Merlini. Ed. W. H. Black, 1830; ed. T. Wright and F. Michel, 1837; ed. J. J. Parry, Illinois University Stud. x, no. 3, 1925.

Studies. [See DNB.; *Ward*, vol. I, p. 203; CHEL. vol. I, pp. 245, 257, 266; Griscom's edn, above.]

Fletcher, R. H. Two Notes on Historia Regum Britanniae. PMLA. xvi, 1901, p. 461.

—— Arthurian Materials in the Chronicles. Harvard Stud. x, 1906.

Jones, W. L. Geoffrey of Monmouth and the Legend of Arthur. Quart. Rev. July 1906.

Leach, H. G. Publication of Prophecies of Merlin. MP. viii, 1911, p. 607.

—— Angevin Britain and Scandinavia. Cambridge, U.S.A. 1921. [P. 130.]

Tausenfreund, E. G. H. Vergil und Gottfried von Monmouth. Halle, 1913.

Feuerhard, P. Geoffrey of Monmouth und das Alte Testament. Halle, 1915.

Bond, R. W. MLR. xi, 1916, p. 347.

Greulich, E. F. Die Arthur-Sage in der Historia Regum Britanniae. Halle, 1916.

Leitzmann, A. Bemerkungen. Archiv, cxxxiv, 1916, p. 373.

Brandenburg, H. Galfrid von Monmouth und die frühmittelenglischen Chronisten. Berlin, 1918.

Entwistle, W. J. Geoffrey of Monmouth and Spanish Literature. MLR.xvii,1922,p.381.

Matter, H. Englische Grundungssagen von Geoffrey of Monmouth bis zur Renaissance. Anglistische Forschungen, lviii, 1922.

Gordon, G. Trojans in Britain. E. & S. ix, 1923, p. 9.

Chambers, Sir E. K. Date. RES. i, 1925, p. 431, iii, 1927, p. 332.

—— Arthur of Britain. 1927. [Pp. 20, 53, 284.]

Parry, J. J. Date of Vita Merlini. MP. xxii, 1925, p. 413.

—— Celtic Tradition and the Vita Merlini. PQ. iv, 1925, p. 193.

Flower, R. RES. ii, 1926, p. 230.

Geoffrey's Purpose in developing Arthur. Speculum, ii, 1927, pp. 33, 317, 448, 449, iii, 1928, p. 16.

(c) Wace

[See G. Paris, Littérature française au Moyen-âge, Paris, 1890, sect. 93; G. Gröber, Grundriss, vol. ii¹, Strasburg, 1902, p. 635.]

Roman de Brut or Geste des Bretons. Ed. Le Roux de Lincy, Rouen, 2 vols. 1836–8.

Morte Arthur. Tr. A. Boyle, 1912 (Everyman's Lib.). [Includes trn of Arthur matter in Wace.]

(d) Layamon's Brut

[*Wells*, pp. 32, 191, 792, 1007, 1052, 1109, 1169, 1212, 1262, 1303, 1346, 1391. See also under Chronicles, pp. 163–5.]

(4) THE ROMANCES IN ENGLISH

(a) Arthour and Merlin

[*Wells*, pp. 41, 768, 1004, 1102, 1385; *Billings*, p. 111.]

MSS. 1, Auchinleck (Nat. Lib. Scotland, 19.2.1); 2, Harley 6223; 3, Lincoln's Inn Lib. 150; 4, Percy Folio (BM. Add. 27879); 5, Douce 236 (Bodleian).

Editions. 1, W. B. D. Turnbull, Abbotsford Club, 1838; 3, 4, 5, J. W. Hales and F. J. Furnivall, Percy Folio Manuscript, 1867–9, vol. i, pp. 417, 420, 479; all MSS, E. Koelbing, Leipzig, 1890.

Selection. J. Zupitza, Übungsbuch, Vienna, 1922.

Abstract. G. Ellis, Specimens of Early English Metrical Romances, 1848, p. 77.

Translation of part. J. L. Weston, Chief Middle English Poets, Boston, 1914, p. 119.

Studies.

Wheatley, H. B. EETS. x, 1865, p. xvi.

Gaster, M. Jewish Sources of and Parallels to Arthur and Merlin. 1887.

Dunlop, J. History of Prose Fiction. Rev. H. Wilson, 2 vols. 1888. [Vol. i, p. 146.]

Mead, W. E. EETS. cxii, 1899, p. lv.

Holthausen, F. Text-notes. Ang. Bbl. xxxi, 1920, p. 198.

(b) Sir Tristrem

[*Wells*, pp. 79, 775, 1105, 1104, 1299; *Billings*, p. 85.]

MS. Auchinleck (Nat. Lib. Scotland, 19.2.1). Ed. Sir W. Scott, Edinburgh, 1804; ed. with Norse, E. Koelbing, Heilbronn, 2 vols. 1878–82; ed. G. P. MacNeill, STS. 1886.

Selections. E. Mätzner, Altenglische Sprachproben, 2 pts. Berlin, 1867–1900; F. Kluge, Lesebuch, Halle, 1904; G. Eyre-Todd, Early Scottish Poetry, Glasgow, 1901; A. Brandl and O. Zippel, Mittelenglische Sprach- und Literaturproben, Berlin, 1917.

Translation. J. L. Weston, Chief Middle English Poets, Boston, 1914, p. 141.

Studies. [*ten Brink*, vol I, p. 238; *Schofield*, p. 208; Histoire littéraire de la France, vol. XIX, p. 687. See also under Tristram, above, p. 132.]

Michel, F. Tristan. Vol. I, 1835.

Bossert, A. Tristan et Iseult. Paris, 1865 [P. 88.]

Heinzel, R. Anzeiger für deutsches Alterthum, VIII, 1882, p. 212, XIV, 1888, p. 272.

Deutschbein, M. Studien zur Sagengeschichte Englands. Cöthen, 1906. [P. 169.]

Skeat, W. W. Romance of Sir Tristram. Scottish Hist. Rev. Oct. 1908.

Henderson, T. F. Scottish Vernacular Literature. Edinburgh, 1910 (3rd edn). [P. 25.]

[See also notes in Scottish Hist. Rev. I, 1904, p. 55; E. Studien, XIII, 1889, p. 133; Ang. XXXIX, 1915, p. 373, XLI, 1917, p. 182, LVIII, 1934, p. 374; verse, Romanic Rev. VII, 1916, pp. 243, 271; Ang. Bbl. XXXIX, 1928, p. 183.]

(c) Ywain and Gawain

[*Wells*, pp. 65, 771, 1103, 1207, 1345, 1386; *Billings*, p. 153.]

MS. Cotton, Galba E IX. Ed. J. Ritson, Ancient English Metrical Romances, 1802, vol. I, p. 1, vol. III, pp. 219, 437; ed. G. Schleich, Leipzig, 1887. [For collation of MS see E. Studien, XII, 1889, p. 139.]

Translation of part. J. L. Weston, Chief Middle English Poets, Boston, 1914, p. 228.

Studies. [*Ward*, vol. I, p. 392; *Schofield*, p. 230. See on French Yvain: W. Foerster, 3rd edn, Halle, 1906; G. Gröber, Grundriss, 2nd edn, Strasburg, 1902, vol. II¹, p. 501; G. Paris, Littérature française au Moyen-âge, Paris, 1890, sect. 57; R. Zenker, Ivainstudien, Halle, 1921.]

Ritson, J. Dissertation on Romance and Minstrelsy. [In Ancient English Metrical Romances, vol. I, 1802.]

Koelbing, E. Reddara Sögur. Strasburg, 1872. [Introduction.]

Steinbach, G. P. Der Einfluss des Crestien de Trois auf die altenglische Literatur. Leipzig, 1886.

Dunlop, J. History of Prose Fiction. Rev. H. Wilson, 2 vols. 1888. [Vol. I, p. 266.]

Schleich, G. Über das Verhältnis der mittelenglischen Romance Ywain und Gawain zu ihrer altfranzösischen Quelle. Berlin, 1889. [Source. See Ang. XII, 1889, p. 479; E. Studien, XV, 1891, p. 429.]

Weston, J. L. Ywain and Gawain and Le Chevalier au Lion. Mod. Lang. Quart. II, 1899, p. 98, III, 1900, p. 194.

Brown, A. C. L. Iwain; Study in Origins of Arthurian Romance. Harvard Stud. VIII, 1903.

Brown, A. C. L. Knight of the Lion. PMLA. XX, 1905, p. 673.

Brodeur, A. G. Grateful Lion. PMLA. XXXIX, 1924, p, 485.

(d) Libeaus Desconus

[*Wells*, pp. 69, 772, 1103, 1207, 1261, 1298, 1386; *Billings*, p. 184.]

MSS. 1, Cotton, Caligula A II; 2, Lincoln's Inn Lib. 150; 3, Royal Lib. Naples XIII B 29 (see T. Wright and J. O. Halliwell[-Phillipps], Reliquiae Antiquae, vol. II, 1843, pp. 58, 65); 4, Ashmole 61 (Bodleian); 5, Lambeth 306; 6, Percy Folio (BM. Add. 27879).

Editions. 1, J. Ritson, Ancient English Metrical Romances, vol. II, 1802, p. 1; C. Hippeau, Le Bel Inconnu, Paris, 1860, p. 241; 6, J. W. Hales and F. J. Furnivall, Percy Folio Manuscript, vol. II, 1867, p. 405; all MSS, M. Kaluza, Leipzig, 1890.

Selection. G. Sampson, Cambridge Book of Prose and Verse, 1924.

Translation. J. L. Weston, Sir Cleges, Sir Libeaus Desconus, 1902.

Studies. [*Ward*, vol. I, p. 400; *Schofield*, p. 226; G. Gröber, Grundriss, Strasburg, 1902, vol. II¹, p. 513. For origin, etc., see E. Studien, I, 1877, pp. 121, 362; Histoire littéraire de la France, vol. XXX, p. 171, especially p. 185; Romania, XV, 1886, p. 1; A. Mennung, Le Bel Inconnu, Halle, 1880; W. H. Schofield, Harvard Stud. IV, 1895. For authorship see G. Sarrazin's edn of Octavian, Heilbronn, 1885, p. XXV; E. Studien, XXII, 1896, p. 331; DNB. under 'Thomas Chestre'; M. Kaluza, Studien, XVIII, 1893, p. 165. See also under Sir Launfal, p. 152 below.]

Magoun, F. P. Source of Sir Thopas. PMLA. XLII, 1927, p. 833.

Dickson, A. PMLA. XLIII, 1928, p. 570.

Trounce, A. McI. The English Tail-Rhyme Romances. Medium Aevum, I, II, III, 1932–4.

(e) Joseph of Arimathie

[*Wells*, pp. 75, 774, 1050, 1103, 1299, 1887; *Billings*, p. 96.]

MS. Vernon (Bodleian 3938). Ed. W. W. Skeat, EETS. 1871.

Studies. [For versification see K. Luick, Ang. XI, 1888, p. 569; *Wells*, p. 800. For dialect, place of origin, see J. R. Hulbert, MP. XIX, 1921, p. 1; R. J. Menner, PMLA. XXXVII, 1922, p. 503.]

Dunlop, J. History of Prose Fiction. Rev. H. Wilson, 2 vols. 1888. [Vol. I, p. 159.]

(f) Sir Gawayne and the Grene Knight

[*Wells*, pp. 54, 770, 953, 1004, 1050, 1102, 1168, 1206, 1260, 1298, 1345, 1385; *Billings*, p. 160; Kittredge, as below. See also under The Pearl Poet, p. 201 below.]

MS. Cotton, Nero A x 4. Ed. Sir F. Madden, Bannatyne Club, 1839; ed. R. Morris, EETS. 1864, rev. 1869, and by Sir I. Gollancz, 1897, 1912; ed. facs. Sir I. Gollancz, EETS. 1922; ed. J. R. R. Tolkien and E. V. Gordon, Oxford, 1925.

Selections. E. Mätzner, Altenglische Sprachproben, 2 pts, Berlin, 1867–1900; F. Kluge, Lesebuch, Halle, 1904; A. S. Cook, Literary Middle English Reader, Boston, 1915; A. Brandl and O. Zippel, Mittelenglische Sprach- und Literaturproben, Berlin, 1917; K. Sisam, Fourteenth Century Verse and Prose, Oxford, 1921; G. Sampson, Cambridge Book of Prose and Verse, 1924.

Translations. (Prose condensed) J. L. Weston, 1898; (literal) E. J. B. Kirtlan, 1912, (prose) 1913; (verse) J. L. Weston, Romance, Vision and Satire, Boston, 1912; (prose) W. A. Neilson and K. G. T. Webster, Chief British Poets, Boston, 1916 (also in trn of Piers Plowman, 1917); (original metre) S. O. Andrew, 1929; (prose) G. H. Gerould, Old English and Medieval Literature, New York, 1929.

Studies. [*ten Brink*, vol. i, p. 337; *CHEL*, vol. i, p. 325: *Ward*, vol. i, p. 487; Histoire littéraire de la France, vol. xxx, p. 71.]

Versification.

Fuhrmann, J. Die alliterirenden Sprachformeln. Kiel, 1886.

Kuhnke, B. Die alliterirende Langzeile. Königsberg, 1899. [Also in M. Kaluza's Studien zur germanischen Alliterationsvers, vol. iv, Weimar, 1900.]

Fischer, J. Die stabende Langzeile. BBA. xi, 1901.

Thomas, J. Die alliterirende Langzeile. Jena, 1908.

ten Brink, B. Stab und Wort im Gawain. SEP. lix, 1920.

Emerson, O. F. Imperfect Lines. MP. xix, 1921, p. 131.

[See also Ang, i, 1878, p. 417, xi, 1888, p. 572, xviii, 1896, p. 83.]

Language

Schwahn, F. Die Conjugation in Sir Gawain. Strasburg, 1884.

Fick, W. Zum mittelenglischen Gedicht von der Perle. Kiel, 1885.

Knigge, F. Die Sprache des Dichters von Sir Gawain. Marburg, 1885.

Kullnick, M. Studien über den Wortschatz in Sir Gawayne. Berlin, 1902.

Wright, E. M. Vocabulary. E. Studien, xxxvi, 1906, p. 209.

Schmittbetz, K. Das Adjektiv. Bonn, 1908. [Also Ang. xxxii, 1909, pp. 1, 163, 359.]

Brett, C. Notes. MLR. viii, 1913, p. 160, x, 1915, p. 188.

Reicke, C. Untersuchungen über den Stil. Königsberg, 1906.

Day, M. Weak Verb. MLR. xiv, 1919, p. 413. [See also Dialect below.]

Text-notes, interpretation.

[JEGP. xxi, 1922, p. 363; TLS. 20, 27 Jan., 3 Feb., 17 March 1927: MLN. xxxvi, 1921, p. 312, xliv, 1929, p. 249; MLR. xiv, 1919, p. 7, xv, 1920, p. 77; E. Studien, xlvii, 1913, p. 311; *Wells*, p. 1206.]

Dialect, place of origin, author, etc.

[J. R. Hulbert, MP. xix, 1921, p. 1; R. J. Menner, PMLA. xxxvii, 1922, p. 503; M. S. Serjeantson. RES. iii, 1927, p. 327].

Trautmann, M. Über die Verfasser und Entstehungszeit einiger alliterirender Gedichte. Leipzig, 1876. [Also Ang. i, 1878, p. 177.]

Thomas, M. C. Sir Gawayne and the Green Knight. Zürich, 1883.

Steinbach, G. P. Der Einfluss des Crestien de Troies auf die altenglische Literatur. Leipzig, 1886. [P. 48.]

Bruce, J. D. Breaking of the Deer. E. Studien, xxxii, 1903, p. 23.

Chambers, R. W. On vv. 697–702. MLR. ii, 1906–7, p. 167.

Hamilton, G. L. Capados and Date. MP. v, 1908, p. 365.

Jackson, I. Sir Gawain as a Garter Poem. Ang. xxxvii, 1913, p. 391.

Hulbert, J. R. Beheading game, lady, green chapel, green lace, pentangle. MP. xiii, 1915, pp. 433, 689.

—— The Name of the Grene Knight. [In Manly Anniversary Studies, Chicago, 1923, p. 12.]

Kittredge, G. L. Gawain and the Green Knight. Cambridge, U.S.A. 1916. [See its bibliography.]

Jahrmann, G. Syr Gawayne and the Grene Knyght und Stuckens Gawân. Die neueren Sprachen, xxvi, 1919, p. 405.

Sundén, K. F. Några Förbisedda Skand. Lånord i Sir Gawayne. Gotenburg, 1920.

von Schaubert, E. Der englische Ursprung von Syr Gawayn and the Grene Knyʒt. E. Studien, lvii, 1923, p. 330.

Barrow, S. F. Medieval Society Romances. New York, 1924. [P. 122.]

Förster, M. Name des Green Knight. Archiv, cxlvii, 1924, p. 194.

Savage, H. L. Significance of Hunting-scenes. JEGP. xxvii, 1928, p. 1.

Savage, H. L. MLN. xlvi, 1931, p. 455; PMLA. xlvi, 1931, p. 169, xlix, 1934, p. 232. [Notes.]

Andrew, S. O. RES. vi, 1930, p. 175. [Text.]

Oakden, J. P. Alliterative Poetry in Middle English. Manchester, 1930, pp. 72, 153, 251, 257, 261.

Buchanan, A. The Irish Framework. PMLA. xlvii, 1932, p. 315.

King, R. W. MLR. xxix, 1934. [Verses 2414 ff.]

Smith, J. H. Gawain's Leap. MLN. xlix, 1934. [Verse 2316.]

Wright, E. M. JEGP. xxxiv, 1935, pp. 157, 339. [Interpretation and vocabulary.]

(g) Awntyrs off Arthure

[Wells, pp. 61, 771, 954, 1004, 1050, 1102, 1206, 1260, 1298, 1344, 1386; Billings, p. 173.]

MSS. 1, Ireland (Hale, Lancs); 2, Thornton (Lincoln Cathedral Lib. A, 5, 2); 3, Douce 324 (Bodleian); 4, Lambeth 491 (see Archiv, lxxxvi, 1891, p. 385).

Editions. 1, J. Robson, Three Early English Metrical Romances, 1842; 2, D. Laing, Select Remains of the Ancient Popular Poetry of Scotland, 1822, rev. J. Small, 1885, rev. W. C. Hazlitt, vol. i, 1895, p. 4; Sir F. Madden, Syr Gawayne, Bannatyne Club, 1839, pp. 95, 326; 3, J. Pinkerton, Scotish Poems, vol. iii, 1792, p. 197; all MSS, F. J. Amours, STS. 1892–7.

Translation. J. L. Weston, Romance, Vision and Satire, Boston, 1912, p. 109.

Studies. [G. Gröber, Grundriss, vol. ii¹, Strasburg, 1902, p. 519; Histoire littéraire de la France, vol. xxx, p. 96; Schofield, p. 218. See also Huchown Discussion, under Morte Arthure, below.]

Trautmann, M. Author. Ang. i, 1878, p. 129.

Lübke, H. Awntyrs of Arthure. MSS., Metre, Author. Berlin, 1883.

Verse. Ang. xii, 1889, p. 452.

Neilson, G. Crosslinks between Pearl and The Awntyrs of Arthure. Scottish Antiquary, xvi, 1902, p. 67.

Athenaeum, 1903, i, pp. 498, 626, 657, 689, 754, 816, ii, p. 221.

Stanza. Romanic Rev. vii, 1916, pp. 243, 271.

Dialect, Place of Origin. J. R. Hulbert, MP. xix, 1921, p. 1; R. J. Menner, PMLA. xxxvii, 1922, p. 503; M. S. Sergeantson, RES. iii, 1927, p. 328.

Holthausen, F. Text-notes. Ang. Bbl. xxxvi, 1925, p. 187.

Andrew, S. O. Huchoun's Works. RES. v, 1929, p. 14.

Oakden, J. P. Alliterative Poetry in Middle English. Manchester, 1930, pp. 113, 217.

Dickins, B. Leeds Stud. no. 2, 1933, p. 62, no. 3, 1934, p. 30; TLS. 21 Dec. 1933, p. 909. [Ireland MS.]

Hooper, A. G. Leeds Stud. no. 3, 1934, p. 37, no. 4, 1935. [Lambeth MS; dialect, author.]

(h) Arthur

[Wells, pp. 35, 767; Billings, p. 190.]

MS. Latin chronicle of British kings, Marquis of Bath. Ed. F. J. Furnivall, EETS. 1864.

Study

Bülbring, K. On Verbs. QF. lxiii, 1889, p. 49.

(i) Morte Arthure (Alliterative)

[Wells, pp. 36, 767, 1004, 1101, 1206, 1260, 1297, 1344, 1384; Billings, p. 181.]

MS. Thornton (Lincoln Cathedral Lib. A, 5, 2). Ed. J. O. Halliwell[-Phillipps], 1847; ed. G. G. Perry and E. Brock, EETS. 1865, new edn, 1871; ed. M. M. Banks, New York, 1900 (notes on glossary, Mod. Lang. Quart. vi, 1906, p. 64); ed. E. Björkman, Heidelberg, 1915.

Selections. R. Wülcker, Lesebuch, 2 pts, Halle, 1874–9; A. Brandl and O. Zippel, Mittelenglische Sprach- und Literaturproben, Berlin, 1917; G. Sampson, Cambridge Book of Prose and Verse, 1924.

Translations. A. Boyle, 1912 (Everyman's Lib.); part, J. L. Weston, Romance, Vision and Satire, Boston, 1912.

Studies. [ten Brink, vol. iii, p. 49; Schofield, p. 253.]

Lübke, H. Awntyrs of Arthure. Berlin, 1883. [P. 30.]

Branscheid, P. Die Quellen. Ang. Anz. viii, 1885, p. 179.

Luick, K. Verse. Ang. xi, 1889, p. 585.

Malory's Morte Darthur. Ed. H. O. Sommer, vol. iii, 1891, p. 148.

Wülcker, R. P. Die Arthursage in der englischen Literatur. Leipzig, 1895. [P. 12.]

Mennicken, F. Versbau und Sprache. BBA. v, 1900.

Neilson, G. Earl of Brittany. Baulked Coronation. N. & Q. 30 Aug., 15, 22 Nov. 1902.

—— Viscount of Rome. Three Dates. Annals. Athenaeum, 27 Dec. 1902; Scottish Antiquary, xvi, 1902; Antiquary, xxxviii, 1902, pp. 73, 229.

Reicke, C. Untersuchungen über dem Stil. Königsberg, 1906.

Griffith, R. H. Malory, Morte Arthure and Fierabras. Ang. xxxii, 1909, p. 389.

Björkman, E. Morte Arthure and its Vocabulary. [In Minneskrift tillägnad Axel Erdmann, Upsala, 1913, p. 343.]

—— Alliterative Text. Ang. xxxix, 1915, p. 253.

Bruce, J. D. Development of the Morte Arthure Theme. Romanic Rev. iv, 1913, p. 403.

Inman, J. A. and Neilson, G. Athenaeum, Sept., Oct., Dec. 1916, Feb. 1917.

Holthausen, F. Names. Textual Criticism. Ang. Bbl. xxxiv, 1923, p. 91, xxxvi, 1925, p. 188.

Andrew, S. O. Dialect. RES. v, 1929, p. 16.

Oakden, J. P. Alliterative Poetry in Middle English. Manchester, 1930, pp. 63, 153, 255.

Cagleson, H. PMLA. xlvii, 1932, p. 344. [Costume.]

Koziol, H. E. Studien, lxvii, 1932, p. 171. [Author.]

O'Loughlin, J. L. N. The Middle English Alliterative Morte Arthure. Medium Aevum, iv, 1935, p. 153.

Huchown Discussion.

[For bibliography see W. Geddie, STS. 1908, p. 40; *Wells*, pp. 400, 826, 1018, 1124, 1271, 310.]

MacCracken, H. N. Summary. PMLA. xxv, 1910, p. 507.

Jusserand, J. J. Literary History of the English People. 3rd edn, vol. i, New York, 1926, p. 526. [Summary.]

Trautmann, M. Ang. i, 1878, p. 109.

Brandes, H. Die mittelenglische Destruction of Troy und ihre Quelle. E. Studien, viii, 1885, p. 410.

McNeill, G. P. Huchown of the Awle Ryale. Scottish Rev. April 1888.

Amours, F. J. Scottish Alliterative Poems in Riming Stanzas. STS. 1892–7. [Introductions.]

Brown, J. T. T. Poems of D. Rate. Scottish Antiquary, xii, 1897, p. 5.

—— Pistill of Susan. Athenaeum, 23 Aug. 1902.

—— Huchown of the Awle Ryale. Glasgow, 1902.

Neilson, G. Sir Hew of Eglintoun and Huchown off the Awle Ryale. Proc. Philosophical Soc. Glasgow, xxxii, 1900–1, p. 111.

—— Crosslinks between Pearl and The Awntyrs of Arthure. Scottish Antiquary, xvi, 1902, p. 67.

Neilson, G. Athenaeum, 1900, 1901, 1902, 1903, 1916, 1917 (see indexes).

—— Three Footnotes. [In Furnivall Miscellany, Oxford, 1901, p. 383.]

—— Huchown of the Awle Ryale. Glasgow, 1902.

—— Early Literary MSS. 1902. [P. 265.]

—— Barbour's Bruce and Buik of Alexander. Scottish Antiquary, xvi, 1902, p. 206. [See *Wells* for criticisms.]

—— Scottish Antiquary, xvii, 1903, p. 51.

Gollancz, Sir I. Recent Theories. Athenaeum, 23 Nov. 1901.

—— CHEL. vol. i, 1907, p. 333. [See also P. Giles, CHEL. vol. ii, 1908, p. 115, 450.]

Millar, J. H. Literary History of Scotland. 1903. [P. 8.]

Henderson, T. F. Scottish Vernacular Literature. Edinburgh, 1910 (3rd edn). [P. 31.]

Björkman, E. E. Studien, xlviii, 1914, p. 171.

Inman, J. A. Athenaeum, Sept. 1916, p. 423.

Andrew, S. O. Huchown's Works. RES. v, 1929, p. 12.

[See too under Pistill of Susan (p. 189 below), Pearl Poet (p. 201 below), Sir Gawayne (p. 135 above), Pearl (pp. 201–2 below), Purity (pp. 202–3 below), Golagrus (p. 139 below), Awntyrs off Arthure (above), Wars of Alexander (p. 143 below), Alexander Buik (p. 144 below), Destruction of Troy (pp. 144–5 below), Barbour's Bruce (pp. 166–7 below), Titus and Vespasian (pp. 157–8 below); and Alliterative Verse, under The Thre Ages, Wynnere, and Piers Plowman Series (pp. 195–6 below).]

(j) Sir Percyvelle of Galles

[*Wells*, pp. 72, 772, 955, 1005, 1103, 1168, 1207, 1298, 1386; *Billings*, p. 125; *Griffith*, below.]

MS. Thornton (Lincoln Cathedral Lib. A, 5, 2). Ed. J. O. Halliwell[-Phillipps], Thornton Romances, 1841, p. 1; ed. F. S. Ellis, 1895 (after Halliwell); ed. J. Campion and F. Holthausen, Heidelberg, 1913.

Abstract. Lady C. Guest, Mabinogion, vol. i, 1849, p. 398; Histoire littéraire de la France, vol. xxx, p. 255; A. Nutt, Studies on the Legend of the Holy Grail, 1888, p. 37.

Translation. J. L. Weston, Chief Middle English Poets, Boston, 1914, p. 236.

Studies. [G. Gröber, Grundriss, vol. ii[1], Strasburg, 1902 p. 504. On verse see Ang. xii, 1889, p. 437; H. Paul, Grundriss der germanischen Philologie, vol. ii[1], Strasburg, 1892, p. 168; Romanic Rev. vii, 1916, pp. 243, 271. See also Harper, Golther, Paris, Strucks, Newell, Woods, Weston, under Perceval, above p. 132.]

Steinbach, G. P. Über den Einfluss des Crestien de Trois auf die altenglische Literatur. Leipzig, 1885.

Ellinger, J. Syntaktische Untersuchungen. Troppau, 1893.

Griffith, R. H. Sir Perceval of Galles. Chicago, 1911. [Sources; see its bibliography.]

Pace, R. B. Source. PMLA. xxxii, 1917, p. 598.

Brown, A. C. L. Grail and English Sir Perceval.
MP. xvi, 1919, p. 553, xvii, 1919, p. 361,
xviii, 1920–1, pp. 201, 661, xxii, 1924,
pp. 79, 113.
Finsterbusch, F. Der Versbau der mittel-
englischen Dichtungen Sir Perceval of
Gales und Sir Degrevant. Vienna, 1919.
Holthausen, F. Text-notes. Ang. xliv, 1920,
p. 78.
Sparnaay, H. Verschmelzung legendarischer
und weltlicher Motive in der Poesie des
Mittelalters. Groningen, 1922.
Bruce, J. D. Evolution of Arthurian Ro-
mance to 1300. 2 vols. Göttingen, 1923–4.
[Vol. i, p. 309.]

(k) Avowynge of King Arthur

[Wells, pp. 64, 771, 1004, 1102, 1261, 1298,
1386; Billings, p. 178.]
MS. Ireland (Hale, Lancs). Ed. J. Robson,
Three Early English Metrical Romances, 1842.
Studies. [Histoire littéraire de la France,
vol. xxx, p. 111. On verse see Romanic Rev.
vii, 1916, pp. 243, 271; SEP. l, 1913, p. 511;
Ang. xxxviii, 1914, p. 268, xxxix, 1915,
p. 274.]
Thomas, M. C. Sir Gawayne and the Grene
Knight. Zürich, 1883.
Kittredge, G. L. On de Garlandia. MLN.
viii, 1893, p. 502.
Greenlaw, E. Vows of Baldwin. PMLA. xxi,
1906, p. 575.
Sergeantson, M. S. Dialect. RES. iii, 1927,
p. 328.
Dickins, B. Leeds Stud. no. 2, 1933, p. 62,
no. 3, 1934, p. 30; TLS. 21 Dec. 1933, p. 909.
[MS.]

(l) Le Morte Arthur (Stanzaic)

[Wells, pp. 48, 769, 1004, 1102, 1206, 1298;
Billings, p. 200.]
MS. Harley 2252. Ed. Roxburghe Club,
1819; ed. F. J. Furnivall, 1864; ed. J. D.
Bruce, EETS. 1903; ed. S. B. Hemingway,
Boston, 1912.
Selections. A. Brandl and O. Zippel, Mittel-
englische Sprach- und Literaturproben, Berlin,
1917; G. Sampson, Cambridge Book of Prose
and Verse, 1924.
Abstract. G. Ellis, Specimens of Early
English Metrical Romances, 1848, p. 143.
Translation of parts. J. L. Weston, Chief
Middle English Poets, Boston, 1914, p. 262;
A. Boyle, Morte Arthur, 1912, p. 95.
Studies. [Schofield, pp. 238, 255; Ward,
vol. i, p. 405. On sources relating to Malory
see Ang. xxiii, 1899, p. 67, xxix, 1905,
p. 529, xxx, 1906, p. 209.]

Weymouth, R. F. Trans. Philolog. Soc. 1860–1
p. 279.
Branscheid, P. Ang. Anz. viii, 1885, p. 220.
Sommer, H. O. Text-notes. Academy, 15
22 Nov. 1890, pp. 450, 479.
Malory's Morte Darthur. Ed. H. O. Sommer
vol. iii, 1891. [Pp. 220, 249.]
Mead, W. E. Selections from Malory. Boston
1897. [Notes.]
Seyferth, P. Sprache und Metrik. BBA
viii. 1902.

(m) Syre Gawane and the Carle
of Carelyle

MS. Porkington 10, Harlech Lib., Bro
gyntyn, Salop. Ed. Sir F. Madden, Sy
Gawayne, Bannatyne Club, 1839, pp. 187
344.
Studies. [Wells, pp. 59, 770, 1004; Billings
p. 215; Histoire littéraire de la France, vo
xxx, p. 68.]
Hulbert, J. R. MP. xiii, 1916, p. 696.
Kittredge, G. L. Gawain and the Gree
Knight. Cambridge, U.S.A. 1916. [Biblic
graphy and index.]

(n) Henry Lovelich's Merlin

MS. Corpus Christi College Cambridge 80
Ed. E. A. Kock, 3 pts, EETS. Ex. Ser. 1904–32
Studies. [Wells, pp. 45, 768, 1385; Billing
p. 123.]
Arthour and Merlin. Ed. E. Koelbing, Leipzig
1890. [Pp. xviii, clxxx.]

(o) Lovelich's History of the Holy Grail

MS. Corpus Christi College Cambridge 80
Ed. with French original, F. J. Furnivall
Seynt Graal, Roxburghe Club, 1861–3; ed
F. J. Furnivall, 4 pts, EETS. Ex. Ser. 1874–
(pt 5, ed. D. Kempe, EETS. Ex. Ser. 1905
see introduction).
Studies. [Wells, pp. 77, 774; Billings,
109.]
Skeat, W. W. Translator. Athenaeum, 2
Nov., 6 Dec. 1902, pp. 684, 758.
Bradley, H. Harry Lovelich. Athenaeum
1 Nov. 1902, p. 587.

(p) Prose Merlin

MS. University Lib. Cambridge. E
H. B. Wheatley, 3 pts, EETS. 1865–9; e
W. E. Mead, 1899. Selection, ed. L. Cranme
Byng, 1930.
Studies. [Wells, pp. 44, 768, 1206, 1385.]
Richter, G. and Stecher, G. Erklärung un
Textkritik. E. Studien, xx, 1895, p. 34
xxviii, 1900, p. 1.

nscombe, A. Hrethel the Great. N. & Q.
28 April 1923, p. 328.

(q) Golagrus and Gawain

[Wells, pp. 63, 771, 1206, 1344, 1386;
illings, p. 168.]

Edinburgh edn,1508 (copy in Nat.Lib. Scot-
nd). Ed. J.Pinkerton,Scotish Poems, vol.iii,
792, p. 65; ed. Sir F. Madden, Syr Gawayne,
annatyne Club, 1839, pp. 131, 336; ed. M.
rautmann, Ang. ii, 1879, p. 395; ed. F. J.
mours, STS. 1892–7; facs. edn, Edinburgh,
327.

Studies. [Histoire littéraire de la France,
ol. xxx, p. 41; Schofield, p. 220. See also
uchown Discussion, under Morte Arthure,
bove p. 137. For notes see Scottish Hist.
ev. April 1904, p. 296; Hist. Rev. i, 1904,
, 55; Ang. Bbl. xxxvi, 1925, p. 185; Ang.
xxvi, 1912, p. 155.]

rautmann,M. Author. Source. Ang. i,1878,
p. 109, ii, 1879, p. 402.
homas, M. C. Sir Gawayne and the Grene
Knight. Zürich, 1883. [P. 87.]
oltemeyer, O. Über die Sprache. Marburg,
1889.
ahn, O. Zur Verbal- und Nominalflexion
bei den schottischen Dichtern. Berlin,
1889.
uick, K. Ang. xii, 1889, p. 438.
earder, J. W. Über den Gebrauch der Praepositionen. Halle, 1894.
eilson, G. History in Golagrus and Gawain.
Proc. Philosophical Soc. Glasgow, 1902.
ettrick, P. J. The Relation of Golagros and
Gawane to the Old French Perceval.
Washington, 1931.

(r) Weddynge of Sir Gawen

[Wells, pp. 67, 771, 1005, 1103, 1168, 1207,
98, 1386; Billings, p. 117; Sumner's edn,
low.]

MS. Rawlinson C 86 (Bodleian). Ed. Sir
Madden, Syr Gawayne, Bannatyne Club,
39, p. 297; ed. L. Sumner, Smith College
ud. v, 1924, p. 4.

Marriage of Sir Gawain. Percy Folio MS
M. Add. 27879). Ed. Sir F. Madden, Syr
awayne, Bannatyne Club, 1839, p. 288; ed.
W. Hales and F. W. Furnivall, Percy Folio
anuscript, vol. i, 1867, p. 105; ed. T. Percy,
liques of Ancient English Poetry, vol. iii,
94, p. 350; ed. J. Ritson, Ancient English
etrical Romances, vol. i, 1802, p. cx; ed.
J. Child, Scottish and English Ballads,
l. i, Boston, 1857, p. 288.

Studies. [Histoire littéraire de la France,
l. xxx, p. 97; Schofield, p. 224.]

Clouston, W. A. Origins and Analogues.
Chaucer Soc., ser. 2, xxii, 1887, p. 483.
Stokes, W. Analogues. Academy, 23 April
1892, p. 399. [See A. Nutt, Academy,
30 April 1892, p. 425.]
Skeat, W. W. Oxford Chaucer. Vol. iii, 1895.
[P. 447.]
Görbing, F. Ballad, The Marriage of Sir
Gawain. Ang. xxiii, 1900, p. 405.
Weston, J. L. Wife of Bath's Tale. Folk-
Lore, xii, 1901, p. 373.
Maynadier, G. H. Wife of Bath's Tale. 1901.
Kittredge, G. L. Gawain and the Green
Knight. Cambridge, U.S.A. 1916. [P. 269.]

(s) Grene Knight

MS. Percy Folio (BM. Add. 27879). Ed.
Sir F. Madden, Syr Gawayne,Bannatyne Club,
1839, pp. 224, 352; ed. J. W. Hales and F. J.
Furnivall, Percy Folio Manuscript, vol. ii,
1867, p. 56.

Studies. [Wells,pp. 58,770,954,1004,1386;
Billings, p. 209.]
Hulbert, J. R. MP. xiii, 1915, pp. 460, 695,
701, 714 ff.
Kittredge, G. L. Gawain and the Green
Knight. Cambridge, U.S.A. 1916. [Pp. 122,
282, 296.]

(t) Turke and Gowin

MS. Percy Folio (BM. Add. 27879). Ed.
Sir F. Madden, Syr Gawayne,Bannatyne Club,
1839, pp. 243, 355; ed. J. W. Hales and F. J.
Furnivall, Percy Folio Manuscript, vol. i,
1867, p. 88.

Studies. [Wells,pp. 59,770,954,1004,1386;
Billings,p.211; Histoire littérairede la France,
vol. xxx, p. 68.]
Hulbert, J. R. MP. xiii, 1915, pp. 697, 703.
Kittredge, G. L. Gawain and the Green
Knight. Cambridge, U.S.A. 1916. [Pp. 118,
200, 274, 296.]

(u) Jeaste of Syr Gawayne

[Wells, pp. 69, 772; Billings, p. 213.]
MS. Douce 261 (Bodleian). Ed. Sir F.
Madden, Syr Gawayne, Bannatyne Club,1839,
pp. 207, 348.
Bennett, R. E. JEGP. xxxiii, 1934, p. 57.
[Sources.]

(v) Lancelot of the Laik

[Wells, pp. 47, 769, 1102; Billings, p. 192.
See also under Lancelot above, p. 131.]
MS. University Lib. Cambridge Kk.1.5.
Ed. J. Stevenson, Maitland Club, 1839; ed.
W. W. Skeat, EETS. 1865, 1870 (rev.); ed.
M. M. Gray, STS., N.S. ii, 1911.

Selection. R. Wülcker, Lesebuch, 2 pts, Halle, 1874–9.

Studies.

Weston, J. L. Legend of Sir Lancelot du Lac. 1901.

—— Three Days' Tournament. 1902.

(w) Percy Folio Ballads

[On the Carle off Carlile, King Arthur's Death, Sir Lancelot du Lake, and The Legend of King Arthur, see *Wells*, index. All are ptd in Percy's Reliques, and in J. W. Hales and F. J. Furnivall, Percy Folio˙ Manuscript, 1867–9.]

(x) Prose Life of Joseph, De Sancto Joseph, Here Begynneth, A Praysyng

[*Wells*, pp. 77, 774, 1299. All are ptd by W. W. Skeat, EETS. XLIV, 1871.]

B. CHARLEMAGNE ROMANCES

(1) THE LEGENDS IN GENERAL

[Wells, pp. 82, 775, 1104, 1207, 1299, 1387; *Billings*, p. 47; *Ward*, vol. I, p. 546.]

Gautier, L. Les Épopées françaises. Paris, 4 vols. 1878–92.

—— Bibliographie des Chansons de Geste. Paris, 1897.

Paris, G. La Littérature française au Moyen-âge. Paris, 1890. [Sects. 15, 18–32.]

—— Histoire poétique de Charlemagne. Paris, 1905 (2nd edn).

Petit de Julleville, L. Histoire de la Langue et de la Littérature françaises. Vol. I, Paris, 1896. [Ch. 2, bibliography, p. 168.]

Gröber, G. Grundriss der romanischen Philologie. Vol. II[1], Strasburg, 1902. [Pp. 447, 461, 535, 792. See its bibliography.]

Ency. Brit. 'Charlemagne.'

(2) THE ENGLISH LEGENDS

[G. Paris, Littérature française au Moyen-âge, Paris, 1890; G. Paris, Histoire poétique de Charlemagne, Paris, 1905; p. 154; Romania, XI, 1882, p. 149, XIII, 1884, p. 598; *Schofield*, p. 146.]

ten Brink, B. Early English Litterature. Vol. I, 1887. [Pp. 122, 124.]

Saintsbury, G. Flourishing of Romance. Edinburgh, 1897. [P. 22.]

Weston, J. L. The Romance Cycle of Charlemagne. 1901. [See its bibliography.]

Ker, W. P. Epic and Romance. 1908 (2nd edn). [Chs. i, iv.]

Bédier, J. Les Légendes épiques. 4 vols. Paris, 1909–13. [Vols. III, IV.]

Kirschoff. Zur Geschichte der Karlssage in der englischen Litteratur. Marburg, 1913.

Leach, H. G. Angevin Britain and Scand-navia. Cambridge, U.S.A. 1921. [P. 235.]

(3) PARTICULAR PHASES AND HEROES

(a) Otuel

[*Wells*, pp. 90, 776, 1299; *Billings*, p. 67.]

MS. Auchinleck (Nat. Lib. Scotlan 19.2.1). Ed. H. W. B. Nicholson, Abbots ford Club, 1836; ed. S. J. Herrtage, EETS Ex. Ser. 1882, p. 65.

Abstract. G. Ellis, Specimens of Earl English Metrical Romances, 1848, p. 237.

Studies. [See Wächter under Roland an Vernagu below. See also Guessard and Mich lant, edn Fr. Otinel, Paris, 1859; L. Gautie Les Épopées françaises, vol. III, Paris, 188 p. 397, and Bibliographie des Chansons c Geste, Paris, 1897, p. 135; G. Gröber, Grun riss, 2nd edn, vol. II[1], Strasburg, 1902, p. 545

Paris, G. Romania, XI, 1882, p. 151.

—— Histoire littéraire de la France. Vc XXVI, p. 269.

—— Histoire poétique de Charlemagne. Par 1905 (2nd edn).

Treutler, H. Die Otinelsage. E. Studien, 1882, p. 97.

Holthausen, G. Text-notes. Ang. XXI, 188 p. 369.

Rajna, P. Romania, XVIII, 1889, p. 35.

Gragger, J. Zur mittelenglischen 'Sir Otue Dichtung. Graz, 1896.

Koeppel, E. Eine historische Anspielun Archiv, CVII, 1901, p. 392.

(b) Roland and Vernagu

[*Wells*, pp. 88, 776, 1104; *Billings*, p. 58.]

MS. Auchinleck (Nat. Lib. Scotlan 19.2.1). Ed. H. W. B. Nicholson, Abbotsfo Club, 1836; ed. S. J. Herrtage, EETS. E Ser. 1882 (notes, Ang. XXI, 1899, p. 366).

Abstract. G. Ellis, Specimens of Ear English Metrical Romances, 1848, pp. 346, 37

Studies. [L. Gautier, Les Épopées française vol. III, Paris, 1882, p. 283, and Bibliograph des Chansons de Geste, Paris, 1897, p. 17 G. Paris, Histoire poétique de Charlemagr Paris, 1905 (2nd edn), pp. 53, 337; Roman IX, 1880, p. 29, XI, 1882, p. 149.]

Wächter, W. Untersuchungen über Rola and Vernagu und Otuel. Berlin, 1885.

Trounce, A. McI. The English Tail-Rhy Romances. Medium Aevum, I, II, III, 1932–

[For metre see M. Kaluza, edn Libea Desconus, Leipzig, 1890, p. lvii. For vei and place see O. Wilda, Über die örtlic Verbreitung der zwölfzeiligen Schweifrei strophe in England, Breslau, 1887.]

(c) Sege of Melayne

[Wells, pp. 89, 776, 1104; Billings, p. 63.]

MS. BM. Add. 31042. Ed. S. J. Herrtage, EETS. Ex. Ser. 1880.

Abstract. G. Ellis, Specimens of Early English Metrical Romances, 1848, p. 357.

Studies. [L. Gautier, Les Épopées françaises, vol. ii, Paris, 1878. pp. 304, 407, and Bibliographie des Chansons de Geste, Paris, 1897, p. 201; Ward, vol. i, p. 953; Romania, xi, 1882, p. 151.]

Dannenberg, B. Metrik und Sprache der Sege of Melayne. Göttingen, 1890.

Holthausen, F. Text-notes. Ang. xl, 1916, p. 402.

Trounce, A. McI. The English Tail-Rhyme Romances. Medium Aevum, i, ii, iii, 1932–4.

(d) Sir Firumbras

[Wells, pp. 86, 776, 1005, 1104, 1207, 1299; Billings, p. 52.]

MS. Ashmole 33 (Bodleian; see W. H. Black, Catalogue of Ashmole MSS, 1845, p. 14). Ed. S. J. Herrtage, EETS. Ex. Ser. 1879.

Selections. J. Zupitza, Übungsbuch, Vienna, 1922; G. E. MacLean, Reader, New York, 1893.

Studies.

Carstens, B. Zur Dialektbestimmung. Kiel, 1884.

Reichel, C. Die mittelenglische Romanze Sir Fyrumbras und ihr Verhältnis zum altfranzösischen und provenzalischen Fierabras. Breslau, 1892.

Jarnik, H. Studien über Fierebrasdichtungen. Halle, 1903.

Griffith, R. H. Malory and Fierebras. Ang. xxxii, 1909, p. 389.

Fischer, W. Relation of vv. 331–759. Archiv, cxlii, 1921, p. 25.

[Notes. E. Studien, xviii, 1900, p. 270; Ang. iv, 1881, p. 308, vii, 1884, p. 160; MLN. xii, 1897, p. 446.]

French Fierebras. Ed. A. Kroeber and G. Servois, Anciens Poètes de la France, Paris, 1860.

Gröber, G. Die handschriftlichen Gestaltungen der Chanson de Geste Fierebras. Leipzig, 1869.

—— Grundriss der romanischen Philologie. Vol. ii¹, Strasburg, 1902, pp. 539, 541, 545, 1194.

Gautier, L. Les Épopées françaises. 4 vols. Paris, 1878–92. [Vol. iii, p. 381.]

—— Bibliographie des Chansons de Geste. Paris, 1897. [P. 97.]

Bédier, J. Composition de Firumbras. Romania, xvii, 1888, p. 22.

Paris, G. La Littérature française au Moyen-âge. Paris, 1890. [Sects. 24, 37.]

—— Histoire poétique de Charlemagne. Paris, 1905 (2nd edn). [P. 154.]

Stokes, W. Irish Version. Revue Celtique, xix, 1898, pp. 14, 118, 252, 364.

(e) Duke Rowlande and Sir Ottuell

[Wells, pp. 91, 776, 1104, 1299; Billings, p. 71.]

MS. BM. Add. 31042. Ed. S. J. Herrtage, EETS. Ex. Ser. xxxv, 1880, p. 53.

Studies. [Ward, vol. i, p. 954.]

Wilda, O. Über die örtliche Verbreitung der zwölfzeiligen Schweifreimstrophe in England. Breslau, 1887.

Engler, H. Quelle und Metrik. Königsberg, 1901.

Holthausen, F. Text-notes. Ang. xl, 1916, p. 397.

Trounce, A. McI. The English Tail-Rhyme Romances. Medium Aevum, i, ii, iii, 1932–4.

(f) Fillingham Otuel and Firumbras

MS. BM. Add. 37492. Ed. M. J. O'Sullivan, EETS. 1935.

Abstract. G. Ellis, Specimens of Early English Metrical Romances, 1848, pp. 357, 373.

Studies. [Wells, pp. 92, 777, 955, 1299; G. Paris, Histoire poétique de Charlemagne, Paris, 1905 (2nd edn).]

O'Sullivan, M. J. Study of the Fillingham Text of Firumbras and Otuel and Roland. Bryn Mawr, 1927.

(g) Song of Roland

[Wells, pp. 92, 777, 1104; Billings, p. 73.]

MS. Lansdowne 388. Ed. S. J. Herrtage, EETS. Ex. Ser. xxxv, 1879, p. 107 (on text, Ang. iv, 1881, p. 317).

Studies.

Schleich, G. Prolegomena ad Carmen de Rolando Anglicanum. Burg, 1879.

—— Beitrag zum mittelenglischen Roland. Ang. iv, 1881, p. 317.

Wichmann, C. A. Das Abhängigkeitsverhältnis des altenglischen Roland. Münster, 1889.

Leach, H. G. Angevin Britain and Scandinavia. Cambridge, U.S.A. 1921. [P. 285.]

Holthausen, F. Text-notes. Ang. li, 1927, p. 16.

Paris, G. Romania, xi, 1882, p. 151.

—— La Littérature française au Moyen-âge. Paris, 1890. [Sect. 33.]

Paris, G. Histoire poétique de Charlemagne. Paris, 1905 (2nd edn). [P. 155.]

Gautier, L. Bibliographie des Chansons de Geste. Paris, 1897. [Pp. 170, 190, 192.]

Gröber, G. Grundriss der romanischen Philologie. Vol. ii¹, Strasburg, 1902, p. 463.

(h) Sowdone of Babylone

[Wells, pp. 84, 775, 1345, 1387; Billings, p. 47.]

MS. J. E. A. Fenwick, Thurlestane House, Cheltenham; copy of same, Douce 175 (Bodleian). Ed. Roxburghe Club, 1854; ed. E. Hausknecht, EETS. Ex. Ser. 1881.

Abstract. G. Ellis, Specimens of Early English Metrical Romances, 1848, p. 379.

Studies. [On French see Wells, p. 775. See also Sir Firumbras, above, p. 141].

Gautier, L. Les Épopées françaises. 4 vols. Paris, 1878–82. [Vol. iii, p. 366.]

Hausknecht, E. Über Sprache und Quelle. Berlin, 1879.

Paris, G. Histoire poétique de Charlemagne. Paris, 1905 (2nd edn). [P. 154.]

Smyser, B. M. Harvard Stud. xiii, 1931, p. 185, xiv, 1932, p. 339. [Author.]

(i) Charles the Grete

Caxton's edn, 1485. Ed. S. J. Herrtage, 2 pts, EETS. Ex. Ser. 1880–1.

(j) Foure Sonnes of Aymon

Caxton's edn, c. 1489. Ed. O. Richardson, 2 pts, EETS. Ex. Ser. 1884–5.

Studies. [Wells, pp. 95, 777, 1104, 1387.] [Dissertations by Erdmann, Olesch, Schumacher, Seeger, Simon, Boldt, Quegwer. Greifswald, 1913. For French version see L. Gautier, Bibliographie des Chansons de Geste, Paris, 1897, p. 158; G. Gröber, Grundriss, vol. ii¹, Strasburg, 1902, p. 547; Revue des Langues Romanes, xlix, 1908, l, 1909, li, 1910, lii, 1911–2.]

(k) Taill of Rauf Coilȝear

[Wells, pp. 94, 777, 1005, 1104, 1345, 1387; Billings, p. 79.]

Robert Lekpreuik's edn, 1572. Ed. D. Laing, Select Remains of Ancient Popular Poetry of Scotland, Edinburgh, 1821, rev. J. Small, Edinburgh, 1882; rev. W. C. Hazlitt, vol. i, 1895, p. 212; ed. S. J. Herrtage, EETS. 1882; ed. W. H. Browne, Baltimore, 1903.

Selections. W. H. Browne, Selections from Early Scottish Poets, Baltimore, 1896, p. 94.

Studies.

Trautmann, M. Der Dichter Huchown. Ang. i, 1878, p. 139.

Paris, G. Romania, xi, 1882, p. 150.

Tonndorf, R. C. Berlin, 1894.

Henderson, T. F. Scottish Vernacular Literature. Edinburgh, 1910 (3rd edn). [P. 76.]

Kittredge, G. L. Sir Gawain and the Green Knight. Cambridge, U.S.A. 1916. [P. 305.]

(l) Huon of Burdeux

De Worde's edn, c. 1534. Ed. Sir S. Lee 4 pts, EETS. Ex. Ser. 1882–7.

Modern rendering. R. Steele, 1895.

Studies. [Wells, pp. 95, 777, 1104.]

Paris, G. La Littérature française au Moyen-âge. Paris, 1890. [Sect. 25.]

Gautier, L. Bibliographie des Chansons de Geste. Paris, 1897. [P. 132.]

Gröber, G. Grundriss der romanischen Philologie. Vol. ii¹, Strasburg, 1902, p. 549.

Ebert, W. Vergleich der beiden Versionen. Halle, 1917.

C. ROMANCES OF ALEXANDER THE GREAT

(1) The Legends in General

[For bibliography and summary see Wells, pp. 98, 778, 1005, 1105, 1208, 1261, 1300, 1345, 1387; Ward, vol. i, p. 94; H. E. Müller, Die Werke des Pfaffen Lamprecht, Munich, 1923 (excellent bibliography); F. P. Magoun, Gests of King Alexander of Macedon, Cambridge, U.S.A. 1929 (excellent bibliography in notes).]

Meyer, P. Alexandre le Grand dans la Littérature du Moyen Âge. 2 vols. Paris, 1886.

Budge, E. A. W. History of Alexander the Great. Cambridge, 1889.

—— Life and Exploits of Alexander the Great. 1896.

Paris, G. La Littérature française au Moyen-âge. Paris, 1890. [Sect. 44.]

Petit de Julleville, L. Histoire de la Langue et de la Littérature françaises. Vol. i, Paris, 1896. [P. 229 (see the bibliography, p. 292).]

Saintsbury, G. Flourishing of Romance. Edinburgh, 1897. [P. 148.]

Gröber, G. Grundriss der romanischen Philologie. Vol. ii¹, Strasburg, 1902, pp. 579, 817.

Ency. Brit. under 'Alexander,' with bibliography.

Schofield, W. H. English Literature from the Norman Conquest to Chaucer. 1906. [P. 298.]

Hamilton, G. L. La Légende d'Alexandre en Angleterre. [In Mélanges offerts à M. A. Thomas, Paris, 1927.]

THE ALEXANDER ROMANCES

THE ALEXANDER ROMANCES 143

(2) Particular Phases

(a) Lyfe of Alisaunder, or Kyng Alisaunder

[*Wells*, pp. 100, 778, 1105, 1208, 1300; F. P. Magoun, Gests of King Alexander, Cambridge, U.S.A. 1929, p. 34.]

MSS. 1, Laud Misc. 622 (Bodleian); 2, Lincoln's Inn L 150; 3, Auchinleck (Nat. Lib. Scotland 19.2.1). Ed. H. Weber, Metrical Romances of the XIII, XIV and XV Centuries, Edinburgh, 1810, vol. I, p. 3 (text-notes, E. Studien, XIII, 1889, p. 138, XVII, 1892, p. 298).

Selections. T. Warton, History of English Poetry, ed. W. C. Hazlitt, vol. II, 1871, p. 206, vol. IV, p. 102; E. Mätzner, Altenglische Sprachproben, 2 pts, Berlin, 1867–1900; R. Wülcker, Lesebuch, 2 pts, Halle, 1874–9; R. Morris, Specimens of Early English, Oxford, 1867; A. Brandl and O. Zippel, Mittelenglische Sprach- und Literaturproben, Berlin, 1917; G. Sampson, Cambridge Book of Prose and Verse, 1924.

Studies.
ten Brink, B. Early English Literature. Vol. I, 1887. [P. 241.]
Meyer, P. Alexandre le Grand dans la Littérature du Moyen Âge. Vol. II, Paris, 1886, p. 294.
Histoire littéraire de la France. Vol. XXIV, p. 501.
Koelbing, E. Arthour and Merlin. Leipzig, 1890, p. lx. [Author.]
Searles, C. MLN. XV, 1900, p. 90.
Hildenbrand, T. Die altfranzösische Roman de Toute Chevalerie und Kyng Alisaunder. Bonn, 1911.
Hamilton, G. L. La Légende d'Alexandre en Angleterre. Paris, 1927. [P. 196.]

[For comparison with French see H. Weisman, edn Lamprecht's Alexander, Frankfort, 1851, vol. I, p. lxxxvi, vol. II, p. 405; and H. Knizel, edn same, 1885, introduction.]

[See also Fragments of Printed Alexander, below, p. 144.]

(b) Alliterative Alexander Fragments

[*Wells*, pp. 102, 778, 1105, 1261, 1300, 1345, 1388; Magoun's edn, below.]

(i) Fragment A, Alisaunder

MS. Bodley Greaves 60. Ed. W. W. Skeat, EETS. Ex. Ser. 1, 1867, p. 177; ed. F. P. Magoun, Gests of King Alexander of Macedon, Cambridge, U.S.A. 1929.

Studies.
Trautmann, M. Über die Verfasser und Entstehungszeit einiger alliterirender Gedichte des Altenglischen. Halle, 1876.

Rosenthal, F. Die alliterierende englische Langzeile. Ang. I, 1878, p. 414.
Luick, K. Die englische Stabreimzeile. Ang. XI, 1889, p. 553.
Deutschbein, M. Zur Entwicklung des englischen Alliterationsverses. Halle, 1902.
Schumacher, K. Studien über den Stabreim. BBA. XI, 1914.
Hulbert, J. R. The West Midland of the Romances. MP. XIX, 1921, p. 1.
Menner, R. J. Sir Gawain and the Green Knight and the West Midland. PMLA. XXXVII, 1922, p. 503.
Oakden, J. P. Alliterative Poetry in Middle English. Manchester, 1930, pp. 47, 153, 247.
Koziol, H. E. Studien, LXVII, 1932, p. 166. [Author.]

(ii) Fragment B, Alexander and Dindimus

MS. Bodley 264. Ed. J. Stevenson, Roxburghe Club, 1849; ed. W. W. Skeat, EETS. Ex. Ser. 1878; ed. F. P. Magoun, as under Fragment A; vv. 1–52, in T. Warton, History of English Poetry, ed. W. C. Hazlitt, vol. IV, 1870, p. 102; ed facs. M. R. James, Oxford, 1933.

Studies. [As under (i) Fragment A, above.]

(iii) Fragment C, Wars of Alexander

MSS. 1, Ashmole 44 (Bodleian); 2, Trinity College Dublin D.4.12 (see E. Studien, III, 1880, p. 531). Ed. J. Stevenson, Roxburghe Club, 1849; ed. W. W. Skeat, EETS. Ex. Ser. 1886.

Studies. [See under (i) Fragment A, above; *Wells*, pp. 104, 105, 778, 779, 1261, 1300; Magoun, edn Fragments A, B, p. 56.]
Meyer, P. Alexandre le Grand. 2 vols. Paris, 1886.
Becker, H. Die Bramahnen in der Alexandersage. Leipzig, 1889.
Hennemann, J. B. Untersuchungen über Wars of Alexander. Berlin, 1889.
Hertz, W. Aristoteles in den Alexanderdichtungen des Mittelalters. Munich, 1889.
Kaluza, M. Strophische Gliederung in der mittelenglischen rein alliterirenden Dichtung. E. Studien, XVI, 1891, p. 169.
Bradley, H. Athenaeum, 22 Dec. 1900, p. 826.
Steffens, H. Versbau und Sprache. BBA. IX, 1901.
Neilson, G. Athenaeum, 21 June 1902, p. 784. [Author.]
Reiche, C. Untersuchungen über den Stil der Morte Arthure. Königsberg, 1906.
Hamilton, G. L. Speculum, II, 1927, p. 113. [Source.]
Andrew, S. O. RES. V, 1929, p. 267. [Dialect, author.]

[See also Huchown Discussion, *Wells*, p.826; and under Morte Arthure, above, p. 137.]

(c) Alexander-Cassamus Fragment

[See *Wells*, pp. 105, 779.]

MS. University Lib. Cambridge Ff.1.6.
Ed. K. Rosskopf, Erlangen, 1911.

Holthausen, F. Text-criticism. E. Studien, LI,
1917, p. 23.

(d) Prose Alexander

MS. Thornton (Lincoln Cathedral Lib.
A, 5, 2). Ed. J. S. Westlake, EETS. 1911. See
Thornton Romances, Camden Soc. 1844,
p. xxvi.

Studies. [*Wells*, pp. 105, 779, 1261, 1300.]
Hamilton, G. L. Speculum, II, 1927, 113.
[Source.]
Magoun, F. P. Gests of King Alexander.
Cambridge, U.S.A. 1929. [P. 56.]

(e) Scottish Alexander Buik

Earl of Dalhousie's (formerly Lord Pan-
mure's) copy of Alexander. Arbuthnet's print,
1580. Ed. with French, D. Laing, Bannatyne
Club, 1831; ed. with French, R. L. G. Ritchie,
4 vols. STS. 1921-9.

Studies. [*Wells*, pp. 105, 778, 1105, 1208,
1300, 1388; Ritchie's edn.]
Hermann, A. Untersuchungen über das
schottische Alexanderbuch. Berlin, 1893.
Scottish N. & Q. July, Aug. Nov. 1895, pp. 17,
46, 85, Feb., May 1896, pp. 132, 187.
Thomas, A. Histoire littéraire de la France.
Vol. XXXVI, pt i, 1924. [Pp. 32-3.]
Magoun, F. P. Gests of King Alexander.
Cambridge, U.S.A. 1929. [P. 28.]
[On French see *Wells*, p. 779.]

(f) Gilbert Hay's Buik

MS. Taymouth Castle. Ed. selections,
A. Hermann, The Forraye of Gadderis. The
Vowis, Berlin, 1900.

Studies. [*Wells*, pp. 106, 779; *Schofield*,
p. 304.]
Hermann, A. The Taymouth MS. Berlin,
1888.
DNB. under 'Hay, Gilbert.'
Magoun, F. P. Gests of King Alexander.
Cambridge, U.S.A. 1929. [P. 29.]

(g) Fragments of Printed Alexander

[*Wells*, pp. 106, 779.]

Edn, c. 1559 (copy in BM.; see A. W. Pollard
and G. R. Redgrave, Short Title Catalogue of
Books printed in England, Scotland and
Ireland, 1926, item 321). Ed. K. Bülbring, E.
Studien, XIII, 1889, p. 145 (see G. L. Kittredge,
E. Studien, XIV, 1890, p. 392).

Magoun, F. P. Gests of King Alexander.
Cambridge, U.S.A. 1929. [P. 34.]

D. ROMANCES OF TROY

(1) THE LEGENDS IN GENERAL

[*Wells*, pp. 106, 780, 1005, 1105, 1208, 1261,
1300, 1388 and edns of pieces below.]

Greif, W. Die mittelalterlichen Bearbeitungen
der Trojanersage. Ausgaben und Abhand-
lungen aus dem Gebiete der romanischen
Philologie, LXI, Marburg, 1886.
Heeger, G. Über die Trojanersage der Britten.
Munich, 1886; Landau, 1891.
Sommer, H. O. Recuyell of the Histories of
Troye. Vol. I, 1894. [P. xlvii.]
Ency. Brit. under 'Troy,' 'Dares,' 'Dictys,'
'Phrygius,' 'Dictys Cretensis,' with biblio-
graphies.
Ward, H. L. D. Catalogue of Romances. Vol.
I, 1883. [P. 1.]
Histoire littéraire de la France. Vol. XXIX,
p. 455.
Schofield, W. H. English Literature from
the Norman Conquest to Chaucer. 1906.
[P. 282.]
Leach, H. G. Angevin Britain and Scandi-
navia. Cambridge, U.S.A. 1921. [P. 133.]
Root, R. K. Chaucer's Troilus and Criseyde.
Princeton, 1926. [P. xxi.]
Parsons, A. E. The Trojan Legend in England.
MLR. XXIV, 1929, pp. 253, 394.

(2) PARTICULAR PHASES

(å) Gest Historiale of the Destruction of Troy

[*Wells*, pp. 108, 780, 1105, 1261, 1301,
1348, 1388.]

MS. Hunterian Museum, University of
Glasgow. Ed. D. Donaldson, EETS. 1869,
1874.

Selections. R. Wülcker, Lesebuch, 2 pts,
Halle, 1874-9; E. Studien, XXIX, 1901, p. 384;
J. Zupitza, Übungsbuch, Vienna, 1922; G. E.
MacLean, Reader, New York, 1893; K. Sisam
Fourteenth Century Verse and Prose, Oxford
1921.

Studies.
Körting, G. Dares und Dictys. Halle, 1874.
Bock, W. Zur Destruction of Troy. Halle
1883. [Language, sources.]
Morley, H. English Writers. 10 vols. 1883-93
[Vol. VI, p. 241.]
Brandes, H. E. Studien, VIII, 1885, p. 398
[Source.]
Greif, W. Die mittelalterlichen Bearbeitungen
der Trojanersage. Marburg, 1886.
Wager, C. H. A. Seege of Troye. New York
1899.
Andrew, S. O. RES. V, 1929, p. 267. [Dialect
author.]

[Author. Ang. i, 1878, p. 123; EETS. i, 1864,
ɔ. ix; E. Studien, viii, 1885, p. 410, xi, 1888,
ɔ. 285.
Compared with Laud Troy-Book. E.
Studien, xxix, 1901, p. 384.
Dialect and Place of Origin. K. Luick, Ang.
xi, 1889, p. 405; K. Reicke, Untersuchungen
über den Stil der Morte Arthure, Königsberg,
1906; J. R. Hulbert, MP. xix, 1921, p. 1; R. J.
Menner, PMLA. xxxvii, 1922, p. 503.]
Oakden, J. P. Alliterative Poetry in Middle
English. Manchester, 1930, pp. 67, 153, 255.
Koziol, H. E. Studien, lxvii, 1932, p. 171.
[Author.]
[See also Huchown Discussion under Morte
Arthure, above, p. 137.]

(b) Seege of Troy

[Wells, pp. 108, 780, 1261, 1301, 1346, 1388;
dns of Wager, Barnicle and Hibler.]

MSS. 1, Harley 525; 2, Arundel xxii;
, Egerton 2862; 4, Lincoln's Inn Lib. 150.
Editions. 1, 4, H. and L. Zietsch, Archiv,
xxii, 1884, p. 11; 1, C. H. A. Wager, New
York, 1899; all MSS, M. E. Barnicle, EETS.
926; 1, 3, 4, L. Hibler-Lebmannsport, Graz,
928.
Studies.
Ward, H. L. D. Catalogue of Romances. Vol. i,
1883.
Zietsch, A. Über Quelle und Sprache
des mittelenglischen Gedichts Seege oder
Batayle of Troye. Göttingen (Kassel), 1883.
Greif, W. Die mittelalterlichen Bearbeitungen
der Trojanersage. Marburg, 1886. [Sects.
168–72.]
Franz, E. T. Über die Quellengemeinschaft
des mittelenglischen Gedichtes Seege oder
Batayle of Troye und des mittelhochdeut-
schen Gedichtes vom trojanischen Kriege
des Konrad von Würzburg. Leipzig, 1888.
Bülbring, K. D. Geschichte der Ablaute der
starken Zeitwörter innerhalb des Süden-
glischen. Strasburg, 1889. [P. 34.]
Lick, W. Zur mittelenglischen Romanz Seege
of Troye. Breslau, 1894.
Sommer, H. O. Recuyell of the Histories of
Troye. Vol. i, 1894. [P. xvii.]
Hibler, L. Methodisches zur Ermittlung des
Schreiberindividualität dargestellt an der
Seege of Troy. Ang. li, 1927, p. 354.
— Die Individualität des A-Schreibers
(MS. Arundel 22). Ang. lx, 1936, p. 39.
Atwood, E. B. Speculum, ix, 1934, p. 379.
[Sources.]

(c) Laud Troy-Book

MS. Laud 590 (Bodleian). Ed. J. E. Wül-
ng, EETS. 1902, 1903.

Studies. [Wells, pp. 109, 780, 1005.]
Greif, W. Die mittelalterlichen Bearbeitungen
der Trojanersage. Marburg, 1886. [Sect.
69.]
Kempe, D. E. Studien, xxix, 1901, p. 1.
Wülfing, J. E. Ang. xxvii, 1904, p. 555,
xxviii, 1905, p. 29; E. Studien, xxix,
1901, p. 374.
Curry, W. C. Judgment of Paris. MLN. xxxi,
1916, p. 114.

(d) Lydgate's Troy-Book

[Wells, pp. 110, 780, 1388.]
Ed. H. Bergen, 4 pts, EETS. Ex. Ser. 1906–
35.
Studies. [ten Brink, vol. ii, p. 224; Ward,
vol. i, pp. 75, 78. DNB. under 'Lydgate.']
Skeat, W. W. Academy, 7 May 1892; N. & Q.
22 Aug., 12 Sept. 1891, pp. 146, 215.
Bergen, H. Description and Genealogy of
MSS. and Prints of Lydgate's Troy-Book.
Munich, 1906.
Wülfing, E. E. Studien, xxix, 1901, p. 382.

(e) Scottish Troy Fragments

[Wells, pp. 110, 780.]
MSS. 1, University Lib. Cambridge
Kk. v. 30, fols. 1 and 304 v.; 2, Douce 148
(Bodleian), fol. 290.
Edition. C. Horstmann, Barbours Legend-
ensammlung, Heilbronn, vol. ii, 1881, p. 215
(see Anzeiger für deutsches Altertum, x, 1885,
p. 334).
Studies.
Prothero, J. W. Memoir of H. Bradshaw.
1888. [P. 133.]
—— Bradshaw's College Papers. 1888.
Bearder, J. W. Über den Gebrauch der Prae-
positionen in der altschottischen Poesie.
Halle, 1894.
[Author, etc. Ang. ix, 1886, p. 493; E.
Studien, x, 1887, p. 373, xxix, 1901, p. 374;
EETS. xxxix, 1869, lvi, 1874.]
[See also Barbour's Bruce, Scottish Legend
Collection.]

(f) Rawlinson Prose Troy Piece

[Wells, pp. 111, 780; Wager, Barnicle,
edns Seege of Troye.]
MS. Rawlinson Misc. D 82 (Bodleian). Ed.
PMLA. xxii, 1907, p. 157; with prose Thebes,
Archiv, cxxx, 1913, pp. 40, 269.

(g) Recuyell of the Histories of Troye

[Wells, pp. 111, 780.]
Ed. H. O. Sommer, 2 vols. 1894.

10

E. ROMANCES OF THEBES

(1) The Legends in General

[*Wells*, pp. 111, 780.]

Constans, L. Légende d'Œdipe. Paris, 1881.
—— Roman de Thèbes. Paris, 1890.
—— Revue des Langues romanes, xxxv, 1893–4, p. 612.
Paris, G. La Littérature française au Moyen-âge. Paris, 1890. [Sect. 47.]
Petit de Julleville, L. Histoire de la Langue et de la Littérature françaises. Vol. i, Paris, 1896. [Pp. 173, 252.]
Gröber, G. Grundriss der romanischen Philologie. Vol. ii¹, Strasburg, 1902, p. 582.
Schofield, W. H. English Literature from the Norman Conquest to Chaucer, 1906. [P. 295.]
Ency. Brit. under 'Thebes, Romances of.'

(2) Particular Phases

(a) Lydgate's Siege of Thebes

[*Wells*, pp. 111, 781, 1346, 1388.]

MSS. Twenty-one or more.

Editions. A. Erdmann, 2 pts, EETS. Ex. Ser. 1911–30; prologue, E. P. Hammond, Ang. xxxvi, 1912, p. 360.

Studies. [*ten Brink*, vol. ii, p. 221; H. Morley, English Writers, vol. vi, 1890, p. 101; *Ward*, vol. i, p. 87; DNB. under 'Lydgate' (bibliography); W. J. Courthope, History of English Poetry, vol. i, 1895, p. 321.]

Koeppel, E. Lydgate's Story of Thebes. Munich, 1884.
Koelbing, E. MS. 25 der Bibliothek des Marquis of Bath. E. Studien, x, 1887, p. 203.
Schick, J. Temple of Glass. EETS. Ex. Ser. 1891. [Date.]
Fiedler, G. Zum Leben Lydgate's. Ang. xv, 1893, p. 391.
Bergen, H. MSS. and Prints of Lydgate's Troy-Book. Bungay, 1906.
MacCracken, H. N. Lydgate Canon. Trans. Philolog. Soc. 1907–9, appendix, and EETS. Ex. Ser. cvii, 1910, introduction.

[For the French see: L. Constans, Légende d'Œdipe, Paris, 1881; Roman de Thèbes, Paris, 1890; Revue des Langues romanes, xxxv, 1893–4, p. 612. Bibliographies in G. Gröber, G. Paris, and Petit de Julleville, as above.]

(b) Rawlinson Prose Siege of Thebes

[*Wells*, pp. 112, 781.]

MS. Rawlinson Misc. D 82 (Bodleian). Ed. Archiv, cxxx, 1913, pp. 40, 269.

F. ROMANCES OF GODFREY OF BOUILLON

(1) The Legends in General

[*Wells*, pp. 95, 777.]

Paris, G. Histoire littéraire de la France [Vol. xxii, p. 350, vol. xxv, p. 507.]
—— Nouvelle Étude sur la Chanson d'Antioche. Paris, 1874.
—— La Littérature française au Moyen-âge Paris, 1890. [Sect. 29.]
Pigeonneau, H. Le Cycle de la Croisade. S Cloud, 1877.
Romania, xxi, 1892, p. 62, xxx, 1901, p. 404 xxiv, 1895, p. 266.
Petit de Julleville, L. Histoire de la Langu et de la Littérature françaises. Paris, 1896 [Ch. ii (see bibliography at p. 169).]
Gautier, L. Bibliographie des Chansons d Geste. Paris, 1897. [P. 77.]
Gröber, G. Grundriss der romanische Philologie. Vol. ii¹, Strasburg, 1902. [Pp 471, 575.]

(2) Particular Phases

(a) Chevalere Assigne

[*Wells*, pp. 96, 777, 1104, 1208, 1299 *Billings*, pp. 228; *Hibbard*, p. 239.]

MS. Cotton, Caligula A ii. Ed. R. Utter son, Roxburghe Club, 1820; ed. Lord Alden ham, EETS. Ex. Ser. 1868.

Studies. [*Ward*, vol. i, p. 708. Verse: E Studien, xvi, 1891, p. 174. Text: Ang. xxi 1899, p. 441. Origin of legend: E. Studien xxix, 1901, p. 337; Zeitschrift für romanisch Philologie, xxi, 1897, p. 176; Romania, xix 1890, p. 314, xxvi, 1897, p. 581.]

Krüger, A. Zur mittelenglischen Chevaler Assigne. Archiv, lxxvii, 1887, p. 169.
Sparnaay, H. Verschmelzung legendarische und weltlicher Motive in der Poesie de Mittelalters. Groningen, 1922.

(b) Helyas, The Knight of the Swan

[*Wells*, pp. 98, 778.]

Edns by De Worde and Copland, early 16t cent. Ptd W. J. Thoms, Collection of Earl Printed Romances, vol. iii, 1828, p. 1; rpt 1 vol. 1904, p. 691. Facs. of De Worde, Grolie Club, New York, 1901.

(c) Godefroy of Boloyne

[*Wells*, pp. 98, 778.]

Caxton's edn, 1481. Ed. M. Colvin, EETS Ex. Ser. 1893.

III. The Non-Cyclic Romances

A. ROMANCES OF ENGLISH HEROES

(1) The Legends in General

[*Wells*, pp. 7, 762, 1003, 1049, 1100, 1167, 204, 1259, 1295, 1343, 1382; *Hibbard*, pp. 81, 56, 214; *Billings*, p. 1.]

en Brink, B. Early English Literature. Vol. I, 1887. [Pp. 148, 225.]
chofield, W. H. English Literature from the Norman Conquest to Chaucer. 1906. [P. 258.]
Ker, W. P. Metrical Romances. CHEL. vol. I, 1907. [Ch. xiii.]
Deutschbein, M. Studien zur Sagengeschichte Englands. Cöthen, 1906.
reek, H. Character in the 'Matter of England' Romances. JEGP. x, 1911, pp. 429, 585; Urbana, 1911.
each, H. G. Angevin Britain and Scandinavia. Cambridge, U.S.A. 1921. [Pp. 234, 324.]

(2) Particular Phases and Heroes

(a) *King Horn*

[*Billings*, p. 1; *Wells*, pp. 8, 762, 1003, 100, 1204, 1295, 1343, 1382; *Hibbard*, p. 81; all, edn below.]

MSS. 1, University Lib. Cambridge g.IV.27, 2; 2, Laud Misc. 180 (Bodleian); , Harley 2253.

Editions. 1, C. Michel, Horn et Rimenhild, aris, 1845; J. R. Lumby, EETS. 1866, ev. G. H. McKnight, 1901; E. Mätzner, Altenglische Sprachproben, pt I, Berlin, 1867, .209; R. Morris, Specimens of Early English, ol. I, Oxford, 1887, p. 237; 2, C. Horstmann, archiv, L, 1872, p. 39 (MS described, Archiv, LIX, 1872, p. 395); 3, J. Ritson, Ancient English Metrical Romances, vol. II, 1802, . 91; all MSS, G. H. McKnight, EETS. 1901; . Hall, Oxford, 1901 (*q.v.* for all earlier materials); critical edn, T. Wissmann, QF. xvi, 876, XLV, 1881. Collation, Anzeiger für eutsches Altertum, IX, 1883, p. 181.

Selections. J. Zupitza, Übungsbuch, Vienna, 874; F. Kluge, Lesebuch, Halle, 1904; A. S. ook, Literary Middle English Reader, Boston, 915; A. Brandl and O. Zippel, Mittelenglsche Sprach- und Literaturproben, Berlin, 917; G. Sampson, Cambridge Book of Prose nd Verse, 1924.

Translations. L. A. Hibbard, Three Middle nglish Romances retold, 1911; J. L. Weston, hief Middle English Poets, Boston, 1914, , 93.

Studies. [ten Brink, vol. I, pp. 149, 227, vol. I, p. 10; *Ward*, vol. I, p. 447; CHEL. vol. I,

1907, p. 304. Verse: T. Wissmann, QF. xvi, 1876, XLV, 1881, and Ang. v, 1882, p. 466; J. M. Schipper, Englische Metrik, pt iii, Bonn, 1881, ch. ix; Ang. Anz. v, 1882, p. 88, VIII, 1895, p. 69; Ang. Bbl. XIII, 1902, p. 332; Hall, edn; and West, Scripture, as below. Textnotes: MLN. VII, 1892, p. 267.]

Wissmann, T. King Horn: Untersuchungen. QF. xvi, 1876.
—— Studien zu King Horn. Ang. IV, 1881 p. 342.
Tamson, G. Vv. 701–4. Ang. xix, 1897 p. 460.
McKnight, G. H. Germanic Elements. PMLA. xv, 1900, p. 221.
Hartenstein, O. Studien zur Hornsage. Kieler Studien, IV, 1902.
Morsbach, L. Die angebliche Originalität des frühmittelenglischen King Horn. [In Festschrift für W. Förster, Halle, 1902, p. 297.]
Northup, C. S. Recent Texts and Studies. JEGP. IV, 1902, p. 529.
Schofield, W. H. Horn and Rimenhild. PMLA. xviii, 1903, p. 1.
Deutschbein, M. Studien zur Sagengeschichte Englands. Cöthen, 1906.
—— Beiträge zur Horn- und Haveloksage. Ang. Bbl. xx, 1909, pp. 16, 55.
West, H. S. Versification of King Horn. Baltimore, 1907.
Heuser, W. Horn und Rigmel (Rimenhild). Ang. xxxi, 1908, p. 105.
Breier, W. Zur Lokalisierung des King Horn. E. Studien, XLII, 1910, p. 307.
Creek, H. Character in the 'Matter of England' Romances. JEGP. x, 1911, pp. 429, 585.
Azzalino, W. Die Wortstellung im King Horn. Halle, 1915.
Funke, O. Zum Verkleidungsmotiv im King Horn. Ang. Bbl. xxxi, 1920, p. 224.
—— E. Studien, LV, 1922, p. 7. [French words.]
Leach, H. G. Angevin Britain and Scandinavia. Cambridge, U.S.A. 1921. [P. 328.]
Töpperwein, A. Sprache und Heimat des mittelenglischen King Horn. [Summary in Jahrbuch der philosophischen Fakultät, Göttingen, 1921, pt I, p. 89.]
Krappe, A. H. Legends of Amicus and Amelius and of King Horn. Leuvensche Bijdragen, xvi, 1924, p. 14.
Leidig, P. Studien zu King Horn. Borna-Leipzig, 1927.
Scripture, E. W. Der Versrhythmus in King Horn. Ang. LII, 1928, p. 382.
Oliver, W. King Horn and Suddene. PMLA. XLVI, 1931, p. 102.
McKeehan, I. P. The Book of the Nativity of St Cuthbert. PMLA. XLVIII, 1933, p. 981.

[On French see *Wells* and *Hibbard*, as above.]

10-2

(b) Horn Childe and Maiden Rimnild

[*Billings*, p. 12; *Wells*, pp. 10, 763, 1100, 1204, 1296; *Hibbard*, p. 97.]

MS. Auchinleck (Nat. Lib. Scotland 19.2.1).

Editions. J. Ritson, Ancient English Metrical Romances, vol. III, 1802, p. 282; C. Michel, Horn et Rimenhild, Paris, 1845, p. 341; J. Caro, E. Studien, XII, 1889, p. 323 (see Ang. XIV, 1891, p. 309); J. Hall, King Horn, Oxford, 1901, p. 179.

Selection. A. Brandl and O. Zippel, Mittelenglische Sprach- und Literaturproben, Berlin, 1917.

Studies. [See under King Horn, above. For author see Romania, XV, 1886, p. 575.]

Schofield, W. H. The Story of Horn and Rimenhild. PMLA. XVIII, 1903, p. 1.

Brunner, K. Romanzen und Volksballaden, Palaestra, CXLVIII, 1925, p. 75.

Leidig, P. Studien zu King Horn. Borna-Leipzig, 1927.

Trounce, A. McI. The English Tail-Rhyme Romances. Medium Aevum, I, II, III, 1932–4.

(c) Hind Horn (Ballad)

[*Wells*, pp. 763, 1100, 1204, 1296.]

Editions. C. Michel, Horn et Rimenhild, Paris, 1845, p. 393; F. J. Child, Ballads, vol. I, Boston, 1882, p. 195.

Selection. A. Brandl and O. Zippel, Mittelenglische Sprach- und Literaturproben, Berlin, 1917.

Studies. [QF. XVI, 1876, p. 121; E. Studien, I, 1877, p. 351, XII, 1889, p. 335; PMLA. XVIII, 1903, p. 1; Romania, XXXIV, 1905, p. 142.]

Nelles, W. C. Journal of American Folk-lore, XXII, 1909, p. 42.

MacSweeney, J. J. MLR. XIV, 1919, p. 210.

Brunner, K. Romanzen und Volksballaden. Palaestra, CXLVIII, 1925, p. 76.

Leidig, P. Studien zu King Horn. Borna-Leipzig, 1927.

(d) King Pontus and the Fair Sidone

[*Billings*, pp. 3, 12; *Wells*, pp. 12, 763.]

MSS. 1, Digby 185 (Bodleian); 2, Douce 384 (Bodleian; fragment).

Edition. PMLA, XII, 1897, p. 1. [See Romania, XXVI, 1897, p. 468; Ang. Bbl. VIII, 1897, p. 197.]

(e) Lay of Havelok

[*Billings*, p. 15; *Wells*, pp. 13, 763, 1003, 1049, 1100, 1204, 1296, 1382; *Hibbard*, p. 103; Skeat and Sisam, edns below.]

MSS. 1, Laud Misc. 108, part II, fol. 20 (Bodleian); 2, University Lib. Cambridg 4407 (19) (4 fragments).

Editions. 1, Sir F. Madden, Roxburghe Club 1828 (with French); W. W. Skeat, EETS. Ex Ser. 1868 (collation, Ang. XIII, 1891, p. 194 Archiv, CVIII, 1902, p. 197), and Oxford, 1902 rev. K. Sisam, Oxford, 1915; F. Holthausen Heidelberg, 1901, 1910, 1928; 2, W. W. Skeat MLR. VI, 1911, p. 455; K. Sisam, edn above p. 103. [See also J. Hall, edn King Horn.]

Selections. R. Morris, Specimens of Earl; English, Oxford, 1867; J. Zupitza, Übungs buch, Vienna, 1874; R. Wülcker, Lesebuch Halle, 1874–9; G. E. MacLean, Reader, Nev York, 1893; O. F. Emerson, Reader, Nev York, 1905; A. S. Cook, Literary Middl English Reader, Boston, 1915; A. Brand and O. Zippel, Mittelenglische Sprach- un Literaturproben, Berlin, 1917; G. Sampson Cambridge Book of Prose and Verse, 1924.

Translations. E. Hickey, 1902; L. A. Hib bard, Three Middle English Romances retold 1911; J.L.Weston,Chief Middle English Poets Boston, 1914, p. 110; F. J. H. Darton, Wonde Book of Old Romance, New York, 1907; A. J Wyatt, 1913.

Studies. [ten Brink, vol. I, pp. 149, 232 DNB. under 'Olaf Sitricson'; Ward, vol. 1 p. 423; H. Morley, English Writers, vol. II 1887, p. 267; Schofield, p. 266; edns by Skea and Sisam. For emendations and notes se Wells, p. 763. Text and explanatory notes Archiv, CVII, 1901, p. 107; Trans. Philolog Soc. 1903–6, p. 161; MLN. VII, 1892, p. 267 XXI, 1906, p. 23; MLR. IV, 1909, p. 91 Archiv, CI, 1898, p. 100; Ang. Bbl. XI, 1900 pp. 306, 359, XII, 1901, p. 146; F. J. Furnivall An English Miscellany, Oxford, 1901, p. 176 E. Studien, XXIX, 1901, p. 368, XXX, 1902 p. 343; Ang. XXIX, 1906, 132; RES. V, 1929 p. 328. On French see Wells and Hibbard a above.]

Ludorff, F. Über die Sprache des altenglische Lay Havelok. Münster, 1874.

Kupferschmidt, M. Die Haveloksage be Gaimar. Romanische Studien, IV, 1879–80 p. 411. [Gaimar and the Lay. See Romania IX, 1880, p. 480.]

Storm, G. Havelok the Dane and the Nors King Olaf Kuaran. E. Studien, III, 1880 p. 533.

Koelbing, E. Amis and Amiloun. Heilbronn 1884. [Introduction.]

Hohmann, L. Über Sprache und Stil des alt englischen Lai Havelok þe Dane. Marburg 1886.

Wohlfeil, P. Lay of Havelok the Dane. Leip zig, 1890.

Hupe, H. Studien. Ang. XIII, 1891, p. 186.

Wittenbrinck, G. Zur Kritik und Rhythmik des altenglischen Lais von Havelok dem Dänen. Burgsteinfurt,1891. [See E. Studien, xvi, 1892, p. 299.]

Ahlström, A. Studier i den Fornfranska Lais-Litteraturen. Upsala, 1892.

Hales, J. W. Folia Litteraria. 1893. [P. 30.] [See Athenaeum, 23 Feb. 1889.]

Gollancz, Sir I. Hamlet in Iceland. 1898.

Putnam, E. K. Lambeth MS. PMLA. xv, 1900, p. 1.

—— Scala-Chronicon Version. Trans. American Philolog. Ass. xxxiv, 1903, p. xci.

Schmidt, F. Zur Heimatbestimmung des Havelok. Göttingen, 1900.

Whistler, C. Saga of Havelok. Saga Book of Viking Club, iii, 1902, p. 395.

Bradley, E. V. 2333. Trans. Philolog. Soc. 1903–4.

Heyman, H. Studies on the Havelok Tale. Upsala, 1903.

van der Gaaf, W. Parliaments held at Lincoln. E. Studien, xxxii, 1903, p. 319.

Brie, F. Zum Fortleben der Havelok-Sage. E. Studien, xxxv, 1905, p. 359.

Zenker, R. Boeve-Amlethus. Berlin, 1905. [Ch. v.]

Deutschbein, M. Studien zur Sagengeschichte Englands. Cöthen, 1906. [P. 96.]

Björkman, E. Nordiska Vikingasagor i England. Nordisk Tidsskrift, 1906, pp. 40, 437.

—— Date. Ang. Bbl. xxviii, 1917, p. 333.

Wolff, A. K. Zur Syntax des Verbums im altenglischen Lay of Havelok the Dane. Leipzig, 1909.

Deutschbein, M. Beiträge zur Horn- und Haveloksage. Ang. Bbl. xx, 1909, pp. 16, 55.

Bugge, A. Havelok and Olaf Tryggvason. Saga Book of Viking Club, vi, 1910, p. 257.

Creek, H. C. Character in the 'Matter of England' Romances. JEGP. x, 1911, pp. 429, 585.

—— Author. E. Studien, xlviii, 1915, p. 193.

Fahnestock, E. Study of Source and Composition of the Old French Lai. Jamaica, New York, 1915.

Beaven, M. King Edward I and the Danes of York. EHR. xxxiii, 1918, p. 1.

Holthausen, F. Text-notes. Ang. xlii, 1918, p. 445.

Leach, H. G. Angevin Britain and Scandinavia. Cambridge, U.S.A. 1921. [P. 324.]

Ashdown, M. Single Combat. MLR. xvii, 1922, p. 113.

Bell, A. Single Combat in the Lai d'Haveloc. MLR. xviii, 1923, p. 22.

—— Le Lai d'Haveloc and Gaimar's Havelok Episode. Manchester, 1926.

Liebermann, G. Havelok and Anlaf. Archiv, cxlvi, 1923, p. 243.

McKeehan, I. P. The Book of the Nativity of St Cuthbert. PMLA. xlviii, 1932, p. 981.

Whiting, B. J. Proverbs in Middle English Romances. Harvard Stud. xv, 1933, p. 111.

(f) Guy of Warwick

[Billings, p. 24; Wells, pp. 15, 764, 1003, 1101, 1204, 1296, 1382; Hibbard, p. 127.]

MSS. 1, 2, Auchinleck (Nat. Lib. Scotland 19.2.1), two versions with Reinbrun; 3, Caius College Cambridge 107; 4, Sloane 1044 (fragment); 5, BM. Add. 14408; 6, University Lib. Cambridge Ff.ii.38; 7, Copland print.

Editions. 1, 2, 5, W. B. D. Turnbull, Abbotsford Club, 1840; 1, 2, 3, 6, J. Zupitza, 5 pts, EETS. Ex. Ser. 1875–91; 4, J. Zupitza, Sitzungsberichte der Wiener Akademie der Wissenschaften, Philosophische Klasse, lxxiv, 1873, p. 623 (see Germania, xxi, 1876, pp. 353, 365; E. Studien, ii, 1879, p. 246); 5, T. Phillips, Middle Hill, 1838; 7, G. Schleich, Palaestra, cxxxix, 1923.

Abstract. G. Ellis, Specimens of Early English Metrical Romances, 1848, p. 188.

Studies. [ten Brink, vol. i, p. 246; Ward, vol. i, pp. 471, 494; DNB; Schofield, pp. 271, 477; Histoire littéraire de la France, vol. xxii, p. 841.]

Zupitza, J. Zur Literaturgeschichte des Guy von Warwick. Vienna, 1873.

Tanner, A. Die Sage von Guy von Warwick. Heilbronn, 1877.

Koelbing, E. Amis and Amiloun und Guy of Warwick. E. Studien, ix; 1886, p. 477.

Wilda, O. Über die örtliche Verbreitung der zwölfzeiligen Schweifreimstrophe in England. Breslau, 1888. [P. 46.]

Reeves, W. So-called Prose Version. MLN. xi, 1896, p. 404.

Liebermann, F. Influence. Archiv, cvii, 1901, p. 107.

Weyrauch, M. Die mittelenglischen Fassungen der Sage von Guy of Warwick. Breslau,1901.

Deutschbein, M. Studien zur Sagengeschichte Englands. Cöthen, 1906. [P. 214.]

Robinson, F. N. Irish Lives of Guy of Warwick. Zeitschrift für celtische Philologie, vi, 1907–8, p. 9.

Mau, P. Gydo und Thyrus. Jena, 1909.

Creek, H. Character in the 'Matter of England' Romances. JEGP, x, 1911, pp. 429, 585.

Crane, R. S. The Vogue of Guy of Warwick. PMLA. xxx, 1915, p. 125.

Hibbard, L. A. Guy of Warwick and Jean Louvet. MP. xiii, 1915, p. 181.

Möller, W. Untersuchungen über Dialektik und Stil und über Verhältnis zu Amis und Amiloun. Königsberg, 1917.

Ashdown, M. Single Combat in Romances.
MLR. xvii, 1922, p. 124.

Trounce, A. McI. The English Tail-Rhyme
Romances. Medium Aevum, i, ii, iii, 1932–
4.

[On Guy and Phillis, Guy and Colbrande,
Guy and Amarant, and Lydgate's Guy see
Wells, p. 165.]

(g) Beues of Hamtoun

[Billings, p. 36; Wells, pp. 21, 765, 1003,
1101, 1205, 1382; Hibbard, p. 115.]

MSS. 1, Auchinleck (Nat. Lib. Scotland
19.2.1); 2, Chetham Lib. Manchester 8009;
3, Caius College Cambridge 175; 4, Egerton
2862 (formerly Duke of Sutherland); 5, Royal
Lib. Naples xiii B 29; 6, University Lib.
Cambridge Ff.ii.38. [See E. Studien, vii,
1884, pp. 191, 198, xiv, 1890, p. 321.]

Editions. 1, W. B. D. Turnbull, Maitland
Club, 1838 (collation, E. Studien, ii, 1878–9,
p. 317); 1, 2, E. Koelbing, 3 pts, EETS. Ex.
Ser. 1885–94.

Selection. G. Sampson, Cambridge Book of
Prose and Verse, 1924.

Analysis. G. Ellis, Specimens of Early
English Metrical Romances, 1848, p. 239.

Translation. L. A. Hibbard, Three Middle
English Romances retold, 1911.

Studies.

Schmirgel, C. Stil und Sprache des mittelenglischen Epos Sir Beves of Hamtoun.
Breslau, 1886.

Koelbing, E. Die Alliteration in Sir Beues of
Hamtoun. E. Studien, xix, 1894, p. 441.

Matzke, J. E. The Legend of St George.
PMLA. xvii, 1902, p. 508, xviii, 1903,
p. 99, xix, 1904, p. 449.

—— Oldest Form of the Beves Legend. MP.
x, 1912, p. 19.

Robinson, F. N. Irish Lives of Guy of Warwick and Beves of Hamtoun. Zeitschrift
für celtische Philologie, vi, 1902–3, p. 10.

Gerould, G. H. The Eustace Legend. PMLA.
xix, 1904, p. 335.

Zenker, R. Boeve-Amlethus. Berlin, 1905.

Deutschbein, M. Studien zur Sagengeschichte
Englands. Cöthen, 1905. [P. 181.]

Creek, H. Character in the 'Matter of
England' Romances. JEGP. x, 1911, pp.
439, 585.

Leach, H. G. Angevin Britain and Scandinavia. Cambridge, U.S.A. 1921. [Pp. 235,
331.]

Crawford, S. J. Sir Bevis of Hamtoun.
Wessex, i, 1930, p. 46.

[On French see Wells, and Hibbard, as
above.]

(h) Richard Coer de Lyon

[Wells, pp. 150, 786, 1006, 1107, 1210,
1302, 1389; Hibbard, p. 147.]

MSS. 1, Auchinleck (Nat. Lib. Scotland
19.2.1; fragments; see E.Studien,vii,1884,pp.
178,190,viii,1885,p.115,xi,1888,p.197,xiii,
1889, p. 138); 2, Egerton 2862 (formerly Duke
of Sutherland); 3, BM. Add. 31042; 4, Harley
4690 (fragments); 5, College of Arms H.D.N.
lviii (see W. H. Black, Catalogue of Arundel
MSS,1829,p.104); 6, Caius College Cambridge
75 (see M. R. James, Catalogue of Library of
Gonville and Caius College, 1907; E. Studien,
xiv, 1890, pp. 321, 337); 7, Douce 228 (Bodleian, fragment).

Editions. Critical edn all MSS, based on 6,
K.Brunner,Vienna,1913; 1,W.B.D.Turnbull
and D. Laing, Owain Miles, Edinburgh, 1837;
E. Koelbing, E. Studien, viii, 1885, p. 115; 6,
most of text, H. Weber, Metrical Romances
of the XIII, XIV, and XV Centuries, vol. ii,
Edinburgh, 1810, p. 148.

Selections. R. Wülcker, Lesebuch, Halle,
1874–9; G. Paris, Romania, xxvi, 1897, pp.
356, 362.

Abstract. G. Ellis, Specimens of Early
English Metrical Romances, 1848, p. 282.

Translation, parts. J. L. Weston, Chief
Middle English Poets, Boston, 1914, pp. 123,
126.

Studies. [ten Brink, vol. i, p. 242; Ward,
vol. i, p. 944; Schofield, p. 314.]

Koelbing, E. Arthour and Merlin. Leipzig,
1890. [P. lx.]

Needler, G. H. Richard Cœur de Lion in
Literature. Leipzig, 1890.

Jentsch, F. Sources. E. Studien, xv, 1891,
p. 161.

Paris, G. Roman de Richard Cœur de Lion.
Romania, xxvi, 1897, p. 353.

Loomis, R. S. Richard Cœur de Lion in
Medieval Art. PMLA. xxx, 1915, p. 509.

Magoun, F. P. Gests of King Alexander of
Macedon. Cambridge, U.S.A. 1929. [P. 28.]

[On French see Wells, and Hibbard.]

(i) Athelston

[Billings, p. 32; Wells, pp. 23, 766, 1049,
1101, 1168, 1205, 1259, 1296, 1383; Hibbard,
p. 143.]

MS. Caius College Cambridge 175. Ed.
C. H. Hartshorne, Ancient Metrical Tales,
1829; ed. T. Wright and J. O. Halliwell
[-Phillipps], Reliquiae Antiquae, vol. ii, 1843,
p. 85; ed. J. Zupitza, E. Studien, xiii, 1889,
p. 331, xiv, 1890, p. 321; ed. Lord F. Hervey,
Corolla S. Eadmundi, 1907, p. 525; ed. A. McI.
Trounce, Philolog. Soc. 1933.

Translation. E. Rickert, Early English
Romances: Friendship, 1908, p. 67.

Studies.

Wilda, O. Über die örtliche Verbreitung der
zwölfzeiligen Schweifreimstrophe in England. Breslau, 1888. [P. 61.]

Zupitza, J. Athelston. E. Studien, xiv, 1890,
p. 321.

Gerould, G. H. Social and Historical Reminiscences. E. Studien, xxxvi, 1906, p. 193.

Hibbard, L. A. A Westminster Legend.
PMLA. xxxvi, 1921, p. 223.

Beug, K. Die Sage von König Athelstan.
Archiv, cxlviii, 1925, p. 181.

Baugh, A. C. A Source. PMLA. xliv, 1929,
p. 377.

Trounce, A. McI. The English Tail-Rhyme
Romances. Medium Aevum, i, ii, iii,
1932–4.

Taylor, G. Leeds Stud. nos. 3, 4, 1934–5.
[Notes.]

[On early ballads on Athelston see H. Paul,
Grundriss der germanischen Philologie, vol. ii[1],
Strasburg, 1909, p. 1087.]

(j) *Gamelyn*

[*Billings*, p. 425; *Wells*, pp. 25, 766, 1205,
1296, 1383; *Hibbard*, p. 156; E. P. Hammond, Chaucer, A Bibliographical Manual,
New York, 1908, p. 425.]

A number of MSS of Canterbury Tales. [See
Hammond, Chaucer, pp. 173, 425; *Hibbard*,
p. 163.] MS Harley 7334: ed. W. W. Skeat,
Oxford Chaucer, vol. iv, 1894, p. 645, vol. v,
p. 477; ed. W. W. Skeat, Oxford, 1884, rev.
1893; Skeat's text, New Rochelle, New York,
1901. Six other MSS, edn in Appendices to
Six-Text Edition of Chaucer, Chaucer Soc.,
Ser. 1, vols. viii–x, xiii, 1869.

Selection. G. Sampson, Cambridge Book of
Prose and Verse, 1924.

Translation. E. Rickert, Early English
Romances: Friendship, 1908, p. 85.

Studies. [ten Brink, vol. ii, p. 183, vol. iii,
p. 271; *Ward*, vol. i, p. 508; *Schofield*, p. 279;
CHEL. vol. ii, 1908, p. 194. For name see
Archiv, cxix, 1907, p. 33, cxxiii, 1909,
p. 23.]

Lindner, F. Tale of Gamelyn. E. Studien, ii,
1879, pp. 94, 321.

Leach, H. G. Angevin Britain and Scandinavia. Cambridge, U.S.A. 1921. [P. 351.]

Brusendorff, A. Chaucer Tradition. Copenhagen, 1925. [Pp. 72, 126.]

Holthausen, F. Ang. Bbl. xl, 1929, p. 57.
[Text-notes.]

Tatlock, J. S. P. PMLA. l, 1935, p. 112.
[Attribution to Chaucer.]

B. BRETON LAIS

(1) THE LEGENDS IN GENERAL

[*Wells*, pp. 124, 783, 1006, 1106, 1209, 1262,
1301. See also G. L. Kittredge, A.J. Phil. vii,
1886, p. 176; EETS. Ex. Ser. xcix, 1906,
p. xxviii; *Schofield*, p. 179; G. Paris, Littérature
française au Moyen-âge, Paris, 1890, sect. 55
(bibliography); Romania, viii, 1879, p. 133,
xiv, 1885, p. 606; L. Petit de Julleville, Histoire
de la Langue et de la Littérature françaises,
vol. i, Paris, 1896, pp. 285, 340; G. Gröber,
Grundriss, vol. ii[1], Strasburg, 1902, pp. 496, 571,
593; Zeitschrift für romanische Philologie,
xxix, 1905, pp. 19, 293, xxx, 1906, p. 698,
xxxii, 1908, pp. 161, 257; K. Warnke, Die Lais
der Marie de France, Halle, 1925 (3rd edn);
definition of lai, H. G. Leach, Angevin Britain
and Scandinavia, Cambridge, U.S.A. 1921,
p. 199.]

(2) PARTICULAR PHASES AND HEROES

(a) *Lai le Freine*

[*Wells*, pp. 126, 783, 1051, 1106, 1209, 1301,
1389; *Hibbard*, p. 294.]

MS. Auchinleck (Nat. Lib. Scotland
19.2.1). Ed. H. Weber, Metrical Romances of
the XIII, XIV and XV Centuries, Edinburgh,
vol. i, 1810, p. 357; ed. H. Varnhagen, Ang.
iii, 1880, p. 415; ed. A. Laurin, Essay on
Language of Lay le Freine, Upsala, 1869;
ed. F. J. Child, English and Scottish Ballads,
vol. ii, Boston, 1886, p. 63; ed. M. Wattie,
Smith College Stud. x, 1929, no. 3.

Abstract. G. Ellis, Specimens of Early
English Metrical Romances, 1848, p. 538.

Translation. E. Rickert, Early English
Romances: Love, 1908, p. 46.

Studies. [ten Brink, vol. i, p. 259; *Schofield*,
p. 192. See also under Breton Lais, above;
also Wilda, Westenholz, Siefken, Wheatley,
et al., in *Wells*, under Eustace-Constance-Florence-Griselda Legends.]

Zupitza, J. E. Studien, x, 1887, p. 41.
Holthausen, F. Ang. xiii, 1891, p. 360.
Guillaume, G. Prologues of The Lay le Freine
and Sir Orfeo. MLN. xxxvi, 1921, p. 458.

(b) *Sir Orfeo*

[*Wells*, pp. 128, 783, 1006, 1050, 1106, 1209,
1262, 1301, 1389; *Hibbard*, p. 195.]

MSS. 1, Auchinleck (Nat. Lib. Scotland
19.2.1); 2, Ashmole 61 (Bodleian); 3, Harley
3810.

Editions. 1, D. Laing, Selected Remains of
Ancient Popular Poetry of Scotland, 1822,
rev. W. C. Hazlitt, vol. i, 1895, p. 64; 1,

compiled from 3, A. S. Cook, Literary Middle English Reader, Boston, 1915, p. 88; K. Sisam, Fourteenth Century Verse and Prose, Oxford, 1921, p. 13; 2, J. O. Halliwell[-Phillipps], Illustrations of the Fairy Mythology of Shakespeare's Midsummer Night's Dream, 1845, p. 36 (rptd W. C. Hazlitt, Fairy Tales, Legends and Romances, 1875, and Scottish Antiquary, XVI, 1902, p. 30); 3, J. Ritson, Ancient English Metrical Romances, vol. II, 1802, p. 248; critical edn, O. Zielke, Breslau, 1880.

Selection. G. Sampson, Cambridge Book of Prose and Verse, 1924.

Translations. J. L. Weston, Chief Middle English Poets, Boston, 1914, p. 133; E. Rickert, Early English Romances: Love, 1908, p. 32; adaptation, E. E. Hunt, Cambridge. U.S.A. 1910.

Studies. [*Ward*, vol. I, p. 171; *Schofield*, p. 184; Histoire littéraire de la France, vol. XXIX, p. 499; G. Gröber, Grundriss, vol. II[1], Strasburg, 1902, p. 593.]

King Orfeo. Ed. F. J. Child, English and Scottish Ballads, vol. I, Boston, 1857, p. 215. [Ballad.]

Kittredge, G. L. AJ. Phil. VII, 1886, p. 176.

Zupitza, J. E. Studien, X, 1887, p. 42.

Foulet, Guillaume. Prologue. MLN. XXI, 1906, p. 46, XXXVI, 1921, p. 458.

Marshall, L. E. Greek Myths in Modern English Poetry. Studi di Filologia moderne, V, 1912, p. 203.

Wirl, J. Orpheus in der englischen Literatur. Vienna, 1913.

Holthausen, F. Ang. XLII, 1918, p. 425. [Textnotes.]

Brunner, K. Palaestra, CXLVIII, 1925, p. 79.

Serjeantson, M. S. RES. III, 1927, p. 330. [Dialect.]

(c) *Emare*

[*Wells*, pp. 129, 783, 1209, 1389; *Hibbard*, p. 23.]

MS. Cotton, Caligula A II (see *Ward*, vol. I, p. 418). Ed. J. Ritson, Ancient English Metrical Romances, vol. II, 1802, p. 183 (collation, E. Studien, XV, 1891, p. 248); ed. A. B. Gough, Old and Middle English Texts, 1901; ed. E. Rickert, EETS. Ex. Ser. 1906.

Studies. [See *Hibbard*, and *Wells*, under Eustace-Constance-Florence-Griselda Legends, and Chaucer's Tales of Clerk and Man of Law.]

Lücke, E. Das Leben der Constance. Ang. XIV, 1891, p. 77.

Gough, A. B. On the Middle English Emare. Kiel, 1900.

—— The Constance Saga. Palaestra, XXIII, 1902.

Ang. Bbl. XIII, 1902, p. 46. [Vv. 49 ff.]

Siefken, O. Der Konstanze-Griseldistypus. Rathenow, 1904.

—— Das geduldige Weib. Leipzig, 1904.

Däumling, H. Studien über den Typus des Mädchens ohne Hände. Munich, 1912.

Trounce, A. McI. The English Tail-Rhyme Romances. Medium Aevum, I, II, III, 1932-4.

(d) *Sir Launfal*

[*Wells*, pp. 131, 783, 1209, 1262, 1301, 1346, 1389; *Billings*, p. 144.]

MS. Cotton, Caligula A II. Ed. Sir H. Ellis, A. Way's trn from Le Grand d'Aussy, vol. II, 1815, p. 298, vol. III, p. 233; ed. J. Ritson, Ancient English Metrical Romances, vol. II, 1802, p. 1 (rptd E. Goldsmid, Edinburgh, 1885); ed. J. O. Halliwell[-Phillipps], Illustrations of the Fairy Mythology of Shakespeare's Midsummer Night's Dream, 1845 (rptd W. C. Hazlitt, Fairy Tales, Legends and Romances, 1875, p. 48); ed. L. Erling, Li Lais de Lanval, Kempten, 1883; ed. M. Kaluza, E. Studien, XVIII, 1893, p. 165.

Selection. G. Sampson, Cambridge Book of Prose and Verse, 1924, p. 238.

Translations. E. Rickert, Early English Romances: Love, 1908, p. 57; J. L. Weston, Chief Middle English Poets, Boston, 1914, p. 204.

[*Studies.* On Thomas Chester see: edns above; DNB.; G. Sarrazin's edn Octovian, Heilbronn, 1885; M. Kaluza's edn Libeaus Desconus, Leipzig, 1890; J. Harris, MLN. XLVI, 1931, p. 24.]

Münster, K. L. C. Untersuchungen zu Thomas Chestre's Launfal. Kiel, 1886.

Kolls, A. F. H. Zur Lanvalsage. Berlin, 1886.

Wilda, O. Über die örtliche Verbreitung der zwölfzeiligen Schweifreimstrophe in England. Breslau, 1887.

Bülbring, K. On Verbs. QF. LXIII, 1889, p. 30.

Schofield, W. H. Lays of Graelent and Launfal. PMLA. XV, 1900, p. 121.

Cross, T. P. Celtic Fée in Launfal. [In Kittredge Anniversary Papers, Boston, 1913, p. 377.]

Trounce, A. McI. The English Tail-Rhyme Romances. Medium Aevum, I, II, III, 1932-4.

(e) *Sir Landeval*

[*Wells*, pp. 133, 784, 1209.]

MS. Rawlinson C 86 (Bodleian). Ed. G. L. Kittredge, AJ. Phil. X, 1889, p. 1; ed. R. Zimmermann, Königsberg, 1900.

Translation. G. Sampson, Cambridge Book of Prose and Verse, 1924, p. 238.

(f) Sir Lambewell

[*Wells*, pp. 133, 784, 1389.]

MS. Percy Folio (BM. Add. 27879). Ed. J. W. Hales and F. J. Furnivall, Percy Folio Manuscript, vol. I, 1867, p. 144; ed. A. F. H. Kolls, Zur Lanvalsage, Berlin, 1886.

(g) Sir Lamwell

[*Wells*, pp. 133, 784, 1262, 1389.]

Ptd fragments. 1, Malone 941 (Bodleian); 2, Douce, II, 95 (Bodleian); 3, University Lib. Cambridge Kk.v.30.

Editions. 1, 2, J. W. Hales and F. J. Furnivall, Percy Folio Manuscript, vol. I, 1867, pp. 522, 533; A. F. H. Kolls, Zur Lanvalsage, Berlin, 1886; 3, F. J. Furnivall, Captain Cox, 1871, p. xxxi, and Robert Laneham's Letter, New Shakspere Soc. 1890.

(h) Sir Degare

[*Wells*, pp. 134, 784, 1106, 1209, 1262, 1302, 1346, 1389; *Hibbard*, p. 301.]

MSS. 1, Auchinleck (Nat. Lib. Scotland 19.2.1; see E. Studien, VII, 1884, p. 185); 2, University Lib. Cambridge Ff.II.38 (some 352 vv.); 3, Egerton 2862 (formerly Duke of Sutherland; see E. Studien, VII, 1884, p. 192); 4, Percy Folio (BM. Add. 27879); 5, Douce 261 (Bodleian); 6, Selden C 39 (Bodleian; print, John King, 1560); 7, print, Copland.

Editions. 1, D. Laing, Abbotsford Club, 1849; 4, J. W. Hales and F. J. Furnivall, Percy Folio Manuscript, vol. III, 1869, p. 16; 7, E. V. Utterson, Select Pieces of Early Popular Poetry, vol. I, 1817, p. 113; all MSS, G. Schleich, Heidelberg, 1929.

Abstract of Copland. G. Ellis, Specimens of Early English Metrical Romances, 1848, p. 574; J. Ashton, Romances of Chivalry, 1890, p. 103.

Studies.

Histoire littéraire de la France. Vol. xxiv, p. 505.

Kaluza, M. Libeaus Desconus. Leipzig, 1890. [P. cliv.]

Slover, C. H. Sire Degarre: a Study. Austin, 1931.

Faust, G. P. Sir Degare. A Study of the Text and Narrative Structure. Princeton, 1935.

(i) Sir Gowther (Robert the Devil)

[*Wells*, pp. 135, 784, 1006, 1106, 1209, 1389; *Billings*, p. 227; *Hibbard*, p. 49.]

MSS. 1, Nat. Lib. Scotland 19.3.1; 2, Royal 17 B xliii.

Editions. 2, E. V. Utterson, Select Pieces of Early Popular Poetry, vol. I, 1817, p. 157; both MSS, K. Breul, Oppeln, 1886. Rpt of

de Worde's Robert the Devil, W. C. Hazlitt, Remains of the Early Popular Poetry of England, vol. I, 1864, p. 217; W. J. Thoms, Collection of Early Prose Romances, 1828, p. 167 (rptd as Early English Romances, 1904; as Early English Prose Romances, 1906).

Studies. [*Ward*, vol. I, p. 416, 419, 728; *Schofield*, p. 187.]

Wilda, O. Über die örtliche Verbreitung der zwölfzeiligen Schweifreimstrophe in England. Breslau, 1887.

Weston, J. L. Three Days' Tournament. 1902.

Ravenal, F. L. Tydorel and Sir Gowther. PMLA. xx, 1905, p. 152.

Crane, R. S. Irish Analogue. Romanic Rev. v, 1914, p. 55.

Ogle, M. Orchard Scene. Romanic Rev. xiii, 1914, p. 37.

Trounce, A. McI. The English Tail-Rhyme Romances. Medium Aevum, I, II, III, 1932-4.

[On Robert the Devil see Breul's edn, and *Hibbard*.]

(j) Earl of Toulous

[*Wells*, pp. 137, 784, 1006, 1106, 1209, 1389; *Hibbard*, p. 35.]

MSS. 1, University Lib. Cambridge Ff.II.38; 2, 3, Ashmole 45 and 61 (Bodleian); 4, Thornton (Lincoln Cathedral Lib. A, 5, 2).

Editions. 1, J. Ritson, Ancient English Metrical Romances, vol. III, 1802, p. 105 (rptd E. Goldsmid, Edinburgh, 1884); critical edn, all MSS, G. Lüdtke, Berlin, 1881.

Translation. E. Rickert, Early English Romances: Love, 1908, p. 80.

Studies.

Child, F. J. English and Scottish Ballads. Vol. II, Boston, 1886, p. 33.

Wilda, O. Über die örtliche Verbreitung der zwölfzeiligen Schweifreimstrophe in England. Breslau, 1887.

Paris, S. Le Roman du Comte de Toulouse. Annales du Midi, xII, 1900, p. 5.

Bolte, J. Bibliographie des litterarischen Vereins in Stuttgart, ccxx, Tübingen, 1901.

Holthausen, F. Text-notes. Ang. Bbl. xxvii, 1916, p. 171.

Trounce, A. McI. The English Tail-Rhyme Romances. Medium Aevum, I, II, III, 1932-4.

C. MISCELLANEOUS ROMANCES

(a) Floris and Blauncheflur

[*Wells*, pp. 139, 785, 1006, 1106, 1209, 1302, 1389; *Hibbard*, p. 184.]

MSS. 1, Auchinleck (Nat. Lib. Scotland 19.2.1); 2, Cotton, Vitellius D III; 3, Egerton 2862 (formerly Duke of Sutherland); 4, University Lib. Cambridge Gg. IV. 27, 2.

Editions. 1, C. H. Hartshorne, Ancient Metrical Tales, 1829; D. Laing, A Peniworth of Witte, Abbotsford Club, 1857; 2, F. Lumby, EETS. 1866; rev. edn, all texts, G. H. Mc-Knight, 1901; 1, 3, A. B. Taylor, Oxford, 1927; critical edn, all texts, E. Hausknecht, Berlin, 1885.

Selection. O. F. Emerson, Reader, New York, 1905.

Translations. E. Rickert, Early English Romances: Love, 1908; F. J. H. Darton, Wonder Book of Old Romance, New York, 1907.

Studies. [*Ward*, vol. I, p. 714. Text: Ang. I, 1878, p. 473, XL, 1916, p. 408; E. Studien, III, 1880, p. 99.]

Paris, G. Romania, XXVIII, 1899, pp. 848, 489, XXXV, 1906, pp. 95, 335.

(b) *Amis and Amiloun*

[*Wells*, pp. 157, 787, 1107, 1210; *Hibbard*, p. 65.]

MSS. 1, Auchinleck (Nat. Lib. Scotland 19.2.1); 2, Douce 326 (Bodleian); 3, Harley 2386; 4, Egerton 2862 (formerly Duke of Sutherland).

Editions. 1, H. Weber, Metrical Romances of the XIII, XIV and XV Centuries, vol. II, Edinburgh, 1810, p. 367; critical edn, all MSS, with French, Latin, Norse, E. Koelbing, Heilbronn, 1884.

Selection. G. Sampson, Cambridge Book of Prose and Verse, 1924, p. 258.

Abstract. G. Ellis, Specimens of Early English Metrical Romances, 1848, p. 584.

Translations. E. Rickert, Early English Romances: Friendship, 1908, p. 1; J. L. Weston, Chief Middle English Poets, Boston, 1914, p. 174; F. J. H. Darton, Wonder Book of Old Romance, New York, 1907.

Studies. [*ten Brink*, vol. I, p. 250; *Ward*, vol. I, p. 674.]

Koelbing, E. Die Überlieferung. PBB. IV, 1877, p. 271, and E. Studien, II, 1878–9, p. 295, v, 1882, p. 465.

Wilda, O. Über die örtliche Verbreitung der zwölfzeiligen Schweifreimstrophe in England. Breslau, 1887.

Ayres, H. M. Faerie Queene and Amis and Amiloun. MLN. xxx, 1915, p. 17. [See its bibliography.]

Holthausen, F. Text-notes. Ang. XLI, 1917, p. 456.

Möller, W. Untersuchungen über Guy of Warwick. Königsberg, 1917. [Relation of strophic part with Amis and Amiloun].

Krappe, A. H. Folk-tale Analogue. MLR. XVIII, 1923, p. 152.

—— Amis and Amiloun and Horn. Leuvensche Bijdragen, XVI, 1924, p. 14.

Trounce, A. McI. The English Tail-Rhyme Romances. Medium Aevum, I, II, III, 1982–4.

[On French see *Wells, Hibbard,* as above.]

(c) *King of Tars*

[*Wells*, pp. 122, 781, 782, 1106, 1209; *Hibbard*, p. 45.]

MSS. 1, Auchinleck (Nat. Lib. Scotland 19.2.1); 2, Vernon (Bodleian 3938); 3, BM. Add. 22288. [On MSS see C. Brown, Register of Middle English Religious Verse, vol. II, 1920, item 745.

Editions. 2, J. Ritson, Ancient English Metrical Romances, vol. II, 1802, p. 156; 1, 2, 3, F. Krause, E. Studien, XI, 1888, p. 33.

Abstract. T. Warton, History of English Poetry, ed. W. C. Hazlitt, vol. II, 1871, p. 176.

Studies. [*Ward*, vol. I, p. 767. Source, notes: Ang. xv, 1892–3, p. 195. Parallels: O. Zielke, edn Sir Orfeo, Berlin, 1880; E. Koelbing, edn Sir Beues, EETS. Ex. Ser. 1885, p. xlv.]

Trounce, A. McI. The English Tail-Rhyme Romances. Medium Aevum, I, II, III, 1932–4.

(d) *Sir Amadace*

[*Wells*, pp. 159, 787, 1006, 1107, 1210, 1262, 1302, 1390; *Hibbard*, p. 73.]

MSS. 1, Auchinleck (Nat. Lib. Scotland 19.2.1); 2, Ireland (Hale, Lancs).

Editions. 1, H. Weber, Metrical Romances of the XIII, XIV and XV Centuries, vol. III, Edinburgh, 1810, p. 241; 2, J. Robson, Three Early English Metrical Romances, 1847, p. 27; both MSS, G. Stephens, Ghost-Thanks, Copenhagen, 1860.

Translation. E. Rickert, Early English Romances: Friendship, 1908, p. 49; J. L. Weston, Chief Middle English Poets, Boston, 1914.

Studies.

Hippe, M. Untersuchungen zu Sir Amadace. Archiv, LXXXI, 1888, p. 141.

Dutz, H. Der Dank der Todten in der Englischen Literatur. Jahresbericht der Staats-Oberrealschule, Troppau, 1894.

Gerould, G. H. The Grateful Dead. Folk-Lore Soc. 1907. [See its bibliography.]

Tatlock, J. S. P. Leuvenoth and the Grateful Dead. MP. XXII, 1924–5, p. 211.

Reinhard, J. R. Fr. Amadas et Ydoine. Paris, 1926; Durham, North Carolina, 1927.

Serjeantson, M. S. Dialect. RES. iii, 1927, p. 328.

Trounce, A. McI. The English Tail-Rhyme Romances. Medium Aevum, i, ii, iii, 1932–4.

Dickins, B. Leeds Stud. no. 2, 1933, p. 62, no. 3, 1934, p. 30; TLS. 21 Dec. 1933, p. 909. [Ireland MS.]

[On French see Reinhard, *Wells*, *Hibbard*.]

(e) The Seven Sages of Rome

[Campbell, edn; *Wells*, pp. 186, 792, 1007, 109, 1211, 1891; *Hibbard*, p. 174.]

MSS. 1, Auchinleck (Nat. Lib. Scotland 19.2.1), Egerton 1995, Arundel 140, University Lib. Cambridge Ff.ii.38, Balliol College Oxford 354; 2, University Lib. Cambridge Dd.i.17; 3, Cotton, Galba E ix, Rawlinson Poetry 175 (Bodleian; see PMLA. xiv, 899, p. 459); 4, Scottish, Asloan (Malahide Castle, Ireland; see E. Studien, xxv, 1898, . 321).

Editions. Auchinleck, parts of Cotton, H. Weber, Metrical Romances of XIII, XIV and XV Centuries, vol. iii, Edinburgh, 1810, p. 1 (collation with MS, E. Studien, vi, 1888, . 443); University Lib. Cambridge Dd.i.17, '. Wright, Percy Soc. 1845 (collation with MS, E. Studien, vi, 1888, p. 448); Cotton, ariants of Rawlinson, Bannatyne Club, 1837; . Campbell, Boston, 1907; Auchinleck (with ariants of Egerton, Arundel, Cambridge Ff., alliol), K. Brunner, EETS. 1933.

Selections. E. Mätzner, Altenglische Sprachroben, pt. i, Berlin, 1867, p. 254; A. S. Cook, iterary Middle English Reader, Boston, 1915, . 141; PMLA. xiv, 1899, pp. 94, 460; Petras, s below, pp. 54, 60; J. O. Halliwell[-Philpps], Thornton Romances, Camden Soc. 344, p. xliii; T. Wright, Percy Soc. 1845, . lxx.

Extracts. G. Ellis, Specimens of Early nglish Metrical Romances, 1848, p. 405.

Modern rendering, parts. J. L. Weston, hief Middle English Poets, Boston, 1914, 281.

Studies. [*Ward*, vol. ii, p. 199.] aris, G. Deux Rédactions des Sept Sages. Paris, 1876. etras, P. Über die mittelenglischen Fassungen der Sage von den Sieben weisen Meistern. Grünberg, 1885. [P. 60.] uchner, G. Historia Septem Sapientum. Erlangen, 1889. — Beiträge zur Geschichte der sieben weisen Meister. Archiv, cxiii, 1904, p. 297. ampbell, K. Study of Romance of the Seven Sages of Rome. Baltimore, 1898, and PMLA. xiv, 1899, p. 1.

Fischer, H. Beiträge zur Literatur der Sieben weisen Meister. Greifswald, 1902.
Campbell, K. Sources of the Story of Sapientes. MLN. xxiii, 1908, p. 202.
Smith, H. A. French Verse Version. Romanic Rev. iii, 1912, p. 1.
Tuttle, A. H. Rimes, Language. MLR. xvi, 1921, p. 166. [See also K. Campbell, MLR. xvii, 1922, p. 289.]
Brunner, K. Die Reimsprache der sogenannten Kentischen Fassung der Sieben weisen Meister. Archiv, cxl, 1920, p. 199.
Krappe, A. H. Studies. Archivum Romanicum, viii, 1924, p. 886, ix, 1925, p. 345, xi, 1927, p. 168, xvi, 1932, p. 271.

(f) Ipomedon

[*Wells*, pp. 146, 785, 1006, 1107, 1210, 1302; *Hibbard*, p. 224.]

MSS. A, Ipomedon, Chetham Lib. 8009 (Manchester); B, Lyfe of Ipomydon, Harley 2252; C, Ipomedon (prose), Marquis of Bath 25.

Editions. H. Weber, Lyfe, Metrical Romances of the XIII, XIV and XV Centuries. vol. ii, Edinburgh, 1810, p. 279; fragments, E. Studien, xiii, 1889, p. 153; all texts, E. Koelbing, Breslau, 1899.

Abstract of Lyfe. G. Ellis, Specimens of Early English Metrical Romances, 1848, p. 505.

Studies. [*Ward*, vol. i, p. 728; Histoire littéraire de la France, vol xxiv, p. 504. On text, language, interpretation: E. Studien, xiv, 1890, pp. 371, 386, xviii, 1894, p. 282, xxxviii, 1914, p. 131; Ang. xl, 1916, p. 412, xli, 1917, p. 463.]

Furnivall, F. J. Captain Cox's Ballads. 1871. [P. cxlii.]
Kirschten, W. Überlieferung und Sprache der Lyfe of Ipomedon. Marburg, 1885.
Seyferth, P. Sprache und Metrik. Le Morte Arthur und sein Verhältniss zu The Lyfe of Ipomedon. Berliner Beiträge zur germanischen und romanischen Philologie, viii, 1895.
Weston, J. L. Three Days' Tournament. 1902.
Carter, C. H. Ipomedon. An Illustration of Romance Origins. [In Haverford Essays, Haverford, 1909, p. 239.]
Barrow, S. F. Medieval Society Romances. New York, 1924. [P. 135.]
Muchnie, H. Coward Knight. PMLA. xliii, 1928–9, p. 327.
Trounce, A. McI. The English Tail-Rhyme Romances. Medium Aevum, i, ii, iii, 1932–4.

(g) Octavian

[*Wells*, pp. 117, 781, 782, 1106, 1208, 1261, 1301, 1388; *Hibbard*, p. 267.]

Version I, Southern

MS. Cotton, Caligula A II. Ed. H. Weber, Metrical Romances of the XIII, XIV, and XV Centuries, vol. III, Edinburgh, 1810, p. 157; G. Sarrazin, with Version II, Heilbronn, 1885.

Version II, Northern

MSS. 1, University Lib. Cambridge Ff. II. 38; 2, Thornton (Lincoln Cathedral Lib. A, 5, 2).

Editions. 1, J. O. Halliwell[-Phillipps], Percy Soc. 1848; 1, 2, G. Sarrazin, Heilbronn, 1885 (with Version I); 1, 2, J. J. Conybeare, 1809 (rptd E. Goldsmid, Aungervyle Soc. 1882).

Studies. [*Ward*, vol. I, p. 762.]

Streve, P. Die Octaviansage. Erlangen, 1884.
Eule, R. Untersuchungen über die nordenglische Version. Halle, 1889.
Kaluza, M. Libeaus Desconus. Leipzig, 1890. [P. clxiii.]
—— Thomas Chestre. E. Studien, XVIII, 1893, p. 165.
DNB. under 'Chestre'.
Siefken, O. Der Konstanze-Griseldistypus. Rathenow, 1904. [P. 40.]
Settegast, F. Floovent und Julian. Halle, 1906.
Brockstedt, G. Floovent-Studien. Kiel. 1907.
Fischer, E. Der Lautbestand der südmittelenglischen Octavian. Anglistische Forschungen, LXIII, 1927.
Kessler, L. Der Prosaroman vom Kaiser Oktavian. Frankfort, 1932.
Trounce, A. McI. The English Tail-Rhyme Romances. Medium Aevum, I, II, III, 1932-4.

[See under Sir Launfal, above, p. 152, Libeaus Desconus, above, p. 134. On French see *Wells* and *Hibbard*.]

(h) William of Palerne

[*Billings*, p. 41; *Wells*, pp. 19, 765, 1003, 1049, 1101, 1204, 1259, 1296, 1344, 1382; *Hibbard*, p. 214.]

MS. King's College Cambridge 13. Ed. Sir F. Madden, Roxburghe Club, 1832; ed. W. W. Skeat, EETS. Ex. Ser. 1867.

Fragment of De Worde's ptd prose. Ptd F. Brie, Archiv, CXVIII, 1907, p. 318.

Selections. H. C. Hartshorne, Ancient Metrical Tales, 1829, p. 256; R. Wülcker, Lesebuch, Halle, 1874-9; R. Morris and W. W.

Skeat. Specimens of Early English, vol. II Oxford, 1894; G. Sampson, Cambridge Book of Prose and Verse, 1924.

Modern rendering. F. J. H. Darton, Wonder Book of Old Romance, New York, 1907.

Studies. [Notes: MLN. VII, 1892, p. 268 Ang. XXVI, 1903, p. 367. Dialect, place o origin: J. R. Hulbert, MP. XIX, 1921-2, p. 1 R. J. Menner, PMLA. XXXVII, 1922, p. 503 M. S. Serjeantson, RES. III, 1927, p. 329.]

Asklöf, I. Essay on William and the Werwolf Upsala, 1872.
Trautmann, M. Über die Verfasser und Ent stehungszeit einiger alliterirender Gedichte Leipzig, 1876.
Kaluza, M. French Source. E. Studien, IV 1881, p. 197.
Schüddekopf, A. Sprache und Dialekt Erlangen, 1886.
Luick, K. Verse. Ang. XI, 1889, p. 566. [Se also Alliterative Verse, p. 196 below.]
Pitschel, E. Zur Syntax. Marburg, 1890.
Smith, K. Werwolf in Literature. PMLA. IX 1894, p. 1.
Kittredge, G. L. Arthur and Gorlagon. Har vard Stud. VIII, 1903, p. 150.
Tibbals, K. Magic in William of Palerne MP. I, 1903-4, p. 355.
Barrow, S. F. Medieval Society Romances New York, 1924. [P. 123.]
McKeehan, I. P. William de Palerne, A Med ieval Best Seller. PMLA. XLI, 1926, p. 787
Hall, V. Irish Version of French. PMLA XLII, 1927, p. 1066.
Oakden, J. P. Alliterative Poetry in Middl English. Manchester, 1930, pp. 55, 158 248.
Koziol, H. E. Studien, LXVII, 1932, p. 167 [Author.]
Whiting, B. J. Harvard Stud. XV, 1933, p 107. [Proverbs.]

[On French see *Wells* and *Hibbard*.]

(i) Sir Isumbras

[*Wells*, pp. 114, 781, 1005, 1105, 1208, 1301 *Hibbard*, p. 1.]

MSS. 1, Caius College Cambridge 17 (A, IX); 2, Thornton (Lincoln Cathedral Lib A, 5, 2); 3, Cotton, Caligula A II (see *Ward* vol. I, pp. 180, 760); 4, Ashmole 61 (Bodleian) 5, Nat. Lib. Scotland 19.3.1; 6, Royal Lib Naples XIII B 29; 7, Gray's Inn, Londo (fragment); 8, University College Oxford 14 (vv. 1-17); 9, MS Malone 941 (Bodleian; pt fragment).

Editions. 2, J. O. Halliwell[-Phillipps Thornton Romances, Camden Soc. 1844, p. 8 (after Halliwell, Kelmscott Press, 1897); 7 C. D'Evelyn, E. Studien, LII, 1918, p. 72; 6

E. Koelbing, E. Studien, III, 1880, p. 200 (see T. Wright and J. O. Halliwell[-Phillipps], Reliquiae Antiquae, vol. II, 1843, pp. 58, 67); 8, E. Studien, XLVIII, 1914–5, p. 329; all MSS, J. Zupitza and G. Schleich, Palaestra, XV, 1901. [See Schleich and *Hibbard* for early ptd texts.]

Summary of Caius. G. Ellis, Specimens of Early English Metrical Romances, 1848, p. 479.

Selection. G. Sampson, Cambridge Book of Prose and Verse, 1924.

Studies. [Date: BBA. XII, 1902, p. 97. On text: Archiv, LXXXVIII, 1892, p. 72, XC, 1893, p. 148].

Sarrazin, G. Octavian. Heilbronn, 1885. [P. xliv.]

Wilda, O. Über die zwölfzeiligen Schweifreimstrophe in England. Breslau, 1887.

Adam, E. EETS. Ex Ser. 1887, p. xxiv.

Gerould, G. H. Eustace Legend. PMLA. XIX, 1904, p. 365, XX, 1905, p. 529.

—— The Grateful Dead. Folk-Lore Soc. 1907.

Murray, J. Eustace Legend. Modern Humanities Research Ass. Bulletin, I, 1927, p. 35.

Krappe, A. H. E. Studien, LXVII, 1932, p. 174. [Armenian parallel.]

Trounce, A. McI. The English Tail-Rhyme Romances. Medium Aevum, I, II, III, 1932–4.

(j) Roberd of Cisyle

[*Wells*, pp. 162, 788, 1006, 1210, 1390; *Hibbard*, p. 58; C. Brown, Register of Middle English Religious Verse, vol. II, 1920, item 1711.]

MSS. 1, Vernon (Bodleian 3938); 2, Trinity College Oxford 57; 3, University Lib. Cambridge Ff.II.38; 4, University Lib. Cambridge Ii.IV.9; 5, Caius College Cambridge 174; 6, Harley 525; 7, Harley 1701; 8, BM. Add. 22283.

Editions. 1, 2, with readings of all MSS, C. Horstmann, Altenglische Legenden, Heilbronn, 1878, p. 209; 3, J. O. Halliwell[-Phillipps], Nugae Poeticae, 1844 (rptd with 6, W. C. Hazlitt, Remains of Early English Popular Poetry, 1864, vol. I, p. 264); 3, 4, 5, C. Horstmann, Archiv, LXII, 1879, p. 416; 6, R. Utterson, priv. ptd, 1839 (rptd with 3, Hazlitt, as above); 7, part with abstract, G. Ellis, Specimens of Early English Metrical Romances, 1848, p. 474; critical edn, R. Nuck, Berlin, 1887.

Translation. F. J. H. Darton, Wonder Book of Old Romance, New York, 1907.

Studies. [*Ward*, vol. I, p. 763, vol. III, pp. 202, 214.]

Gerould, G. H. Saints' Legends. Boston, 1916. [Pp. 252, 369.]

[On French and later versions see *Wells, Hibbard.*]

(k) Sir Eglamour of Artois

[*Wells*, pp. 115, 781, 1005, 1208, 1301; *Hibbard*, p. 275.]

MSS. 1, Thornton (Lincoln Cathedral Lib. A, 5, 2); 2, Cotton, Caligula A II; 3, University Lib. Cambridge Ff.II.38; 4, Egerton 2862 (formerly Duke of Sutherland; one leaf).

Editions. 3, J. O. Halliwell[-Phillipps], Thornton Romances, Camden Soc. 1844, p. 121 (with extracts from Thornton); 1, A. S. Cook, New York, 1911 (*q.v.* for early prints); critical edn, G. Schleich, Palaestra, LIII, 1906. Reprints: Percy Folio MS copy of print, J. W. Hales and F. J. Furnivall, Percy Folio Manuscript, vol. II, 1868, pp. 341, 338; Edinburgh, 1508, D. Laing, edn Golagrus and Gawane, Edinburgh, 1827; c. 1530, J. Hall, Archiv, XCV, 1895, p. 308.

Modern renderings from edn c. 1540. G. Ellis, Specimens of Early English Metrical Romances, 1848, p. 527 (see Laing, above); J. Ashton, Romances of Chivalry, 1890, p. 275.

Studies. [*Ward*, vol. I, pp. 766, 820.]

Adam, E. Eglamour and Torrent. EETS. Ex. Ser. LI, 1887, p. xxvii.

Zielke, A. Untersuchungen über Sir Eglamour. Kiel, 1889.

Schleich, G. Eglamour und Torrent. Archiv, XCII, 1894, p. 343.

Gerould, G. H. Eustace Legend. PMLA. XIX, 1904, p. 439.

Siefken, O. Der Konstanze-Griseldistypus. Rathenow, 1904. [P. 44.]

Rickert, E. Emaré. EETS. Ex. Ser. 1906, p. xlvii.

Baskervill, C. R. Two Plays. MP. XIV, 1916–7, pp. 229, 759.

Murray, J. Eustace Legend. Modern Humanities Research Ass. Bulletin, I, 1927, p. 35.

Trounce, A. McI. The English Tail-Rhyme Romances. Medium Aevum, I, II, III, 1932–4.

(l) Titus and Vespasian, or Destruction of Jerusalem (Couplet Version)

[*Wells*, pp. 153, 786, 1107, 1210, 1346, 1390.]

MSS. 1, BM. Add. 10036; 2, Laud 622 (Bodleian); 3, Douce 78 (Bodleian); 4, Digby 230 (Bodleian); 5, Magdalene College Cambridge, Pepys 37 (new number 2014); 6, Harley 4733; 7, Douce 126 (Bodleian). [On

MSS see *Ward*, vol. I, p. 187; EETS. LXIX, 1878, p. 7; Archiv, CVIII, 1902, p. 199; C. Brown, Register, vol. II, 1920, item 1171.]

Editions. 5, Archiv, CXI, 1903, p. 285, CXII, 1904, p. 25; five MSS, J. A. Herbert, Roxburghe Club, 1905.

Studies. [See Archiv, CXXII, 1909, p. 159.]

Bergau, F. Untersuchungen über Quelle und Verfasser. Königsberg, 1901.

Hulme, W. H. EETS. Ex. Ser. c, 1907, p. xxii and note.

Arvidson, J. M. Language of MS. Pepys 37. Lund, 1916.

[On French see *Wells*, p. 786.]

(m) Sege of Jerusalem, or Distructio Jerusalem (Alliterative Version)

[*Wells*, pp. 155, 786, 1346, 1390.]

MSS. 1, Cotton, Caligula A II; 2, Cotton, Vespasian E XVI; 3, Laud 656 (Bodleian); 4, BM. Add. 31042; 5, University Lib. Cambridge Mm. v.14; 6, Ashburnham CXXX, Art. 5; 7, Lambeth 491.
On MSS see *Ward*, vol. I, pp. 180, 185, 928; Archiv, LXXXVI, 1891, p. 384; C. Brown, Register, vol. II, 1920, item 958.

Editions. 3, G. Steffler, Sege of Jerusalem, Marburg, 1891; E. Koelbing and M. Day, EETS. 1932 (from Laud MS with variants from others).

Studies.

Hales, J. W. and Furnivall, F. J. Percy Folio Manuscript. Vol. III, 1869. [P. xxx.]

Kopka, F. Destruction of Jerusalem. Breslau, 1887.

Reicke, C. Untersuchungen über Morte Arthure. Königsberg, 1906.

Hulbert, J. R. Stud. Phil. XXVIII, 1931, p. 602. [Text.]

(n) Sir Degrevant

[*Wells*, pp. 141, 785, 1006, 1107, 1209; *Hibbard*, p. 306.]

MSS. 1, University Lib. Cambridge Ff.i.6; 2, Thornton (Lincoln Cathedral Lib. A, 5, 2).

Editions. 1, J. O. Halliwell[-Phillipps], Thornton Romances, Camden Soc. 1844, p. 177 (after Halliwell, Kelmscott Press, 1896); 1, 2, K. Luick, Vienna, 1917.

Selections. Halliwell, edn (from Thornton); G. Schleich, E. Studien, XII, 1889, p. 140 (both MSS).

Translation. E. Rickert, Early English Romances: Love, 1908.

Studies. [See E. Studien, III, 1880, p. 100.]

Bülbring, K. Untersuchungen zu mittelenglischer Metrik. SEP. L, 1913.

Medary, M. P. and Brown, A. C. L. Stanzalinking. Romanic Rev. VII, 1916, pp. 243, 271.

Holthausen, F. Text-notes. Ang. XLII, 1918, 78.

Finsterbusch, F. Der Versbau. Vienna, 1919.

(o) Le Bone Florence de Rome

[*Wells*, pp. 133, 781, 782, 1106, 1209, 1301; *Hibbard*, p. 12.]

MS. University Lib. Cambridge Ff.II.38.
Ed. J. Ritson, Ancient English Metrical Romances, vol. III, 1802, p. 46; ed. W. Viëtor and A. Knobbe, text, Marburg, 1893, introduction, 1899.

Studies.

Wenzel, R. Die Fassungen der Sage von Florence de Rome. Marburg, 1890.

Knobbe, A. Über die mittelenglische Dichtung Le Bone Florence. Marburg, 1899.

Siefken, O. Der Konstanze-Griseldistypus. Rathenow, 1904. [P. 34.]

Holthausen, F. Text-notes. Ang. XLI, 1917, p. 497.

Chaytor, H. J. Text of French Fragment. Modern Humanities Research Ass. Bulletin, I, 1927, p. 48.

Trounce, A. McI. The English Tail-Rhyme Romances. Medium Aevum, I, II, III, 1932-4.

[On French see *Wells* and *Hibbard*.]

(p) Sir Cleges

[*Wells*, pp. 160, 787, 1210, 1262, 1302; *Hibbard*, p. 79; McKnight edn, introduction and bibliography.]

MSS. 1, Nat. Lib. Scotland 19.3.1 (formerly Jac. V, 7, 27); 2, Ashmole 61 (Bodleian).

Editions. 1, H. Weber, Metrical Romances of the XIII, XIV, and XV Centuries, vol. I, Edinburgh, 1810, p. 331; 2, G. H. McKnight, Middle English Humorous Tales in Verse, Boston, 1913, p. 38; both MSS, A. Treichel, E. Studien, XXII, 1896, pp. 345, 374.

Translation. J. L. Weston, Sir Cleges, Sir Libeaus Desconus, 1902.

[See J. R. Reinhard, Analogues, Journ. American Folk-Lore, XXXVI, 1925, p. 380, and A. McI. Trounce, The English Tail-Rhyme Romances, Medium Aevum, I, II, III, 1932-4.]

(q) Sir Triamour

[*Wells*, pp. 120, 781, 782, 1208; *Hibbard*, p. 283.]

MSS. 1, University Lib. Cambridge Ff. ii. 38; 2, BM. Add. 27879 (Percy Folio MS); 3, Rawlinson (Bodleian; fragment, 75 vv.).

Editions. 1, J. O. Halliwell[-Phillipps], Percy Soc. 1846; 2, J. W. Hales and F. J. Furnivall, Percy Folio Manuscript, vol. ii, 1868, p. 78. Critical text of vv. 1–132, H. Bauszus, Königsberg, 1902. Copland's print, 593, ptd R. Utterson, Select Pieces of Early Popular Poetry, vol. i, 1817, p. 5.

Abstract of Copland's undated edn (Bodleian). G. Ellis, Specimens of Early English Metrical Romances, 1848, p. 491; J. Ashton, Romances of Chivalry, 1890, p. 171.

Studies. Siefken, O. Das geduldige Weib. Leipzig, 1904. —— Der Konstanze-Griseldistypus. Rathenow, 1904. Trounce, A. McI. The English Tail-Rhyme Romances. Medium Aevum, i, ii, iii, 1932–4.

[On French see *Wells* and *Hibbard*.]

(r) Sir Torrent of Portyngale

[See *Wells*, pp. 117, 781, 782, 1105, 1208; *Hibbard*, p. 279.]

MS. Chetham Lib. 8009 (Manchester; colltion, E. Studien, vii, 1884, p. 344). Ed. J. O. Halliwell[-Phillipps], 1842; ed. E. Adam, EETS. Ex. Ser. 1887. [Fragments of early print in Douce Collection, ptd Halliwell, appendix.]

Studies. [Text. Ang. xvii, 1894–5, p. 401; note, E. Studien, xiii, 1889, p. 136.] Adam, E. Über Sir Torrent of Portyngale. Breslau, 1887. Vilda, O. Über die örtliche Verbreitung der zwölfzeiligen Schweifreimstrophe in England. Breslau, 1887. Schleich, G. Über die Beziehungen von Eglamour und Torrent. Archiv, xcii, 1894, p. 343. Gerould, G. H. Eustace Legend. PMLA. xix, 1904, p. 439. Siefken, O. Der Konstanze-Griseldistypus. Rathenow, 1904. [P. 48.] Spence, L. Dictionary of Medieval Romance. 1913. Holthausen, F. Notes. Ang. xlii, 1918, p. 429. Trounce, A. McI. The English Tail-Rhyme Romances. Medium Aevum, i, ii, iii, 1932–4.

(s) Generydes

[*Wells*, pp. 143, 785, 1209; *Hibbard*, p. 231.]

MSS. 1, Helmingham (Lord Tollemache); 2, Trinity College Cambridge, Gale O, 5, 2.

Editions. 1, F. J. Furnivall, Roxburghe Club, 1866; 2, W. Aldis Wright, EETS. 1873, 1878.

Studies. [Text. E. Studien, xvii, 1892, pp. 23, 49; Ang. i, 1878, p. 481, xxiii, 1900, pp. 125, 249; Archiv, cvi, 1901, p. 351.] Zirwer, O. Untersuchungen zu den beiden mittelenglischen Generydes Romanzen. Breslau, 1889. Holthausen, F. Beiträge zur Textkritik der mittelenglischen Generydes Romanze. Gotenburg, 1898. Settegast, F. Quellenstudien zur Galloromanischen Epik. Leipzig, 1904. [P. 232.]

(t) Parthenope of Blois

[*Wells*, pp. 144, 785, 1107, 1209, 1302; *Hibbard*, p. 200.]

Version I

MSS. 1, University College Oxford C 188; 2, English Poetry C 3 (Bodleian; formerly New College Oxford); 3, Rawlinson, Poet. 14 (Bodleian); 4, Robartes (now Viscount Clifden); 5, BM. Add. 35288; 6, BM. Add. 4860 (18th cent.).

Version II

MS. Vale Royal (Lord Delamere, 308 vv).

Editions. 1, 2, part of 3, W. E. Buckley, Roxburghe Club, 1862; 4, R. Wülker, Ang. xii, 1890, p. 607; Vale Royal, R. C. Nichols, Roxburghe Club, 1873; all MSS, A. T. Bödtker, EETS. Ex. Ser. 1911.

Studies. [*Ward*, vol. i, pp. 698, 707; Ang. xii, 1890, p. 607; E. Studien, xiv, 1890, p. 435.] Koelbing, E. Beiträge zur Geschichte der romantischen Poesie und Prosa des Mittelalters. Berlin, 1876. [P. 80.] Weingärtner, F. Die mittelenglischen Fassungen der Partonopenssage. Breslau, 1888. Barrow, S. K. Medieval Society Romances. New York, 1924. [P. 139.] Leach, H. G. Is Gibbonssaga a Reflection of Partonopeus? [Medieval Studies in Memory of G. S. Loomis, Paris, 1927, p. 113.]

[On foreign versions see *Wells*, *Hibbard*.]

(u) Squyr of Lowe Degre

[*Wells*, pp. 149, 786, 1210; *Hibbard*, p. 263; Mead, edn.]

Texts. 1, Copland's edn, c. 1555–60: ed. J. Ritson, Ancient English Metrical Romances, vol. iii, 1802, p. 145; ed. W. C. Hazlitt, Remains of Early Popular Poetry of England, vol. ii, 1866, p. 21; 2, fragments of de Worde's edn, c. 1520, formerly owned by Mr Christie-Miller, Britwell Court, Burnham, Bucks; 3, Percy Folio MS (BM. Add. 27879): ed. J. W.

Hales and F. J. Furnivall, Percy Folio Manu-
cript, vol. III, 1869, p. 263; all texts, ed.
W. E. Mead, Boston, 1904.

Selection. G. Sampson, Cambridge Book of
Prose and Verse, 1924.

Translation. E. Rickert, Early English
Romances: Love, 1908.

Studies.
Tunk, P. Studien zur The Squyr of Lowe Degre.
Breslau, 1900.
Weyrauch, M. Zur Komposition, Entsteh-
ungszeit, und Beurteilung. E. Studien,
XXXI, 1902, p. 177.
Jefferson, B. L. Note. MLN. XXVIII, 1913,
p. 102.

(v) *Knight of Curtesy*

[*Wells*, pp. 157, 787, 1006, 1210, 1390; *Hibbard*, p. 253; McCausland, edn below.]

Copland's edn, 1568 (Bodleian). Ed. J. Ritson, Ancient English Metrical Romances, vol.
III, 1802, p. 172; ed. W. C. Hazlitt, Remains
of Early Popular Poetry of England, vol. II,
1866, p. 65; ed. E. McCausland, Smith College
Stud. IV, 1922, p. 1.

Translation. E. Rickert, Early English
Romances: Love, 1908, p. 141.

Studies.
Siefken, O. Das geduldige Weib. Leipzig,
1903. [P. 69.]
Lorenz, E. Die Kastellanin von Vergi in der
Literatur Frankreichs, Italiens, etc. Halle,
1909.
Barrow, S. F. Medieval Society Romances.
New York, 1924. [P. 122.]

[See also bibliographies, G. Paris, Littérature
française au Moyen-âge, Paris, 1890, sect. 66;
L. Petit de Julleville, Histoire de la Langue et
de la Littérature françaises, vol. I, Paris, 1896,
p. 343.

(w) *Melusine*

[*Wells*, pp. 156, 787, 1107, 1210, 1302, 1390.]

MS. Royal 18 B II. Ed. A. K. Donald,
EETS. Ex. Ser. 1895.

Studies. [*Ward*, vol. I, p. 687; Literaturblatt
für germanische und romanische Philologie,
1887, p. 346.]

Fairy Melusine and Lusignan family. N. & Q.
21 Oct. 1876, p. 324.
Desaivre, L. La Légend de Mélusine. Niort,
1885.
Köhler, J. Der Ursprung der Melusinersage.
Leipzig, 1895.
Petit de Julleville, L. Histoire de la Langue et
de la Littérature françaises. Vol. I, Paris,
1896. [P. 344.]
Bourdillon, F. W. Huon de Bordeaux and
Melusine. Library, June 1920.

Hoffrichter, L. Die ältesten französischen
Bearbeitungen der Melusine-Sage. Halle,
1928.

[See also Parthenay, below.]

(x) *Parthenay, or Lusignen*

[*Wells*, pp. 156, 787.]

MS. Trinity College Cambridge R, 3, 17.
Ed. W. W. Skeat, EETS. 1866, new edn, 1899.

Abstract. J. Ashton, Romances of Chivalry,
1890, p. 1.

Studies.
Hattendorf, W. Sprache und Dialekt des
spätmittelenglischen 'Romans of Partenay'.
Leipzig, 1887.
[See also Melusine, above.]

(y) *Sir Eger, Sir Grime, and*
Sir Graysteele

[*Hibbard*, p. 312.]

Texts. 1, Percy Folio MS (BM. Add.
27879); ed. J. W. Hales and F. J. Furnivall,
Percy Folio Manuscript, vol. I, 1867, p. 340;
abstract, G. Ellis, Specimens of Early English
Metrical Romances, 1848, p. 546; modern
rendering, E. Rickert, Early English Romances:
Friendship, 1908, p. 137; 2, Eger and Grime,
ptd Aberdeen, 1711, rptd D. Laing, Early
Metrical Tales, Edinburgh, 1826, 1889; 1, 2,
ed. (parallel texts) J. R. Caldwell, Cambridge,
U.S.A. 1933.

[For comparison of versions, notes, gloss,
see G. Reichel, E. Studien, XIX, 1894, p. 1.]

(z) *Roswall and Lillian*

[*Hibbard*, p. 290.]

Texts. 1, Edinburgh, ptd 1663 (in Nat. Lib.
Scotland), ed. O. Lengert, E. Studien, XVI, 1892,
p. 321; 2, ptd c. 1679; 3, ptd Newcastle, n.d.; 4,
Edinburgh, ptd 1775 (Douce, in Bodleian):
abstract, G. Ellis, Specimens of Early English
Metrical Romances, 1848, p. 578; 5, Edinburgh,
ptd 1785; 6, ed. D. Laing, Early Metrical
Tales, Edinburgh, 1826, 1889; modern render-
ing, E. Rickert, Early English Romances:
Love, 1908, p. 116.

[See F. J. Child, English and Scottish
Popular Ballads, vol. V, Boston, 1896, p. 43;
O. Lengert, E. Studien, XVII, 1892, p. 341.]

J. E. W.

II. MIDDLE ENGLISH LITERATURE
TO 1400

[Excluding the Romances (pp. 128–60 above), Chaucer (pp. 208–49 below), and Songs and Lyrics (pp. 267–72 below.]

Narrative Writings: Tales; Chronicles and Prophecies; Sermons and Saints' Legends.

Religious and Didactic Writings: Moral and Religious Instruction; Bible Renderings; Travels; Richard Rolle and Associated Pieces.

Alliterative Pieces: The Thre Ages, Wynnere and the Piers Plowman Series; The Pearl Group.

Wycliffe and Gower: John Wycliffe and Associated Writings; John Gower.

[The references to *Schofield, ten Brink, Ward* and *Wells* are to the manuals by these writers; the full titles will be found on p. 128 above.]

I. TALES

[*Wells*, pp. 164, 788, 955, 1006, 1051, 1107, 1169, 1211, 1302.]

(a) Dame Siriz

[*Wells*, pp. 178, 790, 1108, 1211, 1302, 1346, 1390; McKnight, edn.]

MS. Digby 86 (Bodleian). Ed. T. Wright, Anecdota Literaria, 1844, p. 1; ed. E. Mätzner, Altenglische Sprachproben, pt i, Berlin, 1867, p. 103; ed. J. Zupitza, Übungsbuch, Vienna, 1874; ed. G. H. McKnight, Middle English Humorous Tales in Verse, Boston, 1913, p. 1; ed. A. S. Cook, Literary Middle English Reader, Boston, 1915, p. 141; ed. A. Brandl and O. Zippel, Mittelenglische Sprach- und Literaturproben, Berlin, 1917, p. 118; ed. G. Sampson, Cambridge Book of Prose and Verse, 1924, p. 416.

Studies. [Text: E. Studien, v, 1882, p. 378; MLR. i, 1906, p. 325; Ang. Bbl. xxix, 1918, p. 284; Ang. xxx, 1907, p. 306.]

Schipper, J. Englische Metrik. Bonn, 1881. [Sect. 168.]

Elsner, W. Untersuchungen zu Dame Siris. Berlin, 1887.

—— Zeitschrift für vergleichende Litteraturgeschichte, i, 1887–8, p. 258.

Wolff, E. Untersuchungen über die Geschichte von der Weinenden Hündin. Munich, 1911.

(b) The Vox and the Wolf

[*Wells*, pp. 183, 791, 1108, 1211; McKnight, edn.]

MS. Digby 86 (Bodleian; see W. W. Skeat, Mod. Lang. Quart. iii, 1900, p. 31). Ed. T. Wright, Percy Soc. 1843; ed. T. Wright and J. O. Halliwell[-Phillipps], Reliquiae Antiquae, vol. ii, 1843, p. 272; ed. W. C. Hazlitt, Remains of the Early Popular Poetry of England, vol. i, 1864, p. 58; ed. E. Mätzner, Altenglische Sprachproben, pt i, Berlin, 1867, p. 130; ed. G. H. McKnight, Middle English Humorous Tales in Verse, Boston, 1913, p. 25; ed. A. S. Cook, Literary Middle English Reader, Boston, 1915, p. 188; ed. A. Brandl and O. Zippel, Mittelenglische Sprach- und Literaturproben, Berlin, 1917, p. 114.

Selections. G. Sampson, Cambridge Book of Prose and Verse, 1924, p. 408.

Modern rendering. J. L. Weston, Chief Middle English Poets, Boston, 1914, p. 275.

Studies. [*Ward*, vol. ii, p. 388, vol. iii, p. 31 (see also pp. 39, 44, 47, etc.).]

McKnight, G. H. PMLA. xxiii, 1908, p. 497.

Brett, C. On Words. MLR. xiv, 1919, p. 8.

(c) How the Psalter of Our Lady Was Made

[*Wells*, pp. 168, 789, 955, 956, 1006, 1107.]

MSS. 1, Digby 86 (Bodleian); 2, Auchinleck (Nat. Lib. Scotland 19.2.1); 3, Laud Lat. 95 (Bodleian, lacks beginning); 4, Trinity College Cambridge R, 3, 21.

Editions. 1, C. Horstmann, EETS. cxvii, 1901, p. 776; 1, with variants of 2, C. Horstmann, Altenglishe Legenden, Heilbronn, 1881, p. 220; 2, D. Laing, A Peniworth of Witte Abbotsford Club, 1857; 3, MLN. iv, 1889, p. 274.

(d) Land of Cockaygne

[*Wells*, pp. 228, 798, 1009, 1213, 1304, 1392.]

MS. Harley 913 (Kildare MS). Ed. G. Hickes, Linguarum veterum septentrionalium Thesaurus grammatico-criticus et archaeologicus, vol. i, Oxford, 1703, p. 231; ed. T. Wright, Altdeutsche Blättern, i, 1837, p. 396; ed. F. J. Furnivall, Early English Poems and Lives of Saints, Berlin, 1862, p. 156; ed. E. Mätzner, Altenglische Sprachproben, Berlin, pt i, 1867, p. 147; ed. W. Heuser, Die Kildare Gedichte, Bonn, 1904, p. 141.

Selections. A. S. Cook, Literary Middle English Reader, Boston, 1915, p. 367; G. Sampson, Cambridge Book of Prose and Verse, 1924, p. 304.

Modern renderings. M. H. Shackford, Legends and Satires, Boston, 1913, p. 128; J. L. Weston, Chief Middle English Poets, Boston, 1914, p. 279; abstract, G. Ellis, Specimens of Early English Poetry, vol. i, 1811, p. 82.

Studies.
Wright, T. St Patrick's Purgatory. 1844.
Poeschel, J. Scharaffenland. PBB. v, 1878,
pp. 381, 413.

[The French fabliau is ed. by A. Barbazan,
Fabliaux et Contes, vol. iv, Paris, 1808, p. 175.
See G. Gröber, Grundriss, 2nd edn, vol. ii¹,
Strasburg, 1902, p. 905; Histoire littéraire
de la France, vol. xxiii, p. 149.]

(e) A Peniworþ of Witte

[*Wells*, pp. 179, 790, 1108.]

Version I

MS. Auchinleck (Nat. Lib. Scotland
19.2.1). Ed. D. Laing, A Peniworth of Witte,
Abbotsford Club, 1857; ed. E. Koelbing,
E. Studien, vii, 1884, p.111; variants, ed. Hazlitt below.

Version II. How a Merchande Dyd Hys Wyfe Betray

MSS. 1, University Lib. Cambridge
Ff.ii.38; 2, Harley 5396.

Editions. 1, J. Ritson, Pieces of Ancient
Popular Poetry, 1791, p. 67; with variants of
Auchinleck, ed. W. C. Hazlitt, Remains of
the Early Popular Poetry of England, vol. i,
1864, p. 193; all texts, ed. E. Koelbing,
E. Studien, vii, 1884, p. 111.

Studies. [See E. Studien, viii, 1885, p. 496,
ix, 1886, p. 178, xiii, 1889, p. 135, lv, 1921,
p. 474; Ang. xiv, 1891–2, p. 308. French
version in A. Montaiglon and G. Raynaud,
Recueil Général des Fabliaux, 1878, p. 88.]

(f) The Clerk Who Would See the Virgin

[*Wells*, pp. 169, 789, 1108.]

MS. Auchinleck (Nat. Lib. Scotland
19.2.1). Ed. C. Horstmann, Altenglische
Legenden, Heilbronn, 1881, p. 499.

[See EETS. Ex. Ser. xcvi, 1905, p. 234;
Archiv, lxxxii, 1889, p. 465.]

(g) The Gast of Gy

[*Wells*, pp. 170, 789, 956, 1007, 1108, 1346,
1390.]

Version I (couplets)

MSS. 1, Cotton, Tiberius E vii (see C.
Horstmann, Yorkshire Writers, vol. ii, 1896,
p. 274; EETS. cxlvii, 1913, p. 5); 2, Rawlinson Poet. 175 (Bodleian).

Version II (prose)

MSS. 3, Vernon (Bodleian 3938); 4, Caius
College Cambridge 175 (fragment).

Version III (4-line stanzas)

MS. 5, Magdalene College Cambridge,
Pepys 2125.

Editions. 1, 2, 4, G. Schleich, Palaestra, i,
1898; 1, 3, C. Horstmann, Yorkshire Writers,
vol. ii, 1896, p. 292; Pynson's edn, 1492,
E. Gordon Duff, Athenaeum, 24 Aug. 1901,
p. 254.

[See also Revelation of Purgatory, ed. C.
Horstmann, *op. cit.* i, 383.]

(h) Trentalle Sancti Gregorii

[*Wells*, pp. 172, 789, 956, 1007, 1051, 1108.]

Version I

MSS. 1, Vernon (Bodleian 3938); 2, Cotton,
Caligula A ii; 3, Garrett (Princeton University
Lib.); 4, Lambeth 306; 5, Peniarth (Hengwrt
92; Aberystwyth); 6, Balliol College Oxford
354.

Editions. 1, E. Studien, viii, 1885, p. 275;
2, with variants of 4, EETS. xv, 1866 (rev.),
p. 114; 1, 2, C. Horstmann, EETS. xcviii,
1892, p. 260; 3, E. Studien, xli, 1909–10,
p. 362; 4, EETS. cxvii, 1901, p. 747; critical
text, 1, 2, 4, and University Lib. Cambridge
Kk. ed. A. Kaufmann, Erlanger Beiträge, iii,
1889.

Version II

MSS. 1, Nat. Lib. Scotland, Jac. V, 7, 27
(19.3.1); 2, University Lib. Cambridge
Kk. i. 6; 3, Harley 3810; 4, Porkington 20
(Lord Harlech, Brogynton, Oswestry).

Editions. 1, W. D. B. Turnbull, Vision
of Tundale, Edinburgh, 1843; Ang. xiii,
1890–1, p. 301; 2, ed. Kaufmann, as above;
3, E. Studien, xl, 1909, p. 351.

Studies. [Sources: Ang. xiii, 1890–1, p.
105; J. R. Hulbert, MP. xvi, 1919, p. 485.]
Gerould, G. H. Saints' Legends. Boston, 1916.
[Pp. 230, 367.]

(i) The Smith and His Dame

[*Wells*, pp. 174, 789.]

Copland's edn. Ed. W. C. Hazlitt, Remains
of Early Popular Poetry of England, vol. iii,
1866, p. 201; ed. C. Horstmann, Altenglische
Legenden, Heilbronn, 1881, p. 322.

(j) Vernon Miracles of Mary

[*Wells*, pp. 166, 788, 1169, 1211.]

MS. Vernon (Bodleian 3938). Ed. C.
Horstmann, EETS. xcviii, 1892, p. 138; Archiv,
lvi, 1876, p. 221.

Modern rendering, parts. M. G. Segar,
Medieval Anthology, New York, 1915, pp. 119,
123.

[For sources, etc. see R. W. Tryon, PMLA.
xxxviii, 1923, p. 332.
For other miracles of Mary see *Wells*, pp.
168, 788, 955, 1006, 1107, 1169, 1211.]

(k) *The Eremyte and the Outelawe*

[*Wells*, pp. 174, 789, 906, 1107, 1302, 1390.]
MSS. 1, BM. Add. 37492; 2, BM. Add.
22577 (copy of 1).
Editions. 1, T. Park in Sir S. E. Brydges,
Restituta, vol. IV, 1816, p. 91 (see E. Studien,
XVI, 1892, p. 434); 2, E. Studien, XIV, 1890,
p. 165 (see Ang. XIII, 1890–1, p. 359).
Studies.
Barbazan, A. Chevalier de Barizel. [In Fabliaux et Contes, vol. I, Paris, 1808, p. 208.]
de la Marche, A. L. Légendes et Apologues
d'Etienne de Bourbon, Paris, 1877. [Items
26, 284.]
Crane, T. F. Exempla of Jacques de Vitry.
1890. [Items 72, 165.]
Kittredge, G. L. E. Studien, XIX, 1894,
p. 177.

(l) *Narratio de Virtute Missarum*

[*Wells*, pp. 173, 789.]
MS. Harley 3954. Ed. T. Wright and
J. O. Halliwell[-Phillipps], Reliquiae Anti-
quae, vol. I, 1841, p. 61.

(m) *Child of Bristowe*

[*Wells*, pp. 175, 789, 1007, 1211.]
MS. Harley 2382. Ed. T. Wright, Retrospective Rev., N.S. VI, 1832; ed. C. Hopper,
Camden Soc. 1859; ed. W. C. Hazlitt, Remains of the Early Popular Poetry of England,
vol. I, 1864, p. 110; ed. C. Horstmann, Altenglische Legenden, Heilbronn, 1881, p. 315;
ed. F. J. Child, Cambridge, U.S.A., 1886.

(n) *Merchant and His Son*

MS. University Lib. Cambridge Ff. II. 38.
Ed. J. O. Halliwell[-Phillipps], Nugae Poeticae,
1844, p. 21; ed. W. C. Hazlitt, Remains of the
Early Popular Poetry of England, vol. I, 1864,
p. 132.

II. CHRONICLES AND PROPHECIES

A. CHRONICLES

(1) GENERAL STUDIES

[*Wells*, pp. 190, 792, 956, 1007, 1052, 1109,
1169, 1211, 1262, 1303, 1346, 1391; C. Gross,
Sources and Literature of English History,
1915 (2nd edn).]
Jones, M. L. Latin Chronicles. CHEL. vol. I,
1907. [Pp. 156, 448.]

Curry, W. C. Middle English Ideal of Personal
Beauty in the Chronicles. Baltimore, 1916.
Tout, T. F. The Study of Medieval Chronicles.
John Rylands Lib. Bulletin, VI, 1922,
p. 414.
Poole, R. L. Chronicles and Annals. A Brief
Outline of their Origin and Growth. Oxford,
1926.

(2) INDIVIDUAL CHRONICLES

(a) *Layamon's Brut.*

[*Wells*, pp. 32, 191, 792, 1007, 1109, 1169,
1212, 1262, 1303, 1346, 1391; criticism to 1908,
B. S. Monroe, JEGP. VII, 1908, p. 139; CHEL.
vol. I, 1907, p. 234; DNB.]
MSS. (A) Cotton, Caligula A II; (B) Cotton,
Otho C XIII.
Edition. Both MSS, Sir F. Madden, 3 vols.
1847.
Selections. R. Morris and W. W. Skeat,
Specimens of Early English, vol. I, Oxford,
1885; F. Kluge, Lesebuch, Halle, 1904; O. F.
Emerson, Reader, New York, 1905; A. S.
Cook, Reader, Boston, 1915; A. Brandl and
O. Zippel, Mittelenglische Sprach- und Lite-
raturproben, Berlin, 1917; J. Hall, Selections
from Early Middle English, Oxford, 1920;
J. Hall, Oxford, 1924; G. Sampson, Cambridge
Book of Prose and Verse, 1924.
Studies.
MSS and Text.
Zessach, A. Die beiden Handschriften von
Layamon's Brut und ihr Verhältnis zu
einander. Breslau, 1888.
Luhmann, A. Die Überlieferung von Laya-
mon's Brut. Göttingen, 1905; SEP. XXII,
1906.
E. Studien, III, 1880, p. 269, IV, 1881, p. 96,
v, 1882, p. 373. [Text.]
Kellner, L. V. 13857. Archiv. CXIV, 1905, p. 164.
Monroe, B. S. Studies in Language and Litera-
ture in Celebration of 70th Birthday of J. M.
Hart. New York, 1911. [P. 377.]
Bartels, L. Die Zuverlässigkeit der Hand-
schriften von Layamon's Brut. SEP. XLIX,
1913. [See E. Studien, XLVIII, 1914–5, p. 439;
Ang. Bbl. XXV, 1914, p. 296.]
[Facs. single pages : New Paleographical Soc.
1903–12, Ser. 1, II, pl. 86; Madden edn, vol. I,
pp. xxxv, xxxviii; G. Sampson, Cambridge
Book of Prose and Verse, 1924.]
Versification.
Ang. II, 1879, p. 153; Ang. Anz. v, 1882
p. 111, VIII, 1885, p. 49.
Schipper, J. Englische Metrik. Bonn, 1881.
[Sect. 67.]
—— Grundriss der englischen Metrik. Vienna,
1895. [Sect. 34.]

Guest, E. History of English Rhythms. Ed. W. W. Skeat, 1882. [Index.]

Kluge, F. PBB. IX, 1884, p. 445.

Zetsche, A. W. Über den ersten Theil der Bearbeitung des Roman de Brut. Leipzig, 1887. [Ch. ii.]

Paul's Grundriss der germanischen Philologie. Vol. II¹, Strasburg, 1892, p. 999.

McNary, S. J. Studies in Layamon's Verse. New York, 1904.

Hamelius, P. Rhetorical Structure. [In Mélanges G. Kurth, Liège, 1908.]

Luick, K. Paul's Grundriss der germanischen Philologie. 2nd edn, vol. II¹, Strasburg, 1909, p. 143.

Brandstädter, K. Stabreim und Endreim. Heidelberg, 1912.

Language.

Trans. Philolog. Soc. [Genitive his for -es, 1864, p. 28; plural -es for -en, 1864, p. 57, 1865, p. 75; inorganic h, 1865, p. 90; French spelling, 1895–8, p. 399.]

Ellis, A. J. Early English Pronunciation. Vol. II, Philolog. Soc. 1869. [P. 496.]

Payne, J. Anglo-Norman Words. N. & Q. 10 July 1869, p. 26.

Hadley, J. Possessive Genitive. [In Essays Philological and Critical, 1873, p. 233.]

Callenberg, C. Inflection in Layamon and Orm. Archiv, LVII, 1877, p. 317.

Use of ae. E. Studien, II, 1878, p. 118, III, 1880, p. 403.

Regel, K. Spruch und Bild. Ang. I, 1878, p. 197.

Stratmann, F. H. Das paragogische n. Ang. III, 1880, p. 552.

Sturmfels, A. Altfranzösischer Vokalismus. Ang. VIII, 1885, p. 201.

Bowen, E. W. Open and Close ē. Ang. XVI, 1893–4, p. 380.

Sound ie. AJ. Phil. XV, 1894, p. 58.

Lucht, P. Lautlehre der älteren Layamon-Handschriften. Palaestra, XLIX, 1905.

Böhnke, M. Die Flexion des Verbums. Berlin, 1906.

Lange, H. Das Zeitwort in den beiden Handschriften. Strasburg, 1906.

Luhmann, A. Überlieferung nebst einer Darstellung der lateinischen Vokale und Diphthonge. SEP. XXII, 1906.

Funke, P. Kasussyntax bei Orm und Layamon. Munich, 1907.

Monroe, B. S. French Words. MP. IV, 1907, p. 559.

Hoffmann, P. Das grammatische Genus. SEP. XXXVI, 1909.

Kühl, O. Der Vokalismus der Layamon-Handschrift B. Halle, 1913.

Lichtsinn, P. Der syntaktische Gebrauch des Infinitivs. Kiel, 1913.

Macmillan, M. Wunder ane. MLR. XIII, 1918, p. 480.

Funke, O. E. Studien, LV, 1921, pp. 5, 19, 23. [French words.]

Meissgeier, E. Grammatisches Geschlecht. E. Studien, LVI, 1922, p. 337.

Tatlock, J. S. P. Epic Formulas. PMLA. XXXVIII, 1923, p. 494.

——Layamon's Poetic Style. [In Manly Anniversary Studies, Chicago, 1923, p. 3.]

Sergeantson, M. S. Dialect. RES. III, 1927, p. 320.

Wyld, H. C. Studies in the Diction of Layamon's Brut. Language, VI, 1930, p. 1, IX, 1933, pp. 47, 171, X, 1934, p. 149.

Sources.

PBB. III, 1876, p. 524 (summary, Romania, VII, 1878, p. 148).

Koelbing, E. Arthour and Merlin. Leipzig, 1890. [P. cxxvii.]

Brown, A. C. L. Welsh Traditions. MP. I, 1903, p. 95.

——Table Round before Wace. Harvard Stud. VII, 1900, p. 183 (see Imelmann, p. 23; Romania, XXIX, 1900, p. 634, XXX, 1901, p. 1).

Fletcher, R. H. Layamon and Geoffrey of Monmouth. PMLA. XVIII, 1903, p. 91.

——Harvard Stud. X, 1906, passim.

Imelmann, R. Layamon: Versuch über seine Quellen. Berlin, 1906.

Bruce, J. D. Proper Names. MLN. XXVI, 1911, p. 65.

——Arthur Matter. Romanic Rev. IV, 1913, p. 451.

Miscellaneous.

Krautwald, H. Layamon's Brut verglichen mit Wace's Roman de Brut. Breslau, 1887.

Sayce, A. Y Cymmrodur, X, 1890, p. 207.

Kolbe, M. Schild, Helm und Panzer zur Zeit Layamon's und ihre Schilderung in dessen Brut. Breslau, 1891.

Brut = Chronicle. Academy, 5 March 1892, p. 233.

Vv. 28320 ff. and Hildebrandslied. MLN. XXI, 1906, p. 110.

King Bladud. MLN. XXV, 1910, p. 263, XXVI, 1911, p. 127; New York Nation, 28 Oct. 1909, p. 404.

Seyger, R. Beiträge zu Layamon's Brut. Halle, 1912.

Cook, A. S. Layamon's Knowledge of Runic Inscriptions. Scottish Hist. Rev. XI, 1914, p. 370.

Gillespy, F. L. Layamon's Brut. A Comparative Study of Narrative Art. University of California Publications in Modern Philology, III, 1916, p. 361.

Hinckley, H. B. Date. MP. XVII, 1919–20, p. 247, Ang. LVI, 1932, p. 43.

Cross, T. P. Passing of Arthur. [In Manly Anniversary Studies, Chicago, 1923, p. 284.]

Gordon, G. The Trojans in Britain. E. & S. IX, 1923, p. 9.

Wyld, H. C. Laȝamon as an English Poet. RES. VI, 1930, p. 1.

Tatlock, J. S. P. Irish Costume in Lawman. Stud. Phil. XXVIII, 1931, p. 587.

Loomis, R. S. RES. x, 1934, p. 78. [Notes.]

(b) Robert of Gloucester's Chronicle

[Wells, pp. 195, 794, 1008, 1109, 1169, 1212, 1347, 1391.]

Recension I

MSS. Cotton; Caligula A XI; Harley 201; BM. Add. 19677; and some later.

Recension II

MSS. Trinity College Cambridge R, 4, 26; Digby 205 (Bodleian); University Lib. Cambridge Ee.IV.31; Lord Mostyn (Flintshire) 259; Magdalene College Cambridge, Pepys 2014; and some later.

Editions. T. Hearne, Oxford, 1724, rptd 2 vols. 1810; W. A. Wright, 2 vols. Rolls Ser. 1887.

Selections. E. Mätzner, Altenglische Sprachproben, 2 pts, Berlin, 1867–1900; R. Wülcker, Lesebuch, 2 pts, Halle, 1874–9; R. Morris and W. W. Skeat, Specimens of Early English, vol. II, Oxford, 1894; F. Kluge, Lesebuch, Halle, 1904; Lord F. Hervey, Corolla S. Eadmundi, 1907, p. 360; A. Brandl and O. Zippel, Mittelenglische Sprach- und Literaturproben, Berlin, 1917; G. Sampson, Cambridge Book of Prose and Verse, 1924.

Studies. [ten Brink, vol. I, p. 275; Schofield, p. 358; CHEL. vol. I, 1907, p. 335; DNB. Verse: J. Schipper, Englische Metrik, Bonn, 1881, sect. 114; M. Trautmann, F. Rosenthal, Ang. I, 1878, p. 414, II, 1879, p. 153; T. Wissmann, King Horn, QF. XVI, 1876.]

Ellmer, W. Über die Quellen der Reimchronik Robert's von Gloucester. Halle, 1886; Ang. x, 1887, pp. 1, 291.

Brossmann, K. Über die Quellen der mittelenglischen Chronik des Robert von Gloucester. Striegau, 1887.

Ang. x, 1887–8, p. 308, XVII, 1894–5, p. 70, XXVI, 1903, p. 364.

Bülbring, K. Verbs. QF. LXIII, 1889, p. 16.

Pabst, F. Die Sprache. Berlin, 1889.

—— Die Flexion. Ang. XIII, 1890–1, pp. 202, 245.

Strohmeyer, H. Der Styl. Berlin, 1891.

—— Verhältnis der Handschriften der Reimchronik. Archiv, LXXXVII, 1891, p. 217.

Text-note. MLN. VII, 1892, p. 267.

Liebermann, F. Proverb. Archiv, CXLVI, 1923, p. 243.

Brown, B. D. Robert of Gloucester and Life of Kenelm. MLN. XLI, 1926, p. 13.

(c) Short Metrical Chronicle

[Wells, pp. 198, 794, 1262, 1303, 1347, 1391.]

MSS. 1, University Lib. Cambridge Ff. v. 48; 2, Royal 12 C XII; 3, BM. Add. 19677; Auchinleck (Nat. Lib. Scotland, 19.2.1); 4, University Lib. Cambridge Dd. XIV. 2; 5, College of Arms, LVII; 6, Rawlinson Poet. 145 (Bodleian).

Editions. Royal, J. Ritson, Ancient English Metrical Romances, vol. II, 1802, p. 270 (collation, E. Studien, XV, 1891, p. 249); Auchinleck and Rawlinson, M. C. Carroll and R. Tuve, PMLA. XLVI, 1931, p. 115; all MSS, E. Zettl, EETS. 1935.

Studies.

Bülbring, K. Verbs. QF. LXIII, 1889, p. 15.

Sternberg, R. E. Studien, XVIII, 1893, pp. 1, 356.

Serjeantson, M. S. Dialect. RES. III, 1927, p. 324.

(d) Thomas Bek of Castelford's Chronicle

MS. Göttingen Lib. Codex MS. Hist. 664. [Not edited.]

Studies. [DNB.; Wells, pp. 199, 794.]

Perrin, M. L. Über Thomas Castelford's Chronik. Göttingen, 1890.

Black, S. Ist Thomas Beck der Verfasser der Göttinger Reimchronik? E. Studien, LXIV, 1929, p. 170.

(e) Brut or Chronicles of England

MSS. Some 170 MSS. [See Brie; Wells, below.]

Edition. F. Brie, EETS. 2 pts, 1906–8.

Studies. [Wells, pp. 206, 795, 1008, 1052, 1110, 1170, 1212, 1303.]

Lambeth 491. Archiv, LXXXVI, 1891, p. 383.

Brie, F. Geschichte und Quellen der mittelenglischen Prosachronik The Brute of England. Marburg, 1905.

Kingsford, C. L. English History in 15th Century. Oxford, 1913. [P. 113.]

(f) Robert Mannyng of Brunne's Story

[Wells, pp. 199, 794, 1008, 1109, 1212, 1391.]

MSS. 1, Inner Temple Lib. Petyt No. 511, No. 7; 2, Lambeth 131; 3, Cotton, Julius A v; 4. Lincoln Cathedral Lib.; 5, Rawlinson Misc. 1370 (Bodleian, 176 lines).

Editions. Part II, T. Hearne, Peter Lang-toft's Chronicle, 2 vols. Oxford, 1725; Part I, F. J. Furnivall, 2 vols. Rolls Ser. 1889; Lambeth, beginning, A. W. Zetsche, Ang. IX, 1886, p. 43; Rawlinson, E. Studien, XVII, 1892, p. 166.

Selections. E. Mätzner, Altenglische Sprachproben, 2 pts, Berlin, 1867–1900; R. Wülcker, Lesebuch, 2 pts, Halle, 1874–9; J. Zupitza, Übungsbuch, Vienna, 1874; Lord F. Hervey, Corolla S. Eadmundi, 1907, p. 369; A. Brandl and O. Zippel, Mittelenglische Sprach- und Literaturproben, Berlin, 1917; G. Sampson, Cambridge Book of Prose and Verse, 1924.

Modern rendering, selections. J. L. Weston, Chief Middle English Poets, Boston, 1914, p. 25.

Studies. [*ten Brink,* vol. I, p. 297; CHEL. vol. I, 1907, p. 350; DNB.]

Hellmers, G. H. Über die Sprache von Robert Mannyng of Brunne. Göttingen, 1885.

Zetsche, A. W. Über den ersten Theil der Bearbeitung des Roman de Brut. Leipzig, 1887.

Preussner, O. Robert Mannyng's Übersetzung von Pierre de Langtoft's Chronicle, und ihr Verhältniss zum Originale. Breslau, 1891.

—— Textkritik. E. Studien, XVII, 1892, p. 300.

Thümmig, M. Über die altenglische Übersetzung der Reimchronik Peter Langtoft's durch Robert Manning von Brunne. Leipzig, 1891; Ang. XIV, 1891, p. 1.

Boerner. O. Die Sprache. SEP. XII, 1904.

—— Reimuntersuchungen. SEP. L, 1913, p. 298.

Imelmann, R. Layamon. Berlin, 1906. [P. 104.]

Curry, W. C. MLN. XXXI, 1916, p. 114.

D'Evelyn, C. Use of Methodius. PMLA. XXXIII, 1918, p. 146.

Moore, S. Use of *Do.* MLN. XXXIII, 1918, p. 385.

(g) *Barbour's Bruce*

[*Wells,* pp. 202, 795, 1008, 1110, 1212, 1303, 1392; MacKenzie's edn; W. Geddie, Bibliography of Middle Scots Poets, STS. 1912, p. 61.]

MSS. 1, St John's College Cambridge G, 23; 2, Nat. Lib. Scotland.

Editions. J. Pinkerton, 1790; J. Jamieson, Edinburgh, 1820; C. Innes, Aberdeen, 1856, London, 1868; W. W. Skeat, 4 pts. EETS. Ex. Ser. 1870–9, rptd with corrections, STS. 1893–4; W. M. MacKenzie, 1909 (extensive bibliography).

Selections. E. Mätzner, Altenglische Sprachproben, 2 pts, Berlin, 1867–1900; R. Morris and W. W. Skeat, Specimens of Early English,

vol. II, Oxford, 1894; J. Zupitza, Übungsbuch, Vienna, 1874; G. E. MacLean, Reader, New York, 1893; R. Wülcker, Lesebuch, 2 pts, Halle, 1874–9; O. F. Emerson, Reader, New York, 1915; W. M. MacKenzie, Selections for Schools, 1909; A. S. Cook, Reader, Boston, 1915; F. Kluge, Lesebuch, Halle, 1904; W. A. Neilson and K. G. T. Webster, Chief British Poets, Boston, 1916; G. Eyre-Todd, Early Scottish Poetry, Glasgow, 1891; W. H. Browne, Early Scottish Poets, Baltimore, 1896; A. Brandl and O. Zippel, Mittelenglische Sprach-und Literaturproben, Berlin, 1917; K. Sisam, Fourteenth Century Verse and Prose, Oxford, 1921.

Translations. G. Eyre-Todd, Glasgow, 1907; M. Macmillan, Stirling, 1914. Selections, J. L. Weston, Chief Middle English Poets, Boston, 1914, p. 26.

Studies. [*ten Brink,* vol. III, p. 52; H. Morley, English Writers, vol. VI, 1890, pp. 2, 10, 41, 120; *Schofield,* p. 317; CHEL. vol. II, 1908, pp. 102, 447; Ency. Brit.; DNB.]

Regel, E. Inquiry into Phonetic Peculiarities. Gera, 1877.

Schipper, J. William Dunbar. Berlin, 1884. [P. 14.]

Baudisch, J. Ueber die Charaktere. Marburg, 1886. [See E. Studien, XI, 1888, p. 308.]

Henschel, F. H. Darstellung der Flexionslehre. Leipzig, 1886.

Bain, J. Calendar of Documents Relating to Scotland. Vol. III, Edinburgh, 1888. [P. ix.]

Craigie, W. A. Barbour and Blind Harry. Scottish Rev. XXII, 1893, p. 173.

Kolkwitz, K. P. M. Die Satzgefüge in Barbour's Bruce. Halle, 1893.

Bearder, J. W. Ueber den Gebrauch der Praepositionen. Halle, 1894.

Brown, J. T. T. The Wallace and the Bruce Restudied. BBA. VI. 1900. [For criticisms see *Wells.*]

—— Book of Cupar. Athenaeum, 2, 23 Feb. 1901, pp. 147, 243.

—— Barbour and Buik of Alexander. Scottish Antiquary, XVI, 1902, p. 206.

—— Sword of Bruce. N. & Q. 5, 26 Oct. 9 Nov. 1907, pp. 261, 334, 370.

Neilson, G. and J. T. T. Brown. J. Barbour *vs.* J. Ramsay. Athenaeum, 17, 24 Nov. 1, 8 Dec. 1900, pp. 647, 688, 725, 760.

Neilson, G. J. Barbour. 1900; Trans. Philolog. Soc. 1900. [See E. Studien, XXX, 1902, p. 281; Athenaeum, 9 Feb. 1901, p. 170; Scottish Antiquary, XV, 1901, p. 166; Hist. Rev. 1901, p. 405.]

—— Cornbote. N. & Q., 26 July, 9 Aug. 27 Sept. 1902, pp. 61, 115, 253.

Millar, J. H. Literary History of Scotland. 1903.

Heuser, W. *Ai* und *ei* in der Cambridger Handschrift des Bruce. Ang. xvii, 1904, p. 91.

Henderson, T. F. Scottish Vernacular Literature. Edinburgh, 1910 (3rd edn). [P. 40.]

Williams, O. T. Old English *a*, *ā*, and *ae*. Trans. Philolog. Soc. 1911–4, p. 7.

Maxwell, H. E. Early Chronicles of Scotland. Glasgow, 1912. [P. 234.]

Mühleisen, F. W. Verwandtschaft der Überlieferungen von Barbour's Bruce. Bonn, 1912.

—— Textkritische, metrische und grammatische Untersuchungen von Barbour's Bruce. Bonn, 1912.

Schofield, W. H. The Chief Historical Error in Barbour's Bruce. PMLA. xxxi, 1916, p. 359.

Peter, W. Syntaktischer Gebrauch des Artikels. Kiel, 1923 (summary).

Morris, J. E. The Battle of Bannockburn. History, xvii, 1932, p. 40.

[Legends and Troy Fragments: Ang. ix, 1886, p. 493; E. Studien, x, 1887, p. 373; Athenaeum, 27 Feb. 1897, p. 279. See also Scottish Legend Collection (p. 175 below), Scottish Troy Fragments (p. 145 above), Scottish Alexander Buik (p. 144 above).)]

(h) *Trevisa's Higden's Polychronicon*

[*Wells*, pp. 204, 795, 957, 1008, 1110, 1170, 1212, 1303, 1392; Babington and Lumby, edn; A. J. Perry, EETS clxvii, 1924, introduction; DNB.]

MSS. 1, St John's College Cambridge H, 1; 2, BM. Add. 24194; 3, Harley 1900; 4, Cotton, Tiberius D vii.

Edition. C. Babington and J. R. Lumby, 9 vols. Rolls Ser. 1865–8.

Selections. E. Mätzner, Altenglische Sprachproben, 2 pts, Berlin, 1867–1900; R. Wülcker, Lesebuch, 2 pts, Halle, 1874–9; P. Morris and W. W. Skeat, Specimens of Early English, vol. ii, Oxford, 1894; O. F. Emerson, Reader, New York, 1905; F. Kluge, Lesebuch, Halle, 1904; Lord F. Hervey, Corolla S. Eadmundi, 1907, p. 373; K. Sisam, Fourteenth Century Verse and Prose, Oxford, 1921.

Studies. [CHEL. vol. ii, 1808, pp. 70, 444.] Verbs. QF. lxiii, 1889, p. 37.

Wharton, L. C. On Vegetius. Trans. Philolog. Soc. 1911–4, p. 151.

Pfeffer, B. Die Sprache (Tiberius). Bonn, 1912.

Wilkins, H. J. Was J. Wycliffe a Negligent Pluralist? New York, 1915. [An Appendix, 1916.]

Krapp, G. P. Rise of English Literary Prose. New York, 1916. [P. 20.]

Curry, W. C. MLN. xxxi, 1916, p. 114.

Perry, A. J. Death; Minor Pieces. MLN. xxxiii, 1918, p. 13. [See EETS. clxvii, 1924, introduction.]

Deanesly, M. Lollard Bible. Cambridge, 1920. [Pp. 250, 299.]

Kinkade, B. L. The English Translations of Higden's Polychronicon. Urbana, 1934.

Minor Pieces by Trevisa

Dialogue between Master and Clerk. Ed. J. MacLean, J. Smyth's Lives of the Berkeleys, vol. i, Gloucester, 1883; rptd A. W. Pollard, 15th Century Prose and Verse (Arber's English Garner), 1899, p. 203.

Dialogus inter Militem et Clericum, FitzRalph's Sermon, Methodius Ye Begynnyng. Ed. A. J. Perry, EETS. 1924.

De Proprietatibus Rerum. [Extracts in R. Steele, Medieval Lore, 1893.]

B. PROPHECIES

(1) GENERAL STUDIES

[*Wells*, pp. 220, 797, 957, 1008, 1111, 1170, 1213, 1304, 1347, 1392; *Ward*, vol. i, p. 292.]

Merlin Prophecies. N. & Q. 3 Aug., 14 Sept., 5 Oct., 9 Nov. 1901, pp. 103, 234, 287, 386.

Taylor, R. Political Prophecy in England. New York, 1911. [See its bibliography, and M. H. Dodds, R. W. Bond, MLR. xi, 1916, pp. 276, 346.]

(2) INDIVIDUAL PROPHECIES

(a) *Here Prophecy*

[*Wells*, pp. 221, 797; *Schofield*, p. 368.]

Ed. J. W Hales, Academy, 4 Dec. 1886, p. 380, and Folia Literaria, 1893, p. 55; ed. H. Morley, English Writers, vol. iii, 1889, p. 200.

(b) *Adam Davy's Five Dreams*

[*Wells*, pp. 221, 797, 1008, 1111, 1213; CHEL. vol. i, 1907, p. 355; Taylor, Political Prophecy, p. 92; O. F. Emerson, date, MLR. xxi, 1926, p. 187.]

MS. Laud 622 (Bodleian). Ed. F. J. Furnivall, EETS. lxix, 1878, p. 11; ed. O. F. Emerson, Reader, New York, 1915, p. 227.

Selections. F. Kluge, Lesebuch, Halle, 1904; A. Brandl and O. Zippel, Mittelenglische Sprach- und Literaturproben, Berlin, 1917.

(c) *Prophecy of the Six Kings*

[*Wells*, pp. 222, 797, 1304; *Ward*, vol. i, p. 309; Taylor, Political Prophecy, pp. 4, 48, 99, 157, 160.]

MSS. 1, Cotton, Galba E ix; 2, MSS of Brut of England.

Editions. 1, J. Hall, Poems of Minot, 1907 (2nd edn), p. 101; 2, EETS. cxxxi, 1906, p. 73.

(d) Northern Alliterative Prophecies (Three Pieces)

[*Wells*, pp. 226, 798, 1347, 1393; *Ward*, vol. i, p. 312; Taylor, Political Prophecy, pp. 165, 57. See also As y yod on ay mounday, under Political and Social Lyrics, p. 270.]

MSS. 1, 2, 3, University Lib. Cambridge Kk.i.5; 4, Hatton 56.

Editions. 1, 2, 3, EETS. xlii, 1870, pp. 23, 18, 32; 4, Archiv, cii, 1899, p. 352; all MSS, R. Haferkorn, Leipzig, 1932.

(e) Thomas of Ersseldoune

MSS. 1, Thornton (Lincoln Cathedral Lib. A, 5, 2); 2, University Lib. Cambridge Ff.v.48; 3, Cotton, Vitellius E x; 4, Lansdowne 762; 5, Sloane 2578; scattered fragments elsewhere.

Editions. 2, with collation of 1, 3, R. Jamieson, Popular Ballads and Songs, 1806; 1, supplemented with 2, D. Laing, Select Remains, rev. W. C. Hazlitt, vol. i, 1894, p. 81; 2, J. O. Halliwell[-Phillipps], Illustrations of the Fairy Mythology of Shakespeare's Midsummer Night's Dream, 1845; all MSS, J. A. H. Murray, EETS. 1875; A. Brandl, Berlin, 1880.

Selections. T. Wright and J. O. Halliwell [-Phillipps], Reliquiae Antiquae, vol. i, 1841, p. 30; F. J. Child, English and Scottish Ballads, vol. ii, Boston, 1882, p. 317; A. S. Cook, Reader, Boston, 1915, p. 70; A. Brandl and O. Zippel, Mittelenglische Sprach- und Literaturproben, Berlin, 1917, pp. 133, 134, 137; G. Sampson, Cambridge Book of Prose and Verse, 1924, p. 304.

Studies. [*Wells*, pp. 224, 798, 1009, 1111, 1213; J. A. H. Murray, EETS. 1875; H. Morley, English Writers, vol. iii, 1889, p. 280; *Ward*, vol. i, p. 328; DNB.]

Eyre-Todd, G. Early Scottish Poetry. Glasgow, 1891. [P. 11.]
Ang. xiv, 1891–2, p. 310.
Burnham, J. M. PMLA. xxiii, 1908, p. 375.
Taylor, R. Political Prophecy in England. New York, 1911. [P. 62.]
Saalbach, A. Entstehungsgeschichte der schottischen Volksballade T. Rymer. Halle, 1913.
Stanza. Romanic Rev. vii, 1916, pp. 243, 271.

Flasdieck, H. M. Tom der Reimer. Von keltischen Feen und politischen Propheten. Breslau, 1934.

III. SERMONS AND SAINTS' LEGENDS

[See *Wells*, ch. v, and Supplements.]

Cornelius, R. D. The Figurative Castle. A Study in Mediaeval Allegory with Especial Reference to the Religious Writings. Bryn Mawr, 1930.
Byrne, M. The Tradition of the Nun in Mediaeval England. Washington, 1932.
Van Os, A. B. Religious Visions. The Development of the Eschatological Elements in Mediaeval English Religious Literature. Amsterdam, 1932.

A. THE ALLITERATIVE KATHERINE GROUP

(a) Hali Meidenhad

[*Wells*, pp. 272, 803, 1010, 1113, 1214, 1265 1305, 1395.]

MS. Cotton, Titus D xviii. Ed. O. Cockayne, EETS. 1866, rev. 1920. [See *Wells* for criticisms.]

Studies. [ten Brink, vol. i, pp. 199, 392 Schofield, p. 380; CHEL. vol. i, 1907, p. 229.
Wülcker, R. Language. PBB. i, 1874, p. 209
Murray, J. A. H. and Furnivall, F. J. Academy 10 Aug., 28 Sept. 1889, pp. 89, 206.
Funke, O. E. Studien, lv, 1921, p. 23 [French words.]
Tolkien, J. R. R. Ancrene Wisse and Hali Meiðhad. E. & S. xiv, 1928, p. 104.
Wilson, R. M. Leeds Stud. no. 1, 1932 [Author.]

[See also under Katherine, Juliana, Marherete, below.]

(b) Sawles Warde

[*Wells*, pp. 272, 346, 803, 1113, 1265, 1305 1396.]

MSS. 1, Cotton, Titus D xviii; 2, Roya 17 A xxvii; 3, Bodley 34; 4, (Kentish Arundel lvii (College of Arms).

Editions. 1st version: R. Morris, EETS 1867, p. 245; W. Wagner, Bonn, 1908 F. Kluge, Lesebuch, Halle, 1904, p. 8. Selections: R. Morris and W. W. Skeat, Specimens of Early English, vol. i, Oxford, 1885; A Brandl and O. Zippel, Mittelenglische Sprach und Literaturproben, Berlin, 1917; J. Hall Selections from Early Middle English, Oxford 1920, vol. i, p. 117, vol. ii, p. 492. 2nd version (Kentish): R. Morris, EETS. xxiii, 1866, p. 263 Both versions: R. M. Wilson, Leeds, 1936.

Studies. [*ten Brink*, vol. i, p.204; *Schofield*, p. 386; CHEL. vol. i, 1907, pp. 227, 228, 355.]

Einenkel, E. Author. E. Studien, v, 1882, p. 91. [See also under Katherine, below.]

Vollhardt, W. Der Einfluss der lateinischen geistlichen Literatur auf einige kleinere Schöpfungen der englischen Übergangsperiode. Leipzig, 1888. [P. 26.]

Konrath, M. E. Studien, xii, 1889, p. 459.

Stodte, H. Ueber die Sprache und Heimat der Katharine-Gruppe. Göttingen, 1896.

Williams, I. F. Language. Ang. xxix, 1906, p. 413.

Bartels, L. Die Zuverlässigkeit der Handschriften von Layamons Brut. Halle, 1913.

Powell, C. L. Castle of the Body. Stud. Phil. xvi, 1919, p. 199.

Allen, H. E. MLR. xxviii, 1933, p. 485. [Bodley MS.]

Bethurum, D. The Connection of the Katherine Group with Old English Prose. JEGP. xxxiv, 1935, p. 553.

[See also under Hali Meidenhad above.]

(c) Katherine

[*Wells*, pp. 312, 811, 963, 1013, 1117, 1268, 1307, 1351, 1397.]

MSS. 1, Royal 17 A xxvii; 2, Bodley NE, A, 3, 11; 3, Cotton, Titus D xviii.

Editions. 1, with Latin and variants of 2, 3, E. Einenkel, EETS. 1884 (criticism, Ang. Anz. viii, 1885, p. 175; Deutsche Literaturzeitung, vii, 1881, p. 226; E. Studien, ix, 1886, p. 174); 3, J. Morton, Abbotsford Club, 1841; C. Hardwick, Cambridge Antiquarian Soc. 1849; 1, F. Kluge, Lesebuch, Halle, 1904, p. 64; selection, J. Hall, Selections from Early Middle English, Oxford, 1920, vol. i, p. 128, vol. ii, p. 534.

Studies. [*ten Brink*, vol. i, pp. 199, 392; CHEL. vol. i, 1907, p.229; *Schofield*, p.390. Versification: Ang. Anz. viii, 1885, p. 49; Paul's Grundriss der germanischen Philologie, vol. ii¹, Strasburg, 1892, p. 1003; Ang. v, 1882, p. 91; EETS. lxxx, 1884, p. xxi; J. Schipper, Englische Metrik, Bonn, 1881.]

Einenkel, E. Author. Ang. v, 1882, p. 91. [See also EETS. lxxx, 1884, p. xviii; Ang. v, 1882, p. 86; Deutsche Literaturzeitung, 1882, p. 79; Literaturblatt für germanische und romanische Philologie, xii, 1891, p. 435.]

Bülbring, K. Verbs. QF. lxiii, 1889, p. 3.

Victor, O. Zur Textkritik und Metrik. Bonn, 1912. [Criticism, Ang. Bbl. xxiii, 1912, p.226.]

Gerould, G. H. Saints' Legends. Boston, 1916. [Pp. 208, 364.]

Sergeantson, M. S. Dialect, Royal. RES. iii, 1927, p. 323.

[See also under Hali Meidenhad and Sawles Warde, above. On other Katherine pieces see *Wells*, as above, and C. Brown, Register of Middle English Religious Verse, vol. ii, 1920, index.]

(d) Juliana

[*Wells*, pp. 312, 811, 1013, 1117, 1268, 1307.]

MSS. 1, Royal 17 A xxvii; 2, Bodley 34.

Editions. Both MSS, O. Cockayne and E. Brock, EETS. 1872 (see MLN. vii, 1892, p. 186); R. Morris and W. W. Skeat, Specimens of Early English, vol. i, Oxford, 1885, (see Ang. xxv, 1903, p. 319); J. Hall, Selections from Early Middle English, Oxford, 1920, vol. i, p. 138, vol. ii, p. 543.

Studies. [*ten Brink*, vol. i, pp. 199, 392; *Schofield*, p. 390; CHEL. vol. i, 1907, p. 229. Text: E. Studien, iv, 1881, p. 93; MLN. vii, 1892, p. 267.]

Backhaus, O. Über die Quelle. Halle, 1899.

Kennedy, C. W. Legend of St Juliana. Princeton, 1906.

Bruhnöler, E. Über einige lateinische, englische, französische Fassungen der Julianelegende. Bonn, 1912.

[See also under Hali Meidenhad and Sawles Warde; and Bülbring, Gerould, Sergeantson, under Katherine, above. On other Juliana pieces see *Wells*, as above, and C. Brown, Register, vol. ii, 1920, index.]

(e) Seinte Marherete

[*Wells*, pp. 314, 812, 1013, 1117, 1171, 1216, 1268, 1307, 1397.]

MSS. 1, Royal 17 A xxvii; 2, Bodley 34.

Edition. Both MSS, O. Cockayne, EETS. 1866; F. M. Mack, EETS. 1934.

Studies. [CHEL. vol. i, 1907, p. 229.]

Cockayne, O. Narratiunculae. 1865. [P. 39.]

Vogt, F. Über die Margaretenlegende. PBB. i, 1874, p. 281.

Text. E. Studien, iv, 1881, p. 93.

Brandl, A. English Versions of Margaret Legend. Zeitschrift für die Österreichischen Gymnasien, 1882, p. 686.

Krahl, E. Untersuchungen über vier Versionen der mittelenglischen Margaretenlegende. Berlin, 1889. [Criticism, Ang. xv, 1893, p. 504; Literaturblatt für germanische und romanische Philologie, xii, 1891, p. 158.]

Spencer, F. Development of the Legend of St Margaret. MLN. iv, 1889, p. 393, v, 1890 pp. 121, 141, 213.

Gerould, G. H. Saints' Legends. Boston, 1916. [Pp. 209, 231, 364, 367.]

Gerould, G. H. PMLA. xxxix, 1924, p. 525. [Sources and related matter.]

[See also under Hali Meidenhad and Sawles Warde; Bülbring, Einenkel, Sergeantson, under Katherine. On other Margaret pieces and general legend, see *Wells*, above, and C. Brown, Register, vol. ii, 1920, index.]

B. SERMONS

(1) GENERAL STUDIES

Owst, G. R. Preaching in Medieval England, *c.* 1350–1450. Cambridge, 1926. [See its notes for bibliography.]

—— Literature and Pulpit in Medieval England. Cambridge, 1933.

Horstmann, C. Altenglische Legenden. Heilbronn, 1881. [Introduction.]

Crane, T. F. Medieval Sermon-Books and Stories. Proc. American Philosophical Soc. 1883, no. 114, p. 49.

—— Exempla or Illustrative Stories. 1890.

—— Medieval Story Books. MP. ix, 1911–2, p. 225.

—— Recent Collections of Exempla. Romanic Rev. vi, 1916, p. 219.

Smith, L. T. English Popular Preaching in 14th Century. EHR. vii, 1892, p. 25.

Petit-Dutaillis, C. Les Prédications Populaires. [In Études dédiées à G. Monod, Paris, 1896, p. 373.]

Mosher, J. A. Exemplum in England. New York, 1911. [See its bibliography.]

Little, A. G. Studies in English Franciscan History. Manchester, 1917. [P. 135.]

Deanesly, M. The Lollard Bible. Cambridge, 1920. [Pp. 188, 198.]

Chapman, C. O. Sermons. MLN. xli, 1926, p. 506, xliii, 1928, p. 229; PMLA. xliv, 1929, p. 178.

(2) PARTICULAR COLLECTIONS

(a) Bodley Homilies

[*Wells*, pp. 277, 804.]

MS. Bodley 343. Ed. A. O. Belfour, EETS. 1909 (with trn).

(b) Lambeth Homilies

[*Wells*, pp. 278, 804, 1010, 1114, 1214, 1266, 1306, 1396.]

MS. Lambeth 487. Ed. R. Morris, EETS. 1867 (see E. Studien, xiv, 1890, p. 396). Selections: J. Zupitza, Übungsbuch, Vienna, 1874; R. Morris and W. W. Skeat, Specimens of Early English, vol. i, Oxford, 1885; G. E. MacLean, Reader, New York, 1893; J. Hall, Selections from Early Middle English, Oxford, 1920, vol. i, pp. 76, 79, vol. ii, 1920, pp. 407, 421; selection and Paternoster, G. Sampson, Cambridge Book of Prose and Verse, 1924.

Studies.

Cohn, O. Die Sprache. Berlin, 1880.

Vollhardt, W. Der Einfluss der lateinischen geistlichen Litteratur auf einige kleinere Schöpfungen der englischen Übergangsperiode. Leipzig, 1888. [P. 18.]

Priebsch, R. Otia Merseiana, i, 1889, p. 129; MLR. ii, 1907, p. 138.

Skeat, W. W. Mod. Lang. Quart. ii, 1899, p. 299.

Mosher, J. A. Exemplum in England. New York, 1911. [P. 44.]

Stadlmann, A. Die Sprache der mittelenglischen Predigtsammlung in der Handschrift Lambeth 487. Vienna, 1921.

Funke, O. E. Studien, lv, 1921, p. 23. [French words.]

Allen, H. E. Author. PMLA. xliv, 1929, p. 635.

Wilson, R. M. The Provenance of the Lambeth Homilies, with a New Collation. Leeds Stud. no. 4, 1935.

(c) Trinity College Homilies

[*Wells*, pp. 280, 804, 1010, 1058, 1114, 1266, 1306.]

MS. Trinity College Cambridge B, 14, 52. Ed. R. Morris, EETS. liii, 1873, p. 3 (see E. Studien, xiv, 1890, p. 396); items 15–18, ed. R. Morris and W. W. Skeat, Specimens of Early English, vol. i, Oxford, 1885; items 3, 27, ed. T. Wright and J. O. Halliwell[-Phillipps], Reliquiae Antiquae, vol. i, 1845, p. 125; ed. E. Mätzner, Altenglische Sprachproben, pt ii, Berlin, 1900, p. 42; items 15, 16, ed. J. Hall, Selections from Early Middle English, Oxford, 1920, vol. i, p. 82, vol. ii, p. 427.

Studies.

Krüger, A. Sprache und Dialekt. Göttingen, 1885.

Vollhardt, W. Der Einfluss der lateinischen geistlichen Literatur auf einige kleinere Schöpfungen der englischen Übergangsperiode. Leipzig, 1888. [P. 67.]

E. Studien, xv, 1891, p. 306. [Critical notes.]

Mosher, J. A. Exemplum in England. New York, 1911. [P. 44.]

Strauss, O. Die Sprache der mittelenglischen Predigtsammlung in der Handschrift B. 14. 52 Trinity College, Cambridge. Vienna, 1916 (see Ang. Bbl. xxix, 1918, p. 193; E. Studien, li, 1917–8, p. 250).

Hall, J. Selections from Early Middle English. Oxford, 1920, vol. i, p. 82, vol. ii, p. 427. [On language.]

Funke, O. E. Studien, lv, 1921, p. 23. [French words.]

Ker, N. R. The Scribes of the Trinity Homilies. Medium Aevum, i, 1932, p. 138.

(d) Ormulum

[Wells, pp. 282, 804, 1010, 1058, 1114, 1214, 306, 1396.]

MS. Junius 1 (Bodleian). Collation of MS, E. Studien, i, 1877, p. 1. Ed. R. M. White, Oxford, 1852, rev. R. Holt, 2 vols. Oxford, 878.

Selections. J. Zupitza, Übungsbuch, Vienna, 874; H. Sweet, First Middle English Primer, Oxford, 1884; R. Morris and W. W. Skeat, Specimens of Early English, vol. i, Oxford, 885; G. E. MacLean, Reader, New York, 893; O. F. Emerson, Reader, Boston, 1915; A. Brandl and O. Zippel, Mittelenglische Sprach-und Literaturproben, Berlin, 1917; J. Hall, Selections from Early Middle English, Oxford, 920, vol i, p. 112, vol. ii, p. 479; G. Sampson, Cambridge Book of Prose and Verse, 1924.

Studies. [ten Brink, vol. i, p. 193; Schofield, . 382; H. Morley, English Writers, vol. iii, 889, p. 232; DNB. under 'Orm'; CHEL. ol. i, 1907, pp. 222, 223, 386.

Verse: J. Schipper, Englische Metrik, Bonn, 881, p. 101; Paul's Grundriss, vol. ii¹, Strasurg, 1892, p. 1047; E. Menthel, Ang. Anz. iii, 1885, p. 73; G. Saintsbury, History of English Prosody, vol. i, 1906, p. 38.
Spelling: Ang. Anz. vii, 1884, pp. 94, 208, viii, 1895, p. 371; Academy, 25 Feb. 1890.
Sources: E. Studien, vi, 1883, p. 1.
Author, Name: Archiv, cxvii, 1906, p. 28, xix, 1907, p. 33, cxxiii, 1909, p. 23.]

Conicke, C. H. Notes and Queries. Leipzig, 1853.
Mallenberg, C. Layamon und Orm nach ihren Lautverhältnissen verglichen. Jena, 1876; Archiv, cvii, 1901, p. 317.
Lenrici, E. Orm's Brother. ZDA. xxii, 1878, p. 231.
Laphengst, C. Essay on the Ormulum. Rostock, 1879.
Sachse, R. Die unorganische e. Halle, 1881.
Blackburn, F. A. þ to t. AJ. Phil. iii, 1882, p. 46.
Effer, H. Einfache und doppelte Konsonanten. Berlin, 1885.
Brate, E. Nordische Lehnwörter. PBB. x, 1885, pp. 1, 580.
Lenze, E. Der östmittellandische Dialekt. Cöthen, 1889.
Napier, A. S. Notes on Orthography. Academy, 15 March, 1890, p. 188.
— History of the Holy Rood-Tree. 1894.
Kluge, F. Das französische Element. E. Studien, xxii, 1896, p. 179.
Feyel, F. Der syntaktische Gebrauch des Infinitivs. Meiderich, 1896.
McKnight, G. H. Double Consonants. E. Studien, xxvi, 1899, p. 455.

Holthausen, F. Wel and well. Ang. Bbl. xiii, 1902, p. 16.
Lambertz, P. Die Sprache. Marburg, 1904.
Bülbring, K. Die Schreibung eo. BBA. xvii, 1905, p. 51.
—— Ang. Bbl. xvii, 1906, p. 135.
Bradley, H., Wilson, J. Where written? Athenaeum, 10 May, 14, 21, 28 July 1906, pp. 609, 43, 73, 104.
Reichmann, H. Die Eigennamen. SEP. xxv, 1906.
Funke, O. Kasus-Syntax. Munich, 1907.
Thüns, B. Das Verbum. Leipzig, 1909.
Zenke, W. Syntax und Analyse des Verbums. SEP. xl, 1910.
Deutschbein, M. Quantity Signs. Archiv, cxxvi, 1911, p. 49, cxxvii, 1911, p. 308.
Björkmann, E. Doppelkonsonanten. Ang. xxxvii, 1913, pp. 351, 494.
Laeseke, B. Beitrag zur Stellung des Verbums. Berlin, 1917.
Weinmann, P. Ueber den Gebrauch des Artikels. Berlin, 1920.
Hall, J. Selections from Early Middle English. Vol. ii, Oxford, 1920. [P. 479.]
Deanesly, M. Lollard Bible. Cambridge, 1920. [P. 148.]
Holm, S. Corrections and Additions in Ormulum MS. Upsala, 1922.
Oldendorf, H. Syntax und Analyse des Nomens und Pronomens. Summary in Jahrbuch der philosophischen Fakultät, Göttingen, i, 1922, p. 25.
Flasdieck, H. M. Sprachliche Einheitlichkeit. Ang. xlvii, 1923, p. 289.
Matthes, H. C. Die Einheitlichkeit des Ormulum. Heidelberg, 1933.
—— Ang. lix, 1935, p. 303. [Sources.]
Sisam, K. RES. ix, 1933, p. 1. [Purpose of spelling.]
Hinckley, H. B. The Riddle of the Ormulum. PQ. xiv, 1935, p. 193.

(e) Kentish Sermons

[Wells, pp. 283, 805, 1010, 1114.]

MS. Laud 471 (Bodleian). Ed. R. Morris, EETS. 1872, p. 26; ed. F. Kluge, Lesebuch, 2nd edn, Halle, 1912, p. 12; ed. J. Hall, Selections from Early Middle English, Oxford, 1920, vol. i, p. 214, vol. ii, p. 657; items 1–2, ed. R. Morris and W. W. Skeat, Specimens of Early English, vol. i, Oxford, 1885; item 2, ed. J. Zupitza, Übungsbuch, Vienna, 1874; ed. G. E. MacLean, Reader, New York, 1893; items 4, 5, ed. O. F. Emerson, Reader, New York, 1905.

Studies. [ten Brink, vol. i, p. 283.]

Danker, O. Die Laut- und Flexionslehre der mittelkentischen Denkmäler. Strasburg, 1879.

Reimann, M. Die Sprache der mittelkentischen Evangelien. Berlin, 1883.

Bülbring, K. Verbs. QF. LXIII, 1889, p. 24.

Text-notes. MLN. VII, 1892, p. 267.

Konrath, M. Zur Laut- und Flexionslehre. Archiv, LXXXVIII, 1892, pp. 44, 157, LXXXIX, 1892, p. 153.

Heuser, W. Dialect. Ang. XVII, 1894, p. 82.

von Glahn, N. Zur Geschichte des grammatischen Geschlechts im Mittelenglischen. Anglistische Forschungen, LIII, 1918.

Funke, O. E. Studien, LV, 1921, pp. 4, 24. [French words.]

[On French origin see *Wells*, p. 1114.]

(f) Cotton Vespasian Homilies

[*Wells*, pp. 284, 805, 1010, 1058, 1114.]

MS. Cotton, Vespasian A 22. Ed. R. Morris, EETS. XXXIV, 1868, p. 216 (see E. Studien, XIV, 1890, p. 396); An Bispel, ed. R. Morris and W. W. Skeat, Specimens of Early English, vol. I, Oxford, 1885, ed. J. Hall, Selections from Early Middle English, Oxford, 1920, vol. I, p. 12, vol. II, p. 269.

Studies.

Vollhardt, H. Einfluss der lateinischen geistlichen Literatur. Leipzig, 1888. [P. 24.] [See E. Studien, XIII, 1889, p. 79.]

Text-note. MLN. VII, 1892, p. 267.

Language. Ang. XVII, 1894–5, p. 82.

von Glahn, N. Zur Geschichte des grammatischen Geschlechts. Anglistische Forschungen, LIII, 1918.

(3) PARTICULAR SERMONS

(a) A Lutel Soth Sermun

[*Wells*, pp. 274, 803, 1396; *ten Brink*, vol. I, p. 211.]

MSS. 1, Cotton, Caligula A IX; 2, Jesus College Oxford 29 (Bodleian).

Editions. T. Wright, Percy Soc. XI, 1843, p. 80; R. Morris, EETS. XLIX, 1872, p. 186.

(b) A Sarmun

[*Wells*, pp. 274, 803, 1396.]

MS. Harley 913. Ed. F. J. Furnivall, Early English Poems and Lives of Saints, Berlin, 1862, p. 1; ed. E. Mätzner, Altenglische Sprachproben, pt i, Berlin, 1867, p. 115; ed. W. Heuser, BBA. XIV, 1904, p. 88.

(c) Speculum Gy de Warewyke

[*Wells*, pp. 275, 803, 1350, 1396.]

MSS. 1, Auchinleck (Nat. Lib. Scotland 19.2.1); 2, Royal 17 B XVII; 3, Harley 1731; 4, Harley 525; 5, Arundel 140; 6, University Lib. Cambridge Dd.XI.

Editions. G. L. Morrill, EETS. Ex. Ser 1898; C. Horstmann, Yorkshire Writers, vol II, 1896, p. 24.

Studies.

Weyrauch, M. Die mittelenglischen Fassungen Guy of Warwick. Breslau, 1899.

(d) Sermo in Festo Corporis Christi

[*Wells*, pp. 276, 803.]

MSS. 1, Vernon (Bodleian 3938); 2, University Lib. Cambridge Dd.1; 3, Harley 4196

Editions. All MSS, Archiv, LXXXII, 1889 p. 167; C. Horstmann, EETS. XCVIII, 1892 p. 169. [See EETS. XCVIII, 1892, pp. 198 CXXIII, 1903, p. 309.]

(e) A Luytel Sarmoun of Good Edificacioun

[*Wells*, pp. 275, 803, 1351, 1396.]

MS. Vernon (Bodleian 3938). Ed. C Horstmann, EETS. 1901, p. 476.

(f) Sermon against Miracle Plays

[See *Wells*, pp. 483, 843.]

MS. BM. Add. 24202. Ed. T. Wright an J. O. Halliwell[-Phillipps], Reliquiae Antiquae vol. I, 1841, p. 42; ed. E. Mätzner, Altenglisch Sprachproben, pt ii, Berlin, 1900, p. 222 Selection: A. S. Cook, Reader, Boston, 1915

Studies.

Chambers, Sir E. K. The Medieval Stage Vol. II, Oxford, 1903, p. 102.

Cook, A. S. (New York) Nation, 27 May 1918

(g) Wimbledon's Redde Racionem

[*Wells*, pp. 1057, 1266, 1306.]

MSS. English: Hatton 57 (Bodleian), fo 1; Royal 18 A XVII, fol. 184 v.; Royal 18 XXIII, fol. 39; Harley 2398, fol. 140; Sidne Sussex College Cambridge 74, fol. 168; Corp Christi College Cambridge 357 (ii); BM. Ad 37677; and others. Latin: Caius Colleg Cambridge 334; University Lib. Cambridge Ii.III.8; and others.

Editions. J. Foxe, Acts and Monument vol. III, 1844, p. 292. Hatton, K. F. Sunde A Famous Middle English Sermon, Goteburg, 1925. [For early edns see Owst and BM Catalogue below.]

Studies.

BM. Catalogue and Supplement to same, s. Wimbledon (R.) and Sermon.

James, M. R. A Descriptive Catalogue of th Manuscripts in the Library of Sidne Sussex College, Cambridge. Cambridge 1895.

James, M. R. A Descriptive Catalogue of the Manuscripts in the Library of Gonville and Caius College. 2 vols. and Supplement, Cambridge, 1907–14.

Catalogue of MSS in Old Royal and King's College. Vol. II, 1921, pp. 269, 295.

Owst, G. R. Preaching in Medieval England. Cambridge, 1926. [Index: Wimbledon, Quinquagesimalia.]

(h) *Sermons by Wycliffe and Wycliffites*

[See under John Wycliffe and Associated Writings, p. 203 below.]

C. SAINTS' LEGENDS

(1) GENERAL STUDIES

[*Wells*, pp. 285, 805, 959, 1010, 1058, 1115, 1171, 1214, 1267, 1306.]

Gerould, G. H. Saints' Legends. Boston, 1916. [See its bibliography.]

Horstmann, C. Leben Jesu. Münster, 1873. [Introduction.]

—— Altenglische Legenden. 3 vols. Paderborn, 1875.

—— Sammlung altenglischer Legenden. Heilbronn, 1878.

—— Altenglische Legenden. Neue Folge. Heilbronn, 1881. [Introductions.]

—— EETS. LXXXVII, 1887. [Introduction.]

Lovewell, B. E. Life of St Cecilia. New Haven, 1898. [Bibliography.]

Foster, F. A. Northern Passion. 2 pts, EETS. 1912–3.

Brown, B. Southern Passion. EETS. 1925.

McKeehan, I. P. The Book of the Nativity of St Cuthbert. PMLA. XLVIII, 1933, p. 981.

(2) PARTICULAR COLLECTIONS

(a) *Northern Homily Cycle*

[*Wells*, pp. 287, 805, 959, 1011, 1058, 1115, 1214, 1267, 1306, 1351, 1396; G. H. Gerould, Northern English Homily Collection, Lancaster, Pennsylvania, 1902; G. H. Gerould, Saints' Legends, Boston, 1916.

On MSS. C. Brown, Register of Middle English Religious Verse, vol. II, 1920, index and appendix; G. H. Gerould, Northern English Homily Collection, as above, and Saints' Legends, Boston, 1916, pp. 164, 224, 262; *Wells*, as above; on BM. Add. 38010, Harley 4196, Tiberius see *Ward*, vol. III, pp. 331, 714; on Phillipps 8122 see C. Brown, Register, vol. II, p. 6.]

Editions. MS. Royal College, J. Small, English Metrical Homilies, Edinburgh, 1862; 2 items. E. Mätzner, Altenglische Sprachproben, pt i, Berlin, 1867, p. 278; 2 items,

R. Morris and W. W. Skeat, Specimens of Early English, vol. II, Oxford, 1894, p. 83; Signs of Doom, O. F. Emerson, Reader, New York, 1915.

Legends from various MSS as follows:

Alexius. C. Horstmann, Altenglische Legenden, Heilbron, 1881, p. 174.

Andrew. Selection. O. F. Emerson, Reader, New York, 1915, p. 135.

Barlaam and Josaphat. C. Horstmann, Altenglische Legenden, Paderborn, 1875, p. 226.

Cecilia. B. E. Lovewell, New Haven, 1898; E. Studien, I, 1877, p. 235 (notes, Anzeiger für deutsches Altertum, IV, 1878, p. 252). Trn, J. L. Weston, Chief Middle English Poets, Boston, 1914, p. 72.

Erasmus. Archiv, LXII, 1879, p. 413.

In Festo Corporis Christi. EETS. XCVIII, 1892, p. 169; Archiv, LXXXII, 1889, p. 167.

Miracles of Virgin. R. W. Tryon, PMLA. XXXVIII, 1923, pp. 323, 328.

Nativity. A. Brandl and O. Zippel, Mittelenglische Sprach- und Literaturproben, Berlin, 1917, p. 106.

Northern Passion. F. A. Foster, 2 pts, EETS. 1912–3 (Supplement, 1931). Selections: Archiv, LVII, 1877, p. 78.

Peter and Paul. C. Horstmann, Altenglische Legenden, Heilbronn, 1881, p. 77.

Proprium Sanctorum. Archiv, LXXXI, 1888, pp. 82, 279. Parts: C. Horstmann, Altenglische Legenden, Heilbronn, 1881, p. 1.

Rood, Invencione S. Crucis, De Festo Exaltacionis. EETS. XLVI, 1871, pp. 62, 87, 122.

Theophilus. E. Studien, I, 1877, p. 16. [See E. Studien, I, 1877, p. 186, II, 1878, p. 281; E. Koelbing, Beiträge zur Geschichte der romischen Poesie und Prosa, Breslau, 1870.]

Selections. Ang. XXVII, 1904, p. 290.

Vernon narrationes. Archiv, LVII, 1877, p. 241.

[For other edns see *Wells*, pp. 809 [31] ff.]

Studies. [*ten Brink*, vol. I, p. 290; CHEL. vol. I, 1907, p. 340.]

Horstmann, C. Altenglische Legenden. Paderborn, 1875. [P. iii.]

—— Sammlung altenglischer Legenden. Heilbronn, 1881. [P. lvii.]

Retzlaff, O. Untersuchungen über den Nordischen Legendencyklus. Berlin, 1889.

Weber, O. Language. Berne, 1902. [Small's edn.]

Wetzlar, A. Sprache sowie Glossar [Royal College]. Freiburg, 1907.

Gerould, G. H. Hermit; Oswald. PMLA. XX, 1905, p. 259.

—— Sources. MLN. XXII, 1907, p. 95; E. Studien. XLVII, 1913, p. 84.

Deanesly, M. The Lollard Bible. Cambridge, 1920. [P. 148 (source).]

Aitken, Y. H. Étude sur le Miroir ou les Évangiles des Domnées de Robert de Gretham [with extracts]. Paris, 1922.

Tryon, R. W. Miracles of the Virgin. PMLA. xxxviii, 1923, pp. 323, 328.

Baker, A. T. A Fragment of the Miroir or Évangiles des Domées of Robert de Gretham. Modern Humanities Research Ass. Bulletin, i, 1928, p. 62.

Foster, F. A. Northern Passion. EETS. 1913. [Introduction.]

—— A Study of the Northern Passion. 1914.

Miller, F. H. The Northern Passion and the Mysteries. MLN. xxxiv, 1919, p. 88.

Lyle, M. C. Original Identity of York and Towneley Cycles. Minneapolis, 1919. [See also under York and Towneley Plays in *Wells*, pp. 1137, 1319, and p. 278 below.]

Frank, G. MLN. xxxv, 1920, p. 257, xxxvi, 1921, p. 193, and references there; PMLA. xxxv, 1920, p. 464.

[On French Narrative Passion: G. Frank, MLN. xxxv, 1920, p. 257; H. Theben, Die altfranzösische Passion, Greifswald, 1909; E. Roy, Le Mystère de la Passion, Dijon, 1903, p.27; Foster,*op.cit.*p.49,notes and references.]

(b) *Southern Legend Collection*

[*Wells*, pp. 292, 806, 813, 960, 1011, 1115, 1171, 1214, 1267, 1306, 1351, 1396.]

On MSS. C. Horstmann, Altenglische Legenden, Paderborn, 1875, p. i; Altenglische Legenden, Heilbronn, 1881, p. xliv; EETS. lxxxvii, 1887, p. vii; C. Brown, Register of Middle English Religious Verse, vol. ii, 1920, index; *Wells*, p. 293; on Corpus, Tanner, Ang. i, 1878, p. 392; on Laud, Archiv, xlix, 1872, p. 395; on Stowe, Ang. vii, 1884, p. 405.]

Editions.

Laud 108. C. Horstmann, EETS. 1887. [See Ang. xi, 1888–9, p. 543.]

Harley 2277, various items. F. J. Furnivall, Early English Poems and Lives of Saints. Berlin, 1862.

Bodley 779, later additions. Archiv, lxxxii, 1889, pp. 307, 369.

Advent and Christmas Gospels. C. Horstmann, Altenglische Legenden, Paderborn, 1875, pp. 64, 65.

Alexius. Archiv, li, 1873, p. 101, lvi, 1876, pp. 394, 401.

Barlaam and Josaphat. C. Horstmann, Altenglische Legenden, Paderborn, 1875, pp. 113 (notes, Ang. xiv, 1891–2, p. 318), 215.

Becket. Critical edn, H. Thiemke, Palaestra, cxxxi, 1919; W. H. Black, Percy Soc. 1845;

E. Mätzner, Altenglische Sprachproben, vol i, Berlin, 1867, p. 177. Trn, J. L. Weston Chief Middle English Poets, Boston, 1914 p. 41.

Birth of Jesus. C. Horstmann, Altenglisch Legenden, Paderborn, 1875, p. 64 (see Ang xiv, 1891–2, p. 314); prologue, EETS. lxix 1878, p. 93; with Marriage of Virgin, A Brandl and O. Zippel, Mittelenglisch Sprach- und Literaturproben, Berlin, 1917 pp. 92, 96.

Brandan. T. Wright, Percy Soc. xlviii, 1844 M. Bälz, Die mittelenglische Brandan Legende des Gloucester-Legendars, Berlin 1909; G.Sampson, Cambridge Book of Pros and Verse, 1924, p. 345. Trn, J. L. Weston Chief Middle English Poets, Boston, 1914 p. 57.

Cecilia. B. E. Lovewell, New Haven, 1898 F. J. Furnivall, Chaucer Soc. Ser. 2, x, 1875 p. 208.

Celestyn. Ang. i, 1878, p. 55. [See Ang. xiv 1891–2, p. 310; Gerould, Saints' Legends pp. 228, 367.]

Childhood of Jesus. C. Horstmann, Alteng lische Legenden, Paderborn, 1875, p. 1 Archiv, lxxxii, 1889, p. 107 (see Archiv cxxvii, 1911, p. 318, xlix, 1872, p. 377 E. Studien, ii, 1878–9, p. 115).

Christopher,Dunstan. E.Mätzner,Altenglisch Sprachproben, vol. i, Berlin, 1867, p. 194 171; Jahrbuch für romische und englische Sprache und Literatur, xiv, 1875, p. 32.

Cuthbert. Surtees Soc. lxxxvii, 1891.

Dunstan. R. Morris and W. W. Skeat, Speci mens of Early English, vol. ii, Oxford, 1894 p. 19. Trn, J. L. Weston, Chief Middle English Poets, Boston, 1914, p. 37.

Edmund. Lord F. Hervey, Corolla S. Ead mundi, 1907, p. 362.

Eleven Thousand Virgins. S. B. Liljegren E. Studien, lvii, 1923, p. 85.

Gregory. Archiv, lv, 1876, p. 407.

Guthlac. BBA. xii, 1902, p. 18. [See C. Horst mann, Altenglische Legenden, Paderborn 1875, pp. xxvi, xxxiv; Ang. i, 1878, p 392.]

Juliana. EETS. li, 1872, p. 81; G. Schleich Archiv, cli, 1927, p. 19.

Katherine, Judas. R. Wülcker, Lesebuch, pt i Halle, 1874, pp. 12, 18.

Magdalen. C. Horstmann, Altenglische Le genden, Heilbronn, 1878, p. 148; Archiv, lxviii, 1882, p. 52.

Margaret. EETS. xiii, 1866, p. 24; Archiv, lxxix, 1887, p. 411. [See C. Horstmann, Altenglische Legenden, Heilbronn, 1881, pp. 449, 225.]

Michael. T. Wright, Popular Treatises on Science, 1841, p. 132. [See *Wells*, p. 835 [34].]

Miracles of Virgin. R. W. Tryon, PMLA. xxxviii, 1923, p. 308.

Passion. C. Horstmann, Leben Jesu, Münster, 1873; B. D. Brown, EETS. 1925.

Purgatory of St Patrick. C. Horstmann, Altenglische Legenden, Paderborn, 1875, p. 151. [See St Patrick's Purgatory, below, p. 177.]

Susanna. Ang. i, 1878, p. 85. [For other edns of individual items see Wells, pp. 809 [31] ff., 812 [59] ff.]

Studies. [ten Brink, vol. i, p. 268; Schofield, p. 393; CHEL. vol. i, 1907, p. 338; Horstmann, as above.]

Gerould, G. H. Saints' Legends. Boston, 1916, pp. 151, 223, 360.

Mohr, F. Sprachliche Untersuchungen. Bonn, 1888.

Knörk, O. Untersuchungen über die mittelenglischen Magdalenlegenden, Laud 108. Halle, 1889.

Schmidt, W. Über den Stil (Laud 108). Halle, 1883.

Holthausen, F. Childhood of Jesus (Laud 108). Archiv, cxxxvii, 1918, p. 318.

Heuser, W. Language of Magdalen. Ang. xvii, 1894-5, p. 72.

Brown, B. Kenelm, Gloucester's Chronicle, Origin of Collection. MLN. xli, 1926, p. 13. [See EETS. clxix, 1925, introduction.]

Plenzat, K. Die Theophiluslegende in den Dichtungen des Mittelalters. Berlin, 1926.

Sergeantson, M. S. Dialect. RES. iii, 1927, p. 321.

[For general studies of Brandan, Barlaam and Josaphat, Cecilia, Guthlac, etc., see Wells, p. 806, 1011, 1115, 1214, and ch. v [31] ff., 7].]

(c) Smaller Vernon Collection

MS. Vernon (Bodleian 3938). Ed. items 1-7, with Latin original, C. Horstmann, Altenglische Legenden, Heilbronn, 1878, p. 3; Barlaam and Josaphat, ed. C. Horstmann, Altenglische Legenden, Paderborn, 1875, p. 215; Eufrosyne, ed. E. Studien, i, 1877, p. 300, and C. Horstmann, Altenglische Legenden, Heilbronn, 1878, p. 174.

Studies. [Wells, pp. 304, 808, 1011, 1116.] Horstmann, C. Altenglische Legenden. Heilbronn, 1881, p. lxxxix; Paderborn, 1875, p. xxiv.

Gerould, G. H. Saints' Legends. Boston, 1916. [Pp. 229, 367.]

Hill, R. T. Romanic Rev. x, 1920, p. 159, 191, xii, 1922, p. 44. [Edn of French Euphrosyne.]

(d) Scottish Collection

[Wells, pp. 304, 808, 1011.]

MS. University Lib. Cambridge Gg.ii.6. Ed. C. Horstmann, 2 vols. Heilbronn, 1881-2 (item 29, ptd, C. Horstmann, Altenglische Legenden, Heilbronn, 1881, p. 189); ed. W. M. Metcalfe, STS. 3 vols. 1896; Alexius, Archiv, lxii, 1879, p. 397; Machor, ed. C. Horstmann, Altenglische Legenden, Heilbronn, 1881, p. 189; Cecilia, ed. B. E. Lovewell, New Haven, 1898; Ninian and Machor, ed. W. M. Metcalfe, Paisley, 1906.

Studies. [CHEL. vol. ii, 1908, p. 127. Author: Ang. ix, 1886, p. 493; E. Studien, x, 1887, p. 373; J. Baudisch, Ein Beitrag zur Kenntnis der früher Barbourzugeschriebenen Legendensammlung, Program der öffentlichen Unterrealschule in Wien, 1903.]

Horstmann, C. Altenglische Legenden. Heilbronn, 1881. [P. lxxxix.]

Dublin Rev. April 1887.

Prothero, J. W. Memoir of Henry Bradshaw. 1888. Addendum xii. [P. 143.]

Fiby, H. F. Zur Laut- und Flexionslehre. Brunn, 1889.

Bearder, J. W. Über den Gebrauch der Praepositionen. Halle, 1894.

Gerould, G. H. Saints' Legends. Boston, 1916. [Pp. 176, 363, 182.]

Baum, P. F. Judas. PMLA. xxxi, 1916, p. 531.

[See also Barbour's Bruce, above, pp.166-7; and Huchown Discussion, under Morte Arthure, above, p. 137.]

(e) John Mirk's Festial

MSS. Cotton, Claudius A ii; Bodley, Gough Eccl. Top. 4; Caius College Cambridge 168; Harley 2403; Lansdowne 392; Douce 108 (Bodleian); Douce 60 (Bodleian); Harley 2381.

Editions. T. Erbe, EETS. Ex. Ser. 1905; single items, C. Horstmann, Altenglische Legenden, Heilbronn, 1881, p. cxxiv; Ang. iii, 1880, p. 314.

[See Wells, pp. 301, 807, 1267, 1306, 1397; DNB.; C. Horstmann, Altenglische Legenden, Heilbronn, 1881, p. cviii; Ang. iii, 1880, p. 293; Ward, vol. iii, pp. 681, 705.]

[On separate lives of saints, see Wells, pp. 308, 809. For the alliterative Erkenwald, see under Pearl Group, below, p. 203.]

(3) Particular Legends
(a) Assumption of Mary

[Wells, pp. 330, 815, 1014, 1119.]

MSS.

I. University Lib. Cambridge; 1, Dd.i.1; 2, Ff.ii.38; 3, Gg.iv.27, 2; 4, Harley 2382;

5, BM. Add. 10036; 6, Chetham 8009 (Manchester). [See C. Brown, Register of Middle English Religious Verse, vol. II, 1920, item 1356.] Ed. J. R. Lumby, EETS. XIV, 1866, rev. G. H. McKnight, 1905; critical text, ed. E. Hackauf, Heidelberg, 1902.

E. Studien, III, 1880, p. 93, XXXIII, 1904, p. 179, XXXV, 1905, p. 350. [Notes; sources.] Gierth, F. Über die älteste mittelenglische Version der Assumptio Mariae. Breslau, 1881; rptd E. Studien, VII, 1884, p. 1.

II. Auchinleck (Nat. Lib. Scotland 19.2.1). Ed. E. Studien, VIII, 1885, pp. 427, 448 (see E. Studien, XIII, 1889, p. 358).

III. South Legendary: Harley 2277; Corpus Christi College Cambridge, etc. [See C. Brown, Register, vol. II, 1920, item 1904; EETS. XIV, 1866, 1905 (rev.), p. liii; E. Studien, VIII, 1885, p. 461; C. Horstmann, Altenglische Legenden, Paderborn, 1875, Heilbronn, 1881, introductions; Hackauf, edn as above.]

IV. North Homily: Harley 4196, Cotton, Tiberius E VII. Ed. C. Horstmann, Altenglische Legenden, Heilbronn, 1881, p. 112 (see p. lxxviii).

V. Cursor Mundi, vv. 20065 ff. [See C. Brown, Register, vol. II, 1920, item 2546.] Ed. EETS. LXVI, 1877, pp. 1148, 1602, 1638.

MLN. XXXVI, 1921, p. 238. [Source.]

VI. Phillipps 9803. [See C. Brown, Register, vol. II, 1920, item 204.]

VII. Lambeth 223. [See C. Brown, Register, vol. II, 1920, item 733.]

[On Assumption, see G. H. Gerould, Saints' Legends, Boston, 1916, pp. 212, 365.]

(b) Childhood of Christ

[Wells, pp. 324, 813, 965, 1014, 1118.]
MSS.

I. Harley 3954. Ed. E. Studien, II, 1878–9, p. 117; ed. C. Horstmann, Altenglische Legenden, Heilbronn, 1878, p. 101.

II. Harley 2399. Ed. C. Horstmann, Altenglische Legenden, Heilbronn, 1878, p. 111.

III. BM. Add. 31042. Ed. Archiv, LXXIV, 1885, p. 327.

IV. South Legendary, Laud 108, etc. Ed. Laud, C. Horstmann, Altenglische Legenden, Paderborn, 1875, p. 1. [See Wells, pp. 321, 813 [67]; Southern Legend Collection, above, p. 174.]

Studies.
Reinsch. Die Pseudo-Evangelien von Jesus und Marias Kindheit. Halle, 1879.
Landshoff, H. Kindheit Jesus. Berlin, 1889.

Meyer, P. French Sources. Romania, XVIII 1889, p. 128.
Gast, E. Die beiden Redaktionen. Greifswald, 1909.
Holthausen, F. Zum mittelenglischen Kindheit Jesu (Laud 108). Archiv, CXXVII, 1911 p. 318.
Gerould, G. H. Saints' Legends. Boston, 1916. [Pp. 215, 226, 365.]
Hamilton, G. L. MLN. XXXVI, 1921, p. 239.

(c) Vision of St Paul, or Eleven Pains of Hell

[Wells, pp. 332, 815, 965, 1014, 1119, 1216.]

MSS. 1, Laud 108; 2, Jesus College Oxford 29; 3, Digby 86 (Bodleian); 4, Vernon (Bodleian 3938); 5, Simeon (BM. Add. 22283); 6, Douce 302 (Bodleian); 7, Lambeth 487 (homily 4); 8, BM. Add. 10036. [See C. Brown, Register, vol. II, 1920, index.]

Editions. 1, Archiv, LII, 1874, p. 25; 2, R Morris, EETS. XLIX, 1872, p. 147; 3, Archiv LXII, 1879, p. 403; 4, 5, Horstmann, EETS XCVIII, 1892, p. 251, CXVII, 1901, p. 750 4, EETS. XLIX, 1872, p. 223; E. Studien, I 1877, p. 293; 6, EETS. XLIX, 1872, p. 210; 7 EETS. XXIX, 1867, p. 41; 8, E. Studien, XXII 1896, p. 134.

Studies. [Ward, vol. II, p. 397, etc.; ter Brink, vol. I, p. 213; CHEL. vol. I, 1907 p. 227.]

Meyer, P. Romania, VI, 1877, p. 11, XXIV 1895, p. 357.
—— Notices et Extraits des Manuscrits de la Bibliothèque Nationale. Vol. XXXV, Paris 1897, p. 153.
Brandes, H. Visio S. Pauli. Halle, 1885.
—— E. Studien, VII, 1884, p. 34. [Sources.]
Fritsche, C. Die lateinischen Visionen de Mittelalters. Romanische Forschungen, II 1885–6, p. 247, III, 1886–7, p. 337.
Peters, E. Zur Geschichte der lateinischer Visionslegenden. Romanische Forschungen VIII, 1886, p. 361.
James, M. R. Texts and Studies. Vol. II Cambridge, 1893, p. 3.
Becker, E. Medieval Visions of Heaven and Hell. Baltimore, 1899.
Gröber, G. Grundriss der romanischer Philologie. Vol. II¹, Strasburg, 1902, pp. 21 143, 481, 658, 686.
Huber, M. Beitrag zur Visionsliteratur 3 vols. Metten, 1903–8.
Baake, W. Die Verwendung des Traum motivs in der englischen Dichtung bis au Chaucer. Halle, 1906.
Gerould, G. H. Saints' Legends. Boston 1916. [Pp. 222, 229, 366, 367, 370.]

Willson, E. Medieval English Legends of Visits to the Other-World. Chicago, 1917.

Patch, H. R. Some Elements in Medieval Descriptions of the Otherworld. PMLA. XXXIII, 1918, p. 601.

King, G. G. Vision of Thurkill. Romanic Rev. x, 1919, p. 38.

Hall, J. Selections from Early Middle English. Vol. II, Oxford, 1920, p. 413.

Voigt, W. Beiträge zur Geschichte der Visionsliteratur im Mittelalter. Palaestra, CXLVI, 1924.

[See also under Harrowing of Hell, p. 188.]

(d) St Patrick's Purgatory

[*Wells*, pp. 334, 815, 965, 1014, 1060, 1119, 1216, 1398.]

MSS. Three versions. I. Long couplets: 1, Laud 108 (Bodleian); 2, Egerton 1993; 3, Cotton, Julius D IX; 4, Ashmole 43 (Bodleian); 5, University Lib. Cambridge Add. 3039; 6, Harley 2277, Corpus Christi College Cambridge 145 and cognate South Legendary MSS. II. Tail rime (Owayn Miles): 7, Auchinleck (Nat. Lib. Scotland 19.2.1). III. Short couplets: 8, Cotton, Caligula A II; 9, Brome Hall, Suffolk.

Editions. 1, 2, 4, variants of 3, C. Horstmann, Altenglische Legenden, Paderborn, 1875, p. 151; 8, 7, E. Studien, I, 1877, p. 57; 9, E. Studien, IX, 1886, p. 3; L. T. Smith, Commonplace Book of 15th Century, Norwich, 1886, p. 180; 1, C. Horstmann, EETS. LXXXVII, 1887, p. 199; 7, D. Laing, Owain Miles, Edinburgh, 1837; 6, Royal, J. P. Krapp, Legends of St Patrick's Paradise, Baltimore, 1900, p. 54. Latin text: Romanische Forschungen, VI, 1889, p. 139. [See also under Southern Legend Collection, p. 175.]

Selection. R. Wülcker, Lesebuch, 2 pts, Halle, 1874-9.

Translation. Tail rime: M. H. Shackford, Legends and Satires from Medieval Literature, Boston, 1913, p. 33; J. L. Weston, Chief Middle English Poets, Boston, 1914, p. 83.

Studies. [*Ward*, vol. II. pp. 435, 748.]

Wright, T. St Patrick's Purgatory. 1843.

De Vere, A. Legends of St Patrick. 1872: [Poems.]

Koelbing, E. E. Studien, I, 1877, p. 57. [Author.]

Eckleben, S. Die älteste Schilderung vom Fegefeuer des Heiligen Patricius. Halle, 1885.

Stokes, W. Tripartite Life of St Patrick. Rolls Ser. 1887.

Langlois, E. Origine et Sources du Roman de la Rose. Paris, 1890. [Ch. v.]

Krapp, J. P. Legend of St Patrick's Purgatory: its later Literary History. Baltimore, 1900.

Gröber, G. Grundriss der romanischen Philologie. Vol. II¹, Strasburg, 1902, p. 277.

de Félice, P. L'Autre Monde. Paris, 1906.

Verdeyen, R. and Endepols, J. Tondalus' Visioen en St Patricius' Vagevuur. Hague, 1914, 1917.

van Hamel, A. G. Tondalus' Visioen en Patricius' Vagevuur. Neophilologus, IV, 1919, p. 152.

[See also Becker, Peters, Voigt, under Vision of St Paul, above, p. 176.]

(e) Vision of Tundale

[*Wells*, pp. 335, 816, 1014.]

MSS. 1, Nat. Lib. Scotland 19.3.1; 2, Cotton, Caligula A II; 3, Royal 17 B XLIII; 4, Ashmole 1491 (Bodleian, 2 fragments).

Editions. 3, W. D. B. Turnbull, Edinburgh, 1843; composite text, A. Wagner, Halle, 1893; Cotton, selection, R. Wülcker, Lesebuch, pt ii, Halle, 1879, p. 17. French texts, Friedel and Meyer, Paris, 1907.

Studies. [*Ward*, vol. II, pp. 416, 746.]

Mussafia, A. Sulla visione di Tundalo. Sitzungsber. d. k. Akad. d. Wiss., Phil.-hist. Klasse, LXVII, Vienna, 1871, p. 157.

Wagner, A. Visio Tunugdali. Erlangen, 1882.

—— Zu Tundalusvision. Ang. XX, 1897, p. 452.

Peters, E. Die Vision des Tungdalus. Prgr. des Dorotheenstadt Realgymnasiums, Berlin, 1895.

Becker, E. Medieval Visions. Baltimore, 1899. [P. 81.]

Gröber, G. Grundriss der romanischen Philologie. Vol. II¹, Strasburg, 1902, pp. 277, 401. [On French.]

Gerould, G. H. Saints' Legends. Boston, 1916. [Pp. 248, 369.]

[See also Verdeyen and Endepols, van Hamel, under St Patrick's Purgatory, above.]

IV. MORAL AND RELIGIOUS INSTRUCTION

(a) The Body and the Soul

[*Wells*, pp. 411, 829, 980, 1018, 1068, 1125, 1272, 1311, 1358, 1404.]

Version I

MS. Exeter Book (Cathedral Lib. Exeter). Ed. C. W. M. Grein, Bibliothek der Angelsächsischen Poesie, vol. I, Göttingen, 1857, p. 198; ed. R. Wülker, heliotype reproduction, Leipzig, 1894.

Version II

MS. Worcester Cathedral Lib. (fragments). Ed. T. Phillipps, Fragment of Aelfric's Grammar, 1838; ed. S. W. Singer, Departing Soul's Address to the Body, 1845; ed. E. Haufe, Greifswald, 1880; ed. R. Buchholz, Erlanger Beiträge, vi, 1890; ed. J. Hall, Selections from Early Middle English, Oxford, 1920, vol. i, p. 2, vol. ii, p. 228.

Version III

MS. Bodley 343 (25 vv.). Ed. Archaeologia, xvii, 1814, p. 174; ed. T. Thorpe, Analecta Anglosaxonica, 1846, p. 153; ed. F. L. M. Rieger, Alt- und angelsächsisches Lesebuch, Giessen, 1861, p. 124; ed. A. Schröer, Ang. v, 1882, p. 289; ed. R. Buchholz, Erlanger Beiträge, vi, 1890.

Version IV

MSS. 1, Laud 108 (Bodleian); 2, Auchinleck (Nat. Lib. Scotland 19.2.1); 3, Royal 18 Ax; 4, Vernon (Bodleian 3938); 5, BM. Add. 22283; 6, Digby 102 (Bodleian); 7, BM. Add. 37787. Ed. 1, 4, with Latin, French, T. Wright, Latin Poems Attributed to W. Mapes, Camden Soc. 1841, pp. 334, 340; 2, 1, 4, 6, variants of 5, ed. W. Linow, Erlanger Beiträge, i, 1889, pp. 24, 25, 66, 67, 106; 1, ed. E. Mätzner, Altenglische Sprachproben, pt i, Berlin, 1867, p, 90, and ed. O. F. Emerson, Reader, New York, 1915, p. 47; 3, ed. H. Varnhagen, Ang. ii, 1879, pp. 229; 2, ed. D. Laing, Owain Miles, Edinburgh, 1837.

Version V

MSS. 1, Digby 86 (Bodleian); 2, Trinity College Cambridge B, 14, 39; 3, Harley 2253. [See C. Brown, Register, vol. ii, 1920, item 883.] Ed. 1, E. M. Stengel, Codicem Manu Scriptum Digby 86, Halle, 1871, p. 93; 3, ed. T. Wright, Latin Poems Attributed to W. Mapes, Camden Soc. 1841, p. 346; ed. K. Böddeker, Altenglische Dichtungen des Handschrifts Harley 2253, Berlin, 1878, p. 233.

Version VI

MS. Trinity College Cambridge B, 14, 39, fol. 27 r (22 vv.). [See C. Brown, Register, vol. ii, 1920, item 1429.] Ed. T. Wright, Latin Poems Attributed to W. Mapes, Camden Soc. 1841, p. 322; ed. H. Varnhagen, Ang. iii, 1880, p. 577.

[On MSS. see Ang. ii, 1879, p. 225; C. Brown, Register, vol. ii, 1920, items 228, 883, 1429.]

Translations. C. G. Child, Boston, 1908; J. L. Weston, Chief Middle English Poets, Boston, 1914, p. 304.

Studies. [On general theme and foreign versions see *Wells*, pp. 829, 1018, 1125. See also for the O.E. versions p. 79 above.]

Archiv, xxix, 1861, pp. 205, 321.

Heesch, G. Über Sprache und Versbau. Kiel, 1884.

Wülcker, R. Grundriss zur Geschichte der angelsächsischen Literatur. Leipzig, 1885, p. 231. [Exeter version.]

Bruce. J. D. Contribution to Study. MLN. v, 1890, p. 385.

Holthausen, F. Ang. xiv, 1891–2, p. 321. [Notes; Worcester fragments.]

Kunze, O. Þe desputisoun bitwen þe Bodi and þe Soule. Berlin, 1892. [Text criticism.]

von Glahn, N. Anglistische Forschungen, liii, 1918. [Worcester fragments; grammar.]

Allen, B. On Digby. MLR. xxii, 1927, p. 189.

Allison, T. E. Castell of Perseverance. MLN. xlii, 1927, p. 102.

Oakden, J. P. Alliterative Poetry in Middle English. Manchester, 1930, pp. 41, 43, 120, 137, etc.

(b) Rule of St Benedict

[*Wells*, pp. 365, 820, 1016, 1063, 1121, 1399. See EETS. xc, 1888 and cxx, 1902.]

Common version. MSS. Corpus Christi College Cambridge 178; Corpus Christi College Oxford 197; Cotton, Tiberius A iii (ch. iv); Durham Cathedral Lib. B, 4, 24; Cotton, Titus A iv; Cotton, Faustina A x.

Editions. R. Wülcker, Bibliothek der angelsächsischen Prosa, vol. ii, Cassel, 1885; E. Studien, xxiv, 1898, p. 161.

Wells version. Loose leaves in Chapter Lib. Wells Cathedral. Ed. R. Wülcker, Bibliothek der angelsächsischen Prosa, vol. ii, p. 102; with Winteney, ed. A. Schröer, Halle, 1888.

Interlinear version. MS. Cotton, Tiberius A iii. Ed. H. Logemann, EETS. xc, 1888.

Winteney version. MS. Cotton, Claudius D iii. Ed. with Wells, A. Schröer, Halle, 1888 (collation, E. Studien, xvi, 1892, p. 152).

Northern prose and ritual. MS. Lansdowne 378. Ed. E. A. Kock, EETS. cxx, 1902, pp. 1, 141.

Northern metre. MS. Cotton, Vespasian A xxv. Ed. E. Studien, ii, 1878, p. 60 (see Ang. xiv, 1891–2, p. 302; E. Studien, xxiii, 1897, p. 284); ed. E. A. Kock, EETS. cxx, 1902, pp. 48, 145.

Caxton's abstract. Ed. EETS. cxx, 1902, p. 119.

Studies.

Böddeker, K. Über die Sprache der Benediktinerregel. E. Studien, ii, 1878, p. 344. [Northern metre version.]

Tachauer, J. Die Laute und Flexionen (Winteney). Würzburg, 1900.

Hermanns, W. Lautlehre und Dialektische (Interlinearversion). Bonn, 1906.

Heuser, W. Die Prosaversion der Benediktiner-Regel MS Lansdowne 378. Ang. xxxi, 1908, pp. 276, 398, 543.

Fehr, B. E. Studien, xlvi, 1912–3, p. 337.

Rohr, G. Die Sprache der altenglischen Prosabearbeitungen. Bonn, 1912.

Hagel, F. Zur Sprache der nordenglischen Prosaversion der Benediktiner-Regel. Ang. xliv, 1920, p. 1.

Funke, O. Zur Wortgeschichte der französischen Element im Englischen. E. Studien, lv, 1921, p. 4.

(c) Ancren Riwle

[*Wells*, pp. 361, 820, 972, 1015, 1062, 1120, 1172, 1217, 1269, 1309, 1353, 1399.]

MSS. English: 1, Corpus Christi College Cambridge 402; 2, Cotton, Titus D xviii; 3, Cotton, Nero A xiv; 4, Cotton, Cleopatra C vi; 5, Caius College Cambridge 234 (see Ang. iii, 1880, p. 34; E. Studien, iii, 1880, p. 535, ix, 1886, p. 116, xix, 1894, p. 247); 6, Vernon (Bodleian 3938); 7, Magdalene College Cambridge, Pepys 2498; 8, Lord Robartes (1 leaf; Bodmin, Cornwall). French: Cotton, Vitellius F vii. Latin: Magdalen College Oxford 67; Cotton, Vitellius E vii (fragments). [See also H. E. Allen, MLR. xiv, 1919, p. 209, xvii, 1922, p. 403.]

Editions. 3, with some variants of 2, 4, J. Morton, Camden Soc. 1853 (collation, Jahrbuch für romanische und englische Sprache, xv, 1876, p. 179); 7, J. Påhlsson, The Recluse, Lund, 2 pts, 1911–8 (see E. Studien, li, 1917–8, p. 255; Archiv, clx, 1920, p. 314; Ang. Bbl. xxv, 1914, p. 75); 8, JEGP. ii, 1898, p. 199.

Selections. T. Wright and J. O. Halliwell [-Phillipps], Reliquiae Antiquae, vol. ii, 1843, p. 1; E. Mätzner, Altenglische Sprachproben, pt ii, Berlin, 1900, p. 5; H. Sweet, First Middle English Primer, Oxford, 1884, p. 19; R. Morris and W. W. Skeat, Specimens of Early English, vol. i, Oxford, 1885; O. F. Emerson, Reader, New York, 1915; A. S. Cook, Reader, Boston, 1915; J. Hall, Selections from Early Middle English, vol. i, Oxford, 1920, p. 54, vol. ii, pp. 354, 372; F. Kluge, Lesebuch, Halle, 1904; W. Heuser, Ang. xxx, 1907, p. 108; A. Brandl and O. Zippel, Mittelenglische Sprach- und Literaturproben, Berlin, 1917; G. Sampson, Cambridge Book of Prose and Verse, 1924.

Translation. Morton's edn; rptd King's Classics, 1905, and Medieval Library, 1924.

Studies. [ten Brink, vol. i, p. 200; CHEL. vol. i, 1907, p. 230; Schofield, p. 403.]

Brock, E. Grammatical Forms. Trans. Philolog. Soc. 1865, p. 150.

Wülcker, R. Language. PBB. i, 1874, p. 209.

Bülbring, K. QF. lxiii, 1889, p. 6. [Verbs.]

Bramlette, E. E. Original Language of the Ancren Riwle. Ang. xv, 1892–3, p. 478.

Mühe, T. Über den im MS. Cotton, Titus Text der Ancren Riwle. Göttingen, 1901.

Williams, I. F. Language of the Cleopatra MS. of the Ancren Riwle. Ang. xxviii, 1902, p. 300.

Dahlstedt, A. Word Order. Sundsvall, 1903.

Ostermann, H. Lautlehre der germanischen Wortschatzes. BBA. xix, 1905.

Redepenning, H. Syntaktisches Kapitel. Rostock, 1906.

Heuser, W. Ang. xxx, 1907, p. 103. [Date. Replies: Ang. xxxi, 1908, p. 399; MLR. iv, 1909, p. 433; E. Studien, xxxviii, 1907, p. 453.]

Landwehr, M. Das grammatische Geschlecht. Heidelberg, 1911.

Macaulay, G. C. The Ancren Riwle. MLR. ix, 1914, pp. 63, 145, 324, 463. [Most important.]

Kenyon, J. S. Syntactical Note. MLN. xxix, 1914, p. 127.

McNabb, V. Author. MLR. xi, 1916, p. 1.

—— The Authorship. Rome, 1935.

Allen, H. E. Origin. PMLA. xxxiii, 1918, p. 474; Romanic Rev. ix, 1918, pp. 189, 192. [See B. Fehr, Ang. Bbl. xxxi, 1920, p. 96; G. G. Coulton, MLR. xv, 1920, p. 99.]

—— Some 14th Century Borrowings from Ancren Riwle. MLR. xviii, 1923, p. 1, xix, 1924, p. 95.

—— Further Borrowings. MLR. xxiv, 1929, p. 1.

—— Author. PMLA. xliv, 1929, p. 635.

—— MLR. xxviii, 1933, p. 485. [Author.]

—— PMLA. l, 1935, p. 899. [Identifications.]

Hall, J. Selections from Early Middle English. Vol. i, Oxford, 1920, p. 54, vol. ii, pp. 354, 372.

McNabb, V., Allen, H. E. and Coulton, G. G. Origin. MLR. xv, 1920, p. 406, xvi, 1921, p. 316, xvii, 1922, p. 66.

Dieth, E. Flexivisches und Syntaktisches über das Pronomen. Zurich, 1920.

Funke, O. Zur Wortgeschichte der französischen Element im Englischen. E. Studien, lv, 1921, pp. 16, 19, 24.

Zeise, A. Die Wortschatz. Jena, 1923. [Summary.]

Dymes, D. M. E. Original Language of the Ancren Riwle. E. & S. ix, 1923, p. 31 (see Ang. Bbl. xxxv, 1924, p. 367).

Chambers, R. W., McNabb, V. and Thurston, F. H. RES. i, 1925, p. 4, ii, 1926, pp. 82, 85, 197, 198, 199. [Author; origin.]

Serjeantson, M. S. Dialect of Nero. RES. iii, 1927, p. 323.

Knowles, D. The English Mystics. 1927.

Tolkien, J. R. R. Ancren Wisse and Hali Meiðhad. E. & S. xiv, 1928, p. 104.

Crawford, S. J. The Influence of the Ancren Riwle in the Late Fourteenth Century. MLR. xxv, 1930, p. 191.

Wilson, R. M. Leeds Stud. no. 1, 1932, p. 24. [Connection with Katherine group.]

Ives, D. V. MLR. xxix, 1934, p. 257. [Proverbs.]

(d) Poema Morale

[Wells, pp. 385, 823, 1017, 1064, 1122, 1173, 1218, 1356, 1401.]

MSS. 1, Digby A 4 (Bodleian 1605; see Archiv, cxv, 1905, p. 167); 2, Jesus College Oxford 29 (Bodleian); 3, Trinity College Cambridge 335 (B, 14, 52); 4, Fitzwilliam Museum, Cambridge, McClean 123. 5, 6, Egerton 613 (two texts); 7, Lambeth 487. [On MSS, see C. Brown, Register, vol. ii, 1920, item 786, and MLR. xxi, 1926, p. 249.]

Editions. 5, 6, F. J. Furnivall, Early English Poems and Lives of Saints, Berlin, 1862, p. 22; 6, J. Zupitza, Übungsbuch, Leipzig, 1915, and G. E. MacLean, Reader, 1894, p. 49; 5, EETS. xxxiv, 1868, p. 288; 7, EETS. xxix, 1867, p. 159; 3, EETS. liii, 1873, p. 220; 3, 2, R. Morris and W. W. Skeat, Specimens of Early English, vol. i, Oxford, 1885, p. 194; 2, EETS. xlix, 1872, p. 58; 1, Ang. i, 1878, p. 6; 4, A. C. Paues, Ang. xxx, 1907, p. 217; 7, 3, parts of 6, 5, J. Hall, Selections from Early Middle English, Oxford, 1920, vol. i, p. 30, vol. ii, p. 312; 5, O. F. Emerson, Reader, New York, 1915, p. 176; critical edn, H. Lewin, Halle, 1881, and H. Marcus, Palaestra, cxciv, 1934 (based on Digby MS); Maidstone quotations, C. Brown, MLR. xxi, 1926, p. 249.

Selections. F. Kluge, Lesebuch, Halle, 1904; G. Sampson, Cambridge Book of Prose and Verse, 1924.

Studies. [ten Brink, vol. i, p. 153; CHEL. vol. i, 1907, p. 220; Ang. iii, 1880, p. 32, iv, 1881, p. 406; MLN. i, 1886, p. 14. Language: Ang. xvii, 1894–5, p. 78. Verse: J. Schipper, Englische Metrik, Bonn, 1881, sects. 43, 63, 65; Paul's Grundriss der germanischen Philologie, vol. ii¹, Strasburg, 1892, p. 1047; Ang. Anz. viii, 1885, p. 3.]

Suchier, H. Reimpredigt. Halle, 1879. [Analogues.]

Krüger, A. Sprache und Dialekt (Trinity). Erlangen, 1885.

Gabrielson, A. Le Sermon de Guischart de Beauliu. Upsala, 1909.

—— Guischart de Beauliu's Debt. Archiv, cxxviii, 1912, p. 309.

Jordan, R. Dialect (Lambeth). E. Studien, xlii, 1910, p. 38.

Preusler, W. Syntax. Breslau, 1914.

Allen, H. E. Dependence. Romanic Rev. ix, 1918, p. 181.

Stegen, L. Die Sprachformen und Schreibungen. Jahrbuch der philosophischen Fakultät Göttingen, i, 1921, p. 41.

Walberg, E. Neuphilologische Mitteilungen, xxvi, 1925, p. 87. [On text.]

Moore, S. Ang. liv, 1930, p. 269. [Relations of MSS.]

(e) Proverbs of Alfred

[Wells, pp. 375, 822, 1016, 1064, 1122, 1183, 1217, 1310, 1354, 1400.]

MSS. 1, Jesus College Oxford 29 (Bodleian); 2, Trinity College Cambridge B, 14, 39 (see MLR. v, 1910, p. 282); 3, Cotton, Galba A xix (fragments); 4, Bodley, James 6 (complete copy of Cotton); 5, Maidstone Museum A 13 (see MLR. xxi, 1926, p. 1).

Editions. 1, 2, T. Wright and J. O. Halliwell[-Phillipps], Reliquiae Antiquae, vol. i, 1841, p. 170; R. Morris, EETS. xlix, 1872, p. 102 (see Archiv, lxxxviii, 1802, p. 370); 2, J. M. Kemble, Dialogue of Salomon and Saturnus, 1848, p. 226; 1, 2, 3, W. W. Skeat, Oxford, 1907, E. Borgström, Lund, 1908, 1911, and A. Brandl and O. Zippel, Mittelenglische Sprach- und Literaturproben, Berlin, 1917, p. 145; 1, J. Hall, Selections from Early Middle English, Oxford, 1920, vol. i, p. 18, vol. ii, p. 285; 5, 4, C. Brown, MLR. xxi, 1926, p. 249.

Selections. R. Morris and W. W. Skeat, Specimens of Early English, vol. i, Oxford, 1885, p. 146; J. Zupitza, Übungsbuch, Vienna, 1922; G. Sampson, Cambridge Book of Prose and Verse, 1924.

Translation. J. L. Weston, Chief Middle English Poets, Boston, 1914, p. 289; parts, M. G. Segar, A Medieval Anthology, London, 1916, p. 127.

Studies. [ten Brink, vol. i, p. 151; CHEL. vol. i, 1907, p. 218.]

Wülcker, R. PBB. i, 1874, p. 240; Ang. iii, 1880, p. 370; Ang. Anz. viii, 1885, p. 67.

Gropp, E. On the Language of the Proverbs of Alfred. Halle, 1879.

Schipper, J. Englische Metrik. Bonn, 1881. [Ch. vii.]

Archiv, xc, 1893, p. 141.

Skeat, W. W. Trans. Philolog. Soc. 1895–8, p. 399.

Holthausen, F. Zum mittelenglischen eo. Ang. Bbl. xv, 1904, p. 347.

South, H. P. The Proverbs of Alfred. New York, 1931.

[For other proverbs, see Proverbs of Hendyng, below, p. 183; and Wells, pp. 375, 821, and Supplements.]

(f) Vices and Virtues

[*Wells*, pp. 413, 830, 1019, 1068, 1125, 1219, 1311.]

MS. Stowe 240. Ed. F. Holthausen, EETS. 1888, 1920. Facs. 1 page, Paleographical Soc. Ser. 2, pl. 92. [On other MSS see *Wells*, pp. 1068, 1125, 1219.]

Selections. F. Kluge, Lesebuch, Halle, 1904; J. Hall, Selections from Early Middle English, Oxford, 1920, vol. I, p. 88, vol. II, p. 438.

Studies.

Schmidt, G. Ueber die Sprache und Heimat. Leipzig, 1899.

Traver, H. E. Four Daughters of God. Philadelphia, 1907.

Merrill, E. Dialogue in English Literature. New Haven, 1911. [P. 23.]

Philippsen, M. Die Deklination. Erlangen, 1911.

Meyerhoff, E. Die Verbalflexion. Kiel, 1913.

von Glahn, N. Zur Geschichte des grammatischen Geschlechts. Anglistische Forschungen, LIII, 1918.

Funke, O. Zur Wortgeschichte der französischen Element im Englischen. E. Studien, LV, 1921, p. 23.

Flasdieck, H. E. Studien, LVIII, 1924, p. 1. [Language.]

(g) The Owl and the Nightingale

[*Wells*, pp. 418, 831, 1019, 1069, 1126, 219, 1273, 1311, 1358, 1404; edns by Wells, Atkins.]

MSS. 1, Cotton, Caligula A IX; 2, Jesus College Oxford 29 (Bodleian).

Editions. 1, J. Stevenson, Roxburghe Club, 1838; 1, T. Wright, Percy Soc. 1843; eclectic text, F. H. Stratmann, Krefeld, 1867 (emendations, E. Studien, I, 1877, p. 212); 1, 2, J. E. Wells, Boston, 1907, 1909, 1926; critical text, W. Gadow, Berlin, 1907, Palaestra, XV, 1909; 1, 2, with trn, J. W. H. Atkins, Cambridge, 1922; 1, 2, J. H. G. Grattan and G. F. H. Sykes, EETS. Ex. Ser. 1935.

Selections. E. Mätzner, Altenglische Sprachproben, 2 pts, Berlin, 1867–1900; R. Morris and W. W. Skeat, Specimens of Early English, vol. I, Oxford, 1885, p. 171 (see Ang. XXV, 1902, p. 323); A. S. Cook, Reader, Boston, 1915; A. Brandl and O. Zippel, Mittelenglische Sprach- und Literaturproben, Berlin, 1917; J. Hall, Selections from Early Middle English, Oxford, 1920, vol. I, p. 148, vol. II, p. 553; G. Sampson, Cambridge Book of Prose and Verse, 1924.

Translations. J. L. Weston, Chief Middle English Poets, Boston, 1914; Atkins, edn.

Studies. [H. Morley, English Writers, vol. XI, 1889, p. 331; *ten Brink*, vol. I, p. 214;

W. W. Courthope, History of English Poetry, vol. I, 1895, p. 131; *Schofield*, p. 427; CHEL. vol. I, 1907, p. 238; DNB. under 'Nicholas de Guildford.']

Brandl, A. Spielmannsverhältnisse in frühmittelenglischer Zeit. Sitzungsb. Preuss. Akad. d. Wissensch. 1910, p. xli.

Breier, W. Eule und Nachtigall. SEP. XXXIX, 1910.

Björkmann, E. Archiv, CXXVI, 1911, p. 235. [Author, etc.].

Hinckley, H. B. MP. XVII, 1919–20, p. 247; PMLA. XLIV, 1929, p. 329, XLVI, 1931, p. 93, XLVII, 1932, p. 303; PQ. XII, 1933, p. 339. [Date, author, analogues.]

Kenyon, J. S. MP. XVIII, 1920, p. 55. [Date, etc.]

Knowlton, E. C. Nature in Middle English. JEGP. XX, 1921, pp. 188, 189.

Huganir, K. The Owl and the Nightingale: Sources, Date, Author. Philadelphia, 1931.

Wells, J. E. MLN. XLVIII, 1933, p. 516. [Cotton MS.]

De la Torre Bueno, L. Ang. LVIII, 1934, p. 122. [Date.]

Tupper, F. The Date and Historical Background. PMLA. XLIX, 1934, p. 406.

Text, explanatory notes.

[J. S. Kenyon, JEGP. XI, 1912, p. 572; J. W. H. Atkins, Athenaeum, 20 Jan. 1906, p. 83; F. Holthausen, Ang. Bbl. XXX, 1919, p. 342, XXXIX, 1928, p. 244; E. C. Snyder, MP. XVII, 1920, p. 711; C. Brett, MLR. XIV, 1919, p. 8, XXII, 1927, p. 262; G. G. Coulton, MLR. XVII, 1922, p. 69; M. Ashdown, MLR. XVIII, 1923, p. 337; B. Dickins and J. P. Gilson, TLS. 7 April, 2 June 1927, pp. 251, 408.]

Language.

Noelle, H. Ueber die Sprache. Göttingen, 1870.

Sherman, L. A. Grammatical Analysis. Trans. American Philolog. Ass. 1875, p. 69.

Egge, A. E. Notes. MLN. I, 1886, p. 12.

Bülbring, K. QF. LXIII, 1889, p. 12. [Verbs.]

Kock, A. E. Ang. XXV, 1902, p. 323. [Notes.]

Ebisch, W. Zur Syntax des Verbums. Leipzig, 1905.

Wells, J. E. Accidence. Ang. XXXIII, 1910, p. 252.

—— Accent Markings in Jesus. MLN. XXV, 1910, p. 108.

—— Spelling. MLN. XXVI, 1911, p. 139.

Breier, W. Synthesis und Analysis des Konjunktivs. SEP. L, 1913, p. 251.

Hall, J. Selections from Early Middle English. Vol. II, Oxford, 1920. [P. 253.]

Funke, O. Zur Wortgeschichte der französischen Element im Englischen. E. Studien, LV, 1921, p. 24.

Verse. [See edns, above.]

Schipper, J. Englische Metrik. Bonn, 1881. [Sect. 121.]

Guest, E. History of English Rhythms. Ed. W. W. Skeat, 1882. [P. 427.]

Börsch, J. Ueber Metrik und Poetik. Münster, 1883.

Saintsbury, G. History of English Prosody. Vol. I, 1906. [P. 56.]

Breier, W. E. Studien, XLII, 1910, p. 306. [Verse.]

(h) Cursor Mundi

[Wells, pp. 339, 415, 517, 816, 1014, 1119, 1179, 1180, 1216, 1308, 1398.]

MSS. 1, Cotton, Vespasian A III (most complete); 2, Göttingen University Lib. Theol. 107 (next most complete); 3, Trinity College Cambridge R, 3, 8; 4, Fairfax 14 (Bodleian); 5, BM. Add. 36983 (formerly Bedford); 6, Laud 416 (Bodleian); 7, College of Arms (Arundel) LVII; 8–12, fragments in University Lib. Cambridge Gg.IV.27. 2; Royal College of Physicians, Edinburgh; Rawlinson Poet. 175 (Bodleian); BM. Add. 10036 and 31042. [On MSS, see C. Brown, Register, vol. II, 1920, item 1349; Ward, vol. III, p. 307; Catalogue of Additions, BM. 1900–5, p. 266.]

Editions. R. Morris, 6 pts, EETS. 1874–92.

Selections. R. Morris and W. W. Skeat, Specimens of Early English, vol. II, Oxford, 1894, p. 69; J. Zupitza, Übungsbuch, Vienna, 1922; O. F. Emerson, Reader, New York, 1915; A. Brandl and O. Zippel, Mittelenglische Sprach- und Literaturproben, Berlin, 1917; C. Brown, Religious Lyrics of 14th Century, Oxford, 1924, pp. 39, 37, 44 (see Wells, pp. 1216, 1224, 1226); G. Sampson, Cambridge Book of Prose and Verse, 1924.

Studies. [ten Brink, vol. I, p. 287; H. Morley, English Writers, vol. IV, 1890, p. 121; CHEL, vol. I, 1907, p. 341.]

Hänisch, H. C. W. Inquiry into Sources. Breslau, 1884. [See EETS. XCIX, 1892, CI, 1893.]

Hupe, H. Genealogie und Überlieferung des Handschriften des mittelenglischen Gedichtes Cursor Mundi. Altenburg, 1886. [See E. Studien, XI, 1888, p. 235, XII, 1889, p. 451; Ang. XI, 1888–9, p. 121; Ang. Bbl. I, 1890–1, p. 123.]

Cook, A. S. MLN. VII, 1892, p. 268.

Crow, C. L. Göttingen, 1892. [Metre.]

Barth, C. Wortschatz. Königsberg, 1903.

Ang. XXVI, 1903, p. 365. [Interpretation.]

Hörning, W. Die Schreibung der Handschrift E des Cursor Mundi. Berlin, 1906.

Brown, C. Cursor Mundi and Southern Passion. MLN. XXVI, 1911, p. 15.

Brunner, K. End in BM. Add. MS 31042 Archiv, CXXXII, 1914, p. 316.

Gerould, G. H. Saints' Legends. Boston 1916. [P. 198.]

D'Evelyn, C. Methodius as Source. PMLA XXXIII, 1918, p. 147.

Strandberg, O. Rime-vowels. Upsala, 1919.

Durrschmidt, H. Die Sage von Kain. Bayreuth, 1919. [P. 91.]

Frank, G. Parallels with York, Towneley Plays. MLN. XXXV, 1920, p. 74.

Sources. MLN. XXXVI, 1921, p. 238; Histoire Littéraire de la France, vol. XXXIII p. 364.

Bonnell, J. K. Cain's Jawbone. PMLA XXXIX, 1924, p. 140.

Arend, Z. M. Linking in Cursor Mundi. Trans Philolog. Soc. 1925–30, p. 200.

Menner, J. R. Euhemerism. Speculum, III 1928, p. 246.

Borland, L. Herman's Bible and the Cursor Mundi. Stud. Phil. XXX, 1933, p. 427.

(i) Caligula-Jesus Poems

1, Hwon Holy Chireche Is vnder Uote; 2 Duty of Christians (þeo suþe luue); 3, O Serving Christ (Hwi ne serue we crist?); 4 Doomsday; 5, Death; 6, Long Life; 7, Sign of Death; 8, Saws of St Bede (Sinners Beware); 9, Will and Wit.

MSS. 4, 5, 6, 9. Cotton, Caligula A IX 1–8, Jesus College Oxford 29 (Bodleian); 7 Harley 7322; 8, Digby 86 (Bodleian).

Editions. 1–9, R. Morris, EETS. XLIX, 1872 5, T. Wright, Percy Soc. XI, 1843, p. 70; 6 Ang. I, 1878, p. 410, II, 1879, p. 71, III, 1880 p. 67; EETS. XXIII, 1866, p. 129; 7, T. Wright and J. O. Halliwell[-Phillipps], Reliquiae Antiquae, vol. I, 1841, p. 64, and EETS. 1866, LXV (rev.), p. 253; 8, C. Horstmann, EETS. CXVII 1901, p. 765, and C. Horstmann, Altenglisch Legenden, Heilbronn, 1881, p. 505.

Studies. [Wells, pp. 227, 383, 387, 390–2 395, 504, 798, 823, 824, 825, 848, 1402, Chap vii, and Supplements. Wells, edn Owl and Nightingale, Boston, 1907, 1909, 1926, introduction.]

(j) Bestiary

[Wells, pp. 182, 791, 1007, 1052, 1108, 1211 1302, 1391, q.v. for Physiologus, Bestiaries Bestiary matter.]

MS. Arundel 292, fol. 4. Ed. T. Wright Altdeutsche Blätter, vol. II, 1837, p. 99; ed T. Wright and J. O. Halliwell[-Phillipps] Reliquiae Antiquae, vol. I, 1841, p. 208; ed R. Morris, EETS. XLIX, 1872, p. 1 (see Archiv ʟxxxviii, 1891, p. 265); ed. E. Mätzner, Altenglische Sprachproben, pt i, Berlin, 1867, ɔ. 55; ed. J. Hall, Selections from Early Middle English, Oxford, 1920, vol. i, p. 176, vol. ii, p. 579.

Selections. O. F. Emerson, Middle English Reader, New York, 1915, p. 14; G. Sampson, Cambridge Book of Prose and Verse, 1924, ɔ. 177.

Modern rendering, parts. J. L. Weston, Chief Middle English Poets, Boston, 1914, p. 325; M. H. Shackford, Legends and Satires, Boston, 1913, p. 101.

Studies. [ten Brink, vol. i, p. 196; Schofield, ɔ. 336.]

Schipper, J. Englische Metrik. Bonn, 1881. [Sect. 79.]

Hallbäck, E. S. Language of Middle English Bestiary. Lund, 1905.

(k) Proverbs of Hendyng

[*Wells*, pp. 377, 822, 973, 1016, 1122, 1217, 1271, 1310.]

MSS. 1, Digby 86 (Bodleian); 2, Harley 2253; 3, University Lib. Cambridge Gg.i.1; parts in 4, University Lib. Cambridge 4407–19); 5, St John's College Cambridge F 8 (145); 6, Worcester Cathedral Lib. F 19; 7, Bodley 410; 8, Rawlinson C 670 (Bodleian); 9, Eton College 34; 10, 11, Laud 111 and 213 (Bodleian); and others. [On MSS, see C. Brown, Register, vol. ii, 1920, items 1009, 1298, 1732, 883, 2635; Ang. v, 1882, p. 5; Dover MS, Archiv, cxv, 1905, p. 165.]

Editions. 2, J. M. Kemble, Salomon and Saturnus, 1848, appendix; K. Böddeker, Altenglische Dichtungen des MS. Harley 2253, Berlin, 1878, p. 285; E. Mätzner, Altenglische Sprachproben, pt i, Berlin, 1867, p. 304; R. Morris and W. W. Skeat, Specimens of Early English, vol. ii, Oxford, 1894, p. 35; T. Wright and J. O. Halliwell[-Phillipps], Reliquiae Antiquae, vol. i, 1841, p. 109; 3, 1, with comparison of 2, H. Varnhagen, Ang. iv, 1881, ɔ. 180; 4, W. W. Skeat, MLR. vii, 1912, p. 151; 6, C. Brown, Register, vol. i. 1916, item 451; 7, and others, C. Brown, Register, vol. i, 1916, tems 522, 525, 528; critical edn, G. Schleich, Ang. li, 1927, p. 220, lii, 1928, p. 350.

Selection. G. Sampson, Cambridge Book of Prose and Verse, 1924, p. 406.

Translation. Harley. J. L. Weston, Chief Middle English Poets, Boston, 1914, p. 294.

Studies. [ten Brink, vol. i, p. 313; Schofield, ɔ. 420; CHEL. vol. i, 1907, pp. 219, 363. *Notes*: Romania, xv, 1886, p. 334; EETS. cxlii, 1913, p. 9; on v. 192, G. L. Kittredge, J. Phil. vi, 1885, p. 480; on stanza 75, N. & Q. 10, 24 Nov. 1923, pp. 370, 412.]

Wright, T. Essays on Literature of the Middle Ages. Vol. i, 1846. [Ch. 4.]

Kneuer, K. Die Sprichwörter Hendyng's. Leipzig, 1901.

[For other proverb matter, see *Wells*, pp. 374, 821, and Supplements.]

(l) The Thrush and the Nightingale

[*Wells*, pp. 421, 831, 1126, 1404.]

MSS. 1, Auchinleck (Nat. Lib. Scotland 19.2.1); 2, Digby 86 (Bodleian).

Editions. 1, T. Wright and J. O. Halliwell [-Phillipps], Reliquiae Antiquae, vol. i, 1841, p. 241; W. C. Hazlitt, Remains of the Early Popular Poetry of England, vol. i, 1864, p. 50; collation, E. M. Stengel, Codicem Manu Scriptum Digby 86, Halle, 1871, p. 64; 2, Ang. iv, 1881, p. 207; critical edn, F. Holthausen, Ang. xliii, 1919, p. 52 (see Ang. xliv, 1920, p. 85); C. Brown, English Lyrics of the Thirteenth Century, Oxford, 1932, p. 101.

Studies.

Heider, O. Untersuchungen zur mittelenglischen erotischen Lyrik. Halle, 1905. [P. 17.]

Le Jardin de Plaisance et Fleur de Rhetorique. Société des Anciens Textes français, vol. lx, 1910.

(m) Robert Mannyng's Works

[For Mannyng's Chronicle, see under Chronicles, pp. 165–6 above.]

Handlyng Synne

[*Wells*, pp. 342, 816, 966, 1015, 1060, 1119, 1308, 1399; Septem miracula, *ibid*. pp. 276, 344, 804, 1266, 1305; Englyssh's piece, *ibid*. pp. 344, 351, 816, 818, 966; St John's prose, *ibid*. pp. 966, 1015.]

MSS. 1, Harley 1701; 2, Bodley 415; 3, University Lib. Cambridge Ii.iv.9; 4, Dulwich College, xxiv. [On MSS, see C. Brown, Register, vol. ii, 1920, items 486, 340, 583.]

Editions. 1, with collations of 2, 4, and French, F. J. Furnivall, Roxburghe Club, 1862 and 2 pts, EETS, 1901–3.

Selections. Story in Bodley 6922, C. Horstmann, Altenglische Legenden, Heilbronn, 1881, p. 339; R. Morris and W. W. Skeat, Specimens of Early English, vol. ii, Oxford, 1894; A. S. Cook, Reader, Boston, 1915; O. F. Emerson, Reader, New York, 1915; W. A. Neilson and K. G. T. Webster, Chief Middle English Poets, Boston, 1916; K. Sisam, Fourteenth Century Verse and Prose, Oxford, 1921.

Studies. [ten Brink, vol. i, p. 299; *Ward*, vol. iii, pp. 272, 303, 310; DNB.; CHEL. vol. i, 1907, p. 344.]

Hellmers, G. H. Über die Sprache Robert Mannyngs of Brunne. Göttingen, 1885.

Hales, J. W. On Brymwake. Academy, 8 Jan. 1887, p. 27.

Zupitza, J. Archiv, LXXXII, 1889, p. 206. [Later influence.]

Börner, O. Die Sprache. SEP. XII, 1904.

—— Reimuntersuchung [e vowel]. SEP. L, 1913, p. 298.

Allen, H. E. Manuel des Péchiez. MP. VIII, 1911, p. 434.

—— Mystical Lyrics of Manuel des Péchiez. Romanic Rev. IX, 1912, p. 154.

Kunz, A. Robert Mannyng of Brunne's Handlyng Synne [compared with French]. Königsberg, 1913.

Schlutter, O. B. Ang. XXXVII, 1913, p. 52 (see XXXVIII, 1914, p. 251). [On vv. 9863–66.]

Moore, S. Use of Do. MLN. XXXIII, 1918, p. 385.

Baskervill, C. R. Popular Amusements. Stud. Phil. XVII, 1920, pp. 54, 61, 70.

[See also under Mannyng's Rimed Chronicle, p. 165 above.]

Septem Miracula: Southern version in MSS Vernon (Bodleian 3938), BM. Add. 22283. Ed. EETS. 1892, XCVIII, p. 198, CXXIII, 1903, p. 309; Archiv, LVII, 1877, p. 282 (part), LXXXII, 1889, p. 188 (all). [See Wells, pp. 273, 344, 804; C. Horstmann, Altenglische Legenden, Heilbronn, 1881, pp. lxviii, lxxiii, lxxxii.]

Peter Idley's Instructions to his Son: MS Arundel 20 (and others). Ed. Charlotte D'Evelyn, Boston, 1935. Part ptd W. Heuser, BBA. XIV, 1904, p. 206. [See Wells, pp. 344, 816; Ward, vol. III, p. 313.]

Prose version of French Manuel: MS St John's College Cambridge G 30. [Not ptd.] [See H. E. Allen, MP. XIII, 1916, p. 743, Romanic Rev. VIII, 1917, p. 449.]

Meditations of the Supper of Our Lord

MSS. Harley 1701, 218, 2338; Trinity College Cambridge B, 14, 19; Bodley 415 (2313); BM. Add. 36983 (Bedford); Lambeth 559. [On MSS, see C. Brown, Register, vol. II, 1920, items 160, 398. A prose version is in MS Bodley 789.]

Edition. Harley 1701, variants of Trinity College Cambridge, notes on Bedford, F. J. Furnivall, EETS, 1875.

Studies. [Wells, pp. 358, 819, 1269, 1309; Ward, vol. III, p. 306.]

Hellmers, G. Über die Sprache Robert Mannyngs of Brunne. Göttingen, 1885.

Thien, H. Über die englischen Marienklagen. Kiel, 1906. [P. 32.]

(n) Lay-Folks' Mass-Book

MSS. 1, Nat. Lib. Scotland 19.3.1; 2, Royal 17 B XIII; 3, Corpus Christi College Oxford 155; 4, University Lib. Cambridge Gg.v.31; 5, Gonville and Caius College Cambridge 84; 6, Newnham College Cambridge. [For other MSS see C. Brown, Register, vol. II, 1920, items 806, 2256.]

Editions. 1, W. D. B. Turnbull, Visions of Tundale, Edinburgh, 1843; E. Studien, XXXV, 1905, p. 28; 2, 3, 4, 5, 6, EETS. 1879, p. 1; 2, C. Horstmann, Yorkshire Writers, vol. II, 1896, p. 1; two pieces from 2, F. A. Patterson, Middle English Penitential Lyric, New York, 1911, p. 70; 3, E. Studien, XXXIII, 1904, p. 1.

Studies. [Wells, pp. 355, 818, 970, 1061, 1120, 1269, 1309.]

Wordsworth, C. and Littlehales, H. Old Service Books of the English Church. 1904. [P. 284.]

Deanesly, M. The Lollard Bible. Cambridge, 1920. [P. 212.]

(o) Ayenbite of Inwyt (Dan Michel of Northgate)

[Wells, pp. 345, 817, 966, 1015, 1120, 1216, 1308, 1399.]

MS. Arundel 57. Ed. J. Stevenson, Roxburghe Club, 1855; ed. R. Morris, EETS. 1866.

Selections. E. Mätzner, Altenglische Sprachproben, 2 pts, Berlin, 1867–1900; R. Wülcker, Lesebuch, 2 pts, Halle, 1874–9; J. Zupitza, Übungsbuch, Vienna, 1904; G. E. MacLean, Reader, New York, 1893; R. Morris and W. W. Skeat, Specimens of Early English, vol. II, Oxford, 1894; O. F. Emerson, Reader, New York, 1915; F. Kluge, Lesebuch, Halle, 1904; A. Brandl and O. Zippel, Mittelenglische Sprach- und Literaturproben, Berlin, 1917; C. Brown, Religious Lyrics of 14th Century, Oxford, 1924, p. 49.

Studies. [ten Brink, vol. I, p. 283; CHEL. vol. I, 1907, p. 353; Schofield, pp. 386, 409.]

E. Studien, I, 1877, p. 379, II, 1878, pp. 27, 120; MLN. VII, 1893, p. 268. [Text-notes.]

Evers, R. W. Beiträge zur Erklärung und Textkritik von Dan Michel's Ayenbite of Inwyt. Erlangen, 1888.

Konrath, M. Source of Parallel to Sawles Warde. E. Studien, XII, 1889, p. 459.

Bülbring, K. QF. LXIII, 1889, p. 27. [Verbs.]

Meyer, P. Notice sur le MS. 27 de la Bibliothèque d'Alençon (Somme le Roi). Bulletin de la Société des Anciens Textes français, No. 2, 1892.

Ang. XVII, 1894, p. 79. [Language.]

Child, F. J. Verse as Prose in Ayenbite. MLN. x, 1895, p. 64.

Petersen, K. O. Radcliffe Monographs, xii, 1901.

Förster, M. Die Bibliothek des Dan Michel. Archiv, cxv, 1905, p. 167.

Jensen, H. Die Verbalflexion. Kiel, 1908.

Dolle, R. Graphische und lautliche Untersuchung. Bonn, 1912.

von Glahn, N. Zur Geschichte des grammatischen Geschlechts. Anglistische Forschungen, liii, 1918.

Deanesly, M. The Lollard Bible. Cambridge, 1920. [P. 214.]

Wallenberg, J. K. Vocabulary. Upsala, 1923.

Flasdieck, H. Kentish Ordinalia. Ang. Bbl. xxxix, 1928, p. 359.

(p) Pricke of Conscience

[Wells, pp. 447, 838, 1020, 1129, 1275, 1313, 1361, 1407; H. E. Allen, Writings ascribed to R. Rolle, New York, 1927, p. 372.]

MSS. At least 104, and 5 fragments. [See H. E. Allen, op. cit. p. 372; C. Brown, Register, vol. ii, 1920, index; E. Studien, xxiii, 1887, p. 1; Trans. Philolog. Soc. 1890; Archiv, lxxxvi, 1891, p. 283; MLN. xx, 1905, p. 210; MP. iv, 1906, p. 67; P. Andrae, MSS. of the Pricke of Conscience, Berlin, 1888. Latin MSS, H. E. Allen, MP. xiii, 1916, p. 745.]

Editions. MS Galba, R. Morris, Philolog. Soc. Berlin, 1863; MS Royal couplets and stanzas, Thornton couplets, Rawlinson and Cambridge Dd couplets, C. Horstmann, Yorkshire Writers, vol. ii, 1896, pp. 67, 70, 36, vol. i, 1895, pp. 372, 129 (see 443).

Selections. E. Mätzner, Altenglische Sprachproben, pt i, Berlin, 1867, p. 286; R. Wülcker, Lesebuch, 2 pts, Halle, 1874–9; R. Morris and W. W. Skeat, Specimens of Early English, vol. ii, Oxford, 1894; A. Brandl and O. Zippel, Mittelenglische Sprach- und Literaturproben, Berlin, 1917.

Abstract. H. Morley, English Writers, vol. iv, 1889, p. 264.

Studies.

Köhler, R. Jahrbuch für romanische und englische Sprache, vi, 1864, p. 196.

—— Kleineren Schriften. Vol. iii, Berlin, 1900, no. 26.

Ullmann, J. Speculum Vitae. E. Studien, vii, 1884, p. 415.

Hahn, A. Quellenuntersuchungen zu R. Rolle's englischen Schriften. Berlin, 1900.

Archiv, cvi, 1901, p. 349. [Vv. 7651–86.]

Ang. xxvi, 1903, p. 366. [Interpretation.]

Allen, H. E. Authorship. Radcliffe College Monographs, xv, 1910, p. 115.

Allen, H. E. Speculum Vitae. PMLA. xxxii, 1917, p. 133.

Deanesly, M. The Lollard Bible. Cambridge, 1920. [P. 214.]

Comper, F. M. M. The Life of Richard Rolle. 1928. [P. 217.]

D'Evelyn, C. An East Midland Recension of the Pricke of Conscience. PMLA. xlv, 1930, p. 180.

[See also under Richard Rolle, Life, Canon, Criticism, p. 192 below.]

(q) Distichs of Cato

[Wells, pp. 378, 822, 973, 1122, 1173, 1217.]

MSS.

I. Old English. Cotton, Julius A ii; and others. [See p. 94 above.]

II. Northern couplet version. Bodley 14790 (Rawlinson G 59); Sidney Sussex College Cambridge lxiii. Ed. M. Förster, E. Studien, xxxvi, 1906, p. 4.

III. Four-line stanza version, Little Cato, Great Cato. 1, Vernon (Bodleian 3938); 2, BM. Add. 22283. Ed. 1, M. O. Goldberg, Ang. vii, 1884, p. 167, and F. J. Furnivall, EETS. cxviii, 1901, p. 553.

IV. Six-line stanzas. 1, Bodley 3894; 2, Bodley 29003. Ed. 1, EETS. lxviii, 1878, p. 1667; ed. 2, M. Förster, Archiv, cxlv, 1923, p. 208.

V. Burgh's rime royal. Cato Major, 30 MSS (see C. Brown, Register, vol. ii, 1220, item 533). Ed. University Lib. Cambridge Hh.iv.12, M. Förster, Archiv, cxv, 1905, p. 304, cxvi, 1906, p. 25; ed. Royal 18 D ii, E. Flügel, Ang. xiv, 1892, p. 489. Cato Minor, 19 MSS (see C. Brown, Register, vol. ii, 1920, item 2533). Ed. University Lib. Cambridge Hh.iv.12, M. Förster, Archiv, cxv, 1905, p. 303; Caxton's edn, facsimile, Cambridge, 1906.

VI. Latin version. Tr. W. J. Chase, Madison, 1922.

[On MSS see C. Brown, Register, vol. ii, 1920, items 103, 159, 533, 558, 2533, 2534; EETS. cxvii, 1901, p. 553; Archiv, xcv, 1895, p. 163; E. Studien, vii, 1884, p. 197; EETS. lxix, 1878, p. 99.]

Studies.

Gröber, G. Grundriss der romanischen Philologie. 2nd edn, vol. ii¹, Strasburg, 1902, pp. 381, 383, 482, 863, 1066, 1187.

Schanz, M. Geschichte der römischen Literatur. Munich, 1905 (2nd edn). [P. 38.]

Paul, H. Grundriss der germanischen Philologie. 2nd edn, vol. ii¹, Strasburg, 1909, pp. 1072, 1128.

(r) Charters of Christ

[*Wells*, pp. 369, 821, 1016, 1121, 1217, 1400; Spalding, edn.]

MSS. [See C. Brown, Register, vol. II, 1920, items 1130, 1049, 2644, 716, 2659; Spalding, edn.] Ed. all texts, M. C. Spalding, Bryn Mawr, 1914; ed. Harley 2382, Vernon, Royal EETS. cxvii, 1901, p. 637; ed. Harley 2382, Vernon, Archiv, lxxix, 1887, p. 424; ed. Ashmole 61 and 181, with Latin, M. Förster, Ang. xlii, 1918, p. 192 (see xliii, 1919, p. 194); ed. BM. Add. 5465, B. Fehr, Archiv, cvi, 1901, p. 69; ed. Bodley, Kent Charter 233, N. & Q. 21 Sept. 1901, p. 240.

Studies.
Thien, H. Über die englischen Marienklagen. Kiel, 1906. [P. 82.]
Perrow, E. C. The Last Will and Testament as a Form. Trans. Wisconsin Academy, xvii, 1911–4, p. 682.

(s) The Good Man and the Devil

[*Wells*, pp. 423, 831.]

MSS. 1, Vernon (Bodleian 3938); 2, BM. Add. 22283.

Editions. E. Studien, viii, 1885, p. 259; EETS. xcviii, 1892, p. 329, cxvii, 1901, p. 750.

(t) Lay-Folks' Catechism

[*Wells*, pp. 348[9], 355, 817[9], 818, 967, 970, 1015, 1120, 1269, 1309, 1353, 1399.]

I. Gaystck or Gaytryge version. *MSS.* 1, Thornton (Lincoln Cathedral Lib. A, 5, 2); 2, Rawlinson C, 285 (Bodleian); and others (see C. Brown, Register, vol. II, 1920, item 263). *Editions.* 1, EETS. xxvi, 1867, p. 1; 2, C. Horstmann, Yorkshire Writers, vol. I, 1895, p. 104; 2, EETS. cxviii, 1901, p. 2.

II. Wycliffite version. *MSS.* 1, Lambeth 408; 2, York Minster xvi, l, 12. *Edition.* EETS. cxviii, 1901, p. 3.

Studies.
Wordsworth, C. and Littlehales, H. Old Service Books of the English Church. 1904. [P. 262.]
Baskervill, C. R. MP. xvii, 1919, p. 68.
Deanesly, M. The Lollard Bible. Cambridge, 1920. [P. 141.]

(u) Primer, or Lay-Folks' Prayer-Book

[*Wells*, pp. 356, 819, 970, 1015, 1062, 1120, 399[7], 826[7], 1065[7], 1124[7]; Littlehales, below.]

MSS. 1, University Lib. Cambridge Dd. xi. 82; 2, BM. Add. 17010; 3, St John's College Cambridge G 24; 4, Digby 102 (Bodleian); 5, BM. Add. 39574; and others.

Editions. 1, H. Littlehales, 2 pts, EETS. 1895–7, Ex. Ser. 1903; 2, W. Maskell, Monumenta Ritualia, vol. iii, 1882; 3, H. Littlehales, The Prymer, 2 vols. 1891–2 (with collation of other MSS); 4, J. Kail, Lessons of the Dirige, EETS. cxxiv, 1904; 5, M. Day, EETS. clv, 1917, p. 59.

Studies. [See Littlehales, above.]
Brown, C. Chaucer Soc. ser. 2, xlv, 1910, p. 126; MLN. xxx, 1915, p. 9.
Deanesly, M. The Lollard Bible. Cambridge, 1920. [Pp. 320, 328.]

(v) Castel of Love

[*Wells*, pp. 366, 820, 1016, 1121, 1217, 1309, 1400; C. Brown, Register, vol. II, 1920, items 1016, 2092, 2637.]

A version. MSS. 1, Vernon (Bodley 3938); 2, BM. Add. 22283; 3, Bodleian 29560 (Add. B 107). *Editions.* 1, 2, EETS. xcviii, 1892, p. 355, cxvii, 1901, p. 751; 3, J. O. Halliwell [-Phillipps], Castel of Love, Brixton Hill, 1849. [See EETS. xcviii, 1892, pp. 394, 403.]

B version. MS. Bodleian 6922. Ed. C. Horstmann, Altenglische Legenden, Heilbronn, 1881, p. 349.

C version. MS. Egerton 927. Ed. M. Cooke, R. Grosseteste, Carmina Anglo-Normanica, Caxton Soc. 1852. [See Ang. xiv, 1892, p. 415; EETS. xcviii, 1892, p. 407.]

Studies.
Weymouth, R. E. Trans. Philolog. Soc. viii, 1862–3, p. 48.
Haase, E. Altenglische Bearbeitungen von Grossestestes Chasteau d'Amour. Ang. xii, 1889–90, p. 311.

(w) Abbey of the Holy Ghost

[*Wells*, pp. 368, 821, 1121, 1270, 1309, 1400; H. Traver, Four Daughters of God, Philadelphia, 1907, p. 126; M. Deanesly, The Lollard Bible, Cambridge, 1920, p. 217; H. E. Allen, Writings Ascribed to Richard Rolle, New York, 1927, p. 335.]

MSS. 1, Laud 210 (Bodleian); 2, Vernon (Bodleian 3938); 3, Thornton (Lincoln Cathedral Lib. A, 5, 2); and other MSS.

Editions. 3, G. G. Perry, EETS. xxvi, 1867, p. 48; 3, C. Horstmann, Yorkshire Writers, vol. I, 1895, pp. 321, 337 (with variants from other MSS).

(x) Ypotis, or L'Enfant Sage

[Wells, pp. 425, 832, 981, 1019, 1126, 1358, 1404.]

MSS. 1, Vernon (Bodleian 3938); 2, BM. Add. 22283; 3, Cotton, Caligula A II; 4, Cotton, Titus A XXVI; 5, Arundel 140; 6, Brome (at Brome Hall); 7, English Poetry C, 3 (Bodleian 30516); 8, Rawlinson Q, b, 4 (Bodleian 16032); 9, St John's College Cambridge 29; 10, BM. Add. 36983; 11, Ashmole 750 (Bodleian 6621); 12, Douce 323 (Bodleian 21897); 13, Trinity College Cambridge B, 2, 18 (61); and other MSS (for which see C. Brown, Register, vol. II, 1920, item 140).

Editions. 1 (with variants from 2), C. Horstmann, Altenglische Legenden, Heilbronn, 1881, p. 341; 3 (with variants from 4, 5, 11), C. Horstmann, Altenglische Legenden, Heilbronn, 1881, p. 511; 6, L. T. Smith, A Commonplace Book of the Fifteenth Century, Norwich, 1886 (see also Ang. VII, 1884, p. 317); 7, 8, 9, 10, 13, J. Sutton, PMLA. XXXI, 1916, p. 114; 11, 12, H. Gruber, Berlin, 1887; 13, 10, W. Suchier, L'Enfant Sage, Dresden, 1910, p. 465.

Studies. [See the edns of Suchier, Gruber and Sutton above.]

Gruber, H. Ang. XVIII, 1895, p. 56.
Förster, M. Ang. XLII, 1918, p. 210.

(y) Thomas Usk's Testament of Love

[Wells, pp. 370, 821, 1121, 1270, 1309, 1353, 1400; E. P. Hammond, Chaucer: A Bibliographical Manual, New York, 1908, p. 458.]

Editions. W. Thynne, The Workes of Chaucer, 1532; W. W. Skeat, The Complete Works of Chaucer, vol. VII, Oxford, 1897, p. 1 (see Academy, 11 March 1893, p. 222; Athenaeum, 6, 13 Feb. 1897, pp. 184, 215).

Studies.
Morley, H. English Writers. Vol. v, 1890. [P. 261.]
Skeat, W. W. The Complete Works of Chaucer. Vol. v, Oxford, 1894, p. xii, vol. VII, 1897, p. xviii.
Bradley, H. E. Studien, XXIII, 1897, p. 438.
N. & Q. 26 March 1904, p. 245.
Krapp, J. P. The Rise of English Literary Prose. New York, 1916. [P. 29.]
Bressie, R. The Date of Thomas Usk's Testament of Love. MP. XXVI, 1928, p. 17.
—— A Study of Thomas Usk's The Testament of Love as an Autobiography. Abstracts of Theses. Chicago University, Humanistic Ser. VII, 1931, p. 517.

(z) Book of Cupid, or Cuckoo and Nightingale

[Wells, pp. 423, 831, 1273, 1311, 1404; E. P. Hammond, Chaucer: A Bibliographical Manual, New York, 1908, p. 420.]

MSS. 1, Fairfax 16 (Bodleian); 2, Bodley 638 (Bodleian); 3, University Lib. Cambridge Ff.1.6; 4, Tanner 346 (Bodleian); 5, Selden B 24 (Bodleian).

Editions. E. Vollmer, Berlin, 1898, and BBA. XVII, 1905; W. W. Skeat, The Complete Works of Chaucer, vol. VII, Oxford, 1897, p. 347.

Studies.
Academy, 28 July 1894, p. 67, 2 May 1896, p. 365. [Author.]
Skeat, W. W. The Complete Works of Chaucer. Vol. VII, Oxford, 1897, p. lvii.
Kittredge, G. L. MP. I, 1903, p. 13. [Date, author.]
Cook, A. S. Trans. Connecticut Academy, XX, 1916, p. 214.
Ward, C. E. MLN. XLIV, 1929, p. 217. [Author.]

[For other dialogues (Heart and Eye, Virgin and Christ, Child Jesu and Maistres of the Lawe, Lamentation of Mary to Bernard, Mary and Cross, Christenemon and Jewe, Elucidarium, Maister of Oxenford and Clerke, Diabolus et Virgo) see Wells, pp. 411, 829, and Supplements. For Speculum Christiani, ed. G. Holmstedt, EETS. 1933, see Wells, pp. 1452, 1503.]

V. BIBLE RENDERINGS

[Wells, chs. viii, v B. In addition to items below, see under Richard Rolle, p. 193 and John Wycliffe, p. 204 below.]

(a) Genesis and Exodus

[Wells, pp. 397, 825, 1018, 1124, 1402.]

MS. Corpus Christi College Cambridge 444.

Edition. R. Morris, EETS. 1865 (rev. edn).

Selections. E. Mätzner, Altenglische Sprachproben, 2 pts, Berlin, 1867–1900; R. Morris, Specimens of Early English, Oxford, 1867; J. Zupitza, Übungsbuch, Vienna, 1874; R. Wülcker, Lesebuch, 2 pts, Halle, 1874–9; O. F. Emerson, Middle English Reader, New York, 1915; A. Brandl and O. Zippel, Mittelenglische Sprach- und Literaturproben, Berlin, 1917; J. Hall, Selections from Early Middle English, Oxford, 1920, vol. I, p. 197, vol. II, p. 626.

Studies. [*ten Brink*, vol. I, pp. 197, 391; *Schofield*, p. 374.]

E. Studien, II, 1878–9, p. 120, III, 1880, p. 273, IV, 1881, p. 98, XVI, 1892, p. 429, XVII, 1892, p. 292; Archiv, XC, 1893, pp. 143, 295, CVII, 1901, pp. 317, 386, CIX, 1902, p. 126; Ang. XV, 1892–3, p. 191, XXII, 1899, p. 141; Ang. Anz. VI, 1883, p. 1; MLN. XXVI, 1911, p. 50. [On text.]

Hilmer, H. Die Sprache. Sondershausen, 1876.

Fritsche, A. Ang. V, 1882, p. 60. [Author.]

D'Evelyn, C. PMLA. XXXIII, 1918, p. 146. [Source, Methodius.]

Durrschmidt, H. Die Sage von Kain. Bayreuth, 1919. [P. 86.]

Funke, O. E. Studien, LV, 1921, p. 25. [French words.]

Caro, J. E. Studien, LXVIII, 1933, p. 6. [Notes.]

(b) Harrowing of Hell

[*Wells*, pp. 327, 814, 1014, 1118, 1398; Hulme, below.]

MSS. 1, Digby 86 (Bodleian); 2, Harley 2253; 3, Auchinleck (Nat. Lib. Scotland, 19, 2, 1).

Editions. 1, 2, 3, W. H. Hulme, EETS. Ex. Ser. 1907; 1, 2, 3, H. Varnhagen, Erlangen, 1898; 2, J. P. Collier, Five Miracle Plays, 1836; 2, D. Laing, Owain Miles, Edinburgh, 1837; 2, J. O. Halliwell[-Phillipps], 1840; 2, E. Mall, Breslau, 1871 (with variants from other MSS); 2, A. W. Pollard, English Miracle Plays, Oxford, 1927 (8th edn); 2, K. Böddeker, Altenglische Dichtungen des MS. Harley 2253, Berlin, 1878, p. 264.

Studies.

Ward, Sir A. W. A History of English Dramatic Literature. Vol I, 1899. [P. 90.]

Chambers, Sir E. K. The Medieval Stage. Oxford, 1903. [Vol. I, pp. 80, 83; vol. II, p. 74.]

Young, K. Trans. Wisconsin Academy of Science, Arts and Letters, XVI, 1908–9, p. 889.

Becker, E. J. Die Sage von der Höllenfahrt Christi. Göttingen, 1912.

Kretzmann, P. E. MP. XIII, 1915, p. 49. [Notes.]

Schmidt, K. W. C. Die Darstellung von Christi Höllenfahrt. Marburg, 1915.

Gerould, G. H. Saints' Legends. Boston, 1916. [Pp. 214, 365.]

Hamilton, G. L. MLN. XXXVI, 1921, p. 238.

Curtiss, C. G. Stud. Phil. XXX, 1933, p. 24. [York and Towneley plays.]

(c) Jacob and Josep

[*Wells*, pp. 398, 825, 978, 1018, 1124, 1402.]

MS. Bodley 652 (Bodleian 2306).

Editions. W. Heuser, BBA. XVII, 1905, p. 83; A. S. Napier, Oxford, 1916. [See G. H. Gerould, Saints' Legends, Boston, 1916, p. 223.]

(d) Woman of Samaria

[*Wells*, pp. 408, 828.]

MS. Jesus College Oxford 29.

Editions. EETS. XLIX, 1872, p. 84; J. Zupitza, Übungsbuch, Vienna, 1874; G. E. MacLean, Reader, New York, 1893.

(e) Passion of our Lord

[*Wells*, pp. 409, 828.]

MS. Jesus College Oxford 29.

Edition. EETS. XLIX, 1872, p. 37.

Study.

Wolderich, W. Sprache und Heimat einiger frühmittelenglischen religiösen Gedichte. Halle, 1909.

(f) Gospel of Nicodemus

[*Wells*, pp. 326, 814, 1014, 1060, 1118, 1268, 1308, 1398; Hulme, below.]

MSS. I. Verse: 1, Cotton, Galba E IX; 2, Harley 4196; 3, BM. Add. 32578; 4, Sion College Arc $\frac{L.40.2}{E.25}$. II. Prose: 1, Egerton 2658; 2, Stonyhurst College, B XLIII; 3, Bodleian 207; 4, Salisbury Cathedral Lib. 39; 5, BM. Add. 16165; 6, Magdalene College Cambridge, Pepys 2498; 7, Harley 149; 8, Worcester Cathedral Lib. 172; 9, University Lib. Cambridge Mm.1.29.

Editions. All verse MSS, W. H. Hulme, EETS. Ex. Ser. 1907, and F. Klotz, Königsberg, 1913; 2, C. Horstmann, Archiv, LIII, 1874, p. 389 (see also LVII, 1877, p. 78; readings from 1 at p. 73); 4, Archiv, LXVIII, 1882, p. 207. [The Old English version is ed. W. H. Hulme, PMLA. XIII, 1898, p. 457, and MP. I, 1903–4, pp. 79, 579. For the French version see G. Gröber, Grundriss der romanischen Philologie, vol. II¹, Strasburg, 1902, pp. 656, 934.]

Studies.

Wülcker, R. Evangelium Nicodemi. Paderborn, 1872.

Craigie, W. A. The Gospel of Nicodemus and the York Plays. [Furnivall Miscellany, Oxford, 1901, p. 52.]

Straub, F. Lautlehre der Jungen Nicodemus-Version. Würzburg, 1908.

Young, K. Trans. Wisconsin Academy of Science, Arts, and Letters, XVI, 1908–9, p. 889.

Foster, F. A. EETS. CXLVII, 1913, p. 77. [Influence on Northern Passion.]

Gerould, G. H. Saints' Legends. Boston, 1916. [Pp. 225, 280, 366, 373.]

Miller, F. H. MLN. xxxiv, 1919, p. 88. [Source for plays.]

Lyle, M. C. The Original Identity of the York and Towneley Cycles. Minneapolis, 1919. [See PMLA. xliv, 1929, pp. 313, 319.]

Clark, E. G. The York Plays and the Gospel of Nicodemus. PMLA. xliii, 1928, p. 153.

(g) Surtees Psalter

[*Wells*, pp. 401, 827, 1018, 1066, 1124.]

MSS. 1, Cotton, Vespasian D vii; 2, Egerton 614; 3, Harley 1770; 4, 5, Bodley 425 and 21; 6, Corpus Christi College Cambridge 278. On MSS see C. Brown, Register, vol. ii, 1920, item 1982; Ang. xxix, 1906, p. 385.]

Editions. 1, 2 vols. Surtees Soc. 1843–7; (with variants from 2, 3), C. Horstmann, Yorkshire Writers, vol. ii, 1896, p. 129.

Selections. E. Mätzner, Altenglische Sprachproben, 2 pts, Berlin, 1867–1900; R. Wülcker, Lesebuch, 2 pts, Halle, 1874–9; R. Morris and V. W. Skeat, Specimens of Early English, vol. ii, Oxford, 1894, p. 23; F. Kluge, Lesebuch, Halle, 1904.

Studies.

MLN. vii, 1892, p. 268. [Text-notes.]

Ency. Brit., under 'Psalms.'

Everett, D. MLR. xvii, 1922, p. 337.

Vende, E. Überlieferung zum Psalterium Romanum in England. Halle, 1923.

(h) Prose Psalter

[*Wells*, pp. 402, 827, 1018, 1067, 1124, 1174, 219, 1272, 1311.]

MSS. 1, BM. Add. 17376; 2, Magdalene College Cambridge, Pepys 2498 (see A. C. Paues, E. Studien, xxx, 1902, p. 344); , Trinity College Dublin A, 4, 4.

Edition. K. Bülbring, EETS. 1891.

Selections. O. F. Emerson, Reader, New York, 1915; F. Kluge, Lesebuch, Halle, 904.

Studies.

Paues, A. C. A Fourteenth Century English Biblical Version. 1902. [P. lvi.]

Hirst, T. O. The Phonology of the London MS. Bonn, 1907.

Fogeman, H. Archiv, cxxxiv, 1916, p. 132. [Psalm 90, verse 10.]

Emerson, O. F. MP. xvi, 1918, p. 53. [Psalm 90, verse 10.]

Deanesly, M. The Lollard Bible. Cambridge, 1920. [P. 146.]

Fergeantson, M. S. The Dialect of the Earliest Complete English Prose Psalter. E. Studies, vi, 1924, p. 177.

Dodson, S. Texas University Stud. no. xii, 1932, p. 5.

(i) Rolle's Commentary on the Psalter

[See under Richard Rolle, and Associated Pieces, pp. 193–4 below.]

(j) Rawlinson New Testament Strophic Passages

[*Wells*, pp. 408, 828, 1403.]

MS. Rawlinson, Poet. 175 (F 175; Bodleian).

Edition. Ang. xxvii, 1904, p. 283.

(k) Mayde(n)stone's Seven Penitential Psalms

[*Wells*, pp. 403, 827, 979, 1018, 1067, 1124, 1311, 1357, 1403.]

MSS. 1, Trinity College Dublin 156; 2, Digby 18 (Bodleian) (see EETS. cxxiv, 1904, p. vii); 3, Ashmole 61 (Bodleian); 4, Rawlinson A 389 (Bodleian); 5, BM. Add. 39574; 6, Nat. Lib. Scotland 19, 3, 1; 7, Vernon (Bodleian); 8, BM. Add. 10036; and others (see C. Brown, Register, vol. ii, 1920, items 1215, 1352, 2421, also vol. i, 1916, p. 521.)

Editions. 1, F. S. Ellis, Kelmscott Press, 1894; 2, 3, 4, M. Kaluza, E. Studien, x, 1887, pp. 215, 232; 5, M. Day, EETS. clv, 1917, p. 19; 6 (Psalm 51), F. J. Furnivall, EETS. xv, 1866, p. 279; 7 (Psalm 51), EETS. xcviii, 1892, p. 12; 8 (Psalm 51), EETS. xv, 1866, p. 279.

Selection. R. Morris and W. W. Skeat, Specimens of Early English, vol. ii, Oxford, 1894, p. 231.

Studies.

Wright, T. An Alliterative Poem on the Deposition of Richard II. 1838. [P. vii.]

Adler, M. Berlin, 1885 (also E. Studien, x, 1887, p. 215).

DNB. under 'Maidenstone.'

Deanesly, M. The Lollard Bible. Cambridge, 1920. [Pp. 147, 341.]

[For other treatments of Psalms, see *Wells*, pp. 401, 827, and Supplements, and under Richard Rolle, pp. 193–4 below.]

(l) Susannah, or Pistill of Susan

[*Wells*, pp. 399, 826, 1018, 1271, 1310, 1357, 1402.]

MSS. 1, Vernon (Bodleian 3938); 2, Cotton, Caligula A ii; 3, BM. Add. 22283; 4, Sir Henry Ingilby, Yorkshire; 5, Phillipps 8252 (at Cheltenham).

Editions. 1, D. Laing, Select Remains of Ancient Popular Poetry of Scotland, 1822, rev. W. C. Hazlitt, 1895, vol. I, p. 45; 1, C. Horstmann, Ang. I, 1878, p. 93; 1, C. Horstmann, EETS. cxvii, 1901, p. 626; 1 (with variant readings), F. J. Amours, STS. 1892–7, p. 189; 2, 3, C. Horstmann, Archiv, lxii, 1879, p. 406; 5, C. Horstmann, Archiv, lxxiv, 1885, p. 339; critical text, H. Köster, QF. lxxvi, 1895.

Studies. [ten Brink, vol. iii, p. 50; *Schofield*, p. 465.]

Brade, G. Über Huchowns Pistil of Suet Susane. Breslau, 1892.

Brown, J. T. T. Athenaeum, 23 Aug. 1902, p. 254.

Gerould, G. H. Saints' Legends. Boston, 1916. [Pp. 238, 368.]

Andrew, S. O. Huchown's Works. RES. v, 1929, p. 12. [Dialect.]

[For the Swedish and Danish versions, see Ang. viii, 1885, p. 22; Ang. Bbl. vii, 1907, p. 373; ballad in Percy's Reliques. See also discussion, under Morte Arthure, p. 137 above.]

(m) Bodley New Testament Verse Passages

[*Wells*, pp. 407, 828, 980.]

MS. Bodley 425 (Bodleian 2325).

Edition. Ang. xxix, 1906, p. 396.

(n) Old Testament Strophic Passages

[*Wells*, pp. 398, 826, 1174, 1218, 1357, 1402.]

MSS. 1, Selden Supra 52 (Bodleian); 2, Marquis of Bath 25 (see E. Studien, x, 1887, p. 203).

Editions. 2 (parts), Archiv, lxxix, 1887, p. 447; 1 (part), Ang. xxxi, 1908, pp. 4, 6; 1 (some 6000 lines), H. Kalén, A Middle English Paraphrase of the Old Testament, Göteborgs Högskolas Årsskrift, xxviii, 1923, p. 5.

(o) New Testament Prose Selections

[*Wells*, pp. 405, 828, 1018, 1067, 1125. For MSS see Paues, below.]

Edition. A. C. Paues, A Fourteenth Century English Biblical Version, Cambridge, 1902 (rev. edns without introduction, 1904, 1909).

Selection. A. Brandl and O. Zippel, Mittelenglische Sprach- und Literaturproben, Berlin, 1917.

Studies.

Powell, M. J. EETS. Ex. Ser. cxvi, 1915. [Introduction.]

Deanesly, M. The Lollard Bible. Cambridge, 1920. [P. 304.]

(p) Old Testament Passages in Long Verses

[*Wells*, pp. 398, 826.]

MS. Laud Misc. 622 (Bodleian).

Edition. F. J. Furnivall, EETS. lxix, 1878, pp. 96, 82.

(q) Prose Life of Jesus

[*Wells*, pp. 405, 827, 1219.]

MS. Magdalene College Cambridge, Pepys 2498.

Edition. M. Goates, EETS. clvii, 1919.

Study.

Paues, A. C. A Fourteenth Century English Biblical Version. Cambridge, 1902. [P. lxv.]

(r) Stanzaic Life of Christ

[*Wells*, pp. 1272, 1311, 1377, 1403. On MSS see C. Brown, Register, vol. ii, item 1076.]

MSS. 1, Harley 2250; 2, Harley 3909; 3, BM. Add. 38666.

Edition. F. A. Foster, EETS. 1924.

Study.

Wilson, R. H. Stud. Phil. xxviii, 1931, p. 413. [Connection with Chester plays.]

(s) Pauline Epistles

[*Wells*, pp. 407, 828, 980, 1018, 1125, 1219.]

MS. Corpus Christi College Cambridge 32.

Edition. M. J. Powell, EETS. Ex. Ser. 1915.

Study.

Deanesly, M. The Lollard Bible. Cambridge, 1920. [P. 312.]

VI. Travels

(a) Stations of Rome

[*Wells*, pp. 432, 834, 982, 1070, 1175, 1220, 1405.]

MSS. 1, Cotton, Caligula A ii; 2, Cotton, Vespasian D ix; 3, BM. Add. 37787; 4, Lambeth 306; 5, Cholmondeley, Condover Hall; 6, Porkington 10 (Lord Harlech, Brogyntyn, Oswestry); 7, Vernon (Bodley 3938); 8, BM. Add. 22283. [On MSS see C. Brown, Register, vol. ii, 1920, p. 5 and items 715, 1216, 2641.]

Editions. 1, 4, EETS. xv, 1866, p. 143; 7, 8, 6, EETS. cxvii, 1901, p. 609, xxv, 1867, pp. 1, 30.

Selection. A. S. Cook, Reader, Boston, 1915.

Study.

Hulbert, J. R. Some Medieval Advertisements. MP. xx, 1923, p. 403.

(b) *Stations of Jerusalem*

[*Wells*, pp. 433, 834, 1274, 1312, 1405.]

MSS. 1, Ashmole 61 (Bodleian); 2, William Vey's version (Bodley 565). [On MSS see C. Brown, Register, vol. ii, 1920, items 615, 49.]

Editions. 1, C. Horstmann, Altenglische Legenden, Heilbronn, 1881, p. 355; 2, B. Bandinel, Roxburghe Club, 1857.

[For author, see Scottish Antiquary, xi, 897, p. 145.]

(c) *Travels of Sir John Mandeville*

[*Wells*, pp. 433, 834, 1019, 1070, 1127, 1220, 274, 1312, 1358, 1405; DNB.]

MSS. Some 300, Latin, French, English.

Three English versions. I. Represented by MS Cotton, Titus C xvi. Ed. (from edns of 725, 1727) J. O. Halliwell[-Phillipps], 1839, 866, 1883 (with cuts), rev. J. Ashton, 1887; d. (from MS) P. Hamelius, EETS. 2 pts, 1916; d. (modernised) A. W. Pollard, 1901, 1923; ed. modernised) J. Bramont, 1928 (Everyman's lib.). II. Represented by MS Egerton 1982. Ed. (with French of MS Harley 4383) G. F. Warner, Roxburghe Club, 1889 (see introduction and notes on author, sources, versions, tc.). III. Represented by some defective MSS, as Harley 3954, and others. [See Warner, bove.]

Selections. E. Mätzner, Altenglische Sprachroben, vol. ii, Berlin, 1900, p. 155; R. Wülcker, Lesebuch, Halle, 1874–9; R. Morris and W. W. Skeat, Specimens of Early English, vol. i, Oxford, 1894, p. 164; A. S. Cook, Reader, Boston, 1915; F. Kluge, Lesebuch, Halle, 1904, p. 33; K. Sisam, Fourteenth Century Verse and Prose, Oxford, 1921, pp. 94, 234.

Studies. [See Warner, DNB. and edn above; Cncy. Brit.; H. Morley, English Writers, vol. iv, 1889, p. 279; CHEL. vol. ii, 1908, p. 78, 445.]

chönborn, C. G. Bibliographische Untersuchungen über die Reisebeschreibung. Breslau, 1840.

Wright, T. Early Travels in Palestine. 1848. [P. 127.]

Borgnet, A. and Bormans, S. Les Œuvres de Jean d'Outremeuse. 6 vols. Brussels, 1864–7.

Bormans, S. Bibliophile Belge, 1866, p. 236.

Vogels, J. Verhältnis der italienischen Versionen. Festschrift des Gymnasiums Adolfinum zu Mörs, 1882, p. 37.

—— Die ungedruckten lateinischen Versionen Mandeviles. Crefeld, 1886.

—— Handschriftliche Untersuchungen über die englischen Versionen Mandeviles. Crefeld, 1891.

Nicholson, E. B. Academy, 12 April 1884, p. 261.

Bovenschen, A. Untersuchungen über Johann von Mandevile und die Quellen seiner Reisebeschreibung. Berlin, 1888.

Montégut, E. Revue des Deux Mondes, xcvi, 1889, pp. 277, 547; Heures de Lecture, Paris, 1891, p. 235.

Cordier, H. T'oung Pao. Archives pour l'Histoire, vol. ii, Leyden, 1891. [On French edns.]

Murray, D. John de Berdeus otherwise Sir John Mandevile and the Pestilence. Paisley, 1891 (priv. ptd). [See also his Black Book of Paisley, 1885, for MSS of John de Bourgogne.]

Fife, R. H. Der Wortschatz des englischen Mandevile nach der Versionen der Cottonhandschrift. Leipzig, 1902. [See also AJ. Phil. xxviii, 1907, pt 1.]

Fyvie, J. Some Literary Eccentrics. New York, 1906.

Livre des Merveilles. 2 vols. Bibliothèque Nationale, Paris, 1908. [Reproduction of miniatures.]

Entwistle, W. J. MLR. xvii, 1922, p. 251. [Spanish MS.]

Hinton, J. Stud. Phil. xx, 1923, p. 460. [On ch. v.]

Peebles, R. The Dry Tree. [Vassar Medieval Studies, New Haven, 1923, p. 63.]

Jackson, I. Who was Sir John Mandeville? MLR. xxiii, 1928, p. 466.

Steiner, A. The Date of Composition of Mandeville's Travels. Speculum, ix, 1934, p. 144.

VII. RICHARD ROLLE, AND ASSOCIATED PIECES

A. RICHARD ROLLE (c. 1300–1349)

[A list of Rolle's Latin works will be found below, pp. 307–8.]

(1) GENERAL TREATMENTS

(a) *Bibliography and Summary*

[*Wells*, pp. 444, 837, 983, 1020, 1071, 1129, 1176, 1220, 1274, 1312, 1361, 1407.]

Allen, H. E. Writings Ascribed to Richard Rolle, Hermit of Hampole, and Materials for his Biography. New York, 1927. [See TLS. 22 Nov. 1928, p. 910; N. & Q. 12 May 1928, p. 342.]

(b) *Life of Rolle, etc.*

Breviarium ad Usum Insignis Ecclesiae Eboracensis. Surtees Soc. lxxi, 1880, lxxv, 1883. [Appendix v.]

Officium de Sancto Ricardo de Hampole. Ed. G. G. Perry, EETS. 1866, 1921 (rev. edn); ed. H. Lindkvist, Richard Rolle's Meditatio de Passione, Upsala, 1917 (appendix).

DNB. under 'Rolle, Richard.'

Horstmann, C. Yorkshire Writers. 2 vols. 1895–6.

CHEL. vol. II, 1908, p. 43.

Spurgeon, C. F. E. Mysticism in English Literature. Cambridge, 1913. [P. 116.]

Harford, D. Mending of Life. 1913. [Introduction.]

Clay, R. M. Hermits and Anchorites of England. 1914. [Index.]

Comper, F. M. M. Richard Rolle: The Fire of Love. 1914. [Introduction.]

—— The Life of Richard Rolle. Together with an Edition of his English Lyrics. 1928. [With bibliography.]

Deanesly, M. Incendium Amoris. Manchester, 1915. [Introduction.]

Coleman, C. Catholic World, CVI, 1918, p. 170.

Officium et Miracula. Ed. R. M. Woolley, 1919.

Hodgson, G. E. English Mystics. 1922. [P. 104, Index.]

—— The Sanity of Mysticism. 1926.

Hubbard, H. L. The Amending of Life. A Modern English Version of the Emendatio Vitae. 1922. [Introduction.]

Denis, L. Du Péché à l'Amour Divin. Paris, 1926. [Introduction.]

Oakley, H. H. Quart. Rev. CXLV, 1926, p. 218.

Noetinger, M. The Biography of Richard Rolle. Month, Jan. 1926.

Allen, H. E. Writings Ascribed to Richard Rolle. New York, 1927.

—— Birthplace of Richard Rolle. TLS. 10 Sept. 1931, p. 683.

Knowles, M. D. The English Mystics. 1927.

(c) Manuscripts

Archiv, CX, 1903, p. 113, CIV, 1900, p. 360, CXXXVI, 1917, p. 35; PMLA. XL, 1925, p. 98, XLII, 1927, p. 863; MLR. XVII, 1922, pp. 217, 337, XVIII, 1923, pp. 5, 7, 381.

Floyer, J. K. and Hamilton, S. G. A Catalogue of the Manuscripts in Worcester Cathedral. Oxford, 1906. [See also MP. IV, 1906, p. 67; W. H. Hulme, Western Reserve University Bulletin, XXI, 1918, no. 4.]

Brown, C. A Register of Middle English Religious Verse. 2 vols. Oxford, 1916–20. [Index.]

Allen, H. E. Writings Ascribed to Richard Rolle. New York, 1927.

—— TLS. 17 March 1932, p. 202.

(d) Canon

[Allen, op. cit.; Wells, pp. 447, 837, 983, 1020, 1071, 1220, 401, 827, 1000, 1124, 1174, 1219, 1275, 1312, 1361–2.]

Meditatio de Passione, Speculum Vitæ. E. Studien, VII, 1884, pp. 454, 468, XII, 1889, p. 463; Ang. XV, 1892–3, p. 197; MP. IV. 1906, p. 67.

Horstmann, C. Yorkshire Writers. Vol. II, 1896, p. xxxvi.

Kühn, F. Über die Verfasserschaft der in Horstmanns 'Library' enthaltenen lyrischen Gedichte. Greifswald, 1900.

Schneider, J. P. The Prose Style of Richard Rolle of Hampole. Baltimore, 1906.

Floyer, J. K. and Hamilton, S. G. A Catalogue of the Manuscripts in Worcester Cathedral. Oxford, 1906.

Allen, H. E. The Authorship of Prick of Conscience. Radcliffe Monographs, XV, 1910, p. 115.

Hulme, W. H. Western Reserve University Bulletin, XXI, 1918, no. 4.

(e) Studies

[Wells, as above. See also items under Life, Canon above, and under Editions below.]

E. Studien, III, 1880, p. 406, X, 1887, p. 215.

Hahn, F. K. A. Quellenuntersuchungen zu Richard Rolles englischen Schriften. Berlin, 1900.

Liebermann, F. Archiv, CIV, 1900, p. 360. [MSS.]

Henningsen, H. Über die Wortstellung in den Prosaschriften Richard Rolles. Erlangen, 1911.

Spurgeon, C. F. E. Mysticism in English Literature. Cambridge, 1913.

Krapp, G. P. The Rise of English Literary Prose. New York, 1916. [P. 25.]

Allen, H. E. Romanic Rev. IX, 1918, p. 159.

Hodgson, G. E. English Mystics. 1922. [P. 104.]

—— The Sanity of Mysticism. 1926.

Denis, L. Du Péché à l'Amour Divin. Paris, 1926. [Introduction.]

Gardner, H. L. RES. IX, 1933, p. 129. [Cloud of Unknowing.]

Olmes, A. Sprache und Stil der englischer Mystik des Mittelalters. SEP. LXXVI, 1933.

(f) Editions

Morris, R. Pricke of Conscience. Philolog. Soc. Berlin, 1863.

Perry, G. G. English Prose Treatises. EETS. 1866, 1920.

—— Religious Pieces in Prose and Verse from R. Thornton's MS. EETS. 1867, 1913 (rev. edn).

Bramley, H. R. The Psalter and Certain Canticles by Richard Rolle. Oxford, 1884.

Ullmann, J. Meditations on the Passion. E. Studien, VII, 1884, p. 415.

Horstmann, C. Yorkshire Writers. 2 vols. 1895–6.

Harvey, R. Fire of Love and Mending of Life [Misyn's trn]. EETS. 1896.

Gardner, E. Cell of Self Knowledge. 1910. [Group of prose tracts; modernised spelling.]

Deanesly, M. Incendium Amoris. Manchester, 1915.

Lindkvist, H. Richard Rolle's Meditatio de Passione (MS Uppsala C 494). Upsala, 1917.

Comper, F. M. M. The Life of Richard Rolle. Together with an Edition of his English Lyrics. 1928. [P. 205. Modernised spelling.]

Allen, H. E. English Writings of Richard Rolle, Hermit of Hampole. Oxford, 1931.

(g) Translations

Benson, R. H. A Book of the Love of Jesus. 1904.

Burton, E. Meditations on the Passion. 1906.

Hodgson, G. E. The Form of Perfect Living and Other Prose Treatises. 1910.

Underhill, E. The Book of Contemplation (Divine Cloud). 1912; 1922.

Harford, D. The Mending of Life. 1913.

Comper, F. M. M. Richard Rolle: The Fire of Love; and the Mending of Life. 1914; 1920. [Misyn's trn.]

Pippet, G. Stations of the Cross. 1917.

Hulme, W. H. The Mending of Life. Western Reserve University Bulletin, xxi, no. 4, 1918. [M.E. trn in Worcester Cathedral MS F 172.]

Hubbard, H. L. The Amending of Life. 1922.

Hodgson, G. E. Some Minor Works of Richard Rolle. 1923.

—— The Sanity of Mysticism. 1926. [Appendix.]

Noetinger, M. Scala Perfectionis. Tours, 1923; 1927. [Includes French trn of the Divine Cloud.]

McCann, J. The Cloud of Unknowing. 1924.

Denis, L. Du Péché à l'Amour Divin. Paris, 1926.

Heseltine, G. C. The Fire of Love. 1935.

(2) ENGLISH PIECES ACCEPTED AS BY ROLLE

(a) Form of Perfect Living

[Allen, op. cit. pp. 256, 288; Wells, pp. 449, 838, 984, 1020, 1129, 1275, 1313, 1361, 1407.]

MSS and Editions. Cambridge, Rawlinson, Harley 1022, C. Horstmann, Yorkshire Writers, vol. i, 1895, p. 3; additions in Arundel 507, ibid. vol. i, pp. 412, 416, 417, 419; Seven Gifts portion, Arundel, Thornton, ibid. vol. i, pp. 136, 196; lyrics (modernised), F. M. M. Comper, The Life of Richard Rolle, 1928, p. 224; verse paraphrase, Cotton, Tiberius E vii, Horstmann, op. cit. vol. ii, 1896, p. 283.

Translation. G. E. Hodgson, The Form of Perfect Living and Other Prose Treatises, 1910.

Studies.

Foster, F. A. EETS. cxlvii, 1913, p. 5.

Allen, H. E. MP. xiii, 1916, p. 744.

Cumming, W. P. PMLA. xlii, 1927, p. 863. [MS Ste-Geneviève 3390.]

(b) Ego Dormio

[Allen, op. cit. pp. 246, 307, 308, 290; Wells, pp. 450, 838, 984, 1020, 1221, 1275, 1313, 1361, 1408.]

Editions. C. Horstmann, Yorkshire Writers, vol. i, 1895, pp. 49, 415; two lyrics, F. M. M. Comper, The Life of Richard Rolle, 1928, pp. 228, 231.

Translation. G. E. Hodgson, Some Minor Works of Richard Rolle, 1923.

Studies.

Allen, H. E. Romanic Rev. ix, 1918, p. 159.

Cummings, W. P. PMLA. xlii, 1927, p. 863. [MS Ste-Geneviève 3390.]

(c) Commandment of Love to God

[Allen, op. cit. pp. 251, 308, 309; Wells, pp. 451, 838, 1071, 1129, 1221, 1276, 1313, 1408.]

Edition. C. Horstmann, Yorkshire Writers, vol. i, 1895, p. 61.

Translation. G. E. Hodgson, Some Minor Works of Richard Rolle, 1923.

(d) Meditatio de Passione Domini

[Allen, op. cit. pp. 278, 371; Wells, pp. 451, 838, 1072, 1129, 1276, 1313, 1408.]

Editions. C. Horstmann, Yorkshire Writers, vol. i, 1895, pp. 83, 92; J. Ullmann, E. Studien, vii, 1884, p. 415; H. Lindkvist, Upsala, 1917.

Translations. E. Burton, 1906; (selections) G. Pippet, Stations of the Cross, 1917.

Studies.

Ullmann, J. and Zupitza, J. E. Studien, vii, 1884, pp. 415, 454, xii, 1889, p. 463; Ang. xv, 1892–3, p. 197.

Thien, H. Über die englischen Marienklagen. Kiel, 1906. [P. 29.]

(e) Commentary on the Psalter

[Allen, op. cit. pp. 169, 197; Wells, pp. 401, 827, 1020, 1066, 1124, 1174, 1219, 1271, 1311, 1403.]

Edition. H. R. Bramley, Oxford, 1884.

Studies.

Ang. Anz. viii, 1885, p. 170; E. Studien, x, 1887, p. 112.

Middendorff, H. Studien über Richard Rolle. Magdeburg, 1888.

13

Paues, A. C. A Fourteenth Century English Biblical Version. Cambridge, 1902. [Pp. xxxi, lii. Edns of 1904, 1909, omit introduction.]

Allen, H. E. Radcliffe Monographs, xv, 1910, p. 146.

—— MLR. xviii, 1923, pp. 5, 7. [MS, debt to Ancren Riwle.]

Christ, K. Archiv, cxxxvi, 1917, p. 35. [Vatican MS.]

Deanesly, M. The Lollard Bible. Cambridge, 1920. [P. 144.]

—— Vernacular Books. MLR. xv, 1920, p. 349.

Everett, D. MLR. xvii, 1922, pp. 217, 337, xviii, 1923, p. 381. [MSS, versions.]

Frank, G. PMLA. xl, 1925, p. 98. [Vatican MS.]

Hodgson, G. E. The Sanity of Mysticism. 1926. [P. 151.]

(f) Later Versions of Rolle's Psalter

[Allen, op. cit. pp. 169, 173; Wells, 402, 827, 1067, 1124, 1219, 1311.]

MSS. 1, Trinity College, Cambridge, B, v, 25; 2, Royal 18 cxxvi; and others.

Edition. T. Arnold, Select English Works of John Wyclif, vol. iii, Oxford, 1871, p. 3.

Studies.
Paues, A. C. A Fourteenth Century English Biblical Version. Cambridge, 1902. [Pp. xliii, li.]

Deanesly, M. The Lollard Bible. Cambridge, 1920. [P. 304.]

Everett, D. MLR. xvii, 1922, pp. 217, 337, xviii, 1923, p. 381.

(g) Lyrics

[Allen, op. cit. p. 287; Wells, pp. 451, 452, 838 (ch. xiii, [53]–[57], [58]–[68], [111]–[112], ch. vii [43]), and Supplements.]

MSS. 1, Thornton (Lincoln Cathedral Lib. A, 5, 2); 2, University Lib. Cambridge Dd; 3, Cotton, Galba E ix.

Editions. C. Horstmann, Yorkshire Writers, vol. i, 1895, pp. 72–81, 363–4, 367, 370, vol. ii, 1896, p. 457; F. M. M. Comper, The Life of Richard Rolle, 1928, p. 205. Single lyrics: J. O. Halliwell[-Phillipps], Nugae Poeticae, 1844, p. 39; G. G. Perry, EETS. xxvi, 1867, pp. 72, 79; F. A. Patterson, The Middle English Penitential Lyric, New York, 1911, p. 131; Ang. xxvii, 1904, p. 306; E. Studien, xxi, 1895, p. 201; T. Wright and J. O. Halliwell[-Phillipps], Reliquiae Antiquae, vol. ii, 1843, p. 20.

(3) Pieces sometimes ascribed to Rolle or his Followers

[Allen, op. cit.; Wells, pp. 447, 452, 838, 983, 1020, 1071, 1129, 1175–6, 1220, 1276, 1313, 1362, 1408. For Pricke of Conscience, see under Moral and Religious Instruction, p. 185 above.]

B. WALTER HILTON (d. 1395–6?)

[Wells, pp. 460, 840, 984, 1021, 1072, 1130, 1278, 1315, 1362, 1408.]

(a) Biography and Criticism

[DNB.; CHEL. vol. ii, 1908, p. 299.]

Inge, W. R. Christian Mysticism. 1899. [P. 197.]

—— Studies of English Mystics. 1905. [P. 80.]

Allen, H. E. Radcliffe Monographs, xv, 1910, p. 163.

Spurgeon, C. F. E. Mysticism in English Literature. Cambridge, 1913. [P. 124.]

Deanesly, M. Vernacular Books. MLR. xv, 1920, p. 349.

—— The Lollard Bible. Cambridge, 1920. [P. 218.]

Hodgson, G. E. English Mystics. 1922.

Knowles, M. D. The English Mystics. 1927.

Jones, D. The Minor Works of Walter Hilton. New York, 1929.

(b) Scale of Perfection

[H. E. Allen, Writings Ascribed to Richard Rolle, New York, 1927, pp. 352, 361, 366, index; Hilton; Wells, pp. 460, 840, 984, 1021, 1073, 1130, 1315, 1408.]

Editions. (Modernised) E. Guy, 1869; (modernised) E. Underhill, 1923; (parts) C. Horstmann, Yorkshire Writers, vol. i, 1895, pp. 104, 105, 106. [For MSS see H. E. Allen, MP. xiii, 1916, p. 744; W. H. Hulme, Western Reserve University Bulletin, xxi, 1918, no. 4, p. 23; J. K. Floyer and S. G. Hamilton, Catalogue of Manuscripts in Worcester Cathedral, Oxford, 1906, p. 96; M. Bateson, Catalogue of the Library of Syon Monastery, Isleworth, 1898].

Translations. J. B. Dalgairns, 1870, 1908; (French) M. Noetinger and E. Bouvet, Tours, 1923; (French) M. Noetinger, 1927.

Studies
Lindkvist, H. Richard Rolle's Meditatio de Passione. Upsala, 1917. [P. 19.]

Gardner, H. L. Walter Hilton and The Cloud of Unknowing. RES. ix, 1933, p. 129.

(c) Epistle on Mixed Life

[Allen, op. cit. pp. 36, 197, 364, 366; Wells, pp. 461, 840, 1130, 1362, 1408.]

Editions. C. Horstmann, Yorkshire Writers, vol. I, 1895, p. 264; G. G. Perry, EETS. xx, 1866, p. 19 (rptd 1920).

Translation. J. B. Dalgairns, The Scale of Perfection, 1870, p. 313 (rptd 1908).

Studies.

Schneider, J. P. The Prose Style of Richard Rolle. Baltimore, 1906.

Deanesly, M. The Lollard Bible. Cambridge, 1920. [P. 217.]

(d) Of Angels' Song

[Allen, *op. cit.* pp. 364, 366, 368; *Wells*, pp. 462, 840, 1315.]

Editions. G. G. Perry, EETS. xx, 1866, p. 14; C. Horstmann, Yorkshire Writers, vol. I, 1895, p. 175, vol. II, 1896, p. xli; E. Mätzner, Altenglische Sprachproben, vol. II, Berlin, 1900, p. 133; E. G. Gardner, Cell of Self Knowledge, 1910, p. 61 (Pepwell's text of 1521, modernised spelling).

Translation. G. E. Hodgson, The Sanity of Mysticism, 1926, p. 191.

Studies.

Hodgson, G. E. The English Mystics. 1922. [Pp. 154, 237.]

Underhill, E. The Scale of Perfection. 1923. [Introduction.]

[On other pieces associated with Hilton, see *Wells*, pp. 462, 840, 1278, 1315.]

C. WILLIAM NASSYNGTON (*fl.* 1375)

[*Wells*, pp. 348, 463, 817, 841, 966, 985, 1015, 1021, 1067, 1130, 1172, 1216, 1278, 1315, 1362, 1409; DNB.; CHEL. vol. II, 1908, p. 46.]

(a) Biography and Criticism

Allen, H. E. Radcliffe Monographs, xv, 1910, p. 163.

Horstmann, C. Yorkshire Writers. Vol. II, 1896, p. 274.

Foster, F. A. EETS. CXLVII, 1913, p. 4.

Allen, H. E. PMLA. XXXII, 1917, p. 133.

Deanesly, M. The Lollard Bible. Cambridge, 1920. [P. 215.]

(b) Mirror of Life, or Speculum Vitae

[*Wells*, pp. 348, 817, 966, 1015, 1021, 1067, 1172, 1216, 1279, 1308, 1399.]

Edition. Verses 1–370 (with analysis of whole), E. Studien, VII, 1884, pp. 417, 468. [Collation, E. Studien, XII, 1889, p. 468.]

Studies.

Ullmann, J. E. Studien, VII, 1884, p. 415.

Horstmann, C. Yorkshire Writers. Vol. II, 1896, p. 274.

Allen, H. E. Radcliffe Monographs, xv, 1910, p. 163; PMLA. XXXII, 1917, p. 133.

—— Writings Ascribed to Richard Rolle. New York, 1927, p. 371.

Foster, F. A. EETS. CXLVII, 1913, p. 4.

Watson, G. N. & Q. 22 Nov. 1924, p. 371.

(c) Metrical Form of Living

[*Wells*, pp. 464, 841; H. E. Allen, Writings Ascribed to Richard Rolle, New York, 1927, p. 262.]

Edition. C. Horstmann, Yorkshire Writers, vol. II, 1896, p. 283.

D. JULIANA LAMPIT (JULIAN OF NORWICH)
(1343?–1443?)

[*Wells*, pp. 464, 841, 1021, 1130, 1315; H. E. Allen, Writings Ascribed to Richard Rolle, New York, 1927, pp. 223, 528; DNB.; CHEL. vol. II, 1908, p. 300.]

(a) Biography and Criticism

Blomefield, F. History of Norfolk. 11 vols. 1805–10. [Vol. IV, p. 81.]

Inge, W. R. Studies of English Mystics. 1905. [P. 50.]

Goyau, L. F. Revue des Deux Mondes, XVI, 1913, p. 836.

Spurgeon, C. F. E. Mysticism in English Literature. Cambridge, 1913. [P. 120.]

Clay, R. M. Hermits and Anchorites of England. 1914. [Index.]

(b) Fourteen Revelations of Divine Love

Editions. (Modernised) R. F. S. Cressy, 1670, rptd 1843, 1902; H. Collins, 1877; (modernised) G. Warrack, 1901, 1923.

Translations. All Shall Be Well, 1908 (selections); D. Harford, Comfortable Words for Christ's Lovers, 1911; R. Hudleston, 1927.

Studies.

Hodgson, G. E. English Mystics. 1922. [Pp. 123, 153, and index.]

Maw, M. Buddhist Mysticism. Bordeaux, 1924.

Thouless, R. H. Lady Julian; a Psychological Study. 1924.

Benvenuta, M.. Julian of Norwich. Dublin Rev. CLXXVI, 1925, p. 81.

Knowles, M. D. The English Mystics. 1927.

VIII. THE THREE AGES, WYNNERE, AND THE PIERS PLOWMAN SERIES

A. ALLITERATIVE VERSE

[*Wells*, pp. 240, 800, 1112, 1263, 1304, 1349, 1394.]

Hales, J. W. and Furnivall, F. J. The Percy Folio Manuscript. Vol. III, 1869. [P. xi.]

Ang. I, 1878, pp. 1, 414, v, 1882, p. 240, x, 1887–8, p. 105, xI, 1888–9, pp. 392, 553, xII, 1889–90, p. 437, xIII, 1890–1, p. 140, xv, 1892–3, p. 229, xvIII, 1895–6, p. 83; Ang. Anz. vIII, 1885, p. 49; Ang. Bbl. v, 1904–5, p. 87, xII, 1911–2, p. 33; E. Studien, xvI, 1892, p. 169, xxx, 1902, p. 270, xxxIv, 1904, p. 99; Archiv, cv, 1900, p. 304, cxIII, 1904, p. 183; BBA. xII, 1902, p. 103.

Schipper, J. Englische Metrik. Vol. I, Bonn, 1881. [P. 195.]

Fuhrmann, J. Die alliterierenden Sprachformeln. Hamburg, 1886.

Lawrence, J. Chapters on Alliterative Verse. 1893. [P. 89.]

Kuhnke, B. Die alliterierende Langzeile in Sir Gawayne. Berlin, 1900.

Fischer, J. Die stabende Langzeile in den Werken des Gawaindichters. BBA. xI, 1901, p. 1. [See also Ang. Bbl. xII, 1904, p. 33; BBA. xI, 1901, p. 139.]

Deutschbein, M. Zur Entwicklung des englischen Alliterationsverses. Halle, 1902.

Pilch, L. Umwandlung des altenglischen Alliterationsverses. Königsberg, 1904.

Luick, K. Paul's Grundriss der germanischen Philologie. 2nd edn, vol. II², Strasburg, 1905. [P. 160.]

Reicke, C. Untersuchungen über den Stils der mittelenglischen alliterierenden Gedichte. Königsberg, 1906.

Thomas, J. Die alliterierende Langzeile des Gawayn-Dichters. Coburg, 1908.

Kaluza, M. Englische Metrik in historischer Entwicklung. Berlin, 1909.

Schumacher, K. Studien über den Stabreim. Bonner Studien, xI, 1914.

Menner, R. J. Yale Stud. LxI, 1920, p. xix.

Leonard, W. E. The Scansion of Middle English Alliterative Verse. Wisconsin University Stud. xI, 1920, p. 58.

Emerson, O. F. Imperfect Lines in Pearl and Sir Gawayne. MP. xIx, 1921, p. 131.

Rankin, J. W. Rhythm and Rime before the Norman Conquest. PMLA. xxxvI, 1921, p. 401.

Oakden, J. P. Alliterative Poetry in Middle English. 2 pts. Manchester, 1930–5.

Day, M. Strophic Division in Middle English Alliterative Verse. E. Studien, LxvI, 1931, p. 245.

ulbert, J. R. A Hypothesis concerning the Alliterative Revival. MP. xxvIII, 1931, p. 405.

[See also under Piers Plowman Series (p. 197 below), Pearl Group (p. 201 below), Pearl (p. 201 below), Purity (p. 202 below), Patience (p. 202 below), Erkenwald (p. 203 below), Sir Gawayne (p. 135 above), Pistill of Susan (p. 189 above), Morte Arthure (p. 136 above), Golagrus (p. 139 above), Awn-

tyrs of Arthure (p. 136 above), Wars of Alexander (p. 143 above), Alexander Buik (p. 144 above), Destruction of Troy (p. 144 above), Titus and Vespasian (p. 157 above); and under Huchown Discussion (p. 137 above). The introductions and bibliographies in edns of the works just named are also useful, especially Menner's Purity and Savage's Erkenwald, Yale Stud. LxI, 1920, LxxII, 1926.]

B. ALLITERATIVE PIECES

(a) Parlement of the Thre Ages

[Wells, pp. 241, 800, 957, 1009, 1054, 1112, 1170, 1213, 1263, 1304, 1394.]

MS. BM. Add. 31042. [See Catalogue of the Additional Manuscripts in the British Museum, 1894, under MS 33994.]

Edition. Sir I. Gollancz, Roxburghe Club, 1897; 1915.

Studies. [CHEL. vol. II, 1908, p. 37; Schofield, p. 316.]

Loomis, R. S. The Nine Worthies. MP. xv, 1917–8, p. 211.

Hulbert, J. R. MP. xvIII, 1920, p. 31. [Author, date.]

Roberts, J. H. The Nine Worthies. MP. xIx, 1921–2, p. 297.

Steadman, J. M. MP. xxI, 1923, p. 7. [Author.]

Sergeantson, M. S. RES. III, 1927, p. 331. [Dialect.]

Savage, H. L. MLN. xLIII, 1928, p. 177. ['Lyame.' See also MLN. xLv, 1930, p. 169; JEGP. xxIx, 1930, p. 74.]

Oakden, J. P. RES. x, 1934, p. 200. [By author of Wynnere.]

[See also Huchown Discussion, under Morte Arthure, p. 137 above; and Alliterative Verse, above.]

(b) Wynnere and Wastoure

[Wells, pp. 241, 800, 1054, 1112, 1170, 1213, 1263, 1304, 1394.]

MS. BM. Add. 31042.

Editions. Sir I. Gollancz, Roxburghe Club, 1897 (with Parlement of the Three Ages); Sir I. Gollancz, 1920, 1931 (with modern rendering).

Studies. [CHEL. vol. II, 1908, p. 37.]

Athenaeum, 3, 24 Aug., 7, 14 Sept. 1901, pp. 157, 254, 319, 351. [Date.]

Hulbert, J. R. MP. xvIII, 1920, p. 31. [Author, date.]

Steadman, J. M. MP. xIx, 1921–2, p. 211. [Date.]

—— MP. xxI, 1923, p. 7. [Author.]

—— MLN. xxxvIII, 1923, p. 308. [Text, vocabulary.]

Sergeantson, M. S. RES. III, 1927, p. 331.
[Dialect.]

Anderson, J. M. MLN. XLIII, 1928, p. 47.
[Date.]

Oakden, J. P. RES. x, 1934, p. 200. [By
author of Thre Ages.]

[See also Huchown Discussion, under
Morte Arthure, p. 137 above; and Alliterative
Verse, above.]

(c) Vision concerning Piers Plowman

[*Wells*, pp. 244, 800, 958, 1009, 1055, 1112,
1170, 1213, 1264, 1304, 1349, 1394.]

i. Manuscripts

47 in number. Described by W. W. Skeat,
4 pts, EETS. 1866–84, and in Oxford edn,
vol. II, 1886.

Grouped: *Wells*, pp. 244, 958, 1055; C.
Brown, Register of Middle English Religious
Verse, vol. II, Oxford, 1920, items 880, 881. On
Aberystwyth, MLR. XI, 1916, p. 258. On
A-texts: R.W.Chambers and J.H.G. Grattan,
MLR. IV, 1909, p. 357, XI, 1916, p. 257, XIV,
1919, p. 129; T. A. Knott, MP. XII, 1914–5,
p. 389, XIV, 1916–7, p. 531, XV, 1917–8, p. 23.
On B-texts: E. Blackman, JEGP. XVII, 1918,
p. 489. Facs.: page, Laud 658, W. W. Skeat,
EETS. 1869; page, Laud 581, W. W. Skeat,
Twelve Facsimiles, Oxford, 1892; page,
Trinity College Cambridge B XV 17, W. W.
Greg, Facsimiles of Twelve Manuscripts,
Oxford, 1913; facs. of Ashburnham CXXX in
preparation (2 plates, MP. XXIX, 1932, p. 391).

Chambers, R. W. and Grattan, J. H. G. The
Text of Piers Plowman. MLR. XXVI, 1931,
p. 1.

ii. Editions

A-text: W. W. Skeat, EETS. 1867. B-text:
T. Wright, 1842, rev. 1856, re-ed. 1895;
W. W. Skeat, EETS. 1869; W. W. Skeat,
Prologue, Passus I–VII, 10th edn, Oxford,
1924; J.F.Davis,Prologue,Passus I–VII,1896;
C. D. Pamely, Prologue, Passus V–VII, 1930.
C-text: T. D. Whitaker, 1813: W. W. Skeat,
EETS. 1873. ABC-texts: W. W. Skeat,
Oxford, 1886. [Parallel extracts from 45 MSS,
W. W. Skeat, EETS. 1866. Introduction,
notes, gloss to EETS. edns, W. W. Skeat,
EETS. 1884.]

iii. Selections

R. Wülcker, Lesebuch, 2 pts, Halle, 1874–9;
R. Morris and W. W. Skeat, Specimens of
Early English, vol. II, Oxford, 1894; A. S.
Cook, Reader, Boston, 1915; F. Kluge, Lese-
buch, Halle, 1904; New Rochelle, New York,
1901; C. M. Drennan, 1915; A. Brandl and
O. Zippel, Mittelenglische Sprach- und Litera-
turproben, Berlin, 1917; K. Sisam, Fourteenth
Century Verse and Prose, Oxford, 1921.

iv. Modern Renderings

A-text: Prologue, Passus I–VII, W. A.
Neilson and K. G. T. Webster, Chief British
Poets of the 14th and 15th Centuries, Boston,
1916, p. 48, rptd (with Sir Gawayne), Boston,
1917; (with Prologue of B-text) J. L. Weston,
Romance, Vision, and Satire, Boston, 1912,
pp. 239, 317. B-text: Prologue, Passus I–VII,
K. M. Warren, 1895, 1899, 1913; W. W. Skeat,
1905; A. Burrell, 1912, 1925 (Everyman's
Lib.); D. Attwater, 1930; H. W. Wells, 1935.

v. Argument of poem

Hanscom, E. D. PMLA. IX, 1894, p. 403.

vi. Text

Ang. XV, 1892–3, p. 222; MLR. III, 1908,
p. 171, IV, 1909, p. 357, V, 1910, pp. 1, 340,
XIV, 1919, p. 129; MLN. VII, 1892, p. 268,
XXIII, 1908, pp. 156, 231, XXXII, 1917, p. 57;
Archiv, c, 1898, pp. 155, 334; E. Studien,
V, 1882, p. 150; MP. XII, 1914–5, p. 389.

Chambers, R. W. and Grattan, J. H. G. The
Text of Piers Plowman. MLR. XXVI, 1931,
p. 1.

vii. Language

Bernard, E. William Langland. A Grammatical Treatise. Bonn, 1874.

Kron, R. William Langley's Buch. Erlangen,
1885.

Wandschneider, W. Zur Syntax des Verbums.
Leipzig, 1887.

Teichmann, E. Die Verbalflexion. Aachen,
1887.

Klapprott, L. Das End-e in W. Langland's
Buch. Göttingen, 1890. [Text B.]

Sellert, F. Das Bild. Rostock, 1904.

Jones, H. S. V. Imaginatif. JECP. XIII, 1014,
p. 583.

Hulbert, J. R.. MP. XIX, 1921–2, p. 1.

Menner, R. J. PMLA. XXXVII, 1922, p. 503.

K., A. R. Parked. American Speech, II,
1927, p. 215.

[See also under Authorship Controversy,
below.]

viii. Verse

Hales, J. W. and Furnivall, F. J. The Percy
Folio Manuscript. Vol. III, 1869. [P. xi.]

Rosenthal, F., Luick, K., Teichmann, E.
Ang. I, 1878, p. 414, XI, 1888–9, p. 429,
XIII, 1890–1, p. 140.

Schipper, J. Englische Metrik. Vol. I, Bonn,
1881. [Sect. 95.]

Fischer, J. BBA. XI, 1901, p. 139.

Schneider, A. Die mittelenglische Stabzeile.
BBA. XII, 1902, p. 102.

Luick, K. Paul's Grundriss der germanischen
Philologie. 2nd edn, vol. II², Strasburg,1905.
[P. 141.]

Deakin, M. The Alliteration of Piers Plowman. MLR. IV, 1909, p. 478.

Stewart, G. R. The Meter of Piers Plowman. PMLA. XLII, 1927, p. 113.

[See also under Alliterative Verse, above.]

ix. General Studies

Kron, R. William Langley's Buch. Erlangen, 1885.

Jusserand, J. J. L'Epopée mystique de William Langland. Paris, 1893; tr. Eng. 1894 (rev. edn).

x. Miscellaneous Studies

Burdach, K. Vom Mittelalter zur Reformation. Halle, 1893. [P. 29.]

—— Der Dichter des Ackermann. Berlin, 1926.

Bellezza, P. Langland's Figure des Plowman. E. Studien, XXI, 1895, p. 325.

Academy, 1 Jan. 1898, p. 11. [Source, B XVIII 1–68.]

Hemingway, S. MLN. XXXII, 1917, p. 57. [On B XV 235 ff.]

Tristram, E. E. Piers Plowman in Wallpaintings. Burlington Mag. XXXI, 1917, p. 135.

Hanford, J. H. The Source of Death and Liffe. MP. XV, 1917–8, p. 313; Stud. Phil. XV, 1918, p. 223.

Baum, P. Belling the Cat. MLN. XXXIV, 1919, p. 462.

Wedel, T. The Medieval Attitude toward Astrology. Yale Stud. LX, 1920, p. 121.

Knowlton, E. C. Nature in Middle English. JEGP. XX. 1921, p. 197.

Döring, G. Personennamen in Langland. Leipzig, 1922.

Owst, G. R. The 'Angel' and the 'Goliardeys' of Langland's Prologue. MLR. XX, 1925, p. 270. [See also C. Brett, MLR. XXII, 1927, p. 260.]

Fairchild, H. N. MLN. XLI, 1926, p. 378. [B VI 123–6.]

Withycombe, E. G. The Name Robin Hood. TLS. 7 April 1927, p. 251.

Thomas, G. A. A Study of the Influence of Piers Plowman. Ithaca, 1927.

Devlin, M. A. Date of C-Version. University of Chicago Abstracts of Theses, Humanistic Ser. IV, 1928, p. 317.

Krog, F. Studien zu Chaucer und Langland. Anglistische Forschungen, LXV, 1928.

von Bonsdorff, I. Hankyn or Haukyn? MP. XXVI, 1928–9, p. 57.

Wells, H. W. The Construction of Piers Plowman. PMLA. XLIV, 1929, p. 123.

Bright, A. H. Langland and the Seven Deadly Sins. MLR. XXV, 1930, p. 133.

—— Sources of Piers Plowman. TLS. 24 April 1930, p. 352.

Gaffney, W. The Allegory of the Christ-Knight in Piers Plowman. PMLA. XLVI, 1931, p. 155.

Cargill, O. The Date of the A-Text. PMLA XLVII, 1932, p. 354.

Coghill, N. K. RES. VIII, 1932, p. 303.

—— The Sexcentenary of William Langland London Mercury, XXVI, 1932, p. 40.

—— The Character of Piers Plowman considered from the B Text. Medium Aevum II, 1933, p. 108.

—— Medium Aevum, IV, 1935, pp. 83, 89 [Notes.]

Day, M. 'Mele Tyme of Seintes.' MLR. XXVII, 1932, p. 317.

—— Piers Plowman and Poor Relief. RES VIII, 1932, p. 445.

Sullivan, C. The Latin Insertions and the Macaronic Verse in Piers Plowman. Washington, 1932.

Kirk, R. References to the Law in Piers the Plowman. PMLA. XLVIII, 1933, p. 322.

Carnegy, F. A. R. An Attempt to approach the C-Text. 1934.

—— The Relations between the Social and Divine Order in Piers the Plowman Breslau, 1934.

Kellogg, E. H. Bishop Brunton and the Fable of the Rats. PMLA. L, 1935, p. 57.

[See also the works by J. T. T. Brown and G. Neilson listed under Huchown Discussion p. 137 above.]

xi. Comparisons

Bellezza, P. N. & Q. 4 Aug. 1894, p. 81.

Courthope, W. J. A History of English Poetry. Vol. I, 1895. [Pp. 160, 200 Dante.]

Traver, H. The Four Daughters of God Philadelphia, 1907. [P. 147.]

Owen, D. L. Piers Plowman. A Comparison with French Allegories. 1912; 1915.

Chambers, R. W. Long Will, Dante, and th Righteous Heathen. E. & S. IX, 1923 p. 50.

Iijimo, Ikuzo. Langland and Chaucer Boston, 1925.

Day, M. Duns Scotus and Piers Plowman RES. III, 1927, p. 333.

Adams, M. R. The Use of the Vulgate in Piers Plowman. Stud. Phil. XXIV, 1927 p. 556.

Krog, F. Studien zu Chaucer und Langland Anglistische Forschungen, LXV, 1928.

Cornelius, R. Piers Plowman and the Roma de Fauvel. PMLA. XLVII, 1932, p. 363.

xii. Life, Education, Character, Views, the Times

Günther, E. Englische Leben im 14. Jahrhundert nach The Vision. Leipzig, 1889.

N. & Q., 7 Feb., 8 March, 1891, pp. 108, 285.

Traill, H. D. Social England. Vol. ii, 1898, p. 125.

Hopkins, E. M. The Character and Opinions of William Langland. Kansas University Quart. 1894, p. 284.

—— The Education of William Langland. Princeton College Bulletin, April 1895.

Jack, A. E. Autobiographical Elements in Piers Plowman. JEGP. iii, 1900, p. 393.

Mensendieck, O. Charakterentwicklung und ethisch-theologische Anschauungen. Leipzig, 1900.

Koellreuter, M. Privatleben in England. Zurich, 1908.

Macaulay, G. C. The Name of the Author of Piers Plowman. MLR. v, 1910, p. 195.

Gebhard, H. Langlands und Gowers Kritik der kirchlichen Verhältnisse. Strasburg, 1911.

Keiller, M. M. The Influence of Piers Plowman on the Macro Mankind. PMLA. xxvi, 1911, p. 339.

Cazamian, L. Études de Psychologie littéraire. Paris, 1913.

Görnemann, G. Anglistische Forschungen, xlviii, 1915, p. 121.

Eberhard, O. Der Bauernaufstand vom Jahre 1381 in der englischen Poesie. Anglistische Forschungen, li, 1917.

Chadwick, D. Social Life in the Days of Piers Plowman. Cambridge, 1022.

Bannister, A. T. and Bright, A. H. TLS. 7 Sept. 1922, p. 569, 12 March 1925, p. 172. [Birth-place.]

Bright, A. H. William Langland's Early Life. TLS. 5 Nov. 1925, p. 739, 9 Sept. 1926, p. 596.

—— New Light on Piers Plowman. Oxford, 1928.

Owst, G. R. Literature and Pulpit in Medieval England. Cambridge, 1933.

[See also the edns of Jusserand and Skeat.]

xiii. Authorship Controversy

[For general summary see *Wells*, pp. 250, 302, 958, 1055, 1170, 802, 1009, 1112, 1213, 1264, 1304, 1349, 1394; F. Krog, under Miscellaneous Studies, above.]

Hopkins, E. M. Who wrote Piers Plowman? Kansas University Quart. April 1898.

Jack, A. E. JEGP. iii, 1900, p. 393. [Autobiography.]

Mensendieck, O. Leipzig, 1900 (see under xii above); Zeitschrift für vergleichende Literatur, xviii, 1910, p. 10.

—— JEGP. ix, 1911, p. 404. [Authorship.]

Manly, J. M. MP. iii, 1906, p. 359. [Lost leaf.]

Bradley, H. Athenaeum, 21 April 1906, p. 481. [Misplaced leaf.]

—— The Word 'Moillere' in Piers the Plowman. MLR. ii, 1907, p. 163.

—— Nation (New York), 29 April 1909, p. 436. [Misplaced leaf.]

Manly, J. M. Piers the Plowman and its Sequence. CHEL. vol. ii, 1908, p. 1; (with notes by Manly, H. Bradley, F. J. Furnivall), EETS. Ex. Issue, 1908.

—— The Authorship of Piers Plowman. MP. vii, 1909, p. 83; EETS. Ex. Issue, 1910.

—— MP. xiv, 1917, p. 315. [Marsh's suggestion, 1859, 1860–1.]

Jusserand, J. J. The Work of One or of Five? MP. vi, 1908, p. 271, vii, 1910, p. 289; EETS. Ex. Issue, 1910.

Hall, T. D. Was Langland the Author of C-Text? MLR. iv, 1909, p. 1.

—— Misplaced Lines in Piers Plowman. MP. vii, 1910, p. 327.

Chambers, R. W. and Grattan, J. H. G. The A-text. MLR. iv, 1909, p. 357.

—— MLR. xi, 1916, p. 257. [Reply to Knott.]

—— The Text of Piers Plowman. MLR. xxvi, 1931, p. 1.

Brown, C. and Knott, T. A. Nation (New York), 25 March, 13 May 1909. [Lost leaf.]

Deakin, M. The Alliteration of Piers Plowman. MLR. iv, 1909, p. 478.

Lawrence, W. W. JEGP. viii, 1909, p. 607. [Criticism of Manly.]

Chambers, R. W. The Authorship of Piers Plowman. MLR. v, 1910, p. 1; EETS. Ex. Issue, 1910.

—— The Original Form of the A-Text of Piers Plowman. MLR. vi, 1911, p. 302.

—— The Three Texts and their Grammatical Forms. MLR. xiv, 1919, p. 129.

—— Long Will, Dante, and the Righteous Heathen. E. & S. ix, 1923, p. 50. [See also Ang. Bbl. xxxv, 1912, p. 367.]

Dobson, M. Ang. xxxiii, 1910, p. 391. [Vocabulary of A-text.]

Macaulay, G. C. The Name of the Author of Piers Plowman. MLR. v, 1910, p. 195.

Coulton, G. G. Piers Plowman, One or Five. MLR. vii, 1912, pp. 102, 372.

Owen, D. L. Piers Plowman. A Comparison with French Allegories. 1912; 1915.

Bradley, H. and Rickert, E. Who was John But? MP. xi, 1913, p. 107; MLR. viii, 1913, p. 88.

Moore, S. MP. xi, 1913, p. 177, xii, 1914, p. 19. [Summary of materials.]

Knott, T. MP. xii, 1915, p. 389. [A-version. See also E. Studien, xlix, 1915–6, p. 288.]

—— MP. xiv, 1917, p. 531.

Görnemann, G. Anglistische Forschungen, xlviii, 1915. [Author, origin.]

Adams, M. R. The Use of the Vulgate in Piers Plowman. Stud. Phil. xxiv, 1927, p. 556.

Bright, A. H. New Light on Piers Plowman. Oxford, 1928.

Day, M. The Revisions of Piers Plowman. MLR. xxiii, 1928, p. 1.

Krog, F. Autobiographische oder typische Zahlen in Piers Plowman. Ang. lviii, 1934, p. 318.

Cargill, O. The Langland Myth. PMLA. l, 1935, p. 36.

(d) Pierce the Ploughman's Crede

[Wells, pp. 268, 802, 1009, 1113, 1214, 1395.]

MSS. 1, Royal 18 B xvii; 2, Trinity College Cambridge R, 3, 15.

Editions. 1553 (Glossary by Reynold Wolfe), rptd 1814; T. Wright, 1842 (in edn of Piers Plowman), rev. 1856, 1895; W. W. Skeat, EETS. 1867; W. W. Skeat, Specimens of English, 1394–1579, Oxford, 1892 (6th edn).

Studies. [ien Brink, vol. ii, p. 201; CHEL. vol. ii, 1908, p. 38.]

MLR. iv, 1909, p. 235. [Verse 372.]

N. & Q. 4 May 1867, p. 352.

[See also under Alliterative Verse, p. 196 above.]

(e) Richard the Redeless, or Mum, Sothsegger

[Wells, pp. 269, 803, 1010, 1056, 1113, 1265, 1305, 1395.]

MSS. 1, University Lib. Cambridge Ll.iv.14; 2, BM. Add. 41666 (see R. Steele, TLS. 6 Dec. 1928, p. 965). [Each MS is a fragment.]

Editions. T. Wright, Camden Soc. 1838; T. Wright, Political Poems and Songs, vol. i, Rolls Ser. 1859, p. 368; W. W. Skeat, EETS. liv, 1873, p. 469; W. W. Skeat, Piers Plowman, vol. i, Oxford, 1886, p. 603; EETS. in preparation.]

Translation. (Parts.) A. R. Benham, English Literature to the Death of Chaucer, New Haven, 1916, p. 185.

Studies. [ten Brink, vol. ii, p. 202; CHEL, vol. ii, 1908, p. 35.]

Ziepel, C. The Reign of Richard II. Comments on the Alliterative Poem. Berlin, 1874.

Ang. i, 1878, p. 420, xi, 1889, p. 438. [Verse.]

Athenaeum, 21 April 1906, p. 481. [Title.]

Görnemann, G. Anglistische Forschungen, xlviii, 1915, p. 68. [Author; for criticisms see Wells, p. 1113.]

Bradley, H. Richard the Redeless, iii, 105–6. MLR. xii, 1917, p. 202.

Eberhard, O. Der Bauernaufstand vom Jahre 1381 in der englischen Poesie. Anglistische Forschungen, li, 1917, p. 48.

Snyder, E. C. MP. xvii, 1920, p. 713. [On Prologue, 10.]

Koziol, H. E. Studien, lxvii, 1932, p. 168. [By author of Piers Plowman.]

[See also under Alliterative Verse, p. 196 above.]

(f) Complaint of the Ploughman, or Plowman's Tale

[Wells, pp. 267, 802; E. P. Hammond, Chaucer: A Bibliographical Manual, New York, 1908, pp. 444, 540; CHEL. vol. ii, 1908, p. 39; ten Brink, vol. ii, p. 204.]

Editions. W. Thynne, The Workes of Chaucer, 1542 (2nd edn); T. Wright, Political Poems and Songs, vol. i, Rolls Ser. 1859, p. 304; W. W. Skeat, The Complete Works of Chaucer, vol. vii, Oxford, 1897, p. 149.

Studies.

Athenaeum, 12 July 1902. [Date.]

Irvine, A. S. A Manuscript of The Plowman's Tale. Texas University Stud. no. xii, 1932, p. 27.

(g) Jack Upland

[Wells, pp. 268, 802; CHEL. vol. ii, 1908, p. 39.]

Editions. J. Gough, [c. 1540 or c. 1536]; T. Wright, Political Poems and Songs, vol. ii, Rolls Ser. 1861, p. 16; W. W. Skeat, The Complete Works of Chaucer, vol. vii, Oxford, 1897, p. 191. [No MS extant.]

(h) Reply of Friar Daw Thopias; Rejoinder of Jack Upland

[Wells, pp. 268, 802; CHEL. vol. ii, 1908, p. 40.]

MS. Digby 41 (Bodleian).

Editions. T. Wright, Political Poems and Songs, vol. ii, Rolls Ser. 1861, p. 39; (Daw only) A. S. Cook, Literary Middle English Reader, Boston, 1915, p. 336.

(i) Crowned King

[Wells, pp. 268, 802; CHEL. vol. ii, 1908, p. 40.]

MS. Douce 95 (Bodleian).

Edition. W. W. Skeat, EETS. liv, 1873, p. 523.

(j) Death and Liffe

[Wells, pp. 268, 802, 985, 1009, 1113, 1214, 1305, 1350, 1395; CHEL. vol. ii, 1908, p. 40.]

MS. Percy Folio (BM. Add. 27879).

Editions. J. W. Hales and F. J. Furnivall, Percy Folio Manuscript, vol. iii, 1869, p. 49; J. H. Hanford and J. M. Steadman, Stud. Phil. xv, 1918, p. 223; Sir I. Gollancz, 1930. [Modernised version in E. Arber, Dunbar Anthology, 1901, p. 126.]

Studies.
Ang. Bbl. xxiii, 1912, p. 137.
Steadman, J. M. MLN. xxxii, 1917, p. 499. [Definitions.]
MP. xv, 1918, p. 313. [Sources.]
Holthausen, F. Ang. Bbl. xxxii, 1921, p. 83. [Text-notes.]
Knowlton, E. C. Nature in Middle English. JEGP. xx, 1921, p. 198.
Blau, E. Kiel, 1922.

(k) *Scottish Feilde*

[*Wells*, pp. 268, 802, 1113, 1305, 1350, 1395; CHEL. vol. ii, 1908, p. 40.]

MS. Percy Folio (BM. Add. 27879).
Editions. J. W. Hales and F. J. Furnivall, Percy Folio Manuscript, vol. i, 1867, p. 199; J. Robson, Chetham Soc. Misc. vol. ii, 1855; J. P. Oakden, Chetham Soc. Misc. vol. vi, 1935.

IX. THE PEARL GROUP

(a) *The Pearl Poet*

[*Wells*, pp. 578, 863, 993, 1026, 1138, 1283, 1319, 1370, 1418; Pearl, Patience, Purity, below, and Sir Gawayne and the Grene Knight, above p. 135; introductions and bibliographies in edns of these pieces; Huchown Discussion, under Morte Arthure, p. 137 above; and Alliterative Verse, p. 196 above.]

Trautmann, M. Über Verfasser und Entstehungszeit einiger alliterierenden Gedichte. Halle, 1876. [See also Ang. i, 1878, p. 117.]
Thomas, M. C. Sir Gawayne and the Grene Knight. Zurich, 1883.
Brown, C. The Author of Pearl. PMLA. xix, 1904, p. 115.
Reicke, C. Untersuchungen über den Stil der mittelenglischen alliterierenden Gedichte. Königsberg, 1906.
Gollancz, Sir I. CHEL. vol. i, 1907. [Pp. 320, 472.]
Day, M. The Weak Verb in the Works of the 'Gawain'-Poet. MLR. xiv, 1919, p. 413.
Hulbert, J. R. MP. xix, 1921, p. 1. [On West Midland origin. See also R. J. Menner, PMLA. xxxvii, 1922, p. 503; M. S. Sergeantson, RES. iii, 1927, p. 327.]
Oakden, J. P. Alliterative Poetry in Middle English. Manchester, 1930, pp. 72, 251, 257.
—— The Scribal Errors of MS. Cotton Nero A. x. Library, xiv, 1933, p. 353.
Chapman, C. O. The Musical Training of the Pearl Poet. PMLA. xlvi, 1931, p. 177.
—— The Authorship of the Pearl. PMLA. xlvii, 1932, p. 346.
Koziol, H. E. Studien, lxvii, 1932, p. 170.

[See also DNB. under 'Ralph Strode'; Ency. Brit. under 'Pearl.']

(b) *Pearl*

[*Wells*, pp. 579, 864, 993, 1026, 1082, 1138, 1185, 1229, 1283, 1320.]

MS. Cotton, Nero A x + 4 (once A x). Facs. (179 plates), Sir I. Gollancz, EETS. 1922.
Editions. R. Morris, EETS. 1864, rev. 1869, 1885, 1896, 1901; Sir I. Gollancz, 1891, rev. 1897, 1907, rev. (with trn of Olympia) 1921; C. G. Osgood, Boston, 1906; ed. S. P. Chase *et al.* Boston, 1932.

Selections. A. Brandl and O. Zippel, Mittelenglische Sprach- und Literaturproben, Berlin, 1917; K. Sisam, Fourteenth Century Verse and Prose, Oxford, 1921: G. Sampson, Cambridge Book of Prose and Verse, 1924.

Translations. Sir I. Gollancz (in edns of 1891, 1921); S. W. Mitchell, New York, 1906 (selection, verse); G. G. Coulton, 1906, 1921 (original metre); C. G. Osgood, Princeton, 1907 (prose); S. O. Jewett, New York, 1908 (original metre); J. L. Weston, Romance, Vision, and Satire, Boston, 1912 (original metre); W. A. Neilson and K. G. T. Webster, Chief British Poets of the 14th and 15th Centuries, Boston, 1916 (prose); E. Kirtlan, 1918 (verse); F. Olivero, Milan, 1927 (Italian, prose); S. P. Chase, 1932.

Studies. [*ten* Brink, vol. i, p. 348; CHEL. vol. i, 1907, pp. 320, 472; W. J. Courthope, A History of English Poetry, vol. i, 1895, p. 349; Ency. Brit., under 'Pearl.' See also under Pearl Poet, above.]

Verse. [See also under Alliterative Verse, p. 196 above.]
Trautmann, M. Ang. i, 1878, p. 119.
Schipper, J. Englische Metrik. Vol. i, Bonn, 1881. [Pp. 223, 317, 421.]
—— Grundriss der englischen Metrik. Vienna, 1895. [Sect. 332.]
Fuhrmann, J. Die alliterierenden Sprachformeln. Hamburg, 1886.
Northup, C. S. PMLA. xii, 1897, p. 326.
Luick, K. and Schipper, J. Paul's Grundriss der germanischen Philologie. 2nd edn, vol. ii², Strasburg, 1905. [Pp. 168, 239.]
Saintsbury, G. A History of English Prosody. Vol. i, 1906. [P. 106.]
Romanic Rev. vii, 1916, pp. 243, 271. [Stanza-linking.]
Emerson, O. F. MP. xix, 1921, p. 131. [Imperfect lines.]
—— PMLA. xxxvii, 1922, p. 52.

Language. [See also under Sir Gawayne and the Grene Knight, p. 135 above, especially Schwahn, Knigge, Kullnick, Schmittbetz, Hulbert, Menner, Serjeantson.]

Fick, W. Zum mittelenglischen Gedicht von der Perle. Kiel, 1885.

Tuttle, E. H. Notes on The Pearl. MLR. xv, 1920, p. 298.

Author, Interpretation, etc. [See also under Pearl Poet, above, and edns of Sir Gawayne, Patience, Purity.]

Neilson, G. Crosslinks between Pearl and the Awntyrs. Scottish Antiquary, xvi, 1902, p. 67.

Schofield, W. H. The Nature and Fabric of Pearl. PMLA. xix, 1904, p. 154.

Brown, C. PMLA. xix, 1904, p. 115. [Author, theology.]

Coulton, G. G. In Defence of Pearle. MLR. ii, 1906, p. 39.

Schofield, W. H. Symbolism, Allegory, and Autobiography. PMLA. xxiv, 1909, p. 585.

Chavannes, E. and Pelliot, P. Journal Asiatique, Nov. 1911.

Mead, W. E. Quest, Jan. 1913.

Garrett, R. M. The Pearl, an Interpretation. Seattle, 1918. [See also JEGP. xx, 1921, p. 288; MLN. xxxiv, 1919, p. 42.]

Fletcher, J. JEGP. xx, 1921, p. 1. [Allegory.]

Greene, W. K. PMLA. xl, 1925, p. 814. [Interpretation.]

Madeleva, M. Pearl: A Study in Spiritual Dryness. 1925. [See also MLN. xli, 1926, p. 411.]

Hart, E. Heaven of Virgines. MLN. xlii, 1927, p. 113.

Emerson, O. F. PMLA. xlii, 1927, p. 807. [Notes.]

Cargill, O. and Schlauch, M. Pearl and Its Jeweler. PMLA. xliii, 1928–9, p. 105.

Gordon, E. V. and Onions, C. T. Medium Aevum. i, 1932, p. 126, ii, 1933, p. 165.

Wellek, R. Prague Stud. iv, 1933, p. 1. [Interpretation.]

Day, M. Medium Aevum, iii, 1934, p. 241. [Notes.]

(c) Patience

[Wells, pp. 583, 864, 1026, 1138, 1229, 1283, 1320, 1370, 1418.]

MS. Cotton. Nero A x + 4. Facs. Sir I. Gollancz, EETS. 1922.

Editions. R. Morris, EETS. 1864 (as under Pearl); H. Bateson, Manchester, 1912, rev. 1918; Sir I. Gollancz, 1913.

Selections. J. Zupitza, Übungsbuch, Vienna, 1874; R. Wülcker, Lesebuch, 2 pts, Halle, 1874–9; G. E. MacLean, Reader, New York, 1893; F. Kluge, Lesebuch, Halle, 1904; A. S. Cook, Reader, Boston, 1915; G. Sampson, Cambridge Book of Prose and Verse, 1924.

Translation. (Part.) J. L. Weston, Romance, Vision, and Satire, Boston, 1912, p. 73.

Studies. [See also under Pearl Poet, Purity, Pearl, Sir Gawayne, and edns of same; ten Brink, vol. i, p. 348; CHEL. vol. i, 1907, pp. 323, 472; Schofield, pp. 215, 378.]

Author. [See under Pearl Poet.]

Language. [See under Pearl, Sir Gawayne.]

Verse. [See also under Alliterative Verse, p. 196 above, and Sir Gawayne, p. 135 above.]

Luick, K. Ang. xi, 1889, pp. 392, 553.

Kaluza, M. E. Studien, xvi, 1892, p. 169.

Schipper, J. Grundriss der englischen Metrik. Vienna, 1895. [Sect. 47.]

Trautmann, M. Ang. xvii, 1895, p. 83.

Fischer, J. BBA. xi, 1901.

Interpretation, etc.

E. Studien, iv, 1881, p. 500, xl, 1909, p. 163, xliv, 1911–2, p. 165, xlvii, 1913–4, pp. 133, 313, 316, xlviii, 1914–5, p. 172, xlix, 1915–6, pp. 142, 483; Ang. xi, 1889, p. 583.

Emerson, O. F. Parallels with Tertullian. PMLA. x, 1895, p. 242.

—— More Notes. MLN. xxxi, 1916, p. 1.

Liljegren, S. B. Patience and De Jona. E. Studien, xlviii, 1914–5, p. 337.

Eberhard, O. Die Bauernaufstand vom Jahre 138. in der englischen Poesie. Anglistische Forschungen, li, 1917, p. 83.

(d) Purity (Cleanness)

[Wells, pp. 584, 864, 1026, 1139, 1229, 1283, 1320, 1370, 1418; and edns by Menner, Gollancz.]

MS. Cotton, Nero A x + 4. Facs. Sir I. Gollancz, EETS. 1922.

Editions. R. Morris, EETS. 1864 (as under Pearl); R. J. Menner, Yale Stud. lxi, 1920 (see O. F. Emerson, JEGP. xx, 1921, p. 229); Sir I. Gollancz, 1921 and 1933.

Selections. R. Morris and W. W. Skeat, Specimens of Early English, vol. ii, Oxford, 1894, pp. 151, 161.

Translation. (Part.) J. L. Weston, Romance, Vision, and Satire, Boston, 1912, p. 153.

Studies. [On author, language, verse, see under Pearl Poet, Pearl, Patience, Sir Gawayne (p. 135 above), Alliterative Verse (p. 196 above). See also ten Brink, vol. i, p. 350; CHEL. vol. i, 1907, p. 323.]

Archiv, cvi, 1901, p. 349. [Comestor, source.]

Brown, C. PMLA. xix, 1904, p. 149. [Debt to Mandeville.]

Emerson, O. F. PMLA. xxxiv, 1919, p. 494. [Notes.]

[See also Ang. xxvi, 1903, p. 368; A. T. Bödtker, MLN. xxvi, 1911, p. 127; C. Brett, MLR. x, 1915, p. 188; O. F. Emerson, MLR. x, 1915, p. 373; Sir I. Gollancz, MLR. xiv

1919, p. 152; P. G. Thomas, MLR. xvii, 1922, p. 64, xxiv, 1929, p. 323; H. Bateson, MLR. xiii, 1918, p. 377, xix, 1924, p. 95; H. Bateson, Folk-Lore, xxxiv, 1923, p. 241.]

(e) *Sir Gawayne and the Grene Knight*

[See under Arthurian Romances, p. 135 above.]

(f) *Erkenwald*

[*Wells*, pp. 310, 810, 1012, 1059, 1117, 1215, 1268, 1307, 1351, 1397; edns by Gollancz, Savage.]

MS. Harley 2250.

Editions. C. Horstmann, Altenglische Legenden, Heilbronn, 1881, pp. 265, 527; Sir I. Gollancz, 1922; H. L. Savage, New Haven, 1926.

Translation. Sir I. Gollancz (edn, p. viii).

Studies. [See also discussion of Pearl, Patience, Purity, Sir Gawayne (p. 135 above), Alliterative Verse (p. 196 above), and Huchown, under Morte Arthure (p. 137 above).]

Knigge, F. Die Sprache des Dichters von Sir Gawain und De Erkenwalde. Marburg, 1885.

Gerould, G. H. Saints' Legends. Boston, 1916. [Pp. 237, 368.]

Hulbert, J. R. MP. xvi, 1919, p. 485. [Sources.]

Hibbard, L. A. Erkenbald the Belgian. MP. xvii, 1920, p. 669.

Hulbert, J. R., Menner, R. J., Sergeantson, M. S. MP. xix, 1921, p. 1; PMLA. xxxvii, 1922, p. 503; RES. iii, 1927, p. 326. [Dialect, place of origin.]

Chambers, R. W. E. & S. ix, 1923, p. 65. [Troy matter.]

X. JOHN WYCLIFFE (c. 1320–1384) AND ASSOCIATED WRITINGS

[*Wells*, pp. 410, 465, 828, 841, 1018, 1021, 1068, 1073, 1125, 1130, 1219, 1221, 1272, 1279, 1311, 1315, 1357, 1363, 1403, 1409; CHEL. vol. ii, 1908, pp. 49, 439; Shirley, Lechler, Arnold, and Canon, below.]

(a) *Life of Wycliffe, etc.*

Lewis, J. The Life and Sufferings of John Wiclif. 1720; Oxford, 1820.

Vaughan, R. Life and Opinions of John de Wycliffe, D.D. 1828; 1831.

Shirley, W. W. Fasciculi Zizaniorum Magistri Johannis Wyclif cum Tritico. Rolls Ser. 1858.

Lechler, G. V. Johann von Wiclif und die Vorgeschichte der Reformation. Leipzig, 1873; tr. Eng. 1878, 1884 (rev.), 1903.

Matthew, F. D. English Works of Wyclif. EETS. 1880. [Introduction.]
—— EHR. v, 1890, p. 328.

Buddensieg, R. J. Wicklif, Patriot and Reformator. 1884.
—— Johann Wiclif und seine Zeit. Gotha, 1885.

Athenaeum, 19 July, 1884, p. 82. [Birthplace.]

Loserth, J. Hus und Wiclif. Prague, 1884; tr. Eng. M. J. Evans, 1884.
—— John Wyclif's Activity in Ecclesiastical Politics. EHR. xi, 1896, p. 319.
—— Studien zur Kirchenpolitik Englands im 14. Jahrhundert. Vienna, 1897, 1907. [P. 107.]
—— Neue Erscheinungen der Wiclif-Literatur. Historisches Zeitschrift, xcv, 1905, p. 271.
—— Johann von Wiclif und Robert Grosseteste. Vienna, 1918.

DNB. [With bibliography.]

Sergeant, L. Wyclif, Schoolman and Reformer. 1893.

Petit-Dutaillis, C. Les Prédications populaires. [Études dédiées à G. Monod, Paris, 1896, p. 373.]

Trevelyan, G. M. England in the Age of Wycliffe. 1899; 1900 (3rd edn).

Capes, W. W. The English Church in the 14th and 15th Centuries. 1900. [P. 109.]

Cannon, H. L. The Poor Priests. Washington, 1900. [P. 451.]

Twemlow, J. A. Wycliffe's Preferments and University Degrees. EHR. xv, 1900, p. 529.

Hoare, H. W. H. The Evolution of the English Bible. New York, 1902. [Pp. 63, 321. On 'dominion.']

Gairdner, J. Lollardry and the Reformation in England. 1908.

CHEL. vol. ii, 1908. [Pp. 49, 439.]

Carrick, J. C. Wycliffe and the Lollards. 1908.

Dakin, A. Die Beziehungen John Wycliffe's und der Lollarden zu den Bettelmönchen. 1911.

Wilkins, H. J. Was John Wycliffe a Negligent Pluralist? 1915. [Appendix, Bristol, 1916.]

Cadman, S. P. Three Religious Leaders of Oxford. New York, 1916.

Taylor, H. O. Thought and Expression in the Sixteenth Century. New York, 1920.

Deanesly, M. The Lollard Bible. Cambridge, 1920. [P. 225.]

Shettle, G. T. John Wycliffe of Wycliffe. Leeds, 1922.

Hearnshaw, F. J. C. Social and Political Ideas of Some Great Medieval Thinkers. 1923. [P. 192.]

Workman, H. B. John Wyclif; A Study of the English Medieval Church. Oxford, 1926.

McNeill, J. T. Emphases in Wyclif's Teaching. Journ. of Religion, vii, 1927, p. 447.

Garrod, H. W. TLS. 22 Nov. 1928, p. 909. [Nickname Wyk.]

(b) Canon

[Vaughan, op. cit. vol. II, p. 379; Lechler, op. cit. appendix.]

Shirley, W. W. A Catalogue of the Works by Wyclif. Oxford, 1865.

Arnold, T. Select English Works of John Wyclif. Vol. III, Oxford, 1871, pp. xv, xvii.

Matthew, F. D. English Works of Wyclif. EETS. 1880.

N. & Q. 28 Feb., 2, 23 May, 13 June 1885, pp. 165, 357, 418, 478.

Jones, E. D. Authenticity of Some English Works ascribed to Wycliffe. Ang. xxx, 1907, p. 261.

Deanesly, M. The Lollard Bible. Cambridge, 1920.

(c) Editions of the English Works

[A list of Wycliffe's Latin writings will be found below, pp. 307–11.]

Collected English Wycliffite Writings.

J. H. Todd, Three Treatises by John Wyclif, Dublin, 1851; T. Arnold, Select English Works of John Wyclif, 3 vols. Oxford, 1869–71; F. D. Matthew, English Works of Wyclif, hitherto unprinted, EETS. 1880; H. E. Winn, Select English Writings, Oxford, 1929.

Separate English Wycliffite Pieces.

Treatise of Miraclis Pleyinge. T. Wright and J. O. Halliwell[-Phillipps], Reliquiae Antiquae, vol. I, 1841, p. 42; E. Mätzner, Altenglische Sprachproben, vol. II, Berlin, 1900, p. 222; (modernised) A. H. Benham, English Literature to the Death of Chaucer, New Haven, 1916, p. 525. [See Sir E. K. Chambers, The Medieval Stage, vol. II, Oxford, 1903, p. 102; A. S. Cook, Nation (New York), 27 May 1915, p. 599; G. R. Coffman, PMLA. xxxi, 1916, p. 456.]

Apology for Lollard Doctrines. J. H. Todd, Camden Soc. 1842. [See G. Siebert, Untersuchungen über An Apology, Charlottenburg, 1906.]

Last Age of the Church. J. H. Todd, Dublin, 1840. [See·J. Forshall and F. Madden, The Wycliffite Versions of the Holy Bible, vol. I, Oxford, 1850, p. viii.]

The holi prophete Dauid seith. M. Deanesly, The Lollard Bible, Cambridge, 1920, p. 445 (see pp. 241, 268, 274).

Of Feigned Contemplative Life; De Officio Pastorale. K. Sisam, Fourteenth Century Verse and Prose, Oxford, 1021, pp. 115, 119.

Thirty-Seven Conclusions of Lollards. J. Forshall, Remonstrance against Romish Corruption, 1851; (with Latin) H. F. B. Compston, EHR. xxvi, 1911, p. 738.

Twelve Conclusions of Lollards. H. S. Cronin, EHR. xxii, 1907, p. 292. [See M. Deanesly, The Lollard Bible, Cambridge, 1920, pp. 257, 282, 374.]

Twelve Tracts or Sermons by Purvey. (Item 2.) J. Forshall and F. Madden, The Wycliffite Versions of the Holy Bible, vol. I, Oxford, 1850, p. xiv. [See Deanesly, op. cit. pp. 270, 273, 303.]

[For other pieces in English sometimes ascribed to Wycliffe see Wells.]

(d) Criticism of English Works

Vattier, V. John Wyclyff: sa Vie, ses Œuvres, sa Doctrine. Paris, 1886.

Fürstenau, H. Johann von Wiclifs Lehren von der Einteilung der Kirche und von der Stellung der weltlichen Gewalt. Berlin, 1900.

Rosenkranz, A. E. Wycliffe's ethischsozialische Anschauung. Barmen, 1901.

Heine, D. Wiclif's Lehre vom Güterbesitz. Erlangen, 1903.

Loserth, J. Die ältesten Schreibschriften Wyclifs. Vienna, 1908.

—— Wyclifs Sendschriften, Flugschriften, und kleinere Werke. Vienna, 1910.

Fischer, H. Ueber die Sprache J. Wycliff's. Halle, 1880.

Gasner, E. Über Wyclifs Sprache. Göttingen, 1891.

CHEL. vol. II, 1908. [P. 49.]

Krapp, J. P. The Rise of English Literary Prose. New York, 1916. [P. 32.]

Allen, H. E. Speculum Vitae: Addendum. PMLA. xxxii, 1917, p. 133.

—— Writings Ascribed to Richard Rolle. New York, 1927. [P. 361. MS of Sunday Sermons.]

Deanesly, M. The Lollard Bible. Cambridge, 1920.

[See also Shirley, Arnold, Lechler, Vaughan, Jones, et al. under Canon and Editions. See below under Translations of Bible.]

(e) Wycliffite Translations of the Bible

[Wells, pp. 410, 828, 1018, 1068, 1125, 1219, 1272, 1311. See also M. Deanesly, The Lollard Bible, Cambridge, 1920; A. C. Paues, A Fourteenth Century English Biblical Version, Cambridge, 1902 (with valuable introduction not in edns of 1904, 1909).]

Editions. [Both versions.] J. Forshall and F. Madden, The Wycliffite Versions of the Holy Bible, 4 vols. Oxford, 1850.

ickering, W. 1848. [New Testament, earlier version.]

osworth, J. and Waring, G. Gothic and Anglo-Saxon Gospels, parallel with Tyndale. 1865; 1888 (3rd edn).

xeat, W. W. The New Testament in English. A Version by John Wycliffe revised by J. Purvey about 1388. Oxford, 1879.

— Job, Psalms, Ecclesiastes, Song of Songs. Oxford, 1881.

aw, T. G. and Hall, J. The New Testament in Scots (Nesbet's Purvey, 1520). 3 vols. STS. 1901–4.

ollard, A. W. 15th Century Prose and Verse. 1901 (Arber's English Garner), p. 193. [Part of Prologue, 2nd version.]

eanesly, M. The Lollard Bible. Cambridge, 1920, p. 456 (see pp. 275–8). [Purvey's Epilogue to St Matthew's Gospel.]

Studies. [*ten Brink*, vol. II, pp. 16, 26, 32; HEL. vol. II, 1908, p. 57, 440; Ency. Brit. ider 'Bible'; DNB. under 'Wycliffe,' 'Purvey,' 'Hereford'.]

aass, M. Wyclifs Bibelübersetzung. Archiv, XXIX, 1861, p. 221.

oughton, J. Our English Bible. 1878.

ombert, J. I. English Versions of the Bible. 1883; 1907 (enlarged).

asner, E. Über Wyclifs Sprache. Göttingen, 1891.

orster, E. Wyclif als Übersetzer. Zeitschrift für Kirchengeschichte, XII, 1891, pts 3, 4.

rimm, F. Das syntaktische Gebrauch der Praepositionen bei Wyclif und Purvey. Marburg, 1891.

ager, C. H. A. Pecock's Repressor and the Wycliffite Bible. MLN. IX, 1894, p. 193.

atthew, F. D. The Authorship of the Wycliffite Bible. EHR. x, 1895, p. 91.

oulton, W. F. A History of the English Bible. 1895.

eat, W. W. Trans. Philolog. Soc. 1895–8, p. 212. [Dialect.]

asquet, F. A. The Old English Bible and Other Essays. 1897; 1908.

rr, J. W. Ueber das Verhältnis der Wiclifitischen und der Purvey'schen Bibel-übersetzung zur Vulgata. Leipzig, 1902.

oare, H. W. H. The Evolution of the English Bible. 1902 (2nd edn).

ues, A. C. A Fourteenth Century English Biblical Version. Cambridge, 1902. [Valuable introduction not in edns of 1904, 1909.]

tmann, F. J. Formen und Syntax des Verbums bei Wyclif und Purvey. Weimar, 1902.

ollack, E. Vergleichende Studien zu der Hereford, Wyclif, und Purvey Bibel-übersetzung und der lateinischen Vulgata. Leipzig, 1903.

Smith, H. Syntax der Wyclif-Purvey Übersetzung. Ang. xxx, 1907, p. 413. [See also his Marburg dissertation, 1907.]

Thamm, W. Das Relativpronomen in der Bibelübersetzung Wyclifs und Purveys. Berlin, 1908.

Pollard, A. W. Records of the English Bible. Oxford, 1911.

Tucker, E. C. The Wycliffite Epistle to the Romans compared with the Latin Original. Yale Stud. XLIX, 1914.

Hulme, W. H. Worcester Text of Acts. Western Reserve University Bulletin, XXI, 1918, no. 4, p. 25.

Deanesly, M. The Lollard Bible. Cambridge, 1920. [Pp. 225, 252, 300, 376, 381.]

Kox, M. Studien zur Syntax des Artikels Wyclif's und Purvey's. Kiel, 1922.

[For bibliography and summary of other Bible versions and commentaries, see *Wells*, ch. viii, and Paues and Deanesly, above.]

XI. JOHN GOWER (1330?–1408?)

[G. C. Macaulay, edn, 4 vols. Oxford, 1899–1902, and CHEL. vol. II, 1908, pp. 133, 452 (for criticism, see *Wells*); *Wells*, pp. 585, 865, 994, 1026, 1083, 1139, 1185, 1229, 1283, 1320, 1418.]

(a) Collected Edition

G. C. Macaulay, 4 vols. Oxford, 1899–1902. [For criticism, see *Wells*, p. 865.]

(b) General Treatments

[G. C. Macaulay, as above; *ten Brink*, vol. II, pp. 38, 99, 132; W. J. Courthope, A History of English Poetry, vol. I, 1895, p. 305; H. Morley, English Writers, vol. IV, 1889, pp. 150, 169, 201.]

Ellis, G. Specimens of the Early English Poets. Vol. I, 1801. [P. 169.]

Brydges, Sir S. E. Censura Literaria. Vol. x, 1809. [P. 346.]

—— The British Bibliographer. Vol. II, 1811. [P. 1.]

Quart. Rev. XXVII. 1858, p. 3.

Spies, H. E. Studien, XXVIII, 1900, p. 161 see also JEGP. IV, 1902, p. 118), XXXII, 1903, p. 251, XXXIV, 1904, p. 169.

Snell, F. W. The Age of Chaucer. 1901. [P. 101.]

Ker, W. P. Essays on Medieval Literature. 1905. [P. 101.]

—— English Literature: Medieval. 1912. [P. 221.]

Koellreuter, M. Das Privatleben in England. Zurich, 1908.

Holzknecht, K. J. Literary Patronage in the Middle Ages. Philadelphia, 1923. [Pp. 147, 160.]

Fox, G. C. The Medieval Sciences in the Works of Gower. Princeton, 1931.

(c) Life

[G. C. Macaulay, Oxford edn, vol. IV.]

Leland, J. Commentarii de Scriptoribus Britannicis. Oxford, 1709; rptd Sir S. E. Brydges, Restituta, vol. II, 1816.

Thynne, F. Animadversions. 1599; ed. Chaucer Soc. ser. 2, XIII, 1876.

Todd, H. J. Illustrations of Gower and Chaucer. 1810.

Nicholas, H. N . Retrospective Rev. ser. 2, II, 1827–8, p. 103.

Pauli, R. Confessio Amantis. 1857. [Introduction.]

Bech, L. Ang. v, 1882, p. 313.

Meyer, K. John Gower's Beziehungen zu Chaucer und Richard II. Bonn, 1889.

Lücke, E. Ang. XIV, 1891, pp. 77, 147.

[See also DNB.; N. & Q. 25 Jan. 1902, p. 68, 19 July 1902, p. 59. On tomb see Berthelette's edn of Confessio, 1532, 1534; J. Stow, Survey of London, 1633, p. 450; R. Gough, Sepulchral Monuments, vol. II, 1786, p. 24; G. C. Macaulay, Oxford edn, vol. IV, p. xix; CHEL. vol. II, 1908, p. 134.]

(d) Mirour de l'Omme; Minor French Poems

[G. C. Macaulay, Oxford edn; Wells, pp. 587, 865, 994, 1026, 1139, 1229, 1418.]

Editions. [All poems.] G. C. Macaulay, Oxford edn, vol. I. [Minor poems.] Roxburghe Club, 1850; E. Stengel, Marburg, Ausgaben und Abhandlungen, LXIV, 1886.

Studies.

Mirour.

Academy, 13 April 1895, p. 315, 27 July 1895, p. 71, 3 Aug. 1895, p. 91.

Flügel, E. Ang. XXIV, 1901, p. 437. [Social conditions.]

L'Areine au Mer. Athenaeum, 18 May 1901, p. 632.

Hamilton, G. L. MLN. XIX, 1904, p. 51. [Verse 23449.]

Fowler, R. E. Une Source française des Poèmes de Gower. Maçon, 1905.

Kittredge, G. L. MLN. XXI, 1906, p. 239. [Milton parallel.]

Tatlock, J. S. P. and Kittredge, G. L. Chaucer Soc. ser. 2, XXXVII, 1907, p. 220, XLII, 1909, p. 80. [Date.]

CHEL. vol. II, 1908, pp. 139, 452–4.

Lowes, J. L. Spenser and Gower's Mirour. PMLA. XXIX, 1914, p. 388.

Minor Poems.

Un Traitie, Quixley's Translation. Ed. H. N MacCracken, Yorkshire Archaeologic Journ. XX, 1909, p. 33.

Koeppel, E. Ballades and Chaucer. Studien, XX, 1895, p. 154.

Cohen, H. L. The Ballade. New York, 191 [P. 264.]

(e) Vox Clamantis; Minor Latin Poems

[CHEL. vol. II, 1908, pp. 143, 153, 45 Wells, pp. 589, 865, 1139, 1418.]

Editions. Roxburghe Club, 1850; G. Macaulay, Oxford edn, vol. IV; (minor poem T. Wright, Political Poems and Songs, vol. Rolls Ser. 1859, pp. 346, 356, 360, 417.

Eberhard, O. Der Bauernaufstand vo Jahre 1381 in der englischen Poesie. Ang stische Forschungen, LI, 1917, p. 37.

(f) Confessio Amantis

[G. C. Macaulay, Oxford edn, vol. II, p. 14 Wells, pp. 591, 866, 1026, 1083, 1139, 122 1283, 1320, 1418.]

MSS. [At least 38. See G. C. Macaula Oxford edn, vol. II, p. cxxxviii; H. Spi E. Studien, XXVIII, 1900, p. 200 (see JEG IV, 1902, p. 118), XXXII, 1903, p. 255, XXX 1904, p. 175; Archiv, CX, 1903, p. 103; We p. 1083; N. & Q. 29 May 1926, p. 389.]

Editions. R. Pauli, 1857; G. C. Macaula Oxford edn, vols. II, III; G. C. Macaula EETS. Ex. Ser. 1900, 1901; (selection) Morley, 1889.

Spanish version. A. Birch-Hirschfeld, Le zig, 1909.

Selections. G. C. Macaulay, Oxford, 190 M. W. Easton, Readings in Gower, Ha 1896; R. Wülcker, Lesebuch, 2 pts, Ha 1874–9; E. Mätzner, Altenglische Spra proben, vol. I, Berlin, 1867; R. Morris, a W. W. Skeat, Specimens of Early English, v II, Oxford, 1894; A. S. Cook, Reader, Bost 1915; A. Brandl and O. Zippel, Mittelenglisc Sprach- und Literaturproben, Berlin, 19 W. A. Neilson and K. G. T. Webster, Ch British Poets of the 14th and 15th Centuri Boston, 1916; K. Sisam, Fourteenth Centu Verse and Prose, Oxford, 1921; Cambrid 1927.

Studies. [See also above, General Tre ments.]

Language.

Child, F. J. Observations on the Language Gower's Confessio Amantis. Memoirs American Academy of Arts and Scienc IX, 1867–73, p. 265.

Ellis, A. J. Early English Pronunciation. Vol. III, 1871. [P. 726.]

Tiete, G. Zu John Gower's Confessio Amantis, Lexicalisches. Breslau, 1889.

Fahrenberg, K. Zur Sprache. Archiv, LXXXIX, 1892, p. 389.

Spies, H. Lexicographisches Experiment. Hamburg, 1905.

—— Wörterbucharbeit. Archiv, CXVI, 1906, p. 111.

Förg, B. Die Konjunktionen. Tübingen, 1911.

Eichhorn, E. Das Partizipium. Kiel, 1912.

Steinhoff, E. Über den Gebrauch des Artikels. Heidelberg, 1916.

Kaplan, T. H. Gower's Vocabulary. JEGP. XXXI, 1932, p. 395.

Casson, L. F. Studies in the Diction of the Confessio Amantis. E. Studien, LXIX, 1934, p. 184.

Horton, B. J. C. Notes on the Language of John Gower. E. Studies, XVI, 1934, p. 209.

Verse.

Schipper, J. Englische Metrik. Vol. I, Bonn, 1881. [P. 279.]

Höfer, P. Alliteration bei Gower. Leipzig, 1890.

Skeat, W. W. Some Rimes. Academy, 5 March 1892, p. 230.

Easton, M. W. The Rhymes of Gower's Confessio Amantis. Philadelphia, 1895.

Saintsbury, G. A History of English Prosody. Vol. I, 1906. [P. 319.]

Bihl, J. Wirkungen des Rhythmus. Anglistische Forschungen, L, 1916.

Sources.

Eichinger, J. Die Troja Sage als Stoffquelle. Munich, 1900.

Stollreither, E. Quellen-Nachweise. Munich, 1901.

Hamilton, G. L. PMLA. XX, 1905, p. 179. [Roman de Troie.]

—— MP. IX, 1911–2, p. 323. [Sources, Bk VII.]

—— JEGP. XXVI, 1927, p. 491.

Walz, G. Das Sprichwort. Munich, 1907.

Macaulay, G. C. CHEL. vol. II, 1908. [P. 150.]

Gilbert, A. H. Speculum, III, 1928, p. 84.

Gower and Chaucer.

Hales, J. W. Athenaeum, 24 Dec. 1881, p. 851.

Ang. V, 1882, p. 313.

Meyer, K. Zu Gower's Beziehungen zu Chaucer und Richard II. Bonn, 1889.

Rumbaur, O. Die Geschichte von Appius und Virginia. Breslau, 1890.

Ang. XIV, 1891–2, pp. 77, 147. [Constance.]

Mirour and Prologue. Ang. XXIV, 1901, p. 437.

Hammond, E. P. Chaucer: A Bibliographical Manual. New York, 1908. [Pp. 75, 152, 278.]

Dodd, W. G. Courtly Love in Chaucer and Gower. Boston, 1913.

Garrett, R. M. Confessio Amantis and the Legend of Good Women. JEGP. XXII, 1923, p. 64.

[See also Eichhorn, Bihl, above.]

Miscellaneous.

Flügel, E. Pyramus and Thisbe. Ang. XII, 1889–90, p. 13.

Koellreuter, M. Das Privatleben in England. Zurich, 1908.

Gebhard, H. Langland's und Gower's Kritik der kirchlichen Verhältnisse. Homburg, 1911.

Cook, A. S. Latin Note in Confessio Amantis. Archiv, CXXXII, 1914, p. 395.

Eberhard, O. Der Bauernaufstand vom Jahre 1381 in der englischen Poesie. Anglistische Forschungen, LI, 1917, p. 43.

Wedel, T. O. The Medieval Attitude toward Astrology. New Haven, 1920. [P. 132.]

Knowlton, E. C. Classical Philology, XV, 1920, p. 380. [Genius, allegorical. See also MLN. XXXIX, 1924, p. 89.]

Berndt, E. Nature in Gower. Palaestra, CX, 1923, p. 43.

Pietsch, K. Manly Anniversary Studies, Chicago, 1923, p. 323. [Portuguese original of Spanish text.]

Thomas, G. A. A Study of the Influence of Langland's Piers Plowman and Gower. Ithaca, 1927.

Manly, J. M. On the Question of the Portuguese Translation of Gower's Confessio Amantis. MP. XXVII, 1930, p. 467.

Fox, G. G. The Mediaeval Sciences in the Works of John Gower. Princeton, 1931.

(g) In Praise of Peace

[Wells, pp. 590, 865, 1139, 1418.]

Editions. T. Wright, Political Poems and Songs, vol. II, Rolls Ser. 1861, p. 4; W. W. Skeat, The Complete Works of Chaucer, vol. VII, Oxford, 1897, p. 205; G. C. Macaulay, Oxford edn, vol. IV (on MS, vol. I, p. lxxix).

Studies.

Skeat, W. W. The Chaucer Canon. Oxford, 1900. [P. 100.]

Hammond, E. P. Chaucer: A Bibliographical Manual. New York, 1908. [P. 431.]

Daniels, R. B. Rhetoric in Gower's In Praise of Peace. Stud. Phil. XXXII, 1935, p. 62.

(h) Balade Moral of Gode Counsayle (Passe forthe, thou pilgryme)

[Wells, pp. 590, 865, 1418; CHEL. vol. II, 1908, p. 453.]

MSS. 1, Ashmole 59 (Bodleian); 2, Rawlinson C 86 (Bodleian); 3, BM. Add. 29729.

Edition. K. Meyer and M. Förster, Archiv, CI, 1898, p. 50 (see also CII, 1899, p. 213).

J. E. W.

III. GEOFFREY CHAUCER
(1340?—1400)

General Works: Bibliographies; Collected Editions; Selections; Modernisations and Translations; History of Criticism; Early Criticism and Scholarship; Canon; Chronology; General Studies; Miscellaneous Studies; Science; Influence; Sources; Language; Versification; Biographical Studies.

Minor Poems: ABC; Against Women Unconstant; An Amorous Compleint; Anelida and Arcite; Balade of Compleynt; Book of the Duchesse; Chaucer's Words unto Adam; Compleynt of Mars; Compleynt of Venus; Compleint to His Lady; Compleint to His Purs; Compleynt unto Pite; Former Age; Fortune; Gentilesse; Hous of Fame; Lak of Stedfastnesse; Lenvoy à Bukton; Lenvoy à Scogan; Merciles Beaute; Parlement of Foules; Proverbs; Rosemounde; Truth; Womanly Noblesse.

Longer Works: Romaunt of the Rose; Boethius; Troilus and Criseyde; Legend of Good Women; Astrolabe.

Canterbury Tales: Manuscripts; Editions; Modernisations; Comprehensive Studies; Special Studies; Plan; Fragments and Links; Groups and Motifs; General Prologue; Knight's Tale; Miller's Prologue and Tale; Reeve's Prologue and Tale; Cook's Prologue and Tale; Man of Law's Headlink, Prologue and Tale; Shipman's Prologue, or Man of Law's Endlink; Shipman's Tale; Prioress's Headlink and Tale; Prologue to Sir Thopas, and Sir Thopas; Prologue to Melibeus, and Melibeus; Monk's Prologue and Tale; Nun's Priest's Prologue, Tale, and Epilogue; Physician's Tale; Words of the Host; Pardoner's Prologue, Tale, and Endlink; Wife of Bath's Prologue and Tale; Friar's Prologue and Tale; Summoner's Prologue and Tale; Clerk's Headlink, Prologue and Tale; Merchant's Prologue, Tale, and Epilogue; Squire's Prologue and Tale; Words of the Franklin and Franklin's Tale; Second Nun's Prologue and Tale; Canon's Yeoman's Prologue and Tale; Manciple's Prologue and Tale; Parson's Prologue and Tale, and the Retraction.

I. GENERAL TREATMENTS
A. GENERAL BIBLIOGRAPHY

Hammond, E. P. Chaucer: A Bibliographical Manual. New York, 1908. [Criticism in E. Studien, XLI, 1909–10, p. 136; Ang. Bbl.

xx, 1909, p. 225; JEGP. VIII, 1909, p. 619 Deutsche Literaturzeitung, xxx, 1909 p. 1191; Athenaeum, 6 May 1909, p. 556 MLR. IV, 1909, p. 526; MLN. XXIV, 1909 p. 159; and see Jahresbericht der ger manischen Philologie, xv, 1908, p. 275, xvi 1909, p. 205.] (*Hammond.*)

Wells, J. E. Manual of the Writings in Middle English, 1050–1400. New Haven, 1916. [Six Supplements, 1919, 1923, 1926, 1929, 1932 1935. Summaries of life, canon, chronology and chief facts, and synopses of individual works, with general bibliography and addns to Hammond, complete to July, 1935.] (*Wells.*)

Griffith, D. D. Bibliography of Chaucer 1908–1924. Seattle, 1926. [Addns to Hammond to 1925. On literary, economic social, religious, scientific backgrounds, as well as directly on Chaucer.] (*Griffith.*)

Martin, W. E. A Chaucer Bibliography 1925–1933. Durham, North Carolina, 1935

B. PRINCIPAL EDITIONS OF COMPLETE WORKS

[For fuller list see *Hammond*, p. 114. For edns of single works or groups, see under individual items.]

[Pynson's edn.] 3 pts, 1526. [No general title-page.]

The Workes of Geffray Chaucer. Ed. William Thynne, 1532; 1542; [1590?]; ed. facs W. W. Skeat, 1905 (1532 edn).

The Workes of Geffrey Chaucer. Ed. John Stow, 1561.

The Workes of our Antient and Learned English Poet, Geffrey Chaucer. Ed. Thomas Speght (with notes and glossary), 1598; 1598 (corrected); 1602; 1687.

The Works of Geoffrey Chaucer. Ed. John Urry (with contributions by T. Thomas W. Thomas and G. Dart), 1721.

The Poetical Works. Ed. Sir Harris Nicolas 6 vols. 1845, 1852; rev. R. Morris, 6 vols 1866, 1870, [1872], 1880, 1891, 1893. (Aldine edn.)

The Complete Works. Ed. W. W. Skeat 6 vols. (and a supplementary vol.), Oxford 1894–7. [The standard edn. Referred to as Oxford Chaucer. For criticism see *Hammond*, p. 145.]

The Complete Works. Ed. W. W. Skeat Oxford, 1895. [Text and Glossary. Referred to as Student's Chaucer.]

The Works. Ed. A. W. Pollard, H. F. Heath, M. H. Liddell, Sir W. S. McCormick, 1898. [Globe edn. Referred to as Globe Chaucer.]

The Complete Works. Ed. T. R. Lounsbury, 2 vols. New York, 1901.

The Complete Works. Ed. F. N. Robinson Boston, 1933. (Cambridge edn.)

C. EDITIONS OF SELECTED PIECES

Sweet, H. Second Middle English Primer. Oxford, 1876, 1905 (rev. edn).

Paton, F. N. Selections from Chaucer. 1888.

Robertson, J. L. The Select Chaucer. Edinburgh, 1902.

Greenlaw, E. Selections from Chaucer. Chicago, 1907.

Emerson, O. F. Poems of Chaucer. New York, 1911.

Child, C. G. Selections from Chaucer. Boston, 1912.

MacCracken, H. N. The College Chaucer. New Haven, 1913.

Kaluza, M. Chaucer Handbuch. Leipzig, 1919, 1927.

Neilson, W. A. and Patch, H. R. Selections from Chaucer. New York, 1921.

Legouis, É. Geoffrey Chaucer, Œuvres Choisis. Paris, 1923.

[For earlier selections, see *Hammond*, p. 216; and see under Minor Poems and Canterbury Tales.]

D. MODERNISATIONS AND TRANSLATIONS*

[*Hammond*, p. 220; *Griffith*, p. 24.]

Kynaston, Sir Francis. Amorum Troili et Creseidae. Libri duo priores Anglico-Latini. Oxford, 1635. [Latin rhymed verse.]

Dryden, John. Fables Ancient and Modern; Translated into Verse, from Homer, Ovid, Boccace, & Chaucer: with Original Poems. 1700. [The tales translated from Chaucer are the Knight's Tale, the Nun's Priest's Tale, the Flower and the Leaf, the Wife of Bath's Tale, and the Character of the Parson (imitated and enlarged) from the Prologue.]

Pope, Alexander. Poetical Miscellanies, The sixth Part, Printed for Jacob Tonson. 1709. [January and May, or, the Merchant's Tale: from Chaucer. Included in Ogle and Lipscomb; see below.]

—— Poetical Miscellanies, consisting of Original Poems and Translations publish'd by Mr. Steele. 1714. [The Wife of Bath her Prologue, from Chaucer. Included in Ogle and Lipscomb; see below.]

—— The Temple of Fame: A Vision. 1715; 1736. [Based on The House of Fame.]

Betterton, Thomas. Miscellaneous Poems and Translations by Several Hands, Printed for Bernard Lintot. 1712; 1720; 1722. [(i) Chaucer's Characters, or the Introduction to the Canterbury Tales: (ii) The Miller of Trompington, or, the Reve's Tale from Chaucer. (i) is included in Morell's edn of 1737, in Ogle and in Lipscomb; (ii) is included in Ogle; see below.]

Cobb, Samuel. The Carpenter of Oxford, or, the Miller's Tale, from Chaucer. Attempted in Modern English. To which are added, Two Imitations of Chaucer, By Matthew Prior. 1712. [Cobb's modernisation is included in Ogle; see below.]

'Grosvenor' (*i.e.* Estace Budgell?). The Whimsical Legacy, an Imitation of the Famous Sumner's Tale in Chaucer. Bee, II, 1733. [Included in Ogle and Lipscomb; see below.]

The Canterbury Tales of Chaucer. 1737. [Thomas Morell's edn. Betterton's modernisation of Chaucer's characters, and Dryden's modernisations of The Character of the Parson and The Knight's Tale are rptd in this volume.]

Ogle, George. Gualtherus and Griselda: or the Clerk of Oxford's Tale. From Boccace, Petrarch and Chaucer. To which are added, A Letter to a Friend, with the Clerk of Oxford's Character, &c. The Clerk of Oxford's Prologue from Chaucer. The Declaration, or L'envoy de Chaucer a les Maris de notre Temps, from Chaucer. The Words of our Host, from Chaucer. 1739.

The Canterbury Tales of Chaucer, Modernis'd by Several Hands. 3 vols. 1741; 2 vols. Dublin, 1742. [The 'hands' were George Ogle, the editor of the collection, Thomas Betterton, Samuel Boyse, Henry Brooke, Samuel Cobb, John Dryden, 'Grosvenor,' Jeremiah Markland, Alexander Pope. The following tales were included: Prologue, Knight's Tale, Knight-Miller Link, Miller's Tale, Miller-Reeve Link, Reeve's Tale, Reeve-Cook Link, Cook's Tale, Gamelyn, Man of Law Head-link, Prologue, Tale and End-link, Squire's Tale (with Ogle's conclusion modernised from Spenser), Squire-Franklin link and Merchant Head-link (in one as Prologue to the Merchant's Tale), Merchant's Tale, Wife of Bath's Prologue and Tale, Wife of Bath-Friar Link, Friar's Tale, Friar-Summoner Link, Summoner's Tale, Clerk Head-link and Tale.]

Jackson, Andrew. Matrimonial Scenes: consisting of The Seaman's Tale, The Manciple's Tale, the Character of the Wife of Bath, The Tale of the Wife of Bath and her Five Husbands. All modernized from Chaucer. 1750.

* This section, together with that on Early Criticism and Scholarship, has been contributed by Mrs J. E. Heseltine.

Brooke, Henry. A Collection of the Pieces formerly published by Henry Brooke. 4 vols. 1778. [This contains a rpt of Constantia, or the Man of Law's Tale, first ptd in Ogle, and included again in Lipscomb (see below).]

Penn, John. Poems. 1794. [The Squire's Tale. A Fragment from Chaucer.]

The Canterbury Tales of Chaucer; completed in a Modern Version. 3 vols. Oxford, 1795. [The editor of this collection was William Lipscomb. Modernisations by Ogle, Betterton, Dryden, Pope, Brooke, Markland and Boyse from Ogle's collection of 1741 (see above) are rptd in vols. i, ii and iii, with the exception of the Miller's Tale, Reeve's Tale, Nun's Priest's Tale and Gamelyn, and with occasional alterations in the links due to a different sequence of the tales. Vol. iii also contains the following modernisations by Lipscomb: Franklin's Prologue and Tale, Physician's Tale, Pardoner's Prologue and Tale, Shipman's Prologue and Tale, Shipman-Prioress Link, Prioress's Prologue and Tale, Prioress-Thopas Link, Thopas, Thopas-Melibeus Link, Melibeus, Melibeus-Monk Link, Monk's Tale, Monk-Nun's Priest Link, Nun's Priest's Tale and Endlink, Second Nun's Prologue and Tale, Second Nun-Canon's Yeoman Link, Canon's Yeoman's Tale, Manciple Headlink and Tale. Lipscomb has followed Tyrwhitt's order of the Tales.]

The Squire's Tale. Imitated from Chaucer. Monthly Mag. ii (Supplementary Number), 1796. [Rptd in The Poetical Register and Repository of Fugitive Poetry, 1806.]

Wharton, Richard. Fables: consisting of Select Parts from Dante, Berni, Chaucer and Ariosto. Imitated in English Heroic Verse. 2 vols. 1804–5. [In vol. i there is a modernisation of the Franklin's Tale, with (in a footnote) a modernisation of the description of the Franklin from the Prologue; vol. ii consists of a modernisation and continuation, in six books, of the Squire's Tale.]

Wordsworth, William. Poems by William Wordsworth including Lyrical Ballads and the Miscellaneous Pieces. 3 vols. 1815–20. [Vol. iii contains The Prioress's Tale, from Chaucer. This was rptd in The Poems of Chaucer Modernized, 1841; see below.]

Thurlow, E. H., Baron. Arcita and Palamon: after the excellent Poet, Geoffrey Chaucer. 1822.

Hunt, Leigh. The First Canto of the Squire's Tale of Chaucer, Modernized. Liberal, ii (no. iv), 1823. [Rptd, with revisions, in Stories in Verse, 1855.]

Hunt, Leigh. Death and the Ruffians. A Tale from Chaucer. New Monthly Mag. lxxiv, 1845. [A modernisation of the Pardoner's Tale. Rptd, revised, with a preface, in Stories in Verse, 1855.]

—— Wit and Humour. Selected from the English Poets. 1846. [Includes selections from Chaucer, with a modernised version in prose printed below. The extracts are from the Prologue, Friar's Tale, Pardoner's Tale, Merchant's Tale, Nun's Priest's Tale and Wife of Bath's Tale.]

Kannegiesser, C. L. Gottfried Chaucers Canterburysche Erzählungen. 2 vols. Zwickau, 1827. [In verse. Vol. i, Prologue and Knight's Tale; vol. ii, Franklin's Prologue and Tale, Pardoner's Prologue and Tale, Cook's Tale (i.e. Gamelyn).]

Clarke, C. Cowden. Tales from Chaucer in Prose. Designed chiefly for the use of young Persons. 1833; 1870. [The following are paraphrased: Prologue, Knight's Tale, Man of Law's Tale, Wife of Bath's Tale, Clerk's Tale, Squire's Tale, Pardoner's Tale, Prioress's Tale, Nun's Priest's Tale, Canon's Yeoman's Tale, Cook's Tale (i.e. Gamelyn).]

Griselda, The Clerk's Tale. Re-made from Chaucer. Blackwood's Mag. xli, 1837.

Powell, Thomas. The Nun's Priest's Tale or The Cock and the Fox. Modernised from Chaucer. Monthly Chronicle, vii, Feb. 1841. [C. F. E. Spurgeon, Chaucer Criticism and Allusion, vol. ii, Cambridge, 1925, says this may have been by Leigh Hunt.]

The Poems of Geoffrey Chaucer Modernized. 1841. [The modernisations are by R. H Horne (the editor), Wordsworth, Thomas Powell, Leigh Hunt, Z. A. Z., Robert Bell and Elizabeth Barrett Browning, and include the Prologue, the Cuckoo and the Nightingale, the Legends of Ariadne, Philomene and Phillis, the Manciple's Tale, the Reeve's Tale, the Flower and the Leaf, the Friar's Tale, the Complaint of Mars and Venus, Anelida and Arcite, the Squire's Tale, and the Franklin's Tale.]

The Persoune of a Toun. 1370. His Character from Chaucer by Mr. Dryden, altered and abridged, together with the Persone's Prologue and Tale. By the Persone of a Toun. 1841.

Fiedler, E. Canterburysche Erzählungen. Vol. i, Dessau, 1844. [The Tales of the Knight, Miller, Reeve, Cook and Man of Law in verse. No more pbd.]

Saunders, John. Canterbury Tales from Chaucer. 2 vols. 1845–7. [Prose versions of selected tales, interspersed with lengthy quotations.]

Gomont, H. Geoffrey Chaucer. Paris, 1847. [Extracts from the Prologue and Tales in verse and prose.]

de Chatelain, J. B. Contes de Cantorbery, traduits en vers français. 2 vols. 1857.

Hertzberg, Wilhelm. Geoffrey Chaucer's Canterbury-Geschichten. Uebersetzt in den Versmassen der Urschrift und durch Einleitung und Anmerkungen erläutert. Hildburghausen, 1866.

Clarke, Frederick. The Canterbury Tales of Geoffrey Chaucer: done into Modern English. Vol. I, 1870. [The following are modernised: Prologue, Knight's Tale, Knight-Miller Link, Miller's Tale, Miller-Reeve Link, Reeve's Tale, Reeve-Cook Link, Cook's Tale, Man of Law Headlink, Prologue and Tale, Wife of Bath's Prologue and Tale. No more pbd.]

Tatlock, J. S. P. and MacKaye, P. The Complete Works of Geoffrey Chaucer. New York, 1912, 1914; abridged by C. W. Ziegler, New York, 1922.

[For separate pieces, see under individual items.]

E. HISTORY OF CRITICISM

Koch, J. E. Studien, XLI, 1909–10, p. 113, XLVI, 1912, p. 98, XLVIII, 1914–5, p. 251, LV, 1921, p. 161; Ang. Bbl. XXII, 1911, p. 265, XXV, 1914, p. 327, XXVIII, 1917, p. 152; Germanisch-romanische Monatsschrift I, 1909, p. 490; Ang. XLIX, 1925, pp. 49, 193, 384 (see V. Langhans, Ang. XLIX, 1925, p. 357); introduction to edn of W. A. B. Hertzberg's Canterbury Tales, Berlin, 1925. [On recent criticism.]

Spurgeon, C. F. E. Chaucer devant la Critique en Angleterre et en France. Paris, 1911.

—— Five Hundred Years of Chaucer Criticism and Allusion. 7 pts, Chaucer Soc. 1914–24; 3 vols. Cambridge, 1925.

Lailavoix, L. [Preface to trn of É. Legouis' Geoffrey Chaucer, 1913.]

Schirmer, W. F. Die neueren Sprachen, XXXVI, 1928, pt 1. [On recent criticism.]

F. EARLY CRITICISM AND SCHOLARSHIP (TO 1870)

Caxton, William. [Prohemye to Canterbury Tales, 2nd edn, c. 1484.]

The Workes of Geffray Chaucer newly printed with dyvers workes whiche were never in print before. [Ed. William Thynne,] 1532, 1542, [1545 or 1550?]. [With preface by Sir Brian Tuke in form of dedicatory letter to Henry VIII.]

Gascoigne, George. Certayne Notes of Instruction concerning the making of verse in English. [At the end of The Posies of George Gascoigne, Esquire, 1575. References to Chaucer's rhyme and versification, sigs. T ii, T iii b, U ii b.]

Webbe, William. A Discourse of English Poetrie. 1586.

[Puttenham, George.] The Arte of English Poesie. 1589, pp. 12, 48–50, 54, 62, 69, 71–3, 120, 177, 187–8, 200.

Beaumont, Francis. [Letter to Thomas Speght in Speght's Chaucer; see below.]

The Workes of our Antient and Learned English Poet, Geffrey Chaucer. [Ed. Thomas Speght], 1598, 1602 (with addns), 1687.

Thynne, Francis. Animadversions. 1599; ed. F. J. Furnivall, Chaucer Soc. 1876. [First ptd in H. J. Todd's Illustrations of Gower and Chaucer, 1810.]

Verstegan, Richard. A Restitution of Decayed Intelligence. Antwerp, 1605. [Ch. vii.]

Peacham, Henry. The Compleat Gentleman Fashioning him absolute in the Qualities that may be required in a Noble Gentleman. 1622; 1634; 1661. [Ch. x.]

Brathwait, Richard. A Comment upon the Two Tales of Sir Jeffray Chaucer. The Miller's Tale and The Wife of Bath. 1665.

Rymer, Thomas. A Short View of Tragedy. 1693. [Ch. vii.]

Dryden, John. Fables Ancient and Modern. 1700.

Of the Old English Poets and Poetry. Muses Mercury or Monthly Miscellany, I, June 1707.

Sewell, George. A New Collection of original Poems, never before printed in any Miscellany, by the Author of Sir Walter Raleigh. 1720. [Prefatory verses and preface to The Proclamation of Cupid, and Preface to The Song of Troilus.]

The Works of Geoffrey Chaucer, compared with the Former Editions and many valuable MSS. Out of which, Three Tales are added which were never before Printed; By John Urry: Together with a Glossary. To the Whole is prefixed the Author's Life, and a Preface, giving an Account of this Edition. 1721. [Life by John Dart, Glossary and Preface by Timothy Thomas, both revised by W. Thomas.]

Dart, John. Westmonasterium, or the History and Antiquities of the Abbey Church of St. Peter's, Westminster. 2 vols. 1723, 1742. [A discussion of the authorship of the Ploughman's Tale in vol. I.]

Hearne, Thomas. Robert of Gloucester's Chronicle. 2 vols. 1724. [Vol. II, Appendix iv, A Letter to Mr. Bagford, containing some Remarks upon Geffry Chaucer and his Writings.]

Hearne, Thomas. Remarks and Collections of Thomas Hearne. Oxford Hist. Soc. II–IV, 1886–98. [Extracts from Hearne's diary, with frequent references to study of Chaucer MSS and edns between 1709 and 1713.]

The Canterbury Tales of Chaucer, in the Original, from the Most Authentic Manuscripts; And as they are Turn'd into Modern Language. 1737. [Ed. with a preface, by Thomas Morell. The book contains only the Prologue and the Knight's Tale.]

Ogle, George. Gualtherus and Griselda. 1739. [Preface.]

Biographia Britannica. Vol. II, 1748.

Upton, John. A Letter concerning a New Edition of Spenser's Faerie Queene. 1751. [On Spenser's debt to Chaucer.]

Warton, Thomas. Observations on the Faerie Queene of Spenser. 1754; 1762. [See especially sects. iii–x. The 2nd edn is occasionally expanded.]

—— The History of English Poetry. 4 vols. 1774–81. [Vol. i, sects. xii–xviii on Chaucer, and references in later vols.]

Johnson, Samuel. A Dictionary of the English Language. 2 vols. 1755. [In vol. i, The History of the English Language.]

Gray, Thomas. The Works of Thomas Gray. Ed. T. J. Mathias, 2 vols. 1814. [See vol. II, Metrum, Observations on English Metre, etc.]

Warton, Joseph. An Essay on the Genius and Writings of Pope. The Third Edition, corrected. 2 vols. 1772–82. [Vol. II, sects. vii, viii.]

Tyrwhitt, Thomas. The Canterbury Tales of Chaucer. To which are added, An Essay upon his Language and Versification; an Introductory Discourse; and Notes. 5 vols. 1775–8; 2 vols. Oxford, 1798.

[Neve, Philip.] Cursory Remarks on Some of the Ancient English Poets. 1789.

Ellis, George. Specimens of the Early English Poets. 3 vols. 1801 (2nd edn); 1803; 1811. [Ch. viii of vol. I is on Chaucer, and there are frequent references to him throughout this vol.]

Godwin, William. Life of Geoffrey Chaucer. 2 vols. 1803. [Vol. I, ch. xv, Troilus and Cressida; vol. II, chs. li, lv, Canterbury Tales.]

Southey, Robert. Specimens of the Later English Poets. 3 vols. 1807. [Preface.]

—— The Works of William Cowper. 15 vols. 1835–7. [Vol. II, ch. xii, Sketches of the Progress of English Poetry from Chaucer to Cowper.]

Scott, Sir Walter. The Works of John Dryden. 18 vols. 1808. [See vol. I, pp. 494–503 for criticism of the Fables.]

Nott, G. F. The Works of Henry Howard Earl of Surrey and of Sir Thomas Wyatt the Elder. 2 vols. 1815–6. [Vol. I, A Dissertation on the State of English Poetry before the Sixteenth Century.]

Hazlitt, William. Characters of Shakespear's Plays. 1817. [Troilus and Cressida, p. 83.]

—— Lectures on the English Poets. 1818. [Lecture II, On Chaucer and Spenser, and passages in Lecture III, On Shakespeare and Milton.]

Campbell, Thomas. Specimens of the British Poets; with Biographical and Critical Notices. 7 vols. 1819. [Vol. II.]

The Works of Chaucer. Retrospective Rev. IX, 1824.

Coleridge, S. T. The Table Talk and Omniana. Ed. T. Ashe, 1884. [15 March 1834.]

Hippisley, J. H. Chapters on Early English Literature. 1837, chs. i–vi.

Guest, Edwin. A History of English Rhythms. 2 vols. 1838. [Vol. I, pp. 29–34; vol. II, pp. 237–9, 255–8, 357–9.]

de Lécluze, E. J. Le Pèlerinage de Canterbury, 1328–1400. Revue française, VI, 1838.

D'Israeli, Isaac. Amenities of Literature. 3 vols. 1841. [Vol. I, p. 252.]

Horne, R. H. The Poems of Geoffrey Chaucer Modernized. 1841. [Introduction.]

De Quincey, Thomas. Homer and the Homeridae. Blackwood's Edinburgh Mag. Dec. 1841.

Browning, E. B. The Book of the Poets. Athenaeum, 4 June 1842.

Thoreau, H. D. Homer, Ossian, Chaucer. Dial, IV, 1844. [Rptd in Writings, Riverside Edition, vol. I, Boston, 1894.]

Lowell, J. R. Conversations on some of the Old Poets. Cambridge, U.S.A. 1845. [First Conversation, Chaucer.]

—— Chaucer. North American Rev. July 1870. [Rptd, revised and enlarged, in My Study Windows, 1871, and in Works, Riverside Edition, vol. III, 1890.]

Nicolas, Sir Harris. The Poetical Works of Geoffrey Chaucer with Memoir by Sir Harris Nicolas. 6 vols. 1845, 1866, etc. (Aldine edn.)

Hunt, Leigh. Wit and Humour. Selected from the English Poets. 1846. [Pp. 73–80 on Chaucer's Humour.]

Gomont, H. Geoffrey Chaucer Poète Anglais du XIVe Siècle. Analyses et Fragments. Paris, 1847.

Wright, Thomas. The Canterbury Tales of Geoffrey Chaucer. A New Text. 3 vols. 1847–51; 1853; 1860 (with addns).

Bell, Robert. Works of Chaucer [with Memoir, Introduction, and Notes]. 8 vols. 1854–6; 4 vols. 1878 (rev. edn with preliminary essay by W. W. Skeat).

Ruskin, John. The Harbours of England. 1856. [Pp. 6–8, Chaucer and the sea.]

Sandras, E. G. Étude sur G. Chaucer considéré comme Imitateur des Trouvères. Paris, 1859.

Marsh, G. P. The Origin and History of the English Language. 1862. [Lecture IX, Chaucer and Gower.]

Taine, H. Histoire de la Littérature anglaise. 4 vols., Paris, 1863–4. [Vol. I, ch. iii.]

Hertzberg, Wilhelm. Geoffrey Chaucer's Canterbury-Geschichten. Hildburghausen, 1866. [Preface; an expanded form of an earlier article entitled Geoffrey Chaucer's Leben und schriftstellerischer Charakter in Deutsches Museum, Feb. 1856.]

G. THE CHAUCER CANON

[Hammond, pp. 51, 406, 515; Wells, pp. 617, 869, 1142, 1232, 1323, 1421.]

Skeat, W. W. Oxford Chaucer. Vol. I, pp. lxii, 20, vol. v, p. ix.

—— Minor Poems. Oxford, 1896 (2nd edn), p. vii.

—— The Chaucer Canon. Oxford, 1900. [See Hammond, p. 55.]

Tatlock, J. S. P. The Development and Chronology of Chaucer's Works. Chaucer Soc. 1907, p. 9.

—— Chaucer's Retractions. PMLA. xxviii, 1913, p. 521.

Emerson, O. F. A New Note on the Knight's Tale. [Studies in Celebration of J. M. Hart. New York, 1910.]

Greg, W. W. Attributions in MS. R, 3, 17. MLR. viii, 1913, p. 539.

Campbell, G. H. Chaucer's Prophecy in 1586. MLN. xxix, 1914, p. 195.

Brusendorff, A. The Chaucer Tradition. Copenhagen, 1925, pp. 43, 178, 278, 426, 427, 433, list 151, 445.

Langhans, V. Book of the Leoun; De Contemptu Mundi. Ang. lii, 1928, pp. 113, 325.

Brown, Carleton. Chaucer's Wretched Engendring. PMLA. l, 1935, p. 69. [The 'An Holy Medytacion' attrib. to Lydgate?]

H. CHRONOLOGY OF CHAUCER'S WORKS

[Hammond, p. 70 (see also JEGP. viii, 1909, p. 621); Wells, pp. 623, 869, 994, 1084, 1142, 232, 1323.]

ten Brink, B. Chaucer: Studien zur Geschichte seiner Entwicklung und zur Chronologie seiner Schriften. Münster, 1870.

—— Early English Literature. Vol. ii, 1892, p. 37.

—— E. Studien, xvii, 1892, pp. 1, 189.

Furnivall, F. J. Trial Forewords. 1871. [See also Athenaeum, 1 July, 14 Oct. 1871, pp. 16, 494.]

Koch, J. The Chronology of Chaucer's Writings. Chaucer Soc. 1890.

—— E. Studien, lv, 1921, p. 161; Ang. xlvi, 1922, p. 1.

—— Geoffrey Chaucer's kleinere Dichtungen. Heidelberg, 1928, p. 4.

Skeat, W. W. Oxford Chaucer. Vol. i, p. lxii, vol. ii, p. xxxvii.

Pollard, A. W. A Chaucer Primer. 1903, p. 46.

—— Globe Chaucer. P. xxii.

Lowes, J. L. PMLA. xix, 1904, p. 593, xx, 1905, p. 748, xxiii, 1908, p. 285; MLN. xxvii, 1912, p. 45; MP. viii, 1910–1, pp. 165, 305.

Root, R. K. The Poetry of Chaucer. Boston, 1906, 1922 (rev. edn).

Tatlock, J. S. P. The Development and Chronology of Chaucer's Works. Chaucer Soc. 1907. [Criticism: Ang. Bbl. xx, 1909, p. 129; E. Studien, xli, 1910, p. 405; Nation (New York), 5 March 1908, p. 220.]

Emerson, O. F. Poems of Chaucer. New York, 1911, pp. xviii, xxviii.

Vockrodt, G. Die Reimtechnik Chaucer's als Mittel zur chronologischen Bestimmung seiner in Reimpaar geschriebenen Werke. Halle, 1914.

Tupper, F. PMLA. xxxvi, 1921, p. 219.

Cowling, G. H. Chaucer. 1927, p. 40. [See also RES. ii, 1926, p. 311; J. E. Lineberger, MLN. xlii, 1927, p. 239.]

Langhans, V. Ang. liii, 1929, p. 235. [Dates of prose pieces.]

[See also under individual works.]

I. GENERAL STUDIES

[Hammond, pp. 515, 542; Wells, pp. 599, 867, 1027, 1140, 1230, 1320, 1419; Griffith, p. 27.]

ten Brink, B. Chaucer: Studien zur Geschichte seiner Entwicklung und zur Chronologie seiner Schriften. Münster, 1870.

—— Early English Literature. Vol. ii, 1892, p. 33.

Ward, Sir A. W. Chaucer. 1879. (English Men of Letters Ser.)

Morley, H. English Writers. Vol. v, 1890, p. 83.

Lounsbury, T. R. Studies in Chaucer. 3 vols. New York, 1892.

Brandl, A. Paul's Grundriss der germanischen Philologie. Vol. ii, Strasburg, 1893, p. viii. [Mittelenglische Literatur, sects. 83–96.]

Pollard, A. W. A Chaucer Primer. 1893; 1903 (rev. edn).

Jusserand, J. J. A Literary History of the English People. Vol. i, 1894, p. 267; 1926 (3rd edn).

Courthope, W. J. A History of English Poetry. Vol. I, 1895, p. 247.

Wülcker, R. Geschichte der englischen Literatur. Vol. I, Leipzig, 1896, p. 146.

Snell, F. J. The Fourteenth Century. 1899.

—— The Age of Chaucer. 1901.

Björkmann, E. Geoffrey Chaucer. Stockholm, 1906.

Root, R. K. The Poetry of Chaucer. Boston, 1906, 1922 (rev. edn).

Saintsbury, G. CHEL. vol. II, 1908, p. 156.

Legouis, É. Chaucer. Paris, 1910; tr. Eng. L. Lailavoix, 1913.

—— A History of English Literature. Vol. I, 1926, p. 82.

Ker, W. P. English Literature, Medieval. 1912, ch. 9.

Hadow, G. E. Chaucer and his Times. 1914; 1926.

Edmunds, E. W. Chaucer and his Poetry. 1915.

Kittredge, G. L. Chaucer and his Poetry. Cambridge, U.S.A. 1915.

Langhans, V. Untersuchungen zu Chaucer. Halle, 1918.

—— Zu Chaucers Traumgedichten. Ang. LI, 1927, p. 323.

Kaluza, M. Chaucer Handbuch. Leipzig, 1919.

Jack, A. A. A Commentary on the Poetry of Chaucer and Spenser. Glasgow, 1920.

Coulton, G. G. Chaucer and his England. 1921.

Brendon, J. A. The Age of Chaucer. 1924.

Brusendorff, A. The Chaucer Tradition. Copenhagen, 1925.

Manly, J. M. Some New Light on Chaucer. New York, 1926.

Cowling, G. H. Chaucer. 1927.

French, R. D. A Chaucer Handbook. New York, 1927.

Krog, F. Studien zu Chaucer und Langland. Anglistische Forschungen, LXV, 1928.

Looten, C. Chaucer, ses Modèles, ses Sources, sa Religion. Lille, 1931.

Lowes, J. L. The Art of Geoffrey Chaucer. British Academy Lecture, 1931.

—— Geoffrey Chaucer. 1934.

Chesterton, G. K. Chaucer. 1932.

McNabb, V. Geoffrey Chaucer. A Study in Genius and Ethics. 1934.

[See also DNB. and Ency. Brit. under 'Chaucer.']

J. MISCELLANEOUS STUDIES

[*Hammond*, pp. 515, 542; *Wells*, pp. 867, 1027, 1140, 1230, 1321, 1419; *Griffith*, pp. 33, 36, 40, 42. See also under individual works and sections next following.]

Pollard, A. W. The Development of Chaucer's Genius. Academy, 10 March 1906, p. 227.

Koellreuter, M. Das Privatleben in England nach Chaucer, Gower, und Langland. Halle 1908.

Baskervill, C. R. PMLA. XXVI, 1911, p. 593 [Use of aube.]

Lowes, J. L. Illustrations of Chaucer, chiefly from Deschamps. Romanic Rev. II, 1911 p. 113.

Schofield, W. H. Chivalry in English Literature. Cambridge, U.S.A. 1912, p. 11.

Dodd, W. G. Courtly Love in Chaucer and Gower. Boston, 1913.

Helmeke, T. Beteuerungen und Verwunschungen bei Chaucer. Kiel, 1913.

McCully, B. Chivalry in Chaucer. Trans American Philolog. Ass. XLIV, 1913, p. lxv

Meyer, E. Die Charakterzeichnung be Chaucer. SEP. XLVIII, 1913.

Snell, A. L. F. Chaucer's Comments on hi Methods of Composition. English Journ II, 1913, p. 231.

Heinrich, K. Das geographische Weltbild de späteren englischen Mittelalters. Freiburg 1915.

Berndt, E. Dame Nature in der englische Literatur. Palaestra, CX, 1916, p. 38.

Korsch, H. Chaucer als Kritiker. Berlin, 1916

Tatlock, J. S. P. Chaucer and Wiclif. MI XIV, 1916–7, p. 257,

—— Puns in Chaucer. [Flügel Memoria Volume, Palo Alto, 1916, p. 228.]

Eberhard, O. Der Bauernaufstand vom Jahr 1381 in der englischen Poesie. Anglistisch Forschungen, LI, 1917.

Hayes, J. A Study in Chaucer. Cork, 1917.

Langhans, V. Untersuchungen zu Chaucer Halle, 1918.

Emerson, O. F. Science in Chaucer. MI XVII, 1919–20, p. 287.

—— Chaucer and Medieval Hunting. Ro manic Rev. XIII, 1922, p. 115.

—— Chaucer Essays and Studies. Clevelanc 1930.

Maxfield, E. K. Chaucer and Religious Re form. PMLA. XXXIV, 1919, p. 64.

Benham, A. R. Chaucer and the Renaissance Chaucer and Ovid; Chaucer and Molière South Atlantic Quart. XX, 1921, p. 330.

Cox, S. H. Chaucer's Cheerful Cynicism MLN. XXXVI, 1921, p. 475.

Kellett, E. E. Chaucer as a Critic of Dante London Mercury, IV, 1921, p. 282. [Rpt in Suggestions, Cambridge, 1923.]

Knowlton, E. C. Nature in Middle Englisl JEGP. XX, 1921, p. 186.

Koch, J. Alte Chaucer-Probleme und neu Lösungsversuche. E. Studien, LV, 192. p. 161.

Bregy, K. The Inclusiveness of Chaucer Catholic World, CXV, 1922, p. 304.

Huxley, A. Chaucer. [In On the Margin ,1923

Pieper, W. Das Parlament in der mittelenglischen Literatur. Archiv, cxlvi, 1923,
p. 187.

Wells, W. H. Chaucer as a Literary Critic.
MLN. xxxix, 1924, p. 255.

Lawrence, C. E. The Personality of Geoffrey
Chaucer. Quart. Rev. ccxlii, 1924, p. 315.

Iijima, I. Langland and Chaucer. Boston, 1925.

Kuhl, E. P. Chaucer and the Church. MLN.
xl, 1925, p. 321.

Looten, C. Chaucer et Dante. Revue de
Littérature comparée, v, 1925, p. 545.

Madeleva, M. Chaucer's Nuns and Other
Essays. New York, 1925.

Barry, R. W. Sententiae of Chaucer. Stanford
University Abstracts of Dissertations,
1924–6, p. 91.

Manly, J. M. Chaucer and the Rhetoricians.
British Academy lecture, 1926.

Patch, H. R. Chaucer and Medieval Romance.
[Essays in Memory of Barrett Wendell,
Cambridge, U.S.A. 1926, p. 95.]

—— Chaucer and Lady Fortune. MLR. xxii,
1927, p. 377.

—— Chaucer and the Common People.
JEGP. xxix, 1930, p. 376.

Spencer, T. Chaucer's Hell. Speculum, ii,
1927, p. 177.

Krog, F. Studien zu Chaucer und Langland.
Anglistische Forschungen, lxv, 1928.
[Chaucer and times; development.]

Lüdeke, H. Die Funktionen des Erzählers in
Chaucers epischer Dichtung. SEP. lxxii,
1928.

Chapman, C. O. Chaucer on Preachers and
Preaching. PMLA. xliv, 1929, p. 178.

Getty, A. K. Chaucer's Changing Conceptions of the Humble Lover. PMLA. xliv,
1929, p. 202.

—— The Mediaeval-Modern Conflict in
Chaucer's Poetry. PMLA. xlvii, 1932, p. 385.

Evans, J. Chaucer and Decorative Art. RES.
vi, 1930, p. 408.

Krauss, R., Braddy, H., and Kase, C. R.
Three Chaucer Studies. New York, 1932.

Dempster, G. Dramatic Irony in Chaucer.
Palo Alto, 1932.

Hamilton, M. P. Notes on Chaucer and the
Rhetoricians. PMLA. xlvii, 1932, p. 403.

K. CHAUCER AND SCIENCE

[Griffith, p. 58.]

Brae, A. E. [Edn of Astrolabe, 1870.]

Lounsbury, T. R. Studies in Chaucer. Vol. ii,
New York, 1892, pp. 389, 395.

Skeat, W. W. Oxford Chaucer. Vol. iii.

Browne, H. W. MLN. xxiii, 1908, p. 53.
[Astrology.]

Tatlock, J. S. P. Astrology in Franklin's
Tale. [Kittredge Anniversary Papers,
Boston, 1913, p. 339.]

Lowes, J. L. Nation (New York), 11 Sept.
1913, p. 233; MP. xi, 1914, p. 491; MLN.
xxxi, 1916, p. 185. ['Loveres Maladye.']

Tupper, F. Chaucer's Doctor. Nation (New
York), 26 June 1913, p. 640.

Grimm, F. Astronomical Lore in Chaucer.
Nebraska University Stud. no. 2, 1919.

Emerson, O. F. Opie of Thebes. MP. xvii,
1919–20, p. 287.

Curry, W. C. JEGP. xviii, 1919, p. 593,
xxii, 1923, p. 347; PMLA. xxxv, 1920,
p. 189, xxxvii, 1922, p. 30; MP. xix, 1922,
p. 395; Texas Rev. viii, 1923, p. 307; MLN.
xxxviii, 1923, p. 94; Ang. xlvii, 1923,
p. 213; E. Studien, lviii, 1924, p. 24; PQ.
iv, 1925, p. 1. [Physiognomy, medicine,
astrology, dreams, etc.]

—— Chaucer and the Medieval Sciences. New
York, 1926.

Wedel, T. O. The Medieval Attitude toward
Astrology. Yale Stud. lx, 1920, p. 142.

Farnham, W. E. The Dayes of the Mone.
Stud. Phil. xx, 1923, p. 70.

Damon, S. F. Chaucer and Alchemy. PMLA.
xxxix, 1924, p. 782.

Manly, J. M. Some New Light on Chaucer.
New York, 1926, p. 235.

—— Canterbury Tales. New York, 1928,
p. 132.

[See also under individual works.]

L. INFLUENCE ON SUCCESSORS

[Hammond, pp. 220, 237; Wells, pp. 1140,
1321, 1419; Griffith, pp. 33; C. F. E. Spurgeon,
under History of Criticism, p. 211 above.]

Lounsbury, T. R. Studies in Chaucer. Vol. i,
New York, 1892, ch. 7.

Ainger, A. Lectures and Essays. Vol. ii, 1905,
p. 136.

Tobler, A. Chaucer's Influence on English
Literature. Berlin, 1905.

Saintsbury, G. English Chaucerians. CHEL.
vol. ii, 1908, p. 197.

Gregory Smith, G. Scottish Chaucerians.
CHEL. vol. ii, 1908, p. 239.

Hertwig, D. Der Einfluss von Chaucer's
Canterbury Tales auf die englische
Literatur. Marburg, 1908.

Nadal, T. W. PMLA. xxiii, 1908, p. 646,
xxv, 1910, p. 640. [Spenser.]

Canby, H. S. The Short Story in English.
New York, 1909, p. 78.

Snyder, F. D. MLN. xxv, 1910, p. 78. [Dunbar.]

Hart, W. M. MP. ix, 1911, p. 17. [Hans Sachs.]

Rosenthal, B. Spenser's Verhältniss zu
Chaucer. Berlin, 1911.

Hammond, E. P. Lydgate's Thebes. Ang.
xxxvi, 1912, p. 360.

Brown, C. E. Studien, xlvii, 1913, p. 59.
[Lydgate.]

Long, P. W. From Troilus to Euphues. [Kittredge Anniversary Papers, Boston, 1913, p. 367.]

Schultz, J. R. Sir Walter Scott and Chaucer. MLN. xxviii, 1913, p. 246.

Andrae, A. Ang. Bbl. xxvii, 1916, p. 56. [Longfellow.]

Cook, A. S. MLR. xi, 1916, p. 9. [Skelton.]

Adams, J. Q. MLN. xxxii, 1917, p. 187. [William Goddard.]

Rollins, H. E. Troilus Story from Chaucer to Shakespeare. PMLA. xxxii, 1917, p. 383.

Patch, H. R. MLN. xxxiii, 1918, p. 177. [Spenser, Dekker.]

Berdan, J. Early Tudor Poetry. New York, 1920, p. 48.

Jack, A. A. A Commentary on the Poetry of Chaucer and Spenser. Glasgow, 1920.

Schulze, K. Germanisch-romanische Monatsschrift, viii, 1920, p. 103. [Merchant of Venice.]

Benham, A. R South Atlantic Quart. xx, 1921, p. 330. [Renaissance.]

Golding, L. Saturday Rev. 25 Nov. 1922, p. 782. [Scottish Chaucerians.]

Ord, H. Chaucer the Rival Poet in Shakespeare's Sonnets. New York, 1922.

Root, R. K. Shakespeare misreads Chaucer. MLN. xxxviii, 1923, p. 346. [Merchant of Venice.]

Hammond, E. P. The Nine Syllabled Pentameter Line. MP. xxiii, 1925, p. 129.

Kuhl, E. P. TLS. 5 Nov. 1925, p. 739. [Nashe.]

—— MLN. xliii, 1928, p. 105. [F. Beaumont.]

Cawley, R. R. MLN. xli, 1926, p. 313. [Spenser.]

Koch, J. Ang. l, 1926, p. 104.

Berkelman, R. G. English Journ. xvi, 1927, p. 698. [Masefield.]

Magoun, F. P. MP. xxv, 1927, p. 129. [Spenser, Milton.]

TLS. 25 Aug. 1927, p. 565. [Jane Austen.]

Kellett, E. E. Reconsiderations. Cambridge, 1928.

Robertson, S. MLN. xliii, 1928, p. 105. [Wordsworth.]

Camden, C. RES. vi, 1930, p. 73. [Greene.]

McNeal, T. H. The Clerk's Tale as a Possible Source for Pandosto. PMLA. xlvii, 1932, p. 453.

Wright, L. B. William Painter and the Vogue of Chaucer as a Moral Teacher. MP. xxxi, 1933, p. 165.

Gebhardt, E. R. MLN. xlix, 1934, p. 452. [Jonson.]

M. SOURCES

[Hammond, p. 73; Wells, pp. 868, 1027, 1141, 1231, 1322, 1420; Griffith, p. 42. See also Kittredge, Legouis, Root, under General Studies, above.]

Lounsbury, T. R. Studies in Chaucer, his Life and Writings. Vol. ii, New York, 1892, p. 167.

Skeat, W. W. Oxford Chaucer. Vol. iii, p. 370 (and notes and introductions).

Cipriani, L. PMLA. xxii, 1907, p. 552. [Romance of Rose.]

Root, R. K. Chaucer's Dares. MP. v, 1907, p. 1.

Hinckley, H. B. Notes on Chaucer. Northampton, 1908, pp. 2, 96. [Sercambi, Statius.]

Forsmann, J. Einiges über französische Einflüsse in Chaucers Werken. Deutsche St Annenschule, 1909.

Lowes, J. L. MP. viii, 1910, pp. 165, 305. [Miroir de Mariage.]

—— MLR. v, 1910, p. 33. [French.]

—— MP. xiii, 1915, p. 19, xiv, 1917, p. 705. [Dante.]

—— Classics. Nation (New York), 1916, Supplement 2.

—— PMLA. xxxiii, 1918, p. 302. [Ovide Moralisé. See also S. B. Meech, PMLA. xlvi, 1931, p. 182.]

Morsbach, L., Root, R. K., Tatlock, J. S. P. E. Studien, xlii, 1910, p. 43, xliv, 1911, p. 1; Ang. xxxvii, 1913, p. 69. [Boccaccio.]

Bardelli, M. Qualche Contributo agli Studi sulle Relazioni del Chaucer col Boccaccio. Florence, 1911.

Koeppel, E. Archiv, cxxvi, 1911, p. 180. [De Amicitia.]

Wise, B. A. The Influence of Statius upon Chaucer. Baltimore, 1911.

Legouis, É. Geoffrey Chaucer. 1913, p. 44.

Young, K. Kittredge Anniversary Papers. Boston, 1913, p. 405. [Sercambi.]

—— Chaucer and the Liturgy. MLN. xxx, 1915, p. 97.

Fansler, D. S. Chaucer and the Roman de la Rose. New York, 1914. [See its bibliography.]

Tatlock, J. S. P. MLN. xxix, 1914, p. 97. [Dante.]

—— MP. xviii, 1921, p. 625. [Classics, Boccaccio.]

—— Chaucer and the Legenda Aurea. MLN. xlv, 1930, p. 296.

Tupper, F. Chaucer's Bed's Head. MLN. xxx, 1915, p. 5.

Seibert, H. Chaucer and Horace. MLN. xxxi, 1916, p. 304.

Cummings, H. The Indebtedness of Chaucer's Works to the Italian Works of Boccaccio. Cincinnati University Stud. x, pt 2, 1916.

Jefferson, B. L. Chaucer and the Consolation of Boethius. Princeton, 1917.

Ayres, H. M. Romanic Rev. x, 1919, p. 1. [Seneca.]

Shannon, E. F. MP. xvi, 1919, p. 609. [Lucan.]

Korten, H. Chaucer's literarische Beziehungen zu Boccaccio. Rostock, 1920.

Benham, A. R. South Atlantic Quart. xx, 1921, p. 337. [Ovid.]

Koch, J. Chaucer's Boethiusübersetzung. Ang. xlvi, 1922, p. 1.

—— E. Studien, lvii, 1923, p. 8. [Latin Classics.]

Schinnerl, H. Die Belesenheit Chaucers in der Bibel und der antiken Literatur. Munich, 1923.

Trigona, F. P. Chaucer. Imitatore del Boccaccio. Catania, 1923.

Wrenn, C. L. MLR. xviii, 1923, p. 286. [Horace.]

Mossé, F. Revue Germanique, 1923, p. 283. [Liturgy.]

McGovern, J. B. and Powell, L. F. The Decameron in England. N. & Q. 6, 27 Jan., 3 Feb. 1923, pp. 12, 72, 100.

Farnham, W. E. England's Discovery of the Decameron. PMLA. xxxix, 1924, p. 123.

Landrum, G. W. Chaucer's Use of the Vulgate. PMLA. xxxix, 1924, p. 75.

Schirmer, W. F. Boccaccio's Werke als Quelle G. Chaucers. Germanisch-romanische Monatsschrift, xii, 1924, p. 288.

Schleich, G. Die mittelenglische Umdichtung von Boccaccios de Claris Mulieribus. Palaestra, cxliv, 1924.

Beck, N. B. Chaucer and Boccaccio's Decamerone. Seattle, 1925.

Looten, C. Revue de Littérature comparée, v, 1925, p. 545. [Dante.]

Rand, E. K. Ovid and his Influence. Boston, 1925, p. 145.

Manly, J. M. Chaucer and the Rhetoricians. British Academy Lecture, 1926.

Bethel, J. P. The Influence of Dante on Chaucer's Thought and Expression. Cambridge, U.S.A. 1927.

Praz, M. New Criterion, vi, 1927, pp. 18, 138, 238. [Italy of Trecento.]

Shannon, E. F. Chaucer and the Roman Poets. Cambridge, U.S.A. 1929.

Meech, S. B. Chaucer and an Italian Translation of the Heroides. PMLA. xlv, 1930, p. 110.

McPeek, J. A. S. Did Chaucer know Catullus? MLN. xlvi, 1931, p. 293.

Hankins, J. E. MLN. xlix, 1934, p. 80. [Pervigilium Veneris.]

Coghill, N. K. Chaucer's Debt to Langland. Medium Aevum, iv, 1935, p. 89.

[See also under Gower, p. 207 above, and under individual works.]

N. LANGUAGE

[*Hammond*, pp. 464, 475, 481, 501, 504; *Wells*, pp. 868, 1027, 1141, 1231, 1322, 1420;

Griffith, p. 36. See also under individual writings.]

Tatlock, J. S. P. and Kennedy, A. G. Concordance to the Works of Geoffrey Chaucer, together with the Middle English Version of Le Roman de la Rose. Washington, 1927.

Child, F. J. Observations on the Language of Chaucer. Memoirs of American Academy, N.S. viii, 1863, p. 445.

Ellis, A. J. On Early English Pronunciation. Vol. i, pp. 241, 318, 342, vol. iii, p. 648, EETS. and Chaucer Soc. 1867–88.

Weymouth, R. F. On Early English Pronunciation with Especial Reference to Chaucer. 1874.

ten Brink, B. Chaucer's Sprache und Verskunst. Strasburg, 1884; ed. E. Eckhardt, Leipzig, 1920; tr. M. B. Smith, 1901.

Sweet, H. A History of English Sounds. Oxford, 1888.

Skeat, W. W. Oxford Chaucer. Vol. vi. [Glossary.]

Morsbach, L. Mittelenglische Grammatik. Halle, 1896.

Kaluza, M. Historische Grammatik der englischen Sprache. Berlin, 1900–1.

Jordan, R. Die mittelenglischen Mundarten. Germanisch-romanische Monatsschriften, ii, 1910, p. 124.

Moore, S. Historical Outlines of English Phonology. Ann Arbor, 1919.

—— Historical Outlines of English Phonology and Morphology. Ann Arbor, 1925.

Jespersen, O. Growth and Structure of the English Language. Leipzig, 1923 (4th edn).

Jordan, R. Handbuch der mittelenglische Grammatik. Heidelberg, 1925.

Remus, H. Untersuchungen über den romanischen Wortschatz Chaucer's. Halle, 1903.

—— Die kirchlichen und speziellwissenschaftlichen romanischen Lehnwörter Chaucers. SEP. xiv, 1906.

Wilson, L. R. Chaucer's Relative Construction. Stud. Phil. 1906, p. 1.

Kenyon, J. S. Syntax of the Infinitive in Chaucer. Chaucer Soc. ser. 2, xliv, 1908.

Frieshammer, J. Die sprachliche Form der Chaucerischen Prosa. SEP. xli, 1910.

Borst, E. Zur Stellung des Adverbs. E. Studien, xlii, 1910, p. 339.

Foster, C. H. Chaucer's Pronunciation of *ai, ay, ei, ey*. MLN. xxvi, 1910, p. 76.

Brown, C. Shul and Shal in Chaucer MSS. PMLA. xxvi, 1911, p. 6.

Gerike, F. Das Partizipium Praesentis bei Chaucer. Kiel, 1911.

Flügel, E. Benedicite. [Mätzke Memorial Volume, Palo Alto, 1911.]

Eichhorn, E. Partizipium bei Gower im Vergleich mit Chaucers Gebrauch. Kiel, 1912.

Skeat, W. W. Hit: Tense in Chaucer. N. & Q. 15 June 1912, p. 465.

Helmeke, T. Beteuerungen und Verwünschungen bei Chaucer. Kiel, 1913.

Eitle, H. Die Satzverknüpfung bei Chaucer. Anglistische Forschungen, XLIV, 1914.

—— Die Unterordnung der Sätze bei Chaucer. Tübingen, 1914.

Babcock, C. F. Metrical Use of Inflectional *e*. PMLA. XXIX, 1914, p. 59.

Hüttmann, E. Das Partizipium Praësentis bei Lydgate im Vergleich mit Chaucers Gebrauch. Kiel, 1914.

Wild, F. Die sprachlichen Eigentümlichkeiten der wichtigeren Chaucer-Handschriften. Wiener Beiträge, XLIV, 1915.

Emerson, O. F. Aet—after. MLR. XI, 1916, p. 460. [See also H. Bradley, MLR. XII, 1917, p. 74.]

Sauerbrey, G. Die innere Sprachform bei Chaucer. Halle, 1917.

Nöjd, R. Vocalism of Romanic Words in Chaucer. Upsala, 1919.

von Gross, E. Bildung des Adverbs bei Chaucer. Weimar, 1921.

Juhl, H. Der syntaktische Gebrauch des Infinitivs bei John Lydgate im Vergleich zu dem bei Chaucer und Occleve. Kiel, 1921.

Hittmair, R. Das Zeitwort 'Do' in Chaucers Prosa. Wiener Beiträge, LI, 1923.

Garrett, R. M. Pig's Eye. Dialect Notes, v, 1923, p. 245.

Goffin, R. C. Chaucer and Reason. MLR. XXI, 1926, p. 13.

Manly, J. M. Chaucer and the Rhetoricians. British Academy Lecture, 1926.

—— Canterbury Tales. New York, 1928, p. 88.

Malone, K. MP. XXXII, 1926, p. 483. [Phonology.]

Dew, R. Tamarside Dialect and the Language of Chaucer. Cornhill Mag. Aug. 1927, p. 179.

Hill, M. A. Rhetorical Balance in Chaucer's Poetry. PMLA. XLII, 1927, p. 845.

Heuer, H. Studien zur syntaktischen und stilistischen Funktion des Adverbs bei Chaucer und im Rosenroman. Anglistische Forschungen, LXXV, 1932.

Whiting, B. J. Chaucer's Use of Proverbs. Cambridge, U.S.A. 1934.

[See also under individual pieces.]

O. VERSIFICATION

[*Hammond*, pp. 464, 475, 481, 498, 501; *Wells*, pp. 868, 1027, 1141, 1231, 1322, 1420. *Griffith*, p. 40.]

Schipper, J. Englische Metrik. Vol. I, Bonn, 1881, p. 442.

—— Grundriss der englische Metrik. Leipzig, 1895.

ten Brink, B. [See under Language, above.]

Skeat, W. W. Oxford Chaucer. Vol. VI, p. xxiii.

Hempel, E. Die Silbenmassung in Chaucer's fünftaktigen Verse. Halle, 1898.

Bischoff, O. Ueber zweisilbige Senkung und epische Cäsur bei Chaucer. E. Studien, XXIV, 1898, p. 353, XXV, 1898, p. 339.

Saintsbury, G. A History of English Prosody. Vol. I, 1906, p. 143.

Omond, T. S. English Metrists. Oxford, 1907, p. 239.

Verrier, P. Métrique anglaise. Vol. II, Paris, 1909.

Reger, H. Die epische Cäsur in der Chaucerschule. Bayreuth, 1910.

Licklider, A. H. Chapters on the Metric of the Chaucer Tradition. Baltimore, 1910.

Seeberger, A. Fehlende Auftakt und fehlende Senkung nach der Cäsur in der Chaucerschule. Bayreuth, 1911.

Shannon, E. Chaucer's Use of Octosyllabic Verse. JEGP. XII, 1913, p. 277.

Klee, F. Das Enjambement bei Chaucer. Halle, 1913.

Vockrodt, G. Die Reimteknik bei Chaucer. Halle, 1914.

Joerden, O. Das Verhältnis von Wort-, Satz-, und Vers-Akzent in Chaucers Canterbury Tales. SEP. LV, 1915.

Bihl, J. Die Wirkungen des Rhythmus in der Sprache von Chaucer und Gower. Anglistische Forschungen, L, 1916.

Emerson, O. F. Old French Diphthong *Ei* (*Ey*) and Middle English Metrics. Romanic Rev. VIII, 1917, p. 18.

Beschorner, F. Verbale Reime bei Chaucer. SEP. LX, 1920.

Langhans, V. Der Reimvokal 'e' bei Chaucer. Ang. XLV, 1921, pp. 221, 297.

Hammond, E. P. The Nine-Syllabled Pentameter Line in some Post-Chaucerian MSS. MP. XXIII, 1925, p. 129.

Cowling, G. H. A Note on Chaucer's Stanza. RES. II, 1926, p. 311. [See also his Chaucer, 1927, pp. 66, 193.]

Lineberger, J. E. An Examination of Professor Cowling's New Metrical Test. MLN. XLII, 1927, p. 229.

Buck, H. Chaucer's Use of Feminine Rhyme. MP. XXVI, 1928, p. 13.

Manly, J. M. Canterbury Tales. New York, 1928, pp. 88, 122.

[See also under individual writings.]

II. LIFE OF CHAUCER

[*Hammond*, pp. 1, 305; *Wells*, pp. 608, 869, 994, 1027, 1083, 1141, 1186, 1282, 1284, 1322, 1371, 1420; *Griffith*, p. 10.]

Life-Records [all basic material to 1900]. Chaucer Soc. ser. 2, XII, XIV, XXI, XXXII, 1871–1900.

Kirk, R. E. G. Summary of Life-Records [to 1900]. Chaucer Soc. ser. 2, XXXII, 1900. [Introduction.]

Kuhl, E. P. Index to Life-Records. MP. X, 1913, p. 527.

Nicholas, Sir H. Aldine Chaucer. 1845; 1852; rev. R. Morris, 1866, 1870, etc.

Hales, J. W. DNB. [See Ang. XXI, 1898–9, pp. 245, 257; Athenaeum, 18 Feb. 1905, p. 210.]

Lounsbury, T. R. Atlantic Monthly, XL, 1877, pp. 269, 592; Studies in Chaucer, vol. I, New York, 1892, ch. 2. [Early treatments.]

Morley, H. English Writers. Vol. V, 1890.

Kittredge, G. L. Henry Scogan. Harvard Stud. I, 1892, p. 109.

Bayley, A. R. N. & Q. 15 Feb. 1902, p. 134. [Chaucer, Gloucestershire.]

Furnivall, F. J. Chaucer's Tomb. N. & Q. 9 Jan. 1904, p. 28.

Redstone, V. B. Chaucer-Malyns Family. Suffolk Inst. of Archaeology and Natural History, XII, 1903–6, pt 2; rptd 1905.

—— Chaucer, a Norfolk Man. Academy, 31 Oct. 1908, p. 425.

—— Chaucer's Seals. Athenaeum, 30 May 1908, I, p. 670.

Kern, A. A. Chaucer's Grandfather. N. & Q. 1 July 1905, p. 5.

—— Ancestry of Chaucer. Baltimore, 1906.

—— Records in Close and Patent Rolls. MLN. XXI, 1906, p. 224.

—— Chaucer's Sister. MLN. XXIII, 1908, p. 52.

—— Deschamps' Thureval. MP. VI, 1909, p. 503.

Rye, W. Chaucer, a Norfolk Man. Academy, 10 Sept. 1908, p. 283; Athenaeum, 7 March 1908, p. 290. [See also Athenaeum, 29 Jan. 1881; Chaucer Soc. ser. 2, XXI, 1886, p. 125; Academy, 31 Oct. 1908, p. 425.]

—— Chaucer, a Norfolk Man. Norwich, 1915.

—— TLS. 17 April 1924, p. 240. [Gaunt, Swynford, and Lynn.]

—— Poet Chaucer. TLS. 26 March 1925, p. 228.

—— Chaucer and Lynn. TLS. 24 Feb. 1927, p. 126.

Saintsbury, G. CHEL. vol. II, 1908, p. 156.

Coulton, G. G. Chaucer's Captivity. MLR. IV, 1909, p. 284.

Delachenal, R. Histoire de Charles V. Vol. II, Paris, 1909, p. 241.

Tout, T. F. Mission to Calais, 1360. EHR. XXV, 1910, p. 160.

—— Chapters on the Administrative History of Medieval England. Vol. II, Manchester, 1920, p. 335. [Chaucer at Court.]

Ency. Brit. 11th and later edns.

Emerson, O. F. New Item. MLN. XXVI, 1911, pp. 19, 95. [See also S. Moore, MLN. XXVII, 1912, p. 79.]

—— First Military Service. Romanic Rev. III, 1912, p. 321.

—— Chaucer on his Age. MP. XI, 1913–4, p. 117.

Hulbert, J. R. Chaucer's Official Life. Chicago, 1912.

—— Chaucer and the Earl of Oxford. MP. X, 1912–3, p. 433.

—— Mention of Henry Gisors. MLN. XXXVI, 1921, p. 123.

Moore, S. New Item. MLN. XXVII, 1912, p. 79.

—— Studies in Life-Records. Ang. XXXVII, 1913, p. 1.

—— New Life-Records. MP. XVI, 1918, p. 49, XVIII, 1921, p. 497.

Tatlock, J. S. P. The Duration of Chaucer's Visits to Italy. JEGP. XII, 1913, p. 118.

—— Chaucer and Wiclif. MP. XIV, 1916, p. 157.

Rickert, E. Chaucer and Vache. MP. XI, 1913–4, p. 209.

—— Chaucer and the Inner Temple. [Manly Anniversary Studies, Chicago, 1923, p. 30. See Brusendorff, p. 27, below; Manly, Some New Light, below.]

Kuhl, E. P. Some Friends. PMLA. XXIX, 1914, p. 270.

—— Chaucer Robbed. MLN. XXXVI, 1921, p. 157.

—— My Maistre Bukton. PMLA. XXXVIII, 1923, p. 115.

—— Chaucer and Aldgate. PMLA. XXXIX, 1924, p. 101.

—— Three Documents. MLN. XL, 1925, pp. 442, 511. [Ptd S. Moore, MLR. XXII, 1927, p. 435.]

—— Chaucer and Church. MLN. XL, 1925, p. 321.

Scott, E. J. L. Athenaeum, 6 June 1914, p. 794. [Grandparents, Westminster.]

Hibbard, L. A. Books of de Burley. MLN. XXX, 1915, p. 169.

Cook, A. S. The Historical Background of Chaucer's Knight. Trans. Connecticut Academy. XX, 1916, p. 16.

—— The Last Months of Chaucer's Earliest Patron. Trans. Connecticut Academy, XXI, 1916 p. 1.

—— Trans. Connecticut Academy, XXIII, 1919, pp. 38, 39, 44, 55. [Title 'Sir', mission to Florence in 1372, Swynford-Gaunt liaison, Paon de Roet.]

Tupper, F. Chaucer and Richmond. MLN. XXXI, 1916, p. 350.

—— Chaucer and Lancaster. MLN. XXXII, 1917, p. 54.

—— Chaucer in Ireland. PMLA. XXXVI, 1921, pp. 209, 216. [See A. S. Cook, Trans. Connecticut Academy, XX, 1916, p. 179.]

Jenkins, T. A. Deschamps' Ballade to Chaucer. MLN. xxxiii, 1918, pp. 268, 437. [See also H. Petersen,Neuphilologische Mitteilungen, xxvi, 1925, pts 3, 4.]

Beatty, J. M. Johannes de Chausse Hauberger. MLN. xxxiv, 1919, p. 378.

—— Sir Robert de Assheton. MLN. xxxv, 1920, p. 248; Genealogist, Oct. 1919. [See DNB.]

Farnham, W. E. MLR. xvi, 1921, p. 169. [Scogan, de Nevylle, Chaumpaigne Suit.]

Holzknecht, K. J. Literary Patronage in the Middle Ages. Philadelphia, 1923.

Liebermann, F. Lionel, Chaucer's Gönner. Archiv, cxlv, 1923, p. 258.

Lawrence, C. E. The Personality of Chaucer. Quart. Rev. ccxlii, 1924, p. 317.

Maxfield, E. K. Chaucer and Religious Reform. PMLA. xxxix, 1924, p. 64.

Brusendorff, A. The Chaucer Tradition. Copenhagen, 1925.

Koch, J. [Introduction to edn of Hertzberg's trn of Canterbury Tales, Berlin, 1925.]

Manly, J. M. Some New Light on Chaucer. New York, 1926.

—— Canterbury Tales. New York, 1928, p. 3. [Embodies some material also in next below.]

Manly, J. M. and Rickert, E. TLS. 5 Aug. 1926, p. 549 (see also A. McBain and W. Rye, TLS. 2 Sept. 1926, p. 580); MP. xxiv, 1926–7, pp. 111, 249, 503, xxv, 1927–8, pp. 121, 123, 249, 511; TLS. 19 Aug. 1926; N. & Q. 18 June 1927,p. 434; TLS. 4,11 Aug. and 27 Oct. 1927, pp. 533, 548, 766; TLS. 27 Sept. and 4 Oct. 1928, pp. 684, 707 (see H. W. Garrod and Sir I. Gollancz, TLS. 11, 25 Oct. 1928, pp. 736, 783); MP. xxix,1932, p. 257; TLS. 4 Feb., 20 Oct., 17 Nov., 8 Dec. 1932, pp. 76, 761, 859, 943; TLS. 6 April, 18 May 1933, pp. 248, 348; MLN. xlix, 1934, p. 209; Speculum, ix, 1934, p. 86. [New items.]

Cowling, G. H. Chaucer. 1927.

Roorda, P. Chaucer and Italy. E. Studies, ix, 1927, pts 2, 3.

Wilson, S. C. and Rye, W. The Name Chaucer. TLS. 12, 19 May 1927, pp. 336, 355.

Brooks, E. St J. Chaucer's Mother. TLS. 14 March 1929, p. 209.

Lethaby, W. R., Esdaile, K. A. and Godfrey, W. H. Chaucer's Tomb. TLS. 21, 28 Feb., 7 March 1929, pp. 137, 163, 186.

Krauss, R., Braddy H. and Kase, C. R. Three Chaucer Studies. New York, 1932. [See however review by J. M. Manly, RES. x, 1934, p. 257.]

Braddy, H. New Documentary Evidence concerning Chaucer's Mission to Lombardy. MLN. xlviii, 1933, p. 507.

[On Chaucer and Petrarch see under Clerk's Tale, below. On Lewis Chaucer and Sir Lewis Clifford: G. L. Kittredge, MP. xiv, 1917, p. 513, and i, 1903–4, p. 6, xi, 1913–4, p. 209; M. T. Waugh, Scottish Hist. Rev. xi, 1913–4, pp. 58, 88; J. M. Manly and W. Rye, TLS. 7, 28 June 1928, pp. 430, 486. On Thomas Chaucer: Hammond, pp. 24, 47; Athenaeum, 27 Jan., 3 Feb. 1900, pp. 116, 146, 5 Oct. 1901, p. 455; W. W. Skeat, Oxford Chaucer, vol. i, pp. xlviii, 1; R. E. G. Kirk, Chaucer Soc. 1900, p. li; DNB. under 'Chaucer,' vol. x, p. 158; T. R. Lounsbury, Studies in Chaucer, vol. i, New York, 1891, p. 104; A. S. Cook, Trans. Connecticut Academy, xxiii, 1919, p. 55; A. Brusendorff, The Chaucer Tradition, Copenhagen, 1925, p. 27; J. M. Manly and W. Rye, TLS. 7, 28 June 1928, pp. 430, 486; and especially M. B. Ruud, Thomas Chaucer, Minnesota University Stud. ix, 1926; A. C. Baugh, edn Kirk's Life Records of Thomas Chaucer, PMLA. xlvii, 1932, p. 461, and PMLA. xlviii, 1933, p. 328; R. Krauss, above, MLN. xlvii, 1932, p. 351, and PMLA. xlix, 1934, p. 954; J. M. Manly, TLS. 3 Aug. 1933, p. 525. On Portraits: Hammond, p. 49; M. H. Spielmann, Chaucer Soc. 1900 (criticism, E. Studien, xxx, 1902, p. 445); DNB. under 'Chaucer'; C. F. E. Spurgeon, Chaucer Criticism and Allusion, 3 vols. Cambridge, 1925 (vol. i, frontispiece, vol. ii, p. 9, vol. iii, frontispiece, pt v, p. 16); A. Brusendorff, The Chaucer Tradition, Copenhagen, 1925, frontispiece, pp. 13, 16; J. M. Manly, Some New Light on Chaucer, New York, 1926.]

III. WRITINGS BY CHAUCER

A. MINOR POEMS

[Hammond, pp. 325, 350, 352, 354; Wells, pp. 628, 870, 994, 1027, 1084, 1142, 1188, 1232, 1285, 1323, 1372, 1421; Griffith, pp. 15, 109.]

(1) MANUSCRIPTS

[Hammond, pp. 326, 354; and MLN. xxiii, 1908, p. 20. Introductions, notes, in edns, below.]

Cowling, G. H. Chaucer. 1927, p. 212.

(2) EDITIONS

[Hammond, pp. 350, 352, 354.]

[Parallel-Texts.] Chaucer Soc. 1871 (Duchesse, Pite, Parlement, Mars); Chaucer Soc. 1878 (ABC, Mother of God, Anelida, Former Age, Adam, Hous); Chaucer Soc. 1879 (Legend, Truth, Venus, Scogan, Bukton, Gentilesse, Proverbs, Stedfastnesse, Fortune, Purs); Chaucer Soc. 1880 (supplementary texts for

Parlement, ABC, Anelida, Legend, Mars, Truth, Venus, Gentilesse, Stedfastnesse, Fortune). [See F. J. Furnivall's Trial-Forewords, Chaucer Soc. vi, 1871, x, 1875; I. Marshall and L. Porter's Rime-Index, Chaucer Soc. 1887.]

Odd-Text.] Chaucer Soc. 1871 (Parlement, Prologue to Legend, Balade of Pitee, Cronycle Made by Chaucer); Chaucer Soc. 1880 (ABC, Hous, Legend, Duchesse, Pite, Parlement, Truth, Scogan, Purs); Chaucer Soc. 1886 (Pite, Anelida, Truth, Stedfastnesse, Fortune, Purs, Balade of Pite, Mercilesse Beaute).

One-Text ('Best' text of Parallel-Texts).] Chaucer Soc. 1871 (Duchesse, Pite, Parlement, Mars, ABC with De Guilleville's original); Chaucer Soc. 1880 (Mother of God, Anelida, Former Age, Adam, Hous, Legend, Truth, Venus, Scogan, Bukton, Gentilesse, Proverbs, Stedfastnesse, Fortune, Purs). [See I. Marshall and L Porter's Rime-Index, Chaucer Soc. 1889.]

keat, W. W. Minor Poems. Oxford, 1888, 1896. [ABC, Pite, Duchesse, Mars, Parlement, Merciles Beaute, Anelida, Adam, Hous, Former Age, Fortune, Truth, Gentilesse, Stedfastnesse, Against Women Unconstaunt, Scogan, Bukton, Venus, Purs, Proverbs; with Compleint to His Lady, Amorous Compleint, Balade of Compleynt; 1896 edn adds Rosemounde, Womanly Noblesse, Compleint to My Mortal Foe, Complaint to My Lodesterre.]
—— Oxford Chaucer. Vol. i, pp. 20, 261.
—— Student's Chaucer. Oxford, 1894.
Pollard, A. W. et al. Globe Chaucer.
Koch, J. Geoffrey Chaucer's kleinere Dichtungen. Heidelberg, 1928. [Supplementary notes, Ang. LIII, 1929, p. 1 (see bibliography there). All poems except Troilus and Canterbury Tales.]
Robinson, F. N. Complete Works of Geoffrey Chaucer. Boston, 1933.

Selected Minor Poems

Koch, J. Critical Edition of some Minor Poems. Berlin, 1883.
Bilderbeck, J. B. Selections from the Minor Poems of Chaucer. 1895.
Greenlaw, E. A. Selections from Chaucer. New York, 1908.
Emerson, O. F. Poems of Chaucer. New York, 1911.
MacCracken, H. N. College Chaucer. New Haven, 1913.
Cook, A. S. Literary Middle English Reader. Boston, 1915.
Caluza, M. Chaucer Handbuch. Leipzig, 1919.
Neilson, W. A. and Patch, H. R. Selections from Chaucer. New York, 1921.

Translations

Koch, J. Ausgewählte kleinere Dichtungen Chaucer's. Leipzig, 1880.
Skeat, W. W. The Prologue to the Canterbury Tales, and Minor Poems. 1907.

(3) GENERAL STUDIES

[Hammond, Wells, as cited above under A, p. 220.]

Furnivall, F. J. Trial-Forewords. Chaucer Soc. 1871, 1875.
Würzner, A. Ueber Chaucers lyrische Gedichte. Steyr, 1879.
Capone, G. I Poemi minori di Chaucer. Modica, 1900.
Hammond, E. P. On the Editing of Chaucer's Minor Poems. MLN. xxiii, 1908, p. 20.
Tatlock, J. S. P. MLN. xxix, 1914, p. 97. [Notes.]
Vockrodt, G. Reimtechnik bei Chaucer. Halle, 1914.
Cohen, H. L. The Ballade. New York, 1915, p. 233.
Langhans, V. Untersuchungen zu Chaucer. Halle, 1918.
Voigt, M. Zur Geschichte der Visionliteratur. Palaestra, CXLVI, 1924.
Brusendorff, A. The Chaucer Tradition. Copenhagen, 1925, pp. 178, 433, 445.
Koch, J. Geoffrey Chaucers kleinere Dichtungen. Heidelberg, 1928.

[See the several entries under General Criticism, Canon, Chronology, and Minor Poems, above.]

(4) INDIVIDUAL MINOR POEMS

[On MSS, general bibliography, edns, studies, summary, etc. of individual pieces, see the appropriate headings in Hammond, Wells, and Griffith; also the items listed under Chronology, General Criticism, Canon, and in the several sections under Minor Poems, above. The following are additional separate edns, studies, and notes especially concerned with the individual pieces indicated. For earlier items before 1908, see Hammond.]

(a) ABC

[Hammond, p. 354; Wells, pp. 628, 870, 1084, 1142, 1232, 1323; Griffith, p. 111.]

Root, R. K. The Poetry of Chaucer. Boston, 1906, 1922, p. 57.
Brown, C. MP. ix, 1911–2, p. 1. [Date.]
—— Hours of the Virgin. MLN. xxx, 1915, p. 31.
—— Register of Middle English Religious and Didactic Verse. 2 vols. Bibliog. Soc. 1916–20, index.

Brown, C. Religious Lyrics of the 14th Century. Oxford, 1924.

Tupper, F. MLN. xxx, 1915, p. 9. [Prymer.]

Young, K. MLN. xxx, 1915, p. 97. [Liturgy.]

Langhans, V. Untersuchungen zu Chaucer. Halle, 1918.

Kaluza, M. Chaucer Handbuch. Leipzig, 1919, p. 14.

Landrum, G. PMLA. xxxix, 1924, p. 75. [Vulgate.]

Brusendorff, A. The Chaucer Tradition. Copenhagen, 1925, p. 238.

(b) Against Women Unconstant, or Newfangelnesse

[Hammond, p. 440; Wells, pp. 629, 870, 1142, 1188, 1232; Griffith, p. 127.]

Koch, J. E. Studien, LIII, 1919, p. 162. [Text with German trn.]

Brusendorff, A. The Chaucer Tradition. Copenhagen, 1925, pp. 203, 225, 441.

(c) An Amorous Compleint, or Compleint d'Amours

[Hammond, p. 416; Wells, pp. 629, 870, 1188, 1233.]

Root, R. K. The Poetry of Chaucer. Boston, 1906, 1922 (rev. edn), p. 79.

Brusendorff, A. The Chaucer Tradition. Copenhagen, 1925. pp. 273, 437.

(d) Anelida and Arcite

[Hammond, p. 355; Wells, pp. 630, 870, 1028, 1084, 1142, 1188, 1233, 1285, 1323, 1372, 1421; Griffith, p. 112.]

Cambridge, 1905. [Facs. of Caxton's edn.]

Ker, W. P. Essays on Medieval Literature. 1905, p. 83.

Root, R. K. The Poetry of Chaucer. Boston, 1906, 1922 (rev. edn), p. 68.

Tatlock, J. S. P. The Development and Chronology of Chaucer's Works. Chaucer Soc. 1907, p. 83.

Shannon, E. F. PMLA. xxvii, 1912, p. 461. [Source.]

Cook, A. S. MLN. xxxi, 1916, p. 441. [Ermony.]

Jefferson, B. L. Chaucer and the Consolation of Philosophy of Boethius. Princeton, 1917.

Lowes, J. L. MP. xiv, 1917, p. 725; PMLA. xxxiii, 1918, p. 319. [Dante, Boccaccio, Ovide Moralisé.]

Fabin, M. MLN. xxxiv, 1919, p. 266. [Machaut.]

Kaluza, M. Chaucer Handbuch. Leipzig, 1919, p. 16.

Langhans, V. Ang. XLIV, 1919, p. 226. [Date.

Koch, J. E. Studien, LV, 1921, p. 209, LVI 1922, p. 28; Ang. XLVI, 1922, p. 36 [Date.]

Tupper, F. Chaucer's Tale of Ireland. PMLA xxxvi, 1921, p. 186. [Corinne, ibid. p. 216.

Brusendorff, A. The Chaucer Tradition Copenhagen, 1925, pp. 42, 189, 197 n., 231 259.

Cowling, G. H. RES. ii, 1926, p. 311 [Verse.]

Bush, D. Speculum, iv, 1929, p. 196 [Corinne.]

(e) Balade of Compleynt

[Hammond, p. 410; Wells, pp. 631, 87(1189, 1233.]

Root, R. K. The Poetry of Chaucer. Bostor 1906, 1922 (rev. edn), p. 79.

Brusendorff, A. The Chaucer Traditior Copenhagen, 1925, p. 437. [MS; authen ticity.]

(f) Book of the Duchesse

[Hammond, p. 362; Wells, pp. 631, 876, 99< 1028, 1085, 1142, 1189, 1233, 1323, 142) Griffith, p. 114.]

Lowes, J. L. MP. iii, 1905-6, p. 1. [Vers(1024-9.]

—— Romanic Rev. ii, 1911, p. 121. [Vers 1028.]

—— MP. xi, 1913-4, p. 543; MLN. xxx 1916, p. 185; Nation (New York), 11 Sep 1913, p. 233. ['Hereos.']

—— PMLA. xxxiii, 1918, p. 319. [Ovi Moralisé.]

Root, R. K. The Poetry of Chaucer. Bosto 1906, 1922 (rev. edn), p. 59.

—— MP. xv, 1917-8, p. 2. [Joseph of Exeter

Nadal, T. W. PMLA. xxiii, 1908, p. 64 [Spenser's Daphnaïda.]

Cushman, L. W. University of Californ Chronicle, 1909, p. 252.

Kittredge, G. L. MP. vii, 1909-10, p. 46 PMLA. xxx, 1915, p. 1. [Machaut.]

—— Chaucer and his Poetry. Cambridg U.S.A. 1915, p. 37.

Sypherd, W. O. MLN. xxiv, 1911, p. 4 [Le Songe Vert.]

Emerson, O. F. Romanic Rev. iii, 1912, p. 35 [Notes.]

—— PQ. ii, 1923, p. 81. [Verses 309-1 866-9.]

Legouis, É. Geoffrey Chaucer. 1913, p. 71.

Shannon, E. F. JEGP. xii, 1913, p. 17 [Octosyllabic couplet.]

—— MP. xi, 1913-4, p. 227. [Cave under rock.]

Savage, H. W. MLN. xxxi, 1916, p. 442. [Long Castel.]

Cupper, F. MLN. xxxi, 1916, p. 250. [Allegory.]

—— MLN. xxxii, 1917, p. 54. [Long Castel.]

Jefferson, B. L. Chaucer and the Consolation of Philosophy of Boethius. Princeton, 1917.

Langhans, V. Untersuchungen zu Chaucer. Halle, 1918, p. 253.

Cook, A. S. Th' Emperour Octovian and Augustus. Trans. Connecticut Academy, xxiii, 1919, p. 31.

Kitchel, A. T. Vassar Mediaeval Studies. New Haven, 1923, p. 217. [Machaut.]

Curry, W. C. E. Studien, lviii, 1924, p. 55. [Dreams.]

—— Chaucer and the Medieval Sciences. New York, 1926, p. 236.

Brusendorff, A. The Chaucer Tradition. Copenhagen, 1925, pp. 294, 396, 480.

Crosland, J. MLR. xxi, 1926, p. 380. [Mesure.]

Langhans, V. Ang. li, 1927, p. 323. [On Brusendorff and dream poems.]

Rosenthal, C. L. A Possible Source of Chaucer's Book of the Duchesse: Li Regret de Guillaume by Jehan de la Mote. MLN. xlviii, 1933, p. 511.

Harrison, B. S. Medieval Rhetoric in the Book of the Duchesse. PMLA. xlix, 1934, p. 428.

(g) Chaucer's Words unto Adam

[Hammond, p. 405; Wells, pp. 634, 870, 1028, 1143, 1189, 1233, 1285, 1323; Griffith, . 141.]

Root, R. K. The Poetry of Chaucer. Boston, 1906, 1922 (rev. edn), p. 69.

—— Publications before Printing. PMLA. xxviii, 1913, p. 417.

Kuhl, E. P. Scriveners. MLN. xxix, 1914, p. 263.

Hammond, E. P. Chaucer and Dante and their Scribes. MLN. xxxi, 1916, p. 121.

Kaluza, M. Chaucer Handbuch. Leipzig, 1919, p. 18.

Koch, J. Ang. xlvi, 1922, p. 35. [Date.]

Brusendorff, A. The Chaucer Tradition. Copenhagen, 1925, pp. 57, 276.

Bressie, R., Manly, J. M. and Wagner, B. M. TLS. 9, 16 May, 13 June 1929, pp. 383, 403, 474. [Identity of Adam.]

(h) Compleynt of Mars, or Mars

[Hammond, p. 384; Wells, pp. 635, 870, 1028, 1085, 1143, 1189, 1233, 1285, 1323, 1421; Griffith, p. 126.]

Root, R. K. The Poetry of Chaucer. Boston, 1906, 1922 (rev. edn), p. 63.

Browne, W. H. Chaucer's Astrology. MLN. xxiii, 1908, p. 53.

Legouis, É. Geoffrey Chaucer. 1913, p. 66.

Jefferson, B. L. Chaucer and the Consolation of Philosophy of Boethius. Princeton, 1917.

Langhans, V. Untersuchungen zu Chaucer. Halle, 1918, p. 229.

Kaluza, M. Chaucer Handbuch. Leipzig, 1919, p. 15.

Baskervill, C. R. Songs on the Night Visit. PMLA. xxxvi, 1921, p. 594.

Emerson, O. F. PQ. ii, 1923, p. 82. [Verses 113–4.]

Brusendorff, A. The Chaucer Tradition. Copenhagen, 1925, pp. 42, 183, 231, 261. [See also Ang. li, 1927, p. 323.]

Cowling, G. H. RES. ii, 1926, pp. 311, 405. [Verse; purpose.]

(i) Compleynt of Venus, or Venus

[Hammond, p. 404; Wells, pp. 636, 870, 1028, 1085, 1143, 1189, 1233, 1286, 1324; Griffith, p. 140.]

Piaget, A. Oton de Granson et ses Poésies. Romania, xix, 1890, pp. 237, 403.

Root, R. K. The Poetry of Chaucer. Boston, 1906, 1922 (rev. edn), p. 77.

Cohen, H. L. The Ballade. New York, 1915, p. 236.

Langhans, V. Untersuchungen zu Chaucer. Halle, 1918, p. 246.

Kaluza, M. Chaucer Handbuch. Leipzig, 1919, p. 22.

Brusendorff, A. The Chaucer Tradition. Copenhagen, 1925, pp. 223, 237 (note), 261, 264.

Cowling, G. H. RES. ii, 1926, p. 405. [Purpose.]

(j) Compleint to His Lady, or Balade of Pity

[Hammond, p. 411; Wells, pp. 637, 870, 1028, 1189, 1233, 1421.]

Root, R. K. The Poetry of Chaucer. Boston, 1906, 1922 (rev. edn), p. 68.

Lowes, J. L. MP. xiv, 1916–7, p. 724. [Dante.]

Jefferson, B. L. Chaucer and the Consolation of Philosophy of Boethius. Princeton, 1917.

Brusendorff, A. The Chaucer Tradition. Copenhagen, 1925, pp. 45, 225, 268.

Timmer, B. J. E. Studies, xi, 1929, p. 20. ['Faire rewthelees.']

(k) Compleint to His Purs, or Purs

[Hammond, p. 392; Wells, pp. 637, 870, 1028, 1085, 1143, 1233, 1421; Griffith, p. 130.]

Hammond, E. P. Lament of a Prisoner. Ang. xxxii, 1909, p. 481.

MacCracken, H. N. MLN. xxvii, 1912, p. 228. [On MS Caius College Cambridge 176.]

Cook, A. S. Parallels with de Coucy. Trans. Connecticut Academy, xxiii, 1919, p. 33.

Kaluza, M. Chaucer Handbuch. Leipzig, 1919, p. 22.

Brusendorff, A. The Chaucer Tradition. Copenhagen, 1925, p. 253.

Cowling, G. H. RES. ii, 1926, p. 311. [Verse.]

(l) Compleynt unto Pite

[Hammond, p. 390; Wells, pp. 638, 870, 1028, 1233.]

Critical Edition. B. ten Brink, Essays on Chaucer, pt ii (no. 9), Chaucer Soc. 1874.

Studies.

Bright, J. W. MLN. xvii, 1902, p. 278. [Verses 29–35.]

Root, R. K. The Poetry of Chaucer Boston, 1906, 1922 (rev. edn), p. 58.

Lowes, J. L. MP. xiv, 1916–7, p. 722. [Dante.]

Jefferson, B. L. Chaucer and the Consolation of Philosophy of Boethius. Princeton, 1917.

Cowling, G. H. RES. ii, 1926, p. 311. [On verse.]

(m) The Former Age

[Hammond, p. 367; Wells, pp. 638, 871, 1028, 1085, 1143, 1189, 1233; Griffith, p. 116.]

Root, R. K. The Poetry of Chaucer. Boston, 1906, 1922 (rev. edn), p. 70.

Jefferson, B. L. Chaucer and the Consolation of Philosophy of Boethius. Princeton, 1917.

Koch, J. Ang. xlvi, 1922, p. 44. [Date.]

Brusendorff, A. The Chaucer Tradition. Copenhagen, 1925, p. 293.

(n) Fortune

[Hammond, p. 369; Wells, pp. 639, 871, 1028, 1085, 1143, 1190, 1233; Griffith, p. 116.]

Root, R. K. The Poetry of Chaucer. Boston, 1906, 1922 (rev. edn), p. 71.

Jefferson, B. L. Chaucer and the Consolation of Philosophy of Boethius. Princeton, 1917.

Langhans, V. Untersuchungen zu Chaucer. Halle, 1918, p. 247.

Koch, J. Ang. xlvi, 1922, p. 44. [Date.]

Patch, H. R. The Tradition of the Goddess Fortuna. Smith College Stud. iii, iv, 1922.

Brusendorff, A. The Chaucer Tradition. Copenhagen, 1925, pp. 198, 200 (note), 223, 233, 241, 487, 492.

(o) Gentilesse

[Hammond, p. 371; Wells, pp. 640, 871, 1028, 1190, 1233; Griffith, p. 117.]

Kittredge, G. L. Henry Scogan. Harvard Stud. i, 1892, p. 109.

Lange, H. Zu Scogan. Archiv, cx, 1903, p. 104.

Lowes, J. L. MP. xiii, 1915–6, p. 19. [Convivio.]

Jefferson, B. L. Chaucer and the Consolation of Philosophy of Boethius. Princeton, 1917.

Brusendorff, A. The Chaucer Tradition. Copenhagen, 1925, pp. 225, 232, 254.

Vogt, G. M. Generositas Virtus. JEGP xxiv, 1925, p. 103.

Cowling, G. H. RES. ii, 1926, p. 311. [On verse.]

(p) Hous of Fame

[Hammond, p. 372; Wells, pp. 653, 872, 995, 1029, 1087, 1144, 1192, 1235, 1286, 1324, 1372, 1422; Griffith, p. 117.]

Separate Edition. C. M. Drennan, 1921.

Translation. W. W. Skeat, Oxford, 1907.

Studies.

Ford, H. C. Observations on the Language of Chaucer's Hous of Fame. Lexington Virginia, 1899, 1908.

Bright, J. W. MLN. xvii, 1902, p. 278. [Bk 1, Verses 183–4.]

Root, R. K. The Poetry of Chaucer. Boston, 1906, 1922 (rev. edn), p. 129.

Cipriani, L. PMLA. xxii, 1907, p. 585. [Romance of Rose.]

Sypherd, W. O. Studies in Chaucer's Hous of Fame. Chaucer Soc. 1907.

—— The Completeness of Chaucer's Hous of Fame. MLN. xxx, 1915, p. 65.

Tatlock, J. S. P. The Development and Chronology of Chaucer's Works. Chaucer Soc. 1907, p. 34.

Brandl, A. Anfänge der Autobiographie in England. Sitzungsber. d. kgl. Preuss. Akad. xxxv, 1908, p. 724.

Hamilton, G. L. MLN. xxiii, 1908, p. 63. [Bk 1, verses 358–9.]

Kittredge, G. L. The Date of Chaucer's Troilus. Chaucer Soc. 1908, p. 53.

—— Chaucer and his Poetry. Cambridge U.S.A. 1915, p. 73.

Macaulay, G. C. MLR. iv, 1909, pp. 18, 528. [On bk ii, verses 421 ff.; octosyllabic couplet.]

MacCracken, H. N. Dant in English. Nation (New York), 23 Sept. 1909, p. 276.

Immelmann, R. E. Studien, xlv, 1912, p. 397.

Manly, J. M. What is Chaucer's Hous of Fame? [Kittredge Anniversary Papers Boston, 1913, p. 73.]

Shannon, E. F. MP. xi, 1913–4, p. 230. [Aeolus.]

—— JEGP. xii, 1913, p. 277. [Octosyllabic couplet.]

Fansler, D. S. Chaucer and the Roman de la Rose. New York, 1914, p. 255.

Cook, A. S. Skelton's Garland of Laurel and Chaucer's Hous of Fame. MLR. xi, 1916, p. 9.

Koch, J. E. Studien, l, 1916–7, p. 359. [Meaning; purpose.]

—— Ang. Bbl. xxvii, 1916, p. 139. [Textnotes.]

—— Ang. xlvi, 1922, p. 40, xlix, 1925, p. 214. [Date.]

Tupper, F. JEGP. xvi, 1917, p. 551. [Envy theme.]

Allen, H. E. Romanic Rev. ix, 1918, p. 187. [Bk ii, verse 623.]

Lange, H. Ang. xlii, 1918, p. 345. [Lollius; date.]

Langhans, V. Untersuchungen zu Chaucer. Halle, 1918, p. 78.

—— Ang. li, 1927, p. 323. [Criticism of Brusendorff, below.]

Patch, H. R. MLN. xxxiii, 1918, p. 177. [Influence on Dekker.]

Holthausen, F. Ang. Bbl. xxxi, 1920, p. 137. [Text and metrical notes.]

Jack, A. A. A Commentary on the Poetry of Chaucer and Spenser. Glasgow, 1920, p. 37. [Date; composition.]

Hutchins, C. M. Romania, l, 1924, p. 1. [Bk 1, verse 986.]

Curry, W. C. Chaucer's Science and Art. Texas Rev. viii, 1923, p. 307.

—— Chaucer and the Medieval Sciences. New York, 1926, p. 238. [Dream lore.]

Brusendorff, A. The Chaucer Tradition. Copenhagen, 1925, pp. 148, 237. [On MSS.]

Rand, E. K. Speculum, i, 1926, p. 222. [Bk 1, verses 174 ff., 1455 ff.]

Royster, J. F. Stud. Phil. xxiii, 1926, p. 380. [Bk 1, verses 1277–81.]

Riedel, F. C. JEGP. xxix, 1930, p. 441. [Meaning of poem.]

Teager, F. E. Chaucer's Eagle and the Rhetorical Colours. PMLA. xlvii, 1932, p. 410.

Bronson, B. H. Chaucer's Hous of Fame: Another Hypothesis. Berkeley, 1934.

Sources.

Lowes, J. L. MP. xiii, 1915–6, p. 19, xiv, 1917, pp. 717, 732, 734; PMLA. xxxiii, 1918, p. 324. [Dante, Ovide Moralisé.]

Cummings, H. M. The Indebtedness of Chaucer's Works to the Italian Works of Boccaccio. Cincinnati University Stud. x, pt 2, 1916.

Brown, M. L. MLN. xxxii, 1917, p. 411. [Corbaccio.]

Jefferson, B. L. Chaucer and the Consolation of Philosophy of Boethius. Princeton, 1917.

Root, R. K. MP. xv, 1917, p. 1. [Joseph of Exeter.]

Patch, H. R. Chaucer's Desert. MLN. xxxiv, 1919, p. 321.

Shannon, E. MP. xvi, 1918–9, p. 610. [Lucan.]

Tatlock, J. S. P. MLN. xxxvi, 1921, p. 95. [Eleanor, bk ii, verse 516.]

Koch, J. E. Studien, lvii, 1923, p. 44. [Latin sources.]

Schirmer, W. F. Germanisch-romanische Monatsschrift, xii, 1924, p. 297. [Boccaccio.]

Tuve, R. MLN. xlv, 1930, p. 518. [Guillaume's Pilgrim.]

Whiting, B. J. The Hous of Fame and Renaud de Beaufeu's Li Biaus Desconneüs. MP. xxxi, 1933, p. 196.

[On Lollius, see under Troilus and Criseyde, p. 230 below.]

(q) Lak of Stedfastnesse

[*Hammond,* p. 394; *Wells,* pp. 640, 871, 1028, 1143, 1190, 1234; *Griffith,* p. 120.]

Separate Edition. L. H. Holt, JEGP. vi, 1906–7, p. 419.

Studies.

Root, R. K. The Poetry of Chaucer. Boston, 1906, 1922 (rev. edn), p. 74.

MacCracken, H. N. MLN. xxiii, 1908, p. 212. [On MS.]

Jefferson, B. L. Chaucer and the Consolation of Philosophy of Boethius. Princeton, 1917.

Kaluza, M. Chaucer Handbuch. Leipzig, 1919, p. 20.

Brusendorff, A. The Chaucer Tradition. Copenhagen, 1925, pp. 273, 487, 492.

Cowling, G. H. RES. ii, 1926, p. 311. [On verse.]

(r) Lenvoy à Bukton

[*Hammond,* p. 366; *Wells,* pp. 641, 871, 995, 1028, 1085, 1143, 1190, 1234; *Griffith,* p. 115.]

Root, R. K. The Poetry of Chaucer. Boston, 1906, 1922 (rev. edn), p. 76.

Tatlock, J. S. P. The Development and Chronology of Chaucer's Works. Chaucer Soc. 1907, p. 210.

—— MLN. xxix, 1914, p. 98. [Parallel with John of Salisbury.]

Kittredge, G. L. MLN. xxiv, 1909, p. 14. [Compared with Deschamps.]

Moore, S. and Lowes, J. L. MLN. xxvi, 1911, p. 172, xxvii, 1912, p. 45. [Date.]

Kaluza, M. Chaucer Handbuch. Leipzig, 1919, p. 21.

Kuhl, E. P. PMLA. xxxviii, 1923, p. 115; MLN. xl, 1925, p. 325. ['My Maistre Bukton'; Chaucer and Church.]

Brusendorff, A. The Chaucer Tradition. Copenhagen, 1925, pp. 292, 487.

(s) Lenvoy à Scogan

[*Hammond*, p. 393; *Wells*, pp. 642, 871, 1028, 1086, 1143, 1190, 1234; *Griffith*, p. 133.]

Kittredge, G. L. Henry Scogan. Harvard Stud. I, 1892, p. 109.

—— Alanus de Insulis. MP. VII, 1909–10, p. 483.

Lange, H. Archiv, cx, 1903, p. 104. [Scogan, Court of Love.]

Moore, S. MLN. XXVI, 1911, p. 173. [Date.]

Farnham, W. E. John (Henry) Scogan. MLR. XVI, 1921, p. 120.

—— Scogan's Quem Quaeritis. MLN. XXXVII, 1922, p. 289. [See also N. C. Brooks, MLN. XXXVIII, 1923, p. 57.]

Brusendorff, A. The Chaucer Tradition. Copenhagen, 1925, pp. 201, 289.

Goffin, R. C. MLR. XX, 1925, p. 318. [Verses 47–9 and Cicero.]

Cowling, G. H. RES. II, 1926, p. 311. [On verse.]

French, W. H. The Meaning of Chaucer's Envoy to Scogan. PMLA. XLVIII, 1933, p. 289.

(t) Merciles Beaute

[*Hammond*, p. 436; *Wells*, pp. 642, 871, 1028, 1086, 1143, 1191, 1234; *Griffith*, p. 127.]

Root, R. K. The Poetry of Chaucer. Boston, 1906, 1922 (rev. edn), p. 72.

Lowes, J. L. MLR. V, 1910, p. 33. [Compared with Deschamps.]

Skeat, W. W. MLR. V, 1910, p. 194. [Verse 26.]

Legouis, É. Geoffrey Chaucer. 1913, p. 62.

Koch, J. E. Studien, LIII, 1919, p. 164. [Text; German trn.]

Renwick, W. L. Chaucer's Triple Roundel. MLR. XVI, 1921, p. 322.

Brusendorff, A. The Chaucer Tradition. Copenhagen, 1925, pp. 440, 489.

(u) Parlement of Foules

[*Hammond*, p. 387; *Wells*, pp. 643, 871, 995, 1028, 1086, 1143, 1191, 1234, 1286, 1324, 1372, 1421; *Griffith*, p. 127.]

Separate Edition. C. M. Drennan, 1914.

Modern Rendering. W. W. Skeat, 1907.

Studies.

Cook, A. S. MLN. XXI, 1906, p. 111, XXII, 1907, p. 146. [Verse 353.]

Root, R. K. The Poetry of Chaucer. Boston, 1906, 1922 (rev. edn), p. 65.

—— Joseph of Exeter. MP. XV, 1917, p. 18.

Tatlock, J. S. P. The Development and Chronology of Chaucer's Works. Chaucer Soc. 1907, p. 41.

Moffatt, D. M. Yale Stud. XXXVI, 1908. [Trn, de Lille's Complaint of Nature.]

Emerson, O. F. MP. VIII, 1910–11, p. 45. [The Suitors.]

—— PQ. II, 1923, p. 83. [Verses 204–10; Boccaccio. See also Ang. Bbl. XXII, 1911, p. 374.]

Moore, S. and Emerson, O. F. MLN. XXVI, 1911, pp. 8, 109. [The Suitors.]

Jones, H. S. V. MLN. XXVII, 1912, p. 95. [Verse 693.]

Legouis, É. Geoffrey Chaucer. 1913, p. 82.

Manly, J. M. and Emerson, O. F. What is the Parlement of Foules? SEP. L, 1913, p. 279; JEGP. XIII, 1914, p. 566.

Hammond, E. P. Ang. Bbl. XXV, 1914, p. 234; MLN. XXXI, 1916, p. 121. [Verses 346, 211.]

—— MP. XXIII, 1925, p. 133. [On verse.]

Cummings, H. M. The Indebtedness of Chaucer's Works to the Italian Works of Boccaccio. Cincinnati University Stud. X, pt 2, 1916, p. 13.

Lange, H. What is the Parlement of Foules? Ang. XL, 1916, p. 394.

Shackford, M. H. MLN. XXXI, 1916, p. 507. [Date.]

Farnham, W. E. PMLA. XXXII, 1917, p. 492. [Sources.]

—— The Fowls in Chaucer's Parlement. Wisconsin University Stud. II, 1918, p. 340.

—— Contending Lovers. PMLA. XXXV, 1920, p. 247.

Jefferson, B. L. Chaucer and the Consolation of Philosophy of Boethius. Princeton, 1917.

Lowes, J. L. MP. XIV, 1917, p. 706. [Dante and verses 288 ff., 139–56.]

Langhans, V. Untersuchungen zu Chaucer. Halle, 1918, p. 19.

—— Ang. LI, 1927, p. 323. [Criticism of Brusendorff, below.]

—— Ang. LIV, 1930, p. 25.

Kaluza, M. Chaucer Handbuch. Leipzig, 1919, p. 58.

Rickert, E. MP. XVIII, 1920, p. 1. [New interpretation.]

Knowlton, E. C. Nature in Middle English. JEGP. XX, 1921, p. 186.

Koch, J. Parlement of Foules. E. Studien, LV, 1921, p. 215.

—— Ang. XLVI, 1922, p. 36. [Date.]

—— Ang. XLIX, 1925, p. 212. [Interpretation.]

Tupper, F. Chaucer's Tale of Ireland. PMLA. XXXVI, 1921, p. 197.

Pieper, W. Das Parlament in der mittelenglischen Literatur. Archiv, CXLVI, 1923, pp. 187, 204, 211.

Reid, M. E. Historical Interpretations of the Parlement of Foules. Wisconsin University Stud. XVIII, 1923, p. 60.

Curry, W. C. Texas Rev. VIII, 1923, p. 307. [Science.]

—— E. Studien, LVIII, 1924, p. 55. [On dreams.]

—— Chaucer and the Medieval Sciences. New York, 1926, p. 234. [Dream lore.]

Schirmer, W. F. Germanish-romanische Monatsschrift, XII, 1924, p. 297. [Boccaccio.]

Brusendorff, A. The Chaucer Tradition. Copenhagen, 1925, pp. 165, 286.

Cowling, G. H. RES. II, 1926, p. 311. [On verse.]

McKeehan, I. P. PMLA. XLI, 1926, p. 809. [Purpose.]

Douglas, T. W. MLN. XLIII, 1928, p. 378. [Interpretation.]

Patrick, D. PQ. IX, 1930, p. 61. [Satire.]

Braddy, H. PMLA. XLVI, 1931, p. 1007.

—— The Parlement of Foules. [In R. Krauss, H. Braddy, and C. R. Kase, Three Chaucer Studies, New York, 1932.]

Slaughter, E. E. 'Every Vertu at his Reste.' MLN. XLVI, 1931, p. 448.

Lange, H. Ein neuer Chaucerfund. E. Studien, LXVIII, 1933, p. 174.

(v) Proverbs

[Hammond, p. 449; Wells, pp. 646, 871, 1191, 1234.]

Root, R. K. The Poetry of Chaucer. Boston, 1906, 1922 (rev. edn), p. 78.

Kittredge, G. L. MP. VII, 1909–10, p. 478. [Parallels to verse 4.]

Brusendorff, A. The Chaucer Tradition. Copenhagen, 1925, pp. 225, 284.

(w) Rosemounde

[Hammond, p. 460; Wells, pp. 646, 871, 1143, 1191, 1234, 1286, 1324, 1421; Griffith, p. 132.]

Root, R. K. The Poetry of Chaucer. Boston, 1906, 1922 (rev. edn), p. 72.

Lowes, J. L. Romanic Rev. II, 1911, p. 128. [Verse 20.]

Kaluza, M. Chaucer Handbuch. Leipzig, 1919, p. 19.

Koch, J. E. Studien, LIII, 1919, p. 164. [Text; German trn.]

Brusendorff, A. The Chaucer Tradition. Copenhagen, 1925, p. 439.

Rickert, E. MP. XXV, 1927–8, p. 255. [Occasion.]

(x) Truth

[Hammond, p. 401; Wells, pp. 647, 871, 1029, 1087, 1191, 1234, 1421; Griffith, p. 140.]

Root, R. K. The Poetry of Chaucer. Boston, 1906, 1922 (rev. edn), p. 73.

MacCracken, H. N. MLN. XXIII, 1908, p. 213. [Lambeth text.]

Rickert, E. and Manly, J. M. MP. XI, 1913–4, pp. 209, 226. [Thou Vache. See also J. Koch, Ang. XLVI, 1922, p. 47, XLIX, 1925, p. 238.]

Legouis, É. Geoffrey Chaucer. 1913, p. 68.

Jefferson, B. L. Chaucer and the Consolation of Philosophy of Boethius. Princeton, 1917.

Kittredge, G. L. Lewis Chaucer or Lewis Clifford. MP. XIV, 1917, p. 513. [See also under Life, p. 218 above.]

Koch, J. Ang. XLVI, 1922, p. 47. [Date.]

Brusendorff, A. The Chaucer Tradition. Copenhagen, 1925, pp. 192, 203, 245.

Cowling, G. H. RES. II, 1926, p. 311. [On verse.]

(y) Womanly Noblesse

[Hammond, p. 463; Wells, pp. 647, 871, 1234.]

Root, R. K. The Poetry of Chaucer. Boston, 1906, 1922 (rev. edn), p. 79.

Brusendorff, A. The Chaucer Tradition. Copenhagen, 1925, p. 270. [Exact rpt.]

B. ROMAUNT OF THE ROSE

[Hammond, p. 450; Wells, pp. 648, 872, 1029, 1087, 1144, 1192, 1234, 1286, 1324, 1422; Griffith, p. 130.]

Editions. M. Kaluza, Chaucer Soc. 1891 (with French); W. W. Skeat, Oxford Chaucer, vol. I, pp. 93, 417; F. J. Furnivall, Chaucer Soc. 1911 (rpt of Thynne's edn).

Studies.

Athenaeum, 30 Dec. 1870, p. 721; Academy, 27 April, 1, 8 June, 20 July, 10 Aug. 1878, pp. 365, 489, 512, 66, 143; 8 Sept. 1888, p. 153; 5, 19 July 1890, pp. 11, 51; 18 Aug. 1891, p. 137; 27 Feb., 5 March 1892, pp. 206, 230. [Authorship.]

ten Brink, B. Ang. I, 1878, p. 533; E. Studien, XVII, 1892, p. 9.

Skeat, W. W. Prioress' Tale. 1880 (3rd edn).

—— Essays on Chaucer. Chaucer Soc. 1892, pp. 489, 675.

—— Minor Poems. Oxford, 1896 (2nd edn). [Introduction.]

—— The Chaucer Canon. Oxford, 1900.

Fick, W, and Lindner, F. E. Studien, IX, 1886, pp. 161, 506, XI, 1888, p. 163.

Koch, J. The Chronology of Chaucer's Writings. Chaucer Soc. 1890, p. 7; E. Studien, XXVII, 1900, pp. 61, 227, XXX, 1902, p. 450.

—— E. Studien, LV, 1921, p. 161. [Author.]

—— Ang. XLIX, 1925, p. 205.

Kittredge, G. L. Harvard Stud. I, 1892, p. 1.

Lounsbury, T. R. Studies in Chaucer. Vol. ii, New York, 1892, p. 1.

Kaluza, M. Chaucer und der Rosenroman. Berlin, 1893. [See also Deutsche Literaturzeitung, 1901, p. 863; E. Studien, xx, 1895, p. 338, xxiii, 1897, p. 336, xxiv, 1898, p. 342.]

Schoch, A. D. MP. iii, 1905–6, p. 339. [Summary on author.]

Hinckley, H. B. and Skeat, W. W. Chaucer and Ywaine and Gawaine. Academy, 22 Dec. 1906, p. 640; 26 Jan. 1907, p. 99.

Root, R. K. The Poetry of Chaucer. Boston, 1906, 1922 (rev. edn), p. 45.

Cipriani, L. Romaunt of the Rose and Chaucer. PMLA. xxii, 1907, p. 552.

Lange, H. Ang. xxxv, 1912, p. 338, xxxvi, 1912, p. 479, xxxvii, 1913, p. 146. [Authenticity of Fragment A.]

—— Ang. xxxviii, 1914, p. 477. [Date of A.]

Fansler, D. S. Chaucer and the Romaunt de la Rose. New York, 1914. [See its bibliography.]

Cook, A. S. MLN. xxxi, 1916, p. 442. [Verse 1093, 'fryse.']

—— Chaucer and Venantius Fortunatus. MLN. xxxix, 1924, p. 376.

Jefferson, B. L. Chaucer and the Consolation of Philosophy of Boethius. Princeton, 1917.

Lowes, J. L. Romanic Rev. viii, 1917, p. 383. [Use of de Meun.]

Langhans, V. Untersuchungen zu Chaucer. Halle, 1918, p. 223.

Schöffler, H. Ang. Bbl. xxix, 1918, p. 46. [On verses 1367, 1369.]

Jack, A. A. A Commentary on the Poetry of Chaucer and Spenser. Glasgow, 1920, p. 117.

Snyder, E. D. MP. xvii, 1920, p. 712. [Verses 3807–11.]

Baskervill, C. R. PMLA. xxxvi, 1921, p. 569. [On verses 2640–80.]

Reeves, W. P. MLN. xxxviii, 1923, p. 124. [Verse 1705.]

Landrum, G. Chaucer's Use of the Vulgate. PMLA. xxxix, 1924, p. 75.

Brusendorff, A. The Chaucer Tradition. Copenhagen, 1925, pp. 47, 49, 146.

Thompson, N. M. A Further Study of Chaucer and the Romance of the Rose. Stanford University Abstracts of Dissertations, vol. i, 1927, p. 95.

French Original. [*Hammond*, p. 78.]

Petit de Julleville, L. Histoire de la Langue et de la Littérature françaises. Vol. ii, Paris, 1896, p. 105.

Gröber, G. Grundriss der romanischen Philologie. Vol. ii¹, Strasburg, 1902, pp. 59, 734, 1040.

Warren, F. M. Date and Composition of de Lorris' Roman. PMLA. xxiii, 1908, p. 269.

Langlois, E. Les MSS. du Roman de la Rose. Lille, 1910.

Le Roman de la Rose. Ed. E. Langlois, 5 vols. Société des anciens Textes français, 1920.

C. BOETHIUS

[*Hammond*, p. 360; *Wells*, pp. 650, 872, 995, 1029, 1087, 1144, 1192, 1234, 1324, 1373, 1422; *Griffith*, p. 113.]

Editions. R. Morris, 1868 (from BM. Add. 10340, with collation of Cambridge University Lib. Ii); F. J. Furnivall, Chaucer Soc. 1886 (from Cambridge University Lib. Ii, 3, 21); W. W. Skeat, Oxford Chaucer, vol. i, p. 419, vol. ii, p. vii.

Studies.

Petersen, K. PMLA. xviii, 1903, p. 1. [Source, Trivet.]

James, M. R. A Catalogue of the Manuscripts in the Library of Pembroke College. Cambridge, 1905, p. 195.

Root, R. K. The Poetry of Chaucer. Boston, 1906, 1922 (rev. edn), p. 80.

Warren, F. M. PMLA. xxiii, 1908, p. 269. [Date, composition.]

Fehlauer, F. Die englische Übersetzungen von Boethius' De Consolatione Philosophiae. Berlin, 1909.

Jefferson, B. L. Chaucer and the Consolation of Philosophy of Boethius. Princeton, 1917.

Lowes, J. L. Romanic Rev. viii, 1917, p. 383. [Use of de Meun.]

Kaluza, M. Chaucer Handbuch. Leipzig, 1919, p. 36.

Koch, J. Chaucer's Boethiusübersetzung. Ang. xlvi, 1922, p. 1.

Science, M. TLS. 29 March 1923, p. 199. [Text-note.]

Landrum, G. Chaucer's Use of the Vulgate. PMLA. xxxix, 1924, p. 75.

Brusendorff, A. The Chaucer Tradition. Copenhagen, 1925, p. 174. [Authenticity; MSS.]

Hammond, E. P. Boethius. MLN. xli, 1926, p. 534.

Cline, J. M. The Prose of Chaucer's Boethius. Princeton, 1927.

[For Latin original, see *Hammond*, p. 86; edn by H. F. Stewart and E. K. Rand, New York, 1918; L. Cooper, Concordance of Boethius, Cambridge, U.S.A. 1928.]

D. TROILUS AND CRISEYDE

[*Hammond*, p. 395; *Wells*, pp. 660, 872, 995, 1029, 1088, 1144, 1193, 1235, 1287, 1324, 1373, 1422; *Griffith*, p. 133; Root's edn.]

Manuscripts.

MacCracken, H. N. More Odd Texts. MLN. xxv, 1910, p. 126.

Hammond, E. P. MLN. xxvi, 1911, p. 32. [Burgundian copy.]

Root, R. K. The Manuscripts of Troilus and Criseyde, with 23 Collotype Facsimiles. Chaucer Soc. 1915.

—— The Textual Tradition of Chaucer's Troilus. Chaucer Soc. 1916.

—— Troilus and Criseyde. Princeton, 1926. [Introduction.]

Brusendorff, A. The Chaucer Tradition. Copenhagen, 1925, p. 166.

Koch, J. Ang. xlix, 1925, p. 210.

Editions.

Skeat, W. W. Oxford Chaucer. Vol. ii, pp. xlix, 153, 461.

McCormick, Sir W. S. and Root, R. K. Specimen Extracts from 9 Known Unpublished Manuscripts and from Caxton's and Thynne's First Editions. Chaucer Soc. 1914.

Root, R. K. Princeton, 1926. [From all known MSS.]

Modern Rendering.

G. P. Krapp, New York, 1932.

Studies. [See *Hammond*, p. 395.]

McCormick, Sir W. S. Another Chaucer Stanza. [Furnivall Miscellany, Oxford, 1901, p. 296.]

Tatlock, J. S. P. MP. i, 1903–4, p. 317. [Date. See also J. Koch, E. Studien, xxxvi, 1906, p. 139.]

—— The Development and Chronology of Chaucer's Works. Chaucer Soc. 1907.

—— MLN. xxix, 1914, p. 97. [Bk iii, verse 188, bk iv, verse 788, bk v, verse 1791.]

—— A Welsh Troilus and Cressida. MLR. x, 1915, p. 265.

—— MP. xviii, 1921, p. 623. [Epilogue.]

—— The Date of Troilus. MLN. l, 1935, p. 277.

Root, R. K. The Poetry of Chaucer. Boston, 1906, 1922 (rev. edn), p. 87.

—— Chaucer's Dares. MP. xv, 1917, p. 1.

—— Shakespeare misreads Chaucer. MLN. xxxviii, 1923, p. 346.

Root, R. K. and Russell, H. N. A Planetary Date. PMLA. xxxix, 1924, p. 38.

Cook, A. S. The Character of Criseyde. PMLA. xxii, 1907, p. 531.

Griffin, N. E. Dares and Dictys. Baltimore, 1907.

—— Chaucer's Portrait of Criseyde. JEGP. xx, 1921, p. 39.

Fleschenberg, O. S. Daresstudien. Halle, 1908.

Hamilton, G. L. MLN. xxiii, 1908, p. 127. [Latin hexameters.]

Lowes, J. L. PMLA. xxiii, 1908, p. 285. [Date.]

Lowes, J. L. MP. xi, 1914, p. 544; MLN. xxxi, 1916, p. 185; Nation (New York), 11 Sept. 1913, p. 233. ['Hereos.']

Padelford, F. M. CHEL. vol. ii, 1908, p. 391. [On bk iii, verses 1415–1533, 1695–1712. See also C. R. Baskervill, PMLA. xxxvi, 1921, p. 394.]

Young, K. Origin and Development of the Story of Troilus and Criseyde. Chaucer Soc. 1908.

—— Aspects of the Story of Troilus and Criseyde. Wisconsin University Stud. ii, 1918, p. 367.

—— MLN. xl, 1925, p. 270. [Bk v, verses 1835 ff.]

Kittredge, G. L. The Date of Chaucer's Troilus. Chaucer Soc. 1909.

—— The Pillars of Hercules and Chaucer's 'Trophee.' [Putnam Anniversary Volume, Cedar Rapids, 1909, p. 545.]

—— Chaucer and his Poetry. Cambridge, U.S.A. 1915, p. 108.

Wilkins, E. E. Criseyde. MLN. xxiv, 1909, p. 65.

MacCracken, H. N. More Odd Texts. MLN. xxv, 1910, p. 126.

Brown, C. Contemporary Allusion in Chaucer's Troilus. MLN. xxvi, 1911, p. 208.

Dodd, W. G. Courtly Love in Chaucer and Gower. Boston, 1913.

Long, P. W. From Troilus to Euphues. [Kittredge Anniversary Papers, Boston, 1913, p. 367.]

Meyer, E. Die Charakterzeichnung bei Chaucer. SEP. xlviii, 1913.

Lütgenau, F. E. Studien, l, 1916, p. 63.

Rollins, H. E. The Troilus-Criseyde Story from Chaucer to Shakespeare. PMLA. xxxii, 1917, p. 383.

Tupper, F. JEGP. xvi, 1917, p. 551. [Bk v, verses 1786 ff.]

Hinckley, H. B. MP. xvi, 1918, p. 39. [Bk i, verses 687, 740, 963, 1065, bk ii, verse 188.]

Langhans, V. Untersuchungen zu Chaucer. Halle, 1918, p. 23.

Patch, H. R. Troilus on Predestination. JEGP. xvii, 1918, p. 399.

—— Troilus on Determinism. Speculum, vi, 1931, p. 225.

Emerson, O. F. 'Opie of Thebes Fyn.' MP. xvii, 1919–20, p. 287.

—— PQ. ii, 1923, p. 85. [Bk ii, verses 1228–9.]

Jack, A. A. A Commentary on the Poetry of Chaucer and Spenser. Glasgow, 1920, p. 47.

Baskervill, C. R. PMLA. xxxvi, 1921, p. 593. [Use of aube.]

Read, W. A. JEGP. xx, 1921, p. 397. [Bk i, verse 228.]

Curry, W. C. MLN. xxxvii, 1922, p. 94. [Bk iii, verse 1420.]

Curry, W. C. Destiny in Chaucer's Troilus. PMLA. xlv, 1930, p. 129.

Hibbard, L. A. PQ. i, 1922, p. 222. [Bk iii, verse 733.]

Bullett, G. New Statesman, 30 June 1923, p. 361. [Chaucer and Henryson.]

Murry, J. M. Adelphi, July 1923, p. 151. [Bk i, verses 151–4.]

Pieper, W. Archiv, cxlvi, 1923, pp. 205, 212. [On parliament.]

Barrow, S. F. Medieval Society Romances. New York, 1924, p. 123.

Brusendorff, A. The Chaucer Tradition. Copenhagen, 1925, pp. 59, 165.

Cowling, G. H. RES. ii, 1926, p. 311. [Versification.]

—— Chaucer. 1927, p. 112.

Bonnard, G. RES. v, 1929, p. 323. [Bk v, verse 1637.]

Graydon, J. S. Defense of Criseyde. PMLA. xliv, 1929, p. 141. [See also J. M. Beatty, Stud. Phil. xxvi, 1929, p. 470; J. M. French, PMLA. xliv, 1929, p. 1246.]

Day, M. RES. vi, 1930, p. 73. [Bk v, verse 1637.]

Sources. [*Hammond*, p. 398.]

Broatch, J. W. JEGP. ii, 1898, p. 14. [Indebtedness to Benoit.]

Hamilton, G. L. The Indebtedness of Chaucer to Guido delle Colonne. New York, 1908.

Young, K. MP. iv, 1906, p. 169. [Filocolo.]

—— Wisconsin University Stud. ii, 1918. p. 367. [Courtly Love and Filocolo.]

Cook, A. S. Archiv, cxix, 1907, p. 40. [Bk iii, verses 1 ff.]

—— Romanic Rev. viii, 1917, p. 226. [Bk v, verse 817.]

Wilkins, E. E. MLN. xxiv, 1909, p. 65. [Name Criseyde.]

Kittredge, G. L. MP. vii, 1910, p. 477. [L'Intelligenza.]

—— MLN. xxx, 1915, p. 69. [Machaut.]

—— Lollius. Harvard Stud. in Classical Philology, xxviii, 1917, pp. 47, 92, 110.

Cummings, H. M. The Indebtedness of Chaucer's Works to the Italian Works of Boccaccio. Cincinnati University Stud. x, pt 2, 1916, pp. 1, 50, 153.

Siebert, H. MLN. xxxi, 1916, p. 304. [Horace.]

Jefferson, B. L. Chaucer and the Consolation of Philosophy of Boethius. Princeton, 1917.

Lowes, J. L. MP. xiv, 1917, pp. 710, 715, 719, 721, 731, 733. [Dante.]

—— MP. xiv, 1917, p. 705. [Teseide; Filocolo.]

Root, R. K. MP. xv, 1917, p. 1. [Joseph of Exeter.]

—— Troilus and Criseyde. Princeton, 1926. [Introduction, p. xx.]

Ayres, H. M. Romanic Rev. x, 1919, p. 9 [Seneca.]

Shannon, E. F. MP. xvi, 1919, p. 610. [Lucan and bk v, verse 1792.]

Korten, H. Chaucer's literarische Bezie hungen zu Boccaccio. Rostock, 1920.

Tatlock, J. S. P. MLN. xxxv, 1920, p. 443 [Dante, Guinicelli.]

Wrenn, C. L. MLR. xviii, 1923, p. 286 [Horace.]

Schirmer, W. F. Germanisch-romanisch Monatsschrift, xii, 1924, p. 299. [Boccaccio.

Hinckley, H. B. PQ. vi, 1927, p. 313 [Horace.]

Lewis, C. S. What Chaucer really did to 'I Filostrato.' E. & S. xvii, 1932, p. 56.

[See also trns of Filostrato, by H. M Cummings, Princeton, 1924, and by N. E Griffin and A. B. Myrick, Philadelphia, 1930.

On Lollius. [*Hammond*, pp. 94, 309; MLR iv, 1909, p. 527.]

Broatch, J. W. JEGP. ii, 1898, p. 14.

Hamilton, G. L. The Indebtedness of Chauce to Guido delle Colonne. New York, 1903 p. 1.

Hammond, E. P. MLN. xxii, 1907, p. 51.

Young, K. The Origin and Development o the Story of Troilus and Criseyde. Chauce Soc. 1908, appendix C.

Koch, J. E. Studien, xli, 1909–10, p. 125.

Hathaway, C. M. E. Studien, xliv, 1911–2 p. 161.

Immelmann, R. E.Studien, xlv, 1912, p. 406

Kittredge, G. L. MLN. xxx, 1915, p. 69 Harvard Stud. in Classical Philology xxviii, 1917, p. 47.

Cummings, H. M. The Indebtedness o Chaucer's Works to the Italian Works o Boccaccio. Cincinnati University Stud. x pt 2, 1916, pp. 13, 153.

Lange, H. Ang. xlii, 1918, p. 345.

Korten, H. Chaucer's literarischen Bezie hungen zu Boccaccio. Rostock, 1920, p. 47

Root, R. K. Troilus and Criseyde. Princeton 1926. [Introduction, p. xxxvi.]

Goffin, R. C. TLS. 26 Aug. 1926, p. 564 21 April 1927, p. 280.

On Strode.

Gollancz, Sir I. DNB. under 'Strode.'

—— Pearl. 1921. [Introduction, p. xlvi.]

Brown, C. PMLA. xix, 1904, p. 154.

E. LEGEND OF GOOD WOMEN

[*Hammond*, p. 378; *Wells*, pp. 665, 873, 996 1080, 1089, 1145, 1193, 1235, 1287, 1825 1374, 1422; *Griffith*, p. 121.]

Editions. Parallel Texts, Supplementar Parallel Texts, Odd Texts, Chaucer Soc. 187

1886, 1890; H. Corson, Philadelphia, 1864; W. W. Skeat, Oxford, 1889, Oxford Chaucer, vol. III, pp. xvi, 65, 288.

Modern Rendering. W. W. Skeat, 1907.

Studies. [See *Hammond*, p. 378, for early studies.]

Toynbee, P. Academy, 26 Dec. 1891, p. 588. [Author of Chaucer's 'Book Cleped Valerie.']

Legouis, É. Quel fut le premier composé des deux Prologues? Havre, 1900. [See also E. Studien, xxx, 1902, p. 456; Angl. Bbl. xi, 1900, p. 231.]

Bilderbeck. J. B. Chaucer's Legend of Good Women. 1902.

Kittredge, G. L. Chaucer and Some of his Friends. MP. I. 1903, p. 1.

—— PMLA. xxiv, 1909, p. 343. [Medea, date.]

—— MP. vi, 1908–9, p. 435. [Alceste.]

—— MP. vii, 1910, pp. 471, 482. [Prologue, B 562, Marcia Catoun.]

Tatlock, J. S. P. Dates. MP. I, 1903–4, p. 317.

—— The Development and Chronology of Chaucer's Works. Chaucer Soc. 1907.

—— MLN. xxix, 1914, pp. 99, 100. [Cleopatra's serpent-pit; Ariadne's crown.]

—— Stud. Phil. xviii, 1921, pp. 419, 422. [Source: 'holynesse'; etc.]

Lowes, J. L. Prologue to Legend as Relating to French Marguerite Poems and Filostrato. PMLA. xix, 1904, p. 593.

—— Prologue to Legend in its Chronological Relations. PMLA. xx, 1905, p. 794.

—— JEGP. viii, 1909, p. 513. [Reply to Goddard.]

—— Chaucer's 'Etik.' MLN. xxv, 1910, p. 87.

—— Chaucer and Miroir de Mariage. MP. viii, 1910–1, pp. 165, 305, 331, 334.

—— Kittredge Anniversary Papers. Boston, 1913, p. 95. [The two Prologues; New Testament. See also Ang. Bbl. xxv, 1914, p. 333.]

—— Chaucer and Dante. MP. xiii, 1915–6, p. 19, xiv, 1916–7, p. 714.

—— Ovide Moralisé. PMLA. xxxii, 1917, p. 302.

—— MP. xiv, 1916–7, p. 710, xv, 1917–8, p. 186. [Filocolo; Teseide.]

French, J. C. The Problem of the Two Prologues. Baltimore, 1905.

Goddard, H. C. JEGP. vii, 1907–8, p. 87, viii, 1909, p. 47. [Purpose; a travesty.]

Cook, A. S. MP. vi, 1908–9, p. 475. [On Prologue, verse 334.]

—— Trans. Connecticut Academy, xxiii, 1919, p. 32. [Parallels to verses 125–7.]

Macaulay, G. C. MLR. iv, 1909, p. 18. [Verses 285 ff., 298 ff.]

Root, R. K. PMLA. xxiv, 1909, p. 124. [Legend of Medea.]

—— PMLA. xxv, 1910, p. 228. [Date of Medea.]

Moore, S. MLR. vii, 1912, p. 488. [Prologue; Anne and Richard.]

Hulbert, J. R. Chaucer and the Earl of Oxford. MP. x, 1912–3, p. 433.

Brown, C. Chaucer, Lydgate, and the Legend. E. Studien, xlvii, 1913, p. 59.

—— Chaucer's Serpent-Pit. MLN. xxix, 1914, p. 108.

Dodd, W. G. Courtly Love in Chaucer and Gower. Boston, 1913, p. 154.

Schofield, W. H. Kittredge Anniversary Papers. Boston, 1913, p. 139. [Sea-battle in Cleopatra.]

Jefferson, B. L. JEGP. xiii, 1914, p. 434. [Anne and Alcestis.]

Lange, H., Langhans, V., and Koch, J. Ang. xxxix, 1915, p. 347 (continued Deutsche Literaturzeitung, xxxvii, 1916, p. 891), xli, 1917, pp. 162, 393, xlii, 1918, pp. 142, 352, xliii, 1919, pp. 69, 197, xliv, 1920, pp. 23, 72, 213, 337, 373, 385; E. Studien, lv, 1921, pp. 175, 196, lvi, 1922, p. 36; Ang. xlix, 1925, pp. 178, 216, 267, 357, l, 1926, pp. 62, 70, 104, 106, li, 1927, p. 128, lii, 1928, p. 123, liv, 1930, p. 99, lv, 1931, p. 106. [Controversy on Prologues, etc.]

Siebert, H. Chaucer and Horace. MLN. xxxi, 1916, p. 304.

Tupper, F. The Envy Theme in Prologues and Epilogues. JEGP. xvi, 1917, p. 551.

—— Chaucer's Lady of the Daisies. JEGP. xxi, 1922, p. 293. [See also J. M. Manly, MP. xxiv, 1926–7, p. 257.]

Amy, E. F. The Text of Chaucer's Legend of Good Women. Princeton, 1918.

—— JEGP. xxi, 1922, p. 107. [The MSS.]

Emerson, O. F. MP. xvii, 1919–20, p. 287. [Verses 2668–70.]

Jack, A. A. A Commentary on the Poetry of Chaucer and Spenser. Glasgow, 1920, pp. 71, 840. [Chaucer and stories of women.]

Hibbard, L. A. PQ. i, 1922, p. 222. [Verse 2629.]

Curry, W. C. Hypermnestra and Chaucer's Scientific Method. JEGP. xxii, 1923, p. 347.

—— E. Studien, lviii, 1924, p. 55. [On dreams.]

—— Chaucer and the Medieval Sciences. New York, 1926, p. 286. [Dream lore.]

Garrett, R. M. Cleopatra the Martyr and her Sisters. JEGP. xxii, 1923, p. 64.

Christy, J. Z. N. & Q., 8 Dec. 1923, p. 451. [Prologue, A 145, B 213, Philippa.]

Griffith, D. D. Manly Anniversary Studies, Chicago, 1923, p. 32. [Interpretation.]

Koch, J. E. Studien, lvii, 1923, pp. 29, 37, 45. [Latin sources.]

Whitney, M. P. The Queen of Medieval
Virtues: Largess. [Vassar Medieval Studies,
New Haven, 1923, p. 180.]
Schirmer, W. F. Germanisch-romanische
Monatsschrift, XII, 1924, p. 295. [Boccaccio.]
Connelly, W. Classical Weekly, 13 Oct. 1924,
p. 9. [Ovid's Heroides.]
Holthausen, F. Archiv, CXLVII, 1924, p. 251.
[Ballade, Froissart.]
Schleich, G. Die mittelenglische Umdichtung
von Boccaccio's De Claris Mulieribus.
Palaestra, CXLIV, 1924.
Brusendorff, A. The Chaucer Tradition.
Copenhagen, 1925, pp. 25, 40, 137. [MSS;
author; composition.]
Cowling, G. H. RES. II, 1926, p. 311. [On
B 249–69.]
Rand, E. K. Speculum, I, 1926, p. 222. [Dido,
verse 174.]
Langhans, V. Ang. LI, 1927, p. 323. [On
Brusendorff.]
—— Ang. LII, 1928, p. 325. [Trn of De
Contemptu Mundi.]
Webster, K. G. T. MP. XXV, 1927–8, p. 291.
[Verses 58, 69.]
Ghosh, P. C. MLR. XXVI, 1931, p. 332.
[Cleopatra's death.]
Hamilton, M. P. Chaucer's Marcia Catoun.
MP. XXX, 1933, p. 361.
Hammond, E. P. Chaucer's 'Book of the
Twenty-five Ladies.' MLN. XLVIII, 1933,
p. 514.

F. ASTROLABE

[Hammond, p. 359; Wells, pp. 652, 872, 995,
1029, 1144, 1234, 1286, 1324, 1373, 1422;
Griffith, p. 113.]

Editions. A. E. Brae, 1870; W. W. Skeat,
EETS. Ex. Ser. 1872, Oxford Chaucer, vol. III,
pp. lvii, 175, 352; A. W. Pollard et al. Globe
Chaucer; R. T. Gunther, Chaucer and
Messahalla on the Astrolabe, Oxford, 1930,
1932 (rev.)

Studies.
Furnivall, F. J. Athenaeum, 14 Oct. 1871.
p. 495. [Date.]
Root. R. K. The Poetry of Chaucer. Boston,
1906, 1922 (rev. edn), p. 85.
Moore, S. MP. X, 1912–3, p. 203. [Date.]
Kittredge, G. L. MP. XIV, 1916–7, p. 513.
[Date; Lewis.]
Kaluza, M. Chaucer Handbuch. Leipzig, 1919,
p. 207.
Brusendorff, A. The Chaucer Tradition.
Copenhagen, 1925, p. 175. [MSS; text;
Lewis.]
Manly, J. M., Rye, W., Garrod, H. W. TLS.
7, 28 June, 11 Oct. 1928, pp. 430, 486, 736.
[Lewis.]

Langhans, V. Ang. LIII, 1929, p. 235. [Date.]
Harvey, S. W. Chaucer's Debt to Sacrobosco.
JEGP. XXXIV, 1935, p. 34.

G. CANTERBURY TALES

(1) THE TALES IN GENERAL

[Hammond, p. 150; Wells, pp. 672, 873,
996, 1030, 1090, 1145, 1194, 1236, 1287, 1325,
1374, 1423; Griffith, pp. 19, 65.]

(a) Manuscripts
(i) General

[Hammond, p. 163; Wells, pp. 679, 875,
1030, 1146, 1195, 1236, 1287, 1326, 1374, 1423.]

Skeat, W. W. Oxford Chaucer. Vol. IV, p. vii.
—— The Evolution of the Canterbury Tales.
Chaucer Soc. 1907.
—— The Eight-Text Edition of the Canter-
bury Tales. Chaucer Soc. 1909.
—— The Six-Text Edition of the Canterbury
Tales. With Six Appendices. Chaucer Soc.
1909–11.
—— MLR. V, 1910, p. 430; N. & Q. 12 March
1910, p. 201. [Shipman's, Friar's Prologue.]
Flügel, E. A New Collation of the Ellesmere
MS. Ang. XXX, 1907, p. 401.
Tatlock, J. S. P. The Development and
Chronology of Chaucer's Works. Chaucer
Soc. 1907.
—— MLN. XXIX, 1914, p. 140. [Plimpton MS.]
—— The Canterbury Tales in 1400. PMLA
L, 1935, p. 100.
The Ellesmere Chaucer. 2 vols. Manchester
1911. [Facs. of Ellesmere MS.]
Koch, J. A Detailed Comparison of the 8 MSS
Anglistische Forschungen, XXXVI, 1913, L
1916, p. 323. [Addns, E. Studien, XLVIII
1914–5, p. 259.]
—— E. Studien, XLVII, 1913–4, p. 338
[Text-notes.]
Greg, W. W. Facsimiles of Twelve Manu-
scripts in Trinity College, Cambridge. Ox-
ford, 1913. [One page of R, 3, 3.]
Wild, F. Die sprachlichen Eigentümlich-
keiten der wichtigeren Chaucer-hand-
schriften. Wiener Beiträge, XLIV, 1915.
Piper, E. F. PQ. III, 1924, p. 241, V, 1926
p. 330. [Ellesmere MS.]
Brusendorff, A. The Chaucer Tradition.
Copenhagen, 1925, pp. 53, 63, 93, 106, 126
474.
Spurgeon, C. F. E. Five Hundred Years of
Chaucer Criticism and Allusion. Vol. I
Cambridge, 1925, pp. 26, 33, vol. II
frontispiece. [Three pages facs.]
Marburg, C. Notes on the Cardigan Chaucer
Manuscript. PMLA. XLI, 1926, p. 229.
[See also J. Koch, Ang. XLIX, 1925, p. 220;
Wells, pp. 1146, 1236.]

Cowling, G. H. Chaucer. 1927, p. 212.

Manly, J. M. Canterbury Tales. New York, 1928, pp. 79, 86.

Kilgour, M. PMLA. XLIV, 1929, p. 186. [MS source of Caxton's 2nd edn. See also W. W. Greg, *ibid.* p. 1251.]

Kase, C. R. Observations on the Shifting Positions of Groups G and DE in the MSS. [In R. Krauss, H. Braddy, and C. R. Kase, Three Chaucer Studies, New York, 1932.]

Everett, D. Another Collation of the Ellesmere MS. Medium Aevum, I, 1932, p. 42.

McCormick, Sir W. and Heseltine, J. E. The Manuscripts of Chaucer's Canterbury Tales. A Critical Description of their Contents. Oxford, 1933.

(ii) Harley 7334 Text

[*Hammond*, p. 177; *Wells*, pp. 680, 875, 1195, 1237.]

Chaucer Soc. 1885. [Printed entire.]

Pollard, A. W. Globe Chaucer. P. xxix.

Skeat, W. W. The Chaucer Canon. Oxford, 1900, p. 25.

—— The Eight-Text Edition. Chaucer Soc. 1909.

Tatlock, J. S. P. Chaucer Soc. 1909.

Koch, J. Ang. Bbl. XXII, 1911, p. 267.

Brusendorff, A. The Chaucer Tradition. Copenhagen, 1925, p. 93.

(b) Editions

[For Chaucer Soc. Six-Text and Eight-Text edns, and other texts, see *Hammond*, p. 523.]

Skeat, W. W. Oxford Chaucer. Vols. IV–VI.

—— Student's Chaucer. P. 419.

Pollard, A. W. *et al.* Globe Chaucer. P. 1.

The Ellesmere Chaucer. 2 vols. Manchester, 1911. [Facs. of Ellesmere MS.]

Koch, J. Chaucer's Canterbury Tales nach dem Ellesmere MS. Heidelberg, 1915.

Manly, J. M. Canterbury Tales. New York, 1928. [Parts of several tales omitted.]

Robinson, F. N. Complete Works of Geoffrey Chaucer. Boston, 1933.

[See also *Hammond*, p. 202; *Wells*, pp. 873, 1145, 1325, 1423; *Griffith*, p. 18; and W. W. Greg, The Early Printed Editions of the Canterbury Tales, PMLA. XXXIX, 1924, p. 737. For edns of selected pieces, see under individual items below, and *Hammond*, p. 213.]

(c) Modernisations

[*Hammond*, p. 220; *Wells*, p. 1325, 1423; *Griffith*, p. 24.]

Tatlock, J. S. P. and Mackaye, P. The Complete Works of Geoffrey Chaucer. New York, 1912, 1914; abridged New York, 1923.

(d) Comprehensive Studies

[*Hammond*, p. 150, 523; *Wells*, pp. 672, 874, 996, 1090, 1146, 1194, 1236, 1287, 1325. 1423; *Griffith*, p. 65.]

ten Brink, B. Early English Literature. Vol. II, 1892, p. 138.

Pollard, A. W. A Chaucer Primer. 1893; 1903 (rev. edn).

Skeat, W. W. Oxford Chaucer. Vol. III, p. 371, vol. IV, p. vii, vol. V, p. ix.

Root, R. K. The Poetry of Chaucer. Boston. 1906, 1922 (rev. edn), p. 151.

Björkman, E. Geoffrey Chaucer. Stockholm, 1906.

Legouis, É. Geoffrey Chaucer. 1913, p. 136.

Kittredge, G. L. Chaucer and his Poetry. Cambridge, U.S.A. 1915, p. 146.

Jack, A. A. A Commentary on the Poetry of Chaucer and Spenser. Glasgow, 1920, p. 81.

Brusendorff, A. The Chaucer Tradition. Copenhagen, 1925.

Cowling, G. H. Chaucer. 1927.

French, R. D. A Chaucer Handbook. New York, 1927, p. 193.

Manly, J. M. Canterbury Tales. New York, 1928. [Introduction and notes.]

(e) Special Studies

[*Hammond*, pp. 150, 239, 265. *Wells*, pp. 874, 1030, 1146, 1236, 1325, 1423.]

Hertwig, D. Der Einfluss von Chaucer's Canterbury Tales auf die englische Literatur. Marburg, 1908.

Ewald, W. Der Humor in Chaucer's Canterbury Tales. SEP. XLV, 1911.

Markert, E. Chaucer's Canterbury-Pilger und ihre Tracht. Marburg, 1911.

Meyer, E. Die Charakterzeichnung bei Chaucer. SEP. XLVIII, 1913.

Schofield, W. H. Chivalry in English Literature. Oxford, 1913.

Tatlock, J. S. P. Puns in Chaucer. [Flügel Memorial Volume, Palo Alto, 1916, p. 228.]

Starnes, De W. T. Our Lady of Walsingham. Texas Rev. VII, 1922, p. 306.

Maxfield, E. K. Chaucer and Religious Reform. PMLA. XXXVII, 1922, p. 64.

Landrum, G. W. Chaucer's Use of the Vulgate. PMLA. XXXIX, 1924, p. 75.

Schirmer, W. F. Germanisch-romanische Monatsschrift, XII, 1924, p. 289. [Influence of Boccaccio.]

Looten, C. Les Portraits de Chaucer: leurs Origines. Revue de Littératur comparée, VII, 1927, p. 397.

Manly, J. M. Chaucer and the Rhetoricians. British Academy Lecture, 1927.

Patch, H. R. Chaucer and Lady Fortune. MLR. XXII, 1927, p. 377.

Chapman, C. O. Chaucer on Preachers and Preaching. PMLA. xliv, 1929, p. 178.

Kilgour, M. PMLA. xliv, 1929, p. 186. [MS source of Caxton's 2nd edn.]

Montgomery, F. The Musical Instruments in the Canterbury Tales. Musical Quart. xvii, 1931, p. 439.

[See also under individual items.]

(f) Index of Proper Names and Subjects

Corson, H. Chaucer Soc. 1911; New York, 1911.

(g) General Plan, and its Origin and Development

[*Hammond*, pp. 150, 239, 255, 265, 269; *Wells*, pp. 672, 874–6, 1030, 1146, 1236, 1287, 1325, 1374, 1423.]

Lounsbury, T. R. Studies in Chaucer. Vol. ii, New York, 1892, p. 229.

Skeat, W. W. Oxford Chaucer. Vol. ii, p. xxxvi, vol. iii, pp. 371, 378, 380, 384, vol. v, pp. 4, 19, 129, vol. vi, p. xcix.

—— The Evolution of the Canterbury Tales. Chaucer Soc. 1907.

Fueter, E. Die Rahmenzählung bei Boccaccio und Chaucer. Beiblatt zur allgemeinen Zeitung, 1906, nos. 265–6.

Tatlock, J. S. P. The Duration of the Canterbury Pilgrimage. PMLA. xxi, 1906, p. 478.

—— The Development and Chronology of Chaucer's Works. Chaucer Soc. 1907, p. 132.

—— Chaucer Soc. 1909. [Harl. MS. 7334 and revision.]

—— Boccaccio and the Plan of the Canterbury Tales. Ang. xxxvii, 1913, p. 69.

—— The Canterbury Tales in 1400. PMLA. l, 1935, p. 100.

Root, R. K. The Poetry of Chaucer. Boston, 1906, 1922 (rev. edn), p. 151.

—— Chaucer and the Decameron. E. Studien, xliv, 1911, p. 1.

Hinckley, H. B. Notes on Chaucer. Northampton, 1907, p. 2. [On Sercambi.]

Morsbach, L. Chaucer's Plan. E. Studien, xlii, 1910, p. 43.

Legouis, É. Geoffrey Chaucer. 1913, p. 136.

Young, K. Kittredge Anniversary Papers. Boston, 1913, p. 405.

Jones H. S. V. MP. xiii, 1915–6, p. 45.

Cummings, H. M. The Indebtedness of Chaucer's Works to the Italian Works of Boccaccio. Cincinnati University Stud. x, pt 2, 1916, p. 176.

Korten, H. Chaucer's literarische Beziehungen zu Boccaccio. Rostock, 1920.

Farnham, W. England's Discovery of the Decameron. PMLA. xxxix, 1924, p. 123.

Brusendorff, A. The Chaucer Tradition. Copenhagen, 1925, p. 120.

Manly, J. M. Some New Light on Chaucer. New York, 1926, p. 70.

—— Canterbury Tales. New York, 1928, pp. 67, 74.

Bashe, E. J. The Prologue of the Tale of Beryn. PQ. xii, 1933, p. 1.

Brown, Carleton. The Squire and the Number of the Pilgrims. MLN. xlix, 1934, p. 216.

Morsbach, L. Chaucers Canterbury Tales und das Decameron. Berlin, 1934.

[For illustrations and backgrounds, see especially *Griffith*. See also under individual fragments and tales.]

(h) Fragments and Links, and their Order

[*Hammond*, pp. 155, 158, 165, 166, 241; *Wells*, pp. 675, 677, 874, 875, 1236, 1325, 1374, 1423.]

Furnivall, F. J. A Temporary Preface to the Six-Text Edition of the Canterbury Tales. Chaucer Soc. 1868.

Bradshaw, H. The Skeleton of Chaucer's Canterbury Tales. 1871.

—— Collected Papers. Cambridge, 1889.

Koch, J. The Chronology of Chaucer's Writings. Chaucer Soc. 1890.

—— Anglistische Forschungen, xxxvi, 1913, p. 5.

Skeat, W. W. Academy, 1 Aug. 1891, p. 96 [Order.]

—— Oxford Chaucer. Vol. iii, pp. 374, 379, 434.

—— MLR. v, 1910, p. 430. [Shipman's Prologue.]

ten Brink, B. Early English Literature Vol. ii, 1893, p. 165, vol. iii, 1896, p. 268.

Fleay, F. G. Academy, 26 Oct. 1895, p. 343. [Order.]

Shipley, G. MLN. xi, 1896, p. 290. [Order.]

Root, R. K. The Poetry of Chaucer. Boston, 1906, 1922 (rev. edn), pp. 152, 297.

Tatlock, J. S. P. In Principio. MLN. xxix, 1914, p. 141.

Moore, S. PMLA. xxx, 1915, p. 116. [Position of group C.]

Brusendorff, A. The Chaucer Tradition. Copenhagen, 1925, pp. 69, 73, 119, 120, 121, 123.

Manly, J. M. Canterbury Tales. New York, 1928, pp. 77, 82.

[See also under individual fragments and tales.]

(i) Groups and Motifs

[*Hammond*, pp. 254–61; *Wells*, pp. 683, 876, 996, 1030, 1091, 1146, 1236, 1326, 1424.]

Lowes, J. L. Chaucer and the Miroir de Mariage. MP. VIII, 1910–1, pp. 165, 305.

—— Chaucer and the Seven Deadly Sins. PMLA. XXX, 1915, p. 237.

Moore, S. Date of Chaucer's Marriage Group. MLN. XXVI, 1911, p. 172.

Kittredge, G. L. Chaucer's Discussion of Marriage. MP. IX, 1912, p. 435.

—— Chaucer and his Poetry. Cambridge, U.S.A. 1915, pp. 153, 185.

Tupper, F. St Venus and the Canterbury Pilgrims. Nation (New York), 16 Oct. 1913, p. 354.

—— Chaucer and the Seven Deadly Sins. PMLA. XXIX, 1914, p. 93.

—— Wilful and Impatient Poverty. Nation (New York), 9 July 1914, p. 41.

—— Chaucer's Pardoner's Tavern. JEGP. XIII, 1914, p. 553.

—— The Quarrels of the Canterbury Pilgrims. JEGP. XIV, 1915, p. 256.

—— Chaucer and the Prymer. MLN. XXX, 1915, p. 9.

—— Sinners and Sins. JEGP. XV, 1916, p. 56.

—— The Envy Theme in the Prologues and Epilogues. JEGP. XVI, 1917, p. 551.

Lawrence, W. W. MP. XI, 1913–4, p. 247. [Marriage group.]

Tatlock, J. S. P. Boccaccio and the Plan of the Canterbury Tales. Ang. XXXVII, 1913, p. 94.

Koch, J. Ang. Bbl. XXV, 1914, p. 327, XXVIII, 1917, p. 152. [On Tupper and Lowes. See also Ang. XLIX, 1925, p. 221; E. Studien, XLVI, 1912–3, p. 112.]

Hemingway, S. MLN. XXXI, 1916, p. 479. [Monk and Nun's Priest.]

Kenyon, J. JEGP. XV, 1916, p. 182. [Marriage group.]

Hinckley, H. B. The Debate on Marriage in the Canterbury Tales. PMLA. XXXII, 1917, p. 392.

Curry, W. C. JEGP. XVIII, 1919, p. 593; PMLA. XXXV, 1920, p. 189, XXXVII, 1922, p. 30; MP. XIX, 1921–2, p. 395. [Use of physiognomists, etc.]

—— Chaucer and the Medieval Sciences. New York, 1926.

Manly, J. M. Some New Light on Chaucer. New York, 1926, p. 70.

Brown, Carleton. The Evolution of the Canterbury 'Marriage Group.' PMLA. XLVIII, 1933, p. 1041.

(2) INDIVIDUAL FRAGMENTS AND TALES

(a) Fragment A

[*Hammond*, pp. 150, 265; *Wells*, pp. 689, 876, 1030, 1091, 1146, 1237, 1288, 1326, 1375,

1424; *Griffith*, p. 70; R. K. Root, The Poetry of Chaucer, Boston, 1906, 1922 (rev. edn), p. 160; W. W. Skeat, Oxford Chaucer, vol. III, p. 388.]

(i) General Prologue

[See *Hammond*, *Wells*, under Fragment A, above.]

Annotated Editions.

W. McLeod, 1871; J. Zupitza, Marburg, 1871, Berlin, 1882, 1920; B. ten Brink, Marburg, 1871; A. Monfries, Edinburgh, 1876; E. F. Willoughby, 1881, Chicago, 1907; J. M. D. Meiklejohn, 1882; W. W. Skeat, Oxford, 1891, 1900, 1903, 1906; A. W. Pollard, 1903; C. T. Onions, 1904; H. Van Dyke, New York, 1909; J. A. Wyatt, 1927.

[With Knight's Tale.] S. H. Carpenter, Boston, 1872, 1901; A. J. Wyatt, Cambridge, 1895, 1897, 1899, 1900; W. B. Smith, Cambridge, 1908; F. Mather, Boston, 1908.

[With Nun's Priest's Tale.] A. J. Wyatt, 1904, 1929.

[With Squire's Tale.] A. J. Wyatt, 1903.

[With Knight's and Nun's Priest's Tales.] R. Morris, 1867, rev. W. W. Skeat, Oxford, 1889, 1903; F. J. Mather, Boston, 1898, 1908; M. H. Liddell, New York, 1901, 1902; A. Ingraham, 1902.

[With Prioress's, Nun's Priest's and Pardoner's Tales.] G. H. Cowling, 1934.

Modern Rendering.

Skeat, W. W. 1907.

Studies. [See *Hammond*, p. 265, for early items on sources, date, studies, and notes.]

Schlacht, H. Der gute Pfarrer in der englischen Literatur. Berlin, 1904. [Verses 477 ff.]

Root, R. K. The Poetry of Chaucer. Boston, 1906, 1922 (rev. edn), p. 160.

—— E. Studien, XLIV, 1911–2, p. 1. [Verses 725 ff.]

Cook, A. S. MLN. XXII, 1907, p. 126. [Verse 466.]

—— Beginning the Board in Prussia. JEGP. XIV, 1915, p. 375.

—— Trans. Connecticut Academy, XX, 1916, p. 161. [Verses 51 ff.; historical background.]

—— Romanic Rev. VIII, 1917, p. 224. [Verses 1–8.]

—— MLN. XXXIII, 1918, p. 379; Trans. Connecticut Academy, XXIII, 1919, p. 27. [Verse 386; 'mormal.']

—— Trans. Connecticut Academy, XXIII, 1919, pp. 1, 22, 29. [Verses 1–11 and classics; verse 5 and Dame de Fayel; sources, verses 493–8, 527–8.]

Hammond, E. P. MLN. xxii 1907, p. 51. [Verse 120.]

Hinckley, H. B. Notes on Chaucer. Northampton, 1907, p. 1.

—— MP. xiv, 1916–7, p. 317, xv, 1917–8, p. 56. [Verses 82, 110, 200, 258, 264, 637.]

—— PMLA. xxxiii, 1918, p. xxvii. [Prioress.]

Manly, J. M. A Knight There Was. Trans. American Philolog. Ass. xxxviii, 1907, p. 89.

—— MP. v, 1907–8, p. 201. [Verse 560.]

—— Some New Light on Chaucer. New York, 1926, p. 70. [Pilgrims from actual persons. See also edn of Canterbury Tales, New York, 1928, p. 70.]

—— TLS. 10 Nov. 1927, p. 817. [Prioress.]

Tatlock, J. S. P. The Development and Chronology of Chaucer's Works. Chaucer Soc. 1907, p. 142.

—— MLN. xxix, 1914, p. 141. [Verse 254.]

—— MLN. xxxi, 1916, p. 139. [Verses 509–12.]

—— MP. xiv, 1916–7, p. 257. [Verses 486, 653–62.]

Lowes, J. L. Ang. xxx, 1907, p. 440. [Verse 119.]

—— Romanic Rev. ii, 1911, p. 118. [Verses 262–3, 286, 467.]

—— Romanic Rev. v, 1914, p. 368. [Prioress' Oath.]

Greenlaw, E. and Kittredge, G. L. MLN. xxiii, 1908, pp. 142, 200. [Verse 256.]

Macaulay, G. C. MLR. iv, 1909, p. 15. [Verses 177, 525.]

Kittredge, G. L. MP. vii, 1909–10, p. 475. [Verses 449–52, 475–7, 652.]

—— Chaucer and his Poetry. Cambridge, U.S.A. 1915, p. 146.

Giles, E. Prologue to the Canterbury Tales. Journ. of Education, lxxiii, 1911, pp. 349, 379, 411.

Markert, E. Chaucer's Canterbury-Pilger und ihre Tracht. Würzburg, 1911.

Barnouw, A. J. De Prolog tot de Kantelberg-Vertelligen. Onze Eeuw, 1912, p. 375.

—— Nation (New York), 7 Dec. 1916, p. 540. [Verse 468.]

Jones, H. S. V. PMLA. xxvii, 1912, p. 106. [Clerk.]

Legouis, É. Geoffrey Chaucer. 1913, pp. 136, 206.

Meyer, E. Die Charakterzeichnung bei Chaucer. SEP. xlviii, 1913.

Waugh, M. T. Scottish Hist. Rev. xi, 1913–4, pp. 58, 88. [Verses 43 ff.]

Tupper, F. Nation (New York), 26 June 1913, p. 640. [Verse 411.]

—— The Envy Theme. JEGP. xvi, 1917, p. 551.

Tupper, F. Canterbury Inn. N. & Q. 25 Oct. 1924, p. 301.

Förster, M. Archiv, cxxxii, 1914, p. 399. [Verse 164.]

Young, K. MLN. xxx, 1915, p. 97. [Verses 707–10.]

Hemingway, S. B. MLN. xxxi, 1915, p. 479. [Verses 165 ff.]

Kuhl, E. P. Chaucer's Burgesses. PMLA. xxx, 1915, p. xi.

—— Trans. Wisconsin Academy, xviii, 1916, p. 652. [Verses 361 ff.; date.]

—— PQ. ii, 1923, p. 302. [Verses 118 ff., 146, 147, 164, 160, 125, 129.]

Baum, P. F. MLN. xxxii, 1917, p. 376. [Verses 91, 95.]

—— MLN. xxxvi, 1921, p. 307. [Verse 719.]

Jefferson, B. L. Chaucer and the Consolation of Philosophy of Boethius. Princeton, 1917.

Van Herk, A. Neophilologus, ii, 1917, p. 292. [Verses 164, 253.]

Bruce, J. D. MLN. xxxiv, 1919, p. 118. [Verse 256.]

Curry, W. C. JEGP. xviii, 1919, p. 593. [Pardoner.]

—— PMLA. xxxv, 1920, p. 189. [Reeve, Miller.]

—— MP. xix, 1921–2, p. 395. [Summoner.]

—— MLN. xxxvi, 1921, p. 274. [Verse 385; 'mormal.']

—— PMLA. xxxvii, 1922, p. 30. [Wife of Bath.]

—— JEGP. xxiii, 1924, p. 83. [Man of Law.]

—— PQ. iv, 1925, p. 1. [Physician.]

—— Chaucer and the Medieval Sciences. New York, 1926, pp. 3, 37, 47, 54, 71, 91.

Schulze, K. Germanisch-romanische Monatsschrift, viii, 1920, p. 103. [Verses 445 ff.]

Cummings, H. M. MLN. xxxvii, 1922, p. 86. [Verses 1–7; Boethius.]

Knott, T. A. PQ. i, 1922, p. 1. [Anonymous merchant.]

Koch, J. Ang. xlvi, 1922, p. 37. [Date.]

Law, R. PMLA. xxxvii, 1922, p. 208. [Verse 253.]

Emerson, O. F. PQ. ii, 1923, p. 89. [Verses 163–4; 'preestes thre.']

Goffin, R. C. MLR. xviii, 1923, p. 336. [Verse 323.]

Thompson, J. W. Stud. Phil. xx, 1923, p. 83. [Verse 560.]

Walker, A. S. MLN. xxxviii, 1923, p. 314. [Verses 276–7; date 1385, 1386.]

Knowlton, E. C. JEGP. xxiii, 1924, p. 83. [Man of Law.]

Maxfield, E. K. PMLA. xxxix, 1924, p. 64. [Verses 477 ff.]

Power, E. Medieval People. 1924, p. 59. [Verses 118 ff.]

scher, W. Festschrift für J. Hoops. Heidelberg, 1925, p. 149. [Verses 118 ff.]

vingston, C. H. PMLA. XL, 1925, p. 217. [Verses 124–6.]

adeleva, M. Chaucer's Nuns and Other Essays. New York, 1925. [Verses 118 ff.]

offett, H. Y. PQ. IV, 1925, p. 208. [Verses 587 ff.]

atch, H. R. Characters in Medieval Literature. MLN. XL, 1925, p. 1.

anford, J. H. Speculum I, 1926, p. 38. [Verse 560.]

ckert, E. Harry Bailif. TLS. 12 Dec. 1926.

dgwick, W. B. RES. II, 1926, p. 346. [Verse 58.]

ore, S. MP. XXV, 1927–8, p. 59. [Pardoner.]

ashford, E. H. Nineteenth Century, CIV, 1928, p. 237. [Physician.]

mden, C. PQ. VII, 1928, p. 314. [Burgesses.]

eckmann, E. P. M. MP. XXVI, 1928–9, p. 279. [Verse 673.]

appe, F. S. MLN. XLIII, 1928, p. 176. [Yeoman.]

atter, G. M. MLN. XLIII, 1928, p. 536. [Verse 351.]

hite, F. E. MP. XXVI, 1928–9, pp. 240, 379, XXVII, 1929, p. 123. [Shipman.]

ood-Leigh, K. L. RES. IV, 1928, p. 145. [Franklin.]

yatt, A. J. RES. IV, 1928, p. 439. [Verse 323.]

ost, G. L. MLN. XLIV, 1929, p. 496. [Man of Law.]

ark, T. B. PQ. IX, 1930, p. 312. [Prioress.]

erett, D. 'If Euen-song and Morwe-song Accorde.' RES. VIII, 1932, p. 456.

s, D. V. 'A Man of Religion.' MLR. XXVII, 932, p. 144.

rton, O. E. The Neck of Chaucer's Friar. MLN. XLVIII, 1933, p. 31.

inwright, B. B. Chaucer's Prioress. MLN. XLVIII, 1933, p. 34.

(ii) Knight's Tale

See Hammond, Wells, under Fragment A, 285 above.]

Annotated Editions. [See under General Proue; also W. and R. Chambers, Edinburgh, 6; A. W. Pollard, 1903; R. J. Cunliffe, 5.]

ource. Teseide. Chaucer Soc. ser. 2, III, 8, p. 104.

ollations. Chaucer Soc. ser. 1, IV, 1868 rgin Cambridge, Lansdowne texts); W. W. at. Oxford Chaucer, vol. V, p. 60, vol. III, 92,

arlier Version; Date. B. ten Brink, ucer, Münster, 1870, p. 47; J. Koch, Studien, I, 1877, p. 249; W. W. Skeat, ord Chaucer, vol. I, pp. lxiii, 529, vol. III,

pp. 306, 381, 389; A. W. Pollard, Globe Chaucer, p. xxvi; G. L. Kittredge, MP. I, 1903–4, p. 1; J. L. Lowes, MLN. XIX, 1904, p. 240; PMLA. XX, 1905, p. 841.

Studies. [See Hammond for other earlier items.]

Skeat, W. W. Oxford Chaucer. Vol. III, p. 389, vol. V, p. 60.

Ker, W. P. Essays on Medieval Literature. 1905, p. 87.

Hinckley, H. B. and Skeat, W. W. Academy, 22 Dec. 1906, p. 640, 26 Jan. 1907, p. 99. [Influence of Ywaine and Gawaine.]

Hinckley, H. B. Notes on Chaucer. Northampton, 1907, p. 50.

—— MP. XIV, 1916–7, p. 317, XV, 1917–8, p. 56. [Verses 564, 802, 839, 1052, 1302, 1840, 1945.]

Capone, G. La Novella del Cavaliere e la Teseide. Sassari, 1907, 1909. [Marginalia, 1912.]

Cook, A. S. MLN. XXII, 1907, p. 207. [Verse 810.]

—— Trans. Connecticut Academy, XX, 1916, p. 161. [Verses 1297–1328; suggestion; date.]

—— Trans. Connecticut Academy, XXI, 1916, p. 128. [Verses 1290–4.]

—— MLN. XXXI, 1916, p. 315. [Verse 1311; 'fraknes.']

—— Romanic Rev. IX, 1918, p. 317. [Verses 2012–8.]

—— Trans. Connecticut Academy, XXIII, 1919, p. 30. [Verse 1290.]

Hart, W. M. MLN. XXII, 1907, p. 241. [Verse 1033.]

Tatlock, J. S. P. The Development and Chronology of Chaucer's Works. Chaucer Soc. 1907, pp. 45, 226, 231.

—— MLN. XXIX, 1914, p. 142. [Verse 1529.]

—— Stud. Phil. XVIII, 1921, p. 419. [Source of legend, etc.]

Browne, W. H. Astrology. MLN. XXIII, 1908, p. 53.

Hempl, G., Tatlock, J. S. P. and Mather, F. J. Palamon and Arcite. MLN. XXIII, 1908, p. 127.

Mather, F. J. The Prologue and Knight's Tale. Boston, 1908. [Introduction.]

Gibbs, L. R. and Kittredge, G. L. MLN. XXIV, 1909, p. 197, XXV, 1910, p. 28. [Verses 975–7.]

Macaulay, G. C. MLR. IV, 1909, p. 16. [Verses 297, 309.]

Emerson, O. F. Studies in Celebration of J. M. Hart. New York, 1910. [Date.]

—— MP. XVII, 1919–20, p. 287. [Verses 612–6.]

—— PQ. II, 1923, p. 85. [Verse 121; 'y-bete.']

Gildersleeve, V. C. MLN. xxv, 1910, p. 30. [Sir Aldingar.]

Egg, W. Chaucer's Knight's Tale. Leipzig, 1912.

Hammond, E. P. MLN. xxvii, 1912, p. 92. [Verse 1159.]

Dodd, W. G. Courtly Love in Chaucer and Gower. Boston, 1913.

Klee, H. Das Enjambement bei Chaucer. Halle, 1913. [Date, etc.]

Legouis, É. Geoffrey Chaucer. 1913, p. 119.

MacCracken, H. N. MLN. xxviii, 1913, p. 230. [Verses A 2024–6.]

Meyer, E. Die Charakterzeichnung bei Chaucer. SEP. xlviii, 1913.

Lowes, J. L. Nation (New York), 28 Aug. 1913, p. 233; MLN. xxxi, 1916, p. 185; MP. xi, 1913–4, p. 491. ['Hereos.']

—— MLR. ix, 1914, p. 94. [Verses 1534–9.]

—— MP. xiv, 1916–7, p. 715. [Verses 1329–31; Dante.]

Petersen, O. The Two Noble Kinsmen. Ang. xxxviii, 1914, p. 213.

Williams, W. H. Dryden's Palamon and Arcite and the Knighte's Tale. MLR. ix, 1914, pp. 161, 309.

Robertson, S. Realism in the Knight's Tale. JEGP. xiv, 1915, p. 226.

—— Old English Verse in Chaucer. MLN. xliii, 1928, p. 234.

Cummings, H. M. The Indebtedness of Chaucer's Works to the Italian Works of Boccaccio. Cincinnati University Stud. x, pt 2, 1916.

Jefferson, B. L. Chaucer and the Consolation of Philosophy of Boethius. Princeton, 1917.

Root, R. K. MP. xv, 1917–8, p. 19. [Verses 2062–6; Joseph of Exeter.]

Lange, H. Ang. Bbl. xxix, 1918, p. 139. [Verses 975 ff.]

Schöffler, H. Ang. Bbl. xxix, 1918, p. 42. [Verses 1858 ff.; 'saue.']

Beschorner, F. Verbale Reime bei Chaucer. SEP. lx, 1920.

Vockrodt, G. Reimtechnik bei Chaucer. SEP. lx, 1920.

Curry, W. C. MLN. xxxvi, 1921, p. 272. [Verses 23 ff.]

—— Texas Rev. viii, 1923, p. 307; Ang. xlvii, 1923, p. 213; Chaucer and the Medieval Sciences, New York, 1926, p. 119. [Science; astrology.]

—— Arcite's Intellect. JEGP. xxix, 1930, p. 83.

Koch, J. E. Studien, lv 1921, p. 196. [Palamon and Arcite.]

—— Ang. xlvi, 1922, p. 36. [Date, etc.]

—— Ang. xlix, 1925, p. 208.

Smith, C. A., Tatlock, J. S. P., et al. MLN. xxxvii, 1921, pp. 120, 376, 377, xxxviii, 1923, p. 59, xliv, 1929, p. 182. [Verse 839.]

Hibbard, L. A. PQ. i, 1922, p. 222. [Ver 1566.]

Garrett, R. M. Dialect Notes, v, 1923, p. 24 ['Pig's eye'; verse A 3268.]

Liebermann, F. Theseus Herzogstitel. Archi cxlv, 1923, p. 101.

Patch, H. R. MLN. xxxviii, 1923, p. 6 [Verse 839.]

—— Chaucer and Medieval Romance. [Essa in Memory of Barrett Wendell, Cambridg U.S.A. 1926, p. 101.]

Schirmer, W. F. Germanisch-romanisc Monatsschrift, xii, 1924, p. 298. [Boccacci

Dustoor, P. E. MLR. xxii, 1927, p. 4 [Verses A 1612, 1882, 2153, 2179, 24 2623, 2815, 2892.]

—— TLS. 5 May 1927, p. 318. [Ver A 1462, 2684.]

Fairchild, H. N. Active Arcite, Conte plative Palamon. JEGP. xxvi, 1927, p. 2

Day, M. MLR. xxiii, 1928, p. 208. [Ve A 2625.]

Hulbert, J. R. What was Chaucer's Aim the Knight's Tale? Stud. Phil. xxvi, 19 p. 375.

Baker, C. D. MLN. xlv, 1930, p. 460. [Not

Baum, P. F. MLN. xlvi, 1931, p. 3 [Characterisation.]

Garvin, K. MLN. xlvi, 1931, p. 453. [Tour ment.]

Ackermann, R. W. Tester: Knight's Ta 2499. MLN. xlix, 1934, p. 397.

Wager, W. J. The So-Called Prologue to Knight's Tale. MLN. l, 1935, p. 296.

(iii) Miller s Prologue and Tale

[See Hammond, Wells, under Fragment above p. 235.]

Skeat, W. W. Oxford Chaucer. Vol. p. 395. [Summary, etc.]

Zupitza, J. Archiv, xciv, 1895, p. 4 [Summary; genealogy of story.]

Koelbing, E. Zeitschrift für vergleicher Literaturgeschichte, xii, 1898, p. 4 xiii, 1899, p. 112. [Source.]

Barnouw, A. J. Miller's Tale van Chauc Handelingen van het Zesde Nederlandisc Philologencongres, 1910; MLR. vii, 19 p. 145.

Lowes, J. L. MP. viii, 1910–1, p. 3 [Miroir de Mariage.]

Root, R. K. Chaucer and the Decamer E. Studien, xliv, 1911–2, p. 1.

Tupper, F. JEGP. xiv, 1915, p. 2 [Quarrels.]

Andrae, A. Longfellow and Chaucer. A Bbl. xxvii, 1916, p. 61.

Curry, W. C. PMLA. xxxv, 1920, p. 1 [Reeve, Miller.]

—— Chaucer and the Medieval Scienc New York, 1926, p. 71.

Baum, P. F. MLN. xxxvii, 1922, p. 350. [Analogue.]

Farnham, W. E. The Dayes of the Mone. Stud. Phil. xx, 1923, p. 70.

Manly, J. M. and Arber, A. TLS. 6 Oct., 3 Nov. 1927, pp. 694, 790. [Verse A 3268.]

Brusendorff, A. A Miscellany in Honor of Frederick Klaeber. Minneapolis, 1928. [Verse A 3227.]

Fine, G. The Miller's Tale. A Study of an Unrecorded Manuscript in the John Rylands Library. Manchester, 1933.

(iv) Reeve's Prologue and Tale

[See *Hammond*, *Wells*, under Fragment A, above p. 235.]

Chaucer Soc. ser. 2, vi, 1872. [Sources; analogues.]

Varnhagen, H. E. Studien, ix, 1886, p. 240. [Sources, etc.]

Koeppel, R. Ang. xiv, 1891–2, p. 249. [Sources.]

Skeat, W. W. Oxford Chaucer. Vol. iii, p. 396, vol. v, p. 112.

Perocquigny, J. MLR. iii, 1908, p. 72. [Verse A 4134. See also Revue Germanique, vi, 1910, p. 203.]

Hart, W. M. The Reeve's Tale. PMLA. xxiii, 1908, p. 1.

—— The Narrative Art of the Old French Fabliaux. [Kittredge Anniversary Papers, Boston, 1913, p. 209.]

Tatlock, J. S. P. MLN. xxix, 1914, p. 142. [Simkin's ruse; verse A 4027.]

Tupper, F. JEGP. xiv, 1915, p. 256. [Quarrels.]

Curry, W. C. PMLA. xxxv, 1920, p. 189. [Reeve; Miller.]

—— Chaucer and the Medieval Sciences. New York, 1926, p. 71.

Baum, P. F. MLN. xxxvii, 1922, p. 350. [Verse 135.]

Holthausen, F. Ang. Bbl. xxxiii, 1922, p. 103. [Notes.]

Kuhl, E. Chaucer and the Church. MLN. xl, 1925, p. 337.

Moffett, H. Y. PQ. iv, 1925, p. 298. [Oswald.]

Dieckmann, E. P. M. MP. xxvi, 1928–9, p. 279. [Verse A 4165.]

Dempster, G. JEGP. xxix, 1930, p. 473. [Source of Tale.]

Montgomery, F. PQ. x, 1931, p. 404.

Lange, M. Vom Fabliau zu Boccaccio und Chaucer. Hamburg, 1934.

Tolkien, J. R. R. Chaucer as a Philologist. Trans. Philolog. Soc. 1934, p. 1.

(v) Cook's Prologue and Tale

[See *Hammond*, *Wells*, under Fragment A, above p. 235.]

Skeat, W. W. Oxford Chaucer. Vol. iii, p. 398, vol. v, p. 128.

Root, R. K. The Poetry of Chaucer. Boston, 1906, 1922 (rev. edn), p. 179.

Tupper, F. and Lowes, J. L. PMLA. xxix, 1914, pp. 113, 125, xxx, 1915, p. 237. [Sins motif.]

Curry, W. C. Chaucer and the Medieval Sciences. New York, 1926, p. 47.

(b) Fragment B¹

[*Hammond*, p. 277; *Wells*, pp. 698, 877, 1031, 1147, 1238, 1289, 1327, 1375, 1424; *Griffith*, p. 82; W. W. Skeat, Oxford Chaucer, vol. iii, p. 405, vol. v, p. 132; R. K. Root, The Poetry of Chaucer, Boston, 1906, 1922 (rev. edn), p. 181.]

(i) Man of Law's Headlink, Prologue, and Tale

[See *Hammond*, *Wells*, under Fragment B¹, above.]

Annotated Editions. W. and R. Chambers, Edinburgh, 1883, 1888; R. Morris and W. W. Skeat, Specimens of Early English, Oxford, vol. ii, 1894; W. W. Skeat, Oxford, 1877, 1889 (rev. edn), 1897 (with Pardoner's Tale); W. W. Skeat, Headlink and Prologue, Oxford, 1874, 1898 (with Prioress's Tale, etc.).

Source. Trivet's Chronicles. Originals and Analogues, Chaucer Soc. 1872, p. 1 (and see *ibid.* pp. 57, 71, 221, 365).

Lücke, E. Das Leben Constanze bei Trivet, Gower, und Chaucer. Ang. xiv, 1891–2, pp. 77, 147.

Macaulay, G. C. Gower's Works. Vol. ii, Oxford, 1899, p. 438.

Gough, A. B. On the Middle English Metrical Romance Emare. Kiel, 1900.

—— Constance Saga. Palaestra, xxiii, 1902.

Siefken, O. Der Konstanze-Griseldistypus. Rathenow, 1904.

—— Das geduldige Weib. Leipzig, 1904.

[For Eustace-Constance-Griselda Legend, see also *Wells*, pp. 112, 781, 1005, 1105, 1209; and under Emare, p. 152 above.]

Studies.

Koch, J. The Chronology of Chaucer's Writings. Chaucer Soc. 1890.

—— Ang. xlvi, 1922, p. 40. [Date.]

Koeppel, E. Chaucer and De Contemptu Mundi. Archiv, lxxxiv, 1890, p. 406, lxxxv, 1890, p. 48.

Lounsbury, T. R. Studies in Chaucer. Vol. i, New York, 1892, p. 416, vol. ii, pp. 329, 489.

Skeat, W. W. Oxford Chaucer. Vol. iii, p. 405, vol. v, p. 132.

Tatlock, J. S. P. The Development and Chronology of Chaucer's Works. Chaucer Soc. 1907, p. 172.
—— MLN. xxix, 1914, p. 97. [Verses 782–4; Dante.]
Browne, W. H. MLN. xxiii, 1908, p. 53. [Astrology.]
Kittredge, G. L. and Root, R. K. PMLA. xxiv, 1909, pp. 124, 243, xxv, 1910, p. 228. [Date of Prologue.]
Tupper, F. PMLA. xxix, 1914, pp. 99, 102, 118; Nation (New York), 9 July 1914, p. 41. [Sins motif.]
Lowes, J. L. PMLA. xxx, 1915, p. 310. [On Tupper.]
Jefferson, B. L. Chaucer and the Consolation of Philosophy of Boethius. Princeton, 1917.
Shannon, E. F. MP. xvi, 1918–9, p. 610. [Verses B 400–1; Lucan.]
—— MLN. xxxv, 1920, p. 288. [Verse B 93; Metamorphoseos.]
Curry, W. C. JEGP. xxii, 1923, p. 347. [Astrology.]
—— Texas Rev. viii, 1923, p. 307; JEGP. xxii, 1923, p. 352; Chaucer and the Medieval Sciences, New York, 1926, p. 164. [Science; astrology, etc.]
Farnham, W. E. Stud. Phil. xx, 1923, p. 70. [Astrology.]
Knowlton, E. C. JEGP. xxiii, 1924, p. 83. [Man of Law.]
Landrum, G. PMLA. xxxix, 1924, p. 75. [Vulgate.]
Brusendorff, A. The Chaucer Tradition. Copenhagen, 1925, p. 127. [Verse B 776.]
Livingston, C. H. MLR. xx, 1925, p. 71. ['Askances.']
Schlauch, M. Studies in the Sources of the Man of Law's Tale. New York, 1925.
—— Chaucer's Constance and Accused Queens. New York, 1927.
Cowling, G. H. RES. ii, 1926, p. 311. [Verse.]
Manly, J. M. Some New Light on Chaucer. New York, 1926, p. 131.
Brett, C. MLR. xxii, 1927, p. 264. [Verses B 782 ff.]
Curtiss, J. T. JEGP. xxvi, 1927, p. 24. [Horoscope.]
Cate, W. A. The Problem of the Origin of the Griselda Story. Stud. Phil. xxix, 1932, p. 389.

(ii) Shipman's Prologue, or Man of Law's Endlink

[Hammond, pp. 239, 283; Wells, pp. 702, 878, 1138, 1196, 1238, 1327; Griffith, p. 83.]
Annotated Edition. W. W. Skeat, The Prioress' Tale, Oxford, 1874, 1898.
Studies.
ten Brink, B. Early English Literature. Vol. ii, 1893, p. 172, vol. iii, 1896, p. 268.

Skeat, W. W. Oxford Chaucer. Vol. iii, p. 417 vol. v, p. 165.
—— The Shipman's Prologue. MLR. v, 1910 p. 430. [See also Ang. Bbl. xxii, 1911 p. 280; Ang. xlix, 1925, p. 232.]
Root, R. K. The Poetry of Chaucer. Boston 1906, 1922 (rev. edn), p. 187.
Tatlock, J. S. P. The Development and Chronology of Chaucer's Works. Chaucer Soc. 1907, p. 205.
Goffin, R. C. MLR. xviii, 1923, p. 335 [Verse 1189.]
Brusendorff, A. The Chaucer Tradition Copenhagen, 1925, p. 70. [Original for Yeoman.]
Jones, R. F. A Conjecture on the Wife of Bath's Prologue. JEGP. xxiv, 1925, p. 512
Tupper, F. The Bearings of the Shipman' Prologue. JEGP. xxxiii, 1934, p. 352.

(c) Fragment B[2]

[Hammond, p. 283; Wells, pp. 702–3, 878 997, 1031, 1091, 1147, 1196, 1238, 1289, 1327 1375, 1425; Griffith, p. 83; W.W.Skeat,Oxfor Chaucer, vol. iii, p. 417, vol. v, p. 165; R. K Root, The Poetry of Chaucer, Boston, 1906 1922 (rev. edn), p. 187.]

(i) Shipman's Tale

[See Hammond, Wells, under Fragment B above.]
Karkeek, P. Q. Chaucer Soc. 1884, essay 15 [Shipman and Maudelayne.]
Koch, J. Chaucer Soc. ser. 2, xxvii, 1890 p. 79. [Chronology.]
Skeat, W. W. Oxford Chaucer. Vol. iii pp. 420, 429, vol. v, pp. 38, 168.
Tatlock, J. S. P. The Development and Chronology of Chaucer's Works. Chaucer Soc. 1907, p. 205.
Kittredge, G. L. Chaucer and his Poetry Cambridge, U.S.A. 1915, p. 168.
Spargo, J. W. Chaucer's Shipman's Tale Helsinki, 1930.
[See also under Shipman's Prologue.]

(ii) Prioress's Headlink and Tale

[See Hammond, Wells, under Fragment B above.]
Annotated Editions. R. Morris, Specimen of Early English, Oxford, 1867; W. W. Skea (with Sir Thopas, etc.), Oxford, 1874, 1898 C. M. Drennan, 1914; L. Winstanley, Cam bridge, 1922. [See also under General Pro logue, p. 235 above.]
Studies.
Originals and Analogues. Chaucer So 1875–6, pp. 107, 251, 273.
Lounsbury, T. R. Studies in Chaucer. Vol. i New York, 1892, p. 490.

Skeat, W. W. Oxford Chaucer. Vol. III, p. 421, vol. v, pp. 13, 173.

Lowes, J. L. PMLA. xx, 1905, p. 848. [Date.]

—— Ang. xxxiii, 1910, p. 440. ['Simple and coy.']

—— Romanic Rev. v, 1914, p. 358. [Prioress's Oath. See also *Hammond*, p. 286, and MLN. xxii, 1907, p. 51.]

Brown, C. PMLA. xxi, 1906, p. 486. [Analogues.]

—— MP. iii, 1905–6, p. 467. ['Litel clergeon.' See also E. Studien, xxxvii, 1907, p. 231.]

—— A Study of the Miracle of Our Lady. Chaucer Soc. 1910.

—— MLN. xxxviii, 1923, p. 92. [Latin source.]

Gerould, G. H. MLN. xxiv, 1909, p. 132. [Analogue.]

Canby, H. S. A Study of the Short Story. New York, 1913, p. 5.

Legouis, É. Geoffrey Chaucer. 1913, p. 212.

Kittredge, G. L. Chaucer and his Poetry. Cambridge, U.S.A. 1915, p. 175.

Tupper, F. MLN. xxx, 1915, p. 9. [Prymer.]

Andrae, A. Ang. Bbl. xxvii, 1916, p. 84. [Longfellow.]

Hinckley, H. B. PMLA. xxxiii, 1918, p. xxvii. [Prioress.]

Hart, W. M. Some Old French Miracles. [Gayley Anniversary Papers, Berkeley, 1922, p. 31.]

Power, E. Medieval English Nunneries. Cambridge, 1922.

—— Medieval People. 1924, p. 59.

Kuhl, E. P. PQ. ii, 1923, p. 302. [Prioress.]

Tryon, R. W. The Miracle of Our Lady in Middle English Poetry. PMLA. xxxviii, 1923, p. 308.

Heinrich, M. P. The Canonesses and Education in the Early Middle Ages. St Louis, 1924 (priv. ptd).

Madeleva, M. Chaucer's Nuns and Other Essays. New York, 1925.

Draper, J. W. E. Studien, lx, 1925–6, p. 238. [Verse B 1762.]

Cowling, G. H. RES. ii, 1926, p. 311. [Verse.]

Derocquigny, J. Revue anglo-américaine, v, 1927, p. 160. [Verse B 1687.]

Robertson, S. MLN. xliii, 1928, p. 104. [Verses 57 ff.; Wordsworth.]

[See also under General Prologue, pp. 235–7 above.]

(iii) Prologue to Sir Thopas, and Sir Thopas

[See *Hammond, Wells*, under Fragment B², above.]

Annotated Editions. [With Prioress's Tale.] W. W. Skeat, Oxford, 1874, 1898; L. Winstanley, Cambridge, 1922.

Studies.

Bennewitz, J. Chaucer's Sir Thopas. Halle, 1879. [Relation to sources. See also E. Studien, iv, 1881, p. 339, xi, 1888, p. 495.]

Skeat, W. W. Oxford Chaucer. Vol. III, p. 423, vol. v, p. 182.

Courthope, W. J. A History of English Poetry. Vol. i, 1895, p. 259.

Strong, C. Sir Thopas and Sir Guy. MLN. xxiii, 1907, pp. 73, 102.

Snyder, F. B. MP. vi, 1908–9, p. 133. [Note.]

—— Sir T. Norray and Sir Thopas. MLN. xxv, 1910, p. 78.

Knott, T. A. MP. viii, 1910–1, p. 135. [Mythology.]

Manly, J. M. MP. viii, 1910–1, p. 141. [Stanza-forms.]

—— E. & S. xiii, 1928, p. 52. [Interpretation.]

Nadal, T. W. Spenser's Muiopotmos in Relation to Sir Thopas. PMLA. xxv, 1910, p. 640.

Patterson, R. F. MLR. vii, 1912, p. 376. [Verse B 1915; 'payndemayn.']

Meyer, E. Die Charakterzeichnung bei Chaucer. SEP. xlviii, 1913.

Lange, H. Deutsche Literaturzeitung, xxxvii, 1916, pp. 1299, 1669, 1827. [Interpretation.]

Ayres, H. M. Romanic Rev. x, 1919, p. 1. [Seneca.]

Blau, E. 'Payndemayn.' In Chaucer's Tale of Sir Thopas. Ang. Bbl. xxxi, 1920, p. 237.

Knowlton, E. C. JEGP. xxiv, 1925, p. 90. [Man of Law.]

Magoun, F. P. PMLA. xlii, 1927, p. 833. [Source.]

Fiske, H. S. PQ. vii, 1928, p. 82. [Verses 152–4.]

Ross, W. O. MLN. xlv, 1930, p. 172. [Name 'Thopas'.]

Trounce, A. McI. The English Tail-Rhyme Romances. Medium Aevum, i, 1932, p. 90.

Lawrence, W. W. Satire in Sir Thopas. PMLA. l, 1935, p. 81.

(iv) Prologue to Melibeus, and Melibeus

[See *Hammond, Wells*, under Fragment B², above.]

Brock, E. N. & Q. 9 Jan. 1869, p. 30. [Albertanus Brixiensis.]

Skeat, W. W. Oxford Chaucer. Vol. III, p. 426, vol. v, p. 201.

Tatlock, J. S. P. The Development and Chronology of Chaucer's Works. Chaucer Soc. 1907, p. 188.

Siebert, H. MLN. xxxi, 1916, p. 304. [Horace.]

Jefferson, B. L. Chaucer and the Consolation of Philosophy of Boethius. Princeton, 1917.

16

Cook, A. S. Ménagier de Paris. Romanic Rev. VIII, 1917, p. 219.

Ayres, H. M. Romanic Rev. x, 1919, p. 2. [Seneca.]

Hotson, P. The Tale of Melibeus and John of Gaunt. Stud. Phil. XVIII, 1921, p. 429.

Koch, J. Ang. XLVI, 1922, p. 43. [Date.]

Landrum, G. PMLA. XXXIX, 1924, p. 75. [Vulgate.]

Langhans, V. Ang. LIII, 1929, p. 235. [Date.]

Severs, J. B. The Source of Melibeus. PMLA. L, 1935, p. 92.

(v) Monk's Prologue and Tale

[See *Hammond*, *Wells*, under Fragment B², above, p. 240.]

Annotated Edition. W. W. Skeat (with Prioress's Tale, etc.), Oxford, 1874, 1898.

Studies.

N. & Q. 13 March, 8 May 1897, pp. 205, 369; Archiv, LXXXIV, 1890, p. 416; Ang. XIV, 1891–2, p. 260. [Sources.]

Koch, J. The Chronology of Chaucer's Works. Chaucer Soc. 1890.

—— Ang. XLVI, 1922, p. 39. [Date.]

—— Ang. XLIX, 1925, p. 234. [Date.]

Skeat, W. W. Oxford Chaucer. Vol. II, pp. xxxvii, lvi, vol. III, p. 427, vol. v, p. 224.

Flügel, E. JEGP. I, 1903, p. 126. [Notes.]

Emerson, O. F. MP. I, 1903–4, p. 105. [Notes.]

Tatlock, J. S. P. The Development and Chronology of Chaucer's Works. Chaucer Soc. 1907; MLN. XXI, 1906, pp. 62, 192. [Verses 380–2.]

Gelbach, M. JEGP. VI, 1907, p. 657. [Death of Croesus.]

Kittredge, G. L. Date of Chaucer's Troilus and Other Chaucer Matters. Chaucer Soc. XLII, 1908, p. 41.

—— The Pillars of Hercules and Chaucer's 'Trophee.' [Putnam Anniversary Volume, Cedar Rapids, Iowa, 1909, p. 545.]

MacCracken, H. N. MLN. XXIII, 1908, p. 93. [MS Trinity College Cambridge R, 3, 19.]

Shannon, E. F. Busiris in the Monk's Tale. MP. XI, 1913–4, p. 227.

—— MP. XVI, 1918–9, p. 610. [Verse B 3909–10; Lucan's Pharsalia.]

Tupper, F. and Emerson, O. F. MLN. XXXI, 1916, pp. 11, 142. ['Trophee.']

Jefferson, B. L. Chaucer and the Consolation of Philosophy of Boethius. Princeton, 1917.

Ayres, H. M. Chaucer and Seneca. Romanic Rev. x, 1919, p. 2.

Landrum, G. PMLA. XXXIV, 1919, p. 75. [Vulgate.]

Förster, M. De Casibus Virorum Illustrium in englischer Bearbeitung. Deutsche Literaturzeitung, N.S. I, 1924, pp. 27, 1923.

Crawford, S. J. TLS. 26 June 1924, p. 404. [Verses 3937–48; source.]

Schirmer, W. F. Germanisch-romanische Monatsschrift, XII, 1924, p. 294. [Influence of Boccaccio.]

Brusendorff, A. The Chaucer Tradition. Copenhagen, 1925, pp. 77, 492. [Date.]

Liebermann, F. Archiv, CXLVIII, 1925, p. 96. [Identification of persons.]

Rickert, E. and Richardson, H. G. TLS. 16 Dec. 1926, p. 935, 20 Jan. 1927, p. 44; MP. XXV, 1927–8, p. 79. [Verses B 3083–4; 'Godeleef.']

Babcock, R. W. The Mediaeval Setting of Chaucer's Monk's Tale. PMLA. XLVI, 1931, p. 205.

Norris, D. M. Harry Bailey's 'Corpus Madrian.' MLN. XLVIII, 1933, p. 146.

Spencer, T. The Story of Ugolino in Dante and Chaucer. Speculum, IX, 1934, p. 295.

Braddy, H. The Two Petros. PMLA. L, 1935, p. 69.

(vi) Nun's Priest's Prologue, Tale, and Epilogue

[See *Hammond*, *Wells*, under Fragment B², above, p. 240.]

Annotated Editions. A. W. Pollard, 1908; L. Winstanley, Cambridge, 1915; A. J. Wyatt, 1915; A. S. Cook, Literary Middle English Reader, Boston, 1915, p. 198; R. F. Patterson, 1920; K. Sisam, Oxford, 1927.
[With General Prologue.] A. J. Wyatt, 1904.
[With General Prologue and Knight's Tale.] R. Morris, Oxford, 1867, rev. W. W. Skeat, Oxford, 1889; F. J. Mather, Boston, 1898; M. H. Liddell, New York, 1901, 1902; A. Ingraham, 1902.
[With General Prologue, Prioress's and Pardoner's Tales.] G. H. Cowling, 1934.

Studies.

Originals and Analogues. Chaucer Soc. ser. 2, 1875, pp. 111, 333. [See also, for sources, W. W. Skeat, Academy, 23 July 1887, p. 56; E. P. Dargan, MP. IV, 1906, p. 39.]

Adolphus, A. E. and Skeat, W. W. N. & Q. 14, 28 Sept., 28 Dec. 1907, pp. 202, 252, 514. [Verses 367–71.]

Skeat, W. W. Oxford Chaucer. Vol. III, p. 431, vol. v, p. 247, vol. VI, p. c.

Petersen, K. O. Sources of the Nun's Priest's Tale. Boston, 1898. [See also Romania, XXVIII, 1899, p. 296; E. Studien, XXX, 1902, p. 464.]

Hinckley, H. B. Notes on Chaucer. Northampton, 1907, p. 121.

—— MP. XVI, 1918–9, p. 39. [Verses B 4047–50, 4039–54, 4108, 4243, 4414, 4446, 4573, 4590.]

McKnight, G. H. Medieval Fox and Wolf. PMLA. xxiii, 1908, p. 497.

Kittredge, G. L. MP. vii, 1909–10, p. 489. [De Vinsauf.]

Nadal, T. W. Spenser's Muiopotmos in relation to the Nun's Priest's Tale. PMLA. xxv, 1910, p. 640.

Grandgent, C. H. Chanticleer. [Kittredge Anniversary Papers, Boston, 1913, p. 67.]

MacCracken, H. N. College Chaucer. New Haven, 1913, p. 206. [Epilogue.]

Tupper, F. St Venus. Nation (New York), 16 Oct. 1913, p. 354.

Tatlock, J. S. P. MLN. xxix, 1914, p. 142. [Verses 4372–5, 4565–91, 5471.]

—— Stud. Phil. xviii, 1921, p. 425. [Verse B 4573; 'our.']

Hemingway, S. B. Interpretation. MLN. xxxi, 1916, p. 479.

Van Herk, A. Neophilologus, ii, 1918, p. 292. [Verse B 4008.]

Kenyon, J. S. Notes on the Marriage Group in the Canterbury Tales. JEGP. xv, 1916, p. 282.

Jefferson, B. L. Chaucer and the Consolation of Philosophy of Boethius. Princeton, 1917.

Lecompte, I. C. MP. xiv, 1916–7, p. 737. [Compared with Roman de Renard.]

Brown, C. Mulier est hominis confusio. MLN. xxxv, 1920, p. 479.

Law, R. A. In principio. PMLA. xxxvii, 1922, p. 213.

Emerson, O. F. Notes on Chaucer and some Conjectures. PQ. ii, 1923, p. 89. [Original plan.]

Cook, A. S. MLN. xxxix, 1924, p. 377. [Verses 30–2.]

Curry, W. C. E. Studien, lviii, 1924, p. 24; Texas Rev. viii, 1923, p. 307.

—— Chaucer and the Medieval Sciences. New York, 1926. [Dream lore.]

Hotson, J. L. PMLA. xxxix, 1924, p. 762. [Interpretation.]

Brusendorff, A. 'He Knew Nat Catoun.' [A Miscellany in Honor of Frederick Klaeber, Minneapolis, 1929, p. 320.]

(d) Fragment C

[Hammond, p. 293; Wells, pp. 713, 879, 1031, 1092, 1148, 1239, 1289, 1327, 1375, 1425; Griffith, p. 91; W. W. Skeat, Oxford Chaucer, vol. iii, p. 434, vol. v, p. 260; R. K. Root, The Poetry of Chaucer, Boston, 1906, 1922 (rev. edn), p. 219.]

(i) Physician's Tale

[See Hammond, Wells, under Fragment C, above.]

Rumbauer, O. Die Geschichte von Appius and Virginia in der englischen Literatur. Berlin, 1890, p. 49.

Koeppel, E. Ang. xiv, 1891–2, p. 259. [Note.]

Lounsbury, T. R. Studies in Chaucer. Vol. ii, New York, 1892, p. 279.

Skeat, W. W. Oxford Chaucer. Vol. iii, p. 435, vol. v, p. 260.

Morris, R. Furnivall Miscellany. Oxford, 1901, p. 338. [Physician.]

Kittredge, G. L. MP. i, 1903, p. 5. [Verses 72 ff.; Duchess of Lancaster.]

Tatlock, J. S. P. The Development and Chronology of Chaucer's Works. Chaucer Soc. 1907, p. 150.

Tupper, F. Nation (New York), 26 June 1913, p. 640; PMLA. xxix, 1914, p. 93; MLN. xxx, 1915, p. 5; JEGP. xv, 1916, p. 56. [Sins; interpretations.]

Lowes, J. L. PMLA. xxx, 1915, p. 237. [On Tupper.]

—— 'Loveres Maladye of Hereos.' MP. xi, 1913–4, p. 491. [See also Ang. Bbl. xxv, 1914, p. 332; Nation (New York), 11 Sept. 1913, p. 233; MLN. xxxi, 1916, p. 185.]

Curry, W. C. PQ. iv, 1925, p. 1; Chaucer and the Medieval Sciences, New York, 1926, p. 3. [Science.]

(ii) Words of the Host

[W. W. Skeat, Oxford Chaucer, vol. iii, p. 437, vol. v, p. 264; Wells, pp. 715, 879.]

Annotated Edition. W. W. Skeat (with Tale of Man of Law, etc.). Oxford, 1877, 1889, 1897.

(iii) Pardoner's Prologue, Tale, and Endlink

[See Hammond, Wells, under Fragment C, above.]

Annotated Editions. Tale and Prologue [from 45 MSS and 3 printed texts], Chaucer Soc. 1890, 1892, 1896, 1897, 1898 (and 2 supplements); J. Koch, Berlin, 1902, Chaucer Soc. 1902; R. Morris, Specimens of Early English, Oxford, 1867; O. F. Emerson, Middle English Reader, New York, 1905, 1915, 1921; C. M. Drennan and A. J. Wyatt, 1911; W. W. Skeat (with Man of Law, etc.), Oxford, 1877, 1889, 1897; G. H. Cowling (with General Prologue, etc.), 1934; Carleton Brown, Oxford, 1935.

Sources, Analogues, etc. S. D'Ancona, Romania, iii, 1875, p. 182; R. Morris, Contemporary Rev. 1881, p. 738; H. T. Francis, Academy, 22 Dec. 1883, p. 416, 12 Jan. 1884, p. 30; Originals and Analogues, Chaucer Soc. 1875, pp. 129, 415, 544; G. L. Kittredge, AJ. Phil. ix, 1888, p. 84, MLN. xv, 1900, p. 385; E. Koeppel, Archiv, lxxxiv, 1890, p. 411; H. S. Canby, MP. ii, 1904–5, p. 477.

Studies.

Jusserand, J. J. Chaucer Soc. 1884.

Smith, L. T. EHR. vii, 1892, p. 25.

Kittredge, G. L. Atlantic Monthly, 1893, p. 829.
—— Chaucer and his Poetry. Cambridge U.S.A. 1915, p. 211.
Skeat, W. W. Oxford Chaucer. Vol. II, p. xxxvi, vol. III, p. 438, vol. v, p. 260.
Hinckley, H. B. Notes on Chaucer. Northampton, 1907, p. 157.
—— MP. xvi, 1918, p. 39. [Verses C 406, 953.]
Canby, H. S. The Short Story in English. New York, 1909, p. 72.
—— A Study of the Short Story. New York, 1913, p. 8.
Ayres, H. Romanic Rev. x, 1911, p. 5. [Seneca.]
Hart, W. M. The Pardoner's Tale and Der Dot im Stock. MP. ix, 1911, p. 17.
Lowes, J. L. Romanic Rev. II, 1911, p. 113. [French parallels. See also E. Studien, XLVI, 1912–3, p. 114.]
—— PMLA. xxx, 1915, p. 260. [Sins motif.]
Tupper, F. The Pardoner's Tavern. JEGP. XIII, 1914, p. 553.
—— JEGP. xv, 1916, p. 67. [Sins motif.]
Andrae, A. Ang. Bbl. xxvii, 1916, p. 85. [Notes.]
Hemingway, S. MLN. xxxii, 1917, p. 57. [Verses C 443 ff.]
Curry, W. C. The Secret of Chaucer's Pardoner. JEGP. xviii, 1919, p. 593. [See also Chaucer and the Medieval Sciences, New York, 1926, p. 54.]
Sedgwick, W. B. The Pardoner's Prologue. MLR. xix, 1924, p. 336.
Wells, W. MLN. xL, 1925, p. 58; MP. xxv, 1927–8, p. 163. [Analogues.]
Chapman, C. O. MLN. xLI, 1926, p. 506; PMLA. xLIV, 1929, p. 178. [Sermon.]
Manly, J. M. Some New Light on Chaucer. New York, 1926, p. 122.
Moore, S. MP. xxv, 1927–8, p. 59. [Rouncival.]
Rutter, G. N. MLN. xLIII, 1928, p. 536. [Verses C 350–51.]
Bushnell, N. S. Stud. Phil. xxviii, 1931, p. 450. [Wandering Jew.]
Norris, D. M. Chaucer's Pardoner's Tale and Flanders. PMLA. xLviii, 1933, p. 636.

[See also under General Prologue, pp. 235–7 above.]

(e) Fragment D

[Hammond, p. 296; Wells, pp. 718, 879, 997, 1031, 1092, 1148, 1196, 1239, 1328, 1376, 1425; Griffith, p. 93; W. W. Skeat, Oxford Chaucer, vol. III, p. 445, vol. v, p. 290; R. K. Root, The Poetry of Chaucer, Boston, 1906, 1922 (rev. edn), p. 231.]

(i) Wife of Bath's Prologue and Tale

[See Hammond, Wells, under Fragment D, above.]

Child, F. J. Athenaeum, 3 Dec. 1870, p. 721. [Dante; Corbaccio.]
Chaucer Soc. xvi, 1876, p. 298; Archiv, LXXXIV, 1890, p. 413; Ang. xiv, 1891–2, p. 250. [Use of Jerome.]
Originals and Analogues. Chaucer Soc. 1887, pp. 481, 546.
Derocquigny, J. MLR. III, 1888, p. 72. [Verse 415.]
Toynbee, P. Chaucer's 'Book Cleped Valerie.' Academy, 26 Dec. 1891, p. 588.
ten Brink, B. Early English Literature. Vol. II, 1893, p. 127. [Introduction.]
Maynadier, G. H. The Wife of Bath's Tale, its Sources and Analogues. 1901.
Mead, W. PMLA. xvi, 1901, p. 358. [Sources.]
Rajna, P. Romania, xxxii, 1903, p. 248. [Corbaccio.]
Tatlock, J. S. P. The Development and Chronology of Chaucer's Works. Chaucer Soc. 1907, p. 198.
—— MLN. xxix, 1914, p. 143. [Prologue; verses 800–10.]
Kittredge, G. L. MP. vii, 1910, p. 475, ix, 1911–2, p. 435. [The Wife of Bath; Marriage group.]
Lowes, J. L. Illustrations of Chaucer. Romanic Rev. II, 1911, p. 121.
—— MP. viii, 1910–1, p. 305. [Miroir de Mariage.]
—— MP. xiii, 1915, p. 19. [Dante's Convivio.]
—— PMLA. xxx, 1915, p. 342. [Sins motif.]
—— MP. xv, 1917–8, p. 199. [Macrobius.]
Moore, S. MLN. xxvi, 1911, p. 172. [Date of Marriage group.]
Lawrence, W. W. MP. xi, 1913–4, p. 247. [Marriage group.]
Tupper, F. St Venus. Nation (New York), 16 Oct. 1913, p. 354.
—— PMLA. xxix, 1914, pp. 99, 120. [Sins motif.]
—— JEGP. xv, 1916, p. 95. [Sins interpretations.]
Andrae, A. Ang. Bbl. xxvii, 1916, p. 84. [Longfellow.]
Barnouw, A. J. Nation (New York), 7 Dec. 1916, p. 540. [Verses D 603–4.]
Kenyon, J. S. JEGP. xv, 1916, p. 282. [Marriage group.]
Hinckley, H. B. PMLA. xxxii, 1917, p. 292. [Marriage group.]
Ayres, H. M. Romanic Rev. x, 1919, pp. 5, 7. [Seneca.]

Schulze, K. Germanisch-romanische Monatsschrift, VIII, 1920, p. 103. [Compared with Merchant of Venice.]

Curry, W. C. PMLA. XXXVII, 1922, p. 30; Chaucer and the Medieval Sciences, New York, 1926, p. 91. [On Wife.]

Vogt, G. M. MLN. XXXVII, 1922, p. 339. [Compared with Women Pleased, La Fée Urgèle.]

—— JEGP. XXIV, 1925, p. 102. ['Gentilesse.']

Brusendorff, A. The Chaucer Tradition. Copenhagen, 1925, p. 475. [Verse D 1159.]

Jones, H. S. V. JEGP. XXIV, 1925, p. 512. [Interpretation.]

Rutter, G. M. The Wife of Bath. Western Reserve University Bulletin, XXXIV, 1931, p. 60.

[See also under Groups and Motifs, p. 235 above.]

(ii) Friar's Prologue and Tale

[See *Hammond, Wells*, under Fragment D, above.]

Originals and Analogues. Chaucer Soc. 1872, p. 103. [See also, for sources, Archiv, CX, 1903, p. 427; Ang. XIV, 1891–2, p. 256; Ang. Bbl. XIII, 1902, p. 180.]

Skeat, W. W. Oxford Chaucer. Vol. III, p. 450, vol. V, pp. 24, 322.

—— N. & Q. 12 March 1910, p. 201. [Verse D 1294.]

Lowes, J. L. Romanic Rev. II, 1011, p. 118. [French versions.]

Tupper, F. JEGP. XIV, 1915, p. 256. [Quarrel theory.]

—— JEGP. XV, 1916, p. 73. [Sins motif.]

Tupper, F. and Lowes, J. L. PMLA. XXIX, 1914, p. 112, XXX, 1915, p. 278. [Sins motif.]

Kittredge, G. L. Chaucer and his Poetry. Cambridge, U.S.A. 1915, p. 190.

Andrae, A. Ang. Bbl. XXVII, 1916, p. 85. [Longfellow.]

Jefferson, B. L. Chaucer and the Consolation of Philosophy of Boethius. Princeton, 1917.

Taylor, A. Devil and Advocate. PMLA. XXXVI, 1921, p. 35.

Kuhl, E. P. Chaucer and the Church. MLN. XL, 1925, p. 335.

(iii) Summoner's Prologue and Tale

[See *Hammond, Wells*, under Fragment D, above.]

Originals and Analogues. Chaucer Soc. 1875, p. 135. [See also Ang. XIV, 1891–2, p. 256.]

ten Brink, B. Early English Literature. Vol. II, 1893, p. 160, vol. III, 1896, p. 268. [Original location of tale. See also E. P. Hammond, MP. III, 1905–6, p. 163.]

Tupper, F. and Lowes, J. L.. PMLA. XXIX, 1914, p. 112, XXX, 1915, p. 278. [Sins motif.]

Tatlock, J. S. P. MLN. XXIX, 1914, p. 143. [Verses D 1675–1706, 1854–68.]

Tupper, F. MLN. XXX, 1915, pp. 8, 63. [Jerome; Summoner's Friar.]

—— JEGP. XV, 1916, p. 73. [Sins motif.]

Jefferson, B. L. Chaucer and the Consolation of Philosophy of Boethius. Princeton, 1917.

Stanford, M. JEGP. XIX, 1920, p. 377. [Verses D 1729–31.]

Curry, W. C. MP. XIX, 1921–2, p. 395; Chaucer and the Medieval Sciences, New York, 1926, p. 37. [Summoner's malady.]

—— MLN. XXXVIII, 1923, p. 253. [Verses D 1689 ff.; Dante.]

Brusendorff, A. The Chaucer Tradition. Copenhagen, 1925, p. 134. [Suppression of end.]

Kuhl, E. P. Chaucer and the Church. MLN. XL, 1925, p. 338.

Chapman, C. O. PMLA. XLIV, 1929, p. 178. [On preaching.]

(f) Fragment E

[*Hammond*, p. 302; *Wells*, pp. 725, 879, 997, 1032, 1148, 1197, 1240, 1328, 1376, 1426; *Griffith*, p. 97; W. W. Skeat, Oxford Chaucer, vol. III, p. 453, vol. V, p. 342; R. K. Root, The Poetry of Chaucer, Boston, 1906, 1922 (rev. edn), p. 253.]

(i) Clerk's Headlink, Prologue, and Tale

[See *Hammond, Wells*, under Fragment E, above.]

Annotated Editions. Chaucer Soc. 1899, 1900, 1902 (from 8 MSS); W. and R. Chambers, Edinburgh, 1883, 1888; R. S. Sheppard, C. M. Barrow, E. Winkler, Madras, 1900; K. Sisam, Oxford, 1923; W. W. Skeat (with Prioress's Tale), Oxford, 1874, 1898; L. Winstanley (with Squire's Tale), Cambridge, 1907.

Source. Petrarch's De Obedientia et Fide Uxoria. [Originals and Analogues, Chaucer Soc. 1875, p. 151. See also French fabliau, *ibid.* p. 527.]

[For Eustace-Constance-Griselda legends, see *Wells*, pp. 112, 781, 1005, 1105, 1209; and under Emare, p. 152 above.]

Studies.

Groeneveld, H. Die älteste Bearbeitung der Griseldissage in Frankreich. Marburg, 1886.

von Westenholz, F. Die Griseldissage. Heidelberg, 1888.

Koehler, R. Kleinere Schriften. Vol. II, 1898. [Grisel story.]

Savorini, L. La Leggenda di Griselda. Revista Abruzzese, XV, 1900, pp. 21, 123, 399, 460, 515.

Siefken, O. Der Constanze-Griseldistypus. Rathenow, 1904.

—— Das geduldige Weib. Leipzig, 1904.

Malone, K. Patient Griseldus. Romanic Rev. xx, 1929, p. 340.

Griffith, D. D. The Origin of the Griselda Story. Seattle, 1931.

Le Ménagier de Paris. Ed. J. Pichon, Société des Bibliophiles français, Paris, 1846. *Hammond*, p. 305; B. ten Brink, Chaucer, Münster, 1870, p. 37; F. J. Furnivall, Trial Forewords, 1873, pp. 20, 130; T. R. Lounsbury, Studies in Chaucer, vol. i, New York, 1892, p. 68; J. J. Jusserand, Nineteenth Century, June 1896 (see below, and P. Bellezza, E. Studien, xxiii, 1897, p. 335); E. Flügel, F. J. Mather, Nation (New York), 12, 19 Nov. 1896, pp. 365, 385; MLN. xi, 1896, p. 510. [Did Chaucer meet Petrarch?]

Skeat, W. W. Oxford Chaucer. Vol. iii, p. 453, vol. v, pp. 31, 342.

Koch, J. Chaucer Soc. 1902. [Introduction.]

Kittredge, G. L. Arthur and Gorlagon. Harvard Stud. viii, 1903, p. 241.

—— MP. ix, 1911–2, pp. 440, 444.

—— Chaucer and his Poetry. Cambridge, U.S.A. 1915, p. 193.

Hendrickson, G. L. MP. iv, 1906–7, p. 179. [Boccaccio; high style.]

Adolphus, A. E. N. & Q. 14 Sept. 1907, p. 203. [Verses 106–8.]

Hinckley, H. B. Notes on Chaucer. Northampton, 1907.

—— PMLA. xxxii, 1917, p. 293. [Marriage group.]

Tatlock, J. S. P. Development and Chronology of Chaucer's Works. Chaucer Soc. 1907, p. 156.

Hamilton, G. L. MLN. xxiii, 1908, pp. 169, 171. [Date; 'Petrak.']

Hulton, S. F. The Clerk of Oxford in Fiction. 1909.

Lowes, J. L. MP. viii, 1910–1, p. 333. [Miroir de Mariage.]

—— Romanic Rev. ii, 1911, p. 125. [French illustrations.]

Jones, H. S. V. PMLA. xxvii, 1912, p. 106. [The Clerk.]

Meyer, E. Die Charakterzeichnung bei Chaucer. SEP. xlviii, 1913.

Cook, A. S. Chaucer's Linian. Romanic Rev. viii, 1917, p. 353.

—— Romanic Rev. viii, 1917, p. 210. [Date; use of Ménagier.]

—— Romanic Rev. viii, 1917, p. 222. [Verse 29.]

Cook, A. S. Griselda and Homer's Arete. AJ. Phil. xxxix, 1918, p. 75.

—— The First Two Readers of Petrarch's Tale. MP. xv, 1917–8, p. 633.

Jefferson, B. L. Chaucer and the Consolation of Philosophy of Boethius. Princeton, 1917.

Farnham, W. E. MLN. xxxiii, 1918, p. 193. [Use of Boccaccio.]

—— England's Discovery of the Decameron. PMLA. xxxix, 1924, p. 128.

Glomeau, A. La Mystère de Griselidis. Paris, 1923.

Jusserand, J. J. School for Ambassadors. 1924, appendix. [Verses E 26 ff.; meeting with Petrarch.]

Power, E. Medieval People. 1924, p. 85. [Ménagier's wife.]

Brusendorff, A. The Chaucer Tradition. Copenhagen, 1925, p. 75. [Host's comment.]

Cowling, G. H. RES. ii, 1926, p. 311. [Verse.]

Baldwin, C. S. PMLA. xlii, 1927, p. 109. [Verse E 41.]

Cate, W. A. The Problem of the Origin of the Griselda Story. Stud. Phil. xxix, 1932, p. 389.

Severs, J. B. Chaucer's Source MSS. for the Clerkes Tale. PMLA. xlvii, 1932, p. 431.

(ii) Merchant's Prologue, Tale, and Epilogue

[See *Hammond*, *Wells*, under Fragment E above, p. 245.]

Annotated Edition. K. Sisam (with Clerk's Tale), Oxford, 1923.

Studies.

Originals and Analogues. Chaucer Soc. 1875, pp. 177, 341, 544. [See also Ang Anz. vii, 1884, p. 155; Ang. xiv, 1891–2 p. 257].

Skeat, W. W. Oxford Chaucer. Vol. iii, p. 457 vol. v, p. 353.

Tatlock, J. S. P. The Development and Chronology of Chaucer's Works. Chaucer Soc. 1907, p. 198.

—— Boccaccio and the Plan of the Canterbury Tales. Ang. xxxvii, 1913, p. 96.

—— MLN. xxxii, 1917, p. 373. [Liturgy verses E 1701 ff.]

Holthausen, F. E. Studien, xliii, 1910–1 p. 168. [Sources. See also JEGP. xii, 1913 p. 77.]

Lowes, J. L. MP. viii, 1910–1, p. 168 [Miroir de Mariage.]

Kittredge, G. L. MP. ix, 1911–2, p. 450.

—— Chaucer and his Poetry. Cambridge U.S.A. 1915, p. 201.

Meyer, E. Die Charakterzeichnung bei Chaucer. SEP. xlviii, 1913.

Andrae, A. Ang. Bbl. xxvii, 1916, p. 61 [Longfellow.]

Hinckley, H. B. PMLA. xxxii, 1917, p. 300 [Marriage group.]

—— PQ. iv, 1925, p. 313. [Catullus; verse E 1762–3.]

Jefferson, B. L. Chaucer and the Consolation of Philosophy of Boethius. Princeton, 1917

Knott, T. A. PQ. i, 1922, p. 1. [Anonymous merchant.]

Farnham, W. E. The Merchant's Tale in Chaucer Junior. MLN. XLI, 1926, p. 392.

Magoun, F. P. Ang. LIII, 1929, p. 223. [Verse E 1425.]

Schlauch, M. Chaucer's Merchant's Tale and a Russian Legend of King Solomon. MLN. XLIX, 1934, p. 229.

(g) *Fragment F*

[*Hammond*, p. 310; *Wells*, pp. 732, 880, 997, 1032, 1148, 1197, 1240, 1328, 1426; *Griffith*, p. 101; W. W. Skeat, Oxford Chaucer, vol. III, p. 462, vol. v, p. 370; R. K. Root, The Poetry of Chaucer, Boston, 1906, 1922 (rev. edn), p. 266.]

(i) Squire's Prologue and Tale

[See *Hammond*, *Wells*, under Fragment F, above.]

Annotated Editions. W. and R. Chambers, Edinburgh, 1882; A. W. Pollard, 1899; W. J. Goodrich, Madras, 1899; A. J. Wyatt (with General Prologue), 1903; L. Winstanley (with Clerk's Tale), Cambridge, 1908; W. W. Skeat, with Prioress's Tale, etc.), Oxford, 1874, 1898.

Studies.

Clouston, W. A. Chaucer Soc. 1889. [Sources.]

Holthausen, F. Ang. XIV, 1891–2, p. 320. [Verses F 490–1.]

Koeppel, E. Ang. XIV, 1891–2, p. 257. [Sources.]

Skeat, W. W. Oxford Chaucer. Vol. III, pp. 462, 470, vol. v, p. 370. [See also, for sources, J. M. Manly, PMLA. XI, 1896, p. 349, Nation (New York), 11 June 1896, p. 455.]

Jones, H. S. V. PMLA. XX, 1905, p. 346; JEGP. VI, 1906–7, p. 221; PMLA. XXIII 1908, p. 557; MLN. XXIV, 1909, p. 158. [Cléomadès.]

Hinckley, H. B. Notes on Chaucer. Northampton, 1907, p. 210.

—— Academy, 6 June 1908, p. 866. [Verse F 29; Elpheta.]

—— MLN. XXIII, 1908, p. 157. [Verses 209–13.]

—— MLN. XXIV, 1909, p. 95. [Cléomadès.]

—— MP. XVI, 1918–9, p. 39. [Verse F 250.]

—— PQ. VI, 1928, p. 313. [Verse F 203; Terence.]

Lowes, J. L. Archiv, CXXIV, 1910, p. 132. [Verse F 491.]

—— The Squire's Tale and the Land of Prester John. Washington University Stud. I, pt 2, no. 1, 1913.

Bushnell, A. J. Blackwood's Mag. CLXXXVII, 1910, p. 654. [Names; sources.]

Kittredge, G. L. MP. VII, 1909–10, p. 481. [Verses F 99 ff.; G. de Vinsauf.]

Cook, A. S. Trans. Connecticut Academy, XX, 1916, p. 161.

—— Trans. Connecticut Academy, XXIII, 1919, p. 32. [Verse 57; parallel.]

Baum, P. F. MLN. XXXII, 1917, p. 376. [Verses F 7–8.]

Jefferson, B. L. Chaucer and the Consolation of Philosophy of Boethius. Princeton, 1917.

Tupper, F. Chaucer's Tale of Ireland. PMLA. XXXVI, 1921, pp. 196, 198.

Tatlock, J. S. P. MLN. XXXVIII, 1923, p. 506. [Verses F 490–1.]

Magoun, F. P. Romanic Rev. XVII, 1926, p. 69. [Verses F 253–6; Roman de la Rose.]

Baldwin, C. S. PMLA. XLII, 1927, p. 106. [Verses F 32, 401.]

[See also under Shipman's Prologue, p. 240 above.]

(ii) Words of the Franklin, and Franklin's Tale

[See *Hammond*, *Wells*, under Fragment F, above.]

Originals and Analogues. Chaucer Soc. 1886, p. 289.

Skeat, W. W. Oxford Chaucer. Vol. III, p. 479, vol. v, p. 387.

Schofield, W. H. The Franklin's Tale. PMLA. XIV, 1899, p. 405. [See also *Hammond*, p. 314; P. Rajna, Romania, XXXII, 1903, p. 204.]

Foulet, L. Zeitschrift für romanische Philologie, XXX, 1906, p. 698. [Prologue and Breton lais.]

Hinckley, H. B. Notes on Chaucer. Northampton, 1907, p. 237.

—— PMLA. XXXII, 1917, p. 301. [Marriage group.]

—— MP. XVI, 1918, p. 39. [Verses F 734, 943, 1325.]

Hart, W. M. Haverford Essays. Haverford, U.S.A. 1909, p. 185. [Compared with Breton lais.]

Lowes, J. L. Romanic Rev. II, 1911, p. 125. [Verses F 118–20; French versions.]

—— MP. VIII, 1910–1, p. 324. [Miroir de Mariage.]

—— MP. XIV, 1917, p. 721. [Verses 949–50, 1101; Dante.]

—— MP. XV, 1918, p. 689. [Teseide; Filocolo.]

Aman, A. Der Filiation der Frankeleynes Tale. Munich, 1912.

Hammond, E. P. MLN. XXVII, 1912, p. 91. [Verses 289–90].

Kittredge, G. L. Chaucer's Discussion of Marriage. MP. IX, 1912, p. 457.

—— Chaucer and his Poetry. Cambridge, U.S.A. 1915, p. 204.

Legouis, É. Geoffrey Chaucer. New York, 1913, p. 211.

Meyer, É. Die Charakterzeichnung bei Chaucer. SEP. xlviii, 1913.

Tatlock, J. S. P. Ang. xxxvii, 1913, p. 72. [Boccaccio; plan.]

—— Kittredge Anniversary Papers. Boston, 1913. [Astrology and magic.]

—— The Scene of Chaucer's Franklin's Tale Visited. Chaucer Soc. 1914.

Tupper, F. St Venus. Nation (New York), 16 Oct. 1913, p. 354.

Cummings, H. M. The Indebtedness of Chaucer's Works to the Italian Works of Boccaccio. Cincinnati University Stud. x, pt 2, 1916, p. 181.

Jefferson, B. L. Chaucer and the Consolation of Philosophy of Boethius. Princeton, 1917.

Farnham, W. E. Stud. Phil. xx, 1923, p. 70. [Science.]

Wrenn, C. L. MLR. xviii, 1923, p. 286. [Horace.]

Koch, J. Ang. xlix, 1925, p. 231.

Vogt, G. M. JEGP. xxiv, 1925, p. 102. ['Gentilesse.']

Gerould, G. H. The Social Status of Chaucer's Franklin. PMLA. xli, 1926, p. 262.

Royster, J. F. Magic and Orleans. Stud. Phil. xxiii, 1926, p. 383.

Baldwin, C. S. Cicero on Parnassus. PMLA. xlii, 1927, p. 106.

Schick, J. Die ältesten Versionen von Chaucers Frankeleynes Tale. [In Studia Geiger, Leipzig, 1931, p. 89.]

Harrison, B. S. The Rhetorical Inconsistency of Chaucer's Franklin. Stud. Phil. xxxii, 1935, p. 55.

(h) Fragment G

[*Hammond*, p. 315; *Wells*, pp. 737, 880, 997, 1032, 1093, 1149, 1197, 1241, 1289, 1328, 1376, 1426; *Griffith*, p. 105; W. W. Skeat, Oxford Chaucer, vol. iii, p. 485, vol. v, p. 401; R. K. Root, The Poetry of Chaucer, Boston, 1906, 1922 (rev. edn), p. 277.]

(i) Second Nun's Prologue and Tale

[See *Hammond, Wells*, under Fragment G, above.]

Annotated Edition. W. W. Skeat, The Tale of the Man of Law, Oxford, 1877, 1889, 1897.

Studies.

Originals and Analogues. Chaucer Soc. 1875, p. 189. [See also B. ten Brink, Chaucer, Münster, 1870, p. 130; E. Koelbing, E. Studien, i, 1877, p. 215; F. Holthausen, Archiv, lxxxvii, 1891, pp. 262, 265; W. W. Skeat, Academy, 23 Feb., 30 March 1889, pp. 133, 222.]

Lounsbury, T. R. Studies in Chaucer. Vol. ii, New York, 1892, p. 486.

Kittredge, G. L. Nation (New York), 25 Oct. 1 Nov. 1894, pp. 309, 329; Chaucer Soc 1908, p. 41. [Date.]

Skeat, W. W. Oxford Chaucer. Vol. iii, p. 485 vol. v, p. 401.

Brown, C. MP. ix, 1911-2, p. 1. [Prologue.]

—— MLN. xxx, 1915, p. 231. [Hours o Virgin.]

Lowes, J. L. PMLA. xxvi, 1911, p. 315 xxix, 1914, p. 129. ['Corones Two.']

—— MP. xv, 1917-8, p. 193. [Prologue Alanus; Macrobius.]

MacCracken, H. N. MLN. xxvii, 1912, p. 63 ['Corones Two.']

Tupper, F. PMLA. xxix, 1914, pp. 98, 106 112, etc. [Sins motif. See also J. L. Lowes PMLA. xxx, 1915, p. 288.]

—— MLN. xxx, 1915, p. 9. [Prymer.]

—— JEGP. xv, 1916, p. 77. [Sins motif.]

Gerould, G. H. Saints' Legends. Boston 1916, pp. 239, 369, index.

Jefferson, B. L. Chaucer and the Consolatior of Philosophy of Boethius. Princeton, 1917

Landrum, G. Chaucer's Use of the Vulgate PMLA. xxxix, 1924, p. 75.

Brusendorff, A. The Chaucer Tradition Copenhagen, 1925, p. 131. [Belongs t Second Nun.]

Hammond, E. P. MP. xxiii, 1925-6, p. 148 [Verse.]

Cowling, G. H. RES. ii, 1926, p. 311. [Verse.

Emerson, O. F. PMLA. xli, 1926, p. 252 [Verses 271 ff.; Ambrose.]

Parker, R. E. MLN. xli, 1926, p. 317. ['Corone Two.']

Cornelius, R. D. PMLA. xlii, 1927, p. 1055 ['Corones Two.']

Henshaw, M. MP. xxvi, 1928, p. 15. [Am brose's Preface.]

(ii) Canon's Yeoman's Prologue and Tale

[See *Hammond, Wells*, under Fragment G above.]

Annotated Edition. W. W. Skeat, The Tal of the Man of Law, Oxford, 1877, 1889, 1897

Studies.

Skeat, W. W. Oxford Chaucer. Vol. i p. xxxvii, vol. iii, p. 492, vol. v, p. 414.

Kittredge, G. L. Trans. Royal Soc. Lit. xxx 1910, p. 87.

de Vocht, H. Chaucer and Erasmus. E. Stu dien, xli, 1909-10, p. 387.

Lowes, J. L. Dragon and his Brother. MLN xxviii, 1913, p. 229.

Andrae, A. Ang. Bbl. xxvii, 1916, p. 84 [Longfellow.]

Jefferson, B. L. Chaucer and the Consolatio of Philosophy of Boethius. Princeton, 1917

Richardson, H. G. Trans. Royal Hist. Soc 1922, p. 28.

Emerson, O. F. PQ. ii, 1923, p. 89. [Original plan.]

Damon, F. S. PMLA. xxxix, 1924, p. 782. [Alchemy.]

Baum, P. F. MLN. xl, 1925, p. 152. [Interpretation; date.]

Koch, J. Ang. xlix, 1925, p. 236. [Date.]

Manly, J. M. Some New Light on Chaucer. New York, 1926, p. 235.

(i) Fragment H

[Hammond, p. 317; Wells, pp. 742, 881, 1032, 1149, 1241, 1376, 1426; Griffith, p. 107; W. W. Skeat, Oxford Chaucer, vol. iii, p. 500, vol. v, p. 435; R. K. Root, The Poetry of Chaucer, Boston, 1906, 1922 (rev. edn), p. 283.]

(i) Maniple's Prologue and Tale

[See Hammond, Wells, under Fragment H, above.]

Annotated Edition. W. W. Skeat, The Tale of the Man of Law, Oxford, 1877, 1889, 1897.

Studies.

Furnivall, F. J. Athenaeum, 14 Oct. 1871, p. 495. [Date.]

Originals and Analogues. Chaucer Soc. 1875, pp. 437, 545. [See also Ang. xiii, 1890–1, p. 181, xiv, 1891–2, p. 261; Archiv, lxxxvi, 1891, p. 44.]

Koeppel, E. Ang. xiv, 1891–2, p. 261. [Date.]

Skeat, W. W. Oxford Chaucer. Vol. iii, p. 500, vol. v, pp. 50, 439, 444.

Andrae, A. E. Studien, xlv, 1912, p. 347. [Prologue.]

Koch, J. Ang. Bbl. xxv, 1914, p. 327, xxviii, 1917, pp. 152, 155. [On Tupper.]

Tupper, F. PMLA. xxix, 1914, pp. 99, 101, 109; JEGP. xv, 1916, p. 83. [Sins motif.]

—— JEGP. xiv, 1915, p. 256. [Quarrels motif.]

Lowes, J. L. PMLA. xxx, 1915, p. 330. [Sins motif.]

Siebert, H. MLN. xxxi, 1916, p. 304. [Horace.]

Jefferson, B. L. Chaucer and the Consolation of Philosophy of Boethius. Princeton, 1917.

Root, R. K. MLN. xliv, 1929, p. 493. [Prologue.]

Work, J. A. The Maniple's Prologue. Stud. Phil. xxix, 1932, p. 11.

—— The Positions of the Tales of the Maniple and the Parson. JEGP. xxxi, 1932, p. 62.

(j) Fragment I

[Hammond, p. 318; Wells, pp. 744, 881, 1032, 1093, 1149, 1197, 1241, 1289, 1328, 1376, 1426; Griffith, p. 107; W. W. Skeat, Oxford Chaucer, vol. iii, p. 502, vol. v, p. 444; R. K. Root, The Poetry of Chaucer, Boston, 1906, 1922 (rev. edn), p. 284.]

(i) Parson's Prologue and Tale, and the Retraction

[See Hammond, Wells, under Fragment I, above.]

Annotated Edition. W. W. Skeat, The Tale of the Man of Law, Oxford, 1877, 1889, 1897.

Studies.

Petersen, K. O. The Sources of the Parson's Tale. Boston, 1901.

Schlacht, H. Der gute Pfarrer in der englische.i Literatur. Berlin, 1904.

Spies, H. Festschrift für A. Tobler. Brunswick, 1905, p. 383. [Retraction.]

—— Chaucer's religiöse Grundstimmung und die Echtheit der Parson's Tale. SEP. l, 1913, p. 626. [See also Ang. Bbl. xxv, 1914, p. 84; E. Studien, xxxvii, 1907, p. 227.]

Lowes, J. L. MP. viii, 1910–1, p. 171. [Miroir de Mariage:]

Tatlock, J. S. P. PMLA. xxviii, 1913, p. 521. [Retractions. See also Ang. Bbl. xxv, 1914, p. 327.]

Tupper, F. PMLA. xxix, 1914, pp. 93, 114; JEGP. xv, 1916, p. 90. [Sins motif. See also J. L. Lowes, PMLA. xxx, 1915, p. 237.]

—— MLN. xxx, 1915, p. 11. [A parallel.]

Ayres, H. M. Romanic Rev. x, 1919, p. 3. [Seneca.]

Koch, J. Ang. xlvi, 1922, p. 42. [Date.]

Landrum, G. PMLA. xxxix, 1924, p. 75. [Vulgate.]

Brusendorff, A. The Chaucer Tradition. Copenhagen, 1925, pp. 132, 147, 429. [Authenticity; aim of retraction.]

Chapman, C. O. MLN. xliii, 1928, p. 229; PMLA. xliv, 1929, p. 178. [Sermon quality.]

Work, J. A. Chaucer's Sermon and Retractations. MLN. xlvii, 1932, p. 257.

—— Echoes of the Anathema in Chaucer. PMLA. xlvii, 1932, p. 419.

J. E. W.

3. THE FIFTEENTH CENTURY

I. THE ENGLISH CHAUCERIANS:

LYDGATE, OCCLEVE, HAWES AND OTHERS

A. JOHN LYDGATE (1370?–1450?)

(1) MANUSCRIPTS

[A full discussion of the MSS will be found in the Lydgate Canon appended to H. N. MacCracken's edn of the Minor Poems, 1911.]

(2) SELECTIONS

Minor Poems. Ed. J. O. Halliwell[-Phillipps], Percy Soc. 1840. [Includes London Lackpenny; Moral of Horse, Goose and Sheep; Bycorne and Chichevache; Churl and the Bird; Testament; etc.]

Einige religiöse Gedichte. Ed. O. Maher, Oberpfalz, 1910; Berlin, 1914.

Minor Poems. Ed. H. N. MacCracken, 2 pts, EETS. Ex. Ser. 1911–34. [Includes St Margaret, St Giles, Testament, etc.]

[Other poems are in Thomas Wright, Political Poems and Songs, vol. II, 1861; W. W. Skeat, Complete Works of Chaucer, vol. VII, Oxford, 1897; Sir H. Nicolas, A Chronicle of London, 1827; E. P. Hammond, English Verse between Chaucer and Surrey, Durham, North Carolina, 1927.]

(3) SEPARATE WORKS

Aesop. Ed. P. Sauerstein, Ang. IX, 1885 (from Harl. MS 225); ed. J. Zupitza, Archiv, LXXXV, 1890 (from other MSS).

[Assembly of the Gods.] The Interpretacion of the Names of Goddis and Goddisses. [1498] (de Worde); [n.d.] (de Worde); [1500?] (de Worde); [n.d.] (Pynson); [after 1529] (Redman); 1540; ed. O. L. Triggs, Chicago, 1895 and EETS. 1896 (from Trinity College Cambridge MS); ed. photo. facs. F. Jenkinson, Cambridge, 1906 (from 2nd edn).

A Calendar. Ed. C. Horstmann, Archiv, LXXX, 1888.

On Chaucer and his Troilus. Ed. W. M. Rossetti (in Troilus and Cryseyde, 1873).

Chichevache and Bycorne. [In Old Plays, ed. R. Dodsley, vol. XII, 1780, and Minor Poems, ed. J. O. Halliwell[-Phillipps], 1840.]

The Chorle and the Birde. [1477?] (Caxton); [n.d.] (Caxton); [1493] (Pynson); [n.d.]

(de Worde); [1520] (de Worde); [1550?] (Mychel); [after 1561] (Copland); 1651 (in E. Ashmole's Theatrum Chemicum); ed. M. M. Sykes, Roxburghe Club, 1822; ed. photo. facs. F. Jenkinson, Cambridge, 1906 (from 1st edn); rptd 1929.

[The Complaint of the Black Knight.] The Complainte of a Lovers Lyfe. [n.d.] (de Worde); 1508 (as The mayny or disport of Chaucer in The Knightly Tale of Golagrus and Gawane); 1532 (in Thynne's Works of Chaucer and subsequent edns until discovered to be Lydgate's by Shirley's testimony); ed. E. Krausser, 1896; ed. W. W. Skeat, Complete Works of Chaucer, vol. VII, Oxford, 1897; ed. George Stevenson, STS. 1918 (from 1508 edn).

[Danse Macabre.] The Daunce of Machabree. 1554 (in Fall of Princes); rptd in W. Dugdale's History of St Paul's Cathedral, 1658, and Hans Holbein's Alphabet of Death, 1856; ed. F. Warren and B. White, EETS. 1931.

The Departing of Chaucer. Ed. E. P. Hammond, MP. I, 1903.

Fabula Duorum Mercatorum. Ed. J. Zupitza and G. Schleich, QF. LXXXIII, 1897.

The Falle of Princis. 1494 (Pynson); 1527 (Pynson); 1554 (Tottell); [1555?] (Wayland); ed. Henry Bergen, Carnegie Inst. of Washington, 1923–4, EETS. 1924–7. [See also Proverbs of Lydgate which contain extracts.]

Flour of Curtesye. 1532 (in Thynne's Chaucer and later edns to Chalmers); ed. W. W. Skeat, Complete Works of Chaucer, vol. VII, Oxford, 1897.

On Gloucester's Wedding, and Complaint for my Lady of Gloucester. Ed. E. P. Hammond, Ang. XXVII, 1904.

The Governance of Kings and Princes. [See Secrets of Old Philosophers.]

The Grateful Dead. Ed. A. Beatty (in A New Ploughman's Tale, Chaucer Soc. 1902).

Guy of Warwick. Ed. J. Zupitza, Sitzungsber. d. kgl. Akad. d. Wissensch., Phil.-hist. Kl. LXXIV, Vienna, 1873; ed. F. N. Robinson, Harvard Stud. V, 1896.

The Hystorye Sege and Dystruccyon of Troye. 1513 (Pynson); 1555 (Marshe); 1614 (modernised by T. Heywood as The Life and Death of Hector); ed. Henry Bergen, 4 pts, EETS. Ex. Ser. 1906–35. [See also under Romances of Troy, p. 145 above.]

The Horse the Ghoos and the Sheep. [1477?] (Caxton); [1477–8] (Caxton); [1500] (de Worde); [1500?] (de Worde); 1500 (de Worde); ed. M. M. Sykes, Roxburghe Club, 1822; ed. M. Degenhart, 1900; ed. F. J. Furnivall (in Political, Religious and Love Poems, EETS. 1903); ed. photo. facs. F. Jenkinson, Cambridge, 1906 (from 1500 edn).

King Henry's Triumphal Entry in London. Ed. H. N. MacCracken, Archiv, cxxvi, 1911.

On the Kings of England. Ed. James Gairdner (in The Historical Collections of a Citizen of London in the Fifteenth Century, Camden Soc. 1876).

The Lyf of our Lady. [1484] (2 issues) (Caxton); 1531 (Redman); ed. C. E. Tame (in Early English Religious Literature, 1871–9).

The Lyfe of Seint Albon and the Lyfe of Saint Amphabel. St Albans, 1534; ed. C. Horstmann (in Festschrift der Realschule zu Berlin, Berlin, 1882).

Merita Missae. Ed. T. F. Simmons (in Lay Folks Mass Book, EETS. 1879). [Also contains Venus Mass and extracts from Virtutes Missarum not to be confused with Virtue of the Mass.]

Mummings. Ed. E. P. Hammond (in Mumming at Hertford, Ang. xxxii, 1909); ed. R. Brotanek (in Die englischen Maskenspiele, Vienna, 1902).

New Year's Valentine. Ed. E. P. Hammond, Ang. xxxii, 1909.

Two Nightingale Poems. Ed. O. Glauning, EETS. Ex. Ser. 1900.

The Pilgrimage of the Life of Man. Ed. F. J. Furnivall, EETS. Ex. Ser. 1899–1904; ed. F. J. Furnivall and K. B. Locock, Roxburghe Club, 1905. [For Deguileville himself, see edn by J. J. Sturzinger, Roxburghe Club, 1893.]

The Puerbes [proverbs] of Lydgate. [1515?] (de Worde); [1520?] (de Worde); 1526 (Pynson). [Extracts from Fall of Princes, Loke in Thy Merour, Consulo Quisquis Eris, and Chaucer's Fortune and Truth.]

Queen Margaret's Entry into London. Ed. Carleton Brown, MLR. vii, 1912.

Reason and Sensuality. Ed. E. Sieper, EETS. Ex. Ser. 1901–3.

St Edmund and Fremund. Ed. C. Horstmann (in Altenglische Legenden, 1881); ed. Lord F. Harvey (in Corolla Sancti Eadmundi, 1907).

St Giles. Ed. C. Horstmann (in Altenglische Legenden, 1881); ed. H. N. MacCracken (in Minor Poems, 1911).

St Margaret. Ed. C. Horstmann (in Altenglische Legenden, 1881); ed. H. N. MacCracken (in Minor Poems, 1911).

[Secrets of Old Philosophers.] The Governaunce of Kynges and Prynces. 1511 (Pynson); ed. R. Steele, EETS. Ex. Ser. 1894 (from Sloane MS). [T. Prosiegel's The Book of the Governaunce of Kynges and of Prynces, 1903, corrects this edn and collates with other MSS.]

The Serpent of Division. [n.d.] (fragment) (Treverys); 1559 (Rogers); 1590 (with Gorboduc); ed. H. N. MacCracken, 1911.

[Siege of Thebes.] The Storye of Thebes. [1500?] (de Worde); 1561 (in Stow's Chaucer and later edns to Chalmers); ed. pt i, Axel Erdmann, Chaucer Soc. and EETS. Ex. Ser. 1911; ed. pt ii, Axel Erdmann and E. Ekwall, EETS. 1930; Prologue, ed. E. P. Hammond, Ang. xxxvi, 1912. [See also under Romances of Thebes, p. 146 above.]

Stans Puer ad Mensam. [n.d.] (Caxton); [1545?] (appended to Hugh Rhodes's Book of Nurture); ed. J. O. Halliwell[-Phillipps], and T. Wright (in Reliquiae Antiquae, vol. i, 1841); ed. W. C. Hazlitt (in Early Popular Poetry of England, vol. iii, 1866); ed. F. J. Furnivall (in The Babees Book, EETS. 1868).

Two Tapestry Poems. (a) The Life of St George. (b) The Falls of Seven Princes. Ed. E. P. Hammond, E. Studien, xliii, 1910.

The Temple of Glass. [1477–8] (Caxton); [n.d.] (de Worde); [1500] (de Worde); [n.d.] (de Worde); [1505?] (Pynson); [1530?] (Berthelet); ed. J. Schick, EETS. Ex. Ser. 1891; ed. photo. facs. F. Jenkinson, Cambridge, 1905 (from 1st edn).

The Testament of J. Lydgate. [1515?] (Pynson); rptd in Halliwell's and MacCracken's edns of Minor Poems.

Troy Book. [See History of Troy.]

The Vertue of the Masse. [n.d.] (de Worde); rptd in Fugitive Tracts, vol. iii, 1875.

(4) WORKS ATTRIBUTED TO LYDGATE

Cartae Versificatae. [In Memorials of St Edmund's Abbey, ed. T. Arnold, vol. iii, 1896. Attrib. on internal evidence by Arnold and MacCracken.]

The Child of Bristow. Ed. C. Hopper, Camden Misc. vol. iv, 1859; ed. T. Burke (in The Charm of the West Country, 1913). [Attrib. by Ritson. See also under Tales, p. 163 above.]

The Complaint of Mary Magdalen. 1526 (Pynson); 1561 (in Stow's Chaucer); ed. C. E. Tame, [1871] (as The Lamentation of St Mary Magdalene). [Attrib. in Harl. Catalogue.]

[The Court of Sapience.] De Curia Sapiencie. [1480] (Caxton); 1510 (de Worde); ed. R. Spindler, Leipzig, 1927. [Really by author of The Babees Book? See, however, C. F. Bühler, The Sources of the Court of Sapience, Leipzig, 1932.]

The Lamentation of Our Lady. [Before 1519] (de Worde); ed. C. E. Tame, [1871]. [Attrib. by Ritson, Tanner.]

London Lickpenny. Ed. E. P. Hammond, Ang. xx, 1898; ed. F. Holthausen, Ang. xliii, 1919. [Attrib. by Stowe, Tanner, Ritson.]

The Medecine of the Stomach. [In The Governayle of Helthe, [c. 1489] (Caxton); [n.d.] (de Worde); [c. 1491] (Caxton); ed. W. Blades, 1858. Attrib. in Harl. MS 116, which contains nothing but Lydgate's work.]

The Pilgrimage of the Soul. 1483 (Caxton). [Pt v attrib. by Ritson.]

The Seven Virtues. [1500?]

A Treatise of a Gallant. [1516?] (de Worde). [Attrib. by Bishop John Alcock.]

A Treatise of the Smith. [n.d.] (Copland). [In W. C. Hazlitt, Remains of the Early Popular Poetry of England, vol. iii, 1866. Attrib. by Bale and Ritson.]

(5) Biography and Criticism
(a) General

[Consult introductions to edns mentioned above, especially Schick's Temple of Glass, H. N. MacCracken's Lydgate Canon appended to his edn of Minor Poems; see also Sidney Lee's bibliography in DNB.]

Gattinger, E. Die Lyrik Lydgates. Vienna. 1896.

Reuss, F. Das Naturgefühl bei Lydgate. Archiv, cxxii, 1909.

Hammond, E. P. Chaucer and Lydgate Notes. MLN. xxvii, 1912.

Brown, Carleton. Lydgate and the Legend of Good Women. E. Studien, xlvii, 1913.

Brie, F. Mittelalter und Antike bei Lydgate. E. Studien, lxiv, 1929.

(b) Special Studies

[In alphabetical order of the works discussed.]

Rudolf, Albert. Lydgate und die Assembly of Gods. Berlin, 1909.

Emmerig, O. The Bataile of Agyncourt im Lichte geschichtlicher Quellenwerke. Nuremburg, 1906. [Attributes it to Lydgate.]

Hammond, E. P. The Texts of Lydgate's Danse Macabre. MLN. xxxvi, 1921.

Koeppel, E. Laurents de Premierfait und John Lydgate's Bearbeitung von Boccaccio's De Casibus Virorum Illustrium. Munich, 1885.

Hammond, E. P. A Reproof to Lydgate. MLN. xxvi, 1911. [Rpt of poem censuring passages in Fall of Princes.]

—— Poet and Patron in the Fall of Princes. Ang. xxxviii, 1914.

—— Lydgate and Coluccio Salutati. MP. xxv, 1927. [Passage in Fall of Princes.]

Werner, F. Ein Sammelkapitel aus Lydgate's Fall of Princes. Münchener Archiv, v, 1916.

[Reviews of Bergen's edn of Fall of Princes.] Ang. Bbl. xxxvi, 1925, by E. P. Hammond and M. Förster; Archiv, cxlviii, 1925, by A. Brandl.

Robinson, F. N. On Two MSS. of Lydgate's Guy of Warwick. Harvard Stud. v, 1896.

Lydgates Quelle zu seinem Guy of Warwick. Archiv, cxlvi, 1923.

Brown, Carleton. An Holy Medytacion—By Lydgate? MLN. xl, 1925.

—— Chaucer's Wretched Engendring. PMLA. l, 1935. [Identifies Chaucer's lost work as An Holy Medytacion (hitherto attrib. to Lydgate).]

MacCracken, H. N. In Despite of the Flemings. Ang. xxxiii, 1910.

Rey, Albert. Skelton's Satirical Poems in their relation to Lydgate's Order of Fools. Berne, 1899.

Withington, Robert. Queen Margaret's Entry into London. MP. xiii, 1915.

Schick, J. Kleine Lydgate-studien. Reason and Sensuality. Ang. Bbl. viii, 1897.

Sieper, E. Les Échecs Amoureux und ihre englische Übertragung [i.e. Reson and Sensuallyte]. Weimar, 1898.

Koeppel, E. Lydgate's Story of Thebes—Eine Quellenuntersuchung. Munich, 1884.

MacCracken, H. N. Additional Light on the Temple of Glas. PMLA. xxiii, 1908.

Oakden, J. P. A Note on Lydgate's Verses on the Kings of England. RES. ix, 1933.

(c) Language and Syntax

Reismüller, George. Romanische Lehnwörter bei Lydgate. Leipzig, 1911.

Courmont, André. Studies in Lydgate's Syntax in the Temple of Glass. Paris, 1912.

Babcock, Charlotte F. A Study of the Metrical Use of the Inflectional e in Middle English with Particular Reference to Chaucer and Lydgate. PMLA. xxix, 1914.

Royster, J. F. A Note on Lydgate's Use of the Do Auxiliary. Stud. Phil. xiii, 1916.

Juhl, H. Der syntaktische Gebrauch des Infinitivs bei John Lydgate. Kiel, 1921.

B. THOMAS OCCLEVE or HOCCLEVE
(1368?–1450?)

(1) Manuscripts

Phillips MS 8151.
Durham MS iii. 9.

Ashburnham MS Add. 133.
Harl. MS 4866. (Regiment of Princes.)
Egerton MS 615.
BM. MS Royal 17 D vi.
Sloane MS 1212. (Regiment of Princes.)
BM. Add. MS 24062.

(2) SELECTIONS AND COLLECTIONS

Poems. Ed. G. Mason, 1796.
Works. Vol. i, The Minor Poems, ed. F. J. Furnivall, 1892; vol. ii, The Minor Poems in the Ashburnham MS, ed. Sir I. Gollancz, 1925; vol. iii, The Regiment of Princes and 14 Minor Poems, ed. F. J. Furnivall, 1897 (EETS. Ex. Ser.)

(3) SEPARATE WORKS

The Letter of Cupid. Ed. W. W. Skeat, Works of Chaucer, vol. vii, Oxford, 1897. [Also includes two ballades.]
De Regimine Principum. Ed. T. Wright, Roxburghe Club, 1860.
Tale of Jonathas [in W. Browne's The Shepheards Pipe, 1614]. [Modernised and abridged.]
Of the Virgin and her Sleeveless Garment. Ed. A. Beatty (in A New Ploughman's Tale, Chaucer Soc. 1902.

(4) BIOGRAPHY AND CRITICISM

[The editorial matter of the EETS. Works contains the fullest information and discussion yet given; and something as to him will generally be found in the neighbourhood of notices of Lydgate.]
Bock, F. Metrische Studien zu Hoccleve's Versen. Weilheim, 1900.
MacCracken, H. N. Hoccleve and the Poems from Deguilleville. Nation (New York), 26 Sept. 1907.
Williams, W. H. De Regimine Principum. MLR. iv, 1909.
MacCracken, H. N. Another Poem by Hoccleve? MLN. xxiv, 1909.
Kern, J. H. Hoccleves Verszeile. Ang.xl,1916.
—— Die Datierung von Hoccleve's Dialog. Ang. xl, 1916.
Kern, J. H. Zum Texte einiger Dictungen Thomas Hoccleves. Ang. xxxix, 1916.
Hulbert, J. R. An Hoccleve Item. MLN. xxxvi, 1921.
Kurtz, B. P. The Source of Occleve's Lerne to Dye. MLN. xxxviii, 1923.
—— The Prose of Occleve's Lerne to Dye. MLN. xxxix, 1924.
—— The Relation of Occleve's Lerne to Dye to its Source. PMLA. xl, 1925.

C. BENEDICT BURGH (d. 1483)

The A.B.C. of Aristotle. Ed. F. J. Furnivall (in The Babees Book, EETS. 1868).

A Christemasse Game. Ed. T. Wright (in Specimens of Old Christmas Carols, Percy Soc. 1841); ed. F. J. Furnivall, N. & Q. 16 May 1868.
Parvus Chato. [1477] (Caxton); [1478?] (Caxton); [1480?] (Caxton).
The Boke of Cato. 1558 (Copland). [Contains extra verses.]
Parvus Cato. Magnus Cato. Ed. photo. facs. F. Jenkinson, Cambridge. 1906. [From 1st edn. For recent edns from MS see under Distichs of Cato, p. 185 above.]

D. GEORGE ASHBY (d. 1475)

(1) MANUSCRIPTS

Trinity College Cambridge R.3.19.
Cambridge University Lib. Mm. iv. 42.

(2) EDITIONS

Poems. Ed. Mary Bateson, EETS. Ex. Ser. 1899.
Prisoner's Reflections. Ed. Max Förster, Ang. xx, 1898; ed. F. Holthausen, Ang. xlv, 1921.

(3) CRITICISM

Holthausen, F. George Ashby's Trost in Gefangenschaft. Ang. xliii, 1919.
—— Active Policy of a Prince. Ang. xlv, 1921.

E. HENRY BRADSHAW (d. 1513)

Lyfe of St. Radegunde. [1521?](Pynson); ed. F. Brittain, Cambridge, 1926.
The lyfe of saynt Werburge. 1521 (Pynson); ed. type facs. E. Hawkins, Chetham Soc. 1848; ed. C. Horstmann, EETS. 1887.
[à Wood also mentions a Latin work De Antiquitate urbis Chestriae Chronicon.]

F. GEORGE RIPLEY (d. 1490?), THOMAS NORTON (fl. 1477) AND OTHER ALCHEMISTS

Theatrum Chemicum Britannicum. Ed. Elias Ashmole, 1652.

G. OSBERN BOKENHAM (1393–1447?)

Lyvys of Sayntys. Roxburghe Club, 1835 (from Arundel MS 327); ed. C. Horstmann, Heilbronn, 1883 (as Legenden).

H. STEPHEN HAWES (c. 1475–1530)

(1) EDITIONS

Comfort of Lovers. [1512?] (de Worde).
The Convercyon of Swerers. 1509 (de Worde); [1530?] (Butler); 1551 (Copland); ed. David Laing, Abbotsford Club, 1865.

The Example of Vertu. [1504?] (de Worde); [1520?] (de Worde); 1530.

A Joyfull Medytacyon to all Englande of the Coronacyon of Kynge Henry the Eyght. [1509] (de Worde).

The Passetyme of Pleasure, or the History of Graunde Amoure and la Bel Pucel. [1509] (de Worde); 1517 (de Worde); 1554 (adds 3 verses) (Wayland); 1555 (Tottell); 1555 (Waley); ed. T. Wright, Percy Soc. 1845 (from Tottell's 1555 edn); ed. W. E. Mead, EETS. 1928.

[John Bale attributed to Hawes works entitled The Delight of the Soul (possibly The Pastime of Pleasure), Of the Prince's Marriage, and The Alphabet of Birds, of which nothing is known. The Temple of Glas, attributed to Hawes by Warton, is ascribed by Hawes himself to Lydgate (The Passetyme of Pleasure, ch. xiv).]

(2) BIOGRAPHY AND CRITICISM

Bale, J. Scriptorum Illustrium. [1557.] [P. 632. Hawes is omitted in the edn of 1548.]

à Wood, A. Athenae Oxonienses. Ed. P. Bliss, vol. I, 1813.

Warton, Thomas. The History of English Poetry. Ed. W. C. Hazlitt, vol. I, 1871.

Ames, Joseph. Typographical Antiquities. 1785. [See remarks by Herbert, vol. I, p. 194.]

Minto, W. Characteristics of English Poets. 1874.

Fuhr, K. Lautuntersuchungen zu Stephen Hawes' The Pastime of Pleasure. Marburg, 1891.

Morley, Henry. English Writers. Vol. VII, 1891.

Schick, J. The Temple of Glas. EETS. 1891. [See pp. lxxvi–lxxx.]

ten Brink, B. History of English Literature. Vol. III, 1896.

Burkart, E. A. The Pastime of Pleasure. Critical Introduction to a Proposed New Edition of the Text. 1899.

Zander, F. Stephen Hawes' Passetyme of Pleasure verglichen mit Spenser's Faerie Queene. Rostock, 1905.

Saintsbury, G. A History of English Prosody. Vol. I, 1906.

Natter, H. Untersuchung der Quellen von Stephen Hawes' allegorischem Gedichte 'Pastime of Pleasure.' Passau, 1911.

Berdan, J. M. Early Tudor Poetry. New York, 1920.

Lemmi, C. W. The Influence of Boccaccio on Hawes's Pastime of Pleasure. RES. v, 1929.

Wells, W. Stephen Hawes and the Court of Sapience. RES. VI, 1930.

Bühler, C. F. Kynge Melyzyus and The Pastime of Pleasure. RES. x, 1934.

I. PSEUDO-CHAUCERIAN PIECES

[The following are the most important 15th century poems, other than works by Lydgate and Occleve, that were included in the early edns of Chaucer. They have been rptd in Chaucerian and Other Pieces, ed W. W. Skeat, Oxford, 1897, and summaries of criticism are in E. P. Hammond, Chaucer: A Bibliographical Manual, New York, 1908—referred to as Skeat and Hammond respectively.]

The Assembly of Ladies. [Thynne's Chaucer 1532; Skeat, pp. 380–404; Hammond pp. 408–9.]

[Ros, Sir Richard.] La Belle Dame sans Mercy. [Pynson's Chaucer, 1526; Skeat pp. 299–326; Hammond, pp. 432–3.]

The Court of Love. [Stow's Chaucer, 1561 Skeat, pp. 409–47; Hammond. pp. 418–9.]
  Neilson, W. A. The Origins and Sources of the Court of Love. Harvard Stud. vi 1899.

The Flower and the Leaf. [Speght's Chaucer 1598; Skeat, pp. 361–79; Hammond pp. 423–4.]

[Scogan, Henry.] A Moral Ballade. [Thynne's Chaucer, 1532; Skeat, pp. 237–44; Hammond, p. 455.]
  Farnham, W. E. John (Henry) Scogan MLR. xvi, 1921.

The Tale of Beryn. Ed. F. J. Furnivall and W. G. Stone, Chaucer Soc. 1876. EETS [Urry's Chaucer, 1721; Hammond, p. 412.]

S. R

II. MIDDLE SCOTS WRITERS:
JAMES I, HENRYSON, DUNBAR, GAVIN DOUGLAS AND OTHERS

I. THE MIDDLE SCOTS ANTHOLOGIES
(1) THE MANUSCRIPT COLLECTIONS
(a) Major

Asloan MS. Ed. W. A. Craigie, 2 vols. STS 1923–5. [Written c. 1515 by John Asloan Formerly in possession of the Boswel family at Auchinleck, but since 1882 in tha of R. W. Talbot, afterwards Lord Talbot d Malahide.]

Bannatyne MS. Ed. J. B. Murdoch, 6 vol. Hunterian Club, 1873–1901; ed. W. To Ritchie, 4 vols. STS. 1928–. [Now in Na Lib. Scotland (MS 1.1.6). See Hunteria Club introduction, and Memorials of Georg Bannatyne, Bannatyne Club, 1829.]

Maitland Folio MS. Ed. W. A. Craigie, 2 vols. STS. 1919–27. [Compiled c. 1580 by Sir Richard Maitland of Lethington, Lord Privy Seal of Scotland. Now in Pepysian Lib., Magdalene College, Cambridge.]

Maitland Quarto MS. Ed. W. A. Craigie, STS. 1920. [Written by Sir Richard's daughter Marie in 1586. Contains 42 pieces from Folio MS. Now also in Pepysian collection].

(b) Minor

Makculloch MS. Ed. G. Stevenson, Pieces from the Makculloch and the Gray MSS. together with the Chepman and Myllar Prints, STS. 1918. [A collection of lecture-notes in Latin by Magnus Makculloch at Louvain in 1477, the Scots pieces being written on fly-leaves and blank pages. Now in Laing MSS collection, Edinburgh University.]

Gray MS. Ed. G. Stevenson, STS. 1918. [Written c. 1500 by James Gray, notary public and priest of the diocese of Dunblane. The Scots pieces are interpolated. Now in Nat. Lib. Scotland (MS 34 . 7 . 3).]

(2) The Printed Collections

Chepman and Myllar's Prints. Edinburgh, 1508 (only copy known in Nat. Lib. Scotland); ed. type facs. David Laing, 1827; ed. G. Stevenson, STS. 1918.

Ramsay, Allan. The Ever Green, being a Collection of Scots Poems, wrote by the Ingenious before 1600. 2 vols. Edinburgh, 1724. [Mainly from Bannatyne MS.]

Dalrymple, D. (Lord Hailes). Ancient Scottish Poems. Published from the MS of George Bannatyne, MDLXVIII. Edinburgh, 1770.

Pinkerton, John. Ancient Scotish Poems, never before in print. But now published from the MS Collections of Sir Richard Maitland. 2 vols. Edinburgh, 1786.

Dalyell, J. G. Scottish Poems of the Sixteenth Century. Edinburgh, 1801.

Sibbald, J. Chronicle of Scottish Poetry. 4 vols. Edinburgh, 1802.

Laing, David. Select Remains of the Ancient Popular and Romance Poetry of Scotland. Edinburgh, 1822; ed. John Small, Edinburgh, 1885.

—— Early Scottish Metrical Tales. Edinburgh, 1826; 1889.

The Knightly Tale of Golagrus and Gawane and Other Ancient Poems. Ed. [David Laing], Edinburgh, 1827. [Rpt of Chepman and Myllar poems.]

Ward, T. H. The English Poets. Vol. I (James I, by T. H. Ward; Henryson, by W. E. Henley; Dunbar, by J. Nichol; Gavin Douglas, by A. Lang), 1880.

Ross, J. The Book of Scottish Poems, Ancient and Modern. 2 vols. Paisley, 1882.

Morley, H. English Writers. Vol. VI (James I, Henryson), 1890; vol. VII (Dunbar, Douglas) 1891.

Eyre-Todd, G. Mediaeval Scottish Poetry. Glasgow, 1892.

Gregory Smith, G. Specimens of Middle Scots. Edinburgh, 1902.

Dixon, W. M. The Edinburgh Book of Scottish Verse, 1300–1900. Edinburgh, 1910.

Gray, M. M. Scottish Poetry. From Barbour to James VI. 1935.

II. General Authorities

Warton, T. The History of English Poetry. 3 vols. 1774–81; ed. W. C. Hazlitt, 4 vols. 1871.

Sibbald, J. Chronicle of Scottish Poetry. 4 vols. Edinburgh, 1802.

Irving, D. The Lives of the Scottish Poets. 2 vols. Edinburgh, [1803], 1810 (rev. edn).

—— The History of Scotish Poetry. Ed. J. A. Carlyle, Edinburgh, 1861.

Lives of the Scottish Poets, by the Society of Ancient Scots. Edinburgh, 1822.

Wilson, J. G. The Poets and Poetry of Scotland. 2 vols. in 4, 1876.

ten Brink, B. Geschichte der englischen Literatur. 2 vols. Berlin, 1877–93; tr. Eng. 3 vols. 1883–96.

Ross, J. M. Scottish History and Literature to the Period of the Reformation. Ed. J. Brown, Glasgow, 1884.

Walker, H. Three Centuries of Scottish Literature. 2 vols. Glasgow, 1893.

Henderson, T. F. Scottish Vernacular Literature. 1898; 1910.

Neilson, W. A. The Origins and Sources of the Court of Love. Harvard Stud. VI, 1899.

Gregory Smith, G. The Transition Period. Edinburgh, 1900.

—— Specimens of Middle Scots. Edinburgh, 1902.

—— Scottish Literature: Character and Influence. 1919.

Millar, J. H. A Literary History of Scotland. 1903.

Geddie, W. A Bibliography of Middle Scots Poets. STS. 1912.

Nichols, P. H. Lydgate's Influence on the Aureate Terms of the Scottish Chaucerians. PMLA. XLVII, 1932.

Mackenzie, A. M. An Historical Survey of Scottish Literature to 1714. 1933.

Smith, Janet M. The French Background of Middle Scots Literature. Edinburgh, 1934.

III. PARTICULAR WRITERS

A. JAMES I, KING OF SCOTLAND
(1394–1437)

(1) COLLECTED EDITIONS

Poetical Remains of James the First, King of Scotland. [Ed. William Tytler], Edinburgh, 1783.

The Works of James I, King of Scotland. Perth, 1786. [Pbd R. Morison.]

The Works of James the First, King of Scotland. Ed. W. Tytler, Perth, 1825.

Poetical Remains of James I of Scotland. Ed. C. Rogers, Edinburgh, 1873.

(2) SEPARATE WORKS

(a) The Kingis Quair

(i) Manuscript

Bodleian MS, Arch. Selden, B. 24, fols. 192–211. [Oxford. After 1488.]

(ii) Printed Editions

Chronicle of Scottish Poetry. Ed. J. Sibbald, 4 vols. Edinburgh, 1802. [Vol. I, p. 14. Contains 160 of the 197 stanzas.]

The King's Quair. Ed. Ebenezer Thomson, Ayr, 1815; 1824.

Poetic Remains of the Scotish Kings. Ed. George Chalmers, 1824.

The Kings Quair. Glasgow, 1883. [Ptd 1877.]

The Kingis Quair, together with A Ballad of Good Counsel. Ed. W. W. Skeat, STS. 1884; 1911 (rev. edn).

The Kingis Quair, modernised by W. Mackean. 1886; Paisley, 1908.

The Kingis Quair and the Quare of Jelusy. Ed. A. Lawson, 1910.

Heirefter followis the Quair maid be King James of Scotland the First callit the Kingis Quair and maid quhen his Majestic wes in Ingland. Ed. R. Steele, [1903].

(iii) Critical Studies

[See also General Authorities above, p. 255, especially Irving, Ross and Neilson.]

Wischmann, Walter. Untersuchungen über das Kingis Quair Jakobs I von Schottland. Wismar, 1887.

Bierfreund, T. Palemon og Arcite. Copenhagen, 1891. [A comparative criticism of Boccaccio's Teseide, Chaucer's Knight's Tale, James I of Scotland's Kingis Quair, and Fletcher and Shakespeare's Two Noble Kinsmen.]

Callaghan, J. The Kings Quair. Scots Mag. XIV, 1894.

Jusserand, J. J. Le Roman d'un Roi d'Écosse. Paris, 1895; tr. Eng. (with addns by author), 1896.

—— Jacques Ier d'Écosse fut-il Poète? Étude sur l'authenticité du Cahier du Roi. Paris, 1897. [Rptd from La Revue Historique LXIV, 1897. A complete answer to Brown' criticism.]

Brown, J. T. T. The Authorship of the Kingi Quair. Glasgow, 1896. [Attempts to dis prove James's authorship.]

Brown on The Kingis Quair. Saturday Rev LXXXVII, 1896, p. 55.

Rait, R. S. The Kingis Quair and the New Criticism. Aberdeen, 1898.

(b) Other Poems by, or ascribed to, James I

(i) 'Sen trew Vertew encressis dignytee'

'Sen trew Vertew encressis dignytee' (sometimes entitled Good Counsel). [In Ane Compendious Buik of Godly and Spiritual Songis (The Gude and Godlie Ballatis) 1578; 1600; 1621; ed. D. Laing, Edinburgh 1868 (rptd from 1578 edn); ed. A. F Mitchell, STS. 1897; ed. J. R. Lumby, Rati Raving and other Moral and Religiou Pieces, EETS. 1870; ed. W. W. Skeat, Th Kingis Quair, together with A Ballad o Good Counsel, STS. 1884, 1911 (rev. edn) MS: Cambridge University Lib. Kk.1.5 fol. 5. Second stanza wanting.]

(ii) Peblis to the Play. Christis Kirk on the Grene

A merrie Ballad, called Christ's Kirk on th Green. 1643. [Single folio sheet.]

A Ballad of a Country Wedding. 1660 [Single folio sheet.]

Polemo-Middinia [by William Drummond o Hawthornden?]. Accedit cantilena rustica vulgo inscripta Crists Kirk on the Green Ed. E. G[ibson], Oxford, 1691.

Christ's Kirk on the Green. In three canto [Canto I by James I. Cantos II, III, b A. Ramsay]. Edinburgh, 1718. [See als Poems, by A. Ramsay, 1720, 1722, 1723.]

Christ's Kirk on the Green: Poems in th Scottish Dialect. 1748; [1750]; Glasgow 1768.

Two Ancient Scottish Poems. 1782; Glasgow 1794; Stirling, [1820?]; Falkland, [1821].

Chryste-Kirk on the Greene, supposed to b written by James the First of Scotland attempted in Latin heroic Verse [with text [In Carminum variorum Macaronicorun Delectus, 1813.]

Thomson, A. S. Christ's Kirk on the Green Scottish Notes and Queries, III, 1925.

[For the authorship of these pieces see D. Irving, History of Scotish Poetry, 1861, pp. 142–53; The Kingis Quair, ed. W. W. Skeat, 1884, pp. xvii–xxiii; J. T. T. Brown, The Authorship of the Kingis Quair, 1896, pp. 16–20.]

(iii) The Romaunt of the Rose

Fragment B of the Romaunt of the Rose (ll. 1706–5810). [For Skeat's ascription to James I see Introduction to Oxford Chaucer, pp. 3–6; Chaucer Canon, Oxford, 1900, pp. 75–89; Athenaeum, 22 July 1899.]

(3) BIOGRAPHICAL STUDIES

Memoirs relating to the Restoration of King James I. 1716; Scotia Rediviva, vol. I, [1826]; Tracts illustrative of the Antiquities of Scotland, vol. I, 1836.

Here folowing begynnythe the full lamentable cronycle of the dethe and false murdure of James Stewarde, Kyng of Scotys. Translated out of Latyne into our modern englishe tong by John Shirley [from MS dated 1440]. Glasgow, 1818; Miscellanea Scotica, vol. II, 1818–20. [From this latter work the story was taken by John Galt for The Spaewife, 1823, and by D. G. Rossetti for The King's Tragedy.]

Life and Death of King James the First of Scotland. [Ed. J. Stevenson], Maitland Club, 1837.

Balfour-Melville, E. W. M. James I at Windsor in 1423. Scottish Hist. Rev. April 1928.

—— The English Captivity of James I, King of Scots. Historical Ass. 1929.

B. ROBERT HENRYSON (1425?–1500?)

(1) COLLECTED EDITIONS

The Poems and Fables of Robert Henryson. Ed. David Laing, Edinburgh, 1865.

The Poems of Robert Henryson. Ed. G. Gregory Smith, 3 vols. STS. 1906–14.

The Poems of Robert Henryson. A Revised Text. Ed. W. M. Metcalfe [assisted by T. D. Robb], Paisley, 1917.

Henryson: Selected Fables, The Testament of Cresseid, and Robene and Makyne. Ed. H. M. R. Murray, 1930.

The Poems and Fables of Robert Henryson. Ed. H. M. Wood, Edinburgh, 1933.

(2) SEPARATE WORKS

(a) The Moral Fabillis of Esope

(i) Manuscripts

Harl. MS 3865. [BM. Contains general prologue and 13 fables. 1571.]

Bannatyne MS. [Nat. Lib. Scotland MS 1.1.6. Contains general prologue and 10 fables. 1568.]

Makculloch MS. [Edinburgh University Lib., Laing MSS, no. 149. Contains general prologue and Fable of Cock and Jewel. c. 1500.]

Asloan MS. [Lord Talbot de Malahide. Contains Fable of Two Mice. c. 1515.]

(ii) Printed Editions

The Morall Fabillis of Esope the Phrygian, Compylit in Eloquent, and Ornate Scottis Meter. Edinburgh, 1570. [Only copy known in BM.]

The Fabulous tales of Esope the Phrygian. 1577. [Only copy known was in Sion College Lib., but is now missing.]

The Morall Fables of Esope, the Phrygian. Edinburgh, 1621. ['Neulie revised and corrected.' Unique copy in Nat. Lib. Scotland. Rptd Maitland Club, Edinburgh, 1832, with an unsigned preface by David Irving.]

Henrisone's Fabeln. Ed. A. R. Diebler, Ang. IX, 1866. [Harleian MS.]

(b) Orpheus and Eurydice

[Included in Asloan and Bannatyne MSS, and incomplete in the Chepman and Myllar prints. The last was rptd by D. Laing in the Knightly Tale of Golagrus, Edinburgh, 1827, and in Pieces from the Makculloch and Gray MSS, together with the Chepman and Millar Prints, STS. 1918.]

(c) The Testament of Cresseid

[Appears in Table of Asloan MS, but the leaves on which it was written have been lost.]

The Workes of Geoffray Chaucer. Ed. William Thynne, 1532.

The Testament of Cresseid. Edinburgh, 1593. [Only copy known in BM. Rptd with Robene and Makyne, G. Chalmers, Bannatyne Club, 1824; ed. B. Dickins, Edinburgh, 1925; Cambridge, 1926.]

[The Catalogus Bibliothecae Harleianae (1744–45) records, vol. IV, p. 644, '13734 Henrison's Testament of Cresseid, blackletter 1605,' and, vol. V, p. 378, '12728 Testament of Cresseid, blackletter Edinb. 1611.' These are not now known. See article on Thomas Finlason by J. Aldis, in Trans. Edinburgh Bibliog. Soc. I, 1896.]

The Testament of Cresseid. Printed in the Year, 1663. [Unique copy in Trinity College, Cambridge.]

Chaucerian and Other Pieces. Ed. W. W. Skeat, Oxford, 1897. [Vol. VII of Oxford Chaucer, No. xvii.]

(d) Shorter Poems

(i) Manuscripts

Bannatyne MS. [12 poems, 5 in duplicate.]
Maitland Folio MS. [Pepysian Lib., Magdalene College, Cambridge. Contains 4 poems. c. 1580.]
Makculloch MS. [1 poem and fragment.]
Gray MS. [Nat. Lib. Scotland, MS 34 . 7 . 3. Contains 1 poem. c. 1500.]
Riddell MS. [Chalmers, Auldbar. Contains 1 poem. 1636.]

(ii) Printed Editions

[Two poems (Prais of Age, and Want of Wyse Men) were printed by Chepman and Myllar, Edinburgh, 1508. Several of the poems appear in the collections of Ramsay, Hailes, Sibbald, Pinkerton and Chalmers.]

(3) CRITICAL STUDIES

[See also General Authorities above, p. 255, especially Sibbald, Irving, Ross, Neilson and Gregory Smith.]
Diebler, A. R. Henrisone's Fabeldichtungen. Halle, 1885.
Oliphant, F. R. Robert Henryson. Blackwood's Mag. CXLVIII, 1890.
Saintsbury, G. History of English Prosody. Vol. I, 1906.
Marshall, L. E. Roberto Henryson e la Griseida. Milan, 1910.
Millet, G. The Fortunes of Cressida. New Statesman, 30 June 1923.
Dickins, B. The Testament of Cresseid [note on vv. 45 ff.]. TLS. 11 Dec. 1924.
—— Contributions to the Interpretation of Middle Scots Texts. TLS. 21 Feb. 1924.

C. WILLIAM DUNBAR (1460?–1520?)

(1) MANUSCRIPTS

Bannatyne MS. [Nat. Lib. Scotland, MS 1 . 1 . 6. Contains 60 poems.]
Maitland Folio MS. [Pepysian Lib., Magdalene College, Cambridge. Contains 60 poems and a fragment.]
Asloan MS. [Lord Talbot de Malahide. Contains 5 poems and 2 fragments.]
Makculloch MS. [Edinburgh University Lib., Laing MSS, no. 149. Contains 2 poems.]
Cott. MS Vitell. A XVI, fol. 200. [BM. Contains 1 poem.]
Arundel MS, no. 285, fols. 1, 161, 163. [BM. Contains 3 poems.]
App. to Royal MSS, no. 58, fol. 17 b. [BM. Contains 1 poem.]
Aberdeen Register of Sasines. [Contains 1 poem.]
Reidpath MS. [University Lib. Cambridge, Moore MS Ll . 5 . 10, 1623. Contains 44 poems and 3 fragments.]

(2) EARLY EDITIONS

Chepman and Myllar's Prints. Edinburgh, 1508; ed. G. Stevenson, STS. 1918. [7 poems.]
The Ever Green. Ed. Allan Ramsay, 2 vols. Edinburgh, 1724. [24 poems, freely rendered.]
Ancient Scottish Poems. Ed. D. Dalrymple (Lord Hailes), Edinburgh, 1770. [32 poems from Bannatyne MS.]
Ancient Scotish Poems. Ed. John Pinkerton, 2 vols. 1786. [23 poems.]
Select Poems of Will. Dunbar. Pt I, Perth, 1788. [Pbd R. Morison.]
Chronicle of Scottish Poetry. Ed. J. Sibbald, 4 vols. Edinburgh, 1802. [45 poems.]

(3) COLLECTED EDITIONS

The Poems of William Dunbar. Ed. D. Laing, 2 vols. Edinburgh, 1834. [A selection of poems by the minor Makars was added as a supplementary volume in 1865.]
The Poems of William Dunbar. Ed. John Small, 3 vols. STS. 1884–93. [With contributions by A. J. G. Mackay and W. Gregor.]
The Poems of William Dunbar. Ed. J. Schipper, Denkschriften d. kgl. Akad. d. Wissensch., Phil.-hist. Kl. XL, XLI, Vienna, 1892–4.
Selections from the Poems of an Old Makar, adapted for Modern Readers by H. Haliburton [J. L. Robertson]. 1895.
The Dunbar Anthology, 1401–1508. Being an Anthology of Dunbar and his Contemporaries. Ed. E. Arber, 1901.
The Poems of William Dunbar. Ed. H. B. Baildon, 1907.
The Poems of William Dunbar. Ed. W. M. Mackenzie, Edinburgh, 1932.

(4) SINGLE POEMS

The Thistle and the Rose: a Poem in honour of Margaret, Queen to James IV, King of Scots [with Vertue and Vyce. A poem addrest to James V King of Scots, by J. Bellentyne]. Glasgow, 1750.
Two Married Women and the Widow: translated into English Verse. Edinburgh, 1840.

(5) CRITICAL STUDIES

[See also General Authorities above, p. 255, especially Warton, Sibbald, Irving, Ross and Neilson.]

(a) General

Paterson, J. Life and Poems of Dunbar. Edinburgh, 1860.

Kaufmann, J. Traité de la Langue du Poète écossais William Dunbar, précédé d'une Esquisse de sa Vie et d'un Choix de ses Poèmes. Bonn, 1873.

Schipper, J. William Dunbar. Sein Leben und seine Gedichte. Berlin, 1884.

Mackay, Æ. J. G. William Dunbar, 1460–1520. A Study in the Poetry and History of Scotland. 1889.

Oliphant, F. R. William Dunbar. Blackwood's Mag. CLIV, 1893.

Smeaton, W. H. O. William Dunbar. Edinburgh, 1898.

Nelson, A. S. William Dunbar. GM. CCLXXXVII, 1899.

Mebus, F. Studien zu William Dunbar. Breslau, 1902.

Steinberger, C. Étude sur William Dunbar. Paris, 1908.

Ayres, H. M. 'Theodulus' in Scots [Dunbar, Kennedy, and the Ecloga Theoduli]. MP. XV, 1918.

Powys, Ll. William Dunbar. Freeman, 8 Aug. 1923.

Dickins, B. Contributions to the Interpretation of Middle Scots Texts [Henryson, Dunbar]. TLS. 21 Feb. 1924.

—— Suggested Interpolation of a passage by Kennedy in the Flyting of Dunbar and Kennedy. TLS. 10 July 1924.

William Dunbar. TLS. 10 April 1930.

Jacob, Violet. William Dunbar: An Appreciation. Country Life, 19 March 1931.

Nichols, P. H. William Dunbar as a Scottish Lydgatian. PMLA. XLVI, 1931.

Taylor, R. A. Dunbar. 1932.

(b) Versification

Schipper, J. Altenglische Metrik. 2 vols. Bonn, 1882–8.

McNeil, G. P. Note on the Versification and Metres of Dunbar. [In STS. edn of Dunbar, vol. I, 1884.]

Baildon, H. B. Dissertation on the Rimes in the Authentic Poems of Dunbar. Freiburg, 1899; Trans. Royal Soc. Edinburgh, XXXIX, 1900.

Saintsbury, G. History of English Prosody. Vol. I, 1906.

(c) Imitation

Dunbar, W. Cogitations upon Death; or the Mirrour of Man's Miserie. Aberdeen, 1681 (4th edn); Edinburgh, 1710 (7th edn). [Imitation by a namesake, of Dunbar's Lament for the Makaris.]

D. GAVIN DOUGLAS (1475?–1522)

(1) COLLECTED EDITIONS

Select Works of Gavin Douglas, containing Memoirs of the Author, The Palace of Honour, Prologues to the Aeneid, and a Glossary. Perth, 1787.

The Poetical Works of Gavin Douglas, Bishop of Dunkeld. Ed. John Small, 4 vols. Edinburgh, 1874.

(2) SEPARATE WORKS

(a) The Palise of Honour

[No MSS.]

The Palyce of Honour. [Edinburgh? 1530?] [Fragment of four leaves only. See D. Laing, Adversaria, Bannatyne Club, 1867, p. 19; Poetical Works of G. Douglas, ed. J. Small, vol. I, p. clxx; R. Dickson and J. P. Edward, Annals of Scottish Printing, Cambridge, 1890, pp. 133–5.]

The Palis of Honoure Compyled by Gawyne dowglas Bysshope of Dunkyll. [1553?]

The Palice of Honour. Edinburgh, 1579; rptd R. Morison, together with the Prologues to the Aeneid, Perth, 1787; ed. J. G. Kinnear, Bannatyne Club, 1827.

Scotish Poems, reprinted from Scarce Editions. Ed. J. Pinkerton, 3 vols. 1792. [Rpts 1579 edn.]

Chronicle of Scottish Poetry. Ed. J. Sibbald, 4 vols. Edinburgh, 1802. [Incomplete.]

(b) King Hart

(i) Manuscript

Maitland Folio MS. [Pepysian Lib., Magdalene College, Cambridge.]

(ii) Printed Edition

Ancient Scotish Poems. Ed. John Pinkerton, 2 vols. 1786. [Pinkerton divides the poem, unwarrantably, into two cantos, the first of 53 stanzas, the second of 67.]

(c) Conscience

Maitland Folio MS. [Fols. 192–3.]

(d) Translation of the Aeneid

(i) Manuscripts

Cambridge MS. [Trinity College, Cambridge, Gale's MSS, O . 3 . 12, c. 1525.]

Elphystoun MS. [Edinburgh University Lib. c. 1525.]

Ruthven MS. [Edinburgh University Lib. c. 1535.]

Lambeth MS. [Feb. 1546.]

Longleat MS. [Marquis of Bath. 1547.]

(ii) Printed Editions

The xiii Bukes of Eneados of the famose Poete Virgill Translatet into Scottish metir. 1553.

Virgil's Aeneis translated into Scottish verse. Edinburgh, 1710. [Corrected 'from an excellent manuscript' and 'with a large glossary' and 'the Author's Life and Writings.' The responsible editor was Thomas Ruddiman; the Life is by Bishop John Sage. The MS referred to is the Ruthven.]

The Aeneid of Virgil, Translated into Scottish Verse. [Ed. G. Dundas], 2 vols. Bannatyne Club, 1839. [Rpts Cambridge MS, without prolegomena or notes. Vol. II not pbd.]

[Some of the Prologues have been rptd separately, e.g. by Francis Fawkes, 1752, 1754, and in Original Poems and Translations, 1761; by T. Warton, History of English Poetry, vol. III, 1781; by J. Sibbald, Chronicle of Scottish Poetry, vol. I, 1802.]

(3) CRITICISM

[See also General Authorities above, p. 255 especially Warton, Sibbald, Irving, Ross and Neilson.]

Spelman, Sir H. Glossarium Archaiologicum. 1664. [With a MS glossary to the poems of Gavin Douglas. BM. 12935. k. 5.]

Hunter, W. An Anglo-Saxon Grammar, with an Analysis of the Style of Gavin Douglas. 1832.

Small, J. The Life of Gavin Douglas, Bishop of Dunkeld. Edinburgh, 1874.

Lange, P. Chaucer's Einfluss auf der Original-dichtungen des Schotten Gavin Douglas. Halle, 1882.

Watt, L. M. Douglas's Aeneid. Cambridge, 1920.

Brinton, A. C. Mapheus Vegius and his Thirteenth Book of the Aeneid [with trns of T. Twyne and G. Douglas]. A Chapter on Virgil in the Renaissance. Palo Alto, 1930.

IV. SCOTTISH PROSE

[This list is restricted to works that have been edited. Specimens of Middle Scots, ed. G. Gregory Smith, 1902, contains extracts from most of these works and a bibliography.]

Byssett, Habakkuk. Rolment of Courtis. Ed. Sir P. J. Hamilton-Grierson, 3 vols. STS. 1920–6.

The Chepman and Myllar Prints. 1508; ed. facs. David Laing, 1827; ed. G. Stevenson, STS. 1918. [Includes some prose.]

Craft of Deyng, The Wisdom of Solomon, The Vertewis of the Mess. Ed. J. R. Lumby, Ratis Raving and Other Moral and Religious Pieces, EETS. 1870.

Gau, J. The Richt Vay to the Kingdome of Hevine. Ed. A. F. Mitchell, STS. 1888.

Gilbert of the Haye's Prose Manuscript (A.D. 1456). Ed. J. H. Stevenson, 2 vols. STS. 1901–14.

Irlandia, Johannes de. The Meroure of Wysdome Composed for the Use of James IV, King of Scots, A.D. 1490. Ed. Charles Mac-Pherson, STS. 1926.

Nisbet, Murdoch. The New Testament in Scots [c. 1520.] Ed. T. G. Law, 3 vols. STS. 1901–5.

The Schort Memoriale. Ed. Thomas Thomson, 1827.

The Spectakle of Luf. Ed. David Laing, Bannatyne Misc. vol. II, 1827.

News Out of Scotland. Miscellaneous Collection of Verse and Prose, Sacred and Profane, from the XIV to the XVIII Century. Ed. E. M. Brougham, 1926. [Texts unreliable.]

G. G. S., rev. D. H.

III. ENGLISH PROSE OF THE FIFTEENTH CENTURY:

CAPGRAVE, PECOCK, FORTESCUE, CAXTON, MALORY, BERNERS

A. JOHN CAPGRAVE (1393–1464)

(1) PRINTED WORKS

Nova Legenda Angliae. 1516 (de Worde).

The Chronicle of England. Ed. F. C. Hingeston, Rolls Ser. 1858.

Liber de Illustribus Henricis. Ed. F. C. Hingeston, Rolls Ser. 1858.

The Life of St Katharine. Ed. C. Horstmann (Forewords by J. F. Furnivall), EETS. 1893.

The Lives of St Augustine and St Gilbert of Sempringham and a Sermon. Ed. J. Munro, EETS. 1910.

The Solace of Pilgrimes. Ed. C. A. Mills (Note by H. M. Bannister), British and American Archaeological Soc. of Rome, 1911. [A description of Rome.]

(2) BIOGRAPHY AND CRITICISM

Leland, John. Commentarii de Scriptoribus Britannicis. Ed. A. Hall, Oxford, 1709. [For Latin works.]

Tanner, Thomas. Bibliotheca Britannico-Hibernica. 1748. [See also DNB. for MSS.]

B. REGINALD PECOCK (c. 1395–c. 1460)

(1) PRINTED WORKS

[Book of Faith.] A Treatise proving Scripture to be the Rule of Faith. Ed. Henry Wharton, 1688 (2nd pt and summary of 1st pt only); ed. J. L. Morison, Glasgow, 1909 (whole work). [MS in Trinity College, Cambridge (B 1455).]

The Repressor of Overmuch Blaming of the Clergy. Ed., with Introduction and Bibliography, Churchill Babington, 2 vols. Rolls Ser. 1860. [The standard work on the whole subject of Pecock and his works.]

The Reule of Crysten Religioun. Described by James Gairdner, 1911; ed. W. C. Greet, EETS. 1927. [Pierpont Morgan MS 519.]

The Donet. Ed. E. V. Hitchcock, EETS. 1921. [Bodl. MS 916 collated with The Poore Mennis Myrrour (BM. Add. MS 37788).]

The Folewer to the Donet. Ed., with Introduction on Language and Style, E. V. Hitchcock, EETS. 1924.

[For lost works see Babington's Introduction to The Repressor. Excerpts by H. Wharton from The Poor Men's Mirror or Outdraught of the Donet are in Lambeth MS 594.]

(2) Biography and Criticism

(a) Contemporary Accounts

An English Chronicle. (Cronycullys of England.) [In Three Fifteenth Century Chronicles, ed. James Gairdner, Camden Soc. 1880. Under 1457, for trial and abjuration.]

Chronicle of the Grey Friars. [In Monumenta Franciscana, ed. J. S. Brewer and Richard Howlett, 2 vols. Rolls Ser. 1858–82. Vol. ii, under 1457.]

Gascoigne, Thomas. Loci e Libro Veritatum. Ed. J. E. T. Rogers, Oxford, 1881.

Whethamstede, J. Registrum. Ed. H. T. Riley, 2 vols. Rolls Ser. 1872–3.

(b) Later References and Criticism

Bale, John. Illustrium Majoris Britanniae Scriptorum Summarium. Ipswich, 1548; ed. R. L. Poole and Mary Bateson, Oxford, 1902.

Raynaldus, O. Annalium ecclesiasticorum Baronii Continuatio. 8 vols. Rome, 1646–63. [Under 1459.]

à Wood, A. Historia et Antiquitates Universitatis Oxoniensis. 2 vols. Oxford, 1674; ed. John Gutch, 2 vols. Oxford, 1792–6. [Under 1457.]

Wharton, Henry. Historia de Episcopis et Decanis Londiniensibus. 1695.

Le Neve, John. Fasti Ecclesiae Anglicanae. 1716; ed. T. D. Hardy, 3 vols. Oxford, 1854.

Lewis, John. The Life of Dr Pecock. 1744; Oxford, 1820.

Tanner, Thomas. Bibliotheca Britannico-Hibernica. 1748.

Waterland, Daniel. Works. Ed. W. van Mildert, 10 vols. Oxford, 1823; 6 vols. Oxford, 1856. [Vol. vi, Letters to Lewis. Extracts and bibliography in notes.]

Hook, W. F. Lives of the Archbishops of Canterbury. 12 vols. 1860–76. [Under Stafford and Bourchier.]

Gairdner, James and Spedding, James, Studies in English History. Edinburgh, 1881.

Historical Manuscripts Commission. 12th Report. Appendix. 1891.

Schmidt, F. Studies in the Language of Pecock. Upsala, 1900.

Blackie, E. M. Reginald Pecock. EHR. xxvi, 1911.

Krapp, G. P. Rise of English Literary Prose. Oxford, 1915, pp. 73 ff.

Hannick, E. A. Reginald Pecock. Washington, 1922.

C. SIR JOHN FORTESCUE (c. 1394–c. 1476)

(1) Printed Works

[De Laudibus Legum Angliae.] Prenobilis militis Forescu [sic] de politica administratione et legibus civilibus commentarius. (1546?); 1567; 1573; 1599 (with trn by R. Mulcaster, A learned commendation of the politique lawes of England); ed. John Selden, 1616 (Latin and English); Cincinatti, 1874 (with trn by Francis Gregor).

[The Governance of England.] The Difference between an Absolute and a Limited Monarchy. Ed. Sir J. Fortescue-Aland, 1714; ed. C. Plummer, Oxford, 1885 (the best authority on Fortescue).

The Works of Sir John Fortescue. Ed. Thomas Fortescue, Lord Clermont, 2 vols. 1869. [Contains: De Natura Legis Naturae (1461–3); De Laudibus Legum Angliae (1471); De Titula Edwardi Com. Marchiae; Defensio juris Domus Lancastriae; A Declaration upon Certayn Wrytinges (1471–3); Dialogue between Understanding and Faith (1471), etc.]

(2) Biography and Criticism

Foss, E. The Judges of England. 9 vols. 1848–64. [Vol. iv.]

Skeel, C. A. J. The Influence of the Writings of Sir John Fortescue. Trans. Royal Hist. Soc. x, 1916.

Hearnshaw, F. J. C. The Social and Political Ideas of the Renaissance. 1925, pp. 61–86.

D. WILLIAM CAXTON (1421—1491)

(1) Collected Writings

Caxton's Prologues and Epilogues. Ed. W. J. B. Crotch, EETS. 1928.

(2) Separate Works: Translations, Prologues, Epilogues and Interpolations

Le Fevre, R. The Recuyell of the Histories of Troy. Bruges, 1475 (Caxton); 1502 (de

Worde) (rev.); ed. H. O. Sommer, 2 vols. 1894. [Tr. Caxton with prologue, interpolation, epilogue.]

de Cessolis, J. The Game & Play of the Chess. [1476] (Caxton); [1483] (Caxton); ed. facs. V. Figgins, 1855 (from 2nd edn); ed. W. E. A. Axon, 1883. [Tr. Caxton with dedication, prologue, interpolation, epilogue.]

Le Fevre, R. The History of Jason. [1477] (Caxton); Antwerp, 1492 (Leeu); ed. J. Munro, EETS. Ex. Ser. 1912. [Tr. Caxton with prologue, epilogue.]

Cato, Dionysius. Parvus Cato. [Tr. D. Church?] Magnus Cato. [Tr. Benet Burgh.] [1477] (Caxton); [1478?] (Caxton); [1480?] (Caxton); [after 23 Dec. 1483] (Caxton). [The last edn is first with commentary tr. Caxton.]

Dicts or Sayings of the Philosophers. 1477 (Caxton); [1480?] (Caxton); [1489] (Caxton); 1528 (de Worde); ed. facs. W. Blades, 1877. [Tr. Antony Wydeville, Earl Rivers; colophon by Caxton. See R. Hittmair, Earl Rivers Einleitung zu seiner Übertragung der Weisheitsspräche der Philosophen, Ang. LIX, 1935.]

de Pisan, Christine [du Castel]. Moral Proverbs. [1478] (Caxton); ed. W. Blades, 1859. [Tr. Anthony Wydeville, Earl Rivers. Epilogue by Caxton.]

Boethius. De consolatione philosophiae. [1478?] (Caxton). [Tr. Chaucer. Epilogue by Caxton.]

Cordiale novissimorum. 1479 (Caxton); [1500?] (de Worde). [Tr. Antony Wydeville, Earl Rivers. Epilogue by Caxton.]

Doctrine to learn French and English. [1480] (Caxton); 1497 (de Worde); ed. H. Bradley, EETS. Ex. Ser. 1900. [Trn.]

Higden, R. The Description of Britain. 1480 (Caxton); 1498 (de Worde). [Trevisa's trn of the Polychronicon, ed. and continued by Caxton, with prologue and epilogue.]

—— [Polychronicon.] Cronica. 1482 (Caxton). [Prologue, epilogue, interpolation.]

Vincent of Beauvais. The Mirror of the World. [1481] (Caxton); [1490] (Caxton); ed. O. Prior, EETS. Ex. Ser. 1913. [Trn, prologue, epilogue and interpolation (St Patrick's Purgatory).]

Reynard the Fox. [1481] (Caxton); 1489 (Caxton); 1494 (Pynson); ed. E. Arber, 1880; ed. H. Morley (in Early Prose Romances, 1889); ed. W. S. Stallybrass, 1924. [Trn, prologue, epilogue; and epilogue to 2nd edn.]

Cicero. Tully of Old Age and of Friendship. 1481 (Caxton); 1912. [Trn, prologues, epilogues.]

Godfrey of Bologne. 1481 (Caxton); ed. M. N. Colvin, EETS. Ex. Ser. 1893. [Trn, prologue, epilogue.]

Gower, J. Confessio amantis. 1493 (i.e. 1483) (Caxton). [Prologue, colophon.]

de Voragine, J. The Golden Legend. [1483] (Caxton); [1487?] (Caxton); 1493 (Caxton [de Worde]); 1498 (de Worde); 1503 (Notary); [1510?] (de Worde); 1512 (de Worde); 1527 (de Worde); ed. A. Aspland, 1878; ed. F. S. Ellis, 3 vols. 1892; ed. G. V. O'Neill, 1914 (selection). [Trn, prologue, epilogue, interpolation. See P. Butler, Legenda Aurea: a Study of Caxton's Golden Legend, Baltimore, 1899.]

de la Tour Landry, G. The Knight of the Tower. [1484] (Caxton); ed. T. Wright, EETS. 1868, 1906 (rev. J. Munro); 1902 (selection); ed. G. S. Taylor, 1930. [Trn, prologue, epilogue.]

Aesop. Fables. 1484 (Caxton); ed. J. Jacobs, 2 vols. 1889. [Trn, epilogue.]

Chaucer, G. Canterbury Tales [2nd edn]. [1484?] (Caxton). [Prologue.]

—— [The House of Fame.] The Book of Fame. [1486?] (Caxton).

Order of Chivalry or Knighthood. [1484] (Caxton); ed. A. T. P. Byles, EETS. 1926. [Trn, epilogue.]

Chartier, Alain. The Curial. [1484] (Caxton); ed. P. Meyer and F. J. Furnivall, EETS. Ex. Ser. 1888. [Trn, prologue.]

Charles the Great. 1485 (Caxton); ed. S. J. Herrtage, EETS. Ex. Ser. 1880–1. [Trn, prologue.]

Life of St Winifred. [1485] (Caxton). [Trn.]

Malory, Sir T. Morte d'Arthur. 1485 (Caxton). [Prologue. See below, under Malory.]

Paris and Vienne. 1485 (Caxton); Antwerp, 1492 (Leeu); ed. W. C. Hazlitt, 1868. [Trn, prologue, epilogue.]

Legrand, J. The Royal Book. [1486] (Caxton). [Prologue, epilogue.]

—— The Book of Good Manners. 1487 (Caxton); 1494 (Pynson); ed. F. E. Pearn, 1914 (from Harl. MS 149). [Trn, prologue.]

de Pisan, Christine [du Castel]. Fayts of Arms. [1489] (Caxton); ed. A. T. P. Byles, EETS. 1932. [Trn, prologue, epilogue.]

Blanchardin and Eglantine. [1489] (Caxton); ed. L. Kellner, EETS. Ex. Ser. 1890. [Trn, dedication.]

de Roye, E. Doctrinal of Sapience. 1489 (Caxton). [Trn.]

Four Sons of Aymon. [1489] (Caxton); ed. O. Richardson, 2 vols. EETS. Ex. Ser. 1884–5. [Trn, prologue.]

Art and Craft to know well to Die. [After 15 June 1490] (Caxton); [1500?] (Pynson). [Trn.]

Virgil. Eneydos. [After 22 June 1490] (Caxton); ed. M. T. Culley and F. J. Furnivall, EETS. Ex. Ser. 1890. [Trn, prologue, epilogue.]

Lydgate, John. Life of Our Lady. [1484] (Caxton). [Prologue, epilogue, in verse, by Caxton?]

The Fifteen Oes. [1491] (Caxton). [Epilogue.]

Ars Moriendi. [1491] (Caxton); [1497] (de Worde); 1506 (de Worde); rptd [1868]. [Tr. Caxton?]

Jerome, Saint. Vitas patrum. 1495 (de Worde). [Tr. Caxton.]

Ovid. Six Books of Metamorphoseos. (Met. x–xv.) Ed. G. Hibbert, Roxburghe Club, 1819; ed. S. Gaselee and H. F. B. Brett-Smith, Oxford, 1924. [Tr. Caxton. See A. E. Wilmott, A Study of Caxton's Ovid, 1909. MS hol. (?) Pepys.]

(3) BIOGRAPHY AND CRITICISM

Blades, W. The Life and Typography of William Caxton. 2 vols. 1861–3; 1882 (rev. edn.).

de Ricci, S. A Census of Caxtons. Bibliog. Soc. 1909.

Duff, E. Gordon. William Caxton. Chicago, 1905.

Winship, G. P. William Caxton. 1909.

Fifteenth Century English Books. Bibliog. Soc. 1917.

Aurner, N. S. Caxton: a Study of the Literature of the First English Press. 1926. [With Caxton's prologues, epilogues and interpolations.]

Crotch, W. J. B. Caxton Documents. Library, VIII, IX, 1928.

Thomas, Henry. Wilh. Caxton uyss Engelant. Evidence that the first English printer learned his craft at Cologne. 1928.

Roberts, W. W. William Caxton, Writer and Critic. John Rylands Lib. Bulletin, XIV, 1930 (and separately).

Wiencke, H. Die Sprache Caxtons. Leipzig, 1930.

Byles, A. T. P. William Caxton as a Man of Letters. Library, XV, 1934.

Hittmair, R. Aus Caxtons Vorreden und Nachworten. Leipzig, 1934.

[For further studies of Caxton as a printer see p. 351 below.] A. E.

E. SIR THOMAS MALORY

(1) THE MORTE D'ARTHUR

Le morte Darthur reduced in to englysshe. 1485 (Caxton); 1498 (de Worde); 1529 (de Worde); [1557]; [1585?]; 1634; ed. Sir E. Strachey, 1884 (rev. text); ed. H. O. Sommer, 3 vols. 1889–91; ed. F. J. Simmons, 3 vols. 1893–4; ed. A. W. Pollard, 2 vols. 1900.

(2) BIOGRAPHY AND CRITICISM

Saintsbury, G. The Flourishing of Romance and the Rise of Allegory. Edinburgh, 1897.

Gregory Smith, G. The Transition Period. Edinburgh, 1900.

Ker, W. P. Essays on Medieval Literature. 1905.

Scudder, V. D. The Morte d'Arthur and its Sources. 1917.

Lot, F. Étude sur le Lancelot en Prose. Paris, 1918.

Chambers, Sir E. K. Sir Thomas Malory. English Ass. 1922.

Cooksey, C. F. The Morte d'Arthur. Nineteenth Century, June 1924.

Kittredge, G. L. Sir Thomas Malory. Barnstable, 1925.

Vinaver, E. Le Roman de Tristan et Iseult dans l'Œuvre de Thomas Malory. Paris, 1925.

—— Sir Thomas Malory. Oxford, 1929.

—— Malory's Morte D'Arthur. John Rylands Lib. Bulletin, XIX, 1935. [Winchester MS.]

Loomis, L. H. Arthur's Round Table. PMLA. XLVI, 1926.

Ray, B. K. The Character of Gawain. Dacca University Bulletin, XI, 1926.

Hicks, E. Sir Thomas Malory, his Turbulent Career; a Biography. Cambridge, U.S.A. 1928.

Aurner, N. S. Sir Thomas Malory—Historian? PMLA. XLVIII, 1933.

Stewart, G. R. English Geography in Malory's Morte D'Arthur. MLR. XXX, 1935. [See also under the Arthurian Romances, pp. 130–40 above.] A. E.

F. JOHN BOURCHIER, BARON BERNERS
(1467–1533)

The first [second] volume of sir Johan Froyssart: of the cronycles of England, Fraunce, Spayne. 2 vols. 1523–5; [1545]; ed. G. C. Macaulay, 1895; ed. W. P. Ker, 6 vols. 1901–3; rptd 8 vols. Oxford, 1927–8. [See J. M. B. C. K. de Lettenhove, Froissart, Brussels, 1857.]

The Boke Huon de Bordeuxe. [1534?]; 1601 (3rd edn); ed. Sir S. Lee, 4 pts, EETS. Ex. Ser. 1882–7; ed. R. Steele, 1895 (modernised).

The golden boke of Marcus Aurelius. 1535; 1536; 1539; 1542; 1546; 1553; 1557; 1559; 1566; 1573; 1586; ed. J. M. G. Olivares (in Guevara in England, Berlin, 1916). [Tr. from A. de Guevara through the French version of René Bertant.]

The castell of love. [1540?] (fragment); [1549?]; [1560?]. [Tr. from D. de San Pedro.]

Arthur of lytell Brytayne. [1555?]; [1582]; ed. E. V. Utterson, 1814. A. E.

IV. MISCELLANEOUS AND ANONYMOUS VERSE AND PROSE OF THE FIFTEENTH CENTURY

[This section is in effect a rag-bag into which odds and ends have been collected which did not fit into the other 15th century sections. It makes no pretence to touch more than the fringe of its subject. Moreover several items that might have been included here will be found to be listed, in spite of their later date, in the section on Middle English Literature to 1400 (pp. 161–208 above). Cross-references have not been inserted in such cases.]

(1) COLLECTIONS AND ANTHOLOGIES

[See also the Collections of Selected Pieces and the Collections of Modern Renderings above, p. 114, Songs and Lyrics, pp. 267–70 below, and The Ballads, pp. 272–3 below.]

Select Pieces of Early Popular Poetry. Ed. E. V. Utterson, 2 vols. 1817.

Political Poems of the Reigns of Henry VI and Edward IV. Ed. F. Madden, Archaeologia, xxix, 1842.

Anecdota Literaria. Ed. T. Wright, 1844.

Early English Miscellanies, in Prose and Verse. Ed. J. O. Halliwell[-Phillipps], Warton Club, 1855.

Political Poems and Songs. Ed. T. Wright, Rolls Ser. 1861.

Old English Jest-Books. Ed. W. C. Hazlitt, 3 vols. 1864.

Remains of the Early Popular Poetry of England. Ed. W. C. Hazlitt, 4 vols. 1864–6.

Political, Religious and Love Poems. Ed. F. J. Furnivall, EETS. 1866; 1903 (rev. edn).

Hymns to the Virgin and Christ, The Parliament of Devils, etc. Ed. F. J. Furnivall, EETS. 1867. [Lambeth MS 853.]

Religious Pieces in Prose and Verse. Ed. G. G. Perry, EETS. 1867; 1889 (rev. edn). [Thornton MS, c. 1440.]

The Stacions of Rome, The Pilgrims Sea-Voyage, Clene Maidenhod. Ed. F. J. Furnivall, EETS. 1867.

Early English Meals and Manners. Ed. F. J. Furnivall, EETS. 1868. [Includes: The Babees Book (c. 1475), Aristotle's ABC (c. 1430), Urbanitatis (c. 1460), Stans Puer ad Mensam, The Lytille Childrenes Lytil Boke (c. 1480), The Bokes of Nurture of Hugh Rhodes (temp. Henry VIII) and John Russell (c. 1465), Wynkyn de Worde's Boke of Kervynge (1513), The Booke of Demeanor (1619), The Boke of Curtasye (c. 1435), Seager's Schoole of Vertue (1557).

Ratis Raving and Other Moral and Religious Pieces, in Prose and Verse. Ed. J. R. Lumby, EETS. 1870. [Cambridge University Lib. MS Kk . 1 . 5.]

Jyl of Breyntford's Testament, by Robert Copland, and Other Short Pieces. Ed. F. J. Furnivall, 1871.

Twenty-Six Political and Other Poems. Ed. J. Kail, EETS. 1904. [Bodl. MSS Digby 102 and Douce 322.]

Five Hundred Years of Chaucer Criticism and Allusion. Ed. C. F. E. Spurgeon, 7 pts. Chaucer Soc. 1914–24; 3 vols. Cambridge 1925.

English Verse between Chaucer and Surrey. Ed. E. P. Hammond, Durham, North Carolina, 1927.

The Middle English Stanzaic Versions of the Life of St Anne. Ed. R. E. Parker, EETS. 1927. [For source see Speculum, vii, 1932, p. 106.]

(2) VERSE

Audelay, John. Poems: a Specimen of the Shropshire Dialect in the 15th Century. Ed. J. O. Halliwell[-Phillipps], Percy Soc. 1844. [c. 1420.]

—— Fifteenth Century Carols by John Audelay. Ed. Sir E. K. Chambers and F. Sidgwick, MLR. v, vi, 1910–1.

Poems of John Audelay. Ed. E. K. Whitney, EETS. 1931.

Die me. Umdichtung von Boccaccios 'De Claris Mulieribus.' Ed. G. Schleich, Berlin, 1924. [1433–40.]

Brampton, Thomas. Paraphrase on the Seven Penitential Psalms. Percy Soc. 1842. [1414.]

Poems, written in English, by Charles, Duke of Orleans. Ed. G. W. Taylor, Roxburghe Club, 1827. [Really trns, by an anon English translator, of Charles's French poems. See P. Sauerstein, Berlin, 1893. An edn of Charles's genuine English poems is in preparation for EETS. by R. Steele.]

The Foundation of the Chapel of Walsingham. [1496] (Pynson); rptd H. Huth (Fugitive Tracts written in Verse, vol. ii, 1875).

Idley, Peter. Instructions to his Son. Ed. C. D'Evelyn, Boston, 1935.

Lauder, William. Minor Poems. Ed. F. J. Furnivall, EETS. 1870.

The Libelle of Englyshe Polycye. A Poem on the Use of Sea-Power, 1436. Ed. Sir G. Warner, Oxford, 1926.

Lichfield, William (d. 1447). The Complaint of God to Sinful Man and the Answer of Man. Ed. E. Borgström, Ang. xxxiv, 1911. [See Carleton Brown, Manuscripts of William Lichfield's Complaint of God, E. Studien, xlvii, 1913.]

Metham, John. The Works. Ed. H. Craig, EETS. 1906.

Mirk, John (*fl.* 1403?). Duties of a Parish Priest. Ed. E. Peacock, EETS. 1868; 1902 (rev. edn). [Trn of William de Pagula's Pupilla Oculi. For Mirk's Festial see p. 175 above.]

Palladius on Husbondrie. Ed. B. Lodge and S. J. Herrtage, 2 pts, EETS. 1872–9; ed. M. Liddell, Berlin, 1896. [Trn of *c.* 1420.]

The Parfite Life of Petronylla. [1496] (Pynson); rptd H. Huth (Fugitive Tracts written in Verse, vol. I, 1875).

Ryman, James. Poems. Ed. J. Zupitza, Archiv, LXXXIX, 1892, pp. 167–338.

The Turnament of Totenham. Ed. T. Wright, 1836; ed. W. C. Hazlitt (in Remains of the Early Popular Poetry of England, vol. III, 1864). [For the attribution to Gilbert Pilkington see the articles by Foster, Cargill and Frampton listed under the Towneley Plays, p. 278 below.]

Venus' Mass. Ed. T. F. Simmons (in Lay Folks' Mass Book, EETS. 1879); ed. E. P. Hammond, JEGP. VII, 1908 (as The Lover's Mass). [A parody of the Mass in verse and prose.]

Walton, John (*fl.* 1410). The Boke of Comfort. 1525; ed. M. Science, EETS. 1925. [Trn from Boethius.]

Watton, John. Speculum Christiani. [1486?] (de Machlinia).

(3) PROSE

(a) Chronicles (English and Latin)

[For a fuller list see C. L. Kingsford, English Historical Literature in the Fifteenth Century, Oxford, 1913, and F. J. Starke, Populäre englische Chroniken des 15. Jahrhunderts, Berlin, 1935.]

Arnold, Richard (d. 1521). The Customs of London, otherwise called Arnold's Chronicle. Ed. F. Douce, 1811.

The Brut, or the Chronicles of England. Ed. F. Brie, 2 pts, EETS. 1906–8.

Burton, Thomas of. Chronica monastica de Melsa usque ad Annum 1896. Ed. E. A. Bond, 3 vols. Rolls Ser. 1866–8.

Chronicle of the Rebellion in Lincolnshire. Ed. J. G. Nichols, Camden Misc. vol. I, 1847.

Elmham, Thomas (d. 1440?). Vita et Gesta Henrici Quinti. Ed. T. Hearne, Oxford, 1727.

Fabyan, Robert (d. 1512). The New Chronicles of England and France. 1516 (Pynson); ed. Sir H. Ellis, 1811. [See T. Warton, History of English Poetry, vol. II, 1871.]

Gesta Abbatum (793–1411). 3 vols. Rolls Ser. 1867–9.

Hardyng, John (1378–1465?). English Chronicle in Metre fro the First Begynning of Englande unto the Reigne of Edwarde the Fourth. 1543; ed. Sir H. Ellis, 1812. [See F. Palgrave, Documents and Records illustrating the History of Scotland, 1837.]

Historia Anglicana (1272–1422). Ed. H. T. Riley, 2 vols. Rolls Ser. 1863.

Historia Croylandensis. Ed. Sir H. Savile (in part in Rerum Anglicarum Scriptores, 1596); ed. [J. Fell and W. Fulman] (in Rerum Anglicarum Scriptores Veteres, Oxford, 1684); tr. H. T. Riley, [1847?] (Ingulph's Chronicle); ed. W. de G. Birch, Wisbech, 1883 (The Chronicles of Croyland Abbey). [*c.* 1400. Erroneously attrib. to Ingulph. See W. G. Searle, Ingulf and the Historia Croylandensis, Cambridge Antiquarian Soc. 1894.]

Historia Monasterii S. Augustini Cantuariensis. Ed. C. Hardwick, Rolls Ser. 1858.

Historical Collections of a London Citizen. Ed. J. Gairdner, Camden Soc. 1876. [Includes Gregory's Chronicle.]

Historie of the Arrivall of Edward IV. Ed. J. Bruce, Camden Soc. 1838.

Liber metricus de Henrico Quinto. Ed. C. A. Cole (in Memorials of Henry the Fifth, Rolls Ser. 1858).

Otterbourne, Thomas (*fl.* 1400). Chronicle. [BM. MS Harl. 3648. See T. Hearne, Duo Rerum Anglicarum Scriptores, Oxford, 1732.]

Page, John. The Seige of Rouen. Ed. H. Huscher, Leipzig, 1927. [In verse.]

Rous [or Ross], John (1411?–1491). Historia Regum Angliae. Ed. T. Hearne, 1716. [BM. Cott. MSS Vesp. A XII and Jul. E IV.]

A Short English Chronicle. Ed. J. Gairdner, Three Fifteenth Century Chronicles, Camden Soc. 1880.

Thorne, William (*fl.* 1397). Chronica de Rebus gestis Abbatum S. Augustini Cantuariae. Ed. Sir R. Twysden, Historiae Anglicanae Scriptores, vol. x, 1652.

Walsingham, Thomas (d. 1422). Chronicon Angliae (1328–88). Ed. E. M. Thompson, 1874.

Warkworth, John (d. 1500). Chronicle of the First Thirteen Years of the Reign of Edward IV. Ed. J. O. Halliwell [-Phillipps], Camden Soc. 1839.

Ypodigma Neustriae. Ed. H. T. Riley, Rolls Ser. 1876. [See also DNB.]

(b) Letters

[See also The Political Background, pp. 115–6, and The Social Background, pp. 119–22, above.]

Correspondence of Bekynton. Ed. G. Williams, 2 vols. Rolls Ser. 1872.

Cely Papers. Ed. H. E. Malden, Royal Hist. Soc. 1900.

Original Letters. Ed. Sir H. Ellis, 3 sers. 11 vols. 1825–46.

Epistolae Academiae Oxoniensis. Ed. H. Anstey, Oxford Hist. Soc. 1898.

The Paston Letters. Ed. J. Fenn, 5 vols. 1787–1823; rev. J. Gairdner, 3 vols. 1872–5, 4 vols. 1901, 6 vols. 1904 (expanded); ed. A. D. Greenwood, 1920 (selection). [See H. S. Bennett, The Pastons and their England, Cambridge, 1922.]

Plumpton Correspondence. Ed. T. Stapleton, Camden Soc. 1839.

Stonor Letters. Ed. C. L. Kingsford, 2 vols. Royal Hist. Soc. 1919. [Supplementary letters in Camden Misc. vol. XIII, 1924.]

(c) Other Prose (English)

[See also The Social Background, pp. 119–22, and under Caxton, pp. 261–3, above. For writings in Latin see pp. 280–314 below].

An Alphabet of Tales. An English 15th Century Translation of Alphabetum Narrationum. Ed. M. M. Banks, 2 pts, EETS. 1904–5.

The Earliest Arithmetics in English. Ed. R. Stede, EETS. 1916.

Berners, Dame Juliana (d. 1388?). The Book of Hawking, Hunting and Blasing of Arms. St Albans, 1486; 1496 (adds the Treatyse of Fysshynge); ed. William Blades, 1881 (facs. of 1486 edn); ed. M. G. Watkins, 1880 (Treatyse of Fysshynge only). [See An Older Form of the Treatyse of Fysshynge, ed. T. Satchell, 1883, and Reliquiae Antiquae, ed. T. Wright and J. O. Halliwell [-Phillipps], 2 vols. 1841–3 (vol. I, pp. 149 and 293).]

The Book of Quinte Essence. Ed. F. J. Furnivall, EETS. 1866. [1460–70.]

Dives et Pauper. 1493 (Pynson); 1496 (de Worde). [Dialogue in prose written 1405–10. Attribution to Henry Parker now disproved. See Library, XIV, 1933, p. 299, XV, 1934, p. 31, for MSS, etc.]

The Dyalogus or Communyng betwixt Salomon and Marcolphus. Antwerp, 1492 (Leeu); ed. E. Gordon Duff, 1892. [Trn from Dutch.]

A Fifteenth Century Courtesy Book. Ed. R. W. Chambers, EETS. 1914.

Gesta Romanorum. [1524?] (de Worde); ed. Sir F. Madden, Roxburghe Club, 1838; ed. S. J. Herrtage, EETS. Ex. Ser. 1879 (with notes on MSS); ed. C. Swan and W. Harper, 1891. [Trn of c. 1440. Specimens are in H. Morley, Mediaeval Tales, 1886. On the whole subject see H. Oesterley's study, Berlin, 1872.]

De Imitatione Christi. Ed. J. K.. Ingram, EETS. Ex. Ser. 1893. [Trn of c. 1450. Also includes version by Atkynson and the Lady Margaret, Countess of Richmond and Derby.]

Jacob's Well. Ed. A. Brandeis, Pt 1, EETS. 1900. [c. 1440. Pt 2 in preparation by G. R. Owst.]

Oure Ladyes Myroure. 1530; ed. J. H. Blunt, EETS. 1873.

Lanfranc's Cirurgie. Ed. R. von Fleischhacker, EETS. 1894. [1396 and 1420.]

The Lanterne of Light. Ed. L. M. Swinburn, EETS. 1915. [Early 15th cent. Lollard tract.]

Legenda Aurea. [1483] (Caxton). [15th cent. trn with addns. MSS: BM. Add. 11565, Harl. 4775 and others; Lambeth 72. See on whole subject and for specimens: Pierce Butler, Legenda Aurea, Baltimore, 1899; C. Horstmann, The Early South-English Legendary, EETS. 1887, and his Nova Legenda Angliae, 2 vols. Oxford. 1901.]

The Life of St Ursula, Guiscard and Sigismund. Roxburghe Club, 1818.

The Revelations of Saint Birgitta. Ed. W. P. Cumming, EETS. 1928. [15th cent. trn.]

Secreta Secretorum. Three Prose Englishings, one by J. Yonge, 1428. Ed. R. Steele, EETS. Ex. Ser. 1898.

Three Kings' Sons. Ed. F. J. Furnivall, 1895. [Trn from David Aubert's French, c. 1500.]

The Three Kynges of Coleyn. [1496] (de Worde); ed. C. Horstmann from MSS, EETS. 1886. [Trn, c. 1400, of John of Hildesheim's Historia trium Regum.]

Two Fifteenth-Century Cookery-Books. Ed. T. Austin, EETS. 1888. [c. 1430 and c. 1450.]

The Wright's Chaste Wife. Ed. F. J. Furnivall, EETS. 1865; 1891 (rev. edn). [c. 1462. See W. A. Clouston, Additional Analogues to the Wright's Chaste Wife, EETS. 1886.]

York, Edward, Duke of. The Master of Game. Ed. W. A. and F. Baillie-Grohman, 1904 and 1909.

4. SONGS AND BALLADS

I. SONGS AND LYRICS

(1) GENERAL BIBLIOGRAPHY

(a) Bibliographies

Wells, J. E. A Manual of the Writings in Middle English. New Haven, 1916, and 6 supplements, 1919, 1923, 1926, 1929, 1932, 1935. [Bibliography and summary for each piece in print to 1400: Love and Nature, and Religious Pieces, pp. 485, 843, 985, 1021, 1075, 1132, 1176, 1221, 1279, 1316, 1363, 1410; Political and Social Pieces, pp. 208, 796, 957, 1008, 1052, 1110, 1170, 1212, 1263, 1303, 1348, 1392.] (*Wells.*)

Brown, C. Register of Middle English Religious Verse, 2 vols. Bibliog. Soc. 1916–20. [Lists of MSS and editions of religious Pieces.]

(b) Editions of Groups of Lyrics

[The various selections listed on p. 114, above, should also be consulted.]

Ritson, J. A Select Collection of English Songs. 3 vols. 1783.

—— Ancient Songs. 1790 (for 1792); 2 vols. 1829; rev. W. C. Hazlitt, 1877.

Sandys, W. Christmas Carols, Ancient and Modern. 1833. [Mainly from BM. Add. MSS 5465 and 5665.]

—— Festive Songs, principally of the Sixteenth and Seventeenth Centuries. Percy Soc. 1848.

—— Christmas Tide. 1852.

Wright, T. Songs and Carols. 1836. [Sloane MS 2593.]

—— The Political Songs of England. Camden Soc. 1839; ed. E. Goldsmid, Edinburgh, 1884. [John–Edward III.]

—— Specimens of Old Christmas Carols. Percy Soc. 1841.

—— Specimens of Lyric Poetry, composed in the Reign of Edward the First. Percy Soc. 1842. [Harl. MS 2253.]

—— Religious Songs. [Appended to the Owl and the Nightingale, Percy Soc. 1843.]

—— Songs and Carols, from a Manuscript of the Fifteenth Century. Percy Soc. 1847. [Bodl. MS Eng. Poet. E I.]

—— Songs and Carols, from a Manuscript in the British Museum. Warton Club, 1856. [Sloane MS 2593.]

—— Political Poems and Songs. 2 vols. Rolls Ser. 1859–61. [Edward III–Richard III.]

Wright, T. and Halliwell[-Phillipps], J. O. Reliquiæ Antiquæ. 2 vols. 1841–3.

Madden, Sir F. Political Poems of the Reigns of Henry VI and Edward IV. Archaeologia, XXIX, 1841–2.

Fairholt, F. W. Satirical Songs. Percy Soc. 1842.

Rimbault, E. F. Ancient Poetical Tracts of the Sixteenth Century. Percy Soc. 1842.

Halliwell[-Phillipps], J. O. Early English Miscellanies in Prose and Verse. Warton Club, 1855. [Porkington MS 10, now Harlech 10, at Brogyntyn, Oswestry.]

Furnivall, F. J. Early English Poems and Lives of Saints. Berlin, 1862.

—— Political, Religious and Love Poems. EETS. 1866; 1903 (rev. edn). [Mainly from Lambeth MS 306.]

—— Hymns to the Virgin and Christ, The Parliament of Devils, etc. EETS. 1867; 1895 (rev. edn). [Lambeth MS 853.]

—— Religious Poems from MS Digby 2. Archiv, XCVII, 1896. [See also Archiv, LXXXVI, 1891, p. 290.]

—— Minor Poems of the Vernon Manuscript, Part II. EETS. 1901.

Hazlitt, W. C. Remains of the Early Popular Poetry of England. 4 vols. 1864–6.

Perry. G. G. Religious Pieces in Prose and Verse. EETS. 1867; 1914 (rev. edn). [Thornton MS, c. 1440.]

Morris, R. Old English Homilies. 2 pts, EETS. 1867–8.

Böddeker, K. Altenglische Dichtungen des MS Harleian 2253. Berlin, 1878.

Flügel, E. Liedersammlungen des XVI. Jahrhunderts, besonders aus der Zeit Heinrichs VIII. Ang. XII, XVII, XVIII, XXVI, 1889–1908. [MSS: Balliol 354; BM. Add. 31922; Royal App. 58; etc.]

—— Kleinere Mitteilungen aus Handschriften. Ang. XIV, 1891.

—— Neuenglisches Lesebuch. Halle, 1895.

Jacoby, M. Vier mittelenglische geistliche Gedichte. Berlin, 1890.

Fuller-Maitland, J. A. and Rockstro, W. S. English Carols of the Fifteenth Century. 1891.

Songs and Madrigals of the Fifteenth Century. Plain Song Society, 1891.

Horstmann, C. Minor Poems of the Vernon Manuscript, Part I. EETS. 1892.

—— Yorkshire Writers. 2 vols. 1895–6. [R. Rolle and others.]

Hall, J. Short Pieces from MS Cotton Galba E IX. E. Studien, XXI, 1895.

Fehr, B. Die Lieder des Fairfax MS. Archiv, cvi, 1901, p. 48. [BM. Add. MS 5465.]
—— Die Lieder des Hs Add. 5665. Archiv, cvi, 1901, p. 262.
—— Weitere Beiträge zur englischen Lyrik des 15. und 16. Jahrhunderts. Archiv, cvii, 1901. [MSS: Sloane 2593, 1212, 3501; Harl. 541, 367, 7578.]
—— Die Lieder der Hs Sloane 2593. Archiv, cix, 1902.
Stainer, J. Early Bodleian Music. 2 vols. Oxford, 1901.
The Oxford History of Music. Vols. i and ii, Oxford, 1901–5.
Kail, J. Twenty-Six Political and Other Poems. EETS. 1904. [MSS: Digby 102; Douce 322.]
Heuser, W. Kildare Gedichte. BBA. xiv, 1904. [Harl. MS 913.]
Padelford, F. M. Early Sixteenth Century Lyrics. Boston, 1907.
—— The Songs of Rawlinson MS C 813. 1909.
—— English Songs in MS Selden B 26. Ang. xxxvi, 1912. [c. 1453.]
Chambers, Sir E. K. and Sidgwick, F. Early English Lyrics. 1907; 1912; 1921; 1926. [With bibliography.]
—— —— Fifteenth Century Carols by John Audelay. MLR. v, vi, 1910–11.
Dyboski, R. Songs, Carols and Other Miscellaneous Pieces from Balliol MS 354. EETS. Ex. Ser. 1907.
Quiller-Couch, Sir A. T. Early English Lyrics. Oxford, [1908]. (Select English Classics.)
Root, R. K. Poems from the Garrett MS. E. Studien, xli, 1910.
Jordan, R. Kleinere Dichtungen der Handschrift Harley 8810. E. Studien, xli, 1910.
Patterson, F. A. The Middle English Penitential Lyric. New York, 1911. [With bibliography.]
MacCracken, H. N. Unprinted Texts from the MS Trinity College, Cambridge R.3.21. Archiv, cxxx, 1913. [Temp. Edward IV.]
James, M. R. and Macaulay, G. C. Fifteenth Century Carols and Other Pieces. MLR. viii, 1913.
Rickert, E. Ancient English Christmas Carols, 1400–1700. 1914.
Segar, M. G. Some Minor Poems of the Middle Ages. 1917.
Day, M. Poems of the Wheatley MS. (BM. Add. 39574). EETS. clv, 1917.
Brown, C. Religious Lyrics of the Fourteenth Century. Oxford, 1924.
—— English Lyrics of the Thirteenth Century. Oxford, 1932.
Hammond, E. P. English Verse between Chaucer and Surrey. Durham, North Carolina, 1927.

Comper, F. M. M. Life of Richard Rolle and Lyrics. 1929.
Green, R. L. The Early English Carols. Oxford, 1935.

(c) Modern Renderings

[See also under Richard Rolle, p. 193, above.]

Weston, J. L. The Chief Middle English Poets. Boston, 1914.
Segar, M. G. A Medieval Anthology. 1915.
Adamson, M. R. A Treasury of Middle English Verse. 1930.

(d) General Studies

[Many of the above editions contain important introductions which should be consulted. See also CHEL. vol. ii, 1908, pp. 372, 490.]

ten Brink, B. Geschichte der englischen Literatur. 2 vols. Strasburg, 1877–93; tr. Eng. 3 vols. 1883–96.
Paul, H. Grundriss der germanischen Philologie. Strasburg, 1891–. [Vol. ii, pt 1, 2nd edn.]
Petit de Julleville, L. Histoire de la Langue et de la Littérature francaises. 8 vols. Paris, 1896–1900. [With bibliography.]
Gröber, G. Grundriss der romanischen Philologie. 3 vols. Strasburg, 1888–1902; 2 vols. Strasburg, 1904–6.
Schofield, W. H. English Literature from the Norman Conquest to Chaucer. 1906.
Chambers, Sir E. K. and Sidgwick, F. Some Aspects of Medieval Lyric. [In Early English Lyrics, 1907.]
Reed, E. B. English Lyrical Poetry. New Haven, 1912. [With bibliography.]
Saintsbury, G. Historical Character of English Lyric. Oxford, 1912.
Rhys, E. Lyric Poetry. 1913.
Schelling, F. E. English Lyric. Boston, 1913 [With bibliography.]
Berdan, J. M. Early Tudor Poetry, 1485–1547. New York, 1920.
Kar, G. Thoughts on the Medieval Lyric. Oxford, 1933.
Ritson, J. Ancient Songs. 2 vols. 1790 (for 1792); rev. W. C. Hazlitt, 1877.
Cutts, E. L. Scenes and Characters of the Middle Ages. 1872.
Chambers, Sir E. K. The Medieval Stage. 2 vols. Oxford, 1903. [See vol. i, pp. 23 160, 272, index 'Minstrels.']
Grossmann, W. Frühmittelenglische Zeugnisse über Minstrels. Berlin, 1906.
Duncan, E. The Story of Minstrelsy. New York, 1907.

Brandl, A. Spielmannsverhältnisse im Früh-mittelenglischen. Zeit. Preuss. Akad. d. Wissensch. Berlin, 1911.

(e) Special Studies

Crowest, F. J. The Story of British Music. 1896.

Galpin, F. W. Old English Instruments of Music. 1910.

Gomme, A. B., Lady. The Traditional Games of England. [Dictionary of British Folk-Lore, vol. I, 1894–8.]

Gummere, F. B. The Beginnings of Poetry. New York, 1901.

Liebermann, F. Zu Liedrefrain und Tanz im englischen Mittelalter. Archiv, CXL, 1920, p. 261.

Werner, H. Die Ursprung der Lyrik. Munich, 1924.

Chaytor, H. J. The Troubadours. Cambridge, 1912.

—— Troubadours and England. Cambridge, 1923.

Audiau, J. Les Troubadours et l'Angleterre. Tulle, 1920.

Schipper, J. Englische Metrik in historischer und systematischer Entwickelung darge-stellt. 2 vols. Bonn, 1881–8.

—— A History of English Versification. Oxford, 1910.

Guest, E. History of English Rhythms. Ed. W. W. Skeat, 1882.

Schlüter, A. Ueber die Sprache und Metrik der mittelenglischen Lieder dér MS. 2253. Archiv, LXXI, 1884, pp. 153, 355.

Mayor, J. B. Chapters on English Metre. Cambridge, 1901.

Saintsbury, G. A History of English Prosody. Vol. I, 1906.

Medary, M. P. and Brown, A. C. L. Stanza-Linking. Romanic Rev. VII, 1916, pp. 243, 271.

Sandison, H. E. Chanson d'Aventure in Middle English. Bryn Mawr, 1913. [See its bibliography.]

Spalding, M. C. Middle English Charters of Christ. Bryn Mawr, 1914.

Cohen, H. L. The Ballade. New York, 1915.

Stengel, E. Codicem Manu Scriptum Digby 86. Halle, 1871.

Varnhagen, H. Ang. II, 1879, p. 225, III, 1880, pp. 59, 275, 415, 533, IV, 1881, p. 180. [Notes.]

Lewin, H. Das mittelenglische Poema morale. Halle, 1881.

Schröder, E. Zur Marienlyrik. ZDA. XXV, 1881, p. 127.

Einenkel, E. Eine englische Schriftstellerin des 12. Jahrhunderts. Ang. V, 1882, p. 265.

Trautmann, M. and Menthel, E. Ang. Anz. V, 1882, p. 118, VIII, 1885, p. 60.

Aust, J. Beiträge zur Geschichte der mittel-englischen Lyrik. Archiv, LXX, 1884, p. 253.

Vollhardt, W. Einfluss der lateinischen geist-lichen Literatur auf einige kleinere Schöp-fungen der englischen Übergangsperiode. Leipzig, 1888.

Koelbing, E. Kleine Beiträge. E. Studien, XVII, 1892, p. 296.

Lauchert, F. Über das englischen Marienlied im 13. Jahrhundert. E. Studien, XVI, 1892, p. 124.

Weichardt, C. Die Entwicklung des Natur-gefühls. Kiel, 1900.

Crowne, J. V. Middle English Poems on the Virgin Mary. Catholic University Bulletin, VIII, 1901, p. 309.

Fröhlich, W. De Lamentatione S. Marie. Leipzig, 1902.

Heider, O. Untersuchungen zur mitteleng-lischen erotischen Gedichte. Halle, 1905.

Holthausen, F. Beiträge zur Quellenkunde der mittelenglischen geistlichen Lyrik. Archiv, CXVI, 1906, p. 373.

Thien, H. Über die mittelenglischen Marien klagen. Kiel, 1906. [See its bibliography.]

Marufke, W. Der älteste englische Marien-hymnus. Breslau, 1907.

Taylor, G. C. The English Planctus Mariae. MP. IV, 1907, p. 605. [Bibliography.]

—— The Relations of the English Corpus Christi Play to the Middle English Religious Lyric. MP. V, 1907, p. 1. [Bibliography.]

Wolderich, W. Über die Sprache und Heimat einiger frühmittelenglischen religiösen Ge-dichte der Jesus und Cotton MSS. Halle, 1909.

Müller, A. Mittelenglische geistlichen und weltlichen Lyrik des XIII. Jahrhunderts. SEP. XLIV, 1911.

Corsdress, H. Die Motive der mittelenglischen geistlichen Lyrik. Weimar, 1913.

Benson, L. F. The English Hymn. 1915.

Allen, H. E. Mystical Lyrics of Manuel des Péchiez. Romanic Rev. IX, 1918, p. 154.

Langenfeldt, G. Några Blad ur den Medel-engelska Profanenlyrik före Chaucer. Edda, XI, 1919, p. 18.

Osmond, M. Mystical Poets of the English Church. New York, 1919. [Ch. i.]

Gillman, F. J. The Evolution of the English Hymn. 1927.

Owst, G. R. Literature and Pulpit in Medieval England. Cambridge, 1933.

Brunner, K. Mittelenglische Todesgedichte. Archiv, CLXVII, 1935.

Malone, K. Notes on Middle English Lyrics. ELH. II, 1935.

[See also the studies listed under Rolle's Lyrics, p. 192 above. For works on Carols see *Wells*, p. 1133.]

Wright, T. Latin Poems attributed to W. Mapes. Camden Soc. 1841.

—— Anglo-Latin Satirical Poets. 2 vols. Rolls Ser. 1872.

Ward, H. L. D. Catalogue of Romances in the British Museum. Vol. I, 1883, p. 292.

Haessner, M. Die Goliardendichtung und die Satire im 13. Jahrhundert in England. Leipzig, 1905.

Manitius, M. Die englische Satire des 12. Jahrhunderts. Allgemeine Zeitung, Beilage, 1906, p. 193.

Tucker, S. M. Verse Satire in England before the Renaissance. New York, 1908. [With bibliography.]

Previté-Orton, C. W. Political Satire in English Poetry. Cambridge, 1910.

Taylor, R. Political Prophecy in England. New York, 1911. [With bibliography.]

Dodds, M. H. Political Prophecy in the Reign of King John. MLR. XI, 1916, p. 276.

Eberhard, O. Der Bauernaufstand vom Jahre 1381 in der englischen Poesie. Anglistische Forschungen, LI, 1917.

(2) GROUPS OF POLITICAL AND SOCIAL POEMS

[Only edns of groups are given. See Wells for edns and studies of separate items, and for other pieces, to 1400. Wells, pp. 218, 797 and Supplements.]

[Harley MS. 2253.] The Song against the King of Almaigne, Flemish Insurrection, Execution of Sir Simon Fraser, Elegy on Death of Edward I, The Song of the Husbandman, Against Pride of Ladies, A Song against the Retinues of the Great, Consistory Courts. Ed. T. Wright, The Political Songs of England, 1839; ed. K. Böddeker, Altenglische Dichtungen des MS. Harley 2253, Berlin, 1878.

[Harley MS 913 (Kildare MS).] Song on the Times of Edward II, Pers of Birmingham, Song of Nego, People of Kildare. Ed. W. Heuser, BBA. XIV, 1904.

[Auchinleck MS (Nat. Lib. Scotland 19.2.1).] King's Breaking of Magna Charta, Praise of Women, The Evil Times of Edward II. Ed. T. Wright, The Political Songs of England, 1839.

[Royal MS 12 C XII.] Song on the Times. Ed. T. Wright, Political Poems and Songs, 2 vols. Rolls Ser. 1859–61.

[Cotton MS Cleopatra B II.] Against the Minorite Friars, Against the Friars. Ed. T. Wright, Political Poems and Songs, 2 vols. Rolls Ser. 1859–61; ed. A. S. Cook, Literary Middle English Reader, Boston, 1915.

[Vernon MS (Bodleian 3938).] Death of Edward III, Earthquake of 1382. Ed.

T. Wright, Political Poems and Songs, 2 vols. Rolls Ser. 1859–61. [See Anglistische Forschungen, LI, 1917, p. 351.]

[Harley MSS 536 and 941; Trinity College, Dublin E, 5, 10.] On the Times. Ed. T. Wright, Political Poems and Songs, 2 vols. Rolls Ser. 1859–61; ed. F. W. Fairholt, Satirical Songs, Percy Soc. 1842, p. 44.

[MS of W. Hamper, Deritend House, Birmingham.] King Richard's Ministers. Ed. T. Wright, Political Poems and Songs, 2 vols. Rolls Ser. 1859–61; Archaeologia, XXI, 1827, p. 88.

[Cotton MS Julius A v, fol. 180.] Ballad on Scottish Wars, As y yod on ay mounday. Ed. J. Ritson, Ancient Songs, 1877, p. 35; Langtoft's Chronicle, vol. II, Rolls Ser. 1868 p. 452. [See Wells, pp. 222, 798; H. L. D Ward, Catalogue of Romances in the British Museum, vol. I, 1883, p. 299; J. Hall's edn of Minot, Oxford, 1887, p. 76.]

[Cotton MS Galba E IX.] Siege of Calais Narracio de Domino Denarii, and Minot's Poems (see below). Ed. (first two) T. Wright and J. O. Halliwell[-Phillipps], Reliquiae Antiquae, vol. II, 1843, pp. 21, 108. [See ibid. vol. II, p. 108 for Sir Penny, Caius College Cambridge MS Moore 147. Latin Scottish, French versions in T. Wright Latin Poems attributed to W. Mapes Camden Soc. 1841, pp. 359, 361, 362, 355.

[Digby MS 102 (Bodleian); Douce MS 322 (Bodleian).] Ed. J. Kail, EETS CXXIV, 1904.

(3) LAURENCE MINOT'S LYRICS

MS. Cotton, Galba E IX.

Editions. T. Wright, Political Poems and Songs, vol. I, Rolls Ser. 1859, p. 58; W Scholle, QF. LII, 1882; J. Hall, Oxford 1887, 1915 (3rd edn).

Selections. E. Mätzner, Altenglische Sprachproben, 2 pts, Berlin, 1867–1900; R. Wülcker Lesebuch, 2 pts, Halle, 1874–9; J. Zupitza Übungsbuch, Vienna, 1874; R. Morris and W. W. Skeat, Specimens of Early English vol. II, Oxford, 1894; F. Kluge, Lesebuch Halle, 1904; O. F. Emerson, Reader, New York 1905; A. S. Cook, Reader, Boston, 1915 A. Brandl and O. Zippel, Mittelenglisch Sprach- und Literaturproben, Berlin, 1917 K. Sisam, Fourteenth Century Verse and Prose, Oxford, 1921; G. Sampson, Cambridge Book of Prose and Verse, 1924.

Studies. [See Wells, pp. 215, 797, 1008 1053, 1110, 1213; B. ten Brink, Early English Literature, vol. I, 1883, p. 322; H. Morley English Writers, vol. IV, 1889, p. 258; W. H Schofield, English Literature, 1906, p. 365 CHEL. vol. I, 1907, p. 356; DNB.]

Bierbaum, F. J. Über Laurence Minot und seine Lieder. Halle, 1876.

Dangel, M. Laurence Minot's Gedichte. Königsberg, 1888.

Romanic Rev. VII, 1916, p. 261. [Stanza.]

Snyder, E. C. MP. XVII, 1920, p. 712. [Poems 1 and 2.]

Moore, S. MLN. xxxv, 1920, p. 78. [Life.]

Parker, R. E. On Badding. PMLA. xxxvII, 1922, p. 360.

(4) OTHER SECULAR LYRICS.

[*Wells*, ch. xiii, for full list and for bibliography of each piece.]

Canute Song. Ed. Historia Eliensis, vol. II, Oxford, 1691, p. 26; F. Kluge, Lesebuch, Halle, 1904; J. Zupitza, Übungsbuch, Vienna, 1904; etc.

Cuckoo Song. Ed. J. Ritson, Ancient Songs and Ballads, 2 vols. 1790; ed. (with music), G. Grove, Dictionary of Music and Musicians, 4 vols. 1879–89, 1890; ed. Sir E. K. Chambers and F. Sidgwick, Early English Lyrics, 1907; ed. facs. J. B. Hurry, 1914 (2nd edn).

Mirie It Is, Foweles in the Frith. Ed. J. Stainer, Early Bodleian Music, vol. I, Oxford, 1901, plates 3, 6, vol. II, plates 5, 10; ed. Sir E. K. Chambers and F. Sidgwick, Early English Lyrics, 1907, pp. 3, 5.

College of Arms (Arundel 57) Fragments. Ed. T. Wright and J. O. Halliwell[-Phillipps], Reliquiae Antiquae, vol. II, 1843, p. 19.

Harley MS 2253, 18 lyrics, Alysoun, Johon, Lenten ys come, etc. Ed. T. Wright, Specimens of Lyric Poetry, Percy Soc. 1842; ed. K. Böddeker, Altenglische Dichtungen des MS. Harley 2253, Berlin, 1878. Some in G. Sampson, Cambridge Book of Prose and Verse, 1924; J. Ritson, Ancient Songs and Ballads, 1790; R. Wülcker, Lesebuch, 2 pts, Halle, 1874–9; A. S. Cook, Reader. Boston, 1915.

Bodleian, Rawlinson MS D 913, Fragments. Ed. Ang. xxx, 1907, p. 173.

Various lyrics. Ed. C. Brown, English Lyrics of the Thirteenth Century, Oxford, 1932.

(5) RELIGIOUS LYRICS

[*Wells*, ch. xiii for full list and bibliography of each piece to 1400. MSS and edns, C. Brown, Register of Middle English Religious Verse, 2 vols. Bibliog. Soc., 1916–20.]

Lyrics of St Godric. Ed. Surtees Soc. 1847; ed. J. Hall, Selections from Early Middle English, 2 pts, Oxford, 1920; ed. E. Studien, xi, 1888, p. 401; ed. A. S. Cook, Reader, Boston, 1915, p. 453.

Cotton MS Nero A xiv. On Wel Suiðe God Ureisun, On Lofsong of Ure Lefdi, Lofsong of Ure Lauerde, On God Ureisun of Ure Lefdi. Ed. R. Morris, EETS. xxxiv, 1868, pp. 200, 209, 205, 305.

Cotton MS Caligula A ix and Jesus College, Oxford, MS 29. Ed. T. Wright, Percy Soc. xi, 1843; ed. R. Morris, Old English Miscellany, EETS. 1872.

Tanner MS 169* (Bodleian 9995). Compassio Mariae (fragment). Ed. (with Latin) A. S. Napier, Archiv, LXXXVIII, 1892, p. 181; EETS. CIII, 1894, p. 75; ed. facs. (with music and notes), J. Stainer, Early Bodleian Music, vol. I, Oxford, 1901, plate 5, vol. II, plate 8. [See *Wells*, pp. 519, 850, 1134.]

Harley MS 913 (Kildare MS). Ed. W. Heuser, Kildare Gedichte, BBA. xiv, 1904; ed. F. J. Furnivall, Early English Poems and Lives of Saints, Berlin, 1862.

Phillipps MS 8336. Lyrics of Wm. Herebert. Ed. C. Brown, Religious Lyrics of the Fourteenth Century, Oxford, 1924, p. 15; ed. (part) T. Wright and J. O. Halliwell [-Phillipps], Reliquiae Antiquae, vol. I, 1841, p. 86.

Vernon MS (Bodley 3938). Ed. C. Horstmann, EETS. 2 pts, 1892–1901.

Vernon MSS, Simeon (BM. Add. 22283). Ed. C. Horstmann, EETS. 2 pts, 1892–1901; ed. Ang. vii, 1884, p. 280; ed. F. J. Furnivall, Early English Poems and Lives of Saints, Berlin, 1862.

Merton College Oxford MS 248. Ed. C. Brown, Religious Lyrics of the Fourteenth Century, Oxford, 1924, p. 51.

BM. Add. MS 11307. Meditations on the Passion. Ed. C. D'Evelyn, EETS. 1919.

Nat. Lib. Scotland, MS 18.7.21 (John Grymestone's Book). Ed. C. Brown, Religious Lyrics of the Fourteenth Century, Oxford, 1924, p. 69.

University Lib. Cambridge MS Dd.v.64. R. Rolle, *et al*. Ed. C. Horstmann, Yorkshire Writers, vol. I, 1895, p. 72; ed. F. M. M. Comper, Life of Richard Rolle, 1928, p. 205. [See also under Rolle, p. 192 above.]

Thornton MS (Lincoln Cathedral Lib. A, 5, 2). R. Rolle, *et al*. Ed. Horstmann, Comper, as above. [See also under Rolle, p. 192 above.]

Other lyrics. C. Brown, English Lyrics of the Thirteenth Century. Oxford, 1932.

(6) WILLIAM OF SHOREHAM'S LYRICS

MS. BM. Add. 17376.

Editions. T. Wright, Percy Soc. 1849; M. Konrath, EETS. 1902.

Selections. E. Mätzner, Altenglische Sprachproben, 2 pts, Berlin, 1867–1900; R. Wülcker,

272 THE MIDDLE ENGLISH PERIOD

Lesebuch, 2 pts, Halle, 1874–9; R. Morris and
W. W. Skeat, Specimens of Early English,
vol. ii, Oxford, 1894; A. Brandl and O. Zippel,
Mittelenglische Sprach- und Literaturproben,
Berlin, 1917; G. Sampson, Cambridge Book
of Prose and Verse, 1924; C. Brown, Religious
Lyrics of the Fourteenth Century, Oxford,
1924.

Studies. [See *Wells*, pp. 349, 817, 1015,
1120, 1216, 1309; B. ten Brink, Early English
Literature,vol.i, 1883,p. 281; W. H. Schofield,
English Literature, 1906, p. 387; CHEL. vol. i,
1907, p. 352; J. Schipper, Englische Metrik,
Bonn, 1881, sect. 164.]

Konrath, M. Beiträge zur Erklärung und
Text-kritik des William von Schorham.
Berlin, 1878.

Danker, O. Die Laut- und Flexionslehre der
mittelkentischen Denkmäler. Strasburg,
1879.

Jacoby, M. Vier mittelenglische geistliche
Gedichte aus dem 13. Jahrhundert. Berlin,
1890.

Paues, A. C. A Fourteenth Century Biblical
Version. Cambridge, 1902, p. lvi.

Deanesly, M. The Lollard Bible. Cambridge,
1920. [P. 146, note; biography.]

Seidel, W. William of Shoreham. Laut- und
Formenlehre seiner Gedichte. Leipzig, 1929.
[See also Ang. Bbl. xxxix, 1928, p. 29.]

[On text, language, etc., see Ang. iv, 1881,
p. 200, xvii, 1895, p. 80, xxvi, 1903, p. 365;
E. Studien, ii, 1879, p. 36, iii, 1880, p. 164,
xxi, 1895, p. 153, xlii, 1910, p. 205, xliii,
1911, p. 1, lvii, 1923, p. 307; Literaturblatt
für germanische und romanische Philologie, ii,
1881, p. 60, xi, 1890, p. 372; Anzeiger für
deutsches Alterthum, v, 1879, p. 257; QF.
lxiii, 1889, p. 25; Harvard Stud. i, 1892,
p. 88.] J. E. W. and A. W. R.

II. THE BALLADS

[The following entries deal mainly with the
'popular' ballad. A bibliography of the
'broadside' ballad will be found below, pp.
720–1.]

(1) COLLECTIONS AND EDITIONS OF BALLADS

[Phillips, A. ?] A Collection of Old Ballads.
3 vols. 1723–5.

Ramsay, A. The Ever Green. 2 vols. Edinburgh, 1724.

—— The Tea-Table Miscellany. 3 vols.
1724–7.

Percy, T. Reliques of Ancient English Poetry.
3 vols. 1765; ed. H. B. Wheatley, 3 vols.
1876–7; ed. A. Schroeer, 2 vols. Heilbronn,
1889–93.

[Herd, D.] The Ancient and Modern Scots
Songs. Edinburgh, 1769; 2 vols. 1776.

Evans, T. Old Ballads. 2 vols. 1777–84; ed
R. H. Evans, 4 vols. 1810.

Pinkerton, J. Scottish Tragic Ballads. 1781

—— Select Scotish Ballads. 2 vols. 1783.

Ritson, J. Select Collection of English Songs
3 vols. 1783; ed. T. Park, 3 vols. 1813.

—— Ancient Songs. 2 vols. 1792 (misdated
1790); ed. W. C Hazlitt, 1877.

—— Pieces of Ancient Popular Poetry. 1791
ed. E. Goldsmid, 1884.

—— Scotish Song. 2 vols. 1794.

Johnson, J. The Scots Musical Museum
6 vols. Edinburgh, 1787–1803; ed. W
Stenhouse and D. Laing, 4 vols. 1853.

Scott, Sir Walter. Minstrelsy of the Scottish
Border. 3 vols. Kelso, 1802–3; ed. T. F
Henderson, 4 vols. Edinburgh, 1902.

Jamieson, R. Popular Ballads and Songs
2 vols. Edinburgh, 1806.

Finlay, J. Scottish Historical and Romantic
Ballads. 2 vols. Edinburgh, 1808.

Laing, D. Select Remains of the Ancient
Popular Poetry of Scotland. Edinburgh
1822; ed. J. Small, Edinburgh, 1885.

—— Early Popular Poetry of Scotland and
the Border. 1822–6; ed. W. C. Hazlitt
2 vols. 1895.

Sharpe, C. K. A Ballad Book. Edinburgh
1823; ed. D. Laing, 1880.

Maidment, J. A North Countrie Garland
Edinburgh, 1824.

Motherwell, W. Minstrelsy, Ancient and
Modern. Glasgow, 1827.

Kinloch, G. Ancient Scottish Ballads. 1827.

Buchan, P. Ancient Ballads and Songs of the
North of Scotland. 2 vols. Edinburgh, 1828

Chambers, R. Scottish Ballads and Scottish
Songs. 3 vols. Edinburgh, 1829.

Chappell, W. A Collection of National English
Airs. 1840. [With essay on English Min
strelsy.]

—— Popular Music of the Olden Time. 2 vols
1855–9; ed. H. E. Wooldridge, 2 vols. 1893

Chappell, W. and Ebsworth, J. W. Th
Roxburghe Ballads. 27 pts, 1871–99.

Dixon, J. H. Scottish Traditional Versions of
Ancient Ballads. Percy Soc. 1845.

—— Ancient Poems, Ballads and Songs of the
Peasantry of England. Percy Soc. 1846.

Gutch, J. M. A Lytyll Geste of Robin Hode
2 vols. 1847.

Bell, R. Ancient Poems, Ballads, and Songs
of the Peasantry of England. 1857.

Child, F. J. The English and Scottish Popular
Ballads. 8 vols. Boston, 1857–8; 10 pts
5 vols. Boston, 1882–98. [The 2nd edn i
practically a new work. Vol. v contains
bibliography (pp. 503–65), which, with the
Sources of the Texts (pp. 397–404), the

Titles of Collections of Ballads (pp. 455–68), indexes, lists of ballad-airs and tunes, etc., furnishes a complete apparatus for the student. The 'Cambridge' one-vol. edn (Boston, 1904), ed. H. C. Sargent and G. L. Kittredge, contains one or more versions of each of the 305 in the original collection. The Introduction by G. L. Kittredge, Child's pupil, is the best substitute for the introduction that Child did not live to write for his own work.]

Aytoun, W. E. The Ballads of Scotland. 2 vols. 1858.

Allingham, W. The Ballad Book. 1864.

Hales, J. W. and Furnivall, F. J. Bishop Percy's Folio Manuscript. 3 vols. and supplement, 1867–8.

Veitch, J. History and Poetry of the Scottish Border. 1878; 2 vols. Glasgow, 1893.

Gummere, F. B. Old English Ballads. Boston, 1894.

Sidgwick, F. Popular Ballads of the Olden Time. 4 sers. 1903–12.

Campbell, O. D. and Sharp, C. J. English Folk-Songs from the Southern Appalachians. New York, 1917.

(2) GENERAL CRITICISM

[Many of the collections and edns in the foregoing section contain important introductions or appendices.]

Lang, A. Myth, Ritual and Religion. 2 vols. 1887.

—— Chambers's Cyclopaedia of English Literature. Vol. I, 1901. [Pp. 520 ff.]

Davidson, T. Chambers's Encyclopaedia. Vol. I, 1888. [Under Ballads.]

Brandl, A. Englische Volkspoesie. [In PG. vol. II, 1893, and later edns.]

Child, F. J. Johnson's Cyclopaedia. Vol. I, New York, 1893. [Under Ballads.]

Courthope, W. J. A History of English Poetry. 6 vols. 1895–1910. [Vol. I, ch. 11.]

Gummere, F. B. The Ballad and Communal Poetry. Harvard Stud. v, 1896.

—— The Beginnings of Poetry. 1901.

—— Primitive Poetry and the Ballad. MP. I, 1903.

—— The Popular Ballad. 1907.

Gregory Smith, G. The Transition Period. Edinburgh, 1900. [Ch. vi.]

Heusler, A. Lied und Epos. Dortmund, 1905.

Hecht, H. Neuere Literatur zur englisch-schottischen Balladendichtung. E. Studien, XXXVI, 1906.

Hart, W. M. Ballad and Epic. Harvard Stud. XI, 1907.

—— English Popular Ballads. Chicago, 1916.

Ker, W. P. On the History of the Ballads: 1100–1500. Proc. British Academy, IV, 1909.

Henderson, T. F. The Ballad in Literature. Cambridge, 1912.

Bryant, F. E. A History of English Balladry. Boston, 1913.

Steenstrup, J. C. H. R. The Mediaeval Popular Ballad. Boston, [1914]. [Tr. E. G. Cox.]

Sidgwick, F. The Ballad. 1914.

Gerould, G. H. The Making of Ballads. MP. XXI, 1923.

—— The Ballad of Tradition. Oxford, 1932.

Graves, Robert. The English Ballad. 1927.

(3) SPECIAL STUDIES

Lemcke, L. Die traditionellen schottischen Balladen. Jahrbuch für romanische und englische Literatur, IV, 1862.

Fränkel, L. Zur Geschichte von Robin Hood. E. Studien, XVII, 1887.

Flügel, E. Zur Chronologie der englischen Balladen. Ang. XXI, 1899.

Görbing, F. Beispiele von realisierten Mythen in den englischen und schottischen Balladen. Ang. XXIII, 1900.

Fehr, B. Die formelhaften Elemente in den alten englischen Balladen. Basle, 1900.

Rüdiger, Georg. Zauber und Aberglaube in den englisch-schottischen Volksballaden. Halle, 1907.

Belden, H. M. The Relation of Balladry to Folk-Lore. Journ. American Folk-Lore, XXIV, 1911.

Ehrke, Konrad. Das Geistermotiv in den schottisch-englischen Volksballaden. Marburg, 1914.

Hustvedt, S. B. Ballad Criticism in Scandinavia and Great Britain during the Eighteenth Century. New York, 1916. [With bibliography.]

Rollins, H. E. An Analytical Index to the Ballad Entries, 1557–1709, in the Stationers' Registers. Chapel Hill, 1924.

Wimberley, L. C. Folklore in the English and Scottish Ballads. Chicago, 1928. [With bibliography.]

Humbert, G. Literarische Einflüsse in Schottischen Volksballaden. Versuch einer kritischen Variantenvergleichung. Halle, 1932.

Pound, L. On the Dating of the English and Scottish Ballads. PMLA. XLVII, 1932.

Schmidt, W. Die Entwicklung der englisch-schottischen Volksballaden. Ang. LVII, 1933.

Panke, F. Die schottischen Liebesballaden. Ein Beitrag zur Entstehung von Variantenbildung. Berlin, 1935.

F. S.

5. THE MEDIEVAL DRAMA

General Works: Bibliographies and Histories.
The Liturgical Drama: Surveys and Special Studies; Texts.
The Miracle Plays: General and Special Studies; Collections and Selections; Transitional Pieces; Chester, Coventry, Ludus Coventriae, Towneley and York Plays; Other Plays and Fragments.

[The following sections are principally concerned with the Miracle Plays. For the Moralities see pp. 513–7.]

A. BIBLIOGRAPHIES

Stoddard, F. H. References for Students of Miracle-Plays and Mysteries. Berkeley, 1887. [See review, Ang. XI, 1888.]

Greg, W. W. A List of English Plays written before 1643 and printed before 1700. Bibliog. Soc., 1900.

—— Bibliographical and Textual Problems of the English Miracle Cycles. Library, V, 1914.

Chambers, Sir E. K. The Medieval Stage. 2 vols. Oxford, 1903. [See vol. I, pp. xiii–xlii, for authorities; vol. II, Appendix W, for list of dramatic performances in England; vol. II, Appendix X, for catalogue of English dramatic texts.]

Klein, David. A Contribution to a Bibliography of the Medieval Drama. MLN. xx, 1905. [Additions to Stoddard.]

Wells, J. E. A Manual of the Writings in Middle English. New Haven, 1916, and 6 supplements, 1919, 1923, 1926, 1929, 1932, 1935. [Bibliography to ch. 14.]

Tucker, L. L. and Benham, A. R. A Bibliography of Fifteenth Century Literature. Seattle, 1928. [Pp. 83–98.]

B. GENERAL HISTORIES AND DISCUSSIONS

Mone, F. J. Schauspiele des Mittelalters. Karlsruhe, 1846.

Hase, K. Das geistliche Schauspiel des Mittelalters. Leipzig, 1858; tr. Eng. 1880.

Klein, J. L. Geschichte des Dramas. 13 vols. Leipzig, 1865–86.

Reidt, H. Das geistliche Schauspiele des Mittelalters. Frankfort, 1868.

Sepet, M. Le Drame chrétien au Moyen Âge. Paris, 1878.

Petit de Julleville, L. Histoire du Théâtre en France au Moyen Âge. 4 vols. Paris, 1880–6.

Creizenach, W. Geschichte des neueren Dramas. 5 vols. Halle, 1895–1916.

Mantzius, K. Skuespilkunstens Historie. 5 vols. Copenhagen, 1897–1907; tr. Eng. 5 vols. 1903–21.

Gregory Smith, G. The Transition Period. Edinburgh, 1900.

Tunison, J. S. Dramatic Traditions of the Middle Ages. Chicago, 1907.

Wells, J. E. A Manual of the Writings in Middle English. New Haven, 1916 and 6 supplements, 1919, 1923, 1926, 1929, 1932, 1935. [Ch. 14, Dramatic Pieces.]

Young, Karl. The Drama of the Medieval Church. 2 vols. Oxford, 1933.

C. THE LITURGICAL DRAMA

(1) SURVEYS AND SPECIAL STUDIES

[The works of Sepet, Petit de Julleville, Creizenach and Mantzius in the previous section, and of Ward, Bates, Pollard, Chambers and Davidson below, p. 275, should also be consulted.]

Du Méril, E. Origines Latines du Théâtre moderne. Paris, 1849. [Includes texts.]

Sepet, M. Les Prophètes du Christ. Paris, 1878.

—— Origines catholiques du Théâtre moderne. Paris, 1901.

Milchsack, G. Die lateinischen Österfeiern. Wolfenbuettel, 1880.

Reiners, A. Die Tropen-, Prosen-, und Präfations-Gesänge. Luxemburg, 1884.

Gautier, L. Histoire de la Poésie liturgique au Moyen Âge. Paris, 1886. [Includes texts.]

Frere, W. H. The Winchester Troper. 1894.

Butler, Pierce. A Note on the Origin of the Liturgical Drama. [In Furnivall Miscellany, Oxford, 1901.]

Anz, H. Die lateinischen Magierspiele. Leipzig, 1905.

van der Gaaf, W. The Easter Sepulchre. E. Studien, XXXVII, 1907.

Young, Karl. The Harrowing of Hell in Liturgical Drama. Trans. Wisconsin Academy, XVI, 1909.

—— Observations on the Origin of the Medieval Passion-Play. PMLA. xxv, 1910.

—— The Origin of the Easter Play. PMLA. XXIX, 1914.

Young, Karl. The Dramatic Associations of the Easter Sepulchre. Madison, 1920.
—— Concerning the Origin of the Miracle Play. [In Manly Anniversary Studies, Chicago, 1923.]
—— The Home of the Easter Play. Speculum, I, 1926.
Craig, Hardin. The Origin of the Old Testament Plays. MP. x, 1913.
Jenney, A. M. The Origin of the Old Testament Plays. MP. xiii, 1915.
Kretzmann, P. E. The Liturgical Element in the Earliest Forms of the Medieval Drama. Minneapolis, 1916.
Bonnell, J. K. The Easter Sepulchrum in its Relation to the Architecture of the High Altar. PMLA. xxxi, 1916.
Brooks, N. C. The Sepulchre of Christ in Art and Liturgy. Urbana, 1921.
—— The 'Sepulchrum Christi' and its Ceremonies. JEGP. xxvii, 1928.
Flood, W. H. G. The Irish Origin of the Easter Play. Month, cxli, 1923.

(2) LITURGICAL TEXTS

[See also the collections of Pollard, Adams and Manly below, p. 276.]

Wright, T. Early Mysteries and Latin Poems of the Twelfth and Thirteenth Centuries. 1838.
Coussemaker, E. de. Histoire de l'Harmonie du Moyen Âge. Paris, 1852.
—— Drames liturgiques du Moyen Âge. Paris, 1860.
Lange, K. Die lateinischen Österfeiern. Munich, 1887.
Froning, R. Das Drama des Mittelalters. Stuttgart, 1891.
Gasté, A. Les Drames liturgiques de la Cathédrale de Rouen. Évreux, 1893.
Brooks, N. C. Some New Texts of Liturgical Easter-Plays. JEGP. viii, 1909.
—— Liturgical Easter-Plays from Rheinan MS. JEGP. x, 1911.
Young, Karl. Some Texts of Liturgical Plays. PMLA. xxiv, 1909.
—— A Liturgical Play of Joseph and his Brethren. MLN. xxvi, 1911.
—— Ordo Rachelis. Madison, 1919.
—— A New Version of the Peregrinus. PMLA. xxxiv, 1919.
—— Ordo Prophetarum. Trans. Wisconsin Academy, xx, 1919.
Antichrist and Adam. Tr. S. F. Barrow and W. H. Hulme, Western Reserve Bulletin, xxviii, 1925.
Adam. Tr. E. N. Stone, Seattle, 1926.

D. THE ENGLISH MIRACLE PLAYS

(1) GENERAL TREATMENTS

[See also the general histories of English literature, listed on p. 113 above, especially Warton, Morley, Jusserand, Courthope and Snell.]

Hone, W. Ancient Mysteries Described. 1823.
Sharp, T. A Dissertation on the Pageants or Dramatic Mysteries at Coventry. Coventry, 1825.
Ebert, A. Die englischen Mysterien. Jahrbuch für romanische und englische Literatur, I, 1859.
Meyer, H. Infancy of the English Drama. Hague, 1873.
Ward, Sir A. W. A History of English Dramatic Literature to the Death of Queen Anne. 2 vols. 1875; 3 vols. 1899 (rev. edn).
Genée, R. Die englischen Mirakelspiele und Moralitäten. Berlin, 1878.
Jusserand, J. J. Le Théâtre en Angleterre. Paris, 1878, 1881 (rev. edn).
Collier, J. P. The History of English Dramatic Poetry. 3 vols. 1879.
Zschech, F. Die Anfänge des englischen Dramas. Marienwerder, 1886.
Hohfeld, A. R. Altenglische Kollektivmisterien, Ang. xi, 1889.
Pollard, A. W. English Miracle Plays, Moralities and Interludes. Oxford, 1890, 1927 (8th edn, rev.). [Introduction.]
Davidson, C. Studies in the English Mystery Plays. New Haven, 1892.
—— Concerning English Mystery Plays. MLN. vii, 1892.
Bates, K. L. The English Religious Drama. 1893.
Clarke, S. W. The Miracle Play in England. 1897.
Brandl, Alois. Quellen des weltlichen Dramas in England vor Shakespeare. Q.F. lxxx, 1898. [Introduction.]
Chambers, Sir E. K. The Medieval Stage. 2 vols. Oxford, 1903.
Matthews, Brander. Medieval Drama. MP. I, 1903.
Moore, E. English Miracle Plays and Moralities. 1907.
Gayley, C. M. Plays of our Forefathers, and some of the Traditions upon which they were founded. New York, 1909.
—— The Later Miracle Plays of England. Independent Quart. xii, 1906.
Cron, B. Zur Entwicklungsgeschichte der englischen Misterien Alten Testaments. Marburg, 1913.
Coffman, G. R. A New Theory concerning the Origin of the Miracle Play. Menasha, Wisconsin, 1914.
Manly, J. M. The Miracle Play in Medieval England. Trans. Royal Soc. Lit. vii, 1927.
Withington, R. The Corpus Christi Plays as Dramas. Stud. Phil. xxvii, 1930.

(2) SPECIAL STUDIES

(a) Books

Smith, J. T. English Guilds. The Original Ordinances of more than One Hundred English Guilds. EETS. 1870.

Green, A. S. Town Life in the Fifteenth Century. 2 vols. 1894.

Leach, A. F. Some English Plays and Players. [In Furnivall Miscellany, Oxford, 1901.]

Eckhardt, E. Die lustige Person im älteren englischen Drama. Berlin, 1902.

Gayley, C. M. Representative English Comedies. Boston, 1903. [Introduction.]

Symmes, H. S. Les Débuts de la Critique dramatique en Angleterre. Paris, 1903.

Thien, H. Über die englischen Marienklagen. Kiel, 1906.

Taylor, G. C. The Relation of Lyric and Drama in Medieval England. Chicago, 1907.

Greene, A. An Index of non-Biblical Names in English Mystery Plays. [In Hart Celebrations, Ithaca, 1910.]

Foster, F. A. A Study of the 'Northern Passion' and its Relation to the Cycle Plays. 1914.

Withington, R. English Pageantry; an Historical Outline. 2 vols. Cambridge, U.S.A. 1918–20.

Meier, H. Die Strophenform in den englischen Mysterienspielen. Freiburg, 1921.

Phillips, W. J. Carols and their Connection with Mystery Plays. 1921.

Mill, A. J. Medieval Plays in Scotland. 1927.

Owst, G. R. Literature and Pulpit in Medieval England. Cambridge, 1933.

Chambers, Sir E. K. The English Folk-Play. Oxford, 1933.

(b) Articles in Periodicals

Cushman, L. W. The Devil and the Vice in the English Drama before 1605. Stud. Phil. vi, 1900.

Liebermann, F. Das Osterspiel zu Leicester. Archiv, cvii, 1900.

Gothein, Marie. Die Frau im englischen Drama vor Shakespeare. Sh. Jb. xl, 1904.

Tisdal, F. M. Influence of Popular Custom on Mystery Plays. JEGP. v, 1904.

van der Gaaf, W. Miracles and Mysteries of South East Yorkshire. E. Studien, xxvi, 1906.

Emerson, O. F. Legends of Cain. PMLA. xiv, 1906.

Taylor, G. C. The English Planctus Mariae. MP. iv, 1907.

Craig, Hardin. The Corpus Christi Procession and the Corpus Christi Play. JEGP. xiii, 1913.

—— The Origin of the Old Testament Plays. MP. x, 1913.

Craig, Hardin. The Doomsday Play in England. MP. x, 1913.

—— The Lincoln Cordwainers' Pageant. PMLA. xxxii, 1917.

Coffman, G. R. The Miracle Play in England—Nomenclature. PMLA. xxxi, 1916.

—— The Miracle Play in England. Stud. Phil. xvi, 1919.

Withington, R. The Early 'Royal Entry.' PMLA. xxxii, 1917.

Baskervill, C. R. Some Evidences of Early Romantic Plays in England. MP. xiv, 1917.

—— Dramatic Aspects of Medieval Folk Festivals in England. Stud. Phil. xvii, 1920.

Frank, Grace. Revisions in the English Mysteries. MP. xv, 1918.

Reed, A. W. The Beginnings of the English Secular and Romantic Drama. Shakespeare Ass. 1922.

Moore, J. R. The Tradition of Angelic Singing in English Drama. JEGP. xxii, 1923.

Dustoor, P. E. Some Textual Notes on the English Mystery Plays. MLR. xxi, 1926.

—— Textual Notes on Three Non-Cycle Mystery Plays. MLR. xxiii, 1928.

Collins, F. Music in the Craft Cycles. PMLA. xlvii, 1932.

(3) TEXTS

(a) Collections and Selections

Hawkins, T. The Origin of the English Drama. 3 vols. Oxford, 1773. (*Hawkins.*)

Collier, J. P. Five Miracle Plays. 1886. (*Collier.*)

Marriott, W. A Collection of English Miracle-Plays or Mysteries, containing the Dramas from the Chester, Coventry and Towneley Series, with Candlemas-Day and Bale's God's Promises. Basle, 1838. (*Marriott.*)

Wright, T. and Halliwell[-Phillipps], J. O. Reliquiae Antiquae. 2 vols. 1841–3.

Amyot, T. et al. A Supplement to Dodsley's Old English Plays. 4 vols. 1853. (*Amyot.*)

Pollard, A. W. English Miracle Plays, Moralities and Interludes. Oxford, 1890, 1927 (rev.). (*Pollard.*)

Manly, J. M. Specimens of the Pre-Shakespearean Drama. 2 vols. Boston, 1897–8, 1900–3. (*Manly.*)

Hemingway, S. B. English Nativity Plays. New York, 1909. (*Hemingway.*)

Waterhouse, Osborne. The Non-Cycle Mystery Plays. EETS. Ex. Ser. 1909. (*Waterhouse.*)

Tatlock, J. S. P. and Martin, R. G. Representative English Plays. New York, 1916; 1923. (*Tatlock.*)

Adams, J. Q. Chief Pre-Shakespearean Dramas. Boston, 1924. (*Adams.*)

(b) Transitional Pieces

(i) The Shrewsbury Fragments

Texts. Ed. W. W. Skeat, Academy, 27 Jan. 1890; *Manly*; *Waterhouse*; *Adams.*

Criticism.

Miller, F. H. Metrical Affinities of the Shrewsbury 'Officium Pastorum' and its York Correspondent. MLN. xxxiii, 1918.

(ii) Caiphas

Texts. Ed. T. Wright and J. O. Halliwell [-Phillipps] (in Reliquiae Antiquae, vol. ii, 1843); ed. C. Brown (in Kittredge Anniversary Papers, Boston, 1913).

(iii) Dux Moraud

Texts. Ed. W. Heuser, Ang. xxx, 1908; *Adams.*

(iv) Interludium de Clerico et Puella

Texts. Ed. T. Wright and J. O. Halliwell [-Phillipps] (in Reliquiae Antiquae, vol. i, 1841); ed. Sir E. K. Chambers (in Medieval Stage, vol. ii, 1903); ed. W. Heuser, Ang. xxx, 1908.

(v) Bury St Edmunds Fragment

Text. Ed. J. P. Gilson, TLS. 26 May 1921.

(c) Principal Cycles

(i) Chester Plays

Cycle. Ed. T. Wright, 2 vols. Shakespeare Soc. 1843–7; rptd in *Amyot*, vol. i; ed. H. Deimling and G. W. Mathews, 2 pts, EETS. Ex. Ser. 1893–1916.

One or more plays. Ed. J. H. Markland, Roxburghe Club, 1818; *Collier*; *Marriott*; *Pollard*; *Manly*; ed. H. H. Barne, 1906 (modernised); *Hemingway*; *Adams*; ed. D. Jones, 1928; ed. W. W. Greg, Oxford, 1935 (Antichrist).

Criticism.

Deimling, H. Textgestalt und Kritik. Berlin, 1890.

Ungemacht, H. Die Quellen der fünf ersten Chester Plays. Münich, 1890.

Baugh, A. C. The Chester Plays and French Influence. [In Schelling Anniversary Papers, New York, 1923.]

Mathews, G. W. The Chester Miracle Plays. Liverpool, 1925.

Dustoor, P. E. Textual Notes on the Chester Old Testament Plays. Ang. lii, 1928.

Wilson, R. H. The Stanzaic Life of Christ and the Chester Plays. Stud. Phil. xxviii, 1931.

(ii) Coventry Plays

Shearmen and Tailors' Play. Ed. T. Sharp (a) in Illustrative Papers of the History of Coventry, Coventry, 1817; (b) in A Dissertation on the Coventry Mysteries, Coventry, 1825; *Marriott*; *Manly*; ed. A. W. Pollard (in Fifteenth Century Verse and Prose, 1903); *Adams.*

Weavers' Play. Ed. J. B. Gracie, Abbotsford Club, 1836; ed. F. Holthausen, Ang. xxv, 1902.

Both Plays. Ed. H. Craig, EETS. Ex. Ser. 1902.

Criticism.

Craig, Hardin. Coventry Plays. MLN. xxi, 1918.

Cady, F. W. Towneley, York, and True-Coventry. Stud. Phil. xxvi, 1929.

(iii) Ludus Coventriae, or Hegge Plays

Cycle. Ed. J. O. Halliwell[-Phillipps], Shakespeare Soc. 1841; ed. K. S. Block, EETS. 1922.

One or more plays. Ed. J. Caley, H. Ellis and B. Bandinel (in Dugdale's Monasticon Anglicanum, vol. vi, 1830); *Collier*; *Marriott*; *Pollard*; *Manly*; *Hemingway*; ed. W. W. Greg, Oxford, 1916; *Adams.*

Criticism.

Thompson, E. N. S. The Ludus Coventriae. MLN. xxi, 1906.

Craig, Hardin. Coventry (Hegge) Plays. Athenaeum, 16 Aug. 1913.

—— The Corpus Christi Procession and Play. JEGP. xiii, 1914.

Dodds, M. H. The Problem of the Ludus Coventriae. MLR. ix, 1914.

Swenson, E. L. Inquiry into the Composition and Structure of the Ludus Coventriae. Minneapolis, 1914.

Patch, H. R. The Ludus Coventriae and the Digby Massacre. PMLA. xxxv, 1920.

Hartman, H. The Home of the Ludus Coventriae. MLN. xli, 1926.

Taylor, G. C. The Christus Redivivus of Nicholas Grimald and the Hegge Resurrection Plays. PMLA. xli, 1926.

Clark, T. B. A Theory concerning the Identity and History of the Ludus Coventriae Cycle of Mystery Plays. PQ. xii, 1933.

(iv) Towneley Plays

Cycle. Ed. either J. Rainie, J. Hunter, or J. S. Stevenson, Surtees Soc. 1836; ed. G. England and A. W. Pollard, EETS. Ex. Ser. 1897.

One or more plays. Ed. F. Douce, Roxburghe Club, 1822; *Collier*; *Marriott*; ed. L. T. Smith (in York Plays, Oxford, 1885); *Manly*; *Hemingway*; *Tatlock*; *Adams.*

Criticism.

Skeat, W. W. The Locality of the Towneley Plays. Athenaeum, 2 Dec. 1893.

Koelbing, E. Mak Episode. Zeitschrift für vergleichende Litteraturgeschichte, N.S. XI, 1897.

Peacock, M. H. The Wakefield Mysteries. Ang. XXIV, 1901.

Bunzen, A. Ein Beitrag zur Kritik der Wake-fielder Mysterien. Kiel, 1903.

Hamelius, P. Character of Cain in Towneley Plays. Journ. Comparative Lit. I, 1903.

Gerould, G. H. Roll of the Prima Pastorum. MLN. XIX, 1904.

Traver, H. Relation of Musical Terms in the Shepherds' Play to Date of Composition. MLN. XX, 1905.

Cady, F. W. The Liturgical Basis for the Towneley Mysteries. PMLA. XXIV, 1909.

—— Couplets and Quatrains in Towneley Plays. JEGP. X, 1911.

—— The Wakefield Group in the Towneley Plays. JEGP. XI, 1912.

—— The Towneley Plays. MP. X, 1912.

Foster, F. A. The Mystery Play and the Northern Passion. MLN. XXVI, 1911.

—— Was Gilbert Pilkington Author of Secunda Pastorum? PMLA. XLIII, 1928.

Williams, E. F. The Comic Element in the Wakefield Mysteries. Berkeley, 1914.

Cook, A. S. Another Parallel to the Mak Story. MP. XIV, 1916.

Baugh, A. C. Parallels to the Mak Story. MP. XV, 1918.

Holthausen, F. Studien zu den Towneley Plays. E. Studien, LVIII, 1924.

—— Das Wakefield Spiel von Kain und Abel. E. Studien, LXII, 1927.

Malone, K. A Note on the Towneley Secunda Pastorum. MLN. XL, 1925.

Peacock, M. H. A Note on the Identity of the Towneley Plays with the Wakefield Mys-teries. Ang. Bbl. XXXVI, 1925. [See corre-spondence in TLS. 5 March, 30 April, 7 May 1925.]

Cargill, O. Authorship of the Secunda Pas-torum. PMLA. XLI, 1926.

Dustoor, P. E. Textual Notes on English Mystery Plays. MLR. XXI, 1926.

—— Textual Notes on the Towneley Old Testament Plays. E. Studien, LXIII, 1929.

Wann, Louis. A New Examination of the Manuscript of the Towneley Plays. PMLA. XLIII, 1928.

Carey, M. The Wakefield Group in the Towneley Cycle. Göttingen, 1929.

Frampton, M. G. Gilbert Pilkington once more. PMLA. XLVII, 1932.

—— The Date of the Flourishing of the 'Wakefield Master.' PMLA. L, 1935.

(v) York Plays

Cycle. Ed. L. T. Smith, Oxford, 1885.
One or more plays. Ed. J. Croft (in Excerpta Antiqua, 1797); ed. J. P. Collier, Camden Misc. vol. IV, 1859; Pollard; Manly; Hemingway; Adams.

Criticism.

Hertrich, O. Studien zu den York Plays. Breslau, 1886.

Kamann, P. Die Quellen der York Plays. Ang. X, 1888.

Holthausen, F. The York Plays. Archiv, LXXXV, LXXXVI, 1890–1.

—— Zur Textkritik der York Plays. [In Festgabe für E. Sievers, Halle, 1896.]

—— Zur Erklärung und Textkritik der York Plays. E. Studien, XLI, 1910.

Coblentz, H. Rime-Index to 'Parent Cycle' of York Plays. PMLA. X, 1895.

Koelbing, E. Beiträge zur Erklärung und Text-kritik der York Plays. E. Studien, XX, 1895.

Luick, K. Zur Textkritik der Spiele von York. Ang. XXII, 1899.

Beverley Town Documents. Ed. A. F. Leach, Selden Soc. 1900.

Craigie, W. A. The Gospel of Nicodemus and the York Mystery Plays. [In Furnivall Miscellany, Oxford, 1901.]

Wallis, J. P. R. Crucifixio Christi in the York Cycle. MLR. XII, 1917.

Lyle, M. C. The Original Identity of the York and Towneley Cycles. Minneapolis, 1919.

Moore, J. R. The Tradition of Angelic Singing in English Drama. JEGP. XXII, 1923.

Clark, E. G. The York Plays and the Gospel of Nichodemus. PMLA. XLIII, 1928.

Dustoor, P. E. Textual Notes on the York Old Testament Plays. Ang. LII, 1928.

Frank, Grace. On the Relation between the York and Towneley Plays. PMLA. XLIV, 1929. [See also M. C. Lyle, ibid.]

MacKinnon, E. Notes on the Dramatic Structure of the York Cycle. Stud. Phil. XXVIII, 1931.

Young, Karl. The Records of the York Play of the Pater Noster. Speculum, VII, 1932.

Curtiss, C. G. The York and Towneley Plays on 'The Harrowing of Hell.' Stud. Phil. XXX, 1933.

Mill, A. J. The York Bakers' Play of the Last Supper. MLR. XXX, 1935.

(d) Other Plays and Fragments

(i) Abraham and Isaac (Brome)

Texts. Ed. L. T. Smith, Ang. VII, 1884 (and in A Commonplace Book of the Fifteenth Century, 1886); ed. W. Rye, Norfolk Anti-quarian Misc. vol. III, 1887; Manly; Water-house; Tatlock; Adams.

Criticism.

Hohlfeld, A. R. Two Old English Mystery Plays of Abraham and Isaac. MLN. V, 1890. [Viz. Brome and Chester.]

Harper, C. A. A Comparison between the Brome and Chester Plays of Abraham and Isaac. Cambridge, U.S.A. 1910.

Fort, M. D. The Metres of the Brome and Chester Abraham and Isaac Plays. PMLA. XLI, 1926.

(ii) Abraham and Isaac (Dublin)

Texts. Collier; ed. R. Brotanek, Ang. XXI, 1899; Waterhouse.

(iii) Croxton Play of the Sacrament

Texts. Ed. W. Stokes, Trans. Philolog. Soc. 1861; Manly; Waterhouse; Adams.

(iv) Burial and Resurrection (Bodley)

Texts. Ed. T. Wright and J. O. Halliwell [-Phillipps] (in Reliquiae Antiquae, vol. II, 1843); ed. F. J. Furnivall (in The Digby Plays, 1882 and 1896).

(v) Digby Plays

Complete series. Ed. F. J. Furnivall, New Shakspere Soc. 1882; rptd EETS. Ex. Ser. 1896.

One or more plays. Hawkins; ed. T. Sharp (Ancient Mysteries from the Digby Manuscripts, Abbotsford Club, 1835); Marriott; Manly; Adams.

Criticism.

Schmidt, K. Die Digby-Spiele. Berlin, 1884

(vi) Noah's Ark (Newcastle-upon-Tyne)

Texts. Ed. H. Bourne (in History of Newcastle, 1736); rptd J. Brand (in History of Newcastle, 2 vols. 1789); rptd T. Sharp (in A Dissertation on the Coventry Mysteries, Coventry, 1825); ed. F. Holthausen (in Göteborg's Högskolas Årsskrift, 1897, and separately); ed. R. Brotanek, Ang. XXI, 1899; Waterhouse.

(vii) Adam and Eve (Norwich Grocers' Play)

Texts. Ed. R. Fitch, Norfolk Archaeology, V, 1856 (and separately); Manly; Waterhouse; Adams.

(viii) Cornish Plays

Texts. Ed. D. Gilbert (The Creation of the World, with Noah's Flood, 1827); ed. E. Norris (The Ancient Cornish Drama, 2 vols. Oxford, 1859); ed. W. Stokes (in Beunans Meriasek, The Life of St Meriasek, 1872).

Criticism.

Peter, T. C. The Old Cornish Drama. 1906.

(ix) Stonyhurst Pageants

Text. Ed. C. Brown, Göttingen, 1920.

6. WRITINGS IN LATIN

General Sources and Discussions: Collections of Sources; General Works (including Literary Histories).

Early Writers: Anglo-Norman Period; Reign of Henry II; Thirteenth Century (Franciscans, Dominicans, Other Writers).

Later Writers: Manuals for Preachers; Fourteenth and Fifteenth Centuries (Franciscans, Dominicans, Other Writers).

A. PRINCIPAL COLLECTIONS OF SOURCES

d'Achery, L. Spicilegium sive Collectio veterum aliquot Scriptorum. 13 vols. Paris, 1655–77; 3 vols. Paris, 1723.

Beiträge zur Geschichte der Philosophie des Mittelalters. Texte und Untersuchungen. Ed. C. Baeumker and others, Münster, 1891–. [All works cited as published at Münster belong to this series.]

Brown, E. Fasciculus Rerum expetendarum et fugiendarum. 2 vols. 1690. [Contains works of Woodford, Wyclif, Grosseteste, FitzRalph, etc.]

Dreves, G. M., Blume, C. and Bannister, H. M. Analecta Hymnica Medii Aevi. 55 vols. Leipzig, 1886–1922.

Dreves, G. M. and Blume, C. Ein Jahrtausend lateinischer Hymnendichtung. 2 vols. Leipzig, 1909.

Hauréau, B. Notices et Extraits de quelques Manuscrits latins de la Bibliothèque Nationale. 6 vols. Paris, 1890–3.

Hervieux, L. Les Fabulistes latins. 5 vols. Paris, 1893–9.

Martène, E. and Durand, W. Thesaurus novus Anecdotorum. 5 vols. Paris, 1717.

Notices et Extraits des Manuscrits de la Bibliothèque Nationale (Impériale).

Patrologia Latina. Ed. J. P. Migne, Paris, 1844–.

Rerum Britannicarum Medii Aevi Scriptores (Chronicles and Memorials of Great Britain and Ireland during the Middle Ages). Rolls Ser. 1858–.

Wright, T. Early Mysteries and Other Latin Poems of the Twelfth and Thirteenth Centuries. 1838.

—— The Political Songs of England from the Reign of John to that of Edward II. Camden Soc. 1839.

—— Anglo-Latin Satirical Poets and Epigrammatists of the 12th Century. 2 vols. Rolls Ser. 1872.

B. GENERAL WORKS (INCLUDING LITERARY HISTORIES)

Baeumker, C. Der Platonismus im Mittelalter. [In Studien und Charakteristiken zur Geschichte der Philosophie insbesondere des Mittelalters, Münster, 1927, pp. 139 ff.]

Bale, John. Scriptorum illustrium maioris Brytanniae Summarium. Basle, 1559.

—— Index Britanniae Scriptorum. Ed. R. L. Poole and M. Bateson, Oxford, 1902.

Bateson, M. Medieval England, 1066–1350. 1903.

Baxter, J. H., Johnson, C. and Willard, J. F. An Index of British and Irish Latin Writers, A.D. 400–1520. Archivum Latinitatis Medii Aevi, VII, 1932, pp. 7 ff.

Beddie, J. S. The Ancient Classics in the Mediaeval Libraries. Speculum, V, 1930, pp. 3 ff. [On pp. 17 ff. is a list of the library catalogues A.D. 1050–1250 which have been printed, but are not in T. Gottlieb, Über mittelalterliche Bibliotheken, Leipzig, 1890.]

Cambridge History of English Literature. Vol. I, 1907.

Clerval, A. Les Écoles de Chartres au Moyen Âge. Chartres, 1895.

Cloetta, W. Beiträge zur Litteraturgeschichte des Mittelalters und der Renaissance. 2 vols. Halle, 1890–2.

Coulton, G. G. Five Centuries of Religion. 3 vols. Cambridge, 1923–.

Crump, C. G., Jacob, E. F. *et al.* The Legacy of the Middle Ages. Oxford, 1926.

Davis, H. W. C. *et al.* Mediaeval England. Oxford, 1929. [A new edition, largely rewritten, of F. P. Barnard's Companion to English History (Middle Ages).]

Denholm-Young, N. The Cursus in England. [Oxford Essays in Medieval History presented to H. E. Salter, Oxford, 1934, pp. 68 ff.]

Denifle, H. Quellen zur Gelehrtengeschichte des Predigerordens im 13. und 14. Jahrhundert. Archiv für Litteratur- und Kirchengeschichte des Mittelalters, II, 1886, pp. 165 ff.

—— Quellen zur Gelehrtengeschichte des Carmelitenordens im 13. und 14. Jahrhundert. Archiv für Literatur- und Kirchengeschichte des Mittelalters, V, 1889, pp. 365 ff.

Dictionnaire de la Bible. Vol. II, Paris, 1899. ['Dominicains sur les Saintes Écritures.']

Douais, C. Essai sur l'Organisation des Études dans l'Ordre des Frères Prêcheurs. Paris, 1884.

Dugdale, W. Monasticon Anglicanum. 3 vols. 1655–73; ed. J. Caley, H. Ellis and B. Bandinel, 6 vols. in 8, 1817–30; rptd 1846.

Duhem, P. Le Système du Monde; Histoire des Doctrines cosmologiques de Platon à Copernic. 5 vols. Paris, 1913–7.

von Eicken, H. Geschichte und System der mittelalterlichen Weltanschauung. Stuttgart, 1887.

Felder, H. Geschichte der wissenschaftlichen Studien im Franziskanerorden bis um die Mitte des 13. Jahrhunderts. Freiburg, 1904; tr. French, Paris, 1908.

Formoy, B. E. R. The Dominican Order in England before the Reformation. 1925.

Gilson, É. La Philosophie au Moyen Âge. 2 vols. Paris, 1922.

Glunz, H. H. History of the Vulgate in England from Alcuin to Roger Bacon. Cambridge, 1933. [Pp. 341 ff. give Herbert of Bosham's (d. c. 1186) Prefaces to his revision of the Great Gloss of Peter Lombard. Herbert's works are in Migne, Patrologia Latina, vol. cxc.]

Grabmann, M. Die Geschichte der scholastischen Methode. 2 vols. Freiburg, 1909–11.

Gröber, G. Grundriss der romanischen Philologie. Strasburg, 1888–1902. [Vol. ii, pt i, 1893, Übersicht über die lateinische Literatur von dem VI. Jahrhundert bis 1350.]

Gross, C. Sources and Literature of English History from the Earliest Times to about 1485. Cambridge, U.S.A. 1892, 1915 (rev. edn).

Grunwald, G. Die Geschichte des Gottesbeweise im Mittelalter. Münster, 1907.

Gumbley, W. Provincial Priors and Vicars of the English Dominicans, 1221–1916. EHR. xxxiii, 1918, pp. 243 ff. [Also A. G. Little, ibid. pp. 496 f.]

Haskins, C. H. Studies in Mediaeval Culture. Oxford, 1929.

Histoire littéraire de la France. Paris, 1733–.

Jacob, E. F. Some Aspects of Classical Influence in Medieval England. Vorträge der Bibliothek Warburg, ix, Hamburg, 1932.

Jarrett, B. The English Dominicans. 1921.

Lehmann, P. Bücherliebe und Bücherpflege bei den Karthäusern. [Miscellanea Ehrle, vol. v, Rome, 1924, pp. 364 ff.]

Leyser, P. Historia Poetarum et Poematum medii Aevi. Halle, 1721.

Little, A. G. The Grey Friars in Oxford. Oxford, 1892.

—— Initia Operum quae Saeculis XIII, XIV, XV attribuuntur. Manchester, 1904.

—— Studies in English Franciscan History. Manchester, 1917.

Maître, L. Les Écoles épiscopales et monastiques en Occident avant les Universités (768–1180). Paris, 1886, 1924 (rev. edn).

Mandonnet, P. 'Order of Preachers.' [In Catholic Encyclopedia, 15 vols. New York, 1907–22.]

Manitius, M. Geschichte der lateinischen Literatur des Mittelalters. 3 vols. Munich, 1911–31.

Meyer-Steineg, T. and Sudhoff, K. Geschichte der Medizin. Jena, 1922 (2nd edn).

Moore, N. History of the Study of Medicine in the British Isles. Oxford, 1908.

Morley, H. English Writers. 1893 (3rd edn). [Vols. iii and iv.]

Neuburger, M. and Pagel, J. Handbuch der Geschichte der Medizin. Vol. i, Jena, 1902.

Pits, J. De illustribus Angliae Scriptoribus. Paris, 1619.

Polheim, K. Die lateinische Reimprosa. Leipzig, 1925.

Pollock, F. and Maitland, F. W. The History of English Law before Edward I. 2 vols. Cambridge, 1898 (2nd edn).

Poole, R. L. Illustrations of the History of Medieval Thought and Learning. 1920 (2nd edn).

Potthast, A. Bibliotheca Historica Medii Aevi. 2 vols. Berlin, 1896 (2nd edn).

Power, E. E. Medieval English Nunneries, c. 1250–1535. Cambridge, 1922.

Powicke, F. M. The Medieval Books of Merton College. Oxford, 1931.

Prantl, K. Geschichte der Logik im Abendlande. Leipzig, 1885 (2nd edn). [Vol. ii.]

Quétif, J. and Échard, J. Scriptores Ordinis Praedicatorum. 2 vols. Paris, 1719–21. [New edn in preparation.]

Raby, F. J. E. A History of Christian-Latin Poetry. Oxford, 1927.

—— A History of Secular Latin Poetry in the Middle Ages. 2 vols. Oxford, 1934.

Sandys, Sir J. E. A History of Classical Scholarship from the Sixth Century B.C. to the End of the Middle Ages. 3 vols. Cambridge, 1903–8.

Singer, C. J. From Magic to Science. 1928.

Singer, D. W. Catalogue of Alchemical MSS in Great Britain and Ireland dating from before the XVIth Century. 2 vols. Union Académique Internationale, Brussels, 1928–31.

Tanner, T. Bibliotheca Britannico-Hibernica: sive de Scriptoribus qui in Anglia, Scotia et Hibernia ad Seculi XVII Initium floruerunt. 1748.

Taylor, H. O. The Mediaeval Mind. 2 vols. 1911, 1919 (3rd edn).

Thompson, E. M. The Carthusian Order in England. 1930.

Thorndike, L. History of Magic and Experimental Science. New York, 1923.

Thurot, C. Notices et Extraits de divers MSS latins pour servir à l'Histoire des Doctrines grammaticales au Moyen Âge. [Notices et Extraits des MSS de la Bibliothèque Impériale (Nationale), vol. xxii, 1868, pp. 1 ff.]

Trail, H. D. Social England. Vol. i, 1893.

Ueberweg, F. Grundriss der Geschichte der Philosophie. Vol. ii, Berlin, 1928. [Die patristische und scholastische Philosophie, ed. B. Geyer. Contains valuable bibliographies; referred to below as Ueberweg-Geyer.]

Waddell, H. The Wandering Scholars. 1927; 1932 (rev. edn).

Wadding, L. Scriptores Ordinis Minorum. Rome, 1650; Rome, 1906. [See also J. H. Sbaralea, Supplementum ad Scriptores trium ordinum S. Francisci a Waddingo aliisve descriptos, Rome, 1806; 1908, 1921–.]

—— Annales Minorum. Vols. i–xvi, Rome, 1731–6 (2nd edn).

Walsh, J. J. Medieval Medicine. 1920.

Wilmart, A. Auteurs spirituels et Textes dévots du Moyen Âge latin. Paris, 1932. [Contains articles by Wilmart mentioned below.]

Wright, T. Biographia Britannica Literaria. Vol. ii, 1846.

de Wulf, M. Histoire de la Philosophie Médiévale. 2 vols. Louvain, 1924–5 (5th edn); tr. Eng. 2 vols. 1926. [First pbd 1900.]

—— Philosophy and Civilisation in the Middle Ages. 1922.

Young, K. The Drama of the Medieval Church. 2 vols. Oxford, 1933.

C. THE ANGLO-NORMAN PERIOD

Lanfranc (d. 1089). Opera. Ed. J. A. Giles, 2 vols, Oxford, 1844 (rptd in Migne, Patrologia Latina, vol. cl). [On the doubtful and spurious writings, see Macdonald, Lanfranc, pp. 291 ff.]

Böhmer, H. Die Falschungen des Erzbischofs Lanfranc von Canterbury. Studien zur Geschichte der Theologie und Kirche, viii, 1902.

Tammasia, N. Lanfranco Arcivescovo di Canterbury e la Scuola Pavese. [Mélanges Fitting, vol. ii, Montpellier, 1908, pp. 189 ff.]

Macdonald, A. J. Lanfranc, a Study of his Life, Work and Writing. Oxford, 1926.

—— Eadmer and the Canterbury Privileges. Journ. Theological Stud. xxxii, 1930, pp. 39 ff.

—— Lanfranc of Canterbury. Church Quarterly Rev. cxx, 1935, pp. 241 ff.

Hora, E. Zur Ehrenrettung Lanfranks des Erzbischofs von Canterbury. Theologische Quartalschrift, iii, 1930, pp. 288 ff.

Thompson, S. H. Bishop Gundulf of Rochester and the Vulgate. Speculum, vi, 1931, pp. 468 ff. [Holds that Lanfranc is the author of the Vulgate corrections attrib. to Gundulf.]

Goscelin (d. c. 1099; monk of Canterbury, though born in France). [Biography of St Augustine of Canterbury.] Migne, Patrologia Latina, vol. clv, cols. 14 ff. [For his other biographies see DNB. and Histoire littéraire de la France, vol. viii, pp. 662 ff.]

—— Confortatorius Liber ad Evam inclusam. BM. MS Sloane 3103. [This is the Eve to whom Hilary (see below, p. 284) addressed one of his poems.]

Wilmart, A. Ève et Goscelin. i. Revue Bénédictine, xlvi, 1934, pp. 414 ff.

Godfrey of Cambrai (and Winchester) (d. 1107). Epigrammata. Ed. T. Wright (Anglo-Latin Satirical Poets, vol. ii, pp. 103 ff.).

Anselm (d. 1109). Opera. Migne, Patrologia Latina, vols. clviii–clix. [For other complete and partial edns, see A. Levasti, Sant' Anselmo, referred to below.]

—— Cur Deus homo? Ed. F. Schmitt, Bonn, 1928.

—— Monologion. Ed. F. Schmitt, Bonn, 1929.

—— Proslogion. Ed. F. Schmitt, Bonn, 1931.

—— Epistola de Incarnatione Verbi. Ed. F. Schmitt, Bonn, 1931. [Also A. Wilmart, Le premier ouvrage de S. Anselme contre le trithéisme de Roscelin. Recherches de théologie ancienne et médiévale, iii, 1931, pp. 20 ff.]

—— Fides quaerens intellectum. Ed. A. Koyré, Paris, 1932. [Includes texts and trns of Proslogion, Liber pro insipiente, Liber apologeticus.]

Hasse, F. R. Anselm von Canterbury. Leipzig, 1843.

Church, R. W. Life of St. Anselm. 1870.

Rule, M. Life and Times of St Anselm. 1883.

Rigg, J. M. St Anselm of Canterbury. 1896.

Baeumker, F. Die Lehre Anselms von Canterbury über den Willen und seine Wahlfreiheit. Münster, 1912.

Levasti, A. Sant' Anselmo: Vita e Pensiero. Bari, 1929. [With bibliography.]

—— Skotus Erigena und der hl. Anselm. Philosophisches Jahrbuch, 1929, pp. 506 ff.

Clayton, J. Saint Anselm. A Critical Biography. Milwaukee, 1933.

Lottin, O. La Théorie du libre Arbitre depuis Saint Anselme jusqu'à Saint Thomas d'Aquin. Louvain, 1929.

Betzendörfer, W. Glauben und Wissen bei Anselm von Canterbury. Zeitschrift für Kirchengeschichte, XLVIII, 1929, pp. 854 ff.

Gieselmann, J. Der Abendmahlsbrief des Anselms von Canterbury, ein Werk des Anselm von Laon. Theologische Quartalschrift, III, 1930, pp. 320 ff.

Bliemetzrieden, F. Encore la Lettre d'Anselme de Cantorbéry sur la Cène. Recherches de Théologie ancienne et médiévale, III, 1981, pp. 423 ff. [Criticism of Gieselmann.]

Wilmart, A. La Tradition des Lettres de S. Anselme. Lettres inédites de S. Anselme et de ses Correspondants. Revue Bénédictine, XLIII, 1931, pp. 38 ff.

—— Les Homélies attribués à S. Anselme. Archives d'Histoire doctrinale et littéraire du Moyen-Âge, II, 1927, pp. 1 ff.

Schmitt, F. Eine dreifache Gestalt der 'Epistola de sacrificio azimi et fermentati' des hl. Anselm. Revue Bénédictine, XLVII, 1935, pp. 331 ff.

Van der Plaas, G. Des hl. Anselm 'Cur Deus Homo' auf dem Boden der jüdischchristlichen Polemik des Mittelalters. Divus Thomas, VII, 1929, pp. 446 ff., VIII, 1930, pp. 18 ff.

Druwé, E. La première Redaction du 'Cur Deus Homo' de S. Anselme. Recherches de Science religieuse, XX, 1930, pp. 162 ff. [See also Druwé's Libri sancti Anselmi 'Cur Deus homo' prima Forma inedita, Rome, 1934.]

Rivière, J. Un premier Jet du 'Cur Deus Homo'? Revue des Sciences religieuses, XIV, 1934, pp. 329 ff. [Opposes Druwé.]

Schmitt, F. Zur Entstehungsgeschichte von Anselms 'Cur Deus Homo.' Theologische Revue, XXXIV, 1935, pp. 217 ff.

Dyroff, A. Der ontologische Gottesbeweis des hl. Anselmus in der Scholastik. [Probleme der Gotteserkenntnis, Münster, 1928, pp. 79 ff.]

Abbagnano, N. L'Argomento ontologico di Anselmo di Aosta. Gubbia, 1929.

Beccari, A. Il 'Monologio' di Sant' Anselmo. Convivium, 1929, pp. 431 ff.

Antweiler, A. Anselmus von Canterbury, Monologion und Proslogion. Scholastik, VIII, 1933, pp. 551 ff.

Stolz, A. Zur Theologie Anselms im Proslogion. Catholica, II, 1933, pp. 1 ff.

—— 'Vere esse' im Proslogion des hl. Anselm. Scholastik, IX, 1934, pp. 400 ff.

Stolz, A. Das Proslogion des hl. Anselm. Revue Bénédictine, XLVII, 1935, pp. 331 ff.

Cappuyns, M., L'Argument de Saint Anselme. Recherches de Théologie ancienne et médiévale, VI, 1934, pp. 313 ff.

Gilson, E. Sens et Nature de l'Argument de Saint Anselme. Archives d'Histoire doctrinale et littéraire du Moyen Âge, IX, 1934, pp. 5 ff.

Wilmart, A. Le Recueil des Prières de S. Anselme. [Preface to D. A. Castel, Méditations et Prières de S. Anselme, Maredsous, 1923.]

—— Les Éditions anciennes et modernes des Prières de S. Anselme. Académie des Inscriptions et Belles-Lettres, 1923, pp. 152 ff.

—— Une Prière inédite attribuée à S. Anselme. Revue Bénédictine, XXXV, 1923, pp. 143 ff.

—— La Prière à Notre-Dame et à S. Jean publiée sous le Nom de S. Anselme. La Vie Spirituelle, Supplément, XVIII, 1923, pp. 165 ff.

—— La Tradition des Prières de S. Anselme. Revue Bénédictine, XXXVI, 1924, pp. 52 ff.

—— Les propres Corrections de S. Anselme dans sa grande Prière à la Vierge Marie. Recherches de Théologie ancienne et médiévale, II, 1930, pp. 189 ff.

—— Une Prière au Saint Patron attribuée à S. Anselme. [Auteurs spirituels et Textes dévots du Moyen Âge latin, Paris, 1932, pp. 147 ff.]

—— Le Recueil des Prières adressé par S. Anselme à la Comtesse Mathilde. Ibid. pp. 162 ff.

—— Les Méditations réunies sous le Nom de S. Anselme. Ibid. pp. 173 ff.

—— Prières à sainte Anne, à S. Michel, à S. Martin, censées de S. Anselme. Ibid. pp. 202 ff.

Reginald of Canterbury (d. c. 1109). [Life of St Malchus.] BM. Cott. MS Vesp. E III, and Bodl. MS. Laud. Miscell. 40. [See also Analecta Hymnica, vol. L, pp. 370 ff., for extracts consisting of prayers, etc., mainly in leonine and other rhymed hexameters.]

—— [Other poems.] Ed. T. Wright (Anglo-Latin Satirical Poets, vol. II, pp. 259 ff.).

Liebermann, F. Reginald von Canterbury. Neues Archiv, XIII, 1888, pp. 519 ff.

Gilbert Crispin (d. 1117). [Letters, etc.] Ed. J. A. Robinson (Gilbert Crispin, Abbot of Westminster, Cambridge, 1911).

—— Disputatio Judaei cum Christiano. Migne Patrologia Latina, vol. CLIX.

Holtzmann, W. Zur Geschichte des Investiturstreites. 1. Der Traktat de Simoniacis des Abtes Gilbert von Westminster. Neues Archiv, L, 1933, pp. 246 ff.

Turchill Compotista (*fl.* 1115). Reguncula super abacum. Ed. E. Norducci, Bollettino della Bibliografia e della Storia delle Scienze matematiche e fisiche, xv, 1882. [See R. L. Poole, The Exchequer in the Twelfth Century, Oxford, 1912, pp. 47 ff.]

Herbert de Losinga (d. 1119; bishop of Norwich). [Letters and sermons.] Ed. E. M. Goulburn and H. Symonds (The Life, Letters and Sermons of Bishop Herbert de Losinga, 2 vols. 1878). [Text and trn of sermons, trn only of letters.]
—— Epistolae. Ed. R. Anstruther, Caxton Soc. 1846.

Adelard of Bath (*fl.* 1120). Tractatus de eodem et universo. Ed. H. Willner, Münster, 1903.
—— Regulae abaci. Ed. B. Boncompagni, Bollettino della Bibliografia e della Storia delle Scienze matematiche e fisiche, xiv, 1881, pp. 1 ff.
—— Ezich Elkauresmi per Athelardum Bathoniensem ex arabico sumptus. Ed. (portions) A. A. Björnbo (Festskrift til H. G. Zeuthen, Copenhagen, 1909, pp. 1 ff.); ed. (complete) H. Suter, Die astronomischen Tafeln des Muhammed ibn Mūsā al-Khwārizmī in der Bearbeitung des Maslama ibn Ahmed al-Madjrītī und der lateinischen Uebersetzung des Athelhard von Bath, Kg. Danske Videnskabernes Selskabs Skrifter, vii, pt iii, 1914.
—— Liber ysagogarum Alchorismi in artem astronomicam a magistro Adelardo compositus, Bks 1–3. [In M. Curtze, Abhandlungen zur Geschichte der Mathematik, vol. viii, Leipzig, 1895, pp. 1 ff.]
—— [Euclid's Elements (translated from the Arabic).] Bodl. MS Digby 174.
—— Quaestiones naturales. Louvain, [1480? 1484? 1490?]; ed. M. Müller, Münster, 1934.
—— De cura accipitrum. Vienna (National Bibliothek) MS 2504; Clare College Cambridge MS 15 (incomplete). [See C. H. Haskins, Some Early Treatises on Falconry, in Studies in the History of Mediaeval Science, Cambridge, U.S.A. 1924, 1927, pp. 346 ff.]
—— De opere astrolapsus. Cambridge, Fitzwilliam Museum McClean MS 165; BM. Arundel MS 377 (incomplete).
—— Ysagoga minor Iapharis matematici in astronomiam per Adhelardum Bathoniensem ex arabico sumpta. Bodl. MS Digby 68; BM. Sloane MS 2030.

Adelard of Bath. Liber prestigiorum Thebidis (Elbidis) secundum Ptolomeum et Hermetem per Adhelardum Bathoniensem translatus. Lyons MS 328. ['A treatise on astrological images and horoscopes by Thabit ben Korra,' Haskins, p. 30.]
—— Mappe clavicula. Archaeologia, xxxii, 1847, pp. 183 ff. [Deals 'with the preparation of pigments and other chemical products,' Haskins, p. 30.]

Haskins, C. H. Adelard of Bath. EHR. xxvi, 1911, pp. 491 ff.
—— Adelard of Bath and Henry Plantagenet. EHR. xxviii, 1913, pp. 515 ff.
—— Adelard of Bath. [In Studies in the History of Mediaeval Science, Cambridge, U.S.A. 1924, 1927, pp. 20 ff. The list of Adelard's works given above is taken from this article, which also gives information as to MSS.]
Poole, R. L. The Exchequer in the Twelfth Century. Oxford, 1912, pp. 51 ff.
Thorndike, L. Adelard of Bath and the Continuity of Universal Nature. Nature, xciv, 1915, pp. 616 f.
Bliemetzrieder, F. Adelhard von Bath. Münster, 1935.

Godwin (*fl.* 1120; precentor of Sarum). Meditationes Godwini cantoris Salesberie. Bodl. MS Digby 96.

Eadmer (d. *c.* 1124; monk of Canterbury). Edmeri Cantuariensis Cantoris nova opuscula de sanctorum veneratione et obsecratione. Ed. A. Wilmart, Revue des Sciences religieuses, xv, 1935, pp. 184 ff., 354 ff. [For his historical works, see DNB.]

Hilary (*fl.* 1125). Hilarii Versus et Ludi. Ed. (from Paris MS) J. B. Fuller, New York, 1929. [But reference must still be made to Hilarii Versus et Ludi, ed. J.-J. Champollion-Figeac, Paris, 1838. Emendations of text in E. Herkenrath, Textkritisches zur Apocalypse des Golias, zu Hilarius und zu Walter von Chatillon, Studien zur lateinischen Dichtung des Mittelalters (Ehrengabe für Karl Strecker), ed. W. Stach and H. Walther, Dresden, 1931.]

Gilbert (d. 1134; called the 'Universal,' Bishop of London).

Smalley, B. Gilbertus Universalis, Bishop of London (1128–34), and the Problem of the 'Glossa Ordinaria.' Recherches de Théologie ancienne et médiévale, vii, 1935, pp. 235 ff., viii, 1936, pp. 24 ff.

Walcher of Malvern (d. 1135), Bodl. MS Auct. F . 1 . 9. [Containing 'a set of lunar tables, with explanations, which comprise a cycle of 76 years ending in 1112,' and another treatise in which instead of using 'the clumsy methods of Roman fractions,' he uses 'the degrees, minutes and seconds, and the more exact observations which he has learned, evidently in England, from Petrus Anfusi,' C. H. Haskins, Studies in the History of Mediaeval Science, Cambridge, U.S.A. 1924, 1927, pp. 114–5.]

Osbert of Clare, (d. c. 1136; prior of Westminster). Letters. Ed. E. W. Williamson, Oxford, 1929.

> Robinson, J. A. Westminster in the Twelfth Century: Osbert of Clare. Church Quart. Rev. LXVIII, 1909, pp. 336 ff.
>
> Bloch, M. La Vie de S. Édouard le Confesseur par Osbert de Clare. Analecta Bollandiana, XLI, 1923, pp. 1 ff.
>
> Wilmart, A. Les Compositions d'Osbert de Clare, en honneur de Sainte-Anne. Annales de Bretagne, XXXVII, 1926, pp. 1 ff.
>
> Baugh, A. C. Osbert of Clare, the Sarum Breviary and the Middle English Saint Anne. Speculum, VII, 1932, pp. 106 ff.

Robert of Chester (fl. 1140). [Translation of the Koran.] Basle, 1543. [See also Migne, Patrologia Latina, vol. CLXXXIX, cols. 649 ff.]

—— [Translation of the Iudicia of al-Kindi, and various other translations from the Arabic, references to which are given in C. H. Haskins, Studies in the History of Mediaeval Science, Cambridge, U.S.A. 1924, 1927, pp. 120 ff. Haskins identifies Robert of Chester with the Robert who studied in Spain and was Archdeacon of Pamplona; p. 120.]

Robert Pullen (Pullus) (d. c. 1147; cardinal). Sententiarum theologicarum libri VIII. Paris, 1655. [See Migne, Patrologia Latina, vol. CLXXXVI.]

> Poole, R. L. The Early Lives of Robert Pullen and Nicholas Breakspear. [In Essays in Mediaeval History presented to T. F. Tout, Manchester, 1925.]

Geoffrey of Monmouth (d. c. 1152). Historia Regum Britanniae. Ed. J. A. Giles, 1844; ed. San-Marte (A. Schulz), Halle, 1854; ed. A. Griscom, 1929; ed. E. Faral (in La Légende Arthurienne, vol. III, pt. 1, Paris, 1929).

> Evans, S. Translation of Geoffrey of Monmouth's History. 1903.
>
> Griscom, A. The Date of Composition of Geoffrey of Monmouth's Historia. Speculum, I, 1926, pp. 129 ff.
>
> Nitze, W. A. Geoffrey of Monmouth's King Arthur. Speculum, II, 1927, pp. 317 ff.
>
> Loomis, R. S. .Geoffrey of Monmouth and Arthurian Origins. Speculum, III, 1928, pp. 16 ff.
>
> Parry, J. J. The Chronology of Geoffrey of Monmouth's Historia, bks I and II. Speculum, IV, 1929, pp. 316 ff.
>
> —— The Welsh Texts of Geoffrey of Monmouth's Historia. Speculum, V, 1930, pp. 424 ff.
>
> —— A Variant Version of Geoffrey of Monmouth's Historia. [A Miscellany of Studies in Romance Languages and Literatures presented to Leon E. Kastner, Cambridge, 1932, pp. 364 ff.]
>
> —— Geoffrey of Monmouth and the Date of Regnum Scotorum. Speculum, IX, 1934, pp. 135 ff.
>
> Loomis, L. H. Geoffrey of Monmouth and Stonehenge. PMLA. XLV, 1930.
>
> Tatlock, J. S. P. Certain Contemporaneous Matters in Geoffrey of Monmouth. Speculum, VI, 1931, pp. 206 ff.
>
> Brugger, E. Zu Galfrid von Monmouth's Historia Regum Britanniae. Zeitschrift für französische Sprache und Literatur, LVII, 1933.
>
> Hammer, J. Note on a MS. of Geoffrey of Monmouth's Historia Regum Britanniae. PQ. XII, 1933, pp. 225 ff.

—— Vita Merlini [in verse]. Ed. F. Michel and T. Wright, Paris, 1837 (and in A. F. Gförer, Prophetae veteres pseudepigraphi, Stuttgart, 1840); ed. J. J. Parry, Illinois University Stud. x, 1925, pp. 251 ff.; ed. E. Faral (in La Légende Arthurienne, vol. III, pt I, Paris, 1929, pp. 305 ff.).

> Lot, F. Études sur Merlin. Annales de Bretagne, XV, 1900, pp. 325 ff., 505 ff.
>
> Faral, E. La Légende Arthurienne. Vol. II, pt I, Paris, 1929, pp. 341 ff.
>
> Parry, J. J. The Triple Death in the Vita Merlini. Speculum, V, 1930, pp. 216 f.
>
> Hammer, J. A Commentary on the Prophetia Merlini. Speculum, x, 1935, pp. 3 ff.

Laurence of Durham (d. 1154; prior). Hypognosticon sive memoriales veteris et novi Testamenti. [Extracts in J. Raine, Dialogi Laurentii Dunelmensis, Surtees Soc. 1880, pp. 62 ff.; also in T. Wright, Biographia Britannica Literaria, Anglo-Norman Period, pp. 161 ff.]

—— Dialogorum libri quattuor. Ed. J. Raine, ut sup. [This volume also contains a number of poems of English and Scottish origin of the same period.]

—— Consolatio pro morte amici. BM. MS Cotton Vesp. D. XI. [Extract in Wright, ut sup. p. 164.]

—— Vita sanctae Brigidae. Ed. Acta Sanctorum, Feb. 1, pp. 172 ff.

[On Laurence generally and for MSS see Manitius, Geschichte der lateinischen Literatur des Mittelalters, vol. III, pp. 816 ff., and Raby, Secular Latin Poetry, vol. I, pp. 106 ff.]

Osbern of Gloucester (fl. 1150). Derivationes [grammatical and lexicographical]. Ed. A. Mai (Classici Auctores, vol. VIII, Rome, 1835). [For bibliography, see Manitius, Geschichte der lateinischen Literatur des Mittelalters, vol. III, p. 190.]

Master Walter (of Wimborne; 12th cent.). Poema de Palpone et Assentatore. Ed. T. Wright (Latin Poems attributed to Walter Mapes, 1841, pp. 106 ff.).

D. THE REIGN OF HENRY II
(1154–1189)

(1) GENERAL WORKS

de Ghellinck, J. Le Mouvement théologique du XII⁰ Siècle. Paris, 1914.

Graham, Rose. The Intellectual Influence of English Monasteries between the Tenth and Twelfth Centuries. Trans. Royal Hist. Soc., N.S., XVII, 1903, pp. 22 ff.

Haskins, C. H. Studies in the History of Mediaeval Science. Cambridge, U.S.A. 1924, 1927.

—— The Renaissance of the Twelfth Century. Cambridge, U.S.A. 1927.

—— Some Twelfth Century Writers on Astronomy. [In Studies in the History of Mediaeval Science, pp. 82 ff. References to English writers, such as Michael of Dover (p. 86), Roger of Hereford (p. 87).]

—— A List of Text-Books from the Close of the Twelfth Century. Harvard Stud. XX, 1909, pp. 75 ff. [Revised by Haskins in Studies in the History of Mediaeval Science, pp. 356 ff.]

—— Henry II as a Patron of Literature. [In Essays in Medieval History presented to T. F. Tout, Manchester, 1925.]

—— The Greek Element in the Renaissance of the Twelfth Century. American Hist. Rev. XXV, 1920, pp. 603 ff. [Revised by Haskins in Studies in the History of Mediaeval Science, pp. 140 ff.]

Hunt. R. W. English Learning in the Late 12th Century. Trans. Royal Hist. Soc. 1936, pp. 19 ff.

Stubbs, W. Literature and Learning at the Court of Henry II. [Nos. VI and VII in Seventeen Lectures, Oxford, 1886.]

(2) SCHOLARS AND MEN OF LETTERS

Henry of Huntingdon (d. 1155). Epigrammata. Ed. T. Wright (Anglo-Latin Satirical Poets, vol. II, pp. 163 ff.).

William of Conches (fl. 1154). Philosophia.

Basle, 1531. [Printed in Migne, Patrologia Latina, vol. CLXXXII; for MSS see Thorndike, Magic and Science, vol. II, p. 64.]

—— Dramaticus [or Dragmaticon; dialogue between William and Geoffrey Plantagenet, father of Henry II]. Strasburg, 1567. [For MSS see Thorndike, Magic and Science, vol. II, p. 65. This is a revised version of the Philosophia.]

—— Moralium dogma philosophorum. Ed. Migne, Patrologia Latina, vol. CLXXI, cols. 1007 ff.; ed. J. Holmberg (Das Moralium dogma philosophorum, lateinisch, altfranzösisch und mittelniederfränkisch, Upsala, 1929). [See B. Hauréau, Notices et Extraits, vol. XXXIII, pt i, pp. 257 ff.; J. R. Williams, The Authorship of the Moralium dogma philosophorum, Speculum, VI, 1931, pp. 392 ff.]

Charma, A. Guillaume de Conches. Paris, 1857.

Hauréau, B. Guillaume de Conches. [Singularités historiques et littéraires, Paris, 1894, pp. 231 ff.]

Poole, R. L. Medieval Thought and Learning. 1920. [Pp. 298 ff.]

Wilmart, A. Préface de Guillaume de Conches pour la dernière Part de son Dialogue. Analecta Reginensia, Vatican 1932, pp. 263 ff.

Grabmann, M. Handschriftliche Forschungen und Mitteilungen zum Schriften des Wilhelm von Conches. Bayer. Akad der Wissenschaften, 1935.

Ottaviano, C. Un Brano inedito della 'Philosophia' di Guglielmo di Conches Naples, 1935.

[See also Ueberweg-Geyer, p. 704.]

Aelred, Abbot of Rievaulx (d. 1166). Opera Ed. Migne, Patrologia Latina, vol. CXLV.

—— Sermon on the Saints of Hexham. Ed J. Raine (The Priory of Hexham, vol. I Surtees Soc. 1864, pp. 173 ff.)

—— On the Battle of the Standard. Ed R. Howlett (Chronicles of Stephen, vol. III Rolls Ser. pp. 179 ff.).

Powicke, F. M. Ailred of Rievaulx and his Biographer Walter Daniel. John Rylands Lib. Bulletin, VI, 1921, pp. 310 ff. 452 ff.

Wilmart, A. L'Oraison pastorale de l'Abbé Aelred. Revue Bénédictine XXXVII, 1925, pp. 262 ff.

—— L'Instigateur du Speculum Caritati d'Aelred. Revue d'Ascétique et de Mystique, XIV, 1933, pp. 369 ff., 429 [With text of Aelred's Praefatio and Clausula.]

Harvey, T. E. St Aelred of Rievaulx 1932.

Robert of Melun (d. 1167; bishop of Hereford). [Two books of Sentences.] [Extracts in Grabmann, Die Geschichte der scholastischen Methode, vol. II, pp. 323 ff.]
—— Œuvres: vol. I. Quaestiones de Divina Pagina. Ed. R. M. Martin (Spicilegium sacrum Lovaniense, Louvain, 1932).
Martin, R. M. La Necessité de croire le Mystère de la très sainte Trinité selon Robert de Melun. Revue Thomiste, XXI, 1913, pp. 572 ff.
—— Les Idées de Robert de Melun sur le Péché originel. Revue des Sciences philosophiques et théologiques, VII, 1913, pp. 700 ff., VIII, 1914, pp. 439 ff., IX, 1920, pp. 103 ff., XI, 1922, pp. 390 ff.
—— L'Œuvre théologique de Robert de Melun. Revue d'Histoire ecclésiastique, XVI, 1920, pp. 456 ff.
—— Pro Petro Abaelardo. Un Plaidoyer de Robert de Melun contre Saint Bernard. Revue des Sciences philosophiques et théologiques, XII, 1923, pp. 308 ff.
—— Un Texte intéressant de Robert de Melun. Revue d'Histoire ecclésiastique, XXVIII, 1932, pp. 313 ff.
Anders, F. Die Handschriften der Summa Trinitatis des Robert von Melun. Der Katholik, XCIV, 1914, pp. 267 ff.
—— Die Christologie des Robert von Melun. Forschungen zur christlichen Litteratur- und Dogmengeschichte, XV, 1927, pp. 5 ff.
Pelster, F. Literaturgeschichtliche Beiträge zu Robert von Melun. Zeitschrift für katholische Theologie, LII, 1929, pp. 564 ff.
Bliemetzrieder, F. Robert von Melun und die Schule Anselms von Laon. Zeitschrift für Kirchengeschichte, LIII, 1934, pp. 117 ff.

'Surgens Manerius summo diluculo' (before 1168; anonymous poem). Ed. W. Wattenbach, Anzeiger für Kunde der deutschen Vorzeit, 1875, p. 312; ed. B. Hauréau (Notice sur un Manuscrit de la Reine Christine à la Bibliothèque du Vatican, Notices et Extraits, vol. XXIX, pt ii, p. 325).
Brinkmann, H. Manerius. ZDA., NS., XLVIII, 1923, pp. 194 ff. [With text.]
Lehmann, P. Manerius. ZDA., NS., XLIX, 1924, pp. 237 ff.
Raby, F. J. E. Surgens Manerius summo diluculo. Speculum, VIII, 1933, pp. 204 ff. [With text.]
—— The 'Manerius'-Poem and the Legend of the Swan Children. Speculum, X, 1935, pp. 68 ff.

Thomas Becket (d. 1170). Hymnus de VII gaudiis caelestibus b. Mariae. Analecta Hymnica, vol. XXXI, p. 198. [The satire Ecce sonat in aperto has been ascribed to Becket, but unnecessarily; see A. Hilka and O. Schumann, Carmina Burana, vol. II, pt i, Heidelberg, 1930, p. 17 (text in vol. I, pt i, p. 14).]

Maurice of Kirkham (fl. 1170). MSS. Lincoln College, Oxford, Coll. Lat. 27 and Oxford Bodl. Hatton 92 (Tracts against the Salomites). Extracts in M. R. James, The Salomites, Journ. Theological Stud. XXXV, 1934, pp. 287 ff.

Richard of St Victor (d. c. 1173; canon of St Victor, Paris. According to Alberic of Trois-Fontaines (c. 1241), he was an Englishman, but the tradition of the Abbey makes him a Scot.) Opera. Ed. Migne, Patrologia Latina, vol. CXCVI.
Hauréau, B. Notice sur le Numéro 2590 des MSS. latins de la Bibliothèque Nationale. [Notices et Extraits des MSS. de la Bibliothèque Nationale, XXXIII, pt i, 1890, pp. 235 ff.]
Buonamici, G. Riccardo di S. Vittore. Alatri, 1898.
Grabmann, M. Die Geschichte der scholastischen Methode. Vol. II, Freiburg, 1911, pp. 310 ff.
Ebner, J. Die Erkenntnisslehre Richards von St Victor. Münster, 1917.
Andres, F. Die Stufen der Contemplatio in Bonaventuras Itinerarium mentis in Deum und im Beniamin maior des Richard von St Victor. Franziskanische Studien, VIII, 1921, pp. 189 ff.
Morin, G. Le commentaire sur Nahum du Pseudo-Julien, unc Œuvre de Richard de S.-Victor. Revue Bénédictine, XXXVII, 1925, pp. 404 f.
Ottaviano, C. Riccardo di S. Vittore. Nouvelle Revue Théologique, LXI, 1934, pp. 629 ff.

Achard of Bridlington (d. 1171). De summa Trinitate. Ed. E. Martène and U. Durand (Thesaurus, vol. V, Paris, 1717, pp. 1668 ff.).

Peter of Blois (fl. 1170). Opera. Ed. J. A. Giles, 4 vols. 1846–7, and Migne, Patrologia Latina, vol. CCVII.
—— De amicitia christiana et dilectione Dei et proximi. Ed. M. M. Davy (Un Traité de l'Amour du XIIᵉ Siècle, Paris, 1932).
[Peter's poems are in Giles, vol. IV, pp. 337 ff. He is probably the author of Carmina Burana, nos. 29–31 (see edn by A. Hilka and O. Schumann, vol. II, pt i, Heidelberg, 1930, pp. 47 ff.); no. 63 (38 in Schneller's edn) may also be his. For his poem on the merits of

Wine and Beer, see E. Braunholz, Die Streit-
gedichte Peters von Blois und Roberts von
Beaufeu über den Wert des Weines und
Bieres, Zeitschrift für romanische Philologie,
XLVII, 1927, pp. 32 ff.]
    Robinson, J. A. Somerset Historical
    Essays. 1921, pp. 100 ff.
    Cohn, E. S. The Manuscript Evidence for
    the Letters of Peter of Blois. EHR. XLI,
    1926, pp. 43 ff.

John of Cornwall (*fl.* 1170). Eulogium ad
Alexandrum Papam III [with subtitle,
Quod Christus sit aliquis homo; eulogium
= sound discourse]. Ed. Migne, Patrologia
Latina, vol. CXCIX, cols. 1041 ff. [See DNB.
for other works ascribed to John.]

Robert of Cricklade (*fl.* 1170; chancellor of
Oxford, 1159). Defloratio Pliniana. BM.
MS Royal 15. c. XIV.
    Rück, K. Das Exzerpt der Naturalis
    Historia des Plinius von Robert von
    Cricklade. Sitzungsber. d. kgl. bayer.
    Akad. d. Wissensch. 1902, pp. 195 ff.

John of Salisbury (d. 1180). Policratici Libri
VIII. Ed. C. C. J. Webb, 2 vols. Oxford,
1909.
—— Ioannis Saresberiensis Historiae Ponti-
ficalis quae supersunt. Ed. R. L. Poole,
Oxford, 1927.
—— Ioannis Saresberiensis Episcopi Carno-
tensis Metalogicon Libri IIII. Ed. C. C. J.
Webb, Oxford, 1929.
—— Entheticus de dogmate philosophorum.
Ed. C. Petersen, Hamburg, 1843; ed. J. A.
Giles (in Opera, vol. v, Oxford, 1848,
pp. 239 ff.).
    Schaarschmidt, C. Johannes Saresberi-
    ensis. Leipzig, 1862.
    Poole, R. L. The Masters of the Schools
    at Paris and Chartres in John of Salis-
    bury's Time. EHR. XXXV, 1920, p. 321.
    —— John of Salisbury at the Papal
    Court, 1147–53. EHR. XXXVIII, 1923.
    —— The Early Correspondence of John
    of Salisbury. Proc. British Academy, XI,
    1924.
    Dickinson, J. The Medieval Conception of
    Kingship as developed in the Policraticus
    of John of Salisbury. Speculum, I, 1926,
    pp. 308 ff.
    Rand, E. K. Ioannes Saresberiensis silla-
    bizat. Speculum, I, 1926, pp. 447 f.
    Waddell, H. John of Salisbury. E. & S.
    XIII. 1928.
    Webb, C. C. J. Notes on John of
    Salisbury. EHR. XLVI, 1931, pp.
    260 ff.
    —— John of Salisbury. 1932.
    Lloyd, R. John of Salisbury. Church
    Quarterly Rev. CVIII, 1929, pp. 19 ff.

    Daniels, H. Die Wissenschaftslehre des
    Johannes von Salisbury. Kaldenkirchen,
    1932.
    [See also Ueberweg-Geyer, p. 705.]

Serlo of Wilton (*fl.* 1170).
    Meyer, P. Troisième Rapport sur une
    Mission littéraire en Angleterre et en
    Écosse. Archives des Missions scien-
    tifiques et littéraires, ser. 2, v, 1868,
    pp. 139 ff.
    Hauréau, B. Notice sur un MS. de la
    Reine Christine à la Bibliothèque du
    Vatican. [Notices et Extraits des MSS.
    de la Bibliothèque Nationale, vol. XXIX,
    pt ii, pp. 231 ff.]
    —— Notices et Extraits de quelques
    MSS. Vol. I, pp. 303 ff., vol. II, p. 206.
    —— Poema de partibus orationis.
    Notices sur les Mélanges poétiques
    d'Hildebert de Lavardin. [Notices et
    Extraits des MSS. de la Bibliothèque
    Nationale, vol. XXVIII, pp. 428 ff.]
    —— Notice sur le Numéro 2590 des MSS.
    latins de la Bibliothèque Nationale. *Ibid.*
    vol. XXXIII, pt i, pp. 345 f. [For Serlo's
    commentary on the Lord's prayer.]

Adam du Petit Pont (d. *c.* 1181; bishop of
St Asaph). De arte dialectica. [Extracts
in V. Cousin, Fragments philosophiques,
vol. II, Paris, 1865, pp. 385 ff.]
—— Oratio de utensilibus ad domum regen-
dam [a glossary under the form of a
description]. Ed. M. Haupt, Berichte der
königlichen sächsischen Gesellschaft der
Wissenschaften, 1849, pp. 276 ff.; ed. B.
Hauréau (Notices et Extraits de quelques
MSS., vol. III, pp. 201 ff.).

Daniel of Morley (*fl.* 1175). Philosophia, or
Liber de naturis inferiorum et superiorum.
Ed. K. Sudhoff, Archiv für die Geschichte
der Naturwissenschaften, VIII, 1917, pp. 1 ff.
    Birkenmajer, A. Eine neue Handschrift
    des Liber de naturis inferiorum et su-
    periorum des Daniel von Merlai. Archiv
    für die Geschichte der Naturwissen-
    schaften, IX, pt i, 1920, pp. 45 ff.
    [For bibliography, see C. H. Haskins,
    Studies in the History of Mediaeval
    Science, p. 126, note 39.]

Roger of Hereford (*fl.* 1176). Compotus.
Bodl. MS Digby 40.
—— [Astronomical Tables for the meridian of
Hereford in 1178, BM. Arundel MS 377 and
others given in Haskins, Studies in the
History of Mediaeval Science, p. 125].

Walter the Englishman (*fl.* 1177). [Fables in
verse (Aesop).] Ed. L. Hervieux (Fabulistes
latins, vol. II, pp. 316 ff.); ed. K. McKenzie
and W. Oldfather, Illinois University Stud.
v, 1919, pp. 49 ff.

Ranulf de Glanville (d. 1190). Tractatus de Legibus et Consuetudinibus Angliae. Ed. G. Phillips, Berlin, 2 vols. 1827–8; ed. G. E. Woodbine, New Haven, 1931. [Tr. J. Beames, 1812.]

> Radin, M. Glanvill on the Common Law: Lex terrae and Jus Regni. Pennsylvania University Law Rev. LXXXII, 1933, pp. 26 ff.

Clement of Llanthony (d. c. 1190). Unum ex quattuor [a gospel harmony]. MSS: St John's College Oxford 2; Magdalen College Oxford 160; BM. Royal 4 E II. [See Little, Grey Friars in Oxford, p. 185, note 3; M. Deanesly, Lollard Bible, Cambridge, 1920, p. 177.]

Gervase of Tilbury (fl. 1180). Otia Imperialia. Ed. G. G. Leibnitz (Scriptores Rerum Brunsvicensium, 2 vols. Hanover, 1707–10). [Extracts, ed. J. Stevenson, Radulphi de Coggeshall Chronicon, Rolls Ser. 1875, pp. 419 ff.]

John de Hanville (fl. 1184). Architrenius. Ed. T. Wright (Anglo-Latin Satirical Poets, vol. I, pp. 240 ff.).

Richard FitzNeal, or FitzNigel (d. 1198). Dialogus de Scaccario. Ed. A. Hughes, C. G. Crump and C. Johnson, Oxford, 1902. [Tr. E. F. Henderson, Select Historical Documents of the Middle Ages, 1892, pp. 20 ff.]

Joseph of Exeter (fl. 1190). De Bello Troiano. Frankfurt, 1620, 1675; 1825.

—— Antiocheis. [Fragment in W. Camden, Remaines concerning Britaine, 1870, p. 339; quoted also in T. Wright, Biographia Britannica Literaria, vol. II, p. 406.]

> Jusserand, J. J. De Iosepho Exoniensi vel Iscano [with text of bk I of De Bello Troiano]. Paris, 1877.
> Sedgwick, W. B. The Bellum Troianum of Joseph of Exeter. Speculum, v, 1930, pp. 49 ff., 338.

Walter Map (fl. 1190). De Nugis Curialium. Ed. T. Wright, Camden Soc. 1850; ed. M. R. James, Oxford, 1914.

> Bradley, Henry. Notes on Walter Map's De Nugis Curialium. [Collected Papers, Oxford, 1928, pp. 245 f.]

—— The Latin Poems commonly attributed to Walter Mapes. Ed. T. Wright, Camden Soc. 1841.

[These poems are not by Walter Map, but many of them are of English origin. It is not certain that the Apocalypse of Golias is the work of an English poet; see K. Strecker, Die Apocalypse des Golias, Leipzig, 1928, p. 3. But the Metamorphosis of Golias is probably of English origin; see H. Brinkmann, Die Metamorphosis Goliae und das Streitgedicht Phyllis und Flora, ZDA. L, 1925, pp. 27 ff.

The poems in Wright, pp. 48, 54 and 77 are probably English. The author of the piece on p. 106 seems to have belonged to Wimborne Minster. Manitius, Geschichte der lateinischen literatur des Mittelalters, vol. III, p. 270, is prepared to accept Walter as the author of the poem on p. 54. Walter is certainly the author of the short poem in Giraldus, Opera, vol. I, p. 363; of the Sigillum Walteri Map, in M. R. James, De Nugis Curialium, p. xxxviii; of Lancea Longini, grex albus, ordo nefandus, in Wright, Poems attributed to Walter Mapes, p. xxxv; and of two pieces from which quotations are made in Distinctiones Monasticae (Pitra, Spicilegium Solesmense, vol. III, p. 476, and reproduced in Manitius, op. cit. vol. III, p. 269). For references to other English poems in Wright, op. cit. and in his Political Songs, see K. Strecker, Walter von Chatillon und seine Schule, ZDA. LII, 1927, pp. 161 ff.]

Nigel de Longchamps (Wireker; fl. 1190). Speculum Stultorum and Contra Curiales et Officiales Clericos. Ed. T. Wright (Anglo-Latin Satirical Poets, vol. I, pp. 3 ff.). [Nigel's minor poems are in BM. MS Cotton Vesp. D. XIX, fols. 2 ff.]

> Mozley, J. H. On the Text of the Speculum Stultorum. Speculum, IV, 1929, pp. 430 ff.
> —— On the Text and MSS of the Speculum Stultorum. Speculum, v, 1930, pp. 251 ff.
> —— The Unprinted Poems of Nigel Wireker. Speculum, VII, 1932, pp. 398 ff.
> —— Nigel Wireker or Wetekere? MLR. XXVII, 1932, pp. 314 ff.
> Boutemy, A. The Manuscript Tradition of the Speculum Stultorum. Speculum, VIII, 1933, pp. 510 ff.
> —— A propos d'un MS. du Tractatus contra curiales et officiales clericos de Nigellus de Longchamps. Revue Belge de Philologie et d'Histoire, XIII, 1933, pp. 987 ff.
> —— Sur le 'prologue en prose' et la Date du Speculum Stultorum. Revue de l'Université de Bruxelles, 1934, pp. 67 ff.

Richardus Anglicus (fl. 1196; canonist). Summa de Ordine judiciario. Ed. L. Wahrmund (Quellen zur Geschichte des römischkanonischen Processus im Mittelalter, Innsbruck, 1915).

Gregory the Englishman (end of 13th cent.). Narracio de mirabilibus Rome. Ed. M. R. James, EHR. XXXII, 1917, pp. 531 ff.; ed. F. M. Rushworth, Journ. Roman Stud. IX, 1921, pp. 14 ff.

Geoffrey de Vinsauf (*fl.* 1200). Poëtria Nova. [In E. Faral, Les Arts poétiques du XIIe et du XIIIe Siècle, Paris, 1924, pp. 194 ff. (see also pp. 15 ff. for his life and works); text also in Leyser, Historia Poetarum et Poematum Medii Aevi, pp. 855 ff.]

    Langlois, C. V. Formulaires des Lettres du XIIe, du XIIIe et du XIVe Siècles. [Notices et Extraits des MSS. de la Bibliothèque Nationale, vol. xxxv, pt. ii, pp. 427 ff.]

    Wilmart, A. L'Art poétique de Geoffroi de Vinsauf et les Commentaires de Barthélemy de Pise. Revue Bénédictine, xLI, 1929, pp. 271 ff.

Giraldus Cambrensis (d. *c.* 1220). Opera. Ed. J. S. Brewer, J. F. Dimock and G. F. Warner, 8 vols. Rolls Ser. 1861–91.

    Owen, H. Gerald the Welshman. 1904.

    Coulter, C. C. and Magoun, F. P. Giraldus Cambrensis and Indo-Germanic Philology. Speculum, I, 1926, pp. 104 ff.

    Powicke, F. M. Gerald of Wales. John Rylands Lib. Bulletin, xII, 1928, pp. 389 ff. [Rev. in The Christian Life in the Middle Ages and other Essays, Oxford, 1935, pp. 107 ff.]

    Holmes, U. T. Gerald the Naturalist. Speculum, xI, 1936, pp. 110 ff.

E. THE THIRTEENTH CENTURY

(1) GENERAL WORKS

Chenu, C. D. La Théologie comme Science au XIIIe Siècle: Fishacre et Kilwardby. Archives d'Histoire doctrinale et Littéraire du Moyen Âge, II, 1927, pp. 35 ff.

Daniels, A. Quellenbeiträge und Untersuchungen zur Geschichte der Gottesbeweise im dreizehnten Jahrhundert. Münster, 1909.

Denifle, H. Die Handschriften der Bibelcorrectorien des 13. Jahrhunderts. Archiv für Litteratur- und Kirchengeschichte des Mittelalters, IV, 1888, pp. 263 ff. [These *correctoria* of the Bible text were influenced by Roger Bacon; see Little, English Franciscan History, pp. 213 f.]

Ehrle, F. L'Agostinismo e l' Aristotelismo nella Scolastica del Secolo 13. [From Xenia Tomistica, vol. III, Rome, 1925.]

Faral, E. Le Fabliau latin au Moyen Âge. Romania, I, 1924, pp. 321 ff. [Refers to English 'Comoediae': (a) Baucis and Thraso, ed. H. Hagen, Eine antike Komödie in distischer Nachbildung, Jahrbücher für klassische Philologie, xIV, 1868, pp. 711 ff.; (b) Babio, ed. T. Wright, Early Mysteries and Other Latin Poems of the Twelfth and Thirteenth Centuries. 1838, pp. 65 ff.;

(c) two pieces by Geoffrey de Vinsauf, ed. B. Hauréau, Notices et Extraits des MSS de la Bibliothèque Nationale, xxIX, pt ii, pp. 322 ff. Texts also in G. Cohen, La 'Comédie' Latine en France au XIIe Siècle, 2 vols. Paris, 1981.]

Faral, E. Les Arts poétiques du XIIe et du XIIIe Siècle. Paris, 1924. [See W. B. Sedgwick, Notes and Emendations on Faral's Les Arts poétiques du XIIe et du XIIIe Siècle, Speculum, II, 1927, pp. 331 ff.]

Gasquet, F. A. English Biblical Criticism and English Scholarship in the Thirteenth Century. Dublin Rev. 1898, pp. 1 ff., 356 ff.

Glorieux, P. La Littérature quodlibétique de 1260 à 1320. Kain, 1925. [For addns, see V. Doucet, Maîtres franciscains de Paris, Archivum Franciscanum Historicum, xxVII, 1934, pp. 531 ff.]

—— Comment les Thèses Thomistes furent proscrites à Oxford (1284–1286). Revue Thomiste, x, 1927, pp. 260 ff.

—— Aux Origines du Quodlibet. Divus Thomas, xxxVIII, 1935, pp. 502 ff.

—— Répertoire des Maîtres en Théologie de Paris au XIIIe Siècle. Paris, 1933.

Grabmann, M. Forschungen über die lateinischen Aristotelesübersetzungen des XIII. Jahrhunderts. Münster, 1916.

—— Kurze Mitteilungen über ungedruckte englische Thomisten des 13. Jahrhunderts. Divus Thomas, III, 1925, pp. 211 ff. [For bibliography of English Thomists, see Ueberweg-Geyer, p. 773.]

Lightfoot, J. B. England during the Latter Half of the 13th Century. [In Historical Essays, 1896, pp. 92 ff.]

Little, A. G. The Educational Organisation of the Mendicant Friars in England. Trans. Royal Hist. Soc. vIII, 1894, pp. 49 ff.

—— The Franciscan School at Oxford in the Thirteenth Century. Archivum Franciscanum Historicum, xIX, 1926, pp. 803 ff.

—— The Friars and the Foundation of the Faculty of Theology in the University of Cambridge. [Mélanges Mandonnet, vol. II, Paris, 1930, pp. 389 ff.]

Little, A. G. and Pelster, F. Oxford Theology and Theologians (*c.* A.D. 1282–1302). Oxford, 1934.

Mandonnet, P. La Crise scolaire au Début du XIIIe Siècle et la Fondation de l'Ordre des Frères Prêcheurs. Revue d'Histoire ecclésiastique, xv, 1914, pp. 34 ff.

Rand, E. K. The Classics in the 13th Century. Speculum, IV, 1929, pp. 249 ff.

Rohmer, J. La Théorie de l'Abstraction dans l'École franciscaine d'Alexandre de Halès à Jean Peckham. Archives d'Histoire doctrinale et littéraire du Moyen Âge, III, 1928, pp. 105 ff.

Sedgwick, W. B. The Style and Vocabulary of the Latin Arts of Poetry of the 12th and 13th Centuries. Speculum, III, 1928, pp. 349 ff.

Seppelt, F. X. Der Kampf der Bettelorden an der Universität Paris in der Mitte des 18. Jahrhunderts. Breslau, 1907.

Sharp, D. E. Franciscan Philosophy at Oxford in the 13th Century. Oxford, 1930.

Van den Wyngaert, A. Querelles du Clergé séculier et des Ordres mendiants à l'Université de Paris an XIIIe Siècle. La France Franciscaine, v, 1922, pp. 257 ff.

Wingate, S. D. Mediaeval Latin Versions of the Aristotelian Scientific Corpus with reference to the Biological Works. 1931.

(2) Franciscans

[For lists of Franciscan scholars, see A. G. Little, The Grey Friars in Oxford, Oxford, 1892, pp. 125 ff., and Studies in English Franciscan History, Manchester, 1917. References are given to entries taken from Dr Little's books.]

Amorós, L. La Teologia como Ciencia práctica en la Escuela franciscana en los Tiempos que preceden a Escoto. Archives d'Histoire doctrinale et littéraire du Moyen Âge, IX, 1934, pp. 261 ff. [Many English authors mentioned.]

Bannister, H. M. A Short Notice of some MSS. of the Cambridge Friars, now in the Vatican Library. Collectanea Franciscana, I, pp. 124 ff. (British Society of Franciscan Studies, vol. v, 1914).

James, M. R. The Library of the Grey Friars of Hereford. Collectanea Franciscana, I, pp. 114 ff., 154 ff. (British Society of Franciscan Studies, vol. v, 1914).

—— The List of Libraries prefixed to the Catalogue of John Boston. Collectanea Franciscana, II, p. 37 (British Society of Franciscan Studies, vol. x, 1922). [See also Little, English Franciscan History, pp. 164 f.]

Kingsford, C. L. The Song of Lewes. Oxford, 1893.

Maitland, F. W. A Song on the Death of Simon de Montfort. EHR. XI, 1896, pp. 314 ff.

Bartholomaeus Anglicus (fl. 1230). De proprietatibus rerum. Cologne, [1470?], etc.; Frankfurt, 1601; tr. Eng. c. 1495, and by J. S. Walsh, Medical Life, XL, 1933, pp. 453 ff., 499 ff., 547 ff. [An encyclopaedia of various information.]

Schönbach, A. Des Bartholomaeus Anglicus Beschreibung Deutschlands gegen 1240. Mitteilungen des Instituts für österreichische Geschichtsforschung, XVII, 1906, pp. 54 ff.

Schneider, A. Metaphysische Begriffe des Barth. Anglicus. [Baeumker Festgabe, Münster, 1913, pp. 139 ff.]

Plasmann, T. Bartholomaeus Anglicus. Archivum Franciscanum Historicum, XII, 1919, pp. 68 ff.

Boyar, G. E. S. Bartholomaeus Anglicus and his Encyclopaedia. JEGP. XIX, 1920, pp. 168 ff.

Alexander of Hales (d. 1245). Universae Theologiae Summa. Cologne, 1622. [Also vol. I, Quaracchi, 1924.]

—— Summa de Virtutibus. [See P. Minges, Philosophiegeschichtliche Bemerkungen über die dem Alexander von Hales zugeschriebene Summa de Virtutibus, Baeumker Festgabe, Münster, 1913, pp. 129 ff. On the question of authorship, see also E. Longpré, Thomas d'York, Archivum Franciscanum Historicum, vol. XIX, 1926, pp. 882, note 1.]

Endres, J. A. Des Alexander von Hales' Leben und psychologische Lehre. Philosophisches Jahrbuch, I, 1888, pp. 24 ff., 203 ff., 227 ff.

Guttmann, J. Alexandre de Hales et le Judaïsme. Revue des Études Juives, XIX, 1890, pp. 224 ff.

Picavet, F. Abélard et Alexandre de Hales, Créateurs de la Méthode scolastique. Paris, 1896.

Minges, P. De relatione inter prooemium Summae Alexandri Halensis et prooemium Summae Guidonis Abbatis. Archivum Franciscanum Historicum, VI, 1913, pp. 13 ff.

—— Zur Psychologie des Alexander von Hales. Philosophisches Jahrbuch, 1915, pp. 143 ff.

—— Abhängigkeitsverhältnis zwischen Alexander von Hales und Albert dem Grossen Franziskanische Studien, II, 1915, pp. 208 ff.

Fuchs, J. Die Proprietäten des Seins bei Alexander von Hales. Münich, 1930.

Pelster, F. Forschungen zur Quaestionenliteratur in der Zeit des Alexander von Hales. Scholastik, VI, 1931, pp. 321 ff.

—— Zur Problem der Summa des Alexander von Hales. Gregorianum, XII, 1931, pp. 426 ff.

—— Die Quaestionen des Alexander von Hales. Gregorianum, XIV, 1933, pp. 401 ff.

Imle, F. Die essentiellen Grundlagen des trinitarischen Innenlebens nach Alexander von Hales. [Aus der Geisteswelt des Mittelalters, vol. I, Münster, 1935, pp. 545 ff.]

Dausend, P. H. Das Opusculum super Missam des Fr. Wilhelm von Melitona

19-2

und die entsprechenden Stellen in der Summa theologiae Alexanders von Hales. *Ibid.* pp. 554 ff.

Ferté, J. Rapports de la Somme d'Alexandre de Halès dans son 'De fide' avec Philippe le Chancelier. Recherches de Théologie ancienne et médiévale, VII, 1935, pp. 381 ff. [Further bibliography in Ueberweg-Geyer, pp. 734 f.]

William of Ware (*fl.* 1240). Quaestiones disputatae de immaculata conceptione B.M. Virginis. [Bibliotheca Franciscana Scholastica Medii Aevi, vol. III, Quaracchi, 1904.]
—— Commentary on the Sentences. MSS: Merton College Oxford 103, 104, and others in Little, Grey Friars in Oxford. p. 213. [Extracts in M. Schmaus, Der Liber Propugnatorius des Thomas Anglicus, vol. II, Münster, 1930, pp. 234* ff., and A. Daniels, Wilhelm von Ware über das menschliche Erkennen, Baeumker Festgabe, Münster, 1913, pp. 309 ff. Further bibliography in Schmaus, *op. cit.* vol. II, p. 229* and Ueberweg-Geyer, p. 763.]

Klug, H. Zur Biographie der Minderbrüder Johannes Duns Scotus und Wilhelm von Ware. Franziskanische Studien, II, 1915, pp. 377 ff.
Daniels, A. Zu den Beziehungen zwischen Wilhelm von Ware und Johannes Duns Scotus. Franziskanische Studien, IV, 1917, pp. 221 ff.
Longpré, E. Guillaume de Ware. La France Franciscaine, V, 1922, pp. 71 ff.
Lechner, J. Beiträge zum mittelalterlichen Franziskanerschrifttum, vornehmlich der Oxforder Schule des XIII–XIV Jahrhunderts auf Grund einer Florentiner Wilhelm von Ware-Handschrift. Franziskanische Studien, XIX, 1932, pp. 99 ff.
Bissen, J. M. Question inédite de Guillaume de Ware, O.F.M. sur le Motif de l'Incarnation. Études Franciscains, XLVI, 1934, pp. 218 ff.

William of Nottingham (d. *c.* 1251; provincial minister; 'energetic in furthering the study of theology and in developing the educational organisation of the Franciscans in England,' Little, Grey Friars in Oxford, p. 183). Unum ex quattuor, or De Concordia evangelistarum. [A commentary on the Gospels based on Clement of Llanthony; 'very popular,' Little, p. 185.] MSS: BM. Royal 4 E II (A.D. 1381), and others at Oxford. [For list see Little, p. 185.]

Adam Marsh (d. 1257). Epistolae. Ed. J. S. Brewer (Monumenta Franciscana, vol. I, Rolls Ser. 1858, pp. 77 ff.). [For his other writings see Little, Franciscan School at Oxford, Archivum Franciscanum Historicum, XIX, 1926, p. 36.]

Richard Rufus of Cornwall (Franciscan; *fl.* 1250).

Pelster, F. Zu Richardus Rufus de Cornubia. Zeitschrift für katholische Theologie, XLVIII, 1924, pp. 625 ff.
—— Der älteste Sentenzenkommentar aus der Oxforder Franziskanerschule. Scholastik, I, 1926, pp. 50 ff.
—— Roger Bacons Compendium Studii Theologiae und der Sentenzenkommentar des Richardus Rufus. Scholastik, IV, 1929, pp. 410 ff.
—— Neue Schriften des englischen Franziskaners Richardus Rufus von Cornwall. Scholastik, VIII, 1933, pp. 561 ff., IX, 1934, pp. 256 ff.

Thomas of Eccleston (*fl.* 1250). De adventu fratrum minorum in Angliam. Ed. A. G. Little (Collection d'Études et de Documents sur l'Histoire religieux et littéraire du Moyen Âge, vol. VII, Paris, 1909). [Also ed. J. S. Brewer, Monumenta Franciscana, vol. I, Rolls Ser. 1858, pp. 1 ff.]

Thomas of York (d. *c.* 1260). Sapientiale ['a *summa* of metaphysical problems,' D. E. Sharp, *op. cit.* below, p. 52]. MSS: Vatican Lat. 4301 and 6771; Biblioteca Nazionale, Florence. Conv. Sopp. A 6, 437.
—— Manus quae contra Omnipotentem tenditur.[Treatise against William of S. Amour.] Ed. M. Bierbaum (Bettelorden und Weltgeistlichkeit an der Universität Paris, Franziskanische Studien, 1920, pp. 37 ff.).

Grabmann, M. Die Metaphysik des Thomas von York. [Baeumker Festgabe, Münster, 1913, pp. 181 ff.]
Pelzer, A. Les Versions latines des Ouvrages de Morale conservés sous le Nom d'Aristote en Usage au XIIIe Siècle. Revue Néo-scolastique, 1921, p. 403. [On Thomas's Sapientiale.]
Pelster, F. Thomas von York als Verfasser des Traktats 'Manus quae contra omnipotentem tenditur.' Archivum Franciscanum Historicum, XV, 1922, pp. 3 ff.
Longpré, E. Fr. Thomas d'York. Archivum Franciscanum Historicum, XIX, 1926, pp. 875 ff.
—— Thomas d'York et Matthieu d'Aquasparta. Archives d'Histoire doctrinale et littéraire du Moyen Âge, I, 1926, pp. 270 ff.
Sharp, D. E. Thomas of York. [In Franciscan Philosophy at Oxford, Oxford, 1930, pp. 49 ff.]
Tressera, F. De doctrinis metaphysicis fr. Thomae de Eboraco, O.F.M. Analecta Sacra Tarraconensia, V, 1929, pp. 33 ff.

Thomas Docking (d. *c.* 1270; also called Thomas Good). In IV Libros Sententiarum. Paris, 1505. [For his other works (mainly biblical commentaries) see list in Little, Grey Friars in Oxford, pp. 151 f.]

> Little, A. G. Thomas Docking and his Relations to Roger Bacon. [In Essays in History presented to R. Lane Poole, Oxford, 1927, pp. 301 ff.; contains extracts from Docking's writings.]

Thomas de Hibernia (d. 1270). Promptuarium morale. Ed. L. Wadding (St Anthony of Padua, Concordantiae Morales, Rome, 1624).

Thomas of Bungay (d. *c.* 1275). De celo et mundo. Caius College Cambridge MS 509, § 3 (early 14th cent.). [Little, Grey Friars in Oxford, p. 154.]

Robert of Ware (*fl.* 1268). [Twenty Five Discourses on the Virgin Mary.] London, Gray's Inn MS 7 (13th cent.). [The prologue is autobiographical; extract in Little, Grey Friars in Oxford, p. 212.]

John of Wales (*fl.* 1260–83). [For a list of his works, see Little, Grey Friars in Oxford, pp. 144 ff.; English Franciscan History, pp. 174 ff., 186 (note 1), 231 f. (ptd edns).]

—— Communiloquium [or Summa Collationum ad omne genus hominum]. Venice, 1496; Lyons, 1511; Paris, 1516. [Little, English Franciscan History, p. 176 (note 1); p. 177, 'a collection of informal discourses to all kinds of men.' Extract, ed. L. Thorndike, 'All the World's a Chess-board,' Speculum, VI, 1931, pp. 461 ff.]

—— Compendiloquium. Venice, 1496; Lyons, 1511; Strasburg, 1518. [Little, English Franciscan History, p. 181, 'a compendium of the lives of illustrious philosophers, of their moral sayings, and imitable examples.']

—— Breviloquium de philosophia sive sapientia sanctorum. Venice, 1496; Lyons, 1511; Strasburg, 1518; Louvain, [1485 ?]. [Little, Grey Friars in Oxford, p. 146; English Franciscan History, p. 185, 'a short treatise consisting of extracts from Christian writers.']

—— Breviloquium de virtutibus antiquorum principum et philosophorum. Venice, 1496; Lyons, 1511; Strasburg, 1518; Louvain, [1485 ?]. ['A collection of narrations about the great men of antiquity, illustrating the cardinal virtues of Prudence, Temperance, Fortitude and Justice, "for the benefit and instruction of rulers,"' Little, English Franciscan History, p. 185.]

—— Summa de Penitentia. ['On confession and penance,' Little, English Franciscan History, p. 186.] MSS: BM. Royal 10 A IX (13th cent.); 4 D IV (15th cent.);

Bibliothèque Mazarine Paris 569 (14th cent.); Bibliothèque Publique Falaise 38 (14th cent.; see Little, Grey Friars in Oxford, p. 144).

> Welter, J. T. L'Exemplum dans la Littérature religieuse et didactique du Moyen Âge. Paris, 1927, pp. 172 ff., 233 ff. [For John of Wales's Summa de viciis et virtutibus and his Communiloquium.]

Roger Bacon (d. *c.* 1292). Opera inedita. Ed. J. S. Brewer, Rolls Ser. 1859.

Fr. Rogeri Bacon Compendium Studii Theologiae. Ed. H. Rashdall, British Soc. of Franciscan Stud. 1911.

Roger Bacon, Opus Tertium (part). Ed. A. G. Little, British Soc. of Franciscan Stud. 1912.

Bacon, R. Opus Maius. Ed. J. H. Bridges, 3 vols. Oxford, 1897–1900; tr. R. B. Burke, 2 vols. Philadelphia, 1928.

Opera hactenus inedita Rogeri Baconi. Ed. R. Steele and others. Oxford.

(i) De Viciis contractis in Studio Theologie (1909).

(ii) Communium Naturalium Liber I, partes I, II (1909).

(iii) Communium Naturalium Liber I, partes III, IV (1911).

(iv) Communium Naturalium Liber II, de celestibus, partes I–V (1913).

(v) Secretum Secretorum [with English version of Arabic text, ed. A. S. Fulton; and Anglo-Norman version].

(vi) Compotus Fratris Rogeri; compotus Roberti Grossecapitis Lincolniensis Episcopi; massa compoti Alexandri de Villa Dei (1926).

(vii) Questiones supra undecimum prime Philosophie Aristotelis (Metaphysic XII). Ed. R. Steele and F. M. Delorme (1928).

(viii) Questiones supra libros quatuor Physicorum Aristotelis. Ed. F. M. Delorme and R. Steele (1928).

(ix) De Retardatione Accidentium Senectutis cum aliis Opusculis de Rebus Medicinalibus. Ed. A. G. Little and E. Withington (1928).

(x) Questiones supra libros prime Philosophie Aristotelis (Metaphysica, I, ii, v–x). Ed. R. Steele and F. M. Delorme (1930).

(xi) Questiones supra De Plantis, Metaphysica vetus Aristotelis e codd. vetustissimis. Ed. R. Steele and F. M. Delorme (1932).

(xii) Questiones supra librum de causis, and Liber de causis. Ed. R. Steele and F. M. Delorme (1935).

> Werner, K. Die Kosmologie und allgemeine Naturlehre des Roger Baco. Wiener Sitzungsber. XCIV, 1879.

Held, G. Roger Baco's praktische Philosophie. Jena, 1881.

Poehl, C. Das Verhältnis der Philosophie zur Theologie bei Roger Bacon. Neu-Strelitz, 1893.

Nolan, E. and Hirsch, S. A. The Greek Grammar of Roger Bacon and a Fragment of his Hebrew Grammar. Cambridge, 1902.

Mandonnet, P. Roger Bacon et le Speculum astronomiae (1277). Revue Néoscolastique, XVII, 1910, pp. 313 ff.

—— Roger Bacon et la Composition des trois Opus. Revue Néo-scolastique, XX, 1913, pp. 52 ff., 164 ff.

Hoever, H. Roger Bacons Hylomorphismus als Grundlage seiner philosophischen Anschauungen. Limburg, 1912.

Keicher, O. Der Intellectus Agens bei Roger Bacon. [Baeumker Festgabe, Münster, 1913, pp. 297 ff.]

Baeumker, C. Roger Bacons Naturphilosophie, insbesondere seine Lehre von Materie und Form, Individuation und Universalität. Münster, 1916.

Carton, R. L'Expérience physique chez Roger Bacon. Paris, 1924.

—— L'Expérience mystique de l'Illumination intérieure chez Roger Bacon. Paris, 1924.

—— La Synthèse doctrinale de Roger Bacon. [In É. Gilson, Études de Philosophie médiévale, vols. II, III, V, Paris, 1924.]

Little, A. G. Roger Bacon. Proc. British Academy, XIV, 1928.

Little, A. G. et al. Roger Bacon: Essays. Oxford, 1930. [Covering the whole of Bacon's activities by English and foreign scholars, with a list of Bacon's works by A. G. Little, pp. 373 ff.]

Bovygnes, M. Roger Bacon a-t-il lu des Livres arabes? Archives d'Histoire doctrinale et littéraire du moyen Âge, V, 1930, pp. 311 ff.

Manly, J. M. Roger Bacon and the Voynich MS. Speculum, VI, 1931, pp. 345 ff.

Singer, W. Alchemical Writings of Roger Bacon. Speculum, VII, 1932, pp. 80 ff.

Birkenmajer, A. Avicennas Vorrede zum 'Liber Sufficientiae' und Roger Bacon. Revue Néo-scholastique, XXXVI, 1934, pp. 308 ff.

[For further references see Ueberweg-Geyer, pp. 760 f.]

Richard Middleton (fl. 1283; 'Doctor Solidus,' Little, Grey Friars in Oxford, p. 214). Commentum super quarto Sententiarum. Venice, 1489; [?]; 1507-9, etc.

Richard Middleton. Quodlibeta tria. Venice, 1509; Paris, 1510, 1519, 1529; Brescia, 1591. [For MSS of these and other works see Little, Grey Friars in Oxford, and on Richard see Glorieux, La Littérature Quodlibétique, pp. 267 ff. and bibliography there; also D. E. Sharp, Franciscan Philosophy at Oxford, pp. 211 ff.]

Hocedez, E. Les quaestiones disputatae de Richard de Middleton. [Recherches de Science religieuse, 1916, pp. 498 ff.]

—— Richard de Middleton, sa Vie, ses Œuvres, sa Doctrine. Spicilegium Lovaniense, 1925.

Minges, P. Scotistisches bei Richard de Middleton. Theologische Quartalschrift, 1917, pp. 60 ff.; 1919, pp. 269 ff.

Durst, B. Die Frage der Armenseelanrufung bei Richard von Middletown. Franziskanische Studien, X, 1923, pp. 33 ff. [Extracts, pp. 35 ff.]

Lampen, W. De Patria Ricardi de Mediavilla. Archivum Franciscanum Historicum, XVIII, 1925, pp. 298 ff.

Pelster, F. Die Herkunft des Richard von Mediavilla. Philosophisches Jahrbuch, 1926, pp. 172 f.

Rucker, P. P. Der Ursprung unserer Begriffe nach Richard von Mediavilla. Münster, 1934.

[For further references see Ueberweg-Geyer, pp. 762 f.]

John Pecham (archbishop of Canterbury; 1279–92). Perspectiva Communis. Milan, 1482.

—— Poems [including Philomela praevia]. Analecta Hymnica, vol. L, pp. 592 ff.

—— Canticum pauperis pro dilecto. Bibliotheca Franciscana Ascetica, vol. IV, p. 136.

—— Vier Prosen des Johannes Pecham. Ed. E. Peeters, Franziskanische Studien, IV, 1917, pp. 355 ff.

—— Registrum epistolarum fratris Johannis Peckham. Ed. C. T. Martin, 3 vols. Rolls Ser. 1882–5.

—— Johannis Pecham Tractatus Tres de Paupertate. Ed. C. L. Kingsford, A. G. Little, F. Tocco, British Soc. of Franciscan Stud. 1910. [Contains a bibliography of Pecham's writings, pp. 1 ff., and the poem, Defensio fratrum mendicantium, pp. 148 ff., which Kingsford attributes to Pecham. H. Pflaum, Speculum, VI, 1931, p. 523, thinks it the work of Guy de la Marche.]

—— Johannis Pechami Quaestiones tractantes de anima. Ed. H. Spettmann, Münster, 1918.

Ehrle, F. John Peckham, Über den Kampf des Augustinismus und Aristotelismus in der zweit en Hälfte des XIII.

Jahrhunderts. Zeitschrift für katholische Theologie, XIII, 1889, pp. 172 ff.
Oliger, L. De pueris oblatis in Ord. Min., cum textu hucusque inedito Fr. Joh. Pecham. Archivum Franciscanum Historicum, VIII, 1915, pp. 389 ff.
—— Die theologische Question des Joh. Pecham über die vollkommene Armut. Franziskanische Studien, IV, 1917, pp. 127 ff.
Spettmann, H. Quellencritisches zur Biographie des Johannes Pecham. Franziskanische Studien, II, 1915, pp. 170 ff., 266 ff.
—— Die Psychologie des Iohannes Peckham. Münster, 1919.
—— Die Ethikkommentar des Iohannes Peckham. [Baeumker Festgabe, Münster 1923, pp. 222 ff.]

William de la Mare (d. 1298). [Commentary on the first 2 bks of Bonaventura's Sentences.] MSS: Communal Lib., Todi, 59; Biblioteca Nazionale, Florence, S. Croce, A 2, 727.
—— Correctorium. Strasburg, 1501; ed. in part B. Geyer, Florilegium Patristicum, vol. XIV, Bonn, 1920 (Quaestiones Summae theologiae i, 75–77 una cum Guilelmi de la Mare correctorii art. 25). [See the references in Little, Franciscan School at Oxford, Archivum Franciscanum Historicum, XIX, 1926, pp. 64 f., and P. Glorieux, Les premières Polémiques thomistes, Bibliothèque Thomiste, IX, 1927. The Correctorium was a criticism of the Summa of Aquinas. The Correctorium corruptorii (see below under Richard Clapwell) was an answer to it.]
—— Quaestiones disputatae. Vatican MS Borghes. Lat. 361.
Longpré, E. Guillaume de la Mare. La France Franciscaine, IV, 1921, pp. 288 ff., V, 1922, pp. 289 ff.
—— Guillaume de la Mare. [Dictionnaire de Théologie catholique, ed. A. Vacant and E. Mangenot, vol. VIII, Paris, 1925, cols. 2467 ff.]
Pelster, F. Les Declarationes et les Questiones de Guillaume de la Mare. Recherches de Théologie ancienne et médiévale, III, 1931, pp. 397 ff.
Hufnagel, A. Studien zur Entwicklung des Thomistischen Erkenntnisbegriffes im Anschluss an das Correctorium 'Quare.' Münster, 1935.

Roger Marston (d. after 1298). Quaestio disputata. [In De humanae cognitionis ratione, Quaracchi, 1883, pp. 197 ff.]
—— Fr. Rogeri Marston Quaestiones disputatae de emanatione aeterna, de statu naturae lapsae, et de anima. Quaracchi, 1932. [See also Little, Franciscan School at Oxford, Archivum Franciscanum Historicum, XIX, 1926, pp. 55 ff.]
Daniels, A. Anselmzitate bei dem Oxforder Franziskaner Roger von Marston. Theologische Quartalschrift, XCIII, 1911, pp. 35 ff.
Pelster, F. Roger Marston, O.F.M. Scholastik, III, 1928, pp. 526 ff.
Gilson, E. Roger Marston. Un Cas d'Augustinisme avicennisant. Archives d'Histoire doctrinale et littéraire du Moyen Âge, VIII, 1933, pp. 87 ff.
Guinagh, K. An Unpublished MS. of Rogerius Anglicus. Speculum, IX, 1934, pp. 91 ff.
Belmond, S. La Théorie de la Connaissance d'après Roger Marston. La France Franciscaine, XVII, 1934, pp. 153 ff.
[On Roger, see also de Wulf, Mediaeval Philosophy, vol. II, pp. 147 ff.]

(3) DOMINICANS

John of St Giles (*fl.* 1230; physician to Philip Augustus). Experimenta Johannis de S. Aegidio. Bodl. MS 786. [A collection of medical prescriptions.]
Robert Bacon (d. 1248; Dominican professor at Oxford). [Only lists of his works have survived in Bale, vol. I, p. 295, who refers to a Liber in Sententias Petri Lombardi, among other writings; and in Tanner, p. 62, who refers to a work called Syncategorematica; see DNB., and Quétif-Echard, vol. I, pp. 118 f.]
Richard Fishacre (d. 1248; friend of Robert Bacon). [Commentary on the Sentences of Peter Lombard, in 4 books]. MSS: Oriel College Oxford 31 and 43; Balliol College Oxford 57. [For other works ascribed to him see DNB., and for extracts see R. Martin, La Question de l'Unité de la Forme substantielle dans le premier Collège dominicain d'Oxford, Revue Néo-scolastique, XXII, 1920, pp. 107 ff.]
Pelster, F. Das Leben und die Schriften des Oxforder Dominikanerlehrers Richard Fishacre. Zeitschrift für katholische Theologie, LIV, 1930, pp. 527 ff.
—— Eine HS. mit Predigten des Richard Fischacre. Zeitschrift für katholische Theologie, LVII, 1933, pp. 614 ff.
Sharp, D. E. The Philosophy of Richard Fishacre (d. 1248). New Scholasticism, VII, 1933, pp. 281 ff.
Lottin, O. La Notion du libre Arbitre dans la jeune École dominicaine d'Oxford. Revue des Sciences philosophiques et théologiques, XXIV, 1935, pp. 268 ff. [Fishacre and Kilwardby.]

Robert Kilwardby (d. 1279; Dominican, archbishop of Canterbury). De ortu et divisione philosophiae. [Extracts in Hauréau, Notices et Extraits de quelques MSS latins, vol. v, 116 ff.]
—— De Natura Theologiae. Ed. F. Stegmüller, Münster, 1935.
[For Kilwardby's writings, see F. Tocco, Tractatus (Pechami) contra Fratrem Robertum Kilwardby, in British Soc. of Franciscan Stud. ii, 1910, pp. 91 ff., and Ueberweg-Geyer, p. 764.]
Chenu, M. D. Les Réponses de S. Thomas et de Kilwardby à la Consultation de Jean de Verceil (1271). [Mélanges Mandonnet, vol. i, Paris, 1930, pp. 191 ff.]
—— Le Traité 'De Tempore' de R. Kilwardby. [Aus der Geisteswelt des Mittelalters, vol. ii, Münster, 1935, pp. 854 ff.]
Sharp, D. E. The De Ortu Scientiarum of Robert Kilwardby. New Scholasticism, viii, 1934, pp. 1 ff.
—— The 1277 Condemnation of Kilwardby. New Scholasticism, viii, 1934, pp. 306 ff.
—— Further Philosophical Doctrines of Kilwardby. New Scholasticism, ix, 1935, pp. 39 ff.
Stegmüller, F. Les Questions du Commentaire des Sentences de Robert Kilwardby. Recherches de Théologie ancienne et médiévale, vi, 1934, pp. 55 ff.
—— Robert Kilwardby, O.P. über die Möglichkeit der natürlichen Gottesliebe. Divus Thomas, xxxviii, 1935, pp. 306 ff.
Sommer von Seckendorff, E. Robert Kilwardby und seine philosophische Einleitung 'De Ortu Scientiarum.' Historisches Jahrbuch, lv, 1935, pp. 312 ff.
Doudaine, A. Le 'De Tempore' de Robert Kilwardby, O.P. Recherches de Théologie ancienne et médiévale, xviii, 1936, pp. 94 ff.
—— La Question 'De Necessitate Incarnationis' de Robert Kilwardby, O.P. Recherches de Théologie ancienne et médiévale, xviii, 1936, pp. 97 ff.

Thomas Anglicus (may be Thomas Sutton, *fl*. 1280, but certainly is not Thomas Jorz, or Joyce, d. 1310, prior of Dominicans at Oxford, as DNB. supposes). Liber Propugnatorius super primum librum Sententiarum contra Ioannem Scotum. Venice, 1525.
Schmaus, M. Der Liber Propugnatorius des Thomas Anglicus und die Lehrunterschiede zwischen Thomas von Aquin und Duns Scotus. Münster, 1930.

Richard Clapwell (*fl*. 1286; Dominican Prior at Oxford). Correctorium corruptorii. Strasburg, 1501; Venice, 1501, 1516;

Naples, 1644. [Clapwell has been regarded as author (or joint-author with William of Macclesfield) of this reply to William de la Mare's Correctorium of St Thomas. See de Wulf, Mediaeval Philosophy, vol. ii, p. 44, note 3 and Ueberweg-Geyer, pp. 496 ff.]
Chenu, C. D. La première Diffusion du Thomisme à Oxford. Klapwell et ses 'Notes' sur les Sentences. Archives d'Histoire doctrinale et littéraire du Moyen Âge, iii, 1928, pp. 185 ff.
Pelster, F. Richard von Knapwell, O.P., seine Quaestiones disputatae und sein Quodlibet. Zeitschrift für katholische Theologie, lii, 1928, pp. 473 ff.

William of Hotham (d. 1298; archbishop of Dublin). [For list of works, see Quétif-Echard, vol. i, p. 460; also P. Mandonnet, Siger de Brabant et l'Averroïsme latin au XIIIᵉ Siècle, Freiburg, 1899, p. ciii, note 2; for MS see Paris Bibliothéque Nationale, MS Lat. 15805, quaestiones de quodlibet disputatae a fratre Wuil. de Hozun.]

Thomas of Sutton (*fl*. 1290; Dominican). Quaestiones de Reali Distinctione inter Essentiam et Esse. Ed. F. Pelster, Münster, 1929. [Extracts relating to doctrine of Trinity. In Schmaus, Der Liber Propugnatorius des Thomas Anglicus, vol. ii, pp. 8 ff. See also vol. i, p. xix for MSS of other works.]
Ehrle, F. Thomas de Sutton: sein Leben, seine Quolibet, und seine Quaestiones disputatae. Kempten, 1914. [See also von Hertling Festschrift, 1913.]
Pelster, F. Thomas von Sutton: ein Oxforder Verteidiger der thomistischen Lehre. Zeitschrift für katholische Theologie, xlvi, 1922, pp. 212 ff., 361 ff.
—— Schriften des Thomas von Sutton in der Universitätsbibliothek zu Münster. Zeitschrift für katholische Theologie, xlvii, 1923, pp. 483 ff.
—— Thomas von Sutton, O.P. als Verfasser zweier Schriften über die Einheit der Wesensform. Scholastik, iii, 1928, pp. 411 ff.
Sharp, D. E. Thomas of Sutton, O.P. Revue Néo-scholastique, xxxvii, 1934, pp. 89 ff.

(4) OTHER SCHOLARS AND MEN OF LETTERS

Alfred of 'Sereshel,' or Alfred the Englishman (*fl*. 1200). [Translation of pseudo-Aristotle, De Vegetabilibus.] Barcelona University MS 7.2.6. Ed. E. H. F. Meyer, Leipzig, 1841. [See A. Jourdain, Recherches critiques sur l'Âge et l'Origine des Traductions latines d'Aristote, 2nd edn, Paris, 1843, pp. 106, 430.]

Alfred of ' Sereshel,' or Alfred the Englishman. De motu cordis. Ed. C. Baeumker, Münster, 1923.

Baeumker, C. Die Stellung des Alfred von Sareshel (Alfredus Anglicus) und seiner Schrift de motu cordis in der Wissenschaft des beginnenden XIII. Jahrhunderts. Münchener Sitzungsber. ix, 1913. [See also Haskins, Studies in the History of Mediaeval Science, p. 128, note 48, and references in Baeumker, Der Platonismus im Mittelalter, p. 168, note 74.]

Pelzer, A. Un Source inconnu de Roger Bacon: Alfred de Sareshel, Commentateur des Météorologiques d'Aristote. Archivum Franciscanum Historicum, xii, 1919, pp. 44 ff.

Lacombe, G. Alfredus Anglicus in Metheora. [Aus der Geisteswelt des Mittelalters, vol. i, Münster, 1935, pp. 463 ff. Deals with newly-discovered text of Alfred's commentary on the Meteora.]

Adam of Dryburgh (Master Adam, the Premonstratensian; afterwards a Carthusian; d. c. 1212). Opera. Ed. Migne, Patrologia Latina, vol. cxcviii.

—— De quadripartito exercicio celle. Ed. Migne, Patrologia Latina, vol. cliii, cols. 787 ff. [where it is ascribed to Guigo II, prior of the Grande Chartreuse; on Adam's claim see E. M. Thompson, The Carthusian Order in England, pp. 354 ff.]

Birch, W. de G. Sermones fratris Ade Ordinis Praemonstratensis. Edinburgh, 1901.

Baxter, J. H. Inaugural Lecture. Theology, vi, 1927, pp. 81 ff.

Wilmart, A. Magister Adam Cartusiensis. [Mélanges Mandonnet, vol. ii, Paris, 1930, pp. 145 ff.]

Morin, G. Gloriosus Magister Adam. Revue Bénédictine, xliv, 1932, pp. 179 ff.

Thompson, E. M. A Fragment of a Witham Charterhouse Chronicle and Adam of Dryburgh. John Rylands Library Bulletin, xvi, 1932, pp. 482 ff.

Wilmart, A. Maître Adam Chanoine prémontré devenu chartreux à Witham. Analecta Premonstratensia, ix, 1933, pp. 209 ff.

Alan of Melsa (Prior of Beverley; fl. 1212). Tractatus metricus de Susanna. Ed. J. H. Mozley (Susanna and the Elders; Three Medieval Poems, Studi Medievali, Nuova serie, iii, 1930, pp. 41 ff.).

Alexander Neckham (d. 1217). De naturis rerum and De laudibus divinae sapientiae. Ed. T. Wright, Rolls Ser. 1863. [The De vita monachorum, ed. Wright, Satirical Poets, vol. ii, pp. 175 ff., is probably not by Neckham; B. Hauréau, Journal des Savants, 1882, p. 172, thinks that the author may be Roger of Caen, a monk of Bec.]

Alexander Neckham. Novus Aesopus. Ed. L. Hervieux (Les Fabulistes latins, vol. ii, Paris, 1894, pp. 392 ff.).

—— Novus Avianus. Ed. L. Hervieux (Les Fabulistes latins, vol. iii, pp. 462 ff.).

—— Hymns, etc. Analecta Hymnica, xlviii, pp. 262 ff.

—— Sacerdos ad altare. Ed. C. H. Haskins (A List of Text Books from the Close of the 12th Century, Harvard Stud. xx, 1909, pp. 75 ff.). [Rev. in Studies in the History of Mediaeval Science, pp. 356 ff.]

—— De nominibus utensilium. Ed. T. Wright (A Volume of Vocabularies, 1857, pp. 96 ff.); ed. A. Scheler (Lexicographie latine, Leipzig, 1867).

Hauréau, B. 'Alexander Neckham'. [In Nouvelle Biographie Universelle, 46 vols. Paris, 1852–66.)

—— Mémoires sur deux Écrits intitulés De motu cordis. Mémoires de l'Académie des Inscriptions, xxviii, pt ii, 1876, pp. 317 ff.

Ellis, R. Notes of a Fortnight's Research in the Bibliothèque Nationale of Paris. Journ. Philology, xv, 1886, pp. 241 ff.

—— A Contribution to the History of the Transmission of Classical Literature in the Middle Age, from Oxford MSS. A.J. Phil. x, 1889, p. 159.

Meyer, P. Notices sur les Corrogationes Promethei d'Alexandre Neckham. [Notices et Extraits des MSS, vol. xxxv, pt ii, 1876, pp. 641 ff.]

Mortet, V. Hugue de Fouillou, Pierre le Chantre, Alexandre Neckam, et les Critiques dirigées au XIIme Siècle contre le Luxe des Constructions. [Mélanges d'Histoire offerts à M. Charles Bémont, Paris, 1913, pp. 105 ff.]

Esposito, M. On some Unpublished Poems attributed to Alexander Neckham. EHR. xxx, 1915, pp. 450 ff. [For a correction see F. M. Powicke, Medieval Books of Merton College, Oxford, 1931, p. 173, note.]

[For a list of Neckham's works, see Manitius, Geschichte der lateinischen Literatur des Mittelalters, vol. iii, pp. 784 ff.]

Guy, Prior of Southwick (Augustinian; d. 1217).

Wilmart, A. Un Opuscule sur la Confession composé par Guy de Southwick vers la Fin du XIIe Siècle. Recherches de Théologie ancienne et médiévale, vii, 1935, pp. 337 ff.

Gervase of Melkley (de Saltu Lacteo; *fl.* 1213). Ars versificaria. [Summary in E. Faral, Les Arts poétiques du XIIᵉ et du XIIIᵉ Siècle, Paris, 1924, pp. 328 ff.]

Alberic of London (*fl.* 1217). Scintillarium poesis sive mythologia. Ed. A. Mai (Classici Auctores, vol. III, Rome, 1832, pp. 166 ff.).

Stephen Langton (d. 1228).

> Wilmart, A. L'Hymne et la Séquence du Saint-Esprit. La Vie et les Arts liturgiques, July 1924, pp. 395 ff. [Langton's claim to the authorship of the Veni, sancte Spiritus; see also H. Thurston, Month, June 1913, pp. 602 ff.; Analecta Hymnica, vol. LIV, pp. 237 ff.; Raby, Christian-Latin Poetry, pp. 343 f.]
>
> Powicke, F. M. Stephen Langton. Oxford, 1928. [Langton's Sermons, list of MSS, pp. 168 ff.; his Quaestiones, MSS, pp. 177 ff.; text of his poem Documenta clericorum from Bodl. MS 57, pp. 205 f.; on Langton as poet and his claims to Veni, sancte Spiritus, pp. 45 ff.]
>
> —— Stephen Langton. [In The Christian Life in the Middle Ages and other Essays, Oxford, 1935, pp. 130 ff.]
>
> Lacombe, G. The Questions of Cardinal Stephen Langton. New Scholasticism, III, 1929, pp. 1 ff., 113 ff., IV, 1930, pp. 115 ff.
>
> —— The Authenticity of the Summa of Cardinal Stephen Langton. New Scholasticism, IV, 1930, pp. 97 ff.
>
> Lacombe, G. and Smalley, B. Studies on the Commentaries of Cardinal Stephen Langton. Archives d'Histoire doctrinale et littéraire du Moyen Âge, V, 1930, pp. 5 ff., VI, 1931, pp. 272 ff.
>
> Dulong, M. Étienne Langton, Versificateur. [Mélanges Mandonnet, vol. II, Paris, 1930, pp. 183 ff.]
>
> Gregory, A. L. The Cambridge MS. of the Quaestiones of Stephen Langton. New Scholasticism, IV, 1930, pp. 165 ff.
>
> —— Indices of Rubrics and Incipits of the Principal Manuscripts of the Quaestiones of Stephen Langton. Archives d'Histoire doctrinale et littéraire du Moyen Âge, V, 1930, pp. 221 ff.
>
> Smalley, B. Stephen Langton and the Four Senses of Scripture. Speculum, VI, 1931, pp. 60 ff.
>
> —— Exempla in the Commentaries of Stephen Langton. John Rylands Lib. Bulletin, XVII, 1933, pp. 121 ff.
>
> Major, K. The 'Familia' of Archbishop Stephen Langton. EHR. XLVIII, 1933, pp. 529 ff. [With bibliography of Langton by F. M. Powicke.]

Michael Scot (d. before 1236). Translation of àl-Bitrogi (Alpetragius), de Sphaera. BM. Harl. MS 1.

—— Translation of Aristotle, Historia animalium. Merton College Oxford MS 278.

—— Abbreviatio Avicenne de animalibus.

—— Liber introductorius, liber particularis, Physionomia. [Three treatises on astrology. The last named is also known as De Secretis naturae, ed. R. Foerster, Scriptores Physiognomici, Leipzig, 1893.]

[On Michael Scot, see Haskins, Michael Scot, in Studies in the History of Mediaeval Science, pp. 272 ff. Haskins gives the above and further references to MSS, and valuable bibliographical notes.]

> Brown, J. W. An Inquiry into the Life and Legend of Michael Scot. Edinburgh, 1897.
>
> Haskins, C. H. The Alchemy ascribed to Michael Scot. [In Studies in Mediaeval Science, pp. 148 ff.]

John Holywood (de Sacro Bosco or of Halifax, *fl.* 1230; mathematician). Tractatus de Sphaera. Ferrara, 1472; Paris, 1498. [Many other editions and translations into various languages; a popular text-book of astronomy. For other works see DNB.]

William the Englishman (*fl.*1231; astronomer). Liber tabule que nominatur Saphea [trn of Al-Zarkeli]. Pt i, ed. L. P. E. A. Sédillot (Mémoires sur les Instruments astronomiques des Arabes, Paris, 1844, pp. 185 ff.); pt ii, ed. P. Tannery (Notices et Extraits des MSS. de la Bibliothèque Nationale, vol. XXV, pp. 635 ff.).

William of Drogheda (d. 1245?). Summa Aurea. Caius College Cambridge MSS 54 (31) and 85 (3). Ed. L. Wahrmund (Quellen zur Geschichte des römischkanonischen Processus im Mittelalter, vol. II, pt ii, Innsbruck, 1915).

> Maitland, F. W. William of Drogheda and the Universal Ordinary. EHR. XII, pp. 625 ff., 645 ff. (extracts from William's Summa). [Also in Maitland, Roman Canon Law in the Church of England, 1898, pp. 107 ff.; p. 109 on MSS.]

Odo of Cheriton (d. 1247). Fabulae et Parabolae. Ed. L. Hervieux (Les Fabulistes latins, vol. IV). [See J. T. Welter, L'Exemplum dans la Littérature religieuse et didactique du Moyen Âge, Paris, 1927, pp. 124 ff.; text of sermon, pp. 469 ff.]

Petrus de Hibernia (*fl.* 1240).

> Baeumker, C. Petrus de Hibernia, der Jugendlehrer des Thomas von Aquino und seine Disputation vor König Manfred. Sitzungsber. d. kgl. bayer. Akademie d. Wissensch. VIII, 1920. [The subject of the

disputation was 'utrum membra essent facta propter operaciones vel operaciones essent factae propter membra'; text, pp. 41 ff.]

Grabmann, M. Magister Petrus von Hibernia. Seine Disputation vor König Manfred und seine Aristoteleskommentar. [Mittelalterliches Geistesleben, 1926, pp. 249 ff.]

John of Basingstoke (d. 1252; archdeacon of Leicester, friend of Grosseteste and knew Greek). [See DNB. for his lost works.]

Richard the Englishman (Richard of Wendover and of Salerno; d. 1252). Micrologus [containing five medical treatises: Practica, De Urinis, Anatomia, Repressiva, Prognostica]. Bibliothèque Nationale, Paris, MS 6957. [For other MSS see DNB.]

—— Anatomia. Ed. R. Töpley, Vienna, 1902.

—— Correctorium Alchemiae. Ed. L. Zetzner (Theatrum Chemicum, vol. ii, Strasburg, 1659, pp. 1613 ff.).

—— De signis febrium [part of De signis prognosticis]. [In Opus aureum ac praeclarum, Venice, 1514.]

Stephen of Easton (d. 1252; abbot of Fountains). Meditationes. Ed. A. Wilmart, Revue d'Ascétique et de Mystique, 1929, pp. 368 ff.

—— Exercitium triplex. Ed. A. Wilmart, Revue d'Ascétique et de Mystique, 1930, pp. 355 ff.

Robert Grosseteste (d. 1253). Die philosophischen Werke des Robert Grosseteste. Ed. L. Baur, Münster, 1903.

—— Epistolae. Ed. H. R. Luard, Rolls Ser. 1861.

—— Visio Philiberti [a dialogue between Body and Soul in 'goliardic' verse; it is not improbable that Grosseteste is the author]. Ed. T. G. von Karajan (Frühlingsgabe für Freunde älterer Literatur, Vienna, 1839, pp. 85 ff.); ed. T. Wright (Poems attributed to Walter Mapes, pp. 95 ff.); ed. É du Méril (Poésies populaires latines du Moyen Âge, Paris, 1847, pp. 217 ff.); ed. Florilegium Casinense, vol. iv, 1880, pp. 253 ff.

[See H. Walther, Das Streitgedicht in der lateinischen Literatur des Mittelalters, Munich, 1920, pp. 64 ff. Many of the poems given or referred to in this book are in English MSS.]

Pauli, R. Bischof Grosseteste und Adam Marsch. Tübingen, 1864.

Felten, J. Robert Grosseteste. Freiburg, 1887.

Stevenson, F. S. Robert Grosseteste. 1899.

Baur, L. Das Licht in der Naturphilosophie des Robert Grosseteste. [Festgabe Hertling, 1913, pp. 41 ff.]

Baur, L. Die Philosophie des Robert Grosseteste, Bischofs von Lincoln. Münster, 1917.

Hocedez, E. La Diffusion de la 'Translatio Lincolniensis' du De orthodoxa fide de S. Jean Damascène. Bulletin d'ancienne Littérature et Archéologie chrétienne, 1913, pp. 189 ff.

Minges, P. Robert Grosseteste als Übersetzer der Ethica Nicomachea. Philosophisches Jahrbuch, xxxii, 1919, pp. 230 ff.

James, M. R. Robert Grosseteste on the Psalms. Journ. Theological Stud. xxiii, 1922, pp. 181 ff.

Pelster, F. Zwei unbekannte Traktate des Robert Grosseteste. Scholastik, i, 1926, pp. 572 ff.

Powicke, F. M. Robert Grosseteste and the Nicomachean Ethics. Proc. British Academy, xvi, 1930.

Franceschini, E. Grosseteste's Translation of the Πρόλογος and Σχόλια of Maximus to the Writings of the Pseudo-Dionysius Areopagitica. Journ. Theological Stud. xxxiv, 1932, pp. 355 ff.

—— Roberto Grossetesta e le sue Traduzioni latine. R. Istituto Veneto di Scienza, Lettere, ed Arti, 1933–4.

Thomson, S. H. A Note on Grosseteste's Work of Translation. Journ. Theological Stud. xxxv, 1933, pp. 48 ff.

—— Grosseteste's Topical Concordance of the Bible and the Fathers. Speculum, ix, 1934, pp. 139 ff.

Phelan, G. B. An Unedited Text of Robert Grosseteste on the Subject-matter of Theology. Revue Néo-scolastique, xxxvi, 1934, pp. 172 ff.

John Garland (d. c. 1258). De Mysteriis Ecclesiae. Ed. B. W. Otto (Commentarii critici in Codices bibliothecae Gissensis, Giessen, 1842, pp. 131 ff.). [See also Leyser, Historia Poetarum et Poematum medii aevi, pp. 339 ff.]

—— De Triumphis Ecclesiae. Ed. T. Wright, Roxburghe Club, 1856.

—— [Hymns, etc.] Analecta Hymnica, vol. li, pp. 546 ff.

—— Morale Scolarium. Ed. L. J. Paetow, Berkeley, 1927. [Contains list of Garland's works. See C. H. Haskins, Manuals for Students, in Studies in Mediaeval Culture, pp. 76 ff.]

—— Dictionarius. Ed. T. Wright (A Volume of Vocabularies, 1857, pp. 120 ff.).

—— Poetria magistri Johannis Anglici de arte prosayca metrica et rithmica. Ed. G. Mari, Romanische Forschungen, xiii, 1902, pp. 883 ff.

John Garland. Integumenta Ovidii. Ed. F. Ghisalberti, Messina, 1933.

Zarncke, F. Zwei mittelalterliche Abhandlungen über den Bau rhythmischer Verse. Leipziger Sitzungsber. XXIII, 1871, pp. 34 ff.

Hauréau, B. Les Œuvres de Jean de Garlande. [Notices et Extraits des MSS. de la Bibliothèque Nationale, vol. XXVII, pt ii, pp. 1 ff. See also Faral, Les Arts poétiques du XIIᵉ et du XIIIᵉ Siècle, pp. 40 ff.]

Habel, E. Johannes de Garlandia, ein Schulmann des XIII. Jahrhunderts. Mitteilungen der Gesellschaft für ·deutsche Erziehungs- und Schulgeschichte, 1909, pp. 1 ff., 119 ff.

—— Die Exempla honestae vitae des Johannes de Garlandia. Romanische Forschungen, XXIX, 1911, pp. 131 ff.

Paetow, L. J. The Crusading Ardour of John of Garland. [In The Crusades and other Historical Essays presented to Dana C. Munro, New York, 1928.]

Wilson, E. F. The Georgica Spiritualia of John of Garland. Speculum, VIII, 1932, pp. 358 ff. [Shows that the fragments pbd by F. Novati, in Un Poème inconnu de Gautier de Châtillon, Mélanges Paul Fabre, Paris, 1902, pp. 265 ff., are really excerpts from a religious poem of John of Garland called Georgica Spiritualia.]

Wilmart, A. Commentaire du Distigium de Jean de Garlande. Analecta Reginensia, 1933, pp. 253 ff.

Michael of Cornwall (fl. 1250). Poem against Master Henry of Avranches. MSS: Cambridge Univ. Lib. Ff. VI. 13; Bodl. 851; BM. Cott. Tib. A xx, and Royal 14 C XIII. Ed. A. Hilka [Mittelalterliche Handschriften, Degering Festgabe, Leipzig, 1926, pp. 125 ff.). [For Michael, and Henry of Avranches, who, although of Norman birth, lived much in England and was a court poet, see J. C. Russell, Master Henry of Avranches, Speculum, III, 1928, pp. 34 ff.; list of Henry's poems and MSS, pp. 58 ff. His Comoda gramatice is ed. J. P. Heironimus and J. C. Russell, Two Types of 13th Century Grammatical Poems, Colorado College Publications, no. 158, 1929.]

The Shorter Latin Poems of Master Henry of Avranches relating to England. Ed. J. C. Russell and J. P. Heironimus, Cambridge, U.S.A. 1935. [With list of works and bibliography.]

Gilbert the Englishman (fl. 1250). Compendium Medicinae. Lyons, 1510. [On Gilbert, one of the earliest English writers on medicine, see DNB. where there is also a list of other works ascribed to him.]

Laurence of Somercote (fl. 1254; canon of Chichester). [Treatise on the canonical election of bishops.] Ed. A. von Wretschke, Weimar, 1907.

Henry de Bracton (d. 1268). De legibus et consuetudinibus Angliae. Ed. T. Twiss, 6 vols. Rolls Ser. 1878–83; ed. G. E. Woodbine, 2 vols. New Haven, 1915, 1922, etc.

—— Bracton's Note Book. Ed. F. W. Maitland, 3 vols. 1887.

[For bibliography, see Gross, Sources and Literature of English History, p. 401.]

John of Hoveden (d. 1275). Practica Chilindri. Ed. E. Brock (Essays on Chaucer, Chaucer Soc. vol. II, 1874, pp. 57 ff.).

—— Poems. (1) Meditatio de nativitate passione et resurrectione domini, etc. [Also called Philomena; beginning Ave verbum ens in principio]. Louvain, [c. 1488]; Ghent, 1516; Luxemburg, 1603; ed. C. Blume, Hymnologische Beiträge, IV, Leipzig, 1930. [Extracts in Dreves-Blume, Ein Jahrtausend lateinischer Hymnendichtung, vol. I, Leipzig, 1909, pp. 343 ff.]

(2) Lyra extollens Virginem gloriosam. Analecta Hymnica, vol. XXI, p. 53.

(3) Quinquaginta salutationes beatae virginis. [Extracts in Dreves-Blume, vol. I, p. 348.]

(4) Viola. Ed. F. J. E. Raby, MLR. xxx, 1935, pp. 339 ff.

[The poems as a whole are to be found in BM. MS Nero C IX (14th cent.; almost complete); Bodl. MS Laud. Misc. 368; Bibliothèque Nationale Paris 3757. For extracts and incipits, see Raby, Christian-Latin Poetry, pp. 389 ff.]

Kingsford, C. L. 'John Hoveden.' DNB.

Raby, F. J. E. John of Hoveden. Laudate, XIII, 1935, pp. 87 ff.

Fleta, seu Commentarius Juris Anglici. 1647; 1685.

Fleta, Lib. I. Ed. T. Clarke, 1735. [This work was compiled, c. 1290, in Fleet Prison; based on Bracton.]

Selden, J. Ad Fletam dissertatio. Ed. D. Ogg, Cambridge, 1925.

Anonymous Poems (end of 13th cent.).

(1) De mutatione mala ordinis Cistercii. Ed. W. Meyer (Zwei Gedichte zur Geschichte des Cistercienser Ordens, Nachrichten von der königlichen Gesellschaft der Wissenschaften zu Göttingen, 1908, pp. 396 ff.).

(2) Quondam fuit factus festus. Ibid. pp. 406 ff.

[There is no reason to regard as of English origin any of the poems in the 'Arundel Collection,' edited by W. Meyer, Die Arundel

Sammlung mittellateinischer Lieder, Abhandlungen der königlichen Akademie der Wissenschaften zu Göttingen, 1909.]

F. MANUALS FOR PREACHERS, ETC.

Caplan, H. Medieval Artes Praedicandi. Oxford, 1934. [Supplement, Cornell Studies, 1936.]

Charland, T. Les Auteurs d'Artes Praedicandi au XIII Siècle d'après les Manuscrits. Études d'Histoire littéraire et doctrinale du XIII Siècle, i, 1932.

Crane, T. F. Mediaeval Sermon-Books and Stories. Proc. American Philosophical Soc. xxi, 1883, pp. 49 ff.

—— Mediaeval Sermon-Books and their Study since 1883. Proc. American Philosophical Soc. lvi, 1917, pp. 369 ff.

Davy, M. M. Les Sermons universitaires parisiens de 1230–1231. Paris, 1931. [Texts of sermons by John of St Giles and Richard of Cornwall.]

Deanesly, M. The Lollard Bible. Cambridge, 1920.

Herbert, J. A. Catalogue of Romances in the Department of Manuscripts in the British Museum. Vol. iii, 1910.

Mosher, J. H. The Exemplum in England. New York, 1911.

Owst, G. R. Preaching in Medieval England, an Introduction to Sermon Manuscripts of the Period c. 1350–1450. Cambridge, 1926. [Referred to below as Owst.]

—— Literature and Pulpit in Medieval England. Cambridge, 1933.

Welter, J. T. L'Exemplum dans la Littérature réligieuse et didactique du Moyen Âge. Paris, 1927.

Edmund Rich (d. 1240; archbishop of Canterbury). Speculum Sancti Edmundi (Speculum Ecclesiae). Leyden, 1677; Paris, 1854.

Wallace, W. Life of St Edmund of Canterbury. 1893.

Lacombe, G. La Summa Abendonensis. [Mélanges Mandonnet, vol. ii, Paris, 1930, pp. 163 ff. On Rich and Simon de Henton.]

Liber Exemplorum ad usum praedicantium (c. 1275). [Compiled by an English Friar in Ireland.] Ed. A. G. Little, British Soc. Franciscan Stud. 1908.

Speculum laicorum. Ed. J. T. Welter, Paris, 1914. [Compiled c. 1280 by an English Friar, probably Franciscan; Little, English Franciscan History, p. 138.]

Malachy (fl. 1310; Irish Franciscan). Libellus septem peccatorum mortalium venena eorumque remedia describens, qui dicitur venenum Malachiae. Paris, 1518. [See J. T. Welter, L'Exemplum dans la Littéra-ture religieuse et didactique du Moyen Âge, p. 173.]

Nicole Bozon [Frère Mineur]. Les Contes Moralisés. Ed. L. T. Smith and P. Meyer, Société des Anciens Textes français, 1889. [Compiled in French by an English Franciscan, c. 1320; there is an incomplete Latin version; part of each example is an animal fable; Little, English Franciscan History, p. 139.]

Robert Silke, or Spicer (fl. 1320; Franciscan). Fasciculus morum. MSS: Bodley 187, 332, 410 [and others given in Little, English Franciscan History, pp. 139 ff.].

William Page (de Pagula). Oculus Sacerdotis. MSS: BM. Royal 6 E i and others in Owst, p. 297, note 1. [See also H. W. C. Davis, The Canon Law in England, Zeitschrift der Savigny-Stiftung für Rechtsgeschichte,1913, p. 349.] [Date, c. 1325; a complete 'vademecum' for parsons, Owst, p. 297. There was also a Cilium Oculi Sacerdotis, an anonymous work, see Owst, p. 298, note 4, MSS.]

Gesta Romanorum [c. 1340; probably the work of a Franciscan, to a large extent from English materials, if not actually of English origin]. Ed. H. Oesterley, Berlin, 1872; ed. W. Dick [without the religious application of the stories], Erlangen, 1890; tr. Eng. C. Swan, ed. E. A. Baker, 1924.

Krepinski, M. Quelques Remarques relatives à l'Histoire des Gesta Romanorum. Moyen Âge, xv, 1911, pp. 307 ff., 346 ff.

Welter, J. T. L'Exemplum dans la Littérature religieuse et didactique du moyen Âge. Paris, 1927, pp. 369 ff.

Thomas Walleys (Wallensis; Dominican, d. 1340). Ars Predicandi. MS. Bibliothèque Mazarine Lat. 569 is being edited by M. M. Davy; BM. Harl. 635.

—— De modo componendi sermones cum documentis. MS. Bibliothèque Mazarine Lat. 569; Cambridge University Lib. Gg.vi.20.

Regimen Animarum. BM. Harl. MS 2272. [Owst, pp. 297 f.; c. 1343.]

Robert Holcot (d. 1347; Dominican). Liber de moralizationibus. Venice, 1505; Paris, 1510; Basle, 1586, etc.

—— Liber Sapiencie Salomonis. Basle, 1586.

—— Sermons. BM. MSS Royal 7 C i, Harl. 5369. [Owst, Literature and Pulpit, p. 194, note 1.]

[For other works, see DNB. and on Holcot generally, J. T. Welter, L'Exemplum dans la Littérature religieuse et didactique du Moyen Âge, pp. 360 ff.]

Ranulf Higden (d. 1364). Ars Predicandi. Bodl. MSS 5 and 316. [Owst, pp. 247 and 315, note 2.]

—— Polychronicon. Ed. C. Babington and J. R. Lumby. 9 vols. Rolls Ser. 1865–1886.

John of Tynemouth (d. 1366). Sanctilogium [legends of Saints]. MS Bodl. 240 [and others in J. T. Welter, L'Exemplum dans la Littérature religieuse et didactique du Moyen Âge, p. 161, note 37].

John of Mirfield (Austin canon of S. Bartholomew, Smithfield, c. 1370 [?], Owst, p. 306). Florarium Bartholomei. MSS: Cambridge University Lib. Mm.ii.10; BM. Roy. 7 F xi, and Gray's Inn Lib. 4. [Owst, p.306, note 5, gives a list of some of its 'fresh topical headings.']

Hartley, Sir P. and Aldridge, H. R. Johannes de Mirfeld: his Life and Works. 1936.

Ralph of Acton (fl. 1380). Expositorium. MS John Rylands Lib. Lat. 367.

John de Bromyard (fl. 1390; Dominican). Summa Predicantium. [Ptd Nuremberg, 1485 and lastly at Venice, 1586.] BM. Royal MS 7 E iv. [For other MSS see Owst, p. 68, note 1, and on the Summa generally see J. T, Welter, L'Exemplum dans la Littérature religieuse et didactique du Moyen Âge. pp. 328 ff.]

John Myrc (Mirk; fl. 1403). Manuale Sacerdotum. MSS: Cambridge University Lib. Ff.i.14; York Cathedral Lib. xvi, L 8; Owst, p. 297, note 3. [Others mentioned in DNB.; for his English Instructions for Parish Priests see p. 265.]

Alexander Anglicus (fl. 1429; Fabricius or Carpenter). Destructorium Viciorum. Cologne, 1480, 1485; Nuremberg, 1491, 1500; Paris, 1497, 1500, 1505, 1509, 1516, 1521. ['A vast unoriginal compendium of the vices, boasting an almost unrivalled succession of printed editions down to the year 1521,' Owst, p. 306; date, 1429.]

Thomas Wyngale (fl. 1470; Premonstratensian of W. Dereham). Speculum Juratorum [a summary of virtues and vices]. BM. MS Harl. 148. [See J. T. Welter, L'Exemplum dans la Littérature religieuse et didactique du Moyen Âge, pp. 442 f.]

G. THE 14TH AND 15TH CENTURIES

(1) GENERAL WORKS

Baxter, J. H. Four 'New' Medieval Scottish Authors. Scottish Hist. Rev. xxv, 1928, pp. 90 ff. [Thomas Rossy, bishop of Whithorn, d. 1409; Laurence of Lindores, d. 1437 (see Scottish Hist. Rev. viii, 1910–1 pp. 235 ff.); William Croyser, fl. 1434; Thomas Livingstone, fl. 1440.]

Garrison, F. H. An Introduction to the History of Medicine. Philadelphia, 1913 and 1922 (rev. edn).

Kingsford, C. L. English Historical Literature in the 15th Century. Oxford, 1913.

Michalski, C. Les Courants philosophiques à Oxford et à Paris pendant le XIV Siècle. Bulletin de l'Académie polonaise des Sciences et des Lettres, Cracow, 1921.

—— La Physique nouvelle et les différent Courants philosophiques au XIVe Siècle Bulletin de l'Académie polonaise de Sciences et des Lettres, Cracow, 1928.

Mitchell, R. J. English Students at Padua 1460–75. Trans. Royal Hist. Soc. 1936 pp. 101 ff.

Schum, W. Verzeichnis der Amplonianische Handschriften zu Erfurt. Erfurt, 1887 [For Merton scholars represented in thi collection of 'Oxford dialectical works made by Amplonius at end of 14th cent see F. M. Powicke, The Medieval Books c Merton College, Oxford, 1931, p. 27, note.

Thorndike, L. Science and Thought in th Fifteenth Century. New York, 1929.

Tout, T. F. Literature and Learning in th English Civil Service in the 14th Century Speculum, iv, 1929, pp. 365 ff.

Xiberta, B. M. Le Thomisme de l'École carmélitaine. [Mélanges Mandonnet, vol. Paris, 1930, pp. 441 ff. Especially fc Baconthorpe and Walsingham.]

—— De Scriptoribus scholasticis Saeculi XI ex Ordine Carmelitarum. Louvain, 193 [Includes English Carmelite writers.]

(2) FRANCISCANS

John Duns Scotus (d. 1308). Opera. Ec L. Wadding, 12 vols. Lyons, 1639; rpt Paris, 1891–5.

—— Opus Oxoniense in primum librum Ser tentiarum. Venice, 1472. [And often, unt at Zug in 1702.]

Klein, J. Zur Sittenlehre des Joh. Dur Skotus. Franziskanische Studien, i 1915, pp. 137 ff.

Minges, P. Die Skotische Literatur des 2 Jahrhunderts. Franziskanische Studie iv, 1917, pp. 49 ff., 177 ff.

Landry, B. Duns Scot. Paris, 1922.

Carreras y Artou, J. Ensayo sobre Voluntarismo de J. Duns Scot. Geron 1923.

Pelster, F. Handschriftliches zu Skot mit neuen Angaben über sein Lebe Franziskanische Studien, x, 1923, pp 1

Pelster, F. Eine Münchener Hs. des beginnenden XIV. Jahrhunderts mit einem Verzeichnis von Quaestionen des Duns Scotus und Herveus Natalis. Franziskanische Studien, XVII, 1930, pp. 253 ff.

—— Handschriftliches zur Ueberlieferung der Quaestiones super libros Metaphysicorum und der Collationes des Duns Scotus. Philosophisches Jahrbuch, XLIV, 1931, pp. 79 ff.

Pelzer, A. Le premier Livre des Reportata Parisiensia de Jean Duns Scot. Annales de l'Institut supérieur de Philosophie de Louvain, V, 1923, pp. 449 ff.

Longpré, E. La Philosophie du bienheureux Duns Scot. Paris, 1924. [Criticism of Landry.]

—— Le B. Jean Duns Scot pour le St.-Siège et contre le Gallicanisme, 25–28 Juin, 1303. La France Franciscaine, XI, 1928.

—— Le B. Duns Scot, docteur du Verbe Incarné. Studi francescani, XXX, 1933, pp. 171 ff.

—— Une Réportation inédite du B. Duns Scot: le MS. Ripoll 53. [Aus der Geisteswelt des Mittelalters, vol. II, Münster, 1935, pp. 974 ff.]

Gilson, É. Avicenne et le Point de Depart de Duns Scot. Archives d'Histoire doctrinale et littéraire des Moyen Âge, II, 1927, pp. 89 ff.

Harris, C. R. S. Duns Scotus. 2 vols. Oxford, 1927. [For list of works attributed to Duns Scotus see vol. I, app. I, pp. 313 ff.; full bibliography, vol. I, app. II, pp. 316 ff.]

Balič, C. De Collationibus Joannis Duns Scoti. Bogoslovni Vestnik, IX, 1929, pp. 186 ff.

—— Joannis Duns Scoti Theologiae marianae Elementa. Sibenic, 1933.

Heilig, K. J. Zum Tode des Johannes Duns Scot. Historisches Jahrbuch, XLIX, 1929, pp. 641 ff.

Lampen, W. Joannes Duns Scotus et Sancta Sedes. Quaracchi, 1929.

MacDonagh, H. La Notion d'Être dans la Métaphysique de Jean Duns Scot. Revue Néo-scolastique, XXXI, 1929, pp. 81 ff., 148 ff.

Callebant, A. À propos du bienheureux Jean Duns Scot de Littledean. Archivum Franciscanum Historicum, XXIV, 1931, pp. 305 ff.

Little, A. G. Chronological Notes on the Life of Duns Scotus. EHR. XLVII, 1932, pp. 568 ff.

Kirby, G. T. The Authenticity of the De Perfectione Statuum of Duns Scot. New Scholasticism, VII, 1933, pp. 134 ff.

Luger, F. Die Unsterblichkeitsfrage bei Johannes Duns Scotus, ein Beitrag zur Geschichte der Rückbildung des Aristotelismus in der Scholastik. Vienna, 1933.

Rivière, J. La Doctrine de Scot sur la Rédemption devant l'Histoire et la Théologie. Estudis Franciscans, XLV, 1933, pp. 271 ff.

Kaup, J. Duns Skotus als Vollender der Lehre von der unbefleckten Empfängnis. [Aus der Geisteswelt des Mittelalters, vol. II, Münster, 1935, pp. 991 ff.]

William of Alnwick (fl. 1300; pupil of Duns Scotus). Quaestiones de esse intelligibili. Vatican Lat. MS 1012. [See C. Michalski, Die vielfachen Redaktionen einiger Kommentare zu Petrus Lombardus, Miscellanea Ehrle, vol. I, Rome, 1924, pp. 218 f., and Little, Franciscan School at Oxford, Archivum Franciscanum Historicum, XIX, 1926, pp. 72 f.]

Robert Cowton (fl. 1300). Commentaries on the Sentences. MSS: BM. Royal II B I, II B IV [and others given in Little, Grey Friars in Oxford, p. 222 who says, 'if we may draw any inference from the number of MSS preserved, few works by any Franciscan were in more demand in England in the 14th and 15th centuries'].

Peter Sutton (fl. 1311). [See M. Schmaus, Die Quaestio des Petrus Sutton O.F.M. über die Univokation des Seins, Collectanea Franciscana, III, 1933, pp. 5 ff.]

Richard de Coniton, or Conyngton (Provincial of England, 1310). Tractatus de paupertate contra opiniones Fratris Petri Joannis (Olivi). MS: Florence, Laurentiana, ex Bibl. S. Crucis, Plut. XXXVI, Dext. Cod. XII (late 14th cent.). [See Little, Grey Friars in Oxford, p. 164.]

Douie, D. L. Three Treatises on Evangelical Poverty by Fr. Richard Conyngton, Fr. Walter Chatton and an Anonymous from MS. v, iii, 18, in Bishop Cosin's Library Durham. Archivum Franciscanum Historicum, XXIV, 1931, pp. 341 ff. [On Chatton see D. L. Douie, The Nature and Effect of the Heresy of the Fraticelli, Manchester, 1932, pp. 202 ff.]

John Canon (fl. 1320). [Comment] in libros Octo Physicorum Aristotelis. Padua, 1475; St Albans, 1481; Venice, 1481, etc. [A popular work; see Little, Grey Friars in Oxford, p. 223.]

John of Reading (fl. 1320). In primum librum sententiarum. Biblioteca Nazionale Florence MS D 4, 95. [His Quaestio de Trinitate contained in this MS is edited in M. Schmaus, Der Liber Propugnatorius des

Thomas Anglicus, vol. II, pp. 286* ff.; on John of Reading see E. Longpré, Jean de Reading, in La France franciscaine, 1924, pp. 99 ff.]

Hugh of Newcastle (*fl.* 1322). In primum librum sententiarum. Bibliothèque Nationale Paris Lat. MS 15864.
—— De victoria Christi contra Anti-Christum. Nuremberg, 1471.
  Langlois, C. V. Hugo de Novocastro. [In Essays in Medieval History presented to T. F. Tout, Manchester, 1925, pp. 269 ff.]

Martin of Alnwick (d. 1336; 'Martinus Anglicus'). [See J. Lechner, Beiträge zum Schrifttum des Martinus Anglicus [Martin von Alnwick] O.F.M., Franziskanische Studien, XIX, 1932, pp. 1 ff.]

William of Nottingham (d. 1336; Franciscan). [Commentary on the Sentences, in Caius College MS 300.]
  Meier, L. Wilhelm von Nottingham. Philosophia Perennis. [Festgabe J. Geyser, Regensburg, 1930, pp. 247 ff.]

John de Ridevaus, Rideval or Redovallensis (*fl.* 1330). Ovidii Metamorphoseos fabule ccxviii moraliter exposite. Worcester Cathedral Lib. MS 89 (= 764) [which ascribes it to Jo. Risdevallus; in Cambridge University Lib. MSS i II 20 (15th cent.) and Mm.I.18, § 6 (15th cent.) it is anonymous]. [See Little, Grey Friars in Oxford, p. 171. There are other moral expositions of the Metamorphoses; other works of John de Ridevaus, Little, p. 171.]

Walter Burley (d. *c.* 1345). Liber de vitis et moribus philosophorum et poetarum. Ed. H. Knust, Litterarischer Verein in Stuttgart, 1886.
—— De intentione et remissione formarum. Venice, 1496, 1519.
—— De materia et forma. Oxford, 1500.
—— Comm. in Ethicam Aristotelis. Venice, 1509, 1524.
—— Comm. super IX Lib. Physicorum. Venice, 1509, 1524.
—— Comm. in lib. Posteriorum Analytic. Oxford, 1517.
—— Summa totius logicae. Venice, 1508.
  Baudry, L. Les Rapports de Guillaume d'Occam et de Walter Burleigh. Archives d'Histoire doctrinale et littéraire du Moyen Âge, IX, 1934, pp. 155 ff.

John of Rodington (d. *c.* 1348).
  Lechner, J. Johannes von Rodington, O.F.M., und seine Quodlibet de Conscientia. [Aus der Geisteswelt des Mittel-

alters, vol. II, Münster, 1935, pp. 1125 ff.]
—— Die Quästionen der Sentenzenkommentars des Johannes von Rodington, O.F.M. Franziskanische Studien, XXII, 1935, pp. 232 ff.

William of Ockham (d. *c.* 1349). Expositio aurea super artem veterem. Bologna, 1496.
—— Summa logice. Paris, 1488; Venice, 1522; Oxford, 1675.
—— Quaestiones in octo libros physicorum. Rome, 1637.
—— Summulae in octo libros physicorum. Venice, 1506.
—— Quaestiones in quattuor libros Sententiarum. Lyons, 1495.
—— Quodlibeta septem. Paris, 1487; Strasburg, 1491.
—— De sacramento altaris. De corpore Christi. Strasburg, 1491; Venice, 1516; former ed. T. B. Birch, Burlington, Iowa, 1930.
—— Centiloquium theologicum. Lyons, 1495.
—— Opus nonaginta dierum. Louvain, 1481; Lyons, 1495; ed. M. Goldast (Monarchia, vol. II, Frankfort, 1614, pp. 993 ff.).
—— Epistola ad Fratres Minores [in capitulo apud Assisium congregatos (1334)]. Ed. L. Baudry, Revue d'Histoire franciscaine, III, 1926, pp. 185 ff.; ed. C. K. Brampton, Oxford, 1929.
—— Dialogus inter magistrum et discipulum de Imperatorum et Pontificum potestate. Lyons, 1495; ed. M. Goldast (Monarchia, vol. II, Frankfort, 1614, pp. 398 ff.); ed. C. K. Brampton, Oxford, 1929 (part) and remainder, W. Mulder, Archivum Franciscanum Historicum, XVI, 1923, pp. 469 ff. and XVII, 1924, pp. 72 ff.
—— Tractatus de electione Caroli iv. Ed. C. von Höfler, Abhandlungen der königlichen böhmischen Gesellschaft der Wissenschaften, VI, i, 1868, pp. 14 ff.
—— Defensorium (de paupertate Christi) contra Johannem XXII. Venice, 1513; ed. E. Brown (Fasciculus Rerum expetendarum, vol. II, 1690, pp. 439 ff.).
—— Tractatus adversus errores Johannis XXII. Louvain, 1481; Lyons, 1495; ed. M. Goldast (Monarchia, vol. II, Frankfort, 1614, pp. 957 ff.).
—— De iurisdictione imperatoris in causis matrimonialibus. Heidelberg, 1598; ed. M. Goldast (Monarchia, vol. I, Hanover, 1612, p. 21). [Not certainly by Ockham.]
[The above list is taken almost entirely from Little, Grey Friars in Oxford, pp. 224 ff., where information is also given as to MSS and works which exist only in MS.]
  Hofer, J. Biographische Studien über Wilhelm von Ockham. Archivum Fran-

ciscanum Historicum, vi, 1913, pp. 209 ff., 439 ff., 654 ff.

Pelzer, A. Les 51 Articles de Guillaume Occam censurés en Avignon en 1326. Revue d'Histoire ecclésiastique, xviii, 1922, pp. 240 ff.

McKeon, R. A Note on William of Ockham. Speculum, ii, 1927, pp. 455 f. [With bibliographical indications.]

Moody, E. A. The Logic of William of Ockham. 1935.

Koch, J. Neue Aktenstücke zu dem gegen Wilhelm Ockham in Avignon geführten Prozess. Recherches de Théologie ancienne et médiévale, xviii, 1936, pp. 79 ff.

Hochstetter, E. Studien zur Metaphysik und Erkenntnislehre Wilhelms von Ockham. Berlin, 1927.

Abbagnano, N. Guglielmo di Ockham. Lanciano, 1931.

Moser, S. Grundbegriffe der Naturphilosophie bei Wilhelm von Ockham Philosophie und Grenzwissenschaften, iv, 1932.

Garvens, A. Die Grundlagen der Ethik Wilhelms von Ockham. Franziskanische Studien, xxi, 1934, pp. 243 ff., 360 ff.

Jacob, E. F. Some Notes on Occam as a Political Thinker. John Rylands Lib. Bulletin, xx, 1936.

John Lathbury (fl. 1340). Liber moralium in Threnos Hieremiae. Oxford, 1482.

Thomas Walleys, or Wallensis (d. c. 1350). [Commentary on De Civitate Dei.] Toulouse, 1488. [Uncertainty attaches to some attributions to him; see DNB.]

Adam Wodham, or Godham (d. c. 1358; 'one of the most famous of the later Franciscan schoolmen,' Little, Grey Friars in Oxford, p. 172). Commentarii in iv libros Sententiarum. Paris, 1512. [His work was abbreviated; for MSS of this and other works, Little, p. 173; see also de Wulf, History of Philosophy, vol. ii, pp. 188–9.]

Roger Conway (fl. 1357; 'champion of the mendicants against FitzRalph, archbishop of Armagh,' Little, Grey Friars in Oxford, p. 239). Defensio Religionis Mendicantium, or De confessionibus per regulares audiendis contra informationibus Armachani. Lyons, 1496; Paris, 1511; ed. M. Goldast (Monarchia, vol. ii, Frankfort, 1614, p. 1410).

John Somer (fl. 1380; 'enjoyed a great reputation as an astronomer. Chaucer refers to him in his treatise on the Astrolabe,' Little, Grey Friars in Oxford, p. 244). Tertium opusculum Kalendarii. MSS: BM. Royal 2 B viii (14th cent.) [and others in Little, p. 245].

William Woodford (d. c. 1397; 'determined opponent of the Wicliffites; his works were popular,' Little, Grey Friars in Oxford, pp. 246–7). De sacramento Eucharistiae [or] 72 quaestiones [against Wyclif]. MSS: BM. Royal 7 B iii, § 2 (14th cent.) [and others in Little, p. 247.]

—— De causis condempnacionis articulorum 18 dampnatorum Johannis Wyclif, 1396. Ed. E. Brown (Fasciculus Rerum expetendarum, vol. i, 1690, pp. 190 ff.).

Nicholas of Fakenham (d. c. 1407). Determinatio [and other pieces on the schism]. BM. MS Harl. 3768; ed. F. Bliemetzrieder (Traktat des Minoritenprovinzials von England Fr. Nikolaus de Fakenham (1395) über das grosse abendländische Schisma, Archivum Franciscanum Historicum, i, 1908, pp. 577 ff., ii, 1909, pp. 79 ff.).

(Richard) Tryvytlam, or Trevytham (fl. 1400). [Poem] De Laude Universitatis Oxoniae. Ed. T. Hearne (in Historia Ricardi, vol. ii, Oxford, 1729); ed. H. Furneaux, Oxford Hist. Soc. Collectanea, iii, 1896, pp. 188 ff.

Peter of Candia (of Greek origin, Franciscan, studied at Oxford; elected Pope as Alexander V, 1409).
Ehrle, F. Die Sentenzenkommentar Peters von Candia. Münster, 1925. [This work contains numerous references to English scholars.]

William Russell (fl. 1425; a wayward friar imprisoned for heresy). Super Porphyrii Universalia compendium. Corpus Christi College Oxford MS 126. [Also, probably, Comment. in Aristotelis Praedicamenta in same MS; Little, Grey Friars in Oxford, p. 259.]

Mauritius de Portu, or O'Fihely (of Co. Cork; regent of Franciscan Schools, Milan, 1488; regent doctor in theology at Padua; wrote on Duns Scotus, 'whom he had in so great veneration that he was in a manner besotted with his subtilties,' A. à Wood, Athenae Oxonienses, ed. P. Bliss, vol. i, 1813, pp. 16 ff., where there is a list of his writings, among them an Expositio in quaestiones dialecticas Iohan. Scoti in Isagogen Porphyrii, Ferrara, 1499; Venice, 1512.)

(3) DOMINICANS

William of Macclesfield (d. 1304; cardinal). [For his works see F. Pelster, Scholastik, i, 1926, p. 142; he may be joint-author of the Correctorium corruptorii with Richard Clapwell (see p. 296 above). For literature on Macclesfield see Ueberweg-Geyer, p. 773 and A. M. Walz, S.R.E. Cardinales ex Ord. Praed. assumpti, Analecta Ordinis Praedicatorum, xxxiii, 1922, pp. 225 f.]

20

Thomas de Jorz (d. 1310; cardinal). De paupertate Christi. [See DNB., but several works have been wrongly ascribed to Thomas, and the whole question needs investigation.]

Nicolas Trivet (d. 1328). Expositio in Leviticum. Merton College Oxford MS 188.
—— In libros Augustini de Civitate Dei. MSS: BM. Royal 14 C XIII 8 [and others often joined with work by Thomas Jorz].
—— Quaestiones de causalitate scientiae Dei et concursu divino. Ed. M. Schmaus, Divus Thomas, XXXV, 1932, pp. 185 ff.

[Trivet wrote other theological works and a number of philological works, especially on Seneca (see DNB. for MSS), besides his more famous Annales.]

Ehrle, F. Nicolaus Trivet, sein Leben, seine Quolibet und Quaestiones Ordinariae. [Baeumker Festgabe, Münster, 1923.]

Crathorn (fl. 1341; Oxford scholar). [See J. Kraus, Die Stellung des Oxforder Dominikanlehrers Crathorn zu Thomas von Aquin, Zeitschrift für katholische Theologie, LVII, 1933, pp. 66 ff.; also F. Pelster, Miscellanea Ehrle, vol. I, pp. 330 f. and M. Schmaus, Liber propugnatorius des Thomas Anglicus, pp. 99 f.]

Robert of York (fl. 1348). De aeris impressionibus. Cambridge University Lib. MS Ii.1.1.

Simon de Henton (fl. 1360). Moralia [or] postillae [on the minor prophets]. New College Oxford MS 45.

Walz, P. A. The 'Exceptiones' from the 'Summa' of Simon of Hinton. Angelicum, XIII, 1936, pp. 2 f.

Henry Daniel (fl. 1379; medical writer). De Urinis. Caius College Cambridge MS 180 (213). [Also Liber Uricrisiarum (presumably the treatise otherwise known as De iudiciis urinarum), Caius College Cambridge MS 376 (596).]

Roger Dymock (fl. 1395). Adversus duodecim errores et haereses Lollardorum. Ed. H. S. Cronin, Wyclif Soc. 1922. MSS: Cambridge University Lib. Ii.IV.3; Bibliothèque Nationale Paris 3381.

Thomas Palmer (fl. 1410). De translatione sacrae scripturae in linguam anglicanam. Ed. M. Deanesly, The Lollard Bible, Cambridge, 1920, pp. 418 ff.
—— De adoratione imaginum libellus. Merton College Oxford MS LXVIII. [Contains also De veneratione sanctorum, and De originali peccato.]

Geoffrey the Grammarian, of Lynn (fl. 1440). Promptorium Parvulorum. 1499; 1510, etc.; ed. A. L. Mayhew, EETS. 1908. BM. Harl. MS 221. [A Latin-English Dictionary.] For other works see DNB.]

William Beith (fl. 1480). Commentary on Sentences, etc. [See J. Quétif and J. Échard, Scriptores Ordinis Praedicatorum, vol. I, Paris, 1719, p. 892.]

(4) ROLLE, WYCLIFF AND OTHER SCHOLARS AND MEN OF LETTERS

RICHARD ROLLE OF HAMPOLE (d. 1349).

[For Rolle's English writings see pp. 191–4 above. The following list of his Latin works is from H. E. Allen, Writings ascribed to Richard Rolle, New York, 1927, which describes MSS (pp. 22 ff.) and ptd edns (pp. 9 ff.).]

(a) Early editions.

Explanationes super lectiones beati Job. Oxford, 1483; Paris, 1510.
Speculum spiritualium, additur opusculum Ricardi Hampole de emendatione vitae. Paris, 1510.
De emendatione Peccatoris, per venerabilem Doctorem Richardum Heremitam Anglum. Antwerp, 1533 (with 2 extracts from other works); Cologne, 1535 (with extracts from other works); ed. M. de la Bigne (Magna Bibliotheca Veterum Patrum, vol. XV. Cologne, 1622, pp. 817 ff; rptd 1654, Lyons, 1677 and Cologne, 1694).
D. Richardi in Psalterium Davidicum atque alia quaedam sacrae scripturae monumenta. Cologne, 1536.
D. Richardi enarratio in Threnos. Paris, 1542.

(b) Separate Works. [The early edns referred to are those listed above.]

Super aliquos versus Cantici Canticorum. MSS: Corpus Christi College Oxford 193, Bodl. 861 (and others listed in Allen, pp. 64 ff.). [Portions are ptd, with the account of his conversion from the Incendium amoris, Antwerp, 1533, Cologne, 1535, 1536, 1622 Lyons, 1677.]
Canticum amoris [poem to the Virgin]. MSS: Bodl. Rawlinson C 397; Trinity College Dublin 153.
Judica me Deus [prose; 'a collection of four loosely connected tracts, of which the last three together make up a manual for parish priests,' Allen, p. 93]. MSS: Oxford Laud Misc. 528, BM. Burney 356, Oxford Ashmole 751, Bodl. 861 (and others in Allen, pp 94 ff.).

Melum contemplativorum [mystical treatise in prose]. MSS: Corpus Christi College Oxford 1913; BM. Sloane 2275 (and others in Allen, pp. 114 f.).

Super Lectiones Job in Officio Mortuorum. MSS: Corpus Christi College Oxford 193 (and others in Allen, pp. 130 ff.). [Ptd Oxford, 1483, Paris, 1510, Cologne, 1536.]

Super Threnos Jeremiae. MSS: Bodl. 861; Corpus Christi College Oxford 193; Trinity College Dublin 153. [Ptd Cologne, 1536, Paris, 1542.]

Super Apocalypsim (usque ad cap. VI). MSS: Bodl. 861; BM. Cotton Tib. A xv; Hereford Cathedral O viii i.

Super orationem dominicam. MSS: Bodl. 48, 549, 861 (and others in Allen, pp. 156 f.).

Super symbolum apostolorum. MSS: Bodl. 48, 549, 861 (and others in Allen, pp. 157 f.). [Ptd Cologne, 1535, 1536, 1622, Lyons, 1677.]

Super mulierem fortem. MSS: Trinity College Dublin 153; St John's College Oxford 77 (and others in Allen, p. 159).

De Dei misericordia. MSS: Magdalen College Oxford 71; Trinity College Dublin 321.

[Latin Psalter.] MSS: Bodl. 861; Corpus Christi College Oxford 193 (and others in Allen, pp. 166 ff.). [Ptd Cologne, 1536.]

Super Magnificat. MSS: Bodl. Rawlinson C 397; Hereford Cathedral O viii i (and others in Allen, p. 192).

Super Psalmum xx. MSS: Bodl. 861; Corpus Christi College Oxford 193 (and others in Allen, p. 194).

Liber de amore Dei contra amatores mundi. MSS: Corpus Christi College Oxford 193; BM. Sloane 2275 (and others in Allen, pp. 204 f.).

Incendium Amoris. Ed. M. Deanesly, Manchester, 1915. MSS: Emmanuel College Cambridge 35 (and others in Allen, pp. 213 ff.).

Emendatio Vitae. MSS: Bodl. 16, 43 (and others in Allen, pp. 231 ff.). [Ptd Antwerp, 1533, Cologne, 1535, 1536, 1618, Lyons, 1677, and with alterations Paris, 1510.]

[For works doubtfully or wrongly ascribed to Rolle, see Allen, pp. 312 ff. Critical studies will be found p. 191–3 above.]

John Wyclif (1330?–1384)*

(a) Bibliographies

Loserth, J. Neuere Erscheinungen der Wiclif-Literatur. Historische Zeitschrift, LIII, 1885, pp. 43–62, LXII, 1889, pp. 266–78, xcv, 1905, pp. 271–7.

—— Geschichte des späteren Mittelalters. Munich, 1903, pp. 389–92.

Loserth, J. Wiclif und der Wiclifismus. [In Real-Encyklopädie für protestantische Theologie und Kirche, ed. J. J. Herzog and A. Hauck, vol. xxi, Gotha, 1908. See also vol. xxiv (Ergänzungen), 1913.]

—— Neue Erscheinungen der Wiclif- und Huss-Literatur. Historische Zeitschrift, cxvi, 1916, pp. 271–82.

Workman, H. B. Wyclif. [In Encyclopaedia of Religion, ed. J. Hastings, vol. xii, 1921. A comprehensive view of the literature is more readily obtained from the bibliography to this article than from the selective one in Workman's John Wyclif, vol. i, Oxford, 1926.]

Whitney, J. P. A Note on the Work of the Wyclif Society. [In Essays in History presented to Reginald Lane Poole, ed. H. W. C. Davis, Oxford, 1927.]

Manning, B. L. Wyclif. [In The Cambridge Medieval History, vol. vii, 1932, pp. 900–7.]

(b) Wyclif's Writings

[For Wyclif's English works see pp. 203–5 above.]

(i) Publications of the Wyclif Society (except where otherwise stated).

De Ente sive Summa Intellectualium. Bk i.

1. Tractatus de Ente in communi.
2. Tractatus de Ente primo in communi. Ed. S. H. Thomson (Summa de Ente. Libri primi tractatus primus et secundus, Oxford, 1930).
3. Tractatus purgans errores circa veritates in communi.
4. Tractatus purgans errores circa universalia in communi. Ed. M. H. Dziewicki (De Ente librorum duorum excerpta, 1909). [For the missing pts of chs. 2 and 3 see S. H. Thomson, A 'Lost' Chapter of Wyclif's Summa de Ente, Speculum, iv, 1929, pp. 339–46.]
5. De Universalibus. [Edn by S. H. Thomson in preparation: see his Summa de Ente, p'. ix.]
6. Tractatus de Tempore. [Edn by S. H. Thomson in preparation: see his Summa de Ente, p. ix.]

De Ente sive Summa Intellectualium. Bk ii.

1. Tractatus de Intellectione Dei. Ed. M. H. Dziewicki (De Ente librorum duorum excerpta, 1909).
2. Tractatus de Sciencia Dei. [S. H. Thomson will print this and the three other unprinted tractates of Bk ii. See his Summa de Ente, p. ix.]
3. Tractatus de Volucione Dei. Ed. M. H. Dziewicki (De Ente librorum duorum excerpta, 1909).
4. Tractatus de Personarum Distinccione sive de Trinitate. [Unprinted.]

* The bibliography of Wyclif is by Mr Bernard L. Manning.

5. Tractatus de Ideis. [Unprinted.]
6. Tractatus de Potencia productiva Dei ad Extra. [Unprinted, except a fragment: De Annihilatione (chs. xii–xiv), ed. M. H. Dziewicki, De Ente librorum duorum excerpta, 1909.]

De Ente predicamentali. Ed. R. Beer, 1891. [Beer and Thomson consider this as Pt 5 of Bk I of De Ente sive Summa Intellectualium, reckoning De Universalibus and Tractatus de Tempore as pts 6 and 7. See S. H. Thomson, A 'Lost' Chapter of Wyclif's Summa de Ente, Speculum, IV, 1929, pp. 339–46.]

Summa Theologiae. Bks I, II. Tractatus de Mandatis Divinis. Accedit Tractatus de Statu Innocencie. Ed. J. Loserth and F. D. Matthew, 1922.

Summa Theologiae. Bks III–V. Tractatus de Civili Dominio. Liber primus. Ed. R. L. Poole, 1885. Liber secundus. Ed. J. Loserth, 1900. Liber tertius. Ed. J. Loserth, 2 vols. 1903–4.

Summa Theologiae. Bk VI. De Veritate Sacrae Scripturae. Ed. R. Buddensieg, 3 vols. 1905–7.

Summa Theologiae. Bk VII. Tractatus de Ecclesia. Ed. J. Loserth, 1886.

Summa Theologiae. Bk VIII. Tractatus de Officio Regis. Ed. A. W. Pollard and C. Sayle, 1887.

Summa Theologiae. Bk IX. Tractatus de Potestate Pape. Ed. J. Loserth, 1907.

Summa Theologiae. Bk X. Tractatus de Simonia. Ed. Herzberg-Fränkel and M. H. Dziewicki, 1898.

Summa Theologiae. Bk XI. Tractatus de Apostasia. Ed. M. H. Dziewicki, 1889.

Summa Theologiae. Bk XII. Tractatus de Blasphemia. Ed. M. H. Dziewicki, 1893.

De Compositione Hominis. Ed. R. Beer, 1884.

De Dominio Divino libri tres. Ed. R. L. Poole, 1890. [Includes Richard Fitzralph's De Pauperie Salvatoris, Bks I–IV.]

De Eucharistia et Poenitentia sive de Confessione. Ed. J. Loserth (De Eucharistia Tractatus Maior, 1892).

De Eucharistia Tractatus Maior. Accedit Tractatus de Eucharistia et Poenitentia sive de Confessione. Ed. J. Loserth, 1892.

Dialogus sive Speculum Ecclesie Militantis. Ed. A. W. Pollard, 1886.

Differentia inter Peccatum Mortale et Veniale. Ed. J. Loserth and F. D. Matthew (Tractatus de Mandatis Divinis, 1922).

Logica. Ed. M. H. Dziewicki (Tractatus de Logica, vol. I, 1893).

Logicae continuacio. Tractatus primus et secundus. Ibid.

Logicae continuacio. Tractatus tercius. Ibid. Vols. II, III, 1896–9.

Opus Evangelicum. Bks I, II. De Sermone Domini in Monte. Bks III, IV. De Antichristo. Ed. J. Loserth, 2 vols. 1895–6.

Quaestiones XIII Logicae et Philosophicae. [See Unauthentic and Contested Writings, below, p. 310.]

Questio ad Fratres de Sacramento Altaris. Ed. J. Loserth (De Eucharistia Tractatus Maior, 1892).

Tractatus de Benedicta Incarnatione. Ed. E. Harris, 1886.

Miscellanea Philosophica. Ed. M. H. Dziewicki, 2 vols. 1902–5.
1. De Actibus Animae (in vol. I).
2. De Materia et Forma (in vol. I).

[Of the nine pieces in these volumes these two alone appear to be Wyclif's. See Dziewicki's Introductions and S. H. Thomson, Some Latin Works erroneously ascribed to Wyclif, Speculum, III, 1928, pp. 382–91.]

Opera Minora. Ed. J. Loserth, 1913.
1. Missives and letters:
   (a) Litera missa pape Urbano VI.
   (b) Epistola missa archiepiscopo Cantuariensi.
   (c) Epistola missa episcopo Lincolniensi
   (d) Epistola missa ad simplices sacerdotes.
   (e) De Amore sive ad quinque questiones.
   (f) Litera ad quendam Socium.
   (g) De Peccato in Spiritum Sanctum.
   (h) De Octo Questionibus Pulcris.
   (i) De Fratribus ad Scholares.
2. Conclusiones triginta tres sive de Paupertate Christi.
3. Speculum secularium dominorum.
4. De prelatis contencionum sive de incarcerandis fidelibus.
5. De Fide Catholica.
6. De Ordine Christiano.
7. De Gradibus Cleri Ecclesie.
8. De Servitute Civili et Dominio Seculari
9. De Vaticinacione seu Prophetia.
10. Responsiones ad argumenta Radulfi Strode.
11. Responsiones ad XLIV conclusiones sive ad argucias monachales.
12. Responsiones ad argumenta cuiusdam emuli veritatis.
13. Exposicio textus Matthei xxiii sive De Vae Octuplici.
14. Exposicio textus Matthei xxiv sive De Antichristo.
15. De Oracione Dominica.
16. De Salutacione Angelica.
17. Responsio ad decem questiones magistri Ricardi Strode.
18. Determinacio ad argumenta magistri Outredi de Omesima monachi.

19. Determinacio ad argumenta Wilhelmi Vyrinham. [The second pt is sometimes known separately as De Dominio determinacio contra unum monachum. See J. Loserth, Die ältesten Streitschriften Wiclifs, Sitzungsberichte der Kaiserlichen Akademie der Wissenschaften, Phil.-hist. Klasse, CLX, no. 2, Vienna, 1909.]
20. Labora sicut bonus miles Christi. II Tim. ii. 3.
21. De Graduacionibus sive De Magisterio Christi.

Polemical Works. Ed. R. Buddensieg, 2 vols. 1883. [Contains twenty-six tracts, classified as twenty against the sects, six against the Pope. Buddensieg doubts the authenticity of De Religione Privata I only. Loserth expresses no doubt in his revision of Shirley's Catalogue.]

Vol. I. [Against the sects.]
1. De Fundatione Sectarum.
2. De Ordinatione Fratrum sive De Concordatione Fratrum cum secta simplici Christi sive De Sectis monachorum.
3. De Nova Praevaricantia Mandatorum.
4. De Triplici Vinculo Amoris.
5. De Septem Donis Spiritus Sancti.
6. De Quattuor Sectis Novellis.
7. Purgatorium Sectae Christi.
8. De Novis Ordinibus.
9. De Oratione et Ecclesiae Purgatione.
10. De Diabolo et Membris eius.
11. De Detectione Perfidiarum Antichristi.

Vol. II.
12. De Solutione Satanae.
13. De Mendaciis Fratrum.
14. Descriptio Fratris.
15. De Daemonio Meridiano.
16. De Duobus Generibus Haereticorum.
17. De Religionibus Vanis Monachorum sive de Fundatore Religionis.
18. De Perfectione Statuum.
19. De Religione Privata I.
20. De Religione Privata II.

[Against the Pope.]
21. De Citationibus Frivolis.
22. De Dissensione Paparum sive de Schismate.
23. Cruciata.
24. De Christo et suo Adversario Antichristo.
25. De Contrarietate Duorum Dominorum.
26. Quattuor Imprecationes.

Sermones. 4 vols. Ed. J. Loserth, 1887–90.
I. Super Evangelia Dominicalia.
II. Super Evangelia de Sanctis.
III. Super Epistolas.
IV. Sermones Miscellanei.

(ii) Published otherwise and Unpublished

[For MSS of unpublished works see J. Loserth's revision of W. W. Shirley's Catalogue, Wyclif Soc. 1924.]

Ad Parliamentum Regis. Ed. W. W. Shirley (Fasciculi Zizaniorum, Rolls Ser. 1858, pp. 245–57).
Ad quesita regis et concilii. Ibid. pp. 258–71.
Bonus et utilis tractatus secundum magistrum Johannem. Ed. I. H. Stein, Speculum, VII, 1932, pp. 87–94 (as The Latin Text of Wyclif's Complaint). [See also I. H. Stein, The Wyclif Manuscript in Florence, Speculum, V, 1930, pp. 45–7.]
Contra Killingham Carmelitam. Ed. W. W. Shirley (Fasciculi Zizaniorum, Rolls Ser. 1858, pp. 453–76, 477–80). [Two tracts, one incomplete.]
De Captivo Hispanensi sive De filio comitis de Dene. [Included as ch. vii in De Ecclesia. See above Summa Theologiae, Bk VII.]
Declarationes. Ed. H. T. Riley (Walsingham's Historia Anglicana, vol. I, Rolls Ser. 1863, pp. 357–63).
De Clavibus Ecclesie id est De Potestate Ligandi sive De Clave Celi. Ed. S. H. Thomson, Speculum, III, 1928, p. 251.
De Condemnatione XIX Conclusionum. Ed. W. W. Shirley (Fasciculi Zizaniorum, Rolls Ser. 1858, Appendix, pp. 481–92).
De Dotatione Ecclesiae sive Supplementum Trialogi. Ed. G. V. Lechler (Trialogus, Oxford, 1869).
De Eucharistia conclusiones quindecim. Ed. W. W. Shirley (Fasciculi Zizaniorum, Rolls Ser. 1858, pp. 105–6).
De Eucharistia Confessio. Ibid. pp. 115–32.
De Eucharistia Confessio. Ed. S. H. Thomson, Journ. Theological Stud. XXXIII, 1932, pp. 359–65 (as John Wyclif's 'Lost' De Fide Sacramentorum). [Different from the preceding.]
De Insolubilibus. [Unprinted. Edn by S. H. Thomson in preparation.]
De Juramento Arnaldi. Ed. G. V. Lechler, Johann von Wiclif, vol. II, Leipzig, 1873, pp. 575–9.
De Officio Regis Conclusio. Ed. S. H. Thomson, Speculum, III, 1928, pp. 251–3.
De Versuciis Anti-Christi. Ed. I. H. Stein, EHR. XLVII, 1932, pp. 95–103.
Errare in Materia Fidei quod potuit Ecclesia militans. Ed. S. H. Thomson, Speculum, III, 1928, pp. 248–50.
In omnes Novi Testamenti libros, preter Apocalypsin, Commentarius. [Unprinted.]
Summa de Ente. Libri primi tractatus primus et secundus. Ed. S. H. Thomson, Oxford, 1930.

Tractatus de Officio Pastorali. Ed. G. V.
Lechler, Leipzig, 1863.
Trialogus cum Supplemento Trialogi. Ed.
G. V. Lechler, Oxford, 1869.

(iii) Unauthentic and Contested Writings.

De Imaginibus. [Unprinted. See Loserth's
revision of Shirley's Catalogue, p. 8.]
De Necessitate Futurorum. [Unprinted. See
J. Loserth, Die ältesten Streitschriften
Wiclifs, Sitzungsberichte der Kaiserlichen
Akademie der Wissenschaften, Phil.-hist.
Klasse, CLX, no. 2, Vienna, 1909.]
De Triplici Ecclesia. Ed. S. H. Thomson,
Speculum, III, 1928, pp. 387–91.
Quaestiones XIII Logicae et Philosophicae.
Ed. R. Beer (De Ente predicamentali,
Wyclif Soc. 1891). [See S. H. Thomson,
Speculum, III, 1928, pp. 385–7.]
Super Cantica Canticorum. [Unprinted. See
J. Loserth, Die ältesten Streitschriften
Wiclifs, Sitzungsberichte der Kaiserlichen
Akademie der Wissenschaften, Phil.-hist.
Klasse, CLX, no. 2, Vienna, 1909.]

(c) Modern Works

(i) Biographical

Lewis, J. History of the Life and Sufferings
of John Wicliffe. 1720; Oxford, 1820 (rev.
edn).
Lechler, G. V. Johann von Wiclif und die
Vorgeschichte der Reformation. 2 vols.
Leipzig, 1873; tr. and abridged by P.
Lorimer, [1884].
Burrows, M. Wiclif's Place in History: Three
Lectures. 1882.
Matthew, F. D. The Date of Wyclif's Attack
on Transubstantiation. EHR. V, 1890,
pp. 328–30.
Sergeant, L. John Wyclif. New York, 1892.
(Heroes of the Nations.)
Loserth, J. The Beginnings of Wyclif's
Activity in Ecclesiastical Politics. EHR.
XI, 1896, pp. 319–28.
—— Studien zur Kirchenpolitik Englands im
XIV. Jahrhundert. i. Bis zum Ausbruch des
grossen Schismas (1378). Sitzungsberichte
der Kaiserlichen Akademie der Wissen-
schaften, Phil.-hist. Klasse, CXXXVI, no. 1,
Vienna, 1897. ii. Die Genesis von Wiclifs
Summa Theologiae und seine Lehre vom
wahren und falschen Papsttum. Sitzungs-
berichte der Kaiserlichen Akademie der
Wissenschaften, Phil.-hist. Klasse, CLVI,
no. 6, Vienna, 1908.
Twemlow, J. A. Wycliffe's Preferments and
University Degrees. EHR. XV, 1900, pp.
529–30.
Workman, H. B. The Dawn of the Reformation. Vol. I. The Age of Wyclif. 1901.

Workman, H. B. John Wyclif: a Study of the
English Medieval Church. 2 vols. Oxford, 1926.
Poole, R. L. Wycliffe and Movements for
Reform. 1911.
Cronin, H. S. John Wycliffe, the Reformer,
and Canterbury Hall, Oxford. Trans.
Royal Hist. Soc. ser. 3, VIII, 1914, pp. 55–76.
—— Wycliffe's Canonry at Lincoln. EHR.
XXXV, 1920, pp. 564–9.
Wilkins, H. J. Was John Wycliffe a Negligent
Pluralist? Also John de Trevisa. 1915.
[Appendix, Bristol, 1916.]
Salter, H. E. John Wyclif, Canon of Lincoln.
EHR. XXXV, 1920, p. 98.
Manning, B. L. Wyclif and the House of Herod.
Cambridge Hist. Journ. II, 1926, pp. 66–7.
—— Wyclif. [Cambridge Medieval History,
vol. VII, 1932.]

(ii) Studies on Special Aspects of Wyclif's
Work and Teaching

Loserth, J. Hus und Wiclif. Prague, 1884;
Munich, 1925 (rev. edn); tr. Eng. 1884.
—— Wiclifs Lehre vom wahren und falschen
Papsttum. Historische Zeitschrift, XCIX,
1907, pp. 237–55.
—— Die ältesten Streitschriften Wiclifs.
Studien über die Anfänge der kirchen-
politischen Tätigkeit Wiclifs und die Über-
lieferung seiner Schriften. Sitzungsberichte
der Kaiserlichen Akademie der Wissen-
schaften, Phil.-hist. Klasse, CLX, no. 2,
Vienna, 1909.
—— Johann von Wiclif und Guilelmus
Peraldus. Studien zur Geschichte der
Entstehung von Wiclifs Summa Theologiae.
Sitzungsberichte der Kaiserlichen Akademie
der Wissenschaften, Phil.-hist. Klasse,
CLXXX, no. 3, Vienna, 1917.
—— Johann von Wiclif und Robert Grosse-
teste, Bischof von Lincoln. Sitzungsberichte
der Kaiserlichen Akademie der Wissen-
schaften, Phil.-hist. Klasse, CLXXXVI, no. 2,
Vienna, 1921.
Poole, R. L. Illustrations of the History of
Medieval Thought and Learning. 1920
(rev. edn). [Ch. x. Wycliffe's Doctrine of
Dominion.]
Odložilík, O. Wycliffe's Influence upon Central
and Eastern Europe. Slavonic Rev. VII, 1928–
9, pp. 634–48. [Bibliographical note at end.]
Thomson, S. H. The Philosophical Basis of
Wyclif's Theology. Journ. Religion, XI,
1931, pp. 86–116.

(iii) On the Wyclif Canon

Tanner, T. Bibliotheca Britannico-Hibernica.
Ed. D. Wilkins, 1748.
Shirley, W. W. Catalogue of the Original
Works of John Wyclif. Oxford, 1865; rev.
J. Loserth, Wyclif Soc. [1924].

Loserth, J. Das vermeintliche Schreiben Wiclif's an Urban VI und einige verlorene Flugschriften Wiclif's aus seinen letzten Lebenstagen. Historische Zeitschrift, LXXV, 1895, pp. 476–80.

—— Wiclif's Sendschreiben, Flugschriften, und kleinere Werke kirchenpolitischen Inhalts. Sitzungsberichte der Kaiserlichen Akademie der Wissenschaften, Phil.-hist. Klasse, CLXVI, no. 6, Vienna, 1910.

—— Zur Kritik der Wyclif-Handschriften. Zeitschrift des deutschen Vereins für die Geschichte Mährens und Schlesiens, XX, 1916, pp. 247–57. [Rptd as Zur Verbreitung der Wiclifhandschriften in Böhmen, in Loserth's Huss und Wiclif, rev. edn, Munich, 1925, pp. 193–203.]

Thomson, S. H. Some Latin Works erroneously ascribed to Wyclif. Speculum, III, 1928, pp. 382–91.

—— Three unprinted Opuscula of John Wyclif. Speculum, III, 1928, pp. 248–53.

—— A 'Lost' Chapter of Wyclif's Summa de Ente. Speculum, IV, 1929, pp. 339–46.

—— The Order of Writing of Wyclif's Philosophical Works. [In Českou Minulostí (Festschrift to V. Novotný), Prague, 1929, pp. 146–66.]

—— A Gonville and Caius Wyclif Manuscript. Speculum, VIII, 1933, pp. 197–204.

Stein, I. H. Speculum, V, 1930, pp. 95–7, VI, 1931, pp. 465–8, VIII, 1933, pp. 254–5. [Notes.]

OTHER SCHOLARS AND MEN OF LETTERS

Bernard of Gordon (d. *c*. 1305; perhaps a Scot). Lilium Medicinae. Frankfort, 1617.

Simon of Faversham (1240?–1306; chancellor of Oxford). [See F. M. Powicke, Mélanges F. Lot, 1925, pp. 649 ff., who refers to MSS of his Quaestiones on the Physics and De Anima, bk II.]

Ottaviano, C. Le Quaestiones super Libro Praedicatorum di Simone di Faversham dal MS. Ambrosiano c. 161 inf. Memorie della R. Accademia Nazionale dei Lincei. Classe di Scienze morali storiche e filologiche, ser. 6, III, 1930.

—— Le Opere di Simone di Faversham e la sua Posizione nel Problema degli Universali. Archivio di Filosofia, I, 1931, pp. 15 ff.

Grabmann, M. Die Aristoteleskommentar des Simon von Faversham (†1306). Sitzungsberichte der bayerischen Akademie der Wissenschaften, 1933, fasc. 3.

Sharp, D. Simonis de Faversham Quaestiones super tertium De anima. Archives d'Histoire doctrinale et littéraire du Moyen Âge, IX, 1934, pp. 307 ff.

Ralph de Hengham (d. 1311; chief justice). Summa magna and Summa parva. Ed. W. H. Dunham, Cambridge, 1932.

Henry of Harclay (chancellor of Oxford, 1312). Quaestiones. Vatican Borghes. MS 171.

Pelster, F. Heinrich Harclay, Kanzler von Oxford und seine Quästionen. Miscellanea Ehrle, vol. I, Rome, 1924, pp. 307 ff.

Kraus, J. Die Universalienlehre des Oxforder Kanzlers Heinrich von Harclay in ihrer Mittelstellung zwischen skotistischem Realismus und okkamistischem Nominalismus. Divus Thomas, XI, 1933, pp. 288 ff.

Robert Walsingham (*fl*. 1312; Carmelite). [For list of writings ascribed to him, with extracts and account of his teaching, see B. M. Xiberta, De Scriptoribus scholasticis Saeculi XIV ex Ordine Carmelitarum, Louvain, 1931, pp. 111 ff., and Criterion, IV, 1928, pp. 147 ff., 298 ff.]

John Daston (*fl*. 1320). Rosarium secretissimum philosophorum arcanum comprehendens [and] Visio super artem alchemicam. Ed. J. Manget, Bibliotheca Chemica Curiosa, vol. II, Geneva, 1702.

Walter of Evesham (*fl*. 1320; Benedictine, writer on music). De speculatione Musices. Ed. C. E. H. de Coussemaker (Scriptorum de Musica medii Aevi nova Series, vol. I, Paris, 1864, pp. 182 ff.).

Robert Handlo (*fl*. 1326; writer on music). Regulae. Ed. C. E. H. de Coussemaker (Scriptorum de Musica medii Aevi nova Series, vol. I, Paris, 1864, pp. 383 ff.).

Roger Waltham (d. 1336). Compendium moralis philosophiae. MSS: Bodl. Laud. Misc. 616; Bodl. 2664. ['A series of moral disquisitions on the virtues and duties of princes,' C. L. Kingsford in DNB.]

Richard of Bury (1281–1345; bishop of Durham). Philobiblon. Cologne, 1473; ed. H. Cocheris, Paris, 1856; ed. E. C. Thomas, 1888, 1903 (with trn); ed. A. F. West, New York, 1889; ed. A. Nelson, Stockholm, 1922 [This book is ascribed by some to Robert Holcot, who is said to have written it at Bury's direction.]

de Ghellinck, J. Un Évêque bibliophile au XIVᵉ Siècle. Revue d'Histoire ecclésiastique, XVIII, 1922, pp. 271 ff., XIX, 1923, pp. 157 ff.

John Baconthorpe (d. *c*. 1346; Carmelite, 'Doctor resolutus'). Commentarii in libros I–IV Sententiarum. Paris, 1485; Milan, 1510; Venice, 1526; Cremona, 1618, 1754. [These ptd edns only include bks I and III and the Quaestiones canonicae in bk IV.]

John Baconthorpe. Quodlibeta I–III. Venice, 1527; Cremona, 1618, 1754.

   Xiberta, B. M. De magistro Johanne Baconthorp. Analecta Ordinis Carmelitarum, VI, 1927, pp. 3 ff., 1929, pp. 516 ff.

—— Joan Baconthorp Averroista? Criterion, III, 1927, pp. 45 ff., 296 ff.

—— Joan Baconthorp i el Dogma de la Immaculada Concepció de Maria. Estudis Franciscans, XL, 1928, pp. 89 ff.

—— De Scriptoribus scholasticis Saeculi XIV ex Ordine Carmelitarum. Louvain, 1931, pp. 167 ff. [Incorporates material in articles given above and gives list of Baconthorpe's genuine works and references to MSS. See p. 191 for ptd edns of following minor works: Compendium historiarum et jurium pro defensione institutionis et confirmationis ordinis B. Mariae de monte Carmeli; Speculum de institutione ordinis ad venerationem Virginis Deiparae; Tractatus super regula ordinis Carmelitarum.]

Thomas Bradwardine (c. 1290–1349). Arithmetica et Geometria Speculativa. Paris, 1502–30.

—— De causa Dei. Ed. H. Savile, 1618.

—— De quadratura circuli. Paris, 1495.

—— Tractatus de proportionibus. Paris, 1495.

—— Ars memorativa. Ed. B. Politus (Questio de modalibus, Venice, 1505).

[See also Ueberweg-Geyer, p. 788.]

   Hahn, S. Thomas Bradwardinus und seine Lehre von der menschlichen Willensfreiheit. Münster, 1905.

   Xiberta, B. M. Fragmenta d'una Qüestió inèdita de Tomàs Bradwardine. [Aus der Geisteswelt des Mittelalters, vol. II, Münster, 1935, pp. 1169 ff.]

John Acton, or Ayton (d. 1350). [Commentary on the Ecclesiastical Constitutions of Otho and Ottoboni, papal legates in England in 13th cent.]. [For MSS see DNB.; ptd in W. Lyndewood's Provinciale, Paris, 1501, Oxford, 1679. Acton was a writer on Canon Law; see F. W. Maitland, Roman Canon Law in the Church of England, 1898, pp. 6 ff.]

John Clencock (d. 1352; an Augustinian hermit). In primum librum sententiarum. Erfurt Stadtbücherei MS 2° 117. [On him see F. Ehrle, Die Ehrentitel der scholastischen Lehrer des Mittelalters, Sitzungsberichte d. bayer. Akad. d. Wissensch. 1919, pt 9, p. 38.]

Osbertus Anglicus (fl. 1344; Carmelite). [For MSS of his writings and extracts, see B. M. Xiberta, De Scriptoribus scholasticis Saeculi XIV ex Ordine Carmelitarum, Louvain, 1931, pp. 241 ff.]

John Arderne (b. 1307). De arte phisicali et de cirurgia. Tr. Sir d'Arcy Power (with replica of the Stockholm MS), 1922.

Richard FitzRalph (d. 1360; archbishop of Armagh). Summa de erroribus Armenorum. [or] Summa in Questionibus Armenorum. Paris, 1512. [See M. Deanesly, Lollard Bible, Cambridge, 1920, p. 142, note 1.]

—— De pauperie Salvatoris. Ed. (bks I–IV) R. L. Poole (in appendix to Wyclif's De Dominio Divino, Wyclif Soc. 1890, pp. 257 ff.) [Pp. 264 ff. contain table of contents of remaining three books of the treatise.]

—— Defensorium curatorum. Ed. E. Brown (Fasciculus Rerum expetendarum, vol. II, 1690, pp. 466 ff.).

—— Sermons. BM. Lansdowne MS 393. [See G. R. Owst, Preaching in Medieval England, Cambridge, 1926, p. 10, note 3.]

John de Sheppey (d. 1360; bishop of Rochester). Fabulae. Ed. L. Hervieux (Les Fabulistes latins, vol. IV, Paris, 1899, pp. 417 ff.).

John of Gaddesden (d. 1361). Rosa Medicinae. Pavia, 1492.

   Cholmeley, H. P. John of Gaddesden and the Rosa Medicinae. Oxford, 1912.

   Wulff, W. Rosa Anglica, seu Rosa Medicinae Johannis Anglici, an Early Modern Irish Translation. 1929.

William Heytesbury (fl. 1340–1372; fellow of Merton, chancellor of Oxford). Sophismata. Pavia. 1481.

—— De sensu composito et diviso. Venice, 1494.

—— Consequentiae subtiles. [In R. Strode, Consequentiae, Venice, 1517.]

[See F. M. Powicke, Medieval Books of Merton College, Oxford, 1931, pp. 25 f., and P. Duhem, La Dialectique d'Oxford et la Scholastique italienne, Bulletin italien, XII, 1912, pp. 8 ff.]

William of Rymyngton (chancellor of Oxford; 1372–3). Meditationes. MS Bodl. 801 [and others mentioned by J. McNulty, pp. 243 f. (see below)].

—— Quadraginta quinque conclusiones [and dialogue against Wyclif]. MS Bodl. 158.

—— [Sermons.] MS Bibliothèque Universitaire Paris 790.

   McNulty, J. William of Rymyngton. Yorkshire Archaeological Journ. XXX, 1931, pp. 231 ff. [See also DNB. and H. E. Allen, Writings ascribed to Richard Rolle, New York, 1927, pp. 347 f.]

Robert Rypon of Durham (2nd half of 14th cent.; Benedictine). [Sermons.] BM. MS Harl. 4894. [See Owst, Literature and Pulpit, p. 29.]

John de Burgo (d. 1386; chancellor of Cambridge). Pupilla Oculi. Wolffgang, 1510; Paris, 1518. ['Much less of a preaching manual and much more of the compendium of legal information,' Owst, p. 298.]

Thomas Brunton (d. 1389; Bishop of Rochester). [Sermons.] MS: BM. Harl. 3760. [Owst, Literature and Pulpit, p. 577.]

John Dumbeley (*fl.* 1386). Practica vera alkimica. [Theatrum Chemicum, ed. L. Zetzner, vol. III, Strasburg, 1659, pp. 912 ff.]

Ralph Strode (d. *c.* 1400). Consequentiae. Padua, 1477; Venice, 1517.

—— Obligationes. Venice, 1494.

Poole, R. L. Verses on the Exchequer in the 15th Century (date 1398–1410). EHR. XXXVI, 1921, pp. 58 f.

John Gower (d. 1408; see pp. 205–8 above for his English and French writings). Balades and Other Poems. Ed. Earl Gower, Roxburghe Club, 1818. [3 minor poems.]

—— Vox Clamantis, Chronica Tripertita and some Minor Poems. Ed. H. O. Coxe, Roxburghe Club, 1850.

—— Political Poems. Ed. T. Wright, vol. I, Rolls Ser. 1859. [Chronica Tripertita, pp. 417 ff.; minor poems, pp. 346 ff.]

—— The Complete Works of John Gower. Ed. G. C. Macaulay, vol. III, Oxford, 1902. [Includes all Gower's Latin poems.]

   Meyer, Karl. John Gowers Beziehungen zu Chaucer und König Richard II. Bonn, 1889. [See pp. 67 f. for further minor poems.]

William Sudbury (*fl.* 1400; Benedictine).
   Käppeli, T. Die Tabula des Wilhelm Sudbery, O.S.B. zu den Werken des hl. Thomas von Aquin. Theologische Quartalschrift, xv, 1934, pp. 62 ff.

Walter Diss (*fl.* 1404; Carmelite). Carmen de schismate ecclesiae. Ed. J. M. Lydius (Nicholai de Clemangiis Opera, Leyden, 1613, pp. 31 ff.).

Philip Retingdon (d. 1424; Bishop of Lincoln). [Sermons.] MSS: John Rylands Lib. Lat. 367; Corpus Christi College Oxford 54 [and others mentioned in DNB.].

Thomas Netter of Walden (d. 1430; Carmelite). Doctrinale fidei ecclesiae. Venice 1571.

—— Fasciculi Zizaniorum magistri Johannis Wyclif. Ed. W. W. Shirley, 3 vols. Rolls Ser. 1858.

Oswald de Corda (d. 1437; Carthusian, of Grande Chartreuse, and prior at Perth). Opus pacis. MSS: Basle Univ. F IX 4 [and others mentioned in P. Lehmann, Bücherliebe und Bücherpflege bei den Karthäusern, Miscellanea Ehrle, vol. v, Rome, 1924, p. 374].

William Lyndwood (*fl.* 1430). Provinciale. Oxford, 1482–1679. [On Lyndwood, see F. W. Maitland, Roman Canon Law in the Church of England, 1898, pp. 1 ff.]

James Haldenstone (d. 1443; prior of St Andrews). Letters. Ed. J. H. Baxter (Copiale Prioratus Sancti Andree, Oxford, 1930, pp. 1 ff.).

Thomas Gascoigne (1403–1458; chancellor of Oxford). Dictionarium Theologicum. Lincoln College Oxford MSS 117, 118. [Extracts in J. E. T. Rogers, Loci e Libro Veritatum, Oxford, 1881. For works attrib. to Gascoigne, see DNB.]

Reginald Pecock (d. *c.* 1460; bishop of Chichester). Collectanea quaedam. Ed. J. Foxe (Commentarii Rerum in Ecclesia gestarum, Strasburg, 1554, pp. 119 b ff.). [For Pecock's English works, etc. see p. 260–1 above.]

Gilbert Kymer (d. 1463; dean of Salisbury). Diaetarium de sanitatis custodia. Ed. in part T. Hearne (Liber Niger Scaccarii, Oxford, 1728, pp. 550 ff.).

John Phreas [or Free] (d. 1465). Epistolae. Ed. J. E. Spingarn, New York, 1903 (Unpublished Letters of an English Humanist).

—— Syneseus Cyrenensis de laudibus calvitii. Ed. J. Froben (in Erasmi Moriae Encomium, Basle, 1519 and 1521).

[The verses and epigrams have not been edited.]

John Blacman (*fl.* 1457; Carthusian). Memoir of Henry VI. Ed. M. R. James, Cambridge, 1919. [Pp. xii ff. for prayers to King Henry; see also pp. 51 f., 55 ff. for lists of books belonging to Blacman.]

Sir John Fortescue (d. *c.* 1476 Chief Justice of the King's Bench). Works. Ed. Lord Clermont, 2 vols. 1869. [See also p. 261 above.]

William Wey [or Way] (d. 1476). Itineraria. Ed. G. Williams, Roxburghe Club, 1857.

William Brewyn (*fl.* 1470). [Guide to the Churches of Rome.] MS: Canterbury Cathedral Z.8.33. [Tr. C. E. Woodruff, A XVth Century Guide-Book to the Principal Churches of Rome, 1933.]

John Hauboys (*fl.* 1470). [Treatise on music.] Ed. C. E. H. de Coussemaker (Scriptorum de Musica medii Aevi nova Series, vol. I, Paris, 1864, pp. 403 ff.).

John Ireland (Scottish divine, D.D. Paris 1475; writer in vernacular, see p. 260 above). Esposito, M. An Unpublished Work by John Ireland. EHR.XXXIV,1919,pp.68 ff. [Treatise on the Immaculate Conception of the Blessed Virgin, Trinity College Dublin MS I.5.21 (no. 965 in Abbott, Catalogue of MSS, 1900, p. 164).]

John Hothby (d. 1487). Regulae super proportione. Ed. C. E. H. de Coussemaker (Scriptorum de Musica medii Aevi nova Series, vol. III, Paris, 1869, pp. 328 ff.).
—— De cantu figurato. *Ibid.* pp. 330 ff.
—— Regulae supra contrapunctum. *Ibid.* pp. 333 ff.

Thomas Norton (*fl.* 1477; alchemist). Ordinal. Ed. J. J. Manget (Bibliotheca Chemica Curiosa, Geneva, 1702; rptd Theatrum Chemicum Britannicum, 1928).

Thomas Bradley (d. 1491: Carmelite, Bishop of Dromore). [Prayers.] MS. Harley 211. [Extract in A. Wilmart, Auteurs Spirituels et Textes dévots du Moyen Âge latin, Paris, 1932, p. 555.]

John Shirwood (d. 1494; bishop of Durham). Liber de Ludo Arithmomachia. Rome, 1482. [A game played on boards.]

Allen, P. S. Bishop Shirwood of Durham and his Library. EHR. xxv, 1910, pp. 445ff. [For MSS of Arithmomachia, p. 450.]

John Alcock (d. 1500; bishop of Ely). Mons perfectionis. Westminster, 1497.
—— Gallicantus in sinodo apud Bernwell. 1498.
—— In die Innocentium. Westminster, [?].

F. J. E. R.

THE RENAISSANCE TO THE RESTORATION
1500–1660

1. INTRODUCTION

I. BIBLIOGRAPHIES, COLLECTIONS OF REPRINTS, LITERARY HISTORIES, AND SPECIAL STUDIES

(1) BIBLIOGRAPHICAL WORKS AND GENERAL COLLECTIONS OF REPRINTS

[For the earlier catalogues, and some specialized later ones, see pp. 358–60 below. Collections exclusively of poems and plays are listed in the Poetry and Drama sections below.]

Bale, J. Index Britanniæ Scriptorum. Ed. R. L. Poole and M. Bateson, Oxford, 1902. [Issued in different forms as Illustrium Majoris Britanniæ Scriptorum Summarium, Ipswich [really Wesel], 1548, and as Scriptorum Illustrium Majoris Brytanniæ, Quam Nunc Angliam & Scotiam vocant: Catalogus, Basle, 1557–9.]

Davies, M. Athenæ Britannicæ, or a Critical History of the Oxford and Cambridge Writers and Writings with Those of the Dissenters and Romanists, as Well as Other Authors and Worthies, Both Domestick and Foreign. 6 vols. 1715–6.

Ames, J. Typographical Antiquities; being an Account of Printing in England from 1471 to 1600. 1749; rev. W. Herbert, 3 vols. 1785–90; rev. T. F. Dibdin, 4 vols. (all pbd) 1810–9. [Index by J. A., Bibliog. Soc. 1899.]

Clarke, A. A Bibliographical Dictionary. 6 vols. Liverpool, 1802–4.

Harington, H. and Park, T. Nugæ Antiquæ: being a Miscellaneous Collection of Original Papers, in Prose and Verse; written during the Reigns of Henry VIII, Edward VI, Queen Mary, Elizabeth and King James. 2 vols. 1804.

Brydges, Sir S. E. Censura Literaria. 10 vols. 1805–9, 1815.
—— [and Haslewood, J.] The British Bibliographer. 4 vols. 1810–4.
—— Restituta. 4 vols. 1814–6.
—— Archaica. 2 vols. 1815.
—— Res Literariæ. 3 vols. Naples, 1821–2.

Beloe, W. Anecdotes of Literature and Scarce Books. 6 vols. 1807–12 (vols. I, II rptd 1814).

Park, T. The Harleian Miscellany. 10 vols. 1808–13.

Roxburghe Club. Publications. 1814– .

Triphook, R. Miscellanea Antiqua Anglicana. 2 vols. [1814]–21.

Boswell, Sir A. Frondes Caducæ. 7 vols. Auchinleck, 1816–8.

Camden Society. Publications. Ser. 1, 105 vols. 1838–72. [Descriptive catalogue by J. G. Nichols, 1862, 1872]; New Ser. 57 vols. 1871–97. [Pbns continued by Royal Hist. Soc. 1898–. List and Index, 1840–1924, by H. Hall, 1925.]

Percy Society. Publications. 30 vols. 1840–52.

Wright, T. and Halliwell[-Phillipps], J. O. Reliquiæ Antiquæ. 2 vols. 1841–3.

Parker Society. 55 vols. Cambridge, 1841–54. [General Index by H. Gough, Cambridge, 1855. Republication of the works of the Fathers and early writers of the Reformed English Church.]

Collier, J. P. Shakespeare's Library. A Collection of the Romances, Novels, Poems and Histories used by Shakespeare as the Foundation for his Dramas. 2 vols. [1843]; rev. W. C. Hazlitt, 6 vols. 1875.
—— Illustrations of Early English Popular Literature. 2 vols. 1863–4.
—— A Bibliographical and Critical Account of the Rarest Books in the English Language. 2 vols. 1865; 4 vols. New York, 1866.
—— Illustrations of Old English Literature. 3 vols. 1866.

[MacCray, W. D.] A Manual of British Historians to A.D. 1600. 1845.

Halliwell[-Phillipps], J. O. Contributions to Early English Literature. 6 pts, 1849.
—— The Literature of the Sixteenth and Seventeenth Centuries illustrated by Reprints of very Rare Tracts. 1851.
—— Brief Notices of the Bibliographical Rarities in the Library of J. O. Halliwell, Esq. 1855 (priv. ptd).
—— A Brief List of Some of the Rarer and most Curious Old Book Rarities in the Library of J. O. Halliwell, Esq. West Brompton, 1862 (priv. ptd.)

Hazlitt, W. C. Shakespeare Jest-books. 3 vols. 1864.
—— Handbook to the Popular, Poetical, and Dramatic Literature of Great Britain, from the Invention of Printing to the Restoration. 1867. [Collections and Notes, 1867–1876, 1876; Second Series of Bibliographical Collections and Notes on Early English Literature, 1474–1700, 1882; Third Series, 1887 (Supplements, 1889, 1892); Fourth Series, 1903; Index [1867–89] by G. J. Gray, 1893.]

Hazlitt, W. C. Inedited Tracts, illustrating the Manners, Opinions, and Occupations of Englishmen during the Sixteenth and Seventeenth Centuries. 1868.

—— Fairy Tales, Legends, and Romances, illustrating Shakespeare and Other Early English Writers. 1875.

Early English Text Society. Publications. Original Ser. I–, 1864–; Extra Ser. I–, 1869–.

Jahrbuch der Deutschen Shakespeare-Gesellschaft. Berlin, 1865– [VII–XXXIV, Weimar]. [Shakespeare Bibliographie,1865–. Zuwachs der Bibliothek der Deutschen Shakespeare-Gesellschaft, 1869–. Gesammt Verzeichnis, I–XXX, 1894. Inhalt, XXXI–XXXIX, 1905; XXXV–LVII, 1912. Bücherschau und Zeitschriftenschau, 1900–.]

Rushton, W. L. Shakespeare illustrated by Old Authors. 2 pts, 1867–8.

Spenser Society. Publications. Manchester, 1867–95.

Arber, E. English Reprints. 17 vols. 1868–71.

—— A Transcript of the Registers of the Company of the Stationers of London, 1554–1640 A.D. 5 vols. 1875–94.

—— An English Garner. 8 vols. 1877–90, 1895–6; ed. T. Seccombe, 12 vols. 1903–4. [An Analytical Catalogue of the contents of the two edns issued by John Rylands Lib., Manchester, 1909.]

Ashbee, E. W. Occasional Facsimile Reprints of Rare and Curious Tracts of the Sixteenth and Seventeenth Centuries. 30 pts, 1868–72.

Grosart, A. B. Fuller Worthies' Library. 33 vols. 1868–76.

—— Chertsey Worthies' Library. 13 vols. Edinburgh, 1875–81.

—— Occasional Issues of Unique or very Rare Books. 37 pts, Manchester, 1875–81.

—— Fly-Leaves; or, Additional Notes and Illustrations on Occasional Issues. [Manchester,] 1881.

—— Handlist of Unique or Extremely Rare Elizabethan-Jacobean-Carolian Books. Blackburn, 1884–5.

Hindley, C. The Old Book Collector's Miscellany. 3 vols. 1871–3.

Hunterian Club. Publications. 9 vols. (in 24), Glasgow, 1873–1902.

Boston Public Library. Catalogue of the Barton Shakespeare Collection. Ed. J. M. Hubbard, 2 vols. Boston, 1878–80.

[Ellis, F. S.] The Huth Library. A Catalogue of Printed Books [etc]. 5 vols. 1880.

Bibliotheca Curiosa. Ed. E. Goldsmid, 64 vols. Edinburgh, 1883–8.

British Museum. Catalogue of Books in the Library of the British Museum, printed in England, Scotland and Ireland, and of

Books in English printed abroad to the Year 1640. Ed. G. Bullen, 3 vols. 1884.

British Museum. Catalogue of the Pamphlets, Books, Newspapers, and Manuscripts relating to the Civil War, the Commonwealth, and Restoration. Collected by G. Thomason. 1640–61. Ed. G. K. Fortescue, 2 vols. 1908.

Scottish Text Society. Publications. Ser. 1, 65 vols. Edinburgh, 1884–1918; New Ser. I–, Edinburgh, 1911–.

Tudor Translations. Ed. W. E. Henley, 44 vols. 1892–1909; Second Ser. ed. C. Whibley, I–, 1924–.

Bibliographical Society. Transactions and Monographs. 1893–.

The Isham Reprints. With Bibliographical Preface by C. Edmonds. 2 vols. 1895.

John Rylands Library, Manchester. Catalogue of Books in the John Rylands Library, Manchester, printed in England, Scotland and Ireland, and of Books in English printed abroad to the Year 1640. Ed. E. G. Duff, Manchester, 1895.

Madan, F. The Early Oxford Press, "1468"–1640. Oxford, 1895.

Bibliotheca Lindesiana. Catalogue of English Broadsides, 1505–1897. Aberdeen, 1898. Catalogue of English Newspapers, 1641–1666. Aberdeen, 1901.

Dix, E. R. McC. Catalogue of early Dublin-printed Books, 1601–1700. 4 vols. Dublin, 1898–1905; Supplement, 1912.

Lee, Sir S. A Catalogue of Shakespeareana. 1899.

Betz, L. P. La Littérature comparée. Essai bibliographique. Strasburg, 1900; avec un Index méthodique, par F. Baldensperger, 1904.

Shaw, A. C. Index to the Shakespeare Memorial Library, Birmingham. 3 pts, Birmingham, 1900–3.

Sayle, C. E. Early English Printed Books in the University Library, Cambridge, 1475–1640. 4 vols. Cambridge, 1900–7.

Gayley, C. M. and Scott, F. N. An Introduction to the Methods and Materials of Literary Criticism. Boston, 1901.

Greg, W. W. Catalogue of the Books presented by Edward Capell to Trinity College in Cambridge. Cambridge, 1903.

[Hoe, R.] Catalogue of Books by English Authors who lived before the Year 1700 forming Part of the Library of Robert Hoe. 5 vols. New York, 1903–5.

Aldis, H. G. List of Books printed in Scotland before 1700. Edinburgh Bibliog. Soc. 1904.

Gregory Smith, G. Elizabethan Critical Essays. 2 vols. Oxford, 1904.

Johnston, G. P. A Catalogue of English Pamphlets printed between 1618 and 1700. Edinburgh, 1906.

Gollancz, Sir I. The Shakespeare Classics. 1907–.

Spingarn, J. E. Seventeenth Century Critical Essays. 3 vols. Oxford, 1908–9. [With bibliography.]

Studies in Philology. Recent Literature of the English Renaissance. [Annually in April, nos. by E. Greenlaw and others, XIV–XVIII, 1917–21; by T. S. Graves, XIX–XXII, 1922–5; by H. Craig, XXIII–, 1926–.]

Cole, G. W. Check-List or Brief Catalogue of the Library of Henry E. Huntington. New York, 1919 (priv. ptd.).

—— A Survey of the Bibliography of English Literature, 1475–1640. Papers of Bibliog. Soc. of America, XXIII, pt 2, 1930.

Gerould, J. T. Sources of English History of the Seventeenth Century, 1603–1689. Minneapolis, 1921.

Morgan, R. B. Readings in English Social History from Contemporary Literature. Vol. III, 1485–1603. Cambridge, 1921.

Carpenter, F. I. Reference Guide to Edmund Spenser. Chicago, 1923.

Childs, J. B. Sixteenth-Century Books: a Bibliography of Literature describing Books printed between 1501 and 1601. Papers of Bibliog. Soc. of America, XVII, 1923.

Rollins, H. E. An Analytical Index to the Ballad-Entries (1557–1709) in the Registers of the Company of Stationers of London. Chapel Hill, 1924.

Tawney, R. H. and Power, E. Tudor Economic Documents. 3 vols. 1924.

Bartlett, H. C. Catalogue of Early English Books, chiefly of the Elizabethan Period, collected by W. A. White. New York, 1926.

Pollard, A. W. and Redgrave, G. R. A Short-Title Catalogue of Books printed in England, Scotland and Ireland, and of English Books printed Abroad, 1475–1640. Bibliog. Soc. 1926.

Crane, R. S. and Kaye, F. B. A Census of British Newspapers, 1620–1800. Chapel Hill, 1927.

Kennedy, A. G. A Bibliography of Writings on the English Language. Cambridge, U.S.A. 1927.

Bibliography of British History. Stuart Period, 1603–1714. Ed. G. Davies, Oxford, 1928.

Matheson, C. A Catalogue of the Publications of the Scottish Historical and Kindred Clubs and Societies and of the Papers Relative to Scottish History issued by H.M. Stationery Office, including the Reports of the Royal Commission on Historical Manuscripts, 1908–1927. With a Subject Index. Aberdeen, 1928.

Tucker, L. L. and Benham, A. R. Bibliography of Fifteenth Century Literature. Seattle, 1928.

McGrew, J. F. A Bibliography of the Works on Speech Composition in England during the 16th and 17th Centuries. Quart. Journ. Speech, XV, 1929.

Ebisch, W. and Schücking, L. L. A Shakespeare Bibliography. Oxford, 1931.

Bibliography of British History. Tudor Period, 1485–1603. Ed. C. Read, Oxford, 1933.

The Britwell Handlist, or Short-Title Catalogue of the Principal Volumes to the Year 1800 formerly in the Library of Britwell Court. 2 vols. 1933.

Gebert, C. An Anthology of Elizabethan Dedications and Prefaces. Philadelphia, 1933.

Roberts, M. Elizabethan Prose. 1933.

Brown, Huntington. The Classical Tradition in English Literature. A Bibliography. Harvard Stud. XVIII, 1935.

(2) HISTORIES OF ENGLISH LITERATURE

Walton, I. The Lives of Dr. John Donne, Sir Henry Wotton, Mr. Richard Hooker, Mr. George Herbert. 1651, etc.; ed. A. H. Bullen, 1884; ed. A Dobson, 2 vols. 1898.

Fuller, T. The History of the Worthies of England. 1662, etc.; ed. P. A. Nuttall, 3 vols. 1840.

Aubrey, J. Brief Lives, chiefly of Contemporaries, set down by John Aubrey between the Years 1669 and 1696. Ed. A. Clark, 2 vols. Oxford, 1898.

Leland, J. Commentarii de Scriptoribus Britannicis. Ed. A. Hall, Oxford, 1709.

Warton, T. The History of English Poetry from the Eleventh to the Commencement of the Eighteenth Century. 4 vols. 1774–81, 1824; rev. W. C. Hazlitt, 4 vols. 1871.

Nichols. J. The Progresses and Public Processions of Queen Elizabeth. 3 vols. and vol. IV, pt 1, 1788–1821; 3 vols. 1823.

—— The Progresses, Processions, and Magnificent Festivities of King James I. 4 vols. 1828.

Douce, F. Illustrations of Shakespeare and of Ancient Manners. 2 vols. 1807, 1839.

Drake, N. Shakespeare and his Times. 2 vols. 1817.

Hazlitt, W. Lectures on the English Poets. 1818, etc.

—— Lectures on the Dramatic Literature of the Reign of Elizabeth. 1820, etc.

Willmott, R. E. A. Lives of Sacred Poets. 2 sers. 1834–9.

Coleridge, S. T. The Literary Remains of Samuel Taylor Coleridge. 4 vols. 1836–9, etc.

Coleridge, S. T. Notes and Lectures upon Shakespeare and some of the Old Poets and Dramatists. 2 vols. 1849, etc.

Hallam, H. Introduction to the Literature of Europe in the Fifteenth, Sixteenth and Seventeenth Centuries. 4 vols. 1837–9, etc.

Irving, D. Lives of Scotish Writers. 2 vols. Edinburgh, 1839.

—— The History of Scotish Poetry. Ed. J. A. Carlyle, Edinburgh, 1861.

Ellis, Sir H. Original Letters of Eminent Literary Men of the Sixteenth, Seventeenth and Eighteenth Centuries. Camden Soc. 1843.

Chambers, W. and R. Cyclopædia of English Literature. 2 vols. Edinburgh, 1843–4; rev. R. Carruthers, 4 vols. 1857–60; rev. D. Patrick, 3 vols. 1901–3.

Cattermole, R. Literature of the Church of England. 2 vols. 1844.

Craik, G. L. Sketches of the History of Literature and Learning in England from the Norman Conquest to the Present Day. 3 sers. 1844–5; 2 vols. 1861 (rev. as A Compendious History of English Literature, and of the English Language, from the Norman Conquest).

Hunter, J. New Illustrations of the Life, Studies and Writings of Shakespeare. 2 vols. 1845.

Manning, A. The Household of Sir Thomas More. 1851, etc.

Masson, D. The Life of John Milton. 6 vols. Cambridge, 1859–80. [Index, 1894.]

Spedding, J. Life and Letters of Francis Bacon, Viscount St. Albans. 7 vols. 1861–74.

Taine, H. A. Histoire de la Littérature anglaise. 4 vols. Paris, 1863–4; tr. Eng. 2 vols. Edinburgh, 1871–2.

Rye, W. B. England as seen by Foreigners in the Days of Elizabeth and James I. 1865.

Seebohm, F. The Oxford Reformers. 1867; 1887.

—— The Era of the Protestant Revolution. 1874; 1894.

Whipple, E. P. The Literature of the Age of Elizabeth. Boston, 1869.

Halliwell[-Phillipps], J. O. Illustrations of the Life of Shakespeare in a Discursive Series of Essays. 1874.

—— Outlines of the Life of Shakespeare. Brighton, 1881, etc.

ten Brink, B. Geschichte der englischen Literatur [bis zur Reformation]. 2 vols. Berlin, 1877–93; tr. Eng. 3 vols. 1883–96.

Bayne, P. The Chief Actors in the Puritan Revolution. 1878.

Gosse, Sir E. Seventeenth Century Studies. 1883; 1913.

—— From Shakespeare to Pope. Cambridge, 1885.

—— Jacobean Poets. 1889.

—— The Life and Letters of John Donne. 2 vols. 1899.

Herford, C. H. Studies in the Literary Relations of England and Germany in the Sixteenth Century. Cambridge, 1886.

Bleibtreu, K. Geschichte der englischen Litteratur im Zeitalter der Renaissance und Klassizität. Leipzig, 1887, 1923.

Lupton, J. H. Life of John Colet, Dean of St. Paul's. 1887.

Saintsbury, G. A History of Elizabethan Literature. 1887.

—— The Earlier Renaissance. Edinburgh, 1901.

—— A History of Criticism and Literary Taste. 2 vols. Edinburgh, 1902 and 1912.

—— A History of English Prosody. 2 vols. 1906–8.

Morley, H. English Writers. 11 vols. 1887–95.

Pattison, M. Essays. 2 vols. Oxford, 1889.

Walker, H. Three Centuries of Scottish Literature. 2 vols. Glasgow, 1893.

Jusserand, J. J. Histoire littéraire du Peuple anglais. 2 vols. Paris, 1894–1904; tr. Eng. 3 vols. 1906–9; 3 vols. 1926 (rev. edn).

Traill, H. D. et al. Social England. 6 vols. 1894–1905. [With bibliographies.]

Courthope, W. J. A History of English Poetry. 6 vols. 1895–1910.

Masterman, J. H. B. The Age of Milton. 1897.

Hannay, D. The Later Renaissance. Edinburgh, 1898.

Henderson, T. F. Scottish Vernacular Literature. 1898.

Spingarn, J. E. A History of Literary Criticism in the Renaissance. New York, 1899.

Underhill, J. G. Spanish Literature in the England of the Tudors. New York, 1899. [With bibliography.]

Dowden, E. Puritan and Anglican: Studies in Literature. 1900.

—— Essays Modern and Elizabethan. [1910.]

Gregory Smith, G. The Transition Period. Edinburgh, 1900.

Einstein, L. The Italian Renaissance in England. New York, 1902.

—— Tudor Ideals. New York, 1921.

Seccombe, T. and Allen, J. W. The Age of Shakespeare, 1579–1631. 2 vols. 1903.

Arnold, R. F. Die Kultur der Renaissance. Leipzig, 1904.

Lee, Sir S. Great Englishmen of the Sixteenth Century. 1904; 1907.

—— The Last Years of Elizabeth. [In Cambridge Modern History, vol. III, 1904.]

—— Elizabethan and Other Essays. 1929.

Pollard, A. F. Thomas Cranmer and the English Reformation. 1904; 1926.

Wendell, B. The Temper of the Seventeenth Century in English Literature. Boston, 1904.

Hyde, A. G. George Herbert and his Times. 1905.

Sandys, Sir J. E. Harvard Lectures on the Revival of Learning. Cambridge, 1905.
—— A History of Classical Scholarship. Vol. II, Cambridge, 1908.
Snell, F. J. The Age of Transition. 2 vols. 1905.
Charlanne, L. L'Influence française en Angleterre au XVIIᵉ Siècle. La Vie sociale—la Vie littéraire. Paris, 1906.
Grierson, H. J. C. The First Half of the Seventeenth Century. Edinburgh, 1906.
—— Cross Currents in English Literature of the Seventeenth Century. 1929.
Crawford, C. Collectanea. 2 vols. Stratford-on-Avon, 1906–7.
Omond, T. S. English Metrists. Oxford, 1907.
Swinburne, A. C. The Age of Shakespeare. 1908; 1926.
—— Contemporaries of Shakespeare. 1919; 1926.
Upham, A. H. The French Influence in English Literature from the Accession of Elizabeth to the Restoration. New York, 1908. [With bibliography.]
The Cambridge History of English Literature. Vols. III–VII, 1909–11. [With bibliographies.]
Mackail, J. W. The Springs of Helicon. 1909.
Feuillerat, A. John Lyly. Contribution à l'Histoire de la Renaissance en Angleterre. Cambridge, 1910.
Schelling, F. E. English Literature during the Life Time of Shakespeare. New York, 1910, 1927.
Allen, P. S. The Age of Erasmus. Oxford, 1914.
Robertson, J. M. Elizabethan Literature. 1914.
Waterhouse, G. The Literary Relations of England and Germany in the Seventeenth Century. Cambridge, 1914. [With bibliography.]
Krapp, G. P. The Rise of English Literary Prose. New York, 1915.
Greenlaw, E. An Outline of the Literature of the English Renaissance. Boston, 1916.
Shakespeare's England. An Account of the Life and Manners of his Age. 2 vols. Oxford, 1916. [With bibliographies.]
Burdach, K. Reformation-Renaissance-Humanismus. Berlin, 1918.
Berdan, J. M. Early Tudor Poetry, 1485–1547. New York, 1920.
Wright, T. G. Literary Culture in Early New England, 1620–1730. New Haven, 1920.
Dark, S. The Story of the Renaissance. 1923.
Harrison, G. B. Shakespeare's Fellows: Being a Brief Chronicle of the Elizabethan Age. 1923.
Bullen, A. H. Elizabethans. 1924.
Hudson, W. H. The Story of the Renaissance. New York, 1924.
Legouis, É. and Cazamian, L. Histoire de la Littérature anglaise. Paris, 1924; tr. Eng. 2 vols. 1926–7.
Praz, M. Secentismo e Marinismo in Inghilterra. Florence, 1925.

Smellie, A. The Reformation in its Literature. 1925.
Reed, A. W. Early Tudor Drama: Medwall, the Rastells, Heywood, and the More Circle. 1926.
Salzman, L. F. England in Tudor Times. 1926.
Ascoli, G. La Grande-Bretagne devant l'Opinion française depuis la Guerre de Cent Ans jusqu'à la Fin du XVIᵉ Siècle. Paris, 1927.
—— La Grande-Bretagne devant l'Opinion française au XVIIᵉ Siècle. 2 vols. Paris, 1930.
Blei, F. Frauen und Männer der Renaissance. Hellerau bei Dresden, 1927.
Hanford, J. H. A Milton Handbook. New York, 1927.
Keller, W. and Fehr, B. Englische Literatur von der Renaissance bis zur Aufklärung. 9 pts, Potsdam, 1927–32.
Mangan, J. J. Life, Character and Influence of Desiderius Erasmus, of Rotterdam. 2 vols. 1927.
Kane, E. K. Gongorism and the Golden Age. Chapel Hill, 1928.
Wolff, M. J. Die Renaissance in der englischen Literatur. Bielefeld, 1928.
Clark, G. N. The Seventeenth Century. Oxford, 1929.
Hauser, H. and Renaudet, A. Les Débuts de l'Âge moderne: la Renaissance et la Réforme. Paris, 1929.
Jones, H. S. V. A Spenser Handbook. New York, 1930.
Schirmer, W. F. Der englische Frühhumanismus. Leipzig, 1930.
Smith, P. A History of Modern Culture. Vol. I, The Great Renewal, 1543–1687. New York, 1930.

(3) Works on Special Subjects in the History of English Literature

Farmer, R. An Essay on the Learning of Shakespeare. 1767, etc.
Capell, E. The School of Shakespeare. [Vol. III of Notes and Various Readings, 1779–80.]
Malone, E. A Dissertation on the Three Parts of King Henry VI. 1787.
Willmott, R. E. A. Jeremy Taylor, his Predecessors, Contemporaries and Successors. 1846.
Hamilton, Sir W. Discussions on Philosophy and Literature, Education and University Reform. 1852; 1866.
Walker, W. S. On Shakespeare's Versification. 1854.
Ellis, R. L. General Preface to the Philosophical Works. [Bacon's Works vol. I, 1857.]
Campbell, John, Baron Campbell. Shakespeare's Legal Acquirements. 1859.

Bucknill, J. C. The Medical Knowledge of Shakespeare. 1860.

—— The Mad Folk of Shakespeare. 1867.

Tulloch, J. English Puritanism and its Leaders. Edinburgh, 1861.

—— Rational Theology and Christianized Philosophy in England in the Seventeenth Century. 2 vols. Edinburgh, 1872.

Young, Sir G. History of Greek Literature in England from the earliest Times to the End of the Reign of James I. Cambridge, 1862.

Mullinger, J. B. Cambridge Characteristics in the Seventeenth Century. Cambridge, 1867.

Quick, R. H. Essays on Educational Reformers. 1868; 1902.

Kingsley, C. Plays and Puritans. 1873, etc.

Fleay, F. G. On Metrical Tests as applied to Dramatic Poetry. Trans. New Shakspere Soc. i, 1874.

Pattison, M. Isaac Casaubon. Oxford, 1875, 1892.

Rémusat, C. de. Histoire de la Philosophie en Angleterre depuis Bacon jusqu'à Locke. Paris, 1875.

Beard, C. The Reformation in the Sixteenth Century in its Relation to Modern Thought and Knowledge. 1883.

Stubbes, W. Seventeen Lectures on the Study of Mediaeval and Modern History. Oxford, 1886, 1900.

Cook, A. S. The House of Sleep: A Study in Comparative Literature. MLN. v, 1890.

Kautsky, K. Thomas More und seine Utopia, mit historischer Einleitung. Stuttgart, 1890; tr. Eng. 1927.

Koeppel, E. Studien zur Geschichte der englischen Petrarchismus im XVI. Jahrhundert. Romanische Forschungen, v, 1890.

—— Studien zur Geschichte der italienischen Novelle in der englischen Litteratur des sechzehnten Jahrhunderts. QF. lxx, 1892.

—— Quellen-Studien zu den Dramen Ben Jonsons, John Marstons und Beaumont und Fletchers. Erlangen, 1895.

—— Quellen-Studien zu den Dramen George Chapmans, Philip Massingers und John Fords. QF. lxxxii, 1897.

Schelling, F. E. Poetic and Verse Criticism of the Reign of Elizabeth. Philadelphia, 1891.

Bulthaupt, H. A. Shakespeare und der Naturalismus. Weimar, 1893.

Owen, J. The Skeptics of the French Renaissance. 1893.

Creighton, M. The Tudors and the Reformation. 1896.

Meyer, E. S. Machiavelli and the Elizabethan Drama. Weimar, 1897.

Dewischheit, C. Shakespeare und die Stenographie. Sh. Jb. xxiv. 1898.

Alden, R. M. The Rise of Formal Satire in England. Philadelphia, 1899.

Walton, J. Early History of Legal Studies in England. 1900.

Wendelstein, L. Zur Vorgeschichte des Euphuismus. Halle, 1901.

Spirgatis, M. L. Englische Litteratur auf der Frankfurter Messe von 1561–1620. Leipzig, 1902.

Harrison, J. S. Platonism in English Poetry. New York, 1903.

Anders, H. R. D. Shakespeare's Books. Berlin, 1904.

Canning, A. S. G. Literary Influence in British History. 1904.

Fischer, K. Francis Bacon und seine Schule. [Geschichte der neueren Philosophie, vol. x, Heidelberg, 1904.]

Lee, Sir S. Elizabethan Sonnets: with an Introduction. 2 vols. 1904.

—— Aspects of Shakespeare's Philosophy. [In Shakespeare and the Modern Stage, 1906.]

—— Shakespeare and the Italian Renaissance. British Academy Lecture, 1915.

Benndorf, C. Die englische Pädagogik im 16. Jahrhundert. Vienna, 1905.

Laurie, S. S. Studies in the History of Educational Opinion from the Renaissance. Cambridge, 1905.

Stoll, E. E. Shakespeare, Marston and the Malcontent Type. MP. iii, 1905.

—— Anachronism in Shakespeare Criticism. MP. vii, 1909.

Henriques, G. J. C. George Buchanan in the Lisbon Inquisition. Lisbon, 1906.

Glasgow Quatercentenary Studies. George Buchanan. Glasgow, 1906.

Greg, W. W. Pastoral Poetry and Pastoral Drama. A Literary Inquiry, with special reference to the Pre-Restoration Stage in England. 1906.

—— Principles of Emendation in Shakespeare. British Academy Lecture, 1928.

Zocco, I. Petrarchismo e Petrarchisti in Inghilterra. Palermo, 1906.

Chandler, F. W. The Literature of Roguery. 2 vols. Boston, 1907. [With bibliography.]

Riedner, W. Spensers Belesenheit. Leipzig, 1907.

The British Academy. Papers Read at the Milton Tercentenary. Proc. iii, 1907–8.

Pierce, W. Historical Introduction to the Marprelate Tracts. 1908.

Schücking, L. L. Shakespeare im literarischen Urteil seiner Zeit. Heidelberg, 1908.

—— Die Familie im Puritanismus. Leipzig, 1929.

Watson, F. The English Grammar Schools to 1660: their Curriculum and Practice. Cambridge, 1908.

Watson, F. The Beginnings of the Teaching of Modern Subjects in English. 1909.

Greenlaw, E. The Influence of Machiavelli on Spenser. MP. VII, 1909.

—— Spenser and Lucretius. Stud. Phil. XVII, 1920.

—— The New Science and English Literature in the Seventeenth Century. Johns Hopkins Alumni Mag. XIII, 1926.

Maynadier, H. The Areopagus of Sidney and Spenser. MLR. IV, 1909.

Sheavyn, P. The Literary Profession in the Elizabethan Age. Manchester, 1909.

Fletcher, J. B. A Study of Renaissance Mysticism: Spenser's Foure Hymnes. PMLA. XXVI, 1911.

Merrill, E. The Dialogue in English Literature. New York, 1911.

Cory, H. E. Spenser, the School of the Fletchers, and Milton. Berkeley, 1912.

Schultz, E. Die englischen Schwankbücher bis herab zu 'Dobson's Drie Bobs' (1607). Berlin, 1912.

Wolff, S. L. Greek Romances in Elizabethan Prose Fiction. New York, 1912.

Bewsher, F. W. The Reformation and the Renaissance Compared. 1913.

Burr, G. L. Anent the Middle Ages. American Hist. Rev. XVIII, 1913.

Bailey, M. L. Milton and Jakob Boehme: a Study of German Mysticism in Seventeenth Century England. New York, 1914.

Crane, R. S. The Vogue of Guy of Warwick from the Close of the Middle Ages to the Romantic Revival. PMLA. XXX, 1915.

Kliem, H. Sentimentale Freundschaft in der Shakespeare-Epoche. Jena, 1915.

Padelford, F. M. The Political, Economic, and Social Views of Spenser. JEGP. XIV, 1915.

Adams, E. N. Old English Scholarship in England from 1566–1800. New Haven, 1917.

Powell, C. L. English Domestic Relations, 1487–1653. New York, 1917.

Withington, R. English Pageantry. 2 vols. Cambridge, U.S.A. 1918–20.

Smith, D. N. Characters from the Histories and Memoirs of the Seventeenth Century with an Essay on the Character, and Historical Notes. Oxford, 1919.

Spurgeon, C. F. E. Five Hundred Years of Chaucer Criticism and Allusion. 5 vols. Chaucer Soc. 1919–24; 3 vols. Cambridge, 1925.

Wyndham, G. Essays in Romantic Literature. 1919.

Crane, T. F. Italian Social Customs of the Sixteenth Century and their Influence on the Literatures of Europe. New Haven, 1920.

Osgood, C. G. Spenser's English Rivers. Trans. Connecticut Academy of Arts and Sciences, XXIII, 1920.

Saurat, D. La Pensée de Milton. Paris, 1920; tr. Eng. (as Milton: Man and Thinker), 1925 (rev.).

—— Les Idées philosophiques de Spenser. New Soc. Letters Year Book, I, Lund, 1924.

Taylor, H. O. Thought and Expression in the Sixteenth Century. 2 vols. New York, 1920.

Zeitlin, J. Commonplaces in Elizabethan Life and Letters. JEGP. XIX, 1920.

Croll, M. W. Attic Prose in the Seventeenth Century. Stud. Phil. XVIII, 1921.

—— The Baroque Style in Prose. [In Studies in Honour of Frederick Klaeber, Minneapolis, 1929.]

Huizinga, J. Herfsttijd der Middeleeuwen. Haarlem, 1921; tr. Eng. (as The Waning of the Middle Ages), 1924.

Sisson, C. J. Le Goût public et le Théâtre élisabéthain jusqu'à la Mort de Shakespeare. Dijon, [1921].

Thompson, E. N. S. Mysticism in Seventeenth-Century English Literature. Stud. Phil. XVIII, 1921.

—— Literary Bypaths of the Renaissance. New Haven, 1924.

Clark, D. L. Rhetoric and Poetry in the Renaissance. New York, 1922.

Craig, H. Some Problems of Scholarship in the Literature of the Renaissance, particularly in the English Field. PQ. I, 1922.

—— A Contribution to the Theory of the English Renaissance. PQ. VII, 1928.

—— The Enchanted Glass: the Elizabethan Mind in Literature. New York, 1936.

Smith, P. The Age of the Reformation. 1922.

Willey, B. Tendencies in Renaissance Literary Theory. Cambridge, 1922.

—— The Seventeenth-Century Background. Studies in the Thought of the Age in relation to Poetry and Religion. 1934.

Baskervill, C. R. Bassanio as an Ideal Lover. [In Manly Anniversary Studies in Language and Literature, Chicago, 1923.]

—— The Elizabethan Jig and Related Song Drama. Chicago, 1929.

Benians, S. From Renaissance to Revolution. A Study of the Influence of the Renaissance upon the Political Development of Europe. 1923.

Liljegren, S. B. La Pensée de Milton et Giordano Bruno. Revue de Littérature comparée, III, 1923.

—— The Fall of the Monasteries and the Social Changes in England leading up to the Great Revolution. Lund, 1924.

Brie, F. Deismus und Atheismus in der englischen Renaissance. Ang. XLVIII, 1924.

Camp, C. W. The Artisan in Elizabethan Literature. New York, 1924.

Heidrich, H. John Davies of Hereford (1565?–1618) und sein Bild von Shakespeares Umgebung. Leipzig, 1924.

Schirmer, W. F. Antike, Renaissance und Puritanismus. Munich, 1924.

Seton-Watson, R. W. et al. Tudor Studies [presented to A. F. Pollard]. 1924.

Wells, H. W. Poetic Imagery, Illustrated from Elizabethan Literature. New York, 1924.

Allen, P. S. Erasmus's Services to Learning. British Academy Lecture, 1925.

von Below, G. Über historische Periodisierung, mit besonderem Blick auf die Grenze zwischen Mittelalter und Neuzeit. Archiv für Politik und Geschichte, III, 1925.

Eisinger, F. Das Problem des Selbstmordes in der Literatur der englischen Renaissance. Freiburg, 1925.

Hearnshaw, F. J. C. et al. Social and Political Ideas of some Great Thinkers of the Renaissance and Reformation. 1925.

Kingsford, C. L. Prejudice and Promise in Fifteenth Century England. Oxford, 1925.

Leclère, L. Les Limites chronologiques du Moyen Âge. Revue belge de Philologie et d'Histoire, I, 1925.

Legouis, É. Dans les Sentiers de la Renaissance anglaise. Paris, 1925.

Luick, K. Die Bedeutung der Renaissance für die Entwicklung der englischen Dichtung. Inaugurationsrede. Vienna, 1925.

Modersohn, A. B. Cicero im englischen Geistesleben des 16. Jahrhunderts. Archiv, CXLIX, 1925.

Pompen, A. The English Versions of the Ship of Fools: a Contribution to the History of the Early French Renaissance in England. 1925.

Sencourt, R. Outflying Philosophy. A Literary Study of the Religious Element [in Donne, Browne, Vaughan]. 1925.

Whipple, T. K. Martial and the English Epigram from Sir Thomas Wyatt to Ben Jonson. Berkeley, 1925.

Williams, C. H. England under the Early Tudors. 1925.

Crump, C. G. and Jacob, E. F. The Legacy of the Middle Ages. Oxford, 1926.

Jones, H. S. V. The Faerie Queene and the Medieval Aristotelian Tradition. JEGP. XXV, 1926.

Michelson, H. The Jew in Early English Literature. Amsterdam, 1926.

Pope, E. F. Renaissance Criticism and the Diction of the Faerie Queene. PMLA. XLI, 1926.

Schoell, F. L. Études sur l'Humanisme continental en Angleterre à la Fin de la Renaissance. Paris, 1926.

Bray, R. La Formation de la Doctrine classique en France. Paris, 1927.

Cassirer, E. Individuum und Kosmos in der Philosophie der Renaissance. Leipzig, 1927.

Chaplin, F. K. The Effects of the Reformation on Ideals of Life and Conduct. Cambridge, 1927.

Harrison, G. B. Books and Readers, 1591–4. Library, VIII, 1927.

—— Books and Readers, 1599–1603. Library, XIV, 1933.

Hasselkuss, H. K. Der Petrarchismus in der Sprache der englischen Sonnettdichter der Renaissance. Münster, 1927.

Saxl, F. Antike Götter in der Spätrenaissance. Leipzig, 1927.

Seeger, O. Die Auseinandersetzung zwischen Antike und Moderne in England bis zum Tode Dr. Samuel Johnsons. Leipzig, 1927.

Stammler, W. Von der Mystik zum Barock, 1400–1600. Stuttgart, 1927.

Weisberger, L. A. Machiavelli and Tudor England. Political Science Quart. XLII, 1927.

Allen, J. W. A History of Political Thought in the Sixteenth Century. 1928.

Anderson, R. L. Elizabethan Psychology in Shakespeare's Plays. Iowa City, 1928.

Coulton, G. G. Art and the Reformation. Oxford, 1928.

Gaedick, W. Der weise Narr in der englischen Literatur von Erasmus bis Shakespeare. Leipzig, 1928.

Kempner, N. Raleghs staatstheoretische Schriften; die Einführung des Machiavellismus in England. Leipzig, 1928.

Nathan, W. L. Sir John Cheke und der englische Humanismus. Bonn, 1928.

Ornstein, M. The Rôle of Scientific Societies in the XVII Century. Chicago, 1928.

Praz, M. Machiavelli and the Elizabethans. British Academy Lecture, 1928.

Richardson, C. F. English Preachers and Preaching, 1640–1670. New York, 1928.

Adamson, J. W. The Extent of Literacy in England in the Fifteenth and Sixteenth Centuries. Library, X, 1929.

Albright, E. M. Spenser's Cosmic Philosophy and his Religion. PMLA. XLIV, 1929.

Bundy, M. W. 'Invention' and 'Imagination' in the Renaissance. JEGP. XXIX, 1929.

Frey, D. Gotik und Renaissance als Grundlagen der modernen Weltanschauung. Augsburg, 1929.

Genouy, H. L'Élément pastoral dans la Poésie narrative et le Drame en Angleterre, de 1579 à 1640. Paris, 1929.

Hintze, H. Der nationale und humanitäre Gedanke im Zeitalter der Renaissance. Euphorion, XXX, 1929.

Holmes, E. Aspects of Elizabethan Imagery. Oxford, 1929.

Hoops, R. Der Begriff 'Romance' in der mittelenglischen und frühneuenglischen Literatur. Heidelberg, 1929.

Hughes, M. Y. Virgil and Spenser. Berkeley, 1929.

Kellett, E. E. The Elizabethans. [In the Whirligig of Taste, 1929.]

Kelso, R. The Doctrine of the English Gentleman in the Sixteenth Century. Urbana, 1929.

Shaaber, M. A. Some Forerunners of the Newspaper in England, 1476-1622. Philadelphia, 1929.

Stadelmann, R. Vom Geist des ausgehenden Mittelalters. Halle, 1929.

Thompson, J. W. et al. The Civilization of the Renaissance. Chicago, 1929.

Toffanín, G. Che Cosa fu l'Umanesimo. Florence, 1929.

Wright, F. A. Latin Poetry of the Renaissance. Edinburgh Rev. ccxlix, 1929.

Furlong, P. J. The Renaissance and Individualism. Catholic Hist. Rev. xvi, 1930.

Hauser, H. La Modernité du XVIᵉ Siècle. Paris, 1930.

Hefele, E. Zum Begriff der Renaissance. Historisches Jahrbuch, xlix, 1930.

Herrick, M. T. The Poetics of Aristotle in England. New Haven, 1930.

Latham, M. W. The Elizabethan Fairies: The Fairies of Folklore and the Fairies of Shakespeare. New York, 1930.

Leube, H. Reformation und Humanismus in England. Leipzig, 1930.

Schütt, M. Die englische Biographik der Tudor-Zeit. Hamburg, 1930.

Stauffer, D. A. English Biography before 1700. Cambridge, U.S.A. 1930.

van der Spek, C. The Church and the Churchman in English Literature before 1642. Amsterdam, 1930.

Campbell, L. B. Theories of Revenge in Renaissance England. MP. xxviii, 1931.

Jacob, E. F. Changing Views of the Renaissance. History, Oct. 1931.

Brinkley, R. B. Arthurian Legend in the Seventeenth Century. Baltimore, 1932.

Buckley, G. T. Atheism in the English Renaissance. Chicago, 1932.

Chambers, R. W. The Continuity of English Prose from Alfred to More and his School. EETS. 1932.

Mitchell, W. F. English Pulpit Oratory. 1932. [With bibliography.]

Pearson, L. E. Elizabethan Love Conventions. Berkeley, 1932.

Hoyler, A. Gentleman-Ideal und Gentleman-Erziehung mit besonderer Berücksichtigung der englischen Renaissance. Leipzig, 1933.

Mason, John E. Gentlefolk in the Making. Studies in the History of English Courtesy Literature from 1531 to 1744. Philadelphia, 1935.

Nicolson, M. The 'New Astronomy' and English Literary Imagination. Stud. Phil. xxxii, 1935, MP. xxxii, 1935, ELH. ii, 1935.

White, Harold O. Plagiarism and Imitation during the English Renaissance. Cambridge, U.S.A. 1935.

Williamson, G. Mutability, Decay, and Seventeenth-century Melancholy. ELH. ii, 1935.

Wright, L. B. Middle-Class Culture in Elizabethan England. Chapel Hill, 1935.

H. C.

II. LITERARY RELATIONS WITH THE CONTINENT

General Surveys: Comparative Literature; The Literature of Europe.

Latin Literature of the Renaissance: Philosophy, Theology and Learning; Drama; Miscellaneous Verse; Prose Fiction, Allegory and Satire.

French-English and English-French Relations: General Works; History; Allegory and Satire; Philosophy, Politics, Education; Poetry; Drama; Prose Fiction.

Other Countries: German-English and English-German Relations; Italian-English Relations; Spanish-English Relations; Holland, Russia, Scandinavia.

A. COMPARATIVE LITERATURE IN GENERAL

Rod, É. De la Littérature comparée. Geneva, 1886.

Marsh, A. R. The Comparative Study of Literature. PMLA. xi, 1895.

Texte, J. L'Histoire comparée des Littératures. Revue de Philologie française et de la Littérature, x, 1896.

Gregory Smith, G. Some Notes on the Comparative Study of Literature. MLR. i, 1905.

Routh, H. V. The Future of Comparative Literature. MLR. viii, 1913.

Baldensperger, F. Littérature comparée: le Mot et la Chose. Revue de Littérature comparée, i, 1921.

Campbell, O. J. What is Comparative Literature? [In Essays in Memory of Barrett Wendell, Cambridge, U.S.A. 1926.]

Partridge, E. The Comparative Study of Literature. [In A Critical Medley, Paris, 1926.]

B. THE LITERATURE OF EUROPE IN GENERAL

Riccoboni, L. Réflexions historiques et critiques sur les différents Théâtres de l'Europe. Paris, 1738; tr. Eng. 1741.

Hallam, H. Introduction to the Literature of Europe in the Fifteenth, Sixteenth, and Seventeenth Centuries. 4 vols. 1837-9, etc.

Demogeot, J. Histoire des Littératures étrangères considérées dans leurs Rapports avec le Développement de la Littérature française. Paris, 1884.

Creizenach, W. Geschichte des neueren Dramas. 5 vols. Halle, 1893-1916.

Hannay, D. The Later Renaissance. Edinburgh, 1898.

Saintsbury, G. The Earlier Renaissance. Edinburgh, 1901.

Grierson, H. J. C. The First Half of the Seventeenth Century. Edinburgh, 1906.

—— Cross Currents in English Literature of the Seventeenth Century. 1929.

Kalff, G. Westeuropeesche Letterkunde. Vol. i, Groningen, 1923.

van Tieghem, P. Précis d'Histoire littéraire de l'Europe. Paris, 1925.

Magnus, L. Dictionary of European Literature. 1925.

—— English Literature in its Foreign Relations, 1300-1800. 1927.

C. INTERNATIONAL LATIN LITERATURE

[In this and the following sub-sections 1st edns only have normally been noted. Details of later edns and modern rpts of the English trns will be found, pp. 799-820 below. For further information on the various English originals, adaptations and imitations the appropriate sections below (Poetry, Drama, etc.) should be consulted.]

(1) AUTHORITIES

Spingarn, J. E. A History of Literary Criticism in the Renaissance, with Special Reference to the Influence of Italy in the Formation and Development of Modern Classicism. New York, 1899.

Sandys, Sir J. E. A History of Classical Scholarship. Vol. ii, Cambridge, 1908.

Schoell, F. L. Études sur l'Humanisme continental en Angleterre à la Fin de la Renaissance. Paris, 1926.

Schirmer, W. F. Der englische Frühhumanismus. Leipzig, 1930.

Wright, F. A. and Sinclair, T. A. A History of Later Latin Literature to the End of the Seventeenth Century. 1932.

(2) PHILOSOPHY, THEOLOGY AND LEARNING

Heinrich Cornelius Agrippa von Nettesheim (1486-1535). De Incertitudine et Vanitate Scientiarum. Cologne, 1527; tr. James Sanford, 1569 (as Of the Vanitie and uncertaintie of artes and sciences).

—— De occulta Philosophia Libri tres. Antwerp, 1531; tr. J. F. 1651 (as Three books of occult philosophy).

Giovanni Boccaccio (1313-1375). De Casibus Virorum et Feminarum illustrium Libri IX. [Written c. 1370.]

Lydgate, John. The Fall of Princes or Tragedies of John Bochas. [Written c. 1435, ptd 1494.] [Through the French of Laurent de Premierfait.]

Cavendish, George. Metrical Visions. [First pbd in 1825 by S. W. Singer in vol. ii of The Life of Cardinal Wolsey.]

Lyndsay, Sir David. The Tragicall Death of David Beaton, Bishoppe of Sainct Andrews. [1547.]

Sackville, Thomas, Ferrers, George and Baldwin, William. A Myrroure for Magistrates. 1559.

Jean Calvin (1509-1564). Christianae Religionis institutio. Basle, 1536; tr. T[homas] N[orton], 1561 (as The Institution of Christian Religion).

Johannes Amos Comenius (Komensky) (1592-1671). Janua linguarum reserata. Leszno, 1631; tr. Eng., Latin, French, J. Anchoran, 1639 (as The Gate of Tongues unlocked).

Desiderius Erasmus (1466?-1536). Adagiorum collectanea. Paris, 1500. Adagiorum chiliades. Venice, 1508; tr. Richard Taverner, 1539 (as Proverbes or Adagies gathered out of the Chiliades of Erasmus).

—— Apophthegmatum, sive scite dictorum libri sex. Basle, 1531; tr. Richard Taverner, 1540 (as Flowers of sentencies); tr. Nicolas Udall, 1542 (as Apophthegmes).

—— Colloquiorum formulae. Basle, 1516. [The most popular book of the century. 90 edns to 1546.]

Pylgremage of Pure Devotyon [Peregrinatio religionis ergo]. Tr. [c. 1536].

Two Dyaloges [Cyclops and De rebus ac vocabulis]. Tr. Edmonde Becke, Canterbury, [1550].

A Mery dialogue declaringe the propertyes of shrowde shrewes and honest wyves [Conjugium]. Tr. 1557.

Diversoria. Tr. E. H[ake?], 1566.

Seven Dialogues both pithie and profitable. Tr. W[illiam] B[urton], 1606.

Lyly, John. Euphues and his Ephoebus. [The Euphues, the Anatomy of Wit, [1578].]

Desiderius Erasmus. De civilitate morum puerilium libellus. Antwerp, 1526; tr. Robert Whitinton, 1532.

—— De contemptu mundi epistola. Louvain, 1521; tr. T. Paynell, 1533.

—— Enchiridion militis christiani. Antwerp, 1503. [75 edns to 1545.]

    A booke called in Latin Enchiridion militis christiani and in English the Manual of the Christian Knight. [Tr. W. Tyndale?] 1533.

    Hansom weapon of a chrysten knight. Tr. 1538.

—— Moriae encomium. Paris, 1509; tr. Sir Thomas Chaloner, 1549 (as The praise of Folie).

—— Paraphrasis in quatuor evangelia et acta apostolorum. Basle, 1524.

    The first Tome of the Paraphrase of Erasmus upon the newe Testamente. Tr. Nicolas Udall, 1548.

    The seconde tome or volume of the Paraphrase upon the newe testament. Tr. Myles Coverdale and J. Olde, 1549.

—— Querela pacis. Basle, 1516.

    The Complaint of Peace. Tr. T. Paynell, 1559.

    Bibliotheca Erasmiana. Répertoire des Œuvres d'Érasme. 3 vols. Ghent, 1893.

    Bang, W. and de Vocht, H. Klassiker und Humanisten: John Lyly und Erasmus. E. Studien, xxxvi, 1906.

    de Vocht, H. De Invloed van Erasmus op de Engelsche Tooneel-literatuur der XVIᵉ en XVIIᵉ Eeuwen. Pt i, Shakespeare Jest-books, Lyly. Ghent, 1908.

    —— The Earliest English Translations of Erasmus' Colloquia 1536–1566. Louvain, 1928.

Marsilio Ficino (1433–1499). Theologia platonica de immortalitate animae. [Florence? c. 1482.]

—— In Platonis libros argumenta et commentaria. Symposium. Florence, 1483–4.

    Spenser, Edmund. Hymnes in honour of Love and Beautie.1596. [Written c.1580.]

    Harrison, J. S. Platonism in English Poetry of the Sixteenth and Seventeenth Centuries. New York. 1903.

    Schroeder, K. Platonismus in der englischen Renaissance vor und bei Thomas Eliot. Berlin, 1920.

    Schoell, F. L. Les Emprunts de G. Chapman à Marsile Ficin. Revue de Littérature comparée, iii, 1923.

    Dannenberg, F. Das Erbe Platons bis zur Bildung Lylys. Berlin, 1931.

Jeronymo Osorio da Fonseca (1506–1580). De nobilitate civili libri duo; De nobilitate christiana libri tres. Lisbon, 1542; tr. William Blandie, 1576 (as The five Bookes of Hieronimo Osorius, contayning a discussion of civile and Christian nobilitie).

Hugo Grotius (1583–1645). De jure belli et pacis. Paris, 1625; tr. Clement Barksdale, 1654 (as The illustrious Hugo Grotius of the law of Warre and Peace).

Daniel Heinsius (1580–1655). De tragoediae constitutione. Leyden, 1611.

    Jonson, Ben. Timber; or, Discoveries made upon men and matter. 1641; ed. M. Castelain, Paris, 1906.

    Spingarn, J. E. The Sources of Jonson's Discoveries. MP. ii, 1905.

Philipp Melanchthon (1497–1560). Apologia Confessionis Augustanae. Wittenberg,1531; tr. 1536 (as The Apologie of the Confessyon of the Germaynes).

—— Historia de vita et actis M. Lutheri. Wittenberg, [1547?]; tr. 1561 (as The hystory of the lyfe and actes of M. Luther).

—— Moralis philosophiae epitome. Wittenberg, 1539; tr. J. G[oodale], [1550] (as A civile nosegay wherein is contayned not onylye the offyce and dewty of all magistrates and judges but of all subjectes).

Aureolus Philippus Paracelsus, or Theophrastus Bombast von Hohenheim (1493–1541). De natura rerum libri septem. Basle, 1570; tr. F. J. 1650.

—— De summis naturae mysteriis libri tres. Basle, 1570; tr. R. Turner, 1656 (as Paracelsus, Of the supreme mysteries of nature).

Francesco Patrizi (1413–1492). De regno et regis institutione. Paris, 1518; tr. Eng. (in part) Sir Thomas Elyot, 1531 (in The Boke named the Governour).

Count Giovanni Pico della Mirandola (1463–1494). Omnia Opera. Bologna, 1496.

—— Regulae XII partim excitantes, partim dirigentes hominem in pugna spirituali. Bologna, 1496.

    Twelve rules of a Christian Lyfe. Tr. Sir Thomas More, [1510?].

    The rules of a Christian Lyfe. Tr. Sir Thomas Elyot, 1534.

    H., W. Twelve Rules, And Weapons Concerning the Spirituell Battell. 1589.

—— Vita [by his nephew, Giovanni Francesco Pico]. Bologna, 1496; tr. Sir Thomas More, [1510?] (as The lyfe of Johan Picus Erle of Myrandula with dyvers epystles and other werkes of ye said Johan Picus).

[General influence on Spenser's Faerie Queene (1590) and Henry Reynolds' Mythomystes (1632). See also under Ficino.]

Pierre de la Ramée (Ramus) (1515–1572). Dialecticae Partitiones. Paris, 1543.

    The Logicke of P. Ramus Martyr newly

translated per M. Roll Makylmenaeum Scotum. 1574.

The Art of Logick. Tr. Anthony Wotton, 1626.

P. Ramus his Dialectica in two bookes. Tr. R. F[age], 1632.

Jacob Sprenger and Henricus Institoris (Krämer). Malleus maleficarum. Strasburg, 1486.

> Scot, Reginald. Discoverie of Witchcraft. 1584.
> James I. Daemonologie. Edinburgh, 1597.

[See the special bibliography of the literature of witchcraft, pp. 893–4 below.]

Juan Luis Vives (1492–1540). De instructione feminae christianae. Bruges, 1523; tr. Richard Hyrde, 1540 (as The Instruction of a Christen woman).

—— Introductio ad sapientiam. Bruges, 1524; tr. Richard Morison, 1540 (as An introduction to wysdome).

—— De officio mariti. Bruges, 1528; tr. Thomas Paynell [1553?] (as The office and duetie of an husband).

(3) DRAMA

George Buchanan (1506–1582). Jephthes sive Votum, Tragoedia. Paris, 1554.

> Jephté, tragédie traduicte du Latin par Fl[orent] Ch[rétien]. Orléans, 1567.
> Jephthes, ein christlich Tragoedia durch H. Nicephorum mit Reimen verteutschet. Brunswick, 1604.

—— Baptistes, sive Calumnia, Tragoedia. 1578. [Written 1543.]

> Baptistes of Dooper, Treuerspel getrocken uyt de Latijnsche Vaersen van G. Buchanan door J. de Decker. Amsterdam, 1656.
> Hume Brown, C. George Buchanan, Humanist and Reformer. Edinburgh, 1890.

[See also pp. 901–2 below.]

Gulielmus Fullonius (Gnaphaeus: 1493–1568). De Filio Prodigo comoedia Acolasti titulo inscripta. Hague, 1529.

> Johannis Palsgravi Londiniensis Ecphrasis Anglica in Comoediam Acolasti. The Comedye of Acolastus translated into oure Englysshe tongue. 1540.

Georgius Macropedius (c. 1475–1558). Rebelles. 's Hertozenbosch, 1535.

Christophorus Stymmelius. Studentes. Frankfort, 1549. [28 edns to 1662.]

> Gascoigne, George. The Glasse of Government. 1575.
> [Richards, Thomas?] Misogonus. [MS 1577. Ptd in Quellen des weltlichen Dramas in England, ed. A. Brandl, QF. LXXX, 1898.]

Johannes Ravisius Textor (c. 1480–1524). Dialogi. Paris, 1536. [Includes Juvenis, Pater, Uxor; and Thersites.]

> A new Enterlude called Thersytes. [c. 1537.]
> Ingelend, Thomas. A pretie Enterlude: called The Disobedient Child. [1570?]

Thomas Kirchmayer (Naogeorg: 1511–1563). Pammachius. Wittenberg, 1538. [Eng. trn (lost) by John Bale.]

> Bale, John. Kynge Johan. [Written c. 1540.]
> Foxe, John. Christus Triumphans. 1556. [Tr. French (1562), and English (1579) by John Day.]
> Herford, C. H. The Literary Relations of England and Germany in the Sixteenth Century. Cambridge, 1886.
> Holthausen, F. Studien zum älteren englischen Drama. E. Studien, XXXI, 1901.

(4) MISCELLANEOUS VERSE

Hieronymus Angerianus (fl. 1520). Erotopaegnion. Paris, [c. 1520].

> Fletcher, Giles. Licia. 1593.

Mathias Casimir (Sarbiewski: 1595–1640). Lyricorum libri IV, Epodon liber unus alterq. Epigrammatum. Antwerp, 1632.

> The Odes of Casimire. Tr. G. H. 1646.
> Sherburne, Sir Edward. Salmacis. 1651.

Friedrich Dedekind (d. 1598). Grobianus. Frankfort, 1549.

> F., R. The Schoole of Slovenrie: or Cato turned wrong side outward. 1605.
> Dekker, Thomas. The Gul's Horn-booke. 1609.
> Grobiana's Nuptials. [c. 1610.]
> Bergmeier, F. Dedekinds Grobianus in England. Greifswald, 1904.
> Rühl, Ernst. Grobianus in England. Berlin, 1904.

Johannes Baptista Spagnuolus Mantuanus (1448–1516). Bucolica. Paris, 1513.

> The Eglogs of the poet B. Mantuan. Tr. George Turbervile, 1567.
> The Bucolics of Baptist Mantuan in ten Eclogues. Tr. T. Harvey, 1656.
> Barclay, Alexander. Egloges. [c. 1514]; ed. Beatrice White, EETS. 1928.
> Googe, Barnabe. Eglogs, Epytaphes and Sonettes. 1563.
> Spenser, Edmund. The Shepheardes Calender. 1579.
> Mustard, W. P. Eclogues of Baptista Mantuanus. Baltimore, 1911.

John Owen (1560–1622). Epigrammatum Libri Tres. 1606. Liber singularis. 1607. Libri Tres. 2 vols. 1612.

> Epigrams of that most wittie and worthie Epigrammatist Mr. John Owen, Gentleman. Tr. John Vicars, 1619.

Hayman, Robert. Quodlibets, Epigrams
and other small parcels. 1628.
Pecke, Thomas. Parnasi Puerperium: or,
some Wellwishes to Ingenuity. 1659.
Ancumanus, Bernhardus Nicaeus. Rosa-
rium Das ist Rosengarten. Emden, 1641.
Titz, Johann Peter. Florilegii Oweniani
Centuria. Danzig, 1643.
Schultz, Simon. Centuria Epigrammatum
e Martialis et Oweni Libris selectorum.
Danzig, 1644.
Löber, Valentin. Epigrammatum Oweni
Drey Bücher. Hamburg, 1651.
—— Teutschredender Owenus. Ham-
burg, 1652.

[For the extraordinary popularity of Owen
in Germany see Erich Urban, Owenus und
die deutschen Epigrammatiker des XVII.
Jahrhunderts, Berlin, 1900. See also p. 859
below.]

Marcellus Palingenius (Pietro Angelo Man-
zolli: 1501?–1543?). Zodiacus Vitae. Venice,
[c. 1531.]
The first six Books of the Most Christian
Poet, Marcellus Palingenius called the
Zodiak of Lyfe. Tr. Barnabe Googe, 1561.
Johannes Secundus (1511–1536). Basia et
alia quaedam. Leyden, 1539.
Crane, D. Johannes Secundus, his Life,
Work and Influence on English Literature.
Leipzig, 1931.
Aeneas Sylvius (Enea Silvio Piccolomini:
1405–1464). De curialium miseriis epistola.
Milan, 1473.
Barclay, Alexander. Egloges. [c. 1514.]
Mustard, W. P. Aeneae Silvii de curia-
lium miseriis epistola. Baltimore, 1928.

(5) Prose Fiction, Allegory, and Satire

John Barclay (1582–1621). Euphormionis
Lusinini Satyricon. [London?], 1603. Pars
secunda. Paris, 1607.
[For trns, etc., see Jules Dukas, Étude
bibliographique et littéraire sur le
Satyricon de Jean Barclay, Paris, 1880,
and pp. 859–60 below.]
—— Icon animorum. 1614.
Icon animorum. The Mirroure of the
Minds, Englished by Thomas May. 1633.
Icon animorum. Auss dem Lateinischen
ins Teutsche aussgesetzet durch Johann
Seyferten von Ulm. Bremen, 1649.
[For other trns, etc., see Albert
Collignon, Le Portrait des Esprits (Icon
Animorum) de Jean Barclay, Nancy,
1906.]
—— Argenis. Paris, 1621. [40 edns to 1693.]
Barclay His Argenis. Tr. Kingsmill Long,
1625.

John Barclay His Argenis. Tr. Sir Robert
Le Grys and Thomas May, 1629.
Johann Barclaijens Argenis Deutsch
gemacht durch Martin Opitzen. Breslau,
1626.
Becker, P. A. Johann Barclay, 1582–1621.
Zeitschrift für vergleichende Literatur-
geschichte, xv, 1904.
Schmidt, K. F. John Barclay. Argenis.
Eine literarhistorische Untersuchung.
I. Ausgaben der Argenis, ihrer Fort-
setzungen und Übersetzungen. Berlin,
1904.

[Joseph Hall?] (1574–1656). Mundus Alter et
Idem. Auth: Mercurio Britannico. Frank-
fort, [1605?]
Utopiae Pars II. Mundus alter et idem.
Die heutige newe alte Welt. Erstlich in
Lateinischer Sprach gestellt durch Herrn
Albericum Gentilem in Engelland. Nun
aber verteutscht Durch Gregorium
Hyemsmensium [i.e. Wintermonat]. Leip-
zig, 1613.
Sir Thomas More (1478–1535). Libellus vere
aureus, de optimo reip. statu deque nova
Insula Utopia. Louvain, 1516, etc.
A fruteful and pleasaunt worke of the
beste state of a publyque weale, and of
the newe yle called Utopia: written in
Latyne by Sir Thomas More, Knyght,
and translated into Englyshe by Raphe
Robynson. 1551.
Von der wunderbarlichen Innsel Utopia
genant, das ander Buch. Tr. Claudius
Cantiuncula, Basle, 1524.
De optimo Reipublicae Statu, Libellus
vere aureus. Ordentliche und Auss-
führliche Beschreibung Der überaus
herrlichen Insul Utopia. Tr. Gregorius
Hyemsmensius [i.e. Wintermonat], Leip-
zig, 1612.
La republica nuovamente ritrovata, del
governo dell' isola Eutopia. Tr. A. F.
Doni, Venice, 1548.
De Utopie. Nu eerst overghesedt in neder
Duytsche. Antwerp, 1562.
La description de l'Isle d'Utopie. Tr.
J. le Blond, Paris, 1550.
Rabelais, François. Pantagruel. Lyons,
[1532?].
Brüggemann, F. Utopie und Robin-
sonade. [In Untersuchungen zu Schnabels
Insel Felsenburg, Weimar, 1914.]
Kautsky, K. Thomas More und seine
Utopia. Mit historischer Einleitung.
Stuttgart, 1890; tr. Eng. 1927.
The Utopia of Sir Thomas More. Ralph
Robinson's Translation, with an Intro-
duction and Bibliography by A. Guth-
kelch. 1910.

D. GENERAL FOREIGN INFLUENCE ON ENGLISH LITERATURE

Jusserand, J. J. The English Novel in the Time of Shakespeare. 1890.

Koeppel, E. Quellenstudien zu den Dramen Ben Jonsons, John Marstons, und Beaumont und Fletchers. Erlangen, 1895.

—— Quellenstudien zu den Dramen George Chapmans, Philip Massingers and John Fords. QF. LXXXII, 1897.

Brandl, A. Quellen des weltlichen Dramas in England vor Shakespeare. QF. LXXX, 1898.

Worman, E. J. Alien Members of the Book Trade during the Tudor Period. Bibliog. Soc. 1906.

Tucker, T. G. The Foreign Debt of English Literature. 1907.

Schelling, F. E. Elizabethan Drama, 1558–1642. 2 vols. Boston, 1908.

—— Foreign Influences in Elizabethan Plays. New York, 1923.

Harris, W. J. The First Printed Translations into English of the Great Foreign Classics. [1909.]

Wallace, C. W. The Evolution of the English Drama up to Shakespeare. Berlin, 1912.

Baker, E. A. The History of the English Novel. Vol. I (The Age of Romance from the Beginning to the Renaissance), 1924.

Hayes, G. R. Antony Munday's Romances of Chivalry. Library, VI, 1925, VII, 1926.

Wolff, M. J. Die Renaissance in der englischen Literatur. Bielefeld, 1928.

Aronstein, P. Das englische Renaissancedrama. Leipzig, 1929.

Henderson, G. D. Foreign Religious Influences in Seventeenth Century Scotland. Edinburgh Rev. April 1929.

Scott, J G. Les Sonnets élisabéthains: les Sources et l'Apport personnel. Paris, 1929.

Quellen des Shakespeare in Novellen, Märchen und Sagen. Ed. T. Echtermeyer, L. Henschel, and K. Simrock, Berlin, 1831; Bonn, 1870.

Shakespeare's Library: a Collection of the Romances, Novels, Poems, and Histories used by Shakespeare as the Foundation of his Dramas. Ed. J. P. Collier, 2 vols. 1843; rev. W. C. Hazlitt, 6 vols. 1875.

Gericke, R. Shakespeares Hamlet-Quellen: Saxo-Grammaticus, Belleforest, und The Hystorie of Hamblett. Leipzig, 1881.

Ohle, R. Shakespeares Cymbeline und seine romanischen Vorläufer. Berlin, 1890.

Anders, H. R. D. Shakespeare's Books. A Dissertation on Shakespeare's Reading and the Immediate Sources of his Works. Berlin, 1904.

Fischer, R. Shakespeares Quellen in der Originalsprache und Deutsch, herausgegeben im Auftrag der deutschen Shakespeare-Gesellschaft. II. Quellen zu Romeo und Julia. Bonn, 1922.

Keller, W. Shakespeare als Überarbeiter fremder Dramen. Sh. Jb. LVIII, 1922.

Gollancz, Sir I. The Sources of Hamlet; with an Essay on the Legend. 1926.

[See also Works, ed. J. O. Halliwell[-Phillips], 1853-65.]

E. SPECIAL LITERARY RELATIONS

(1) THE LITERARY RELATIONS OF ENGLAND AND FRANCE.

(a) General

Barclay, Alexander. Introductorie to write and to pronounce French. 1521.

Dewes (or Du Guez), Giles. An Introductorie for to learne to rede, to pronounce, and to speake French trewly. [1532?]

Palsgrave, John. L'esclaircissement de la langue francoyse. 1530. [Includes a survey of French literature.]

Holyband, Claudius (Claude de Sainliens). Treasurie of the French Tongue. 1580; 1593 (enlarged as A Dictionarie French and English).

Eliot, John. Ortho-Epia Gallica. Eliots Fruits for the French. 1593.

    Yates, F. The Importance of John Eliot's Ortho-Epia Gallica. RES. VII, 1931.

Dallington, Sir Robert. A method for Travell. 1606.

Cotgrave, Randle. A Dictionarie of the French and English Tongues. 1611.

Michiels, Alfred. Histoire des Idées littéraires en France. Brussels, 1848 (3rd edn).

Michel, F. Les Écossais en France et les Français en Écosse. Paris, 1862.

Smiles, Samuel. The Huguenots; their Settlements, Churches, and Industries in England and Ireland. 1867; 1889 (6th edn).

de Schickler, Baron F. Les Églises du Refuge en Angleterre, 1547–1685. Paris, 1892.

Haudecœur, A. Jeanne d'Arc dans la Littérature et devant l'Opinion en Angleterre. Rheims, 1895.

Littleboy, A. L. Relations between French and English Literature in the Sixteenth and Seventeenth Centuries. 1895.

Jusserand, J. J. French Ignorance of English Literature in Tudor Times. Nineteenth Century, April 1898.

Bastide, C. Huguenot Thought in England. Journ. of Comparative Lit. I, 1903.

Upham, A. H. The French Influence in English Literature from the Accession of Elizabeth to the Restoration. New York, 1908.

Lee, Sir S. The French Renaissance in England. An Account of the Literary Relations of England and France in the 16th Century. Oxford, 1910.

Lambley, K. The Teaching and Cultivation of the French Language in England during Tudor and Stuart Times. Manchester, 1920.

Mathorez, J. Note sur les Intellectuels écossais en France au XVIe Siècle. Bulletin du Bibliophile, March 1919.

Bibliographie de la Littérature anglaise traduite en français. Le Navire d'Argent, June 1925.

Ascoli, Georges. La Grande-Bretagne devant l'Opinion française depuis la Guerre de Cent Ans jusqu'à la Fin du XVIe Siècle. Paris, 1927. [With bibliography.]

—— La Grande-Bretagne devant l'Opinion française au XVIIe Siècle. 2 vols. Paris, 1930. [With bibliography.]

(b) History

Philippe de Commines (1445–1509). Cronique et hystoire faicte et composée par feu messire Phelippe de Commines. Paris, 1523.

The Historie of Philip de Commines, Knight. Tr. T. Danett, 1596.

Estienne Perlin. Description des royaulmes d'Angleterre et d'Escosse. Paris, 1558.

Jean de Serres (c. 1540–1598). Mémoires de la troisième guerre civile. [Paris?], 1568–9.

Inventaire général de l'histoire de France. Paris, 1597.

The Three Parts of Commentaries of the Civill Warres of Fraunce. Tr. Thomas Timms, 1574. The fourth Parte, 1576.

The Lyfe of the most godly Jasper Colignie Shatilion. Tr. Arthur Golding, 1576.

A General Inventorie of the History of Fraunce. Tr. Edward Grimeston, 1607.

Simon Goulart (1543–1628). Premier [etc.] Recueil des choses mémorables advenues sous la Ligue. Geneva, 1587–99.

—— Histoires admirables de notres temps. Paris, 1600.

Admirable and memorable histories containing the wonders of our time. Tr. Edward Grimeston, 1607.

(c) Allegory and Satire

Pierre Gringoire (c. 1475–1544). Le chasteau de labour. Paris, 1499.

Barclay, Alexander. The Castell of Laboure. Paris, [1503?].

Jean Le Maire de Belges (1473–c. 1548). Le Temple d'Honneur et de vertu. [c. 1503.]

Barclay, Alexander. The description of the Toure of Vertue. 1513.

François Rabelais (c. 1490–1553). Pantagruel. Lyons, [1532?]. Gargantua. Lyons, [1535?].

The First [Second] Book of the works of Mr. F. Rabelais containing five books of the Lives of Gargantua and his Sonne Pantagruel. Tr. Sir Thomas Urquhart, 2 vols. 1653.

François Rabelais. Pantagruéline Prognostication. Lyons, 1533.

Pantagruel's Prognostication. Tr. Democritus Pseudomantis, 1620. [No copy extant?]

Nashe, Thomas. Have with you to Saffron-Walden, or Gabriel Harvey's Hunt is up. 1596.

Brown, H. Rabelais in English Literature. Cambridge, U.S.A., 1933.

[Antoine de la Sale ?] (c. 1398–c. 1461). Les quinze joyes de mariage. [c. 1450; ptd. c. 1480.]

[Tofte, R.?] The Batchelor's Banquet. 1603; ed. F. P. Wilson, Oxford, 1929.

La Satyre Ménippée. [Tours?], 1594. [By Pierre Le Roy and others.)

A Pleasant Satyre—A Satyre Menippized. 1595.

Pompen, A. The English Versions of the Ship of Fools: a Contribution to the History of the Early French Renaissance in England. 1925.

(d) Philosophy, Politics, Education, etc.

Jacques Amyot (1513–1593). Vies des hommes illustres. Paris, 1559.

The lives of the most noble Grecians and Romans compared together by Plutarch. Tr. (from the French of Amyot) Sir Thomas North, 1579.

Jean Bodin (c. 1530–1596). Les six livres de la République. Paris, 1576.

The six bookes of a Commonweale. Tr. Richard Knolles, 1606.

Jean Chapelain (1595–1674). [Preface to Marino's Adone.] 1623.

D'Avenant, Sir W. Preface to Gondibert. Paris, 1650.

René Descartes (1596–1650). Discours de la Méthode. Leyden, 1637.

A Discourse of a method for the well guiding of reason. Tr. 1649.

Joachim du Bellay (1524–1560). Deffense et Illustration de la Langue française. Paris, 1549.

Mulcaster, Richard. The First Part of the Elementarie. 1582.

François de la Noue (1531–1591). Discours politiques et militaires. Basle, 1587.

The Politicke and militarie discourses. Tr. E. A[ggas], 1587.

Pierre de la Primaudaye (b. 1545?). L'Académie françoise. Paris, 1577.

The French Academie. Tr. T. B[owes?], 1586.

Michel de Montaigne (1533–1592). L'Apologie de Raimond Sebond. [In Essais, Bordeaux, 1580.]

  Ralegh, Sir W. The Sceptick. 1651.

—— Essais. Bordeaux, 1580.
The Essays or Morall, Politicke and Millitarie Discourses of Lo: Michaell de Montaigne. Tr. John Florio, 1603.

  Bacon, Sir Francis. Essayes. 1597.
  Cornwallis, Sir William. Essayes. 1600.
  Robertson, J. M. Montaigne and Shakspere. 1897; 1909.
  Dieckow, F. A. F. John Florios englische Übersetzung der Essais Montaignes und Lord Bacons, Ben Jonsons und Robert Burtons Verhältnis zu Montaigne. Strasburg, 1903.
  Routh, H. V. The Origins of the Essay compared in French and English Literatures. MLR. xv, 1920.
  Selby, F. G. Bacon and Montaigne. Criterion, Jan. 1925.
  Taylor, G. C. Shakespeare's Debt to Montaigne. Cambridge, U.S.A. 1925.
  Zeitlin, J. The Development of Bacon's Essays with Special Reference to the Question of Montaigne's Influence upon them. JEGP. xxvii, 1928.
  Türck, Susanne. Shakespeare und Montaigne. Berlin, 1930.

Sir Francis Bacon (Viscount St Albans) (1561–1626). Essayes. 1597; 1612; 1625. Tr. French Sir G. Chevalier, 1619; J. Baudoin, Paris, 1621. [Baudoin also tr. De sapientia veterum, 1619.]

  Rémusat, C. de. Bacon: sa Vie, son Temps, sa Philosophie, et son Influence jusqu'à nos Jours. Paris, 1857.

(e) Lyrical Poetry

(i) The Sonnet

[The principal models for the English sonneteers enumerated below were Marot, Ronsard, Du Bellay, and Desportes. See also p. 339, England and Italy.]

Spenser, Edmund. The Visions of Bellay. [In J. van der Noodt's Theatre for Worldlings, 1569.]

  Koeppel, E. Visions of Petrarch and Visions of Bellay. E. Studien, xv, 1891.

—— The Ruins of Rome. 1591. [See Joachim du Bellay, Les Antiquitez de Rome, 1558.]

—— Amoretti. 1595.

Watson, Thomas. The Ἑκατομπαθία, or Passionate Centurie of Love. [1582.] The Tears of Fancie, or Love Disdained. 1593.

Sidney, Sir Philip. Astrophel and Stella. 1591.

Daniel, Samuel. Delia. 1592. [See Maurice Scève, Délie, 1544.]

Constable, Henry. Diana. 1592. [See Philippe Desportes, Diane, 1573.]

Barnes, Barnabe. Parthenophil and Parthenophe. 1593.

Lodge, Thomas. Phillis. 1593. [See Vauquelin de la Fresnaye: Foresteries, 1555; Idylles, 1605.]

Fletcher, Giles. Licia. 1593.

Percy, William. Coelia. 1594.

Zepheria. 1594.

Drayton, Michael. Idea's Mirrour. 1594. [See Claude de Pontoux, L'Idée, 1579.]

C., E. Emaricdulfe. 1595.

Barnfield, Richard. Cynthia with certaine sonnets. 1595.

Griffin, Bartholomew. Fidessa. 1596.

Linche, Richard. Diella. 1596.

Smith, William. Chloris. 1596.

Tofte, Robert. Laura. 1597.

Shakespeare, William. Sonnets. 1609. [Written before 1600.]

Kastner, L. E. The Scottish Sonneteers and the French Poets. MLR. iii, 1908.

—— The Elizabethan Sonneteers and the French Poets. MLR. iii, 1908.

—— Wyatt and the French Sonneteers. MLR. iv, 1909.

Scott, J. G. Les Sonnets élisabéthains. Le Sources et l'Apport personnel. Paris, 1929.

(ii) General

Joachim du Bellay. Recueil de Poésie. Paris, 1549. L'Olive. Paris, 1549. Les Antiquite de Rome. Paris, 1558. Les Regrets. Paris, 1558. Les jeux rustiques. Paris, 1558. [See Spenser, etc., above.]

Philippe Desportes. Diane. Paris, 1573. Amours d'Hippolyte. Paris, 1573. [See Constable, Daniel, Drayton, Lodge, and Spenser above.]

  Kastner, L. E. Spenser's Amoretti and Desportes. MLR. iv, 1909.

—— Suckling and Desportes. MLR. v 1910, vi, 1911.

Gilles Durant (1550–1605). Le zodiac amoureux Paris, 1587.

  Chapman, George. The Amorous Zodiacke. 1595.

Clément Marot (1496–1544). Elegie sur Mm Loise de Savoye. Paris, 1531.

—— Complaincte d'un Pastoureau Chrestien Paris, 1532.

—— Eglogue au Roy. Paris, 1532.

  Spenser, Edmund. Shepheards Calendar 1579.

—— Les Visions de Petrarque. Lyons, 1539

  Spenser, Edmund. Visions of Petrarch [Written 1569.]

Pierre de Ronsard (1524–1585). Odes. Paris, 1550. Amours. Paris, 1552. Hymnes. Paris, 1555. Œuvres. Paris, 1560. [For general influence see under (i) above.]

Soothern, John. Pandora. 1584.

Drummond, William. Poems. Edinburgh, 1616.

Kastner, L. E. Drummond of Hawthornden and the Poets of the Pléiade. MLR. IV, 1909.

—— Drummond of Hawthornden and the French Poets of the Sixteenth Century. MLR. V, 1910.

Hoffmann, O. Studien zu Alexander Montgomerie. E. Studien, xx, 1895.

The Pléiade and the Elizabethans. Edinburgh Rev. April 1907.

Laumonier, P. Ronsard et l'Écosse. Revue de Littérature comparée, IV, 1924.

Grubb, M. Lodge's Borrowing from Ronsard. MLN. XLV, 1930.

Melin de Saint-Gelais (1491–1558). Œuvres. Lyons, 1547.

Koeppel, E. Sir Thomas Wyatt und Melin de Saint-Gelais. Ang. XIII, 1891.

Kastner, L. E. Saint-Amant and the English Poets. MLR. XXVI, 1931.

Dowland, Robert. A Musicall Banquet Furnished with varietie of delicious Ayres, Collected out of the best Authors in English, French, Spanish, and Italian. 1610.

Hume, Tobias. The First Part of Ayres, French, Pollish, and others. 1605.

(f) Epic Poetry

Guillaume de Saluste, Seigneur du Bartas (1544–1590). La Muse chrétienne. Bordeaux, 1573.

—— La Semaine ou Création du monde. Paris, 1578.

—— La seconde Semaine. Paris, 1584.

The Historie of Judith. Tr. T. Hudson, 1584. [From La Muse chrétienne.]

Bartas his divine weekes and workes. Tr. J. Sylvester, 1605–7. [Pts appeared 1590–8.]

Weller, P. J. Sylvesters englische Übersetzung der religiösen Epen des Du Bartas. Tübingen, 1902.

James I of England and VI of Scotland. His Majesties Poetical exercises at vacant houres. Edinburgh, 1591.

Drayton, Michael. Moyses in a map of his miracles. 1604.

Ashton, H. Du Bartas en Angleterre. Paris, 1908. [For Drayton, Donne, N. Breton, Sir J. Davies, and J. Davies of Hereford.]

Taylor, G. C. Milton's Use of Du Bartas. Cambridge, U.S.A. 1934.

Huon of Bordeaux. [12th cent.; prose, 1454.]

Fletcher, J. B. Huon of Bordeux and the Faerie Queene. JEGP. II, 1899.

McArthur, J. R. The Influence of Huon of Burdeux upon the Faerie Queene. JEGP. IV, 1903.

(g) Psalms, Hymns, Sermons, Theology, etc.

Clément Marot. Psaumes. Strasburg, 1539.

Théodore de Bèze (1519–1605). Traduction en vers français des psaumes omis par Marot. Geneva, 1553.

Sternhold, T. Certayne Psalms. 1548.

Sternhold, T., Hopkins, J. et al. The Whole Booke of Psalmes. 1562.

Whittingham, William, et al. Psalter. 1556. Scots Psalter. 1564.

Philippe de Mornay, Seigneur du Plessis-Marly (1549–1623). Traité de la vérité de la religion chrétienne. Antwerp, 1581.

A woorke concerning the trewnesse of the Christian religion. Begunne to be translated by Sir Philip Sidney and finished by Arthur Golding. 1587.

—— Discours de la vie et de la mort. Lausanne, 1576.

The defense of Death done into English by E[dward] A[ggas]. 1576.

A discourse of Life and Death. Tr. Mary Herbert, Countess of Pembroke, 1592.

Buckley, G. T. The Indebtedness of Sir John Davies' Nosce teipsum to Philip Mornay's Trunesse of the Christian Religion. MP. XXIV, 1927.

Joseph Hall. Characters of Vertues and Vices. 1608.

Caracteres de vertus et de vices. Tr. [J. L. de Tourval?], Paris, 1619.

—— Solomon's Divine Arts. 1609.

Les arts divins de Salomon. Tr. Th. J[aquemot], Geneva, 1632.

(h) Drama

(i) Influence of French Dramatists

Pierre Corneille (1606–1684). Le Cid. Paris, 1636; tr. Joseph Rutter, 1637.

—— Horace. Paris, 1639; tr. Sir William Lower, 1656.

—— Polyeucte. Paris, 1640; tr. Sir William Lower, 1655.

Robert Garnier (c. 1545–c. 1600). Cornélie. Paris, 1574.

Pompey the Great, his faire Cornelia's Tragedy. Tr. Thomas Kyd, 1595. [1st edn, anon., 1594.]

—— Marc-Antoine. Paris, 1578.

The Tragedie of Antonie. Tr. Mary Herbert, Countess of Pembroke, 1590.

Daniel, Samuel. Cleopatra. 1594. Philotas. 1605.

Greville, Fulke. Alaham; Mustapha. [1609.] [Both written before 1600.]

Alexander, Sir William. The Monarchicke Tragedies. 1607.

Witherspoon, A. M. The Influence of Robert Garnier on Elizabethan Drama. New Haven, 1924.

Young, Karl. The Influence of French Farce upon the Plays of John Heywood. MP. II, 1904.

Schelling, F. E. Elizabethan Drama, 1558–1642. 2 vols. Boston, 1908.

Ristine, F. H. English Tragi-comedy, its Origin and History. New York, 1910.

Mill, A. J. The Influence of the Continental Drama on Lyndsay's Satyre of the Thrie Estaitis. MLR. xxv, 1930.

(ii) French Historical Sources of English Plays

Pierre-Victor Palma Cayet (1525–1610). Chronologie septennaire. Paris, 1605.

—— Chronologie novennaire. Paris, 1608.

Massinger, Philip. Believe as you list. 1631.

Chapman, George. Bussy d'Ambois. 1607. Revenge of Bussy d'Ambois. 1613. [See Jean de Serres, Inventaire général and Grimeston's trn, above, and Pierre Matthieu, Histoire des troubles en France sous Henri III et Henri IV, 1594.]

—— The Conspiracie and Tragedie of Charles, Duke of Byron. 1608.

Boas, F. S. The Sources of Chapman's The Conspiracy of Byron and The Revenge of Bussy d'Ambois. Athenaeum, 10 Jan. 1903.

Chapman, George and Shirley, James. The Tragedie of Chabot, Admirall of France. 1639; ed. E. Lehmann, Philadelphia, 1906. [Source: Étienne Pasquier, Recherches de la France, 1560–1621.]

Drayton, Michael and Dekker, Thomas. The Civil Wars in France. 1598. [Lost.]

Marlowe, Christopher. The Massacre at Paris. [c. 1592.]

Webster, John. The Guise. 1601. [Lost.]

(iii) English History in French Tragedy

Jean de la Serre (1600–1665). Thomas Morus, ou le triomphe de la foi et de la constance. Paris, 1641.

Antoine de Montchrétien (c. 1570–1621). L'Escossaise. Rouen, 1601.

Lawrence, W. J. Early French Players in England. Ang. xxxII, 1909.

Lancaster, H. C. French Dramatic Literature in the Seventeenth Century. Baltimore, 1929.

(i) Prose Fiction

Vital d'Audiguier. Histoire tragicomique de nostre temps sous les noms de Lysandre et de Caliste. Paris, 1615.

Fletcher, John and Massinger, Philip. The Lovers Progress. 1623.

Pierre Boaistuau (d. 1566) and François de Belleforest (1530–1583). XVIII histoires extraictes des œuvres italiennes de Bandel, et mises en langue françoise. Paris, 1559.

Painter, William. Palace of Pleasure. 1566. [See also Section (3), England and Italy.]

Gautier de Costes de la Calprenède. Cassandre. Paris, 1642–5.

Cassandra. Tr. Sir C. Cotterell, 1652.

—— Cléopâtre. Paris, 1647–58.

Hymen's Praeludia, being the first part of Cleopatra. Tr. R. Loveday, 1652. [Completed by various hands, 1654–9.]

Philippe Desportes. Amours de Diane. Paris, 1573. [Sonnets.]

Lodge, T. Rosalynde. Euphues' Golden Legacie. 1590.

Marin Leroy de Gomberville (1600–1674). Polexandre. Paris, 1629; tr. W. Browne, 1647.

Huon de Bordeaux. [Written 1454, ptd 1513.]

Here begynnethe the Boke Huon de Bordeuxe. Tr. Sir John Bourchier, Baron Berners, [1534?].

Olivier de la Marche (c. 1426–1502). Le chevalier délibéré. 1483.

The Resolved Gentleman. Tr. Sir Lewis Lewkenor [from the Spanish version of Hernando de Acuña], 1594.

Marguerite de Navarre (1492–1549). Heptaméron (Histoires des amants fortunez). Paris, 1558; tr. R. Codrington, 1654.

Painter, W. Palace of Pleasure. 1566.

Jacques Yver. Le printemps d'Iver. Paris, 1572.

W[otton], H[enry]. A Courtlie Controversie of Cupid's Cautels. 1578.

Honoré d'Urfé (1568–1625). L'Astrée. Pt I, Paris, 1607. Pt II, Paris, 1610. Pt III, Paris, 1619. Pts IV and V (by B. Baro), Paris, 1627.

Astrea. Tr. by a Person of quality, 1657–8.

Fletcher, John. Monsieur Thomas. 1639. [Written c. 1613.]

—— The Tragedie of Valentinian. [Written before 1614.]

Jusserand, J. J. The English Novel in the Time of Shakespeare. 1890.

Robert Greene. Pandosto: the Triumph of Time. 1588. Tr. French G. L. Regnault, 1615, and Du Bail, 1626.

> La Serre, Jean de. Pandoste, ou la princesse malheureuse. Paris, 1631.

Sir Philip Sidney. The Countesse of Pembrokes Arcadia. 1590.

> Larcadie de la Comtesse de Pembrok Premiere Partie. Traduicte par un Gentil-homme François. Seconde Partie. Traduicte par D. Geneviefve Chappelain. Paris, 1625. [There is another trn by J. Baudouin and G. Chappuis, 1624.]
> Mareschal, Antoine. La cour bergère. Paris, 1640.
> Lancaster, H. C. Sidney, Galaut, La Calprenède: an Early Instance of the Influence of English Literature upon French. MLN. XLII, 1927.

von Wurzbach, W. Geschichte des französischen Romans. Vol. I, Heidelberg, 1912.

(2) The Literary Relations of England and Germany

(a) General (including German Switzerland)

Ascham, Roger. A Report and Discourse of the affaires of Germany. [1570].

> Katterfeld, A. Roger Ascham, sein Leben und die Werke mit besonderer Berücksichtigung der Berichte über Deutschland aus den Jahren 1550–1553. Strasburg, 1879. [See also, for Germany in general, Fynes Moryson, An Itinerary, 1617; Charles Hughes, Shakespeare's Europe, 1903; and Thomas Coryat, Crudities, 1611.]

Elze, Karl. Die englische Sprache und Literatur in Deutschland. Dresden, 1864.

Schaible, K. H. Geschichte der Deutschen in England von den ersten germanischen Ansiedlungen in Britannien bis zum Ende des 18. Jahrhunderts. Strasburg, 1885.

Herford, C. H. Studies in the Literary Relations of England and Germany in the Sixteenth Century. Cambridge, 1886.

Jacobs, H. E. The Lutheran Movement in England. 1891.

Vetter, T. Englische Flüchtlinge in Zürich während der ersten Hälfte des XVI. Jahrhunderts. Zürich, 1894.

—— Litterarische Beziehungen zwischen England und der Schweiz im Reformationszeitalter. Zürich, 1901.

Spirgatis, M. L. Englische Literatur auf der Frankfurter Messe von 1561–1620. Leipzig, 1902.

Koeppel, E. Deutsche Strömungen in der englischen Literatur. Strasburg, 1910.

Waterhouse, G. The Literary Relations of England and Germany in the Seventeenth Century. Cambridge, 1914.

Price, L. M. English-German Literary Influences. Bibliography and Survey. Berkeley, 1919–20.

—— The Reception of English Literature in Germany. Berkeley, 1932.

Morgan, B. Q. Bibliography of German Literature in English Translation. Madison, 1922.

Koszul, A. Les Relations entre l'Alsace et l'Angleterre au XVIe Siècle. Revue de Littérature comparée, IX, 1929.

(b) Legends

(i) The Faust Cycle

Historia von D. Johann Fausten, dem weitbeschreyten Zauberer und Schwartzkünstler. Frankfort, 1587.

> The Historie of the damnable life, and deserved death of Doctor John Faustus according to the true Copie printed at Franckfort, and translated into English by P. F. Gent. 1592. [Earlier edn 1588?]
> The Second Report of Doctor John Faustus, containing his appearances, and the deedes of Wagner. Written by an English Gentleman student in Wittenberg. 1594. [Rpt of both trns, ed. W. Rose, 1925.]

Marlowe, Christopher. The Tragicall History of Dr Faustus. [1601?]; 1604. [Acted 1592.]

Greene, Robert. The Honorable Historie of frier Bacon, and frier Bungay. 1594.

Barnes, Barnabe. The Divil's Charter. 1607.

The Merry Devill of Edmonton. 1608.

> Marlowe's Dr Faustus and Greene's Friar Bacon and Friar Bungay. Ed. Sir A. W. Ward, 1878; 1901 (4th edn).
> Delius, F. Marlowe's Faust und seine Quelle. Göttingen, 1881.
> Diebler, A. Faust und Wagner-Pantomimen in England. Ang. VII, 1884.
> Schröder, K. R. Textverhältnisse und Entstehungsgeschichte von Marlowes Faust. Berlin, 1909.

(ii) Miscellaneous

Sebastian Münster (1489–1552). Cosmographia, d.h. Beschreibung aller Länder. Basle, 1543.

> A Briefe Collection and compendious extract of strange and memorable thinges,

gathered out of the Cosmography of S. Munster. 1572.

The wrathful judgment of God upon Bishop Hatto. 1586. [Ballad.]

The Comical History of the Costlie Whore. 1633.

Wunderbarlicher Bericht, von einem Juden, aus Jerusalem Bürtig, Ahasuerus genanndt. Schleswig, 1564.

Wonderful strange newes out of Germanie of a Jewe that hath lived wandringe ever since the Passion of our Saviour Christ. 1612. [Ballad.]

Zirus, W. Der ewige Jude in der Dichtung, vornehmlich in der englischen und deutschen. Leipzig, 1928.

Fortunatus und seine Söhne. Augsburg, 1509; rptd H. Günther, 1914 (in Neudrucke deutscher Literaturwerke des 16. und 17. Jahrhunderts).

The right pleasant and variable Tragical history of Fortunatus. Tr. Thomas Churchyard, 1612.

Dekker, Thomas. The Pleasant Comedie of Old Fortunatus. 1600.

(c) Polemical Dialogues and Tracts

Niklas Manuel (1484–1530). Die Krankheit der Messe. [c. 1527.]

Roy, William and Barlow, Jerome. Rede me and be not wrothe. 1528.

Hans Sachs (1494–1576). Disputation zwischen einem Chorherrn und einem Schuhmacher. [Nuremberg?] 1524.

Scoloker, Anthony. Goodly dysputacion between a Christen shomaker and a Popysshe Person translated out of the German Tongue into Englysshe. 1548.

John Bon and Mast Parson. 1548.

(d) Satires and Jest-books

Sebastian Brant (1457–1521). Das Narren schyff. Basle, 1494. Tr. Latin Jacob Locher (1497); French Pierre Riviere (1497) and Jehan Droyn (1498).

Barclay, Alexander. The Shyp of Folys of the Worlde. Translated out of Laten, Frenche, and Doche into Englysshe tonge. 1509.

Watson, Henry. The Shyppe of Fooles, translated out of frenche. 1509.

Fraustadt, F. Über das Verhältnis von Barclays Ship of Fools zur lateinischen, französischen und deutschen Quelle. Breslau, 1894.

Pompen, A. The English Versions of the Ship of Fools. 1925.

Cock Lorell's Bote. [c. 1510.]

Skelton, John. The Bowge of Court. [c. 1520.]

Rey, Albert. Skelton's Satirical Poems in their Relation to Lydgate's Order of Fools, Cock Lorell's Bote, and Barclay's Ship of Fools. Berne, 1899.

Copland, Robert. Hye Way to the Spyttell-House. [c. 1535.]

Tarlton, Richard. Jigge of a Horse loade of Fooles. [c. 1588.]

Ein kurtzweilig lesen von Dyl Eulenspiegel. Strasburg, 1515.

[Andrewe, Lawrence ?]. Tyll Howleglas. Antwerp (Doesborch), [c. 1520].

[Copland, William.] Here beginneth a merye Jest of a man called Howleglass. [1528?]

Brie, F. Eulenspiegel in England. Berlin, 1903.

Der Pfaff vom Kahlenberg. Strasburg, [c. 1500–20].

[Andrewe, Lawrence?] The Parson of Kalenborowe. Antwerp (Doesborch), [c. 1520].

Bruder Rausch. [Numerous edns from about 1550.]

Freer Rush. 1568.

Dekker, Thomas. If this be not a good Play, the Divell is in it. 1612.

(e) Hymns, Sermons, Theology, etc.

Martin Luther (1483–1546). Von der Freyheyt eyniss Christen menschen. Wittenberg, 1520.

A Treatise touching the Libertie of a Christian. Tr. James Bell, 1579.

—— Geistliche Lieder. Erfurt, 1524.

Coverdale, Miles. Goostly Psalmes and Spiritual Songs. [c. 1535.]

Gude and Godlie Ballates. Edinburgh, 1567.

Special and chosen sermons, collected out of his writings and preachings. Tr. W. G[ace], 1578.

—— Tischreden oder Colloquia. Eisleben, 1566.

Dris Martini Lutheri Colloquia Mensalia: or Dr. Martin Luther's Divine Discourses at his Table, &c. Tr. Henry Bell, 1652.

Jakob Boehme (1575–1624). Schriften. Amsterdam, 1675. [First work: Aurora, oder Morgenröthe im Aufgang, written 1612.]

Two Theosophicall Epistles. 1645.

The Epistles of Jacob Behmen aliter, Teutonicus Philosophus. 1649.

Mercurius Teutonicus; or A Christian Information concerning the last Times. 1649.

The High and Deep Searching out of the Threefold Life of Man. Tr. John Sparrow, 1650; rptd C. J. Barker, 1909 (with

Bibliography listing trns by John Sparrow, John Ellistone, and Humphrey Blunden).
Hotham, Durand. The Life of Jacob Behmen. 1654.
Closs, Karl. Jakob Böhmes Aufnahme in England. Archiv, cxlviii, 1925.
Daniel Dyke (d. 1614). The Mystery of Self-Deceiving. 1614.
Nosce Teipsum: Das grosse Geheimnis des Selbbetrugs übersetzet durch D. H. P. Basle, 1638.
Joseph Hall. Heaven upon Earth. 1606.
Joseph Hallens Himmel auf Erden. Breslau, 1632.
—— Characters of Vertues and Vices. 1608.
Vorbildung der Tugenden und Untugenden durch den W. H. N. N. Emden, 1628. [Two further trns in 1652 and 1685.]
[For a full list of English theological works current in German trn see G. Waterhouse, The Literary Relations of England and Germany in the Seventeenth Century, Cambridge, 1914.]

(f) Philosophy, Politics, etc.

Francis Bacon. Essays. 1597; 1612; 1625.
von Stubenberg, Johann Wilhelm. Getreue Reden: die Sitten-, Regiments- und Hauslehre betreffend. Nuremberg, 1654.

(g) Lyrical Poetry

Bohm, W. Englands Einfluss auf G. R. Weckherlin. Göttingen, 1893. [Exaggerates English influence.]
Fischer, H. Georg Rudolf Weckherlin's Gedichte. Tübingen, 1893, 1907.

(h) Drama and Stage

(i) Plays Dealing with Contemporary Events

Glapthorne, Henry. The Tragedy of Albertus Wallenstein. 1639.
Gryphius, Andreas. Ermordete Majestät oder Carolus Stuardus König von Gross Britannien. Breslau, 1657.

(ii) General English Influence on Germany

Englische Comedien und Tragedien. Leipzig, 1620 and 1624.
Liebeskampff, oder Ander Theil der Englischen Comödien und Tragödien. 1630.
Trautmann, K. Englische Komödianten in Nürnberg bis zum Abschlusse des dreissigjährigen Krieges, 1593–1648. Archiv für Litteraturgeschichte, xiv, 1886.
Creizenach, W. Die Schauspiele der englischen Komödianten. Berlin, [1889].
Bolte, Johannes. Die Singspiele der englischen Komödianten und ihrer Nachfolger in Deutschland. Hamburg, 1893.

Schmidt, Erich. Das Verhältnis der deutschen Volksschauspiele zu Marlowes Tragical History of Dr Faustus. [In Sitzungsberichte der preussischen Akademie der Wissenschaften, 1900.]
Robertson, J. G. Zur Kritik Jacob Ayrers. Mit Rücksicht auf Hans Sachs und die englischen Komödianten. Leipzig, 1902.
Herz, E. Englische Schauspieler und englisches Schauspiel zur Zeit Shakespeares in Deutschland. Hamburg, 1903.
Schoenwerth, R. Die niederländischen und deutschen Bearbeitungen von Thomas Kyd's Spanish Tragedy. Berlin, 1903.
Baesecke, A. Das Schauspiel der englischen Komödianten in Deutschland. Halle, 1935.

(i) Prose Fiction

Sir Philip Sidney. The Countesse of Pembrokes Arcadia. 1590; ed. (with the addns of Sir William Alexander and Richard Beling) E. A. Baker, 1907.
Arcadia der Gräffin von Pembrock übersetzt durch Valentinum Theocritum von Hirschberg. Frankfort, 1629.
Arcadia der Gräfin von Pembrock übersehen und gebessert: die Gedichte aber und Reymen gantz anderst gemacht und übersetzt von M. O. V. B. [Martin Opitz von Boberfeld]. Frankfort, 1638.
Brunhuber, K. Sir Philip Sidneys Arcadia und ihre Nachläufer. Nuremberg, 1903.

(3) THE LITERARY RELATIONS OF ENGLAND AND ITALY

(a) General

Niccolò Machiavelli (1469–1527). Istorie Florentine. Florence, 1532.
The Florentine Historie. Tr. T[homas] B[edingfield], 1595.
Francesco Guicciardini (1482–1540). Istoria d'Italia. Florence, 1561.
The Historie of Guicciardin, conteining the Warres of Italie. Tr. Sir Geoffrey Fenton, 1579.
Thomas, William. The Historie of Italie. 1549.
—— Principal Rules of the Italian Grammer. 1550.
Florio, John. A worlde of wordes. 1598.
Chambrun, Comtesse de. Giovanni Florio. Un Apôtre de la Renaissance anglaise à l'Époque de Shakespeare. Paris, 1921.
Spampanato, V. Giovanni Florio. Un' Amico del Bruno in Inghilterra. Critica, 20 May, 20 Sept. 1923.
Yates, F. A. John Florio. Cambridge, 1934.
Dallington, Robert. A Survey of the Grand Duke's State of Tuscany in the yeare of our Lord 1596. 1605.

22

Murray, J. A. The Influence of Italian on English Literature during the Sixteenth and Seventeenth Centuries. Le Bas Prize Essay. Cambridge, 1886.

Scott, M. A. Elizabethan Translations from the Italian: the Titles of such Works now first collected and arranged with Annotations. PMLA. x–xiv, 1895–9; New York, 1916.

Fränkel, L. Romanische, insbesondere italienische Wechselbeziehungen zur englischen Literatur. Ein 'Repertorium auf Grund neuer Veröffentlichungen (1894–6). Erlangen, 1900.

Einstein, L. The Italian Renaissance in England. New York, 1902.

Wolff, S. L. Robert Greene and the Italian Renaissance. E. Studien, xxxvii, 1907.

Crane, T. F. Italian Social Customs of the Sixteenth Century and their Influence on the Literature of Europe. New Haven, 1920.

Schoell, F. L. Les Mythologistes italiens de la Renaissance et la Poésie élisabéthaine. Revue de Littérature comparée, iv, 1924.

Praz, Mario. Secentismo e Marinismo in Inghilterra: J. Donne, R. Crashaw. Florence, 1925.

Ady, C. M. Italian Influences on English History during the Period of the Renaissance. History, ix, 1925.

Bouvy, E. A travers cinq Siècles de Littérature italienne. Paris, 1926.

Jeffrey, Violet M. John Lyly and the Italian Renaissance. Paris, 1929.

(b) *Philosophy, Politcs, Education, etc.*

Giordano Bruno (1548?–1600). Spaccio della Bestia trionfante. 1584.

Carew, Thomas. Coelum Brittanicum. 1634.
Elton, O. Giordano Bruno in England. [In Modern Studies, 1907.]

Baldassare Castiglione (1478–1529). Il libro del Cortegiano. Venice, 1528.

The Courtyer of Count Baldessar Castilio done into Englyshe by Thomas Hoby. 1561.
Ascham, R. The Scholemaster. 1570.
On Civyle and uncivyle life. 1579 (reissued 1586 as The English Courtier and the Countrey-gentleman).
Cleland, J. 'Ηρωπαιδεία or the institution of a Nobleman. 1607.

Giambattista Giraldi Cinthio (1504–1573). Tre dialoghi della vita civile. Monte-Regale, 1565.

A Discourse of Civill life. Tr. Lodowick Bryskett, 1606. [Written c. 1586.]

Ludovico Cornaro (1467–1566). Discorsi della vita sobria. Padua, 1558.

A Treatise of Temperance and Sobriety. Tr. George Herbert, 1634.

Giovanni della Casa (1503–1556). Il Galateo. Florence, 1560.

Galateo. Tr. R. Peterson, 1576.

Antonio Francesco Doni (1513–1574). La Filosofia morale. Venice, 1552.

The morall philosophy: drawn out of the ancient writers. A work first compiled in the Indian tongue, Englished out of the Italian by Thomas North. 1570.

Stefano Guazzo (1530–1593). La civil conversatione. Venice, 1574.

Civille Conversation divided into four books, the first three translated out of French by G. Pettie. The fourth translated out of Italian by B. Young. 1581–6.

Niccolò Machiavelli. Libro dell' arte della guerra. Florence, 1521.

The Arte of Warre. Tr. Peter Whitehorne, 1560.
—— Il Principe. Rome, 1531. [Written 1514.]
Nicholas Machiavel's Prince. Tr. E[dward] D[acres], 1640.
[Machiavelli's reputation in England was not so much due to this late trn as to the hostile pamphlet of I. Gentillet, Discours sur les moyens de bien gouverner et maintenir en bonne paix un royaume. Contre N. Machiavel le Florentin (1576), which was translated by Simon Patericke in 1602 as A Discourse upon the means of well-governing a kingdom against Nicholas Machiavell the Florentine.]

Ellinger, G. Thomas Morus und Machiavelli. [In Vierteljahrsschrift für Kultur und Litteratur der Renaissance, 1884.]
Kempner, N. Raleghs staatstheoretische Schriften. Leipzig, 1928.
Praz, Mario. Machiavelli and the Elizabethans. British Academy, 1928.

Count Giovanni Pico della Mirandola. Commento sopra una canzona de amore da H. Benivieni. Bologna, 1496.

A Platonick Discourse on Love. Tr. T. Stanley, 1651.

Harrison, J. S. Platonism in English Poetry of the Sixteenth and Seventeenth Centuries. New York, 1903.

Annibal Romei. Discorsi. Ferrara, 1586.

The Courtiers Academie. Tr. J. K[eper], [1598].

Francesco Sansovino (1521–1586). Concetti Politici. Venice, 1578.

The Quintessence of Wit. Tr. Robert Hichcock, 1590.

Ludovico Castelvetro (1505–1571). La poetica d'Aristotele vulgarizzata. Vienna, 1570.

Torquato Tasso (1544–1595). Discorsi dell' Arte Poetica. Venice, 1587.

LITERARY RELATIONS WITH THE CONTINENT

Giacomo Mazzoni (1548–1598). Della Difesa della commedia di Dante. Cesena, 1573.

Milton, John. Of Education. 1644.

(c) Allegory, Satire, etc.

Luigi Alamanni (1495–1556). Opere Toscane. Lyons, 1532.

Wyatt, Sir Thomas. Of the Courtier's Life written to John Poins. 1557.

Pietro Aretino (1492–1557). Poesie burlesche, Comedie, Lettere. Venice, 1538–57.

Nashe, Thomas. Apologie of Pierce Pennylesse. 1592.

Ludovico Ariosto (1474–1533). Satire. Venice, 1557.

Satires in seven famous discourses. Tr. [Robert Tofte?], 1608.

Trajano Boccalini (1556–1613). Ragguagli di Parnaso. Venice, 1612; tr. Henry Carey, Earl of Monmouth, 1656.

Suckling, Sir John. A Session of the Poets. 1637.

[Wither, George?] Great Assises holden in Parnassus. 1645.

Sheppard, Samuel. Socratic Session. 1651.

Brotanek, R. Trajano Boccalinis Einfluss auf die englische Litteratur. Archiv, cxi, 1903.

Serafino dell' Aquila (1466–1500). Strambotti. Venice, 1504.

Wyatt, Sir Thomas. Epigrams. 1557.

Cecchini, A. Serafino Aquilano e l'Influenza della Lirica italiana sulla Lirica inglese del 1500. Aquila, 1934.

(d) Lyrical Poetry

Francesco Petrarca (1304–1374). Sonnetti, Trionfi, etc. Venice, 1470.

Songes and Sonettes, written by the ryght honorable Lorde Henry Haward late Earle of Surrey, and other. 1557. [Tottel's Miscellany.]

The Tryumphes of Fraunces Petrarcke. Tr. Henry Parker, Baron Morley, [1565].

Turbervile, George. Epitaphs, Epigrams, Songs and Sonets. 1567.

Howell, Thomas. The Arbor of Amitie. 1568. New Sonets and pretie pamphlets. 1568. Devises, for his owne exercise, and his Friends pleasure. 1581.

Gascoigne, George. A Hundreth sundrie Flowres. [1573].

Watson, Thomas. The ʽΕΚΑΤΟΜΠΑΘΙʼΑ or Passionate Centurie of Love. 1582.

Sidney, Sir Philip. Astrophel and Stella. 1591.

Spenser, Edmund. Amoretti. 1595.

[See also the writers of sonnets enumerated under England and France, p. 332. It is frequently impossible to distinguish between French and Italian influence.]

Madrigales translated of foure, five and sixe parts, chosen out of divers excellent Authors. 1588.

Musica Transalpina. The Second Booke of Madrigalles translated out of sundrie Italian Authors. 1597.

Morley, Thomas. Canzonets. Or little Short Songs to Four Voyces; Collected out of the best and approved Italian Authors. 1597.

—— Madrigals to five voices. Collected out of the best approved Italian authors. 1598.

Watson, Thomas. The first sett of Italian Madrigalls Englished. 1590.

Dowland, John. The first book of Songs or Airs. 1596.

Giambattista Marino (1569–1625). Rime. Venice, 1602.

Crashaw, Richard. Steps to the Temple. 1646.

Sherburne, Sir Edward. Salmacis. 1651.

Stanley, Thomas. Poems. 1651.

Luigi Tansillo (1510–1568). Le Lacrime di San Pietro. Venice, 1560.

Southwell, Robert. St Peter's Complaint. 1595.

Fehse, H. Henry Howard, Earl of Surrey. Ein Beitrag zur Geschichte des Petrarchismus in England. Chemnitz, 1883.

Lentzner, C. A. Die Geschichte des Sonettes in England. Leipzig, 1886.

Koeppel, E. Studien zur Geschichte des englischen Petrarchismus im XVI. Jahrhundert. Romanische Forschungen, v, 1890.

Noble, J. A. The Sonnet in England. 1893.

De Marchi, L. L' Influenza della Lirica italiana sulla Lirica inglese nel Secolo XVI. Nuova Antologia, LVIII, 1895.

Zocco, I. Petrarchismo e Petrarchisti in Inghilterra. Palermo, 1906.

Kastner, L. E. Thomas Lodge as an Imitator of the Italian Poets. MLR. II, 1907.

—— On the Italian and French Sources of Drummond of Hawthornden. MLR. VI, 1911.

—— The Italian Sources of Daniel's 'Delia.' MLR. VII, 1912.

—— The Italian and Spanish Sources of William Drummond of Hawthornden. [In Miscellanea di Studi critici in Onore di Crescini, Cividale, 1927.]

Wolff, M. J. Shakespeare und der Petrarkismus. Die neueren Sprachen, III, 1920.

Lea, K. M. Conceits. MLR. XX, 1925.

Praz, Mario. Secentismo e Marinismo in Inghilterra. Florence, 1925.

Walker, A. Italian Sources of the Lyrics of Thomas Lodge. MLR. XXII, 1927.

Hasselkuss, H. K. Der Petrarkismus in der Sprache der englischen Sonettdichter der Renaissance. Münster, 1927.

Meozzi, A. Il Petrarchismo europeo. Parte prima. Pisa, 1934.

22-2

(e) Epic Poetry

Ludovico Ariosto. Orlando Furioso. Ferrara, 1516.

Orlando Furioso in English Heroical Verse. Tr. Sir J. Harington, 1591.

Greene, Robert. Orlando Furioso. 1594. [Play.]

Spenser, Edmund. The Faerie Queene. Bks I–III, 1590; bks IV–VI, 1595–6.

Warton, T. On Spenser's Imitations of Ariost. 1754.

Dodge, R. E. N. Spenser's Imitations from Ariosto. PMLA. XII, 1897, XXXV, 1920.

Croce, B. Ariosto, Shakespeare and Corneille. Tr. D. Ainslie, 1921.

Kynaston, Sir Francis. Leoline and Sydanis. 1642.

Chamberlayne, W. Pharonnida. 1659.

Matteo Maria Boiardo (c. 1434–1494). Orlando Innamorato. Scandiano, 1480.

Orlando Innamorato. The three first Bookes. Tr. R[obert] T[ofte], 1598.

Dante Alighieri (1265–1321). La Divina Commedia. Foligno, 1472.

König, W. Shakespeare und Dante. Sh. Jb. VII, 1872.

Koeppel, E. Dante in der englischen Literatur des XVI. Jahrhunderts. Zeitschrift für vergleichende Litteraturgeschichte, III, 1890.

Borinski, K. Dante und Shakespeare. Ang. XVIII, 1896.

Gardner, E. Dante and Shakespeare. Dublin Rev. April 1902.

Sills, K. C. M. Wyatt and Dante. Journ. Comparative Lit. IV, 1903.

Toynbee, P. Dante in English Literature from Chaucer to Cary. 1909.

—— Britain's Tribute to Dante in Literature and Art: a Chronological Record of 540 Years. Oxford, 1921.

—— The Earliest References to Dante in English Literature. [In Miscellanea di Studi in onore di Arturo Graf, Bergamo, 1903.]

Farinelli, Arturo. Dante in Spagna, Francia, Inghilterra, Germania. Turin, 1922.

Galimberti, Alice. Dante nel Pensiero inglese. Florence, 1922.

Giambattista Marino. La Strage degli Innocenti. Rome, 1633.

The Suspicion of Herod. Tr. Richard Crashaw, 1646.

Torquato Tasso. Gerusalemme Liberata. Parma, 1581.

Godfrey of Bulloigne; or the Recoverie of Hierusalem. Cantos I–V. Tr. R. C[arew], 1594.

Godfrey of Bulloigne. Tr. Edward Fairfax, 1600.

Blanchard, H. S. Imitations from Tasso in the Faerie Queene. Berkeley, 1925.

Bullock, W. L. Carew's Text of the Gerusalemme Liberata. PMLA. XLV, 1930.

Pope, E. V. The Critical Background of the Spenserian Stanza. MP. XXIII, 1926.

Lemmi, C. W. The Influence of Trissino on the Faerie Queene. PQ. VII, 1928.

Levinson, R. B. Spenser and Bruno. PMLA. LXIII, 1928.

(f) Drama

Ludovico Ariosto. Gli Suppositi. 1509 (prose); ptd Venice, 1525.

—— I Suppositi. 1519 (verse); ptd Venice, 1542.

Supposes. Tr. George Gascoigne, 1566.

Hieronimo Bisaccioni. I Falsi Pastori. [c. 1575]; ptd Verona, 1605.

Jeffery, V. M. Italian Influence in Fletcher's Faithful Shepherdess. MLR. XXI, 1926.

Giambattista Giraldi Cinthio. Orbecche. Venice, 1541. [General influence on European tragedy.]

Ludovico Dolce (1508–1568). Giocasta. Venice, 1549.

Gascoigne, George and Kinwelmershe, Francis. Jocasta. Ed. J. W. Cunliffe, Boston, 1906. [Acted 1566.]

Antonio Francesco Grazzini (1503–1583). La Spiritata. Venice, 1582.

The Bugbears. 1561; ed. C. Grabau, Archiv, XCVIII, XCIX, 1897.

Gian Battista Guarini (1537–1612). Il Pastor Fido. Venice, 1590.

Il Pastor Fido; Or The Faithful Shepheard. Tr. [Edward Dymock], 1602; tr. Sir Richard Fanshawe, 1647.

Daniel, Samuel. The Queenes Arcadia. 1605.

Fletcher, John. The Faithfull Shepheardesse. [1610?]

Luigi Pasqualigo. Il Fedele. Venice, 1574.

Fedele and Fortunio. The Deceipts in Love. Tr. A. Munday, 1584.

Anello Paulillo. Il Giuditio di Paride. Naples, 1566.

Peele, George. The Araygnement of Paris. 1584.

Alessandro Piccolomini (1508–1578). Alessandro. Venice, 1586.

Chapman, George. May-Day. 1611.

Torquato Tasso. Aminta. Venice, 1581.

Fraunce, Abraham. The Lamentations of Amyntas for the death of Phillis. 1587. [In part from Thomas .Watson's Latin adaptation, Amyntas, 1585.]

Torquato Tasso's Aminta. Tr. [Henry Reynolds], 1628.

Daniel, Samuel. The Queenes Arcadia. 1605.

Randolph, Thomas. Amyntas, or The Impossible Dowry. 1638. [Also influenced by Giovanni Donato Cuccheti's La Pazzia, 1581.]

Giovanni Giorgio Trissino (1478–1550). Sofonisba. Rome, 1524. [General influence on English tragedy, e.g. Sackville and Marlowe.]

König, W. Shakespeare und Giordano Bruno. Sh. Jb. xi, 1876.

Meyer, E. Machiavelli and the Elizabethan Drama. Weimar, 1897.

Schücking, L. Studien über die stofflichen Beziehungen der englischen Komödie zur italienischen bis Lilly. Halle, 1901.

Shands, H. A. Massingers The Great Duke of Florence und seine Quellen. Halle, 1902.

Gerhardt, E. Massingers Duke of Milan und seine Quellen. Halle, 1905.

Greg, W. W. Pastoral Poetry and Pastoral Drama. 1906.

Cunliffe, J. W. The Influence of Italian on Early Elizabethan Drama. MP. iv, 1907.

Reyher, P. Les Masques anglais. Étude sur les Ballets et la Vie de Cour en Angleterre, 1512–1640. Paris, 1909.

Bond, R. W. Early Plays from the Italian. Oxford, 1911.

Welsford, Enid. The Italian Influence on the English Court Masque. MLR. xviii, 1923.

Jeffery, V. M. Italian and English Pastoral Drama of the Renaissance. MLR. xix, 1924.

Rebora, P. L' Italia nel Dramma inglese (1558–1642). Milan, 1925.

Smith, W. Italian Actors in Elizabethan England. MLN. xliv, 1929.

Gargano, G. S. Machiavelli e il Machiavelismo nel Teatro elisabethiano. Marzocco, 13 July 1930.

Lothian, J. M. Shakespeare's Knowledge of Aretino's Plays. MLR. xxv, 1930.

(g) Prose Fiction

Matteo Bandello (1480–1561). Novelle. Lucca, 1554–73.

Boaistuau, P. and Belleforest, F. de. XVIII histoires extraictes des œuvres italiennes de Bandel. Paris, 1559.

Painter, William. The Palace of Pleasure. 2 vols. 1566–7.

Fenton, Sir Geoffrey. Certaine Tragicall Discourses. 1567. [From the French of Boiastuau and Belleforest.]

The Tragicall Historye of Romeus and Juliet written first in Italian by Bandell. Tr. Ar[thur] B[roke], 1562.

Shakespeare, W. Romeo and Juliet. 1597. [For the sources of Shakespeare's plays see section D, General Foreign Influence on English Literature, p. 330.]

Heywood, Thomas. A Woman kilde with Kindness. 1607.

—— The Royall King and the Loyall Subject. 1637.

Marston, John. The Insatiate Countesse. 1613.

Markham, G. and Machin, L. The Dumbe Knight. 1607.

Webster, John. The Dutchesse of Malfy. 1612.

Edward III. 1596.

Kiesow, K. Die verschiedenen Bearbeitungen der Novelle von der Herzogin von Amalfi des Bandello in der Litteratur des XVI. und XVII. Jahrhunderts. Ang. xvii, 1894.

Koeppel, E. Studien zur Geschichte der italienischen Novelle in der englischen Litteratur des XVI. Jahrhunderts. QF. lxx, 1892.

Giovanni Boccaccio (1313–1375). Decamerone. 1353; ptd 1470.
The Decameron, containing an hundred pleasant novels. Tr. 1620.

Painter, W. The Palace of Pleasure. 2 vols. 1566–7.

Wilmot, Robert, et al. The Tragedie of Gismund of Salerne. [Written 1567.]

Pettie, George. A Petite Pallace of Pettie his Pleasure. 1576.

Whetstone, G. Rock of Regard. 1576.

Riche, B. Riche his Farewell to the Militarie Profession. 1581.

Turbervile, G. Tragical Tales, translated by Turbervile in time of his Troubles out of sundry Italians. 1587.

Greene, R. Perimedes the Blacksmith. 1588.

Marston, John. Parasitaster, or the Fawne. 1606.

Beaumont, Francis. The Triumph of Love. [c. 1612.]

Shirley, James. The Royall Master. 1638.

Shakespeare, W. All's well that ends well. [Written before 1598.]

—— Filocopo. [Written c. 1341.]
A pleasant disport entitled Philocopo. Tr. H. G[rantham], 1566.

—— L'Amorosa Fiammetta. [Written c. 1344.]
Amorous Fiammetta fyrst written in Italian by Master John Boccace and now done into English by B. Giovanno del M. Temp. [Bartholomew Young of the Middle Temple]. 1587.

Giambattista Giraldi Cinthio. Hecatommithi. Monte-Regale, 1565.

An Heptameron of Civill Discourses. Tr. George Whetstone, 1582.

Whetstone, G. Promos and Cassandra. 1578.

Greene, R. The Scottish History of James IV. 1594.

Shakespeare, W. Measure for Measure. [Written c. 1604.] Othello. [Written c. 1604.]

Massinger, Philip, and another. The Lawes of Candy. [Written c. 1620.]

Giacomo Sannazaro (1458–1530). Arcadia. Venice, 1502.

Sidney, Sir Philip. The Countess of Pembrokes Arcadia. 1590.

Brunhuber, K. Sir Philip Sidney's Arcadia und ihre Nachläufer. Nuremberg, 1903.

Genouy, H. L''Arcadia' de Sidney dans ses Rapports avec l''Arcadia' de Sannazaro et la 'Diana' de Montemayor. Montpellier, 1928.

(h) Sermons

Bernadino Ochino (1487–1564). Prediche. Venice, 1545.

Sermons. Tr. R. Argentine, Ipswich, 1548.

Fourteen Sermons. Tr. Anne Cooke, [1550?].

(4) THE LITERARY RELATIONS OF ENGLAND WITH SPAIN AND PORTUGAL

(a) General

Beale, Robert. Rerum hispanicarum scriptores. Frankfort, 1579.

Corro, Antonio. Reglas gramaticales para aprender la lengua española y francesa. Oxford, 1586.

A Spanish Grammar with certeine rules teaching both the Spanish and French tongues, together with a Spanish dictionary. Tr. John Thorius, 1590.

Acosta, José de. Historia Natural y Moral de las Indias. Seville, 1590.

Perceval, Richard and D'Oylie, Thomas. Bibliotheca hispanica. 1591. [Grammar and dictionary. Second edn by John Minsheu, 1599.]

Stepney, William. The Spanish Schoolmaster conteyning 7 dialogues. 1591.

Landmann, F. Der Euphuismus, sein Wesen, seine Quelle, seine Geschichte. Giessen, 1881.

Bahlsen, L. Spanische Quellen der englischen Litteratur besonders Englands zu Shakespeares Zeit. Zeitschrift für vergleichende Litteraturgeschichte, VI, 1893.

Fitzmaurice-Kelly, J. History of Spanish Literature. New York, 1898.

—— The Relations between Spanish and English Literature. Liverpool, 1910.

Underhill, J. G. Spanish Literature in the England of the Tudors. New York, 1899.

Hume, M. A. S. Spanish Influence on English Literature. 1905.

—— Some Spanish Influences in Elizabethan Literature. Trans. Royal Soc. Lit. XXIX, 1909.

Schevill, R. On the Influence of Spanish Literature on English in the Early Seventeenth Century. Romanische Forschungen, XX, 1907.

Thomas, H. English Translations of Portuguese books before 1680. Library, VII, 1926.

(b) Philosophy, Politics, Education, etc.

Federico Furió Ceriol. Consejo y consejeros de principes. Antwerp, 1559.

A very briefe and profitable Treatise, declaring howe many counsels and what manner of counselers a prince that will gouerne well ought to have. Tr. Thomas Blundeville (from the Italian version of Alfonso de Ulloa), 1570.

Bartolomé Felipe. Tratado del consejo y de los consejeros de los principes. Coimbra, 1584.

The Counsellor, a treatise of counsels and counsellers of princes. Tr. John Thorius, 1589.

Antonio de Guevara (1474–1546). Libro del emperador Marco aurelio con relox de principes. Valladolid, 1529.

The Golden Boke of Marcus Aurelius. Tr. (from the French version of René Bertaut: Livre dore de Marc Aurele, 1531) Sir John Bourchier, Baron Berners, 1534. [One of the most popular books of the century in England.]

The Diall of Princes. Tr. (from the French of Bertaut, 1540) Sir Thomas North, 1557.

Lyly, John. Euphues, the Anatomy of Wit. 1578.

—— Euphues and his England. 1580.

—— Aviso de privados y doctrina de cortesanos. Valladolid, 1539.

The favoured Courtier. Tr. (from a French version) Sir Thomas North, 1568.

—— Epistolas familiares. Valladolid, 1539–45.

Familiar Epistles. Tr. Edward Hellowes, 1574.

Golden Epistles, gathered as well out of the Remaynder of Guevaraes workes as other Authors, Latine, Frenche, and Italian. Tr. Sir Geoffrey Fenton (mainly from Seigneur de Guttery's Epîtres dorées, 1556), 1575.

Antonio de Guevara. Menosprecio de la corte y alabanza de la aldea. Valladolid, 1539.

    A Dispraise of the life of a Courtier. Tr. (from the French version of Antoine Alaigre, 1544) Sir Francis Bryan, 1548.

    The Praise and Happiness of the Countrie Life. Tr. Henry Vaughan, 1651.

    Thomas, H. The English Translations of Guevara's Works. [In Estudios eruditos in Memoriam de Adolfo Bonilla, vol. II, Madrid, 1930.]

Juan Huarte. Examen de ingenios. Baeza, 1575.

    The examination of men's wits. Tr. (from the Italian version of Camillo Camilli, 1582) R[ichard] C[arew], 1594.

Francisco de Valdés. Espejo y disciplina militar. Brussels, 1586.

    The Serjeant Major. Tr. John Thorius, 1590.

(c) Allegory and Satire

Francisco de Quevedo Villegas (1580–1645). Sueños. Barcelona, 1627.

—— Discurso de todos los diablos o infierno enmendado. Barcelona, 1627.

    Hell reformed; or a glasse of favourites in a vision. Tr. 1641.

—— Historia de la vida del Buscon llamado don Pablos exemplo de vagamundos y espejo de tacaños. Saragossa, 1626.

    The life and adventures of Buscon the witty Spaniard. [With] The Provident Knight. Tr. J. D. 1657.

Diego Hernandez de San Pedro. Carcel de Amor. Seville, 1492.

    The Castell of Love. Tr. (from a French version) John Bourchier, Baron Berners, [1540?].

(d) Sermons, Theology, etc.

Diego de Estella (1524–1578). Tratado de la vanidad del mundo. Salamanca, 1574.

    Contempt of the world and the vanitie thereof. Tr. (probably from an Italian version) G. C. [Douay?], 1584.

    Methode unto mortification, called heretofore the contempt of the world and the vanitie thereof. Tr. Thomas Rogers, 1586.

Luis de Granada (1504?–1588). Memorial de la vida christiana. Salamanca, 1566.

    A Memoriall of a Christian life. Tr. [Richard Hopkins], Rouen, 1586.

—— Libro de la oracion y consideracion. Salamanca, 1567.

    Of Prayer and Meditation. Tr. [Richard Hopkins], Paris, 1582.

    Granados Devotion. Tr. (probably from a French version) [Francis Meres], 1598.

Antonio de Guevara. Monte Calvario. Salamanca, 1542.

    The Mount of Calvarie. Tr. bk I, 1595; bk II, 1597.

Juan de Valdés (c. 1500–1541). Ciento i Diez Conçideraçiones. [c. 1540.] [Suppressed by the Inquisition.]

    The hundred and ten Considerations of Signior John Valdesso. Tr. (from an Italian version, 1550, with a Letter and 'Briefe Notes' by George Herbert) Nicholas Ferrar, Oxford, 1638.

(e) Drama

'Tirso de Molina' (Gabriel Téllez; 1585–1648) El Castigo del Pensèque. Madrid, 1627.

    Shirley, James. The Opportunitie. 1640. [Acted 1634.]

Fernando de Rojas. Tragicomedia de Calisto y Melibea (La Celestina). Burgos, 1499. [A novel in dialogue form.]

    A new comodye Of an Enterlude wherein is shewed the bewte and good properties of women. [c. 1530.] [Attrib. to John Rastell.]

    The Spanish Bawd represented in Celestina; or the Tragick Comedy of Calisto and Melibea. Tr. James Mabbe, 1631.

    The delightful History of Celestina the fair daughter to the King of Thessalie. Tr. (from a French version) [W. Barley?], 1596.

    Rosenbach, A. W. S. The Influence of the Celestina in the Early English Drama. Sh. Jb. xxxix, 1903.

Lope de Vega (1562–1635). Don Lope de Cardona. Madrid, 1618.

    Shirley, James. The Young Admirall. 1637. [Acted 1633.]

Frey, Albert R. William Shakespeare and alleged Spanish Prototypes. New York Shakespeare Soc. 1886.

Stiefel, A. L. Die Nachahmung spanischer Komödien in England unter den ersten Stuarts. Romanische Forschungen, v, 1890.

—— Die Nachahmung spanischer Komödien in England. Archiv, xcix. 1897.

Koeppel, E. Quellen-Studien zu den Dramen Ben Jonsons, John Marstons, und Beaumont und Fletchers. Erlangen, 1895.

Koch, Max. Shakespeare und Lope de Vega. E. Studien, xx, 1895.

Grossmann, R. Spanien und das elisabethanische Drama. Hamburg, 1920.

(f) Prose Fiction

Mateo Aleman. Guzman de Alfarache. Madrid, 1599.

    The Rogue; or The Life of Guzman d'Alfarache. Tr. [James Mabbe], 1622.

    Fletcher, John and Massinger, Philip. The Little French Lawyer. [c. 1619.]

Palmerin de Oliva. Salamanca, 1511. Tr. Anthony Munday. Pt I, 1588; pt II, 1597. [From the French and Italian versions of Jean Mangin (1546) and Mambrino de Roseo (1544).]

Don Polindo. Toledo, 1526.

    Palladino of England. Tr. (from the French version of Claude Collet, 1555) A. Munday, 1588.

Miguel de Cervantes Saavedra (1547–1616). Don Quijote. Madrid, 1605–15.

    The History of the Valorous and Wittie Knight Errant Don Quixote of the Mancha. Tr. [Thomas Shelton], 1612.

    Beaumont, Francis and Fletcher, John. The Knight of the Burning Pestle. 1613.

    —— —— The Coxcombe. [Written c. 1610.]

    Field, Nathaniel. Amends for Ladies. [Written c. 1611.]

    Davenport, Robert. The City Nightcap. 1624.

    Rosenbach, A. S. N. The Curious Impertinent in English Dramatic Literature. MLN. xvii, 1902.

—— Novelas exemplares. Madrid, 1613.

    Fletcher, John. Rule a Wife and have a Wife. [Written c. 1624.]

    —— The Chances. [Written c. 1625.]

    Fletcher, John and Shirley, James. Loves Pilgrimage. 1635.

    Massinger, Philip. The Renegado. 1630.

    Middleton, Thomas and Rowley, William. The Spanish Gipsie. 1653.

—— Trabajos de Persiles y Sigismunda. Madrid, 1617. Tr. 1619.

    Fletcher, John and Massinger, Philip. The Custome of the Countrey. [Written c. 1620.]

    Fitzmaurice-Kelly, J. Cervantes in England. British Academy, 1905.

    Ford, J. D. M. and Lansing, R. Cervantes. A Tentative Bibliography. Cambridge, U.S.A. 1931.

Gonzalo de Cespedes y Meneses. Poema tragico del Español Gerardo. Madrid, 1615. [Prose romance.]

    Gerardo the Unfortunate Spaniard. Tr. Leonard Digges, 1622.

    Fletcher, John. The Spanish Curate. [Written c. 1622.]

    Fletcher, John and Rowley, William. The Maid in the Mill. [Written 1623.]

Jeronimo Fernandez. Don Belianis de Grecia. Madrid, 1547.

    The Honour of chivalrie, set downe in the historie of the magnanimous and heroike Don Bellianis. Tr. L. A. 1598.

Juan de Flores. Historia de Cerisel y Mirabella. Seville, 1524.

    Fletcher, John. Women Pleas'd. [Written c. 1620.]

Luis Hurtado (c. 1520–1579). Palmerin de Inglaterra. Pt I, Toledo, 1547; pt II, 1548.

    Palmerin of England. Tr. (from the French version of Jacques Vincent, 1552–3) A. Munday, 1581.

Diego Fernandes Lisboa. Palmerin de Inglaterra. Pt III, Lisbon, 1587.

    Palmerin of England, Part III. Tr. (from the Italian version of Mambrino de Roseo, 1558) A. Munday, 1595.

Diego Hurtado de Mendoza (1503–1575). Lazarillo de Tormes. Burgos, 1554.

    The Pleasant History of Lazarillo de Tormes. Tr. David Rowland, 1586.

Segunda Parte del Lazarillo de Tormes. Antwerp, 1555.

    The most pleasant Historie of Lazarillo de Tormes. Pt II. Tr. W[illiam] P[histon], 1596.

    Nashe, Thomas. The Unfortunate Traveller, or the Life of Jacke Wilton. 1594.

Pedro Mexia (1496?–1552). Silva de varia leccion. Seville, 1542.

    The Forest or collection of historyes. Tr. (from the French version of Claude Gruget, 1552) Thomas Fortescue, 1571.

Garcia Ordoñez de Montalvo. Amadis de Gaula. Saragossa, 1508. [Written c. 1465.]

    The Treasurie of Amadis of Fraunce. Tr. (from a French version: Thresor de tous les livres d'Amadis de Gaule, Antwerp, 1560) Thomas Paynell, 1568.

    The first Book of Amadis of Gaule. Tr. (from the French version of Nicholas d'Herberay des Essarts, 1540–1552) Anthony Munday, 1589. The Second Booke of Amadis de Gaule. 1595. The Ancient and Honourable History of Amadis de Gaule (The First—Fourth Booke). 1619.

    Baret, Eugène. De l'Amadis de Gaule et de son Influence sur les Mœurs et la Littérature au XVIe et au XVIIe Siècle. Paris, 1873.

Juan Perez de Montalban (1602–1638). Sucesos y Prodigios de Amor. Madrid, 1624.

    Aurora & the Prince. Tr. T[homas] S[tanley], 1647.

Jorge de Montemayor. Los siete libros de la Diane de Jorge de Montemayor. Valencia, '1542' [1559?].

    Perez, Alonzo. Diana. Alcala, 1564. [Continuation of above.]

    Polo, Gaspar Gil. Diana Enamorada. Valencia, 1564. [Continuation of above.]

Diana. Tr. Bartholomew Yong, 1598. [Completed 1583.]

Sidney, Sir Philip. The Countess of Pembroke's Arcadia. 1590.

Shakespeare. Two Gentlemen of Verona. [Written c. 1594.]

Harrison, T. P. Bartholomew Yong, Translator. MLR. xxi, 1926.

—— The Faerie Queene and the Diana. PQ. ix, 1930.

Diego Hernandez de San Pedro. Tratado de Arnalte y Lucenda. Burgos, 1491.

The pretie and wittie Historie of Arnalte and Lucenda. Tr.(from the Italian version of Bartolomeo Miraffi, 1570) Claudius Hollyband, 1575.

Antonio de Torquemada. Jardin de Flores curiosas. Salamanca, 1570.

The Spanish Mandevile of Miracles. Tr. Ferdinand Walker, 1600.

Francisco Vasquez de Ciudad Rodrigo. Primaleon y Polendos. Salamanca, 1512.

Primaleon of Greece. Tr. Anthony Munday (from the French versions of François Vernassol (Pt i, 1550) and Gabriel Chapuis (Pt ii, 1577)), 1589.

Primaleon y Polendos. Pt iii, Toledo, 1528. History of Palmendos. Tr. (from the French version of G. Chapuis, 1579) A. Munday, 1589.

Heckmann, T. Massingers The Renegado und seine spanischen Quellen. Halle, 1905.

Utter, —. The Beginnings of the Picaresque Novel in England. Harvard Monthly, April 1906.

Chandler, F. W. The Literature of Roguery. 2 vols. Boston, 1907.

Thomas. H. Spanish and Portuguese Romances of Chivalry. Cambridge, 1920.

Habel, U. Die Nachwirkung des pikaresken Romans in England. Breslau, 1930.

(g) Miscellaneous Verse

Luis Vas de Camoens(1524–1580). Os Lusiadas. Lisbon, 1572. [Begun 1547.]

Lusiads, or Portugals Historicall Poem. Tr. Sir Richard Fanshawe, 1655.

Juan Boscan-Almogaver (c. 1500–1544). Ero y Leandro. Lisbon, 1543.

Fraunce, Abraham. Arcadian Rhetoricke. 1584. [Quotes from Boscan and Garcilasso de la Vega.]

Stanley, Thomas. Poems. 1651.

Luis de Gongora y Argote (1561–1627). Obras en verso. Madrid, 1627.

Stanley, Thomas. Poems. 1651.

Thomas, H. Three Translators of Gongora and other Spanish Poets during the XVII Century. Revue Hispanique, xlviii, 1920.

Jorge de Montemayor. Diana. Valencia, 1542.

Googe, Barnabe. Eglogs, Epytaphes and Sonettes. 1563.

Iñigo Lopez de Mendoza (1398–1458). Proverbios. 1494.

Diaz de Toledo, Pedro. Glosas. 1494.

The Proverbs of Sir James Lopes de Mendoza, marques of Santillana, with the paraphrase of D. Peter Diaz of Toledo. 1579.

(5) The Literary Relations of England with Other Countries

Fletcher, John and Massinger, Philip. Sir John van Olden Barnevelt. [Written 1619. Founded on the events of May 1619.]

Hall, Joseph. Contemplations upon the Holy storie. 8 vols. 1612–26.

Contemplationes Sionis Door E. Schuttenium in Neder-duytsch vertaelt. Amsterdam, 1642.

Sidney, Sir Philip. Defence of Poesie. 1595. [Written before 1583.]

Rodenburg, T. Eglentiers Poëtens Borstweringh. Amsterdam, 1619.

Pienaar, W. J. B. Edmund Spenser and Jonker Jan van der Noot. E. Studies, viii, 1926.

Bense, J. F. Anglo-Dutch Relations from the Earliest Times to the Death of William III. Hague, 1926.

Simmons, E. J. English Literature and Culture in Russia (1553–1840). Cambridge, U.S.A. 1935.

Seaton, E. Literary Relations of England and Scandinavia in the Seventeenth Century. Oxford, 1935.   G. W.

III. BOOK PRODUCTION AND DISTRIBUTION

The Accessory Crafts: Paper; Handwriting; Bookbinding; Illustration of Books.

Printing and Publishing: Types and Ornaments; Printing Practice; Authors and Publication.

Printers and Booksellers: General Works; London Printers and Booksellers; The Provinces; Scotland; Ireland; Wales; English Printing Abroad; Importation of Books; Regulation of the Book Trade; Lists of Books.

Libraries and Book-Collectors.

A. PAPER

[Throughout the period the bulk of the English paper supply came from abroad; works dealing with foreign watermarks which occur on papers used in England are therefore included below.]

Sotheby, S. L. The Typography of the XVth Century, being Specimens together with their Watermarks. 1845.

—— Principia Typographica to which is added an Attempt to elucidate the Character of the Paper Marks of the Period. 3 vols. and supplement, 1858.

Hunter, Joseph. Specimens of Marks used by the Early Manufacturers of Paper,. as exhibited in Documents in the Public Archives of England. Archaeologia, XXXVII, 1857.

Patent Office. Abridgements of Specifications relating to the Manufacture of Paper, Pasteboard and Papier Mâché. 1858.

—— Abridgements of Specifications relating to cutting, folding and ornamenting Paper, etc. Pt II, 1636–1866. 1879 (2nd edn).

Jenkins, Rhys. Paper Making in England, 1588–1788. Library Ass. Record, II, 1900, III, 1901, IV, 1902. [Rptd in Collected Papers, Newcomen Soc. 1936.]

Duff, E. Gordon. English Printing on Vellum to the End of 1600. Lancashire Bibliog. Soc. 1902.

Briquet, C. M. Les Filigranes. 4 vols. Paris, 1907; 4 vols. Berlin, 1929. [Although the only English watermark here recorded is that of John Tate (see the colophon to Wynkyn de Worde's Bartholomaeus, De Proprietatibus Rerum, 1496) it is indispensable for identifying the sources of English paper supply before 1600.]

Aitken, P. H. Some Notes on the History of Paper. Trans. Bibliog. Soc. XIII, 1914.

Le Clert, Louis. Le Papier: Recherches et Notes pour servir à l'Histoire du Papier, principalement à Troyes et aux Environs depuis le XIVe Siècle. 2 vols. Paris, 1926.

Heawood, Edward. The Position on the Sheet of Early Watermarks. Library, IX, 1929.

—— Sources of English Paper Supply. Library, X, 1929–30, XI, 1930–1.

B. HANDWRITING

Steffens, F. Lateinische Palaeographie. 4 pts, Freiburg (Switzerland), 1903–10; tr. French, Paris, 1910.

(1) BEFORE THE INVENTION OF PRINTING

Scriveners' Company. The Case of the Free Scriveners of London: set forth in a Report from a Committee of the Court of Assistants of the Company of Scriveners, London: to the Masters, Wardens and Assistants of the Company. At their Court, holden the 23d day of June, 1748. 1749. [Rptd in facs. about 1890.]

Kirchoff, Albrecht. Handschriftshändler des Mittelalters. Leipzig, 1853.

Wattenbach, W. Das Schriftswesen im Mittelalter. Leipzig, 1871; Leipzig, 1896 (3rd edn).

Bradley, J. W. Dictionary of Miniaturists, Illuminators, Calligraphers and Copyists. 3 vols. 1887–9.

Skeat, W. W. Twelve Facsimiles of Old English Manuscripts. Oxford, 1892.

Madan, Falconer. Books in Manuscript. 1893.

Johnson, Charles and Jenkinson, Hilary. English Court Hand, A.D. 1066 to 1500. 2 vols. Oxford, 1912.

Greg, W. W. Facsimiles of Twelve Early English Manuscripts in the Library of Trinity College Cambridge. Oxford, 1913.

Millar, E. G. English Illuminated Manuscripts of the XIVth and XVth Centuries. Paris, 1928.

(2) CONTEMPORARY WRITING MANUALS 1571–1660

Baildon, John and De Beauchesne, John. A Booke containing divers sortes of hands, as well the English as the French secretarie. 1570; 1571; 1590; 1591; 1602; 1615.

Billingsley, Martin. The Pen's Excellencie, or the secretarie's delighte. [1618.]

Gething, Richard. Calligraphotechnia, or the Art of Faire Writing. 1619; 1642.

—— Chirographia. 1645; 1664 (as Gething's Redivivus).

Brown, David. The new invention intituled Calligraphia; or the Art of faire writing. St Andrews, 1622.

Davies, John. The Writing Schoole-Master. 1636 (16th edn).

Cocker, Edward. Art's Glory, or the Penman's Treasure. 1657.

—— The Pen's Transcendencie or Faire Writing's Labyrinth. 1657.

—— Pen's Triumph. 1658.

Gery, Peter. Gerii viri in arte scriptoria quondam celeberrimi opera. 1659.

(3) HISTORY AND BIBLIOGRAPHY OF HANDWRITING AFTER 1500

Massey, William. The Origin and Progress of Letters. 1763. [The 2nd pt consists of biographies of English writing masters arranged alphabetically.]

Strange, E. F. The Early English Writing Masters. Bibliographica, III, 1897.

Jenkinson, Hilary. English Current Writing and Early Printing. Trans. Bibliog. Soc. XIII, 1915.

—— Elizabethan Handwritings. A Preliminary Sketch. Library, III, 1923.

—— The Later Court Hands in England. 2 vols. Cambridge, 1926.

Thompson, Sir E. M. Handwriting. [In Shakespeare's England, vol. I, Oxford, 1916.]

Byrne, M. St C. Elizabethan Handwriting for Beginners. RES. I, 1925.

McKerrow, R. B. The Capital Letters in Elizabethan Handwriting. RES. III, 1927.

Tannenbaum, S. A. Problems in Shakespeare's Penmanship. New York, 1927.

—— The Handwriting of the Renaissance. New York, 1930.

Heal, Ambrose. The English Writing Masters and their Copy-Books: a Biographical Dictionary and a Bibliography. Cambridge, 1931.

Judge, C. B. Specimens of Sixteenth-Century Handwriting. Cambridge, U.S.A. 1936.

(4) THE AUTHENTICITY OF INDIVIDUAL HANDS

Nichols, J. G. Autographs of Royal, Noble and Remarkable Personages from the Reign of Richard II to Charles II. 1829.

[Turner, Dawson.] Guide to the Historian towards the Verification of MSS. by Reference to Engraved Facsimiles of Handwriting. Yarmouth, 1848.

Sotheby, S. L. Ramblings in the Elucidation of the Autograph of Milton. 1861.

Hardy, W. J. The Handwriting of the Kings and Queens of England. 1893.

Thompson, Sir E. M. Autograph MSS. of Anthony Munday. Trans. Bibliog. Soc. XIV, 1915–7.

—— Shakespeare's Handwriting. Oxford, 1916.

English Literary Autographs. 1550–1660. Pt I, Dramatists; pt II, Poets; pt III, Prose Writers. Ed. W. W. Greg with J. P. Gilson, Hilary Jenkinson, R. B. McKerrow, A. W. Pollard, Oxford, 1925–32.

C. BOOKBINDING

Mejer, Wolfgang. Bibliographie der Buchbinderei-Literatur. Leipzig, 1925.

A generall note of the prises for binding all sorts of bookes. 1619. [Broadside; Soc. Antiquaries, Catalogue by Lemon (see below, p. 360), no. 171.]

To the most Honorable Assembly of the Commons House of Parliament: the binders of bookes in London doe most humblie shew, complaining of the Company of the Goldbeaters and of their monopoly of the importation and sale of gold foliat. [1621.] [Broadside; Soc. Antiquaries, Lemon, no. 186.]

To the most Honorable Assembly of the Commons in the house of Parliament: the Binders of Bookes in London doe most humblie shew, That George Withers, Gent. hath lately composed a Book. which he calleth The Songs and hymns of the Church; and complaining of the grievance that, according to his privilege, no Psalm Book, Bible, Testament, or other service book should be bound and sold, unless the said Songs and Hymns were bound up with them. [1624.] [Soc. Antiquaries, Lemon, no. 225.]

A generall Note of the prises of binding all sorts of Bookes. [18 June 1646.] [BM. (Thomason Tracts) 669, fol. 10 (60).]

Burlington Fine Arts Club. Catalogue of the Exhibition of Bookbindings. 1891.

Prideaux, S. T. An Historical Sketch of Bookbinding. 1893.

Holmes, R. R. Specimens of Royal, Fine and Historical Bookbinding selected from the Royal Library, Windsor Castle. 1893.

Weale, W. H. J. Bookbindings and Rubbings of Bookbindings in the National Art Library South Kensington. 2 vols. 1894–8.

Fletcher, W. Y. English Bookbindings in the British Museum. 1895.

Davenport, C. J. Royal English Bookbindings. 1896.

—— Little Gidding Bindings. Bibliographica, II, 1896.

—— English Embroidered Bookbindings. 1899.

—— Thomas Berthelet, Royal Printer and Bookbinder to Henry VIII. Caxton Club, Chicago, 1901.

—— English Heraldic Book-stamps. 1909. [A copy with much necessary annotation and correction by E. Gordon Duff is in Cambridge University Lib.]

Gibson, Strickland. Some Notable Bodleian Bindings, XIIth to XVIIIth Centuries. Oxford, 1901–4.

—— Early Oxford Bindings. Bibliog. Soc. 1903.

Gray, G. J. The Earlier Cambridge Stationers and Bookbinders and the First Cambridge Printer. Bibliog. Soc. 1904.

—— Queen Elizabeth and Bookbinding. Library, VII, 1916.

Bagford, John. Notes on Bookbinding. Ed. C. J. Davenport. Trans. Bibliog. Soc. VII, 1904.

Skipton, H. P. K. The Life and Times of Nicholas Ferrar [of Little Gidding]. 1907.

Duff, E. Gordon. The Bindings of Thomas Wotton. Library, I, 1910.

—— Scottish Bookbinding, Armorial and Artistic. Trans. Bibliog. Soc. XVII, 1917–9.

Weale, W. H. J. and Taylor, Lawrence. Early Stamped Bookbindings in the British Museum. 1922.

Goldschmidt, E. P. Gothic and Renaissance Bookbindings. 2 vols. 1928.

Hobson, G. D. English Bookbinding before 1500. Cambridge, 1929.

—— Bindings in Cambridge Libraries. Cambridge, 1929.

D. THE ILLUSTRATION OF BOOKS

Chatto, W. A. and Jackson, J. A Treatise on Wood Engraving. 1861.

Pollard, A. W. Early Illustrated Books. 1893.

—— Woodcuts in English Plays printed before 1660. Library, I, 1900.

—— Some Notes on English Illustrated Books. Trans. Bibliog. Soc. VI, 1901.

Fagan, L. A. History of Engraving in England. 3 pts, 1893.

Colvin, Sir Sidney. Early Engraving and Engravers in England, 1545–1695. 1905.

Salaman, M. C. Old Engravers of England, 1540–1800. [1906.]

British Museum. Catalogue of Engraved British Portraits in the British Museum. 6 vols. 1908–25.

Chubb, Thomas. The Printed Maps in the Atlases of Great Britain and Ireland, 1579–1870. 1927.

Hodnett, E. English Woodcuts, 1480–1535. Bibliog. Soc. 1935.

E. TYPES, ORNAMENTS, &c.

Bigmore, E. C. and Wyman, C. W. A Bibliography of Printing. 3 vols. 1880–6.

Reed, T. B. A History of the Old English Letter Foundries. 1887.

Duff, E. Gordon. Early English Printing, a Series of Facsimiles of all the Types used in England during the XVth Century. 1896.

Sayle, C. E. Initial Letters in Early English Printed Books. Trans. Bibliog. Soc. VII, 1902–4.

Proctor, Robert. The French Royal Greek Types and the Eton Chrysostom. Trans. Bibliog. Soc. VII, 1902–4.

Steele, Robert. The Earliest English Music Printing: a Description and Bibliography of English Printed Music to the Close of the Sixteenth Century. Bibliog. Soc. 1903.

Greg, W. W. Notes on the Types, Borders, etc. used by Thomas Berthelet. Trans. Bibliog. Soc. VIII, 1904–6.

Dix, E. R. McC. The Ornaments used by John Franckton, Printer at Dublin. Trans. Bibliog. Soc. VIII, 1904–6.

—— The Initial Letters and Factotums used by John Franckton, Printer in Dublin. Library, II, 1922.

British Museum. Squire, W. B. Catalogue of the Printed Music published between 1487 and 1800. 2 vols. 1912.

McKerrow, R. B. Printers' and Publishers' Devices in England and Scotland 1485–1640. Bibliog. Soc. 1913.

McKerrow, R. B. and Ferguson, F. S. Title-Page Borders used in England and Scotland, 1485–1640. Bibliog. Soc. 1932. [Additions, Library, XVII, 1936.]

Updike, D. B. Printing Types, their History, Forms and Use. 2 vols. Cambridge, U.S.A. 1922.

Lynam, E. W. The Irish Character in Print, 1571–1923. Library, IV, 1924.

Plomer, H. R. English Printers' Ornaments. 1924.

Osborne, L. E. The Whitchurch Compartment in London and Mexico. Library, VIII, 1928.

Isaac, Frank. English and Scottish Printing Types, 1501–1535 and 1508–1541 [1535–58; 1552–8]. 2 vols. Bibliog. Soc. 1930–2. [A series of facs. showing all the types used during this period.]

—— English Printers' Types of the Sixteenth Century. 1936.

Johnson, A. F. A Catalogue of Engraved and Etched English Title-pages to 1691. Bibliog. Soc. 1934.

—— Type Designs: their History and Development. 1934.

—— Sources of Roman and Italic Types used by English Printers in the XVIth Century. Library, XVII, 1936.

Davies, Hugh W. Devices of the Early Printers, 1457–1560. 1935.

F. PRINTING PRACTICE

Hornschuch, Jerome. Ὀρθοτυπογραφια; Instructio operas typographicas correcturis. Leipzig, 1608.

Moxon, Joseph. Mechanick Exercises. 1677–1683; ed. T. L. De Vinne, 2 vols. New York, 1896. [The section on Printing occupies the second part.]

Carleton, G. M. The Elizabethan Compositor. Columbia University Graduate Record, pt II, Jan.-Feb. 1906.

Hart, Horace. On the Red Printing in the 1611 Bible. Library, II, 1911. [See also additional note by R. B. McKerrow on pp. 323–7 of same vol.]

Simpson, Percy. Shakespearian Punctuation. Oxford, 1911.
—— Proof-Reading in the Sixteenth, Seventeenth and Eighteenth Centuries. 1935.
McKerrow, R. B. The Use of the Galley in Elizabethan Printing. Library, II, 1922.
—— Elizabethan Printers and the Composition of Reprints. Library, V, 1925.
—— An Introduction to Bibliography for Literary Students. Oxford, 1927.
—— The Elizabethan Printer and Dramatic Manuscripts. Library, XII, 1931.
Greg, W. W. An Elizabethan Printer and his Copy. Library, IV, 1925.
—— A Proof Sheet of 1606. Library, XVII, 1937.
Rushforth, Marjorie. Two John Taylor Manuscripts at Leonard Lichfield's Press. Library, XI, 1931.
Bone, G. Extant MSS. printed from by Wynkyn de Worde. Library, XII, 1931.
Brooke, C. F. T. Elizabethan Proof Corrections in the First Part of the Contention (1600), with Facsimiles. Huntington Lib. Bulletin, Nov. 1931.
Willoughby, E. E. The Printing of the First Folio. Bibliog. Soc. 1933.
Tillotson, G. and A. Pen and Ink Corrections in Mid.-XVIIth Century Books. Library, XIV, 1933.
Jackson, W. A. Counterfeit Printing in Jacobean Times. Library, XV, 1934.
Allen, D. C. Some Contemporary Accounts of Renaissance Printing Methods. Library, XVI, 1936.

G. AUTHORS AND PUBLICATION

Robinson, Richard. Eupolemia. 1603; ed. G. M. Vogt, Stud. Phil. Oct. 1924. [See also R. B. McKerrow, GM. ccc, April 1906. An account of his literary earnings.]
Furnivall, F. J. Pynson's Contracts with Horman and Palsgrave. Trans. Philolog. Soc. 1867.
Hazlitt, W. C. Prefaces, Dedications and Epistles from Early English Books 1540–1701. 1874 (priv. ptd).
Wheatley, H. B. The Dedication of Books to Patron and Friend. 1887.
Sheavyn, Phoebe. The Literary Profession in the Elizabethan Age. Manchester, 1909.
Nichol Smith, D. Authors and Patrons. [In Shakespeare's England, vol. II, Oxford, 1916.]
Albright, E. M. Notes on the Status of Literary Property, 1500–1545. MP. XVII, 1919.
—— Dramatic Publication in England, 1580–1640. New York, 1927.
Holzknecht, K. J. Literary Patronage in the Middle Ages. Philadelphia, 1924.

H. GENERAL HISTORICAL WORKS

Smyth, Richard. The Obituary of Richard Smyth, Secondary of the Poultry Compter, London: being a Catalogue of all such Persons as he knew in their Life: extending from 1627 to 1674. Ed. Sir Henry Ellis, Camden Soc. 1849.
Ames, Joseph. Typographical Antiquities: being an Historical Account of Printing in England; with some Memoirs of our Antient Printers and a Register of the Books printed by them from the Year 1471 to 1600. 1749; rev. William Herbert, 3 vols. 1785–90; rev. T. F. Dibdin, 4 vols. 1810–9. [See An Index to Dibdin's Edition of the Typographical Antiquities first compiled by Joseph Ames, with some References to the Intermediate Edition by William Herbert, Bibliog. Soc. 1899.]
Ellis, Sir Henry. Copies of Original Papers Illustrative of the Management of Literature by Printers and Stationers in the Middle of the Reign of Queen Elizabeth. Archaeologia, XXV, 1834.
Timperley, C. H. A Dictionary of Printers. 1839; 1842 (as An Encyclopaedia of Literary and Typographical Anecdote).
Masson, David. The Life of John Milton. 6 vols, 1859–80. [Vol. I rev. 1881.]
Rogers, J. E. T. A History of Agriculture and Prices in England. 7 vols. Oxford, 1866–1902. [See vol. IV, ch. 20 and vol. V, ch. 22, for prices of books, paper, etc.]
Bradshaw, Henry. Collected Papers. Cambridge, 1889.
Arber, Edward. A Transcript of the Register of the Company of Stationers of London. 5 vols, 1875–90 (priv. ptd).
Roberts, William. The Earlier History of English Bookselling. 1889; 1892.
Duff, E. Gordon. The Stationers at the Sign of the Trinity. Bibliographica, I, 1895.
—— The Printers, Stationers and Booksellers of London from 1476 to 1535. Cambridge, 1906.
—— Early Chancery Proceedings concerning Members of the Book Trade. Library, VIII, 1907.
—— Notes on Stationers from the Lay Subsidy Rolls of 1523–4. Library, IX, 1908.
—— The Fifth Edition of Burton's Anatomy of Melancholy. Library, IV, 1924.
Two References to the English Book Trade circa 1525. Bibliographica, I, 1895.
Plomer, H. R. Notices of Printers and Printing in the State Papers. Bibliographica, II, 1896.
—— The Long Shop in the Poultry. Bibliographica, II, 1896.

Plomer, H. R. New Documents relating to English Printers and Publishers of the XVIth Century. Trans. Bibliog. Soc. IV, 1896–8.

—— A Short History of English Printing, 1476–1898. 1900; [1920] (rev. edn).

—— Notices of English Stationers in the Archives of the City of London. Trans. Bibliog. Soc. VI, 1900–1.

—— The King's Printing House under the Stuarts. Library, II, 1901.

—— St Paul's Cathedral and its Bookselling Tenants. Library, III, 1902.

—— Abstracts from the Wills of English Printers and Stationers from 1492 to 1650. Bibliog. Soc. 1903.

—— A Secret Press at Stepney in 1596. Library, IV, 1903.

—— Secret Printing during the Civil War. Library, V, 1904.

—— Westminster Hall and its Booksellers. Library, VI, 1905.

—— Bishop Bancroft and a Catholic Press. Library, VIII, 1907.

—— Some Notes on the Latin and Irish Stocks of the Company of Stationers. Library, VIII, 1907.

—— Some Notices of Men connected with the English Book Trade from the Plea Rolls of Henry VIII. Library, I, 1910.

—— Some Early Booksellers and their Customers. Library, III, 1912.

—— Bibliographical Notes from the Privy Purse Expenses of Henry VII. Library, IV, 1913.

—— Some Elizabethan Book Sales. Library, VII, 1916.

—— Wynkyn de Worde and his Contemporaries. 1925.

Putnam, G. H. Books and their Makers during the Middle Ages: A Study of the Conditions of the Production and Distribution of Literature from the Fall of the Roman Empire to the Close of the XVIIth Century. 2 vols. New York, 1897.

Wheatley, H. B. The Prices of Books: an Inquiry into the Changes in the Prices of Books which have occurred in England at Different Periods. 1898.

—— Signs of Booksellers in St Paul's Churchyard. Trans. Bibliog. Soc. IX, 1906–8.

Welch, C. St Paul's Cathedral and its Early Literary Associations. Trans. London and Middlesex Archaeological Soc. I, 1905.

—— The City Printers. Trans. Bibliog. Soc. XIV, 1915–7.

Worman, E. J. Alien Members of the Book Trade during the Tudor Period. Being an Index to those whose Names occur in the Returns of Aliens, Letters of Denization,

and Other Documents published by the Huguenot Society. Bibliog. Soc. 1906.

Steele, R. L. Printers and Books in Chancery. Library, X, 1909.

Aldis, H. G. The Book Trade, 1557–1625. CHEL. vol. IV, 1909.

—— Book Production and Distribution, 1625–1800. CHEL, vol. XI, 1915.

—— The Printed Book. Cambridge, 1916.

Mumby, F. A. The Romance of Bookselling: a History from the Earliest Times to the XXth Century. 1910; 1930 (rev. edn).

Pollard, A. W. Records of the English Bible. 1911.

—— Shakespeare's Fight with the Pirates. 1917; Cambridge, 1920 (rev.).

McKerrow, R. B. Booksellers, Printers and Stationers. [In Shakespeare's England, vol. II, Oxford, 1916.]

Lathrop, H. B. The First English Printers and their Patrons. Library, III, 1923.

Sellers, Harry. Italian Books printed in England before 1640. Library, V, 1925.

Steele, Robert. The King's Printers. Library, VII, 1927.

Ferguson, F. S. Relations between London and Edinburgh Printers and Stationers (–1640). Library, VIII, 1928.

Judge, C. B. Elizabethan Book-Pirates. Cambridge, U.S.A. 1934.

Jackson, W. A. A London Bookseller's Ledger of 1535. Colophon (New York), Spring 1936.

Byron, H. J. Some Exchequer Cases involving Members of the Book Trade, 1534–58. Library, XVI, 1936.

I. INDIVIDUAL PRINTERS AND BOOKSELLERS

Duff, E. Gordon. Hand-Lists of English Printers, 1501–1556. Pt I. Wynkyn de Worde, Julian Notary, R. & W. Faques, John Skot. Bibliog. Soc. 1895.

Duff, E. Gordon, Plomer, H. R. and Proctor, R. Hand-Lists of English Printers, 1501–1556. Pt II. R. Pynson, R. Copland, J. Rastell, P. Treveris, R. Bankes, L. Andrewe, W. Rastell, T. Godfray, J. Byddell. Bibliog. Soc. 1896.

Duff, E. Gordon, Greg, W. W., McKerrow, R. B. and Pollard, A. W. Hand-Lists of English Printers, 1501–1556. Pt III. T. Berthelet, J. Butler, J. Herford, T. Gibson, J. Nicholson, R. Grafton, J. Mayler, T. Raynalde, W. Middleton, R. Kele, R. Lant, R. Wolfe. Bibliog. Soc. 1905.

Duff, E. Gordon, Plomer, H. R. and Pollard, A. W. Hand-Lists of English Printers, 1501–1556. Pt IV. H. Pepwell, R. Redman, R. Wyer, T. Petyt, E. Whitchurch, J. Cawood, N. Hyll, J. Day, R. Jugge, W. Powell, W. Copland, R. Tottel. Bibliog. Soc. 1913.

Duff, E. Gordon. A Century of the English Book Trade: Short Notices of all Printers, Stationers, Bookbinders, 1457 to 1557. Bibliog. Soc. 1905.

Plomer, H. R. A Dictionary of the Booksellers and Printers who were at Work in England, Scotland and Ireland from 1641 to 1667. Bibliog. Soc. 1907.

McKerrow, R. B. A Dictionary of the Printers and Booksellers in England, Scotland and Ireland, and of Foreign Printers of English Books, 1557–1640. Bibliog. Soc. 1910.

(1) *William Caxton.*

Middleton, Conyers. The Origin of Printing in England. Cambridge, 1735.

Lewis, John. The Life of Caxton. 1737.

Blades, William. The Life and Typography of William Caxton. 2 vols. 1861–3; 1877 (as The Biography); 1882 (rev. edn); 1897.

Duff, E. Gordon. William Caxton. Caxton Club, Chicago, 1905.

de Ricci, Seymour. A Census of Caxtons. Bibliog. Soc. 1909.

Plomer, H. R. William Caxton. 1925.

Aurner, N. S. Caxton. 1926.

Caxton's Prologues and Epilogues. Ed. W. J. B. Crotch, EETS. 1928. [Important preliminary summary of recently discovered material.]

Pollard, A. W. The New Caxton Indulgence. Library, ix, 1929.

Crotch, W. J. B. Caxton's Son-in-law. Library, ix, 1929.

(2) *William de Machlinia.*

Smith, George. William de Machlinia: the Primer on Vellum printed by him in London about 1484. 1929.

(3) *Richard Pynson.*

Plomer, H. R. Richard Pynson v. Henry Squyer. Trans. Bibliog. Soc. vi, 1902–4.

—— Two Law-suits of Richard Pynson. Library, x, 1909.

—— Richard Pynson, Glover and Printer. Library, iii, 1923.

Pynson's Dealings with John Russhe. Library, ix, 1918.

(4) *Wynkyn de Worde.*

Plomer, H. R. Wynkyn de Worde and his Contemporaries. 1925.

Bone, Gavin. Extant MSS. printed from by Wynkyn de Worde. Library, xii, 1931.

(5) *John Rastell.*

Plomer, H. R. John Rastell and his Contemporaries. Bibliographica, ii, 1896.

Reed, A. W. John Rastell, Printer, Lawyer, Venturer, Dramatist and Controversialist. Trans. Bibliog. Soc. xvii, 1917–9.

(6) *William Rastell.*

Reed, A. W. The Editor of Sir Thomas More's English Works: William Rastell. Library, iv, 1924.

—— Early Tudor Drama: Medwall, the Rastells, Heywood and the More Circle. 1926.

(7) *Thomas Berthelet.*

Davenport, C. J. Thomas Berthelet, Printer and Bookbinder to Henry VIII. Caxton Club, Chicago, 1901.

Rose-Troup, F. Two Book Bills of Catherine Parr. Library, ii, 1911.

(8) *Robert Wyer.*

Plomer, H. R. Robert Wyer, Printer and Bookseller. Bibliog. Soc. 1897.

Lathrop, H. B. Some Rogueries of Robert Wyer. Library, v, 1914.

(9) *Reyner Wolfe.*

Sayle, C. E. Reyner Wolfe. Trans. Bibliog. Soc. xiii, 1913–5.

(10) *Richard Grafton.*

Kingdon, J. A. Incidents in the Lives of Thomas Poyntz and Richard Grafton. 1895 (priv. ptd).

—— Richard Grafton, Citizen and Grocer of London. A Sequel to Poyntz and Grafton. 1901 (priv. ptd).

Sisson, C. J. Grafton and the London Grey Friars. Library, xi, 1931.

(11) *John Wayland.*

Byrom, H. J. John Wayland—Printer, Scrivener and Litigant. Library, xi, 1931.

(12) *John Day.*

Nichols, J. G. John Day, the Printer. GM. cii, 1832.

(13) *Robert Copland.*

Plomer, H. R. Robert Copland, Printer and Translator. Trans. Bibliog. Soc. iii, 1896.

(14) *Richard Tottel.*

Plomer, H. R. Richard Tottel. Bibliographica, iii, 1897.

Byrom, H. J. Richard Tottel—His Life and Work. Library, viii, 1928.

(15 *Hugh Singleton.*

Byron, H. J. Spenser's First Printer, Hugh Singleton. Library, xiv, 1933.

(16) *William Pickering.*

Gray, G. J. William Pickering, the Earliest Bookseller on London Bridge, 1556–1571. Trans. Bibliog. Soc. IV, 1896–98.

(17) *Henry Denham.*

Plomer, H. R. Henry Denham, Printer. Library, X, 1909.

(18) *Henry Bynneman.*

Plomer, H. R. Henry Bynneman, Printer, 1566–1583. Library, IX, 1908.

(19) *Thomas East.*

Plomer, H. R. Thomas East, Printer. Library, II, 1901.

(20) *John Wolfe.*

Hoppe, H. R. John Wolfe, Printer and Publisher, 1579–1601. Library, XIV, 1933.

(21) *Thomas Chard.*

Jahn, Robert. Letters and Book-Lists of Thomas Chard, 1583–4. Library, IV, 1924.

(22) *Richard Field.*

Kirwood, A. E. M. Richard Field, Printer. Library, XII, 1931.

(23) *Eliot's Court Printing House.*

Plomer, H. R. The Eliot's Court Printing House, 1584–1674. Library, II, 1922.
—— The Eliot's Court Press, Decorative Blocks and Initials. Library, III, 1923.

(24) *Peter Short.*

Thompson, S. P. Peter Short, Printer and his Marks. Trans. Bibliog. Soc. IV, 1896–98.

(25) *Nicholas Ling.*

Hebel, J. W. Nicholas Ling and England's Helicon. Library, V, 1925.

(26) *Edward Blount.*

Lee, Sir Sidney. An Elizabethan Bookseller. Bibliographica, I, 1895.

(27) *Edward Allde.*

McKerrow, R. B. Edward Allde as a Typical Trade Printer. Library, X, 1930.

(28) *William Jaggard.*

Jaggard, William. Shakespeare's Publishers: Notes on the Tudor-Stuart Period of the Jaggard Press. Liverpool, 1907.
Willoughby, E. E. A Printer of Shakespeare. The Books and Times of William Jaggard. 1934.

(29) *Thomas Walkley.*

Simpson, Percy. Walkley's Piracy of Wither's Poems in 1620. Library, VI, 1926.

(30) *Thomas Brudenell.*

Plomer, H. R. A Printer's Bill in the XVIIth Century. Library, VII, 1906.

(31) *Humphrey Moseley.*

Reed, J. C. Humphrey Moseley, Publisher. Proc. Oxford Bibliog. Soc. II, 1928.

(32) *George Thomason.*

The Will of George Thomason. Library, X, 1909. [See also G. K. Fortescue, Introduction to the Catalogue of the Thomasson Tracts in the British Museum (see below, p. 360).]

J. PROVINCIAL PRINTERS AND BOOKSELLERS

Humphreys, A. L. A Handbook to County Bibliography. 1917.
Cotton, Henry. Typographical Gazetteer. 2 sers. Oxford, 1831 (2nd edn); 2 sers. Oxford, 1866.
Allnutt, W. H. Notes on Printers and Printing in the Provincial Towns of England and Wales. 1879. [Gives an alphabetical list of towns, specifying date, printer, book and reference.]
—— English Provincial Presses. Bibliographica, II, 1896.
Duff, E. Gordon. The English Provincial Printers, Stationers and Bookbinders to 1557. Cambridge, 1912.
Bloom, J. H. English Tracts, Pamphlets, and Printed Sheets, issued in Suffolk, Leicester, Stafford, Warwick and Worcester, 1473–1650. 2 vols. 1922–3.
Plomer, H. R. and Peddie, R. A. Stephen Bulkley, Printer. Library, VIII, 1907.
Hawkes, A. J. The Birchley Hall Secret Press. Library, VII, 1927. [See rejoinder by C. A. Newdigate, below p. 355.]

(1) *Marprelate Press.*

Pierce, W. An Historical Introduction to the Marprelate Tracts. 1908.
—— John Penry, his Life, Times and Writings. 1923.
Wilson, J. D. A New Tract from the Marprelate Press. Library, X, 1909.

(2) *Cambridge.*

Bradshaw, Henry. On the Books printed by John Siberch at Cambridge in 1521–2. [Introduction facs. Henry Bullock's Oratio, Cambridge, 1886.]
Bowes, Robert. Biographical Notes on the [Cambridge] University Printers. Cambridge Antiquarian Soc. Communications, V, 1886.

Bowes, Robert. A Catalogue of Books printed at, or relating to the University, Town or County of Cambridge, 1521–1893. With Bibliographical and Biographical Notes. Cambridge, 1894. [Index by E. J. Worman, Cambridge, 1894.]

Gray, G. J. The Earlier Cambridge Stationers and Bookbinders, and the First Cambridge Printer. Bibliog. Soc. 1904.

—— John Siberch, the First Cambridge Printer, 1521–1522. Cambridge, 1921.

—— The Cambridge University Press and John Siberch. Library, VIII, 1928.

Bowes, R. and Gray, G. J. John Siberch; Bibliographical Notes, 1886–1905. Cambridge, 1906.

Roberts, S. C. A History of the Cambridge University Press, 1521–1921. Cambridge, 1921.

Barnes, G. R. A List of Books printed in Cambridge at the University Press, 1521–1800. Cambridge, 1935.

(3) *Chester.*

Stewart-Brown, R. A Chester Bookseller's Lawsuit of 1653. Library, IX, 1929.

—— The Stationers, Booksellers, and Printers of Chester. Trans. Hist. Soc. Lancs. and Cheshire, LXXXIII, 1934.

(4) *Devonshire.*

Dredge, J. I. Devon Booksellers of the XVIIth and XVIIIth Centuries. Plymouth, 1885–91 with 3 supplements (priv. ptd).

(5) *Exeter.*

Plomer, H. R. An Exeter Bookseller [John Gropall], his Friends and Contemporaries. Library, VIII, 1917.

(6) *Ipswich.*

Beck, F. G. M. A New Ipswich Book of 1548. Library, X, 1909.

(7) *Newcastle.*

Welford, Richard. Early Newcastle Typography. 1639–1800. Newcastle-on-Tyne, 1907. [Rptd from Archaeologia Aeliana, III, 1907.]

(8) *Manchester.*

Earwaker, J. P. Notes on the Booksellers of Manchester prior to 1700. Trans. Lancashire and Cheshire Antiquarian Soc. VI, 1888.

(9) *Oxford.*

The Day-book of John Dorne. Ed. Falconer Madan, Oxford Hist. Soc. Collectanea, I, 1885.

Madan, Falconer. The Early Oxford Press '1468'–1640. Oxford, 1895.

—— Oxford Literature, 1450–1640 and 1641–1650. Oxford, 1912. [Really vol. II of the preceding book.]

Madan, Falconer. Oxford Literature, 1651–80. Oxford, 1931.

—— A Chart of Oxford Printing, '1468'–1900. Bibliog. Soc. 1904.

Gibson, Strickland. Abstracts from the Wills and Testamentary Documents of Binders, Printers and Stationers of Oxford, from 1493 to 1638. Bibliog. Soc. 1907.

Lindsay, T. M. An Oxford Bookseller [John Dorne] in 1520. Glasgow, 1907.

Duff, E. Gordon. A Bookseller's Accounts *circa* 1510. Library, VIII, 1907.

(10) *St Albans.*

Blades, William. Some Account of the Typography of St. Albans in the XVth Century. 1860 (priv. ptd).

(11) *Shrewsbury.*

Allnutt, W. H. The King's Printer at Shrewsbury. Library, I, 1900.

Lloyd, L. C. The Book Trade in Shropshire. Trans. Shropshire Arch. and Nat. Hist. Soc. XLVIII, 1935–6.

(12) *Warrington.*

Rylands, W. H. Booksellers in Warrington, 1639 to 1657. With the Full List of the Contents of a Stationer's Shop there in 1647. Proc. Hist. Soc. Lancashire and Cheshire, XXXVII, 1888.

(13) *Winchester.*

Piper, A. C. The Book Trade in Winchester, 1549–1789. Library, VII, 1916.

(14) *Worcestershire.*

Burton, J. R. Early Worcestershire Printers and Books. Associated Architectural Socs. Reports, XXIV, Lincoln, 1897.

(15) *York.*

Davies, R. A Memoir of the York Press. Westminster, 1868.

K. SCOTTISH PRINTERS AND BOOKSELLERS

Aldis, H. G. A List of Books printed in Scotland before 1700. Edinburgh Bibliog. Soc. 1904.

Reid, J. Bibliotheca Scoto-Gadelica. Glasgow, 1832.

Dickson, Robert and Edmond, J. P. Annals of Scottish Printing from the Introduction of the Art in 1507 to the Beginning of the XVIIth Century. Cambridge, 1890.

Edmond, J. P. Bibliographical Gleanings: 1890–1893. Being Additions and Corrections to the Annals of Scottish Printing. Papers Edinburgh Bibliog. Soc. I, 1896.

Mackay, Sheriff. A Short Note of the Local Presses of Scotland; with a List of Books relating to Fife. Papers Edinburgh Bibliog. Soc. III, 1899.

Maclean, Donald. Typographia Scoto-Gadelica, or Books printed in the Gaelic of Scotland, [1567–1914]. Edinburgh, 1915.

(1) *Aberdeen.*

Edmond, J. P. The Aberdeen Printers: Edward Raban to James Nicol, 1620–1736. Aberdeen, 1886.

—— Last Notes on the Aberdeen Printers. Aberdeen, 1888.

Duff, E. Gordon. The Early Career of Edward Raban, afterwards First Printer at Aberdeen. Library, II, 1922.

Johnstone, J. F. K. and Robertson, A. W. Bibliographia Aberdonensis: being an Account of Books relating to or printed in the Shires of Aberdeen, Banff, Kincardine, or written by Natives or Residents, or by Officers, Graduates or Alumni of the Universities of Aberdeen. Vol. I [–1640], vol. II [1641–1700]. Third Spalding Club, Aberdeen, 1929–30.

(2) *Edinburgh.*

Inventory of Work done for the State by His Majesty's Printer in Scotland [Evan Tyler] 1642–1647. Edinburgh, 1815.

Lee, John. Memorial for the Bible Societies of Scotland, containing Remarks on the Complaint of His Majesty's Printer against the Marquess of Huntly and others. With an Appendix of Original Papers. Edinburgh, 1824. [Also: Additional Memorial, Edinburgh, 1826; and W. J. Couper, An Index to Principal Lee's Memorial for the Bible Societies of Scotland, Glasgow, 1918.]

Collection of the Wills of Printers and Stationers in Edinburgh between the Years 1577 and 1687. Bannatyne Misc. II, 1836.

Dobson, W. T. The History of the Bassandyne Bible. Edinburgh, 1887.

Edmond, J. P. Notes on the Inventories of Edinburgh Printers, 1577–1603. Papers Edinburgh Bibliog. Soc. I, 1896.

Cowan, William. Andro Hart and his Press: 1601–1639. With a Hand-list of Books. Papers Edinburgh Bibliog. Soc. I, 1896.

Aldis, H. G. Thomas Finlason and his Press; 1604–1627. With a Hand-list of Books. Papers Edinburgh Bibliog. Soc. I, 1896.

(3) *Glasgow.*

Graham, M. The Early Glasgow Press. Glasgow, 1906.

Couper, W. J. The Origins of Glasgow Printing. Edinburgh, 1911.

Murray, David. Printing in Glasgow, 1638–1742. Records Glasgow Bibliog. Soc. II, 1913.

A Century of Books printed in Glasgow, 1638–1686, shown in the Kelvingrove Galleries, Glasgow, June, 1918. Records Glasgow Bibliog. Soc. V, 1920.

Maclehose, James. The Glasgow University Press, 1638–1931. Glasgow, 1931.

(4) *St Andrews.*

Bushnell, G. H. Catalogue of the Productions of the Early Presses at St Andrews. St Andrews, 1926.

—— The Life and Work of Edward Raban, St Andrews' most Famous Printer. St Andrews, 1928.

L. IRISH PRINTING

[For Irish Type, and for ornaments, etc., used by John Franckton see also p. 348.]

Dix, E. R. McC. Irish Provincial Printing prior to 1701. Library, II, 1901.

—— List of Books, Pamphlets, etc. printed wholly or partly in Irish. Dublin, 1905.

—— A List of Irish Towns and the Dates of the Earliest Printing in each. Dublin, 1909 (2nd edn).

Dottin, G. Les Livres Irlandais imprimés de 1571 à 1820. Paris, 1910.

(1) *Dublin.*

Dix, E. R. McC. The Earliest Dublin Printing [1551–1600]. Dublin, 1901; 1932 (rev. as Printing in Dublin prior to 1601).

—— List of Books, etc. printed in Dublin 1601–1700. 4 pts and supplement, Dublin, 1898–1912.

—— The Earliest Dublin Printers and the Company of Stationers of London. Trans. Bibliog. Soc. VII, 1902–4.

—— Humfrey Powell, the First Dublin Printer. Proc. Royal Irish Academy, XXVII, 1908.

—— William Kearney, the Second Dublin Printer. Proc. Royal Irish Academy, XXVIII, 1910.

—— [Isaac Grover.] An old Dublin Stationer's Will and Inventory. Library, II, 1911.

(2) *Cork.*

Dix, E. R. McC. List of Books, etc. printed in the City of Cork in the XVIIth and XVIIIth Centuries. 13 pts, Cork, 1904. [Rptd from Journ. Cork Hist. and Archaeological Soc.]

M. WELSH PRINTING

[There was no printing in Wales until 1718, but there are several works of importance dealing with printing in Welsh prior to 1660.]

Williams, Moses. Cofrestr o'r holl Lyfrau Printjedig gan mwyaf a gyfansoddwyd yn y Jaith Gymraeg, neu a gyfjeithwyd iddi hyd y Flwyddyn 1717. 1717; rptd Welsh Bibliog. Soc. Carmarthen, 1912.

Rowlands, William. Cambrian Bibliography [1546–1800] edited and enlarged by D. Silvan Evans. Llanidloes, 1869.

Davies, W. Ll. Welsh Books entered in the Stationers' Registers, 1554–1708. Journ. Welsh Bibliog. Soc. II, Carmarthen, 1921.

Short-Title List of Welsh Books, 1546–1700. Journ. Welsh Bibliog. Soc. II, Carmarthen, 1921–2.

N. ENGLISH PRINTING ABROAD

Duthilloeuil, H. R. Bibliographie Douaisienne. Douai, 1842 (rev. edn).

Frère, Édouard. Des Livres de Liturgie des Églises d'Angleterre imprimées à Rouen dans les XVme et XVIme Siècles. Rouen, 1867.

Dexter, H. C. Congregationalism of 300 Years. 1879.

Theux de Montjardin, X. de. Bibliographie Liégeoise. Bruges, 1885 (rev. edn).

Gillow, Joseph. A Literary and Biographical History, or Bibliographical Dictionary of English Catholics [1534–1900]. 5 vols. 1885–1902.

Proctor, Robert. Jan Van Doesborgh, Printer at Antwerp. An Essay in Bibliography. Bibliog. Soc. 1894.

Pollard, A. W. English Books printed Abroad. Trans. Bibliog. Soc. III, 1896.

Bled, O. Les Jésuites anglais à Saint Omer. St Omer, 1897.

Haudecœur, W. G. La Conservation providentielle du Catholicisme en Angleterre, ou Histoire du Collège Anglais. Rheims, 1898.

Wilson, J. D. Richard Schilders and the English Puritans. Trans. Bibliog. Soc. XI, 1909–11.

Steele, Robert. Notes on English Books printed Abroad, 1525–1548. Trans. Bibliog. Soc. XI, 1909–11.

—— Hans Lufft of Marburg. Library, II, 1911.

Plomer, H. R. The Protestant Press in the Reign of Queen Mary. Library, I, 1910.

Newdigate, C. A. Notes on the XVIIth Century Printing Press of the English College at St Omer. Library, X, 1919.

—— Birchley—or St Omers. Library, VII, 1927. [A rejoinder to A. J. Hawkes (see above, p. 352).]

Harris, Rendel and Jones, S. K. The Pilgrim Press: a Bibliographical and Historical Memorial of the Books printed at Leyden by the Pilgrim Fathers. Cambridge, 1922.

Kronenberg, M. E. Notes on English Printing in the Low Countries, 1491–1540. Library, IX, 1929.

Isaac, Frank. Egidius van der Erve and his English Printed Books. Library, XII, 1931.

O. THE IMPORTATION OF BOOKS

[For the Catalogues of Frankfort Fair books, probably imported by John Bill, 1617–1627, see below, p. 358.]

Plomer, H. R. The Importation of Books into England in the XVth and XVIth Centuries. Library, IV, 1924.

—— The Importation of Low Country and French Books into England, 1480 and 1502–3. Library, IX, 1929.

Fetherstone, Henry. Catalogus Librorum in diversis Locis Italiae emptorum. 1628.

Martine, Robert. Catalogus Librorum ex Italia. 1633.

—— Catalogus Librorum ex Roma, Venetiis aliisque Italiae Locis. 1635.

Catalogus Librorum in diversis Italiae Locis emptorum. Anno 1636. qui Londini in Caemeterio Sancti Pauli ad Insigne Rosae prostant venales. 1637. [This catalogue has been variously assigned to George Thomason, Octavian Pulleyn and Robert Martine.]

Martine, Robert. Catalogus Librorum ex praecipuis Italiae Emptoriis selectorum. 1639.

—— Catalogus Librorum e diversis Europae Regionibus congestorum. 1640.

—— Catalogue des diverses Livres Francoises, recueillées dans la France. 1640. [Trinity College, Dublin.]

—— Catalogus libb. ex Italiæ Emporiis Selectorum. 1650. [Trinity College, Dublin.]

Whitaker, Richard. Catalogus Librorum quos de Nundinis Francofurtensibus autumnalibus Anni 1645, ac alibi comparavit Rich. Whitakerus, bibliopola Londinensis: apud quem jam prostant venales. 1645. [There is a copy in the Bibliothek des Borsenvereins at Leipzig.]

Thomason, George. Catalogus Librorum diversis Italiae Locis emptorum. 1647.

Martin, John and Allestrye, James. The Library of Joannes Riolan. 1655.

Pulleyn, Octavian. Catalogus Librorum in omne Genere insignium. 1657.

P. THE REGULATION OF THE BOOK TRADE

(1) GENERAL PRIMARY AUTHORITIES

[The original documents from which many of the compilations listed below are abridged are still preserved in the Public Record Office in Chancery Lane, London. The most useful guide to the various types of document there preserved is M. S. Giuseppi, A Guide to the Manuscripts preserved in the Public Record Office, 2 vols. 1923–4.]

Nicolas, Sir Harris. Proceedings and Ordinances of the Privy Council of England. Vol. VII (1540–2), 1837.

Acts of the Privy Council of England. New Ser. [1542–1621], ed. J. R. Dasent, etc. 37 vols. 1890–1930.

Redgrave, G. R. The Privy Council in its Relation to Literature and Printing. Trans. Bibliog. Soc. VII, 1902–4.

Calendar of Letters and Papers, Foreign and Domestic, of the reign of Henry VIII (1509–1547). Ed. J. S. Brewer and J. R. Gairdner, 21 vols. in 34, 1862–1910; vol. I, new edn, 3 pts, 1920.

Calendar of State Papers, Domestic Series, of the reigns of Edward VI, Mary, Elizabeth and James I preserved in the Public Record Office (1547–1625). Ed. R. Lemon and M. A. E. Green, 12 vols. 1856–72.

Calendar of State Papers, Domestic Series, of the reign of Charles I (1625–1649). Ed. J. Bruce, W. D. Hamilton and S. C. Lomas, 23 vols. 1858–97.

Calendar of State Papers, Domestic Series, of the Commonwealth (1649–1660). Ed. M. A. E. Green, 13 vols. 1875–86.

[Star Chamber: many important cases concerning the regulation of printing were heard in the Star Chamber. Those that have been printed are cited below, but the greater part remain in MS. The best list of these is given in A Study of the Court of Star Chamber by Cora Scofield, Chicago, 1900. See also: Public Record Office, List of Proceedings in the Court of Star Chamber, vol. I (1485–1558), 1901.]

[British Museum: Department of MSS. Add. MS 326, no. 7; see also Harl. MS 6265, no. 19.] [These contain the proceedings against Stephen Vallenger in 1582, for distributing seditious books.] [Star Chamber.]

Rushworth, John. Historical Collections of Private Passages of State, Weighty Matters in Law, Remarkable Proceedings in Five Parliaments, 1618–1648. 8 vols. 1659–1701; 8 vols. 1721 (best edn). [Star Chamber.]

Reports of Cases in the Star Chamber and Court of High Commission. Ed. S. R. Gardiner, Camden Soc. 1886. [This covers for the Star Chamber, Easter Term 1631 to Trinity Term 1632; for the Court of High Commission, Oct. 1631–June 1632.]

Steele, Robert. A Bibliography of Royal Proclamations, 1485–1714. With an Historical Essay. [Bibliotheca Lindesiana: Catalogue of the Printed Books (of James Lindsay, Earl of Crawford), vols. V and VI, Aberdeen, 1910.]

Halliwell[-Phillipps], J. O. A Collection of Ancient Documents respecting the Office of the Master of the Revels. 1870.

Herbert, Sir Henry. Dramatic Records of Sir Henry Herbert, Master of the Revels, 1623–1673. Ed. J. Q. Adams, New Haven, 1917.

Marcham, Frank. The King's Office of Revels, 1610–1622. 1925.

(2) THE STATIONERS' COMPANY

[A considerable amount of material will be found in the introductions and appendices to Arber's Transcript of the Stationers' Register (see below, p. 358).]

The Orders, Rules and Ordinances made by the Mystery of Stationers of London. 1678. [Rptd with addns 1692. This edn rptd in facs. about 1860.]

The Charters and Grants of the Company now in Force. 1741; 1825.

Nichols, John. The Stationers' Company. [Literary Anecdotes of the XVIIIth Century, vol. III, pp. 545–607, 1812.]

Nichols, J. G. Historical Notices of the Worshipful Company of Stationers of London. 1864.

A Sketch of the History and Privileges of the Company. 1871.

Rivington, C. R. The Records of the Worshipful Company of Stationers of London. Westminster, 1883. [Rptd in Trans. Middlesex Archaeological Soc. VI, 1885, and in Arber's Transcript of the Registers, vol. v.]

—— A Short Account of the Worshipful Company of Stationers. 1903 (priv. ptd). [Mainly rptd from Notes on the Stationers' Company, Library, IV, 1903.]

—— A Brief Account of the Worshipful Company of Stationers. [1910.]

Index to Liber A of the Records of the Company of Stationers. 1902 (priv. ptd).

Catalogue of the Records at Stationers' Hall. Library, VI, 1926.

Records of the Court of the Stationers' Company, 1576 to 1602 from Register B. Ed. W. W. Greg and E. Boswell, Bibliog. Soc. 1930.

Pollard, Graham. The Company of Stationers before 1557. Library, XVIII, 1937.

(3) CONTEMPORARY MATERIAL

[See for various documents BM. Harl. MS 5910 passim (e.g. fols. 86, 105–9, 123).]

Ordinances decreed [in Star Chamber] for reformation of divers disorders in printing and uttering of Bookes. 1566. [Soc. Antiquaries, Lemon, no. 57.]

Barker, Christopher. A Note of the State of the Company of Printers, Booksellers, and Bookebynders, December 1582. [MS among the Burghley Papers, BM. Lansdowne MSS, vol. xLVIII, no. 82 (fol. 189), ptd in Archaeologia, xxv, 1834.]

To the Right Reverend and Right Honourable the Lords Spirituall and Temporal assembled in Parliament, An Abstract of the General Grievances of the poore Freemen and Journey-men Printers oppressed, and kept in servile bondage all their lives by the Unlawful Ordinances of the Master and Wardens of the Company which they fortifie only by a warrant dormant. [March 1614 ?] [Broadside: Bagford Collection; also Soc. Antiquaries, Lemon, no. 214; Arber, Transcript of the Stationers' Register, vol. iv, p. 525.]

An Abstract of His Majestie's Letters Patents granted unto Roger Wood and Thomas Symcocke for the sole printing of paper and parchment on the one side. 1620. [Broadside.]

Wither, George. The Schollers Purgatory, discovered in the Stationers' Commonwealth. Imprinted for the Honest Stationers. [1625?] [Rptd in Miscellaneous Works of George Wither, 1st Collection, Spenser Soc. 1872.]

The Humble Petition of the Stationers, Printers and Booksellers of the Citie of London, on the introduction of a bill reducing the Printers to a certain number, and for the avoiding of unskilful Printers. [13 Feb. 1631 ?] [Soc. Antiquaries, Lemon, no. 312.]

A Decree of the Starre-Chamber concerning Printing, made July 11, 1637. 1637. [Rptd in Memoirs of Thomas Hollis, 2 vols. 1780.]

An Order made by the House of Commons, 29 Jan. that the Printers doe neither print nor reprint any thing without the name and consent of the Author. [1641.] [Broadside: BM. Thomason Tracts E, 207 (2).]

[Sparke, Michael.] Scintilla, or a light broken into darke warehouses, with observations on the monopolies of seaven severall patents and two charters. Practised and performed by a mistery of some printers, sleeping stationers and combining booksellers. 1641. [Rptd in Arber's Transcript, vol. iv, and in T. H. Darlow and H. F. Moule, Historical Catalogue of the Printed Editions of Holy Scripture in the Library of the British and Foreign Bible Society, vol. i, 1903, pp. 189 ff.]

A New Discovery of the prelate's tyranny in their late prosecutions of Mr William Pryn, Dr John Bastwick and Mr Henry Burton. 1641.

The Petition of the printers of London. [March 1642.] [BM. Thomason Tracts 669, f. 4 (79).]

The London Printer's Lamentation. 1642.

An Ordinance of the Lords and Commons for Prohibiting the Printing of any lying Pamphlet. 1642.

A Briefe Relation of Certain Passages at the censure of Dr Bastwick, Mr Burton and Mr Prynne. 1643. [Rptd in Harleian Misc. vol. iv, 1809.]

A Particular of the Names of the Licensers appointed by the House of Commons for printing. [14 June 1643.]

An Order of the Lords and Commons for Regulating of Printing and suppressing the great abuses in printing libels. Also authorising the Master and Wardens of the Stationers' Company to make diligent search, seize and carry away all such Books &c. 1643.

Milton, John. Areopagitica; or a Plea for the Liberty of Unlicensed Printing. 1644.

To the High Court of Parliament. The Petition of the Masters and Workmen Printers of London. [1645?] [Broadside: Bagford Collection.]

An Ordinance of the Lords and Commons against Unlicensed or scandalous pamphlets, and for better regulating of Printing. 1647.

An Order of the Commons prohibiting the Printing of Lying Pamphlets. 1647.

To the Commons. The Petition of firm friends to the Parliament [in favour of 'the unrestricted freedom of printing']. [18 Jan. 1649.]

Ball, W. A Brief Treatise concerning the regulating of Printing, humbly presented to the Parliament of England. 1651.

The Beacon set on fire; or the Humble Information of certain stationers. 1652.

[Sparks, Michael.] A Second Beacon fired by Scintilla. 1652.

The Beacons Quenched. 1652.

[Cheynell, Francis.] The Beacon Flameing. 1652.

A Second Beacon Fired. 1654.

Goodwin, John. A Fresh Discovery of the High-Presbyterian Spirit; or, the Quenching of the Second Beacon Fired. 1654.

Orders of the Lord Protector for putting into execution the Laws made against Printing unlicensed Books. 1655.

To Parliament. The Petition of the Workmen-Printers, Freemen of the City of London. [14 April 1659.] [Against the monopoly of printing Bibles, possessed by Henry Hills and John Field.]

The London Printer, his lamentation; or the Press Oppressed or Overpressed. 1660. [Rptd in Harleian Misc. vol. iii, 1809.]

(4) HISTORICAL ACCOUNTS

Strype, John. The Life and Acts of John Whitgift. 2 vols. 1717–8; 3 vols. Oxford, 1822 (rev. edn).

[Hart, W. H.] Index Expurgatorius Anglicanus. 5 pts, 1872–8.

Gardiner, S. R. Documents relating to the Proceedings against William Prynne in 1634 and 1637 with a Biographical Fragment by the late John Bruce. Camden Soc. 1877.

Farber, J. A. Books condemned to be Burnt. 1892.

Axon, W. E. A. The Licensing of Montagu's Miscellanea Spiritualia, [1648]. Library, II, 1901.

Plomer, H. R. Some Dealings of the Long Parliament with the Press. Library, X, 1909.

Fowell, Frank and Palmer, Frank. Censorship in England. 1913.

Pollard, A. W. The Regulation of the Book Trade in the XVIth Century. Library, VII, 1916.

Klein, A. J. Intolerance in the Reign of Queen Elizabeth. Boston, 1917.

Reed, A. W. The Regulation of the Book Trade before the Proclamation of 1538. Trans. Bibliog. Soc. XV, 1917–9.

Feasey, E. I. The Licensing of The Mirror for Magistrates. Library, III, 1923.

Kuhl, Ernest. The Stationers' Company and Censorship, 1599–1601. Library, IX, 1929.

McKerrow, R. B. Richard Robinson's Eupolemia and the Licensers. Library, XI, 1931.

Clyde, W. M. The Struggle for the Freedom of the Press from Caxton to Cromwell. 1934.

Q. LISTS OF BOOKS

[The best general list of English books before 1641 is the Short-Title Catalogue (see p. 360 below), and for English books before 1500, Gordon Duff's XVth Century English Books, 1917. For the period 1641–60 the most useful general list is the Catalogue of the Thomason Collection in the BM.]

(1) CONTEMPORARY

Arber, Edward. Contemporary Lists of Books produced in England. Bibliographica, III, 1897.

Growoll, A. Three Centuries of English Book Trade Bibliography. Dibdin Club, New York, 1903. [This contains an important bibliography of general publishing trade catalogues by Wilberforce Eames.]

Cole, G. W. A Survey of the Bibliography of English Literature, 1475–1640. Bibliog. Soc. of America Papers, XXIII, 1930.

Besterman, T. The Beginnings of Systematic Bibliography. Oxford, 1935.

Arber, Edward. A Transcript of the Register of the Company of Stationers of London, 1554–1640. 5 vols. 1875–94 (priv. ptd).

Eyre, G. E. Briscoe. A Transcript of the Registers of the Worshipful Company of Stationers of London, from 1640 to 1709. 3 vols. Roxburghe Club, 1913.

Rollins, H. E. An Analytical Index to the Ballad Entries (1557–1709) in the Registers of the Company of Stationers of London. Chapel Hill, North Carolina, 1924.

(a) General Trade Catalogues

Maunsell, Andrew. The First [Second] Part of the Catalogue of English printed bookes: which concerneth such matters of Diuinitie, as have bin either written in our owne Tongue, or translated out of anie other language: and have bin published, to the glory of God, and edification of the Church of Christ in England. Gathered into Alphabet, and such Method as it is, by Andrew Maunsell, Bookseller. 1595. [The 2nd pt deals with technical books; no more was pbd.]

Jaggard, William. A Catalogue of such English Bookes as lately have bene, and now are in Printing for Publication. From the ninth day of October, 1618, untill Easter Terme. [The only copy known is in the Bodleian.]

Catalogus Universalis pro Nundinis Francofurtensibus Vernalibus, de anno M.DC.XVII. 1617. [There are, for some years at least, three different issues of this catalogue; and their relationship to each other and to the official Catalogue of the Frankfort Fair has never been worked out. It was continued to the Autumn of 1628. It is probably only an abbreviated rpt of the official Fair catalogue; but from Autumn 1622 to Autumn 1626 there was added a supplement called 'Books printed in English since the last Vernal Mart.']

A Catalogue of certaine Books, which have been published and (by Authoritie) Printed in England, both in Latin and English, since the yeare 1626, untill November this present yeare 1631. Now published for supply since the intermission of the English Catalogue, with intention hereafter to publish it exactly every yeare. 1631. [No continuation has been found.]

[London, William.] A Catalogue of the most vendible Books in England, Orderly and Alphabetically Digested; under Heads of Divinity, History, Physick and Chirurgery, Law, Arithmetick, Geometry, Astrologie,

Dialling, Measuring Land and Timber, Gageing, Navigation, Merchandize, Limning, Military Discipline, Heraldry, Fortification and Fireworks, Husbandry, Gardening, Romances, Poems, Playes, &c. with Hebrew, Greek and Latin Books for Schools and Scholars. 1658. [This is the second issue of William London's Catalogue. It was first issued in the previous year. To this 1658 issue was added 'A Supplement of New Books, come forth since August 1st, 1657 till June 1st, 1658, which is intended to be continued from Year to Year, beginning at June 1st, 1658, where this ends.' Nevertheless all that appeared was 'A Catalogue of New Books By Way of Supplement to the Former. Being such as have been printed from that time, till Easter Term, 1660. London. 1660.']

(b) Particular Trade Catalogues

A Note of the severall sortes of Bookes in the Ware-houses of the Kings Majesties Printing House [*i.e.* of Robert Barker and John Bill]. [1620.] [Broadside: Soc. Antiquaries, Lemon, no. 174.]

A Catalogue of the most approved Divinity Books, which have been printed or reprinted about twenty years past, and continued down to this present year. 1655. 1655 (John Rothwell). [2nd edn 1657; Supplement, August, 1660.]

A Catalogue of Books printed for John Martin, Jam. Allestry and Thom. Dicas: and are to be sold at the Bell in St Paul's Church-yard. [1660.]

[Information on the trade catalogues of Plays, added at the end of various books by Humphrey Moseley, William Leake, etc., will be found in Appendices I and II to W. W. Greg, A List of Masques, Pageants, etc., Bibliog. Soc. 1902, and of some Oxford publishers in F. Madan, Oxford Books, vol. III (see above p. 353).

(c) Bibliographies

Leland, John. Commentarii de Scriptoribus Britannicis. Ed. Anthony Hall, Oxford, 1709. [A better edn is that of Thomas Hearne, in vol. v of his edn of Leland's Collectanea, Oxford, 1715, rptd 1770 and again in 1774.]

Bale, John. Illustrium Majoris Britanniae Scriptorum Summarium in quinque centurias divisum. Ipswich [really Wesel], 1548.

—— Scriptorum Illustrium maioris Britanniae Catalogus. 2 pts, Basle, 1557-9.

——Index Britanniae Scriptorum quos collegit J. Baleus. Ed. R. L. Poole and Mary Bateson, Oxford, 1902.

Pits, John. Relationum Historicarum de Rebus Anglicis. Vol. I, Paris, 1619. [No more was pbd. It is usually cited as De Illustribus Angliae Scriptoribus.]

James, Thomas. Index Generalis librorum prohibitorum a pontificiis. Oxford, 1627.

Ware, Sir James. De Scriptoribus Hiberniae. Dublin, 1639. [Tr. Walter Harris in his edn of Ware's Works, 1746.]

Crowe, William. Catalogue of our English Writers on the Old and New Testaments. 1668. [This was first pbd under another title in 1663; it is really an enlarged edn of Verneuil's work (see below under Bodleian, p. 362).]

Gore, Thomas. Catalogus plerumque omnium authorum qui de re heraldica scripserunt. Oxford, 1668, 1674 (enlarged).

Cooper, William. A Catalogue of Chymicall Books. [At the end of The Philosophical Epitaph of W. C. Esq. 1673.]

(2) Modern Lists

[See also pp. 317–9 above.]

(a) Bibliographies

Tanner, Thomas. Bibliotheca Britannico-Hibernica. 1748.

Watt, R. Bibliotheca Britannica; or a General Index to British and Foreign literature. 4 vols. Edinburgh, 1824. [Two vols. under authors, and two under subjects.]

Lowndes, W. T. The Bibliographer's Manual of English Literature. 4 vols. 1834; rev. H. G. Bohn, 11 vols. 1857–64.

Collier, J. P. A Bibliographical and Critical Account of the Rarest Books in the English Language. 2 vols. 1865.

Hazlitt, W. C. Handbook to the Popular, Poetical and Dramatic Literature of Great Britain, from the Invention of Printing to the Restoration. 1876.

—— Collections and Notes, 1867–1876. 1876.

—— Collections and Notes: 2nd Series. 1882.

—— Collections and Notes: 3rd and Final Series. 1887.

—— Supplement to 3rd Series. 1889.

—— 2nd Supplement to 3rd Series. 1892.

—— Collections and Notes. 4th Series. 1903.

Gray, G. J. General Index to Hazlitt's Handbook and Collections (1867–1889). 1893.

Hoskins, Edgar. Horae Beatae Mariae Virginis: or Sarum and York Primers, with Kindred Books, and Primers of the Reformed Roman Use. 1901.

Duff, E. Gordon. XVth Century English Books. A Bibliography of Books and Documents printed in England and of Books for the English Market printed Abroad. Bibliog. Soc. 1917.

Bosanquet, E. F. English Printed Almanacks and Prognostications. A Bibliographical History to the year 1600. Bibliog. Soc. 1917. [Addenda, Library, VIII, 1928, XVIII, 1937.]

Pollard, A. W., Redgrave, G. R. *et al.* A Short-Title Catalogue of Books printed in England Scotland and Ireland, and of English Books printed Abroad, 1475–1640. Bibliog. Soc. 1926.

(b) Catalogues of Libraries and Exhibitions

Steevens, George. A Catalogue of the Curious and Valuable Library which will be sold by Auction by Mr King. 1800.

Reed, Isaac. A Catalogue of the Curious and Extensive Library which will be sold by Auction by Messrs King and Lochée. 1807.

[Griffith, A. F.] Bibliotheca Anglo-Poetica. 1815.

Heber, Richard. Bibliotheca Heberiana. 13 pts, 10 April 1834–22 Feb. 1837.

Malone, Edmond. Catalogue of the Early English Poetry and other Works, illustrative of the British Drama, collected by Edmond Malone, and now preserved in the Bodleian Library. Oxford, 1836.

Douce, Francis. Catalogue of the Books and Manuscripts bequeathed to the Bodleian Library. Oxford, 1840.

Corser, Thomas. Collectanea Anglo-Poetica. 11 vols. Manchester, 1860–83. [The later vols. ed. James Crossley.]

Dyce, Alexander. A Catalogue of the Printed Books and Manuscripts bequeathed to the South Kensington Museum. 2 vols. 1875.

Bullen, George. Caxton Celebration, 1877. Catalogue. 1877.

[Ellis, F. S.] The Huth Library. A Catalogue of the Printed Books [etc.]. 5 vols. 1880. [Sale Catalogue, 12 pts, Sotheby's, 12 June, 1911–27 Feb. 1922.]

British Museum. Catalogue of Books printed in England, Scotland and Ireland, and of Books in English printed abroad, to the year 1640. Ed. George Bullen, 3 vols. 1884. [The subject indexes are still valuable; and the cross references are useful in using the Short-Title Catalogue.]

Katalog der Bibliothek des Borsenvereins der Deutschen Buchhandler. 2 vols. in 3, Leipzig, 1885–1902.

Society of Antiquaries. Catalogue of a Collection of Printed Broadsides in the possession of the Society of Antiquaries. Compiled by Robert Lemon. 1886.

Grolier Club. Catalogue of Original and Early Editions of some of the Poetical and Prose Works of English Writers from Langland to Wither. New York, 1894.

Grolier Club. Catalogue of Original and Early Editions of some of the Poetical and Prose Works of English Writers from Wither to Prior. 3 vols. New York. 1905.

Duff, E. Gordon. Catalogue of Books in the John Rylands Library, Manchester, printed in England, Scotland and Ireland, and of Books in English printed abroad to the End of the Year 1640. Manchester, 1895.

Cambridge University Library. Early English Printed Books in the University Library, Cambridge, 1475–1640. Ed. C. E. Sayle, 4 vols. Cambridge, 1900–7. [This is the fullest catalogue extant which arranges English books to 1640 under their printers.]

Greg, W. W. A Catalogue of the Books presented by Edward Capell to the Library of Trinity College, Cambridge. Cambridge, 1903. [Shakespeariana.]

British Museum: Thomason Collection. Catalogue of the Pamphlets, Books, Newspapers and Manuscripts relating to the Civil War, the Commonwealth and Restoration, 1640–1661. Ed. G. K. Fortescue, 2 vols. 1908. [This is the most valuable catalogue that there is for the period, and though by no means complete, it is the nearest approach to a sequel to the Short-Title Catalogue.]

Madan, Falconer. Notes on the Thomason Collection of Civil War Tracts. Bibliographica, III, 1897.

Cole, G. W. A Catalogue of Books consisting of English Literature and Miscellanea including many Original Editions of Shakespeare forming part of the Library of E. D. Church. 2 vols. New York, 1909.

Lindsay, J. L. (Earl of Crawford). Bibliotheca Lindesiana. Vols. I–IV, Printed Books. Aberdeen, 1910.

Catalogue of an Exhibition of Books, &c. illustrative of the History and Progress of Printing and Bookselling in England, 1477–1800. Held at Stationers' Hall, 25–29 June 1912. By the International Association of Antiquarian Booksellers. 1912.

Christie-Miller, W. H. [Auction Catalogues of the Britwell Court Library. 21 pts, Sotheby's, 15 Aug. 1916–25 July 1927.]

St Bride Foundation. Catalogue of the Technical Reference Library of Works on Printing and the Allied Arts [by R. A. Peddie]. 1919.

Foxcroft, A. B. Catalogue of English Books and Fragments, 1477–1535, in the Public Library of Victoria. Melbourne, 1933.

R. LIBRARIES AND BOOK-COLLECTING

James, Thomas. Ecloga Oxonio-Cantabrigiensis tributa in libros duos. 1600. [A catalogue of the manuscripts in the college libraries of Oxford and Cambridge.]

Botfield, Beriah. Notes on the Cathedral Libraries of England. 1849.

Edwards, Edward. Memoirs of Libraries. 2 vols. 1859. [Part of vol. I, 2nd edn, Newport, I. of W., ptd 1885, privately issued, 1901.]

Plomer, H. R. References to Books in the Reports of the Historical MSS. Commissioners. Bibliographica, III, 1897.

Clark, J. W. The Care of Books. Cambridge, 1909 (2nd edn).

Streeter, B. H. The Chained Library. A Survey of Four Centuries in the Evolution of the English Library. 1931.

[Much useful information (particularly on the provenance of important MSS) may also be gleaned from the catalogues compiled by M. R. James, for the various Cambridge Colleges and for Aberdeen University, Lambeth Palace, Westminster Abbey, Hereford Cathedral, Eton College, the John Rylands Library Manchester (Western MSS) and Mr Pierpoint Morgan.]

(1) BEFORE THE DISSOLUTION OF THE MONASTERIES

(a) General

Bury, Richard d'Aungerville de (bishop of Durham). Philobiblon: Tractatus pulcherrimus de amore librorum. Cologne, 1473; ed. Thomas James, Oxford, 1599; ed. A. F. West, 3 vols. Grolier Club, New York, 1889; tr. Eng. J. B. Inglis, 1832 and E. C. Thomas, 1888.

Bisticci, Vespasiano da. Vite di Huomini illustri del Secolo xv. Ed. L. Frati. 2 vols. Bologna, 1892–93; tr. Eng. 1926.

Merryweather, F. S. Bibliomania in the Middle Ages. 1849; ed. H. B. Copinger, 1933.

Becker, G. Catalogi Bibliothecarum antiqui. Bonn, 1885. [This gives in full all catalogues then known up to 1300. From 1300 to 1500 it gives references to where they may be found.]

Gottlieb, Theodor. Ueber mittelalterliche Bibliotheken. Leipzig, 1890. [Gives useful addns to Edwards, Memoires of Libraries.]

Plomer, H. R. Books mentioned in Wills. Trans. Bibliog. Soc. VII, 1902–4.

Gasquet, F. A. Some Notes on Medieval Monastic Libraries. [In Old English Bible and other Essays, 1908.]

Savage, E. A. Old English Libraries. 1911. [Contains a useful list of library catalogues before 1525.]

(b) Particular Libraries

[Arranged alphabetically under Towns.]

(1) Bretton Priory.

Hunter, Joseph. English Monastic Libraries. A Catalogue of the Library of the Priory of Bretton in Yorkshire. Notices of the Libraries belonging to other Religious Houses. 1831.

(2) Bury St Edmunds.

James, M. R. On the Abbey of St. Edmund at Bury. Cambridge Antiquarian Soc. 1895.

(3) Canterbury.

James, M. R. The Ancient Libraries of Canterbury and Dover. Cambridge, 1903.

(4) Coventry.

[The Accessions Book (c. 1600–1610) of the Coventry Grammar School Library is in the Cambridge University Lib.]

(5) Dover.

Haines, C. R. The Library of Dover Priory; its Catalogue and Extant Volumes. Library, VIII, 1928.

[See also under Canterbury above.]

(6) Durham.

Catalogi Veteres Librorum Ecclesiae Cathedralis Dunelm. Catalogues of the Library of Durham Cathedral, at various periods from the Conquest to the Dissolution, including catalogues of the Abbey of Hulne, and of the MSS. preserved in the Library of Bp Cosin. Ed. James Raine and Beriah Botfield, Surtees Soc. 1838.

(7) Oxford, Merton College.

Allen, P. S. Early Documents connected with the Library of Merton College, Oxford. Library, IV, 1924.

Garrod, H. W. The Library Regulations of a Medieval College. Library, VIII, 1928.

Powicke, F. M. The Mediaeval Books of Merton College. Oxford, 1931.

(8) Peterborough.

James, M. R. Lists of MSS. formerly in Peterborough Abbey Library. With Preface and Identifications by M. R. James. Supplement no. v to Trans. Bibliog. Soc. 1926.

(9) Sion College, London.

Bateson, Mary. Catalogue of the Library of Sion College, Isleworth. 1898.

(10) York.

James, M. R. The Catalogue of the Library of the Augustinian Friars at York. Now first edited from the MS. at Trinity College, Dublin. [In Fasciculus Ioanni Willis Clark dicatus, Cambridge, 1909.]

(11) *John Tiptoft, Earl of Worcester* (d. 1470).

Mitchell, R. J. A Renaissance Library: the Collection of John Tiptoft. Library, xviii, 1937.

(2) 1540–1660

(a) General

Leland, John. The laboryouse journey & serche of J. Leylande for Englandes antiquitees, geuen of hym as a newe yeares gyfte to Kynge Henry the VIII, with declaracyons enlarged by J. Bale. 1549.

—— Collectanea. Ed. Thomas Hearne, 6 vols. Oxford, 1715; rptd 1770, 1774.

—— Itinerary. Ed. Lucy Toulmin Smith, 5 vols. 1907–8.

Clarke, A. L. John Leland and Henry VIII. Library, ii, 1912.

Jacob, Louys. Traicté des Plus Belles Bibliotheques Publiques & Particulieres qui ont esté & qui sont à present dans le monde. 2 pts, Paris, 1644. [England occupies pp. 242–307.]

Durie, John. The Reformed Librarie Keeper, whereunto is added the description of one of the chiefest libraries in Germanie [*i.e.* Wolfenbüttel]. 1650.

Naudé, Gabriel. Instructions concerning the erecting of a Library now interpreted by John Evelyn. 1661. [Originally pbd in French, Paris, 1628.]

Beloe, William. Anecdotes of Literature and Scarce Books. 6 vols. 1807–14.

Edwards, Edward. Libraries and Founders of Libraries. 1864.

—— The Lives of the Founders of the British Museum, 1570–1870. 1870.

Garnett, Richard. Librarianship in the XVIIth Century. [In Essays in Librarianship and Bibliography, 1899.]

The Literature of Libraries in the XVIIth and XVIIIth Centuries. Ed. J. C. Dana and H. W. Kent, 6 pts, Chicago, 1906. [Reprints of Naudé, Durie, etc.]

Abrahams, I. and Sayle, C. E. The Purchase of Hebrew Books by the English Parliament in 1647. Trans. Jewish Hist. Soc. of England, viii, 1914.

(b) Public and Semi-public Libraries

[Arranged alphabetically under towns.]

(1) Bury St Edmunds.

Bartholomew, A. T. and Gordon, Cosmo. On the Library at King Edward VI School, Bury St Edmunds. Library, i, 1910.

(2) Cambridge, University Library.

Sayle, C. E. Annals of Cambridge University Library. Library, vi, 1915.

(3) Cambridge, Corpus Christi College.

James, M. R. A Descriptive Catalogue of the MSS. in the Library of Corpus Christi College, Cambridge. 2 vols. Cambridge, 1909–12.

(4) Cambridge, Peterhouse.

James, M. R. A Descriptive Catalogue of the MSS. in the Library of Peterhouse, with an Essay on the History of the Library by J. W. Clark. Cambridge, 1899.

(5) Canterbury Cathedral.

Beazeley, M. History of the Chapter Library of Canterbury Cathedral. Trans Bibliog. Soc. viii, 1904–6.

(6) Dublin, Trinity College.

Abbott, T. K. The Book of Trinity College Dublin (1591–1891). Dublin, 1892. [Ch. 7.]

(7) Durham Cathedral.

Hughes, H. D. A History of Durham Cathedral Library. Durham, 1925.

(8) Leicester.

Deedes, Cecil and Stocks, J. E. and J. L. The Old Town Hall Library of Leicester. Oxford, 1919.

(9) London, Royal College of Physicians.

Merrett, Christopher. Museum Harveianum. 1660.

(10) London, Sion College.

Spencer, John. Catalogus Universalis Librorum omnium in Bibliotheca Collegii Sionii apud Londinensis. 1650.

Reading, William. The History of the Ancient and Present State of Sion College, and of the London Clergy's Library there. 1724.

Milman, W. H. Some Account of Sion College in the City of London, and its Library. [1880.]

(11) Norwich, City Library.

Stephen, G. A. Three Centuries of a City Library: an Historical and Descriptive Account of the Norwich Public Library, Established 1608. Norwich, 1917.

(12) Oxford, the Bodleian.

Catalogues: [under faculties] ed. Thomas James, 1605; [alphabetical] ed. Thomas James, 1620; [Appendix to 1620] ed. John Rous, 1635; [of Biblical Commentaries] ed. John Verneuil, 1635; [2nd edn of Verneuil (in English)] ed. John Verneuil, 1642.

Bodley, Sir Thomas. The Life of, written by Himself [in 1609]. Oxford, 1647. [Rptd with addns as Trecentale Bodleianum, Oxford, 1913.]

Bodley, Sir Thomas. Reliquiae Bodleianae. Ed. T. Hearne, 1703.

—— The Letters of, to Thomas James. Ed. G. W. Wheeler, Oxford, 1926.

Macray, W. D. The Annals of the Bodleian Library. 1868; Oxford, 1890 (with addns).

Wheeler, G. W. The Earliest Catalogues of the Bodleian Library. Oxford, 1928 (priv. ptd).

(13) Saint Andrews.

Inventories of Buikis in the Colleges of Sanct Androis [1588–1612]. Maitland Club Misc. vol. i, pt ii, Edinburgh, 1833.

(14) Worcester Cathedral.

Floyer, J. K. A Thousand Years of a Cathedral Library. Reliquary, Jan. 1901.

Wilson, J. M. The Library of Printed Books in Worcester Cathedral. Library, ii, 1912.

(c) Individual Collectors

Quaritch, Bernard. Contributions towards a Dictionary of English Book Collectors. 13 pts, 1892–9.

Elton, C. I. and M. A. The Great Book Collectors. 1893.

Fletcher, W. Y. English Book Collectors. 1902.

De Ricci, Seymour. English Collectors of Books and MSS. and their Marks of Ownership, 1559–1900. Cambridge, 1930.

(1) John Bale (1495–1563).

McCusker, Honor. Books and MSS. formerly in the Possession of John Bale. Library, xvi, 1935.

(2) John Clement (d. 1572).

Reed, A. W. John Clement and his Books. Library, vi, 1926.

(3) Matthew Parker (1504–1575).

Strype, John. The Life and Acts of Matthew Parker. 1711; 3 vols. Oxford, 1821.

Correspondence. Ed. John Bruce, Parker Soc. 1853.

James, M. R. The Sources of Archbishop Parker's Collection of MSS. at Corpus Christi College, Cambridge with a Reprint of the Catalogue of Thomas Markaunt's Library. Cambridge Antiquarian Soc. 1899.

Pearce, E. C. Matthew Parker. Library, vi, 1926.

(4) Clemens Little (d. 1580).

Catalogus Librorum [left to the City of Edinburgh to start the University Library]. Maitland Club Misc. vol. i, pt ii, Edinburgh, 1833.

(5) Stephen Vallenger (d. 1581).

Plomer, H. R. Stephen Vallenger. Library, ii, 1901.

(6) Sir William More (1520–after 1576).

Evans, John. Extracts from the Private Account-Book of Sir William More. Archeologia, xxxvi, 1855.

(7) Francis Russell, Earl of Bedford (1527?–1585).

Byrne, M. St C. and Thomson, G. S. 'My Lord's Books' [1584]. RES. vii, 1931.

(8) William Cecil, Baron Burghley (1520–1598).

Bibliotheca Illustris: sive catalogus variorum librorum quorum auctio habebitur Londini Nov 21, 1687. per T. Bentley & B. Walford. [This sale catalogue contains Burghley's library in the main; though some later books have been added.]

(9) John Dee (1527–1608).

The Private Diary of Dr John Dee, and the Catalogue of his Library of Manuscripts. Ed. J. O. Halliwell [-Phillipps], Camden Soc. 1842.

James, M. R. Lists of Manuscripts formerly owned by Dr John Dee. Supplement No. 1 to Trans. Bibliog. Soc. 1921.

(10) James I (1566–1625).

The Library of James VI. 1578–83. From a Manuscript in the Hand of Peter Young, his Tutor. Ed. G. F. Warner, Scottish Hist. Soc. Edinburgh, 1893.

(11) Henry Savile of Banke (1568–1617).

Gilson, J. P. The Library of Henry Savile of Banke. Trans. Bibliog. Soc. ix, 1906–8.

(12) William Drummond of Hawthornden (1585–1649).

Auctarium Bibliothecae Edinburgenae. Edinburgh, 1627; rptd Edinburgh, 1815. [A catalogue of a gift of 500 books to Edinburgh University.]

(13) James Ussher, Archbishop of Armagh (1581–1656).

Works. Ed. C. R. Elrington and J. H. Todd, 17 vols. Dublin, 1847–64. [Particularly the Life of Ussher by Elrington in vol. i.]

(14) John Williams, Archbishop of York (1582–1650).

Hacket, John (bishop of Lichfield). Scrinia Reserata: a Memorial Offer'd to the Great Deservings of John Williams. 1693.

(15) Sir James Ware (1594–1666).

Librorum Manuscriptorum in Bibliotheca Jacobi Waraei, Equitis Catalogus. Dublin, 1648.

(16) Humfrey Dyson (fl. 1640).

Steele, Robert. Humfrey Dyson. Library, 1910.

(17) *Richard Smyth* (1590–1675).

Bibliotheca Smithiana: sive catalogus librorum Horum Auctio habebitur Londini, May 15, 1682. per R. Chiswell. [This is a sale catalogue; the collection was started by Humfrey Dyson.]

Duff, E. Gordon. The Library of Richard Smith. Library, VIII, 1907.

(18) *Edward Gwynn* (d. 1645?).

Jackson, W. A. Edward Gwynn. Library, XV, 1934.

(19) *Edward Conway, Earl of Conway.*

Plomer, H. R. A Cavalier's Library. Library, V, 1904.

(20) *John Evelyn* (1620–1706).

Keynes, Geoffrey. John Evelyn as a Bibliophile. Library, XII, 1931.   H. G. P.

IV. EDUCATION

General Works: Historical Surveys; Early Works on Education; Illustrative Matter.

The Universities: General Works; Oxford; Cambridge.

The Schools: General Works; Particular Schools.

Other Aspects: School Books and Text Books; The Doctrine of Courtesy; Education of Women and Girls.

[Most of the historical works and similar books of reference in this list are not confined in range to the period 1500–1660. As a rule, their titles are not repeated in the sections which deal with the years beyond 1660.

The list of school books is not exhaustive; such books are recorded in great numbers in the Short Title Catalogue [STC.]. The books here named are either representative of their class at the time, or are works which aimed at improving the current practice. The 'Other Text Books' relate to studies which were not being pursued in the schools of the time, nor were they all written for university students. Their real place is in association with the 'doctrine of courtesy,' a mode of education foreign to schools and universities, the education practised in courts, in great households, in special 'academies' and by private instructors of a non-academic kind.]

A. HISTORICAL WORKS

(1) GENERAL

Adamson, J. W. A Short History of Education. Cambridge, 1919, 1930 (rev.).

Boyd, William. The History of Western Education. 1921.

Cambridge History of English Literature. Vol. III, ch. xix; vol. v, ch. xiv; vol. vii, ch. xiv; vol. ix, ch. xv; Cambridge, 1908–12.

Corcoran, T. Studies in the History of Classical Teaching, Irish and Continental, 1500–1700. 1911.

—— State Policy in Irish Education, 1536–1816. 1916.

Courthope, W. J. A History of English Poetry. 6 vols. 1895–1910.

De Montmorency, J. E. G. State Intervention in English Education. Cambridge, 1902.

Fuller, T. The History of the Worthies of England. 1662; ed. P. A. Nuttall, 3 vols. 1840.

Hallam, H. Introduction to the Literature of Europe. 4 vols. 1837–9. [Vol. II, ch. i.]

Kerr, J. Scottish Education, School and University from Early Times to 1908. Cambridge, 1910.

Laurie, S. S. Studies in the History of Educational Opinion from the Renaissance. Cambridge, 1903.

Leach, A. F. Educational Charters and Documents, 598–1909. Cambridge, 1911.

Quick, R. H. Essays on Educational Reformers. 1868; 1888 (rev.).

Sandys, Sir J. E. A History of Classical Scholarship. 3 vols. Cambridge, 1903–8.

Schmidt, C. A. *et al.* Geschichte der Erziehung. 6 vols. Stuttgart, 1884–1902. [Vol. III.]

Strong, John. A History of Secondary Education in Scotland. Oxford, 1909.

Strype, John. Works, with General Index. 27 vols. Oxford, 1821–40.

Turner, G. Lyon. Original Records of Early Nonconformity under Persecution and Indulgence. 2 vols. 1911.

Watson, Foster. The Beginnings of the Teaching of Modern Subjects in England. 1909.

—— List of Research and Literary Works. 1913.

Watson, Foster, *et al.* Encyclopaedia and Dictionary of Education. 4 vols. 1921–2. [Historical entries.]

Wodehouse, Helen. A Survey of the History of Education. 1924.

(2) 1500–1660

Adamson, J. W. Pioneers of Modern Education, 1600–1700. Cambridge, 1905, 1921 (rev. edn).

—— The Extent of Literacy in England in the Fifteenth and Sixteenth Centuries. Library, X, 1929.

Arber, E. A Transcript of the Registers of the Company of Stationers of London 1554–1640, A.D. 5 vols. 1875–94 (priv. ptd).

Benndorf, C. Die englische Pädagogik im 16. Jahrhundert: Elyot, Ascham, und Mulcaster. Vienna, 1905.

Bradshaw, H. Collected Papers. Cambridge, 1889.

Calendar of State Papers, Domestic Series, 1547–1601. 5 vols. 1856–69.

Cambridge Modern History. Vol. i, chs. xvi, xvii, 1902; vol. v, ch. xxiii, 1908.

Craig, H. The Enchanted Glass: the Elizabethan Mind in Literature. New York, 1936.

Drane, A. T. Christian Schools and Scholars to the Council of Trent. Rev. W. Gumbley, 1924.

Edgar, John. History of Early Scottish Education. Edinburgh, 1893.

Einstein, L. The Italian Renaissance in England. New York, 1902.

Erasmus, Desiderius. The Epistles. Tr. and ed. F. M. Nichols, 3 vols. 1901–18.

—— Opus Epistolarum. Ed. P. S. and H. M. Allen, Oxford, 1906– .

Fischer, T. A. Drei Studien zur englischen Literaturgeschichte. Gotha, 1892. [Ascham.]

Guilday, Peter. The English Catholic Refugees on the Continent, 1558-1795. Vol. i, Colleges and Convents in the Low Countries. 1914.

Harrison, William. Elizabethan England. Ed. L. Withington, [1899].

Katterfeld, A. Roger Ascham. Sein Leben und seine Werke. Strasburg, 1879.

Keatinge, M. W. The Great Didactic of John Amos Comenius. 1896.

Klaehr, T. Leben und Werke Richard Mulcasters. Dresden, 1893.

Leach, A. F. English Schools at the Reformation, 1546–8. 1896.

Petre, E. Notices of the English Colleges and Convents established on the Continent. Norwich, 1849.

Watson, Foster. Religious Refugees and English Education. 1911.

—— Mulcaster and his 'Elementarie.' Educational Times, Jan. 1893.

—— Notices of some Early English Writers on Education. U.S. Bureau of Education, Reports, 1901, vol. i; 1902, vol. i; 1903, vol. i. Washington, 1902–5.

Wood, N. The Reformation and English Education. 1931.

Woodward, W. H. Studies in Education during the Age of the Renaissance. Cambridge, 1906.

Wright, L. B. Middle-Class Culture in Elizabethan England. Chapel Hill, 1935.

B. WORKS ON EDUCATION

Ascham, R. The Scholemaster Or plaine and perfite way of teachyng children to understand, write, and speake, in Latin tong, but specially purposed for the private brynging up of youth in Gentlemen and Noblemens houses. 1570; ed. J. E. B. Mayor, 1863.

Ascham, R. Toxophilus, The schole of shootinge conteyned in two bookes. 1545.

Bacon, Francis (Viscount St Albans). The Two Bookes of the Advancement of Learning. 1605; ed. W. Aldis Wright, Oxford, 1876.

—— New Atlantis. 1627. [Trn in H. Morley, Ideal Commonwealths, 1885.]

Bonner, Edmund. An Honest Godlye Instruction for bringing up of children. 1555.

Brinsley, John. Ludus Literarius: or the Grammar Schoole: shewing how to proceede from the first entrance into learning to the highest perfection required in the Grammar Schooles. 1612; 1627; ed. E. T. Campagnac, Liverpool, 1917.

—— A consolation for our Grammar Schooles: or a faithfull incouragement for laying of a sure foundation of all good learninge in our Schooles. 1622.

Bulwer, John. Philocophus art to Heare what any man speaks by the moving of his lips. 1648.

Caius, John. De pronunciatione Graecae et Latinae linguae cum scriptione nova Libellus. 1574.

Comenius (Jan Amos Komensky). Opera Didactica Omnia. Amsterdam, 1657.

—— Conatuum Comenianorum Praeludia. Ed. S. Hartlib, Oxford, 1637.

—— Reverendi Viri J. A. Comenii Pansophiae Prodromus. 1639. [Preface by Hartlib.]

—— A Reformation of Schooles. Tr. S. Hartlib, 1642.

—— School of Infancy. With Sketch of Author's Life [by D. Benham]. 1858.

—— John Amos Comenius: Life and Educational Works. By S. S. Laurie. 1881; Cambridge, 1887 (rev.). [See R. F. Young, Comenius in England, 1932.]

Cowley, Abraham. A Proposition for the Advancement of Experimental Philosophy. 1661; [rptd in Cowley's Essays, ed. A. R. Waller, Cambridge, 1906].

Dury, John. The Reformed School. [1649?]

—— The Reformed Librarie Keeper, with a Supplement to the Reformed School. 1650.

Elyot, Sir Thomas. The Education or Bringinge up of Children. [1535?] [Tr. from περὶ παίδων ἀγωγῆς, which has been ascribed to Plutarch.]

[Gott, Samuel.] Novae Solymae libri sex. 1648; tr. and ed. W. Begley, 2 vols. 1902.

Hake, Edward. 'A Touchestone for this time present, a perfect Rule' for parents and schoolmasters. 1574.

Harrington, James. The Commonwealth of Oceana. 1656; ed. Henry Morley, 1887.

Hartlib, Samuel. A Description of the famous Kingdom of Macaria. 1641.

Hoole, Charles. A New Discovery of the Old Art of teaching schoole in four small treatises. 1660; ed. E. T. Campagnac, Liverpool, 1913.

Hyde, Edward (Earl of Clarendon). A Collection of several Tracts of Edward Hyde. Ed. T. Woodward, 1727. [Education, pp. 285–348.]

Kempe, William. The Education of Children in Learning. 1587.

Lyster, J. A Rule how to bring up Children. 1588.

Milton, John. Of Education: to Master Samuel Hartlib. 1644; ed. Oscar Browning, Cambridge, 1883.

Mulcaster, Richard. Positions. 1581; ed. R. H. Quick, 1888.

Petty, William. The Advice to Mr S. Hartlib for the Advancement of some particular parts of Learning. 1648; rptd Harleian Misc. vol. VI, 1808.

Reynolds, E. Sermon touching the Use of Humane Learning. 1658.

Sturmius, J. A ritch Storehouse or Treasurie for Nobilitye and Gentlemen which in Latine is called Nobilitas literata. Tr. Eng. T. B[rowne], 1570.

Watt, R. Bibliotheca Britannica. 4 vols. Edinburgh, 1824. [Education, 1477–1820 in vol. III.]

Wotton, Sir Henry. Reliquiae Wottonianae. [4th edn 1685 includes A Survey of Education.]

C. ILLUSTRATIVE MATTER AND SOURCES

Allen, William. An Apologie and true Declaration of the institution and endevours of the two English Colleges in Rome [and] in Rhemes. Mons, 1581.

Ascham, Roger. Epistolarum libri IV; accedunt J. Sturmii aliorumque ad Ascham epistolae. Oxford, 1703.

—— Epistolae Jo. Sturmii et ceterorum ad Rogerum Aschamum nec non alia Angliae lumina. Ed. J. H. Acker, Jena, 1712.

Bedell, William (bishop of Kilmore). A True Relation of the Life and Death of William Bedell. Ed. T. W. Jones, Camden Soc. 1872.

—— Two Biographies, Letters, etc. Ed. E. S. Shuckburgh, Cambridge, 1902.

Bodley, Sir Thomas. Life written by himself. Oxford, 1647.

James, T. Catalogus librorum bibliothecae publicae quam T. Bodleius in Academia Oxoniensi nuper instituit. Oxford, 1605.
Macray, W. D. The Annals of the Bodleian Library, Oxford, 1598–1867. 1868.
Pietas Oxoniensis, in Memory of Sir Thomas Bodley, Knt., and the Foundation of the Bodleian Library. Oxford, 1902.

Bramston, Sir John. Autobiography. Camden Soc. 1845.

Burgon, J. W. The Life and Times of Sir Thomas Gresham. 2 vols. 1839.

Camden, W. Annales Rerum Anglicarum et Hibernicarum Regnante Elizabetha, ad annum MDLXXXIX. 2 vols. 1615–27.

Chambers, M. C. E. Life of Mary Ward. Ed. H. D. Coleridge, 2 vols. 1882–5.

Cheke, Sir J. The Hurt of Sedition. 1549.

—— The Gospel according to St Matthew translated. Also VII Original Letters of Sir J. Cheke. 1843.
S[trype], J[ohn]. The Life of Sir John Cheke. 1698.

Churton, Ralph. Life of Alexander Nowell, Dean of St Paul's. Oxford, 1809.

Clark, J. W. The Care of Books. Cambridge, 1901.

Dafforne, Richard. The Apprentices Time entertainer. 3 pts, 1640.

D'Ewes, Sir Simonds. Autobiography. Ed. J. O. Halliwell[-Phillipps], 2 vols. 1845.

—— Diary. Ed. J. H. Marsden (in College Life in the Time of James I, 1851).

Ellis, Sir H. Original Letters of Eminent Literary Men of the Sixteenth, Seventeenth and Eighteenth Centuries. Camden Soc. 1843.

Ferrar of Little Gidding. [See T. Hearne, and J. E. B. Mayor.]

Feuillerat, A. John Lyly, Contribution à l'Histoire de la Renaissance en Angleterre. Cambridge, 1910.

Fletcher, G. De Literis antiquae Britanniae. Cambridge, 1633.

Frere, W. H. and Kennedy, W. M. Visitation Articles and Injunctions of the Period of the Reformation. 1910. [See Index sub vocibus 'scholars,' 'school,' 'schole publice,' 'schoolmaster,' 'Cambridge University,' 'Oxford University.']

Fripp, E. I. Shakespeare Studies. Oxford, 1930.

Fripp, E. I. and Savage, R. Minutes and Accounts of Stratford upon Avon, 1552–1620. 3 vols. Dugdale Soc, 1921–6. [Vol. III.]

Gardiner, D. The Oxinden Letters (1607–1642). 1933. [Education of boys and girls.]

Gasquet, F. A. Henry VIII and the English Monasteries. 1899.

—— The Canterbury Claustral School. [In Old English Bible, 1908, pp. 225–6.]

Hacket, John. Scrinia reserata: a memorial of John Williams, D.D. 1693.

Hartlib, Samuel.
Dircks, H. Biographical Memoir. 1865.
Turnbull, G. H. Samuel Hartlib: Life and Relation to J. A. Comenius. Cambridge, 1920.

Hearne, T. Reliquiae Hearnianae. Collected with notes by P. Bliss. 2 vols. 1857.
—— Peter Langtoft's Chronicle. 2 vols. Oxford, 1725. [A miscellany including the Ferrars of Little Gidding and Wallis's account of his own education.]
Heywood, Oliver. The Autobiography and Diaries. Ed. J. Horsfall Turner, 4 vols. 1882–5.
Huarte, Juan. Examen de Ingenios, The Examination of Men's Wits, Englished by R. C. 1594. [An edn of 1616 runs 'translated out of the Spanish tongue by M. Camillo Camili, Englished out of his Italian by R. C,' i.e. Richard Carew.]
Kingsford, C. L. Prejudice and Promise in Fifteenth Century England. Oxford, 1925.
Knox, T. F. Records of the English Catholics under the Penal Laws. 2 vols. 1878–82.
Lever, Thomas. Three fruitfull Sermons. 1550; rptd E. Arber, 1870.
Lupton, J. H. A Life of John Colet. 1887; 1909 (rev.).
Madan, F. The Early Oxford Press, a Bibliography of Printing and Publishing at Oxford, '1468'–1640. Oxford Hist. Soc. 1895.
Maitland, F. W. Roman Canon Law in the Church of England. 1898.
Martindale, Adam. Life, by himself. Ed. R. Parkinson, Chetham Soc. 1845.
Mayor, J. E. B. Nicholas Ferrar. Two Lives. Cambridge, 1855.
—— Life and Death of William Bedell. Cambridge, 1871.
Mead, D. M. Diary of Lady Margaret Hoby (1599–1605). 1930.
Milton, John. Private Correspondence and Academic Exercises. Ed. and tr. P. B. and E. M. W. Tillyard, Cambridge, 1932.
Pollard, A. F. England under the Protector Somerset. 1900.
Gregory Smith, G. Elizabethan Critical Essays. 2 vols. Oxford, 1904.
Smith, L. P. The Life and Letters of Sir Henry Wotton. 2 vols. Oxford 1907.
Smith, Sir Thomas. De Republica Anglorum. The maner of Governement or policie of the Realme of England. 1583; ed. L. Alston and F. W. Maitland, Cambridge, 1906.
—— De recta et emendata Linguae Graecae Pronuntiatione. Paris, 1568.
Sturmius, Joannes.
    Collard, F. La Pédagogie de Sturm. [In Mélanges d'Histoire offerts à Charles Moeller, Louvain, 1914.]
    Schmidt, Charles. La Vie et les Travaux de Jean Sturm. Strasburg, 1855.
    [See also Art. 'Sturm' in Rein's Encyclopädisches Handbuch der Pädagogik, vol. ix, 1909.]

Memoirs of the Verney Family. Ed. F. and M. Verney, 4 vols. 1892–9. [See vol. iii, chs. iii and x; vol. iv, ch. x.]
Wallis, John. [See under Hearne above.]
Ward, J. The Lives of the Professors of Gresham College, to which is prefixed the Life of the Founder, Sir T. Gresham. 2 vols. 1740.
Warton, T. The Life of Sir T. Pope, Founder of Trinity College, Oxford. 1772; 1780 (enlarged).
Wilson, J. D. The Schoolmaster in Shakespeare's Plays. Trans. Royal Soc. Lit. ix, 1930.

D. THE UNIVERSITIES

(1) GENERAL WORKS

Anderson, P. J. Fasti Academiae Mariscallanae Aberdonensis, 1593–1860. 2 vols. Aberdeen, 1889–97.
    Studies in the History and Development of the University of Aberdeen. Aberdeen, 1906.
Antimartinus, sive Monitio cuiusdam Londinensis ad adolescentes utriusque Academiae contra Martin Marprelate. 1589.
Boas, F. S. University Drama in the Tudor Age. Oxford, 1914.
—— Shakespeare and the Universities. Oxford, 1923.
Boreman, Robert. Παιδεία-Ορίαμβος. The Triumph of Learning and of Truth, an answer to four quaeries. Whether there be any need of Universities? [etc.] 1653; rptd Harleian Misc. vol. i, 1808, pp. 505 ff.
Buck, Sir George. The Third Universitee of England. 1615. [In an Appendix to J. Stow's Annales or General Chronicle of England, pp. 958–988 of E. Howes' edn of 1615.]
Coutts, J. Glasgow University, History from its Foundation in 1451 to 1909. Glasgow, 1909.
Craufurd, T. The History of the University of Edinburgh from 1580 to 1646. Edinburgh, 1808.
Dell, William (Master of Caius College, Cambridge, 1649–1660). The Tryal of Spirits whereunto is added The right Reformation of Learning, Schools and Universities according to the state of the Gospel. 1653; rptd 1759. [Anticipated University extension.]
—— The Stumbling Stone. 1653.
Grant, Sir Alexander. The Story of the University of Edinburgh during its First Three Hundred Years. 2 vols. 1884. [See Edinburgh Rev. clix, 1884.]
H[all], J[ohn]. A humble motion to Parliament concerning Advancement of Learning and Reform of the Universities. 1649.

Hobbes, Thomas. Leviathan. 1651; ed. A. R.
Waller, Cambridge, 1904.
—— Tracts of Mr. Thos. Hobbs of Malmes-
bury. I, Behemoth. 1682. [In English
Works, ed. Sir W. Molesworth, vol. VI,
1839–46.]
Kendall, George. Sancti Sanciti, The Common
Doctrine of the Perseverance of the Saints
as also an Appendix in answer to Master
[John] Horne [of King's Lynn] goring all
Universitie Learning. 1654. [The appendix
bears title, A Fescue for a Horne Book or an
Apology for University Learning as neces-
sary for Country Preachers.]
Moore Smith, G. C. College Plays performed
in the University of Cambridge. 1923.
Motives for the Present Founding of an Uni-
versity in London. By a Lover of his
Nation. 1647.
Poole, Matthew. A Model for the maintaining
of students of choice abilities at the Uni-
versity. 1658. [Prefatory letter by Richard
Baxter.]
Sancroft, William. Collectanea Curiosa re-
lating to the Antiquities of the Universities
of Oxford and Cambridge chiefly from the
MSS. of Archbishop Sancroft. Ed. John
Gotch, 2 vols. Oxford, 1781.
Scheme of a New College (after the manner of
an University) designed at Rippon in
Yorkshire 4th July, 1604. [See Francis
Peck, Desiderata Curiosa, 1779, C. 7, no.
20.]
Sedgwick, Joseph. Ἐπισκόπου Διδακτικός,
Learning's necessity to an able minister of
the Gospel. 1653.
—— Sermon at St. Maries in Cambridge
May 1st, 1653. [With] Appendix wherein
Mr. Del's Stumbling-stone is briefly repli'd
unto. And a fuller Discourse of the use of
Universities and Learning. 1653.
Sprat, Thomas. History of the Royal Society
of London for the Improving of Natural
Knowledge. 1667.
Stow, John and Strype, John. A Survey of
the Cities of London and Westminster.
2 vols. 1720. [Gresham College, vol. I, ch.
xxii; vol. II, Appendix pp. 2 ff, 18 ff.]
Trinity College, Dublin. The Book of Trinity
College, Dublin [Annals, 1591–1891]. Belfast, 1892.
[Ward, Seth.] Vindiciae Academiarum, containing some briefe Animadversions upon
Mr. Webster's book stiled The Examination
of Academies, together with an appendix
concerning what M. Hobbs and M. Dell
have published on this argument. By H. D.
Preface by N. S. [John Wilkins]. Oxford,
1654.
Waterhous[e], Edward. An humble Apologie
for Learning and Learned Men. 1653.

Webster, John. Academiarum Examen,
wherein is discussed the Matter, Method
and Customs of Academick and Scholastic
Learning and the insufficiency thereof laid
open; and also some expedient for the
Reforming of Schools. 1654.

(2) OXFORD

(a) Oxford Colleges

College Histories Series. 1900–. [Various
authors.]
The College Monographs. 1906. [Various
authors.]
Statutes of the Colleges of Oxford, with Royal
Patents of Foundation. 3 vols. Oxford
1853.
Chalmers, Alexander. History of the Colleges
[and] Halls of Oxford. Oxford, 1810.
Clark, A. The Colleges of Oxford: their History
and Traditions. 1891.

(1) All Souls.
Burrows, M. Worthies of All Souls: four Centuries of English History illustrated from
the College Archives. 1874.

(2) Brasenose.
Brasenose College Register 1509–1909. Oxford, 1909.
Madan, F. et al. Brasenose College Quatercentenary Monographs. 2 vols. Oxford, 1909.
Brasenole Ale: Poems presented annually by
the Butler. Ed. J. Prior, 1857.

(3) Christ Church.
Tom Tower, Christ Church; Letters of Sir C
Wren to Dr Fell. Ed. W. D. Caröe, 1923.

(4) Corpus.
Fowler, Thomas. History of Corpus Christi
College. Oxford, 1893.
Ward, G. R. M. The Foundation Statutes of
Bishop Fox for Corpus Christi College, 1517.
1843.

(5) Exeter.
Boase, C. W. Exeter College Register, etc. with
History of the College. 1879.
—— Register of Exeter College with Historical
Documents. Oxford, 1894.

(6) Magdalen.
Register of Members: (i) ed. J. R. Bloxam
7 vols. Oxford, 1853–85; (ii) ed. W. D
Macray, 6 vols. Oxford, 1894–1909.

(7) Merton.
Allen, P. S. and Garrod, H. W. Merton
Muniments. Oxford, 1928.
Brodrick, G. C. Memorials of Merton College
with Biographical Notices of the Wardens
and Fellows. Oxford Hist. Soc. IV, 1885.

Percival, E. F. The Foundation Statutes of Merton with Ordinances of Archbishops Peckham, Chicheley and Laud. 1847.

Registrum Annalium Collegii Mertonensis, 1483–1521. Ed. H. E. Salter, Oxford, 1923.

(8) Oriel.

Richards, G. C. and Salter, H. E. The Dean's Register of Oriel, 1446–1661. Oxford, 1926.

Shadwell, C. L. and Salter, H. E. Oriel College Records. Oxford, 1926.

(9) Pembroke.

Macleane, D. A History of Pembroke College, anciently Broadgates Hall. Oxford Hist. Soc. 1897.

(10) Queen's.

Magrath, J. R. Queen's College, Oxford. 2 vols. Oxford, 1921.

—— Liber Obituarius. Oxford, 1910.

(11) Wadham.

Gardiner, R. B. Wadham College Registers, 1613–1719. 1889.

—— The Letters of Dorothy Wadham, 1609–1618. Oxford, 1904.

Jackson, Sir T. G. Wadham College, its Foundation, Architecture, History. Oxford, 1893.

(b) Oxford University

Ackermann, R. History of the University of Oxford, its Colleges, Halls and Public Buildings [by W. Combe]. 1814.

Allibond, John. Rustica Academiae Oxoniensis nuper Reformatae Descriptio in Visitatione Fanatica. 1648. [Tr. E. Ward, 1717; rptd in Somers Tracts, vol. v, 1810, pp. 503 ff.]

Anstey, H. Munimenta Academica: or Documents Illustrative of Academical Life and Studies at Oxford. 2 pts, Rolls Ser. 1868.

—— Epistolae Academicae Oxonienses. Life and Studies in the 15th Century. 2 vols. 1898.

Aubrey, John. Letters written by Eminent Persons. 2 vols. in 3, 1813.

Ayliffe, J. The antient and present state of the university of Oxford. 2 vols. 1714.

Bagshaw, William. A Short Censure of the book of W[illiam] P[rynne] entitled, The University of Oxford. 1648.

Boase, C. W. and Clark, A. The Register of the University of Oxford. 5 vols. Oxford Hist. Soc. 1884–9.

[Brandon, J.] The Oxonian Antippodes or the Oxford Anty-Parliament. 1644.

Brodrick, G. C. A History of the University of Oxford. 1886.

Burrows, M. The Register of the Visitors of the University of Oxford, 1647–58. [An] Account of the University during the Commonwealth. Camden Soc. 1881.

Caius, Thomas. Vindiciae antiquitatis Academiae Oxoniensis contra J. Caium Cantabrigiensem. Ed. T. Hearne, 2 vols. Oxford, 1730. [With 'notes relating to the Ferrars of Gidding Parva.']

The sworne Confederacy between the Convocation at Oxford and the Tower of London. 1647.

Enactments in Parliament especially concerning the Universities of Oxford and Cambridge, Winchester, Eton and Westminster [1363–1912]. Ed. L. L. Shadwell, 4 vols. Oxford Hist. Soc. 1912.

Foster, Joseph. Alumni Oxonienses, 1500–1886. 8 vols. Oxford, 1887–91.

Griffiths, John and Shadwell, C. L. The Laudian Code of Statutes, 1636. Oxford, 1888.

Gunther, R. W. T. Early Science in Oxford. 4 vols. Oxford, 1923–5. [Vols. iii, iv, 17th cent.]

Hall, Thomas. Vindiciae Literarum, the Schools guarded. 1654.

Lang, Andrew. Oxford. Brief Historical and Descriptives Notes. 1882.

Langbaine, Gerard. The Foundation of the Universitie of Oxford. 1651.

Madan, F. Rough List of MS Materials Relating to the History of Oxford in the Printed Catalogues of the Bodleian and College Libraries. Oxford, 1887.

Mallet, C. E. A History of the University of Oxford. 3 vols. 1924–7.

Maxwell-Lyte, H. C. A History of the University of Oxford to 1530. 1886.

Pattison, Mark. Essays. Ed. H. Nettleship, 2 vols. Oxford, 1889. [A Chapter of University History (1630–1687) and Oxford Studies, in vol. i.]

Plummer, C. Elizabethan Oxford. Oxford Hist. Soc. 1886.

Prynne, W. The University of Oxford's Plea refuted. 1647.

Quiller-Couch, L. M. Reminiscences of Oxford, by Oxford Men, 1559–1850. Oxford Hist. Soc. 1892.

Reasons of present judgement of the University of Oxford concerning the Solemn League and Covenant. Oxford, 1647.

Salter, H. E. Mediaeval Archives of the University of Oxford. 2 vols. Oxford, 1920–1.

Sundry Things from several hands concerning the University of Oxford [including a 'Model for a College Reformation': Christ Church is meant], 1659. Harleian Misc. ed T. Park, vol. vi, 1810.

Twyne, Brian. Antiquitatis Academiae Oxoniensis Apologia in tres libros. Oxford, 1608.

à Wood, A. Athenae Oxonienses. 2 vols. 1691–2; ed. P. Bliss, 4 vols. 1813–20.

à Wood, A. The History and Antiquities of the Colleges and Halls in the University of Oxford. Oxford, 1786.
—— The History and Antiquities of the University of Oxford. Ed. J. Gutch, 2 vols. Oxford, 1792–6.
—— Life and Times of, 1632–95, described by Himself. Ed. A. Clark, 5 vols. Oxford, 1889–1900.

(3) CAMBRIDGE

(a) *Cambridge Colleges*

College Histories Series. 1900–. [Various authors.]
The College Monographs. 1906. [Various authors.]
Wilson, J. Memorabilia Cantabrigiae. 1803.

(1) *Gonville and Caius.*

Venn, John. Annals of Gonville and Caius College. 1904.
Venn, J., Roberts, E. S. and Gross, E. J. Biographical History of Gonville and Caius College, 1349–1897. 4 vols. Cambridge, 1897–1912.

(2) *Christ's.*

Lloyd, A. H. Early History of Christ's College, Cambridge. 1934.
Rackham, H. Early Statutes of Christ's College with the Statutes of God's House. Cambridge, 1927.
Biographical Register of Christ's College, 1505–1905, and of God's House, 1448–1505. Ed. J. Peile, 2 vols. Cambridge, 1910–3.
Cooper, C. H. Memoir of Margaret, Countess of Richmond and Derby. Ed. J. E. B. Mayor, Cambridge, 1874.

(3) *Clare.*

[Forbes, M. D.] Clare College, 1326–1926. 2 vols. Cambridge, 1928–30.
Wardale, J. R. Clare College Letters and Documents. Cambridge, 1903.

(4) *Corpus.*

Masters, R. History of the College of Corpus Christi and the B. Virgin Mary. 2 vols. Cambridge, 1753; Cambridge, 1831 (with a Continuation by John Lamb).

(5) *Emmanuel.*

Dillingham, W. Vita L. Chadertoni una cum vita J. Usserii. Cambridge, 1700.
Shuckburgh, E. S. Laurence Chatterton, D.D.; translated from a Latin Memoir. Richard Farmer, D.D.: an Essay. Cambridge, 1884.

(6) *King's.*

Heywood, J. and Wright, T. The Ancient Laws of the Fifteenth Century for King's College, Cambridge, and for the Public School of Eton College. 1850.

(7) *Pembroke.*

Attwater, A. Pembroke College: A Short History. Cambridge, 1936.

(8) *Peterhouse.*

Walker, T. A. Biographical Register of Peterhouse Men, 1284–1616. 2 pts, Cambridge, 1927–30.
—— Admissions to Peterhouse. Cambridge, 1912.

(9) *Queens'.*

Searle, W. G. The History of the Queens' College of St Margaret and St Bernard in the University of Cambridge. Cambridge Antiquarian Soc. 1867–71.

(10) *St Catharine's.*

Jones, W. H. S. A History of St Catharine's College. Cambridge, 1936.
Philpott, H. Documents relating to St Catharine's College, Cambridge. Cambridge, 1861.

(11) *St John's.*

Baker, T. History of the College of St John the Evangelist, Cambridge. Ed. J. E. B. Mayor, 2 vols. Cambridge, 1869.
Hessels, J. H. Founding of Collegium Sancti Johannis Evangelistae. Early Statutes. Cambridge, 1918.
Howard, H. F. An Account of the Finances of the College of St John the Evangelist. Cambridge, 1935.
Mayor, J. E. B. Early Statutes of the College of St John. Cambridge, 1859.
Seward, A. C. Collegium Divi Johannis Evangelistae, 1511–1911. 1911 (priv. ptd).

(12) *Trinity.*

Ball, W. R. R. Cambridge Papers. 1918.
Ball, W. R. R. and Venn, J. A. Admissions to Trinity College, 1546–1900. 5 vols. Cambridge, 1913–16.

(b) *Cambridge University*

Ackermann, R. A History of the University of Cambridge: its Colleges, Halls and Public Buildings [by W. Combe]. 1815.
Caius, Joannes. De antiquitate Cantabrigiensis Academiae. 1568.
—— Historiae Cantabrigiensis Academiae ab Urbe condita Liber. 1574.
—— Works. Ed. J. Venn and E. S. Roberts, Cambridge, 1912.
Carter, E. History of the University of Cambridge to 1753 with a Particular Account of each College and Hall. 1753.
Clark, J. W. Cambridge: Brief Historical and Descriptive Notes. 1881.
—— Letters Patent of Elizabeth and James the First, addressed to the University of Cambridge. Ed. J. W. Clark, Cambridge, 1892.

Collection of Statutes for the University and the Colleges of Cambridge. [Ed. J. Heywood,] 1840.

Cooper, C. H. and T. Athenae Cantabrigienses. 2 vols. Cambridge, 1858–61.

Documents Relating to the University and Colleges of Cambridge. 3 vols. 1852. [Prepared for the Royal Commission of 1850–2.]

Dyer, G. History of the University and Colleges of Cambridge. 2 vols. 1814.

Fuller, Thomas. The History of the University of Cambridge. [In Church History of Britain, 1655. Ed. separately J. Nichols, 1840.]

Grace Books, 1454–1589. Ed. S. M. Leathes, M. Bateson, W. G. Searle and J. Venn, Cambridge, 1907–10.

Heywood, J. and Wright, T. Cambridge University Transactions during the Puritan Controversies of the 16th and 17th Centuries. 2 vols. 1854.

Lamb, J. A Collection of Letters, Statutes, and other Documents, from the MS Library of Corpus Christi College, Illustrative of the History of the University of Cambridge from A.D. MD to MDLXXII. 1838.

Langbaine, G. The Founding of the Universitie of Cambridge. 1651.

Mullinger, J. Bass. A History of the University of Cambridge: from the Earliest Times to the Close of the Platonist Movement. 3 vols. Cambridge, 1873–1911.

—— A History of the University of Cambridge. 1888.

—— Cambridge Characteristics in the 17th Century. 1867.

Neale, C. M. The Early Honours Lists (1498 to 1746–7) of the University of Cambridge. 1909.

Parker, Matthew. De Antiquitate Britannicae Ecclesiae. Ed. Samuel Drake, 1729. [Includes Academiae Historia Cantabrigiensis.]

P[arker], R[ichard]. Σκελετὸς Cantabrigiensis, Collegiorum Umbratilis Delineatio. [1622.] [Tr. 1721 as The History and Antiquities of the University of Cambridge. In Two Parts.]

Peacock, George. Observations on the Statutes of the University of Cambridge. 1841.

Robinson, Matthew. Autobiography. Ed. J. E. B. Mayor, Cambridge, 1856.

Sheppard, J. T. Richard Croke, a Sixteenth Century Don. Cambridge, 1919.

Venn, J. and Venn, J. A. Alumni Cantabrigienses. Pt I (to 1751). 4 vols. Cambridge, 1922–7.

[See also Enactments in Parliament under Oxford, p. 369 above.]

E. SCHOOLS

(1) GENERAL WORKS

Barnes, A. S. The Catholic Schools of England. 1926.

Carlisle, N. A Concise Description of the Endowed Grammar Schools in England and Wales. 2 vols. 1818.

Christie. R. C. The Old Church and School Libraries of Lancashire. Chetham Soc. 1885.

Conybeare, John (Schoolmaster at Molton, Devon, 1580, and at Swimbridge, 1594), Letters and Exercises of. Ed. F. C. Conybeare, 1905.

Enactments in Parliament. [See p. 369.]

Gascoigne, George. The Glasse of Governement. 1575. [Grammar-school studies.]

Grant, James. History of the Burgh and Parish Schools of Scotland. 1876.

Hazlitt, W. C. Schools, School-Books and Schoolmasters. 1888.

Knight, L. S. Welsh Independent Grammar Schools to 1600. Newtown, [1926].

Leach, A. F. Schools. Ency. Brit. 11th edn, 1911.

—— The Schools of Mediaeval England. 1915. [Contains a very full list of Leach's writings.]

—— Early Yorkshire Schools. 2 vols. Yorkshire Archaeological Soc. 1899–1903. [York, Beverley, Ripon, Pontefract, Howden, Northallerton, Acaster, Rotherham, Giggleswick, Sedbergh.]

—— Milton as Schoolboy and Schoolmaster. British Academy Lecture, 1908.

Minchin, J. G. C. Our Public Schools, their Influence on English History. 1901.

Motter, T. H. V. The School Drama in England. 1929.

Nedham, Marchamont. A Discourse concerning schools and schoolmasters. 1663.

Public Schools Inquiry Commission. Report of the Commissioners appointed to Enquire into Certain Colleges and Schools. 4 vols. 1864.

Sandys, Sir J. E. Schools and School-Books. [In Shakespeare's England, 2 vols. 1916.]

Schools Inquiry Commission. Report of the Commissioners appointed to Inquire into the Education given in the Schools of England [other than the Public Schools]. 21 vols. and 1 vol. of maps, 1867–8.

Staunton, Howard. The Great Schools of England. 1869.

Stow, John, and Strype, John. A Survey of the Cities of London and Westminster. 2 vols. 1720. [Public Schools of London, vol. I, ch. xxv, pp. 162–73; Disputations, vol. I, p. 124; Christ's Hospital, vol. I, pp. 174 ff.; Jesuit Schools in the Savoy, vol. II, pp. 107 f.; Westminster School, vol. II, pp. 8 f.; Tenison's School, vol. II, p. 73.]

Stowe, A. M. English Grammar Schools in the Reign of Queen Elizabeth. New York, 1908.
Watson, Foster. The Old Grammar Schools. Cambridge, 1916.
—— The English Grammar Schools to 1660: their Curriculum and Practice. Cambridge, 1908.

(2) Particular Schools

Ackermann, R. A History of the Colleges of Winchester, Eton and Westminster. 1816.

Abingdon.

Preston, A. E. The Church and Parish of St Nicholas, Abingdon. Oxford, 1929.

Birmingham.

Carter, W. F. and Barnard, E. A. B. The Records of King Edward's School, Birmingham. 3 vols. Dugdale Soc. 1924–33.

Bury St Edmunds.

Bury St Edmunds Grammar School. Library, I, 1910.

Canterbury School.

Leach, A. F. Times, 12 Sept. 1896, 7 Sept. 1897; Guardian, 12, 19 Jan. 1898; Times, 4, 6, 10 Jan. 1911.
Woodruff, C. E. and Cape, H. J. Schola Regia Cantuariensis: The King's School. 1908.

Charterhouse.

Bearcroft, P. Historical Account of Thomas Sutton Esq. and of his Foundation in Charter-House. 1737.
Brown, W. H. Charterhouse, Past and Present. Hospital and School. 1879.
Taylor, W. F. The Charterhouse of London. 1912.
Tod, A. H. Charterhouse. 1900.
Wilmot, E. P. E. and Streatfield, E. C. Charterhouse, Old and New. 1895.

Christ's Hospital.

Annals of Christ's Hospital from its Foundation. By a Blue. 1867.
Howes, John. The John Howes Manuscript, a Brief Note of the Order and Manner of the First Erection of the Three Royal Hospitals of Christ's, etc. Ed. W. Lemprière, 1904.
List of University Exhibitioners, 1566–1885. 1885.
Pearce, E. H. Annals of Christ's Hospital. 1908 (2nd edn).

Downside.

Birt, H. N. Downside. The History of St Gregory's School from its Commencement at Douay. 1902.

Dulwich.

Ormiston, T. L. Dulwich College Register, 1619–1926. [1926.]

Eton College.

Benson, A. C. Fasti Etonenses: Biographical History of Eton. Eton, 1899.
Brock, A. Clutton. Eton. 1900.
[Collins, W. L.] Etoniana, Ancient and Modern. Edinburgh, 1865.
Cust, L. History of Eton College. 1899.
Heywood, J. and Wright, T. The Ancient Laws of the Fifteenth Century for King's College, Cambridge, and for the Public School of Eton College. 1850.
Maxwell-Lyte, H. C. A History of Eton College, 1440–1910. 1873; 1911 (4th edn).
Sterry, W. Annals of the King's College of our Lady of Eton beside Windsor. 1898.
Thackeray, F. St J. Eton College Library. Eton, 1881.

Felsted.

Foundation Deeds of Felsted School. Ed. A. Clark, Oxford, 1916.

Guildford.

Williamson, G. C. The Royal Grammar School of Guildford, 1509. 1929.

Hadleigh.

[Hawkins, W.] Apollo Shroving, composed for the Schollars of the Free School of Hadleigh. [1627.]

Harrow.

The Harrow School Register, 1571–1800. Ed. W. T. J. Gunn, 1934.
Padmore, George, and the Harrow Vestry. Orders, Statutes and Rules to be Observed and Kept by the Free Grammar School at Harrow Founded by John Lyon 1590. 1833.
Scott, E. J. L. Records of the Grammar School. Harrow, 1886.
Thornton, P. M. Harrow School. 1885.
Williams, J. F. Harrow. 1901.

Hartlebury.

Robertson, D. The Old Order Book of Hartlebury Grammar School. Worcestershire Hist. Soc. 1904.

Leeds.

Price, A. C. A History of Leeds Grammar School from its Foundation. Leeds, 1919.

Magdalen.

Bayley, A. R. Magdalen College School, N. & Q. 8 July 1905–18 May 1907.

Manchester.

Latin Verses, etc. by Scholars of Manchester Grammar School 1640 and 1750–1800. Ed. A. A. Mumford, Chetham Misc. vol. IV, 1921.
Mumford, A. A. Manchester Grammar School. 1515–1915. 1919.

Whatton, W. R. History of the Foundation
in Manchester of the Free Grammar School.
4 vols. Manchester, 1828–48.

Merchant Taylors'.

Clode, C. M. The Early History of the Guild
of Merchant Taylors. 2 pts, 1888 (priv.
ptd).
—— Memorials of the Guild of Merchant
Taylors. 1875 (priv. ptd).
Merchant Taylors' School: its Origin, History
and Present Surroundings. 1930. [Various
contributors.]
Robinson, C. J. Register of the Merchant
Taylors' School, 1562–1874. 2 vols. Lewes,
1882–3.
Sayle, R. T. D. Annals of Merchant Taylors'
School Library. Library, xvi, 1935.
Wilson, H. B. The History of Merchant-
Taylors' School from its Foundation to the
Present Time. 2 pts, 1812–4.

Oakham.

Sargant, W. L. The Book of Oakham School.
Cambridge, 1928.

Perse.

Gray, J. M. A History of the Perse School,
Cambridge. Cambridge, 1921.

Repton.

Macdonald, Alec. A Short History of Repton.
1929.
Repton School Register, 1557–1922. Ed.
Minna Messiter, 2 pts, Repton, 1910–22.
Repton School Register, 1620–1894. Ed. F. C.
Hipkins, 1895.

Rugby.

Bettinson, G. H. Rugby School. Birmingham,
1930.
Bradby, H. C. Rugby. 1900.
Rouse, W. H. D. History of Rugby School.
1898.

Sedbergh.

Clarke, H. L. and Weech, N. W. History of
Sedbergh School, 1525–1925. Sedbergh,
1925.
Platt, A. E. The History of the Parish and
Grammar School of Sedbergh. 1876.
Sedbergh School Register, 1546–1895. Ed.
Bernard Wilson, Leeds, 1895.

Shrewsbury.

Blakeway, J. B. History of Shrewsbury
School. Shrewsbury, 1889.
Fisher, G. W. and Spencer Hill, J. Annals of
Shrewsbury School. 1899.
Oldham, J. B. Shrewsbury School Library.
Library Assoc. Record, vi, 1928.

St Paul's.

Gardiner, R. B. Admission Registers from
1748 to 1876. 1884. [Contains biographical
notices and notes on the earlier masters and
scholars of the school from the foundation.]
Leach, A. F. (with a Rejoinder by A. S.
Lupton). Journ. Education, June 1904, July,
Aug., Sept., 1909; Times, 2, 12 April 1904.
—— Archaeologia, lxii, 1910.
McDonnell, M. F. J. A History of St Paul's
School. 1909.

Stratford on Avon.

Leach, A. F. Shakespeare's School. Journ.
Education, Jan., March 1908. [See E. I.
Fripp and R. Savage, p. 366 above, and
Arthur Gray, A Chapter in the Early Life
of Shakespeare: Polesworth in Arden, Cam-
bridge, 1926.]

Tonbridge.

Rivington, S. History of Tonbridge School
from 1553. 1869.

Wakefield.

Peacock, H. M. History of the Free Grammar
School of Wakefield. 1892.

Warwick.

Leach, A. F. History of Warwick School. 1906.

Worcester.

Leach, A. F. Early Education in Worcester.
685–1770. Worcestershire Hist. Soc. 1913.

Westminster.

Airy, R. Westminster. 1902.
Barker, G. F. R. Memoirs of Richard Busby
(1606–1695). 1895.
Barker, G. F. R. and Stenning, A. H. Record
of Old Westminsters. A Biographical List
from the Earliest Times to 1927. 2 vols.
1928.
Forshall, F. H. Westminster School. 1884.
Leach, A. F. The Origin of Westminster
School. Journ. Education, Jan. 1905.
—— Nicholas Udall. Ency. Brit. 11th edn,
1910–11.
Sargeaunt, J. Annals of Westminster School.
1898.
Tanner, E. Westminster School. A History.
1934.
Welch, Joseph. A List of Scholars of St Peter's
College, Westminster, as they were Elected
to Christ Church College, Oxford, and
Trinity College, Cambridge, from 1561 to the
Present Time. [1788]; rev. 'By an old King's
Scholar,' 1852.

Winchester.

Adams, H. C. Wykehamica: a History of
Winchester College and Commoners from
the Foundation. 1878.

Chitty, H. Chaplains of Winchester College, 1417–1542. 1914.

Cook, A. K. About Winchester College: to which is prefixed De Collegio Wintoniensi by Robert Matthew. 1917.

Holgate, C. W. and Chitty, H. Winchester Long Rolls, 1653–1721. Winchester, 1899.
—— Winchester Long Rolls, 1723–1812. Winchester, 1904.

Kirby, T. F. Annals of Winchester College from the Foundation in the year 1382 to the Present Time. 1892.
—— Winchester Scholars: a List of the Wardens, Fellows and Scholars of St Mary College of Winchester. 1888.

Leach, A. F. A History of Winchester College. 1899.

Warner, R. F. Winchester. 1900.

Winchester College, 1393–1893. By Old Wykehamists. 1893.

Wolverhampton.

Mander, G. P. History of Wolverhampton Grammar School. Wolverhampton, 1913.

York.

Leach, A. F. Fortnightly Rev. Nov. 1892.

Raine, Angelo. History of St Peter's School. York, 1926.

Victoria History of the Counties of England:
Bedford. Vol. II, 1908, pp. 149–85.
Berkshire. Vol. II, 1907, pp. 245–84.
Buckingham. Vol. II, 1908, pp. 147–221.
Derby. Vol. II, 1907, pp. 207–81.
Durham. Vol. I, 1905, pp. 365–413.
Essex. Vol. II, 1907, pp. 501–64.
Gloucester. Vol. II, 1907, pp. 313–448.
Hampshire and the Isle of Wight. Vol. II, 1903, pp. 250–408.
Hertford. Vol. II, 1908, pp. 47–102.
Huntingdon. Vol. II, 1932.
Lancashire. Vol. II, 1908, pp. 561–614.
Lincoln. Vol. II, 1906, pp. 421–92.
Northampton. Vol. II, 1906, pp. 201–88.
Nottingham. Vol. II, 1910, pp. 179–250.
Rutland. Vol. I, 1908, pp. 259–300.
Somerset. Vol. II, 1911, pp. 435–65.
Suffolk. Vol. II, 1907, pp. 301–55.
Surrey. Vol. II, 1905, pp. 155–242.
Sussex. Vol. II, 1907, pp. 397–440.
Warwick. Vol. II, 1910, pp. 179–250.
Worcester. Vol. IV, 1924, pp. 473–540.
York. Vol. I, 1907, pp. 415–500.

F. SCHOOL BOOKS AND OTHER TEXT BOOKS

[For a long list of school books, 1500–1900, see Bernard Quaritch, A Catalogue (No. 464) of Early School Books, 1932. The section 'Scholars and Scholarship', pp. 852–63 below, will also be found to supplement the following lists.]

Watson, Foster. The Curriculum and Text Books of the English Schools in the First Half of the 17th Century. Trans. Bibliog. Soc. VI, 1901; 1903.

(1) SCHOOL BOOKS

Busby, Richard. A Short Institution of Grammar. 1647.
—— An English Introduction to the Latin Tongue. 1659.

Farnaby, T. Systema grammaticum. 1641.

Harmar, John. Praxis grammatica. 1623.

Holt, John. Lac Puerorum: Mylke for Children. [1510?] (de Worde); 1520 (Pynson). ['Much used' (A. à Wood). Two copies survive in BM.; fragments at Oxford and Cambridge.]

Horman, William. Vulgaria. 1519; rptd M. R. James, Oxford, 1926.

Lily, William. Absolutissimus de octo orationis partium Constructione Libellus. Basle, 1515. [With John Colet and Erasmus.]
—— Joannis Coleti Theologi, olim decani Divi Pauli Editio: una cum quisbusdam G. Lilii Grammatices Rudimentis. 1534. [With Colet, the source of the Eton Latin Grammar. See Stanbridge below.]
—— An Introduction to the Eyght Partes of Speche compiled and sette forthe by the commaundement of Henry VIII. 1542. [The compilation is attrib. to 'certain learned men meet for such a purpose'; but the earlier work of Stanbridge, Colet and Lily was liberally drawn upon.]

> Danes, John. A Light to Lilie. 1637.
> Granger, Thomas. Syntagma grammatica or an easie explanation of Lilie's Grammar. 1616.
> Hayne (or Haine), William. Lilies Rules construed. 1642.
> Hoole, Charles. Lily's Latin Grammar fitted for the use of schools. 1651.

Linacre, Thomas. Rudimenta Grammatices diligenter castigata denuo. [*c.* 1523–4.]

Plimpton, G. A. The Education of Shakespeare illustrated from School Books in Use in his Time. 1933.

Shaw, A. E. The Earliest Latin Grammars in English. Trans. Bibliog. Soc. V, 1899.

Shirley, James. Via ad Latinam complanata. 1649.
—— Manductio or a leading of children by the hand through the principles of grammar. 1660.

Stanbridge, John. The Accidence of mayster Stanbridges owne makynge. [Rouen, 1505.] [Many edns after Stanbridge's death (1510) with title, Accidentia.]
—— Vulgaria Stanbrigi. 1508.
—— Vocabula. 1510.
—— Parvulorum Institutio. [Before 1513.]

Whittinton, Robert. Declinationes nominum. [1515?]; 1517 (as Editio Roberti Whittentoni Grammatices). [14 other edns by 1533. The edns of Whittinton's school grammar books fill more than 4 columns in A. W. Pollard and G. R. Redgrave, A Short-Title Catalogue of Books printed in England, 1475–1640, 1926.]
—— The Vulgaria of John Stanbridge and the Vulgaria of Robert Whittinton. Ed. B. White, EETS. 1933.

Woodward, Ezekias. A childes patrimony. 1640.
—— Vestibulum or a manuduction towardes a faire edifice. 1640.
—— A Light to Grammar. 1641.

The Gate of Tongues Series. [Introduced by William Bathe; the plan of the series is explained in the title-page of William Bathe, Janua Linguarum sive modus quo patefit aditus ad omnes linguas intelligendas. In qua totius linguae Vocabula quae frequentiora et fundamentalia sunt, continentur, nullo repetito, 1623. Original edn, Salamanca, 1611. English edns of 1615, 1623 have an English trn by W. Welde.]

Barbier, Jean. Janua Linguarum Quadrilinguis, or a Messe of Tongues: Latine, English, French and Spanish. 1617.
Comenius (J. A. Komensky). Porta Linguarum trilinguis [Latin, English, French] reserata: The Gate of Tongues unlocked. 1631. [This is the first English version of an original dated 4 March 1631; see Comenius, Opera Didactica Omnia, Amsterdam, 1657, p. 254.]
Comenius, J. A., Horn, T. and Robothan, T. The Gate of Tongues unlocked. 1643. [Trn.]
Grave, Jean de. The Pathway to the Gate of Tongues. 1633.
Hartlib, Samuel. True and readie Way to learn the Latin Tongue. 1654.

Cordier, Maturin. Colloquiorum scholasticorum Libri IV ad pueros in sermone Latino paulatim exercendos. Lyons, 1564. Tr. Charles Hoole, 1657 (as School Colloquies, English and Latine).
—— Corderius Dialogues. Translated Grammatically. By John Brinsley. 1614; 1625; 1636.
Culmann, Leonhard. Sententiae pueriles. Leipzig, 1544. Tr. Charles Hoole, 1658 (as Sentences for Children).
Erasmus, D. Adagia. Venice. 1508. [Many later edns.]
—— Colloquiorum Formulae [more familiarly, Colloquia]. Basle, 1516, 1523 (and other later and enlarged edns).
Hermes Anglo-Latinus or directions for young Latinists to speak Latin purely. 1639.

Murray, David. Some Early Grammars and other School Books in Use in Scotland. Glasgow Royal Philosophical Soc. 2 pts, 1905–6.
Stockwood, John. A Bartholomew fairing for Parentes. 1589.
—— Disputatiuncularum grammaticalium Libellus. 1598; 1619 (4th edn). [School disputations.]
Vives, J. L. Exercitatio Linguae Latinae. Paris, 1539. Tr. Foster Watson, 1908 (as Tudor Schoolboy Life).

Catho [Cato] pro pueris. 1513. [STC.: the first of 24 entries, 1513–1636, of the Moral Distichs attrib. to 'Cato.']
Comenius, J. A. Orbis sensualium Pictus. Nuremberg, 1658. Tr. Charles Hoole, 1659 (as Comenius's Visible World or a Picture and Nomenclature of all the chief things).
Ockland, C. Anglorum Praelia, ab anno domini 1327 usque ad annum 1558. Carmine summatim perstricta. 1580.
—— De pacatissimo Angliae statu imperante Elizabetha compendiosa Narratio. Haec duo Poëmata, Regiae Majestatis Consiliarii in omnibus hujus regni Scholis praelegenda pueris praescripserunt. 2 pts, 1582.
Terentius Christianus: utpote comediis sacris transformatus: quo purissimi sermonis elegantia linguam exornet et politis moribus ac insigni pietate mentem imbuat. Cologne, 1591; 1607.
Vergil, Polydore. Angliae Historiae Libri XXVI. Basle, 1534. [An Act of the Privy Council, 1582, ordered the book to be read in schools.]
Whytyngton (Whittinton), Robert. A lytel booke of good manners for children: into the englishe tonge. 1532. [Tr. from Erasmus, De civilitate morum puerilium, 1526.]

Baret, J. An Alvearie: or triple Dictionarie, in Englishe, Latin, and French. [1573.]
Cooper, T. Thesaurus Linguae Romanae et Britannicae. 1565; 1578.
Elyot, Sir Thomas. The Dictionary of Syr T. Elyot. 1538.
Gregory, Francis. Greek-Latin Lexicon. 1654.
Leuins, P. Manipulus Vocabularum. 1570.
Ortus [Hortus] Vocabulorum. Westminster, 1500. [8 other edns by 1532.]
Rider, John. Bibliotheca Scholastica: a double Dictionary. Oxford, 1589. [Latin-English, English-Latin.]
Thomas, Thomas. Dictionarium linguae Latinae et Anglicanae. [1588?]
Withal, John. A shorte Dictionarie for Yonge Beginners gathered of good authors. 1562.

Camden, William. Institutio graecae grammatices. 1595.

Caninius, Angelus. 'Ελληνισμός in quo quicquid vetustissimi scriptores praecipiunt facili modo exponuntur. Paris, 1555; 1613. [Charged two shillings in an Eton bill of 1613.]

Cheke, Sir John. De Pronunciatione Graecae linguae Disputationes cum Stephano Wintoniensi Episcopo. Basle, 1555.

Dugard, William. Rudimenta graecae linguae. 1656.

Grant, Edward. τῆς 'Ελληνικῆς Γλώσσης σταχυολογία: Graecae linguae Spicilegium. 1575.

Lubin, Eilhard. Clavis graecae linguae. 1620.

Robertson, W. The First Gate to the Holy Tongue [Hebrew]. The Second Gate. 2 pts, [1654].

Shirley, James. 'Εισαγωγή sive Introductorium Complectens colloquia familiaria, Aesopi fabulas et Luciani selectiores mortuorum Dialogos. 1656.

Stockwood, J. Progymnasma Scholasticum h. e. Epigrammatum Graecorum ex Anthologia. 1597.

Grotius, Hugo. Baptizatorum puerorum Institutio. Ed. N. Grey and John Hales, 1647. [Metrical version by Francis Goldsmith, Greek by Christopher Wase, Biblical proofs by Grey.]

Nowell, Alexander. A Catechism or first instruction of Christian religion. 1570.

—— Catechismus sive prima institutio disciplinaque pietatis Christianae. 1570. Tr. Greek, 1573.

—— Catechismus parvus pueris primum Latine qui ediscatur proponendus in scholis. 1573.

Primers of 1535, 1539, 1545. Three Primers put forth in the reign of Henry VIII. Oxford, 1848 (2nd edn).

Barton, W. The Art of Rhetorik concisely handled. 1634.

Clarke, John. Dux Oratorius. 1653.

—— Formulae Oratoriae in usum scholarum. 1632 (4th edn).

Cox, L. The arte or crafte of Rhethoryke. [1524.]

Farnaby, Thomas. Index Rhetoricus. 1625.

—— Troposchematologia: maximam partem ex Indice Rhetorico Farnabii deprompta: additis insuper Anglicanis exemplis. 1648.

Fraunce, A. The Arcadian Rhetorike: or the praecepts of Rhetorike made plaine by examples. [1584.]

Gregory, Francis. Instruction concerning the Art of Oratory for the use of schools. 1659.

Guarna, Andreas. Grammaticale Bellum Nominis et Verbi Regum, de principalitate orationis inter se contendentium. Strasburg,

1512. Tr. Eng. W. Hayward, 1569 (as Bellum Grammaticale, A Discourse of great war and dissention betwene two worthy Princes, the Noune and the Verbe contending for the chief place or dignity in Oration).

Mulcaster, Richard. The First Part of the Elementarie which entreateth chefelie of the right writing of our English tung. 1582; ed. E. T. Campagnac, Oxford, 1925.

Peacham, H. The Garden of Eloquence, conteyning the figures of Grammar and Rhetorick. 1577.

Rainolde, R. A booke called the Foundacion of Rhetorike. 1563.

Sherry, R. A treatise of Schemes & Tropes gathered out of the best Grammarians & Orateurs, written fyrst in Latin by Erasmus of Roterodame. [1550.]

Susenbrotus, Joannes. Epitome Troporum ac Schematum et grammaticorum et rhetorum. Zurich, [1540?]. [London edns, 1562, 1570, 1608, 1621, 1627, 1635.]

Wilson, Sir Thomas. The rule of reason, conteining the Arte of Logique. 1551.

—— The Arte of Rhetorique, for the use of all suche as are studious of eloquence. 1553; rptd Oxford, 1909 (from 1584 edn).

A. B. C. both in Latyn and Englishe. Being a Facsimile Reprint of the Earliest Extant English Reading Book. Ed. E. S. Shuckburgh, 1889. [Before 1538.]

A new booke of spelling. 1610.

Bullokar, William. A Booke at Large for the Amendment of Orthographie for English Speech. 1580. [See T. Warton, A History of English Poetry, ed. W. C. Hazlitt, vol. IV, 1871, p. 250.]

Butler, Charles. The English Grammar or the Institution of letters, syllables and woords in the English tung. Oxford, 1634.

Clement, F. The Petie Schole of spelling and writing in English, with an English orthographie. 1587.

[Cooke, E.] The Englishe Scholemaister. 1596.

Cotgrave, R. A Dictionarie of the French and English Tongues. 1611; 1632; 1650; 1660; 1673.

Daines, Simon. Orthoepia anglicana: or the first part of the English grammar. 1640.

Greaves, Paul. Grammatica anglicana. Cambridge, 1594.

Hart, John. An Orthographie. 1569.

—— A methode or comfortable beginning for all unlearned to read English. 1570.

Hewes, John. A perfect Survey of the English tongue. 1624.

Lloyd, Richard. The Schoolmaster's Auxiliaries to read and write English dexterously [and] Latin in prose and verse. 1653–4.

Poole, Joshua. The English Accidence. 1655.
—— The English Parnassus or a help to English poesy. 1657.
Robertson, George. Learning's Foundation firmly laid in a short method of teaching to read English. 1651.
Wharton, J. A new English grammar. 1655.
Field, E. M. The Child and his Book. Some Account of the History and Progress of Children's Literature in England. [1891.]
Tuer, A. W. History of the Horn-Book. 2 vols. 1896.
—— Forgotten Children's Books. 1898–9.

(2) OTHER TEXT BOOKS

[These deal with subjects not usually taught in schools during this period.]

Bales, Peter. The writing schoolemaster. 1589.
—— The arte of brachygraphie: the order of orthographie: the key of kalygraphie. 1590.
Bright, T. Characterie. 1588.
Davies, John. The Writing Schoole-master. 1636 (16th edn).
Folkingham, William. Brachigraphy: or the art of short writing. 1620.
Gething, Richard. Calligraphotechnica: or the art of faire writing. 1619.
Willis, J. Stenography. 1602. [Many later edns.]
De la Mothe, G. The French Alphabet teaching in a very short time, by a most easie way, to pronounce French naturally, to reade it perfectly, to write it truly. Together with the Treasure of the French tongue. 2 pts, 1595–6.
Desainliens, Claude [Claudius Hollyband]. The French Littelton: a most easie way to learne the frenche tongue. 1566.
—— The French Schoolemaister. 1573. [Many later edns before 1640. New edn 'corrected and enriched' by Jas. Giffard, 1660. See A. W. Pollard, Trans. Bibliog. Soc. xiii, 1915, and A. E. M. Kirwood, Library, xii, 1931.]
—— The pretie and wittie historie of Arnalt and Lucenda with certain rules and dialogues for the learner of the Italian tong. 1575.
—— Claudii a Sancto Vinculo de pronuntiatione linguae gallicae libri duo. 2 pts, 1580.
—— Campo di Fior or else the flourie field of foure languages Latine, French, English but chiefly of the Italian tongue. 1583.
Duwes, Giles. An Introductorie for to lerne Frenche. [1534?] [Other edns doubtfully assigned to 1539, 1540, 1545.]
Florio, J. A Worlde of Wordes, Italian and English. 1598. [See F. A. Yates, John Florio, Cambridge, 1934, on Tudor and later modern language tutors.]
Palsgrave, John. Lesclarcissement de la langue francoyse. 2 pts, 1530.
Percyvall, Richard. Bibliotheca Hispanica containing a grammar with a dictionarie in Spanish, English and Latin. 2 pts, 1591.
Wodroephe, John. The Spared Houres of a Souldier in his Travels or the True Marrowe of the French Tongue with two rare and excellent Books of Dialogues. Dort, 1623; 1625.

Minsheu, John. Ἡγεμὼν εἰς τὰς γλώσσας id est Ductor in Linguas, the Guide to Tongues. In undecim linguis. 1617; 1626.
—— The Guide into the Tongues with their agreement and consent one with another, as also their etymologies [and] derivations of all the most part of words in eleven languages. 1627. [The languages are English, Welsh, Dutch, German, French, Italian, Spanish, Portuguese, Latin, Greek, Hebrew.]
Fox, G., Stubs, J. and Furley, B. A Battle-Door for Teachers and Professors to learn Singular and Plural. Also examples in several languages. In this Book are contained several bad unsavoury Words gathered forth of certain School-Books, which have been taught Boyes in England, which is a Rod and a Whip to School-Masters who teach such Books. 1660.

Barton, W. Arithmeticke abreviated. 1634.
Billingsley, Sir Henry. The Elements of Geometrie of Euclide of Megara. Faithfully (now first) translated into the Englishe Toung. [1570.] [Preface by John Dee on the mathematical sciences and their application, with 'certaine new Secrets, Mathematicall and Mechanicall.' The first English Euclid.]
Blagrave, John. The Mathematical Jewel. 1585.
Dansie, John. A mathematicall manuel. 1627.
Gray, Dionis. The Storehouse of Brevitie in woorkes of Arithmetike. 1577.
Harpur, John. The Jewell of Arithmetick. 1617.
Hill, Thomas. The Arte of vulgar Arithmeticke. 1592. [The title-page of the 1600 edn indicates the purposes of all the arithmetical and mathematical books then written—purposes with which the school had no concern. Hill describes the art of vulgar arithmetic as 'a knowledge pleasant for Gentlemen, commendable for Capteines and Soldiers, profitable for Merchants, and generally necessary for all estates and degrees'.]
An Introduction for to lerne to recken with the Pen. 1539. [As opposed to the counting board.]

An Introduction of Algorisme. 1574. [Rev. from previous item.]

Lyte, Henry. The Art of Tens or decimall arithmeticke. 1619.

Napier, John. Mirifici logarithmorum canonis Descriptio. Edinburgh, 1614.

Oughtred, William. Arithmeticae Institutio; totius Mathematicae Clavis. 1631.

—— The Key of the Mathematicks new Forged and Filed. 1647.

    Cajori, F. William Oughtred. Chicago, 1916.

Recorde, Roberte. The Ground of Artes, teaching the woorke and practise of Arithmetike both in whole numbres and fractions etc. [c. 1542]. [This is the date of the 1st edn given by D. E. Smith, Rara Arithmetica (1908), p. 213. The edn which he describes is of 1558. See also A. De Morgan, Arithmetical Books, p. 22. Like many of these early mathematical works, the 1558 title-page has a drawing of a teacher and a group of pupils and, as always, these pupils are grown men.]

—— The Whetstone of Witte, which is the seconde parte of Arithmetike: containyng thextraction of Rootes, the Cossike practise [i.e. Algebra] with the rule of Equation; and the woorkes of Surde Nombres. 1557.

—— Record's Arithmetick augmented by M. John Dee [and John Mellis]. 1658.

—— Pathway to Knowledge. 1551. [The 'enunciations' of Euclid, bks I–IV, with practical applications.]

—— The Castle of Knowledge. (Containing the explication of the sphere, both celestiall and materiall.) 1556.

Steele, R. The Earliest Arithmetics in English. EETS. 1922.

—— Early Printed English Books on Arithmetic. Trans. Bibliog. Soc. IV, 1898.

Tap, J. Pathway to Knowledge. The Whole Art of Arithmeticke. 1613.

Tonstall, Cuthbert. De Arte Supputandi Libri IV. 1522. [The earliest English-printed book on arithmetic; the work is in Latin. Tonstall, in his dedicatory epistle to Thomas More, explains that the book is written in order to facilitate honest dealing between buyer and seller.]

Wythers, S. A briefe chronicle of the foure principall empyres. 1563. [A trn of Sleidanus's De IV Summis Imperiis.]

G. THE DOCTRINE OF COURTESY

Babees Book, the Bokes of Nurture of Hugh Rhodes and John Russell. Ed. F. J. Furnivall, EETS. 1868.

Blundeville, T. M. Blundeville his Exercises, containing Six Treatises in Cosmographie,

Astronomie, and Geographie as also in the Arte of Navigation. 1594. [Containing eight treatises.]

Brathwait, Richard. The English Gentleman: containing sundry excellent rules of every Gentleman of selecter ranke. 1630.

—— The English Gentleman and the English Gentlewoman. 1641.

Casa, Giovanni della. Il Galateo. Florence, 1560.

    Galateo done into English by R. Peterson. 1576; ed. H. J. Reid, 1892 (priv. ptd); ed. J. E. Spingarn, Boston, 1914. [See Waker below.]

Castiglione, Baldassare. Il Cortegiano. Venice, 1528.

    The Courtyer divided into foure books done into Englyshe by Thomas Hoby. 1561; ed. Sir Walter Raleigh, 1900.

Cleland, James. Ἡρωπαιδεία or the institution of a young noble man. Oxford, 1607, 1612 (as The instruction of a young nobleman.)

Cuningham, W. The Cosmographical Glasse conteinyng the pleasant Principles of Cosmographie, Geographie, Hydrographie or Navigation. 1559.

Cyvile and uncyvile Life: a discourse where is disputed what order of lyfe best beseemeth a gentleman. 1579. [Re-issued 1586 as The English Courtier and the cuntrey Gentleman. See Guazzo below.]

Digges, Leonard and Thomas. An Arithmetical Militare Treatise named Stratioticos for the Profession of a Soldiour. 1572. [Arithmetic, algebra; military discipline; camps and their governance.]

Elyot, Sir Thomas. The Boke named the Governour. 1531; ed. H. H. S. Croft, 2 vols. 1880; ed. Foster Watson, 1907 (Everyman's Lib.).

Ferne, Sir John. The Blazon of Gentrie. 1586.

Furnivall, F. J. Education in Early England. EETS. 1867.

—— Manners and Meals in the Olden Time. EETS. 1868. [A miscellany containing Stans Puer ad Mensam, two Bokes of Nurture, Bokes of Kervynge, of Curtasye, the Schoole of Vertue, etc., all of 15th and 16th cents.]

Gent, J. B. Heroick Education. 1656.

Gerbier, Sir Balthazar (of the Academy at Bethnal Green). The Interpreter of the Academie for Forrain Languages and all Noble Sciences, and Exercises, concerning Military Architecture or Fortifications. 1648.

—— Treatie of Fortifications. The Interpreter, etc. 1648.

—— The First Lecture concerning Navigation read publickly at Sir Balthazar Gerbier's Academy at Bednal-Greene. 1649.

Gerbier, Sir Balthazar. A Series of Six Lectures read publickly at [Gerbier's] Academy. 1649–50. [Cosmography, navigation, the creation of the world (lecture by Henry Walker), fortification, the art of speaking well.]

—— A Public Lecture on all the Languages, Arts, Sciences, and Noble Exercises, which are taught in Sr Balthazar Gerbier's Academy. 1650.

Gilbert, Sir Humphrey. Queene Elizabethes Achademy. 1572; rptd EETS. Ex. Ser. 1869.

Greville, Fulke (Baron Brooke). The Life of the renowned Sr Philip Sidney. 1652; ed. N. Smith, Oxford, 1907.

Guazzo, Stefano. La civil conversatione. Venice, 1577.
Civile Conversation. [Trn of bks I to III by George Pettie (1581), of bk IV by B. Young, 1586.] Ed. Sir E. Sullivan, 2 vols. 1925.

Guevara, Antonio de. The Diall of Princes, Englysshed out of the Frenche by Thomas North. 1557.

—— Libro del emperador Marco aurelio con relox de principes. Valladolid, 1529.

—— The Dial of Princes (with the famous booke of Marcus Aurelius). Englished by T. North. 2 pts, 1568.

—— The Diall of Princes. Select Passages, with an Introduction and a Bibliography by K. N. Colville. 1919.

Herbert, Edward (Baron Herbert of Cherbury). The Life, written by himself. 1764; ed. Sir S. Lee, 1886.

Higford, William. The Institution of a Gentleman. 3 pts, 1660.

Humphrey, Laurence. The Nobles: or Of Nobilitye. 1561.

Hutchinson, Lucy. Memoirs of the Life of Colonel Hutchinson. Ed. Julius Hutchinson, 1806; ed. Sir C. H. Firth, 1906.

The Institucion of a Gentleman. 1555.

Kelso, Ruth. The Doctrine of the English Gentleman in the Sixteenth Century. Urbana, 1929.

K[epers], J. The Courtiers Academie. [1598.] [Tr. from the Discorsi of Annibale Romei.]

Kynaston, Francis. The constitutions of the Museum Minervae [in Covent Garden, London]. 1636.

La Primaudaye, Pierre de. L'Académie françoise. Paris, 1577.
Bowes, J[erome?]. The French Academy. 1577.
The French Academie, wherin is discoursed the institution of maners. Tr. Eng. T[homas] B[owes? or Thomas Beard?]. 1586.
The French Academie fully finished in foure bookes. 4 pts, 1618.

Lyly, J. Euphues and his Ephoebus. [In Euphues, The Anatomy of Wit, 1578.]

M[arkham], G[ervase]. The Gentlemans Academie or the Booke of S. Albans reduced into a better method. 1595.

Mason, John E. Gentlefolk in the Making. Studies in the History of English Courtesy Literature. Philadelphia, 1935.

Mathematical and Military Lecture in Leadenhall. [c. 1582.] [See Strype's Stow, vol. I, p. 125, 1720. Virtually an Officers Training Corps.]

Milton, John. Of Education. 1644.

Overend, G. H. A. A Prince's School Books. Library, II, 1890. [James VI, aet. 10.]

Peacham, Henry. The Compleat Gentleman, fashioning him absolut in the most necessary and commendable Qualities concerning Minde or Body that may be required in a Noble Gentleman. 1622; ed. G. S. Gordon, Oxford, 1906 (from 1634 edn).

—— The Gentleman's Exercise for drawing all manner of Beasts. 1612.

Percy, Henry (Duke of Northumberland). Advice to his Son. Ed. G. B. Harrison, 1930.

Philibert de Vienne. The Philosopher of the Court, Englished by George North. 1575.

Randolph, Thomas. The Drinking Academy. Ed. S. A. Tannenbaum, and Hyder E. Rollins, 1930. [A satire on the Courtly Academics.]

Russell, John. The Boke of Nurture folowyng England's Gise. [See Babees Book above.]

Saviolo, V. Vincentio Saviolo his Practise. 2 pts, 1595.

[Segar, Sir William.] The Booke of Honor and Armes. 1590.

Segar, Sir William. Honor, Military and Civill. 1602.

Selden, J. Titles of Honour. 1614.

Sidney, Sir P. The Correspondence between Sir Philip Sidney and H. Languet with Notes and a Memoir of Sidney. Ed. S. A. Pears, 1845.

W[aker], N[athaniel]. The Refined Courtier or a correction of several indecencies crept into civil conversation. 1663. [Translation and abridgement of Il Galateo of Giovanni della Casa.]

H. EDUCATION OF WOMEN AND GIRLS

Ballard, G. Memoirs of several Ladies of Great Britain. Oxford, 1752.

Brathwait, Richard. The English Gentlewoman drawne out to the full body: expressing what habiliments do best attire her. 1631.

Bruts, G. M. The necessarie, fit and convenient education of a yong gentlewoman. Tr. W. P. 1598.

Cavendish, Margaret (Duchess of Newcastle). A True Relation of the Life of. Ed. Sir S. E. Brydges, 1814. [Rptd from Natures Pictures, 1656.]

Gosynhill, Edward. The Prayse of all Women, called Mulierum Pean. [1542?]
—— The vertuous scholehous of ungracious women. [1550.]
—— The Schole house of Women. 1572.

M[arkham], G[ervase]. The English Hous-Wife, containing the inward and outward Vertue which ought to be in a Compleat Woman, as her Skill in Physic, Cookery, Extraction of Oyles, Ordering of great feastes. 1631.

Mulcaster, Richard. Positions. 1581; ed. R. H. Quick, 1887.

Watson, Foster. Vives and the Renascence Education of Women. 1912.

Wright, L. B. The Reading of Renaissance English Women. Stud. Phil. xxviii, 1931.

J. W. A.

V. THE SOCIAL BACKGROUND

Social Life in General: Bibliographies; Anthologies; Collections of Public Documents; Topographical Surveys and Descriptions; Letters, Diaries, Autobiographies, Memoirs and Miscellaneous Private Documents; Modern Studies and Surveys.

Particular Aspects of Social Life: London and the Life of the Town; The Art of War; Navigation and Seamanship; Agriculture and Gardening; The Fine Arts; Sports and Pastimes; Heraldry; Cookery Books.

[Aspects of English social life are also reflected in the following sections: Education (pp. 364–80 above); Minor Popular Literature (pp. 712–21 below); Character-Books and Essays (pp. 721–6 below); News-Sheets and News-Books (pp. 736–63 below); Books of Travel (pp. 763–98 below); and Science and Pseudo-Science (pp. 879–94 below). An attempt has been made not to duplicate these sections here and they should constantly be borne in mind.]

A. SOCIAL LIFE IN GENERAL

(1) BIBLIOGRAPHIES

[Hart, W. H.] Index Expurgatorius Anglicanus. 5 pts, 1872–8. [A *catalogue raisonné* of books prohibited in England, 1523–1681.]

Shakespeare's England. An Account of the Life and Manners of his Age. 2 vols. Oxford, 1916. [Ed. Sir Sidney Lee and C. T. Onions. Each ch. has a bibliography.]

Bibliography of British History, Stuart Period, 1603–1714. Ed. G. Davies, Oxford, 1928.

Bibliography of British History, Tudor Period, 1485–1603. Ed. C. Read, Oxford, 1933.

(2) ANTHOLOGIES

[For more specialized items the list of Collections of Reprints, pp. 317–9 above, should be consulted.]

Social England Illustrated. Ed. A. Lang, 1903. (Arber's English Garner.)
Tudor Tracts, 1532–1588. Ed. A. F. Pollard, 1903. (English Garner.)
Stuart Tracts, 1603–93. Ed. Sir C. H. Firth, 1903. (English Garner.)
Life in Shakespeare's England. A Book of Elizabethan Prose. Ed. J. D. Wilson, Cambridge, 1911.
Readings in English Social History to 1837. Ed. R. B. Morgan, 1923.
Tudor Economic Documents. Ed. R. H. Tawney and Eileen Power, 3 vols. 1924.
England in Shakespeare's Day. Ed. G. B. Harrison, 1928.

(3) COLLECTIONS OF PUBLIC DOCUMENTS

[The principal collections are listed under Sources in the section on The Political Background, pp. 396–400 below. It has not seemed necessary to repeat these here and the following list is only to be regarded as supplementary.]

A Booke containing all such Proclamations as were published during the Raigne of the Late Queene Elizabeth. Ed. Humphrey Dyson, 1618.

A Collection of Ordinances and Regulations for the Government of the Royal Household. Soc. Antiquaries, 1790.

A Complete Collection of State Trials. Ed. T. B. Howell, 34 vols. 1809.

Accounts of Revels at Court, under Elizabeth and James. Ed. Peter Cunningham, Shakespeare Soc. 1842.

Calendar of State Papers, Domestic Series. Henry VIII. Ed. J. S. Brewer, J. Gairdner and R. H. Brodie, 21 vols. 1862–1910. Edward VI, Mary, Elizabeth, and James I. Ed. R. Lemon and M. A. E. Green, 12 vols. 1856–72. Charles I. Vols. i–xii (1625–38), ed. J. Bruce, 1858–69; vol. xiii (1638–9), ed. J. Bruce and W. D. Hamilton, 1871; vols. xiv–xxii (1639–49), ed. W. D. Hamilton, 1873–93; Addenda (1639–49), ed. W. D. Hamilton and S. C. Lomas, 1897. Commonwealth and Protectorate (1649–60). Ed. M. A. E. Green, 15 vols. 1875–86.

Lancashire and Cheshire Wills and Inventories. Ed. J. G. Piecope, 3 pts, Chetham Soc. 1857–61.

A Selection of the Wills of Eminent Persons, preserved in the Prerogative Court of Canterbury, 1495–1695. Ed. J. G. Nichols and J. Bruce, Camden Soc. 1863.

State Trials, Political and Social. Ed. H. L. Stephen, 4 vols. 1899–1902.

Bibliotheca Lindesiana. A Bibliography of Royal Proclamations, 1485–1714. Ed. Robert Steele, 2 vols. Oxford, 1910.

The Official Papers of Sir Nathaniel Bacon of Stiffkey, Norfolk, as Justice of the Peace, 1580–1620. Ed. H. W. Saunders, Royal Hist. Soc. 1915.

(4) TOPOGRAPHICAL SURVEYS AND DESCRIPTIONS

[A very much fuller list will be found in the section 'Descriptions of the British Isles', pp. 773–7 below. The following list has been restricted to titles not appearing there.]

A Relation or rather a True Account of the Isle of England about the Year 1500. Ed. and tr. from Italian C. A. Sneyd, Camden Soc. 1847.

Leland, John. The Laboryouse Journey and Serche of J. Leylande for Englandes Antiquites. 1549.

—— The Itinerary. Ed. T. Hearne, 9 vols. Oxford, 1710–2; ed. L. T. Smith, 5 vols. 1906–10.

—— J. Lelandi de Rebus Britannicis Collectanea. Ed. T. Hearne, 6 vols. Oxford, 1715.

Perlin, Estienne. Description des Royaulmes d'Angleterre et d'Escosse. Paris, 1558; ed. R. Gough, 1775.

Smith, William. The Particular Description of England. 1588; ed. H. B. Wheatley and E. W. Ashbee, 1879.

Hentzner, Paulus. Itinerarium Germaniae; Galliae; Angliae; Italiae. Nuremberg, 1612; ed. and tr. Horace Walpole, 1797 (English section only, as Travels in England during the Reign of Queen Elizabeth).

Moryson, Fynes. An Itinerary (containing his Ten Yeares Travell through Germany, Bohmerland, France, England, Scotland and Ireland). 3 pts, 1617; 4 vols. Glasgow, 1907–8 (adds pt IV).

Zeiller, M. Itinerarii Galliae et Magnae Britanniae. 2 pts, Strasburg, 1634.

(5) LETTERS, DIARIES, AUTOBIOGRAPHIES, MEMOIRS AND MISCELLANEOUS PRIVATE DOCUMENTS[1]

(a) *Collections of Letters, Diaries, Memoirs, etc.*

[A few minor historical, or professedly historical, works are included here. The principal contemporary annals and histories are listed under Sources in the section on The Political Background, pp. 396–400 above, and have not been repeated; but they should not be overlooked as they contain much incidental social information.]

Foxe, John. Actes and Monuments. 1563; ed. J. Pratt, 8 vols. 1877.

Naunton, Sir Robert. Fragmenta Regalia, or Observations on Queen Elizabeth her Times and Favorites. 1641; ed. Sir Walter Scott, Edinburgh, 1808; ed. E. Arber, 1870.

Wilson, Arthur. The History of Great Britain, being the Life and Reign of James I. 1653.

Cabala, sive Scrinia Sacra. Mysteries of State and Government in Letters of illustrious Persons. 2 pts, 1654.

Fuller, Thomas. The Church-History of Britain. 1655; ed. J. S. Brewer, 6 vols. Oxford, 1875–8.

—— The History of the Worthies of England. 1662; ed. J. Nichols, 2 vols. 1811.

Finett, Sir John. Finetti Philoxenis. Ed. J. Howell, 1656.

Winstanley, William. England's Worthies. 1660.

Lloyd, D. Memoirs of Excellent Personnages. 1668.

Walton, Izaak. The Lives of Donne, Wotton, Hooker, Herbert. 1670; ed. A. Dobson, 2 vols. 1898.

à Wood, Anthony. Athenae Oxonienses. 2 vols. 1691–2; ed. P. Bliss, 6 vols. 1813–20.

Bohun, Edmund. The Character of Queen Elizabeth. 1693.

Strype, John. Annals of the Reformation. 2 pts, 1709–8; 4 vols. Oxford, 1824 (enlarged).

A Collection of Letters from the Original Manuscripts. Ed. L. Howard, 2 vols. 1753.

Harington, Sir John, et al. Nugae Antiquae. Ed. H. Harington, 2 vols. 1769–75; ed. T. Park, 2 vols. 1804.

A Collection of Original Royal Letters written by King Charles the First and Second, King James the Second, and the King of Bohemia; together with Original Letters written by Prince Rupert, Charles Louis Count Palatine, the Duchess of Hanover, and several other distinguished Persons; from 1619 to 1665. Ed. Sir George Bromley, 1787.

Secret Memoirs of the Court of James I. [Ed. Sir Walter Scott], 2 vols. Edinburgh, 1811. [Contains: F. Osborne's Traditional Memoirs; Sir A. Weldon's Court and Character of James; Sir W. Sanderson's Aulicus Coquinariae; Sir E. Peyton's Divine Catastrophe of the House of Stuart.]

Original Letters illustrative of English History. Ed. Sir Henry Ellis, 3 sers 11 vols. 1825–46.

—— Original Letters of Eminent Literary Men of the Sixteenth, Seventeenth and Eighteenth Centuries. Camden Soc. 1843.

[1] This section has been revised by Miss M. Coate.

Wiffen, J. H. The Historical Memoirs of the House of Russell. 2 vols. 1833.

The Loseley Manuscripts. Ed. A. J. Kempe, 1835. [From Henry VIII to James I.]

Queen Elizabeth and her Times: Original Letters. Ed. T. Wright, 2 vols. 1838.

Goodman, Godfrey. The Court of King James the First. Ed. J. S. Brewer, 2 vols. 1839.

Plumpton Correspondence. A Series of Letters written in the Reigns of Edward IV, Richard III, Henry VII, and Henry VIII. Ed. T. Stapleton, Camden Soc. 1839.

The Zurich Letters, comprising the Correspondence of several English Bishops during the Early Part of the Reign of Queen Elizabeth. Ed. and tr. H. Robinson, 3 sers. Parker Soc. 1842–8.

The Rutland Papers. Original Documents Illustrative of the Courts and Times of Henry VII and Henry VIII. Ed. W. Jerdan, Camden Soc. 1842.

Letters of the Kings of England. Ed. J. O. Halliwell[-Phillipps]. 2 vols. 1846.

The Court and Times of James the First; being a Series of Historical and Confidential Letters. Ed. R. F. Williams, 2 vols. 1848.

The Court and Times of Charles the First; illustrated by Authentic and Confidential Letters. Ed. R. F. Williams, 2 vols. 1848.

Devereux, W. B. Lives and Letters of the Devereux, Earls of Essex, 1540–1646. 2 vols. 1853.

The Stanley Papers. Ed. F. R. Raines, 3 pts, Chetham Soc. 1853–67.

Letters and Papers of the Verney Family down to 1639. Ed. J. Bruce, Camden Soc. 1853.

Memoirs of the Verney Family, 1642–96. Ed. Lady F. P. and Lady M. M. Verney, 4 vols. 1892–9; 2 vols. 1904 (rev. and abridged).

Trevelyan Papers. Ed. J. P. Collier, Sir W. C. Trevelyan and Sir C. L. Trevelyan, 3 pts, Camden Soc. 1857–72.

Court and Society from Elizabeth to Anne. From the Papers at Kimbolton. Ed. W. D. Montagu, Duke of Manchester, vol. I, 1864.

Rye, W. B. England as seen by Foreigners in the Days of Elizabeth and James the First. Comprising Translations of the Journals of the Two Dukes of Wirtemberg in 1592 and 1610. With Extracts from the Travels of Foreign Princes and Others. 1865.

Report of the Royal Commission on Historical Manuscripts. 1870–.

> Fourth Report. Appendix. The Manuscripts of the Earl of Denbigh at Newnham Paddox. 1874. [Family letters, temp. James I–Civil War.]
> Calendar of the Manuscripts of the Marquis of Salisbury at Hatfield. 15 pts, 1883–1930.
> Tenth Report. Appendix, pt VI. On the Manuscripts of Philip Playdell Bouverie, Esq. 1887.
> Thirteenth Report. Appendix, pt II. On the Manuscripts of the Duke of Portland at Welbeck. Vol. I, 1891. [Nelson Collection of 17th cent. letters, etc.]
> Fifteenth Report. Appendix, pt II. The Manuscripts of J. Eliot Hodgkin, Esq. of Richmond, Surrey. 1897. [Letters and documents, 1597–1788.]
> Fifteenth Report. Appendix, pt VII. The Manuscripts of the Duke of Somerset. 1898. [Letters of Seymour family from 1552.]
> Report on the Manuscripts of the Duke of Buccleuch and Queensberry. Vol. I, 1899. [Winwood Papers and Montagu Papers, 1483–1758.]
> Report on Manuscripts in Various Collections. Vol. II, 1903. [Sir George Wombwell's MSS include Narrative of Robert Pylkington, temp. Henry VIII; and household account books, 1571–1582.]
> Report on Manuscripts in Various Collections. Vol. III, 1904. [W. Clarke-Thornhill's MSS include correspondence of Sir Thomas Tresham, temp. Elizabeth.]
> Report on the Manuscripts of Lord Middleton of Wollaton Hall, Nottinghamshire. 1911. [Household accounts of Willoughby family, 1509–1603; and Collections of Cassandra Willoughby, 1702 (from older letters).]

Longleat Papers. Ed. J. E. Jackson, Wiltshire Archaeological and Natural History Mag. XIV, 1874, XVIII, 1878, XIX, 1880.

Records of the English Province of the Society of Jesus. Ed. H. Foley, 7 vols. 1877–83. [Especially for the letters of Father Anthony Rivers, fl. 1601–6.]

Yorkshire Diaries and Autobiographies in the Seventeenth and Eighteenth Centuries. Ed. C. Jackson, Surtees Soc. 1877. [Includes Captain Adam Eyre's Diary, 1646–8 and the autobiography of John Shawe, Vicar of Rotherham, 1608–1664 (first ptd by J. Broadley, 1824).]

Smith, John. The Berkeley Manuscripts. The Lives of the Berkeleys from 1066 to 1618. Ed. Sir J. Maclean, 3 vols. Bristol and Gloucestershire Archaeological Soc. 1883–5.

Beaumont Papers. Letters relating to the Family of Beaumont of Whitley, Yorkshire. Ed. W. D. Macray, Roxburghe Club, 1884.

Hall, Hubert. Society in the Elizabethan Age. 1886. [Appendix II, The Darrell Papers.]

Jeayes, I. H. Descriptive Catalogue of the Charters and Muniments at Berkeley Castle. 1892.

Aubrey, John. Brief Lives. Ed. A. Clark, 2 vols. Oxford, 1898.

Sitwell, Sir George. Letters of the Sitwells and Sacheverells. 2 vols. Scarborough, 1900–1. [Especially for George Sitwell, d. 1667.]

Bedingfield Papers. Diaries and Memoirs of the Bedingfields of Oxburgh, in the 17th and 18th Centuries. Catholic Record Soc. Miscellamea, vol. VI, 1909.

Six North Country Diaries. Ed. J. C. Hodgson, 2 pts. Surtees Soc. 1910–5. [Includes the diaries of Sir William Brereton (1635) and John Ashton (1639).]

Allen, P. S. Some Sixteenth Century Manuscript Letter-books. Trans. Bibliog. Soc. XII, 1911–3.

Letts, Malcolm. Three Foreigners in London, 1584–1618. Cornhill Mag. Aug. 1920, Sept. 1922.

Letters of the Fifteenth and Sixteenth Centuries. Ed. R. C. Anderson, Southampton Record Soc. 1921–2.

English Diaries. Ed. Arthur Ponsonby, 1923. [Extracts from 19 diaries between 1549 and 1660.]

More English Diaries. Ed. Arthur Ponsonby, 1927. [Extracts from 8 diaries, 1586–1660.]

The Fugger News-Letters, 1568–1605. Ed. Victor von Klarwill. Tr. Eng. 1924.

The Fugger News-Letters. Second Series, 1568–1605. Ed. Victor von Klarwill. Tr. Eng. 1926.

The Elizabethan Home Discovered in 2 Dialogues. Ed. M. St C. Byrne, [1925]; 1930 (rev. edn.). [Selections from Claudius Hollyband's (Claud Desainliens) French Scholemaister, French Littleton, and Campo di Fior; and from Pierre Erondelle's French Garden.]

Calendar of Wynn (of Gwydir) Papers, 1515–1690. 1926.

Literae vivorum eruditorum ad F. Craneveldium, 1522–1528. Ed. H. de Vocht, Louvain, 1928.

Orlebar, F. St J. Orlebar Chronicles, 1553–1733. 1930.

As the Foreigner saw us. Ed. M. Letts, 1935.

(b) Private Letters, Diaries, Autobiographies, Contemporary Memoirs, etc.

[In roughly chronological order based upon the subject-matter. Dates following a name are of birth and death; dates at the end of an entry are of the period covered.]

Cavendish, George. The Negotiations of Thomas Woolsey. 1641; ed. F. S. Ellis, 1899.

Roper, William. The Mirrour of Vertue in Wordly Greatness; or the Life of Syr T. More [1478–1535]. Paris, 1626.

Opus Epistolarum Des. Erasmi Roterodami [1466?–1536]. Ed. P. S. and H. M. Allen, 7 vols. Oxford, 1906–.

The Letters of Stephen Gardiner [1483?–1555]. Ed. J. A. Muller, Cambridge, 1933.

Letters of Richard Fox, 1486–1527. Ed. P. S. and H. M. Allen, Oxford, 1929.

The Northumberland Household Book. The Regulations and Establishment of the Household of Henry Algernon Percy, 5th Earl of Northumberland, began A.D. 1512. Ed. T. Percy, 1770.

Starkey, Thomas [1499?–1538]. England in the Reign of King Henry the Eighth. Pt I. Starkey's Life and Letters. Ed. S. J. Herrtage, EETS. Ex. Ser. 1878.

The Durham Household Book. From Pentecost 1530 to Pentecost 1534. Ed. J. Raine, Surtees Soc. 1844.

Correspondence of Edward, third Earl of Derby. Ed. T. N. Toller, Chetham Soc. 1890. [1533–1540.]

Correspondence of Matthew Parker. Letters by and to him, 1535 to 1575. Ed. J. Bruce and T. T. Perowne, Parker Soc. 1853.

The Second Book of the Travels of Nicander Nucius of Corcyra. Ed. J. A. Cranmer, Camden Soc. 1841.

Strype, John. The Life of the Learned Sir Thomas Smith [1513–1577]. 1698; Oxford, 1820. [Includes letters.]

Ascham, Roger [1515–1568]. Familiarium Epistolarum Libri tres. [1576]; ed. W. Elstob, Oxford, 1703.

A Booke of the Travaile and Lief of me, Thomas Hoby. Ed. Edgar Powell, Camden Misc. vol. X, 1902. [1547–1564.]

Narratives of the Days of the Reformation, chiefly from the Manuscripts of John Foxe [1516–1587], with two Contemporary Biographies of Archbishop Cranmer. Ed. J. G. Nichols, Camden Soc. 1859.

Burgon, J. W. The Life and Times of Sir Thomas Gresham [1519?–1579]. 2 vols. 1839. [Includes letters.]

Nares, Edward. Memoirs of the Life and Administration of William Cecil, Lord Burghley [1520–1598]. 3 vols. 1828–31. [Includes letters, etc.]

The Life of Mr. William Whittingham, Deane of Durham [1524?–1579]. Ed. M. A. E. Green, Camden Misc. vol. VI, 1871.

The Literary Remains of Edward VI. Ed. J. G. Nichols, 1857. [Includes diary, 1549–1552.]

The Diary of H. Machyn, Citizen and Merchant Taylor of London. Ed. J. G. Nichols, Camden Soc. 1848. [1550–1563.]

The Correspondence of Matthew Hutton, Archbishop of York [1529–1606]. Ed. J. Raine, Surtees Soc. 1843.

Staehlin, Karl. Sir Francis Walsingham [1530?–1590] und seine Zeit. Vol. I (all pbd), Heidelberg, 1908. [Includes letters.]

The Correspondence of Robert Bowes of Ashe [1535?–1597]. Ed. J. Stevenson, Surtees Soc. 1841.

The Autobiography and Personal Diary of Dr Simon Forman. Ed. J. O. Halliwell [-Phillipps], 1849. [1552–1602.]

The Private Diary of Dr John Dee and the Catalogue of his Library of Manuscripts. Ed. J. O. Halliwell[-Phillipps], Camden Soc. 1842. [1554–1601.]

Queen Elizabeth and a Swedish Princess. Being an Account of the Visit of Princess Cecilia of Sweden to England in 1565. From the Original Manuscripts of James Bell. Ed. E. Seaton, 1926.

The Spending of the Money of Robert Nowell of Reade Hall, Lancaster, 1568–80. Ed. A. B. Grosart (in The Towneley Hall Manuscripts, 1877).

Journal of Sir Francis Walsingham. Ed. C. T. Martin, Camden Misc. vol. VI, 1871. [1570–1583.]

Letter-book of Gabriel Harvey, A.D. 1573–1580. Ed. E. J. L. Scott, Camden Soc. 1884.

The Memoirs of Sir James Melville [1535–1617]. Ed. G. Scott, 1683; ed. H. F. Stewart, 1929.

Nicolas, Sir N. H. Memoirs of the Life and Times of Sir Christopher Hatton [1540–1591]. 1847. [Includes letters.]

—— Life of William Davison [1541?–1608], Secretary of State. 1823. [Includes letters.]

Edwards, Edward. The Life of Sir Walter Ralegh [1552?–1618]. 2 vols. 1868. [Includes letters.]

Laneham, Robert. A Letter; wherein the Entertainment at Killingworth Castle, is signified. [1575]; ed. F. J. Furnivall, New Shakspere Soc. 1890.

Richard Broughton's Devereux Papers. Ed. H. E. Malden, Camden Misc. vol. XIII, 1924. [1575–1601.]

Letters written by John Chamberlain [1553–1627] during the Reign of Queen Elizabeth. Ed. Sarah Williams, Camden Soc. 1861.

Greville, Fulke (Baron Brooke). The Life of the Renowned Sir Philip Sidney[1554–1586]. 1652; ed. N. Smith, Oxford, 1907.

The Correspondence between Sir Philip Sidney and H. Languet. Ed. S. A. Pears, 1845; ed. W. A. Bradley, Boston, 1912.

The Life of Sir Thomas Bodley [1545–1613] written by Himself [in 1609]. Oxford, 1647; rptd Oxford, 1913 (as Trecentale Bodleianum).

Reliquiae Bodleianae. Ed. T. Hearne, Oxford, 1703.

The Letters of Sir Thomas Bodley to Thomas James. Ed. G. W. Wheeler, Oxford, 1926.

Journey through England and Scotland made by Liupold von Wedel. Ed. G. von Bülow, Trans. Royal Hist. Soc. IX, 1895. [1584–5.]

Newdigate-Newdegate, Lady A. E. Gossip from a Muniment Room: Passages in the Lives of Anne and Mary Fytton, 1574–1618. 1897.

Letters of Philip Gawdy of West Harling, Norfolk. Ed. I. H. Jeayes, Roxburghe Club, 1906. [1579–1616.]. [See also Hist. MSS Commission, 1885, for Gawdy MSS.]

The Diary of Philip Wyot. [MS, 1586–1608. Extracts in More English Diaries, ed. Arthur Ponsonby, 1927.]

Memoirs of the Life of Robert Carey [1560?–1639] written by himself. Ed. John, Earl of Cork and Orrery, 1759; ed. G. H. Powell, 1905. [To 1626.]

Letters and Life of Francis Bacon [1561–1626], including all his Letters, Speeches, Tracts, State Papers, Memorials, Devices. Ed. James Spedding, 7 vols. 1861–4. [Vols. VIII–XIV of The Works of Francis Bacon, 1857–74.]

Two Elizabethan Puritan Diaries, by Richard Rogers and Samuel Ward. Ed. M. M. Knappen, Chicago, 1933.

Coningsby, Sir Thomas. Journal of the Siege of Rouen, 1591. Ed. J. G. Nichols, Camden Misc. vol. I, 1847.

The House and Farm Accounts of the Shuttleworths of Gawthorpe Farm. Ed. J. Harland, 4 vols. Chetham Soc. 1856–8. [1582–1621.]

Letters from Sir Robert Cecil [1563?–1612] to Sir George Carew. Ed. Sir J. Maclean, Camden Soc. 1864.

The Journal of Sir Roger Wilbraham. Ed. H. S. Scott, Camden Misc. vol. x, 1902. [1593–1616.]

Breunings von Buchenbach, H. J. Relation über seine Sendung nach England im Jahr 1595. Ed. A. Schlossberger, Stuttgart, 1863.

Montague, Anthony, Viscount. A Booke of Orders and Rules. Sussex Archaeological Collections, VII, 1854. [1595.]

Correspondence of Sir Henry Unton, Ambassador from Queen Elizabeth to Henry IV, King of France in the Years 1591 and 1592. Ed. J. Stevenson, Roxburghe Club, 1847.

The Unton Inventories. Ed. J. G. Nichols, Berkshire Ashmolean Soc. 1844. [1596–1620.]

Robinson, Richard. Eupolemia, Archippus and Panoplia. 1603; ed. R. B. McKerrow, GM. ccc, 1906; ed. G. M. Vogt, Stud. Phil. XXI, 1924.

Diary of Lady Margaret Hoby, 1599–1605. Ed. Dorothy M. Meads, 1930.

Cecil, Algernon. A Life of Robert Cecil, first Earl of Salisbury [1563?–1612]. 1915. [Includes letters.]

The Edmondes Papers. A Selection from the Correspondence of Sir Thomas Edmondes [1563?–1639]. Ed. G. G. Butler, Roxburghe Club, 1913.

During the Persecution. Autobiography of Father John Gerard [1564–1637] of the Society of Jesus. Tr. and ed. G. R. Kingdon, 1886.

Life and Letters of Sir Henry Wotton [1568–1639]. Ed. L. P. Smith, 2 vols. Oxford, 1907.

The Autobiography of Phineas Pett [1570–1647]. Ed. W. G. Perrin, Navy Records Soc. 1918.

Liber Famelicus of Sir James Whitelocke [1570–1632]. Ed. J. Bruce, Camden Soc. 1858.

A True Relation of the Life and Death of William Bedell, Bishop of Kilmore [1571–1642]. Ed. T. W. Jones, Camden Soc. 1872. [By his son William Bedell.]

Speculum Episcoporum; or the Lyfe and Death of D. William Bedell. Ed. E. S. Shuckburgh (with A True Relation, letters, etc.), Cambridge, 1902. [By his son-in-law, Alexander Clogy.]

Thomas Platters des Jüngeren Englandfahrt im Jahre 1599. Ed. H. Hecht, Halle, 1929.

Bayly, Lewis. The Practise of Piety. 1612.

Jonson, Ben [1573?–1637]. Conversations with Drummond. Ed. D. Laing, Shakespeare Soc. 1842; ed. R. F. Patterson, 1923.

The History of the Troubles of William Laud [1573–1645], Archbishop of Canterbury. Wrote by himself. To which is prefixed the Diary of his Own life. [Ed. Henry Wharton], 1695; ed. W. Scott and T. Bliss (in Works, vols. III and IV, Oxford, 1847–60).

Diary of the Journey of Philip Julius, Duke of Stettin-Pomerania, through England in the Year 1602. Ed. G. von Bülow and W. Powell, Trans. Royal Hist. Soc. VI, 1892.

Gosse, Sir E. The Life and Letters of John Donne [1573–1631]. 2 vols. 1899.

Bradley, E. T. Life of the Lady Arabella Stuart [1575–1615]. 2 vols. 1889. [Includes letters.]

Mathew, A. H. and Calthrop, A. The Life of Sir Tobie Matthew [1577–1655]. 1907. [Includes letters.]

The Diary of John Manningham. Ed. J. Bruce, Camden Soc. 1868. [1602–1603.]

Diary of Walter Yonge, written at Colyton and Axminster, Co. Devon. Ed. G. Roberts, Camden Soc. 1848. [1604–1628.]

Parr, Richard. Life of James Usher [1581–1656], late Lord Archbishop of Armagh. 1686.

The Life of Edward Lord Herbert of Cherbury [1583–1648] written by himself. Ed. H. Walpole, 1764; ed. Sir S. Lee, 1886, 1907 (rev. edn). [To 1624.]

Duncon, J. The Holy Life and Death of the Lady Letice Vi-Countess Falkland [1585–1639]. 1648; 1908.

W[illis], R. Mount Tabor. Or Private Exercises of a Penitent Sinner. 1639.

The Diary of John Young [1585–1654], Dean of Winchester. Ed. F. R. Goodman, 1928.

Life and Letters of Mr Endymion Porter [1587–1649]. Ed. Dorothea Townshend, 1897.

Lives of Lady Anne Clifford [1590–1676], and of her Parents, summarized by herself. Ed. J. P. Gilson, Roxburghe Club, 1916.

The Diary of Lady Anne Clifford. Ed. V. Sackville West, 1923. [1603–1619.]

Foster, John. Sir John Eliot [1592–1632]. 2 vols. 1864. [Contains numerous letters from Eliot and Sir Bevil Grenville.]

The Diary of Walter Powell. Ed. J. A. Bradney, Bristol, 1907. [1606–1654.]

The Oxinden Letters, 1607–1642. Ed. D. Gardiner, 1933.

Lismore Papers. By Richard Boyle, Earl of Cork. Ed. A. B. Grosart, 10 vols. 1886–8. [Contains Earl of Cork's diary from 1611–1643 and letters to and from him.]

Letters from George, Lord Carew [1555–1629], to Sir Thomas Roe. Ed. Sir J. Maclean, Camden Soc. 1860. [1615–7.]

The Diary of the Rev. Ralph Josselin. Ed. E. Hockliffe, Royal Hist. Soc. 1908. [1616–1683.]

The Journal of Nicholas Assheton of Downham with Notes from the Life of John Bruen. Ed. F. R. Raines, Chetham Soc. 1848. [1617–1618.]

Nicholas Ferrar [1592–1637]. Two Lives by his Brother John and by Doctor Jebb. Ed. J. E. B. Mayor, Cambridge, 1855.

The Life of Mr Robert Blair [1593–1666], Minister of St Andrews, containing his Autobiography, 1593–1636. Ed. T. M'Crie, Wodrow Soc. Edinburgh, 1898.

Herbert, George [1593–1633]. A Priest to the Temple, or, the Countrey Parson. [In Remains, 1652]; ed. H. C. Beeching, Oxford, 1898.

The Life and Original Correspondence of Sir George Radcliffe [1593–1657]. Ed. T. D. Whitaker, 1810.

The Nicholas Papers. Correspondence of Sir Edward Nicholas [1593–1669], Secretary of State. Ed. G. F. Warner, 3 vols. Camden Soc. 1886–97. [Vol. IV, Royal Hist. Soc.]

Birch, Thomas. The Life of Henry Prince of Wales, Eldest Son of James I. 1760. [Includes letters.]

The Rawdon Papers; consisting of Letters to and from Dr J. Bramhall [1594–1663], Primate of Ireland. Ed. E. Berwick, 1819.

The Correspondence of John Cosin, Bishop of Durham [1594–1672]. Ed. G. Ormsby, 2 pts, Surtees Soc. 1869–72.

Howell, James [1594?–1666]. Epistolae Ho-Elianæ. Familiar Letters Domestic and Forren. 1645; ed. J. Jacobs, 2 vols. 1890.

Wilson, Arthur [1595–1652]. Observations of God's Providence in the Tract of my Life. Ed. F. Peck (in Desiderata Curiosa, vol. II, 1735); ed. P. Bliss (with The Inconstant Lady, Oxford, 1814).

Green, M. A. E. The Life of Elizabeth, Electress Palatine and Queen of Bohemia [1596–1662]. 1909. [Includes letters.]

The Letters and Journals of Robert Baillie [1599–1662]. 2 vols. Edinburgh, 1775; ed. D. Laing, 3 vols. Bannatyne Club, 1841–2.

Correspondence of the Family of Hatton being chiefly letters addressed to Christopher first Viscount Hatton, A.D. 1601–1704. Ed. E. M. Thompson, 2 vols. Camden Soc. 1878.

The Letters of Dorothy Wadham, 1609–1618. Ed. R. B. Gardiner, Oxford, 1904.

The Private Correspondence of Jane, Lady Cornwallis, 1613–1644. 1842.

The Relations of Sydnam Poyntz. Ed. A. T. S. Goodrick, Royal Hist. Soc. 1908. [1624–1636.]

Private Letters from the Earl of Strafford to his third Wife. Ed. R. M. Milnes, Philobiblon Soc. Misc. vol. I, 1854. [1635–1637.]

Letters of King Charles the First to Queen Henrietta Maria in 1646. Ed. J. Bruce, Camden Soc. 1856.

The Private Correspondence between King Charles I and Sir Edward Nicholas; also between Sir Edward Hyde and Sir Richard Browne. [In Evelyn's Diary, ed. W. Bray and H. B. Wheatley, vol. IV, 1879.]

Letters of Queen Henrietta Maria. Ed. M. A. E. Green, 1857.

Letters of the Lady Brilliana Harley. Ed. T. T. Lewis, Camden Soc. 1854. [1625–1643.]

The Diary of Thomas Crosfield [b. 1602], Fellow of Queen's College, Oxford. Ed. F. S. Boas, Royal Soc. Lit. 1935.

Lilly, William [1602–1681]. The History of his Life and Times. 1715; 1822.

Diary of John Rous, Incumbent of Santon Downham, Suffolk. Ed. M. A. E. Green, Camden Soc. 1856. [1625–1642.]

Private Memoirs of Sir Kenelm Digby [1603–1665]. Written by himself. [Ed. Sir N. H. Nicholas], 1827.

The Autobiography [to 1636] and Correspondence [to 1649] of Sir Simonds D'Ewes [1602–1650]. Ed. J. O. Halliwell [-Phillipps], 2 vols. 1845. [From 1619.]

Marsden, J. H. College Life in the Time of James I. 1851. [Based upon a diary of Sir S. D'Ewes.]

Sir Thomas Isham's Diary. Ed. Walter Rye, Trans. Royal Hist. Soc. 1907. [Includes Sir John Isham's diary for 1626.]

[Walsingham, Edward.] Life of Sir John Digby [1605–1675]. Ed. G. Bernard, Camden Misc. vol. XII, 1910.

Memoirs Biographical and Historical, of Bulstrode Whitelocke [1605–1675]. Ed. R. H. Whitelocke, 1860.

The Life of Marmaduke Rawdon of York [1610–1669]. Ed. R. Davies, Camden Soc. 1863.

Autobiography of Thomas Raymond [c. 1610–c. 1681) and Memoirs of the Family of Guise of Elmore, Gloucestershire. Ed. G. Davies. Royal Hist. Soc. 1917.

The Autobiography of Sir John Bramston. Ed. Lord Braybrooke, Camden Soc. 1845. [1611–1700.]

Hutchinson, Lucy. Memoirs of the Life of Colonel Hutchinson [1615–1664]. To which is prefixed the Life of Mrs Hutchinson [1620–?] written by herself. 1806; ed. Sir C. H. Firth, 2 vols. 1885 and 1906.

Reliquiae Baxterianae or Mr Richard Baxter's Narrative of the most Memorable Passages of his Life and Times. Ed. M. Sylvester, 1696; ed. J. M. Lloyd Thomas, 1925 (selection). [1615–1691.]

Military Memoir of Colonel John Birch [1616–1691], by Roe, his Secretary. Ed. J. and T. W. Webb, Camden Soc. 1873.

Letters and Speeches of Oliver Cromwell. Ed. Thomas Carlyle, 2 vols. 1845; rev. S. C. Lomas, 2 vols. 1904.

The Memoirs of Sir George Courthop [1616–1685]. Ed. S. C. Lomas, Camden Misc. vol. XI, 1907.

Memoirs of the Life of that Learned Antiquary Elias Ashmole [1617–1692] drawn up by himself. Ed. C. Burman, 1717; ed. R. T. Gunther, Oxford, 1927.

Memoirs of Edmund Ludlow [1617?–1692]. 3 vols. Vivay, 1698–9; ed. C. H. Firth, 2 vols. Oxford, 1894.

The Autobiography of Lady Halkett [1622–1699]. Ed. J. G. Nichols, Camden Soc. 1875. [1622–1655.]

The Diary and Correspondence of Dr John Worthington. Ed. J. Crossley and R. C. Christie, 3 pts, Chetham Soc. 1847–86. [1632–1637.]

The Correspondence of Dr Basire, 1634–1675. Ed. W. N. Darnell, 1831.

Matthew, Sir Tobie [1577–1655]. The Life of Lady Lucy Knatchbull. Ed. D. Knowles, 1932. [Written 1642.]

The Life of Adam Martindale [1623–86] written by himself. Ed. R. Parkinson, Chetham Soc. 1845.

Cavendish, Margaret (Duchess of Newcastle) [1624?–1674]. A True Relation of the Birth, Breeding, and Life of, written by herself. [In Nature's Pictures, 1656; ed. Sir S. E. Brydges, 1814.]

—— The Life of William Cavendish, Duke of Newcastle [1592–1676]. 1667; ed. Sir C. H. Firth, 1886 (with above).

Letters written by Margaret, Duchess of Newcastle, to her Husband. Ed. R. W. Goulding, Roxburghe Club, 1909.

Memoirs of Thomas Papillon of London, Merchant [1623–1702]. Ed. A. F. W. Papillon, Reading, 1887.

The Journal of George Fox [1624–91]. 2 vols. 1694–8; ed. Norman Penney, 2 vols. Cambridge, 1911.

Memoirs of Lady Fanshawe [1625–1680]. Ed. Sir N. H. Nicholas, 1829; ed. H. C. Fanshawe, 1907.

Autobiography of Mary Countess of Warwick [1625–1678]. Ed. T. C. Croker, Percy Soc. 1848.

Memoirs of the Life of Ambrose Barnes [1627–1710]. Ed. W. H. D. Longstaffe, Surtees Soc. 1867.

The Obituary of Richard Smyth, Secondary of the Poultry Compter, London, being a Catalogue of All such Persons as he knew in their Life, 1627 to 1674. Ed. Sir H. Ellis, Camden Soc. 1849.

The Autobiography of Matthew Robinson [1628–1694]. Ed. J. E. B. Mayor, 1856.

The Autobiography of Mrs. Alice Thornton. Ed. C. Jackson, Surtees Soc. 1875. [1629–1669.]

The Autobiography and Diaries of Oliver Heywood [1630–1702]. Ed. J. H. Turner, 4 vols. 1882–5.

Memoirs of the Reign of Charles the First. Ed. J. G. W. Johnson, 2 vols. 1848. [To 1642.] [The Fairfax Correspondence.]

Memorials of the Civil War: comprising the Correspondence of the Fairfax Family. Ed. R. Bell, 2 vols. 1849. [To 1660.]

Rural Economy in Yorkshire in 1641, being the Farming and Account Books of H. Best. Ed. C. B. Robinson, Surtees Soc. 1857.

Diaries and Letters of Philip Henry, 1631–1696. Ed. M. H. Lee, 1882.

Turner, Sir James. Memoirs of his Own Life and Times [1632–70]. Ed. I. Thomson, Bannatyne Club, 1829.

Autobiography of Captain John Hodgson [d. 1684]. Ed. Sir Walter Scott, Edinburgh, 1806; ed. J. H. Turner, 1882.

Monckton Papers. Ed. E. Peacock, Philobiblon Soc. Misc. vol. xv, 1884. [Includes Sir Philip Monckton's Memoir, *temp.* Civil War.]

The Life, Diary [1643–1686] and Correspondence [1635–1686] of Sir William Dugdale. Ed. W. Hamper, 1827.

The Autobiography of H. Newcome [1627–1695]. Ed. R. Parkinson, 2 vols. Chetham Soc. 1852.

Autobiography of Joseph Lister of Bradford [1627–1709]. Ed. T. Wright, 1842.

Hopton, Sir Ralph. Bellum Civile. Narrative of his Campaigns in the West, 1642–1644. Ed. C. E. N. Chadwyck Healey, Somerset Records Soc. 1902.

Clarke Papers. Selections from the Papers of William Clarke, 1647–1660. Ed. C. H. Firth, 4 vols. Camden Soc. 1891–1901.

The Diary of Henry Townshend of Elmley Lovett, 1640–1663. Ed. J. W. W. Bund, 4 pts, Worcestershire Hist. Soc. 1915–20.

The Flemings in Oxford. Vol. I, 1650–1680. Ed. J. R. Magrath, Oxford Hist. Soc. XLIV, 1904.

Memoirs illustrative of the Life and Writings of John Evelyn, comprising his Diary from 1641 to 1705–6 and his Letters [1642–1704]. Ed. W. Bray, 2 vols. 1818; ed. H. B. Wheatley, 3 vols. 1906.

Slingsby, Sir Henry. Original Memoirs, written during the Great Civil War. Ed. Sir Walter Scott, Edinburgh, 1806.

—— The Diary of Sir Henry Slingsby, of Scriven, Bart. Ed. D. Parsons, 1836. [1638–1648.]

Bayley, A. R. The Civil War in Dorset, 1642–1660. 1910.

Cary, Henry. Memorials of the Great Civil War in England. 2 vols. 1842. [Ptd from the Tanner MSS in the Bodleian.]

The Journal of William Dowsing. [Ed. R. Loder], 1786; ed. C. H. E. White, Ipswich, 1885. [1643–1644.]

Christie, W. D. Life of Anthony Ashley Cooper, 1st Earl of Shaftesbury. 2 vols. 1871. [Includes diary, 1646–1650.]

Webb, J. Memorials of the Civil War in Herefordshire. Ed. T. W. Webbe, 2 vols. 1879.

Diary of John Ward, Vicar of Stratford-upon-Avon (1648–1679). Ed. C. Severn, 1839.

The Hamilton Papers: being Selections from Letters of the Duke of Hamilton, relating to 1638–1650. Ed. S. R. Gardiner, Camden Soc. 1880.

Conway Letters. The Correspondence of Anne, Viscountess Conway, Henry More, and their Friends, 1642–1684. Ed. M. H. Nicolson, New Haven, 1930.

Memoires by Sir John Hinton Physitian In Ordinary to his Majesties Person. 1679. [1642–1660.]

Letters from Dorothy Osborne [1627–1695] to Sir William Temple. Ed. E. A. Parry, 1888; ed. G. C. Moore Smith, Oxford, 1928.

The Life and Times of Anthony Wood [1632–1695] described by himself. Ed. A. Clarke, 5 vols. Oxford, 1889–1900.

Diary of Thomas Burton. 1656–1659. Ed. G. T. Rutt, 4 vols. 1828. [Parliamentary proceedings.]

The Memoirs of Sir John Reresby [1634–1689]. 1734; ed. A. Watt, 1904.

Loveday, Robert. Letters Domestick and Forrein, occasionally distributed in Subjects Philosophicall Historicall Morall. 1659.

Forde, Thomas. Faenestra in Pectore. Or, Familiar Letters. 1660.

Autobiography and Anecdotes by William Taswell, 1651–1682. Ed. G. P. Elliott, Camden Misc. vol. ii, 1853.

(6) MODERN STUDIES AND SURVEYS

(a) General Works

Shakespeare's England. An Account of the Life and Manners of his Age. 2 vols. Oxford, 1916. [Ed. Sir Sidney Lee and C. T. Onions. Includes, besides the sections listed separately below, Travel, The Home, Authors and Patrons, Rogues and Vagabonds.]

Strutt, Joseph. Worda Angelcynnan: or a Compleat View of the Manners of England. 3 vols. 1775–6.

Douce, F. Illustrations of Shakespeare, and of Ancient Manners. 2 vols. 1807.

Brand, John. Observations on Popular Antiquities. 2 vols. 1813; rev. W. C. Hazlitt, 3 vols. 1870.

Drake, Nathan. Shakespeare and his Times. 2 vols. 1817.

Aikin, Lucy. Memoirs of the Court of Queen Elizabeth. 1818.

—— Memoirs of the Court of King James the First. 2 vols. 1822.

—— Memoirs of the Court of King Charles the First. 2 vols. 1833.

Thornbury, G. W. Shakespeare's England. 2 vols. 1856.

Roberts, G. The Social History of the Southern Counties of England. 1856.

Dyer, T. F. T. British Popular Customs. 1876.

—— Old English Social Life as told by the Parish Registers. 1898.

Ashton, J. Humour, Wit and Society of the 17th Century. 1883.

Hall, Hubert. Society in the Elizabethan Age. 1886.

Traill, H. D. et al. Social England. 6 vols. 1893–7; 6 vols. 1901–4 (rev. edn). [Vol. iii, Henry VIII to Elizabeth; vol. iv, James I to Anne.]

Einstein, Lewis. The Italian Renaissance in England. New York, 1902.

—— Tudor Ideals. New York, 1921.

'Godfrey, Elizabeth.' Home Life under the Stuarts, 1603–49. 1903.

—— Social Life under the Stuarts. 1904.

Schelling, F. E. The Queen's Progress and other Elizabethan Sketches. [1904.]

Stephenson, H. T. The Elizabethan People. New York, 1910.

Abrams, Annie. English Life and Manners in the Later Middle Ages. 1913.

Bastide, C. The Anglo-French Entente in the Seventeenth Century. 1914.

Quennell, H. and M. History of Everyday Things in England. 2 vols. 1919. [Vol. ii.]

Taylor, H. O. Thought and Expression in the 16th Century. 2 vols. New York, 1920. [Vol. ii.]

Coate, M. Social Life in Stuart England. 1924.

Byrne, M. St C. Elizabethan Life in Town and Country. 1925.

Hartley, D. and Elliot, M. Life and Work of the People of England. 2 vols. 1925. [Collection of contemporary illustrations.]

Salzman, L. F. England in Tudor Times. 1926.

Harrison, G. B. An Elizabethan Journal: being a Record of those Things most talked of during the Years 1591–1594. 1928.

—— Elizabethan England. 1930.

—— A Second Elizabethan Journal, 1595–1598. 1931.

—— A Last Elizabethan Journal, 1599–1603. 1933.

(b) Special Studies

Nichols, J. Illustrations of the Manners and Expences of Antient Times in England from the Accompts of Churchwardens. 1797.

Fairholt, F. W. Lord Mayors' Pageants with Specimens of the Pamphlets published by the City Poets. 2 pts, Percy Soc. 1843–4.

Wright, T. History of Domestic Manners and Sentiments in England. 1862.

Early English Meals and Manners: the Boke of Norture of John Russell, the Bokes of Kervynge, Curtasye and Demeanor, the Babees Book, Urbanitatis, etc. Ed. F. J. Furnivall, EETS. 1868. [Introduction.]

Early English Treatises and Poems on Education, Precedence and Manners. Ed. F. J. Furnivall, EETS. Ex. Ser. 1869.

Jessopp, A. One Generation of a Norfolk House. Norwich, 1879.

—— Origin and Growth of English Towns. [In Historical Studies, 1893.]

Harris, G. Domestic Everyday Life, Manners and Customs in this Country to the End of the Eighteenth Century. Trans. Royal Hist. Soc. ix, 1881.

Cunningham, W. The Growth of English Industry and Commerce in Modern Times. Cambridge, 1882; 3 vols. Cambridge, 1922–1 (rev. edn).

Vatke, E. F. T. Culturbilder aus Alt-England. Berlin, 1887.

Wheatley, H. B. The Dedication of Books. 1887.

Smith, E. Foreign Visitors in England. 1889.

Child-Marriages and -Divorces, Trothplights, etc. Chester Depositions, 1561–6. Ed. F. J. Furnivall, EETS. 1897. [Introduction.]

Chambers, Sir E. K. The Medieval Stage. 2 vols. Oxford, 1903.

—— The Elizabethan Stage. 4 vols. Oxford, 1923.

[Mines of incidental social information, especially for the Court.]

Ware, S. L. The Elizabethan Parish in its Ecclesiastical and Financial Aspects. Baltimore, 1908.

Sheavyn, Phoebe. The Literary Profession in the Elizabethan Age. Manchester, 1909.

—— Writers and the Publishing Trade, circa 1600. Library, VII, 1906.

—— Patrons and Professional Writers under Elizabeth and James I. Library, VII, 1906.

Bates, E. S. Touring in 1600. Boston, 1911.

Carriages and Coaches. Ed. R. Straus, 1912.

Aydelotte, Frank. Elizabethan Rogues and Vagabonds. Oxford, 1913.

Howard, Clare. English Travellers of the Renaissance. 1913.

Kennedy, W. P. M. Parish Life under Queen Elizabeth. 1914.

Powell, C. L. English Domestic Relations, 1487–1653. New York, 1917.

Jones, P. van B. The Household of a Tudor Nobleman. Urbana, 1917.

Withington, Robert. English Pageantry: an Historical Outline. 2 vols. Cambridge, U.S.A. 1918–20.

Wilson, Violet A. Queen Elizabeth's Maids of Honour. 1922.

—— Society Women of Shakespeare's Time. 1924.

Liljegren, S. B. The Fall of the Monasteries and the Social Changes in England leading up to the Great Revolution. Lund, 1924.

Parkes, Joan. Travel in England in the Seventeenth Century. 1925.

Ascoli, Georges. La Grande-Bretagne devant l'Opinion français depuis la Guerre de Cent Ans jusqu'à la Fin du XVIe Siècle. Paris, 1927.

—— La Grande-Bretagne devant l'Opinion française au XVIIe Siecle. 2 vols. Paris, 1930.

Wilson, F. P. The Plague in Shakespeare's London. Oxford, 1927.

B. PARTICULAR ASPECTS OF SOCIAL LIFE

(1) LONDON AND THE LIFE OF THE TOWN

[For the London prisons, rogues and vagabonds, etc. see below, pp. 717–8.]

Agas, Ralph. Civitas Londinum. A Survey of the Cities of London and Westminster. [1591?]; ed. facs. W. H. Overall, 1874.

Stow, John. A Survay of London. 1598; 1603 (rev.); rev. and continued by J. Strype, 2 vols. 1720; ed. C. L. Kingsford, 3 vols. Oxford, 1908–27.

The Great Frost; Cold Doings in London. 1608; rptd A. Lang (Social England Illustrated, 1903).

Bartholomew Faire. 1641; ed. C. Hindley (The Old Book Collector's Miscellany, vol. III, 1873).

P[eacham], H. The Art of Living in London. 1642; rptd Harleian Miscellany, vol. IX, 1812.

Ogilvy, John and Morgan, William. A Large and Accurate Map of the City of London. 1677; ed. facs. Charles Welch, London and Middlesex Archaeological Soc. 1895.

Malcolm, J. P. Anecdotes of the Manners and Customs of London to 1700. 2 vols. 1811.

Cunningham, Peter. A Handbook for London. 2 vols. 1849.

Morley, Henry. Memoirs of Bartholomew Fair. 1859.

'Larwood, Jacob.' The Story of the London Parks. 2 vols. [1872].

Wheatley, H. B. London Past and Present. 3 vols. 1891.

Besant, Sir Walter. London. 1892.

—— Westminster. 1895.

—— South London. 1899.

—— East London. 1901.

—— London in the Time of the Stuarts. 1903.

—— London in the Time of the Tudors. 1904.

Ordish, T. F. Shakespeare's London. 1897.

Stephenson, H. T. Shakespeare's London. New York, 1905.

Duval, Georges. Londres au Temps de Shakespeare. Paris, 1907.

Page, William. History of London. 1909–. (Victoria County Histories.)

Salaman, M. C. London Past and Present. Studio, 1916.

Harben, H. A. A Dictionary of London. 1918.

(2) THE ART OF WAR

Cockle, M. J. W. A Bibliography of English Military Books up to 1642. 1900.

Whitehorne, Peter. The Arte of Warre. 2 pts, 1560–2; 1574; 1588. [From Machiavelli.]

—— Onosandro Platonico, of the Generall Captaine, and of his Office. 1563.

Sadler, J. The Foure Bookes of Martiall Policye. [1572.] [From Flavius Vegetius Renatus.]

Rich, Barnabe. A right Exelent Dialogue betwene Mercury and an English Souldier. [1574.]

—— A Pathway to Military Practise. 1587.

—— A Souldiers Wishe to Britons Welfare. 1604.

P[roctor], T[homas]. Of the Knowledge and Conducte of Warres. 1578.

Digges, Leonard and Thomas. An Arithmeticall Militare Treatise, named Stratioticos. 1579; 1590.

[Hales, John?] A Discourse of the Common Weal. 1581; ed. E. Lamond, Cambridge, 1893.

Bourne, William. The Arte of Shooting in Great Ordnaunce. 1587; 1643.

A[ggas], E. The Politicke and Militarie Discourses of the Lord de la Noue. 1587 (1588).

Smythe, Sir John. Certen Discourses concerning the Formes and Effects of Divers Sortes of Weapons. 1590.

Williams, Sir Roger. A Briefe Discourse of Warre. 1590 (bis); rptd E. Arber (English Garner, vol. v, 1882).

Garrard, William. The Arte of Warre. Rev. R. Hitchcock, 1591.

Knyvett, Sir Thomas. The Defence of the Realme. 1596.

Hoby, Sir Edward. Theorique and Practise of Warre. 1597. [From B. de Mendoza's Spanish.]

Barret, Robert. The Theorike and Practike of Moderne Warres. 1598.

Smith, Thomas. The Arte of Gunnerie. 2 pts, 1600; 1628; 1643.

Norton, Robert. The Gunner, shewing the whole Practice of Artillerie. 1628.

Knevet, Ralph. Στρατιωτικόν, or a Discourse of Militarie Discipline. 1628.

C[ruso], J[ohn]. Militarie Instructions for the Cavallrie. Cambridge, 1632.

—— The Arte of Warre, or Militarie Discourses. By the Lord of Praissac. 2 pts, Cambridge, 1639.

Barriffe, William. Military Discipline; or, the Young Artillery-man. 1635; 1639.

Hexham, H. The Principles of the Art Militarie, practised in the Warres of the Netherlands. 1637.

Ward, Robert. Animadversions of Warre. 1639.

M., R. A Compleat Schoole of Warre; or, a Direct Way for the Ordering and Exercising of a Foot Company. 1642.

Fisher, Thomas. Warlike Directions; or, the Souldiers Practice. 1643 (2nd edn). [A drill book.]

Elton, R. The Compleat Body of the Art Military. 1650; 1659. [Infantry drill.]

Grose, F. Military Antiquities. 1801.

Meyrick, S. R. A Critical Inquiry into Antient Armour. 3 vols. 1824.

Hewitt, J. Ancient Armour and Weapons. 3 vols. Oxford, 1855–60.

ffoulkes, C. Armour and Weapons. Oxford. 1909.

—— European Arms and Armour in the University of Oxford. 1912.

Fortescue, Sir J. W. A History of the British Army. 13 vols. 1899–1930. [Vol. i.]

Fortescue, Sir J. W. and Dillon, Viscount. The Army: Military Serivce. and Equipment. [In Shakespeare's England, 2 vols. Oxford, 1916.]

(3) NAVIGATION AND SEAMANSHIP

Admiralty Library. Subject Catalogue of Printed Books. Pt i. Historical Section. Ed. W. G. Perrin, 1912.

Callender, G. A. R. Bibliography of Naval History. 2 pts, 1924–5.

Manwaring, G. E. Bibliography of British Naval History. 1930.

Eden, Richard. The Arte of Navigation. 1561; 1572; 1579; 1584; 1589; 1596; 1609; 1615. [From Martin Cortes.]

Bourne, William. A Regiment for the Sea. [1574]; [1576?]; 1577; 1580; 1587; 1592; 1596; 1611; 1620; 1631.

Frampton, J. The Arte of Navigation. 1581; 1595. [From Pedro de Medina.]

Davis, John. The Seamans Secrets. 1594 (no copy extant?); 1607; 1626; 1633; rptd 1880.

—— The Worldes Hydrographical Discription. 1595. [Maps and charts.]

Smith, Captain John. An Accidence, or the Path-way to Experience for Young Seamen. 1626; 1636; 1653 (expanded as Seaman's Grammar).

Norwood, Richard. The Seamans Practice. 1637; 1659; 1662.

Saltonstall, C. The Navigator. 1642; [1660?].

Manwayring, Sir Henry. The Sea-mans Dictionary. 1644; 1670; ed. G. E. Manwaring, Navy Records Soc. 1920. [Written c. 1625.]

Potter, R. Pathway to Perfect Sailing. 1644.

Monson, Sir W. Naval Tracts [in A Collection of Voyages, ed. A. and J. Churchill, vol. iii, 1732]; ed. M. Oppenheim, 5 vols. Navy Records Soc. 1902–14.

Bourne, H. R. Fox. English Seamen under the Tudors (1485–1603). 2 vols. 1868.

State Papers relating to the Defeat of the Spanish Armada. 2 vols. Navy Records Soc. 1894.

Oppenheim, M. A History of the Administration of the Royal Navy, 1509–1660. 1896.

Corbett, J. S. Drake and the Tudor Navy. 2 vols. 1898.
 — England in the Mediterranean, 1603–1713. 2 vols. 1904.
Robinson, C. N. and Leyland, J. The British Tar. 1909.
Whall, W. B. Shakespeare's Sea Terms Explained. 1910.
Laughton, L. G. C. The Navy: Ships and Sailors. [In Shakespeare's England, 2 vols. Oxford, 1916.]

(4) AGRICULTURE AND GARDENING

Rohde, E. S. The Old English Gardening Books. 1924. [Contains bibliography.]

[Fitzherbert, John?] The Booke of Husbandrie. [1523?]; [1525?]; [1535?]; [1541?]; [1547?]; 1548; [1555?]; [1560?]; 1562; 1568, etc.; ed. W. W. Skeat, English Dialect Soc. 1882.
 — The Boke of Surveyinge and Improvements. 1523; 1526; [1535?]; 1539; [1545?]; 1546; [1548?]; [1555?]; 1567, etc.
'Mountain, Didymus' [i.e. Thomas Hill]. A most Briefe and Pleasaunt Treatyse, teachynge how to dresse, sowe, and set a Garden. 1563; 1568; 1572; 1574; 1579; 1586; 1591; 1608.
 — A Pleasaunt Instruction of the Parfit Ordering of Bees. 1568.
 — The Gardeners Labyrinth. 1577; 1578; 1586; 1594; 1608. [Completed by Henry Dethick.]
Mascall, Leonard. A Booke of the Arte and Maner, howe to plant and graffe all Sortes of Trees. [1572]; 1575; 1582; 1590; 1592; 1596. [From French.]
 — The Husbandlye Ordring and Governmente of Poultrie. 1581.
Tusser, Thomas. Five hundreth Pointes of Good Husbandry. 1573 (and 17 edns to 1638); ed. W. Payne and S. J. Herrtage, English Dialect Soc. 1878.
Scot, Reginald. A Perfite Platforme of a Hoppe Garden. 1574; 1576; 1578.
Googe, Barnaby. Foure Bookes of Husbandry, collected by M. Conradus Heresbachius. 1577; 1578; 1586; 1596; 1601; 1614; 1631 (enlarged by Gervase Markham).
Harrison, William. A Description of England. [In R. Holinshed, Chronicles, 1578 and 1587; ed. bks II and III F. J. Furnivall, 3 vols. New Shakspere Soc. 1877–1909.]
[Hales, John?] A Discourse of the Common Weal. 1581; ed. E. Lamond, 1893.
Cogan, Thomas. The Haven of Helthe. 1584; 1588; 1596; 1605; 1612; 1636.
B[ellot], J[acques]. The Booke of Thrift, containing a Perfite Order to profit Lands. 1589.

The Orchard and the Garden. 1594; 1596; 1602.
Platt, Sir Hugh. The Jewell House of Art and Nature. Containing Divers Inventions, together with Experimentes in the Art of Husbandry, Distillation, and Moulding. 1594.
 — Sundrie New and Artificiall Remedies against Famine. 1596.
 — The New and Admirable Arte of setting Corne. 1600; 1601.
 — Floraes Paradise, beautified and adorned with Sundry Sorts of Delicate Fruites and Flowers. 1608.
Surflet, R. Maison Rustique or the Countrie-farme. 1600; 1606; rev. Gervase Markham, 1616. [Tr. from French of C. Estienne.]
Gardiner, Richard. Profitable Instructions for the Manuring, Sowing, and Planting of Kitchin Gardens. 1603.
F., N. The Fruiterers Secrets. 1604.
Butler, Charles. The Feminine Monarchie; or, a Treatise concerning Bees. Oxford, 1609; 1619; Oxford, 1634.
Standish, Arthur. The Commons Complaint. The Generall Destruction and Waste of Woods in this Kingdome. 1611 (3 edns); 1612.
 — New Directions of Experience to the Commons Complaint for the Planting of Timber and Fire-wood. 1613; 1614; 1615.
C., R. An Olde Thrift newly Revived. The Manner of Planting, Preserving, and Husbanding Yong Trees. 1612.
Markham, Gervase. The English Husbandman. 2 vols. 1613–4; 1635 (bis). [Farming and gardening.]
 — Cheape and Good Husbandry. 1614; 1616; 1623; 1631.
 — The Country Housewifes Garden. 1617.
 — Markhams Farwell to Husbandry. 1620; 1625; 1631; 1638.
 — The Country-mans Recreation, or the Art of Planting, Grafting and Gardening. 1640.
W., E. [i.e. T. Wood?] A Garden of Flowers. 2 pts, Utrecht, 1615. [Tr. from C. de Passe.]
Lawson, William. A New Orchard and Garden. 2 pts, 1618; 1623; 1629; ed. E. S. Rohde, 1927.
Harward, Simon. A most Profitable New Treatise of the Art of propagating Plants, in Lawson's New Orchard. 1623.
Parkinson, John. Paradisi in Sole, Paradisus terrestris. 1629; 1656; rptd 1904.
Weston, Sir Richard. A Discourse of Husbandrie used in Brabant and Flanders. Ed. Samuel Hartlib, 1605 (for 1650); 1652.

Donaldson, John. Agricultural Biography. 1854.

Rogers, J. E. T. A History of Agriculture and Prices in England (1259–1582). 7 vols. Oxford, 1866–1902.

—— Six Centuries of Work and Wages. 2 vols. Oxford, 1884.

Smith, C. Roach. The Rural Life of Shakespeare. 1870.

Ellacombe, H. N. The Plant-lore and Gardencraft of Shakespeare. 1878.

Seebohm, Frederick. The English Village Community. 1883.

Hazlitt, W. C. Gleanings in Old Garden Literature. 1887.

Prothero, R. E. (Baron Ernle). The Pioneers and Progress of English Farming. 1888.

—— Agriculture and Gardening. [In Shakespeare's England, 2 vols. Oxford, 1916.]

Blomfield, Sir R. The Formal Garden in England. 1892. [With F. I. Thomas.]

Amherst, Alicia. A History of Gardening in England. 1895.

Hasbach, W. A History of the English Agricultural Labourer. Tr. Eng. 1908.

McDonald, D. Agricultural Writers, 1200–1800. 1908.

Arber, A. Herbals, their Origin and Evolution. Cambridge, 1912.

(5) THE FINE ARTS

(a) Painting, Sculpture and Engraving

H[aydock], R[ichard]. A Tracte containing the Artes of curious Paintinge, carvinge & buildinge. Oxford, 1598. [From G. P. Lomazzo.]

Peacham, Henry. The Art of Drawing with the Pen, and Limming in Water Colours. 1606.

Evelyn, John. Sculptura, or the History of Chalcography. 1662; ed. C. F. Bell, Oxford, 1906.

Walpole, Horace. Anecdotes of Painting in England. 4 vols. 1762–71; ed. R. Wornum, 3 vols. 1849.

Colvin, Sir Sidney. Early Engravings and Engravers in England (1545–1695). 1905.

Williamson, G. C. The History of Portrait Miniatures. 2 vols. 1907.

Spielmann, M. H. British Portrait Painting to the Opening of the Nineteenth Century. 2 vols. 1910.

Baker, C. H. C. Lely and the Stuart Portrait Painters before and after Van Dyck. 2 vols. 1912.

Cust, Lionel. Painting, Sculpture, and Engraving. [In Shakespeare's England, 2 vols. Oxford, 1916.]

Designs by Inigo Jones for Masques and Plays at Court. Ed. P. Simpson and C. F. Bell, Walpole Soc. 1924.

Baker, C. H. C. and Constable, W. G. English Painting of the Sixteenth and Seventeenth Centuries. 1930.

(b) Music

[For collections of songs, madrigals, etc. see below pp. 481 ff.]

Morley, Thomas. A Plaine and Easie Introduction to Practicall Musicke. 1597.

Ravenscroft. Thomas. A Briefe Discourse of Musicke. 1614.

Playford, John. A Brief Introduction to the Skill of Musick for Song and Viol. 1654 (and 15 edns to 1700).

Nagel, W. Geschichte der Musik in England. 2 vols. Strasburg, 1894–7.

Davey, Henry. A History of English Music. 1895.

Naylor, E. W. Shakespeare and Music. 1896; 1931.

Oxford History of Music. Ed. W. H. Hadow. 6 vols. Oxford, 1901–5. [Vols. II and III.]

Walker, Ernest. A History of Music in England. Oxford, 1907.

Galpin, F. W. Old English Instruments of Music. 1910.

Cowling, G. H. Music on the Shakespearian Stage. Cambridge, 1913.

Borren, Charles van den. Sources of Keyboard Music in England. Tr. Eng. [1914].

Squire, W. Barclay. Music. [In Shakespeare's England, 2 vols. Oxford, 1916.]

Fellowes, E. H. The English Madrigal Composers. Oxford, 1921.

(c) Architecture

Shute, John. The First and Chief Groundes of Architecture. 1563; 1584.

The First Booke of Architecture. 5 pts, 1611. [Tr. through Dutch from Sebastiano Serlio, Architettura, 1551.]

Wotton, Sir Henry. The Elements of Architecture. 1624; ed. S. T. Prideaux, 1903.

Kip, J. and Knyff, L. Britannia Illustrata. 1709.

Campbell, C. Vitruvius Britannicus. 2 vols. 1715. [Illustrations.]

Nash, Joseph. The Mansions of England in the Olden Time. 4 vols. 1839–49; ed. C. Holme, 1905.

Gotch, J. A. Architecture of the Renaissance in England. 2 vols. 1891–4. [With W. T. Brown.]

—— Early Renaissance Architecture in England (1500–1625). 1901; 1914 (rev.).

—— The Growth of the English House. 1909.

—— Architecture. [In Shakespeare's England, 2 vols. Oxford, 1916.]

Blomfield, Sir Reginald. History of Renaissance Architecture (1500–1800). 2 vols. 1897.

Garner, Thomas and Stratton, Arthur. The Domestic Architecture of England during the Tudor Period. 2 vols. 1908.

Stratton, Arthur. The English Interior. 1920.

Jackson, Sir T. G. The Renaissance of Roman Architecture. 2 vols. Cambridge, 1922. [Vol. II.]

(d) The Lesser Arts

Vallance, A. Art in England during the Elizabethan and Stuart Periods. Studio, Spring No. 1908.

Litchfield, F. Illustrated History of Furniture. 1892.

Macquoid, P. A History of English Furniture. 3 vols. 1904–8. [Vol. I.]

Macquoid, P. and Edwards, R. Dictionary of English Furniture. 3 vols. 1924–7.

Jourdain, M. English Decoration and Furniture (1500–1650). 1924.

Jewitt, L. The Ceramic Art of Great Britain. 2 vols. 1878.

Thomson, W. G. A History of Tapestry. 1906.
—— Tapestry Weaving in England. 1914.

Smith, H. Clifford. Jewellery. 1908.

Strutt, Joseph. Dress and Habits of the People of England. 2 vols. 1796–9; ed. J. R. Planché, 2 vols. 1842.

Fairholt, F. W. Costume in England, till the Close of the Eighteenth Century. 1846; rev. H. A. Dillon, 2 vols. 1885.

Calthorpe, D. C. English Costume. 4 vols. 1906. [Vol. III, Tudor and Stuart.]

Ashdown, C. C. British Costume during Nineteen Centuries. 1910.

Kelly, F. M. and Schwabe, R. A Short History of Costume and Armour. 1931.

(6) Sports and Pastimes

(a) Horsemanship and Farriery

Huth, F. N. Works on Horses and Equitation. A Bibliographical Record of Hippology. 1887.

The Proprytees and Medycynes for Hors. [1500?] (de Worde.)

Blundeville, Thomas. The Fower Chiefyst Offices belonging to Horsmanshippe. 2 pts, 1565–6; [1570?]; 1580; 1593; 1597; 1609.
—— A Newe Booke, containing the Arte of Ryding, and Breakinge Great Horses. [1560?]; 1580; 1597. [From Federico Grisone, Ordini di Cavalcare.]

Malbie, Sir Nicholas. Remedies for Diseases of Horses. 1574 (anon.). [Probably not by Malbie.]
—— A Plaine and Easie Way to remedie a Horse that is foundered in his Feete. 1576; 1583; 1594.

Astley, J. The Art of Riding, set foorth out of Xenophon and Gryson. 1584.

Bedingfield, Thomas. The Art of Riding. 1584. [Abbrev. from Claudio Corte, Il Cavallerizzo.]

Clifford, Christopher. The Schoole of Horsmanship. 1585.

Mascall, L. The First Booke of Cattell, wherein is shewed the Government of Oxen, Kine, Calves, and how to use Bulls and other Cattell to the Yoake and Fell; the Second Booke intreating of the Government of Horses. 1587; 1591; 1596; 1600; 1605; 1610.

Markham, Gervase. A Discource of Horsmanshippe. 1593; 1595; 1597; 1599; 1606.
—— How to trayne and teach Horses to amble. 1605.
—— Cavalarice; or the English Horseman. 1607; 1617.
—— A Cure for all Diseases in Horses. 1610; 1616 (as Markhams Method).
—— Markhams Maister-peece. Or, what doth a Horse-man lacke. 1610; 1623; 1631; 1636.
—— Countrey Contentments, in two Bookes. 1615; 1623; 1631; 1633. [Bk I includes The Whole Art of riding Great Horses.]
—— Markhams Faithfull Farrier. 1629; 1630; Oxford, 1631; 1635; 1638.
—— The Complete Farriar. 1639.
—— The Perfect Horseman. Ed. Launcelot Thetford, 1655.
—— The Gentleman's Accomplish'd Jockey. 1722.

C., L. W. A verie Perfect Discourse, how to know the Age of a Horse, and the Diseases that breed in him. 1601; 1602; 1610; 1624; 1630.

Morgan, Nicholas. The Perfection of Horse-Manship. 1609.

Baret, Michael. An Hipponomie or the Vineyard of Horsemanship. 1618.

The Horsemans Honour. 1620. [Sometimes attrib. to G. Markham.]

Browne, T. Fiftie Years Practice: or an Exact Discourse concerning Snaffle-riding. 1624.

Berenger, Richard. The History and Art of Horsemanship. 2 vols. 1771.

Madden, D. H. The Diary of Master William Silence. A Study of Shakespeare and Elizabethan Sport. 1897.

Gilbey, Sir Walter. The Great Horse. 1899.

Sieveking, A. F. Horsemanship, with Farriery. [In Shakespeare's England, 2 vols. Oxford, 1916.]

(b) Hunting, Coursing, Hawking, Fowling, Angling

[Dansey, W.] Arrian on Coursing. 1831. [Includes a bibliography of early works on hunting and coursing.]

Westwood, T. and Satchell, T. Bibliotheca Piscatoria. 1883. [Supplement, 1901.]

Harting, J. E. Bibliotheca Accipitraria; A Catalogue of Books relating to Falconry. 1891.

A Bibliography of Fishes. Ed. B. Dean, C. R. Eastman, E. W. Gudges and A. W. Henn. 3 vols. New York, 1916–23.

Schwerdt, C. F. G. R. Hunting, Hawking, Shooting. 3 vols. 1928.

Turbervile, George. The Booke of Faulconrie or Hauking. 1575; 1611.

—— The Noble Arte of Venerie or Hunting. 1575 (anon.); 1611; rptd Oxford, 1908.

A Perfect Booke for keepinge of Sparhawkes or Goshawkes. Ed. J. E. Harting, 1886. [Written c. 1575.]

Googe, Barnabe. Foure Bookes of Husbandry, Collected by M. Conradus Heresbachius. 1577, etc.; rev. Gervase Markham, 1631 (as The Whole Art of Husbandry). [Bk iv treats of Angling.]

M[ascall], L[eonard]. A Booke of Fishing with Hooke & Line. 1590; 1600.

Cockaine, Sir Thomas. A Short Treatise of Hunting. 1591; ed. E. Cokayne, Roxburghe Club, 1897; ed. facs. W. R. Halliday, Shakespeare Ass. 1932.

Manwood, J. A Brefe Collection of the Lawes of the Forest. [1592]; 1598; 1615.

Markham, Gervase. The Gentlemans Academie. Or, the Booke of S. Albans: compiled by Juliana Barnes, and now reduced into a Better Method, by G. M. 1595.

—— The English Husbandman. 2 pts, 1613–4; 1635 (bis). [Pt ii contains a Discourse of the Generall Art of Fishing; ed. H. G. Hutchinson, 1927.]

—— Cheape and Good Husbandry. Together with the Making of Fish-ponds, and the Taking of all Sorts of Fish. 1614, etc.

—— The Pleasures of Princes. A Discourse of Fishing. 1614.

—— Countrey Contentments, in two Bookes. 1615, etc. [Bk i contains the Arts of Hunting, Hawking, etc.]

—— Hungers Prevention: or, the Whole Arte of Fowling. 1621.

—— The Young Sportsman's Instructor. In Angling, Fowling, Hawking, Hunting, ordering Singing Birds, Hawks, Poultry, Coneys, Hares, and Dogs, and how to cure them. By G. M., n.d.; rptd 1820; ed. S. Gamidge, Worcester, n.d.

Gryndall, William. Hawking, Hunting, Fowling, and Fishing, with the True Measures of Blowing. 1596.

Taverner, John. Certaine Experiments concerning Fish and Fruite. 1600.

D[ennys], J[ohn]. The Secrets of Angling. 1613; 1630; ed. E. Arber (in An English Garner, vol. i, 1870); ed. E. M. Goldsmid (in

Bibliotheca Curiosa, 1885]. [Verse. G. Markham turned it into prose in Countrey Contentments, 1623 (2nd edn).]

S., T. A Jewell for Gentrie. Being all the Arts belonging to Hawking, Hunting, Fowling and Fishing. Together with all the True Measures for winding of the Horne. 3 pts, 1614. [Based on Book of St Albans.]

Latham, Simon. Lathams Falconry: or the Faulcons Lure and Cure. 1615; 1633.

—— Lathams New and Second Booke of Faulconry. 1618.

Bert, Edmund. An Approved Treatise of Hawkes and Hawking. 1619.

Barker, Thomas. The Art of Angling. 1651; 1653; 1654; 1657; rptd 1820.

Walton, Izaak. The Compleat Angler. 1653. [For later edns see below p. 830.]

Wase, Christopher. Cynegeticon. A Poem of Hunting by Grotius. Englished and Illustrated. 1654.

Harting, J. E. The Ornithology of Shakespeare. 1871.

Ellacombe, H. N. Shakespeare as an Angler. 1883.

Madden, D. H. The Diary of Master William Silence. A Study of Shakespeare and Elizabethan Sport. 1897.

Aldis, H. G. Writers on Country Pursuits and Pastimes. CHEL. vol. iv. 1909.

Shakespeare's England. 2 vols. Oxford, 1916. [Includes Hunting by Sir J. W. Fortescue; Falconry by Gerald Lascelles; Coursing, Fowling and Angling by A. F. Sieveking.]

(c) Archery, Fencing and Duelling

Ascham, Roger. Toxophilus, the Schoole of Shootinge. 1545; 1571; 1589; ed. E. Arber, Birmingham, 1868.

Smythe, Sir John. Certain Discourses concerning Weapons. 1590.

Neade, William. The Double-armed Man. 1625.

Markham, Gervase. The Art of Archerie. 1634.

Wood, William. The Bowman's Glory. 1682.

Longman, C. J. and Walrond, H. Archery. 1894. (Badminton Lib.). [With bibliography.]

Rushton, W. L. Shakespeare an Archer. 1897.

Walrond, H. Archery. [In Shakespeare's England, 2 vols. Oxford, 1916.]

Thimm, C. A. Bibliography of Fencing and Duelling. 1896.

[Segar, Sir W.?] The Booke of Honor and Armes. 1590.

Sutcliffe, Matthew. The Practice, Proceedings and Lawes of Armes. 1593.

Vincentio Saviolo, His Practise. 2 pts, 1595–4.

Silver, George. Paradoxes of Defence, wherein is proved the True Grounds of Fight to be in the Short Auncient Weapons. 1599; ed. facs. J. D. Wilson, Shakespeare Ass. 1933.
—— Brief Instructions upon my Paradoxes of Defence. Ed. Cyril Matthey, 1898.

Selden, John. The Duello or Single Combat. 1610.

A Brief of Two Proclamations and his Majesty's Edict against Duels. 1613.

Bacon, Francis (Viscount St Albans). The Charge touching Duells. 1614.

Worke for Cutlers; or a Merry Dialogue betweene Sword, Rapier and Dagger. 1615; ed. A. F. Sieveking, 1904.

Favyn, André. The Theater of Honour and Knighthood. 1623.

Castle, Egerton. Schools and Masters of Fence. 1885; 1892 (rev. edn).

Sieveking, A. F. Fencing and Duelling. [In Shakespeare's England, 2 vols. Oxford, 1916.]

(d) Dancing

[Copland, Robert?] The Maner of Dauncynge of Bace Daunces after the Use of Fraunce. 1521.

Elyot, Sir Thomas. The Boke named The Governour. 1531, etc.; ed. H. H. S. Croft, 1880.

Ascham, Roger. The Scholemaster. 1570, etc.; ed. J. E. B. Mayor, 1863; ed. E. Arber, 1895.

Mulcaster, Richard. Positions wherein those Circumstances are examined Necessarie for the Training up of Children. 1581.

Davies, Sir John. Orchestra. 1596; ed. E. Arber (English Garner, vol. v, 1882). [Verse.]

James I. Βασιλικὸν Δῶρον. Edinburgh, 1599; Edinburgh, 1603; 1603 (5 edns); 1604.

Peacham, Henry. The Compleat Gentleman. 1622; 1627; 1634; ed. G. S. Gordon, Oxford, 1906.

P[layford], J[ohn]. The English Dancing-Master. 1651 (and 9 edns to 1700).

Strutt, Joseph. Glig-Gamena Angel-Deod, or the Sports and Pastimes of the People of England. 1801; ed. J. C. Cox, 1903.

Grove, Lilly. Dancing. 1895. (Badminton Lib.)

Naylor, E. W. Shakespeare and Music. 1896.

Vuillier, G. A History of Dancing. 2 vols. 1898.

Sharp, Cecil. The Country Dance Book. 6 pts, 1909–22.

Sieveking, A. F. Dancing. [In Shakespeare's England, 2 vols. Oxford, 1916.]

(e) Miscellaneous Games and Sports

Erasmus, Desiderius. Colloquia. Basle, 1529, etc.; tr. Eng. N. Bailey, 1725. [Lusus Pueriles.]

Elyot, Sir Thomas. The Governour. 1531, etc.; ed. H. H. S. Croft, 1880.

Vives, J. L. Linguae Latinae Exercitatio. Basle, 1539, etc.; tr. and ed. Foster Watson, 1908.

Rowbothum, James. The Pleasaunt and Wittie Playe of the Cheasts. 1562; 1569; 1597. [From French of Damiano da Odemira.]

Digby, Everard. De Arte Natandi. 1587; tr. Eng. Christopher Middleton, 1595.

Wilson, George. The Commendation of Cockes and Cock-fighting. 1607.

Markham, Gervase. The Pleasures of Princes or Good Mens Recreations. 1614. [Section on cock-fighting.]

Saul, Arthur. The Famous Game of Chesse-Play. 1614; [1620?]; 1640.

Annalia Dubrensia. [Poems] upon the Yeerely Celebration of Mr. Robert Dovers' Olympick Games upon the Cotswold-Hill. Ed. M. Walbancke, 1636; ed. A. B. Grosart, Manchester, 1877.

Stokes, William. The Vaulting Master. Oxford, 1652.

Cotton, Charles. The Compleat Gamester. 1674, etc.; ed. C. H. Hartmann, 1930.

Holme, Randle. The Academy of Armoury. 1688.

Strutt, Joseph. Glig-Gamena Angel-Deod, or the Sports and Pastimes of the People of England. 1801; ed. J. C. Cox, 1903.

Blaine, D. P. An Encyclopaedia of Rural Sports. 1840.

Hore, J. P. The History of Newmarket and the Annals of the Turf [to 1700]. 3 vols. 1886.

Govett, L. A. The King's Own Book of Sports. History of the Declarations of James I as to Sports on Sunday, etc. 1890.

Gomme, Lady A. B. The Traditional Games of England, Scotland, and Ireland. 2 vols. 1894–8.

Hackwood, F. W. Old English Sports. 1907.

Sieveking, A. F. Games. [In Shakespeare's England, 2 vols. Oxford, 1916.]

Lee, Sir Sidney. Bear baiting, Bullfighting, and Cockfighting. [In Shakespeare's England, 2 vols. Oxford, 1916.]

(7) HERALDRY

Moule, T. Bibliotheca Heraldica Magnae Britanniae. 1822.

Gatfield, G. Guide to Printed Books and Manuscripts relating to Heraldry and Genealogy. 1892.

Legh, Gerard. The Accedens of Armory. 1562; 1568; 1576; 1591; 1597; 1612.

Bossewell, John. Workes of Armorie. 1572; 1597.

R[obinson, R.] A Rare, True and Proper Blazon of Colours in Armoryes and Ensigns. [1583.] [Tr. from French.]

Ferne, Sir John. The Blazon of Gentrie. 1586.

[Segar, Sir William?] The Booke of Honor and Armes. 1590.

Segar, Sir William. Honor Military and Civill. 1602.

Wyrley, William. The True Use of Armorie. 1592.

B[olton], E[dmund]. The Elements of Armories. 1610.

Guillim, John. A Display of Heraldrie. 1610; 1632; 1638.

Milles, Thomas. The Catalogue of Honor. 1610.

Holland, Henry. Baziliωlogia. Effigies of All our English Kings with their Armes. 1618.

Brooke, Ralph. A Catalogue and Succession of the Kings, Princes, Dukes, Marquesses, Earles, and Viscounts of this Realme with their Armes, Wives, and Children. 1619; 1622.

Peacham, Henry. The Compleat Gentleman. 1622, etc.; ed. G. S. Gordon, Oxford, 1906.

Favyn, André. The Theater of Honour and Knighthood. 1623.

Dalloway, James. Inquiries into the Origin and Progress of the Science of Heraldry in England. 1793.

Noble, Mark. A History of the College of Arms. 1804.

von Mauntz, Alfred. Heraldik im Dienste der Shakspear-Forschung. Berlin, 1903.

Nason, A. H. Heralds and Heraldry in Ben Jonson's Plays. New York, 1907.

Barron, Oswald. Heraldry. [In Shakespeare's England, 2 vols. Oxford, 1916.]

(8) COOKERY BOOKS, ETC.

The Boke of Cokery. 1500 (Pynson).

The Boke of Kervynge. 1508; 1513; [1560?]; 1613; ed. F. J. Furnivall, Roxburghe Club, 1866, EETS. 1868.

Hervet, Gentian. Xenophon's Treatise of Householde. 1532; 1537; 1544; [1550?]; 1557; 1573.

Boorde, Andrew. A compendyous Regyment or a Dyetary of Helth. [1542?]; 1567 (for 1547); 1562; 1576; ed. F. J. Furnivall, EETS. Ex. Ser. 1870.

Rhodes, Hugh. The Boke of Nurture for Men Servants and Children. [1545?]; [1550?]; [1564?]; 1568; [1568?]; 1577.

A Proper Newe Booke of Cookerye. 1558; ed. F. Frere, Cambridge, 1913.

Turner, William. A New Boke of the Natures of All Wines. 1568. [Extracts in Social England Illustrated, ed. A. Lang, 1903.]

Dawson, Thomas. The Good Huswifes Jewell; Rare Devises for Conseites in Cookerie. 1587.

K[yd], T. The Householders Philosophie: whereunto is anexed a Dairie Booke. 1588. [Tr. from Tasso.]

Buttes, Henry. Dyets Dry Dinner. 1599.

Platt, Sir Hugh. Delightes for Ladies, to adorne their Persons, Tables, Closets and Distillatories. 1602 (and 9 edns to 1636).

A Closet for Ladies and Gentlewomen, or, the Art of Preserving, Conserving, and Candying. 1608 (and 6 edns to 1636).

Murrell, John. A New Booke of Cookerie. 1615; 1617.

— A Daily Exercise for Ladies and Gentlewomen. 1617. [Preserving.]

May, R. The Accomplisht Cook. 1660; 1678; 1685.

Digby, Sir Kenelm. The Closet of Sir Kenelme Digbie opened: whereby is discovered several Ways for making of Metheglin, Sider, Cherry-wine, etc. Together with Directions for Cookery. 1677, etc.; ed. Anne Macdonell, 1910.

A Plain Plantain: Country Wines, Dishes and Herbal Cures, from a 17th Century Household Receipt Book. Ed. R. G. Alexander, 1923.

Walford, C. Early Laws and Customs in Great Britain regarding Food. Trans. Royal Hist. Soc. VIII, 1880.

Hazlitt, W. C. Old Cookery Books and Ancient Cuisine. 1886.

Oxford, A. W. English Cookery Books to the Year 1850. Oxford, 1913.

VI. THE POLITICAL BACKGROUND

Political History (Contemporary sources, Later works): General Works; 1485–1547; 1547–1603; 1603–1660.

Constitutional History: General Works; Parliament; The Council.

[The following lists should be supplemented by Bibliography of British History, Tudor Period, 1485–1603, ed. C. Read, Oxford, 1933, and the companion work Bibliography of British History, Stuart Period, 1603–1714, ed. G. Davies, Oxford, 1928.]

A. POLITICAL HISTORY

(1) GENERAL AND MISCELLANEOUS

(a) Sources

[This section contains sources that are too general or miscellaneous to fit into any of the three divisions 1485–1547, 1547–1603, 1603–1660.]

Holinshed, Raphael. Chronicles. 2 vols. 1577; ed. Sir Henry Ellis, 6 vols. 1807–8.

Stow, John. The Chronicles of England. [First appeared in this permanent form 1580. Many rpts with addns down to 1631. Later edns called 'Annales.']

Cabala, sive Scrinia sacra. 1654; 1691 (best edn). [Miscellaneous state papers.]

Foedera, Conventiones, Literae. Ed. T. Rymer and R. Sanderson, 20 vols. 1704–32. [Stops in 1654.]

Memorials of Affairs of State in the Reigns of Q. Elizabeth and K. James collected [chiefly] from the Original Papers of Sir R. Winwood. Ed. Edmund Sawyer, 3 vols. 1725.

Desiderata curiosa. Ed. Francis Peck, 2 vols. 1732–5; 2 vols. in 1, 1779 (best edn). [Miscellaneous collection of material.]

The Harleian Miscellany: or a Collection of Pamphlets and Tracts. Ed. William Oldys, 8 vols. 1744–6; ed. J. Malham, 12 vols. 1808–11; ed. T. Park, 10 vols. 1808–13.

Letters and Memorials of State in the Reigns of Queen Mary, Queen Elizabeth, King James, King Charles I from the Originals at Penshurst. Ed. Arthur Collins, 2 vols. 1746. [Commonly called Sydney Papers.]

A Collection of Scarce and Valuable Tracts. 16 vols. 1748–52; ed. Sir Walter Scott, 13 vols. 1809–15. [Known as Somers tracts.]

Birch, T. An historical view of the negotiations between the Courts of England, France and Brussels, 1592–1617. 1749.

Miscellaneous [Hardwicke] State Papers from 1501 to 1726. 2 vols. 1778.

Illustrations of British History. Ed. E. Lodge, 3 vols. 1791; 3 vols. 1838. [Has Talbot Papers.]

The State Papers and Letters of Sir Ralph Sadler. Ed. A. Clifford (with notes by Sir Walter Scott), 2 vols. Edinburgh, 1809; 3 vols. 1908. [See also Letters and Negotiations of Sir Ralph Sadler, Ambassador of Henry VIII to Scotland, Edinburgh, 1720.]

Original Letters from the British Museum and Other Collections. Ed. Sir Henry Ellis, 11 vols. 1824–46.

Archives ou Correspondance inédite de la Maison d'Orange-Nassau. Ser. 1 and 2. Ed. G. Groen van Prinsterer, 9 vols. Leyden, 1835–47; 5 vols. Utrecht, 1857–62. [Valuable for Anglo-Dutch relations, 1560–1688.]

The Egerton Papers, a Collection of Public and Private Documents of Elizabeth and James I. Ed. J. P. Collier, Camden Soc. 1840.

Letters of the Kings of England. Ed. J. O. Halliwell [-Phillipps], 2 vols. 1846.

Bacon, Francis (Viscount St Albans). Collected Works. Ed. J. Spedding, R. L. Ellis and D. D. Heath, 14 vols. 1857–74.

Calendar of State Papers and Manuscripts relating to English Affairs existing in the Archives and Collections of Venice. 1202–1603, 12 vols. 1864–98; 1603–66, 25 vols. 1900–33. [Valuable until 1557, after which there is no Venetian representative in England till 1602, and later.]

Tudor Tracts, 1532–1588. Ed. A. F. Pollard, 1903. (English Garner.)

Ward, Sir A. W. Historical and Political Writings. I. State Papers and Letters. II. Histories and Memoirs. CHEL. vol. VII, 1911.

(b) Later Works

[The most succinct account is in the Cambridge Modern History: more continuous narratives are in Ranke or Innes and Trevelyan (listed, p. 401). Froude writes as a partisan but virulent criticism has not seriously impaired the value of his detailed account of the critical years 1529–88.]

Hume, David. The History of England from the Invasion of Julius Caesar to the Revolution in 1688. 8 vols. 1763. [Originally issued in pts, 1754–7. Continued by Smollett to 1760 and by T. S. Hughes to 1835.]

Lingard, John. A History of England to 1688. 8 vols. 1819–30; 10 vols. 1849 (rev. edn).

Devereux, W. B. Lives and Letters of the Devereux, Earls of Essex, 1540–1646. 2 vols. 1853.

Froude, J. A. History of England from the Fall of Wolsey to the Defeat of the Spanish Armada. 12 vols. 1856–70; 8 vols. 1862–4 (rev. edn).

von Ranke, Leopold. Englische Geschichte, vornehmlich im sechzehnten und siebzehnten Jahrhundert. 7 vols. Berlin, 1859–68; tr. Eng. 6 vols. Oxford, 1875.

Motley, J. L. History of the United Netherlands, 1584–1619. 4 vols. 1860–7.

Seeley, Sir J. R. The Growth of British Policy. 2 vols. Cambridge, 1895.

Bagwell, R. Ireland under the Tudors. 3 vols. 1885–90. [Continued in Ireland under the Stuarts, 1603–1660, 2 vols. 1909.]

Figgis, J. N. The Theory of the Divine Right of Kings. Cambridge, 1896, 1914 (enlarged).

Brown, P. Hume. History of Scotland to the Present Time. 3 vols. Cambridge, 1899–1909, 1911.

Cambridge Modern History. Ed. Sir A. W. Ward, G. W. Prothero, and Stanley Leathes, Cambridge, 1902–6. [Vols. I–IV.]

Innes, A. D. England under the Tudors. 1905, etc.

Pollard, A. F. Factors in Modern History. 1907; 1926.

Smith, L. P. The Life and Letters of Sir Henry Wotton. 2 vols. Oxford, 1907.

Tudor Studies presented to Albert Frederick Pollard. Ed. R. W. Seton-Watson, 1924.

(2) 1485–1547

(a) Sources

[For Henry VII, Pollard's selection will suffice as an introduction. For Henry VIII the Letters and Papers overshadow all other sources, but the Chronicles of Wriothesley and Hall are both valuable.]

Hall, Edward. The Union of the Two Noble and Illustre Famelies York and Lancaster. 1542; ed. Sir Henry Ellis, 1809; ed. Charles Whibley, 2 vols. 1904. [Best contemporary history of Henry VIII's reign.]

Memorials of King Henry the Seventh. Ed. J. Gairdner, Rolls Ser. 1858.

Calendar of Letters, Dispatches and State Papers relating to the Negotiations between England and Spain preserved in the Archives of Simancas and elsewhere. 11 vols. in 17, 1862–1916. [1485–1553.]

Letters and Papers Foreign and Domestic of the Reign of Henry VIII. 21 vols. 1862–1910; 2nd edn, vol. I, 1920. [Includes many documents outside PRO. Supersedes State Papers during the Reign of Henry the Eighth, 11 vols. 1830–52, which prints selected correspondence in extenso.]

Records of the Reformation, the Divorce, 1527–33. Ed. Nicholas Pocock, 2 vols. Oxford, 1870.

Materials for a History of the Reign of Henry VII from Documents in the Public Record Office. Ed. W. Campbell, 2 vols. Rolls Ser. 1873–7.

Wriothesley, Charles. A Chronicle of England. Ed. W. D. Hamilton, 2 vols. Camden Soc. 1875–7.

The Reign of Henry VII from Contemporary Sources. Ed. A. F. Pollard, 3 vols. 1913–4.

(b) Later Works

[Fisher is the best modern work, and supplies a useful bibliography. Probably Busch is the best introduction and has a detailed bibliography. Bacon's Henry VII is well worth reading: modern lives are by Gairdner and Temperley. Pollard's studies of Wolsey and Henry VIII are valuable, if biased.]

Bacon, Francis. The Historie of the Raigne of King Henry the Seventh. 1622; ed. J. R. Lumby, 1876.

Herbert, Edward (Baron Herbert of Cherbury). The Life and Raigne of King Henry the Eighth. 1649; rptd 1741.

Brewer, J. S. The Reign of Henry VIII to the Death of Wolsey. 2 vols. 1884.

Gairdner, James. Henry the Seventh. 1889.

Busch, W. England unter den Tudors. Vol. I (all pbd), Stuttgart, 1892; tr. Eng. 1895.

Merriman, R. B. The Life and Letters of Thomas Cromwell. 2 vols. Oxford, 1902.

Pollard, A. F. Henry VIII. 1902; 1905 (with references).

—— Wolsey, 1929.

Fisher, H. A. L. Political History of England. Vol. v, 1485–1547. 1906.

Temperley, Gladys. Henry VII. 1914.

(3) 1547–1603

(a) Sources

[The sources for 1547–1603 are more voluminous than for the earlier period. There is no collection similar to the Letters and Papers, but the various Calendars of State Papers become of increasing importance as they become more detailed. The correspondence of Burghley and the letters ptd by Forbes, Birch, Wright and Tytler are of the first importance Camden's is the best contemporary history but it is doubtful whether he should be regarded as an independent authority.]

Camden, William. Annales Rerum anglicarum et hibernicarum regnante Elizabetha. 1615–27; ed. Thomas Hearne, 3 vols. 1717.

Digges, Sir Dudley. The Compleat Ambassador or Two Treaties of the Intended Marriage of Qu: Elizabeth. 1655.

A full view of Public Transactions in the Reign of Q. Elizabeth. Ed. Patrick Forbes, 2 vols. 1740–1. [State papers chiefly 1558–63.]

Memoirs of Queen Elizabeth from 1581 till her Death. From the Papers of Anthony Bacon Ed. Thomas Birch, 2 vols. 1754.

Memoirs of the Life of Robert Cary. 1759 ed. Sir Walter Scott, Edinburgh, 1808.

The Progresses of Queen Elizabeth. Ed. John Nichols, 4 vols. 1788–1821; 3 vols. 1823.

Queen Elizabeth and her Times. Ed. T Wright, 2 vols. 1838. [Letters of Burghley Leicester, Walsingham, etc.]

England under the Reigns of Edward VI and Mary. Ed. P. F. Tytler, 2 vols. 1839 [Original letters.]

Correspondence of Robert Dudley, Earl of Leycester, during his Government of the Low Countries. Ed. John Bruce, Camden Soc. 1844.

Letters written by John Chamberlain. Ed Sarah Williams, Camden Soc. 1861. [New letters.]

Calendar of State Papers, Foreign Series 1547–87. 25 vols. (including Addenda fo 1583). 1861–1931.

Calendar of State Papers, Domestic Series. Vols. I and II, 1547–90, 1856–65; vols. III–VI, 1591–1603 and Addenda, 2 vols. 1867–72.

Literary Remains of King Edward VI. Ed. J. G. Nichols, Roxburghe Club, 1857.

Historical Manuscripts Commission. Salisbury MSS. 15 vols. 1883–1930. [Contains many official papers of Burghley and Robert Cecil, some of which are ptd in Samuel Haynes and W. Murdin's Collection of State Papers of Burghley, 2 vols. 1740–59. See also Hist. MSS Commission 3rd–7th Reports.]

Troubles Connected with the Prayer Book of 1549. Ed. Nicholas Pocock, Camden Soc. 1884.

Relations politiques des Pays-Bas et de l'Angleterre sous le Règne de Philippe II, 1555–1579. Ed. J. M. B. C. Baron Kervyn de Lettenhove, 11 vols. Brussels, 1882–1900.

Calendar of Letters and State Papers, relating to English Affairs preserved principally in the Archives of Simancas. 4 vols. 1892–9. [Incomplete and confined to Simancas.]

(b) Later Works

[Pollard's book is the best for the whole section and has a good bibliography. There have been no detailed studies of the reigns of Edward VI and Mary since Froude's (see p. 397), but Pollard's Protector Somerset and Stone's Mary I supply new facts as well as new points of view. Read and Cheyney furnish impartial and learned accounts of the political history of Elizabeth's reign.]

Nicolas, Sir N. H. Life of William Davison, Secretary of State to Queen Elizabeth. 1823.

Burgon, J. W. Life and Times of Sir Thomas Gresham. 2 vols. 1839.

Russell, F. W. Kett's Rebellion in Norfolk. 1859.

Edwards, Edward. The Life of Sir Walter Ralegh. 2 vols. 1868.

Creighton, Mandell. Queen Elizabeth. 1896.

Hume, Martin. The Year after the Armada, and Other Studies. 1896.

—— The Great Lord Burghley. 1898; 1906.

—— Treason and Plot. Struggles for Catholic Supremacy in the Last Years of Elizabeth. 1901.

Pollard, A. F. England under Protector Somerset. 1900.

—— Political History of England. Vol. VI, 1547–1603. 1910.

Stone, J. M. The History of Mary I. 1901.

Staehlin, Karl. Sir Francis Walsingham und seine Zeit. Vol. I (all pbd), Heidelberg, 1908. [Useful down to 1573.]

Rose-Troup, Frances. The Western Rebellion of 1549. 1913.

Cheyney, E. P. A History of England from the Defeat of the Armada to the Death of Elizabeth. 2 vols. New York, 1914–26.

Cecil, Algernon. A Life of Robert Cecil, First Earl of Salisbury. 1915.

Read, Conyers. Mr Secretary Walsingham and the Policy of Queen Elizabeth. 3 vols. Oxford, 1925.

Muller, J. A. Stephen Gardiner and the Tudor Reaction. New York, 1926.

(4) 1603–1660

(a) Sources

(i) General

[The Calendar of State Papers, Domestic, covers the whole period and is much more detailed than the corresponding volumes for the previous century. The Venetian Calendar (listed p. 397 above) has reached 1666 and should be consulted throughout. Rushworth's Collections are partly based on state papers and private information and partly on pamphlets and newspapers, so should be used with caution. His parliamentary bias can be corrected from Clarendon, whose History and papers are the most valuable source for the civil wars.]

Baker, Sir R. A Chronicle of the Kings of England. 1641. [Edns after 1660 have a valuable continuation to that year by E. Phillips.]

Rushworth, J. Historical Collections of Private Passages of State. 7 vols. 1659–1701; 8 vols. 1721. [Covers 1618–49.]

Hyde, Edward (Earl of Clarendon). The History of the Rebellion. 3 vols. Oxford, 1702–4; ed. B. Bandinel, 7 vols. Oxford, 1849; ed. W. D. Macray, 6 vols. Oxford, 1888. [For critical estimate see Sir C. H. Firth in EHR. XIX, 1904.]

State Papers collected by Edward, Earl of Clarendon. Ed. R. Scrope and T. Monkhouse, 3 vols. Oxford, 1767–86. [Covers 1621–60. The Calendar of these and other Clarendon state papers at the Bodleian Lib. is ptd as far as 1657, ed. W. D. Macray, 3 vols. Oxford, 1869–76.]

Calendar of State Papers, Domestic Series, James I. 4 vols. 1857–9, with Addenda 1580–1625, 1872; Charles I. 22 vols. 1858–93, with Addenda 1625–49, 1897; 1649–60, 13 vols. 1875–86.

Stuart Tracts 1603–93. Ed. Sir C. H. Firth, 1903. (English Garner.)

(ii) 1603–1642

[The contemporary view of James I and the events of his reign can be studied in the Secret History and the Court and Times. For the reign of Charles newsletters are available in the Court and Times and Strafford's Letters. D'Ewes gives the Puritan's comments on events: his criticisms should be compared with those of Warwick and Clarendon (listed p. 399 above).]

An Impartial Collection of the Great Affairs of State. Ed. J. Nalson, 2 vols. 1682–3. [Covers 1638–42: see Hist. MSS Commission, Portland MSS, vol. i.]

Warwick, Sir Philip. Memoires of the Reigne of King Charles I. 1701; ed. Sir Walter Scott, Edinburgh, 1813.

The Earl of Strafforde's Letters and Despatches. Ed. W. Knowler, 2 vols. 1739; Dublin, 1740.

Secret History of the Court of James the First. Ed. Sir Walter Scott, 2 vols. Edinburgh, 1811. [Reprints 17th cent. histories.]

The Progresses of James I. Ed. J. Nichols, 4 vols. 1828.

The Autobiography [to 1636] and Correspondence [to 1649] of Sir Simonds D'Ewes. Ed. J. O. Halliwell[-Phillipps], 2 vols. 1845.

The Court and Times of James the First. Ed. R. F. Williams, 2 vols. 1848. [Newsletters. A similar collection exists for Charles I, 2 vols. 1848.]

Memoirs of the Reign of Charles the First. Ed. G. W. Johnson, 2 vols. 1848. [Continued in Memorials of the Civil War, ed. R. Bell, 2 vols. 1849. The four vols. often classed together as the Fairfax Correspondence.]

Historical Manuscripts Commission. Cowper MSS, vols. i–ii, 1888. [Papers of Sir John Coke.]

(iii) 1642–1660.

[For the first civil war Vicars and Sprigge are valuable for students without access to the newspapers and pamphlets on which these contemporaries based their narratives. For events in 1647 and later the Clarke Papers, with their detailed introductions, are of the greatest value. Thurloe is the main authority for the Protectorate: Ludlow for the opposition to it. The Life of Colonel Hutchinson reveals the more rigid type of Puritan.]

Vicars, John. Englands Parliamentarie-chronicle. 3 pts, 1644–6. [A history of the first civil war.]

Sprigge, J. Anglia rediviva; England's Recovery: being the History of the Army under Sir Thomas Fairfax. 1647; rptd Oxford, 1854.

Heath, J. A Brief Chronicle of the Late Intestine Warr [1637–63]. 1663; 1676.

Newcastle, Margaret, Duchess of. The Life of William Cavendish, Duke of Newcastle. 1667; ed. Sir C. H. Firth. 1886.

Grumble, T. The Life of General Monck, Duke of Albemarle. 1671.

Whitelocke, B. Memorials of the English Affairs. 1682; ed. 4 vols. Oxford, 1853.

Memoirs of Edmund Ludlow. 3 vols. Vivay, 1698–9; ed. Sir C. H. Firth, 2 vols. Oxford, 1894.

Walker, Sir Edward. Historical Discourses. 1705. [Valuable for campaigns of 1644–5, and 1650, and for treaty of Newport.]

A Collection of Original Letters and Papers concerning the Affairs of England, 1641–60. Ed. T. Carte, 2 vols. 1739. [Ormonde Papers.]

A Collection of the State Papers of John Thurloe. Ed. T. Birch, 7 vols. 1742.

Original Letters and Papers of State, 1649–1658. Ed. J. Nickolls, 1743. [Usually called Milton State Papers.]

Memoirs of the Life of Colonel Hutchinson by his Widow [Lucy Hutchinson]. Ed. J. Hutchinson, 1806, etc.; ed. Sir C. H. Firth, 1906.

Cromwelliana. Ed. M. Stace, 1810. [Extracts from newspapers, 1642–58.]

Select Tracts relating to the Civil Wars in England. Ed. Francis, Baron Maseres, 2 vols. 1815 and 1826.

Memorials of the Great Civil War, 1646–52. Ed. H. Cary, 2 vols. 1842.

Oliver Cromwell's Letters and Speeches. Ed. T. Carlyle, 2 vols. 1845, etc; ed. S. C. Lomas, 3 vols. 1904.

The Nicholas Papers. Correspondence of Sir Edward Nicholas, 1641–60. Ed. G. F. Warner, 4 vols. Camden Soc. 1886–1920.

Clarke Papers. Ed. C. H. Firth, 4 vols. Camden Soc. 1891–1901.

(b) Later Works

[Trevelyan furnishes the best account of the period on a moderate scale and has an interesting survey of the condition of England in 1603. Gardiner covers 1603–56 with unrivalled thoroughness, and is continued till 1658 by Firth. For 1658–60 there is nothing better than Guizot.]

Memoirs of Prince Rupert and the Cavaliers. Ed. E. B. G. Warburton, 3 vols. 1849.

Guizot, F. P. G. History of Richard Cromwell and the Restoration. Tr. Eng. A. R. Scoble, 2 vols. 1856.

Forster, J. Sir John Eliot. 2 vols. 1864.

Gardiner, S. R. History of England, 1603–42. 10 vols. 1883–4. [Pbd 1863–82, two vols. at a time, with separate titles. Continued to 1656 in History of the Great Civil War, 3 vols. 1886–91, rev. edn 4 vols. 1893, and in History of the Commonwealth and Protectorate, 3 vols. 1894–1901, rev. edn 4 vols. 1903.]

Firth, Sir C. H. Oliver Cromwell and the Rule of the Puritans. New York, 1900; 1923.
—— Cromwell's Army. 1902; 1921.
—— The Last Years of the Protectorate, 1656–8. 2 vols. 1909.
Trevelyan, G. M. England under the Stuarts. 1904, etc.
Scott, Eva. The King in Exile. 1905. [Charles II, 1646–54; continued in The Travels of King Charles II, 1654–60, 1907.]
Montague, F. C. The History of England, 1603–1660. 1907.
Abbott, W. C. A Bibliography of Oliver Cromwell. Cambridge, U.S.A. 1929.

(5) CONSTITUTIONAL HISTORY

(a) General and Miscellaneous

[General constitutional history is best studied in the two works by J. R. Tanner, and in the introductions to Prothero and Gardiner. Maitland has one survey at 1509 and another at 1625, while Medley supplies the handiest reference book.]

Smith, Sir Thomas. De Republica Anglorum. The Maner of Governement or Policie of the Realme of England. 1583; ed. L. Alston and F. W. Maitland, Cambridge, 1906.
Hallam, H. The Constitutional History of England from the Accession of Henry VII to the Death of George II. 2 vols. 1827, etc.
Anson, Sir W. R. Law and Custom of the Constitution. 2 pts, Oxford, 1886–92; ed. M. L. Gwyer: Vol. I, Parliament, 1922. Vol. II, The Crown, pt I, 1907, pt II, 1908.
The Constitutional Documents of the Puritan Revolution, 1625–1660. Ed. S. R. Gardiner, Oxford, 1889 and 1906.
Select Statutes and other Constitutional Documents, 1558–1625. Ed. G. W. Prothero, Oxford, 1894 and 1913.
Medley, D. J. A Student's Manual of English Constitutional History. Oxford, 1894 and 1925.
Holdsworth, Sir W. S. The History of English Law. 3 vols. 1903–9; 9 vols. 1924–6.
Maitland, F. W. The Constitutional History of England. Cambridge, 1908.
Tanner, J. R. Tudor Constitutional Documents, 1485–1603, with an Historical Commentary. Cambridge, 1922. [Continued in: Constitutional Documents of the Reign of James I, Cambridge, 1930.]
—— English Constitutional Conflicts of the Seventeenth Century, 1603–1689. Cambridge, 1928.
Evans, F. M. G. The Principal Secretary of State, 1558–1680. Manchester, 1923.

(b) Parliament

[The general history of parliament may be found in Anson or Medley—listed in (a) above —and Pollard. For 1485–1603 there is Read, Bibliography; afterwards recourse may be had to Davies, Bibliography. (See for both p. 396 above.)]

Journals of the House of Lords, 1509–1660. Vols. I–X.
Journals of the House of Commons, 1547–1660. Vols. I–VII.
Historical Collections; or an Exact Account of the Proceedings of the Four Last Parliaments of Q. Elizabeth. Collected by Heywood Townshend, 1680.
The Journals of all the Parliaments during the Reign of Queen Elizabeth. Ed. Sir Simonds D'Ewes, 1682.
The Parliamentary or Constitutional History of England [to 1660]. 24 vols. 1751–62. [Commonly called the Old Parliamentary History: valuable for extracts from pamphlets.]
The Parliamentary History of England. Ed. William Cobbett, vols. I–III, 1806–8.
Statutes of the Realm. Published by Command. Ed. Sir T. E. Tomlins, vols. II–V, 1816–9.
Diary of Thomas Burton, 1656–9. Ed. J. T. Rutt, 4 vols. 1828.
Historical Manuscripts Commission. Reports I–VII. 1870–9. [House of Lords MSS, 1450–1665. Drafts of bills, lists of committees, petitions, etc. with Laud's visitation, 1636 (4th Rep.), and letters of Charles I captured at Naseby (1st Rep.).]
Return of the Names of every Member returned to serve in each Parliament. 2 vols. 1878. Indexes, c. 1891. [Commonly called Official Returns of Members of Parliament.]
Pike, L. O. A Constitutional History of the House of Lords. 1894.
Firth, Sir C. H. The House of Lords during the Civil War, 1603–60. 1910.
McIlwain, C. H. The High Court of Parliament. New Haven, 1910.
Acts and Ordinances of the Interregnum, 1642–60. Ed. Sir C. H. Firth and R. S. Rait, 3 vols. 1911.
Pollard, A. F. The Evolution of Parliament. 1920; 1926.
The Commons' Debates for 1629. Ed. W. Notestein and F. H. Relf, Minneapolis, 1921. [Introduction valuable as a guide to sources for parliamentary debates, 1603–60.]
The Journal of Sir Simonds D'Ewes, 1640–1. Ed. Wallace Notestein, New Haven, 1923.
Notestein, W. The Winning of the Initiative by the House of Commons. Proc. British Academy, 1926.

26

Notes of the Debates in the House of Lords. Ed. F. H. Relf, Camden Soc. 1929. [Concerns 1621, 1625, 1628.]

(c) *The Council*

[Pollard describes the council under the Tudors, Turner under the Stuarts; Adair supplies a guide to the conciliar sources for both periods.]

Proceedings and Ordinances of the Privy Council of England. Vol. vii, 1540–2. 1837.

Acts of the Privy Council of England, 1542–1625. 45 vols. 1890–1933.

Scofield, C. L. A Study of the Court of Star Chamber. Chicago, 1900.

Select Cases before the King's Council in the Star Chamber commonly called the Court of the Star Chamber, 1477–1544. Ed. I. S. Leadam, 2 vols. Selden Soc. 1903–11.

Skeel, C. A. J. The Council in the Marches of Wales. 1904.

Bibliotheca Lindesiana. A Bibliography of Royal Proclamations, 1485–1714. Ed. Robert Steele, 2 vols. Oxford, 1910.

Reid, R. R. The King's Council of the North. 1921.

Pollard, A. F. The Council, Star Chamber and Privy Council under the Tudors. EHR. xxxvii, 1922, xxxviii, 1923.

Adair, E. R. The Sources for the History of the Council, 1485–1714. 1924.

Turner, E. R. The Privy Council of England, 1603–1784. 2 vols. Baltimore, 1927–8.

G. D.

2. THE POETRY

I. GENERAL INTRODUCTION

MISCELLANIES, ANTHOLOGIES, CRITICAL SURVEYS

(1) MISCELLANIES AND REPRESENTATIVE BALLAD-COLLECTIONS, 1557–1660

[Song-collections are listed pp. 481 ff. below.]

Case, A. E. A Bibliography of English Poetical Miscellanies, 1521–1750. Bibliog. Soc. 1935.

The Courte of Venus. [1549.] [Three fragments (of apparently two edns) are known: Bodleian, Folger, University of Texas. See C. C. Stopes, Shakespeare's Industry, chs. xxi–xxiii, 1916; A. K. Foxwell, Poems of Wiat, vol. II, pp. 171–3, 1913; R. H. Griffith and R. A. Law, TLS. 5 July 1928, 26 Dec. 1929, 4 Sept. 1930, and Texas University Stud. no. 10, 1930.]

Songes and Sonettes, written by the ryght honorable Lorde Henry Haward late Earle of Surrey, and other. Apud Richardum Tottel. 5 June 1557 (rptd J. P. Collier, Seven English Poetical Miscellanies, 1867); 31 July 1557 (two settings with omissions and addns); 1559 (bis); 1565; 1567; 1574; 1585; 1587.

> Songes and Sonettes. 1717 (Edmund Curll).
> Poems of Henry Howard, Earl of Surrey. With the Poems of Sir Thomas Wiat. Ed. George Sewell, 1717.
> The Praise of Geraldine, (A Florentine Lady.) Being, the Love Poems of Surrey. Also The Poetical Recreations of Sir Thomas Wyate. 1728 (Henry Curll).
> Songs and Sonnettes. Ed. Thomas Percy, 1763–1808. [Unpbd, the edn being destroyed by fire in 1808. See C. J. Brooks, E. Studien, LXVIII, 1934, pp. 424 ff.; A. Koszul, Bulletin de la Faculté des Lettres de Strasbourg, 1935, pp. 193 ff.].
> Songs and Sonnets. Ed. G. F. Nott, [1814?] [Unpbd, the edn being destroyed by fire. Copies in BM.]
> Tottel's Miscellany. Ed. E. Arber, 1870.
> Tottel's Miscellany (1557–1587). Ed. H. E. Rollins, 2 vols. Cambridge, U.S.A. 1928–9.
> [See H. R. Plomer, Richard Tottel, Bibliographica, III, 1897; W. W. Greg, Tottel's Miscellany, Library, v, 1904; H. J. Byrom, Richard Tottel—his Life and Work, Library, VIII, 1927; H. J. Byrom. Tottel's Miscellany, 1717–1817, RES. III, 1927; George Sherburn, Songes and Sonnettes,

TLS. 24 July 1930; H. J. Byrom, The Case for Nicholas Grimald as Editor of Tottel's Miscellany, MLR. XXVII, 1932; H. E. Rollins, Tottel's Miscellany and John Hall, TLS. 14 Jan. 1932. See also below under Grimald, p. 437, Surrey, pp. 412 f., Wyatt, pp. 411 f..]

A Hundreth sundrie Flowres. By George Gascoigne. [1573.] [B. M. Ward's edn, 1926, and his article in RES. IV, 1928, argue for multiple authorship. See also under Gascoigne, pp. 414 f. below.]

The Paradyse of daynty devises, aptly furnished, with sundry pithie and learned inventions. By Richard Edwards [and others]. 1576. [99 poems, thirteen of them in no later edn.]

> The Paradyse of daynty devises. Conteyning sundry pithy preceptes, learned Counsels, and excellent inventions. 1578 (rptd J. P. Collier, Seven English Poetical Miscellanies, 1867. 98 poems, one of which appears in no later edn. Possibly a rpt of a lost 1577 edn); 1580 (101 poems, four of them in no later edn); 1585 (103 poems, seven of which are new); [1590?]; 1596 (bis); 1600; 1606.
> The Paradise of Dainty Devices Reprinted from the First Edition, 1576. With Additional Pieces from the Editions of 1580 & 1600. Ed. Sir S. E. Brydges, 1810 (re-issued 1812). [For a proposed American rptd based on Brydges see Philobiblion, I, 1862.]
> The Paradise of Dainty Devices (1576–1606). Ed. H. E. Rollins, Cambridge, U.S.A. 1927.
> [See R. A. D. Lithgow, The Paradise of Dainty Devises, Trans. Royal Soc. Lit. XVII, 1895; C. C. Stopes, Shakespeare's Industry, ch. xx, 1916; D. T. Starnes, The Sources of Poems in The Paradise of Dainty Devices, PQ. VI, 1927.]

Flowers of Epigrammes. By Timothy Kendall. 1577; rptd type facs. Spenser Soc. 1874. [Poems by Kendall, Turbervile, Grimald, and others. See H. B. Lathrop, MLN. XLIII, 1928, pp. 223–9.]

A gorgious Gallery, of gallant Inventions. By divers worthy workemen and joyned together by T. P[roctor]. 1578; ed. Thomas Park (Heliconia, vol. I, 1815); rptd Henry Ellis (Three Collections of English Poetry, Roxburghe Club, 1845); rptd J. P. Collier (Seven English Poetical Miscellanies, 1867); ed. H. E. Rollins, Cambridge, U.S.A. 1926.

26-2

H. his Devises. By Thomas Howell [and others]. 1581; ed. A. B. Grosart (Howell's Poems, Manchester, 1879); ed. Sir W. Raleigh, Oxford, 1906.

A Handefull of pleasant delites. By Clement Robinson, and divers others. 1584 (fragments of two other edns in BM. and Huntington Lib.); ed. T. Park (Heliconia, vol. II, 1815); ed. E. Arber (English Scholar's Lib. no. 3, 1878); ed. type facs. Spenser Soc. 1871; ed. H. E. Rollins, Cambridge, U.S.A. 1924; ed. Arnold Kershaw, 1926. [See H. E. Rollins, The Date, Authors, and Contents of A Handful of Pleasant Delights, JEGP. XVIII, 1919, and MLN. XLI, 1926.]

A Banquet of Dainty Conceits. Written by A[nthony]. M[unday]. 1588; rptd Harleian Misc. vol. IX, 1812.

Brittons Bowre of Delights. 1591; 1597; ed. H. E. Rollins, Cambridge, U.S.A. 1933. [By Nicholas Breton and others.]

The Phoenix Nest. Built up with the most rare workes of Noble men, woorthy Knights, &c. Set foorth by R. S. 1593; ed. T. Park (Heliconia, vol. II, 1815); rptd J. P. Collier (Seven English Poetical Miscellanies, 1867); ed. Hugh Macdonald, 1926; ed. H. E. Rollins, Cambridge, U.S.A. 1931. [See Sir E. Gosse, Sunday Times, 24 April 1927.]

The Garland of Good Will. Written by T[homas]. D[eloney]. 1631; 1659; 1678; 1686; [1690?]; [1696?]; [1700?]; [1709?]. [Poems by Raleigh, Breton, Shakespeare (?), and others. Apparently registered S.R. 5 March 1593. The 1631 edn is rptd in F. O. Mann's Deloney, 1912; the 1678 edn rptd J. H. Dixon, Percy Soc. 1851, with addns from the edn of *c.* 1709.]

The Arbor of amorous Devises. By N. B. Gent. [and others]. 1597; ed. H. E. Rollins, Cambridge, U.S.A. 1937. [Imperfect Capell copy rptd A. B. Grosart's Breton, vol. I, 1879. The first edn now lost, issued in 1594.]

Politeuphuia; wits commonwealth. By John Bodenham. 1597; 1598; 1650; 1653; 1655 ('17th edn'); 1674; 1688, etc. [A dictionary of prose and some verse quotations.]

The Passionate Pilgrime. By W. Shakespeare. 1599. [Contains poems by Barnfield, Marlowe, Raleigh, and others. See under Shakespeare, below, p. 581.]

Englands Helicon. 1600; 1614 (with addns); ed. Sir S. E. Brydges and J. Haslewood (British Bibliographer, vol. III, 1812); rptd J. P. Collier (Seven English Poetical Miscellanies, 1867); ed. A. H. Bullen, 1887, 1899; ed. Hugh Macdonald, 1925 (see correspondence in TLS. 23, 30 April, 7, 14, 21 May 1925); ed. H. E. Rollins, 2 vols. Cambridge, U.S.A. 1935. [See J. W. Hebel, Nicholas Ling and England's Helicon, Library, v, 1924; H. E. Rollins, England's Helicon and Henry Chettle, TLS. 1 Oct. 1931.]

Englands Parnassus: Or The choysest Flowers of our Moderne Poets. 1600 (at least four distinct impressions, some with, some without, the initials or name of the editor, Robert Allott); ed. T. Park (Heliconia, vol. III, 1815); rptd J. P. Collier (Seven English Poetical Miscellanies, 1867); ed. Charles Crawford, 1913. [See Charles Crawford, Englands Parnassus, N. & Q. 2 May 1908–26 June 1909.]

Bel-vedere Or The Garden of the Muses. [Collected by John Bodenham.] 1600; 1610 (as The Garden of the Muses); rptd Spenser Soc. 1875. [See Charles Crawford, E. Studien, XLIII, 1911.]

Strange Histories, Of Kings, Princes, Dukes, &c. By Thomas Deloney. 1602; rptd F. O. Mann (Deloney's Works, 1912).

> Strange Histories. Principally by Thomas Deloney. From the Edition of 1607. Ed. [J. P. Collier], Percy Soc. 1841. [Probably originally issued before 1600, when Deloney died. Other edns of 1612, 1631, greatly changed. Title of 1674 edn changed to The Royal Garland of Love and Delight.]

A Poetical Rapsody Containing, Diverse Sonnets, Odes, Elegies, Madrigalls, and other Poesies. 1602 (176 poems); 1608 (240 poems); 1611 (248 poems); 1621 (247 poems, three of those first appearing in 1602 edn being omitted); ed. Sir S. E. Brydges, 3 vols. 1814, 1816–17 (Lee Priory Press); ed. Sir N. H. Nicolas, 2 vols. 1826; ed. A. H. Bullen, 2 vols. 1890–1; ed. H. E. Rollins, 2 vols. Cambridge, U.S.A. 1931-2. [See G. C. Moore Smith and Charles Best, RES. I, 1925; H. E. Rollins, A. W. and A Poetical Rhapsody, Stud. Phil. XXIX, 1932.]

A Crowne-Garland of Goulden Roses. By Richard Johnson. 1612; ed. William Chappell, Percy Soc. 1842. [The BM. has a 1631 edn, the addns of which are duplicated in the 1659 edn rptd Chappell, Percy Soc. 1845. Other edns 1683, 1692.]

The Golden Garland of Princely Pleasures and Delicate Delights. By Richard Johnson. 1620 (3rd edn); 1690.

Loves Garland, or Posies for Rings, Handkerchers, and Gloves. 1624; rptd J. O. Halliwell[-Phillipps] (Literature of the Sixteenth and Seventeenth Centuries, 1851); rptd E. Arber (English Garner, vol. I, 1877); ed. J. R. Brown, 1883.

Pick, Samuel. Festum Voluptatis, or The Banquet of Pleasure. 1639. [The entire contents are lifted from A Poetical Rapsody; Breton, John Davies, and Others. See H. E. Rollins, Samuel Pick's Borrowings, RES. VII, 1931.

Witts Recreations. 1640.
Wit's Recreations Augmented. 1641; 1645; 1650; 1654; 1663; 1667; 1683; rptd T. Park (in Musarum Deliciae, 2 vols. 1817, [1874]).

Songs and Poems of Love and Drollery. By T[homas]. W[eaver]. 1654.

Wits Interpreter, the English Parnassus. By John Cotgrave. 1655; 1662; 1671.

Choyce Drollery: Songs & Sonnets. 1656; ed. J. W. Ebsworth, Boston, Lincs. 1876.

Wit and Drollery, Jovial Poems. 1656; 1661; 1682. [By J. Smith, Sir J. Mennis, and others.]

Sportive Wit: the Muses Merriment. By C. J., B. J., W. T., [and others]. 1656.

Parnassus Biceps: or, Several Choice Pieces of Poetry. By Abraham Wright. 1656; ed. G. Thorn-Drury, 1927.

Poole, Joshua. The English Parnassus, or A Helpe to English Poesie. 1657; 1677.

Wit Restor'd In severall Select Poems. 1658; rptd T. Park (in Musarum Deliciae, 2 vols. 1817, [1874]).

(2) Anthologies: Poems and Ballads

[For sonnet-anthologies see p. 428 below; for anthologies of 17th cent. poetry see p. 440.]

A Collection of Old Ballads. 3 vols. 1723–5; rptd [1872]. [Ed. (?) Ambrose Philips: see S. B. Hustvedt, TLS. 6, 13 Dec. 1923.]

The Hive. A Collection of the most Celebrated Songs. 2 vols. 1724.

The Compleat Academy of Complements. To which is added, A compleat Collection of choice Songs and merry Catches. 1729.

A Collection of Bacchanalian Songs. 1729.

The Choice: Being a Collection of 250 Celebrated Songs. 1729; 3 vols. 1732–3 (enlarged).

A Collection of Loyal Songs Written against the Rump Parliament, 1639–1661. 2 vols. 1731.

A Complete Collection of Old and New English and Scotch Songs. 4 vols. 1735–6.

Cooper, Elizabeth. The Muses Library. 1737.

Bacchus and Venus: A Collection of near 200 Witty Songs and Catches. 1737.

The Merry Companion: or, Universal Songster. 1739.

The Lark, containing above 470 Songs. 1740.

The Siren. A choice collection of Songs. [1740?]

The Nightingale. Containing a Collection of 492 Songs. 1742.

The Aviary: Or, Magazine of British Melody. A Collection of 1344 Songs. [1750?]

The Buck's Bottle Companion: Being a Complete Collection of Humourous, Bottle, and Hunting Songs. 1775.

Ellis, George. Specimens of the Early English Poets. 1790; 3 vols. 1801; 3 vols. 1803 (rev.).

Nugae Antiquae. Ed. T. Park, 2 vols. 1804. [First edn, by Henry Harington, 2 vols. 1769, 1775; 2nd edn rev. 3 vols. 1779; 3rd edn, 3 vols. 1792.]

Evans, Thomas. Old Ballads, Historical and Narrative. Ed. R. H. Evans, 4 vols. 1810. [1st edn, 2 vols. 1777; 2nd edn, 4 vols. 1784.]

Headley, Henry. Select Beauties of Ancient English Poetry. 2 vols. in 1, 1810. [First edn, 2 vols. 1787.]

Park, Thomas. Heliconia. Comprising a Selection of English Poetry of the Elizabethan Age. 3 vols. 1815.

Ballads, and other Fugitive Poetical Pieces from the Collections of Sir James Balfour. Edinburgh, 1834.

Collier, J. P. Old Ballads from Early Printed Copies. Percy Soc. 1840.

—— Eight Ballads, from the Original Blackletter Copies. 1846 (priv. ptd).

—— A Book of Roxburghe Ballads. 1847.

—— Broadside Black-letter Ballads. 1868 (priv. ptd).

—— Twenty-five Old Ballads and Songs: from MSS. 1869. [Spurious: see N. & Q. 18 May 1895.]

Wright, Thomas. Political Ballads Published in England during the Commonwealth. Percy Soc. 1841.

—— Songs and Ballads chiefly of the Reign of Philip and Mary. Roxburghe Club, 1860. [See MLN. xxxiv, 1919.]

Ellis, Henry. Three Collections of English Poetry of the Latter Part of the Sixteenth Century. Roxburghe Club, 1845.

Farr, Edward. Select Poetry Chiefly Devotional of the Reign of Queen Elizabeth. 2 vols. Parker Soc. 1845.

Hannah, John. Poems by Sir Henry Wotton, Sir Walter Raleigh, and Others. 1845.

—— The Courtly Poets from Raleigh to Montrose. 1870.

—— Poems of Raleigh, Wotton, and Other Courtly Poets, 1540–1650. 1875; 1892.

Rimbault, E. F. A Little Book of Songs and Ballads. 1851.

Child, F. J. English and Scottish Ballads. 8 vols. Boston, 1857–8 and 1864.

Halliwell[-Phillipps], J. O. Thomas Deloney. Three Old Ballads on the Spanish Armada. 1860.

—— Those Songs and Poems from England's Helicon Connected with Shakespeare. 1865.

Wilkins, W. W. Political Ballads of the Seventeenth and Eighteenth Centuries. 2 vols. 1860.

Huth, Henry. Ancient Ballads and Broadsides Published in the Sixteenth Century. Philobiblon Soc. 1867. [Re-issued as A Collection of 79 Black-letter Ballads, J. Lilly, 1867.]

Furnivall, F. J. and Morfill, W. R. Ballads from MSS. 2 vols. Ballad Soc. 1868–73.

Chappell, W. and Ebsworth, J. W. Roxburghe Ballads. 9 vols. Ballad Soc. 1869–97.

[Hazlitt, W. C.] Inedited Poetical Miscellanies, 1584–1700. 1870.

Furnivall, F. J. Love-poems and Humourous Ones. Ballad Soc. 1874.

Boeddeker, K. Englische Lieder und Balladen aus dem 16. Jahrhundert. Jahrbuch für romanische und englische Sprache, xiv, xv, 1875–6.

Ebsworth, J. W. Bagford Ballads. 2 vols. Ballad Soc. 1878.

Linton, W. J. Rare Poems of the Sixteenth and Seventeenth Centuries. New Haven, 1882; London, 1883.

Ashton, John. Humour, Wit and Satire of the Seventeenth Century. 1883.

—— A Century of Ballads. 1888.

Goldsmid, E. Quaint Gleanings from Ancient Poetry. Edinburgh, 1884.

Bullen, A. H. Poems, Chiefly Lyrical, from Romances and Prose-Tracts of the Elizabethan Age. 1890.

Schelling, F. E. A Book of Elizabethan Lyrics. Boston, 1895.

—— A Book of Seventeenth Century Lyrics. Boston, 1899.

Carpenter, F. I. English Lyric Poetry, 1500–1700. 1897; 1906.

Farmer, J. S. Merry Songs and Ballads Prior to 1800. 5 vols. 1897.

Arber, Edward. The Surrey and Wyatt Anthology, 1509–1547. 1900.

—— The Spenser Anthology, 1548–1591. 1899.

—— The Shakespeare Anthology, 1592–1616. 1899.

—— The Jonson Anthology, 1617–1637. 1899.

—— The Milton Anthology, 1638–1674. 1899.

Symons, Arthur. A Sixteenth-Century Anthology. 1905; 1925.

Padelford, F. M. Early Sixteenth Century Lyrics. Boston, 1907.

Clark, Andrew. Shirburn Ballads, 1585–1616. 1907. [See Journ. American Folk-Lore, xxx, 1917.]

Firth, Sir C. H. Naval Songs and Ballads. Navy Records Soc. 1908.

Collmann, H. L. Ballads and Broadsides chiefly of the Elizabethan Period. Roxburghe Club, 1912.

Brougham, E. M. V. Corn from Olde Fieldes. [1918.]

—— News out of Scotland: Being a Miscellaneous Collection of Verse and Prose. 1926.

Massingham, H. J. A Treasury of Seventeenth Century English Verse. 1919.

Rollins, H. E. Old English Ballads, 1553–1625. Cambridge, 1920.

—— A Pepysian Garland, 1595–1639. Cambridge, 1922.

—— Cavalier and Puritan. Ballads of the Great Rebellion. New York, 1923.

—— The Pack of Autolycus. Cambridge, U.S.A. 1927.

—— The Pepys Ballads. 8 vols. Cambridge, U.S.A. 1929–32.

Rohde, E. S. The Old-World Pleasaunce: An Anthology. 1925.

Ault, Norman. Elizabethan Lyrics. 1925.

—— Seventeenth Century Lyrics. 1928.

Duncan, Edmondstoune. Lyrics from the Old Song Books. 1927.

Hammond, E. P. English Verse between Chaucer and Surrey. Durham, North Carolina, 1927.

Judson, A. C. Seventeenth-Century Lyrics. Chicago, 1927.

Draper, J. W. A Century of Broadside Elegies of the Seventeenth Century. 1928.

Peacock, W. English Verse. Vol. i, 1928.

Campbell, K. W. Anthology of English Poetry: 16th and 17th Centuries. 1929.

Hebel, J. W. and Hudson, H. H. Poetry of the English Renaissance, 1509–1660. New York, 1929.

Chambers, Sir E. K. The Oxford Book of Sixteenth Century Verse. 1932.

Reed, E. B. Christmas Carols of the Sixteenth Century. Cambridge, U.S.A. 1932.

Grierson, H. J. C. and Bullough, G. The Oxford Book of Seventeenth Century Verse. 1934.

Green, R. L. The Early English Carols. Oxford, 1935.

(3) Criticism, Biography, Bibliography

(a) Books

Warton, Thomas. The History of English Poetry. Vol. iii, 1781; ed. W. C. Hazlitt, vol. iv, 1871.

Brydges, Sir S. E. Censura Literaria. 10 vols. 1805–9 and 1815.

—— The British Bibliographer. 4 vols. 1810–4.

—— Restituta. 4 vols. 1814–6.

[Fry, John.] Pieces of Ancient Poetry. Bristol, 1814.

Collier, J. P. Extracts from the Registers of the Stationers' Company. 2 vols. Shakespeare Soc. 1848–9.

—— A Bibliographical and Critical Account of the Rarest Books in the English Language. 2 vols. 1865 (re-issued New York, 1866).

Halliwell[-Phillipps], J. O. A Catalogue of Ballads and Poems. Presented to the Chetham Library. 1851.

—— A Catalogue of an Unique Collection of Ancient English Broadside Ballads. 1856. [The Euing collection, now at Glasgow University.]

Chappell, William. Popular Music of the Olden Time. 2 vols. [1855–9]; ed. H. E. Wooldridge, 2 vols. 1893.

Corser, Thomas. Collectanea Anglo-Poetica. 5 vols. in 11, Chetham Soc. 1860–83.

Lemon, Robert. Catalogue of a Collection of Broadsides in the Possession of the Society of Antiquaries. 1866.

Arber, Edward. A Transcript of the Stationers' Registers. 5 vols. 1875–94.

Bullen, A. H. Carols and Poems. 1886.

Saintsbury, George. A History of Elizabethan Literature. 1887, etc.

—— A History of English Prosody. Vols. I, II, 1906–8.

Bibliotheca Lindesiana, Catalogue of English Ballads. 1890 (priv. ptd).

Courthope, W. J. A History of English Poetry. Vol. II, 1897 and 1904, vol. III, 1903.

Erskine, John. The Elizabethan Lyric. New York, 1903 and 1905.

Sievers, Richard. Thomas Deloney. Eine Studie über Balladenliteratur der Shakspere-Zeit. Berlin, 1904.

Körting, G. Grundriss der Geschichte der englischen Litteratur. Münster, 1905 (4th edn).

Zocco, Irene. Petrarchismo e Petrarchisti in Inghilterra. Palermo, 1906.

Schelling, F. E. English Literature during the Lifetime of Shakespeare. New York, 1910; 1927 (rev. edn).

Reed, E. B. English Lyrical Poetry. New Haven, 1912.

Hustvedt, S. B. Ballad Criticism in Scandinavia and Great Britain. New York, 1916.

Scott, M. A. Elizabethan Translations from the Italian. Boston, 1916.

Berdan, J. M. Early Tudor Poetry. New York, 1920.

De Ricci, Seymour. The Book Collector's Guide. Philadelphia, 1921.

Rollins, H. E. An Analytical Index to the Ballad-Entries in the Stationers' Registers. Chapel Hill, North Carolina. 1924. [Ptd also in Stud. Phil. xxi, 1924.]

Wells, H. W. Poetic Imagery Illustrated from Elizabethan Literature. New York, 1924.

Whipple, T. K. Martial and the English Epigram from Sir Thomas Wyatt to Ben Jonson. Berkeley, 1925.

Bartlett, H. C. Catalogue of Early English Books collected by W. A. White. New York, 1926. [Many of these items are now in the Harvard College Lib.]

Baskervill, C. R. The Elizabethan Jig. Chicago, 1929.

Genouy, H. L'Élément pastoral dans la Poésie narrative et le Drame en Angleterre de 1579 à 1640. Paris, 1929.

Shaaber, M. A. Some Forerunners of the Newspaper in England, 1476–1622. Philadelphia, 1929.

Bush, Douglas. Mythology and the Renaissance Tradition in English Poetry. Minneapolis, 1933.

(b) Articles

E., B. Ballads [in BM. Add. MS 15225]. GM. xxxiv, 1850.

Hazlitt, W. C. A Catalogue of Early English Miscellanies formerly in the Harleian Library. Camden Misc. vol. v, 1862.

Chappell, W. Some Account of an Unpublished Collection of Songs and Ballads by King Henry VIII and his Contemporaries. Archaeologia, xli, 1867.

Langton, Robert. The Black-letter Ballads in the Free Reference Library, Manchester. Trans. Lancs. and Cheshire Antiquarian Soc. II, 1884.

Koeppel, Emil. Studien zur Geschichte des englischen Petrarchismus im sechzehnten Jahrhundert. Romanische Forschungen, v, 1889.

Flügel, E. Liedersammlungen des XVI. Jahrhunderts, besonders aus der Zeit Heinrichs VIII. Ang. xii, 1889, xxvi, 1903.

de Marchi, Luigi. L'Influenza della Lirica italiana sulla Lirica inglese nel Secolo XVI. Nuova Antologia, lviii, 1895.

The Elizabethan Lyric. Quart. Rev. cxcvi, 1902.

Swaen, A. E. H. Notes on some Old Songs. Archiv, cxxi, 1908.

—— Notes on Ballads. Neophilologus, iii, 1918.

—— Ballads, Tunes and Dances in Nash's Works. Neophilologus, v, 1920.

Firth, Sir C. H. The Ballad History of the Reigns of the Later Tudors. Trans. Royal Hist. Soc. iii, 1909.

—— The Ballad History of the Reign of James I. Trans. Royal Hist. Soc. v, 1911.

—— The Reign of Charles I. Trans. Royal Hist. Soc. vi, 1912. [A ballad-history.]

—— Ballads and Broadsides. [In Shakespeare's England, vol. II, Oxford, 1917 and 1926. With a valuable bibliography.]

Rollins, H. E. The Black-letter Broadside
Ballad. PMLA. xxxiv, 1919.
von Schaubert, E. Zur Geschichte der Black-
letter Broadside Ballad. Ang. L, 1927.
Tannenbaum, S. A. Unfamiliar Versions of
some Elizabethan Poems. PMLA. xLv,
1930.
Campbell, L. B. The Christian Muse. Hun-
tington Lib. Bulletin, Oct. 1935.
Hughey, R. The Huntington Manuscript at
Arundel Castle and Related Documents.
Library, xv, 1935.
H. E. R.

II. THE TUDOR POETS

SKELTON, BARCLAY, WYATT, SURREY,
A MIRROR FOR MAGISTRATES, GASCOIGNE,
BRETON, SPENSER, SIDNEY, GREVILLE,
SOUTHWELL, DANIEL, DRAYTON, DAVIES
OF HEREFORD, CAMPION, WOTTON, SIR
JOHN DAVIES, BARNFIELD

JOHN SKELTON (1460?–1529)

(1) COLLECTED WORKS

Pithy pleasaunt and profitable workes of
maister Skelton, Poete Laureate. Nowe
collected and newly published. 1568. [List
of contents headed 'Workes of Skelton
newly collected by I. S.' Mainly from
latest edns of works previously ptd separately; omits Dyvers Balettys, Replycacion
agaynst certayne yong scolers and Magnyfycence; adds miscellaneous pieces, Latin
and English; includes works not by Skelton
—'A parable by William Cornishe in ye
Fleete,' and 'The boke of Three Fooles M.
Skelton Poete Laureate gave to my Lorde
Cardynall' (chs. xlix, l, xlviii of Henry
Watson's version of the Ship of Fools).]
Pithy Pleasaunt and Profitable Workes of
Maister Skelton, Poete Laureate to King
Henry the VIIIth. 1736. [Inaccurate
rpt of Workes, 1568; 'edited by J. Bowle,
the stupidest of all two-legged animals'
(Gifford, pencil note cited by Dyce). The
1736 edn was rptd in Chalmers' English
Poets, vol. II, 1810 (review by Southey,
Quarterly Rev. xi, 1814, p. 484).]
The Poetical Works of John Skelton: with
Notes, and some Account of the Author and
his Writings. Ed. A. Dyce. 2 vols. 1843.
[Standard edn; text based usually on
earliest 16th cent. edns, with collation of
later rpts and of MSS; adds Against
Garnesche from MS Harley 367, and from
various sources a number of minor pieces,
sometimes of doubtful authenticity; introduction, with bibliography and documented

biography, and reprint of Merie Tales of
Skelton; full notes, textual and explanatory.]
The Complete Poems of John Skelton,
Laureate. Ed. P. Henderson, 1931. [Text,
modernized in spelling, based on Dyce.]

(2) SELECTIONS

A Selection from the Poetical Works of John
Skelton. Ed. W. H. Williams, 1902.
Poems by John Skelton. Ed. R. Hughes,
1924.

(3) SEPARATE WORKS

Here begynneth a lytell treatyse named the
bowge of courte. [By 1500] (de Worde);
[after 1501] (de Worde).
A ballade of the scottysshe kynge. [1513]
(R. Faukes) (anon.); ed. facs. J. Ashton,
1882. [Expanded version ptd in Certayne
bokes.]
A ryght delectable tratyse upon a goodly
Garlande or Chapelet of Laurell studyously
dyvysed at Sheryflotton Castell. 1523
(R. Faukes).
Here Folowythe dyvers Balettys and dyties
solacyous. [c. 1525–30] (J. Rastell?). [Con-
tains: My darlyng dere my daysy floure, The
auncient acquaintance madam betwen us
twayn, Knolege aquayntance resort favour
with grace, Cuncta licet cecidisse putas dis-
crimina rerum, Go pytyous hart rasyd with
dedly wo.]
Skelton Laureate agaynste a comely Coy-
strowne that curyously chawntyd And
curryshly cowntred Agaynste the .ix.
Musys. [c. 1525–30] (J. Rastell?). [Includes
also: Skelton Laureat uppon a deedmans
hed, Womanhod wanton ye want.]
A replycacion agaynst certayne yong scolers.
[c. 1528] (Pynson). [Preceded by Latin
dedication to Wolsey.]
Magnyfycence. A goodly interlude and a
mery. [1529–32] (J. Rastell or P. Treveris);
ed. Sir J. Littledale, Roxburghe Club, 1821;
ed. R. L. Ramsay, EETS. 1908; ed. facs.
J. S. Farmer, 1910 (Tudor Facsimile
Texts).
Here after foloweth a lytell boke called Collyn
Clout. [1532–7] (Thomas Godfray); [1542–
6] (R. Kele); [1554–5?] (J. Wyghte);
variant issue: T. Marshe); [?] (A. Kytson;
variants: A. Veale, J. Wallye).
Here after foloweth the boke of Phyllyp
Sparowe. [1542–6] (R. Kele); [1551–5] (J.
Wyght; variant: R. Toy); [?] (A. Kitson;
variants: A. Veale, J. Walley).
Here after foloweth a lytell boke, which hath
to name, why come ye nat to courte.
[1542–6] (R. Kele); [1551–5] (J. Wyght;
variant: R. Toy); [?] (A. Kytson; variants:
A. Veale, J. Wallye).

Here after foloweth certayne bokes whose names here after shall appere Speke Parrot The deth of the noble prince Kyng Edwarde the fourth. A treatyse of the Scottes. Ware the Hawke The Tunnyng of Elynour Rummynge. [1542–8] (H. Tab); [c. 1554] (J. Kynge and T. Marche); [?] (J. Day). [Between Ware the Hawke and Elynour Rummynge occur minor pieces not mentioned on the title-page: Skeltonis Apostrophat ad divum Iohannem decollatum, All nobyll men of this take hede (occurs also at the beginning of editions of Why come ye nat to courte?), How every thyng must have a tyme, Prayer to the father of hevyn, To the seconde parson, To the holy gooste. The authorship of the Time and Trinity verses, and of Edward IV, is questioned by F. Brie, E. Studien, xxxvii, 1907.]

A Myrroure for Magistrates. 1559; 1563; 1571; 1574; 1587, etc. [Includes, with attribution to Skelton, How king Edward through his surfeting and untemperate life, sodainly died in the mids of his prosperity.]

Christmas Carolles. [1542–6] (R. Kele); ed. photo-facs. E. B. Reed, Huntington Lib. 1932. [Includes Vexilla regis; but there is no certainty that this version of the hymn, ptd by Dyce from P. Bliss, Bibliographical Miscellanies, 1818, is the Skelton version mentioned in Garlande of Laurell, l. 1420.]

(4) MANUSCRIPTS

Against Christopher Garnesche. BM. Harley 367, fols. 101–9.

Speke Parrot. BM. Harley 2252, fols. 133–40. [Contains much, ptd by Dyce, which is not in Certayne bokes nor in Workes, 1568.]

Collyn Clout. BM. Harley 2252, fols. 147–53.

The profecy of Skelton 1529. BM. Lansdowne 762, fol. 75 (71). [Fragment of Collyn Clout, ptd by Dyce, vol. i, p. 329.]

Why come ye nat to courte? Bodley Rawlinson C. 813, fols. 36–43. [Incomplete; ptd by J. Zupitza, Archiv, lxxxv, 1890, pp. 429–36.]

The Garlande of Laurell. BM. Cotton Vitellius E. x., fols. 206 (200)–225 (217). [Imperfect; only MS signatures (in sixes) A, D and E extant. Basis of the text given by E. P. Hammond, English Verse between Chaucer and Surrey, Durham, North Carolina, 1927, pp. 342–60.]

Skelton Laureat upon the dolorus dethe and much lamentable chaunce of the mooste honorable Erle of Northumberlande. BM. Royal 18. D. ii. fols. 165–6. [Ptd by T. Percy, Reliques of Ancient English Poetry, 2nd edn, vol. i, 1767, pp. 93–104.]

Lament for Edward IV. (a) BM. Harley 4011, fols. 169–70. [Like Currer MS used by Dyce, contains stanza not in Certayne bokes or Workes, 1568.] (b) BM. Add. 29729, fols. 8–9. [Transcript by Stowe in 1558 edn of works of Lydgate; in heading and colophon of Edward IV elegy 'Lidgate' deleted and 'Skelton' substituted. Skelton's authorship of the poem—of which a version appeared in Certayne bokes, in Workes, 1568, and in Myrroure for Magistrates, 1559—has been questioned.]

Manerly Margery Mylk and Ale. BM. Add. 5465 ('Fairfax MS.'), fols. 96 (109)–99 (112). [With music by 'Willm. Cornyssh junior'.]

Masteres Anne. Trinity College, Cambridge, R. 3. 17, flyleaf. [Ptd by F. Brie, with ascription to Skelton, E. Studien, xxxvii, 1907, pp. 29–30, and by L. J. Lloyd, RES. v, 1929, p. 304.]

The Rose both White and Rede. Public Record Office, Treasury of the Receipt of the Exchequer, B. 2. 8. [Letters and Papers of Henry VIII, vol. ii, pt ii (1515–8), p. 1518. Ptd by Dyce, vol. i, pp. ix–xi; independently by C. C. Stopes, Athenaeum, 2 May 1914, p. 625.]

To the Trinity. BM. Add. 20059, flyleaf. [Some difference from version in Certayne bokes and Workes, 1568.]

Of Tyme. BM. Egerton 2402, fol. 230. [Adds eight lines not in Certayne bokes and Workes, 1568; see TLS. 20 Sept. 1934, 17 Jan. 1935.]

[Prose trn of Diodorus Siculus.] Corpus Christi College, Cambridge, 357. [Unpublished; 7+249 folios. From Poggio's Latin version (as six books) of the Bibliotheca Historica, Bks i–v; imperfect, breaking off in Poggio's Bk v (at Bk iv, ch. 19 of the Greek text).]

[Moral treatise in Latin.] BM. Add. 26787. [Dedicated to Prince Henry, dated 28 Aug. 1501; with epigram to prince 'quando insignitus erat dux Eboracensis'; presumably the Methodos Skeltonidis Laureati (Praecepta moralia) formerly in Lincoln Cathedral (see T. Tanner, Bibliotheca Britannico-Hibernica, 1748), and the Speculum Principis described in Garlande of Laurell, ll. 1226–32; ptd by F. M. Salter, Speculum, ix, 1934.]

Salve plus decies quam sunt momenta dierum. BM. Add. 4787, fol. 224 (226). [Minor differences from form in Workes, 1568.]

I liber et propera regem tu pronus adora. Corpus Christi College, Cambridge, 432, fols. i^b–iii. [See M. R. James, Catalogue, vol. ii, pp. 338–9.]

Qui trahis ex domiti ramum pede dive leonis. Cambridge University Lib. Ee. v. 18, fol. 52. [Ptd by F. Brie, E. Studien, xxxvii, 1907, p. 28, from the Catalogue, vol. ii, p. 178.]

Wofully araide. (a) BM. Harley 4012, fol. 109. [Ptd in part by F. Brie, E. Studien, xxxvii, 1907, pp. 23–4.] (b) BM. Add. 5465 ('Fairfax MS.'), fols. 63 (76)–67 (80) [with music by 'Willm. Cornyssh junior'], and fols. 73 (86)–77 (90) [with music by 'Browne']. (c) Flyleaf of Heber copy of (pseudo-) Boetius de disciplina scholarium, Daventrie, 1496. ['Explicit quod Skelton'; used by Dyce; ptd by W. de G. Birch, Athenaeum, 29 Nov. 1873, p. 679.] [Identification of the extant Wofully Araide with the poem mentioned in Garlande of Laurell, l. 1418, is highly uncertain; see F. Brie, E. Studien, xxxvii, 1907, pp. 22–5.]

How darest thow swere or be so bold also. Trinity College, Cambridge, O. 2. 53, fol. 66. [Ptd by F. Brie, E. Studien, xxxvii, 1907, pp. 31–2, with speculation that it is a fragment of the Recule ageinst Gaguyne mentioned in Garlande of Laurell, l. 1187; also in RES. v, 1929, p. 303 by L. J. Lloyd, who challenges Brie's identification.]

Lament on Parting. (a) (Petyously constraynyd am I). BM. Royal Appendix 58, fols. 19 (17)–21 (19). [With music; at end, 'Quod docter Coper'; ptd by E. Flügel, Ang. xii, 1889, pp. 266–7, as part of preceding poem.] (b) (Peteually constraynd am I.) Flyleaf of Heber copy of (pseudo-) Boetius de disciplina scholarium, Daventrie, 1496. [Shorter version; ptd by W. de G. Birch, with attribution to Skelton, Athenaeum, 29 Nov. 1873, p. 679, whence rptd by J. Ashton (Ballade of the scottysshe Kynge, p. 19) and by A. Koelbing (Zur Charakteristik John Skelton's, p. 161). The attribution to Skelton, based solely on its proximity in the Heber pseudo-Boethius to Wofully Araide, and the biographical glozings, seems unwarranted.]

(5) BIOGRAPHY AND CRITICISM

Merie Tales Newly Imprinted and made by Master Skelton Poet Laureat. [1567?]; rptd A. Dyce (Poetical Works of Skelton, vol. i, 1843); rptd W. C. Hazlitt (Old English Jest Books, vol. ii, 1864).

Bale, J. [Autograph notebook (Bodley, Cod. Seld. supra 64, fols. 69b, 96a); ed. R. L. Poole and M. Bateson as Index Britanniae Scriptorum, 1902.]

—— Scriptorum Britanniae Catalogus. 1557–9, pp. 651–2. [The basis of later accounts up to Dyce.]

Fuller, T. Worthies of England. 1662. [Norfolk, p. 257.]

à Wood, A. Athenae Oxonienses. 1691; ed. P. Bliss, vol. i, 1813, pp. 49–54.

Blomefield, F. History of Norfolk. 1739; vol. i, 1805.

Tanner, T. Bibliotheca Britannico-Hibernica. 1748, pp. 675–6.

Warton, T. The History of English Poetry. Vol. ii, 1778, pp. 336–63; ed. W. C. Hazlitt, vol. iii, 1871, pp. 268–90.

Retrospective Rev. vi, 1822, pp. 337–53.

Dyce, A. [To the rich biographical introduction prefixed to his edn of Skelton in 1843 later investigators have added little.]

GM. Sept. 1844, pp. 227–47. [Detailed review of Dyce's edn, with notes about Christopher Garnesche.]

Quarterly Rev. lxxiii, 1844, pp. 510–36.

Bradley, H. Two Puzzles in Skelton. Academy, 1 Aug. 1896. [Solution of number-cyphers in Ware the Hauke and Garlande of Laurell.]

Hooper, J. Skelton Laureate. GM. Sept. 1897.

Rey, A. Skelton's Satirical Poems in their relation to Lydgate's Order of Fools, Cocke Lorell's Bote, and Barclay's Ship of Fools. Berne, 1899.

Koelbing, A. Zur Charakteristik John Skelton's. Stuttgart, 1904.

—— Barclay and Skelton. CHEL. vol. iii, 1909.

Thümmel, A. Studien über John Skelton. Leipzig, 1905.

Brie, F. Skelton-Studien. E. Studien, xxxvii, 1907.

—— Zwei verlorene Dichtungen von John Skelton. Archiv, cxxxviii, 1919. [Conjectures about theme and treatment.]

Dodds, M. H. Early Political Plays. Library, iv, 1913. [Magnyfycence.]

Se Boyar, G. E. Skelton's Replycacion. MLN. xxviii, 1913.

Berdan, J. M. On the Dating of Skelton's Satires. PMLA. xxix, 1914.

—— Speke Parrot, an Interpretation. MLN. xxx, 1915.

—— Early Tudor Poetry. New York, 1920.

Cook, A. S. Skelton's Garland of Laurel and Chaucer's Hous of Fame. MLR. xi, 1916.

Dunbabin, R. L. Notes on Skelton. MLR. xii, 1917.

Westlake, H. F. TLS. 27 Oct. 1921. [Westminster lease, 1518: 'in quo tenemento Johannes Skelton laureatus modo habitat.']

Hammond, E. P. English Verse between Chaucer and Surrey. Durham, North Carolina, 1927. [Annotated text of Garlande of Laurell (based on MS Cotton Vitellius E. x, and on Faukes' edn), preceded by critical note on Skelton and 'select bibliography'.]

Stearns, H. The Date of the Garlande of Laurell. MLN. xliii, 1928.

—— John Skelton and Christopher Garnesche. MLN. xliii, 1928.

Blunden, E. John Skelton, TLS. 20 June 1929. [Collected in Votive Tablets, 1931.]

Lloyd, L. J. A Note on Skelton. RES. v, 1929.

—— John Skelton and the New Learning. MLR. xxiv, 1929.

Pollard, A. F. Wolsey. 1929.

Gordon, I. A. Skelton's Philip Sparrow and the Roman Service-Book. MLR. xxix, 1934.

Salter, F. M. Skelton's Speculum Principis. Speculum, ix, 1934.

Edwards, H. L. R. John Skelton: a Genealogical Study. RES. xi, 1935.

Nelson, W. PMLA. li, 1936. [Speak, Parrot; quarrel with Wolsey.] F. W. B.

ALEXANDER BARCLAY (1475?–1552)

(1) WRITINGS

The Castell of Labour. Paris, [1503?] (A Vérard); [1505?] (Pynson); 1506 (imperfect copy in Bodley); 1506 (de Worde); ed. type facs. A. W. Pollard, Roxburghe Club, 1905 (from de Worde's 1506 edn with French text of 1501). [Tr. from Pierre Gringore, Le chasteau de labour.]

The Shyp of Folys of the Worlde. Translated out of Laten, Frenche, and Doche into Englysshe tonge. 1509 (Pynson); 1570 (Cawood); ed. T. H. Jamieson, 2 vols. Edinburgh, 1874. [Tr. from Sebastian Brant, Das Narren schyff, Basle, 1494, but mainly through Jacob Locher's Latin and Pierre Rivière's French versions. An English prose trn by Henry Watson also appeared in 1509, rptd 1517. For details as to German, Latin, Low German, French and Dutch edns of Brant, see CHEL. vol. iii, pp. 478–9, 1909.]

The Egloges of Alexander Barclay prest whereof the fyrst thre conteyneth the myseryes of courters and courtes of all prynces in generall. [1515?] (de Worde); [?] (Herforde); [1548] (Powell). [Eclogues i–iii. Based on Aeneas Sylvius, Tractatus de curialium miseriis, but in pastoral form suggested by Mantuan.]

The boke of Codrus and Mynalcas. [1521] (Pynson). [Eclogue iv. From Mantuan.]

The fyfte Eglog of Alexandre Barclay of the cytezen and uplondyshman. [1521] (de Worde); ed. F. W. Fairholt, Percy Soc. 1847. [From Mantuan.]

Certayne Egloges of Alexander Barclay, Priest. [Appended to Cawood's edn of Ship of Fools, 1570.] Rptd type facs. Spenser Soc. 1885; ed. Beatrice White, EETS. 1928.

The famous cronycle of the warre agaynst Jugurth. [1520] (Pynson); [1525] (Pynson); rev. Thomas Paynell, 1557. [Tr. from Sallust.]

The lyfe of the blessed martyr Saynte Thomas. [1520] (Pynson). [Anon., attrib. by Bale.]

The introductory to wryte and to pronounce Frenche. 1521 (Copland).

A ryght frutefull treatyse, intituled the myrrour of good maners, translate into englysshe. [1523] (Pynson). [Appended to Cawood's edn of Ship of Fools, 1570.] Rptd type facs. Spenser Soc. 1885 (from Cawood's edn). [From Dominicus Mancinus' Latin.]

(2) CRITICAL WORKS AND ARTICLES

Jamieson, T. H. Notice of the Life and Writings of Alexander Barclay. 1874 (priv. ptd).

Herford, C. H. Studies in the Literary Relations of England and Germany in the Sixteenth Century. Cambridge, 1886. [Ch. vi.]

Reissert, O. Die Eklogen des Alexander Barclay. Neuphilologische Beiträge, Hanover, 1886.

Sommer, H. O. Erster Versuch über die englische Hirtendichtung. Marburg, 1888. [Pp. 33–41.]

Fraustadt, F. Über das Verhältnis von Barclay's 'Ship of Fools' zur lateinischen, französischen und deutschen Quelle. Breslau, 1894.

Koelbing, Arthur. Barclay and Skelton. CHEL. vol. iii, 1909.

Mustard, W. P. Notes on the Egloges of Alexander Barclay. MLN. xxiv, 1909.

Berdan, J. M. Alexander Barclay, Poet and Preacher. MLR. viii, 1913.

—— Early Tudor Poetry. New York, 1920. [Pp. 237–56.]

Schultz, J. R. The Life of Alexander Barclay. JEGP. xviii, 1919.

—— Alexander Barclay and the Later Eclogue Writers. MLN. xxxv, 1920.

—— The Method of Barclay's Eclogues. JEGP. xxxii, 1933.

Pompen, A. The English Versions of The Ship of Fools. 1925.

White, B. The Eclogues of Alexander Barclay. EETS. 1928. [Introduction.]

Pyle, F. 'The Barbarous Metre of Barclay.' MLR. xxxii, 1937. B. W.

SIR THOMAS WYATT (1503?–1542)

(1) WRITINGS

Tho. wyatis translatyon of Plutarckes boke of the Quyete of mynde. [1528] (Pynson); ed. facs. C. R. Baskervill, Cambridge, U.S.A. 1931.

Certayne Psalmes chosen out of the Psalter of David commonly called the vii penytentiall Psalmes, drawen into Englyshe meter by sir Thomas Wyat knyght, whereunto is added a prologe of the auctore before every Psalme very pleasant and profettable to the Godly reader. 1549.

Songes and Sonettes, written by the ryght honorable Lorde Henry Haward late Earle of Surrey, and other. Apud Richardum Tottel. 1557 (5 June); 1557 (31 July) (two settings with omissions and addns); 1559 (*bis*); 1565; 1567; 1574; 1585; 1587; ed. E. Arber, 1870, etc.; ed. H. E. Rollins, 2 vols. Cambridge, U.S.A. 1928–9. [For other edns and discussions see p. 401 above.]

Poems of Henry Howard, Earl of Surrey. With the Poems of Sir Thomas Wiat. Ed. George Sewell, 1717.

The Works of Henry Howard Earl of Surrey and of Sir Thomas Wyatt the Elder. Ed. G. F. Nott, 2 vols. 1815–6.

The Poetical Works of Sir Thomas Wyatt. Ed. R. Bell, 1854.

The Poems of Sir Thomas Wiat. Ed. A. K. Foxwell, 2 vols. 1913.

The Poetry of Sir Thomas Wyatt. A Selection and a Study. Ed. E. M. W. Tillyard, 1929.

(2) Critical Works and Articles

Simonds, W. C. Sir Thomas Wyatt and his Poems. Strasburg, 1889.

Koeppel, E. Sir Thomas Wyatt und Melin de Saint-Gelais. Ang. xiii, 1891.

Bapst, Edmond. Deux Gentilshommes—Poètes de la Cour de Henry VIII. Paris, 1891.

Flügel, E. Die handschriftliche Überlieferung der Gedichte von Sir Thomas Wyatt. Ang. xviii, 1896.

Kastner, L. E. The Elizabethan Sonneteers and the French Poets. MLR. iii, 1908.

Berdan, J. M. and Kastner, L. E. Wyatt and the French Sonneteers. MLR. iv, 1909. [A discussion.]

Foxwell, A. K. A Study of Sir Thomas Wyatt's Poetry. 1011.

Stopes, C. C. Shakespeare's Industry. 1916.

Hammond, E. P. Poems signed by Sir Thomas Wyatt. MLN. xxxvii, 1922.

Padelford, F. M. The Scansion of Wyatt's Early Sonnets. Stud. Phil. xx, 1923.

Whipple, T. K. Martial and the English Epigram from Sir Thomas Wyatt to Ben Jonson. Berkeley, 1925.

Tillyard, E. M. W. The Poetry of Sir Thomas Wyatt. A Selection and a Study. 1929.

Griffith, R. H. and Law, R. A. A Boke of Ballets and The Courte of Venus. Texas University Stud. no. 10, 1930.

Chambers, Sir E. K. Sir Thomas Wyatt and some Collected Studies. 1933.

Hayes, A. McH. Wyatt's Letters to his Son. MLN. xlix, 1934.

[The works of Berdan, Courthope, Koeppel, Marchi, Saintsbury, Scott, Warton and Zocco listed in the General section above, pp. 406–7, should also be consulted.]   H. J. B.

HENRY HOWARD, EARL OF SURREY
(1517?–1547)

(1) Poems

Songes and Sonettes, written by the ryght honorable Lorde Henry Haward late Earle of Surrey, and other. Apud Richardum Tottel. 1557 (5 June); 1557 (31 July) (two settings with omissions and addns); 1559 (*bis*); 1565; 1567; 1574; 1585; 1587; ed. E. Arber, 1870 etc.; ed. H. E. Rollins, 2 vols. Cambridge, U.S.A. 1928–9. [For other edns see p. 401 above.]

Certain Bokes of Virgiles Aeneaeis turned into English meter by the right honorable lorde, Henry Earle of Surrey. Apud Ricardum Tottel. 1557; rptd Roxburghe Club, 1814.

Poems of Henry Howard, Earl of Surrey. With the Poems of Sir Thomas Wiat. Ed. George Sewell, 1717.

The Works of Henry Howard Earl of Surrey and of Sir Thomas Wyatt the Elder. Ed. G. F. Nott, 2 vols. 1815–6.

Poetical Works of Henry Howard, Earl of Surrey, Minor Contemporaneous Poets and Thomas Sackville, Lord Buckhurst. Ed. R. Bell, 1854.

The Poems of Henry Howard, Earl of Surrey. Ed. F. M. Padelford, Seattle, 1920 and 1928 (rev. edn).

Surrey's Fourth Boke of Vergill. Ed. H. Hartman, 1933.

(2) Critical Works and Articles

Schroeer, A. Über die Anfänge des Blankverses in England. Ang. iv, 1881.

Fehse, Hermann. Henry Howard, Earl of Surrey. Ein Beitrag zur Geschichte des Petrarchismus in England. Chemnitz, 1888.

Emerson, O. F. The Development of Blank Verse. A Study of Surrey. MLN. iv, 1889.

Bapst, Edmond. Deux Gentilshommes—Poètes de la Cour de Henry VIII. Paris, 1891.

Fest, O. Über Surreys Virgilübersetzung, nebst Neuausgabe des vierten Buches nach Tottels Originaldruck und der bisher ungedruckten Hs. Hargrave 205 [BM.]. Berlin, 1903.

Imelmann, R. Zu den Anfängen des Blankverses: Surrey's Aeneis in ursprünglicher Gestalt. Sh. Jb. xli, 1905.

Padelford, F. M. The Manuscript Poems of Henry Howard, Earl of Surrey. Ang. xxix, 1906.

Willcock, G. D. A hitherto Uncollated Version of Surrey's Translation of the Fourth Book of the Aeneid. MLR. xiv, 1919, xv, 1920, xvii, 1922.

Hudson, H. H. Surrey and Martial. MLN. xxxviii, 1923.

[The works of Berdan, Courthope, Koeppel, Marchi, Saintsbury, Scott, Warton and Zocco, listed in the General section above pp. 406–7 should be consulted. See also under Wyatt above.] H. J. B.

A MIRROR FOR MAGISTRATES

(1) EDITIONS

A memorial of suche Princes, as since the tyme of King Richard the seconde, have been unfortunate in the Realme of England. [The title-page, all that was ptd, of Wayland's projected edn of 1554, preserved on fol. xl of Wayland's edn of Lydgate's Fall of Princes.]

A Myrroure For Magistrates. Wherein maye be seen by example of other, with howe grevous plages vices are punished: and howe frayle and unstable worldly prosperitie is founde, even of those, whom Fortune seemeth most highly to favour. 1559 (Thomas Marshe). [Ed. William Baldwin. For the list of contributors in this and the next edn see J. W. Cunliffe's table, CHEL. vol. iii, pp. 514–5, 1909.]

A Myrrour for Magistrates. 1563 (Thomas Marshe). [Ed. William Baldwin. Adds tragedy of Somerset apparently accidentally omitted in 1559 edn, and a second part consisting of 8 lives.]

A Myrrour for Magistrates. Newly corrected and augmented. 1571 (Thomas Marshe). [Corrects the mistakes of arrangement in 1563 edn.]

The First parte of the Mirour for Magistrates, containing the falles of the first infortunate Princes of this lande: From the comming of Brute to the incarnation of our saviour. 1574 (Thomas Marshe). [Ed. John Higgins. Includes 16, in some copies 17, new prechristian lives only, all by Higgins. Rptd 1575.]

The Last parte of the Mirour for Magistrates. Newly corrected and amended. 1574 (Thomas Marshe). [Combines Baldwin's two pts. Rptd 1575 and 1578 (which adds the tragedies of Eleanor Cobham and Humphrey, duke of Gloucester, both by George Ferrers).]

The seconde part of the Mirrour for Magistrates, containing the falle of the infortunate Princes of this Lande. From the Conquest of Caesar, unto the commying of Duke William the Conquerour. 1578 (Richard Webster). [By Thomas Blenerhasset. Includes 12 tragedies from A.D. 44 to 1066.]

The Mirour for Magistrates: Newly imprinted, and with the addition of divers Tragedies enlarged. 1587 (Henry Marsh, being the assigne of Thomas Marsh). [Ed. John Higgins. Combines the First parte of 1574 and the Last parte of 1578, adding 23 new lives by Higgins (to A.D. 209), Sir Nicholas Burdet (by Higgins), two poems by Francis Dingley of Munston, and Cardinal Wolsey (by Thomas Churchyard).]

A Mirour for Magistrates: Being a true chronicle historie of the untimely falles of such unfortunate Princes and men of note, as have happened since the first entrance of Brute into his Iland, untill this our latter Age. Newly enlarged with a last part, called A Winter nights Vision, being an addition of such Tragedies, especially famous, as are exempted in the former Historie, with a Poem annexed, called Englands Eliza. 1610 (Felix Kyngston) (re-issued under fresh titles 1619, 1620, 1621). [Ed. Richard Niccols. Combines with omissions, addns and alterations the seconde part of 1578 (Blenerhasset's) with Higgins's 1587 edn. The original issue contained a dedication to Henry, Prince of Wales, which was carefully suppressed, only one copy apparently having survived. See Notes on Sales, TLS. 22 Sept. 1921.]

Mirror for Magistrates. Ed. (with useful introduction) Joseph Haslewood, 3 vols. 1815. [Text of 1587, collated with the other edns.]

The Complaint of Henry Duke of Buckingham. Ed. (from Sackville's MS, with Induction) M. Hearsey, New Haven, 1936.

(2) CRITICAL WORKS AND ARTICLES

Warton, Thomas. The History of English Poetry. Vol. iii, 1781, pp. 209–82.

Trench, W. F. A Mirror for Magistrates: Its Origin and Influence. 1898 (priv. ptd).

—— William Baldwin. Mod. Lang. Quart. i, 1899.

Davies, J. A Mirror for Magistrates, considered with Special Reference to the Sources of Sackville's Contributions. Leipzig, 1906.

Cunliffe, J. W. A Mirror for Magistrates. CHEL. vol. iii, 1909.

Feasey, E. I. The Licensing of the Mirror for Magistrates. Library, III, 1922.
—— William Baldwin. MLR. xx, 1925.
Bush, D. Classical Lives in The Mirror for Magistrates. Stud. Phil. xxII, 1925.
Farnham, W. John Higgins' Mirror and Locrine. MP. xxIII, 1926.
—— The Miror for Magistrates and Elizabethan Tragedy. JEGP. xxv, 1926.
—— The Progeny of A Mirror for Magistrates. MP. xxIX, 1932.
Hearsey, M. Thomas Sackville. TLS. 18 April 1929.
—— The MS. of Sackville's Contribution to the Mirror for Magistrates. RES. VIII, 1932.
Davies, G. Mirror for Magistrates. TLS. 23 July 1931.
Campbell, L. B. Mirror for Magistrates. TLS. 30 June 1932.
—— Humphrey Duke of Gloucester and Elinor Cobham in the Mirror for Magistrates. Huntington Lib. Bulletin, April 1934.
—— The Suppressed Edition of A Mirror for Magistrates. Huntington Lib. Bulletin, Nov. 1934.
Jackson, W. A. Wayland's Edition of the Mirror for Magistrates. Library, xIII, 1932.
Taylor, M. A. Lord Cobham and the Mirror for Magistrates. Shakespeare Ass. Bulletin, VIII, 1933.
Case, A. E. A Bibliography of English Poetical Miscellanies. Bibliog. Soc. 1935. [Collations, etc. pp. 2–7.]
Pyle, F. A Mirror for Magistrates. TLS. 28 Dec. 1935. [Criticism of L. B. Campbell.]

J. W. C.

GEORGE GASCOIGNE (1542?–1577)

(1) COLLECTED WORKS

The pleasauntest workes of George Gascoigne Esquyre: His Flowers, Hearbes, Weedes, the Fruites of Warre, the Comedie called Supposes, the Tragedie of Jocasta, the Steele glasse, the Complaint of Phylomene, the Story of Ferdinando Jeronimi and the pleasure at Kenelworth Castle. 1587 (also issued as The Whole woorkes).
The Complete Poems of George Gascoigne. Ed. W. C. Hazlitt, 2 vols. 1869–70. [Includes Glass of Government, Posies, Pleasures at Kenilworth, Steel Glass, and prints from BM. MSS: The Grief of Joye, Certeyne Elegies, and The Tale of Hemetes the heremyte.]
The Works of George Gascoigne. Ed. J. W. Cunliffe, 2 vols. Cambridge, 1907–10. [Includes all the works listed below.]

(2) SEPARATE WORKS
(a) Original Editions

A Hundreth sundrie Flowers. [1573]. [Supposes, Jocasta, A discourse of the adventures passed by Master F. J., Gascoignes voyage into Hollande, Dan Bartholomew of Bathe, and shorter poems.]
The Posies of George Gascoigne. Corrected, perfected, and augmented by the Author. 1575 (2 issues). [Substantially the same as A Hundreth sundrie Flowres, but adds Dulce bellum inexpertes, The fruite of Fetters, and Certayne notes of Instruction concerning the making of verse or ryme in English. The order of the poems is completely changed.]
The Glasse of Government. A tragicall Comedie. 1575 (2 issues).
The Stele Glas. A Satyre. 1576.
A Delicate Diet, for daintie mouthde Droonkardes. 1576.
The Spoyle of Antwerpe. 1576.
The Droomme of Doomes day. Translated. 1576.
The Princelye pleasures, at the Courte at Kenelwoorth. 1576. [The last known copy, in Birmingham Public Lib., has been destroyed by fire. A reprint was made in 1821.]
The Wyll of the Devil. [1577?] (anon.). [Generally attrib. to Gascoigne.]
The Queenes Majesties Entertainment at Woodstock. 1585. [The unique copy in BM. has lost the first 4 pages including the title-page. Includes the Tale of Hemetes the Heremyte which Gascoigne translated into Latin, French and Italian, and a comedy which is sometimes attrib. to him.]

(b) Modern Editions and Reprints

Jocasta: A Tragedie written in Greeke by Euripides, translated and digested into Acte by George Gascoygne and Francis Kinwelmershe. Ed. F. J. Child (Four Old Plays, Cambridge, U.S.A. 1848); ed. J. W. Cunliffe, Boston, 1906 (Belles Lettres ser.).
Supposes: A Comedie written in the Italian tongue by Ariosto, Englished. Ed. T. Hawkins (The Origin of the English Drama, vol. III, Oxford, 1773); ed. J. W. Cunliffe, Boston, 1906 (Belles Lettres ser.); ed. R. W. Bond (Early Plays from the Italian, Oxford, 1911).
A Hundreth Sundrie Flowres. Ed. B. M. Ward, 1926. [Omits Jocasta, Supposes and part of prose sections of The Adventures of Master F. J.]

he Glass of Government. Ed. photo. facs. J. S. Farmer, [1914]. (Tudor Facsmile Texts.)

he Steele Glas and The Complaynt of Philomene. Ed. E. Arber, 1868.

he tale of Hemetes the heremyte Pronounced before the Q. Majesty at Woodstock. Ed. J. Nichols from MS (in Progresses of Queen Elizabeth, vol. I, 1788). [BM. Royal MS 18 A XLVIII.]

he Queenes Majesties Entertainment at Woodstock. Ed. A. W. Pollard, 1903 and 1910; ed. J. W. Cunliffe, PMLA. XXVI, 1911.

(3) COMMENDATORY PIECES, ETC.

Turbervile, George.] The Noble Arte of Venerie or Hunting. 1575. [Includes George Gascoigne in the commendation of the noble Arte of Venerie.]

Bedingfeld, Thomas. Cardanus Comforte, translated. 1576. [Includes George Gascoigne to the reader of this Booke.]

Gilbert, Sir Humphrey. A Discourse of a Discoverie for a new Passage to Cataia. 1576. [Includes George Gascoigne Esquire to the Reader, and A Prophetical Sonnet of the same George Gascoine.]

Holliband [i.e. Desainliens], Claudius. The Frenche Littleton. 1566 (for 1576?). [Includes George Gascoigne Squire in commendation of this booke.]

Fleming, Abraham. Synesius Encomium calvitii. 1579. [Fleming appended to his trn, The pleasant tale of Hemetes the Heremite, both in Latine and Englishe.]

(4) BIOGRAPHY AND CRITICISM

Whetstone, George. A Remembraunce of the wel imployed life and godly end of George Gaskoigne Esquire. 1577; ed. E. Arber (with The Steele Glas, 1868).

Hunter, Joseph. Chorus Vatum Anglicanorum. Vol. I, 1838. [MS in BM. Add. 24487.]

Arber, Edward. Chronicle of the Life, Works and Times of Gascoigne. 1868. [In his edn of The Steele Glas.]

Herford, C. H. Gascoigne's Glass of Government. E. Studien, IX, 1886.

—— Studies in the Literary Relations of England and Germany in the Sixteenth Century. Cambridge, 1886, pp. 149–63.

Schelling, F. E. The Life and Writings of George Gascoigne. Boston, 1893.

Cunliffe, J. W. George Gascoigne. CHEL. vol. III, 1909.

Ward, B. M. George Gascoigne and his Circle. RES. II, 1926. [See also F. E. Teager, RES. VII, 1931, p. 330.]

—— The Death of Gascoigne. RES. II, 1926.

—— The Will of John Bacon. RES. III, 1927. [For Gascoigne's wife.]

Ward, B. M. Further Research on A Hundreth Sundrie Flowres. RES. IV, 1928.

Ambrose, Genevieve. George Gascoigne. RES. II, 1926, XIII, 1937.

Cawley, R. R. George Gascoigne and the Siege of Famagusta. MLN. XLIII, 1928.

Bradner, L. The First English Novel: A Study of George Gascoigne's Adventures of Master F. J. PMLA. XLV, 1930.

Hankins, J. E. A Note on Gascoigne's Biography. MP. XXX, 1932.

Bowers, F. T. Notes on Gascoigne's A hundreth Sundrie Flowers and The Posies. Harvard Stud. XVI, 1934.

Prouty, C. T. Gascoigne in the Low Countries. RES. XII, 1936.

J. W. C.

NICHOLAS BRETON (1545?–1626?)

(1) COLLECTED WORKS

The Works in Verse and Prose of Nicholas Breton. Ed. A. B. Grosart, 2 vols. 1879 (priv. ptd). (Chertsey Worthies' Lib.)

A Mad World My Masters and Other Prose Works by Nicholas Breton. Ed. Ursula Kentish-Wright, 2 vols. 1929. [15 pieces.]

(2) WRITINGS IN VERSE

A Smale Handfull of Fragrant Flowers. 1575 (' by N.B.'); ed. T. Park (in Heliconia, vol. I, 1815). [Often attrib. to Breton, but more probably by Nathaniel Baxter.]

A Floorish upon Fancie. 1577 (' by N. B.'); 1582 (with addns); ed. T. Park (in Heliconia, vol. I, 1815).

The Workes of a Young Wyt Trust up with a Fardell of Pretie Fancies. 1577.

Brittons Bowre of Delights. 1591; 1597; ed. H. E. Rollins, Cambridge, U.S.A. 1933. [Only partly Breton's, including his Amoris Lachrimae for the Death of Sir Philip Sidney, and some short pieces.]

The Pilgrimage to Paradise, joyned with the Countesse of Pembrookes Love. Oxford, 1592.

A Solemne Passion of the Soules Love. 1595 (appended to the anon. prose Marie Magdalens Love); 1598; 1622; 1623.

The Arbour of Amorous Devises. 1597. [Only partly Breton's. See p. 404 above.]

Pasquils Mad-cap and Mad-cappes Message. 1600 (anon.); 1626.

The Second Part of Pasquils Mad-cap, intituled the Fooles-cap. 1600.

Pasquils Mistresse. 1600.

Pasquils Passe and Passeth not. 1600.

Melancholike Humours. 1600; ed. Sir S. E. Brydges, 1815; ed. G. B. Harrison, 1929.

No Whippinge nor Trippinge. 1601 (anon.); ed. Charles Edmonds (in Isham Reprints, 1895).

A Divine Poem, divided into Two Partes: the Ravished Soule, and the Blessed Weeper, 1601.

An Excellent Poeme, upon the Longing of a Blessed Heart. 1601; ed. Sir S. E. Brydges, 1814.

Olde Mad-cappes New Gally-mawfry. 1602.

The Mothers Blessing. 1602; 1621.

The Passion of a Discontented Minde. 1602 (anon.); 1621; ed. J. P. Collier (in Illustrations of Old English Literature, vol. i, 1866). [Possibly not Breton's. Sir S. Lee attrib. to Southwell.]

The Soules Harmony. 1602; 1635.

A True Description of Unthankfulnesse. 1602.

The Passionate Shepheard. 1604 (anon.); ed. F. Ouvry, 1877 (priv. ptd).

The Soules Immortal Crowne devided into Seaven Dayes Workes. 1605.

The Honour of Valour. 1605.

Honest Counsaile. A Merrie Fitte of a Poetical Furie. 1605.

Cornu-copiae. Pasquils Nightcap. 1612; 1623. [Possibly not Breton's. A. B. Grosart attrib. to William Fennor.]

I would and would not. 1614 ('by B.N.').

The Hate of Treason, with a Touch of the Late Treason. 1616('by N.B.'); ed. A. B. Grosart (in Works, from MS as An Invective against Treason).

The Countess of Pembrook's Passion. Ed. J. O. Halliwell[-Phillipps] (in A Brief Description of the Plymouth Manuscripts, 1853); ed. R. G. B., 1862 (from another MS as A Poem on Our Saviour's Passion, and attrib. to Countess of Pembroke).

(3) WRITINGS IN PROSE

The Wil of Wit, Wits Wil, or Wils Wit. 1597; 1599; 1606; ed. J. O. Halliwell[-Phillipps], 1860. [Stationers' Register, 1580. Includes: 1. A Discourse betwixt Wit and Will; 2. The Authors Dreame; 3. The Scholler and the Souldiour; 4. The Miseries of Mavillia; 5. The Praise of Virtuous Ladies; 6. A Dialogue between Anger and Patience; 7. A Phisitions Letter; 8. A Farewell.]

Wits Trenchmour in a Conference had betwixt a Scholler and an Angler. 1597.

Auspicante Jehova. Maries Exercise. 1597.

The Figure of Foure, or a Handfull of Sweet Flowers. 1631. [S.R., 1597.]

The Figure of Foure. The Second Part. 1623 (by 'N.B.'); 1636; 1654.

The Strange Fortune of Two Excellent Princes. 1600.

A Poste with a Madde Packet of Letters. 1602; 1603 ('enlarged'); 1606 ('second Part'); 1607; 1609; 1620; [1623?]; 1630; 1633; 1634; 1637.

Wonders Worth the Hearing. 1602.

A Dialogue Full of Pithe and Pleasure: between Three Phylosophers. 1603.

A Merrie Dialogue betwixt the Taker and Mistaker. 1603; 1635 (as A Mad World my Masters).

Grimellos Fortunes. 1604 ('by B.N.'); ed E. G. Morice, Bristol, 1936.

I pray you be not Angrie. 1605; 1624; 1632

An Old Mans Lesson and a Young Mans Love 1605; ed. (with Grimellos Fortunes) E. G Morice, Bristol, 1936.

Choice, Chance and Change, or Conceites in their Colours. 1606 (anon.); ed. A. B Grosart, Manchester, 1881.

A Murmurer. 1607.

Divine Considerations of the Soule, concerning the Excellencie of God and the Vilenesse of Man. 1608.

Wits Private Wealth, Stored with Choice Commodities. 1612; 1613; 1615; 1629 1639.

Characters upon Essaies Morall, and Divine 1615; ed. Sir S. E. Brydges (in Archaica vol. i, 1815).

The Good and the Badde, or Descriptions of the Worthies and Unworthies of this Age 1616; 1643 (as Englands Selected Charac ters).

Crossing of Proverbs: Crosse-Answeres and Crosse-Humours. 2 pts, 1616 ('by B.N.') [1620?] ('corrected with Additions').

Machiavells Dogge. 1617 (anon.). [See F. T Bowers, An Addition to the Breton Canon MLN. xlv, 1930.]

Conceited Letters newlie laid Open. 1618 1632.

The Court and Country, dialogue-wise between a Courtier and a Country-man. 1618; ed W. C. Hazlitt (Inedited Tracts, 1868).

Strange News out of Divers Countries. 162: (signed B. N.).

Fantasticks serving for a Perpetuall Prognos tication. 1626 (signed N. B.).

[Character of Queen Elizabeth.] Ed. John Nichols (in The Progresses and Public Pro cessions of Queen Elizabeth, 3 vols. 1788- 1807).

(4) BIOGRAPHY AND CRITICISM

Kuskop, T. F. C. Nicholas Breton und seine Prosaschriften. Leipzig, 1902.

Greenough, C. N. Nicholas Breton, Character Writer and Quadrumaniac. [In Kittredge Anniversary Papers, Boston, 1913.]

Bullen, A. H. Breton. [In Elizabethans 1924.]

Crawford, Charles. Greenes Funeralls, 1594 and Nicholas Breton. Stud. Phil. Ex. Ser i, 1929.

Monroe, N. E. Nicholas Breton as a Pamphle teer. Philadelphia, [1929].

Blunden, E. Nicholas Breton's Prose. [In Votive Tablets, 1931.]

EDMUND SPENSER (1552?–1599)

(1) Bibliographies and Concordances

Osgood, C. G. A Concordance to the Poems of Spenser. Washington, 1915.

Whitman, C. H. A Subject Index to the Poems of Edmund Spenser. New Haven, 1918.

Carpenter, F. I. A Reference Guide to Edmund Spenser. Chicago, 1923. [Supplement by D. F. Atkinson, Baltimore, 1937.]

Parrot, Alice. A Critical Bibliography of Spenser from 1923 to 1928. Stud. Phil. xxv, 1928.

Johnson, F. R. A Critical Bibliography of the Works of Edmund Spenser printed before 1700. Baltimore, 1933.

Wurtsbaugh, J. Two Centuries of Spenserian Scholarship, 1609–1805. Baltimore, 1936.

(2) Works

(a) Collections

The Faerie Queen: The Shepheards Calendar: Together with the other Works of England's Arch-Poët, Edm. Spenser: Collected into one Volume, and carefully corrected. 1611–12–13; 1617.

The Works of that Famous English Poet, Mr Edmond Spenser. 1679.

Works. Ed. John Hughes, 5 vols. 1715, 1750. [Essays.]

Works. Ed. H. J. Todd, 8 vols. 1805; 1856, etc. [Notes.]

Poetical Works. Ed. F. J. Child, 5 vols. Boston, 1855, etc. [Notes.]

Works. Ed. J. Payne Collier, 5 vols. 1862, etc. [Notes.]

Complete Works. Ed. R. Morris and J. W. Hales, 1869, etc. (Globe edn.)

Complete Works. Ed. A. B. Grosart, 9 vols. 1882–94. [Essays by various hands. Unfinished.]

Poetical Works. Ed. R. E. N. Dodge, Boston, 1908. (Cambridge edn). [Notes.]

Poetical Works. Ed. J. C. Smith and E. de Selincourt, 3 vols. Oxford, 1909–10 (with bibliographical and textual notes); Oxford, 1912 (with Spenser-Harvey letters, abridged textual notes, and essay by E. de Selincourt).

Works. Ed. W. L. Renwick, 4 vols. 1928–34. [Notes. Incomplete, omitting Faerie Queen, but including all the other poems and State of Ireland.]

Works. Ed. E. Greenlaw, C. G. Osgood and F. M. Padelford, 8 vols. Baltimore, 1932– . (Variorum edn).

(b) Separate Poetical Works

A Theatre, wherein be represented the miseries and calamities that follow the Voluptuous Worldlings. Devised by S. John vander Noodt. 1569; rptd photo. facs. New York, 1936. [Contains 'Epigrams' and 'Sonets' by Spenser; revised versions in Complaints, 1591.]

The Shepheardes Calender Conteyning twelve Aeglogues proportionable to the twelve monethes. 1579 (anon.); 1581; 1586; 1591; 1597; rptd Theodore Bathurst, 1653 (with Latin trn); ed. photo. facs. H. O. Sommer, 1890; ed. C. H. Herford, 1895 (introduction and notes).

The Faerie Queene. Books i–iii. 1590. [For later edns see below.]

Complaints. Containing sundrie small Poemes of the Worlds Vanitie. By Ed. Sp. 1591. [Contains: The Ruines of Time; The Teares of the Muses; Virgils Gnat; Prosopopoia, or Mother Hubberds Tale; The Ruines of Rome, by Bellay; Muiopotmos, or the Fate of the Butterflie; Visions of the Worlds Vanitie; Petrarches Visions Muiopotmos is dated 1590.]

Daphnaïda. An Elegie upon the death of the noble and vertuous Douglas Howard. By Ed. Sp. 1591; 1596 (with Fowre Hymnes).

To M. Gabriell Harvey. [In Harvey's Foure Letters, 1592. The Sonnet is dated 1586.]

Amoretti and Epithalamion. 1595; ed. Sir S. Lee (in Elizabethan Sonnets, 1904); ed. C. Van Winkle, New York, 1926 (Epithalamion only); rptd photo. facs. 1927.

Colin Clouts Come home againe. [Astrophel.] 1595. [Contains also poems on death of Philip Sidney by other hands. 'The Doleful Lay of Clorinda,' ostensibly by the Countess of Pembroke, has been attrib. to Spenser.]

[Commendatory sonnet prefixed to Nennio, Or a Treatise of Nobility. Written by Sir John Baptista Nenna of Bari. Done into English by William Jones, 1595.]

The Faerie Queene. Disposed into twelve bookes, Fashioning xii. Morall vertues. Books i–vi. 2 vols. 1596. [For later edns see below.]

Fowre Hymnes. [Daphnaïda.] 1596; ed. L. Winstanley, Cambridge, 1907 (Hymnes only).

Prothalamion Or A Spousall Verse in honour of the double mariage of the Ladie Elizabeth and the Ladie Katherine Somerset. 1596.

Upon the Historie of George Castriot. [In Historie of George Castriot. Newly translated out of French by Z. I., 1596.]

[Commendatory sonnet prefixed to The Commonwealth and Government of Venice. Written by the Cardinal Gaspar Contareno, and translated by Lewis Lewkenor, 1599.]

The Faerie Queene. 1609 (first edn of fragments of Book VII); ed. R. Church, 1758 (notes); ed. J. Upton, 1758 (notes); ed. T. J. Wise, 1895–7; ed. Kate M. Warren, 1897–1900 (notes); ed. J. C. Smith, Oxford, 1909 (see Works above). Book I: ed. G. W. Kitchin, Oxford, 1867; ed. L. Winstanley, Cambridge, 1915. Book II: ed. G. W. Kitchin, Oxford, 1887; ed. L. Winstanley, Cambridge, 1914. Book V: ed. A. B. Gough, Oxford, 1918. [These have Introductions and notes.]

Fragments. [In Ware's edn of View of Ireland, 1633. See under Prose Works below.]

(c) Prose Works

Three Proper, and wittie, familiar Letters. [Two other, very commendable Letters.] 1580. [By Gabriel Harvey and Edmund Spenser. Portions ed. G. Gregory Smith, Elizabethan Critical Essays, vol. I, Oxford, 1904.]

Axiochus. A most excellent Dialogue, written in Greeke by Plato. Translated out of Greek by Edw. Spenser. 1592; ed. F. M. Padelford, Baltimore, 1934.

A View of the Present State of Ireland. Ed. Sir James Ware, Dublin, 1633. [MSS in BM. (3); Bodley (2); University Lib. Cambridge (3); Lambeth; Trinity College, Dublin; Record Office.]

(3) BIOGRAPHY AND CRITICISM

(a) Books and Chapters in Books

Webbe, W. A Discourse of English Poetrie. 1586.

Jortin, J. Remarks on Spenser's Poetry. 1734. [Expanded in Tracts Critical, Philological, and Miscellaneous, 1790.]

Warton, T. Observations on The Faerie Queene. 1754; 1762 (enlarged).

Hurd, R. Letters on Chivalry and Romance. 1762.

Hazlitt, W. Lectures on the English Poets. 1818.

Malone, E. Shakespeare's Works. Vol. II, 1821.

Coleridge, S. T. Literary Remains. Vol. I, 1836. [Lecture III of course delivered 1818.]

Hunt, Leigh. Imagination and Fancy. 1844.

Craik, G. L. Spenser and his Poetry. 3 vols. 1845.

Fleay, F. G. Guide to Chaucer and Spenser. 1877.

Church, R. W. Spenser. 1879. (English Men of Letters ser.)

de Vere, Aubrey. Essays. 1887.

Dowden, E. Transcripts and Studies. 1888.

Legouis, É. Quomodo Spenserus Versum heroicum renovarit ac refecerit. Paris, 1896.

Legouis, É. Edmund Spenser. Paris, 1923. [In French.]

—— Edmund Spenser. 1926. [In English. Part tr. from the preceding.]

Greg, W. W. Pastoral Poetry and Pastoral Drama. 1906.

Mackail, J. W. The Springs of Helicon. 1909.

Cory, H. E. The Critics of Edmund Spenser. Berkeley, 1911.

Dixon, W. M. English Epic and Heroic Poetry. 1912.

Higginson, J. J. Spenser's Shepherd's Calendar in Relation to Contemporary Affairs. New York, 1912.

Palmer, G. H. Formative Types in English Poetry. Boston, 1918.

Jack, A. A. A Commentary on Chaucer and Spenser. Glasgow, 1920.

Renwick, W. L. Edmund Spenser: an Essay on Renaissance Poetry. 1925.

Henley, Pauline. Spenser in Ireland. Cork, 1928.

Hughes, M. Y. Virgil and Spenser. Berkeley, 1929.

Bhattacherje, M. Studies in Spenser. Calcutta, 1929.

—— Platonic Ideas in Spenser. Calcutta, 1935.

Jones, H. S. V. A Spenser Handbook. New York, 1930.

Wyld, H. C. Spenser's Diction and Style in Relation to those of Later English Poetry. [In A Grammatical Miscellany offered to Otto Jespersen, Copenhagen, 1930.]

Greenlaw, E. Studies in Spenser's Historical Allegory. Baltimore, 1932.

Millican, C. B. Spenser and the Table Round. Cambridge, U.S.A. 1932.

Davis, B. E. C. Edmund Spenser. Cambridge, 1933.

Spens, Janet. Spenser's Faerie Queene. An Interpretation. 1934.

Stein, H. Studies in Spenser's Complaints. New York, 1934.

Lewis, C. S. The Allegory of Love. Oxford, 1936.

(b) Articles in Periodicals

Spenser and Lucretius. Edinburgh Rev. CLXI, 1885.

Koeppel, E. Spenser's Verhältniss zu Tasso. Ang. XI, 1889.

Dodge, R. E. N. Spenser's Imitations from Ariosto. PMLA. XII, 1897, XXXV, 1920.

Fletcher, J. B. Areopagus and Pléiade. Journ. Germanic Philology, II, 1899.

—— A Study in Renaissance Mysticism. PMLA. XXVI, 1911.

—— The Painter of the Poets. Stud. Phil. XIV, 1917.

Greenlaw, E. The Shepheardes Calender. PMLA. xxvi, 1911; Stud. Phil. xi, 1913.
—— Some Old Religious Cults in Spenser. Stud. Phil. xx, 1923.
Padelford, F. M. Spenser and the Puritan Propaganda. MP. xi, 1913.
—— The Political, Economic and Social Views of Spenser. JEGP. xvi, 1917.
Jones, H. S. V. Spenser's Defence of Lord Grey. Illinois University Stud. v, 1919.
Mustard, W. P. E. K.'s Classical Allusions. MLN. xxxiv, 1919.
Osgood, C. G. Spenser's English Rivers. Trans. Connecticut Academy, xxiii, 1920.
—— Spenser and the Enchanted Glass. Johns Hopkins Alumni Mag. xix, 1930.
Renwick, W. L. The Critical Origins of Spenser's Diction. MLR. xvii, 1922.
Hughes, M. Y. Spenser and the Greek Pastoral Triad. Stud. Phil. xx, 1923.
—— Spenser's Palmer. ELH. ii, 1935.
Plomer, J. B. Spenser's Handwriting. MP. xxi, 1923.
Covington, F. F. Spenser's Use of Irish History in the View of the Present State of Ireland. Texas University Stud. iv, 1924.
Saurat, D. Les Idées philosophiques de Spenser. Yearbook Lund Soc. Letters, i, 1924.
Taylor, A. E. Spenser's Knowledge of Plato. MLR. xix, 1924.
Welply, W. H. Edmund Spenser: Some New Discoveries. N. & Q. 21 June, 12 July 1924.
—— Edmund Spenser: Being an Account of some Recent Researches into his Life and Lineage. N. & Q. 13 Feb.–9 April 1932.
—— More Notes on Edmund Spenser. N. & Q. 12, 19 Aug. 1933.
Blanchard, H. H. Spenser and Boiardo. PMLA. xl, 1925.
Davis, B. E. C. The Text of Spenser's Complaints. MLR. xx, 1925.
Landrum, G. W. Spenser's Use of the Bible. PMLA. xli, 1926.
Notcutt, H. C. The Faerie Queene and its Critics. E. & S. xii, 1926.
Wilson, F. P. Spenser and Ireland. RES. ii, 1926.
Hewlett, J. H. Interpreting a Spenser-Harvey Letter. PMLA. xlii, 1927.
Scott, J. G. Sources of Spenser's Amoretti. MLR. xxii, 1927.
Knowlton, E. C. The Genii of Spenser. Stud. Phil. xxv, 1928.
Sandison, H. E. Arthur Gorges. PMLA. xliii, 1928.
Hamer, D. Spenser's Marriage. RES. ix, 1931.
Byron, H. J. Edmund Spenser's First Printer. Library, xiv, 1933.

Judson, A. C. A Biographical Sketch of John Young, Bishop of Rochester. Indiana University Stud. xxi, 1934.
Stirling, B. The Philosophy of Spenser's 'Garden of Adonis.' PMLA. xlix, 1934.
Jenkins, R. Newes out of Munster. A Document in Spenser's Hand. Stud. Phil. xxxii, 1935.   W. L. R.

SIR PHILIP SIDNEY (1554–1586)

(1) COLLECTED WORKS AND SELECTIONS

The Countesse of Pembrokes Arcadia. Now the third time published with sundry new additions [i.e. Certaine Sonets; The Defence of Poesie; Astrophel and Stella; Her most Excellent Majestie walking in Wansteet Garden]. 1598; Edinburgh, 1599; 1605; 1613 (with addn of A Dialogue betweene two Shepherds); Dublin, 1621 (contains supplement by Sir W. Alexander); 1623; 1627 (contains A Sixth Booke by R. B[eling], dated 1628); 1629 ('with the supplement of a defect by Sir W. A. Whereunto is now added a sixth Booke, by R. B.'); 1633; 1638 ('with a twofold supplement: the one by Sir W. A.; the other, by Mr Johnstoun'); 1655 ('with his Life and Death; a brief Table of the principal heads, and som other new Additions' [i.e. A Remedie for Love]); 1662; 1674.
The Works in Prose and Verse. The Fourteenth Edition. 3 vols. 1725–4; Dublin, 1739.
The Miscellaneous Works and Letters. Ed. W. Gray, Oxford, 1829; Boston, 1860; 1893.
The Complete Poems. Ed. A. B. Grosart, 2 vols. 1873.
The Complete Poetical Works. Ed. A. B. Grosart, 3 vols. 1877.
Astrophel and Stella und Defense of Poesie. Ed. E. Flügel, Halle, 1889.
The Defence of Poesie; A Letter to Queen Elizabeth; A Defence of Leicester. Ed. G. E. Woodberry, Boston, 1908.
The Complete Works. Ed. A. Feuillerat, 4 vols. Cambridge, 1912–26.

(2) SEPARATE WORKS

A Woorke concerning the trewnesse of the Christian Religion. By Philip of Mornay, Lord of Plessie Marlie. Begunne to be translated into English by Sir Philip Sidney and finished by Arthur Golding. 1587; 1592; 1604; 1617.
The Countesse of Pembrokes Arcadia. 1590 (the New Arcadia only); 1593 ('Now since the first edition augmented and ended', the end supplied from the Old Arcadia); ed. photo. facs. (1590) O. Sommer, 1891; ed.

E. A. Baker, 1907 (modernized, with the addns of Sir William Alexander and Richard Beling).

Syr P. S. His Astrophel and Stella. Wherein the excellence of sweete Poesie is concluded. To the end of which are added sundry other rare Sonnets of divers Noble men and Gentlemen. 1591 (Newman).

Sir P. S. His Astrophel and Stella. Wherein the excellence of sweete Poesie is concluded. 1591 (Newman).

Syr P. S. His Astrophel and Stella. Wherein the excellence of Sweete Poesie is concluded. To the end of which are added sundry other rare Sonnets of divers Noble men and Gentlemen. [1591] (Lownes).

Astrophel and Stella. Ed. E. Arber (An English Garner, vol. I, 1877); ed. A. W. Pollard, 1888; ed. Sir S. Lee (in Elizabethan Sonnets, vol. I, 1904); ed. M. Wilson, New York, 1931.

The Defence of Poesie. 1595 (Ponsonby); 1595 (Olney, as An Apologie for Poetrie); ed. [J. Warton], 1787 (The Defence of Poesy); ed. A. S. Cook, Boston, 1890 (The Defence of Poesy); ed. E. S. Shuckburgh, Cambridge, 1891 (An Apologie for Poetrie); ed. J. C. Collins, Oxford, 1907 (An Apologie for Poetrie); rptd photo. facs. 1928 (The Defence of Poesie).

Defence of Robert Dudley, Earl of Leicester. [In A. Collins, Letters and Memorials of State, 1746.]

The Psalms of David. Begun by Sir P. Sidney and finished by the Countess of Pembroke. [In Early English Poets, vol. VIII, 1823.]

The Correspondence of Sir Philip Sidney and H. Languet. Ed. S. A. Pears, 1845; ed. W. A. Bradley, Boston, 1912.

(3) Biography and Criticism
(a) Books

Greville, Fulke (Baron Brooke). Life of Sir Philip Sidney. 1652; ed. N. Smith, Oxford, 1907.

Collins, A. Letters and Memorials of State. 1746.

Zouch, T. Memoirs of the Life and Writings. 1808.

Saint-Marc Girardin. Cours de Littérature Dramatique. Vol. III, Paris, 1843.

Crossley, J. Sir Philip Sidney and the Arcadia. 1853.

[Davis, S. M. H.]. The Life and Times of Sir Philip Sidney. Boston, 1859.

Bourne, H. R. F. A Memoir of Sir Philip Sidney. 1862; 1891 (as Sir Philip Sidney, Type of English Chivalry).

Lloyd, J. The Life of Sir Philip Sidney. 1862.

Quossek, C. Sidneys 'Defence of Poesy' und die Poetik des Aristotles. Crefeld, 1880.

Symonds, J. A. Sir Philip Sidney. 1886. (English Men of Letters ser.)

Jusserand, J. J. Le Roman anglais au Temps de Shakespeare. Paris, 1887; tr. Eng. 1890.

Morley, E. The Works of Sir Philip Sidney. 1901. (The Quain Essay.)

Brunhuber, K. Sir Philip Sidneys Arcadia und ihre Nachläufer. Nuremberg, 1903.

Lee, Sir S. Great Englishmen of the XVIth Century. 1904.

Sinning, N. F. W. 'Cupid's Revenge' von Beaumont und Fletcher und Sidneys Arcadia. Halle-Wittemberg, 1905.

Greg, W. W. Pastoral Poetry and Pastoral Drama. 1906.

Hill, H. W. Sidney's Arcadia and the Elizabethan Drama. Reno, 1908.

Addleshaw, P. Sir Philip Sidney. 1909.

Wolff, S. L. The Greek Romances in Elizabethan Prose Fiction. New York, 1912.

Greenlaw, E. Sidney's Arcadia as an Example of Elizabethan Allegory. [In Kittredge Anniversary Papers, Boston, 1913.]

—— The Captivity Episode in Sidney's Arcadia. [In Manly Anniversary Studies, Chicago, 1923.]

Wallace, M. W. The Life of Sir Philip Sidney. Cambridge, 1915.

Brie, F. Sidneys Arcadia. QF. CXXIV, 1918.

Genouy, H. L''Arcadia' de Sidney dans ses rapports avec l''Arcadia' de Sannazaro et la 'Diana' de Montemayor. Montpellier, 1928.

Zandvoort, R. W. Sidney's Arcadia. A Comparison between the Two Versions. Amsterdam, 1929.

Scott, J. G. Les Sonnets élisabéthains. Paris, 1929. [Ch. ii.]

Wilson, Mona. Sir Philip Sidney. 1931.

Denkinger, E. M. Immortal Sidney. New York, 1932.

Osborn, A. W. Sir Philip Sidney en France. Paris, 1932.

Goldman, M. S. Sir Philip Sidney and the Arcadia. Urbana, 1934.

Myrick, K. O. Sir Philip Sidney as a Literary Craftsman. Cambridge, U.S.A. 1935.

Warren, C. H. Sir Philip Sidney. 1936.

(b) Articles in Periodicals

'C.' The Arcadia Unveiled. N. & Q. 6, 20, 27 June 1863. [See F. Howard's reply, N. & Q. 22 Aug. 1863.]

Fletcher, J. B. Areopagus and Pleiade. JEGP. II, 1898.

Crawford, C. Webster and Sir Philip Sidney. N. & Q. 17 Sept., 1, 15, 29 Oct., 12 Nov. 1904.

Maynadier, H. The Areopagus of Sidney and Spenser. MLR. iv, 1909.

Dobell, B. New Light on Sidney's Arcadia. Quarterly Rev. ccxi, 1909.

Long, P. W. Spenser and Sidney. Ang. xxxviii, 1914.

Greenlaw, E. Shakespeare's Pastorals. Stud. Phil. xiii, 1916.

Brie, F. Umfang und Ursprung der poetischen Beseelung in der Englischen Renaissance bis zu Sidney. E. Studien, l, 1916–7.

Harkness S. The Prose Style of Sir Philip Sidney. Wisconsin University Stud. ii, 1918.

Whigan, R. G. and Emerson, O. F. Sonnet Structure in Sidney's Astrophel and Stella. Stud. Phil. xviii, 1921.

Behler, M. Die Beziehungen zwischen Sidney und Spenser. Archiv, cxlvi, 1923.

Harrison, T. P. A Source of Sidney's Arcadia. Texas University Stud. no. 6, 1926.

—— The Relations of Spenser and Sidney. PMLA. xlv, 1930.

Lancaster, H. C. Sidney, Galaut, La Calprenède. MLN. xlii, 1927.

Danchin, F. C. Les deux Arcadies de Sir Philip Sidney. Revue Anglo-Américaine, v, 1927.

Praz, M. Sidney's Original Arcadia. London Mercury, xv, 1927.

Whitney, L. Concerning Nature in the Countess of Pembroke's Arcadia. Stud. Phil. xxiv, 1927.

Wallace, M. W. The Reputation of Sir Philip Sidney. Johns Hopkins Alumni Mag. xvii, 1928.

Hainsworth, G. L'Arcadie de Sidney en France. Revue de Littérature comparée, x, 1930.

Briggs, W. D. Political Ideas in Sidney's Arcadia. Stud. Phil. xxviii, 1931, xxix, 1932.

Denkinger, E. M. The Arcadia and 'the fish Torpedo faire.' Stud. Phil. xxviii, 1931.

Hanford, J. H. and Watson, S. R. Personal Allegory in the Arcadia. MP. xxx, 1934.

Banks, T. H. Astrophel and Stella. PMLA. l, 1935.

Hudson, H. H. Penelope Devereux as Sidney's Stella. Huntington Lib. Bulletin, April 1935.   A. F.

FULKE GREVILLE, BARON BROOKE
(1554–1628)

(1) COLLECTED WORKS

Certaine learned and elegant workes of the Right Honourable Fulke, Lord Brooke, written in his youth and familiar exercise with Sir Philip Sidney. 1633.

The Remains of Sir Fulk Grevill Lord Brooke: Being Poems of Monarchy and Religion: Never before Printed. 1670. [Contains Poems, Alaham, Mustapha, Caelica, a Letter to an Honourable Lady, a Letter of Travell.]

The Works in Verse and Prose Complete of the Lord Brooke. Ed. A. B. Grosart, 4 vols. 1870. (Fuller Worthies' Lib.)

The Friend of Sir Philip Sidney: Selections from the Works of Fulke Greville. Ed. A. B. Grosart, 1894.

(2) SEPARATE WORKS

The Tragedy of Mustapha. 1609.

The life of the renowned Sr Philip Sidney. 1652; ed. Sir S. E. Brydges, 2 vols. Lee Priory, 1816; ed. N. Smith, Oxford, 1907.

Caelica. Ed. M. F. Crow (Elizabethan Sonnet-Cycles, vol. [iv], 1898). [First ptd in Workes, 1633.]

(3) BIOGRAPHY AND CRITICISM

Bolton, E. Hypercritica. 1622; ed. in part J. E. Spingarn (Seventeenth Century Critical Essays, vol. i, Oxford, 1908).

Croll, M. The Works of Fulke Greville. Philadelphia, 1903.

Cushman, R. N. Concerning Fulke Greville's Tragedies, Alaham and Mustapha. MLN. xxiv, 1909.

Bullen, A. H. Elizabethans. 1924. [Essay on Greville.]

Kuhl, E. P. Contemporary Politics in Elizabethan Drama: Fulke Greville. PQ. vii, 1928.

Scott, J. G. Les Sonnets élisabéthains. Paris, 1929. [Ch. iii.]

Rice, W. G. The Sources of Fulke Greville's Alaham. JEGP. xxx, 1931.

Bullough, G. Fulk Greville. MLR. xxviii, 1933.

Purcell, J. M. Astrophel and Stella and Greville's Caelica. PMLA. l, 1935.

Ellis-Fermor, U. M. The Jacobean Drama, 1936.

ROBERT SOUTHWELL (1561?–1595)

[For Southwell's writings in prose see p. 685 below.]

(1) COLLECTED POEMS

Poetical Works. Ed. W. B. Turnbull (with Memoir), 1856.

Complete Poems. Ed. A. B. Grosart (with Memorial-introduction and Notes), 1872. (Fuller Worthies' Lib.)

Complete [Poetical] Works. [1886.]

The Book of Robert Southwell. Ed. C. M. Hood, Oxford, 1926. [Shorter poems.]

(2) SEPARATE POETICAL WORKS

Saint Peters complaynt. With other poems. 1595 (*bis*; anon.); 1597; 1599; Edinburgh, [1600?], 1602 ('Newly augmented. With other poems'); [1602?]; 1615.

Mæoniæ, Or, Certaine excellent Poems and spirituall Hymnes: omitted in the last impression of Peters Complaint. All composed by R. S. 1595 (*bis*).

A Foure-Fould Meditation of the foure last things. Composed in a Divine Poeme. By R. S. 1606; ed. C. Edmonds (Isham Reprints, no. 4, 1895).

S. Peters Complaint and Saint Mary Magdalens Funerall Teares. With sundry other selected and devout poems. [St Omer], 1616, 1620.

St Peters Complainte, Mary Magdal. teares. Wth other workes. 1620; 1630; Edinburgh, 1634; 1636.

St. Peter's Complaint, and Other Poems. Ed. (with a biography) W. J. Walter, 1817.

(3) BIOGRAPHY AND CRITICISM

Possoz, Alexis. Vie du Père Southwell. Paris, 1866.

Macleod, J. G. Robert Southwell as Scholar, Poet, and Martyr. Month, Dec. 1877.

Thurston, Herbert. An Unknown Poem of Father Southwell. Month, Oct. 1894.

—— Father Southwell the Euphuist. Month, Feb. and March, 1895.

Praz, Mario. Robert Southwell's Saint Peter's Complaint and its Italian Source. MLR. xix, 1924.

Morton, R. A. An Appreciation of Robert Southwell. Philadelphia, 1929.

Robbie, H. J. L. The Authorship of A Fourefold Meditation. RES. v, 1929. [Not by Southwell?]

Janelle, P. Robert Southwell the Writer. A Study in Religious Inspiration. Clermont-Ferrand, 1935. [Bibliography, pp. 306–23.]

Mangam, C. R. Robert Southwell and the Council of Trent. Revue anglo-américaine, xii, 1935.

SAMUEL DANIEL (1563?–1619)

(1) BIBLIOGRAPHY

Sellers, H. A Bibliography of the Works of Samuel Daniel. Proc. Oxford Bibliog. Soc. ii, 1928–30. [Supplementary Note, *ibid.* p. 341.]

(2) COLLECTED WORKS

Poeticall Essayes. 1599. [Contains five books of Civil Wars; Musophilus; Letter from Octavia to Marcus Antonius; Cleopatra; Complaint of Rosamund.]

Works Newly augmented. 1601 (re-issued 1602). [Contains six books of Civil Wars; Musophilus; Letter from Octavia; Cleopatra; Rosamond; Delia.]

Certaine Small Poems Lately Printed: with the Tragedie of Philotas. 1605. [Contains Letter from Octavia; Cleopatra; Rosamond; Ulisses and the Syren; Philotas.]

Certaine Small Workes heretofore divulged & now againe corrected and augmented. 1607. [Contains Philotas; Letter from Octavia; Cleopatra; Rosamond; Ulisses; Musophilus; Queenes Arcadia; Funerall Poeme upon the Earle of Devonshire.]

Certaine Small Workes heretofore divulged and now againe corrected and augmented. 1611. [Contains Philotas; Letter from Octavia; Cleopatra; Rosamond; Ulisses; Musophilus; Queenes Arcadia; Funerall Poeme; Delia.]

Whole Workes in Poetrie. 1623. [Contains Civile Wares; Letter from Octavia; Funerall Poeme; Panegyrike congratulatorie; Certaine epistles; Musophilus; Rosamond; Delia; 'To the Angell Spirit of Sr Phillip Sidney'; Letter to a worthy Countesse; 'To James Montague, Lord Bishop of Winchester'; Philotas; Hymens Triumph; Ulysses; Queenes Arcadia; Twelve Goddesses; Cleopatra.]

The Poetical Works of Mr Samuel Daniel. 1718.

The Complete Works in Verse and Prose. Ed. A. B. Grosart, 5 vols. 1885–96.

Poems and A Defence of Ryme. Ed. A. C. Sprague, Cambridge, U.S.A. 1930.

(3) SEPARATE WORKS

The Worthy Tract of Paulus Jovius, Containing a Discourse of Imprese. 1585.

Syr P. S. His Astrophel and Stella. To the end of which are added, sundry other rare Sonnets of divers Noblemen and Gentlemen. 1591. [Newman's surreptitious edn. Of the 28 sonnets ascribed to Daniel, 24 reappeared in Delia.]

Delia. With the complaint of Rosamond. 1592 (*bis*); 1594 (as Delia and Rosamond augmented, and adds Cleopatra); 1598; ed. A. Esdaile, 1908 (with Drayton's Idea). [J. P. Collier produced a type facs. of Rosamond in 1870.]

First Fowre Bookes of the civile wars. 1595.

Panegyrike Congratulatory delivered to the Kings most excellent majesty. Also certaine Epistles. With a Defence of Ryme. [1603] (folio); 1603 (octavo). [The Certaine Epistles are addressed to Sir T. Egerton, Lord H. Howard, the Countess of Cumberland, the Countess of Bedford, Lady Anne Clifford, the Earl of Southampton.]

The True Discription of a Royall Masque. 1604
(Allde). [First and surreptitious edn of the
Vision of the Twelve Goddesses.]
The Vision of the 12. Goddesses. 1604 (Water-
son); ed. E. Law, 1880.
The Queenes Arcadia. 1606.
Funerall Poeme vppon the Death of the Earle
of Devonshyre. [1606?]
Tragedie of Philotas. 1607. [Contains Philo-
tas; Panegyrike congratulatorie; Certaine
epistles; Defence of Ryme.]
Civile Wares, corrected and continued. 1609.
[Eight books: the complete poem.]
Order and Solemnitie of the Creation of
Prince Henrie, Prince of Wales: whereunto
is annexed the Royall Maske [Tethys Fes-
tival, by Daniel]. 1610.
First Part of the Historie of England. 1612;
1613.
Hymens Triumph. 1615.
Collection of the Historie of England. [1618?];
1621; 1626; 1634; 1650; 1685.
The prayse of private life. [In Letters and
Epigrams by Sir John Harington, ed. N. E.
McClure, Philadelphia, 1930.]
Defence of Rhyme. Rptd J. Haslewood
(Ancient Critical Essays, vol. II, 1815); ed.
G. Gregory Smith (Elizabethan Critical
Essays, vol. II, Oxford, 1904); rptd G. B.
Harrison, 1925.

(4) BIOGRAPHY AND CRITICISM

(a) Books

Fuller, T. History of the Worthies of England.
1662. [Somersetshire, p. 28.]
à Wood, Anthony. Historia et Antiquitates
Universitatis Oxoniensis. 1674. [Sig.
Dddddd 4.]
—— Athenæ Oxonienses. 1691. [Sig. Bb 1,
column 379.]
Introductory Memoir. [In Poetical Works of
Mr. Samuel Daniel, 1718.]
Oldys, W. Life of Daniel. [In E. Cooper's
Muses' Library, 1737.]
Hunter, J. Chorus Vatum Anglicanorum.
1845. [BM. Add. MS 24489, vol. III.]
Grosart, A. B. Introduction and Notes. [In
Complete Works of Daniel, 1885–96.]
Scott, J. G. Les Sonnets élisabéthains. Paris,
1929. [Ch. VIII.]

(b) Articles in Periodicals

Moorman, F. W. Shakespeare's History-
Plays and Daniel's Civile Wars. Sh. Jb.
XL, 1904.
Ruutz-Rees, C. Some Debts of Samuel Daniel
to Du Bellay. MLN. XXIV, 1909.
Kastner, L. E. The Italian Sources of Daniel's
Delia. MLR. VII, 1912.

Sellers, H. Samuel Daniel: Additions to the
Text. MLR. XI, 1916.
—— Two New Letters of Samuel Daniel.
TLS. 24 March 1927.
Daniel, M. S. An Elizabethan Wordsworth
[i.e. S. Daniel]. Dublin Rev. CLXXVI, 1925.
Brettle, R. E. Samuel Daniel and the
Children of the Queen's Revels, 1604–5.
RES. III, 1927.
                                          H. S.

MICHAEL DRAYTON (1563–1631)

[Considerably more detailed bibliographies
will be found in CHEL. vol. IV, 1909, and
Oliver Elton, An Introduction to Michael
Drayton, Spenser Soc. 1895.]

(1) COLLECTED WORKS

Poems: By Michaell Draiton Esquire. 1605
(contains: The Barrons warres; Englands
heroicall epistles; Idea (sonnets); Legends
of Robert, Matilda, and Gaveston); 1608
('Newly corrected'); 1610; 1613; [1615?];
[1619] (with engraved title-page reading
'Poems collected into one volume'. Adds:
Odes; Legend of Cromwell; The Owle;
Eglogues; and The Man in the Moone.
Re-issued 1620); 1630 (contains only Barons
Warres; Englands heroicall epistles; Legends
of Robert, Matilda, Gaveston and Cromwell; Idea); 1637 (as Poems collected into
one volume); rptd Spenser Soc. 1888 (from
1st edn).
The Works of Michael Drayton, Esq. 1748;
1753.
Poems. Ed. J. P. Collier, Roxburghe Club,
1856.
Complete Works. Ed. R. Hooper, 3 vols.
1876. [Incomplete, contains only Polyol-
bion and Harmony of the Church.]
Complete Works. Ed. J. W. Hebel, 5 vols.
Oxford, 1931.

(2) SEPARATE WORKS

(a) Original Editions

The Harmonie of the Church, containing
spirituall songes and holy hymnes. 1591
(re-issued 1610 as A Heavenly Harmonie);
ed. A. Dyce, Percy Soc. 1843.
Idea. The Shepheards Garland, fashioned in
nine eglogs. 1593; ed. type facs. J. P.
Collier, [1870?]. [It is not clear whether the
word 'Idea' is a part of the title or the
head-ornament, but the sonnet-sequence of
that name is not included.]
Ideas Mirrour. Amours in quaterzains. 1594.
Matilda, the fair and chaste daughter of the
Lord R. Fitzwater. 1594 (bis).

Peirs Gaveston. [1594?]; [1595?]. [Rptd in rev. form in The Tragicall Legend of Robert, 1596.]

Endimion and Phoebe. Ideas Latmus. 1595; ed. type facs. J. P. Collier, [1870?]; ed. J. W. Hebel, Oxford, 1925.

Mortimeriados. The lamentable civell warres of Edward the second and the Barrons. 1596 (re-issued [1596?]); 1603 (re-written as The Barrons Wars, and adds Idea, 67 sonnets).

The Tragicall Legend of Robert, Duke of Normandy; with the Legend of Matilda the chast; and the Legend of Piers Gaveston. 1596.

Englands Heroicall Epistles. 1597; 1598 ('Newly enlarged'); 1600 ('Newly corrected: with Idea'); 1602, etc.

The first part of the true and honorable historie, of the life of Sir John Oldcastle. 1600; ed. [Sir W. Scott] (Ancient British Drama, vol. I, 1810); ed. C. F. Tucker Brooke (Shakespeare Apocrypha, Oxford, 1908); rptd photo. facs. Malone Soc. 1908. [In collaboration with Munday, Hathway and Wilson.]

To the Majestie of King James. A gratulatorie poem. 1603.

Moyses in a Map of his Miracles. 1604.

The Owle. 1604 (bis).

A Paean Triumphall. 1604; rptd J. Nichols (Progresses of King James, vol. I, 1828).

Poems Lyrick and pastorall: Odes, Eglogs, The man in the Moone. [1606?]

The Legend of great Cromwel. 1607 (re-issued 1609 as The Historie of the Life and Death of the Lord Cromwell). [Rptd in the Mirror for Magistrates, 1610.]

Polyolbion. [1612] (18 songs, re-issued 1613); 1622 (2 parts, 30 songs, as A Chorographi-call Description of Great Britain, pt II, re-issued 1622); rptd Spenser Soc. 1890.

The Battaile of Agincourt; the Miseries of Queene Margarite; Nimphidia; the Quest of Cinthia; the Shepheards Sirena; the Moone-Calfe; Elegies upon sundry occasions. 1627; 1631. [Not the Ballad of Agincourt but a long poem in ottava rima.]

The Muses Elizium, being ten Nymphalls; Noahs Floud; Moses, his birth and miracles [i.e. Moyses in a Map of his Miracles]; David and Golia. 1630; rptd Spenser Soc. 1892.

(b) Modern Selections

Select Poems. Ed. E. Sanford (Works of the British Poets, vol. II, 1819).

Selections from the Poems of Michael Drayton. Ed. A. H. Bullen, 1883.

The Barons' Wars; Nymphidia; and Other Poems. Ed. H. Morley, 1887.

A Selection from the Poetry of Samuel Daniel and Michael Drayton. Ed. H. C. Beeching, 1899.

Poems. 1905.

Minor Poems. Ed. C. Brett, 1907.

The Battaile of Agincourt. Ed. Richard Garnett, 1893.

Idea. In Sixty-three Sonnets. Ed. E. Arber (English Garner, vol. VI, 1883); ed. M. F. Crow (Elizabethan Sonnet-Cycles, vol. [III], 1897); ed. Sir S. Lee (Elizabethan Sonnets, vol. II, 1904); ed. A. Esdaile, 1908 (with Daniel's Delia).

[Nymphidia.] The History of Queen Mab; or, the Court of Fairy. 1751.

Nymphidia: the Court of Fairy. Ed. Sir S. E. Brydges, 1814; ed. J. Gray, 1896 (with The Muses Elizium); ed. H. F. B. Brett-Smith, Oxford, 1921; ed. J. C. Squire, 1924.

[Nymphidia and Polyolbion.] Select Works of the English Poets. Ed. R. Southey, 1831.

The Quest of Cynthia. 1922.

(8) Biography and Criticism

Elton, Oliver. An Introduction to Michael Drayton. Spenser Soc. 1895. [Bibliography.]

—— Michael Drayton: a Critical Study. 1905.

Probst, Albert. Daniels 'Civil Wars' und Draytons 'Barons' Wars', eine Quellenstudie. Strasburg, 1902.

Whittaker, L. Drayton as a Dramatist. PMLA. XVIII, 1903.

—— The Sonnets of Michael Drayton. MP. I, 1904.

Child, H. H. Michael Drayton. CHEL. vol. IV, 1909.

Claassen, W. Draytons England's Heroicall Epistles, eine Quellenstudie. Leipzig, 1913.

Numeratzky, Willy. Michael Draytons Be-lesenheit und literarische Kritik. Berlin, 1915.

Long, E. Drayton's Eighth Nymphal. Stud. Phil. XIII, 1916.

Adams, J. Q. Michael Drayton's To the Virginia Voyage. MLN. XXXIII, 1918.

McKerrow, R. B. The Supposed Calling-in of Drayton's Harmony of the Church, 1591. Library, I, 1919.

von Schaubert, Else. Draytons Anteil an Heinrich VI, 2. und 3. Teil. Köthen, 1920.

—— Zu der Frage nach Draytons Anteil an Shakespeares Heinrich VI. E. Studien, LVI, 1922.

Cawley, R. R. Drayton and the Voyagers. PMLA. XXXVIII, 1923.

—— Drayton's Use of Welsh History. Stud. Phil. XXII, 1925.

Hebel, J. W. The Surreptitious Editions of Michael Drayton's Peirs Gaveston. Library, IV, 1923.
—— Drayton's Sirena. PMLA. XXXIX, 1924.
—— Drayton and Shakespeare. MLN. XLI, 1926.
Jenkins, R. Drayton s Relation to the School of Donne, as revealed in the Shepheards Sirena. PMLA. XXXVIII, 1923.
—— The Source of Drayton's Battle of Agincourt. PMLA. XLI, 1926.
—— Drayton's Sirena again. PMLA. XLII, 1927.
Keller, Wolfgang. Noch einmal Draytons angebliche Mitarbeit an Heinrich VI. E. Studien, LVII, 1923.
Bullen, A. H. Drayton. [In Elizabethans, 1924.]
Finney, C. L. Drayton's Endimion and Phoebe and Keats' Endymion. PMLA. XXXIX, 1924.
Lucas, F. L. Michael Drayton. [In Authors Dead and Living, 1926.]
Gourvitch, I. The Welsh Element in the Poly-Olbion. RES. IV, 1928.
—— Drayton's Debt to Geoffrey of Monmouth. RES. IV, 1928.
—— A Note on Drayton and Philemon Holland. MLR. XXV, 1930.
Scott, J. G. Les Sonnets élisabéthains. Paris, 1929. [Ch. x.]
Constable, K. M. Drayton and the Holland Family. MLR. XXVI, 1931.   J. W. H.

JOHN DAVIES OF HEREFORD
(1565?–1618?)

(1) WORKS

Mirum in modum. A glimpse of Gods glorie and the soules shape. 1602.
Microcosmos. The discovery of the little world. 1603.
Bien Venu. Greate Britaines welcome to the Danes. 1606.
Summa Totalis: an addition to Mirum in Modum. 1607.
The Holy Roode. 1609.
Humours Heav'n on Earth; with the Civile Warres of Death and Fortune. As also, The Triumph of Death: or, the picture of the Plague as it was in 1603. 1609.
Wittes Pilgrimage through a world of amorous sonnets, soule-passions, and other passages. [1610?]
The Scourge of Folly, consisting of satyricall epigramms, and others in honor of many noble Persons, together with a pleasant Descant upon most English Proverbes. [1611?]. [Including the Scourge for Paper-Persecutors (Papers Complaint).]

The Muses Sacrifice, or divine meditations. 1612. [With 'Rights of the living and the dead: being a proper appendix to the precedent meditations.']
The Muses-Teares for the losse of Henry, Prince of Wales; with Times sobs for the death of his darling; and lastly, his epitaphs. Where-unto is added, Consolatory straines. 1613.
A Select Second Husband for Sir Thomas Overburie's Wife, now a matchlesse widow. 1616. [Containing also 'Divers elegies touching the death of Sir Thomas Overburie, Mirum in modum, and Speculum proditori.']
Wits Bedlam where is had whipping-cheer to cure the mad. 1617.
A Scourge for Paper-Persecutors. By J. D. With a continu'd just Inquisition of the same subiect, by A. H[olland?]. 1625. [Verse satires. Rptd from the Scourge of Folly, 1611.]
Ψαλμὸς Θεῖος, or a Divine Psalme. Whereunto is annexed an Elogie upon the Patron [pattern, i.e. the Scriptures], with certaine Divine Epigrams. 1652.
The Complete Works. Ed. A. B. Grosart, 1878. (Chertsey Worthies' Lib.)

(2) BIOGRAPHY AND CRITICISM

Fuller, T. History of the Worthies of England. 1662.
à Wood, Anthony. Athenæ Oxonienses. 1691.
Hunter, J. Chorus Vatum Anglicanorum. 1838–54. [BM. Add. MSS 24487–24492.]
Grosart, A. B. Introduction. [In Complete Works of Davies, 1878.]
Heidrich, Hans. John Davies of Hereford und sein Bild von Shakespeares Umgebung. Berlin, 1924.
Anderson, R. L. A French Source for John Davies of Hereford's System of Psychology. PQ. VI, 1927.   H. S.

THOMAS CAMPION (1567–1620)

(1) COLLECTED EDITIONS

The Works of Dr. Thomas Campion. Ed. A. H. Bullen, 1889.
Fifty Songs. Ed. J. Gray, 1896.
Lyric Poems. Ed. E. Rhys, [1896].
Songs and Masques, with Observations in the Art of English Poesy. Ed. A. H. Bullen, 1903.
Songs. Astolat Press, 1904.
Poetical Works (in English). Ed. P. S. Vivian, [1907]. (Muses' Lib.)
Campion's Works. Ed. P. S. Vivian, 1909.

(2) SEPARATE WORKS

Poemata: Ad Thamesin; Fragmentum Umbrae; Liber Elegiarum; Liber Epigrammatum. 1595.

A Booke of Ayres, set foorth to be song to the Lute, Orpherian, and Base Violl, by Philip Rosseter Lutenist. 1601. [The words by Campion.]

Observations in the Art of English Poesie. 1602; rptd J. Haslewood (Ancient Critical Essays, vol. II, 1815); ed. G. Gregory Smith (Elizabethan Critical Essays, vol. II, Oxford, 1904); rptd G. B. Harrison, 1925 (with Daniel's Defence of Rhyme).

The Discription of a Maske, presented before the Kinges Majestie at White-Hall, on Twelfth Night last, in honour of the Lord Hayes, and his Bride. Other small Poemes are adjoyned. 1607; ed. K. Talbot, 1924.

Two Bookes of Ayres. The First contayning divine and morall songs: the Second, Light conceits of lovers. [1610.] [Words and music by Campion.]

A Relation of the late Royall Entertainment given by the Lord Knowles, at Cawsome-House the Description of the Lords Maske, presented in the Banquetting-house on the Mariage night of the Count Palatine and the Ladie Elizabeth. 1613.

Songs of Mourning: bewailing the untimely death of Prince Henry. 1613.

The Description of a Maske: presented in the Banqueting roome at Whitehall, at the Mariage of the Earle of Somerset and the Lady Frances Howard. Whereunto are annexed divers choyse Ayres. 1614.

The Third and Fourth Booke of Ayres. [1617?] [Words and music by Campion.]

Epigrammatum libri II; Vmbra; Elegiarum liber unus. 1619.

A New Way of Making Fowre-parts in Counter-point. [1620?]

(3) BIOGRAPHY AND CRITICISM

Vivian, P. S. Thomas Campion. CHEL. vol. IV, 1909.

MacDonagh, T. Thomas Campion and the Art of English Poetry. 1913.

Lynd, R. Thomas Campion. Athenaeum, 26 Sept. 1919.

Flood, W. H. G. Thomas Campion: his Irish Ancestry. Music Student, Aug. 1920.

Gosse, Sir E. Thomas Campion. Music Student, April, 1920. [A tercentenary notice.]

Savage, Henry. Thomas Campion and his 'Dark Lady'. Bookman's Journ. 16 and 23 April 1920.
H. S.

SIR HENRY WOTTON (1568–1639)

(1) COLLECTED WORKS

Poems. Ed. A. Dyce, Percy Soc. 1842.

Poems by Sir Henry Wotton, Sir Walter Raleigh and Others. Ed. J. Hannah, 1845, etc.

(2) SEPARATE WORKS

The elements of Architecture. 1624; ed. S. T. Prideaux, 1903.

Ad regem e Scotia reducem Henrici Wottoni plausus et vota. 1633.

A parallel betweene Robert late Earle of Essex and George late Duke of Buckingham. 1641; ed. Sir S. E. Brydges, 1814.

A short view of the life and death of George Villiers Duke of Buckingham. 1642; rptd Harleian Misc. vol. VIII, 1744.

A panegyrick of king Charles; being observations upon the inclination, life, and government of our sovereign lord the King. 1649.

Reliquiae Wottonianae; or a collection of lives, letters, poems; with characters of sundry personages: and other incomparable pieces of language and art. Ed. (with life) Izaak Walton, 1651; 1654 (with addns); 1672; 1685 (adds letters to Lord Zouch).

The State of Christendom; or a most exact and curious discovery of many secret passages and hidden mysteries of the Times. 1657.

Letters to Sir Edmund Bacon. 1661.

Letters and Dispatches from Sir Henry Wotton, 1617–1620. Ed. George Tomline, Roxburghe Club, 1850.

(3) BIOGRAPHY AND CRITICISM

Walton, Izaak. The Life of Sir Henry Wotton. 1670. [First ptd in Reliquiae Wottonianae, 1651.]

Ward, Sir A. W. Sir Henry Wotton: a Biographical Sketch. 1898.

Smith, L. P. The Life and Letters of Sir Henry Wotton. 2 vols. Oxford, 1907.

Asquith, H. H. Sir Henry Wotton. With some General Reflections on Style in English Poetry. English Ass. 1919.

SIR JOHN DAVIES (1569–1626)

(1) COLLECTED WORKS

The Poetical Works of Sir John Davies published from a Corrected Copy formerly in the Possession of Mr Thompson. 1773.

The Works in Verse and Prose [including hitherto unpublished manuscripts]. Ed. A. B. Grosart, 3 vols. 1869–76. (Fuller Worthies' Lib.)

The Complete Poems. Ed. A. B. Grosart, 2 vols. 1876. (Fuller Worthies' Lib.)

The Works. Ed. H. Morley, 1889.

(2) POEMS

Epigrammes and elegies by J. D[avies] and C. M[arlowe]. 2 pts, Middelburg, [1590?]; rptd C. Edmonds (Isham Reprints, 1870).

Orchestra or a Poeme of Dauncing Judicially proving the true observation of time and measure, in the Authenticall and laudable use of Dauncing. 1596; rptd E. Arber (English Garner, vol. v, 1882); ed. R. S. Lambert, 1922.

Orchestra or A Poeme expressing the Antiquitie and Excellencie of Dauncing. In a Dialogue betweene Penelope and one of her Wooers. Not finished. 1622 (appended to Nosce teipsum).

Hymnes of Astraea in acrosticke verse. 1599. 1618; 1622 (appended to Nosce teipsum); rptd (from 1599 edn) E. Arber (English Garner, vol. v, 1882).

Nosce teipsum. This oracle expounded in two elegies. 1. Of humane knowledge. 2. Of the soule of man and the immortalitie thereof. 1599; 1602 ('newly corrected'); 1608; 1619; 3 pts, 1622 (includes Hymnes of Astraea and Orchestra); ed. Nahum Tate, 1697, etc.; rptd, 2 pts, Dublin (as A Poem on the immortality of the soul, with essay by T. Sheridan and Historical Relations concerning Ireland); rptd (from 1599 edn) E. Arber (English Garner, vol. v, 1882); rptd H. Morley, 1890.

(3) OTHER WRITINGS

[For Davies's historical writings see p. 837 below.]

Sir Martin Mar-people his coller of esses. 1590.

A discoverie of the true causes why Ireland was never entirely subdued untill the beginning of his Majesties happie raigne. 1612 (re-issued 1613), etc.

A new post: with soveraigne salve to cure the worlds madnes. 1620; [1625?] (as Reasons moane).

(4) BIOGRAPHY AND CRITICISM

Woolrych, H. W. Lives of Eminent Serjeants-at-Law. 2 vols. 1869.

Sneath, E. H. Philosophy in Poetry. A Study of Nosce Teipsum. New York, 1903.

Seemann, Margarete. Sir John Davies, sein Leben und seine Werke. Vienna. 1913.

Ramsay, M. P. Les Doctrines médiévales chez Donne. 1917; 1924 (rev. edn).

Holmes, M. D. The Poet as Philosopher. A Study of Nosce Teipsum. 1921.

Bredvold, L. I. The Sources used by Davies in Nosce Teipsum. PMLA. xxxviii, 1923.

Buckley, G. T. The Indebtedness of Sir John Davies' Nosce Teipsum to Philip Mornay's Trunesse of the Christian Religion. MP. xxv, 1927.

Tilley, M. P. The Comedy Lingua and Sir John Davies's Nosce Teipsum. MLN. xliv, 1929.

RICHARD BARNFIELD (1574–1627)

(1) COLLECTED WORKS

Poems. Ed. A. B. Grosart, 1876. (Fuller Worthies' Lib.)

Some Longer Elizabethan Poems. Ed. A. H. Bullen, 1903. (English Garner.) [Reprints first edns of all Barnfield's works except Greenes funeralls.]

(2) SEPARATE WORKS

The Affectionate Shepheard. Containing the Complaint of Daphnis for the love of Ganymede. 1594 (anon.); ed. J. O. Halliwell [-Phillipps], Percy Soc. 1842.

Greenes funeralls. 1594 (signed R. B.); ed. R. B. McKerrow, 1911; rptd [1923].

Cynthia. With certaine Sonnets, and the Legend of Cassandra. 1595; rptd Beldornie Press, Ryde, Isle of Wight, 1841.

The Encomion of Lady Pecunia: Or The praise of Money. 1598; 1605 (as Lady Pecunia).

The Complaint of Poetrie, for the Death of Liberalitie. 1598 (anon.).

The Combat betweene Conscience and Covetousnesse, in the minde of Man. 1598 (anon.).

Poems: In divers humors. 1598; 1605; ed. A. Boswell, Roxburghe Club, 1816; ed. J. P. Collier (Illustrations of Old English Literature, 1866).

(3) CRITICISM

Henneman, J. B. Barnfield's Ode: 'As it fell upon a day'. [In Furnivall Miscellany, Oxford, 1901.]

III. THE ELIZABETHAN SONNETEERS

A. MISCELLANIES CONTAINING SONNETS

Songes and Sonettes. 1557; ed. E. Arber, 1870; ed. H. E. Rollins, 2 vols. Cambridge, U.S.A. 1928–9. [Tottel's Miscellany.]

A Hundreth sundrie Flowres. [1573]; ed. B. M. Ward, 1926. [G. Gascoigne and others.]

The Paradyse of daynty devises. 1576; ed. H. E. Rollins, Cambridge, U.S.A. 1927. [R. Edwards and others.]

A gorgious Gallery, of Gallant Inventions. 1578; ed. H. E. Rollins, Cambridge, U.S.A. 1926. [T. Proctor and others.]

A Handefull of pleasant delites. 1584; ed.
H. E. Rollins, Cambridge, U.S.A. 1924.
[C. Robinson and others.]
The Phoenix Nest. 1593; ed. H. E. Rollins,
Cambridge, U.S.A. 1931.
The Passionate Pilgrim. 1599; ed. facs. Sir S.
Lee, Oxford, 1905.
Englands Helicon. 1600; ed. A. H. Bullen,
1887; ed. H. E. Rollins, Cambridge, U.S.A.
1935.
A Poetical Rapsody. 1602; ed. A. H. Bullen,
2 vols. 1890–1; ed. H. E. Rollins, Cam-
bridge, U.S.A. 1931–2. [F. Davison and
others.]

B. MODERN REPRINTS AND ANTHOLOGIES

[The fullest collections are those of Crow,
1896, and Lee, 1904.]

Park, T. Heliconia. Comprising a Selection of
English Poetry of the Elizabethan Age.
3 vols. 1815.
Collier, J. P. Seven English Poetical Miscel-
lanies printed between 1557 and 1602. 1867.
[The above Miscellanies except Hundreth
Sundrie Flowres and The Passionate Pilgrim.]
Arber, E. An English Garner. 8 vols. 1877–
96.
Main, D. M. A Treasury of English Sonnets.
1880. [Notes.]
—— Three Hundred English Sonnets. Edin-
burgh, 1884. [Notes.]
Bullen, A. H. Lyrics from the Song-books of
the Elizabethan Age. 1887. [Introduction,
etc.]
—— More Lyrics from the Song-books of the
Elizabethan Age. 1888.
—— Lyrics from the Song-books of the
Elizabethan Age. 1889–90. [A selection from
the two preceding volumes.]
—— Poems, chiefly Lyrical, from Romances
and Prose-tracts of the Elizabethan Age.
1890.
Dircks, W. H. Cavalier and Courtier Lyrists.
1884; 1890.
Garrett, E. H. Elizabethan Songs in Honour
of Love and Beauty. 1891; 1893.
Schelling, F. E. Elizabethan Lyrics. Boston,
1895. [Introduction, etc.]
Crow, M. F. Elizabethan Sonnet-Cycles.
4 vols. 1896–8. [Introductions.]
Carpenter, F. I. English Lyric Poetry, 1500–
1700. 1897; 1925. [Introduction.]
Quiller-Couch, Sir A. T. English Sonnets. 1897.
[Introduction and Notes.]
Dennis, J. English Lyrics from Spenser to
Milton. 1898. [Introduction.]
Nichols, J. B. B. A Little Book of English
Sonnets. 1899; 1903. [Introduction and
notes.]

Saintsbury, G. Seventeenth Century Lyrics.
1900.
—— Minor Caroline Poets. 3 vols. Oxford,
1905–21. [Introductions.]
Briscoe, J. P. Tudor and Stuart Love-Songs.
1902.
Lee, Sir S. Elizabethan Sonnets. 2 vols. 1904.
[Rpt of Arber's English Garner, with addns.
Introduction.]
Meynell, A. A Seventeenth Century Anthology.
1904. [Introduction.]
Symons, A. A Sixteenth Century Anthology.
[1905]; 1925. [Introduction and short
notes.]
—— A Pageant of Elizabethan Poetry. 1906.
[Introduction and Notes.]
Braithwaite, W. S. Book of Elizabethan
Verse. 1906. [Introduction and Notes.]
Carrington, F. The Queen's Garland. 1907.
—— The King's Lyrics. 1907.
Padelford. F. M. Early Sixteenth Century
Lyrics. Boston, 1907. [Introduction, etc.]
Young, W. T. An Anthology of the Poetry of
the Age of Shakespeare. Cambridge, 1910.
[Sonnets, pp. 183–217.]
Barter, A. Treasury of Elizabethan Lyrics.
1910. [Introduction.]
—— Treasury of Caroline Lyrics. 1924.
[Introduction.]
Robertson, W. The Golden Book of English
Sonnets. 1913; 1922.
Massingham, H. J. A Treasury of Seventeenth
Century Verse, 1616–1660. 1919. [Intro-
duction and Notes.]
Grierson, H. J. C. Metaphysical Lyrics and
Poems of the Seventeenth Century, Donne
to Butler. Oxford, 1921.
Mavor, D. Elizabethan Lyrics, selected from
the Miscellanies. 1921. [Introduction, etc.]
B., B. A Garland of Elizabethan Sonnets.
1923.
Hartog, W. G. The Kiss in English Poetry.
1923.
Legouis, É. Dans les Sentiers de la Renaissance
anglaise. Paris, 1925. [Trns into French.]
Ault, N. Elizabethan Lyrics from the Original
Texts. 1925.
—— Seventeenth Century Lyrics. 1928.
[Notes.]
Judson, A. C. Seventeenth Century Lyrics.
Chicago, 1927. [Notes.]
Chambers, Sir E. K. The Oxford Book of
Sixteenth Century Verse. 1932.

C. GENERAL WORKS ON THE ELIZA-BETHAN SONNET

(a) Sources for the Elizabethan Sonnets

Saintsbury, G. The Earlier Renaissance. 1901.
[Bibliographical notes on the chief anthologies of Latin verse of the Renaissance.]

Vaganay, H. Le Sonnet en Italie et en France au XVIᵉ Siècle. Lyons, 1903. [Chronological lists of sonnets pbd in Italy and France.]

Lachèvre, F. Bibliographie des Recueils collectifs de Poésies. XVIᵉ Siècle. Paris, 1922.

The Greek Anthology. Florence, 1494. [Collected by Maximus Planudes; ed. A. I. Lascaris.]

Anacreontis Carmina. Paris, 1586, etc.

*Gherus, Ranutius' [i.e. Janus Gruterus]. Delitiae cc Italorum poetarum, Delitiae c poetarum Belgicorum, Delitiae c poetarum Gallorum. Frankfort, 1608-14.

(b) Critical Works on Foreign Petrarchists

(i) Italian

Flamini, F. La Lirica toscana del Rinascimento. Pisa, 1891.

—— Studi di Storia letteraria italiana e straniera. Leghorn, 1895.

—— Il Cinquecento. Milan, 1902. [With bibliography.]

Monnier, P. Le Quattrocento. 2 vols. Paris, 1901.

(ii) French

Bourciez, É. Les Mœurs polies et la Littérature de Cour sous Henri II. Paris, 1886.

Pieri, M. Le Pétrarquisme au XVIᵉ Siècle. Marseilles, 1896.

Jasinski, M. Histoire du Sonnet en France. Douai, 1903.

Tilley, A. The Literature of the French Renaissance. 2 vols. Cambridge, 1904.

Vianey, J. Le Pétrarquisme en France au XVIᵉ Siècle. Montpellier, 1909. [With bibliography.]

Laumonier, P. Ronsard, Poète lyrique. Paris, 1909. [With bibliography.]

Lefranc, A. Écrivains français de la Renaissance. Le Platonisme et la Littérature en France. Paris, 1914.

Raymond, M. L'Influence de Ronsard, 1550-1585. 2 vols. Paris, 1927. [Bibliographical notes of books dealing with the French Petrarchists.]

(c) Critical Works on the Elizabethan Sonnet

(i) Books

Torraca, F. Gli Imitatori stranieri di J. Sannazaro. Rome, 1882.

Lentzner, C. A. Die Geschichte des Sonettes in England. Leipzig, 1886.

Littleboy, A. L. Relations between French and English Literature in the Sixteenth and Seventeenth Centuries. 1895.

Windschied, K. Die englische Hirtendichtung von 1579-1625. Halle, 1895.

Lee, Sir S. Life of Shakespeare. 1898, etc.

—— The French Renaissance in England. Oxford, 1910.

Einstein, L. The Italian Renaissance in England. New York, 1902, etc. [With bibliography.]

Segrè, C. Studi Petrarcheschi. Florence, 1903.

Maiberger, M. Studien über den Einfluss Frankreichs auf die Elisabethanische Literatur, die Lyrik in der 2. Hälfte des XVI. Jahrhunderts. Frankfort, 1903.

Erskine, J. The Elizabethan Lyric. New York, 1903. [With bibliography.]

Harrison, J. S. Platonism in English Poetry of the Sixteenth and Seventeenth Centuries. New York, 1903 and 1915. [With bibliography.]

Zocco, I. Petrarchismo e Petrarchisti in Inghilterra. Palermo, 1906.

Charlanne, L. L'Influence française en Angleterre au XVIIᵉ Siècle. Paris, 1906.

Greg, W. W. Pastoral Poetry and Pastoral Drama. 1906.

Upham, A. H. The French Influence in English Literature from the Accession of Elizabeth to the Restoration. New York, 1908 and 1911. [With bibliography.]

Schelling, F. E. The English Lyric. 1913.

Cruse, A. B. Elizabethan Lyrists and their Poetry. 1913.

Scott, M. A. Elizabethan Translations from the Italian. Boston, 1916.

Berdan, J. M. Early Tudor Poetry. New York, 1920.

Bullen, A. H. Elizabethans. 1924.

Hasselkuss, H. K. Der Petrarkismus in der Sprache der englischen Sonettdichter der Renaissance. Münster, 1927.

Scott, J. G. Les Sonnets élisabéthains. Paris, 1929. [With bibliographical notes and chronological lists of Italian, French, and English Petrarchists.]

(ii) Articles

Rathery, E. J. B. Relations intellectuelles entre la France et l'Angleterre. Revue contemporaine, 1855 and 1856. [Pbd also in book form, Paris, 1856.]

Isaac, H. Wie weit geht die Abhängigkeit Shakespeares von Daniel als Lyriker? Sh. Jb. XVII, 1882.

Cook, A. S. The Elizabethan Invocations to Sleep. MLN. IV, 1889.

Koeppel, E. Die englischen Tasso-Übersetzungen des 16. Jahrhunderts. Ang. XI, XII, XIII, 1889-91.

—— Studien zur Geschichte des englischen Petrarchismus im 16. Jahrhundert. Romanische Forschungen, V, 1890.

Koeppel, E. Zu Astrophel and Stella. Ang. XIII, 1891.

De Marchi, L. L' influenza della Lirica italiana sulla Lirica inglese nel Secolo XVI. Nuova Antologia, LVIII, 1895.

Kastner, L. E. Thomas Lodge. Athenaeum, 22 and 29 Oct. 1904.

—— Lodge as an Imitator of the Italian Poets. MLR. II, 1907.

—— Elizabethan Sonneteers and the French Poets. MLR. III, 1908.

—— Scottish Sonneteers and the French Poets. MLR. III, 1908.

—— Spenser's Amoretti and Desportes. MLR. IV, 1909.

—— The Italian Sources of Daniel's Delia. MLR. VII, 1912.

Klein, D. Foreign Influence on Shakespeare's Sonnets. Sewanee Rev. XIII, 1905.

Fitzmaurice-Kelly, J. Note on Three Sonnets [by Spenser, F. de la Torre, and Tasso]. Revue hispanique, XIII, 1906.

Collins, J. C. The Literary Indebtedness of England to France. Fortnightly Rev. Aug. 1908.

Wolff, M. J. Petrarkismus und Antipetrarkismus in Shakespeares Sonetten. E. Studien, XLIX, 1916.

Alden, R. M. The Lyrical Conceit of the Elizabethans. Stud. Phil. XIV, 1917.

—— Lyrical Conceits of the Metaphysical Poets. Stud. Phil. XVII, 1920.

Moore Smith, G. C. Charles Best. RES. I, 1925.

Schirmer, W. F. Das Sonett in der englischen Literatur. Ang. XXXVII, 1925.

Scott, J. G. The Sources of Giles Fletcher's Licia. MLR, XX, 1925.

—— A Latin Version of a Sonnet of Constable's. MLR. XX, 1925.

—— Encore un Imitateur de Desportes. Revue de Littérature comparée, V, 1925. [J. C., the author of Alcilia.]

—— Parallels to Three Elizabethan Sonnets. MLR. XXI, 1926. [Astrophel and Stella, xvii, xxv; Phillis, xxxix.]

—— The Names of the Heroines of Elizabethan Sonnet-Sequences. RES. II, 1926.

—— Minor Elizabethan Sonneteers and their Greater Predecessors. RES. II, 1926.

—— The Sources of Watson's Tears of Fancie. MLR. XXI, 1926.

—— The Sources of Spenser's Amoretti. MLR. XXII, 1927.

Lea, K. M. Conceits of Elizabethan and Jacobean Poetry. MLR, XX, 1925.

Potter, G. R. Milton's Early Poems. The School of Donne, and the Elizabethan Sonneteers. PQ. VI, 1927.

Walker, A. Italian Sources of Lyrics of Thomas Lodge. MLR. XXII, 1927.

Vaganay, H. Les Sonnets élisabéthains. Revue de Littérature comparée, April 1934. [French sources.]

D. INDIVIDUAL SONNETEERS

[Biographical and critical material will generally be found in the Introductions of the modern edns cited.]

SIR T. WYATT (1503?–1542)
[See pp. 411–2 above.]

HENRY HOWARD, EARL OF SURREY (1517?–1547)
[See pp. 412–3 above.]

GILES FLETCHER THE ELDER (1549?–1611)
(a) Sonnets
Licia, or poems of love. 1593; ed. A. B. Grosart, Manchester, 1870; ed. E. Arber (An English Garner, vol. VIII, 1896); ed. M. F. Crow (Elizabethan Sonnet-Cycles, 1896); ed. Sir S. Lee (Elizabethan Sonnets, vol. II, 1904).

(b) Other Writings
Of the Russe Common Wealth. 1591.

(c) Criticism
Scott, J. G. The Sources of Giles Fletcher's Licia. MLR. XX, 1925. [Repeated with examples of borrowings in Les Sonnets élisabéthains by the same writer.]

EDMUND SPENSER (1552–1599)
[See pp. 417–9 above.]

HENRY LOK (1553?–1608?)
(a) Sonnets
Sonnet to King James. [Prefixed to Essayes of a prentise, 1591.]
The first parte of christian passions. 1593. [No copy extant.]
Ecclesiastes whereunto are annexed sundrie Sonets of Christian Passions heretofore printed with other affectionate Sonets of a feeling Conscience [and Sonets of the Author to Divers collected by the printer]. 1597; rptd A. B. Grosart (Miscellanies of the Fuller Worthies' Lib. vol. II, 1871).

(b) Criticism
Scott, J. G. Les Sonnets élisabéthains. Paris 1929. [Ch. xiii.]

SIR PHILIP SIDNEY (1554–1586)
[See pp. 419–21 above.]

FULKE GREVILLE, BARON BROOKE (1554–1628)

[See p. 421 above.]

ALEXANDER MONTGOMERY (1556?–1610?)

[See p. 898 below.]

THOMAS WATSON (1557?–1592)

(a) Sonnets

The ʻΕκατομπαθία or passionate centurie of love. [1582]; rptd E. Arber, 1870, 1895. [Not in strict sonnet-form.]

The tears of fancie, or, love disdained. 1593; rptd E. Arber, 1870; rptd Sir S. Lee (Elizabethan Sonnets, vol. I, 1904).

(b) Other Works

Sophoclis Antigone. 1581. [A Latin trn.]

Amynta T. Watsoni. 1585; tr. Eng. A. Fraunce, 1587, 1588, 1589, 1596 (as The lamentations of Amyntas).

Helenae raptus. 1586. [A Latin trn from Coluthus.]

The first sett of Italian madrigalls Englished. 1590; ed. F. I. Carpenter, JEGP. II, 1899.

Meliboeus, sive ecloga in obitum F. Walsinghami. 1590.

An Eglogue upon the death of the Right Honourable Sir Francis Walsingham. 1590. [A trn by Watson himself of the previous item.]

Amyntae gaudia. 1592; tr. Eng. J. T. 1594 (as An ould fashioned love).

(c) Criticism

Carpenter, F. I. Thomas Watson's Italian Madrigals Englished. JEGP. II, 1899.

Scott, J. G. The Sources of Watson's Tears of Fancie. MLR. XXI, 1926.

—— Les Sonnets élisabéthains. Paris, 1929. [Ch. iv.]

JOHN SOOWTHERN

(a) Sonnets

Pandora, the musyque of the beautie of his mistresse Diana. 1584.

(b) Criticism

Lee, Sir S. Elizabethan Sonnets. Vol. I, 1904. [Introduction.]

Scott, J. G. Les Sonnets élisabéthains. Paris, 1929. [Ch. i.]

THOMAS LODGE (1558?–1625)

[See pp. 527–9 below.]

SAMUEL DANIEL (1562–1619)

[See pp. 422–3 above.]

HENRY CONSTABLE (1562–1613)

(a) Sonnets

Sonnet. [Prefixed to King James' Poetical Exercises, 1591.]

Diana. 1592. [23 sonnets.]

Diana, augmented with divers Quatorzains of honourable and learned personages. 1594; rptd Sir J. Littledale, Roxburghe Club, 1818; rptd E. Arber (English Garner, vol. II, 1879); rptd M. F. Crow (Elizabethan Sonnet-cycles, 1896); rptd J. Gray, 1897 (selections only); rptd Sir S. Lee (Elizabethan Sonnets, vol. II, 1904); rptd W. Jerrold (Pastorals and Sonnets, Hull, 1906). [The first two decades are the same as sonnets in the 1592 Diana. Decade III, sonnets ii to viii, and Decade IV, Sonnet ix, are by Sidney.]

Four Sonnets to Sir P. Sidney's Soul. [Prefixed to Apologie for Poetry, 1595.]

Sonnet. [Prefixed to E. Bolton's Elements of Armory, 1610.]

The Harleian Miscellany. Ed. T. Park, vol. IX, 1812, p. 489. [Includes sonnets of Constable 'from the original MSS.' These comprise the following sonnets of the 1594 Diana: Decades I and II, Decade III, sonnet i, and Decade IV, sonnets i, ii, iii, and vi, Decade VIII, sonnet v. Park's edn contains, besides seven sonnets to Queen Elizabeth and King James, seven to various ladies, seven 'upon sundry occasions,' four funeral sonnets (already ptd), and a last sonnet to Lady Arabella Stuart.]

Spiritual Sonnets. Ed. T. Park (Heliconia, vol. II, 1815).

Diana, the Sonnets and Poems of H. Constable. Ed. W. C. Hazlitt, 1859. [Re-edition of Park's work, with a rearrangement of the sonnets and exclusion of Decade IV, sonnet vi and Decade VIII, sonnet v (of the 1594 Diana). The Spiritual Sonnets are included in Hazlitt's volume.]

Elizabethan Sonnet-cycles. Ed. M. F. Crow, 1896. [Rpt of the 1594 Diana together with 12 love-sonnets presumably addressed also to Diana (the latter already ptd by Park and Hazlitt).]

(b) Other Works

Englands Helicon. 1600. [Includes 4 pastoral poems by Constable.]

(c) Criticism

Kastner, L. E. Elizabethan Sonneteers and the French Poets. MLR. III, 1908.

Scott, J. G. A Latin Version of a Sonnet of Constable's. MLR. XX, 1925.

—— Les Sonnets élisabéthains. Paris, 1929. [Ch. ix.]

MICHAEL DRAYTON (1563–1631)

[See pp. 423–5 above.]

WILLIAM FOWLER

(a) Sonnets

Sonnet. [Prefixed to James VI's Essayes of A Prentise, Edinburgh, 1584.]
Sonnet. [Prefixed to T. Hudson's Historie of Judith, Edinburgh, 1584.]
Sonet. [Prefixed to James VI's His Majesties Poeticall Exercises, Edinburgh, 1591.]
Epitaphe upon the death of Sir John Seton of Barns. [?]
An Epitaphe upon the Death of M. Robert Bowes. [1597.]
A Funeral Sonet [on] Elizabeth Douglas. [?]
The Works of William Fowler. Ed. H. W. Meikle, STS. 1914. [Includes: The Tarantula of Love; A Sonnet-sequence; Of Death; Miscellaneous Sonnets.]

(b) Critical and biographical

Stevenson, G. The Works of Alexander Montgomery. STS. 1910. [Introduction.]
Kastner, L. E. The Poems of William Drummond of Hawthornden. STS. 1913. [Introduction.]
Scott, J. G. Les Sonnets élisabéthains. Paris, 1929. [Appendix.]

JOHN STEWART OF BALDYNNEIS

(a) Sonnets

Poems. Ed. T. Crockett, STS. 1913. [Includes several sonnets among Rapsodies of the Author's youthfull braine.]

(b) Critical and biographical

Stevenson, G. The Works of Alexander Montgomery. STS. 1910. [Introduction.]
Scott, J. G. Les Sonnets élisabéthains. Paris, 1929. [Appendix.]

WILLIAM SHAKESPEARE (1564–1616)

[See pp. 581–3 below.]

JOHN DAVIES OF HEREFORD (1565?–1618)

[See p. 425 above.]

KING JAMES VI AND I (1566–1625)

[See p. 897 below.]

SIR WILLIAM ALEXANDER, EARL OF STIRLING (1567?–1640)

(a) Sonnets

Aurora, containing the first fancies of the Authors youth. 1604; ed. L. E. Kastner and H. B. Charlton (The Poetical Works of Sir W. Alexander, vol. II, STS. 1929).

(b) Other Works

The Tragedie of Darius. Edinburgh, 1603.
A Paraenesis to the Prince. 1604.
The Monarchick Tragedies. 1604. [Croesus and Darius.]
The Monarchick Tragedies, Croesus, Darius, The Alexandraean, Julius Caesar. 1607; 1616.
An elegie on the death of Prince Henrie. Edinburgh, 1612.
Doomesday. Edinburgh, 1614.
An encouragement to colonies. 1624 (re-issued 1630 as The mapp of New-England).
Recreations with the Muses. 1637.
The Poetical Works of Sir W. Alexander. Ed. R. Alison, 3 vols. Glasgow, 1870–2.
The Poetical Works of Sir W. Alexander. Ed. L. E. Kastner and H. B. Charlton, 2 vols. STS. 1921–9. [With bibliography of Alexander's works.]
[See also under James I, p. 897 below.]

(c) Criticism

Beumelburg, H. Sir William Alexander als dramatischer Dichter. Halle, 1880.
Kastner, L. E. The Scottish Sonneteers and the French Poets. MLR. III, 1908.

SIR JOHN DAVIES (1569–1626)

[See pp. 426–7 above.]

BARNABE BARNES (1569?–1609)

(a) Sonnets

Parthenophil and Parthenophe. 1593; ed. A. B. Grosart (The Poems of Barnabe Barnes, 1875); ed. E. Arber (English Garner, vol. v, 1882); ed. Sir S. Lee (Elizabethan Sonnets, vol. I, 1904); ed. M. H. Dodds (Ten Poems from Parthenophil and Parthenophe, Tynemouth, 1929).
A Divine Centurie of Spiritual Sonnets. 1595; ed. T. Park (Heliconia, vol. II, 1815); ed. A. B. Grosart (in Barnes' Poems, 1875).

(b) Other Writings

[Dedicatory poems and letters.] [Ptd by Grosart, Introduction to Barnes' Poems, 1875.]
Foure Books of Offices. 1606.
The Divil's Charter, a tragedie. 1607; ed. R. B. McKerrow (Bang's Materialien, vol. VI Louvain, 1904); rptd photo. facs. 1913 (Tudor Facsimile Texts). [Extracts by A. B. Grosart in Barnes' Poems, 1875, and by C. H. Herford, Literary Relations of England and Germany, Cambridge, 1886.]

(c) Criticism

Dowden, E. Academy, 2 Sept. 1876.
Kastner, L. E. Elizabethan Sonneteers and the French Poets. MLR. iii, 1908.
Bayley, A. R. Barnabe Barnes. N. & Q. 12 April 1924.
Scott, J. G. Les Sonnets élisabéthains. Paris, 1929. [Ch. v.]
[See also p. 640 below.]

JOHN DONNE (1573–1630)

[See pp. 441–4 below.]

RICHARD BARNFIELD (1574–1627)

[See p. 427 above.]

WILLIAM PERCY (1575–1648)

(a) Sonnets

Sonnets to the fairest Coelia. 1594; ed. Sir S. E. Brydges, Lee Priory, Kent, 1818; ed. A. B. Grosart, Manchester, 1877; ed. E. Arber, (English Garner, vol. vi, 1883); ed. Sir S. Lee (Elizabethan Sonnets, vol. ii, 1904).

(b) Other Works

Madrigal. [In Barnes' Foure Books of Offices, 1606.]
The cuck-queanes and cuckolds errants, or the bearing down the Inne; a comedye. The Fairy Pastoral, or Forest of Elves. Ed. J[oseph] H[aslewood], Roxburghe Club, 1824.
[The following are still unprinted (MSS in BM.):
Arabia sitiens, or a dream of a dry year. 1601.
The Aphrodisial or Sea Feast. 1602.
A Country's Tragedy in Vacuniam or Cupid's sacrifice. 1602.
Necromantes or the two supposed heads. 1602.]

(c) Criticism

Scott, J. G. Les Sonnets élisabéthains. Paris, 1929. [Ch. xii.]
Dodds, M. H. N. & Q. 13 June, 4, 25 July, 3, 10 Oct. 1931.
—— A Dreame of a Drye Yeare. JEGP. xxxii, 1933.

RICHARD LYNCHE (LINCHE)

(a) Sonnets

Diella, certaine sonnets. 1596 (signed 'R. L., Gentleman'); ed. E. Utterson, 1841; ed. E. Arber (English Garner, vol. vii, 1883); ed. A. B. Grosart, Manchester, 1877; ed. Sir S. Lee (Elizabethan Sonnets, vol. ii, 1904).

(b) Other Works

The Fountaine of Ancient fiction done out of Italian into English. 1599.
An Historical Treatise of the travels of Noah into Europe done into English. 1601.

(c) Criticism

Scott, J. G. Minor Elizabethan Sonneteers and their Greater Predecessors. RES. ii, 1926.
—— Les Sonnets élisabéthains. Paris, 1929. [Ch. xii.]

WILLIAM SMITH

(a) Sonnets

Chloris. 1596; ed. A. B. Grosart, Manchester, 1877; ed. E. Arber (English Garner, vol. viii, 1896); ed. M. F. Crow (Elizabethan Sonnet-cycles, 1896); ed. Sir S. Lee (Elizabethan Sonnets, vol. ii, 1904).

(b) Criticism

Scott, J. G. Minor Elizabethan Sonneteers and their Greater Predecessors. RES. ii, 1926.
—— Les Sonnets élisabéthains. Paris, 1929. [Ch. xii.]

BARTHOLOMEW GRIFFIN (d. 1602)

(a) Sonnets

Fidessa, more chaste than kind. 1596; ed. P. Bliss, 1815; ed. A. B. Grosart (Occasional Issues, Manchester, 1876); ed. E. Arber (English Garner, vol. v, 1882); ed. M. F. Crow (Elizabethan Sonnet-cycles, 1896); ed. Sir S. Lee (Elizabethan Sonnets, vol. ii, 1904).

(b) Criticism

Dowden, E. The Passionate Pilgrim. Shakespeare Quarto Facs. 1883. [Introduction, pp. xii, xiii, xx.]
Scott, J. G. Minor Elizabethan Sonneteers and their Greater Predecessors. RES. ii, 1926.
—— Les Sonnets élisabéthains. Paris, 1929. [Ch. xii.]

ROBERT TOFTE (d. 1620)

(a) Sonnets

Laura: the toyes of a traveller. 1597; ed. E. Arber (English Garner, vol. viii, 1896); ed. Sir S. Lee (Elizabethan Sonnets, vol. ii, 1904). [Not in strict sonnet-form.]

(b) Other Writings

Alba, the months minde of a melancholy lover, [followed by Certaine divine poems by R. T. Gent.]. 1598; ed. A. B. Grosart, Manchester, 1880.

Two tales from Ariosto. 1597.

Orlando inamorato, three first books. 1598.

A controversy between the two Tassi, Of marriage and wiving, done into English by R. T. Gent. 1599.

Ariosto's Satires by Gervase Markham [really by Tofte]. 1608; 1611 (anon.).

Honour's Academy translated from the French of Nicolas de Montreux. 1610.

Varchi's Blason of Jealousie, translated by R. T. 1615. [See Harvard Stud. xviii, 1935, pp. 47 ff.]

(c) Criticism

Halliwell[-Phillipps], J. O. Some Account of Tofte's Alba. 1865.

Collier, J. P. Bibliographical Catalogue. Vol. ii, 1870, p. 437.

Scott, J. G. Les Sonnets élisabéthains. Paris, 1929. [Ch. xii.]

WILLIAM DRUMMOND OF HAWTHORNDEN (1585–1649)

[See pp. 444–5 below.]

GEORGE WITHER (1588–1667)

[See pp. 446–9 below.]

WILLIAM BROWNE (1591–1643?)

[See p. 449 below.]

GEORGE HERBERT (1593–1633)

[See pp. 451–3 below.]

WILLIAM HABINGTON (1605–1654)

[See p. 453 below.]

SONNET-SEQUENCES BY ANONYMOUS WRITERS

Zepheria. 1594; ed. Sir S. Lee (Elizabethan Sonnets, vol. ii, 1904).

Emaricdulfe. 1595 (signed E. C.); ed. C. Edmonds, Roxburghe Club, 1881 (in A Lamport Garland).   J. G. S.

IV. MINOR TUDOR VERSE

[In this and the succeeding sections no attempt has been made to duplicate titles or writers entered elsewhere. The following omissions in particular should be noted: Miscellanies (pp. 403–5 above), Sonneteers (pp. 427–34), Epigrammatists and Formal Satirists (pp.479–81), Song-Books (pp.481–6), Versions of the Psalms (pp. 677–9), and the popular satirical verse listed in the sections on Pamphleteers and Miscellaneous Writers (pp. 704–12) and Minor Popular Literature (pp. 712–21).]

WILLIAM BALDWIN

[See under A Mirror for Magistrates, pp. 413–4 above.]

THOMAS BLENERHASSET (1550?–1625?)

[See under A Mirror for Magistrates, pp. 413–4 above.]

ARTHUR BROKE (d. 1563)

The tragicall historye of Romeus and Juliet, written first in Italian by Bandell. 1562; 1567; 1587; ed. P. A. Daniel, New Shakspere Soc. 1875; rptd 1890; ed. J. J. Munro, 1908 (Shakspeare Classics). [See also under Shakespeare's Romeo and Juliet, pp. 557–8 below.]

J. C.

Alcilia. Philoparthens Loving Follie. 1595; ed. W. Wagner, Sh. Jb. x, 1875; ed. A. B. Grosart, Manchester, 1879.

Alcilia. Philoparthens loving Folly: Whereunto is added, Pigmalions Image [by J. Marston]: With the Love of Amos and Laura [by S. Page]. And also, Epigrammes, by Sir J[ohn] H[arington] and others. 2 pts, 1613; 3 pts, 1619; 1628; rptd E. Arber (English Garner, vol. iv, 1882).

GEORGE CAVENDISH (1500–1561?)

Metrical Visions. [In Life of Cardinal Wolsey, ed. S. W. Singer, 2 vols. 1825, etc. Extracts, with criticism, in English Verse between Chaucer and Surrey, ed. E. P. Hammond, Durham, North Carolina, 1927. See also p. 824 below.]

GEORGE CHAPMAN (1559?–1634)

[See under Drama, pp. 609–11 below.]

BARTHOLOMEW CHAPPELL

The garden of prudence. 1595.

THOMAS CHURCHYARD (1520?–1604)

The Thre first bookes of Ovids De Tristibus, translated into Englishe. 1572; 1578; 1580; rptd Roxburghe Club, 1816.

The Firste part of Churchyardes Chippes, contayning twelve severall Labours. 1575; 1578; rptd J. P. Collier, [1870?].

A Lamentable, and pitifull Description, of the wofull warres in Flaunders since the foure last yeares of the Emperor Charles the fifth his raigne. With a briefe rehearsall of many things done since that season, untill this present yeare, and death of Don John. 1578.

A Discourse of the Queenes Majesties entertainement in Suffolk and Norffolk: with a description of many things then presently seene. Devised by Thomas Churchyarde; Gent. with divers shewes of his own invention sette out at Norwich: and some rehearsal of hir Highnesse retourne from Progresse. Whereunto is adjoyned a commendation of Sir Humfrey Gilberts ventrous journey. [1578]; rptd 1851.

The Miserie of Flaunders, calamitie of Fraunce, Misfortune of Portugall, Unquietness of Ireland, Troubles of Scotlande: And the blessed state of Englande. 1579; rptd 1876.

A generall rehearsall of warres, wherein is five hundred severall services of land and sea: as sieges, battailes, skirmiches, and encounters. A thousande gentle mennes names, of the best sort of warriours. A praise and true honour of Souldiours: A proofe of perfite Nobilitie. A triall and first erection of Heraldes: A discourse of calamitie. And joyned to the same some Tragedies and Epitaphes, as many as was necessarie for this firste booke. [1579.]

A light Bondell of livly discourses called Churchyardes Charge, presented as a Newe yeres gifte to the right honourable, the Earle of Surrie, in whiche Bondell of verses is sutche varietie of matter, and severall inventions, that maie bee as delitefull to the Reader, as it was a Charge and labour to the writer. 1580; rptd J. P. Collier, [1870?].

The Worthiness of Wales: Wherein are more then a thousand severall things rehearsed: some set out in prose to the pleasure of the Reader, and with such varietie of verse for the beautifying of the Book, as no doubt shal delight thousands to understand. 1587; rptd 1776; rptd Spenser Soc. 1876.

A Sparke of Frendship and warm Good-Will, that shows the Effect of true Affection, and unfolds the Fineness of this World. Whereunto is joined, the Commodity of sundry Sciences, and the Benefit that Paper bringeth, with many rare Matters rehearsed in the same. With a Description and Commendation of a Paper-Mill, now of late set up (near the Town of Dartford) by an High German, called M. Spilman, Jeweller to the Queen's most excellent Majesty. 1588; rptd Harleian Misc. vol. III, 1774, vol. II, 1809.

A Handefull of gladsome Verses, given to the Queene's Majesty at Woodstocke this Prograce. Oxford, 1592; rptd H. Huth and W. C. Hazlitt (Fugitive Tracts, Ser. 1, 1875).

Churchyards Challenge. 1593.

The Mirror of Man, and manners of Men. 1594; rptd Sir A. Boswell (Frondes Caducae, vol. II, Auchinleck, 1816). [First ptd in somewhat different form c. 1552; as A Myrrour for Man.]

A musicall consort of Heavenly harmonie (compounded out of manie parts of Musicke) called Churchyards Charitie. 1595; rptd Sir A. Boswell (Frondes Caducae, vol. IV, Auchinleck, 1817). [Includes a Praise of Poetrie.]

A Sad and solemne funerall of the right honorable Sir Francis Knowles, Knight, Treasurer of the Queenes Majesties Houshold, one of her privie councell, and Knight of the most honorable Order of the Garter. 1596; rptd T. Park (Heliconia, vol. II, 1815).

The Fortunate Farewel to the most forward and noble Earle of Essex, one of the honorable privie Counsel, Earle high Marshal of England, Master of the horse, Master of the ordinance, Knight of the garter, and Lord Lieutenant general of all the Queenes Majesties forces in Ireland. 1599.

Sorrowfull Verses made on [the] death of our most Soveraigne Lady Queene Elizabeth, my Gracious Mistresse. [1603.]

Churchyards good will. Sad and heavy Verses, in the nature of an Epitaph, for the losse of the Archbishop of Canterbury, lately deceased, Primate and Metropolitane of all England. 1604; rptd T. Park (Heliconia, vol. III, 1815); rptd H. Huth and W. C. Hazlitt (Fugitive Tracts, Ser. 2, 1875).

[For Churchyard's shorter pieces see DNB. and A. G. Chester, MLN, LII, 1937, pp. 180–3. His contributions to A Mirror for Magistrates are listed in CHEL. vol. III, 1909, pp. 514–5. See also H. W. Adnitt, Thomas Churchyard, 1520–1604, Shrewsbury, [1884], and in Trans. Shropshire Archaeological and Natural History Soc. III, 1880; B. B. Gamzue, Elizabeth and Literary Patronage, PMLA. XLIX, 1934; A. G. Chester, Thomas Churchyard's Pension, PMLA. L, 1935.]

PETER COLSE

Penelopes Complaint: or a Mirror for wanton Minions. 1596; ed. A. B. Grosart, Manchester, 1880.

ANTHONY COPLEY (1567–1607?)

Wits fittes and fancies; also Loves owle. 1595; 1596; 1614 (bis).

A Fig for Fortune. 1596; rptd Spenser Soc. 1883.

[For Copley's tracts in prose against the Jesuits, see DNB.]

ROGER COTTON

A Direction to the waters of lyfe. 1590; 1592; 1610 (as A Direct Way). [Prose.]

An Armor of Proofe, brought from the Tower of David, to fight against Spannyardes, and all enimies of the trueth. 1596.

A Spirituall Song. Drawen out of the holy Scriptures. 1596.

The Courte of Venus

The Court of Venus. [See p. 403 above.]

THOMAS CUTWODE

Caltha Poetarum: or the Bumble Bee. 1599; rptd Roxburghe Club, 1815.

WALTER (1541?–1576) AND ROBERT (1566–1601) DEVEREUX, EARLS OF ESSEX

The Poems of Thomas Lord Vaux; Edward Earl of Oxford; Robert Earl of Essex; and Walter Earl of Essex. Ed. A. B. Grosart, Fuller Worthies' Misc. vol. IV, 1872.

JOHN DICKENSON

Arisbas, Euphues amidst his slumbers: Or Cupids Journey to Hell. 1594. [Prose.]
The Shepheardes Complaint. A passionate Eclogue, written in English Hexameters: Whereunto are annexed other conceits. [1596.]
Greene in Conceipt. New raised from his grave to write the Tragique Historie of faire Valeria of London. 1598.
Prose and Verse by John Dickenson. Ed. A. B. Grosart, Manchester, 1878.

SIR EDWARD DYER (d. 1607)

The Writings in Verse and Prose of Sir Edward Dyer, Knt. Ed. A. B. Grosart, 1872.
[See R. M. Sargent, At the Court of Queen Elizabeth: the Life and Lyrics of Sir Edward Dyer, Oxford, 1935, and B. M. Wagner, New Poems by Sir Edward Dyer, RES. XI, 1935.]

THOMAS EDWARDS

Cephalus and Procris. Narcissus. Aurora musae amica. 1595; ed. W. E. Buckley, Roxburghe Club, 1882.
[See C. C. Stopes, Thomas Edwards, Author of Cephalus and Procris, MLR. XVI, 1921.]

GEORGE FERRERS (1500?–1579)

[See under A Mirror for Magistrates, pp. 413–4 above.]

WILLIAM FORREST

A New Ballade of the Marigolde. 1553; rptd T. Park (Harleian Misc. vol. X, 1813).
The History of Grisild the Second. Ed. W. D. Macray, Roxburghe Club, 1875. [Includes Oration consolatorye to Marye oure Queene, and specimens of Forrest's other works.]

[A versification of the Pater Noster and the Te Deum by Forrest is ptd in Foxe's Actes and Monuments, 1563, pp. 1139–40, and an extract from the Pleasaunt Poesye of Princelie Practise is given in England in the Reign of King Henry the Eighth. Part I. Starkey's Life and Letters, ed. S. J. Herrtage, EETS. 1878. For Forrest's MSS see CHEL. IV, 1909, 476.]

ABRAHAM FRAUNCE (fl. 1587–1633)

The Lamentations of Amintas for the death of Phillis. Paraphrastically translated out of Latine [i.e. T. Watson's Amyntas] into English hexameters. 1587; 1588 ('corrected'); 1589; 1596.
Abrahami Fransi Insignium, Armorum, Emblematum, Hieroglyphicorum, et Symbolorum Explicatio. 1588.
The Lawiers Logike, exemplifying the praecepts of Logike by the practice of Lawe. 1588.
The Arcadian Rhetorike, or the Precepts of Rhetorike made plaine by examples. 1588.
The Countesse of Pembrokes Yvychurch. 1591. [Trns in English hexameters of Tasso's Aminta, Watson's Amyntas, Virgil's Alexis, and the beginning of Heliodorus' Aethiopica.]
The Countesse of Pembrokes Emanuel. Conteining the nativity, passion, buriall, and resurrection of Christ: with certaine Psalmes. All in English hexameters. 1591; ed. A. B. Grosart (Miscellanies of Fuller Worthies' Lib. vol. III, 1871).
The third part of the Countesse of Pembrokes Yvychurch: entituled, Amintas Dale. Wherein are the most conceited tales of the pagan gods in English hexameters. 1592. [A prose romance with verse interspersed.]
Victoria, a Latin comedy by Abraham Fraunce. Ed. G. C. Moore Smith (Bang's Materialien, vol. XIV, Louvain, 1906).

BERNARD GARTER

The tragicall and true historie which happened betweene two English lovers. Written by Ber. Gar. 1565; 1568.
The joyfull receavinge of the Quenes majestie into Norwiche. [1578]; [1578?]. [Includes a masque by Garter and Henry Goldingham; rptd J. Nichols, Progresses of Queen Elizabeth, vol. II, 1823.]
The commody of the most vertuous and Godlye Susanna. 1578; ed. B. I. Evans and W. W. Greg, Malone Soc. 1937.
A New Yeares Gifte, prepared by B. G. 1579. [Verse and prose.]

HUMFREY GIFFORD

A Posie of Gilloflowers, eche differing from other in colour and odour, yet all sweete. 1580; ed. F. J. H. Darton, 1933. [Prose (mainly trns from Italian) and verse.]
The Poems. Ed. A. B. Grosart, Fuller Worthies' Lib. Misc. 1870.
The Complete Poems and Translations in Prose. Ed. A. B. Grosart, 1875.

BARNABE GOOGE (1540–1594)

Eglogs, Epytaphes and Sonettes. 1563; ed. E. Arber, 1871.

The Zodiake of Life written by the Godly and zealous Poet Marcellus Pallingenius stellatus, wherein are conteyned twelve Bookes disclosing the haynous Crymes & wicked vices of our corrupt nature. Newly translated into Englishe verse. 1565; 1576 (rev.); 1588. [Bks I–III, 1560; bks I–VI, 1561.]

The Popish Kingdome, or Reigne of Antichrist, written by Thomas Naogeorgos [Kirchmayer]. 1570; 1577; ed. R. C. Hofe, 1880.

Foure Bookes of Husbandrie, collected by Conradus Heresbachius. 1577; 1578; 1586; 1596; 1601; 1614, etc.

The Proverbs of the noble Sir James Lopez de Mendoza. 1579.

[See T. P. Harrison, Googe's 'Eglogs' and Montemayor's 'Diana.' Texas University Stud. v, 1925.]

NICHOLAS GRIMALD (1519?–1562?)

Christus Redivivus. Comoedia Tragica. Cologne, 1543; ed. J. M. Hart, PMLA. XIV, 1899.

Archipropheta, Tragoedia. Cologne, 1548.

A preservative, or triacle, agaynst the poyson of Pelagius, lately revived, & styrred up agayn, by the furious secte of the Annabaptistes. By William Turner. [1551.] [Contains verses by Nicholas Grimald.]

Marcus Tullius Ciceroes thre bokes of duties, to Marcus his sonne, turned oute of latine into english. 1556.

Nicolai Grimoaldi viri doctis. In P. V. Maronis quatuor libros Georgicorum in oratione soluta Paraphrasis elegantissimus. 1591.

[For Grimald's contributions to Tottel's Miscellany, see p. 403 above. See also L. R. Merrill, The Life and Poems of Nicholas Grimald, New Haven, 1925; H. H. Hudson, Grimald's Translations from Beza, MLN. XXXIX, 1924; G. C. Taylor, The Christus Redivivus and the Hegge Resurrection Play, PMLA. XLI, 1926; G. P. Shannon, Nicholas Grimald's Heroic Couplet and the Latin Elegiac Distich, PMLA. XLV, 1930; H. J. Byrom, The Case for Nicholas Grimald as Editor of Tottel's Miscellany, MLR. XXVII, 1932.]

MATTHEW GROVE

The most famous and Tragicall Historie of Pelops and Hippodamia. Whereunto are adjoyned sundrie pleasant devises, Epigrams, songes and sonnettes. 1587.

Poems. Ed. A. B. Grosart, 1878.

[Guistard and Sismond.] Certaine worthye Manuscript Poems, of great antiquitie, reserved long in the studie of a Northfolke Gentleman. And now first published by J. S. 1597. [A version of the Tancred-Sigismund story.]

JOHN HEYWOOD (1497?–1580?)

[See under Drama, pp. 518–9 below.]

JOHN HIGGINS (fl. 1570–1602)

[See under A Mirror for Magistrates, pp. 413–4 above.]

ROBERT HOLLAND (1557–1622?)

The Holie Historie of our Lord gathered into English meter. 1594. [For Holland's writings in Welsh see DNB.]

THOMAS HOWELL

The Arbor of Amitie, wherin is comprised pleasant Poëms and pretie Poesies. 1568.

New Sonets, & pretie pamphlets. Newly augmented, corrected & amended. [1567–8?]

Howell, His Devises, for his owne exercise, and his Friends pleasure. 1581; ed. Sir Walter Raleigh, [Oxford], 1906.

The Poems of Thomas Howell (1568–81). Ed. A. B. Grosart, 1879 (in vol. VIII of Occasional Issues).

[The Fable of Ovid treting of Narcissus, with a Moral ther unto, 1560 (signed T. H.) has also been assigned to Howell, but without much probability.]

ALEXANDER HUME (1560?–1609)

[See under Scottish Literature, p. 896 below.]

KING JAMES VI AND I (1566–1625)

[See under Scottish Literature, p. 897 below.]

WILLIAM LAUDER (1520?–1573)

[See under Scottish Literature, p. 897 below.]

EDWARD LEWICKE

The most wonderful and pleasaunt History of Titus and Gisippus, drawen into English metre. 1562.

SIR DAVID LINDSAY (1490?–1555)

[See under Scottish Literature, pp. 897–8 below.]

THOMAS LODGE (1558?–1625)

[See under Drama, pp. 527–9 below.]

CHRISTOPHER MARLOWE (1564–1593)

[See under Drama, pp. 531–3 below.]

ALEXANDER MONTGOMERIE (1556?–1610?)
[See under Scottish Literature, p. 898 below.]

SIR THOMAS MORE (1478–1535)
[See under Humanists, p. 667 below.]

ANTHONY MUNDAY (1553–1633)
[See under Drama, pp. 535–7 below.]

WILLIAM NEVILL (1497–c. 1540)
The Castell of Pleasure. [1517?] (de Worde); 1518 (Pepwell); ed. R. D. Cornelius, EETS. 1930. [Extracts in English Verse between Chaucer and Surrey, ed. E. P. Hammond, Durham, North Carolina, 1927.]

HENRY PARKER, BARON MORLEY
(1476–1556)
The tryumphes of Fraunces Petrarcke. [After 1553]; rptd Roxburghe Club, 1887. [Extracts, criticism, etc. in English Verse between Chaucer and Surrey, ed. E. P. Hammond, Durham, North Carolina, 1927.]

GEORGE PEELE (1558?–1597?)
[See under Drama, pp. 526–7 below.]

THOMAS PEEND
The pleasant fable of Hermaphroditus and Salmacis. 1565.

HENRY PETOWE
The Second Part of Hero and Leander, conteyning their further Fortunes. 1598.
Philocasander and Elanira, the faire Lady of Britaine. 1599.
Elizabetha quasi vivens. Elizas Funerall. By H. P. 1603; rptd Harleian Misc. vol. x, 1813; rptd J. Nichols (Progresses of Queen Elizabeth, vol. III, 1823).
Englands Caesar. His Majesties most Royall Coronation. 1603; rptd Harleian Misc. vol. x, 1813; rptd J. Nichols (Progresses of James I, vol. I, 1828).
[For Petowe's tracts in prose see DNB. See also G. P. Shannon, Petowe's Continuation of Hero and Leander, MLN. XLIV, 1929, and A. T. Crathern, A Romanticized Version of Hero and Leander, MLN. XLVI, 1931.]

The Pilgrims Tale
The Pilgrims Tale. [A pseudo-Chaucerian fragment appended to The Courte of Venus (see p. 403 above); rptd F. J. Furnivall in his edn of Francis Thynne's Animadversions, Chaucer Soc. 1876.]

THOMAS POWELL (1572?–1635?)
Loves Leprosie. 1598; ed. E. F. Rimbault, Percy Soc. vol. VI, 1842.

The Passionate Poet. With a Description of the Thracian Ismarus. 1601.
Vertues Due, or a true Modell of the Life of Katherine Howard, late Countess of Nottingham. By T. P. 1603; ed. C. Edmonds (in A Lamport Garland, Roxburghe Club, 1881). [For Powell's prose see DNB.]

SIR WALTER RALEGH (1552?–1618)
[See pp. 827–9 below.]

THOMAS ROGERS (1574?–1609?)
Celestiall Elegies of the Goddesses and the Muses. 1598; ed. facs. C. Edmonds (A Lamport Garland, Roxburghe Club, 1881). [Sonnets.]
Leicester's Ghost. [Appended to the two 1641 edns of the anon. Leicester's Commonwealth. Written c. 1605; a rime royal narrative.]
[See F. B. Williams, Thomas Rogers of Bryanston, an Elizabethan Gentleman-of-Letters, Harvard Stud. XVI, 1934.]

FRANCIS SABIE
Pans Pipe, Three pastorall Eglogues, in English Hexameter. With other Poetical Verses delightfull. 1595.
The Fisher-mans Tale. 1595.
Floras Fortune, the second part of the Fishermans Tale. 1595 (signed F. S.). [Greene's Pandosto in blank verse.]
Adams Complaint. The Olde Worldes Tragedie David and Bathsheba. 1596.

THOMAS SACKVILLE, EARL OF DORSET
(1536–1608)
[See under A Mirror for Magistrates, pp. 413–4 above and p. 523 below under Drama.]

ALEXANDER SCOTT (1525?–1584)
[See under Scottish Literature, p. 899 below.]

THOMAS STORER (1571–1604)
Life and Death of Thomas Wolsey, Cardinall. 1599; rptd T. Park (Heliconia, vol. II, 1815); rptd Oxford, 1826.

GEORGE TURBERVILE (1540?–1598?)
Epitaphes, Epigrams, Songs and Sonets, with a Discourse of the Friendly affections of Tymetes to Pyndara his Ladie. Newly corrected with additions. 1567; 1570; rptd J. P. Collier, [1867]. [For Turbervile's sources see T. K. Whipple, Martial and the English Epigram, Berkeley, 1925, and H. B. Lathrop, MLN. XLIII, 1928, pp. 223–9.]
The Heroycall Epistles of the Learned Poet Publius Ovidius Naso; with Aulus [Angelus] Sabinus Aunsweres to certaine of the same. 1567; [1569]; [1570?]; [1580?]; 1600; [1605]; ed. F. S. Boas, 1928.

The Eglogs of the Poet Mantuan turned into English verse. 1567; 1572; 1594; 1597.
A plaine Path to perfect Vertue. Translated into English [from Mancinus]. 1568.
The Booke of Faulconrie or Hauking. Collected out of the best Aucthors. 1575; 1611 (rev.).
The Noble Art of Venerie or Hunting. Translated out of the best Authors. [1575] (anon.); 1611.
Tragical Tales, translated by Turbervile. In time of his troubles, out of sundrie Italian, with the Argument and Lenvoye to eche Tale. 1587; rptd Edinburgh, 1837.

[See E. Koeppel, Die englische Tasso-Übersetzungen des 16. Jahrhunderts. D. George Turbervile's Verhältniss zur italienischen Litteratur, Ang. XIII, 1891; H. E. Rollins, New Facts about George Turbervile, MP. xv, 1918, and R. Pruvost, The Source of Tragical Tales, nos. 2, 5 and 8, RES. x, 1934.

THOMAS TUSSER (1524?–1580)

A hundreth good pointes of husbandrie. A hundreth good pointes, of good husbandry, maintaineth good household, with huswifry. House-keping and husbandry, if it be good: must love one another, as cousinnes in blood. The wife to, must husband as well as the man: or farewel thy husbandry, doe what thou can. 1557; rptd 1810.
  A hundrethe good points of husbandrie, lately maried unto a hundrethe good points of Huswifry newly corrected and amplified. 1571.
  Five hundreth points of good husbandry united to as many of good huswiferie, first devised, & nowe lately augmented with diverse approved lessons concerning hopps & gardening. 1573; 1577.
  Five hundred pointes of good Husbandrie, corrected, better ordered, and newly augmented to a fourth part more. 1580.
  Tusser Redivivus: Being Part of Mr. Thomas Tusser's Five Hundred Points of Husbandry. 1710.
  The last will and testament of Thomas Tusser Now First Printed. To which is added, His Metrical Autobiography, &c. 1846.
  Fiue Hundred Pointes of Good Husbandrie. Ed. W. Payne and S. J. Herrtage, English Dialect Soc. 1878; ed. D. Hilman, 1931; ed. D. Hartley, 1931.

WILLIAM VALLANS

A Tale of two Swannes. Wherein is comprehended the original encrease of the river Lee, commonly called Ware River: together with the Antiquitie of sundrie Places and Townes seated upon the same. 1590; rptd T. Hearne (Leland's Itinerary, vol. v, Oxford, 1710).

THOMAS, BARON VAUX (1510–1556)

The Poems of Thomas Lord Vaux; Edward Earl of Oxford; Robert Earl of Essex; and Walter Earl of Essex. Ed. A. B. Grosart, Fuller Worthies' Misc. vol. IV, 1872.

EDWARD DE VERE, EARL OF OXFORD (1550–1604)

The Poems of Thomas Lord Vaux: Edward Earl of Oxford; Robert Earl of Essex; and Walter Earl of Essex. Ed. A. B. Grosart, Fuller Worthies' Misc. vol. IV, 1872.
The Poems of Edward de Vere, Seventeenth Earl of Oxford. Ed. J. T. Looney, 1921.

[See B. M. Ward, The Seventeenth Earl of Oxford, 1928. For the Oxford-Shakespeare controversy see below under Shakespeare, p. 546.]

WILLIAM WARNER (1558?–1609)

Pan his Syrinx, or Pipe, compact of seven reedes. [1584.] [Prose tales.]
  Syrinx, or a seavenfold historie. Newly perused and amended. 1597.
Albions England, or historicall map of the same Island. In verse and prose. 1586. [Bks I–IV.]
  The First and Second parts of Albions England. 1589. [Bks I–VI.]
  Albions England: the third time corrected and augmented. 1592. [Bks I–VIII.]
  Albions England: a continued historie of the same kingdome. 1596; 1597. [Bks I–XII.]
  Albions England. Whereunto is also newly added an Epitome of the whole Historie of England. 1602. [Bks I–XIII.]
  A Continuance of Albions England. 1606. [Bks XIV–XVI.]
  Albions England. 1612. [Sixteen Books, with the prose Breviate of the true Historie of Æneas and Epitome.]
Menæcmi. A pleasant and fine conceited comædie taken out of the most excellent wittie poet Plautus. 1595; rptd 1779 (in Six Old Plays); 1875 (in vol. v of J. P. Collier's Shakespeare's Library, 2nd edn, ed. W. C. Hazlitt); 1905 (with the Comedy of Errors); ed. W. H. D. Rouse, 1912 (The Shakespeare Classics).

[See R. R. Cawley, Warner and the Voyagers, MP. XIX, 1922.]

ARTHUR WARREN

The poore Mans Passions: and Poverties Patience. 1605.

GEORGE WHETSTONE (1544?–1587)

The Rocke of Regard, being all the invention, collection and translation of George Whetstone Gent. 1576; rptd J. P. Collier, [1867]. [68 pieces, mainly in verse and consisting of tales tr. from Italian.]

A Remembraunce of the wel imployed life and godly end of George Gaskoigne, Esquire. [1578?]; rptd Bristol, 1815; ed. E. Arber (Gascoigne's Works, 1868).

The Right Excellent And Famous Historye Of Promos and Cassandra. 1578. [For later edns see p. 520 below.]

A Remembrance of the woorthie life of Sir Nicholas Bacon. [1579?]. [Rptd with the poems (listed below) on Dyer, the Earl of Sussex and Sidney, by Sir A. Boswell, Frondes Caducae, vol. I, Auchinleck, 1816.]

An Heptameron of Civill Discourses. Containing: The Christmas Exercise of sundrie Gentlemen and Gentlewomen. 1582; 1593 (as Aurelia). [Prose trns from Cinthio, etc., including The rare Historie of Promos and Cassandra (rptd J. P. Collier, Shakespeare's Library, vol. II, 1843, and rev. W. C. Hazlitt, vol. III, 1875).]

A Remembraunce of Sir James Dier. [1583.]

A Remembraunce of the Life of Thomas, Erle of Sussex. 1583.

A Mirour for Magistrates of Cyties. 1584 (reissued 1586 as The Enemie to Unthryftiness). [Prose.]

The honorable Reputation of a Souldier. 1585; Leyden, 1586 (with Dutch trn). [Prose; military anecdotes from the classics.]

A mirror of Treue Honnour exposing the life of Francis, Earl of Bedford. 1585; rptd T. Park (Heliconia, vol. II, 1815).

The English Myrror. 1586. [Prose; historical incidents.]

Sir Philip Sidney, his honourable life, his valiant death and true vertues. [1587?]

The Censure of a loyall Subject. 1587 (reissued n.d.); rptd J. P. Collier (Illustrations of Early English Popular Literature, vol. I, 1863). [Prose.]

[See M. Eccles, Whetstone's Death, TLS. 27 Aug. 1931.]

'HENRY WILLOBY'

Willobie his Avisa. Or, the true Picture of a modest Maid, and of a Chast and constant wife. In Hexameter verse. 1594; 1605 ('The fourth time corrected and augmented,' 2nd and 3rd edns are believed to have been ptd 1596, 1599); 1635; ed. A. B. Grosart, Manchester, 1880; ed. G. B. Harrison, 1926.

JAMES YATES

The Castell of Courtesie, whereunto is adjoyned the Holde of Humilitie, with the Chariot of Chastitie thereunto annexed. Also A Dialogue between Age and Youth and other matters herein conteined. 1582. [The hould of humilitie also issued separately.]

H. J. B.

V. THE JACOBEAN AND CAROLINE POETS

ANTHOLOGIES AND GENERAL STUDIES

[This section is intended only to supplement, for the 1603–1660 period, the list of Miscellanies, Anthologies, Critical Surveys, 1500–1660, pp. 403–8 above, which should be referred to.]

(1) ANTHOLOGIES

Farr, Edward. Select Poetry, chiefly Sacred, of the Reign of James the First. Cambridge, 1847.

Palgrave, F. T. The Treasury of Sacred Song. 1889.

Brooke, W. T. Fletcher's Christ's Victory and Triumph, and Inedited Sacred Poems of the Sixteenth and Seventeenth Centuries. [1888.]

Saintsbury, George. Minor Poets of the Caroline Period. 3 vols. Oxford, 1905–21.

Grierson, H. J. C. Metaphysical Lyrics and Poems of the Seventeenth Century. Oxford, 1921.

Howarth, R. G. Minor Poets of the Seventeenth Century: Suckling, Carew, Lord Herbert. 1931. (Everyman's Lib.)

Quennell, P. Aspects of Seventeenth Century Verse. 1933.

Grierson, H. J. C. and Bullough, G. The Oxford Book of Seventeenth Century Verse. 1934.

(2) GENERAL STUDIES

Brydges, Sir S. E. Censura Literaria. 10 vols. 1805–9, 1815. Restituta. 4 vols. 1814–6.

Willmott, R. A. Lives of Sacred Poets. First Series. 1834.

Macdonald, George. England's Antiphon. 1874.

Gosse, Sir Edmund. From Shakespeare to Pope. 1885.

—— The Jacobean Poets. 1894.

Abbey, C. J. Religious Thought in Old English Verse. 1892.

Dowden, Edward. Puritan and Anglican: Studies in Literature. 1900.

Harrison, J. S. Platonism in English Poetry of the Sixteenth and Seventeenth Centuries. New York, 1903.

Wendell, Barrett. The Temper of the Seventeenth Century in English Literature. 1906.

Clutton-Brock, A. The Fantastic School of English Poetry. [In Cambridge Modern History, vol. IV, Cambridge, 1906.]

Hutchinson, F. E. The Sacred Poets. CHEL. vol. VII, 1911.

Moorman, F. W. Cavalier Lyrists. CHEL. vol. VII, 1911.

Thompson, A. H. Writers of the Couplet. CHEL. vol. VII, 1911.

—— The Mystical Element in English Poetry. E. & S. VIII, 1922.

Saintsbury, George. Lesser Caroline Poets. CHEL. vol. VII, 1911.

Spurgeon, C. F. E. Mysticism in English Literature. 1913.

Jones, Rufus. Spiritual Reformers of the Sixteenth and Seventeenth Centuries. 1914.

Inge, W. R. English Religious Poetry. Trans. Royal Soc. Lit. XXXIII, 1915.

Quiller-Couch, Sir A. T. Studies in Literature. First Series. Cambridge, 1918.

Shafer, Robert. The English Ode to 1660. Princeton, 1918.

Seventeenth Century Verse. TLS. 26 Feb. 1920.

Alden, R. M. The Lyrical Conceits of the Metaphysical Poets. Stud. Phil. XVII, 1920.

Thompson, E. N. S. Mysticism in Seventeenth Century English Literature. Stud. Phil. XVIII, 1921.

Eliot, T. S. The Metaphysical Poets. [In Homage to John Dryden, 1924.]

Nethercot, A. H. The Reputation of the Metaphysical Poets during the Seventeenth Century. JEGP. XXIII, 1924.

—— The Reputation of the Metaphysical Poets during the Age of Pope. PQ. IV, 1925.

—— The Reputation of the Metaphysical Poets during the Age of Johnson. Stud. Phil. XXII, 1925.

Grierson, H. J. C. The Background of English Literature. 1925.

—— Cross-currents in Seventeenth Century Literature. 1929.

Lea, K. M. Conceits. MLR. XX, 1925.

The Margin of Philosophy. TLS. 5 Nov. 1925.

Read, Herbert. The Nature of Metaphysical Poetry. [In Reason and Romanticism, 1926.]

—— Phases of Poetry. 1929.

Schelling, F. E. Devotional Poetry in the Reign of Charles I. [In Shakespeare and 'Demi-Science,' Philadelphia, 1927.]

Emperor, J. B. The Catullian Influence in English Lyric Poetry, 1600–1690. Missouri University Stud. III, 1928.

Williamson, George. The Donne Tradition: English Poetry from Donne to Cowley. Cambridge, U.S.A. 1930.

Friederich, W. P. Spiritualismus und Sensualismus in der englischen Barocklyrik. Vienna, 1932.

Bennett, Joan. Four Metaphysical Poets: Donne, Herbert, Vaughan, Crashaw. Cambridge, 1934.

Leishman, J. B. The Metaphysical Poets: Donne, Herbert, Vaughan, Traherne. Oxford, 1934.

Sharp, R. L. Some Light on Metaphysical Obscurity and Roughness. Stud. Phil. XXXI, 1934.

Smith, James. On Metaphysical Poetry. [In Determinations, ed. F. R. Leavis, 1934.]

Leavis, F. R. English Poetry in the Seventeenth Century. Scrutiny, IV, 1935.

Wallerstein, R. C. The Development of the Rhetoric and Metre of the Heroic Couplet, especially in 1625–1645. PMLA. L, 1935.

DONNE, SANDYS, PHINEAS FLETCHER, DRUMMOND, GILES FLETCHER, WITHER, BROWNE, HERRICK, KING, QUARLES, HERBERT, CAREW, HABINGTON, DAVENANT, WALLER, SUCKLING, CRASHAW, DENHAM, COWLEY, LOVELACE, MARVELL, VAUGHAN, TRAHERNE.

JOHN DONNE (1573–1631)

(1) BIBLIOGRAPHY

Keynes, Geoffrey. A Bibliography of the Works of John Donne. Baskerville Club, 1914; Cambridge, 1932 (rev. edn).

(2) COLLECTED WORKS

The Works of John Donne. Ed. Henry Alford, 6 vols. 1839. [The only modern rpt of a majority of the Sermons. A few letters, poems, and the Devotions are included. The text, unfortunately, is worthless.]

The Complete Poetry and Selected Prose. Ed. John Hayward, 1929, 1930 (rev. edn).

(3) POEMS

(a) *Collected Poems*

Poems by J. D. with elegies on the author's death. 1633; 1635 (contains additional poems of which only 17 are by Donne); 1639; 1649 (re-issued 1650 with 13 additional pieces); 1669 (adds 5 poems).

Poems on Several Occasions. 1719.

Poetical Works. Edinburgh, 1779. (Bell's edn.)

Complete Poems. Ed. A. B. Grosart, 2 vols. 1872. (Fuller Worthies' Lib.)

Poems from the Edition of 1633. Ed. C. E. Norton, 2 vols. Grolier Club, New York, 1895.

Poems. Ed. Sir E. K. Chambers, with Introduction by George Saintsbury, 2 vols. 1896, etc. (Muses' Lib.)

Poems. Ed. H. J. C. Grierson, 2 vols. Oxford, 1912; 1 vol. Oxford, 1929 (without commentary). [The standard edn.]

Poems. Ed. John Hayward. [In Complete Poetry and Selected Prose, 1930.]

Poems. Ed. H. I'A. Fausset, 1931. (Everyman's Lib.)

(b) Selected Poems

Koren-bloemen. Van Constantin Huygens. Amsterdam, 1658 and 1672. [Contains *inter alia* 19 poems by Donne tr. into Dutch.]

[Selections from Donne will be found in the Collections of Anderson, 1793; Chalmers, 1810; Campbell, 1819; Sanford, 1819; Southey, 1831; etc.]

(c) Separate Poems and Occasional Pieces

Ben Jonson his Volpone Or the foxe. 1607. [Contains lines to Jonson.]

Coryat's Crudities. 1611. [Three pieces by Donne among the Panegyricke Verses.]

An Anatomy of the World. Wherein, by occasion of the untimely death of Mistris Elizabeth Drury the frailty and the decay of this whole world is represented. 1611.

The First Anniversary, anatomie of the World. The Second Anniversarie, Of the progres of the Soule. 1612; 1621; 1625; rptd photo. facs. (from 1621 edn) New York, 1927.

A Second Booke of Ayres by William Corkine. 1612. [Two poems by Donne set to music.]

Lachrymae Lachrymarum. By Joshua Sylvester. 1613 (3rd edn). [Donne's Elegy on Prince Henry.]

An Elegy by John Donne. Ed. Sir E. K. Chambers, RES. VII, 1931. [From Holgate MS, Morgan Lib. New York.]

[A full examination of the MS books in which important texts of the poems are preserved will be found in Poems, ed. H. J. C. Grierson, vol. II, 1912.]

(4) PROSE WORKS
(a) Separate Works and Occasional Pieces

Pseudo-martyr. Wherein out of certaine Propositions and Gradations, This Conclusion is evicted. That those which are of the Romane Religion in this Kingdome, may and ought to take the Oath of Allegeance. 1610.

Conclave Ignati. Sive ejus in nuperis inferni comitiis Inthronisatio. [1611] (12mo and 4to); 1680.

Ignatius his Conclave: or His Inthronisation in a late Election in Hell. 1611; 1626; 1634; 1653; rptd J. Hayward (in Complete Poetry and Selected Prose, 1930).

A Wife Now The Widdow of Sir Thomas Overbury. Whereunto are added many witty Characters &c. 1614 (2nd edn). [Contains Donne's Newes from the very Country. Ptd in Poems, 1650, and subsequent edns.]

Sir Thomas Overbury His Wife. The eleventh Impression. 1622. [Contains Donne's News from the very Country; An Essay of Valour; The true Character of a Dunce.]

Devotions upon Emergent Occasions. 1624 (*bis*); 1626; 1634; 1638; rptd 1840 (Pickering); ed. J. Sparrow, 1923 (standard edn); rptd [1925] (Abbey Classics).

Juvenilia, or certaine paradoxes and problemes. 1633 (*bis*); ed. G. Keynes, 1923.

Paradoxes, problems, essays, characters, with Ignatius his Conclave. 1652.

Biathanatos. A declaration of that paradoxe, or thesis, that Self-homicide is not so Naturally Sinne, that it may never be otherwise. [1646]; 1648; 1700; ed. photo. facs. J. W. Hebel, New York, 1930. [For an examination of this work see J. Adams, An Essay concerning Self-Murther, 1700; and C. Moore, A full enquiry into the subject of Suicide, 1790.]

Essayes in Divinity, interwoven with meditations and prayers. 1651.

Essays in Divinity. Ed. A. Jessopp, 1855.

The Courtier's Library, or Catalogus Librorum Aulicorum Etc. Ed. and tr. E. M. Simpson, 1930. [This *jeu d'esprit* was first ptd among the miscellaneous pieces in Poems, 1650.]

(b) Sermons

Sermon on Judges xx. 15. 1622 (3 issues). [The text is corrected after the second issue to Judges v. 20.]

Sermon on Acts i. 8. Preached to the Honourable Company of the Virginian Plantation. 1622; 1624.

Encænia. The feast of dedication. Celebrated at Lincolnes Inne, in a Sermon there upon Ascension day. 1623.

First Sermon preached to King Charles. 1625.

A sermon preached to the King's Mtie at Whitehall. 1626.

A sermon of commemoration of the Lady Danvers. 1627.

Death's duell, or, A Consolation to the Soule, against the dying Life, and living Death of the Body. 1632; 1633 (3 issues); rptd J. Hayward (Complete Poetry and Selected Prose, 1930).

Six sermons upon severall occasions. 1634. [These were rptd in Fifty Sermons, 1649.]

Sapientia Clamitans. 1638. [Contains Donne's Sermon of Valediction at my going into Germany—no. 19 in the vol. of 26 sermons, 1660, with important textual differences.]

LXXX Sermons. 1640. [Contains Walton's Life of Donne.]

Fifty Sermons. 1649.

XXVI Sermons. 1660 (3 issues).

Sermons. Ed. H. Alford. [In Works, 6 vols. 1839.]

Selected Passages. Ed. L. P. Smith, 1919.

Sermon on Psalm 38, v. 9. Now first printed. 1921 (priv. ptd); rptd E. M. Simpson (Study of Prose Works, 1924).

Ten Sermons. Ed. G. Keynes, 1923.

Sermon of Valediction at his Going into Germany, 1619. Ed. E. M. Simpson, 1933.

(c) Letters

Letters to severall persons of honour. 1651; 1654; rptd facs. New York, 1910.

Cabala. Mysteries of State &c. 1654. [Contains 2 letters by Donne.]

Walton, Izaak. Life of Donne. 1658. [Contains 5 letters.]

—— Life of Herbert. 1670. [Contains 4 letters.]

A collection of letters, made by Sir Tobie Mathew: 1660; 1692. [Contains 31 letters.]

The Loseley Manuscripts. Ed. A. J. Kempe, 1835. [Contains 10 letters.]

Gosse, Sir E. The Life and Letters of John Donne. 2 vols. 1899. [The standard edn. A new edn of the letters, ed. I. A. Shapiro, is in preparation.]

Simpson, E. M. A Study of the Prose Works. 1924. [Contains 32 unpublished letters from the Burley MS.]

Letter to Sir G. More. London Mercury, xiii, 1925. [From Loseley MSS.]

Complete Poetry and Selected Prose. Ed. J. Hayward, 1930. [Contains 3 unpublished letters.]

Letter to Sir Nicholas Carew. [Ptd for the first time from MS, Cambridge, U.S.A. 1930.]

(5) Biography and Criticism
(a) Books

Jonson, Ben. Conversations with Drummond of Hawthornden. Ed. R. F. Patterson, 1923.

Walton, Izaak. Life. 1658. [Rptd in Walton's Lives, 1670, 1675, etc. The most fully annotated edn is 1852, ed. T. E. Tomlins.]

Johnson, S. Life of Cowley. [In Lives of the Poets, vol. i, 1781; ed. G. B. Hill, vol. i, Oxford, 1905.]

Coleridge, S. T. Literary Remains. Vols. i, iii, 1836–8.

Dowden, E. New Studies in Literature. 1895. [Contains an essay on Donne.]

Jessopp, A. John Donne. 1897.

Gosse, Sir E. Life and Letters. 2 vols. 1899.

Ashton, H. Du Bartas en Angleterre. Paris, 1908.

Ramsay, M. Les Doctrines médiévales chez Donne. 1917; 1924 (rev. edn).

Fausset, H. I'A. John Donne. [1924.]

Simpson, E. M. A Study of the Prose Works of John Donne. Oxford, 1924.

Praz, Mario. Secentismo e Marinismo in Inghilterra. Florence, 1925.

Bredvold, L. I. Studies in Shakespeare, Milton and Donne. Vol. i, Ann Arbor, 1925.

Legouis, P. Donne the Craftsman. Paris, 1928.

Williamson, G. The Donne Tradition. Cambridge, U.S.A. 1930.

Spencer, T. et al. A Garland for John Donne. Cambridge, U.S.A. 1932.

Coffin, C. M. John Donne and the New Philosophy. New York, 1937.

(b) Articles

[A complete list of articles on Donne will be found in the 2nd edn of Keynes' Bibliography.]

Chambers, Sir E. K. Donne, Diplomatist and Soldier. MLR. v, 1910.

Simpson (Spearing), E. M. Donne's Sermons and their Relation to his Poetry. MLR. vii, 1912.

—— A Chronological Arrangement of Donne's Sermons. MLR. viii, 1913.

—— John Donne and Overbury's Characters. MLR. xviii, 1923.

—— Two Manuscripts of Paradoxes and Problems. RES. iii, 1927.

—— A Note on Donne's Punctuation. RES. iv, 1928.

—— More Manuscripts of Donne's Paradoxes and Problems. RES. x, 1934.

Moore Smith, G. C. Donniana. MLR. viii, 1913.

Belden, H. M. JEGP. xiv, 1913. [Review of Grierson's edn.]

Picavet, F. Medieval Doctrines in the Works of Donne and Locke. Mind, xxvi, 1917.

Sampson, John. A Contemporary Light upon John Donne. E. & S. vii, 1921.

Bredvold, L. I. The Naturalism of Donne in relation to some Renaissance Traditions. JEGP. xxii, 1923.

Sparrow, John. On the Date of Donne's 'Hymne to God my God.' MLR. xix, 1924.

—— Donne's Table-Talk. London Mercury, xviii, 1928.

—— Donne and Contemporary Preachers. E. & S. xvii, 1931.

De Havilland, M. Two Unpublished Manuscripts of Donne. London Mercury, xiii, 1925.

Wilder, M. L. Did Jonson write 'The Expostulation' attributed to Donne? MLR. XXI, 1926.

Robbie, H. J. L. RES. III, IV, 1927-8. [Undescribed Donne MSS.]

Wilson, F. P. The Early Life of Donne. RES. III, 1927.

Wood, H. H. A Seventeenth Century Manuscript of Poems by Donne and Others. E. & S. XVII, 1931.

Shapiro, I. A. The Text of Donne's Letters. RES. VII, 1931.

Hughes, M. Y. The Lineage of 'The Extasie.' MLR. XXVII, 1932.

—— Kidnapping Donne. [In CaliforniaEssays in Criticism, ser. 2, Berkeley, 1934, which also includes G. R. Potter, Donne's Discovery of Himself.]

Doggett, F. A. Donne's Platonism. Sewanee Rev. XLII, 1934.

Williamson, G. The Libertine Donne. PQ. XIII, 1934.

G. L. K. and J. H.

GEORGE SANDYS (1577-1643)

(1) POEMS

The first five books of Ovid's Metamorphoses. 1621 (bis). [No copy known. See Sir S. E. Brydges, Censura Literaria, vol. VI, 1805, p. 132.]

Ovid's Metamorphosis Englished by G. S. 1626; 1628; Oxford, 1632 (rev. and with 'An essay to the Translation of Virgil's Aenis'); 1638; 1640; 1656.

A Paraphrase upon the Psalmes. By G. S. 1636.

A Paraphrase upon the Divine Poems. 1638; 1648; 1676. [An enlarged edn of the preceding.]

Christ's Passion. A Tragedie. 1640 (bis); 1687. [From Hugo Grotius.]

A Paraphrase upon the Song of Solomon. By G. S. 1641.

Selections from the Paraphrases, with memoir [by H. J. Todd]. 1839.

The Poetical Works of George Sandys. Ed. R. Hooper, 2 vols. 1872.

(2) PROSE WORKS

A Relation of a Journey. 1615; 1621; 1627; 1632; 1637; 1652 (as Sandys Travailes); 1658; 1673; rptd 1864. Tr. Dutch, Amsterdam, 1653; German, Frankfort, 1669. [Selections in Purchas his Pilgrimes, pt ii, 1625, and J. Harris, Navigantium Bibliotheca, vols. I, II, 1705. Tr. Dutch, Amsterdam, 1653 and 1665; German, Frankfort, 1669.]

Sacrae Heptades, by G. S. 1626. [Doubtfully ascribed to Sandys.]

(3) BIOGRAPHY AND CRITICISM

Hooper, R. The Poetical Works of Sandys. Vol. I, 1872. [Introduction.]

T. H. B.

PHINEAS FLETCHER (1582-1650)

(1) COLLECTED WORKS

The Poems. Ed. A. B. Grosart, 4 vols. 1869. (Fuller Worthies' Lib.)

The Poetical Works of Giles and Phineas Fletcher. Ed. F. S. Boas, 2 vols. Cambridge, 1908-9.

(2) SEPARATE WORKS

Locustae, vel pietas Jesuitica. (The Locusts or Apollyonists.) 2 pts, [Cambridge], 1627.

Brittain's Ida written by that renowned Poët Edmond Spencer. 1628. [Really by Fletcher.]

Sicelides A Piscatory. As it hath beene Acted in King's Colledge, in Cambridge. 1631 (anon.). [Variant texts in BM. Add. MS 4453 and Bodley, Rawlinson Poet. MS 214.]

Joy in Tribulation, or Consolations for Afflicted Spirits. 1632.

The Way to Blessedness, a treatise on the First Psalme. 1632.

Sylva Poetica. Cambridge, 1633.

The Purple Island: or the Isle of Man: together with Piscatorie Eclogs and other Poetical Miscellanies. 2 pts, Cambridge, 1633. [Purple Island rptd 1783; Piscatory Eclogs, ed. A. F. Tytler, Edinburgh, 1771.]

Elisa or An Elegie Upon the Unripe Decease, of Sr Antonie Irby. Cambridge, 1633.

A Father's Testament. Written long since for the benefit of the particular relations of the author. 1670.

Venus & Anchises—Britain's Ida—and other Poems. Ed from MS Ethel Seaton, Royal Soc. Lit. 1926.

(3) CRITICISM

Cory, H. E. Spenser, the School of the Fletchers and Milton. Berkeley, 1912.

Waibel, Karl. Phineas Fletcher's Purple Island. E. Studien, LVIII, 1924.

Langdale, A. B. Phineas Fletcher. New York, 1937.

WILLIAM DRUMMOND OF HAWTHORNDEN (1585-1649)*

(1) COLLECTED WORKS

The History of Scotland, from the year 1423. until the year 1542. With several memorials of state, during the reign of James VI and Charles I. 1655; 1681 (re-issued 1682). [Virtually a collected edn of Drummond's prose; includes Cypresse Grove, various political tracts and selected letters. Preface by 'Mr. Hall of Grayes Inn.']

---

* The bibliographies of Drummond, Giles Fletcher, Browne, Herrick and King have been revised by Mr G. Tillotson.

Poems, by that most famous Wit, William Drummond of Hawthornden. 1656 (re-issued 1659 as The most Elegant and Elabourate Poems of that Great Court Wit Mr William Drummond). [Preface by Edward Phillips. Contains most of the poems previously pbd and 35 new poems, two of which are probably not Drummond's.]

The Works of William Drummond, of Hawthornden. Consisting of those which were formerly Printed, and those which were design'd for the Press. Now Published from the Author's Original Copies. Edinburgh, 1711. [Ed. John Sage and T. Ruddiman. Adds about 40 poetical pieces and hymns, many of doubtful authenticity, various prose tracts and papers, a selection of Drummond's correspondence, and a memoir by Bishop Sage.]

The Poems of William Drummond. 1790; 1791.

The Poems. Ed. [T. Maitland and D. Irving], Maitland Club, 1832.

The Poems. Ed. P. Cunningham, 1833.

The Poetical Works. Ed. W. B. Turnbull, 1856 and 1890.

The Poems. Ed. W. C. Ward, 2 vols. 1894. (Muses' Lib.)

The Poetical Works, with 'A Cypresse Grove.' Ed. L. E. Kastner, 2 vols. STS. and Manchester, 1913. [Standard edn.]

(2) SEPARATE WORKS

Teares on the Death of Meliades. Edinburgh, 1613; Edinburgh, 1614 (3rd edn).

Mausoleum or, the choisest flowres of the Epitaphs, written on the Death of Prince Henrie. Edinburgh, 1613; rptd D. Laing (Fugitive Scottish Poetry of the Seventeenth Century, ser. 1, Edinburgh, 1853). [3 contributions by Drummond.]

Poems by William Drummond of Hawthornden. [Edinburgh? 1614?] (priv. ptd for distribution to Drummond's friends?); Edinburgh, 1616 (expanded and rev. as Poems: Amorous, Funerall, Divine, Pastorall, in Sonnets, Songs, Sextains, Madrigals).

Forth Feasting. A Panegyricke to the Kings Most Excellent Majestie. Edinburgh, 1617; Edinburgh, 1618 (in The Muses Welcome [to King James], ed. J. Adamson, with a new sonnet by Drummond prefixed).

Flowres of Sion. To which is adjoyned his Cypresse Grove. [Edinburgh], 1623; Edinburgh, 1630 (adds 4 poems).

Auctarium bibliothecae Edinburgenae. 1627.

The Entertainment of the high and mighty Monarch Charles King of Great Britaine, into his auncient and royall citie of Edinburgh. Edinburgh, 1633.

To The Exequies of the Honourable Sr Antonye Alexander, Knight. A Pastorall Elegie. Edinburgh, 1638.

Polemo-Medinia inter Vitarvam et Nebernam. [Edinburgh, 1642–49?] (anon.); Edinburgh, 1684; ed. E. Gibson, Oxford, 1691 (with attribution to Drummond).

(3) BIOGRAPHY AND CRITICISM

Conversations of Ben Jonson with William Drummond of Hawthornden. Ed. D. Laing, Shakespeare Soc. 1842; ed. R. F. Patterson, 1923.

Laing, D. A Brief Account of the Hawthornden Manuscripts in the Possession of the Society of Antiquaries of Scotland; with Extracts, containing Unpublished Letters and Poems of William Drummond. Trans. Soc. Antiquaries of Scotland, IV, 1831.

Masson, David. Drummond of Hawthornden. 1873.

Maclean, C. M. Alexander Scott, Montgomerie, and Drummond of Hawthornden as Lyric Poets. 1915.

Simpson, P. The Genuineness of the Drummond Conversations. RES. II, 1926.

Greene, G. S. Drummond's Borrowings from Donne. PQ. XI, 1932.

Wallerstein, R. C. The Style of Drummond in its Relation to his Translations. PMLA. XLVIII, 1933.

Joly, A. William Drummond de Hawthornden. Lille, 1935.

[For articles on Drummond's borrowings from French and Italian poetry, see pp. 332 and 339 above.]

GILES FLETCHER, THE YOUNGER
(1588?–1623)
(1) COLLECTED WORKS

The Poems. Ed. A. B. Grosart, 1868. (Fuller Worthies' Lib.)

The Complete Poems. Ed. A. B. Grosart, 1876.

The Poetical Works of Giles and Phineas Fletcher. Ed. F. S. Boas, 2 vols. Cambridge, 1908–9.

(2) SEPARATE WORKS

Sorrowes Joy Or a Lamentation for our late deceased Soveraigne Elizabeth, with a triumph for the prosperous succession of our gratious King, James. Cambridge, 1603.

Christs Victorie, and Triumph in Heaven, and Earth, over, and after death. 2 pts, Cambridge, 1610; Cambridge, 1632 (re-issued Cambridge, 1640); rptd 1783 (with The Purple Island); rptd 1824 (with life and extracts from G. Herbert); ed. R. Catter-

mole and H. Stebbing (in Sacred Poetry of the Seventeenth Century, 1835); ed. [W. T. Brooke], [1888].
The Reward of the Faithfull. 1623. [Prose.]

(3) CRITICISM

Cory, H. E. Spenser, the School of the Fletchers, and Milton. Berkeley, 1912.

GEORGE WITHER (1588–1667)

(1) BIBLIOGRAPHIES

Sidgwick, F. The Poetry of Wither. Vol. I, 1902, pp. xlvii–lvi.
Grolier Club. Contributions to English Bibliography. Vol. III, New York, 1905, items 1013–1076.

(2) COLLECTED WORKS

The Workes of Master George Wither. Containing Satyrs, Epigrams, Eclogues, Sonnets, and Poems. Whereunto is annexed a Paraphrase on the Creed and the Lords Prayer. 1620. [Pirated. Contains A Satyre; Epithalamia; W. Browne's Shepheards Pipe with the Eclogues by C. Brooke, J. Davis, and Wither's (?) To his Melissa; The shepheards Hunting; Fidelia and other verses.]
Juvenilia. A Collection of those Poems which were heretofore imprinted, and written by George Wither. 1622 (re-issued 1626); 1633; rptd 3 pts, Spenser Soc. 1871. [Abuses Stript and Whipt, The Scourge, Epigrams, Prince Henries Obsequies, A Satyre, Epithalamia, Shepheards Hunting; 1633 edn and some copies of 1622 add Wither's Motto, Faire-Virtue and some minor verse.]
Ecchoes from the Sixth Trumpet. Reverberated by A Review of Neglected Remembrances: Abreviating Precautions and Predictions heretofore published at several Times. 1666 (re-issued 1668, as Nil Ultra: or the Last Works of Captain George Wither, and 1669, as Fragmenta Prophetica. Or, the Remains of George Wither). [Excerpts from Wither's prophetic poems connected by short prose paragraphs, and some new verse.]
Extracts from Juvenilia. Ed. 'Aretephil' [Alexander Dalrymple], 1785. [With running commentary.]
Select Lyrical Passages. Written about 1622. Ed. Sir S. E. Brydges, [1815].
Juvenilia. Ed. [J. M. Gutch], 4 vols. [Bristol, 1820]. [Includes several of the other early pieces besides Juvenilia.]
Miscellaneous Works. 6 vols. Spenser Soc. 1872–3. [These make, together with the other Spenser Soc. reprints, practically a complete edn of Wither.]
The Poems. Ed. H. Morley, 1891.

The Poetry. Ed. (with important biographical introduction) F. Sidgwick, 2 vols. 1902.
Four Scarce Poems of George Wither. Ed. J. M. French, Huntington Lib. Bulletin, Nov. 1931.

(3) SEPARATE WORKS

Epithalamia: or Nuptiall Poems [on the marriage of Frederick, Count Palatine and the Princess Elizabeth]. 1612; 1633.
Prince Henries Obsequies or mournefull Elegies upon his Death. 1612; 1622; 1633.
Abuses Stript, and Whipt. Or Satirical Essaies, Divided into two Bookes. Also the Scourge. Epigrams. 1613 (at least 4 edns); 1614; 1615; 1617. [Sidgwick suggests a suppressed edn 1611; but see Grolier Club comment, Contributions to English Bibliography, vol. III, 1905, item 1014.]
Shepheards Pipe. 1614. [By W. Browne; but contains Wither's 'Thirsis and Alexis' and 'Another Eclogue' (rptd as Eclogues v and iv of Shepheards Hunting), as well as 'To his Melisa' which may be Wither's.]
A Satyre: dedicated to his most excellent Majestie. 1614; 1615 (at least 2 edns); 1616.
Fidelia. 1615; 1617; 1619; rptd Sir S. E. Bridges, 1815; rptd (from 1615 edn) E. Arber (English Garner, vol. VI, 1883).
The Shepheards Hunting: being certain Eclogues written during the time of the Authors Imprisonment in the Marshalsey. 1615 (3 edns); rptd Sir S. E. Brydges, [1814]; rptd R. Southey (in Select Works of the British Poets, 1831).
A Preparation to the Psalter. 1619; rptd Spenser Soc. 1884.
Exercises upon the first psalme. 1620; rptd Spenser Soc. 1882.
The Songs of the Old Testament, Translated into English Measures. 1621.
Wither's Motto. Nec habeo, nec Careo, nec Curo. [London], 1621 (re-issued n.d. with engraved title-page); 1621 (engraved title-page); 1621 (with Postscript; at least 2 edns); 1633; rptd Sir S. E. Brydges (in Restituta, vol. I, 1814).
Faire-Virtue, The Mistresse of Phil'arete. A Miscelany of Epigrams, Sonnets, Epitaphs, etc. 1622 (re-issued twice 1622 with new title-pages—once perhaps as part of Juvenilia); 1626; 1633; rptd Sir S. E. Brydges, 1818; rptd E. Arber (English Garner, vol. IV, 1882).
The Hymnes and Songs of the Church. Translated and Composed by G. W. 1623 (bis); [1623?] (bis); ed. E. Farr (Library of Old Authors, 1856); rptd Spenser Soc. 1881.
The Schollers Purgatory, Discovered in the Stationers Common-wealth, and described in a Discorse Apologeticall. [1625?]

Britain's Remembrancer. Containing a Narration of the Plague lately past; a declaration of the mischiefs present, and a Prediction of Judgments to come. 1628; rptd 2 pts, Spenser Soc. 1880. [Extracts rptd: 1643, both as Mr Wither his Prophesie and as Wither's Remembrancer; 1691, in A Collection of many Wonderful Prophecies; 1734, in A Warning to the Inhabitants of Europe.]

The Psalmes of David Translated into Lyrick-Verse. Illustrated, with a short Argument, and a briefe Prayer, or Meditation; before, & after, every Psalme. Netherlands, 1632; rptd 2 pts, Spenser Soc. 1881.

A Collection of Emblemes, ancient and moderne. 4 bks, 1635 (Bks 2–4 dated 1634; various issues same year).

The Nature of Man written in Greek by Nemesius. Englished. 1636 (re-issued 1657).

A new song of a young mans opinion of the difference between good and bad women. [Before 1640.] [Broadside.]

Halelujah or, Britans Second Remembrancer bringing to Remembrance (in praisefull and Poenitentiall Hymns, Spirituall Songs, and Morall Odes) Meditations, advancing the glory of God, in the practise of Pietie and Vertue; and applyed to easie Tunes, to be sung in Families, etc. Composed in a three-fold Volume, by George Wither. The first, containo Hymns Occasionall. The second, Hymns Temporary. The third, Hymns Personall. That all Persons, according to their Degrees, and Qualities, may at all Times, and upon all eminent Occasions, be remembered to praise God; and to be mindfull of their Duties. One woe is past, the second, passing on; Beware the third, if this, in vain be gone. 1641; ed. E. Farr (Library of Old Authors, 1856); rptd 3 pts, Spenser Soc. 1879.

Campo-Musae, or the Field-Musings of Captain George Wither, touching his Military Ingagement for the King and Parliament, the justnesse of the same, and the present distractions of these Islands. 1643 (bis); 1644; 1661.

Se Defendendo. A Shield, and Shaft, against Detraction. ['13 March 1643,' Thomason.]

Mercurius Rusticus: or, A Countrey Messenger. Informing divers things for the furtherance of those proceedings which concerne the Publique Peace and Safety. [1643] (anon.).

Wither's prophesie of the downfal of Antichrist. 1644.

Letters of Advice: touching the Choice of Knights and Burgesses for the Parliament. ['2 Nov. 1644', Thomason.]

Vox Pacifica: a Voice tending to the Pacification of God's wrath. 1645.

Justitiarius justificatus. The Justice justified. ['13 April 1646', Thomason.]

Opobalsamum Anglicanum: an English Balme, lately pressed out of a shrub, and spread upon these papers. 1646.

Major Wither's Disclaimer: being a Disavowment of The Doubtfull Almanack. Lately published in the name of the said Major Wither. ['8 Jan. 1646,' Thomason.]

What Peace to the wicked? By a Free-man, though a Prisoner. 1646 (anon.). [Attrib. to Wither by Thomason.]

Amygdala Britannica, Almonds for Parrets. Composed, heretofore, by a well-knowne Moderne Author. 1647 (anon.). [Attrib. to Wither by Thomason.]

Carmen Expostulatorium: Or, a timely Expostulation with those both of the City of London and the Present Armie [who have attempted to renew civil war]. 1647.

The Tired Petitioner. 1647. [Excerpts in Ecchoes, 1666.]

A Si Quis, or Queries. 1648. [Excerpts in Ecchoes, 1666.]

Prosopopoeia Britannica: Britans Genius, or, Good-Angel, personated. Discovered, by Terrae-Filius. 1648.

Carmen-Ternarium Semi-Cynicum. [1648–9.]

A thankful Retribution. 1649. [Excerpts in Ecchoes, 1666.]

Carmen Eucharisticon: A Private Thank-Oblation [for the deliverance of England from Irish rebels]. 1649. [Composed 29 Aug.]

Respublica Anglicana or the Historie of Parliament in their late Proceedings. The Author G: W: 1650.

Three grains of Spirituall Frankincense. 1651.

British Appeals, with Gods Mercifull Replies, on the behalfe of the Common-wealth of England. 1651 (re-issued same year at least once).

A Timely Caution. 1652.

The dark Lantern, containing a dim Discoverie. 1653 (with A Perpetuall Parliament).

Westrow Revived. A Funerall Poem without Fiction. 1653.

The Modern States-man. By G. W. Esq. 1654. ['18 Nov. 1653,' Thomason.]

To the Parliament of the Common-wealth. The humble Petition of George Wither Esq. [1654]. [Broadside.]

The Protector. A Poem briefly illustrating the Supereminency of that Dignity. 1655.

Vaticinium Causuale. A Rapture occasioned by the Deliverance of the Protector from a desperate Danger. 1655.

Boni ominis Votum: a good omen to the next Parliament. 1656.

A Cause Allegorically Stated. 1657. [Excerpts in Ecchoes, 1666.]

A Suddain Flash Timely Discovering, Some Reasons wherefore, the stile of Protector, should not be deserted by these Nations. By Britans Remembrancer. 1657.

The Petition, and Narrative of Geo. Wither Esq; concerning his many grievances. ['1658,' Thomason.]

Epistolium–Vagum–Prosa–Metricum: or, an Epistle at Randome. 1659.

A Cordial Confection, to strengthen their Hearts whose Courage begins to fail. 1659.

Salt upon Salt: made out of certain ingenious Verses upon the late Storm and the Death of his Highness ensuing. 1659.

Speculum Speculativum: or, a Considering-Glass; being an Inspection into the present and late sad Condition of these Nations. 1660 (3 edns).

Furor-Poeticus (i.e.) Propheticus. By G. W. Esq;. 1660.

Fides-Anglicana. Or, a Plea for the Publick-Faith of these Nations. 1660. [Concludes with a list by Wither of his works—including many never ptd and some lost in MS.]

Predictions of the Overthrow of Popery. 1660.

An Improvement of Imprisonment, Disgrace, Poverty, into Real Freedom; Honest Reputation; Perdurable Riches. 1661.

Joco-Serio. Strange News, of a Discourse between two dead Giants. G. W. 1661. [A retort to A Dialogue between Colbrant and Brandamore.]

A Triple Paradox: Affixed to a Counter-mure raised against the World, the Flesh and the Devil. 1661.

The Prisoners Plea: humbly offered in a Remonstrance; with a Petition annexed, to the Commons of England. 1661.

Paralellogrammaton. An Epistle to the three Nations of England, Scotland, and Ireland. 1662.

A Proclamation in the Name of the King of Kings, to all the Inhabitants of the Isles of Great Brittain. 1662 (re-issued same year with Sig. A re-set).

Verses intended to the King's Majesty. 1662 (bis).

The Modern States-man. By G. W. Esq. 1663.

Tuba-Pacifica. Seasonable Praecautions, whereby is sounded forth a Retreat from the War intended between England and the United-Provinces. 1664.

A Memorandum to London, occasioned by the Pestilence. 1665. [Includes 'Warning-piece to London', and 'Single Sacrifice offered to Almighty God'.]

Meditations upon the Lords Prayer. 1665. [Pp. 189–90, five stanzas omitted from Warning Piece to London.]

Three Private Meditations. 1665; 1666.

Sigh for the Pitchers [upon the engagement expected 31 May 1666 with the Dutch]. 1666; 1666 (title corrected to Sighs).

Divine Poems (by way of Paraphrase) on the Ten Commandments. 1688 (re-issued 1728).

The strange and wonderful Prophecy, was taken out of an old Manuscript, by Capt. George Withers; and printed in the Year, 1646. 1689. [1646 edn apparently not extant.]

The tired Petitioner. n.d. [Excerpts in Ecchoes from the Sixth Trumpet, 1666 (see p. 446 above).]

Vox Vulgi: a poem in censure of the Parliament of 1661. Ed. (from MS) W. D. Macray, 1880.

The History of the Pestilence (1625). Ed. (from Magdalene College Cambridge MS, perhaps autograph) J. M. French, Cambridge, U.S.A. 1932.

(4) CONJECTURAL ATTRIBUTIONS

The two incomparable Generalissimo's of the world briefly described. [1644?] [Signed G. W.]

The Great Assises Holden in Parnassus by Apollo. 1645. [Attrib. to Wither by T. Hearne and A. Dalrymple (see A. à Wood, Athenae Oxonienses, ed. P. Bliss, vol. III, 1815, p. 773); J. W. Ebbsworth disputes the attribution.]

Articles presented against this Parliament. By Terrae-Filius. 1648.

Vaticinium Votivum: or, Palaemon's Prophetick Prayer. [1649] (re-issued same year with cancel).

An Allarum from Heaven, or, a Memento to the great Councell. By G. W. 1649. [Attrib. in Grolier Club Contributions, vol. III, item 1055.]

[See also under News-Books, 1641–1659, pp. 751 ff. below, for some other conjectural attributions.]

(5) BIOGRAPHY AND CRITICISM

Aubrey, J. Brief Lives. Ed. A. Clark, 2 vols. Oxford, 1898.

à Wood, A. Athenae Oxonienses. Ed. P. Bliss, vol. III, 1813.

Lamb, Charles. The Poetical Works of George Wither. [In Works, 1818.]

Swinburne, A. C. Miscellanies. 1886. [Includes essay on Lamb's marginalia in a copy of Gutch's Juvenilia.]

Simpson, P. Walkley's Piracy of Wither's Poems in 1620. Library, VI, 1925.

Firth, Sir C. H. George Wither. RES. II, 1926.

French, J. M. George Wither in Prison. PMLA. XLV, 1930.

Anderson, P. B. George Wither and the 'Regalia.' PQ. XIV, 1935.

Borowski, B. Die Anspielung auf Avians Fabel 'De cupido et invido' in Withers 'Abuses stript and whipt.' Ang. LIX, 1935.

G. T.

WILLIAM BROWNE OF TAVISTOCK (1590?–1645?)

(1) COLLECTED WORKS

The Works of William Browne; containing Britannia's Pastorals, The Shepherd's Pipe, The Inner Temple Masque, and Other Poems. Ed. W. Thompson [and T. Davies], 3 vols. 1772.
The Whole Works. Ed. W. C. Hazlitt, 2 vols. 1868–9. (Roxburghe Lib.)
The Poetical Works. Ed. G. Goodwin, with an Introduction by A. H. Bullen, 2 vols. 1894. (Muses' Lib.)

(2) SEPARATE WORKS

An Elegie on the never inough bewailed Death [of Henry, Prince of Wales]. 1613.
Britannia's Pastorals. Bk I: 1613. Bks I (rev.), II: 1616; 1625; rptd R. Southey (Select Works of the British Poets, 1831); ed. W. Thompson, 1845. Bk III (incomplete): ed. (from MS) T. C. Croker, Percy Soc. 1852.
Inner Temple Masque. [Acted 13 Jan. 1614; first ptd in Works, 1772.]
Shepheards Pipe. 1614; 1620 (as part of Wither's Works).
Original Poems never before published. Ed. (from BM. Lansdowne MS 777) Sir S. E. Brydges, 1815.

(3) BIOGRAPHY AND CRITICISM

Moorman, F. W. William Browne. His Britannia's Pastorals. QF. LXXXI, 1897.
Sidney, P. 'The Subject of All Verse': being an Enquiry into the Authorship of a Famous Epitaph. 1907.
Candy, H. C. H. On the First Two Editions of Book I of Britannia's Pastorals. Library, IX, 1918.
Tillotson, G. A Manuscript of William Browne. RES. VI, 1930. [Further Note, VII, 1931.]
—— Towards a Text of Browne's Britannia's Pastorals. Library, XI, 1930.

ROBERT HERRICK (1591–1674)

(1) ORIGINAL EDITION

Hesperides: or, The Works both Humane & Divine of Robert Herrick Esq. 1648. [Includes, with separate title and pagination, His Noble Numbers: or, his pious pieces, Wherein (amongst other things) he sings the Birth of his Christ: and sighes for his Saviours suffering on the Crosse, 1647.]

(2) COLLECTED POEMS

The Works of Robert Herrick. Ed. (with biography) [T. Maitland], 2 vols. Edinburgh, 1823; 2 vols. 1825 (as The Poetical Works).
Hesperides, or Works Both Human And Divine. Ed. H. G. Clarke, 2 vols. 1844.
Hesperides, or the works both humane and divine of Robert Herrick Esq. Ed. S. W. S[inger], 2 vols. 1846; 2 vols. Boston, 1856.
Hesperides; or, Works Both Human And Divine, of Robert Herrick. Ed. G. T. F., 1852.
The Poetical Works of Robert Herrick. Ed. E. Walford, 1859.
Hesperides the poems and other remains of Robert Herrick. Ed. W. C. Hazlitt, 2 vols. 1869 and 1890.
The Complete Poems of Robert Herrick. Ed. A. B. Grosart, 3 vols. 1876.
Robert Herrick. The Hesperides and Noble Numbers. Ed. A. W. Pollard, with Preface by A. C. Swinburne, 2 vols. 1891. (Muses' Lib.)
The Poetical Works of Robert Herrick. Ed. G. Saintsbury, 2 vols. 1893.
The Poetical Works of Robert Herrick. Ed. F. W. Moorman, Oxford, 1915; 1921 (text only).
The Poetical Works of Robert Herrick. Ed. Humbert Wolfe, 4 vols. 1928.

(3) SELECTED POEMS

Witts Recreations. 1650 (4th edn). [Many of Herrick's poems included.]
Select Poems from the Hesperides, or Works Both Human And Divine, of Robert Herrick, Esq. Ed. J. N[ott], Bristol, [1810].
Chrysomela. A Selection from the Lyrical Poems of Robert Herrick. Ed. F. T. Palgrave, 1877.
Selections from the Poetry of Robert Herrick. Ed. Austin Dobson, [1882].
Herrick, his Flowers. Oxford, 1891. [Ptd by H. Daniel.]
Selections from the Poetry of Robert Herrick. Ed. E. E. Hale, Boston, 1895.
Robert Herrick. Ed. Henry Newbolt, 1923.

(4) BIOGRAPHY AND CRITICISM

Gosse, Sir E. Robert Herrick. [In Seventeenth Century Studies, 1883.]
Hale, E. E. Die chronologische Anordnung der Dichtungen Robert Herricks. Halle, 1892.
Thomson, John. Indexes to the First Lines and to the Subjects of the Poems of Robert Herrick. Bulletin of the Free Library of Philadelphia, III, 1901.

29

Pollard, A. W. A List of Variations in Three Copies of the Original Edition of Herrick's Hesperides. Library, IV, 1903.

Moorman, F. W. Robert Herrick. A Biographical and Critical Study. 1910.

Nixon, P. Herrick and Martial. Classical Philology, v, 1910.

Delattre, F. Robert Herrick. Contribution à l'Étude de la Poésie lyrique en Angleterre au dix-septième Siècle. Paris, 1912.

Mandel, Leon. Robert Herrick, the Last Elizabethan. Çhicago, 1927.

Blunden, E. Herrick. [In Votive Tablets, 1931.]

Roeckerath, N. Der Nachruhm Herricks und Wallers. Leipzig, 1931.

Aiken, P. The Influence of the Latin Elegists on Herrick. Orono, 1932.

Ault, N. Herrick and Song-Books. TLS. 20 April 1933.

Easton, E. I. M. Youth Immortal. A Life of Robert Herrick. Boston, 1934.

MacLeod, M. A Concordance to the Poems of Robert Herrick. New York, 1936.

HENRY KING (1592–1669)

(1) WRITINGS

Elegy upon K. Charles I. 1649.

A Groane at the Funerall of Charles the First. 1649 (re-issued 1649 as A Deepe groane).

Psalmes of David Turned into Meter. 1651 (re-issued 1654); 1671.

Poems, Elegies, Paradoxes, and Sonnets. 1657 (re-issued with addns 1664, and as by Ben Jonson 1700).

Sacred Poems. Ed. J. Hannah, Oxford, 1843.

English Poems. Ed. L. Mason, New Haven, 1914.

Minor Caroline Poets. Ed. George Saintsbury, vol. III, Oxford, 1921. [King's English poems and critical introduction.]

The Poems. Ed. John Sparrow, 1925. [Bibliography by G. Keynes.]

[For King's sermons see p. 698 below.]

(2) BIOGRAPHY AND CRITICISM

Mason, L. The Life and Works of Henry King. Trans. Connecticut Academy, XVIII, 1913.

Simpson, P. The Bodleian Manuscripts of Henry King. Bodleian Quart. Record, v, 1929.

FRANCIS QUARLES (1592–1644)

(1) COLLECTED WORKS

Collected Works, in Prose and Verse. Ed. A. B. Grosart, 3 vols. 1880–1. (Chertsey Worthies' Lib.)

(2) POETICAL WORKS

A Feast of Wormes. Set forth in a poeme of the History of Jonah. And Pentelogia. 1620.

Hadassa: or The History of Queene Ester. 1621.

Job Militant: with Meditations. 1624.

Sions Elegies, Wept by Jeremie the Prophet, and periphras'd. 1624.

Sions Sonets. Sung by Solomon, and periphras'd. 1625.

Argalus and Parthenia. 1629.

An Alphabet of Elegies, upon the death of doctor Ailmer. 1630.

Divine Poems. 1630; 1634 ('Newly Augmented'). [Includes all the above except Argalus and Parthenia, which is secular.]

The Historie of Samson. 1631.

Divine Fancies: digested into epigrammes, meditations, and observations. 1632.

Emblemes. 1635; 1639; 1643; ed. G. Gilfillan, 1857; ed. W. W. Wilkins, 1859.

Hieroglyphikes of the life of Man. 1638. [From 1639 printed commonly with Emblemes.]

Sighes at the contemporary deaths of the Countesse of Cleaveland and Mistrisse Cicily Killegrue. 1640.

Solomons Recantation, entituled Ecclesiastes, paraphrased. With a short relation of the author's Life [by his widow, Ursula]. 1645; 1648; rptd 1732.

The Shepheards Oracles: delivered in certain Eglogues. 1646; 1679. [One Eclogue was printed off, perhaps as a specimen, in 1644. Copy in Bodleian.]

The Virgin Widow. A Comedie. 1649; 1656. [Prose and verse.]

(3) PROSE WORKS

Enchyridion. 1640; 1641 (enlarged).

Observations concerning Princes and States. 1642.

Judgement and Mercy for afflicted Soules. 2 pts, 1646. [The 2nd pt had already appeared in 1644 in a pirated edn, as Barnabas and Boanerges; or Wine and Oyle for afflicted Soules. This version was rptd as well as Ursula Quarles's.]

The Loyall Convert. Oxford, 1644 (anon.). [A pirated edn has Oxford 1643 on title-page, but was probably ptd in London in 1644. Both the Oxford and London edns were rptd.]

The Whipper Whipt. 1644 (anon.). [Without printer's name or place.]

The New Distemper. Oxford, 1645.

The Profest Royalist in his quarrel with the times: maintained in three Tracts. Oxford, 1645. [Rpt of the above.]

(4) CRITICISM

Nethercot, A. H. The Literary Legend of Francis Quarles. MP. xx, 1923.

Ustick, W. L. Later Editions of Quarles' Enchiridion. Library, ix, 1928.

Beachcroft, T. O. Quarles—and the Emblem Habit. Dublin Rev. CLXXXVIII, 1930.

Haight, G. S. The Publication of Quarles' Emblems. Library, xv, 1934.

—— The Sources of Quarles' Emblems. Library, xvi, 1935.

—— Francis Quarles in the Civil War. RES. XII, 1936.

Praz, M. Studi sul Concettismo. Milan, 1934.

F. E. H.

GEORGE HERBERT (1593–1633)

(1) BIBLIOGRAPHY

Palmer, G. H. A Herbert Bibliography. Cambridge, U.S.A. 1911. [Useful but incomplete, being in the main a description of books collected by the compiler.]

(2) COLLECTED WORKS

Works. With a preface by W. Pickering, and annotations of S. T. Coleridge. 2 vols. 1835–6; 1846; 1859. [Includes A Paradox from Rawlinson MSS in Bodleian Library, 17 Latin letters from the Orator's book at Cambridge, Latin poems, Oley's and Walton's lives.]

Works. Ed. R. A. Willmott, 1854.

The Complete Works. Ed. A. B. Grosart, 3 vols. 1874. (Fuller Worthies' Lib.) [Uses for the first time the Williams MS, and prints from it 6 English poems and two sets of Latin poems, and from Playford's Psalms and Hymns (1671) some psalms attributed to Herbert.]

The English Works newly arranged and annotated by George Herbert Palmer. 3 vols. 1905 and 1907. [The first serious attempt to discover the chronological order of the poems and to deal thoroughly with difficulties of interpretation. Contains a photograph of a pencil drawing on vellum by R. White.]

Works. Ed. F. E. Hutchinson. [In preparation.]

(3) LATIN AND GREEK COMPOSITIONS

Epicedium Cantabrigiense, in Obitum Henrici Principis Walliae. Cambridge, 1612. [Contains 2 Latin poems by Herbert.]

Lacrymae Cantabrigienses, in Obitum Reginae Annae. Cambridge, 1619. [Contains 1 Latin poem by Herbert.]

Oratio habita coram Dominis Legatis. [With Eng. trn. In True Copies of all the Latine Orations, made at Cambridge on the 25 and 27 of Februarie last past, 1623.]

Oratio quâ Principis Caroli reditum ex Hispaniis celebravit Georgius Herbert. Cambridge, 1623.

Memoriae Francisci, Baronis de Verulamio, Sacrum. 1626. [Contains 1 Latin poem by Herbert.]

A Sermon of Commemoration of the Lady Danvers by John Donne. Together with other conmemorations of her, called Parentalia: by her sonne G. Herbert. 1627. [19 poems in Latin and Greek.]

Ecclesiastes Solomonis. By J[ames] D[uport]. 1662. [Contains, with separate title-page, Herbert's Musae Responsoriae, ad Andreae Melvini Anti-Tami-Cami-Categoriam.]

(4) ENGLISH WORKS

(a) *The Temple*

[Tanner MS 307 in Bodleian Lib. is the copy licensed for the press by the Cambridge Vice-Chancellor and his assessors. It is not in Herbert's hand.]

The Temple, Sacred Poems and Private Ejaculations. Cambridge, 1633 (three copies are known to exist of an undated issue of the first edn, with a different title-page. For a description see A Catalogue of the Huth Library, lot 3598, June 1913, and Palmer's Herbert Bibliography, p. 20); Cambridge, 1633 (type reset, but the only important textual difference is in the first line of 3rd stanza of The Church-Porch); Cambridge, 1634, 1635, 1638, 1641 (6th edn. From this edn onwards The Synagogue (anon.), by Christopher Harvey is commonly bound up with The Temple. There are two different edns with 'seventh' on the title-page; one is undated, and was probably ptd at London before 1656; the other, London, 1656, follows the earlier edns line for line, but includes for the first time an elaborate Table or index of 30 pages); 1660; 1667; 1674 (includes Walton's Life and portrait by R. White; re-issued 1695 with new title-page and re-setting of first 6 preliminary leaves); 1678 (some copies have date 1679); 1703 (with portrait re-engraved by J. Sturt, White's pupil); 1709.

Select Parts of Mr Herbert's Sacred Poems. 1773. [Prepared by John Wesley, who also adapted some of Herbert's poems for his hymn-books. Interesting as the only reprinting of Herbert's poems traced between 1709 and 1799, except for the inclusion of The Church-Porch, The Sacrifice and Dotage in John Wheeldon's Sacred Prolusions, 1773.]

The Temple. Bristol, 1799.

Herbert's Poems with his Country Parson and Walton's Life. 1806; 1809. [From this date e ,ns are numerous, often with Walton's Life, and sometimes with The Country Parson. The more important only are given below.]

The Temple. Lowell, Mass. 1834 (first American edn); ed. G. Gilfillan, 1853; ed. C. C. Clarke, 1863; ed. A. B. Grosart, 1876, 1891 (rev. edn); ed. type facs. A. B. Grosart, 1876 (from undated Huth copy of 1st edn); ed. type facs. T. F. Unwin, 1876 (from BM. dated copy of 1st edn; re-issued 1882 with essay by J. H. Shorthouse); ed. R. A. Willmott, 1880; ed. E. Rhys, 1885; ed. E. C. S. Gibson, 1899; ed. A. R. Waller, 1902 (with A Priest to the Temple); ed. W. Alexander, [1904]; ed. A. Waugh, 1907; ed. Francis Meynell, 1927 (from Bodleian MS).

(b) Prose Works

Hygiasticon in three treatises. 1634(bis); 1636; 1678 (as The Temperate Man). [The second, A Treatise of Temperance and Sobrietie, by Luigi Cornaro (1475–1566), was tr. by Herbert from Lessius' Latin version, 1613: see Mayor's Nicholas Ferrar, p. 51.]

The Hundred and Ten Considerations of Signior John Valdesso. Oxford, 1638. [Juan de Valdés (1500–1541) wrote in Spanish. Ferrar tr. from the Italian version (first ptd in 1550), and Herbert contributed a Letter and 'Briefe Notes.' A garbled edn, unfortunately followed in some rpts, was ptd at Cambridge in 1646. Rpt of 1638 edn ed. F. Chapman, 1905.]

Witts Recreations. With a thousand out-Landish Proverbs. 1640. [With separate title-page, Outlandish Proverbs Selected by Mr G. H. Re-issued separately as Jacula Prudentum. Or, Outlandish Proverbs, Selected by Mr George Herbert, 1651. The ascription to Herbert is discussed in N. & Q. 31 Jan. and 14 Feb. 1857. See also H. G. Wright below.]

Herbert's Remains. 1652. [Ed. Barnabas Oley. Prints for the first time A Priest to the Temple (the larger part of the book), and adds Jacula Prudentum, Apothegmes, and A Prefatory View of the Authour's Life (anon; by Barnabas Oley). Jacula Prudentum has a separate title-page dated 1651, but it differs in type from the separate edn of 1651 and is much enlarged.]

A Priest to the Temple, or, The Countrey Parson his Character, and Rule of Holy Life. 1671 (with a new Preface by B[arnabas] O[ley]); 1675; 1701; 1806; 1807, etc.; ed. H. C. Beeching, 1898.

(5) BIOGRAPHY AND CRITICISM

(a) Books

Herbert, Edward (Baron Herbert of Cherbury). Autobiography. Strawberry Hill, 1764; ed. Sir S. Lee, 1886 and 1907 (rev. edn).

—— Poems English and Latin. Ed. G. C. Moore Smith, Oxford, 1923.

Walton, Izaak. The Life of Mr George Herbert. 1670. [Included also, with separate title-page, in collected Lives, 1670; the type is reset, and the text is less correct than in the separately ptd Life. Some corrections are made for the next appearance of the Life, appended to the 1674 edn of The Temple, and others for the 1675 edn of Lives.]

Coleridge, S. T. Biographia Literaria. 1817. [Chs. xix, xx.]

Nicholas Ferrar. Two Lives. Ed. J. E. B. Mayor, Cambridge, 1855.

Daniell, J. J. Life of George Herbert. 1893 (anon.); 1898 (with author's name); 1902. [Contains ecclesiastical documents overlooked by previous biographers.]

Beeching, H. C. Religio Laici. 1902.

Hyde, A. G. George Herbert and his Times. 1906.

More, P. E. Shelburne Essays. Fourth Series. Princeton, 1906.

Clutton-Brock, A. More Essays on Books. 1921.

Mann, Cameron. A Concordance to the English Poems of George Herbert. Boston, 1927.

(b) Articles in Periodicals

Addison, Joseph. False Wit. Spectator, 7 May 1711.

Herbert's Poems. Retrospective Rev. III, 1821.

Smith, I. Gregory. George Herbert. Christian Remembrancer, July 1862.

George Herbert. TLS. 22 Dec. 1905.

George Herbert. TLS. 1 April 1920.

Moore Smith, G. C. Wordsworth and George Herbert. N. & Q. 13 Jan. 1923.

Lucas, F. L. George Herbert. Life and Letters, Dec. 1928.

Beachcroft, T. O. Nicholas Ferrar and George Herbert. Criterion, XII, 1932.

Eliot, T. S. George Herbert. Spectator, 12 March 1932.

Anderton, H. I. George Herbert. TLS. 9 March 1933.

George Herbert, 1593–1633. TLS. 2 March 1933.

Parson Herbert. Times, 3 March 1933.

Hutchinson, F. E. George Herbert. A Tercentenary. Nineteenth Century, March 1933.

Sparrow, J. The Text of George Herbert. TLS. 14 Dec. 1933.

Blunden, E. George Herbert's Latin Poems. E. & S. xix, 1934. [For corrections see A. Brulé, Revue anglo-américaine, Oct. 1934, pp. 49–51.]

Wright, H. G. Was George Herbert the Author of Jacula Prudentum? RES. xi, 1935.

F. E. H.

THOMAS CAREW (1598?–1639?)

(1) ORIGINAL EDITIONS

Cœlum Britannicum. A Masque at Whitehall. 1634 (anon.) (re-issued with corrections same year).

Poems. By Thomas Carew Esquire. One of the Gentlemen of the Privie-Chamber, and Sewer in Ordinary to His Majesty. [Ed. Aurelian Townsend?] 1640 (includes, with separate title but continuous pagination, Cœlum Britannicum, 1640;) 1642 ('revised and enlarged'; adds 8 poems, 1 by Waller); 1651 (as Poems, With a Maske; adds 3 poems); 1671 (as Poems, Songs and Sonnets, Together with a Masque).

(2) COLLECTED EDITIONS

Poems, Songs, and Sonnets: together with a Masque. Ed. [T. Davies?], 1772.

The Works of Thomas Carew. Ed. [T. Maitland], Edinburgh, 1824.

The Poems of Thomas Carew. 1845.

The Poems of Thomas Carew. Ed. W. C. Hazlitt, 1870.

The Poems and Masque of Thomas Carew. Ed. J. W. Ebsworth, 1893.

The Poems of Thomas Carew. Ed. A. Vincent, 1899. (Muses' Lib.)

(3) SELECTION

A Selection from the Poetical Works of Thomas Carew. Ed. John Fry, 1810.

(4) CRITICISM

Quiller-Couch, Sir A. T. Thomas Carew. [In Adventures in Criticism, 1896.]

Powell, C. L. New Material on Thomas Carew. MLR. xi, 1916.

WILLIAM HABINGTON (1605–1654)

Castara. 2 pts, 1634 (anon.); 1635 ('corrected and augmented.' Adds 3 prose characters and 26 poems. Author's name at head of commendatory verses); 1639–40 (adds a 3rd pt, with new title-page: character 'A Holy Man' and 22 poems, mostly religious); ed. C. A. Elton, Bristol, [1812]; rptd R. Southey (Select Works of the British Poets, 1831); ed. E. Arber, 1870, 1895 (with collation of the 3 original edns).

The Queene of Arragon. A Tragi-Comedie. 1640; rptd Dodsley's Old Plays, vol. x, 1744, ed. W. C. Hazlitt, with memoir, vol. xiii, 1875; ed. R. Thyer, 1759. [See Samuel Butler's Remains, ed. Thyer, vol. i, p. 185, 1759.]

The Historie of Edward the Fourth. 1640. [Rptd (attrib. to John Habington) in W. Kennett's Complete History of England, vol. i, 1706. Compiled, it is said, from the materials of his father, Thomas Habington, or Abington, antiquary.]

Observations upon Historie. 1641.

[Commendatory verses by Habington are in several books, e.g. in the 1647 folio of Beaumont and Fletcher, and in Jonsonus Virbius, 1638, where the name is given as W. Abington. There is a poem addressed to the author of Castara in Witts Recreation, 1640, and another in Malone MS 18, fol. 68 in Bodleian Lib.]

F. E. H.

SIR WILLIAM DAVENANT (1606–1668)

(1) COLLECTED WORKS

The Works of Sr William D'avenant Kt Consisting of Those which were formerly Printed, and Those which he design'd for the Press: Now published out of the Authors Originall Copies. 1673.

(2) POEMS

(a) Collected Poems

Madagascar, with other poems. 1638; 1648.

Select Works of the British Poets. Ed. R. Southey, 1831. [Gondibert and selections from the non-dramatic poems.]

(b) Individual Poems

Gondibert: an Heroick Poem. 1651 (8° and 4°).

A Panegyrick to his Excellency the Lord Generall Monck. 1659. [Folio sheet.]

Poem, upon His Sacred Majesties Return. 1660.

Poem, to the King's Most Sacred Majesty. 1663.

[London, King Charles his Augusta, 1648, though ascribed to Davenant in the printer's epistle, is not by him.]

(3) PROSE WORKS

A Discourse upon Gondibert. Paris, 1650 (also issued as The Preface to Gondibert); ed. J. E. Spingarn (Seventeenth Century Critical Essays, vol. ii, Oxford, 1908).

(4) Plays and Masques

(a) Collected Plays

The Works of Sr William Davenant. 1673. [Rpts the already pbd plays, often with considerable alterations, and adds: The Playhouse to be Let; Law against Lovers; News from Plymouth; The Distresses; The Siege; The Fair Favourite.]

The Dramatic Works of Sir William D'Avenant, with Prefatory Memoir and Notes. Ed. J. Maidment and W. H. Logan, 5 vols. Edinburgh, 1872–4. (Dramatists of the Restoration.)

(b) Separate Works

The Tragedy of Albovine, King of the Lombards. 1629.

The Cruell Brother. A Tragedy. As it was presented, at the private House, in the Blacke-Fryers: By His Majesties Servants. 1630.

The Just Italian. Lately presented in the private house in Blacke Friers, By his Majesties Servants. 1630.

The Temple of Love. A Masque. 1634 (for 1635).

The Platonick Lovers. A Tragæ comedy. Presented at the private House in the Black-Fryers, By his Majesties Servants. 1636; 1665 (with The Witts).

The Witts. A Comedie, presented at the Private House in Black Fryers, by his Majesties Servants. 1636; 1665 (with The Platonick Lovers, as Two Excellent Plays); ed. I. Reed (Dodsley's Old Plays, vol. viii, 1780); ed. Sir W. Scott (Ancient British Drama, vol. i, 1810); ed. J. P. Collier (Dodsley's Old Plays, vol. viii, 1825–7).

The Triumphs of the Prince D'Amour. A masque Presented by His Highnesse at His Pallace in the Middle Temple. 1635 (for 1636).

Britannia Triumphans: A Masque, Presented at White Hall by the Kings Majestie. 1637 (for 1638).

Luminalia or the Festivall of Light, Personated in a masque at Court By the Queenes Majestie and her Ladies. 1637 (for 1638); ed. A. B. Grosart (Miscellanies of Fuller Worthies Lib. vol. iv, 1872).

Salmacida Spolia. A Masque Presented by the King and Queenes Majesties, at White-hall. 1639 (for 1640): rptd W. R. Chetwood (Select Collection of Old Plays, Dublin, 1750); ed. H. A. Evans (English Masques, 1879).

The Unfortunate Lovers: A Tragedie; As it was lately Acted with great applause at the private House in Black-Fryers; By His Majesties Servants. 1643; 1649.

Love and Honour. Presented by His Majesties Servants at the Black-Fryers. 1649; ed. J. W. Tupper, Boston, 1909 (Belles Lettres Ser.).

The Siege of Rhodes Made a Representation by the Art of Prospective in Scenes, And the Story sung in Recitative Musick. At the back part of Rutland-House in the upper end of Aldersgate-Street, London. 1656; 1659 ('At the Cock Pit in Drury Lane'); 1663 (rev. and expanded as The Siege of Rhodes: The First and Second Part. As they were lately Represented at the Duke of York's Theatre in Lincolns-Inn-Fields); 1670.

The first days Entertainment at Rutland House, by Declamations and Musick: After the Manner of the Ancients. 1657.

The Cruelty of the Spaniards in Peru. Exprest by Instrumentall and Vocal Musick, and by Art of Perspective in Scenes, &c. 1658.

The History of Sr Francis Drake. Pt 1 (all ptd), 1659.

The Rivals. A Comedy. Acted by His Highness the Duke of York's Servants. 1668.

The Man's the Master: a Comedy. 1669.

The Tempest, or the Enchanted Island. A Comedy. As it is now Acted at his Highness the Duke of York's Theatre. 1670; ed. M. Summers (Shakespearian Adaptations, 1922). [In collaboration with John Dryden.]

Macbeth. With all the Alterations, Amendments, Additions, and New Songs. 1674 (bis); 1687; 1695; 1697; 1710.

(5) Biography and Criticism

Certain Verses Written By severall of the Authors Friends; To Be Re-Printed with the Second Edition of Gondibert. 1653.

Hurd, R. Q. Horatii Flacci epistola ad Augustum. To which is added a discourse concerning poetical imitation. 1751.

Aikin, J. and A. L. Miscellaneous Pieces in Prose. 1773. [Gondibert, pp. 138–89.]

Elze, K. Sir William Davenant. Sh. Jb. iv, 1869.

Campbell, K. The Source of the Siege of Rhodes. MLN. xiii, 1898.

—— The Source of Davenant's Albovine. JEGP. iv, 1902.

—— Notes on D'Avenant's Life. MLN. xviii, 1903.

Firth, Sir C. H. Sir William Davenant and the Revival of Drama during the Protectorate. EHR. xviii, 1903.

Gronauer, G. Sir William Davenant's Gondibert. Munich, 1911.

Hooper, E. S. The Authorship of Luminalia and Notes on some Other Poems of Sir William D'Avenant. MLR. viii, 1913.

Thaler, Alwin. Thomas Heywood, D'Avenant, and The Siege of Rhodes. PMLA. xxxix, 1924.

Spencer, Hazelton. D'Avenant's Macbeth and Shakespeare's. PMLA. xl, 1925.

Richardson, W. R. Sir William Davenant as American Colonizer. ELH. i, 1934.

Harbage, A. Sir William Davenant. Philadelphia, 1935. [Includes bibliography.]

EDMUND WALLER (1606–1687)

(1) Poems

(a) Collected Poems

Poems. 1645 (3 edns); 1664; 1668; 1682; 1686; 1693, etc.

Divine Poems. 1685.

The Second Part of Mr. Waller's Poems. 1690; 1705; 1711; 1712; 1722. [The anon. Preface is generally attrib. to Francis Atterbury.]

The Works of Edmund Waller, Esq., in Verse and Prose. Ed. E. Fenton, 1729, 1730, 1758.

The Works of Waller in verse and prose, with life. 1772.

The Poetical Works of Waller and Denham. Ed. G. Gilfillan, Edinburgh, 1857.

Poems. Ed. G. Thorn-Drury, 1893; 2 vols. 1901. (Muses' Lib.) [The authoritative edn.]

(b) Individual Poems

Rex Redux. Cambridge, 1633. [Contains Waller's To the King on his return.]

A Paraphrase upon the Divine Poems, by G. S[andys]. 1638. [Contains Waller's To George Sandys.]

Jonsonus Virbius. 1638. [Contains Waller's Upon Ben Johnson.]

Poems. By Thomas Carew. 1642 (2nd edn). [Contains Waller's To my Lord Admiral.]

Witts Recreations. 1645 (3rd edn). [Contains the following poems of Waller, some under different titles indicated in brackets: To Amoret, 'Amoret! the Milky Way'; To Phyllis, 'Phyllis! why should we delay' (The Cunning Curtezan); The Fall (The Reply); Of the marriage of the Dwarfs (On the Two Dwarfs that were married); The Bud; On the Discovery of a Lady's Painting (On a patch'd up Madam); Of Loving at First Sight (The Reply to the Contrary); The Self-banished (The Melancholy Lover); To a Friend of their loves (The Variable Lover); To Zelinda (The Ladyes Slave); To the Mutable Fair (The Reply); On a Brede of divers colours; Chloris and Hylas (On the approaching Spring); Go, lovely Rose! (On

the Rose); Under a Lady's Picture (To be ingraven under the Queen's Picture); To one married to an old Man (To the Wife being marryed to that old man).]

Oratio in Gymnasio Patavino. [1646.] [Contains Waller's Verses to Dr George Rogers.]

A Discourse upon Gondibert. Paris, 1650. [Contains Waller's To Sir William Davenant. Rptd with Gondibert, 1651.]

Ayres and Dialogues. 1653. [Contains the following poems of Waller, some under different titles indicated in brackets: The Bud; To a Lady singing (To the same Lady singing); While I listen to thy Voice. Vol. ii, 1655 contains Waller's To Chloris, 'Chloris! since first' (To a Lady, more affable); Go, lovely Rose!]

Poems by Francis Beaumont Gent. 1653. [Contains Waller's 'Say, lovely Dream' (taken from Waller's Poems, 1645); Of Loving at First Sight; To the Mutable Fair; Song, 'Behold the Brand of Beauty tossed.']

Grati Falisci Cynegeticon by Christopher Wase. 1654. [Contains Waller's To Mr Wase.]

History of the Wars of Flanders, by H. Carey. 1654. [Contains Waller's Ad Comitem Monumetensem.]

A Panegyrick to my Lord Protector. 1655 (bis).

An Essay on Lucretius, by J. Evelyn. 1656. [Contains Waller's To his friend, Master Evelyn.]

A Prospective of the Naval Triumph, by Busenello. 1658. [Contains Waller's To Sir Thos. Higgons.]

Upon the late Storme, and of the death of his Highnesse. [1658]; 1659 (in Three Poems upon the Death of his late Highnesse).

The Passion of Dido. 1658; 1679. [By Waller and Sidney Godolphin.]

To the King, upon his Majesties happy return. [1660.]

To my Lady Morton. 1661.

A Poem on St James's Park. 1661.

To the Queen, upon her Majesty's Birthday. 1663.

Pompey the Great. A Tragedy. Translated out of French by Certain Persons of Honour. 1664. [Act i by Waller.]

Upon her Majesty's New Buildings. 1665.

Three Plays, by Sir William Killigrew. 1665. [Contains Waller's To Mr. Killigrew, under the title Of Pandoras not being approved.]

Instructions to a Painter for the Drawing of the Posture and Progress of his Majesties Forces at Sea. 1666.

Historical Applications by George, first Earl of Berkeley. 1666. [Contains Waller's To a Friend of the Author.]

Of the Lady Mary. 1677.

Horace's Art of Poetry made English, by the Earl of Roscommon. 1680. [Contains Waller's Upon the Earl of Roscommon's translation.]
The Maid's Tragedy, Altered. 1690.
[Neve, Philip.] Cursory Remarks on Some of the Ancient English Poets. 1789. [Contains Waller's When he was at sea; In Answer to one who writ against a Fair Lady.]
English Poets. Ed. A. Chalmers, 1810. [Contains Waller's To the Prince of Orange; On Mrs Higgons.]

(2) PROSE WORKS
Speech against Prelates Innovations. 1641.
Mr. Waller's Speech in the Painted Chamber 6 July 1641, 1641
Speech, 4 July 1643. 1643.
The Workes of Edmund Waller in this Parliament. 1645.

(3) BIOGRAPHY AND CRITICISM
(a) Books
Stockdale, P. Life of Waller. 1772.
Johnson, Samuel. Lives of the Poets. Vol. I, 1781; ed. G. B. Hill, vol. I, Oxford, 1905.
Cartwright, J. Sacharissa. 1893.
Beeching, H. C. An English Miscellany. 1901.
Thorn-Drury, G. The Poems of Waller. 1901. [Introduction.]
Chew, B. Essays and Verses about Books. New York, 1926 (priv. ptd).

(b) Articles in Periodicals
Aldington, R. Note on Waller's Poems. Living Age, CCCXII, 1922.
Grierson, H. J. C. Poems by Waller. TLS. 29 Dec. 1927.
Lloyd, C. Waller as a Member of the Royal Society. PMLA. XLIII, 1928.
Roeckerath, N. Der Nachruhm Herricks und Wallers. Leipzig, 1931.
de Beer, E. S. An Uncollected Poem by Waller. RES. VIII, 1932.
Riske, E. T. Waller in Exile. TLS. 13 Oct. 1932.   T. H. B.

SIR JOHN SUCKLING (1609–1642)
(1) ORIGINAL EDITIONS
Aglaura. 1638 (anon.). [Rptd in Fragmenta Aurea.]
The Discontented Colonell. [1640?] [Rptd in Fragmenta Aurea as Brennoralt.]
The Coppy of a Letter written to the Lower House of Parliament. 1641.
Fragmenta Aurea. A Collection of all the Incomparable Peeces written By Sir John Suckling. 1646 (contains, each with separate title and pagination, Poems, Aglaura, The Goblins, Brennoralt, all dated 1646); 1648

(in 4 pts, as in 1646 edn, but each dated 1648); 1658 (continuous pagination, but adds, with separate title and pagination, The Last Remains of Sir John Suckling, 1659. This includes, with separate titles and pagination but continuous signatures, Letters to Several Persons of Honor, The Sad One. A Tragedy, both dated 1659).

(2) COLLECTED EDITIONS
The Works of Sir John Suckling. 1676; 1696 (contains, with separate titles but continuous pagination, the 4 plays, each dated 1694); 1709; 1719; Dublin, 1766; 2 vols. 1770.
The Poems, Plays and other remains of Sir John Suckling. Ed. W. C. Hazlitt, 2 vols. 1874; 2 vols. 1892 (rev. edn).
The Works of Sir John Suckling. Ed. A. H. Thompson, 1910.

(3) SELECTIONS
Selection from the Works of Sir John Suckling. Ed. A. Suckling, 1836.
[The Goblins is rptd in Dodsley's Old Plays, vol. VII, 1744, and later edns.]

(4) CRITICISM
Kastner, L. E. Suckling and Desportes. MLR. V, VI, 1910–1.
Lynch, K. M. The Social Mode of Restoration Comedy. New York, 1927.

RICHARD CRASHAW
(1612 or 1613–1649)
[A full account of all MSS is given in L. C. Martin's edn of Works, pp. liv–lxxxi. This edn records also the first appearance of all occasional pieces.]

(1) ORIGINAL EDITIONS
Epigrammatum Sacrorum Liber. Cambridge, 1634. [The Dedication is signed R. C.]
Steps to the Temple. Sacred Poems, With other Delights of the Muses. 1646; 1648 ('second Edition wherein are added divers pieces not before extant').
Carmen Deo Nostro, Te Decet Hymnus, Sacred Poems, Collected, Corrected, Augmented. By R.C. Paris, 1652. [Ed. the poet's friend, Thomas Car, alias Miles Pinkney. Three engravings are probably by Crashaw.]
A Letter from Mr. Crashaw to the Countess of Denbigh, Against Irresolution and Delay in matters of Religion. [1653.] [No printer's name or date. A contemporary hand has written 1653, and G. Thomason, a previous owner of the unique copy in BM., has added 'Sept: 23' above the year. It differs widely from the version in Carmen, 1652: see Martin, pp. 236, 348, 446.]

Steps to the Temple, The Delights of the Muses, and Carmen Deo Nostro. The Second Edition. 1670. [Grosart, vol. II, p. viii, records an undated re-issue of the above, with 'The Third Edition' on the title-page, but it has not been traced.]

Poemata et Epigrammata. Editio Secunda, Auctior & emendatior. Cambridge, 1670 (re-issued with fresh title-page 1674).

(2) LATER EDITIONS

Epigrammata Sacra Selecta, cum Anglica Versione. Sacred epigrams Englished. 1682. [Crashaw is not named, but all the Latin epigrams are his. The anon. trns are by Clement Barksdale.]

R. Crashaw's Poetry, with some account of the author by P[eregrine] P[hillips]. 1787. [Selections.]

Select Beauties of Ancient English Poetry. Ed. H. Headley, vol. I, 1787. [Prints all Sospetto d'Herode, except Argomento and the first four stanzas.]

The Suspicion of Herod. Kensington, 1834.

Poetical Works. Ed. G. Gilfillan, 1857. [Based on 1670 edn.]

Complete Works. Ed. W. B. Turnbull, 1858.

Complete Works. Ed. A. B. Grosart, 2 vols. 1872–3; with supplement, 1887–8. (Fuller Worthies' Lib.)

Poems. Ed. C. Cowden Clarke, [1881].

English Poems. Ed. E. Hutton, 1899.

Poems. Ed. A. R. Waller, Cambridge, 1904. [More complete collection of English, Latin and Greek poems than ptd till then.]

Poems. Ed. J. R. Tutin, with Introduction by H. C. Beeching. [1905.] (Muses' Lib.)

Poems, English Latin and Greek. Ed. L. C. Martin, Oxford, 1927. [The most authoritative text. Contains some hitherto unptd poems and new biographical matter.]

(3) BIOGRAPHY AND CRITICISM
(a) Books

Bargrave, John (1610–1680). Alexander VII and the College of Cardinals. Camden Soc. 1867.

Pope, A. Works. Ed. W. Elwin, vol. VI, pp. 116–8, 1871. [Letter to H. Cromwell, 17 Dec. 1710.]

Gosse, Sir E. Seventeenth Century Studies. 1883.

Thompson, Francis. Collected Works. Vol. III, 1913.

The Minor Poems of Joseph Beaumont. Ed. E. Robinson, 1914. [For parallels between Beaumont and Crashaw.]

Chalmers, Lord. Richard Crashaw: 'Poet and Saint.' [In In Memoriam Adolphus W. Ward, Cambridge, 1924.]

Praz, Mario. Secentismo e Marinismo in Inghilterra. Florence, 1925.

Eliot, T. S. For Lancelot Andrewes. 1928.

Wallerstein, R. C. Richard Crashaw. A Study in Style and Poetic Development. Madison, 1935.

(b) Articles in Periodicals

Richard Crashaw's Poems. Retrospective Rev. I, 1820.

McCarthy, D. F. Crashaw and Shelley. N. & Q. 5 June 1858.

Mayor, J. E. B. Crashaw and Shelley. N. & Q. 26 June 1858.

Sharland, E. C. Richard Crashaw and Mary Collet. Church Quart. Rev. Jan. 1912.

Martin, L. C. A Crashaw and Shelley Parallel. MLR. XI, 1916.

—— A hitherto unpublished Poem of Richard Crashaw. London Mercury, June 1923. [Epithalamium.]

Comfrey, B. A Note on Richard Crashaw. MLN. XXXVI, 1921.

Williams, I. A. Epitaphs on a Husband and Wife. London Mercury, Feb. 1923.

An Italian Critic on Donne and Crashaw. TLS. 17 Dec. 1925. [Review of Praz.]

Crashaw's Poetical Works. TLS. 17 Dec. 1927.

Hutchinson, F. E. Richard Crashaw. Church Quart. Rev. April, 1928.

Tholen, W. Richard Crashaw, ein englischer Dichter und Mystiker der Barockzeit. Das neue Ufer, XLVIII, 1928.

Warren, A. Crashaw and Peterhouse. TLS. 18 Aug. 1931, 3 Nov. 1932.

—— Crashaw and St Teresa. TLS. 25 Aug. 1932.

—— The Mysticism of Crashaw. Church Quart. Rev. CXVI, 1933.

—— Crashaw's Epigrammata Sacra. JEGP. XXXIII, 1934.

—— The Reputation of Crashaw in the Seventeenth and Eighteenth Centuries. Stud. Phil. XXXI, 1934.

—— Richard Crashaw. MP. XXXII, 1935.

Beachcroft, T. O. Crashaw—and the Baroque Style. Criterion, XIII, 1934.
F. E. H.

SIR JOHN DENHAM (1615–1669)

(1) POEMS
(a) Collected Poems

Poems and Translations. 1668; 1671; 1684; 1703; 1709; 1719; Glasgow, 1755; 1769; Glasgow, 1771.

The Poetical Works of Waller and Denham. Ed. G. Gilfillan, Edinburgh, 1857.

The Poetical Works of Denham. Ed. T. H.
Banks, New Haven, 1928. [The authoritative edn.]

(b) Individual Poems

The Sophy. 1642.
Coopers Hill. 1642; 1643; 1650; 1655 (rev.,
1st authorized edn); 1709. Latine Reddi-
tum, Oxford, 1676.
Mr. Hampdens Speech. 1643 (anon.). [Rptd
in Rump, 1662.]
Comedies and Tragedies by Beaumont and
Fletcher. 1647. [Contains Denham's On
Mr John Fletchers Works among the pre-
fatory poems.]
Il Pastor Fido, by Richard Fanshawe. 1648.
[Contains Denham's To Sir Richard Fan-
shaw among the prefatory poems. Rptd
with Coopers Hill, 1650.]
Lachrymae Musarum. 1650. [Contains Den-
ham's Elegie upon Hastings.]
Certain Verses to be reprinted with Gondibert.
1653. [Contains poems by Denham.]
The Destruction of Troy. 1656 (anon.)
Panegyrick on Monck. 1659 (anon.)
A Relation of a Quaker. 1659 (anon.)
Prologue to his Majesty at the first Play at the
Cock-pit. 1660 (anon.).
Rump. 1662. [Contains Denham's To the Five
Members; A Western Wonder; A Second
Western Wonder.]
Several Copies of Verses on the Death of
Cowley. 1667. [Contains Denham's On
Mr Abraham Cowley, also issued separately.]
The Famous Battel of the Catts. 1668 (anon.).
[Denham's authorship uncertain.]
Cato Major. 1669; 1710.
The British Princes, by Edward Howard. 1669.
[Contains Denham's To Howard among the
prefatory poems.]
Horace, by Corneille. 1678. [Fifth act tr.
by Denham.]
Chorus Poetarum. 1694. [Contains Denham's
To his Mistress.]
A Version of the Psalms. 1714.
Fifth Part of Miscellany Poems. 1716. [Con-
tains a portion of The Sophy, entitled
Verses.]

(2) Prose Works

The Anatomy of Play. 1651 (anon.)

(3) Works Attributed to Denham

The Lawrel and the Ax. [?]
Madam Semphronia's Farewel. [?]
A Letter sent to William Laud. 1641 (anon.).
Upon her Majesty's New Buildings. 1665.
[Waller.]
Second Advice to a Painter. 1667.
Second and Third Advice to a Painter. 1667.
Directions to a Painter. 1667.

The True Presbyterian. 1680.
His M—y's speech. [Contained in Bibliotheca
Curiosa, ed. E. Goldsmid, Edinburgh, 1885.]

(4) Biography and Criticism

à Wood, Anthony. Athenae Oxonienses. 2 vols.
Oxford, 1691–2; ed. P. Bliss, 6 vols. 1813–
20.
Johnson, Samuel. Lives of the Poets. Vol. I,
1781; ed. G. B. Hill, vol. I, Oxford,
1905.
Aubrey, J. Brief Lives. Ed. A. Clark, 2 vols.
Oxford, 1898.
Banks, T. H. The Poetical Works of Denham.
New Haven, 1928. [Introduction.]

T. H. B.

ABRAHAM COWLEY (1618–1667)

(1) Bibliography

Loiseau, Jean. Abraham Cowley, sa Vie, son
Œuvre. Paris, 1931. [A detailed bibliography will be found on pp. 655–87.]

(2) Collected Works

The Works of Mr Abraham Cowley. Consisting
of Those which were formerly Printed: and
Those which he Design'd for the Press.
1668 (also re-issued with corrections); 1669;
1672; 1674; 1678; 1680; 1681; 1684; 1688;
1693; 1700; 3 vols. 1707–8; 3 vols. 1710–1;
3 vols. 1721. [Reprints: the Poems of
1656 and the Verses of 1663, the latter with
some additional pieces; the Proposition of
1660; the Vision of 1661 (as A Discourse by
way of Vision). And adds from MS Several
Discourses by way of Essays, in Verse and
Prose. T. Sprat's An Account of the Life
and Writings of Mr. Abraham Cowley is
prefixed. The 1680 and most of the later
edns add The Second Part of the Works.
1688 adds commendatory verses, 1693 adds
Cutter of Coleman Street, 1700 has an ode
'Never before Printed'; 1707–8, etc. add
the Third Part of the Works.]
The Second Part of the Works of Mr. Abraham
Cowley. Being what was Written and
Published by himself in his Younger Years.
The Fourth Edition. 1681; 1682; 1684.
[Reprints: the poems in Poeticall Blossomes
(adding 3 poems to 'Sylva' and omitting
1 poem); Loves Riddle; Naufragium
Joculare.]
The Second and Third Parts of the Works of
Mr. Abraham Cowley. The Third [part] con-
taining his six books of Plants now made
English [by J. O., C. Cleve, N. Tate and
Aphra Behn]. 1689; 1700; 1708; 1711;
1721.

The Complete Works in Verse and Prose of Abraham Cowley. Ed. A. B. Grosart, 2 vols. Edinburgh, 1881. (Chertsey Worthies' Lib.)

The English Writings of Abraham Cowley. Ed. A. R. Waller, 2 vols. Cambridge, 1905–6.

(3) SELECTIONS

Poems of Mr. Cowley and Others composed into Song By William King Organist of New Colledge. Oxford, 1668. [16 poems by Cowley, 15 from The Mistress.]

Songs set by Signior Pietro Reggio. [1680.] [Contains 33 songs from 'Anacreontiques' and The Mistress.]

Select Works in Verse and Prose With a Preface and Notes by the Editor [R. Hurd]. 2 vols. 1772; 2 vols. Dublin, 1772; 3 vols. 1777 (enlarged).

Cowley's Prose Works. Ed. J. R. Lumby, Cambridge, 1887; rev. A. Tilley, Cambridge, 1923.

Abraham Cowley: the Essays and Other Prose Writings. Ed. A. B. Gough, Oxford, 1915.

The Mistress with Other Select Poems. Ed. John Sparrow, 1926.

(4) ENGLISH WORKS

(a) Poems

Poeticall Blossomes. 1633 ('by A. C.'); 1636 ('enlarged'; adds Sylva, or, Divers Copies of Verses); 1637.

Satyre against Separatists. 1642 ('by A. C.'); 1660; 1675. [Not by Cowley?]

Satyre, The Puritan and the Papist. By a Scholler in Oxford. 1643 (anon., but rptd as Cowley's in Wit and Loyalty Reviv'd, 1682); rptd Somers Tracts, vol. v, 1811.

The Mistress: or, several copies of love-versès. 1647.

The Foure Ages of England. 1648; 1675; 1705. [Ascribed to Cowley on title-page, but disowned by him in the Preface to Poems, 1656.]

Poems. 1656. [Contains: Preface; Miscellanies; The Mistress; Pindarique Odes; Davideis.]

Ode, upon the Blessed Restoration and Returne of his sacred Majestie, Charles the Second. 1660.

Verses lately written upon several occasions. 1663. [A note by the publisher refers to an unauthorized Dublin edn of 1663; but no copy appears to be extant.]

Poem on the late Civil War. 1679. [Extensive fragment.]

(b) Other Writings

Loves Riddle. A Pastorall Comaedie. 1638.

The Guardian. A Comedie. 1650.

A Proposition for the Advancement of Experimental Philosophy. 1661.

A Vision, concerning his late pretended Highness, Cromwell the Wicked. 1661 (also issued as The Visions and Prophecies concerning England, Scotland, and Ireland, of Ezekiel Grebner); rptd Harleian Misc. vol. v, 1745, 1808, 1810.

Cutter of Coleman-Street; a Comedy. 1663.

(5) LATIN WORKS

Naufragium Joculare, comedia. 1638.

A Couleii Plantarum Libri duo. 1662.

A. Couleii Poemata Latina. 1668; 1678. [Contains: a shortened Latin version of Sprat's Life; the contents of Plantarum Libri duo; 4 more Libri Plantarum; Miscellanea.]

(6) BIOGRAPHY AND CRITICISM

Johnson, Samuel. The Lives of the Poets. Vol. I, 1781; ed. G. B. Hill, vol. I, Oxford, 1905.

Gosse, Sir E. Seventeenth Century Studies. 1883.

Firth, Sir C. H. Abraham Cowley at the Restoration. Academy, 7 Oct. 1893.

Macbride, J. M. A Study of Cowley's Davideis. JEGP. II, 1901.

Shafer, Robert. The English Ode. Princeton, 1918.

Moore Smith, G. C. Abraham Cowley and Lord Falkland. N. & Q. 15 Oct. 1921.

Nethercot, A. H. The Relation of Cowley's 'Pindarics' to Pindar's Odes. MP. XIX, 1921.

—— The Reputation of Abraham Cowley. PMLA. XXXVIII, 1923.

—— Abraham Cowley's Discourse concerning Style. RES. II, 1926.

—— Abraham Cowley as Dramatist. RES. IV, 1928.

—— The Letters of Abraham Cowley. MLN. XLIII, 1928.

—— The Essays of Abraham Cowley. JEGP. XXIX, 1930.

—— Abraham Cowley. The Muse's Hannibal. Oxford, 1931.

Sparrow, John. The Text of Cowley's Mistress. RES. III, 1927.

—— The Text of Cowley's Satire The Puritan and the Papist. Ang. LVIII, 1934.

Loiseau, Jean. Abraham Cowley, sa Vie, son Œuvre. Paris, 1931.

—— Abraham Cowley's Reputation in England. Paris, 1931.

Wiley, A. N. The Prologue and Epilogue to the Guardian. RES. x, 1934.

J. S.

RICHARD LOVELACE (1618-1657?)

(1) COLLECTED POEMS

Lucasta. The Poems of Richard Lovelace. In Two Parts. Ed. S. W. S[inger], 1817-8: [Originally issued as vols. I and IV of Select Early English Poets.]

Lucasta. The Poems of Richard Lovelace, Esq. Ed. W. C. Hazlitt, 1864 and 1897.

Lucasta. I. Epodes, Odes, Sonnets, Songs, Etc. II. Posthume Poems. Ed. Harold Child, 1904.

Lucasta. The Poems of Richard Lovelace, Esquire. Ed. W. L. Phelps, 2 vols. Chicago, 1921.

The Poems of Richard Lovelace. Ed. C. H. Wilkinson, 2 vols. Oxford, 1925; 1 vol. Oxford, 1930. [Standard edn.]

(2) SEPARATE WORKS

Lucasta: Epodes, Odes, Sonnets, Songs, &c. to which is added Amarantha, a Pastorall. By Richard Lovelace, Esq. 1649 (3 issues).

Lucasta. Posthume Poems of Richard Lovelace Esq. 1659. [Ed. D. P. Lovelace. Includes, with separate title and pagination but continuous signatures, Elegies Sacred To the Memory of the Author, 1660.]

(3) BIOGRAPHY AND CRITICISM

[Brydges, Sir S. E.] Remarks on English Bards. GM. LXI, 1791, LXII, 1792.

Lovelace's Lucasta. Retrospective Rev. IV, 1821.

Hartmann, C. H. The Cavalier Spirit, and its Influence on the Life and Work of Richard Lovelace. 1925.

Judson, A. C. Who was Lucasta? MP. XXIII, 1925.

Wilkinson, C. H. The Poems of Richard Lovelace. Vol. I, Oxford, 1925. [Introduction.]

ANDREW MARVELL (1621-1678)

(1) BIBLIOGRAPHIES

[The best bibliographies of Marvell will be found in H. M. Margoliouth, Marvell's Poems and Letters, vol. I, pp. 206-14, Oxford, 1927; and in P. Legouis, André Marvell, Poète, Puritain, Patriote, pp. 451-87, Paris, 1928.]

(2) COLLECTED WORKS

Miscellaneous Poems by Andrew Marvell, Esq. 1681. [In all but two known copies the three Cromwell poems have been cancelled.]

The Works of Andrew Marvell. Ed. T. Cooke, 2 vols. 1726; 1772. [Poems, Satires and a few letters.]

The Works of Andrew Marvell. Ed. E. Thompson, 3 vols. 1776. [Poems, Satires Prose Works and letters.]

The Poetical Works of Andrew Marvell. Boston, 1857; 1870; Boston, 1878 (in The Poetical Works of Milton and Marvell) [1881 or 1882].

The Complete Works in Verse and Prose of Andrew Marvell. Ed. A. B. Grosart, 4 vols. 1872-5. (Fuller Worthies' Lib.)

Poems and Satires of Andrew Marvell. Ed G. A. Aitken, 2 vols. 1892; 1901. (Muses Lib.)

The Poems and Some Satires of Andrew Marvell. Ed. E. Wright, 1904.

Miscellaneous Poems by Andrew Marvell, Esq 1923.

The Poems and Letters of Andrew Marvell Ed. H. M. Margoliouth, 2 vols. Oxford, 1927 [Complete except for Prose Works.]

(3) SELECTED WORKS

[For anthologies, in which Marvell's poem have had an important place, see Legouis bibliography, pp. 473-5. For Poems of Affairs of State, in which Marvell's satire were included, see Margoliouth's bibliography pp. 209-12.]

(4) SEPARATE WORKS

(a) Poetry

An Elegy upon the Death of my Lord Francis Villiers. [1648.] [Only one copy known anon.; attribution not conclusively proved

The First Anniversary of the Government Under His Highness The Lord Protector 1655.

The Character of Holland. 1665; 1672.

(b) Prose

The Rehearsal Transpros'd: Or, Animadversions Upon a late Book, Intituled A Preface Shewing What Grounds there a of Fears and Jealousies of Popery. 1672 1672 ('The second Edition, corrected' 1672 ('The second Impression, with Additions and Amendments').

The Rehearsall Transpros'd: The Second Part Occasioned by Two Letters. Answered b Andrew Marvel. 1673; 1674. [Only two copies of the 1674 edn have been reported in the possession of Mr F. P. Wilson and Mr H. M. Margoliouth.]

Mr. Smirke; Or the Divine in Mode: Being Certain Annotations, upon the Animadversions on the Naked Truth. Together with a Short Historical Essay, concerning General Councils, Creeds, and Impositions, in Matters of Religion. 1676. [A Short Historical Essay was re-issued separately, 1680; 1687; 1703

An Account of the Growth of Popery And
Arbitrary Government in England. Amsterdam, 1677 (re-issued 'Amsterdam'
[1678]); tr. French, Hamburg, 1680.
Remarks Upon a Late Disingenuous Discourse Writ by one T. D. Under the pretence De ˉCausa Dei, and of Answering
Mr. John Howe's Letter and Postscript of
God's Prescience,&c. By a Protestant.1678.

[For prose pamphlets attrib. on inadequate
evidence to Marvell see Legouis' bibliography,
pp. 467–71.]

(5) BIOGRAPHY AND CRITICISM

Miège, G. A Relation of Three Embassies
From his Sacred Majestie Charles II To The
Great Duke of Muscovie, The King of
Sweden, and The King of Denmark.
Written by an Attendant on the Embassies.
1669.
à Wood, A. Athenae Oxonienses. 2 vols.
Oxford,1691–2; ed. P. Bliss,6 vols.1813–20.
Cooke, T. Life. [Prefixed to his edn (see
above), 1726.]
Biographia Britannica. Vol. v, 1760.
Thompson, E. Life. [Prefixed to his edn (see
above), 1776.]
Landor, W. S. Imaginary Conversations.
5 vols. 1824–9.
Dove, J. The Life of Andrew Marvell, the
Celebrated Patriot: with Extracts and
Selections from his Prose and Poetical
Works. 1832.
Coleridge, H. The Life of Andrew Marvell.
Hull, 1835. [The Dove-Coleridge life also
appeared, with considerable variations, in
Biographia Borealis, 1833, and Lives of
Illustrious Worthies of Yorkshire, 1835.]
Aubrey, J. Brief Lives. Ed. A. Clark, 2 vols.
Oxford, 1898. [Marvell in vol. II.]
Beeching, H. C. The Lyrical Poems of
Andrew Marvell. National Rev. July 1901.
Birrell, A. Andrew Marvell. 1905. (English
Men of Letters Ser.)
Poscher, R. Andrew Marvells poetische
Werke. Vienna, 1908.
Andrew Marvell Tercentenary Celebration.
Descriptive Catalogue of Exhibits. Hull,
1921.
Andrew Marvell. Tercentenary Tributes.
1922.
Margoliouth, H. M. Marvell: Some Bio-
graphical Points. MLR. XVII, 1922.
—— Marvell in Rome. TLS. 5 June 1924.
Legouis, P. Andrew Marvell: Further Bio-
graphical Points. MLR. XVIII, 1923.
—— Marvell's Maniban. RES. II, 1926.
—— André Marvell, Poète, Puritain, Patriote.
Paris,1928. [The only thorough biographical
and critical work on Marvell.]

Eliot, T. S. Andrew Marvell. [In Homage to
John Dryden, 1924.]
Sackville-West, V. Andrew Marvell. 1929.
Empson, W. Marvell's 'Garden.' [In Versions
of Pastoral, 1935.]
H. M. M.

HENRY VAUGHAN (1622–1695)

(1) COLLECTED WORKS

Complete Works. Ed. A. B. Grosart,
4 vols. 1870–1. (Fuller Worthies' Lib.)
[Includes also the poems of Thomas
Vaughan.]
Works. Ed. L. C. Martin, 2 vols. Oxford, 1914.
[The most complete edn, with full *apparatus
criticus*.]

(2) ORIGINAL EDITIONS

Poems, with the tenth Satyre of Juvenal
Englished. 1646.
Silex Scintillans: Sacred Poems and Private
Ejaculations. 1650.
Olor Iscanus. Select Poems, and Translations,
formerly written. Published by a Friend.
1651 (re-issued 1679). [The preface is dated
'Newton by Usk this 17. of Decemb. 1647.'
The prose trns are of two discourses by
Plutarch, one by Maximus Tyrius (all three
from John Reynolds's Latin versions of the
Greek originals), and The Praise and Happi-
nesse of the Countrie-Life, written in
Spanish by Antonio de Guevara, but
probably tr. from the Latin version of 1633.]
The Mount of Olives: or, Solitary Devotions.
With a Discourse of Man in Glory by
Anselm, done into English. 1652.
Flores Solitudinis. Collected in his Sicknesse
and Retirement. 1654. [Trns of two Latin
discourses by Johan: Euseb: Nierembergius;
of The World Condemned by Eucherius,
bishop of Lyons; and The Life of Paulinus,
bishop of Nola (mostly a trn).]
Silex Scintillans. The second Edition, in two
Books. 1655. [The unsold sheets of the
1650 volume (= Bk I) are used, except for
a new title-page and for the resetting of the
four pages containing Isaac's Marriage,
which is revised.]
Hermetical Physick. By Henry Nollius.
Englished. 1655. [Trn of Heinrich Nolle's
Systema Medicinae Hermeticae Generale,
1613.]
Thalia Rediviva: The Pass-Times and Diver-
sions of a Countrey-Muse, in choice Poems.
With some learned Remains of Eugenius
Philalethes. 1678. [Eugenius Philalethes is
his twin-brother Thomas, who died in 1666.
See The Works of Thomas Vaughan, ed.
A. E. Waite, 1919 and p. 886 below.]

(3) LATER EDITIONS

Spiritual Songs. 1706. [W. Carew Hazlitt (quoted in Chambers's edn, vol. II, p. lxi) mentions the existence of this edn, but was unable to trace it.]

Silex Scintillans, with Memoir by H. F. Lyte. 1847; Boston, 1856; 1858; 1883. [Contains also Pious Thoughts from Thalia Rediviva.]

Silex Scintillans. Ed. typ. facs. [of 1650 edn] W. Clare, 18ᴜ5.

Secular Poems. Ed. J. R. Tutin, Hull, 1893.

Poems. Ed. Sir E. K. Chambers, with Introduction by H. C. Beeching, 2 vols. [1896]. (Muses' Lib.)

Poems. Ed. Sir I. Gollancz, 1900.

The Mount of Olives, Man in Darkness, and Life of Paulinus. Ed. L. I. Guiney, 1902.

Poems. Ed. E. Hutton, 1904.

Silex Scintillans. Ed. W. A. L. Bettany, [1905]. [Contains the fullest list of parallels with Herbert.]

Henry Vaughan and Andrew Marvell: The Best of Both Worlds. A Choice from their Poems by Francis Meynell. [1918.]

Poems, and Essay from The Mount of Olives and Two Letters. Ed. F[rancis] M[eynell], 1924.

(4) BIOGRAPHY AND CRITICISM

(a) Books

Brown, John. Horae Subsecivae. Ser. 1, 1858.

Shairp, J. C. Sketches in History and Poetry. 1887.

Guiney, L. I. A Little English Gallery. New York, 1894.

Palgrave, F. T. Landscape in Poetry. 1897.

Letters of Oxford Welshmen. Ed. photo. facs. R. Ellis, Oxford, 1903.

Spens, Janet. Two Periods of Disillusion. 1909.

Johnson, Lionel. Post Liminium: Essays and Critical Papers. 1911.

Hodgson, G. E. A Study in Illumination. [1914.]

Heide, Anna von der. Das Naturgefühl in der englischen Dichtung im Zeitalter Miltons. Heidelberg, 1915.

Clutton-Brock, A. More Essays on Books. 1921.

Loudon, K. M. Two Mystic Poets. 1922. [Crashaw and Vaughan.]

Sencourt, R. Out-flying Philosophy. 1925.

Lucas, F. L. Authors Dead and Living. 1926.

Blunden, E. On the Poems of Henry Vaughan. With his Principal Latin Poems translated into English Verse. 1927.

More, P. E. New Shelburne Essays. Vol. I, Princeton, 1928.

Holmes, Elizabeth. Henry Vaughan and the Hermetic Philosophy. Oxford, 1932.

Morgan, G. E. F. Life of Henry Vaughan. [In preparation.]

(b) Articles in Periodicals

Vaughan's Olor Iscanus. Retrospective Rev. III, 1821.

Henry Vaughan. Macmillan's Mag. LXIII, 1890.

Sichel, Edith. Henry Vaughan, Silurist. Monthly Rev. April 1903.

Vaughan and Herrick. Athenaeum, 12 June 1915.

The Poetry of Henry Vaughan. TLS. 15 July 1915.

Brett-Smith, H. F. B. Vaughan and D'Avenant. MLR. XI, 1916.

Bensly, E. Notes on Henry Vaughan. MLR. XIV, 1919.

Henry Vaughan. TLS. 20 April 1922.

Merrill, L. R. Vaughan's Influence upon Wordsworth's Poetry. MLN. XXXVII, 1922.

Judson, A. C. Cornelius Agrippa and Henry Vaughan. MLN. XLI, 1926.

—— Henry Vaughan as a Nature Poet. PMLA. XLII, 1927.

—— The Source of Henry Vaughan's Ideas concerning God in Nature. Stud. Phil. XXIV, 1927.

Eliot, T. S. The Silurist. Dial, Sept. 1927.

Martin, L. C. Vaughan and Cowper. MLR. XXII, 1927.

Morgan, G. E. F. Henry Vaughan, Silurist. TLS. 3 Nov. 1932.

Clough, W. O. Henry Vaughan and the Hermetic Philosophy. PMLA. XLVIII, 1933.

Smith, A. J. Some Relations between Henry Vaughan and Thomas Vaughan. Papers of Michigan Academy, XVIII, 1933. [See also R. M. Wardle, PMLA. II, 1936.]

F. E. H.

THOMAS TRAHERNE (1637?–1674)

(1) WORKS

Roman Forgeries. By a faithful son of the Church of England. 1673.

Christian Ethicks, or divine morality opening the way to Blessedness. 1675. [Contains 8 poems.]

A serious and patheticall Contemplation of the Mercies of God. 1699 (anon., but identified by Dobell). [Ed. by the Nonjuror, Geo. Hickes, with some account of the unnamed author by a friend. Contains 3 rhymed poems.]

The Poetical Works. Now first published
from the Original Manuscripts. Ed. Bertram
Dobell, 1903 and 1906.

Centuries of Meditations. Now first printed
from the Author's Manuscript. Ed. B.
Dobell, 1908 and 1928 (rev. edn).

Traherne's Poems of Felicity. Edited from
the MS. by H. I. Bell. 1910. [The MS
(BM. Burney 392) was prepared for the
press, probably by the poet's brother
Philip. It contains 39 poems which are not
in Dobell's volumes. There are considerable
variations in the 23 poems which appear in
both MS collections.]

The Poetical Works. Ed. G. I. Wade, 1932.
[The poems ptd in 1903, but in the spelling
of the MSS, plus the poems from the
Burney MS.]

Felicities of Thomas Traherne. Ed. Sir A. T.
Quiller-Couch, 1935.

(2) BIOGRAPHY AND CRITICISM

Dobell, B. An Unknown Seventeenth Century
Poet. Athenaeum, 7, 14 April 1900.
[Dobell's first announcement of his dis-
covery.]

Jones, W. L. Traherne and the Religious
Poetry of the Seventeenth Century. Quart.
Rev. Oct. 1904.

Quiller-Couch, Sir A. T. From a Cornish
Window. Cambridge, 1906.

Willcox, L. E. A Joyous Mystic. North
American Rev. June 1911.

Fleming, W. K. Mysticism in Christianity.
1913.

Lock, Walter. An English Mystic. Constructive Quart. Dec. 1913.

Herman, E. The Meaning and Value of Mysticism. 1916.

Proud, J. W. Traherne and Theophilus
Gale. Friends' Quart. Examiner, April
1916.

Willett, G. E. Traherne: an Essay. 1919.

Correspondence. TLS. 29 Sept., 6, 20, 27 Oct.
1927.

Thompson, E. N. S. The Philosophy of Thomas
Traherne. PQ. VIII, 1929.

Beachcroft, T. O. Traherne and the Cambridge Platonists. Dublin Rev. April
1930.

—— Traherne, and the Doctrine of Felicity.
Criterion, IX, 1930.

Wade, G. I. The Manuscripts of the Poems of
Traherne. MLR. XXVI, 1931.

—— Thomas Traherne as 'Divine Philosopher.' Hibbert Journ. XXXII, 1934.

—— Traherne and the Spiritual Value of
Nature Study. London Quart. Rev. CLIX,
1934.
F. E. H.

VI. JOHN MILTON (1608–1674)

(1) BIBLIOGRAPHIES, ETC.

A Verbal Index to Milton's Paradise Lost:
Adapted to Every Edition but the First.
1741.

Prendergast, G. L. A Complete Concordance
to the Poetical Works of Milton. Madras,
1857–9.

Cleveland, C. D. A Complete Concordance to
the Poetical Works of John Milton. 1867.

Lenox Library, New York City. Collation of
the Different Editions of the Works of
Milton. New York, 1881.

The First Edition of the Paradise Lost. Book-
lore, III, 1886. [On the nine variations of
the title-page.]

Anderson, J. P. Bibliography. [In R.
Garnett's Life, 1890.]

British Museum. Catalogue of Printed Books.
Milton. 1892.

Bradshaw, J. A Concordance to the Poetical
Works of John Milton. 1894.

Almack, E. A Bibliography of the King's
Book, or Eikon Basilike. 1896.

Lockwood, L. E. Lexicon to the English
Poetical Works of John Milton. New York,
1907.

Milton, 1608–1674. Facsimile of the Autographs and Documents in the British
Museum. 1908.

Milton Tercentenary. Catalogue of Exhibits
[in Stoke Newington Public Library].
9 Dec. 1908. 1908.

Williamson, G. C. The Portraits, Prints and
Writings of John Milton, Exhibited at
Christ's College, Cambridge, 1908. Cam-
bridge, 1908.

Pollard, A. W. The Bibliography of Milton.
Library, X, 1909.

Thompson, E. N. S. John Milton. A Topical
Bibliography. New Haven, 1916.

Gilbert, A. H. A Geographical Dictionary of
Milton. New Haven, 1919.

Cooper, L. A Concordance of the Latin,
Greek, and Italian Poems of John Milton.
Halle, 1923.

Granniss, R. S. The Beverly Chew Collection
of Milton Portraits. New York, 1926.

Stevens, D. H. Reference Guide to Milton
from 1800 to the Present Day. Chicago, 1930.

Fletcher, H. F. Contributions to a Milton
Bibliography, 1800–1930. Urbana, 1931.

(2) COLLECTED WORKS

[In 1833 R. Fletcher wrote introductions to
the volumes of prose and poetry pbd in that
year. These were frequently rptd in stereotype,
one printing appearing in Paris about 1836.
The prose collection was incomplete, and no
editing or notes gave value to the texts.]

The Works of John Milton in Verse and Prose. Ed. J. Mitford, 8 vols. 1851

The Student's Milton. Being the Complete Poems of John Milton with the Greater Part of His Prose Works, with New Translations of His Italian, Latin, and Greek Poems. Ed. F. A. Patterson, New York, 1930. [The same editor has general charge of the Columbia University edn of the Complete Works, to be pbd in 18 vols. 1930–6. The poetry, 2 vols. in 3 pts, New York, 1930, has variants in the texts issued in Milton's life and new trns.]

(3) POEMS
(a) Collected Poems

Poetical Works. Together with Explanatory Notes on Each Book of the Paradise Lost, and a Table never before Printed. Ed. P[atrick] H[ume], 5 pts, 1695. [Pbd also, without Hume's notes, with Paradise Regained and Samson Agonistes.]

Poetical Works. Paradise Lost. Seventh Edition. Paradise Regain'd. To which is added Samson Agonistes and Poems upon Several Occasions. Fourth Edition. 2 vols. 1705.

Poetical Works. 2 vols. 1707. [Includes P.L., 8th edn, vol. I; P.R., 5th edn, and Poems upon Several Occasions, 4th edn, vol. II.]

Poetical Works. 2 vols. 1720. [Includes Addison's essays and Of Education. Other edns, 1721 and 1727.]

[Poetical Works.] 2 vols. 1725. [Includes P.L., 12th edn, vol. I; P.R., S.A., Poems on Several Occasions, and Of Education, 6th edn, vol. II.]

[Poetical Works.] 2 vols. 1727. [Includes P.L., 13th edn, vol. I; P.R., S.A., and Poems on Several Occasions, 7th edn, vol. II.]

[Poetical Works.] 2 vols. 1730. [Includes P.L., 14th edn, vol. I; P.R., S.A., and Poems on Several Occasions, 7th edn, corrected, vol. II.]

Poetical Works. 2 vols. 1731. [Of Education in vol. II.]

[Poetical Works.] 3 vols. 1746–7. [Includes Fenton's Life and Of Education.]

[Poetical Works.] Ed. J. Hawkey, 2 vols. Dublin, 1747–52.

Poetical Works, with Notes of Various Authors. Ed. T. Newton, 3 vols. 1749–52.

[Poetical Works.] 2 vols. 1751. [Includes Of Education.]

[Poetical Works.] 2 vols. 1753. [Includes Of Education.]

[Poetical Works.] 2 vols. 1758. [Newton's text. Other edns, 1758, 1759, 1760, 1763, 1766.]

[Poetical Works.] 2 vols. Edinburgh, 1762. [With preface, glossary, and life. Another edn, 1767.]

Poetical Works. 4 vols. 1770, 1773.

[Poetical Works.] 4 vols. 1773. (British Poets.)

Poetical Works. 4 vols. 1776. [Newton's text, Addison's essays, and life.]

Poems. Ed. S. Johnson, 3 vols. 1779. (Works of the English Poets.)

Poetical Works. 2 vols. 1790.

Poetical Works. 3 vols. 1794–7. [Hayley's Life.]

[Poetical Works.] 2 vols. 1795 and 1796. [Fenton's Life and Johnson's criticism.]

Poetical Works. 2 vols. 1795 and 1796. [Newton's text, Addison's essays, and life.]

Poetical Works. Ed. J. Aikin, 3 vols. 1805.

Poetical Works. With the Principal Notes of Various Commentators. Ed. H. J. Todd, 6 vols. 1801; 7 vols. 1809 (with addns and a verbal index), 1826, 1834, and 1842. [Life in vol. I.]

Life and Poetical Works with Notes by William Cowper. Ed. W. Hayley, 4 vols. Chichester, 1810. [Includes trn of Andreini's Adamo.]

Poetical Works, with Notes of Various Authors; to Which Is Prefixed Newton's Life. Ed. E. Hawkins, 4 vols. 1824.

Poetical Works, with Cowper's Translations. 3 vols. 1826.

Poetical Works. Ed. J. Mitford, 3 vols. 1832. (Aldine Edition.)

Poetical Works. Ed. Sir S. E. Brydges, 6 vols. 1835.

Poetical Works. Ed. H. Stebbing, 1839.

Poetical Works of Milton, Thomson, and Young. Ed. H. F. Cary, 1841.

Poetical Works. With a Memoir by J. Montgomery, 2 vols. 1843.

Poetical Works. Ed. C. D. Cleveland, Philadelphia, 1853. [With verbal index.]

Poetical Works. Ed. G. Gilfillan, 2 vols. Edinburgh, 1853.

Poems. Ed. T. Keightley, 2 vols. 1859.

English Poems. Ed. R. C. Browne, 2 vols. 1866; 1894 (with notes by H. Bradley).

Poetical Works. Ed. D. Masson, 3 vols. 1874 and 1890 (rev. edn). [Also in Golden Treasury ser. 2 vols. 1874, and in Globe ser. 1877.]

Poetical Works. Ed. J. Bradshaw, 3 vols. 1878.

Complete Poetical Works. Ed. W. V. Moody, Boston, [1899]; 1924 (rev. edn, with new trns). (Cambridge Poets.)

The Cambridge Milton for Schools. Ed. A. W. Verity, 10 vols. Cambridge, 1891–6. [Rev. edn of P.L. 1910.] (Pitt Press ser.)

Poetical Works. Ed. H. C. Beeching, 1900.

Poetical Works. Ed. W. A. Wright, Cambridge, 1903.

Poetical Works. Ed. Sir W. Raleigh, 1905.

[Poetical Works.] Ed. Sir H. Newbolt, [1924].

The Poems of John Milton, Arranged in Chronological Order. Ed. H. J. C. Grierson, 2 vols. 1925.

Poems in English by John Milton, with Illustrations by William Blake. 2 vols. 1926.

(b) Selections

Poems of Mr. John Milton, both English and Latin, Compos'd at several times. Printed by his true Copies. 1645; photo. facs. 1924; type facs. Oxford, 1924.

Poems, &c. upon several occasions. By Mr. John Milton: Both English and Latin, &c. Composed at several times. With a small Tractate of Education to Mr. Hartlib. 1673.

L'Allegro and Il Penseroso. Glasgow, 1751.

Milton's Italian Poems translated and addressed to a gentleman of Italy. 1776. [Tr. J. Langhorne.]

Poems upon Several Occasions: English, Italian, and Latin, with Translations. Ed. T. Warton, 1785; 1791 (with addns).

Latin and Italian Poems of Milton Translated by W. Cowper. Ed. W. Hayley, 1808.

The Latin and Italian Poems. Tr. J. G. Strutt, 1814.

Sonnets. Ed. M. Pattison, 1883. [Other edns: A. Sampson, New York, 1886; A. W. Verity, Cambridge, 1895; J. S. Smart, with original notes and new biographical data, Glasgow, 1921; Bristol, 1929.]

Minor Poems. Ed. W. J. Rolfe, New York, 1887.

[Minor Poems.] Ed. O. Elton, 5 vols. Oxford, 1893–1900. [Il Penseroso, 1890; L'Allegro, 1893; Arcades and Sonnets, 1893; Comus, 1898; Lycidas, 1900.]

Facsimile of the Manuscript of Milton's Minor Poems Preserved in the Library of Trinity College. Ed. W. A. Wright, Cambridge, 1899.

Lyric and Dramatic Poems. Ed. M. W. Sampson, New York, 1901.

Minor English Poems. Ed. H. C. Beeching, 1903; 1923.

Milton: Poetry and Prose; with Essays by Johnson, Hazlitt, and Macaulay. Ed. B. G. Madan, Oxford, 1920.

Selections from the Prose and Poetry. Ed. J. H. Hanford, Boston, [1923].

Nativity Ode; Lycidas; Sonnets. Ed. W. Bell, New York, 1929.

The Latin Poems of John Milton. Ed. W. MacKellar, New Haven, 1930.

The Cambridge Manuscript of John Milton. Lycidas and Some of the Other Poems. Ed. photo. facs. F. A. Patterson, Facs. Text Soc. 1933.

Paradise Regained, the Minor Poems, and Samson Agonistes. Ed. M. Y. Hughes, New York, 1937.

(c) Separate Publications

An Epitaph on the Admirable Dramaticke Poet, W. Shakespeare. [Part of the introductory matter to the Second Folio, 1632. Written in 1630. Also in the Folios of 1664 and 1685, and in Shakespeare's Poems of 1640.]

Examen Poeticum Duplex. 1698. [Contains 4 of the early Latin poems.]

On the Morning of Christ's Nativity. With Illustrations by William Blake and a Note by G. Keynes. Cambridge, 1923.

A Maske Presented at Ludlow Castle, 1634: On Michaelmasse night, before the Right Honorable, John Earle of Bridgewater. 1637. [Edns by H. J. Todd, Canterbury, 1798, 1799; H. B. Sprague, New York, 1876; A. W. Verity, Cambridge, 1891; O. Elton, Oxford, 1893; ed. facs. New York, 1903; rptd type facs. Cambridge, 1906; Lady Alix Egerton, 1910; D. Figgis, 1926. Stage adaptations are listed in the bibliographies. Tr. Italian Polidori, 1802, and with notes, 1809.]

Lycidas. [In Justa Edouardo King naufrago, ab Amicis mœrentibus, amoris et μνείας χάριν, Cambridge, 1638; rptd Dublin, 1835, with entire volume; ed. C. S. Jerram, 1874; ed. O. Elton, 1893. Tr. Latin W. Hog, 1694, F. A. Paley, 1374; Greek J. Plumtre, Cambridge, 1797.]

Epitaphium Damonis. [1639?]; rptd (with trn) W. W. Skeat, Cambridge, 1933. [Unique copy in BM.]

[Sonnet to Henry Lawes.] [In Choice Psalmes, put into Musick for three voices. Compos'd by Henry and William Lawes, 1648.]

Paradise lost. A Poem Written in Ten Books By John Milton. Licensed and Entred according to Order. 1667. [On variations in the title-pages of copies dated 1667, 1668, and 1669 see Wright's edn of the Poetical Works, A. W. Pollard, Library, x, 1909, and the BM. catalogue.]

Paradise Lost. A Poem in Twelve Books. The Author John Milton. The Second Edition. Revised and Augmented by the same Author. 1674; 3rd edn, 1678; 4th edn (Bentley and Tonson), 1688; 5th edn (Tonson alone), 1691; 1692; 1695. [Pbd by Tonson with other poems from 1695: e.g. 1705 (7th edn of P.L.); 1720 (with Addison's essays); 1725 (with Fenton's Life); 1738 (15th edn of P.L.).]

Paradise Lost in Ten Books. The Text Exactly Reproduced from the First Edition of 1667. 1873.

Paradise Lost as Originally Published, being a Facsimile Reproduction of the First Edition. Introd. D. Masson, 1877.

30

The Manuscript of Milton's Paradise Lost, Book I. Ed. Helen Darbishire, Oxford, 1931. [MS in J. P. Morgan Lib. New York.]

[Paradise Lost has been ed. by: P. Hume, 1695; R. Bentley, 1732; T. Newton, 1749; Capel Lofft, Bury St. Edmunds, 1792; J. B. Williams, 1824; J. Prendeville, 1840; H. Stebbing, 1848; R. H. Shepherd, 1873; D. Masson, 1877; R. Vaughan, 1882; A. W. Verity, 1910; G. H. Cowling and H. F. Hallett, 1926; M. Y. Hughes, New York, 1935. Also in many collected edns of the poems as listed. Among the trns are: Latin (paraphrase), W. Hog, 1690; M. Bold, Bk I, 1702; J. Trapp, 1741; W. Dobson, 1750. French, Dupré de Saint Maur, 1729; L. Racine, 1775; J. Mosneron, 1787; J. de Lille, 1805; Chateaubriand, 1836; Pongerville, 1838. Swedish, Oxenstierna, 1815. Dutch, J. van Zanten, 1728; 1798–1811; ten Kate, 1875. German, Berge, 1682; Bodmer, 1732; Bürde, 1792; Pries, Bk I, 1807, and complete, 1813; Bruckbräu, 1828; Eitner, 1865. Italian, Rolli, 1735; Mariottini, 1796; Martinengo, 1801; Papi, 1811; Sorelli, 1820. Spanish, J. de Escoquiz, 1812; Juan Mateos, 1914. Portuguese, Targini, Paris, 1823. Hebrew, Salkinson, Vienna, 1871. Greek, Casdagli, 1887. Other trns are noted in the bibliographies listed.]

Paradise Regain'd. A Poem. In IV Books. To which is added Samson Agonistes. 1671 (for 1670); 2nd edn, 1680; 3rd edn, 1688 (uniform with Tonson's folio of P.L.).

Paradise Regained, Samson Agonistes, and Poems. Ed. T. Newton, 1752 (rptd eight times). [Other edns: C. Dunster, 1795; C. S. Jerram, 1877; W. H. D. Rouse, 1897; L. C. Martin, Oxford, 1925. A French trn, with other of Milton's poems, was pbd in 1730.]

Samson Agonistes. 1671 (pbd with Paradise Regained, with a separate title-page); 2nd edn, 1681; 3rd edn, 1688. [Edns: J. C. Collins, Oxford, 1883; C. S. Jerram, 1890; H. M. Percival, 1890; A. W. Verity, Cambridge, 1892; Sir E. K. Chambers, 1897; C. T. Onions, 1905.]

(4) PROSE
(a) Collected Prose

A Complete Collection of the Historical, Political, and Miscellaneous Works of Milton. 3 vols. 1694–8. [Ed. J. Toland. Second volume, Amsterdam = London.]

The Works of John Milton. 1697. [Prose.]

A Complete Collection of the Historical, Political, and Miscellaneous Works of John Milton, containing Several Original Papers of His never before Published. Ed. T. Birch, 2 vols. 1738 and 1753 (enlarged).

Prose Works. Ed. C. Symmons, 7 vols. 1806.

The Prose Works, with New Translations and an Introduction by G. Burnett. 2 vols. 1809.

Prose Works. Ed. R. Fletcher, 1833. [Index in 1838 edn.]

Prose Works. Ed. R. W. Griswold, 2 vols. Philadelphia, 1845.

Prose Works. Ed. J. A. St John, 5 vols. [1848]–81. (Bohn's Lib.)

Private Correspondence and Academic Exercises. Ed. and tr. P. B. and E. M. W. Tillyard, Cambridge, 1932.

(b) Selections

Weber, G. John Miltons prosaische Schriften über Kirche, Staat und öffentliches Leben seiner Zeit. Historisches Taschenbuch, 1852–3.

Autobiography of John Milton: or Milton's Life in His Own Words. Ed. J. G. Graham, 1872.

An Introduction to the Prose and Poetical Works of John Milton, Comprising All the Autobiographic Passages of His Works. Ed. H. Corson, 1899.

[Selections, ed. as follows: F. Jenks, Boston, 1826; Edinburgh, 1836; J. A. St John, 1836; S. Manning, 1862; J. G. Graham, 1870; R. Garnett, 1893; L. E. Lockwood, 1911; B. G. Madan, Oxford, 1920; M. W. Wallace, 1925 (World's Classics); W. Haller, 1927; C. E. Vaughan, 1927 (Everyman's Lib.).]

(c) Separate Publications

Of Reformation Touching Church Discipline In England: And the Causes that hitherto have hindered it; Two bookes, written to a Freind. [May,] 1641; ed. W. T. Hale, New Haven, 1916.

Of Prelatical Episcopacy, and Whither it may be deduc'd from the Apostolical times by vertue of those Testimonies which are alledg'd to that purpose in some late Treatises: One whereof goes under the Name of James Archbishop of Armagh. [June,] 1641.

Animadversions upon the Remonstrant's Defence, against Smectymnuus. [July,] 1641.

The Reason of Church-government Urg'd against Prelaty. By Mr. John Milton. In two Books. 1641. [Feb. 1642.]

An Apology Against a Pamphlet call'd A Modest Confutation of the Animadversions upon the Remonstrant against Smectymnuus. [March,] 1642.

The Doctrine and Discipline of Divorce: restor'd to the good of both sexes, From the bondage of Canon Law, and other mistakes, to Christian freedom, guided by the Rule of Charity. [Aug.] 1643.

The Doctrine and Discipline of Divorce: Restor'd to the good of both Sexes, From the bondage of Canon Law, and other mistakes, to the true meaning of Scripture in the Law and Gospel compar'd. Now the second time revis'd and much augmented. 1643. [Feb. 1644. With a signed introductory letter 'To the Parliament.' Twice rptd 1645.]

Of Education. To Master Samuel Hartlib. [No title-page. Licensing entry 4 June 1644.] Rptd 1673; ed. O. Browning, Cambridge, 1883; ed. E. E. Morris, 1895; ed. O. M. Ainsworth, New Haven, 1928.

The Judgement Of Martin Bucer, concerning Divorce. Writt'n to Edward the sixt, in his second Book of the Kingdom of Christ. And now Englisht. [July,] 1644. [Anon., but has Milton's name in the text.]

Areopagitica; A Speech of Mr. John Milton For the Liberty Of Unlicenc'd Printing, To the Parlament of England. [Nov.] 1644; ed. J. W. Hales, Oxford, 1882; ed. H. Morley, 1886; ed. J. R. Lowell, 1890; ed. R. C. Jebb, 1918; ed. W. Haller, 1927.

Tetrachordon: Expositions Upon the foure chief places in Scripture which treat of Mariage, or nullities in Mariage. By the former Author, J. M. [March,] 1645.

Colasterion: A Reply to A nameless answer against The Doctrine and Discipline of Divorce. By the former Author, J. M. [March,] 1645.

Observations upon the Articles of Peace with the Irish Rebels, on the letter of Ormond to Col. Jones, and the Representation of the Presbytery at Belfast. 1649.

The Tenure of Kings and Magistrates. The Author. J. M. [Feb.] 1649; ed. W. T. Allison, New York, 1911.

ΕΙΚΟΝΟΚΛΆΣΤΗΣ, In Answer to a Book Intitl'd ΕΊΚΩ'Ν ΒΑΣΙΛΙΚΗ', The Portrature of his Sacred Majesty in his Solitudes and Sufferings. The Author I. M. [Oct.] 1649.

ΕΙΚΟΝΟΚΛΆΣΤΗΣ, in Answer to a Book Intitl'd The Portrature of his Sacred Majesty in his Solitudes and Sufferings. Publish'd now the Second time, and much Enlarg'd. 1650; rptd Amsterdam [London], 1690.

Joannis Miltoni Angli Pro Populo Anglicano defensio, contra Claudii anonymi, alias Salmasii, Defensionem Regiam. 1650. [Before 25 March 1651. Six edns and a Dutch trn appeared during 1651.] Editio emendatior. 1651. Editio correctior et auctior, ab autore denuo recognita. 1658; tr. J. Washington, 1692.

A Letter written to a Gentleman in the Country, touching the Dissolution of the late Parliament and the Reasons thereof. 1653.

Joannis Miltoni Angli pro Populo Anglicano Defensio secunda. Contra infamem libellum anonymum cui titulus, Regii sanguinis clamor ad cœlum adversus parricidas Anglicanos. [May,] 1654; ed. G. Crantzius, Hague, 1654; tr. R. Fellowes, 1806, and F. Wrangham, 1816.

Joannis Miltoni pro se Defensio contra Alexandrum Morum Ecclesiasten Libelli famosi, cui titulus, Regii sanguinis clamor ad cœlum adversus Parricidas Anglicanos, authorem recte dictum. 1655.

Scriptum dom. Protectoris contra Hispanos. [26 Oct. 1655.] 1655; tr. [James Thomson?] 1738.

Literae ab Olivaro protectore ad sacram regiam majestatem Sueciae. 1656.

A Treatise of Civil power in Ecclesiastical causes; shewing that it is not lawfull for any power on earth to compell in matters of religion. The author J. M. [Feb.] 1659.

Considerations touching the likeliest means to remove Hirelings out of the Church. The author J. M. [Aug.] 1659; rptd 1839.

Brief Notes upon a late Sermon, Titl'd, The Fear of God and the King; Preach'd, and sinc Publish'd, By Matthew Griffith, D.D. and Chaplain to the late King. 1660.

The Present Means and Brief Delineation of a Free Commonwealth, easy to be put in Practice and without Delay, in a letter to General Monk. 1660.

The Readie and Easie Way to Establish a Free Commonwealth, and the Excellence thereof Compar'd with the inconveniences and dangers of readmitting kingship in this nation. The author J. M. [Feb.–April,] 1660; ed. E. M. Clark, New Haven, 1915.

Accedence Commenc't Grammar, Supply'd with Sufficient Rules for the use of such as, Younger or Elder, are desirous, without more trouble than needs, to attain the Latin tongue. By John Milton. 1669.

The History of Britain, That Part especially now call'd England. 1670; ed. F. Maseres, 1818.

Joannis Miltoni Angli, Artis Logicae plenior Institutio, ad Petri Rami Methodum Concinnata. Adjecta est Praxis Annalytica et Petri Rami Vita. Libris duobus. 1672.

Of True Religion, Hæresie, Schism, Toleration, And what best means may be us'd against the growth of Popery. The Author J.M. 1673.

A Declaration. Or Letters Patents of the Election of this present King of Poland, John the Third, Elected on the 22nd of May, last past, Anno Dom. 1674. Now faithfully translated from the Latin Copy. 1674.

Joannis Miltoni Angli, Epistolarum Familiarum Liber Unus: Quibus accesserunt, Ejusdem, jam olim in Collegio Adolescentis,

Prolusiones Quaedam Oratoriae. 1674; tr. J. Hall, Philadelphia, 1829.

Literae Pseudo-Senatus Anglicani, Cromwellii reliquorumque Perduellium nomine ac jussu conscriptae a Joanne Miltono. 1676; 1690.

Mr. John Milton's Character of the Long Parliament and Assembly of Divines. In MDCXLI. Omitted in his other Works, and never before Printed, And very seasonable for these times. 1681; rptd Harleian Misc. vol. v, 1810.

A Brief History of Moscovia and of other less known Countries lying eastward of Russia as far as Cathay. By John Milton. 1682; ed. Prince D. S. Mirsky, 1929.

Milton's Republican Letters, or a Collection of such as were written by command of the late Commonwealth of England. 1682.

Letters of State, Written by Mr. John Milton. From the year 1649 Till the year 1659. To Which is added, An Account of his Life [by E. Phillips]. Together with several of his Poems; And a Catalogue of his Works, never before Printed. 1694; ed. H. Fernow, Hamburg, 1903.

A Discourse on the Harmony of the Spheres as delivered in a Latin thesis by Mr. J. Milton; and translated [by F. Peck]. 1740.

Original Letters and Papers of State addressed to Oliver Cromwell concerning the affairs of Great Britain from the year 1649 to 1658. Ed. J. Nickolls, 1743.

Joannis Miltoni Angli de Doctrina Christiana Libri Duo Posthumi, quos ex schedis manuscriptis deprompsit et typis mandari primus curavit C. R. Sumner. 1825; tr. C. R. Sumner, 1825.

Last Thoughts on the Trinity, extracted from A Treatise on Christian Doctrine. 1828.

Original Papers, Illustrative of the Life and Writings of John Milton, Including Sixteen Letters of State Written by Him. Now First Published. Ed. W. D. Hamilton, Camden Soc. 1859.

A Common-place Book of John Milton. Reproduced by the Autotype Process. Ed. A. J. Horwood, 1876, Camden Soc. 1876, and 1877 (rev. edn).

(5) BIOGRAPHY AND CRITICISM

(a) Books

Hall, J. A Humble Remonstrance. 1641.

Smectymnuus. A Modest Confutation of a Slanderous and Scurrilous Libell, entituled Animadversions. 1642.

Du Moulin, P. Regii Sanguinis Clamor ad Coelum adversus Parricidas Anglicanos. Hague, 1652 and 1653.

Filmer, Sir R. Observations concerning the Originall of Government upon Mr. Hobs Leviathan, Mr. Milton against Salmasius, etc. 1652.

Harrington, J. The Censure of the Rota upon Mr Milton's Book entitled The Ready and Easie Way. 1660; rptd Harleian Misc. vol. iv, 1809.

Salmasius, C. de. Claudii Salmasii ad Johannem Miltonum Responsio. Dijon, 1660.

A Proclamation for calling in and suppressing of Two Books written by John Milton; the one intituled Johannis Miltoni Angli, pro Populo Anglicano Defensio, and the other Εικονοκλάστης. 13 Aug. 1660. (Thomason Tracts.)

[L'Estrange, R.] No Blind Guides, in Answer to a Seditious Pamphlet of J. Milton's intituled Brief Notes upon a Late Sermon titl'd, the Fear of God and the King. 1660.

Phillips, E. Theatrum poetarum Anglicanorum. 1675; ed. Sir S. E. Brydges, 1800.

Toland, J. The Life of Milton. 1699; 1761; rptd Cleveland, 1924 (with E. Fenton's Life).

—— Amyntor, or a Defence of Milton's Life. 1699; 1761.

Addison, J. [Notes upon the Twelve Books of Paradise Lost.] Spectator, 5 Jan.–3 May 1712.

Ellwood, T. The History of the Life of. 1714; ed. C. G. Crump, 1900; ed. S. Graveson, 1906.

Clarke, S. Some Reflections on That Part of a Book called Amyntor, or the Defence of Milton's Life, Which Relates to the Writings of the Primitive Fathers. 1731.

[Routh, B.] Lettres critiques sur le Paradis Perdu, et Reconquis de Milton. 1731.

Bentley, R. Dr. Bentley's emendations on the twelve books of Paradise Lost. 1732.

Meadowcourt, R. A Critique on Milton's Paradise Regained. 1732.

—— A Critical Dissertation with Notes, on Paradise Regained. 1748.

Pearce, Z. A Review of the Text of Milton's Paradise Lost. 1732 and 1733. [On Bentley's edn.]

Richardson, J. (father and son). Explanatory Notes and Remarks on Milton's Paradise Lost. 1734.

Bodmer, J. J. Critische Abhandlung von dem Wunderbaren in der Poesie in einer Vertheidigung des Gedichtes J. Miltons von dem verlohrnen Paradiese. Zürich, 1740.

Peck, F. New Memoirs of the Life and Poetical Works of Mr. John Milton. 1740.

Richardson, R. Zoilomastix; or a Vindication of Milton from the Charges of W. Lauder. 1747.

Lauder, W. An Essay on Milton's Use and Imitation of the Moderns in his Paradise Lost. 1750.

—— A Letter to the Rev. Mr. Douglas, Occasioned by His Vindication of Milton. 1751.

—— Delectus Auctorum sacrorum Miltono facem praelucentium. 1752.

Douglas, J. Milton Vindicated from the Charge of Plagiarism Brought against Him by Mr. Lauder. 1751.

Neve, P. A Note on the Disinterment of Milton's Coffin. 1770.

Johnson, S. Lives of the Poets. 4 vols. 1781. [Milton's Life, ed. Sir C. H. Firth, Oxford, 1888. In complete edn of G. B. Hill and H. S. Scott, 3 vols. Oxford, 1905, etc.]

Darby, S. A Letter to T. Warton, on His Late Edition of Milton's Juvenile Poems. 1785.

Burney, C. Remarks on the Greek Verses of Milton. [1790.]

D'Israeli, I. Curiosities of Literature. 7 vols. 1791–1834. [Milton items *passim*.]

Dunster, C. Considerations on Milton's Early Reading and the Prima Stamina of His Paradise Lost. 1800.

Mosneron, J. Vie de Milton. Paris, 1804.

Mortimer, C. E. An Historical Memoir of the Poetical Life of John Milton. 1805.

Todd, H. J. Some Account of the Life and Writings of John Milton. 1809. [Vol. i. of Poetical Works.]

Aubrey, J. Brief Lives. 2 vols. 1813; ed. A. Clark, Oxford, 1890.

à Wood, A. Fasti Oxonienses. Ed. P. Bliss, vol. i, 1815, pp. 480–6.

Godwin, W. Lives of Edward and John Philips. To Which Are Added: i. Collections for the Life of Milton by John Aubrey; ii. The Life of Milton. By Edward Philips. 1815.

Scolari, F. Saggio di Critica sul Paradiso Perduto. Venice, 1818.

Landor, W. S. Imaginary Conversations. 5 vols. 1824–9; ed. C. G. Crump, 1891.

—— Last Fruit off an Old Tree. 1853.

Channing, W. E. Remarks on the Character and Writings of John Milton. Boston, 1826.

Cann, C. A Scriptural and Allegorical Glossary to Milton's Paradise Lost. [1828.]

Ivimey, J. John Milton, His Life and Times, Religious and Political Opinions. 1833.

Brydges, Sir S. E. Milton. [1835.]

Coleridge, S. T. Literary Remains. 2 vols. 1836.

—— Seven Lectures on Shakespeare and Milton. Ed. J. P. Collier, 1856.

Geoffroy, A. Étude sur les Pamphlets politiques et religieux de Milton. Paris, 1848.

Hunter, J. Milton. A Sheaf of Gleanings after His Biographers and Annotators. 1850.

Marsh, J. F. Papers Connected with the Affairs of Milton and His Family. Chetham Soc. Misc. 1851.

—— Notice of the Inventory of the Effects of Mrs. Milton, Widow of the Poet. Liverpool, 1855.

—— On the Engraved Portraits and Pretended Portraits of Milton. Liverpool, 1860.

De Quincey, T. Collected Works. 16 vols. 1853–60. [Vol. vi, pp. 31–52; vol. x, pp. 79–98. Based on pbns in Blackwood's Mag. in 1842.]

Masson, D. Essays: Biographical and Critical. Cambridge, 1856.

—— The Life of John Milton: Narrated in Connexion with the Political, Ecclesiastical, and Literary History of His Time. 7 vols. 1859–94. [Vol. i, rev. 1881.]

des Essarts, E. De veterum poetarum tum Graeciae, tum Romae apud Miltonem imitatione. Paris, 1858.

Hamilton, W. D. Original Papers Illustrative of the Life and Writings of John Milton. Camden Soc. 1859.

Keightley, T. Life, Opinions, and Writings of John Milton. 1859.

Liebert, G. Milton. Studien zur Geschichte des englischen Geistes. Hamburg, 1860.

Lotheissen, F. Studien über John Miltons poetische Werke. Budingen, 1860.

Macaulay, T. B. Miscellaneous Writings. 1860. [Imaginary conversation of Cowley and Milton.]

Sotheby, S. L. Ramblings in the Elucidation of the Autograph of Milton. 1861.

Scherer, E. Études critiques sur la Littérature contemporaine. Paris, 1863–5; tr. Eng. 1891.

Wiese, L. Miltons Verlorenes Paradies. Berlin, 1863.

von Treitschke, H.. Milton. Historische und politische Aufsätze. Leipzig, 1865, pp. 69–122.

de Guerle, E. Milton, sa Vie et ses Œuvres. Paris, 1868.

Pauli, R. Aufsätze zur englischen Geschichte. Leipzig, 1869.

Jebb, R. C. Milton's Areopagitica. A Commentary. [1872.]

Münch, W. Die Entstehung des Verlorenen Paradieses. Cleve, 1874.

Lowell, J. R. Milton. [In Among My Books, ser. 2, Boston, 1876.]

Stern, A. Milton und seine Zeit. 2 vols. Leipzig, 1877–9.

Arnold. M. Mixed Essays. 1879.

—— Essays in Criticism. Ser. 2, 1888.

Bagehot, W. Milton. [In Literary Studies, 2 vols. 1879.]

Brooke, S. A. Milton. 1879. (Classical Writers.)

Gosse, Sir E. Studies in the Literature of Northern Europe. 1879. [Vondel and Milton.]

Pattison, M. Milton. 1879. (English Men of Letters Ser.)

Hodgson, S. H. Outcast Essays. 1881.

Ademello, A. La Leonora di Milton e di Clemente IX. Milan, [1885].

Edmundson, G. Milton and Vondel. 1885.

Birrell, A. Obiter Dicta. Ser 2, 1887.

Dowden, E. Transcripts and Studies. 1888.

—— Puritan and Anglican: Studies in Literature. 1900.

Garnett, R. Life of John Milton. 1890. [Bibliography by J. P. Anderson.]

Jenny, G. Miltons Verlorenes Paradies in der deutschen Literatur des 18. Jahrhunderts. St Gallen, 1890.

Meyer, J. B. Miltons pädagogische Schriften und Aüsserungen. Langensalza, 1890.

Criticisms on Paradise Lost. Ed. A. S. Cook, Boston, 1892.

Rost, W. Die Orthographie der ersten Quarto-ausgabe von Miltons 'Paradise Lost.' Leipzig, 1892.

Schlesinger, A. Der Natursinn bei John Milton. Leipzig, 1892.

Bridges, Robert. Milton's Prosody. Oxford, 1893. [Rev. edn, 1901; with A Chapter on Accentual Verse, and Notes, 1921.]

Hales, J. W. Folia Literaria. 1893.

Hübler, F. Milton und Klopstock mit besonderer Berücksichtigung des 'Paradise Lost' und des Messias. Reichenberg, 1893–5.

Vodoz, J. An Essay on the Prose of John Milton. Zürich, 1895.

Gurteen, S. H. The Epic of the Fall of Man. A Comparative Study of Caedmon, Dante, and Milton. New York, 1896.

Orchard, T. N. The Astronomy of Paradise Lost. 1896; 1913 (rev. edn).

Masterman, J. H. The Age of Milton. 1897.

Trent, W. P. John Milton: a Short Study of his Life and Works. New York, 1899.

Osgood, C. G. The Classical Mythology of Milton's English Poems. New York, 1900.

Raleigh, Sir Walter. Milton. 1900.

Scott, A. M. Über das Verhältnis von Drydens 'State of Innocence' zu Miltons 'Paradise Lost.' Halle, 1900.

Brown, G. D. Syllabification and Accent in the Paradise Lost. Baltimore, 1901.

Scheifers, B. On the Sentiment for Nature in Milton's Poetical Works. Eisleben, 1901.

Thomas, W. De epico apud Joannem Miltonium Versu. Paris, 1901.

Scrocca, A. Studio critico sul Paradiso Perduto del Milton. Naples, [1902].

Downing, J. Testimonies and Criticisms relating to the Life and Works of John Milton. St Austell, 1903.

Buff, F. Miltons 'Paradise Lost' in seinem Verhältnisse zur Aeneide, Ilias, und Odyssee. Munich, 1904.

Telleen, J. M. Milton dans la Littérature française. Paris, 1904.

Collins, J. C. Miltonic Myths and their Authors. [In Studies in Poetry and Criticism, 1905.]

Williamson, G. C. Milton. 1905.

Allodoli, E. Giovanni Milton e l'Italia. Prato, 1907.

Woodhull, M. The Epic of Paradise Lost: Twelve Essays. New York, 1907.

Papers Read at the Milton Centenary, 1908. British Academy Proc. III, 1907–8. [Papers by Sir F. Bridge, O. Elton, W. J. Courthope, E. Dowden, Sir C. H. Firth, R. C. Jebb, A. F. Leach, G. Meredith, J. G. Robertson, Sir A. W. Ward.]

Milton Memorial Lectures, 1908. Ed. P. W. Ames, 1909. [Essays by G. C. Williamson, W. H. Hadow, E. H. Coleridge, W. E. A. Axon, E. H. Pember, G. Saintsbury, H. G. Rosedale, E. Dowden, Sir Edward Braybrook, A. Vambéry.]

Chauvet, P. La Religion de Milton. Paris, 1909.

Hudson, W. H. Milton and his Poetry. 1909.

Morton, E. P. The Technique of English Non-dramatic Blank Verse. Chicago, 1910.

Gajšek, S. Milton und Caedmon. Leipzig, 1911.

Saintsbury, G. Milton. CHEL. vol. VII, 1911.

Visser, M. Miltons Prosawerken. Rotterdam, 1911.

Hübener, G. Die stilistische Spannung in Miltons 'Paradise Lost.' Halle, 1913.

Sampson, A. Studies in Milton. New York, 1913.

Spaeth, S. G. Milton's Knowledge of Music. Weimar, 1913.

Bailey, M. L. Milton and Jakob Boehme: a Study of German Mysticism in Seventeenth-Century England. New York, 1914.

Pizzo, E. Milton's Verlorenes Paradies im deutschen Urteile des 18. Jahrhunderts. Berlin, 1914.

Thompson, E. N. S. Essays on Milton. New Haven, 1914.

Bailey, J. C. Milton. 1915.

Good, J. W. Studies in the Milton Tradition. Urbana, 1915.

Baker, A. T. Milton and Chateaubriand. Manchester, 1919.

Liljegren, S. B. Studies in Milton. Lund, 1919.

Lindelöf, U. Milton. Helsingfors, 1920.

Mutschmann, H. Der andere Milton. Bonn, 1920.

Mutschmann, H. Studies concerning the Origin of Paradise Lost. Dorpat, 1924.
—— Further Studies concerning the Origin of Paradise Lost. Dorpat, 1934.
Saurat, D. Blake and Milton. Bordeaux, 1920.
—— La Pensée de Milton. Paris, 1920.
—— Milton: Man and Thinker. New York, 1925.
—— Milton et le Matérialisme chrétien en Angleterre. Paris, 1928.
Havens, R. D. The Influence of Milton on English Poetry. Cambridge, U.S.A. 1922.
Douady, J. La Création et le Fruit défendu selon Milton. Paris, 1923.
Visiak, E. H. Milton Agonistes; a Metaphysical Criticism. 1923.
Candy, H. C. H. Some Newly-discovered Stanzas Written by John Milton on Engraved Scenes Illustrating Ovid's Metamorphoses. 1924.
Herford, C. H. Dante and Milton. Manchester, 1924.
Langdon, I. Milton's Theory of Poetry and Fine Art. New Haven, 1924.
Schirmer, W. F. Antike, Renaissance und Puritanismus. Munich, 1924.
Hanford, J. H. Samson Agonistes and Milton in Old Age. [In Studies in Shakespeare, Milton, and Donne, New York, 1925.]
—— A Milton Handbook. New York, 1926, 1933 (rev.).
Fletcher, H. F. Milton's Semitic Studies and Some Manifestations of them in his Poetry. Chicago, 1926.
—— Grierson's Suggested Date for Milton's Ad Patrem. [In Scott Anniversary Papers, Chicago, 1929.]
—— The Use of the Bible in Milton's Prose. Urbana, 1930.
—— Milton's Rabbinical Readings. Urbana, 1930.
Kreipe, C. E. Milton's Samson Agonistes. Halle, 1926.
Larson, M. A. The Modernity of Milton. Chicago, 1927.
Stevens, D. H. Milton Papers. Chicago, 1927.
Albrecht, W. Über das Theatrum Poetarum von Miltons Neffen Edward Phillips. Leipzig, 1928.
Agar, H. Milton and Plato. Princeton, 1928.
Smith, R. M. The Variant Issues of Shakespeare's Second Folio and Milton's First Published Poem; a Bibliographical Problem. Bethlehem, Pennsylvania, 1928.
Ullrich, H. Deutsche Milton-Übersetzungen vom 18. Jahrhundert bis zur Gegenwart. Stuttgart, 1928.
Stoll, E. E. Poets and Playwrights: Shakespeare, Jonson, Spenser, Milton. Minneapolis, 1930.

Tillyard, E. M. W. Milton. 1930.
—— Milton: L'Allegro and Il Penseroso. English Ass. Lecture, 1932.
Grierson, H. J. C. A Note upon the Samson Agonistes of Milton and Samson of 'Heilige Wraeck' by Vondel. [In Mélanges à Baldensperger, Paris, 1930.]
Oras, A. Milton's Editors and Commentators from Patrick Hume to Henry John Todd (1695–1801). Dorpat, 1931.
Bush, D. Mythology and the Renaissance Tradition in English Poetry. Minneapolis, 1932.
Darbishire, H. The Early Lives of Milton. 1932. [Rpts of the 6 early lives.]
Raymond, D. N. Oliver's Secretary: John Milton in an Era of Revolt. New York, 1932.
Scherpbier, H. Milton in Holland. Amsterdam, 1933.
Brown, Eleanor G. Milton's Blindness. New York, 1934.
Macaulay, Rose. Milton. 1934.
Taylor, G. C. Milton's Use of Du Bartas. Cambridge, U.S.A. 1934.
Belloc, H. Milton. 1935.
Empson, W. Milton and Bentley. [In Some Versions of Pastoral, 1935.]

(b) Articles in Periodicals

Barker, E. H. Error in Milton's Latinity Noticed. Classical Journ. VII, 1812.
Macaulay, T. B. Milton. Edinburgh Rev. LXXXIV, 1825.
Channing, W. E. Remarks on the Character and Writings of John Milton; Occasioned by the Publication of Christian Doctrine. Christian Examiner (Boston), III, 1826.
Emerson, R. W. Milton. North American Rev. XLVII, 1838. [Rptd in Essays from North American Review, New York, 1879.]
De Quincey, T. Life of Milton. Blackwood's Mag. XLVI, 1839.
Masson, D. The Three Devils: Luther's, Milton's, and Goethe's. Fraser's Mag. XXX, 1844.
Clarke, H. Milton's Genealogy. N. & Q. 19 March 1859.
A Miltonic Controversy. [Newspaper cuttings dealing with a poem entitled An Epitaph, attrib. to Milton by H. Morley, 1868.] [BM. 11826 . k . 16.]
Owen, R. Milton and Galileo. Fraser's Mag. LXXIX, 1869.
Bayne, P. John Milton. Contemporary Rev. XXII, 1873.
Symonds, J. A. The Blank Verse of Milton. Fortnightly Rev. XXII, 1874.
Axon, W. E. A. Milton's Comus and Fletcher's Faithful Shepherdess. Manchester, 1882.

Edmundson, G. Milton and Vondel. Academy, 31 Oct., 21 Nov. 1885.

Harris, H. Was Paradise Lost Suggested by the Mystery Plays? MLN. x, 1895.

Kuhns, O. Dante's Influence on Milton. MLN. XIII, 1898.

Gosse, Sir E. The Milton Manuscripts at Trinity. Atlantic Monthly, LXXXV, 1900.

Stephen, Sir L. New Lights on Milton. Quarterly Rev. CXCIV, 1901.

Parsons, E. S. The Earliest Life of Milton. EHR. XVII, 1902.

Neilson, W. A. Nova Solyma: a Romance Attributed to Milton. MP. I, 1903–4. [On W. Begley's edn, 2 vols. 1902.]

Cooper, L. The Abyssinian Paradise in Coleridge and Milton. MP. III, 1906.

Münch, W. Ein italienischer Vorgänger Miltons. Neueren Sprachen, XIII, 1906.

Thomas, W. Milton's Heroic Line Viewed from an Historical Viewpoint. MLR. II, III, 1907–8.

—— Le Sentiment de la Nature dans Milton. Revue germanique, VII, 1911.

Christ's College Mag. XXIII, 1908. [Milton Tercentenary. Contributions by E. J. Dent. C. R. Fay, J. W. Hales, J. W. Mackail, J. Peile, C. Sayle, W. W. Skeat, T. N. Toller.]

Cook, A. S. Notes on Milton's Ode on the Morning of Christ's Nativity. Trans. Connecticut Academy of Arts and Sciences, xv, 1909.

Havens, R. D. The Early Reputation of Paradise Lost. E. Studien, XL, 1909.

Hanford, J. H. The Pastoral Elegy and Milton's Lycidas. PMLA. xxv, 1910.

—— The Dramatic Element in Paradise Lost. Stud. Phil. XIV, 1917.

—— The Temptation Motive in Milton. Stud. Phil. xv, 1918.

—— Milton and the Return to Humanism. Stud. Phil. XVI, 1919.

—— The Date of Milton's De Doctrina Christiana. Stud. Phil. XVII, 1920.

—— The Arrangement and Order of Milton's Sonnets. MP. XVIII, 1921.

—— The Chronology of Milton's Private Studies. PMLA. XXXVI, 1921.

—— Milton and the Art of War. Stud. Phil. XVIII, 1921.

—— The Manuscript of Paradise Lost. MP. xxv, 1928.

Jones, S. K. The Authorship of Nova Solyma. Library, I, 1910.

Kittredge, G. L. Milton and Roger Williams. MLN. xxv, 1910.

Lockwood, L. E. Milton's Corrections to the Minor Poems. MLN. xxv, 1910.

Roberts, W. W. Chateaubriand and Milton. MLR. v, 1910.

Erskine, J. The Theme of Death in Paradise Lost. PMLA. XXXII, 1917.

Greenlaw, E. A Better Teacher than Aquinas. Stud. Phil. XIV, 1917.

—— Spenser's Influence on Paradise Lost. Stud. Phil. XVII, 1920.

Ramsay, R. L. Morality Themes in Milton's Poetry. Stud. Phil. xv, 1918.

Thompson, E. N. S. Milton's Of Education. Stud. Phil. xv, 1918.

—— Milton's Prose Style. PQ. XIV, 1935.

Gilbert, A. H. The Cambridge Manuscript and Milton's Plans for an Epic. Stud. Phil. XVI, 1919.

—— Milton and the Mysteries. Stud. Phil. XVII, 1920.

—— The Problem of Evil in Paradise Lost. JEGP. XXII, 1923.

Stevens, D. H. The Order of Milton's Sonnets. MP. XVII, 1919.

Glicksman, H. Lowell on Milton's Areopagitica. MLN. xxxv, 1920.

—— The Sources of Milton's History of Britain. Wisconsin University Stud. XI, 1920.

Sherburn, G. W. The Early Popularity of Milton's Minor Poems. MP. XVII, 1919–20.

Liljegren, S. B. Bemerkungen zur Biographie Miltons. E. Studien, LIV, 1920.

Fischer, W. Der alte und der neue Milton. Germanisch-romanische Monatsschrift, x, 1922.

Rand, E. K. Milton in Rustication. Stud. Phil. XIX, 1922.

Madan, F. F. Milton, Salmasius and Dugard. Library, IV, 1923.

Bredvold, L. I. Milton and Bodin's Heptaplomeres. Stud. Phil. XXI, 1924.

Larson, M. A. The Influence of Milton's Divorce Tracts on Farquhar's Beaux Stratagem. PMLA. XXXIX, 1924.

Nicolson, M. H. The Spirit World of Milton and More. Stud. Phil. XXII, 1925.

—— Milton and Hobbes. Stud. Phil. XXIII, 1926.

—— Milton and the Conjectura Cabbalistica. PQ. VI, 1927.

—— Milton and the Telescope. ELH. II, 1935.

Saurat, D. Milton and the King's Prayer. RES. I, 1925.

Thaler, A. The Shakesperian Element in Milton. PMLA. XL, 1925.

Garrod, H. W. Milton's Lines on Shakespeare. E. & S. XII, 1926.

Peers, E. A. Milton in Spain. Stud. Phil. XXIII, 1926.

Haller, W. Before Areopagitica. PMLA. XLII, 1927.

Magoun, F. P. The Chaucer of Spenser and Milton. MP. xxv, 1927.

Moore, C. A. Miltoniana (1679–1741). MP. xxiv, 1927.

Fletcher, H. F. Milton and Rashi. JEGP. xxvii, 1928.

—— Nathaniel Lee and Milton. MLN. xliv, 1929.

—— Milton and Ben Gerson. JEGP. xxix, 1930.

Grierson, H. J. C. John Milton. Criterion, vii, 1928.

Martin, B. The Date of Milton's First Marriage. Stud. Phil. xxv, 1928.

Baldwin, E. C. Some Extra-Biblical Semitic Influences upon Milton's Story of the Fall of Man. JEGP. xxviii, 1929.

Helsztyński, S. Milton in Poland. Stud. Phil. xxvi, 1929.

Riley, E. H. Milton's Tribute to Vergil. Stud. Phil. xxvi, 1929.

Siebert, T. Wahrheit und Wahrhaftigkeit bei Milton. E. Studien, lxiv, 1929.

—— Untersuchungen über Miltons Kunst vom psychologischen Standpunkt aus. Ang. liv, 1930.

—— Egozentrisches in Miltons Schreibweise mit besonderer Berücksichtigung des Satan in 'Paradise Lost.' Ang. lv, 1931.

Blunden, E. Milton and the New Consciousness. Nation and Athenaeum, 26 April 1930.

Dorian, D. C. Milton's 'two-handed engine.' PMLA. xlv, 1930.

Dustoor, P. E. Legends of Lucifer in Early English and in Milton. Ang. liv, 1930.

Read, A. W. Disinterment of Milton's Remains. PMLA. xlv, 1930.

Sorsby, Arnold. On the Nature of Milton's Blindness. British Journ. of Ophthalmology, xiv, 1930.

Bush, D. Notes on Milton's Classical Mythology. Stud. Phil. xxviii, 1931.

Whaler, J. The Miltonic Simile. PMLA. xlvi, 1931.

Wright, B. A. Milton's First Marriage. MLR. xxvi, xxvii, 1931–2.

Candy, H. C. H. Milton's Autographs. Library, xiii, 1932.

Lewis, C. S. A Note on Comus. RES. viii, 1932.

Stoll, E. E. Milton a Romantic. RES. viii, 1932.

Darbishire, H. The Chronology of Milton's Handwriting. Library, xiv, 1933.

Wilmer, W. H. The Blindness of Milton. JEGP. xxxii, 1933.

French, J. M. A New Letter by John Milton. PMLA. xlix, 1934.

—— An Action against Milton. TLS. 21 Dec. 1935, 14 March 1936.

Leavis, F. R. Milton's Verse. Scrutiny, ii, 1934.

Sewell, A. Milton's De Doctrina Christiana. E. & S. xix, 1934.

Wolfe, D. M. Milton, Lilburne, and the People. MP. xxxi, 1934.

Kelley, M. Milton and the Third Person of the Trinity. Stud. Phil. xxxii, 1935.

—— Milton's Debt to Wolleb's Compendium Theologiae Christianae. PMLA. l, 1935.

Parker, W. R. Some Problems in the Chronology of Milton's Early Poems. RES. xi, 1935.

Parsons, E. S. The Authorship of the Anonymous Life of Milton. PMLA. l, 1935.

Williamson, G. Milton and the Mortalist Heresy. Stud. Phil. xxxii, 1935.

Wyld, H. C. The Significance of -'n and -en in Milton's Spelling. E. Studien, lxx, 1935.

D. H. S.

VII. MINOR JACOBEAN AND CAROLINE VERSE, 1603–1660

[In this list (*Saintsbury*) printed after any title indicates that the work in question will be found in Minor Poets of the Caroline Period, ed. G. Saintsbury, 3 vols. Oxford, 1905, 1906, 1921. The following omissions should be noted: Miscellanies (listed pp. 403–5 above); Epigrammatists and Formal Satirists (pp. 479 ff. below); Song-Books (pp. 481–6 below); Scottish Poetry (pp. 896–900 below). Cross references have also not been entered to the popular verse which is listed in the sections on Pamphleteers and Miscellaneous Writers (pp. 704–12 below) and Minor Popular Literature (pp. 712–21 below), and to versifications of the Psalms (pp. 677–9 below). The poetical works listed here are the more important poems and collections of their authors and do not always represent the whole of their poetic output.]

JOHN ABBOT

Jesus praefigured; or a Poeme of the Holy Name. 1623.

CHARLES ALEYN (d. 1640)

The Battailes of Crescey, and Poictiers. 1631.
The historie of Henrie the Seventh. 1638.

JOHN ANDREWES

The Anatomie of Basenesse. 1615; ed. A. B. Grosart, Fuller Worthies' Misc. vol. ii, 1871.

JOHN AUSTIN (1613–1669)

Devotions in the Antient Way of Offices. Paris, 1668; ed. R. F. Littledale, 1869. [Includes hymns.]

ROBERT AYLETT (1583–1655?)

Divine and Moral Speculations. 1654.
Devotions. 1655.
[See Huntington Lib. Bulletin, Oct. 1936.]

SIR ROBERT AYTON (OR AYTOUN) (1570–1638)
Poems. Bannatyne Misc. vol. I, 1827; ed.
C. Rogers, 1871 (adds memoir and Latin
poems).

THOMAS BANCROFT

The Gluttons Feaver. 1633.
Two Bookes of Epigrammes and Epitaphs.
1639.
The Heroical Lover or Antheon and Fidelta.
1658.
[See W. Charvat, PMLA. XLVII, 1932, pp.
753–8.]

WILLIAM BARKSTED

Mirrha the Mother of Adonis. 1607.
Hiren. 1611.
Poems. Ed. A. B. Grosart, 1876.

ROBERT BARON (1630–after 1655)

'ΕΡΟΤΟΠΑΙΓΝΙΟΝ or the Cyprian Academy.
1647 (re-issued 1648). [A romance; prose
and verse.]
Pocula Castalia. 1650.
[For Baron's dramatic works see p. 640
below. See also K. C. Slagle, Robert Baron,
Cavalier Poet, N. & Q. 12 Oct. 1935.]

ROBERT BARRET

The Sacred Warr. [MS in Bodleian. Written
1603–6.]
[For Barret's Theorike of Warres see p. 390
above.]

WILLIAM BASSE

Sword and Buckler. 1602.
Three Pastoral Elegies. 1602.
Great Brittaines Sunnes-set. Oxford, 1613;
rptd facs. Oxford, 1872.
The Pastorals and Other Workes. Ed. J. P.
Collier, Oxford, 1870. [Prepared for pbn
1653, but not ptd.]
Works. Ed. R. W. Bond, 1893.

SIR JOHN BEAUMONT (1583–1627)

Bosworth Field, with a Taste of the Varitey of
other Poems. 1629; 1710; rptd A. Chalmers
(English Poets, vol. VI, 1810); ed. A. B.
Grosart, 1869 (Fuller Worthies Lib.)

JOSEPH BEAUMONT (1616–1699)

Psyche, or Love's Mysterie, displaying the
Intercourse betwixt Christ and the Soule.
1648; 1651; ed. C. Beaumont, Cambridge,
1702 (with corrections and 4 new cantos).
Original Poems in English and Latin. Ed. J. G.
[probably John Gee], Cambridge, 1749.
[Selection.]
Poems. Ed. A. Chalmers (English Poets, vol.
VI, 1810).

Poetical Works. Ed. A. B. Grosart, 2 vols.
1877–80. (Chertsey Worthies Lib.)
The Minor Poems. Ed. [from the autograph
MS] Eloise Robinson, 1914.

THOMAS BEEDOME (d. 1641?)

Poems. Divine and Humane. 1641.
Select Poems. Ed. F. Meynell, 1928.

EDWARD BENLOWES (1603?–1676)

Theophila or Loves Sacrifice. 1652. (Saints-
bury.)
The Summary of Wisedome. 1657. (Saints-
bury.)
[See C. Niemeyer, RES. XII, 1936; H.
Jenkins, MLR. XXXII, 1937.]

WILLIAM BOSWORTH (1607–1650)

The chast and Lost Lovers, Arcadius and
Sepha. 1651. (Saintsbury.)

ANNE BRADSTREET (1612–1672)

The tenth Muse lately sprung up in America.
1650; Boston, 1678; rptd 1758.
Works. Ed. J. H. Ellis, Charlestown, 1867;
New York, 1932.
Poems. Ed. F. E. Hopkins, New York, 1897.
[See O. Wegelin, A List of Editions of the
Poems of Anne Bradstreet, with Several
Additional Books relating to her, American
Book Collector, IV, 1933.]

RICHARD BRATHWAITE (1588?–1673)

[See pp. 711–2 below.]

ALEXANDER BROME (1620–1666)

The Cunning Lovers. A Comedy. As it was
Acted at the private House in Drury Lane.
1654.
Poems upon several occasions. 1660.
Songs and other poems. 1661; 1664; 1668;
rptd A. Chalmers (English Poets, vol. VI,
1810).
The Poems of Horace, by Several Persons,
1666; 1671; 1680. [Ed. and largely tr. by
Brome.]

PATRICK CARY

Poems, from a Manuscript written in the
Time of Oliver Cromwell. 1771. [MS dated
1651.]
Trivial Poems, and Triolets. Ed. Sir Walter
Scott, 1820. [The whole, of which the 1771
edn gave only a part.] (Saintsbury.)

WILLIAM CARTWRIGHT (1611–1643)

[See p. 655 below.]

MARGARET CAVENDISH, DUCHESS OF
NEWCASTLE (1624?–1673)

[See p. 642 below.]

JOHN CHALKHILL (*fl.* 1600)

Thealma and Clearchus. 1683; ed. S. W.
Singer, 1820. (*Saintsbury.*) [Preface by Izaak
Walton.]

ROBERT CHAMBERLAIN (b. 1607)

Nocturnall Lucubrations. Whereunto are
added Epigrams and Epitaphs. 1638.
Conceits, Clinches, Flashes, and Whimsies.
1639; 1640 (with changes, as Jocabella).

WILLIAM CHAMBERLAYNE (1619–1689)

Love's Victory. 1658; 1678 (as Wits led by the
Nose); ed. S. W. Singer, 1820.
Pharonnida. 1659; ed. S. W. Singer, 1820.
(*Saintsbury.*)
England's Jubile. 1660. (*Saintsbury.*)

SIR ROBERT CHESTER (1566?–1640?)

Loves Martyr. 1601 (re-issued 1611 as The
Annals of Great Brittaine); ed. A. B. Grosart,
Occasional Issues, vol. VII, 1878 (and New
Shakspere Soc.). [Appendix contains
poems by Shakespeare, Jonson, Chapman,
etc.]
Poems by Sir John Salusbury and Robert
Chester. Ed. Carleton Brown, EETS. Ex.
Ser. 1914 (and Bryn Mawr, 1913).

JOHN CLEVELAND (1618–1658)

The character of a London diurnal with severall
select poems. 1647. [Rptd many times in
1647 and 1648. The poems are not all by
Cleveland.]
Poems By J. C. with additions. 1651; 1653;
1654; 1657; 1659, etc.
J. Cleaveland Revived: Poems, Orations,
Epistles; And other of his Genuine Incom-
parable Pieces, never before publisht. 1659,
etc.
Clievelandi Vindiciae; Or, Clieveland's Genuine
Poems, Orations, Epistles, &c. Purged from
the many False & Spurious Ones. To which
are added many never Printed before. 1677.
Poems. Ed. J. M. Berdan, New Haven, 1911.
(*Saintsbury.*)
[See bibliographical note in Saintsbury,
vol. III, pp. 12–18, and S. V. Gapp, Notes on
John Cleveland, PMLA. XLVI, 1931. For
Cleveland's 'characters' see p. 723 below,
and for his news-books, pp. 731–63.]

SIR ASTON COKAYNE (1608–1684)

[See p. 642 below.]

ANNE COLLINS

Divine Songs and Meditations. 1653.

THOMAS COLLINS

The Penitent Publican. 1610.
The Teares of Love. 1615.

JOHN COLLOP

Poesis Rediviva. 1656. [See J. Drinkwater,
A Book for Bookmen, 1926.]

RICHARD CORBET (1582–1635)

Certain elegant Poems. 1647, etc. [Amplified
in later edns.]
Poetica Stromata, by R. C. [Hague?] 1648.
[Poems rptd in Chalmers' English Poets,
vol. V, 1810. See J. E. V. Crofts, A Life of
Bishop Corbett, E. & S. x, 1924.]

RALPH CRANE

The Workes of Mercy, both Corporeall and
Spirituall. 1621; [1625?] as (The Pilgrimes
New-yeares-Gift).

THOMAS CRANLEY

Amanda, or the Reformed Whore. 1635 (re-
issued 1639, as The Converted Courtezan);
priv. rptd F. Ouvry, 1869.

HUGH CROMPTON

Poems. Being a fardle of Fancies. 1657.
Pierides, or the Muses Mount. [1658?]

SAMUEL CROSSMAN (1624?–1684)

The Young Mans Meditation. Sacred Poems.
1664; rptd 1863.

GEORGE DANIEL (1616–1657)

Poems. Ed. A. B. Grosart, Boston, Lincs.
1878.

JAMES DAY

A new Spring of Divine Poetrie. 1637.

E[DMUND] E[LYS] (1634?–1707?)

Dia Poemata. 1655.
Divine Poems. 1658; 1659.
Miscellanea. Oxford, 1662.

MILDMAY FANE, EARL OF WESTMORLAND
(d. 1666)

[See p. 644 below.]

SIR RICHARD FANSHAWE (1608–1666)

[See p. 644 below.]

OWEN FELLTHAM (1602?–1668)

Lusoria, or Occasional Pieces. [Appended to
Resolves, 1661 (8th edn). See also p. 725
below.]

CHARLES FITZ-GEFFRY (1575?–1638)

Sir Francis Drake. 1596; ed. Sir S. E. Brydges,
Lee Priory, 1819.
The Blessed Birthday celebrated: also Holy
Transportations. 1634; 1636; 1654.

Complete Poems. Ed. A. B. Grosart, 1881.
(Chertsey Worthies' Lib.)

[See G. C. Moore Smith, Charles Fitzgeffrey, Poet and Divine, MLR. xv, 1919.]

ROBERT FLETCHER

Ex otio Negotium, or, Martial his epigrams translated. With sundry Poems and Fancies. 1656.

THOMAS FORDE (*fl.* 1647–61)

[See p. 726 below.]

THOMAS FULLER (1608–1661)

[See p. 835 below.]

SIDNEY GODOLPHIN (1610–1643)

The Passion of Dido for Aeneas. 1658; 1679. [Completed by Waller.]
The Poems. Ed. W. Dighton, Oxford, 1931. (*Saintsbury.*)

ROBERT GOMERSAL (1602–1646?)

The Levite's Revenge. 1628; 1633 (in Poems).
The Tragedie of Lodovick Sforza Duke of Millan. 1628; 1633 (in Poems, with separate title-page); ed. B. R. Pearn, Louvain, 1933 (Bang's Materialien, N.S. vol. viii).
Poems. 1633.

JOHN HAGTHORPE

Divine Meditations, and Elegies. 1622; ed. Sir S. E. Brydges, 1817 (selection, as Hagthorpe Revived).
Visiones rerum. 1623.

JOHN HALL (1627–1656)

Poems. Cambridge, 1646; ed. Sir S. E. Brydges, 1816 (selection). (*Saintsbury.*)
Hierocles upon the Golden verses of Pythagoras englished. 1657. [Includes An account of the author, by John Davies, of Kidwelly.]

[For Hall's essays see p. 726 below; for his version of Longinus see p. 804.]

WILLIAM HAMMOND (b. 1614)

Poems. By W. H. 1655; ed. Sir S. E. Brydges, 1816. (*Saintsbury.*)

PATRICK HANNAY

The Nightingale. Sheretine and Mariana [etc.]. 1622; ed. E. V. Utterson, 1841; ed. D. Laing, Hunterian Club, 1875. (*Saintsbury.*)

CHRISTOPHER HARVEY (1597–1663)

The Synagogue. 1640; 1647 (enlarged). [Often rptd with G. Herbert's The Temple from 1641, though with separate title-page and pagination.]

ROBERT HEATH

Clarastella. 1650.

[See also pp. 481, 726 below.]

EDWARD HERBERT, BARON HERBERT OF CHERBURY (1583–1648)

Occasional Verses. 1665.
Poems. Ed. J. C. Collins, 1881; ed. G. C. Moore Smith, Oxford, 1923.

[For Herbert's prose see pp. 841–2 and 875 below.]

THOMAS HEYWOOD (d. 1650?)

[See p. 625 below.]

BÁRTEN HOLYDAY (1593–1661)

[See p. 697 below.]

NICHOLAS HOOKES (1628–1712)

Amanda. 1653; rptd 1923.
Miscellanea Poetica. 1653.

JAMES HOWELL (1594?–1666)

[See pp. 832–3 below.]

SIR FRANCIS HUBERT (d. 1629)

The Deplorable Life and Death of Edward the Second. 1628 (re-issued 1629).

PATHERICKE JENKYN (or JENKYNS)

Amorea. 1661.

THOMAS JORDAN (1612?–1685)

[See p. 646 below.]

RALPH KNEVET (1600–1671)

[See p. 647 below.]

SIR FRANCIS KYNASTON (1587–1642)

Amorum Troili ët Creseidae. Libri duo priores Anglico-Latini. Oxford, 1635. [Chaucer in rhymed Latin.]
Leoline and Sydonis. Cynthiades. 1642. (*Saintsbury.*)

WILLIAM LATHUM

Phyala Lachrymarum. 1634.

[See L. B. Marshall, RES. viii, 1932, pp. 37–43, and TLS. 29 Sept. 1932, p. 687.]

LEONARD LAWRENCE

Arnalte and Lucenda. 1639.

WILLIAM LEE (d. 1645)

Songs of Sion. Hamburg, 1620; ed. A. B. Grosart, Fuller Worthies' Misc. 1871.

SIR WILLIAM LEIGHTON

Vertue Triumphant. 1603.
The Teares of a Sorrowfull Soule. 1613.

CHRISTOPHER LEVER

A Crucifixe. 1607.
Queene Elizabeths Teares. 1607; ed. A. B. Grosart, Fuller Worthies' Misc. 1870 (with A Crucifixe).

MARTIN LLUELYN (1616–1681)

Men-Miracles. With other Poemes. 1646 (re-issued 1656); 1661 (as The marrow of the Muses); 1679.
[See R. Wallerstein, Martin Lluelyn, Cavalier and 'Metaphysical,' JEGP. xxxv, 1936.]

SHAKERLEY MARMION (1602–1639)

[See p. 647 below.]

HUMPHREY MILL

Poems occasioned by a melancholy Vision. 1639.
A Nights Search. 1640. [Second pt 1646 and 1652.]

HENRY MORE (1614–1687)

[See p. 875 below.]

THOMAS NABBES (1605–1641?)

[See p. 648 below.]

RICHARD NICCOLS (1584–1616)

The Cuckow. 1607.
A Mirour for Magistrates. Newly enlarged with a last part called A Winter Nights Vision. 1610. [The enlargement by Niccolls.]
The Three Sisters Teares. 1613.
The Furies. With Vertue's Encomium; or, the Image of Honour. 1614; rptd Harleian Miscellany, vol. x, 1808 (with Monodia: or, Waltham's Complaint, 1615.)
Londons Artillery. 1616.
Sir Thomas Overburies Vision. 1616; rptd Harleian Miscellany, vol. vii, 1744, etc.; ed. J. Maidment, Hunterian Club, 1873.
The Beggers Ape. 1627; rptd photo. facs. New York, 1936.

SAMUEL PAGE (1574–1630)

The Love of Amos and Laura. [In Alcilia, 1613, 1619, 1628; ed. A. B. Grosart, 1879.]

CLEMENT PAMAN (fl. 1660)

[Short poems often found in 17th cent. MSS but apparently never collected. See BM. and Bodley MS catalogues. One piece ptd N. Ault, Seventeenth Century Lyrics, 1928.]

THOMAS PESTEL (1584?–1659?)

Sermons and Devotions. 1659.
[See H. A. Buchan, Thomas Pestell's Poems in MS. Malone 14, Bodleian Quart. Record, vii, 1933.]

'PHILANDER'

Tarquin and Lucretia. 1660; 1669.

THOMAS PHILIPOT (d. 1682)

Poems. 1646.
Aesop's Fables. 1665; 1666; 1687; 1703.

SAMUEL PICK

Festum Voluptatis. 1639.
[See H. E. Rollins, Samuel Pick's Borrowings. RES. vii, 1931, and p. 405 above.]

EDMUND PRESTWICH

Hippolytus, Translated out of Seneca. Together with divers other Poems. 1651.

JOHN QUARLES (1624–1665)

Fons Lachrymarum, or a Fountain of Tears. 1648; 1649; 1655; 1677.
Regale Lectum Miseriae, or a Kingly Bed of Miserie. 1648; 1649; 1658; 1659; 1660; 1679.
Gods Love and Mans Unworthiness. 1651; 1655 (with Divine Meditations).
Divine Meditations upon several Subjects. 1655; 1663; 1671; 1679.
The Banishment of Tarquin, or the Reward of Lust. [Appended to Shakespeare's Rape of Lucrece, 1655.]
The History of the most vile Dimagoras. 1658.
A Continuation of the History [by Francis Quarles] of Argalus and Parthenia. 1659.

THOMAS RANDOLPH (1605–1635)

[See p. 658 below.]

NATHANIEL RICHARDS (1612?–1654?)

The Celestiall Publican. 1630; 1632 (as Poems, Divine, Morall, and Satyricall); 1641 (enlarged).
The Tragedy of Messallina The Roman Emperesse. As it hath beene Acted by the Company of his Majesties Revells. 1640; ed. A. R. Skemp (Bang's Materialien, vol. xxx, Louvain, 1908).

THOMAS ROBINSON

The Life and Death of Mary Magdalene. Ed. H. O. Sommer, EETS. Ex. Ser. 1899. [Written c. 1620.]

ALEXANDER ROSS (1591–1654)

Three Decads of Divine Meditations. [1620.]
Mel Heliconium. 1642.
[For Ross's prose see pp. 877 and 883 below.]

JOHN SALTMARSH (d. 1647)

[See p. 699 below.]

SAMUEL SHEPPARD

The times Displayed. 1646.
The Faerie King. [Bodley MS Rawl. Poet. 28.]
The Loves of Amandus and Sophronia. 1650.
Epigrams theological, philosophical, and romantick. 1651.
[See Hyder E. Rollins, Samuel Sheppard and his Praise of Poets, Stud. Phil. xxxiv, 1927; and see p. 867 below.]

JAMES SHIRLEY (1596–1666)
[See p. 639 below.]

JAMES SMITH (1605–1667)
[Verses in collections pbd by Smith and Sir J. Mennis: Witts Recreations, 1640 (rptd 1817); Musarum Deliciae, 1655 (rptd 1817); Wit Restored, 1658 (rptd 1817).]

THOMAS STANLEY (1625–1678)
Poems and Translations. 1647 (priv. ptd); 1651 (as Poems); 1652; 1656 (in John Gamble's Ayres and Dialogues); ed. Sir S. E. Brydges, 1814 (from 1651 edn); ed. L. I. Guiney, Hull, 1907; rptd 1923 (only trns from Joannes Secundus). (*Saintsbury.*)
[For Stanley's The History of Philosophy, 1655–62, see p. 878 below, and p. 863 for his trns from Anacreon, Bion, Moschus, Secundus, Ausonius, etc.]

MATTHEW STEVENSON
Occasion's Offspring. 1645; 1654.
The Twelve Moneths. 1661; rptd 1928.
Bellum Presbyteriale. 1661.
Florus Britannicus. 1662.
Poems. 1665; 1673 (as Poems: or, a Miscellany); 1673 (as Norfolk Drollery); 1685 (as The Wits).
The Wits Paraphras'd. 1680.

SIR JOHN STRADLING (1563–1637)
Beati Pacifici: a Divine Poem. 1623.
Divine Poems. 1625; rptd A. B. Grosart, 1883.

WILLIAM STRODE (1602–1645)
Poetical Works. Ed. B. Dobell, 1907.
[See also p. 659 below.]

JOSHUA SYLVESTER (1563–1618)
Lachrimae Lachrimarum. 1612; 1613.
The Sacred Workes gathered into one Volume. 1620.
Works. Ed. A. B. Grosart, 1880. (Chertsey Worthies' Lib.)
[For Sylvester's trns from Saluste Du Bartas see p. 818 below.]

JOHN TATHAM
[See p. 658 below.]

JEREMY TAYLOR (1613–1667)
[See pp. 700–2 below.]

AURELIAN TOWNSEND (1583?–1643)
Albion's Triumph. 1631. [Masque.]
Tempe Restored. 1631 (for 1632). [Masque.]
Poems. [In various miscellanies.]
Poems and Masks. Ed. Sir E. K. Chambers, 1912.

HENRY TUBBE (1618–1655)
Meditations Divine & Morall by H. T. 1659; 1682; ed. G. C. Moore Smith, Oxford, 1915 (selections).

THOMAS WASHBOURNE (1606–1687)
Divine Poems. 1654.
Poems. Ed. A. B. Grosart, 1868. (Fuller Worthies' Lib.)

ROWLAND WATKYNS
Flamma sine Fumo: or, Poems without Fictions. 1662.
[See L. B. Marshall, TLS. 29 Sept. 1932, p. 687.]

JOHN WEEVER (1576–1632)
Agnus Dei. 1601; 1603; 1606; 1611.
The Mirror of Martyrs. 1601; rptd Roxburghe Club, 1873.
[For Weever's epigrams and satires see p. 480 below.]

NATHANIEL WHITING (*fl.* 1629–1663)
Le Hore di recreatione, or the pleasant historie of Albino and Bellama. By N. W. 1637 (re-issued 1638; also 1639 as The most pleasante historie of Albino and Bellama). (*Saintsbury.*)

LADY MARY WROTH
The Countesse of Mountgomeries Urania. 1621. [Prose romance with verses interspersed.]   L. C. M.

VIII. EMBLEM BOOKS

Astry, Sir J. The Royal Politician, represented in One Hundred Emblems. 1700; 1725 (enlarged). [From the Spanish of Diego de Saavedra Fajardo.]
Ayres, Philip (1638–1712). Emblems of Love. In four Languages. 1683. [Three issues about the same date, one being undated. Rptd, with some only of the illustrations, in G. Saintsbury's Minor Caroline Poets, vol. II, Oxford, 1906.]
Bunyan, John. A Book for Boys and Girls. 1686. [Rptd sometimes under the title, Divine Emblems. Ed. type facs. John Brown, 1889.]
Farley, Robert. Lychnocausia, Lights Morall Emblems. 1638; rptd 1860. [Latin and English.]
Harvey, Christopher (1597–1663). Schola Cordis in 47 Emblems. 1647, etc.; ed. A. B. Grosart, (1874 Fuller Worthies' Lib.) [Anon., and sometimes attrib. to Quarles. It is adapted from Benedictus von Haeften's book with the same title.]

Hawkins, Henry (1572?–1646). Partheneia Sacra. By H. A. Rouen, 1633 (anon.) [In English.]

H[all], J[ohn]. Emblems with Elegant Figures. [1648.]

Hugo, Herman. Pia Desideria. Englished by Edmund Arwaker. Antwerp, 1686 and 1690.

Paradin, Claudius. The Heroicall Devises. Translated out of Latin by P. S. 1591.

Peacham, Henry (1576?–1643?). Minerva Britanna: or a Garden of Heroycal Devises. 1612.

—— The Mirrour of Majestie. 1618; rptd Holbein Soc. 1870.

Peyton, Thomas (1595–1626). The Glasse of Time in the first Age. 1620.

—— The Glasse of Time in the second Age. 1623; rptd New York, 1886 (with first Age).

Quarles, Francis. [See p. 450 above.]

Sterry, Thomas. A Rot amongst the Bishops, set forth in lively Emblems. 1641; rptd 1838.

Thynne, Francis (1545?–1608). Emblemes and Epigrames. Ed. F. J. Furnivall, EETS. 1876. [Written in 1600, but probably never ptd.]

Whitney, Geffrey (1548?–1601?). A Choice of Emblemes, gathered out of sundrie writers, Englished and moralized. 2 pts, Leyden, 1585. [See below for H. Green's rpt.]

Willet, Andrew (1562–1621). Sacrorum Emblematum Centuria una. Cambridge, [1596?] [Latin, with English rendering.]

Wither, George. A Collection of Emblemes, ancient and modern. 1635.

Wyrley, William (1565–1618). The True Use of Armorie. 1592.

Books and Articles on Emblem-Writing
(a) Books

Alciati Emblematum Fontes Quatuor. Flumen Abundans. Ed. photo. facs. H. Green, 2 vols. Holbein Soc. 1870–1. [Reproduction, with annotation, of the four principal early edns, Augsburg, 1531; Paris, 1534; Venice, 1546; Lyons, 1551. This popular work, constantly enlarged, and ptd in many countries, set the vogue.]

Mignault, Claude. Syntagma de Symbolis. Antwerp, 1581.

Menestrier, C. F. L'Art des Emblèmes. Paris, 1584.

Daniel, Samuel. The Worthy Tract of Paulus Jovius of Rare Inventions called Imprese. 1585. [Ragionamento sopra i motti e designi, Rome, 1555.]

Fraunce, Abraham. Insignium, Armorum, Emblematum Explicatio. 1588.

Drummond, William. Of Impreses. [In Works, Edinburgh, 1711.]

Blount, Henry. The Art of Making Devises. 1650. [From the French of Henri Estienne.]

Moral Emblems from Jacob Cats and Robert Farlie. Ed. R. Pigot, 1860.

Green, Henry. Whitney's Choice of Emblemes. Type facs. rpt (with a dissertation, essays and notes). 1866. [A valuable repertory of all information about emblem-books.]

—— Shakespeare and the Emblem Writers. 1870.

—— Andrea Alciati and his Books of Emblems. 1872.

Sears, G. E. A Collection of the Emblem Books of Alciati in the Library of. New York, 1888 (priv. ptd).

Thompson, E. N. S. Literary Bypaths of the Renaissance. New Haven, 1924.

(b) Articles in Periodicals

Redgrave, G. R. Emblems and Impresas. Bibliophile, III, 1909.

—— Daniel and the Emblem Literature. Trans. Bibliog. Soc. XI, 1912.

Thomas, H. Ayres' Emblemata Amatoria. Library, I, 1910.

Floyer, J. K. Some Emblem Books and their Writers. Cornhill Mag. Sept. 1921.

Praz, Mario. Stanley, Sherburne and Ayres as Translators and Imitators. MLR. xx, 1925.

—— The English Emblem Literature. E. Studies, XVI, 1934.

Fucilla, J. G. De Morte et Amore. PQ. XIV, 1935. [Alciato's influence.]   F. E. H.

IX. EPIGRAMMATISTS AND FORMAL SATIRISTS

[To 1640 only. For popular verse satire the section on Popular Literature, pp. 712–21 below, should be consulted.]

(1) Modern Studies

Collier, J. P. The Poetical Decameron. 2 vols. Edinburgh, 1820. [3rd, 4th and 5th conversations.]

Shade, O. Satiren und Pasquille aus der Reformationszeit. Hanover, 1856.

Alden, R. M. The Rise of Formal Satire in England. Philadelphia, 1899.

Whipple, T. K. Martial and the English Epigram from Sir Thomas Wyatt to Ben Jonson. Berkeley, 1925.

Lathrop, H. B. Janus Cornarius's Selecta Epigrammata Graeca and the Early English Epigrammatists. MLN. XLIII, 1928.

(2) COLLECTIONS OF EPIGRAMS AND SATIRES

Crowley, Robert. One and Thirtye Epigrammes. 1550; ed. J. M. Cowper, EETS. Ex. Ser. 1872.

John Heywoodes woorkes. A dialogue conteynyng the number of the effectual proverbes in the Englishe tongue, compact in a matter concernynge two maner of maryages. With one hundred of Epigrammes; and three hundred of Epigrammes upon three hundred proverbs: and a fifth hundred of Epigrams. Whereunto are now newly added a syxt hundred of Epigrams. 1562; ed. J. S. Farmer, Early English Drama Soc. 1906. [For other edns see under Heywood (1497?–1580?), pp. 518–9 below.]

Drant, Thomas (d. 1578?). A Medicinable Morall, that is the two bookes of Horace his Satyres englyshed. Also epigrammes. 1566.

Turbervile, George (1540?–1610). Epitaphes, Epigrams, Songs and Sonets. 1567. [See also under Turbervile, p. 438 above.]

Gascoigne, George (1525?–1577). The Stele Glas. A Satyre. 1576. [See also under Gascoigne pp. 414–5 above.]

Kendall, Timothy. Flowres of Epigrammes out of sundrie the moste singular authours. 1577.

Epigrammes and elegies by J. D[avies] and C. M[arlowe]. 2 pts, Middelburg, [1590?]. [See also under Sir John Davies (1569–1626), pp. 426–7 above.]

Donne, John (1573–1631). Satires. [In Poems, 1633, etc. See also pp. 441–4 above.]

Lodge, Thomas (1558?–1625). A Fig for Momus: containing pleasant Varietie, included in Satyres, Eclogues and Epistles. 1595. [See also under Lodge, pp. 527–9 below.]

Hall, Joseph (1574–1656). Virgidemiarum. Sixe Bookes. First three bookes of Toothlesse Satyrs. 1597; 1598; 1602.

—— Virgidemiarum. Sixe Bookes, three last bookes of byting Satyres. 1598; 1599. [Both pts are rptd in the various edns of Hall's Works: ed. J. Pratt, 1808; ed. P. Hall, Oxford, 1837; ed. P. Winter, 1863. Also in Complete Poems, ed. A. B. Grosart, Manchester, 1879. See S. M. Salyer, Stud. Phil. xxv, 1928, pp. 149–70.]

[Guilpin, Edward.] Skialetheia or a Shadowe of Truth in certain Epigrams and Satyres. 1598; rptd A. B. Grosart, 1878.

Marston, John (1575?–1634). The Metamorphosis of Pygmalion's Image, and certain Satyres. 1598 (anon.).

Marston, John. The Scourge of Villanie, three Bookes of Satyres. 1598. [See M. S. Allen, The Satire of John Marston, Columbus, Ohio, 1920, and pp. 627–8 below.]

Rankins, William. Seaven Satyres applyed to the weeke. 1598.

Tyro, T. Tyros Roring Megge. Planted against the walles of Melancholy. 1598.

Bastard, Thomas (1566–1618). Chrestoleros: Seven bookes of Epigrammes. 1598; rptd A. B. Grosart, 1880.

Barnfield, Richard (1574–1627). Encomion of Lady Pecunia. 1598. [See also p. 427 above.]

Weever, John (1576–1632). Epigrammes in the oldest Cut and Newest Fashion. 1599; ed. R. B. McKerrow, 1911.

—— Faunus and Melliflora; or, the original of our English satyres. 1600.

M., T. Micro-cynicon. Sixe Snarling Satyres. 1599. [Sometimes attrib. to Thomas Middleton, more probably Thomas Moffat.]

Goddard, William. A Mastif Whelp, with other ruff-Island-like Currs fetcht from amongst the Antipodes. [Dort? 1599.]

—— A Neaste of Waspes latelie found out and discovered in the Low Countreys. 1615; ed. C. H. Wilkinson, Oxford, 1921.

—— A Satyricall Dialogue, or a sharplye-invective Conference betweene Alexander the Great and that trulye woman-hater Diogynes. [Dort? 1616?]

Rowlands, Samuel (1570?–1630?). The letting of humours blood in the Head Vaine. 1600.

—— Humors Looking-glasse. 1608 (anon., sometimes attrib. to Rowlands). [See also under Rowlands, pp. 707–8 below.]

Thynne, Francis. Emblemes and Epigrames. Ed. F. J. Furnivall, EETS. 1876. [Written 1600.]

Breton, Nicholas (1545?–1626?). Pasquils Mad-Cappe and his Message. 1600.

—— Pasquils Foolescap. 1600.

—— Pasquils Mistresse, or the Worthy and Unworthy Woman. 1600.

—— Pasquils Passe and Passeth Not. 1600. [See also under Breton, pp. 415–7 above.]

C., J. Epigrams served up in fifty-two several dishes. [c. 1604.]

Woodhouse, Peter. The Flea. 1605; rptd 1877.

P[arrot], H[enry]. The Mous-Trap. 1606.

—— Epigrams. 1608.

—— Laquei Ridiculosi, or Springes to catch Woodcocks. 1613.

—— The Mastive, or Young-Whelpe of the Old-Dogge. Epigrams and Satyres. 1615.

—— VIII Cures for the Itch. Characters, Epigrams, Epitaphs. 1626. [See M. C. Pitman, The Epigrams of Henry Peacham and Henry Parrot, MLR. xxix, 1934.]

W[alkington], T. (d. 1621). The Optick Glasse of Humors. 1607; Oxford, [1631?]; 1639.

West, Richard. The Court of Conscience or Dick Whippers Sessions. 1607.

—— A Century of Epigrams. 1608.

Epigrams or Humours Lottery. 1608.

[Tofte, Robert (1562–1620).] Ariostos Satyres. 1608; 1611. [Ascribed on title-page to G. Markham, without warrant.]

Heath, John. Two Centuries of Epigrammes. 1610.

Sharpe, Roger. More fooles yet. 1610. [Epigrams.]

Scot, Thomas. Philomythie or Philomythologie. Wherein outlandish birds, beasts and fishes are taught to speake true English verse. 2 pts, 1610; 1616 (enlarged); 1622.

—— The second part of Philomythie. 1625.

Davies, John, of Hereford (1565?–1618?). The Scourge of Folly. [1611?] [See also under Davies, p. 425 above.]

Taylor, John (1580–1653). The Sculler, or Gallimawfry of Sonnets, Satyres and Epigrams. 1612.

—— Epigrammes, being ninety in number, besides two new made Satyres. 1651. [See also under Taylor, pp. 708–11 below.]

Wither, George (1588–1667). Abuses Stript and Whipt. 1613. [See also under Wither, p. 446–9 above.]

Freeman, Thomas. Rubbe and a Great Cast: Epigrams. (Runne and a Great Cast.) 2 pts, 1614.

C., R. The Times Whistle: or A New Daunce of Seven Satires and other Poems. [1614?]; ed. J. M. Cowper, EETS. 1871.

Brathwaite, Richard (1588?–1673). A Strappado for the Divell. Epigrams and Satyres. 1615.

—— Natures Embassie: or, the Wilde-mans Measures: Danced naked by twelve Satyres. 1621. [See also under Brathwaite, pp. 711–2 below.]

Anton, Robert. The Philosophers Satyrs. 1616 (re-issued 1617 as Vices Anotimie).

Harington, Sir John (1561–1612). The most elegant and witty Epigrams of. 1618. [See also under Harington, p. 705 below.]

Jonson, Ben (1573?–1637). Epigrams. [In Works, 1616.] [See also under Jonson, pp. 613–9 below.]

Hutton, Henry. Follies Anatomie or Satyres and Satyricall Epigrams with a Compendious History of Ixions Wheele. 1619; rptd E. F. Rimbault, Percy Soc. 1842.

[Wroth, Sir Thomas.] The Abortive of an Idle Hour, or a century of Epigrams. 1620.

Peacham, Henry (1576?–1643?). Thalia's Banquet furnished with newly devised epigrammes. 1620. [See under Parrot above for criticism.]

Martyn, Joseph. Newe Epigrams, having in their Company a mad Satyre. 1621.

Hayman, Robert. Quodibets, lately come over from New Britaniola. 3 pts, 1628.

Epigrammes. [Paris, c. 1630?] [Anti-Protestant.]

Randolph, Thomas (1605–1635). Aristippos or, The Joviall Philosopher. 1630. [See also under Randolph, p. 658 below.]

Epigrammes, mirrour of New Reformation. 1634.

Chamberlain, Robert (b. 1607). Nocturnall Lucubrations. Whereunto are added Epigrams and Epitaphs. 1638.

—— Conceits, Clinches, Flashes, and Whimsies. 1639; 1640 (with changes, as Jocabella).

Bancroft, Thomas. Two Bookes of Epigrammes and Epitaphs. 1639.

X. SONG BOOKS

A. GENERAL LITERATURE

Prescott, O. Form or Design in Vocal Music Musical World, LXI, 1881.

Tiersot, J. Histoire de la Chanson populaire en France. Paris, 1889.

Vogel, E. Biblioteca della Musica vocale italiana di Genere profano, stampata dal 1500 al 1700. Berlin, 1892.

Einstein, A. The Madrigal. Musical Quart. Oct. 1924.

Vatielli, M. E. The Growth of the Dramatic Madrigal. Sackbut, Dec. 1926.

Dent, E. J. The Musical Form of the Madrigal. Music and Letters, July 1930.

Flower, D. On Music Printing, 1473–1701. Book Collectors' Quart. Oct. 1931.

[See also articles on song, madrigal, and part-song in Grove's Dictionary of Music.]

B. LITERATURE ON ENGLISH SONG BOOKS, ETC.

Rimbault, E. F. Bibliotheca Madrigaliana. 1847.

Chappell, W. Old English Popular Music. Ed. H. E. Wooldridge, 2 vols. 1893.

Nagel, W. Geschichte der Musik in England. 2 vols. Strasburg, 1894–7.

Cox, F. A. English Madrigals in the Time of Shakespeare. 1899.

Becker, O. Die englischen Madrigalisten William Byrd, Thomas Morley und John Dowland. Bonn, 1901.

Parry, Sir C. H. H. Music of the 17th Century. [In Oxford History of Music, vol. III, 1902.]

Bolle, W. Die gedruckten englischen Liederbücher bis 1600. Weimar, 1903.

Steele, R. R. The Earliest English Music Printing. Bibliog. Soc. 1903. [With full indexes, etc.]

Kidson, F. A Study of Old English Song and Popular Melody prior to the 19th Century. Musical Quart. Oct. 1915.

Fellowes, E. H. Elizabethan Madrigals. Proc. Soc. Antiquaries, 1919–20.

—— The English Madrigal Composers. Oxford, 1921.

—— The English Madrigal School. 1924. [An introduction to the collection of that title, pbd separately.]

—— The English Madrigal. Oxford, 1925.

Bridge, Sir J. F. Twelve Good Musicians from John Bull to Henry Purcell. 1920.

Davey, H. History of English Music. 1921 (rev. edn).

'Warlock, P.' (P. Heseltine). On Editing Elizabethan Songs. Musical Times, July 1922.

—— The English Ayre. 1926.

—— The Editing of Old English Songs. Sackbut, Feb.–March 1926.

Pulver, J. A Dictionary of Old English Music and Musical Instruments. 1923.

—— Musical Life in Tudor England. Sackbut, March 1924.

—— A Biographical Dictionary of Old English Music. 1927.

Walker, E. History of English Music. 1924 (rev. edn).

Flood, W. H. G. Early Tudor Composers. 1925.

Van den Borren, C. The Aesthetic Value of the English Madrigal. Proc. Musical Ass. 1925–6.

Dent, E. J. Foundations of English Opera. A Study of Musical Drama in England during the Seventeenth Century. Cambridge, 1928.

Gibbon, J. M. Melody and the Lyric from Chaucer to the Cavaliers. 1930.

Wooldridge, H. E. The Polyphonic Period. Part II. [In Oxford History of Music, vol. II, 1932 (2nd edn).]

Ainsworth, E. G. Stanzas of the Orlando Furioso in English Collections of Madrigals. RES. VII, 1931.

C. COLLECTIONS

Chappell, W. Popular Music of the Olden Time. 2 vols. [1855–9].

Flügel, E. Liedersammlungen des XVI. Jahrhunderts. Ang. XII, 1889.

The Oriana Collection of Early Madrigals, British and Foreign. 100 pts, 1905–16.

Fellowes, E. H. The English Madrigal School. 36 vols. 1913–24.

—— The English School of Lutenist Song-Writers. Ser. 1, 15 vols. 1920–5, Ser. 2, 12 vols. 1925–7.

—— English Madrigal Verse. 1920; 1929.

'Warlock, P.' and Wilson, P. English Ayres, 1598–1612. Transcribed and edited by P. Warlock and P. Wilson. 1922, etc.

'Warlock, P.' (P. Heseltine.) The First (Third) Book of Elizabethan Songs that were originally composed for One Voice to sing and Four Stringed Instruments to accompany. Transcribed from 16th and Early 17th Century MSS. 1926.

——Giles Earle his Booke. 1932. [Words only.]

D. SEPARATE SONG BOOKS

XX songes, IX of IIII partes and XI of thre partes. 1530 (Wynkyn de Worde); ed. (words only) E. Flügel, Ang. XII, 1889. [Containing songs by John Taverner, Thomas Ashwell, Robert Jones the elder, Robert Cowper, John Gwynneth, Wm. Cornyshe, Richard Pygott, Robert Fayrfax and Thos. Stretton.]

THOMAS WHYTHORNE (b. 1528)

Songes of three, fower, and five voyces. 1571. Duos, or songs for two voyces. 1590. [See 'P. Warlock' (P. Heseltine), Thomas Whythorne, 1927.]

Musica Transalpina. Madrigales translated out of foure, five and sixe parts, chosen out of divers excellent Authors, with the first and second part of La Verginella, made by Maister Byrd. 1588.

WILLIAM BYRD (1543–1623)

Collected Madrigals. Ed. E. H. Fellowes, 1920. (English Madrigal School, vols. XIV–XVI.)

Psalms, Sonets, & songs of sadnes & pietie. 1588; 1590.

Songs of sundrie natures, some of gravitie, and others of myrth. Lately made and composed into Musicke of 3. 4. 5. and 6. parts. 1589; 1610; ed. G. E. P. Arkwright, 1892–3 (Old English Edition, nos. 6–9).

Psalmes, songs, and sonnets: some solemne, others joyfull. Fit for voyces and viols of 3. 4. 5. and 6. parts. 1611.

[See also Musica Transalpina, 1588; The Teares or Lamentacions of a Sorrowfull Soule, 1614; E. H. Fellowes, William Byrd, 1923; S. Grew, William Byrd, Musical Times, Oct. 1922; V. Ricci, Il Tricentenario del Compositore William Byrd, Rivista Musicale Italiana, 1924; The Byrd Tercentenary [articles by W. B. Squire, J. A. Fuller-Maitland, E. H. Fellowes, and Gerald Cooper], Chesterian, June 1923; F. Howes, William Byrd, 1928.]

THOMAS WATSON (1557?–1592)

The first sett, of Italian Madrigalls Englished. 1590. [See also under the Sonneteers, p. 431 above.]

THOMAS MORLEY (1557–1606?)

Collected Madrigals. Ed. E. H. Fellowes, 1913. (English Madrigal School, vols. I–IV.)

Canzonets and madrigals for 3 and 4 voices. Ed. W. W. Holland and W. Cooke, [1808?].

Canzonets or little short songs to three voyces. 1593; 1606 (with additional songs); 1631.

Madrigalls to foure voyces. The first booke. 1594; 1600 (with 2 additional songs).

The first booke of Canzonets to two voyces. 1595; 1619.

The first booke of Balletts to five voyces. 1595; 1600; ed. E. F. Rimbault, Musical Antiquaries Soc. 1842.

Canzonets or little short Songs to foure voyces: celected out of the best and approv'd Italian authors. 1595.

Canzonets or little short Aers to five and sixe voices. 1597.

A Plaine and Easie Introduction to Practicall Musicke, with new songs. 1597; 1608.

Madrigals to five voyces Celected out of the best approved Italian authors. 1598.

The First Booke of Ayres. 1600; ed. E. H. Fellowes, 1932 (English School of Lutenist Song Writers, ser. 2, vol. XVI).

[See also The Triumphes of Oriana, 1601; E. H. Fellowes, Musical Opinion, Sept. 1916; W. H. G. Flood, Musical Times, March 1927.]

JOHN MUNDY (1560?–1630)

Songs and Psalmes composed into 3. 4. and 5. parts. 1594. [Madrigals included in Songs and psalmes, ed. E. H. Fellowes, 1924 (English Madrigal School, vol. xxxv). See also The Triumphes of Oriana, 1601.]

JOHN DOWLAND (1563–1626)

Collected Madrigals. Ed. E. H. Fellowes, 1920–5. (English School of Lutenist Song Writers, ser. 1, vols. I, II, V, VI, X–XII, XIV.)

Fifty Songs. Ed. E. H. Fellowes, 1925.

The first booke of Songes or Ayres of fowre parts. 1597; 1600; 1606; 1613; ed. (with life of Dowland) W. Chappell, Musical Antiquaries Soc. 1844.

The seconde booke of Songs or Ayres. 1600.

The third and last booke of Songs or Aires. 1603.

A Pilgrimes Solace. Wherein is contained Musicall Harmonie of 3. 4. and 5. parts. 1612.

[See also A Musicall Banquet, 1610; E. H. Fellowes, Songs of Dowland, 1929, and Musical Opinion, Dec. 1929; P. Heseltine, A Note on John Dowland, Musical Times, March 1926, Aug. 1927; W. H. G. Flood, Musical Times, June 1927; M. Dowling, Library, March 1932.]

Musica Transalpina. The second booke of madrigalles to 5. & 6. voyces, translated out of sundrie Italian Authors. 1597. [A sequel to Musica transalpina, 1588.]

GEORGE KIRBYE (1565?–1634)

The first set of English Madrigalls. 1597; ed. E. H. Fellowes, 1922 (English Madrigal

School, vol. XXIV). [See also The Triumphes of Oriana, 1601.]

NATHANIEL PATRICK (or PATTRICK) (1560?–1595)

Songes of Sundrye Natures. 1597. [See W. H. G. Flood, Musical Times, Sept. 1926.]

THOMAS WEELKES (1575?–1623)

Madrigals to 3. 4. 5. & 6. voyces. 1597; ed. E. J. Hopkins, Musical Antiquaries Soc. 1843; ed. E. H. Fellowes, 1916 (English Madrigal School, vol. IX).

Ballets and madrigals to five voyces. 1598; 1608; ed. G. E. P. Arkwright, 1895 (Old English Edition, nos. 13–5); ed. E. H. Fellowes, 1916 (English Madrigal School, vol. X).

Madrigals of 5. and 6. parts. 1600; ed. E. H. Fellowes, 1916 (English Madrigal School, vol. XI).

Madrigals of 6. parts. 1600; ed. E. H. Fellowes, 1916 (English Madrigal School, vol. XII).

Ayeres or Phantasticke Spirites for three voices. 1608; ed. G. E. P. Arkwright, 1895–6 (Old English Edition, nos. 16–7).

[See also The Triumphes of Oriana, 1601; The Teares or Lamentacions of a Sorrowfull Soule, 1614; E. H. Fellowes, Proc. Musical Ass. 1915–6, pp. 117 ff.]

JOHN WILBYE (1574–1638)

Collected Madrigals. Ed. E. H. Fellowes, 1914. (English Madrigal School, vols. VI, VII.)

The first set of English Madrigals to 3. 4. 5. and 6. voices. 1598; ed. J. Turle, Musical Antiquaries Soc. 1840–1.

The second set of Madrigals. 1609; ed. G. W. Budd, Musical Antiquaries Soc. 1846.

[See also The Triumphes of Oriana, 1601; The Teares or Lamentacions of a Sorrowfull Soule, 1614; E. H. Fellowes, Proc. Musical Ass. 1914–5, pp. 55 f.]

MICHAEL CAVENDISH (1565?–1628)

[Airs, including eight madrigals for five voices; the title is unknown.] 1598. [See also The Triumphes of Oriana, 1601.]

GILES FARNABY (1560?–1600)

Canzonets to fowre voyces, with a Song of eight parts. 1598; ed. E. H. Fellowes, 1922 (English Madrigal School, vol. XX). [See W. H. G. Flood, Musical Times, July 1926.]

JOHN BENNET

Madrigalls to foure voyces. 1599; ed. E. J. Hopkins, Musical Antiquaries Soc. 1845; ed. E. H. Fellowes, 1922 (English Madrigal School, vol. XXIII). [See also The Triumphes of Oriana, 1601.]

JOHN FARMER (1565?–1605?)

The first set of English Madrigals. 1599; ed. E. H. Fellowes, 1913 (English Madrigal School, vol. VIII). [See also The Triumphes of Oriana, 1601; W. H. G. Flood, Musical Times, March 1926.]

ROBERT JONES, the younger
(b. *c.* 1575)

The first booke of Songes & Ayres of foure parts. 1600; ed. E. H. Fellowes, 1925 (English School of Lutenist Song Writers, ser. 2, vol. v).

The second Booke. 1601; ed. E. H. Fellowes, 1926 (English School of Lutenist Song Writers, ser. 2, vol. VI).

The first set of Madrigals. 1607; ed. E. H. Fellowes, 1924 (English Madrigal School, vol. XXXV).

Ultimum vale or the third booke of ayres. 1608; ed. E. H. Fellowes, 1926 (English School of Lutenist Song Writers, ser. 2, vol. VII).

A Musicall Dreame. Or the fourth booke of ayres. 1609; ed. E. H. Fellowes, 1927 (English School of Lutenist Song Writers, ser. 2, vol. VIII).

The Muses Garden for Delights, or the fift Booke of Ayres. 1610; ed. W. B. Squire, 1926; ed. E. H. Fellowes, 1927 (English School of Lutenist Song Writers, ser. 2, vol. IX).

[See also The Triumphes of Oriana, 1601; The Teares or Lamentacions of a Sorrowfull Soule, 1614; E. H. Fellowes, The Text of the Song-books of Robert Jones, Music and Letters, Jan. 1927; P. Heseltine, Robert Jones and his Prefaces, Musical Times, Feb.–March 1923; W. H. G. Flood, Musical Times, July 1928.]

THOMAS CAMPION (1567–1620)

[See pp. 425–6 above.]

The Triumphes of Oriana, to 5. and 6. voices: composed by diverse severall aucthors. 1601; ed. W. Hawes, 1814; ed. L. Benson, 1905 (Oriana Collection of Early Madrigals); ed. E. H. Fellowes, 1923 (English Madrigal School, vol. XXXII). [Containing songs by Thos. Morley, the editor, Michael East, Daniel Norcome, John Mundy, Ellis Gibbons, John Bennet, John Hilton the elder, George Marson, Richard Carlton, John Holmes, Richard Nicolson, Thos. Tomkins, Michael Cavendish, Wm. Cobbold, John Farmer, John Wilbye, Thos. Hunt, Thos. Weelkes, George Kirbye, Robert Jones, Edward Johnson, John Lisley and John Milton, father of the poet.]

RICHARD CARLTON (1557?–1638?)

Madrigals to five voyces. 1601; ed. E. H. Fellowes, 1923 (English Madrigal School, vol. XXVII). [See also The Triumphes of Oriana, 1601; W. H. G. Flood, Musical Times, Aug. 1928.]

PHILIP ROSSETER (1572?–1623)

A Booke of Ayres, set foorth to be song to the Lute, Orpherian and Base Violl. 1601. [Selections, ed. E. H. Fellowes, 1923 (English School of Lutenist Song Writers, ser. 1, vols. VIII, IX); further selections, with Campion, ed. E. H. Fellowes, 1922–4 (English School of Lutenist Song Writers, ser. 1, vols. IV, XIII).] [See W. H. G. Flood, Musical Times, Dec. 1927.]

THOMAS BATESON (*c.* 1570–*c.* 1630)

Collected Madrigals. Ed. E. H. Fellowes, 1922 (English Madrigal School, vols. XXI, XXII).

The first set of English Madrigales to 3. 4. 5. and 6. voices. 1604; ed. E. F. Rimbault, Musical Antiquaries Soc. 1846.

The second set of Madrigales to 3. 4. 5. and 6. Parts. 1618.

MICHAEL EAST (or ESTE) (1580?–1640)

Collected Madrigals. Ed. E. H. Fellowes, 1923 (English Madrigal School, vols. XXIX–XXXI).

Madrigales to 3. 4. and 5. parts. 1604.

The Second Set of Madrigales. 1606.

The Third Set of Bookes. 1610.

The Fourth Set of Bookes. 1619.

The Fift Set of Bokes. 1618.

The Sixt Set of Bokes. 1624.

The Seventh Set of Bookes. 1638.

[See also The Triumphes of Oriana, 1601.]

THOMAS GREAVES

Songes of sundrie kindes. 1604; ed. E. H. Fellowes, 1924 (English Madrigal School, vol. XXXVI).

TOBIAS HUME (d. 1645)

The first part of Ayres, French, Pollish and others together. 1605.

FRANCIS PILKINGTON (1562?–1638)

The first booke of Songs or Ayres of 4. parts. 1605; ed. G. E. P. Arkwright, 1897–8 (Old English Edition, vols. 18–20); ed. E. H. Fellowes, 1922–5 (English School of Lutenist Song Writers, ser. 1, vols. VII, XV).

The first set of Madrigals and Pastorals. 1613; ed. E. H. Fellowes, 1923 (English Madrigal School, vol. XXV).

The second set of Madrigals and Pastorals. 1624; ed. E. H. Fellowes, 1923 (English Madrigal School, vol. XXVI).

[See also The Teares or Lamentacions of a Sorrowfull Soule, 1614.]

RICHARD ALISON (or ALLISON)

An Howres Recreation in Musicke, apt for Instrumentes and Voyces. 1606; ed. E. H. Fellowes, 1924 (English Madrigal School, vol. XXXIII). [See W. H. G. Flood, Musical Times, Sept. 1928.]

JOHN BARTLET

A Book of Ayres with a Triplicitie of Musicke. 1606; ed. E. H. Fellowes, 1925 (English School of Lutenist Song Writers, ser. 2, vol. x).

JOHN COOPER (or COPRARIO) (1580?–c. 1650?)

Funeral Teares. For the death of the Right Honorable the Earle of Devonshire. 1606.
Songs of Mourning: bewailing the untimely death of Prince Henry. 1613.
[See also The Teares or Lamentacions of a Sorrowfull Soule, 1614; J. Pulver, Giovanni Coprario alias John Cooper, Monthly Musical Record, April 1927.]

JOHN DANYEL (1564?–1625?)

Songs for the Lute Viol and Voice. 1606; ed. E. H. Fellowes, 1926 (English School of Lutenist Song Writers, ser. 2, vol. XIII). [See P. Heseltine, Musical Times, April 1925; W. H. G. Flood, Musical Times, March 1928.]

THOMAS FORD (1580?–1648)

Musicke of Sundrie Kindes, set forth in two Bookes. 1607. Airs to the lute, ed. E. H. Fellowes, 1921 (English School of Lutenist Song Writers, ser. 1, vol. III). [See also The Teares or Lamentacions of a Sorrowfull Soule, 1614.]

HENRY YOULL

Canzonets to three voyces. 1608; ed. E. H. Fellowes, 1923 (English Madrigal School, vol. XXVIII).

ALFONSO FERRABOSCO, the younger (1580?–1628)

Ayres. 1609; ed. E. H. Fellowes, 1927 (English School of Lutenist Song Writers, ser. 2, vol. xv).

THOMAS RAVENSCROFT (1583?–1633?)

Pammelia. Musickes Miscellanie. Or Mixed Varietie of Pleasant Roundelayes and delightfull Catches. 1609; 1618; ed. 'P. Warlock' (P. Heseltine), 1928. [Collected by T. Ravenscroft.]
Deuteromelia: or the Second part of Musicks melodie. 1609. [Collected by T. Ravenscroft.]
Melismata. Musicall Phansies. 1611. [Collected by T. Ravenscroft.]

A Brief Discourse of the true (but neglected) use of Charact'ring the Degrees by their Perfection, Imperfection, and Diminution in Measurable Musicke. 1614. [With songs by Ravenscroft, John Bennet and Edward Piers.]
[See J. Mark, Musical Times, Oct. 1924.]

WILLIAM CORKINE

Collected Airs. Ed. E. H. Fellowes, 1926 (English School of Lutenist Song Writers, ser. 2, vol. XIII).
Ayres, to sing and play to the Lute and Basse Viol. 1610.
The second book of Ayres. 1612.

A Musicall Banquet. 1610. [Compiled by Robert Dowland. Containing songs by Antony Holborne, J. Dowland, D. Batchelar, R. Martin, R. Hales, Tesseir and others.]

JOHN MAYNARD

The XII Wonders of the World. Set and composed for the Violl de Gambo, the Lute and the Voyce. 1611.

ORLANDO GIBBONS (1583–1625)

The first set of Madrigals and Mottets of 5. parts. 1612; ed. Sir G. Smart, Musical Antiquaries Soc. 1841; ed. E. H. Fellowes, 1914 (English Madrigal School, vol. v). [See also The Teares or Lamentacions of a Sorrowfull Soule, 1614; E. H. Fellowes, Orlando Gibbons, 1925; W. H. G. Flood, Musical Times, April 1929.]

HENRY LICHFILD

The first set of Madrigals of 5. Parts. 1613; ed. E. H. Fellowes, 1922 (English Madrigal School, vol. XVII).

JOHN WARD (d. c. 1640)

The first set of English Madrigals. 1613; ed. E. H. Fellowes, 1922 (English Madrigal School, vol. XIX). [See also The Teares or Lamentacions of a Sorrowfull Soule, 1614.]

The Teares or Lamentacions of a Sorrowfull Soule: Composed with Musicall Ayres and Songs. Set foorth by Sir William Leighton Knight. 1614. [Containing songs by Sir W. Leighton, John Wilbye, John Dowland, John Milton, R. Johnson, Thos. Ford, E. Hooper, R. Kindersley, N. Gyles, J. Coprario, J. Bull, W. Byrd, F. Pilkington, T. Lupo, R. Jones, M. Peerson, O. Gibbons, T. Weelkes, John Ward, A. Ferrabosco, T. Thopull.]
Sacred motets or anthems for four and five voices by W. Byrde and his contemporaries [from The Teares or Lamentacions of a Sorrowfull Soule]. Ed. Sir J. F. Bridge, 1922.

JOHN AMNER (d. 1641)

Sacred Hymnes, of 3. 4. 5. and 6. parts. 1615.

GEORGE MASON and JOHN EARSDEN

The Ayres that were sung and played, at Brougham Castle in Westmerland, in the Kings Entertainment. 1618.

THOMAS VAUTOR (b. c. 1590?)

The First Set: beeing Songs of divers Ayres and Natures. 1619; ed. E. H. Fellowes, 1924 (English Madrigal School, vol. XXXIV).

MARTIN PEERSON (1580?–1650)

Private Musicke, or the first booke of Ayres and Dialogues. 1620.
Mottects or Grave Chamber Musique. 1620.
[See also The Teares or Lamentacions of a Sorrowfull Soule, 1614.]

JOHN ADSON (d. 1640?)

Courtly Masquing Ayres, Composed to 5. and 6. Parts. 1621.

JOHN ATTEY (d. 1640?)

The first booke of Ayres of foure parts. 1622; ed. E. H. Fellowes, 1926 (English School of Lutenist Song Writers, ser. 2, vol. XVI).

THOMAS TOMKINS (1573?–1656)

Songs of 3. 4. 5. and 6. parts. 1622; ed. E. H. Fellowes, 1922 (English Madrigal School, vol. XVIII).

JOHN HILTON, the younger (1599–1657)

Ayres, or, Fa Las for three voyces. 1627; ed. J. Warren, Musical Antiquaries Soc. 1844.
Catch that, catch can, or A Choice Collection of Catches, Rounds & Canons. 1652; 1658 (rev. and enlarged by J. Playford); 1663 further enlarged).

WALTER PORTER (1590?–1659)

Madrigales and Ayres. Of two, three, foure and five Voyces. 1632.
Mottets of Two Voyces. 1657.

HENRY LAWES (1595–1662)

Comedies and tragi-comedies, with other poems by Mr. William Cartwright. The ayres and songs set by Mr. Henry Lawes. 1651.
Ayres and Dialogues for One, Two, and Three Voyces. The First Booke. 1653; The second book of Ayres and Dialogues. 1655; The third book. 1658 (re-issued 1669 as the third bk of The Treasury of Musick). [Selections from the first and second bks were issued by Playford in 1669, both as Select Ayres and

Dialogues, The second book and as bk 2 of The Treasury of Musick. See also Select Musicall Ayres, 1652; The Second Booke of Ayres, 1652; Select Musicall Ayres and Dialogues, 1653.]

Select Musicall Ayres, and Dialogues, for one and two Voyces. Published by John Playford. 1652. [Containing songs by J. Wilson, C. Colman, H. Lawes, W. Webb, W. Smegergill, R. Johnson, W. Lawes, N. Lanneare, J. Taylor, R. Smith.]
The Second Booke of Ayres. Published by John Playford. 1652. [Containing songs by N. Lanneare, C. Colman, W. Webb, W. Lawes, H. Lawes, W. Smegergill.]
Select Musicall Ayres and Dialogues, in Three Bookes. Published by John Playford. 1653. [Containing most of the songs ptd in the two preceding works, with the addn of a third bk of 15 songs by Webb, Lanneare; Wilson, W. Lawes, and W. Tompkins. Enlarged edn 1659, entitled Select Ayres and Dialogues for One, Two, and Three Voyces. Containing works by the following additional composers: Lady Deering, J. Goodgroome, J. Cobb, Playford, Jenkins, S. Ives. Re-issued 1669 as bk I of The Treasury of Musick.]

JOHN GAMBLE (d. 1687)

Ayres and Dialogues (To be Sung to the Theorbo-Lute or Base-Violl). 1656.
Second book of Ayres and Dialogues. 1659.

JOHN PLAYFORD (1623–1686?)

A Brief Introduction to the Skill of Musick: for Song and Viol. 1658; 1660 (enlarged); 1662 (a third book added). [12 further edns before 1700. See G. R. Hayes, Introduction to the Skill of Music, Musical Opinion, Feb. 1926; J. Pulver, Playford's Introduction to the Skill of Music, Monthly Music Record, July 1922.]
[See also Select Musicall Ayres, 1652; The Second Booke of Ayres, 1652; Select Musicall Ayres, 1653; W. B. Squire, Music and Letters, July 1923; F. Kidson, John Playford and 17th Century Music Publishing, Musical Quart. Oct. 1918; W. C. Smith, Unnoticed Catalogues of Early Music, Musical Times, July-Aug. 1926.]

JOHN WILSON (1595–1673)

Cheerfull Ayres or Ballads. 1660. [See also Select Musicall Ayres, 1652; The Second Booke of Ayres, 1652; Select Musicall Ayres, 1653.]   R. A. W.

3. THE DRAMA

I. GENERAL INTRODUCTION

BIBLIOGRAPHIES, COLLECTIONS OF PLAYS, GENERAL HISTORY AND CRITICISM

A. BIBLIOGRAPHIES AND DICTIONARIES OF PLAYS AND DRAMATISTS

[The earliest dramatic bibliographies are the booksellers' catalogues of: Richard Rogers and William Ley (appended to The Careless Shepherdess, 1656); Edward Archer (The Old Law, 1656); Francis Kirkman (Tom Tyler, 1661 and, expanded, Nicomede, 1671). These, and the dramatic entries in some publishers' lists of the same time, have been appended by W. W. Greg to A List of Masques, Bibliog. Soc. 1902. Greg's Notes on Dramatic Bibliographers, Malone Soc. Collections, vol. I, pts 4 and 5, 1911, vol. II, pt 3, 1931, provides a critical discussion of the 17th and 18th century lists of pre-Restoration plays. In addition to the bibliographies listed below the general bibliographies of the literature of the period (see pp. 317–9 above) should be consulted. A fuller list of the 18th and 19th century dictionaries and catalogues will be found in vol. II of this work.]

Phillips, Edward. Theatrum Poetarum. 1675; rev. [Sir S. E. Brydges], 1800.

Winstanley, William. Lives of the most Famous English Poets. 1687.

Langbaine, Gerard. Momus Triumphans. 1688 (re-issued as A New Catalogue of English Plays).

–––– An Account of the English Dramatick Poets. Oxford, 1691; rev. C. Gildon et al. [1698] (as The Lives and Characters of the English Dramatick Poets; re-issued 1699).

J[acob], G[iles]. The Poetical Register. 1719 (re-issued 1723).

[Mottley, John.] A Compleat List of All the English Dramatic Poets. [Appended to Thomas Whincop's Scanderberg, 1747.]

[Baker, D. E.] The Companion to the Play-House. 2 vols. 1764; rev. Isaac Reed, 2 vols. 1782 (as Biographia Dramatica); rev. Stephen Jones, 3 vols. in 4, 1812.

C[apell], E[dward]. Notitia Dramatica; or, Tables of Ancient Playes. [1774?] [Rptd in Notes and Various Readings, vol. III, 1783.]

Halliwell[-Phillipps], J. O. A Dictionary of Old English Plays. 1860.

Lowe, R. W. A Bibliographical Account of English Theatrical Literature. 1888.

Hazlitt, W. C. A Manual for the Collector and Amateur of Old English Plays. 1892.

Greg, W. W. A List of English Plays written before 1643 and printed before 1700. Bibliog. Soc. 1900.

–––– A List of Masques, Pageants, etc., supplementary to A List of English Plays. Bibliog. Soc. 1902. [The standard handlists.]

Chambers, Sir E. K. The Mediaeval Stage. 2 vols. Oxford, 1903. [Vol. II, Appendix x provides a critical catalogue of the miracle plays, moralities and interludes now extant.]

–––– The Elizabethan Stage. 4 vols. Oxford, 1923. [Chs. xxiii and xxiv, Playwrights (biographical notes, works and critical material) and Anonymous Work. Appendices K (Academic Plays), L (Printed Plays), M (Lost Plays), and N (Manuscript Plays) should also be consulted.]

Schelling, F. E. Elizabethan Drama. 2 vols. Boston, 1908. [Vol. II contains a detailed bibliographical summary.]

Reyher, Paul. Bibliographie des Ballets de 1603 à 1640. [In Les Masques anglais, pp. 518–32, Paris, 1909.]

Creizenach, Wilhelm. Verlorengegangene englische Dramen aus dem Zeitalter Shakespeares. Sh. Jb. LIV, 1918. [Supplements and completes Schelling's list.]

Sibley, G. M. The Lost Plays and Masques, 1500–1642. Ithaca, 1933.

Barrett, W. P. Chart of Plays, 1584 to 1623. Shakespeare Ass. 1934.

Harbage, A. Elizabethan and Seventeenth-Century Play Manuscripts. PMLA. L, 1935.

B. COLLECTIONS OF PLAYS

[Collections of the so-called Shakespeare Apocrypha and of Shakespeare's dramatic sources have generally been omitted. A list will be found under Shakespeare, pp. 576 and 583 below. The contents of most of the earlier collections are given in W. C. Hazlitt, A Manual for the Collector of Old English Plays, p. 267, 1892. The later collections are given in Sir E. K. Chambers, The Elizabethan Stage, vol. III, p. 205, 1923.]

Dodsley, Robert. A Select Collection of Old Plays. 12 vols. 1744; ed. Isaac Reed, 12 vols. 1780; ed. O. Gilchrist [and J. P. Collier], 12 vols. 1825–7; ed. W. C. Hazlitt, 15 vols. 1874–6. [Hazlitt's Dodsley, the standard edn, contains 83 plays: vol. I, Interlude of the Four Elements, Calisto and

Melibaea, Everyman, Hickscorner, The Pardoner and the Friar, The World and the Child, God's Promises, The Four P.P., Thersites; vol. ii, Interlude of Youth, Lusty Juventus, Jack Juggler, Nice Wanton, History of Jacob and Esau, Disobedient Child, Marriage of Wit and Science; vol. iii, New Custom, Ralph Roister Doister, Gammer Gurton's Needle, The Trial of Treasure, Like will to Like; vol. iv, Damon and Pithias, Appius and Virginia, Cambyses, The Misfortunes of Arthur, Jeronimo; vol. v, The Spanish Tragedy, Cornelia, Soliman and Perseda, Life and Death of Jack Straw; vol. vi, The Conflict of Conscience, Rare Triumphs of Love and Fortune, The Three Ladies of London, Three Lords and Three Ladies of London, A Knack to know a Knave; vol. vii, Tancred and Gismunda, Wounds of Civil War, Mucedorus, The Two Angry Women of Abington, Look about you; vol. viii, Summer's Last Will and Testament, Downfall of Robert Earl of Huntington, Death of Robert Earl of Huntington, Contention between Liberality and Prodigality, Grim the Collier of Croydon; vol. ix, How to choose a Good Wife from a Bad, The Return from Parnassus, Wily Beguiled, Lingua, Miseries of Enforced Marriage; vol. x, The Revenger's Tragedy, The Dumb Knight, The Merry Devil of Edmonton, Ram-Alley, The Second Maiden's Tragedy, Englishmen for My Money; vol. xi, A Woman is a Weathercock, Amends for Ladies, Green's Tu Quoque, Albumazar, The Hog hath lost his Pearl, The Heir; vol. xii, The Old Couple, A Woman never Vexed, The Ordinary, The London Chanticleers, The Shepherd's Holiday, The True Trojans, The Lost Lady; vol. xiii, A Match at Midnight, The City Nightcap, The City-Match, The Queen of Arragon, The Antiquary; vol. xiv, The Rebellion, Lust's Dominion, Andromana, Lady Alimony, The Parson's Wedding; vol. xv, Elvira, The Marriage Night, The Adventures of Five Hours, All Mistaken, Historia Histrionica.] (*Hazlitt's Dodsley.*)

[Chetwood, W. R.] A Select Collection of Old Plays. Dublin, 1750.

Hawkins, T. The Origin of the English Drama. 3 vols. Oxford, 1773.

[Nichols, John.] Six Old Plays on which Shakespeare founded his Measure for Measure. Comedy of Errors. The Taming of the Shrew. King John. King Henry IV and King Henry V. King Lear. 2 vols. 1779.

Lamb, Charles. Specimens of English Dramatic Poets. 1808; ed. Sir I. Gollancz, 2 vols. 1893.

[Scott, Sir Walter.] Ancient British Drama. 3 vols. 1810. (*Ancient British Drama.*)

[Dilke, C. W.] Old English Plays. 6 vols. 1814–5. [Supplements Dodsley.]

The Old English Drama. 2 vols. 1825. [Pbd by Hurst, Robinson, & Co., and A. Constable, but most of the plays have the separate imprint of C. Baldwyn, 1824, who is sometimes referred to as the editor.]

Collier, J. P. Five Old Plays. 1828; 1833. [Issued as a supplement to Collier's Dodsley.]

—— Five Old Plays. Roxburghe Club, 1851. [A different collection from that of 1828.]

The Old English Drama. 3 vols. 1830. [Pbd by Thomas White, who was perhaps the editor.]

C[hild], F. J. Four Old Plays. Cambridge, U.S.A. 1848.

Amyot, T. *et al.* A Supplement to Dodsley's Old English Plays. 4 vols. 1853. [The plays were originally issued separately in the Publications of the Shakespeare Soc. 1841–53.]

Keltie, J. S. The Works of the British Dramatists. 1870.

Hazlitt, W. C. Shakespeare's Library. Second Edition. Part 1, 4 vols.; part 2, 2 vols. 1875. [Pt 1 is based on Collier's Shakespeare's Library; pt 2 on Nichols and Amyot.]

Simpson, Richard. The School of Shakspere. 2 vols. 1878.

Bullen, A. H. A Collection of Old English Plays. 4 vols. 1882–5.

—— Old English Plays. New Ser. 3 vols. 1887–90.

The Mermaid Series. 1887–1909. [Selected plays by various editors; includes Beaumont and Fletcher, Chapman, Dekker, Ford, Greene, Heywood, Jonson, Marlowe, Massinger, Middleton, Shirley, Webster and Tourneur, and Nero and other Plays (Nero, 1624; Porter's Two Angry Women of Abington; Day's Parliament of Bees, and Humour out of Breath; Field's Woman is a Weathercock, and Amends for Ladies).]

Pollard, A. W. English Miracle Plays, Moralities and Interludes. Oxford, 1890; Oxford, 1927 (rev. edn). [Selected scenes.]

The Temple Dramatists. 1896–1906. Ser. 2, 1933–. [Single plays by various editors, including Beaumont and Fletcher (The Faithful Shepherdess, The Knight of the Burning Pestle, Philaster), Dekker (Old Fortunatus), Ford (The Broken Heart), Heywood (A Woman Killed with Kindness), Jonson (Every Man in his Humour), Kyd (The Spanish Tragedy), Marlowe (Doctor Faustus, Edward II), Marston (The Malcontent), Massinger (A New Way to

Pay Old Debts), Peele (The Arraignment of Paris), Tourneur (The Revenger's Tragedy), Udall (Ralph Roister Doister), Webster (The Duchess of Malfi, The White Devil), and Arden of Feversham, Edward III, The Merry Devil of Edmonton, Selimus, The Two Noble Kinsmen, The Return from Parnassus.]

Manly, J. M. Specimens of Pre-Shakespearean Drama. 2 vols. Boston, 1897–8, 1900–3. (*Manly.*)

Evans, H. A. English Masques. 1897. (Warwick Lib.)

Jahrbuch der deutschen Shakespeare-Gesellschaft. 1897–. [Includes at intervals from vol. xxxiii plays by various editors. Vol. xxxiii, Wilson's Cobbler's Prophecy; vol. xxxv, Shakespeare's Richard II; vol. xxxvi Wager's The Longer Thou Livest; vol. xxxvii, The Wars of Cyrus; vol. xxxviii, Jonson's Every Man in his Humour; vol. xl, Lupton's All for Money; vol. xliii, Wapull's The Tide Tarrieth No Man; vol. xlvi, Lumley's Iphigenia; vols. xlvii, xlviii, Caesar and Pompey.]

Brandl, Alois. Quellen des weltlichen Dramas in England vor Shakespeare. Ein Ergänzungsband zu Dodsley's 'Old English Plays.' QF. lxxx, 1898. (*Brandl.*)

Baker, G. P. *et al.* The Belles Lettres Series. Section iii. The English Drama. Boston, 1902–15. [Selected plays of Beaumont and Fletcher, Chapman, Dekker, Ford, Gascoigne, Jonson and Webster in separate volumes by various editors.]

Bang, W. *et al.* Materialien zur Kunde des älteren englischen Dramas. Louvain, 1902–. [First Ser. includes, besides other material, the following plays in facs. in the order issued: Henry Chettle and John Day, The Blind Beggar of Bednall Green, ed. from 1659 quarto W. Bang; The King and Queenes Entertainement at Richmond, ed. from 1656 quarto W. Bang and R. Brotanek; Thomas Heywood, Pleasant Dialogues and Drammas, ed. from 1637 octavo W. Bang; Everyman, rptd from Skot's edn at Britwell W. W. Greg; Godly Queene Hester, ed. from 1561 quarto W. W. Greg; Barnabe Barnes, The Devil's Charter, ed. from 1607 quarto R. B. McKerrow; Ben Jonson, Dramas, rptd from 1616 folio W. Bang, 2 pts; Pedantius, ed. G. C. Moore Smith; Ben Jonson, Every Man in his Humor, rptd from 1601 quarto W. Bang and W. W. Greg; Ben Jonson, Sad Shepherd, ed. W. W. Greg; The Enterlude of Youth, with fragments of the Playe of Lucres and of Nature, ed. W. Bang and R. B. McKerrow; The Queen, ed. from 1653 quarto W. Bang; Abraham Fraunce, Victoria, ed. from MS

G. C. Moore Smith; Ben Jonson, Every Man out of his Humor, rptd from Holmes' 1600 quarto W. Bang and W. W. Greg; Ben Jonson, Every Man out of his Humour, rptd from Linge's 1600 quarto W. Bang and W. W. Greg; Anthony Brewer, The Love-Sick King, ed. from 1655 quarto A. E. H. Swaen; Thomas Dekker, Satiro-Mastix, rptd from 1602 edn H. Scherer; Ben Jonson, The Fountain of Self-Love, rptd from 1601 quarto W. Bang and L. Krebs; John Ford's Dramatic Works, rptd from quartos W. Bang, pt 1; Everyman, rptd (from Skot's edn *penes* A. H. Huth) W. W. Greg; John Bale, Kynge Johan, ed. from MS W. Bang; Sir Gyles Goosecappe, ed. from 1606 quarto W. Bang and R. Brotanek, pt 1; Everyman, rptd W. W. Greg from Pynson fragments; Nathaniel Richards, Tragedy of Messalina, ed. A. R. Skemp; Samuel Daniel, The Tragedy of Cleopatra, rptd M. Lederer from 1611 edn; A Newe Interlude of Impacyente Poverte, ed. from 1560 quarto R. B. McKerrow; How a Man may chuse a Good Wife from a Bad, ed. A. E. H. Swaen; Edward Sharpham, The Fleire, ed. from 1607 quarto H. Nibbe; John Mason, The Turke, ed. from 1610 and 1632 quartos J. Q. Adams; John Studley's Translation of Seneca's Agamemnon and Medea, ed. from 1566 octavos E. M. Spearing; Ben Jonson, A Tale of a Tub, rptd H. Scherer from 1640 edn; William Heming, The Jewes Tragedy, ed. from 1662 quarto H. A. Cohn; Jasper Heywood's Translations of Seneca's Troas, Thyestes and Hercules Furens, ed. from 1559, 1560 and 1561 octavos H. de Vocht; William Sampson, Vow-Breaker, ed. H. Wallrath; Thomas May, Tragedy of Julia Agrippina, ed. F. E. Schmid. New Ser. 1928– includes: John Ford, Dramatic Works, rptd from quartos H. de Vocht, pt ii; Simon Baylie, The Wizard, ed. from MS H. de Vocht; Lust's Dominion, ed. from 1657 edn J. le G. Brereton; Robert Gomersall, The Tragedie of Lodovick Sforsa, ed. from 1628 quarto B. R. Pearn.] (*Bang.*)

Gayley, C. M. *et al.* Representative English Comedies. 3 vols. New York, 1903–14. [Includes, with some general discussions, the following plays with full critical introductions: vol. i, John Heywood, Play of the Wether, Mery Play betweene Johan Johan, Tyb, etc., ed. A. W. Pollard; Nicholas Udall, Ralph Roister Doister, ed. Ewald Flügel; William Stevenson, Gammer Gurton's Needle, ed. Henry Bradley; John Lyly, Alexander and Campaspe, ed. G. P. Baker; George Peele, The Old Wives' Tale, ed. F. B. Gummere; Robert Greene,

Honourable Historie of Frier Bacon, ed. C. M. Gayley; Henry Porter, The Two Angry Women of Abington, ed. C. M. Gayley. Vol. II, Ben Jonson, Every Man in His Humour, ed. C. H. Herford; Epicoene, ed. C. M. Gayley; The Alchemist, ed. G. A. Smithson; Eastward Hoe, ed. J. W. Cunliffe; The Merry Devill of Edmonton, ed. J. M. Manly. Vol. III, Thomas Dekker, The Shoemakers Holiday, ed. A. F. Lange; Thomas Middleton, The Spanish Gipsie, ed. H. B. Clarke; John Fletcher, Rule a Wife and have a Wife, ed. George Saintsbury; Philip Massinger, A New Way to pay Old Debts, ed. Brander Matthews; Richard Brome, The Antipodes, ed. G. P. Baker; James Shirley, The Royall Master, ed. Sir A. W. Ward.] (Gayley.)

Farmer, J. S. Early English Dramatists. 12 vols. Early English Drama Soc. 1905–8. [Includes the 5 following collections.]

—— Six Anonymous Plays. First Series (c. 1510–1537). Early English Drama Soc. 1905.

—— Six Anonymous Plays (Second Series). Early English Drama Soc. 1906.

—— Anonymous Plays (3rd Series). Early English Drama Soc. 1906.

—— 'Lost' Tudor Plays, with some others. Early English Drama Soc. 1907.

—— Five Anonymous Plays (Fourth Series). Early English Drama Soc. 1908.

—— The Museum Dramatists. Early English Drama Soc. 1906–. [Single plays with notes and introductions.]

—— Tudor Facsimile Texts. 143 vols. 1907–14. [Farmer's Hand List to the Tudor Facsimile Texts, 1914, includes several plays that were never issued. Some of the plays have been re-issued as Old English Plays, Student's Facsimile Edition. Plays in alphabetical order: Thomas Lupton, All for Money, 1578; R. B., Apius and Virginia, 1575; Arden of Feversham, 1592; P. Massinger, Believe As Ye List (from MS); The Birth of Merlin, 1662; J. Day, The Blind Beggar of Bednal Green, 1659; T. D., The Bloody Banquet, 1620; Caesar and Pompey, 1607; Calisto and Melibea, [1530?]; T. Preston, Cambyses, King of Persia, [1584?]; The Castle of Perseverance (from MS); J. Bale, The Chief Promises of God, 1538; Clyomon and Clamydes, 1599; R. Wilson, The Cobbler's Prophecie, 1594; N. Woodes, The Conflict of Conscience, 1581; The Contention between Liberality and Prodigality, 1602; The Contention betwixt York and Lancaster, 1594; R. Edwards, Damon and Pithias, 1571; A. Munday, The Death of Robert, Earl of Huntington, 1601; B. Barnes, The Devil's Charter, 1607; C.

Marlowe and T. Nashe, Dido, Queene of Carthage, 1594; T. Ingelend, The Disobedient Child, [1560?]; C. Marlowe, Doctor Faustus, 1604; A. Munday, The Downfall of Robert, Earl of Huntington, 1601; G. Chapman, etc., Eastward Hoe, 1605; W. Haughton, Englishmen for My Money, 1616; Everyman, [1500–6?]; Every Woman in Her Humor, 1609; Fair Em, 1631; The Fair Maid of Bristow, 1605; The Famous Victories of Henry the Fifth, 1598; T. Sackville and T. Norton, Ferrex and Porrex, [1570?]; R. Greene, Friar Bacon and Friar Bungay, 1594; W. S., Gammer Gurton's Needle, 1575; [J. Rastell], Gentleness and Nobility, [1527?]; George a Greene, 1599; R. Wilmot, etc., Gismond of Salerne (from MS); G. Gascoigne, The Glass of Government, 1575; J. Cooke, Greene's Tu-quoque, 1614; Grim, the Collier of Croydon, 1662; Histrio-Mastix, 1610; H. Chettle, Hoffman, 1631; S. S., The Honest Lawyer, 1616; J. Pickering, Horestes, 1567; How a Man May Choose a Good Wife from a Bad, 1602; Impatient Poverty, 1560; Jack Drum's Entertainment, 1601; Jack Juggler, 1563; Jacob and Esau, 1568; Johan the Evangelist, [1565?]; A. Munday, John-a-Kent and John-a-Cumber (from MS); J. Heywood, John John the Husband, [1533?]; King Darius, 1565; King Edward the Third, 1596; King Leir, 1605; W. Shakespeare, King Richard the third, 1597; A Knack to Know an Honest Man, 1596; A Knack to Know a Knave, 1594; A Larum for London, 1602; U. Fulwell, Like Will to Like, 1587; The Life and Death of Jack Straw, 1593; The Life and Death of Captain Thomas Stukeley, 1605; L. Wager, The Life and Repentance of Mary Magdalene, 1567; Locrine, 1595; The London Prodigal, 1605; W. Wager, The Longer Thou Livest, [1568?]; Look About You and Be Not Wroth, 1600; T. Lodge and R. Greene, A Looking Glass for London, 1598; R. Wever, Lusty Juventus, 1540; J. Skelton, Magnificence, [1530]; Mankind (from MS); The Marriage of Wit and Science, [1570?]; [J. Lyly], Maid's Metamorphosis, 1600; The Merry Devil of Edmonton, 1608; Mind, Will and Understanding (from MS); G. Wilkins, The Miseries of Enforced Marriage, 1607; T. Hughes, The Misfortunes of Arthur, 1587; Mucedorus, 1598; H. Medwall, Nature, [1530?]; [J. Rastell], The Nature of the Four Elements, 1519; Nero, 1607; New Custom, 1573; Nice Wanton, 1560, [1565?]; S. R., The Noble Soldier, 1634; T. Dekker and J. Webster, Northward Hoe, 1607; J. Heywood, The Pardoner and the Frere, [1521?]; H. Chettle, etc., Patient Grissil,

1603; The Pedler's Prophecy, 1595; The
Pilgrimage to Parnassus (from MS); J.
Heywood, The Play of Love, 1533; J. Hey-
wood, Play of the Weather, 1533; G. Whet-
stone, Promos and Cassandra, 1578; W. S.,
The Puritan, 1607; L. Barry, Ram Alley,
1611; Respublica (from MS); The Return
from Parnassus, 2 pts (from MS and 1606);
Richard Duke of York, 1600; T. Middleton
and T. Dekker, The Roaring Girl, 1611; Sir
Gyles Goosecappe, 1606; M. Drayton, etc.,
Sir John Oldcastle, 1600; A. Munday, etc.,
Sir Thomas More (from MS); T. Dekker and
J. Webster, Sir Thomas Wyat, 1607; Solimon
and Perseda, 1599 (really from an 1815
forgery); Swetnam, 1620; The Taming of a
Shrew, 1594; R. Wilmot, etc. Tancred and
Gismund, 1591; J. Bale, The Temptations
of Our Lord, 1538; Thersytes, [1537?];
Thomas Lord Cromwell, 1602; R. Wilson,
The Three Ladies of London, 1584; J. Bale,
The Three Laws, 1538; R. Wilson, The
Three Lords and Three Ladies of London,
1590; G. Wapull, The Tide Tarrieth No
Man, 1576; Tom Tyler and his Wife, 1661;
The Trial of Treasure, 1567; The Trouble-
some Reign of King John, 1591; The Trial
of Chivalry, 1605; H. Porter, The Two
Angry Women of Abington, 1599; R. Yaring-
ton, Two Lamentable Tragedies, 1601; R.
Armin, Two Maids of More-Clacke, 1609;
The Two Merry Milkmaids, 1620; J.
Fletcher and W. Shakespeare, The Two
Noble Kinsmen, 1634; Two Wise Men,
1619; R. A., The Valiant Welshman, 1615;
S. Brandon, The Virtuous Octavia, 1598; A
Warning for Fair Women, 1599; The Wars
of Cyrus, 1594; The Weakest goeth to the
Wall, 1600; Wealth and Health, [1558?];
T. Dekker and J. Webster, Westward Hoe,
1607; S. Rowley, When you see me you
know me, 1613; Wily Beguiled, 1606; The
Wisdom of Doctor Dodypoll, 1600; J.
Redford, Wit and Science (from MS); The
Wit of a Woman, 1604; J. Heywood, Witty
and Witless (from MS); The World and the
Child, 1522; A Yorkshire Tragedy, 1608;
Youth, [1520?], [1557], [1562?]. (TFT.)

Greg, W. W. et al. The Malone Society
Reprints. 1907–. [Facs. rpts, often with
critical introductions, in order of publication: G. Peele, The Battle of Alcazar, 1594;
R. Greene, The History of Orlando Furioso,
1594; The Interlude of Johan the Evangelist, [1560?]; The Interlude of Wealth and
Health; [1557?] The History of King Leir,
1605; [J. Rastell?], The Interlude of Calisto
and Melebea, [1527?]; W. S., The Tragedy
of Locrine, 1595; A. Munday, etc., The Life
of Sir John Oldcastle, 1600; [R. Greene?],
The Tragical Reign of Selimus, 1594; G.

P[eele], The Old Wives Tale, 1595; J. Phillip,
The Play of Patient Grissell, [1566?]; Iphi-
genia at Aulis, tr. Lady Lumley (from MS);
S. Brandon, The Virtuous Octavia, [1598];
[A. Munday?], Fidele and Fortunio, the Two
Italian Gentlemen, 1585 (imperfect); The
Second Maiden's Tragedy (from MS); G.
Peele, The Arraignment of Paris, 1584; Tom
Tyler and his Wife, 1661; T. Lodge, The
Wounds of Civil War, 1594; A Knack to Know
an Honest Man, 1596; The Birth of Hercules
(from MS); R. B., Apius and Virginia, 1575;
G. Peele, King Edward the First, 1593; The
Comedy of George a Green, 1599; The
Tragedy of Caesar's Revenge, [1606?]; The
Book of Sir Thomas More (from MS);
G. Peele, The Love of King David and Fair
Bethsabe, 1599; H. Porter, The Two Angry
Women of Abington, 1599; The Weakest
goeth to the Wall, 1600; Wily Beguiled,
1606; W. Haughton, Englishmen for My
Money, 1616; The Resurrection of Our Lord
(from imperfect MS); Cleomon and Clamy-
des, 1599; Look about You, 1600; A Larum
for London, 1602; The Contention between
Liberality and Prodigality, 1602; The Wit
of a Woman, 1604; Lady E[lizabeth]
C[ary], The Tragedy of Mariam, 1613;
R. Wilson, The Cobler's Prophecy, 1594;
The Pedlar's Prophecy, 1595; R. Wilmot,
etc., The Tragedy of Tancred and Gismund,
1591; The Tragedy of Tiberius, 1607; The
Welsh Embassador (from MS); B. J[onson],
Every Man out of His Humour, 1600
(Holme's first edn); R. Greene, The Scottish
History of James the Fourth, 1598; J. M[ar-
ston], Antonio and Mellida and Antonio's
Revenge, 1602; The Christmas Prince (from
MS); A. Munday, John a Kent and John a
Cumber (from MS); T. Kyd, The Spanish
Tragedy with Additions, 1602; C. Marlowe,
Edward the Second, 1594; R. G[reene],
Alphonsus King of Aragon, 1599; R. Greene,
Friar Bacon and Friar Bungay, 1594; P.
Massinger, Believe as You list (from MS);
Fair Em, [1593?]; Edmond Ironside, or,
War hath made All Friends (from MS); G.
Chapman, The Blind Beggar of Alexandria,
1598; P. Massinger, The Parliament of Love
(from MS); C. Marlowe, The Massacre of
Paris, [1594?]; The True Tragedy of Richard
III, 1594; The First Part of the Reign of King
Richard II, or, Thomas of Woodstock (from
MS); The Two Noble Ladies (from MS); The
Rare Triumphs of Love and Fortune, 1589; J.
Bale, King Johan (from MS); T. Lodge and
R. Greene, A Looking-Glass for London and
England, 1594; W. Mountfort, The Launch-
ing of the Mary (from MS); Jack Juggler,
[1562?]; J. Lyly, Alexander and Campaspe
1584.

The following fragmentary plays have been rptd in the Malone Soc. Collections: pt. 1, 1907, Love Feigned and Unfeigned, a fragmentary morality; The Prodigal Son, a fragmentary interlude ptd *c.* 1530; pt 2, 1908, Robin Hood and the Sheriff of Nottingham, [*c.* 1475]; A Play of Robin Hood for May-Games; The Play of Lucrece, a fragmentary interlude; pt 3, 1909, Albion Knight, an imperfect morality; Temperance and Humility, a fragmentary morality; pts 4 and 5, 1911, The Cruel Debtor, a fragmentary morality; vol. II, pt 2, 1923, The Cruel Debtor, a further fragment; vol. II, pt 3, 1931, Somebody and Others, or the Spoiling of Lady Verity (fragment). The Malone Soc. has also pbd documents, etc. of theatrical interest.] (*Malone Soc.*)

Brooke, C. F. T. The Shakespeare Apocrypha. Oxford, 1908. [14 plays that have been ascribed to Shakespeare.]

Thorndike, A. H. The Minor Elizabethan Drama. I. Pre-Shakespearean Tragedies; II. Pre-Shakespearean Comedies. 2 vols. [1910]. (Everyman's Lib.)

Bond, R. W. Early Plays from the Italian. Oxford, 1911.

Neilson, W. A. The Chief Elizabethan Dramatists. Boston, 1911.

Cunliffe, J. W. Early English Classical Tragedies. Oxford, 1912.

Schelling, F. E. *et al.* Masterpieces of the English Drama. New York, 1912–. [Similar to the Mermaid Ser.]

—— Typical Elizabethan Plays. New York, 1926, 1931 (enlarged).

Tatlock, J. S. P. and Martin, R. G. Representative English Plays. New York, 1916; 1923.

Adams, J. Q. Chief Pre-Shakespearean Dramas. Boston, 1924. (*Adams.*)

Oliphant, E. H. C. Shakespeare and his Fellow Dramatists. 2 vols. New York, 1929.

Rylands, G. Six Elizabethan Tragedies. 1931.

Brooke, C. F. T. and Paradise, N. B. English Drama, 1580–1642. Boston, 1933.

Spencer, H. Elizabethan Plays. Boston, 1933.

Baskervill, C. R., Heltzel, V. B. and Nethercot, A. H. Elizabethan and Stuart Plays. New York, 1934.

Boas, F. S. Five Pre-Shakespearean Comedies (Early Tudor Period). 1934. (World's Classics.)

McIlwraith, A. K. Five Elizabethan Comedies. 1934. (World's Classics.)

C. DRAMATIC HISTORY AND CRITICISM

(1) GENERAL SURVEYS

[The earliest accounts of the Tudor-Stuart drama are in the dictionaries of dramatists and plays of the 17th and 18th centuries (see p. 487 above) and the general histories of English literature (see pp. 319–21 above). Only the more important of these are included here.]

Langbaine, Gerard. An Account of the English Dramatick Poets. Oxford, 1691.

[Baker, D. E.] The Companion to the Play-House. 2 vols. 1764; rev. Isaac Reed, 2 vols. 1782 (as Biographia Dramatica); rev. Stephen Jones, 3 vols. in 4, 1812.

Warton, Thomas. The History of English Poetry. 4 vols. 1774–81; ed. W. C. Hazlitt, 4 vols. 1871.

Drake, N. Shakespeare and his Times. 1817.

Collier, J. P. The History of English Dramatic Poetry to the Time of Shakespeare, and Annals of the Stage to the Restoration. 3 vols. 1831; 3 vols. 1879 (rev. edn).

Genest, John. Some Account of the English Stage, from 1660 to 1830. 10 vols. Bath, 1832.

Mézières, A. Prédécesseurs et Contemporains de Shakespeare. Paris, 1863.

—— Contemporains et Successeurs de Shakespeare. Paris, 1864.

Klein, J. L. Geschichte des Dramas. 13 vols. in 15, Leipzig, 1865–86. [Vols. XII and XIII.]

Hazlitt, W. C. Handbook to the Popular and Dramatic Literature of Great Britain. 1867.

—— The English Drama and Stage, 1543–1664. Illustrated by Documents, Treatises and Poems. 1869. (Roxburghe Lib.)

Ward, Sir A. W. A History of English Dramatic Literature to the Death of Queen Anne. 2 vols. 1875; 3 vols. 1899 (rev. edn).

Jusserand, J. J. Le Théâtre en Angleterre jusqu'aux Prédécesseurs immédiats de Shakespeare. Paris, 1878; Paris, 1881.

Proelss, R. Geschichte des neueren Dramas. 3 vols. Leipzig, 1880–3. [Vol. II.]

Symonds, J. A. Shakspere's Predecessors in the English Drama. 1884; 1900 (rev. edn).

Fleay, F. G. A Chronicle History of the London Stage, 1559–1642. 1890.

—— A Biographical Chronicle of the English Drama, 1559–1642. 2 vols. 1891.

Creizenach, W. Geschichte des neueren Dramas. 5 vols. Halle, 1893–1916 (vols. I–II rev. 1911–23). [Vols. IV and V tr. Eng. 1916 (as The English Drama in the Age of Shakespeare).]

Courthope, W. J. A History of English Poetry. 6 vols. 1895–1910. [Vol. IV.]

Boas, F. S. Shakspere and his Predecessors. 1896.

—— An Introduction to Tudor Drama. Oxford, 1933.

Brandl, A. Quellen des weltlichen Dramas in England vor Shakespeare. QF. LXXX 1898. [Introduction.]

Seccombe, T. and Allen, J. W. The Age of Shakespeare (1579–1631). 2 vols. 1903. [Vol. II.]

Matthews, B. The Development of the Drama. New York, 1904.

Crawford, C. Collectanea. 2 vols. Stratford-on-Avon, 1906–7.

Thorndike, A. H. Tragedy. Boston, 1908.

—— English Comedy. New York, 1929.

Schelling, F. E. Elizabethan Drama, 1558–1642. 2 vols. Boston, 1908.

—— Elizabethan Playwrights. A Short History of the English Drama to 1642. 1925.

Cambridge History of English Literature. Vols. V and VI, Cambridge, 1910.

Brooke, C. F. T. The Tudor Drama. A History of English Drama to the Retirement of Shakespeare. 1912.

Wallace, C. W. The Evolution of the English Drama up to Shakespeare. Berlin, 1912.

Spens, Janet. Elizabethan Drama. 1922.

Harrison, G. B. Shakespeare's Fellows; being a Brief Chronicle of the Shakespearean Age. 1923.

—— The Story of Elizabethan Drama. Cambridge, 1924.

Nicoll, A. British Drama. An Historical Survey. 1925.

Reed, A. W. Early Tudor Drama. 1926.

Mackenzie, A. M. The Playgoer's Handbook to the English Renaissance Drama. 1927.

Eckhardt, Eduard. Das englische Drama im Zeitalter der Reformation und der Hochrenaissance. Berlin, 1928.

—— Das englische Drama der Spätrenaissance. Shakespeares Nachfolger. Berlin, 1929.

Sisson, C. J. The Elizabethan Dramatists, except Shakespeare. 1928.

Aronstein, Philipp. Das englische Renaissancedrama. Leipzig, 1929.

Le Théâtre élizabéthain. Cahiers du Sud, X, 1933. [Contributions by H. G. Barker, T. S. Eliot, W. Empson, A. Koszul, etc.]

Ellis-Fermor, U. M. The Jacobean Drama. An Interpretation. 1936.

Harbage, A. Cavalier Drama. New York, 1936.

(2) Special Studies

(a) *The Dramatic Forms*

Singer, H. W. Das bürgerliche Trauerspiel in England. Leipzig, 1892.

Seifert, J. Die Wit- und Science-Moralitäten. Karolinenthal, 1892.

Fischer, R. Zur Kunstentwicklung der englischen Tragödie bis zu Shakespeare. Strasburg, 1893.

Winscheid, K. Die englische Hirtendichtung von 1597–1675. 1895.

Chambers, Sir E. K. English Pastorals. 1895. [Introduction.]

Evans, H. A. English Masques. 1897. [Introduction.]

Churchill, G. B. and Keller, Wolfgang. Die lateinischen Universitätsdramen Englands in der Zeit der Königin Elisabeth. Sh. Jb. XXXIV, 1898. [Supplemented by L. B. Morgan, Sh. Jb. XLVII, 1911.]

Thorndike, A. H. The Pastoral Element in the English Drama before 1605. MLN. XIV, 1900.

—— Court Masques and the Drama. PMLA. XV, 1906.

Schelling, F. E. The English Chronicle Play. New York, 1902.

Brotanek, Rudolf. Die englischen Maskenspiele. Vienna, 1902.

Chase, L. N. The English Heroic Play. New York, 1903.

Child, C. G. The Rise of the Heroic Play. MLN. XIX, 1904.

Laidler, J. History of Pastoral Drama in England until 1700. E. Studien, XXXV, 1905.

Greg, W. W. Pastoral Poetry and Pastoral Drama. 1906.

Ballweg, Oscar. Das klassizistische Drama zur Zeit Shakespeares. Heidelberg, 1909.

Reyher, Paul. Les Masques anglais (1512–1640). Paris, 1909.

Ristine, F. H. English Tragi-comedy. New York, 1910.

Thompson, E. N. S. The English Moral Plays. New Haven, 1910.

Bayne, Ronald. Masque and Pastoral. CHEL. vol. VI, 1910.

Boas, F. S. University Plays. CHEL. vol. VI, 1910.

—— University Drama in the Tudor Age. Oxford, 1914.

Cunliffe, J. W. Early English Classical Tragedies. Oxford, 1912. [Introduction.]

McConaughty, J. L. The School Drama. 1913.

Baskervill, C. R. Some Evidence for Early Romantic Plays in England. MP. XIV, 1916.

—— The Elizabethan Jig and related Song Drama. Chicago, 1929.

Simpson, Percy. The Masque. [In Shakespeare's England, vol. II, Oxford, 1916.]

Ellison, L. M. The Early Romantic Drama at the English Court. Chicago, 1917.

Kastner, L. E. and Charlton, H. B. The Poetical Works of Sir William Alexander, Earl of Sterling. 2 vols. STC. and Manchester, 1921–9. [Vol. I includes detailed survey of Senecan drama.]

Reed, A. W. The Beginnings of the English Secular and Romantic Drama. Shakespeare Ass. lecture, 1922.

Moore Smith, G. C. College Plays performed in the University of Cambridge. Cambridge, 1923.

Welsford, Enid. The Court Masque. Cambridge, 1927.

Genouy, H. L'Élément pastoral dans la Poésie narrative et le Drame en Angleterre de 1579 à 1640. Paris, 1929.

Motter, T. H. V. The School Drama in England. 1929.

(b) Sources and Influences

[The section Literary Relations with the Continent, pp. 325–45 above, should also be consulted.]

Herford, C. H. Studies in the Literary Relations of England and Germany in the Sixteenth Century. Cambridge, 1886.

Stiefel, A. L. Die Nachahmung spanischer Komödien in England unter den ersten Stuarts. Romanische Forschungen, v, 1890.

Koeppel, E. Studien zur Geschichte der italienischen Novelle in der englischen Litteratur des sechzehnten Jahrhunderts. QF. LXX, 1892.

—— Quellen-Studien zu den Dramen Ben Jonsons, John Marstons, und Beaumont und Fletchers. Erlangen, 1895.

—— Zur Quellen-Kunde der Stuarts-Dramen. Archiv, XCVII, 1896.

—— Quellen-Studien zu den Dramen George Chapmans, Philip Massingers und John Fords. QF. LXXXII, 1897.

—— Studien über Shakespeares Wirkung auf zeitgenössische Dramatiker. *Bang.* vol. IX, 1905.

—— Ben Jonsons Wirkung auf zeitgenössische Dramatiker. Heidelberg, 1906.

Bahlsen, L. Spanische Quellen der dramatischen Litteratur besonders Englands zu Shakespeares Zeit. Zeitschrift für vergleichende Litteraturgeschichte, VI, 1893.

Cunliffe, J. W. The Influence of Seneca on Elizabethan Tragedy. 1893.

—— Italian Prototypes of Masque and Dumbshow. PMLA. XXII, 1907.

—— The Influence of Italian on Early Elizabethan Drama. MP. IV, 1907.

Meyer, E. Machiavelli and the Elizabethan Drama. Berlin, 1897.

Smith, H. Pastoral Influence in English Drama. 1897.

Underhill, J. G. Spanish Literature in the England of the Tudors. New York, 1899.

Schücking, L. L. Studien über die stofflichen Beziehungen der englischen Komödie zur italienischen bis Lilly. Halle, 1901.

Ballmann, O. Chaucers Einfluss auf das englische Drama. Ang. XXV, 1902.

Rosenbach, A. S. W. The Curious Impertinent in English Dramatic Literature. MLN. XVII, 1902.

—— The Influence of the Celestina in the Early English Drama. Sh. Jb. XXXIX, 1903.

Ott, A. Die italienische Novelle im englischen Drama von 1600 bis zur Restauration. Zürich, 1904.

Fitzmaurice-Kelly, J. Cervantes in England. British Academy Lecture, 1905.

Bang, W. and de Vocht, H. Klassiker und Humanisten als Quelle älterer Dramatiker. E. Studien, XXXVI, 1906.

Manly, J. M. The Influence of the Tragedies of Seneca upon Early English Drama. [Prefixed to F. J. Miller, Tragedies of Seneca translated into English Verse, Chicago, 1907.]

Upham, A. H. The French Influence in English Literature from the Accession of Elizabeth to the Restoration. New York, 1908.

Watt, L. M. Attic and Elizabethan Tragedy. 1908.

Smith, W. Italian and Elizabethan Comedy. MP. V, 1908.

—— The Commedia dell' Arte. New York, 1912.

Ballweg, O. Das klassizistische Drama zur Zeit Shakespeares. Heidelberg, 1909.

Smith, R. M. Froissart and the English Chronicle Play. 1915.

Scott, M. A. Elizabethan Translations from the Italian. Boston, 1916.

Villey, P. Montaigne et les Poètes dramatiques anglais du Temps de Shakespeare. Revue d'Histoire littéraire, XXIV, 1917.

Grossman, R. Spanien und das elisabethanische Drama. Hamburg, 1920.

Lucas, F. L. Seneca and Elizabethan Tragedy. Cambridge, 1922.

Schelling, F. E. Foreign Influences in Elizabethan Plays. New York, 1923.

Gargano, G. S. Scapigliatura italiana a Londra. Florence, 1923.

—— Machiavelli e il Machiavelismo nel Teatro elisabethiano. Marzocco, 13 July 1930.

Welsford, Enid. The Italian Influence on the English Court Masque. MLR. XVIII, 1923.

Witherspoon, A. M. The Influence of Robert Garnier on Elizabethan Drama. New Haven, 1924.

Jeffrey, V. M. Italian and English Pastoral Drama of the Renaissance. MLR. XIX, 1924.

Rebora, P. L'Italia nel Dramma inglese (1558–1642). Milan, 1925.

Wright, L. B. The Scriptures and the Elizabethan Stage. MP. XXVI, 1928.

Lea, K. M. Italian Popular Comedy. A Study in the Commedia dell' Arte, 1560–1620, with Special Reference to the English Stage. 2 vols. Oxford, 1934.

Simpson, P. The Theme of Revenge in Elizabethan Tragedy. British Academy Lecture, 1935.

(c) Character Types

Graf, H. Der Miles Gloriosus im englischen Drama bis zur Zeit des Bürgerkrieges. Schwerin, 1891.

Meyer, E. Machiavelli and the Elizabethan Drama. Berlin, 1897.

Churchill, G. B. Richard the Third up to Shakespeare. Berlin, 1900.

Cushman, L. W. The Devil and the Vice in the English Dramatic Literature before Shakespeare. Halle, 1900.

Eckhardt, E. Die lustige Person im älteren englischen Drama. Berlin, 1902.

—— Die Dialekt- und Ausländertypen des älteren englischen Dramas. Bang, vols. XXVII, XXX, 1910–1.

Schelling, F. E. Some Features of the Supernatural as represented in Plays of the Reigns of Elizabeth and James. MP. I, 1903.

Ankenbrand, H. Die Figur des Geistes im Drama der englischen Renaissance. Munich, 1906.

Peers, E. A. Elizabethan Drama and its Mad Folk. Cambridge, 1914.

Boyer, C. V. The Villain as Hero in Elizabethan Tragedy. 1914.

Stonex, A. B. The Usurer in the Elizabethan Drama. PMLA. XXXI, 1916.

Zandvoort, R. W. The Messenger in the Early English Drama. E. Studies, III, 1921.

Busby, O. M. Studies in the Development of the Fool in the Elizabethan Drama. 1923.

Camp, C. W. The Artisan in Elizabethan Literature. New York, 1924.

Cardozo, L. J. The Contemporary Jew in the Elizabethan Drama. Amsterdam, 1925.

McIntyre, C. F. The Later Career of the Elizabethan Villain-Hero. PMLA. XL, 1925.

Van der Spek, C. The Church and the Churchman in English Dramatic Literature before 1642. Amsterdam, 1930.

Myers, A. M. Representation and Misrepresentation of the Puritan in Elizabethan Drama. Philadelphia, 1931.

Clough, W. O. The Broken English of Foreign Characters of the Elizabethan Stage. PQ. XII, 1933.

Bowers, F. T. The Audience and the Revenger of Elizabethan Tragedy. Stud. Phil. XXXI, 1934.

Withington, R. 'Vice' and 'Parasite'. A Note on the Evolution of the Elizabethan Villain. PMLA. XLIX, 1934.

Yearsley, M. Doctors in Elizabethan Drama. 1934.

Vandiver, E. P. The Elizabethan Dramatic Parasite. Stud. Phil. XXXII, 1935.

(d) Structure and Composition

Carpenter, F. I. Metaphor and Simile in the Minor Elizabethan Drama. Chicago, 1895.

Schwab, H. Das Schauspiel im Schauspiel zur Zeit Shakespeares. Vienna, 1896.

Hubbard, F. G. Repetition and Parallelism in the Earlier Elizabethan Drama. PMLA. XX, 1905.

—— A Type of Blank Verse Line found in the Earlier Elizabethan Drama. PMLA. XXXII, 1917.

Foster, F. A. Dumb Show in Elizabethan Drama before 1620. E. Studien, XLIV, 1911.

Friedland, L. S. Dramatic Unities in England. JEGP. X, 1911.

Buland, M. The Presentation of Time in the Elizabethan Drama. New York, 1912.

Alden, R. M. The Use of Comic Material in the Tragedy of Shakespeare and his Contemporaries. JEGP. XIII, 1914.

Fansler, H. E. The Evolution of Technic in Elizabethan Tragedy. Chicago, 1914.

Freeburg, V. O. Disguise Plots in Elizabethan Drama. New York, 1915.

Muncaster, M. The Use of Prose in Elizabethan Drama. MLR. XIV, 1919.

Winslow, O. E. Low Comedy as a Structural Element in English Drama to 1642. Chicago, 1926 (priv. ptd).

Boas, F. S. The Play within the Play. Shakespeare Ass. 1927.

Forsythe, R. S. Comic Effects in Elizabethan Drama. Quart. Journ. University of North Dakota, XVII, 1927.

Templeman, W. D. The Place of the Lyric in Elizabethan Drama before 1600. Western Reserve Bulletin, XXX, 1927.

Fenton, D. The Extra-Dramatic Moment in Elizabethan Plays before 1616. Philadelphia, 1930.

Macdonald, J. F. The Use of Prose in English Drama before Shakespeare. Toronto University Quart. II, 1933.

Bradbrook, M. C. Themes and Conventions of Elizabethan Tragedy. Cambridge, 1935.

Kreider, P. V. Elizabethan Comic Character Conventions as revealed in the Comedies of George Chapman. Ann Arbor, 1935.

Spencer, T. Death and Elizabethan Tragedy. Cambridge, U.S.A. 1936.

(e) Collaboration and Authorship

Fleay, F. G. On Metrical Tests as applied to Dramatic Poetry. Trans. New Shakspere Soc. I, 1874.

Thompson, E. N. S. Elizabethan Dramatic Collaboration. E. Studien, XL, 1909.

Oliphant, E. H. C. Problems of Authorship in Elizabethan Dramatic Literature. MP. VIII, 1911.

—— The Plays of Beaumont and Fletcher. New Haven, 1927.

—— How not to play the Game of Parallels. JEGP. XXVIII, 1929.

—— Collaboration in Elizabethan Drama. PQ. VIII, 1929.

Farnham, W. E. Colloquial Contractions in Beaumont, Fletcher, Massinger, and Shakespeare as a Test of Authorship. PMLA. XXXI, 1916.

Sykes, H. D. Sidelights on Shakespeare. Stratford-on-Avon, 1919.

—— Sidelights on Elizabethan Drama. 1924.

Chelli, M. Étude sur la Collaboration de Massinger avec Fletcher et son Groupe. Paris, 1926.

Lawrence, W. J. Early Dramatic Collaboration. [In Pre-Restoration Stage Studies, Cambridge, U.S.A. 1927.]

—— Those Nut-Cracking Elizabethans. 1935. ['Bad Quartos'; Double Titles; Massinger's Punctuation, etc.]

(f) Miscellaneous Studies

Penniman, J. H. The War of the Theatres. Boston, 1897.

Small, R. A. The Stage-Quarrel between Jonson and the so-called Poetasters. Breslau, 1899.

Olson, B. The Morris Dance in Drama before 1640. Quart. Journ. University of North Dakota, X, 1920.

Sisson, C. J. Le Goût public et le Théâtre élisabéthain. Dijon, [1921].

Sugden, E. H. A Topographical Dictionary to the Works of Shakespeare and his Fellow Dramatists. Manchester, 1925.

Lawrence, W. J. Pre-Restoration Stage Studies. Cambridge, U.S.A. 1927. [Includes papers on: Early Composite Plays; The Rise and Progress of the Complex-Disguise Play; The Origin of the Substantive Theatre Masque; Early Prompt-Books and what they reveal.]

—— The Dedication of Early English Plays. Life and Letters, III, 1929.

Bald, R. C. 'Assembled' Texts. Library, XII, 1931.

Lindabury, R. V. A Study of Patriotism in the Elizabethan Drama. Princeton, 1931.

Russell, H. K. Elizabethan Dramatic Poetry in the Light of Natural and Moral Philosophy. PQ. XII, 1933.

Wright, L. B. The Reading of Plays during the Puritan Revolution. Huntington Lib. Bulletin, Nov. 1934.

Gilbert, A. H. Logic in the Elizabethan Drama. Stud. Phil. XXXII, 1935.

Hart, A. Play Abridgement (Length of Plays; Time Allotted for Representation; Acting Versions). [Rptd from RES. VIII, X, 1932–4, in Shakespeare and the Homilies, Melbourne, 1935.]

Sharpe, R. B. The Real War of the Theatres. Shakespeare's Fellows in Rivalry with the Admiral's Men, 1594–1603. Boston, 1935.

Linthicum, M. C. Costume in the Drama of Shakespeare and his Contemporaries. Oxford, 1936.

(3) AESTHETIC CRITICISM

[The bulk of contemporary criticism was concerned with the morality of the drama. On this the section, The Puritan Attack on the Theatre, pp. 507–13 below, should be consulted. Excerpts are given in David Klein, Literary Criticism from the Elizabethan Dramatists, New York, 1910, and in Sir E. K. Chambers, The Elizabethan Stage, vol. IV, Appendix C, Oxford, 1923. An extensive bibliography is provided in H. S. Symmes, Les Débuts de la Critique dramatique en Angleterre jusqu'à la Mort de Shakespeare, Paris, 1903. The section, Literary Criticism, pp. 863–8 below, should also be consulted.]

Dryden, John. Essays. Ed. W. P. Ker, 2 vols. Oxford, 1903.

Rymer, Thomas. The Tragedies of the last Age Consider'd and Examin'd. 1678.

—— A Short View of Tragedy. 1693.

Lamb, Charles. Specimens of English Dramatic Poets. 1808; ed. Sir I. Gollancz, 2 vols. 1893.

von Schlegel, A. W. Vorlesungen über dramatische Kunst. Heidelberg, 1809–11; tr. Eng. 1846.

Hazlitt, William. Lectures on the Dramatic Literature of the Age of Elizabeth. 1818.

Coleridge, S. T. Literary Remains. Vols. I and II, 1836.

—— Notes and Lectures upon Shakespeare and some of the Old Poets and Dramatists. Ed. Sara Coleridge, 2 vols. 1849.

Taine, H. A. Histoire de la Littérature anglaise. 4 vols. Paris, 1863–4; tr. Eng. 2 vols. 1872.

Lowell, J. R. The Old English Dramatists. Boston, 1892.

Swinburne, A. C. The Age of Shakespeare. 1908.

—— Contemporaries of Shakespeare. 1919.

Symons, Arthur. Studies in the Elizabethan Drama. 1920.

Eliot, T. S. The Sacred Wood. 1920.

—— Elizabethan Essays. 1934.

Barrill, E. W. Heredity as Fate in Greek and Elizabethan Drama. JEGP. XIX, 1920.

Archer, William. The Old Drama and the New. 1923.

[Woolf, Virginia.] Notes on an Elizabethan Play. TLS. 5 March 1925. [Rptd in The Common Reader, 1925.]

Empson, W. Double Plots. [In Some Versions of Pastoral, 1935.]

Knights, L. C. Drama and Society in the Age of Jonson. 1937.

II. THEATRES AND ACTORS

General Works: Bibliographies; Original Sources; Histories, Surveys and General Discussions.

Special Aspects: Censorship and Governmental Supervision; Plays at Court; Public and Private Theatres; Companies and Actors; Staging, Production, Theatrical Structure and Management.

[The subject-matter of this section is comprehensively covered in Sir E. K. Chambers, The Elizabethan Stage, 4 vols. Oxford, 1923, referred to as *Chambers*. For the earlier period there is the companion work, Sir E. K. Chambers, The Mediaeval Stage, 2 vols. Oxford, 1903, and after 1642 there is Leslie Hotson, The Commonwealth and Restoration Stage, Cambridge, U.S.A. 1928. For the years between 1616 and 1642 the best general history is J. T. Murray, English Dramatic Companies, 1558–1642, 2 vols. 1910.]

A. BIBLIOGRAPHIES AND DICTIONARIES

Lowe, R. W. A Bibliographical Account of English Theatrical Literature. 1888.

Chambers, Sir E. K. The Mediaeval Stage. 2 vols. Oxford, 1903.

—— The Elizabethan Stage. 4 vols. Oxford, 1923. [Both of these works are preceded by a useful 'List of Authorities' and the various chapters each have a detailed 'Bibliographical Note.' The Shakespeare Ass. has pbd an Index to this and the following work by B. White, 1934.]

—— William Shakespeare. 2 vols. Oxford, 1930. [The 'Bibliographical Notes' to chs. ii and iii supplement those in The Elizabethan Stage.]

Thorndike, A. H. Shakespeare's Theater. New York, 1916. [Contains bibliography.]

Adams, J. Q. Shakespearean Playhouses. Boston, [1917.] [Contains bibliography.]

Nungezer, Edwin. A Dictionary of Actors and of Other Persons associated with the Public Representation of Plays in England before 1642. New Haven, 1929.

Ebisch, Walther and Schücking, L. L. A Shakespeare Bibliography. Oxford, 1931. [Pp. 119–35, Shakespeare's Stage and the Production of his Plays.]

B. ORIGINAL SOURCES

(1) PUBLIC DOCUMENTS

Manuscripts Preserved in the Muniment Room at Loseley House. Ed. A. J. Kempe, 1835.

Extracts from the Accounts of the Revels at Court, in the Reigns of Queen Elizabeth and King James I. Ed. P. Cunningham, Shakespeare Soc. 1842. [See E. Law, Some Supposed Shakespeare Forgeries, 1911; C. C. Stopes, The Seventeenth Century Accounts of the Masters of the Revels, Shakespeare Ass. 1922; W. J. Lawrence, MLR. xix, 1924; D. B. T. Wood, RES. i, 1925; S. A. Tannenbaum, Shakespeare Forgeries in the Revels Accounts, New York, 1928.]

Calendar of State Papers. Domestic Series. Edward VI, Mary, Elizabeth, and James I: ed. R. Lemon and M. A. Everett Green, 12 vols. 1856–72. Charles I: ed. J. Bruce and W. D. Hamilton, 18 vols. 1858–97. Commonwealth and Protectorate: ed. M. A. Everett Green, 15 vols. 1875–86.

Notices Illustrative of the Drama and other Popular Amusements, chiefly in the Sixteenth and Seventeenth Centuries, extracted from the Chamberlain's Accounts and other Manuscripts of the Borough of Leicester. Ed. W. Kelly, 1865.

A Collection of Ancient Documents respecting the Office of Master of the Revels, and other Papers relating to the Early English Theatre. [Ed. J. O. Halliwell-Phillipps], 1870.

Transcript of the Registers of the Company of Stationers, 1554–1640. Ed. E. Arber, 5 vols. 1875–94.

Overall, W. H. and H. C. Analytical Index to the Series of Records known as the Remembrancia. Preserved among the Archives of the City of London, 1579–1664. 1878.

Middlesex County Records. Ed. J. C. Jeaffreson, 4 vols. 1887–1902; ed. W. J. Hardy, 1905–.

Acts of the Privy Council of England. New Series. Ed. J. R. Dasent, 32 vols. 1890–1907.

Calendar of the Patent Rolls. 1891–1908.

Dramatic Records of the City of London. The Remembrancia. Ed. Sir E. K. Chambers and W. W. Greg, Malone Soc. Collections, vol. i, 1907.

Dramatic Records from the Lansdowne Manuscripts. Ed. Sir E. K. Chambers and W. W. Greg, Malone Soc. Collections, vol. i, 1908.

Documents relating to the Office of the Revels in the Time of Queen Elizabeth. Ed. A. Feuillerat, *Bang*, vol. xxi, 1908.

Dramatic Records from the Patent Rolls. Company Licences. Ed. Sir E. K. Chambers and W. W. Greg, Malone Soc. Collections, vol. i, 1909.

Dramatic Records from the Privy Council Register, 1603–1642. Ed. Sir E. K. Chambers and W. W. Greg, Malone Soc. Collections, vol. i, 1911.

Dramatic Records from the Privy Council Register. James I and Charles I. Ed. C. C. Stopes, Sh. Jb. xlviii, 1912.

Documents relating to the Revels at Court in the Time of King Edward VI and Queen Mary. Ed. A. Feuillerat, *Bang*, vol. xliv, 1914.

Dramatic Records of the City of London: The Repertories, Journals and Letter Books. Ed. A. J. Mill and Sir E. K. Chambers, Malone Soc. Collections, vol. ii, 1931.

Dramatic Records: The Lord Chamberlain's Office. Ed. E. Boswell and Sir E. K. Chambers, Malone Soc. Collections, vol. ii, 1931.

(2) PRIVATE DOCUMENTS

Stow, John. A Survey of London. 1598; 1603 (rev. edn); rev. J. Strype, 2 vols. 1720; ed C. H. Kingsford, 3 vols. Oxford, 1908–27 (from 1603 edn).

Hentzner, Paulus. Itinerarium Germaniae; Galliae; Angliae; Italiae. Nuremburg, 1612; tr. Horace Walpole, 1797.

Moryson, Fynes. An Itinerary. 1617; rptd Glasgow, 1907–8.

Flecknoe, Richard. A Short Discourse of the English Stage. [Appended to Love's Kingdom, 1664.] Rptd W. C. Hazlitt (English Drama and Stage, 1869); ed. J. E. Spingarn (Critical Essays of the Seventeenth Century, vol. ii, Oxford, 1908).

[Wright, James.] Historia Histrionica: an Historical Account of the English Stage. In a Dialogue of Plays and Players. 1699; rptd *Hazlitt's Dodsley*, vol. xv; ed. facs. E. W. Ashbee, 1872; ed. A. Lang (Social England Illustrated, 1903).

Downes, John. Roscius Anglicanus, or, an Historical Review of the Stage. 1708; ed. J. Knight, 1886; ed. M. Summers [1928].

Wilkinson, R. Londina Illustrata. 2 vols. 1819.

The Alleyn Papers. A Collection of Original Documents Illustrative of the Life and Times of Edward Alleyn. Ed. J. P. Collier, Shakespeare Soc. 1843.

The Diary of Philip Henslowe, from 1591 to 1609. Ed. J. P. Collier, Shakespeare Soc. 1845.

The Diary of Henry Machyn, Citizen and Merchant Taylor of London, 1550 to 1563. Ed. J. G. Nichols, Camden Soc. 1848.

Autobiography and Personal Diary of Dr. Simon Forman, 1552 to 1602. Ed. J. O. Halliwell[-Phillipps], 1849.

Rye, W. B. England as seen by Foreigners in the Days of Elizabeth and James the First. Comprising Translations of the Journals of the two Dukes of Wirtemberg in 1592 and 1610. With Extracts from the Travels of Foreign Princes and Others. 1865.

Diary of John Manningham, of the Middle Temple, 1602–3. Ed. J. Bruce, Camden Soc. 1868.

Warner, G. F. Catalogue of the Manuscripts and Muniments of Alleyn's College of God's Gift at Dulwich. 1881.

Diary of the Journey of Philip Junius, Duke of Stettin-Pomerania, through England in the Year 1602. Ed. G. von Bülow and W. Powell, Trans. Royal Hist. Soc., N.S., vi, 1892.

Henslowe's Diary. Pt i, Text; pt ii, Commentary. Ed. W. W. Greg, 1904–8.

Henslowe Papers. Being Documents Supplementary to Henslowe's Diary. Ed. W. W. Greg, 1907.

[See T. W. Baldwin, Posting Henslowe's Accounts, JEGP. xxvi, 1927.]

Four Letters on Theatrical Affairs. Ed. Sir E. K. Chambers, Malone Soc. Collections, vol. ii, 1923.

Boas, F. S. Crosfield's Diary and the Caroline Stage. Fortnightly Rev. cxvii, 1925.

Thomas Platters, des Jüngeren, Englandfahrt im Jahre 1599. Ed. H. Hecht, Halle, 1929.

Greg, W. W. Dramatic Documents from the Elizabethan Playhouses. Stage Plots, Actor's Parts, Prompt Books. 2 vols. Oxford, 1931.

C. HISTORIES, SURVEYS AND GENERAL DISCUSSIONS

Malone, Edmond. Historical Account of the Rise and Progress of the English Stage and of the Economy and Usages of the Ancient Theatres in England. 1790. [Also included in Malone's edn of Shakespeare, vol. i, 1790, and, expanded and rev., in J. Boswell's Third Variorum Shakespeare, 1821.]

Chalmers, George. An Account of the Rise and Progress of the English Stage. [In An Apology for the Believers in the Shakespeare Papers, 1797, and enlarged in A Supplemental Apology for the Believers in the Shakespeare Papers, 1799.]

Collier, J. P. The History of English Dramatic Poetry to the Time of Shakespeare, and Annals of the Stage to the Restoration. 3 vols. 1831; 3 vols. 1879 (rev. edn).

Collier, J. P. New Facts regarding the Life of Shakespeare. 1835.
—— New Particulars regarding the Works of Shakespeare. 1836.
—— Farther Particulars regarding Shakespeare and his Works. 1839.
[These works abound in forgeries, of which some are analysed in C. M. Ingleby, A Complete View of the Shakespere Controversy, 1861.]
Hazlitt, W. C. The English Drama and Stage under the Tudor and Stuart Princes, 1543–1664. Illustrated by a Series of Documents, Treatises and Poems. 1869.
Fleay, F. G. Shakespeare Manual. 1876; 1878 (rev. edn).
—— Introduction to Shakespearian Study. 1877.
—— On the Actor Lists, 1578–1642. Trans. Royal Hist. Soc. IX, 1881.
—— On the History of Theatres in London, 1576–1642. Trans. Royal Hist. Soc. X, 1882.
—— A Chronicle History of the Life and Work of William Shakespeare. 1886.
—— A Chronicle History of tne London Stage, 1559–1642. 1890.
—— A Biographical Chronicle of the English Drama, 1559–1642. 2 vols. 1891.
Jusserand, J. J. Le Théâtre en Angleterre depuis la Conquête jusqu'aux Prédécesseurs immédiats de Shakespeare. Paris, 1878; Paris, 1881 (rev. edn).
Halliwell-Phillipps, J. O. Outlines of the Life of Shakespeare. 1881; 2 vols. 1890 (rev. edn).
Firth, Sir C. H. The Suppression of the Drama during the Protectorate and Commonwealth. N. & Q. 18 Aug. 1888.
Creizenach, Wilhelm. Geschichte des neueren Dramas. 5 vols. Halle, 1893–1916. [Vols. IV, V.]
Lee, Sir Sidney. Life of William Shakespeare. 1898; 1922 (rev. edn).
Small, R. A. The Stage-quarrel between Ben Jonson and the so-called Poetasters. Breslau, 1899.
Chambers, Sir E. K. The Mediaeval Stage. 2 vols. Oxford, 1903.
—— The Elizabethan Stage. 4 vols. Oxford, 1923. [To 1616.]
Wallace, C. W. The Children of the Chapel at Blackfriars, 1597–1603. Lincoln, Nebraska, 1908.
—— The Evolution of the English Drama up to Shakespeare. Berlin, 1912.
Gildersleeve. V. C. Government Regulation of the Elizabethan Drama. New York, 1908.
Murray, J. T. English Dramatic Companies, 1558–1642. 2 vols. 1910.

Lawrence, W. J. The Elizabethan Playhouse and Other Studies. Stratford-on-Avon, 1912.
—— The Elizabethan Playhouse. Second Ser. Stratford-on-Avon, 1913.
—— Pre-Restoration Stage Studies. Cambridge, U.S.A. 1927.
Archer, William and Lawrence, W. J. The Playhouse. [In Shakespeare's England, vol. II, Oxford, 1916.]
Thorndike, A. H. Shakespeare's Theater. New York, 1916.
Adams, J. Q. Shakespearean Playhouses. A History of English Theatres from the Beginnings to the Restoration. Boston [1917].
Rollins, H. E. A Contribution to the History of the English Commonwealth Drama. Stud. Phil. XVIII, 1921.
—— The Commonwealth Drama: Miscellaneous Notes. Stud. Phil. XX, 1923.
Boas, F. S. Shakespeare and the Universities. Oxford, 1923.
Hotson, Leslie. The Commonwealth and Restoration Stage. Cambridge, U.S.A. 1928.
Sharpe, R. B. The Real War of the Theatres. Shakespeare's Fellows in Rivalry with the Admiral's Men, 1594–1603. Boston, 1935.

D. CENSORSHIP AND GOVERNMENTAL SUPERVISION

[See *Chambers*, vol. I, The Revels Office, pp. 71–105, The Control of the Stage, pp. 236–348.]

Gildersleeve, V. C. Government Regulation of the Elizabethan Drama. New York, 1908.
Feuillerat, Albert. Le Bureau des Menusplaisirs et la Mise en Scène à la Cour d'Élisabeth. Louvain, 1910.
Graves, T. S. The Court and the London Theatres during the Reign of Queen Elizabeth. Menasha, Wisconsin, 1913.
Acts of the Privy Council of England. New Ser. Ed. J. R. Dasent, 32 vols. 1890–1907.
Dramatic Records from the Privy Council Register, 1603–1642. Ed. Sir E. K. Chambers and W. W. Greg, Malone Soc. Collections, vol. I, 1911.
Dramatic Records from the Privy Council Register. James I and Charles I. Ed. C. C. Stopes, Sh. Jb. XLVIII, 1912.
Percy, E. The Privy Council under the Tudors. 1907.
Hornemann, C. Das Privy Council von England zur Zeit der Königin Elisabeth. Hanover, 1912.
Adair, E. R. The Sources for the History of the Council in the Sixteenth and Seventeenth Centuries. 1924.

Documents relating to the Office of the Revels in the Time of Queen Elizabeth. Ed. A. Feuillerat, *Bang*, vol. xxi, 1908.

Documents relating to the Revels at Court in the Time of King Edward VI and Queen Mary.Ed.A.Feuillerat,*Bang*,vol.xliv,1914.

Adams, J. Q. The Dramatic Records of Sir Henry Herbert, Master of the Revels, 1623–73. New Haven, 1917.

The King's Office of the Revels, 1610–1622. Fragments of Manuscripts. Ed. F. Marcham and J. P. Gilson, 1925.

Chambers, Sir E. K. Notes on the History of the Revels Office under the Tudors. 1906.

—— The Elizabethan Lords Chamberlain. Malone Soc. Collections, vol. i, 1907.

Stopes, C. C. The Seventeenth Century Accounts of the Masters of the Revels. Shakespeare Ass. 1922.

Marcham, F. The King's Office of the Revels. RES. ii, 1926.

Eccles, M. Sir George Buc, Master of the Revels. [In Thomas Lodge and Other Elizabethans, ed. C. J. Sisson, Cambridge, U.S.A. 1933.]

Simpson, Richard. The Political Use of the Stage in Shakespeare's Time. Trans. New Shakspere Soc. pt ii, 1874.

—— The Politics of Shakespeare's Historical Plays. Trans. New Shakspere Soc. pt ii, 1874.

Gardiner, S. R. The Political Element in Massinger. Trans. New Shakspere Soc. 1875–6.

Lee, Sir Sidney. The Topical Side of the Elizabethan Drama. Trans. New Shakspere Soc. 1887–92.

—— Elizabethan England and the Jews. Trans. New Shakspere Soc. 1887–92.

Graves, T. S. Some Allusions to Religious and Political Plays. MP. ix, 1912.

—— The Political Use of the Stage during the Reign of James I. Ang. xxxviii, 1914.

E. PLAYS AT COURT, MASQUES, PAGEANTS, ETC.

[See *Chambers*, vol. i, The Court, Pageantry, The Mask, The Court Play, pp. 1–235; vol. iii, Staging at Court, pp. 1–46. For works on the Italian and French court stages see *Chambers*, vol. iii, p. 19.]

Nichols, John. The Progresses and Public Processions of Queen Elizabeth. 4 vols. 1788–1821; 3 vols. 1823.

—— The Progresses, Processions, and Magnificent Festivities of King James I. 4 vols. 1828.

Nichols, J. G. London Pageants. 1837.

Fairholt, F. W. History of Lord Mayors' Pageants. Percy Soc. 1843–4.

—— The Civic Garland. 1845.

Cunningham, P. and Collier, J. P. Inigo Jones, a Life; and Five Court Masques. Shakespeare Soc. 1848.

Kelly, W. Royal Progresses and Visits to Leicester. 1884.

Stopes, C. C. William Hunnis. Sh. Jb. xxvii, 1892.

—— William Hunnis and the Revels of the Chapel Royal. *Bang*, vol. xxix, 1910.

Evans, H. A. English Masques. 1897.

Brotanek, R. Die englischen Maskenspiele. Vienna, 1902.

Chambers, Sir E. K. Court Performances before Queen Elizabeth. MLR. ii, 1906.

—— Court Performances under James I. MLR. iv, 1909.

Helmholtz-Phelan, A. A. The Staging of the Court Drama to 1595. PMLA. xxiv, 1909.

Reyher, P. Les Masques anglais. Paris, 1909.

Feuillerat, Albert. Le Bureau des Menus-plaisirs et la Mise en Scène à la Cour d'Élisabeth. Louvain, 1910.

Lawrence, W. J. The Mounting of the Carolan Masques. [In The Elizabethan Playhouse, Stratford-on-Avon, 1912.]

Wallace, C. W. The Evolution of the English Drama up to Shakespeare. Berlin, 1912.

Graves, T. S. The Court and the London Theatres during the Reign of Queen Elizabeth. Menasha, Wisconsin. 1913.

Sullivan, Mary. Court Masques of James I. 1913.

Boas, F. S. University Drama in the Tudor Age. Oxford, 1914.

Withington, Robert. English Pageantry, an Historical Outline. 2 vols. Cambridge, U.S.A. 1918–20.

Thaler, Alwin. The Players at Court. JEGP. xix, 1920.

Designs by Inigo Jones for Masques and Plays at Court. Ed. P. Simpson and C. F. Bell, Walpole and Malone Socs. 1924.

Bradner, Leicester. Stages and Stage Scenery in Court Drama before 1558. RES. i, 1925.

Steele, M. S. Plays and Masques at Court during the Reigns of Elizabeth, James, and Charles. New Haven, 1926.

F. PUBLIC AND PRIVATE THEATRES

[See *Chambers*, vol. ii, The Public Theatres, pp. 353–474, The Private Theatres, pp. 475–517. The chief London maps have been reproduced by the London Topographical Society and on a smaller scale by G. E. Mitton, Maps of Old London (1908). Some are also given as illustrations in G. P. Baker, The Development of Shakespeare as a Dramatist (1907). They are classified by W. Martin, A Study of Early Map-Views of London, Antiquary, xlv, 1909, and in The Site of the Globe Playhouse of Shakespeare, Surrey Archaeological Collections, vol. xxiii, 1910.]

THEATRES AND ACTORS

Ellis, Henry. The History and Antiquities of the Parish of Saint Leonard Shoreditch and Liberty of Norton Folgate. 1798.

'Hood, Eu.' [i.e. Joseph Haslewood]. Of the London Theatres. GM. LXXXIII–LXXXVI, 1813–6. [Rptd Gentleman's Magazine Lib. xv, 1904.]

Tomlins, T. E. Origin of the Curtain Theatre and Mistakes Regarding it. Shakespeare Soc. Papers, vol. I, 1844,

Cunningham, Peter. The Whitefriars, the Salisbury Court, and the Duke's Theatres. Shakespeare Soc. Papers, vol. IV, 1849.

Rendle, W. The Bankside, Southwark, and the Globe. 1877. [Appended to Harrison's Description, ed. F. J. Furnivall, pt II, New Shakspere Soc. 1878.]

—— Old Southwark and its People. 1878.

—— The Playhouses at Bankside in the Time of Shakespeare. Walford's Antiquarian, VII, VIII, 1885.

Rendle, W. and Newman, P. The Inns of Old Southwark and their Associations. 1888.

Greenstreet, James. The White Friars Theatre in the Time of Shakespeare. Trans. New Shakspere Soc. I, 1888.

—— The Blackfriars Playhouse: its Antecedents. Athenaeum, 17 July 1886, 7 Jan. 1888.

—— The Blackfriars Theatre in the Time of Shakespeare. Athenaeum, 7, 12 April 1888.

Gaedertz, K. T. Zur Kenntnis der altenglischen Bühne. Bremen, 1888. [Publishes John de Witt's description and plan of the Swan.]

Ordish, T. F. Early London Theatres [in the Fields]. 1894.

Wallace, C. W. Old Blackfriars Theatre. Fresh Discovery of Documents. Times, 11 Sept. 1906.

—— The Children of the Chapel at Blackfriars (1597–1603). Nebraska University Stud. VIII, 1908.

—— Shakespeare in London. Fresh Documents on the Poet and his Theatres. Times, 2, 4 Oct. 1909.

—— Three London Theatres of Shakespeare's Time. Nebraska University Stud. IX, 1909. [The Red Bull, The Fortune, The Bear Garden.]

—— The Swan Theatre and the Earl of Pembroke's Servants. E. Studien, XLIII, 1911.

—— The Evolution of the English Drama up to Shakespeare, with a History of the First Blackfriars Theatre. Berlin, 1912.

—— Advance Sheets from Shakespeare, the Globe, and Blackfriars. Stratford-on-Avon, 1909; Sh. Jb. XLVI, 1910.

—— The First London Theatre. Nebraska University Stud. XIII, 1913.

Wallace, C. W. New Light on Shakespeare. Times, 30 April and 1 May 1914.

Archer, William. The Fortune Theatre, 1600. Sh. Jb. XLIV, 1908.

Stopes, C. C. Burbage's Theatre. Fortnightly Rev. July 1909.

—— Burbage and Shakespeare's Stage. 1913.

Martin, W. The Site of the Globe Playhouse of Shakespeare. 1910; Surrey Archaeological Soc. Collections, vol. XXIII, 1910.

Feuillerat, Albert. The Origin of Shakespeare's Blackfriars Theatre. Sh. Jb. XLVIII, 1912.

—— Blackfriars Records. Malone Soc. Collections, vol. II, 1913.

Lawrence, W. J. New Facts about the Blackfriars. [In The Elizabethan Playhouse, Stratford-on-Avon, 1912.]

—— The Elizabethan Private Playhouse. Criterion, IX, 1930. [Rptd in Those Nut-Cracking Elizabethans, 1935.]

Graves, T. S. A Note on the Swan Theatre. MP. IX, 1912.

Braines, W. W. Holywell Priory and the Site of the Theatre, Shoreditch. London County Council, 1915.

—— The Site of the Theatre, Shoreditch. London Topographical Record, XI, 1917.

—— The Site of the Globe Playhouse, Southwark. 1921; 1924 (enlarged).

Thorndike, A. H. Shakespeare's Theater. New York, 1916.

Adams, J. Q. Shakespearean Playhouses. A History of English Theatres from the Beginnings to the Restoration. Boston, [1917].

—— The Housekeepers of the Globe. MP. XVII, 1919.

Graves, T. S. Notes on the Elizabethan Theatres. Stud. Phil. XVII, 1920.

—— Richard Rawlidge on London Playhouses. MP. XVIII, 1920.

—— Some References to Elizabethan Theatres. Stud. Phil. XIX, 1922.

The Site of the Globe Playhouse. London County Council, 1921.

Hubbard, George. On the Site of the Globe Playhouse of Shakespeare. 1923.

Sisson, C. J. The Theatres and Companies. [In A Companion to Shakespeare Studies, ed. H. Granville-Barker and G. B. Harrison, Cambridge, 1934.]

G. THE COMPANIES AND THE ACTORS

(1) THE COMPANIES

(a) *The Boy Companies*

[See *Chambers*, vol. II, pp. 1–76, where references will also be found to the Children of Windsor; Westminster School; Eton College; Merchant Taylors' School.]

(i) General Works

Albrecht, A. Das englische Kindertheater. Halle, 1883.

Lyly, John. Endymion. Ed. G. P. Baker, New York, 1894. [Introduction.]

Maas, H. Die Kindertruppen. Göttingen, 1901.

—— Äussere Geschichte der englischen Theatertruppen in dem Zeitraum von 1559 bis 1642. Bang, vol. xix, 1907.

Chambers, Sir E. K. Court Performances before Queen Elizabeth. MLR. ii, 1906.

—— Court Performances under James I. MLR. iv, 1909.

Murray, J. T. English Dramatic Companies. 2 vols. 1910.

Nairn, J. A. Boy Actors under the Tudors and Stewarts. Trans. Royal Soc. Lit. xxxiii, 1913.

Hillebrand, H. N. The Child Actors. Urbana, 1926.

Aronstein, P. Die englischen Knabentheater und ihr Drama. Die neueren Sprachen, xxxv, 1927.

(ii) The Children of Paul's

Simpson, W. S. Gleanings from Old Saint Paul's. 1889.

Bumpus, J. S. The Organists and Composers of St Paul's Cathedral. 1891.

McDonnell, M. F. J. A History of St Paul's School. 1909.

Leach, A. F. St Paul's School. Journ. Education, xxxi, 1909.

—— St Paul's School before Colet. Archaeologia, lxii, 1910.

Flood, W. H. G. Master Sebastian. Musical Antiquary, iii, iv, 1911–3.

Hillebrand, H. N. Sebastian Westcote, Dramatist and Master of the Children of Paul's. JEGP. xiv, 1915.

Reed, A. W. John Heywood. Library, viii, ix, 1917–8.

(iii) The Children of the Chapel and of the Queen's Revels

Rimbault, E. F. The Old Cheque Book of the Chapel Royal. Camden Soc. 1872.

Stopes, C. C. W. Hunnis. Sh. Jb. xxvii, 1892.

—— W. Hunnis, the Dramatist. Athenaeum, 31 March 1900.

—— Mary's Chapel Royal and her Coronation Play. Athenaeum, 9 Sept. 1905.

—— W. Hunnis and the Revels of the Chapel Royal. Bang, vol. xxix, 1910.

Durand, W. Y. Notes on Richard Edwards. JEGP. iv, 1902.

—— Some Errors concerning Richard Edwards. MLN. xxiii, 1908.

Wallace, C. W. The Children of the Chapel at Blackfriars (1597–1603). Nebraska University Stud. viii, 1908.

—— Shakespeare and his London Associates. Nebraska University Stud. x, 1910.

—— The Evolution of the English Drama up to Shakespeare. Berlin, 1912.

Manly, J. M. The Children of the Chapel Royal and their Masters. CHEL. vol. vi, 1910.

Feuillerat, A. The Origin of Shakespeare's Blackfriars Theatre. Sh. Jb. xlviii, 1912.

—— Blackfriars Records. Malone Soc. Collections, vol. ii, 1913.

Flood, W. H. G. Queen Mary's Chapel Royal. EHR. xxxiii, 1918.

Hillebrand, H. N. The Early History of the Chapel Royal. MP. xviii, 1920.

(iv) The Children of the King's Revels

Greenstreet, J. The Whitefriars Theatre in the Time of Shakespeare. Trans. New Shakspere Soc. pt iii, 1889.

Hillebrand, H. N. The Children of the King's Revels at Whitefriars. JEGP. xxi, 1922.

(b) The Adult Companies

[See *Chambers*, vol. ii, pp. 77–260.]

Greenstreet, James. Documents relating to the Players at the Red Bull, Clerkenwell, and the Cockpit in Drury Lane in the Time of James I. Trans. New Shakspere Soc. 1880–5.

Maas, Hermann. Äussere Geschichte der englischen Theatertruppen in dem Zeitraum von 1559 bis 1642. Bang, vol. xix, 1907.

Wallace, C. W. Three London Theatres of Shakespeare's Time. Nebraska University Stud. ix, 1909. [The Red Bull Company, etc.]

—— The Swan Theatre and the Earl of Pembroke's Servants. E. Studien, xliii, 1910–1.

—— Shakespeare and his London Associates as revealed in recently discovered Documents. Nebraska University Stud. x, 1910.

—— The First London Theatre. Nebraska University Stud. xiii, 1913.

Murray, J. T. English Dramatic Companies, 1558–1642. Vol. i, London Companies; vol. ii, Provincial Companies. 1910.

Chambers, Sir E. K. Plays of the King's Men in 1641. Malone Soc. Collections, vol. i, 1911.

—— Elizabethan Stage Gleanings. RES. i, 1925.

Thaler, Alwin. The Elizabethan Dramatic Companies. PMLA. xxxv, 1920.

Baldwin, T. W. The Organization and Personnel of the Shakespearean Company. Princeton, 1927.

(c) Court Performances and Provincial·Tours

Cunningham, Peter. Extracts from the Accounts of the Revels at Court. Shakespeare Soc. 1842.

Halliwell-Phillipps, J. O. The Visits of Shakespeare's Company of Actors to the Provincial Cities and Towns of England. Brighton, 1887.

Murray, J. T. English Dramatic Companies in the Towns outside of London, 1550–1600. MP. ii, 1905.

Chambers, Sir E. K. Court Performances before Queen Elizabeth. MLR. ii, 1906.

—— Court Performances under James I. MLR. iv, 1909.

Thaler, Alwin. The Players at Court, 1564–1642. JEGP. xix, 1920.

—— The Travelling Players in Shakespeare's England. MP. xvii, 1920.

—— Strolling Players and Provincial Drama after Shakspere. PMLA. xxxvii, 1922.

—— Faire Em (and Shakespeare's Company?) in Lancashire. PMLA. xlvi, 1931.

Tillotson, G. Othello and the Alchemist at Oxford in 1610. TLS. 20 July 1933.

(d) English Actors Abroad

[See Chambers, vol. ii, The International Companies, pp. 261–94.]

Cohn, Albert. Shakespeare in Germany in the Sixteenth and Seventeenth Centuries. 1865.

—— Englische Komödianten in Köln (1592–1656). Sh. Jb. xxi, 1886.

—— König Lear 1692 und Titus Andronicus 1699 in Breslau aufgeführt. Sh. Jb. xxiii, 1888.

Tittman, Julius. Die Schauspiele der englischen Komödianten in Deutschland. Leipzig, 1880.

Meissner, Johannes. Die englischen Komödianten in Österreich. Sh. Jb. xix, 1884.

Trautmann, Karl. Englische Komödianten in Nürnberg bis zum Schlusse des 30jährigen Krieges (1593–1648). Ein englischer Springer am Hofe zu Turin (1665). Eine Augsburger Lear-Aufführung (1665). Englische Komödianten in Ulm, 1602. Archiv für Literaturgeschichte, xiv, xv, 1886–7.

Bolte, Johannes. Englische Komödianten in Dänemark und Schweden. Sh. Jb. xxiii, 1888.

—— Englische Komödianten in Münster und Ulm. Sh. Jb. xxxvi, 1900.

—— Die Singspiele der englischen Komödianten und ihrer Nachfolger in Deutschland, Holland und Skandinavien. Hamburg, 1893.

—— Das Danziger Theater im 16. und 17. Jahrhundert. Hamburg, 1895.

Creizenach, Wilhelm. Die Schauspiele der englischen Komödianten. Berlin, [1889].

Meyer, C. F. Englische Komödianten am Hofe des Herzogs Philipp Julius von Pommern-Wolgast. Sh. Jb. xxxviii, 1902.

Herz, Emil. Englische Schauspieler und englisches Schauspiel zur Zeit Shakespeares in Deutschland. Hamburg, 1903.

Brandl, Alois. Englische Komödianten in Frankfurt. Sh. Jb. xl, 1904.

Harris, C. The English Comedians in Germany before the Thirty Years' War: the Financial Side. PMLA. xxii, 1907.

Yates, F. A. English Actors in Paris during the Lifetime of Shakespeare. RES. i, 1925.

Fredén, Gustaf. A propos du Théâtre anglais en Allemagne. L'Auteur inconnu des 'Comédies et Tragédies anglaises' de 1620. Revue de Littérature comparée, viii, 1928.

Lea, K. M. English Players at the Swedish Court. MLR. xxvi, 1931.

(e) Foreign Actors in England

Smith, Winifred. Italian and Elizabethan Comedy. MP. v, 1908.

—— The Commedia dell' Arte. New York, 1912.

—— Italian Actors in Elizabethan England. MLN. xliv, 1929.

Lawrence, W. J. Early French Players in England. [In the Elizabethan Playhouse, Stratford-on-Avon, 1912.]

Chambers, Sir E. K. Italian Players in England. TLS. 12 May 1921.

(2) The Actors

[See Chambers, vol. ii, pp. 295–352.]

Collier, J. P. Memoirs of the Principal Actors in the Plays of Shakespeare. Shakespeare Soc. 1846. [Rev. in History of English Dramatic Poetry, vol. iii, 1879.]

Wallace, C. W. Gervase Markham, Dramatist. Sh. Jb. xlvi, 1910.

Chambers, Sir E. K. Two Early Player-Lists. Malone Soc. Collections, vol. i, 1911.

Simpson, Percy. Actors and Acting. [In Shakespeare's England, vol. ii, Oxford, 1916.]

Graves, T. S. Women on the Pre-Restoration Stage. Stud. Phil. xxii, 1925.

Gaw, Alison. Actors' Names in Basic Shakespearean Texts, with Special Reference to Romeo and Juliet and Much Ado. PMLA. xl, 1925.

Denkinger, E. M. Actors' Names in the Register of St Botolph Aldgate. PMLA. xli, 1926.

Harrison, G. B. Shakespeare's Actors. Shakespeare Ass. 1927.

Nungezer, Edwin. A Dictionary of Actors and of Other Persons Associated with the Public Representation of Plays in England before 1642. New Haven, 1929.

Bentley, G. E. New Actors of the Elizabethan Period. MLN. XLIV, 1929.

—— Records of Players in the Parish of St Giles, Cripplegate. PMLA. XLIV, 1929.

Collier, J. P. Memoirs of Edward Alleyn. 1841.

—— A Collection of Original Documents Illustrative of the Life and Times of Edward Alleyn. 2 vols. Shakespeare Soc. 1843.

Young, William. The History of Dulwich College. With a Life of Edward Alleyn. 2 vols. Edinburgh, 1889.

Greg, W. W. Edward Alleyn. Shakespeare Ass. 1927.

Gray, A. K. Robert Armine, the Foole. PMLA. XLII, 1927.

Stopes, C. C. Burbage and Shakespeare's Stage. 1913.

Boswell, Eleanore. 'Young Mr Cartwright.' MLR. XXIV, 1929.

Gaw, Allison. John Sincklo as one of Shakespeare's Actors. Ang. XLIX, 1926.

Halliwell[-Phillipps], J. O. Tarlton's Jests and News out of Purgatory. With Notes and some Account of the Life of Tarlton. Shakespeare Soc. 1844.

H. STAGING AND PRODUCTION, AND THE STRUCTURE AND CONDUCT OF THE THEATRES

(1) GENERAL WORKS

Creizenach, Wilhelm. Geschichte des neueren Dramas. 5 vols. Halle, 1893–1916. [Vol. IV.]

Mantzius, Karl. Skuespilkunstens Historie. 5 vols. Copenhagen, 1897–1907; tr. Eng. 6 vols. 1903–21.

Child, H. H. The Elizabethan Theatre. CHEL. vol. VI, 1910.

Lawrence, W. J. The Elizabethan Playhouse and other Studies. Stratford-on-Avon, 1912. [Includes essays on: The Evolution and Influence of the Elizabethan Playhouse; the Situation of the Lords' Room; Title and Locality Boards on the Pre-Restoration Stage; Music and Song in the Elizabethan Theatre.]

—— The Elizabethan Playhouse and other Studies. Ser. 2, Stratford-on-Avon, 1913. [Includes essays on: Light and Darkness in the Elizabethan Theatre; Windows on the Pre-Restoration Stage; The Origin of the Theatre Programme; Early Systems of Admission.]

Lawrence, W. J. Pre-Restoration Stage Studies. Cambridge, U.S.A. 1927. [The Inn-Yard Play; The Practice of Doubling; The Elizabethan Stage Jig; 'Hamlet' as Shakespeare staged it; The Elizabethan Nocturnal; Stage Traps in the Early English Theatre; Illusion of Sounds in the Elizabethan Theatre; Elizabethan Stage Realism; Characteristics of Platform Stage Spectacle; Elizabethan Stage Properties; etc.]

—— The Physical Conditions of the Elizabethan Public Playhouse. Cambridge, U.S.A. 1927.

—— Those Nut-Cracking Elizabethans. 1935. [Use of Animals; Supers; Bearers for the Dead; Bells; Stage Furniture; etc.]

Thorndike, A. H. From Outdoors to Indoors on the Elizabethan Stage. [In Kittredge Anniversary Papers, Boston, 1913.]

—— Shakespeare's Theater. New York, 1916.

(2) THE STRUCTURE AND APPEARANCE OF THE THEATRES

[See Chambers, vol. II, pp. 518–57.]

[Representations of the interiors of playhouses:
1. Arend van Buchell's copy of a drawing by Johannes de Witt of the Swan, [c. 1596].
2. A small engraving in a compartment of the title-page of W. Alabaster, Roxana, 1632.
3. A very similar engraving on the title-page of N. Richards, Messalina, 1640.
4. An engraved frontispiece to Francis Kirkman's edns, 1672 and 1673, of The Wits, or Sport upon Sport.]

Gaedertz, K. T. Zur Kenntnis der altenglischen Bühne. Bremen, 1888.

Wheatley, H. B. On a Contemporary Drawing of the Interior of the Swan Theatre. Trans. New Shakspere Soc. 1888.

Archer, William. A Sixteenth-Century Playhouse. Universal Rev. I, 1888.

—— The Stage of Shakespeare. Tribune, 10 Aug. 1907.

—— The Fortune Theatre, 1600. Tribune, 12 Oct. 1907; Sh. Jb. XLIV.

—— The Swan Drawing. Tribune, 11 Jan. 1908.

—— The Elizabethan Stage. Quart. Rev. CCVIII, 1908.

Genée, R. Über die scenischen Formen Shakespeares in ihrem Verhältnisse zur Bühne seiner Zeit. Sh. Jb. XXVI, 1891.

Logeman, H. Johannes de Witt's Visit to the Swan Theatre. Ang. XIX, 1897.

Brandl, A. Shakespeares dramatische Werke. Tr. Schlegel und Tieck, ed. A. Brandl, 10 vols. Leipzig, [1897–9]. [Introduction.]

—— Quellen des weltlichen Dramas in England vor Shakespeare. QF. LXXX, 1898. [Introduction.]

Kilian, E. Die scenischen Formen Shakespeares in ihrer Beziehung zu der Aufführung seiner Dramen auf der modernen Bühne. Sh. Jb. xxxvi, 1900.

Grabau, C. Zur englischen Bühne um 1600. Sh. Jb. xxxviii, 1902.

Lawrence, W. J. Some Characteristics of the Elizabethan-Stuart Stage. E. Studien, xxxii, 1902.

—— Night Performances in the Elizabethan Theatres. E. Studien, xlviii, 1915.

—— New Light on the Elizabethan Theatre. Fortnightly Rev. May 1916.

—— A Forgotten Playhouse Custom of Shakespeare's Day. [In A Book of Homage, 1916.]

Brodmeier, Cecil. Die Shakespeare-Bühne nach den alten Bühnenweisungen. Jena, 1902; Weimar, 1904.

Bang, W. Zur Bühne Shakespeares. Sh. Jb. xl, 1904.

Keller, Wolfgang. Nochmals zur Bühne Shakespeares. Sh. Jb. xl, 1904.

Tolman, A. H. Shakespeare's Stage and Modern Adaptations. [In The Views about Hamlet, Boston, 1906.]

—— Alternation in the Staging of Shakespeare's Plays. MP. vi, 1909.

Hale, E. E. The Influence of Theatrical Conditions on Shakespeare. MP. i, 1904.

Proelss, R. Von den ältesten Drucken der Dramen Shakespeares. Leipzig, 1905.

Baker, G. P. Hamlet on an Elizabethan Stage. Sh. Jb. xli, 1905.

—— Elizabethan Stage Theories. TLS. 3 Nov. 1905.

Moenkemeyer, P. Prolegomena zu einer Darstellung der englischen Volksbühne zur Elisabeth- und Stuart-Zeit nach den alten Bühnenweisungen. Göttingen, 1905.

Wegener, Richard. Die Bühneneinrichtung des Shakespeareschen Theaters nach den zeitgenössischen Dramen. Halle, 1907.

Chambers, Sir E. K. The Stage of the Globe. [The Works of William Shakespeare, vol. x, Stratford-on-Avon, 1907.]

Godfrey, W. H. An Elizabethan Playhouse. Architectural Rev. xxiii, 1908.

—— A Scale Model of the Fortune Theatre. Architectural Rev. xxxi, 1912. [See also Architects' and Builders' Journal, Aug. 1911.]

Schelling, F. E. The Elizabethan Playhouse. Proc. Philadelphia Numismatic and Antiquarian Soc. 1908.

Albright, V. E. The Shakespearian Stage. New York, 1909.

—— Percy's Plays as Proof of the Elizabethan Stage. MP. xi, 1913.

Skemp, A. R. Some Characteristics of the English Stage before the Restoration. Sh. Jb. xlv, 1909.

Creizenach, W. Bühnenwesen und Schauspielkunst. [Geschichte des neueren Dramas, vol. iv, Halle, 1909.]

Neuendorff, B. Die englische Volksbühne im Zeitalter Shakespeares nach den Bühnenanweisungen. Berlin, 1910.

Adams, J. Q. The Four Pictorial Representations of the Elizabethan Stage. JEGP. x, 1911.

Eichler, Albert. Die frühneuenglische Volksbühne. 2 pts, Germanisch-romanische Monatsschrift, iii, 1911.

Forestier, A. The Fortune Theatre Reconstructed. Illustrated London News, 12 Aug. 1911.

Evans, M. B. An Early Type of Stage. MP. ix, 1912.

Bell, H. Contributions to the History of the English Playhouse. Architectural Record, 1913.

Reynolds, G. F. William Percy and his Plays. MP. xii, 1914.

Brereton, J. le G. De Witt at the Swan. [In A Book of Homage, 1916.]

Hartmann, Georg. Die Bühnengastin in Shakespeares Dramen als Ausdruck von Gemütsbewegungen. Sh. Jb. lxix, lxx, 1924.

Borcherdt, H. H. Der Renaissancestil des Theaters, ein Prinzipieller Versuch. Halle, 1926.

(3) Production and Stage Management: Costume, Scenery, Properties, Music, Jigs, Variety Entertainment, Extemporal Acting, etc.

[See *Chambers*, vol. iii, Staging in the Theatres: Sixteenth Century, pp. 47–102; Staging in the Theatres: Seventeenth Century, pp. 103–54.]

(a) General Works

Elze, Karl. Eine Aufführung im Globus-Theater. Sh. Jb. xiv, 1879.

Koeppel, E. Die unkritische Behandlung dramaturgischer Angaben in den Shakespeare-Ausgaben. E. Studien, xxxiv, 1904.

Kaulfuss-Diesch, C. H. Die Inszenierung des deutschen Dramas an der Wende des 16. und 17. Jahrhunderts. 1905.

Reynolds, G. F. Some Principles of Elizabethan Staging. 2 pts, Chicago, 1905; MP. ii, 1905.

—— What we know of the Elizabethan Stage. MP. ix, 1911–2.

Baker, G. P. The Development of Shakespeare as a Dramatist. New York, 1907.

Aronstein, Philipp. Die Organisation des englischen Schauspiels im Zeitalter Shakespeares. Germanisch-romanische Monatsschrift, ii, 1910.

Pilch, Leo. Shakespeare als Regisseur. Zeitschrift für französischen und englischen Unterricht, x, 1911.

Reese, G. H. Studien und Beiträge zur Geschichte der englischen Schauspielkunst im Zeitalter Shakespeares. Jena, 1911.

Poel, W. Shakespeare in the Theatre. 1915.

—— Some Notes on Shakespeare's Stage and Plays. 1916.

Dickinson, T. H. Some Principles of Shakespeare Staging. [In Wisconsin Shakespeare Studies, 1916.]

Rhodes, R. C. The Stagery of Shakespeare. Birmingham, 1922.

Isaacs, J. Production and Stage-Management at the Blackfriars Theatre. Shakespeare Ass. Lecture, 1933.

(b) Costume, Scenery and Properties

Reynolds, G. F. 'Trees' on the Stage of Shakespeare. MP. iv, 1907.

Stopes, C. C. Elizabethan Stage Scenery. Fortnightly Rev. June 1907.

James I at Oxford in 1605. Property Lists from the University Archives. Ed. F. S. Boas and W. W. Greg, Malone Soc. Collections, vol. i, 1909.

Wallace, C. W. Globe Theatre Apparel. [1909] (priv. ptd).

Keith, W. G. The Designs for the First Movable Scenery on the English Stage. Burlington Mag. xxv, 1914.

Lawrence, W. J. The Elizabethan Stage Throne. Texas Rev. Jan. 1918.

—— Bells on the Elizabethan Stage. Fortnightly Rev. July 1924.

Graves, T. S. The Devil in the Playhouse. South Atlantic Quart. xix, 1920.

Campbell, L. B. Scenes and Machines on the English Stage during the Renaissance. Cambridge, 1923.

Wright, L. B. Elizabethan Sea Drama and its Staging. Ang. li, 1927.

Winninghoff, Elisabeth. Das Theaterkostüm bei Shakespeare. Münster, 1928.

(c) Music, Jigs and Variety Entertainments

Cowling, G. H. Music on the Shakespearian Stage. 1913.

Arkwright, G. E. P. Elizabethan Choirboy Plays and their Music. Proc. Musical Ass. 1914.

Graves, T. S. The Ass as Actor. South Atlantic Quart. xv, 1916.

—— The Elizabethan Trained Ape. MLN. xxxv, 1920.

Strunk, W. The Elizabethan Showman's Ape. MLN. xxxii, 1917.

Lawrence, W. J. Horses on the Elizabethan Stage. TLS. 5 June 1919.

Lawrence, W. J. He's for a Jig or —. TLS. 3 July 1919.

—— Music in the Elizabethan Theatre. Musical Quart. vi, 1920.

Ogilvie, Janet. Heard 'Off': Stage Noises in the Elizabethan Theatre. English Rev. xlv, 1927.

Wright, L. B. Animal Actors on the English Stage before 1642. PMLA. xlii, 1927.

—— Juggling Tricks and Conjuring on the English Stage before 1642. MP. xxiv, 1927.

—— Stage Duelling in the Elizabethan Theatre. MLR. xxii, 1927.

—— Variety Entertainment by Elizabethan Strolling Players. JEGP. xxvi, 1927.

—— Variety-show Clownery on the Pre-Restoration Stage. Ang. lii, 1928.

—— Vaudeville Dancing and Acrobatics in Elizabethan Plays. E. Studien, lxiii, 1928.

—— Madmen as Vaudeville Performers on the Elizabethan Stage. JEGP. xxx, 1931.

Baskervill, C. R. The Elizabethan Jig and Related Song Drama. Chicago, 1929.

Moore, J. R. The Songs of the Public Theaters in the Time of Shakespeare. JEGP. xxviii, 1929.

Pearn, B. R. Dumb-Show in Elizabethan Drama. RES. xi, 1935.

(d) Extemporal Acting

Lawrence, W. J. Shakespeare and the Italian Comedians. TLS. 11 Nov. 1920.

Graves, T. S. Some Aspects of Extemporal Acting. Stud. Phil. xix, 1922.

Wright, L. B. Will Kemp and the Commedia dell' Arte. MLN. xli, 1926.

Marschall, Wilhelm. Das 'Sir Thomas Moore'-Manuskript und die englische Commedia dell' Arte. Ang. lii, 1928.

—— Die neun Dichter des Hamlet. Heidelberg, [1928].

Lea, K. M. Italian Popular Comedy. 2 vols. Oxford, 1934.

(4) The Conduct of the Theatres: Finance, Organization, etc.

[See Chambers, vol. i, The Actors' Economics, pp. 348–88.]

Maas, Hermann. Äussere Geschichte der englischen Theatertruppen in dem Zeitraum von 1559–1642. Bang, vol. xix, 1907. [3rd essay.]

Wallace, C. W. The Globe and Blackfriars Systems of Finance. TLS. 2 and 9 Oct. 1909.

—— Shakspere and the Blackfriars. Century Mag. Sept. 1910.

Baskervill, C. R. The Custom of Sitting on the Elizabethan Stage. MP. viii, 1911.

Graves, T. S. A Note on the Swan Theatre. MP. ix, 1912.

—— The Court and the London Theaters during the Reign of Queen Elizabeth. Menasha, Wisconsin, 1913.

—— The Origin of the Custom of Sitting on the Stage. JEGP. xiii, 1914.

—— Night Scenes in the Elizabethan Theatres. E. Studien, xlvii, 1914. [See also W. J. Lawrence, E. Studien, xlviii, 1915.]

—— Organized Applause. South Atlantic Quart. xix, 1920.

Thaler, Alwin. Shakespeare's Income. Stud. Phil. xv, 1918.

—— Playwrights' Benefits and Interior Gathering in the Elizabethan Theatre. Stud. Phil. xvi, 1919.

—— The 'Free-list' and Theatre Tickets in Shakespeare's Time and After. MLR. xv, 1920.

—— Shakspere to Sheridan. A Book about the Theatre of Yesterday and To-day. Cambridge, U.S.A. 1922.

—— Minor Actors and Employees in the Elizabethan Theatre. MP. xx, 1922.

Rhodes, R C. Shakespeare's Prompt Books. i. Stage-Directions. ii. The Curtains. TLS. 21 and 28 July, 1921.

Holzknecht, K. J. Theatrical Billposting in the Age of Elizabeth. PQ. i, 1923.

Wilson, F. P. Ralph Crane, Scrivener to the King's Players. Library, viii, 1927.

Baldwin, T. W. The Organization and Personnel of the Shakespearian Company. Princeton, 1927.

(5) MISCELLANEOUS STUDIES

Foster, F. A. Dumb Show in Elizabethan Drama before 1620. E. Studien, xliv, 1911.

Graves, T. S. The 'Act Time' in Elizabethan Theatres. Stud. Phil. xii, 1915.

Greg, W. W. 'Bad' Quartos outside Shakespeare. Alcazar and Orlando. Library, x, 1919.

—— Two Elizabethan Stage Abridgements, the Battle of Alcazar and Orlando Furioso. Oxford, 1923.

—— The Evidence of Theatrical Plots for the History of the Elizabethan Stage. RES. i, 1925.

—— Act-divisions in Shakespeare. RES. iv, 1928.

—— Dramatic Documents from the Elizabethan Playhouses. Stage Plots, Actors' Parts, Prompt Books. 2 vols. Oxford, 1931.

Engelen, Julia. Die Schauspieler-Ökonomie in Shakespeares Dramen. Münster, 1926.

Sack, Maria. Darstellerzahl und Rollenverteilung bei Shakespeare. Leipzig, 1928.

Hunter, Sir Mark. Act- and Scene-division in the Plays of Shakespeare. RES. ii, 1926. [See also J. D. Wilson, RES. iii, 1927.]

Wilson, J. D. 'They sleepe all the Act.' RES. iv, 1928.

Lawrence, W. J. Act-intervals in Early Shakespearian Performances. RES. iv, 1928.

van Dam, B. A. P. Alleyn's Player's Part of Green's Orlando Furioso, and the Text of the Quarto of 1594. E. Studies, xi, 1929.

Hart, A. The Time allotted for Representation of Elizabethan and Jacobean Plays. RES. vii, 1932.

III. THE PURITAN ATTACK UPON THE STAGE

[Bibliographies of the subject will be found in E. N. S. Thompson, Controversy between the Puritans and the Stage, New York, 1903; N. S. Symmes, Les Débuts de la Critique Dramatique, Paris, 1903; and Sir E. K. Chambers, Elizabethan Stage, vol. iv, pp. 187–259, Oxford, 1923, where significant portions of many of the documents are rptd, while R. W. Lowe, Bibliographical Account of English Theatrical Literature, 1888, may also be referred to. A complete list of Prynne's works is contained in S. R. Gardiner, Documents relating to William Prynne, Camden Soc. 1877.]

(1) MANUSCRIPTS

Field, Nathaniel. Feild the Players Letter to Mr Sutton Preacher att St Mary Overs 1616. [Calendar of State Papers, Domestic, James I, lxxxix, no. 105; rptd J. O. Halliwell[-Phillipps], The Remonstrance of Nathan Field, 1865; and in his Illustrations of the Life of Shakespeare, vol. i, app. xxiii, 1874.]

Gager, William. [His letters to Rainolds on the subject of stage plays are to be seen at Oxford in the libraries of Corpus Christi College (MS ccclii, 6) and of University College (MS J 18). Reprints in part by F. S. Boas, and K. Young, see (3) below.]

Remembrancia, a series of records preserved in the office of the Town Clerk of the City of London. [All the documents in this series, bearing upon the stage, have been rptd by the Malone Soc. (Collections, pt i). The City's Letter Books, which extend to 1590, the Journals of the Common Council and the Repertories of the Court of Aldermen, all hitherto unexplored, are likely to contain material of interest. Such of the Burghley Papers, among the Lansdowne MSS at the BM., as deal with the stage have also been rptd in the Malone Society's Collections.]

(2) CONTEMPORARY PAMPHLETS AND OTHER MATERIAL ILLUSTRATING THE SUBJECT

The Actors Remonstrance, or Complaint: For The silencing of their profession, and banishment from their severall Play-houses. In which is fully set downe their grievances for their restraint; especially since Stage-playes, only of all publike recreations are prohibited; the exercise at the Beares Colledge, and the motions of Puppets being still in force and vigour. 1643; rptd W. C. Hazlitt, English Drama and Stage, pp. 200–65, 1869; rptd C. Hindley, Miscellanea Antiqua Anglicana, vol. III, 1873.

Agrippa. Henrie Cornelius Agrippa, of tne Vanitie and uncertaintie of Artes and Sciences, Englished by Ja. San. Gent. 1569; 1575.

Alley, William. ΠΤΩΧΟΜΥΣΕΙΟΝ. The poore mans Librarie. 2 vols. 1565, 1570.

Ascham, Roger. The Scholemaster. 1570.

Babington, Gervase. A very fruitfull Exposition of the Commaundements by way of Questions and Answeres for greater plainnesse. 1583; rptd in part F. J. Furnivall, Stubbes's Anatomy of Abuses, pt I, pp. 75*–93*, New Shakspere Soc. 1879.

Beard, Thomas. The Theatre of God's Judgments translated out of the French and augmented. 1597; 1612.

Bodin, Jean. Les six livres de la Republique. Paris, 1576; tr. Eng. R. Knolles, 1606.

Brome, Alexander. Rump: or an exact Collection of the choycest Poems and Songs relating to the late Times. 1662. [Contains the Players Petition to the Parliament, which is rptd in W. C. Hazlitt, English Drama and Stage, pp. 272–5, 1869.]

Bucer, Martin. Scripta Anglicana. Basle, 1577. [Ch. 54, De honestis ludis, rptd H. S. Symmes, Les Débuts, 1903.]

Case, John. Speculum Moralium Quaestionum in Universam Ethicen Aristotelis, Authore Magistro Johanne Caso Oxoniensi, olim Collegii Divi Johannis Praecursoris Socio. Oxford, 1585; 1589. [Extract in Sir E. K. Chambers, Elizabethan Stage, vol. IV, p. 228, 1923.]

Chettle, Henry. Kind-harts Dreame. Conteining five Apparitions, with their Invectives against abuses raigning. [1593.]

Coke, Sir Edward. The Lord Coke His Speech and Charge. With a discoverie of the Abuses and Corruption of officers. 1607.

Crashawe, William. The Sermon Preached at the Crosse, Feb. xiiij. 1607.

Elyot, Sir Thomas. The Boke named the Governour. 1531; ed. H. H. S. Croft, 2 vols. 1880.

Fenton, Sir Geoffrey. Certain tragicall discourses written out of Frenche and Latin. 1567.

—— A forme of Christian pollicie gathered out of French. 1574. [Partially rptd H. S. Symmes, Les Débuts, 1903.]

Ferrarius. A woorke of Joannes Ferrarius Montanus, touchynge the good orderynge of a common weale. Englished by William Bavande. 1559. [Partially rptd H. S. Symmes, Les Débuts, 1903.]

Field, John. A godly exhortation, by occasion of the late judgement of God shewed at Parris-garden, the thirteenth day of Januarie; where were assembled by estimation; above a thousand persons, whereof some were slaine; & of that number, at the least, as is crediblie reported, the thirde person maimed and hurt. Given to all estates for their instruction, concerning the keeping of the Sabboth day. 1583.

Field, Nathaniel. [See (1) above.]

Gager, William. [See (1) above.]

G[ainsford?], T[homas?]. The rich Cabnit furnished with a Varietie of exquisite Discriptions, exquisite Characters, witty Discourses, and delightful Histories. 1616. [Partially rptd W. C. Hazlitt, English Drama and Stage, pp. 228–30, 1869.]

Gosson, Stephen. The Schoole of Abuse, Conteining a plesaunt invective against Poets, Pipers, Plaiers, Jesters, and such like caterpillers of a commonwelth; setting up the Flagge of Defiance to their mischievous exercise, & overthrowing their Bulwarkes, by Prophane Writers, Naturall reason, and common experience. 1579; 1587; rptd Sir Walter Scott, Somers Tracts, 2nd edn, vol. III, pp. 552–74, 1809–15; rptd J. P. Collier, Shakespeare Soc. (with Thomas Heywood's Apology for Actors) 1841; ed. E. Arber, 1895.

—— The Ephemerides of Phialo, devided into three Bookes. The first, A method which he ought to follow that desireth to rebuke his freend, when he seeth him swarve: without kindling his choler, or hurting himselfe. The second, A Canuazado to Courtiers in foure pointes. The thirde, The defence of a Curtezan overthrowen. And a short Apologie of the Schoole of Abuse, against Poets, Pipers, Players & their Excusers. 1579; 1586. [Rptd (extracts and An Apologie of the Schoole of Abuse) E. Arber, 1895 (with The Schoole of Abuse).]

—— Playes confuted in five Actions, Proving that they are not to be suffred in a Christian common weale, by the waye both the Cavils of Thomas Lodge and the Play of Playes, written in their defence, and other objections of Players frendes, are truely set downe and directlye aunsweared. [1582.] [Rptd in W. C. Hazlitt, English Drama and Stage, pp. 159–218, 1869.]

Gosson, Stephen. The Trumpet of Warre. A Sermon preached at Paules Crosse, the seventh of Maie, 1598. [Rptd (extracts) with Pleasant Quippes, 1847.]

—— Pleasant Quippes for Upstart New-fangled Gentlewomen. 1596 (anon.); rptd E. F. Rimbault, 1841; rptd Totham, 1847.

G[reene?], J[ohn?]. A Refutation of the Apology for Actors. Divided into three briefe Treatises. Wherein is confuted and opposed all the chiefe Groundes and Arguments alleaged in defence of Playes: And withall in each Treatise is deciphered Actors, 1. Heathenish and Diabolicall institution. 2. Their ancient and moderne indignitie. 3. The wonderfull abuse of their impious qualitie. 1615.

Greene, Robert. Greenes Never too late. Or a Powder of Experience sent to all Youthfull Gentlemen. 1590.

Harvey, Gabriel. Three proper and wittie, familiar Letters, touching the Earthquake in April last, lately passed between two Universitie men. 1580. [Rptd A. B. Grosart, Harvey's Works, 3 vols. 1884.]

Heywood, Thomas. An Apology for Actors. Containing three briefe Treatises. 1. Their Antiquity. 2. Their ancient Dignity. 3. The true use of their quality. 1612; 1658 (as The Actors Vindication). [Rptd Sir Walter Scott, Somers Tracts, 2nd edn, vol. III, pp. 574–600, 1809–15; rptd J. P. Collier, Shakespeare Soc. 1841.]

Lake, Osmund. A Probe Theologicall: Or, The First Part of the Christian Pastors Proofe of his learned Parishioners Faith. Wherein is handled, the Doctrine of the Law for the knowledge of it, with such profitable questions, as aptly fall in at every branch of the Law. 1612.

Laneham, Robert. A Letter: Whearin, part of the entertainment untoo the Queenz Majesty at Killingwoorth Castl, in Warwik Sheer in this Soomerz Progress 1575. iz signified. [1575.] [Rptd F. J. Furnivall, Captain Cox, his Ballads and Books, Ballad Soc. 1871.]

Lodge, Thomas. Honest Excuses. [A Defence of Poetry, music and stage-plays in reply to Stephen Gosson's School of Abuse.] [Probably pbd in the late summer of 1579. Suppressed by authority. No title-page or preface. Rptd David Lang, A Defence of Poetry, Shakespeare Soc. 1853; rptd Sir E. Gosse, Complete Works of Thomas Lodge, Hunterian Club, 1883; rptd G. Saintsbury, Elizabethan and Jacobean Pamphlets, 1892.]

Lodge, Thomas. An Alarum against Usurers. Containing tryed experiences against worldly abuses. Hereunto are annexed the delectable historie of Forbonius and Prisceria: with the lamentable complaint of Truth over England. 1584. [Rptd David Laing (with A Defence), Shakespeare Soc. 1853; rptd Sir E. Gosse, Complete Works of Lodge, 1883.]

Lupton, Donald. London and the Countrey Carbonadoed and Quartred into severall Characters. 1632. [Rptd Harleian Misc. vol. IX, 1808; rptd J. O. Halliwell[-Phillipps], Books of Characters, 1857.]

Mariana, Juan de. Tratado contra los Juegos Públicos. [Rptd in Obras, Biblioteca de Autores Españoles, 2 vols. Madrid, 1854.]

—— De Rege et Regis Institutione. Toledo, 1599.

Nashe, Thomas. The Anatomie of Absurditie: Contayning a breefe confutation of the slender imputed prayses to feminine perfection, with a short description of the severall practises of youth, and sundry follies of our licentious times. No lesse pleasant to be read, then profitable to be remembered, especially of those, who live more licentiously, or addicted to a more nyce stoycall austeritie. 1589. [Rptd R. B. McKerrow, Nashe's Works, vol. I, 1904.]

—— Pierce Penilesse his supplication to the Divell. Describing the overspreading of Vice, and suppression of Vertue. Pleasantly interlac'd with variable delights: and pathetically intermixt with conceipted reproofes. 1592. [Rptd R. B. McKerrow, Nashe's Works, vol. I, 1904.]

Newes from the North. Otherwise called the conference between Simon Certain and Pierce Plowman. Faithfully collected and gathered by T. F. Student. 1585.

Newton, Thomas. A Treatise, touching Dyceplay and prophane Gaming. Wherein, as Godly recreations and moderate disportes bee Christianly allowed and learnedly defended: so, all vaine, ydle, unlawfull, offensive, and prophane Exercises, bee sharply reproved and flatly condemned. Written in Latine by Lambertus Danaeus. 1586.

North, Thomas. The Diall of Princes. Compiled by the reverende father in God, Don Anthony of Guevara, Bysshop of Guadix. Preacher and Cronicler, to Charles the fyft Emperour of Rome. Englysshed oute of the Frenche. 1557.

Northbrooke, John. Spiritus est vicarius Christi in terra. A Treatise wherein Dicing, Dauncing, Vaine playes or Enterluds with other idle pastimes &c. commonly used on the Sabboth day, are reproved by the Authoritie of the word of God and auntient

writers. Made Dialoguewise. [1577]; 1579.
[Rptd J. P. Collier, Shakespeare Soc.
1843.]

Orders Appointed to be executed in the Cittie
of London, for setting roges and idle persons
to worke, and for releefe of the poore. [?]

An Ordinance of the Lords and Commons
Assembled in Parliament, for The utter
suppression and abolishing of all Stage-
Playes and Interludes. With the Penalties
to be inflicted upon the Actors and Spectators herein exprest. Die Veneris 11
Februarii. 1647. Ordered by the Lords,
Assembled in Parliament, That this Ordinance for the suppression of Stage-Playes,
shall be forthwith printed and published.
1647.

Overbury, Sir Thomas. A Wife Now The
Widdow of Sir Thomas Overburye. Being
A most exquisite and singular Poem of the
choice of a Wife. Whereunto are added
many witty Characters, and conceited
Newes, written by himselfe and other
learned Gentlemen his friends. 1614.
[Rptd E. F. Rimbault, Miscellaneous works
of Sir Thomas Overbury, 1856. 'An Ex-
cellent Actor' [attrib. John Webster]. See
Gwendolen Murphy, Bibliography of English
Character-Books, 1925, pp. 18–9, and H. D.
Sykes and A. F. Bourgeois, N. & Q. 1913–5.
A reply to Stephens' sketch, see below
p. 511.]

Certaine Propositions offered to the Consideration of the Honourable Houses of Parliament. 1642. [Rptd in Antiquarian Repertory, vol. iii, 1808.]

Prynne, William. Histriomastix. The Players
Scourge, or, Actors Tragœdie, Divided into
Two Parts. Wherein it is largely evidenced,
by divers Arguments, by the concurring
Authorities and Resolutions of sundry texts
of Scripture: of the whole Primitive Church,
both under the Law and Gospell; of 55
Synodes and Councels; of 71 Fathers and
Christian Writers, before the yeare of our
Lord 1200; of above 150 foraigne &
domestique Protestant and Popish Authors,
since: of 40 Heathen Philosophers, Historians, Poets; of many Heathen, many
Christian Nations, Republiques, Emperors,
Princes, Magistrates; of sundry Apostolicall, Canonicall, Imperiall Constitutions;
and of our owne English statutes, Magistrates, Universities, Writers, Preachers.
That popular Stage-playes (the very
Pompes of the Divell which we renounce in
Baptisme, if we beleeve the Fathers) are
sinfull, heathenish, lewde, ungodly Spec-
tacles, and most pernicious Corruptions;
condemned in all ages, as intolerable Mischiefes to Churches, to Republickes, to the

manners, mindes, and soules of men. And
that the Profession of Play-poets, of Stage-
players; together with the penning, acting,
and frequenting of Stage playes, are unlawfull, infamous and misbeseeming Christians.
All pretences to the contrary are here likewise fully answered; and the unlawfulness
of acting or beholding Academicall Enterludes, briefly discussed; besides sundry
other particulars concerning Dancing,
Dicing, Health-drinking, etc. of which the
Table will informe you. By William Prynne,
an Utter-Barrester of Lincolnes Inne.
[Quotations from Cyprian, Lactantius,
Chrysostom and Augustine.] 1633. [Answers
to Prynne did not appear until after
the Restoration, e.g. Sir Richard Baker,
Theatrum Redivivum in answer to Prynne's
Histriomastix, 1662. Another edn, with
different title-page: Theatrum Triumphans,
1670.]

Prynne, William. Mr William Prynn His
Defence of Stage-Plays, or a Retractation
of a former Book of his called Histrio-
Mastix, 1649. [A forgery. Rptd in W. C.
Hazlitt, English Drama and Stage, pp. 267–
71, 1869.]

—— The Vindication of William Prynne,
Esquire, from some scandalous papers and
imputations newly printed and published
to traduce and defame him in his reputation from the King's Head in the Strand.
Jan. 10. 1648. [A broadside. Rptd J. P.
Collier, Poetical Decameron, 2 vols. 1820;
rptd W. C. Hazlitt, English Drama and
Stage, p. 271, 1869.].

Rainolds, John. Th' overthrow of Stage-
Playes, By the way of controversie betwixt
D. Gager and D. Rainoldes, Wherein all
the reasons that can be made for them are
notably refuted; th' objections aunswered,
and the case so cleared and resolved, as that
the judgement of any man, that is not froward
and perverse, may easilie be satisfied. Wherein is manifestly proved, that it is not onely
unlawfull to bee an Actor, but a beholder of
those vanities. Whereunto are added also
and annexed in th' end certaine latine
Letters betwixt the sayed Maister Rainoldes, and D. Gentiles, Reader of the Civill
Law in Oxford. Concerning the same matter.
1599. [No printer's name or place. Some
copies (a second edn?) are imprinted
'Middleburgh, by Richard Schilders 1600,'
and the type in those copies dated 1599 is
undoubtedly his. Another edn: At Oxford,
Printed by John Lichfield, Printer to the
famous Universitie, 1629.]

Rankins, William. A Mirrour of Monsters:
Wherein is plainely described the manifold
vices & spotted enormities, that are caused

by the infectious sight of Playes, with the description of the subtile slights of Sathan, making them his instruments. 1587.

Rawlidge, Richard. A Monster lately found out and discovered or the Scourging of Tipplers. 1627.

A Second & third Blast of retrait from plaies and Theatres: the one whereof was sounded by a reverend Byshop dead long since: the other by a worshipful and zealous Gentleman now alive: One showing the filthiness of plaies in times past; the other the abhomination of Theatres in the time present: both expresly proving that the Commonweale is nigh unto the cursse of God; wherein either plaiers be made of, or theatres maintained. Set forth by Anglo-phile Eutheo. 1580. [Rptd W. C. Hazlitt, English Drama and Stage, pp. 96–155, 1869.]

A Short Treatise against Stage-Playes. [Middelburgh?] 1625. [Rptd W. C. Hazlitt, English Drama and Stage, pp. 231–52, 1869.]

Sidney, Sir Philip. An Apologie for Poetrie. 1595.

The Stage-Players Complaint. In a pleasant Dialogue betweene Cane of the Fortune, and Reed of the Friers. Deploring their sad & solitary conditions for want of Imployment. In this heavie and contagious time of the Plague in London. 1641.

Stephens, John. Satyrical Essayes, Characters, and others, or Accurate and quick Descriptions, fitted to the life of their Subjects. 1615. [Rptd J. O. Halliwell [-Phillipps], Books of Characters, 1857. See above, T. Overbury, and Sir E. K. Chambers, Elizabethan Stage, vol. iv, p. 255, 1923.]

Stockwood, John. A Sermon Preached at Paules Crosse on Barthelmew day, being the 24. of August. 1578. Wherein, besides many other profitable matters meete for all Christians to follow, is at large prooved, that it is the part of all those that are fathers, householders, and Scholemaisters, to instruct all those under their governement, in the word and knowledge of the Lorde. [1578.]

Stubbes, Philip. A fearefull and terrible Example of Gods juste judgement, executed upon a lewde Fellow, who usually accustomed to sweare by Gods Blood, which may be a caveat to all the whole world, that they blaspheme not the name of their God by swearing. [1581?] [Rptd J. P. Collier, Broadside Blackletter Ballads, printed in the 16th and 17th Centuries, 1868.]

—— Two wunderfull and rare Examples. Of the undeffered and present approching judgement of the Lord our God: the one upon a wicked and pernitious blasphemer

of the name of God, and servant to one Maister Frauncis Pennell, Gentleman, dwelling at Boothbie, in Lincolnshire, three myles from Granthan. The other upon a woman, named Joane Bowser, dwelling at Donnington, in Leicester, to whome the Divill verie straungely appeared, as in the discourse following, you may reade. In June last 1581. [1581?] (contains rpt of A fearfull and terrible Example). [Rptd J. P. Reardon, Shakespeare Soc. Papers, vol. iv, p. 71, 1848.]

Stubbes, Philip. The Anatomie of Abuses: Containing A Discoverie, or briefe summarie, of such Notable Vices and imperfections, as now raigne in many Christian Countreyes of the Worlde: but (especiallie) in a verie famous Ilande called Ailgna: Together, with most fearefull Examples of Gods Judgementes, executed upon the wicked for the same, as well in Ailgna of late, as in other places elsewhere. Verie Godly, to be read of all true Christians, everie where; but most needfull, to be regarded in Englande. Made dialogue-wise. 1583; 1595 (5th edn). [Rptd F. J. Furnivall, New Shakspere Soc. 1877–9.]

—— The Second part of the Anatomie of Abuses, conteining The display of Corruptions, with a perfect description of such imperfections, blemishes, and abuses, as now reigning in everie degree, require reformation for feare of Gods vengeance to be powred upon the people and countrie, without speedie repentance and conversion unto God: made dialoguewise. [1583.] [Rptd F. J. Furnivall, New Shakspere Soc. 1882.]

—— The intended Treason, of Doctor Parrie: and his complices, Against the Queenes moste Excellent Majestie. With a Letter sent from the Pope to the same effect. [1585.] [Rptd J. P. Reardon, Shakespeare Soc. Papers, vol. iii, Art. iv, p. 15, 1847.]

—— A Christal Glasse for Christian Women: Contayning An excellent Discourse, of the godly life and Christian death of Mistresse Katherine Stubbes who departed this life in Burton uppon Trent, in Staffordshire, the 14 day of December, 1590. 1591; 1647 (6th or 7th edn). [Rptd (partially) F. J. Furnivall, New Shakspere Soc. 1879.]

—— A perfect Pathway to Felicitie, Conteining godly Meditations, and praiers, fit for all times, and necessarie to be practized of all good Christians. 1592. [Rptd (partially) F. J. Furnivall, New Shakspere Soc. 1879.]

—— A Motive to good workes. Or rather, To true Christianitie indeede. Wherein by the waie is shewed, how farre wee are behinde, not onely our fore-fathers in good workes, but also many other creatures in the endes of our creation: with the difference betwixt the pretenced good workes of the Anti-christian Papist, and the good workes of the Christian Protestant. 1593.

A Treatise of Daunses, wherein it is showed, that they are as it were accessories and dependants (or things annexed) to whore-dom: where also by the way is touched and proved, that Playes are joyned and knit to-gether in a ranck or rowe with them. 1581.

A true reporte of the death and martyrdome of M. Campion Jesuite and priest observid and written by a catholike priest, which was present thereat. [Douay, 1582?]

Twyne, Thomas. Phisicke against Fortune, as well prosperous, as adverse, conteyned in two Bookes. Whereby men are instructed with lyke indifferencie to remedie theyr affections, as well in tyme of the bryght shynyng sunne of prosperitie, as also of the foule lowryng stormes of adversitie. Written in Latine by Frauncis Petrarch, a most famous Poet, and Oratour. And now first Englished. 1579.

Wager, Lewis. A New Enterlude, never be-fore this tyme imprinted, entreating of the Life and Repentaunce of Marie Magdalene: not only godlie, learned and fruitefull, but also well furnished with pleasaunt myrth and pastime, very delectable for those which shall heare or reade the same. 1566; 1567; rptd F. Ives Carpenter, Chicago, 1902.

Whetstone, George. A Mirour for Mage-strates of Cyties. Representing the Ordi-naunces, Policies, and diligence, of the Noble Emperour, Alexander (surnamed) Severus, to suppresse and chastise the notorious Vices noorished in Rome, by the superfluous nomber of Dicing-houses, Tavarns, and common Stewes: Suffred and cheerished, by his beastlye Predecessour, Heluogabalys, with sundrie grave Orations: by the said noble Emperor, concerning Reformation. And Hereunto, is added, A Touchstone for the Time: Containing: many perillous Mischiefes, bred in the Bowels of the Citie of London: By the Infection of some of these Sanctuaries of Iniquitie. 1584.

White, Thomas. A Sermon Preached at Pawles Crosse on Sunday the thirde of November 1577. in the time of the Plague. 1578.

Wither, George. Abuses Stript, and Whipt: or Satirical Essayes. 1613 (4 edns).

(3) MODERN AUTHORITIES, EDITIONS AND WORKS OF REFERENCE

Boas, F. S. A 'Defence' of Oxford Plays and Players. Fortnightly Rev. LXXXVIII, 1907.

Boas, F. S. University Drama in the Tudor Age. Oxford, 1914. [Especially ch. x on Gager, Rainoldes, and the Oxford plays.]

Chambers, Sir E. K. Notes on the History of the Revels Office under the Tudors. 1906.
—— Elizabethan Stage. 4 vols. Oxford, 1923. [Vol. I, pp. 236–68; vol. IV, pp. 184–259.]

Collier, J. P. History of English Dramatic Poetry and Annals of the Stage. 3 vols. 1831; 3 vols. 1879 (rev.).

Creizenach, W. Geschichte des neueren Dramas. 5 vols. Halle, 1893–1916.

Cullen, C. Puritanism and the Stage. Proc. Royal Philosophical Soc. Glasgow, XLIII, 1911–2.

Dasent, J. R. Acts of the Privy Council of England, 1542–1604. 32 vols. 1890–1907.

Feuillerat, A. Documents relating to the Office of the Revels in the Times of King Edward VI and Queen Mary. Bang, vol. XLIV, 1914.
—— Documents relating to the Office of the Revels in the Time of Queen Elizabeth. Bang, vol. XXI, 1908.

Fleay, F. G. Biographical Chronicle of the English Drama. 1891.
—— Chronicle History of the London Stage. 1890.
—— Shakespeare and Puritanism. Ang. VII, 1884.

Furnivall, F. J. Philip Stubbes's Anatomy of Abuses in Shakspere's Youth. With Intro-duction and Notes. New Shakspere Soc. 1879.
—— Shakspere's England. William Harri-son's Description of England. New Shak-spere Soc. 1876.
—— Captain Cox, his Ballads, and Books, or Robert Laneham's Letter. Ballad Soc. 1871; 1907 (Shakespeare Lib.).

Gardiner, S. R. Documents relating to the Proceedings against William Prynne in 1634 and 1637, with a Biographical Frag-ment by the late John Bruce. Camden Soc. 1877.

Gildersleeve, Virginia C. Government Regu-lation of the Elizabethan Drama. New York, 1908.

Gosse, Sir E. Thomas Lodge. [In Seventeenth Century Studies, 1883, etc.]

Graves, T. S. Notes on Puritanism and the Stage. Stud. Phil. XVIII, 1921.

Grierson, H. J. C. Cross Currents in English Literature of the Seventeenth Century. 1929.

Grindal, E. The Remains of. Parker Soc. 1843.

Halliwell[-Phillipps], J. O. Tarlton's Jests and News out of Purgatory. Shakespeare Soc. 1844.
—— Illustrations of the Life of Shakespeare. Pt I, 1874.

Halliwell[-Phillipps], J. O. Outlines of the Life of Shakespeare. 2 vols. 1882.

Harington, Sir John. Nugae Antiquae. Ed. H. Harington, with illustrative notes by T. Park, 2 vols. 1804.

Harrison, W. Harrison's Description of England. Being Books II and III of his Description of Britaine and England. Ed. from the first two edns of Holinshed's Chronicle (1577, 1587), with introduction, F. J. Furnivall, 3 pts and Supplement, New Shakspere Soc. 1877–8; 1908 (with addns by C. C. Stopes, pt IV (Supplement). [Also Select Edition, by L. Withington, with Furnivall's Introduction, 1902.]

Hazlitt, W. C. The English Drama and Stage. 1869. [Indispensable for its rpts of documents, pamphlets, and treatises.]

Hutchinson, J. Memoirs by his widow, Lucy. Ed. Sir C. H. Firth, 1906.

Kingsley, C. Plays and Puritans. 1873.

Lodge, T. Complete Works. Ed. Sir E. Gosse, 12 vols. Hunterian Club, Glasgow, 1873–9.

Lounsbury, T. R. A Puritan Censor of the Stage [Prynne]. Yale Rev. XII, 1923.

Lowe, R. W. A Bibliographical Account of English Theatrical Literature. 1888.

Malone Society Collections. Pts I, II, 1907–8. [A very important help to any study of the city's attack. All documents from the Remembrancia and the Burghley papers, dealing with the stage, are carefully rptd.]

Nash, Thomas. The Works of. Ed. R. B. McKerrow, vols. I–III, 1904–5.

Ordish, T. F. Early London Theatres (in the Fields). 1894.

Parker, M. The Correspondence of. Ed. J. Bruce and T. T. Perowne, Parker Soc. 1852.

Analytical Index to the Series of Records known as the Remembrancia, preserved among the Archives of the city of London. A.D. 1579–1664. 1878.

Selden, John. Opera Omnia. Ed. David Wilkins, 3 vols. in 6, 1726.

—— Table Talk. Ed. S. H. Reynolds, Oxford, 1892.

Simpson, R. The Political Use of the Stage in Shakespere's Time. Trans. New Shakspere Soc. pt II, 1874.

Calendar of State Papers. Domestic Series. Reigns of Edward VI, Mary, Elizabeth, 1547–1589. Ed. R. Lemon, 1856. Reign of James I. Ed. M. A. Everett Greene, 1857–69.

A complete Collection of State Trials. Ed. T. B. Howell, 34 vols. 1809. [Vol. III contains Proceedings against William Prynne.]

Symmes, H. S. Les Débuts de la Critique dramatique en Angleterre jusqu'à la Mort de Shakespeare. Paris, 1903. [Deals only incidentally with the subject of this chapter but throws fresh light upon it. Contains a useful bibliography and reprints important passages from Bucer, Fenton and Ferrarius.]

Taylor, G. C. Another Renaissance Attack on the Stage. PQ. IX, 1930.

Thompson, E. N. S. The Controversy between the Puritans and the Stage. Yale Studies in English. New York, 1903. [Despite inaccuracies and the author's ultra-puritan sympathies, this book, the only monograph covering the whole ground, should prove of great service to the student. A useful review of it by W. W. Greg appeared in MLR. I, 1906.]

Ward, Sir A. W. History of English Dramatic Literature. 3 vols. 1899. [Especially vol. I, pp. 456–62; vol. III, pp. 206–9, 229–47.]

Wilson, J. D. The Title of Lodge's Reply to Gosson's School of Abuse. MLR. III, 1908.

—— Anthony Munday, Pursuivant and Pamphleteer. MLR. IV, 1909.

Wright, T. Queen Elizabeth and her Times. 2 vols. 1838.

Young, K. [Rainoldes'] Letter to Thomas Thornton. [In Shakespeare Studies, by Members of the Department of English of the University of Wisconsin, 1916.]

—— William Gager's Defence of the Academic Stage. Trans. Wisconsin Academy of Sciences, Arts, and Letters, no. 18, 1916. [Gager's Momus, portions of the correspondence between Gager and Rainoldes, and all of Gager's long letter of 31 July 1592. See also F. S. Boas, University Drama.]

J. D. W., rev. E. N. S. T.

IV. THE MORALITIES

[In this and the following sections an attempt has been made to record the whole extant dramatic output of the period now in print. Undramatic dialogues and translations not intended for the stage have, however, generally been omitted. The italicized abbreviations (*Adams, Brandl, Malone Soc., TFT.*, etc.) refer to collections of plays, the full titles of which will be found, pp. 488–92 above.]

A. CRITICAL STUDIES

Seifert, J. Die Wit- und Science-Moralitäten des 16. Jahrhunderts. Karolinenthal, 1892.

Bolte, J. Der Teufel in der Kirche. Zeitschrift für vergleichende Litteraturgeschichte, XI, 1897.

Cushman, L. W. The Devil and Vice in English Dramatic Literature before Shakespeare. Halle, 1900. [See also review in Anzeiger für deutsches Alterthum, xxvii, 1901.]

Eckhardt, E. Die lustige Person im älteren englischen Drama. Berlin, 1902.

—— Die metrische Unterscheidung von Ernst und Komik in den englischen Moralitäten. E. Studien, lxii, 1927.

Haslinghuis, E. J. De Duivel in het Drama der Middeleeuwen. Leyden, 1912.

Moore, J. R. Ancestors of Autolycus in the English Moralities and Interludes. Washington University Stud. ix, 1922.

Allison, T. E. The Paternoster Play and the Origin of the Vice. PMLA. xxxix, 1924.

Withington, R. The Development of the 'Vice.' [In Essays in Memory of Barrett Wendell, Cambridge, U.S.A. 1926.]

Wright, L. B. Social Aspects of some Belated Moralities. Ang. liv, 1930.

[See also the general works of Brandl, Chambers, Collier, Creizenach, Ward and Warton listed above, pp. 492–3.]

B. PRE-TUDOR MORALITIES

The Macro Plays. (Mankind; Wisdom, who is Christ; the Castell of Perseverance.) Ed. F. J. Furnivall and A. W. Pollard, EETS. Ex. Ser. 1904; *TFT*. 1907.

The Castell of Perseverance. Ed. in part A. W. Pollard (English Miracle Plays, 1890, 1927). [See under Macro Plays above.]

Mankind. Ed. in part A. W. Pollard (English Miracle Plays, 1890, 1927); *Manly*, vol. i; *Brandl*; ed. J. S. Farmer ('Lost' Tudor Plays, 1907); *Adams*. [See under Macro Plays above.]

    Keiller, M. M. The Influence of Piers Plowman in Mankind. PMLA. xxvi, 1911.

    Mackenzie, W. R. A New Source of Mankind [Four Daughters of God]. PMLA. xxvii, 1912.

    Smart, W. K. Some Notes on Mankind. MP. xiv, 1917. [Dates 1465–74.]

    —— Mankind and the Mumming Plays. MLN. xxxii, 1917.

Wisdom, who is Christ. Ed. W. B. D. Turnbull, Abbotsford Club, 1837 (as Mind, Will and Understanding); ed. F. J. Furnivall (in Digby Plays, New Shakspere Soc. 1882). [See under Macro Plays above. See also W. K. Smart, Some English and Latin Sources and Parallels, Madison, 1912. (Dates 1460–3.)]

The Pride of Life. [Fragment.] Ed. J. Mills, Proc. Royal Soc. Antiquaries of Ireland, 1891; *Brandl*. [See F. Holthausen, Pride of Life, Archiv, cviii, 1901.]

C. EARLY TUDOR MORALITIES

JOHN BALE (1495–1563)

The Dramatic Writings of John Bale. Ed. J. S. Farmer, 1907.

[God's Promises.] A Tragedye or enterlude manyfestyng the chefe promyses of God unto man. Compyled 1538. [1547?]; 1577; 1578; rptd R. Dodsley (Select Collection of Old Plays, vol. i, 1744, 1780, 1825); *Hazlitt's Dodsley*, vol. i; *TFT*. 1908.

[John Baptist.] A Briefe Comedy or Enterlude of Johan Baptystes. Compyled m.d. xxxviii. n.d. (no copy traceable); rptd Harleian Misc. vol. i, 1744, 1808.

[Temptation.] A brefe Comedy or enterlude concernynge the temptacyon of our Lorde. Compyled m.d.xxxviii. [1548?]; rptd A. B. Grosart, Miscellanies of Fuller Worthies Lib. vol. i, 1870; *TFT*. 1909.

[Three Laws.] A Comedy concernynge thre lawes, of nature, Moses, and Christ. Compyled m.d.xxxviii. [1548?]; 1562; ed. A. Schroeer, Ang. v, 1882; *TFT*. 1908.

Kynge Johan. Ed. J. P. Collier, Camden Soc. 1838; *Manly*, vol. i, ed. W. Bang, *Bang*, vol. xxv, 1909; ed. J. H. P. Pafford, *Malone Soc.* 1931. [Written 1534–47. MS in Huntington Lib. See C. E. Cason, Additional Lines to Bale's Kynge Johan, JEGP. xxvii, 1928.]

[For Bale's Summarium, see p. 317 above. For his numerous controversial works, see the selection by H. Christmas, Parker Soc. 1849, and C. H. and T. Cooper, Athenae Cantabrigienses, 1858–61. See also H. McCusker, Books and Manuscripts formerly in the Possession of John Bale, Library, xvi, 1935.]

SIR DAVID LINDSAY (1490–1555)

Ane Satyre of the Thrie Estaits. Edinburgh, 1602. [See under Lindsay, pp. 897–8 below.]

HENRY MEDWALL

Nature. [1530?] (W. Rastell); *Brandl*; *Bang*, vol. xii, 1905; (facs. fragment) ed. J. S. Farmer ('Lost' Tudor Plays, 1907); *TFT*. 1908. [Written 1486–1500. For Medwall's Fulgens and Lucres see below, p. 517.]

JOHN RASTELL (1470?–1536)

A new interlude and a mery of the nature of the .iiii. elements. [1519] (anon.); rptd Percy Soc. 1848; *Hazlitt's Dodsley*, vol. i; ed. T. Fischer, Marburg, 1903; ed. J. S. Farmer (Six Anonymous Plays, 1905); *TFT*. 1908. [For Calisto and Melibea, and Gentylnes & Nobylyte, see p. 517 below.]

JOHN REDFORD (d. 1547)

Wyt and Scyence. Ed. J. O. Halliwell[-Phillipps], Shakespeare Soc. 1848; *Manly*, vol. i; ed. J. S. Farmer ('Lost' Tudor Plays, 1907); *TFT*. 1908; *Adams*. [BM. Add. MS 15233 (probably autograph). Written late in Henry VIII's reign. See J. Seifert, Prague, 1892; C. R. Baskervill, Mummers' Wooing Plays in England, MP. xxi, 1923; S. A. Tannenbaum, Editorial Notes on Wit and Science, PQ. xiv, 1935.]

JOHN SKELTON (1460?–1529)

Magnyfycence. [1529?] [See under Skelton, p. 408 above.]

R. WEVER

An Enterlude called lusty Juventus. [1565?] (Copland); [1565?] (Veale); [1570?] (Awdely); ed. T. Hawkins (Origin of English Drama, vol. i, 1773); *Hazlitt's Dodsley*, vol. ii; ed. J. S. Farmer, Early English Drama Soc. 1905; *TFT*. 1907 (Awdely's edn).[Written 1547–53. Stationers' Register, 1560.]

ANONYMOUS PLAYS

[Albyon Knight.] [1566?] (fragment); ed. J. P. Collier, Shakespeare Soc. Papers, vol. i, 1844; rptd W. W. Greg, Malone Soc. Collections, vol. i, 1909. [S.R. 1566, written c. 1560.]
[The Summoning of Everyman.] [1509–19] (4 edns, 2 by Pynson, 2 by J. Skot); ed. T. Hawkins (Origin of English Drama, vol. i, 1773); ed. K. Goedeke, Hanover, 1865 (with masterly introduction on history of theme); *Hazlitt's Dodsley*, vol. i; ed. H. Logeman, Ghent, 1892 (with Dutch text); ed. K. H. de Raaf, Groningen, 1897; ed. A. W. Pollard (Fifteenth Century Prose and Verse, 1903); ed. F. Sidgwick, 1902; ed. M. J. Moses, New York, 1903 (original introduction); ed. J. S. Farmer, Early English Drama Soc. 1905 and 1906 (Museum Dramatists); *Bang*, vol. iv, 1904 (Skot's edn), vol. xxiv, 1909 (Skot's other edn), vol. xxviii, 1910 (2 Pynson fragments); *TFT*. 1912; ed. J. S. Tatlock and R. G. Martin (Representative English Plays, 1916, 1923); *Adams*.

Holthausen, F. and Koelbing, E. Brief Notes. E. Studien, xxi, 1895.
Sidgwick, F. Everyman. N. & Q. 7 Feb. 1903.
Roersch, A. Elckerlijk-Everyman. Archiv, cxiii, 1904.
Bang, W. Zu Everyman. E. Studien, xxxv, 1905.
Manly, J. M. Elckerlijk-Everyman: Question of Priority. MP. viii, 1910. [See F. A. Wood, *ibid*.]

Bates, E. P. Everyman and the Talmud. Athenaeum, 29 Nov. 1913. [See M. J. Landa, Athenaeum, 6 Dec. 1913.]
A new enterlude, drawen oute of the holy scripture, of godly queene Hester. 1561; ed. J. P. Collier (Early English Popular Literature, vol. i, 1863); ed. A. B. Grosart, 1870; ed. W. W. Greg, *Bang*, vol. v, 1904 (excellent introduction); ed. J. S. Farmer (Anonymous Plays, ser. 2, 1906). [Written 1525–9.]
Hyckescorner. [1512?] (de Worde); [?] (J. Waley); ed. T. Hawkins (Origin of English Drama, vol. i, 1773); *Hazlitt's Dodsley*, vol. i; *Manly*, vol. i; ed. J. S. Farmer (Six Anonymous Plays, 1905); *TFT*. 1908.
A new enterlude of Impacient Poverte. [1560?]; 1560; ed. J. S. Farmer ('Lost' Tudor Plays, 1907); *TFT*. 1907 (dated edn); ed. R. B. McKerrow, *Bang*, vol. xxxiii, 1911 (dated edn). [Written 1545–52.]
The Interlude of Johan the Evangelyst. [1560?]; *Malone Soc*. 1907; *TFT*. 1907.
A Preaty Interlude called, Nice wanton. 1560; [1565?]; *Hazlitt's Dodsley*, vol. ii; *Manly*, vol. i; *TFT*. 1908, 1909 (both edns). [Written *temp*. Edward VI or Mary.]
Respublica. Ed. J. P. Collier (Illustrations of English Literature, vol. i, 1886); *Brandl*; ed. L. A. Magnus, EETS. Ex. Ser. 1905 (inaccurate text); ed. J. S. Farmer ('Lost' Tudor Plays, 1907); *TFT*. 1908. [MS dated 1553.]
The Resurrection of Our Lord. Ed. J. D. Wilson and B. Dobell, *Malone Soc*. 1912. [Written 1530–60. Perhaps by Bale?]
[Somebody, Avarice and Minister.] [c. 1550] (fragment); ed. S. R. Maitland (A List of some of the Early Printed Books at Lambeth, 1843); ed. facs. W. W. Greg, Malone Soc. Collections, vol. ii, 1931 (as Somebody and Others). [Tr. from French Protestant morality, La Vérité Cachée.]
[Temperance and Humility.] [c. 1530.] Ed. W. W. Greg, Malone Soc. Collections, vol. i, 1909. [Fragment.]
An enterlude of Welth, and Helth. [1558?]; *TFT*. 1907; ed. W. W. Greg and P. Simpson, *Malone Soc*. 1907; ed. J. S. Farmer ('Lost' Tudor Plays, 1907); ed. F. Holthausen, Kiel, 1908 (rev. edn 1922). [S.R. 1557, probably written a year or two earlier. See Sir M. Hunter, MLR. iii, 1907; A. E. H. Swaen, E. Studien, xli, 1910.]
A propre newe Interlude of the Worlde and the chylde, otherwyse called (Mundus & Infans). 1522; ed. Roxburghe Club, 1817; ed. J. P. Collier (Dodsley's Old Plays, vol. xii, 1827); *Hazlitt's Dodsley*, vol. i; *Manly*, vol. i; *TFT*. 1909. [See H. N. MacCracken, A Source of Mundus et Infans, PMLA. xxiii, 1908.]

Thenterlude of Youth. [1520?] (fragment, de Worde?); [1557] (J. Waley); [1562?] (Copland); ed. S. R. Maitland (de Worde fragment, in A List of some of the Early Printed Books at Lambeth, 1843); ed. J. O. Halliwell[-Phillipps],1849; *Hazlitt's Dodsley*, vol. II; ed. W. Bang and R. B. McKerrow. *Bang*, vol. XII, 1905; *TFT*. 1908–9 (all 3 edns). [Written early Henry VIII's reign.]

D. ELIZABETHAN MORALITIES

ULPIAN FULWEL

An Enterlude Intituled Like wil to like quod the Devel to the Colier. 1568; [*c*. 1570]; 1587; *Hazlitt's Dodsley*, vol. III; ed. J. S. Farmer, Early English Drama Soc. 1906; *TFT*. 1909 (1587 edn).

THOMAS GARTER

The commody of the most vertuous and Godlye Susanna. 1578; ed. B. I. Evans and W. W. Greg, *Malone Soc.* 1937. [See B. I. Evans, TLS. 2 May 1936, p. 372.]

THOMAS LUPTON

A Moral and Pitieful Comedie, Intituled, All for Money. 1578; ed. J. O. Halliwell [-Phillipps] (Literature of Sixteenth and Seventeenth Centuries, 1851); ed. E. Vogel, Sh. Jb. XL, 1904; *TFT*. 1910.

LEWIS WAGER

A new Enterlude, never before this tyme imprinted, entreating of the Life and Repentance of Marie Magdalene. 1566 (re-issued 1567); ed. F. I. Carpenter, Chicago, 1902 and 1904 (rev. edn); *TFT*. 1908 (1567 issue). [See R. Imelman's review of Carpenter's edn, Archiv, CXI, 1903.]

W. WAGER

A very mery and Pythie Commedie, called, The longer thou livest, the more foole thou art. [1569]; ed. A. Brandl, Sh. Jb. XXXVI, 1900; *TFT*. 1910.
A Comedy or Enterlude intituled, Inough is as good as a feast. [1565?]; ed. facs. S. de Ricci, New York, 1920.
[The Cruel Debtor.] 1566 (fragments); ed. F. J. Furnivall, Trans. New Shakespere Soc. 1878; ed. W. W. Greg, Malone Soc. Collections, vol. I, 1911, vol. II, 1923. [S.R. entry to Wager. R. Imelmann, Archiv, CXI, 1903, p. 209, argues for Lewis Wager.]

GEORGE WAPULL

The Tyde tarryeth no Man. 1576; ed. J. O. Halliwell[-Phillipps] (Literature of the Sixteenth and Seventeenth Centuries, 1851); ed. E. Vogel, Sh. Jb. XL, 1904; *TFT*. 1910.

ROBERT WILSON (d. 1600)

A right excellent and famous Comoedy called the three Ladies of London. 1584 ('Written by R. W.'); 1592 (variant text); ed. J. P. Collier (Five Old Plays, Roxburghe Club, 1851); *Hazlitt's Dodsley*, vol. VI; *TFT*. 1911.
The Pleasant and Stately Morall, of the three Lords and three Ladies of London. 1590 ('by R. W.'); ed. J. P. Collier (Five Old Plays, Roxburghe Club, 1851); *Hazlitt's Dodsley*, vol. VI; *TFT*. 1912. [See H. Fernow, Hamburg, 1885.]
The Coblers Prophesie. 1594; ed. W. Dibelius, Sh. Jb. XXXIII, 1897; *TFT*. 1911; ed. A. C. Wood, *Malone Soc.* 1914.
[For Wilson see S. R. Golding, N. & Q. 7, 14 April 1928.]

NATHANIEL WOODES

An excellent new Comedie Intituled: The Conflict of Conscience. 1581; ed. J. P. Collier (Five Old Plays, Roxburghe Club, 1851); *Hazlitt's Dodsley*, vol. VI, *TFT*. 1911. [See C. Wine, PMLA. L, 1935.]

ANONYMOUS PLAYS

A Pleasant Comedie Shewing the contention betweene Liberalitie and Prodigalitie. 1602; *Hazlitt's Dodsley*, vol. VIII; *TFT*, 1912; ed. W. W. Greg, *Malone Soc.* 1913. [Acted before Queen Elizabeth 1600, probably a revision of an earlier work. See H. N. Hillebrand, Sebastian Westcote and Liberalitie and Prodigalitie, JEGP. XIV, 1915.]
A Pretie new Enterlude both pithie & pleasaunt of the Story of Kyng Daryus. 1565; 1577; ed. J. O. Halliwell[-Phillipps], 1860; *Brandl*; ed. J. S. Farmer (Anonymous Plays, ser. 3, 1906); *TFT*. 1907, 1909 (both edns).
[Love Feigned and Unfeigned.] Ed. A. Esdaile, Malone Soc. Collections, vol. I, 1908. [Fragmentary MS in BM. See E. B. Daw, PMLA. XXXII, 1917.]
A new and Pleasant enterlude intituled the mariage of Witte and Science. [1570?]; *Hazlitt's Dodsley*, vol. II; *TFT*. 1909; photo. facs. 1020.
The Marriage of Wit and Wisdom. Ed. J. O. Halliwell[-Phillipps], Shakespeare Soc. 1846; *TFT*. 1909. [MS *c*. 1579. Perhaps by the Francis Merbury whose name is appended to the epilogue. See S. A. Tannenbaum, PQ. IX, 1930; M. P. Tilley, Shakespeare Ass. Bulletin, X, 1935.]
A new Enterlude No less wittie: then pleasant, entituled new Custome. 1573; ed. R. Dodsley (Collection of Old Plays, vol. I, 1744); *Hazlitt's Dodsley*, vol. III; ed. J. S. Farmer (Anonymous Plays, ser. 3, 1906); *TFT*. 1908. [Written after 1561.]

The Pedlers Prophecie. 1595; *TFT*. 1911; ed.
W. W. Greg, *Malone Soc*. 1914. [Sometimes
attrib. to Robert Wilson. For date see G. L.
Kittredge, Harvard Stud. XVI, 1934.]
Ane verie excellent and delectabill Treatise
intitulit Philotus. Edinburgh, 1603 and
1612; ed. J. W. Mackenzie, Bannatyne
Club, 1835. [See also p. 900 below.]
A new and mery Enterlude, called the Triall of
Treasure. 1567; ed. J. O. Halliwell[-Phil-
lipps], Percy Soc. 1850; *Hazlitt's Dodsley*,
vol. III; ed. J. S. Farmer (Anonymous Plays,
ser. 3, 1906); *TFT*. 1908
[R. Willis, Mount Tabor, 1639, describes a
lost morality, The Cradle of Security. See
J. O. Halliwell[-Phillipps], Outlines of the Life
of Shakespeare, vol. I, 1887. A lost Protestant
morality, of which one character was a
'Colyer', is discussed by A. Feuillerat, MLR.
IX, 1914.]

W. C., *rev*. A. W. R.

V. THE EARLY COMEDIES

MEDWALL, RASTELL, HEYWOOD, UDALL
AND THEIR CONTEMPORARIES

[The italicized abbreviations used in this
section (*Adams, Bang, Gayley, TFT*., etc.)
refer to collections of plays, the full titles of
which will be found, pp. 488–92 above.]

I. CRITICAL AND HISTORICAL STUDIES

Bale, John. Illustrium majoris Britanniae
Scriptorum Summarium. 1548; ed. R. L.
Poole and Mary Bateson, 1902.
Cunningham, Peter. Extracts from the Ac-
counts of Revels at Court in the Reigns of
Queen Elizabeth and King James. Shake-
speare Soc. 1842.
Symonds, J. A. Shakspere's Predecessors in
the English Drama. 1884; 1900 (rev. edn).
Collins, J. C. The Predecessors of Shake-
peare. [In Essays and Studies, 1895.]
Gayley, C. M. An Historical View of the
Beginnings of English Comedy. *Gayley*,
vol. I (Introduction).
Chambers, Sir E. K. The Medieval Stage. 2 vols.
Oxford, 1903. [Vol. II, Appendix X, Texts of
Medieval Plays and Early Tudor Interludes,
contains valuable bibliography.]
—— Court Performances before Queen Eliza-
beth. MLR. II, 1906.
—— Notes on the History of the Revels Office
under the Tudors. 1906.
Feuillerat, A. Documents relating to the
Office of the Revels in the Time of Queen
Elizabeth. *Bang*, vol. XXI, 1908.
—— Documents relating to the Office of the
Revels in the Time of King Edward VI and
Queen Mary. *Bang*, vol. XLIV, 1914.

Bond, R. W. Early Plays from the Italian.
Supposes, The Buggbears, Misogonus. Ox-
ford, 1911. [Introduction.]
Wallace, C. W. The Evolution of the English
Drama up to Shakespeare. Berlin, 1912.
Brooke, C. F. T. The Tudor Drama. 1912.
Boas, F. S. University Drama in the Tudor
Age. Oxford, 1914.
Moore Smith, G. C. The Academic Drama at
Cambridge. Malone Soc. Collections, vol. II,
1923.
Reed, A. W. Early Tudor Drama: Medwall,
the Rastells, Heywood, and the More Circle.
1926.
Greg, W. W. Notes on some Early Plays.
Library, XI, 1930.
[See also the general surveys of Collier,
Fleay, Creizenach, Brandl, Ward, Schelling,
etc., listed in the General Introduction,
pp. 492–3 above.]

II. HENRY MEDWALL (*temp*. Henry VII)

A godely interlude of Fulgens Cenatoure of
Rome. Lucres his doughter. Gayus flaminius
& Publi[us]. Corneli[us] of the disputacyon
of noblenes. [c. 1515] (J. Rastell); ed. W.
Bang and R. B. McKerrow, *Bang*, vol. XII,
1905 (fragment); rptd facs. S. de Ricci,
New York, 1920; ed. F. S. Boas and A. W.
Reed, Oxford, 1926 (see review in Revue
anglo-américaine, June 1927). [See L. B.
Wright, MLN. XLI, 1926, and C. R. Basker-
vill, Conventional Features of Medwall's
Fulgens and Lucres, MP. XXIV, 1927. For
Medwall's morality Nature see above p. 514.]

III. JOHN RASTELL (1470–1536)

[Calisto and Melebea.] A new comodye in
englysh in maner Of an enterlude ryght
elygant & full of craft of rethoryk. [c. 1527]
(J. Rastell) (anon.); *Hazlitt's Dodsley*, vol. I;
ed. J. S. Farmer (Six Anonymous Plays,
1905); ed. W. W. Greg, *Malone Soc*. 1908;
ed. H. W. Allen, 1908 (with The Spanish
Bawd); *TFT*. 1909. [See A. W. S. Rosenbach, The Influence of the Celestina in
the Early English Drama, Sh. Jb. XXXIX,
1903, and A. W. Reed, Early Tudor Drama,
1926, who shows Rastell's hand in the
trn.]
Of Gentylnes & Nobylyte: a dyaloge betwen
the marchaunt, the Knyght & the plowman.
[c. 1527] (J. Rastell)(anon.); rptd J. H. Burn,
1829; ed. J. S. Farmer, Early English Drama
Soc. 1908; *TFT*. 1908. [See C. F. T. Brooke,
MLR. VI, 1911; E. C. Dunn, MLR. XII, 1917;
A. W. Reed, Early Tudor Drama, 1926, who
ascribes the play to Rastell.]
[For Rastell's Nature of the Four Elements
see under the Moralities, p. 514 above.]

IV. JOHN HEYWOOD (1497?–1580?)

(a) Collected Plays

The Dramatic Writings of John Heywood. Ed. J. S. Farmer, Early English Drama Soc. 1905.

(b) Separate Plays

A mery play Betwene Johan Johan the husbande Tyb his wyfe & Syr Jhān the preest. 1533 (W. Rastell); rptd Chiswick Press, [1819?]; *Brandl*; ed. A. W. Pollard, *Gayley*, vol. I; ed. J. S. Farmer (Two Tudor Shrew Plays, 1908); *TFT*. 1907; *Adams*.

A mery Play betwene the pardoner and the frere, the curate and neybour Pratte. 1533 (W. Rastell); ed. F. J. Child (Four Old Plays, 1848); *Hazlitt's Dodsley*, vol. I; ed. in part A. W. Pollard (English Miracle Plays, 1890, 1927); ed. J. S. Farmer, 1906; *TFT*. 1907.

A play of love, A new and mery enterlude concerning pleasure and payne in love. 1533 (W. Rastell); [?] (Waley); *Brandl*; *TFT*. 1909 (Waley's edn). [See W. W. Greg, Archiv, CVI, 1901.]

The play of the wether. A new and a very mery enterlude of all maner wethers. 1533 (W. Rastell); [?] W. Rastell; [?] (Awdeley); [?] (Kytson); *Brandl*; ed. A. W. Pollard, *Gayley*, vol. I; *TFT*. 1908, 1909 (1533 and Awdeley's edns); *Adams*. [See F. Holthausen, Archiv, CXVI, 1906 and J. Q. Adams, MLN. XXII, 1907.]

The playe called the foure P.P. A new and a very mery enterlude of A palmer. A pardoner. A potycary. A pedler. [1543–7] (Myddylton); [?] (Copland); 1569; rptd R. Dodsley (Collection of Old Plays, vol. I); *Ancient British Drama*, vol. I; *Hazlitt's Dodsley*, vol. I; *Manly*, vol. I; *TFT*. 1908 (Myddylton's edn); *Adams*.

Wytty and Wytless. Ed. F. W. Fairholt, Percy Soc. 1846 (abridged as A Dialogue on Wit and Folly); *TFT*. 1909. [BM. MS Harl. 367.]

(c) Non-Dramatic Works

[A Dialogue conteining the number in effect of all the proverbes in the English tongue.] [1549?] (signed J. H. Unique copy in BM. lacks everything before sig. c); 1561 ('Newly oversene and somewhat augmented').

An hundred Epigrammes. 1550.

Two hundred Epigrammes, upon the hundred proverbes, with a thyrde hundred newely added. 1555.

A fourth hundred of Epygrams, Newly invented. 1560.

John Heywoodes woorkes. A dialogue conteynyng the number of the effectual proverbes in the Englishe tongue. With one hundred of Epigrammes; and three hundred of Epigrammes upon three hundred proverbs; and a fifth hundred of Epigrams. Whereunto are now newly added a syxt hundred of Epigrams. 1562; 1566; 1576; 1587; 1598; rptd Spenser Soc. 1867; ed. J. Sharman, 1874; ed. J. S. Farmer, 1906 (with three ballads and a birthday poem [1534] to Princess Mary).

The Spider and the Flie. 1556; rptd Spenser Soc. 1894 (with Introduction by Sir A. W. Ward). [See J. Haber, John Heywood's The Spider and the Flie, Weimar, 1900.]

(d) Biography and Criticism

Pitseus, J. Relationum Historicarum de Rebus Anglicis Tomus Primus. Paris, 1619.

Fairholt, F. W. Some Account of John Heywood and his Interludes. 1846. [Prefixed to Percy Soc. edn of Wit and Folly; contains long selections from Heywood's other interludes.]

Calendar of State Papers, Domestic Series, of the reigns of Edward VI, Mary and Elizabeth. Vol. I, 1547–80, ed. R. Lemon; vol. VII, Addenda, 1566–79, ed. M. A. Everett Green, 1856 ff.

Calendar of Letters and Papers of the Reign of Henry VIII. Ed. J. S. Brewer and J. Gairdner, 1862 ff.

Sharman, J. The Proverbs of John Heywood. 1874. [Introduction.]

Swoboda, W. John Heywood als Dramatiker. Vienna, 1888.

Brandl, A. Quellen des weltlichen Dramas. QF. LXXX, 1898. [Introduction, pp. xlvii–lv.]

Pollard, A. W. Critical Essay. [Prefixed to his edn of Wether and Johan Johan in *Gayley*, 1903.]

Young, K. The Influence of French Farce upon the Plays of John Heywood. MP. II, 1904–5.

Holthausen, F. Zu Heywood's Wetterspiel. Archiv, CXVI, 1906.

Bang, W. Acta Anglo-Lovaniensia. John Heywood und sein Kreis. E. Studien, XXXVIII, 1907.

Graves, T. S. The Heywood Circle and the Reformation. MP. X, 1913.

—— On the Reputation of John Heywood. MP. XXI, 1923.

Hillebrand, H. N. On the Interludes attributed to John Heywood. MP. XII, 1915.

—— John Heywood. MP. XIII, 1916.

Baskervill, C. R. John Heywood. MP. XIII, 1916.

Reed, A. W. John Heywood and his Friends. Library, VIII, 1917.

—— The Canon of John Heywood's Plays. 1918.

—— Early Tudor Drama. 1926.

Bolwell, R. W. Life and Works of John Heywood. New York, 1922.

V. NICHOLAS UDALL (1505–1556)

(a) Dramatic Works

Ralph Roister Doister. [1577?] (anon., unique copy at Eton has no title-page or colophon, but S.R. 1577); ed. T. Briggs, 1818; ed. F. Marshall, 1821; ed. T. White (Old English Drama, vol. I, 1830); ed. W. D. Cooper, Shakespeare Soc. 1847; ed. E. Arber, 1869; *Hazlitt's Dodsley*, vol. III; *Manly*, vol. II; ed. W. H. Williams and P. A. Robins, 1901 (Temple Dramatists); ed. E. Flügel, *Gayley*, vol. I; ed. J. S. Farmer (Dramatic Writings of Nicholas Udall, Early English Drama Soc. 1906) and 1907 (Museum Dramatists); ed. C. G. Child, 1913; *Adams*; ed. W. W. Greg, *Malone Soc.* 1935.

[Ezechias, a play performed before Elizabeth in 1564, is not extant, but is described by Abraham Hartwell in Regina Literata, 1565. See A. R. Moon, TLS. 19 April 1928.]

(b) Other Writings

Floures for Latine spekynge selected and gathered out of Terence, and the same translated in to Englysshe. 1533 (preface dated 1535); 1538; 1544; 1560; rev. John Higgins, 1575; 1581.

Apopthegmes, that is to saie, Prompte Saiynges, compiled in Latin by Erasmus. 1542; 1564.

The first tome or volume of the paraphrase of Erasmus upon the newe testament. 1548; 1551.

A Discourse or Traictise concernynge the Sacrament of the Lordes Supper. [1550?]. [From P. M. Vermigli.]

Compendiosa totius anatomie delineatio. 1553 (re-issued 1557, and with addns 1559). [From Thomas Geminus; an English version.]

Verses and Ditties Made at the Coronation of Queen Anne. Ed. J. Nichols (Progresses of Queen Elizabeth, vol. I, 1788); ed. F. J. Furnivall (Ballads from Manuscripts, Ballad Soc. 1870); ed. E. Arber (English Garner, vol. II, 1879; English only). [English and Latin verses by Udall and John Leland.]

An answer to the articles of the comoners of Devonsheir and Cornwall. Ed. N. Pocock (Troubles connected with the Prayer Book of 1549, Camden Soc. 1884).

(c) Biography and Criticism

The Loseley Manuscripts. Ed. A. J. Kempe, 1836.

Walter, M. Beiträge zu Ralph Royster Doyster. E. Studien, v, 1882.

Graf, H. Der Miles Gloriosus im englischen Drama bis zur Zeit des Bürgerkrieges. Schwerin, 1891.

Hales, J. W. The Date of the First English Comedy. E. Studien, XVIII, 1893.

Flügel, E. Nicholas Udall's Dialogues and Interludes. [In Furnivall Miscellany, Oxford, 1901.]

The Birthe of Hercules. Ed. M. W. Wallace, 1903. [Introduction.]

Williams, W. H. Ralph Roister Doister. E. Studien, XXXVI, XXXVII, 1906–7.

—— Ralph Roister Doister and The Wasps. MLR. VII, 1912.

Maulsby, D. L. The Relation between Udall's Roister Doister and the Comedies of Plautus and Terence. E. Studien, XXXVIII, 1907.

Hinton, J. Source of Ralph Roister Doister. MP. XI, 1913.

Chislett, W. Ralph Roister Doister. MLN. XXIX, 1914.

Dudok, G. Ralph Roister Doister. Did its Author write Jacke Juggler? Neophilologus, I, 1915.

Reed, A. W. Nicholas Udall and Thomas Wilson. RES. I, 1925.

Baldwin, T. W. and Linthicum, M. C. The Date of Ralf Roister Doister. PQ. VI, 1927.

Byrom, H. J. Some Lawsuits of Nicholas Udall. RES. XI, 1935.

VI. OTHER COMEDIES

RICHARD EDWARDS (1523?–1566)

The excellent Comedie of two the most faithfullest Freendes, Damon and Pithias. Newly Imprinted, as the same was shewed before the Queenes Majestie, by the Children of her Graces Chappell. 1571; 1582; rptd R. Dodsley (Collection of Old Plays, vol. I, 1744); ed. Sir S. E. Brydges, 1810; *Ancient British Drama*, vol. I; *Hazlitt's Dodsley*, vol. IV; ed. J. S. Farmer, Early English Drama Soc. 1906; *TFT*. 1908 (1571 edn). [See C. W. Wallace, The Children of the Chapel at Blackfriars, 1597–1603, Lincoln, Nebraska, 1908; W. Y. Durand, JEGP. IV, 1901–2 and MLN. XXIII, 1908; R. W. Bond, Lyly's Works, vol. II, pp. 238–41, 1902; L. Bradner, Life and Poems of Richard Edwards, New Haven, 1927; C. M. Newlin, Some Sources, MLN. XLVII, 1932.]

[Palamon and Arcyte, Edwards's other play, is not extant, but summary of plot 'in two Parts' is given by J. Bereblock in his Commentarii, rptd C. Plummer (in Elizabethan Oxford, Oxford Hist. Soc. 1887). See W. Y. Durand, Palaemon and Arcyte, Progue, Marcus Geminus, and the

Theatre in which they were acted, as described by John Bereblock (1566), PMLA. xx, 1909. H. E. Rollins, RES. iv, 1928, prints from MS An Elegie on the Death of a Sweetheart, which appears to have been sung in Pt ii.

For The Paradyse of daynty devises, 1576, which was 'devised and written for the most part' by Edwards, see p. 403 above, and for the fragmentary collection of stories attrib. to him, p. 728 below.]

THOMAS INGELEND

A pretie and Mery new Enterlude: called the Disobedient Child. [1570?]; ed. J. O. Halliwell[-Phillipps], Percy Soc. 1848; *Hazlitt's Dodsley*, vol. ii; ed. J. S. Farmer (Dramatic Writings of Richard Wever and Thomas Ingelend, 1905); *TFT*. 1908. [See F. Holthausen, Studien zum älteren englischen Drama, E. Studien, xxxi, 1902, which contains a comparison of The Disobedient Child with the Dialogue of Textor on which it is based.]

JOHN PHILLIP

The Commodye of pacient and meeke Grissill. [?] (S.R. 1566 and 1569); ed. R. B. McKerrow and W. W. Greg, *Malone Soc.* 1909. [See A. E. H. Swaen, Some Notes on Pacient Grissill, E. Studien, xxii, 1896.]

[WILLIAM STEVENSON?]

A Ryght Pithy, Pleasaunt an[d] merie Comedie: Intytuled Gammer gurtons Nedle: Played in Christes Colledge in Cambridge. Made by Mr. S. Mr. of Art. 1575; rptd T. Johnson, 1661; rptd R. Dodsley (Collection of Old Plays, vol. i, 1744); ed. T. Hawkins (Origin of English Drama, vol. i, 1773); *Ancient British Drama*, vol. i; *Manly*, vol. ii; ed. H. Bradley, *Gayley*, vol. i; *TFT*. 1910; ed. H. F. B. Brett-Smith, Oxford, 1920. [On authorship see H. Bradley, Athenaeum, 6 Aug. 1898; C. H. Ross, MLN. vii, 1892 and Ang. xix, 1896; F. S. Boas, University Drama in the Tudor Age, 1914.]

GEORGE WHETSTONE (1544?–1587?)

The Right Excellent And Famous Historye Of Promos and Cassandra: Devided into two Commical Discourses. 1578; rptd [J. Nichols], 1779 (Six Old Plays, vol. i); ed. W. C. Hazlitt (Shakespeare's Library, vol. vi, 1875); ed. Sir I. Gollancz, Oxford, 1909 (Shakespeare Classics); *TFT*. 1910.

[See F. E. Budd, Rouillet's Philamira and Whetstone's Promos and Cassandra, RES. vi, 1930. For Whetstone's other writings see p. 440 above.]

ANONYMOUS PLAYS

The Bugbears. Ed. C. Grabau, Archiv, xcviii, xcix, 1897; ed. R. W. Bond (Early Plays from the Italian, 1911). [Lansdowne MS 807, fols. 55–77. Tr. (by John Jeffere?) from A. F. Grazzini, La Spiritata, 1561. See C. Grabau, Quellenuntersuchung, Archiv, xcix, 1897.]

The Historie of the two valiant Knights, Syr Clyomon Knight of the Golden Sheeld: And Clamydes the White Knight. 1599; ed. A. Dyce (Peele's Dramatic Works, 1839 and 1861); ed. A. H. Bullen (Peele's Works, 1882); ed. W. W. Greg, *Malone Soc.* 1913; *TFT*, 1913. [Peele's name is written in an old hand on the title-page of one of the extant copies. but it is probably by 'some such person as Richard Edwards' (A. H. Bullen). See L. Kellner, E. Studien, xiii, 1889; G. L. Kittredge, JEGP. ii, 1898, who ascribes to Thomas Preston; H. Morley, English Writers, vol. ix, pp. 238–45, 1895, who summarizes plot.]

An excellent and pleasant Comedie, termed after the name of the Vice, Common Condicions. [1576]; [?] (fragment); *Brandl* (2nd edn); ed. J. S. Farmer (2nd edn, in Five Anonymous Plays, 1908); ed. photo. facs. C. F. T. Brooke, New Haven, 1915 (from 1st edn). [See Brandl's introduction, pp. cxii–cxviii, and W. Worall, MLR. xiii, 1918.]

The Rare Triumphs of Love and Fortune. 1589; ed. J. P. Collier (Five Old Plays, Roxburghe Club, 1851); *Hazlitt's Dodsley*, vol. vi; ed. W. W. Greg, *Malone Soc.* 1930.

A mery geste of Robyn Hoode and of hys lyfe, wyth a newe playe for to be played in Maye games. [1560?]; ed. J. Ritson (Robin Hood, vol. ii, 1795); ed. F. J. Child (English and Scottish Popular Ballads, vol. iii, 1888); *Manly*, vol. ii; ed. facs. W. W. Greg, Malone Soc. Collections, vol. i, 1908 (with fragment, c. 1475, Robin Hood and the Sheriff of Nottingham, also ptd in *Manly*, vol. i).

A new Enterlude called Thersytes. [c. 1537]; ed. J. Haslewood, Roxburghe Club, 1820 (Two Interludes); ed. F. J. Child (Four Old Plays, 1848); *Hazlitt's Dodsley*, vol. i; rptd facs. E. W. Ashbee, 1876; ed. in part A. W. Pollard (English Miracle Plays, 1890, 1927); ed. J. S. Farmer (Six Anonymous Plays, 1905); *TFT*. 1912. [See F. Holthausen, Studien zum älteren englischen Drama, E. Studien, xxxi, 1902, which compares Thersites with the Dialogus of Textor on which it is based; A. R. Moon, Library, vii, 1926, who assigns to Udall.]

Tom Tyler and his Wife, An Excellent Old Play, As it was Printed and Acted about a hundred Years ago. 1661; ed. F. E. Schelling, PMLA. xv, 1900; ed. J. S. Farmer (Two Tudor Shrew Plays, 1906, and Six Anonymous Plays, ser. 2, 1906); ed. G. C. Moore Smith and W. W. Greg, *Malone Soc.* 1910; *TFT*. 1912.

VII. School and Prodigal Son Plays

A. CRITICAL STUDIES

Herford, C. H. Studies in the Literary Relations of England and Germany in the Sixteenth Century. Cambridge, 1886.

Cloetta, W. Beiträge zur Litteraturgeschichte des Mittelalters und der Renaissance. 2 pts, Halle, 1890–2.

Bolte, J. Lateinische Litteraturdenkmäler des XV. und XVI. Jahrhunderts. Berlin, 1891.

Bahlmann, P. Die lateinischen Dramen von Wimpheling's Stylpho bis zur Mitte des sechzehnten Jahrhunderts, 1480–1550. Münster, 1893.

—— Die Erneuerer des antiken Dramas und ihre ersten dramatischen Versuche, 1314–1478. Münster, 1896.

Sargeaunt, J. Annals of Westminster School. 1898.

Watson, Foster. The English Grammar Schools to 1660. Their Curriculum and Practice. 1898.

Fisher, G. W. Annals of Shrewsbury School. 1899.

Maxwell-Lyte, H. C. History of Eton College, 1440–1898. 1899 (3rd edn).

Leach, A. F. Some English Plays and Players. [In Furnivall Miscellany, Oxford, 1901.]

Scott, E. J. L. Accounts of the Westminster Play, 1564 and 1616. Athenaeum, 14 Feb. 1903. [Heautontimoroumenos and Miles Gloriosus.]

Wallace, M. W. The Birthe of Hercules. 1903. [An edn of an anonymous MS trn of the Amphitruo (*c.* 1610) with an introduction on Roman comedy in England.]

Roeder, A. Menechmi und Amphitruo im englischen Drama. Leipzig, 1904.

Maulsby, D. L. The Relation between Udall's Roister Doister and the Comedies of Plautus and Terence. E. Studien, xxxviii, 1907.

Woodruff, C. E. and Cape, H. J. Schola Regia Cantuariensis: a history of Canterbury School, commonly called the King's School. 1908.

Wilson, J. D. Euphuism and The Prodigal Son. Library, x, 1909.

Wilson, H. B. The History of Merchant-Taylors' School from its Foundation to the Present Time. 2 pts, 1912–4.

Motter, T. H. V. The School Drama in England. 1929.

B. THE PLAYS

George Gascoigne (1525?–1577)

The Glasse of Government. 1575. [See p. 414 above.]

Thomas Ingelend

The Disobedient Child. [1570?] [See p. 520 above.]

John Palsgrave (d. 1554)

Johannis Palsgravi Londoniensis ecphrasis Anglica in comoediam Acolasti. The Comedye of Acolastus translated into oure englysshe tongue. 1540; ed. P. L. Carver, EETS. 1937. [Tr. from G. Gnaphaeus. See P. L. Carver, Library, xiv, 1934.]

Nicholas Udall (1505–1556)

Ralph Roister Doister. [1567?] [See p. 519 above.]

Anonymous Pieces

A new enterlude for chyldren to playe, named Jacke Jugeler. 1563; [1565?]; [?]; rptd J. Haslewood, Roxburghe Club, 1820 (Two Interludes); ed. F. J. Child (Four Old Plays, 1848); ed. A. B. Grosart (Fuller Worthies' Misc. vol. iv, 1873); *Hazlitt's Dodsley*, vol. ii; rptd facs. E. W. Ashbee, 1876; ed. J. S. Farmer (Anonymous Plays, ser. 3, 1907); *TFT*. 1912; ed. W. H. Williams, Cambridge, 1914; ed. E. L. Smart and W. W. Greg, *Malone Soc.* 1934; ed. (3rd edn) B. I. Evans and W. W. Greg, *Malone Soc.* 1937. [See W. H. Williams, MLR. vii, 1912; G. C. Moore Smith, MLR. x, 1915; G. Dudok, Neophilologus, i, 1915.]

A newe mery and wittie Comedie or Enterlude, newly imprinted, treating upon the Historie of Jacob and Esau. 1568; *Hazlitt's Dodsley*, vol. ii; ed. J. S. Farmer (Six Anonymous Plays, ser. 2, 1906); *TFT*. 1908. [See C. C. Stopes, Athenaeum, 28 April 1900, who attributes to William Hunnis.]

Misogonus. *Brandl*; ed. J. S. Farmer (Six Anonymous Plays, ser. 2, 1906); ed. R. W. Bond (Early Plays from the Italian, 1911). [Mutilated MS at Chatsworth dated 1577. See G. L. Kittredge, Misogonus and Laurence Johnson, JEGP. iii, 1901; W. Bang, Ralph Roister Doister, Literaturblatt für germanische und romanische Philologie, xxiii, 1902; S. A. Tannenbaum, Shaksperian Scraps, New York, 1933 (confirming Kittredge's attribution to Laurence Johnson).]

Nice Wanton. 1560. [See under Early Tudor Moralities, p. 515 above.]

[The Prodigal Son.] [c. 1530.] [A black-letter fragment, rptd Malone Soc. Collections, vol. I, 1907, where it is identified as founded, like Ingelend's The Disobedient Child, on Textor's dialogue Juvenis, Pater, Uxor.]

Terens in englysh. The translacyon out of Latin into englysh of the furst comedy of tyrens callyd Andria. [1520?]

Thersytes. [1537?] [See p. 520 above.]

F. S. B., *rev.* A. W. R.

VI. THE EARLY TRAGEDIES

[The section University Plays, pp. 654–63 below, should be consulted for Latin and academic tragedies. The italicized abbreviations (*Manly*, *TFT.*, etc.) refer to collections of pla;ys, the full titles of which will be found on pp. 488–92 above.]

I. CRITICAL AND HISTORICAL STUDIES

Cunliffe, J. W. The Influence of Seneca on Elizabethan Tragedy. 1893.

—— The Influence of Italian on Early Elizabethan Drama. MP. IV, 1907.

—— Early English Tragedy. CHEL. vol. v, 1910.

—— Early English Classical Tragedies: Gorboduc or Ferrex and Porrex, Jocasta, Gismond of Salerne, The Misfortunes of Arthur. Oxford, 1912. [Introduction.]

Churchill, G. B. Richard the Third up to Shakespeare. Berlin, 1900.

Schelling, F. E. The English Chronicle Play. New York, 1902. [List of plays, pp. 276–86.]

Reynolds, G. F. Some Principles of Elizabethan Staging. MP. II, III, 1905.

Hubbard, F. G. Repetition and Parallelism in the Earlier Elizabethan Drama. PMLA. xx, 1905.

Moorman, F. W. The Pre-Shakespearean Ghost. MLR. I, 1906.

Chambers, Sir E. K. Court Performances before Queen Elizabeth. MLR. II, 1907.

Manly, J. M. The Influence of the Tragedies of Seneca upon Early English Drama. [Prefixed to F. J. Miller's trn of Seneca's tragedies, Chicago, 1907.]

Durand, W. Y. Palaemon and Arcyte, Progne, Marcus Geminus, and the Theatre in which they were acted, as described by John Bereblock (1566). PMLA. xx, 1909.

Ristine, F. H. English Tragicomedy: Its Origin and History. New York, 1910.

Brooke, C. F. T. The Tudor Drama. 1912.

Spearing, E. M. The Elizabethan Translations of Seneca's Tragedies. Cambridge, 1912.

Wallace, C. W. The Evolution of the Englis h Drama up to Shakespeare. Berlin, 1912.

Boas, F. S. University Drama in the Tudor Age. Oxford, 1914.

Ellison, L. M. The Early Romantic Drama at the English Court. Chicago, 1917.

Lucas, F. L. Seneca and Elizabethan Tragedy. Cambridge, 1922.

Reed, A. W. The Beginnings of English Secular and Romantic Drama. English Ass. Lecture, 1922.

Eliot, T. S. Seneca, his Tenne Tragedies. 2 vols. 1927. [Introduction.]

II. TRANSLATIONS FROM SENECA

A. COLLECTED TRANSLATIONS

Seneca His Tenne Tragedies, Translated into Englysh. 1581; ed. J. Leigh, Spenser Soc. 1887; ed. T. S. Eliot, 2 vols. 1927.

[The collection includes the 7 plays given below, together with Thebais (tr. Thomas Newton), Hippolytus (tr. John Studley), and Hercules Oetaeus (tr. Studley). Newton (1542?–1607) was the editor. See E. M. Spearing, MLR. IV, 1908.]

B. INDIVIDUAL PLAYS

JASPER HEYWOOD (1535?–1598)

The Sixt Tragedie of the most grave and prudent author, Lucius, Anneus, Seneca, entituled Troas. 1559 (*bis*); [1560?]; ed. H. de Vocht, *Bang.* vol. XLI, 1913. [For notes see W. W. Greg, Library, XI, 1930, pp. 162–70.]

The seconde Tragedie of Seneca entituled Thyestes. 1560; ed. H. de Vocht, *Bang,* vol. XLI, 1913.

The first Tragedie of Lucius Anneus Seneca, intituled Hercules Furens. 1561; ed. H. de Vocht, *Bang,* vol. XLI, 1913.

ALEXANDER NEVYLE (1544–1614)

The Lamentable Tragedie of Oedipus the Sonne of Laius Kyng of Thebes. 1563. [See E. M. Spearing, MLR. xv, 1920.]

T[HOMAS] N[UCE] (d. 1617)

The ninth Tragedie of Lucius Anneus Seneca, called Octavia. [1566.]

JOHN STUDLEY (b. *c.* 1547)

The Eyght Tragedie of Seneca. Entituled Agamemnon. 1566; ed. E. M. Spearing, *Bang,* vol. XXXVIII, 1913.

The seventh Tragedie of Seneca, Entituled Medea. 1566; ed. E. M. Spearing, *Bang,* vol. XXXVIII, 1913.

III. OTHER TRAGEDIES

JANE, LADY LUMLEY

Iphigenia in Aulis. Ed. H. H. Child, *Malone Soc.* 1909; ed. G. Becker, Sh. Jb. XLVI, 1910. [BM. MS Reg. 15 A. ix. Date *c.* 1555.]

HENRY CHEKE

[Free Will.] A certayne Tragedie wrytten fyrst in Italian, by F. N. B[assano]. [1561?]

THOMAS NORTON (1532–1584) AND THOMAS SACKVILLE (1536–1608)

The Tragedie of Gorboduc, whereof three Actes were wrytten by Thomas Norton, and the two laste by Thomas Sackvyle. Sett forthe as the same was shewed before the Quenes most excellent Majestie, in her highnes Court of Whitehall, the .xviii. day of January, Anno Domini 1561. By the Gentlemen of Thynner Temple in London. 1565; [1570?] (as The Tragidie of Ferrex and Porrex); 1590 (as Gorboduc); rptd R. Dodsley (Collection of Old Plays, vol. II, 1744); rptd T. Hawkins (Origin of English Drama, vol. II, 1773); ed. W. D. Cooper, Shakespeare Soc. 1847; ed. R. W. Sackville-West (Works of Sackville, 1850); ed. L. T. Smith, Heilbronn, 1883; *Manly*, vol. II; ed. J. S. Farmer, Early English Drama Soc. 1906; *TFT.* 1908; ed. H. A. Watt, Madison, 1910; ed. J. W. Cunliffe (Early English Classical Tragedies, Oxford, 1912). [See L. H. Courtney, N. & Q. 6 Oct. 1860; F. Koch, Halle, 1881; H. Schmidt, Seneca's Influence upon Gorboduc, MLN. II, 1887; E. Koeppel, E. Studien, XVI, 1891; H. A. Watt, Wisconsin University Bulletin, 1910; S. A. Small, The Political Import of Gorboduc, PMLA. XLVI, 1931; and the introductions to the edns given above.]

JOHN PICKERING

A Newe Enterlude of Vice Conteyninge, the Historye of Horestes with the cruell revengment of his Fathers death, upon his one naturall Mother. 1567; ed. J. P. Collier (Illustrations of Old English Literature, vol. II, 1866); *Brandl*; *TFT.* 1910. [See F. Brie, E. Studien, XLVI, 1912.]

THOMAS PRESTON

A lamentable Tragedie, mixed full of plesant mirth, containing the life of Cambises king of Percia. [1570?]; [1585?]; rptd T. Hawkins (Origin of English Drama, vol. I, 1778);

Hazlitt's Dodsley, vol. IV; *TFT.* 1910. [See M. P. Tilley, Shakespeare and his Ridicule of Cambyses, MLN. XXIV, 1909; D. C. Allen, A Source, MLN. XLIX, 1934; M. C. Linthicum, The Date, PMLA. XLIX, 1934.]

RICHARD EDWARDS (1523?–1566)

Damon and Pithias. 1571. [See p. 519 above.]

GEORGE GASCOIGNE (1525?–1577) AND FRANCIS KINWELMERSH (d. 1580?)

Jocasta. [Acted 1566; for edns see p. 414 above.]

R. B.

A new Tragicall Comedie of Apius and Virginia. 1575; rptd C. W. Dilke (Old English Plays, vol. V, 1815); ed. J. P. Collier (Dodsley's Old Plays, vol. XIII, 1826); *Hazlitt's Dodsley*, vol. IV; ed. J. S. Farmer, Early English Drama Soc. 1908; *TFT.* 1908; ed. R. B. McKerrow, *Malone Soc.* 1911.

GEORGE WHETSTONE (1544?–1587?)

Promos and Cassandra. 1578. [See p. 520 above.]

THOMAS HUGHES

Certaine devises and shewes presented to her Majestie by the Gentlemen of Grayes-Inne at her Highnesse Court in Greenewich. 1587. [Includes The Misfortunes of Arthur, by Hughes. Rptd J. P. Collier (Five Old Plays, 1828 and 1833); *Hazlitt's Dodsley*, vol. IV; ed. H. C. Grumbine, Berlin, 1900; *TFT.* 1911; ed. J. W. Cunliffe (Early English Classical Tragedies, Oxford, 1912). See E. H. Waller, A Possible Interpretation of The Misfortunes of Arthur, JEGP. XXIV, 1925.]

ROBERT WILMOT, HENRY NOEL (d. 1597) R. STAFFORD, G. AL., AND CHRISTOPHER HATTON (1540–1591)

The Tragedie of Tancred and Gismund. Compiled by the Gentlemen of the Inner Temple, and by them presented before her Majestie. Newly revived and polished according to the decorum of these daies. By R. W. 1591; rptd R. Dodsley (Collection of Old Plays, vol. XI, 1744); *Hazlitt's Dodsley*, vol. VII; *TFT.* 1912. [The first version, Gismond of Salern, is extant in 2 MSS which have been collated and ptd in *Brandl*, *TFT.* 1912, and J. W. Cunliffe's Early English Classical Tragedies, Oxford, 1912. See J. W. Cunliffe, PMLA. XXI, 1906, and A. Klein, The Decorum of these Days, PMLA. XXXIII, 1918.]

J. W. C.

VII. THE LATER ELIZABETHAN DRAMATISTS

LYLY, KYD, PEELE, LODGE, GREENE, MARLOWE, NASHE

JOHN LYLY (1554?–1606)

(1) COLLECTED WORKS

The Complete Works. Ed. R. W. Bond, 3 vols. Oxford, 1902.

(2) THE PLAYS

(a) Collected Editions

Sixe Court Comedies. Ed. E. Blount, 1632. [Contains: Endimion, Alexander and Campaspe, Sapho and Phao, Gallathea, Midas, Mother Bombie.]

The Dramatic Works. Ed. F. W. Fairholt, 2 vols. 1858, 1892.

(b) Separate Plays

A moste excellent Comedie of Alexander, Campaspe, and Diogenes, Played beefore the Queenes Majestie on new yeares day at night, by her Majesties children, and the children of Poules. 1584 (3 edns, all anon., 2nd and 3rd as Campaspe; headlines in all edns, A tragicall Comedie of Alexander and Campaspe); 1591; rptd R. Dodsley (Collection of Old Plays, vol. II, 1744); Ancient British Drama, vol. I; Manly, vol. II; ed. G. P. Baker, Gayley, vol. I; ed. W. W. Greg, Malone Soc. 1933.

Sapho and Phao, Played beefore the Queenes Majestie on Shrovetewsday, by her Majesties Children, and the Boyes of Paules. 1584; 1591.

Endimion, The Man in the Moone. Playd before the Queenes Majestie at Greenewich on Candlemas day at night, by the Chyldren of Paules. 1591 (anon.); rptd [C. W. Dilke] (Old English Plays, vol. II, 1814); ed. G. P. Baker, 1894.

Gallathea. As it was playde before the Queenes Majestie at Greene-wiche, on New-yeeres day at Night. By the Chyldren of Paules. 1592 (anon.).

Midas. Plaied Before the Queenes Majestie Upon Twelfe Day At night. By the Children of Paules. 1592 (anon.); rptd [C. W. Dilke] (Old English Plays, vol. I, 1814).

Mother Bombie. As it was sundrie times plaied by the Children of Powles, London. 1594 (anon.); rptd [C. W. Dilke] (Old English Plays, vol. I, 1814).

The Woman in the Moone. As it was presented before her Highnesse. 1597.

Loves Metamorphosis. A Wittie and Courtly Pastorall. First playd by the Children of Paules, and now by the Children of the Chappell. 1601.

[The Maydes Metamorphosis, 1600, and several anon. entertainments and fragments of entertainments have also been assigned to Lyly, but without much plausibility.]

(3) OTHER WRITINGS

Euphues. The Anatomy of Wit. [1578]; [1579] ('corrected and augmented'); 1579; 1580.

Euphues and his England. 1580 (3 edns). [Both parts.] 2 vols. 1581; 1582; 1585; ed. E. Arber, 1868, 1895; ed. M. W. Croll and H. Clemons, 1916.

A Whip for an Ape: Or Martin displaied. [1589] (also issued as Rythmes against Martin Marre-Prelate) (anon.); rptd I. D'Israeli (Quarrels of Authors, vol. III, 1814). [Possibly by Lyly.]

Pappe with a Hatchet. Alias, A figge for my Godsonne. Or Cracke me this nut. Or A Countrie cuffe. that is, a sound boxe of the eare, for the idiot Martin. [1589] (anon.); rptd J. Petheram, 1844; ed. G. Saintsbury (Elizabethan and Jacobean Pamphlets, 1892). [Probably by Lyly.]

(4) BIOGRAPHY AND CRITICISM

(a) General

Bond, R. W. John Lyly: Novelist and Dramatist. Quart. Rev. CLXXXIII, 1896.

—— The Complete Works. 3 vols. Oxford, 1902. [Introduction.]

Wilson, J. D. John Lyly. Cambridge, 1905. [See A. Feuillerat's review, MLR. I, 1906.]

Feuillerat, A. John Lyly. Contribution à l'Histoire de la Renaissance en Angleterre. Cambridge, 1910.

Jeffrey, V. M. John Lyly and the Italian Renaissance. Paris, 1929.

(b) Studies of the Plays

Halpin, N. J. Oberon's Vision in Midsummer Night's Dream illustrated by a Comparison with Lyly's Endymion. Shakespeare Soc. 1843.

Hense, C. C. John Lyly und Shakespeare. Sh. Jb. VII, 1872, VIII, 1873.

Goodlet, J. Shakespeare's Debt to John Lyly. E. Studien, V, 1882.

Steinhäuser, K. John Lyly als Dramatiker. 1884.

Sprenger, R. Zu John Lilly's Campaspe. E. Studien, XVI, 1892.

Spingarn, J. E. The Date of Lyly's Endymion. Athenaeum, 4 Aug. 1894. [Replies by F. G. Fleay and R. W. Bond, 11 Aug. 1894.]

Baker, G. P. John Lyly. Gayley, vol. I.

Bond, R. W. Lyly's Doubtful Poems. Athenaeum, 9 May 1903.

Koeppel, E. Zu John Lyly's Alexander und Campaspe. Archiv, cx, 1903.

Greg, W. W. On the Authorship of the Songs in Lyly's Plays. Mod. Lang. Quart. I, 1905. [See also W. J. Lawrence, TLS. 20 Dec. 1923, W. W. Greg, TLS. 3 Jan. 1924, J. R. Moore, PMLA. xlii, 1927, R. W. Bond, RES. vi, vii, 1930–1.]

Long, P. W. The Purport of Lyly's Endymion. PMLA. xxiv, 1909, MP. viii, 1911.

Brie, F. Lyly und Greene. E. Studien, xlii, 1910.

Lindsay, David (Earl of Crawford and Balcarres). John Lyly. Bulletin John Rylands Lib. viii, 1924.

Golding, S. R. The Authorship of The Maid's Metamorphosis. RES. ii, 1926.

(c) Euphues and Euphuism

Morley, H. Euphuism. Quart. Rev. cix, 1861.

Weymouth, R. F. Analysis of Euphuism and its Elements. Trans. Philolog. Soc. 1870–2.

Landmann, F. Shakespeare and Euphuism. Trans. New Shakspere Soc. 1880–5.

—— Der Euphuismus, sein Wesen, seine Quelle, seine Geschichte. Giessen, 1881.

—— Euphues: John Lyly. Heilbronn, 1887.

Hart, J. M. Euphuism. Columbus, 1889.

Koeppel, E. Studien zur Geschichte der italienischen Novelle in der englischen Litteratur des sechzehnten Jahrhunderts. QF. lxx, 1892.

Child, C. G. John Lyly and Euphuism. Erlangen, 1894.

Moore, J. M. A Study of Euphuism. Liverpool, 1896.

Bang, W. and de Vocht, H. Klassiker und Humanisten: John Lyly und Erasmus. E. Studien, xxxvi, 1906.

Whipple, T. K. Isocrates and Euphuism. MLR. xi, 1916.

Tilley, M. P. Elizabethan Proverb Love in Lyly's Euphues, and in Pettie's Petite Pallace. New York, 1926.

—— Euphues and Ovid's Heroical Epistles. MLN. xlv, 1930.

Pruvost, R. Réflexions sur l'Euphuisme. Revue anglo-américaine, Oct. 1930.

Torretta, L. L' Italofobia di John Lyly e i Rapporti dell' Euphues col Rinascimento italiano. Giornale storico della Letteratura italiana, ciii, 1934.

THOMAS KYD (1558–1594)

(1) Collected Works

The Works of Thomas Kyd. Ed. F. S. Boas, 1901. [With biographical and critical Introduction.]

(2) Particular Works

Cornelia. 1594 (re-issued 1595 as Pompey the Great, his faire Corneliaes Tragedie: effected by her Father and Husbandes downe-cast, death and fortune. Written in French by that excellent poet Ro. Garnier; and translated into English); rptd R. Dodsley (Collection of Old Plays, vol. xi, 1744); *Hazlitt's Dodsley*, vol. v; ed. H. Gassner, Munich, 1894.

The Spanish Tragedie. Newly corrected and amended of such grosse faults as passed in the first impression. [1594?] (anon.); 1594; 1599; 1602 ('Newly corrected, amended, and enlarged with new additions of the Painters part, and others, as it hath of late been divers times acted'); 1602; 1610; 1615; 1618; 1623; 1633; rptd R. Dodsley (Collection of Old Plays, vol. ii, 1744); rptd T. Hawkins (Origin of English Drama, vol. ii, 1773); *Ancient British Drama*, vol. i; *Hazlitt's Dodsley*, vol. v; *Manly*, vol. ii; ed. J. Schick, 1898 (Temple Dramatists); ed. J. Schick, Berlin, 1901; ed. W. W. Greg, *Malone Soc.* 1925 (1602 edn).

The Householders Philosophy. [By Torquato Tasso] and now translated by T. K. 1588.

The Truth of the most wicked and secret murder of John Brewen. 1592; ed. J. P. Collier (Illustrations of Early English Popular Literature, vol. i, 1863).

Fragments. [In England's Parnassus, 1600.] [The following anon. plays (see pp. 538–9 below) have also been assigned to Kyd: Arden of Feversham; The Contention of York and Lancaster; Edward III; Jeronimo; Leir; The Rare Triumphs of Love and Fortune; Soliman and Perseda; The Taming of a Shrew; The True Tragedy of Richard III; as well as a lost Hamlet and Shakespeare's Titus Andronicus.]

(3) Biography and Criticism

(a) Books

Widgery, W. H. The First Quarto Edition of Hamlet. 1880.

Markscheffel, K. Thomas Kyds Tragödien. Weimar, 1885.

Schroeer, A. Über Titus Andronicus. Marburg, 1891.

Sarrazin, G. Thomas Kyd und sein Kreis. Berlin, 1892.

Fleischner, G. O. Bemerkungen über Thomas Kyd's 'Spanish Tragedy.' Dresden, 1896.

Boas, F. S. The Works of Thomas Kyd. 1901. [Introduction.]

Schoenwerth, R. Die niederländischen und deutschen Bearbeitungen von Thomas Kyd's 'Spanish Tragedy.' Berlin, 1903.

Michael, A. O. Der Stil in Thomas Kyds Originaldramen. Berlin, 1905.

Crawford, C. A Concordance to the Works of Thomas Kyd. *Bang*, vol. xv, 1906–10.

—— Collectanea. 2 vols. Stratford-on-Avon, 1906–7.

Fitzgerald, J. The Sources of the Hamlet Tragedy. 1909.

(b) Articles

Sarrazin, G. Die Entstehung der Hamlet-Tragödie. Ang. xii, xiii, 1890, 1891.

—— Der Verfasser von 'Soliman and Perseda.' E. Studien, xv, 1891.

Koeppel, E. Soliman and Perseda. E. Studien, xvi, 1892.

Worp, J. A. Die Fabel der 'Spanish Tragedy.' Sh. Jb. xxix, 1894.

Schick, J. Thomas Kyd's Todesjahr. Sh. Jb. xxxv, 1899.

Bang, W. Kyds Spanish Tragedy. E. Studien, xxviii, 1900.

Moorman, F. W. The Pre-Shakespearian Ghost. MLR. i, 1906.

Brereton, J. le G. Notes on the Text of Kyd. E. Studien, xxxvii, 1907.

Allen, J. The Lost Hamlet of Kyd. Westminster Rev. clxx, 1908.

Wiehl, K. Thomas Kyd und Soliman und Perseda. E. Studien, xliv, 1912.

Lawrence, W. J. Soliman and Perseda. MLR. ix, 1914.

Gray, H. D. The First Quarto Hamlet. MLR. x, 1915, PMLA. xlii, 1927.

—— Reconstruction of a Lost Play. PQ. vii, 1928.

Brown, F. K. Marlowe and Kyd. TLS. 2 June 1921. [See also F. S. Boas, TLS. 30 June 1921.]

Brandl, A. Kyd an den Privy Council über Marlowe. Archiv, cxlii, 1921.

Baldwin, T. W. On the Chronology of Thomas Kyd's Plays. MLN. xl, 1925.

—— Thomas Kyd's Early Company Connections. PQ. vi, 1927.

Forsythe, R. S. Notes on the Spanish Tragedy. PQ. v, 1926. [See also W. P. Mustard, *ibid.*]

Bowers, F. T. Kyd's Pedringano: Sources and Parallels. Harvard Stud. xiii, 1931.

Baker, H. Ghosts and Guides: Kyd's Spanish Tragedy and the Medieval Tragedy. MP. xxxiii, 1935.   U. M. E.-F.

GEORGE PEELE (1557?–1596)

(1) COLLECTED WORKS

The Works of George Peele. Ed. A. Dyce, 3 vols. 1828–39.

The Dramatic and Poetical Works of Robert Greene and George Peele. Ed. A. Dyce, 1861; 1879.

The Plays and Poems. Ed. H. Morley, 1887.

The Works of George Peele. Ed. A. H. Bullen, 2 vols. 1888.

(2) PLAYS AND MASQUES

The Araygnement of Paris A Pastorall. Presented before the Queenes Majestie, by the Children of her Chappell. 1584 (anon.); ed. O. Smeaton, 1905 (Temple Dramatists); ed. H. H. Child, *Malone Soc.* 1910.

The Famous Chronicle of king Edwarde the first, sirnamed Edward Longshankes, with his returne from the holy land. Also the life of Lleuellen rebell in Wales. Lastly, the sinking of Queene Elinor, who sunck at Charingcrosse, and rose againe at Pottershith, now named Queenehith. 1593; 1599; ed. J. P. Collier (Dodsley's Old Plays, vol. xi, 1827); ed. W. W. Greg, *Malone Soc.* 1911.

The Battell of Alcazar, fought in Barbarie, betweene Sebastian king of Portugall, and Abdelmelec king of Morocco. With the death of Captaine Stukeley. As it was sundrie times plaid by the Lord high Admirall his servants. 1594 (anon.); ed. W. W. Greg, *Malone Soc.* 1907.

The Old Wives Tale. A pleasant conceited Comedie, played by the Queenes Majesties players. 1595. ('by G. P.'); ed. F. B. Gummere, *Gayley*, vol. i; ed. W. W. Greg, *Malone Soc.* 1908.

The Love of King David and Fair Bethsabe. With the Tragedie of Absalon. As it hath ben divers times plaied on the stage. 1599; rptd T. Hawkins (Origin of English Drama, vol. ii, 1773); *Manly*, vol. ii; ed. W. W. Greg, *Malone Soc.* 1912.

The Hunting of Cupid. Ed. W. W. Greg, Malone Soc. Collections, vol. i, 1911. [Fragmentary excerpts in the commonplace book of William Drummond of Hawthornden. The original edn (Stationers' Register, 1591) is lost.]

Two Elizabethan Stage Abridgments: The Battle of Alcazar and Orlando Furioso. Ed. W. W. Greg, *Malone Soc.* 1922.

[The following anon. plays (see pp. 537–9, 651–4, below) have also been partially or wholly assigned to Peele: Alphonsus of Germany, Captain Thomas Stukeley, Clyomon and Clamydes, Contention of York and Lancaster, George a Greene, Histriomastix, Jack Straw, Troublesome Reign of King John, Knack to Know a Knave, Leir, Locrine, Mucedorus, Soliman and Perseda, Taming of a Shrew, True Tragedy of Richard III, Wily Beguiled, Wisdom of Dr Dodipoll, and Shakespeare's Henry VI.]

(3) Pageants, Poems and Other Writings

The Device of the Pageant borne before Woolstone Dixi Lord Maior of the Citie of London. 1585; rptd Harleian Miscellany, vol. x, 1813; ed. J. Nichols (Progresses of Elizabeth, vol. ii, 1823); ed. F. W. Fairholt (Lord Mayors' Pageants, Percy Soc. 1843).

A Farewell. Entituled to the famous and fortunate Generalls of our English forces: Sir John Norris & Syr Frauncis Drake Knights, and all theyr brave and resolute followers. Whereunto is annexed: A tale of Troy. 1589. [The Tale of Troy was rptd with rev. text 1604; no copy now extant but text in Dyce's (1861) and Bullen's edns of Works.]

An Eglogue. Gratulatorie. Entituled: To the right honorable, and renowned Shepheard of Albions Arcadia: Robert Earle of Essex and Ewe, for his welcome into England from Portugall. 1589.

Polyhymnia Describing, The Honourable Triumph at Tylt, before her Majestie. 1590.

Descensus Astraeae. The Device of a Pageant, borne before M. William Web, Lord Maior of the Citie of London. [1591]; rptd Harleian Miscellany, vol. x, 1813; ed. F. W. Fairholt (Lord Mayors' Pageants, Percy Soc. 1843).

The Honour of the Garter. Displaied in a Poeme gratulatorie: Entitled to the worthie and renowned Earle of Northumberland. [1593.]

Merrie Conceited Jests of George Peele. 1607; 1627; 1657; 1671; ed. W. C. Hazlitt (Shakespeare Jest-Books, vol. ii, 1864); ed. C. Hindley (Old Book Collector's Miscellany, vol. i, 1871).

Anglorum Feriae. Englandes Hollydayes beginninge the 38 yeare of the Raign of our Soveraigne Ladie [1595]. Ed. R. Fitch, Ipswich [c. 1830]. [BM. Add. MS. 21432.]

(4) Biography and Criticism

Kellner, L. Sir Clyomon and Sir Clamides. E. Studien, xiii, 1889.

Schelling, F. E. The Source of Peele's Arraignment of Paris. MLN. viii, 1893.

Odell, G. C. D. Peele as a Dramatist. Bibliographer, ii, 1903.

Bayley, A. R. Peele as a Dramatic Artist. Oxford Point of View, 15 Feb. 1903.

Gummere, F. B. George Peele. *Gayley*, vol. i.

Sarrazin, G. Zur Biographie und Characteristik von George Peele. Archiv, cxxiv, 1910.

Cheffaud, P. H. George Peele. Paris, 1913.

Sykes, H. D. Sidelights on Shakespeare. Stratford-on-Avon, 1919.

—— The Authorship of A Knack to Know a Knave. N. & Q. 31 May, 17 June 1924.

Sykes, H. D. Peele's Borrowing from Du Bartas. N. & Q. 15, 22 Nov. 1924.

—— Sidelights on Elizabethan Drama. 1924.

Jeffery, V. M. Italian and English Pastoral Drama. 2. Source of Peele's Arraignment of Paris. MLR., xix, 1924.

Greg, W. W. A Collier Mystification. RES. i, 1925.

Jones, G. The Intention of Peele's Old Wives' Tale. Aberystwyth Stud. vii, 1925.

Gilbert, A. H. The Source of Peele's Arraignment of Paris. MLN. xli, 1926.

Larsen, T. The Canon of Peele's Works. MP. xxvi, 1928.

—— The Early Years of George Peele. Trans. Royal Soc. of Canada, xxii, 1928.

—— The Father of George Peele. MP. xxvi, 1928.

—— George Peele in the Chancellor's Court. MP. xxviii, 1930.

—— The Growth of the Peele Canon. Library, xi, 1930.

—— The Date of Peele's Old Wives' Tale. MP. xxx, 1932.

—— A Bibliography of the Writings of George Peele. MP. xxxii, 1934. [Lost works, contributions to miscellanies, etc., census of extant copies; ignores doubtful plays.]

Sampley, A. M. The Text of Peele's David and Bethsabe. PMLA. xlvi, 1831.

—— Verbal Tests for Peele's Plays. Stud. Phil. xxx, 1033.

Dowling, H. M. The Date and Order of Peele's Plays. N. & Q. 11, 18 March 1933. [Other Peele articles, N. & Q. 11 Feb., 27 May, 21 Oct. 1933.]

THOMAS LODGE (1557–8?–1625)

(1) Collected Works

The Complete Works. Ed. Sir E. Gosse, 4 vols. Hunterian Club, Glasgow, 1883. [Omits trns.]

The Complete Works. Ed. A. Walker. [In preparation.]

(2) Plays

The Wounds of Civill War. Lively set forth in the true Tragedies of Marius and Scilla. As it hath beene publiquely plaide in London, by the Lord high Admirall his Servants. 1594; ed. J. P. Collier (Dodsley's Old Plays, vol. viii, 1825); *Hazlitt's Dodsley*, vol. vii; ed. J. D. Wilson, *Malone Soc.* 1910.

A Looking Glasse for London and England. Made by Thomas Lodge Gentleman, and Robert Greene. In Artibus Magister. 1594; 1598; 1602; n.d.; 1617; *TFT.* 1914; ed. W. W. Greg, *Malone Soc.* 1932. [See also under Greene below.]

[The following anon. plays (see pp. 537–9, 651–4 below) have been wholly or partially assigned to Lodge: An Alarum for London, The Contention of York and Lancaster, George a Greene, Leir, Mucedorus, Selimus, Sir Thomas More, The Troublesome Reign of King John, A Warning for Fair Women, together with Greene's James IV and Shakespeare's Henry VI.]

(3) OTHER WRITINGS

[A Defence of Poetry, Music, and Stage Plays.] [1579?]; ed. D. Laing, Shakespeare Soc. 1853. [A reply to S. Gosson's Schoole of Abuse. Extracts rptd in Elizabethan Critical Essays, ed. G. Gregory Smith, vol. i, Oxford, 1904.]

An Alarum against Usurers: [with] the delectable historie of Forbonius and Prisceria [and] the lamentable Complaint of Truth over England. 1584; ed. D. Laing, Shakespeare Soc. 1853.

Scillaes Metamorphosis: Enterlaced with the unfortunate love of Glaucus: with sundrie other Poems and Sonnets. 1589 (re-issued 1610 as A most pleasunt Historie of Glaucus and Scilla); rptd S. W. S[inger], Chiswick, 1819.

Rosalynde. Euphues golden legacie. 1590; 1592; 1596; 1598; 1604; 1609; 1612 (as Euphues Golden Legacie); 1623; 1634; 1642; ed. F. G. Waldron, 1802; ed. W. C. Hazlitt, 1875; ed. H. Morley, 1887; ed. W. W. Greg, 1907; ed. E. C. Baldwin, Boston, 1923.

Catharos. Diogenes in his Singularitie. 1591 ('By T. L.').

The Famous, true and historicall life of Robert second Duke of Normandy. 1591 ('By T. L. G.').

Euphues Shadow, the Battaile of the Sences [with] the Deafe mans Dialogue. 1592.

The Life and Death of william Long beard, with manye other histories. 1593; ed. J. P. Collier (Illustrations of Old English Literature, vol. ii, 1866).

Phillis: Honoured with Pastorall Sonnets, Elegies, and amorous delights. [With] the tragicall complaynt of Elstred. 1593; ed. M. F. Crow (Elizabethan Sonnet-Cycles, vol. i, Chicago, 1896); ed. Sir S. Lee (selection in Elizabethan Sonnets, vol. ii, 1904).

A fig for Momus: Containing Satyres, Eclogues, and Epistles. 1595; ed. Sir A. Boswell (Frondes Caducae, no. 3, Auchinleck, 1817).

The Divel conjured. 1596 (signed T. L.).

A Margarite of America. 1596; ed. J. O. Halliwell[-Phillipps], 1859; ed. G. B. Harrison, 1927 (with Greene's Menaphon).

Wits Miserie, and the Worlds Madnesse. 1596 (signed T. L.).

Prosopopeia Containing the Teares of the Mother of God. 1596 (signed T. L.).

The Flowers of Lodowicke of Granado. 1601 ('by T. L.'). [Trn of Michael ab Isselt's Flores Lodovici Granatensis.]

The Famous and Memorable Workes of Josephus. 1602; 1609; 1620; 1632; 1640; 1655; 1670; 1683; 1693.

A Treatise of the Plague. 1603.

The Workes of Lucius Annaeus Seneca. 1614; 1620; 1632. [Selections: ed. W. Clode, 1888; ed. W. H. D. Rouse, 1899 (Temple Classics).]

A Learned Summary Upon the famous Poem of William of Saluste Lord of Bartas. Translated out of French. 1621 ('by T. L.'); 1637; 1638.

The Poore Mans Talentt. Ed. Sir E. Gosse (Complete Works, vol. iv, 1883). [From the Norfolk-Collier MS; another MS is BM. Add. 34212.]

(4) BIOGRAPHY AND CRITICISM

Ingleby, C. M. Was Thomas Lodge an Actor? 1868.

—— Thomas Lodge and the Stage. N. & Q. 7 Feb., 23 May 1885.

Gosse, Sir E. Thomas Lodge. [In Seventeenth Century Studies, 1885; rptd from the introduction to his edn of The Complete Works.]

Carl, R. Über Thomas Lodge's Leben und Werke. Ang. x, 1887.

Koeppel, E. Studien zur Geschichte der italienischen Novelle. Strasburg, 1892. [Ch. xiv.]

Alden, R. M. The Rise of Formal Satire in England. Philadelphia, 1899. [Pp. 90–7.]

Kastner, L. E. Thomas Lodge as an Imitator of the French Poets. Athenaeum, 22, 29 Oct. 1904.

—— Thomas Lodge as an Imitator of the Italian Poets. MLR. ii, 1907.

Hart, H. C. Greene and Lodge. N. & Q. 17 March 1906. [On Greene's hand in Rosalynde.]

Arkle, A. H. The Flowers of Lodowicke of Granada. N. & Q. 31 March 1906.

Wilson, J. D. The Missing Title of Lodge's Reply to Gosson's School of Abuse. MLR. iii, 1908.

Lee, Sir S. The French Renaissance in England. 1910. [Pp. 231–4, 242–3, 260, 455–62.]

Scott, J. G. Les Sonnets élisabéthains. Paris, 1929. [Ch. vi.]

Walker, A. Italian Sources of Lyrics of Thomas Lodge. MLR. xxii, 1927.

—— Some Sources of the Prose Pamphlets of Thomas Lodge. RES. viii, 1932.

—— The Life of Thomas Lodge. RES. ix, x, 1933–4.

Paradise, N. B. Thomas Lodge. New Haven, 1931. [With bibliography.]

Sisson, C. J. Thomas Lodge and other Elizabethans. Cambridge, U.S.A. 1933.

Tenney, E. A. Thomas Lodge. Ithaca, 1935.

A. W.

ROBERT GREENE (1558–1592)

(1) Collected Works

The Dramatic Works, to which are added his Poems. Ed. A. Dyce, 2 vols. 1831.

The Poems of Robert Greene and Christopher Marlowe. Ed. R. Bell, 1856; 1876.

The Dramatic and Poetical Works of Robert Greene and George Peele. Ed. A. Dyce, 1861; 1879.

The Life and Complete Works in Prose and Verse. Ed. A. B. Grosart, 15 vols. 1881–6. (Huth Lib.)

The Plays and Poems. Ed. J. C. Collins, 2 vols. Oxford, 1905. [See reviews by W. W. Greg, MLR. i, 1905–6, and R. A. Law, MLN, xxii, 1907.]

The Complete Plays. Ed. T. H. Dickinson, 1909. (Mermaid Ser.)

(2) Plays

(a) Plays known to be by Greene

The Historie of Orlando Furioso One of the twelve Pieres of France. As it was plaid before the Queenes Majestie. 1594; 1599; ed. W. W. Greg, Malone Soc.

The Honorable Historie of frier Bacon, and frier Bongay. As it was plaid by her Majesties servants. 1594; 1630; 1655; ed. J. P. Collier (Dodsley's Old Plays, vol. viii, 1826); ed. Sir A. W. Ward (Old English Drama, 1878); ed C. M. Gayley, Gayley, vol. i; TFT. 1914; ed. W. W. Greg, Malone Soc. 1926.

The Scottish Historie of James the fourth, slaine at Flodden. Entermixed with a pleasant Comedie, presented by Oboram king of Fayeries: As it hath bene sundrie times publikely plaide. 1598; Manly, vol. ii; ed. A. E. H. Swaen and W. W. Greg, Malone Soc. 1921.

The Comicall Historie of Alphonsus King of Aragon. As it hath bene sundrie times Acted. Made by R. G. 1599; ed. W. W. Greg, Malone Soc. 1926.

A Looking Glasse for London and Englande. Made by Thomas Lodge Gentleman, and Robert Greene. In Artibus Magister. 1594; 1598; 1602; 1617; TFT. 1914; ed. W. W. Greg, Malone Soc. 1932.

Two Elizabethan Stage Abridgments: The Battle of Alcazar and Orlando Furioso. Ed. W. W. Greg, Malone Soc. 1922.

(b) Plays ascribed to Greene

The First part of the Tragicall raigne of Selimus. As it was playd by the Queenes Majesties Players. 1594 (anon.); 1638; ed. A. B. Grossart, 1898 (Temple Dramatists); ed. W. Bang, Malone Soc. 1908. [Six passages are assigned to Greene in Robert Allot's Englands Parnassus, 1600.]

[The following anon. plays (see pp. 537–9, 651–4 below) have also been wholly or partially ascribed to Greene: The Contention of York and Lancaster, Edward III, Fair Em, George a Greene, The Troublesome Reign of King John, A Knack to Know a Knave, The Thracian Wonder, Leir, Locrine, Mucedorus, The Taming of a Shrew, Thomas Lord Cromwell, as well as Shakespeare's Titus Andronicus and Henry VI.]

(3) Novels and Pamphlets

Mamillia. A Mirrour or looking-glasse for the Ladies of Englande. 1583; 1593.

Arbasto, The Anatomie of Fortune. 1584; 1594; 1617; 1626.

Gwydonius. The Carde of Fancie. 1584; 1587; 1593; 1608; ed. G. Saintsbury (Shorter Novels, vol. i, 1929 (Everyman's Lib.)).

Morando: The Tritameron of Love. 1584; 1587.

The Myrrour of Modestie. 1584.

Planetomachia. 1585.

Euphues his censure to Philautus. 1587.

Penelopes Web. 1587; 1601.

Alcida: Greenes Metamorphosis. 1588; 1617.

Pandosto. The Triumph of Time. 1588 (running title, The Historie of Dorastus and Fawnia); 1607; 1609; 1614; 1619; 1629, etc.; ed. P. G. Thomas, 1907.

Perimedes the Blacksmith. 1588.

Ciceronis Amor. Tullies Love. 1589; 1592; 1597; 1601; 1605; 1609; 1611; 1616; 1628.

Menaphon. Camillas alarum to slumbering Euphues. 1589; 1599; 1605; 1616 (as Arcadia or Menaphon); 1632; ed. G. B. Harrison, 1927 (with Lodge's A Margarite for America).

The Spanish Masquerado. 1589.

Greenes never too late. 1590; 1600; 1607; 1611; 1616; [1620?]; 1621; [1630?]; 1631, etc.

Franciscos Fortunes: or The second Part of Greenes Never too late. 1590.

Greenes mourning garment. 1590; 1597; 1616.

Greenes farewell to folly. 1591; 1617.

A maydens dream; upon the death of Sir Christopher Hatton. 1591.

A Notable Discovery of Coosnage. 1591; ed. J. O. Halliwell[-Phillipps], 1859; ed. G. B. Harrison, 1923.

34

The second part of conny-catching. 1592; ed. G. B. Harrison, 1923 (with A notable discovery).

The thirde and last part of Conny-catching. 1592 (signed R. G.); ed. G. B. Harrison, 1923.

A disputation betweene a hee conny-catcher and a shee conny-catcher. 1592; ed. G. B. Harrison, 1923 (with The thirde part).

The blacke bookes messenger. 1592; ed. G. B. Harrison, 1924. [See The defence of conny catching. By Cuthbert Cunny-catcher. 1592; ed. J. E. Adlard, 1859; ed. G. B. Harrison, 1924 (with The blacke bookes messenger).]

Philomela. The Lady Fitzwaters nightingale. 1592; 1615; 1631; rptd Sir S. E. Brydges (Archaica, vol. I, 1815).

A quip for an upstart courtier. 1592; ed. C. Hindley (Old Book Collector's Miscellany, vol. III, 1873).

Greenes, groats-worth of witte, bought with a million of Repentance. 1592; 1596; 1600; 1616; 1617; 1621; 1629; 1637, etc.; ed. Sir S. E. Brydges, Lee Priory, 1813; ed. C. Hindley (Old Book Collector's Miscellany, vol. I, 1871); ed. C. M. Ingleby (Shakspere Allusion Books, pt I, New Shakspere Soc. 1874); ed. G. B. Harrison, 1923.

The Repentance of Robert Greene Maister of Artes. 1592; ed. G. B. Harrison, 1923 (with Greenes, Groatsworth).

Mamillia. The second part of the triumph of Pallas. 1593.

Greenes Orpharion. Wherein is discovered a musicall concorde of pleasant Histories. 1599.

(4) Biography and Criticism

Bernhardi, W. Robert Greenes Leben und Schriften. Leipzig, 1874.

Brown, J. M. An Early Rival of Shakespeare. 1877.

Simpson, R. Account of Robert Greene. [In The School of Shakespeare, vol. II, 1878.]

Storojenko, N. The Life of Robert Greene. [In Works, ed. A. B. Grosart, vol. I, 1881.]

Creizenach, W. Zu Greenes James the Fourth, Ang. VIII, 1885.

Herford, C. H. Greene's Romances and Shakespeare. Trans. New Shakspere Soc. 1888.

Conrad, H. Robert Greene als Dramatiker. Sh. Jb. XXIX, 1894.

Gayley, C. M. Robert Greene, his Life and the Order of his Plays. Gayley, vol. I.

Woodberry, G. E. Greene's Place in Comedy. Gayley, vol. I.

Ehrke, K. Robert Greenes Dramen. Greifswald, 1904.

Schelling, F. E. The Queen's Progress. [1904].

Collins, J. C. The Plays and Poems of Robert Greene. 2 vols. Oxford, 1905. [Introduction.]

Koeppel, E. Locrine und Selimus. Sh. Jb. XLI, 1905.

Wolff, S. L. Robert Greene and the Italian Renaissance. E. Studien, XXXVII, 1907.

Chandler, F. W. The Literature of Roguery. 2 vols. Boston, 1907. [Vol. I, ch. iii.]

Brie, F. Lyly und Greene. E. Studien, XLII, 1910.

Dewar, R. Robert Greene. Reading College Rev. VI, 1914.

Jordan, J. C. Robert Greene. New York, 1915. [With bibliography.]

Cole, G. W. Bibliography—a Forecast. Trans. Bibliog. Soc. of America, XIV, 1920.

McCallum, J. D. Greene's Friar Bacon and Friar Bungay. MLN. XXXV, 1920.

McKerrow, R. B. Greene and Gabriel Harvey. TLS. 8 March 1923.

Harrison, G. B. Shakespeare's Fellows. 1923.

Gore, R. G. Concerning Repetitions in Greene's Romances. PQ. III, 1924.

Round, P. Z. Greene's Materials for Friar Bacon and Friar Bungay. MLR. XXI, 1926.

South, H. P. The Upstart Crow. MP. XXV, 1927.

van Dam, B. A. P. Alleyn's Player's Part of Greene's Orlando Furioso and the Text of the Q of 1594. E. Studies, XI, 1929.

—— Greene's Alphonsus. E. Studies, XIII, 1931.

—— Greene's James IV. E. Studies, XIV, 1932.

Camden, C. Chaucer and Greene. RES. VI, 1930.

Sykes, H. D. Robert Greene and George a Greene. RES. VII, 1931, IX, 1933.

Baskervill, C. R. A Prompt Copy of A Looking Glass for London and England. MP. XXX, 1932.

Hudson, R. Greene's James IV and Contemporary Allusions to Scotland. PMLA. XLVII, 1932.

McNeal, T. H. The Clerk's Tale as a Possible Source for Pandosto. PMLA. XLVII, 1932.

Sanders, C. Robert Greene and the Harveys. Bloomington, 1932.

—— Robert Greene and his 'Editors.' PMLA. XLVIII, 1933.

Bald, R. C. The Locrine and George-a-Greene. Title-page Inscriptions. Library, XV, 1934.

Jenkins, H. On the Authenticity of Greene's Groatsworth of Wit and The Repentance of Robert Greene. RES. XI, 1935.

CHRISTOPHER MARLOWE (1564-1593)

(1) BIBLIOGRAPHY, THE CANON, ETC.

Heinemann, W. A Bibliography of Marlowe's Dr Faustus. 1884.
Foard, J. T. The Joint Authorship of Marlowe and Shakespeare. GM. CCLXXXVIII, 1900.
Crawford, C. The Marlowe Concordance. *Bang*, vol. XXXIV, N.S. II, V, VI, VII, 1911-32.
Brooke, C. F. T. The Marlowe Canon. 1922.
Wells, W. The Authorship of Julius Caesar. 1923.

(2) COLLECTED EDITIONS

The Works of Christopher Marlowe. [Ed. G. Robinson,] 3 vols. 1826.
The Works of Christopher Marlowe, with Notes and some Account of his Life and Writings. Ed. A. Dyce, 3 vols. 1850; 1 vol. 1858.
The Works of Christopher Marlowe. Ed. F. Cunningham, 1870.
The Works of Christopher Marlowe. Ed. A. H. Bullen, 3 vols. 1885.
Christopher Marlowe. Ed. Havelock Ellis, 1887, etc. (Mermaid Ser.)
The Works of Christopher Marlowe. Ed. C. F. T. Brooke, Oxford, 1910.
Christopher Marlowe. Ed. W. L. Phelps, New York, 1912. [The plays only.]
The Works and Life of Christopher Marlowe. Ed. R. H. Case, 6 vols. 1930-3. [Life and Dido, ed. C. F. T. Brooke, 1930; Tamburlaine, ed. U. M. Ellis-Fermor, 1930; The Jew of Malta and The Massacre at Paris, ed. H. S. Bennett, 1931; Edward II, ed. H. B. Charlton and R. D. Waller, 1933; Doctor Faustus, ed. F. S. Boas, 1932; Poems, ed. L. C. Martin, 1931.]

(3) PLAYS

Tamburlaine the Great. Divided into two Tragicall Discourses, as they were sundrie times shewed upon stages in the Citie of London. By the Lord Admyrall, his servantes. 1590; 1593; 1597; 1605-6; ed. K. Vollmöller, Heilbronn, 1885.
The Troublesome reigne and lamentable death of Edward the second, King of England. As it was sundrie times publiquely acted in the cittie of London, by the Earle of Pembroke his servants. 1594; 1598; 1612; 1622; rptd R. Dodsley (Collection of Old Plays, vol. II, 1744); ed. W. Wagner, Hamburg, 1871; ed. F. G. Fleay, 1873 and 1877; ed. O. W. Tancock, Oxford, 1879 and 1899; ed. A. W. Verity, 1896 (Temple Dramatists); ed. W. D. Briggs, 1914; ed. W. W. Greg, *Malone Soc.* 1925.

The Tragedie of Dido Queene of Carthage: Played by the Children of her Majesties Chappell. Written by Christopher Marlowe, and Thomas Nash, Gent. 1594; rptd Old English Drama, vol. II, 1825; ed. A. B. Grosart (Works of Nash, vol. VI, 1885); ed. R. B. McKerrow (Works of Nash, vol. II, 1904); *TFT.* 1914.
The Massacre at Paris: With the Death of the Duke of Guise. As it was plaide by the Lord high Admirall his servants. [1600?]; ed. W. W. Greg, *Malone Soc.* 1928.
The Tragicall History of D. Faustus. As it hath been acted by the Earle of Nottingham his servants. Written by Ch. Marl. 1604; 1609; 1611; 1616; 1619; 1620; 1624; 1631; 1663; rptd [C. W. Dilke] (Old English Plays, vol. I, 1814); ed. W. Wagner, 1877; ed. Sir A. W. Ward, 1878, etc.; ed. H. Morley, 1883; ed. H. Breyman, Heilbronn, 1885; ed. Sir I. Gollancz, 1897 (Temple Dramatists); ed. W. Modlem, 1912; *TFT.* 1914.
The Famous Tragedy of the Rich Jew of Malta. As it was played before the King and Queene, in His Majesties Theatre at White-Hall, by her Majesties Servants. 1633; ed. I. Reed (Dodsley's Old Plays, vol. VIII, 1780); ed. A. Wagner, Heilbronn, 1889.

[The following anon. plays (see pp. 537-9 below) have also been wholly or partially ascribed to Marlowe: An Alarum for London, Arden of Feversham, The Contention of York and Lancaster, Edward III, Locrine, Lust's Dominion, Selimus, The Taming of a Shrew, The Troublesome Reign of King John, and Shakespeare's Titus Adronicus, Henry VI and Richard III.]

(4) POEMS

(a) Collected Edition

The Poems of Robert Greene and Christopher Marlowe. Ed. R. Bell, 1856 and 1876.

(b) Separate Works

All Ovids Elegies: 3. Bookes. By C. M. Epigrams by J.[ohn] D.[avies]. Middelburg, [1595?-1640] (4 edns); ed. C. Edmonds (Isham Reprints, 1870); rptd 1925.
Certaine of Ovids Elegies. Middelburg, [1595?-1640] (*bis*); rptd [1830?]; rptd 1925.
Hero and Leander. 1598; 1598 (with Chapman's continuation); 1600; 1606; 1609; 1613; 1617; 1622; 1629; 1637; ed. Sir S. E. Brydges (Restituta, vol. II, 1815); rptd 1820; ed. S. W. Singer (Select Early English Poets, vol. VIII, 1821).
Lucans First Booke translated line for line. 1600.
I walked along a stream. [In Englands Parnassus, pp. 480-1, 1600.]

The Passionate Shepherd to his Love. [In Englands Helicon, pp. 3–4, 1614.]

(5) BIOGRAPHY AND CRITICISM

(a) Books

Beard, T. The Theatre of Gods Judgements. 1597.

Vaughan, W. The Golden Grove. 1600.

Malone, E. The Plays and Poems of William Shakespeare. Vols. I, II, III, 1821.

von Bodenstedt, F. M. Marlowe und Greene als Vorläufer Shakespeares. Brunswick, 1858.

—— Shakespeares Zeitgenossen und ihre Werke. Vol. III, Berlin, 1860.

Graf, A. Il Fausto di Cristoforo Marlowe. [In Studii drammatici, Turin, 1878.]

Verity, A. W. Marlowe's Influence on Shakespeare. 1886.

Faligan, E. De Marlovianis Fabulis. Paris, 1887.

—— Histoire de la Légende de Faust. Paris, 1888.

Lewis, J. G. Christopher Marlowe. 1890.

Dasent, J. R. Acts of the Privy Council of England. 1901. [Vol. XXIV, 1592–3.]

Boas, F. S. The Works of Thomas Kyd. 1901. [Introductory and supplementary documents.]

—— Marlowe and his Circle. Oxford, 1929.

Tzschaschel, C. Marlowe's 'Edward II' und seine Quelle. Halle, 1902.

Ingram, J. H. Christopher Marlowe and his Associates. 1904.

Brereton, J. le G. The Case of Francis Ingram. [In Elizabethan Dramatists, Sidney, 1905–6.]

Crawford, C. Collectanea. Vol. I, Stratford-on-Avon, 1906.

Eliot, T. S. Notes on the Blank Verse of Christopher Marlowe. [In The Sacred Wood, 1920.]

Thimme, M. Marlowe's 'Jew of Malta', Stil- und Echtheitsfragen. Halle, 1921.

Brooke, C. F. T. The Reputation of Christopher Marlowe. 1922.

Hotson, J. L. The Death of Christopher Marlowe. 1925.

Ellis-Fermor, U. M. Christopher Marlowe. 1927.

Robertson, J. M. Marlowe: A Conspectus. 1931.

Eccles, M. Christopher Marlowe in London. Cambridge, U.S.A. 1934.

Bradbrook, M. C. Themes and Conventions of Elizabethan Tragedy. Cambridge, 1935.

(b) Articles

Maitland, H. Faustus. Blackwood's Mag. July 1817.

Broughton, J. Of the Dramatic Writers who preceded Shakespeare. GM. Jan., Feb., March, April, June, 1830. [Five articles on Marlowe.]

von Leitner, P. Über den Faust von Marlowe. Jahrbuch für Drama, I, 1837.

de Careil, A. F. Les Trois Fausts. Revue Politique et Littéraire, June 1877.

Herford, C. H. and Wagner, A. Marlowe's Source of his Tamburlaine. Academy, 20 Oct. 1883.

Lee, Sir S. Another New Fact about Marlowe. Athenaeum, 18 Aug. 1894.

Nicklin, I. A. Marlowe's Gaveston. Free Rev. V, 1896.

Logeman, H. Notes on Dr Faustus. Recueil de Travaux, Université de Gand, 1898.

—— The Name of Marlowe's Murderer. Ang. XXXVIII, 1914.

Ewig, W. Shakespeare und Marlowes Hero und Leander. Ang. XXII, 1899.

Brereton, J. le G. Notes on the Text of Marlowe. Ang. Bbl. XVI, 1905.

—— Marlowe: some Textual Notes. MLR. VI, 1911.

Marquardsen, A. Marlowes Kosmologie. Sh. Jb. XLI, 1905.

Moore Smith, G. C. Marlowe at Cambridge. MLR. IV, 1909.

Brooke, C. F. T. On the Date of the First Edition of Marlowe's Edward II. MLN. XXIV, 1909.

– —— A Prototype of Marlowe's Jew of Malta. TLS. 8 June 1921.

—— Marlowe's Versification and Style. Stud. Phil. XIX, 1922.

—— Notes on Marlowe's Doctor Faustus. PQ. XII, 1933.

Danchin, F. C. En Marge de la Seconde Partie de Tamburlaine. Revue germanique, VIII, 1912.

—— Quelques Documents concernant les Dramaturges Thomas Kyd et Christophe Marlowe. Revue germanique, IX, 1913–14.

Baker, G. P. Dramatic Technique in Marlowe. E. & S. IV, 1913.

Brown, F. K. Marlowe and Kyd. TLS. 2 June 1921.

Boas, F. S. Marlowe and Kyd. TLS. 30 June, 14 July 1921.

Brandl, A. Kyd an den Privy Council über Marlowe. Archiv, CXLII, 1921.

Seaton, E. Marlowe and his Authorities. TLS. 16 June 1921.

—— Marlowe's Map. E. & S. X, 1924.

—— Fresh Sources for Marlowe. RES. V, 1929.

—— Marlowe, Robert Poley, and the Tippings. RES. V, 1929.

—— Robert Poley's Ciphers. RES. VII, 1931.

Simpson, P. The 1604 Text of Marlowe's Dr Faustus. E. & S. VII, 1921.

Burchardt, C. Christopher Marlowe. Edda, xviii, Christiania, 1922.
Briggs, W. D. On a Document concerning Marlowe. Stud. Phil. xx, 1923.
—— Marlowe's Faustus. MLN. xxxviii, 1923.
Holthausen, F. Zur vergleichenden Märchen- und Sagenkunde. Ang. Bbl. xxxiv, 1923.
Symons, A. A Note on the Genius of Marlowe. English Rev. April 1923.
Thaler, A. Churchyard and Marlowe. MLN. xxxviii, 1923.
Berdan, J. M. Marlowe's Edward II. PQ. iii, 1924.
Rosenberg, W. L. Marlowes Faustus und Goethes Faust. Neue Zeitung, vii, 1925.
Herrington, H. W. Christopher Marlowe— Rationalist. [In Essays in Memory of Barrett Wendell, Cambridge, U.S.A. 1926.]
Moore, H. Gabriel Harvey's References to Marlowe. Stud. Phil. xxiii, 1926.
Spence, L. The Influence of Marlowe's Sources on Tamburlaine. MP. xxiv, 1926, PMLA. xlii, 1927.
Bush, D. The Influence of Marlowe's Hero and Leander on Early Mythological Poems. MLN. xlii, 1927.
—— Notes on Marlowe's Hero and Leander. PMLA. xliv, 1929.
Gray, A. K. Some Observations on Christopher Marlowe, Government Agent. PMLA. xliii, 1928.
Camden, C. Marlowe and Elizabethan Psychology. PQ. viii, 1929.
Flasdieck, H. M. Zur Datierung von Marlowe's Faust. E. Studien, lxiv, lxv, 1929–30.
Thorp, W. The Ethical Problem in Marlowe's Tamburlaine. JEGP. xxix, 1930.
Praz, M. Christopher Marlowe. E. Studies, xiii, 1931.
Boas, F. S. and Hall, E. V. Richard Baines, Informer. A New Sidelight on Marlowe. Nineteenth Century, cxii, 1933.
De Kalb, E. Robert Poley's Movements as a Messenger of the Court, 1588–1601. RES. ix, 1933.
Adams, J. Q. The Massacre at Paris Leaf. Library, xiv, 1934.
Mills, L. J. The Meaning of Edward II. MP. xxxii, 1934.
van Dam, B. A. P. The Collier Leaf [of Massacre at Paris]. E. Studies, xvi, 1934.
—— Marlowe's Tamburlaine. E. Studies, xvi, 1934.
Eccles, M. Marlowe in Kentish Tradition. N. & Q. 13–27 July 1935.　U. M. E.-F.

THOMAS NASHE (1567–1601?)

(1) COLLECTED WORKS

The Complete Works. Ed. A. B. Grosart, 6 vols. 1881–5. (Huth Lib.)

The Works. Ed. R. B. McKerrow, 5 vols. 1904–10.

(2) THE PLAYS

A pleasant Comedie, called Summers last Will and Testament. 1600; ed. J. P. Collier (Dodsley's Old Plays, vol. ix, 1826); Hazlitt's Dodsley, vol. viii.
[For The Tragedie of Dido Queene of Carthage: Played by the Children of her Majesties Chapel. Written by Christopher Marlowe, and Thomas Nash, Gent. 1594, see under Marlowe, above. Nashe may also have contributed to the anon. A Knack to Know a Knave, 1594.

(3) PAMPHLETS AND NOVELS

The anatomie of absurditie. 158'; ed. J. P. Collier (Illustrations of Old English Literature, vol. iii, 1866).
Pierce Penilesse his supplication to the divell. 1592; (3 edns); 1593; 1595; ed. J. P. Collier, Shakespeare Soc. 1842 (and in Miscellaneous Tracts, 1870).
Strange newes, of the intercepting certaine letters. 1592 (re-issued 1593 under same title and as The apologie of Pierce Penilesse); ed. J. P. Collier (Miscellaneous Tracts, 1870).
Christs teares over Jerusalem. 1593 (re-issued 1594); 1613; ed. Sir S. E. Brydges (Archaica, vol. i, 1815).
The terrors of the night. 1594.
The unfortunate traveller. 1594 (bis, 2nd edn 'Newly corrected'); ed. Sir E. Gosse, 1892; ed. S. C. Chew, New York, 1926; ed. H. F. B. Brett Smith, Oxford, 1927.
Have with you to Saffron-Walden. 1596; ed. J. P. Collier (Miscellaneous Tracts, 1870).
Nashes lenten stuffe, the praise of red herring. 1599; rptd Harleian Misc. vol. vi, 1745, vol. ii, 1809, vol. vi, 1810; rptd C. Hindley (Old Book Collector's Miscellany, vol. i, 1871).
The choise of valentines. Ed. J. S. Farmer, 1899. [Not in Grosart; in subscribers' copies only of McKerrow.]
To the gentlemen students of both universities. [Preface to Menaphon, 1589, by R. Greene; see p. 529 above.]
Somewhat to reade for them that list. [Preface to Astrophel and Stella, 1591, by Sir P. Sidney; see pp. 419–20 above.]
[For the Marprelate tracts conjecturally ascribed to Nashe see p. 692 below.]

(4) BIOGRAPHY AND CRITICISM

Cunningham, P. New Facts in the Life of Nashe. Shakespeare Soc. Papers, iii, 1847.

Nicholson, M. D. The Date of Summer's Last Will and Testament. Athenaeum, 10 Jan. 1891.

Cunliffe, J. W. Nash and the Earlier Hamlet. PMLA. xxi, 1906.

Piehler, A. Thomas Nash und seine Streitschriften. Leipzig, 1907.

Upham, A. H. The French Influence in English Literature. New York, 1908.

Harman, E. G. Gabriel Harvey and Thomas Nashe. 1923.

Mustard, W. P. Notes on Thomas Nash's Works. MLN. xl, 1925.

Coffman, G. R. A Note on Shakespeare and Nash. MLN, xlii, 1927.

Salyer, S. M. Hall's Satires and the Harvey-Nashe Controversy. Stud. Phil. xxv, 1928.

Brown, Huntington. Rabelais in English Literature. Cambridge, U.S.A. 1933.

Allen, D. C. The Anatomie of Absurditie. Stud. Phil. xxxii, 1935.

A. K. McI.

VIII. THE MINOR ELIZABETHAN DRAMA, 1580–1603

[No attempt has been made to duplicate here either the section of University Plays (pp. 654–68 below) or the Minor Jacobean and Caroline Drama (pp. 640–54 below). The latter includes several plays possibly written in the Elizabethan period though pbd later. The italicized abbreviations (*Hazlitt's Dodsley*, *TFT.*, etc.) refer to the collections of plays listed pp. 488–92 above.]

SIR WILLIAM ALEXANDER, EARL OF STIRLING (1576?–1640)

[See p. 432 above.]

SAMUEL BRANDON

The Tragicomoedi of the vertuous Octavia. 1598; ed. R. B. McKerrow, *Malone Soc.* 1909; *TFT.* 1912.

HENRY CHETTLE (1560?–1607?)

(a) Plays

The Downfall of Robert, Earle of Huntington. Acted by the Earle of Notingham, Lord high Admirall of England, his Servants. 1601; ed. J. P. Collier (Five Old Plays, 1828, 1833); *Hazlitt's Dodsley*, vol. viii; *TFT.* 1913. [With Munday.]

The Death of Robert, Earle of Huntington. Acted by the Earle of Notingham, Lord high Admirall of England, his Servants. 1601; ed. J. P. Collier (Five Old Plays, 1828, 1833); *Hazlitt's Dodsley*, vol. viii; *TFT.* 1913. [With Munday.]

The Pleasant Comodie of Patient Grissill. As it hath beene sundrie times lately plaid by the Earle of Nottingham (Lord high Admirall) his servants. 1603; ed. J. P. Collier, Shakespeare Soc. 1841; ed. A. B. Grosart (Dekker's Works, vol. v, 1886); G. Hübsch, Erlangen, 1893; *TFT.* 1911. [With W. Haughton and T. Dekker.]

The Tragedy of Hoffman or A Revenge for a Father, As it hath bin divers times acted with great Applause, at the Phenix in Druery-lane. 1631; ed. H. B. L[eonard], 1852; ed. R. Ackermann, 1894; *TFT.* 1913.

The Blind-Beggar Of Bednal-Green. 1659. [See under Day below.]

[The greater number of Chettle's plays and collaborations, as recorded in Henslowe's diary, have been lost; The Trial of Chivalry, The Weakest Goeth to the Wall, Hand A in Sir Thomas More and Yarington's Two Lamentable Tragedies have been ascribed to him.]

(b) Other writings

Kind harts dreame. [1593]; ed. E. F. Rimbault, Percy Soc. 1842; ed. C. M. Ingleby (Shakspere Allusion-Books, pt 1, New Shakspere Soc. 1874); rptd G. B. Harrison, 1923.

Piers Plainnes seaven yeres prentiship. 1595.

Englandes mourning garment. [1603]; rptd Harleian Misc. vol. iii, 1809; ed. C. M. Ingleby (Shakspere Allusion-Books, pt 1, New Shakspere Soc. 1874).

(c) Criticism

Delius, N. Chettle's Hoffman und Shakespeare's Hamlet. Sh. Jb. ix, 1874.

Thorndike, A. H. The Relations of Hamlet to Contemporary Revenge Plays. PMLA. xvii, 1902.

Sykes, H. D. The Dramatic Work of Henry Chettle. N. & Q. 7 April–19 May 1923.

Jones, F. L. The Trial of Chivalry. A Chettle Play. PMLA. xli, 1926.

Jenkins, Harold. The Life and Work of Henry Chettle. 1934.

SAMUEL DANIEL (1563?–1619)

[For Daniel's tragedies (Cleopatra, Philotas), pastorals (The Queenes Arcadia, Hymens Triumph), and masks (The Vision of the 12. Goddesses, Tethys Festival), see p. 422 above. The Maydes Metamorphosis, 1600 (anon.), has also been ascribed to him.]

JOHN DAY (c. 1574–c. 1640)

The Complete Works of John Day. Ed. A. H. Bullen, 1881.

The Ile of Guls. As it hath been often playd in the blacke Fryars, by the Children of the Revels. 1606 (*bis*); 1633.

The Travailes of The three English Brothers. Sir Thomas, Sir Anthony, Mr Robert Shirley. As it is now play'd by her Majesties Servants. 1607. [The dedication signed John Day, William Rowley and George Wilkins.]

Humour out of breath. A Comedie Divers times latelie acted, By the Children Of the Kings Revells. 1608; ed. J. O. Halliwell [-Phillipps], 1860; ed. A. Symons (Nero and Other Plays, 1888). [See M. E. Borish, Harvard Stud. XVI, 1934.]

Law-Trickes or, Who Would Have Thought It. As it hath bene divers times Acted by the Children of the Revels. 1608. [See M. E. Borish, MP. XXXIV, 1937.]

The Parliament of Bees, With their proper Characters. 1641; ed. A. Symons (Nero and Other Plays, 1888). [Lansdowne MS 725 is a variant text.]

The Blind-Beggar Of Bednal-Green, With The merry humor of Tom Strowd the Norfolk Yeoman, as it was divers times publickly acted by the Princes Servants. 1659; ed. W. Bang, Bang, vol. I, 1902; TFT. 1914. [With Chettle.]

[See A. C. Swinburne, Contemporaries of Shakespeare, 1919, and H. D. Sykes, The Dramatic Work of Chettle, N. & Q. 7 April–19 May 1923. The following anon. plays have also been ascribed to Day: Edward IV, The Fair Maid of Bristol, The Maid's Metamorphosis, The Noble Soldier, the Parnassus trilogy, Lust's Dominion and Yarington's Two Lamentable Tragedies.]

MICHAEL DRAYTON (1563–1631)

The first part Of the true and honorable historie, of the life of Sir John Oldcastle. 1600. [With Munday, Richard Hathway and Wilson.]

[For general bibliography of Drayton's works, see pp. 428–5. Edward IV, The London Prodigal, The Merry Devil of Edmonton, Sir Thomas More, and Thomas Lord Cromwell (see pp. 539,652 below) have also been partially or wholly ascribed to him.]

FULKE GREVILLE, BARON BROOKE (1554–1628)

[See p. 421 above.]

WILLIAM HAUGHTON (c. 1575–1605)

English-Men For my Money: Or, A pleasant Comedy, called, A Woman will have her Will. 1616; 1626; 1631; rptd C. Baldwyn (Old English Drama, vol. I, 1825); Hazlitt's Dodsley, vol. x; TFT. 1911; ed. W. W. Greg, Malone Soc. 1912; ed. A. C. Baugh, 1917.

Grim the Collier of Croyden: or, The Devil and his Dame: With the Devil and St Dunstan. [Included, as 'by I. T.', in GratiaeTheatrales, 1662.] Ancient British Drama, vol. III; Hazlitt's Dodsley, vol. VII; TFT. 1912.

The Pleasant Comodie of Patient Grissill. 1603. [See under Chettle above.]

[See W. J. Lawrence, Englishmen for my Money, RES. I, 1925, and H. D. Sykes, The Authorship of Grim the Collier of Croydon, MLR. XIV, 1919. Haughton may also have collaborated in Marlowe's Lust's Dominion and Yarington's Two Lamentable Tragedies.]

ANTHONY MUNDAY (1553–1663)

(a) Plays

Fedele and Fortunio. The deceites in Love: excellently discoursed in a very pleasaunt and fine conceited Comoedie, of two Italian Gentlemen. Translated out of Italian, and set downe according as it hath beene presented before the Queenes moste excellent Majestie. 1585 (anon.); ed. P. Simpson, Malone Soc. 1909; ed. F. Flügge, Archiv, CXXIII, 1909. [From L. Pasqualigo. Chapman and Gosson have also been suggested as the translator.]

The first part Of the true and honorable historie, of the Life of Sir John Oldcastle. 1600; ed. C. F. T. Brooke (in The Shakespeare Apocrypha, Oxford, 1908); ed. P. Simpson, Malone Soc. 1908; TFT. 1911. [With Drayton, Hathway and Wilson.]

The Downfall of Robert, Earle of Huntington. Acted by the Right Honourable, the Earle of Notingham, Lord high Admirall of England, his servants. 1601; ed. J. P. Collier (Five Old Plays,1828,1833); Hazlitt's Dodsley, vol. VIII; TFT. 1913. [With Chettle.]

The Death of Robert, Earle of Huntington. Acted by the Right Honourable, the Earle of Notingham, Lord high Admirall of England, his servants. 1601; ed. J. P. Collier (Five Old Plays,1828,1833); Hazlitt's Dodsley, vol. VIII; TFT. 1913. [With Chettle.]

John a Kent and John a Cumber. A Comedy. Printed from the Original Manuscript. Ed. J. P. Collier, Shakespeare Soc. 1851; TFT. 1912; ed. M. St C. Byrne, Malone Soc. 1923. [Autograph MS in Huntington Lib. (HM 500).]

Sir Thomas More. A Play. Now first printed. Ed. A. Dyce, Shakespeare Soc. 1844; ed. A. F. Hopkinson, 1902 (priv. ptd); ed. C. F. T. Brooke (in The Shakespeare Apocrypha, Oxford, 1908); TFT. 1910; ed. W. W. Greg, Malone Soc. 1911. [BM. Harleian MS 7368. See also under Shakespeare, p. 576 below.]

[The Weakest Goeth to the Wall, 1600 (see under anon. plays, p. 538 below) has also been ascribed to Munday.]

(b) Other Original Writings

The Mirrour of Mutabilitie, or Principall part of the Mirrour for Magistrates. Selected out of the sacred Scriptures by A. M. 1579. [Verse.]

A View of Sundry Examples, Reporting many straunge Murthers. [1580?]

The Paine of Pleasure. 1580. [Verse. Stationers' Register 1578.]

Zelauto. The Fountaine of Fame. 1580. [Verse and prose.]

The True Reporte of the Prosperous Successe which God gave unto our souldiours in Ireland. [1581] (signed A. M.).

A Breefe Discourse of the Taking of Edmund Campion. 1581.

A Courtly Controversie betweene Loove and Learning betweene a Ladie and a Gentleman of Scienna. 1581.

A Discoverie of Edmund Campion and his Confederates. Published by A. M. 1582.

A Breefe Aunswer made unto two Seditious Pamphlets. 1582.

A Breefe and True Reporte of the Execution of Certaine Traytours. Gathered by A. M. 1582.

The English Romayne Lyfe. 1582; 1590; rptd Harleian Misc. vol. VII, 1744, 1808; ed. G. B. Harrison, 1925.

A Watch-woord to Englande, to beware of traytours. 1584 (bis.; signed A. M.).

A Banquet of Daintie Conceits. Written by A. M. 1588; rptd Harleian Misc. vol. IX, 1744, 1812. [Verse. S.R. 1584.]

The Triumphes of re-united Britannia. Performed in honor of Sir Leonard Holliday Lorde Mayor. 1605; rptd J. Nichols (The Progresses of James I, vol. I, 1828).

Camp-bell: or The Ironmongers Faire Feild. [1609.] [Pageant at the installation of Sir T. Campbell as Lord Mayor.]

Londons Love, to the Royal Prince Henrie, meeting him on the River of Thames. 1610 (anon.); rptd J. Nichols (The Progresses of James I, vol. II, 1828).

A Briefe Chronicle, of the Successe of Times, from the Creation of the World, to this instant. 1611.

Chruso-thriambos. The Triumphes of Golde. At the Inauguration of Sir James Pemberton Lord Maior. Devised and Written by A. M. 1611.

Himatia-Poleos. The Triumphs of olde Draperie at the enstalment of Sr. Thomas Hayes Lord Maior. Devised and written by A. M. 1614.

Metropolis Coronata, the Triumphes of Ancient Drapery in a second Yeeres performance. In Honour of Sir John Jolles Lord Maior. Devised, and written by A. M. 1615; rptd J. Nichols (The Progresses of James I, vol. III, 1828).

Chrysanaleia: The Golden Fishing. Applauding the advancement of Mr John Leman to the dignitie of Lord Maior. 1616; rptd J. Nichols (The Progresses of James I, vol. III, 1828); ed. J. G. Nichols, 1884 (as The Fishmongers' Pageant, 1616).

Sidero-Thriambos. Or Steele and Iron Triumphing. Applauding the advancement of Sir Sebastian Harvey to the dignitie of Lord Maior. Devised and written by A. M. 1618.

The Triumphs of the Golden Fleece. Performed at the enstaulment of Mr. Martin Lumley in the Maioraltie. 1623.

(c) Translations

Palmerin D'Oliva. Written in the Spanish, Italian and French, and from them turned into English. 1588; 1597; 1597 (The Second Part of Palmerin d'Oliva); 1615 (pt 1; re-issued 1616); 1616 (pt 2); 1637 (both pts).

The Famous, pleasant, and variable Historie, of Palladine of England. Translated out of French. 1588.

The Declaration of the Lord de la Noue, upon his taking Armes. Truely translated by A. M. 1589.

The Honorable, pleasant and rare conceited Historie of Palmendos. Translated out of French. 1589; 1633; 1653.

[The First Book of Amadis of Gaule.] [1590] (title-page missing in only extant copy); 1619 (The Ancient, Famous and Honourable History of Amadis de Gaule. Written in French by the Lord of Essars, Nicholas de Herberay).

The Masque of the League and the Spanyard discovered. Faythfully translated out of the French coppie. 1592 (signed A. M.; re-issued 1605 as Falshood in Friendship).

Archaioplutos. Or the Riches of Elder Ages. Written in French by Guil. Thelin, Lord of Gutmont and Morillonuilliers. 1592.

Gerileon of England. The second Part of his Historie. Written in French by Estienne de Maisonneufve. 1592.

The Defence of Contraries. Paradoxes against common opinion. Translated out of French by A. M. 1593 (re-issued anon. 1602, as Paradoxes against common Opinion). [From Charles Estienne.]

The First Booke of Primaleon of Greece. 1595 (first 4 sheets only by Munday); 1596 (The second Booke of Primaleon of Greece. Translated out of French by A. M.); 1619 (bks i–iii, 'Translated out of French and Italian by A. M.').

[The First Part of Palmerin of England.] [1596] (title-page missing in only extant copy); 1596 (The Seconde Part, of the no less rare, then excellent and stately Historie, of Palmerin of England. Translated out of French by A. M.); 1602 (pt 3); 1609 (pt 1; re-issued 1639); 1616 (pt 2). [S.R. 1581.]

A breefe Treatise of the vertue of the Crosse. Translated out of French. 1599.

The Strangest Adventure that ever happened. Containing a discourse concerning the King of Portugall Don Sebastian. All first done in Spanish, then in French. 1601 (signed A. M.); rptd Harleian Misc. vol. IV, 1809.

The True knowledge of a mans owne selfe. Written in French by Monsieur du Plessis, Lord of Plessie Marly. 1602.

A True and admirable Historie, of a Mayden of Consolens, in Poictiers. 1603 (signed A. M.)

The Dumbe Divine Speaker. Written in Italian by Fra. Giacomo Affinati d' Acuto Romano. And truelie translated by A. M. 1605.

The Conversion of a most Noble Lady of Fraunce. Truely translated out of French. 1608.

(d) Biography and Criticism

Wilson, J. D. Anthony Munday, Pamphleteer and Pursuivant. MLR. IV, 1909.

Byrne, M. St C. Anthony Munday and his Books. Library, I, 1921.

—— Anthony Munday's Spelling as a Literary Clue. Library, IV, 1923.

Hayes, G. Anthony Munday's Romances of Chivalry. Library, VI, 1925.

—— Anthony Munday's Romances: a Post-script. Library, VII, 1926.

Aronstein, P. Ein dramatischer Kunsthand-werker. Archiv, CXLIX, 1926.

Turner, C. Anthony Munday: an Elizabethan Man of Letters. Berkeley, 1928. [With bibliography.]

Ashton, J. W. John a Kent and John a Cumber. PQ. VIII, 1929; MLN. XLVIII, 1933; PMLA. XLIX, 1934.

WILLIAM PERCY (1575–1648)

[See p. 433 above.]

HENRY PORTER

The Pleasant Historie Of, the two angrie women of Abington. As it was lately playde by the right Honorable the Earle of Notting-ham, Lord High Admirall his servants. 1599 (*bis*); *Hazlitt's Dodsley*, vol. VII; ed. C. M. Gayley, *Gayley*, vol. I; *TFT*. 1911; ed. W. W. Greg, *Malone Soc.* 1912.

[See E. H. C. Oliphant, PMLA. XLIII, 1928; L. Hotson, The Adventure of the Single Rapier, Atlantic Monthly, CXLVIII, 1931 (on Porter's death).]

SAMUEL ROWLEY (d. 1624)

When You See Me, You know me. Or the famous Chronicle Historie of king Henrie the Eight, with the birth and vertuous life of Edward Prince of Wales. As it was playd by the high and mightie Prince of Wales his servants. 1605; 1613; 1621; 1632; ed. K. Elze, Dessau, 1874; *TFT*. 1912.

The Noble Souldier. Or, A Contract Broken, Justly Reveng'd. A Tragedy. Written by S. R. 1634; rptd A. H. Bullen (Old English Plays, vol. I, 1882); *TFT*. 1913. [Probably with Day and Dekker.]

[See H. D. Sykes, Sidelights on Elizabethan Drama, 1924, who ascribes to Rowley The Famous Victories of Henry V, the prose scenes in The Taming of a Shrew, the clowning passages in Greene's Orlando, and the prose scenes of Wily Beguiled. Rowley was also responsible, with William Bird, for the additions to Marlowe's Faustus. See also B. Lloyd, The Noble Soldier and The Welsh Ambassador, RES. III, 1927.]

MARY SIDNEY, COUNTESS OF PEMBROKE (1561–1621)

A Discourse of Life and Death. Written in French by Ph. Mornay. Antonius, A Tragoedie written also in French by Ro. Garnier Both done in English by the Countesse of Pembroke. 1592.

The Tragedie of Antonie. 1595; ed. A. Luce, Weimar, 1897.

[See F. B. Young, Mary Sidney, Countess of Pembroke, 1912.]

ROBERT YARINGTON

Two Lamentable Tragedies. The one, of the Murther of Maister Beech a Chaundler in Thames-streete, and his boye, done by Thomas Merry. The other of a Young childe murthered in a Wood by two Ruffins, with the consent of his Unckle. By Rob. Yarington. 1601; rptd A. H. Bullen (Old English Plays, vol. IV, 1885); *TFT*. 1913.

[See R. A. Law, Yarington's Two Lamentable Tragedies, MLR. v, 1910. Yarington is perhaps a pseudonym; Chettle, Day and Haughton have been suggested as the authors. See however B. M. Wagner, MLN. XLV, 1930, pp. 147–8.]

ANONYMOUS PLAYS (1580–1603)

Fedele and Fortunio. 1585. [See under Munday, p. 535 above.]

The Troublesome Raigne of John King of England. As it was (sundry times) publikely acted by the Queenes Majesties Players, in the honourable Citie of London. 1591;

1611; 1622; rptd J. Nichols, 1779 (Six Old Plays, vol. II); ed. W. C. Hazlitt (Shakespeare's Library, vol. V, 1875); rptd facs. F. J. Furnivall, 1888 (from 1591 edn); ed. F. J. Furnivall and J. Munro, *TFT*. 1911; 1913 (Shakespeare Classics). [See H. D. Sykes, Sidelights on Shakespeare, Stratford-on-Avon, 1919, who ascribes to Peele, and under Shakespeare, p. 560 below.]

The Tragedye of Solyman and Perseda. [1592?]; 1599; rptd type facs. [1815] (as 1599); *Hazlitt's Dodsley*, vol. V; ed. F. S. Boas (Works of Kyd, 1901); *TFT*. 1912 (from 1815 reprint). [See under Kyd, p. 526 above.]

The Lamentable and True Tragedie of M. Arden of Feversham in Kent. 1592. [See under Shakespeare, p. 579 below.]

The Life and Death of Jacke Straw, A notable Rebell in England: Who was kild in Smithfield by the Lord Maior of London. 1593 (colophon 1594); 1604; *Hazlitt's Dodsley*, vol. V; ed. H. Schütt, 1901; *TFT*. 1911. [By Peele? See F. Holthausen, Kieler Studien, II, 1901.]

The First Part of the Contention betwixt the two famous Houses of Yorke and Lancaster. 1594. [See also under Shakespeare, pp. 552–3 below.]

A most pleasant and merie new Comedie intituled, A knacke to knowe a knave. Newlie set foorth, as it hath sundrie tymes bene played by Ed. Allen and his Companie. With kemps applauded Merrimentes of the men of Goteham in receiving the king into Goteham. 1594; ed. J. P. Collier (Five Old Plays, Roxburghe Club, 1851); *Hazlitt's Dodsley*, vol. VI; *TFT*. 1911.

The First part of the Tragicall raigne of Selimus. 1594. [See under Greene, p. 529 above.]

A Pleasant Conceited Historie, called The taming of a Shrew. As it was sundry times acted by the Right Honorable the Earle of Pembrook his servants. 1594. [See under Shakespeare, p. 555 below.]

The True Tragedie of Richard the Third: As it was played by the Queenes Majesties Players. 1594; ed. B. Field, Shakespeare Soc. 1844; ed. W. C. Hazlitt (Shakespeare's Library, vol. VI, 1875); ed. W. W. Greg, *Malone Soc*. 1929. [See G. B. Churchill, Richard the Third up to Shakespeare, Berlin, 1900; L. F. Mott, Foreign Politics in an Old Play, MP. XIX, 1921.]

The Warres of Cyrus King of Persia. Played by the children of her Majesties Chappell. 1594; ed. W. Keller, Sh. Jb. XXXVII, 1901; *TFT*. 1911. [By Richard Farrant (*fl*. 1564–80)? See W. J. Lawrence, TLS. 11 Aug. 1921.]

The Lamentable Tragedie of Locrine. Newly set forth, overseene and corrected. By W. S. 1595. [See under Shakespeare, p. 579 below.]

The True Tragedie of Richard Duke of Yorke, and the death of good King Henrie the Sixt, with the whole contention betweene the two Houses Lancaster and Yorke, as it was sundrie times acted by the Earle of Pembroke his servants. 1595. [See under Shakespeare, pp. 552–3 below.]

The Raigne of King Edward the Third: As it hath bin sundrie times plaied about the Citie of London. 1596. [See under Shakespeare, p. 577 below.]

A Pleasant Conceited Comedie, called, A knacke to know an honest Man. As it hath beene sundrie times plaied about the Citie of London. 1596; ed. H. de Vocht, *Malone Soc*. 1910; *TFT*. 1912.

The Famous Victories of Henry the fifth: containing the Honourable Battell of Agincourt. As it was plaide by the Queenes Majesties Players. 1598; 1617; rptd [J. Nichols,] 1779 (Six Old Plays, vol. II); ed. W. C. Hazlitt (Shakespeare's Library, vol. V, 1875); rptd facs. P. A. Daniel, 1887; *TFT*. 1913. [See also under Shakespeare, p. 563 below.]

A Most pleasant Comedie of Mucedorus. Newly set foorth, as it hath bin sundrie times plaide in the honorable Cittie of London. 1598. [See under Shakespeare, p. 579 below.]

A Pleasant Conceyted Comedie of George a Greene, the Pinner of Wakefield. As it was sundry times acted by the servants of the Earle of Sussex. 1599; rptd R. Dodsley (Collection of Plays, vol. I, 1744, vol. III, 1780, 1825); *Ancient British Drama*, vol. I; ed. F. W. Clarke, *Malone Soc*. 1911; *TFT*. 1913. [Also in collected edns of Greene (see p. 529 above).]

A Pleasant Commodie, called Look about you. As it was lately played by the Lord High Admirall his Servantes. 1599; *Hazlitt's Dodsley*, vol. VII; *TFT*. 1912; ed. W. W. Greg, *Malone Soc*. 1013 [See F. L. Jones, PMLA. XLIV. 1929.]

A warning for Faire Women. Containing, The most tragicall and lamentable murther of Master George Sanders of London, Marchant. As it hath beene lately diverse times acted by the Lord Chamberlaine his Servantes. 1599; rptd R. Simpson (School of Shakespeare, vol. II, 1878); *TFT*. 1912.

The Weakest Goeth to the Wall. As it hath bene sundry times plaide by the Earle of Oxenforde, Lord great Chamberlaine of England his servants. 1600; 1618; *TFT*. 1911; ed. W. W. Greg, *Malone Soc*. 1912.

The Wisdome of Doctor Dodypoll. As it hath bene sundrie times Acted by the Children of Powles. 1600; ed. A. H. Bullen (Collection of Old English Plays, vol. III, 1884); *TFT*. 1912. [See E. Koeppel, Shakespeare's 'Julius Caesar' und die Entstehungszeit des anonymen Dramas 'The Wisdom of Doctor Dodypoll', Sh. Jb. XLIII, 1907.]

The First and Second Parts of King Edward the Fourth. As it hath divers times been publikely played by the Earle of Derbie his servants. 1600; 1605; 1613; 1619; 1626; ed. B. Field, Shakespeare Soc. 1842. [See also under Heywood, p. 623 below.]

The Maydes Metamorphosis. As it hath beene sundrie times Acted by the Children of Powles. 1600; ed. A. H. Bullen (Collection of Old English Plays, vol. I, 1882); ed. R. W. Bond (Works of Lyly, vol. III, 1902); *TFT*. 1912.

Jacke Drums Entertainment: Or The Comedie Of Pasquill and Katherine. As it hath bene sundry times plaide by the Children of Powles. 1601; 1616 (re-issued 1618); ed. R. Simpson (School of Shakespeare, vol. II, 1878); *TFT*. 1912.

A Pleasant conceited Comedie, Wherein is shewed how a man may chuse a good Wife from a bad. 1602. [See under Heywood, p. 623 below.]

Alarum for London, or The Siedge of Antwerpe. As it hath been playde by the Lord Chamberlaine his Servants. 1602; ed. R. Simpson, 1872; *TFT*. 1912; ed. W. W. Greg, *Malone Soc.* 1913.

Il Pastor Fido: Or the Faithfull Shepheard. Translated out of Italian into English. 1602; 1633. [By John Dymocke?]

The True Chronicle Historie of the whole life and death of Thomas Lord Cromwell. Written by W. S. 1602. [See under Shakespeare, p. 580 below.]

A Pleasant Comedie of Faire Em, the Millers Daughter of Manchester. As it was sundry times publiquely acted by the Lord Strange his Servants. [1605?] [See under Shakespeare, p. 579 below.]

The First Part of Jeronimo. With the Warres of Portugall, and the life and death of Don Andraea. 1605; *Ancient British Drama*, vol. I; *Hazlitt's Dodsley*, vol. IV; ed. F. S. Boas (Works of Kyd, 1901). [See K. Wiehl, Thomas Kyd und die Autorschaft von Jeronimo, E. Studien, XLIV, 1912, and under Kyd, p. 525 above.]

The Famous Historye of the life and death of Captaine Thomas Stukeley. As it hath beene Acted. 1605; rptd R. Simpson (School of Shakespeare, vol. I, 1878); *TFT*. 1911. [See J. Q. Adams, JEGP. XV, 1916.]

The True Chronicle History of King Leir, and his three daughters, Gonorill, Ragan, and Cordella. As it hath beene divers and sundry times lately acted. 1605; rptd J. Nichols, 1779 (Six Old Plays, vol. II); ed. W. C. Hazlitt (Shakespeare's Library, vol. VI, 1875); ed. W. W. Greg, *Malone Soc.* 1907; ed. Sir S. Lee, 1909 (Shakespeare Classics); ed. R. Fischer (Quellen zu König Lear, Bonn, 1914). [See H. D. Sykes, Sidelights on Shakespeare, Stratford-on-Avon, 1919, and under Shakespeare, p. 571 below.]

Lusts Dominion; Or, The Lascivious Queen. A Tragedie. Written by Christopher Marlowe, Gent. 1657; ed. C. W. Dilke (Old English Plays, vol. I, 1814); *Hazlitt's Dodsley*, vol. XIV; ed. J. le G. Brereton, *Bang*, N.S. V, 1931. [Not by Marlowe; Brereton ascribes to Dekker, as does H. D. Sykes, Sidelights on Elizabethan Drama, 1924.]

Sir Thomas More. [BM. MS Harl. 7368. See under Shakespeare, pp. 576–7 below.]

Edmund Ironside The English King. A trew Chronicle History called War hath made all friends. Ed. Eleanor Boswell, *Malone Soc.* 1927. [BM. Egerton MS 1994, fols. 97–118. See F. S. Boas, Shakespeare and the Universities, 1923, and M. H. Dodds, MLR. XVIII, 1924.]

The tragedy of Thomas of Woodstock. Ed. J. O. Halliwell[-Phillipps], 1870 (as A Tragedy of King Richard the Second); ed. W. Keller, Sh. Jb. XXXV, 1899 (as Richard II, Part I); ed. W. P. Frijlinck, *Malone Soc.* 1929 (as The First Part of the Reign of King Richard the Second, or Thomas of Woodstock). [BM. Egerton MS 1994, fols. 161–185 b. See A. H. Bullen, A Collection of Old English Plays, vol. II, 1885; F. S. Boas, Shakespeare and the Universities, 1923; B. Lloyd, Jonson and Thomas of Woodstock, TLS. 17 July 1924.]

IX. WILLIAM SHAKESPEARE
(1564–1616)

The Bibliography of Shakespeare: General Bibliographies; Shakespeare Societies and Periodicals.

The Life and Personality of Shakespeare: Shakespeare's Life (The Documents; The Principal Biographies; Special Studies); Shakespeare's Personality and Interests (General Studies; Education; Religion, Philosophy and Psychology; The Supernatural; The State, Society and Contemporary Politics; The Law; Natural History and Medicine; Shakespeare's Geographical Knowledge; Other Interests); The Shakespeare-Bacon Controversy and Similar Theories (The Baconian Theory; The Derby Theory; The Oxford Theory).

The Works of Shakespeare: Collected Works (The Four Folios; The Principal Later Editions; Extracts and Vulgarisations); Plays included in the Folio (I, II, III Henry the Sixth; Richard the Third; The Comedy of Errors; Titus Andronicus; The Taming of the Shrew; The Two Gentlemen of Verona; Love's Labour's Lost; Romeo and Juliet; Richard the Second; A Midsummer Night's Dream; King John; The Merchant of Venice; I, II Henry the Fourth; Much Ado About Nothing; Henry the Fifth; Julius Caesar; As You Like It; Twelfth Night; Hamlet; The Merry Wives of Windsor; Troilus and Cressida; All's Well that Ends Well; Measure for Measure; Othello; King Lear; Macbeth; Anthony and Cleopatra; Coriolanus; Timon of Athens; Cymbeline; The Winter's Tale; The Tempest; Henry the Eighth); Plays excluded from the Folio (Sir Thomas More; Edward the Third; Pericles; The Two Noble Kinsmen; Other Ascribed Plays); The Poems (Venus and Adonis; Lucrece; The Passionate Pilgrim; The Phoenix and Turtle; The Sonnets; A Lover's Complaint).

The Criticism of Shakespeare: Technical Criticism (Sources and Influences; Transmission of the Text, Chronology, Authenticity and Related Problems; Textual Criticism; Language, Vocabulary, Style and Prosody); Aesthetic Criticism (Anthologies of Shakespearian Criticism; History of Shakespearian Criticism; Principal Critics to 1800; Nineteenth and Twentieth Centuries—Trends in Shakespearian Criticism, General Criticism, Special Studies); Shakespeare's Influence (Adaptations and Influence in England; France; Germany and Australia; Other Countries).

[This section is deeply indebted to the bibliographies of Jaggard, Bartlett, and Ebisch and Schücking, and to the Bibliographical Notes in Chambers.]

I. THE BIBLIOGRAPHY OF SHAKESPEARE

A. GENERAL BIBLIOGRAPHIES

[Current literature is covered by the Shakespeare-Jahrbuch, the Bulletin of the Shakespeare Association of America, the Annual Bibliography of English Language and Literature (Modern Humanities Research Association), The Year's Work in English Studies (English Association), the English Association Bulletin, and, for periodicals, by the Review of English Studies.]

Jaggard, William. Shakespeare Bibliography: a Dictionary of Every Known Issue of the Writings of Our National Poet and of Recorded Opinion thereon in the English Language. Stratford-on-Avon, 1911. [Arranged alphabetically. A very full skeleton hand-list.] (*Jaggard.*)

Bartlett, Henrietta C. Mr. William Shakespeare. Original and Early Editions of His Quartos and Folios, His Source Books and those containing Contemporary Notices. New Haven, 1922. [Very thorough and reliable within its limits.] (*Bartlett.*)

Chambers, Sir E. K. William Shakespeare. A Study of Facts and Problems. 2 vols. Oxford, 1930. [Each chapter is preceded by a valuable critical Bibliographical Note. A skeleton List of Books will be found in vol. II pp. 409–25.] (*Chambers.*)

Ebisch, Walther and Schücking, Levin L. A Shakespeare Bibliography. Oxford, 1931. [A classified hand-list—with occasional brief critical notes—of recent edns, books and articles to 1929. Supplement (1930–35), Oxford, 1937.] (*Ebisch and Schücking.*)

[Wilson, John.] Catalogue of All the Books, Pamphlets, etc. relating to Shakespeare. 1827.

Halliwell[-Phillipps], J. O. Shakespeariana. A Catalogue of the Early Editions of Shakespeare's Plays and of the Commentaries and Other Publications Illustrative of His Works. 1841.

Thimm, Franz. Shakespeariana from 1564 to 1864. An Account of the Shakespearian Literature of England, Germany, France, and Other European Countries, with Bibliographical Introductions. 1865; 1872 (rev. edn).

Jahrbuch der Deutschen Shakespeare-Gesellschaft. Berlin [later Weimar], 1865–. [In progress. Includes a biennial Shakespeare-Bibliographie.]

Hubbard, J. M. Catalogue of the Works of William Shakespeare and Shakespeariana in the Barton Collection of the Boston Public Library. 2 vols. Boston, 1878–80.

British Museum. Catalogue of Printed Books. William Shakespeare. 1897.

Lee, Sir Sidney. A Catalogue of Shakespeariana. 1899.

—— A Shakespeare Reference Library. English Ass. 1910; rev. Sir E. K. Chambers, 1925.

Greg, W. W. A List of English Plays written before 1643 and printed before 1700. Bibliog. Soc. 1900.

—— Catalogue of the Books presented by Edward Capell to the Library of Trinity College in Cambridge. Cambridge, 1903.

Greg, W. W. A Descriptive Catalogue of the Early Editions of the Works of Shakespeare preserved in the Library of Eton College. Oxford, [1909].

Shaw,, A. C. Birmingham Free Libraries: Index to the Shakespeare Memorial Library. 3 pts, Birmingham, 1900–3.

Scherzer, Jane. American Editions of Shakespeare, 1753–1866. PMLA. xxii, 1907.

Pollard, A. W. Shakespeare Folios and Quartos, 1594–1685. 1909.

Katalog der Bibliothek der Deutschen Shakespeare-Gesellschaft. Weimar, 1909.

Aldis, H. G., Moorman, F. W., Walder, Ernest and Robertson, J. G. Shakespeare. CHEL. vol. v, 1910.

A Catalogue of the Shakespeare Exhibition held in the Bodleian Library to commemorate the Death of Shakespeare. Oxford, 1916.

Bartlett, H. C. Catalogue of the Exhibition of Shakespeareana held at the New York Public Library in Commemoration of the Tercentenary of Shakespeare's Death. New York, 1917.

Herford, C. H. A Sketch of Recent Shakespearean Investigation, 1893–1923. 1923. [Critical survey.]

Gollancz, Sir Israel. In Commemoration of the First Folio Tercentenary. A Resetting of the Preliminary Matter of the First Folio, with a Catalogue of Shakespeareana exhibited in the Hall of the Company of Stationers. 1923.

Guide to the MSS. and Printed Books exhibited in Celebration of the Tercentenary of the First Folio. 1923. [BM. Ed. A. W. Pollard.]

Specimens of Shakespeareana in the Bodleian Library at Oxford. Oxford, 1927.

A Companion to Shakespeare Studies. Ed. H. Granville-Barker and G. B. Harrison, Cambridge, 1934. ['Reading List' with comments, pp. 347–68.]

Ford, H. L. Shakespeare, 1700–1740. A Collation of the Editions and Separate Plays. Lavorrick, 1935 (priv. ptd).

B. SHAKESPEARE SOCIETIES AND PERIODICALS

[See F. S. Boas, Shakespeare Societies, Past and Present, Shakespeare Rev. i, 1928.]

Shakespeare Society. 1841–52. [48 publications, 1841–53. For titles see *Jaggard*, pp. 606–7.]

Deutsche Shakespeare-Gesellschaft. 1864–. [Jahrbuch, Berlin, 1865–.]

New Shakspere Society. 1874–86. [27 publications. For titles and contents see *Jaggard*, pp. 228–31.]

New York Shakespeare Society. 1885–. [13 publications, New York, 1885–1903. For titles see *Jaggard*, p. 232.]

Shakespeare Association. 1917–. [18 pamphlets, Oxford, 1917–35. For titles see *Ebisch and Schücking*, p. 171. Also publishes texts, facsimiles and critical studies.]

Shakespeare Association of America. 1926–. [Annual Bulletin, New York, 1926–.]

Shakespeare Review. Stratford-on-Avon, 1928–.

II. THE LIFE AND PERSONALITY OF SHAKESPEARE

A. SHAKESPEARE'S LIFE

[*Ebisch and Schücking*, pp. 23–32; *Chambers*, vol. i, chs. i–iii.]

(1) THE DOCUMENTS

[*Chambers*, vol. ii, Appendix A.]

Lambert, D. H. Cartae Shakespeareanae. Shakespeare Documents. A Chronological Catalogue of Extant Evidence. 1904.

Neilson, W. A. and Thorndike, A. H. The Facts about Shakespeare. New York, 1913, 1931 (rev.).

Brooke, C. F. T. Shakespeare of Stratford. A Handbook for Students. New Haven, 1926.

Butler, Pierce. Materials for the Life of Shakespeare. Chapel Hill, North Carolina, 1932.

[The principal forgeries are listed in *Chambers*, vol. ii, Appendix F. For the literature provoked by the forgeries of Ireland and Collier, and the alleged forgeries of Cunningham, see *Ebisch and Schücking*, pp. 24–6, and the following:]

Stamp, A. E. The Disputed Revels Accounts. Shakespeare Ass. 1930.

Klein, D. The Case of Forman's 'Booke of Plaies.' PQ. xi, 1932.

Tannenbaum, S. A. More about the Forged Revels Accounts. New York, 1932.

—— Shaksperian Scraps and Other Elizabethan Fragments. New York, 1933. [Various Collier forgeries.]

(2) THE PRINCIPAL BIOGRAPHIES

[The early biographical notes of Fuller, Aubrey, etc. are listed below, p. 592.]

Rowe, Nicholas. Some Account of the Life, &c. of Mr William Shakespear. [Prefixed to his edn of The Works, 1709.]

Drake, Nathan. Shakespeare and his Times. 2 vols. 1817.

Malone, Edmond. Life of Shakespeare. [Third variorum edn, vol. II, 1821.]

Collier, J. P. New Facts regarding the Life of Shakespeare. 1835.

—— New Particulars regarding the Works of Shakespeare. 1836.

—— Traditionary Anecdotes of Shakespeare. 1838.

—— Further Particulars regarding Shakespeare and his Works. 1839.

—— Life of Shakespeare. 1844.

Knight, Charles. William Shakespere. 1843.

Halliwell [-Phillipps], J. O. The Life of William Shakespeare. 1848; 1853.

—— Illustrations of the Life of Shakespeare. 1874.

—— Outlines of the Life of Shakespeare. Brighton, 1881; 1887 (final revision).

Dowden, Edward. Shakspere, A Critical Study of his Mind and Art. 1874.

Elze, Karl. William Shakespeare. Halle, 1876; tr. Eng. 1888.

Ingleby, C. M. Shakespeare, the Man and the Book. 2 vols. 1877–81.

Fleay, F. G. A Chronicle History of the Life and Work of William Shakespeare. 1886.

Brandes, Georg. William Shakespeare. 2 vols. Copenhagen, 1896; tr. Eng. 2 vols. 1898.

Sarrazin, Gregor. William Shakespeares Lehrjahre. Weimar, 1897.

Lee, Sir Sidney. A Life of William Shakespeare. 1898; 1925 (final revision). [The DNB. article is also by Lee.]

Rolfe, W. J. A Life of William Shakespeare. Boston, 1904.

Raleigh, Sir Walter. Shakespeare. 1907. (English Men of Letters Ser.)

Saintsbury, George. Shakespeare, Life and Plays. CHEL. vol. v, 1910; ed. H. Waddell, Cambridge, 1934.

Smeaton, Oliphant. Shakespeare, his Life and Work. [1912.] (Everyman's Lib.)

Brandl, Alois. Shakespeares Leben-Umwelt-Kunst. Berlin, 1922.

Alden, R. M. Shakespeare. New York, 1922, 1932 (rev. O. J. Campbell).

Adams, J. Q. A Life of William Shakespeare. Boston, 1923.

Lamborn, E. A. G. and Harrison, G. B. Shakespeare, the Man and his Stage. 1923.

Longworth-Chambrun, Clara. Shakespeare, Acteur-Poète. Paris, 1926; tr. Eng. New York, 1927.

Smart, J. S. Shakespeare: Truth and Tradition. 1928.

Chambers, Sir E. K. William Shakespeare. A Study of Facts and Problems. 2 vols. Oxford, 1930; 1933 (abridged by C. Williams). [Index by B. White, Shakespeare Ass. 1934.]

Wilson, J. D. The Essential Shakespeare. Cambridge, 1932.

Harrison, G. B. Shakespeare at Work, 1592–1603. 1933.

Parrott, T. M. William Shakespeare: a Handbook. New York, 1934.

[Biographical chapters are also included in many of the general critical studies listed below, pp. 594–5, as well as in the introductory matter to the principal collected edns (see pp. 548–51 below).]

(3) SPECIAL STUDIES

Hunter, J. New Illustrations of Shakespeare. 1845.

Green, C. F. The Legend of Shakespeare's Crab-Tree. 1857; 1862.

Wise, J. R. Shakespeare, his Birthplace and its Neighbourhood. 1861.

Bracebridge, C. H. Shakespeare No Deer-Stealer. 1862.

French, G. R. Shakespeareana Genealogica. 1869.

Blacker, Carola. Stratford-on-Avon and Shakespeare. Sh. Jb. XXXII, 1896.

Yeatman, J. P. The Gentle Shakespeare. 1896; 1904 (rev. edn).

Stopes, C. C. Shakespeare's Warwickshire Contemporaries. Stratford-on-Avon, 1897, 1907 (expanded).

—— Shakespeare's Family, being a Record of the Ancestors and Descendants of William Shakespeare, with Some Account of the Ardens. 1901.

—— Shakespeare's Fellows and Followers. A Special Set of Facts collected from the Lord Chamberlain's Papers. Sh. Jb. XLVI, 1910.

—— Burbage and Shakespeare's Stage. 1913.

—— Shakespeare's Environment. 1914; 1918 (expanded).

—— The Life of Henry, Third Earl of Southampton. Cambridge, 1922.

—— Early Records illustrating the Personal Life of Shakespeare. [In Shakespeare and the Theatre, Shakespeare Ass. 1927.]

Elton, C. I. William Shakespeare, his Family and Friends. Ed. A. H. Thompson, 1904.

Gray, J. W. Shakespeare's Marriage. 1905.

Haney, J. L. The Name of William Shakespeare. A Study in Orthography. Philadelphia, 1906.

Spielmann, M. H. On the Portraits of Shakespeare. [Stratford Town Shakespeare, vol. x, 1907.]

—— Shakespeare's Portraiture. [In Studies in the First Folio, Shakespeare Ass. 1924.]

Tannenbaum, S. A. The Shakspere Coat-of-Arms. New York, 1908.

—— A New Study of Shakspere's Will. Stud. Phil. XXIII, 1926.

Kingsley, R. G. Shakespeare in Warwickshire. Nineteenth Century, LXVII, 1910.

Law, Ernest. Shakespeare as a Groom of the Chamber. 1910.

Wallace, C. W. Shakespeare and his London Associates. Nebraska University Stud. x, 1910.

—— New Shakespeare Discoveries. Harper's Mag. CXX, 1910.

—— Shakespeare's Money Interest in the Globe Theater. Century Mag. LXXX, 1910.

—— Shakespeare and the Blackfriars. Century Mag. LXXX, 1910.

Thaler, Alwin. Shakespeare's Income. Stud. Phil. xv, 1918.

Fehr, Bernhard. Shakespeare and Coventry. Ang. Bbl. XXXI, 1920.

Longworth-Chambrun, Clara. Giovanni Florio. Paris, 1921.

Savage, Richard and Fripp, E. I. Minutes and Accounts of the Corporation of Stratford-upon-Avon, 1553–1620. Dugdale Soc. 1921–.

Fripp, E. I. Master Richard Quyny. Oxford, 1924.

—— Shakespeare's Stratford. Oxford, 1928.

—— Shakespeare's Haunts near Stratford. Oxford, 1929.

—— Shakespeare Studies. 1930.

Brooke, C. F. T. Shakespeare's Moiety of the Stratford Tithes. MLN. XL, 1925.

Gray, Arthur. A Chapter in the Early Life of Shakespeare. Cambridge, 1926.

Salzmann, L. F. Shakespeare and the Quarter Sessions. London Mercury, Nov. 1926.

Addy, S. O. Shakespeare's Will: the Stigma Removed. N. & Q. 16 Jan., 6 Feb. 1926.

—— Shakespeare's Marriage. N. & Q. 23, 30 Oct. 1926.

—— The Proving of Shakespeare's Will. N. & Q. 22 Oct. 1927.

—— Shakespeare's Puritan Relations. N.&Q. 21 April 1928.

Farnam, H. W. Shakespeare's Economics. New Haven, 1931.

Hotson, Leslie. Shakespeare versus Shallow. 1931.

[For Shakespeare's handwriting, see p. 586 below. For discussions of his education, his religion, his travels, his professions, etc., the following section, Shakespeare's Personality and Interests, should be consulted.]

B. SHAKESPEARE'S PERSONALITY AND INTERESTS

[*Ebisch and Schücking*, pp. 32–44.]

(1) GENERAL STUDIES

Bagehot, Walter. Shakespeare the Man. [In Literary Studies, vol. I, 1879, etc.]

Smith, Goldwin. Shakespeare the Man. Toronto, 1899.

Stephen, Sir Leslie. Shakespeare the Man. [In Studies of a Biographer, 4 vols. 1898–1902.]

Bradley, A. C. Shakespeare the Man. [In Oxford Lectures on Poetry, 1909.]

Harris, Frank. The Man Shakespeare. New York, 1909.

Lee, Sir Sidney. The Impersonal Aspect of Shakespeare's Art. English Ass. Lecture, 1909.

Dowden, Edward. Is Shakespeare Self-revealed? [In Essays, Modern and Elizabethan, 1910.]

Masson, David. Shakespeare Personally. Ed. Rosaline Masson, 1914.

Beeching, H. C. The Benefit of the Doubt. [In A Book of Homage to Shakespeare, Oxford, 1916.]

—— The Character of Shakespeare. British Academy Lecture, 1917.

Brewster, W. T. The Restoration of Shakespeare's Personality. [In Columbia University Shakespearian Studies, 1916.]

Mackail, J. W. Shakespeare after Three Hundred Years. British Academy Lecture, 1916.

Richter, Helene. Shakespeare der Mensch. Leipzig, 1923.

Harman, E. G. The 'Impersonality' of Shakespeare. 1925.

(2) EDUCATION

[The general section on Education, pp. 364–80 above, should also be consulted.]

Baynes, T. S. What Shakespeare learnt at School. [In Shakespeare Studies, 1894.]

Leach, A. F. English Schools at the Reformation. 1896.

Watson, Foster. The Curriculum and Text-Books of English Schools in the Seventeenth Century. Trans. Bibliog. Soc. VI, 1902.

Bayley, A. R. Shakespeare's School. N. & Q. 26 Oct. 1907, 22 April 1916.

Blach, S. Shakespeares Lateingrammatik. Lilys Grammatica Latina. Sh. Jb. XLIV, XLV, 1908–9.

Sandys, Sir J. E. Education. [In Shakespeare's England, vol. I, Oxford, 1916.]

Pollen, J. H. A Shakespeare Discovery: his School-master afterwards a Jesuit. Month, CXXX, 1917.

Stevenson, W. H. Shakespeare's School-master and Handwriting. TLS. 8 Jan. 1920.

Plimpton, George. The Education of Shakespeare. Illustrated from the Schoolbooks in Use at his Time. 1933.

(3) RELIGION, PHILOSOPHY AND PSYCHOLOGY

Fleay, F. G. Shakespeare and Puritanism. Ang. VII, 1884.

Carter, Thomas. Shakespeare, Puritan and Recusant. Edinburgh, 1897.

Bowden, H. S. and Simpson, Richard. The Religion of Shakespeare. 1899.

Moulton, R. G. The Moral System of Shakespeare. New York, 1903.

Beeching, H. C. On the Religion of Shakespeare. [In Shakespeare's Works, Stratford Town edn, vol. x, 1907.]

Lee, Sir Sidney. Aspects of Shakespeare's Philosophy. [In Shakespeare and the Modern Stage, 1907.]

Dowden, Edward. Elizabethan Psychology. [In Essays, Modern and Elizabethan, 1910.]

Bundy, M. W. Shakespeare and Elizabethan Psychology. JEGP. XXIII, 1924.

Jones, Sir Henry. The Ethical Idea in Shakespeare. [In Essays on Literature and Education, ed. H.J.W.Hetherington, 1924.]

Craig, Hardin. Shakespeare's Depiction of Passions. PQ. IV, 1925.

—— Shakespeare and Formal Logic. [In Klaeber Studies, Minneapolis, 1929.]

Schücking, L. L. Shakespeares Persönlichkeitsideal. Neue Jahrbücher für Wissenschaft und Jugendbildung, III, 1927.

Fripp, E. I. The Religion of Shakespeare's Father. Hibbert Journ. XXVI, 1928.

Anderson, R. L. Elizabethan Psychology and Shakespeare's Plays. Iowa City, 1928.

Campbell, L. B. Shakespeare's Tragic Heroes. Cambridge, 1930.

(4) THE SUPERNATURAL

[The section on Science and Pseudo-Science, pp. 879–94 below, should also be consulted.]

Lewes Lavater: Of Ghostes and Spirites walking by Nyght, 1572. Ed. J. D. Wilson and May Yardley, Shakespeare Ass. 1929. [Introduction and appendix.]

Reginald Scot: The Discoverie of Witchcraft. 1584; ed. B. Nicholson, 1886. [Introduction.]

Spalding,T.A.Elizabethan Demonology. 1880.

Dyer, T. F. T. Folk-Lore of Shakespeare. [1883.]

Jaggard, W. Folklore, Superstition and Witchcraft in Shakespeare. A Bibliography. 1896.

Nutt, Alfred. The Fairy Mythology of Shakespeare. 1900.

Wilson, William. Shakespeare and Astrology. Boston, 1903.

Gibson, J. P. Shakespeare's Use of the Supernatural. Cambridge, 1908.

Lucy, Margaret. Shakespeare and the Supernatural. Liverpool, 1908.

Stewart, H. H. The Supernatural in Shakespeare. 1908.

Notestein, Wallace. A History of Witchcraft in England, 1558–1718. Washington, 1911.

Clark, Cumberland. Shakespeare and Science. Birmingham, 1929.

—— Shakespeare and the Supernatural. 1932.

Kittredge, G. L. Witchcraft in Old and New England. Cambridge, U.S.A. 1929.

Latham, M. W. Elizabethan Fairies. New York, 1930.

(5) THE STATE, SOCIETY AND CONTEMPORARY POLITICS

von Hofmannsthal, Hugo. Shakespeares Könige und grosse Herren. Sh. Jb. XLI, 1905.

Tolstoi, L. N. Shakespeare. Hanover, 1906; tr. Eng. 1907.

Lee, Sir Sidney. Shakespeare and Patriotism. [In Shakespeare and the Modern Stage, 1907.]

—— Shakespeare and Public Affairs. Contemporary Rev. CIV, 1913.

Tupper, Frederick. The Shakespearean Mob. PMLA. XXVII, 1912.

Tolman, A. H. Is Shakespeare Aristocratic? PMLA. XXIX, 1914.

Gayley, C. M. Shakespeare and the Founders of Liberty in America. New York, 1917.

Raleigh, Sir Walter. Shakespeare and England. British Academy Lecture, 1918.

Chambers, R. W. The Expression of Ideas—particularly Political Ideas—in the Three Pages and in Shakespeare. [In Shakespeare's Hand in The Play of Sir Thomas More, Cambridge, 1923.]

Marriott, J. A. R. Shakespeare and Politics. Cornhill, Dec. 1927.

Schelling, F. E. The Common Folk of Shakespeare. [In Shakespeare and 'Demi-Science,' Philadelphia, 1927.]

Charlton, H. B. Shakespeare, Politics, and Politicians. English Ass. Lecture, 1929.

Ward, B. M. Shakespeare and the Anglo-Spanish War (1585–1604). Revue anglo-américaine, April 1930.

Harrison, G. B. Shakespeare's Topical Significances. TLS. 13, 20 Nov. 1930.

(6) THE LAW

Rushton, W. L. Shakespeare a Lawyer. 1858.

—— Shakespeare's Legal Maxims. 1859; 1907.

—— Shakespeare's Testamentary Language. 1869.

—— Shakespeare Illustrated by the Lex Scripta. 1870.

Campbell, John (Baron Campbell). Shakespeare's Legal Acquirements. 1859.

Devecmon, W. C. In re Shakespeare's Legal Acquirements. New York Shakespeare Soc. 1899.

Allen, Charles. Notes on the Bacon-Shakespeare Question. Boston, 1900.

Collins, J. C. Was Shakespeare a Lawyer? [In Studies in Shakespeare, 1904.]

White, E. J. Commentaries on the Law in Shakespeare. St Louis, 1911.

Greenwood, Sir G. G. Shakespeare's Law and Latin. 1916.

—— Shakespeare's Law. 1920.

Underhill, A. Law. [Shakespeare's England, vol. i, Oxford, 1916.]

Barton, Sir D. P. Links between Shakespeare and the Law. 1929.

Keeton, G. W. Shakespeare and his Legal Problems. 1930.

(7) NATURAL HISTORY AND MEDICINE

Patterson, Robert. The Natural History of the Insects mentioned in Shakespeare's Plays. 1838.

Bucknill, J. C. The Medical Knowledge of Shakespeare. 1860.

—— The Mad Folk of Shakespeare. 1867.

Beisley, Sidney. Shakspere's Garden. 1864.

Harting, J. E. The Ornithology of Shakespeare. 1871.

Ellacombe, H. N. The Plant-Lore and Garden Craft of Shakespeare. Exeter, [1878]; 1884.

Phipson, Emma. The Animal-Lore of Shakespeare's Time. 1883.

Moyes, J. Medicine and Kindred Arts in the Plays of Shakespeare. Glasgow, 1896.

Seager, H. W. Natural History in Shakespeare's Time. 1896.

Dowden, Edward. Shakespeare as a Man of Science. [In Essays, Modern and Elizabethan, 1910.]

Cartaz, A. La Toxicologie dans les Drames de Shakespeare. Paris, 1911.

Robin, P. A. The Old Physiology in English Literature. 1911.

Geikie, A. The Birds of Shakespeare. 1916.

Savage, F. G. The Flora and Folk-Lore of Shakespeare. Cheltenham, 1923.

Singleton, Esther. The Shakespeare Garden. 1923.

Somerville, H. Madness in Shakespearian Tragedy. 1929.

Luce, M. .Shakespeare and Botany. [In Man and Nature, 1935.]

Rohde, E. S. Shakespeare's Wild Flowers, Fairy Lore, Gardens, Herbs, Gatherers of Simples and Bee Lore. 1935.

(8) SHAKESPEARE'S GEOGRAPHICAL KNOWLEDGE

(including his alleged travels)

Sugden, E. H. A Topographical Dictionary to the Works of Shakespeare and his Fellow Dramatists. Manchester, 1925.

Elze, Karl. Shakespeares mutmassliche Reisen. Sh. Jb. VIII, 1873.

Elze, Theodor. Italienische Skizzen zu Shakespeare. Sh. Jb. XIII, XIV, XV, 1878–80.

—— Venezianische Skizzen zu Shakespeare. Munich, 1899.

Sarrazin, Gregor. Shakespeare in Mantua? Sh. Jb. XXIX, 1894.

—— Neue italienische Skizzen zu Shakespeare. Sh. Jb. XXXVI, 1900.

—— Shakespeare in Mailand? Sh. Jb. XLVI, 1910.

Stefansson, J. Shakespeare at Elsinore. Contemporary Rev. LXIX, 1896.

Bristol, F. M. Shakespeare and America. Chicago, 1898.

Keller, Wolfgang. Zu Shakespeares italienische Reise. Sh. Jb. XXXV, 1899.

Koeppel, E. War Shakespeare in Italien? Sh. Jb. XXXV, 1899.

Logeman, Henri. Shakespeare et Helsingör. [In Mélanges Paul Fredericy, Brussels, 1904.]

Lawrence, W. J. Was Shakespeare ever in Ireland? Sh. Jb. XLII, 1906.

Sullivan, E. Shakespeare and the Waterways of North Italy. Nineteenth Century, LXIV, 1908.

—— Shakespeare and Italy. Nineteenth Century, LXXXIII, 1918.

Collison-Morley, Lacy. Shakespeare in Italy. Stratford-on-Avon, 1916.

Smart, J. S. Shakespeare's Italian Names. MLR. XI, 1916.

Tilley, M. P. Shakespeare and Italian Geography. JEGP. XVI, 1917.

Nulli, Attilio. Shakespeare in Italia. Milan, 1918.

Eagle, R. A. Shakespeare and Italy. Nineteenth Century, XCIII, 1923.

Jeffery, V. M. Shakespeare's Venice. MLR. XXVII, 1932.

(9) OTHER INTERESTS

Thoms, W. J. Was Shakespeare ever a Soldier? [In Three Notelets on Shakespeare, 1865.]

Ellacombe, H. N. Shakespeare as an Angler. 1883.

Naylor, E. W. Shakespeare and Music. With Illustrations from the Music of the 16th and 17th Centuries. 1896.

Rushton, W. L. Shakespeare an Archer. 1897.

Madden, D. H. The Diary of Master William Silence. A Study of Shakespeare and Elizabethan Sport. 1897.

von Mauntz, A. Heraldik im Diensten der Shakespeare-Forschung. Berlin, 1903.

Loewe, H. Shakespeare und die Waldmannskunst. Sh. Jb. XL, 1904.

Brown, Carleton. Shakespeare and the Horse. Library, III, 1912.

Matthews, Brander. Shakespeare as an Actor. North American Rev. 1912.

Herford, C. H. Shakespeare and the Arts. John Rylands Lib. Bulletin, XI, 1927.

Rothery, G. C. The Heraldry of Shakespeare. 1930.

Thorp, M. F. Shakespeare and the Fine Arts. PMLA. XLVI, 1931.

C. THE SHAKESPEARE-BACON CONTROVERSY AND SIMILAR THEORIES

[*Ebisch and Schücking*, pp. 182–6. The following is a very brief selection from the immense literature upon the subject.]

(1) THE BACONIAN THEORY

Bacon, Delia S. The Philosophy of the Plays of Shakespeare Unfolded. 1857.

Greenwood, Sir G. G. The Shakespeare Problem Restated. 1908.

—— In re Shakespeare, Beeching v. Greenwood. 1909.

—— Is there a Shakespeare Problem? 1916.

Beeching, H. C. William Shakespeare, Player, Playmaker, and Poet. A Reply to Mr. George Greenwood. 1908.

Lang, Andrew. Shakespeare, Bacon, and the Great Unknown. 1912.

Robertson, J. M. The Baconian Heresy. A Confutation. 1913.

Baxter, J. T. The Greatest of Literary Problems. The Authorship of the Shakespeare Works. Boston, 1915. [With bibliography.]

Hookham, George. Will o' the Wisp, or the Elusive Shakespeare. Oxford, 1921.

Young, K. The Shakespeare Skeptics. North American Rev. CCXV, 1922.

Connes, Georges. Le Mystère Shakespearien. Paris, 1926.

Spurgeon, C. F. E. The Use of Imagery by Shakespeare and Bacon. RES. IX, 1933.

(2) THE DERBY THEORY

Lefranc, Abel. Sous le Masque de 'William Shakespeare'. 2 vols. Paris, 1918–9.

Lee, Sir Sidney. More Doubts about Shakespeare. Quart. Rev. CCXXXII, 1919.

Castelain, Maurice. Shakespeare ou Derby? Revue germanique, I, 1920.

(3) THE OXFORD THEORY

Looney, J. T. 'Shakespeare' identified in Edward de Vere, the 17th Earl of Oxford. 1920.

Ward, B. M. The Seventeenth Earl of Oxford. 1928.

Connes, Georges. Du Nouveau sur de Vere. Revue anglo-américaine, VI, 1928.

Allen, Percy. Shakespeare and Chapman as Topical Dramatists. 1929.

—— The Case for Edward de Vere, 17th Earl of Oxford, as 'W. Shakespeare'. 1930.

—— The Oxford-Shakespeare Case Corroborated. 1931.

Rendall, G. H. Shakespeare Sonnets and Edward de Vere. 1930.

—— Shake-speare: Handwriting and Spelling. 1931.

III. THE WORKS OF SHAKESPEARE

A. COLLECTED WORKS

(1) THE FOUR FOLIOS

[*Bartlett*, pp. 50–4; *Ebisch and Schücking*, pp. 50–2; *Chambers*, vol. I, pp. 126–7.]

(a) The First Folio.

Mr. William Shakespeares Comedies, Histories, & Tragedies. Published according to the True Originall Copies. [Droeshout portrait.] London Printed by Isaac Jaggard, and Ed. Blount: 1623. [Colophon: Printed at the Charges of W. Jaggard, Ed. Blount, J. Smethweeke, and W. Aspley, 1623. The arrangement of the preliminary leaves varies in different copies. There are also occasional textual variations, e.g. Hamlet p. 278, Othello p. 333, due to corrections in the press. Ed. John Heming and Henry Condell, and contains: The Tempest; The Two Gentlemen of Verona; The Merry Wives of Windsor; Measure for Measure; The Comedy of Errours; Much Adoo about Nothing; Loves Labour Lost; Midsommer Nights Dreame; The Merchant of Venice; As You Like It; The Taming of the Shrew; Alls Well that Ends Well; Twelfe-Night; The Winters Tale; King John; Richard the Second; First part of Henry the Fourth; Second part of Henry the Fourth; Henry the Fift; First part of Henry the Sixt; Second part of Henry the Sixt; Third part of Henry the Sixt; Richard the Third; King Henry the Eight; Troylus and Cressida; Coriolanus; Titus Andronicus; Romeo and Juliet; Timon of Athens; Julius Caesar; Macbeth; Hamlet, Prince of Denmarke; King Lear; Othello, the Moore of Venice; Anthony and Cleopatra; Cymbeline.

Reprints: E. and J. Wright, 1807–8; Lionel Booth, 3 vols. 1864; Howard Staunton, photolithographic facs. 1866; J. O. Halliwell-Phillipps, reduced facs. 1876; Sir Sidney Lee, facs. Oxford, 1902; facs. 1910 (Methuen).

Studies: Sir Sidney Lee, Census of Extant Copies of the First Folio, Oxford, 1902 (also ptd in Lee's facs. edn, Oxford, 1902), and Notes and Additions to the Census, Oxford, 1906 (also in Library, VII, 1906); W. W. Greg, The Bibliographical History of the First Folio, Library, IV, 1903; G. W. Cole, The First Folio. A Further Word regarding the Correct Arrangement of its Preliminary Leaves, New York, 1909; Wolfgang Keller, Shakespeares literarisches Testament, E. Studien, L, 1916, Die Anordnung von Shakespeares Dramen in der ersten Folio-Ausgabe, Sh. Jb. LVI, 1920, and Shakespeare, Ben Jonson und die Folio, Sh. Jb. LX, 1924; Hans Hecht, Shakespeares Testament und die Vorrede der Schauspieler zur ersten Folio, Germanisch-romanische Monatsschrift, X, 1922; R. C. Rhodes, Shakespeare's First Folio, Oxford, 1923; A. W. Pollard, The Foundations of Shakespeare's Text, British Academy Lecture, 1923; Studies in the First Folio, ed. Sir Israel Gollancz, Shakespeare Ass., 1924 (includes: J. D. Wilson, The Task of Heminge and Condell; Sir Sidney Lee, A Survey of First Folios; W. W. Greg, The First Folio and Its Publishers); Max Förster, Zum Jubiläum der Shakespeare-Folio, Zeitschrift für Bücherfreunde, XVI, 1924; E. E. Stoll, On the Anniversary of the Folio (in Shakespeare Studies, New York, 1927).]

(b) The Second, Third and Fourth Folios.

Mr. William Shakespeares Comedies, Histories, and Tragedies. Published according to the true Originall Coppies. The second Impression. [Droeshout portrait.] London, Printed by Tho. Cotes, for Robert Allot, and are to be sold at his shop at the signe of the blacke Beare in Pauls Church-yard. 1632. [Some copies have one 'p' in 'Copies.' Others have John Smethwick, Richard Hawkins, William Aspley, or Richard Meighen for Allot. Reprint: facs. 1909 (Methuen). Studies: C. A. Smith, The Chief Differences between the First and Second Folios, E. Studien, XXX, 1902; R. M. Smith, The Variant Issues of Shakespeare's Second Folio and Milton's first published English Poem, Bethlehem, Pennsylvania, 1928.]

Mr. William Shakespeares Comedies, Histories, and Tragedies. Published according to the true Original Copies. The Third Impression. [Droeshout portrait.] London, Printed for Philip Chetwinde, 1663. [First issue of the Third Folio. Some copies are without the portrait.]

Mr. William Shakespear's Comedies, Histories, and Tragedies. Published according to the true Original Copies. The third Impression. And unto this Impression is added seven Plays, never before Printed in Folio. viz. Pericles Prince of Tyre. The London Prodigall. The History of Thomas Ld. Cromwell. Sir John Oldcastle Lord Cobham. The Puritan Widow. A Yorkshire Tragedy. The Tragedy of Locrine. London, Printed for P.C. 1664. [Second issue of the Third Folio with the seven additional plays. Reprint: facs. 1905 (Methuen).]

Mr. William Shakespear's Comedies, Histories, And Tragedies. Published according to the true Original Copies. Unto which is added, Seven Plays, Never before Printed in Folio: Viz. Pericles Prince of Tyre. The London Prodigal. The History of Thomas Lord Cromwel. Sir John Oldcastle Lord Cobham. The Puritan Widow. A Yorkshire Tragedy. The Tragedy of Locrine. The Fourth Edition. London, Printed for H. Herringman, E. Brewster, and R. Bentley, at the Anchor in the New Exchange, the Crane in St. Pauls Church-Yard, and in Russel-Street Covent-Garden. 1685. [Also found with two other imprints. Reprint: facs. 1904 (Methuen).]

(2) THE PRINCIPAL LATER EDITIONS

[See W. S. Brassington, Handlist of Collective Editions of Shakespeare's Works published before 1800, Stratford-on-Avon, 1898; H. B. Wheatley, Shakespeare's Editors from 1623 to the 20th Century, Trans. Bibliog. Soc. XIV, 1915–7; Allardyce Nicoll, The Editors of Shakespeare from First Folio to Malone (in Studies in the First Folio, Shakespeare Ass. 1924); H. L. Ford, Shakspeare, 1700–1740. A Collation of the Editions and Separate Plays, Lavorrick, 1935 (priv. ptd). Also Jaggard, pp. 498–558; Ebisch and Schücking, pp. 53–8; Chambers, vol. I, ch. ix. For adversaria, etc. see below, pp. 587–8].

Rowe, Nicholas. The Works of Mr. William Shakespear. Revis'd and Corrected, with an Account of the Life and Writings of the Author. 6 vols. 1709. [A 7th vol., including the poems and critical essays by Charles Gildon, followed in 1710, probably without authority. It was, however, rptd in the 3rd issue of Rowe's 2nd edn, 9 vols. 1714. See A. Jackson, Rowe's Edition of Shakespeare, Library, x, 1930.]

Pope, Alexander. The Works of Shakespear. Collated and Corrected. 6 vols. 1725–3. [A supplementary 7th vol. of the poems, ed. George Sewell, followed in 1725.] Rptd 8 vols. Dublin, 1725–6; 10 vols. 1728; 10 vols. 1728 (corrected and adding Pericles and the spurious plays); 9 vols. 1731 (plays only); 8 vols. 1734–6 (plays only); 9 vols. 1635 (for 1735; plays only); 16 vols. Glasgow, 1752–7; 8 vols. Glasgow, 1766; 9 vols. Birmingham, 1768. [See T. R. Lounsbury, The First Editors of Shakespeare (Pope and Theobald), 1906; Hans Schmidt, Die Shakespeare-Ausgabe von Pope, Giessen, 1912.]

Theobald, Lewis. The Works of Shakespeare. Collated with the Oldest Copies, and Corrected; with Notes, Explanatory and Critical. 7 vols. 1733; 7 vols. Dublin, 1739; 8 vols. 1740; 8 vols. 1752; 8 vols. 1757; 8 vols. 1762; 8 vols. 1767; 12 vols. 1772; 8 vols. 1773; 12 vols. [1777?]. [Plays only. See J. C. Collins, The Porson of Shakespearean Critics (in Essays and Studies, 1895); T. R. Lounsbury, The First Editors of Shakespeare (Pope and Theobald), 1906; R. F. Jones, Lewis Theobald, New York, 1919; Wendel Mertz, Die Shakespeare-Ausgabe von Theobald, Giessen, 1925.]

Hanmer, Sir Thomas. The Works of Shakespear. Carefully revised and corrected. 6 vols. Oxford, 1744–3 (re-issued 1744–6); 6 vols. 1745; 9 vols. 1747; 9 vols. 1748; 9 vols. 1750–1; 9 vols. 1760; 6 vols. Oxford, 1770–1 (also 1771; adds Theobald's and Capell's variant readings, Pope's preface, Rowe's life, new notes by Percy, Warton and John Hawkins, and Collins's verse epistle). [Plays only.]

Warburton, William. The Works of Shakespear. The Genuine Text, collated with all the Former Editions and then corrected and emended, is here settled; being restored from the Blunders of the First Editors, and the Interpolations of the Two Last: with a Comment and Notes, Critical and Explanatory, by Mr. Pope and Mr. Warburton. 8 vols. 1747; 8 vols. Dublin, 1747. [Plays only.]

[Blair, Hugh.] The Works of Shakespear. In which the Beauties observed by Pope, Warburton, and Dodd are pointed out. 8 vols. Edinburgh, 1753 (re-issued London, 1753); 8 vols. Edinburgh, 1761; 8 vols. Edinburgh, 1769 (bis); 8 vols. Edinburgh, 1771; 8 vols. [1771?]. [Plays only.]

Johnson, Samuel. The Plays of William Shakespeare. With the Corrections and Illustrations of Various Commentators, to which are added Notes. 8 vols. 1765; 10 vols. Dublin, 1766; 8 vols. 1768.

Steevens, George. Twenty of the Plays of Shakespeare. Being the Whole Number printed in Quarto during His Life-Time, or before the Restoration; collated where there were Different Copies and publish'd from the Originals. 4 vols. 1766. [Midsummer Night's Dream, 1600; Merry Wives, 1619, 1630, 1602; Much Ado, 1600; Merchant of Venice, 1600; Love's Labour's Lost, 1631; Taming of the Shrew, 1631; King Lear, 1608; King John, 1611; King Richard the Second, 1615; King Henry the Fourth, 1613; King Henry the Fourth Second Part, 1600; King Henry the Fifth, 1608; King Henry the Sixth [n.d.]; King Richard the Third, 1612; Titus Andronicus, 1611; Troilus and Cressida, 1609; Romeo and Juliet, 1597 and 1609; Hamlet, 1611; Othello, 1622; Sonnets, 1609; King Lear [Leir], 1605.]

[Capell, Edward.] Mr. William Shakespeare His Comedies, Histories, and Tragedies, set out by Himself in Quarto or by the Players His Fellows in Folio and now faithfully republish'd with an Introduction. Whereunto will be added, in some Other Volumes, Notes Critical and Explanatory and a Body of Various Readings. 10 vols. 1767–8. [The promised Notes and Various Readings did not appear until 1779–83 (3 vols.), though a first part came out in [1774].]

Johnson, Samuel and Steevens, George. The Plays of William Shakespeare, With the Corrections and Illustrations of Various Commentators; to which are added Notes by Samuel Johnson and George Steevens. With an Appendix [by Richard Farmer]. 10 vols. 1773. [Based upon Johnsons edn.]

[Steevens, George.] The Plays of William Shakespeare. With the Corrections and Illustrations of Various Commentators; to which are added Notes by Samuel Johnson and George Steevens. The Second Edition, revised and augmented. 10 vols. 1778. [Includes Malone's Attempt to Ascertain the Order in which the Plays attributed to Shakespeare were Written. Malone also added a Supplement, 2 vols. 1780, with notes, the first draft of his History of the Stage, and the poems and doubtful plays. He added a further Appendix in 1783.]

[Reed, Isaac.] The Plays of William Shakespeare. With the Corrections and Illustrations of Various Commentators; to which are added Notes by Samuel Johnson and George Steevens. Third Edition, revised and augmented by the Editor of Dodsley's Collection of Old Plays. 10 vols. 1785. [Includes notes by Malone.]

Malone, Edmond. The Plays and Poems of William Shakespeare, collated verbatim with the most Authentick Copies. With the Corrections and Illustrations of Various Commentators, to which are added, an Essay on the Chronological Order of his Plays; an Essay relative to Shakespeare and Jonson; a Dissertation on the Three Parts of King Henry VI; an Historical Account of the English Stage; and Notes by E. Malone. 10 vols. 1790.

[Steevens, George.] The Plays of William Shakespeare. With the Corrections and Illustrations of Various Commentators. To which are added Notes by Samuel Johnson and George Steevens. The Fourth Edition. Revised and augmented with a Glossarial Index. 15 vols. 1793.

The Plays and Poems of William Shakespeare. Corrected from the latest and best London Editions, with Notes, by Samuel Johnson. To which are added, A Glossary and the Life of the Author. 8 vols. Philadelphia, 1795–6. [First American edn.]

Wagner, C. The Dramatic Works of Shakespeare. 8 vols. Brunswick, 1797–1801. [First continental edn.]

Reed, Isaac. The Plays of William Shakespeare. With the Corrections and Illustrations of Various Commentators. To which are added, Notes by Samuel Johnson and George Steevens. Fifth Edition. Revised and augmented by Isaac Reed, with a Glossarial Index. 21 vols. 1803. [First variorum edn. Embodies Steevens's last corrections.]

[Bowdler, Thomas.] The Family Shakespeare. 4 vols. Bath, 1807. [20 plays.]

Reed, Isaac. The Plays of William Shakespeare. With the Corrections and Illustrations of Various Commentators. To which are added Notes by Samuel Johnson and George Steevens. Revised and augmented by Isaac Reed. Sixth Edition. 21 vols. 1813. [Second variorum edn.]

[Boswell, James.] The Plays and Poems of William Shakespeare, with the Corrections and Illustrations of Various Commentators, comprehending a Life of the Poet, and an Enlarged History of the Stage. 21 vols. 1821. [Third variorum edn. Based upon Malone's edn and his MS collections.]

Harness, W. The Dramatic Works. 8 vols. 1825.

Singer, S. W. The Dramatic Works. 10 vols. 1826. [Includes Life by C. Symmons.]

Campbell, Thomas. The Dramatic Works. 1838. [With Life and Remarks.]

Knight, Charles. The Pictorial Edition of the Works. 8 vols. 1838–43; 8 vols. 1864–7. [Introductory notices, notes, variant readings, glossary, biography, music to the songs and many wood engravings. Knight was also responsible for several later edns.]

Collier, J. P. The Works. The Text formed from an entirely New Collation of the Old Editions. With the Various Readings, Notes, a Life of the Poet, and a History of the Early English Stage. 8 vols. 1842–4; 8 vols. 1844–53; 6 vols. 1858 (as Comedies, Histories, Tragedies, and Poems); 8 vols. 1878 (as Plays and Poems). [The forged Notes and Emendations from Early Manuscript Corrections in a Copy of the Folio, 1632 were issued as a supplemental vol. in 1853.]

Verplanck, G. C. Shakespeare's Plays, with His Life, Critical Introductions and Notes, Original and Selected. 3 vols. New York, [1844]–7.

Hudson, H. N. The Works. 11 vols. Boston, 1851–6.

—— The Complete Works. 20 vols. Boston, 1880–1. (Harvard edn.)

Halliwell[-Phillipps], J. O. The Works. The Text formed from a New Collation of the Early Editions: to which are added All the Original Novels and Tales on which the Plays are founded; Copious Archaeological Annotations; an Essay on the Formation of the Text; and a Life of the Poet. 16 vols. 1853–65.

Delius, Nicolaus. Shakespeares Werke. 2 vols. Elberfeld, 1854; 7 vols. Elberfeld, 1882.

Lloyd, W. W. Dramatic Works. 10 vols. 1855–6. [Based on Singer's edn, with new Life and Critical Essays.]

Dyce, Alexander. The Works. The Text revised. 6 vols. 1857; 9 vols. 1864–7 (adds Glossary); 10 vols. 1895–1901. [Life, notices of early edns, account of the plays.]

White, R. G. The Works. 12 vols. Boston, 1857–66.

—— The Riverside Shakespeare. 3 vols. Boston, 1883.

Staunton, Howard. The Plays. 3 vols. 1858–60; 6 vols. 1860; 6 vols. 1894.

Cowden Clarke, Mary. Shakespeare's Works. 2 vols. New York, 1860; 4 vols. 1864 (with C. Cowden Clarke's assistance).

Clark, W. G., Glover, J. and Wright, W. A. The Works. 9 vols. Cambridge, 1863–6; 9 vols. 1891–3 (rev.). [The 'Cambridge' Shakespeare; the 'Globe' edn, based upon it, 1 vol. 1864, etc.]

Marsh, J. B. The Reference Shakespeare. 1864. [Plays only.]

Clark, W. G. and Wright, W. A. Shakespeare's Select Plays. 10 vols. Oxford, 1868–83. (Clarendon Press edn.)

Furness, H. H. and Furness, H. H. jr. A New Variorum Edition of the Works of Shakespeare. Philadelphia, 1871–. [The fullest of all edns of the plays. The following vols. have appeared: Romeo and Juliet; Macbeth; Hamlet, 2 vols.; King Lear; Othello; Merchant of Venice; As You Like It; Tempest; Midsummer Night's Dream; Winter's Tale; Much Ado; Twelfth Night; Love's Labour's Lost; King Richard III; Antony and Cleopatra; Julius Caesar; King John; Cymbeline; Coriolanus; Henry IV.] (New Variorum).

Rolfe, W. J. The Works. 40 vols. New York, 1871–96.

Furnivall, F. J. The Leopold Shakespeare. 1877.

Furnivall, F. J. et al. Plays and Poems in Quarto. Facsimiles. 43 vols. 1880–91.

Dowden, Edward. The Works. 12 vols. 1882–3. (Parchment Lib.)

The Plays. 13 vols. 1886–91. [Falcon edn. Separate plays by various editors including H. C. Beeching, A. C. Bradley, Sir E. K. Chambers, O. Elton.] (Falcon.)

Irving, Sir Henry and Marshall, F. A. The Henry Irving Shakespeare. 8 vols. 1888–90, 1906. [With stage history of each play.]

Morgan, Appleton, et al. The Comedies, Histories and Tragedies. 22 vols. New York Shakespeare Soc. 1888–1906. [Parallel texts of the plays from the Quartos and Folio.] (Bankside.)

Verity, A. W. The Pitt Press Shakespeare. 13 vols. Cambridge, 1890–1905. [Incomplete. Much Ado, ed. G. Sampson, 1923.]

Craig, W. J. The Oxford Shakespeare. [1891], etc. [Also in 3 vols. with general introduction by A. C. Swinburne and separate introductions to the various plays and poems by E. Dowden.]

The Warwick Shakespeare. 13 vols. 1893–8. [Incomplete. Separate plays by various editors including F. S. Boas, Sir E. K. Chambers, C. H. Herford, G. C. Moore Smith, etc.] (Warwick.)

Gollancz, Sir Israel. The Temple Shakespeare. 40 vols. 1894–6, etc.

Craig, W. J., Case, R. H. et al. The Arden Shakespeare. 37 vols. 1899–1924. [The best annotated edn of the separate plays. W. O. Brigstocke, All's Well; J. W. Holme, As You Like It; Henry Cunningham, Comedy of Errors, Macbeth, Midsummer Night's Dream; W. J. Craig and R. H. Case, Coriolanus; Edward Dowden, Cymbeline, Hamlet, Romeo and Juliet; Michael Macmillan, Julius Caesar; R. P. Cowl and A. E. Morgan, 1 Henry IV; R. P. Cowl, 2 Henry IV; H. A. Evans, Henry V; H. C. Hart and C. K. Pooler, 1, 2, 3 Henry VI; C. K.

Pooler, Henry VIII, Merchant of Venice, Sonnets and Poems; I. B. John, King John, Richard II; A. H. Thompson, Richard III; H. C. Hart, Love's Labour's Lost, Merry Wives, Measure for Measure, Othello; W. J. Craig, King Lear; G. R. Trenery, Much Ado; K. Deighton, Pericles, Timon of Athens, Troilus and Cressida; R. W. Bond, Taming of the Shrew, Two Gentlemen; Morton Luce, Tempest, Twelfth Night; H. B. Baildon, Titus Andronicus; F. W. Moorman, Winter's Tale.] (Arden.)

Herford, C. H. The Works. 10 vols. 1899–1900. (Eversley edn.)

Henley, W. E. and Raleigh, Sir W. The Works. 10 vols. 1901–4. (Edinburgh Folio edn.)

Porter, Charlotte and Clarke, H. A. The Complete Works. 13 vols. New York, 1903–8. [Pembroke edn. Introduction by J. C. Collins.]

—— William Shakespeare. First Folio Edition. 40 vols. New York, 1903–12. [American First Folio edn. Plays only.]

Neilson, W. A. The Complete Dramatic and Poetic Works. Boston, 1906. (Cambridge edn.)

Bullen, A. H. The Works. 10 vols. Stratford-on-Avon. 1907. [Stratford Town edn. Includes: Henry Davey, Memoir of Shakespeare; J. J. Jusserand, Ben Jonson's Views on Shakespeare's Art; Robert Bridges, On the Influence of the Audience; H. C. Beeching, On the Religion of Shakespeare, and On the Sonnets; Sir E. K. Chambers, The Stage of the Globe; M. H. Spielmann, Portraits of Shakespeare.]

Furnivall, F. J. and Boswell-Stone, W. G. The Old Spelling Shakespeare. 17 vols. 1907–12. [Incomplete.]

Gordon, G. S. Nine Plays: Merchant of Venice, Midsummer Night's Dream, As You Like It, The Tempest, King Richard II, King Henry V, Julius Caesar, Hamlet, and Macbeth. Oxford, 1908.

Lee, Sir Sidney. The Works. 20 vols. 1910. (Caxton edn.)

Neilson, W. A., Thorndike, A. H. et al. The Tudor Shakespeare. 40 vols. New York, 1911–3. (Tudor.)

Herford, C. H. et al. Heath's Shakespear. [1915]–. (Heath.)

Cross, W. L., Brooke, C. F. T., et al. The Yale Shakespeare. 40 vols. New Haven, 1918–28. [C. B. Tinker, Comedy of Errors; K. Young, Two Gentlemen; G. V. Santvoord, Merry Wives; C. F. T. Brooke, Much Ado, 1, 2, 3 Henry VI, Coriolanus; W. L. Cross and C. F. T. Brooke, Love's Labour's Lost; W. H. Durham, Midsummer Night's Dream, Romeo and Juliet, Measure for Measure; W. L. Phelps, Merchant of Venice, King

Lear; J. R. Crawford, As You Like It, Hamlet, Richard III; H. T. E. Perry, Taming of the Shrew; G. H. Nettleton, Twelfth Night; F. E. Pierce, Winter's Tale; L. M. Buell, Richard II; S. B. Hemingway, 1, 2 Henry IV, Cymbeline; R. D. French, Henry V, Comedy of Errors; S. T. Williams, Timon of Athens, King John; L. Mason, Julius Caesar, Othello; C. M. Lewis, Macbeth; H. S. Canby, Antony and Cleopatra; E. B. Reed, Sonnets; A. M. Witherspoon, Titus Andronicus; J. M. Berdan and C. F. T. Brooke, Henry VIII; A. E. Case, All's Well; A. R. Bellinger, Pericles; N. B. Paradise, Troilus and Cressida; Albert Feuillerat, Venus and Adonis and the Other Poems.] (*Yale*.)

Quiller-Couch, Sir A. T. and Wilson, J. D. The Works of Shakespeare. Cambridge, 1921–. [New Cambridge edn. The following vols. have appeared: Tempest, Two Gentlemen, Merry Wives, Measure for Measure, Comedy of Errors, Much Ado, Love's Labour's Lost, Midsummer Night's Dream, Merchant of Venice, As You Like It, Taming of the Shrew, All's Well, Twelfth Night, Winter's Tale, Hamlet, King John.] (*New Cambridge*.)

Granville-Barker, H. The Players' Shakespeare. 1923–.

Farjeon, H. The Works of Shakespeare. 7 vols. 1929–34. (Nonesuch Press edn.)

Ridley, M. R. The New Temple Shakespeare. 39 vols. 1934–6.

Boas, G. The New Eversley Shakespeare. 1935–.

(3) EXTRACTS AND VULGARISATIONS

[For the adaptations of Shakespeare's plays by Dryden, Otway, Garrick, etc. the particular plays should be consulted in *Jaggard*. The Bankside Restoration Shakespeare, ed. J. A. Morgan, New York Shakespeare Soc. 1898–1908, reprints the more important. A full list of the various selections from Shakespeare will be found in *Jaggard*, pp. 560–84.]

[Allot, Robert.] Englands Parnassus, or the Choysest Flowers of our Moderne Poets. 1600. [Includes 79 extracts from Shakespeare.]

Gildon, Charles. The Most Beautiful Topics, Descriptions, and Similes that occur throughout Shakespeare's Plays. [In The Complete Art of Poetry, 2 vols. 1718.]

Dodd, William. The Beauties of Shakespear, regularly selected from each Play. With a General Index, digesting them under Proper Heads. 2 vols. 1752; 2 vols. 1757 (with addns); 2 vols. Dublin, 1773; 3 vols. 1780 ('with the Author's Last Corrections'), etc.

Lamb, Charles [and Mary]. Tales from Shakespeare, designed for the Use of Young Persons. 2 vols. 1807, 1810, 1816, 1822, etc.

Shakespeare Anthology: Poems, Poetical Passages, Lyrics. 1936. (Nonesuch Press.)

B. THE PLAYS

[Arranged in the chronological order of composition adopted in *Chambers*.]

(1) THE QUARTOS

[*Chambers* has a Table of Quartos, vol. II, pp. 394–6.]

Collection of Lithographic Facsimiles of the Early Quarto Editions of the Separate Works of Shakespeare by E. W. Ashbee. Ed. J. O. Halliwell[-Phillipps], 48 vols. 1862–76.

Shakspere Quarto Facsimiles. Issued under the Superintendence of F. J. Furnivall, 43 vols. 1880–9. [Photo-lithographic facsimiles by William Griggs with introductions by various editors.]

Fleay, F. G. Tabular View of the Quarto Editions of Shakespeare's Works, 1593–1630. Trans. New Shakspere Soc. I, 1874.

Wagner, Albrecht. Eine Sammlung von Shakespeares Quartos in Deutschland. Ang. xxv, 1902.

Wheatley, H. B. Post-Restoration Quartos of Shakespeare's Plays. Library, IV, 1913.

Bartlett, Henrietta and Pollard, A. W. A Census of Shakespeare's Plays in Quarto, 1594–1709. New Haven, 1916. [See also Henrietta Bartlett, First Editions of Shakespeare's Quartos, Library, XVI, 1935.]

Greg, W. W. On Certain False Dates in Shakespearian Quartos. Library, IX, 1908.

Jaggard, William. False Dates in Shakespearian Quartos. Library, X, 1909.

Neidig, W. J. The Shakespeare Quartos of 1619. MP. VIII, 1910.

—— False Dates on Shakespeare Quartos. Century Mag. LXXX, 1910.

Huth, A. H. and Pollard, A. W. On the Supposed False Dates in Certain Shakespeare Quartos. Library, I, 1910.

(2) THE PLAYS INCLUDED IN THE FOLIO OF 1623

[I, II, III Henry the Sixth; Richard the Third; The Comedy of Errors; Titus Andronicus; The Taming of the Shrew; The Two Gentlemen of Verona; Love's Labour's Lost; Romeo and Juliet; Richard the Second; A Midsummer Night's Dream; King John; The Merchant of Venice; I, II Henry the Fourth; Much Ado about Nothing; Henry the Fifth; Julius Caesar; As You Like It; Twelfth Night; Hamlet; The Merry Wives of Windsor; Troilus and Cressida; All's Well that Ends

Well; Measure for Measure; Othello; King Lear; Macbeth; Antony and Cleopatra; Coriolanus ; Timon of Athens; Cymbeline; The Winter's Tale; The Tempest; Henry the Eighth.]

I, II, III Henry the Sixth

[*Jaggard*, pp. 342–6; *Bartlett*, pp. 121–3; *Ebisch and Schücking*, pp. 196–8; *Chambers*, vol. I, pp. 273–93.]

The First part of the Contention betwixt the two famous Houses of Yorke and Lancaster, with the death of the good Duke Humphrey: And the banishment and death of the Duke of Suffolke, and the Tragicall end of the proud Cardinall of Winchester, with the notable Rebellion of Jacke Cade: And the Duke of Yorkes first claime unto the Crowne. London. Printed by Thomas Creed, for Thomas Millington, and are to be sold at his shop under Saint Peters Church in Cornwall. 1594. [Facsimile: F. J. Furnivall, 1891.]

The First part of the Contention betwixt the two famous houses of Yorke and Lancaster. 1600.

The true Tragedie of Richard Duke of Yorke, and the death of good King Henrie the Sixt, with the whole contention betweene the two Houses Lancaster and Yorke, as it was sundrie times acted by the Right Honourable the Earle of Pembroke his servants. Printed at London by P[eter] S[hort] for Thomas Millington, and are to be sold at his shoppe under Saint Peters Church in Cornwal. 1595. [Facsimile: T. Tyler, 1891.]

The True Tragedie of Richarde Duke of Yorke, and the death of good King Henrie the sixt. 1600.

The Whole Contention betweene the two Famous Houses, Lancaster and Yorke. With the Tragicall ends of the good Duke Humfrey, Richard Duke of Yorke, and King Henrie the sixt. Divided into two Parts: And newly corrected and enlarged. Written by William Shakespeare, Gent. Printed at London, for T[homas] P[avier]. [1619.] [Facsimile: F. J. Furnivall, 2 pts, 1886.]

Modern editions: C. W. Thomas, New York, 1892 [2 Henry VI] (*Bankside*: parallel texts of Contention and F 1); A. Morgan, New York, 1892 [3 Henry VI] (*Bankside*: parallel texts of True Tragedie and F 1); H. C. Hart, 3 pts, 1909–10 (*Arden*); C. F. T. Brooke, 3 pts, New Haven, 1918–23 (*Yale*).

Shakspere's Holinshed. Ed. W. G. Boswell-Stone, 1896; 1907.

Malone, Edmond. A Dissertation on the Three Parts of King Henry VI, tending to show that these Plays were not originally written by Shakespeare. 1787; 1792 (expanded). [Rptd in third variorum Shakespeare, ed. J. Boswell, vol. XVIII, 1821.]

Knight, Charles. An Essay on the Three Parts of King Henry VI, and King Richard III. [In Pictorial Shakespeare, vol. VII, 1843.]

White, R. G. An Essay on the Authorship of the Three Parts of King Henry VI. [In his edn of Shakespeare, vol. VII, Boston, 1859.]

Ulrici, Hermann. Christopher Marlowe und Shakespeares Verhältnis zu ihm. Sh. Jb. I, 1865.

Fleay, F. G. Who wrote Henry VI? Macmillan's Mag. XXXIII, 1875.

Lee, Jane. On the Authorship of the 2nd and 3rd Parts of Henry VI, and their Originals. Trans. New Shakspere Soc. 1876.

Phipson, Emma. The Natural History Similes in Henry VI. Trans. New Shakspere Soc. pt 3, 1877–9.

Delius, Nicolaus. Zur Kritik der Doppeltexte des Shakespeareschen King Henry VI (Part II–III). Sh. Jb. XV, 1880.

Henneman, J. B. The Episodes in Shakespeare's 1 Henry VI. PMLA. XV, 1900.

Courthope, W. J. On the Authenticity of Some of the Early Plays Assigned to Shakespeare. [In A History of English Poetry, vol. IV, 1903.]

Schmidt, Karl. Margareta von Anjou vor und bei Shakespeare. Berlin, 1906.

Conrad, Hermann. Entstehung des 2. und 3. Teiles von Shakespeares Heinrich VI. Zeitschrift für französischen und englischen Unterricht, VIII, 1909.

Krecke, G. Die englischen Bühnenbearbeitungen von Shakespeares 'King Henry VI.' Rostock, 1911.

Brooke, C. F. T. The Authorship of the 2nd and 3rd Parts of King Henry VI. Trans. Connecticut Academy, XVII, 1912.

Seyferth, Paul. In welchem Verhältnis steht H6B zu 'The Contention' und H6C zu 'The True Tragedie'? Ang. XL, 1916.

Gray, H. D. The Purport of Shakespeare's Contribution to 1 Henry VI. PMLA. XXXII, 1917.

Pollard, A. W. The York and Lancaster Plays in the Shakespeare Folio. TLS. 19, 26 Sept. 1918.

von Schaubert, E. Drayton's Anteil an Heinrich VI, 2. und 3. Teil. Cöthen, 1920.

Keller, Wolfgang. Noch einmal Draytons angebliche Mitarbeit an Heinrich VI. E. Studien, LVII, 1923.

Alexander, Peter. 2 Henry VI and the Copy for The Contention. 1594. TLS. 9 Oct. 1924.

Alexander, Peter. 3 Henry VI and Richard, Duke of York. TLS. 13 Nov. 1924.

—— Shakespeare's Henry VI and Richard III. Cambridge, 1929. [Introduction by A. W. Pollard.]

Kingsford, C. L. Fifteenth Century History in Shakespeare's Plays. [In Prejudice and Promise in Fifteenth Century England, 1925.]

Gourvitch, J. Drayton and Henry VI. N. & Q. 18, 25 Sept. 1926.

Gaw, Allison. The Origin and Development of 1 Henry VI in Relation to Shakespeare, Marlowe, Peele, and Greene. Los Angeles, 1926.

Chambers, Sir E. K. The Relation of the Contention to 2 and 3 Henry VI. Proc. Oxford Bibliog. Soc. II, 1926.

—— Actors' Gag in Elizabethan Plays. TLS. 8 March 1928.

van Jan, Eduard. Das literarische Bild der Jeanne d'Arc (1429–1926). Halle, 1928.

Doran, Madeleine. Henry VI, Parts II and III, their Relation to the Contention and the True Tragedy. Iowa City, 1928.

van Dam, B. A. P. Shakespeare Problems nearing Solution. Henry VI and Richard III. E. Studies, XII, 1930. [A review of P. Alexander's book.]

Greer, C. A. The York and Lancaster Quarto-Folio Sequence. PMLA. XLVIII, 1933.

McKerrow, R. B. A Note on Henry VI, Part II, and The Contention of York and Lancaster. RES. IX, 1933.

King, L. The Use of Hall's Chronicles in the Folio and Quarto Texts of Henry VI. PQ. XIII, 1934.

Richard the Third

[*Jaggard*, pp. 368–77; *Bartlett*, pp. 19–22; *Ebisch and Schücking*, pp. 198–200; *Chambers*, vol. I, pp. 294–305.]

The Tragedy of King Richard the third. Containing, His treacherous Plots against his brother Clarence: the pittiefull murther of his iunocent [*sic*] nephewes: his tyrannicall usurpation: with the whole course of his detested life, and most deserved death. As it hath beene lately Acted by the Right honourable the Lord Chamberlaine his servants. At London Printed by Valentine Sims, for Andrew Wise, dwelling in Paules Chuch-yard [*sic*], at the Signe of the Angell. 1597 (anon.). [Facsimiles: J. O. Halliwell[-Phillipps], 1863; P. A. Daniel, 1886.]

The Tragedie of King Richard the Third. By William Shake-speare. 1598 (ed. facs. J. O. Halliwell[-Phillipps], 1867); 1602 ('Newly augmented,' but in fact identical with the earlier edns; ed. facs. J. O. Halliwell [-Phillipps], 1865, P. A. Daniel, 1888); 1605 (ed. facs. J. O. Halliwell[-Phillipps], 1863); 1612 (ed. facs. J. O. Halliwell[-Phillipps], 1871); 1622 (ed. facs. P. A. Daniel, 1889); 1629; 1634.

Modern editions: W. A. Wright, Oxford, 1880; E. A. Calkins, New York, 1891 (*Bankside*: parallel texts of Q 1 and F 1); G. Macdonald, 1896 (*Warwick*); A. H. Thompson, 1907 (*Arden*); H. H. Furness, jr., Philadelphia, 1908 (*New Variorum*); J. R. Crawford, New Haven, 1927 (*Yale*).

Shakspere's Holinshed. Ed. W. G. Boswell-Stone, 1896; 1907.

Oechelhäuser, Wilhelm. Essay über Richard III. Sh. Jb. III, 1868.

Fischer, Kuno. Shakespeares Charakterentwicklung Richards III. Heidelberg, 1868 and 1889.

Delius, Nicolaus. Über den ursprünglichen Text des King Richard III. Sh. Jb. VII, 1872.

Fleay, F. G. Who wrote Henry VI? Macmillan's Mag. XXXIII, 1875.

Spedding, James. On the Corrected Edition of Richard III. Trans. New Shakspere Soc. 1875.

Pickersgill, E. H. On the Quarto and Folio of Richard III. Trans. New Shakspere Soc. 1875.

Koppel, R. Textkritische Studien über Shakespeares Richard III. und King Lear. Dresden, 1877.

Schmidt, Alexander. Quartos und Folio von Richard III. Sh. Jb. xv, 1880. [Rptd in Gesammelte Abhandlungen, Berlin, 1889.]

Lowell, J. R. Shakespeare's Richard III. [In Latest Literary Essays and Addresses, 1891.]

Churchill, G. B. Richard III up to Shakespeare. Berlin, 1900.

Hammond, E. P. The Tent Scene in Richard III. MLN. XVII, 1902.

Schmidt, K. Margareta von Anjou vor und bei Shakespeare. Berlin, 1906.

Pape, Otto. Über die Entstehung der ersten Quarto von Shakespeares Richard III. Erlangen, 1906.

—— Die erste Quarto von Richard III ein stenographische Raubdruck. Archiv für Stenographie, LVII, 1906.

Wood, A. I. P. The Stage History of Shakespeare's King Richard III. New York, 1909.

Koeppel, E. Shakespeares Richard III, und Senecas Troades. Sh. Jb. XLVII, 1911.

Wilhelm, Friedrich. Zu Seneca und Shakespeare. Archiv, CXXIX, 1912.

Law, R. A. Richard the Third, Act I, Scene 4. PMLA. XXVII, 1912.

Moriarty, W. D. The Bearing on Dramatic Sequence of the Varia in Richard III and King Lear. MP. x, 1913.

Campbell, O. J. A Dutch Analogue of Richard III, 1651. [In Shakespeare Studies by Members of the University of Wisconsin, Madison, 1916.]

—— The Position of The roode en witte Roos in the Saga of King Richard III. Madison, 1919.

Goetze, Gertrud. Die Richard-Anna-Szene in Shakespeares Richard III. Ang. XLI, 1917.

Pollard, A. W. The York and Lancaster Plays in the First Folio. TLS. 19, 26 Sept. 1918.

Robertson, J. M. The Authorship of Richard III. [In The Shakespeare Canon, vol. I, 1922.]

Babcock, R. W. An Introduction to the Study of the Text of Richard III. Stud. Phil. XXIV, 1927.

Alexander, Peter. Shakespeare's Henry VI and Richard III. Cambridge, 1929.

Greer, C. A. The Relation of Richard III to The True Tragedy of Richard Duke of York and The Third Part of Henry VI. Stud. Phil. XXIX, 1932.

Begg, E. Stud. Phil. XXXII, 1935. [Hall, Holinshed.]

Patrick, D. L. The Textual History of Richard III. Palo Alto, 1936.

The Comedy of Errors

[*Jaggard*, pp. 294–6; *Ebisch and Schücking*, pp. 194–5; *Chambers*, vol. I, pp. 305–12.]

Mr. William Shakespeares Comedies, Histories, & Tragedies. 1623. ['The Comedie of Errors' occupies pp. 85–100 of the Comedies.]

Modern editions: A. Morgan, New York, 1894 (*Bankside*); H. Cunningham, 1906 (*Arden*); Sir A. T. Quiller-Couch and J. D. Wilson, Cambridge, 1922 (*New Cambridge*); R. D. French, New Haven, 1926 (*Yale*).

Rouse, W. H. D. The Menaechmi, the Original of Shakespeare's 'Comedy of Errors.' The Latin Text together with the Elizabethan Translation. 1912. (Shakespeare Classics.)

von Friesen, H. Bemerkungen zu den Altersbestimmungen für einige Stücke von Shakespeare. Sh. Jb. II, 1867.

Isaac, H. Shakespeares Comedy of Errors und die Menächmen des Plautus. Archiv, LXX, 1883.

Gröne, J. Zwei neuentdeckte Quellen zu Shakespeares 'Comedy of Errors.' Sh. Jb. XXIX, 1894.

Roeder, K. Menechmi und Amphitruo im englischen Drama bis zur 1661. Leipzig, 1904.

Lang, Friedrich. Shakespeares 'Comedy of Errors' in englischer Bühnenbearbeitung. Rostock, 1909.

Robertson, J. M. The Authorship of The Comedy of Errors. [In The Shakespeare Canon, vol. II, 1923.]

Gill, E. M. A Comparison of the Characters in The Comedy of Errors with those in the Menaechmi. Texas University Stud. v, 1925.

Gaw, Allison. The Evolution of the Comedy of Errors. PMLA. XLI, 1926.

Baldwin, T. W. William Shakespeare adapts a Hanging. Princeton, 1931.

Charlton, H. B. Shakespeare's Recoil from Romanticism. John Rylands Lib. Bulletin, Jan .1931.

Titus Andronicus

[*Jaggard*, pp. 474–6; *Bartlett*, pp. 15–6; *Ebisch and Schücking*, pp. 191–3; *Chambers*, vol. I, pp. 312–22.]

The Most Lamentable Romaine Tragedie of Titus Andronicus: As it was Plaide by the Right Honourable the Earle of Darbie, Earle of Pembrooke and Earle of Sussex their Servants. London, Printed by John Danter, and are to be sold by Edward White & Thomas Millington, at the little North doore of Paules at the signe of the Gunne. 1594 (anon.). [The only copy known, now *penes* H. C. Folger, was discovered in Sweden in 1905.]

The most lamentable Romaine Tragedie of Titus Andronicus. 1600 (ed. facs. J. O. Halliwell[-Phillipps], 1867, A. Symons, 1885); 1611 (as The Most Lamentable Tragedie).

German version: Eine sehr klägliche Tragoedia von Tito Andronico und der hoffertigen Kayserin (in Engelische Comedien und Tragedien, 1620). Rptd W. Creizenach (in Die Schauspiele der englischen Komödianten, Berlin, 1889).

Dutch version: Vos, Jan. Aran en Titus, af Wraak en Weerwraak. 1641.

Modern editions: A. Morgan, New York, 1890 (*Bankside*: parallel texts of Q 2 and F 1); H. B. Baildon, 1904 (*Arden*); A. M. Witherspoon, New Haven, 1926 (*Yale*).

Kurz, Hermann. Zu Titus Andronicus. Sh. Jb. v, 1870.

Halliwell-Phillipps, J. O. Memoranda on Titus Andronicus. 1879.

Cohn, Albert. König Lear 1692 und Titus Andronicus 1699 in Breslau aufgeführt. Sh. Jb. XXIII, 1888.

Morgan, J. A. Shakespeareana. Vol. VI, New York, 1888.

Schroeer, Arnold. Über Titus Andronicus. Zur Kritik der neuesten Shakspereforschung. Marburg, 1891.

Koeppel, E. Beiträge zur Geschichte des elisabethanischen Dramas. IV. Titus Andronicus. E. Studien, XVI, 1892.

Varnhagen, H. Zur Vorgeschichte der Fabel von Shakespeares Titus Andronicus. E. Studien, XIX, 1894.

Grosart, A. B. Was Robert Greene substantially the Author of Titus Andronicus? E. Studien, XXII, 1896.

Sarrazin, Gregor. Germanische Heldensage in Shakespeares Titus Andronicus. Archiv, XCVII, 1896.

Crawford, Charles. The Date and Authenticity of Titus Andronicus. Sh. Jb. XXXVI, 1900.

Fuller, H. de W. The Sources of Titus Andronicus. PMLA. XVI, 1901.

Baker, G. P. 'Titus and Vespacia' and 'Titus and Ondronicus' in Henslowe's Diary. PMLA. XVI, 1901.

Robertson, J. M. Did Shakespeare write Titus Andronicus? A Study in Elizabethan Literature. 1905.

—— An Introduction to the Study of the Shakespeare Canon, proceeding on the Problem of Titus Andronicus. 1924. [An enlargement of the above.]

Keller, Wolfgang. Die neuaufgefundene Quarto des 'Titus Andronicus' von 1594. Sh. Jb. XLI, 1905.

Schreckhas, R. Über Entstehungzeit und Verfasser des 'Titus Andronicus.' Rostock, 1906.

Greg, W. W. Henslowe's Diary. Vol. II, 1908. [P. 159.]

—— Titus Andronicus. MLR. XIV, 1919.

Dibelius, Wilhelm. Zur Stoffgeschichte des Titus Andronicus. Sh. Jb. XLVIII, 1912.

Gray, H. D. The Authorship of Titus Andronicus. [In Flügel Memorial Volume, Palo Alto, 1916.]

—— Titus Andronicus Once More. MLN. XXXIV, 1919.

—— The Titus Andronicus Problem. Stud. Phil. XVII, 1920.

—— Shakespeare's Share in Titus Andronicus. PQ. V, 1926.

Brooke, C. F. T. Titus Andronicus and Shakespeare. MLN. XXXIV, 1919.

Parrott, T. M. Shakespeare's Revision of Titus Andronicus. MLR. XIV, 1919.

Granger, F. Shakespeare and the Legend of Andronicus. TLS. 1 April 1920. [See also subsequent correspondence.]

Symons, Arthur. Titus Andronicus and the Tragedy of Blood. [In Studies in the Elizabethan Drama, 1920.]

Rhodes, R. C. Titus and Vespasian. TLS. 17 April 1924. [See also subsequent correspondence.]

Chambers. Sir E. K. The First Illustration to Shakespeare. Library, V, 1925.

Clark, E. G. Titus and Vespasian. MLN. XLI, 1926.

Gray, A. K. Shakespeare and Titus Andronicus. Stud. Phil. XXV, 1928.

Bolton, J. S. G. The Authentic Text of Titus Andronicus. PMLA. XLIV, 1929.

—— Titus Andronicus: Shakespeare at Thirty. Stud. Phil. XXX, 1933.

McKerrow, R. B. A Note on Titus Andronicus. Library, XV, 1934.

The Taming of the Shrew

[*Jaggard*, pp. 456–62; *Ebisch and Schücking*, pp. 208–10; *Chambers*, vol. I, pp. 322–8.]

A Pleasant Conceited Historie, called The taming of a Shrew. As it was sundry times acted by the Right honorable the Earle of Pembrook his servants. Printed at London by Peter Short and are to be sold by Cutbert Burbie. at his shop at the Royall Exchange. 1594 (facsimiles: J. O. Halliwell [-Phillipps], 1876; F. J. Furnivall, 1886; *TFT*. 1912; reprints: T. Amyot, 1844; F. S. Boas, 1908); 1596; 1607. [Alternatively held to be the source or a 'bad quarto' of the F 1 play.]

A Wittie and Pleasant Comedie Called The Taming of the Shrew. As it was acted by his Majesties Servants at the Blacke Friers and the Globe. Written by Will. Shakespeare Printed by W. S. for John Smethwicke, and are to be sold at his Shop in Saint Dunstones Churchyard under the Diall. 1631. [Rptd from F 1.]

Modern editions: A. R. Frey, New York, 1888 (*Bankside*: parallel texts of A Shrew and F1); R. W. Bond, 1904 and 1929 (*Arden*); H. T. E. Perry, New Haven, 1921 (*Yale*); Sir A. T. Quiller-Couch and J. D. Wilson, Cambridge, 1928 (*New Cambridge*).

Hickson, S. The Taming of the Shrew. N. & Q. 26 Jan., 9 Feb., 30 March 1850.

Delius, Nicolaus. Shakespeares Taming of the Shrew. Elberfeld, 1864.

Köhler, Reinhold. Zu Shakespeares 'The Taming of the Shrew.' Sh. Jb. III, 1868.

Fleay, F. G. On the Authorship of The Taming of the Shrew. Trans. New Shakspere Soc. 1874.

Urbach, R. Das Verhältnis des Shakespeareschen Lustspiels 'The Taming of the Shrew' zu seinen Quellen. Rostock, 1877.

Weilen, Alexander von. Shakespeares Vorspiel zu der Widerspänstigen Zähmung. Frankfort, 1884.

Tolman, A. H. Shakspere's Part in The Taming of the Shrew. Strasburg, 1891.

—— What has become of Shakespeare's Play 'Love's Labour's Won'? Chicago, 1902.

Tolman, A. H. Views about Hamlet. Boston, 1904. [Reprints the above.]

Bolte, Johannes. Eine Parallele zu Shakespeares 'The Taming of the Shrew.' Sh. Jb. xxvii, 1892.

Schomburg, E. H. The Taming of the Shrew. Halle, 1904.

Kuhl, E. P. Shakespeare's Purpose in dropping Sly. MLN. xxxvi, 1921.

—— The Authorship of The Taming of the Shrew. PMLA. xl, 1925.

Robertson, J. M. Marlowe and Comedy. [In The Shakespeare Canon, vol. ii, 1923.]

Sykes, H. D. The Authorship óf The Taming of a Shrew, The Famous Victories of Henry V, and the Additions to Marlowe's Faustus. Shakespeare Ass. Pamphlet, 1919. [Rptd in Sidelights on Elizabethan Drama, 1924.]

Alexander, Peter. The Taming of a Shrew. TLS. 16 Sept. 1926.

Ashton, F. H. The Revision of the Folio Text of The Taming of the Shrew. PQ. vi, 1927.

van Dam, B. A. P. The Taming of a Shrew. E. Studies, x, 1928.

Charlton, H. B. The Taming of the Shrew. John Rylands Lib. Bulletin, July 1932.

The Two Gentlemen of Verona

[*Jaggard*, pp. 483–4; *Ebisch and Schücking*, p. 195; *Chambers*, vol. i, pp. 329–31.]

Mr. William Shakespeares Comedies, Histories, & Tragedies. 1623. [ˈThe Two Gentlemen of Verona' occupies pp. 20–38 of the Comedies.]

Modern editions: R. W. Bond, 1906 (*Arden*); Sir A. T. Quiller-Couch and J. D. Wilson, Cambridge, 1921 (*New Cambridge*); K. Young, New Haven, 1924 (*Yale*).

Fleay, F. G. On the Date and Composition of The Two Gentlemen of Verona. Trans. New Shakspere Soc. 1874. [With comment by F. J. Furnivall.]

Zupitza, Julius. Über die Fabel in Shakespeares Beiden Veronesern. Sh. Jb. xxiii, 1888.

Latham, Grace. Julia, Silvia, Hero, and Viola. Trans. New Shakspere Soc. pt 3, 1887–92.

Sarrazin, Gregor. Der Räuberwald in der Lombardei. Sh. Jb. xxxix, 1903.

Bründel, H. F. Shakespeares 'Two Gentlemen of Verona' in englischer Bühnenbearbeitung. Rostock, 1909.

Norpoth, Hugo. Metrisch-chronologische Untersuchung von Shakespeares 'Two Gentlemen of Verona.' Bonn, 1916.

Robertson, J. M. The Authorship of The Two Gentlemen of Verona. [In The Shakespeare Canon, vol. ii, 1923.]

Campbell, O. J. The Two Gentlemen of Verona and Italian Comedy. [In Michigan Studies in Shakespeare, Milton and Donne, New York, 1925.]

Harrison, T. P. Concerning The Two Gentlemen of Verona and Montemayor's Diana. MLN. xli, 1926.

Charlton, H. B. Romanticism in Shakespearian Comedy. John Rylands Lib. Bulletin, July 1930.

Wales, J. G. Shakespeare's Use of English and Foreign Elements in the Setting of the Two Gentlemen of Verona. Trans. Wisconsin Academy, xxvii, 1932.

Small, S. A. The Ending of The Two Gentlemen of Verona. PMLA. xlviii, 1933.

Love's Labour's Lost

[*Jaggard*, pp. 378–80; *Bartlett*, pp. 24–5; *Ebisch and Schücking*, pp. 193–4; *Chambers*, vol. i, pp. 331–8.]

A Pleasant Conceited Comedie Called, Loves labors lost. As it was presented before her Highnes this last Christmas. Newly corrected and augmented By W. Shakespere. Imprinted at London by W[illiam] W[hite] for Cutbert Burby. 1598. [Facsimiles: J. O. Halliwell[-Phillipps], 1869; F. J. Furnivall, 1880.]

Loves Labours lost. A Wittie And Pleasant Comedie, As it was Acted by his Majesties Servants at the Blacke-Friers and the Globe. Written By William Shakespeare. 1631.

Modern editions: H. H. Furness, Philadelphia, 1904 (*New Variorum*); I. H. Platt, New York, 1906 (*Bankside*: parallel texts of Q1 and F1); H. C. Hart, 1906 (*Arden*); H. B. Charlton, 1917 (*Heath*); Sir A. T. Quiller-Couch and J. D. Wilson, Cambridge, 1923 (*New Cambridge*); W. L. Cross and C. F. T. Brooke, New Haven, 1925 (*Yale*).

von Friesen, H. Bemerkungen zu den Altersbestimmungen für einige Stücke von Shakespeare. 3. Love's Labour's Lost. Sh. Jb. ii, 1867.

Halliwell-Phillipps, J. O. Memoranda on Love's Labour's Lost. 1879.

Lee, Sir Sidney. A New Study of Love's Labour's Lost. GM. xxv, 1880.

Fleay, F. G. Shakespeare and Puritanism. Ang. vii, 1884.

Pater, Walter. Love's Labour's Lost. [In Appreciations, 1889, etc.]

Sarrazin, Gregor. Die Entstehung von Shakespeares Verlorener Liebesmüh. Sh. Jb. xxxi, 1895.

McClumpha, C. F. Parallels between Shakespeare's Sonnets and Love's Labour's Lost. MLN. xv, 1900.

de Perott, J. Eine spanische Parallele zu 'Love's Labour's Lost.' Sh. Jb. XLIV, 1908.

Schult, F. Bühnenbearbeitungen von Shakespeare's 'Love's Labour's Lost.' Rostock, 1910.

Phelps, J. Father Parsons in Shakespeare. Archiv, CXXXIII, 1915.

Charlton, H. B. A Textual Note on Love's Labour's Lost. Library, VIII, 1917.

—— A Disputed Passage in Love's Labour's Lost. MLR. XII, 1917.

—— The Date of Love's Labour's Lost. MLR. XIII, 1918.

Robertson, J. M. Love's Labour's Lost. [In Shakespeare and Chapman, 1917.]

Gray, H. D. The Original Version of Love's Labour's Lost. Palo Alto, 1918.

Roberts, J. H. The Nine Worthies. MP. XIX, 1921–2.

Gray, A. K. The Secret of Love's Labour's Lost. PMLA. XXXIX, 1924.

Campbell, O. J. Love's Labour's Lost re-studied. [In Michigan Studies in Shakespeare, Milton and Donne, New York, 1925.]

Bayley, A. R. Or Mons, the Hill. N. & Q. 6, 13 June, 1925.

Granville-Barker, H. Prefaces to Shakespeare. Ser. 1, 1927.

Eichler, Albert. 'Love's Labour's Lost' und 'As You Like It' als Hofaufführungen. E. Studien, LXIV, 1929.

Taylor, R. The Date of Love's Labour's Lost. New York, 1932.

Yates, F. A. A Study of Love's Labour's Lost. Cambridge, 1936.

Boughner, D. G. Don Armado as a Gallant. Revue anglo-américaine, Oct. 1935.

Romeo and Juliet

[*Jaggard*, pp. 442–50; *Bartlett*, pp. 22–4; *Ebisch and Schücking*, pp. 202–5; *Chambers*, vol. I, pp. 338–47.]

An Excellent conceited Tragedie of Romeo and Juliet. As it hath been often (with great applause) plaid publiquely, by the right Honourable the L. of Hunsdon his Servants. London, Printed by John Danter. 1597. [Facsimile: H. A. Evans, 1886. Reprints: P. A. Daniel, New Shakspere Soc. 1874; W. A. Wright (Cambridge Shakespeare, vol. IX, 1893). Modern edition: F. G. Hubbard, Madison, 1924.] (The 'bad' quarto.)

The Most Excellent and lamentable Tragedie, of Romeo and Juliet. Newly corrected, augmented, and amended: As it hath bene sundry times publiquely acted, by the right Honourable the Lord Chamberlaine his Servants. London Printed by Thomas Creede, for Cuthbert Burby, and are to be sold at his shop neare the Exchange. 1599.

[Facsimile: H. A. Evans, 1886. Reprint: P. A. Daniel, New Shakspere Soc. 1874. Modern edition: P. A. Daniel, New Shakspere Soc. 1875.] (The 'good' quarto.)

The Most Excellent and Lamentable Tragedie, of Romeo and Juliet. 1609; n.d. (2 issues of title, 2nd adding 'Written by W. Shakespeare,' ed. facs. H. A. Evans, 1887); 1637.

German version: Romio und Julietta. [Ptd A. Cohn, Shakespeare in Germany, 1865, with trn, from Vienna Hofbibliothek MS 13107.]

Modern editions: T. Mommsen, Oldenburg, 1859 (parallel texts of Q1 and Q2); H. H. Furness, Philadelphia, 1871 and 1909 (*New Variorum*); P. A. Daniel, New Shakspere Soc. 1874 (parallel texts of Q1 and Q2); B. R. Field, New York, 1889 (*Bankside*: parallel texts); E. Dowden, 1900 (*Arden*); W. H. Durham, New Haven, 1917 (*Yale*).

Brooke's Romeus and Juliet. Ed. J. J. Munro, 1908. (Shakespeare Classics.)

Pace-Sanfelice, G. The Original Story of Romeo and Juliet. 1868.

Daniel, P. A. Brooke's Romeus and Juliet and Painter's Rhomeo and Julietta. New Shakspere Soc. 1875.

Schulze, K. P. Die Entwicklung der Sage von Romeo und Julia. Sh. Jb. XI, 1876.

—— The Jolly Goshawk. Sh. Jb. XIII, 1878.

Fleay, F. G. Romeo and Juliet. Macmillan's Mag. XXXVII, 1877.

Spalding, T. A. On the First Quarto of Romeo and Juliet. Trans. New Shakspere Soc. 1878.

Gericke, Robert. Romeo und Juliet nach Shakespeares Manuskript. Sh. Jb. XIV, 1879.

Delius, Nicolaus. Brookes episches und Shakespeares dramatisches Gedicht von Romeo und Juliet. Sh. Jb. XVI, 1881.

Dowden, E. Romeo and Juliet. [In Transcripts and Studies, 1888.]

Cohn, Albert. Adrian Sevin's Bearbeitung der Sage vom Romeo und Julia. Sh. Jb. XXIV, 1889.

Fränkel, Ludwig. Untersuchungen zur Entwicklungsgeschichte des Stoffes von Romeo und Julia. Zeitschrift für vergleichende Litteraturgeschichte, III, IV, 1890–1.

—— Shakespeare und das Tagelied. Hanover, 1893.

—— Neue Beiträge zur Geschichte des Stoffes von Shakespeares 'Romeo and Juliet.' E. Studien, XIX, 1894.

McClumpha, C. F. Shakespeare's Sonnets and Romeo and Juliet. Sh. Jb. XL, 1904.

Fuller, H. de W. Romeo and Juliette. MP. IV, 1906.

Smith, W. A Comic Version of Romeo and Juliette. MP. VII, 1909.

Hemingway, S. B. The Relation of A Midsummer Night's Dream to Romeo and Juliet. MLN. xxvi, 1911.

Gray, H. D. Romeo, Rosaline, and Juliet. MLN. xxix, 1914.

Schöttner, Adolf. Über die mutmassliche stenographische Entstehung der ersten Quarto von Shakespeares Romeo und Julia. Leipzig, 1918.

Wilson, J. D. and Pollard, A. W. The 'Stolne and Surreptitious' Shakespearian Texts. Romeo and Juliet (1597). TLS. 14 Aug. 1919.

Fischer, Rudolf. Quellen zu Romeo und Julia. Bonn, 1922.

Robertson, J. M. Romeo and Juliet. [In The Shakespeare Canon, vol. iii, 1925.]

Tilley, M. P. A Parody of Euphues in Romeo and Juliet. MLN. xli, 1926.

Hjort, G. The Good and Bad Quartos of Romeo and Juliet and Love's Labour's Lost. MLR. xxi, 1926.

van Dam, B. A. P. Did Shakespeare revise Romeo and Juliet? Ang. li, 1927.

Law, R. A. On Shakespeare's Changes of his Source Material in Romeo and Juliet. Texas University Stud. ix, 1929.

Moore, O. H. Le Rôle de Boaistuau dans le Développement de la Légende de Roméo et Juliette. Revue de Littérature comparée, Oct. 1929.

Granville-Barker, H. Prefaces to Shakespeare. Ser. 2, 1930.

Hauvette, H. La Morte vivante. Paris, 1933.

Richard the Second

[*Jaggard*, pp. 362–8; *Bartlett*, pp. 16–9; *Ebisch and Schücking*, p. 201; *Chambers*, vol. i, pp. 348–56.]

The Tragedie of King Richard the second. As it hath beene publikely acted by the right Honourable the Lorde Chamberlaine his Servants. London Printed by Valentine Simmes for Androw Wise, and are to be sold at his shop in Paules church yard at the signe of the Angel. 1597 (anon.). [Facsimiles: J. O. Halliwell[-Phillipps], 1862; W. A. Harrison, 1888.]

The Tragedie of King Richard the second. By William Shake-speare. 1598 (ed. facs. J. O. Halliwell[-Phillipps], 1869); 1598 (ed. facs. A. W. Pollard, 1916); 1608 (re-issued 1608 as 'With new additions of the Parliament Sceane, and the deposing of King Richard,' though the earlier issue also contains the new scene; ed. facs. J. O. Halliwell[-Phillipps], 1858, 1870, 1871, W. A. Harrison, 1888); 1615 (ed. facs. J. O. Halliwell[-Phillipps], 1870); 1634 (ed. facs. P. A. Daniel, 1887).

Modern editions: Sir E. K. Chambers, 1891 (*Falcon*); A. Waites, New York, 1892 (*Bankside*: parallel texts of Q1 and F1); C. H. Herford, 1893 (*Warwick*); I. B. John, 1912, 1925 (*Arden*); L. M. Buell, New Haven, 1921 (*Yale*).

Shakespeare's Holinshed. Ed. W. G. Boswell-Stone, 1896; 1907.

Die Quarto und Folio von Richard II. Sh. Jb. xv, 1880.

Elze, Karl. Alexandrines in The Winter's Tale and King Richard II. Halle, 1882.

—— Notes on King Richard II. E. Studien, xii, 1889.

Plomer, H. R. An Examination of Some Existing Copies of Hayward's King Henrie IV. Library, iii, 1902.

Moorman, F. W. Shakespeare's History-Plays and Daniel's Civile Wars. Sh. Jb. xl, 1904.

Allwardt, Wilhelm. Die englischen Bühnenbearbeitungen von Shakespeares King Richard II. Rostock, 1909.

Swinburne, A. C. Richard II. [In Three Plays of Shakespeare, 1909.]

Eidam, Christian. Über die Einleitung in Shakespeares Richard II. Die neueren Sprachen, xix, 1911–2.

Pollard, A. W. The Tragedy of King Richard II. 1916. [Introduction to facs. of Q3.]

Kohler, Josef. Die Staatsidee Shakespeares in Richard II. Sh. Jb. liii, 1917.

Robertson, J. M. The Authorship of Richard II. [In The Shakespeare Canon, vol. ii, 1923.]

Chambers, Sir E. K. The Date of Richard II. RES. i, 1925.

Albright, E. M. Shakespeare's Richard II and the Essex Conspiracy. PMLA. xlii, 1927.

—— Shakespeare's Richard II, Hayward's History of Henry IV and the Essex Conspiracy. PMLA. xlvi, 1931.

Kuhl, E. P. Shakespeare and Hayward. Stud. Phil. xxv, 1928.

Heffner, R. Shakespeare, Hayward and Essex. PMLA. xlv, 1930.

A Midsummer Night's Dream

[*Jaggard*, pp. 408–16; *Bartlett*, pp. 32–3; *Ebisch and Schücking*, pp. 206–8; *Chambers*, vol. i, pp. 356–63.]

A Midsommer nights dreame. As it hath beene sundry times publickely acted, by the Right honourable, the Lord Chamberlaine his servants. Written by William Shake-speare. Imprinted at London, for Thomas Fisher, and are to be soulde at his shoppe, at the Signe of the White Hart, in Fleete-streete. 1600. [Facsimiles: J. O. Halliwell[-Phillipps], 1864; J. W. Ebsworth, 1880.]

A Midsommer nights dreame. As it hath beene sundry times publikely acted, by the Right Honourable, the Lord Chamberlaine his servants. Written by William Shakespeare. Printed by James Roberts, 1600 [for 1619]. [Facsimiles: J. O. Halliwell[-Phillipps], 1865; J. W. Ebsworth, 1880.]

Modern editions: W. Reynolds, New York, 1890 (*Bankside*: parallel texts of Q1 and F1); H. H. Furness, Philadelphia, 1895 (*New Variorum*); Sir E. K. Chambers, 1897 (*Warwick*); H. Cunningham, 1905 (*Arden*); W. H. Durham, New Haven, 1918 (*Yale*); Sir A. T. Quiller-Couch and J. D. Wilson, Cambridge, 1924 (*New Cambridge*).

Sidgwick, Frank. The Sources and Analogues of A Midsummer Night's Dream. 1908. (Shakespeare Classics.)

Halliwell[-Phillipps], J. O. An Introduction to Shakespeare's Midsummer Night's Dream. 1841.
—— Illustrations of the Fairy Mythology of Shakespeare's Midsummer Night's Dream. Shakespeare Soc. 1845.
—— Memoranda on Shakespeare's Midsummer Night's Dream. 1879.

Halpin, N. J. Oberon's Vision in the Midsummer Night's Dream illustrated by a Comparison with Lyly's Endymion. Shakespeare Soc. 1843.

Elze, Karl. Zum Sommernachtstraum. Sh. Jb. III, 1868.

Kurz, Hermann. Nachlese. 2. Zum Sommernachtstraum. Sh. Jb. IV, 1869.

Krauss, Fritz. Eine Quelle zu Shakespeares Sommernachtstraum. Sh. Jb. XI, 1876.

ten Brink, B. Über den Sommernachtstraum. Vortrag. Sh. Jb. XIII, 1878.

Proescholdt, L. On the Sources of Shakespeare's Midsummer Night's Dream. Halle, 1878.

Schmidt, Alexander. Die ältesten Ausgaben des Sommernachtstraums. Königsberg, 1881.

Finkenbrink, G. An Essay on the Date, Plot and Sources of Shakespeare's A Midsummer Night's Dream. Part I: On the Date. Mühlheim, 1884.

Gaedertz, K. T. Zur Kenntnis der altenglischen Bühne. Bremen, 1888.

Flügel, E. Pyramys and Tysbe. Ang. XII, 1889.

Hart, G. Die Pyramus-und-Thisbe-Saga. Passau, 1889.

Würzner, A. Die Orthographie der beiden Quarto-Ausgaben von Shaksp3res Sommernachtstraum. Vienna, 1893.

Sarrazin, Gregor. Die Abfassungszeit des Sommernachtstraums. Archiv, XCV, 1895.
—— Szenerie und Staffage in Sommernachtstraum. Archiv, CIV, 1900.

Fränkel, L. Vor-Shakespearesches Pyramus and Thisbe-Stück? Sh. Jb. XXXIII, 1897.

Tobler, R. Shakespeares Sommernachtstraum und Montemayors Dramen. Sh. Jb. XXXIV, 1898.

Vollhardt, W. Die Beziehungen des Sommernachtstraums zum italienischen Schäferdrama. Leipzig, 1899.

von Westenholz, F. P. Shakespeares 'Gewonnene Liebesmüh.' Beilage zur Allgemeine Zeitung, 14 Jan. 1902.

Reich, Hermann. Der Mann mit dem Eselskopf. Ein Mimodrama vom klassischen Altertum verfolgt bis auf Shakespeare. Sh. Jb. XL, 1904.

Thiselton, A. E. Some Textual Notes on A Midsummer Night's Dream. 1904.

Greg, W. W. On Certain False Dates in Shakespearian Quartos. Library, IX, 1908.

Hemingway, S. B. The Relation of Midsummer Night's Dream to Romeo and Juliet. MLN. XXVI, 1911.

Chambers, Sir E. K. The Occasion of A Midsummer Night's Dream. [In A Book of Homage to Shakespeare, 1916.]

Lawrence, W. J. Shakespeare from a New Angle. Studies, VIII, 1919.
—— The Date of A Midsummer Night's Dream. TLS. 9 Dec. 1920.
—— A Plummet for Bottom's Dream. Fortnightly Rev. CXVII, 1922. [Rptd in Shakespeare's Workshop, Oxford, 1928.]

Lefranc, A. La Réalité dans 'A Midsummer Night's Dream.' [In Mélanges Bernard Bouvier, Paris, 1920.]

Rickert, Edith. Political Propaganda and Satire in A Midsummer Night's Dream. MP. XXI, 1923.

Eichler, Albert. Das Hofbühnenmässige in Shakespeares 'Midsummer Night's Dream.' Sh. Jb. LXI, 1925.

Priestley, J. B. Bully Bottom. [In The English Comic Characters, 1925.]

Spencer, Hazelton. A Nice Derangement. MLR. XXV, 1930.

Genouy, H. Considérations sur le 'Midsummer Night's Dream.' Revue de l'Enseignement des Langues vivantes, XLIX, 1932.

van Kranendonk, A. G. Spenserian Echoes in A Midsummer Night's Dream. E. Studies, XIV, 1932.

Charlton, H. B. A Midsummer Night's Dream. John Rylands Lib. Bulletin, XVII, 1933.

King John

[*Jaggard*, pp. 350–4; *Ebisch and Schücking*, pp. 210–1; *Chambers*, vol. I, pp. 364–7.]

Mr. William Shakespeares Comedies, Histories, & Tragedies. 1623. ['The Life and Death of King John' occupies pp. 1–22 of the Histories.]

Modern editions: F. G. Fleay, 1878; A. Morgan, New York, 1892 (*Bankside*: parallel texts); G. C. Moore Smith, 1900 (*Warwick*); I. B. John, 1907 (*Arden*); H. H. Furness, jr. Philadelphia, 1919 (*New Variorum*); S. T. Williams, New Haven, 1927 (*Yale*); J. D. Wilson, Cambridge, 1936 (*New Cambridge*).

The Troublesome Raigne of John King of England. 1591. The Second part of the troublesome Raigne of King John. 1591 (facsimiles: F. J. Furnivall, 2 pts, 1888; J. S. Farmer, *TFT*. 1911. Reprint: F. J. Furnivall and J. Munro, 1913); 1611 (as The First and second Part); 1622.

Rose, E. Shakespeare as an Adapter. Macmillan's Mag. XXXVIII, 1878.

Kopplow, Georg. Shakespeares 'King John' und seine Quellen. Kiel, 1900.

Moore Smith, G. C. Shakespeare's King John and The Troublesome Raigne. [In Furnivall Miscellany, 1901.]

Kerrl, Anna. Die metrischen Unterschiede von Shakespeares 'King John' und 'Julius Caesar.' Bonn, 1913.

Liebermann, Felix. Shakespeare als Bearbeiter des 'King John.' Archiv, CXLII, CXLIII, 1921–2.

Harrison, G. B. Shakespeare's Topical Significances. I. King John. TLS. 13 Nov. 1930.

The Merchant of Venice

[*Jaggard*, pp. 393–402; *Bartlett*, pp. .30–2; *Ebisch and Schücking*, pp. 211–3; *Chambers*, vol. I, pp. 368–75.]

The most excellent Historie of the Merchant of Venice. With the extreame crueltie of Shylocke the Jewe towards the sayd Merchant, in cutting a just pound of his flesh: and the obtayning of Portia by the choyse of three chests. As it hath beene divers times acted by the Lord Chamberlaine his Servants. Written by William Shakespeare. At London, Printed by J[ames] R[oberts] for Thomas Heyes, and are to be sold in Paules Church-yard, at the signe of the Greene Dragon. 1600. [Facsimiles: J. O. Halliwell[-Phillipps], 1870; F. J. Furnivall, 1887.]

The Excellent History of the Merchant of Venice. With the extreme cruelty of Shylocke the Jew towards the saide Merchant, in cutting a just pound of his flesh. And the obtaining of Portia, by the choyse of three Caskets. Written by W. Shakespeare. Printed by J. Roberts, 1600 (for 1619; ed. facs. J. O. Halliwell[-Phillipps], 1865, F. J. Furnivall, 1880); 1637 (re-issued 1652).

Modern editions: W. Reynolds, New York, 1888 (*Bankside*: parallel texts of Q1 and

F1); H. H. Furness, Philadelphia, 1888 (*New Variorum*); C. K. Pooler, 1905 and 1927 (*Arden*); W. L. Phelps, New Haven, 1923 (*Yale*); Sir A. T. Quiller-Couch and J. D. Wilson, Cambridge, 1926 (*New Cambridge*).

Elze, Karl. Zum Kaufmann von Venedig. Sh. Jb. VI, 1871.

Smith, L. T. The Bond-Story in the Merchant of Venice. Trans. New Shakspere Soc. 1875.

Lee, Sir Sidney. The Original of Shylock. GM. XXIV, 1880.

—— Elizabethan England and the Jews. Trans. New Shakspere Soc. 1888.

Grätz, H. Shylock in der Sage, im Drama und in der Geschichte. Krotoschin, 1880, 1888.

Bolte, Johannes. Jakob Rosefeldt's Moschus, eine Parallele zum Kaufmann von Venedig. Sh. Jb. XXI, 1886.

—— Der Jude von Venetien. Die älteste deutsche Bearbeitung des 'Merchant of Venice' [um 1690]. Sh. Jb. XXII, 1887.

—— Zur Shylock-Fabel. Sh. Jb. XXVII, 1892.

Clouston, W. A. Shylock and his Predecessors. Academy, 18 June, 6 Aug. 1887.

Hales, J. W. Shakespeare and the Jews. EHR. IX, 1894.

Dimock, A. The Conspiracy of Dr. Lopez. EHR. IX, 1894.

Mory, E. Marlowes Jude von Malta und Shakespeares Kaufmann von Venedig. Basle, 1897.

Eberstadt, Rudolf. Der Shylockvertrag und sein Urbild. Sh. Jb. XLIV, 1908.

Stoll, E. E. Shylock. JEGP. X, 1911. [Enlarged in Shakespeare Studies, New York, 1927.]

Brie, Friedrich. Zur Entstehung des Kaufmanns von Venedig. Sh. Jb. XLIX, 1913.

Creizenach, Wilhelm. Betrachtungen über den Kaufmann von Venedig. Sh. Jb. LI, 1915.

Baskervill, C. R. Bassanio as an Ideal Lover. [In Manly Anniversary Studies, Chicago, 1923.]

van Dam, B. A. P. The Text of the Merchant of Venice. Neophilologus, XIII, 1927.

Small, S. A. Shaksperean Character Interpretation: The Merchant of Venice. Göttingen, 1927.

—— 'The Jew.' MLR. XXVI, 1931.

Brown, B. D. Medieval Prototypes of Lorenzo and Jessica. MLN. XLIV, 1929.

Tretiak, A. The Merchant of Venice and the Alien Question. RES. V, 1929.

Granville-Barker, H. Prefaces to Shakespeare. Ser. 2, 1930.

Schlauch, Margaret. The Pound of Flesh Story in the North. JEGP. XXX, 1931.

Cardozo, J. L. The Background of Shakespeare's Merchant of Venice. E. Studies, XIV, 1932.

Roth, C. The Background of Shylock. RES. IX, 1933.

Wood, F. T. The Merchant of Venice in the Eighteenth Century. E. Studies, XV, 1933.

Charlton, H. B. Shakespeare's Jew. John Rylands Lib. Bulletin, XVIII, 1934.

Wilson, J. H. Granville's 'Stock-Jobbing Jew.' PQ. XIII, 1934.

Draper, J. W. MP. XXXIII, 1935. [Usury.]

I, II Henry the Fourth

[*Jaggard*, pp. 327–35; *Bartlett*, pp. 25–9; *Ebisch and Schücking*, pp. 214–5; *Chambers*, vol. I, pp. 375–84.]

Part I

[There are 4 leaves in the Folger collection which J. O. Halliwell[-Phillipps] considered to be a portion of the first and hitherto unknown edition of the First Part of Henry 4th, published by Wise early in the year 1598.']

The History of Henrie the fourth; With the battell at Shrewsburie, betweene the King and Lord Henry Percy, surnamed Henrie Hotspur of the North. With the humorous conceits of Sir John Falstalffe. At London, Printed by P. S[hort] for Andrew Wise, dwelling in Paules Churchyard, at the signe of the Angell. 1598. [Facsimiles: J. O. Halliwell[-Phillipps], 1866; H. A. Evans, 1881.]

The History of Henrie the Fourth; With the battell at Shrewsburie, betweene the King and Lord Henry Percy, surnamed Henry Hotspur of the North. With the humorous conceits of Sir John Falstalffe. Newly corrected by W. Shake-speare. 1599 (ed. facs. J. O. Halliwell[-Phillipps], 1861); 1604 (ed. facs. J. O. Halliwell[-Phillipps], 1871); 1608 (ed. facs. J. O. Halliwell[-Phillipps], 1867); 1613 (ed. facs. J. O. Halliwell[-Phillipps], 1867); 1622; 1632; 1639; 1700.

Modern editions: W. H. Fleming, New York, 1890 (*Bankside*: parallel texts); R. P. Cowl and A. E. Morgan, 1914 and 1923 (*Arden*); S. B. Hemingway, New Haven, 1917 (*Yale*), and Philadelphia, 1936 (*New Variorum*).

Part II

The Second part of Henrie the fourth, continuing to his death, and coronation of Henrie the fift. With the humours of sir John Falstaffe, and swaggering Pistoll. As it hath been sundrie times publikely acted by the right honourable, the Lord Chamberlaine his servants. Written by William Shakespeare. London Printed by V[alentine] S[immes] for Andrew Wise, and William Aspley. 1600. [III, i, originally omitted, is found in some copies in a cancel sheet of 6 leaves. Facsimiles: J. O. Halliwell[-Phillipps], 1866; H. A. Evans, 1882.]

Modern editions: W. H. Fleming, New York, 1890 (*Bankside*: parallel texts); S. B. Hemingway, New Haven, 1921 (*Yale*); R. P. Cowl, 1923 (*Arden*).

Parts I and II

King Henry the Fourth. Printed from a Contemporary Manuscript, circa 1610. Ed. J. O. Halliwell[-Phillipps], Shakespeare Soc. 1845. [The Dering MS, 'a compilation in a 17th century hand of scenes from Q5 of Part I and Q of Part II, probably for private performance, with alterations in the hand of Sir Edward Dering (1598–1644) of Surrenden, Kent' (*Chambers*).]

The Famous Victories of Henry the fifth; containing the Honourable Battell of Agincourt. 1598; ed. facs. P. A. Daniel, 1887.

Shakspere's Holinshed. Ed. W. G. Boswell-Stone, 1896; 1907.

Halliwell[-Phillipps], J. O. On the Character of Sir John Falstaff, as originally exhibited by Shakespeare in the Two Parts of King Henry IV. 1841.

Gairdner, J. On the Historical Element in Shakespeare's Falstaff. Fortnightly Rev. XIX, 1873. [Rptd in J. Gairdner's and J. Spedding's Studies in English History, Edinburgh, 1881.]

Hagena, K. Remarks on the Introductory Scene of 2 Henry IV. Trans. New Shakspere Soc. 1878.

Solly-Flood, F. The Story of Prince Henry of Monmouth and Chief-Justice Gascoign. Trans. Royal Hist. Soc. III, 1886.

Sarrazin, Gregor. Falstaff, Pistol, Nym und ihre Urbilder. [In Kleine Shakespeare-Studien, Berlin, 1902.]

Moorman, F. W. Shakespeare's History-Plays and Daniel's Civile Wars. Sh. Jb. XL, 1904.

Baeske, Wilhelm. Oldcastle-Falstaff in der englischen Literatur bis zu Shakespeare. Berlin, 1905.

Ainger, A. Sir John Falstaff. [In Lectures and Essays, 1905.]

Bradley, A. C. The Rejection of Falstaff. [In Oxford Lectures on Poetry, 1909.]

Harcourt, L. W. The Two Sir John Falstaffs. Trans. Royal Hist. Soc. IV, 1910.

Wrage, W. Englische Bühnenbearbeitungen von Shakespeares King Henry IV, Part I. Rostock, 1910.

Kingsford, C. L. The First English Life of Henry V. 1911.

Ax, H. The Relation of Shakespeare's Henry IV to Holinshed. Freiburg, 1912.

Stoll, E. E. Falstaff. MP. XII, 1914. [Rptd in Shakespeare Studies, New York, 1927.]

Cunliffe, J. W. The Character of Henry V as Prince and King. [In Columbia Shakespearian Studies, New York, 1916.]

Baker, H. T. The Two Falstaffs. MLN. xxxiv, 1919.

Tolman, A. H. Why did Shakespeare create Falstaff? PMLA. xxxiv, 1919.

Pollard, A. W. The Variant Settings in 2 Henry IV and their Spellings. TLS. 21 Oct. 1920.

Monaghan, James. Falstaff and his Forebears. Stud. Phil. xviii, 1921.

Spargo, J. W. An Interpretation of Falstaff. Washington University Stud. ix, 1922.

Morgan, A. E. Some Problems of Shakespeare's Henry IV. Shakespeare Ass. Pamphlet, 1924.

Cowl, R. P. Some Literary Allusions in Henry IV. TLS. 26 March 1925.

—— Echoes of Henry IV in Elizabethan Drama. TLS. 22 Oct. 1925.

—— Some 'Echoes' in Elizabethan Drama of Shakespeare's King Henry IV, Parts i and ii, considered in Relation to the Text of those Plays. Helsingfors, 1926.

—— King Henry IV and Other Plays. An Experiment with 'Echoes.' 1927.

—— Notes on the Text of King Henry IV. 1927.

—— Sources of the Text of King Henry IV. 1929.

Priestley, J. B. Falstaff and his Circle. [In The English Comic Characters, 1925.]

Morris, J. E. The Date of Henry IV. TLS. 28 Jan. 1926.

Bowling, W. G. The Wild Prince Hal in Legend and Literature. Washington University Stud. xiii, 1926.

Knowlton, E. C. Falstaff Redux. JEGP. xxv, 1926.

Law, R. A. Structural Unity in the Two Parts of Henry IV. Stud. Phil. xxiv, 1927.

Newdigate, B. H. Falstaff, Shallow and the Stratford Musters. London Mercury, xv, 1927.

Schücking, L. L. The Quarto of King Henry IV, Part ii. TLS. 25 Sept. 1930.

Taylor, M. A. Shakespeare and Gloucestershire. RES. vii, 1931.

Hartmann, Herbert. Prince Hal's 'Shew of Zeale.' PMLA. xlvi, 1931.

Cazamian, Louis. The Humor of Falstaff. Johns Hopkins Alumni Mag. xxiii, 1933.

Knights, L. C. Notes on Comedy. Scrutiny, ii, 1933.

Charlton, H. B. Falstaff. John Rylands Lib. Bulletin, xix, 1935.

Elson, J. J. The Non-Shakespearean Richard II and Henry IV, Part i. Stud. Phil. xxxii, 1935.

Hart, A. Was the Second Part of King Henry the Fourth censored? [In Shakespeare and the Homilies, Melbourne, 1935.]

Purcell, J. M. N. & Q. 1 June 1935. [Date.]

Much Ado About Nothing

[*Jaggard*, pp. 418–21; *Ebisch and Schücking*, pp. 221–2; *Chambers*, vol. i, pp. 384–8.]

Much adoe about Nothing. As it hath been sundrie times publikely acted by the right honourable, the Lord Chamberlaine his servants. Written by William Shakespeare. London Printed by V. S[immes] for Andrew Wise, and William Aspley. 1600. [Facsimiles: J. O. Halliwell[-Phillipps], 1865; P. A. Daniel, 1886.]

Modern editions: W. H. Fleming, New York, 1889 (*Bankside*: parallel texts); H. H. Furness, Philadelphia, 1899 (*New Variorum*); F. S. Boas, 1916; C. F. T. Brooke, New Haven, 1917 (*Yale*); Sir A. T. Quiller-Couch and J. D. Wilson, Cambridge, 1923 (*New Cambridge*); G. R. Trenery, 1924 (*Arden*); A. G. Newcomer, 1929.

Collier, J. P. Dogberry and his Associates. Shakespeare Soc. Papers, i, 1844.

Brae, A. E. Collier, Coleridge and Shakespeare. 1860.

Weichberger, Konrad. Die Urquelle von Shakespeares 'Much ado about Nothing.' Sh. Jb. xxxiv, 1898.

Sarrazin, Gregor. Die Abfassungszeit von Viel Lärm um nichts. Sh. Jb. xxxv, 1899.

Scott, M. A. The Book of the Courtyer: a Possible Source of Benedick and Beatrice. PMLA. xvi, 1901.

Holleck-Weithmann, Fritz. Zur Quellenfrage von Shakespeares Lustspiel 'Much ado about Nothing.' Heidelberg, 1902.

Mason, Lawrence. A New Stage-direction for Much Ado, Act i, Sc. 1. MP. xi, 1913–4.

Wolff, M. J. Zur Geschichte des Stoffes von 'Much Ado about Nothing.' E. Studien, xlviii, 1914–5.

Brereton, J. le G. Much Adoe, iv. i. 145–60. RES. iv, 1928.

Law, R. A. Notes on Shakespeare's Much Ado. Texas University Stud. xii, 1932.

Wales, J. G. Shakespeare's Use of English and Foreign Elements in the Setting of Much Ado. Trans. Wisconsin Academy, xxviii, 1933.

Gaw, A. Is Shakespeare's Much Ado a Revised Earlier Play? PMLA. l, 1935.

Henry the Fifth

[*Jaggard*, pp. 336–41; *Bartlett*, pp. 29–30; *Ebisch and Schücking*, pp. 216–7; *Chambers*, vol. i, pp. 388–96.]

The Cronicle History of Henry the fift, With his battell fought at Agin Court in France. Togither with Auntient Pistoll. As it hath bene sundry times playd by the Right honorable the Lord Chamberlaine his servants. London Printed by Thomas

WILLIAM SHAKESPEARE

563

Creede, for Tho. Millington, and John Busby. And are to be sold at his house in Carter Lane, next the Powle head. 1600. [Facsimiles: J. O. Halliwell[-Phillipps], 1867; A. Symons, 1886. Reprints: B. Nicholson, New Shakspere Soc. 1875; W. A. Wright (Cambridge Shakespeare, vol. IX, 1893).]

The Chronicle History of Henry the fift, With his battell fought at Agin Court in France. Together with Auntient Pistoll. As it hath bene sundry times playd by the Right honorable the Lord Chamberlaine his servants. 1602 (ed. facs. J. O. Halliwell [-Phillipps], 1867); 1608 (for 1619: ed. facs. J. O. Halliwell[-Phillipps], 1870, A. Symons, 1886).

Modern editions: B. Nicholson and P. A. Daniel, New Shakspere Soc. 1877 (parallel texts of Q1 and F1); W. G. Boswell-Stone, New Shakspere Soc. 1880; H. P. Stokes, New York, 1892 (*Bankside*: parallel texts); G. C. Moore Smith, 1896 (*Warwick*); H. A. Evans, 1903 (*Arden*); E. Roman, Marburg, 1908 (parallel texts of Q1, Q3 and F1); R. D. French, New Haven, 1918 (*Yale*).

The Famous Victories of Henry the fifth: containing the Honourable Battell of Agincourt. 1598. [See p. 538 above.]

Shakspere's Holinshed. Ed. W. G. Boswell-Stone, 1896; 1907.

Nicholson, Brinsley. The Relation of the Quarto to the Folio Version of Henry V. Trans. New Shakspere Soc. 1879.

Sarrazin, Gregor. Nym und Ben Jonson. Sh. Jb. XL, 1904.

Kabel, Paul. Die Sage von Heinrich V bis zu Shakespeare. Berlin, 1908.

Wilson, J. D. Martin Marprelate and Shakespeare's Fluellen. Library, III, 1912.

Wielert, A. Quartos und Folios von Shakespeares 'Henry V.' Königsberg, 1913.

Brereton, J. le G. Shakespeare's Wild Irishman. MLR. XII, 1917.

Pollard, A. W. and Wilson, J. D. The 'Stolne and Surreptitious' Shakespearian Texts: Henry V (1600). TLS. 13 March, 1919.

Gould, G. A New Reading of Henry V. English Rev. XXIX, 1919.

Price, H. T. The Text of Henry V. Newcastle-under-Lyme, 1920.

—— The Quarto and Folio Texts of Henry V. PQ. XII, 1933.

Robertson, J. M. The Origination of Henry V. [In The Shakespeare Canon, vol. I, 1922.]

Kraner, Werner. Die Entstehung der ersten Quarto von Shakespeares Heinrich V. Leipzig, 1924.

Wallis, N. H. Some Aspects of Shakespeare's Richard II and Henry V. [In The Ethics of Criticism, 1924.]

Craig, Hardin. The Relation of the First Quarto Version to the First Folio Version of Shakespeare's Henry V. PQ. VI, 1927.

Poel, William. The Five Act Divisions in Henry V. TLS. 6 Oct. 1927.

Ward, B. M. The Famous Victories of Henry V: its Place in Elizabethan Dramatic Literature. RES. IV, 1928.

Albright, E. M. The Folio Version of Henry V in Relation to Shakespeare's Times. PMLA. XLIII, 1928.

Simison, B. D. A Source for the First Quarto of Henry V. MLN. XLVI, 1931.

—— Stage-Directions: a Test for the Playhouse Origin-of the First Quarto Henry V. PQ. XI, 1932.

Radoff, M. L. The Influence of the French Farce in Henry V and The Merry Wives. MLN. XLVIII, 1933.

Law, R. A. Holinshed as Source for Henry V and King Lear. Texas University Stud. XIV, 1934.

Okerlund, G. The Quarto Version of Henry V as a Stage Adaptation. PMLA. XLIX, 1934.

Julius Caesar

[*Jaggard*, pp. 319–26; *Bartlett*, pp. 46–8; *Ebisch and Schücking*, pp. 218–21; *Chambers*, vol. I, pp. 396–401.]

Mr. William Shakespeares Comedies, Histories, & Tragedies. 1623. ['The Life and death of Julius Caesar' occupies pp. 109–30 of the Tragedies.]

Julius Caesar. A Tragedy. 1684; [?]; [?]; [?]; [?]; 1691. [See H. Bartlett, Library, IV, 1913.]

Modern editions: A. D. Innes, 1893 (*Warwick*); Sir M. Hunter, 1900; M. Macmillan, 1902 (*Arden*); F. H. Sykes, 1909; H. H. Furness, jr., Philadelphia, 1913 (*New Variorum*); L. Mason, New Haven, 1919 (*Yale*).

Shakespeare's Plutarch. Ed. C. F. T. Brooke. Vol. I: containing the Main Sources of Julius Caesar. 1909. (Shakespeare Classics.)

Craik, G. L. The English of Shakespeare, illustrated in a Philological Commentary on his Julius Caesar. 1857, etc.

Fleay, F. G. Julius Caesar. Trans. New Shakspere Soc. 1874.

Delius, Nicolaus. Shakespeares Julius Caesar und seine Quellen in Plutarch. Sh. Jb. XVII, 1882.

Simpson, P. The Date of Shakespeare's Julius Caesar. N. & Q. 11 Feb., 18 March 1899.

Koeppel, E. Shakespeares Julius Caesar und die Entstehungszeit des anonymen Dramas 'The Wisdom of Dr. Dodypoll.' Sh. Jb. XLIII, 1907.

36-2

Kannengiesser, Paul. Ein Doppelredaktion in Shakespeares Julius Caesar. Sh. Jb. XLIV, 1908.

Keller, Wolfgang. Zwei Bemerkungen zu Julius Caesar. Sh. Jb. XLV, 1909.

MacCallum, M. W. Shakespeare's Roman Plays and their Background. 1910.

Ayres, H. M. Shakespeare's Julius Caesar in the Light of some other Versions. PMLA. XXV, 1910.

Sarrazin, Gregor. Shakespeare und Orlando Pescetti. E. Studien, XLVI, 1913.

Boecker, Alexander. A Probable Italian Source of Shakespeare's Julius Caesar. New York, 1913.

Kerrl, Anna. Die metrischen Unterschiede von Shakespeares 'King John' und 'Julius Caesar.' Bonn, 1913.

Faggi, Adolfo. Il Giulio Cesare di Shakespeare. Rome, 1916.

Tassin, A. de V. Julius Caesar. [In Columbia Shakespearian Studies, New York, 1916.]

Robertson, J. M. The Origination of Julius Caesar. [In The Shakespeare Canon, vol. I, 1922.]

Wells, William. The Authorship of Julius Caesar. 1923.

Shackford, M. H. Julius Caesar and Ovid. MLN. XLI, 1926.

Woelcken, F. Shakespeares 'Julius Caesar' und Marlowes 'Massacre at Paris.' Sh. Jb. LXIII, 1927.

Oliphant, E. H. C. The Plays of Beaumont and Fletcher. New Haven, 1927.

—— Beaumont and Fletcher. TLS. 23 Feb. 1928.

Granville-Barker, H. Prefaces to Shakespeare. Ser. 1, 1927.

Shestov, Leo. The Ethical Problem in Julius Caesar. New Adelphi, June 1928.

Hunter, Sir Mark. Politics and Character in Shakespeare's Julius Caesar. [In Essays by Divers Hands,Trans.RoyalSoc.Lit.x,1931].

Morsbach, L. Shakespeares Cäsarbild. Heidelberg, 1935.

As You Like It

[*Jaggard*, pp. 280–92; *Ebisch und Schücking*, pp. 222–3; *Chambers*, vol. I, pp. 401–4.]

Mr. William Shakespeares Comedies, Histories, & Tragedies. 1623. ['As you Like it' occupies pp. 185–207 of the Comedies.]

Modern editions: H. H. Furness, Philadelphia, 1890 (*New Variorum*); J. W. Holme, 1914 (*Arden*); J. R. Crawford, New Haven, 1919 (*Yale*); Sir A. T. Quiller-Couch and J. D. Wilson, Cambridge, 1926 (*New Cambridge*).

Lodge's Rosalynde, being the Original of Shakespeare's 'As You Like it.' Ed. W. W. Greg, 1907. (Shakespeare Classics.)

Delius, Nicolaus. Lodges 'Rosalynde' und Shakespeares 'As You Like it.' Sh. Jb. VI, 1871.

Boswell-Stone, W. G. Shakespere's As You Like it and Lodge's Rosalynde compared. Trans. New Shakspere Soc. 1882.

Zupitza, Julius. Die mittelenglische Vorstufe von Shakespeares 'As You Like it.' Sh. Jb. XXI, 1886.

Herford, C. H. Shakespeare's Masters and As You Like it. 1890.

Thorndike, A. H. The Relation of As You Like it to Robin Hood Plays. JEGP. IV, 1901.

Stoll, E. E. Shakspere, Marston, and the Malcontent Type. MP. III, 1905–6.

Conrad, Hermann. Die Erzählung von Gamelyn als Quelle zu Shakespeares 'As You Like it.' Sh. Jb. XLVI, 1910.

Bibelje, W. Die englischen Bühnenbearbeitungen von Shakespeares 'As You Like it.' Rostock, 1911.

Rea, J. D. Jaques in Praise of Folly. MP. XVII, 1919.

Landau, L. Some Parallels to Shakespeare's 'Seven Ages.' JEGP. XIX, 1920.

Tolman, A. H. Shakespeare's Manipulation of his Sources in As You Like it. MLN. XXXVII, 1922.

Priestley, J. B. Touchstone. [In The English Comic Characters, 1925.]

Eichler, Albert. 'Love's Labour's Lost' und 'As You Like it' als Hofaufführungen. E. Studien, LXIV, 1929.

Newdigate, B. H. Harington, Jaques and Touchstone. TLS. 3, 10 Jan. 1929.

Deutschbein, M. Shakespeares Kritik an Montaigne in 'As You Like it.' Neuphilologische Monatsschrift, v, 1934.

Draper, J. W. Orlando, and the Younger Brother. PQ. XIII, 1934.

Campbell, O. J. Jaques. Huntington Lib. Bulletin, Oct. 1935.

Fink, Z. S. PQ. XIV, 1935. [Jaques.]

Kreider, P. V. Shakespeare Ass. Bulletin, x, 1935. [Literary satire.]

Twelfth Night

[*Jaggard*, pp. 478–82; *Ebisch and Schücking*, pp. 223–4; *Chambers*, vol. I, pp. 404–7.]

Mr. William Shakespeares Comedies, Histories, & Tragedies. 1623. ['Twelfe-Night, or what you will' occupies pp. 255–75 of the Comedies; ed. facs. J. D. Wilson, 1928.]

Modern editions: A. D. Innes, 1895 (*Warwick*); H. H. Furness, Philadelphia, 1901 (*New Variorum*); M. Luce, 1906, 1929 (*Arden*); G. H. Nettleton, New Haven, 1922 (*Yale*); Sir A. T. Quiller-Couch and J. D. Wilson, Cambridge, 1930 (*New Cambridge*).

Rich's Apolonius and Silla, an Original of Shakespeare's Twelfth Night. Ed. M. Luce, 1912. (Shakespeare Classics.)

Fleay, F. G. On the Date and Composition of Twelfth Night. Trans. New Shakspere Soc. 1874.

Coote, C. H. Shakspere's 'New Map' in Twelfth Night. Trans. New Shakspere Soc. 1878.

Conrad, Hermann. Über die Entstehungszeit von Was ihr wollt. Sh. Jb. XXXI, 1895.

—— Zu den Quellen von Shaksperes 'Twelfth Night.' E. Studien, XLVI, 1912.

Meissner, H. Die Quellen zu Shakespeares Was ihr wollt. Lyck, 1895.

Logeman, H. Johannes de Witt's Visit to the Swan Theatre. Ang. XIX, 1897.

de Perott, J. Noch eine eventuelle Quelle zum Heiligen Dreikönigsabend. Sh. Jb. XLVI, 1910.

Tilley, M. P. The Organic Unity of Twelfth Night. PMLA. XXIX, 1914.

Gollancz, Sir Israel. Malvolio. [In A Book of Homage to Shakespeare, 1916.]

Archer, William. The Two Twelfth Nights. Fortnightly Rev. CX, 1918.

Symons, Arthur. Twelfth Night. [In Studies in the Elizabethan Drama, 1920.]

Priestley, J. B. The Illyrians. [In The English Comic Characters, 1925.]

Chambers, Sir E. K. Shakespeare: A Survey. 1925. [Pp. 178 ff.]

Bradley, A. C. Feste the Jester. [In A Miscellany, 1929.]

Wilson, J. D. Twelfth Night and the Gunpowder Plot. TLS. 13 June 1929.

Thaler, A. The Original Malvolio? Shakespeare Ass. Bulletin, VII, 1932.

Mueschke, P. and Fleisher, J. Jonsonian Elements in the Comic Underplot of Twelfth Night. PMLA. XLVIII, 1933.

Draper, J. W. Olivia's Household. PMLA. XLIX, 1934.

Wright, L. B. A Conduct Book for Malvolio. Stud. Phil. XXXI, 1934.

Hamlet

[*Jaggard*, pp. 306–18; *Bartlett*, pp. 35–9; *Ebisch and Schücking*, pp. 224–38; *Chambers*, vol. I, pp. 408–25.]

The Tragical Historie of Hamlet Prince of Denmarke By William Shake-speare. As it hath beene diverse times acted by his Highnesse servants in the Cittie of London: as also in the two Universities of Cambridge and Oxford, and elsewhere. At London printed for N[icholas] L[ing] and John Trundell. 1603. [Facsimiles: J. O. Halliwell[-Phillipps], 1866; F. J. Furnivall, 1880. Reprints: W. A. Wright (Cambridge Shake-

speare, vol. IX, 1893); F. G. Hubbard, Madison, 1920; G. B. Harrison, 1924; Cambridge, U.S.A. 1931.]

The Tragicall Historie of Hamlet, Prince of Denmarke. By William Shakespeare. Newly imprinted and enlarged to almost as much againe as it was, according to the true and perfect Coppie. At London, Printed by J[ames] R[oberts] for N[icholas] L[ing] and are to be sold at his shoppe under Saint Dunstons Church in Fleet-street. 1604 (in some copies 1605). [Facsimiles: J. O. Halliwell[-Phillipps], 1867; F. J. Furnivall, 1880.]

The Tragedy of Hamlet Prince of Denmarke. By William Shakespeare. 1611; [1630?]; 1637; 1676 (*bis*); 1683; 1695 (2 issues); 1703 (*bis*).

German version: Tragoedia der bestrafte Bruder-mord oder: Prinz Hamlet aus Dännemark. Ed. H. A. O. Reichard (Olla Podrida, vol. II, 1781); ed. A. Cohn (with Eng. trn in Shakespeare in Germany, 1865); ed. W. Creizenach (Schauspiele der englischen Komödianten, 1889). [MS in Library of Gotha, dated 1710.]

Modern editions: S. Timmins, 1860 (parallel texts of Q1 and Q2); H. H. Furness, Philadelphia, 1877 (*New Variorum*); E. P. Vining, New York, 1890 (*Bankside*: parallel texts of Q1 and F1); W. Viëtor, Marburg, 1891, 1913 (parallel texts of Q1, Q2, F1); Sir E. K. Chambers, 1894 (*Warwick*); E. Dowden, 1899, 1928 (*Arden*); J. D. Wilson, Cambridge, 1934, 1936 (*New Cambridge*).

Shakespeares Hamlet-Quellen: Saxo Grammaticus, Belleforest und The Hystorie of Hamlet. Ed. R. Gericke and M. Moltke, Leipzig, 1881.

Hamlet in Iceland. Ed. Sir I. Gollancz, 1898.

Corpus Hamleticum. Hamlet in Sage und Dichtung, Kunst und Musik. Ed. J. Schick, 3 vols. Berlin, 1912–Leipzig, 1933.

The Sources of Hamlet. Ed. Sir I. Gollancz, 1926. (Shakespeare Classics.)

Latham, R. G. Two Dissertations on the Hamlet of Saxo Grammaticus. 1872.

Marshall, F. A. A Study of Hamlet. 1875.

Silberschag, Karl. Shakespeares Hamlet, seine Quellen und politischen Beziehungen. Sh. Jb. XII, 1877.

Herford, C. H. and Widgery, W. H. The First Quarto Edition of Hamlet, 1603. 1880.

Nicholson, Brinsley. Kemp and the Play of Hamlet.—Yorick and Tarlton. Trans. New Shakspere Soc. 1880.

Tanger, Gustav. The First and Second Quartos and the First Folio of Hamlet. Trans. New Shakspere Soc. 1880.

Tanger, Gustav. Hamlet, nach Shakespeares Manuskript. Ang. IV, 1881.

—— 'Der bestrafte Brudermord' und sein Verhältnis zu Shakespeares Hamlet. Sh. Jb. XXIII, 1888.

Conrad (Isaac), Hermann. Hamlets Familie. Sh. Jb. XVI, 1881.

—— Die Hamlet-Periode in Shakespeares Leben. Archiv, LXXIII, LXXIV, LXXV, 1885–6.

—— Shakespeares Selbstbekenntnisse. Hamlet und sein Urbild. Stuttgart, 1897.

Fleay, F. G. Neglected Facts on Hamlet. E. Studien, VII, 1884.

Creizenach, Wilhelm. Die Tragödie 'Der bestrafte Brudermord' und ihre Bedeutung für die Kritik des Shakespeareschen Hamlet. Leipzig, 1887.

—— 'Der bestrafte Brudermord' and its Relation to Shakespeare's Hamlet. MP. II, 1904.

—— Hamletfragen. Sh. Jb. XLII, 1906.

Sarrazin, Gregor. Die Entstehung der Hamlet-Tragödie. Ang. XII, XIII, XIV, 1889–92.

—— Thomas Kyd und sein Kreis. Berlin, 1892.

—— Das Personal von Shakespeares Hamlet und der Hof Friedrichs II von Dänemark. E. Studien, XXI, 1895.

—— Der Name Ophelia. E. Studien, XXI, 1895.

Leo, F. A. Rosenkrantz und Güldenstern. Sh. Jb. XXV, XXVI, 1890–1.

Loening, Richard. Die Hamlet-Tragödie Shakespeares. Stuttgart, 1893.

Elton, Oliver. Shakespeare's Hamlet. 1894. [With trn of Saxo Grammaticus.]

Corbin, John. The Elizabethan Hamlet. 1895.

—— The German Hamlet and the Earlier English Versions. Harvard Stud. V, 1896.

Tolman, A. H. A View of the Views about Hamlet. PMLA. XIII, 1898. [Rptd in The Views about Hamlet, and Other Essays, Boston, 1904.]

MacCallum, M. W. The Authorship of the Early Hamlet. [In Furnivall Miscellany, 1901.]

Schick, Josef. Die Entstehung des Hamlet. Sh. Jb. XXXVIII, 1902.

Thorndike, A. H. The Relation of Hamlet to Contemporary Revenge Plays. PMLA. XVII, 1902.

Evans, M. B. Der bestrafte Brudermord. Sein Verhältnis zu Shakespeares Hamlet. Bonn, 1902 and 1910 (enlarged).

—— 'Der bestrafte Brudermord' and its Relation to Shakespeare's Hamlet. MP. II, 1905.

Bradley, A. C. Hamlet. [In Shakespearean Tragedy, 1904.]

Logeman, H. Shakespeare et Helsingör. [In Mélanges Paul Fredericq, Brussels, 1904.]

von Westenholz, F. P. Die Hamlet-Quellen. E. Studien, XXXIV, 1904.

Zenker, Rudolf. Boeve-Amlethus. Das altfranzösische Epos von Boeve de Hamtone und der Ursprung der Hamletsage. Berlin, 1905.

Jack, A. E. Thomas Kyd and the Ur-Hamlet. PMLA. XX, 1905.

Stoll, E. E. Shakespeare, Marston and the Malcontent Type. MP. III, 1906.

—— Hamlet. An Historical and Comparative Study. Minneapolis, 1919.

—— Hamlet the Man. English Ass. Lecture, 1935.

Cunliffe, J. W. Nash and the Earlier Hamlet. PMLA. XXI, 1906.

Lewis, C. M. The Genesis of Hamlet. New York, 1907.

Eichhoff, T. Versuch einer praktischen Hamlet-Kritik. Ang. XXX, 1907.

McKerrow, R. B. Works of Nashe. Vol. IV, 1908. [Note on preface to Menaphon.]

Allen, J. L. The Lost Hamlet of Kyd. Westminster Rev. CLXX, 1908.

Fitzgerald, J. D. The Sources of the Hamlet Tragedy. 1909.

Reed, E. B. The College Element in Hamlet. MP. VI, 1909.

Huizinga, J. Rosenkranz und Güldenstern. Sh. Jb. XLVI, 1910.

Greg, W. W. The Hamlet Quartos. MLR. V, 1910.

—— Hamlet's Hallucination. MLR. XII, 1917.

—— The Hamlet Texts and Recent Work in Shakespeare Bibliography. MLR. XIV, 1919.

—— Principles of Emendation in Shakespeare. British Academy Lecture, 1928.

—— What happens in Hamlet. MLR. XXXI, 1936.

Jones, Ernest. The Œdipus-Complex as an Explanation of Hamlet's Mystery. American Journ. Psychology, XXI, 1910.

—— A Psycho-analytic Study of Hamlet. 1922.

Pündter, E. Englische Hamlet-Darsteller und -Darstellung im 17. und 18. Jahrhundert. Munich, 1912.

von Gersdoff, W. Vom Ursprung des deutschen Hamlets. Sh. Jb. XLVIII, 1912.

Wolff, M. J. Zur Urhamlet. E. Studien, XLV, 1912.

—— Italienisches bei Shakespeare. E. Studien, LIV, 1920.

Gollancz, Sir Israel. The Name Polonius. Archiv, CXXXII, 1914.

—— Polonius. [In A Book of Homage to Shakespeare, 1916.]

Murray, Gilbert. Hamlet and Orestes. Oxford, 1914.

—— The Classical Tradition in Poetry. Oxford, 1927.

Gray, H. D. The First Quarto of Hamlet. MLR. x, 1915.

—— Did Shakespeare write a Tragedy of Dido? MLR. xv, 1920.

—— Thomas Kyd and the First Quarto of Hamlet. PMLA. xlii, 1927.

—— Reconstruction of a Lost Play. PQ. vii, 1928.

—— The Date of Hamlet. JEGP. xxxi, 1932.

van Dam, B. A. P. Are there Interpolations in the Text of Hamlet? [In A Book of Homage to Shakespeare, 1916.]

—— The Text of Shakespeare's Hamlet. 1924.

Wilson, J. D. The Copy for Hamlet, 1603. Library, ix, 1918.

—— The Hamlet Transcript, 1593. Library, ix, 1918. [These two articles were issued together in book form, 1918.]

—— The Parallel Plots in Hamlet. MLR. xiii, 1918.

—— The Play Scene in Hamlet restored. Athenaeum, July, Aug., Oct., Nov. 1918.

—— Spellings and Misprints in the Second Quarto of Hamlet. E. & S. x, 1924.

—— The Manuscripts of Shakespeare's Hamlet, and the Problems of its Transmission. 2 vols. Cambridge, 1934.

—— What happens in Hamlet. Cambridge, 1935.

Hubbard, F. G. The 'Marcellus' Theory of the First Quarto of Hamlet. MLN. xxxiii, 1918.

—— The Readings of the First Quarto of Hamlet. PMLA. xxxviii, 1923.

Robertson, J. M. The Problem of Hamlet. 1919.

—— Hamlet once more. 1923.

Lawrence, W. W. The Play-Scene in Hamlet. JEGP. xiv, 1919.

Ferguson, E. L. The Play-Scene in Hamlet. MLR. xiv, 1919.

Eliot, T. S. Hamlet. [In The Sacred Wood, 1920.]

Østerberg, V. Studier over Hamlet-Texterne. Copenhagen, 1920.

—— Prince Hamlet's Age. Copenhagen, 1924.

Jones, H. M. The King in Hamlet. Austin, Texas, 1921.

Winstanley, Lilian. Hamlet and the Scottish Succession. 1921.

—— Hamlet and the Essex Conspiracy. Aberystwyth Stud. vi, vii, 1924–5.

Clutton-Brock, Arthur. Shakespeare's Hamlet. 1922.

Spencer, Hazelton. Hamlet under the Restoration. PMLA. xxxviii, 1923.

—— Seventeenth-Century Cuts in Hamlet's Soliloquies. RES. ix, 1933.

Fox, W. S. Lucian in the Grave-Scene of Hamlet. P,Q. ii, 1923.

Malone, Kemp. The Literary History of Hamlet. Heidelberg, 1923.

—— On the Etymology of Hamlet. PQ. iv, 1925; RES. iii, 1927, iv, 1928.

de Groot, H. Hamlet, its Textual History. Amsterdam, 1923.

Lawrence, W. J. The Ghost in Hamlet. Nineteenth Century, xcv, 1924. [Rptd in Shakespeare's Workshop, Oxford, 1928.]

——The Date of Hamlet. TLS. 8 April 1926. [Rptd in Shakespeare's Workshop, Oxford, 1928.]

—— Hamlet as Shakespeare staged it. Johns Hopkins Alumni Mag. xiv, 1926. [Rptd in Pre-Restoration Stage Studies, Cambridge, U.S.A. 1927.]

—— The Mystery of the Hamlet First Quarto. Criterion, v, 1927. [Rptd in Shakespeare's Workshop, Oxford, 1928.]

—— The Pirates of Hamlet. Criterion, viii, 1929.

—— The Dumb Show in Hamlet. Life and Letters, v, 1930.

Diamond, W. Wilhelm Meister's Interpretation of Hamlet. MP. xxiii, 1925.

Clark, Cumberland. A Study of Hamlet. Stratford-on-Avon, 1926.

Conrad, B. R. Hamlet's Delay. PMLA. xli, 1926.

O'Sullivan, M. I. Hamlet and Dr. Timothy Bright. PMLA. xli, 1926.

Bradby, G. F. The Problems of Hamlet. 1928. [Rptd in Short Studies in Shakespeare, 1929.]

Santayana, George. Hamlet. Life and Letters, i, 1928.

Schücking, L. L. Zum Problem der Überlieferung des Hamlet-Textes. Leipzig, 1931.

—— The Churchyard-Scene an Afterthought? RES. xi, 1935.

—— Der Sinn des Hamlet. Leipzig, 1935.

Waldock, A. J. A. Hamlet. A Study in Critical Method. Cambridge, 1931.

Widmann, Wilhelm. Hamlets Bühnenlaufbahn. Shakespeare-Gesellschaft, 1932.

Chapman, J. A. Hamlet. 1932.

Bowers, F. T. Alphonsus, Emperor of Germany and the Ur-Hamlet. MLN. xlviii, 1933.

Childs, R. de S. Influence of the Court Tragedy on the Play Scene in Hamlet. JEGP. xxxii, 1933.

Richards, I. T. The Meaning of Hamlet's Soliloquy. PMLA. xlviii, 1933.

Walley, H. R. The Dates of Hamlet and Marston's The Malcontent. RES. ix, 1933.

—— Shakespeare's Conception of Hamlet. PMLA. xlviii, 1933.

Craig, Hardin. Hamlet's Book. Huntington Lib. Bulletin, Nov. 1934.

Draper, J. W. The Elder Hamlet and the Ghost. Shakespeare Ass. Bulletin, ix, 1934.

Draper, J. W. Revue anglo-américaine, Oct. 1934; PQ. xiv, 1935; Sh. Jb. lxxi, 1935; E. Studien, lxix, 1935; Revue de Littérature comparée, April 1935. [Character-studies.]

Stone, G. W. Garrick's Long Lost Alteration of Hamlet. PMLA. xlix, 1934.

Weigelin, E. Hamlet-Studien. Stuttgart, 1934.

Bullough, G. 'The Murder of Gonzago.' MLR. xxx, 1935.

Brock, J. H. E. The Dramatic Purpose of Hamlet. Cambridge, 1935.

Hart, A. The Vocabulary of the First Quarto of Hamlet. RES. xii, 1936.

[For further items, see A. A. Raven, A Hamlet Bibliography and Reference Guide, Chicago, 1936.]

The Merry Wives of Windsor

[*Jaggard*, pp. 404–8; *Bartlett*, pp. 33–5; *Ebisch and Schücking*, pp. 217–8; *Chambers*, vol. i, pp. 425–38.]

A Most pleasaunt and excellent conceited Comedie, of Syr John Falstaffe, and the merrie Wives of Windsor. Entermixed with sundrie variable and pleasing humors, of Syr Hugh the Welch Knight, Justice Shallow, and his wise Cousin M. Slender. With the swaggering vaine of Auncient Pistoll, and Corporall Nym. By William Shakespeare. As it hath bene divers times Acted by the right Honorable my Lord Chamberlaines servants. Both before her Majestie, and elsewhere. London Printed by T. C[reede] for Arthur Johnson, and are to be sold at his shop in Powles Churchyard, at the signe of the Flower de Leuse and the Crowne. 1602. [Facsimiles: J. O. Halliwell[-Phillipps], 1866; P. A. Daniel, 1881; W. W. Greg, Oxford. 1910. Reprints: J. O. Halliwell[-Phillipps], Shakespeare Soc. 1842; W. A. Wright (Cambridge Shakespeare, vol. ix, 1893).]

A Most pleasant and excellent conceited Comedy, of Sir John Falstaffe, and the merry Wives of Windsor. With the swaggering vaine of Ancient Pistoll, and Corporal Nym. Written by W. Shakespeare. 1619 (ed. facs. J. O. Halliwell [-Phillips], 1866); 1630; 1664.

Modern editions: A. Morgan, New York, 1888 (*Bankside*: parallel texts); H. C. Hart, 1904 (*Arden*); Sir A. T. Quiller-Couch and J. D. Wilson, Cambridge, 1921 (*New Cambridge*); G. van Santvoord, New Haven, 1922 (*Yale*).

Halliwell[-Phillipps], J. O. An Account of the Only Known Manuscript of Shakespeare's Plays. 1843.

Vollhardt, W. Ein italienischer Falstaff. Studien zur vergleichenden Literaturgeschichte, vii, 1907.

Bruce, J. D. Two Notes on The Merry Wives. MLR. vii, 1912.

Friedrich, Paul. Studien zur englischen Stenographie im Zeitalter Shakespeares. Leipzig, 1914.

Robertson, J. M. The Problem of The Merry Wives of Windsor. Shakespeare Ass. 1917.

Pollard, A. W. and Wilson, J. D. The 'Stolne and Surreptitious' Shakespearian Texts. The Merry Wives of Windsor (1602). TLS. 7 Aug. 1919.

Forsythe, R. S. A Plautine Source of The Merry Wives of Windsor. MP. xviii, 1920.

—— The Merry Wives of Windsor. Two New Analogues. PQ. vii, 1928.

Schücking, L. L. The Fairy Scene in The Merry Wives in Folio and Quarto. MLR. xix, 1924.

Campbell, O. J. The Italianate Background of The Merry Wives of Windsor. [In Michigan Essays and Studies, Ann Arbor, 1932.]

Radoff, M. L. MLN. xlviii, 1933. [Influence of French farces.]

Crofts, J. E. V. Shakespeare and the Post-Horses. Bristol, 1937.

Troilus and Cressida

[*Jaggard*, pp. 476–8; *Bartlett*, pp. 40–1; *Ebisch and Schücking*, pp. 239–40; *Chambers*, vol. i, pp. 438–49.]

The Historie of Troylus and Cresseida. As it was acted by the Kings Majesties servants at the Globe. Written by William Shakespeare. London Imprinted by G. Eld for R. Bonian and H. Walley, and are to be sold at the spred Eagle in Paules Churchyeard, over against the great North doore. 1609. [Facsimile: J. O. Halliwell[-Phillipps], 1871.]

The Famous Historie of Troylus and Cresseid. Excellently expressing the beginning of their loves, with the conceited wooing of Pandarus Prince of Licia. Written by William Shakespeare. London Imprinted by G. Eld for R. Bonian and H. Walley, and are to be sold at the spred Eagle in Paules Church-yeard, over against the great North doore. 1609. [Second issue with new title and epistle inserted. Facsimiles: J. O. Halliwell[-Phillipps], 1863; H. P. Stokes, 1886.]

Modern editions: A. Morgan, New York, 1889 (*Bankside*: parallel texts); K. Deighton, 1906 (*Arden*); J. S. P. Tatlock, New York, 1912 (*Tudor*); N. B. Paradise, New Haven, 1927 (*Yale*).

Eitner, Karl. Die Troilus-Fabel und die Bedeutung des letzten Aktes von Shakespeares Troilus und Cressida. Sh. Jb. iii, 1868.

Hertzberg, W. Die Quellen der Troilus-Sage in ihrem Verhältnis zu Shakespeares Troilus und Cressida. Sh. Jb. VI, 1871.

Fleay, F. G. On the Composition of Troilus and Cressida. Trans. New Shakspere Soc. 1874.

Ulrici, Hermann. Ist Troilus und Cressida 'comedy' oder 'tragedy' oder 'history'? Sh. Jb. IX, 1874.

Herford, C. H. Troilus and Cressida and Euphues, his Censure to Philautus. Trans. New Shakspere Soc. 1888.

Stache, E. Das Verhältnis von Shakespeares Troilus and Cressida zu Chaucers gleichnamigen Gedicht. Nordhausen, 1893.

Small, R. A. The Stage-quarrel between Ben Jonson and the so-called Poetasters. Breslau, 1899.

Boyle, Robert. Troilus and Cressida. E. Studien, xxx, 1902.

Acheson, Arthur. Shakespeare and the Rival Poet. 1903.

Koeppel, Emil. Studien über Shakespeares Wirkung auf zeitgenössische Dramatiker. *Bang*, vol. IX, 1905.

Adams, J. Q. Timon of Athens and the Irregularities in the First Folio. JEGP. VII, 1908.

Young, Karl. The Origin and Development of the Story of Troilus and Criseyde. Chaucer Soc. 1908.

Griffin, N. E. Un-Homeric Elements in the Story of Troy. JEGP. VII, 1908.

Tatlock, J. S. P. The Siege of Troy in Elizabethan Literature, especially in Shakespeare and Heywood. PMLA. xxx, 1915.

—— The Welsh Troilus and Cressida and its Relation to the Elizabethan Drama. MLR. x, 1915.

—— The Chief Problem in Shakespeare. Sewanee Rev. XXIV, 1916.

Hanford, J. H. A Platonic Passage in Shakespeare's Troilus and Cressida. Stud. Phil. XIII, 1916.

Lawrence, W. W. The Love-story in Troilus and Cressida. [In Columbia Shakespearian Studies, New York, 1916.]

Rollins, H. E. The Troilus-Cressida Story from Chaucer to Shakespeare. PMLA. XXXII, 1917.

Robertson, J. M. Shakespeare and Chapman. 1917.

Campbell, O. W. Troilus and Cressida. A Justification. London Mercury, IV, 1921.

Guha, P. K. The Problem of Shakespeare's Troilus and Cressida. Dacca University Bulletin, IX, 1926.

Alexander, Peter. Troilus and Cressida, 1609. Library, IX, 1928.

All's Well That Ends Well

[*Jaggard*, pp. 281–2; *Ebisch and Schücking*, pp. 241–2; *Chambers*, vol. I, pp. 449–52.]

Mr. William Shakespeares Comedies, Histories, & Tragedies: 1623. ['All is well, that Ends well'—running title: 'Alls Well, that ends Well'—occupies pp. 230–54 of the Comedies.]

Modern editions: W. O. Brigstocke, 1904, 1929 (*Arden*); A. E. Case, New Haven, 1926 (*Yale*); Sir A. T. Quiller-Couch and J. D. Wilson, Cambridge, 1929 (*New Cambridge*).

von Friesen, H. Bemerkungen zu den Altersbestimmungen für einige Stücke von Shakespeare. Sh. Jb. II, 1867.

Elze, Karl. Ende gut, alles gut. Sh. Jb. VII, 1872.

Fleay, F. G. On All's Well. Trans. New Shakspere Soc. 1874.

von der Hagen, H. Über die altfranzösische Vorstufe des Shakespeareschen Lustspiels Ende gut, alles gut. Halle, 1879.

Delius, Nicolaus. Shakespeare's All's Well that Ends Well and Paynter's Giletta of Narbonne. Sh. Jb. XXII, 1887.

Boyle, Robert. All's Well that Ends Well and Love's Labour's Won. E. Studien, XIV, 1890.

Thiselton, A. E. Some Textual Notes on All's Well that Ends Well. 1900.

von Westenholz, F. P. Shakespeares 'Gewonnene Liebesmüh.' Allgemeine Zeitung, I, 1902.

Tolman, A. H. What has become of Shakespeare's Play 'Love's Labour's Won'? Chicago, 1902.

Kellner, L. Exegetische Bemerkungen zu 'All's Well that Ends Well.' Sh. Jb. LIII, 1917.

Lawrence, W. W. The Meaning of All's Well that Ends Well. PMLA. XXXVII, 1922.

—— Shakespeare's Problem Comedies. New York, 1931.

Robertson, J. M. All's Well that Ends Well. [In The Shakespeare Canon, vol. III, 1925].

Hastings, W. T. Shakespeare Ass. Bulletin, x, 1935. [Notes.]

Measure For Measure

[*Jaggard*, pp. 391–3; *Ebisch and Schücking*, pp. 240–1; *Chambers*, vol. I, pp. 452–7.]

Mr. William Shakespeares Comedies, Histories, & Tragedies. 1623. ['Measure for Measure' occupies pp. 61–84 of the Comedies.]

Modern editions: H. C. Hart, 1905, 1925 (*Arden*); Sir A. T. Quiller-Couch and J. D. Wilson, Cambridge, 1922 (*New Cambridge*); W. H. Durham, New Haven, 1926 (*Yale*).

Whetstone's Historie of Promos and Cassandra. Ed. Sir I. Gollancz, 1909. (Shakespeare Classics.)

Foth, K. Shakespeares Mass für Mass und die Geschichte von Promos und Cassandra. Sh. Jb. XIII, 1878.

Pater, Walter. Measure for Measure. [In Appreciations, 1889.]

K., L. L. The Plot of Measure for Measure. N. & Q. 29 July 1893.

Sarrazin, Gregor. Neue italienische Skizzen zu Shakespeare. 1. Herzog Vincentio in Mass für Mass und sein Urbild, Herzog Vincentio Gonzaga. Sh. Jb. XXXI, 1895.

Thiselton, A. E. Some Textual Notes on Measure for Measure. 1901.

Legouis, É. Shakespeare: Mesure pour Mesure. Revue des Cours et Conférences, XVIII, 1910.

Law, Ernest. The First-Night Performance of Measure for Measure. Times, 26 Dec. 1910.

Suddard, Mary. Measure for Measure as a Clue to Shakespeare's Attitude towards Puritanism. [In Studies and Essays, Cambridge, 1912.]

Albrecht, Louis. Neue Untersuchungen zu Shakespeares Mass für Mass. Berlin, 1914.

Crawford, J. P. W. A Sixteenth Century Spanish Analogue of Measure for Measure. MLN. XXXV, 1920.

Symons, Arthur. Measure for Measure. [In Studies in the Elizabethan Drama, 1920.]

Gould, G. A New Reading of Measure for Measure. English Rev. XXXVI, 1923.

Robertson, J. M. The Problem of Measure for Measure. [In The Shakespeare Canon, vol. II, 1923.]

Koszul, A. La Technique dramatique de Shakespeare, étudiée dans le premier Acte de 'Measure for Measure.' Revue de l'Enseignement des Langues vivantes, XLIV, 1927.

Falconer, J. A. Shakespeare's Lost Chance. Neophilologus, XIV, 1928.

Durham, W. H. Measure for Measure as Measure for Critics. [In California Essays in Criticism, Berkeley, 1929.]

Wilson, R. H. The Mariana Plot of Measure for Measure. PQ. IX, 1930.

Lawrence, W. W. Shakespeare's Problem Comedies. New York, 1931.

Othello

[*Jaggard*, pp. 421–9; *Bartlett*, pp. 43–5; *Ebisch and Schücking*, pp. 246–7; *Chambers*, vol. I, pp. 457–63.]

The Tragoedy of Othello, The Moore of Venice. As it hath beene diverse times acted at the Globe, and at the Black-Friers, by his Majesties Servants. Written by William Shakespeare. London, Printed by N[icholas] O[kes] for Thomas Walkley, and are to be sold at his shop, at the Eagle and Child, in Brittans Bursse. 1622. [Facsimiles: J. O. Halliwell[-Phillipps], 1864; H. A. Evans, 1885.]

The Tragoedy of Othello, The Moore of Venice. 1630 (ed. facs. H. A. Evans, 1885); 1655; 1681; 1687; 1695; 1705.

Modern editions: H. H. Furness, Philadelphia, 1886 (*New Variorum*); T. R. Price, New York, 1890 (*Bankside*: parallel texts); H. C. Hart, 1903, 1928 (*Arden*); A. Schroeer, Heidelberg, 1909 (parallel texts); L. Mason, New Haven, 1918 (*Yale*); C. H. Herford, 1920 (*Warwick*).

Turnbull, W. R. Othello, a Critical Study. Edinburgh, 1892.

Moulton, R. G. Othello as a Type of Plot. Trans. New Shakspere Soc. 1887–92.

Bobsin, O. Shakespeares Othello in englischer Bühnenbearbeitung. Rostock, 1904.

Bradley, A. C. Othello. [In Shakespearean Tragedy, 1904.]

Swinburne, A. C. Othello. [In Three Plays of Shakespeare, 1909.]

Law, Ernest. Othello on All Hallows Day, 1604. Times, 31 Oct. 1910.

de Fonblanque, E. M. The Italian Sources of Othello. Fortnightly Rev. XCVI, 1911.

Stoll, E. E. Othello, an Historical and Comparative Study. Minneapolis, 1915.

—— Othello the Man. Shakespeare Ass. Bulletin, IX, 1934.

Brooke, C. F. T. The Romantic Iago. Yale Rev. VII, 1918.

Radebrecht, Friedrich. Shakespeares Abhängigkeit von John Marston. Cöthen, 1918.

Whitney, Lois. Did Shakespeare know 'Leo Africanus'? PMLA. XXXVII, 1922.

Krappe, A. H. A Byzantine Source of Shakespeare's Othello. MLN. XXXIX, 1924.

Winstanley, Lilian. Othello as the Tragedy of Italy. 1924.

Bullock, W. A. The Sources of Othello. MLN. XL, 1925.

Gilbert, A. H. Scenes of Discovery in Othello. PQ. V, 1926.

Tesch, Albert. Zum Namen Desdemona. Germanisch-romanische Monatsschrift, XVII, 1929.

Knight, G. W. The Style of Othello. Fortnightly Rev. April 1929.

Draper, J. W. 'Honest Iago.' PMLA. XLVI, 1931.

—— 'This Poor Trash of Venice.' JEGP. XXX, 1931.

—— Captain General Othello. Ang. LV, 1931.

—— Othello and Elizabethan Army Life. Revue anglo-américaine, IX, 1932.

—— Desdemona: a Compound of Two Cultures. Revue de Littérature comparée, XIII, 1933.

Cameron, K. W. Othello, Quarto 1, Reconsidered. PMLA. xlvii, 1932.
—— The Text of Othello. An Analysis. PMLA. xlix, 1934.
Kelcy, A. Notes on Othello. PQ. xii, 1933.
Wales, J. G. Trans. Wisconsin Academy, xxix, 1935. [Setting.]

King Lear

[*Jaggard*, pp. 354–62; *Bartlett*, pp. 39–40; *Ebisch and Schücking*, pp. 242–5; *Chambers*, vol. i, pp. 463–70.]

M. William Shak-speare: His True Chronicle Historie of the life and death of King Lear and his three Daughters. With the unfortunate life of Edgar, sonne and heire to the Earle of Gloster, and his sullen and assumed humor of Tom of Bedlam: As it was played before the Kings Majestie at Whitehall upon S. Stephans night in Christmas Hollidayes. By his Majesties servants playing usually at the Gloabe on the Bancke-side. London, Printed for Nathaniel Butter, and are to be sold at his shop in Pauls Church-yard at the signe of the Pide Bull neere St. Austins Gate. 1608. [Sheets D, E, F, G, K are found in corrected and uncorrected forms (see W. W. Greg, RES. i, 1925, p. 469). Facsimiles: J. O. Halliwell[-Phillipps], 1868; P. A. Daniel, 1885.]

M. William Shake-speare, His True Chronicle History of the life and death of King Lear, and his three Daughters. With the unfortunate life of Edgar, sonne and heire to the Earle of Glocester, and his sullen and assumed humour of Tom of Bedlam. 1608 (for 1619; ed. facs. J. O. Halliwell[-Phillipps], 1867, P. A. Daniel, 1885); 1655.

Modern editions: H. H. Furness, Philadelphia, 1880 (*New Variorum*); A. A. Adee, New York, 1890 (*Bankside*: parallel texts); W. Viëtor, Marburg, 1892 (parallel texts); W. J. Craig, 1901, 1927 (*Arden*); D. Nichol Smith, 1902 (*Warwick*); W. L. Phelps, New Haven, 1917 (*Yale*).

The True Chronicle History of King Leir, and his three daughters, Gonorill, Ragan, and Cordella. 1605; rptd facs. *Malone Soc.* 1907; *TFT.* 1910; ed. Sir S. Lee, 1909 (Shakespeare Classics).
Shakspere's Holinshed. Ed. W. G. Boswell-Stone, 1896, 1907.
Quellen zu König Lear. Ed. R. Fischer, Bonn, 1914.
Delius, Nicolaus. Über den ursprünglichen Text des 'King Lear.' Sh. Jb. x, 1875.
Koppel, Richard. Textkritische Studien über Shakespeares 'Richard III' und 'King Lear.' Dresden, 1877.

Koppel, Richard. Verbesserungsvorschläge zu den Erläuterungen und der Textlesung des Lear. Berlin, 1899.
Fleay, F. G. The Date and Text of King Lear. Robinson's Epitome of Literature, 1 Aug. 1879.
Schmidt, Alexander. Zur Textkritik des 'King Lear.' Ang. iii, 1880.
Price, T. R. King Lear. A Study of Shakspere's Dramatic Method. PMLA. ix, 1894.
Sampson, M. W. On the Date of King Lear. Mod. Lang. Quart. v, 1902.
Bradley, A. C. King Lear. [In Shakespearean Tragedy, 1904.]
Bode, Emil. Die Learsage vor Shakespeare. Göttingen, 1904.
Perrett, Wilfrid. The Story of King Lear from Geoffrey of Monmouth to Shakespeare. Berlin, 1904.
Law, R. A. On the Date of King Lear. PMLA. xxi, 1906.
—— Holinshed as Source for Henry V and King Lear. Texas University Stud. xiv, 1934.
Greg, W. W. On Certain False Dates in Shakespearian Quartos. Library, ix, 1908.
Merriman, R. B. On the Date of King Lear. Athenaeum, 23 May 1908.
Swinburne, A. C. King Lear. [In Three Plays of Shakespeare, 1909.]
Cunnington, R. H. The Revision of King Lear. MLR. v, 1910.
Moriarty, W. D. The Bearing on Dramatic Sequence of the Varia in Richard III and King Lear. MP. x, 1913.
Schücking, L. L. Eine Anleihe Shakespeares bei Tourneur. E. Studien, l, 1916.
Radebrecht, Friedrich. Shakespeares Abhängigkeit von John Marston. Cöthen, 1918.
Winstanley, Lilian. Macbeth, King Lear and Contemporary History. Cambridge, 1922.
Craig, Hardin. The Ethics of King Lear. PQ. iv, 1925.
Sievers, Eduard. Shakespeares Anteil am King Lear. [In Anglica, vol. ii, Leipzig, 1925.]
Granville-Barker, H. Prefaces to Shakespeare. Ser. 1, 1927.
Blunden, Edmund. Shakespeare's Significances. Shakespeare Ass. Lecture, 1929.
Doran, M. The Text of King Lear. Palo Alto, 1931.
—— Elements in the Composition of King Lear. Stud. Phil. xxx, 1933.
—— The Quarto of King Lear and Bright's Shorthand. MP. xxxiii, 1935.
Ashton, J. W. The Wrath of King Lear. JEGP. xxxi, 1932.
Kelcy, A. Notes on King Lear. PQ. xi, 1932.
Adams, J. Q. The Quarto of King Lear and Shorthand. MP. xxxi, 1933.

Greg, W. W. The Function of Bibliography in Literary Criticism illustrated in a Study of the Text of King Lear. Neophilologus, XVIII, 1933.

Kreider, P. V. Gloucester's Eyes. Shakespeare Ass. Bulletin, VIII, 1933.

Stoll, E. E. Kent and Gloster. Life and Letters, IX, 1933.

Bransom, J. S. H. The Tragedy of King Lear. Oxford, 1934.

Harrison, G. B. The Background to King Lear. TLS. 28 Dec. 1935.

van Dam, B. A. P. The Text of Shakespeare's Lear. Bang, N.S. vol, x, 1935.

Macbeth

[*Jaggard*, pp. 381–91; *Ebisch and Schücking*, pp. 247–50; *Chambers*, vol. I, pp. 471–6.]

Mr. William Shakespeares Comedies, Histories, & Tragedies. 1623. ['The Tragedy of Macbeth' occupies pp. 131–51 of the Tragedies.]

Macbeth: A Tragedy. 1673.

Modern editions: W. G. Clark and W. A. Wright, Oxford, 1869; H. H. Furness, Philadelphia, 1873, rev. H. H. Furness, jr., 1903 (*New Variorum*); Sir E. K. Chambers, 1893 (*Warwick*); J. M. Manly, 1896; M. H. Liddell, 1903; H. Conrad, 1907; H. Cunningham, 1912, 1928 (*Arden*); C. M. Lewis, New Haven, 1918 (*Yale*).

Shakspere's Holinshed. Ed. W. G. Boswell-Stone, 1896, 1907.

Delius, Nicolaus. Shaksperes Macbeth. Bremen, 1841.

Hales, J. W. On the Porter in Macbeth. Trans. New Shakspere Soc. 1874.

Fleay, F. G. Macbeth. Trans. New Shakspere Soc. 1874.

—— Davenant's Macbeth and Shakespeare's Witches. Ang. VII, 1884.

Spalding, T. A. On the Witch-Scenes in Macbeth. Trans. New Shakspere Soc. 1877–9.

Sarrazin, Gregor. Shakespeares Macbeth und Kyds Spanish Tragedy. E. Studien, XXI, 1895.

Stopes, C. C. Shakespeare's Materials for Macbeth. Athenaeum, 25 July 1896.

—— The Scottish and English Macbeth. [In Shakespeare's Industry, 1897.]

Chambers, D. L. The Metre of Macbeth. Princeton, 1903.

Bradley, A. C. Macbeth. [In Shakespearean Tragedy, 1904.]

Kröger, Ernst. Die Sage von Macbeth bis zu Shakespere. Berlin, 1904.

Brandl, A. Die Vorgeschichte der Schicksalsschwestern in Macbeth. Sitzungsber. Preuss. Akad. Wiss. Berlin, 1919. [Rptd in Liebermann Festgabe, Halle, 1921.]

Lawrence, W. J. The Mystery of Macbeth. Fortnightly Rev. CXIII, 1920. [Rptd in Shakespeare's Workshop, Oxford, 1928.]

Symons, Arthur. Macbeth. [In Studies in the Elizabethan Drama, 1920.]

Winstanley, Lilian. Macbeth, King Lear, and Contemporary History. Cambridge, 1922.

Bald, R. C. Macbeth and the 'Short' Plays. RES. IV, 1928.

Kittredge, G. L. Witchcraft in Old and New England. Cambridge, U.S.A. 1929. [Ch. 1.]

Knight, G. W. Macbeth and the Nature of Evil. Hibbert Journ. Jan. 1930.

Curry, W. C. 'Tumbling Nature's Germens. Stud. Phil. XXIX, 1932.

—— The Demonic Metaphysics of Macbeth. Stud. Phil. XXX, 1933.

—— Macbeth's Changing Character. JEGP. XXXIV, 1935.

Tonge, M. Black Magic and Miracles in Macbeth. JEGP. XXXI, 1932.

Thaler, A. The Lost Scenes of Macbeth. PMLA. XLIX, 1934.

Antony and Cleopatra

[*Jaggard*, pp. 282–5; *Ebisch and Schücking*, pp. 250–1; *Chambers*, vol. I, pp. 476–8.]

Mr. William Shakespeares Comedies, Histories, & Tragedies. 1623. ['Anthony and Cleopater'—running title: 'The Tragedy of Anthony and Cleopatra'—occupies pp. 340–68 of the Tragedies.]

Modern editions: R. H. Case, 1906, 1930 (*Arden*); H. H. Furness, jr., Philadelphia, 1907 (*New Variorum*); H. S. Canby, New Haven, 1921 (*Yale*).

Shakespeare's Plutarch. Ed. C. F. T. Brooke. Vol. II: containing the Main Sources of Antony and Cleopatra and of Coriolanus. 1909. (Shakespeare Classics.)

Vatke, Theodor. Shakespeares Antonius und Kleopatra und Plutarchs Biographie des Antonius. Sh. Jb. III, 1868.

Adler, Fritz. Das Verhältnis von Shakespeares 'Antony and Cleopatra' zu Plutarchs Biographie des Antonius. Halle, 1895; Sh. Jb. XXXI, 1895.

Bradley, A. C. Shakespeare's Antony and Cleopatra. [In Oxford Lectures on Poetry, 1909.]

MacCallum, M. W. Shakespeare's Roman Plays and their Background. 1910.

Bayfield, M. A. A Study of Shakespeare's Versification. Cambridge, 1920.

Symons, Arthur. Antony and Cleopatra. [In Studies in the Elizabethan Drama, 1920.]

Gundolf, Friedrich. Antonius und Cleopatra. Sh. Jb. LXII, 1926.

Schücking, L. L. Die Characterprobleme bei Shakespeare. Leipzig, 1927.

Simpson, Lucie. Shakespeare's Cleopatra. Fortnightly Rev. CXXIX, 1928.

Stoll, E. E. Cleopatra. MLR. XXIII, 1928. [Rptd in Poets and Playwrights, Minneapolis, 1930.]

Granville-Barker, H. Prefaces to Shakespeare. Ser. 2, 1930.

Coriolanus

[*Jaggard*, pp. 296–300; *Ebisch and Schücking*, pp. 251–2; *Chambers*, vol. I, pp. 478–80.]

Mr. William Shakespeares Comedies, Histories, & Tragedies. 1623. ['The Tragedy of Coriolanus' occupies pp. 1–30 of the Tragedies.]

Modern editions: Sir E. K. Chambers, 1898 (*Warwick*); G. S. Gordon, Oxford, 1912; W. J. Craig and R. H. Case, 1922 (*Arden*); C. F. T. Brooke, New Haven, 1924; H. H. Furness, jr., Philadelphia, 1928 (*New Variorum*).

Shakespeare's Plutarch. Ed. C. F. T. Brooke. Vol. II: containing the Main Sources of Antony and Cleopatra and of Coriolanus. 1909. (Shakespeare Classics.)

Halliwell[-Phillipps], J. O. A Hint on the Date of Coriolanus. Trans. New Shakspere Soc. 1874.

Delius, Nicolaus. Shakespeares Coriolanus in seinem Verhältnis zum Coriolanus des Plutarch. Sh. Jb. XI, 1876.

Büttner, Richard. Zu Coriolan und seiner Quelle. Sh. Jb. XLI, 1905.

MacCallum, M. W. Shakespeare's Roman Plays and their Background. 1910.

Bradley, A. C. Coriolanus. British Academy Lecture, 1912. [Rptd in A Miscellany, 1929.]

Murry, J. M. A Neglected Heroine of Shakespeare. London Mercury, v, 1922. [Rptd in Countries of the Mind, 1922.]

Tolman, A. H. The Structure of Shakespeare's Tragedies, with Special Reference to Coriolanus. MLN. XXXVII, 1922.

Hayhurst, C. H. A History of the Text of Coriolanus. Chicago, 1924.

Timon of Athens

[*Jaggard*, pp. 471–4; *Ebisch and Schücking*, pp. 252–3; *Chambers*, vol. I, pp. 480–4.]

Mr. William Shakespeares Comedies, Histories, & Tragedies. 1623. ['Timon of Athens'—head title: 'The Life of Tymon of Athens'—occupies pp. 80–[99] of the Tragedies.]

Modern edition: K. Deighton, 1905, 1929 (*Arden*).

Delius, Nicolaus. Über Shakespeares Timon of Athens. Sh. Jb. II, 1867.

Tschischwitz, B. Timon von Athen. Ein kritischer Versuch. Sh. Jb. IV, 1869.

Müller, Adolf. Über die Quellen, aus denen Shakespeare den Timon von Athen entnommen hat. Jena, 1873.

Fleay, F. G. On the Authorship of Timon of Athens. Trans. New Shakspere Soc. 1874.

Kullmann, Georg. Shakespeares Anteil an dem unter seinem Namen veröffentlichen Trauerspiele Timon. Archiv für Litteraturgeschichte, XI, 1882.

Wendlandt, Wilhelm. Shakespeares Timon von Athen. Sh. Jb. XXIII, 1888.

Bradley, A. C. King Lear and Timon. [In Shakespearean Tragedy, 1904.]

Clemons, W. H. The Sources of Timon. Princeton University Bulletin, XV, 1904.

Adams, J. Q. Timon of Athens and the Irregularities of the First Folio. JEGP. VII, 1908.

—— The Timon Plays. JEGP. IX, 1910.

Conrad, Hermann. Shakesperes Timon. Zeitschrift für vergleichende Litteraturgeschichte, XVII, 1909.

Wright, E. H. The Authorship of Timon of Athens. New York, 1910.

Robertson, J. M. Shakespeare and Chapman. 1917.

Wells, W. Timon of Athens. N. & Q. 5 June 1920.

Parrott, T. M. The Problem of Timon of Athens. Shakespeare Ass. Pamphlet, 1923.

Sykes, H. D. The Problem of Timon. N. & Q. 4 Aug.–15 Sept. 1923. [Rptd in Sidelights on Elizabethan Drama, 1924.]

Wecter, Dixon. Shakespeare's Purpose in Timon of Athens. PMLA. XLIII, 1928.

Bond, R. W. Lucian and Boiardo in Timon of Athens. MLR. XXV, 1930.

Draper, J. W. The Theme of Timon of Athens. MLR. XXIX, 1934.

Cymbeline

[*Jaggard*, pp. 301–3; *Ebisch and Schücking*, pp. 254–5; *Chambers*, vol. I, pp. 484–7.]

Mr. William Shakespeares Comedies, Histories, & Tragedies. 1623. ['Cymbeline King of Britaine'—running title: 'The Tragedie of Cymbeline'—occupies pp. 369–99 of the Tragedies.]

Modern editions: C. M. Ingleby, 1886; A. J. Wyatt, 1897 (*Warwick*); E. Dowden, 1903 (*Arden*); H. H. Furness jr., Philadelphia, 1913 (*New Variorum*); S. B. Hemingway, New Haven, 1924 (*Yale*).

Shakspere's Holinshed. Ed. W. G. Boswell-Stone, 1896, 1907.

Leonhardt, B. Über die Quellen Cymbelines. Ang. VI, 1883.

Leonhardt, B. Über Beziehungen von Beaumont und Fletcher's Philaster zu Shakespeares Hamlet und Cymbeline. Ang. VIII, 1885.

—— Schlusswort zu Cymbeline. Ang. VIII, 1885.

Levy, S. Eine neue Quelle zu Shakespeares Cymbeline. Ang. VII, 1884.

—— Noch einmal die Quellen Cymbelines. Ang. VIII, 1885.

Elze, K. A Letter to C. M. Ingleby on Cymbeline. Ang. VIII, 1885.

ten Brink, B. Zu Cymbeline. Ang. IX, 1886.

Boodle, R. W. The Original of Cymbeline. N. & Q. 19 Nov. 1887.

—— Die Quelle zu Cymbeline. Sh. Jb. XXIII, 1888.

Ohle, R. Shakespeares Cymbeline und seine romanischen Vorläufer. Leipzig, 1890.

Reich, Hermann. Zur Quelle des Cymbeline. Sh. Jb. XLI, 1905.

Brie, F. Eine neue Quelle zum Cymbeline. Sh. Jb. XLIV, 1908.

Lücke, Friedrich. Über Bearbeitungen von Shakespeares Cymbeline. Rostock, 1909.

de Perott, J. Der Prinzenraub aus Rache. Sh. Jb. XLV, 1909.

Brandl, Alois. Imogen auf den Aran-Inseln. Sh. Jb. LIII, 1917.

Robertson, J. M. The Interlude in Cymbeline. [In Shakespeare and Chapman, 1917.]

Lawrence, W. W. The Wager in Cymbeline. PMLA. XXXV, 1920.

Reyher, Paul. La Date de Cymbeline. Revue anglo-américane, II, 1925.

Kellner, Leon. Cymbeline. Eine textkritische Studie. [In Anglica, vol. II, Leipzig, 1925.]

Granville-Barker, H. Prefaces to Shakespeare. Ser. 2, 1930.

Lancaster, H. C. Hermione's Statue. Stud. Phil. XXIX, 1932.

The Winter's Tale

[*Jaggard*, pp. 490–4; *Ebisch and Schücking*, pp. 255–6; *Chambers*, vol. I, pp. 487–90.]

Mr. William Shakespeares Comedies, Histories, & Tragedies. 1623. ['The Winters Tale' occupies pp. 277–303 of the Comedies.]

Modern editions: H. H. Furness, Philadelphia, 1898 (*New Variorum*); F. W. Moorman, 1912 (*Arden*); F. E. Pierce, New Haven, 1918 (*Yale*); Sir A. T. Quiller-Couch and J. D. Wilson, Cambridge, 1931 (*New Cambridge*).

Greene's Pandosto, or Dorastus and Fawnia, being the Original of Shakespeare's Winter's Tale. Ed. P. G. Thomas, 1907. (Shakespeare Classics.)

Caro, J. Die historischen Elemente in Shakespeares Sturm und Wintermärchen. E. Studien, II, 1879.

Delius, Nicolaus. Greenes Pandosto und Shakespeares Winter's Tale. Sh. Jb. XV, 1880.

Elze, Karl. Alexandrines in The Winter's Tale and King Richard II. Halle, 1882.

Boas, F. Der Sturm und das Wintermärchen in ihrer symbolischen Bedeutung. Stettin, 1882.

Boyle, R. Shakespeares Wintermärchen und Sturm. St Petersburg, 1885.

Bolte, Johannes. Zur Schlusszene des Wintermärchens. Sh. Jb. XXVI, 1891.

von Lippmann, Edmund. 'Die Küste von Böhmen.' Sh. Jb. XXVII, 1892.

Mount, C. D. Sir Philip Sidney and Shakespeare. N. & Q. 22 April 1893.

Koeppel, Emil. Ein Vorbild für Shaksperes Statue der Hermione. Archiv, XCVII, 1896.

Fränkel, Ludwig. Der Streit um die Küste von Bohemia im Wintermärchen. Sh. Jb. XXXIV, 1898.

Fries, K. Quellenstudien zu Shakespeares Wintermärchen. Neue Jahrbücher für Pädagogik, VI, 1900.

Kralik, Richard. Shakespeares Böhmen im Wintermärchen. Sh. Jb. XXXVII, 1901.

Conrad, Hermann. Das Wintermärchen als Abschluss von Shaksperes Denken und Schaffen. Preussische Jahrbücher, CXXX, 1907.

Jusserand, J. J. The Winter's Tale. 1907. [Rptd in The School for Ambassadors, 1924.]

Krause, H. Umarbeitungen und Bühneneinrichtungen von Shakespeare's 'The Winter's Tale.' Rostock, 1913.

de Perott, Josef. Die Hirtendichtung des Feliciano de Silva und Shakespeares Wintermärchen. Archiv, CXXX, 1913.

Møller, Niels. Shakespeare ved sit Arbeide. Særlig i Winter's Tale. Edda, VI, 1916.

Symons, Arthur. The Winter's Tale. [In Studies in the Elizabethan Drama, 1920.]

Tannenbaum, S. A. Textual and Other Notes on The Winter's Tale. PQ. VII, 1928.

The Tempest

[*Jaggard*, pp. 462–70; *Ebisch and Schücking*, pp. 256–9; *Chambers*, vol. I, pp. 490–4.]

Mr. William Shakespeares Comedies, Histories, & Tragedies. 1623. ['The Tempest' occupies pp. 1–19 of the Comedies.]

Modern editions: H. H. Furness, Philadelphia, 1892 (*New Variorum*); F. S. Boas, 1897 (*Warwick*); M. Luce, 1902, 1926 (*Arden*); W. Vickery, Rowfant Club, 1911; C. B. Tinker, New Haven, 1918 (*Yale*); Sir A. T. Quiller-Couch and J. D. Wilson, Cambridge, 1921 (*New Cambridge*).

Jakob Ayrer: Dramen. Ed. A. von Keller, Stuttgart, 1865.

Malone, Edmond. An Account of the Incidents from which the Title and Part of Shakespeare's Tempest were derived, and its True Date ascertained. [First Variorum Shakespeare, vol. xv, 1803.]

Chalmers, G. Another Account of the Incidents from which the Title and Part of Shakespeare's Tempest were derived. 1815.

Hunter, J. A Disquisition on the Scene, Origin, Date, etc. of Shakespeare's Tempest. 1839.

Thoms, W. J. On the Connexion between the Early English and Early German Drama, and on the Probable Origin of Shakespeare's Tempest. [Colburn's] New Monthly Mag. LXI, 1841.

Meissner, Johannes. Untersuchungen über Shakespeares Sturm. Dessau, 1872.

Brae, A. E. Prospero's Clothes-Line. Trans. Royal Soc. Lit. x, 1874.

Landau, Marcus. Le Fonti della Tempesta di W. Shakespeare. Nuova Antologia, Sept. 1878.

Caro, J. Die historischen Elemente in Shakespeares Sturm und Wintermärchen. E. Studien, II, 1879.

Boyle, R. Shakespeares Wintermärchen und Sturm. St Petersburg, 1885.

Boodle, R. W. The Original of Cymbeline and possibly of The Tempest. N. & Q. 19 Nov. 1887.

Garnett, Richard. The Date and Occasion of The Tempest. Universal Rev. III, 1889.

Swaen, A. E. H. Caliban. E. Studien, xxI, 1895.

Newell, W. W. The Sources of Shakespeare's Tempest. Journ. American Folk-Lore, xvI, 1903.

de Perott, Josef. The Probable Source of the Plot of Shakespeare's Tempest. Worcester, U.S.A. 1905.

—— Die Magelönen- und die Sturmfabel. Sh. Jb. XLVII, 1911.

Sarrazin, Gregor. Neue italienische Skizzen zu Shakespeare. 7. Die Vertreibung des Herzogs Prospero. Sh. Jb. XLII, 1906.

Becker, Gustav. Zur Quellenfrage von Shakespeares Sturm. Sh. Jb. XLIII, 1907.

Lee, Sir Sidney. The Call of the West. Scribner's Mag. XLII, 1907.

—— The American Indian in Elizabethan England. Scribner's Mag. XLII, 1907.

—— Caliban's Visits to England. Cornhill Mag. xxxIV, 1913.

Neri, F. Scenari delle Maschere in Arcadia. Città di Castello, 1913.

Kelsey, R. M. Indian Dances in The Tempest. JEGP. xIII, 1914.

Gilbert, A. H. The Tempest, Parallelism in Characters and Situations. JEGP. xIv, 1915.

Gayley, C. M. Shakespeare and the Founders of Liberty in America. New York, 1917.

Robertson, J. M. The Masque in the Tempest. [In Shakespeare and Chapman, 1917.]

—— The Masque in The Tempest. TLS. 31 March 1921.

Bell, R. The Topography of the Tempest. Contemporary Rev. cxII, 1917.

Rea, J. D. A Source for the Storm in the Tempest. MP. xvII, 1919.

—— A Note on the Tempest. MLN. xxxv, 1920.

Ward, Sir A. W. Shakespeare and the Makers of Virginia. Proc. British Academy, 1919.

Gray, H. D. The Sources of the Tempest. MLN. xxxv, 1920.

—— Some Indications that the Tempest was revised. Stud. Phil. xvIII, 1921.

Lawrence, W. J. The Masque in the Tempest. Fortnightly Rev. cxII, 1920.

—— Shakespeare avrebbe tratto il Soggetto di La Tempesta da Scenari italiani? Le Lettere, II, 1923.

Law, Ernest. Shakespeare's Tempest as originally produced at Court. Shakespeare Ass. Pamphlet, [1921].

Still, C. Shakespeare's Mystery Play. 1921.

Lefranc, Abel. L'Origine d'Ariel. [In Cinquantenaire de l'École Pratique des Hautes Études, 1921.]

Chambers, Sir E. K. The Integrity of The Tempest. RES. I, 1925.

Longworth-Chambrun, Clara. Revue de Littérature comparée, v, 1925. [French influences.]

Eichler, A. Shakespeares The Tempest als Hofaufführung. [In Festgabe für Karl Luick, Marburg, 1925.]

Cawley, R. R. Shakspere's Use of the Voyagers in the Tempest. PMLA. XLI, 1926.

Fouquet, Karl. Jakob Ayrers Sidea, Shakespeares 'Tempest' und das Märchen. Marburg, 1929.

Bushnell, N. S. Natural Supernaturalism in The Tempest. PMLA. XLVII, 1932.

Knight, G. W. The Shakespearian Tempest. 1932.

Stoll, E. E. The Tempest. PMLA. XLVII, 1932.

Curry, W, C. Sacerdotal Science in Shakespeare's The Tempest. Archiv, cLXVIII, 1935.

Wilson, J. D. The Meaning of the Tempest. Newcastle, 1936. [Lecture.]

Henry the Eighth

[*Jaggard*, pp. 346–50; *Ebisch and Schücking*, pp. 259–60; *Chambers*, vol. I, pp. 495–8.]

Mr. William Shakespeares Comedies, Histories, & Tragedies. 1623. ['The Life of King Henry the Eight'—head title: 'The Famous History of the Life of King Henry the Eight'—occupies pp. 205–32 of the Histories.]

Modern editions: D. Nichol Smith, 1899 (*Warwick*); C. K. Pooler, 1915 (*Arden*); J. M. Berdan and C. F. T. Brooke, New Haven, 1925 (*Yale*).

Shakspere's Holinshed. Ed. W. G. Boswell-Stone, 1896 and 1907.

S[pedding], J[ames]. On the Several Shares of Shakspere and Fletcher in the Play of Henry VIII. GM. xxxiv, 1850; Trans. New Shakspere Soc. 1874.

Hickson, S. A Confirmation of Mr. Spedding's Paper on the Authorship of Henry VIII. N. & Q. 24 Aug. 1850; Trans. New Shakspere Soc. 1874.

Elze, Karl. Zu Heinrich VIII. Sh. Jb. ix, 1874.

Delius, Nicolaus. Fletchers angebliche Beteiligung an Shakespeares 'King Henry VIII.' Sh. Jb. xiv, 1879.

Zeitlin, W. Shakespeares King Henry VIII und Rowleys 'When you see me, you know me.' Ang. iv, 1881.

Boyle, Robert. Über die Echtheit Heinrichs VIII. von Shakespeare. St Petersburg, 1884.

—— King Henry VIII. An Investigation into the Origin and Authorship of the Play. Trans. New Shakspere Soc. 1885.

—— Beaumont, Fletcher and Massinger. E. Studien, x, 1887.

Fleay, F. G. Mr. Boyle's Theory as to Henry VIII. Athenaeum, 14 March 1885.

Oliphant, E. H. C. The Works of Beaumont and Fletcher. E. Studien, xv, 1891.

—— The Plays of Beaumont and Fletcher. New Haven, 1927.

Thorndike, A. H. The Influence of Beaumont and Fletcher on Shakespeare. Worcester, U.S.A. 1901.

Conrad, Hermann. 'Henry VIII,' Fletchers Werk, überarbeitet von Shakespeare. E. Studien, lii, 1918.

Sykes, H. D. King Henry VIII. [In Sidelights on Shakespeare, Stratford-on Avon, 1919.]

Symons, Arthur. The Question of Henry VIII. [In Studies in the Elizabethan Drama, 1920.]

Ege, Karl. Shakespeares Anteil an Heinrich VIII. Sh. Jb. lviii, 1922.

Flood, W. H. G. The Date of the Production of Henry VIII. Month, cxl, 1922.

Nicolson, M. H. The Authorship of Henry VIII. PMLA. xxxvii, 1922.

Maxwell, Baldwin. Fletcher and Henry VIII. [In Manly Anniversary Studies, Chicago, 1923. See also his review of Sykes, MP. xxiii, 1926.]

Lawrence, W. J. The Stage Directions in King Henry VIII. TLS. 18 Dec. 1930.

Alexander, Peter. Conjectural History, or Shakespeare's Henry VIII. E. & S. xvi, 1931.

(3) The Plays Excluded from the Folio

[Sir Thomas More, Edward the Third, Pericles, The Two Noble Kinsmen, and Other Ascribed Plays.]

(a) Collected Editions

[For a fuller list see Sir E. K. Chambers, Elizabethan Stage, vol. iii, p. 204, 1923.]

Pseudo-Shakspere'sche Dramen. Ed. N. Delius, 5 pts, Elberfeld, 1854–74.

Pseudo-Shakespearian Plays. Ed. K. Warnke and L. Proescholdt, 5 pts, Halle, 1883–8.

Shakespeare's Doubtful Plays. Ed. A. F. Hopkinson, 3 vols. 1891–5.

The Shakespeare Apocrypha. Ed. C. F. T. Brooke, Oxford, 1908. [14 plays in old spelling. Detailed introduction.]

(b) General Discussions

von Vincke, G. Die zweifelhaften Stücke Shakespeares. Sh. Jb. viii, 1873.

Elze, Karl. Notes on Elizabethan Dramatists. Halle, 1880.

Sachs, R. Die Shakespeare zugeschriebenen zweifelhaften Stücke. Sh. Jb. xxvii, 1892.

Hopkinson, A. F. Essays on Shakespeare's Doubtful Plays. 1900. [Rptd from his edn of the plays, 1891–5.]

Moorman, F. W. Plays of Uncertain Authorship attributed to Shakespeare. CHEL. vol. v, 1910.

Petersen, Ottomar. Pseudoshakespearesche Dramen. Ang. xxxvii, 1913.

Sykes, H. D. Sidelights on Shakespeare. Stratford-on-Avon, 1919.

Sir Thomas More

[*Ebisch and Schücking*, pp. 277–8; *Chambers*, vol. i, pp. 499–515.]

The Booke of Sir Thomas Moore. [MS: BM. Harleian 7368.] Ed. A. Dyce, Shakespeare Soc. 1844; ed. A. F. Hopkinson, 1902; ed. C. F. T. Brooke (Shakespeare Apocrypha, Oxford, 1908); ed. photo. facs. J. S. Farmer, TFT. 1910; ed. W. W. Greg, Malone Soc. 1911.

Simpson, Richard. Are there any Extant MSS. in Shakespeare's Handwriting? N. & Q. 1 July 1871.

Spedding, James. Shakespeare's Handwriting. N. & Q. 21 Sept. 1872.

—— On a Question concerning a Supposed Specimen of Shakespeare's Handwriting. [In Reviews and Discussions, 1879.]

Nicholson, Brinsley. The Plays of Sir Thomas More and Hamlet. N. & Q. 29 Nov. 1883.

Hall, A. Shakespeare's Handwriting. 1899.

Baskervill, C. R. Some Parallels to Bartholomew Fair. MP. VI, 1908.

Greg, W. W. Autograph Plays by Anthony Munday. MLR. VIII, 1913.

—— Shakespeare's Hand once more. TLS. 24 Nov., 1 Dec. 1927.

—— T. Goodal in Sir Thomas More. PMLA. XLIV, 1929.

Schücking, L. L. Das Datum des pseudo-shakespeareschen Thomas More. E. Studien, XLVI, 1913.

—— Shakespeare and Sir Thomas More. RES. I, 1925.

Thompson, Sir E. M. Shakespeare's Handwriting. Oxford, 1916.

Simpson, Percy. The Play of Sir Thomas More, and Shakespeare's Hand in it. Library, VIII, 1917.

Green, A. The Apocryphal Sir Thomas More and the Shakespeare Holograph. American Journ. Philology, XXXIX, 1918.

Oliphant, E. H. C. Sir Thomas More. JEGP. XVIII, 1919.

Lawrence, W. J. Was Sir Thomas More ever acted? TLS. 1 July 1920.

Stevenson, W. H. Shakespeare's Schoolmaster and Handwriting. TLS. 8 Jan. 1920.

Byrne, M. St C. Anthony Munday and his Books. Library, I, 1921.

Shakespeare's Hand in The Play of Sir Thomas More. Cambridge, 1923. [Contributions by A. W. Pollard, W. W. Greg, Sir E. M. Thompson, J. D. Wilson, and R. W. Chambers.]

Greenwood, Sir George. The Shakespeare Signatures and Sir Thomas More. 1924.

van Dam, B. A. P. The Text of Shakspeare's Hamlet. 1924.

Harrison, G. B. The Date of Sir Thomas More. RES. I, 1925.

Pollard, A. W. Verse Tests and the Date of Sir Thomas More. RES. I, 1925.

Tannenbaum, S. A. Shakspere's Unquestioned Autographs and the Addition to Sir Thomas Moore. Stud. Phil. XXII, 1925.

—— The Booke of Sir Thomas Moore. New York, 1927.

—— Problems in Shakspere's Penmanship. New York, 1927.

—— More about the Booke of Sir Thomas Moore. PMLA. XLIII, 1928.

Sievers, Eduard. Shakespeares Anteil am 'King Lear.' [In Anglica, vol. II, Leipzig, 1925.]

Acheson, Arthur. Shakespeare, Chapman et Sir Thomas More. Revue anglo-américaine, III, 1926.

Marschall, Wilhelm. Das Sir Thomas Moore-Manuskript und die englische Commedia dell' Arte. Ang. LII, 1928.

Golding, S. R. Robert Wilson and Sir Thomas More. N. & Q. 7, 14 April 1928.

Spurgeon, Caroline. Imagery in the Sir Thomas More Fragment. RES. VI, 1930.

Chambers, R. W. Some Sequences of Thought in Shakespeare and in the 147 Lines of Sir Thomas More. MLR. XXVI, 1931.

Schütt, M. Die Quellen des 'Book of Sir Thomas More.' E. Studien, LXVIII, 1933.

Collins, D. C. On the Date of Sir Thomas More. RES. X, 1934.

Edward the Third

[*Jaggard*, pp. 326–7; *Bartlett*, pp. 59–60; *Ebisch and Schücking*, pp. 273–4; *Chambers*, vol. I, pp. 515–8.]

The Raigne of King Edward the third: As it hath bin sundrie times plaied about the Citie of London. 1596. [Facsimile: J. S. Farmer, *TFT*. 1910.]

The Raigne of King Edward the Third. 1599.

Modern editions: E. Capell (Prolusions, 1760); N. Delius (Pseudo-Shakspere'sche Dramen, pt 1, Elberfeld, 1854); K. Warnke and L. Proescholdt, Halle, 1886; G. C. Moore Smith, 1897 (Temple Dramatists); C. F. T. Brooke (Shakespeare Apocrypha, Oxford, 1908).

von Friesen, H. Edward III, angeblich ein Stück von Shakespeare. Sh. Jb. II, 1867.

Collier, J. P. King Edward III, a Historical Play by William Shakespeare. Maidenhead, 1874.

Teetgen, Alexander. Shakespeare's King Edward III. 1875.

Swinburne, A. C. Note on the Historical Play of King Edward III. GM. XXIII, 1879.

von Vincke, G. König Eduard III.—ein Bühnenstück? Sh. Jb. XIV, 1879.

Phipson, E. King Edward III. Trans. New Shakspere Soc. 1889.

Liebau, Gustav. König Eduard III. von England und die Gräfin von Salisbury. Heidelberg, 1900.

—— König Eduard III. im Lichte europäischer Poesie. Heidelberg, 1901.

Smith, R. M. Edward III. A Study of the Authorship. JEGP. X, 1911.

Platt, A. Edward III and Shakespeare's Sonnets. MLR. VI, 1911.

Golding, S. R. The Authorship of Edward III. N. & Q. 5 May 1928.

Østerberg, V. The 'Countess-Scenes' of Edward III. Sh. Jb. LXV, 1929.

Hart, A. The Vocabulary of Edward III. [In Shakespeare and the Homilies, Melbourne, 1935.]

Pericles

[*Jaggard*, pp. 430–3; *Bartlett*, pp. 41–3; *Ebisch and Schücking*, pp. 260–2; *Chambers*, vol. I, pp. 518–28.]

The Late, And much admired Play, Called Pericles, Prince of Tyre. With the true Relation of the whole Historie, adventures, and fortunes of the said Prince: As also, The no lesse strange, and worthy accidents, in the Birth and Life, of his Daughter Mariana. As it hath been divers and sundry times acted by his Majesties Servants, at the Globe on the Banck-side. By William Shakespeare. Imprinted at London for Henry Gosson, and are to be sold at the signe of the Sunne in Pater-noster row, &c. 1609. [Facsimiles: J. O. Halliwell[-Phillipps], 1862; P. Z. Round, 1886; Sir S. Lee, Oxford, 1905.]

The Late, And much admired Play, Called Pericles, Prince of Tyre. 1609 (title identical with Q1, differentiated by 'Eneer Gower' for 'Enter Gower' on sig. A 2. Facsimiles: J. O. Halliwell[-Phillipps],1871; P.Z. Round,1886); 1611 (facs.J.O. Halliwell[-Phillipps], 1871); 1619; 1630 (2 issues); 1635.

Modern editions: A. Morgan, New York, 1891 (*Bankside*: parallel texts); K. Deighton, 1907, 1925 (*Arden*); A. R. Bellinger, New Haven, 1925 (*Yale*).

Wilkins, George. The Painfull Adventures of Pericles Prince of Tyre. Being the true History of the Play of Pericles, as it was lately presented by the worthy and ancient Poet John Gower. 1608; ed. T. Mommsen, Oldenburg, 1857.

Delius, Nicolaus. Über Shakespeares Pericles, Prince of Tyre. Sh. Jb. III, 1868.

Fleay, F. G. On the Play of Pericles. Trans. New Shakspere Soc. 1874.

Boyle, Robert. Pericles. E. Studien, v, 1882.
—— On Wilkins's Share in the Play called Shakspere's Pericles. Trans. New Shakspere Soc. 1882.

Elze, Karl. Notes and Conjectural Emendations on Antony and Cleopatra and Pericles. E. Studien, IX, 1886.

Smyth, A. H. Shakespeare's Pericles and Apollonius of Tyre. Philadelphia, 1898.

Baker, H. T. The Authorship of Pericles, v. i, 1–101. MLN. XXII, 1907.
—— The Relation of Shakspere's Pericles to George Wilkins's Novels. PMLA. XXIII,1908.

Thomas, D. L. On the Play Pericles. E. Studien, XXXIX, 1908.

Garrett, R. M. Gower in Pericles. Sh. Jb. XLVIII, 1912.

Graves, T. S. On the Date and Significance of Pericles. MP. XIII, 1916.

Steinhäuser, Karolina. Die neueren Anschauungen über die Echtheit von Shakespeares Pericles. Heidelberg, 1918.

Sykes, H. D. Wilkins and Shakespeare's Pericles, Prince of Tyre. [In Sidelights on Shakespeare, Stratford-on-Avon, 1919.]

Crosse, G. Pericles on the Stage. N. & Q. 7 May 1921.

Gray, H. D. Heywood's 'Pericles' revised by Shakespeare. PMLA. XL, 1925.

Østerberg, V. Grevinden af Salisbury og Marina af Shakespeare. Copenhagen, 1926.

Cowl, R. P. The Authorship of Pericles and the Date of The Life and Death of Lord Cromwell. 1927.

Allen, Percy. Shakespeare, Jonson and Wilkins as Borrowers. 1928.

Spiker, S. George Wilkins and the Authorship of Pericles. Stud. Phil. XXX, 1933.

The Two Noble Kinsmen

[*Jaggard*, pp. 484–6; *Ebisch and Schücking*, pp. 275–6; *Chambers*, vol. I, pp. 528–32.]

The Two Noble Kinsmen: Presented at the Blackfriers by the Kings Majesties servants, with great applause: Written by the memorable Worthies of their time; Mr. John Fletcher, and Mr. William Shakspeare. Gent. Printed at London by Tho. Cotes, for John Waterson: and are to be sold at the signe of the Crowne in Pauls Churchyard. 1634. [Facsimile: J. S. Farmer, *TFT*. 1910. Reprint: H. Littledale, New Shakspere Soc. 1876.]

Fifty Comedies and Tragedies. Written by Francis Beaumont and John Fletcher, Gentlemen. 1679.

Modern editions: W. W. Skeat, 1875; H. Littledale, New Shakspere Soc. 1885; W. J. Rolfe, New York, 1891; C. H. Herford, 1897 (Temple Dramatists); C. F. T. Brooke (Shakespeare Apocrypha, Oxford, 1908).

Spalding, W. A Letter on Shakespere's Authorship of The Two Noble Kinsmen. Edinburgh, 1833. [Rptd Trans. New Shakspere Soc. 1876.]

Hickson, Samuel. The Shares of Shakespeare and Fletcher in The Two Noble Kinsmen. Westminster Rev. XLVII, 1847. [Rptd with addns by F. G. Fleay and F. J. Furnivall, Trans. New Shakspere Soc. 1874.]

Delius, Nicolaus. Die angebliche Shakespeare-Fletcher'sche Autorschaft des Dramas 'The Two Noble Kinsmen.' Sh. Jb. XIII, 1878.

Boyle, Robert. Shakespeare und die Beiden edlen Vettern. St Petersburg, 1880; E. Studien, IV, 1881.

Boyle, Robert. On Massinger and The Two Noble Kinsmen. Trans. New Shakspere Soc. 1882.

Bierfreund, Theodor. Palamon og Arcite. Copenhagen, 1891.

Oliphant, E. H. C. The Works of Beaumont and Fletcher. E. Studien, xv, 1891.

—— The Plays of Beaumont and Fletcher. New Haven, 1927.

Thorndike, A. H. The Influence of Beaumont and Fletcher on Shakespeare. Worcester, U.S.A. 1901.

Durand, W. Y. Notes on Richard Edwardes. JEGP. iv, 1902.

Petersen, Ottomar. The Two Noble Kinsmen. Ang. xxxviii, 1914.

Sykes, H. D. The Authorship of The Two Noble Kinsmen. MLR. xi, 1916. [Rptd in Sidelights on Shakespeare, Stratford-on-Avon, 1919.]

Lawrence, W. J. New Light on The Two Noble Kinsmen. TLS. 14 July 1921. [See also subsequent correspondence.]

Cruikshank, A. H. Massinger and The Two Noble Kinsmen. Oxford, 1922.

Gray, H. D. Beaumont and The Two Noble Kinsmen. PQ. ii, 1923.

Ege, Karl. Der Anteil Shakespeares an 'The Two Noble Kinsmen.' Sh. Jb. lix, 1924.

Bradley, A. C. Scene-endings in Shakespeare and in The Two Noble Kinsmen. [In A Miscellany, 1929.]

Hart, A. Shakespeare and the Vocabulary of The Two Noble Kinsmen. [In Shakespeare and the Homilies, Melbourne, 1935.]

Other Plays that have been Ascribed to Shakespeare

[*Ebisch and Schücking*, pp. 272–7; *Chambers*, vol. i, pp. 532–42.]

The lamentable and true tragedie of M. Arden of Feversham in Kent. 1592; 1599; 1633; ed. Edward Jacob, Feversham, 1770 (ascribes to Shakespeare); ed. A. H. Bullen, 1887; ed. R. Bayne, 1897 (Temple Dramatists); ed. C. F. T. Brooke (Shakespeare Apocrypha, Oxford, 1908). [See Charles Crawford, Sh. Jb. xxxix, 1903; H. D. Sykes, Sidelights on Shakespeare, Stratford-on-Avon, 1919.

The Birth Of Merlin: Or, The Childe hath found his Father. Written by William Shakespear, and William Rowley. 1662; ed. N. Delius (Pseudo-Shakspere'sche Dramen, pt 3, Elberfeld, 1856); ed. K. Warnke and L. Proescholdt (Pseudo-Shakespearian Plays, pt 4, Halle, 1887); ed. A. F. Hopkinson (Shakespeare's Doubtful Plays, vol. ii, 1892); ed. C. F. T. Brooke

(Shakespeare Apocrypha, Oxford, 1908). [See F. A. Howe, MP. iv, 1906; William Wells, MLR. xvi, 1921.]

A pleasant commodie of faire Em, the millers daughter of Manchester: With the love of William the conqueror. [1605?]; 1631; ed. N. Delius (Pseudo-Shakspere'sche Dramen, pt 5, Elberfeld, 1874); ed. K. Warnke and L. Proescholdt (Pseudo-Shakespearian Plays, pt i, Halle, 1883); ed. A. F. Hopkinson (Shakespeare's Doubtful Plays, vol. iii, 1895); ed. C. F. T. Brooke (Shakespeare Apocrypha, Oxford, 1908); ed. W. W. Greg, *Malone Soc.* 1927. [See Karl Elze, Sh. Jb. xv, 1880; G. Steinschneider, Das pseudo-Shakspere'sche Drama 'Fair Em,' Prowsnitz, 1892; Paul Lohr, 'Le Printemps d'Yver' und die Quelle zu 'Fair Em,' Munich, 1912.]

The Lamentable Tragedie of Locrine, the eldest sonne of King Brutus. Newly set foorth, overseene and corrected, By W. S. 1595; ed. A. F. Hopkinson (Shakespeare's Doubtful Plays, vol. ii, 1892); ed. C. F. T. Brooke (Shakespeare Apocrypha, Oxford, 1908); ed. R. B. McKerrow, *Malone Soc.* 1908. [See Rudolf Brotanek, Ang. Bbl. xi, 1900; Charles Crawford, N. & Q. 26 Jan.–18 May 1901; W. S. Gaud, MP. i, 1904; E. Koeppel, Sh. Jb. xli, 1905; T. Erbe, Die Locrinesage, Halle, 1904; Alfred Neubner, König Lokrin, Berlin, 1908.]

The London Prodigall. By William Shakespeare. 1605; *Ancient British Drama*, vol. i; ed. A. F. Hopkinson (Shakespeare's Doubtful Plays, vol. ii, 1893); ed. C. F. T. Brooke (Shakespeare Apocrypha, Oxford, 1908).

A Most pleasant Comedie of Mucedorus, the Kings Sonne of Valentia. 1598; 1610; 1611; 1613; 1615 ('Amplified with new additions'); 1618; 1619; 1621; [1626?]; 1629; 1631; 1634; 1639; ed. J. P. Collier, 1824; ed. N. Delius (Pseudo-Shakspere'sche Dramen, pt 4, Elberfeld, 1874); *Hazlitt's Dodsley*, vol. vii; ed. K. Warnke and L. Proescholdt, Halle, 1878; ed. A. F. Hopkinson (Shakespeare's Doubtful Plays, vol. ii, 1893); ed. C. F. T. Brooke (Shakespeare Apocrypha, Oxford, 1908). [See Wilhelm Wagner, Sh. Jb. xi, 1876, xiv, 1879; Karl Elze, Sh. Jb. xv, 1880 and E. Studien, vi, 1883; E. Soffé, Ist Mucedorus ein Schauspiel Shakespeares? Brünn, 1887; W. W. Greg, Sh. Jb. xl, 1904.]

The Puritaine Or The Widdow of Watling-streete. Written by W. S. 1607; *Ancient British Drama*, vol. i; ed. A. F. Hopkinson (Shakespeare's Doubtful Plays, vol. iii, 1895); ed. C. F. T. Brooke (Shakespeare Apocrypha, Oxford, 1908). [See A. H. Bullen, Works of Thomas Middleton, 1885 (Introduction).]

The first part Of the true and honorable historie, of the life of Sir John Old-castle, the good Lord Cobham. 1600; 1600 (for 1619, 'Written by William Shakespeare'); *Ancient British Drama*, vol. I; ed. A. F. Hopkinson (Shakespeare's Doubtful Plays, vol. III, 1894); ed. C. F. T. Brooke (Shakespeare Apocrypha, Oxford, 1908); ed. P. Simpson, *Malone Soc.* 1908. [See Wilhelm Baeske, Oldcastle-Falstaff bis zu Shakespeare, Berlin, 1905. See also p. 535 above.]

The True Chronicle Historie of the whole life and death of Thomas Lord Cromwell. Written by W. S. 1602; 1613; *Ancient British Drama*, vol. I; ed. A. F. Hopkinson (Shakespeare's Doubtful Plays, vol. I, 1891); ed. C. F. T. Brooke (Shakespeare Apocrypha, Oxford, 1908). [See Willy Streit, Jena, 1904.]

A Yorkshire Tragedy. Written by W. Shakspeare. 1608; 1619; *Ancient British Drama*, vol. I; ed. A. F. Hopkinson (Shakespeare's Doubtful Plays, vol. I, 1891); ed. C. F. T. Brooke (Shakespeare Apocrypha, Oxford, 1908). [See H. D. Sykes, JEGP. XVI, 1917, and Sidelights on Shakespeare, Stratford-on-Avon, 1919.]

C. THE POEMS

The Poems of Shakespeare, edited with an Introduction and Notes by George Wyndham. 1898.

The Poems and Sonnets of Shakspere. With an Introduction by Edward Dowden. 190?.

Shakespeare's Poems and Pericles. Collotype Facsimiles, with Introduction and Bibliographies by Sidney Lee, of the Earliest Editions. 5 vols. Oxford, 1905.

Sachs, R. Shakespeares Gedichte. Sh. Jb. XXV, 1890.

Reimer, Hans. Der Vers in Shakespeares nichtdramatischen Werken. Bonn, 1908.

Groos, Karl and Netto, Ilse. Psychologisch-statistische Untersuchungen über die visuellen Sinneseindrücke in Shakespeares lyrischen und epischen Dichtungen. E. Studien, XLIII, 1910.

Saintsbury, George. Shakespeare: Poems. CHEL. vol. v, ch. 9, 1910.

Farr, H. Notes on Shakespeare's Printers and Publishers. Library, III, 1923.

Furness, H. K. A Concordance to Shakespeare's Poems. Philadelphia, 1874.

Venus and Adonis

[*Jaggard*, pp. 486–9; *Bartlett*, pp. 3–6; *Ebisch and Schücking*, p. 269; *Chambers*, vol. I, pp. 543–5.]

Venus and Adonis. Vilia miretur vulgus: mihi flavus Apollo Pocula Castalia plena mini-

stret aqua. London Imprinted by Richard Field, and are to be sold at the signe of the white Greyhound in Paules Church-yard. 1593. [Facsimiles: J. O. Halliwell[-Phillipps], 1867; A. Symons, 1886; Sir Sidney Lee, Oxford, 1905 (with bibliography).]

Venus and Adonis. 1594 (rev. edn); [1594–6?] (only extant copy, *penes* H. C. Folger, lacks title); 1596; 1599 (type facs. 1870); 1599; 1602; 1617; 1620; Edinburgh, 1627; 1630; [1630–6?] (only extant copy, in Bodleian, lacks title); 1636.

Modern editions: G. Wyndham, 1898; C. K. Pooler, 1911, 1927 (*Arden*); A. Feuillerat, New Haven, 1927 (*Yale*).

Reardon, J. P. Shakespeare's Venus and Adonis and Lodge's Scilla's Metamorphosis. Shakespeare Soc. Papers, III, 1847.

Morgan, J. A. Venus and Adonis, a Study of Warwickshire Dialect. New York Shakespeare Soc. 1885, 1900.

Wuerzner, Alois. Die Orthographie der ersten Quarto-Ausgaben von Shakespeares 'Venus and Adonis' und 'Lucrece' Vienna, 1887.

Dürnhöfer, M. Shakespeares Venus und Adonis im Verhältnis zu Ovids Metamorphosen und Constables Schäfergesang. Halle, 1890.

Sarrazin, Gregor. Die Abfassungszeit von Shakespeares Venus und Adonis. E. Studien, XIX, 1894.

Brown, Carleton. Shakespeare and the Horse. Library, III, 1912.

Marschall, Wilhelm. Shakespeares Orthographie. Ang, LI, 1927.

Spencer, Hazleton. Shakespeare's Use of Golding in Venus and Adonis. MLN. XLIV, 1929.

Lucrece

[*Jaggard*, pp. 441–2; *Bartlett*, pp. 6–9; *Ebisch and Schücking*, p. 270; *Chambers*, vol. I, pp. 545–7.]

Lucrece. London. Printed by Richard Field, for John Harrison, and are to be sold at the signe of the white Greyhound in Paules Churhyard [*sic*]. 1594. [Running-title, 'The Rape of Lucrece'. Facsimiles: J. O. Halliwell[-Phillipps], 1867; F. J. Furnivall, 1886; Sir Sidney Lee, Oxford, 1905 (with bibliography).]

Lucrece. 1598; 1600; 1607; 1616 (as The Rape of Lucrece); 1624; 1632; 1655 (adds J. Quarles, The Banishment of Tarquin).

Modern editions: G. Wyndham, 1898; C. K. Pooler, 1911, 1927 (*Arden*).

Wuerzner, Alois. Die Orthographie der ersten Quarto-Ausgaben von Shakespeares 'Venus and Adonis' und 'Lucrece.' Vienna, 1887.

Ewig, W. Shakespeares Lucrece. Eine literar-historische Untersuchung. Ang. xxii, 1899; Kiel, 1899.

Vordieck, A. Parallelismus zwischen Shakespeares Macbeth und seiner epischen Dichtung Lucrece. Neisse, 1901.

Marschall, Wilhelm. Shakespeares Orthographie. Ang. li, 1927.

—— Das 'Argument' zu Shakespeares Lucrece. Ang. liii, 1929.

The Passionate Pilgrim

[*Jaggard*, pp. 429–30; *Bartlett*, pp. 9–10; *Ebisch and Schücking*, p. 270; *Chambers*, vol. i, pp. 547–8.]

The Passionate Pilgrime. By W. Shakespeare. At London Printed for W. Jaggard, and are to be sold by W. Leake, at the Grey-hound in Paules Churchyard. 1599. [Second title on C3, 'Sonnets To sundry notes of Musicke'. Facsimiles: type facs. C. Edmonds, 1870; E. Dowden, 1883; Sir Sidney Lee, Oxford, 1905.]

The Passionate Pilgrime Or Certaine Amorous Sonnets, betweene Venus and Adonis, newly corrected and augmented. By W. Shakespeare. The third Edition. Whereunto is newly added two Love-Epistles, the first from Paris to Hellen, and Hellens answere backe againe to Paris. 1612. [2nd edn not known. The Epistles are by T. Heywood. Some copies are found without Shakespeare's name, possibly, it is thought, owing to Heywood's protest in his Apology for Actors, 1612, against the piracy.]

Modern edition: C. K. Pooler, 1911, 1927 (*Arden*).

Höhnen, A. Shakespeare's Passionate Pilgrim. Jena, 1867.

Halliwell-Phillipps, J. O. The Passionate Pilgrim. [In Outlines, vol. i, p. 401, 1890.]

Kuhl, E. P. Shakespeare and the Passionate Pilgrim. MLN. xxxiv, 1919.

The Phoenix and Turtle

[*Jaggard*, p. 471; *Bartlett*, pp. 10–11; *Chambers*, vol. i, pp. 549–50.]

Loves Martyr: Or, Rosalins Complaint. Allegorically shadowing the truth of Love, in the constant Fate of the Phoenix and Turtle. A Poeme translated out of the Italian by Robert Chester. To these are added some new compositions of severall moderne Writers whose names are subscribed to their severall workes, upon the first subject: viz. the Phoenix and Turtle. London Imprinted for E[dward] B[lount]. 1601; 1611 (as The Anuals of great Brittaine); rptd A. B. Grosart, New Shakspere Soc. 1878.

Halliwell[-Phillipps], J. O. Some Account of Chester's Love's Martyr. 1865.

Furnivall, F. J. On Chester's Love's Martyr: Essex is not the Turtle-Dove of Shakspere's Phoenix and the Turtle. Trans. New Shakspere Soc. pt iii, 1877–9.

Fairchild, A. H. R. The Phoenix and Turtle. A Critical and Historical Interpretation. E. Studien, xxxiii, 1904.

Brown, Carleton. Poems by Sir John Salusbury and Robert Chester. EETS. Ex. Ser. 1914.

The Sonnets

[*Jaggard*, pp. 452–6; *Bartlett*, pp. 11–2; *Ebisch and Schücking*, pp. 263–9; *Chambers*, vol. i, pp. 555–76.]

Shake-speares Sonnets. Never before Imprinted. At London By G. Eld for T. T[horpe] and are to be solde by John Wright, dwelling at Christ Church gate. 1609. [Some copies have William Aspley instead of John Wright. Appended is A Lovers complaint. By William Shakespeare. Facsimiles: T. Tyler, 1886; Sir S. Lee, Oxford, 1905; 1925 (J. Cape); 1926 (N. Douglas).]

Poems: Written by Wil. Shake-speare. Gent. 1640. [Includes the sonnets and A Lover's Complaint, and interspersed among them the full contents of The Passionate Pilgrim of 1612, together with some other poems, most of which are not attrib. to Shakespeare. Rptd 1885 (A. R. Smith).]

Modern editions: E. Dowden, 1881; T. Tyler, 1890 and 1899; G. Wyndham, 1898 (with Poems); S. Butler, 1899; C. C. Stopes, 1904; H. C. Beeching, 1904; A. H. Bullen, 1905; W. H. Hadow, Oxford, 1907; C. M. Walsh, 1908; R. M. Alden, Boston, 1916 (variorum); C. K. Pooler, 1918 (*Arden*); E. B. Reed, New Haven, 1923 (*Yale*); T. G. Tucker, Cambridge, 1924; C. F. T. Brooke, New York, 1936.

Boaden, James. On the Sonnets of Shakespeare, identifying the Person to whom they were addressed and elucidating Several Points in the Poet's History. 1837. [Originally published GM. cii, 1832.]

Brown, C. A. Shakespeare's Autobiographical Poems. 1838.

Delius, Nicolaus. Über Shakespeares Sonette. Sh. Jb. i, 1865.

Massey, Gerald. Shakespeare's Sonnets, never before interpreted, his Private Friends identified, together with a recovered Likeness of himself. 1866.

—— The Secret Drama of Shakespeare's Sonnets. 1872; 1888.

von Friesen, H. Über Shakespeares Sonette. Sh. Jb. iv, 1869.

Brown, H. The Sonnets of Shakespeare solved. 1870.

Goedeke, K. Über die Shakespeare Sonette. Deutsche Rundschau, III, 1877.

Hertzberg, W. Eine griechische Quelle zu Shakespeares Sonetten. Sh. Jb. XIII, 1878.

Spalding, T. A. Shakespeare's Sonnets. GM. XX, 1878.

Isaac [Conrad], Hermann. Zu den Sonetten Shaksperes. Archiv, LIX–LXII, 1878–9.

—— Wie weit geht die Abhängigkeit Shakespeares von Daniel als Lyriker? Sh. Jb. XVII, 1882.

—— Die Sonett-Periode in Shakespeares Leben. Sh. Jb. XIX, 1884.

—— Shaksperes Selbstbekenntnisse. Hamlet und sein Urbild. Stuttgart, 1897.

Stengel, E. Bilden die ersten 126 Sonette Shakespeares einen Sonettzyklus, und welches ist die ursprüngliche Reihenfolge derselben? E. Studien, IV, 1881.

Krauss, Fritz. Die Schwarze Schöne der Shakespeare-Sonette. Sh. Jb. XVI, 1881.

Leo, F. A. Hilfsmittel bei Untersuchungen über Shakespeares Sonette. Sh. Jb. XXIII, 1888.

Stopes, C. C. Shakespeare's Sonnets. Sh. Jb. XXV, 1890.

—— The Date of Shakespeare's Sonnets. Athenaeum, 19, 26 March 1898.

—— Mr. W. H. Athenaeum, 4 Aug. 1900.

von Mauntz, Alfred. Shakespeares lyrische Gedichte. Sh. Jb. XXVIII, 1893.

—— Einige Glossen zu Shakespeares Sonett 121. Ang. XIX, 1897.

Sarrazin, Gregor. Die Entstehung von Shakespeares 'Love's Labour's Lost.' Sh. Jb. XXXI, 1895.

—— Shakespeares Lehrjahre. Eine literarhistorische Studie. Weimar, 1897.

—— Wortechos bei Shakespeare. Sh. Jb. XXXIII, XXXIV, 1897–8.

—— Zu Sonett CIV. Sh. Jb. XXXIV, 1898.

—— Aus Shakespeares Meisterwerkstatt. Stilgeschichtliche Studien. Berlin, 1906.

Archer, William. Shakespeare's Sonnets. Fortnightly Rev. LXII, 1897.

Newdigate, Lady Newdigate. Gossip from a Muniment-Room. 2 vols. 1897–8.

Lee, Sir Sidney. Shakespeare and the Earl of Pembroke. Fortnightly Rev. LXIX, 1898.

—— A Life of William Shakespeare. 1898; 1925 (rev. edn).

—— Ovid and Shakespeare's Sonnets. Quart. Rev. CCX, 1909.

Tyler, Thomas. The Herbert-Fitton Theory of Shakespeare's Sonnets. 1898.

McClumpha, C. F. Shakespeare's Sonnets and Love's Labour's Lost. MLN. XV, 1900.

McClumpha, C. F. Shakespeare's Sonnets and A Midsummer Night's Dream. MLN. XVI, 1901.

—— Shakespeare's Sonnets and Romeo and Juliet. Sh. Jb. XL, 1904.

Filon, Augustin. Les Sonnets de Shakespeare. Revue des Deux Mondes, LXXI, 1901.

Acheson, Arthur. Shakespeare and the Rival Poet. 1903.

—— Mistress Davenant, the Dark Lady of Shakespeare's Sonnets. 1913.

—— Shakespeare's Sonnet Story, 1592–8. 1922.

Hughes, C. Willobie his Avisa. 1904.

Bates, E. S. The Sincerity of Shakespeare's Sonnets. MP. VIII, 1910–1.

Mackail, J. W. Shakespeare's Sonnets. [In Lectures on Poetry, 1911.]

de Montmorency, J. E. G. The 'Other Poet of Shakespeare's Sonnets. Contemporary Rev. CI, 1912.

Alden, R. M. The Quarto Arrangement of Shakespeare's Sonnets. [In Kittredge Anniversary Papers, Boston, 1913.]

—— The 1640 Text of Shakespeare's Sonnets. MP. XIV, 1916–7.

Gray, H. D. The Arrangement and the Date of Shakespeare's Sonnets. PMLA. XXX, 1915.

Wolff, M. J. Petrarkismus und Antipetrarkismus in Shakespeares Sonetten. E. Studien, XL, 1915–6.

—— Shakespeare und der Petrarkismus. Die neueren Sprachen, XXVIII, 1921.

Ord, Hubert. Chaucer and the Rival Poet in Shakespeare's Sonnets. 1921.

Poel, William, et al. Shakespeare and the Davenants. TLS. 2 June–4 Aug. 1921.

Redin, Mats. The Friend in Shakespeare's Sonnets. E. Studien, LVI, 1922.

Forrest, H. T. S. The Five Authors of 'Shake-speares Sonnets.' 1923.

Emerson, O. F. Shakespeare's Sonnetteering. Stud. Phil. XX, 1923.

Fort, J. A. The Two Dated Sonnets of Shakespeare. Oxford, 1924.

—— The Time-Scheme of Shakespeare's Sonnets. Nineteenth Century, C, 1926.

—— Thorpe's Text of Shakespeare's Sonnets. RES. II, 1926.

—— The Story contained in the Second Series of Shakespeare's Sonnets. RES. III, 1927.

—— Further Notes on Shakespeare's Sonnets. Library, IX, 1928.

—— The Date of Shakespeare's 107th Sonnet. Library, IX, 1929.

—— A Time-Scheme for Shakespeare's Sonnets. 1929.

—— The Order and Chronology of Shakespeare's Sonnets. RES. IX, 1933.

Bray, Sir Denys. The Original Order of Shakespeare's Sonnets. 1925.

Bray, Sir Denys. The Art-Form of the Elizabethan Sonnet Sequence and Shakespeare's Sonnets. Sh. Jb. LXIII, 1927.

Fischer, Rudolf. Shakespeares Sonette (Gruppierung, Kunstform). Ed. K. Brunner, Vienna, 1925.

Sievers, Eduard. Shakespeares Anteil am 'King Lear.' [In Anglica, vol. II, Leipzig, 1925.]

Harrison, G. B. Willobie his Avisa. 1926. [Introduction.]

—— The Mortal Moon. TLS. 29 Nov. 1928.

Robertson, J. M. The Problems of the Shakespear Sonnets. 1926.

Marschall, W. Aus Shakespeares poetischen Briefwechsel. Heidelberg, 1926.

—— Das Zentralproblem der Shakespeare Sonette. Ang. LI, 1927.

Beckwith, Elizabeth. On the Chronology of Shakespeare's Sonnets. JEGP. XXV, 1926.

Spira, Theodor. Shakespeares Sonette in Zusammenhang seines Werkes. Königsberg, 1929.

Scott, J. G. Les Sonnets élisabéthains. Les Sources et l'Apport personnel. Paris, 1929. [Ch. XIV.]

Murry, J. M. Concerning Sonnet 107. New Adelphi, March 1929.

Douglas, Lord Alfred. The True History of Shakespeare's Sonnets. 1933.

Kellner, L. Shakespeares Sonette. E. Studien, LXVIII, 1933.

Mattingly, G. The Date of Shakespeare's Sonnet CVII. PMLA. XLVIII, 1933.

Dannenberg, F. Shakespeares Sonette: Herkunft, Wesen, Deutung. Sh. Jb. LXX, 1934.

Knights, L. C. Revaluations. V. Shakespeare's Sonnets. Scrutiny, III, 1934.

Empson, W. They that have Power. [In Some Versions of Pastoral, 1935.]

Archer, C. 'Thou' and 'You' in the Sonnets. TLS. 27 June 1936.

Nisbet, U. The Onlie Begetter. 1936.

A Lover's Complaint

[For edns see under Sonnets, p. 581 above.]

Delius, Nicolaus. Shakespeare's A Lover's Complaint. Sh. Jb. XX, 1885.

Sarrazin, Gregor. Über Shakespeares Klage der Liebenden. [In Kleine Shakespeare-Studien, Breslau, 1902.]

Mackail, J. W. A Lover's Complaint. E. & S. III, 1912.

Robertson, J. M. Shakespeare and Chapman. A Thesis of Chapman's Authorship of A Lover's Complaint and his Origination of Timon of Athens. 1917.

IV. THE CRITICISM OF SHAKESPEARE

A. TECHNICAL CRITICISM

A Companion to Shakespeare Studies. Ed. H. Granville-Barker and G. B. Harrison, Cambridge, 1934. [C. J. Sisson, The Theatres and Companies; H. Granville-Barker, Shakespeare's Dramatic Art; G. Rylands, Shakespeare the Poet; G. D. Willcock, Shakespeare and Elizabethan English; E. J. Dent, Shakespeare and Music; A. L. Attwater, Shakespeare's Sources; B. Dobrée, Shakespeare and the Drama of his Time; A. W. Pollard, Shakespeare's Text; T. S. Eliot and J. Isaacs, Shakespearian Criticsm; J. Isaacs, Shakespearian Scholarship; H. Child, Shakespeare in the Theatre to the Present Time.]

(1) SOURCES AND INFLUENCES

[*Ebisch and Schücking*, pp. 61–79.]

(a) Collections of Shakespeare's Sources

[Lennox, Charlotte.] Shakespear Illustrated, or, the Novels and Histories on which the Plays of Shakespear are founded. 3 vols. 1753–4, 1756.

[Nichols, John.] Six Old Plays on which Shakespeare founded his Measure for Measure. Comedy of Errors. The Taming of the Shrew. King John. King Henry IV and King Henry V. King Lear. 2 vols. 1770.

Capell, Edward. The School of Shakespeare. [Notes and Various Readings to Shakespeare, vol. III, 1783.]

Echtermayer, T., Henschel, L., and Simrock, K. Quellen des Shakespeare in Novellen, Märchen und Sagen. 3 pts, Berlin, 1831; 2 pts, Bonn, 1870.

Collier, J. P. Shakespeare's Library. A Collection of the Romances, Novels, Poems and Histories, used by Shakespeare as the Foundation of his Dramas. 2 vols. [1843], 1850; rev. W. C. Hazlitt, 6 vols. 1875 (adding the plays).

Halliwell[-Phillipps], J. O. The Works of William Shakespeare. 16 vols. 1853–65. [Includes 'all the original novels and tales on which the plays are founded.']

Hazlitt, W. C. Shakespeare's Jest-Books. 3 vols. 1864.

—— Fairy Tales, Legends, and Romances illustrating Shakespeare and Other Early English Writers. 1875.

Furness, H. H. and H. H. jr. A New Variorum Edition of the Works of Shakespeare. Philadelphia, 1871–. [Reprints with each play its source or sources. 19 plays have been issued.]

Skeat, W. W. Shakespeare's Plutarch. 1875.
Leo, F. A. Four Chapters of North's Plutarch. 1878.
Boswell-Stone, W. G. Shakspere's Holinshed. 1896; 1907.
Gollancz, Sir Israel, et al. The Shakespeare Classics. 11 vols. 1907–13. [For individual titles see under separate plays.]
Schubring, Paul. Shakespeares italienische Novellen. Berlin, 1920.
Nicoll, A. and J. Holinshed's Chronicles as used in Shakespeare's Plays. 1927. (Everyman's Lib.)

(b) Modern Studies

[Additional references will be found in the general section, Literary Relations with the Continent, pp. 325–45 above.]

(i) General Studies

Farmer, Richard. Essay on the Learning of Shakespeare. Cambridge, 1767 and 1767 (expanded). [Rptd in D. Nichol Smith, Eighteenth Century Essays on Shakespeare, Glasgow, 1903.]
Anders, H. R. D. Shakespeare's Books. Berlin, 1904.
Stopes, C. C. Shakespeare's Industry. 1916.
Thorndike, A. H. Shakespeare as a Debtor. New York, 1916.
Wheatley, H. B. Shakespeare as a Man of Letters. Trans. Bibliog. Soc. xiv, 1919.
Bartlett, H. C. Mr. William Shakespeare: Original and Early Editions of his Quartos and Folios, his Source Books and those containing Contemporary Notices. New Haven, 1922. [A bibliography. Source-books, pp. 85–135.]
Kellett, E. E. Shakspere as a Borrower. [In Suggestions, Cambridge, 1923.]
Schelling, F. E. Foreign Influences in Elizabethan Plays. New York, 1923.

(ii) Classical Influences

Stapfer, Paul. Shakespeare et l'Antiquité. 2 vols. Paris, 1879–80, 1884; tr. Eng. 1880.
Delius, Nicolaus. Klassische Reminiszenzen in Shakespeares Dramen. Sh. Jb. xviii, 1883.
Cruikshank, A. H. The Classical Attainments of Shakespeare. [In Noctes Shakespearianae, 1887.]
Root, R. K. Classical Mythology in Shakespeare. New York, 1903.
Collins, J. C. Shakespeare as a Classical Scholar. [In Studies in Shakespeare, 1904.]
Watt, L. M. Attic and Elizabethan Tragedy. 1908.

Theobald, William. The Classical Element in the Shakespeare Plays. Ed. R. M. Theobald, 1909.
Bush, Douglas. Notes on Shakespeare's Classical Mythology. PQ. vi, 1927.

Rick, Leo. Shakespeare und Ovid. Sh. Jb. lv, 1919.
Coulter, C. C. The Plautine Tradition in Shakespeare. JEGP. xix, 1920.
Cunliffe, J. W. The Influence of Seneca on Elizabethan Tragedy. 1893.
Lucas, F. L. Seneca and Elizabethan Tragedy. Cambridge, 1922.

(iii) Contemporary Continental Influences

Murray, J. R. The Influence of Italian upon English Literature during the Sixteenth and Seventeenth Centuries. Cambridge, 1886.
Underhill, J. G. Spanish Literature in the England of the Tudors. New York, 1899.
Upham, A. H. The French Influence in English Literature from the Accession of Elizabeth to the Restoration. New York, 1908.
Lee, Sir Sidney. Shakespeare and the Italian Renaissance. British Academy Lecture, 1915.
Thomas, H. Shakespeare and Spain. Oxford, 1922.
Rébora, Piero. L'Italia nel Dramma inglese (1558–1642). Milan, 1925.

Lothian, J. M. Shakespeare's Knowledge of Aretino's Plays. MLR. xxv, 1930.
Beyersdorff, Robert. Giordano Bruno und Shakespeare. Sh. Jb. xxvi, 1891.
König, Wilhelm. Shakespeare und Dante. Sh. Jb. vii, 1872.
Meyer, Edward. Machiavelli and the Elizabethan Drama. Heidelberg, 1897.
Sarrazin, Gregor. Shakespeare und Orlando Pescetti. E. Studien, xlvi, 1913.

Feis, Jacob. Shakespeare and Montaigne. 1884.
Robertson, J. M. Montaigne and Shakespeare. 1897.
Hooker, E. R. The Relation of Shakespeare to Montaigne. PMLA. xvii, 1902.
Collins, J. C. Shakespeare and Montaigne. [In Studies in Shakespeare, 1904.]
Villey, Pierre. Montaigne and Shakespeare. 1916.
Taylor, G. C. Shakespeare's Debt to Montaigne. Oxford, 1925.
König, Wilhelm. Über die Entlehnungen Shakespeares, insbesondere aus Rabelais und einigen italienischen Dramatikern. Sh. Jb. ix, 1874.

Harrison, T. P. Shakespeare and Montemayor's Diana. Austin, 1926.

(iv) Contemporary English Influences

Gatch, K. H. Shakespeare's Allusions to the Older Drama. PQ. VII, 1928.

Thorndike, A. H. The Influence of Beaumont and Fletcher on Shakespeare. Worcester, U.S.A. 1901.

Robertson, J. M. Shakespeare and Chapman. 1917.

Tynan, J. L. The Influence of Greene on Shakespeare's Early Romance. PMLA. XXVII, 1912.

Zeeveld, W. G. The Influence of Hall on Shakespeare's English Historical Plays. ELH. III, 1936.

Aronstein, Philipp. Shakespeare und Ben Jonson. E. Studien, XXXIV, 1904.

Hense, C. C. John Lilly und Shakespeare. Sh. Jb. VII, VIII, 1872–3.

Goodlet, John. Shakespeare's Debt to John Lilly. E. Studien, V, 1882.

Verity, A. W. The Influence of Christopher Marlowe on Shakespeare's Earlier Style. Cambridge, 1886.

Stern, Alfred. Shakespeare und Marlowe. Archiv, CLVI, 1929.

Radebrecht, Friedrich. Shakespeares Abhängigkeit von John Marston. Cöthen, 1918.

Schücking, L. L. Eine Anleihe Shakespeares bei Tourneur. E. Studien, L, 1916.

Starnes, D. T. Shakespeare and Elyot's Governour. Austin, 1927.

Hart, A. Shakespeare and the Homilies. [In Shakespeare and the Homilies, Melbourne, 1935.]

Rushton, W. L. Shakespeare and The Arte of English Poesie. Liverpool, 1909.

Hermann, E. Shakespeare und Spenser. [In Drei Shakespeare-Studien, Erlangen, 1879.]

Luce, M. Spenser and Shakespeare. [In Man and Nature, 1935.]

Craig, Hardin. Shakespeare and Wilson's Arte of Rhetorique. Stud. Phil. XXVIII, 1931.

(v) Influence of the Bible

Wordsworth, C. On Shakespeare's Knowledge and Use of the Bible. 1864; 1892.

Carter, Thomas. Shakespeare and Holy Scripture. 1905.

Burgess, W. The Bible in Shakespeare. New York, 1918.

Noble, R. Shakespeare's Biblical Knowledge. 1935.

(vi) Miscellaneous Influences

Green, Henry. Shakespeare and the Emblem Writers. 1870.

Brie, Friedrich. Shakespeare und die Impresa-Kunst seiner Zeit. Sh. Jb. L, 1914.

Jente, R. The Proverbs of Shakespeare. Washington University Stud. XIII, 1926.

(2) Transmission of the Text, Chronology, Authenticity, and Related Problems

(a) The Transmission of the Text

[*Ebisch and Schücking*, pp. 44–8; *Chambers*, vol. I, chs. 4, 5, 6. The list that follows is restricted to writings immediately concerned with Shakespeare and should be supplemented by the section on Book Production and Distribution, pp. 345–64 above.]

(i) Printing and Publishing

Blades, William. Common Typographical Errors, with Especial Reference to the Text of Shakespeare. Athenaeum, 27 Jan. 1872.

—— Shakespeare and Typography. 1872.

van Dam, B. A. P. and Stoffel, C. William Shakespeare: Prosody and Text. Leyden, 1900.

van Dam, B. A. P. The Text of Shakespeare's Hamlet. 1924.

—— Textual Criticism of Shakespeare's Plays. E. Studies, VI, 1925.

Pollard, A. W. Shakespeare Folios and Quartos. 1909.

—— King Richard II. A New Quarto. 1916.

—— The Manuscripts of Shakespeare's Plays. Library, VII, 1916.

—— Shakespeare's Fight with the Pirates. Cambridge, 1920.

—— The Foundations of Shakespeare's Text. British Academy Lecture, 1923.

Pollard, A. W. and Bartlett, H. C. A Census of Shakespeare's Plays in Quarto. 1916.

Pollard, A. W. and Wilson, J. D. The 'Stolne and Surreptitious' Shakespearian Texts. TLS. 9, 16 Jan. 1919.

—— What follows if Some of the Good Quarto Editions of Shakespeare's Plays were printed from his Autograph Manuscripts? Trans. Bibliog. Soc. XV, 1920.

Wilson, J. D. The Copy for Hamlet, 1603. 1918.

—— The Tempest. Cambridge, 1921. [General introduction to New Cambridge Shakespeare.]

—— Spellings and Misprints in the Second Quarto of Hamlet. E. & S. X, 1924.

Rhodes, R. C. Shakespeare's Prompt Books. TLS. 21, 28 July 1921.

Lawrence, W. J. The Theory of Assembled Texts. TLS. 11 Jan. 1923.

—— The Secret of 'The Bad Quartos.' Criterion, April 1931.

Simpson, Percy. The Bibliographical Study of Shakespeare. Proc. Oxford Bibliog. Soc. I, 1923.

Kellner, Leon. Restoring Shakespeare. A Critical Analysis of the Misreadings in Shakespeare's Works. Leipzig, 1925.

Albright, E. M. Dramatic Publication in England, 1580–1640. New York, 1927. [With bibliography.]

Greg, W. W. Principles of Emendation in Shakespeare. British Academy Lecture, 1928.

(ii) Shakespeare's Printers and Publishers

Plomer, H. R. The Printers of Shakespeare's Plays and Poems. Library, VII, 1906.

Farr, Henry. Notes on Shakespeare's Printers and Publishers. Library, III, 1923.

Kirwood, A. E. M. Richard Field, Printer, 1589–1604. Library, XII, 1931.

Willoughby, E. E. The Printing of the First Folio. Bibliog. Soc. 1933.

(iii) Shorthand and Shakespeare's Text

Levy, Matthias. Shakespeare and Shorthand. 1884.

—— William Shakespeare and Timothe Bright. 1910.

Dewischeit, Curt. Shakespeare und die Stenographie. Sh. Jb. XXXIV, 1898.

Friedrich, P. Studien zur englischen Stenographie im Zeitalter Shakespeares. Leipzig, 1914.

Price, H. T. The Text of Henry V. Newcastle-under-Lyme, 1920.

van Dam, B. A. P. The Text of Shakespeare's Hamlet. 1924.

Kraner, W. Zur englischen Kurzschrift im Zeitalter Shakespeares. Das Jane-Seager-Manuskript. Sh. Jb. LXVII, 1931.

Matthews, W. Shorthand and the Bad Shakespeare Quartos. MLR. XXVII, 1932. [Postscript, MLR. XXVIII, 1933.]

—— Peter Bales, Timothy Bright and William Shakespeare. JEGP. XXXIV, 1935.

—— Shakespeare and the Reporters. Library, XV, 1935.

(iv) Shakespeare's Handwriting

[*Chambers*, vol. I, pp. 499–515. For general works on Elizabethan handwriting see pp. 346–7 above.]

Simpson, Richard. Are there any Extant Manuscripts in Shakespeare's Handwriting? N. & Q. 1 July 1871.

Spedding, James. Shakespeare's Handwriting. N. & Q. 21 Sept. 1872.

Thompson, Sir E. M. Shakespeare's Handwriting. Oxford, 1916.

—— Shakespeare's Handwriting. [In Shakespeare's England, vol. I, Oxford, 1916.]

—— Two Pretended Autographs of Shakespeare. Library, VIII, 1917.

Tannenbaum, S. A. Shakspere's Unquestioned Autographs and the Addition to Sir Thomas More. Stud. Phil. XXII, 1925.

—— Problems in Shakespeare's Penmanship. New York, 1927.

(b) The Chronology of the Plays

[*Ebisch and Schücking*, pp. 187–8; *Chambers*, vol. I, pp. 243–74. See also under Prosody, p. 590 below.]

Malone, Edmond. An Attempt to ascertain the Order in which the Plays attributed to Shakespeare were written. [In Steevens's edn of the Works, 1778; rev. in Malone's edn 1790 and again in the 3rd variorum edn, 1821.]

Hurdis, James. Cursory Remarks upon the Arrangement of the Plays of Shakespeare. 1792.

Chalmers, George. The Chronology of Shakespeare's Dramas. [In A Supplemental Apology, 1799.]

Furnivall, F. J. The Succession of Shakspere's Works and the Use of Metrical Tests in settling it. 1874.

Ingram, J. K. On the 'Weak Endings' of Shakespeare. Trans. New Shakspere Soc. 1874.

Fleay, F. G. Metrical Tests as applied to Dramatic Poetry. Trans. New Shakspere Soc. I, 1874.

—— Metrical Tests applied to Shakespeare. [In C. M. Ingleby, Shakespeare, the Man and the Book, vol. II, 1881.]

Stokes, H. P. An Attempt to determine the Chronological Order of Shakespeare's Plays. 1878.

Pulling, F. S. The 'Speech-Ending' Test applied to Twenty of Shakespeare's Plays. Trans. New Shakspere Soc. 1879.

Schipper, J. Shakespeares Blankvers. [In Englische Metrik, pt II, Bonn, 1888.]

ten Brink, Bernhard. Shakspere. Strasburg, 1893, 1894. [2nd lecture.]

Sarrazin, Gregor. Zur Chronologie von Shakespeares Jugenddramen. Sh. Jb. XXX, 1894.

—— Chronologie von Shakespeares Dichtungen. Sh. Jb. XXXII, 1896.

—— William Shakespeares Lehrjahre. Weimar, 1897.

Conrad, Hermann. Metrische Untersuchungen zur Feststellung der Abfassungszeit von Shakespeares Dramen. Sh. Jb. XXXI, 1896.

—— Kennen wir Shaksperes Entwicklungsgang? Preussische Jahrbücher, CXXII, 1905.

—— Eine neue Methode der chronologischen Shakespeare-Forschung. Germanisch-romanische Monatsschrift, I, 1909.

Ward, Sir A. W. Chronological Order of Shakspere's Plays. [In History of English Dramatic Literature, vol. ii, 1899.]

Ekwall, E. Die Shakespeare-Chronologie. Germanisch-romanische Monatsschrift, iii, 1911.

(c) Authenticity and Related Problems

[*Chambers*, vol. i, pp. 205–42.]

Hoffmann, F. H. Über die Beteuerungen in Shakespeares Dramen. Halle, 1894.

Thompson, E. N. S. Elizabethan Dramatic Collaboration. E. Studien, xl, 1908.

Oliphant, E. H. C. Shakespeare's Plays: An Examination. MLR. iii, iv, 1908–9.

—— Collaboration in Elizabethan Drama. PQ. viii, 1929.

—— The Shakespeare Canon. Quart. Rev. cclix, 1932.

Manly, J. M. Cuts and Insertions in Shakespeare's Plays. Stud. Phil. xiv, 1917.

Robertson, J. M. Shakespeare and Chapman. 1917.

—— The Shakespeare Canon. 4 pts, 1922–32.

—— An Introduction to the Study of the Shakespeare Canon. 1924.

Keller, Wolfgang. Shakespeare als Überarbeiter fremder Dramen. Sh. Jb. lviii, 1922.

Chambers, Sir E. K. The Disintegration of Shakespeare. British Academy Lecture, 1924.

—— The Unrest in Shakespearean Studies. Nineteenth Century, li, 1927.

Gaw, Allison. Actors' Names in Basic Shakespearean Texts. PMLA. xl, 1925.

Lawrence, W. J. Early Dramatic Collaboration: A Theory. [In Pre-Restoration Stage Studies, Cambridge, U.S.A. 1927.]

—— Shakespeare's Workshop. Oxford, 1928. [Includes: Shakespeare's Lost Characters, and A New Shakespearean Test.]

Bald, R. C. Macbeth and the 'Short' Plays. RES. iv, 1928.

Hart, A. The Number of Lines in Shakespeare's Plays. RES. viii, 1932.

(3) Textual Criticism

[See also the preceding section.]

The Works of William Shakespeare. Ed. W. G. Clark, J. Glover and W. A. Wright, 9 vols. Cambridge, 1863–8, etc. [Preface provides a succinct account of previous textual criticism.]

Walder, Ernest. Shakespearean Criticism, Textual and Literary, from Dryden to the End of the 18th Century. Bradford, 1895.

Walder, Ernest. The Text of Shakespeare. CHEL. vol. v, 1910.

Lounsbury, T. R. The First Editors of Shakespeare (Pope and Theobald). 1906. [Pbd New York, as The Text of Shakespeare, its History from the Quartos to Theobald, 1906.]

Theobald, Lewis. Shakespeare Restored; or, a Specimen of the Many Errors as well committed as unemended by Mr. Pope in his Late Edition of this Poet. Designed to restore the True Reading of Shakespeare in All the Editions ever yet printed. 1726; 1740.

Upton, John. Critical Observations on Shakespeare. 1746; Dublin, 1747; 1748 (rev. edn with preface on Warburton's edn).

Grey, Zachary. A Word or Two of Advice to William Warburton; a Dealer in Many Words. 1746.

—— A Free and Familiar Letter to William Warburton. 1750.

—— Remarks upon a Late Edition of Shakespeare [*i.e.* Warburton's], with a Defence of Sir Thomas Hanmer. [1751]; 1752 (as Examination of a Late Edition).

—— Critical, Historical, and Explanatory Notes on Shakespeare with Emendations of the Text and Metre. 2 vols. 1754.

Edwards, Thomas. A Supplement to Mr Warburton's Edition of Shakespeare. Being the Canons of Criticism and Glossary collected from the Notes in that Celebrated Work. 1748 (*bis*); 1753 (rev. Edwards and Richard Roderick as Canons of Criticism); 1753; 1758; 1765 (adds Roderick's Remarks on Shakespear).

Holt, John. An Attempte to rescue that Aunciente English Poet Maister Williaume Shakespere from the Maney Errours faulsely charged on him by certaine Newfangled Wittes. 1749; 1750 (as Remarks on The Tempest).

[Nichols, Philip.] The Castrated Letter of Sir Thomas Hanmer in the Sixth Volume of Biographia Britannica. 1763. [Exposes Warburton's treatment of Hanmer.]

Heath, Benjamin. A Revisal of Shakespeare's Text, wherein the Alterations introduced into it by the more Modern Editors and Critics are particularly considered. 1765.

Kenrick, William. A Review of Doctor Johnson's New Edition of Shakespeare: in which the Ignorance, or Inattention, of that Editor is exposed. 1765.

—— A Defence of Mr Kenrick's Review. 1766.

Tyrwhitt, Thomas. Observations and Conjectures upon some Passages of Shakespeare. Oxford, 1766.

Capell, Edward. Notes and Various Readings to Shakespeare. [1774] (Part the First); 3 vols. 1779–83 (extended, and with addns by John Collins).

Ritson, Joseph. Remarks, Critical and Illustrative, on the Text and Notes of the Last Edition of Shakespeare. 1783. [On the Johnson-Steevens-Reed-Malone edn of 1778.]

—— The Quip Modest; a Few Words by Way of Supplement to Remarks, occasioned by the Republication of that Edition. 1788 (re-issued 1788, with rev. preface, toning down the abuse of Steevens).

—— Cursory Criticisms on the Edition of Shakespeare published by Edmond Malone. 1792.

Mason, J. M. Comments on the Last Edition of Shakespeare's Plays. 1785. [On the Johnson-Steevens-Reed-Malone edn of 1778.]

—— Comments on the Plays of Beaumont and Fletcher. With an Appendix containing some Further Observations on Shakespeare, extended to the Late Editions of Malone and Steevens. 2 pts, 1797–8.

—— Comments on the Several Editions of Shakespeare's Plays, extended to those of Malone and Steevens. Dublin, 1807.

Malone, Edmond. A Letter to Richard Farmer relative to the Edition of Shakespeare published in 1790, and some Late Criticisms on that Work. 1792 (bis). [Replies to Ritson's Cursory Criticisms.]

Seymour, E. H. Remarks, Critical, Conjectural, and Explanatory, upon the Plays of Shakespeare, resulting from a Collation of the Early Copies, with that of Johnson and Steevens, edited by Isaac Reed. 2 vols. 1805.

Pye, H. J. Comments on the Commentators on Shakespear. 1807.

Douce, Francis. Illustrations of Shakespeare and of Ancient Manners. 2 vols. 1807; 1 vol. 1839.

Nichols, John. Illustrations of the Literary History of the Eighteenth Century. 8 vols. 1817–58. [Vol. ii includes correspondence of Theobald, Thirlby and Warburton on Shakespeare.]

Collier, J. P. Reasons for a New Edition of Shakespeare's Works. 1841.

—— Notes and Emendations to the Text of Shakespeare's Plays, from Early Manuscript Corrections in a Copy of the Folio of 1632. 1852.

Dyce, Alexander. Remarks on Mr Collier's and Mr Knight's Editions. 1844.

[Spalding, W.] Recent Editions of Shakespeare. Edinburgh Rev. LXXXI, 1845. [On Knight's edns.]

Bodham, Charles. Criticism applied to Shakspere. 1846.

—— The Text of Shakespeare. [In Cambridge Essays, 1856.]

Knight, Charles. Old Lamps, or New? A Plea for the Original Editions of the Text of Shakspere. 1853.

Walker, W. S. A Critical Examination of the Text of Shakespeare. Ed. W. N. Lettsom, 3 vols. 1860.

Ingleby, C. M. The Still Lion. An Essay towards the Restoration of Shakespeare's Text. 1867; 1875 (enlarged as Shakespeare Hermeneutics).

Daniel, P. A. Notes and Conjectural Emendations of certain Doubtful Passages in Shakespeare's Plays. 1870.

Bulloch, J. Studies on the Text of Shakespeare. 1878.

Vaughan, H. H. New Readings and New Renderings of Shakespeare's Tragedies. 3 vols. 1878–86. [King Henry VIII, King Richard III, Cymbeline.]

Gould, George. Corrigenda and Emendations of the Text of Shakspere. 1881; 1884.

Morgan, J. A. Some Shakespearean Commentators. Cincinnati, 1882.

van Dam, B. A. P. and Stoffel, C. William Shakespeare, Prosody and Text. Leyden, 1900.

Elton, Oliver. Recent Shakespearian Criticism. [In Modern Studies, 1907.]

Stewart, C. D. Some Textual Difficulties in Shakespeare. New Haven, 1914.

Pollard, A. W. The Foundations of Shakespeare's Text. Proc. British Academy, XI, 1923.

Kellner, Leon. Restoring Shakespeare. A Critical Analysis of the Misreadings in Shakespeare's Works. Leipzig, 1925.

Greg, W. W. Principles of Emendation in Shakespeare. British Academy Lecture, 1928.

Adams, J. Q. Elizabethan Playhouse Manuscripts and their Significance for the Text of Shakespeare. Johns Hopkins Alumni Mag. XXI, 1932.

McKerrow, R. B. The Treatment of Shakespeare's Text by his Earlier Editors. British Academy Lecture, 1933.

(4) LANGUAGE, VOCABULARY, STYLE AND PROSODY

(a) Shakespeare's Language

[Ebisch and Schücking, pp. 79–85. See also A. G. Kennedy, A Bibliography of Writings on the English Language, New Haven, 1927.]

(i) General Works

Walker, W. S. A Critical Examination of the Text of Shakespeare, with Remarks on his Language. 3 vols. 1860.

Abbott, E. A. A Shakespearian Grammar. 1869, etc.

Franz, Wilhelm. Shakespeare-Grammatik. Halle, 1898–1900; Heidelberg, 1924.

—— Orthographie, Lautgebung und Wortbildung in den Werken Shakespeares mit Ausspracheproben. Heidelberg, 1905.

Tilley, M. P. Some Evidence in Shakespeare of Contemporary Effort to refine the Language of the Day. PMLA. xxxi, 1916.

Bradley, Henry. Shakespeare's English. [In Shakespeare's England, vol. ii, Oxford, 1916.]

Jespersen, Otto. Shakespeare and the Language of Poetry. [In Growth and Structure of the English Language, Leipzig, 1926.]

Langworthy, C. A. A Verse-Sentence Analysis of Shakespeare's Plays. PMLA. xlvi, 1931.

Willcock, G. B. Shakespeare as a Critic of Language. Shakespeare Ass. Pamphlet, 1934.

Mackie, W. S. Shakespeare's English. MLR. xxxi, 1936.

(ii) Pronunciation and Orthography

Ellis, A. J. On Early English Pronunciation with Especial Reference to Shakespere and Chaucer. 5 vols. EETS. Ex. Ser. 1867–89.

Viëtor, Wilhelm. Shakespeare's Pronunciation. 2 vols. Marburg, 1906.

Zachrisson, R. E. Shakespeares Uttal. Upsala, 1914.

Pollard, A. W. Elizabethan Spelling as a Literary and Bibliographical Clue. Library, iv, 1923.

Wilson, J. D. Bibliographical Links between the Three Pages [of Sir Thomas More] and the Good Quartos. [In Shakespeare's Hand in the Play of Sir Thomas More, Cambridge, 1923.]

Sievers, Eduard. Shakespeares Anteil am King Lear. [In Anglica, vol. ii, Leipzig, 1925.]

Marschall, Wilhelm. Shakespeares Orthographie. Ang. li, 1927.

(iii) Punctuation

Simpson, Percy. Shakespearian Punctuation. Oxford, 1911.

—— The Bibliographical Study of Shakespeare. Oxford Bibliog. Soc. i, 1923.

Pollard, A. W. Shakespeare's Fight with the Pirates. Cambridge, 1917, 1920.

Sullivan, Sir E. Punctuation in Shakespeare. Nineteenth Century, xc, 1921.

The Works of Shakespeare. Ed. Sir A. T. Quiller-Couch and J. D. Wilson, Cambridge, 1921–. [See Wilson's note in The Tempest.]

Alden, R. M. The Punctuation of Shakespeare's Printers. PMLA. xxxix, 1924.

Fries, C. C. Shakespearian Punctuation. [In Studies in Shakespeare, Milton and Donne, New York, 1925.]

Jenkinson, Hilary. Notes on the Study of English Punctuation of the Sixteenth Century. RES. ii, 1926.

Isaacs, J. A Note on Shakespeare's Dramatic Punctuation. RES. ii, 1926.

Alexander, Peter. Shakespeare's Punctuation. TLS. 17 March 1932.

Thorndike, A. H. Parentheses in Shakespeare. Shakespeare Ass. Bulletin, ix, 1934.

(b) Shakespeare's Vocabulary

(i) General Works

Ekwall, Eilert. Shakspere's Vocabulary. Its Etymological Elements. Upsala, 1903.

Franz, W. Die Wortbildung bei Shakespeare. E. Studien, xxxv, 1905.

Whall, W. B. Shakespeare's Sea Terms Explained. Bristol, 1910.

Bastide, Charles. La France et les Français dans le Théâtre de Shakespeare. Edda, vi, 1916.

Gordon, George. Shakespeare's English. SPE. 1928.

(ii) Dialects

Huntley, R. W. A Glossary of the Cotswold Gloucestershire Dialect. 1869.

Northall, G. F. A Warwickshire Word-Book. English Dialect Soc. 1896.

Morgan, Appleton. A Study in Warwickshire Dialect. New York Shakespeare Soc. 1900.

Förster, Max. Die kymrischen Einlagen bei Shakespeare. Germanisch-romanische Monatsschrift, xii, 1924.

(iii) Concordances, Glossaries, Dictionaries, etc.

Nares, Robert. A Glossary, or, Collection of Words, Phrases, Names, and Allusions to Customs, Proverbs, etc. [in] Shakespeare and his Contemporaries. 1822; rev. J. O. Halliwell[-Phillipps] and Thomas Wright, 2 vols. 1859. [See TLS. 1 June 1922.]

Clarke, M. C. The Complete Concordance to Shakspere. 1870 (rev. edn).

Schmidt, Alexander. Shakespeare-Lexicon. Vollständiger englischer Sprachschatz mit allen Wörtern, Wendungen und Satzbildungen in den Werken des Dichters. Berlin, 1874–5; rev. G. Sarrazin, 2 vols. Berlin, 1902.

Bellamy, G. S. The New Shaksperian Dictionary of Quotations. 1875.

Dyce, Alexander. A Glossary to the Works of William Shakespeare. Rev. H. Littledale, 1902.

Bartlett, John. A New and Complete Concordance to Shakespeare. 1906.

Foster, John. A Shakespeare Word-Book. [1908.]

Edwardes, Marian. A Pocket Lexicon and Concordance to Shakespeare. 1909.

Cunliffe, R. J. A New Shakespearian Dictionary. 1910.

Onions, C. T. A Shakespeare Glossary. Oxford, 1911.

Skeat, W. W. A Glossary of Tudor and Stuart Words, especially from the Dramatists. Rev. A. L. Mayhew, Oxford, 1914.

Kellner, Leon. Shakespeare-Wörterbuch. Leipzig, 1922.

Stokes, F. G. A Dictionary of the Characters and Proper Names in Shakespeare. 1924.

(c) Shakespeare's Style

Spalding, William. A Letter on Shakespeare's Authorship of The Two Noble Kinsmen, and on the Characteristics of Shakespeare's Style, and the Secret of his Supremacy. Edinburgh, 1833; New Shakspere Soc. 1876.

Rushton, W. L. Shakespeare's Euphuisms. 1871.

—— Shakespeare and The Arte of English Poesie. Liverpool, 1909.

Clarke, C. C. and M. C. The Shakespeare Key, unlocking the Treasures of his Style. 1879.

Sharpe, H. The Prose in Shakespeare's Plays. Trans. New Shakspere Soc. 1885.

Sarrazin, Gregor. Wortechos bei Shakespeare. Sh. Jb. xxxiii, xxxiv, 1897–8.

—— Aus Shakespeares Meisterwerkstatt. Stilgeschichtliche Studien. Berlin, 1906.

Kellett, E. E. Some Notes on a Feature in Shakspere's Style. [In Suggestions, Cambridge, 1923.]

Michels, Wilhelm. Barockstil bei Shakespeare und Calderón. Frankfort, 1928. [Rptd in Revue Hispanique, 1929.]

Rylands, G. W. H. Notes and Quotations Preparatory to a Study of Shakespeare's Diction and Style. [In Words and Poetry, 1928.]

Spurgeon, C. F. E. Leading Motives in the Imagery of Shakespeare's Tragedies. Shakespeare Ass. Lecture, 1930.

—— Shakespeare's Iterative Imagery, (1) as Undersong, (2) as Touchstone. British Academy Lecture, 1931.

—— Shakespeare's Imagery and what it tells us. Cambridge, 1935.

Clemen, W. Shakespeares Bilder, ihre Entwicklung und ihre Funktionen im dramatischen Werk. Bonn, 1935.

Empson, W. Timon's Dog. Life and Letters, xv, 1936. [Shakespeare's imagery.]

(d) Shakespeare's Prosody

Walker, W. S. On Shakespeare's Versification. 1854.

Bathurst, Charles. Remarks on the Difference in Shakespeare's Versification in Different Periods of his Life. 1857.

Fleay, F. G. On Metrical Tests as applied to Dramatic Poetry. Trans. New Shakspere Soc. i, 1874.

Ingram, J. K. On the Weak Endings of Shakespeare. Trans. New Shakspere Soc. i, 1874.

Pulling, F. S. The Speech-Ending Test applied to Twenty of Shakespeare's Plays. Trans. New Shakspere Soc. 1877–9.

van Dam, B. A. P. and Stoffel, C. William Shakespeare, Prosody and Text. Leyden, 1900.

van Dam, B. A. P. The Text of Shakespeare's Hamlet. 1924. [Chs. 6 and 7.]

Bayfield, M. A. Shakespeare's Versification and the Early Texts. TLS. 13 June 1918.

—— Abbreviations in Shakespeare's Prose. TLS. 20 June 1918.

—— A Study of Shakespeare's Versification. Cambridge, 1920.

Young, Sir George. Shakespeare as a Metrist. [In English Prosody on Inductive Lines, Cambridge, 1928.]

B. AESTHETIC CRITICISM

[Ebisch and Schücking, pp. 139–147. A fuller bibliography is R. W. Babcock, A Preliminary Bibliography of Eighteenth-Century Criticism of Shakespeare, Stud. Phil., Ex. Ser. i, 1929.]

(1) ANTHOLOGIES OF SHAKESPEARIAN CRITICISM
(including the Allusion-Books)

Blount, Sir T. P. De Re Poetica, or Remarks upon Poetry. 1694.

Garrick, David. Testimonies to the Genius and Merits of Shakespeare. [Appended to Garrick's Ode on Shakespeare, 1769.]

Steevens, George. Detached Pieces of Criticism. [Appended to the Johnson-Steevens edns of Shakespeare's Works of 1778, 1785 and 1793.]

Ingleby, C. M. Shakespeare's Centurie of Prayse. New Shakspere Soc. 1874; rev. L. T. Smith, New Shakspere Soc. 1879.

Furnivall, F. J. Allusions to Shakspere, A.D. 1592–1693: Supplement to Shakspere's Centurie of Prayse. New Shakspere Soc. 1880.

—— Some Three Hundred Fresh Allusions to Shakspere from 1594 to 1694. New Shakspere Soc. 1886.

Nichol Smith, D. Eighteenth Century Essays on Shakespeare. Glasgow, 1903. [With detailed introduction.[

—— Shakespeare Criticism. 1916. (World's Classics.)

Hughes, C. E. The Praise of Shakespeare. An English Anthology. 1904.

Warner, Beverley. Famous Introductions to Shakespeare's Plays. New York, 1906. [Rowe to Malone.]

Munro, John. The Shakspere Allusion-Book. A Collection of Allusions from 1591 to 1700, originally compiled by C. M. Ingleby, Miss L. Toulmin Smith, and by F. J. Furnivall, and now re-edited. 2 vols. 1909; rev. Sir E. K. Chambers, 2 vols. Oxford, 1932.

—— More Shakespeare Allusions. MP. xiii, 1916.

[Thorn-Drury, George.] Some Seventeenth Century Allusions to Shakespeare. 1920.

—— More Seventeenth Century Allusions to Shakespeare. 1924.

Bartlett, H. C. Mr. William Shakespeare. Original and Early Editions, Source Books and those containing Contemporary Notices. New Haven, 1922. [A bibliography.]

(2) THE HISTORY OF SHAKESPEARIAN CRITICISM

Knight, Charles. A History of Opinion on the Writings of Shakspere. [Cabinet edn of Shakespeare, supplementary vol. 1847.]

Hallam, G. Contributions to a History of Shakespearean Criticism. [In Shakespeariana, New York Shakespeare Soc. ix, 1892.]

Walder, Ernest. Shakespearean Criticism, Textual and Literary, from Dryden to the End of the Eighteenth Century. Bradford, 1895.

Hamelius, Paul. Die Kritik in der englischen Literatur des 17. und 18. Jahrhunderts. Leipzig, 1897.

Morton, E. P. Shakspere in the Seventeenth Century. JEGP. i, 1897.

Sheran, W. H. Early Critics of Shakespeare. Catholic World, lxvi, 1897.

Lounsbury, T. R. Shakespeare as a Dramatic Artist, with an Account of his Reputation at Various Periods. New York, 1901.

—— Shakespeare and Voltaire. New York, 1902.

—— The Text of Shakespeare, its History from the Quartos to Theobald. New York, 1906.

Gloede, O. Shakespeare in der englischen Litteratur des 17. und 18. Jahrhunderts. Doberan, 1902.

Brandl, Alois. Edward Young. Ein Beitrag zur Geschichte der Shakespeare-Kritik des 18. Jahrhunderts. Sh. Jb. xxxix, 1903.

Bradley, A. C. Eighteenth-Century Estimates of Shakespeare. Scottish Hist. Rev. i, 1904.

Evans, H. A. A Shakespearian Controversy of the Eighteenth Century. Ang. xxviii, 1905.

Adler, J. Zur Shakespeare-Kritik des 18. Jahrhunderts. (Die Shakespeare-Kritik in Gentleman's Magazine.) Königsberg, 1906.

Johnson, C. F. Shakespeare and his Critics. Boston, 1909.

Dowden, Edward. Some Old Shakespearians. [In Essays, Modern and Elizabethan, 1910.]

Gundolf, Friedrich. Shakespeare und der deutsche Geist. Berlin, 1911, 1914.

Götz, H. J. Die komischen Bestandteile von Shakespeares Tragödien in der Kritik Englands. Giessen, 1917.

Tolman, A. H. The Early History of Shakespeare's Reputation. [In Falstaff and Other Shakespearean Topics, New York, 1925.]

Raysor, T. M. The Study of Shakespeare's Characters in the 18th Century. MLN. xlii, 1927.

Looten, Camille. La première Controverse internationale sur Shakespeare entre l'Abbé Le Blanc et W. Guthrie. Lille, 1927.

Nichol Smith, D. Shakespeare in the Eighteenth Century. Oxford, 1928.

Babcock, R. W. A Preliminary Bibliography of Eighteenth Century Criticism of Shakespeare. Stud. Phil., Ex. Ser. i, 1929.

—— The Genesis of Shakespeare Idolatry 1766–1799. Chapel Hill, 1931.

Ralli, Augustus. A History of Shakespearian Criticism. 2 vols. Oxford, 1932.

Pillai, V. K. A. Shakespeare Criticism from the Beginnings to 1765. 1933.

Lovett, D. Shakespeare as a Poet of Realism in the Eighteenth Century. ELH. ii, 1935.

Henderson, W. A. et al. Addison's Knowledge of Shakespeare. N. & Q. 19 Aug., 9 Sept. 1893.

Child, Mary. Mr. Spectator and Shakespeare. Library, vi, 1905.

Neumann, J. H. Shakespearean Criticism in the Tatler and Spectator. PMLA. xxxix, 1924.

Raleigh, Sir Walter. Johnson on Shakespeare. 1908.

Jusserand, J. J. Ben Jonson's Views on Shakespeare's Art. [In Stratford Town Shakespeare, vol. x, 1907.]

Carver, P. L. The Influence of Maurice Morgann. RES. vi, 1930.

Lee, Sir Sidney. Pepys and Shakespeare. Fortnightly Rev. lxxxv, 1906. [Rptd in Shakespeare and the Modern Stage, 1907.]

Babcock, R. W. William Richardson's Criticism of Shakespeare. JEGP. xxviii, 1929.

(3) THE PRINCIPAL CRITICS TO 1800

[This list includes the more important early allusions and some of the prefaces to edns of Shakespeare. It should, however, be supplemented by the list of edns given above, pp. 547–51, many of which contain critical prefaces and notes, and by the section on Textual Criticism, pp. 587–8 above, much of which is not wholly textual. Most of the earlier items, or selections from them, will be found rptd in the Anthologies listed above, p. 590. *Chambers*, vol. II, Appendixes A and B, reprints the contemporary allusions and later biographical scraps.]

Greene, Robert. Greenes, Groats-worth of witte, bought with a million of Repentance. 1592.

Chettle, Henry. Kind-Harts Dreame. [1593.]
—— Englandes Mourning Garment. [1603.] [Verse.]

H., T. Oenone and Paris. 1594. [Verse. See J. D. Parsons, Earliest Critical Notice of Shakespeare, N. & Q. 20 July 1929.]

Willobie, H. Willobie His Avisa. 1594; ed. C. Hughes, 1904; ed. G. B. Harrison, 1926. [Verse.]

C[ovell], W[illiam]. Polimanteia. 1595.

Edwards, Thomas. Cephalus and Procris. 1595. [Verse.]

Meres, Francis. Palladis Tamia. Wits Treasury, Being the Second part of Wits Commonwealth. 1598.

Barnefield, Richard. A Remembrance of some English Poets. [Verse. In The Encomion of Lady Pecunia, 1598.]

Weever, John. Ad Gulielmum Shakespeare. [Verse. In Epigrammes in the oldest cut, and newest fashion, 1599.]

Davies, John. To our English Terence, Mr. Will. Shakespeare. [Verse. In The Scourge of Folly, Consisting of Satyricall Epigramms, and others, 1611.]

Freeman, Thomas. To Master W. Shakespeare. [Verse. In Rubbe, and A great Cast, 1614.]

Jonson, Ben. To the memory of my beloved, The Author Mr. William Shakespeare: And what he hath left us. [Verse. Prefixed to the 1623 folio.]
—— De Shakespeare nostrati. [In Timber: or, Discoveries, 1641.]

Holland, Hugh. Upon the Lines and Life of the Famous Scenick Poet, Master William Shakespeare. [Verse. Prefixed to the 1623 folio.]

Heminge, John and Condell, Henrie. To the great Variety of Readers. [Prefixed to the 1623 folio.]

Digges, Leonard. To the Memorie of the deceased Author, Maister W. Shakespeare. [Verse. Prefixed to the 1623 folio.]

Milton, John. An Epitaph on the Admirable Dramatic Poet, W. Shakespeare. [Verse. Prefixed to 1632 folio. See H. W. Garrod, E. & S. XII, 1926.]

S., I. M. On worthy Master Shakespeare and his Poems. [Verse. Prefixed to the 1632 folio.]

Basse, William. On Mr. William Shakespeare. [Verse. First ptd in Donne's Poems, 1633.]

An Elegie on the Death of that famous Writer and Actor, Mr. William Shakespeare. [Verse. Appended to the Poems of 1640.]

Winstanley, W. English Worthies. 1660; 1684.
—— The Lives of the Most Famous English Poets. 1687.

Baker, Sir R. Theatrum Redivivum. 1662.

Fuller, Thomas. The History of the Worthies of England. 1662. [Under Warwickshire.]

Newcastle, Margaret Cavendish, Duchess of. CCXI Sociable Letters. 1664. [Letter CXXIII.]

Pepys, Samuel. Diary [1659–69]. Ed. Richard, Lord Braybrooke, 2 vols. 1825.

Evelyn, John. Diary [1641–1706]. Ed. William Bray, 2 vols. 1818.

Dryden, John. Of Dramatick Poesie, An Essay. 1668.
—— Troilus and Cressida. 1679. [Preface.]

Phillips, Edward. Theatrum Poetarum. 1675.

Rymer, Thomas. The Tragedies of the Last Age Considered. 1678.
—— A Short View of Tragedy. 1693.

Aubrey, John. Brief Lives. Ed. A. Clark, 2 vols. Oxford, 1898. [Written c. 1681.]

Lee, Nathaniel. Lucius Junius Brutus. 1681. [Preface.]

Langbaine, Gerard. Momus Triumphans. 1688.
—— An Account of the English Dramatic Poets. 1691; rev. C. Gildon, 1699.

Dennis, John. The Impartial Critic. 1692; 1697.
—— The Comical Gallant. 1702. [Preface.]
—— An Essay on the Genius and Writings of Shakespeare. 1711; 1712.

Some Reflections on Mr Rymer's Short View of Tragedy, and an Attempt at a Vindication of Shakespear. [In Miscellaneous Letters and Essays, ed. Charles Gildon, 1694.]

Drake, J. Historia Anglo-Scotica. 1703.

Douglas, Hypolitus, Earl of. Secret History of Mackbeth. 1708.

Rowe, Nicholas. Some Account of the Life, &c. of Mr. William Shakespear. [Prefixed to his edn of The Works, 1709.]

Steele, Sir Richard and Addison, Joseph. The Tatler. 1709–11.
—— The Spectator. 1711–12.

Gildon, Charles. An Essay on the Art, Rise, and Progress of the Stage. [In 1710 edn of Poems.]
—— Remarks on the Plays of Shakespeare. [In 1710 edn of Poems.]

Pope, Alexander. The Works of Shakespear. Vol. I, 1725. [Preface.]

Theobald, Lewis. Shakespeare Restored. 1726.

Roberts, John. An Answer to Mr. Pope's Preface. 1729.

Some Account of the Present State of the British Islands, with a Notice of Shakspeare. 1734.

Some Remarks on the Tragedy of Hamlet. 1736. [Perhaps by Sir T. Hanmer. See however C. D. Thorpe, MLN. xLIX, 1934, pp. 493–8.]

Peck, F. Explanatory and Critical Notes on divers Passages of Shakespeare's Plays. [Appended to New Memoirs of Milton, 1740.]

Morris, Corbyn. An Essay towards fixing the true Standards of Wit and Humour. 1744. [On Falstaff.]

Johnson, Samuel. Miscellaneous Observations on Macbeth. 1745.

—— Proposals for Printing Shakspear. 1756.

—— The Plays of William Shakespeare. Vol. i, 1765. [Preface.]

Upton, J. Critical Observations on Shakespeare. 1746; 1748.

Guthrie, W. Essay on English Tragedy, with Remarks on the Abbé Le Blanc's Observations on the English Stage. 1747;1749;1757.

Edwards, Thomas. A Supplement to Mr. Warburton's Edition—being the Canons of Criticism. 1747; 1748; 1750; 1753; 1757; 1758; 1765.

Whalley, Peter. Enquiry into the Learning of Shakespeare. 1748.

Holt, J. An Attempte to Rescue that Aunciente English Poet. 1749; 1750.

—— Proposals for Publishing an Edition of Shakespeare. 1750.

Miscellaneous Observations on the Tragedy of Hamlet. 1752.

[Lennox, Charlotte.] Shakespear Illustrated, or, the Novels and Histories on which the Plays of Shakespear are founded. 3 vols. 1753–4, 1756.

Hume, David. History of England. 1754. [Appendix to the Reign of James I.]

—— Four Dissertations. 1757.

Roderick, R. Remarks on Shakespear. [In T. Edwards, Canons of Criticism, 1758 (6th edn).]

Heath, B. A Revisal of Shakespeare's Text. 1765.

Steevens, George. Proposals for an Edition of Shakespeare. 1766.

Tyrwhitt, T. Observations and Conjectures upon some Passages of Shakespeare. 1766.

Farmer, Richard. Essay on the Learning of Shakespeare. Cambridge, 1767; 1767 (enlarged); 1799.

—— Shakespeariana. 1798.

[Warner, Richard.] A Letter to David Garrick, Esq., concerning a glossary to the plays of Shakespeare, to which is annexed a Specimen. 1768.

Montagu, Elizabeth. Essay on the Genius and Writings of Shakespear. 1769; 1770; 1772; 1773; 1778; 1785; 1810.

Hall, J. Illustrations of Shakespeare. 1773.

Capell, Edward. Notes and Various Readings to Shakespeare. 3 vols. [1774]–83.

P[rescot], K. Shakespeare, An Essay. 1774.

Richardson, W. A Philosophical Analysis and Illustration of Some of Shakespeare's Remarkable Characters. 1774 (bis); 1775; 1780; 1784; 1786; 1797; 1798; 1812.

—— Essays on Shakespeare's Dramatic Characters of Richard III, King Lear, and Timon of Athens. 1784; 1785; 1786; 1797; 1798; 1812.

—— Essays on Shakespeare's Dramatic Character of Sir John Falstaff and on his Female Characters. 1789; 1797; 1798; 1812.

[Gentleman, F.] Introduction to Shakespeare's Plays. [In Bell's edn, 1774.]

Griffith, Elizabeth. The Morality of Shakespeare's Drama. 1775; 1777.

Mortimer, J. H. Shakespeare's Characters. 1775.

Pilon, F. An Essay on the Character of Hamlet. 1777. [As performed by Henderson.]

Morgann, Maurice. An Essay on the Dramatic Character of Falstaff. 1777; 1820; 1825; ed. W. A. Gill, 1912.

Jordan, J. Original Collections on Shakespeare and Stratford. [1780]; 1864.

—— The Families of Shakespeare and Hart. [1790]; 1865.

Felton, S. Imperfect Hints Toward a New Edition of Shakespeare. 1782; 1787.

[Jackson, William.] Thirty Letters on various Subjects. 2 vols. 1783. [2 letters on Shakespeare.]

Davies, T. Dramatic Miscellanies. 3 vols. 1783–4, 1785.

Whately, T. Remarks on some of the Characters of Shakspeare. 1785; 1808; 1839.

Kemble, J. P. Macbeth Reconsidered. 1786.

Becket, A. A Concordance to Shakespeare. 1787.

Robertson, T. Hamlet. Trans. Edinburgh Soc. xi, 1788.

Stack, R. Falstaff. Trans. Irish Academy, ii, 1788.

Ayscough, S. Index to the Remarkable Passages and Words of Shakespeare. 1790.

Mason, George. Collection of English Words used by Shakespeare. 1790.

Hurdis, J. Cursory Remarks upon the Arrangement of the Plays of Shakespeare. 1792.

Whiter, W. Specimen of a Commentary on Shakespeare. 1794.

Plumptre, James. Observations on Hamlet being an Attempt to prove it Indirect Censure on Mary Queen of Scots. 1796.

Plumptre, James. Appendix to Observations on Hamlet. 1797.

Essays by a Society of Gentlemen, at Exeter. 1796. [Includes: On Literary Fame and the Historical Characters of Shakespeare; An Apology for the Character and Conduct of Iago; An Apology for the Character and Conduct of Shylock. By Richard Hole?]

(4) THE NINETEENTH AND TWENTIETH CENTURIES

(a) Discussions of the Trends in Shakespearian Criticism

Doumic, René. Shakespeare et la Critique française. Revue des Deux Mondes, LXXIV, 1904.

Elton, O. Recent Shakespeare Criticism. [In Modern Studies, 1907.]

Stoll, E. E. Anachronism in Shakespeare Criticism. MP. VII, 1910.

—— Modern Sceptical Criticism of Shakespeare. Sewanee Rev. XXXV, 1928.

Herford, C. H. The German Contribution to Shakespeare. [In A Book of Homage, Oxford, 1916.]

—— A Sketch of Recent Shakespearean Investigation, 1893–1923. 1923.

Chambers, Sir E. K. The Disintegration of Shakespeare. British Academy Lecture, 1924.

—— The Unrest in Shakespearean Studies. Nineteenth Century, LI, 1927.

Haines, C. M. Shakespeare in France. Criticism, Voltaire to Victor Hugo. Oxford, 1925.

Small, S. A. The Return to Shakespeare. The Historical Realists. Baltimore, 1927.

Greenlaw, Edwin. Recent Trends in Shakespeare Criticism. Shakespeare Ass. of America Bulletin, II, 1927.

Legouis, Émile. La Réaction contre la Critique romantique de Shakespeare. E. & S. XIII, 1928.

Wilson, J. D. Idolatry and Scepticism in Shakespearian Studies. Criterion, July 1930.

—— Thirteen Volumes of Shakespeare: A Retrospect. MLR. XXV, 1930.

Alexander, Peter. Conjectural History, or Shakespeare's Henry VIII. E. & S. XVI, 1931.

Robertson, J. M. The State of Shakespeare Study: A Critical Conspectus. 1931.

Connes, Georges. État présent des Études Shakespeariennes. Paris, 1932.

de Reul, Paul. La 'désintégration' de Shakespeare. Brussels, 1932.

Knights, L. C. How Many Children had Lady Macbeth? Cambridge, 1933.

Sisson, C. J. The Mythical Sorrows of Shakespeare. British Academy Lecture, 1934.

(b) General Criticism

Douce, Francis. Illustrations of Shakespeare. 2 vols. 1807; 1839.

Schlegel, A. W. Vorlesungen über dramatische Kunst und Literatur. Heidelberg, 1809–11; tr. Eng. 1846.

Hazlitt, William. Characters of Shakespeare's Plays. 1817, etc.; ed. W. C. Hazlitt, 1873.

Drake, Nathan. Shakespeare and his Times. 2 vols. 1817.

—— Memorials of Shakespeare by Various Writers. 1828.

Tieck, Ludwig. Das Buch über Shakespeare. Ed. H. Lüdeke, Halle, 1920.

Guizot, François. De Shakespeare et de la Poésie dramatique. Paris, 1822.

—— Shakespeare et son Temps. Paris, 1852; tr. Eng. 1852.

Jameson, Anna. Shakespeare's Heroines. 2 vols. 1832, etc.

Ulrici, Hermann. Über Shakespeares dramatische Kunst. Halle, 1839, etc.; tr. Eng. 1846, 2 vols. 1876.

Coleridge, S. T. Notes and Lectures upon Shakespeare and some of the Old Poets and Dramatists. Ed. Sara Coleridge, 2 vols. 1849, etc.

Gervinus, G. G. Shakespeare. 4 vols. Leipzig, 1849–50, etc.; tr. Eng. 2 vols. 1862.

Knight, Charles. Studies of Shakespeare. 1851.

Maginn, William. Shakespeare Papers. Pictures Grave and Gay. 1859; 1860 (enlarged).

Mézières, A. Shakespeare, ses Œuvres et ses Critiques. Paris, 1860.

De Quincey, Thomas. Shakespeare: a Biography. Edinburgh, 1864. [Reprints On the Knocking at the Gate in Macbeth (first ptd 1823) and the article on Shakespeare in Ency. Brit., 7th edn, 1838.]

Hugo, Victor. William Shakespeare. Paris, 1864; tr. Eng. 1864.

Dowden, Edward. Shakspere. A Critical Study of his Mind and Art. 1874, etc.; ed. W. D. Howe, New York, 1918.

—— A Shakspere Primer. 1877.

—— Introduction to Shakespeare. 1893.

Fleay, F. G. Shakespeare Manual. 1876; 1878.

—— Introduction to Shakespearian Study. 1877.

—— Chronicle History of the Life and Work of William Shakespeare. 1886.

Elze, Karl. Abhandlungen zu Shakespeare. Halle, 1877; tr. Eng. 1888.

Swinburne, A. C. A Study of Shakespeare. 1880.

—— Three Plays of Shakespeare. 1909. [Lear, Othello, Richard II.]

Hales, J. W. Notes and Essays on Shakespeare. 1884.

Moulton, R. G. Shakespeare as a Dramatic Artist. Oxford, 1885, etc.
—— The Moral System of Shakespeare. 1903.
White, R. G. Studies in Shakespeare. Boston, 1885.
Delius, Nicolaus. Abhandlungen zu Shakespeare. 2 vols. Berlin, 1889.
ten Brink, Bernhard. Shakspere. Fünf Vorlesungen. Strasburg, 1893, 1894; tr. Eng. 1895.
Brandes, Georg. William Shakespeare. Copenhagen, 1896, etc; tr. Eng. 2 vols. 1896.
Boas, F. S. Shakspere and his Predecessors. 1896.
Fleming, W. H. Shakespeare's Plots. A Study in Dramatic Construction. New York, 1902.
Bradley, A. C. Shakespearean Tragedy. Lectures on Hamlet, Othello, King Lear, Macbeth. 1904.
Collins, J. C. Studies in Shakespeare. 1904.
Brooke, A. Stopford. On Ten Plays of Shakespeare. 1905; 1920.
—— Ten More Plays of Shakespeare. 1913; 1920.
Luce, Morton. A Handbook to the Works of William Shakespeare. 1906.
Tolstoy, L. N. Shakespeare. New York, 1906, etc.
Baker, G. P. The Development of Shakespeare as a Dramatist. New York. 1907.
Raleigh, Sir Walter. Shakespeare. 1907. (English Men of Letters Ser.)
Figgis, Darrell. Shakespeare, a Study. 1911.
Masefield, John. William Shakespeare. [1911.] (Home University Lib.)
—— Shakespeare and Spiritual Life. Oxford, 1924. (Romanes Lecture.)
Matthews, Brander. Shakspere as a Playwright. New York, 1913.
Shakespearean Studies. Ed. B. Matthews and A. H. Thorndike, New York, 1916.
A Book of Homage to Shakespeare. Ed. Sir I. Gollancz, Oxford, 1916.
Kittredge, G. L. Shakspere. An Address. Cambridge, U.S.A. 1916.
Stopes, C. C. Shakespeare's Industry. 1916.
Quiller-Couch, Sir A. T. Shakespeare's Workmanship. 1918, etc.
Croce, Benedetto. Ariosto, Shakespeare e Corneille. Bari, 1920; tr. Eng. 1921.
Dyboski, Roman. Rise and Fall in Shakespeare's Dramatic Art. Shakespeare Ass. Lecture, 1923.
Chambers, Sir E. K. Shakespeare, a Survey. 1925.
Granville-Barker, Harley. From 'Henry V' to 'Hamlet.' British Academy Lecture, 1925.
—— Prefaces to Shakespeare. 2 sers. 1927–30.
—— Associating with Shakespeare. Shakespeare Ass. Lecture, 1932.

Tolman, A. H. Falstaff and Other Shakespearean Topics. New York, 1925.
Eliot, T. S. Shakespeare and the Stoicism of Seneca. Shakespeare Ass. Lecture, 1927. [Rptd in Elizabethan Essays, 1934.]
Haines, C. M. The Development of Shakespeare's Stagecraft. Shakespeare Ass. Lecture, 1927.
Lewis, Wyndham. The Lion and the Fox: the Rôle of the Hero in the Plays of Shakespeare. 1927.
Schelling, F. E. Shakespeare and 'Demi-Science.' Philadelphia, 1927.
Stoll, E. E. Shakespeare Studies. New York, 1927.
—— Poets and Playwrights. Minneapolis, 1930.
—— Art and Artifice in Shakespeare. New York, 1933.
Nicoll, Allardyce. Studies in Shakespeare. 1928. [Hamlet, Othello, Lear, Macbeth.]
Gundolf, Friedrich. Shakespeare. Sein Wesen und Werk. 2 vols. Berlin, 1928–9.
Bailey, John. Shakespeare. 1929.
Bradby, G. F. Short Studies in Shakespeare. 1929.
Knight, G. W. Myth and Miracle. An Essay on the Symbolism of Shakespeare. [1929.]
—— The Wheel of Fire. Essays in Interpretation of Shakespeare's Sombre Tragedies. 1930.
—— The Imperial Theme: Further Interpretations of Shakespeare's Tragedies. Oxford, 1932.
Wilson, J. D. The Elizabethan Shakespeare. British Academy Lecture, 1929.
—— The Essential Shakespeare. Cambridge, 1932.
Abercrombie, Lascelles. A Plea for the Liberty of Interpreting Shakespeare. British Academy Lecture, 1930.
Mackail, J. W. The Approach to Shakespeare. Oxford, 1930.
Aspects of Shakespeare. (British Academy Lectures on Shakespeare.) 1933.
Drinkwater, John. Shakespeare. 1933.
Smith, Logan Pearsall. On Reading Shakespeare. 1933.
Squire, Sir J. C. Shakespeare as a Dramatist. 1935.
Ellis-Fermor, U. M. The Jacobean Drama. 1936.
Murry, J. M. Shakespeare. 1936.

(c) Special Studies

(i) Characterisation and Character-Types

[A list of studies of the various character-types in Elizabethan drama generally will be found on p. 495 above.]

1. *General Studies.*
Wright, E. H. Reality and Inconsistency in Shakespeare's Characters. New York, 1916.

38-2

Schücking, L. L. Die Charakterprobleme bei Shakespeare. Leipzig, 1919, 1927; tr. Eng. New York, 1922.

Wales, J. G. Character and Action in Shakespeare. Wisconsin University Stud. XVIII, 1923.

Young, Karl. Samuel Johnson on Shakespeare, One Aspect. Wisconsin University Stud. XVIII, 1924.

Stoll, E. E. Shakespeare Studies. New York, 1927.

Campbell, L. B. Shakespeare's Tragic Heroes, Slaves of Passion. Cambridge, 1930.

2. *Shakespeare's Women, Ghosts, Fools Foreigners and Kings.*

Jameson, Anna B. Shakespeare's Heroines. 1832, etc.

Heine, Heinrich. Shakespeares Mädchen und Frauen. [In Sämtliche Werke, vol. v, Leipzig, 1839.]

Ruskin, John. Sesame and Lilies. 1865, etc.

Martin, Helena F. On Some of Shakespeare's Female Characters. 1885.

Harris, Frank. The Women of Shakespeare. New York, 1912.

Gray, H. D. The Evolution of Shakespeare's Heroine. JEGP. XII, 1913.

Kellett, E. E. Shakspere's Amazons. [In Suggestions, Cambridge, 1923.]

Mackenzie, A. M. The Women in Shakespeare's Plays. 1924.

Moorman, F. W. Shakespeare's Ghosts. MLR. I, 1906.

Stoll, E. E. The Objectivity of the Ghosts in Shakespeare. PMLA. XXII, 1907.

—— The Ghosts. [In Shakespeare Studies, New York, 1927.]

Wood, F. T. The Supernatural in Shakespearean Drama. Revue anglo-américaine, IX, 1932.

Johnson, Lionel. The Fools of Shakespeare. [In Noctes Shakesperianae, Winchester College Shakespeare Soc. 1887; rptd in Post Liminium, 1911.]

Davey, S. Fools, Jesters, and Comic Characters in Shakespeare. Trans. Royal Soc. Lit. XXIII, 1902.

Scholderer, Victor. The Development of Shakespeare's Fools. Library, X, 1909.

Bastide, Charles. La France et les Français dans le Théâtre de Shakespeare. Edda, VI, 1916.

Hughes, A. E. Shakespeare and his Welsh Characters. Shakespeare Ass. 1918.

Harries, F. J. Shakespeare and the Welsh. 1919.

Friedlander, Gerald. Shakespeare and the Jew. 1921.

Pater, Walter. Shakespeare's English Kings. [In Appreciations, 1889.]

von Hofmannsthal, Hugo. Shakespeares Könige und grosse Herren. Sh. Jb. XLI, 1905.

Stobart, J. C. Shakespeare's Monarchs. 1926.

Henneke, Agnes. Shakespeares englische Könige. Sh. Jb. LXVI, 1930.

3. *Other Character-Types.*

Stoll, E. E. Criminals in Shakespeare and in Science. MP. X, 1912.

—— The Criminals. [In Shakespeare Studies, New York, 1927.]

Tupper, Frederick. The Shakespearean Mob. PMLA. XXVII, 1912.

Kellett, E. E. Shakespeare's Children. [In Suggestions, Cambridge, 1923.]

Wilson, J. D. The Schoolmaster in Shakespeare's Plays. [In Essays by Divers Hands, Trans. Royal Soc. Lit. IX, 1930.]

McPeek, J. A. S. Shakspere and the Fraternity of Unthrifts. Harvard Stud. XIV, 1932.

Quiller-Couch, Sir A. T. Paternity in Shakespeare. British Academy Lecture, 1932.

Small, S. A. Shakespeare's Coxcomb Characters. Shakespeare Ass. Bulletin, VIII, 1933.

Wood, F. T. Shakespeare and the Plebs. E. & S. XVIII, 1933.

Frasure, L. D. Shakespeare's Constables. Ang. LVIII, 1934.

Toole, M. M. Shakespeare's Courtiers. Shakespeare Ass. Bulletin, IX, 1934.

(ii) The Influence of Theatrical Conditions

Hale, E. E. The Influence of Theatrical Conditions on Shakespeare. MP. I, 1904.

Bradley, A. C. Shakespeare's Theatre and Audience. [In Oxford Lectures on Poetry, 1909.]

Schmidt, J. E. Shakespeares Dramen und sein Schauspielerberuf. Berlin, 1914.

Sisson, C. J. Le Goût public et le Théâtre élisabéthain jusqu'à la Mort de Shakespeare. Dijon, [1921].

Granville-Barker, H. The Stagecraft of Shakespeare. Fortnightly Rev. CXX, 1926.

Cowling, G. H. Shakespeare and the Elizabethan Stage. Shakespeare Ass. Lecture, 1927.

Isaacs, J. Shakespeare as a Man of the Theatre. Shakespeare Ass. Lecture, 1927.

Harrison, G. B. Shakespeare's Actors. Shakespeare Ass. Lecture, 1927.

Bridges, Robert. The Influence of the Audience on Shakespeare's Drama. Oxford, 1927. [Collected Essays, vol. I.]

Bradbrook, M. C. Elizabethan Stage Conditions. A Study of their Place in the Interpretation of Shakespeare's Plays. Cambridge, 1932.

Spencer, Hazelton. How Shakespeare staged his Plays. Some Notes on the Dubiety of Non-Textual Evidence. Johns Hopkins Alumni Mag. xx, 1932.

Sprague, A. C. Shakespeare and the Audience. Cambridge, U.S.A. 1935.

(iii) Special Aspects of Shakespeare's Dramatic Technique

Daniel, P. A. Time Analysis of the Plots of Shakespeare's Plays. Trans. New Shakspere Soc. 1877–9.

Arnold, M. le R. The Soliloquies of Shakespeare. New York, 1911.

Stoll, E. E. Hamlet and Iago. [In Kittredge Anniversary Papers, Boston, 1913.]

—— The Comic Method. [In Shakespeare Studies, New York, 1927.]

Alden, R. M. The Use of Comic Material in the Tragedy of Shakespeare and his Contemporaries. JEGP. xiii, 1914.

Scholes, P. A. The Purpose behind Shakespeare's Use of Music. Proc. Musical Ass. 1917.

Koppel, Richard. Das Primitiv in Shakespeares Dramatik. Berlin, 1918.

Schücking, L. L. Die Handlungsbegründung. [In Die Charakterprobleme bei Shakespeare, Leipzig, 1919.]

Thaler, Alwin. Shakspere and the Unhappy Happy Ending. PMLA. xlii, 1927. [Rptd in Shakspere's Silences, 1929.]

—— Shakspere's Silences. Cambridge, U.S.A. 1929.

Matheson, B. S. The Invented Personages in Shakespeare's Plays. Philadelphia, 1933.

Draper, J. W. Court vs. Country in Shakespeare's Plays. JEGP. xxxiii, 1934.

—— Mistaken Identity in Shakespeare's Comedies. Revue anglo-américaine, April 1934.

Kreider, P. V. The Mechanics of Disguise in Shakespeare's Plays. Shakespeare Ass. Bulletin, ix, 1934.

Raysor, T. M. The Aesthetic Significance of Shakespeare's Handling of Time. Stud. Phil. xxxii, 1935.

Spedding, James. On the Division of the Acts in Lear, Much Ado, and Twelfth Night. Trans. New Shakspere Soc. 1877–9.

Hunter, Sir Mark. Act and Scene Division in the Plays of Shakespeare. RES. ii, 1926.

Wilson, J. D. Act- and Scene-Divisions in the Plays of Shakespeare. RES. iii, 1927.

Greg, W. W. Act-Divisions in Shakespeare. RES. iv, 1928.

Willoughby, E. E. The Heading Actus Primus, Scaena Prima, in the First Folio. RES. iv, 1928.

(iv) The Dramatic Types

1. *Tragedy.*

Bradley, A. C. Shakespearean Tragedy. Lectures on Hamlet, Othello, King Lear, Macbeth. 1904.

MacCallum, M. W. Shakespeare's Roman Plays and their Background. 1910.

Klein, M. Form und Aufbau der Tragödien Macbeth, Othello, Lear, Hamlet. Ang, lvi, 1932.

Draper, J. W. The Realism of Shakespeare's Roman Plays. Stud. Phil. xxx, 1933.

2. *Historical Plays.*

Courtenay, T. P. Commentaries on the Historical Plays of Shakespeare. 2 vols. 1840, 1861.

Simpson, Richard. The Politics of Shakespeare's Historical Plays. Trans. New Shakspere Soc. 1874.

—— On the Political Use of the Stage in Shakespeare's Time. Trans. New Shakspere Soc. 1874.

Warner, B. E. English History in Shakespeare's Plays. New York, 1894, 1903.

Davey, S. The Relation of Poetry to History, with Special Reference to Shakespeare's Historical Plays. Trans. Royal Soc. Lit. xxiv, 1903.

Moorman, F. W. Shakespeare's History-Plays and Daniel's Civile Wars. Sh. Jb. xl, 1904.

Marriott, J. A. R. English History in Shakespeare. 1918. [Rptd from Fortnightly Rev. cvi, cvii, cviii, 1916–7.]

Pollard, A. W. The York and Lancaster Plays. TLS. 20, 27 Sept. 1918.

Steinitzer, Alfred. Shakespeares Königsdramen. Munich, 1922.

Hearnshaw, F. J. C. Shakespeare as Historian. Contemporary Rev. cxxiv, 1923.

Stobart, J. C. Shakespeare's Monarchs. 1926.

Henneke, Agnes. Shakespeares englische Könige. Sh. Jb. lxvi, 1930.

3. *Comedy.*

Dowden, Edward. Shakespeare as a Comic Dramatist. *Gayley*, vol. ii, 1903.

Ker, W. P. A Note on the Form of Shakespeare's Comedies. Edda, vi, 1916.

Charlton, H. B. A Note on Shakespeare's Romantic Comedies. [In Anglica, vol. ii, Leipzig, 1924.]

Quiller-Couch, Sir A. T. Shakespeare's Comedies. [In Studies in Literature, Ser. 3, Cambridge, 1929.]

Lawrence, W. W. Shakespeare's Problem Comedies. New York, 1931.

4. *Other Types*.

Cunliffe, J. W. The Masque in Shakespeare's Plays. Archiv, cxxv, 1910.

Greenlaw, Edwin. Shakespeare's Pastorals. Stud. Phil. xiii, 1916.

Morsbach, Lorenz. Shakespeares Prologe, Epiloge und Chorus-Reden. Berlin, 1929.

5. *Miscellaneous Elements in Shakespeare's Plays*.

Moorman, F. W. The Interpretation of Nature in English Poetry from Beowulf to Shakespeare. Strasburg, 1905.

Hanford, J. H. Suicide in the Plays of Shakespeare. PMLA. xxvii, 1912.

Sullivan, Sir E. What Shakespeare saw in Nature. Nineteenth Century, lxxiii, 1913.

Pyre, J. F. A. Shakespeare's Pathos. [In Wisconsin Shakespeare Studies, 1916.]

Herford, C. H. The Normality of Shakespeare, illustrated in his Treatment of Love and Marriage. English Ass. Lecture, 1920. [Rptd in Shakespeare's Treatment of Love and Marriage and Other Essays, 1921.]

Grierson, Helen. Friendship in Shakespeare's Plays. Contemporary Rev. Nov. 1921.

Luce, M. Nature in Shakespeare. Nineteenth Century, xcii, 1922.

—— Love in Shakespeare. Nineteenth Century, xcvi, 1924.

Kellett, E. E. Some Medievalisms in Shakspere. [In Suggestions, Cambridge, 1923.]

—— Shakspere and Marriage. [In Suggestions, Cambridge, 1923.]

Noble, Richmond. Shakespeare's Use of Song. Oxford, 1923.

—— Shakespeare's Songs and Stage. Shakespeare Ass. Lecture, 1927.

Legouis, Émile. The Bacchic Element in Shakespeare's Plays. British Academy Lecture, 1926.

Rannie, D. W. Scenery in Shakespeare's Plays and Other Studies. Oxford, 1926.

Schücking, L. L. Die Familie bei Shakespeare. E. Studien, lxii, 1927.

Knight, G. W. The Theme of Romantic Friendship in Shakespeare. Holborn Rev. Oct. 1929.

Stoll, E. E. 'Reconciliation' in Tragedy: Shakespeare and Sophocles. Toronto University Quart. iv, 1934.

Draper, J. W. Political Themes in Shakespeare's Later Plays. JEGP. xxxv, 1936.

C. SHAKESPEARE'S INFLUENCE

(1) SHAKESPEARIAN ADAPTATIONS AND SHAKESPEARE'S LITERARY INFLUENCE IN ENGLAND

[The principal adaptations are listed in *Bartlett*, pp. 71–82. They have been collected in the Bankside Restoration Shakespeare, ed. J. A. Morgan, New York Shakespeare Soc. 1898–1908. For treatises on particular adaptations see *Ebisch and Schücking* under the separate plays.]

(a) *The Stage-History of Shakespeare's Plays and the Shakespearian Adaptations*

[The general histories of the stage, pp. 498–9 should also be consulted.]

Genest, John. Some Account of the English Stage, 1660 to 1830. 10 vols. Bath, 1832.

Stage Adaptations of Shakespeare. Cornhill, viii, 1863.

von Vincke, G. Bearbeitungen und Aufführungen Shakespearescher Stücke vom Tode des Dichters bis zum Tode Garricks. Sh. Jb. ix, 1874.

—— Shakespeare auf der englischen Bühne seit Garrick. Sh. Jb. xxii, 1887.

Hudson, W. H. Early Mutilators of Shakespeare. Poet Lore, iv, 1892.

Kilbourne, F. W. Stage Versions of Shakespeare before 1800. Poet Lore, xv, 1904.

—— Alterations and Adaptations of Shakespeare. Boston, 1906.

Egan, M. E. Imitators of Shakespeare. [In The Ghost in Hamlet, Chicago, 1906.]

Finck, H. F. Shakespearean Operas. Nation (New York), 23 March 1916.

Squire, W. B. Shakespearean Operas. [In A Book of Homage, 1916.]

Pollard, A. W. The Improvers of Shakespeare. Library, xiv, 1916.

Odell, G. C. D. Shakespeare from Betterton to Irving. 2 vols. New York, 1920.

Sharp, R. F. Travesties of Shakespeare's Plays. Library, i, 1920.

Summers, Montague. Shakespeare Adaptations. Boston, 1922. [Introduction.]

Spencer, Hazelton. Improving Shakespeare. PMLA. xli, 1926.

—— Shakespeare Improved. Cambridge, U.S.A. 1927.

Williams, J. D. E. Sir Wm. Davenant's Relation to Shakespeare. Strasburg, 1905.

Spencer, Hazelton. Davenant's Macbeth and Shakespeare's. PMLA. xl, 1925.

Delius, Nicolaus. Dryden und Shakespeare. Sh. Jb. iv, 1869.

Nicoll, Allardyce. Dryden as an Adapter of Shakespeare. Shakespeare Ass. Lecture, 1922.

Child, H. The Shakespearian Productions of John Philip Kemble. Shakespeare Ass. Pamphlet, 1935.

(b) Shakespeare's Literary Influence

Koeppel, Emil. Studien über Shakespeares Wirkung auf zeitgenössische Dramatiker. Bang, vol. ix, 1905.

Cowl, R. P. Echoes of Henry the Fourth in Elizabethan Drama. TLS. 22 Oct. 1925.

—— Some Echoes in Elizabethan Drama of Shakespeare's King Henry the Fourth. 1927.

Jones, F. L. Echoes of Shakespeare in Later Elizabethan Drama. PMLA. xlv, 1930.

Sutherland, J. R. Shakespeare's Imitators in the Eighteenth Century. MLR. xxviii, 1933.

Du Bois, A. E. Shakespeare and 19th-Century Drama. ELH. i, 1934.

Thaler, Alwin. Shakspere and Sir Thomas Browne. [In Shakspere's Silences, Cambridge, U.S.A. 1929.]

—— The Shakespearean Element in Milton. PMLA. xl, 1925. [Enlarged in Shakspere's Silences, Cambridge, U.S.A. 1929.]

Elliott, G. R. Shakespeare's Significance for Browning. Ang. xxxii, 1909.

Dibelius, Wilhelm. Dickens und Shakespeare. Sh. Jb. lii, 1916.

Murry, J. M. Keats and Shakespeare. Oxford, 1925.

Spurgeon, C. F. E. Keats's Shakespeare. Oxford, 1925.

Taylor, G. C. Shakspere and Milton again. Stud. Phil. xxiii, 1926.

Garrod, H. W. Milton's Lines on Shakespeare. E. & S. xii, 1926.

Rothbarth, Margarethe. Pope and Shakespeare. Ang. xxxix, 1916.

Brewer, J. W. Shakespeare's Influence on Sir Walter Scott. Boston, 1925.

(2) Shakespeare Abroad

Robertson, J. G. The Knowledge of Shakespeare on the Continent at the Beginning of the Eighteenth Century. MLR. i, 1906.

—— Shakespeare on the Continent. CHEL. vol. v, 1910.

Herford, C. H. A Sketch of the History of Shakespeare's Influence on the Continent. John Rylands Lib. Bulletin, ix, 1925.

(i) France*

(a) Histories and Studies

(i) General

1. Books.

Michiels, A. Histoire des Idées littéraires en France. Brussels, 1842.

Lacroix, A. De l'Influence de Shakespeare sur le Théâtre français. Brussels, 1856.

Pellissier, G. Le Drame Shakespearien en France. [In Essais de Littérature contemporaine, Paris, 1893.]

Jusserand, J. J. Shakespeare en France. Paris, 1898; tr. Eng. 1899.

Baldensperger, F. Esquisse d'une Histoire de Shakespeare en France. [In Études d'Histoire littéraire, ser. 2, Paris, 1910.]

Haines, C. M. Shakespeare in France. Shakespeare Ass. 1925.

2. Articles.

Engel, J. Shakespeare in Frankreich. Sh. Jb. xxxiv, 1898.

(ii) Special Periods

Seventeenth Century

Jusserand, J. J. Allusions to Shakespeare. Revue critique d'Histoire et de Littérature, 14 Nov. 1887.

Texte, J. Sur la première Mention du Nom de Shakespeare dans un Ouvrage imprimé en français. Revue d'Histoire littéraire, 15 Oct. 1894.

Eighteenth Century

1. Books.

Lotheissen, F. Literatur und Gesellschaft in Frankreich zur Zeit der Revolution. Weimar, 1872.

Kühn, C. Ueber Ducis in seiner Beziehung zu Shakespeare. Jena, 1875.

Morandi, L. Voltaire contro Shakespeare, Baretti contro Voltaire. Rome, 1882; Città di Castello, 1884 (rev. and enlarged).

Penning, G. E. Ducis als Nachahmer Shakespeares. Bremen, 1884.

Ballantyne, A. Voltaire's Visit to England. 1893.

Lion, H. Les Tragédies et les Théories dramatiques de Voltaire. Paris, 1896.

Lounsbury, T. R. Shakespeare and Voltaire. New York, 1902.

Cushing, M. G. P. le Tourneur. New York, 1909.

Van Tieghem, P. L'Année littéraire (1754–90) comme Intermédiaire en France des Littératures étrangères. Paris, 1917.

* The section on Shakespeare in France has been compiled by Professor Albert Feuillerat.

Hunter, A. C. Un Introducteur de la Littéra-
ture anglaise en France: J. B. Suard. Paris,
1925.
Sonet, É. Voltaire et l'Influence anglaise.
Rennes, 1926.
Chase, C. B. The Young Voltaire. New York,
1926.
Looten, C. La première Controverse inter-
nationale sur Shakespeare entre l'Abbé Le
Blanc et W. Guthrie. Lille, 1927.
Dargan, E. P. The Question of Voltaire's
Primacy in establishing the English Vogue.
[Mélanges Baldensperger, Paris, 1930.]

2. *Articles.*

Blaze de Bury, H. Shakespeare et Voltaire.
Revue des deux Mondes, 15 Aug. 1873.
[Rptd in Tableaux Romantiques de Lit-
térature et d'Art, Paris, 1878.]
König, W. Voltaire und Shakespeare. Sh. Jb.
x, 1875.
Rosières, R. La Littérature en France de
1750 à 1800. Revue politique et littéraire,
19 Aug. 1882. [Rptd in Recherches sur la
Poésie contemporaine, Paris, 1896.]
Collins, J. C. Voltaire in England. Cornhill
Mag. xlvi, 1882. [Included in extended
form in Bolingbroke, a Historical Stndy,
and Voltaire in England, 1886. Again rev.
and pbd with other essays in Voltaire,
Montesquieu and Rousseau in England,
1908.]
Humbert, C. Voltaire ein Bewunderer Shakespeares. Neue Jahrbücher für Philologie
und Pädagogik, cxxxiii, cxxxiv, Leipzig,
1886.
Faguet, É. Voltaire critique de Shakespeare.
Revue des Cours et Conférences, 15 Nov.
1900.
Dubedout, E. J. Shakespeare and Voltaire.
MP. iii, 1905.
Robertson, J. G. The Knowledge of Shakespeare on the Continent at the Beginning of
the Eighteenth Century. MLR. i, 1906.
Dargan, E. P. Shakespeare and Ducis. MP.
x, 1912.
Briese, W. Shakespeares 'Julius Cæsar' und
'La Mort de César' von Voltaire. Zeit-
schrift für französischen und englischen
Unterricht, xv, 1916.
Finch, M. B. and Peers, E. A. Walpole's Rela-
tions with Voltaire. MP. xviii, 1920.

Nineteenth Century
1. *Books.*
Gautier, T. Histoire de l'Art dramatique en
France. Paris, 1858-9.
Reymond, W. Corneille, Shakespeare et
Goethe. Étude sur l'Influence Anglo-
germanique en France au XIXe Siècle.
Berlin, 1864.

Wattendorff, L. Essai sur l'Influence que
Shakespeare a exercée sur la Tragédie
Romantique française. Pt 1, Coblenz,
1888.
—— Essay on the Influence which Shake-
speare exercised on the French Romantic
Tragedy. Pt 2, Coblenz, 1889.
Fricke, E. Der Einfluss Shakespeares auf
Mussets Dramen. Basle, 1901.
Latreille, C. G. Sand et Shakespeare. Annales
Internationales d'Histoire. Congrès de Paris.
Sect. vi, Histoire comparée des Littératures.
Paris, 1901.
Le Roy, A. L'Aube du Théâtre Romantique.
Paris, 1904.
Gunnell, D. Stendhal et l'Angleterre. Paris,
1908.
Borgerhoff, J. L. Le Théâtre anglais à Paris
sous la Restauration. Paris, 1913.
Girard, H. Émile Deschamps. Paris, 1921.
Draper, F. M. W. The Rise and Fall of the
French Romantic Drama, with Special
Reference to the Influence of Shakespeare,
Scott and Byron. 1923.
Larat, J. La Tradition et l'Exotisme dans
l'Œuvre de Ch. Nodier. Paris, 1923.
Reynaud, L. Le Romantisme. Ses Origines
Anglo-germaniques. Paris, 1926.
Sessely, A. Influence de Shakespeare sur A.
de Vigny. Berne, 1928.
Keys, A. C. Les Adaptations musicales de
Shakespeare en France jusqu'en 1870.
Paris, 1933.

2. *Articles.*
Renard, G. L'Influence de l'Angleterre sur la
France depuis 1830. Nouvelle Revue,
15 Aug. 1885.
Latreille, C. Un Épisode de l'Histoire de
Shakespeare en France. Revue d'Histoire
littéraire de la France, xxiii, 1916.
Carré, J. M. Maeterlinck et les Littératures
étrangères. Revue de Littérature com-
parée, vi, 1926.

(b) *Translations*
(i) Complete Works
Shakespeare, traduit de l'Anglois par P. Le
Tourneur, le Comte de Catuelan et J.
Fontaine-Malherbe. 20 vols. Paris, 1776-
82; rev. F. Guizot, F. de Barante and
A. P[ichot], 13 vols. Paris, 1821.
Œuvres Complètes. Tr. M. F. Michel, 3 vols.
Paris, 1839.
Œuvres Complètes. Tr. B. Laroche, 2 vols.
1839-40; 7 vols. Paris, 1842-3.
Œuvres Complètes. Tr. F. V. Hugo, 18 vols.
Paris, 1859-66.
Œuvres Complètes. Tr. É. Montégut, 10 vols.
Paris, 1867-73.

L'Année Littéraire. Paris, 1754–90.
Grimm, F. M. and Diderot, D. Correspondance littéraire. Paris, 1812; ed. Tourneux, 1877.

(iii) 1779–1819

de Rivarol, A. De l'Universalité de la Langue française. Paris, 1785. [In Œuvres, vol. II, Paris, 1808.]
Chénier, M. J. Lettre sur Jules César. [1788. In A. Chénier, Œuvres posthumes, Paris, 1826.]
La Harpe, F. J. Cours de Littérature. Paris, 1799.
—— Correspondance littéraire avec le Grand Duc de Russie. Paris, 1801.
de Staël, Madame. De la Littérature. Paris, 1800.
de Chateaubriand, F. R. Shakspeare. Mercure de France, 1801. [In Œuvres complètes, vol. VIII, Paris, 1836–9. Incorporated in Essai sur la Littérature anglaise (1836), vol. XXXIII, 1836–9.]
[Dupin, C.] Lettre à Milady Morgan sur Racine et sur Shakespeare. Paris, 1818.
Geoffroy, J. L. Cours de Littérature dramatique. Paris, 1819–20.

(iv) 1820–1848
1. *Books*.

Guizot, F. P. G. Sur la Vie et les Œuvres de Shakespeare. [In Œuvres complètes, Paris, 1821.]
'Stendhal' [Henri Beyle]. Racine et Shakespeare. 2 vols. Paris, 1823–5.
Hugo, V. Cromwell. Paris, 1827. [Préface.]
Villemain, A. F. Essai littéraire sur Shakespeare. [In Nouveaux Mélanges historiques et littéraires, Paris, 1827. Rptd in rev. form in Études de Littérature ancienne et étrangère, Paris, 1846.]
Deschamps, É. Études françaises et étrangères. Paris, 1828.
Duport, P. Essais littéraires sur Shakespeare. 2 vols. Paris, 1828; tr. Eng. 1834.
de Vigny, A. Othello. Paris, 1830. [Préface (1829).]
—— Seconde Préface d'Othello. Paris, 1839.
Chasles, P. Caractères et Paysages. Paris, 1833.
de Barante, A. G. P. B. Mélanges historiques et littéraires. Paris, 1835. [Rptd under the title Études littéraires et historiques, Paris, 1858.]
de Chateaubriand, F. R. Essai sur la Littérature anglaise. Paris, 1836. [Œuvres complètes, vol. XXXIII, Paris, 1836–9. Partly pbd in Revue des deux Mondes, 1 Jan. 1836.]
Dumas, A. Sur le Génie de Shakespeare. [Preface to B. Laroche's trn, Paris, 1839.]

Saint-Marc Girardin. Cours de Littérature dramatique. Paris, 1843.

2. *Articles*.

Buchon, J. A. Biographie de Shakespeare et Coup d'œil général sur le caractère distinctif de son Génie. Revue Encyclopédique, XI, July, 1821.
Le Globe. 1824–30. [Especially the 28 articles by C. Magnin, 1827–8, that are rptd in his Causeries et Méditations, Paris, 1843.]
'Morlaix, A.' [L. de Wailly]. Sonnets de Shakespeare. Revue des deux Mondes, 15 Dec. 1834.
Chasles, P. Cervantès et Shakespeare. Revue de Paris, N.S. XIII, 1835.

(v) 1849–1870
1. *Books*.

Chasles, P. Études sur Shakespeare, Marie Stuart et l'Arétin. Paris, 1851. [Rptd in L'Angleterre au XVIe Siècle, Paris, 1879.]
—— Études contemporaines. Paris, 1867.
de Sainte-Beuve, A. Causeries du Lundi. Paris, 1851–62.
Guizot, F. P. G. Shakespeare et son Temps. Paris, 1852; tr. Eng. 1852.
Lemoinne, J. Études critiques et biographiques. Paris, 1852.
Janin, J. Histoire de la Littérature dramatique. Paris, 1853.
Lucas, H. Curiosités dramatiques et littéraires. Paris, 1855.
Mézières, A. Shakespeare. Ses Œuvres et ses Critiques. Paris, 1860.
Rio, A. F. Shakespeare. Paris, 1864. [Rptd with a new title: Shakespeare Catholique, Paris, 1875.]
Hugo, V. W. Shakespeare. Paris, 1864; tr. Eng. 1864.
de Lamartine, A. Shakespeare et son Œuvre. Paris, 1864; [tr. Eng. in Biography and Portraits of Some Celebrated People, 1866.]
Taine, H. Histoire de la Littérature anglaise. Paris, 1864.
Büchner, A. Les Comédies de Shakespeare. Paris, 1865.
Schérer, E. Études critiques sur la Littérature contemporaine. Vol. III, Paris, 1866; tr. Eng. G. Saintsbury, 1891.
Courdaveaux, V. Caractères et Talents. Paris, 1867.
—— Études sur la Littérature ancienne et moderne. Paris, 1867.
Jullien, B. Shakespeare considéré comme Poète dramatique. Paris, 1867.
Brierre de Boismont, A. Shakespeare. Études médico-psychologiques sur les Hommes célèbres. Paris, 1869.

2. Articles.

Montégut, É. Types modernes en Littérature: Hamlet. Revue des deux Mondes, 1 April 1856. [Rptd in Types littéraires et Fantaisies esthétiques, Paris, 1882.]

—— Une Hypothèse sur la Tempête. Revue des deux Mondes, 1 Aug. 1865. [Rptd in Essais sur la Littérature anglaise, Paris, 1883.]

Chasles, P. Shakespeare's Sonnets, Athenaeum, 25 Jan. 1862, Feb.–May, 1867.

Blaze de Bury, H. Shakespeare et ses Musiciens. Revue des deux Mondes, 15 May 1867. [Rptd in Tableaux Romantiques de Littérature et d'Art, Paris, 1878.]

—— Hamlet et ses Commentateurs depuis Goethe. Revue des deux Mondes, 15 March, 1868. [Rptd in Tableaux Romantiques.]

(vi) 1871–1914

1. Books.

Gomont, H. Le César de Shakespeare. Étude historique et littéraire. Paris, 1874.

Lichtenberger, E. De Carminibus Shakesperiensibus cum nova Thorpianae inscriptionis interpretatione. Paris, 1877.

Büchner, A. Hamlet le Danois. Paris, 1878.

Stapfer, P. Shakespeare et l'Antiquité. Molière, Shakespeare et la Critique allemande. 2 vols. Paris, 1879–80; tr. Eng. 1880.

Bourget, P. Études et Portraits. Vol. i, Paris, 1889.

Darmesteter, J. Shakespeare. Paris, 1889.

Pinloche, A. De Shakesperii Hamleto et germanica tragoedia quæ inscribitur: Der bestrafte Brudermord. Paris, 1890.

Legouis, É. [Introduction to his Pages Choisies, Paris, 1899.]

Duval, G. La Vie véridique de Shakespeare. Paris, 1900.

Jusserand, J. J. Histoire littéraire du Peuple anglais. Vol. ii, Paris, 1904; tr. Eng. 1906.

Pellissier, G. Shakespeare et la Superstition Shakespearienne. Paris, 1914.

Richepin, J. A travers Shakespeare. Paris, 1914.

2. Articles.

Onimus, E. La Psychologie médicale dans les Drames de Shakespeare. Revue des deux Mondes, 1 April 1876.

Reinach, T. Hamlet. Nouvelle Revue, i, 1879.

Copin, A. Les Sonnets de Shakespeare. Revue d'Art dramatique, Nov.–Dec. 1887.

Bouchor, M. Shakespeare au Théâtre. Revue de Paris, 1 Sept. 1895.

Pilon, E. Les Fêtes Athéniennes: Les Sites Shakespeariens. Revue d'Art dramatique, 5 Feb. 1898.

Coquelin, C. Molière et Shakespeare. Grande Revue, 1 Jan. 1901.

Filon, A. Les Sonnets de Shakespeare. Revue des deux Mondes, 15 April 1901.

Delacour, A. La Religion de Shakespeare. Mercure de France, xli, Feb. 1902.

Brémond, A. La Légende de Shakespeare. Études, xcii, July–Sept. 1902.

Bellaigue, C. Shakespeare et la Musique. Revue des deux Mondes, 15 May 1903.

Castelain, M. Shakespeare et Ben Jonson. Revue Germanique, iii, Jan., April, 1907.

(vii) 1915–1931

1. Books.

Longworth-Chambrun, Clara. G. Florio, un Apôtre de la Renaissance. 1921.

—— Shakespeare Acteur-Poète. Paris, 1926; tr. Eng. New York.

Feuillerat, A. Shakespeare: Œuvres Choisies. Paris, 1922. [Introduction.]

'Fagus' [G. Faillet]. Essai sur Shakespeare. Amiens, 1923.

Jusserand, J. J. School for Ambassadors. 1924.

Looten, C. Shakespeare et la Religion. Paris, 1924.

Marie, A. A la Recherche de Shakespeare. Paris, 1924.

de Pourtalès, G. De Hamlet à Swann. Paris, 1924.

Legouis, É. The Bacchic Element in Shakespeare's Plays. British Academy Lecture, 1926; tr. French, Revue anglo-américaine, Dec. 1926.

Fréjaville, G. Les Travestis de Shakespeare. Paris, 1930.

Gillet, L. Shakespeare. Paris, 1931.

2. Articles.

Brémond, H. Les Généraux de Shakespeare. Correspondant, 25 April 1916.

Chevrillon, A. Shakespeare et l'Ame anglaise. Revue de Paris, 15 May 1916. [Rptd in his Trois Études de Littérature anglaise, Paris, 1921; tr. Eng. 1923.]

Vigouroux, A. La Pathologie mentale dans les Drames de Shakespeare. Annales médicopsychologiques, ser. 10, x, 1918.

Bastide, C. Shakespeare et les Idées politiques de son Temps. Revue des Sciences politiques, xlvi, 1923.

Longworth-Chambrun, Clara. Shakespeare, Southampton et la Conjuration d'Essex. Revue anglo-américaine, iii, Oct. 1925.

Berthelot, R. La Sagesse Shakespearienne. Revue de Métaphysique et de Morale, xxiii, April, 1926. [Rptd in La Sagesse de Shakespeare et de Goethe, Paris, 1930.]

Legouis, É. La Réaction contre la Critique romantique de Shakespeare. E. & S. XIII, 1928.

(d) The Authenticity Question
1. Books.

Demblon, C. Lord Rutland est Shakespeare. Paris, 1912.
—— L'Auteur d'Hamlet et son Monde. Paris, 1914.
—— L'Auteur d'Hamlet et son Œuvre. Paris, 1914.
Lefranc, A. Sous le Masque de 'Wm. Shakespeare.' 2 vols. Paris, 1918–9.
—— La Réalité dans le 'Songe d'une Nuit d'Eté.' [In Mélanges Bouvier, Geneva, 1920.]
—— L'Origine d'Ariel. [In Mélanges, Cinquantenaire de l'École des Hautes Études, Paris, 1921.]
—— Le Secret de Wm. Stanley. Brussels, 1923.
—— Hélène de Tournon et l'Ophélie d'Hamlet. Paris, 1926.
Connes, G. Le Mystère Shakespearien. Paris, 1926. [First pbd in Revue des Cours et Conférences, XXVI–XXVII, Jan. 1925–March 1926.]

2. Articles.

Villemain, J. Un Procès littéraire. Bacon contre Shakespeare. L'Instruction publique, Revue des Lettres, 31 Aug.–7 Sept. 1878.
Büchner, A. Shakespeare ou Bacon. Revue Britannique, LXI, May, 1885.
de Raynal, M. Une Controverse littéraire. Shakespeare et Bacon. Correspondant, 25 Aug. 1888.
Boubée, J. . Shakespeare ou Bacon? Études, 20 May, 5 June, 5 July 1903.
Boulenger, J. L'Affaire Shakespeare. Revue de Paris, 1 Feb. 1919. [Rptd in book form 1919.]
Lefranc, A. Du Nouveau sur Shakespeare. Le Secret du 'Songe d'une Nuit d'Été.' L'Opinion, 16, 23 Oct. 1920. [See Illustration, 30 Oct. 1920.]
—— Du Nouveau sur Shakespeare. A Propos des 'Joyeuses Commères.' L'Opinion, 5, 12 Feb. 1921.
Cartier, H. Un Problème d'Histoire et de Cryptographie. Mercure de France, 1 Dec. 1921, 15 Feb., 1 March, 1, 15 Sept. 1922.
—— Le Mystère Bacon-Shakespeare. Mercure de France, 1 Feb., 15 April, 1 July 1923.
Speckman, M. A. W. and Cartier, H. Le Chiffre de Bacon. Mercure de France, 1 Feb. 1922.
Feuillerat, A. Shakespeare est-il Shakespeare? Revue des deux Mondes, 1 Nov. 1922.
de Pourtalès, G. N'y aurait-il plus d'Affaire Shakespeare? Revue Hebdomadaire, 16 Dec. 1922.

Speckman, M. A. W. Les Méthodes de Cryptographie de Fr. Bacon. Mercure de France, 15 Aug. 1924.

(ii) Germany and Austria
(a) Modern Studies
(i) General

Koberstein, August. Shakespeare in Deutschland. Sh. Jb. I, 1865.
Genée, Rudolph. Geschichte der Shakespeareschen Dramen in Deutschland. Leipzig, 1870.
Oehlmann, Wilhelm. Shakespeares Wert für unsere nationale Literatur. Sh. Jb. V, 1870.
Richter, K. A. Beiträge zum Bekanntwerden Shakespeares in Deutschland. 3 pts, Breslau, 1909–12.
Brandl, Alois. Shakespeare and Germany. British Academy, [1913].
Price, L. M. English-German Literary Influences. Bibliography and Survey. Berkeley, 1920.
Förster, Max. Shakespeare und Deutschland. Sh. Jb. LVII, 1921.
Kahn, L. W. Shakespeares Sonette in Deutschland. Berne, 1935.

(ii) Special Periods

Cohn, Albert. Shakespeare in Germany in the 16th and 17th Centuries. 1865.
Hense, C. C. Deutsche Dichter in ihrem Verhältnis zu Shakespeare. Sh. Jb. V, VI, 1870–1. [The Sturm und Drang period and Goethe, Schiller, Kleist, Tieck.]
Suphan, B. Shakespeare im Anbruch der klassischen Zeit unserer Literatur. Sh. Jb. XXV, 1890.
Walther, E. Der Einfluss Shakespeares auf die Sturm- und Drangperiode unserer Literatur. Chemnitz, 1890.
Joachimi-Dege, Marie. Deutsche Shakespeare-Probleme im 18. Jahrhundert und im Zeitalter der Romantik. Leipzig, 1907.
Böhtlingk, A. Shakespeare und unsere Klassiker. I: Lessing und Shakespeare. II: Goethe und Shakespeare. III: Schiller und Shakespeare. 3 vols. Leipzig, 1909–10.
Gundelfinger [Gundolf], F. Shakespeare und der deutsche Geist vor dem Auftreten Lessings. Heidelberg, 1911. [Enlarged in Shakespeare und der deutsche Geist, Berlin, 1911, etc.]
Richter, K. A. Shakespeare in Deutschland, 1739–1770. Oppeln, 1912.

(iii) Particular Authors

Götzinger, Ernst. Das Shakespeare-Büchlein des Armen Mannes im Toggenburg [Ulrich Bräker] vom Jahre 1780. Sh. Jb. XII, 1877.

Schneider, Karl. H. W. von Gerstenberg als Verkünder Shakespeares. Sh. Jb. LVIII, 1922.

Friedrich, Ernst. Gottsched—Shakespeare—Tolstoi. Die neueren Sprachen, XXIV, 1917.

Leo, F. A. Shakespeare und Goethe. Sh. Jb. XXIV, 1889.

Wagner, C. B. Shakespeares Einfluss auf Goethe. Halle, 1890.

Huther, A. Goethes Götz von Berlichingen und Shakespeares historische Dramen. Cottbus, 1893.

Böhtlingk, A. Goethe und Shakespeare. Leipzig, 1909.

Eckert, H. Goethes Urteile über Shakespeare. Göttingen, 1918.

Leitzmann, Albert. Dodd's 'Beauties of Shakespeare' als Quelle für Goethe und Herder. Sh. Jb. LV, 1919.

Bartmann, H. Grabbes Verhältnis zu Shakespeare. Münster, 1908.

Dolin, Wilhelm. Grillparzers Shakespeare-Studien. Sh. Jb. LI, 1915.

Gross, Edgar. Grillparzers Verhältnis zu Shakespeare. Sh. Jb. LI, 1915.

Braun, Hans. Grillparzers Verhältnis zu Shakespeare. Munich, 1916.

Alberts, Wilhelm. Hebbels Stellung zu Shakespeare. Berlin, 1908.

Schalles, E. A. Heines Verhältnis zu Shakespeare. Berlin, 1904.

Zinkernagel, Franz. Herders Shakespeare-Aufsatz. Bonn, 1912.

Corssen, Meta. Kleists und Shakespeares dramatische Gestalten. Sh. Jb. LVIII, 1922.

—— Kleist und Shakespeare. Weimar, 1930.

Jacobowski, L. Klinger und Shakespeare. Freiburg, 1891.

Rauch, H. Lenz und Shakespeare. Freiburg, 1892.

Meisnest, F. W. Lessing und Shakespeare. PMLA. XIX, 1904.

Kettner, Gustav. Lessing und Shakespeare. Neue Jahrbücher für das klassische Altertum, XIX, 1907.

Walzel, Oskar. Der Kritiker Lessing und Shakespeare. Sh. Jb. LXV, 1929.

Fischer, B. Otto Ludwigs Trauerspielplan 'Der Sandwirt von Passeier' und sein Verhältnis zu den 'Shakespeare-Studien.' Greifswald, 1916.

Stern, Alfred. Moses Mendelssohn und Shakespeare. Neue Schweizer Rundschau, 1929.

Ludwig, Albert. Nietzsche und Shakespeare. Sh. Jb. LVI, 1920.

Engel, F. Spuren Shakespeares in Schillers dramatischen Werken. Magdeburg, 1901.

Nussberger, Max. Schiller als politischer Dichter. Shakespeare und das deutsche Drama. Basle, 1919.

Gebhard, Richard. Shakespeare und Schopenhauer. Sh. Jb. XLVII, 1911.

Želak, Dominik. Tieck und Shakespeare. Leipzig, 1902.

Lüdeke, Henry. Ludwig Tiecks Shakespeare-Studien. Frankfurt, 1917.

—— Ludwig Tieck und das alte englische Theater. Frankfurt, 1922.

Deetjen, Werner. Goethe und Tiecks elisabethanische Studien. Sh. Jb. LXV, 1929.

Hüttmann, W. C. F. Weisse und seine Zeit in ihrem Verhältnis zu Shakespeare. Bonn, 1912.

(b) The Translations

(i) Modern Studies

Assmann, C. Shakespeare und seine deutschen Übersetzer. Liegnitz, 1843.

Genée, Rudolph. Geschichte der Shakespeareschen Dramen in Deutschland. Leipzig, 1870.

von Vincke, G. Zur Geschichte der deutschen Shakespeare-Übersetzungen. Sh. Jb. XVI, XVII, 1881–2.

Schroeer, Arnold. Über Shakespeare-Übersetzungen. Die neueren Sprachen, XVI, 1909.

Drews, W. König Lear auf der deutschen Bühne im 17. und 18. Jahrhundert. Berlin, 1932.

Mensel, E. H. Die erste deutsche Romeo-Übersetzung. Northampton, Massachusetts, 1933.

(ii) The Principal Translations

[For the trns of individual plays see Ludwig Unflad, Die Shakespeare-Literatur in Deutschland, Munich, 1880.]

Wieland, C. M. Shakespeares theatralische Werke. 8 vols. Zürich, 1762–6. [Prose. See Marcus Simpson, Eine Vergleichung der Wielandschen Shakespeare-Übersetzung mit dem Originale, Munich, 1898; Ernst Stadler, Wielands Shakespeare, Strasburg, 1910; F. W. Meisnest, Wieland's Translation of Shakespeare, MLR. IX, 1914.]

Eschenburg, J. J. William Shakespears Schauspiele. 13 vols. Zürich, 1775–82. [Prose.]

—— Willhelm Shakespears Schauspiele. 22 vols. Strasburg, 1778–Mannheim, 1783. [See Hermann Uhde-Bernays, Der Mannheimer Shakespeare, Berlin, 1902; H. Schrader, Eschenburg und Shakespeare, Marburg, 1911.]

Schlegel, A. W. Shakespeares dramatische Werke. 8 vols. Berlin, 1797–1801. [Vol. IX added 1810. Only 17 plays. See Michael Bernays, Zur Entstehungsgeschichte des

Schlegel'schen Shakespeare, Leipzig, 1872; Rudolf Genée, A. W. Schlegel und Shakespeare, Berlin, 1903; B. Assmann, Studien zur A. W. Schlegelschen Shakespeare-Übersetzung. Die Wortspiele, Dresden, 1906.]

Voss, J. H., Heinrich and Abraham. Shakespeares Schauspiele. 9 vols. Leipzig, 1818–29.

Benda, J. W. O. Shakespeares dramatische Werke. 19 vols. Leipzig, 1825–6.

Schlegel, A. W. Shakespeares dramatische Werke. Rev. Ludwig Tieck, 9 vols. Berlin, 1825–33.

Schlegel, A. W. and Tieck, Ludwig. Shakespeares dramatische Werke. 12 vols. Berlin, 1839–40. [See Michael Bernays, Der Schlegel-Tiecksche Shakespeare, Sh. Jb. I, 1865; W. Wetz, Zur Beurteilung der Schlegel-Tieckschen Shakespeare-Übersetzung, E. Studien, XXVIII, 1900; Alois Brandl, Ludwig Fulda, Paul Heyse und Adolf Wilbrandt über die Schlegel-Tiecksche Shakespeare-Übersetzung, Sh. Jb. XXXVII, 1901; F. Deibel, Dorothea Schlegel, Greifswald, 1904; Henry Lüdeke, Zur Tieckschen Shakespeare-Übersetzung, Sh. Jb. LV, 1919; Ludwig Tiecks erste Shakespeare-Übersetzung (1794), Sh. Jb. LVII, 1921; Ludwig Tieck und das alte englische Theater, Frankfurt, 1922; Walther Fischer, Ludwig Tiecks Shakespeare, Die neueren Sprachen, XXXIV, 1926.]

Ortlepp, Ernst. W. Shakespeares dramatische Werke. 16 vols. Stuttgart, 1838–9.

Böttger, A. et al. W. Shakespeares sämtliche dramatische Werke. 12 vols. Leipzig, 1839.

Keller, Adelbert and Rapp, Moriz. William Shaksperes dramatische Werke. 37 vols. Stuttgart, 1843–7.

Schlegel, A. W. and Tieck, Ludwig. Shakespeares dramatische Werke. Rev. H. Ulrici, 12 vols. Deutsche Shakespeare-Gesellschaft, Berlin, 1867–71; ed. Richard Gosche and Benno Tschischwitz, 8 vols. Berlin, 1877; rev. Michael Bernays, 12 vols. Berlin, 1891; ed. Alois Brandl, 10 vols. Leipzig, 1897–9; rev. Hermann Conrad, 5 vols. Stuttgart, 1905; ed. Wolfgang Keller, 5 vols. Berlin, 1912; ed. Julius Bab, 9 vols. Stuttgart, 1923; ed. L. L. Schücking and E. von Schaubert, 10 vols. Munich, 1925–9.

Dingelstedt, F. et al. Shakespeare in deutscher Übersetzung. 10 vols. Hildburghausen, 1867.

Bodenstedt, Friedrich, et al. William Shakespeares dramatische Werke. 9 vols. Leipzig, 1867–71.

Gundolf, Friedrich. Shakespeare in deutscher Sprache. 10 vols. Berlin, 1908–23.

Rothe, Hans. Neue Shakespeare-Übersetzung. Munich, 1922–.

(c) Criticism

Morhof, D. G. Unterricht von der Teutschen Sprache und Poesie. Kiel, 1682.

Cramer, J. F. Vindiciae Nominis Germanici, contra quosdam Obtrectatores Gallos. Amsterdam, 1694.

Acta Eruditorum. Leipzig, 1695.

Feind, B. Gedanken von der Opera. Gedichte I. Stade, 1708.

Allgemeines historisches Lexicon. Ed. J. F. Buddens, vol. IV, Leipzig, 1709.

Der Vernünfftler. Hamburg, 1713. [No. 85.]

Compendiöses Gelehrten-Lexicon. Ed. J. B. Mencke, Leipzig, 1715.

Bentheim, H. L. Engelländischer Kirch- und Schulen-Staat. Leipzig, 1732 (2nd edn.)

Bodmer, J. J. Miltons Verlust des Paradieses. Zürich, 1732. [Preface.]

—— Critische Abhandlung von dem Wunderbaren in der Poesie. Zürich, 1740.

—— Critische Betrachtungen der poetischen Gemählde der Dichter. Zürich, 1741.

von Borck, K. W. Versuch einer gebundenen Übersetzung des Trauerspiels vom Tode des Julius Caesar. Berlin, 1741.

Gottsched, J. C. Beyträge zur kritischen Historie der deutschen Sprache. Leipzig, 1741. [Vol. VII.[

Schlegel, J. E. Vergleichung Shakespears und Andreas Gryphs. [In Gottsched's Beyträge, vol. VII, 1741.]

Neuer Büchersaal der schönen Wissenschaften und freyen Künste. Leipzig, 1744–9.

Lessing, G. E. Beiträge zur Historie und Aufnahme des Theaters. 1750.

—— Theatralische Bibliothek. 1758.

—— Briefe, die neueste Literatur betreffend. No. 17, 16 Feb. 1759.

—— Hamburgische Dramaturgie. Nos. 12, 15, 73, 1767–8.

Neue Erweiterungen der Erkenntnis und des Vergnügens. Frankfort, 1753 (Life of Shakespeare); 1756 (trn of scenes from Richard III).

Neue Probestücke der englischen Schaubühne. Basle, 1758. [Trn of Romeo and Juliet.]

von Gerstenberg, H. W. Briefe über Merkwürdigkeiten der Literatur. Nos. 14–18, Schleswig, 1766–7.

von Goethe, J. W. Zum Schäkespars Tag. 1771.

—— Götz von Berlichingen. 1773.

—— Wilhelm Meisters Lehrjahre. 1795–6.

—— Romeo und Julie für das Theater bearbeitet. 1812.

—— Shakespeare und kein Ende. 1815.

Herder, J. G. Shakespear. [In Von deutscher Art and Kunst, Hamburg, 1773.]

Lenz, J. M. R. Anmerkungen übers Theater nebst angehängtem übersetztem Stuck Shakespeares, Amor vincit omnia [Love's Labour's Lost]. Leipzig, 1774.

Eschenburg, J. J. Über Shakespeare. Zürich, 1787.

Schlegel, A. W. Etwas über William Shakespeare bei Gelegenheit Wilhelm Meisters. Die Hoven, IV, 1796.

—— Über Shakespeares Romeo und Julia. Die Hoven, x, 1797.

—— Über dramatische Kunst und Literatur. Heidelberg, 1809–11. [Lectures XXII–XXVII.]

Tieck, J. L. Der Sturm. Nebst einer Abhandlung über Shakespeares Behandlung des Wunderbaren. Berlin, 1796.

—— Kritische Schriften. Vol. IV, Leipzig, 1852.

—— Das Buch über Shakespeare. Ed. Henry Lüdeke, Halle, 1920.

Schlegel, F. Die Griechen und Römer. Neustrelitz, 1797.

—— Geschichte der alten und neuen Literatur. Vienna, 1815.

von Schiller, J. F. Macbeth. 1801.

—— Othello. 1805. [Based on H. Voss's trn.]

Hegel, G. W. F. Vorlesungen über Asthetik. Berlin, 1875–8.

Heine, H. Shakespeares Mädchen und Frauen. [In Sämmtliche Werke, vol. v, Leipzig, 1839.]

Ulrici, H. Über Shakespeares dramatische Kunst und sein Verhältnis zu Calderon und Goethe. Halle, 1829.

Gervinus, G. G. Shakespeare. 4 vols. Leipzig, 1849–50.

—— Händel und Shakespeare. Leipzig, 1868.

Delius, N. Der Mythus von William Shakespeare. Bonn, 1851.

—— Über das englische Theaterwesen zu Shakespeares Zeit. Bonn, 1853.

—— Abhandlungen zu Shakespeare. 2 sers. Elberfeld, 1878–88.

Immermann, K. Theaterbriefe. Berlin, 1851.

Mommsen, Tycho. Marlow und Shakespeare. Eisenach, 1854.

—— Romeo und Juliet. Oldenburg, 1859.

Kreyssig, F. Vorlesungen über Shakespeare. 3 vols. Berlin, 1858.

Vischer, F. T. Kritische Gänge. Neue Folge. Stuttgart, 1861.

—— Shakespeare-Vorträge. 6 vols. Berlin, 1899–1905.

von Friesen, H. Shakespearestudien. 3 vols. Vienna, 1864–76.

—— Briefe über Shakespeares Hamlet. Leipzig, 1864.

Tschischwitz, B. Shakspere-Forschungen. Halle, 1868.

Ludwig, Otto. Shakespeare-Studien. Leipzig, 1871.

Bodenstedt, F. Shakespeares Frauencharaktere. Leipzig, 1875.

Werder, K. Vorlesungen über Shakespeares Hamlet. Berlin, 1875.

—— Vorlesungen über Shakespeares Macbeth. Berlin, 1885.

Elze, Karl. William Shakespeare. Halle, 1876.

—— Abhandlungen zu Shakespeare. Halle, 1877.

ten Brink, Bernhard. Shakespeare. Fünf Vorlesungen. Strasburg, 1893.

Sarrazin, Gregor. William Shakespeares Lehrjahre. Weimar, 1897.

Schücking, L. L. Shakespeare im literarischen Urteil seiner Zeit. Heidelberg, 1898.

—— Die Charakterprobleme bei Shakespeare. Leipzig, 1919.

Wolff, M. J. William Shakespeare. Studien und Aufsätze. Leipzig, 1903.

—— Shakespeare. Der Dichter und sein Werk. 2 vols. Munich, 1908.

Wetz, Wilhelm. Die Lebensnachrichten über Shakespeare. Heidelberg, 1912.

Brandl, Alois. Shakespeares Leben—Umwelt—Kunst. Berlin, 1922.

Richter, Helene. Shakespeare der Mensch. Leipzig, 1923.

Gundolf, Friedrich. Shakespeare. Sein Wesen und Werk. 2 vols. Berlin, 1928–9.

(iii) Other Countries

[Translations and critical writings are omitted.]

Greece

Boltz, A. Shakespeare in Griechenland. Sh. Jb. XI, 1876.

Wagner, Wilhelm. Shakespeare in Griechenland. Sh. Jb. XII, 1877.

Holland

Loffelt, A. Nederlandsche Navolgingen van Shakespeare en van de oude engelsche Dramatici in de 17. Eeuw. Nederlandsch Spectator, 1868.

Moltzer, H. E. Shakespeare's Invloed op het nederlandsch Tooneel der zeventiende Eeuw. Groningen, 1874.

Arnold, T. J. I. Shakespeare in de Nederlandsche Letterkunde en op het Nederlandsch Tooneel. Bibliographische Adversaria, IV, 1879. [Also separately, Hague, 1879.]

—— Shakespeare-Bibliography in the Netherlands. Bibliographische Adversaria, IV, 1879. [Also separately, Hague, 1879.]

Pennink, B. Nederland en Shakespeare. Hague, 1936.

Hungary

Greguss, A. Shakespeare in Ungarn. Budapest, 1879.

Berzeviczy, Albert. Shakespeare és a Magyar Nemzetlélek. Magyar Shakespeare-Tár, VIII, 1896.

Bayer, J. Shakespeare Drámái Hazánkban. 2 vols. Budapest, 1909. [A full Hungarian bibliography of Shakespeare.]

Riedl, .Friedrich. Shakespeare és a Magyar Irodalom. Budapest, 1916.

Császár, Elemér. Shakespeare és a Magyar Költészet. Budapest, 1917.

Haraszti, Z. Shakespeare in Hungary. Boston, 1929.

India

Legouis, É. La Révolte de L'Inde contre Shakespeare. Revue anglo-américaine, Feb. 1925.

Sisson, C. J. Shakespeare in India. Shakespeare Ass. 1926.

Shahani, R. G. Shakespeare through Eastern Eyes. 1932.

Menon, C. N. Shakespeare's Tragedies through Indian Eyes. Madras, 1934.

Italy

Reforgiato, Vinzenzo. Shakespeare e Manzoni. Catania, 1908.

Bellezza, P. Shakespeare e Manzoni. Milan, 1927.

Japan

Walter, Erwin. Shakespeare in Japan. Sh. Jb. LI, 1915.

Poland

Bernacki, L. S. A. Poniatowski als Shakespeare-Übersetzer. Sh. Jb. XLII, 1906.

Calina, Josephine. Shakespeare in Poland. Shakespeare Ass. 1923.

Portugal

Condamin, J. Un royal Traducteur de Shakespeare, Louis, Roi de Portugal. [In Études et Souvenirs, Paris, 1883.]

Michaëlis de Vasconcellos, C. Shakespeare in Portugal. Sh. Jb. XV, 1880.

Roumania

Beza, Marcu. Shakespeare in Roumania. Shakespeare Ass. 1931.

Russia

Pokrowskij, Michael. Puschkin und Shakespeare. Sh. Jb. XLIII, 1907.

Lirondelle, André. Catherine II, Élève de Shakespeare. Revue Germanique, IV, 1908.
—— Shakespeare en Russie (1748–1840). Paris, 1912.

Gebhard, Richard. Ivan Turgenjew in seinen Beziehungen zu Shakespeare. Sh. Jb. XLV, 1909.

Friedrichs, Ernst. Shakespeare in Russland. E. Studien, L, 1916.

Simmons, E. J. Catherine the Great and Shakespeare. PMLA. XLVII, 1932.
—— English Literature and Culture in Russia. Cambridge, U.S.A. 1935.

Scandinavia

Bolin, Wilhelm. Zur Shakespeare-Literatur Schwedens. Sh. Jb. XV, 1880.

Palmblad, H. V. E. Shakspere and Strindberg. Germanic Rev. III, 1928.

Tonstad, Trygve. Wergeland og Shakespeare. Edda, XXVIII, 1928.

Molin, Nils. Shakespeare och Sverige intill 1800. Gothenburg, 1931.

Rubow, P. V. Shakespeare paa Dansk. Copenhagen, 1932.
—— Studier over danske Shakespeare-Oversaettelser. Acta Philologica Scandinavica, VIII, 1933.

Serbia

Popović, V. Shakespeare in Serbia. 1928.

Spain

Ruppert y Ujaravi, R. Shakespeare en España. Madrid, 1920.

Schütt, Maria. Hat Calderón Shakespeare gekannt? Die Quellen von Calderóns La Cisma de Inglaterra? Sh. Jb. LXI, 1925.

Par, Alfonso. Contribución a la Bibliografía española de Shakespeare. Barcelona, 1930.
—— Shakespeare en la Literatura española. 2 vols. Madrid, 1935.

Switzerland

Vetter, Theodor. Shakespeare und die deutsche Schweiz. Sh. Jb. XLVIII, 1912.

The United States

Churchill, G. B. Shakespeare in America. Sh. Jb. XLII, 1906.

Cairns, W. B. Shakespeare in America. Edda, VI, 1916.

Thorndike, A. H. Shakespeare in America. British Academy Lecture, 1927.

Harrison, R. C. Walt Whitman and Shakespeare. PMLA. XLIV, 1929.

Furness, C. J. Walt Whitman's Estimate of Shakespeare. Harvard Stud. XIV, 1932.

X. THE JACOBEAN AND CAROLINE DRAMATISTS

CHAPMAN, MIDDLETON, JONSON, DEKKER,
HEYWOOD, MARSTON, TOURNEUR,
WEBSTER, MASSINGER, BEAUMONT
AND FLETCHER, ROWLEY,
FORD, SHIRLEY

[The italicised abbreviations used in this section (*Bang, Gayley, TFT.*, etc.) refer to the collections of plays listed above, pp. 488–92.]

GEORGE CHAPMAN (1559?–1634)

(1) COLLECTED WORKS

The Comedies and Tragedies of George Chapman. [Ed. R. H. Shepherd,] 3 vols. 1873. [Omits Eastward Ho.]

The Works of George Chapman. Ed. R. H. Shepherd, 3 vols. 1874–5, 1889. [Includes The Second Maiden's Tragedy, Two Wise Men and All the Rest Fools, Alphonsus, The Ball, and Revenge for Honour, in addition to the plays listed below. Vols. II, III include the trns and poems. Vol. III has an Introduction by A. C. Swinburne (later issued separately).]

George Chapman. Ed. W. L. Phelps, 1895. (Mermaid Ser.) [Contains All Fools, Bussy D'Ambois, The Revenge of Bussy D'Ambois, The Conspiracy, and the Tragedy of Charles Duke of Byron.]

The Plays and Poems of George Chapman. Ed. T. M. Parrott, 2 vols. 1910–4. [Vol. III (The Poems) has not been issued. Includes, in addition to plays listed below, Alphonsus, The Ball, Revenge for Honour and Sir Giles Goosecap.]

(2) PLAYS

The Blinde begger of Alexandria, most pleasantly discoursing his variable humours in disguised shapes full of conceite and pleasure. As it hath beene sundry times publickly acted in London, by the right honorable the Earle of Nottingham, Lord high Admirall his servantes. 1598; ed. W. W. Greg, *Malone Soc.* 1928.

A pleasant Comedy entituled: An Humerous dayes Myrth. As it hath been sundrie times publikely acted by the right honourable the Earle of Nottingham Lord high Admirall his servants. By G. C. 1599.

Eastward Hoe. As It was playd in the Black-friers. By The Children of her Majesties Revels. Made by Geo: Chapman. Ben Jonson. Joh. Marston. 1605 (*bis*); rptd R. Dodsley (Collection of Old Plays, vol. IV, 1744, 1780, 1825); *Ancient British Drama*, vol. II; ed. F. E. Schelling, Boston, 1904 (Belles Lettres Ser.); ed. J. W. Cunliffe, *Gayley*, vol. II; *TFT.* 1914; ed. J. H. Harris,

New Haven, 1926. [Also included in collected edns of Marston (see p. 627).]

Al Fooles. A Comedy, Presented at the Black Fryers, And lately before his Majestie. 1605; ed. I. Reed (Dodsley's Old Plays, vol. IV, 1780); *Ancient British Drama*, vol. II; ed. J. P. Collier (Dodsley's Old Plays, vol. IV, 1825); ed. T. M. Parrott, Boston, 1907 (Belles Lettres Ser.).

Monsieur D'Olive. A Comedie, as it was sundrie times acted by her Majesties children at the Blacke-Friers. 1606; ed. C. W. Dilke (Old English Plays, vol. III, 1814).

The Gentleman Usher. 1606; ed. T. M. Parrott, Boston, 1907 (Belles Lettres Ser.).

Bussy D'Ambois: A Tragedie: As it hath been often presented at Paules. 1607 (re-issued 1608) (anon.); 1641 (re-issued, 1646, 1657); ed. C. W. Dilke (Old English Plays, vol. III, 1814); ed. F. S. Boas, Boston, 1905 (Belles Lettres Ser.).

The Conspiracie, And Tragedie Of Charles Duke of Byron, Marshall of France. Acted lately in two playes, at the Black-Friers. 1608; 1625.

May-Day. A witty Comedie, divers times acted at the Blacke Fryers. 1611; ed. C. W. Dilke (Old English Plays, vol. IV, 1814).

The Widdowes Teares. A Comedie. As it was often presented in the blacke and white Friers. 1612; rptd R. Dodsley (Collection of Old Plays, vol. VI, 1744, 1780, 1825).

The Revenge Of Bussy D'Ambois. A Tragedie. As it hath beene often presented at the private Play-house in the White-Fryers. 1613; ed. F. S. Boas, Boston, 1905 (Belles Lettres Ser.).

The Warres Of Pompey and Caesar. Out of whose events is evicted this Proposition. Only a just man is a freeman. 1631 (re-issued 1631 and 1653).

The Tragedie of Chabot Admirall of France. As it was presented by her Majesties Servants, at the private House in Drury Lane. Written by George Chapman, and James Shirly. 1639; ed. E. Lehman, Philadelphia, 1906. [Apparently a revision by Shirley of a play written by Chapman *c.* 1613.]

[In addition to Munday's Fedele and Fortunio (see p. 535 above), Shirley's The Ball (see p. 639 below), and parts of several of Shakespeare's plays, the following anon. plays (listed pp. 651–3 below) have been wholly or partially assigned to Chapman: Alphonsus Emperour of Germany, The Distracted Emperor, Sir Giles Goosecap, Histriomastix, Revenge for Honour, The Second Maiden's Tragedy, Time's Triumph, Two Wise Men.]

(3) MASQUE

The Memorable Masque Of The Two Honourable Houses Or Innes of Court; the Middle Temple, and Lyncolnes Inne. As It Was Performed Before the King, at White-hall on Shrove-Munday at night; being the 15. of Febr. 1613. At the Princely Celebration Of the most royall Nuptials of the Palsgrave, and his thrice gratious Princesse Elizabeth, etc. With a description of their march on horse-backe to the Court, from the Maister of the Rolls his house: with all their right Noble consorts, and most showfull attendants. Invented, and fashioned, with the ground, and speciall structure of the whole worke: By our Kingdomes most Artfull and Ingenious Architect Innigo Jones. Supplied, Applied, Digested, and written, By Geo. Chapman. [1613?] (*bis*); ed. J. Nichols (Progresses of James I, vol. II, 1828).

(4) TRANSLATIONS

(a) Homer

Seaven Bookes of the Iliades of Homere, prince of Poets. Translated according to the Greeke in judgement of his best Commentaries. 1598. [Bks I, II, VII–XI.]
Achilles Shield. Translated as the other seven Bookes of Homer, out of his eighteenth booke of Iliades. 1598.
Homer, Prince of Poets, translated according to the Greeke in twelve Bookes of his Iliads. [1610?] (re-issued 1611). [Reprints the 7 bks of 1598 and adds III–VI and XII.]
The Iliads of Homer, Prince of Poets. Never before in any language truely translated. With a Comment uppon some of his chiefe places. [1611]; ed. R. Hooper, 2 vols. 1857; rptd H. Morley, 1883. [Adds bks XIII–XXIV and substitutes new versions of I and part of II.]
Homers Odysses. [1614?] [Bks I–XII.]
Twenty-four Bookes of Homers Odisses. [1615?]; ed. R. Hooper, 2 vols. 1857; rptd 2 vols. 1897 (Temple Classics). [Adds bks XIII–XXIV to a re-issue of the previous item.]
The Whole Works of Homer, Prince of Poets, in his Iliads and Odysses. [1616] (re-issues of the edns of [1611] and [1615?] with new general title-page); rptd 1904; rptd 2 vols. Oxford, 1930.
The Crowne of all Homers Workes, Batrachomyomachia Or the Battaile of Frogs and Mise. His Hymn's and Epigrams. [1624?] (also issued in The Whole Works); rptd 1818; ed. R. Hooper, 1858.

(b) Other Writers

Petrarchs Seven Penitentiall Psalmes, paraphrastically translated, with other Philosophicall Poems, and a Hymne to Christ upon the Crosse. 1612.
The Divine Poem of Musaeus, first of all bookes, translated according to the Originall. 1616.
The Georgicks of Hesiod; Translated Elaborately out of the Greek. 1618.
A Justification Of A Strange Action of Nero in burying with a solemne funerall one of the cast Hayres of his Mistresse Poppaea: Also a just reproofe of a Romane smell-Feast, being the fifth Satyre of Juvenall translated. 1629.

(5) OTHER WRITINGS

Σκιὰ νυκτός. The Shadow of Night: Containing Two Poeticall Hymnes. 1594 ('by G. C.'); rptd A. Acheson (in Shakespeare and the Rival Poet, 1903).
Ovids Banquet of Sence. A Coronet for his Mistresse Philosophie, and his amorous Zodiacke. With a translation of a Latin coppie written by a Fryer [Walter Map]. 1595; 1639; rptd A. Acheson (in Shakespeare and the Rival Poet, 1903). [The trn, The Amorous Contention of Phillis and Flora, was rptd in 1598 as by R. S. (= Richard Stapleton?) who may be the author.]
Euthymiae Raptus; or the Teares of Peace. With Interlocutions. 1609; rptd A. Acheson (in Shakespeare and the Rival Poet, 1903).
An Epicede or Funerall Song: on the Death of Henry Prince of Wales. 1612; rptd Sir S. E. Brydges, 1818.
Andromeda Liberata. Or, the Nuptials of Perseus and Andromeda. 1614.
A free and offenceles justification of Andromeda liberata. 1614.
Eugenia: or true nobilities trance; for the death of William Lord Russell. 1614 (priv. ptd?).
Pro Vere Autumni Lachrymae. Inscribed to the immortal memorie of Sir Horatio Vere. 1622.
[For Chapman's continuation of Marlowe's Hero and Leander, see p. 531 above.]

(6) BIOGRAPHY AND CRITICISM

Bodenstedt, T. Chapman in seinem Verhältniss zu Shakespeare. Sh. Jb. I, 1865.
Swinburne, A. C. George Chapman: a Critical Essay. 1875. [Also as introduction to The Works, ed. R. H. Shepherd, vol. III; rptd in The Age of Shakespeare, 1908.]
Koeppel, E. Quellenstudien zu den Dramen George Chapman's, Philip Massinger's und John Ford's. QF. LXXXII, 1897.

Stiefel, A. L. George Chapman und das italienische Drama. Sh. Jb. xxxv, 1899.

Dobell, B. Newly discovered Documents of the Elizabethan and Jacobean Periods. Athenaeum, 23, 30 March, 6, 13 April 1901.

Boas, F. S. The Sources of Chapman's The Conspiracy of Byron and The Revenge of Bussy d'Ambois. Athenaeum, 10 Jan. 1903.

Acheson, A. Shakespeare and the Rival Poet, with Sundry Poetical Pieces by George Chapman bearing on the Subject. 1903.

—— Shakespeare, Chapman and Sir Thomas More. 1931.

Lohff, A. George Chapman. Berlin, 1903.

Stoll, E. E. On the Dates of some of Chapman's plays. MLN. xx, 1905.

Brereton, J. le G. Hermes, 16 Oct. 1905. [Review of F. S. Boas' edns of Bussy d'Ambois and The Revenge of Bussy d'Ambois.]

Parrott, T. M. Notes on the Text of Chapman's Plays. Ang. xxx, 1907. [See also MLR. iii, iv, 1908.]

Schoell, F. L. George Chapman and the Italian Neo-Latinists of the Quattrocento. MP. xiii, 1916.

—— Les Emprunts de G. Chapman à Marsile Fiein. Revue de Littérature comparée, iii, 1923.

—— Études sur l'Humanisme continental en Angleterre à la Fin de la Renaissance. Paris, 1926.

Robertson, J. M. Shakespeare and Chapman. A Thesis of Chapman's Authorship of A Lover's Complaint and his Origination of Timon of Athens. 1917.

Ferguson, A. S. The Plays of George Chapman. MLR. xiii, xv, 1918–20.

Bullen, A. H. Chapman. [In Elizabethans, 1924.]

Spens, J. Chapman's Ethical Thought. E. & S. xi, 1924.

Solve, N. D. Stuart Politics in Chapman's Tragedy of Chabot. Ann Arbor, 1928.

Engel, C.-E. Les Sources du Bussy d'Amboise de Chapman. Revue de Littérature comparée, xii, 1932.

Janish, W. Die erste englische Übersetzung der Homerischen Hymnen. Mitteilungen des Vereins klassischer Philologen in Wien, viii, 1933.

George Chapman. TLS. 10 May 1934.

Ellis, Havelock. George Chapman. With Illustrative Pieces. 1934.

Bartlett, P. Chapman's Revisions in his Iliads. Stud. Phil. xxxii, 1935.

Craig, H. Ethics in the Jacobean Drama. [In Essays in Dramatic Literature: the Parrott Presentation Volume, Princeton, 1935.]

Kennedy, C. W. Political Theory in the Plays of George Chapman. Ibid.

Smith, J. Revaluations (vii): George Chapman. Scrutiny, iv, 1935.

Ellis-Fermor, U. M. The Jacobean Drama. 1936.

Sisson, C. J. Lost Plays of Shakespeare's Age. Cambridge, 1936. [For Chapman's lost play The Old Joiner of Aldgate.]

THOMAS MIDDLETON (1570?–1627)

(1) COLLECTED WORKS

Works. Ed. A. Dyce, 5 vols. 1840.

Works. Ed. A. H. Bullen, 8 vols. 1885–6. [The standard edn.]

Thomas Middleton. (Mermaid Ser.) Vol. i, ed. A. C. Swinburne, 1887. [Contains A Trick to catch the old one; The Changeling; A Chaste Maid in Cheapside; Women beware Women; The Spanish Gipsy.] Vol. ii, ed. Havelock Ellis, 1890. [Contains The Roaring Girl, The Witch, A Fair Quarrel, The Mayor of Queenborough, The Widow.]

The Spanish Gipsy and All's Lost by Lust. Ed. E. C. Morris, Boston, 1908. (Belles Lettres Ser.)

Thomas Middleton. Ed. M. W. Sampson, 1915. [Contains Mickaelmas Term, A Trick to Catch the Old One, A Fair Quarrel, The Changeling.]

(2) PLAYS

Blurt Master-Constable. Or The Spaniards Night-walke. As it hath bin sundry times privately acted by the Children of Paules. 1602 (anon.); rptd W. R. Chetwood (Select Collection of Old Plays, 1750).

The Phoenix, As It hath beene sundry times Acted by the Children of Paules, And presented before his Majestie. 1607 (anon.); 1630.

Michaelmas Terme. As it hath been sundry times acted by the Children of Paules. 1607 (anon.); 1630.

A Tricke to Catch the Old-one. As it hath beene often in Action, both at Paules, and the Black-Fryers. Presented before his Majestie on New-yeares night last. Composde by T. M. 1608 (re-issued 1608); 1616; ed. C. W. Dilke (Old English Plays, vol. v, 1814); rptd Old English Drama, vol. iii, 1830.

The Famelie of Love. Acted by the Children of his Majesties Revells. 1608 (anon.).

A Mad World, My Masters. As it hath bin lately in Action by the Children of Paules. Composed by T. M. 1608; 1640; Ancient British Drama, vol. ii.

Your five Gallants. As it hath beene often in Action at the Black-friers. [1608?]

A Game at Chesse. As it was Acted nine days to gether at the Globe on the Bank side. [1625] (3 edns, first re-issued with date 1625) (anon.); ed. R. C. Bald, Cambridge, 1929. [MSS: BM. Lansdowne 490; Bridgewater House; Trinity College, Cambridge.]

A Chast Mayd In Cheape-side. A Pleasant conceited Comedy never before printed. As it hath beene often acted at the Swan on the Banke-side, by the Lady Elizabeth her Servants. 1630.

Two New Plays, viz. More Dissemblers besides Women. A Comedy. Women beware Women. A Tragedy. 1657; ed. C. W. Dilke (Old English Plays, vols. IV, V, 1815).

No Wit (Help) Like A Womans. A Comedy. 1657 (re-issued 1677 as The Counterfeit Bridegroom).

The Mayor of Quinborough: A Comedy. As it hath been often Acted at Black-Fryars, By His Majesties Servants. 1661; rptd R. Dodsley (Collection of Old Plays, vol. XI, 1745, 1780, 1827).

Any Thing For A Quiet Life. A Comedy. Formerly Acted at Black-Fryers, by His late Majesties Servants. 1662. [With Webster?]

A Tragi-Coomodie, Called the Witch; Long since acted by His Ma^{ttes} Servants at the Black-Friers. 1778. [First ptd from a MS discovered by Isaac Reed, now in the Bodleian Lib.]

The Honest Whore. 1604. [With Dekker. See under Dekker, p. 619 below.]

The Roaring Girle. Or Moll Cut-Purse. As it hath lately beene Acted on the Fortune-stage by the Prince his Players. Written by T. Middleton and T. Dekkar. 1611; Ancient British Drama, vol. II; TFT. 1914.

A Faire Quarrell. As it was Acted before the King and divers times publikely by the Prince his Highnes Servants. Written By Thomas Midleton and William Rowley Gentl. 1617 (re-issued 1617 'With new Additions'); 1622.

The Widdow A Comedie. As it was Acted at the private House in Black-Fryers, by His late Majesties Servants. Written by Ben: Johnson. John Fletcher. Tho: Middelton. Gent. 1652. [Principally by Middleton.]

The Changeling: As it was Acted at the Privat house in Drury-Lane, and Salisbury Court. Written by Thomas Midleton and William Rowley. Gent. 1653; (re-issued 1668); ed. C. W. Dilke (Old English Plays, vol. IV, 1815).

The Spanish Gipsie. As it was Acted at the Privat House in Drury-Lane, and Salisbury Court. Written by Thomas Midleton and William Rowley Gent. 1653; 1661; ed. C. W. Dilke (Old English Plays, vol. IV, 1815); ed. H. B. Clarke, Gayley, vol. III.

The Excellent Comedy, called The Old Law: Or A new way to please you. By Phil. Massinger. Tho. Middleton. William Rowley. Acted before the King and Queene at Salisbury House, and at severall other places. 1656.

[In addition to Beaumont and Fletcher's Wit at Several Weapons (see p. 633 below) and Tourneur's The Revenger's Tragedy (see p. 628), the following anon. plays (see pp. 651–3) have been wholly or partially ascribed to Middleton: The Birth of Merlin, The Bloody Banquet, The Puritan, The Second Maiden's Tragedy.]

(3) MASQUES AND PAGEANTS

The Magnificent Entertainment: Given to King James, Queene Anne his wife, and Henry Frederick the Prince, upon the day of his Majesties Tryumphant Passage (from the Tower) through his Honourable Citie (and Chamber) of London, being the 15. of March, 1603. As well by the English as by the Strangers: With the speeches and Songes, delivered in the severall Pageants. Mart. 1604. [To this Middleton contributed only the speech of Zeal.]

The Triumphs of Truth. A Solemnity unparalleld for Cost, Art and Magnificence, at the Confirmation and Establishment of that Worthy and true Nobly-minded Gentleman, Sir Thomas Middleton, Knight; in the Honorable Office of his Majesties Lieuetenant, the Lord Maior of the thrice Famous City of London. 1613 (re-issued with addns in the same year); rptd J. Nichols (Progresses of James I, vol. II, 1828).

[Running Stream Entertainment.] [Appended to re-issue of The Triumphs of Truth, 1613.] Ed. J. Nichols (Progresses of James I, vol. II, 1828).

Civitatis Amor. The Cities Love. An entertainment by water, at Chelsey, and Whitehall. 1616.

The Tryumphs of Honour and Industry. A solemnity at the establishment of G. Bowles, Lord Maior. 1617.

The Inner-Temple Masque. Or Masque of Heroes. Presented (as an Entertainment for many worthy Ladies:) By Gentlemen of the same Ancient and Noble House. 1619.

The Triumphs of Love and Antiquity. An honourable solemnitie at the establishment of Sir W. Cockayn, Lord Maior. 1619.

A Courtly Masque; The Device called, The World tost at Tennis. As it hath beene divers times Presented to the Contentment of many Noble and Worthy Spectators: By the Prince his Servants. Invented, and set downe, By Tho: Middleton & William Rowley Gent. 1620.

Honorable Entertainments, Compos'de for the Service of this Noble Citie. Some of which were fashion'd for the Entertainment of the Lords of his Majesties most Honorable Privie Counsell, upon the Occasion of their late Royall Employment. 1621.

The Sunne in Aries. A noble solemnity at the establishment of Ed. Barkham, Lord Maior. 1621.

[The Triumphs of Honor and Virtue. A noble solemnitie at the establishment of P. Proby, Lord Maior.] 1622.

An Invention performed for the Service of ye Right honorable Edward Barbham, L. Mayor of the Cittie of London. 1623.

The Triumphs of Integrity. A noble solemnity at the establishment of M. Lumley, Lord Maior. 1623.

The Triumphs of Health and Prosperity. A noble solemnity at the inauguration of Cuthbert Hacket, Lord Maior. 1626.

(4) OTHER WORKS

The Wisdome of Solomon Paraphrased. 1597 (bis).

Micro-cynicon. Sixe Snarling Satyres. 1599 ('By T.M.').

The Blacke Booke. 1604 ('by T.M.').

Father Hubburds Tales: Or The Ant, And the Nightingale. 1604 (anon.); 1604 (as The Ant and the Nightingale, by T.M.) (bis).

Sir Robert Sherley, sent ambassadour in the name of the King of Persia to Sigismond the third, King of Poland, his royal entertainment. 1609.

The Peace-Maker: Or, Great Brittaines Blessing. 1618.

The Mariage Of The Old And New Testament. 1620. [Dedication signed By Tho. Middleton, Chronologer for the Honourable Citie of London.]

(5) BIOGRAPHY AND CRITICISM

Wiggin, P. G. An Enquiry into the Authorship of the Middleton-Rowley Plays. Boston, 1897.

Jung, H. Das Verhältniss Thomas Middletons zu Shakspere. Munich, 1904.

Morris, E. C. The Allegory in Middleton's A Game at Chesse. E. Studien, xxxviii, 1907.

—— On the Date and Composition of The Old Law. PMLA. xvii, 1909.

Symons, Arthur. Middleton and Rowley. CHEL. vol. vi, 1910. [Rptd in his Studies in the Elizabethan Drama, 1920.]

Withington, R. English Pageantry. 2 vols. Cambridge, U.S.A. 1918–20.

Grossman, R. Spanien und das elizabethanische Drama. Hamburg, 1920.

Lawrence, W. J. Early Substantive Masques. TLS. 8 Dec. 1921.

Sykes, H. D. Sidelights on Elizabethan Drama. 1924.

Lloyd, B. A Minor Source of The Changeling. MLR. xix, 1924.

Dunkel, W. D. The Dramatic Technique of Thomas Middleton in his Comedies of London Life. Chicago, 1925.

—— The Authorship of Anything for a Quiet Life. PMLA. xliii, 1928.

—— The Authorship of The Puritan. PMLA. xlv, 1930.

—— The Authorship of The Revenger's Tragedy. PMLA. xlvi, 1931.

—— Did not Rowley merely revise Middleton? PMLA. xlviii, 1933.

Oliphant, E. H. C. The Bloodie Banquet, a Dekker-Middleton Play. TLS. 17 Dec. 1925.

—— The Authorship of The Revenger's Tragedy. Stud. Phil. xxiii, 1926. [Attributes to Middleton.]

Eliot, T. S. Thomas Middleton. [In For Lancelot Andrewes, 1928.]

Wagner, B. M. New Allusions to A Game at Chesse. PMLA. xliv, 1929.

Eccles, M. Middleton's Birth and Education. RES. vii, 1931.

Bald, R. C. Middleton's Civic Employments. MP. xxxi, 1933.

—— The Sources of Middleton's City Comedies. JEGP. xxxiii, 1934.

—— The Chronology of Middleton's Plays. MLR. xxxii, 1937.

Dowling, M. A Note on Moll Cutpurse—'The Roaring Girl.' RES. x, 1934.

Hoole, W. S. Thomas Middleton's Use of Imprese in Your Five Gallants. Stud. Phil. xxxi, 1934.

Bradbrook, M. C. Themes and Conventions of Elizabethan Tragedy. Cambridge, 1935.

Christian, M. G. Middleton's Acquaintance with the Merrie Conceited Jests of George Peele. PMLA. l, 1935.

Ellis-Fermor, U. M. The Jacobean Drama. 1936.

F. E. S.

BEN JONSON (1572–1637)

(1) BIBLIOGRAPHY

Nicholson, B. Ben Jonson's Folios and the Bibliographers. N. & Q. 18 June 1870.

—— On the Conjoint Proprietorship in Ben Jonson's Works. N. & Q. 18 March 1871.

Greg, W. W. A List of English Plays written before 1643. Bibliog. Soc. 1900.

—— A List of Masques, Pageants, etc. Bibliog. Soc. 1902. [The introduction discusses the 1616 Folio.]

Greg, W. W. The First Edition of Ben Jonson's Every Man Out of his Humour. Library, I, 1920. [Supplementary notes, II, p. 49, III, p. 57.]

—— The Riddle of Jonson's Chronology. Library, VI, 1926.

—— Was there a 1612 Quarto of Epicœne? Library, xv, 1934.

van Dam, B. A. P. and Stoffel, C. The Authority of the Ben Jonson Folio of 1616. Ang. XXVI, 1903.

Aitken, G. B. Ben Jonson's Works. N. & Q. 29 May 1909.

Marcham, F. Thomas Walkley and the Ben Jonson 'Works' of 1640. Library, XI, 1931. [Supplementary article by W. W. Greg.]

Ford, H. L. Collation of the Ben Jonson Folios, 1616–31–1640. 1932.

(2) COLLECTED WORKS

The Workes of Benjamin Jonson. 1616. [Contains:
Every Man In his Humour. (Chamberlain's, Curtain, 1598.)
Every Man Out of his Humour. (Chamberlain's, Globe, 1599.)
Cynthias Revels, or The Fountaynn of Selfe-Love. (Chapel Children, Blackfriars, 1600.)
Poëtaster, or His Arraignment. (Chapel Children, Blackfriars, 1601.)
Sejanus his Fall. (King's, Globe, 1603.)
Volpone, or The Foxe. (King's, Globe, 1605.)
Epicœne, or The silent Woman. (Revels Children, Whitefriars, 1609.)
The Alchemist. (King's, Globe, 1610.)
Catiline his Conspiracy. (King's, Globe, 1611.)
Epigrammes. (S.R. 15 May 1612.)
The Forrest.
Part of the Kings Entertainment [on his state-entry into London, 15 March 1604].
A Panegyre on the Happie Entrance of James [to open Parliament, 19 March 1604].
Entertainments and Masques. 1603–1616. (See section (4) below.)]

The Workes of Benjamin Jonson. 1640. [The first vol. reprints 1616. The second vol. contains:
Bartholmew Fayre. 1631. (Lady Elizabeth's, Hope, 31 Oct. 1614.)
The Divell is an Asse. 1631 [in some copies 1641]. (King's, Blackfriars, autumn 1616.)
The Staple of Newes. 1631. (King's, Blackfriars, Feb. 1625.)
The Magnetick Lady: or, Humors Reconcil'd. (King's, Blackfriars, licensed 12 Oct. 1632.)
A Tale of a Tub. (Queen Henrietta's, Cockpit, licensed 7 May 1633.) ·

The Sad Shepherd: or, A Tale of Robin-Hood. 1641. (Three acts only.)
Masques. 1617–1631. (See section (4) below.)
Underwoods.
Entertainments. 1633–4. (See section (4) below.)
Mortimer his Fall. (One scene only.)
Horace, his Art of Poetrie.
The English Grammar.
Timber: or Discoveries.]

The Works of Ben Jonson. 1692; 1716. [Adds The New Inn, Leges Convivales.]

Works. Ed. P. Whalley, 7 vols. 1756. [Adds The Case is Altered.]

Works. Ed. W. Gifford, 9 vols. 1816; rptd F. Cunningham [with occasional corrections], 3 vols. 1871, 9 vols. 1875.

Works. Ed. Barry Cornwall, 1838.

Ben Jonson's Dramen nach der Folio 1616. Ed. W. Bang, 2 pts, Bang, vol. VII, 1905–8.

Works. Ed. H. C. Hart. 2 vols. 1906. [Incomplete.]

Ben Jonson. Ed. C. H. Herford and P. Simpson, 6 vols. (to be completed in 10), Oxford, 1925–37.

(3) PLAYS

Four Select Plays: Silent Woman, Volpone, Catiline, Alchemist [with Shadwell's Timon of Athens]. [Advertised in the Post-boy, 16 March 1710.]

Ben Johnson's Plays in Two Volumes. Dublin, 1729. [Volpone, Catiline, Bartholomew Fair, Sejanus, Epicœne, Every Man In and Out of his Humour, Alchemist.]

The Three Celebrated Plays of Ben Johnson. 1732. [Fox, Alchemist, Silent Woman.]

Plays. Glasgow, 1766. [Volpone, Alchemist, Epicœne.]

Plays and Poems. Ed. H. Morley, 1885. [Alchemist, Volpone, Epicœne, Sad Shepherd.]

Dramatic Works and Lyrics. Ed. J. A. Symonds, 1886. [A selection.]

Ben Jonson. Ed. B. Nicholson (introduction by C. H. Herford), 3 vols. 1893–4. (Mermaid Ser.) [Every Man In and Out of his Humour, Poetaster, Bartholomew Fair, Cynthia's Revels, Sejanus, Volpone, Epicœne, Alchemist.]

The Complete Plays. Ed. F. E. Schelling, 2 vols. 1910. (Everyman's Lib.)

Ben Jonson. Ed. E. Rhys, New York, 1915. [Every Man In his Humour, Volpone, Epicœne, Alchemist.]

Every Man Out of his Humor. 1600 (3 quarto edns). (Stationers' Register, 8 April.)
Facs. rpt of Quarto 1, ed. W. W. Greg and F. P. Wilson, Malone Soc. 1920.
Facs. rpt of Quartos 2 and 3, ed. W. Bang and W. W. Greg, Bang, vols. XVI, XVII, 1907.

Œuvres Dramatiques. Tr. G. Duval, 8 vols. Paris, 1908–9.

Collection Shakespeare. Ed. A. Koszul, Paris, 1922—.

(ii) Smaller collections and selections

Le Théâtre Anglois. [Tr. P. A. de La Place], 8 vols. 1745.

Chefs-d'Œuvre de Shakespeare. Tr. A. Bruguière de Sorsum. Rev. M. de Chênedollé, 2 vols. Paris, 1826.

Chefs-d'Œuvre de Shakespeare traduits par les plus célèbres Littérateurs sous la Direction de D. O'Sullivan. 3 vols. Paris, 1836–9.

Legouis, É. Pages Choisies des Grands Écrivains: Shakespeare. Paris, 1899.

Œuvres Choisies. Traduction et Notice par G. Roth. 3 vols. Paris, 1918.

Œuvres Choisies. Traduction Nouvelle par A. Feuillerat. Les Cent Chefs-d'Œuvre Étrangers. 2 vols. Paris, 1922.

(iii) Separate Plays

[Lack of space has made it impossible to give a list of the translations of separate plays. For these the reader is referred to: A. Dubeux, Les Traductions françaises de Shakespeare (Études Françaises, Société des Professeurs français en Amérique, 15e Cahier, 1928).]

(iv) The Poems

Poèmes et Sonnets. Traduits en Vers français par E. Lafond. Paris, 1856.

Sonnets. Traduits en Vers français par A. Copin. Paris, 1888. [Partly pbd in Revue d'Art Dramatique, 1887–8.]

Sonnets. Traduits en Sonnets français par F. Henry, Paris, 1900.

Sonnets. Essai d'une Interprétation en Vers français par Ch. M. Garnier. Cahiers de la Quinzaine, 23 Dec. 1906, 31 Mar. 1907. [Rptd in rev. form in Collection Shakespeare, 1922.]

Les Poèmes Intimes et le Pèlerin Passionné. Tr. A. Doysié, Paris, 1919.

Vénus et Adonis. Tr. E. Godefroy, Paris, 1921. [First ptd in Vers et Prose, XI, XII, 1907–8.]

Sonnets. Tr. É. Le Brun, Paris, [1927].

(c) Criticism
(i) Before 1728

Boyer, A. The Compleat French Master [1700?]; [1705?]; 1710.

Le Spectateur ou le Socrate Moderne, tr. de l'Anglois. Amsterdam, 1714; 1716–8; 1722–30. [Translator's note.]

Dissertation sur la Poésie Anglaise. Journal Littéraire. Hague, 1717.

(ii) 1728–1778

Prévost, A. F. Mémoires d'un Homme de Qualité. Paris, 1728.

—— Le Pour et le Contre. Paris, 1733, etc. [Articles on Shakespeare, 1738, etc.]

Voltaire, F. A. de. Essai sur la Poésie épique. Paris, 1728.

—— Œdipe. Paris, 1730. [Préface.]

—— Brutus. Paris, 1731. [Préface: Discours sur la Tragedie à Mylord Bolingbroke.]

—— Zaïre. Paris, 1733. [Épitre Dedicatoire.]

—— Lettres Philosophiques. Lettres sur les Anglais. Basle, 1734; ed. G. Lanson, 1909; tr. Eng. 1733.

—— La Mort de César. Paris, 1736. [Préface.]

—— Sémiramis. Paris, 1749. [Dissertation sur la Tragédie.]

—— Appel à toutes les Nations de l'Europe. Paris, 1761. [Rptd with a new title: Du Théâtre anglais par Jerôme Carré in Contes de Guillaume Vadé, Paris, 1764.]

—— Observations sur le J. César de Shakespeare. [Preface to Commentaires sur Médée et le Cid, in Théâtre de P. Corneille, Paris, 1764.]

—— Questions sur l'Encyclopédie (Art dramatique, Goût, etc.). 1770–1. [Included in Dictionnaire Philosophique, ed. Kehl, Paris, 1784–90.]

—— Lettre à l'Académie française. Paris, 1776.

—— Irène. Paris, 1778. [Lettre à l'Académie.]

Riccoboni, L. Réflexions historiques et critiques sur les différents Théâtres de l'Europe. Paris, 1738.

Le Blanc, Abbé. Lettres d'un François. 3 vols. Hague, 1745; Amsterdam, 1751.

La Place, P. A. de. Discours sur le Théâtre anglois. [In Théâtre anglois, Paris, 1745.]

Hénault, Président. Nouveau Théâtre françois: François II. Paris, 1747. [Préface.]

Chauffepié, J. G. de. Nouveau Dictionnaire historique. Vol. IV, Amsterdam, 1750, etc.

Fiquet du Bocage. Lettres sur le Théâtre anglois. 2 vols. Paris, 1752.

Journal Étranger. Dec. 1755.

d'Arnaud, F. T. de Baculard. Supplément à la 1ère Edition du Comte de Comminges, Second Discours Préliminaire. Hague, 1765.

Suard, J. B. A. Essai historique sur l'Origine et les Progrès du Drame anglais. Observations sur Shakespeare. [In Variétés littéraires, 4 vols. Paris, 1768.]

Marmontel, J. F. de. Chefs-d'œuvre dramatiques. Discours sur la Tragédie. 1773.

Journal Anglais, I, 1775.

Mercier, S. De la Littérature et des Littérateurs. Paris, 1778.

Diderot, D., d'Alembert, J. et al. Encyclopédie. Paris, 1750, etc.

Every Man In his Humor. 1601. (S.R. 4 and 14 Aug. 1600.)

Facs. rpt of Quarto, ed. C. Grabau, Sh. Jb. xxxviii, 1902; ed. W. Bang and W. W. Greg, *Bang*, vol. x, 1905.

Facs. rpt of Quarto and Folio, ed. H. H. Carter, New Haven, 1921.

Folio text of 1616, ed. Sir W. Scott (Modern British Drama, vol. iii, 1811); ed. H. B. Wheatley, 1877; ed. W. M. Dixon, 1896 (Temple Dramatists); ed. H. Maas, Rostock, 1901; ed. W. A. Neilson, 1911 (Chief Elizabethan Dramatists); ed. C. H. Herford, *Gayley*, vol. ii; ed. P. Simpson, Oxford, 1919; ed. R. S. Knox, 1923; ed. G. B. Harrison, 1926.

The Fountaine of Selfe-Love. Or Cynthias Revels. 1601. (S.R. 23 May.)

Facs. rpt, ed. W. Bang and L. Krebs, *Bang*, vol. xxii, 1908.

Folio text, ed. A. C. Judson, New Haven, 1912.

Poetaster or The Arraignment. 1602. (S.R. 21 Dec. 1601.)

Facs. rpt of Quarto, ed. H. de Vocht, *Bang*. N.S. vol. ix, 1934.

Folio text, ed. H. S. Mallory, New Haven, 1905; ed. J. H. Penniman [with Satiromastix], Boston, 1913. (Belles Lettres Ser.)

Sejanus his fall. 1605. (S.R. 2 Nov. 1604.)

Folio text, ed. W. D. Briggs, Boston, 1911 (Belles Lettres Ser.); ed. W. A. Neilson, 1911 (Chief Elizabethan Dramatists).

Volpone Or The Foxe. 1607. (Preface dated 11 Feb.)

Quarto text, ed. V. O. Sullivan, 1898; ed. facs. H. de Vocht, *Bang*, N.S. vol. xi, 1935.

Folio text, 1709; 1714, 1749; ed. Sir W. Scott (Modern British Drama, vol. iii, 1811); Old English Drama, vol. i, 1830; ed. H. B. Wilkins, Paris, 1906; ed. W. A. Neilson, 1911 (Chief Elizabethan Dramatists); ed. J. D. Rea, New Haven, 1919; ed. F. E. Schelling, New York, 1926 (Typical Elizabethan Plays).

The Case is Alterd. 1609. (S.R. 26 Jan., 20 July.)

Chicago, 1902; ed. W. E. Selin, New Haven, 1919.

Catiline his Conspiracy. 1611; 1635; 1674.

Folio text, ed. L. H. Harris, New Haven, 1916.

The Alchemist. 1612. (S.R. 3 Oct. 1610.)

Quarto text, photo. facs. Noel Douglas Replicas, 1927, and New York, 1935.

Folio text, ed. Sir W. Scott (Modern British Drama, vol. iii, 1811); ed. C. M. Hathaway, New York, 1903; ed. H. C. Hart, 1903; ed. F. E. Schelling [with Eastward Hoe], Boston, 1903 (Belles Lettres Ser.); ed. W. A. Neilson, 1911 (Chief

Elizabethan Dramatists); ed. G. A. Smithson, *Gayley*, vol. ii.

Epicœne, or The Silent Woman. 1620. (S.R. 20 Sept. 1610.)

Folio text, 1739; Old English Drama, vol. iii, 1830; ed. A. Henry, New York, 1906; ed. C. M. Gayley, *Gayley*, vol. ii; rptd 1925.

Bartholomew Fair. Ed. C. S. Alden, New York, 1904.

The Devil is an Ass. Ed. W. S. Johnson, New York, 1905.

The Staple of News. Ed. De Winter, New York, 1905.

The Newe Inne, or The light Heart. 1631; ed. G. B. Tennant, New York, 1908.

The Magnetic Lady, or Humours Reconciled. Ed. W. H. Peck, New York, 1914.

A Tale of a Tub. Ed. H. Scherer, *Bang*, vol. xxxix, 1913; ed. F. M. Snell, 1915.

The Sad Shepherd, or A Tale of Robin Hood, with a Continuation by F. G. Waldron. 1783.

Ben Jonson's Sad Shepherd, with Waldron's Continuation. Ed. W. W. Greg, *Bang*, vol. xi, 1905.

The Sad Shepherd. Ed. F. E. Schelling, New York, 1926 (Typical Elizabethan Plays); ed. J. L. Potts, Cambridge, 1929.

[For Eastward Hoe in which Jonson collaborated with Chapman and Marston, see under Chapman, p. 609 above.]

(4) MASQUES AND ENTERTAINMENTS

[The 1616 Folio contains:

Part of the Kings Entertainment, and A Panegyre. 15 and 19 March 1604.

Entertainment at Althrope. [The Satyr.] 25 June 1603.

Entertainment at Highgate. [The Penates.] 1 May 1604.

Entertainment of the King of Denmark. 24 July 1606.

Entertainment at Theobalds. 22 May 1607.

The Queenes Masques. (1) Of Blacknesse, (2) of Beautie. 6 Jan. 1605, 10 Jan. 1608.

Hymenæi. 5 Jan. 1606.

Lord Haddington's Masque. [The Hue and Cry after Cupid.] 9 Feb. 1608.

The Masque of Queenes. 2 Feb. 1609.

The Speeches at Prince Henries Barriers. 6 Jan. 1610.

Oberon, the Faery Prince. 1 Jan. 1611.

Love Freed from Ignorance and Folly. 3 Feb. 1611.

Love Restored. 6 Jan. 1612.

A Challenge at Tilt. 1 Jan. 1614.

The Irish Masque. 23 Dec. 1613.

Mercury Vindicated from the Alchemists. 6 Jan. 1615.

The Golden Age Restored. 1 and 6 Jan. 1616.

The 1640 Folio rpts the preceding, and adds in vol. II:

Christmas his Masque. 25 Dec. 1616.
Lord Hay's Masque. [Lovers Made Men.] 22 Feb. 1617.
The Vision of Delight. 6 and 19 Jan. 1617.
Pleasure Reconciled to Vertue. 6 Jan. 1618.
For the Honour of Wales. 17 Feb. 1618.
Newes from the New World Discover'd in the Moone. 6 Jan. 1621.
The Metamorphos'd Gypsies. 3 and 5 Aug. and Sept. 1621.
The Masque of Augures. 6 Jan. and 5 May 1622.
Time Vindicated. 6 Jan. 1623.
Neptunes Triumph. Planned for 6 Jan. 1624.
Pans Anniversarie. 6 Jan. and 29 Feb. 1620.
The Masque of Owles. 19 Aug. 1624.
The Fortunate Isles. 9 Jan. 1625.
Loves Triumph through Callipolis. 9 Jan. 1631.
Chloridia. 22 Feb. 1631.
Entertainment at Welbeck. May 1633.
Loves Wel-come at Bolsover. 30 July 1634.]

Nichols, J. The Progresses, Processions and Magnificent Festivities of King James the First. 4 vols. 1828. [Rpts all the masques and entertainments.]
Masques and Entertainments. Ed. H. Morley. 1890.

Evans, H. A. English Masques. 1897. [10 masques.]

Part of King James his Royall Entertainment. Also, a briefe Panegyre of his Majesties Entrance to Parliament. 1604. (S.R. 19 March.)
Entertainment of the Queene and Prince at Althrope. 1604. [Added to the preceding.]
Hymenæi. 1606.
The Characters of two Royal Masques. The one of Blacknesse, The other of Beautie. 1608 (S.R. 21 April); ed. J. P. Collier (Five Court Masques, Shakespeare Soc. 1848).
The Description of the Masque celebrating the Marriage of John, Lord Ramsey, Viscount Haddington. 1608; ed. F. E. Schelling, New York, 1926 (Typical Elizabethan Plays).
The Masque of Queenes. 1609 (S.R. 12 Feb.); ed. J. P. Collier (Five Court Masques, Shakespeare Soc. 1848); ed. G. Chapman, photo. facs. with Inigo Jones's designs, 1930.
Lovers made Men. 1617.
The Masque of Augures. 1621.
Time Vindicated. 1623.
The Fortunate Isles and their Union. [1624.]
Neptunes Triumph for the returne of Albion. [1625.]

Loves Triumph through Callipolis. 1630.
Chloridia. 1630.
The Masque of Gypsies. 1640; ed. G. W. Cole, New York, 1931. [See section (5) below.]
Entertainment at the Christening of Charles Cavendish, May 1620. Monthly Mag. 1817. [From BM. Harley MS 4955.]

(5) POEMS

[The 1616 Folio contains the Epigrams, the Forest. Rptd 1640. The 1640 Folio adds the Underwoods, Horace's Art of Poetry.]

Execration against Vulcan, Epigrams. 1640. [Imprimatur 14 Dec. 1639.]
Horace's Art of Poetry, Masque of Gypsies, Epigrams. 1640. [Imprimatur 21 Feb.]

[Occasional Poems not ptd in the Folios are prefixed to:

Palmer, T. The Sprite of Trees and Herbs. 1599. [See N. & Q. 28 Sept. 1895.]
Breton, N. Melancholic Humours. 1600.
Holland, H. Pancharis. 1603.
Wright, T. The Passions of the Mind. 1604 (2nd edn).
Fletcher, J. The Faithful Shepherdess. [1609–10.]
Coryat, T. Crudities. 1611.
Juvenal and Persius. Ed. T. Farnaby, 1612.
Seneca's Tragedies. Ed. T. Farnaby, 1613.
Stephens, J. Cinthia's Revenge. 1613.
Brooke, C. The Ghost of Richard III. 1614.
The Husband. 1614.
Browne, W. Britannia's Pastorals. 1616.
Hesiod. Tr. G. Chapman, 1618.
Aleman's Rogue. Tr. J. Mabbe, 1623.
Shakespeare, W. Works. 1623.
Warre, T. The Touchstone of Truth. 1624.
Lucan. Tr. T. May, 1627.
Drayton, M. The Battle of Agincourt. 1627.
Beaumont, J. Bosworth Field. 1629.
Brome, R. The Northern Lass. 1632.
Sutcliffe, A. Meditations of Man's Mortality. 1633.
Stafford, A. The Female Glory. 1635.
Rutter, J. The Shepherd's Holy-day. 1635.
Annalia Dubrensia [in honour of Captain Dover]. 1636.]
Poems. Ed. R. Anderson, 1793; ed. A. Chalmers, 1810.
Selections. Ed. E. Sandford, 1819; ed. H. Bennett, 1907.
Underwoods. Cambridge, 1905.
Briggs, W. D. Ben Jonson's Third Ode to Himself. Athenaeum, 13 June 1914.
—— Recovered Lines of Ben Jonson. MLN. xxix, 1914. [The conclusion of Forest, xii.]
Horace: on the Art of Poetry. Ed. E. H. Blakeney, 1928. [With Jonson's rendering.]

(6) Prose Works

[The 1640 Folio contains The English Grammar, Discoveries.]

(a) The English Grammar

The English Grammar. Ed. A. V. Waite, 1909; ed. S. Gibson, 1928.

(b) Discoveries

Observations on Poetry and Eloquence. Ed. J. Warton, 1757 (with Sidney's Apology).
Timber, or Discoveries. Ed. H. Morley, 1892; ed. F. E. Schelling, 1892; ed. Sir I. Gollancz, 1898; ed. M. Castelain, Paris, [1906]; ed. G. B. Harrison, 1923.

(c) Letters

[Collected in Ben Jonson, ed. C. H. Herford and P. Simpson, vol. I, 1925.]
A Collection of Letters. Ed. T. Matthew, 1660. [One letter, p. 328.]
Drummond, W. Works. 1711. [One letter, p. 154.]
The Gentleman's Magazine. Vol. LVI, pt I, 1786 (one letter); vol. LXVI, pt I, 1796 (four letters from Harley MS. 4955).
Dobell, B. Newly Discovered Documents of the Elizabethan and Jacobean Periods. Athenaeum, 30 March, 13 April 1901. [Three letters.]
Simpson, P. Ben Jonson and Cecilia Bulstrode. TLS. 6 March 1930. [One letter.]

(7) Biography and Criticism

Dekker, T. Satiro-mastix. Or the untrussing of the Humorous Poet. 1602.
Heads of a Conversation betwixt Ben Johnson and William Drummond. [Drummond's Works, 1711.]
Notes of Ben Jonson's Conversations with William Drummond. Ed. D. Laing, Archæologica Scotica, IV, 1833; Shakespeare Soc. 1842; rptd Gifford's Jonson, ed. F. Cunningham, vol. III, 1871.
Ben Jonson's Conversations with William Drummond. Ed. P. Sidney, 1906; ed. R. F. Patterson, 1923; ed. G. B. Harrison, 1923.
Stainer, C. L. Jonson and Drummond, their Conversations. An 18th Century Forgery. Oxford, 1925.
Simpson, P. The Genuineness of the Drummond Conversations. RES. II, 1926.

Taylor, J. A Funeral Elegy upon the Death of B. Jonson, Poet. 1637.
Jonsonus Virbius, or The Memory of Ben Jonson Revived by the Friends of the Muses. Ed. B. Duppa, 1638.
Davenant, Sir W. To Doctor Duppa. An acknowledgment for his collection, in Honour of Ben Johnson's memory. [In Madagascar; with other Poems, 1638.]

Fuller, T. The History of the Worthies of England. [Westminster, p. 243.] 1662; ed. J. Nichols, vol. II, p. 112, 1811.
Aubrey, J. Lives of Eminent Persons. Ed. A. Clark, Oxford, 1898.
Chetwood, W. R. Memoirs of the Life and Writings of Ben Jonson. Dublin, 1756.
Penniman, J. H. The War of the Theatres. Boston, 1897.
Small, R. A. The Stage-quarrel between Ben Jonson and the so-called Poetasters. Breslau, 1899.
Herford, C. H. Ben Jonson and the Cardinal Duperron. MLR. IV, 1908.
Chambers, Sir E. K. Ben Jonson and the Isle of Dogs. MLR. IV, 1909.
Briggs, W. D. On certain Incidents in Ben Jonson's Life. MP. XI, 1913.
—— The Birth-date of Ben Jonson. MLN. XXXIII, 1918.
Adams, J. Q. The Bones of Ben Jonson. Stud. Phil. XVI, 1919.
Bradley, J. F. and Adams, J. Q. The Jonson Allusion-book, 1597–1700. New Haven, 1922.
Noyes, R. G. Ben Jonson on the English Stage, 1660–1776. Cambridge, U.S.A. 1936.
Dryden, J. Examen of the Silent Woman. [In An Essay of Dramatick Poesie, 1668.]
Hazlitt, W. On Shakespeare and Ben Jonson. [In Lectures on the English Comic Writers, 1819.]
Coleridge, S. T. Notes on Ben Jonson. [In Literary Remains, vol. I, 1836.]
von Baudissin, W. Ben Jonson und seine Schule. 2 vols. Leipzig, 1836.
Schmidt, A. Essay on the Life and Dramatic Writings of Ben Jonson. Danzig, 1847.
Symonds, J. A. Ben Jonson. 1886.
Swinburne, A. C. A Study of Ben Jonson. 1889.
Herford, C. H. Ben Jonson. DNB. vol. XXX, 1892.
Aronstein, P. Ben Jonson. Heidelberg, 1906.
Castelain, M. Ben Jonson, l'Homme et l'Œuvre. Paris, 1907.
Thorndike, A. H. Ben Jonson. CHEL. vol. VI, 1910.
Gregory Smith, G. Ben Jonson. [1919.] (English Men of Letters Ser.)
Eliot, T. S. The Sacred Wood. 1920.
Huxley, A. On the Margin. 1923.
Palmer, J. Ben Jonson. 1934.
Walker, R. S. Ben Jonson's Lyric Poetry. Criterion, XIII, 1934.
Knights, L. C. Tradition and Ben Jonson. Scrutiny, IV, 1935.
Ellis-Fermor, U. M. The Jacobean Drama. 1936.
Hoffschulte, H. Ueber Ben Jonson's ältere Lustspiele. Münster, 1894.

Woodbridge, E. Studies in Jonson's Comedy. Boston, 1898.

Baskerville, C. R. English Elements in Jonson's Early Comedy. Texas University Bulletin, no. 178, 1911.

Kerr, M. The Influence of Ben Jonson on English Comedy. Philadelphia, 1912.

Briggs, W. D. The Influence of Jonson's Tragedy on the XVIIth Century. Ang. xxxv, 1912.

Grossmann, H. Ben Jonson als Kritiker. Berlin, 1898.

Crawford, C. Ben Jonson's Method of Composing Verse. [Collectanea, vol. i, Stratford, 1906.]

Howell, A. C. A Note on Ben Jonson's Literary Methods. Stud. Phil. xxviii, 1931.

Nason, A. H. Heralds and Heraldry in Ben Jonson's Plays. New York, 1907.

Lindsey, E. S. The Music in Ben Jonson's Plays. MLN. xliv, 1929.

Upton, J. Remarks on three Plays of Ben Jonson. 1749. [Volpone, Epicœne, Alchemist.]

Saegelken, C. Ben Jonson's Römerdramen. Bremen, 1880.

Koeppel, E. Quellenstudien zu den Dramen Ben Jonson's, John Marston's, und Beaumont und Fletcher's. Erlangen, 1895.

—— Ben Jonson's Wirkung auf zeitgenössische Dramatiker. Heidelberg, 1906.

Schelling, F. E. Ben Jonson and the Classical School. Baltimore, 1898.

Reinsch, H. Ben Jonson's Poetik und seine Beziehungen zu Horaz. Naumburg, 1898.

Hofmiller, J. Die ersten sechs Masken Ben Jonson's in ihrem Verhältnis zur antiken Literatur. Freising, 1901.

Bang, W. Ben Jonson und Castiglione's Cortegiano. E. Studien, xxxvi, 1906.

Birck, P. Literarische Anspielungen in den Werken Ben Jonson's. Strasburg, 1908.

Brown, H. Ben Jonson and Rabelais. MLN. xliv, 1929.

Gebhardt, E. R. Ben Jonson's Appreciation of Chaucer. MLN. xlix, 1934.

Gilchrist, O. G. An Examination of the Charges of Ben Jonson's Enmity towards Shakespeare. 1808.

—— A Letter to W. Gifford. 1811.

[Cartwright, R.] Shakespeare and Jonson: Dramatic versus Wit Combats. 1864.

Herpich, C. A. Shakespeare and Ben Jonson: did they quarrel? N. & Q. 12 April 1902.

Aronstein, P. Shakespeare und Ben Jonson. E. Studien, xxxiv, 1904.

Sarrazin, G. Nym und Ben Jonson. Sh. Jb. xl, 1904.

Castelain, M. Shakespeare et Ben Jonson. Revue Germanique, iii, 1907.

Jusserand, J. J. Ben Jonson's Views on Shakespeare's Art. [In Shakespeare Head edn of Shakespeare, vol. x, Stratford, 1907.]

Keller, W. Shakespeare, Ben Jonson und die Folio von 1623. Sh. Jb. lix, lx, 1924.

Gray, A. How Shakespeare 'Purged' Jonson. Cambridge, 1928.

Mueschke, P. and Fleisher, J. Jonsonian Elements in the Comic Underplot of Twelfth Night. PMLA. xlviii, 1933.

Simpson, P. Field and Ben Jonson. N. & Q. 19 Oct. 1895.

—— Ben Jonson on Chapman. TLS. 3 March 1932.

Hart, H. C. Ben Jonson, Gabriel Harvey and Nash. N. & Q. 14 March, 11 April, 2 May, 27 June, 29 Aug., 3, 31 Oct., 21 Nov., 19 Dec. 1903, 14 May 1904.

Osborn, L. B. Ben Jonson and Hoskyns. TLS. 1 May 1930.

Warren, A. Pope and Ben Jonson. MLN. xlv, 1930.

Stanger, H. Der Einfluss Ben Jonsons auf Ludwig Tieck. Studien zur vergleichenden Litteraturgeschichte, i, ii, 1901–2.

Fischer, W. Tieck als Ben Jonson-Philologe. Sh. Jb. lxii, 1926.

Crawford, C. Ben Jonson's Case is Altered: its Date. N. & Q. 16 Jan. 1909.

Buff, A. The Quarto Edition of Every Man In his Humour. E. Studien, i, 1877.

Nicholson, B. On the Dates of the Two Versions of Every Man In his Humour. Antiquary, vi, 1882.

Holthausen, F. Die Quelle von Ben Jonsons Volpone. Ang. xii, 1889.

Adams, J. Q. The Sources of Ben Jonson's Volpone. MP. ii, 1904.

Graves, T. S. Jonson's Epicœne and Lady Arabella Stuart. MP. xiv, 1917.

Campbell, O. J. The Relation of Epicœne to Aretino's Il Marescalco. PMLA. xlvi, 1931.

Vogt, A. Catiline und ihre Quellen. Halle, 1905.

Holstein, E. Verhältnis von Ben Jonson's 'Devil is an Ass' und John Wilson's Belphegor zu Machiavelli's Novelle vom Belfagor. 1901.

Kittredge, G. L. James I and The Devil is an Ass. MP. xi, 1911.

Garnett, R. Ben Jonson's probable Authorship of Scene 2, Act iv, of Fletcher's Bloody Brother. MP. ii, 1905.

Crawford, C. Ben Jonson and the Bloody Brother. Sh. Jb. xli, 1905.

Aronstein, P. Fletcher's 'Love's Pilgrimage' und Ben Jonson's 'The New Inn.' E. Studien, XLIII, 1911.

Smith, K. F. On the Source of Ben Jonson's Song, 'Still to be Neat'. AJ. Phil. XXIX, 1908.

Gollancz, Sir I. Ben Jonson's Ode to the Phœnix and the Turtle. TLS. 8 Oct. 1925.

Johnston, G. B. Notes on Jonson's Execration against Vulcan. MLN. XLVI, 1931.

Spingarn, J. E. The Sources of Jonson's Discoveries. MP. II, 1905.

Simpson, P. Tanquam Explorator: Jonson's Method in the Discoveries. MLR. II, 1907.

Clark, D. L. The Requirements of a Poet. MP. XVI, 1918. [Discoveries, Sect. 130.]

Briggs, W. D. Studies in Ben Jonson, vols. I–V. Ang. XXXVII–XXXIX, 1913–6.

—— On Jonson's Classical Borrowings: The New Inn, MP. X, 1913; Underwoods, MP. XV, 1917; Epigrams and Forest, Classical Philology, XI, 1906; Plays, MLN. XXXI, 1916; Cynthia's Revels, Flügel Memorial vol. 1916.

P. S.

THOMAS DEKKER (1572?–1632)

(1) DRAMATIC WORKS

(a) Collected Plays

The Dramatic Works of Thomas Dekker. [Ed. R. H. Shepherd], 4 vols. 1873.

Thomas Dekker. Ed. E. Rhys, 1887, etc. (Mermaid Ser.). [The Shoemaker's Holiday; The Honest Whore, 2 pts; Old Fortunatus; The Witch of Edmonton.]

(b) Separate Plays

The Pleasant Comedie of Old Fortunatus. As it was plaied before the Queenes Majestie this Christmas, by the Right Honourable the Earle of Nottingham, Lord high Admirall of England his Servants. 1600; ed. C. W. Dilke (Old English Plays, vol. III, 1815); ed. H. Scherer, Munich, 1901; ed. O. Smeaton, 1906 (Temple Dramatists).

The Shomakers Holiday. Or The Gentle Craft. With the humorous life of Simon Eyre, shoomaker, and Lord Maior of London. As it was acted before the Queenes most excellent Majestie on New-yeares day at night last, by the right honourable the Earle of Notingham, Lord high Admirall of England, his servants. 1600 (anon.); 1610; 1618; 1624; 1631; 1657; ed. H. Fritsche, Thorn, 1862; ed. K. Warnke and C. Proescholdt, Halle, 1886; ed. A. F. Lange, Gayley, vol. III; ed. J. R. Sutherland, 1928.

Satiro-mastix. Or The untrussing of the Humorous Poet. As it hath bin presented publikely, by the Right Honorable, the

Lord Chamberlaine his Servants; and privately, by the Children of Paules. 1602; ed. T. Hawkins (Origin of English Drama, vol. III, Oxford, 1773); ed. H. Scherer, Bang, vol. XX, 1907; ed. J. H. Penniman, Boston, 1913 (Belles Lettres Ser.). [With Marston?]

The Honest Whore, With, The Humours of the Patient Man, and the Longing Wife. 1604; 1605; 1615; 1616; 1635; ed. I. Reed (Dodsley's Old Plays, vol. III, 1780); Ancient British Drama, vol. I; ed. J. P. Collier (Dodsley's Old Plays, vol. III, 1825). [See M. Baird, The Early Editions of the Converted Courtezan, or Honest Whore, Library, X, 1929. With Middleton.]

North-Ward Hoe. Sundry times Acted by the Children of Paules. By Thomas Decker, and John Webster. 1607; TFT. 1914. [Also included in some edns of Webster (see p. 620 below).]

The Famous History of Sir Thomas Wyat. With the Coronation of Queen Mary, and the coming in of King Philip. As it was plaied by the Queens Majesties Servants. Written by Thomas Dickers, And John Webster. 1607; 1612; ed. W. J. Blew (Two Old Plays, 1876); TFT. 1914. [Also included in some edns of Webster.]

West-Ward Hoe. As it hath beene divers times Acted by the Children of Paules. Written by Tho: Decker, and John Webster. 1607; TFT. 1914. [Also included in some edns of Webster.]

The Whore Of Babylon. As it was acted by the Princes Servants. 1607.

If It Be Not Good, The Divel is in it. A New Play, As It Hath Bin lately Acted, with great applause, by the Queenes Majesties Servants: At the Red Bull. 1612.

The Second Part Of The Honest Whore, With The Humors of the Patient Man, the Impatient Wife: the Honest Whore, persuaded by strong Arguments to turne Curtizan againe: her brave refuting those Arguments. And lastly, the Comicall Passages of an Italian Bridewell, where the Scæne ends. 1630; ed. I. Reed (Dodsley's Old Plays, vol. III, 1780); Ancient British Drama, vol. I; ed. J. P. Collier (Dodsley's Old Plays, vol. III, 1825). [With Middleton.]

A Tragi-Comedy: Called, Match mee in London. As it hath beene often Presented; First, at the Bull in St. Johns-street; And lately, at the Private-House in Drury-Lane, called the Phœnix. 1631.

The Wonder Of A Kingdome. 1636; ed. C. W. Dilke (Old English Plays, vol. II, 1814). [With Day?]

[For Patient Grissill (with Chettle and Haughton) see p. 534 above; for The Roaring

Girle (with Middleton) see p. 612; for The Virgin Martir (with Massinger) see p. 630; for The Witch of Edmonton (with Ford and W. Rowley) see p. 636; for The Sun's-Darling (with Ford) see p. 637; for The Noble Souldier (with Day and S. Rowley?) see p. 537. There is good ground for connecting Dekker with the following anon. plays (pp. 539, 651): Sir Thomas More, Lusts Dominion, The Bloodie Banquet. More hazardous attributions are: Captaine Thomas Stukeley, The Weakest Goeth to the Wall, The Distracted Emperor, The London Prodigall. Dekker has also been assigned the songs in the 1632 edn of Lyly's plays (see p. 525).]

(c) Pageants and Masques

The Magnificent Entertainment: Given to King James, Queen Anne his wife, and Henry Frederick the Prince, upon the day of his Majesties Tryumphant Passage (from the Tower) through his Honourable Citie (and Chamber) of London, being the 15. of March, 1603. As well by the English as by the Strangers: With the speeches and Songes, delivered in the severall Pageants. 1604 (3 edns); Edinburgh, 1604; ed. Sir W. Scott (Somers Tracts, vol. III, 1810); ed. J. Nichols (Progresses of James I, vol. I, 1828). [With contributions by Jonson and Middleton, but mainly Dekker's.]

Troia-Nova Triumphans. London Triumphing, Or, The Solemne, Magnificent, and Memorable Receiving of that worthy Gentleman, Sir John Swinerton Knight, into the Citty of London, after his Returne from taking the Oath of Maioralty at Westminster, on the Morrow next after Simon and Judes day, being the 29. of October, 1612. All the Showes, Pageants, Chariots of Triumph, with other Devices, (both on the Water and Land) here fully expressed. 1612; ed. F. W. Fairholt (Lord Mayors' Pageants, vol. II, 1844).

Brittannia's Honor: Brightly Shining in severall Magnificent Shewes or Pageants, to Celebrate the Solemnity of the Right Honorable Richard Deane, At his Inauguration into the Maioralty of the Honourable Citty of London, on Wednesday, October the 29th. 1628. At the particular Cost, and Charges of the Right Worshipfull, Worthy, and Ancient Society of Skinners. 1628.

Londons Tempe, Or, The Feild of Happines. In which Feild are planted severall Trees of Magnificence, State and Bewty, to Celebrate the Solemnity of the Right Honorable James Campebell, At his Inauguration into the Honorable Office of Praetorship, or

Maioralty of London, on Thursday the 29 of October, 1629. All the particular Inventions, for the Pageants, Showes of Triumph, both by Water and land being here fully set downe, At the sole Cost, and liberall Charges of the Right worshipfull Society of Ironmongers. [1629]; ed. F. W. Fairholt (Lord Mayors' Pageants, vol. II, 1844).

(2) NON-DRAMATIC WORKS

(a) Collected Edition

Non-Dramatic Works of T. Dekker. Ed. A. B. Grosart, 5 vols. 1884–6. (Huth Lib.) [The only attempt at a collected edn. Reprints the following: vol. I, The Wonderfull yeare; vol. II, The Seven deadly Sinnes, Newes from Hell, The Double PP., The Guls Hornebooke, Jests to make you Merie; vol. III, Dekker his Dreame, The Belman of London, Lanthorne and Candle-light, A Strange Horse-Race; vol. IV, The Dead Tearme, Worke for Armourers, The Ravens Almanacke, A Rod for Run-awayes; vol. V, Foure Birds of Noahs Arke. For Canaans Calamitie and The Batchelars Banquet (rptd in vol. I) see (3) below.]

(b) Pamphlets in Prose and Verse

The Wonderfull yeare. Wherein is shewed the picture of London, lying sicke of the Plague. 1603 (anon.); [2 edns before 1607]; ed. J. Morgan (Phœnix Britannicus, 1731); ed. G. B. Harrison, 1924; ed. F. P. Wilson (The Plague Pamphlets of Thomas Dekker, Oxford, 1925).

Newes from Graves-end: Sent to Nobody. 1604 (anon.); ed. F. P. Wilson (The Plague Pamphlets of Thomas Dekker, Oxford, 1925). [On the London plague of 1603. Verse, with a long preface in prose.]

The Meeting of Gallants at an Ordinarie: Or, The Walkes in Powles. 1604 (anon.); ed. J. O. Halliwell[-Phillipps], Percy Soc. 1841; ed. F. P. Wilson (The Plague Pamphlets of Thomas Dekker, Oxford, 1925). [On the London plague of 1603. In verse and prose.]

The Double PP. A Papist in Armes. Bearing Ten severall Sheilds. Encountred by the Protestant. At Ten severall Weapons. A Jesuite Marching before them. 1606. [A verse attack on the Roman Catholics. Dekker's authorship is proved by a printed leaf with a dedicatory poem to Sir Henry Cock preserved in a unique copy formerly at Britwell Court.]

Newes From Hell; Brought by the Divells Carrier. 1606; 1607 (rev. as A Knights Conjuring. Done in earnest: Discovered in Jest); ed. E. F. Rimbault, Percy Soc. 1842 (1607 edn). [A satire on London's vices inspired by Nashe's Pierce Pennilesse.]

The Seven deadly Sinnes of London: Drawne in seven severall Coaches, Through the seven severall Gates of the Citie Bringing the Plague with them. 1606; ed. J. P. Collier (Illustrations of Old English Literature, vol. II, 1866); ed. E. Arber, 1879; rptd Cambridge, 1905; ed. H. F. B. Brett-Smith, Oxford, 1922.

Jests to make you Merie: With the Conjuring up of Cock Watt, (the walking Spirit of Newgate) to tell Tales: Unto which is Added, the miserie of a Prison, and a Prisoner. And a Paradox in praise of Serjeants. Written by T. D. and George Wilkins. 1607.

The Dead Tearme. Or, Westminsters Complaint for long Vacations and short Termes. Written in manner of a Dialogue betweene the two Cityes London and Westminster. 1608.

The Belman Of London. Bringing to light the most notorious villanies that are now practised in the Kingdome. 1608 (4 edns with slight changes) (anon.); 1616; 1640; ed. O. Smeaton, [1905] (Temple Classics). [Mainly a cento compiled from pamphlets on beggars and coney-catchers by Awdeley, Harman, Greene, and Rowlands.]

Lanthorne and Candle-light. Or The Bell-mans second Nights walke. In which Hee brings to light, a Broode of more strange Villanies, then ever were till this yeare discovered. 1608; 1609; 1612 (with many addns and some omissions as O per se O, Or A new Cryer of Lanthorne and Candle-light. Being an Addition, or Lengthening, of the Bell-mans Second Night-walke); 1616 (with new chapters on prisons as Villanies Discovered by Lanthorne and Candle-light, and the helpe of a New Cryer called O per se O); 1620 (with slight addns); 1632 (with addns and omissions as English Villanies Six Severall Times Prest to Death by the Printers); 1638 (as English Villanies Seven Severall Times Prest to Death by the Printers); 1648 (as English Villanies Eight Severall Times Prest to Death by the Printers); ed. O. Smeaton, [1905] (Temple Classics).

The Ravens Almanacke Foretelling of a Plague, Famine, and Civill Warre. 1609. [A parody on prognostications.]

Foure Birds of Noahs Arke: Viz. 1. The Dove. 2. The Eagle. 3. The Pellican. 4. The Phoenix. 1609; ed. F. P. Wilson, Stratford-on-Avon, 1924. [A devotional work.]

The Guls Horne-booke. 1609; ed. J. Nott, Bristol, 1812; ed. G. Saintsbury (Elizabethan and Jacobean Pamphlets, 1892); ed. R. B. McKerrow, 1904; ed. O. Smeaton, [1905] (Temple Classics). [A satire on the Jacobean gallant. The early chapters are indebted to Frederick Dedekind's Grobianus, 1549, tr. Eng. R. F., as The Schoole of Slovenrie or Cato turnd wrong side outward, 1605.]

Worke For Armorours: Or, The Peace is Broken. Open warres likely to happin this yeare 1609: God helpe the Poore, The rich can shift. 1609. [An allegorical description of the rising of poverty against wealth.]

A Strange Horse-Race, At the end of which, comes in The Catch-Poles Masque. And After That The Bankrouts Banquet: Which done, the Divell, falling sicke, makes his last will and Testament, this present yeare. 1613.

The Artillery Garden, a Poem dedicated to the Honour of those Gentlemen who (there) practize Military Discipline. 1616. [This poem, known to William Oldys, cannot now be found.]

Dekker his Dreame. In which, beeing rapt with a Poeticall Enthusiasme, the great Volumes of Heaven and Hell to Him were opened, in which he read many Wonderfull Things. 1620; ed. J. O. Halliwell[-Phillipps], 1860. [Mostly in verse.]

A Rod for Run-awayes. Gods Tokens, Of his fcareful Judgements, sundry wayes pronounced upon this City, and on severall persons, both flying from it, and staying in it. 1625; 1625 (with addns and omissions); ed. F. P. Wilson (The Plague Pamphlets of Thomas Dekker, Oxford, 1925).

Looke Up and see Wonders. A miraculous Apparition in the Ayre, lately seene in Barke-shire at Bawlkin Greene neere Hatford. 1628 (anon.). [A pamphlet attrib. to Dekker by F. P. Wilson, The Plague Pamphlets of Thomas Dekker, Oxford, 1925, p. 249.]

Warres, Warres, Warres. 1628. [A verse pamphlet in praise of war and of the officers of the Artillery Garden.]

London Looke Backe, at that Yeare of Yeares 1625. And Looke Forward, upon this Yeare, 1630. 1630 (anon.); ed. F. P. Wilson (The Plague Pamphlets of Thomas Dekker, Oxford, 1925).

The Blacke Rod: And the White Rod. (Justice and Mercie.) Striking, and Sparing, London. 1630; ed. F. P. Wilson (The Plague Pamphlets of Thomas Dekker, Oxford, 1925).

Penny-Wise Pound-Foolish. Or, a Bristow Diamond, set in two Rings, and both Crack'd. 1631 (anon.); ed. W. Bang, *Bang,* vol. xxiii, 1908. [A version with English and Italian settings of the old story A Pennyworth of Wit.]

[Dekker also wrote dedicatory verses to Anthony Munday in The Third and last part of Palmerin of England, 1602, and in A True and admirable Historie, of a Mayden of Consolens, 1603; to Stephen Harrison in The Archs of Triumph Erected in honor of the High and mighty prince, James, 1604; to John Taylor the Water-Poet in Taylors Urania, or his Heavenly Muse, 1615; to Richard Brome in The Northerne Lasse, a Comœdie, 1632.]

(3) Biography and Criticism

Corser, T. Collectanea Anglo-poetica. Chetham Soc. 1873.

Herford, C. H. Studies in the Literary Relations of England and Germany in the Sixteenth Century. Cambridge, 1886. [For Grobianus, the Guls Horne-booke and the Fortunatus legend.]

Kupka, P. Über den dramatischen Vers Thomas Dekkers. Halle, 1893.

Small, R. A. The Stage-Quarrel between Jonson and the so-called Poetasters. Breslau, 1899. [For Satiro-mastix.]

Bang, W. Dekker-Studien. E. Studien, xxviii, 1900.

Rühl, E. Grobianus in England. Berlin, 1904.

Greg, W. W. On the Authorship of the Songs in Lyly's Plays. Mod. Lang. Quart. i, 1905. [Ascribes to Dekker. But see R. W. Bond, RES. vi, vii, 1930–1.]

—— 'The Honest Whore' or 'The Converted Courtezan.' Library, xv, 1934.

Stoll, E. E. The Influence of Jonson on Dekker. MLN. xxi, 1906.

Henslowe Papers. Ed. W. W. Greg, 1907. [Contains 2 letters to Edward Alleyn. Facs. of one of them in English Literary Autographs, ed. W. W. Greg, 1925.]

Swinburne, A. C. Thomas Dekker. [In The Age of Shakespeare, 1908.]

Pierce, F. E. The Collaboration of Webster and Dekker. New Haven, 1909.

—— The Collaboration of Dekker and Ford. Ang. xxxvi, 1912.

Hunt, Mary L. Thomas Dekker. New York, 1911.

—— Geffray Mynshul and Thomas Dekker. JEGP. xi, 1912.

Mann, F. O. T. Deloney's Works. Oxford, 1912. [Introduction, on the authorship of Canaans Calamitie.]

Aydelotte, F. Elizabethan Rogues and Vagabonds. Oxford, 1913. [For Dekker's rogue pamphlets and their sources.]

Spender, C. The Plays of Thomas Dekker. Contemporary Rev. Sept. 1916.

Wilson, F. P. Three Notes on Thomas Dekker. MLR. xv, 1920.

—— The Batchelars Banquet. Oxford, 1929. [Introduction, on the authorship of this adaptation of Les Quinze Joyes de Mariage.]

Ovaa, W. A. Dekker and The Virgin Mary. E. Studies, iii, 1921.

Bullen, A. H. Dekker. [In Elizabethans, 1924.]

Law, R. A. The Shoemakers' Holiday and Romeo and Juliet. Stud. Phil. xxi, 1924.

Sisson, C. J. Keep the Widow Waking, a Lost Play by Dekker. Library, vii, 1927. [Expanded in Lost Plays of Shakespeare's Age, Cambridge, 1936. See also G. B. Harrison, Library, x, 1930.]

Chandler, W. K. The Sources of the Characters in The Shoemakers' Holiday. MP. xxvii, 1928.

—— The Topography of Dekker's The Shoemakers' Holiday. Stud. Phil. xxvi, 1929.

Potter, R. Three Jacobean Devil Plays. Stud. Phil. xxviii, 1931. [For If It Be Not Good.]

Thieme, H. Zur Verfasserfrage des Dekkerschen Stückes 'Old Fortunatus.' Leipzig, 1934.

Ellis-Fermor, U. M. The Jacobean Drama. 1936.

Taylor, W. J. Thomas Dekker and the 'Overburian' Characters. MLR. xxxi, 1936.

· W. P. B. and F. P. W.

THOMAS HEYWOOD (1574?–1641)

(1) Bibliography

Clark, A. M. A Bibliography of Thomas Heywood. Proc. Oxford Bibliog. Soc. i, 1925.

(2) Collected Plays

The Dramatic Works of Thomas Heywood. Ed. J. P. Collier and B. Field, 2 vols. Shakespeare Soc. 1842–51. [Contains only: Edward IV, 2 pts; If you know not me, 2 pts; The Fair Maid of the Exchange; A Woman killed with Kindness; The Golden Age; The Silver Age; The Fair Maid of the West, 2 pts; The Royal King and the Loyal Subject; Fortune by Land and Sea.]

The Dramatic Works of Thomas Heywood. Ed. R. H. Shepherd, 6 vols. 1874. [Includes all the plays listed below, except How a Man may choose a Good Wife, Nobody and Somebody, Dick of Devonshire, The Captives.]

Thomas Heywood, Ed. A. W. Verity, 1888, etc. (Mermaid Ser.) [A Woman killed with Kindness; The Fair Maid of the West, pt 1; The English Traveller; The Wise Woman of Hogsdon; The Rape of Lucrece.]

(3) Separate Plays

The First and Second partes of King Edward the Fourth. Containing His mery pastime with the Tanner of Tamwoorth, as also his love to fayre Mistresse Shoare. As it hath divers times been publiquely played by the Right Honorable the Earle of Derby his servants. 1599 (anon.); 1600; 1605; 1613; 1619; 1626; ed. facs. S. de Ricci, 1922.

A pleasant conceited Comedie. Wherein is shewed how a man may chuse a good Wife from a bad. As it hath bene sundry times Acted by the Earle of Worcesters Servants. 1602 (anon.); 1605; 1608; 1614; 1621; 1630; 1634; rptd C. Baldwin (Old English Drama, vol. i, 1825); Hazlitt's Dodsley, vol. ix; ed. A. E. H. Swaen, Bang, vol. xxxv, 1912; TFT. 1912.

If you know not me, You know no bodie: Or, The troubles of Queene Elizabeth. 1605 (anon.); 1606; 1608; 1610; 1613; 1623; 1632; 1639; ed. W. J. Blew, 1876; ed. M. Doran, Malone Soc. 1935.

The Second Part of, If you know not me, you know no bodie. With the building of the Royall Exchange: And the famous Victorie of Queene Elizabeth, in the Yeare 1588. 1606 (anon.); 1609 (as The Second Part of Queene Elizabeths troubles. Doctor Paries treasons. With the Humors of Hobson and Tawney-cote); 1623; 1633; ed. M. Doran, Malone Soc. 1935.

No-body, and Some-body. With the true Chronicle Historie of Elydure, who was fortunately three severall times crowned King of England. The true Coppy thereof, as it hath beene acted by the Queens Majesties Servants. [1606] (anon.); ed. A. Smith, 1877; ed. R. Simpson (School of Shakespeare, vol. i, 1878); TFT. 1911. [Tr. German in Englische Comedien und Tragedien, 1620; ed. F. Bischoff, Niemand und Jemand in Graz im Jahre 1608, Mitteilungen des historischen Vereins für Steiermark, xlvii, 1899. Tr. German L. Tieck, ed. J. Bolte, Sh. Jb. xxix, 1894.]

The Fayre Mayde of the Exchange: With The pleasaunt Humours of the Cripple of Fanchurch. 1607 (anon.); 1625; 1637.

A Woman kilde with Kindnesse. 1607; 1617 ('The third Edition. As it hath beene often times Acted by the Queenes Majest. Servants'); rptd R. Dodsley (Collection of Old Plays, vol. iv, 1744); ed. I. Reed (Dodsley's Old Plays, vol. vii, 1780); Ancient British

Drama, vol. ii; ed. Sir A. W. Ward, 1897 (Temple Dramatists); ed. K. L. Bates, Boston, 1917 (Belles Lettres Ser.).

The Rape of Lucrece. A True Roman Tragedie. With the severall Songes in their apt places, by Valerius, the merrie Lord amongst the Roman Peeres. Acted by her Majesties Servants at the Red Bull, neere Clarkenwell. 1608; 1609; 1614; 1630; 1638 ('revised, and sundry Songs before omitted, now inserted in their right places'); rptd C. Baldwin (Old English Drama, vol. i, 1825).

The Golden Age: or The lives of Jupiter and Saturne, with the defining of the Heathen Gods. As it hath beene sundry times acted at the Red Bull, by the Queenes Majesties Servants. 1611 (certain copies have 'deifying' for 'defining' in the title).

The Silver Age, Including. The love of Jupiter to Alcmena: The birth of Hercules. And The Rape of Proserpine. Concluding, With the Arraignement of the Moone. 1613. [BM. Egerton MS 1994 includes Callisto or the Escapes of Jupiter, made up of scenes from The Golden and Silver Ages.]

The Brazen Age, The first Act containing, The death of the Centaure Nessus, The Second, The Tragedy of Meleager: The Third The Tragedy of Jason and Medea: The Fourth. Vulcans Net. The Fifth. The Labours and death of Hercules. 1613.

The Foure Prentises. of London. With the Conquest of Jerusalem. As it hath bene diverse times Acted, at the Red Bull, by the Queenes Majesties Servants. 1615; 1632; ed. I. Reed (Dodsley's Old Plays, vol. vi, 1780); Ancient British Drama, vol. iii; ed. J. P. Collier (Dodsley's Old Plays, vol. vi, 1825).

The fair Maid Of The West. Or, A Girle worth gold. The first part. As it was lately acted before the King and Queen, with approved liking. By the Queens Majesties Comedians. Written by T. H. 1631; ed. K. L. Bates, Boston, 1917 (Belles Lettres Ser.).

The fair Maid Of the West. The second part. 1631.

The Iron Age: Contayning the Rape of Hellen: The Siege of Troy: The Combate betwixt Hector and Ajax: Hector and Troilus slayne by Achilles: Achilles slaine by Paris: Ajax and Ulisses contend for the Armour of Achilles: The Death of Ajax, &c. 1632.

The Second Part of the Iron Age: Which contayneth the death of Penthesilea, Paris, Priam, and Hecuba: The burning of Troy: The deaths of Agamemnon, Menelaus, Clitemnestra, Hellena, Orestes, Egistus, Pillades, King Diomed, Pyrhus, Cethus, Synon, Thersites, &c. 1632.

The English Traveller. As it hath beene Publikely acted at the Cock-pit in Drury-lane: By Her Majesties servants. 1633; ed. C. W. Dilke (Old English Plays, vol. VI, 1815); ed. F. A. Gebke (Die englische Bühne zu Shakespeare's Zeit, vol. II, 1890).

The late Lancashire Witches. A well received Comedy, lately Acted at the Globe on the Banke-side, by the Kings Majesties Actors. Written, By Thom. Heywood, and Richard Broome. 1634; rptd L. Tieck (Shakespeare's Vorschule, vol. I, 1823); ed. J. O. Halliwell [-Phillipps], 1853.

A Pleasant Comedy, called A Mayden-head well lost. As it hath beene publickly Acted at the Cocke-pit in Drury-lane. By her Majesties Servants. 1634; rptd C. Baldwin (Old English Drama, vol. II, 1824).

A Challenge for Beautie. As it hath beene sundry times Acted, By the Kings Majesties Servants: At the Blacke-friers, and at the Globe on the Banke-side. 1636; ed. C. W. Dilke (Old English Plays, vol. VI, 1815).

Loves Maistresse: or, The Queens Masque. As it was three times presented before their two excellent Majesties, within the space of eight dayes; In the presence of sundry Forraigne Ambassadors. Publikely Acted by the Queens Comœdians, At the Phœnix in Drury-lane. 1636; 1640 (2 edns, both 'The Second Impression, corrected by the Author'); rptd T. Wilkins, 1792; rptd C. Baldwin (Old English Drama, vol. II, 1825); ed. E. M. Goldsmid, Edinburgh, 1886 (in Bibliotheca Curiosa); ed. H. M. Blake, 1910.

The Royall King, and The Loyall Subject. As it hath beene Acted with great Applause by the Queenes Majesties Servants. 1637; ed. C. W. Dilke (Old English Plays, vol. VI, 1815); ed. K. W. Tibbals, 1906.

The Wise-woman Of Hogsdon. A Comedie. 1638.

Fortune by Land and Sea. A Tragi-Comedy. As it was Acted by the Queens Servants. Written by Tho. Haywood and William Rowly. 1655; ed. J. E. Walker, 1899.

Dick of Devonshire. Ed. A. H. Bullen (Collection of Old English Plays, vol. II, 1883). [BM. Egerton MS 1994.]

The Captives; or The Lost Recovered. Ed. A. H. Bullen (Collection of Old English Plays, vol. IV, 1885); ed. A. C. Judson, 1921. [BM. Egerton MS 1994.]

[For Heywood's share in Appius and Virginia, 1654, The Famous History of Sir Thomas Wyat, 1607, The Famous Tragedy of the Rich Jew of Malta, 1633, Henry Shirley's Martyr'd Souldier, 1638, and A Yorkshire Tragedy, 1608, and the original form of The Miseries of Enforced Marriage, 1607, see A. M. Clark, A Bibliography of Thomas Heywood, Proc.Oxford Bibliog.Soc.I, 1925. Heywood's hand or 'finger' has also been suggested in Shakespeare's Pericles (see p. 578) and the anon. George a Greene (p. 538) and Thomas Lord Cromwell (p. 539).]

(4) PAGEANTS

Londons Jus Honorarium. Exprest in sundry Triumphs, pagiants, and shews: At the Initiation or Entrance of the Right Honourable George Whitmore, into the Maioralty. 1631.

Londini Artium & Scientiarum Scaturigo. Or, Londons Fountaine of Arts and Sciences. Exprest at the Initiation of the Right Honorable Nicholas Raynton into the Maiorty. 1632.

Londini Emporia, or Londons Mercatura at the Inauguration of the Right Honorable Ralph Freeman into the Maiorty. 1633.

Londini Sinus Salutis, or, Londons Harbour of Health, and Happinesse at the Initiation of the Right Honourable, Christopher Clethrowe, Into the Maioralty. 1635.

Londini Speculum: or, Londons Mirror, at the Initiation of the right Honorable Richard Fenn, into the Mairolty. 1637.

Porta pietatis, or, The Port or Harbour of Piety at the Initiation of the Right Honourable Sir Maurice Abbot Knight, into the Maioralty. 1638; rptd F. W. Fairholt (Lord Mayor's Pageants, vol. x, Percy Soc. 1843-4).

Londini Status Pacatus: or, Londons Peacable Estate at the Innitiation of the right Honourable Henry Garway, into the Majoralty. 1639. [The pageants for 1631, 1635, 1637, 1638 and 1639 are rptd in R. H. Shepherd's edn of The Dramatic Works, vols. IV and V, 1874. F. W. Fairholt rptd the pageant for 1638 and gave full descriptions of those for 1632 and 1633 in Lord Mayors' Pageants, vol. x, Percy Soc. 1843-4.]

(5) PROSE

The Two most worthy and Notable Histories which remaine unmained to Posterity: (viz:) The Conspiracie of Cateline, undertaken against the government of the Senate of Rome, and The Warre which Jugurth for many yeares maintained against the same State. Both written by C. C. Salustius. 1608 (anon.); ed. C. Whibley, 1924 (Tudor Translations).

An Apology For Actors. Containing three briefe Treatises. 1 Their Antiquity. 2 Their ancient Dignity. 3 The true use of their quality. 1612; [1658] (as The Actors Vindication); rptd Somers Tracts, vol. I, 1750; ed. Sir W. Scott (Somers Tracts, vol. III, 1810); ed. J. P. Collier, Shakespeare Soc. 1841; ed. Sir E. K. Chambers (condensed in Elizabethan Stage, vol. IV, 1923).

Γυναικεῖον: or, Nine Bookes of Various History. Concerninge Women; Inscribed by yᵉ names of yᵉ Nine Muses. 1624; 1657 (as The Generall Historie of Women).

Englands Elizabeth: Her Life and Troubles, During her Minoritie, from the Cradle to the Crowne. 1631; Cambridge, 1632, 1641.

Philocothonista, or, the Drunkard, Opened, Dissected, and Anatomized. 1635.

The Wonder of this Age: or, The Picture of a Man living, who is One hundred Fifty two yeeres old, and upward. This 12th day of November. 1635 (anon.).

The three Wonders of this Age. 1636.

The New-yeeres gift: Presented at Court, from the Lady Parvula to the Lord Minimus, (commonly called Little Jeffery) Her Majesties Servant, with a Letter Written by Microphilus. 1636 (signed T.H.); 1638.

A True Discourse of the Two infamous upstart Prophets, Richard Farnham Weaver of White-Chappell, and John Bull Weaver of Saint Butolphs Algate, now Prisoners. As also of Margaret Tennis now Prisoner. Written by T. H. 1636.

A Curtaine Lecture: As it is read By a Countrey Farmers wife to her Good man. By a Countrey Gentlewoman or Lady to her Esquire or Knight. By a Souldiers wife to her Captain or Lieutenant. By a Citizens or Tradesmans wife to her husband. By a Court Lady to her Lord. Concluding with an imitable Lecture read by a Queene to her Soveraigne Lord and King. 1637 (signed T. H.).

The Phœnix of these late times: Or the life of Mr Henry Welby, Esq. 1637 (bis).

A True Description of His Majesties Royall Ship, Built this yeare 1637, at Wooll-witch in Kent. Published by Authoritie. 1637; 1638 (with addns). [An extract in The Common-wealths Great Ship Commonly called the Soveraigne of the Seas, 1653.]

A True Relation, of the Lives and Deaths of the two most Famous English Pyrats, Purser, and Clinton; who lived in the Reigne of Queene Elizabeth. 1639 (anon.).

The Exemplary Lives and memorable Acts of nine of the most worthy Women of the World: Three Jewes. Three Gentiles. Three Christians. Written by the Author of the History of Women. 1640.

A Revelation of Mʳ· Brightmans Revelation. In A Dialogue betweene a Minister of the Gospell, and a Citizen of London, whereby it is manifest, that Mr Brightman was a true Prophet. 1641 (anon.).

Brightmans Predictions and Prophesies. 1641 (anon.).

The Black Box of Roome opened. From whence are revealed, the Damnable Bloody Plots, Practises, and behaviour of Jesuites, Priests, Papists, and other Recusants in Generall. 1641 (anon.).

The Life of Merlin, Sirnamed Ambrosius. His Prophesies, and Predictions Interpreted; Being a Chronographicall History of all the Kings, from Brute to the Reigne of our Royall Soveraigne King Charles. 1641; 1651 (as Merlins Prophesies and Predictions Interpreted). [An extract in Seven Severall Strange Prophesies, 1642; Nine Notable Prophesies, 1644; and Twelve Strange Prophesies, [n.d.].]

A New plot discovered, practised by an assembly of Papists, for the deliverance of William Waller, alias Walker, alias Ward, alias Slater, a Jesuite, which was hang'd, drawn, and quartered revealed by John Hodgskins a Porter, by a Letter. 1641 (anon.).

A Dialogue or accidental discourse Betwixt Mr Alderman Abell, and Richard Kilvert, the two maine Projectors for Wine, and also Alderman Abels wife, &c. 1641 (anon.).

The Rat-trap: Or, The Jesuites taken in their owne Net, &c. 1641 (anon.).

Machiavels Ghost. As he lately appeared to his deare Sons, the Moderne Projectors. Printed by authority. 1641 (anon.); 1641 (as Machiavel. As He lately appeared). [An extract in Hogs Caracter of a Projector, 1642, etc.]

The Famo[us] and Remarkable Hist[ory of] Sir Richard Whittingto[n, Three] times Lord Maior of Lon[don.] Written by T. H. 1656; 1678; [1680?].

(6) MISCELLANEOUS VERSE

Troia Britanica: or, Great Britaines Troy. 1609. [Extracts in The Passionate Pilgrim, 1612, and Poems: written by Wil. Shakespeare. Gent. 1640.]

A Funerall Elegie, Upon the death of Henry, Prince of Wales. Written by Thomas Heywood. 1613. [Ptd in Three Elegies on the most lamented Death of Prince Henrie, 1613.]

A Marriage Triumphe. In Memorie of the happie Nuptials betwixt the High and Mightie Prince Count Palatine. And the most Excellent Princesse the Lady Elizabeth. 1613; rptd J. P. Collier, Percy Soc. 1842; ed. E. M. Goldsmid, Aungervyle Soc. 1884.

Publii Ovidii Nasonis de Arte Amandi or, The Art of Love. [n.d.] [Other edns under various titles n.d. (bis) and 1662 (?), 1667, 1672, 1677, 1682, 1705.]

40

A Funeral Elegie, upon King James. 1625.
The Hierarchie of the blessed Angells. 1635.
Pleasant Dialogues and Dramma's, selected
out of Lucian, Erasmus, Textor, Ovid, &c.
1637; ed. W. Bang, *Bang*, vol. III, 1903.
[R. H. Shepherd includes most of Pleasant
Dialogues and Dramas in the Dramatic
Works, vol. VI, 1874.]
The life and death of Queene Elizabeth.
Written in Heroicall Verse. 1639 (anon.).
Reader, Here you'l plainly see Judgement
perverted By these three: A Priest, A Judge,
A Patentee. 1641.

[For modern edns of Heywood's miscellaneous prose and verse, for works edited by
him, for his commendatory verses, for his lost
works, and for the Heywood Apocrypha, see
A. M. Clark, A Bibliography of Thomas
Heywood, Proc. Oxford Bibliog. Soc. I, 1925.]

(7) BIOGRAPHY AND CRITICISM

Gosse, Sir E. Seventeenth Century Studies.
1883, etc.
—— The Jacobean Poets. 1894, etc.
—— Books on the Table. 1921.
Marshall, F. A Woman killed with Kindness.
Theatre, 1 April 1887.
Swinburne, A. C. The Historical and Classical
Plays of Thomas Heywood. Nineteenth
Century, XXXVII, 1890.
—— The Romantic and Contemporary Plays
of Thomas Heywood. Nineteenth Century,
XXXVIII, 1890. [Both rptd in The Age of
Shakespeare, 1908.]
Sprenger, R. Kleine Bemerkungen. Thomas
Heywood. E. Studien, XIX, 1894.
van Dam, B. A. P., and Stoffel, C. The Fifth
Act of Thomas Heywood's Queen Eliza-
beth: Second Part. Sh. Jb. XXXVIII, 1902.
Kämpfer, O. Das Verhältnis von Thomas
Heywood's 'The Royal King and the Loyal
Subject' zu Painter's 'Palace of Pleasure.'
Halle, 1903.
Bolte, J. Eine Hamburger Aufführung von
'Nobody and Somebody.' Sh. Jb. XLI, 1905.
Brereton, J. le G. Notes on the Text of
Thomas Heywood. [Elizabethan Drama.
Notes and Studies, Sydney, 1906.]
Grierson, H. J. C. The First Half of the
Seventeenth Century. Edinburgh, 1906.
Budig, W. Untersuchungen über 'Jane Shore.'
Rostock, 1908.
Thomas, D. L. On the Play Pericles. E.
Studien, XXXVIII, 1908.
Baskervill, C. R. The Sources and Analogues
of How a Man may Choose a Good Wife
from a Bad. PMLA. XXIV, 1909.
Hibbard, L. A. The Authorship and Date of
the Fayre Maide of the Exchange. MP.
VII, 1910.

Martin, R. G. A New Source for A Woman
Killed with Kindness. E. Studien, XLIII,
1911.
—— Is the Late Lancashire Witches a Re-
vision? MP. XIII, 1915.
—— Notes on Thomas Heywood's Ages.
MLN. XXXIII, 1918.
—— A New Specimen of the Revenge Play.
MP. XVI, 1918.
—— A Critical Study of Thomas Heywood's
Gunaikeion. Stud. Phil. XX, 1923.
—— The Sources of Heywood's If You Know
Not Me, You Know Nobody, Part I. MLN.
XXXIX, 1924.
Oliphant, E. H. C. Problems of Authorship
in Elizabethan Dramatic Literature. MP.
VIII, 1911.
Adams, J. Q. Thomas Heywood and How a
Man may Choose a Good Wife from a Bad.
E. Studien, XLV, 1912.
—— Shakespeare, Heywood and the Classics.
MLN. XXXIV, 1919.
Andrews, C. E. The Authorship of The Late
Lancashire Witches. MLN. XXVIII, 1913.
[Rptd in Richard Brome: A Study of his
Life and Works, New York, 1913.]
Aronstein, P. Thomas Heywood. Ang.
XXXVII, 1913.
—— Die Verfasserschaft des Dramas 'The
Fair Maid of the Exchange.' E. Studien,
XLV, 1915.
Brooke, R. The Authorship of the Later
Appius and Virginia. MLR. IX, 1913.
[Rptd in shorter form in John Webster and
the Elizabethan Drama, 1916.]
Gilbert, A. H. Thomas Heywood's Debt to
Plautus. JEGP. XII, 1913.
Tatlock, J. S. P. The Siege of Troy in Eliza-
bethan Literature, especially in Shake-
speare and Heywood. PMLA. XXX, 1915.
Winkler, A. Thomas Heywood's 'A Woman
Killed with Kindness' und das Ehebruchs-
drama seiner Zeit. Leipzig, 1915.
Frost, M. M. Thomas Heywood's Indebted-
ness to Stow. MLR. XI, 1916.
Jewell, R. Thomas Heywood's The Fair Maid
of the West. [In Studies in English Drama,
First Series, ed. Allison Gaw, New York,
1917.]
Clark, A. M. The Authorship of Appius and
Virginia. MLR. XVI, 1921.
—— Thomas Heywood as a Critic. MLN.
XXXVII, 1922.
—— Thomas Heywood's Art of Love Lost and
Found. Library, III, 1922.
—— Lydgate's Troy Book. TLS. 2 Oct.
1924.
—— A Marlowe Mystification. TLS. 16 July
1925.
—— A Bibliography of Thomas Heywood.
Proc. Oxford Bibliog. Soc. I, 1925.

Clark, A. M. Thomas Heywood: Playwright and Miscellanist. Oxford, 1931. [The standard authority.]

Velte, M. The Bourgeois Element in the Dramas of Thomas Heywood. Mysore,1922.

Sykes, H. D. Sidelights on Elizabethan Drama. 1924.

—— Thomas Heywood's Authorship of King Edward IV. N. & Q. 12 Sept. 1925.

Gray, H. D. Heywood's Pericles, Revised by Shakespeare. PMLA. XL, 1925.

—— Appius and Virginia: by Webster and Heywood. Stud. Phil. XXIII, 1926.

Greg, W. W. The Escapes of Jupiter; an Autograph Play of Thomas Heywood. Berlin, 1925.

—— English Literary Autographs, 1550–1650. Pt I (Dramatists), 1925.

Lloyd, B. Thomas Heywood and the N.E.D. TLS. 4 March 1926.

Cromwell, O. Thomas Heywood: A Study in the Elizabethan Drama of Everyday Life. New Haven, 1928.

Wright, L. B. Notes on Thomas Heywood's Later Reputation. RES. IV, 1928.

—— Heywood and the Popularising of History. MLN. XLIII, 1928.

Giordano-Orsini, G. N. The Copy for If you know not me, you know no bodie, Part I. TLS. 4 Dec. 1930.

—— Thomas Heywood's Play on The Troubles of Queen Elizabeth. Library, XIV, 1933.

Rice, W. G. The Moroccan Episode in Thomas Heywood's The Fair Maid of the West. PQ. IX, 1930.

Rouse, C. A. Was Heywood a Servant of the Earl of Southampton? PMLA. XLV, 1930.

[Eliot, T. S.] Thomas Heywood. TLS. 30 July 1931. [Rptd in Selected Essays, 1932, and Elizabethan Essays, 1934.]

Martin, M. T. If You Know Not Me and The Famous Historie of Sir Thomas Wyatt. Library, XIII, 1932.

A. M. C.

JOHN MARSTON (1575?–1634)

(1) COLLECTED WORKS

Tragedies and Comedies collected into one volume. Viz. 1. Antonio and Mellida. 2. Antonio's Revenge. 3. The Tragedie of Sophonisba. 4. What You Will. 5. The Fawne. 6. The Dutch Courtezan. Ed. W. Sheares, 1633 (re-issued as The Workes of Mr John Marston).

The Works of John Marston. Ed. J. O. Halliwell[-Phillipps], 3 vols. 1856.

The Poems of John Marston (1598–1601). Ed. A. B. Grosart, Manchester, 1879.

The Works of John Marston. Ed. A. H. Bullen, 3 vols. 1887.

The Plays of John Marston. Ed. H. H. Wood, 3 vols. Edinburgh, 1934– .

(2) PLAYS

The History of Antonio and Mellida. The first part. As it hath beene sundry times acted, by the children of Paules. Written by J. M. 1602; ed. C. W. Dilke (Old English Plays, vol. II, 1814); ed. W. W. Greg, Malone Soc. 1921.

Antonios Revenge. The second part. As it hath beene sundry times acted, by the children of Paules. Written by J. M. 1602; ed. C. W. Dilke (Old English Plays, vol. II, 1814); ed. W. W. Greg, Malone Soc. 1921.

The Malcontent. 1604 (bis); 1604 ('With the Additions played by the Kings Majesties servants. Written by Jhon Webster'); Ancient British Drama, vol. II; ed. G. B. Harrison, 1933 (Temple Dramatists). [Also included in some edns of Webster (see p. 629 below).]

The Dutch Courtezan. As it was playd in the Blacke-Friars, by the Children of her Majesties Revels. 1605.

Parasitaster, Or The Fawne, As It Hath Bene Divers times presented at the blacke Friars, by the Children of the Queenes Majesties Revels. 1606; 1606 ('now corrected of many faults, which by reason of the Author's absence were let slip in the first edition'); ed. C. W. Dilke (Old English Plays, vol. II, 1814).

The Wonder of Women Or The Tragedie of Sophonisba, as it hath beene sundry times Acted at the Blacke Friers. 1606.

What You Will. 1607.

The Insatiate Countesse. A Tragedie: Acted at White-Fryers. 1613; 1616; 1631 (2 issues, one as 'Written by William Barksteed'). [Probably a fragment by Marston written up by Barksted (see p. 474 above).]

[Marston collaborated with Jonson and Chapman in Eastward Ho (see p. 609) and probably took some share (see pp. 651–3) in the anon. Histriomastix and Jack Drum's Entertainment, and less certainly in An Alarum for London, The Distracted Emperor, The London Prodigal, The Puritan, and Dekker's Satiromastix.]

(3) MASQUE

The hoble Lorde & Lady of Huntingdons Entertainement of theire right Noble Mother Alice: Countesse Dowager of Darby the first night of her honors arrivall att the house of Ashby. [MS at Bridgewater House. Extracts in Works of Milton, ed. H. J. Todd, vol. V, 1801, and Progresses of James I, ed. J. Nichols, vol. II, 1828.]

40-2

(4) OTHER WORKS

The Metamorphosis of Pigmalions Image. And Certaine Satyres. 1598 (as by W. Kinsayder); 1613, etc. (appended to J. C.'s Alcilia); ed. J. Bowle (Miscellaneous Pieces of Poesie, 1764); rptd Waltham St Lawrence, 1927.

The Scourge of Villanie. Three bookes of Satyres. 1598 (as by W. Kinsayder); 1599 (with addns); ed. J. Bowle (Miscellaneous Pieces of Poesie, 1764); ed. G. B. Harrison, 1925.

[Verses by Marston are contained in the Appendix to Sir Robert Chester's Love's Martyr, 1601, under the title A Narration and Description of a most exact wondrous Creature, arising out of the Phœnix and Turtle Dove's ashes.]

(5) BIOGRAPHY AND CRITICISM

von Scholten, W. Metrische Untersuchungen zu Marston's Trauerspielen. Halle, 1886.

Aronstein, P. John Marston als Dramatiker. E. Studien, xx, xxi, 1893.

Deighton, K. Marston's Works. Conjectural Readings. 1893.

Koeppel, E. Quellenstudien zu den Dramen Ben Jonson's, John Marston's, und Beaumont und Fletcher's. Erlangen, 1895.

Small, R. A. The Authorship and Date of the Insatiate Countess. Harvard Stud. v, 1896.

—— The Stage-Quarrel between Ben Jonson and the so-called Poetasters. Breslau, 1899. [See also, on this subject, the articles by H. C. Hart in N. & Q. 14 March, 11 April, 2 May 1903.]

Penniman, J. H. The War of the Theatres. Boston, 1897.

von Wurzbach, W. John Marston. Sh. Jb. xxxiii, 1897.

Winckler, C. John Marston's litterarische Anfänge. Breslau, 1903.

—— Marston's Erstlingswerke und ihre Beziehungen zu Shakespeare. E. Studien, xxxiii, 1904.

Holthausen, F. Die Quellen von Marston's 'What You Will.' Sh. Jb. xli, 1905.

Stoll, E. E. Shakspere, Marston, and the Malcontent Type. MP. iii, 1906.

Crawford, C. Collectanea. Ser. 2, Stratford-on-Avon, 1907.

Allen, M. S. The Satire of John Marston. Columbus, 1920.

Beckwith, E. A. On the Hall-Marston Controversy. JEGP. xxv, 1926.

Brettle, R. E. Bibliographical Notes on some Marston Quartos and Early Collected Editions. Library, viii, xii, 1927–31.

—— John Marston, Dramatist, at Oxford. RES. iii 1927.

Brettle, R. E. John Marston, Dramatist. Some New Facts about his Life. MLR. xxii, 1927.

—— Marston born in Oxfordshire. MLR. xxii, 1927.

Upton, A. W. Allusions to James I and his Court in Marston's Fawn and Beaumont's Woman Hater. PMLA. xliv, 1929.

Adams, J. Q. Eastward Hoe and its Satire against the Scots. Stud. Phil. xxviii, 1931.

Davenport, A. Some Notes on References to Joseph Hall in Marston's Satires. RES. ix, 1933.

Walley, H. R. The Dates of Hamlet and Marston's The Malcontent. RES. ix, 1933.

[Eliot, T. S.] John Marston. TLS. 26 July 1934. [Rptd in Elizabethan Essays, 1934.]

Spencer, T. John Marston. Criterion, xiii, 1934.

Ellis-Fermor, U. M. The Jacobean Drama. 1936.

CYRIL TOURNEUR (1575?–1626)

(1) COLLECTED WORKS

The Plays and Poems. Ed. J. Churton Collins, 2 vols. 1878.

Webster and Tourneur. Ed. J. A. Symonds, 1888, etc. (Mermaid Ser.) [The Atheist's Tragedy, The Revenger's Tragedy.]

The Complete Works. Ed. Allardyce Nicoll, 1930.

(2) PLAYS

The Revengers Tragædie. As it hath beene sundry times Acted, by the Kings Majesties Servants. 1607 (anon.); 1608; rptd R. Dodsley (Collection of Old Plays, vol. iv, 1744, 1780, 1825); Ancient British Drama, vol. ii; Hazlitt's Dodsley, vol. x; ed. A. H. Thorndike (Webster and Tourneur, New York, 1912); ed. G. B. Harrison, 1934 (Temple Dramatists).

The Atheist's Tragedie: Or The honest Man's Revenge. As in divers places it hath often beene Acted. 1611 (re-issued 1612).

[Tourneur has also been assigned a share (see pp. 651–3) in the anon. The Distracted Emperor and The Second Maiden's Tragedy, and (see p. 633) in Beaumont and Fletcher's The Honest Man's Fortune.]

(3) OTHER WORKS

The Transformed Metamorphosis. 1600.

A Funerall Poeme. Upon the Death of Sir Francis Vere, Knight. 1609 (anon.).

A Griefe On the Death of Prince Henrie. 1613. [Part of Three Elegies on the most lamented Death of Prince Henrie.]

The Character of Robert Earle of Salesburye. [MSS in BM. etc.]

(4) Criticism

Thorndike, A. H. Hamlet and Contemporary Revenge Plays. PMLA. xvii, 1902.
Stoll, E. E. John Webster. 1905. [Pp. 105–16; Appendix i.]
Swinburne, A. C. Cyril Tourneur. [In The Age of Shakespeare, 1908.]
Schücking, L. L. Eine Anleihe Shakespeares bei Tourneur. E. Studien, l, 1916–7.
Wenzel, P. Cyril Tourneurs Stellung in der Geschichte des englischen Dramas. Breslau, 1918.
Sykes, H. D. The Revenger's Tragedy; The Second Maiden's Tragedy. N. & Q. Sept. 1919.
Oliphant, E. H. C. The Authorship of The Revenger's Tragedy. Stud. Phil. xxiii, 1926. [Attributes to Middleton.]
—— Tourneur and Mr T. S. Eliot. Stud. Phil. xxxii, 1935.
[Eliot, T. S.] Cyril Tourneur. TLS. 13 Nov. 1930. [Rptd in Elizabethan Essays, 1934.]
Bradbrook, M. C. Themes and Conventions of Elizabethan Tragedy. Cambridge, 1935.
Ellis-Fermor, U. M. The Imagery of The Revengers Tragedie and The Atheists Tragedie. MLR. xxx, 1935.
—— The Jacobean Drama. 1936.

F. L. L.

JOHN WEBSTER (1580?–1625)

(1) Collected Works

Works. Ed. A. Dyce, 4 vols. 1830; 1 vol. 1857 (rev. edn).
Dramatic Works. Ed. W. C. Hazlitt, 4 vols. 1857 and 1897.
Works. Ed. F. L. Lucas, 4 vols. 1927. [With detailed introduction and bibliography. See also the reviews by W. W. Greg, RES. iv, 1928, and M. Praz, E. Studies, x, 1928.]
Webster and Tourneur. Ed. J. A. Symonds, 1888, etc. (Mermaid Ser.) [The White Devil and The Duchess of Malfi.]
The White Devil and The Duchess of Malfy. Ed. M. W. Sampson, Boston, 1904. (Belles Lettres Ser.)
Webster and Tourneur. Ed. A. H. Thorndike, New York, 1912. [The White Devil, The Duchess of Malfi and Appius and Virginia.]

(2) Plays

The White Divel, Or, The Tragedy of Paulo Giordano Ursini, Duke of Brachiano, With The Life and Death of Vittoria Corombona the famous Venetian Curtizan, Acted by the Queenes Majesties Servants. 1612; 1631; 1665; 1672; rptd R. Dodsley (Collection of Plays, vol. vi, 1744, 1780, 1825); Ancient British Drama, vol. iii; ed. G. B. Harrison, 1933 (Temple Dramatists).

The Tragedy Of The Dutchesse Of Malfy. As it was Presented privatly, at the Black-Friers; and publiquely at the Globe, By the Kings Majesties Servants. The perfect and exact Coppy, with diverse things Printed, that the length of the Play would not beare in the Presentment. 1623; 1640; 1678; [?]; ed. C. E. Vaughan, 1896 (Temple Dramatists); ed. F. Allen, 1921.
The Devils Law-case. Or, When Women goe to Law, the Devill is full of Businesse. A new Tragecomoedy. The true and perfect Copie from the Originall. As it was approovedly well Acted by her Majesties Servants. 1623.
Appius and Virginia. A Tragedy. 1654 (reissued 1659); 1679; ed. C. W. Dilke (Old English Plays, vol. v, 1815). [Really by Heywood?]
A Cure for a Cuckold. A Pleasant Comedy. 1661 (anon.); ed. Sir E. Gosse, 1885 (main plot only as Love's Graduate). [With Rowley.]

[For The Malcontent (with Marston) see p. 627; for The Famous History of Sir Thomas Wyat (with Dekker) see p. 619; for West-Ward Hoe (with Dekker) see p. 619; for North-Ward Hoe (with Dekker) see p. 619; for Anything for a Quiet Life (with Middleton?) see p. 612; for The Faire Maide of the Inne (with Massinger and Ford?) see p. 633. Tourneur's The Revenger's Tragedy and the anon. The Weakest Goeth to the Wall (see p. 538) have also been assigned to Webster. For The Thracian Wonder see p. 653 below.]

(3) Other Works

A Monumental Columne, Erected to the living Memory of the ever-glorious Henry, late Prince of Wales. 1613. [Also as part of Three elegies on the most lamented Death of Prince Henrie.]
New Characters (Drawne to the life) of severall persons, in severall qualities. 1615 (anon.). [At the end of the Sixth Impression of Overbury's Characters.]
Monuments of Honor. Celebrated in the Honorable City of London, at the sole Munificent charge and expences of the Right Worthy and Worshipfull Fraternity of the Eminent Merchant-Taylors, at the Confirmation of John Gore in the High Office of his Majesties Lieutenant over this His Royall Chamber. 1624.

(4) Criticism

Gnoli, D. Vittoria Accoramboni. Florence, 1870.
Gosse, Sir E. John Webster. [In Seventeenth Century Studies, 1883.]

Kiesow, K. Die verschiedenen Bearbeitungen der Novelle von der Herzogin von Amalfi des Bandello in der Literatur des XVI. und XVII. Jahrhunderts. Ang. xvii, 1895.

Greg, W. W. Webster's White Devil. Mod. Lang. Quart. iii, 1900.

Stoll, E. E. John Webster. 1905.

Morellini, D. Giovanna d' Aragona, Duchessa d'Amalfi. Cesena, 1906.

Crawford, C. Collectanea. 2 sers. Stratford-on-Avon, 1906–7. [Contains articles on Webster's borrowings from Sidney, Montaigne, etc.]

Tischner, F. Die Verfasserschaft der Webster-Rowley-Dramen. Marburg, 1907.

Krusius, P. Eine Untersuchung der Sprache J. Webster's. Halle, 1908.

Swinburne, A. C. John Webster. [In The Age of Shakespeare, 1908.]

Pierce, F. E. The Collaboration of Webster and Dekker. New Haven, 1909.

Stork, C. W. William Rowley. All's Lost by Lust and A Shoemaker, A Gentleman. Philadelphia, 1910. [Introduction.]

Sykes, H. D. An Attempt to determine the Date of Webster's Appius and Virginia. N. & Q. 24, 31 May, 14 June, 26 July 1913.

—— Was Webster a Contributor to Overbury's Characters? N. & Q. 24 April, 1, 8, 15 May 1915.

—— Sidelights on Elizabethan Drama. 1924.

Brooke, R. John Webster and the Elizabethan Drama. 1916.

Archer, W. The Duchess of Malfi. Nineteenth Century, lxxxvii, 1920.

Clark, A. M. The Authorship of Appius and Virginia. MLR. xvi, 1921.

—— Thomas Heywood. Oxford, 1931. [For Appius and Virginia.]

Olivero, F. La Duchessa di Amalfi di John Webster. Rivista d' Italia, March 1925. [Rptd in Studi Britannici, Turin, 1931.]

Gray, H. D. Appius and Virginia. By Heywood and Webster. Stud. Phil. xxiv, 1927.

—— A Cure for a Cuckold by Heywood, Rowley and Webster. MLR. xxii, 1927.

Haworth, P. English Hymns and Ballads and Other Studies in Popular Literature. 1927.

Wagner, B. M. New Verses by John Webster. MLN. xlvi, 1931.

Edwards, W. A. John Webster. [In Determinations, ed. F. R. Leavis, 1934.]

Bradbrook, M. C. Themes and Conventions of Elizabethan Tragedy. Cambridge, 1935.

Ellis-Fermor, U. M. The Jacobean Drama. 1936.

F. L. L.

PHILIP MASSINGER (1583–1640)

(1) Collected Works

The Dramatic Works. Ed. T. Coxeter, 4 vols. 1759 (re-issued 1761 with introduction by T. Davies).

The Dramatick Works. Ed. J. Monck Mason, 4 vols. 1779. [With an introduction by T. Davies.]

The Plays. Ed. W. Gifford, 4 vols. 1805 (prints from MS The Parliament of Love), 1813, 1840, etc. [With an essay on the dramatic writings of Massinger by J. Ferriar.]

The Dramatic Works of Massinger and Ford. Ed. Hartley Coleridge, 1840, 1848, 1851.

Plays. From the Text of W. Gifford. With the addition of, Believe as you list. Ed. F. Cunningham, 1868, etc.

Philip Massinger. Ed. A. Symons, 2 vols. 1887–9, etc. (Mermaid Ser.). [The Duke of Milan; A New Way to pay Old Debts; The Great Duke of Florence; The Maid of Honour; The City Madam; The Roman Actor; The Fatal Dowry; The Guardian; The Virgin Martyr; Believe as you list.]

Philip Massinger. Ed. L. A. Sherman, New York, 1912. [The Roman Actor; The Maid of Honour; A New Way to pay Old Debts; Believe as you list.]

(2) Plays

The Virgin Martir, A Tragedie. As it hath bin divers times publickely Acted with great Applause, By the servants of his Majesties Revels. Written by Phillip Messenger and Thomas Deker. 1622; 1631; 1651; 1661; ed. J. S. Keltie (Works of the British Dramatists, 1827).

The Duke Of Millaine. A Tragædie. As it hath beene often acted by his Majesties servants, at the blacke Friers. 1623; 1638; rptd T. Dibdin, 1816 (London Theatre); ed. T. W. Baldwin, Lancaster (Pennsylvania), 1918.

The Bond-Man: An Antient Storie. As it hath been often Acted at the Cock-pit in Drury-lane: by the most Excellent Princesse, the lady Elizabeth her Servants. 1624; 1638; rptd Modern British Drama, vol. i, 1804; ed. B. T. Spencer, Princeton, 1932.

The Roman Actor. A Tragædie. As it hath divers times beene Acted, at the private Play-house in the Black-Friers, by the Kings Majesties Servants. 1629; ed. W. L. Sandidge, Princeton, 1929.

The Picture. A Tragecomedie, As it was often presented at the Globe, and Blacke-Friers Play-houses, by the Kings Majesties servants. 1630; rptd R. Dodsley (Collection of Old Plays, vol. viii, 1744).

The Renegado, A Tragæcomedie. As it hath
beene often acted by the Queenes Majesties
servants, at the private Play-house in
Drurye-Lane. 1630.

The Emperour Of The East. A Tragæ-
Comœdie. The Scæne Constantinople. As
it hath bene divers times acted, at the
Black-friers, and Globe Play-houses, by the
Kings Majesties Servants. 1632.

The Fatall Dowry: A Tragedy. As it hath
beene often Acted at the Private House in
Blackefryers, by his Majesties Servants.
Written by P. M. and N. F. 1632; rptd.
Modern British Drama, vol. I, 1804; ed.
C. L. Lockert, Lancaster (Pennsylvania),
1918. [With Nathaniel Field.]

The Maid of Honour. As It Hath Beene Often
Presented at the Phœnix in Drurie-Lane,
by the Queenes Majesties Servants. 1632;
rptd 1829 (Cumberland's British Theatre).

A New Way To Pay Old Debts A Comœdie
As it hath beene often acted at the Phœnix
in Drury-Lane, by the Queenes Majesties
servants. 1633; rptd R. Dodsley (Collection
of Old Plays, vol. VIII, 1744); rptd Modern
British Drama, vol. I, 1804; ed. N. Deighton,
1893; ed. C. Stronach, 1904; ed. A. H.
Cruickshank, Oxford, 1926.

The Great Duke Of Florence. A Comicall
Historie. As it hath beene often presented
by her Ma^tles Servants at the Phœnix in
Drurie Lane. 1636; ed. J. M. Stockholm,
Baltimore, 1933.

The Unnaturall Combat. A Tragedie. The
Scæne Marsellis. As it was presented by
the Kings Majesties Servants at the Globe.
1639; rptd R. Dodsley (Collection of Old
Plays, vol. VIII, 1744); ed. R. S. Telfer,
Princeton, 1932.

Three New Plays; viz.

The Bashful Lover. A Tragi-Comedy. As
it hath been often Acted at the Private-
House in Black-Friers, by His late
Majesties Servants. 1655.

The Guardian, A Comical-History. As it
hath been often acted at the Private-
House in Black-Friars, by his late
Majesties Servants. 1655; rptd R. Dodsley (Collection of Old Plays, vol. VIII,
1744).

A very Woman, Or the Prince of Tarent. A
Tragi-Comedy. As it hath been often
acted at the Private-House in Black-
Friars, by his late Majesties Servants.
1655.

Never Printed before. 1655.

The City-Madam, A Comedie. As it was acted
at the private House in Black Friers. 1658;
1659; rptd R. Dodsley (Collection of Old
Plays, vol. VIII, 1744); ed. R. Kirk, Princeton, 1934.

Believe as you list. Ed. T. C. Croker, Percy
Soc. 1849; TFT. 1907 (facs. of MS); ed.
C. J. Sisson, Malone Soc. 1928. [Egerton
MS 2828.]

The Parliament of Love. Ed. K. M. Lea,
Malone Soc. 1928. [Dyce MS 39.]

(3) POEMS

The Copie of a Letter written upon occasion to
the Earle of Pembrooke Lo: Chamberlaine.
Ed. A. B. Grosart, E. Studien, XXVI, 1899;
ed. P. Simpson, Athenaeum, 8 Sept. 1906;
ed. A. H. Cruickshank (Philip Massinger,
Oxford, 1920). [c. 1615–1623. Trinity College, Dublin MS G. 2. 21, pp. 554–7.]

A Newyeares Guift presented to my Lady and
M:^rs the then Lady Katherine Stanhop now
Countesse of Chesterfeild. Ed. A. B. Gro-
sart, E. Studien, XXVI, 1899; ed. P. Simpson,
Athenaeum, 8 Sept. 1906; ed. A. H. Cruick-
shank (Philip Massinger, Oxford, 1920).
[c. 1615–1623. Trinity College, Dublin MS.
G. 2. 21, pp. 557–9.]

To my Honorable Freinde Sir Francis Fol-
jambe knight and Baronet. Ed. W.
Gifford (Massinger's Plays, 1813 (2nd edn)).
[Autograph inscription in Dyce copy of The
Duke of Milan, 1623. Facs. in Handbook of
the Dyce and Forster Collections, 1880, p.
21.]

Londons Lamentable Estate, in any great
Visitation. [1625? Bodleian MS Rawl. Poet.
61, fols. 71^r–76^r. See F. P. Wilson, Library,
VII, 1926, p. 199.]

The Virgins Character. Ed. A. K. McIlwraith,
RES. IV, 1928. [c. 1625–1630. MS Harleian
6918, fols. 52^r–54^r.]

To my Judicious and Learned friend the
Author upon his ingenious poem The
Gratefull Servant. [J. Shirley, The Grate-
full Servant, 1630. Rptd in Massinger's
Dramatic Works, ed. T. Coxeter, 1759, etc.]

Sero, sed Serio. To the right honourable my
most singular good Lord and Patron Philip
Earle of Pembrooke and Montgomerye,
Uppon the deplorable and untimely death
of his Sonne Charles. Ed. T. Coxeter
(Massinger's Dramatic Works, 1759), etc.
[1635. MS Royal 18 A. xx, fols. 1^r–4^r.]

To his Sonne, upon his Minerva. [Date uncertain. Prefixed to The Innovation of
Penelope and Ulysses, by James Smith, in
Wit Restor'd in severall Select Poems,
1658. Rptd T. Coxeter, Massinger's Dramatic Works, 1759, etc.]

(4) BIOGRAPHY AND CRITICISM

Fleay, F. G. On Metrical Tests as applied to
Dramatic Poetry [Fletcher, Beaumont,
Massinger]. Trans. New Shakspere Soc. I,
1874.

Gardiner, S. R. The Political Element in Massinger. Contemporary Rev. Aug. 1876. [Rptd Trans. New Shakspere Soc. I, 1875–6.]

Boyle, R. On Beaumont, Fletcher and Massinger. E. Studien, v, VII–X, 1882, 1884–7.

Swinburne, A. C. Philip Massinger. Fortnightly Rev. July 1889. [Rptd in Contemporaries of Shakespeare, 1919.]

Oliphant, E. H. C. The Works of Beaumont and Fletcher. E. Studien, XIV–XVI, 1890–2.

—— Shakspere's Plays: an Examination. MLR. III, IV, 1908–9.

—— The Plays of Beaumont and Fletcher. New Haven, 1927.

—— The Plays of Beaumont and Fletcher: Some Additional Notes. PQ. IX, 1930.

Lowell, J. R. Massinger and Ford. [In Latest Literary Essays and Addresses, 1891.]

Koeppel, E. Quellen-Studien zu den Dramen George Chapman's, Philip Massinger's und John Ford's. QF. LXXXII, 1897.

Stephen, Sir L. Philip Massinger. [In Hours in a Library, vol. II. 1899.]

von Wurzbach, W. Philip Massinger. Sh. Jb. XXXV–XXXVI, 1899–1900.

Raebel, K. Massinger's Drama, 'The Maid of Honour,' in seinem Verhältniss zu Painter's 'Palace of Pleasure.' Halle, 1901.

Morris, E. C. On the Date and Composition of The Old Law. PMLA. XVII, 1902.

Shands, H. A. Massinger's 'The Great Duke of Florence' und seine Quellen. Halle, 1902.

Gerhardt, E. P. Massinger's 'The Duke of Milan' und seine Quellen. Halle, 1905.

Beck, C. Philip Massinger, 'The Fatall Dowry.' Einleitung zu einer neuen Ausgabe. Bayreuth, 1906.

Cruickshank, A. H. Philip Massinger. Oxford, 1920.

—— Massinger and The Two Noble Kinsmen. Oxford, 1922.

Eliot, T. S. Philip Massinger. [In The Sacred Wood, 1920.]

Thorn-Drury, G. A Little Ark. 1921. [Contains a biographical poem addressed to Massinger by Henerie Parker.]

Frijlinck, W. P. [Preface to her edn of Sir J. van Olden Barnevelt, Amsterdam, 1922.]

Greg, W. W. Autograph Corrections in The Duke of Milan. Library, IV, 1923.

—— More Massinger Corrections. Library, V, 1924. [See also A. H. Cruickshank, ibid.]

Sykes, H. D. Sidelights on Elizabethan Drama. 1924.

Chelli, M. Le Drame de Massinger. Lyon, 1924.

—— Étude sur la Collaboration de Massinger avec Fletcher et son Groupe. Paris, 1926.

Makkink, H. J. Philip Massinger and John Fletcher: a Comparison. Rotterdam, 1927.

Lawrence, W. J. The Renegado. TLS. 24 Oct. 1929. [Late seventeenth century adaptation in MS.]

—— Massinger's Punctuation. Criterion, XI, 1932. [Rptd in Those Nut-Cracking Elizabethans, 1935.]

McIlwraith, A. K. Did Massinger revise The Emperour of the East? RES. IV, 1929.

—— Some Bibliographical Notes on Massinger. Library, XI, 1930.

—— On the Date of A New Way to Pay Old Debts. MLR. XXVIII, 1933.

Ball, R. H. Massinger and the House of Pembroke. MLN. XLVI, 1931.

Steiner, A. Massinger's The Picture, Bandello, and Hungary. MLN. XLVI, 1931.

Eccles, M. Arthur Massinger. TLS. 16 July 1931.

Jones, F. L. An Experiment with Massinger's Verse. PMLA. XLVII, 1932.

Rice, W. G. The Sources of Massinger's The Renegado. PQ. XI, 1932.

Spencer, B. T. Philip Massinger. [In Seventeenth-Century Studies, ed. R. Shafer, Princeton, 1933.]

McManaway, J. G. Philip Massinger and the Restoration Drama. ELH. I, 1934.

A. K. Mc I.

FRANCIS BEAUMONT (1585?–1616) AND JOHN FLETCHER (1579–1625)

(1) BIBLIOGRAPHIES

Potter, A. C. A Bibliography of Beaumont and Fletcher. Cambridge, U.S.A. 1890. [See also for particular plays B. Leonhardt, Ang. XIX, XX, XXIII, XXIV, XXVI, 1896–1903, and the bibliographies prefixed to the individual plays in A. H. Bullen's Variorum Edition, 1904–12.]

(2) COLLECTED WORKS

Comedies and Tragedies written by Francis Beaumont and John Fletcher, Gentlemen. Never printed before, And now published by the Authors Originall Copies. 1647. [Contains the following plays: The Mad Lover; The Spanish Curat; The Little French Lawyer; The Custome of the Countrey; The Noble Gentleman; The Captaine; Beggars Bush; The Coxcombe; The False One; The Chances; The Loyall Subject; The Lawes of Candy; The Lovers Progres; The Island Princesse; The Humorous Lieutenant; The Nice Valour, or, the Passionate Mad-man; The Maid in the Mill; The Prophetesse; The Tragedie of Bonduca; The Sea Voyage; The double Marriage; The Pilgrim; The Knight of Malta; The Womans Prize: or, the Tamer Tamed; Loves Cure or, the Martiall Maide; The Honest mans Fortune; The Queene of Corinth; Women pleas'd; A Wife for a Moneth; Wit At severall Weapons; The Tragedie of Valentinian; The Faire Maide of the Inne; Loves Pilgrimage; The Maske of the Gentlemen of Grayes-Inne, and the Inner-Temple, at the Marriage of the Prince and Princesse Palatine of Rhene; Foure Playes (or Morall Representations) in one.

The 34 plays included in the above list were all previously unprinted. The Masque of the Inner Temple and Grayes Inn had been ptd c. 1613. The Wild-Goose Chase was omitted because the copy of it had gone astray. When recovered, it was pbd separately in folio, 1652.]

Fifty Comedies and Tragedies. Written by Francis Beaumont and John Fletcher, Gentlemen. Published by the Authors Original Copies, the Songs to each play being added. 1679. [Contains 52 plays (including The Coronation) and The Masque.]
The Works of Beaumont and Fletcher in seven volumes. 1711.
The Works of Mr Francis Beaumont and Mr John Fletcher. In ten volumes. Collated with all the former editions and corrected. With notes. By the late Mr Theobald, Mr Seward and Mr Sympson. 1750.
The Dramatick Works of Beaumont and Fletcher. [Ed. G. Colman], 10 vols. 1778.
The Dramatic Works of Ben Jonson and Beaumont and Fletcher, the latter from the Text and with the Notes of G. Colman. 4 vols. 1811.
The Works of Beaumont and Fletcher in Fourteen Volumes; with an Introduction and Explanatory Notes by H. Weber. 1812. [The Faithful Friends appears first in this edn.]
The Works of Beaumont and Fletcher. With an Introduction by George Darley. 2 vols. 1840. [Text of Weber, with addns in The Humorous Lieutenant from Dyce's Demetrius and Enanthe, 1830.]
The Works of Beaumont and Fletcher: the Text formed from a New Collation of Early Editions. With Notes and a Biographical Memoir. By A. Dyce. 11 vols. 1843–6.
Beaumont et Fletcher traduits par Ernest Lafond. Paris, 1865. [The Two Noble Kinsmen, Valentinian, Rollo, The Little French Lawyer.]
The Works of Francis Beaumont and John Fletcher. Variorum Edition. 1904–12. [To have been completed in 12 vols. of which four only were pbd. The plays are separately edited, with introductions and notes, by

various editors (P. A. Daniel, R. W. Bond, W. W. Greg, R. B. McKerrow, J. Masefield, M. Luce, C. Brett, R. G. Martin and Sir E. K. Chambers), under the general direction of A. H. Bullen. Vol. i: The Maid's Tragedy; Philaster; A King and No King; The Scornful Lady; The Custom of the Country. Vol. ii: The Elder Brother; The Spanish Curate; Wit without Money; The Beggar's Bush; The Humorous Lieutenant. Vol. iii: The Faithful Shepherdess; The Mad Lover; The Loyal Subject; Rule a Wife and have a Wife; The Laws of Candy. Vol. iv: The False One; The Little French Lawyer; Valentinian; Monsieur Thomas; The Chances.]
Beaumont and Fletcher. Ten Plays. Ed. J. St Loe Strachey, 2 vols. 1904. (Mermaid Ser.)
Beaumont and Fletcher. Ed. A. Glover and A. R. Waller, 10 vols. Cambridge, 1905–12, [A rpt of the folio of 1679, with collation of all the previously ptd texts.]
Beaumont and Fletcher. Select Plays. Ed. G. P. Baker, 1911. (Everyman's Lib.)

(3) SEPARATE PLAYS

The Woman Hater. As it hath beene lately Acted by the Children of Paules. 1607 (2 issues); 1648 ('As it hath beene Acted by his Majesties Servants. Written by John Fletcher Gent.'; re-issued 1649 as The Woman Hater, Or The Hungry Courtier. A Comedy, Written by Francis Beaumont And John Fletcher, Gent.).
The Faithfull Shepheardesse. By John Fletcher. [1609?]; 1629; 1634; 1656; 1665; ed. F. W. Moorman, 1896 (Temple Dramatists).
The Knight of the Burning Pestle. 1613; 1635 ('As it is now Acted by Her Majesties Servants at the Private House in Drury Lane. Written by Francis Beaumont and John Fletcher'); ed. F. W. Moorman, 1898 (Temple Dramatists); ed. H. S. Murch, New Haven, 1908; ed. R. M. Alden, Boston, 1910 (Belles Lettres Ser.); ed. W. T. Williams, 1924; ed. M. J. Sargeaunt, 1928; ed. J. K. Peel, 1929.
The Masque of the Inner Temple and Grayes Inne: Grayes Inne And The Inner Temple, Presented Before his Majestie, the Queenes Majestie, the Prince, Count Palatine and the Lady Elizabeth their Highnesses, in the Banquetting house at White-hall on Saturday the twentieth day of Februarie, 1612. [1613?] (2 issues, one, 'By Francis Beaumont, Gent.'); ed. J. Nichols (Progresses of James I, vol. ii, 1828).

Cupids Revenge. As it hath beene divers times Acted by the Children of her Majesties Revels. By John Fletcher. 1615; 1630 ('Written by Fran. Beaumont & Jo. Fletcher Gentlemen'); 1635.

The Scornful Ladie. A Comedie. As it was Acted by the Children of Her Majesties Revels in the Blacke Fryers. Written by Fra. Beaumont and Jo. Fletcher, Gent. 1616; 1625; 1630; 1635; 1639; 1651 (bis); 1677.

A King and No King. Acted at the Globe, by his Majesties Servants: written by Francis Beaumont and John Flecher. 1619; 1625; 1631; 1639; 1655; 1661; 1676; 1693; ed. R. M. Alden, Boston, 1910 (Belles Lettres Ser.).

The Maides Tragedy. As it hath beene divers times Acted at the Blacke-friers by the Kings Majesties Servants. 1619; 1622; 1630 ('Written by Francis Beaumont, and John Fletcher Gentlemen'); 1638; 1641; 1650 (for 1660?); 1661; 1686; 1704; 1717, etc.; ed. A. H. Thorndike, Boston, 1906 (Belles Lettres Ser.); ed. C. Morley, 1929.

Phylaster. Or, Love lyes a Bleeding. Acted at the Globe by his Majesties Servants. Written by Francis Baymont and John Fletcher, Gent. 1620; 1622; 1628; 1634; 1639; 1652; [1663]; 1687; 1717, etc.; ed. F. S. Boas, 1898 (Temple Dramatists); ed. A. H. Thorndike, Boston, 1906 (Belles Lettres Ser.).

The Tragedy of Thierry King of France, and his Brother Theodoret. As it was diverse times acted at the Blacke-Friers by the Kings Majesties Servants. 1621; 1648 ('Written by John Fletcher Gent'; re-issued 1649 as 'Written by Fracis Beamont, And John Fletcher Gent.').

Henry VIII. [First ptd in the Shakespeare folio, 1623; for later edns see under Shakespeare, p. 575 above.]

The Two Noble Kinsmen: Presented at the Blackfriers by the Kings Majesties servants, Written by the memorable Worthies of their time; Mr John Fletcher, and Mr William Shakespeare, Gent. 1634; ed. H. Littledale, New Shakspere Soc. 1876; ed. C. H. Herford, 1897 (Temple Dramatists); TFT. 1910. [Also included in collections of the Shakespeare Apocrypha (see p. 578).]

The Elder Brother A Comedie. Acted at the Blacke Friers, by his Majesties Servants. Printed according to the true copie. Written by John Fletcher Gent. 1637; 1651 ('Written by Francis Beaumont, And John Fletcher Gent.'); 1661; 1678; ed. W. H. Draper, 1916.

Wit With-Out Money. A Comedie, As it hath beene Presented at the private house in Drurie Lane, by her Majesties Servants. Written by Francis Beamont, and John Flecher. Gent. 1639; 1661; 1718.

Monsieur Thomas. A Comedy. Acted at the Private House in Blacke Fryers. The Author, John Fletcher, Gent. 1639 (re-issued n.d. c. 1661·as Fathers Own Son).

The Bloody Brother. A Tragedy. By B. J. F. 1639; Oxford, 1640 (as The Tragœdy of Rollo Duke of Normandy. Acted by His Majesties Servants. Written by John Fletcher Gent); 1718 (as The Bloody Brother, or Rollo, A Tragedy. Written by Mr Francis Beaumont, And Mr John Fletcher).

Rule A Wife And have a Wife. A Comoedy. Acted By His Majesties Servants. Written by John Fletcher Gent. Oxford, 1640; 1696; 1697; 1717; 1728, etc.; ed. G. Saintsbury, Gayley, vol. III.

The Night-Walker, Or The Little Theife. A Comedy, As it was presented by her Majesties Servants, at the Private House in Drury Lane. Written by John Fletcher. Gent. 1640; 1661.

The Coronation A Comedy. 1640. [See Shirley, p. 638.]

The Wild-Goose Chase. A Comedie. As it hath been Acted with Singular Applause at the Black-Friers: Being the Noble, Last, and Onely Remaines of those Incomparable Drammatists, Francis Beaumont, And John Fletcher, Gent. Retriv'd for the publick delight of all the Ingenious; And private Benefit of John Lowin And Joseph Taylor, Servants to His late Majestie. By a Person of Honour. 1652.

The Widdow A Comedie. As it was Acted at the private House in Black-Fryers, by His late Majesties Servants. Written by Ben: Johnson. John Fletcher, Tho: Middleton, Gent. Printed by the Originall Copy. 1652.

The Beggars Bush. Written by Francis Beaumont And John Fletcher, Gentlemen. 1661; 1717; 1761, etc. (altered as The Royal Merchant, and The Merchant of Bruges).

The Chances, A Comedy: As it was Acted At The Theater Royal. Corrected and Altered by a Person of Honour [Duke of Buckingham]. 1682; 1692; 1705; 1773 (altered by Garrick).

The Humorous Lieutenant, Or Generous Enemies, A Comedy: As it is now Acted by His Majesties Servants, At The Theatre-Royal in Drury-Lane. 1697; ed. A. Dyce, 1830 (as Demetrius and Enanthe, Being the Humorous Lieutenant, pbd from a MS dated 1625).

The Loyal Subject, or The Faithful General. [1700?]; 1717; 1748.

The Island Princess. 1717. [Altered for the stage 1669, 1687, etc.]

Valentinian. 1717. [Altered for the stage 1690, 1719.]

A Wife for a Month. 1717.

The Custom of the Country. 1717.

The Pilgrim. 1718. [Altered 1700, 1789, etc.]

Love's Cure, or The Martial Maid. 1718.

Bonduca. 1718. [Altered for the stage, 1696, 1778, etc.]

The Spanish Curate. 1718.

Sir John van Olden Barnavelt. Ed. A. H. Bullen (Old English Plays, vol. II, 1884); ed. W. P. Frijlinck, Amsterdam, 1922.

The Faire Maide of the Inne. Ed. F. L. Lucas (Works of Webster, vol. IV, 1927).

(4) POEMS

Salmasis and Hermaphroditus. 1602 (anon.); rptd Shakespeare Soc. 1847. [By Beaumont.]

Certain Elegies done by sundrie excellent wits (Fr. Beau., M. Dr., N. H.) with satyres and epigrames. 1618; rptd 1843.

Poems. By Francis Beaumont. 1640 (containing Salmacis and Hermaphroditus, Remedie of Love, Elegy to Lady Markham, and other poems, some certainly not by Beaumont); 1653 (with addns; re-issued 1660 as Poems. The Golden Remains of Francis Beaumont & John Fletcher).

Verses by Francis Beaumont. TLS. 15 Sept. 1921.

Songs and Lyrics from the Plays of Beaumont and Fletcher. Ed. E. H. Fellowes, 1928.

(5) BIOGRAPHY AND CRITICISM

Mason, J. Monck. Comments on the Plays of Beaumont and Fletcher. 1798.

Hickson, S. The Shares of Shakespeare and Fletcher in The Two Noble Kinsmen. Westminster Rev. XCII, 1847. [Rptd in Trans. New Shakspere Soc. I, 1874.]

Salmacis and Hermaphroditus not by Francis Beaumont. Shakespeare Soc. Papers, III, 1847.

Spedding, J. On the Several Shares of Shakespeare and Fletcher in Henry VIII. GM. Aug. 1850. [Rptd Trans. New Shakspere Soc. I, 1874.]

Fleay, F. G. On Metrical Tests as applied to Dramatic Poetry. Pt II. Fletcher, Beaumont and Massinger. Trans. New Shakspere Soc. I, 1874.

—— Chronology of the Plays of Fletcher and Massinger. E. Studien, IX, 1886.

Swinburne, A. C. Beaumont and Fletcher. Ency. Brit. 9th edn, 1875. [Rptd in Studies in Prose and Poetry, 1894.]

—— The Earlier Plays of Beaumont and Fletcher. English Rev. May 1910.

Boyle, R. Beaumont, Fletcher and Massinger. E. Studien, v, VII, VIII, IX, x, 1882–7.

—— Shakespeare und die beiden Vettern. E. Studien, IV, 1881.

Macaulay, J. C. Francis Beaumont, a Critical Study. 1883.

Macaulay, G. C. Beaumont and Fletcher. CHEL. vol. VI, 1910.

Symonds, J. A. Some Notes on Fletcher's Valentinian. Fortnightly Rev. Sept. 1886.

Oliphant, E. H. C. The Works of Beaumont and Fletcher. E. Studien, XIV, XV, XVI, 1890–2.

—— The Plays of Beaumont and Fletcher. An Attempt to determine their Respective Shares and the Shares of Others. New Haven, 1927.

—— The Plays of Beaumont and Fletcher: some Additional Notes. PQ. IX, 1930.

Bahlsen, L. Spanische Quellen der dramatischen Litteratur besonders Englands zu Shakespeares Zeit. Zeitschrift für vergleichende Litteratur, VI, 1893. [The Maid in the Mill and A Wife for a Month.]

Koeppel, E. Quellen-Studien zu den Dramen Ben Jonson's, John Marston's, und Beaumont und Fletcher's. Erlangen, 1895.

Thorndike, A. H. The Influence of Beaumont and Fletcher on Shakespeare. Worcester, Massachusetts, 1901.

Rosenbach, A. S. N. The Curious Impertinent in English Dramatic Literature. MLN. XVII, 1902.

Garnett, R. Ben Jonson's probable Authorship of Scene 2, Act IV of Fletcher's Bloody Brother. MP. II, 1905.

Hatcher, O. L. John Fletcher, a Study in Dramatic Method. Chicago, 1905.

—— The Sources of Fletcher's Monsieur Thomas. Ang. XXX, 1907.

Brereton, J. le G. Marginalia on Beaumont and Fletcher. Elizabethan Dramatists. Pts III, IV. Sydney, 1906.

De Perrott, J. Beaumont and Fletcher and The Mirrour of Knighthood. MLN. XXII, 1907.

Aronstein, P. Die Moral des Beaumont-Fletcherschen Dramas. Ang. XXXI, 1908.

—— Fletchers 'Love's Pilgrimage' und Ben Jonsons 'The New Inn.' E. Studien, XLIII, 1910–11.

Crawford, C. Ben Jonson and The Bloody Brother. Sh. Jb. XLI, 1908.

Thompson, E. N. S. Elizabethan Dramatic Co-operation. E. Studien, XL, 1908.

Alden, R. M. An Introduction to Beaumont and Fletcher's Plays. [Prefixed to Belles Lettres Ser. edn of The Knight of the Burning Pestle and A King and No King, Boston, 1910.]

Case, R. H. Beaumont and Fletcher. Quarterly Rev. CCXX, 1914.

Gayley, C. M. Beaumont the Dramatist. New York, 1914.

Frijlinck, W. P. The Tragedy of Sir John Van Olden Barnavelt. Amsterdam, 1922. [Introduction.]

Wells, W. The Authorship of Julius Caesar. 1923.

Schutt, J. H. Beaumont and Fletcher's Philaster. E. Studies, VI, 1924.

Sykes, H. D. Sidelights on Elizabethan Drama. 1924.

John Fletcher. TLS. 20 Aug. 1925.

Chelli, M. Étude sur la Collaboration de Massinger avec Fletcher et son Groupe. Paris, 1926.

Harrison, T. P. A Probable Source of Beaumont and Fletcher's Philaster. PMLA. XLI, 1926.

Jeffery, V. M. Italian Influence in Fletcher's Faithful Shepherdess. MLR. XXI, 1926.

Sprague, A. C. Beaumont and Fletcher on the Restoration Stage. Cambridge, U.S.A. 1926.

Greg, W. W. Nathan Field and the Beaumont and Fletcher Folio of 1679. RES. III, 1927.

Wilson, J. H. The Influence of Beaumont and Fletcher on Restoration Drama. Columbus, 1928.

Lindsey, E. S. The Original Music for Beaumont's Play, The Knight of the Burning Pestle. Stud. Phil. XXVI, 1929.

Tannenbaum, S. A. A Hitherto Unpublished John Fletcher Autograph. JEGP. XXVIII, 1929; PQ. XIII, 1934.

Upton, A. W. Allusions to James I and his Court in Marston's Fawn and Beaumont's Woman Hater. PMLA. XLIV, 1929.

Ward, C. E. Note on Beaumont and Fletcher's Coxcomb. PQ. IX, 1930.

Koszul, A. Beaumont et Fletcher, et le Baroque. Cahiers du Sud, X, 1933.

Maxwell, B. Notes towards Dating Fletcher's Wit Without Money. PQ. XII, 1933.

—— The Date of The Pilgrim. PQ. XIII, 1934.

—— The Woman's Prize. MP. XXXII, 1935.

—— The Date of Fletcher's The Nightwalker. MLN. L, 1935.

Bond, R. W. On Six Plays in 'Beaumont and Fletcher, 1679.' RES. XI, 1935. [Comments by E. H. C. Oliphant, RES. XII, 1936, pp. 197–202.]

Ellis-Fermor, U. M. The Jacobean Drama. 1936.

F. E. S.

WILLIAM ROWLEY (1585?–1642?)

(1) WORKS

A Search for Money. Or The lamentable complaint for the losse of the wandring Knight, Mounsieur l'Argent. Or Come along with me, I know thou lovest money. Dedicated to all those that lack money. 1609; rptd Percy Soc. 1840. [A pamphlet.]

A New Wonder, A Woman Never Vext. A Pleasant Conceited Comedy: sundry times Acted: never before printed. 1632; ed. C. W. Dilke (Old English Plays, vol. V, 1815); Hazlitt's Dodsley, vol. XII.

A Match at Mid-Night. A Pleasant Comœdie: As it hath been Acted by the Children of the Revells. Written by W. R. 1633; Ancient British Drama, vol. II; Hazlitt's Dodsley, vol. XII.

A Tragedy Called All's Lost By Lust. Divers times Acted by the Lady Elizabeth's servants. And now lately by her Majesties Servants, at the Phoenix in Drury Lane. 1633; ed. E. P. Morris, Boston, 1907 (Belles Lettres Ser.); ed. C. W. Stork, Philadelphia, 1910.

A Merrie and Pleasant Comedy: Never before Printed, called A Shoo-maker a Gentleman. As it hath beene sundry times Acted at the Red Bull and other Theaters. Written by W. R. Gentleman. 1638; ed. C. W. Stork, Philadelphia, 1910.

Fortune By Land and Sea. A Tragi-Comedy. As it was Acted by the Queens Servants. Written by Tho. Haywood. And William Rowly. 1655; ed. J. E. Walker, 1899.

The Witch of Edmonton A known true story. Composed into A Tragi-Comedy By divers well-esteemed Poets; William Rowley, Thomas Dekker, John Ford, etc. Acted by the Princes Servants, often at the Cock-Pit in Drury-Lane, once at Court. 1658. [Included in collected edns of Ford (see below).]

The Birth Of Merlin: Or The Child hath found his Father: Written by William Shakespear, and William Rowley. 1662; ed. T. E. Jacob, 1889; TFT. 1910. [Also included in collections of the Shakespeare Apocrypha (see p. 576).]

[For The Old Law (with Massinger and Middleton), see Middleton, p. 612; for The Changeling (with Middleton), see p. 612; for The Spanish Gipsie (with Middleton), see p. 612; for The World Tost at Tennis (with Middleton), sec p. 612; for The Travailes of The Three English Brothers (with Day), see Day, p. 535; for A Cure For A Cuckold (with Webster), see Webster, p. 629. Other ascriptions to Rowley are the anon. The Troublesome Reign of King John (see p. 537) and The Thracian Wonder (see p. 653), Shakespeare's Pericles, and Beaumont and Fletcher's The Captain, The Coxcomb, and Wit at Several Weapons (see pp. 632–4).]

(2) CRITICISM

[See also under Middleton, p. 613 above.]

Howe, F. A. The Authorship of The Birth of Merlin. MP. IV, 1906.

Thompson, E. N. S. Elizabethan Dramatic Collaboration. E. Studien, XL, 1908.

Stork, C. W. William Rowley. Philadelphia, 1910. [Introduction.]

Wells, W. The Birth of Merlin. MLR. XVI, 1921. [Attributes to Beaumont and Fletcher.]

Gray, H. D. A Cure for a Cuckold. MLR. XXII, 1927.

Dickson, M. J. William Rowley. TLS. 28 March 1928.

F. E. S.

JOHN FORD (1586–1639)

(1) Collected Works

The Dramatic Works of John Ford. Ed. H. Weber, 2 vols. Edinburgh, 1811.

The Dramatic Works of John Ford [with] Fame's Memorial. Ed. W. Gifford, 2 vols. 1827; rev. A. Dyce, 3 vols. 1869; rev. A. H. Bullen, 3 vols. 1895.

The Dramatic Works of Massinger and Ford. Ed. Hartley Coleridge, 1840, etc.

John Ford. Ed. Havelock Ellis, [1888], etc. (Mermaid Ser.) [Contains The Lover's Melancholy, 'Tis Pity, The Broken Heart, Love's Sacrifice, and Perkin Warbeck.]

John Forde's Dramatic Works. Ed. W. Bang and H. de Vocht, *Bang*, vols. XXIII, N.S. I, 1908, 1927.

(2) Plays

The Lovers Melancholy. Acted At The Private House in the Blacke Friers, and publikely at the Globe by the Kings Majesties servants. 1629.

The Broken Heart. A Tragedy. Acted By the Kings Majesties Servants at the private House in the Black-Friers. Fide Honor. 1633; ed. O. Smeaton, 1906 (Temple Dramatists); ed. S. P. Sherman, Boston, 1915 (Belles Lettres Ser.). [Fide Honor is an anagram for Iohn Forde.]

Loves Sacrifice. A Tragedie Received Generally Well. Acted by the Queenes Majesties Servants at the Phœnix in Drury-lane. 1633.

Tis Pitty Shees a Whore. Acted by the Queenes Majesties Servants, at The Phœnix in Drury-Lane, 1633; rptd R. Dodsley (Collection of Old Plays, vol. v, 1744); ed. I. Reed (Dodsley's Old Plays, vol. VIII, 1780); ed. S. P. Sherman, Boston, 1915 (Belles Lettres Ser.).

The Chronicle Historie Of Perkin Warbeck. A Strange Truth. Acted (sometimes) by the Queenes Majesties Servants at the Phœnix in Drurie lane. Fide Honor. 1634; ed. J. P. Pickburn and J. le G. Brereton, 1896; ed. M. C. Struble, Seattle, 1926.

The Fancies, Chast and Noble: Presented By The Queenes Majesties Servants, At the Phœnix in Drury-lane. Fide Honor. 1638.

The Ladies Triall. Acted By both their Majesties Servants at the private house in Drury Lane. Fide Honor. 1639.

The Sun's-Darling: A Moral Masque: As it hath been often presented at Whitehall, by their Majesties Servants; and after at the Cock-pit in Drury Lane. Written by John Foard and Tho. Decker Gent. 1656 (re-issued twice in 1657).

[For The Witch of Edmonton (with Dekker and William Rowley), see p. 636; for The Queen (an anon. play that has been assigned to Ford), see p. 653.]

(3) Other Works

Fames Memoriall, Or The Earle of Devonshire Deceased: With his honourable life, peacefull end, and solemne Funerall. 1606; rptd [Sir S. E. Brydges], Lee Priory, 1810.

Honor Triumphant. Or The Peeres Challenge, by Armes defensible, at Tilt, Turney, and Barriers. In Honor of all faire Ladies, and in defence of these foure positions following. 1. Knights in Ladies service have no freewill. 2. Beauty is the mainteiner of valour. 3. Faire Lady was never false. 4. Perfect lovers are onely wise. Mainteined by Arguments. Also The Monarches meeting: Or The King of Denmarkes welcome into England. 1606; rptd Shakespeare Soc. 1843.

A Line Of Life. Pointing at the Immortalitie of a Vertuous Name. 1620; rptd Shakespeare Soc. 1843.

(4) Criticism

Wolff, M. John Ford, ein Nachahmer Shakespeares. Heidelberg, 1880.

Hannemann, H. L. E. Metrische Untersuchungen zu John Ford. Halle, 1886.

Swinburne, A. C. John Ford. [In Essays and Studies, 1888.]

Koeppel, E. Quellenstudien zu den Dramen George Chapmans, Philip Massingers und John Fords. QF. LXXXII, 1897.

Bang, W. John Forde und Parthenios von Nikaia. E. Studien, XXXVI, 1906.

Sherman, S. P. Forde's Contribution to the Decadence of the Drama. *Bang*, vol. XXIII, 1908.

—— Stella and The Broken Heart. PMLA. XXIV, 1909.

—— A New Play by Ford. MLN. XXIII, 1909. [The Queene.]

Pierce, F. E. The Collaboration of Dekker and Ford. I, The Authorship of The Sun's Darling. II, The Authorship of The Witch of Edmonton. Ang. XXXVI, 1912.

Sykes, H. D. Sidelights on Elizabethan Drama. 1924.
—— The Authorship of The Witch of Edmonton. N. & Q. 18, 25 Dec. 1926.
Lloyd, B. An Inedited MS. of Ford's Fame's Memorial. RES. i, 1925.
—— An Unprinted Poem by John Ford. RES. i, 1925.
Struble, M. C. The Indebtedness of Ford's Perkin Warbeck to Gainsford. Ang. xlix, 1925.
[Woolf, Virginia.] Notes on an Elizabethan Play. TLS. 5 March 1925. [Rptd in The Common Reader, 1925.]
[Eliot, T. S.] John Ford. TLS. 5 May 1932. [Rptd in Elizabethan Essays, 1934.]
Sargeaunt, M. J. John Ford at the Middle Temple. RES. viii, 1932.
—— Writings ascribed to John Ford by Joseph Hunter in Chorus Vatum. RES. x, 1934.
—— John Ford. Oxford, 1935.
Cochnower, M. E. John Ford. [In Seventeenth Century Studies, ed. R. Shafer, Princeton, 1933.]
Ellis-Fermor, U. M. The Jacobean Drama. 1936.

F. E. S.

JAMES SHIRLEY (1596–1666)

(1) COLLECTED WORKS

Dramatic Works and Poems. Ed. W. Gifford and A. Dyce, 6 vols. 1833.
James Shirley. Ed. Sir E. Gosse, 1888, etc. (Mermaid Ser.) [The Witty Fair One, The Traitor, Hyde Park, The Lady of Pleasure, The Cardinal, The Triumph of Peace.]

(2) PLAYS

The Wedding. As It Was Lately Acted by her Majesties Servants, at the Phenix in Drury-Lane. 1629; 1633; 1660.
The Gratefull Servant. A Comedie. As it was lately presented with good applause in the private House in Drury-Lane, By her Majesties Servants. 1630; 1637; [1661?].
The Schoole Of Complement. As It Was Acted by her Majesties Servants at the Private house in Drury Lane. By J. S. 1631; 1637; 1667 (as Love Tricks: or, the School of Complements).
Changes: Or, Love in a Maze. A Comedie, As it was presented at the Private House in Salisbury Court, by the Company of His Majesties Revels. 1632.
The Wittie Faire One. A Comedie. As it was presented at the Private House in Drury Lane. By her Majesties Servants. 1633.

The Bird In A Cage. A Comedie. As it hath beene Presented at the Phoenix in Drury-Lane. 1633.
The Traytor, A Tragedie. Acted By her Majesties Servants. 1635.
Hide Park, A Comedie, As it was presented by her Majesties Servants, at the private house in Drury Lane. 1637.
The Gamester. As It Was Presented by her Majesties Servants At the private House in Drury-Lane. 1637.
The Young Admirall. As It Was Presented By her Majesties Servants, at the private house in Drury Lane. 1637.
The Example. As It Was Presented by her Majesties Servants At the private House in Drury-Lane. 1637.
The Lady Of Pleasure. A Comedie, As it was Acted by her Majesties Servants, at the private House in Drury Lane. 1637.
The Dukes Mistris, As It Was Presented by her Majesties Servants, At the private House in Drury-Lane. 1638.
The Royall Master; As it was Acted in the new Theater in Dublin: And Before the Right Honorable the Lord Deputie of Ireland, in the Castle. 1638; ed. Sir A. W. Ward, Gayley, vol. iii.
The Maides Revenge. A Tragedy. As it hath beene Acted at the private house in Drury Lane, by her Majesties Servants. 1639.
Loves Crueltie. A Tragedie, As it was presented by her Majesties Servants, at the private House in Drury lane. 1640.
The Opportunitie A Comedy, As it was presented by her Majesties Servants, at the private House in Drury Lane. 1640 (re-issued n.d.).
The Coronation A Comedy. As it was presented by her Majesties Servants at the private House in Drury Lane. Written by John Fletcher, Gent. 1640. [Licensed to Shirley in February 1635 and claimed by him in 1652.]
The Constant Maid. A Comedy. 1640; 1661 (as Love will finde out the Way; re-issued 1667 as The Constant Maid, or Love will finde out the Way).
St Patrick For Ireland. The first Part. 1640.
The Humorous Courtier. A Comedy, As it hath been presented at the private house in Drury-Lane. 1640.
A Pastorall Called The Arcadia. Acted by her Majesties Servants at the Phoenix in Drury Lane. 1640.
An Excellent Comedy, Called, The Prince of Priggs Revels: Or, The Practises of that grand Thief Captain James Hind, Relating Divers of his Pranks and Exploits, never heretofore published by any. Repleat with various Conceits, and Tarltonian Mirth, suitable to the subject. Written by J.S. 1651.

Six New Playes, viz.

The Brothers, A Comedie, As It was Acted at the private House In Black Fryers. 1652.

The Doubtful Heir. A Tragi-comedie, As It was Acted at the private House In Black Friers. 1652.

The Imposture A Tragi-Comedie, As It was Acted at the private House In Black Fryers. 1652.

The Cardinal, A Tragedie, As It was acted at the private House In Black Fryers. 1652.

The Sisters, A Comedie, As It was acted at the private House in Black Fryers. 1652.

The Court Secret, A Tragi-Comedy: Never Acted, But prepared for the Scene at Black-Friers. 1653.

All written by James Shirley. 1653.

The Polititian, A Tragedy, Presented at Salisbury Court By Her Majesties Servants. 1655.

The Gentleman Of Venice A Tragi-Comedie Presented at the Private house in Salisbury Court by her Majesties Servants. 1655.

Honoria And Mammon. Scene Metropolis, or New-Troy. Whereunto is added the Contention of Ajax and Ulisses, for the Armour of Achilles. As it was represented by young Gentlemen of quality at a private entertainment of some Persons of Honour. 1659 (re-issued twice n.d.).

The Ball, A Comedy, As it was presented by her Majesties Servants, at the private House in Drury Lane. Written by George Chapman -and James Shirly. 1639. [Rptd in collected edns of Chapman (see p. 609 above).]

The Tragedie Of Chabot Admirall Of France. As it was presented by her Majesties Servants, at the private House in Drury Lane. Written by George Chapman, and James Shirly. 1639; ed. E. Lehman, Philadelphia, 1906.

[There is no reason for attributing Andromana: Or The Merchant's Wife to Shirley, except that it was pbd, in 1660, as by 'J. S.' Lewis Theobald's Double Falsehood, 1728, may have been based upon a lost MS play by Shirley.]

(3) MASQUES, ETC.

A Contention For Honour And Riches. By J. S. 1633.

The Triumph Of Peace. A Masque, presented by the Foure Honourable Houses, Or Innes of Court. Before the King and Queenes Majesties, in the Banquetting-house at White Hall, February the third, 1633. 1633 (3 edns).

The Triumph Of Beautie. As it was personated by some young Gentlemen, for whom it was intended, at a private Recreation. 1646. [Appended to Poems.]

Cupid and Death. A Masque. As it was Presented before his Excellencie, the Embassadour of Portugal, Upon the 26. of March, 1653. Written by J. S. 1653; 1659.

The Contention Of Ajax and Ulysses, For The Arms of Achilles. As it was nobly represented by young Gentlemen of Quality, at a private Entertainment of some persons of Honour. Written by James Shirley. 1659.

(4) OTHER WORKS

Poems. 1646. [Contains 1. Verses on various Subjects. 2. Narcissus, or The Self Lover. 3. Several Prologues and Epilogues. 4. The Triumph of Beautie.]

Via Ad Latinam Linguam Complanata. The Way made plain to the Latine Tongue. The Rules composed in English and Latine Verse: For the greater Delight and Benefit of Learners. 1649; 1651 (as Grammatica Anglo-Latina).

The Rudiments of Grammar. The Rules composed in English Verse, For the greater Benefit and delight of young beginners. 1656; 1660 (enlarged as Manductio: Or, A leading of Children by the Hand Through The Principles of Grammar).

The True Impartial History and Wars Of The Kingdom of Ireland. 1693. [Epistle to Reader signed J. S.]

A Little Ark containing Sundry Pieces of Seventeenth Century Verse. Ed. G. Thorn-Drury, 1921. [Contains An Ode upon the Happy Return of King Charles II to his Long wishing Nation, May 29 1660, by James Shirley Gent.]

(5) BIOGRAPHY AND CRITICISM

Life and Writings of James Shirley. Quart. Rev. XLIX, 1833.

Fleay, F. G. Annals of the Careers of James and Henry Shirley. Ang. VIII, 1885.

Swinburne, A. C. James Shirley. Fortnightly Rev. XLVII, 1890. [Rptd in Contemporaries of Shakespeare, 1919.]

Ritter, O. Shirley's Amor und Tod. E. Studien, XXXII, 1903.

Baskervill, C. R. The Source of the Main Plot in Shirley's Love Tricks. MLN. XXIV, 1909.

Forsythe, R. S. Shirley's Plays in their Relation to the Elizabethan Drama. New York, 1914.

Parlin, H. T. Shirley's Comedy of London Life. University of Texas Bulletin, no. 371, 1914.

Nason, A. H. James Shirley, Dramatist. A Biographical and Critical Study. New York, 1915.

Baugh, A. C. Some New Facts about Shirley. MLR. xvii, 1922.

—— Further Facts about James Shirley. RES. vii, 1931.

Summers, M. A Restoration Prompt-Book [Shirley's The Sisters]. [In Essays in Petto, 1928.]

Clark, W. S. The Relation of Shirley's Prologue to Orrery's The General. RES. vi, 1930.

Howarth, R. G. A Manuscript of James Shirley's Court Secret. RES. vii, viii, 1931–2.

—— Some Unpublished Poems of James Shirley. RES. ix, 1933.

—— Shirley's Cupid and Death. TLS. 15 Nov. 1934.

MacMullan, H. The Sources of Shirley's St Patrick for Ireland. PMLA. xlviii, 1933.

F. E. S.

XI. THE MINOR JACOBEAN AND CAROLINE DRAMA, 1603–1660

[This period is covered by A. Harbage, Cavalier Drama, New York, 1936. For academic plays see pp. 654–63 below. The italicised abbreviations (Bang, TFT., etc.) refer to the collections of plays listed above, pp. 488–92.]

ROBERT ARMIN (1565?–1610)

The History of the two Maids of More-clacke, With the life and simple maner of John in the Hospitall. Played by the Children of the Kings Majesties Revels. 1609; ed. A. B. Grosart (The Works of Robert Armin, Actor, 1605–1609, 1880); TFT. 1913. [See A. K. Gray, Robert Armine, the Foole, PMLA. xlii, 1927; J. M. Murry, A 'Fellow' of Shakespeare: Robert Armin, New Adelphi, March 1928.]

BARNABE BARNES (1570?–1609)

(a) Play

The Divils Charter: A Tragædie Conteining the Life and Death of Pope Alexander the sixt. As it was plaide before the Kings Majestie, upon Candlemasse night last: by his Majesties Servants. But more exactly reved, corrected, and augmented since by the Author. 1607; ed. R. B. McKerrow, Bang, vol. vi, 1904; TFT. 1913.

(b) Biography and Criticism

Knight, J. Barnabe Barnes. Athenaeum, 20 Aug. 1904.

Swaen, A. E. H., Moore Smith, G. C. and McKerrow, R. B. Notes on The Devil's Charter by Barnabe Barnes. MLR. i, 1906.

Swaen, A. E. H. Notes on The Devil's Charter. MLR. ii, 1907.

Bayley, A. R. N. & Q. 12 April 1924.

Eccles, M. Barnabe Barnes. [In Thomas Lodge and Other Elizabethans, ed. C. J. Sisson, Cambridge, U.S.A. 1933.]

[See also under the Sonneteers, pp. 432–3 above.]

ROBERT BARON (1630–after 1659)

'ΕΡΟΤΟΠΑΙΓΝΙΟΝ, or the Cyprian Academy. 1647 (re-issued 1648). [A romance incorporating the pastoral Gripus and Hegio, or the Passionate Lovers, and the masque Deorum Dona, the latter with a separate title-page dated 1647.]

An Apologie for Paris. For rejecting of Juno, and Pallas, and presenting of Ate's golden ball to Venus. 1649. [Prose dialogue.]

Mirza. A Tragedie, really acted in Persia in the last age. Illustrated with Historical Annotations. [1655.]

[See G. C. Moore Smith, Robert Baron, N. & Q. 3, 10, 17, 24 Jan., 14 March 1914; J. F. Bradley, Robert Baron's Tragedy of Mirza, MLN. xxxiv, 1919; K. C. Slagle, N. & Q. 12 Oct. 1935. See also The Drinking Academy, under Thomas Randolph, p. 658 below, and p. 474 above.]

DAVID, LORD BARRY (1585–1610)
[wrongly designated Lodowick Barry]

Ram-Alley: Or Merrie-Trickes. A Comedy Divers times here-to-fore acted. By the Children of the Kings Revels. Written by Lo: Barrey. 1611; 1636; 1639; ed. I. Reed (Dodsley's Old Plays, vol. v, 1780); Ancient British Drama, vol. ii; ed. J. P. Collier (Dodsley's Old Plays, vol. v, 1825); Hazlitt's Dodsley, vol. x; TFT. 1913. [See J. Q. Adams, Lordinge (alias Lodowick) Barry, MP. ix, 1912; W. J. Lawrence, The Mystery of Lodowick Barry, Stud. Phil. xiv, 1917.]

SIMON BAYLIE

The Wizard. Ed. (from Durham Cathedral MS and BM. Add. MS 10306) H. de Vocht, Bang, N.S. vol. iv, 1930. [Written 1603–25.]

DAUBRIDGECOURT BELCHIER (1580?–1621)

Hans Beer-Pot his invisible comedie of See me, and See me not. Acted in the Low Countries, by an honest Company of Health-Drinkers. 1618.

SIR WILLIAM BERKELEY (1609–1677)

The Lost Lady. A Tragy Comedy. 1638; 1639; ed. R. Dodsley (Collection of Old Plays, vol. x, 1744); *Hazlitt's Dodsley*, vol. XII. [See The Love Letters of Dorothy Osborne to Sir William Temple, ed. Sir I. Gollancz, 1903, Letter lxvi.]

LADY ELIZABETH BRACKLEY and LADY JANE CAVENDISH (collaborated *c.* 1645)

The Concealed Fansyes. Ed. N. C. Starr, PMLA. XLVI, 1931. [The MS (Bodley Rawl. Poet. 16) contains a second piece by the same authors, called A Pastorall.]

ANTHONY BREWER (d. 1624?)

The Love-sick King, An English Tragical History: with The Life and Death of Cartesmunda, the fair Nun of Winchester. 1655; 1680 (as The Perjured Nun); rptd W. R. Chetwood (A Select Collection of Old Plays, 1750); ed. A. E. H. Swaen, *Bang*, vol. XVIII, 1907. [See A. E. H. Swaen, The Date of Brewer's Love-sick King, MLR. III, 1908 (reviewed by J. Q. Adams, MLN. XXIII, 1908); M. H. Dodds, Edmond Ironside and The Love-sick King, MLR. XIX, 1924.]

T[HOMAS] B[REWER?] (*fl.* 1624)

The Countrie Girle. A Comedie. As it hath beene often Acted with much applause. 1647. [See E. H. C. Oliphant, MP. VIII, 1911; Retrospective Rev. ser. 2, II, 1828.]

ALEXANDER BROME (1620–1666)

[See p. 474 above.]

RICHARD BROME (d. 1652?)

(a) *Collected Plays*

The Dramatic Works of Richard Brome. Ed. R. H. Shepherd, 3 vols. 1873.

(b) *Separate Plays*

The Northern Lasse, A Comoedie. As it hath beene often Acted with good Applause, at the Globe, and Black Fryers. By his Majesties Servants. 1632; 1663; 1684.

The Sparagus Garden: A Comedie. Acted in the yeare 1635. by the then Company of Revels, at Salisbury Court. 1640.

The Antipodes: A Comedie. Acted in the yeare 1638. by the Queenes Majesties Servants, at Salisbury Court in Fleet-street. 1640; ed. G. P. Baker, *Gayley*, vol. III.

A Joviall Crew: Or, The Merry Beggars. Presented in a Comedie, at The Cock-pit in Drury-Lane, in the year 1641. 1652; 1661; 1684; rptd R. Dodsley (Collection of Old Plays, vol. VI, 1744); ed. I. Reed (Dodsley's Old Plays, vol. x, 1780); *Ancient British*

Drama, vol. III; ed. J. P. Collier (Dodsley's Old Plays, vol. x, 1827).

Five New Playes, (Viz.): The Madd Couple well matcht, The Novella, The Court Begger, The City Witt, The Damoiselle. 1653. [Ed. Alexander Brome.]

The Queenes Exchange, A comedy Acted with generall applause at the Black-Friers By His Majesties Servants. 1657 (in BM. copy 644.d.35 altered to 1656); 1661 (re-issued as The Royall Exchange).

Five new Playes, viz. The English Moor, or The Mock-Marriage. The Love-Sick Court, or The Ambitious Politique. Covent Garden Weeded. The New Academy, or The New Exchange. The Queen and Concubine. 1659. [Ed. Alexander Brome.]

[For The Late Lancashire Witches, 1634 (with Heywood), see above, p. 624.]

(c) *Biography and Criticism*

Symonds, J. A. [Review of The Dramatic Works of Richard Brome.] Academy, 21 March 1874.

Faust, E. K. R. Richard Brome. Ein Beitrag zur Geschichte der englischen Litteratur. Halle, 1887.

Swinburne, A. C. Richard Brome. Fortnightly Rev. 1892. [Rptd in Contemporaries of Shakespeare, 1919.]

Koeppel, E. QF. LXXXII, 1897. [For source of The Queen and Concubine.]

Allen, H. F. A Study of the Comedies of Richard Brome, especially as Representative of Dramatic Decadence. 1912.

Andrews, C. E. Richard Brome: A Study of his Life and Works. New Haven, 1913.

Thaler, A. Was Richard Brome an Actor? MLN. XXXVI, 1921.

Aronstein, Philipp. Das englische Renaissance-drama. Leipzig, 1929.

Sharpe, R. B. The Source of Brome's The Novella. Stud. Phil. xxx, 1933.

WILLIAM BROWNE OF TAVISTOCK (1591–1643?)

[For Browne's Inner Temple Masque see above, p. 449.]

HENRY BURKHEAD

Cola's Furie, or Lirenda's Miserie. Kilkenny, 1645; 1646.

[For The Female Rebellion, see under Anonymous Plays below, p. 652.]

H[ENRY] B[URNELL]

Landgartha. A Tragie-Comedy, as it was presented in the new Theater in Dublin, with good applause, being an Ancient story. 1641.

THOMAS CAMPION (1567–1620)

[For Campion's masques see above, p. 426.]

THOMAS CAREW (1598?–1639?)

[For Carew's masque Cœlum Britannicum see above, p. 453.]

LODOWICK CARLELL (1602–1675)

The Deserving Favorite. As it was lately Acted, first before the Kings Majestie, and since publikely at the Black-Friers. By his Majesties Servants. 1629; 1659; ed. (with biographical memoir) C. H. Gray, 1905.

Arviragus and Philicia. As it was acted at the Private House in Black-Fryers by his Majesties Servants. The first and second Part. 1639 (anon.).

The Passionate Lovers, A Tragi-Comedy. The First and Second Parts. Twice presented before the King and Queens Majesties at Somerset-House, and very often at the Private House in Black-Friars, with great Applause, By his late Majesties Servants. 1655 (8vo); 1655 (4to).

Two New Playes. Viz. 1. The Fool would be a Favourit: or, The Discreet Lover. 2. Osmond, the Great Turk: or, The Noble Servant. As they have been often acted by the Queen's Majesty's Servants, with great applause. 1657; ed. A. Nicoll, 1926.

Heraclius Emperour Of the East. A Tragedy. Written in French by Monsieur de Corneille. Englished by Lodowick Carlell, Esq. 1664.

GEORGE CARTWRIGHT

The Heroick-Lover, or, The Infanta of Spaine. 1661. [According to dedication to Charles II, 'penn'd many years ago.']

WILLIAM CARTWRIGHT (1611–1643)

[See p. 655 below.]

LADY E[LIZABETH] C[ARY] (1586–1639)

The Tragedy of Mariam. 1613; ed. A. C. Dunstan and W. W. Greg, Malone Soc. 1914. [Written 1602–5. See A. C. Dunstan, Examination of two English Dramas, Königsberg, 1908.]

HENRY CARY, VISCOUNT FALKLAND (d. 1633)

The Marriage Night. 1664; Hazlitt's Dodsley, vol. xv.

[For the blank-verse poem The History of King Edward II, supposed to be writ by Henry Viscount Faulkland, 1680, see D. A. Stauffer, The Parrott Presentation Volume, Princeton, 1935, pp. 289–314, who attributes to Elizabeth Cary.]

MARGARET CAVENDISH, DUCHESS OF NEWCASTLE (1623–1674)

Playes written by the Thrice Noble, Illustrious and Excellent Princess, The Lady Marchioness of Newcastle. 1662. [Contains the following plays, all unacted: Loves Ad-ventures (2 pts); Several Wits: The wise Wit, the wild Wit, the cholerick Wit, the humble Wit; Youths Glory and Deaths Banquet (2 pts); The Lady Contemplation (2 pts); Wits Cabal (2 pts); The Unnatural Tragedie; The Publick Wooing; The Matrimonial Trouble (2 pts); Natures Three Daughters, Beauty, Love, and Wit (2 pts); The Religious; The Comical Hash; Bell in Campo (2 pts); The Apocriphal Ladies; The Female Academy.]

Plays, Never before Printed. 1668. [Contains the following plays, all unacted: The Sociable Companions; or, The Female Wits; The Presence; The Bridals; The Convent of a Pleasure; and 'A Piece of a Play'.]

[See H. T. E. Perry, The First Duchess of Newcastle and her Husband as Figures in Literary History, Cambridge, U.S.A. 1921, and p. 842 below.]

WILLIAM CAVENDISH, DUKE OF NEWCASTLE (1593–1676)

The Country Captaine And the Varietie, Two Comedies, Written by a Person of Honor. Lately presented by his Majesties Servants, at the Black-Fryers. 1649. [The plays have separate title-pages, that of The Country Captaine bearing the imprint of Samuel Browne, English bookseller at the Hague. The Country Captaine was ed. by A. H. Bullen from BM. MS Harl. 7650 and assigned to Shirley under the title Captain Underwit, Old English Plays, vol. II, 1883.]

The Humorous Lovers. A Comedy, Acted by His Royal Highnes's Servants. 1677.

The Triumphant Widow, or the Medley of Humours. A Comedy, Acted by His Royal Highnes's Servants. 1677.

A Pleasante & Merrye Humor off a Roge. Ed. F. Needham (Welbeck Miscellany, no. 1, 1935).

R[OBERT] C[HAMBERLAIN] (1607?–after 1660)

The Swaggering Damsell. A Comedy. 1640.

WILLIAM CHAMBERLAYNE (1619–1689)

[See p. 475 above.]

SIR ASTON COKAYNE (1608–1684)

(a) Collected Plays

The Dramatic Works of Sir Aston Cokain. Ed. J. Maidment and W. H. Logan, Edinburgh, 1874.

(b) Separate Plays

The Obstinate Lady: A New Comedy. 1657; 1658 (in A Chain of Golden Poems); 1662 (in Poems, bis); 1669 (in Choice Poems Of Several Sorts).

Trapolin. 1658 (in A Chain of Golden Poems); 1662 (in Poems, *bis*); 1669 (in Choice Poems Of Several Sorts). [Comedy.]

The Tragedy of Ovid. 1662 (in Poems, *bis*); 1669 (in Choice Poems Of Several Sorts).

(c) Poems

A Chain of Golden Poems. 1658; 1662 (as Poems, *bis*); 1669 (as Choice Poems Of Several Sorts). [Contains A Masque Presented at Bretbie, 1639.]

(d) Criticism

Spaeman, H. Aston Cokains Werke. Münster, 1923.

Lea, K. M. Sir Aston Cokayne and the Commedia dell' Arte. MLR. xxiii, 1928.

Burns, M. The Devil of a Duke. TLS. 18 July 1929.

JOHN COOKE (*fl.* 1612)

Greene's Tu quoque, or, The Cittie Gallant. As it hath beene divers times acted by the Queenes Majesties Servants. 1614 (ed. Thomas Heywood); 1622; [?]; rptd R. Dodsley (Collection of Old Plays, vol. iii, 1744); ed. I. Reed (Dodsley's Old Plays, vol. vii, 1780); *Ancient British Drama*, vol. ii; ed. J. P. Collier (Dodsley's Old Plays, vol. vii, 1825); *Hazlitt's Dodsley*, vol. xi; *TFT.* 1913.

ABRAHAM COWLEY (1618–1667)

[See p. 459 above.]

ROBERT COX (d. 1655)

Actæon and Diana, with a Pastorall Story of the Nymph Oenone; Followed by the severall conceited humors Of Bumpkin, the Huntsman. Hobbinall, the Shepheard. Singing Simpkin. And John Swabber the Seaman. Printed for the use of the Author Robert Cox. [1655]; 1656 (with the additional 'droll,' Simpleton the Smith). [Rptd in parts in The Wits, or Sport upon Sport, 1662; 1672. Pt 2, 1673 (*bis*); rptd W. R. Chetwood (Collection of Old English Plays, 1750); ed. J. J. Elson, Ithaca, 1932 (with 3 drolls by Cox not included in The Wits). See H. E. Rollins, Contribution to the History of the English Commonwealth Drama, Stud. Phil. xvii, 1921, xx, 1923; TLS. 3, 10, 24 Aug. 1922.]

ROBERT DABORNE (d. 1628)

(a) Collected Plays

Robert Daborne's Plays. Ed. A. E. H. Swaen, Ang. xx, xxi, 1898–9.

(b) Separate Plays

A Christian turn'd Turke: or, The Tragicall Lives and Deaths of the two Famous Pyrates, Ward and Dansiker. As it hath beene publickly Acted. 1612.

The Poor-Mans Comfort. A Tragi-Comedy, As it was divers times Acted at the Cock-pit in Drury lane with great applause. 1655. [BM. MS Egerton 1994.]

[Daborne has also been conjecturally assigned a share in Beaumont and Fletcher's Cupid's Revenge, The Honest Man's Fortune, and Thierry and Theodoret.]

(c) Biography and Criticism

Malone, E. The Plays and Poems of William Shakespeare. With a Life of the Poet and an Enlarged History of the Stage. Vol. iii, 1821.

Collier, J. P. Alleyn Papers: Original Documents illustrative of the Life of Edward Alleyn, and of the Early Stage. 1843.

Bullen, A. H. A Collection of Old English Plays. Vol. ii, 1882.

Boyle, R. Daborne's Share in the Beaumont and Fletcher Plays. E. Studien, xxvi, 1899.

Greg, W. W. Henslowe Papers: being Documents supplementary to Henslowe's Diary. 1907.

Boas, F. S. Shakespeare and the Universities. 1923.

Flood, W. H. G. Fennor and Daborne at Youghal in 1618. MLR. xx, 1925.

Chelli, Maurice. Étude sur la Collaboration de Massinger avec Fletcher et son Groupe. Paris, 1926.

Oliphant, E. H. C. The Plays of Beaumont and Fletcher. New Haven, 1927.

SIR WILLIAM DAVENANT (1606–1668)

[See p. 454 above.]

ROBERT DAVENPORT (d. after 1651?)

(a) Collected Plays

The Works of Robert Davenport. Ed. A. H. Bullen (Old English Plays, vol. iii, 1890).

(b) Separate Plays

A Pleasant and Witty Comedy: Called, A New Tricke to Cheat the Divell. Written by R. D. Gent. 1639.

King John and Matilda, A Tragedy. As it was Acted with great Applause by Her Majesties Servants at the Cock-pit in Drury Lane. 1655; 1662.

The City-Night-Cap: Or, Crede quod habes, & habes. A Tragi-Comedy. As it was Acted with great Applause, by Her Majesties Servants, at the Phœnix in Drury Lane. 1661; rptd R. Dodsley (Collection of Old Plays, vol. ix, 1744); ed. I. Reed (Dodsley's Old Plays, vol. xi, 1780); *Ancient British Drama* vol. iii; ed. J. P. Collier (Dodsley's Old

Plays, vol. XI, 1827); *Hazlitt's Dodsley*, vol. XIII. [See Retrospective Rev. IV, 1821; A. C. Swinburne, Robert Davenport (in Contemporaries of Shakespeare, 1919); J. C. Jordon, Davenport's The City Nightcap and Greene's Philomela, MLN. XXVI, 1921; E. Eckhardt, A New Trick to Cheat the Devil, Ang. LIX, 1935.]

SIR JOHN DENHAM (1615–1669)

[See p. 458 above.]

SIR WILLIAM DENNY (1603?–1676)

The Sheepheard's Holiday. Ed. (from BM. Add. MS 34065) W. C. Hazlitt (Huth's Inedited Poetical Miscellanies, 1584–1700, 1870).

GEORGE GERBIER D'OUVILLY

The False Favorite Disgraced and The Reward of Loyalty. A Tragi-Comedy. 1657. [Unacted.]

THOMAS DRUE (or DREW) (*fl.* 1623)

The Life of the Dutches of Suffolke. As it hath beene divers and sundry times acted, with good applause. 1631. [See W. J. Lawrence, Found, a Missing Jacobean Dramatist, TLS. 23 March 1922 and 12 July 1923; J. K. Neill, Thomas Drue's Dutches of Suffolke and the Succession, MLN. XLVIII, 1933. Drue has been suggested as also the author of The Bloody Banquet.]

MILDMAY FANE, EARL OF WESTMORLAND (*c.* 1600–1665)

(a) Plays

Six Comedies performed at the Earl of Westmorland's seat at Apethorpe, co. Northampton by the children and servants of the family. Raguaillo D'Oceano, 1640; Candy Restored, 1640 [1641]; Tyme's Trick upon the Cards, 1641 [1642]; The Change, 1642; Vertue's Triumph, 1644; De Pugna Animi, 1650. [BM Add. MS 34221.]
Don Phoeba's Triumph. [Huntington Lib. MS HM 770.]

(b) Other Writings

Otia Sacra. 1648 (priv. ptd). [Poems.]
The Poems of Mildmay Fane, Earl of Westmorland. Ed. A. B. Grosart, Manchester, 1879.
Fugitive Verses. [See Hist. MSS Commission, Earl of Westmorland MSS, 10th Report, 1885.]

(c) Criticism

Harbage, A. An Unnoted Caroline Dramatist. Stud. Phil. XXXI, 1934.
Leech, C. A 'Drame of Ease.' TLS.,11 Jan. 1936.

SIR RICHARD FANSHAWE (1608–1666)

(a) Plays

Il Pastor Fido, The faithfull Shepherd. A Pastorall Written in Italian by Baptista Guarini, And now Newly Translated. 1647 (anon.); 1648 ('With An Addition cf divers other Poems'); 1664; 1676; 1692; 1736.
La Fida Pastora [i.e. Fletcher's Faithful Shepherdess]. Comoedia Pastoralis. Autore F. F. Anglo-Britanno. Adduntur nonnulla varii argumenti carmina ab eodem. 1658.
Querer por solo querer. To love only for Love sake. A Dramatick Romance, by Antonio de Mendoza, Paraphrased in English Anno 1654. 1670; 1671.

(b) Other Writings

Selected Parts Of Horace, Prince of Lyricks. Concluding With a Piece out of Ausonius, and another out of Virgil. Now newly put into English. 1652.
The Lusiad, Or, Portugals Historicall Poem. 1655. [From Camoens.]
Original Letters of his Excellency Sir Richard Fanshawe, during his Embassies in Spain and Portugal. 2 vols. 1701–24.
Memoirs of Lady Fanshawe, to which are added Extracts from the Correspondence of Sir Richard Fanshawe. Ed. Sir H. Nicolas, 1829; ed. B. Marshall, 1905; ed. E. J. Fanshawe, 1907.
Historical Manuscripts Commission. The Manuscripts of J. M. Heathcote of Conington Castle. Ed. S. C. Lomas, Norwich, 1899. [Includes Fanshawe's correspondence.]
The Fourth Book of Vergil's Aeneid. Ed. A. L. Irvine, Oxford, 1929.

(c) Criticism

Mackail, J. W. Sir Richard Fanshawe. Trans. Royal Soc. Lit. 1909. [Rptd in Studies of English Poets, 1926.]
Harbage, A. Fanshawe and Hobbes's Leviathan. TLS. 30 June 1932.

NATHAN FIELD (1587–1620?)

(a) Plays

A Woman is a Weather-cocke. A New Comedy, As it was acted before the King in White-Hall. And divers times Privately at the White-Friers, By the Children of her Majesties Revels. 1612; ed. J. P. Collier (Five Old Plays, 1828); rptd T. White (Old English Drama, vol. II, 1830); *Hazlitt's Dodsley*, vol. XI; ed. A. W. Verity (Nero and Other Plays, 1888).

Amends for Ladies. A Comedie. As it was acted at the Blacke-Fryers, both by the Princes Servants, and the Lady Elizabeths. 1618 (bis); 1639 ('With the merry prankes of Moll Cut-Purse: Or, the humour of roaring'); ed. J. P. Collier (Five Old Plays, 1828); rptd T. White (Old English Drama, vol. ii, 1830); *Hazlitt's Dodsley*, vol. xi; ed. A. W. Verity (Nero and Other Plays, 1888).

[Field has also been conjecturally assigned a share in some of the Beaumont and Fletcher plays (see pp. 632–6 above), among others, Bonduca, Cupid's Revenge, The Honest Man's Fortune, Thierry and Theodoret, and Four Plays in One, as well as in the anon. The Distracted Emperor (Charlemagne) (see p. 652) and in Massinger's The Fatal Dowry (see p. 631).]

(b) Biography and Criticism

Halliwell[-Phillipps], J. O. The Remonstrance of Nathaniel Field addressed to a Preacher in Southwark, who had been arraigning against the Players at the Globe Theatre, in the Year 1616. Now first edited from the Original Manuscript. 1865.

Fleay, F. G. Annals of the Career of Nathaniel Field. E. Studien, xiii, 1890.

Beck, C. Philip Massinger, "The Fatall Dowry,' Einleitung zu einer neuen Ausgabe. Bayreuth, 1906.

Fischer, H. Nathaniel Fields Komödie 'Amends for Ladies.' Kiel, 1907.

Sykes, H. D. Nathaniel Field's Work in the Beaumont and Fletcher Plays. N. & Q. 19, 26 Feb., 5, 12 March 1921. [Rptd in Sidelights on Elizabethan Drama, 1924.]

Baldwin, T. W. Nathaniel Field and Robert Wilson. MLN. xli, 1926. [See TLS. 8, 15 April, 27 May, 3 June 1926 for criticism of J. J. O'Neill and W. W. Greg and Baldwin's reply.]

Chelli, Maurice. Étude sur la Collaboration de Massinger avec Fletcher et son Groupe. Paris, 1926.

Greg, W. W. Nathan Field and the Beaumont and Fletcher Folio of 1679. RES. iii, 1927.

Brinkley, R. F. Nathan and Nathaniel Field. MLN. xlii, 1927.

—— Nathan Field, the Actor-Playwright. New Haven, 1928.

Oliphant, E. H. C. The Plays of Beaumont and Fletcher. New Haven, 1927.

—— A Note [on F. L. Fenton, MLN. xlii, 1927]. MLN. xliii, 1928.

Lawrence, W. J. A Puzzling Point in A Woman is a Weathercock. TLS. 12 July 1928.

Aronstein, P. Das englische Renaissancedrama. Leipzig, 1929.

THOMAS FORDE (fl. 1647–61)
[See p. 726 below.]

SIR RALPH FREEMAN (1590?–1655)
Imperiale, A Tragedie. 1639 (signed R. F.); 1640; 1645. [See C. C. Gumm, Sir Ralph Freeman's Imperiale, in Studies in English Drama, ser. 1, ed. Allison Gaw, New York, 1917.]

HENRY GLAPTHORNE
(1610–after 1643)

(a) Collected Works
The Plays and Poems of Henry Glapthorne. Ed. [R. H. Shepherd], 2 vols. 1874.

(b) Plays
Argalus and Parthenia. As it hath been Acted at the Court before their Majesties: And At the Private-House in Drury-Lane, By their Majesties Servants. 1639.

The Tragedy of Albertus Wallenstein, Late Duke of Fridland, and Generall to the Emperor Ferdinand the second. The Scene, Egers. And acted with good Allowance at the Globe on the Banke-side, by his Majesties Servants. 1639; 1640; rptd C. Baldwin (Old English Drama, vol. ii, 1825).

The Hollander. A Comedy written 1635. Acted at the Cock-pit in Drury lane, by their Majesties Servants, with good allowance. And at the Court before both their Majesties. 1640.

Wit in a Constable. A Comedy written 1639. Acted at the Cock-pit in Drury-Lane, by their Majesties Servants, with good allowance. 1640.

The Ladies Priviledge. As it was Acted with good allowance at the Cock-pit in Drury-lane, And before their Majesties at White-Hall twice. By their Majesties Servants. 1640; rptd C. Baldwin (Old English Drama, vol. ii, 1825).

The Lady Mother. Ed. A. H. Bullen (Old English Plays, vol. ii, 1883). [BM. MS Egerton 1994.]

[For Revenge for Honour, see anonymous plays below, p. 653.]

(c) Criticism
Retrospective Rev. x, 1824, pp. 122–59.

Adams, J. Q. Some Notes on Henry Glapthorne's Wit in a Constable. JEGP. xiii, 1914.

Sykes, H. D. Glapthorne's Play: The Lady Mother. N. & Q. 29 Dec. 1923.

Walter, J. L. TLS. 19 Sept. 1936, p. 748.

THOMAS GOFFE (1591–1629)

The Raging Turke; or, Bajazet the Second. A Tragedie written by Thomas Goffe, of Christ-Church in Oxford, and Acted by the Students of the same house. 1631.

The Couragious Turke, Or, Amurath the First. A Tragedie. Written by Thomas Goffe of Christ-Church in Oxford, and Acted by the Students of the same House. 1632.

The Tragedie of Orestes, Written by Thomas Goffe of Christs Church in Oxford: And Acted by the Students of the same House. 1633.

Three Excellent Tragœdies. Viz. The Raging Turk. The Couragious Turk. And The Tragœdie of Orestes. The second Edition, carefully corrected by a friend of the Authors. 1656.

The Careless Shepherdess. A Tragi-Comedy Acted before the King & Queene, And at Salisbury-Court. 1656.

[See W. J. Lawrence, Goffe's The Careless Shepherdess, MLR. xiv, 1919, and The Authorship of The Careless Shepherdess, TLS. 24 July 1924; A. Thaler, Thomas Goffe's Præludium, MLN. xxvi, 1921; A. Harbage, TLS. 20 June 1936.

FRANCIS GOLDSMITH (1613–1655)

Hugo Grotius, his Sophompaneas, or Joseph. A Tragedy. With Annotations. 1652.

ROBERT GOMERSALL (1602–1646?)

[See p. 476 above.]

JOHN GOUGH

The Strange Discovery: A Tragi-Comedy. 1640 (bis).

WILLIAM HABINGTON (1605–1654)

[See p. 453 above.]

S[AMUEL] H[ARDING] (1616?–1670?)

Sicily and Naples, or, The Fatall Union. A Tragœdy. 1640.

WILLIAM HAWKINS (1600?–1637)

Apollo Shroving Composed for the Schollars of the Free-schoole of Hadleigh in Suffolke. And acted by them on Shrove-tuesday, 1626. [1627] (anon); ed. H. G. Rhoads, Philadelphia, 1936.

[Hawkins also pbd several collections of Latin verse.]

WILLIAM HEMING (1602–after 1634)

(a) Plays

The Fatal Contract, A French Tragedy. As it was Acted with great Applause by her Majesties Servants. 1653; 1654; 1661; 1687 (as The Eunuch); ed. O. Junge, Strasburg, 1912.

The Jewes Tragedy, or, Their Fatal and Final Overthrow by Vespatian and Titus his Son. Agreeable To the Authentick and Famous History of Josephus. 1662; ed. H. A. Cohn, Bang, vol. xl, 1913.

(b) Poems

The Time Poets. Ed. J. J. Parry, JEGP. xix, 1920.

William Hemminge's Elegy on Randolph's Finger. Ed. G. C. Moore Smith, Oxford, 1923.

(c) Biography and Criticism

Adams, J. Q. William Heminge and Shakespeare. MP. xii, 1914.

Heming's Time Poets. TLS. 24 May 1923.

Bentley, G. E. Players in the Parish of St Giles in the Fields. RES. vi, 1930.

FRANCIS JAQUES

The Queene of Corsica. A Tragedy. Written By Fran: Jaques Anno Dom: 1642. [BM. MS Lansdowne 807, ff. 1–28.]

JOHN JONES

Adrasta: Or, The Woman's Spleene, And Loves Conquest. A Tragi-comedie. Never Acted. 1635.

THOMAS JORDAN (1612?–1685)

Poetical varieties. 1637. [For Jordan's numerous later books of verse see DNB.]

Cupid his Coronation. In a Mask As it was Presented with good Approbation at the Spittle diverse tymes by Masters and yong Ladyes that were theyre scholers, in the year 1654. written by Thomas Jordan. [Bodley MS. Rawl. B. 165.]

Fancy's Festivals: a Masque. As it hath been privately presented by many civil persons of quality. And now at their requests newly printed. 1657. [A dramatic medley incorporating Cupid his Coronation.]

The Walks of Islington and Hogsdon, with The Humours of Woodstreet-Compter. A Comedy, As it was Acted 19. days together, with extraordinary Applause. 1657; [1663] (as Tricks of Youth, or The Walks of Islington and Hogsdon, with The Humours of Woodstreet-Compter).

Bacchus Festival: or, A New Medley: being a Musical Representation at the Entertainment of his Excellency the Lord General Monk at Vintners Hall, 12 April 1660. 1660.

A new droll: or The Counter Scuffle. The Second Part. 1663.

Money is an Asse A Comedy, As it hath been Acted with good Applause. 1668. [See G. Thorn-Drury, Jordan's Money is an Ass, RES. i, 1925. Jordan wrote the London civic pageants every year from 1671 to 1684.]

HENRY KILLIGREW (1613–1700)

The Conspiracy A Tragedy, As it was intended for the Nuptialls, of the Lord Charles Herbert, and the Lady Villers. 1638; 1653 (as Pallantus and Eudora).

THOMAS KILLIGREW (1612–1683)

The Prisoners and Claracilla. Two Tragæ-Comedies. As they were presented at the Phœnix in Drury-Lane, by her M^{tles} Servants. 1641.

Comedies, and Tragedies. 1664. [Includes, each with separate title-page and all dated 1663 except the two last which are dated 1664: (1) The Princess: Or, Love at first Sight; (2) The Parson's Wedding; (3) The Pilgrim; (4) The First Part of Cicilia and Clorinda, Or, Love in Arms; (5) The Second Part of Cicilia and Clorinda; (6) Thomaso, Or, The Wanderer; (7) The Second Part of Thomaso; (8) The First Part of Bellamiva her Dream; Or, The Love of Shadows; (9) The Second Part of Bellamira her Dream; (10) Claricilla; (11) The Prisoners. The Parson's Wedding is rptd in R. Dodsley's Collection of Old Plays, vol. IX, 1744, vol. XI, 1780, 1827, *Ancient British Drama*, vol. II, and *Hazlitt's Dodsley*, vol. XIV, and ed. M. Summers, Restoration Comedies, 1921. See A. Harbage, Thomas Killigrew, Cavalier Dramatist, Philadelphia, 1930.]

JOHN KIRKE (d. 1642?)

The Seven Champions of Christendome. Acted at the Cocke-pit, and at the Red-Bull in St. John's Streete, with a generall liking. 1638; rptd T. White (Old English Drama, vol. III, 1830); ed. G. E. Dawson, Western Reserve University Bulletin, XXXII, 1929. [See W. J. Lawrence, John Kirke, The Caroline Actor-Dramatist. Stud. Phil. XXI, 1924.]

R. K[IRKHAM]

Alfrede or Right Reinthron'd. Being a Tragicomedie. 1659. [Bodley MS Rawl. Poet. 80.]

RALPH KNEVET (1600–1671)

(a) *Play*

Rhodon and Iris. A Pastorall, as it was Presented at the Florists Feast in Norwich May 3. 1631. 1631.

(b) *Other Writings*

Στρατιωτικόν, or a discourse of militarie discipline. 1628.

Funerall elegies; to the memory of Lady Paston [etc.]. 1637.

A Gallery to the Temple. Lyricall Poems upon Sacred Occasions. [BM. Add. MS 27447.]

SIR WILLIAM LOWER (1600?–1662)

The Phaenix in her flames. A Tragedy. 1639.

Polyeuctes, Or The Martyr. A Tragedy. 1655. [From Corneille.]

Horatius: A Roman Tragedie. 1656. [From Corneille.]

The Enchanted Lovers: A Pastoral. Hague, 1658 (re-issued 1661 and in Three New Playes, 1661); ed. W. B. Gates (The Dramatic Works and Translations of Sir William Lower, Philadelphia, 1932).

The Noble Ingratitude. A Pastoral-Tragi-Comedy. Hague, 1659 (re-issued 1661 in Three New Playes). [From Quinault.]

The Amourous Fantasme, A Tragi-Comedy. Hague, 1660 (re-issued 1661 in Three New Playes). [From Quinault.]

Don Japhet of Armenia. [BM. Add. MS 28723. From Scarron.]

Three Dorothies, or Jodelet Boxed. [MS formerly in Skeffington Hall. From Scarron.]

JAMES MABBE (1572–1642?)

The Spanish Bawd, represented in Celestina, or the Tragicke-Comedy of Calisto and Melibea. 1631 (anon.); ed. H. W. Allen; rptd 1923. [From the Spanish of Fernando de Rojas.]

LEWIS MACHIN (*fl.* 1608)

[See p. 706 below.]

COSMO MANUCHE (or MANUCCI)

The Just General: A tragi-Comedy. 1652.

The Bastard: a Tragedy. 1652 (anon.). [Usually assigned to Manuche, probably in error.]

The Loyal Lovers: a Tragi-comedy. 1652.

The Feast. [*c.* 1664. MS Castle Ashby, Northampton, and MS Worcester College, Oxford.]

The Banish'd Shepheardess. [Huntington Lib. MS EL 8395 (holograph).]

[For other MS plays by Manuche see DNB. Supplement 1, and the corrective note in the Index and Epitome. See also B. M. Wagner, MS Plays of the 17th Century, TLS. 4 Oct. 1934.]

GERVASE MARKHAM (1568?–1637)

[See p. 706 below.]

SHAKERLEY MARMION (1603–1639)

(a) *Collected Works*

The Dramatic Works of Shakerley Marmion. Ed. J. Maidment and W. H. Logan, 1875.

(b) Plays

Hollands Leaguer. An Excellent Comedy As it hath bin lately and often Acted with great applause, by the high and mighty Prince Charles his Servants; at the private house in Salisbury Court. 1632.

A Fine Companion. Acted before the King and Queene at White-Hall, And sundrie times with great applause at the private House in Salisbury Court, By the Prince his Servants. 1633.

The Antiquary. A Comedy, Acted by Her Majesties Servants at the Cock-Pit. 1641; ed. R. Dodsley (Collection of Old Plays, vol. VII, 1744); ed. I. Reed (Dodsley's Old Plays, vol. x, 1780); *Ancient British Drama*, vol. x; ed. J. P. Collier (Dodsley's Old Plays, vol. x, 1826); *Hazlitt's Dodsley*, vol. XIII.

The Soddered Citizen. Ed. (from MS in private hands) J. H. P. Pafford and W. W. Greg, *Malone Soc.* 1936. [Really by John Clavell?]

JOHN MASON (b. 1582)

The Turke. A Worthie Tragedie. As it hath bene divers times acted by the Children of his Majesties Revels. 1610; 1632 (as An Excellent Tragedy of Mulleasses the Turke, and Borgias Governour of Florence); ed. J. Q. Adams, *Bang*, vol. XXXVII, 1913. [See G. C. Moore Smith, John Mason and Edward Sharpham, MLR. VIII, 1913.]

JOHN MASON (fl. 1648)

Princeps Rhetoricus or πιλομαχια. The Combat of Caps. 1648. [An academic allegory performed at a boys' school in Surrey, 21 Dec. 1647. See S. C. Northrup, On a School Play of 1648, E. Studien, XLV, 1913.]

THOMAS MAY (1595–1650)

The Heire an excellent Comedie. As it was lately Acted by the Company of the Revels. 1622; 1633 (*bis*); rptd R. Dodsley (Collection of Old Plays, vol. VII, 1744); ed. I. Reed (Dodsley's Old Plays, vol. VIII, 1780); *Ancient British Drama*, vol. I; ed. J. P. Collier, Dodsley's Old Plays, vol. VIII, 1825; *Hazlitt's Dodsley*, vol. XI.

The Tragedy of Antigone, The Theban Princesse. 1631.

The Tragedie of Cleopatra Queen of Ægypt. Acted 1626. 1639; 1654 (with Agrippina Empress of Rome, as Two Tragedies).

The Tragedy of Julia Agrippina; Empresse of Rome. By T. M. Esq. 1639; 1654 (with Cleopatra Queene of Ægypt, as Two Tragedies); ed. F. E. Schmid, *Bang*, vol. XLIII, 1914.

The Old Couple. A Comedy. 1658; rptd R. Dodsley (Collection of Old Plays, vol. VII, 1744); ed. I. Reed (Dodsley's Old Plays, vol. x, 1780); *Ancient British Drama*, vol. III; ed. J. P. Collier (Dodsley's Old Plays, vol. x, 1826); *Hazlitt's Dodsley*, vol. XII.

[See A. G. Chester, Thomas May: Man of Letters, Philadelphia, 1932. This notes the German dissertations on May, and provides a complete bibliography. See also C. H. Wilkinson, RES. XI, 1935, pp. 195–8. For the historical and political works see p. 839 below.]

JASPER MAYNE (1604–1672)

The Citye Match. A Comoedye. Presented to the King and Queene at White-Hall. Acted since at Black-Friers by His Majesties Servants. 1639 (anon.); 1658 and 1659 (with The Amorous Warre, as Two Plaies); 1659; rptd R. Dodsley (Collection of Old Plays, vol. x, 1744); ed. I. Reed (Dodsley's Old Plays, vol. x, 1780); *Ancient British Drama*, vol. II; ed. J. P. Collier (Dodsley's Old Plays, vol. IX, 1825); *Hazlitt's Dodsley*, vol. XIII.

The Amorous Warre. A Tragi-Comœdy. 1648 (anon.); 1658 and 1659 (with The City Match, as Two Plaies); 1659.

[For Mayne's sermons see p. 698 below.]

THOMAS MERITON (b. 1638)

The Wandring Lover. A Tragy-Comedie Being Acted severall times privately at sundry places by the Author and his friends with Great Applause. 1658.

Love and War, A Tragedy. 1658.

WALTER MONTAGU (1603?–1677)

The Shepheard's Paradise. A Comedy. Privately Acted before the Late King Charles by the Queen's Majesty, and Ladies of Honour. 1629 (for 1659; re-issued with date corrected).

WALTER MOUNTFORT (fl. 1632)

The Launchinge of the Mary or The Seamans honest wyfe. Ed. J. H. Walter and W. W. Greg, *Malone Soc.* 1933. [BM. MS Egerton 1994. See A. H. Bullen, Old English Plays, vol. II, 1882; F. S. Boas, Shakespeare and the Universities, 1923.]

THOMAS NABBES (1605–1641)

(a) Collected Plays

Plays, Masques, Epigrams, Elegies, and Epithalamiums. 1639.

The Works of Thomas Nabbes. Ed. A. H. Bullen. [In Old English Plays, N.S. vols. I and II, 1887.]

(b) Separate Plays

Hannibal and Scipio. An Historicall Tragedy Acted in the yeare 1635. by the Queenes Majesties Servants, at their Private house in Drury-Lane. 1637; 1639 (in Plays, Masques).

Microcosmus. A Morall Maske, Presented with generall liking, at the private house in Salisbury Court. 1637; 1639 (in Plays, Masques); ed. R. Dodsley (Collection of Old Plays, vol. v, 1744); ed. I. Reed (Dodsley's Old Plays, vol. IX, 1780); Ancient British Drama, vol. II; ed. J. P. Collier (Dodsley's Old Plays, vol. IX, 1825).

Covent-Garden: A Pleasant Comedie: Acted in the yeare, MDCXXXII. By the Queenes Majesties Servants. 1638; 1639; 1639 (in Plays, Masques).

A Presentation Intended for the Prince his Highnesse on his Birthday, the 29 of May, 1638. 1638; 1639; 1639 (in Plays, Masques).

The Springs Glorie. Vindicating Love by temperance. Moralized in a Maske. With other Poems, Epigrams, Elegies, and Epithalamiums. 1638 (re-issued 1639); 1639 (in Plays, Masques).

Totenham-Court. A Pleasant Comedie: Acted in the Yeare MDCXXXIII. At the private House in Salisbury-Court. 1638; 1639 (bis); 1639 (in Plays, Masques); 1709.

The Bride, A Comedie. Acted in the yeere 1638. at the private house in Drury-lane by their Majesties Servants. 1639 (in Plays, Masques); 1640.

The Unfortunate Mother: A Tragedie. Never acted; but set downe according to the intention of the Author. 1639 (in Plays, Masques); 1640.

(c) Criticism

Swinburne, A. C. Thomas Nabbes. [In Contemporaries of Shakespeare, 1919.]

Lawrence, W. J. Early Substantive Masques. TLS. 8 Dec. 1921.

Koch, J. Thomas Nabbes, ein zu wenig beachteter Dichter. Ang. XLVII, 1923.

—— Echte und 'unechte' Masken. E. Studien, LVIII, 1924.

THOMAS NEWMAN

The Two First Comedies of Terence called Andria, and the Eunuch newly Englished. Fitted for Schollers Private Action in their Schooles. 1627.

WILLIAM PEAPS

Love In it's Extasie: Or, The large Prerogative. A kind of Royall Pastorall written long since. 1649.

EDMUND PRESTWICH

Hippolytus. 1651. [A rhymed trn from Seneca.]

The Hectors: or the False Challenge. A Comedy Written in the Year MDCLV. The Scene London. 1656 (anon.). [Attrib. to Prestwich by Phillips and Winstanley.]

FRANCIS QUARLES (1592–1644)

[See p. 450 above.]

THOMAS RAWLINS (1620?–1670)

The Rebellion: A Tragedy: As it was acted nine dayes together, and divers times since with good applause, by his Majesties Company of Revells. 1640 (re-issued 1654?); Ancient British Drama, vol. III; Hazlitt's Dodsley, vol. XIV.

[HENRY REYNOLDS]

Torquato Tasso's Aminta Englisht. To this is added Ariadne's Complaint in imitation of Anguillara. 1628.

NATHANIEL RICHARDS (1612?–1654?)

[See p. 477 above.]

WILLIAM RIDER

The Twins. A Tragi-Comedy. Acted at the Private House in Salisbury Court, with general Applause. 1655.

JOSEPH RUTTER

The Shepheards Holy-Day. A Pastorall Tragi-Comaedie. Acted Before Both their Majesties At White-Hall, by the Queenes Servants. With an Elegie on the death of the most noble Lady, the Lady Venetia Digby. 1635 (signed J. R.); Hazlitt's Dodsley, vol. XII.

The Cid, A Tragi comedy, out of French made English: And acted before their Majesties at Court, and on the Cock-pit Stage in Drury-lane by the servants to both their Majesties. 1637; 1650 ('Corrected and Amended'). [From Corneille.]

The Second Part of the Cid. 1640.

WILLIAM SAMPSON (1590?–1636?)

The true Tragedy Of Herod and Antipater: With the Death of faire Marriam. According to Josephus, the learned and famous Jew. As it hath beene of late, divers times publiquely Acted (with great Applause) at the Red Bull, by the Company of his Majesties Revels. Written by Gervase Markham and William Sampson Gentlemen. 1622 (bis). [See A. M. Silbermann, Untersuchungen über die Quellen, Würzburg, 1929. See also under Lady Elizabeth Cary, p. 642 above.]

The Vow Breaker. Or, The Faire Maide of Clifton. In Notinghamshire as it hath beene divers times Acted by severall Companies with great applause. 1636; ed. H. Wallrath, *Bang*, vol. XLII, 1914.

GEORGE SANDYS (1578–1644)

[See p. 444 above.]

LEWIS SHARPE

The Noble Stranger. As it was Acted at the Private House in Salisbury Court, by her Majesties Servants. 1640.

EDWARD SHARPHAM (1576–1608)

The Fleire. As it hath beene often played in the Blacke-Fryers by the Children of the Reuells. 1607; 1610; 1615; 1631; ed. H. Nibbe, *Bang*, vol. XXXVI, 1912.

Cupids Whirligig, As it hath bene sundry times Acted by the Children of the King's Majesties Revels. 1607; 1611; 1616; 1630; ed. A. Nicoll, 1926.

[See G. C. Moore Smith, Edward Sharpham, N. & Q. 11 July 1908, and John Mason and Edward Sharpham, MLR. vol. VIII, 1913; M. W. Sampson, The Plays of Edward Sharpham in Studies in Language and Literature in Celebration of the 70th Birthday of J. M. Hart, New York, 1910; C. Leech, The Plays of Edward Sharpham, RES. XI, 1935.]

SIR EDWARD SHERBURNE (1618–1702)

[See vol. II of this work.]

HENRY SHIRLEY (d. 1627)

The Martyr'd Souldier: As it was sundry times Acted with generall applause at the Private house in Drury lane, and at other publicke Theaters. By the Queenes Majesties servants. 1638; ed. A. H. Bullen (Old English Plays, vol. I, 1882). [See A. M. Clark, Thomas Heywood, Playwright and Miscellanist, Oxford, 1931; F. G. Fleay, Annals of the Careers of James and Henry Shirley, Ang. VIII, 1885.]

J[ONATHON] S[IDNAM] (*fl.* 1630–1655)

Filli Di Sciro. Or Phillis of Scyros. An Excellent Pastorall. 1655. [From Bonarelli.]

Il Pastor Fido. [BM. Add. MS 29493. From Guarini.]

W[ENTWORTH?] SMITH (*fl.* 1601–23)

The Hector of Germaine, or the Palsgrave, Prime Elector. A New Play, an Honourable Hystorie. As it hath beene publikely Acted at the Red Bull, and at the Curtaine, by a Companie of Young men of this Citie. With new Additions. 1615; ed. L. W. Payne, Philadelphia, 1906.

JOHN STEPHENS (*fl.* 1615)

Cinthias Revenge: or Maenanders Extasie. 1613. [See P. Simpson, The Authorship and Original Issue of Cinthia's Revenge, MLR. II, 1907.]

SIR JOHN SUCKLING (1609–1642)

[See p. 456 above.]

GILBERT SWINHOE

The Tragedy of The Unhappy Fair Irene. 1658.

ROBERT TAILOR (*fl.* 1614)

The Hogge hath lost his Pearle. A Comedy. Divers times Publikely acted, by certaine London Prentices. 1614; rptd R. Dodsley (Collection of Old Plays, vol. III, 1744); ed. I. Reed (Dodsley's Old Plays, vol. VI, 1780); *Ancient British Drama*, vol. III; ed. J. P. Collier (Dodsley's Old Plays, vol. VI, 1825); *Hazlitt's Dodsley*, vol. XI. [See E. N. Albright, A Stage Cartoon of the Mayor of London in 1613, in Manly Anniversary Studies, Chicago, 1923.]

SIR GILBERT TALBOT (*fl.* 1657)

Fillis of Sciros. [BM. Add. MS 12128 (autograph); another copy, Bodley MS Rawl. Poet. 130. From Bonarelli.]

JOHN TATHAM (d. 1664)

(a) Collected Plays

Dramatic Works. Ed. J. Maidment and W. H. Logan, Edinburgh, 1879.

(b) Separate Plays

Love Crownes the End. A Pastorall presented by the Scollers of Bingham in the County of Nottingham, in the yeare 1632. 1640 (in Fancies Theater); 1657 (in new edn of preceding entitled The Mirrour of Fancies).

The Distracted State. A tragedy. Written in the Yeer 1641. By J. T. 1651.

The Scots Figgaries: or A Knot of Knaves. A Comedy. 1652.

The Rump: Or The Mirrour of the late Times, A New Comedy, Acted at Dorset-Court. 1660; 1661 ('Newly Corrected, with Additions').

[Tatham wrote the London civic pageants yearly from 1657 to 1664.]

(c) Poems

Fancies Theater. 1640; 1657 (as The Mirrour of Fancies).

Ostella. 1650.

AURELIAN TOWNSEND (*fl.* 1601–43)

[For Townsend's masques see above, p. 478.]

C[HRISTOPHER] W[ASE] (1625?–1690)

Electra. 1649. [From Sophocles.]

GEORGE WILKINS (*fl.* 1605–1608)

(a) Play

The Miseries of Inforst Mariage. As it is now playd by his Majesties Servants. 1607; 1611; 1629; 1637; ed. I. Reed (Dodsley's Old Plays, vol. v, 1780); *Ancient British Drama*, vol. ii; ed. J. P. Collier (Dodsley's Old Plays, vol. v, 1825); *Hazlitt's Dodsley*, vol. ix; *TFT.* 1913.

[Wilkins probably wrote Acts 1, 2 of Shakespeare's Pericles; he has also been assigned scenes in Shakespeare's Timon of Athens and the anon. The Yorkshire Tragedy.]

(b) Other Writings

Three Miseries of Barbary: plague, famine, civill warre. [1606?]
Jests to make you Merie. 1607. [With Dekker.]
The Painfull Adventures of Pericles Prince of Tyre. 1608; ed. T. Mommsen, Oldenburg, 1857.

(c) Criticism

Sykes, H. D. Sidelights on Shakespeare. 1919.
Golding, S. R. Day and Wilkins as Collaborators. N. & Q. 12, 19 June 1926.
Allen, P. Shakespeare, Wilkins and Jonson as Borrowers. 1928.
Clark, A. M. Thomas Heywood, Playwright and Miscellanist. Oxford, 1931.
Spiker, S. George Wilkins and the Authorship of Pericles. Stud. Phil. xxx, 1933.

LEONARD WILLAN (*fl.* 1649–1670)

Astræa, or, True Love's Myrrour. a Pastoral. 1651.
Orgula: or the Fatall Error. a Tragedy Composed by L. W. 1658. [See M. L. Birkett, Five Minor Poets, TLS. 29 Sept. 1932.]

[For Willan's version of Aesop see p. 799 below.]

ARTHUR WILSON (1595–1652)

The Inconstant Ladie. Acted at Blackfriers. The Scæne Burgundie. Ed. (from Bodley MS Rawl. Poet. 9 or 128) P. Bliss, Oxford, 1814.
The Swisser. Acted at the Blackfriers, 1631. Ed. (from BM. Add. MS 36759) A. Feuillerat, Paris, 1904.
The Corporal. [Bodley MS Douce c. 2. An early 18th century fragment of Wilson's lost play, ending in Act ii, Scene 1; for earlier fragments of this play, see B. M. Wagner, MS. Plays of the 17th Century, TLS. 4 Oct. 1934.]

[See Wilson's God's Providence in the Tract of my Life, ed. F. Peck (Desiderata Curiosa, vol. ii, 1735); W. R., Arthur Wilson's play The Swisser, Athenaeum, 14 Feb. 1903. See also p. 838 below.]

ANONYMOUS PLAYS

The Tragedy of Alphonsus Emperour of Germany. As it hath been very often Acted at the Privat house in Black-Friers. By George Chapman Gent. 1654; ed. K. Elze, Leipzig, 1867; ed. H. F. Schwarz, New York, 1913. [Also included in collected edns of Chapman (see p. 609 above), though almost certainly not his. See H. D. Sykes, Sidelights on Elizabethan Drama, 1924 (who assigns to Peele), and F. T. Bowers and T. Starck, Harvard Stud. xv, 1933, pp. 147–89.]
Andromana, the Merchant's Wife. By J. S. 1660; rptd R. Dodsley (Collection of Old Plays, vol. xi, 1744); ed. I. Reed (Dodsley's Old Plays, vol. xi, 1780); *Ancient British Drama*, vol. iii; *Hazlitt's Dodsley*, vol. xiv.
The Tragedy of Sir John Van Olden Barnavelt. Ed. (from BM. Add. MS 18653) A. H. Bullen (Old English Plays, vol. ii, 1883); ed. W. P. Frijlinck, Amsterdam, 1922. [See S. C. Chew, Lycidas and the Play of Barnavelt, MLN. xxxviii, 1923.]
The Bloodie Banquet. A Tragedie. By T. D. 1620 (for 1630?); 1639; *TFT.* 1914. [See E. H. C. Oliphant and W. W. Greg, TLS. 17, 24 Dec. 1925.]
The Famous Tragedie of King Charles I. Basely Butchered. 1649.
Marcus Tullius Cicero. That Famous Roman Orator his Tragedy. 1651.
The Tragedie of Claudius Tiberius Nero, Rome's greatest Tyrant. Truly represented out of the purest Records of those times. 1607; *TFT.* 1913; ed. W. W. Greg, *Malone Soc.* 1914.
The Costlie Whore. A Comicall Historie, Acted by the Companie of the Revels. 1633; ed. A. H. Bullen (Old English Plays, N.S. vol. ii, 1887). [See W. J. Lawrence and Walter Worrall, MLR. xvii, 1922.]
A Cure for a Cuckold. A pleasant Comedy. As it hath been several times Acted with great Applause. Written by John Webster and William Rowley. 1661 (also issued with The Thracian Wonder, with a general title-page: Two New Playes, 1661). [The attribution of authorship has been generally denied; see under Webster above, p. 630.]
The Cyprian Conqueror, or The Faithless Relict. [BM. MS Sloane 3709. See J. Q. Adams, MLN. xxiii, 1908.]
Dick of Devonshire. Ed. (from BM. MS Egerton 1994) A. H. Bullen (Old English Plays, vol. ii, 1883).
The disloyal favourite, or the tragedy of Mettellus. [Bodley MS Rawl. D. 1361, ff. 285–306.]

The Distracted Emperor. A Tragi-Comedy. Ed. A. H. Bullen (Old English Plays, vol. III, 1884); ed. F. L. Schoell, 1920. [BM. MS Egerton 1994. The play, which has no title in the MS, is sometimes called Charlemagne. See F. L. Schoell, Un Drame élisabéthain anonyme, Charlemagne, Revue germanique, VIII, 1912; F. S. Boas, Shakespeare and the Universities, 1923.]

Everie Woman in her Humor. 1609; ed. A. H. Bullen (Old English Plays, vol. IV, 1885); TFT. 1913. [See J. Q. Adams, Every Woman in Her Humour and The Dumb Knight, MP. x, 1913.]

The Extravagant Shepherd. A Pastorall Comedie. By T. R. 1654. [From Thomas Corneille.]

The Faire Maide of Bristow. As it was plaide at Hampton, before the King and Queenes most excellent Majesties. 1605; ed. A. H. Quinn, Philadelphia, 1902; TFT. 1912. [See Sh. Jb. XXXI, 1895, for a German trn by L. Tieck, ed. J. Bolte. See also J. le G. Brereton, Notes on The Fair Maid of Bristowe, MLR. III, 1907.]

The Fayre Mayde of the Exchange. 1607. [See under Heywood, p. 623 above.]

The Fary Knight, or Oberon the Second. [c. 1640. Folger Shakespeare Lib. MS 46. 1.]

The Faithful Friends. [Dyce MS 10. Ptd in Weber's and Dyce's edns of Beaumont and Fletcher (see p. 633 above).]

The Fatall Maryage or A second Lucreatya. [BM. MS Egerton 1994. See A. H. Bullen, Old English Plays, vol. II, 1882; W. W. Greg, Dramatic Documents from the Elizabethan Playhouses, vol. I, 1931.

The Female Rebellion. Ed. Alexander Smith, 1872. [Hunterian Museum MS. Another copy, Bodley MS Tanner 466, contains a coeval note to the initialled H. B. ascribing the play to Henry Birkhead. This may well be a mistake for Burkhead.]

The Argument of the Pastorall of Florimene, with the Description of the Scœnes and Intermedii. Presented before the Kings Majesty in the Hall at Whitehall the 21. of December. 1635.

The Ghost Or The Woman wears the Breeches. A Comedy Written in the Year MDCXL. 1653.

The Gossip's Braule; or, The Women weare the Breeches. A mock Comedy. 1655.

The Governor. A Tragi Comedy. 1656. [BM. Add. MS 10419. Not the play by Sir Cornelius Formido once in the Warburton Collection.]

The Tragical History of Guy, Earl of Warwick. Written by B. J. 1661.

Histrio-Mastix. Or, the Player whipt. 1610; ed. R. Simpson (The School of Shakespeare,

vol. II, 1878); TFT. 1912. [See F. Hoppe, Histriomastix-Studien, Breslau, 1906. See also under Marston, p. 627 above.]

The Honest Lawyer. Acted By The Queenes Majesties Servants. Written by S. S. 1616; TFT. 1914.

The King and Queenes Entertainement at Richmond. In a Masque. Oxford, 1636; ed. W. Bang and R. Brotanek, Bang, vol. II, 1903.

The Knave in Graine, New Vampt. A witty Comedy, Acted at the Fortune many dayes together with great Applause. Written by J. D. Gent. 1640.

Lady Alimony, or the Alimony Lady, an excellent pleasant new Comedy, duly authorized, daily acted, and frequently followed. 1659; Hazlitt's Dodsley, vol. XIV.

The London Chaunticleres. A Witty Comoedy, Full of Various and Delightfull Mirth. Often Acted with Great Applause And never before Published. 1659; Hazlitt's Dodsley, vol. XII.

The London Prodigall. 1605. [See under Shakespeare, p. 579 above.]

Loves Changelinges Change. [BM. MS Egerton 1994. See A. H. Bullen, Old English Plays, vol. II, 1882; F. S. Boas, Shakespeare and the Universities, 1923.]

Love's Victorie. Ed. (from MS in private hands probably identical with Huntington Lib. MS HM 600) J. O. Halliwell[-Phillipps] (Brief Description of the Ancient & Modern Manuscripts Preserved in the Public Library, Plymouth: To which are added some fragments of Early Literature hitherto Unpublished, 1853).

The Marriage Broker, or The Pander. By M. W. [In Gratiae Theatrales, or, A choice Ternary of English plays. Composed upon especial occasions by several ingenious persons, 1662. A collection of three plays, including Haughton's Grim the Collier of Croyden; and Thorney Abbey. All appear to be old plays, with texts sophisticated.]

The Merry Devill of Edmonton. As it hath beene sundry times Acted, by his Majesties Servants, at the Globe. 1608; 1612; 1617; 1626; 1631; 1655; Hazlitt's Dodsley, vol. x; ed. H. Walker, 1897 (Temple Dramatists); TFT. 1911; ed. J. M. Manly, Gayley, vol. II. [Also included in the Shakespeare Apocrypha collections (see p. 576 above) to whom the play was assigned in the Stationers' Register entry for 1653.]

Nebuchadnezzars Fierie Furnace. Ed. (from BM. MS Harl. 7578) M. Rösler, Bang, N.S. vol. XII, 1936. [By Joshua Sylvester?]

The Tragedy of Nero. Newly Written. 1624; 1633; ed. (from BM. MS Egerton 1994) A. H. Bullen (Old English Plays, vol. I,

1882); ed. H. P. Horne (Nero and Other Plays, 1888). [See A. H. Bullen, Old English Plays, vol. II, 1882; W. G. Rutherford, The Anonymous Play of Nero, Athenaeum, 3 Nov. 1906; R. S. Forsythe, An Indebtedness of Nero to the 3rd Part of King Henry VI, MLN. xxv, 1910; F. E. Schmid, Die Tragödie Nero und Thomas May, *Bang*, vol. XLIII, 1914; F. S. Boas, Shakespeare and the Universities, 1923.]

No-Body and Some-Body. [1606?] [See under Heywood, p. 623 above.]

The Partiall Law. Ed. (from MS, now Folger Shakespeare Lib. MS 553. 1) B. Dobell, 1908.

Pelopidarum Secunda. [BM. MS Harl. 5110. A tragedy in English acted at Winchester College.]

The Prince of Priggs Revels; or, the Practices of that grand Thief, Captain James Hind. By J. S. 1651.

The Puritaine Or The Widdow of Watling-streete. 1607. [See under Shakespeare, p. 579 above.]

The Queen, Or The Excellency Of Her Sex. An Excellent old Play. Found out by a Person of Honour, and given to the Publisher, Alexander Goughe. 1653; ed. W. Bang, *Bang*, vol. XIII, 1906. [Bang attributes to Ford, as does H. D. Sykes, Sidelights on Elizabethan Drama, 1924.]

The Rebellion of Naples, or the Tragedy of Massenello Commonly so called: But Rightly Tomaso Aniello di Malfa Generall of the Neopolitans. Written by a Gentleman who was an eye-witness where this was really acted upon that bloudy State the streets of Naples. MDCXLVII. 1649. [Dedication signed T. B.]

Revenge for Honour: A Tragedie, by George Chapman. 1654. [Included in some of the collected edns of Chapman (see p. 609 above), though the ascription to him is probably incorrect. See H. D. Sykes, N. & Q. 20 May 1916; C. F. Beckingham, RES. xi, 1935; F. T. Bowers, MLN. LII, 1937.]

The Second Maiden's Tragedy. Ed. C. Baldwin (Old English Drama, vol. I, 1824); ed. R. H. Shepherd (Chapman's Works, vol. III, 1875); *Hazlitt's Dodsley*, vol. x; ed. W. W. Greg, *Malone Soc.* 1909. [BM. MS Lansdowne 807, f. 29. See W. Nicholson, MLN. xxvII, 1912.]

Sir Gyles Goosecappe. Knight. A Comedie presented by the Chil: of the Chappell. 1606; 1636; ed. A. H. Bullen (Old English Plays, vol. III, 1884); ed. W. Bang and R. Brotanek, *Bang*, vol. XXVI, 1909; *TFT.* 1912; ed. T. M. Parrott (The Comedies of George Chapman, 1914). [See G. L. Kittredge, Notes on Elizabethan Plays,

JEGP. I, 1898; T. M. Parrott, The Authorship of Sir Giles Goosecap, MP. IV, 1906.]

Swetnam, The Woman-hater, Arraigned by Women. A new Comedie, Acted at the Red Bull, by the late Queenes Servants. 1620; ed. A. B. Grosart, 1880; *TFT.* 1914.

Tell Tale. [Dulwich College MS. See G. F. Warner, Catalogue of Dulwich College, 1881; A. H. Bullen, Old English Plays, vol. II, 1882.]

Thorney Abbey. By T. W. 1662. [In Gratiae Theatrales; see above, under The Marriage Broker. See E. H. C. Oliphant, MP. VIII, 1910.]

The Thracian Wonder. A Comical History. Written by John Webster and William Rowley. 1661. [Almost certainly not by either Webster or Rowley. See J. Q. Adams, MP. III, 1906; J. le G. Brereton, MLR. II, 1906; O. L. Hatcher, MLN. xxIII, 1908. Issued with A Cure for a Cuckold (see above) as Two New Playes.]

[Time's Triumph.] [BM. MS Egerton 1994, ff. 212–223. A titleless dramatic allegory dated 5 Aug. 1643. See J. D. Jump, RES. xI, 1935, pp. 186–91, who traces it in part to Chapman.]

Titus. Or the Palm of Christian Courage to be exhibited by the Scholars of the Society of Jesus at Kilkenny. A.D. 1644. Waterford, 1644.

The True Tragi-Comedie formarly acted at court and now revived by ane eie witnes. [BM. Add. MS 25348. A treatment of the divorce of Robert Carr and Lady Frances Howard; written after 1634.]

The History of the tryall of Chevalry, With the life and death of Cavaliero Dicke Bowyer. As it hath bin lately acted by the right Honourable the Earle of Darby his servants. 1605; ed. A. H. Bullen (Old English Plays, vol. III, 1884); *TFT.* 1912. [See C. R. Baskervill, Sidney's Arcadia and The Trial of Chivalry, MP. x, 1912; F. L. Jones, PMLA. xLI, 1926.]

A Pleasant Comedie Called The Two Merry Milke-maids. Or, The best words weare the Garland. As it was Acted before the King, with generall Approbation, by the Companie of the Revels. By I. C. 1620; 1661; *TFT.* 1914.

The Two Noble Ladies. Ed. (from BM. MS Egerton 1994) R. G. Rhoads and W. W. Greg, *Malone Soc.* 1930. [See A. H. Bullen, Old English Plays, vol. II, 1882; F. S. Boas, Shakespeare and the Universities, 1923.]

Two Wise Men and all the rest fooles: Or A comicall morall, censuring the follies of this age, as it hath beene diverse times acted. 1619; *TFT.* 1913. [Also rptd in The Works of George Chapman, ed. R. H. Shepherd, 1874–5, 1889.]

Tyranicall-Government Anatomized: or, A Discourse concerning Evil-Councellors. Being The Life and Death of John the Baptist. 1643; ed. J. T. T. Brown (George Buchanan Glasgow Quatercentenary Studies, Glasgow, 1907). [A trn of Buchanan's Baptistes, sometimes attrib. to Milton.]

The Valiant Scot. By J. W. Gent. 1637. [Tragedy. See T. Hach, Über das Drama The Valiant Scot, Erlangen, 1901; J. L. Carver, The Valiant Scot, in Studies in English Drama, ser. 1, ed. A. Gaw, New York, 1917.]

The Valiant Welshman, Or The True Chronicle History of the life and valiant deedes of Caradoc the Great, King of Cambria, now called Wales. As it hath beene sundry times Acted by the Prince of Wales his servants. Written by R. A. Gent. 1615; 1663; ed. V. Kreb, Munich, 1902; *TFT*. 1913. [See W. J. Lawrence, Welsh Portraiture in Elizabethan Drama, TLS. 9 Nov. 1922, and Welsh Song in Elizabethan Drama, TLS. 7 Dec. 1922; H. D. Sykes, The Dramatic Work of Henry Chettle, N. & Q. 7 April, 19 May 1923.]

The Wasp. [MS at Alnwick Castle; *Malone Soc.* edn in preparation.]

The Welsh Ambassador. Ed. W. W. Greg and H. Littledale, *Malone Soc.* 1921. [Cardiff Public Lib. MS. See B. Lloyd, The Noble Soldier and The Welsh Ambassador, RES. III, 1927, and K. M. Lea, edn of The Parliament of Love, *Malone Soc.* 1928.]

Whimsies of Senor Hidalgo, or The Masculine Bride. [BM. MS Harl. 5152.]

The White Ethiopian. [BM. MS Harl. 7313.]

Wine, Beere, and Ale. Together by the Eares. A Dialogue Written first in Dutch by Gallobelgicus and faithfully translated by Mercurius Britannicus. 1629; 1630 (enlarged as Wine, Beere, Ale, and Tobacco Contending for Superiority); 1658; rptd J. O. Halliwell[-Phillipps], 1854; ed. J. H. Hanford, Stud. Phil. XII, 1915. [Not a trn but an original interlude, suited to actual performance.]

A Pleasant Comoedie, Wherein is merily shewen: The wit of a Woman. 1604; *TFT*. 1912; ed. W. W. Greg, *Malone Soc.* 1913.

The World's Idol, or Plutus the God of Wealth. By H. B. B. 1659. [From Aristophanes.]

[Xamolxis and Perindo.] [BM. Add. MS 29496. A titleless play of the 17th century.]

A Yorkshire Tragedy. 1608. [See under Shakespeare, p. 580 above.]

A. M. C. and A. H.

XII. UNIVERSITY PLAYS, 1500–1642

A. GENERAL AUTHORITIES

Courtney, W. L. Oxford Plays down to the Restoration. N. & Q. 11 Dec. 1886.

Plummer, C. Elizabethan Oxford. Reprints of Rare Tracts. Oxford Hist. Soc. 1887.

The Latin Plays acted before the University of Cambridge. Retrospective Rev. XII, 1825.

Lee, M. L. Narcissus. A Twelfe Night Merriment. 1893. [The Introduction contains a list of Oxford plays.]

Churchill, G. B. and Keller, W. Die lateinischen Universitäts-Dramen Englands in der Zeit der Königin Elizabeth. Mit Vorwort von A. Brandl. Sh. Jb. XXXIV, 1898. [This article is referred to in the present bibliography as Sh. Jb. XXXIV.]

Greg, W. W. Pastoral Poetry and Pastoral Drama. 1906.

Gofflot, L. V. Le Théâtre au Collège du Moyen Age à nos Jours. Paris, 1907.

Moore Smith, G. C. Notes on some English University Plays. MLR. III, 1908.

—— Plays performed in Cambridge Colleges before 1585. [In Fasciculus J. W. Clark dicatus, 1909.]

—— The Academic Drama at Cambridge: Extracts from College Records. Malone Soc. Collections, vol. II, 1923.

—— College Plays performed in the University of Cambridge. Cambridge, 1923.

Boas, F. S. and Greg, W. W. James I at Oxford in 1605; Property Lists from the University Archives. Malone Soc. Collections, vol. I, 1909.

Boas, F. S. University Plays. CHEL. vol. VI, 1910.

—— University Drama in the Tudor Age. 1914.

—— Shakespeare and the Universities. [1923.]

Morgan, L. B. The Latin University Drama. Sh. Jb. XLVII, 1911. [A supplement to the article by G. B. Churchill and W. Keller, mentioned above. It contains an account of 13 Latin plays, some of which however do not seem to be of Oxford or Cambridge origin.]

B. ENGLISH UNIVERSITY DRAMATISTS AND PLAYS

[The following list includes the English and Latin plays written before 1642, preserved in ptd form, or in MSS which can be verified as still extant. Plays known only by allusion are not recorded, except in a few cases of special importance. Other lost plays and plays dating after 1642 are recorded in G. C. Moore Smith's College Plays Performed in the University of Cambridge, 1923.]

WILLIAM ALABASTER (1567–1640)

Roxana Tragoedia olim Cantabrigiae acta in Col. Trin. 1632.

Roxana Tragoedia a plagiarii unguibus vindicata, aucta, & agnita ab Authore Gulielmo Alabastro. 1632. [MSS: Trinity College Cambridge R.17.10; University Lib. Cambridge Ff.II.9; Lambeth Palace 838; Emmanuel College Cambridge III.1.17. Synopsis in Sh.Jb.xxxiv, pp.252–5. Source: La Dalida, Tragedia nova di Luigi Groto, Cieco di Hadria, 1567. See B. Dobell, The Sonnets of William Alabaster, Athenaeum, 26 Dec. 1903.]

THOMAS ATKINSON (1600–1639)

Homo. [BM. Harl. MS 6925. Contains dedication to Laud, as President of St John's College, Oxford, by the author, Thomas Atkinson.]

HENRY BELLAMY (b. 1604)

Iphis, Comœdia Latina, Autore Henrico Bellamy. [Bodl. MS Lat. Misc. 1.17. Dedicated to Juxon, President of St John's College, Oxford.]

SAMUEL BERNARD (1591–1657)

Andronicus Comnenus. [BM. Sloane MS 1767. A Latin tragedy. See Sh. Jb. xxxiv, p. 256 and B. Morgan, Sh. Jb. xlvii, 1911, p. 78.]

JOHN BLENCOWE (b. 1609)

Mercurius sive Literarum Lucta. [MS in St John's College Oxford. See F. S. Boas, Recently recovered MSS at St John's College, Oxford, MLR. xi, 1916.]

SAMUEL BROOKE (d. 1632)

Adelphe. [Trinity College Cambridge MS R.3.9, 'Comoedia in Collegii Trin. aula bis publice acta. Authore Dno Dre Brooke Coll. Trin.' Also, R.10.4, with prologue dated 1662. Source: G. B. della Porta, La Sorella.]

Melanthe: Fabula Pastoralis, acta cum Jacobus, Magnæ Brit. Franc. et Hiberniæ Rex, Cantabrigiam suam nuper inviserat, ibidemque musarum atque animi gratia dies quinque commoraretur. Egerunt Alumni Coll. San. et individuæ Trinitatis Cantabrigiæ. 1615; ed. J. S. G. Bolton, 1928. [A copy of 1615 edn in the Bodleian contains the cast in MS.]

Scyros. [MSS: Trinity College Cambridge R.3.6, 'Fabula Pastoralis acta coram Principe Charolo et comite Palatino mensis Martii 30 [for 3º] A.D. 1612. Authore Dre Brooke Coll. Trin.'; R.3.37, R.10.4, R.17.10, and O.3.4; Emmanuel College Cambridge III.1.17; University Lib.

Cambridge Ee.v.16; Shipdham Church, Thetford. Source: G. de Bonarelli, Filli di Sciro, favola pastorale, Ferrara, 1607.]

ROBERT BURTON (1577–1640)

[See pp. 829–30 below.]

WILLIAM CARTWRIGHT (1611–1643)

The Royall Slave. A Tragi-Comedy. Presented to the King and Queene by the Students of Christ-Church in Oxford. August 30, 1636. Presented since to both their Majesties at Hampton-Court by the Kings Servants. Oxford, 1639 (re-issued 1640). [BM. Add. MS 41616. Bought at Petworth sale, 1928. See W. G. Rice, Sources of William Cartwright's Royal Slave, MLN. xlv, 1930.]

Comedies, Tragi-Comedies, With other Poems, By Mr. William Cartwright, late Student of Christ-Church in Oxford, and Proctor of the University. The Ayres and Songs set by Mr Henry Lawes, Servant to his late Majesty in his Publick and Private Musick. 1651. [The plays included are: The Lady Errant. The Royall Slave. The Ordinary. The Siedge or Love's Convert. The Royall Slave is the second play in this vol. with the imprint 'The Third edition,' 1651. The Ordinary is rptd in the four edns of Dodsley, in vols. x, x, x, and xii, respectively, and in Ancient British Drama, vol. iii.]

JOHN CHRISTOPHERSON (d. 1558)

Ἰεφθάτ. Ed. F. H. Forbes and W. O. Sypherd, Newark, Delaware, [1929] (with English trn). [MSS: Trinity College Cambridge O.1.37; St John's College Cambridge 284.]

Iephthe. [A Latin version of the above. MS Bodl. Tanner 466, fols. 126–53. See B. M. Wagner, TLS. 26 Sept. 1929; F. S. Boas, TLS. 30 Jan. 1930.]

ABRAHAM COWLEY (1618–1667)

[See p. 459 above.]

JOSEPH CROWTHER

[Cephalus and Procris]. [MS in St John's College Oxford, without title. A Latin play dedicated to Juxon. See F. S. Boas, Recently recovered MSS at St John's College, Oxford, MLR. xi, 1916.]

AQUILA CRUSO (fl. 1614–8)

Euribates Pseudomagus. [Emmanuel College Cambridge MS III.1.17. See Sh.Jb.xxxiv, p. 318.]

SAMUEL DANIEL (1562–1619)

The Queenes Arcadia. 1606. [See pp. 422–3 above.]

RICHARD EDWARDS (1523?–1566)
[See pp. 519–20 above.]

JASPER FISHER

Fuimus Troes Æneid, 2. The True Trojanes,
Being A Story of the Britaines valour at the
Romanes first invasion: Publikely repre-
sented by the Gentlemen Students of
Magdalen Colledge in Oxford. 1633; rptd
Hazlitt's Dodsley, vol. XII.

PHINEAS FLETCHER (1582–1650)

Sicelides A Piscatory. As it hath beene Acted
in Kings Colledge, in Cambridge. 1631.
[See p. 444 above.]

EDWARD FORSET (1553–1630)

Pedantius. Comoedia, Olim Cantabrig. Acta
in Coll. Trin. Numquàm antehàc Typis
evulgata. 1631; ed. G. C. Moore Smith, Bang,
vol. VIII, 1905. [Caius College Cambridge
MS 62, with the title 'Pædantius comoedia
acta in Collegio Sanctæ et individuæ
Trinitatis authore Mro Forcet'; also in
Trinity College Cambridge MS R. 17 (9),
apparently a copy of the Caius MS. Synopsis
in Sh. Jb. XXXIV, pp. 279–81, preceded by
critical remarks, including the theory that
Holofernes was derived from Pedantius.
See Sir John Harington: Orlando Furioso
in English Heroical Verse, 1591 (contains
incidental references to the play); Gabriel
Harvey: Rhetor, 1577; Smithus; vel
Musarum Lachrymae, 1578; Χαῖρε vel
Gratulationes Valdenses, 1578; Three
Proper and Wittie familiar letters, 1580
(phrases from these works are introduced
into the play); Thomas Nashe: Have with
you to Saffron Walden, 1596; Strange
Newes, 1593. Here Nashe speaks of 'M.
Winkfield's [i.e. Anthony Wingfield's]
Comoedie of Pedantius in Trinity College';
G. C. Moore Smith: Letter in TLS. 10 Oct.
1918 (proves Forset's authorship of the
play); Notes on some English University
Plays, MLR. III, 1908 (supplementary notes
on Pedantius).]

ABRAHAM FRAUNCE (fl. 1587–1633)
[See p. 436 above.]

WILLIAM GAGER (fl. 1580–1609)

Dido. [MS in the library of Christ Church,
Oxford. An imperfect MS, BM Add. MS
22583, has been ptd in The Works of
Christopher Marlowe, ed. A. Dyce, Appendix
3 (1858). Synopsis of BM. MS in Sh. Jb.
XXXIV, p. 238.]
Meleager Tragoedia nova. Bis publice acta in
aede Christi Oxoniae. Oxford, 1592. [Synop-
sis in Sh. Jb. XXXIV, pp. 234–6.]

Panniculus Hippolyto Senecae Tragoediae
assutus. 1591. [Ptd as an appendix to
Meleager.]
Oedipus. [BM. Add. MS 22583 (imperfect).
Synopsis in Sh. Jb. XXXIV, pp. 236–7.]
Ulysses Redux. Tragoedia Nova. In aede
Christi Oxoniae publice Academicis recitata,
octavo Idus Februarii 1591/2. Oxford,
[1592]. [Synopsis in Sh. Jb. XXXIV, pp.
239–41.]
    A Letter of William Gager to Dr John
    Rainolds, dated 'the laste of Julye 1592.'
    Corpus Christi College Oxford MS 352.
    A Letter of Dr J. Rainolds to an unknown
    friend, dated Feb. 6, 1591/2. Corpus
    Christi College Oxford MS 352.
    Rainolds, John. Th' Overthrow of Stage-
    playes. 1599; 1629.
    Boas, F. S. A Defence of Oxford Plays
    and Players. Fortnightly Rev. August,
    1907. [Contains an account, with ex-
    tracts, of Gager's letter to Rainolds.]
    [Ward, R.] Fucus Histriomastix. Ed.
    G. C. Moore Smith, 1909. [Pp. 98–9.]
    Young, K. William Gager's Defence of
    the Academic Stage. Trans. Wisconsin
    Academy, XVIII, 1916. [Prints Gager's
    letter to Rainolds in full.]
    Brooke, C. F. T. William Gager to Queen
    Elizabeth. Stud. Phil. XXIX, 1932.

THOMAS GOFFE (1591–1629)
[See p. 646 above.]

WILLIAM GOLDINGHAM (d. 1589)

Herodes. [University Lib. Cambridge MS
Mm.I.24. Synopsis in Sh. Jb. XXXIV,
pp. 243–4.]

NICHOLAS GRIMALD (1519–1562)
[See p. 437 above.]

MATTHEW GWYNNE (1558?–1627)

Nero Tragœdia Nova Matthaeo Gwinne Med.
Doct. Collegii Divi Praecursoris apud
Oxonienses Socio collecta è Tacito, Sue-
tonio, Dione, Seneca. 1603. [There was
another issue, with a different dedication,
later in the year, and a third in 1639.
Synopsis in Sh. Jb. XXXIV, pp. 268–71.]
Vertumnus sive Annus Recurrens Oxonii
XXIX Augusti, Anno, 1605. Coram Jacobo
Rege, Henrico Principe, Proceribus. A
Joannensibus in Scena recitatus ab uno
scriptus, Phrasi Comica propè Tragicis
Senariis. 1607. [Appended to the play are
the Latin hexameters greeting James as a
descendant of Banquo, recited in front of
St John's College by three youths attired as
Nymphs. As the verses are signed M. G.,
they are evidently from Gwynne's pen.]

JOHN HACKET (1592–1670)

Loiola. Scena est Amsterodami: à vesperâ ad vesperam peraguntur omnia. 1648. [MSS: Trinity College Cambridge R.17.9, 'authore d^{no} Hackett,' and R.17.10 (imperfect); BM. Add. MS 26709 (without title, and imperfect); Durham Cathedral Hunter MSS (Quarto 26.1); Shipdham Church, Thetford.]

PETER HAUSTED (d. 1645)

The Rival Friends. A Comœdie, As it was Acted before the King and Queens Majesties, when out of their princely favour they were pleased to visite their Universitie of Cambridge, upon the 19. day of March. 1631. Cryed downe by Boyes, Faction, Envie, and confident Ignorance, approv'd by the judicious, and now exposed to the publique censure, by the Authour, Pet. Hausted M^r in Artes of Queenes Colledge. 1632. [A copy in BM. contains the cast in MS.]

Senile Odium. Comœdia Cantabrigiæ publicè Academicis recitata in Collegio Reginali ab ejusdem Collegii juventate. Lusimus innocui. 1633. [MS in Longleat Lib.]

WALTER HAWKESWORTH (d. 1606)

Labyrinthus. Comoedia, habita A.D. 1622, coram Sereniss. Rege Jacobo, in Academia Cantabrigiensi. 1636. [MSS: University Lib. Cambridge Ee.v.16 (which contains, after the Prologue the statement 'Authore Mro. Haukesworth Trinitatis Collegii quondam socio'); Trinity College Cambridge R.3.6, with statement, 'Authore M^{ro} Hauksworth'; St John's College Cambridge J,8; Lambeth, 838; Bodl. Douce 43 and 315; Trinity College Cambridge R.3.9; Shipdham Church, Thetford. Synopsis in Sh. Jb. xxxiv, pp. 309–13; source: G. B. della Porta's La Cintia.]

Leander. [MSS: Trinity College Cambridge R.3.9., 'Authore M^{ro} Haukesworth, Collegii Trinitatis olim Socio Acta est secundo A.D. 1602. comitiis Baccalaureorum primo acta est A.D. 1598,' gives the texts and casts at both performances; BM. Sloane 1762, which also gives the two texts and casts; St John's College Cambridge J, 8; Emmanuel. College Cambridge I.2.30; Bodl. Rawl. Misc. 341; University Lib. Cambridge Ee.v.16; Lambeth 838 (imperfect); Shipdham Church, Thetford. Synopsis in Sh. Jb. xxxiv, pp. 305–8; source: G. B. della Porta's La Fantesca.]

BARTEN HOLYDAY (1593–1661)

Τεχνογαμία: Or the Marriages of the Arts. A Comedie. Written by Barten Holyday, Master of Arts, and Student of Christ-Church in Oxford, and acted by the Students of the same House before the Universitie, at Shrovetide. 1618; 1630. [See J. Nichols, Progresses of James I, vol. IV, 1828, pp. 1109–12. For Holyday's trns of Horace and Persius see pp. 803,805 below.]

LEONARD HUTTEN (1557?–1632)

Bellum Grammaticale, sive Nominum Verborumque discordia civilis Tragico-Comoedia. Summo cum applausu olim apud Oxonienses in Scaenam producta. 1635; ed. A. Hume, Edinburgh, 1658 and 1698; ed. R. Spencer, 1726 and 1729; ed. J. Bolte (with William Gager's prologue and epilogue, etc. in Andrea Guarnas Bellum Grammaticale und seine Nachahmungen, Berlin, 1908). [For synopsis see Sh. Jb. xxxiv, pp. 273–5. An adaptation of Guarna's Bellum Grammaticale. For Hutten's authorship see F. S. Boas, University Drama in the Tudor Age, 1914, p. 256. For trns and other adaptations of Guarna's work in England see F. S. Boas, CHEL. vol. VI, 1910, pp. 482–3.]

WILLIAM JOHNSON (1534–1614)

Valetudinarium. [MSS: Emmanuel College Cambridge I.2.32, 'Comoedia acta coram Academicis Febr. 6° 1637. Authore M^{ro} Guill. Johnson Coll. Regin. Soc.'; University Lib. Cambridge Dd.III.73; St John's College Cambridge S, 59 (imperfect).]

THOMAS LEGGE (1535–1607)

Richardus Tertius. [MSS: University Lib. Cambridge Mm.IV.40, dated Comitiis Bacchalaureorum A.D. 1579/80; Caius College Cambridge 62 (formerly 125), where it is described as 'tragoedia trium vesperum, Habita in Collegio Divi Johannis Evangelistae, Comitiis Bacchalaureorum Anno 1573' (a mistake for 1579); Emmanuel College Cambridge I.3.19, with list of actors, confirming the date 1579/80; Clare College Cambridge Kk.3.12, dated 'comitiis Bacchal. 1579'; Bodl. Tanner 306 (first 'actio' only) with note 'Acted in St John's Hall before the Earle of Essex 17 March, 1582' (date probably mistaken); BM. Harl. 2412 and 6926. Ptd Shakespeare Soc. 1844, and in Hazlitt-Collier, Shakespeare's Library, vol. II, 1875. See G. B. Churchill, Richard III bis Shakespeare, 1897 (enlarged in Palaestra, x, 1900); G. C. Moore Smith, Notes on some English University Plays, MLR. III, 1908; Sh. Jb. xxxiv, p. 258.]

JASPER MAYNE (1604–1672)

[See p. 648 above.]

ROBERT MEAD (1616–1653)

The Combat of Love and Friendship, a Comedy, As it hath formerly been presented by the Gentlemen of Ch. Ch. in Oxford. By Robert Mead sometime of the same Colledge. 1654.

PETER MEASE (*fl.* 1618–27)

Adrastus parentans sive Vindicta. Tragœdia. [BM. Add. MS 10417. Source: Herodotus, bk. I, ch. 35. See G. C. Moore Smith, Notes on some English University Plays, MLR. III, 1908.]

WILLIAM MEWE (*fl.* 1620–50)

Pseudomagia. [MSS: Emmanuel College Cambridge, I.3.16, 'Authore Mro Mewe Cant. Col. Emman.'; Trinity College Cambridge R.17.10.]

THOMAS NEALE (1614–1646?)

The Warde, a tragicomedy, 16 Sept. 1637. Ed. J. A. Mitchell, Philadelphia. 1937. [Bodl. MS Rawl. Poet. 79. This MS contains a number of works written by Neale between 1637 and 1644.]

PHILIP PARSONS (1594–1653)

Atalanta. [BM. Harl. MS 6924. Contains dedication in Latin elegiacs to Laud, as President of St John's College, Oxford, signed by the author.]

THOMAS RANDOLPH (1605–1635)

Aristippus; or, the Joviall Philosopher: Demonstrativelie prooving, that Quartes, Pintes, and Pottles, Are sometimes necessary Authours in a Scholers Library. Presented in a private Shew. To which is added, The Conceited Pedler. 1630 (*bis*); 1631; 1635; [?]. [BM. MS Sloane 2531, 16, with variants from printed text.]

The Jealous Lovers. A Comedie presented to their gracious Majesties at Cambridge, by the Students of Trinity-Colledge. Written by Thomas Randolph, Master of Arts, and Fellow of the House. Cambridge, 1632; 1634; 1640.

Poems with the Muses Looking-Glasse: and Amyntas. By Thomas Randolph Master of Arts, and late Fellow of Trinity Colledge in Cambridge. 1638. [This volume was ed. by Robert Randolph, the poet's brother. The 2nd edn, enlarged, 1640, includes the 1640 edn of The Jealous Lovers. Aristippus, to which The Conceited Pedler is added, does not appear till the 4th edn. The 5th edn was reached by 1664. The Muse's Looking Glass was rptd in the earlier three edns of *Dodsley*,

in vols. VI, IX, IX respectively; and in *Ancient British Drama*, vol. II. For a full discussion of Amyntas see W. W. Greg's Pastoral Poetry and Pastoral Drama, 1906.]

Hey for Honesty, Down with Knavery. Πλουτοφθαλμία Πλουτογαμία. A pleasant Comedie, entitled Hey for Honesty, Down with Knavery. Translated out of Aristophanes his Plutus, by Tho. Randolph. Augmented and Published by F. J. 1651. [An adaptation, and not merely a trn.]

The Drinking Academy. Ed. H. E. Rollins, PMLA. XXXIX, 1924; ed. H. E. Rollins and S. A. Tannenbaum, Cambridge, U.S.A. 1930. [Assigned by G. C. Moore Smith, RES. VI, 1930, to Robert Baron, but see reply by Rollins, PMLA. XLVI, 1931. MS in Huntington Lib., HM 91.]

Poetical and Dramatic Works. Collected and ed. W. C. Hazlitt, 2 vols. 1875.

[See Retrospective Rev. vol. VI, 1822; K. Kottas, Thomas Randolph, sein Leben und seine Werke, Vienna, 1909; C. L. Day, Thomas Randolph's Part in the Authorship of Hey for Honesty, PMLA. XLI, 1926, and New Poems by Randolph, RES. VIII, 1932; G. C. Moore Smith, The Canon of Randolph's Dramatic Works, RES. I, 1925, and Thomas Randolph, British Academy, 1927.]

THOMAS RANDOLPH and RICHARD BRAITHWAIT (?) (1588?–1673)

Cornelianum Dolium. Comœdia lepidissima optimorum judiciis approbata, et theatrali coryphæo, nec immerito, donata, palma chorali apprime digna Auctore T. R. ingeniosissimo hujus aevi Heliconis. 1638. [Assigned by W. C. Hazlitt to Thomas Riley of Trinity College, Cambridge, but the publisher's 'T. R.' is doubtless Thomas Randolph, who may have drafted the play, which appears to have been completed by Richard Braithwait. See G. C. Moore Smith, Canon of Randolph's Dramatic Works, RES. I, 1925, and J. Crossly, N. & Q. 2 Nov. 1861. Source: G. Boccaccio, Decameron, 2nd Story of Seventh Day. See European Mag. XXXVII, 1800, pp. 343–4, 439.]

J. RICKETS (*fl.* 1625–33)

Byrsa Basilica seu Regale Excambium à Sereniss. Reginâ Elizabethâ in personâ suâ sic insignitum; Anno Dom: 1570. Mense Januar: 23° die, Monumentum Mercuriale D.D. Thomae Greshami Militis et Negotiatoris Regii; qui suis solidis sumptibus e solo erexit, dicavitque tam Mercatori quam Mercurio. [Bodl. MS Tanner 207. The name of the author is on the last leaf. Synopsis in Sh. Jb. XXXIV, pp. 281–5.]

GEORGE RUGGLE (1575–1622)

Ignoramus. Comœdia coram Regia Majestate Jacobi Regis Angliæ. Impensis J. S. 1630; 1630 ('Secunda editio auctior & emendatior. Una cum Argumentis unicuique Scenæ præpositis, ut melius totius fabulæ scopus, qui aliter obscurior est, intelligatur'); [?] ('Editio Tertia, locis sexcentis emendatior. Cum Eorum supplemento quæ, causidicorum municipalium reverentia, hactenus desiderabantur. Autore M^{ro} Ruggle, Aulæ Clarensis A. M.'); 1659; 1668; 1707; 1731; Dublin, 1736; 1737; ed. Sir J. S. Hawkins, 1787. [MSS: Douce 43; Bodl. Tanner 306; BM. Harl. 6869 (imperfect) and 7042, fol. 245 (cast only); and reference to MS, 'possibly Mr Ruggle's copy' formerly at Clare Hall.]

Ignoramus: A Comedy As it was several times Acted with extraordinary Applause, before the Magisty of King James With a Supplement which (out of respect to the Students of the Common Law) was hitherto wanting. Written in Latine by R. Ruggles sometimes Master of Arts in Clare Colledge in Cambridge. And Translated into English by R. C[odrington] sometimes Master of Arts in Magdalen Colledge in Oxford. 1662.

The English Lawyer, a Comedy, acted at the Royal Theatre; written by Edward Ravenscroft, Gent. 1678.

An English Prologue and Epilogue to the Latin Comedy of Ignoramus. With a Preface and Notes Relative to Modern Times and Manners. By George Dyer, Late of Emmanuel College, Cambridge. 1797. [Written for the performance of the play at Westminster School in 1794.]

[Sources: G. B. della Porta, La Trappolaria, 1596; John Cowell, The Interpreter, 1607. See J. B. Mullinger, The University of Cambridge, vol. II, 1884, pp. 529–40, which contains an analysis of the plot of the play; B. M. Wagner, John Rhodes and Ignoramus, RES. v, 1929.]

JOHN SADLER (1615–1674)

Masquerade du Ciel. Presented to the great Queen of the little world: a Celestial Map of the heavenly bodies the years 1639, 1640 by J. S. of Emmanuel college, Cambridge. 1640.

GEORGE SALTERNE (b. 1568)

Tomumbeius sive Sultanici in Aegypto Inperii Eversio. Tragoedia nova auctore Georgio Salterno Bristoensi. [Bodl. MS Rawl. Poet. 75. Synopsis in Sh. Jb. XXXIV, pp. 247–9.]

JOSEPH SIMEON (or SIMONS) (1594–1671)

Fratrum Concordia Sæva seu Zeno. Rome, 1648.

Leo Armenus sive Impietas Punita. [Included with Zeno in J. Simonis, Tragœdiæ quinque quarum duæ postremæ nunc primum lucem vident, Liège, 1657; 1680; 1697. MSS of both plays in University Lib. Cambridge Ii.VI.35, and of Zeno in BM. Harl. 5024, and St John's College, Cambridge. Simeon was Provincial of the Jesuits, and lived chiefly in Rome and Liège. Zeno, according to the Retrospective Rev. XII, 1825, p. 5, was acted at Cambridge in 1631, but G. C. Moore Smith (College Plays, 1923, p. 96) considers that 'anno 1631 acta' in the University Lib. Cambridge MS refers to a performance at Douay or some other place abroad.]

THOMAS SNELLING (b. 1614)

Thibaldus sive Vindictae Ingenium Tragoedia. Oxford, 1640 (re-issued as Pharamus sive Libido Vindex, Hispanica tragoedia, 1650). [See J. Bolte, Die Oxforder Tragödie Thibaldus, Sh. Jb. XXVII, 1892; F. Madan, The Early Oxford Press, 1895, p. 223; Anthony à Wood, Athenae Oxonienses, ed. P. Bliss, vol. III, 1813, p. 275.]

THOMAS SPARROWE

Confessor. [Bodl. MS Rawl. Poet. 77. Thomas Sparrowe, who dedicates the play to an unnamed Bishop, matriculated as a pensioner of St John's College, Cambridge, on 22 March 1630, and graduated B.A. in 1633. See G. C. Moore Smith, Notes on some English University Plays, MLR. III, 1908.]

WILLIAM STEVENSON (?) (*fl.* 1553–60)

Gammer Gurtons Nedle. 1575. [See p. 520 above.]

WILLIAM STRODE (1602–1645)

The Floating Island: A Tragi-Comedy, Acted before his Majesty at Oxford, Aug. 29. 1636. By the Students of Christ-Church. Written by William Strode, late Orator of the University of Oxford, the Aires and Songs set by Mr Henry Lawes, servant to his late Majesty in his publick and private Musick. 1655; ed. B. Dobell (Poetical Works of William Strode, 1907).

EDMUND STUB

Fraus Honesta. Comœdia Cantabrigiæ olim acta, authore Magistro Stubbe, Collegii Trinitatis Socio. 1632. [MSS: Trinity College Cambridge R.17.10, 'Acta erat haec Comedia decimo die Febr. A.D. 1618'

and R.17.9; Emmanuel College Cambridge
III.1.17, with cast of the play, and note,
apparently in a different hand, 'Scæna est
Florentiæ decimo die Februarii, 1616'; BM.
Harl. 2296 (without title). See G. C. Moore
Smith, Notes on some English University
Plays, MLR. III, 1908.]

THOMAS TOMKIS (*fl.* 1607)

Lingua: Or the Combat of the Tongue, and the
five Senses, For Superiority. A pleasant
Comœdie. 1607; 1617; 1622; 1657; [?];
ed. I. Reed (Dodsley's Old Plays, vol. v,
1780); ed. J. P. Collier (Dodsley's Old Plays,
vol. v, 1825); *Hazlitt's Dodsley*, vol. IX;
TFT. 1913. [See F. S. Boas, Macbeth and
Lingua, MLR. IV, 1909; F. G. Fleay, Shakespeariana, March 1885; F. J. Furnivall,
Sir John Harington's Shakespeare Quartos,
N. & Q. 17 May 1890, who gives an account
of a list of volumes and single copies of plays
belonging to Harington from BM. Add. MS
27632. On fol. 30 Harington mentions 'The
combat of Lingua made by Thom. Tomkis
of Trinity Colledge in Cambridge.' See also
N. & Q. 9 Aug. 1890; Retrospective Rev. II,
1820, pp. 270 ff.; G. C. Moore Smith, Notes
on some English University Plays, MLR.
III, 1908; M. P. Tilley, The Comedy 'Lingua'
and Du Bartas' La Sepmaine, MLN. XLII,
1927, and The Comedy 'Lingua' and Sir
John Davier's Nosce Teipsum, MLN. XLIV,
1929.]

Albumazar. A Comedy presented before the
Kings Majestie at Cambridge, the ninth of
March, 1614. By the Gentlemen of Trinitie
Colledge. 1615 (*bis*); 1634 (*bis*) ('Newly
revised and corrected by a speciall Hand');
1668. [Source: G. B. della Porta, L' Astro-
logo, 1606; rptd in *Ancient British Drama*,
vol. II, and in *Hazlitt's Dodsley*, vol. XI. See
Albumazar, a Comedy, N. & Q. 3, 31 March,
14 April 1866, 24 Aug. 1867.]

NICHOLAS UDALL (1505–1556)

Ezechias. [Performed before Elizabeth in the
chapel of King's College, Cambridge, 3 Aug.
1564. See p. 519 above.]

SIR FRANCIS VERNEY (1584–1615)

The tragedye of Antipoe. [Bodl. MS Eng.
Poet. e. 5. Dedicated to King James I by
'Yoͬ graces most affectionaͭᵉ servant to
command Francis Verney.' See G. C. Moore
Smith, Notes on some English University
Plays, MLR. III, 1908.]

THOMAS VINCENT (d. 1633)

Paria. Acta coram sereniss. Rege Carolo:
Authore Tho. Vincent, Trin. Colleg. Socio.
1648. [Emmanuel College Cambridge MS
I.3.16, 'Acta coram sereniss. Rege Carolo.

Mar. 3. 1627. Ab hora undecima ad quin-
tam.' Source: Eusebio Luchetti, Le due
Sorelle Rivali, Venice, 1609. See T.
Odinga, Thomas Vincent's Paria, E.
Studien, XVI, 1892, who prints Vincent's
prefatory English abstract of the plot of
this Latin play; G. C. Moore Smith, College
Plays, 1923, p. 97.]

ROBERT WARD (?) (*fl.* 1623–42)

Fucus Histriomastix. Ed. G. C. Moore Smith,
1909. [MSS: Lambeth Palace 838 and Bodl.
Rawl. Poet. 21. 'Probably written by Robert
Ward and acted at Queens' College, Cambridge, in Lent 1623' (Moore Smith). On the
performance before James I at Newmarket
see verses by H. Molle, ptd by G. C. Moore
Smith, Cambridge Rev. 5 May 1910.]

NATHANIEL WIBOURNE (d. 1613)

Machiavellus. [Bodl. Douce MS 234 (imperfect;
dated 'Anno Dmni. 1597. Decemb. 9').
The attribution of the authorship to Wi-
bourne, Fellow of St John's College, Cambridge, is in Douce's handwriting. Synopsis
in Sh. Jb. XXXIV, pp. 300–2.]

GEORGE WILDE (1610–1665)

Eumorphus sive Cupido Adultus. Comœdia.
Acta A Joañensibus Oxoñ Feb. 5º 1634.
Authore Georgio Wilde ejusdᵐ Coll. Soc. et
LL. Bacc. [BM. Add. MS 14047.]
Loves Hospitall. As it was acted before the
Kinge & Queens Majestyes by the Students
of Sᵗ Jo. Baptists Coͫl in Oxoñ: Augustii
29º 1636. Authore Georgio Wilde LL: Bac.
[BM. Add. MS 14047.]
The Converted Robber. A Pastorall Acted by
Sᵗ Johns College. 1637. [Also in BM. Add.
MS 14047, and probably by Wilde, though
it does not contain his name.]

RALPH WORSELEY (d. 1590)

Synedrium, id est, Consessus animalium vide-
licet collectio mor[a]e comoediae aut pocius
tragoediae descriptum. [In Latin prose.
Imperfect.]
Synedrii, id est consessus animalium inscripta
tragoedia. A.D. 1553. Mense Novembris
14 die. Finis. 27 die. Febr. 1554. Per me
Radulphum Worselaeum. [In Latin verse.
Trinity College Cambridge MS O.3.25. Both
plays are dramatic paraphrases of W. Caxton's Historye of Reynart the foxe (1481).
See F. S. Boas, University Drama in the
Tudor Age, 1914, Appendix 2.]

CHRISTOPHER WREN (1591–1658)

ΦΥΣΙ-ΠΟΝΟ-ΜΑΧΙΑ. [A Latin Comedy dedicated to J. Buckeridge, President of St
John's College, Oxford, by the author, the
father of Sir Christopher Wren. Bodl. MS 30.]

RICHARD ZOUCH (1590–1661)
Fallacy or The Troubles of great Hermenia.
Aug: 13: 1631. R. Z. [BM. Harl. MS 6869.
Ptd, with some changes, under the title of
The Sophister. A Comedy, 1639.]

C. ANONYMOUS PLAYS

[Absalon]. [BM. Stowe MS 957. The MS does
not contain the title or the author's name,
and the play is probably not the Absalon of
Thomas Watson, Master of St John's
College, Cambridge, eulogised by Roger
Ascham in The Scholemaster. See F. S.
Boas, University Drama in the Tudor Age,
1914, Appendix I. Synopsis in Sh. Jb.
XXXIV, pp. 230–2.]
The tragedy of Amurath, 3rd tyrant of the
Turkes, as it was publickly presented to the
University of Oxford by the Students of
Christchurch, Mathew's day, 1618. [His-
torical MSS Commission Report, vol. I, p.
49.]
Andronicus: A Tragedy, Impieties Long
Successe, or Heavens Late Revenge. 1661.
[The printer's preface states that the play
'was born some eighteen years since in
Oxford,' so that it probably dates from just
before the Civil War.]
Antoninus Bassianus Caracalla. [Bodl. MS
Rawl. C, 590. A Latin tragedy. Synopsis
in Sh. Jb. XXXIV, pp. 265–7.]
A Merrie Dialogue, Betweene Band, Cuffe, and
Ruffe: Done by an excellent Wit, And
Lately acted in a shew in the famous
Universitie of Cambridge. 1615; 1615 (as
Exchange Ware at the Second hand, viz.
Band, Ruffe and Cuffe. Adds an intro-
ductory dialogue); 1661 (as A Merrie
Dialogue, etc., and without introductory
dialogue); rptd T. Park (Harleian Misc.
vol. x, 1813) (with Prologue from MS,
apparently at Eshton Hall, Yorks, 'which
is said to have been acted at Oxford, Feb.
24, 1646'); rptd J. O. Halliwell[-Phillipps]
(Contributions to Early English Literature,
1849); rptd C. Hindley (Miscellanea Antiqua
Anglicana, vol. II, 1871). [BM. Add. MS
23723, lacks introduction.]
The Birthe of Hercules. Ed. M. W. Wallace,
1903; ed. R. W. Bond, Malone Soc. 1910.
[BM. Add. MS 28722. G. C. Moore Smith,
College Plays, 1923, p. 108, suggests that
Richard Bernard, of Christ's College, Cam-
bridge, the translator of Terence, was the
author. Source: Plautus's Amphitruo.]
The Tragedie of Caesar's Revenge. [?]; 1607
(as The Tragedie of Caesar and Pompey. Or
Caesars Revenge. Privately acted by the
Students of Trinity Colledge in Oxford); ed.
F. S. Boas, Malone Soc. 1911. [See T. M.

Parrott, MLR. v, 1910; H. M. Ayres,
PMLA. xxx, 1915; W. Mühlfeld, Sh. Jb.
XLVII, XLVIII, 1911–2.]
[The Christmas Prince.] A true and faithfull
relation of the risinge and fall of Thomas
Tucker, Prince of Alba Fortunata, Lord St
Johns &c., with all the occurrents which
happened throughout his whole domination.
[MS in library of St John's College, Oxford
(1607–8), which includes the following plays
of unknown authorship: Ara Fortunae;
Saturnalia; Philomela; Time's Complaint;
The Seven Dayes of the Weeke; Philomathes;
Ira seu Tumulus Fortunae; Periander. The
narrative part of the MS, and the play, The
Seven Dayes of the Weeke, are printed in
Miscellanea Antiqua Anglicana, vol. I, 1816,
under the title, The Christmas Prince, As it
was exhibited in the University of Oxford, in
the year 1607. P. Bliss, the editor, attributed
by mistake The Christmas Prince to Griffin
Higgs who has a MS poem in Latin on Sir
Thomas White in the same vol. Rptd in
full, ed. F. S. Boas and W. W. Greg, Malone
Soc. 1923. See F. E. Schelling, The Queen's
Progress, and other Elizabethan Sketches,
1904; A. Harbage, The Authorship of the
Christmas Prince, MLN. L, 1935.]
Cancer: Comoedia. 1648 (with Loiola, Stoicus
Vapulans and Paria). [Source: L. Salviati,
Il Granchio, Florence, 1606 (2nd edn). See
G. C. Moore Smith, College Plays, 1923,
p. 99.]
Club Law A Comedy Acted in Clare Hall,
Cambridge, about 1599–1600. Now printed
for the first time. Ed. G. C. Moore Smith,
1907. [St John's College Cambridge MS
S, 62 (imperfect). See W. W. Greg, MLR.
IV, 1909 (review of Moore Smith's edn);
T. Fuller, History of the University of
Cambridge, 1655, pp. 31–3.]
Clytophon. [Emmanuel College Cambridge
MS III.1.17. A Latin Comedy. At end of
MS, 'Guli. Bretonus possessor, Gul. Ainse-
worthus Scriptor.' Ainseworth was probably
the scribe, not the author. See Sh. Jb.
XXXIV, pp. 317–8.]
Fatum Vortigerni Seu miserabilis vita et exitus
Vortigerni regis Britanniae una complectens
adventum Saxonum sive Anglorum in
Britanniam. [BM. Lansdowne MS 723.
Synopsis in Sh. Jb. XXXIV, pp. 260–4,
preceded by critical remarks. By Thomas
Carleton and acted at Douay 1619? See
W. H. McCabe, TLS. 15 Aug. 1935, p. 513.]
Fraus Pia. [BM Sloane MS 1855. A Latin
comedy. See G. C. Moore Smith, Notes on
some English University Plays, MLR. III,
1908.]
Grobiana's Nuptialls. [Bodl. MS 30. Acted at
St John's College, Oxford.]

Hispanus. [Bodl. Douce MS 234, 'Summus histriodidascalus Mr Pratt. In diem comitialem anno dni 1596.' From cast appears to have been acted at St John's College Cambridge. Pratt may be the author, or [M]orrell, whose name, mutilated, is at bottom of first page. Synopsis in Sh. Jb. xxxiv, pp. 298–300.]

Hymenæus. A Comedy acted at St John's College, Cambridge. Now first printed. Ed. G. C. Moore Smith, 1908. [MSS: Caius College Cambridge 62, and St John's College Cambridge S, 45 (both perfect, but without title). From cast it appears to have been acted at St John's, March 1579. Synopsis in Sh. Jb. xxxiv, pp. 289–91, preceded by critical remarks. Source: G. Boccaccio, Decameron, 10th Story of Fourth Day.]

[Jovis et Junonis nuptiae.] [Trinity College Cambridge MS R. 10. 4 (perfect, but without title). A Latin mythological play.]

Laelia. Ed. G. C. Moore Smith, Cambridge, 1910. [Lambeth Palace MS 838. Synopsis in Sh. Jb. xxxiv, pp. 292–4. See also pp. 286–7. Source: Gl' Ingannati (contained in the volume entitled Comedia del Sacrificio degli Intronati, 1537). See C. Estienne, Les Abusez, Comedie faite à la mode des anciens Comiques, premièrement composée en langue Tuscane & nommée Intronati, depuys traduite en Francoys par Charles Estienne, 1549; H. H. Furness, Twelfth Night (The Variorum Shakespeare), 1901, who gives, pp. 341–59, a trn of the chief scenes in Gl' Ingannati, and pp. 359–61, an English version of the synopsis of Laelia in Sh. Jb.; G. C. Moore Smith, MLR. xxiii, 1928.]

Mercurius Rusticans, comœdia, cujus scena est Hinxey. [Bodl. MS Wood D, 18.]

Microcosmus. [In Trinity College Cambridge MS R. 10. 4. A Latin Cambridge play. See G. C. Moore Smith, College Plays, 1923, pp. 108–9.]

Narcissus A Twelve Night Merriment played by youths of the parish at the College of S. John the Baptist in Oxford, A.D. 1602. Ed. M. L. Lee, 1893. [Bodl. MS Rawl. Poet. 212. See C. H. Collister, Narcissus Plays distinguished, MLN. xx, 1905.]

Nottola. [Bodl. Douce MS 47. A Latin comedy.]

The Parnassus Trilogy

(i) The Plays

The Returne from Parnassus: Or The Scourge of Simony. Publiquely acted by the Students in Saint Johns Colledge in Cambridge. 1606 (bis); ed. T. Hawkins (The Origin of the English Drama, vol. iii,

Oxford, 1773); Ancient British Drama, vol. i; Hazlitt's Dodsley, vol. ix; ed. E. Arber, 1880; ed. O. Smeaton, 1905 (Temple Dramatists); TFT. 1912. [MS once in Halliwell-Phillipps collection; now Folger Shakespeare Lib. 448. 12?]

The Pilgrimage to Parnassus with the Two Parts of the Return from Parnassus. Three Comedies performed in St John's College, Cambridge, A.D. MDXCVII–MDCI. Ed. (from MSS) W. D. Macray, 1886; TFT. 1912. [Includes: The Pilgrimage to Parnassus (Bodl. MS Rawl. D, 398, no. 72); The Return from Parnassus, Pt i (Bodl. MS Rawl. D, 398, no. 72); The Return from Parnassus, Pt ii (as ptd in 1606).]

(ii) Criticism

Corney, B. The Return from Parnassus: Its Authorship. N. & Q. 12 May 1866.

Bullen, A. H. The Works of John Day. 1881. [Introduction.]

Mullinger, J. B. The University of Cambridge. Vol. i, 1884.

Hales, J. W. Academy, 19 March 1887. [Review of Macray's edn.]

—— Three Elizabethan Comedies. Macmillan's Mag. May 1887.

Fleay, F. G. A Biographical Chronicle of the English Drama. 2 vols. 1891.

Sarrazin, G. Thomas Kyd und sein Kreis. Berlin, 1892.

Ward, Sir A. W. History of English Dramatic Literature. 3 vols. 1899. [Vol. ii includes a communication from Sir I. Gollancz in favour of Day's authorship.]

Moore Smith, G. C. The Parnassus Plays. MLR. x, 1915.

Golding, S. R. The Parnassus Plays. N. & Q. 19 Nov. 1927.

Parthenia. Comoedia pastoralis. [Emmanuel College Cambridge MS I.3.16. Synopsis in Sh. Jb. xxxiv, pp. 320–2. Source: L. Groto, Il Pentimento Amoroso, Venice, 1576.]

Pastor Fidus. [MSS: University Lib. Cambridge Ff.ii.9, and Trinity College Cambridge R.3.37. The Cambridge University MS has a note 'Il pastor fido, di signor Guarini recitata in Collegio Regali Cantabrigiæ.' It has a prologue in the form of a dialogue between Prologus and Argumentum. The Trinity College MS adds, after the title, 'Tragicomoedia Pastoritia.' It has the prologue, slightly adapted, of the second version of Leander. Below the title, in red ink, is 'Guliel. Quarles.' Synopsis of the Prologue in the Cambridge University MS in Sh. Jb. xxxiv, p. 319. Source: G.-B. Guarini, Il Pastor fido, tragi-comedia pastorale, Venice, 1590. See W. W. Greg,

Pastoral Poetry and Pastoral Drama, 1906, pp. 194–210, 242–7, 252 (note).]

Pathomachia: or the Battell of Affections. Shadowed by a faigned Siedge of the Citie Pathopolis. Written some yeeres since, and now first published by a Friend of the deceased Author. 1630. [Has the running title 'Love's Loode-Stone.' MSS: BM. Harl. 6869; Bodl. Eng. Misc. e. 5 (imperfect). See G. C. Moore Smith, Notes on some English University Plays, MLR. III, 1908.]

Perfidus Hetruscus. [Bodl. MS Rawl. C, 787. Synopsis in Sh. Jb. XXXIV, pp. 250–2.]

[Psyche et Filii ejus.] [Bodl. MS Rawl. Poet. 171. A Latin allegorical play. See G. C. Moore Smith, Notes on some English University Plays, MLR. III, 1908.]

Romeus et Julietta. [BM. MS Sloane 1775, pp. 242–9 and 251–2 (imperfect). See H. de W. Fuller, Romeo and Juliette, MP. IV, 1906–7. (Contains a synopsis of the fragment and discusses its provenance.)]

Sapientia Salomonis: Drama Comicotragicum. [BM. Add. MS 20061. This MS was for a performance by Westminster boys before the Queen and Princess Cecilia of Sweden (see article in The Observer, 7 Dec. 1919). The play was acted at Trinity College, Cambridge, in 1565–6. Synopsis, with prefatory critical remarks, in Sh. Jb. XXXIV, pp. 224–9, also 323. Source: Xystus Betuleius: Drama comico-tragicum: Sapientia Salomonis, 1555.]

Senilis Amor. [Bodl. MS Rawl. Poet. 9 (imperfect). Dated 1635. May be by P. Hausted, author of Senile Odium. See L. B. Morgan, Sh. Jb. XLVII, 1911, p. 82.]

Silvanus. [Bodl. MS Douce 234. A Latin comedy. 'Acta haec fabula 13º Januarii an. dmi. 1596.' The cast shows the performance was at St John's College, Cambridge. F. Rollinson, who played the title-part, may have been the author. Synopsis in Sh. Jb. XXXIV, pp. 295–7.]

Solymannidæ Tragœdia. [BM. Lansdowne MS 723. After dramatis personae is added: 'Solymanidæ/Lugubris exitus Mustaphæ & G[angeri]/1581 Martii 5º.' Synopsis in Sh. Jb. XXXIV, pp. 245–6.]

Stoicus Vapulans. Olim Cantabrigiæ actus in Collegio S. Johannis Evangelistæ Ab ejus-dem Collegii Juventute. 1648. [An allegorical comedy acted at St John's College, Cambridge, at Christmastide, 1618. See College Life in the Time of James the First, as illustrated by an Unpublished Diary of Sir Symonds D'Ewes, 1851, pp. 61–2.]

Susenbrotus Comoedia. Acta Cantabrigiæ in Collegio Trin. coram rege Jacobo & Carolo principe. anno 1615. [Bodl. MS Rawl. Poet. 195, fol. 79. Another MS of the play with the title Fortunia, from the name of the heroine, is in the possession of the Earl of Ellesmere. See G. C. Moore Smith, College Plays, 1923, p. 101.]

Timon. A Play. Now first printed. Ed. A. Dyce, Shakespeare Soc. 1842. [Victoria and Albert Museum MS Dyce 52.]

A Pleasant Comedie, Called Wily Beguilde. The Chiefe Actors be these: A poore Scholler, a rich Foole, and a Knave at a shifte. 1606; 1623; 1630; 1635; [?]; ed. T. Hawkins (The Origin of the English Drama, vol. III, Oxford, 1773); *Hazlitt's Dodsley*, vol. IX; ed. W. W. Greg, *Malone Soc.* 1912; *TFT.* 1912. [See F. S. Boas, The Works of Thomas Kyd, 1901, Introduction, pp. xciv–xcv; G. Sarrazin, Thomas Kyd und sein Kreis, 1892. pp. 75–7 (both the above discuss Kyd's influence on the play); M. Baldwin, Stud. Phil. XIX, 1922, who suggests that the play is a revision of the lost Wylie Beguylie acted at Merton College, Oxford in 1567.]

Worke for Cutlers. Or, A Merry Dialogue Betweene Sword, Rapier, and Dagger. Acted in a Shew in the famous Universitie of Cambridge. 1615; rptd T. Park (Harleian Misc. vol. X, 1813); rptd C. Hindley (Miscellanea Antiqua Anglicana, vol. II, 1872); ed. A. F. Sieveking, 1904. [Sieveking argues in favour of the authorship of Thomas Heywood.]

Zelotypus. [MSS: Emmanuel College Cambridge III.1.17; Trinity College Cambridge R.3.9. From the cast given in both MSS it appears to have been acted at St John's College, Cambridge, in 1606. See G. C. Moore Smith, Notes on some English University Plays, MLR. III, 1908. Synopsis in Sh. Jb. XXXIV, pp. 313–7.]

F. S. B.

4. RELIGIOUS PROSE: CONTROVERSIAL AND DEVOTIONAL

I. HUMANISTS AND REFORMERS

LINACRE, ERASMUS, COLET, MORE, TINDALE, GARDINER, LATIMER, COVERDALE, CRANMER, LUPSET, FISH, ELYOT, RIDLEY, PARKER, CAIUS, PONET, ASCHAM, WILSON, FULKE

[For a more detailed bibliographical survey, especially of the minor figures, H. Gough, A General Index to the Publications of the Parker Society, Parker Soc. 1855, will be found useful.]

GENERAL STUDIES

Seebohm, Frederic. The Oxford Reformers of 1498: Colet, More, Erasmus. 1867; 1887.

Dixon, R. W. History of the Church of England from the Absolution of the Roman Jurisdiction. 6 vols. 1878–1902.

Morley, Henry. English Writers. Vol. VII, 1891. [Useful bibliographies.]

Wakeman, H. O. An Introduction to the History of the Church of England. 1896; rev. S. L. Ollard, 1914.

Gairdner, James. A History of the English Church in the 16th Century. From Henry VIII to Mary. 1902.

—— Lollardry and the Reformation. 4 vols. 1908–13.

Einstein, Lewis. The Italian Renaissance in England. New York, 1902.

—— Tudor Ideals. New York, 1921.

Gasquet, F. A. The Bibliography of some Devotional Books printed by the Earliest English Printers. Trans. Bibliog. Soc. VII, 1902–4.

—— Cardinal Pole and his Early Friends. 1927.

Frere, W. H. A History of the English Church in the Reigns of Elizabeth and James I, 1558–1625. 1904.

Opus Epistolarum Des. Erasmi Roterodami. Ed. P. S. and H. M. Allen, 8 vols. Oxford, 1906–34.

Allen, P. S. Some Sixteenth Century Manuscript Letter-books. Trans. Bibliog. Soc. XII, 1911–3.

—— The Age of Erasmus. Oxford, 1914.

Chamberlain, A. B. Hans Holbein. 1913.

Berdan, J. M. Early Tudor Poetry (1485–1547). New York, 1920.

Taylor, H. O. Thought and Expression in the Sixteenth Century. 2 vols. New York, 1920–1.

McFarlane, H. B. Cardinal Pole. Oxford, 1924.

Reed, A. W. Early Tudor Drama: Medwall, the Rastells, and the More Circle. 1926.

—— John Clement and his Books. Library, VI, 1926.

Life and Letters of Richard Fox (1486–1527), Founder of Corpus Christi College. Ed. P. S. and H. M. Allen, Oxford, 1930.

JOHN FISHER (1459?–1535)

[See pp. 681–2, 684 below.]

THOMAS LINACRE (1460?–1524)

(1) WORKS

Linacri Progymnasmatia. [1512?]. [A Latin grammar written for Colet's school, but not adopted.]

De Emendata Structura Latini Sermonis libri sex. 1524.

The Rudiments of Grammar. 1524.

[For Linacre's trns and edns of Greek and Latin medical works see bibliography in H. Morley, English Writers, vol. VII, 1891, p. 323, and p. 887 below.]

(2) BIOGRAPHY

Johnson, J. N. The Life of Thomas Linacre. Ed. R. Graves, 2 vols. 1835.

Burrows, Sir Montagu. Linacre's Catalogue of Books belonging to Grocyn with a Memoir of Grocyn. Collectanea Oxford Hist. Soc. II, 1890.

Osler, Sir William. Thomas Linacre. Cambridge, 1908.

DESIDERIUS ERASMUS (1466?–1536)

[This is not a bibliography of Erasmus, but of Erasmus in England. For further information the following should be consulted: Répertoire des Œuvres d'Érasme, 3 vols. Bibliotheca Erasmiana, Ghent, 1893; Bibliographie des Œuvres d'Érasme, 7 vols. Bibliotheca Erasmiana, Ghent, 1897–1908.]

(1) COLLECTED WORKS

Opera omnia. Ed. J. Le Clerc, 10 vols. Leyden, 1703–6.

The Epistles of Erasmus from his Earliest Letters to his Fifty-First Year. Ed. F. M. Nichols, 3 vols. 1901–18. [English trns.]

Opus Epistolarum Des. Erasmi Roterodami. Ed. P. S. and H. M. Allen, 8 vols. Oxford, 1906–34.

(2) Selected Works

Selections from Erasmus, principally from his Epistles. Ed. P. S. Allen, Oxford, 1908 and 1918.

(3) English Translations to 1640

(a) The Colloquies

The Earliest English Translations of Erasmus' Colloquia, 1536–1566. Ed. Henry de Vocht, Louvain, 1928. [Excellent introduction and: (1) A Mery Dialogue; (2) Two Dyaloges; (3) A Dialoge or Communication; (4) One Dialogue, or Colloquye.]

A Dialoge or Communication of Two Persons intituled the Pylgremage of Pure Devotyon. [1540?]

A very Pleasaunt and Fruitful Diologe called the Epicure. 1545.

Becke, Edmonde. Two Dyaloges, one called Polyphemus, the other dysposyng of thinges and names. Canterbury, [1550].

A Mery Dialogue, declaryng the Propertyes of Shrowde Shrewes, and Honest Wyves. 1557.

H[ake?], E. One Dialogue, or Colloquye (entituled Diversoria). 1566.

B[urton], W. Seven Dialogues both Pithie and Profitable. 1606 (re-issued as Utile dulce); 1624.

(b) Other Writings

[Roper, Margaret.] A Devout Treatise upon the Pater Noster. [1526?]

[Roy, W. ?] An Exhortation to the Diligent Studye of Scripture. [Antwerp], 1529; [1540?]

Taverner, R. A ryght Frutefull Epystle in Laude of Matrymony. [1530?]

—— Commonplaces of Scripture ordrely set forth. 1538.

—— Proverbes or Adagies with Newe Addicions. 1539 (bis); 1545; 1550; 1552; 1569.

—— Flores aliquot Sententiarum ex variis collecti Scriptoribus. 1540; 1547; 1550; [1556?]. [Latin and English.]

An Epystell unto Christofer Bysshop of Basyle concernyng the Forbedinge of Eatynge of Flesshe. [1530?]

A Treatise perswadynge a Man patiently to suffre the Deth of his Frende. [1532.]

Whytyngton, R. De Civilitate Morun (sic) puerilium: a Lytell Book of Good Maners for Chyldren. 1532; 1540; 1554. [Latin and English.]

A Sermon. [1532?] [On the marriage at Cana.]

Bellum Erasmi, translated into Englyshe. 1533 (for 1534).

Paynell, T. De Contemptu Mundi. 1533.

—— The Complaint of Peace. 1559.

[Tyndale, William?] A Booke called in Latyn Enchiridion and in Englysshe the Manuall of the Christen Knyght. 1533; 1534 (as Enchiridion Militis Christiani, newly corrected); [1540?]; 1541; 1544; 1548; [1550?]; 1576; rptd 1905 (from 1533 edn). [See J. A. Gee, Tindale and the 1533 English Enchiridion of Erasmus, PMLA. XLIX, 1934.]

A Playne and Godly Exposytion of the Commune Crede and of the .X. Commaundementes. [1533]; [1533?].

An Epistle concernynge the Veryte of the Sacrament of Christes Body. [1535?]

A Lytle Treatise of the Maner of Confession. [1535?]

The Paraphrase of Erasmi upon the Epistle of Paule unto Titus. [1535?]

An Exposicyon of the XV Psalme. 1537.

Preparation to Deathe. 1538; 1543.

[A Sermon of the Chylde Jesus.] [1540?] [The unique copy in BM. is without its title-page.]

A Scorneful Image or Monstrus Shape of a Marvelous Strange Fygure called, Sileni Alcibiadis. [?]

Udall, Nicholas. Apopthegmes, that is to saie, Prompte Saiynges. 1542; 1564; rptd 1877.

[——]. The First Tome of the Paraphrase of the Newe Testament. 1548.

Coverdale, Miles. A Shorte Recapitulacion of Erasmus Enchiridion. [Antwerp?], 1545.

Coverdale, Miles and Olde, J. The Seconde Tome of the Paraphrase upon the newe Testament. 1549.

Chaloner, Sir T. The Praise of Folie. 1549; [1560?]; 1577.

Lesse, N. The Censure and Judgement of Erasmus: whyther Dyvorsemente stondeth with the Lawe of God. [1550?]

A Comfortable Exhortation agaynst the Chaunces of Death. 1553.

The Epistle sente unto Conradus Pelicanus. 1554.

L[eigh], N. Modest Means to Marriage. 1568.

Adagia in Latine and English. Aberdeen, 1622.

(4) Biography and Criticism

Jortin, J. The Life of Erasmus. 2 vols. 1758–60.

Seebohm, F. The Oxford Reformers of 1498: Colet, More, Erasmus. 1867; 1887.

Drummond, R. B. Erasmus, his Life and Character as shown in his Correspondence and Works. 2 vols. 1873.

Jebb, R. C. Erasmus. Cambridge, 1890. [Rptd in Essays and Addresses, 1907.]

Froude, J. A. Life and Letters of Erasmus. 1894.

de Vocht, H. De Invloed van Erasmus op de engelsche Tooneel-literatuur der XVIᵉ en XVIIᵉ Eeuwen. I. Shakespeare Jest Books —Lyly. Ghent, 1908.
Allen, P. S. The Age of Erasmus. 1914.
—— Erasmus's Services to Learning. British Academy Lecture, 1925.
Murray, R. H. Erasmus and Luther: Their Attitude to Toleration. 1920.
Savage, H. J. The First Visit of Erasmus to England. PMLA. xxxvii, 1922.
Smith, Preserved. Erasmus, a Study of his Life, Ideals, and Place in History. New York, 1923.
—— A Key to the Colloquies of Erasmus. Cambridge, U.S.A. 1927.
Thomson, J. A. K. Erasmus in England. Vorträge der Bibliothek Warburg, 1930–1.

JOHN COLET (1467?–1519)

(1) WORKS

Oratio habita ad Clerum in Convocatione Anno 1511. [1512]; tr. Eng. (by Thomas Lupset?) [1530?] (bis); ed. J. H. Lupton (in Life of John Colet, 1887).
Libellus de Constructione. 1513.
Aeditio una cum quibusdam G. Lilii Grammatices Rudimentis. 1527; 1534; Antwerp, 1535; [Antwerp, 1535] (as Paules Accidence); Antwerp, 1536.
A ryght Frutefull Monycion concerning the ordre of a good chrysten mannes lyfe. 1534; 1563; 1577.
Opus de Sacramentis Ecclesiae. Ed. J. H. Lupton, 1867.
Two Treatises on Hierarchies of Dionysius. Ed. and tr. J. H. Lupton, 1869.
An Exposition of St Paul's Epistle to the Romans. Ed. and tr. J. H. Lupton, 1873.
An Exposition of St Paul's First Epistle to the Corinthians. Ed. and tr. J. H. Lupton, 1874.
Letters to Radulphus on the Mosaic Account of the Creation. Ed. and tr. J. H. Lupton, 1876. [Also includes shorter works by or attrib. to Colet.]

(2) BIOGRAPHIES

Erasmus, Desiderius. The Lives of Jehan Vitrier and John Colet. Ed. and tr. J. H. Lupton, 1883.
Knight, Samuel. The Life of Dr. John Colet. 1724; Oxford, 1823.
Seebohm, F. The Oxford Reformers of 1498: Colet, More, Erasmus. 1867; 1887.
Lupton, J. H. Life of John Colet. 1887; 1909.
Marriott, Sir J. A. R. The Life of John Colet. 1933.

SIR THOMAS MORE (1478–1535)
[A fuller bibliography by A. Guthkelch will be found appended to G. Sampson's edn of Utopia, 1910.]

(1) THE UTOPIA

(a) Latin Text

Libellus vere aureus de optimo reip. statu, deque nova Insula Utopiae cura P. Aegidii nunc primum editus. [Louvain, 1516]; Paris, [1517?]; Basle, 1518 (bis). [The Latin text accompanies Lupton's and Sampson's edns of Robinson's trn.]

(b) Ralph Robinson's Translation

A fruteful and pleasaunt work of the newe yle called Utopia translated into Englyshe by Raphe Robynson. 1551; 1556; 1597; 1624; 1639; ed. T. F. Dibdin, 1808; ed. E. Arber, 1869; ed. J. R. Lumby, 1879; ed. J. H. Lupton, Oxford, 1895 (includes Latin text and additional trns); ed. G. Sampson and A. Guthkelch, 1910 (with Latin text). Finely printed edns: Kelmscott Press, 1893 (foreword by William Morris); Ashendene Press, 1906; Golden Cockerel Press, 1929 (introduction by A. W. Reed).

(c) Other Translations

[Burnet, Gilbert.] Utopia: written in Latin by Sir Thomas More. 1684; rptd H. Morley, 1885; ed. Sir Sidney Lee, 1906 (with the poems).
[Cayley, Sir Arthur.] Memoirs of Sir Thomas More; with a new translation of his Utopia, his History of King Richard III, and his Latin Poems. 2 vols. 1808.
[Also tr. Valerian Paget, 1909, and G. C. Richards, 1923. For French, German, Italian, Spanish and Dutch trns see Guthkelch's bibliography, pp. 435–6.]

(d) Critical Studies

Kautsky, Karl. Thomas More und seine Utopia. Mit historischer Einleitung. Stuttgart, 1890; tr. Eng. H. J. Stenning, 1927.
Dudok, G. Sir Thomas More and his Utopia. Amsterdam, 1923.
Reed, A. W. Sir Thomas More. [In Social and Political Ideas of the Renaissance and the Reformation, ed. F. J. C. Hearnshaw, 1925.]
Chambers, R. W. The Saga and Myth of Sir Thomas More. British Academy Lecture, 1927.
Dermenghem, G. E. Thomas Morus et les Utopistes de la Renaissance. Paris, 1927.
The Fame of Blessed Thomas More. Ed. R. W. Chambers, 1929. [Essays by R. Knox, H. Belloc, G. K. Chesterton, etc.]

Campbell, W. E. More's Utopia and his Social Teaching. 1930.

(2) THE LATIN WORKS

(a) Collected Editions

Thomae Mori lucubrationes. Basle, 1563. [A collection of those Latin works which had already been pbd separately, together with letters on More's life, character and death.]

Thomae Mori Omnia opera. Louvain, 1565 and 1566. [First appearance of the Latin text of More's History of King Richard III.]

Thomae Mori Opera omnia. Sumptibus C. Genschii. Frankfort, 1689. [Based on the earlier collections, with additional *elogia*.]

(b) Separate Works

Luciani compluria opuscula ab Erasmo & Thoma Moro in latinorum linguam traducta. [Paris, 1506]; Paris, 1514; Venice, 1516 (with addns by Erasmus); Venice, 1517; Basle, 1528, etc. [More was responsible for: (1) Cynicus; (2) Menippus, seu Necromantia; (3) Philopseudes, seu incredulus; (4) Tyrannicida, with the Declamatio Mori de eodem.]

Epigrammata Thomae Mori pleraque e Graecis versa. Basle, 1518 and 1520.

Thomae Mori Epistola ad Germanum Brixium. 1520. [An answer to G. Brixii Antimorus, Paris, 1520.]

Eruditissimi viri G. Rossei opus quo repellit Lutheri calumnias. 1523. [Rosseus was More's pseudonym. See 'Thomas Morus in Lutherum' in the Louvain edn of the Latin works, 1565.]

Epistola T. Mori ad Academiam Oxon. Oxford, 1633. [Reproaching the University for the neglect of the Greek language.]

(3) THE ENGLISH WORKS

(a) Collected Editions and Selections

The workes of Sir Thomas More wrytten by him in the Englysh tonge. 1557; ed. facs. with modernised version W. E. Campbell, with introductions by R. W. Chambers and notes and introductions by A. W. Reed, 2 vols. 1931–. [This collection was ed. by More's nephew, W. Rastell.]

The Wisdom and Wit of Blessed Thomas More; being Extracts from such of his Works as were written in English. Ed. T. E. Bridgett, 1892.

Sir Thomas More: Selections from his English Works and from the Lives by Erasmus and Roper. Ed. P. S. and H. M. Allen, Oxford, 1924.

(b) Separate Works

A mery jest how the sergeant would lerne to play the frere. [1510?] (Julian Notary).

The lyfe of Johan Picus Erle of Myrandula. [1510?] (J. Rastell); [1510?] (de Worde); ed. J. M. Rigg, 1890 (from de Worde's text).

The supplycacyon of soulys. Agaynst the supplycacyon of beggars. [1530] (W. Rastell). [An answer to Simon Fish.]

A dyaloge of syr Thomas More of ymages, praying to sayntys, othere thynges touchyng the pestylent sect of Luther and Tyndale. 1529 (J. Rastell); 1530 (W. Rastell, 'newly oversene'). [See William Tyndale, An answere unto Sir Thomas Mores dialoge, [1530], ed. Parker Soc. 1850.]

The confutacyon of Tyndales answere. 1532 (W. Rastell). [Bks I–III.]

The second parte of the confutacion of Tyndals answere. 1533 (W. Rastell).

The debellacyon of Salem and Bizance. 1533 (W. Rastell).

The apologye of syr T. More knyght. 1533 (W. Rastell); ed. A. I. Taft, EETS. 1929.

Syr Thomas Mores answere to the poysoned booke which [W. Tyndale] hath named the Souper of the Lorde. 1534 (W. Rastell).

A dialoge of comfort against tribulacion. 1553 (Tottell).

[Versions of More's History of King Richard III originally appeared in the chronicles of Hardyng and Hall. There are modern edns by S. W. Singer, 1821, and, with omissions, J. R. Lumby, 1883. For an examination of the authorship see articles by R. W. Chambers and W. A. G. Doyle-Davidson in Campbell's edn of the English Works, vol. I, 1931.]

(4) THE MORE CIRCLE

Rastell, John (1470?–1536). The Pastime of People. 1529; ed. T. F. Dibdin, 1811. [A history of England with remarkable woodcuts.]

—— A newe boke of purgatory. 1530.

[For the plays assigned to Rastell (The Four Elements, Gentleness and Nobility, and Calisto and Meliboea) see above, pp. 514, 517. For his activities as law printer, compiler of law books, and controversialist, see A. W. Reed, Early Tudor Drama, 1926.]

Frith, John. A disputacion of Purgatorye whiche answereth unto Sir Thomas More. [London? 1533.]

—— A boke made by J. F., prisoner in the tower of London. Münster, 1533.

Smythe, Walter. Twelve Merry jests of the widow Edith. 1525 (J. Rastell); ed. W. C. Hazlitt (Shakespeare Jest-Books, vol. III, 1864). [Amusing references to More household.]

Roy, William. Rede me and be not wroth. [1526]; ed. E. Arber, 1871. [See A. Koszul, Was Bishop William Barlowe Friar Jerome Barlowe? RES. IV, 1928.]

Watson, Foster. Vives and the Renaissance Education of Women. 1912. [Interesting notes on More and his household.]

Life and Works of Thomas Lupset. Ed. J. A. Gee, New Haven, 1928.

Literae Virorum eruditorum ad F. Crane-veldium, 1522–1528. Ed. H. de Vocht, Louvain, 1928.

(5) BIOGRAPHIES

[For the Tudor lives see R. W. Chambers, British Academy Lecture, 1927.]

Harpsfield, N. The Life and Death of Sir Thomas Moore. Ed. (from MSS) E. V. Hitchcock, EETS. 1932. [Includes The Continuity of English Prose from Alfred to More, a Life of Harpsfield, and Notes—all by R. W. Chambers; and Appendices, containing various biographical fragments.]

Stapleton, T. Tres Thomae. Douai, 1588; tr. Eng. P. E. Hallett, 1928. [St Thomas, Thomas à Becket, Thomas More.]

Roper, W. The Mirrour of Vertue in Worldly Greatnes; or, the life of Sir Thomas More. Paris, 1625, etc.; ed. E. V. Hitchcock, EETS. 1935.

Ba., Ro. Ed. (from MS) C. Wordsworth (Ecclesiastical Biography, vol. II, 1810).

More, Cresacre. The life and death of Sir T. More, written by M. T. M. [Paris, 1631?]; ed. J. Hunter, 1828.

Mackintosh, Sir James. Lardner's Cabinet Cyclopaedia. 1830.

Seebohm, Frederic. The Oxford Reformers of 1498: Colet, More, Erasmus. 1867; 1887.

Bridgett, T. E. Life and Writings of Blessed Thomas More. 1887.

Hutton, W. H. Sir Thomas More. 1895.

Brémond, Henri. Sir Thomas More. Tr. Eng. H. Child, 1904.

Routh, E. M. G. Sir Thomas More and his Friends. 1934.

Chambers, R. W. Thomas More. 1935.

Cecil, A. A Portrait of Thomas More. 1936.

[For the play, The Booke of Sir Thomas Moore, see pp. 576–7 above. For works containing references to More see Guthkelch's bibliography, pp. 429–31.]

WILLIAM TINDALE (d. 1536)

(1) WORKS

The Obedience of a Christen Man. [Antwerp?], 1528; 1535; [1548]; [?]; [1548?]; [1550?] (bis); 1561.

The Parable of the Wicked Mammon. [Antwerp], 1528; 1536; [1541?]; 1547; [1548] ('corrected'); 1549; 1528 (for 1550?); [1560?].

An Answere unto Sir T. More's Dialoge. [Antwerp? 1530.]

The Practyse of Prelates, whether the Kynges Grace may be separated from hys Quene. [Antwerp?] 1530; 1548; [1549?].

An Exposicion upon the v. VI. VII. Chapters of Mathew. [Antwerp? 1530?]; [?]; 1548; [1550?] ('corrected').

The Exposition of the Fyrste Epistle of Seynt Jhon. [Antwerp], 1531.

The Supper of the Lorde. [Antwerp?], 1533; [?]; 1533; [1548?] (3 edns).

A fruitefull and Godly Treatise Expressing the Right Institution of the Sacraments. [1533?]; [1548?] (as A briefe declaration).

A Pathway to the Holy Scripture. [153–] (anon.); [1534?]; 1564.

The Testament of W. Tracie, Esquier, expounded. 1535.

The Exposition of the Epistles of St Jhon. 1538.

A Compendious Introduccion unto the pistle to the Romayns. [?]

The Whole Works of W. Tyndall, J. Frith and Doct. Barnes. 2 vols. 1573–2. [Preface by Fox.]

Doctrinal Treatises and Introductions to Different Portions of the Holy Scriptures. Ed. H. Walter, Parker Soc. 1848. [Contains The Parable of the Wicked Mammon and The Obedience of a Christian Man.]

Tyndale's Expositions and Practice of Prelates. Ed. H. Walter, Parker Soc. 1849.

An Answer to Sir Thomas More's Dialogue. The Supper of the Lord, and Wm Tracy's Testament expounded. Ed. H. Walter, Parker Soc. 1850.

[For Tindale's biblical trns see below, p. 675. See also under Erasmus and More above.]

(2) BIOGRAPHY

Demaus, R. William Tyndall. A Biography. 1871; rev. R. Lovett, 1886. [See also under More above and under the Bible, pp. 672–4 below.]

STEPHEN GARDINER (1483?–1555)

(1) WORKS

Stephani Winton. Episcopi De Vera Obedientia Oratio. 1535; Strasburg, 1536; Hamburg, 1536; tr. Eng. 1553 (3 edns).

A Declaration of Such True Articles as George Joye hath gone about to confute. 1546 (bis).

A Detection of the Devils Sophistrie, wherwith he robbeth the Unlearned People, of the True Byleef, in the Sacrament of the Aulter. 1546 (bis).

An Explication and Assertion of the True Catholique Fayth, touchyng the moost Blessed Sacrament of the Aulter. [Rouen, 1551].

Obedience in Church & State: Three Political Tracts by Stephen Gardiner. Ed. P. Janelle, Cambridge, 1930. [Prints from MS a tract on Fisher's execution (1535) and an answer to Bucer (1541); and reprints De Vera Obedientia, 1535, and the English trn of 1553.]

The Letters of Stephen Gardiner. Ed. J. A. Muller, Cambridge, 1933.

(2) Biography

Muller, J. A. Stephen Gardiner and the Tudor Reaction. 1926.

HUGH LATIMER (1485?–1555)
(1) Works

Concio quam habuit Pater H. Latimer in Conventu Spiritualium. [1537]; tr. Eng. 1537 (bis); 1537 (for 1538).

A notable sermon of Maister Hughe Latimer, preached in the Shroudes at Paules Churche. 1548 (bis); [?]; ed. E. Arber, 1868. [The Plough Sermon.]

The fyrste Sermon of Mayster Hughe Latimer, preached before the Kinges Majestie at Westminster. [1549] (3 edns.); ed. E. Arber, 1869.

The Seconde [Third, Fourth, Fifth, Sixth, Seventh] Sermon preached before the Kynges Majestic. [1549] (bis); 1562 (as The Seven Sermons).

A most Faithfull Sermon preached before the Kynges Majestye. [1550]; [1550?].

A Sermon preached at Stamford. [1550.]

Certain Sermons made before Katherine, duchess of Suffolk. Ed. Augustine Bernher, 1552; 1562.

Twenty Seven Sermons preached by Hugh Latimer. 1562. [Preface by Thomas Some.]

Frutefull Sermons by Hugh Latimer. 3 pts, 1571–5; 1578; 1584; 1596; 1607. [38 sermons.]

Seven sermons made upon the Lordes Prayer. 1572.

The Sermons of Master Hugh Latimer. 2 vols. 1758. [With life.]

Sermons of Hugh Latimer arranged. With Life. Ed. John Watkins, 2 vols. 1824.

Latimer's Sermons. Ed. G. E. Corrie, Parker Soc. 1844.

Sermons and Remains of Hugh Latimer. Ed. G. E. Corrie, Parker Soc. 1845.

Sermons. Ed. H. C. Beeching, [1906]. (Everyman's Lib.)

(2) Biographies and Studies

Becon, Thomas. The Jewel of Joye. [1553.] [Latimer's preaching.]

Demaus, R. Hugh Latimer. A Biography. 1869; 1881 (rev. edn).

Tulloch, J. Leaders of the Reformation. 1883.

Carlyle, R. W. and A. J. Hugh Latimer. 1900.

Ryle, J. C. Bishops Latimer and Ridley. 1925.

MILES COVERDALE (1488–1568)

Goostly Psalmes. [1539?]

The Order that the Churche in Denmarke doth use. [1550?]

Certain most Godly Letters of such True Saintes as gave their Lyves. 1564.

Writings of Myles Coverdale. Ed. G. Pearson, Parker Soc. 1844.

Remains of Myles Coverdale. Ed. G. Pearson, Parker Soc. 1846.

[For Coverdale's trn of the Bible see p. 675 below. For his other trns see under Erasmus above, Satires on Women (p. 716 below) and Calvin (p. 811 below).]

THOMAS CRANMER (1489–1556)
(1) Works

Cathechismus. That is to say; a Shorte Instruction into Christian Religion. 1548 (bis); [?].

A Defence of the True and Catholike Doctrine of the Sacrament. 1550 (3 edns); 1557 (rev.); ed. C. H. H. Wright, 1907; tr. Latin Sir J. Cheke, 1553.

An Answer unto a Crafty and Sophistical Cavillation devised by Stephen Gardiner. 1551; 1580 ('revised and corrected by the Archbishop').

A Confutation of Unwritten Verities. Translated and set forth by E. P. 1558; 1582.

The Remains of Thomas Cranmer. Ed. H. Jenkyns, 4 vols. Oxford, 1833.

Writings and Disputations of Thomas Cranmer relative to the Sacrament of the Lord's Supper. Ed. J. E. Cox, Parker Soc. 1844. [Includes life.]

Miscellaneous Writings and Letters of Thomas Cranmer. Ed. J. E. Cox, Parker Soc. 1846.

(2) Biographies and Studies

Strype, John. Memorials of Thomas Cranmer. 1694.

Dixon, R. W. History of the Church of England. 6 vols. 1884–1902. [Full and sympathetic treatment of Cranmer.]

Mason, A. J. Thomas Cranmer. 1898.

Pollard, A. F. Thomas Cranmer and the English Reformation. 1904; 1926.

Bolwell, R. W. The Life and Works of John Heywood. New York, 1921. [Ch. ii.]

Smyth, C. H. Cranmer and the Reformation under Edward VI. Cambridge, 1926.

Deane, A. C. Life of Thomas Cranmer. 1927.

THOMAS LUPSET (1495–1530)

The sermon of doctor Colete made to the Convocacion at Paulis. [1530?] (bis). [The trn is anon. but is probably by Lupset.]

A treatise of charite. 1533 (anon.); 1535; 1539.

A compendious and a very fruteful treatyse, teachynge the waye of Dyenge well. 1534; 1541.

An exhortation to yonge men, perswadinge them to walke in the pathe way that leadeth to honeste and goodnes. 1535; 1538; 1544.

A Sermon of Saint Chrysostome: translated into Englishe. 1542.

Tho. Lupsets workes. 1546; 1560.

The Life and Works of Thomas Lupset with a Critical Text of the Original Treatises [i.e. 2nd, 3rd and 4th items above] and the Letters. Ed. J. A. Gee, New Haven, 1928. [See pp. 157–74, Bibliography and Canon of Lupset's Works, for other writings that have been ascribed to Lupset.]

RICHARD WHITFORD (fl. 1495–1555?)

[See below p. 685.]

SIMON FISH (d. 1531)

A supplicacyon for the beggars. [1529?]; ed. F. J. Furnivall, EETS. Ex. Ser. 1871; ed. E. Arber, Birmingham, 1878.

The Summe of the holye scripture and ordynance of Christen teachyng. [Antwerp], 1529; n.p. [1529?]; [1535?] (bis); [1547]; 1548; [1550?]. [Tr. from Dutch.]

A supplication of the Poore Commons, wnere-unto is added the Supplication of Beggers. 2 pts [1546].

SIR THOMAS ELYOT (1499?–1546)

(1) WORKS

The Boke named the Governour. 1531; 1537; 1544; 1546; 1553; 1557; 1565; 1580; ed. H. H. S. Croft, 2 vols. 1880 (with important introduction on Elyot's life and works); ed. F. Watson, 1907 (Everyman's Lib.).

Of the Knowledge which maketh a Wise Man. 1533; 1534; [after 1548?].

Pasquil the Playne, a Dialogue on Talkativeness and Silence. 1533 (bis); 1540; Rome, [1552?].

A Swete and Devoute Sermon of Holy Saynte Ciprian of the Mortalitie of Man. [With] The Rules of a Christian Lyfe made by Picus Erle of Mirandula. 1534; 1539. [Trns.]

The Doctrinal of Princes. [1534] (bis); [1548?]. [Tr. from Isocrates.]

The Education or Bringinge up of Children. [1535?]; [1550?]. [Tr. from Plutarch.]

How one may take Profyte of his Enmyes. [1535?] (anon.). [Tr. from Plutarch.]

The Dictionary of Syr Thomas Elyot. 1538; 1545 (as Bibliotheca Elyotae); rev. T. Cooper, 1548; 1552; 1559.

The Castel of Helth. 1539; 1541 (bis) ('corrected'); 1541 (for 1544?); 1541 (for 1548–9?); 1547; [1559?]; [1560?]; 1561; 1572; 1580; [1580?]; 1587; 1595; rptd facs. New York, 1937.

The Bankette of Sapience. 1539; 1542; 1545; 1557; 1564.

The Image of Governance compiled of the Actes of Alexander Severus. 1541; 1544; 1549; 1556.

The Defence of Good Women. 1545.

A Preservative agaynste Deth. 1545.

(2) BIOGRAPHY AND CRITICISM

Benndorf, C. Die englische Pädagogik im 16. Jahrhundert: Elyot, Ascham, und Mulcaster. Vienna, 1905.

Pollard, A. F. Sir Thomas More and Sir Thomas Elyot. TLS. 17 July 1930.

Starnes, D. T. Sir Thomas Elyot and the Sayings of Philosophers. Texas University Stud. XIII, 1933.

NICHOLAS RIDLEY (1500?–1555)

(1) WORKS

A Brief Declaracion of the Lordes Supper. [Zurich?], 1555; ed. F. H. Moule, 1895.

Certen Godly, Learned and Comfortable Conferences betwene D. N. Ridley and M. H. Latymer. [Zurich], 1556 (bis); 1574 (with The Lordes Supper). [Includes A Treatise agaynst the Errour of Transubstantiation.]

A Frendly Farewel, which Master Doctor Ridley did write, unto all his True Lovers and Frendes in God, a Litle before that he suffred. 1559.

A Pituous Lamentation of the Miserable Estate of the Churche of Christ in Englande in the Time of the Late Revolt from the Gospel. 1566; [?].

Works. Ed. H. Christmas, Parker Soc. 1843.

(2) BIOGRAPHIES

Ryle, J. C. Bishops Latimer and Ridley. 1925.

Merrill, L. R. The Life and Poems of Nicholas Grimald. New Haven, 1925. [Introduction.]

MATHEW PARKER (1504–1575)

(1) WORKS

How we ought to take the Death of the Godly. A Sermon made in Cambridge at the Buriall of the Noble Clerck D. M. Bucer. [1551?]; [1570?].

A Briefe Examination of a certaine Declaration. [1566.]

The Whole Psalter translated into English Metre. [1567?]

De Antiquitate Britannicae Ecclesiae Cantuariensis, cum Archiepiscopis ejusdem 70. [1572] (anon.); ed. S. Drake, 1729.

An Admonition to All Suche as shall intende to enter the State of Matrimony. 1574; 1594; [1605?]; 1620.

The Correspondence of Matthew Parker. Ed. J. Bruce and T. T. Perowne, Parker Soc. 1853.

[Parker also edited a sermon of Aelfric's, the Anglo-Saxon version of the Gospels, and the following chroniclers: Asser, Matthew of Westminster, Matthew Paris, Thomas Walsingham.]

(2) BIOGRAPHIES

Strype, John. The Life and Acts of Matthew Parker. 1711; 3 vols. Oxford, 1821.

Kennedy, W. M. Life of Archbishop Parker. 1908.

Pearce, E. C. Matthew Parker. Library, VI, 1925.

Greg, W. W. Books and Bookmen in the Correspondence of Archbishop Parker. Library, XVI, 1935.

JOHN CAIUS (1510–1573)

A Boke, or Counseill against the Disease called the Sweate, or Sweatyng Sicknesse. 1552. [Latin and English.]

De Antiquitate Cantabrigiensis Academiae Libri duo. 1568; 1574.

De Canibus Britannicis liber unus; De rariorum animalium et stirpium historia; de libris propriis. 3 pts, 1570. [Pt I, tr. Eng. A. Fleming as Of English Dogges, 1576.]

De Pronunciatione Grecae & Latinae Linguae cum Scriptione nova Libellus. 1574.

Historiae Cantabrigiensis Academiae Liber. 1574.

The Works of John Caius. Ed. E. S. Roberts, Cambridge, 1912. [With Memoir of Caius by John Venn.]

[Caius also edited and translated into Latin Galen's works (see p. 888 below).]

JOHN PONET (or POYNET) (1514?–1556)

A tragoedie or dialoge of the unjuste primacie of the Bishop of Rome. 1549; ed. C. E. Plumptre, 1899. [Tr. from Bernardino Ochino.]

ROGER ASCHAM (1515–1568)

(1) COLLECTED WORKS

The English Works of Roger Ascham. Ed. James Bennet, 1761; rev. J. G. Cochrane, 1815.

The Whole Works of Roger Ascham. Ed. J. A. Giles, 4 vols. in 3, 1865–4.

English Works: Toxophilus, Report of the Affaires of Germany, The Scholemaster. Ed. W. Aldis Wright, Cambridge, 1904.

(2) SEPARATE WORKS

Toxophilus, the Schole of Shootinge conteyned in Two Bookes. 1545; 1571 ('newlye perused'); 1589; ed. J. Walters, Wrexham, 1788; ed. E. Arber, Birmingham, 1868.

A Report and Discourse of the Affaires and State of Germany. [1570?]; 1570.

The Scholemaster, or Plain and Perfite Way of teachyng Children the Latin Tong. 1570; 1571 (bis); 1571 (for 1573); 1589; ed. J. Upton, 1711 and 1743 (rev. edn); ed. J. E. B. Mayor, 1863; ed. E. Arber, Birmingham, 1869; ed. J. Holzamer, Vienna, 1881.

Familiarium Epistolarum Libri tres. [1576]; 1578 (rev.); 1581; 1590; Hanover, 1602; ed. E. G[rant], Hanover, 1610; ed. W. Elstob, Oxford, 1703.

Apologia pro Cæna dominica. Themata. Expositiones in epistolas Pauli ad Titum & Philemonem. 1577.

(3) CRITICAL STUDIES

Katterfeld, A. Roger Ascham. Sein Leben und seine Werke. Strasburg, 1879.

Quick, R. H. Essays on Educational Reformers. 1888.

Fischer, T. A. Drei Studien zur englische Literaturgeschichte. Gotha, 1892.

Benndorf, C. Die englische Pädagogik im 16. Jahrhundert: Elyot, Ascham, und Mulcaster. Vienna, 1905.

Radford, L. B. Roger Ascham. Quart. Rev. CCLVI, 1931.

THOMAS LEVER (1521–1577)

[See p. 682 below.]

THOMAS WILSON (1525?–1581)

(1) WORKS

The Rule of Reason, conteining the Arte of Logique set forthe in Englishe. 1551; 1552; 1553 (for 1554); 1563; 1567 (for 1584?); 1580.

The Arte of Rhetorique for the Use of all suche as are Studious of Eloquence sette forth in Englishe. 1553 (for 1554); 1560 ('Newlie sette forthe again'); 1562; 1563; 1567; 1580; 1584; 1585; ed. G. H. Mair, Oxford, 1909 (from 1560 edn).

The Three Orations of Demosthenes in Favour of the Olynthians with those his Fower Orations against King Philip of Macedonie. 1570.

A Discourse upon Usurye. 1572; 1584; ed. R. H. Tawney, 1925.

Vita et Obitus duorum Fratrum Hen. et Car. Brandoni. 1551 (re-issued n.d.). [In collaboration with Walter Haddon.]

(2) CRITICISM

Reed, A. W. Nicholas Udall and Thomas Wilson. RES. I, 1925.

Wagner, R. H. The Text and Editions of Wilson's Arte of Rhetorique. MLN. XLIV, 1929.

—— Wilson and his Sources. Quart. Journ. Speech, XV, 1929.

WILLIAM FULKE (1538–1589)

A defense of the sincere and true translations of the holie scriptures into the English tong. 3 pts, 1583; 1617; 1633; ed. N. C. Hartshorne, Parker Soc. 1843.

A. W. R.

II. THE ENGLISH BIBLE

(1) CATALOGUES AND BIBLIOGRAPHIES

Cotton, H. A List of Editions of the Bible and Parts thereof in English, from the Year MDV. to MDCCCXX. Oxford, 1821; 1852.

—— Rhemes and Doway. Oxford, 1855. [Deals fully with the R.C. edns.]

Orme, W. Bibliotheca Biblica. Edinburgh, 1824.

Horne, T. H. A Manual of Biblical Bibliography. 1839.

Wilson, L. Bibles, Testaments, Psalms and Other Books of the Holy Scriptures in English, in the Collection of Lea Wilson. 1845.

Shea, J. G. A Bibliographical Account of Catholic Bibles printed in the United States. New York, 1859.

O'Callaghan, E. B. A List of Editions of the Holy Scriptures and Parts thereof, printed in America previous to 1860. Albany, 1861.

Loftie, W. J. A Century of Bibles, or the Authorised Version from 1611 to 1711. 1872.

Stevens, H. The Bibles in the Caxton Exhibition, 1877. 1878.

Lovett, R. The English Bible in the John Rylands Library, 1525–1640. 1899.

Darlow, T. H. and Moule, H. F. Historical Catalogue of the Printed Editions of Holy Scripture in the Library of the British and Foreign Bible Society. 2 vols. (in 4 pts), 1903–11. [Vol. I (English), 1903, contains full descriptions of all the important edns. Cited below in section (4) as HC.]

Milligan, G. Notes on the Euing Collection of Bibles. Records of Glasgow Bibliog. Soc. IV, 1914.

Pollard, A. W. and Redgrave, G. R. A Short-title Catalogue of Books printed in England, Scotland, and Ireland, and of English Books printed abroad 1475–1640. Bibliog. Soc. 1926. [This contains the fullest list of Bible edns down to 1640. Cited below in section (4) as STC.]

[Most of the great libraries of England and America and some smaller or private libraries contain notable collections of English Bibles. Useful illustrated guides to special Bible exhibitions have been pbd by the British Museum, the British and Foreign Bible Soc., Glasgow University Lib., the John Rylands Lib. (Manchester), and other libraries. Some of the books in section (2) contain lists of Bible edns.]

(2) GENERAL WORKS

Lewis, J. A Complete History of the Several Translations of the Holy Bible and New Testament into English. 1731 (prefixed to the earliest ptd edn of the Wycliffite N.T.); 1739; 1818.

Newcome, W. An Historical View of the English Biblical Translations. Dublin, 1792.

Anderson, C. The Annals of the English Bible. 2 vols. 1845; 1862 (rev. edn); abridged by S. I. Prime, New York, 1849.

Conant, H. C. The English Bible. New York, 1856; rev. T. J. Conant, New York, 1881.

Westcott, B. F. A General View of the History of the English Bible. 1868; 1872; rev. W. Aldis Wright, 1905. [The standard work on the subject.]

Blunt, J. H. A Plain Account of the English Bible. 1870.

Dore, J. R. Old Bibles. 1876; 1888.

Eadie, J. The English Bible. 2 vols. 1876.

Moulton, W. F. The History of the English Bible. 1878; rev. J. H. and W. F. Moulton, jun. [1911].

Stoughton, J. Our English Bible. 1878.

Condit, B. The History of the English Bible. New York, 1882.

Mombert, J. I. A Hand-book of the English Versions of the Bible. New York, 1883; 1890; 1907; 1931. [See Athenaeum, 18 April and 2 May 1885.]

Schaff, P. A Companion to the Greek Testament and the English Version. New York, 1883. [Includes chs. on the Authorized and Revised Versions.]

Smyth, J. Paterson. How we got our Bible. 1886; 1889; 1899; 1906.

Edgar, A. The Bibles of England. Paisley, 1889.

Lovett, R. The Printed English Bible, 1525–1885. 1894; 1909.

Pattison, T. H. The History of the English Bible. 1894.

Kenyon, Sir F. G. Our Bible and the Ancient Manuscripts. 1895; 1912. [Includes a ch. on the English ptd Bible.]

—— The English Versions of the Bible. [The History of Christianity in the Light of Modern Knowledge, 1929, pp. 639–49.]

Milligan, G. The English Bible: a Sketch of its History. 1895; 1907.

—— [Article on English Versions in vol. IV of J. Hastings' Dictionary of the Bible, Edinburgh, 1900–4. See also articles by J. H. Lupton on English Versions, and by Ll. J. M. Bebb on Continental Versions, in the Extra vol.]

—— The New Testament and its Transmission. 1932.

Ayres, S. G. and Sitterly, C. F. The History of the English Bible studied by the Library Method. New York, [1898].

Hoare, H. W. The Evolution of the English Bible. 1901; 1902; 1911 (as Our English Bible).

Barker, H. English Bible Versions. New York, 1907.

Price, I. M. The Ancestry of our English Bible. Philadelphia, 1907.

Heaton, W. J. Our own English Bible. 3 vols. 1910 3.

Bevan, J. O. Our English Bible. 1911.

Brown, J. The History of the English Bible. Cambridge, 1911.

Canton, W. The Bible and the English People. 1911; 1914 (rev. as The Bible and the Anglo-Saxon People).

Girdlestone, R. B. Our English Bible. 1911.

Jayne, A. G. The Bible in English. [1911.]

Payne, J. D. The English Bible. 1911.

Pollard, A. W. Records of the English Bible: the Documents relating to the Translation and Publication of the Bible in English, 1525–1611. Oxford, 1911. [Indispensable to students.]

Penniman, J. H. A Book about the English Bible. New York, 1919; 1931.

Guppy, H. A Brief Sketch of the History of the Transmission of the Bible down to the Revised English Version of 1881–95. Manchester, 1925.

Baikie, J. The English Bible and its Story. 1928.

Scott, W. The Story of our English Bible. 1929.

(3) Special Studies

Sparke, M. Scintilla, or a Light broken into darke Warehouses. 1641. [This tract, which throws a flood of light on the prices of Bibles and the general bookselling trade in the early 17th century, is rptd in E. Arber's Transcript of the Registers of the Stationers' Company, vol. IV, pp. 35–8, and in the Bible Society's Historical Catalogue, vol. I, pp. 189–94.]

Kilburne, W. Dangerous Errors in several late printed Bibles. 1659. [Rptd in W. J. Loftie's A Century of Bibles, 1872.]

Lee, J. Memorial for the Bible Societies in Scotland. Edinburgh, 1824. Additional Memorial. Edinburgh, 1826. [See Index by W. J. Couper, Glasgow, 1918.]

—— Remarks on the complaint of His Majesty's Printers against the Bible Societies. Edinburgh, 1824. [These deal with the Bible monopoly, incorrect edns, etc.]

Petty, W. T. An Essay upon the Influence of the Translation of the Bible upon English Literature. 1830.

Bagster, S. The English Hexapla, exhibiting the Six Important English Translations of the New Testament Scriptures: Wiclif, 1380; Tyndale, 1534; Cranmer, 1539; Genevan, 1557; Anglo-Rhemish, 1582; Authorised, 1611; preceded by an Historical Account [by S. P. Tregelles] of the English Translations. [1841]; [1872] (with historical account by J. Stoughton).

MacCulloch, J. M. Literary Characteristics of the Holy Scriptures. Greenock, 1845 and 1847.

Roger, C. A Collation of the Principal English Translations with an Historical Account of the English Versions, with Memoirs of the Principal Translators. 1847.

Walter, H. Doctrinal Treatises and Introductions to Different Portions of the Holy Scriptures. By William Tyndale. Parker Soc. 1848.

Halsey, L. J. The Literary Attractions of the Bible. New York, 1859 (3rd edn).

Marsh, G. P. Lectures on the English Language. New York, 1863 (4th edn).

Wordsworth, C. Shakespeare's Knowledge and Use of the Bible. 1864; 1892.

Fry, F. A Description of the Great Bible, 1539, and the Six Editions of Cranmer's Bible, 1540 and 1541, also of the Editions in Large Folio of the Authorized Version printed in 1611, 1613, 1617, 1634, 1640. 1865.

—— The Bible by Coverdale MDXXXV. 1867.

—— A Bibliographical Description of the Editions of the New Testament, Tyndale's Version. 1878.

Wright, W. Aldis. The Bible Word-book. 1866; 1884. [A useful glossary of archaic words and phrases in the A.V. and the Book of Common Prayer. The Preface mentions earlier works on the same subject. See also A Select Glossary of Bible Words, by A. L. Mayhew, 1891.]

Wright, W. Aldis. The Hexaplar Psalter. Cambridge, 1911. [Contains the Psalms in six versions: Coverdale (1535), Great Bible (1539), Geneva (1560), Bishops' (1568), A.V. (1611), R.V. (1885).]

Scrivener, F. H. A. The Cambridge Paragraph Bible of the Authorized English Version, with the Text Revised by a Collation of its Early and Other Principal Editions and a Critical Introduction prefixed. Cambridge, 1873.

—— The Authorized Edition of the English Bible (1611), its Subsequent Reprints and Modern Representatives. Cambridge, 1884.

Bradshaw, H. Godfried van der Haghen (G. H.), the Publisher of Tindale's Own Last Edition of the New Testament in 1534–35. Bibliographer, Dec. 1881. [Rptd in Collected Papers of Henry Bradshaw, Cambridge, 1889.]

Arber, E. An Apology, made by George Joy, to satisfy, if it may be, W. Tindale. Birmingham, 1882. [No. 13 of The English Scholar's Library. Rptd from the unique copy in Cambridge University Lib. of G. Joye's defence of himself against Tindale's charges.]

Cheney, J. L. The Sources of Tindale's New Testament. Ang. VI, 1883.

Dobson, W. T. History of the Bassandyne Bible, the First printed in Scotland. Edinburgh, 1887.

Smith, W. E. A Study of the Great 'She' Bible (1613 or 1611). 1890. [Rptd from Library, II, 1890.]

Cook, A. S. The Bible and English Prose Style. Boston, 1892.

—— Biblical Quotations in Old English Prose Writers. 2 vols. 1898; New York, 1903.

—— The Authorised Version and its Influence. CHEL. vol. IV, 1909.

—— The Authorized Version of the Bible and its Influence. New York, 1910.

Moulton, R. G. The Literary Study of the Bible. 1896; 1912.

König, E. Stilistik, Rhetorik, Poetik in Bezug auf die biblische Litteratur. Leipzig, 1900.

Carleton, J. G. The Part of Rheims in the Making of the English Bible. Oxford, 1902.

Prothero, R. E. (Baron Ernle). The Psalms in Human Life. 1903, etc.

Swearingen, G. F. Die englische Schriftsprache bei Coverdale. Mit einem Anhang über ihre weitere Entwicklung in den Bibelübersetzungen bis zu der Authorized Version 1611. Berlin, 1904.

Carter, T. Shakespeare and Holy Scripture. 1905.

Williams, J. M. Roman Catholic and Protestant Bibles compared. New York, 1905.

Gardiner, J. H. The Bible as English Literature. 1906.

Howorth, H. H. The Origin and Authority of the Biblical Canon in the Anglican Church. Journ. Theological Stud. Oct. 1906, pp. 1–40. [Gives the history of the Apocrypha in the English versions.]

Slater, J. R. The Sources of Tyndale's Version of the Pentateuch. Chicago, 1906.

Whitney, J. P. Reformation Literature in England. CHEL. vol. III, 1909.

Cleaveland, E. W. A Study of Tindale's Genesis compared with the Genesis of Coverdale and of the Authorized Version. New York, 1911.

Taylor, A. The Bible and English Life. [1911.]

von Dobschütz, E. The Influence of the Bible on Civilisation. Edinburgh, 1914. [See the same writer's article, Bible in the Church, in J. Hastings' Encyclopaedia of Religion and Ethics, 1908–21.]

Gruber, L. F. The Truth about the so-called 'Luther's Testament in English', Tyndale's New Testament. St Paul, Minnesota, 1917. [Rptd from Lutheran Church Rev. Oct. 1916 and April–May 1917. Rev. as The First English New Testament and Luther: the Real Extent to which Tyndale was dependent upon Luther as a Translator, Burlington, Iowa, 1928.]

Moffatt, J. The Bible in Scots Literature. 1924.

Guppy, H. William Tindale and the Earlier Translators of the Bible into English. Manchester, 1925.

Fletcher, H. F. The Use of the Bible in Milton's Prose. New York, 1929.

Mellone, S. H. The Bible and English Literature. Ency. Brit. 14th edn, 1929.

Innes, K. E. The Bible as Literature. 1930.

Coleman, E. D. The Bible in English Drama: an Annotated List. New York, 1931.

Dinsmore, C. A. The English Bible as Literature. 1931.

Eason, C. The Circulation of the Douay Bible in Ireland. Dublin, 1931.

[For certain special points, e.g. the omission of the Apocrypha, marginal notes and references, misprints, Bible monopoly, original prose versions since 1611, patents to print, prices, etc., consult the index to general subjects at the end of vol. IV of the Bible Society's Historical Catalogue, and many of the works mentioned above.]

(4) The Translations

The Golden Legend. [An English trn of the Legenda Aurea of Jacobus de Voragine, containing nearly the whole of the Pentateuch, and a considerable part of the Gospels, with mediaeval glosses. Ptd by W. Caxton at Westminster: (1) [after 20 Nov. 1483], (2) [1487?]; etc. STC. 24873–80.] Ed. F. S. Ellis, 7 vols. 1900 (Temple Classics).

Tindale's version. The Cologne fragment. [P. Quentell? Cologne, 1525.] [The first attempt made by W. Tindale to publish the trn of the N.T. prepared by himself with some help from W. Roy. Perhaps no more than sigs. A–K (40 leaves). Represented only by the Grenville copy in the British Museum, which contains sigs. A–H, without title-leaf, i.e. 31 leaves, ending at Matt. xxii. 12. STC. 2823; HC. 1.] Ed. photo. facs. E. Arber, 1871; ed photo. facs. A. W. Pollard, Oxford, 1926.

Tindale's New Testament. [P. Schoeffer, Worms, 1525 or 1526.] [The first edn definitely known to have been completed. STC. 2824; HC. 2. Two copies: (1) in the Baptist College Lib. Bristol, wanting only the title-leaf, (2) in St Paul's Cathedral Lib., very imperfect.] Ed. (with memoir) G. Offor, 1836; ed. facs. F. Fry, Bristol, 1862.

[Some early edns have been lost. Those extant include the following: (a) ptd at Antwerp by the Widow of Christoffel of Endhoven (i.e. Christoffel van Ruremund), Aug. 1534, and again 9 Jan. 1535; (b) corrected by Tindale himself, ptd at Antwerp by M. Emperowr [i.e. de Keyser], Nov. 1534, and again [M. de Keyser? for Govaert van der Haghen], 1534–5; (c) with strange spellings [Hans van Ruremund, Antwerp], 1535 and again [1535?]; (d) 7 edns in 1536, including one ascribed to T. Godfray, London, apparently the earliest edn of the N.T. ptd in England. STC. 2825–35; HC. 5, 6, 8–12. For later edns down to 1566 see catalogues and Fry's bibliography. The Nov. 1534 edn was rptd S. Bagster, The English Hexapla, [1841] and [1872].]

Tindale's Pentateuch. Hans Luft, Malborow [i.e. Marburg] in the land of Hesse [identified by M. E. Kronenberg with Johannes Hoochstraten of Antwerp: see Library, IX, 1928, pp. 153–9], 17 Jan. 1530. [A rev. edn of Genesis with a re-issue of the other books appeared in 1534. STC. 2350–1; HC. 3.] Ed. (with collations and prolegomena) J. I. Mombert, New York, 1884.

Tindale's Jonah. [M. de Keyser, Antwerp? 1531?] [STC. 2788; HC. 4. Only one copy (British Museum) known.] Ed. facs. F. Fry, Bristol, 1863.

[Tindale also translated the liturgical 'Epistles' taken from the O.T., which were ptd for the first time as an appendix to the Nov. 1534 edn of his N.T. Before his death in Oct. 1536 he seems to have carried his trn of the O.T. as far as Chronicles (or Nehemiah). All

Tindale's work, with the exception of Jonah, the O.T. Epistles (and Nehemiah, if he translated it), was incorporated in Matthew's Bible of 1537 (see below), the remaining books being supplied from Coverdale's version.]

G. Joye's translations of (1) Isaiah, 10 May 1531, (2) Jeremiah, Lamentations and the Song of Moses, May 1534, (3) Psalms, Aug. 1534; apparently all printed at Antwerp. [STC. 2777–8, 2372. For Joye's unauthorised correction of Tindale's New Testament see above: the second of his two edns, includes his own trn of the O.T. Epistles. See Library, Jan. 1905, p. 19.]

Coverdale's Bible. [Christopher Froschouer, Zurich?] 4 Oct. 1535. [The first ptd English Bible. See L. A. Sheppard, The Printers of the Coverdale Bible, 1535, Library, XVI, 1935. STC. 2063; HC. 7. Rptd S. Bagster, 1838; and again, with memoir of Coverdale added, 1847. The Psalter rptd W. A. Wright, The Hexaplar Psalter, 1911.]

[Other edns: (a) J. Nycolson, Southwark, 1537, folio and 4to, the earliest English Bibles ptd in England; (b) C. Froschouer, Zurich, for A. Hester, London, 16 Aug. 1550; re-issued by R. Jugge in 1553. For edns of the N.T. down to 1550 see catalogues.]

Matthew's Bible. Printed at Antwerp for R. Grafton and E. Whitchurch, London, 1537. [Thomas Matthew is commonly treated as a pseudonym of John Rogers, the editor of this Bible, which, welding together the work of Tindale and Coverdale (see above), may be considered the real primary version of the English Bible. STC. 2066; HC. 17.]

[Other edns: Ed. E. Becke, J. Day and W. Seres, 17 Aug. 1549; T. Raynalde and W. Hyll, 31 Oct. 1549; N. Hyll for others, 6 May 1551.]

Taverner's Bible. J. Byddell for T. Berthelet, London, 1539. [STC. 2067; HC. 24. See also HC. 66.]

Great Bible. [F. Regnault, Paris, and] R. Grafton and E. Whitchurch, London, 1539. [A revision by Coverdale of Matthew's Bible. STC. 2068; HC. 25. The N.T. rptd S. Bagster, The English Hexapla, [1841] and [1872]. The Psalter rptd W. A. Wright, The Hexaplar Psalter, 1911. The Prayer Book version of the Psalter is taken from the Great Bible.]

[An edn in smaller folio appeared in April 1540, and this was followed by six large folio edns in 1540–1, the first of which was the earliest to include Cranmer's prologue. STC. 2069–76; HC. 29–31, 34–7. For other edns down to 1569 see catalogues.]

Whittingham's Testament. C. Badius, Geneva, 10 June 1557. [An independent version due to one translator, who is assumed to be William Whittingham. The earliest English N.T. ptd in roman type and with verse divisions. STC. 2871; HC. 76. The N.T. rptd S. Bagster, The English Hexapla, [1841] and [1872]; and also separately, [1842], facs.]

Geneva Bible. R. Hall, Geneva, 1560. [Tr. Whittingham and other English refugees at Geneva. The earliest English Bible ptd in roman type and with verse divisions. STC. 2093; HC. 77. The Psalter rptd W. A. Wright, The Hexaplar Psalter, 1911.]

[Other edns of the Bible: Geneva, 1561–2, 1568–70; 1576 (bis, ptd by C. Barker, London, the first produced in England); 1577 (bis); 1578; Edinburgh, 1576–9 (the Bassandyne Bible, the earliest English Bible ptd in Scotland); etc. (including the earliest English Bible ptd at Cambridge, 29 May 1591). Edns of the N.T.: Geneva, 1560; C. Barker, London, 1575, 1575–6, 1576 (first revised by L. Tomson), etc. Between 1560 and 1644 at least 140 edns appeared of the Geneva Bible or N.T.: see catalogues.]

Bishops' Bible. R. Jugge, London, 1568. [STC. 2099; HC. 89. The Psalter rptd W. A. Wright, The Hexaplar Psalter, 1911.]

[Corrected edns appeared in 1569 (4to) and 1572 (folio). For other edns of the Bible down to 1602, and of the N.T. down to 1617, see catalogues.]

Douai-Rheims Bible. N.T., J. Fogny, Rheims, 1582; O.T., L. Kellam, 2 vols. Douai, 1609–10. [The Roman Catholic version, prepared by Gregory Martin and other English refugees in France. STC. 2884, 2207; HC. 134, 231. The N.T. rptd S. Bagster, The English Hexapla, [1841] and [1872].]

[Other edns: N.T., 1600, 1621, 1633; O.T., 1635. According to Cotton, not a single edn of this R.C. version of the Bible was pbd between 1635 and 1750. For reprints and 'confutations' of the Rheims N.T. by W. Fulke (1589, etc.) and T. Cartwright (1618) see HC. 156 and 282.]

King James' Bible, or the Authorized Version. R. Barker, London, 1611. [STC. 2216; HC. 240. An 'exact reprint page for page' was issued by the Oxford University Press, 1833. A literal rpt, with a list of variations between the 'two issues of 1611', ed. W. A. Wright, 5 vols. Cambridge, 1909. In commemoration of the tercentenary of the Authorized Version the Oxford University Press issued two special edns: (1) photo. facs., slightly reduced, of the original

black-letter edn of 1611; (2) a reproduction in roman type of the same book; both with a bibliographical introduction by A. W. Pollard.]

[Corrected edns: Cambridge, 1629, 1638, 1762; Oxford, 1769. The earliest English Bible ptd at Oxford was issued in 1673–5. For the problem of the early edns and other special points see catalogues and various books mentioned above, especially A. W. Pollard's Records.]   H. F. M.

III. THE PRAYER BOOK

(1) EDITIONS

The Booke of the Common Prayer and Administracion of the Sacramentes, and other Rites and Ceremonies of the Churche: after the use of the Churche of England. 1549, etc. (for later edns see STC. nos. 16268–16278); ed. H. B. Walton and P. G. Medd, 1869; ed. J. Parker, Oxford, 1883; rptd W. B., 1888. [See also under next item.]

The Boke of Common Prayer and Administracion of the Sacramentes and other Rites and Ceremonies in the Churche of Englande. 1552, etc. (for later edns see STC. 16280–16290); ed. J. Parker, Oxford, 1883; rptd W. B., 1888; ed. H. J. Wotherspoon, Edinburgh, 1905. [Edns of the 1549 and the 1552 versions together: E. Cardwell, Oxford, 1838; J. Ketley, Parker Soc. 1844; E. C. S. Gibson, 1910 (Everyman's Lib.).]

The Boke of Common Praier and Administration of the Sacramentes, and other Rites and Ceremonies in the Churche of Englande. 1559, etc. (for later edns to 1640 see STC. nos. 16292–16422); rptd W. B., 1890.

The Booke of Common Prayer, and Administration of the Sacraments. And other parts of divine service for the use of the Church of Scotland. 1637, etc.; rptd P. Hall (in Reliquiae Liturgicae, vol. I, Bath, 1847); ed. facs. J. Dowden, Edinburgh, 1884; ed. J. Cooper, Edinburgh, 1904.

The Book of Common-Prayer And Administration Of the Sacraments and other Rites & Ceremonies Of the Church, According to the Use Of the Church of England. 1662, etc.; rptd 1848; ed. J. H. Blunt, 1866, 1903 (rev. edn).

Facsimile of the Black-letter Prayer-book [1636], containing Manuscript Alterations and Additions made in 1661 'out of which was fairly written' the Book of Common Prayer [of 1662]. 1871.

Facsimile of the Original Manuscript of the Book of Common Prayer [of 1662]. 1891.

Liturgiae Britannicae; or the Several Editions of the Book of Common Prayer together with the Liturgy of the Church of Scotland. Ed. W. Keeling, 1842, 1851.

(2) HISTORIES AND SPECIAL STUDIES

Sparrow, A. A Rationale upon the Book of Common Prayer of the Church of England. 1657; ed. J. H. N[ewman], Oxford, 1839.

Cardwell, E. A History of Conferences and Other Proceedings connected with the Revision of the Book of Common Prayer from 1558 to 1690. Oxford, 1840.

Hall, P. Reliquiae Liturgicae. Documents connected with the Liturgy of the Church of England. 5 vols. Bath, 1847.

—— Fragmenta Liturgica. Documents illustrative of the Liturgy of the Church of England. 7 vols. Bath, 1848.

Parker, J. The First Prayer-Book of Edward VI compared with the Successive Revisions of the Book of Common Prayer. Oxford, 1877.

Gasquet, F. A. and Bishop, E. Edward VI and the Book of Common Prayer. 1890; 1928 (rev. edn).

Batiffol, P. Histoire du Bréviaire romain. Paris, 1893; tr. Eng. 1898.

Dowden, J. The Workmanship of the Prayer Book in its Literary and Liturgical Aspects. 1899.

—— Further Studies in the Prayer Book. 1908.

Procter, F. and Frere, W. H. A New History of the Book of Common Prayer. 1901; 1905 (rev. edn).

Gee, H. The Elizabethan Prayer-Book and Ornaments. 1902.

Swete, H. B. Church Services and Service Books before the Reformation. 1905.

Brightman, E. The English Rite. 1915.

Brightman, E. and Mackenzie, K. D. The History of the Book of Common Prayer down to 1662. [In Liturgy and Worship, ed. W. K. L. Clarke, 1932. A useful bibliography supplements the present list.]

Dodge, J. G. The Litany in English. Berkeley, 1922.

IV. VERSIONS OF THE PSALMS

[The primary authorities for the subject are J. Julian, Dictionary of Hymnology, 1925 and J. Holland, Psalmists of Britain, 2 vols. 1843.]

Aleph, Johan. The Psalter of David. Strasburg. 1530. [A prose trn of 150 Psalms based on the Psalmorum Libri Quinque of Martin Bucer.]

Joye, George. David's Psalter. Antwerp, 1534. [A prose trn of 150 Psalms based on the Latin of Felix Pratensis. See C. Anderson, Annals of the English Bible, 1862.]

Croke, Sir John. Thirteen Psalmes. [1536?]; ed. Percy Soc. 1843. [A verse trn of Ps. 6, 32, 38, 51, 102, 130, 143, 19, 13, 43, 139, 91, 31. v. 1–6. See Sir A. Croke, Early English Poetry, vol. II, pp. 56–7, Percy Soc. 1843.]

Coverdale, Miles. Goostly Psalmes and Spirituall Songes. [1539?]; ed. G. Pearson, Parker Soc. 1846. [A metrical trn of Ps. 2, 11, 13, 24, 45, 50, 67, 123, 127, 129, 133, 136, 147 (Vulgate numbering), shewing indebtedness in some places to the German hymn-writers. See Julian, Dictionary of Hymnology, p. 442; A. F. Mitchell, The Wedderburns and their Work, Edinburgh, 1867, pp. 31–4.]

—— A Paraphrasis upon all the Psalmes of David. 1539. [Prose trn of 150 Psalms made from the Latin of Johannes Campensis; assigned by Bale in Illustres Britanniae Scriptores to Coverdale.]

'Basille, Theodore' (i.e. Thomas Becon). David's Harpe. 1542; ed. Parker Soc. 1843. [A prose trn of Ps. 116, v. 10–9, with exposition. See Holland, Psalmists of Britain, vol. I, pp. 127 ff.]

Howard, Henry (Earl of Surrey). [Verse trns of Ps. 55, 73, 88, 8. See Holland, vol. I, pp. 85–6.]

Wiat, Sir Thomas. Certayne Psalmes. 1549; ed. J. Nott, 1816. [A verse trn of the Penitential Psalms (Ps. 6, 32, 38, 51, 102, 130, 143) in lyric form, shewing considerable indebtedness to the Italian prose paraphrases of Pietro Aretino. See A. K. Foxwell, Poems of Sir Thomas Wiat, 2 vols. 1913.]

Crowley, Robert. The Psalter of David. [?] [A metrical trn of 150 Psalms, based on the Latin Biblia Sacrosancta of Leo Judas.]

Sternhold, Thomas, and others. Certayne Psalmes [later The Whole Booke of Psalmes]. [1549]; 1549; 1551 (bis); 1553; Geneva, 1556; 1560; 1561 (bis); 1562; 1563; 1564 (bis); Edinburgh, 1564; 1565 (bis); Edinburgh, 1565; 1566; 1567; 1569; Geneva, 1569; 1570; 1572; etc. [Annual edns until close of 16th cent. after which it was rptd at intervals until commencement of the 18th cent. Of these edns the first contained 19 Psalms by Sternhold, a later edn in the same year 37 by Sternhold and 7 by John Hopkins; 1556 edn an additional 7 by William Whittingham; first complete edn 1561. This metrical version of the Psalter was intended for public use, and was licensed for use in the churches by

Edward VI and Elizabeth. See Sir S. E. Brydges, Censura Literaria, vol. x, 1805, pp. 4–21; T. Warton, History of English Poetry, vol. IV, 1871, pp. 136–7; Julian, Dictionary of Hymnology, p. 857 under Old Version. The share of the various contributors to the complete edn was as follows: Sternhold, Thomas: Ps. 1–17, 19, 20, 21, 25, 28, 29, 32, 34, 41, 43, 44, 49, 63, 68, 73, 78, 103, 120, 123, 128.

Hopkins, John: Ps. 24, 27, 30, 33, 35, 36, 38, 39, 40, 42, 45, 46, 47, 48, 50, 52, 54, 55, 57–62, 64, 65, 69–72, 74, 76, 77, 79–99. See Brydges, vol. x, p. 10; Julian, p. 861.

Whittingham, William: Ps. 23, 37, 50, 51, 67, 71, 114, 115, 119, 121, 124, 127, 129, 130, 133, 137. See Brydges, vol. x, p. 11; Julian, p. 161.

Kethe, William: Ps. 27, 36, 47, 54, 58, 62, 70, 85, 88, 90, 91, 94, 100, 101, 104, 107, 111, 112, 113, 122, 125, 126, 134, 138, 142. See Brydges, vol. x, p. 11; Julian, p. 623 (William Kethe), p. 1022 (Scottish Hymnody).

Norton, Thomas: Ps. 51, 53, 75, 101, 102, 105, 106, 108, 109, 110, 115, 116, 117, 129, 136, 138–145, 147, 149, 150. See Julian, p. 862.

Marckant, John: Ps. 118, 131, 132, 135. See Julian, p. 862.

Pullain, John: Ps. 148, 149. See Brydges, vol. x, p. 11; Julian, p. 861.]

Hall, John. Courte of Vertue. 1550; 1565. [A metrical version of Ps. 25, 34, 54, 65, 113, 114, 115, 130, 137, 140, 145, with a verse prologue to each Psalm.]

Hunnis, William. Certayne Psalmes. 1550. [A verse trn of Ps. 51, 56, 57, 113, 117, 147, intended for musical setting.]

—— Seven Sobs of a Sorrowful Soule for Sinne. 1585; 1597; 1600; Edinburgh, 1621; 1629. [A verse trn of amazing prolixity of the Penitential Psalms.]

Seager, Francis. Certaine Psalmes. 1553. [A metrical version set to music of Ps. 88, 31, 51, 112, 130, 138, 140, 141, 143, 144, 145, 146, 147, 149, 43, 64, 120, 70.]

Parker, Matthew. The Whole Psalter translated into English Metre. [1556?] [A metrical version of 150 Psalms with musical settings, characterised by great diversity of metre. See T. Warton, History of English Poetry, vol. IV, 1871, pp. 143–7.]

Wedderburn, John. Gude and Godlie Ballatis. Edinburgh, 1567, 1578, 1600, 1621; ed. A. F. Mitchell, STS. 1897. [A metrical version of Ps. 2, 12, 13, 15, 23, 31, 33, 37, 51, 64, 67, 77, 79, 83, 91, 104, 115, 124, 128, 130, 137, 145. See A. F. Mitchell, The Wedderburns and their Work, Edinburgh, 1867, and p. 903 below.]

Golding, Arthur. Psalms of David. 1571. [A prose version of 150 Psalms with Calvin's commentary to same.]

Gascoigne, George. De Profundis. [A lyrical rendering of Ps. 130 contained in A Hundreth Sundrie Flowres, 1573, 1575, 1587. See Holland, vol. I, p. 182.]

Rogers, Thomas. A Golden Chaine. 1579; 1587. [Some 71 short poems composed principally of a collection of verses from the Psalms, arranged according to subject matter.]

Gilbie, Anthony. The Psalmes of David. 1581; 1590. [A prose paraphrase of 150 Psalms based on Theodore Beza.]

Stanyhurst, Richard. [Verse trns of Ps. 1, 2, 3, 4, in various classical metres, appended to The first foure bookes of Virgil his Aeneis, Leyden, 1582. See Holland, vol. I, pp. 187–9.]

Sidney, Sir Philip and the Countess of Pembroke. The Psalmes of David translated into Divers and Sundry Kindes of Verse. Written 1587? Ed. S. W. Singer, 1823; ed. A. Feuillerat (Complete Works of Sidney, vol. III, Cambridge, 1923). [A verse trn in various metres of 150 Psalms, Ps. 1–43 being the work of Sidney and the rest of his sister. See Holland, vol. I, pp. 194–200; A. Feuillerat, Complete Works of Sidney, vol. III, pp. viii–ix.]

Fraunce, Abraham. Certaine Psalmes of David. [A verse trn in English Hexameters of Ps. 1, 6, 8, 29, 38, 5, 73, 104 contained in The Countess of Pembroke's Emmanuel, 1591. See Holland, vol. I, pp. 224–6.]

Lok, Henry. Sundry Psalms of David. [A trn in sonnet form of Ps. 27, 71, 119, 121, 130, in Sundry Christian Passions, 1597. See Holland, vol. I, pp. 228–9.]

Verstegan, Richard. Odes in Imitation of the Seaven Penitential Psalmes. Antwerp, 1601. [A verse trn of Ps. 6, 32, 37, 51, 102, 130, 143. See J. Fitzmaurice-Kelly, New Rev. July, 1897.]

Dod, Henry. Certaine Psalmes of David. 1603; 1620 (as Al the Psalmes of David). [The earlier edn contained a metrical version of Ps. 104, 111, 120, 122, 124, 125, 126, 130. See Holland, vol. I, pp. 247–50.]

Grymeston, Elizabeth. Odes in Imitation of the seven Paenitentiall Psalmes. 1604; 1610. [Verse trns in seven different metres of the Penitential Psalms. See Sir S. E. Brydges, Censura Literaria, vol. IV, 1805, pp. 39–42.]

Montgomery, Alexander. The Mindes Melodie. Edinburgh, 1606. [A metrical version of Ps. 1, 4, 6, 15, 19, 23, 43, 57, 91, 101, 117, 121, 125, 128. See Holland, vol. I, pp. 241–2.]

Hall, Joseph. Some fewe of David's Psalms metaphrased for a taste of the reste. 1607; 1624. [A metrical version of Ps. 1–10 intended for singing to the traditional tunes. See Holland, vol. II, pp. 27–9.]

Ainsworth, Henry. The Booke of Psalmes. Amsterdam, 1612; 1617; 1632; Amsterdam, 1644. [A metrical version of 150 Psalms with musical setting.]

Davies, John. The Doleful Dove. [A verse trn of the Penitential Psalms contained in The Muses Sacrifice, 1612.]

Leighton, Sir William. Seaven Psalmes of David's Repentance. [A verse trn of the Penitential Psalms contained in Teares or Lamentations of a Sorowful Soul, 1613.]

Sandys, Sir Edwin. Fifti select Psalmes of David. 1615. [A metrical version, set to music, of Ps. 1, 2, 8, 15–7, 19–22, 25, 32, 34, 36, 37, 40, 42, 44, 45, 49–51, 67–9, 73, 79, 82, 84, 90, 92, 94, 100, 101, 103, 104, 107, 110–2, 118, 119, 122, 128, 130, 137, 139, 141, 145, 146. See Holland, vol. I, pp. 270–1.]

Milton, John. [Verse trn of Ps. 114, 136, 1623; Ps. 80–8, 1648; Ps. 1–8, 1653. All these are included in Poems in English and Latin, 1673. See Holland, vol. II, pp. 39–41.]

Bacon, Francis. Certaine Psalmes. 1625; 1765. [A verse trn of Ps. 1, 12, 90, 104, 126, 137, 149, in various metres, dedicated to George Herbert. See Holland, vol. I, pp. 267–8.]

Top, Alexandre. Book of Prayses. Amsterdam, 1629. [A prose version of 150 Psalms purporting to be made direct from the Hebrew.]

James I. The Psalms. Oxford, 1631; 1636; 1637; Edinburgh, 1712. [A metrical version of 150 Psalms intended for use with the Scottish Book of Common Prayer: largely, if not entirely, the work of William Alexander, Earl of Stirling. See Holland, vol. I, pp. 251–8, 259–86.]

Wither, George. The Psalmes of David. [Netherlands?], 1632; rptd 2 pts, Spencer Soc. 1881. [A verse trn of 150 Psalms. See Holland, vol. II, pp. 6–11.]

H[erbert?], G[eorge?] [A verse trn of Ps. 3, 4, 6, 7, 1, 2, 5, in H. Playford's Psalmes and Hymnes in Solomn Musick, 1671. See Holland, vol. I, pp. 279.]

Fletcher, Phineas. Certain of the Royal Prophets Psalmes.. [A verse trn of Ps. 1, 42, 63, 127, 130, 137, contained in the Poetical Miscellanies ptd with The Purple Island, Cambridge, 1633. See Holland, vol. II, p. 16.]

Goodridge, Richard. The Psalmes. 1634. [A metrical version of 150 Psalms with 100 variant versions. See Holland, vol. II, p. 53.]

Hawkins, John. Paraphrase upon the seaven Penitential Psalmes. [Douai?], 1635. [A prose version of the Penitential Psalms tr. from the Italian of Pietro Aretino.]

S[andys], G[eorge]. A Paraphrase upon the Psalmes. 1636; 1638; 1648; 1676. [A verse trn of 150 Psalms in various metres with musical settings. See Holland, vol. I, pp. 282–8.]

B[rathwait], R[ichard]. The Psalmes of David. 1638. [A metrical version of 150 Psalms based on Arias Montanus. See Julian, p. 923.]

Slatyer, William. Psalmes of David. 1643; 1652. [A metrical version in four languages (Greek, Latin, English, Hebrew) of Ps. 1–22, with musical settings by Thomas Campion, etc. See Holland, vol. I, pp. 301–3.]

Barton, William. The Book of Psalms. 1644; 1645; 1646; 1654; 1682; 1691; 1705. [A metrical version of 150 Psalms with appendix of variant lines. See Holland, vol. II, pp. 18–21.]

Boyd, Zachary. The Psalmes of David. Glasgow, 1646; 1648. [A metrical version of 150 Psalms with interlinear prose version. See Holland, vol. II, pp. 23–6.]

Crashaw, Richard. [Verse trns of Ps. 23, 137, in Steps to the Temple, 1648 (2nd edn). See Holland, vol. II, pp. 12–4.]

Roberts, Francis. The Book of Praises. [A metrical version of 150 Psalms embodied in his Clavis Bibliorum, 1649, 1656, 1657, 1665, 1675. See Holland, vol. II, pp. 60–3.]

Vaughan, Henry. [Verse trn of Ps. 121, in Silex Scintillans, 1650; Ps. 104, 45, added to 2nd edn, 1655. See Holland, vol. II, pp. 100–1.]

White, John. David's Psalms. 1654. [A verse trn of 150 Psalms based upon the Authorised Version and the Latin of Tremellius. See Holland, vol. II, pp. 67–8.]   F. H.

V. SERMONS AND DEVOTIONAL WRITINGS: FISHER TO DONNE

(1) HISTORY OF PREACHING

(a) General History

Broadus, J. A. Lectures on the History of Preaching. 1876.

Rothe, R. Geschichte der Predigt. Bremen, 1881.

Ker, J. Lectures on the History of Preaching. 1888.

Hauck-Herzogs Realencyklopädie. Vol. xv, Leipzig, 1896 (3rd edn); tr. Eng. 1908. [Art. 'Predigt' by M. Schian.]

Hering, H. Geschichte der Predigt. Berlin, 1897.

Dargan, E. C. A History of Preaching. 2 vols. 1905–13.

(b) Preaching in Mediaeval England

Neale, J. M. Mediaeval Preachers. 1856.

Baring-Gould, S. Post-Mediaeval Preachers. 1865.

Gasquet, F. A. The Old English Bible, and other Essays. 1897.

—— The Eve of the Reformation. 1900.

Owst, G. R. Preaching in Mediaeval England: an Introduction to Sermon Manuscripts of the Period c. 1350–1450. Cambridge, 1926.

—— Literature and Pulpit in Medieval England. Cambridge, 1933.

Chambers, R. W. The Continuity of English Prose from Alfred to More. EETS. 1932.

(c) For the Period of the English Reformation

Haweis, J. O. W. Sketches of the Reformation, taken from the contemporary pulpit. 1844.

Coleridge, S. T. Notes on English Divines. Ed. D. Coleridge, 2 vols. 1853.

Tulloch, J. Leaders of the Reformation. 1859; 1883 (enlarged edn).

Masters in English Theology. Ed. A. Barry, 1877.

Classic Preachers of the English Church. Ed. J. E. Kempe, 2 sers. 1877–8.

Dixon, R. W. History of the Church of England. 6 vols. 1878–1902. [Gives special attention to the preachers.]

Taylor, W. M. The Scottish Pulpit from the Reformation. 1887.

Blaikie, W. G. The Preachers of Scotland from the Sixth to the Nineteenth Century. 1888.

Brown, John. Puritan Preaching in England. 1900.

White, H. C. English Devotional Literature (Prose), 1600–1640. Madison, 1931.

Mitchell, W. F. English Pulpit Oratory from Andrewes to Tillotson. 1932. [Contains a useful bibliography.]

(d) Sixteenth Century Writers on Methods of Preaching

Erasmus, Desiderius. Des. Erasmi Rot. Ecclesiastae sive de ratione concionandi libri quatuor. Basle, 1535; tr. Eng. 1797.

Polanus, Amandus. De concionum sacrarum methodo. Basle, 1574.

de la Ramée, P. The Logike of P. Ramus, newly translated. 1574.

Gerardus, Andreas ('Hyperius'). The Practis of Preaching. Englished by J. Ludham. 1577.

Osiander, L. De ratione concionandi. Tübingen, 1582.

Perkins, William. Prophetica, sive de sacra ratione concionandi. 1592; tr. Eng. 1606.

Sutcliffe, Matthew. De recta Studii Theologici ratione. 1602.

(2) SERMONS

Adams, Thomas (fl. 1612–1653). The Workes, being the Summe of his Sermons. 1629; ed. J. Angus, 3 vols. 1861. [Selection, ed. J. Brown, Cambridge 1909.]

Alcock, John (1430–1500; bishop of Ely). Sermo. Qui habet aures. [n.d.] (bis). [In English.]

Andrewes, Lancelot (1555–1626; bishop of Winchester). The wonderfull combate betweene Christ and Satan, opened in seven sermons. 1592 (anon.); 1627.

—— Sermon on good Friday last before the King [on Lam. i. 12]. 1604.

—— Concio latine habita coram regia majestate, 5 Aug. 1606. 1610. [English version added to XCVI Sermons, 1641 (4th edn).]

—— A sermon before the King concerning the right of calling assemblies. 1606. Tr. Latin, 1608; Dutch, Leyden, 1610.

—— A sermon on Christmas Day, 1609. [Gal. iv. 4, 5.] 1610.

—— A sermon on Christmas Day, 1610. [Lk. ii. 10, 11.] [1611.] [Rptd with above as Two Sermons. Of the Birth of Christ, 1610.]

—— A sermon before His majestie at Holdenbie. [1 Chr. xvi. 22.] 1610.

—— Scala Coeli: nineteene sermons concerning prayer. 1611.

—— A sermon on Easter-day. [Ps. cxviii. 22.] 1611.

—— A sermon on Easter-day. [Phil. ii. 8–11.] 1614.

—— A sermon preached the fift of November, 1617. 1618.

—— A sermon on Easter-day. [1 Cor. xi. 16.] 1618.

—— A sermon on Easter-day. [Jn. xx. 11–16.] 1620.

—— XCVI Sermons. Ed. W. Laud and J. Buckeridge, 1629; 1631 (another issue with date 1632); 1635; 1641; 1661; ed. J. P. Wilson, 5 vols. 1841–3.

—— Opuscula quaedam posthuma. 1629. [Includes Latin sermons.]

—— The Moral Law expounded. Whereunto is annexed 19 sermons upon Prayer. Also 7 sermons on our Saviours Tentations. 1642.

—— Sacrilege a snare: a sermon ad clerum. [Prvbs. xx. 25.] Translated [from Latin]. 1646.

—— Ἀποσπασμάτια Sacra; posthumous and orphan Lectures. 1657.

[See also biographies by R. L. Ottley, 1894, A. Whyte, 1896, and D. Macleane, 1910; a lecture by R. W. Church in Masters in English Theology, 1877; a lecture by J. H. North in Classic Preachers, ser. 2, 1878; and T. S. Eliot, For Lancelot Andrewes, 1928.]

Bancroft, Richard (1544–1610; archbishop of Canterbury). A Sermon at Paules Crosse, 9 Feb. 1588. [1589.]

Becon, Thomas (1512–1567). A new Postil conteinyng sermons upon all the sonday gospelles. 2 vols. 1566; 1567.

Bilson, Thomas (1547–1616; bishop of Winchester). The effect of certaine sermons touching full redemption. 1599.

—— A sermon before the King and Queen at their coronations, July 25, 1603. 1603; 1604.

Boys, John (1571–1625; dean of Canterbury). An Exposition of the Dominicall Epistles and Gospels. 1610.

—— An Exposition of the Festivall Epistles and Gospels. 1613.

—— Remaines, containing sundry Sermons. 1631.

Bradford, John (1510?–1555). A Sermon of repentaunce. [1553]; 1558; 1619; 1623.

—— Two notable Sermons, the one of Repentance [i.e. the preceding] and the other of the Lordes supper. 1574.

Broughton, Hugh (1549–1612). An Exposition upon the Lords Prayer, preached at Oatelands, Aug. 13, 1603. [1603?]

—— The works of the great Albionean divine. Ed. J. Lightfoot, 4 vols. 1662.

Bruce, Robert (1554–1631). Sermons upon the Sacrament of the Lords Supper: preached in the Kirk of Edinburgh. Edinburgh, [1590?].

—— Sermons preached in the Kirk of Edinburgh. Edinburgh, 1591.

—— The Way to True Peace and Rest. Delivered at Edinborough in XVI sermons. 1617. [An English rendering of the two preceding volumes which are in Scottish.]

—— Sermons, reprinted from the Original Editions of 1590 and 1591, with Collections for his Life by R. Wodrow. Ed. W. Cunningham, Wodrow Soc. 1843.

—— Robert Bruce's Sermons on the Sacrament done into English, with a Biography. Ed. J. Laidlaw, 1901.

Cole, Thomas (d. 1571). A sermon at Maydstone the fyrste sonday in Lent. 1553.

—— A Sermon before the Queene, March 1, 1564. 1564.

Colet, John (1467?–1519). [See p. 666 above.]

Cowper, William (1568–1619; bishop of Galloway). Two Sermons preached in Scotland before the King. 1618.

Denison, John (d. 1629). The Heavenly Banquet, set forth in seven Sermons. 1619; 1631.

—— Foure Sermons: the blessednesse of peace-makers. 1620.

—— The sinners acquittance: three sermons. 1624.

Dering, Edward (1540?–1576). A Sermon preached at the Tower of London the xi day of December 1569. [1570?] (3 edns) (anon.); 1584; 1589.

—— A Sermon preached before the Quenes Majestie the 25 Februarie, anno 1569. [1570?], etc. (12 edns by 1603).

—— Maister Derings Workes. 4 pts, 1590; 1597 (enlarged edn); 1614.

Donne, John (1573–1630). [See pp. 441–4 above.]

[The following refer especially to Donne's preaching:

Lightfoot, J. B. Lecture I. [In Classic Preachers of the English Church, 1877.]

Beeching, H. C. Religio Laici. 1902.

Simpson, E. M. A Study of the Prose Works of John Donne. 1924.

Hayward, J. [In A Garland for John Donne, ed. T. Spencer, Cambridge, U.S.A. 1931.]

Sparrow, J. Donne and Contemporary Preachers. E. & S. xvi, 1931.

Sparrow, J. and Hutchinson, F. E. Theology, March 1931.]

Drant, Thomas (d. 1578?). Two Sermons preached, the one at S. Maries Spittle on Tuesday in Easter week 1570, and the other at the Court at Windsor Jan. 8, 1569. [1570?]

—— A sermon concernyng almes geving, preached at S. Maries Spittle. [1572?]

Fisher, John (1459?–1535; bishop of Rochester). The fruytfull saynges of Davyd in the seven penytencyall psalmes. Devyded in seven sermons. 1508; 1509 (bis); 1510; [1515?]; [1518?]; 1525; 1529; 1555; rptd 1714; ed. J. E. B. Mayor, EETS. 1876; ed. K. Vaughan, 1888; ed. J. S. Phillimore, 2 vols. 1914.

—— Sermon in the Cathedrall chyrche of saynt Poule, the body beynge present of kynge Henry the VII, the x day of Maye, MCCCCCix. 1509 (bis).

—— A mornynge remembraunce had at the moneth mynde of the noble prynces Margarete. [1509]; ed. T. Baker, 1708; ed. J. Hymers, 1840; ed. J. E. B. Mayor, EETS. 1876; ed. C. R. Ashbee, 1906.

—— A sermon agayn the pernicyous doctryn of Martin luuther [12 May 1521]. [1521?] (bis); [1528?]; 1554; 1556; tr. Latin R. Pace, Cambridge, 1521. [For Pace see J. Wegg, Richard Pace, 1932.]

—— A Sermon had at Paulis, upon quinquagesom sonday, concernynge certayne heretickes. [11 Feb. 1525.] [1525–6]. [This sermon is sometimes confused with the preceding item. It is not included in any modern edn. The BM. copy (C. 53 b. 15) has several corrections, made in a contemporary hand, not Fisher's, but perhaps at his instance. See G. J. Gray, Fisher's Sermons against Luther, 1912.]

Fisher, John. Two fruytfull sermons. 1532. [Both on Matt. v. 20.]

—— Opera Omnia. Würzburg, 1597. [Latin works only.]

—— The English Works, now first collected by J. E. B. Mayor. Pt i (all pbd), EETS. Ex. Ser. 1876.

    Kerker, M. John Fisher, sein Leben und Wirken. Tübingen, 1860.

    Baumstark, R. John Fisher. Freiburg, 1879.

    Bridgett, T. E. Life of Fisher. 1888; 1890.

    van Ortroy, F. Vie du bienheureux Martyr Jean Fisher: Texte anglais et Traduction latine du XVIe Siècle. (Analecta Bollandiana, x, xii.) Brussels, 1893.

    Fischer-Treuenfeld, R. Lord Johan Fyssher. 1894.

    Bayne, R. The Life of Fisher, transcribed from MS Harleian 6382. EETS. Ex. Ser. 1921.

Fitzjames, Richard (d. 1522; bishop of London). Sermo die lune in ebdomada Pasche. [c. 1495]; ed. photo. facs. F. J. H. Jenkinson, Cambridge, 1907. [In English.]

Gilpin, Bernard (1517–1583). A sermon preached in the court at Greenewich the firste Sonday after the Epiphanie, 1552, by B. G. 1581; 1630. [Rptd in the 1636 edn of G. Carleton's Life of Gilpin, and in Life by W. Gilpin, 1752.]

[For an appreciation see J. B. Lightfoot, Leaders in the Northern Church, 1890.]

Gosson, Stephen (1554–1624). The Trumpet of Warre. Preached at Paules Crosse, May 7, 1598. [1598.]

Gouge, William (1578–1653). Πανοπλια του Θεου. The Whole-Armor of God. 1616.

Greenham, Richard (1535?–1594?). Two learned and godly Sermons. 1595.

—— Works. Ed. H[enry] H[olland], 1599, etc. (5 edns by 1612).

Grindal, Edmund (1519?–1583; archbishop of Canterbury). A Sermon at the ffuneral solemnitie of Ferdinandus the late emperour. 1564. Tr. Latin J. Fox, 1564. [Rptd in Remains, ed. W. Nicholson, Parker Soc. 1843.]

Harpsfield, John (1516–1578). Concio habita coram Patribus et clero in ecclesia Paulina Londini, Oct. 26, 1553. 1553.

—— A Sermon or Homelie upon Saint Andrewes daye. 1556.

Hooker, Richard (1554–1600). [See pp. 685–8 below.]

Hooper, John (d. 1555; bishop of Worcester). A funerall oratyon made the xiiii day januarii, 1549. 1549.

—— An oversighte and deliberacion uppon the prophet Jonas, comprehended in seven Sermons. [1550] (bis); 1560.

Hooper, John. Early Writings. Ed. S. Carr, Parker Soc. 1843.

Hutchinson, Roger (d. 1555). The Image of God, or laie mans booke. 1550; 1560 (bis); 1573; 1580 ('Newly corrected').

—— A faithful declaration of Christes holy supper, in three sermons preached at Eaton Colledge, 1552. 1560.

—— Works. Ed. J. Bruce, Parker Soc. 1842.

Jewel, John (1522–1571; bishop of Salisbury). The Copie of a Sermon pronounced at Paules Crosse the second Sondaye before Easter, 1560. [1560.]

[Jewel's famous challenge was first given in a sermon at Paul's Cross on 26 Nov. 1559; it was repeated in substance in a Court sermon on 17 March 1560, and at Paul's Cross again on 31 March. It was ptd, 'as nere as the authour could call it to remembraunce' on 10 May following, as above. The ensuing controversy led to Jewel's Apologia Ecclesiae Anglicanae, 1562.]

—— Certaine sermons preached before the Queene and at Paules Crosse. 1583 (bis); 1603.

—— A sermon made in Latine in Oxenforde. Tr. R. V. [1586?]

—— Seven godly sermons; never before imprinted. 1607.

—— Works. With Life [by D. Featley]. 1609; 1611.

—— Works. Ed. J. Ayre, 4 vols. Parker Soc. 1845–50; ed. R. W. Jelf, 8 vols. 1848.

Knox, John (1505–1572). A Sermon [on Isai. xxvi, 13] preached in the Church of Edenbrough, 19 Aug. 1565. For the which the said John Knoxe was inhibite. 1566. [Date on title-page, but no place of printing or printer's name. The sermon is ptd in Knox's Historie of the Reformation, ed. D. B[uchanan], 1644, and in Collected Works, ed. D. Laing, vol. vi, 1864.]

Latimer, Hugh (1485?–1555). [See p. 669 above.]

Lever, Thomas (1521–1577). A fruitfull Sermon made in Poules churche in the Shroudes the seconde daye of February. Anno M.D. and fiftie. 1550 (also issued n.d.).

—— A sermon preached the fourth Sundaye in Lente before the kynges majestie. M.CCCCC.l. [1550.] [Arber in his rpt points out that some issues have 'the thyrd Sonday' on the title-page, but that the sermon deals with the Gospel for the Fourth Sunday in Lent.]

—— A sermon preached at Pauls Crosse the xiiii day of December. Anno M.D.L. [1550] (bis).

—— Three fruitfull sermons made 1550 and now newlie perused by the aucthour. 1572; rptd E. Arber, 1870, etc.

Longland, John (1473–1547?; bishop of Lincoln). Tres Conciones. [c. 1527.] [Includes also Quinque Sermones. The Conciones were delivered in 1519, 1525 and 1527; the five Sermons, delivered in English in Lent 1517, are here in a Latin trn, probably by Thomas Caius. According to DNB., the Sermons were ptd by Pynson in 1517, but no copy can be traced. See S. R. Maitland, Early Printed Books at Lambeth, 1843, pp. 230–2, 243.]

—— A Sermond made be for the Kynge at Rychemunte, uppon good fryday, MCCCCCXXXVI. [1535?] [The date of delivery is inconsistent with that of the next entry, and W. G. Hiscock (TLS. 31 Dec. 1931) gives reasons for assigning this sermon to 1535. Copy in Trinity College, Cambridge.]

—— A Sermond spoken before the Kynge at Grenwiche uppon Good fryday, M.D. XXXVI. [1536?]

—— A Sermonde made before the Kynge at grenewiche, upon good Fridaye, MDXXXVIII. [1538.]

Perkins, William (1558–1602). Exposition upon the whole Epistle of Jude, containing 66 sermons. 1606.

—— Exposition of Christ's Sermon in the Mount. Cambridge, 1608.

—— The Works gathered into one volume. Cambridge, 1603; 3 vols. Cambridge, 1608, etc.

Playfere, Thomas (1561?–1609). The whole sermons gathered into one volume. 1623.

Rainolds (or Reynolds), John (1549–1607). A sermon upon part of the eighteenth psalm preached to the Scholars of Oxford. 1586; 1613.

—— The prophecie of Obadiah opened in sondry sermons. 1613. [Ed. W. Hinde, after Reynolds's death, apparently from Hinde's own notes.]

—— The discovery of the Man of Sinne, first preached to the Universitie & Cittie of Oxon. Ed. W. H[inde], 1614.

—— The Prophesie of Haggai interpreted in sundry Sermons. Never before printed. 1649.

[See Hallam's appreciation of Reynolds in History of European Literature, pt ii, ch. 2, 1837–9.]

Rollock, Robert (1555?–1599). Certaine sermons upon severall places of the epistles of Paul. 1599.

—— Lectures upon the Epistle to the Colossians. 1603.

—— Lectures upon the Epistles to the Thessalonians. 1606.

—— Lectures upon the History of the Passion. 1616.

Rollock, Robert (1555?–1599). Select Works, with the XVII Century Life by H. Charteris. Ed. W. M. Gunn, 2 vols. Wodrow Soc. 1844–9.

Sandys, Edwin (1516?–1588; archbishop of York). Sermons. 1585; 1616; ed. J. Ayre, Parker Soc. 1841.

Smith, Henry (1550?–1591). The Examination of Usurie in two sermons, taken by characterie, & after examined. 1591. [With a short preface, signed, Thine H. S.]

[These and several other sermons of Smith were ptd in the author's lifetime, or immediately after his death, and for over thirty years after his death there was a remarkably large output of his sermons, singly, in small sets, and in collected edns. On the use of shorthand for taking down sermons, see Foster Watson, The English Grammar Schools, 1908.]

—— The Sermons gathered into one volume. 1592; ed. Thomas Fuller, with a short memoir, 1657; 1675; rptd 2 vols. 1866–7.

—— A Selection of the Sermons. Ed. John Brown, Cambridge, 1908.

Tunstall, Cuthbert (1474–1559; bishop of Durham). A Sermon made upon Palme sondaye last past. 1539.

Udall, John (1560?–1592). Amendment of life: three sermons. 1584; 1588.

—— Obedience to the Gospell: two sermons. 1584; 1588.

—— Peter's Fall: two sermons. 1584; [1590?].

—— The true remedie against famine and warres: five sermons. [1588.]

—— The combate betwixt Christ and the Devill. Foure sermons. [1588?]

Watson, Thomas (1513–1584; bishop of Lincoln). Twoo notable sermons before the Quene concernynge the reall presence. 1554.

—— Holsome and Catholyke doctryne concerninge the seven Sacramentes, in shorte sermons, x Feb. 1558. 1558 (bis). [Also a surreptitious edn in same month, and another on 7 June. Modernised edn, T. E. Bridgett, 1876.]

Whitgift, John (1530?–1604; archbishop of Canterbury). A godlie Sermon preached before the Queen, March 26, 1574. 1574; rptd 1714.

—— Sermon preached at Pauls Crosse, Nov. 17, 1583. 1589.

—— Works. Ed. J. Ayre, 3 vols. Parker Soc. 1851–3.

(3) DEVOTIONAL WRITINGS

The abbaye of the holy Ghost. [c. 1496]; [c. 1500]; ed. photo. facs. F. J. H. Jenkinson, Cambridge, 1907.

Alcock, John. Mons perfeccionis, the hyll of perfeccyon. 1496; 1497; [1498]; 1501.

Alcock, John. Desponsacio virginis xpristo. An exhortation to relygyouse systers. [c. 1496]; [?].

Andrewes, Lancelot. The Private Devotions. Translated from the Greek. 1647.

—— A Manual of the Private Devotions. Translated out of a fair Greek MS. by R. D[rake]. 1648; 1674. [This differs considerably from the preceding book which had another editor.]

—— Preces Privatae, Graece et Latine. Ed. John Lamphire, 1675.

—— The Devotions translated from the Greek by J. H. N[ewman]. 1842. From the Latin by J. M. Neale. 1844; rptd 1920.

—— The Greek Devotions. Ed. P. G. Medd, 1892. Newly done into English by P. G. Medd, 1899.

—— The Devotions, Greek and Latin. Ed. H. Veale, 1895.

—— Preces Privatae. Tr. with Introduction and Notes F. E. Brightman, 1903.

—— A Manual of directions for the Sick. Tr. (from a Greek MS) R. D[rake], 1648.

Babington, Gervase (1550–1610). A briefe Conference betwixt mans Frailty and Faith. 1583, etc. (5 edns by 1602).

—— The Workes. 1615, etc. (4 edns by 1637).

Bayly, Lewis (d. 1632; bishop of Bangor). The Practise of Pietie. 1613 (3rd edn, earlier edns not traced, and 45 edns by 1640); ed. G. Webster, 1842. Tr. French, 1625; German, 1629; Welsh, 1630; Polish, 1647.

Becon, Thomas. Davids harpe ful of armony. By Theodore Basille [pseudonym]. 1542.

—— The floure of godlye prayers. 1551.

—— The pomander of prayer. 1558 (anon.), etc. (5 edns by 1578). [Another book with this title was ptd by de Worde in 1530.]

—— Worckes. 3 vols. 1560–4; ed. J. Ayre, 3 vols. Parker Soc. 1843–4.

Betson, Thomas. A ryght profytable treatyse. [c. 1500]; ed. photo. facs. F. J. H. Jenkinson, Cambridge, 1905.

Bradford, John. A godlye medytacyon. 1559.

—— Godlie meditations upon the Lordes prayer. 1562.

—— Godly meditations upon the ten commaundementes. 1567; 1578.

—— Writings. Ed. A. Townsend, Parker Soc. 1853.

Bull, Henry (d. 1575?). Christian praiers and holie meditations, gathered by H. B. 1566, etc. (6 edns by 1596); rptd Parker Soc. 1842.

Byfield, Nicholas (1579–1622). The Marrow of the Oracles of God. 1620, etc. (11th edn, 1640).

Catharine [Parr], queen of England (1512–1548). Prayers stirryng the mynd unto heauenly medytacions. 1545, etc. (11 edns by 1559).

Colet, John. A ryght frutefull monycion concerning the ordre of a good chrysten mannes lyfe. 1534; 1563; 1577.

Cowper, William. Three heavenly treatises. 1609.

—— Workes. 1623; 1626; 1629–8.

Day, Richard (1552–1607?). A booke of Christian Prayers, collected out of the auncient writers. 1578; 1581; 1590; 1608. [Included in Private Prayers put forth by Authority during the Reign of Queen Elizabeth, ed. W. K. Clay, Parker Soc. 1851. Based on a book of prayers ptd by his father, John Day, in 1569.]

Donne, John. [See pp. 441–4 above.]

Elyot, Sir Thomas (1490?–1546). A swete and devoute sermon of saynte ciprian of mortalitie of man. The rules of a christian lyfe made by Picus erle of Mirandula, bothe translated into englyshe by syr T. E. 1534; 1539. [The same trns appear in the collected Workes of Thomas Lupset (1546), who died in 1530.]

Fisher, John. A spirituall consolation to hys sister Elizabeth. The wayes to perfect Religion. A sermon preached upon a good Friday. [1535]; 1577; Paris, 1640; ed. J. E. B. Mayor, EETS. 1876; ed. D. O'Connor, 1903 (modernised). [Latin version of the sermon in Opera, Würzburg, 1597.]

—— A godlie treatisse declaryng the benefites of prayer. Written in latin fourtie yeres past and lately translated. [1560]; 1577; tr. R. A[nthony] B[att], Paris, 1640. [Modernised version of 1640 trn, 1887.]

The Lives of Women Saints. Ed. C. Horstmann, from a MS compiled c. 1610–5, EETS. 1886.

Lupset, Thomas (1495–1530). [See p. 670 above.]

More, Sir Thomas (1478–1535). [See pp. 666–8 above.]

Norden, John (fl. 1600). A pensive mans practise. 1584.

—— A Progresse of Pietie. 1596; rptd Parker Soc. 1847.

P[arsons], R[obert] (1546–1610). The first parte of the booke of the Christian Exercise appertayning to resolution. [Rouen], 1582; [Rouen?], 1585 (with additions as A Christian Directorie, guiding men to their salvation, commonly called the Resolution, with Reproofe of the falsified edition published by E. Buny). [Edmund Bunny ed. in 1584 a protestant version of which there were many edns in the following years. See H. Thurston, Catholic Writers and Elizabethan Readers, rptd from The Month, 1894–5.]

Horæ Beatæ Mariæ Virginis or Sarum and York Primers with Kindred Books and Primers of the Reformed Roman Use. Ed. Edgar Hoskins, 1901.

Rogers, Thomas (d. 1616). Of the Imitation of Christ, Three bookes, translated. 1580. [Many edns to 1640.]
—— A pretious booke of heavenlie meditations, called a private talke of the soule with God. Written, as some think, by S. Augustine. 1581. [From 1592 usually ptd with the above.]
—— Saint Augustines Praiers in the English tong. Whereunto is annexed Saint Augustines Psalter translated. 1581. [Supposititious works of St Augustine.]
—— Soliloquium Animae, the sole-talke of the soule. 1592. [From St Thomas à Kempis.]
Simon, 'the anker of London wall' (fl. 1512–29). The fruyte of redempcyon, compyled in Englysshe. 1514; 1517; 1530; 1532.
Southwell, Robert (1561?–1595). [For poetical works see pp. 421–2 above.]
—— Marie Magdalens funerall teares. 1594; n.d.; 1609.
—— The Triumphs over Death: or, a consolatorie Epistle. 1595; 1596 (bis); rptd Sir S. E. Brydges (in Archaica, vol. I, 1815); ed. from MSS J. W. Trotman, 1914.
—— An Humble Supplication to Her Majestie. 1595.
—— A short Rule of Good Life. Newly set forth, according to the authors direction, before his death. [London?, 1598?] (bis); St Omer, 1622.
—— An Epistle of Comfort to the Reverend Preistes. Paris, [1604?] (anon.); 1605; [St Omer?], 1616.
—— Hundred Meditations on the Love of God. Ed. from Stonyhurst MS J. Morris, 1873. [Tr. from Diego de Estella.]
—— The Prose Works. Ed. W. J. Walter, 1828.
  Poetical Works. 1872. (Fuller Worthies' Lib.) [Memoir by A. B. Grosart.]
  Thurston, H. Catholic Writers. 1895. [Rptd from The Month, 1894–5.]
  Diego de Estella and Robert Southwell. TLS. 20, 27 Nov. 1930.
  Janelle, P. Robert Southwell the Writer. Clermont-Ferrand, 1935.
Sutton, Christopher (1565?–1629). Disce Mori. 1600, etc. (9 edns by 1626); ed. J. H. N[ewman], 1839.
—— Godly Meditations upon the most holy Sacrament. 1601, etc. (5 edns by 1635); ed. J. H. N[ewman], 1838.
—— Disce Vivere. 1602, etc. (8 edns by 1634); ed. J. H. N[ewman], 1839.
Whitford, Richard (fl. 1495–1555?). The Psalter of Jesus. 1529; [1545?]; Antwerp, 1575; 1583, etc. (some ptd at Douai); ed. W. Raynal, 1872; rptd 1908. [Attrib. to Whitford. It is also found at the end of a

Salisbury Primer, ptd by Y. Bonhomme, Paris, 1532. For earlier authority, see The Psalter of Jesus: from a MS of 15th century. Preface signed H. G[ough], 1885. Also, written apparently without knowledge of H. G.'s tract, Jesu's Psalter: what it was at its origin, by S. H. Sole, 1888.]
—— A werke for housholders. 1530; 1533.
—— A werke of preparacion. A werke for housholders. 1531 (an undated issue also).
—— The folowynge of Cryste. Bks I–III. [1531?]. Bk IV. [1532?]; [1535?], etc. [Based on the trn of St Thomas à Kempis by W. Atkynson, 1503–4.]
—— The Pype, or Tonne, of the lyfe of perfection. 1532. [See S. R. Maitland, Early Printed Books at Lambeth, 1843, p. 193.]
Woolton, John (1535?–1594; bishop of Exeter). The Christian Manuell. 1576; rptd Parker Soc. 1851.
—— The Castell of Christians beseeged. 1577.

F. E. H.

VI. RICHARD HOOKER (1554–1600)

(1) BIBLIOGRAPHY

[The fullest account of the extant MSS and of the changes in the text of succeeding edns, and the best discussion of the authenticity of the last three bks of the Polity, are in J. Keble's edn of Hooker's Works (rev. edn, 1888). This is supplemented by F. Paget's Introduction to the Fifth Book (rev. edn, 1907) and by Houk's edn of Bk VIII, 1931.]

(2) COLLECTED EDITIONS

Of the lawes of ecclesiasticall politie. Certayne divine tractates, and other godly sermons. 6 pts, 1617–6–8; 1622; 1632–1; 1638.
Works. Ed. with Life, J. Gauden, 1662.
Works. With Life by I. Walton, 1666, etc.
Works. Ed. W. S. Dobson, 2 vols. 1825.
Works. Ed. B. Hanbury, 3 vols. 1830. [Rpts A Christian Letter and Covel's Defence.]
Works. Ed. John Keble, 3 vols. Oxford, 1836; rev. R. W. Church and F. Paget, Oxford, 1888. [With much supplementary matter, much of it hitherto unprinted.]

(3) EDITIONS OF THE POLITY

Of the lawes of ecclesiasticall politie. Eyght Bookes. [n.d.] [Entered at Stationers' Hall, eight bks, 29 Jan. 1592–3 (Arber, vol. II, p. 295). Pbd in 1594 (Walton and Strype), or perhaps 1593 (Houk). The editio princeps gives headings of eight bks, but contains only I–IV.]

The fift booke. 1597. [The last to appear in Hooker's lifetime. Bodley MS Add. C 165, with corrections in Hooker's hand, was used by the printers for Bk v. See Simpson, below.]

Books i–v. 1604. [Though styled 2nd edn, strictly is a 2nd edn of i–iv only, as Bk v is unchanged from 1597, and the vol. is not continuously paged (Paget, p. 318).]

Books i–v. 1611. [Reset, and with continuous pagination.]

The sixth and eighth books, according to the most authentique copies. 1648; 1651. [From imperfect copies. In the preface of 1648 (modified in 1651) there is an allusion to the danger of 'counterfeit copies' (*i.e.* in MS) being in circulation. Already John Spenser's To the Reader in edn of 1604 had referred to the 'dismembered' state of surviving copies of the last three bks, although the author 'lived till he saw them perfected.']

Works. Ed. J. Gauden, 1662. [Includes Bk vii for first time, and adds to the end of Bk viii 8 folio pages hitherto unprinted except for some passages included in Nicholas Bernard's Clavi Trabales, 1661.]

Works. Ed. J. Keble, 1836. [Bk viii ptd from a fuller and better arranged MS (C.3.11, Trinity College, Dublin). Keble also detached the last two pages of Bk viii, as ptd by Gauden and subsequent editors, because he believed them to be misplaced, and ptd them as Appendix ii, 'Supposed fragment of a sermon on civil obedience.' He also questioned whether Bk vi, although in his judgment Hooker's, belonged to the Polity, because its contents did not correspond closely with Hooker's description of Bk vi in the 1594 edn or with the Notes on Bk vi supplied to Hooker by his former pupils, George Cranmer and (Sir) Edwin Sandys (ptd in Keble's edn: MS at Corpus Christi College, Oxford).]

Book i. With Introduction and Glossary by R. W. Church, 1868.

Book v. With Prolegomena and Appendices by R. Bayne, 1902.

Book viii. With Introduction by R. A. Houk, New York, 1931.

Paget, F. An Introduction to the Fifth Book. 1899; 1907 (rev. edn).

Simpson, P. Proof-reading by English Authors of the XVI and XVII Centuries. Proc. Oxford Bibliog. Soc. ii, pt i, 1927. [Special attention to the 'unrivalled' MS of Bk v in the Bodleian.]

(4) Sermons and Tractates

A learned and comfortable sermon of the certaintie of faith. Oxford, 1612. [On Habakkuk, i, 4, first pt].

A learned discourse of Justification. Oxford, 1612, 1613 (corrected), 1631. [On Habakkuk, i, 4, second pt.]

The answere to a supplication preferred by Mr Walter Travers to the Privie Counsell. Oxford, 1612. [On the connection of Travers's appeal to the Privy Council with Hooker's two preceding sermons, see Walton's Life.]

A learned sermon of the nature of pride. Oxford, 1612. [On Habakkuk, ii, 4. Keble ptd for the first time a large addn to this sermon from MS B.1.13 folio, Trinity College, Dublin.]

A remedie against sorrow and feare, delivered in a funerall sermon. Oxford, 1612.

Two sermons upon part of S. Judes epistle. Oxford, 1614. [Keble is less convinced about the genuineness of these two sermons than about anything else bearing Hooker's name; if they are his, Paget thinks they are a very early work, but Paget (p. 327) gives reasons against an early date. All the above items were ed. by Henry Jackson, under the supervision of John Spenser, President of Corpus Christi College.]

A discovery of the causes of these contentions concerning Church-government: out of the fragments of Richard Hooker. [In Certain briefe treatises concerning the government of the Church, Oxford, 1641. This composite volume was probably prepared by, or under the direction of, Archbishop Ussher. Keble, who prints A discovery as Appendix ii to Bk viii of the Polity, is doubtful of its being Hooker's.]

Mr Hookers judgment of regal power in matters of religion. [In Nicholas Bernard's Clavi Trabales, 1661. The editor of this composite volume, formerly Ussher's chaplain, ptd Mr Hookers judgment from MSS that had belonged to the archbishop. It includes pts of Bk viii which had not appeared in the versions of 1648 and 1651, but which are represented, although with variations of wording and order, in Gauden's edn of 1662.]

A sermon of Richard Hooker found in the study of Bishop Andrews. [Ptd as an appendix to Walton's Life of Dr Sanderson, 1678.]

(5) Contemporary Controversy and Criticism

[See also the bibliography on the Marprelate Controversy, pp. 688–94 below.]

[Bacon, Francis.] Considerations touching the better pacification of the Church. 1604 (3 edns); 1640; 1689.

Bacon, Francis. An advertisement touching the controversies of the Church. 1640. [Written in 1589. Paget (p. 157) thinks that Hooker saw this in MS.]

Bancroft, R. Daungerous positions under pretence of reformation. 1593 (anon.); 1640; ed. R. G. Usher, Camden Soc. 1905.

—— A survay of the pretended holy discipline. 1593 (anon.).

Bilson, T. The perpetual governement of Christes church. 1593; 1610; 1611 (a Latin version, enlarged); ed. R. Eden, Oxford, 1842.

Bridges, J. A defence of the government established in the church of Englande. 1587.

[Cartwright, T.] A seconde Admonition to the Parliament. [Wandsworth, 1572]; [Leipzig], 1617. [For the first Admonition, see Field and Wilcox, below.]

—— A replye to an answere made of M. Doctor Whitgift. [Wandsworth, c. 1574.]

—— The second replie agaynst Maister Whitgiftes second answere. By T. C. [Zurich], 1575.

—— The rest of the second replie. [n.p.], 1577.

—— A briefe apologie against M. Sutcliffe. [Middelburg], 1596.

—— A christian letter of certaine English protestants unto Mr R. Hoo. [Middelburg, 1599.] [Hooker ptd no answer to this attack on the Polity, but Keble ptd in 1836 extensive fragments of an intended answer from MS B.1.13, Trinity College, Dublin, as well as annotations in Hooker's hand in a copy of A Christian Letter at Corpus Christi College, Oxford.]

Covell, W. A just and temperate defence of the five books of Ecclesiastical Policie against a letter of certain English protestants. 1603. [Rptd in Hanbury's edn of Works.]

Cranmer, George. Concerning the new Church discipline, a letter to R. H. [n.p.] 1642. [Written in 1598. Commonly ptd after Walton's Life in edns of Hooker.]

[Fenner, Dudley.] A defence of the godlie ministers against the slaunders of D. Bridges. [Middelburg], 1587.

[Field, John and Wilcox, Thomas?] An Admonition to the Parliament. [Wandsworth, 1572] (bis).

[Fulke, W.] A declaration, containing the desires of all those ministers that seek Discipline and Reformation. 1584. [B. Brook, Lives of the Puritans, vol. I, p. 388, says that this work was by Fulke, though Fenner's name is prefixed.]

Jewel, J. Apologia Ecclesiae Anglicanae. 1562; tr. Eng. 1562.

Orders and Dealings in the Church of Northampton (drawn up 5 June 1571). State Papers Domestic, vol. LXXIII, p. 38. [Ptd in Strype's Annals of the Reformation.]

Querimonia Ecclesiae. 1592.

[Sandys, Edwin.] A relation of the state of religion. 1605 (3 edns). [Ptd without the author's leave. It was burnt on 7 Nov. 1605 by order of the High Commission, perhaps at Sandys's request. Copies with the author's autograph corrections in BM. and Bodley. From the BM. corrected copy a new edn, under the title Europae Speculum, or a View or Survey of the state of religion, was ptd at The Hague in 1629, and was frequently rptd.]

Saravia, Hadrianus. De diversis ministrorum gradibus. 1590; tr. Eng. 1591.

—— Defensio tractationis de diversis gradibus. 1594.

Sutcliffe, M. A treatise of ecclesiasticall discipline. 1590–1.

Travers, Walter. Ecclesiasticae disciplinae explicatio. La Rochelle, 1574 (anon.); tr. Eng. (probably by T. Cartwright, under the title A full and plaine Declaration of ecclesiasticall discipline), [Zurich], 1574, Geneva, 1580.

—— A defence of the ecclesiastical discipline, against a replie of Maister Bridges. 1588 (anon.).

—— A supplication made to the Privy Counsel. Oxford, 1612. [Commonly ptd in edns of Hooker.]

Whitgift, J. An answere to a certen libel intituled An admonition to the Parliament. 1572; 1573 ('augmented').

—— The defense of the aunswere to the admonition. 1574.

Fuller, T. Church-History of Britain. 1655.

Strype, John. Annals of the Reformation. 2 pts, 1709–8. [Enlarged in succeeding edns up to 1737.]

—— The Life and Acts of John Whitgift. 2 pts, 1718–7. [The above two works, together with other collections of Strype, were rptd at Oxford, with a general index, in 21 vols. 1812–28.]

Neal, Daniel. The History of the Puritans. 4 vols. 1732–8.

Brook, Benjamin. The Lives of the Puritans. 3 vols. 1813.

Frere, W. H. The English Church in the reigns of Elizabeth and James I. 1904.

Dale, R. W. History of English Congregationalism. Completed and edited by A. W. W. Dale. 1907.

Usher, R. G. The Reconstruction of the English Church. 1910.

Pearson, A. F. Scott. Thomas Cartwright and Elizabethan Puritanism. Cambridge, 1925.

(6) BIOGRAPHY AND CRITICISM

(a) Biographical Writings

[Letters and other MSS of Hooker at Corpus Christi College, Oxford, are catalogued in H. O. Coxe's Catalogue of Oxford MSS, pt 2, 1852.]

Gauden, John. Life. [In his edn of Hooker's Works, 1662.]

Walton, Izaak. The Life of Mr Rich. Hooker. 1665. [Prefixed to most edns of Hooker from 1666, and included in Walton's Lives from 1670. Written at Archbishop Sheldon's suggestion, partly to correct the errors in Gauden's recent Life, and also to suggest caution about the imperfection of Bks vi–viii in the state in which they had survived.]

à Wood, Anthony. Athenae Oxonienses. 2 vols. 1691–2.

Prince, John. Danmonii Orientales Illustres: or, The Worthies of Devon. 1701. [Based mainly on Walton for Hooker.]

Keble, John. Editor's Preface. [In his edn of Works, 1836. Walton's Life is included, with many corrections and addns.]

Fowler, T. History of Corpus Christi College, Oxford. 1893.

Staley, V. Richard Hooker. 1907.

Thomas, V. Richard Hooker's College Life. N. & Q. 23 March 1861. [Books owned by Hooker.]

(b) Criticism

Hoadly, B. The Original of Civil Government discussed. 1709.

Swift, J. The Tatler, no. 230, 1710.

Warburton, W. The Alliance between Church and State. 1736.

Landor, W. S. Imaginary Conversations. [Ser. 1,] 1825. [Vol. ii.]

Hallam, H. Introduction to the Literature of Europe. 4 vols. 1837–9.

Wordsworth, Christopher. Christian Institutes. 4 vols. 1837.

D'Israeli, I. Amenities of Literature. 1841.

Coleridge, S. T. Notes on English Divines. Ed. D. Coleridge, 2 vols. 1853.

Maurice, J. F. D. A History of Moral and Metaphysical Philosophy. 1862.

Sack, C. H. Richard Hooker von den Gesetzen des Kirchenregiments. Heidelberg, 1868.

Ruskin, J. Modern Painters. 1869. [Vol. ii.]

Hunt, J. Religious Thought in England from the Reformation. 1870. [Vol. i.]

de Rémusat. C. F. M. Histoire de la Philosophie en Angleterre. Paris, 1875

Masters in English Theology. Ed. A. Barry, 1877.

Stephen, Sir J. F. Horae Sabbaticae. 1892. [Vol. i.]

Dowden, E. Puritan and Anglican. 1900.

Robertson, A. Regnum Dei. 1901.

Beeching, H. C. Religio Laici. 1902.

Figgis, J. N. Cambridge Modern History. 1904. [Vol. iii.]

—— From Gerson to Grotius. Cambridge, 1907, 1916 (rev.).

Galante, A. La Teoria delle Relazioni fra lo Stato e la Chiesa. Leipzig, 1908. (Festschrift Emil Friedberg).

Foakes-Jackson, F. J. CHEL. vol. iii, 1909.

Wicksteed, P. H. The Reactions between Dogma and Philosophy. 1920.

Thornton, L. S. Richard Hooker: a Study of his Theology. 1924.

Sykes, Norman. Richard Hooker. [In The Social and Political Ideas of the XVI and XVII Centuries, ed. F. J. C. Hearnshaw, 1926.]

Allen, J. W. A History of Political Thought in the XVI Century. 1928.

Michaelis, G. Richard Hooker als politischer Denker. Berlin, 1933.

F. E. H.

VII. THE MARPRELATE CONTROVERSY

(1) BIBLIOGRAPHIES

[The best bibliographies are contained in the late W. Pierce's Historical Introduction to the Marprelate Tracts (1908) and The Marprelate Tracts (1911). For references to cognate literature E. Arber's Introductory Sketch to the Martin Marprelate Controversy (1879) is still of great value. For the history of the Presbyterian movement whose left wing is represented by Marprelate, for information regarding original documents and for an account of the Puritan press and other kindred and contemporary writings, Professor A. F. Scott Pearson's Thomas Cartwright and Elizabethan Puritanism (1925) is indispensable.]

(2) MANUSCRIPTS

[Most of the manuscript authorities have been ptd or cited by Arber, Pierce and Pearson. For references to MSS relating to Udall, Penry and Waldegrave after their flight to the north, see Pierce's John Penry (1923) and Pearson, op. cit. Many contemporary Puritan papers are contained in Dr A. Peel's edn of The Seconde Parte of a Register (1915).]

(3) THE MARPRELATE TRACTS

(a) The Epistle

Oh read over D. John Bridges, for it is a worthy worke: Or an epitome of the fyrste Booke of that right worshipfull volume, written against the Puritanes, in the defence of the noble cleargie, by as worshipfull a prieste, John Bridges, Presbyter, Priest or elder, doctor of Divillitie, and Deane of Sarum. Wherein the arguments of the puritans are wisely prevented, that when they come to answere M. Doctor, they must needes say something that hath bene spoken. Compiled for the behoofe and overthrow of the Parsons, Fyckers, and Currats, that have lernt their Catechismes and are past grace: By the reverend and worthie Martin Marprelate gentleman, and dedicated to the Confocationhouse. The Epitome is not yet published, but it shall be when the Bishops are at convenient leysure to view the same. In the meane time, let them be content with this learned Epistle. Printed oversea, in Europe, within two furlongs of a Bounsing Priest, at the cost and charges of M. Marprelate, gentleman. [Secretly ptd by Waldegrave, East Molesey, Oct. 1588; rptd J. Petheram, 1842; E. Arber, 1880; W. Pierce, 1911.]

(b) The Epitome

Oh read over [as in the Epistle], bene spoken. Compiled for the behoofe and overthrow of the unpreaching Parsons, Fyckers, and Currats, that have lernt their Catechismes, and are past grace: By the reverend and worthie Martin Marprelat gentleman, and dedicated by a second Epistle to the Terrible Priests. In this Epitome, the foresaide Fickers, etc. are very insufficiently furnished, with notable inabilitie of most vincible reasons, to answere the cavill of the puritanes. And lest M. Doctor should thinke that no man can write without sence but his selfe, the senceles titles of the several pages, and the handling of the matter throughout the Epitome, shewe plainely, that beetleheaded ignoraunce must not live and die with him alone. Printed on the other hand of some of the Priests. [Secretly ptd by Waldegrave, Fawsley, Nov. 1588; rptd J. Petheram, 1843; W. Pierce, 1911.]

(c) The Mineralls

Certaine Minerall and Metaphisicall Schoolpoints, to be defended by the reverende Bishops, and the rest of my cleargie masters of the Convocation house, against both the universities, and al the reformed Churches in Christendome. Wherin is layd open the very Quintessence of all Catercorner divinitie. And with all, to the preventing of the Cavels of these wrangling Puritans, the persons by whom, and the places where these misteries are so worthely maintayned, are for the most part, plainly set downe to the view of all men, and that to the ternall prayse of the most reverend Fathers. [Broadside secretly ptd by Waldegrave at Coventry before 20 Feb. 1589; rptd W. Pierce, 1911.]

(d) Hay any Worke for Cooper

Hay any worke for Cooper: Or a briefe Pistle directed by waye of an hublication to the reverende Byshopps, counselling them, if they will needs be barrelled up, for feare of smelling in the nostrels of her Majestie & the State, that they would use the advise of reverend Martin, for the providing of their Cooper. Because the reverend T. C. (by which misticall letters is understood, eyther the bounsing Parson of Eastmeane, or Tom Coakes his Chaplaine) to bee an unskilfull and a beceytfull tubtrimmer. Wherein worthy Martin quits himselfe like a man I warrant you, in the modest defence of his selfe and his learned Pistles, and makes the Coopers hoopes to flye off, and the Bishops Tubs to leake out of all crye. Penned and compiled by Martin the Metropolitane. Printed in Europe, not farre from some of the Bounsing Priestes. [Secretly ptd by Waldegrave at White Friars, Coventry, March 1589; rptd under title Reformation no enemie, 1641; under proper title, 1642; J. Petheram, 1845; W. Pierce, 1911.]

(e) Martin Junior or Theses Martinianae

Theses Martinianae: That is, Certaine Demonstrative Conclusions, sette downe and collected (as it should seeme) by that famous and renowmed Clarke, the reverend Martin Marprelate the great: serving as a manifest and sufficient confutation of al that ever the Colledge of Catercaps with their whole band of Clergie-priests, have, or can bring for the defence of their ambitious and Antichristian Prelacie. Published and set foorth as an after-birth of the noble Gentleman himselfe, by a pretty stripling of his, Martin Junior, and dedicated by him to his good neame and nuncka, Maister John Kankerbury: How the yongman came by them, the Reader shall understande sufficiently in the Epilogue. In the meane time, whosoever can bring mee acquainted with my father, Ile bee bounde hee shall not loose his labour. Printed by the assignes of Martin Junior,

44

without any priviledge of the Catercaps. [Secretly ptd by John Hodgkins at the Priory, Wolston, July 1589; rptd W. Pierce, 1911.]

(f) Martin Senior or The Just Censure

The just censure and reproofe of Martin Junior. Wherein the rash and undiscreete headines of the foolish youth, is sharply mette with, and the boy hath his lesson taught him, I warrant you, by his reverend and elder brother, Martin Senior, sonne and heire unto the renowmed Martin Marprelate the Great. Where also, least the springall shold be utterly discouraged in his good meaning, you shall finde, that hee is not bereaved of his due commendations. [Secretly ptd by John Hodgkins at the Priory, Wolston, July, 1589; rptd W. Pierce, 1911.]

(g) The Protestatyon

The Protestatyon of Martin Marprelat. Wherin not with standing the surprizing of the printer, he maketh it known unto the world that he feareth, neither proud priest, Antichristian pope, tiranous prellate, nor godlesse catercap: but defiethe all the race of them by these presents and offereth conditionally, as is farthere expressed hearin by open disputation to apear in the defence of his caus aginst them and theirs. Which chaleng if they dare not maintaine aginst him: then doth he alsoe publishe that he never meaneth by the assitaunce of god to leave the assayling of them and theire generation untill they be uterly extinguised out of our church. Published by the worthie gentleman D. martin marprelat D. in all the faculties primat and metroPolitan. [After the seizure of the main Puritan press and the arrest of Hodgkins and his assistants at Manchester this tract was secretly and very imperfectly ptd probably in Sept. 1589 at ? Wolston; rptd W. Pierce, 1911.]

(4) Contemporary Writings

Fulke, W.] A Briefe and plaine declaration, concerning the desires of all those faithfull Ministers, that have and do seeke for the Discipline and reformation of the Church of Englande. Which may serve for a just Apologie, against the false accusations and slanders of their adversaries. 1584. [Written as early as 1573, this book was pbd, without the author's knowledge or sanction, by the Puritans, who added a preface to it and gave it the running headline A Learned Discourse of Ecclesiasticall Government. It was generally referred to as 'A Learned Discourse.'

It must be carefully distinguished from A Full and Plaine Declaration (1574), with which many scholars have confused it.] A Commission sente to the Pope, Cardynales, Bishops, Friers, Monkes, with all the rable of that Viperous Generation by the highe and mighty Prince, and king Sathanas the Devill of Hell. 1586.

Bridges, John. A Defence of the government established in the Church of Englande for ecclesiasticall matters. Contayning an answere unto a Treatise called The Learned Discourse of Eccl. Government, otherwise intituled, A briefe and plaine declaration, etc. Comprehending likewise an answer to the arguments in a Treatise named The judgement of a most Reverend and Learned man from beyond the Seas, etc. Answering also the argumentes of Calvine, Beza and Danaeus, with other our Reverend learned Bretheren, besides Caenales and Bodinus, both for the regiment of women, and in defence of her Majestie, and of all other Christian Princes supreme Government in Ecclesiasticall causes, Against the Tetrarchie that our Brethren would erect in every particular congregation, of Doctors, Pastors, Governors and Deacons, with their severall and joynt authoritie in Elections, Excommunications, Synodall Constitutions and other Ecclesiasticall matters. 1587. [This is the book against which the first Marprelate Tracts were directed.]

Fenner, Dudley. A Defence of the godlie Ministers, against the slaunders of D. Bridges, contayned in his answere to the Preface before the Discourse of Ecclesiasticall governement, with a Declaration of the Bishops proceding against them. 1587. [The Preface vindicated is that placed by the Puritans before Fulke's Briefe and Plaine Declaration or A Learned Discourse. According to the rpt in A parte of a register this Defence was written by Fenner 'a moneth before his death'. Probably ptd by Schilders, Middelburg.]

Penry, John. A Treatise Containing The Aequity of An Humble Supplication Which is to be Exhibited unto Hir Gracious Majesty And this high Court of Parliament in the behalfe of the Countrey of Wales, that some order may be taken for the preaching of the Gospell among those people. Oxford, 1587; ed. A. J. Grieve, Congregational Hist. Soc. 1905.

—— Th' Appellation of John Penri unto the Highe court of Parliament, from the bad and injurious dealing of th'Archb. of Canterb. & other his colleagues of the high commission: Wherin the complainant, humbly submitting himselfe and his cause unto the determination of this honorable assembly: craveth nothing els, but either release from trouble and persecution, or just tryall. 1589. [Dedication dated 7 March. Secretly ptd probably by Waldegrave.]

Penry, John. A Briefe Discovery of the Untruthes and Slanders (Against the True Governement of the Church of Christ) contained in a Sermon, preached the 8. of Februarie 1588. by D. Bancroft, and since that time, set forth in Print, with additions by the said Authour. This Short Answer may serve for the clearing of the truth, untill a larger confutation of the Sermon be published. [Probably ptd by Waldegrave in Edinburgh, 1590.]

Udall, John. The state of the Church of Englande, laide open in a conference betweene Diotrephes a Bishop, Tertullus a Papist, Demetrius an usurer, Pandocheus an In-keeper, and Paule a Preacher of the word of God. [Secretly ptd by Waldegrave, April, 1588; rptd in A parte of a register, c. 1592; E. Arber, 1879.]

—— A Demonstration of the trueth of that Discipline which Christe hath prescribed in his worde for the governement of his Church, in all times and places, untill the ende of the worlde. [Secretly ptd by Waldegrave on the Marprelate press at East Molesey, about August, 1588; rptd in A parte of a register, c. 1592; E. Arber, 1880.]

[Travers, Walter.] A Defence of the Ecclesiasticall Discipline ordayned of God to be used in his Church. Against a Replie of Maister Bridges to a brief and plain Declaration of it which was printed in 1584. Which replie he termeth, A Defence of the government established in the Church of Englande, for Ecclesiasticall matters. 1588. [Probably ptd by Schilders, Middelburg. See J. D. Wilson, Trans. Bibliog. Soc. XI, 1912.]

Bancroft, Richard. A sermon preached at Paules Crosse the 9. of Februarie, being the first Sunday in the Parleament, Anno 1588. by Richard Bancroft D. of Divinitie, and Chaplaine to the right Honorable Sir Christopher Hatton. Wherein some things are now added which then were omitted, either through want of time or default of memory. 1588 (bis). [Entered at Stationers' Hall, 3 March 1589; rptd Bibliotheca Scriptorum Ecclesiae Anglicanae, 1709.]

—— Daungerous Positions and Proceedings, published and practised within this Iland of Brytaine and under pretence of Reformation, and for the Presbiteriall Discipline. 1593.

—— A survay of the Pretended Holy Discipline. Contayning the beginnings, successe, parts, proceedings, authority, and doctrine of it: with some of the manifold, and materiall repugnances, varieties and uncertainties in that behalfe. Faithfully gathered, by way of historicall narration, out of the bookes and writinges, of principall favourers of that platforme. 1593.

C., T. (i.e. Thomas Cooper, bishop of Winchester). An Admonition to the people of England: Wherein are answered, not onely the slaunderous untruethes, reprochfully uttered by Martin the Libeller, but also many other Crimes by some of his broode, objected generally against all Bishops, and the chiefe of the Cleargie, purposely to deface and discredite the present state of the Church. 1589 (3 edns); rptd J. Petheram, 1847; E. Arber, 1882.

A Dialogue wherein is laid open, the tyrannicall dealing of L. Bishopps against Gods children: with certaine points of doctrine, wherein they approve themselves (according to D. Bridges his judgement) to be truely the Bishops of the Divell. [Probably ptd on Waldegrave's press shortly after April, 1589; rptd under the title The character of a Puritan and his Gallimaufrey of the Antichristian clergie; prepared with D. Bridges Sawce for the present time to feed on. By the worthy Gentleman D. Martin Mar-Prelat, 1643.]

Mar-Martine.

I know not why a trueth in rime set out
Maie not as well mar Martine and his mates,
As shamelesse lies in prose-books cast about
Marpriests, & prelates, and subvert whole states.
For where truth builds & lying overthroes,
One truth in rime, is worth ten lies in prose.

[Seven pp. of doggerel priv. ptd, c. May, 1589. Partly rptd among Doubtful Works in Works of John Lyly, ed. R. W. Bond, vol. III, 1902.]

Marre Mar-Martin: or Marre-Martins medling, in a manner misliked.

Martins vaine prose, Marre-Martin doth mislike,
Reason (forsooth) for Martin seekes debate:
Marre-Martin will not so; yet doth his patience strike:
Last verse, first prose, conclude in one selfe hate:
Both maintaine strife, unfitting Englands state.
Martin, Marre-Martin, Barrow joyned with Browne
Shew zeale: yet strive to pull Religion downe.

[Priv. ptd probably in London, c. June, 1589. Rptd Sir S. E. Brydges, Censura Literaria, 1805–9, vol. II, art. lxxiii.]

44-2

Anti-Martinus, sive Monitio cujusdam Londonensis, ad Adolescentes utriusque Academiae, contra personatum quendam rabulam, qui se Anglicè Martin Marprelat Hoc est, Martinum Μαστιγάρχον ἢ μισάρχον, vocat. 1589. [Signed at end Totus Vester A. L. Entered at Stationers' Hall, 3 July 1589.]

A Counter-cuffe given to Martin Junior: by the venturous, hardie, and renowned Pasquill of England, Cavaliero. Not of olde Martins making, which newlie knighted the Saints in Heaven, with rise up Sir Peter and Sir Paule; but lately dubd for his service at home in the defence of his Country, and for the cleane breaking of his staffe upon Martins face. Printed betweene the skye and the grounde. Within a myle of an Oake, and not many fieldes of, from the unpriviledged Presse of Ass-ignes of Martin Junior. 1589 (bis) (priv. ptd August, 1589); rptd Nashe's Works, ed. A. B. Grosart, Huth Lib. vol. I, 1883; ed. R. B. McKerrow, vol. I, 1904. [By Nashe?]

Martins Months minde, That is A certaine report, and true description of the Death and Funeralls, of olde Martin Marreprelate, the great makebate of England and father of the Factious. Contayning the cause of his death, the manner of his buriall, and the right copies both of his Will, and of such Epitaphs, as by Sundrie his dearest friends, and other of his well willers were framed for him.

Martin the ape, the dronke, and the madde

The three Martins are, whose workes we have had,

If Martin the fourth come, after Martins so evill

Nor man, nor beast comes, but Martin the devill. 1589.

[Priv. ptd, London, c. Aug. 1589; rptd Nashe's Works, ed. A. B. Grosart, vol. I, 1883. It has been suggested that the author of this was also the author of An Almond for a Parrat, but was not Pasquil.]

M. Some laid open in his colours: Wherein the indifferent Reader may easily see, howe wretchedly and loosely he hath handeled the cause against M. Penri. Done by an Oxford man, to his friend in Cambridge. [Secretly ptd by Waldegrave c. Aug. 1589. The last page is signed I.G. By Job Throkmorton?]

A Whip for an Ape: Or Martin displaied. [Priv. ptd c. Oct. 1589. Also pbd from the same type under title Rythmes against Martin Marre-Prelate. Ascribed to John Lyly. Rptd I. D'Israeli, Quarrels of Authors, vol. III, 1814; The Bibliographical Miscellany, No. 5, 20 March 1854; Lyly's Works, ed. R. W. Bond, vol. III, 1902.]

[Nashe, Thomas?] The Returne of the renowned Cavaliero Pasquill of England, from the other side the Seas, and his meeting with Marforius at London upon the Royall Exchange. Where they encounter with a little houshold talke of Martin and Martinisme, discovering the scabbe that is bredde in England, and conferring together about the speedie dispersing of the golden Legende of the lives of the Saints. If my breath be so hote that I burne my mouth, suppose I was Printed by Pepper Allie. 1589. [Dated at the end '20 Octobris'; rptd Nashe's Works, ed. A. B. Grosart, vol. I, 1883; ed. R. B. McKerrow, vol. I, 1904.]

—— An Almond for a Parrat, Or Cutbert Curry-knaves Almes. Fit for the knave Martin, and the rest of those impudent Beggers, that can not be content to stay their stomakes with a Benefice, but they will needes breake their fastes with our Bishops. Rimarum sum plenus. Therefore beware (gentle Reader) you catch not the hicket with laughing. Imprinted at a Place, not farre from a Place, by the Assignes of Signior Some-body and are to be sold at his shoppe in Trouble-knave Street, at the signe of the Standish. [1590] (priv. ptd); rptd J. Petheram, 1846; Works of Thomas Nashe, ed. R. B. McKerrow, among Doubtful Works, vol. III, 1905.

—— The Firste Parte of Pasquils Apologie. Wherein he renders a reason to his friendes of his long silence: and gallops the fielde with the Treatise of Reformation lately written by a fugitive John Penrie. Printed where I was and where I will bee readie by the helpe of God and my Muse, to send you the May-game of Martinisme for an intermedium, betweene the first and seconde part of the apologie. 1590. [Priv. ptd in London. Dated at end, 2 July.

A reply to Penry's A Treatise Wherein is Manifestlie Proved, That Reformation and Those that sincerely favor the same, are unjustly charged to be enemies unto hir Majestie, and the State, which was ptd by Waldegrave in Scotland c. April, 1590; rptd Nashe's Works, ed. A. B. Grosart, vol. I, 1883, ed. R. B. McKerrow, vol. I, 1904.]

[Lyly, John]. Pappe with a Hatchet. Alias, A figge for my God sonne. Or Cracke me this nut. Or A Countrie cuffe. that is, a sound boxe of the eare, for the idiot Martin to hold his peace, seeing the patch will take no warning. Written by one that dares call a dog, a dog, and made to prevent Martins dog daies. Imprinted by John Anoke, and John Astile, for the Baylive of Withernam, cum privilegio perennitatis, and are to bee sold at the signe of the crab tree cudgell in twackcoate lane. [Priv. ptd in London, c. Nov. 1589; rptd J. Petheram, 1844; Elizabethan and Jacobean Pamphlets, ed. G. Saintsbury, 1892; Lyly's Works, ed. R. W. Bond, vol. III, 1902.]

A Myrror for Martinists, And all other Schismatiques, which in these daungerous daies doe breake the godlie unitie, and disturbe the Christian peace of the Church. 1590. [Entered at Stationers' Hall, 22 Dec. 1589.]

Wright, Leonard. A Friendly Admonition to Martine Marprelate and his Mates. 1590. [Entered at Stationers' Hall, 19 Jan.]

Plaine Percevall the Peace-Maker of England. Sweetly indevoring with his blunt persuasions to botch up a Reconciliation between Mar-ton and Mar-tother. Compiled by lawful art. [The authorship has been ascribed to one of the Harvey brothers. Pbd early in 1590; rptd J. Petheram, 1860.]

[Harvey, Richard.] A Theologicall Discourse of the Lamb of God and His Enemies: Contayning a briefe Commentarie of Christian faith and felicitie, together with a detection of old and new Barbarisme, now commonly called Martinisme. Newly published both to declare the unfayned resolution of the wryter in these present controversies, and to exercise the faithfull subject in godly reverence and dutiful obedience. 1590.

A petition directed to her most excellent Majestie, wherein is delivered 1. A meane howe to compound the civill dissension in the church of England. 2. A proofe that they who write for Reformation, doe not offend against the stat. of 23 Eliz. ci, and therefore till matters bee compounded, deserve more favour. [Probably written by a lawyer, c. 1591.]

A parte of a register, contayninge sundrie memorable matters, written by divers godly and learned in our time, which stande for and desire the reformation of our Church, in Discipline and Ceremonies, accordinge to the pure worde of God, and the Lawe of our Lande. [Without date or place, but c. 1592. Schilders, Middelburg, has been suspected as the printer, but Bancroft thought the work was imported from Scotland.]

Sutcliffe, Matthew. An Answere to a Certaine Libel supplicatori, or rather Diffamatory, and also to certaine Calumnious Articles and Interrogatories, both printed and scattered in secret corners, to the slaunder of the Ecclesiasticall state, and put forth under the name and title of a Petition directed to her Majestie. Wherein not onely the frivolous discourse of the Petitioners is refuted, but also the accusation against the Disciplinarians his clyents justified, and the slaunderous cavils at the present governement

disciphered. 1592. [Dedicatory epistle dated 20 Dec.]

Sutcliffe, Matthew. An Answere unto a certaine calumnious letter published by M. Job Throkmorton, entitled A defence against the slanders of M. Sutcliffe, wherein the vanitie both of the defence of himselfe and the accusation of others is manifestly declared. 1595.

Harvey, Gabriel. An Advertisement for Papp-Hatchett. [Dated 5 Nov. 1589, but pbd as second book of Pierces Supererogation, 1593; rptd Sir S. E. Brydges, Archaica, vol. II, 1815; ed. A. B. Grosart, Harvey's Works, Huth Lib. vol. II, 1884.]

Throkmorton, Job. The Defence of Job Throkmorton against the slaunders of Maister Sutcliffe, taken out of a Copye of his owne hande as it was written to an honorable Personage. 1594. [In this book Throkmorton denies that he is Martin Marprelate. Probably ptd by Schilders, Middelburg.]

Bacon, Francis. An Advertisement touching the Controversies of the Church of England. [Pbd in Bacon's Resuscitatio, 1657; rptd Bacon's Works, ed. J. Spedding, 1857–74; ed. E. Arber, Introductory Sketch, 1879.]

(5) MODERN WORKS

Strype, J. Annals of the Reformation. 2 pts, 1709–8; 4 vols. 1725–31 (complete); 4 vols. Oxford, 1824.

—— Life of John Whitgift. 2 pts, 1718–7; Oxford, 1822.

Brook, B. The Lives of the Puritans. 3 vols. 1813.

D'Israeli, I. Quarrels of Authors. 3 vols. 1814.

Neal, D. The History of the Puritans. 3 vols. 1837.

Petheram, J. Reprints of The Epistle, The Epitome, Hay any Worke, Pappe with a Hatchet, An Almond for a Parrat, An Admonition to the People of England, Plaine Percevall. 1842–7.

Maskell, W. History of the Martin Marprelate Controversy. 1845.

Arber, Edward. An Introductory Sketch to the Martin Marprelate Controversy. 1878. [Reprints: Diotrephes, Demonstration of Discipline, The Epistle, Admonition to the People of England.]

Dexter, H. M. The Congregationalism of the Last Three Hundred Years, as seen in its Literature. New York, 1880.

Grosart, A. B. The Works of Thomas Nashe. 1883.

—— The Works of Gabriel Harvey. 1884.

Saintsbury, G. Elizabethan and Jacobean Pamphlets. 1892.

Allnutt, W. H. The Marprelate Press, 1588–89. Bibliographica, II, 1896.

Bond, R. W. The Complete Works of John Lyly. 3 vols. Oxford, 1902.

Lee, Sir Sidney. The Last Years of Elizabeth. [In The Cambridge Modern History, III, 1904. Also in DNB. on Penry, Throkmorton, Udall, Waldegrave.]

Frere, W. H. The English Church in the Reigns of Elizabeth and James I. 1904. [Vol. v of W. R. W. Stephens and W. Hunt's History of the English Church.]

McKerrow, R. B. The Works of Thomas Nashe. 5 vols. 1904–10.

Wilson, J. D. A Date in the Marprelate Controversy. Library, VIII, 1907.

—— The Marprelate Controversy. CHEL. vol. III, 1909.

—— Richard Schilders and the English Puritans. Trans. Bibliog. Soc. XI, 1912.

Pierce, W. An Historical Introduction to the Marprelate Tracts. 1908.

—— The Marprelate Tracts. 1911.

—— John Penry, his Life, Times and Writings. 1923.

Peel, Albert. The Seconde Parte of a Register. 2 vols. Cambridge, 1915.

Bonnard, G. La Controverse de Martin Marprelate. Geneva, 1916.

Pearson, A. F. Scott. Thomas Cartwright and Elizabethan Puritanism. Cambridge, 1925.

—— Church and State: Political Aspects of Sixteenth Century Puritanism. Cambridge, 1928.

McCorkle, J. N. Note concerning Mistress Crane and the Martin Marprelate Controversy. Library, XII, 1931.

J. D. W., *rev.* A. F. S. P.

VIII. THE CAROLINE DIVINES, 1620–1660

(1) CRITICAL AND HISTORICAL WORKS

Calamy, Edmund. An Abridgment of Mr Baxter's History of his Life and Times; with an Account of many others of those worthy ministers who were ejected at the Restoration. 1702; 2 vols. 1713; rev. S. Palmer, 3 vols. 1802–3 (as The Nonconformists' Memorial).

Neal, Daniel. The History of the Puritans (1517–1688). 4 vols. 1732–8; 5 vols. 1793–7.

Crosby, Thomas. The History of the English Baptists. 4 vols. 1738.

Brook, Benjamin. The Lives of the Puritans. 3 vols. 1813.

Bloom, J. H. Pulpit Oratory in the Time of James the First. 1831.

Wilmott, R. A. Jeremy Taylor, his Predecessors, Contemporaries, and Successors. 1846.

Coleridge, S. T. Notes on English Divines. Ed. D. Coleridge, 2 vols. 1853.

Hunt, J. Religious Thought in England to the End of the 18th Century. 3 vols. 1870–3.

Tulloch, J. Rational Theology and Christian Philosophy in England in the Seventeenth Century. 2 vols. Edinburgh, 1872.

Barclay, R. The Inner Life of the Religious Societies of the Commonwealth. 1876.

Stoughton, J. History of Religion in England (1640–1850). 6 vols. 1881.

Drysdale, A. H. History of the Presbyterians in England. 1889.

Wakeman, H. O. The Church and the Puritans, 1570–1660. 1889.

Stephen, Sir J. F. Horae Sabbaticae. Ser. 1, 1892.

Brown, John. Puritan Preaching in England. 1900.

Dowden, E. Puritan and Anglican. 1900.

Campagnac, E. T. The Cambridge Platonists. Oxford, 1901. [Introduction.]

Hutton, W. H. The English Church from the Accession of Charles I to the Death of Anne. 1903.

—— Caroline Divines. CHEL. vol. VII, 1911.

Braithwaite, W. C. The Beginnings of Quakerism (1647–1660). 1912.

Tatham, G. A. B. Puritans in Power [1640–1660]. 1913.

Powicke, F. J. The Cambridge Platonists. A Study. 1926.

Richardson, C. F. English Preachers and Preaching, 1640–1670. New York, 1928.

Grierson, H. J. C. Cross Currents in English Literature of the Seventeenth Century. 1929.

Jones, R. F. The Attack on Pulpit Eloquence in the Restoration. JEGP. XXX, 1931.

White, H. C. English Devotional Literature (Prose), 1600–1640. Madison, 1931. [Bibliography, pp. 271–94.]

Mitchell, W. F. English Pulpit Oratory from Andrewes to Tillotson. 1932. [Bibliography, pp. 401–73.]

[For general works on preaching see pp. 679–80 above.]

(2) CONTEMPORARY TREATISES ON PREACHING

Wilkins, John. Ecclesiastes; or, a discourse concerning the Gift of Preaching as it falls under the Rules of Art. 1646, etc. (7 edns by 1679).

[Chappell, William.] Methodus Concionandi. 1648; tr. Eng. 1656 (as The Preacher, Or, The Art and Method of Preaching).

Bowles, Oliver. De Pastore Evangelico Tractatus. 1649.

Prideaux, John. Scholasticae Theologiae Syntagma Mnemonicum. Oxford, 1651, 1660.

Wright, Abraham. Five Sermons, In Five Several Styles Or Waies of Preaching. 1656. [Includes 2 genuine sermons by Andrewes and Hall, and 3 parodies—of Mayne and Cartwright, of the Presbyterians, and of the Independents.]

Price, William. Ars Concionandi. Amsterdam, 1657.

Eachard, John. The Grounds and Occasions of the Contempt of the Clergy. 1670, etc. (9 edns by 1685); rptd E. Arber (English Garner, vol. vii, 1883).

A[rdene], J. Directions concerning the Matter and Stile of Sermons. 1671.

Glanvill, Joseph. An Essay concerning Preaching, written for the Direction of a Young Divine. 1678.

—— A Seasonable Defence of Preaching, and the Plain Way of it. 1678.

(3) The Principal Divines

[This section has been restricted to writers who were born between 1575 and 1620. The older men who survived into the Caroline period have already been listed in Sermons and Devotional Writings: Fisher to Donne (pp. 679–85 above), and the younger men who had begun to publish before 1660 will be found among the Restoration Divines in vol. ii of this work. No cross references have been included to these sections, or to Scholars and Scholarship (pp. 852–63 below) which will be found partly to overlap this section.]

Baker, David [Augustin] (1575–1641). Sancta Sophia, or Directions for the Prayer of Contemplation. Extracted out of more than xl Treatises by Augustin Baker And Methodically digested by Serenus Cressy. 2 vols. Douai, 1657; ed. N. Sweeney, 1876.

—— The Confessions of Augustin Baker. Ed. J. McCann, 1922.

—— The Cloud of Unknowing and other Treatises by an English Mystic of the Fourteenth Century. With a Commentary on the Cloud by Augustin Baker. Ed. J. McCann, 1924.

—— A Spirituall Life in a Secular State being an Addition to the Abridgment of a Spirituall Life. 1927.

Sweeney, J. N. The Life and Spirit of Father Augustine Baker. 1861.

Baxter, Richard (1615–1691). The Saint's Everlasting Rest: or a Treatise of the blessed state of the Saints in their enjoyment of God in Glory. 1650; 1651 ('corrected and enlarged'); 1652; 1653; 1654; 1656; 1658; 1659; 1662; 1669; 1671; 1677; 1688; ed. W. Young, 1907.

Baxter, Richard (1615–1691). Gildas Salvianus; the Reformed Pastor. 1656; 1657 ('with an appendix'); 1680.

—— A Call to the Unconverted to Turn and Live and Accept of Mercy. 1657, etc. (13th edn, 1669).

—— The Life of Faith, as it is the Evidence of things unseen. A Sermon preached before the King at White-Hall. 1660; 1670 (very much enlarged).

—— Poetical Fragments: Heart-Imployment with God and itself. 1681; 1689; 1699 (includes Additions to the Poetical Fragments, 1700); rptd 1821.

—— Mr Richard Baxter's Paraphrase on the Psalms of David in metre, with other Hymns. 1692.

—— Reliquiae Baxterianae: or Mr Richard Baxter's Narrative of the most Memorable Passages in his Life and Times. Ed. M. Sylvester, 1696; abridged by J. M. L. Thomas, 1925.

[For Baxter's other writings, over a hundred in all, see A. B. Grosart, Annotated List of the Writings of Richard Baxter, 1868 (priv. ptd), and A. G. Matthews, The Works of Richard Baxter. An Annotated List, 1933 (priv. ptd).]

Powicke, F. J. A Life of the Rev. Richard Baxter (1615–1660). 1924.

—— The Reverend Richard Baxter. Under the Cross (1660–91). 1926.

Brinsley, John (1600–1665). The Healing of Israel's Breaches; in six Sermons. 1641.

—— The Saints Solemne Covenant with their God; a sermon. 1644.

Brownrig, Ralph (1592–1659; Bishop of Exeter). Fourty Sermons. 1661; 2 vols. 1665–4 (vol. ii = Twenty Five Sermons); 2 vols. 1674 (as Sixty-five Sermons); 2 vols. 1685.

—— Twenty Five Sermons. 1664. [Rptd with Fourty Sermons.]

Burton, Henry (1578–1648). Israels fast; or a meditation upon Josh. vii, 6. 1628 (bis).

—— The seven vials or a briefe and plaine Exposition upon Revelation. 1628.

—— For God, and the King. The summe of Two Sermons. 1636 (bis).

—— A most godly sermon shewing the necessity of selfe-denyall and humiliation, in regard of the present plague. 1641.

—— England's Bondage and Hope of Deliverance. 1641. [Sermon before Parliament.]

Calamy, Edmund (1600–1666). The Noble-Mans Patterne. 1643. [Sermon before House of Lords.]

—— An Indictment Against England because of her selfe-murdering divisions. 1645. [Sermon.]

—— Englands Antidote against the Plague of Civil Warre. 1645. [Sermon.]

Calamy, Edmund (1600–1666). The Fixed Saint held forth in a Farewell Sermon. 1662. [Also ptd with the final sermons of other prominent non-conformists (Baxter, Case, Jacomb, Manton, Watson, etc.) as An Exact Collection of Farewell Sermons, 1662.]
—— Eli Trembling for fear of the Ark. Oxford, 1663. [Calamy was committed to Newgate for preaching this sermon.]
Cartwright, William (1611–1643). An Offspring of Mercy issuing out of the Womb of Cruelty: A Passion sermon preached at Christ's Church in Oxford. 1652.
    Goffin, R. C. The Life and Poems of William Cartwright. Cambridge, 1918.
Cheynell, Francis (1608–1665). Sions Memento, and Gods Alarum. 1643. [Sermon before House of Commons.]
—— Chillingworthi Novissima; or the sicknesse, heresy, death, and buriall of William Chillingworth. 1644.
—— The Man of Honour described. 1645. [Sermon before Parliament.]
Chillingworth, William (1602–1643). The Religion of Protestants a Safe Way to Salvation. Oxford, 1638 (bis); 1664; 1674; 1684; 1687, etc.
—— The Works. 1704; 1719 (7th edn); 1727; 1742 (with Life by T. Birch); 3 vols. 1820; 3 vols. Oxford, 1838.
    Plumptre, E. H. William Chillingworth. [In Masters in English Theology, ed. A. Barry, 1877.]
Cosin, John (1594–1672; Bishop of Durham). A Collection of Private Devotions, in the practice of the ancient Church, called the Houres of Prayer. 1627, etc. (at least 7 edns by 1676).
—— A Scholastical History of the Canon of the Holy Scripture. 1657; 1672; 1683.
—— Historia Transubstantionis Papalis. 1675; tr. Eng. 1676 (rptd in Tracts for the Times, vol. I,. 1834, and ed. J. S. Brewer, with Memoir, 1840).
—— Regiae Angliae Religio Catholica. Ed. T. Smith (appended to the life of Cosin in Vitae quorundam eruditissimorum Virorum, 1707); ed. W. Wekett, 1729 (from another MS); ed. F. Meyrick, 1853; tr. Eng. 1870.
—— The Works. Ed. J. Sansom, 5 vols. Oxford, 1843–55. (Lib. of Anglo-Catholic Theology).
—— The Correspondence of John Cosin. Ed. G. Ornsby, 2 vols. Surtees Soc. 1869–72.
Cressy, Hugh Paulin [Serenus] (1605–1674). Exomologesis; or, a faithful narrative of the Conversion into Catholique Unity of Hugh Paulin de Cressy. Paris, 1647; Paris, 1653.
—— The Church History of Britanny from the beginning of Christianity to the Norman Conquest. [Rouen], 1668.

Cudworth, Ralph (1617–1688). [See p. 877 below.]
Dell, William (d. 1664). The Building and Glory of the truely Christian and Spiritual Church. 1646. [Sermon before Fairfax and his officers at Marston.]
—— Right Reformation. 1646. [Sermon before House of Commons.]
—— Several Sermons and Discourses. 1652; 1709; rptd 2 vols. 1817.
—— The Stumbling Stone; wherein the University is reproved by the Word of God. 1653. [Sermon in answer to Sydrach Simpson.]
Downame, George (d. 1634; Bishop of Derry). The Christian Arte of Thriving. 1620. [Sermon.]
—— A Godly and Learned Treatise of Prayer. Cambridge, 1640.
    Dredge, J. I. Dr. George Downame. Manchester, 1881.
Edwards, Thomas (1595–1645). Gangraena; or, a Catalogue and Discovery of many of the errours of the sectaries of this time. 3 pts, 1646 (3 edns).
Ferrar, Nicholas (1592–1637). The Story Books of Little Gidding, being the Religious Dialogues recited in the Great Room, 1631–1632. Ed. E. C. Sharland, 1899.
    MacDonough, T. M. Brief Memoirs of Nicholas Ferrar. Chiefly collected from a Narrative by Dr. Turner. 1837.
    Nicholas Ferrar: Two Lives, by his Brother John, and by Dr. Jebb. Ed. J. E. B. Mayor, Cambridge, 1885.
    Carter, T. T. Nicholas Ferrar; his Household and his Friends. 1892.
    Acland, J. E. Little Gidding and its Inmates in the Time of Charles I. 1903.
    Skipton, H. P. K. The Life and Times of Nicholas Ferrar. 1907.
Frank, Mark (1613–1664). LI Sermons. 1672; ed. W H. M., 2 vols. Oxford, 1849.
Fuller, Thomas (1608–1661). [See pp. 835–6 below.]
Gauden, John (1605–1662; Bishop of Exeter). The Love of Truth and Peace. 1641. [Sermon before House of Commons.]
—— A Sermon Preached before the Honourable House of Commons Novemb. 29, 1640. 1641.
—— Three Sermons Preached upon Severall Publike Occasions. 1642.
—— Funerals Made Cordials. 1658. [Funeral sermon for Robert Rich.]
—— A sermon preached in the Temple-Chappel, at the Funeral of Dr. Brounrig. 1660.
—— ΜΕΓΑΛΕΙΑ ΘΕΟΥ. Gods great Demonstrations. 1660. [Sermon before House of Commons.]

Gauden, John (1605–1662; Bishop of Exeter). Anti-Baal-Berith; or The Binding of the Covenant and all Covenanters to their good behaviors. 1661.

[For Eikon Basiliké, which is now generally attrib. to Gauden, see E. Almack, A Bibliography of the King's Book, 1896.]

Gunning, Peter (1614–1684; Bishop of Ely). A Contention for Truth in two several publique disputations betweene Mr. Gunning and Mr. Denne in the Church of St Clement-Danes. 1638.

—— Schism Unmask'd, or a late conference between Mr. Peter Gunning and Mr. John Pierson on the one part, and two disputants of the Romish Persuasion on the other. Paris, 1658.

—— The Paschal, or Lent Fast, Apostolical and Perpetual with an appendix containing an answer to the objections of the Presbyterians against the Fast of Lent. 1662; ed. C. P. Eden, Oxford, 1845.

Hakewill, George (1578–1649). King Davids Vow for Reformation. Delivered in twelve sermons before the Prince. 1621.

—— A Comparison between the Dayes of Purim and that of the Powder treason. Oxford, 1626.

[For Hakewill's philosophical writings see p. 875 below.]

Hales, John (1584–1656). Golden Remaines of the ever memorable Mr. John Hales. 1659; 1673 (enlarged); 1677; 1688.

—— Sermons preached at Eton. 1660; 1673.

—— The Works. Ed. D. Dalrymple, 3 vols. Glasgow, 1765.

Hall, Joseph (1574–1656; Bishop of Norwich). Mundus Alter et Idem, sive Terra Australis ante hac semper incognita. Auth: Mercurio Britannico. Frankfort, [1605?]; Hanover, 1607; Utrecht, 1643; ed. H. J. Anderson, 1908. Tr. Eng. J. H[ealey], [1609?] (ed. H. Brown, Cambridge, U.S.A. 1937); German, 1613.

—— Meditations and Vowes Divine and Morall. 1605; 1606 (enlarged); 1607; 1609; 1616; 1621.

—— Contemplations upon the principall passages of the Holy storie. 8 vols. 1612–26; ed. C. Wordsworth, 1871.

—— The Works. 3 vols. 1625–62 (vol. I rptd 1628, 1633, 1634, 1647); ed. J. Pratt, 10 vols. 1808; ed. P. Hall, 12 vols. Oxford, 1837–9; ed. P. Wynter, 10 vols. Oxford, 1863.

—— Episcopacie by Divine Right. 3 pts, 1640.

—— The Complete Poems. Ed. A. B. Grosart, Manchester, 1879.

[For Hall's other writings see p. 480 above and pp. 722, 841 below.]

Jones, John. Bishop Hall, his Life and Times. 1826.

Lewis, G. A Life of Joseph Hall. 1886.

Salyer, S. M. Renaissance Influences in Hall's Mundus. PQ. VI, 1927.

Hall, Thomas (1610?–1665). The Pulpit Guarded. 1651 (3 edns).

—— Vindiciae Literarum; the Schools Guarded. 1655.

—— Funebria Florae; the Downfall of May-Games. 1660; 1661.

Hammond, Henry (1605–1660). A Practical Catechism. 1645; 1646 (enlarged), etc. (13th edn, 1691).

—— The Christians Obligations to Peace and Charity with ix Sermons more. 1649; 1652 ('corrected').

—— A Paraphrase and Annotations upon the New Testament. 1653; 1671; 1675; 1702, etc.

—— A Paraphrase and Annotations upon the books of the Psalms. 1659.

—— Sermons. 1664; 1675.

—— The Works. Ed. W. Fulman, 4 vols. 1684.

—— The Miscellaneous Theological Works. Ed. N. Pocock, 3 vols. Oxford, 1847–50.

Fell, John. The Life of Dr Henry Hammond. 1661; rptd C. Wordsworth (Ecclesiastical Biography, vol. IV, 1810).

Perry, G. G. Life of Henry Hammond. [1862.]

Hardy, Nathaniel (1618–1670). Justice triumphing: or, the spoylers spoyled: laid forth in a gratulatory sermon for the glorious delivery from the barbarous Powder Plot, Nov. 5, 1646. 1647 (bis); 1656.

—— A divine prospective: representing the just mans peacefull end. In a funeral sermon on Sir John Gay. 1649; 1654; 1660.

—— Love and Fear, the inseparable twins of a blest matrimony: characterized in a sermon occasioned by the late Nuptials between Wm. Christmas and Elizabeth Adams. 1653; 1658.

—— Lamentation, Mourning and Woe; sighed forth in a sermon preached the next Lords-Day after the dismal fire in the city of London. 1666.

Herbert, George (1593–1632). [See pp. 451–3 above.]

Hildersham, Arthur (1563–1632). Lectures upon the fourth of John. 1629; 1632 ('corrected and enlarged'); 1647.

Holyday, Barten (1593–1661). Motives to a Good Life; in ten sermons. Oxford, 1657.

—— A Survey of the World, in ten books. Oxford, 1661. [Poem.]

[For Holyday's Τεχνογαμία see p. 657 above; his trns from Horace and Persius will be found pp. 803, 805 below.]

Hoyle, Joshua (d. 1654). Jehojadahs Justice against Mattan, Baal's priest. Preacht upon the occasion of a Speech utter'd upon Tower-Hill. 1645. [An arraignment of Laud.]

Ingelo, Nathaniel (1621?–1683). The Perfection, Authority, and Credibility of the Holy Scriptures. 1659 (bis). [Sermon before Cambridge University.]

—— Bentivolio and Urania. 1660 (bis); 1673; 1682. [An allegorical romance.]

Jackson, Thomas (1579–1640). Nazareth and Bethlehem, and Mankinds Comfort. Two Sermons. Oxford, 1617.

—— Divine Sermons. Oxford, 1637.

—— A Collection of the Works. Ed. B. O[ley], 3 pts, 1653–7; 3 vols. 1673; rptd 12 vols. Oxford, 1844.

King, Henry (1592–1669). A Sermon preached at Paul's Crosse, upon occasion of that false report touching the supposed apostasie of John King, late Lord Bishop of London. 1621.

—— Two Sermons preached at White-Hall in Lent. 1627.

—— An Exposition upon the Lord's Prayer, delivered in certaine sermons. 1628; 1634.

—— A Sermon preached at the funeral of Bryan [Duppa] lord Bishop of Winchester. 1662.

[For King's poems see p. 450 above.]

Laud, William (1573–1645; Archbishop of Canterbury). The Archbishop of Canterbury's Speech, or, His Funeral Sermon Preacht by Himself on the Scaffold on Tower-Hill, on Friday the 10 of January, 1644. All faithfully written by John Hinde. 1644; 1660; rptd Harleian Misc. vol. VIII, 1744, 1808. [Another version, first ptd Oxford, 1644, is rptd in Somers Tracts, vol. IV, 1809.]

—— Seven Sermons preached upon severall Occasions. 1651.

—— The History of the Troubles and Tryal of William Laud. Wrote by himself. [Ed. H. Wharton], 1695. [Includes some of Laud's other writings.]

—— The Second Volume of the Remains of William Laud. Ed. H. and E. Wharton, 1700.

—— The Works. Ed. W. Scott and J. Bliss, 7 vols. Oxford, 1847–60.

Heylin, Peter. Cyprianus Anglicus. 1668.
Mozley, J. B. Lectures and Theological Papers. 1883.
Hutton, W. H. William Laud. 1895.
Duncan-Jones, A. S. Archbishop Laud. 1927.
Coffin, R. P. T. William Laud. New York, 1930.

Leighton, Robert (1611–1684; Archbishop of Glasgow). Sermons published after his death from his Papers. 1692.

—— Expository Works and other Remains revised by Philip Doddridge. 2 vols. Edinburgh, 1748.

—— Remains, consisting of all the Unpublished Pieces left by him to the Diocese of Dunblane. With his Life by G. Jerment. 1814.

—— The Genuine Works. To which is prefixed the Life of the Author by E. Middleton. 4 vols. 1819.

—— The Whole Works. Ed. W. West, 6 vols. 1869–75.

—— The Whole Works. Ed. J. N. Pearson, New York, 1874.

Tulloch, J. Archbishop Leighton. [In Scottish Divines, 1505–1872, Edinburgh, 1883.]
Knox, E. A. Robert Leighton. 1930.

Love, Christopher (1618–1651). Englands Distemper, set forth in a sermon preacht on the first day of the treaty. 1645; 1651.

—— Grace: The Truth and Growth Thereof. The summe and substance of fifteen Sermons. 1652; 1657.

—— Heaven's Glory, Hell's Terror Or Two Treatises. 2 pts, 1653.

—— A Treatise of Effectual Calling and Election, in xvi Sermons. 1653.

—— The Combate between the Flesh and Spirit being the summe and substance of xxvii. Sermons. To which is added the Christians Directory in xv. Sermons. 2 pts, 1654; 2 pts, 1658.

Marshall, Stephen (1594?–1655). A Peace Offering to God: a sermon preached to the House of Commons at their publique thanksgiving for the Peace. 1641.

—— Reformation and Desolation: or a sermon. Preached to the House of Commons. 1642.

—— A Sacred Panegyrick: or a Sermon of Thanksgiving preached to the two Houses of Parliament. 1644.

—— A Sacred Record to be made of Gods mercies to Zion. A Thanksgiving Sermon preached to the two Houses of Parliament June 19, 1645. Being the Day of their Publick Thanksgiving for the Victory in Naseby-field. [1645.]

—— The Power of the Civil Magistrate in matters of Religion vindicated. In a Sermon preached before Parliament. 1657.

Mayne, Jasper (1604–1672). A Sermon Concerning Unity and Agreement. Preached at Carfax Church in Oxford. 1646; 1647.

—— A Sermon against False Prophets, preached in Oxford, shortly after the surrender of that garrison. 1646.

Mayne, Jasper (1604–1672). A late Printed Sermon Against False Prophets, Vindicated by Letter, From the causeless Aspersions of Mr. Francis Cheynell. 1647.
—— A Sermon Against Schisme. Preacht in the Church of Wattlington in Oxford-shire, with some Interruptions, September 11, 1652. At a publick dispute held there, Between Jasper Mayne, D.D. And one —. 1652.
—— A Sermon Preached at the Consecration of Herbert [Croft] Lord Bishop of Hereford. 1662.
[For Mayne's plays see p. 648 above.]
Moore, John (1595?–1657). The Crying Sin of England of not caring for the Poor, wherein Inclosure is Arraigned: being two sermons. 1653.
More, Gertrude (1606–1633). The Holy Practises of a Devine Lover, Or The Sainctly Ideots Devotions. Paris, 1657; ed. H. L. Fox, 1909.
    Collins, Henry. Life of Dame Gertrude More. 1877.
More, Henry (1614–1687). [See pp. 875–6 below.]
Morley, George (1597–1684; Bishop of Winchester). A modest advertisement concerning the present controversie about Church Government. 1641.
—— A Letter concerning the Death of Lady Capel. 1654.
—— A Sermon preached at the Magnificent Coronation of Charles the IId. 1661.
—— Epistola ad Virum Clarissimum D. Cornelium Triglandium. 1663.
—— Several Treatises, written upon several occasions. 1683.
Owen, John (1616–1683). Ουρανων Ουρανια. The Shaking and Translating of Heaven and Earth. A sermon preached to the House of Commons. 1649.
—— A Complete Collection of the Sermons. [Ed. J. Asty], 1721. [Includes a sermon preached 31 Jan. 1649 and a funeral sermon for Henry Ireton.]
—— The Works. Ed. T. Russell, 28 vols. 1826. [Includes W. Orme's Memoirs of the Life, Writings and Religious Connexions of John Owen, first pbd 1820.]
Palmer, Herbert (1601–1647). The Glasse of God's Providence. 1644. [Sermon before Parliament.]
—— Memorials of Godlinesse and Christianitie. 3 pts, 1644–5, etc. (10th edn, 1670); ed. A. B. Grosart, Edinburgh, 1865. [Pt ii is sometimes incorrectly ascribed to Francis Bacon.]
—— The Duty and Honours of Church-Restorers. 1646. [Sermon before House of Commons.]

Pearson, John (1613–1686; Bishop of Chester). An Exposition of the Creed. 1659, etc. (at least 8 edns by 1704); ed. T. Chevallier and R. Sinker, Cambridge, 1882.
—— Vindiciae Epistolarum S. Ignatii. 1672; ed. E. Churton, 2 vols. Oxford, 1852.
—— The Minor Theological Works. Ed. E. Churton, 2 vols. Oxford, 1844.
—— Bishop Pearson's Five Lectures on the Acts of the Apostles. Ed. J. R. Crowfoot, Cambridge, 1851.
[Pearson also wrote prefaces for Meric Casaubon's edn of Hierocles, 1655, and The Golden Remains of John Hales, 1659.]
    Cheetham, S. [In Masters in English Theology, ed. A. Barry, 1877.]
Peters, Hugh (1598–1660). Gods Doings and Mans Duty. 1646 (bis). [Sermon before Parliament.]
—— A Sermon preached before his Death. 1660.
Preston, John (1587–1628). Sermons preached before his Majestie, and upon other speciale occasions. 1630; 1631 (bis); 1634; 1637.
—— Life Eternall Or, A Treatise Of the knowledge of the Divine Essence. Delivered in xviii. Sermons. 1631 (bis); 1632; 1634.
—— Foure Godly and Learned Treatises. 1633 (3rd edn); 1636.
Reynolds, Edward (1599–1676; Bishop of Norwich). An Explication of the fourteenth Chapter of the Prophet Hosea, in several sermons. 1658.
—— A Sermon touching the Use of Humane Learning, preached at the funeral of John Langley, late school-master at Pauls School in London. 1658.
—— The Comfort and Crown of Great Actions. 1658. [Sermon before the East India Company.]
—— A Sermon Preached before the Peers November 7, 1666. Being a Day of Solemn Humiliation for the Continuing Pestilence. 1666.
—— The Whole Works. [Ed. J. R. Pitman,] 6 vols. 1826. [With a Life by R. Chalmers.]
Saltmarsh, John (d. 1647). Poemata Sacra, Latinè et Anglicè scripta. Cambridge, 1636.
—— Holy Discoveries and Flames. 1640; rptd 1811.
—— Perfume against the Sulpherous Stinke of the Snuffe of the light for Smoak. 1646.
—— Sparkles of Glory, or some Beams of the Morning-Star. 1647; rptd 1811, 1847.
Sancroft, William (1617–1693; Archbishop of Canterbury). Occasional Sermons. With some Remarks of his Life and Conversation, in a Letter to a Friend. 1694 (re-issued 1703).

Sancroft, William (1617–1693; Archbishop of Canterbury). Familiar Letters to Sir Henry North, to which is prefixed some Account of his Life and Character. 1757.

D'Oyly, G. The Life of William Sancroft. 2 vols. 1821.

Sanderson, Robert (1587–1663; Bishop of Lincoln). Ten Sermons. 1627; 1632 (enlarged as Twelve Sermons); 1637 (enlarged as Twelve Sermons: whereunto are added two sermons more); 1656 (enlarged as Twenty Sermons); 1657 (rptd from 1637 edn as Fourteen Sermons); 1671 (enlarged as xxxiv Sermons); 1674; 1681 (enlarged as xxxv Sermons, with Walton's Life); 1686 (re-issued 1689); ed. R. Montgomery, 2 vols. 1841.

—— The Works. Ed. W. Jacobson, 6 vols. Oxford, 1854.

Walton, Izaak. The Life of Dr. Sanderson. 1678.

Lewis, G. Robert Sanderson. 1924.

[For Sanderson's philosophical works see p. 874 below.]

Sheldon, Gilbert (1598–1677; Archbishop of Canterbury). Davids Deliverance and Thanksgiving. A Sermon preached before the King. Being the Day of Solemn Thanksgiving for the Happy Return of His Majesty. 1660.

Sibbes, Richard (1577–1635). Bowels Opened: Or, a Discovery of the Neare and Deare Love, Union and Communion betwixt Christ and the Church. Delivered in divers Sermons. 1632; 1641.

—— Light from Heaven. In foure Treatises. 1638.

—— An Exposition of the Third Chapter of the Epistle of St. Paul to the Philippians [and other sermons]. 1639; 1647.

—— Beames of Divine Light Breaking forth from severall places of holy Scripture. In xxi Sermons. 1639.

—— The Glorious Feast of the Gospel in divers Sermons. 1650.

—— The Complete Works. Ed. A. B. Grosart, 6 vols. 1862–3.

Spurstow, William (1605–1666). England's patterne and duty in its monthly fasts. 1643. [Sermon before Parliament.]

—— England's Eminent Judgments. 1644. [Sermon before House of Lords, 5 Nov. 1644.]

—— Death and the Grave no Bar to Believers Happinesse. 1656. [Funeral sermon for Lady Vyner.]

Sterry, Peter (1613–1672). The Spirit Convincing of Sinne. 1645; 1646. [Sermon before House of Commons.]

—— The Clouds in which Christ Comes. 1648. [Sermon before House of Commons.]

Sterry, Peter (1613–1672). The Teachings of Christ in the Soul. 1648. [Sermon before House of Lords.]

—— The Commings Forth of Christ opened in a sermon before Parliament for the victories obtained in Ireland. 1650.

—— England's Deliverance From the Northern Presbytery, A Thanksgiving Sermon. 1652. [Before Parliament.]

—— The Way of God with His People in these Nations; a thanksgiving sermon for the victory over the Spaniards. 1657. [Before House of Lords.]

—— The True Way of Uniting the People of God in These Nations. 1660. [Sermon.]

—— A Discourse of the Freedom of the Will. 1675.

—— The Rise, Race, And Royalty of the Kingdom of God in the Soul of Man. Opened in several Sermons. 1683.

—— The Appearance of God to Man in the Gospel. 1710.

Pinto, V. de S. Peter Sterry. A Biographical and Critical Study with Passages selected from his Writings. Cambridge, 1934.

Steward, Richard (1593?–1651). Catholique Divinity: or the most solid and sententious expressions of the primitive doctors. 1657.

—— Golden remains; or three sermons. 1661.

—— A Discourse of episcopacy and sacrilege by way of letter. Written in 1646. 1683.

Pocock, N. Life of Richard Steward. 1908.

Strode, William (1602–1645). A Sermon preached at a Visitation held at Lin in Norfolk. 1660.

—— Poetical Works. Ed. B. Dobell, 1907.

[For Strode's The Floating Island see p. 659 above.]

Taylor, Jeremy (1613–1667; Bishop of Down). A Sermon Preached In Saint Maries Church in Oxford. Upon the Anniversary of the Gunpowder-Treason. Oxford, 1638.

—— Of The Sacred Order, And Offices of Episcopacy, By Divine Institution, Apostolicall Tradition, & Catholike practice. Oxford, 1642 (re-issued London, 1647).

—— A Discourse concerning Prayer Ex tempore, or, By pretence of the Spirit. 1646 (anon.); 1647; 1649 (enlarged as An Apology For Authorised and Set Forms of Liturgie).

—— A new and easie Institution of Grammar. 1647. [In collaboration with William Wyatt.]

—— ΘΕΟΛΟΓΙΑ 'ΕΚΛΕΚΤΙΚΗ. A Discourse of The Liberty of Prophesying. 1647.

—— Treatises of 1. The Liberty of Prophesying. 2. Prayer Ex Tempore. 3. Episcopacie. Together with A Sermon preached at Oxon. 1648.

Taylor, Jeremy (1613–1667; Bishop of Down). The Great Exemplar of Sanctity and Holy Life according to Christian Institution. 1649; 1653; 1657; 1667, etc.

—— A Funerall Sermon, Preached At the Obsequies of the Right Honble and most vertuous Lady, The Lady Frances, Countesse of Carbery. 1650.

—— The Rule and Exercises of Holy Living. 1650; 1651; 1654 (4th edn); 1656, etc. (19th edn, 1703); ed. A. R. Waller, 2 vols. 1900.

—— The Rule and Exercises of Holy Dying. 1651; 1652; 1655. [Subsequently rptd with Holy Living.]

—— xxviii Sermons Preached at Golden Grove. Together with A Discourse of the Office Ministeriall. 1651; 1655; 1668.

—— A short Catechism for The institution of Young Persons in the Christian Religion. To which is added, An Explication of the Apostolical Creed. 1652.

—— A Discourse of Baptisme, Its Institution, and Efficacy upon all Believers. 1652; 1653.

—— Two Discourses 1. Of Baptisme. 2. Of Prayer Ex tempore. 1653.

—— xxv Sermons Preached At Golden-Grove. 1653; 1655; 1668.

—— ENIAYTOΣ. A Course of Sermons for All the Sundaies Of the Year. 1653; 1655 (enlarged); 1668 (enlarged); 1678 (enlarged).

—— The Real Presence and Spirituall of Christ in the Blessed Sacrament. 1654.

—— The Golden Grove or, A Manuall of Daily Prayers and Letanies, Fitted to the dayes of the Weeke. 1655; 1659 (4th edn), etc. (21st edn, 1703).

—— Unum Necessarium or, The Doctrine and Practice of Repentance. 1655.

—— A further Explication of The Doctrine of Original Sin. 1656.

—— Deus Justificatus. Two Discourses of Original Sin. 1656.

—— A Discourse of the Nature, Offices and Measures of Friendship. 1657; 1657 (as The Measures and Offices of Friendship); 1662; 1671; 1675; 1684; rptd 1920.

—— ΣΥΜΒΟΛΟΝ ΗΘΙΚΟΠΟΛΕΜΙΚΟΝ. Or A Collection of Polemical and Moral Discourses. 1657; 1674 (3rd edn, enlarged).

—— A Collection of offices or Forms of Prayer in Cases Ordinary and Extraordinary. 1658.

—— A Sermon preached at the Funerall of Sr. George Dalston. 1658.

—— The Worthy Communicant or A Discourse of the Nature, Effects, and Blessings consequent to the worthy receiving of the Lords Supper. 1660 (re-issued 1661); 1667; 1674 (adds a Sermon by Taylor).

Taylor, Jeremy (1613–1667; Bishop of Down). Ductor Dubitantium, or The Rule of Conscience In all her general measures. 2 vols. 1660; 1671; 1676; 1696; 2 vols. 1725 (abridged by R. Barcroft).

—— A Sermon Preached at the Consecration of two Archbishops and ten Bishops, in the Cathedral in Dublin. Dublin, 1660; 1663.

—— A Sermon Preached At the opening of the Parliament of Ireland. 1661.

—— Rules and Advices To the Clergy Of the Diocese of Down and Connor. Dublin, 1661 (bis); 1663.

—— Via Intelligentiae. A Sermon Preached to the University of Dublin. 1662.

—— A Sermon Preached in Christ-Church, Dublin: at the Funeral of The Arch-bishop of Armagh: with A Narrative of his whole Life. Dublin, 1663; 1663; 1663 ('Enlarged').

—— The Righteousness Evangelicall Describ'd. The Christians Conquest Over the Body of Sin. Fides Formata, or Faith working by Love. In Three Sermons. Dublin, 1663; 1663.

—— ΕΒΔΟΜΑΣ ΕΜΒΟΛΙΜΑΙΟΣ, A Supplement to the ENIAYTOΣ, Or Course of Sermons for the whole year: Being Seven Sermons Preached since the Restauration. 1663 (re-issued 1664).

—— ΧΡΙΣΙΣ ΤΕΛΕΙΩΤΙΚΙΙ. A Discourse of Confirmation. Dublin, 1663; 1664.

—— A Dissuasive from Popery To the People of Ireland. Dublin, 1664 (re-issued London, 1664); 1668 (enlarged).

—— ΔΕΚΑΣ ΕΜΒΟΛΙΜΑΙΟΣ, A Supplement to the ENIAYTOΣ: Being Ten Sermons Preached since the Restauration. 1667.

—— The Second Part of the Dissuasive from Popery: In Vindication of the First Part. 1667.

—— B. Taylor's Opuscula. The Measures of Friendship. With Additional Tracts. 1675.

—— Christ's Yoke an Easy Yoke, And yet, The Gate to Heaven a Strait Gate. In two excellent Sermons. 1675.

—— The Whole Works. Ed. (with Life and critique) R. Heber, 15 vols. 1822; rev. C. P. Eden, 10 vols. 1847–54.

—— On The Reverence Due to the Altar. Now first printed. Ed. J. Barrow, Oxford, 1848.

—— The Poems and Verse-Translations of Jeremy Taylor. Ed. A. B. Grosart, 1870. (Fuller Worthies' Lib. Misc.)

—— The Golden Grove. Selected Passages from the Sermons and Writings of Jeremy Taylor. Ed. L. P. Smith, Oxford, 1930.

[For books to which Taylor contributed and books which have been attrib. to him see the bibliography by R. Gathorne-Hardy in The

Golden Grove, ed. L. P. Smith, Oxford, 1930, and TLS. 15 Sept. 1932.]

    Wilmott, R. A. Jeremy Taylor, his Predecessors, Contemporaries, and Successors. 1846.

    May, E. H. A Dissertation of the Life, Theology and Times of Dr Jeremy Taylor. 1892.

    Gosse, Sir E. Jeremy Taylor. 1904. (English Men of Letters Ser.)

    Worley, G. Jeremy Taylor: a Sketch of his Life and Times. 1904.

    Brown, W. J. Jeremy Taylor. 1925.

    Nicolson, M. H. New Material on Jeremy Taylor. PQ. VIII, 1930.

Taylor, Thomas (1576–1633). A Mappe of Rome. Preached in five Sermons on occasion of the Gunpowder Treason. 1619; 1620; 1634.

—— A Man in Christ, or: A new Creature. To which is added a Treatise, containing Meditations from the Creatures. 1628; 1629 ('corrected'); 1632; 1635.

Thorndike, Herbert (1598–1672). Epitome Lexici Hebraici, Rabinici et Arabici. 1635.

—— Of the Government of Churches, a discourse pointing at the Primitive Form. Cambridge, 1641; 1649; ed. D. Lewis, 1841.

—— Of Religious Assemblies and the Public Service of God. Cambridge, 1642.

—— A Discourse of the Right of the Church in a Christian State. 1649; ed. J. S. Brewer, 1841.

—— A Letter concerning the Present State of Religion amongst us. 1656.

—— An Epilogue to the Tragedy of the Church of England. 1659.

—— The Due Way of composing the differences on foot. 1660; 1662; 1687.

—— Just Weights and Measures. 1662. [Rptd with The Due Way, 1662, 1687.]

—— A Discourse of the Forbearance or the Penalties, which a Due Reformation requires. 1670.

—— De Ratione ac Jure finiendi Controversias Ecclesiae Disputatio. 1670.

—— Theological Works. 6 vols. Oxford, 1844–56. (Lib. of Anglo-Catholic Theology.) [Includes 8 pieces left in MS. Vols. III–VI, ed. A. W. Haddan; life and bibliography in vol. VI.]

Tombes, John (1603?–1676). Fermentum Pharisaeorum. 1643. [Sermon.]

—— Jehovah Jireh: or Gods providence in delivering the Godly. Opened in two sermons in Bristol of thanksgiving for the deliverance of that citie from the Invasion without, and the Plot of Malignants within. 1643.

Tombes, John (1603?–1676). Anthropolatria, Or, The Sinne of Glorying in Eminent Ministers of the Gospel. 1645. [Sermon.]

Ussher, James (1581–1656; Archbishop of Armagh). The Soveraignes Power and the Subjects Duty; a sermon at Christ Church. Oxford, 1644.

—— The Rights of Primogeniture; or the excellency of royall authority; a sermon before His Majesty, upon the anniversary of his Birth-Day. 1648.

—— Eighteen Sermons preached in Oxford, 1640. 1659; 1660 (re-issued 1662).

—— The Whole Works. Ed. C. R. Elrington and J. H. Todd, 17 vols. Dublin, 1847. [For Ussher's other writings see pp. 857–8 below.]

    Parr, Richard. The Life of James Usher, late Lord Archbishop of Armagh. 1686. [Contains 323 letters to or from Ussher.]

    Wright, W. B. The Ussher Memoirs. Dublin, 1889.

    Carr, J. A. The Life and Times of James Ussher, Archbishop of Armagh. 1895.

Vines, Richard (1600?–1656). The Hearse of the Renowned Earle of Essex. 1646. [Funeral sermon.]

Wallis, John (1616–1703). Theological Discourses [and sermons]. 2 pts, 1692. [For Wallis's other writings see p. 877 below.]

Walton, Brian (1600–1661; Bishop of Chester). B. Waltoni Introductio ad Lectionem Linguarum Orientialium. 1655 (bis); rptd 1821.

—— The Considerator Considered. 1659. [A reply to John Owen.]

    Todd, H. J. Memoirs of the Life and Writings of Walton. 2 vols. 1821.

    Barnes, W. E. Brian Walton. [In Studies in Memory of A. W. Ward, Cambridge, 1924.]

Ward, Seth (1617–1689; Bishop of Salisbury). Vindiciae Academiarum. Oxford, 1654.

—— Against Resistance of Lawful Powers: a sermon. 1661.

—— The Christians Victory over Death. A sermon at the Funeral of the Duke of Albemarle. 1670.

—— A Sermon Against the Anti-Scripturists. Also Another concerning Infidelity. Preached at White-Hall. 2 pts, 1670.

—— An Apology for the Mysteries of the Gospel, a sermon. 1673.

    Pope, Walter. Life of Seth, Lord Bishop of Salisbury. 1697.

Whichcote, Benjamin (1609–1683). [See p. 879 below.]

Wilkins, John (1614–1672; Bishop of Chester). The Discovery of a World in the Moone. 1638 (anon.); 2 pts, 1640.

Wilkins, John (1614–1672; Bishop of Chester). Mercury, Or, The Secret Messenger. 1641; 1694.

—— Ecclesiastes; or, a discourse concerning the Gift of Preaching as it falls under the Rules of Art. 1646; 1647; 1651; 1656; 1659; 1669; 1679.

—— Mathematicall Magick. In two books. 1648; 1680.

—— A Discourse concerning the Beauty of Providence in all the Rugged Passages of it. 1649; 1704 (7th edn).

—— A Discourse concerning the gift of Prayer. 1653; 1704 (8th edn); tr. French, 1665.

—— An Essay towards a Real Character and a Philosophical Language. 1668. [For this work see O. Funke, Zum Weltsprachenproblem in England im 17. Jahrhundert, Heidelberg, 1929.]

—— Of the Principles and Duties of Natural Religion. [Ed. I. Ibbotson,] 2 pts, 1675; 1722–3 (8th edn). [Preface by Tillotson.]

—— Sermons preached upon several occasions before the King at Whitehall. 1677; 1680; 1682 (with Preface by Tillotson); 1701.

—— The Mathematical and Philosophical Works. With a Short Life of the Author. 1708; rptd 2 vols. 1802.

Henderson, P. A. W. The Life and Times of John Wilkins. 1910.

Worthington, John (1618–1671). Ὑποτύπωσις ὑγιαινόν των λόγων. A Form of Sound Words: or a Scripture Catechism; shewing what a Christian is to believe and practise in order to Salvation. 1673, etc. (7 edns by 1733).

—— The Great Duty of Self-Resignation to the Divine Will. 1675; 1689; rptd Bristol, 1823.

—— The Doctrines of the Resurrection and the Reward to come, considered as the grand Motives to an Holy Life. 1690.

—— Charitas Evangelica: a Discourse of Christian Love. 1691.

—— Forms of Prayer for a Family. 1693; 1721.

—— Miscellanies, also a Collection of Epistles; with the Author's Character by Archbishop Tillotson. 1704.

—— Select Discourses. 1725; rptd 1826.

—— Diary and Correspondence of Dr John Worthington. Ed. J. Crossley, 2 vols. Chetham Soc. 1847–86.

[For works edited and translated by Worthington see the bibliography pbd by the Chetham Soc. in 1885.]

Young, Thomas (1587–1655). Hopes Incouragement pointed at. 1644. [Sermon before House of Commons.]

C. F. R. and F. J. P.

5. POPULAR AND MISCELLANEOUS PROSE

I. PAMPHLETEERS AND MISCELLANEOUS WRITERS

BARNABE RICH (1540?–1617)

(1) WRITINGS

A right Exelent and pleasant Dialogue, betwene Mercury and an English Souldier. [1574.]

Allarme to England, fore-shewing what Perilles are procured, where the People live without Regard of Martiall Lawe. 1578 (*bis*); 1625 (abbreviated by G. M[arcelline?] as Vox Militis).

Riche his Farewell to Militarie profession. 1581; 1606 (with addns); ed. J. P. Collier, Shakespeare Soc. 1846. [A collection of romances.]

The Straunge and Wonderfull Adventures of Don Simonides. 1581.

The True Report of a Late Practise enterprised by a Papist. 1582.

The Second Tome of the Travailes and Adventures of Don Simonides. 1584.

The Famous Hystory of Herodotus. 1584 ('by B. R.') (bks 1–2); ed. A. Lang, 1888 (bk 2 only); ed. L. Whibley, 1926 (Tudor Translations, ser. 2). [The attribution to Rich is not certain.]

A Pathway to Military Practise. 1587.

The Adventures of Brusanus, Prince of Hungaria. 1592.

Greenes Newes both from Heaven and Hell. 1593 ('by B. R.'); ed. R. B. McKerrow, 1911 (with Greenes Funeralls, by R. B., 1594, also sometimes attrib. to Rich).

A Martiall Conference, pleasantly discoursed between Two Souldiers only practised in Finsbury Fields. 1598.

A Souldiers Wishe to Britons Welfare. 2 pts, 1604 (pt 2, The Fruites of Long Experience).

Faultes Faults, and Nothing else but Faultes. 1606 (re-issued 1616 as My Ladies Looking Glasse).

A Short Survey of Ireland truely discovering who hath armed that People with Disobedience. 1069 (*i.e.* 1609).

Roome for a Gentleman, or the Second Part of Faultes collected for the True Meridian of Dublin. 1609

A New Description of Ireland, wherein is described the Disposition of the Irish. 1610 (re-issued anon. 1624 as A New Irish Prognostication).

A True and a Kinde Excuse in Defence of that Booke, intituled a Newe Description of Irelande. 1612.

A Catholicke Conference betweene Syr Tady MacMareall and Patricke Plaine. 1612.

The Excellency of Good Women. 1613.

Opinion Diefied, discovering the Ingins, Traps, and Traynes that are set to catch Opinion. 1613.

The Honestie of this Age. 1614; 1615; 1616; ed. Peter Cunningham, Percy Soc. 1844.

The Irish Hubbub or, the English Hue and Crie. 1617; 1619; 1622.

Barnaby Rich's 'Remembrances of the State of Ireland, 1612', with Notices of Other Manuscript Reports, by the same Writer, on Ireland. Ed. C. L. Falkiner, Royal Irish Academy, 1906.

(2) BIOGRAPHY AND CRITICISM

Ghall, S. Barnabe Rich and Ireland. Dublin Mag. Sept. 1926.

Pruvost, R. The Beginnings of Barnabe Rich's Military Career. RES. ix, 1933.

Starnes, D. T. Barnabe Rich's Sappho Duke of Mantona: a Study in Elizabethan Story-Making. Stud. Phil. xxx, 1933.

NICHOLAS BRETON (1545?–1656?)

[See pp. 415–7 above.]

GABRIEL HARVEY (1545?–1630?)

(1) COLLECTED WORKS

The Complete Works. Ed. A. B. Grosart, 3 vols. 1884–5 (priv. ptd).

(2) SEPARATE WORKS

Three proper, and wittie, familiar letters. 1580; ed. E. de Selincourt (in Complete Poetical Works of Edmund Spenser, Oxford, 1912).

Foure letters, and certaine sonnets: especially touching Robert Greene. 1592; ed. Sir S. E. Brydges (Archaica, vol. ii, 1815); ed. G. B. Harrison, 1922.

Pierces supererogation or a new prayse of the Old Asse. 1593; ed. Sir S. E. Brydges (Archaica, vol. ii, 1815).

A new letter of notable contents. 1593; ed. Sir S. E. Brydges (Archaica, vol. ii, 1815)

The trimming of Thomas Nash Gentleman, by the high-tituled patron Don Richardo de Medico campo. 1597. [Doubtfully attrib. to Harvey.]

The Letter Book of Gabriel Harvey. Ed. E. J. L. Scott, Camden Soc. 1884.

Marginalia. Ed. G. C. Moore Smith, Stratford-upon-Avon, 1913.

[For Harvey's Latin writings, and the works of his brothers John and Richard, see R. B. McKerrow, Works of Thomas Nashe, vol. v, 1910, pp. 163–75.]

(3) CRITICISM

D'Israeli, Isaac. Quarrels of Authors. 1814.

Brydges, Sir S. E. Restituta. Vol. III, 1814–6.

Collier, J. P. Miscellaneous Tracts. 1870.

Morley, Henry. Hobbinol. [In Clement Marot and Other Studies, vol. II, 1871.]

Moore Smith, G. C. Pedantius. Louvain, 1905. (Bang's Materialien, vol. VIII.) [Introduction.]

—— Printed Books with Gabriel Harvey's Autograph or MS Notes. MLR. XXVIII, 1933, XXIX, 1934.

Berli, H. Gabriel Harvey, der Dichterfreund und Kritiker. Zürich, 1913.

Caldwell, J. R. Dating a Spenser-Harvey Letter. PMLA. XLI, 1926.

Moore, H. Gabriel Harvey's References to Marlowe. Stud. Phil. XXIII, 1926.

Tannenbaum, S. A. Some Unpublished Harvey Marginalia. MLR. xxv, 1930.

Camden, C. Some Unnoted Harvey Marginalia. PQ. XIII, 1934.

Johnson, F. R. The First Edition of Gabriel Harvey's Foure Letters. Library, xv, 1934.

THOMAS LODGE (1558?–1625)

[See pp. 527–9 above.]

ROBERT GREENE (1560–1592)

[See pp. 529–30 above.]

HENRY CHETTLE (1560?–1607?)

[See p. 534 above.]

SIR JOHN HARINGTON (1561–1612)

(1) WRITINGS

Orlando Furioso in English Heroical Verse. 1591; 1607; 1634. [A Preface, or rather a Briefe Apologie of Poetrie, rptd Joseph Haslewood (Ancient Critical Essays, vol. II, 1815), and G. Gregory Smith (Elizabethan Critical Essays, vol. II, Oxford, 1904).]

A New Discourse of a Stale Subject, called the Metamorphosis of Ajax. Written by Misa-cnos to his Friend Philostilpnos. 1596 (3 edns). [With two supplements, also issued separately: (1) An Anatomie of the Metamorphosed Ajax. 1596 ('by T. C.'); (2) An Apologie. I. Or rather a Retraction. 1596 (anon.) (bis).]

Ulysses upon Ajax. Written by Misodiaboles to his Friend Philaretes. 1596 (anon.) (bis); rptd with Metamorphosis, Anatomy and Apology, Chiswick, 1814; ed. with Metamorphosis, Anatomie and Apologie, P. Warlock and J. Lindsay, 1927.

The Englishmans Doctor. Or, The Schoole of Salerne. 1607; 1608; 1609; 2 pts, 1617; 1624; rptd 1830; ed. F. R. Packard and F. H. Garrison, 1922. [Verse trn of Schola Salernitana.]

Epigrams both Pleasant and Serious. 1615.

The most Elegant and Wittie Epigrams of Sir John Harington. 4 bks, 1618; 1625; 1633. [Bk IV reprints 1615 Epigrams.]

A Briefe View of the State of the Church of England. Ed. J. Chetwind, 1653.

Nugae Antiquae: being a Miscellaneous Collection of Original Papers in Prose and Verse. Ed. Henry Harington, 2 vols. 1769–75; ed. T. Park, 2 vols. 1804.

The Letters and Epigrams of Sir John Harington. Ed. N. E. McClure, Philadelphia, 1930.

(2) CRITICISM

Collier, J. P. The Poetical Decameron. 2 vols. Edinburgh, 1820.

Raleigh, Sir Walter. Sir John Harington. [In Some Authors, Oxford, 1923.]

Moore Smith, G. C., McClure, N. E., and Harlow, V. T. TLS. 10 March, 19 May, 14 July, 27 Oct. 1927.

Kirwood, A. E. The Metamorphosis of Ajax and its Sequels. Library, XII, 1931.

THOMAS NASHE (1567–1600?)

[See pp. 533–4 above.]

GERVASE MARKHAM (1568?–1637)

(1) WORKS

[A full-dress bibliography of Markham's works is badly needed; the following list may be supplemented from the DNB. and the Bibliographical Society's Short-Title Catalogue. Titles followed by a reference to the Stationers' Register only are of works not known to be now extant.]

A discource of horsmanshippe. 1593.

Thyrsis and Daphne. By Gervis Mackwm. [S.R. 23 April 1593.]

The gentlemans academie. Or, the booke of S. Albans: compiled by Juliana Barnes, and now reduced into a better method, by G. M. 1595.

The most honorable tragedie of Sir Richard Grinvile, Knight. 1595; ed. E. Arber, The Last Fight of the Revenge at Sea, 1871. [Poem.]

The poem of poems; or Sions muse; contayning the divine song of King Salomon.
1595.

Devoreux. Vertues teares for the losse of King
Henry III of Fraunce. Translated by
Jervis Markham. 1597.

The teares of the beloved: or, the lamentations
of Saint John. 1600; ed. A. B. Grosart,
Miscellanies of the Fuller Worthies' Lib.
vol. II, 1871.

Marie Magdalens lamentations. 1601; ed.
A. B. Grosart, Miscellanies of the Fuller
Worthies' Lib. vol. II, 1871.

How to trayne and teach horses to amble.
1605.

Cavelarice, or the English horseman. 1607.

The English Arcadia alluding his beginning
from Sir Philip Sydnes ending. Pt 1, 1607;
pt 2, 1613.

Rodomonths infernall, or the divell conquered.
Ariastos conclusions of the marriage of
Rogero with Bradamanth, translated by
G. M. 1607. [S.R. 15 Sept. 1598.]

The dumbe knight. A pleasant Comedy, acted
sundry times by the children of his Majesties
Revels. 1608 (3 edns); 1633; ed. R. Dodsley
(Collection of Old Plays, vol. VI, 1744;
rev. I. Reed, vol. IV, 1780; rev. J. P.
Collier, vol. IV, 1825; rev. W. C. Hazlitt,
vol. X, 1875); ed. Sir Walter Scott (Ancient
British Drama, vol. II, 1810). [With Lewis
Machin, who signs preface.]

The famous whore, or noble curtizan. 1609;
ed. F. Ouvry, 1868.

A cure for all diseases in horses. 1610; 1616
(as Markhams method).

Markhams maister-peece. Or, what doth a
horse-man lacke. 1610.

Hobsons horse-load of letters: or a president
for epistles. 1613.

The English husbandman. Bk I, 1613. Bk II
(as The Pleasures of Princes), 1614.

The Pleasures of Princes, or, Good Men's
Recreations. 1614; 1635; ed. in part H. G.
Hutchinson, 1927 (The Art of Angling).
[Angling and cock-fighting.]

Cheap and good husbandry for the well-
ordering of all beasts, and fowles. 1614.
[Rptd in A way to get wealth, 1631.]

Countrey contentments, in two bookes. 1615.
[Bk I, The whole art of riding great horses;
Bk II, The English huswife. Book II rptd as
Countrey contentments, or the English
huswife, 1623. Books I and II rptd in A way
to get wealth, as Country contentments:
or, the husbandmans recreations, 1631.]

Maison rustique, or, the countrey farmer. By
Charles Stevens, and John Liebault. Translated by Richard Surflet. Reviewed, corrected, and augmented. By Gervase Markham. 1616.

The country housewifes garden. 1617; 1631
(in A way to get wealth).

Conceyted letters, newly layde open. The per-
fections or arte of episteling. 1618. [? by
Markham.]

The horsemans honour. 1620. [? by Markham.]

Markhams farewell to husbandry. 1620; 1631
(in A way to get wealth).

Verus pater, or health of body. [S.R. 4 May
1620.]

Wittes only wealth. [S.R. 4 May 1620.]

Death triumphant. [S.R. 16 Nov. 1621.]

Hungers prevention: or, the whole arte of
fowling. 1621.

A second parte to the mothers blessing, or
a cure against misfortunes. [S.R. 7 May
1622.]

The true Tragedy Of Herod and Antipater:
With the Death of faire Marriam. As it hath
beene Acted at the Red Bull. By Gervase
Markham and William Sampson. 1622 (bis).

Honour in his perfection. 1624.

The inrichment of the Weald of Kent. 1625;
1631 (in A way to get wealth).

The souldiers accidence. 1625; 1639 (in The
souldiers exercise).

The souldiers grammar. Pt I, 1626; pt II,
1627; 1639 (in The souldiers exercise).

Markhams faithfull farrier. 1629.

A way to get wealth. 1631. [Contains I.
Cheape and good husbandry; II and III.
Country contentments, parts 1 and 2; IV.
The inrichment of the weald of Kent; V.
Markhams farewell to husbandry; VI.
A new orchard and garden (by William
Lawson).]

The whole art of husbandrie, by C. Heresbach,
translated by B. Googe, 1577, enlarged by
Gervase Markham. 1631.

The art of archerie. 1634.

The complete farriar. 1639.

The souldiers exercise: in three bookes [sc.
with The souldiers accidence and The
souldiers grammar]. 1639.

The country-mans recreations. 1640.

The perfect horseman; or, the experienc'd
secrets of Mr Markham's fifty years practice. Published by Launcelot Thetford.
1655.

The husbandman's jewel, directing how to
improve the land. 1707.

The compleat husbandman. 1707.

The gentleman's accomplish'd jockey. 1722.

The young sportsman's instructor. n.d.;
rptd 1820; ed. S. Gamidge, Worcester, n.d.

(2) DOUBTFUL WORKS

A health to the gentlemanly profession of
serving-men. 1598; rptd W. C. Hazlitt
(Inedited Tracts, 1868).

The newe metamorphosis. [BM. Add. MSS 14824–6. Attrib. to Markham by J. H. N. Lyon, A Study of The newe metamorphosis, New York, 1919, but cf. review by G. C. M[oore] S[mith], MLR. xvi, 1921 and see under John Marston, p. 628 above.]

Ariostos satyres, by Gervase Markham. 1608. [By Robert Tofte?]

The pastoralls of Julietta. 1610. [By Robert Tofte?]

A schoole for yonge schollers. [S.R. 26 Sept. 1615.]

Vox militis, by G. M. 1625. [Attrib. to Markham by P. Bliss, MS note in Bodleian copy, but by DNB. to G. Marcelline.]

(3) Biography and Criticism

Ritson, J. Bibliographia Poetica. 1802.

Brydges, Sir S. E. Censura Literaria. 10 vols. 1805–9.

—— Restituta. 1814. [Vol. ii, p. 469.]

Markham, D. F. History of the Markham Family, 1854.

Landau, M. Die Dramen von Herod und Marianne. Zeitschrift für vergleichende Litteraturgeschichte, vi, 1895–6.

Wallace, C. W. Gervase Markham, Dramatist. Sh. Jb. xlvi, 1910.

Adams, J. Q. Every Woman in Her Humour and The Dumb Knight. MP. x, 1913.

Markham, Sir Clements R. Markham Memorials. 1913.

Lyon, J. H. N. A Study of The newe metamorphosis. New York, 1919.

Silbermann, A. M. Untersuchungen über die Quellen des Dramas 'The True Tragedy of Herod and Antipater.' Würzburg, 1929.

A. K. McI.

THOMAS DEKKER (1570?–1641)

[See pp. 619–22 above.]

SAMUEL ROWLANDS (1570?–1630?)

(1) Collected Works

The Complete Works of Samuel Rowlands. Ed. Sir Edmund Gosse, with Notes and Glossary by S. J. Herrtage, 3 vols. Hunterian Club, 1880. [Omits A Theater of Delightfull Recreation, and The Bride and includes the spurious Martin Mark-all. Ave Caesar was added separately in 1888.]

The Four Knaves. Ed. E. F. Rimbault, Percy Soc. 1842. [Includes The Knave of Clubs; The Knave of Hearts; More Knaves yet.]

(2) Writings in Verse

[The majority of Rowlands's writings originally appeared under the initials S. R.]

The Betraying of Christ. Judas in Despaire. 1598 (bis).

The Letting of Humours Blood in the Head-Vaine. 1600; [before 1603] (as Humours Ordinarie); 1607; 1611 (as The Letting); 1613; ed. Sir Walter Scott, Edinburgh, 1814.

Tis Merrie when Gossips Meete. 1602; 1609; 1619 (with additional songs as Well met Gossip); 1627; rptd 1818 (Chiswick Press).

Ave Caesar. God save the King. 1603; ed. W. C. Hazlitt (in Fugitive Poetical Tracts, ser. 2, 1875).

Looke to it; for, Ile stabbe ye. 1604 (bis); ed. E. V. Utterson, 1841.

Hell's Broke Loose. 1605.

A Theater of Delightfull Recreation. 1605. [Only extant copy in Folger Lib., Washington.]

A Terrible Battell betweene Time and Death. [1606?]

Diogines Lanthorne. 1607; [1608]; 1628; 1631; 1634.

Democritus, or Doctor Merry-man his Medicines. [1607]; 1609 (rev. and reduced as Doctor Merrie-Man); 1616; 1618; 1623; 1627.

Humors Looking Glasse. 1608; ed. J. P. Collier, 1870.

The Famous Historie of Guy Earl of Warwick. 1609; 1632; 1635.

A Whole Crew of Kind Gossips All met to be Merry. 1609; 1613 ('enlarged').

The Knave of Clubbes. 1609; 1611; [1611]; ed. E. V. Utterson, 1841. [First ptd 1600 as Tis Merry when Knaves Meet—no copies extant.]

The Knave of Harts. Haile Fellow well met. 1612 (anon.); 1613; ed. E. V. Utterson, 1840.

More Knaves yet? The Knaves of Spades and Diamonds. [1613]; ed. E. V. Utterson, 1841.

Sir Thomas Overbury, or the Poysoned Knights Complaint. [1614.]

A Fooles Bolt is soon shott. 1614.

The Melancholie Knight. 1615; ed. E. V. Utterson, 1841.

The Bride. 1617; ed. A. C. Porter, Boston, 1905.

A Sacred Memorie of the Miracles Wrought by Jesus Christ. 1618.

The Night-Raven. 1620; 1624; 1634; ed. E. V. Utterson, 1880.

A Paire of Spy-Knaves. [1620?].

Good Newes and Bad Newes. 1622; ed. E. V. Utterson, 1841; ed. J. P. Collier.

(3) Writings in Prose

Greenes Ghost Haunting Conie-Catchers. 1602; 1626; ed. J. O. Halliwell[-Phillipps], 1860.

Martin Mark-all, Beadle of Bridewell; his Defence. 1610; ed. A. V. Judges (in The Elizabethan Underworld, 1930). [Probably not by Rowlands but Samuel Rid.]

Heavens Glory, seeke it. 1628; 3 pts, 1639 (as
A most Excellent Treatise of the Way to
seek Heavens Glory). [By Samuel Rowland,
who may be different from Samuel Rowlands.]

(4) BIOGRAPHY AND CRITICISM

Gosse, Sir Edmund. Samuel Rowlands. [In
Seventeenth Century Studies, 1883, rptd
from The Complete Works.]

JOHN TAYLOR (1578–1653)

(1) COLLECTED WORKS

All the Workes of John Taylor the Water
Poet Beeing 63 in Number Corrected,
Revised. 1630; rptd 3 pts, Spenser Soc.
1868–9.
Works of John Taylor the Water Poet not
included in the Folio Volume of 1630. 5 pts,
Spenser Soc. 1870–8.
The Old Book Collector's Miscellany. Ed.
Charles Hindley, 3 vols. 1871–3. [Vol. II
contains 6 and vol. III 14 pieces by Taylor.]
Works of John Taylor the Water-Poet. Ed.
Charles Hindley, 1872. [21 pieces. Has
useful Introduction and List of the Works
written by, or accredited to, John Taylor.]
Early Prose and Poetical Works of John
Taylor the Water Poet. 1888. [13 pieces.]

(2) INDIVIDUAL WORKS

(a) *Writings in Verse*

Great Britaine All in Blacke. For the In-
comparable Losse of Henry, our Late
Worthy Prince. 1612.
The Sculler, rowing from Tiber to Thames.
1612; 1614 (as Taylors Water-worke).
[Sonnets, Satyres, Epigrams.]
The Eighth Wonder of the World, or Coriats
Escape from his Supposed Drowning. 1613.
The Nipping or Snipping of Abuses. 1614.
Verbum Sempiternae. 2 pts, 1614 (pt 2,
Salvator Mundi); 1616 (corrected). [A
thumb-bible of verse summaries of the Old
and New Testaments. See W. Johnston, A
Bibliography of the Thumb Bibles of John
Taylor, 1910; W. M. Stone, The Thumb
Bibles of John Taylor, Brookline, U.S.A.
[1928].]
A Cast over the Water given gratis to William
Fennor, the Rimer from London. [1615.]
Faire and Fowle Weather. 1615.
Taylors Revenge. 1615. [Satire on W. Fen-
nor.]
The Booke of Martyrs. 1617 (anon.); 1631;
1639. [A thumb-book.]
A Kicksy Winsey: or a Lerry Come-Twang:
where-in John Taylor hath satyrically
suited 800 of his Bad Debters. 1619; 1624
(rev. as The Scourge of Basenesse).

An English-mans Love to Bohemia. 1620.
Fill Gut and Pinch Belly. 1620. [Broad-
side.]
The Muses Mourning: or, Funerall Sonnets on
the Death of John Moray. [1620?]
The Colde Tearme or the Metamorphosis of
the River of Thames. [1621] (anon.). [Pos-
sibly by Taylor.]
A Shilling, or the Travailes of Twelve-pence.
[1621]; 1635 (as The Travels of Twelve-
pence).
The Subjects Joy for the Parliament. [1621.]
[Broadside.]
Superbiae Flagellum, or the whip of Pride.
1621.
Taylors Goose, describing the Wilde Goose.
1621.
Taylors Motto: et habeo, et careo, et curo.
1621.
An Arrant Thiefe. With a Comparison be-
tweene a Thiefe and a Booke. 1622; 1625;
1635.
A Common Whore with all these Graces
Grac'd. 1622; 1625; 1635.
The Great O Toole. 1622; 1623 (with A verry
Merry Wherry-ferry-voyage).
A Memoriall of all the English Monarchs.
1622; 1630 (expanded).
Sir Gregory Nonsence his Newes from No
Place. 1700 (*i.e.* 1622).
Taylors Farewell to the Tower-bottles. 1622.
A verry Merry Wherry-Ferry-Voyage. 1622;
1623 (with O Toole the Great).
The Water-cormorant his Complaint. 1622.
[Satires.]
Honour conceal'd, strangely reveal'd; or the
Worthy Praise of Archibald Armstrong.
1623.
The Praise and Vertue of a Jayle, and Jaylers.
1623.
The Praise of Cleane Linnen. 1624.
Taylors Pastorall: or the Noble Antiquitie of
Shepheards. 1624. [Mainly verse.]
True Loving Sorrow attired in a Robe of
Griefe upon the Funerall of the Duke of
Richmond and Lennox. 1624. [Broadside.]
For the Sacred Memoriall of Charles Howard,
Earle of Nottingham. 1625 (anon.).
A Living Sadness, in Duty Consecrated to the
Memory of our Late Soveraigne James.
[1625].
A Funerall Elegie in Memory of Lancelot,
Bishop of Winchester. 1626.
A Warning for Swearers. 1626 (and with The
Fearefull Summer, 1625); 1629 (as Christian
Admonitions). [Broadside.]
A Dogge of War, or the Travels of Drunkard.
[1628?]; rptd 1927. [Mainly verse.]
The Churches Deliverances. 1630.
A Meditation on the Passion. 1630. [Broad-
side.]

The Suddaine Turne of ffortunes Wheale. [1631]; ed. (from MS) J. O. Halliwell-[Phillipps] (Contributions to Early English Literature, 1849).

Taylor on Thame Isis: or the Description of the Thame and Isis. 1632.

The Couches Overthrow. [1635?] (anon.). [Black-letter ballad, perhaps by Taylor.]

A most Horrible, Terrible, Tollerable, Termagant Satyre. [1635.] [Characters.]

The Olde Old very Olde Man: or the Age and Long Life of Thomas Parr. 1635; 1635 (adds Postscript); rptd 1774 (Harleian Misc. vol. VII); rptd 1794 (Curious Tracts, ed. J. Caulfield).

A Funerall Elegie upon the Death of B. Jonson, Poet. 1637 (anon.).

A Sad and Deplorable Loving Elegy to the Memory of M. Richard Wyan. 1638. [Broadsheet.]

Differing Worships, or, the Oddes, betweene some Knights Service and Gods. Or Tom Nash his Ghost. 1640.

The Complaint of M. Tenter-hooke the Projector, and Sir Thomas Dodger the Patentee. 1641. [Broadsheet.]

The Irish Footman's Poetry. Or George the Runner against Henry the Walker, in Defence of John the Swimmer. 1641 (anon.); rptd W. C. Hazlitt (Fugitive Tracts, ser. 2, 1875).

A Pedlar and a Romish Priest. 1641. [Based on Sir James Sempill's Pack Man's Paternoster.]

A Swarme of Sectaries. 1641.

A Reply as True as Steele to A Swarme of Sectaries. 1641. [Attacks H. Walker.]

The Apprentices Advice to the XII Bishops. 1642.

A Delicate, Dainty, Damnable Dialogue betweene the Devill and a Jesuite. 1642.

Heads of all Fashion. 1642 (anon.); rptd E. W. Ashbee, 1871.

Mad Fashions, Od Fashions, all out of Fashion. 1642; rptd E. W. Ashbee, 1871.

A Plea for Prerogative. By Thorny Ailo: alias, John Taylor. 1642.

Truth's Triumph in the Gracious Preservation of the King. 1643.

Aqua-Musae: or, Cacafogo, Cacadaemon, Captain George Wither wrung in the Withers. [Oxford, 1644?]

Mad Verse, Sad Verse, Glad Verse and Bad Verse. [Oxford, 1644.]

Rebells Anathematized. Oxford, 1645.

The Kings most Excellent Majesties Wellcome to his owne House. 1647.

'ΙΠΠ-ΑΝΘΡΩΠΟΣ: or, an Ironicall Expostulation for the horse of the Lord Mayor of London. 1648 (anon.).

Taylors Arithmetike. [1650?]; 1650; 1653.

Alterations Strange. 1651.

Epigrammes: besides, Two New made Satyres. 1651.

The Impartiallest Satyre that ever was seen. 1652 (anon.).

Misselanies. 1652.

The Certain Travailes of an Uncertain Journey. [1653.]

Nonsence upon Sence. [1653?]

The Essence of Nonsence upon Sence. [1653.]

A Dreadful Battle between a Taylor and a Louse. 2 pts, [1654?]. [Black-letter ballad, perhaps by another J. Taylor.]

(b) Writings in Prose

Odcombs Complaint: or Coriats Funerall Epicedium. 1613.

The Dolphins Danger and Deliverance. [1616?] [Sea-fight with 6 Turkish men-of-war.]

Three Weekes, Three Daies, and Three Houres Observation and Travel, from London to Hamburgh. 1617.

Master Thomas Coriat To his Friends in England. 1618 (anon.).

Jack a Lent: his Beginning and Entertainment. 1620 (bis).

The Life and Death of the Virgin Mary. 1620; 1622.

The Praise of Hemp-seed. With the Voyage of Mr Roger Bird and the Writer hereof in a Boat of Brown-paper, to Quinborough in Kent. 1620; 1623.

The Unnaturel Father: or a Cruel Murther committed by one John Rowse. 1621.

The World runnes on Wheeles. 1623; 1635.

An Armado, or Navye, of 103 Ships & Other Vessels; who have the Art to sayle by Land as well as by Sea. 1627 (bis); 1635.

A Famous Fight at Sea. 1627. [The English and Dutch against the Portuguese.]

Wit and Mirth. 1629; 1635 (abridged); ed. W. C. Hazlitt (Old English Jest Books, vol. III, 1864).

The Great Eater of Kent, or Part of the Exploits of Nicholas Wood. 1630.

Master Thomas Coriats Commendations to his Friends in England. 1630.

The Complaint of Christmas and the Teares of Twelfetyde. 1631.

The Triumphs of Fame and Honour, at the Inauguration of R. Parkhurst into the Office of Lord Maior. 1634.

A Brave, Memorable and Dangerous Sea-fight foughten neere the Road of Tittawan in Barbary. 1636.

The Honorable, and Memorable Foundations within Ten Shires. Also, a Relation of the Wine Tavernes. 1636.

The Carriers Cosmographie. Or a Briefe Relation of the Innes in, and neere London. 1637; ed. E. W. Ashbee, 1869 (Occasional Facsimile Reprints); ed. E. Arber, 1877 (English Garner, vol. I).

Taylors Feast: conteyning Twenty-seaven Dishes. 1638.

Divers Crabtree Lectures. 1639.

A Juniper Lecture: Second Impression. 1639; 1652.

A Brave and Valiant Sea Fight. 1640; 1640 (as A Valorous and Perillous Sea-fight).

The Hellish Parliament being a Counter-Parliament to this in England. 1641.

The Liar. 1641 (anon.).

Religious Enemies. 1641.

Some Small and Simple Reasons by Aminadab Blowes against the Liturgy. 1641 (anon.). [Perhaps not Taylor's.]

A Tale in a Tub, by My-heele Mendsoale. 1641 ('by J. T.').

To the Right Honorable Assembly the Petition of the Watermen. 1641; 1642.

An Apology for Private Preaching. [1642] ('by T. J.').

An Honest Answer to the Late Apologie for Private Preaching. [1642] ('by T. J.').

A Cluster of Coxcombs, the Donatists, Publicans, Disciplinarians, Anabaptists, and Brownists. 1642.

The Devil turn'd Round-head. [1642] (anon.).

An Humble Desired Union betwene Prerogative and Priviledge. 1642.

John Taylors Manifestation against Joshua Church. 1642.

Rare Physick for the Church Sick of an Ague. 1642.

A Seasonable Lecture disburthened from Henry Walker. Taken in Short Writing by Thorny Ailo. 1642. [Thorny Ailo = anagram of John Taylor.]

The Whole Life and Progresse of Henry Walker. 1642.

The Conversion, Confession, Contrition of a Rebellious Round-head. 1643.

An Intercepted Letter sent to London from a Spie at Oxford. 1643.

A Letter sent to London from a Spie at Oxford. By Thorny Ailo. 1643.

Love One Another: a Tub Lecture, preached at a Conventicle by John Alexander, a Joyner. [1643] (anon.). [Possibly not Taylor's.]

Mercurius Aquaticus; or, the Water-Poets Answer to Mercurius Britannicus. 1643.

A Preter-pluperfect Spick and Span New Nocturnall. [Oxford, 1643.]

Ad Populum. 1644.

Crop-Eare Curried, or, Tom Nash his Ghost, declaring the Pruining of Prinnes Two Last Parricidicall Pamphlets. [Oxford], 1644.

The Generall Complaint of the Commons. [1644?] ('by Jo-Ta.').

John Taylor being yet Unhanged, sends Greeting, to John Booker. 1644.

Mercurius Infernalis. 1644.

No Mercurius Aulicus. [Oxford], 1644.

The Causes of the Diseases of this Kingdom. [Oxford], 1645.

A most Learned Speech by Miles Corbet, revised. [Oxford, 1645.]

Oxford besiedged, surprised, taken. 1645 ('by Io-Ta.').

A Briefe Relation of the Idiotismes of Miles Corbet. By Antho. Roily. 1646. [Antho. Roily = anagram of John Taylor.]

The Complaint of Christmas. [Oxford, 1646.]

The Noble Cavalier Caracterised, and a Rebellious Caviller Cauterised. [1647?]

A Recommendation to Mercurius Morbicus [i.e. H. Walker]. 1647 (anon.).

The World turn'd upside down. 1647.

The Wonder of a Kingdom. 1648.

Mercurius Melancholicus for King Charles the Second. 1649.

The Number and Names of all the Kings of England and Scotland. 1649; 1650.

A Late Weary Merry Voyage from London to Gravesend to Cambridge. 1650.

Mercurius Pacificus. [1650] (anon.). [Perhaps not Taylor's.]

Ale Ale-vated into the Ale-titude. 1651; 1652; 1653; 1656. [Includes Randolph's verses, The ExAle-tation of Ale.]

Ranters of Both Sexes. 1651.

Christmas in & out. 1652.

Newes from Tenebris. 1652.

The Names of all the Dukes, Marquesses, &c. 1653.

[For other news-books that have been conjecturally attrib. to Taylor, see pp. 757–60 below.]

(c) *Writings in Mixed Prose and Verse*

Laugh and be Fat, or a Commentary upon the Odcombyan Banket. [1612.]

Heavens Blessing and Earths Joy. Or, a True Relation of the Al-beloved Mariage of Frederick & Elizabeth. 2 pts, 1613; rptd 1809 (Somers Tracts, ed. Sir W. Scott, vol. III); rptd 1828 (Progresses of James I, ed. J. Nichols, vol. II).

A Briefe Remembrance of all the English Monarchs from the Normans Conquest. 1618 (bis); 1622. [Engraved portraits, with prose and verse.]

The Pennyles Pilgrimage, or the Moneylesse Perambulation of John Taylor, from London to Edenborough. 1618.

Taylor his Travels: from London to Prague. 1620.

The Praise, Antiquity and Commodity of Beggery, Beggars and Begging. 1621.

A New Discovery by Sea, With a Wherry from London to Salisbury. 1623.

Prince Charles his Welcome from Spain. 1623.

The Fearefull Summer: or Londons Calamitie. Oxford, 1625; Oxford, 1625 ('enlarged'); 1636.

A Bawd. 1635.

Taylors Travels and Circular Perambulation. 1636; 1636 (as John Taylor the Water-poets Travels through London). [A catalogue of the London taverns.]

Drinke and Welcome: or the Historie of the Drinks in Use now. By Haldrick Van Speagle, Translated. 1637; ed. E. W. Ashbee, 1871 (Occasional Facsimile Reprints).

Bull, Beare, and Horse. 1638.

Part of this Summers Travels. Or News from Hell, Hull and Hallifax. [1640?]

Englands Comfort, and Londons Joy: expressed in the Royall Entertainment of King Charles at his Returne from Scotland. 1641.

John Taylors Last Voyage with a Scullers Boate from London to Hereford. 1641.

A Full and Compleat Answer against the Writer of A Tale in a Tub. By Thorny Ailo, Annagram. 1642.

Tailors Travels, from London, to the Isle of Wight. 1648; rptd J. O. Halliwell[-Phillipps], 1851 (Literature of Sixteenth and Seventeenth Centuries Illustrated).

John Taylors Wandering, to see the Wonders of the West. 1649; rptd facs. E. W. Ashbee, 1869.

A Short Relation of a Long Journey round Wales. [1653]; rptd J. O. Halliwell[-Phillipps], 1852.

(3) Criticism

Thorp, Willard. John Taylor, Water Poet. Texas Rev. VIII, 1922.

Dow, R. B. The Life and Times of John Taylor, with a Bibliography of his Writings. Harvard Summaries of Theses (1931), pp. 218–23.

RICHARD BRATHWAITE (1588?–1673)

The Golden Fleece. Whereto bee Annexed Two Elogies, Narcissus Change and Aesons Dotage. 1611.

The Poets Willowe, or the Passionate Shepheard. 1614; 1620.

The Prodigals Teares: or His fare-well to Vanity. 1614; 1620. [Moral treatise.]

The yong mans gleanings. Gathered Out of divers Fathers. By R. B. Gent. 1614.

The Schollers Medley, or an Intermixt Discourse upon Historicall and Poeticall Relations. 1614; 1638 (as A Survey of History; re-issued 1651).

Loves Labyrinth, or the True Lovers Knot. 1615 (also issued with A Strappado for the Divell).

A Strappado for the Divell. Epigrams and Satyres. 2 pts, 1615 (pt 2, Loves Labyrinth); ed. J. W. Ebsworth, Boston, 1878.

Disputatio inauguralis. Jus potandi exponet Blasius Multibibus. [Leipzig, 1616?]; 1617; 1626; tr. German, Leipzig, 1616. [Englished as A Solemn Joviall Disputation, 1617.]

A Solemn Joviall Disputation of Drinking. 2 pts, 1617 (anon.) (pt 2, The Smoaking Age, with the Life and Death of Tobacco). [The English version of Disputatio inauguralis.]

The Good Wife: Or, A rare one Amongst Women. By Musophilus. 1618. [Also appended to Patrick Hannay, A Happy Husband, 1618.]

Remains after Death: including Divers Memorable Observances. 1618. [Also appended to Patrick Hannay, A Happy Husband, 1618.]

A New Spring Shadowed in Sundry Pithie Poems. By Musophilus. 1619.

Essaies upon the Five Senses, with a Pithie One upon Detraction. 1620; 1635; ed. Sir S. E. Brydges (in Archaica, vol. II, 1815).

Natures Embassie: or the Wilde-Mans Measures. 5 pts, 1621; 1623 (for 1621, with The Shepherds Tales); 1626 (with The Shepherds Tales Revived); ed. J. W. Ebsworth, Boston, 1877. [A collection of poems.]

Panedone, or Health from Helicon. 1621.

The Shepheards Tales. 1621; 1626 (rev.).

Times Curtaine Drawne, or the Anatomie of Vanitie. 2 pts, 1621.

Querela Clientis; Medela Patientis. [1620–30?] [Miscellaneous pieces in Latin.]

The English Gentleman: containing Sundry Excellent Rules. 1630; 1633 (rev.); 1641 (with The English Gentlewoman; re-issued 1652, 1655, 1656, as Times Treasury).

The English Gentlewoman Drawne out to the Full Body. 1631; 1641 (with The English Gentleman).

Whimzies or a New Cast of Characters. By Clitus-Alexandrinus. 2 pts, 1631 (pt 2, A Cater-Character Throwne out of a Box); ed J. O. Halliwell[-Phillipps], 1859.

Novissima Tuba. By Musophilus. 1632; 1633. [A sacred poem in Latin; tr. Eng. John Vicars, The Last Trumpet: or a Sixfold Christian Dialogue, 1635.]

A Strange Metamorphosis of Man. 1634 (anon). [Not certainly Brathwaite's.]

Anniversaries upon his Panarete. 1634 (anon.). [Verses in memory of his wife.]

Anniversaries upon his Panarete. The Second Anniders. 1635 (anon.).

Raglands Niobe, or Eliza's Elegie. 1635. [In memoriam Elizabeth, Lady Herbert.]

The Arcadian Princesse; or the Triumph of Justice. 1635. [Tr. from Italian of M. Silesio.]

The Fatall Nuptiall: Or, Mournefull Marriage, Relating, The drowning of 47. persons. 1636. [In verse.]

The Lives of all the Roman Emperors. 1636 (signed R. B.).

A Spirituall Spicerie: containing Sundrie Sweet Tractates. 1638. [Prose and verse.]

The Psalmes of David and of Other Holy Prophets Paraphrased. By R. B. 1638.

Barnabees Journall under the Names of Mirtilus and Faustulus, Shadowed. By Corymbaeus. [1638]; ed. J. H[aslewood], 1818 and 1876 (rev. W. C. Hazlitt); ed. D. B. Thomas, 1933. [English and Latin verse.]

An Epitome of All the Lives of the Kings of France. Translated by R. B. 1639.

Ar't Asleepe Husband? A Boulster Lecture. By Philogenes Panedonius. 1640.

The Two Lancashire Lovers, or the Excellent History of Philocles and Doriclea. By Musaeus Palatinus. 1640.

The Penitent Pilgrim. 1641; rptd 1847; ed. G. E. Watts, 1897 (abridged).

Astraea's Tears. 2 pts, 1641 (anon.; pt 2, Panaretees Triumph, 1641). [Elegy on Brathwaite's godfather, Sir Richard Hutton.]

Mercurius Britanicus. [1641?] (bis); rptd Somers Tracts, ed. Sir W. Scott, vol. v, 1809. [2 English versions, neither apparently by Brathwaite, pbd 1641.]

A Mustur Roll of the Evill Angels. By R. B. Gent. 1655 (also issued as Capitall Hereticks); 1659. [Account of the principal heretics.]

Lignum Vitae. 1658. [Latin verse.]

The Honest Ghost, or a voice from the Vault. 1658 (anon.). [Satire.]

Panthalia: or the Royal Romance. By Castalio Pomerano. 1659 (anon.). [Sometimes attrib. to Brathwaite, but the portrait found in some copies is not his.]

To his Majesty upon his happy arrivall in our late discomposed Albion. 1660.

The Chimneys Scuffle. 1662 (anon.). [Satire.]

Tragi-Comoedia, Cui in titulum inscribitur Regicidium. 1665.

The Captive Captain: Or The Restrain'd Cavalier. 1665 (signed R. B.). [Medley of prose and verse.]

A Comment upon Two Tales of our Ancient Poet Sir Jeffray Chaucer by R. B. 1665; ed. C. F. E. Spurgeon, Chaucer Soc. 1901.

The History of Moderation. By Hesychius Pamphilus. 1669 (re-issued as The Trimmer, 1684).

[For Brathwaite's life and writings see Haslewood's edns of Barnabees Journall and M. W. Black, Richard Brathwait, Philadelphia, 1928; both contain bibliographies.]

II. MINOR POPULAR LITERATURE

TRACTS, PAMPHLETS, JEST-BOOKS, BURLESQUES, BROADSIDE BALLADS, ETC.

[The ensuing lists are merely intended as representative selections. First editions only have been cited.]

I. BIBLIOGRAPHIES

Beloe, W. Anecdotes of Literature and Scarce Books. 6 vols. 1807–12.

Ames, Joseph and Herbert, W. Typographical Antiquities. Ed. T. F. Dibdin, 4 vols. 1810–9.

Collier, J. P. A Bibliographical and Critical Account of the Rarest Books in the English Language. 2 vols. 1865.

Hazlitt, W. C. Handbook to the Popular, Poetical and Dramatic Literature of Great Britain. 1867. [Supplements, index, etc. 1876–1903.]

II. COLLECTIONS OF TRACTS

[For other titles see p. 380 above.]

Peck, F. Desiderata Curiosa. 2 vols. 1732–5.

The Harleian Miscellany: a Collection of Scarce, Curious, and Entertaining Pamphlets and Tracts. Ed. W. Oldys, with preface by S. Johnson, 8 vols. 1744–6; ed. T. Park, 10 vols. 1808–13.

Collection of Scarce and Valuable Tracts. 16 vols. 1748–52; ed. Sir W. Scott, 13 vols. 1809–15. [Somers Tracts.]

Brydges, Sir S. E. Archaica, containing a Reprint of Scarce Old English Prose Tracts. 2 vols. 1815.

Triphook, R. Miscellanea Antiqua Anglicana. 7 pts, 1816.

Utterson, E. V. Select Pieces of Early Popular Poetry. 2 vols. 1817.

Halliwell[-Phillipps], J. O. Contributions to Early English Literature. 6 pts, 1849.

—— The Literature of the Sixteenth and Seventeenth Centuries Illustrated by Reprints of very Rare Tracts. 1851.

Collier, J. P. Illustrations of Early English Popular Literature. 2 vols. 1863–4.

—— Illustrations of Old English Literature. 3 vols. 1866.

Hindley, Charles. Miscellanea Antiqua Anglicana. The Old Book Collector's Miscellany. 3 vols. 1871–3.

Hazlitt, W. C. Fugitive Tracts, Written in Verse. 2 sers. 1875. [1493–1700.]

Arber, Edward. An English Garner. 8 vols. 1877–90; ed. T. Seccombe, 12 vols. 1903–4.

Edmonds, C. The Isham Reprints. 2 vols. 1895.

Harrison, G. B. The Bodley Head Quartos. 15 vols. 1923–6. [Reprints of Elizabethan and Jacobean pamphlets, etc.]

III. GENERAL SOCIAL SATIRES

Cocke Lorelles Bote. [1510?]; ed. E. F. Rimbault, Percy Soc. 1843.

A Treatise of a Galaunt. [1510?]; ed. J. O. Halliwell[-Phillipps], 1860; ed. W. C. Hazlitt (in Early English Popular Poetry, vol. III, 1864). [Sometimes attrib. to Lydgate.]

Boorde, Andrew. The Fyrst Boke of the Introduction of Knowledge. 1542; ed. F. J. Furnivall, EETS. Ex. Ser. 1870.

Brinkelow, Henry. The Lamentacion of a Christian against the Citie of London. [1542] (under pseud. R. Mors); ed. J. M. Cowper, EETS. Ex. Ser. 1874.

—— The co-Plaint of Roderyck Mors for the Redresse of Certeyn Wycked Lawes. [1548?] (anon.); ed. J. M. Cowper, EETS. Ex. Ser. 1874.

Colin Blowbols Testament. Ed. J. O. Halliwell[-Phillipps] (in Nugae Poeticae, 1844); ed. W. C. Hazlitt (in Early English Popular Poetry, vol. I, 1864).

Hill, Thomas. The Shaking of the Sheets or the Dance of Death. Ed. W. Chappell (in Popular Music of the Olden Time, vol. I, 1855).

Hake, Edward. A Touchestone for this Time Present. 1574.

—— Newes out of Powles Churcheyarde. [1579]; ed. C. Edmonds, 1872 (Isham Reprints).

—— An Oration conteyning an Expostulation. 1587.

—— Of Golds Kingdome, and this Un-helping Age. 1604.

The Wyll of the Devil. [1577?]; ed. J. P. Collier (in Illustrations of Early English Popular Literature, vol. I, 1863); ed. F. J. Furnivall, 1871.

Northbrooke, John. Spiritus est Vicarius Christi in Terra. A Treatise wherein Dicing, Dauncing, Vaine Plaies or Enterludes are reproved. [1577?]; 1579; ed. J. P. Collier, Shakespeare Soc. 1843.

Gosson, Stephen. The Schoole of Abuse, con-teining a Pleasaunt Invective against Poets, Pipers, Plaiers, Jesters, and such like Caterpillers of a Commonwelth. 1579; 1587; ed. J. P. Collier, Shakespeare Soc. 1841; ed. E. Arber, 1868.

—— Quippes for Upstart, Newfangled Gentlewomen. 1595 (anon.).

[Walker, Gilbert] A Manifest Detection of Dice-play. [1580?]; ed. J. O. Halliwell [-Phillipps], Percy Soc. 1850; ed. A. V. Judges (Elizabethan Underworld, 1930).

Salter, Thomas. A Contention between three Brethren; that is to say, the Whoremonger, the Drunkarde and the Dice-Player. 1581.

W[ilcox], T. A Glasse for Gamesters. 1581.

Stafford, W. Compendious or Briefe Examina-tion of Certayne Ordinary Complaints. 1581; ed. F. D. Matthew and F. J. Furnivall, New Shakspere Soc. 1876.

Stubbes, Philip. The Anatomie of Abuses. 2 pts, 1583; ed. F. J. Furnivall, 2 pts, New Shakspere Soc. 1877–82.

Newton, T. True and Christian Friendshippe. 1586. [Tr. from Lambert Daneau: Includes A Right Excellent Invective against Dice-Play.]

R[ankins], W. The English Ape, the Italian Imitation, the Foote-steppes of Fraunce. 1588.

Tarltons Newes out of Purgatorie. 1590; ed. J. O. Halliwell[-Phillipps], Shakespeare Soc. 1844.

Tell-Trothes New Yeare's Gift and the Passionate Morrice. 1593. J. Lane's Tom Tell-Troths Message, and his Pens Com-plaint. 1600. T. Powell's Tom of All Trades. Or the Plain Path-way to Preferment. 1631. The Glasse of Godly Love (by J. Rogers?). Ed. F. J. Furnivall, New Shak-spere Soc. 1876.

B[anchieri], A[driano]. The Noblenesse of the Asse. 1595.

C[lerke?], W. Polimanteia, or the Meanes to judge of the Fall of a Commonwealth. Whereunto is added, A Letter from England to Cambridge, Oxford, Innes of Court. Cambridge, 1595. [Letter rptd A. B. Grosart, Elizabethan England, Manchester, 1881.]

Maroccus extaticus. Or, Bankes Bay Horse in a Trance. 1595; ed. E. F. Rimbault (in Early English Poetry, Percy Soc. 1844). [Verse.]

The Hospitall of Incurable Fools. 1600. [Tr. from T. Garzoni.]

The Meeting of Gallants at an Ordinarie, or the Walkes in Powles. 1604; ed. J. O. Halliwell[-Phillipps], Percy Soc. 1841.

Pimlyco. Or Runne Red-cap. 1609; ed. facs. A. H. Bullen (in Antient Drolleries, vol. II, Oxford, 1890).

Rowley, William. A Search for Money, or the Lamentable Complaint for the Losse of the Wandring Knight, Mounsieur l'Argent. 1609; ed. Percy Soc. 1840.

J[ohnson], R[ichard]. Looke on me, London. I am an Honest Englishman, ripping up the Bowels of Mischief, lurking in thy

Suburbs and Precincts. 1613; ed. J. P. Collier (in Illustrations of Early English Popular Literature, vol. II, 1864).

Carey, Walter. The Present State of England expressed in this Paradox, Our Fathers were very Rich with Little, and we Poore with Much. 1626.

Prynne, W. Healthes Sicknesse, or a Discourse proving the Drinking of Healthes to be Sinfull. 1628.

—— The Unloveliness of Love-locks. 1628.

Lupton, Donald. London and the Countrey Carbonadoed. 1632.

The Hunting of the Hare; with her Last Wyll and Testament. [1635?] [Ballad.]

Peacham, Henry. The Worth of a Peny: or a Caution to keep Money. 1647 (for 1641?); ed. A. Lang (in Social England Illustrated, 1903).

Hall, Thomas. Comarum ἀκοσμεια. The Loathsomenesse of Long Haire. 1654.

IV. Jest-Books, Comic Dialogues, Burlesques, etc.

Esdaile, Arundell. A List of English Tales and Prose Romances printed before 1740. 2 pts, Bibliog. Soc. 1912.

Thoms, W. J. Early English Prose Romances. 3 vols. 1858.

Hazlitt, W. C. Shakespeare Jest-Books. 3 vols. 1864. [Reprints 15 of the ensuing collections.]

Morley, Henry. Early Prose Romances. 1889.

Smith, Walter. XII Mery Jests of the Wyddow Edyth. 1525; 1573; ed. W. C. Hazlitt (in Shakespeare Jest-Books, vol. III, 1864).

A C. Mery Tales. [1525?]; [1535?]; ed. W. C. Hazlitt (in Shakespeare Jest-Books, vol. I, 1864); ed. H. Oesterley, 1866; ed. facs. W. C. Hazlitt (from 1535 edn).

A Merye Jest of a Man that was called Howleglas. [1528?]; ed. K. Mackenzie, 1860; ed. F. Ouvry, 1867.

Tales, and Quick Answers, very Mery and Pleasant to Rede. [1535?]; ed. W. C. Hazlitt (in Shakespeare Jest-Books, vol. I, 1864).

[Barnes, ?] The Treatyse Answerynge the Boke of Berdes. [1548?]; ed. F. J. Furnivall, EETS. Ex. Ser. 1870. [A reply to a lost tract by Andrew Boorde.]

The Sack-Full of Newes. 1673; ed. W. C. Hazlitt (in Shakespeare Jest-Books, vol. II, 1864). [Stationers' Register, 1557.]

Scoggin, his Jestes. 1613; ed. W. C. Hazlitt (in Shakespeare Jest-Books, vol. II, 1864). [1565-6.]

Skelton, John. Merie Tales. [1567]; ed. A. Dyce (in his edn of Skelton, 1843); ed. W. C. Hazlitt (in Shakespeare Jest-Books, vol. II, 1864).

The Historie of Frier Rush. 1620; ed. H. Morley (in Early Prose Romances, 1889). [1568-9. Based on an old Danish tale. See Robert Priebsch, Die Grundfabel und Entwicklungsgeschichte der Dichtung von Bruder Rausch, Untersuchungen und Quellen, vol. I, Prague, 1908.]

Sanford, James. The Garden of Pleasure: contayninge most Pleasante Tales, Worthy Deedes and Witty Sayings. 1573. [Tr. from Ludovico Guicciardini.]

The Life and Pranks of Long Meg of Westminster. 1582; ed. C. Hindley (in The Old Book Collector's Miscellany, vol. II, 1872).

Phist[on]. W. The Welspring of Wittie Conceites. 1584. [Tr. from Italian.]

The Cobler of Caunterburie. [1590]; 1630 (as The Tincker of Turvey); ed. J. O. Halliwell [-Phillipps], Shakespeare Soc. 1844; ed. F. Ouvry, 1862 (priv. ptd).

Ferris, Richard. The Most Dangerous and Memorable Adventure of Richard Ferris, who undertoke to rowe by Sea to Bristowe. 1590; rptd A. Lang (in Social England Illustrated, 1903).

Barckley, Sir Richard. A Discourse of the Felicitie of Man: or his Summum Bonum. 1598.

'Snuffe, C. de C.' [i.e. John Singer]. Quips upon Questions, or a Clownes Conceite. 1600.

Kemp, William. Kemp's Nine Daies Wonder, Performed in a Daunce from London to Norwich. 1600; ed. A. Dyce, Camden Soc. 1840; ed. A. Lang (in Social England Illustrated, 1903); ed. G. B. Harrison, 1923 (Bodley Head Quartos); ed. A. C. Ward (in A Miscellany of Tracts, 1927).

[Corrozet, Gilles.] Memorable Conceits of Divers Personages. 1602.

Jacke of Dover, his Quest for the Veriest Foole in England. 1604; 1615 (as Jacke of Dovers Merry Tales); cd. T. Wright, Percy Soc. 1842; ed. W. C. Hazlitt (in Shakespeare Jest-Books, vol. II, 1864).

Pasquils Jests, mixed with Mother Bunches Merriments. 1604; ed. W. C. Hazlitt (in Shakespeare Jest-Books, vol. III, 1864).

Newes from Graves End. 1604. [J. P. Collier assigns to Dekker.]

Terilo, William. A Piece of Friar Bacons Brazen-heads Prophesie. 1604; ed. J. O. Halliwell[-Phillipps], Percy Soc. 1844.

Newes from Rome also certaine Prophecies of a Jew called Cabel Shilock. 1606. [See N. & Q. 24 July 1909.]

Merrie Conceited Jests of George Peale. 1607; ed. W. C. Hazlitt (in Shakespeare Jest-Books, vol. II, 1864); ed. C. Hindley, 1869.

Johnson, Richard. The Pleasant Conceites of Old Hobson. 1607; ed. J. O. Halliwell [-Phillipps], Percy Soc. 1843; ed. W. C. Hazlitt (in Shakespeare Jest-Books, vol. III, 1864).

—— The Pleasant Walkes of Moore-fields. 1607; ed. J. P. Collier (in Illustrations of Early English Popular Literature, vol. II, 1864).

D[ekker?], T. and Wilkins, George. Jests to make you Merie. 1607.

Armin, Robert. A Nest of Ninnies. 1608; ed. J. P. Collier (in Fools and Jesters, Shakespeare Soc. 1842).

Certaine Conceyts and Jeasts. [Appended to The Philosophers Banquet, 1609]; ed. W. C. Hazlitt (in Shakespeare Jest-Books, vol. III, 1864).

Tarlton's Jests. 1638; ed. J. O. Halliwell [-Phillipps], Shakespeare Soc. 1844; ed. W. C. Hazlitt (in Shakespeare Jest-Books, vol. II, 1864); ed. facs. E. W. Ashbee, [1876?] (priv. ptd). [S.R. 1609.]

Cobbes Prophecies. 1614; ed. facs. A. H. Bullen (Antient Drolleries, vol. I, Oxford, 1890).

Willet, R. Merry Jests, concerning Popes, Monks and Friers. 1617. [Tr. from N.S.]

[Fcnnor, William?] Pasquils Palinodia, and his Progresse to the Taverne. 1619; ed. J. P. Collier (in Illustrations of Old English Literature, vol. I, 1866).

Westward for Smelts, or the Waterman's Fare of Mad Merry Western wenches whose Tales are Sweet, and will much content you. Written by Kinde Kit of Kingstone. 1620; ed. J. O. Halliwell[-Phillipps], 1848.

Painter, William. Chaucer new Painted. [1623.] [Versified proverbs, riddles, anagrams, etc.]

Gratiae ludentes; Jests from the Universities. 1628.

Robin Good-fellow, his Mad Prankes and Merry Jestes. 2 pts, 1628; ed. J. P. Collier, Percy Soc. 1841; ed. J. O. Halliwell[-Phillipps] (Illustrations of Fairy Mythology, Shakespeare Soc. 1845); ed. W. C. Hazlitt (Fairy Mythology of Shakespeare, 1875).

Taylor, John. Wit and Mirth. 1629; ed. W. C. Hazlitt (in Shakespeare Jest-Books, vol. III, 1864).

B., A. The Merry Tales of the Mad Men of Gottam. 1630; ed. J. O. Halliwell[-Phillipps], 1840; ed. W. C. Hazlitt (in Shakespeare Jest-Books, vol. III, 1864). [By Andrew Boorde?]

[Chamberlain, Robert.] Conceits, Clinches, Flashes, and Whimzies. 1639; ed. J. O. Halliwell[-Phillipps], 1860; ed. W. C. Hazlitt (in Old English Jest-Books, vol. III, 1864).

S., S. Paradoxes or Encomions in the Praise of being lowsey, Treachery, Nothing, Beggary. 1653.

Gayton, E. Wit Revived. 1655.

Here's Jack in a Box, that will Conjure the Fox. 1656.

Cox, R. Actaeon and Diana. 1656.

Mirth in abundance. 1659.

The Hangman's joy. 1660.

F[ord], E. Fair Play in the Lottery. 1660.

A Choice Banquet of Witty Jests. 1660.

Ashton, J. Humour, Wit and Satire of the Seventeenth Century. 1883.

Herford, C. H. Studies in the Literary Relations of England and Germany in the Sixteenth Century. Cambridge, 1886.

Clouston, W. A. The Book of Noodles: Stories of Simpletons; or, Fools and their Follies. 1888.

de Vocht, Henry. De Invloed van Erasmus op de engelsche Tooneel-literatuur der XVIe en XVIIe Eeuwen. I, Shakespeare Jest-Books—Lyly. Ghent, 1908.

Stiefel, A. L. Zum Einfluss des Erasmus auf die englische Literatur. Archiv, CXXIV, 1910. [Jest-Books.]

Schulz, Ernest. Die englischen Schwankbücher bis 1607. Berlin, 1912.

Field, J. E. The Myth of the Pent Cuckoo. 1913.

V. COLLECTIONS OF QUOTATIONS AND MAXIMS

Taverner, Richard. The garden of wysdom. 1539. [See C. R. Baskervill, Stud. Phil. XXIX, 1932, pp. 149–59.]

Baldwin, William. A Treatise of Morall Phylosophie; contaynyng the sayinges of the wyse. 2 pts, 1547.

Blage, Thomas. A Schoole of wise conceyts. 1569.

Florio, Giovanni. Florio his Firste Fruites. 1578.

Crewe, Thomas. The Nosegay of morall philosophie. 1580.

Bodenham, John. Politeuphuia. Wits Commonwealth. 1597. [Actually compiled by Nicholas Ling, but generally attrib. to his patron Bodenham. See F. B. Williams, John Bodenham, Stud. Phil. XXXI, 1934.]

Meres, F. Palladis Tamia; Wits Treasury. 1598. [The section 'Poetrie' rptd, ed. D. C. Allen, Urbana, 1933.]

Allott, Robert. Wits Theater of the Little World. 1599.

[Wrednott, William.] Palladis Palatium. 1604.

Breton, Nicholas. Wits Private Wealth.
1612.
The Country-mans new Commonwealth.
1647.

VI. RIDDLES

The Demaundes Joyous. 1511; ed. C. H.
Hartshorne (in Ancient Metrical Tales,
1829); ed. J. Timbs (in The Literary World,
1839).
[The Boke of a Hundred Riddles.] [1530?]
Delectable Demaundes and Pleasant Ques-
tions. [1566.] [Tr. from Alain Chartier.]
The Riddles of Heraclitus and Democritus.
1598.
The Booke of Meery Riddles. 1629; ed. J. O.
Halliwell[-Phillipps], 1866.

VII. TRACTS AND SATIRES ON WOMEN AND MARRIAGE

The Payne and Sorowe of Evyll Maryage.
[1509?] [Tr. from Golias de Conjuge non
ducenda.]
Walter, William. The Spectacle of Lovers; a
Lytell Controvers Dyalogue bytwene Love
and Councell. [1520?]
The Boke of Mayd Emelyn. [1525]; ed. E. F.
Rimbault (in Ancient Poetical Tracts,
Percy Soc. 1842); ed. W. C. Hazlitt (in
Early English Popular Poetry, vol. IV,
1864).
[Copland, Robert.] A Complaynt of them
that be to soone maryed. 1535.
——— The Complaynte of them that ben to
late maryed. [1535?]; ed. J. P. Collier (in
Illustrations of Early English Popular
Literature, vol. I, 1863).
——— Gyl of Braintfords Testament. [1560?];
ed. F. J. Furnivall, 1871 (priv. ptd).
Bansley, Charles. A Treatyse shewing the
Pryde of Women. [1540?]; ed. J. P. Collier,
[1841]. [Verse.]
Coverdale, Myles. Christen State of Matry-
monye, wherein Housbandes and Wyfes
may lerne to kepe House together with
Love. 1541. [Tr. from Heinrich Bullinger.]
Gosynhill, Edward. The Prayse of all Women,
called Mulierum Pean. [1542?]
——— The Vertuous Scholehous of Ungracious
Women. [1550?] (anon.).
——— A Dialogue bytwene the Commune
Secretary and Jalowsye touching Harlottes.
[1560?] (anon.)
Vaughan, Robert. A Dialogue Defensyve for
Women. 1542.
Elyot, Sir Thomas. The Defence of Good
Women. 1545.
Knox, John. The First Blast of the Trumpet
against the Monstruous Regiment of
Women. [Geneva], 1558.

The Schole howse of Women. 1560; ed. E. V.
Utterson (Select Pieces of Early Popular
Poetry, 2 vols. 1817); ed. W. C. Hazlitt
(Early English Popular Poetry, vol. IV,
1864). [Incorrectly attrib. to Edward
Gosynhill.]
More, Edward. A Lytle and Bryefe Treatyse
called the Defence of Women, made
agaynste the Schole-howse of Women.
1560; ed. E. V. Utterson (in Select Pieces
of Early Popular Poetry, 2 vols. 1817).
The Deceyte of Women, to the Instruction
and Ensample of All Men, yonge and olde.
[1560?]; ed. F. Brie, Archiv, CLVI, 1929.
The Proude Wyves Pater Noster. 1560; ed.
W. C. Hazlitt (in Early English Popular
Poetry, vol. IV, 1864).
Evans, Lewis. A New Balet entituled how to
wyve well. 1561.
Pyrrye, C. The Prayse and Dysprayse of
Women. [1569?]
A Merry Jeste of a Shrewde and Curste Wyfe
lapped in Morrelles Skin. [1580?]; ed.
Shakespeare Soc. 1844; ed. W. C. Hazlitt
(in Early English Popular Poetry, vol. IV,
1864).
The Taming of a Shrew. Ed. J. Ritson (in
Ancient Songs and Ballads, vol. II, 1829).
[Ballad.]
[Tofte, Robert?] The Batchelars Banquet.
1603; ed. F. P. Wilson, Oxford, 1929. [Based
on Les Quinze Joyes de Mariage.]
G., J. An Apologie for Women-kinde. 1605.
Swetnam, Joseph. The Arraignment of Lewd,
Idle, Froward and Inconstant Women.
1617.
Speght, Rachel. A Mouzell for Melastomus.
Or an Answere to that Pamphlet made by
Jo. Sw[etnam]. The Arraignement of
Women. 1617.
Heale, William. An Apologie for Women.
1619.
Newstead, Christopher. An Apology for
Women. 1620.
Ferrers, Richard. The Worth of Women, a
Poem. 1622.
The Parliament of Women. 1640.
H., I. A strange Wonder. 1642.
Strong, James. Joanereidos. 1645.
Nevile, Henry. The Parliament of Ladies.
1647.
——— The Ladies, a second time assembled in
Parliament. 1647.
——— Newes from the New Exchange: or the
Commonwealth of Ladies, drawn to the life.
1650.
The City-Dames' petition in the behalfe of the
Cavaliers. 1647.
The Divell a Married Man, or the Divell hath
met with his Match. 1647. [A tale tr. from
Macchiavelli.]

Hey Hoe for a Husband, or the Parliament of
Maides. 1647.
Women will have their Will. 1648.
A Dialogue between Mistris Macquerella, a
suburb bawd, Mrs Scolapendra, a noted
curtezan, and Mr Pimpinello an usher, etc.
Pittifully bemoaning the tenour of the Act
now in force against adultery and fornica-
tion. 1650.
Gerbier, Charles. Elogium Heroinum. 1651.
Fleetwood, E. The glory of Women. 1652.
[Tr. from H. C. Agrippa.]
A Brief Anatomie of Women. 1653.
The Citie Matrons. 1654.
The Gossip's Braule. 1655.
Thorowgood, G. Pray be not Angry; or, the
Woman's New Law; with their several votes,
orders, rules and precepts to the London
Prentices. 1656.
The Parliament of Women. 1656.
Now or Never; or, a new Parliament of
Women assembled. 1656.
An Invective against the Pride of Women.
1657.
B., W. The Yellow Book. 1658 (2nd edn).
—— A New Trial of the Ladies. 1658 (2nd
edn).
The Crafty Whore. 1658.
Philalethes, Mercurius. Select City Quaeries.
1660.

Lancher, L. J. Satires et Diatribes contre les
Femmes, l'Amour et le Mariage. Paris,
1860.
Tobler, A. Proverbia quae dicuntur super
Natura Feminarum. Zeitschrift für roma-
nische Philologie, ix, 1885.
[Gay, Jules]. Bibliographie des principaux
Ouvrages relatifs à l'Amour, aux Femmes,
au Mariage. Rev. J. Lemonnyer, 4 vols.
Paris, 1893–1900.

VIII. Rogue Pamphlets and Prison Tracts, etc.

[See also the bibliography appended to
F. W. Chandler, The Literature of Roguery,
2 vols. Boston, 1907; and W. C. Hazlitt, A
Tentative Catalogue of Our Prison Literature, Bibliographer, vi, 1884.]

A. 1500–1640
The Rogues and Vagabonds of Shakespeare's
Youth. Ed. E. Viles and F. J. Furnivall,
EETS. 1869; New Shakspere Soc. 1880.
[1. Awdeley's Fraternitye; 2. Harman's
Caveat; 3. Haben's (or Heyberdine's) A
Sermon in Praise of Thieves; 4. parts of The
Groundworke of Coney-catching.]
The Elizabethan Underworld: A Collection of
Tudor and Early Stuart Tracts and Ballads.
Ed. A. V. Judges, 1930.

[Awdeley, John.] The Fraternitye of Vaca-
bondes. 1565; ed. E. Viles and F. J. Furni-
vall, EETS. 1869.
Harman, Thomas. A Caveat or Warening for
Commen Cursetors vulgarly called Vaga-
bones. 1567; ed. E. Viles and F. J. Furni-
vall, EETS. 1869; ed. A. V. Judges (in The
Elizabethan Underworld, 1930).
Hutton, Luke. The Blacke Dogge of Newgate.
[1596?]; ed. A. V. Judges (in The Eliza-
bethan Underworld, 1930).
—— Luke Hulton's Lamentation. 1598; ed.
A. V. Judges (in The Elizabethan Under-
world, 1930).
S[harpham?], E. The Discoverie of the
Knightes of the Poste. 1597.
The Life and Death of Gamaliel Ratsey, a
Famous Thief. [1605]; ed. J. P. Collier (in
Illustrations of Old English Literature,
vol. iii, 1866); ed. facs. (with Ratseis Ghost)
S. H. Atkins, Shakespeare Ass. 1935.
Ratseis Ghost, or the Second Part of his
Madde Pranks. [1605]; ed. facs. H. B.
Charlton, Manchester, 1933.
R[owlands], S[amuel]. Martin Mark-all,
Beadle of Bridewell. 1610; ed. A. V. Judges
(in The Elizabethan Underworld, 1930).
[Also attrib. to Samuel Rid.]
Rid, Samuel. The Art of Jugling. 1612; 1614.
The Severall Notorious and Lewd Cousonages
of John West and Alice West. 1613.
Fennor, William. The Compters Common-
Wealth. 1617; ed. A. V. Judges (in The
Elizabethan Underworld, 1930).
[Mynshull, Geffray]. Certaine Characters and
Essayes of Prison and Prisoners. 1618.
The Oeconomy of the Fleete or an Apological
Answeare of A. Harris, late Warden there,
unto XIX. Articles sett forth against him
by the Prisoners. Ed. A. Jessopp, Camden
Soc. 1879. [1621.]
Wither, George. The Schollers Purgatory.
[1625?]
Clavell, John. Recantation of an ill led Life,
or a Discoverie of the High-way Law. 1628.
Wickins, Nathan. Wood Street Compter's
Plea for its Prisoner. 1638.

B. 1640–1660
(1) Tracts on Prisons and Admini-stration of Law
L., W. The Courts of Justice Corrected and
Amended, or The Corrupt Lawyer Untrust,
Lash'd and Quasht. 1642.
Bagwell, William. The Distressed Merchant
and the Prisoners comfort in distresse.
1645.
A Looking-Glasse for all proud, ambitious,
covetous and corrupt Lawyers. 1646.

Robins, Robert. A Whip for the Marshall's Court. 1647.

P., Theophilus. Salus Populi desperately ill of a languishing Consumption. 1648.

Jones, John. The Crie of Bloud. 1651.

—— Every Mans Case; or, Lawyers Routed. 1652.

March, John. Amicus Reipublicae. 1651.

Miscellanea Magna. The Second Century. 1653. [A list of satirical misinterpretations of Latin legal phrases.]

Leach, Edmund. The Down-Fall of the Unjust Lawyers. 1653.

Multum in parvo: or a summary narrative on behalfe of prisoners captived for debt. 1653.

Rogers, John. Sagrir. Or Doomes-day drawing nigh, with Thunder and Lightening to Lawyers. 1653.

A New Case put to an Old Lawyer. 1656. [Satire.]

Cole, William. A Rod for the Lawyers, who are hereby declared to be the grand robbers and deceivers of the nation. 1659.

Pryor, William and Turner, Thomas. The Out-Cries of the Poor, Oppressed and Imprisoned. 1659.

Adis, Henry. A Fannaticks Letter sent out of the Dungeon of the Gate-House Prison of Westminster. 1661.

(2) ROGUE PAMPHLETS AND BURLESQUES

Frogges of Egypt, or the Catterpillars of the Commonwealth truly dissected and laid open. 1641.

Wonderful Newes from Wood-Street Counter. 1642.

F[idge], G[eorge]. The English Gusman; or the History of that unparallel'd thief James Hind. 1652.

A Pill to purge Melancholy. 1652.

Hinds Elder Brother, or the Master Thief Discovered, being a Relation of the Life of Major Thomas Knowls. 1652.

B., J. The Knight Errant: being a witty, notable and true relation of the strange adventures of Sir William Hart. 1652.

S., R. The Counter-Scuffle. 1653.

Gayton, Edmund. Pleasant Notes upon Don Quixot. 1654.

—— Wil: Bagnal's Ghost. 1655.

The Witty Rogue arraigned, condemned and executed. Or, the history of that incomparable thief Richard Hainam. 1656.

The Devils Cabinet broke open; or, A New Discovery of the High-way Thieves. 1657.

[Head, Richard?] The Catterpillers of this Nation Anatomized. 1659.

—— The English Rogue, described in the life of Meriton Latroon. 1665.

C. STUDIES AND SURVEYS

Langford, J. A. Prison Books and their Authors. 1861.

Ashton, J. The Fleet, its Rivers, Prison and Marriages. 1888.

Chandler, F. W. The Literature of Roguery. 2 vols. Boston, 1907.

Aydelotte, Frank. Elizabethan Rogues and Vagabonds. Oxford, 1913.

IX. TOBACCO PAMPHLETS

[See W. Bragge, Bibliotheca Nicotiana, Birmingham, 1880, and F. W. Fairholt, Tobacco: its History and Associations, 1859.]

Frampton, John. Joyfull News out of the Newe Founde Worlde. [1577]; rptd 1925. [Tr. from Nicolas Monardes.]

C[hute], A[nthony]. Tobaco. The Distinct and Severall Opinions of the Phisitions. 1595. [See R. J. Kane, Anthony Chute, Thomas Nashe, and the First English Work on Tobacco, RES. VII, 1931.]

Buttes, Henry. Dyets Dry Dinner. 1599.

A New And Short Defense of Tabacco. 1602.

[Beaumont, Sir John.] The Metamorphosis of Tabacco. 1602.

H., J. Work for Chimney-Sweepers, or a Warning for Tabacconists. 1602.

A Defence of Tabacco: with a Friendly Answer to the Late Printed Booke called Worke for Chimney-Sweepers. 1602.

King James I. A Counter Blaste to Tobacco. 1604; 1616; ed. E. Arber, 1895.

G[ardiner], E[dmund]. The Triall of Tabacco. 1610.

Perfuming of Tobacco and the Great Abuse Committed in it. 1611.

Barclay, William. Nepenthes, or the Vertues of Tobacco. Edinburgh, 1614; ed. Spalding Club Misc. vol. I, 1841.

T., C. An Advice how to plant Tobacco in England. 1615.

Deacon, John. Tobacco Tortured, or the Filthie Fume of Tobacco Refined. 1616.

Sylvester, Joshua. Tobacco Battered & the Pipes Shattered by a Volley of Holy Shot. [1617.] [Verse.]

Rich, Barnabe. The Irish Hubbub, or the English Hue and Crie. 1617.

Brathwaite, Richard. The Smoaking Age, or the Man in the Mist. [Appended to A Solemn Joviall Disputation, 1617.]

Bretnor, T. Opiologia; or a Treatise concerning Opium. 1618. [Tr. from Angelo Sala.]

Bennett, Edward. A Treatise touching the Inconveniences that Tobacco hath brought into this Land. [1620?]

Venner, Tobias. A Briefe and Accurate Treatise concerning the Taking of the Fume of Tobacco. 1621.

Thorius, Raphael. Hymnus Tabaci. 1626.

X. Moral and Political Tracts and Pamphlets

A. 1500–1640

Vox Populi Vox Dei. Ed. W. C. Hazlitt (in Early English Popular Poetry, vol. III, 1864). [1515–20.]

[Copland, Robert.] The Hye Way to the Spyttel Hous. [1536?]; ed. W. C. Hazlitt (in Early English Popular Poetry, vol. IV, 1864); ed. A. V. Judges (in The Elizabethan Underworld, 1930).

Crowley, Robert. An Informacion and Peticion agaynst the Oppressours of the Pore Commons. [1548.]

—— The Voyce of the Laste Trumpet. 1549.

—— One and Thyrtye Epigrammes. 1550.

—— The Way to Wealth. 1550.

—— Pleasure and Payne, Heaven and Hell. 1551.

—— The Select Works of Robert Crowley. Ed. J. M. Cowper, EETS. Ex. Ser. 1872. [Includes all the above.]

The Booke in Meeter of Robin Conscience. [1550?]; ed. J. O. Halliwell[-Phillipps] (in Contributions to English Literature, 1849); ed. W. C. Hazlitt (in Early English Popular Poetry, vol. III, 1864).

Newes come from Hell. 1565. [Attacks usurers.]

Mosse, M. The Arraignment and Conviction of Usurie. 1505.

Usurie Araigned and Condemned. 1625. [For other usury pamphlets, see p. 845 below.]

B. CIVIL WAR PAMPHLETS AND BROADSIDES

[Many thousands of pamphlets and fly-sheets were produced 1640–60. In the present bibliography only a few illustrations are recorded. See Catalogue of Thomason Tracts, BM., 1908; Rump: or an exact collection of the choycest Poems and songs relating to the Late Times from Anno 1639 to Anno 1661, 1662. See also C. W. Previté-Orton, Political Satire in English Poetry, Cambridge, 1910; T. Wright, Political Ballads published in England during the Commonwealth, Percy Soc. 1841, and History of Grotesque and Caricature, 1865.]

(1) Satires on Political Characters

A Description of the Passage of Thomas late Earle of Strafford over the River of Styx. 1641.

A Dialogue, or, Rather a Parley betweene Prince Ruperts Dogge whose name is Puddle, and Tobies Dog whose name is Pepper. 1643. [For numerous other sarcasms on Prince Rupert's dog see Catalogue of Thomason Tracts.]

A true and strange Relation of a Boy who was entertained by the Devill about Crediton. 1645.

Blacke Tom his speech to the House. 1647. [Ballad upon Fairfax and his Army.]

Whitehall Fayre; or, Who buyes good Penni-worths of Barkstead. 1648. [Satire in verse on Col. John Barkstead, formerly goldsmith in the Strand.]

The World in a Maize, or Oliver's Ghost. 1659. [Satire in prose and verse.]

Nelson, Abraham. A Perfect Description of Antichrist and his false Prophet. Written in 1654. 1660.

Haslerig and Vain; or, A dialogue between them in the Tower of London. 1660.

Hugh Peters last Will and Testament. 1660.

Brethren in Iniquity. 1660. [Titchburne and Ireton.]

A Rope for Pol; or a hue and cry after Marchemont Nedham, the late scurrulous news-writer. 1660.

B., F. The Character of Sr. Arthur Haslerig. 1661.

Verax, Philadelphus. The Knavish Merchant. 1661. [Attack on Richard Neave in defence of Thomas Crocker.]

The Pretended Saint and the Prophane Libertine. 1661. [Robert Titchburne and Henry Marten.]

(2) Mock Testaments

The Late Will and Testament of the Doctors Commons. 1641.

A true Inventory of the goods and chattels of Superstition. 1642.

B., J. The last Will and Testament of Superstition. 1642.

The last Will and Testament of P. Rupert, 1645; Charing Crosse, 1646; Sir John Presbyter, 1647; Sir James Independent, 1647; Tom Fairfax, 1648; Richard Brandon, 1649; Philip Herbert who dyed of fooleage, 1650; James Hynd, 1651.

Mercurius Democritus, his last Will and Testament. 1652.

(3) Pamphlets on King Charles

Symmons, Edward. A Vindication of King Charles. 1648. [An answer to The Kings Cabinet Opened: or, Certain Packets of Secret Letters and Papers, written with the Kings own Hand, and taken in his Cabinet at Nasby Field, 14 June 1645.]

Howell, J. The Instruments of a King. .1648.

Wotton, Sir H. A Panegyrick of King Charles. 1649.

Quarles, John. Regale Lectum Miseriae. 1649.

The Confession of Richard Brandon. 1649.

B[rome], R[ichard]. Lachrymae Musarum. 1649.

Philipps, Fabian. King Charles the First no Man of Blood but a Martyr for his People. 1649.

A Dialogue: or, a Dispute between the late Hangman [R. Brandon] and Death. 1649.

[Cleveland, John.] Majestas Intemerata. 1649.

The Princely Pellican. 1649.

The None-Such Charles. 1651.

A New Conference between the Ghosts of King Charles and Oliver Cromwell. By Adam Wood. 1659.

(4) TRACTS AGAINST CHRISTMAS

Taylor, John. The Complaint of Christmas. [Oxford, 1646.]

H., T. A Ha! Christmas. 1647.

Younge, Richard. A Touchstone to try whether we be Christians in name onely, or Christians in deed. 1648.

Palmer, George. The Lawfulness of the Celebration of Christs Birth-day debated. 1648.

Reading, John. Christmas Revived. 1660.

(5) TRACTS ON PAST HISTORY

Cotton, Sir Robert. The Troublesome Life and Raigne of King Henry the Third. 1642.

The true Coppy of the Complaint of Roderyck Mors. 1642.

W[alker], G[eorge]. Anglo-Tyrannus. 1650.

Chamberlain, E. The late Warre parallel'd. Or, a brief relation of the five years civil warres of Henry the Third. 1660.

(6) EXPOSURES AND REFLECTIONS ARISING OUT OF THE WAR

J[ordan], T[homas]. A Diurnall of Dangers. 1642. [Satire on contemporary Diurnalls.]

Newes, True Newes, Laudable Newes, Citie Newes, Court News, Countrey Newes. 1642. [Satire.]

A Remonstrance of Londons Occurrences. 1643.

Edwards, Thomas. Gangraena. 3 pts, 1646.

A fresh Whip for all scandalous Lyers [i.e. the 'Diurnall-Writer' and the 'Perfect Occurrence Writer']. 1647.

Mercurius Anti Mercurius. 1648.

F[orde], T[homas]. Lusus Fortunae. 1649.

The Hue and Cry after those rambling proto-notaries of the times, Mercurius Elencticus, Britanicus, Melancholicus and Aulicus. 1651.

(7) PEACE PAMPHLETS

A Cure for the State. 1640. [Satire in the form of a medical prescription.]

Maddison, Sir Ralph. Englands Looking In and Out. 1640. [On the financial and commercial condition of the country.]

Morton, Thomas. Englands Warning-Piece. 1642.

Prynne, W. A Soveraign Antidote to prevent, appease and determine our unnaturall Civill Warres and Dissentions. 1642.

The Virgins Complaint for the losse of their Sweet-Hearts by these present Wars, and keeping their Virginities against their wills. 1643.

Taylor, John. The Causes of the Diseases and Distempers of this Kingdom. [Oxford,] 1645.

Study to be quiet. 1647.

Jennings, Theodore. The Right Way to Peace. 1647.

Levitt, William. The Samaritans Box newly opened. 1647.

Homes, Nathaniel. Plain Dealing. 1652.

Herbert, Sir Percy. Certaine Conceptions or Considerations. 1652.

XI. BROADSIDE BALLADS

[See also pp. 272–3 above.]

A. REPRINTS AND CATALOGUES OF COLLECTIONS

The Harleian Miscellany. Ed. W. Oldys, 8 vols. 1744–6; ed. T. Park, 10 vols. 1808–13.

Collier, J. P. Old Ballads. Percy Soc. 1840.

—— A Book of Roxburghe Ballads. 1847.

—— Broadside Black-letter Ballads printed in the Sixteenth and Seventeenth Centuries. 1868.

—— Twenty-five Old Ballads. 1869 (priv. ptd).

Wright, T. Political Ballads published in England during the Commonwealth. Percy Soc. 1841.

—— Songs and Ballads. 1860. [From MS Ashmole, temp. Philip and Mary.]

Chappell, W. Popular Music of the Olden Time. 2 vols. 1855–9 and 1893.

Chappell, W. and Ebsworth, J. W. The Roxburghe Ballads. 9 vols. Ballad Soc. 1869–99.

Halliwell[-Phillipps], J. O. A Catalogue of an Unique Collection of Ancient Broadside Ballads. 1856. [A sale catalogue.]

Wilkins, W. W. Political Ballads of the Seventeenth and Eighteenth Centuries. 2 vols. 1860.

Mackay, C. Cavalier Songs and Ballads, 1642–1684. 1863.

Lemon, R. Catalogue of a Collection of Broadsides. Soc. Antiquaries, 1866.

Huth, Henry. Ancient Ballads and Broadsides published in England in the Sixteenth Century. Philobiblon Soc. 1867. [The Helmingham-Daniel-Huth-BM. collection.]

Morfill, W. R. Ballads from Manuscripts. Ballad Soc. 1873.

Bibliotheca Lindesiana. Catalogue of English Ballads. 1890. [Collection of the Earl of Crawford.]

Clark, Andrew. The Shirburn Ballads, 1585–1616. 1907. [From the Bodleian.]

Fortescue, G. K. Catalogue of the Pamphlets collected by George Thomason, 1640–1661. 2 vols. BM. 1908.

Catalogue of the Fifty Manuscripts and Printed Books bequeathed by A. H. Huth. BM. 1912. [No. 50 is the vol. containing the Heber-Daniel-Huth-BM. half of the Helmingham collection.]

Collmann, H. L. Ballads and Broadsides, chiefly of the Elizabethan Period, now at Britwell Court. Roxburghe Club, 1912. [The Heber-Britwell-Huntington half of the Helmingham collection.]

Rollins, H. E. Old English Ballads, 1553–1625, chiefly from Manuscripts. Cambridge, 1920.

—— A Pepysian Garland, 1595–1639. Cambridge, 1922.

—— Cavalier and Puritan, 1640–1660. New York, 1923.

B. SINGLE BALLAD-WRITERS

WILLIAM GRAY (*fl.* 1535–51)

[See E. W. Dormer, 'Gray of Reading.' Sixteenth-Century Controversialist and Ballad-Writer, Reading, 1923.]

WILLIAM ELDERTON

[See H. E. Rollins, William Elderton, Elizabethan Actor and Ballad-writer, Stud. Phil. XVII, 1920.]

CLEMENT ROBINSON

A Handful of Pleasant Delights. 1584; ed. H. E. Rollins, Cambridge, U.S.A., 1924; ed. A. Kershaw, 1927.

THOMAS DELONEY

The Works. Ed. F. O. Mann, Oxford, 1912.

The Garland of Goodwill. 1631; ed. J. H. Dixon, Percy Soc. 1851. [S.R. 1593.]

Sievers, R. Thomas Deloney. Berlin, 1904.

MARTIN PARKER

[See H. E. Rollins, Martin Parker, MP. XVI, 1919.]

C. GENERAL HISTORY AND CRITICISM

Firth, Sir C. H. The Ballad History of the Reigns of King Henry VII and Henry VIII. Trans. Royal Hist. Soc. II, 1908, III, 1909.

Esdaile, Arundell. Autolycus' Pack. Quart. Rev. April, 1913.

—— The British Museum: the Collections. [In The Uses of Libraries, ed. E. A. Baker, 1927.]

Rollins, H. E. The Black-letter Broadside Ballad. PMLA. XXXIV, 1919.

—— An Analytical Index of the Ballad-entries in the Registers of the Company of Stationers. Chapel Hill, North Carolina, 1924.

XII. JIGS

Sievers, Richard. Thomas Deloney. Eine Studie über Balladenlitteratur der Shakspere-Zeit. Berlin, 1904.

Baskervill, C. R. The Elizabethan Jig and Related Song Drama. Chicago, 1929. [Prints the following: A Jigge for the Ballad-mongers; A new Northern Jigge. The Soldiers Farewel to his love; A Country new Jigge between Simon and Susan; A mery new Jigge. Or, the pleasant wooing betwixt Kit and Pegge; Clods Carroll: or, A proper new Jigg; The Souldiers delight in the North: Or, A New North-countrey Jigge; The New Scotch-Jigg: Or, The Bonney Cravat; The Second Part of the new Scotch Jigg: Or, Jenny's Reply, To Johnny's Cravat; A Pleasant Jigg Betwixt Jack and his Mistress; The West-Country Jigg: Or, Love in Due Season; The West-Country Jigg: Or, A Trenchmore Galliard; The Soldiers Catch: Or, The Salisbury Jigg; A Spanish Gentleman and an English Gentlewoman; The Merry Wooing of Robin and Joan; The North Country lovers; A merry discourse [between the Tinker and Joan]; A Droll from Jordan's London's Resurrection to Joy and Triumph; The Wooing of Nan; Rowlands god sonne; Singing Simpkin; Frauncis new Jigge (Attowell's Jig); The Black Man; The Cheaters Cheated, by Thomas Jordan; and several Dutch and German jigs of English origin.]

III. CHARACTER-BOOKS AND ESSAYS

(1) CHARACTER-BOOKS

(a) *Bibliography*

Murphy, Gwendolen. A Bibliography of English Character-Books, 1608–1700. Oxford, 1925.

(b) *Collections of Characters*

Books of Characters. Ed. J. O. Halliwell [-Phillipps], 1857.

Character Writings of the Seventeenth Century. Ed. Henry Morley, 1891.

A Cabinet of Characters. Ed. Gwendolen Murphy, Oxford, 1925.

(c) General Criticism

Baldwin, E. C. Ben Jonson's Indebtedness to the Greek Character-Sketch. MLN. xvi, 1901.
—— The Relation of the English Character to its Greek Prototype. PMLA. xviii, 1903.
—— The Relation of the Seventeenth Century Character to the Periodical Essay. PMLA. xix, 1904.
—— A Suggestion for a New Edition of Butler's Hudibras. PMLA. xxvi, 1911.
Gordon, G. S. Theophrastus and his Imitators. [In English Literature and the Classics, Oxford, 1912.]
Thompson, E. N. S. Character Books. [In Literary Bypaths of the Renaissance, New Haven, 1924.]
—— Character-Books and Familiar Letters. [In The Seventeenth-Century English Essay, Iowa City, 1926.]
[Criticism on individual character-writers, even on Earle, is to be found only in the modern edns of their works, and in collections of characters, rather than in separate articles.]

(d) Individual Books of Characters

Hall, Joseph. Characters of Vertues and Vices. 1608 (bis) (24 characters); 1621 (as Meditations and Vowes to p. 682, from then on as Characters of Vertues and Vices); rptd (in Hall's Works) 1625, 1628, 1647, 1808, 1837, 1863; tr. French, Paris, 1610 and 1619, Geneva, 1634; versified by Nahum Tate, 1691.
Overbury, Sir Thomas. A Wife Now the Widdow of Sir Thomas Overburye. Whereunto are added many witty Characters. 1614 (2nd edn of A Wife; adds 21 characters); 1614 (30 characters); 1614 (31 characters); 1615 (as New and Choise Characters. 73 characters, of which 32 are by John Webster. See G. Murphy, Bibliography); 1616 (as Sir Thomas Overburie His Wife, With New Elegies upon his (now knowne) untimely death. Whereunto are annexed new Newes and Characters. 72 characters); 1616 (73 characters); 1616 (81 characters); 1618; 1622 (82 characters); [Dublin], 1626; 1627; 1628; 1630; 1632; 1638; 1655; 1664; rptd 1756 (in The Miscellaneous Works in Verse and Prose); ed. E. F. Rimbault, 1856 (in The Miscellaneous Works in Prose and Verse; from 1616 edn); ed. W. J. Paylor, Oxford, 1936. [See also C. E. Gough, The Life and Characters of Sir Thomas Overbury, Norwich, 1909.

The 1622 edn contains A Dunce by John Donne, rptd in Paradoxes, Problems, Essayes, Characters by Dr. Donne, 1652, which contains also A Scot.]
Breton, Nicholas. Characters upon Essaies Morall and Divine. 1615. [18 characters.]
—— The Good and the Badde, or Descriptions of the Worthies and Unworthies of this Age. 1616 (50 characters); 1643 (as England's Selected Characters; 28 characters, 23 rptd, 5 new).
—— Fantasticks: Serving for a Perpetuall Prognostication. 1626 (36 characters). Selections: M. Stevenson. The Twelve Moneths. 1661 (12 characters from Fantasticks 1626 are here adapted); 1927 (The Twelve Moneths (ed. Brian Rhys, 12 characters rptd from Fantasticks, 1626)). [See also A. B. Grosart's edn of Breton's Works, 1879.]
Stephens, John. Satyrical Essayes Characters and Others. Or Accurate and quick Descriptions fitted to the life of their Subjects. 1615 (43 characters); 1615 (as Essayes and Characters Ironicall and Instructive; 50 characters. Re-issued 1631 as New Essayes and Characters).
[Mynshul, Geffray]. Certaine Characters and Essayes of Prison and Prisoners Compiled by Novus Homo A Prisoner in the King's Bench. 1618 (7 characters, 9 essays); 1618 (as Essayes and Characters of a Prison and Prisoners. Written by G. M.); 1638; rptd Edinburgh, 1821 (from 2nd edn).
P[arrot?], H[enry?] viii. Cures for the Itch. Characters. Epigrams. Epitaphs. By H. P. 1626. [13 characters.]
Earle, John. Micro-cosmographie. Or, A Peece of the World Discovered; in Essayes and Characters. Newly Composed for the Northerne parts of this Kingdome. 1628 (54 characters); 1628; 1628 (printed by Stansby for Allot); 1628 (not extant?); 1629 (77 characters); 1630; 1633 (78 characters); 1638; 1650 (3rd edn rptd); 1650 (74 characters, 1–54 as in previous edn, 55–74 from 5th edn); 1664 (78 characters); 1669; 1732; 1740; 1786 (74 characters, from 2nd 1650 edn); ed. P. Bliss, 1811 (78 characters); ed. Edward Arber, 1868; ed. H. Morley, 1889; ed. S. West, Cambridge, 1897; ed. S. T. Irwin, Bristol, 1897; ed. W. H. D. Rouse, 1899 (Temple Classics); Cambridge, 1903; 1904; ed. G. Murphy, Golden Cockerel Press, 1928; ed. H. Osborne, 1933. Selections: A True Description of the Pot-Companion Poet. Also A Character of the Swil-bole Cook, 1642; The Character of a Tavern, 1675; A Gallery of Portraits, Dublin, 1813 (32 portraits adapted from Earle); A Book of Characters: Selected from the writings of

Overbury, Earle and Butler, Edinburgh, 1865 (67 characters from Earle; re-issued as The Mirror of Character, Edinburgh, 1869). Tr. Latin, Leyden, 1654 (52 characters), 1662 and 1669; French, Louvain, 1671 (94 characters, 52 from Earle).

M., R. Micrologia. Characters, or Essayes, of Persons, Trades, and Places, offered to the City and Country. By R. M. 1629. [16 characters.]

Brathwaite, Richard. Whimzies: or, A New Cast of Characters, 1631; ed. J. O. Halliwell [-Phillipps], 1859. [24 characters plus 4 (the four have a section-title A Cater-Character).]

—— The Captive-Captain: or The Restrain'd Cavalier. 1665. [11 characters.]

[Other scattered characters, in A Strappado for the Divell, 1615 (3 characters); in Essaies upon the Five Senses, 1620 (1 character); in The English Gentleman, 1630 and in The English Gentlewoman, 1631 (1 character in each).]

L[enton], F[rancis]. Characterismi: or, Lentons Leasures. Expressed in Essayes and Characters, never before written on. 1631 (41 characters); 1632; 1636 (as Lentons Leisures Described, in divers Moderne Characters, by Francis Lenton, Her Majesties Poet); 1653 (as Lentons Characters: or Witty and ingenious Descriptions of Severall Professions, presented to all judicious Readers); 1663 (as Characters: or Wit and the World in their Proper Colours). [See L. S. Willis, Francis Lenton, Queen's Poet, Philadelphia, 1931.]

Saltonstall, Wye. Picturae Loquentes. Or, Pictures drawne forth in Characters. 1631 (26 characters); 1635 (38 characters).

Lupton, Donald. London and the Countrey Carbonadoed and Quartered into severall Characters. 1632 (36 characters); rptd Aungervyle Soc. Edinburgh, 1883.

—— The Quacking Mountebanck, or The Jesuite turn'd Quaker. 1655.

A Strange Metamorphosis of Man, transformed into a Wildernesse. Deciphered in Characters. 1634 (40 characters).

J[ordan], T[homas]. Pictures of Passions, Fancies, and Affections. Poetically Deciphered in variety of Characters. 1641. [19 characters.]

[Heywood, Thomas]. Machiavel as he lately appeared to his deare Sons the Moderne Projectors. 1641 (also issued as Machiavels Ghost; 1 character plus 9 short sketches of 'particular' projectors); 1642 (extract as Hogs Caracter of a Projector).

[Heywood's A True Discourse of the Two Prophets, 1636, and Troia Britannica, 1609, also contain 1 character each.]

Browne, Humphry. A Map of the Microcosme, or A Morall Description of Man. Newly compiled into Essayes. 1642. [18 characters.]

Fuller, Thomas. The Holy State. The Profane State. By Thomas Fuller. Cambridge, 1642 (48 characters); 1648; 1652; 1663; rptd 1840 and 1884 (9 characters and the Lives omitted). Selection: The Marvellous Wisdom and Quaint Conceits of Thomas Fuller, abridged by A. L. J. Gosset, 1893.

The Upright Protestant. 1643 (1 character); 1645 (as The Character of a believing Christian); 1648 (as A Believing Christian on M 4v–O 4 of The Remaines of the Right Honorable Francis Lord Verulam).

Cleveland, John. The Character of a London Diurnal. 1644 (*bis*); 1647 (3 edns).

—— The Character of a Moderate Intelligencer. With some Select Poems, by J. C. 1647.

—— The Character of a Country Committee-man, with the Eare-marke of a Sequestrator. 1649.

—— A Character of a Diurnal-Maker. By J. C. 1654 (*bis*).

[Cleveland's characters rptd: (1) Two characters, the London-Diurnal and the Country-Committee-man, in his Poems, 1651 (*bis*), 1653 (*bis*). (2) Three characters, the above two and the Diurnal-Maker in his Poems, 1654, 1657, 1659, 1661, 1662, 1665, 1669, and in Clievelandi Vindiciae: or, Clieveland's Genuine Poems &c, 1677. (3) The Puritan (verse) in J. Cleaveland Revived, 1659, 1660, 1662, 1668. (4) The 3 prose, and 1 verse characters in The Works of Mr John Cleveland, 1687.]

F[orde], T[homas]. The Times Anatomiz'd, in severall characters. 1647. [30 characters.]

A fresh Whip for all scandalous Lyers, or, A true description of the two eminent Pamphliteers, or squib-tellers of this Kingdome. 1647. [2 characters.]

Flecknoe, Richard. Miscellania, or, Poems of all sorts, with divers other Pieces. 1653. [4 characters.]

—— Enigmaticall Characters, All Taken to the Life, from severall Persons, Humours, & Dispositions. 1658 (69 characters; re-issued 1665 as Fifty-Five Enigmatical Characters); 1665 (as Sixty-nine Enigmatical Characters; 69 characters as in 1658); 1665 (as Richard Flecknoe's Ænigmatical Characters; 78 characters, 22 new).

—— Heroick Portraits with other Miscellany Pieces. 1660. [4 portraits, 15 characters.]

—— A Farrago of several Pieces. 1666. [6 characters.]

Flecknoe, Richard. A Collection of the choicest Epigrams and Characters of Richard Flecknoe. 1673 (63 characters, 19 new); 1677 (as Seventy eight Characters, of so many Vertuous and Vi-tious Persons; 63 characters, 2 being new).

(e) Controversial Characters

The True Character of an Untrue Bishop. 1641.

Lucifers Lacky, or the Devils new Creature. Being the true Character of a dissembling Brownist. 1641.

The Lively Character of the Malignant Partie. 1642.

A Puritane set forth in his Lively Colours: Or, K. James his description of a Puritan. Whereunto is added, The Round-heads Character, with the Character of an Holy Sister. 1642. [3 characters.]

T., G. Roger the Canterburian. Or the Character of a Prelaticall Man. 1642.

A Description of the Round-Head and Rattle Head [in verse]. 1642.

The Anatomy of the Separatists, alias, Brownists. 1642.

May, Thomas. The Character of a Right Malignant. 1644.

A Character of an Anti-Malignant. 1644.

A New Anatomie, or Character of a Christian or Round-head. 1645.

The True Character of Mercurius Aulicus. 1645.

The Character of an Oxford Incendiary. 1645.

Geree, John. The Character of an Old English Puritan, or Non-conformist. 1646 (bis); 1649; 1672 (re-issued 1673 as The Character of the Sober Non-Conformist).

The Character of an Agitator. 1647.

A Recommendation to Mercurius Morbicus. Together with a fair character upon his worth. 1647.

An Agitator Anotomiz'd, or The Character of an Agitator. 1648.

The Character of a Phanatique. 1660.

A Briefe Description or Character of the Religion and Manners of the Phanatiques in General. 1660.

The Character of a Presbyter, or Sʳ John Anatomized. 1660.

(f) The Chief Books, other than Character-Books, which contain Characters

M., W. The Man in the Moone, Telling Strange Fortunes, or The English Fortune-teller. 1609. [13 characters.] Adaptation: The Wandering-Jew, Telling Fortunes to Englishmen. 1640. [18 characters, 6 from The Man in the Moone.]

Adams, Thomas. Mystical Bedlam, or The World of Mad-Men. 1615. [2 characters.]
—— Diseases of the Soule. 1616. [18 characters.]
[These two books rptd in The Workes of Tho: Adams, 1629, 1861.]

H[eath], J[ohn]. The House of Correction: or, Certain Satyricall Epigrams. Together with a few Characters, called Par Pari. 1619. [9 characters.]

Habington, William. Castara. The second Edition. 1635 (3 characters); 1640 (4 characters); rptd Bristol, 1812 (from 1640 edn); ed. E. Arber, 1870.

North, Dudley (Baron North). A Forest of Varieties. 1645 (10 characters); 1659 (as A Forest Promiscuous of Several Seasons Productions).

Wortley, Francis. Characters and Elegies. 1646. [9 characters.]

Herbert, George. Herbert's Remains. 1652 (about 12 characters); 1671; 1675; 1701.

Gayton, E. Wil: Bagnal's Ghost. In his perambulation of the Prisons of London. 1655. [4 characters.]

[Sprigg, W.?] Philosophicall Essayes. Oxford, 1657. [5 characters.]

Osborn, Francis. A Miscellany of Sundry Essayes, Paradoxes and Characters. 1659. [4 characters.]

Ellis, Clement. The Gentile Sinner, or, England's Brave Gentleman: Characterized. Oxford, 1660 (25 characters); 1661; 1664; 1668; 1672; 1679; 1690.

G. M.

(2) Essays

[The following list, which is by no means complete, has not been restricted to the essay proper but also includes representative specimens of such kindred forms, as the maxim, the meditation, the 'vow' or 'resolve,' the paradox, etc. On the whole subject see E. N. S. Thompson, The Seventeenth-Century English Essay, Iowa City, 1926. First editions only have been recorded of works listed elsewhere in the Bibliography and cross-references have not been included for writers, like Brathwaite and Mynshul, who appear in other subdivisions of this section.]

D[aunce?], E[dward]. The Prayse of Nothing. 1585. [See R. M. Sargent, The Authorship of The Prayse of Nothing, Library, XII, 1931, which explodes the older attribution to Sir Edward Dyer.]

Churchyard, Thomas. A Sparke of Friendship and Warm Good-Will. 1588; rptd Harleian Misc. vol. II, 1809.

Segar, Sir William. The Booke of Honor and Armes. 1590.

Remedies against Discontentment, drawn into Severall Discourses. By Anonymus. 1596.

Bacon, Francis. Essayes. 1597. [For later edns, reprints and criticism see pp. 868–71 below.]

Tyro, T. Tyros Roving Megge. 1598.

Greenham, Richard. The Works. Ed. H. H[olland], 1599 (*bis*); 1601; 1605; 1612. [Especially the 'Grave Counsels' in pt 2.]

James I. Βασιλικὸν Δῶρον. Devided into three bookes. Edinburgh, 1599. [For reprints see p. 911 below.]

Cornwallis, Sir William. Essayes. 2 pts, 1600–1, 1606–10 ('Newly enlarged'); 1632–1 ('Newlie corrected by H. O.').

—— Discourses upon Seneca the Tragedian. 1601.

—— Essayes or rather Encomions. 1616.

—— Essays of Certaine Paradoxes. 1616 (anon.); 1617 (adds Essayes or rather Encomions).
[For Cornwallis see P. B. Whitt, RES. VIII, 1932, and R. E. Bennett, Cornwallis's Use of Montaigne, PMLA. XLVIII, 1933. Harvard Stud. XIII, 1931, pp. 219–40, prints 4 MS paradoxes by Cornwallis.]

Johnson, Robert. Essaies, or rather Imperfect Offers. 1601; 1607; 1613; 1638 (as Johnsons Essayes).

H[ynd?], J[ohn?]. The Mirrour of Worldly Fame. 1603; rptd Harleian Misc. vol. II, 1809.

Digges, Thomas and Dudley. Foure Paradoxes, or Politique Discourses. 1604.

Grymeston, Elizabeth. Miscelanea. Meditations. Memoratives. 1604; [1606?] (*bis*); [1608?] (*bis*); [1610?].

Hall, Joseph. Meditations and Vowes, Divine and Morall. 1605.

—— Contemplations upon the Principal Passages of the Holy Story. 8 vols. 1612–26.

—— Occasional Meditations. 1630. [For reprints see p. 697 above.]

Rich, Barnabe. Faultes, Faults, and nothing Else but Faultes. 1606.

Walkington, Thomas. The Opticke Glasse of Humors. 1607; Oxford [1631?]; 1639.

Breton, Nicholas. Divine Considerations of the Soule. 1608.

—— Characters upon Essaies Morall and Divine. 1615.

T[uvil], D[aniel]. Essaies Politicke and Morall. 1608.

—— Essayes, Morall and Theologicall. 1609; 1629 (as Vade Mecum).

—— The Dove and the Serpent. 1614.

—— Asylum Veneris, or a Sanctuary for Ladies. 1616.

Stafford, Anthony. Meditations and Resolutions, Moral, Divine, Politicall. 1612.

T[uke], T[homas]. New Essayes: Meditations and Vowes. 1614.

Stephens, John. Satyrical Essayes Characters and Others. 1615.

R[ous], F[rancis]. Meditations of Instruction, of Exhortation, of Reproofe. 1616.

The Rich Cabinet, furnished with varietie of excellent discriptions, exquisite charracters, witty discourses, and delightful histories, disgested alphabetically into common places. 1616.

[Mynshul, Geffray.] Certaine Characters and Essayes of Prison and Prisoners. 1618.

Brathwaite, Richard. Essaies upon the Five Senses. 1620.

[Brydges, Grey (Baron Chandos).] Horae Subsecivae. Observations and Discourses. 1620.

Mason, William. A Handful of Essaies. 1621.

Felltham, Owen. Resolves Divine, Morall, Politicall. [1623?]; 1628. Resolves, a Second Centurie. 1628. Resolves, a Duple Century. 1628–9; 1631; 1634; 1635; 1636; 1647; ed. J. Cumming, 1806; ed. O. Smeaton, 1904 (Temple Classics). [For Feltham see Retrospective Rev. x, 1824, and M. D. Cornu, University of Washington Digests of Theses (1914–31), Seattle, 1931, pp. 139–42.]

Donne, John. Devotions upon Emergent Occasions. 1624.

—— Essayes in Divinity, interwoven with meditations and prayers. 1651.

—— Paradoxes, problems, essays, characters, with Ignatius his Conclave. 1652. [For rpts and criticism see pp. 441–4 above.]

Robinson, John. Observations Divine and Morall. 1625 (re-issued 1628 as New Essayes); 1629; 1638 (as Essayes).

Henshaw, Joseph. Horae Succisivae; or, Spare-houres of Meditations. 1631 (2nd edn); 1632; 1635; 1640.

Culverwel, Ezekiel. Time well Spent in Sacred Meditations, Divine Observations, Heavenly Exhortations. 1634; 1635.

Warwick, Arthur. Spare-Minutes; or, Re-solved Meditations. 1634 (2nd edn, *bis*); 1635 (4th edn); 1636; 1637; 1640; ed. W. J. Loftie, 1881.

Austin, William. Devotionis Augustinianae Flamma, or, Certaine Devout, Godly, and Learned Meditations. 1635; 1637.

Person, David. Varieties, or a Surveigh of rare and excelent Matters. 1635.

Peacham, Henry. The Truth of our Times. Revealed out of one Mans Experience by Way of Essay. 1638.

—— The Valley of Varietie: or, Discourse fitting for the Times. 1638.

Quarles, Francis. Enchyridion. 1640.
—— Judgement and Mercy for afflicted Soules. 1646. [For rpts see pp. 450–1 above.]
Jonson, Ben. Timber: or, Discoveries. [In The Works of Benjamin Jonson, vol. II, 1641. For rpts and criticism see pp. 613–9 above.]
Fuller, Thomas. The Holy State. The Profane State. Cambridge, 1642.
—— Good Thoughts in Bad Times. Exeter, 1645.
—— Good Thoughts in Worse Times. 1647.
—— Mixt Contemplations in Better Times. 1660.
[See pp. 835–6 below for rpts and criticism.]
Ralegh, Sir Walter. The Prince or Maxims of State. 1642. [For rpts see p. 827 below.]
Palmer, Herbert. Memorials of Godlinesse and Christianitie. 3 pts, 1644–5; 1655 (5th edn); 1657 (7th edn); 1670 (10th edn); ed. A. B. Grosart, Edinburgh, 1865. [Pt ii also rptd in Bacon's Remaines, 1648; for a refutation of Bacon's authorship see Grosart's edn.]
Howell, James. Epistolae Ho-Elianae. Familiar Letters Domestic and Forren. 4 vols. 1645–55. [For rpts see p. 832 below.]
[North, Dudley (Baron North).] A Forest of Varieties. 1645. [Poems, essays, letters and characters.]
Hall, John (1627–1656). Horae Vacivae, or Essays. Some Occasional Considerations. 1646.
—— Paradoxes by J. de la Salle. 1653 (reissued 1656 as Paradoxes by John Hall).
[For Hall and his writings see P. S. Havens, A Tract long attributed to Milton, Huntington Lib. Bulletin, Nov. 1934. For the poems see p. 476 above.]
Montagu, Walter. Miscellanea Spiritualia: or Devout Essaies. 1648; 1654.
F[orde], T[homas]. Lusus Fortunae: The Play of Fortune: continually Acted by the severall Creatures on the Stage of the World. 1649.
—— Virtus Rediviva, a Panegyrick on our late King Charles the I., attended with severall other Pieces from the same Pen. 1661. [Contains, with separate pagination but continuous signatures, the following pieces, each dated 1660 and 'By Tho. Forde': (1) Virtus Rediviva; (2) A Theatre of Wits, Ancient and Modern. Represented in a Collection of Apothegmes; (3) Faenestra in Pectore. Or, Familiar Letters; (4) Love's Labyrinth; or, The Royal Shepherdess: a Tragi-comedie; (5) Fragmenta Poetica: or, Poetical Diversions. The five pieces were also issued separately, and the whole collection is sometimes found with the following alternative title: A Theatre of Wits,

Ancient and Modern. Attended with severall other ingenious Pieces from the same Pen.]
[For Forde see J. Q. Adams, Thomas Forde's Love's Labyrinth, in J. M. Hart Studies, New York, 1910.]
Cottoni posthuma. 1651. [Sir Robert Bruce Cotton's remains, edited by James Howell, and containing essays ascribed by Howell (almost certainly wrongly) to Sir Philip Sidney and Sir Francis Walsingham.]
Herbert, Sir Percy. Certaine Conceptions or Considerations upon the strange change of Peoples dispositions and actions in these latter times. 1652.
Harflete, Henry. A Banquet of Essayes, Fetcht out of Famous Owens Confectionary. 1653. [Essays suggested by the Latin epigrams of John Owen.]
[Master, William.] Λόγοι Εὔκαιροι, Essayes and Observations Theologicall & Morall. 1653.
S., S. Paradoxes, or Encomions in the praise of being Lowsey, Treachery, Blindnesse. The Emperor Nero. Madnesse. 1653.
Whitlock, Richard. ΖΩΟΤΟΜΙ´Α, or, Observations on the Present Manners of the English. 1654; 1664. [See G. Williamson, PQ. xv, 1936.]
Wotton, Sir Henry. Aphorisms of Education. [In Reliquiae Wottonianae, 1654 (2nd edn). For rpts, etc. see p. 426 above.]
C[ulpeper], T[homas]. Morall Discourses and Essays upon Severall Select Subjects. 1655.
The Surfeit. To ABC. 1656.
[Sprigg, William.] Philosophicall Essayes with Brief Adviso's. Oxford, 1657.
Two Essays of Love and Marriage. 1657.
H[eath], R[obert]. Paradoxical Assertions and Philosophical Problems. 1659. [For Heath's Clarastella see p. 476 above.]
Osborn, Francis. A Miscellany of Sundry Essayes, Paradoxes and Problematical Discourses, Letters and Characters. 1659.
T., H. Meditations Divine and Morall. 1659.

IV. PROSE FICTION

History and Criticism. Collections of Reprints. Original Works of Fiction. Translations of Works of Known Authorship. Translations of Anonymous Works.

A. HISTORY AND CRITICISM

Warton, Thomas. The History of English Poetry. 4 vols. 1774–81; rev. W. C. Hazlitt, 4 vols. 1871. [Prefatory dissertation on the Origin of Romantic Fiction in Europe.]
Dunlop, J. C. The History of Fiction. 3 vols. Edinburgh, 1814; rev. J. H. Wilson, 2 vols. 1888.

Murray, J. A. The Influence of Italian on English Literature during the XVIth and XVIIth Centuries. Cambridge, 1886.

Ashton, J. Romances of Chivalry. 1887.

Jusserand, J. J. Le Roman au Temps de Shakespeare. Paris, 1887; tr. Eng. 1890, 1899 ('enlarged by the author').

Morley, H. English Writers. 11 vols. 1887–95. [Vol. x.]

Koeppel, E. Studien zur Geschichte der italienischen Novelle in der englischen Litteratur des sechzehnten Jahrhunderts. QF. LXX, 1892.

Rennert, H. A. Spanish Pastoral Romance. Baltimore, 1892.

Bahlsen, L. Spanische Quellen der englischen Litteratur besonders Englands zu Shakespeares Zeit. Zeitschrift für vergleichende Litteraturgeschichte, VI, 1893.

Raleigh, Sir W. The English Novel. 1894; 1929 (rev. edn).

Courthope, W. J. A History of English Poetry. 6 vols. 1895–1910. [Vol. II.]

Warren, F. M. History of the Novel previous to the Seventeenth Century. New York, 1895.

Chandler, F. W. Romances of Roguery. Pt 1 (Picaresque Novel in Spain), New York, 1899. [With bibliography.]

—— The Literature of Roguery. 2 vols. Boston, 1907. [With bibliography.]

Cross, W. L. The Development of the English Novel. New York, 1899. [With bibliography.]

Underhill, J. G. Spanish Literature in the England of the Tudors. New York, 1899.

Stoddard, F. H. The Evolution of the English Novel. New York, 1900.

Wendelstein, L. Zur Vorgeschichte des Euphuismus. Halle, 1901.

Reynier, G. Le Roman sentimental avant L'Astrée. Paris, 1908.

—— Les Origines du Roman réaliste. Paris, 1912.

Upham, A. H. The French Influence in English Literature from Elizabeth to the Restoration. New York, 1908.

Canby, H. S. The Short Story in English. New York, 1909. [Ch. vi, The Short Story in the Renaissance; ch. vii, The Elizabethan Novella. With bibliography.]

Morgan, C. E. The Rise of the Novel of Manners: a Study of English Prose Fiction between 1600 and 1740. New York, 1911.

Esdaile, A. A List of English Tales and Prose Romances printed before 1740. Bibliog. Soc. 1912.

Schulz, E. Die englischen Schwankbücher bis herab zu 'Dobson's Drie Bobs' (1607). Berlin, 1912.

Tieje, A. J. The Expressed Aim of the Long Prose Fiction from 1579 to 1740. JEGP. XI, 1912.

—— The Critical Heritage of Fiction in 1579. E. Studien, XLVII, 1913.

—— The Theory of Characterization in Prose Fiction prior to 1740. Minneapolis, 1916.

Wolff, S. L. The Greek Romances in Elizabethan Prose Fiction. New York, 1912. [With bibliography.]

Long, P. W. From Troilus to Euphues. [In Kittredge Anniversary Papers, Boston, 1913.]

Prys, J. Der Staatsroman des 16. und 17. Jahrhunderts. Würzburg, 1913.

Saintsbury, G. The English Novel. 1913.

Scott, M. A. Elizabethan Translations from the Italian. New York, 1916.

Savage, H. J. Italian Influence in English Fiction. PMLA. XXXII, 1917.

Thomas, H. Spanish and Portuguese Romances of Chivalry. Cambridge, 1920. [With bibliography.]

Prothero, R. E. (Baron Ernle). The Light Reading of our Ancestors. 1927.

Baker, E. A. The History of the English Novel. Vol. II (The Elizabethan Age and After), 1929. [With select bibliography.]

Hoops, R. Der Begriff 'Romance' in der mittelenglischen und frühneuenglischen Literatur. Heidelberg, 1929.

Habel, U. Die Nachwirkung des picaresken Romans in England, von Nash bis Fielding. Breslau, 1930.

Haviland, T. P. The Roman de Longue Haleine on English Soil. Philadelphia, 1931. [With bibliography.]

Brinkley, R. F. Arthurian Legend in the Seventeenth Century. Baltimore, 1932.

Darton, F. J. H. Children's Books in England. Cambridge, 1932.

Leavis, Q. D. Fiction and the Reading Public. 1932.

Lovett, R. M. and Hughes, H. S. The History of the Novel in England. Boston, 1932.

Rolfe, F. On the Bibliography of Seventeenth-Century Prose Fiction. PMLA. XLIX, 1934.

B. COLLECTIONS OF REPRINTS

Early English Prose Romances. Ed. W. J. Thoms, 3 vols. 1827–8, 1858 (rev.); [1907] (omitting Thoms's introductions but adding 4 additional pieces and essay by H. Morley).

Shakespeare's Library. A Collection of the Romances, Novels, Poems and Histories, used by Shakespeare as the Foundation of his Dramas. Ed. J. P. Collier, 2 vols. [1843], 1850; rev. W. C. Hazlitt, 6 vols. 1875.

Shakespeare's Jest-Books. Ed. W. C. Hazlitt, 3 vols. 1864.

Fairy Tales, Legends, and Romances illustrating Shakespeare and Other Early English Writers. Ed. W. C. Hazlitt, 1875.

Spanish Short Stories of the Sixteenth Century in Contemporary Translation. Ed. J. B. Trend, 1928. (World's Classics.)

Shorter Novels. Vol. I (Elizabethan and Jacobean). Ed. G. Saintsbury, 1929. (Everyman's Lib.)

Elizabethan Tales. Ed. E. J. O'Brien, 1936.

C. ORIGINAL WORKS OF FICTION

[The following list has been restricted to works originally written in English first printed between 1500 and 1660. For Latin romances by English writers pp. 859–61 of the section Scholars and Scholarship below should be referred to, though English translations of such works will be found immediately below. The expression 'Prose Fiction' has deliberately been interpreted in the widest possible sense, but no attempt has been made to duplicate the section on Jest-Books, pp. 714–5 above, and other border-line types may have been inadvertently omitted. With these reservations both this list and the following list of Translations are intended to be complete. Both sections are heavily indebted to A. Esdaile, A List of English Tales and Prose Romances printed before 1740, Bibliog. Soc. 1912.]

The deceyte of Women, to the instruction and ensample of all men, newly corrected. [1547]; [1561?]; ed. F. Brie, Archiv, CLVI, 1929.

A lyttle treatyse called the Image of Idlenesse, conteynynge certayne matters moved betwene Walter Wedlocke and Bawdin Bacheler. [1559]; 1574 ('corrected and augmented').

Baldwin, William. A Marvellous Hystory intituled Beware The Cat. 1561; 1570; 1584; 1652.

Painter, William. The Palace of Pleasure Beautified, adorned and well furnished, with Pleasaunt Histories and excellent Novelles, selected out of divers good and commendable authors. 2 vols. 1566–7; 2 vols. 1569; 2 vols. 1575 ('Eftsones perused corrected and augmented'); ed. J. Jacobs, 3 vols. 1890; ed. H. Miles, 4 vols. 1930.

Tilney, Edmund. A briefe and pleasant discourse of duties in Mariage, called the Flower of Friendshippe. 1568 (bis); 1571; 1577.

Edwards, Richard. [A collection of short comic stories in prose.] 1570 (no copy extant); [1620–30?] (fragment).

[Gascoigne, George.] A pleasant discourse of the adventures of master F. J. [In A Hundreth sundrie Flowers, 1573, ed. B. M. Ward, 1926. Rev. and transferred to an Italian setting in A Hundreth sundrie Flowres, 1575. See L. Bradner, The First English Novel, PMLA. XLV, 1930, and p. 414 above.]

—— The Pleasant tale of Hemetes the Hermite. [First ptd as by Abraham Fleming appended to Fleming's A Paradox Proving Baldnesse better than bushie haire, 1579 (from Synesius). For later edns see p. 415 above.]

Rich, Barnabe. A Right Exelent and pleasant Dialogue, betwene Mercury and an English Souldier: Bewtified with sundry worthy Histories. 1574.

—— Riche his Farewell to Militarie profession: conteinyng verie pleasant discourses fit for a peaceable tyme. 1581; 1606 ('Newly augmented'); ed. J. P. Collier, Shakespeare Soc. 1846. [See D. T. Starnes, Barnabe Rich's Sappho Duke of Mantona: a Study in Elizabethan Story-making, Stud. Phil. XXX, 1933.]

—— The straunge and wonderfull adventures of Don Simonides, a gentilman Spaniarde. 1581.

—— The Second Tome of the Travailes and adventures of Don Simonides, enterlaced with varietie of Historie. 1584.

—— The Adventures of Brusanus, Prince of Hungaria. 1592.

Pettie, George. A Petite Pallace of Pettie his pleasure: Contayning many pretie Hystories, by him set foorth in comely colours and most delightfully discoursed. [1576]; [1578?]; [1580?]; 1608; 1613; ed. Sir I. Gollancz, 2 vols. 1908; ed. H. Miles, 4 vols. 1930. [For Pettie's sources see D. Bush, JEGP. XXIII, 1924, XXVII, 1928.]

Whetstone, George. The Rocke of Regard, being all the invention, collection and translation of George Whetstone Gent. 1576. [Mainly, but not wholly, verse.]

—— An Heptameron of Civill Discourses. Containing: The Christmasse Exercise of sundrie Gentlemen and Gentlewomen. 1582; 1593 (as Aurelia).

Grange, John. The Golden Aphroditis [with] certaine Metres upon sundry poyntes, as also divers Pamphlets in prose. 1577; rptd photo. facs. New York, 1936. [See H. E. Rollins, Harvard Stud. XVI, 1934, pp. 177–98.]

Lyly, John. Euphues. The Anatomy of Wit. [1578.]

—— Euphues and his England. 1580. [For rpts and criticism see pp. 524–5 above.]

C., H. The Forrest of Fancy. Wherein is conteined very prety Apothegmes and pleasaunt histories, both in meeter and prose. 1579. [See Sir S. E. Brydges, Restituta, vol. III, 1816.]

Gosson, Stephen. The Ephemerides of Phialo. 1579; 1586.

Gifford, Humphrey. A Posie of Gilloflowers. 1580. [Includes short stories. For rpts see p. 436 above.]

Munday, Anthony. Zelauto. The Fountaine of Fame. Erected in an Orcharde of Amorous Adventures. 1580. [See also p. 537 above.]

Saker, Austen. Narbonus. The Laberynth of Libertie. 2 vols. 1580.

The Life and Pranks of Long Meg of Westminster. 1582; 1620; 1635; 1636; rptd C. Hindley (The Old Book Collector's Miscellany, vol. II, 1872).

Greene, Robert. Mamillia. A Mirrour or looking-glasse for the Ladies of Englande. 1583.

—— Arbasto, The Anatomie of Fortune. 1584.

—— Gwydonius. The Carde of Fancie. 1584.

—— Morando the Tritameron of Love. 1584 (pt 1 only); 2 pts, 1587.

—— The Myrrour of Modestie. By R. G. 1584.

—— Planetomachia. 1585.

—— Euphues his Censure to Philautus. 1587.

—— Penelopes Web. 1587.

—— Pandosto. The Triumph of Time [running title: The Historie of Dorastus and Fawnia]. 1588.

—— Perimedes the Blacke-Smith. 1588.

—— Ciceronis Amor. Tullies Love. 1589.

—— The Spanish Masquerado. 1589.

—— Menaphon Camilla's alarum to slumbering Euphues. 1589.

—— The Black Bookes Messenger. Laying Open the Life and Death of Ned Browne by R. G. 1592.

—— Philomela. The Lady Fitzwaters Nightingale. 1592.

—— The second part of the triumph of Pallas. 1593.

—— Greene's Orpharion. Wherin is discovered a musicale concorde of pleasant Histories. 1599.

—— Alcida Greenes Metamorphosis. 1617. [S.R. 1588.]

[For rpts and criticism see pp. 529–30 above.]

Melbancke, Brian. Philotimus. The Warre betwixt Nature and Fortune. 1583. [See H. E. Rollins, Stud. Phil. Ex. Ser. I, 1929, pp. 40–57, and M. P. Tilley, Stud. Phil. XXVII, 1930, pp. 186–214.]

Averell, William. A Dyall for dainty Darlings. 1584; 1590 (expanded as Foure notable Histories).

Lodge, Thomas. An Alarum against Usurers. Heereunto are annexed the delectable historie of Forbonius and Prisceria. 1584.

—— Rosalynde. Euphues golden legacie. 1590.

—— The Famous, true and historicall Life of Robert second Duke of Normandy. By T. L. G. 1591.

—— Euphues Shadow, the Battaile of the Sences. 1592.

—— The Life and Death of William Long beard, with manye other histories. 1593.

—— A Margarite of America. 1596.

[For rpts, etc. see pp. 527–9 above.]

Warner, William. Pan his Syrinx, or Pipe, Compact of seven Reedes: including in one, seven Tragical and Comicall Arguments. [1584]; 1597 ('Newly perused and amended').

C., W. The Adventures of Ladie Egeria. [1585?]

The Cobler of Caunterburie, Or An Invective against Tarltons Newes out of Purgatorie. 1590; 1608; 1614; 1630 (as The Tincker of Turvey).

R[obarts], H[enry]. A Defiance to Fortune. Proclaimed by Andrugio, noble Duke of Saxony. Whereunto is adjoyned the honorable Warres of Galastino, Duke of Millaine. 1590.

—— Phaeander, The Mayden Knight. 1595; 1617 (4th edn, enlarged).

—— Honours Conquest. Wherin is conteined the famous Hystorie of Edward of Lancaster. With the famous victories performed by the knight, of the unconquered Castel. 1598.

—— Haigh for Devonshire. A pleasant Discourse of sixe gallant Marchants of Devonshire. 1600.

[See L. B. Wright, Henry Robarts: Patriotic Propagandist and Novelist, Stud. Phil. XXIX, 1932.]

Sidney, Sir Philip. The Countesse of Pembrokes Arcadia. 1590. [For rpts and critical studies see pp. 419–20 above.]

M., Jo. Philippes Venus. Wherein is pleasantly discoursed Sundrye fine and wittie arguments of the Gods and Goddesses for the expelling of wanton Venus. 1591.

Fraunce, Abraham. The third part of the Countesse of Pembrokes Yvychurch: entituled, Amintas Dale. 1592.

Johnson, Richard. The nine Worthies of London. 1592.

—— The Most famous History of the Seaven Champions of Christendome. 2 pts, 1596–7; 2 vols. 1608; 2 vols. [1616] ('Whereunto is added by the first Author, the true manner of their deaths'); 1623; 2 vols. [1626], [1639].

Johnson, Richard. The most pleasant History of Tom a Lincolne, That renowned Souldier, the Red-Rose Knight. 1631 (6th edn); 1635; 1655; ed. W. J. Thoms (Early English Prose Romances, vol. II, 1828, etc.). [Stationers' Register, 1599, and pt 2, 1607.]
—— The Pleasant Conceites of Old Hobson the merry Londoner. 1607; 1634; 1640.
—— The History of Tom Thumbe, the Little. 1621.
C[hettle], H[enry]. Kind Harts Dreame. [1593.]
—— Piers Plainnes seaven yeres Prentiship. 1595.
[For rpts, etc. see p. 534 above.]
D[ickenson], J[ohn]. Arisbas, Euphues amidst his slumbers: Or Cupids Journey to Hell. 1594.
—— Greene in Conceipt. New raised from his grave to write the Tragique Historie of faire Valeria of London.
[For rpts see p. 436 above.] 1598.
Nashe, Thomas. The Unfortunate Traveller. Or, The life of Jacke Wilton. 1594; 1594 ('Newly corrected and augmented'). [See also pp. 533–4 above.]
Forde, Emanuel. The Most Pleasant Historie of Ornatus and Artesia. [1595?]; 1607; 1619; 1634; 1650; ed. P. Henderson, 1930.
—— Parismus, The Renoumed Prince of Bohemia. 2 vols. 1598–9 (vol. II, Parismenos); 2 vols. 1608–9 (vol. II, 3rd edn 'amended'); 2 vols. 1615, 1630, 1636, 1649; 1657. [Extracts in The Birth of Romance, ed. R. B. Johnson, 1928.]
—— The Famous Historie of Montelyon. 1633; 1663; 1668; 1671; 1673; 1677, etc.
G[oodwin], T[homas] P[ope]. The Moste Pleasaunt Historye of Blanchardine Sonne to the King of Friz; & the faire Lady Eglantine. 2 vols. 1595; 1597.
Parry, Robert. Moderatus, The most delectable and famous Historie of the Blacke Knight. 1595.
Beard, Thomas. The Theatre of Gods Judgements: Or, A Collection of Histories out of Sacred, Ecclesiasticall and prophane Authors. 1597; 1612; 1631 (enlarged); 1648.
Breton, Nicholas. The Miseries of Mavillia. [In The Wil of Wit, 1597.]
—— The Strange Fortunes of Two Excellent Princes. 1600.
—— Grimellos Fortunes. 1604.
[For rpts, etc. see pp. 415–7 above.]
Middleton, Christopher. The Famous Historie of Chinon of England. With the worthy Atchievement of Sir Lancelot du Lake, and Sir Tristram du Lions. 1597; ed. W. E. Mead, EETS. 1925.

Deloney, Thomas. The Gentle Craft. A most merry and pleasant Historie. 2 pts, 1598 (no perfect copy extant); 1627 (pt 1 only, as A Discourse containing many matters of delight; 1635; 1639 (pt 2, 'Newly corrected and augmented'); 1648 (pt 1, 'Set forth with pictures'); 1652; ed. A. F. Lange, Berlin, 1903; ed. W. H. D. Rouse, 1926.
—— The Pleasant History of John Winchcomb, in his younger yeares called Jack of Newberie. 1619 (8th edn); 1626 (10th edn); 1630; 1633; 1637; ed. J. O. Halliwell [-Phillipps], 1859; ed. W. H. D. Rouse, 1920; ed. G. Saintsbury (in Shorter Novels, vol. I, 1929, Everyman's Lib.). [S.R. 1597.]
—— Thomas of Reading. Or, The sixe worthy yeomen of the West. 1612 (4th edn); 1623; 1632; 1636; ed. W. J. Thoms (in Early English Prose Romances, vol. I, 1827, etc.); ed. W. H. D. Rouse, 1920; ed. G. Saintsbury (in Shorter Novels, vol. I, 1929, Everyman's Lib.).
—— The Works of Thomas Deloney. Ed. F. O. Mann, Oxford, 1912.
[For biography and criticism see R. Sievers, Thomas Deloney, eine Studie über Balladen-Literatur der Shakspere-Zeit, Berlin, 1904, and A. Chevalley, Thomas Deloney; le Roman des Métiers au Temps de Shakespeare, Paris, 1926. See also H. E. Rollins, PMLA. L, 1935, pp. 679–86.]
C[hambers], R[obert]. Palestina. Florence (really London?), 1600.
The Heroicall Adventures of the Knight of the Sea. Comprised in the Historie of Prince Oceander. 1600.
Dekker, Thomas. The Wonderfull Yeare. [1603?]
—— A Knights Conjuring. [1607.]
[For rpts etc. see pp. 619–22 above.]
H[ynd], J[ohn]. The most excellent Historie of Lysimachus and Varrona, daughter to Syllanus, Duke of Hypatia, in Thessalia. 1604.
—— Eliosto Libidinoso: Described in two Bookes Wherein their imminent dangers are declared who [guide] their life by Affection. 1606.
Jacke of Dover. His Quest of Inquirie, or His privy search for the veriest Foole in England. 1604; 1608; 1615 (as Jacke of Dovers merry tales).
The First and Second part of the History of the famous Euordanus Prince of Denmark. With the strange Adventures of Iago Prince of Saxonie: And of both theyr severall fortunes in Love. 1605.
Dobson, George. Dobson's Drie Bobbes: Sonne and Heire to Skoggin. 1607.
Markham, Gervase. The English Arcadia, Alluding his beginning from Sir Philip Sydnes ending. 1607.

Markham, Gervase. The Second and Last Part of the First Booke of the English Arcadia. 1613.

Wilkins, George. The Painfull Adventures of Pericles Prince of Tyre. Being the true History of the Play of Pericles, as it was lately presented. 1608; ed. T. Mommsen, Oldenburg, 1857.

The Famous & renowned History of Morindos a King of Spaine; Who maryed with Miracola a Spanish Witch. 1609.

Anton, Robert. Moriomachia. 1613; ed. G. Becker, Archiv, cxxII, 1909.

V[alens], W. The Honourable Prentice: Or, This Taylor is a man. Shewed in the life and death of Sir John Hawkewood. 1615 (re-issued 1616).

Gainsford, Thomas. The Historie of Trebizond. In foure Bookes. 1616.

Westward for Smelts. Or, The Water-mans Fare of mad-merry Western wenches, whose Tales will much content you. Written by Kinde Kit of Kingstone. 1620.

Reynolds, John. The Triumphs of Gods Revenge, against the crying, and execrable Sinne of Murther: In thirty severall Tragicall Histories. 3 vols. 1621–3; 1629 (only The First Booke); 6 vols. 1635–4; 1639 (re-issued 1640); 1657–6.

—— The Flower of Fidelitie. Displaying In a Continuate Historie, The various Adventures of Three Foraign Princes. 1650; 1660. [Much verse interspersed.]

Wroth, Lady Mary. The Countesse of Montgomeries Urania. 1621.

B[eling], R[ichard]. A Sixth Booke to the Countesse of Pembrokes Arcadia. Dublin, 1624. [For rpts see under Sidney, p. 419 above.]

Bacon, Francis (Viscount St Albans). The New Atlantis. [In Sylva Sylvarum, 1626. See also p. 869 below.]

Kennedy, John. The Historie of Calanthrop and Lucilla. Edinburgh, 1626; 1631.

B[ernard], R[ichard]. The Isle of Man: Or, The Legall Proceeding in Man-shire against Sinne. 1627 (4th edn, 'much enlarged'); 1628; 1630 (7th edn); 1632; 1635 (10th edn); 1640; 1648; 1659. [See M. Müller, The Isle of Man (1626). Eine literargeschichtliche Untersuchung, Markneukirchen, 1933.]

The Famous Historie of Fryer Bacon. 1627; 1629; [1631]; 1640; 1661; 1666; 1679, etc.; ed. W. G. Thoms (in Early English Prose Romances, vol. I, 1827, etc.).

Brewer, Thomas. The Life and Death of the merry Devill of Edmonton. 1631.

The Pinder of Wakefield: Being the merry History of George a Greene. 1632; 1633; ed. W. J. Thoms (Early English Prose Romances, vol. II, 18 etc.).

Goodman, Nicholas. Hollands Leaguer: or an Historical Discourse of the Life and Actions of Dona Britanica Hollandia. 1632.

The Famous History of George Lord Fauconbridge Bastard son of Richard Cordelion King of England. 1635.

Bettie, W. The Historie of Titana and Theseus. 1636.

Crofts, Robert. The Lover: or, Nuptiall Love. 1638.

Godwin, Francis. The Man in the Moone: or a discourse of a Voyage thither. 1638; 1657.

Rivers, George. The Heroinae: or The lives of Arria, Paulina, Lucrecia, Dido, Theutilla, Cypriana, Arctaphila. 1639.

S., J. Clidamas, or the Sicilian Tale. 1639.

Brathwaite, Richard. Art asleepe Husband? 1640.

—— The Penitent Pilgrim. 1641. [See also p. 712 above.]

H[owell], J[ames]. Δενδρολογια. Dodona's Grove, or, The Vocall Forest. 1640. [Second Part, 1650. See also p. 832 below.]

The Pleasant History of Cawwood the Rooke, or the Assembly of Birds. 1640; 1656.

Johnson, John. The Academy of Love describing the folly of younge men, & the fallacy of women. 1641.

C., W. The First Part Of The Renowned Historie of Fragosa King of Aragon. 2 vols. 1646; 1656.

Baron, Robert. ΕΡΟΤΟΠΑΙΓΝΙΟΝ Or the Cyprian Academy. 1647 (re-issued 1648).

—— An Apologie for Paris. For rejecting of Juno, and Pallas, and presenting of Ate's golden ball to Venus. 1649.

Nevile, Henry. The Parliament of Ladies. Or Divers remarkable passages of Ladies in Spring-Garden, in Parliament Assembled. 1647 (bis).

—— The Ladies, a Second Time, Assembled in Parliament. 1647.

—— Newes from the New Exchange, or, the Commonwealth of Ladies. 1650.

Bayly, Thomas. Herba Parietis: or, The Wall-Flower, As it grew out of the Prison of London, called Newgate. Being a History which is partly True, Partly Romantick, Morally Divine. 1650.

Sheppard, Samuel. The Loves of Amandus and Sophronia. Inriched with Odes and Sonnets. 1650.

Beware the Beare. The strange but pleasing History of Balbulo and Rosina. 1650.

The Famous History of Stout Stukley: or His valiant Life and Death. [c. 1650.]

The Pleasant History of King Henry the Eighth and the Abbot of Reading. [c. 1650.]

Charleton, Walter. The Ephesian and Cimmerian Matrons: two remarkable Examples of the Power of Love and Wit. [1651?] 1659 (only The Ephesian Matron).

F[idge], G[eorge]. Hind's Ramble, or, The Description of his manner and course of life. 1651.

—— The English Gusman; or, the History of that Unparallel'd Thief James Hind. 1652. [Abridged as Wit for Money, c. 1652.]

W[eamys], A[nne]. A Continuation of Sir Philip Sydney's Arcadia. 1651.

Cloria and Narcissus. A Delightfull and New Romance, Imbellished with divers Politicall Notions. 2 vols. 1653.

Boyle, Roger (Earl of Orrery). Parthenissa: A Romance. In Six Tomes. 4 vols. Waterford, 1654–5 (re-issued 1655); 1654 (pt 1 only). The Last Part. The Fifth Tome. 1656. The Last Part. The Sixth Tome. 1669. Complete. 1676.

Triana, Or a Threefold Romanza of Mariana Paduana Sabina. 1654 (re-issued 1664 and erroneously ascribed to Thomas Fuller).

Crouch, H[umphrey]. A New and Pleasant History of unfortunate Hodg of the South. 1655.

P[rice], L[aurence]. The Witch of the Woodlands: Or, The Coblers New Translation. 1655.

Theophania: or severall Modern Histories Represented by way of Romance: and Politickly Discours'd upon, by an English Person of Quality. 1655.

Cavendish, Margaret (Duchess of Newcastle). Natures Pictures Drawn by Fancies Pencil to the Life. 1656. [Stories in prose and verse.]

H., T. The Famous and Remarkable History of Sir Richard Whittington. 1656.

Harrington, James. The Common-Wealth of Oceana. 1656; 1658; ed. H. Morley, 1887; ed. S. B. Liljegren, Lund, 1924. [See also p. 878 below.]

Holland, Samuel. Don Zara Del Fogo: A Mock-Romance. 1656.

The Most Pleasant History of Bovinian. Being An Addition to [Deloney's] Crispine and Crispianus. 1656.

M., T. The Life of a Satyrical Puppy called Nim. Who worrieth all those Satyrists he knowes, and barkes at the rest. 1657. [Sometimes, but almost certainly incorrectly, attrib. to Thomas May. Listed in Humphrey Moseley's (the publisher's) catalogue, 1656, as by W. D.]

Panthalia: or the Royal Romance. By Castalio Pomerano. 1659. [Often attrib. either to Brathwaite or Howell, but the portrait found in some copies is not theirs.]

D. TRANSLATIONS INTO ENGLISH

[The sections Literary Relations with the Continent (pp. 325–45 above) and Translations into English (pp. 799–822 below) will be found to supplement the following lists.]

(a) Translations of Works of Known Authorship

ACHILLES TATIUS
[See p. 799 below.]

MATEO ALEMÁN
[See p. 809 below.]

BARTHÉLÉMI ANEAU
Ἀλέκτωρ. The Cock. Containing the first part of the Historie of the valorous Squire Alector. 1590.

APULEIUS
[See p. 799 below.]

LUCA ASSARINO
La Stratonica; or The Unfortunate Queen. 1651.

VITAL D'AUDIGUIER
D., W. Lisander and Calista, a tragi-comical History. 1621; 1627 (as A Tragi-Comicall History); 1635; 1652.

B[arwick], W. Love and Valour: Celebrated in the person of the Author, by the name of Adraste. 1638.

BANDELLO
[See p. 810 below.]

JOHN BARCLAY
[See pp. 810–1 below.]

FRANÇOIS DE BELLEFOREST
The Hystorie of Hamblet. 1608. [Rptd in 1907 edn of Early English Prose Romances, ed. W. J. Thoms.]

BIDPAI
[See p. 811 below.]

GIOVANNI FRANCESCO BIONDI
Hayward, Ja[mes]. Eromena, or, Love and Revenge. Divided into six Books. 1632.

—— Donzella Desterrada, or, The Banish'd Virgin. Divided into three Books And Englished by J. H. 1635.

G., R. Coralbo. A New Romance. 1655.

FRANÇOIS LE METEL DE BOISROBERT
G., W. (William Duncomb?). The Indian history of Anaxander and Orazia. 1657.

JEAN PIERRE CAMUS
Du Verger, S. Admirable Events. Together with morall Relations. 1639.

Diotrephe. Or, An Historie of Valentines. 1641.

Wright, James. The Loving Enemie, Or, A famous true History. 1650.
—— Nature's Paradox: Or, The Innocent Impostor. A Pleasant Polonian History: Originally Intituled Iphigenes. 1652.

Jennings, John. Elise, or Innocencie Guilty. A New Romance. 1655.

FRANCESCO CARMENI

Nissena, an Excellent New Romance: Now Englished by an Honorable Anti-Socordist. 1653.

JEAN DE CARTIGNY

Goodyear, William. The Voyage of the Wandering Knight. 1581; 1607; [1609?]; [1626?]; 1650.

NICOLAS CAUSSIN

P., G. The Unfortunate Politique. Oxford, 1639.

RENÉ DE CERIZIERS

T[asborough], J[ohn]. Innocency Acknowledg'd in The Life and Death of S. Genovefa Countesse Palatin of Trevers. Ghent, 1645.

Lower, Sir William. The Innocent Lady, or the Illustrious Innocence. 1654; 1656 (as The Triumphant Lady).
—— The Innocent Lord; Or, The Divine Providence. Being The incomparable History of Joseph. 1655.

CERVANTES

[See p. 812 below.]

GONZALO CESPEDES Y MENESES

Digges, Leonard. Gerardo the Unfortunate Spaniard, or a Patterne for Lascivious Lovers. 1622; 1653.

CHRISTINE DE PISAN

[Anslay, B.] The boke of the Cyte of Ladyes. 1521.

W[yer], R. The C. Hystoryes of Troye. [1540?]

FRANCESCO COLONNA

D[allington?], R. Hypnerotomachia. The Strife of Love in a Dreame. 1592; ed. A. Lang, 1891.

GUIDO DELLE COLONNE

Paynell, Thomas. The faythfull and true storye of the destruction of Troye. 1553.

CYRANO DE BERGERAC

[See p. 813 below.]

JEAN DESMARETS DE SAINT SORLIN

Ariana. 1636; 1641.

HENRI ESTIENNE

C[arew?], R. A World of Wonders. 1607 (re-issued Edinburgh, 1608).

JUAN DE FLORES

Histoire de Aurelio et Isabelle In foure langagies, Frenche, Italien, Spanishe, and Inglishe. Antwerp, 1556; Brussels, 1608.

A Paire of Turtle Doves: or, the Tragicall History of Bellora and Fidelio. 1606.

CARLOS GARCIA

M., W. The Sonne of the Rogue, or, the Politick Theefe. 1638; 1650 (as Lavernae, or the Spanish Gipsy).

GIOVANNI BATTISTA GIRALDI (CINTHIO)

[See p. 813 below.]

JEAN OGIER DE GOMBAULD

Hurst, Richard. Endimion, An Excellent Fancy. 1639.

MARIN LE ROY, SIEUR DE GOMBERVILLE

Browne, William. The History of Polexander: in Five Bookes. 1647 (re-issued 1648?).

SIMON GOULART

Grimeston, Edward. Admirable and Memorable Histories containing the wonders of our time. 1607.

LODOVICO GUICCIARDINI

[See p. 814 below.]

JOSEPH HALL

H[ealey], J[ohn]. The Discovery of a New World, or A Description of the South Indies. [1609?]; ed. H. Brown, Cambridge, U.S.A. 1937.

HELIODORUS

[See p. 802 below.]

GAUTIER DE COSTES DE LA CALPRENÈDE

[See p. 815 below.]

OLIVIER DE LA MARCHE

Lewkenor, Lewes. The Resolved Gentleman. Translated out of Spanishe. 1594. [From the version of Hernando de Acuña.]

FRANCISCO DE LAS COVERAS

The History of Don Fenise. 1651. [From the French version.]

LONGUS

[See p. 804 below.]

GIOVANNI FRANCESCO LOREDANO

Cokaine, Sir Aston. Dianea: an Excellent New Romance. 1654.

S., J. The Life of Adam. 1659.

LUCIAN

[See p. 804 below.]

MACCHIAVELLI

The Divell a married man, or, The Divell hath met with his Match. [1647.]

MARGUERITE DE NAVARRE

B., A. The Queene of Navarres Tales. Containing, Verie pleasant Discourses of fortunate Lovers. 1597.

Codrington, Robert. Heptameron, or the History of the Fortunate Lovers. 1654.

PEDRO MEXÍA

Fortescue, Thomas. The Foreste or Collection of Histories, dooen out of Frenche. 1571; [1576]. [From the French version of Claude Gruget.]

JUAN PEREZ DE MONTALBAN

S[tanley], T[homas]. Aurora & the Prince. 1647; 1650.

P., E. The Illustrious Shepherdess. The Imperious Brother. 2 pts, 1656.

JORGE DE MONTEMAYOR

[See p. 816 below.]

NICOLAS DE MONTREUX

T[ofte], R[obert]. Honours Academie. Or the Famous Pastorall of the faire Shepheardesse, Julietta. 1610.

SIR THOMAS MORE

[See p. 666 above.]

DIEGO ORTUÑEZ DE CALAHORRA

[See p. 817 below.]

ENEA SILVIO PICCOLOMINI (AENEAS SILVIUS)

The goodlie history of the Ladye Lucres of Scene in Tuskane. [1550?]; 1560; 1567.

PLUTARCH

Sanford, James. The Amorous and Tragicall Tales of Plutarch. Whereunto is annexed the Hystorie of Cariclea and Theogenes, and the sayings of the Greeke Philosophers. 1567.

FRANCISCO DE QUEVEDO VILLEGAS

M., E. Hell Reformed or A Glasse for Favorites. 1641.

The Life and Adventures of Buscon The Witty Spaniard. To which is added, The Provident Knight. 1657.

RABELAIS

[See p. 818 below.]

DIEGO HERNANDEZ DE SAN PEDRO

[See p. 814 below.]

GILBERT SAULNIER, SIEUR DU VERDIER

The Love and Armes of the Greeke Princes. Or, The Romant of Romants. 3 pts, 1640.

MADELEINE DE SCUDÉRY

[See p. 819 below.]

MARIANO SILESIO

Brathwaite, Richard. The Arcadian Princesse; Or, The Triumph of Justice. 1635.

CHARLES SOREL

[Davies, John.] The Extravagant Shepherd. The Anti-Romance: or, the History of the Shepherd Lyris. 1653; 1654.

The Comical History of Francion. 1655.

JOSÉ TEIXEIRA

The Strangest Adventure that ever happened. Containing a discourse concerning the King of Portugall Dom Sebastion. 1601.

HONORÉ D'URFÉ

[See p. 819 below.]

LOPE DE VEGA

The Pilgrime of Casteele. 1621; 1623.

(b) Translations of Anonymous Works

Robert the devyll. [1502?] (bis); ed. W. J. Thoms (Early English Prose Romances, vol. I, 1827, etc.).

The dystruccyon of Jherusalem by Vaspazian and Tytus. [1505?]; [1509–16]; 1528.

[Copland, Robert.] Kynge Apollyn of Thyre. 1510; [1594?] (as The Patterne of painefull Adventures); 1607; ed. facs. E. W. Ashbee, 1870. [From the French.]

—— The hystory of the noble Helyas knyght of the swanne newly translated out of frensshe. 1512; ed. W. J. Thoms (Early English Prose Romances, vol. III, 1828, etc.).

[Joseph of Arimathea.] A treatyse taken out of a boke Which somtyme Theodosius the Emperour founde of Joseph of Arimathy. [1510?]

The noble hystory of the moost excellent and myghty prynce Ponthus of Galyce & lytell Brytayne. 1511; 1548.

The hystorye of Olyver of Castylle, and of the fayre Helayne doughter unto the kynge of Englande. 1518.

A lyttel story that was of a trwethe done in the lande of Gelders of a mayde that was named Mary of Nemmegen that was the dyvels paramoure. Antwerp, [1518?]; ed. H. M. Ayres and A. J. Barnouw, Cambridge, U.S.A. 1932.

This matter treateth of a merchantes wyfe that afterwarde went lyke a man and was called Frederyke of Jennen. Antwerp, 1518; [1520?]; [1560?].

Virgilius. This boke treath of the lyfe of Virgilius and of his deth and many mervayles that he dyd in his lyfe tyme. Antwerp, [1518?]; [1561?]; ed. W. J. Thoms (Early English Prose Romances, vol. ii, 1828, etc.).

Thystorye of the .vii. Wyse Maysters of rome. [1520?]; [1555?]; 1633 ('newly corrected'); 1653.

[Copland, William?] A merye Jest of a man called Howleglas. [1528?]; [1530?]; [1560?]. [See F. Brie, Eulenspiegel in England, Berlin, 1903.]

Bourchier, John (Baron Berners). The Boke Huon de Bordeuxe. [1534?]; 1601 (3rd edn); ed. Sir S. Lee, 3 pts, EETS. Ex. Ser. 1882–7; ed. R. Steele, 1895 (modernised).

—— Arthur of Brytayn. The hystory of Arthur of lytell Brytayne, translated out of frensshe. [1555?]; [1582]; ed. E. V. Utterson, 1814.

The Dialoges of Creatures Moralysed. [Antwerp, 1535.]

The hystorye of Gesta Romanorum. 1557; rev. R. Robinson, 1595; 1600; 1602; 1610; [1640?]; 1648.

The Hystory of the two valyaunte brethren Valentyne and Orson, sonnes unto the Emperour of Greece. [1565?]; [1570?]. [Abridgement, 1637, 1649.]

The Historie of Frier Rush: how he came to a house of Religion to seeke service. 1620; 1626; 1629; 1659; ed. W. J. Thoms (Early English Prose Romances, vol. i, 1827, etc.). [S.R. 1569. From the German.]

Amadis of Gaul. [See p. 809 below.]

Lazarillo de Tormes. [See p. 815 below.]

S[myth], R[obert]. Straunge, Lamentable, and Tragicall Hystories. Translated out of French. 1577.

The Gallant, delectable and pleasaunt Hystorie of Gerileon of Englande. Composed in the Frenche Tongue, by Steven De Maison Neufve Bordelois. 1583. [S.R. 1577.]

W[otton], H[enry]. A Courtlie controversie of Cupids Cautels: Conteyning five Tragicall Histories. Translated out of French as neare as our English phrase will permit. 1578.

Munday, Anthony. Palmerin d'Oliva, the Mirrour of Nobilitie. 2 pts, 1588–97; 1615; 2 pts, 1616; 2 vols. 1637; 1653. [Of the various sequels, versions (either by Munday or anon.) appeared of Palmendos, Primaleon, Palladine, and Palmerin of England.]

—— The Second Part of the History of Gerileon of England. 1592.

F., P. The Historie of the damnable life, and deserved death of Doctor John Faustus. 1592; 1608; 1618; 1622; 1636; 1648; ed. W. Rose, 1925. [The Second Report of Doctor John Faustus, 1594 (bis). Both rptd in Early English Prose Romances, ed. W. J. Thoms, vol. iii, 1828, etc.]

[Barley, William?] The delightful History of Celestina the Faire; daughter to the king of Thessalie. 1596. [From the French.]

M[arkham], J[arvis] (i.e. Gervase). The most Famous and renowned Historie of that woorthie and illustrous knight Mervine, Sonne to Oger the Dane. 1612. [S.R. 1596. From the French.]

A., L. The Honour of Chivalrie. Set downe in the most Famous Historie of the Magnanimous and Heroike Prince Don Bellianis. Englished out of Italian. 1598; 1650.

The True History of the late and Lamentable Adventures of Don Sebastian, King of Portugal. 1602; rptd Harleian Misc. vol. iv, 1809. [A Continuation of the lamentable and admirable Adventures of Don Sebastian, 1603, rptd Harleian Misc. vol. v, 1810.]

The Antient, True, and admirable History of Patient Grissel. Written in French. 1607; 1619.

Churchyard, Thomas. The right pleasant and variable Tragical history of Fortunatus. 1612. [From the German.]

The History of the Birth, Travels, Strange Adventures, and Death of Fortunatus. [1650?]. [S.R. 1615. From the Dutch.]

Hart, Alexander. The True History of the Tragicke loves of Hipolito and Isabella Neapolitans. 1628; 1633. [From Les amours tragiques d'Hypolite et Isabelle, Paris, 1610 (by Mcslicr?).]

—— The Tragi-Comicall History of Alexto And Angelica. 1640.

Celestina. [See p. 812 below.]

The Fortunate, the Deceived, and the Unfortunate Lovers. 1632. [From the Italian.]

H., Sir T. A Saxon Historie, of the Admirable Adventures of Clodoaldus and his Three Children. Translated out of French. 1634.

Godwin, Paul. Histoire Des Larrons, or the History of Theeves. Written in French, and Translated out of the Originall. 1638.

The History of Philoxypes and Polycrite. Englished out of French. 1652.

C[odrington], R[obert]. The Troublesome and Hard Adventures in Love. Written in Spanish by Michael Cervantes. 1652. [From the Spanish, but not from Cervantes.]

Choice Novels, and Amorous Tales, written by the most Refined Wits of Italy. Newly translated. 1652.

Kirkman, Francis. The Loves and Adventures of Clerio and Lozia. Written Originally in French. 1652; 1655.

E. I.

V. NEWS-SHEETS AND NEWS-BOOKS

The Beginnings, 1500–1640: Pamphlets and Broadsides; Single-Sheet Corantos; The Earliest News-Periodicals; Semi-Annual Foreign Histories; Modern Works.

Civil Wars and Commonwealth, 1641–1659: General Authorities; Biographies of Particular Journalists; Bibliographies and Catalogues; The News-Books.

I. 1500–1640

(1) PAMPHLETS AND BROADSIDES

[Soon after the introduction of printing, and almost a hundred and fifty years before the evolution of the newspaper, reports of news— each, as a rule, dealing with a single event— were printed and offered for sale in these forms. After the middle of the sixteenth century, they became numerous. The titles cited below are representative of their variety.]

(a) *News Published by the State*

[The object in publishing official declarations on current matters of state was quite as much to lead public opinion as to inform it, but these documents, whether accurate or not, frequently contained a great deal of information not otherwise available in print, and were sometimes issued with so much weight of authority as to become 'news' in themselves.]

The determinations of the universities of Italy and Fraunce, that it is so unlefull for a man to marie his brothers wyfe, that the pope hath no power to dispence therwith. [1531.] [Pbd also in Latin.]

Answere made by the kynges hyghnes to the Petitions of the rebelles in Yorkeshire. 1536.

A protestation made for the kynge of Englande that neyther his hyghenes, nor his prelates, neyther any other prynce, or prelate, is bounde to come to the pretended councell, that Paule byshoppe of Rome, indicted at Mantua. 1537.

A declaration, conteynyng the just causes of this present warre with the Scottis. 1542.

The saying of John late Duke of Northumberlande uppon the scaffolde. [1553.]

A declaration of the Quenes Majestie. Conteyning the causes which have constrayned her to arme certaine of her Subjectes. 1562; rptd Harleian Misc. ed. T. Park, vol. III, p. 185, 1809.

The copie of a letter concernyng the credit of the late published detection of the doynges of the Ladie Marie of Scotland. [1572]; rptd Harleian Misc. ed. T. Park, vol. III, p. 561, 1809.

A particular declaration of the traiterous affection borne against her Majesty by Edmund Campion, Jesuite. 1582; rptd Phœnix Britannicus, ed. J. Morgan, vol. I, p. 481, 1732.

The Execution of Justice in England against certeine stirrers of sedition. 1583 (*bis*); tr. Latin, Dutch, French, and Italian; rptd Harleian Misc. ed. T. Park, vol. II, p. 137, 1808–13.

A Declaration of the causes mooving the Queene of England to give aide to the people in the Lowe Countries. 1585 (2 issues); tr. Latin, Dutch, French, and Italian; rptd Somers Tracts, ed. Sir W. Scott, vol. I, p. 410, 1809.

The Copie of a Letter to the Earle of Leycester. [Signed R. C.] 1586; tr. French; rptd Somers Tracts, ed. Sir W. Scott, vol. I, p. 224, 1809.

Her majesties most Princelie answere, delivered on the last day of November 1601: taken verbatim in writing by A. B. 1601.

[Bacon, Francis.] A declaration of the Treasons by Robert late earle of Essex. 1601; rptd E. A. Abbott, Bacon and Essex, 1877.

The Kings Majesties Speech in Parliament, the 19. March 1603. 1604; rptd Political Works of James I, ed. C. H. McIlwain, 1918.

Articles of peace Concluded at London the 18. August 1604. 1605.

His majesties speach in this last Session of Parliament, as neere his very words as could be gathered at the instant. 1605 (*bis*); tr. Latin; rptd Harleian Misc. ed. T. Park, vol. IV, p. 245, 1809.

A true and perfect relation of the proceedings against Garnet and his Confederats. 1606 (3 issues).

The kings majesties Speach To the Lords and Commons the xxj. of March. 1609. [1609]; rptd Political works of James I, ed. C. H. McIlwain, 1918.

A declaration of the demeanor of Sir Walter Raleigh. 1618 (3 edns); rptd Harleian Misc. ed. T. Park, vol. III, p. 18, 1808–9.

His majesties declaration of the causes which moved him to dissolve the last parliament. 1628 [*i.e.* 1629].

His Majesties Declaration, concerning His Proceedings with His Subjects of Scotland. 1640.

(b) Controversial and Polemical Tracts containing News

[Pamphlets published from interested and personal motives and intended as propaganda were often useful as well for the news they contained, especially before the booksellers had caught the idea of carrying on a trade in printed news or when they dealt with subjects the booksellers dared not handle.]

Sex que elegantissime epistole quarum tris a Sixto Quarto ad Venetiarum ducem totidemque ab ipso Duce conscripte sunt. [1483]; rptd facs. G. Bullen, 1892.

The promisse of matrimonie. [1486]; rptd facs. E. Picot and H. Stein, Recueil de Pièces historiques, Paris, 1923.

The actes of the disputacion in the cowncell of the Empyre at Regenspurg. [Antwerp?], 1542.

The Supplicacion: That the nobles and comons of Osteryke made unto kyng Ferdinandus. [1543?]

The Communication betwene my lord Chauncelor and judge Hales. [Rouen, 1553]; rptd Harleian Misc. ed. T. Park, vol. III, p. 174, 1809.

A Warnyng for Englande Conteynyng the horrible practises of the Kyng of Spayne in the Kyngdome of Naples. 1555.

An edict of the French King conteining a prohibition of al exercise of any other religion then of the catholique, the apostolique and the Romaine. Louvain, 1568.

A request presented to the Kyng of Spayn, by the inhabitantes of the Lowe countreyes protesting that they will live according to the reformation of the Gospell: the xxii. of June. 1578. [1578.]

Ellyot, George. A very true report of the apprehension of Edmond Campion. 1581; rptd A. F. Pollard, Tudor Tracts (Arber's English Garner), p. 451, 1903.

[Allen, William.] A Briefe Historie of the Glorious Martyrdom of xii Reverend Priests. 1582; rptd J. H. Pollen, 1908.

A true report of the late apprehension of John Nicols. Rheims, 1583.

B., I. The copy of a letter lately written by a Spanishe gentleman to his friend in England. [Printed abroad,] 1589.

A relation of the King of Spaines receiving in Valliodolid, and in the Inglish College of the same towne, in August 1592. [Printed abroad?] 1592.

Newes from Spayne and Holland conteyning. An information of Inglish affayres in Spayne. [Printed abroad?] 1593.

An extract Translated out of the French Copie, and taken out of the Registers of the French Kings Privie Councell. [1600?] [Broadside.]

An apologie of the Earle of Essex, against those which tax him to be the hinderer of peace. 1603.

Sir Francis Bacon his apologie, in certaine imputations concerning the late Earle of Essex. 1604 (bis); 1605; rptd E. A. Abbott, Bacon and Essex, 1877.

A faithfull report of proceedings anent the assemblie at Aberdeen 2 July 1605. [Middelburg,] 1606.

A record of some worthy proceedings: in the Howse of Commons in the late Parliament. [Amsterdam?] 1611; rptd Somers Tracts, ed. Sir W. Scott, vol. II, p. 148, 1809.

To the kings most excellent majeste, The humble Petition and information of sir Lewis Stucley, touching Sir Walter Raleigh. 1618; rptd Harleian Misc. ed. T. Park, vol. III, p. 63, 1809.

Harrison, John. A short relation of The departure of Prince Frederick from Heydelberg towards Prague. Dordrecht, 1619.

[Scott, Thomas.] Vox Populi, or Newes from Spayne. [Gorcum?] 1620 (4 edns); rptd Somers Tracts, ed. Sir W. Scott, vol. II, p. 508, 1809. [A forgery.]

A declaration set forth by the Protestants in France. La Rochelle, 1621.

A courante of newes from the East India. 1622.

A true relation of the Unjust and barbarous proceedings against the English at Amboyna in the East-Indies, by the Neatherlandish governour. 1624 (4 edns).

[Du Mats de Montmartin, Esau.] An admirable discovery of an horrible attempt; slaunderously fathered upon those of Rochell. 1624.

The protestation of the noblemen, ministers, and commons, at the Mercate Crosse of Edinburgh, the 4. of Julii. [Edinburgh,] 1638.

The protestation of the Generall Assembly of the Kirke of Scotland the 18. of December. 1638. Edinburgh, 1639.

(c) News Published for Profit by the Bookselling Trade

(i) News of Public Affairs

Hereafter ensue the trewe encountre or Batayle lately don betwene Englande and Scotlande. [1513]; rptd John Ashton, The Earliest known Printed English Ballad, 1882.

The copye of the Submissyon of Oneyll which he made to the Kynges Majestie at Grenewych the .xxiiii. daye of September. [1542.] [Broadside.]

The late expedicion in Scotlande under the Erle of Hertforde. 1544; rptd A. F. Pollard, Tudor Tracts (Arber's English Garner), p. 37, 1903.

Patten, William. The Expedicion into Scotlande of the Duke of Soomerset. 1548; rptd A. F. Pollard, Tudor Tracts (Arber's English Garner), p. 53, 1903.

Proctor, John. The historie of wyates rebellion. 1554 (*bis*); rptd A. F. Pollard, Tudor Tracts (Arber's English Garner), p. 199, 1903.

Elder, John. The Copie of a letter sent in to Scotlande, of the arivall and marryage of Philippe, Prynce of Spaine, to Marye Quene of England. [1555.]

The copie of the P[u]blication of the trewse made betwene Kynge Henry second, Themeperour: and the Kyng of Ingland. [1556.] [Broadside.]

Kyrkh[am], W. Joyfull Newes for true Subjectes, to God and the Crowne, The Rebelles are cooled, their Bragges be put downe. [1570]; rptd Joseph Lilly, A Collection of 79 Black Letter Ballads, p. 231, 1867. [Broadside. Typical of a very large class of ballads appearing on the heels of public events of all kinds which, while they were undoubtedly prompted by public interest in such events and alluded directly to them, seldom contained much of the kind of information one would call news. Few of them are mentioned in these lists.]

The Severall Confessions, of Thomas Norton, and Christopher Norton: who suffred at Tiburne, May. xxvii. 1570. [1570]; rptd Phœnix Britannicus, ed. J. Morgan, vol. I, p. 419, 1732.

Partridge, I. The ende and Confession of John Felton. Who suffred for highe Treason the .viii. of August 1570. [1570]; rptd Phœnix Britannicus, ed. J. Morgan, vol. I, p. 415, 1732.

A declaration of the lyfe and Death of John Story. 1571; rptd Harleian Misc. ed. T. Park, vol. III, p. 100, 1809.

The Confession and declaration of Robert sharpe, of the Familie of Love, at Pawles Crosse the .xii. of June. 1575. [1575]; rptd H. L. Collmann, Ballads and Broadsides, no. 83, 1912. [Broadside.]

Newe newes contayning A shorte rehersall of the late enterprise of certaine Rebelles of Ireland. 1579.

Churchyard, Thomas. A Moste true Reporte of James Fitz Morrice Death. [1579?]

—— A plaine or moste true report of a daungerous service by English men & other worthy souldiours, for the takyng of Macklin. 1580.

M., A. The true reporte of the successe which God gave unto our English Souldiours in Ireland. [1581] (2 issues).

S., M. The Araignement, and Execution, of a Traitour, named Everalde Ducket, alias Hauns. 1581.

M[unday], A[nthony]. A Breefe discourse of the taking of Edmund Campion and divers other Papistes, in Barkeshire. 1581.

—— A breefe and true reporte, of the Execution of certaine Traytours at Tiborne, the xxviii. and xxx. of Maye. 1582. 1582.

B., R. The severall Executions & confessions, of John Slade & John Bodye: Two notorious Traitours. [1583.]

Lingham, John. A true Relation of all suche Englishe Captaines and Lieuetenants, as have been slaine in the lowe Countries. 1584.

Churchyard, Thomas. A Scourge for Rebels: Wherin are many notable services truly set out. 1584.

M., W. A True Discourse of the late Battaile fought betweene our En[g]lishmen, and the Prince of Parma, the 15. of November 1585. 1585.

Mote, Humphrey. The Primrose of London with her valiant adventure on the Spanish coast. 1585; rptd E. W. Ashbee, Occasional Facsimile Reprints, no. 20, 1871.

The Life and end of Thomas Awfeeld and Thomas Webley: Executed the 6. of July. 1585. [1585.]

The Scottish queens Burial at Peterborough, upon Tuesday, being Lammas Day 1587. [1587]; rptd A. F. Pollard, Tudor Tracts (Arber's English Garner), p. 475, 1903.

D., T. A briefe report of the militarie services done in the Low Countries, by the Erle of Leicester. 1587.

D[eloney], T[homas]. A joyfull new Ballad, declaring the happie obtaining of the great Galleazzo. 1588; rptd A. F. Pollard, Tudor Tracts (Arber's English Garner), p. 485, 1903.

A true Discourse of the Armie which the King of Spaine caused to bee assembled against England. 1588.

The copie of a letter sent out of England to don Bernardin Mendoza, Ambassadour in France for Spaine, declaring the state of England. Whereunto are adjoyned certaine advertisements, concerning the losses happened to the Spanish navie. 1588; rptd Harleian Misc. ed. T. Park, vol. I, p. 142, 1808.

Orders set downe by the Duke of Medina, General of the Kings Fleet, to be observed in the voyage toward England. 1588; rptd Harleian Misc. ed. T. Park, vol. I, p. 115, 1808.

A briefe Treatise. Discovering the offences of the late 14. Traitors condemned the 26. of August. 1588.

A true report of the inditement and Execution of John Weldon, William Hartley, and Robert Sutton: Who suffred for high Treason the fifth of October. 1588.

de M., D. F. R. An answer to the untruthes, published in Spaine, in glorie of their supposed victorie against our English navie. 1589. Tr. Spanish.

Bigges, Walter. A Summarie and true Discourse of Sir Francis Drakes West Indian voyage. 1589.

A true Coppie of a Discourse written by a Gentleman, employed in the late Voyage of Spaine and Portingale. 1589; rptd J. P. Collier, Miscellaneous Tracts, vol. III, 1870.

A True Recitall touching the death of Thomas Bales, a Seminarie Priest. 1590.

A Particuler, of the yeelding uppe of Zutphen, and the beleagering of Deventer. 1591.

The true Reporte of the service in Britanic. Performed by Sir John Norreys. 1591.

True newes From one of Sir Fraunces Veres Companie. 1591.

Newes from Sir Roger Williams. 1591.

The honorable actions of Edward Gleinham against the Spaniards, and the Holy League, in foure sundrie fightes. 1591; rptd 1820.

The Valiant and most laudable fight in the Straights, by the Centurion, against five Spanish Gallies. 1591.

Ralegh, Sir Walter. A Report of the Truth of a fight Betwixt the Revenge and an Armada of the king of Spaine. 1591; rptd E. Arber, 1871.

The sea-mans Triumph. Declaring the takinge of the great Carrick, lately brought to Dartmouth. 1592; rptd E. W. Ashbee, Occasional Facsimile Reprints, no. 27, 1871.

Newes from Brest. A Diurnal of al that Sir John Norreis hath doone. 1594.

R[oberts], H[enry]. Newes from the Levane Seas. 1594; rptd J. P. Collier, Illustrations of Old English Literature, vol. I, 1866.

Monings, Edward. The Landgrave of Hessen his receiving of her Majesties Embassador. 1596.

A true credible report of a great fight at sea between certaine ships of England and five ships of warre of the king of Spaines. [1600.]

Extremities Urging Sir Fra. Veare to offer the late Anti-parle with the Arch-duke Albertus. 1602 (3 edns).

Mansel, Sir Robert. A true report of the service done upon certaine Gallies passing through the Narrow Seas. 1602.

E., I. A letter from a Souldier in Ireland touching the Victorie of her Majesties Forces. 1602.

The copie of his majesties letter, sent the 26. of June 1604: signifying his pleasure to the Commons House of Parliament. 1604.

To the king's majestie. The humble Petition of two and Twentie Preachers, in London and the suburbs thereof. [1604.] [Broadside.]

Hamond, Tho[mas]. The Late Commotion of certaine Papists in Herefordshire. 1605.

W., T. The araignment and execution of the late traytors. 1606; rptd Harleian Misc. ed. T. Park, vol. III, p. 131, 1808–13.

A True Report of the Araignment of a Popish Priest, named Robert Drewrie. 1607; rptd Harleian Misc. ed. T. Park, vol. III, p. 38, 1809.

The Over-throw of an Irish rebell, Sir Carey Adoughertie. 1608.

Newes From Lough-foyle in Ireland. 1608 (bis).

Remonstrances made by the Kings Majesties ambassadour, unto the French King. 1615.

[Roberts, Henry.] A True Relation of a Fight, performed by two small Shippes of London against Six great Galles of Tunes. [1616.]

A relation of the late entertainment of the Lord Roos his Majesties Embassador to the King of Spaine. 1617.

A Fight at Sea, Famously fought by the Dolphin of London. 1617; rptd C. R. Beazley, Voyages and Travels (Arber's English Garner), vol. II, p. 213, 1903.

The speech of sir Dudley Carleton ambassadour for the king of Great Britaine, made in the Estates generall of the Low countries. 1618.

Gainsforde, Th[omas]. The true exemplary, and remarkable history of the Earle of Tirone. 1619.

B[utton], I. Algiers voyage in a journall. 1621.

M., A. A relation of the passages of our English companies since their first departure to Germanie. 1621.

A relation Strange and true, of a ship of Bristol named the Jacob, taken by the Turkish Pirats. 1622.

The famous and wonderful recoverie of the Exchange, from the Turkish pirates. 1622; rptd Sir C. H. Firth, Stuart Tracts (Arber's English Garner), p. 247, 1903.

A journall and Relation of the action which Edward Lord Cecil did undertake upon the coast of Spaine, 1625, 1626 (bis).

Taylor, John. A famous Fight at Sea. 1627; rptd Works of John Taylor, vol. II, Spenser Soc. 1869.

Sir Benjamin Rudierd his speech in behalfe of the Clergie. 1628.

The Copies of two Speeches in Parliament. [1628.]

The king's speech in parlament, June 7. 1628. [1628.] [Broadside.]

H[eywood], T[homas]. A true discourse of the two infamous upstart prophets, Richard Farnham and John Bull. 1636; 1642.

Crowne, William. A true relation of the travels of Thomas Lord Howard, Earle of Arundell and Surrey, Ambassadour to Ferdinando, Emperour of Germanie. 1637.

The Arivall and Intertainementes of the Embassador From the Emperour of Morocco. 1637.

A briefe relation Of certain passages in the Starre-Chamber June 14th. 1637. 1637; 1638; rptd Harleian Misc. ed. T. Park, vol. IV, p. 12, 1809.

Heywood, Thomas. A True Description of His Majesties Royall Ship, Built this yeare 1637. 1637 (bis); 1653.

Lenthall, William. Mr. Speaker his speech to his Majestie in Parliament. 1640.

Articles exhibited in parliament against William Archbishop of Canterbury. 1640.

A list of the colonels, as also the names of ships, captaines and lieutenants that are now set forth under the command of the Earle of Northumberland. [1640.]

Mr. Speakers Speech with His Majesties Speech to Parliament at the passing of the Bill for Tonnage and Poundage. 1641.

The Confession of a Papist Priest, who was hanged at Tiburne. 1641. [Broadside.]

Sad News from the Seas. Being a relation of tne losse of the Merchant Royall. 1641.

An exact Relation of a battell fought by the Lord Moore against the rebels in Ireland. 1641.

The last and best Newes from Ireland, 3 to 17 November. 1641.

Bloody Newes from Norwich; or, a relation of a bloody attempt of the Papists to consume the city by fire. 1641.

(ii) News of Royalties, the Court, and other Eminent Persons

The traduction & mariage of the princesse Kateryne [of Aragon]. [1501.]

The solempnities and triumphes doon at the spousells of the kyngs doughter. [1508]; tr. Latin; rptd J. Gairdner, Camden Misc. vol. IX, 1895.

[Lyly, William.] Of the tryumphe and the uses that Charles themperour & and the kyng of England were saluted with passyng through London. [1522.]

The maner of the tryumphe at Caleys and Bulleyn. [1532] (bis); rptd A. F. Pollard, Tudor Tracts (Arber's English Garner), p. 1, 1903.

The noble tryumphaunt Coronation of Quene Anne. [1533]; rptd A. F. Pollard, Tudor Tracts (Arber's English Garner), p. 9, 1903.

The Passage of our most drad Soveraigne Lady Quene Elyzabeth to westminster the daye before her Coronacion. 1558 [i.e. 1559] (bis); 1603 (2 issues); rptd A. F. Pollard, Tudor Tracts (Arber's English Garner), p. 365, 1903.

La[neham], R[obert]. A Letter whearin part of the entertainment untoo the Queenz Majesty at Killingwoorth Castle is signified. [1575]; rptd F. J. Furnivall, Ballad Soc. 1871 and 1907.

Gar[ter], Ber[nard]. The joyfull Receyving of the Queenes Majestie, into Norwiche. 1578 (bis); rptd J. Nichols, Progresses and Public Processions of Queen Elizabeth, vol. II, p. 136, 1823.

Goldwel, Henry. A briefe declaration of the shews performed before the French Ambassadours. [1581]; rptd J. Nichols, Progresses and Public Processions of Queen Elizabeth, vol. II, p. 310, 1823.

The honorable entertainement gieven to the Queenes majestie at Elvetham. 1591; rptd R. W. Bond, Complete Works of John Lyly, vol. I, p. 431, 1902.

A living remembrance of Master Robert Rogers, Leatherseller of London deceased. [1601]; rptd H. L. Collmann, Ballads and Broadsides, no. 79, 1912. [Broadside. The only example listed here of the numerous metrical 'epitaphs' of the period, which, partaking somewhat of the nature of obituary notices, may have had some little interest as news.]

Chettle, Henry. Englandes Mourning Garment: in memorie of Elizabeth. To which is added the manner of her Funerall. 1603 (2 issues); rptd Harleian Misc. ed. T. Park, vol. III, p. 524, 1809.

P[etowe], H[enry]. Elizabetha quasi vivens, Elizas Funerall. 1603 (bis); rptd Harleian Misc. ed. T. Park, vol. X, p. 333, 1813.

The True Narration of the Entertainment of his Majestie, from Edenbrough till London. 1603; rptd Sir C. H. Firth, Stuart Tracts (Arber's English Garner), p. 11, 1903.

Dugdale, Gilbert. The Time Triumphant, declaring the arival of King James, his Coronation at Westminster. 1604; rptd Sir C. H. Firth, Stuart Tracts (Arber's English Garner), p. 69, 1903.

[Dekker, Thomas.] The Magnificent Entertainment: given to King James upon his Passage through London. 1604 (3 edns); rptd J. Nichols, Progresses of James the First, vol. I, p. 337, 1828.

[Daniel, Samuel.] The true description of a Royall Masque. Presented at Hampton Court. And Personated by the Queenes Majestie, attended by Eleven Ladies of Honour. 1604.

Roberts, H[enry]. The most royall and Honourable entertainment of Christiern the fourth. 1606; rptd Harleian Misc. ed. T. Park, vol. IX, p. 431, 1812.

Nixon, Anthony. The three English brothers. 1607 (2 issues).

The Order and Solemnitie of the Creation of Prince Henrie Prince of Wales. 1610; rptd Somers Tracts, ed. Sir W. Scott, vol. II, p. 183, 1809.

Chapman, George. An epicede or Funerall Song: On the Death of Henry Prince of Wales. With The Funeralls of the same Prince. 1612; 1613.

[Campion, Thomas.] A relation of the late royall entertainment given by the Lord Knowles. 1613.

The marriage of the two great princes, Fredericke Count Palatine and the Lady Elizabeth. With the showes and fire-workes upon the water. 1613 (2 edns); rptd J. Nichols, Progresses of James the First, vol. II, p. 536, 1828.

The magnificent princely entertainment given to Frederick Count Palatine and the Lady Elizabeth. 1613.

The Charterhouse with the last will and Testament of Thomas Sutton. 1614.

Middleton, Tho[mas]. Civitatis amor. The Cities Love. An entertainment by water, At the receiving of Charles, To bee created Prince of Wales. 1616; rptd Works, ed. A. H. Bullen, vol. VII, p. 269, 1885.

A true relation and journall of the entertainment given to Prince Charles by the King of Spaine at Madrid. 1623 (2 issues); rptd J. Nichols, Progresses of James the First, vol. IV, p. 818, 1828.

La Peña, Juan Antonio de. A relation of the royall Festivities at Madrid To Honour the Espousall of the Prince of Wales, with the Infanta Maria. 1623; rptd J. Nichols, Progresses of James the First, vol. IV, p. 889, 1828.

A true discourse of the Contract and Mariage of Charles, King of Great Britaine, and the Lady Henrietta of Burbon. 1625.

Peeke, Richard. Three to One, being an English Spanish Combat with an English quarter Staffe against three Spanish Rapiers. [1626]; rptd Sir C. H. Firth, Stuart Tracts (Arber's English Garner), p. 275, 1903.

Taylor, John. The Great Eater of Kent. 1630; rptd C. Hindley, Old Book Collector's Miscellany, vol. III, 1873.

(iii) Sensational News

This horryble monster is cast of a Sowe in Eestlande in Pruse. [1531.] [Broadside.]

The copye of the wordes, that lorde Sturton spake at his Death as his Confession. 1557 (bis); rptd G. J. Gray, Trans. Bibliog. Soc. IV, 1898. [Broadside.]

[Pilkington, James.] The true report of the burnyng of the steple and churche of Poules in London. 1561; rptd A. F. Pollard, Tudor Tracts (Arber's English Garner), p. 401, 1903.

D., Jhon. A discription of a monstrous Chylde, borne at Chychester. 1562; rptd Joseph Lilly, A Collection of 79 Black Letter Ballads, p. 201, 1867. [Broadside.]

R., C. The true discription of this marveilous straunge fishe. 1569; rptd Joseph Lilly, A Collection of 79 Black Letter Ballads, p. 145, 1867.

Knel, T[homas], jr. A declaration of such tempestious Fluddes as hath been in divers places of England. 1570; rptd G. J. Gray, Trans. Bibliog. Soc. IV, 1898.

S., D. A true reporte of an horrible murther, doen by Jhon Kynnestar. 1573; rptd W. C. Hazlitt, Fugitive Tracts, ser. 1, 1875.

G[olding], A[rthur]. A briefe discourse of the late murther of George Saunders. 1573; 1577; rptd R. Simpson, School of Shakespeare, vol. II, p. 220, 1878.

Fleming, Abraham. A Straunge and terrible Wunder wrought in the parish Church of Bongay. [1577]; rptd 1820.

E[lderton], W[illiam]. A newe Ballade, declaryng the shootyng of the Gunne at the Courte. [1579]; rptd Harleian Misc. ed. T. Park, vol. x, p. 272, 1811. [Broadside.]

A notable and prodigious Historie of a Mayden who neither eateth, drinketh, nor sleepeth, and yet liveth. 1589.

The most dangerous and memorable adventure of Richard Ferris, from Tower Wharfe in a small Wherry Boate to Bristowe. 1590; rptd A. Lang, Social England Illustrated (Arber's English Garner), p. 101, 1903.

R., W. The Most horrible and tragicall murther of John Lord Bourgh. 1591; rptd J. P. Collier, Illustrations of Early English Popular Literature, vol. I, 1863.

Newes from Scotland of Doctor Fian a notable Sorcerer. [1591] (3 edns); rptd G. B. Harrison, Bodley Head Quartos, [1926].

Kydde, Th[omas]. The trueth of the murthering of John Brewen. 1592; rptd J. P. Collier, Illustrations of Early English Popular Literature, vol. I, 1863.

Darrell, John. A true Narration of the Vexation by the Devil, of 7. persons in Lancashire. 1600; rptd Somers Tracts, ed. Sir W. Scott, vol. III, 1809.

Two most unnaturall and bloodie Murthers. 1605; rptd J. P. Collier, Illustrations of Early English Popular Literature, vol. I. 1863.

The Life and Death of Gamaliell Ratsey, a famous theefe. [1605]; rptd J. P. Collier, Illustrations of Old English Literature, vol. III, 1866.

Strange fearful & true newes, which hapned at Carlstadt, in Croatia. [1606.]

Jones, William. Gods warning to his people of England. By the great overflowing of the Waters or Floudes. 1607 (bis); rptd Harleian Misc. ed. T. Park, vol. III, p. 379, 1809.

The Apprehension and execution of Elizabeth Abbot for a cruell murther. 1608; rptd Harleian Misc. ed. T. Park, vol. x, p. 436, 1813.

Two monstrous births in Devon and Plymouth. 1608; rptd Harleian Misc. ed. T. Park, vol. x, p. 462, 1813.

Potts, Thomas. The wonderfull discoverie of witches in Lancaster. 1613; rptd Somers Tracts, ed. Sir W. Scott, vol. III, p. 95, 1809.

R., A. True and wonderfull. A discourse relating a strange serpent (or dragon). 1614; rptd C. H. Hindley, Old Book Collector's Miscellany, vol. II, 1873.

The Lieutenant of the Tower his speech and repentance, at the time of his death. [1615] (bis); rptd Harleian Misc. ed. T. Park, vol. v, p. 546, 1810.

The Just Downfall of Weston, M. Turner, and Franklin for the murder of Sir Tho: Overbury. [1616.]

Platte, T. Anne Wallens Lamentation, For the Murthering of her husband. [1616]; rptd H. E. Rollins, Pepysian Garland, Cambridge, 1922. [Broadside.]

The Wonderfull Battell of Starelings: Fought at Corke in Ireland. 1622; rptd Phoenix Britannicus, ed. J. Morgan, vol. I, p. 250, 1732.

B[edford], Th[omas]. A true and certaine relation of a strange birth at Stone-house. 1635; rptd C. H. Hindley, Old Book Collector's Miscellany, vol. II, 1873.

A Marvellous Murther, Committed upon George Drawnefield. [1638?]; rptd H. E. Rollins, Pack of Autolycus, Cambridge, 1927. [Broadside.]

A certaine Relation of the hog-faced Gentlewoman. 1640; rptd E. W. Ashbee, Occasional Facsimile Reprints, no. 16, 1871.

Murther, Murther, or, a bloody relation how Anne Hamton murthered her husband. 1641; rptd C. H. Hindley, Old Book Collector's Miscellany, vol. II, 1873.

The Marine Mercury. Or a true relation of the strange appearance of a Man-Fish in the river Thames. 1642.

(iv) News from Foreign Parts

[Nearly all of these, which represent a very large class of newsbooks, were translated from books published abroad.]

[Caorsin, Gulielmus.] [The Siege of Rhodes.] Translated by Johan Kay. [1482?]; rptd H. W. Fincham, Caoursin's Account of the Siege of Rhodes in 1480, 1926.

Of the new landes founde by the messengers of the kynge of portyngale. [Antwerp, 1520?]; rptd E. Arber, The First Three English Books on America, p. xxiii, 1895.

The tryumphant vyctory of the imperyall mageste agaynst the turkes. 1532.

Vyllagon, Nicholas. A lamentable and piteous treatise of themperour Charles the V. and his army. 1542; rptd Harleian Misc. ed. T. Park, vol. IV, p. 533, 1809.

Newes concernynge the general councell holden at Trydent. [1549.]

A true declaration of the voyadge of M. John Haukins to Guynea and the West Indies. 1569; rptd C. R. Beazley, Voyages and Travels (Arber's English Garner), vol. I, p. 91, 1903.

Varamund, Ernest [i.e. François Hotman]. A true and plaine report of the Furious outrages of Fraunce. 'Striveling,' (really London?), 1573; tr. Latin; rptd Harleian Misc. ed. T. Park, vol. VII, p. 336, 1811.

Gilbert, Sir Humphrey. A discourse of a discoverie for a new passage to Cataia. 1576.

[Gascoigne, George.] The Spoyle of Antwerpe, Faithfully reported by a True Englishman who was present at the same. [1577?]; rptd A. F. Pollard, Tudor Tracts (Arber's English Garner), p. 419, 1903.

The strange and marveilous Newes lately come from Chyna. [1577?]; rptd Sir S. E. Brydges, Censura Literaria, vol. VI, p. 126, 1805–9.

C., W. The true reporte of the Skirmish fought betwene the States of Flaunders, and Don Joan. [1578?]

A briefe discourse of the assault, committed upon William Prince of Orange. 1582 (bis); rptd Somers Tracts, ed. Sir W. Scott, vol. I, p. 382, 1809.

P., G. The true report of the death, of William of Nassawe. Middelburg, 1584; rptd Harleian Misc. ed. T. Park, vol. III, p. 200, 1809.

Studley, Christopher. Treason Pretended against the king of Scots. 1585; rptd Harleian Misc. ed. T. Park, vol. VII, p. 50, 1811.

The whole and true discourse of the enterprises against Henry de Valois. 1589; rptd Harleian Misc. ed. T. Park, vol. IV, p. 240, 1809.

A journall, or Briefe report of the late service in Britaigne, by the Prince de Dombes. 1591.

R[oberts], H[enry]. Lancaster his Allarums in Brasill. [1595.]

Newes from Rome, Venice, and Vienna, touching the present proceedinges of the Turkes against the Christians. 1595. [An early example (for England) of a budget of news from various places, later known in England as a coranto.]

Newes from divers countries. As, From Spaine, Antwerpe, Collin, Venice, Rome. 1597.

A briefe and true Declaration of the sicknesse and death of the King of Spaine. 1599; rptd Harleian Misc. ed. T. Park, vol. II, p. 395, 1809.

The Earle of Gowries conspiracie against the Kings Majestie of Scotland. 1600; 1603; rptd Somers Tracts, ed. Sir W. Scott, vol. I, p. 508, 1809.

[Teixeira, José.] The True Historie of the adventures of Don Sebastian King of Portugall. 1602; rptd Harleian Misc. ed. T. Park, vol. IV, p. 423, 1809.

A letter written to the East Indian marchants in London: containing the estate of the East Indian fleete. 1603.

The terrible and deserved death of Francis Ravilliack for the murther of the French King. 1610; rptd Harleian Misc. ed. T. Park, vol. VI, p. 607, 1810.

A true declaration of the arrivall of Cornelius Haga ambassador for the United Netherlands, at Constantinople. 1613; rptd Harleian Misc. ed. T. Park, vol. VIII, p. 404, 1811.

The true description of the execution of justice upon Sir John van Olden Barnevelt. 1619.

A relation Containing the manner of the Election and Coronation of Ferdinand the Emperour, in Francford. 1620.

A True Relation of the Bloody Execution of some chief Statesmen in Prague. 1621; rptd Harleian Misc. ed. T. Park, vol. VII, p. 320, 1811.

True copies of the insolent letter written by the Great Turke for denouncing of warre against Poland. 1621; rptd Somers Tracts, ed. Sir W. Scott, vol. II, p. 462, 1809.

A journall or daily register of the Siege of Berghen-up-Zoome. 1622.

Pellham, Edward. Gods power and providence: shewed in the preservation of eight Englishmen left in Green-land. 1631; rptd Hakluyt Soc. 1855.

The great and famous battel of Lutzen, betweene the King of Sweden and Walstein. 1633.

A true and perfect Relation of the Victorie gained by Philip, King of Spaine against Lewis the French King. 1641.

(2) Single-Sheet Corantos

[These were budgets of news from various continental news-centres, originally, no doubt, extracted from letters. Four series of them, appearing approximately weekly, were published in English at various Dutch cities in 1620 and 1621. The earliest known part of each series is listed below; for the full list (except the fourth entry below) see M. A. Shaaber, Some Forerunners of the Newspaper in England, Philadelphia, 1929 (Appendix). In September and October 1621, after the Dutch series had apparently ceased, the series printed in London appeared. These six London corantos have a good claim to be called the first English newspapers. The series of news-books which commenced the following May (see next section), to which that title is usually awarded, differs from them only in format and was probably issued by the same bookseller. Of the 33 single-sheet corantos known to exist, 24 have been rptd in facs. by W. P. Van Stockum, jr, The First Newspapers of England printed in Holland, Hague, 1914.]

[Coranto without title.] Imprinted at Amsterdam by George Veseler, A°. 1620. The 2. of Decemember [sic]. [15 other issues with Veseler's name are known.]

Courante, Or, Newes from Italy and Germany. Printed at Amsterdam [by Broer Jonson?] the 9. of Aprill, 1621. [One other similar issue without a name and six more with Jonson's imprint are also known.]

Newes from the Low Countries. Printed at Altmore [i.e. Alkmaar] by M H, July 29. 1621.

Corrant or newes from Italie, Germanie, France, and other places. From Altmore by M H August 6. 1621. [No others with this imprint on record.]

Corante, or, newes from Italy, Germany, Hungaria, Polonia, France, and Dutchland. Imprinted at the Hage by Adrian Clarke, the 10. of August. 1621. [No other with this imprint on record.]

Corante, or, newes from Italy, Germany, Hungarie, Spaine and France. London Printed for N. B. [Nicholas Bourne?] September the 24. 1621.

Corante, or weekely newes from Italy [&c.]. the 30. of Septemb. 1621.

Corant or weekly newes. October 2. 1621.

Corante, or weekely newes. the 6. of October. 1621.

Corant or weekly newes. October the 11. 1621.

Corant or weekly newes. October the 22. 1621.

(3) The Earliest News-Periodicals

[All confined to foreign news.]

(a) The First English 'Newspaper'

[The word newspaper is something of a misnomer because it had not come into use at this time and the numbers of this first newsperiodical were ptd as quarto pamphlets. In content they are quite like the single-sheet corantos ptd at London and may be regarded as their successor. 11 issues ptd for Nicholas Bourne and Thomas Archer between 23 May and 9 September 1622 have survived, and entries in the Stationers' Register give evidence of six more.]

A Currant of generall newes Dated the 14th of may last [1622]. [This, presumably the first number, is known only from the S.R. entry on 18 May 1622 (Arber's Transcript, vol. IV, p. 68).]

The 23. of May. Weekely Newes from Italy, Germanie, Hungaria, Bohemia, the Palatinate, France, and the Low Countries. Translated out of the Low Dutch Copie. 1622.

The 30. of May. Weekly newes from Italy, Germanie, [etc.]. 1622.

Good newes from Alsasia and the Palatinate, the fift of June. 1622.

The true copies of two especiall letters sent from the Palatinate. Printed this 21. of June. 1622.

The Safe arrivall of Christian duke of Brunswick Unto the king of Bohemiah. Printed this third of July. 1622.

A true relation of the proceedings of the Bavarian and Spanish forces before the City Heydelburgh. Printed the 11. of Julii. 1622.

The surprisall of two imperial townes by Count Mansfield. Printed this nineteenth of July. 1622.

August 11. 1622. A remonstration unto the French King. 1622.

The 13. of August 1622. The post of the prince, which advises us the taking of Steen Bergh. And Relates all the late Newes of Europe. 1622.

The 2 of September. Two great battailes very lately fought. 1622.

The Ninth of September. 1622. Count Mansfields proceedings since the last battaile. 1622.

[The issue of 9 Sept. seems to have offended the authorities and Bourne and Archer published no more until that of 27 Sept. which was 'Printed for Nathaniel Butter and Thomas Archer.' This signifies a merger of Bourne and Archer's periodical with that which Butter and his associates had been publishing since 5 June or earlier (see below), and it may have been commanded by the government. Henceforth Butter and Bourne are the leading partners in the enterprise.]

The 27. of September. A relation of letters, and other advertisements of Newes. Printed for Nathaniel Butter, and Thomas Archer. 1622.

The 4. of Octob: 1622. A true relation of the affaires of Europe. Printed for Nathaniel Butter, and Nicholas Bourne. 1622.

October 15. 1622. Novo 1. A relation of the late occurrents which have happened in Christendome. Printed for Butter and Bourne. 1622.

October 15. 1622. No. 2. A continuation of the affaires of the Low-Countries. Printed for Butter and Barth. Downes. 1622.

[From this point forward, since the publishers have hit on the idea of numbering their issues, the parts of this periodical are easier to identify. In the issue of 4 Oct. and No. 2 of 15 Oct. the style and arrangement of the news change noticeably as an 'editor' takes the newsbooks in hand. Except for the fact that in 1625 the publishers used the pseudonym of Mercurius Britannicus instead of their own names, the periodical seems to have continued without change, not always very prosperously, until it was ordered to stop by the Court of Star Chamber, 17 Oct. 1632.]

(b) Butter's Periodical

[Between 5 June and 25 Sept. 1622 Butter (sometimes in association with William Sheffard or Bartholomew Downes) pbd 8 periodical newsbooks which are known to-day and S.R. give evidence of 3 or 4 more. This series was merged with Bourne and Archer's on 27 Sept. (see above).]

More news from the Palatinate, the second time imprinted June the 5. Printed for N. Butter and W. Sheffard. 1622.

A letter sent from Maynhem concerning the late defeate given the Duke of Brunswicke. Whereunto is added a Couranto of other newes this 20. of June. For Butter. 1622.

The certaine newes of this present weeke this second of August. For Butter. 1622.

[13 Aug. For Butter, 1622.]

The fourth of September. Newes from sundry places, both forraine and domestique. For Butter. 1622.

The 14. of September. A relation of many memorable Passages since the 4. of this Moneth. For Butter, Downes, and Shefford. 1622.

The 20th. of September. The Newes which now arrive from divers parts. For Butter and Sheffard. 1622.

The 25. of September. Newes from most parts of Christendome. For Butter and Sheffard. 1622.

(c) Newsbooks Published by Sheffard, Newbery, and Downes

[While these newsbooks were undoubtedly pbd in emulation of those issued by Bourne and Archer and by Butter, there are scarcely enough of them to warrant calling them a third periodical. Entries in S.R. (Arber's

Transcript, vol. IV, pp. 78, 80) indicate that Sheffard and Downes pbd one, perhaps two, more. On 14 September Sheffard and Downes joined forces with Butter (see above).]

The 18 of June. Weekely Newes from Italy, Germanie, Hungaria, Bohemia, the Palatinate, and the Low Countries. For Nathaniel Newbery and William Sheffard. 1622.

The relation of all the last passages of the warres in the Palatinate. Printed this eighteenth of July. For Newbery and Sheffard. 1622.

(d) Thomas Walkley's Periodical

A journall of all the proceedings of the Duke of Buckingham in the Isle of Ree. 1627.

A continued journall. August 17. 1627. [Four more numbers are known to have been pbd.]

(e) Archer's Periodical

[A number of newsbooks pbd by Thomas Archer (sometimes in association with Benjamin Fisher) in 1624, 1625 and 1628 arouses the suspicion that he broke away from the Butter-Bourne syndicate and tried, possibly at two different times, to publish a newsperiodical of his own.]

Septemb. 9. Numb. 23. A continuation of the former newes. [1624.] [In another issue the title reads: Septemb. 10. Numb. 23. Extraordinary newes. Both issues are numbered 32 on the second leaf.]

October 11. Number 2. Two wonderful and lamentable accidents. 1624.

November the 10. Number the 5. In this weekes newes is Related [etc.]. 1625 (for 1624).

Novem 24. Num. 7. The weekely Newes. 1624.

[Date and number cut off.] A continuation of all the principall occurrences. 1625.

Aug. 7. Num. 6. The continuation of our weekly Newes. 1628.

August 15. Num. 7. The Continuation of our weekly Newes. 1628.

(4) SEMI-ANNUAL FOREIGN HISTORIES

[When the weekly newsbooks were suppressed in October 1632, Butter and Bourne resorted to issuing their news in semi-annual volumes.]

[Watts, William.] The Swedish intelligencer. The first part. 1632 (3 edns). The Second Part. 1632 (2 issues). The Third Part. Unto which is added The Fourth Part. 1633.

The continuation of the German history. The Fifth Part. 1633.

The history of the present Warres of Germany. A sixt part. 1634.

A supplement to the sixth part of the Germane history. 1634.

[C., N.] The German history continued. The Seventh Part. 1634.

—— The modern history of the world. The eighth Part. 1635.

—— Numb. primo. The principall passages of Germany, Italy, France, and other places. 1636 (2 issues).

—— Num. 2. The continuation of the actions in the upper Germanie. 1637.

—— Diatelesma. Nu. 3. 1637. The second part. 1638. The fifth part. 1639.

[On 20 December 1638, by royal warrant, Butter and Bourne were granted the privilege of publishing foreign news for 21 years. The publication of the weekly newsbooks was immediately resumed, but the privilege was soon nullified by events which threw the news-publishing field wide open. Weekly newsbooks devoted to foreign news continued to appear irregularly throughout the greater part of the next twenty years.]

(5) MODERN WORKS
(a) Books

Timperley, C. H. Encyclopaedia of Literary and Typographical Anecdote. 1842.

Bourne, H. R. Fox. English Newspapers. 2 vols. 1887.

Bücher, Carl. Industrial Evolution. Tr. S. M. Wickett, New York, 1901. ['The genesis of journalism,' pp. 215–43, traces the rise of printed newsbooks and sheets out of written newsletters on the continent.]

Muddiman, J. G. A History of English Journalism to the Foundation of the Gazette. 1908. [Pbd under the pseudonym 'J. B. Williams.']

Firth, C. H. Ballads and Broadsides. [In Shakespeare's England, 2 vols. Oxford, 1916.]

McKerrow, R. B. Booksellers, Printers, and the Stationers' Trade. [In Shakespeare's England, 2 vols. Oxford, 1916.]

Rollins, H. E. Old English Ballads. Cambridge, 1920. [This collection of ballads, as well as the next four contains a valuable introduction.]

—— A Pepysian Garland. Cambridge, 1922.

—— Cavalier and Puritan. New York, 1923.

—— The Pack of Autolycus. Cambridge, U.S.A. 1927.

—— The Pepys Ballads. 8 vols. Cambridge, U.S.A. 1929–32.

Notestein, Wallace, and Relf, F. H. Commons Debates for 1629. Minneapolis, 1921.

Harlow, A. F. Old Post Bags. New York, 1928.

Harrison, G. B. An Elizabethan Journal. 1928.
—— A Second Elizabethan Journal. 1931.
—— A Last Elizabethan Journal, 1599–1603. 1933.
Shaaber, M. A. Some Forerunners of the Newspaper in England, 1476–1622. Philadelphia, 1929.
Morison, Stanley. The English Newspaper. Cambridge, 1932.

(b) Articles in Periodicals

Firth, Sir C. H. The Ballad History of the Reigns of Henry VII and Henry VIII. Trans. Royal Hist. Soc. ii, 1908.
—— The Ballad History of the Reigns of the Later Tudors. Trans. Royal Hist. Soc. iii, 1909.
—— Ballad History of the Reign of James I. Trans. Royal Hist. Soc. v, 1911.
Barwick, G. F. Corantos. Library, iv, 1913.
Esdaile, Arundell. Autolycus' Pack: the Ballad Journalism of the Sixteenth Century. Quart. Rev. ccxviii, 1913.
'Williams, J. B.' [i.e. J. G. Muddiman]. The Earliest English Corantos. Library, iv, 1913.
Rollins, H. E. The Black-letter Broadside Ballads. PMLA. xxxiv, 1919.
Shaaber, M. A. The History of the First English Newspaper. Stud. Phil. xxix, 1932.

(c) Bibliographical Works

Ames, Joseph. Typographical Antiquities; augmented by William Herbert; and enlarged by Thomas F. Dibdin. 4 vols. 1810–19.
Lemon, Robert. Catalogue of a Collection of Printed Broadsides in the Possession of the Society of Antiquaries. 1866.
Hazlitt, W. C. Hand-Book to the Popular, Poetical, and Dramatic Literature of Great Britain. 1867.
—— Collections and Notes, 1867–76. 1876. Ser. 2, 1882. Ser. 3, 1887. Supplements, 1889, 1892. Ser. 4, 1903.
Arber, Edward. A Transcript of the Registers of the Company of Stationers of London; 1554–1640. 5 vols. 1875–94.
British Museum. Catalogue of Books in English, to the Year 1640. 3 vols. 1884.
[Sayle, C. E.] Early English Printed Books in the University Library Cambridge (1475 to 1640). 4 vols. Cambridge, 1900–7.
['Williams, J. B.' i.e. J. G. Muddiman]. The Times Tercentenary Handlist of English and Welsh Newspapers, Magazines and Reviews. 1920.
Rollins, H. E. An Analytical Index to the Ballad-entries (1557–1709) in the Registers of the Company of Stationers of London. Stud. Phil. xxi, 1924.

Pollard, A. W. and Redgrave, G. R. A Short-title Catalogue of English Books, 1475–1640. Bibliog. Soc. 1926.
Crane, R. S. and Kaye, F. B. A Census of British Newspapers and Periodicals, 1620–1800. Chapel Hill, North Carolina, 1927.

(d) Books on Governmental Regulation of the Press

Hart, W. H. Index Expurgatorius Anglicanus. 5 pts, 1872–8.
Paterson, James. The Liberty of the Press, Speech, and Public Worship. 1880. [Chs. iii, v.]
Stephen, Sir J. F. A History of the Criminal Law of England. 3 vols. 1883. [Vol. ii, ch. xxiv.]
Duff, E. Gordon. A Century of the English Book Trade. 1905.
Putnam, G. H. The Censorship of the Church of Rome. 2 vols. New York, 1907. [Vol. ii, chs. viii, ix.]
Dictionary of Printers and Booksellers, 1557–1640. Ed. R. B. McKerrow, 1910.
Pollard, A. W. Shakespeare's Fight with the Pirates. Cambridge, 1917.
Salmon, L. M. The Newspaper and Authority. New York, 1923.
Reed, A. W. Early Tudor Drama. [1926.]
Albright, E. M. Dramatic Publication in England, 1580–1640. New York, 1927.

M. A. S.

II. 1641–1659

(1) GENERAL AUTHORITIES

(a) Original Sources now Printed

Journals of the House of Lords (1628–1649). Vols. iv–x.
Journals of the House of Commons (1640–1659). Vols. ii–vii.
Acts and Ordinances of the Interregnum. Ed. Sir C. H. Firth and R. S. Rait, 3 vols. 1911.
Calendar of State Papers. Domestic Series. Charles I. Vols. xvii–xxiii (1641–9), ed. W. D. Hamilton, 1882–97.
Calendar of State Papers. Domestic Series. The Commonwealth. Vols. i–xiii (1649–60), ed. M. A. E. Green, 1875–86.
Thurloe, John. A Collection of State Papers. Ed. T. Birch, 7 vols. 1742.
A Transcript of the Registers of the Stationers Company (1641–1708). Ed. G. E. Briscoe Eyre [and H. R. Plomer], 3 vols. Roxburghe Club, 1912–3.

(b) Contemporary Pamphlets

Jonson, Ben. The Staple of News. 1631.
Old Newes Newly Revived: or, the discovery of all the Occurrences happened since the

beginning of Parliament between Mr Inquisitive, a Country Gentleman, and Master Intelligencer, a Newsmonger. [June] 1641.

A Presse full of Pamphlets. [April] 1642.

J[ordan], T[homas]. A Diurnall of Dangers. [14 Aug.] 1642.

A Remonstrance of Londons Occurrences. [31 Jan.] 1643.

[Parker, Henry.] Humble Remonstrance of the Company of Stationers. [April] 1643; rptd E. Arber (Transcript of the Registers of the Company of Stationers, vol. i, 1875, pp. 584–8).

A Letter from Mercurius Civicus to Mercurius Rusticus; or, Londons Confession but not repentance. Oxford, [25 Aug.]. 1643.

[Featley, Daniel.] Sacra Nemesis, the Levites Scourge; or, Mercurius Britan-Civicus disciplined. [1 Aug.] 1644.

M[ilton], J[ohn]. Areopagitica. [24 Nov.] 1644.

[Cleveland, John.] The Character of a London Diurnall. [Oxford, Jan.] 1645. [Rptd in Poems, 1659, etc.]

[Wither, George.] The Great Assizes holden in Parnassus by Apollo. [11 Feb.] 1645; rptd Spenser Soc. 1885.

A Character of the New Oxford Libeller in answer to his Character of a London Diurnall. [11 Feb.] 1645.

The Oxford Character of a London Diurnall examined and answered. [31 March] 1645.

[Pecke, Samuel?] A Full Answer to a scandalous pamphlet intituled 'A Character of a London Diurnall.' [10 April] 1645.

[Taylor, John.] Rebels Anathematized and Anatomized. Oxford, [25 May] 1645; rptd Spenser Soc. 1884.

The Cavaliers Diurnall written by Adventure. [31 March 1647.]

[Cleveland, John.] A Character of a Moderate Intelligencer. [29 April] 1647.

A True Diurnall with some Perfect Occurrences, Weekly and Moderate Intelligence. [31 May] 1647.

A Fresh Whip for all Scandalous Lyers; or a True Description of the Two Eminent Pamphleteers, or Squibtellers of this Kingdome. [9 Sept.] 1647.

Mercurius Diabolicus; or Hells Intelligencer. the author Democritus Junior. [29 Sept.] 1647.

Welcome, most welcome Newes. Mercurius Retrogradus, one of the Fraternity who is come on Earth to visit and salute his dear Brethren, viz. Mercurius Aulicus, Britanicus, Aquaticus, Melancholicus, Morbicus, Moderator. [15 Oct.] 1647.

Hinc Illae Lacrimae, or the Impietie of Impunitie. [23 Dec.] 1647.

Loyalty Speaks Truth; or, A Conference of the Grand Mercuries, Pragmaticus, Melancholicus and Elencticus. [10 Jan.] 1648.

[Harris, John?] Mercurius Anti-Mercurius communicating all Humours, Conditions, Forgeries and Lyes of Mydas-eared newsmongers. [4 April] 1648.

A Muzzle for Cerberus and his three whelps Mercurius Elencticus, Bellicus and Melancholicus, by Mercurio-Mastix Hibernicus. [20 June] 1648.

Hermes Straticus or a Scourge for Elencticus and the Royall Pamphleteers. 17 Aug. 1648.

[Hackluyt, John?] Mercurius Anti-Mercurius. No. 1, 19 Sept.–No. 3, 2 Oct. 1648. [Also attrib. to John Harris.]

[Howell, James.] A Trance; or, News from Hell, brought to towne by Mercurius Acheronticus. [11 Dec.] 1648.

The Hue and Cry after those rambling protonotaries of the times, Mercurius Elencticus, Britanicus, Melancholicus and Aulicus. [7 Feb.] 1651.

[Sheppard, Samuel?] Mercurius Mastix. Faithfully Lashing all Scouts, Posts, Spys, and others who cheat the Commonwealth. No. 1, 27 Aug. 1652.

[Sheppard], S[amuel]. The Weepers; or, The Bed of Snakes Broken. [13 Sept.] 1652.

[Cleveland, John.] A Character of a Diurnall Maker. [28 Nov.] 1653. [Rptd in Poems, 1659, etc.]

(c) Modern Works

Chalmers, George. The Life of Thomas Ruddiman. 1794.

Wright, Thomas. Political Ballads published in England during the Commonwealth. Percy Soc. 1841.

Hunt, F. K. The Fourth Estate. Contributions towards a History of Newspapers and of the Liberty of the Press. 2 vols. 1850.

Andrews, A. A. A History of British Journalism. 2 vols. 1859.

Hart, W. H. Index Expurgatorius Anglicanus. 5 pts, 1872–8.

Paterson, J. The Liberty of the Press, Speech and Public Worship. 1880.

Jackson, Mason. The Pictorial Press, its Origin and Progress. 1885.

Bourne, H. R. Fox. English Newspapers. 2 vols. 1887.

Plomer, H. R. Notices of Printers and Printing in the State Papers. Bibliographica, ii, 1896, pp. 204–26.

'Williams, J. B.' [i.e. J. G. Muddiman]. The Newsbooks and Letters of News of the Restoration. EHR. April 1908.

—— A History of English Journalism to the Foundation of the Gazette. 1908.

'Williams, J. B.' The Beginnings of English Journalism. CHEL. vol. VII, 1911.

Notestein, W. and Relf, F. H. Commons Debates for 1629. Minneapolis, 1921. [Introduction.]

McCutcheon, R. P. The Beginnings of Book Reviewing in English Periodicals. PMLA. XXXVII, 1922.

Rollins, H. E. Cavalier and Puritan. New York, 1923.

Thompson, E. N. S. Literary Bypaths of the Renaissance. New Haven, 1924. [Ch. iii, War Journalism of the XVIIth Century.]

Griffith, R. H. Some Unrecorded Newsbooks. TLS. 11 Dec. 1924.

Morison, Stanley. The English Newspaper. Some Account of the Physical Development of Journals published in London between 1622 and the Present Day. Cambridge, 1932.

Richardson, Mrs Herbert. The Old English Newspaper. English Ass. 1933.

Clyde, W. M. The Struggle for the Freedom of the Press from Caxton to Cromwell. St Andrews, 1934.

(2) BIOGRAPHIES OF PARTICULAR JOURNALISTS

Aubrey, John. Brief Lives. Ed. A. Clark, 2 vols. Oxford, 1898.

à Wood, Anthony. Athenae Oxonienses. 2 vols. Oxford, 1691–2; 2 vols. 1721; ed. P. Bliss, 4 vols. 1813–20.

Plomer, H. R. A Dictionary of Booksellers and Printers, 1641–1667. Bibliog. Soc. 1907.

SIMEON ASHE (A Continuation of True Intelligence, 1644).

[Barwick, John.] Querela Cantabrigiensis. Oxford, [1 April] 1646.

THOMAS AUDLEY (Mercurius Britanicus, 1643–4).

[Taylor, John.] Mercurius Aquaticus: or the Water Poet's Answer to all that shall be written by Mercurius Britanicus. Oxford, [18 Jan.] 1644. [This was the first pamphlet of a long controversy between Taylor and John Booker.]

Mercurius Anti-Britanicus; or, The Second Part of the King's Cabinet Vindicated. [Oxford, Aug.] 1645.

SIR JOHN BERKENHEAD (Mercurius Aulicus, 1643–5).

The Recantation of Mercurius Aulicus; or Berkenhead's Complaint. [14 March] 1644.

The True Character of Mercurius Aulicus. 1645.

Biographia Britannica. Vol. II, 1780, pp. 324–6.

EDWARD BOWLES (A Faithful Relation of The Scottish Army, 1644).

Calamy, E. The Nonconformist's Memorial. Ed. S. Palmer, vol. III, 1803, pp. 455–8.

JOHN CLEVELAND (Mercurius Pragmaticus, 1647).

A Character of the New Oxford Libeller in answer to his Character of a London Diurnall. [11 Feb.] 1645.

Lake, John. [Life prefixed to] Clievelandi Vindiciae. 1677.

Percy, Thomas. Biographia Britannica. Vol. III, 1784, pp. 628–33.

JOHN DILLINGHAM (The Parliament Scout, 1643–5; The Moderate Intelligencer, 1645–9).

The Copy of a Letter written from Northampton. [6 Feb.] 1646.

WALTER FROST (A Brief Relation, 1649).

Mercurius Elencticus. 5 Nov. 1649.

JOHN HACKLUYT (Mercurius Melancholicus, 1647–8, etc.).

Mercurius Melancholicus. No. 2, 2 June 1649. [A counterfeit attrib. to John Taylor.]

JOHN HALL (Mercurius Brittanicus, 1648, etc.).

[Wharton, Sir George.] Mercurius Elencticus. Nos. 27–29, 34, May–July 1648.

D[avies], J[ohn]. [Memoir prefixed to] Hierocles upon the Golden Verses of Pythagoras. Tr. John Hall, 1657.

JOHN HARRIS (Mercurius Militaris, 1648, etc.).

[Crouch, John.] Mercurius Fumigosus. 30 Nov., 13 Dec. 1654.

The Speech of Major John Harris at the place of execution. [Sept.] 1660.

JOHN MILTON (Mercurius Politicus, 1650–2).

Masson, David. The Life of John Milton. 8 vols. 1859–80 (rev. edn of vol. I, 1881).

'Williams, J. B.' [i.e. J. G. Muddiman]. John Milton, Journalist. Oxford and Cambridge Rev. XVIII, 1912.

HENRY MUDDIMAN (The Parliamentary Intelligencer, 1659).

Muddiman, J. G. The King's Journalist. 1923.

MARCHAMONT NEEDHAM (Mercurius Britanicus, 1644–6; Mercurius Pragmaticus, 1648; Mercurius Politicus, 1650–60).

[Taylor, John.] Rebells Anathematized and Anatomized. Oxford, [25 May] 1645.

Mercurius Anti-Britanicus, or the Second Part of the King's Cabinet Vindicated. [Oxford, Aug.] 1645.

Wortley, Sir Francis. Characters and Elegies. 1646, p. 26.

Match me these two; or the conviction and arraignment of Britannicus and Lilburne. [29 July] 1647.

[Cleveland, John?] The Committee Man's Complaint. [26 Aug.] 1647.

—— The Poor Committee Man's Accompt avouched by Britannicus. [26 Aug.] 1647.

—— The Character of Mercurius Politicus. [14 Aug.] 1650.

—— The Second Character of Mercurius Politicus. [23 Oct.] 1650.

Kilburne, William. A New Years Gift for Mercurius Politicus. [29 Dec.] 1659. [Broadside.]

The Downefall of Mercurius Britannicus-Pragmaticus-Politicus, and three headed Cerberus. [9 April 1660.]

A Dialogue between Thomas Scot and Marchamont Nedham. [1660.]

[L'Estrange, Sir Roger.] A Rope for Pol, or a Hue and Cry after Marchamont Nedham. [7 Sept.] 1660.

Wright, Thomas. Political Ballads. Percy Soc. 1841, pp. 56–63.

SAMUEL PECKE (*A Perfect Diurnal*, 1642–55, etc.).

A Fresh Whip for all Scandalous Lyers. [9 Sept.] 1647.

JOHN RUSHWORTH (*The London Post*, 1647, etc.).

[Crouch, John.] The Man in the Moon. 24 Oct. 1649.

JOHN SALTMARSH (*Perfect Occurrences*, 1646).

Fuller, Thomas. The History of the Worthies of England. 1662, p. 212.

SAMUEL SHEPPARD (*Mercurius Pragmaticus*, 1647, etc.).

The Metropolitan Nuncio. No. 3, 13 June 1649.

GEORGE SMITH (*The Scotish Dove*, 1643–6).

The Scotish Dove sent out the last time. [25 Dec.] 1646.

JOHN STREATER (*Observations upon Aristotle*, 1654).

Secret Reasons of State. [23 May] 1659.

JOHN TAYLOR (*Mercurius Melancholicus* [counterfeit], 1647, etc.).

Hindley, C. [Introduction to Taylor's] Works. 1872.

HENRY WALKER (*Perfect Occurrences*, 1647–9, etc.).

[Taylor, John.] The Whole Life and Progress of Henry Walker the Ironmonger. 1642; rptd C. Hindley (Old Book Collector's Miscellany, vol. III, 1873).

A Fresh Whip for All Scandalous Lyers. [7 Sept.] 1647.

A Recommendation to Mercurius Morbicus. [6 Oct.] 1647. [Attrib. to Martin Parker or John Taylor.]

à Wood, Anthony. Athenae Oxonienses. Ed. P. Bliss, vol. II, 1815, column 71.

'Williams, J. B.' [*i.e.* J. G. Muddiman]. Henry Walker, Journalist of the Commonwealth. Nineteenth Century, March 1908.

SIR GEORGE WHARTON (*Mercurius Elencticus*, 1647–9).

[Hall, John?] The Late Story of Mr William Lilly. [2 Feb.] 1648.

(3) COMMENTS UPON PARTICULAR NEWS-BOOKS

A Continuation of the True Diurnall (pbd H. Blunden) (1642).

Griffith, R. H. The Second English Newspaper. TLS. 4 Dec. 1924.

Mercurius Aulicus (1643–5).

A Letter from a minister in his Excellence his Army by way of prevention to Mercurius Aulicus and his complices. [18 April] 1643. [Perhaps by Edward Bowles.]

A Copy of a Letter written by Mr Stephen Marshall. [17 May] 1643.

An Antidote against the malignant influence of Mercurius (surnamed) Aulicus. 2 Sept. 1643.

An Answer to Mercurius Aulicus. [*c*. 15 Dec.] 1643.

Anti-Aulicus. [No. 1, 6 Feb. 1644]; [No. 2, 8 Feb. 1644.]

The Recantation of Mercurius Aulicus; or Berkinhead's Complaint. [14 March] 1644.

Mercurius Aulico-Mastix; or, The Whipping Mercury. No. 1, 12 April 1644.

[Cheynell, Francis.] Aulicus his Dream. [15 May] 1644 (*bis*).

The True Character of Mercurius Aulicus. 1645.

News from Smith the Oxford Jaylor with the arraignment of Mercurius Aulicus for his notorious libelling against State and Kingdome. [5 Feb.] 1645.

A Whip for an Ape: or Aulicus his Whelp worm'd for feare he should run mad and byte Brittanicus. [29 Aug.] 1645.

Mercurius Britanicus (1643–6).

Britanicus Vapulans; or The Whipping of poor British Mercury by Mercurius Urbanus, younger brother to Aulicus. No. 1, 4 Nov. 1643; [continued as] Mercurius Urbanus. [No. 2], 9 Nov. 1643; [No. 3, n.d.]. [Attrib. to Daniel Featley.]

[Taylor, John.] Mercurius Aquaticus; or the Water Poet's Answer to all that shall be written by Mercurius Britanicus. [18 Jan.] 1644. [This pamphlet involved Taylor in a lengthy controversy with John Booker.]

A Checke to Britanicus. [14 Feb.] 1644. [Attrib. to William Prynne.]

A Check to the Checker of Britanicus. [24 Feb.] 1644. [Attrib. to John Saltmarsh.]

Ruperts Sumpter and Private Cabinet rifled by way of dialogue between Mercurius Britannicus and Mercurius Aulicus. [20 July] 1644.

Mercurius Anti-Britannicus. [Oxford, 4 Aug. 1645.]

Mercurius Britannicus, his Apologie to all well-affected People. [11 Aug.] 1645.

Mercurius Anti-Britannicus; or, Part of the King's Cabinet vindicated from the aspersions of Mercurius Britannicus. [Oxford, 11 Aug.], 1645.

Aulicus his hue and Cry sent forth after Britanicus. [13 Aug.] 1645. [Attrib. to Francis Cheynell.]

Mercurius Anti-Britannicus; or, The Second Part of the King's Cabinet vindicated. [18? Aug. 1645.]

[Wortley, Sir Francis.] Britannicus his Blessing. Britanicus his Welcome. Cambridge, [17 Jan.] 1646. [Rptd as Mercurius Britanicus his Welcome to Hell: with the Devill's Blessing to Britanicus, [25 Feb.] 1647; also rptd in Wortley's Characters and Elegies, [15 July] 1646.]

Mercurius Britannicus his Vision being a reply to a pamphlet termed Britanicus his Welcome to Hell. [25 March] 1647. [Attrib. to Marchamont Needham.]

Mercurius Civicus (1643–6).

A Letter from Mercurius Civicus to Mercurius Rusticus; or, Londons Confession but not repentance. Oxford, [25 Aug.] 1643.

Plomer, H. R. An Analysis of the Civil War Newspaper Mercurius Civicus. Library, VI, 1905.

Mercurius Democritus (1652–3; 1659).

Mercurius Democritus, his last will and testament. [16 Sept.] 1652.

Newes from Tenebris; or preterpluperfect nocturnall or night Worke. 1652. [Attrib. to John Taylor.]

A Hue and Cry after Mercurius Democritus and The Wandering Whore. 1662.

Mercurius Melancholicus (1647–9).

Mercurius Anti-Melancholicus. No. 1, 24 Sept. 1647.

Mercurius Morbicus (1647).

A Recommendation to Mercurius Morbicus. [6 Oct.] 1647. [Attrib. to John Taylor or Martin Parker.]

Mercurius Politicus (1650–60).

[Cleveland, John?] The Character of Mercurius Politicus. [14 Aug.] 1650.

—— The Second Character of Mercurius Politicus. [23 Oct.] 1650.

Webster, John. The Picture of Mercurius Politicus. [12 Oct.] 1653.

Mercurius Pragmaticus (1647–50).

Mercurius Anti-Pragmaticus. No. 1, 19 Oct. 1647–No. 19, 3 Feb. 1648.

The Publick Adviser (1657).

[Needham, Marchamont.] The Office of Publick Advice newly set up. [14 May] 1657.

Speciall Passages and Certaine Informations (pbd H. Blunden, 1642–3).

Mercurius Civicus. 8 June 1643.

The Weekly Information from the Office of Intelligence (1657).

[Williams, Oliver.] A Prohibition to all Persons who have set up any offices called by the names of Addresses, Publique Advice, or Intelligence in London. [26 May] 1657.

(4) LISTS OF NEWS-BOOKS AND NEWS-
PAPERS

(a) *Bibliographies*

Chalmers, George. A Chronological List of Newspapers from the Epoch of the Civil Wars. [In The Life of Thomas Ruddiman, 1794, Appendix 6.]

Nichols, John. Literary Anecdotes of the XVIIIth Century. 9 vols. 1812–5. [Vol. IV, pp. 38–97; Additions, vol. VIII, pp. 494–9.]

Timperley, C. H. An Encyclopaedia of Literary and Typographical Anecdote. 1842.

Bullen, George [and Rayner, W.]. Caxton Celebration Catalogue. 1877, pp. 225–46.

'Williams, J. B.' [i.e. J. G. Muddiman]. The History of English Journalism to the Foundation of the Gazette. 1908. [Appendix D.]

Madan, Falconer. Oxford Books. Vol. II (1641–50), Oxford, 1912.

Crane, R. S. and Kaye, F. B. A Census of British Newspapers and Periodicals, 1620–1800. Chapel Hill, North Carolina, 1927. [Pt ii.]

(b) *Lists of Extant Files*

British Museum. Catalogue of Printed Books. Periodical Publications. 2 vols. 1899–1900.

[Edmonds, J. P.] Bibliotheca Lindesiana [belonging to the Earl of Crawford and Balcarres]. Collations and Notes. No. V, 1901 (priv. ptd).

British Museum. Catalogue of the Thomason Tracts. 2 vols. 1908.

Yale University. A List of Newspapers in the Yale University Library. New Haven, 1916.

[Muddiman, J. G.] The Tercentenary Handlist of English and Welsh Newspapers, Magazines and Reviews. 1920.

Crane, R. S. and Kaye, F. B. A Census of British Newspapers and Periodicals, 1620–1800. Chapel Hill, North Carolina, 1927. [Pt i.]

Gabler, A. J. Check List of English Newspapers and Periodicals before 1801 in the Huntington Library. Huntington Lib. Bulletin, no. 2, Nov. 1931.

[Stewart, Andrew.] Catalogue of an Exhibition Illustrating the History of the English Newspaper from the Library of the Press Club, London, 1932.

Milford, R. T. and Sutherland, D. M. A Catalogue of English Newspapers and Periodicals in the Bodleian Library 1622–1800. Proc. Oxford Bibliog. Soc. IV, 1936.

(5) THE NEWS-BOOKS, 1641–59

[For the purpose of the following list a news-book is defined as a pamphlet containing current news, or comment thereon, issued or intended to be issued periodically. The presence of a serial number printed on the pamphlet is accepted as evidence of intention to issue periodically. Sometimes a single pamphlet has sequels which develop into a numbered series (e.g. 19 Aug. 1642); and in such cases the pamphlets at the beginning, though unnumbered and with varying titles, have been included if they are clearly part of one series. The pamphlets of Irish news in 1642, though often listed as news-books, have been omitted from this list as they do not fall within the scope of the present definition. In no case has the title only of a pamphlet been taken as a criterion of its being a news-book.

Of many of the entries in this list there exist different forms under the same title and date. These are usually called counterfeits; but they fall into three distinct classes. (i) Where the same title, numbering, text and imprint have been set up differently throughout, it has been referred to as a *reprint*. Most reprints have the names of two printers in the imprint; and presumably arose from the double setting up required to print a large edition in a short time. (ii) Where the same title and imprint occur with a different text, it has been referred to as a *counterfeit*. Their object was often political. In the present list the use of this term has been restricted to this form of variant. (iii) Where the title is the same, but the text and the imprint differ, it has been referred to as

an *imitation*. Only one case has so far been noticed in which the same title and text are found with a different imprint (A Continuation of the True Diurnall of Passages in Parliament. No. 2, 24 Jan. 1642. Sold by Stationers). When alterations have been made in what is the same setting of type, it has been referred to as an *issue*.

Ptd = printed by; pbd = published by or sold for. These indications have been added to distinguish different forms or series of similar titles. They are intended to identify the particular piece listed, and they refer to the imprint thereon whether false or not. Where adequate evidence is known to the compiler of this list, authorship has been indicated without qualification: but the phrase 'attrib. to' has been used in the absence of such knowledge. A few attributions have been suggested with the phrase 'perhaps by.' All news-books with the exception of two noted in 1654 were issued in small quarto. An asterisk has been used to distinguish entries which derive solely from the bibliographies listed above in section (4) (*a*). All other entries are derived from personal examination or from the catalogues listed in section (4) (*b*), where the files are available for corroboration. Any numbers, dates, or imprints here given which are not printed on the news-books themselves have been enclosed in square brackets.

All dates are recorded in the new style irrespective of that ptd on the news-book. The dates given are the days of issue in so far as they are ascertainable. Thus the run of a periodical in this list is not dated from the earliest date mentioned in the text of the earliest issue as in so many catalogues, but from the latest date in the earliest issue to the latest date in the last. Where the news mentioned has taken place in London, the latest date is assumed to be that of the issue of the news-book. Where the latest date concerns an event outside London, or where there is no date at all, the manuscript dates of the Thomason Collection or other contemporary notes have been supplied within square brackets.

It is not always simple to decide if one paper is a continuation of another, or to judge how far the identity of a news-book may survive a change of title or printer or suspension for varying periods. In general it has been considered more accurate to adopt in this list a more conservative attitude than that of the British Museum General Catalogue and most previous bibliographies. To mitigate the misconceptions arising from this, cross-references have been added. Under the date on which any title first appears in this list there have been noted the dates of all similar titles, supposed continuations, revivals, imitations or counterfeits. Under the date of each subsequent appearance of the same title is noted the date of its earliest appearance together with the dates of its immediate predecessor or continuation and any counterfeits of this particular series that are separately entered.]

The Heads of Severall Proceedings in this Present Parliament. [No. 1], 29 Nov. 1641. [Continued as] The Heads of Severall proceedings in both Houses of Parliament. [No. 2], 6 Dec.; [No. 3 not extant]; [continued as] Diurnall Occurrences, or, The Heads of Severall proceedings in both Houses of Parliament. [No. 4], 20 Dec. 1641–[No. 9], 24 Jan. 1642; No. 4, 31 Jan.– No. 6, 14 Feb. 1642. [The subtitle varies slightly, that of Jan. 31 reading 'or, The last Weekes Proceedings in both Houses of Parliament.' All pbd John Thomas, but 20 Dec. with T. B. and 3, 10 Jan. with Nathaniel Butter.] (Cf. 20 Dec. 1641, 17 Jan., 23 May 1642).

The Diurnall, or, The Heads of All the Proceedings in Parliament. [No. 1], 13 Dec.– [No. 3], 26 Dec. 1641. [No. 1 pbd J. W. and T. B.; Nos. 2, 3 pbd John Wright.]

The Diurnall Occurrances: or, The Heads of Proceedings in Parliament. [No. 1], 20 Dec. 1641. [Pbd T. Bates and F. Coules (2 issues).] (Cf. 29 Nov. 1641, 17 Jan. 1642.)

Diurnal Occurrances, Touching the dayly Proceedings in Parliament. [No. 1], 25 Dec. 1641; [No. 2], 3 Jan.; [No. 3], 10 Jan. 1642. [No. 1 no imprint; Nos. 2, 3 pbd John Hammond. No. 2 rptd Edinburgh, 1642.]

Diurnall Occurrences in Parliament. [No. 1], 2 Jan.; [No. 2], 10 Jan.; [No. 3], 17 Jan. 1642. [No. 1, no imprint; Nos. 2, 3 pbd William Cooke.] (Cf. 17 Jan., 6 June 1642.)

The Passages in Parliament. [No. 1], 10 Jan. 1642. [Pbd Nathaniel Butter.]

Diurnal Occurrences or, The Heads of Proceedings in both Houses of Parliament. [No. 1 not extant]; [No. 2], 17 Jan.–No. 6, 14 Feb. 1642. [Pbd John Greensmith.] (Cf. 29 Nov., 20 Dec. 1641.)

The Diurnall Occurrances in Parliament. [No. 1], 17 Jan.; No. 2, 24 Jan.–No. 6, 14 Feb. 1642. [Pbd F. Coules and T. Banks.] (Cf. 20 Dec. 1641; 2 Jan., 6 June 1642.)

A True Diurnall of The Last Weeks Passages in Parliament. No. 1, 17 Jan. 1642; [continued as] A Continuation of the true Diurnall of Passages in Parliament. No. 2, 24 Jan.–No. 11, 28 March 1642. [Nos. 1, 2 pbd Humphrey Blunden; Nos. 3–11, no imprint. There is a counterfeit of No. 11.] (Cf. 24 Jan., 31 Jan., 28 Feb. 1642.)

The Diurnal Occurrences, or Proceedings in the Parliament the last weeke. [No. 1], 17 Jan. 1642; [No. 2 not extant]; [continued as] A True Diurnall Occurrences; or, Proceedings in the Parliament this last weeke. No. 3, 31 Jan. 1642. [No. 1 pbd John Burroughes; No. 3 pbd F. L. and George Thompson.] (Cf. 7 Feb., 21 March 1642.)

A True Diurnall, or the Passages in Parliament. No. 2, 24 Jan. 1642[–?]; [perhaps continued as] A True Diurnall of the Passages in Parliament. [?–]; No. 10, 21 March; [No. 11, 28 March 1642]. [No. 2 pbd Humphrey Tuckey; No. 10, no imprint.] (Cf. 17 Jan., 24 Jan., 31 Jan., 28 Feb., 14 March, 28 March 1642.)

A Continuation of the True Diurnall of Passages in Parliament. [No. 2], 24 Jan. 1642 [–?]. [Pbd George Hutton.] (Cf. 17 Jan., 24 Jan., 28 Feb. 1642.)

A Continuation of the True Diurnall of Passages in Parliament. No. 2, 24 Jan. 1642 [–?]. ['Sold by Stationers.' This has the same text as No. 2 of A True Diurnall (No. 1, 17 Jan. 1642).]

A True Diurnall of the Last Weeks Passage in both Houses of Parliament. No. 2, 24 Jan. 1642[–?]. [No imprint.] (Cf. 17 Jan., 21 Jan., 28 Feb., 14 March 1642.)

A True Diurnall of the Last Weekes Passages in Parliament. No. 3, 31 Jan. 1642. [Pbd John Wright.] (Cf. 17 Jan., 24 Jan., 28 Feb., 14 March 1642.)

A Perfect Diurnall of the Passages in Parliament. [No. 1], 31 Jan.–No. 12, 4 April 1642. [Nos. [1]–[8] have neither number nor imprint; Nos. 9–12 pbd William Cook. There are two settings of the same text for Nos. 9 (mis-numbered 7) and 11. By Samuel Pecke.] (Cf. 20 June, 11 July, 23 July, 1 Aug., 29 Aug., 12 Sept. 1642 (2), 3 July 1643, 16 July, 17 Dec. 1649, 22 July 1650, 8 May 1654, 21 Feb. 1660.)

The True Diurnal Occurrances, or the Heads of the Proceedings of Both Houses of Parliament. [No. 1], 7 Feb.; [No. 2], 14 Feb. 1642. [Pbd John Hammond. No. 1 by R. P.; No. 2 by J[ohn] B[ond].] (Cf. 17 Jan., 28 March 1642.)

A Continuation of the true Diurnall, of all the Passages in Parliament. No. 7, 28 Feb.–No. 11, 28 March 1642. [No imprint; imitation of No. 10 (pbd R. Wood); counterfeit of No. 11 with different text.] (Cf. 17 Jan. 1642, etc.)

A Continuation of the true Diurnall Occurrences in Parliament. No. 3, 7 March 1642 [?–No. 11, 28 March 1642.] [No imprint.] (Cf. 17 Jan. 1642, etc.)

A Continuation of the true Diurnall of Proceedings in Parliament. No. 9, 14 March; No. 10, 21 March; [No. 11 ,28 March 1642]. [No imprint.]

A True Diurnal of the Passages in Parliament. [No. 1], 14 March; [No. 2], 21 March; [? No. 3, 28 March 1642]. [No imprint.] (Cf. 24 Jan. 1642.)

A Continuation of the true Diurnall Occurrences and passages in both Houses of Parliament. No. 10, 21 March; No. 11, 28 March 1642. [No imprint.] (Cf. 17 Jan., 7 Feb., 7 March 1642.)

*A Continuation of the weekly Occurrences in Parliament. [No. ?], 23 May 1642.

*Remarkable Occurrences from the High Court of Parliament. [No. ?], 23 May 1642; [probably continued as] The Heads of All the Proceedings in both Houses of Parliament. [No. ?], 30 May 1642[-?]. [Pbd J. Smith and A. Coe.] (Cf. 29 Nov. 1641.)

Some Special Passages from London, Westminster, Yorke [etc.]. No. 2, 24 May; No. 3, 31 May; No. 1, 2 June–No. 11, 9 Aug. 1642, [The towns mentioned in the title vary. It is probable that there are two different series running under this title. No. 1 pbd Thomas Baker; No. 10 (Aug. 1), pbd R. O. and G. D.] (Cf. 16 Aug. 1642.)

Diurnall Ocurrences in Parliament. [No. 1], 6 June; No. 2, 13 June; [No. 3], 20 June; [No. 4], 25 June 1642. [Pbd F. Coles and T. Banks; imitations of Nos. [1–3] without No. or imprint.]

Remarkeable Passages in Parliament. [No. 1], 6 June 1642. (Cf. 12 Sept. 1642, 2 Nov. 1643.)

A Perfect Diurnall of the Passages in Parliament. No. 1, 20 June–No. 9, 15 Aug. 1642. [Nos. 1–3 'London printed'; Nos. 4–6 pbd William Cooke; Nos. 7–9 pbd William Cooke 'at Furnifalls Inne Gate.' By Samuel Pecke.] (Cf. 31 Jan. 1642, etc.) [Eight distinct series under this title in 1642 are listed separately in their chronological places, but fourteen imitations of single nos. have been grouped together in the next entry.]

A Perfect Diurnall of the Passages in Parliament [imitations]. [Unnumbered], 11 July 1642 (pbd William Rodgers); [unnumbered], 18 July (pbd Robert Williamson); [unnumbered], 19 July (no imprint); [unnumbered], 25 July (pbd John Thomas); [unnumbered], 25 July (2 issues pbd J. G. and R. W.); No. 7, 1 Aug. (pbd John Jonson); No. 9, 15 Aug. (ptd Thomas Fawcet for T. C.); No. 14, 19 Sept. (pbd Walt. Cook and Robert Woodner); No. 14, 19 Sept.; No. 15, 26 Sept. (both pbd Walt. Cook and Robert Woody); No. 17 [thus for 16], 3 Oct. (pbd William Cookes); No. 18 [thus for 17], 10 Oct. (pbd Walter Cooke and Robert Wood); No. 17 [thus for 20], 31 Oct. 1642 (pbd T. F. for Wil. Cooke).

A Perfect Diurnall of the Passages in Parliament. [Unnumbered], 11 July 1642; [unnumbered], 25 July; [unnumbered], 1 Aug.; No. 8, 8 Aug.; No. 9, 15 Aug. 1642. [First 4 nos. pbd William Cook; Nos. 8, 9, pbd William Cook 'at Furnivals Inne.'] (Cf. 31 Jan., 20 June 1642.)

A True and Perfect Diurnall of all the Chiefe Passages in Lancashire. No. 1, 9 July 1642. [Pbd T. U.]

A Current. [?], 12 July 1642[-?].

A Perfect Diurnall of the Passages in Parliament. No. 6, 25 July–No. 9, 15 Aug. 1642. [Pbd Thomas Cook.] (Cf. 31 Jan., 20 June 1642.)

A Diurnall and Particular of the last weekes daily Occurrents. [No. 1], [26] July [1642]. [Pbd D. C.]

A Perfect Diurnall of the Passages in Parliament. [Unnumbered], 1 Aug.; No. 8, 8 Aug. 1642–No. 54, 19 June 1643. [The first no. and No. 8 pbd Robert Wood: from No. 9 on, pbd Walter Cook and Robert Wood, but the spelling of the first name varies on Nos. 9–12. Later ptd R. Austin and A. Coe for Walter Cook and Robert Wood and sold by T. Bates. Counterfeits of No. 14, 19 Sept. and No. 19, 24 Oct.–No. 26, 12 Dec. 1642. Rpts of Nos. 29, 31, 2, 16 Jan. 1643.] (Cf. 31 Jan., 20 June 1642.)

A Continuation of the True Diurnall of Passages in Parliament. No. 1, 15 Aug. 1642. [Pbd T. Paine and M. Simmons.] (Cf. 17 Jan. 1642, etc.)

An Exact and True Diurnall of the Proceedings in Parliament. [No. 1], 15 Aug.–[No. 4], 5 Sept. 1642. [Pbd W. Cooke, except [No. 2] pbd Thomas Cooke.]

Some Speciall and Considerable Passages from London, Westminster, [etc.]. No. 1, 16 Aug. 1642; [continued as] Some Speciall Passages from divers parts, &c. No. 2, 23 Aug. 1642; [continued as] Speciall Passages and certain informations from severall places. No. 3, 30 Aug. 1642–No. 44, 13 June 1643. [Pbd Humphrey Blunden. There is an imitation of No. 2, 23 Aug. and counterfeits of Nos. 19 and 20, 20 and 27 Dec. 1642.] (Cf. 24 May, 13 Sept. 1642, 19 July 1643.)

A True Relation of Certaine Speciall and Remarkable Passages. [No. 1], 19 Aug. 1642. [Continued as] Certaine Speciall and Remarkable Passages from both Houses of Parliament. [No. 2], 23 Aug.; [No. 3], 26 Aug. 1642; [continued as] A Continuation of Certaine Speciall and Remarkable Passages. No. 4, 30 Aug. 1642–No. 59, 13 Oct. 1643[-?]. [No. 1 pbd F. Leach; No. 2 on, pbd F. Leach and F. Coles. Came out twice a week, with two exceptions, until the second week in Oct. 1642. By Samuel

Pecke.] (Cf. 8 Oct., 14 Oct. (twice), 11 Nov., 24 Nov. 1642, 5 Jan., 10 July 1644, 26 Sept. 1645, 9 June 1647.)

A Perfect Diurnall of the Passages in Parliament. No. 11, 29 Aug.–No. 15, 3 Oct. 1642. [Pbd Will. Cooke. There is a rpt of No. 13, 12 Sept. 1642.] (Cf. 31 Jan., 20 June 1642.)

A True and Perfect Diurnall of the passages in Parliament. No. 11, [6 Sept. 1642]. [Pbd H. Blundell.]

Remarkable Passages, or a Perfect Diurnall of the weekly proceedings in both Houses of Parliament. No. 1, 12 Sept. 1642. [Pbd M. Walbank and J. W.] (Cf. 6 June 1642, 8 Nov. 1643.)

A Perfect Diurnall of the Passages in Parliament. [All unnumbered.] 12 Sept. 1642 (pbd William Cooke); 19 Sept. (pbd Robert Wood, Wil. Cooke); 26 Sept.; [3 Oct.]; 10 Oct. (both pbd Wil. Cooke); 17 Oct. 1642 (pbd William Cooke at Furnivals Inne). (Cf. 31 Jan., 20 June 1642.)

A Perfect Diurnall of the Passages in Parliament. No. 13, 12 Sept. 1642–No. 53, 19 June 1643. [Ptd F. Leach and I. Okes, pbd F. Coles. There are rpts of No. 16, 3 Oct.; No. 18, 17 Oct.; No. 27, 19 Dec. 1642; No. 32, 23 Jan. 1643; No. 36, 20 Feb.; and No. 37, 27 Feb. 1643. By Samuel Pecke.] (Cf. 31 Jan., 20 June 1642.)

Quotidian Occurrences in and about London. [Unnumbered], 12 Sept. 1642.

Englands Memorable Accidents. [No. 1, 12 Sept.]; [No. 2], 19 Sept. 1642–No. 19, 16 Jan. 1643. [Pbd Stephen Bowtell.]

Speciall Passages and Certain Informations. No. 1, 13 Sept. 1642. [Ptd R. Austin and A. Coe.] (Cf. 16 Aug. 1642.)

A Continuation of our Weekly Intelligence from His Majesties Army. [Unnumbered], 16 Sept. 1642.

A Perfect Relation, or Summarie. No. 1, 19 Sept.; No. 2, 12 Oct. 1642. [Ptd F. Coles.]

A Continuation of True and Special Passages. [Unnumbered], 29 Sept. 1642. [Pbd William Cook.]

Certain Speciall and Remarkable Passages of the Proceedings in both Houses of Parliament. [No. 1], 6 Oct. 1642. [Pbd T. B.] (Cf. 19 Aug. 1642.)

A Continuation of Certaine Speciall and Remarkable Passages. No. 13, 8 Oct.; No. 14, 12 Oct.; No. 15, 14 Oct. 1642–No. 52, 16 June; [No. 53, 23 June 1643]. [The first 3 nos. pbd Robert Wood; from No. 21, 1 Dec. 1642 on, pbd Walter Cooke and Robert Wood.] (Cf. 19 Aug. 1642.)

Weekly Intelligence from severall Parts of this Kingdome. [No. 1], 11 Oct.; [No. 2], 18 Oct. 1642. [Pbd R. Howes.]

A Continuation of Certaine Speciall and Remarkable Passages. No. 15, 14 Oct. 1642. [Pbd John Wright.] (Cf. 19 Aug. 1642.)

A Continuation of Certaine Speciall and Remarkable Passages. No. 1, 14 Oct. 1642. [Pbd Marke Walbank.] (Cf. 19 Aug. 1642.)

A Collection of Speciall Passages. [Unnumbered], 2 Nov. 1642. [Pbd F. Coles.]

A Continuation of Certaine Speciall and Remarkable Passages. [All unnumbered.] 11 Nov., 18 Nov., 24 Nov. 1642. [Pbd John White.] (Cf. 19 Aug., 14 Oct. 1642.)

A Continuation of Certaine Speciall and Remarkable Passages. [Unnumbered], 24 Nov. 1642. [Pbd I. Coule.] (Cf. 19 Aug. 1642.)

A Grand Diurnall of the passages in Parliament. No. 1, 28 Nov. 1642. (Pbd J. Field.)

A Continuation of the most remarkable Passages in both Houses of Parliament, by G. H. [No. 1], 3 Dec. 1642. [Ptd R. Herne.]

The Kingdomes Weekly Intelligencer sent abroad to prevent misinformation. [No. 1], 3 Jan. 1643–[No. 332], 9 Oct. 1649. [Nos. 187–98 omitted. Counterfeits: No. 24 [thus for 4], 24 Jan. 1643: No. 22, 6 June; No. 23, 13 June 1643; [unnumbered], 13 June 1643 (pbd Peter Cole). Attrib. to Richard Collings.]

The Oxford Diurnall communicating the intelligence and affaires of the Court to the rest of the Kingdome. No. 1, 7 Jan. 1643. [Oxford.]

Mercurius Aulicus, communicating the intelligence and affairs of the Court to the rest of the Kingdome. [No. 1], 8 Jan. 1643–[No. 118], 7 Sept. 1645. [Oxford. With some interruptions after No. 99, 24 Nov. 1644. By Sir John Berkenhead, but by Peter Heylin in Aug. and Sept. 1643 and June 1644. Counterfeit: [No. 40], 7 Oct. 1643.]

Mercurius Aulicus [etc. London reprints]. [No. 2], 14 Jan. 1643–[No. 8], 25 Feb.; [No. 10], 11 March; [No. 40], 7 Oct. 1643; [No. 53], 6 Jan. 1644–[No. 57], 3 Feb.; [No. 64], 23 March; [No. 70], 4 May; [No. 72], 18 May; [No. 75], 8 June; [No. 80], 13 July; [No. 84], 10 Aug.; [No. 88], 7 Sept.; [No. 94], 10 Oct.; [No. 96], 2 Nov.; [No. 98], 16 Nov.; [No. 99], 23 Nov. 1644. [Several of these have different text from the corresponding nos. ptd at Oxford.] (Cf. 3 Feb. 1648, 7 Aug. 1648, 21 Aug. 1649, 20 March 1654.)

Certaine Informations. No. 1, 23 Jan. 1643–No. 57, 21 Feb. 1644. [By William Ingler.]

The Daily Intelligencer of Court, City and Countrey. No. 1, 30 Jan. 1643.

Mercurius Civicus. London's Intelligencer, or truth really imparted. No. 1, 11 May 1643–No. 183, 10 Dec. 1646. [Attrib. to Richard Collings.]

Mercurius Rusticus, or the Countries Complaint. [No. 1], 20 May 1643–No. 21, 16 March 1644. [Oxford. Issued irregularly; rptd 1647 (as Angliae Ruina), 1685, 1723, 1732. By Bruno Ryves.] (Cf. 26 Oct. 1643, 12 Nov. 1647.)

A Coranto from Beyond the Sea. No. 1, 9 June 1643.

The Parliaments Scouts Discovery. No. 1, 16 June 1643. [Attrib. to John Dillingham.]

The Parliament Scout communicating his Intelligence to the Kingdome. No. 1, 27 June; No. 2, 6 July 1643–No. 85, 30 Jan. 1645. [By John Dillingham.]

A Perfect Diurnall of Some Passages in Parliament and from other parts of this Kingdom. No. 1, 3 July 1643–No. 323, 8 Oct.; No. 324, 12 Nov. 1649. [Pbd F. Coles and Laurence Blaicklock. There are rpts of practically the whole series; and a counterfeit of No. 161, 31 Aug. 1646, and probably others. By Samuel Pecke.] (Cf. 31 Jan. 1642.)

A Weekly Accompt, or Perfect Diurnall. No. 1, 10 July 1643. [Attrib. to Daniel Border.] (Cf. 3 Aug., 6 Sept. 1643, 25 May, 1 June 1659.)

Wednesday's Mercury, or Speciall Passages and certain Informations. No. 1, 19 July 1643; [continued as] The Speciall Passages Continued. No. 2, 22 July; No. 3, 28 July; [continued as] Wednesday's Mercury; or, the Speciall Passages and Certain Informations. No. 4, 2 Aug. 1643. [Ptd T. P[aine] and M. S[immons].] (Cf. 16 Aug. 1642.)

A Weekly Accompt of certain special and remarkable passages from both Houses of Parliament. No. [1], 3 Aug. 1643. [Ptd Bernard Alsop.] (Cf. 10 July 1643.)

Mercurius Britanicus communicating the affairs of Great Britaine. No. 1, 29 Aug. 1643–No. 130, 18 May 1646. [None issued between 9 and 30 Sept. 1644. Counterfeits; No. 27, 18 March–No. 29, 1 April 1644, and probably others. Nos. 1–51 by Thomas Audley; Nos. 52–130 by Marchamont Needham.] (Cf. 24 June 1647, 7 April, 23 May 1648, 4 May 1649, 26 July 1652, 23 May 1653.)

The Weekly Account. No. 1, 6 Sept. 1643–No. 17, 29 April 1647; [continued as] The Perfect Weekly Account. No. 18, 5 May 1647–No. 52, 28 Dec. 1647; No. 1, 5 June 1648. [There is a new series numbering each January. Ptd B. Alsop. Attrib. to Daniel Border.] (Cf. 10 July 1643, 29 March 1648, 17 July 1650.)

The True Informer continuing a collection of the most speciall and observable passages. No. 1, [23 Sept. 1643]–No. 67, 22 Feb. 1645. [Attrib. to Henry Whalley.] (Cf. 26 April 1645, 28 Aug. 1651, 6 Jan. 1654.)

New Christian Uses upon the Weekly True Passages. No. 1, 7 Oct. 1643. [Attrib. to George Smith.]

The Scottish Mercury. [Unnumbered], [13 Oct. 1643.] [By George Smith.]

The Scotch Intelligencer, Relating the Weekly News from Scotland, the Court and other places. [No. 1], 17 Oct.; [No. 2], 25 Oct. 1643.

The Scotish Dove sent out and returning. No. 1, 20 Oct. 1643–No. 161, 26 Nov. 1646; [continued as] The Scotish Dove sent out the last time. [1 no., 25 Dec. 1646]. [By George Smith.]

Mercurius Rusticus, or a Countrey Messenger. [No. 1], [26 Oct. 1643]. [By George Wither.] (Cf. 20 May 1643.)

The Welch Mercury, communicating remarkable intelligence and true news. No. 1, 28 Oct.–No. 3, 11 Nov. 1643[–?]; [probably continued as] The British Mercury; or, The Welch Diurnall. [?–]; No. 6, 3 Dec. 1643[–?]. [Ptd W. Ley and G. Lindsay.]

Mercurius Cambro-Britannus, The British Mercury or the Welch Diurnall. [No. 1, 30 Oct.]–No. 4, 20 Nov. 1643–No. 8, 24 Jan. 1644. [Ptd B. Alsop. None issued between 5 Dec. 1643 and 13 Jan. 1644.]

The Compleate Intelligencer and Resolver. [No. 1], 2 Nov.; No. 2, 7 Nov.–No. 5, 28 Nov. 1643. [Attrib. to George Smith.]

Informator Rusticus; or, The Country Intelligencer. No. 1, 3 Nov. 1643. [Attrib. to Henry Walker.]

Britanicus Vapulans; or, The Whipping of poor British Mercury by Mercurius Urbanus, younger brother to Aulicus. No. 1, 4 Nov. 1643; [continued as] Mercurius Urbanus. [No. 2], 9 Nov. 1643; [No. 3, n.d.]. [Attrib. to Daniel Featley.]

Remarkable Passages. No. 1, 8 Nov.–No. 8, 29 Dec. 1643. [Pbd A. Coe.] (Cf. 6 June 1642.)

The Kingdomes Weekly Post with his packet of letters, publishing his message to the City and the Countrey. No. 1, 9 Nov. 1643–No. 10, 10 Jan. 1644. [Attrib. to John Rushworth.] (Cf. 15 Oct. 1645, 5 Jan. 1648.)

A Continuation of Certain Speciall and Remarkable Passages. No. 1, 5 Jan.–No. 18, 2 May 1644. [Ptd F. C[oules] for F. Leach. By Samuel Pecke.] (Cf. 19 Aug. 1642.)

Occurrences of Certain Speciall and Remarkable Passages. [No. 1, 5 Jan.]; No. 2, 12 Jan.–No. 21, 24 May 1644; [continued as] Perfect Occurrences of Parliament. No. 22, 31 May 1644–[3rd ser.] No. 10, 6 March 1646; [continued as] Perfect Occurrences of both Houses of Parliament. No. 11, 13

March 1646–No. 53, 1 Jan. 1647; [continued as] Perfect Occurrences of Every Dayes Journall in Parliament. No. 1, 8 Jan. 1647–No. 145, 12 Oct. 1649. [Pbd Andrew Coe, Jane Coe. Attrib. to John Saltmarsh to 1646. From 8 Jan. 1647 by Henry Walker.] (Cf. 6 Feb. 1654.)

Mercurius &c. [No. 1], 17 Jan.; No. 2, 6 Feb. 1644; [continued as] Mercurius Veridicus. No. 3, 13 Feb.–No. 11, 10 April 1644. (Cf. 19 April 1645, 21 April 1648.)

The Spie. Communicating Intelligence from Oxford. No. 1, 30 Jan.–No. 22, 25 June 1644. [By Durant Hotham.]

Anti-Aulicus. [No. 1], [6 Feb.]; [No. 2], [8 Feb. 1644].

Mercurius Anglicus, or a Post from the North. No. 1, 7 Feb. No. 2, 20 Feb. 1644. [Pbd T. B.] (Cf. 3 Aug. 1648, 1 Oct. 1650.)

A Faithfull Relation of the late Occurrences and Proceedings of the Scotish Army. [No. 1], 21 Feb. 1644[–?]; [continued as] The Late Proceedings of the Scottish Army. [–?]; No. 4, 21 March 1644[–?]; [continued as] Intelligence from the Scottish Army. No. 6, 14 April 1644; [continued as] Extract of Letters. No. 7, 30 April 1644; [continued as] Intelligence from the South Borders of Scotland. No. 8, 13 May 1644. [Pbd R. Bostock and S. Gellibrand. By Edward Bowles.]

The Military Scribe. No. 1, 27 Feb.–No. 6, 2 April 1644.

Britains Remembrancer of the most remarkable passages in both Kingdomes. No. 1, 19 March–No. 3, 2 April 1644.

Mercurius Aulico-Mastix; or, The Whipping Mercury. No. 1, 12 April 1644. [Ptd G. Bishop.]

A True and Perfect Journall of the Warres in England. No. 1, 16 April; No. 2, 30 April 1644.

The Weekly News from Forraigne Parts Beyond the Seas. No. 1, 1 May; No. 2, 6 May; No. 3, 13 May 1644.

The Flying Post. No. 1, 10 May 1644.

A Particular Relation of the Successes of the Earl of Manchesters Army. [No. 1], 6 [10] May 1644; [continued as] A Continuation of True Intelligence from the Earl of Manchester's Army. No. 2, 1 [4] June 1644; [continued as] A Particular Relation of the most remarkable occurrences from the united forces in the North. No. 3, 10 [13] June 1644; [continued as] A Continuation of True Intelligence from the Earl of Manchesters Army. No. 4, 17 [21] June–No. 7, 16 [20] Aug. 1644. [Pbd Thomas Underhill. By Simeon Ashe and William Good.]

Cheife Heads of Each Dayes Proceedings in Parliament. [No. 1], 15 May 1644.

An Exact Diurnall. No. 1, 22 May 1644; [continued as] A Diary, or an Exact Journal. No. 2, 31 May–No. 88, 22 Jan. 1646; No. 1, 29 Jan.–No. 6, 5 March 1646. (Cf. 17 July 1647, 29 Sept. 1651.]

Le Mercure Anglois. No. 1, [7 June]; No. 2, 13 June; No. 3, 10 July 1644–No. 63, 13 Nov. 1645; No. 1, 20 Nov. 1645–No. 65, 15 April 1647; [?–]No. 4, 29 July 1647–No. 73, 14 Dec. 1648[–?]. [Attrib. to John Cotgrave.]

The Court Mercurie communicating the most remarkable passages of the Kings Armie. No. 1, 2 July–No. 15, 16 Oct. 1644. [Attrib. to John Cotgrave.]

A Continuation of Certain Speciall and Remarkable Passages. No. 1, 10 July–No. 4, 1 Aug. 1644. [Perhaps by Samuel Pecke.] (Cf. 19 Aug. 1642.)

The London Post. No. 1, 6 Aug. 1644–No. 30 [31], 8 April 1645. [Attrib. to John Rushworth and Gilbert Mabbott.] (Cf. Dec. 31, 1646.)

*The Countrey Messenger; or, The Faithfull Foot post. No. 1, 20 Sept. 1644.

The Countrey Foot-post. No. 1, 2 Oct. 1644; [continued as] The Countrey Messenger. No. 2, 11 Oct. 1644. [Attrib. to John Rushworth.]

Perfect Passages of Each Dayes Proceedings in Parliament. No. 1, 23 Oct. 1644–No. 71, 4 March 1646. (Cf. 5 July 1650.)

Januaries Account. [No. 1], [? 1 Feb. 1645]; [continued as] The Monthly Account. No. 2, [1 March 1645]; [continued as] The General Account. [No. 3], [31 March 1645]. [Monthly. Pbd Richard Harper.]

The Moderate Intelligencer Impartially communicating Martiall Affaires to the Kingdome of England. No. 1, 6 March 1645–No. 237, 4 Oct. 1649. [By John Dillingham.] (Cf. 29 June 1648, 24 May, 5 June 1649, 8 Dec. 1652, 26 April, 9 May 1653, 23 Feb. 1654.)

The Weekely Post-Master. No. 1, 15 April–No. 4, 6 May 1645.

Mercurius Veridicus, or True Informations. No. 1, 19 April 1645–No. 35, 6 Jan. 1646; No. [3], 17 Jan.–No. 10, 7 March 1646. (Cf. 17 Jan. 1644.)

A Perfect Declaration. No. 1, 26 April 1645; [continued as] The True Informer containing a perfect collection of the Proceedings in Parliament. No. 2, 3 May 1645–No. 45, 7 March 1646. [Attrib. to Henry Whalley.] (Cf. 23 Sept. 1643.)

The Parliaments Post. No. 1, 13 May–No. 21, 7 Oct. 1645.

The Exchange Intelligencer. No. 1, 15 May–No. 8, 18 July 1645.

Heads of Some Notes of the Citie Scout. No. 4, 19 Aug.–No. 10, 30 Sept. 1645; [continued as] The City Scout. No. 11, 7 Oct.–No. 16, 11 Nov. 1645.

Mercurius Anti-Britannicus [Oxford]. [No. 1], [4 Aug.]–[No. 3], [18 Aug. 1645].

A Continuation of Certaine Speciall and Remarkable Passages. No. 1, 26 Sept. 1645–No. 24, 6 March 1646. [By Samuel Pecke.] (Cf. 19 Aug. 1642.)

The Kingdomes Weekly Post. [No. 1], 15 Oct.–[No. 10], 16 Dec. 1645. [Attrib. to John Harris.] (Cf. 9 Nov. 1643.)

A Packet of Letters from Sir Thomas Fairfax his Quarters. No. 1, 30 Oct. 1645. (Cf. 26 June 1646, 18 March 1648.)

The Kingdomes Scout. No. 1, 2 Dec.–No. 3, 16 Dec. 1645.

Mercurius Academicus [Oxford]. [No. 1], 20 Dec. 1645–[No. 14], 21 March 1646. [Attrib. to Richard Little, or Thomas Swadlin.] (Cf. 15 April 1648.)

The Citties Weekly Post. [No. 1], 22 Dec. 1645–No. 11, 3 March 1646.

The Phoenix of Europe or the Forraine Intelligencer. No. 1, 16 Jan. 1646. [By W. Pendred.]

The Moderate Messenger. No. 1, 3 Feb.–No. 4, 3 March 1646. (Cf. 23 Feb. 1647, 30 April 1649, 7 Feb. 1653.)

An Exact and True Collection of the Weekly Passages. [No. 1], [26 Feb.]; [No. 2], [? March 1646].

The Westerne Informer. No. 1, 7 March 1646.

Generall News from All Parts of Christendome. No. 1, 12 May; No. 2, 26 May 1646.

The Packet of Letters. [No. 1], 26 June 1646. [Pbd Thomas Bates.] (Cf. 30 Oct. 1645, 18 March 1648.)

Papers sent from the Scotts Quarters. No. 1, 14 Oct. 1646; [continued as] A Continuation of Papers [etc.]. No. 2, 28 Oct. 1646; [continued as] A Continuation of a journall of passages of the Parliament and other papers [etc.]. No. 3, 5 Nov.–No. 6, 26 Nov. 1646. [By Samuel Pecke; supplements to A Perfect Diurnal.]

The Military Actions of Europe. No. 1, 27 Oct.; No. 2, 2 Nov. 1646.

Mercurius Candidus. No. 1, 20 Nov. 1646 [–?]. [Attrib. to John Harris.] (Cf. 28 Jan. 1647.)

Diutinus Britanicus. No. 1, 2 Dec.; No. 2, 8 Dec. 1646; [continued as] Mercurius Diutinus (not Britanicus). No. 3, 16 Dec. 1646; [continued as] Mercurius Diutinus. No. 4, 23 Dec. 1646–No. 11, 10 Feb. 1647. [By Thomas Audley.]

The London Post. No. 1, 31 Dec. 1646–No. 9, 26 Feb. 1647. [Attrib. to John Rushworth and Gilbert Mabbott.] (Cf. 6 Aug. 1644.)

England's Remembrancer of London's Integritie. No. 1, [19 Jan.]; No. 2, [11 Feb. 1647].

Mercurius Candidus. No. 1, 28 Jan. 1647. [Attrib. to Samuel Pecke.]

The Moderate Messenger. No. 22, 23 Feb. 1647. [Only number.]

A Continuation of Certaine Speciall and Remarkable Passages. [No. 1], 9 June–No. 13, 17 Sept. 1647. [By Samuel Pecke.] (Cf. 19 Aug. 1642.)

Mercurius Britanicus. No. 1, 24 June–No. 3, 8 July 1647. [Ptd B. W.]

The Armies Post. No. 1, 8 July 1647.

A Diarie or an Exact Journall of the Proceedings of the Treaty betwixt the Parliament and the Army. No. 1, 17 July–No. 3, 29 July 1647. (Cf. 22 May 1644.)

A Perfect Summary of Chiefe Passages in Parliament. [No. 1], 26 July–No. 11, 6 Oct. 1647. (Cf. 19 Feb., 9 Oct. 1648, 29 Jan. 1649.)

The Moderne Intelligencer. No. 1, 19 Aug.–No. 7, 30 Sept. 1647. (Cf. 3 Sept. 1651.)

Mercurius Melancholicus. [No. 1], n.d.; No. 2, 11 Sept. 1647–No. 59, 8 Oct. 1648. [By John Hackluyt.] (There is a reprint of [No. 1].)

Mercurius Melancholicus [counterfeits]. No. 1, 11 Sept. 1647; No. 2, 11/17 Sept.; No. 3, 11/18 Sept.; No. 4, 25 Sept. (2 issues); No. 45, 23 July 1648 (2 issues)–No. 52, 21 Aug. 1648, excepting No. 47, 17 July; No. 58–62 (in one number), 21 Nov. 1648. [Attrib. to Martin Parker and John Taylor.] (Cf. 28 July 1648, 1 Jan. 1649, 31 May 1649.)

Mercurius Morbicus or Newes from Westminster and other parts. No. 1. 2. 3. (one number), [20 Sept.]; No. 4, 27 Sept. 1647. [By Henry Walker.]

Mercurius Pragmaticus communicating Intelligence from all parts. No. 1, 21 Sept. 1647–No. 28, 28 March 1648; No. 1, 4 April 1648–[No. 53], 8 May 1649. [By John Cleaveland and Samuel Sheppard; in 1648 by Marchamont Needham.] (Cf. 24 April, 17 Sept. 1649, 10 June 1651, 25 May, 6 July 1652, 25 May 1653, 30 Aug. 1658, 20 June, 6 Sept., 30 Dec. 1659.)

Mercurius Pragmaticus [rpts]. [1st ser.] No. 6, 26 Oct. 1647; No. 7; No. 10; No. 11; No. 16, 3 Jan. 1648; [2nd ser.] No. 7, 16 May 1648.

Mercurius Pragmaticus [counterfeits]. [1st ser.], No. 2, 28 Sept.; No. 9; No. 10; No. 11, 30 Nov. 1647; No. 18, 18 Jan. 1648; [2nd ser.], No. 7, 16 May; No. 19, 8 Aug. 1648; No. 20, 15 Aug.; No. 20, 12 Sept. 1648–No. 22; No. 23 [for 24]; No. 24 [for 25]; No. 38; No. 39; No. 43; [No. 51]; [No. 52], 1 May 1649.

Mercurius Anti-Melancholicus. No. 1, 24 Sept. 1647.

Mercurius Clericus or Newes from Syon communicated to all who love (and seek) the Peace of Jerusalem. No. 1, 24 Sept. 1647.

Mercurius Clericus or Newes from the Assembly of their last III years in the Holy Convocation at Westminster. No. 1, [25 Sept. 1647].

Mercurius Medicus or a Soveraigne Salve for these sick times. No. 1, [11 Oct.]; No. 2, 22 Oct. 1647. [By Henry Walker.]

Mercurius Anti-Pragmaticus. No. 1, 19 Oct. 1647–No. 19, 3 Feb. 1648.

Mercurius Elencticus communicating the unparallell'd proceedings at Westminster. [No. 1], 5 Nov. 1647–No. 59, 9 Jan. 1649. [By Sir George Wharton and Samuel Sheppard. (There are counterfeits of No. 36, 2 Aug. and of No. 46, 11 Oct. 1648.)] (Cf. 7 Feb., 13 Feb., 28 Feb., 11 April, 1 May, 7 May 1649, 22 April 1650, 10 June 1651, 25 May, 6 July 1652.)

Mercurius Populi. No. 1, 11 Nov. 1647.

Mercurius Rusticus. No. 1, [12 Nov.]–No. 5, 10 Dec. 1647. (Cf. 20 May 1643.)

Mercurius Bellicus. No. 1, 22 Nov. 1647–No. 27, 26 July 1648. [Suspended from 29 Nov. 1647–14 Feb. 1648. By Sir John Berkenhead.]

Mercurius Vapulans. [No. 1], [27 Nov. 1647]; No. 2, n.d.

The Kingdom's Weekly Post. No. 1, 5 Jan.–No. 10, 9 March 1648. [Attrib. to Daniel Border.]

Heads of Chiefe Passages in Parliament. No. 1, 12 Jan.–No. 3, 26 Jan. 1648; [continued as] Kingdoms Weekly Account of Heads of Chiefe Passages in Parliament. No. 4, 2 Feb.–No. 11, 22 March 1648. [Attrib. to Henry Whalley.]

Mercurius Dogmaticus. No. 1, 13 Jan.–No. 4, 3 Feb. 1648. [Attrib. to Samuel Sheppard.]

Mercurius Aulicus againe communicating intelligence from all parts. No. 1, 3 Feb.–No. 15, 18 May 1648. [Nos. 7–9, 10–12, 10–13, and 12–14 formed each one number. Attrib. to Samuel Sheppard.] (Cf. 8 Jan. 1643.)

A Perfect Summarie of Chiefe Passages in Parliament. No. 1, 19 Feb. 1648. (Cf. 26 July 1647.)

Packets of Letters. No. 1, 18 March–No. 37, 28 Nov. 1648. [Irregular; supplements to Perfect Occurrences. By Henry Walker.] (Cf. 30 Oct. 1645.)

Westminster Projects; or, The Mystery of Darby House discovered. [No. 1], [23] March 1648; [continued as] Tricks of State; or more Westminster Projects. [No. 2], 18 April 1648; [–?]; [continued as] Windsor Projects and Westminster Practices. [No. 4], [15 May 1648]; [continued as] Westminster Projects; or, the Mystery of Iniquity

of Darby-House Discovered. No. 5, [6 June]; No. 6, [23 June] 1648.

Mercurius Insanus Insanissimus. [No. 1, ?]; No. 2, [27 March]; No. 3, [17 April 1648]–No. 7, n.d.

The Perfect Weekly Account. No. 1, 29 March 1648–[unnumbered], 10 Oct. 1649. [By 'B. D.'] (Cf. 6 Sept. 1643.)

Mercurius Brittanicus communicating his most remarkable intelligence unto the Kingdome. No. 1, 7 April 1648. [No imprint. By John Hall.] (Cf. 29 Aug. 1643, 23 May 1648.)

Mercurius Critticus. No. 1, 13 April–No. 3, 4 May 1648. [Attrib. to John Crouch.]

Mercurius Academicus. No. 1, 15 April 1648. [Attrib. to Thomas Swadlin.] (Cf. 20 Dec. 1645.)

Mercurius Veridicus communicating Intelligence from all parts of Great Britaine. No. 1, 21 April–No. 3, 8 May 1648. (Cf. 17 Jan. 1644.)

Mercurius Militaris communicating intelligence from the Saints dissembled at Westminster. No. 1, 28 April 1648. (Cf. 10 Oct. 1648, 24 April, 29 May 1649.)

Mercurius Urbanicus; or, Newes from London and Westminster. [Unnumbered], 9 May 1648.

Mercurius Gallicus. No. 3, [12 May 1648].

Mercurius Publicus Communicating emergent occurrences. No. 1, [15 May]–No. 3, 29 May 1648.

The Parliament-Kite or the Tell Tale Bird. No. 1, 15 May–No. 15, 31 Aug. 1648.

Mercurius Britanicus alive again. No. 1, 16 May 1648; [continued as] Mercurius Britanicus giving a perfect accompt. No. 2, 23 May–No. 12, 1 Aug. 1648; [continued as] Mercurius Britanicus stating the affairs. No. 13, 16 Aug. 1648. (Cf. 29 Aug. 1643.)

Mercurius Honestus or Newes from Westminster. No. 1, [19 May] 1648; No. 2, [25 May 1648].

Mercurius Censorius. No. 1, 1 June–No. 3, 20 June 1648. [Attrib. to John Hall.]

Mercurius Domesticus. No. 1, [5 June 1648].

New News, Strange News, True News. [No. 1], [15] June 1648.

Mercurius Psitacus or the Parroting Mercury. No. 1, 12 June–No. 9, 7 Aug. 1648.

The Parliaments Vulture. No. 1, 22 June 1648.

A Perfect Diary of Passages of the Kings Army. [No. 1], [26 June 1648].

The Moderate communicating martial affaires to the Kingdome of England. No. 171, 29 June–No. 173, 13 July 1648; No. 1, 18 July 1648–No. 63, 25 Sept. 1649. [Attrib. to Gilbert Mabbott.] (Cf. 6 March 1645.)

The Parliaments Scriche Owle. No. 1, [29 June]–No. 3, 14 July 1648.

A Wonder. A Mercury without a Lye in's Mouth. [No. 1], [6 July 1648].

Mercurius Scoticus. No. 1, [19 July 1648]. [Attrib. to Sir George Wharton.] (Cf. 30 Sept. 1651.)

Mercurius Melancholicus; or Newes from Westminster and the head quarters. No. 1, 28 July 1648. [Attrib. to John Crouch.] (Cf. 11 Sept. 1647.)

The Royall Diurnall. No. 1, 31 July–No. 5, 29 Aug. 1648. [Attrib. to Samuel Sheppard.] (Cf. 25 Feb. 1650.)

Mercurius Anglicus. No. 1, 3 Aug. 1648. (Cf. 7 Feb. 1644.)

Mercurius Aulicus communicating intelligence from all parts of the Kingdome. [No. 1], [7 Aug.]–No. 4, [28 Aug. 1648]. (Cf. 8 Jan. 1643.)

Mercurius Aquaticus. [No. 1], 11 Aug. 1648. [Attrib. to John Taylor.]

The Colchester Spie. No. 1 [11 Aug.]; No. 2, 17 Aug.; [No. 3, 28 Aug.], 1648. [2 issues of No. 1.]

Hermes Straticus, or a Scourge for Elencticus. No. 1, 17 Aug. 1648.

Mercurius Fidelicus. No. 1, 24 Aug.; No. 2, 31 Aug. 1648.

The Parliament Porter or the Door Keeper of the House of Commons. No. 1, 4 Sept.–No. 4, 25 Sept. 1648.

Mercurius Catholicus. No. 1, [15 Sept.]; No. 2, 11 Dec. 1648. [Attrib. to Thomas Budd.]

Mercurius Anti-Mercurius. No. 1, 19 Sept.– No. 3, 2 Oct. 1648. [Perhaps by John Hackluyt, also attrib. to John Harris.]

The Treaty Traverst. No. 1, 26 Sept. 1648.

Mercurio Volpone or the Fox. No. 1, 5 Oct.; No. 2, 12 Oct. 1648.

A Perfect Summary. [No. 1], 9 Oct. 1648. (Cf. 26 July 1647.)

Mercurius Militaris or The Armies Scout. No. 1, 10 Oct.–No. 5, 21 Nov. 1648. [Attrib. to John Harris.] (Cf. 8 Nov. 1648, 28 April 1648).

The True Informer or Monthly Mercury being the certain intelligence of Mercurius Militaris. No. 1, [7 Oct.] 8 Nov. 1648. [Monthly.]

Mercurius Pacificus. [No. 1], [8 Nov. 1648]. [Attrib. to John Taylor.] (Cf. 24 May 1649.)

Martin Nonsence His Collections. No. 1, 27 Nov. 1648.

A Declaration collected out of the Journals of both Houses of Parliament. No. 1, 6 Dec.– No. 3, 20 Dec. 1648; [continued as] Heads of a Diarie. No. 4, 27 Dec. 1648–No. 6, 9 Jan. 1649. [By Henry Walker.]

*Passages concerning the King, the army, city and Kingdom. No. 1, 6 Dec. 1648.

Mercurius Impartialis or an Answer to that Treasonable Pamphlet Mercurius Militaris, together with the Moderate. No. 1, 12 Dec. 1648. [Attrib. to Sir George Wharton.]

Mercurius Melancholicus communicating the generall affaires of the Kingdome. No. 1, 1 Jan.–No. 3, 12 Jan. 1649. [Attrib. to John Hackluyt.] (Cf. 11 Sept. 1647, 28 July 1648, 31 May 1649.)

A Perfect Narrative of the Whole Proceedings of the High Court of Justice in the Tryal of the King. No. 1, 23 Jan. 1649; [continued as] A Continuation of the Narrative [etc.]. No. 2, 25 Jan.; No. 3, 29 Jan. 1649. [There is a rpt of No. 2.]

The Armies Modest Intelligencer. [No. 1], 26 Jan.–No. 3, 8 Feb. 1649; [continued as] The Armies Weekly Intelligencer. No. 4, 15 Feb.; No. 5, 22 Feb. 1649.

A Perfect Summary of Exact Passages. No. 1, 29 Jan.–No. 9, 26 March 1649; [continued as] A Perfect Summary of an Exact Diarye. No. 10, 3 April–No. 27, 1 Oct. 1649. [Attrib. to Theodore Jennings. No. 9 is entitled A Perfect Collection [etc.]; No. 22 reverts to the original form.] (Cf. 26 July 1647.)

The Kingdomes Faithfull Scout. No. 1, 2 Feb. 1649; [continued as] The Kingdomes Faithfull and Impartiall Scout. No. 2, 9 Feb. No. 37, 12 Oct. 1649. [Attrib. to Daniel Border. No. 5 reverts to the style of No. 1.]

Mercurius Elencticus communicating the un-parallell'd proceedings at Westminster. No. 1, 7 Feb. 1649. [Attrib. to Sir George Wharton.] (Cf. 5 Nov. 1647, 13, 28 Feb. 1649.)

Mercurius Elencticus communicating the un-parallell'd proceedings at Westminster. No. 56, 13 Feb. 1649. (Cf. preceding entry.)

Mercurius Elencticus communicating intelligence from all parts. No. 69, 28 Feb. 1649. (Cf. preceding entries.)

The Impartiall Intelligencer. No. 1, 7 March –No. 29, 19 Sept. 1649.

A Modest Narrative of Intelligence Fitted for the Republique of England and Ireland. No. 1, 7 April–No. 25, 22 Sept. 1649.

Mercurius Elencticus communicating the un-parallell'd proceedings of the rebells at Westminster. No. 1, 11 April 1649. [Attrib. to Samuel Sheppard.] (Cf. 5 Nov. 1647, 7, 13, 28 Feb., 1, 7 May 1649.)

The Man in the Moone Discovering a World of Knavery under the Sunne. [No. 1], 16 April 1649–No. 56, 5 June 1650. [By John Crouch.]

Mercurius Philo-Monarchicus. No. 1, 17 April; [unnumbered], 21 May 1649.

Continued Heads of Perfect Passages. No. 1, 20 April–No. 5, 18 May 1649. [Pbd A. Coe.]

Mercurius Pragmaticus (For King Charles II). 2 pars. No. 1, 24 April 1649–No. 53, 28 May 1650. [Counterfeits: No. 4, 15 May 1649– No. 10, 26 June; No. 14, 24 July 1649.] (Cf. 21 Sept. 1647, 17 Sept. 1649.)

Mercurius Militaris or The People's Scout. No. 1, 24 April–No. 3, [8 May 1649]. [There is a rpt of No. 2.] (Cf. 28 April 1648.)

England's Moderate Messenger. No. 1, 30 April–No. 11, 9 July 1649; [continued as] The Moderate Messenger. No. 12, 16 July–No. 22, 24 Sept. 1649. [Attrib. to Daniel Border.] (Cf. 3 Feb. 1646.)

Mercurius Elencticus communicating the un-parralell'd proceedings of the rebbells at Westminster. No. 1, 1 May–No. 27, 5 Nov. 1649. (Cf. 5 Nov. 1647, 11 April, 7 May 1649.)

Mercurius Brittanicus communicating intelligence from all parts, and handling the humours and conceits of Mercurius Pragmaticus. No. 1, 4 May–No. 7, 5 June 1649. [Attrib. to Gilbert Mabbott.] (Cf. 29 Aug. 1643.)

Mercurius Elencticus (For King Charls II.) communicating intelligence from all parts. Pars [2]. No 1, 7 May 1649. (Cf. 5 Nov. 1647, 24 April, 1 May 1649.)

A Moderate Intelligence impartially communicating martial affairs to the Kingdom of England. No. 1, 24 May; No. 2, 31 May 1649. [Pbd Robert White.] (Cf. 6 March 1645.)

Mercurius Pacificus. No. 1, 25 May; No. 2, 31 May 1649. [Attrib. to John Taylor.] (Cf. 8 Nov. 1648.)

Mercurius Republicus. No. 1, 29 May 1649.

Mercurius Militaris or Times only Truth-Teller. No. 1, 29 May 1649; [continued as] The Metropolitan Nuncio. No. 1, 6 June; No. 3, 13 June 1649. [Attrib. to John Hackluyt.] (Cf. 28 April 1648.)

Mercurius Melancholicus for King Charls the Second. No. 1, 31 May; No. 2, 7 June 1649. [Attrib. to John Taylor.] (Cf. 11 Sept. 1647.)

Mercurius Verax or Truth appearing after seaven yeares Banishment. [No. 1], [4 June 1649].

*The Moderate Intelligencer. No. 1, 5 June 1649[–?]. [Attrib. to John Dillingham.] (Cf. 6 March 1645.)

The Moderate Mercury. No. 1, 21 June; No. 2, 28 June 1649.

A Perfect Diurnall of Passages in Parliament. No. 1, 16 July; No. 2, 23 July 1649. [Pbd Robert Wood. Imitations of the paper started on 3 July 1643.] (Cf. 31 Jan. 1642.)

A Tuesdaies Journall. No. 1, 24 July–No. 4, 21 Aug. 1649. [By Henry Walker.]

Mercurius Carolinus. No. 1, 26 July 1649.

The Armies Painfull-Messenger. No. 1, 2 Aug. 1649.

Great Britaines Paine-full Messenger Affording true notice of all affaires. No. 1, 16 Aug.–No. 3, 30 Aug. 1649. [Attrib. to A. Ford.]

Mercurius Aulicus (For King Charls II). [No. 1], 21 Aug.–No. 3, 4 Sept. 1649. (Cf. 8 Jan. 1643.)

Mercurius Hybernicus. No. 1, 6 Sept. 1649.

Mercurius Pragmaticus for King Charls II. No. 1, 17 Sept. 1649; No. 2, 24 Sept. 1649 [–?]. (Cf. 21 Sept. 1647, 24 April 1649.)

A Briefe Relation of some affaires and transactions Civill and Military, both Forraigne and Domestique. No. 1, 2 Oct. 1649–No. 56, 1 Oct.; No. 57, 22 Oct. 1650. [By Walter Frost.]

Severall Proceedings in Parliament. No. 1, 9 Oct. 1649–No. 186, 21 April 1653; [continued as] Severall Proceedings of State Affaires. No. 187, 28 April 1653–No. 261, 28 Sept. 1654; [continued as] Severall Proceedings of Parliament. No. 262, 5 Oct. 1654–No. 278, 25 Jan. 1655; [continued as] Several Proceedings of State Affaires. No. 279, 1 Feb.–No. 282, 22 Feb. 1655; [continued as] Perfect Proceedings of State Affaires. No. 283, 1 March–No. 313, 27 Sept. 1655. [By Henry Scobell and Henry Walker.] (Cf. 26 July 1653.)

A Very Full and Particular Relation. No. 6, [31 Oct. 1649]. [Pbd M. Simmons. A supplement to A Briefe Relation.]

A Perfect and more particular relation. No. 2, [19 Nov. 1649]. [Pbd F. Leach.]

A Perfect Diurnall of Some Passages and Proceedings of and in relation to the Armies. No. 1, 17 Dec. 1649–No. 302, 24 Sept. 1655. [By John Rushworth and Samuel Pecke. Counterfeits: No. 138, 2 Aug.–No. 140, 16 Aug. 1652.] (Cf. 31 Jan. 1642.)

The Royall Diurnall (for King Charls II). No. 1, 25 Feb.–No. 7, 15 April; No. 1, 22 April; No. 2, 30 April 1650. (Cf. 31 July 1648.)

Mercurius Elenticus (for King Charles the II.). No. 1, 22 April–No. 7, 3 June 1650. (Cf. 5 Nov. 1647.)

Mercurius Politicus comprising the summ of all intelligence. No. 1, 13 June 1650–No. 615, 12 April 1660. [Attrib. to John Hall and Marchamont Needham until Jan. 1653; by M. Nedham until the end except from 13 May–16 Aug. 1659 when it is by John Canne. Supervised by John Milton until Jan. 1653; by John Thurloe from Feb. 1653 to May 1659.]

Nouvelles Ordinaires de Londres. [No. 1, ? June 1650]–No. 186, 22 Jan.–No. 229, 5 Nov. 1654; [probably suspended 1661–2]–No. 567, 3 May 1663 [–?]. [Attrib. to Jean de l'Écluse in 1663.]

The Impartial Scout. No. 53, 28 June 1650–No. 66, 27 Sept. 1653. [Attrib. to Daniel Border.]

Perfect Passages of every Daies Intelligence. No. 1, 5 July 1650–No. 80, 31 Dec. 1652; [continued as] The Moderate Publisher of every Dayes Intelligence. No. 81, 21 Jan.–No. 94, 22 April 1653; No. 140, 29 April–No. 149, 9 Sept. 1653. [Ptd J. Clowes. Counterfeit: No. 8S [sic], 28 Jan. 1653 (ptd E. Neile. By Henry Walker.] (Cf. 16 Oct. 1644, 31 Oct. 1651, 14 Oct. 1653, 20 Jan. 1654.)

The Perfect Weekly Account. [No. 59], 17 July–No. 70, 26 Sept. 1650. [Ptd B. Alsop.] (Cf. 6 Sept. 1643, 29 March 1648.)

A Perfect Diurnal of Some Passages of Parliament. No. 324, 22 July; No. 325, 29 July 1650. [Ptd W. Hunt for F. Coales, L. Chapman, and L. Blaiklock. Imitations of the periodical started 17 Dec. 1649.] (Cf. 31 Jan. 1642.)

The Weekly Intelligencer of the Commonweaith. No. 1, 23 July 1650–[2nd ser. No. 6], 25 Sept. 1655. [Attrib. to Richard Collings.] (Cf. 10 May, 26 July 1659.)

True Intelligence from the Head Quarters. No. 1, 23 July–No. 3, 7 Aug. 1650.

The Best and most Perfect Intelligencer. No. 1, 8 Aug. 1650. [Attrib. to William Huby.]

Mercurius Anglicus. No. 1, 1 Oct. 1650. [Attrib. to Henry Walker.] (Cf. 7 Feb. 1644.)

The Faithfull Scout. No. 1, 3 Jan. 1651–No. 102, 31 Dec. 1652; No. 103, 11 Feb.–No. 108, 18 March 1653[–?]; [continued as] The Armies Scout. [?–]No. 114, 30 April–[No. 119], 3 June 1653; [continued as] The Faithfull Scout. No. 115, 10 June 1653–No. 246, 28 Sept. 1655. [Ptd Robert Wood. Attrib. to Daniel Border.] (Cf. 29 April 1659.)

A Perfect Account of the Daily Intelligence. [No. 1, 15 Jan. 1651]–No. 3, 29 Jan. 1653–No. 246, 26 Sept. 1655. ['By B. D.']

Mercurius Pragmaticus Revived and from the shades of his Retirement return'd again. No. 1, 10 June 1651 [continued as] Mercurius Elencticus. No. 2, 17 June–No. 4, 1 July 1651; [continued as] Mercurius Scommaticus. No. 1, 8 July 1651. [Attrib. to Samuel Sheppard.] (Cf. 21 Sept., 5 Nov. 1647.)

Several Letters from Scotland. No. 1, 15 [23] July 1651. [Ptd F. Neile.]

The Armies Intelligencer. No. 1, 5 Aug. 1651.

The True Informer. No. 1, 28 Aug. 1651. [Pbd F. N.] (Cf. 23 Sept. 1643.)

The Modern Intelligencer. No. 5, 3 Sept. 1651. [Attrib. to Henry Walker.] (Cf. 19 Aug. 1647.)

The Diary. No. 1, 29 Sept.–No. 6, 3 Nov. 1651. [Ptd Bernard Alsop.] (Cf. 22 May 1644.)

Mercurius Scoticus or the Royal Messenger. No. 2, 30 Sept. 1651. [Attrib. to Francis Nelson.] (Cf. 19 July 1648.)

Perfect Particulars of Every Daies Intelligence. No. 39, 31 Oct. 1651. [Ptd F. Neile. An Imitation of Perfect Passages.] (Cf. 5 July 1650.)

The French Intelligencer. No. 1, 25 Nov. 1651–No. 26, 18 May 1652. [Ptd Robert Wood. Attrib. to Daniel Border.]

Mercurius Bellonius. No. 1, 4 Feb.–No. 5, 3 March 1652. [Ptd J. C. Attrib. to John Crouch.]

The Dutch Spy. No. 1, 24 March–No. 3, 7 April 1652.

Mercurius Democritus or a true and perfect Nocturnall communicating wonderfull news of the World in the Moon. No. 1, 8 April–No. 21, 25 Aug. 1652; [continued as] The Laughing Mercury. No. 22, 8 Sept.–No. 30, 3 Nov. 1652; [continued as] Mercurius Democritus. No. 31, 10 Nov. 1652–No. 81, 9 Nov. 1653. [By John Crouch.] (Cf. 25 Jan. 1654, 3 May 1659.)

Mercurius Phreneticus. No. 2, [8 April]–No. 4, [22 April 1652]. [Attrib. to Samuel Sheppard.] (Cf. 19 July 1652.)

Mercurius Zeteticus. [No. 1], [22 April 1652].

The French Occurrences. No. 1, 17 May 1652–No. 40, 3 Jan. 1653. [Pbd George Horton.]

Mercurius Pragmaticus. No. 1, 25 May–No. 6, 30 June 1652. [Attrib. to Samuel Sheppard.] (Cf. 21 Sept. 1647, 6 July 1652.)

Mercurius Heraclitus. No. 1, 28 June–No. 3, 12 July 1652. [Pbd J. C. and D. W. By John Crouch.]

Mercurius Pragmaticus. No. 1, 6 July 1652. [By Marchamont Needham.] (Cf. 21 Sept. 1647, 25 May 1652.)

Mercurius Phreneticus. No. 1, 19 July 1652. [Attrib. to Samuel Sheppard.]

Mercurius Britannicus. No. 1, 26 July–No. 23, 28 Dec. 1652. [The first 5 nos. by Marchamont Needham. There is a counterfeit of No. 21, 14 Dec. Pbd Robert Wood.]

Mercurius Cinicus or a true and perfect intelligence. No. 1, 11 Aug. 1652.

Mercurius Mastix, Faithfully lashing all Scouts, Mercuries, Posts, Spys and others who cheat the Commonwealth. No. 1, 27 Aug. 1652. [By Samuel Sheppard.]

*The Dutch Intelligencer. No. 1, 8 Sept. 1652.

The Flying Eagle. No. 1, 4 Dec. 1652–No. 5, 1 Jan. 1653. [Ptd T. Fawcet for A. P.]

The Moderate Intelligencer. No. 166, 8 Dec.–No. 169, 29 Dec. 1652. [Pbd Robert Wood. Attrib. to John Dillingham.] (Cf. 5 June 1649, 26 April 1653.)

The Moderate Messenger. No. 1, 7 Feb.–No. [5], 14 March 1653. [Pbd George Horton.]

The Faithful Post. No. 89, 1 April–No. 93, 29 April 1653; No. 131, 6 May–No. 140, 8 July 1653; No. 120, 15 July–No. 126, 2 Sept. 1653. [During April and May pbd G. Horton; 3 June, pbd R. Eeles; 10–24 June, pbd T. L.; 8 July–2 Sept. pbd R. E. An offshoot from The Faithfull Scout.]

The Faithfull Post [counterfeits]. No. 116, 14 June–No. 123, 2 Aug. 1653. [5, 12 July, no imprint; the rest pbd G. Horton.] (Cf. 3 Jan. 1651, 9 Nov. 1653, 11 Jan. 1654.)

Moderate Occurrences. No. 1, 5 April–No. 9, 31 May 1653. [Pbd George Horton.]

The Moderate Intelligencer. No. 175, 26 April 1653. [Ptd Robert Wood.]

The Moderate Intelligencer. No. 1, 9 May –No. 17, 29 Aug. 1653. (Cf. 6 March 1645, 23 Feb. 1654.)

Mercurius Britannicus. No. 2, 23 May–No. 10, 20 June 1653. [Pbd George Horton.]

Mercurius Pragmaticus. No. 1, 25 May–No. 8, 13 July 1653. [Ptd Matthew Mede.] (Cf. 21 Sept. 1647.)

The Daily Proceedings. [No. 1], [17 June 1653.]

Mercurius Rhadamanthus. [No. 1], [27 June]– No. 5, 25 July 1653.

The True and Perfect Dutch Diurnall. No. 1, 3 July; No. 2, 26 July 1653. [Pbd Tho. Lock.] (Cf. 10 Jan. 1654.)

Severall Proceedings of Parliament. No. 1, 26 July–No. 21, 13 Dec. 1653. [Ptd John Field.]

The Loyal Messenger. No. 1, 10 Aug. 1653. [Pbd George Horton.]

The Newes or the Ful Particulars of the last Fight. No. 1, 12 Aug. 1653.

The Moderate Publisher of Every Dayes Intelligence. No. [1], 14 Oct. 1653–No. 12, 13 Jan. 1654. [Pbd J. C[lowes] and T. W.] (Cf. 5 July 1650, 20 Jan. 1654.)

Great Brittain's Post. No. 136, 9 Nov. (ptd R. Wood); No. 151, 21 Dec.; No. 152, 28 Dec. 1653. [Pbd G. Horton.] (Cf. 1 April 1653, 11 Jan. 1654.)

The True Informer. No. 1, 6 Jan.; [No. 2], 13 Jan. 1654; [continued as] The True and Perfect Informer. [No. 3], 20 Jan. 1654. [Ptd T. Lock.] (Cf. 23 Sept. 1643.)

The True and Perfect Dutch Diurnall. No. 3, 10 Jan. 1654–No. 15, 22 May 1654. [Ptd T. Lock.] (Cf. 3 July 1653.)

The Politique Post. [Unnumbered], 11 Jan. 1654; [continued as] The Grand Politique Post. No. 127, 17 Jan.; No. 127, 24 Jan.; No. 164, 15 Feb.; No. 172, 11 April 1654; [continued as] The Weekly Post. No. 174, 18 April 1654–No. 245, 17 Sept. 1655. [Pbd G. Horton.] (Cf. 1 April, 9 Nov. 1653, 10 May 1659.)

The Moderate Publisher of Every Dayes Intelligence. No. 1, 20 Jan. 1654; [continued as] Certain Passages of Every Dayes Intelligence. No. 2, 27 Jan. 1654–[3rd ser.] No. 4, 28 Sept. 1655. [Ptd F. Neile.] (Cf. 5 July 1650, 14 Oct. 1653.)

Mercurius Democritus. No. 82, 25 Jan.–No. 86, 22 Feb. 1654. [Pbd George Horton; J. Crouch and T. W.] (Cf. 8 April 1652.)

The Loyal Intelligencer. No. 73, 30 Jan. 1654. [Pbd G. Horton.]

The Politique Informer. No. 1, 30 Jan.; No. 2, 6 Feb. 1654. [Ptd R. Wood.]

Perfect Occurrences. No. 1, 6 Feb.–No. 5, 23 June 1654.

The Moderate Intelligencer. No. 165, 23 Feb. –No. 177, 10 May 1654. [Pbd G. Horton. Counterfeits: No. 171, 5 April; No. 172, 12 April; No. 174, 26 April 1654 (all ptd R. Wood).] (Cf. 6 March 1645, 9 May 1654.)

Mercurius Poeticus. [No. 1, 1 March]; No. 2, 8 March[–No. 5, 29 March, 1654]. [Attrib. to Marchamont Needham.]

Mercurius Nullus, or the Invisible Nuncio. [No. 1], [13 March], 1654; [No. 2], [20 March], 1654.

Mercurius Aulicus. No. 1, 20 March–No. 3, 3 April 1654. (Cf. 8 Jan. 1643.)

The Loyal Messenger or Newes from Whitehall. No. 4, 10 April 1654. [Pbd R. Moon. Probably by John Streater.]

Observations Historical, Political and Philosophical upon Aristotle's First Book of Political Government, together with a narrative of State-Affaires in England, Scotland and Ireland. No. 1, 11 April–No. 11, 4 July 1654. [Pbd R. Moone. Folio. By John Streater.]

Perfect Diurnall Occurrences of Certain Military Affairs. No. 1, 8 May 1654; [continued as] A Perfect Diurnall; or, Occurrences of Certain Military Affairs. No. 2, 15 May–No. 28, 30 Oct. 1654. (Cf. 31 Jan. 1642.)

Perfect and Impartial Intelligence together with A Politick Commentary on the Life of Caius Julius Caesar. No. 1, [16 May]–No. 3, 2 June 1654. [Pbd R. Moon. Perhaps by John Streater.]

The Weekly Abstract. No. 1, 3 June–No. 3, 19 June 1654. [Folio.]

Mercurius Fumigosus. No. 1, 7 June 1654– No. 70, 3 Oct. 1655. [By John Crouch.]

Mercurius Jocosus or the merrie Mercurye. [No. 1], 21 July–[No. 3], 4 Aug. 1654. [Attrib. to Thomas Lock.]

The Observator, with a Summary of Intelligence. No. 1, 31 Oct.; No. 2, 7 Nov. 1654. [By Marchamont Needham.]

The Publick Intelligencer. No. 1, 8 Oct. 1655– No. 225, 9 April 1660. [By Marchamont

Needham except from 13 May to 16 Aug. 1659 when it was by John Canne. Under the supervision of John Thurloe until May 1659.]

The Publick Adviser. No. 1, 26 May–No. 19, 28 Sept. 1657. [By Marchamont Needham. The first paper devoted entirely to advertising.]

The Weekly Information from the Office of Intelligence. No. 1, 20 July 1657. [By Oliver Williams. Also an advertising paper.]

Mercurius Pragmaticus. No. 1, 30 Aug. 1658. [? = 6 Sept. 1659.] (Cf. 21 Sept. 1647.)

The Faithful Scout. No. 1, 29 April–No. 11, 9 July 1659; [continued as] The National Scout. No. 12, 16 July 1659; [continued as] The Loyall Scout. [Unnumbered], 22 July 1659–No. 36, 6 Jan. 1660–?–No. 78, 17 June 1660. [Pbd G. Horton. Attrib. to Daniel Border.] (Cf. 3 Jan. 1651.)

Mercurius Democritus communicating faithfully the affairs both in City and Countrey. No. 2, 3 May 1659; [perhaps continued as] Mercurius Democritus or a perfect Nocturnall. No. 1, 10 May–No. 13, 16 Aug. 1659. [By John Crouch.] (Cf. 8 April 1652.)

The Weekly Post. No. 1, 10 May 1659–No. 42, 21 Feb. 1660[–?]. [Pbd G. Horton. Attrib. to Daniel Border.] (Cf. 11 Jan. 1654.)

The Weekly Intelligencer of the Commonwealth. No. 1, 10 May–No. 30, 6 Dec. 1659 [–?]. [Attrib. to R. Collings.] (Cf. 23 July 1650.)

The Moderate Informer. [No. 1], 19 May; [No. 2], 25 May 1659. [Attrib. to Marchamont Needham.]

*The Weekly Account, on the establishment of a free state. No. 1, 25 May 1659. (Cf. 6 Sept. 1643.)

The Weekly Account Faithfully Representing, The most Remarkable Passages in Parliament. No. 1, 1 June 1659. [Ptd E. Alsop.] (Cf. 6 Sept. 1643.)

Mercurius Pragmaticus. [Unnumbered], [20 June 1659]. (Cf. 2 Sept. 1647.)

A Particular Advice from the Office of Intelligence. No. 1, 30 June–No. 51, 30 Dec. 1659; [continued as] An Exact Accompt of the Daily Proceedings in Parliament. No. 53, 6 Jan.–No. 104, 6 July 1660[–?]. [After the first few issues numbered consecutively with Occurrences from Foreign Parts. By Oliver Williams and others.]

Occurrences from Foreign Parts. No. 1, 5 July 1659–No. 88, 18 May 1660[–?]. [After the first few issues numbered consecutively with A Particular Advice. By Oliver Williams and others.]

*The Weekly Intelligencer of the Commonwealth. No. 1, 26 July 1659. (Cf. 23 July 1650, 10 May 1659.)

Mercurius Pragmaticus communicating his Weekly Intelligence. No. 1, 6 Sept. 1659. [Pbd H. Marsh.] (Cf. 21 Sept. 1647, 30 Aug. 1658.)

The Parliamentary Intelligencer. No. 1, 26 Dec. 1659–No. 53, 31 Dec. 1660; [continued as] The Kingdomes Intelligencer. No. 1, 7 Jan. 1661–31 Aug. 1663. [New series number each year. By Henry Muddiman and Giles Dury.]

*The Loyall Scout. No. 1, 26 Dec. 1659.

Mercurius Pragmaticus Impartially communicating the true state of affairs. No. 2, 30 Dec. 1659. (Cf. 21 Sept. 1647, 6 Sept. 1659.)

H. G. P.

VI. BOOKS OF TRAVEL

General Collections, Histories and Geographical Collections. Europe and the Mediterranean Countries. Farther Africa and Asia. America. Critical-Historical Works and Bibliographies.

(1) GENERAL WORKS

(a) Collections and Histories of Travel

Pietro Martire d'Anghiera. The Decades of the newe worlde of West India, Conteyning the navigations and conquestes of the Spanyardes, translated into Englysshe by Rycharde Eden. 1555; ed. Edward Arber (in The First Three English Books on America, Birmingham, 1885). [In part from the De Orbe novo Decades, Alcalá, 1516, and the De nuper repertis insulis, Basle, 1521; and from other sources concerning both East and West Indies.]

—— The History of Travayle in the West and East Indies, and other countreys lying eyther way, towardes the fruitfull and rych Moluccaes. Newly set in order, augmented, and finished by Richarde Willes. 1577. [Adding to Peter Martyr a large Pt II from other sources.]

—— De Orbe novo Petri Martyris Anglerii Decades octo. Labore & industria Richardi Hakluyti. Paris, 1587. [Second edn of the complete work, originally Alcalá, 1530.]

—— De Novo Orbe, or the Historie of the West Indies, Contayning the acts and adventures of the Spanyardes. Whereof three, have been formerly translated into English, by Richard Eden, whereunto the other five, are newly added by M[ichael] Lok. 1612; [1625?]; 1812 (in A Selection of Curious, Rare, and Early Voyages).

Richard Hakluyt. Divers voyages, touching the discoverie of America. 1582. [See Voyages to America, Section (4) (a) below, p. 786.]

—— The principall Navigations, Voiages and Discoveries of the English nation, made by Sea or over Land, to the most remote and farthest distant Quarters of the earth. 1589; 3 vols. 1598–1600 (as The principal Navigations, Voiages, Traffiques and Discoveries); 4 vols. 1809–12 (as Hakluyt's Collection of the Early Voyages, Travels, and Discoveries of the English Nation); 16 vols. Edinburgh, 1884–90 (as Principal Navigations of the English Nation); 12 vols. Hakluyt Soc. Ex. Ser. 1903–5; 8 vols. 1908 (as Hakluyt's Voyages, Everyman's Lib., partial). [Continued in Purchas, 1625.]

Antonio Galvam. The Discoveries of the World from their first originall unto the yeere of our Lord 1555. Briefly written in the Portugall tongue by Antonie Galvano: Corrected, quoted, and now published in English by Richard Hakluyt. 1601; 1745 (in Harleian Voyages, vol. II); 1812 (in A Selection of Curious, Rare, and Early Voyages); ed. C. R. D. Bethune, Hakluyt Soc. 1862. [From the Tratado de todos os descobrimentos, Lisbon, 1563.]

Samuel Purchas. Hakluytus Posthumus or Purchas his Pilgrimes. Contayning a History of the World, in Sea voyages, and lande-Travells, by Englishmen & others. 4 vols. 1625; 20 vols. Hakluyt Soc. Ex. Ser. Glasgow, 1905–7; tr. Dutch (partial), Amsterdam, 1655.

Giovanni Battista Ramusio. Primo Volume delle Navigationi e Viaggi. Venice, 1550, 1554, 1563, 1588, 1606 and 1613. Secondo Volume. Venice, 1559, 1574, 1583 and 1606. Terzo Volume. Venice, 1556, 1565, 1606.

Theodore de Bry. Collectiones Peregrinationum in Indiam Orientalem et Indiam Occidentalem, XXV Partibus Comprehensae. Frankfort, 1590–1634. [In Latin and German, some in French and English.]

Levinus Hulsius. Sammlung von Sechs und Zwanzig Schiffahrten in verschiedene fremde Lände. Nuremberg, etc., 1598–1650. [In German and Latin.]

Awnsham and John Churchill. A Collection of Voyages and Travels, Some now first Printed from original Manuscripts. 6 vols. 1704–32, 1732, 1744–6; 8 vols. 1752.

John Harris. Navigantium atque Itinerantium Bibliotheca: Or, A Compleat Collection of Voyages and Travels. 2 vols. 1705, 1744–8 and 1764.

Pieter van der Aa. Verzameling der gedenkwaardigste reysen naar Oost en West Indies. 28 vols. Leyden, 1706–7; 8 vols. Leyden, 1727 (as De Aanmerkenswaardigste Zee- en Land-reizen der Portugeezen, Spanjaarden, Engelsen en allerhande Natien).

William Oldys. The Harleian Miscellany: A Collection of Scarce, Curious, and Entertaining Pamphlets and Tracts. Selected from the Library of Edward Harley, Second Earl of Oxford. 8 vols. 1744–6; ed. T. Park, 10 vols. 1808–13; 12 vols. 1808–11. [Park's edition cited below.]

Thomas Osborne. A Collection of Voyages and Travels, consisting of authentic writers in our own tongue. Compiled from the Library of the late Earl of Oxford. 2 vols. 1745; 2 vols. 1747. [Referred to below as Harleian Voyages.]

Thomas Astley. A New General Collection of Voyages and Travels: Consisting Of the most Esteemed Relations, which have been hitherto published in any Language. 4 vols. 1745–7. Tr. German (as vols. I–VII of J. J. Schwabe, Allgemeine Historie der Reisen, Leipzig, 1747–74); French (as vols. I–IX of Abbé Prévost, Histoire des Voyages, 20 vols. Paris, 1746–89, and 25 vols. Amsterdam, 1747–89).

John Pinkerton. A General Collection of the Best and Most Interesting Voyages and Travels in all Parts of the World. 17 vols. 1808–14.

A Selection of Curious, Rare, and Early Voyages, and Histories of Interesting Discoveries, chiefly Published by Hakluyt, or at his Suggestion, but not included in his Celebrated Compilation. Ed. R. H. Evans, 1812. [Also issued as vol. v of Hakluyt's Voyages.]

Peter Force. Tracts and Other Papers, Relating Principally to the Origin, Settlement, and Progress of the Colonies in North America. 4 vols. Washington, 1836–46; 2 vols. Rochester, New York, 1898–9 (in part, as American Colonial Tracts).

Hakluyt Society Publications. 1847–.

Edward Arber. An English Garner. 8 vols. 1877–97; 12 vols. 1903–4. [In the 2nd edn most of the relevant pieces are grouped together as Voyages and Travels, ed. C. R. Beazley, 2 vols. 1903. Cited below as Arber.]

E. J. Payne. Voyages of the Elizabethan Seamen. Select Narratives from the Principal Navigations of Hakluyt. 2 vols. Oxford, 1880 and 1893; 1907.

Navy Records Society Publications. 1894–.

F. C. Danvers and W. Foster. Letters Received by the East India Company from its Servants in the East, 1602–1617. 6 vols. 1896–1902.

Original Narratives of Early American History. Ed. J. F. Jameson, 18 vols. New York, 1906–17.

Massachusetts Historical Society. Americana Series, Photostat Reproductions. Boston, 1919–.

The Broadway Travellers. Ed. Sir Edward Denison Ross and Eileen Power, 1926–.

Argonaut Press Classics of Travel and Exploration. Ed. N. M. Penzer, 1926–.

(b) Geographical Descriptions

Bartholomaeus Anglicus. De proprietatibus rerum. [Cologne, 1470?], etc. [No Latin edns in England.]

—— Bartholomeus de proprietatibus rerum. [Tr. John de Trevisa], [Westminster, 1495?]; 1535; 1582 (as Batman uppon Bartholome, His Booke De Proprietatibus Rerum; with addns by Stephan Batman).

[Gauthier or Gossouin de Metz?] The Mirrour of the World or thymage of the same. [1481]; [1490]; [1529?]; ed. O. H. Prior, EETS. Ex. Ser. 1913. [Written c. 1245? Tr. William Caxton from the Image du Monde.]

Ranulf Higden. Mappa Mundi or Description of the World. [Bk I of the Polychronicon, tr. John de Trevisa, 1377.] 1482; 1495; 1527. [Latin original ed. C. Babington, 9 vols. Rolls Ser. 1865–86. For English portion, see below, p. 773.]

Proclus Diadochus. De Sphaera, sive circulis coelestibus libellus. Venice, 1499 (with Latin trn by Thomas Linacre); Leipzig, [1500?]; Vienna, 1511; Paris, 1534, etc.

—— The Descripcion of the Sphere or Frame of the worlde. Englysshed by me Wyllyam Salysburye [1550.]

—— Procli Sphaera. Ed. John Bainbridge, 1620. [Greek and Latin.]

Roger Barlow. A Brief Summe of Geographie. Ed. E. G. R. Taylor, Hakluyt Soc. 1932. [1541. BM. Royal MS 18 B xxviii. Tr. from Martin Fernandez de Enciso, Suma de geographia, Seville, 1519, 1530 and 1546.]

Sebastian Münster. A treatyse of the newe India, with other new founde landes and Ilandes, as well eastwarde as westwarde. Translated out of Latin into English. By Rycharde Eden. 1553; ed. Edward Arber (in The First Three English Books on America, Birmingham, 1885). [From portions of Bk v of the Cosmographia universalis, Basle, 1550, etc.]

—— A Briefe Collection and compendious extract of straunge and memorable thinges gathered out of the Cosmographye of Sebastian Munster. 1572; 1574. [Anon. compilation.]

Joannes Boemus. The Discription of the Contrey of Aphrique. the fyrst part of the worlde. Translated out of Frenche into Englyshe by Wyllyam Prat. 1554. [From the first book of the Repertorium Librorum Trium De Omnium Gentium Ritibus, Augsburg, 1520; later as Omnium Gentium Mores, Leges, & Ritus; French edns; 1540, 1542, 1547.]

—— The Fardle of facions conteining the aunciente maners, customes, and Lawes, of the peoples enhabiting the two partes of the earth, called Affrike and Asie. 1555; 1812 (in A Selection, etc.). [Tr. William Watreman.]

—— A Discoverie of the countries of Tartaria, Scithia, & Cataya, by the North-East: With the manners, fashions, and orders which are used in those countries. Set foorth by John Frampton. 1580. [From Boemus via Francisco Thamara, El libro de las Costumbres de todas las gentes del Mundo, Antwerp, 1556.]

—— The Manners, Lawes, and Customes of All Nations. 1611. [Tr. complete E. Aston, and including other material.]

William Cuningham. The Cosmographical Glasse; conteinyng the principles of Cosmographie, Geographie, Hydrographie, or Navigation. 1559.

Caius Plinius Secundus. A Summarie of the Antiquities, and wonders of the worlde, abstracted out of the sixtene first bookes of Plinie, translated oute of French by I. A. [1566]; 1585 and 1587 (as The Secrets and wonders of the world). [From Pierre de Changy, Paris, 1559.]

—— The Historie of the World. Commonly called, The Naturall Historie of C. Plinius Secundus. Translated into English by Philemon Holland. 2 vols. 1601, 1634 (re-issued 1635).

Dionysius Periegetes. The Surveye of the World, or Situation of the Earth, so muche as is inhabited. now englished by Thomas Twine. 1572. [Greek edn, Eton [1607?]; Cambridge, 1633. Commentary (Latin) by William Hill, 1658.]

George Buchanan. De Sphaera fragmentum. [In Franciscanus et Fratres, [Geneva?], 1584 and 1585.]

—— Sphaera; Georgii Buchanani Scoti quinque libris descripta. Herborn, 1586, 1587, 1617. [In Franciscanus et Fratres, [n.p.] 1594; Heidelberg, 1604 and 1609. In Poemata omnia, Edinburgh, 1615; Leyden, 1621; Saumur, 1621; Leyden, 1628; Amsterdam, 1641, 1657, 1665 and 1676; Edinburgh, 1677; 1686; Amsterdam, 1687. In Opera Omnia, Edinburgh, 1715; Leyden, 1725.]

Pomponius Mela. The worke of Pomponius Mela. The Cosmographer, concerninge the Situation of the world. Translated out of Latine By Arthur Golding. 1585; 1590 (combined with next item).

Julius Solinus. The excellent and pleasant worke of Julius Solinus Polyhistor. Translated out of Latin into English, by Arthur Golding. 1587; 1590 (combined with preceding item, as The Rare and Singuler worke of Pomponius Mela).

Guillaume de Saluste Seigneur du Bartas. The Colonies of Bartas. With the Commentary of S. G. S. [Tr. William Lisle], 1598; 1625 (in his Part of Du Bartas, English and French); 1637 (in Foure Bookes of Dubartas in French and English). [From La Seconde Semaine ou Enfance du Monde, Paris, 1584, etc. Also tr. Joshua Sylvester in The Second Weeke, or childhood of the world, 1598, and in Bartas his Devine Weekes and Workes, 1605, 1608, 1611, 1613, 1621, 1633, and 1641. Also tr. Thomas Winter in The Second Day of the First Week, 1603.]

The Theatre of the Earth. Containing very short and compendious descriptions of all countries, gathered out of the chiefest cosmographers, both ancient and modern, and disposed in alphabeticall order. 1599; 1601.

[George Abbot.] A Briefe Description of the whole worlde. Wherein Is Particularly described, all the Monarchies, Empires, and kingdomes of the same. 1599; 1600; 1605; 1608; 1617; 1620; 1624; 1636; 1664.

Giovanni Botero. The Travellers Breviat, or An historicall description of the most famous kingdomes in the World. 1601; 1601 (as The Worlde, or, an historicall description); 1603 (as An Historicall description); 1608 (as Relations of the most famous kingdomes); 1611; 1616; 1630. [Tr. Robert Johnson from Le relazioni universali, Rome, 1592, etc.]

—— A Treatise, Concerning the causes of the magnificencie and greatnes of Cities, done into English by Robert Peterson. 1606. [From the Tre libri delle cause della grandezza delle città, Ferrara, 1589, etc.]

—— The Cause of the Greatnesse of Cities. 1635. [Tr. Sir T. Hawkins from the same.]

Abraham Ortelius. Abraham Ortelius his epitome of the Theater of the Worlde. 1603; [1610]. [From the Latin, Epitome, Antwerp, 1589, etc.]

—— Theatrum Orbis Terrarum Abrahami Orteli Antverp. Geographi Regii. The Theatre of the Whole World. 1606. [From the Latin, Antwerp, 1570, etc.]

Robert Stafforde. A Geographicall and Anthologicall description of all the Empires and Kingdomes, both of Continent and Ilands in this terrestriall Globe. 1607; 1618; 1618; 1634.

Richard Zouche. The Dove: or Passages of Cosmography. 1613; ed. Richard Walker, Oxford, 1839. [Verse.]

Samuel Purchas. Purchas his Pilgrimage. or Relations of the World and the Religions observed in All Ages And places discovered. 1613; 1614; 1617; 1626.

Edward Brerewood. Enquiries Touching the Diversity of Languages, and Religions through the cheife parts of the world. 1614; 1622; 1625 (in Purchas his Pilgrimes); 1635; 1674. Tr. French, Paris, 1640 and 1663; Latin, Frankfort, 1650 and 1659.

Pierre d'Avity. The Estates, Empires, and Principallities of the World. Represented by ye description of countries, maners of inhabitants. Translated out of French by E[dward] Grimstone 1615. [From Les Empires, Royaumes, Estats, et Principautez du Monde, Paris, 1614, etc.]

Peter Heylyn. Microcosmus, Or A Little Description Of The Great World. A Treatise Historicall, Geographicall, Politicall, Theologicall. Oxford, 1621, 1625, 1627, 1629, [1630?], 1633, 1636, and 1639. [Enlarged to make the next item.]

—— Cosmographie in four Bookes contayning the Chorographie & Historie of the whole World, and all the Principall Kingdomes, Provinces, Seas, and Isles Thereof. 1652; 1657; 1660; 1665; 1666; 1669; 1670; 1682; 1703.

Nathanaell Carpenter. Geography delineated forth in two Bookes. Containing the sphaericall and topicall Parts thereof. Oxford, 1625 and 1635.

William Pemble. A Briefe Introduction to Geography containing a Description of the Grounds, and Generall Part thereof. Oxford, 1630; 1635; 1635 (in The Workes of W. Pemble); Oxford, 1658; Oxford, 1659, 1669, 1675, 1685 (in The Workes).

John Speed. A Prospect of the Most Famous Parts of the World Viz. Asia, Affrica, Europe, America. 1631; 1646; 1668; 1676 (with The Theatre of Great Britain).

Gerard Mercator. Historia mundi: or Mercators Atlas. Containing his cosmographicall Description of the Fabricke and Figure of the World. Englished by W. S[altonstall]. 1635; 1637; [1639?]. [Original Latin, Düsseldorf, 1595, etc.]

—— Atlas or a Geographicke description of the Regions, Countries and Kingdomes of the worlde. 2 vols. Amsterdam, 1636, 1638 and 1641. [Tr. Henry Hexham.]

Ephraim Pagitt. Christianographie, Or The Description of the multitude and sundry sorts of Christians in the World not subject to the Pope. 1635; 1636; 1640.
—— A Relation of the Christians in the World. 1639.
Lewes Roberts. The Merchants Mappe of Commerce: Wherein, the Universall Manner and Matter of Trade, is compendiously handled. 1638; 1671; 1677; 1700.
Petrus Bertius. Breviarium totius Orbis Terrarum. Oxford, 1651, 1663 (in Tractatus duo Mathematici); Oxford, 1657 (in Philippi Cluverii Introductionis in Universam Geographiam; see below). [First pbd Leyden, 1624.]
Diodorus Siculus. The History of Diodorus Siculus. Containing all that is Most Memorable and of greatest Antiquity in the first Ages of the World Until the War of Troy. Done into English by H[enry] C[ogan]. 1653.
Alexander Ross. ΠΑΝΣΕΒΕΙΑ, or, A View of all Religions in the World: With the several Church-Governments, from the Creation, to these times. Together with a Discovery of all known Heresies, in all Ages and Places. 1653; 1655; 1658; 1664; 1696; [1780?]. Tr. Dutch, Amsterdam, 1663 and 1671; French, Amsterdam, 1666 and 1669; German, Amsterdam, 1667, Nuremberg, 1701 and 1717.
Tommaso Campanella. A Discourse Touching the Spanish Monarchy. Wherein We have a Politicall Glasse, representing each particular Country. 1654; [1660?] (as Advice to the King of Spaine). [Tr. Edmund Chilmead from the De Monarchia Hispanica discursus, Amsterdam, 1640, etc.]
Samuel Clarke. A Geographicall Description of all the Countries in the knowne World as also of the Chiefest Cittyes, Famousest Structures, Greatest Ruins, Strangest Fountaines. 1657; 1671; 1689.
Philippus Cluverius. Introductionis in Universam Geographiam, tam Veterem quam Novam, Libri VI. Accessit P. Bertii Breviarium Orbis Terrarum. Oxford, 1657; tr. Eng. Oxford, 1657 (as An Introduction into Geography, both Ancient and Moderne, comprised in sixe bookes). [First pbd Leyden, 1624.]
Robert Fage. A Description of The whole Worlde, with Some General Rules touching the use of the Globe, Wherein Is contained the situation of several Countries. 1658.
R. P. A Geographicall Description Of The World. Describing Europe, Asia, Africa, and America. With all its Kingdoms, Countries, and Common-Wealths. [Appended to Dionysius Petavius, The History Of The World: Or, An Account of Time, 1659.]
Tho[mas] Porter. A Compendious View or Cosmographical, and Geographical Description of the whole World. Wherein is shewed the situation of the several Countries, and Islands. 1659.

(2) Europe and the Mediterranean Countries

(a) Travels and Voyages

Informacion for pylgrymes unto the holy londe. [1498]; 1524; rptd Roxburghe Club, Edinburgh, 1824; ed. facs. E. G. Duff. 1893. [In part from William Wey, Itineraries to Jerusalem, c. 1460, ptd Roxburghe Club, Edinburgh, 1857.]
The Pylgrymage of Sir Richarde Guylforde [1506–1507] towardes Jherusalem. 1511; ed. Sir Henry Ellis, Camden Soc. 1851.
Rychard Torkyngton. The Pylgrymage of Sir Rychard Torkyngton Person of Mulberton in Norffolke. And how he went towardys Jherusalem. Ed. W. J. Loftie, 1884. [1517–8. BM. Add. MSS 28561 and 28562.]
Robert Langton. The pylgrimage of M. Robert Langton clerke to saynt James in Compostell. 1522; ed. E. M. Blackie, Cambridge, U.S.A. 1924.
Nicolas Durand de Villegagnon. A lamentable and piteous Treatise, wherin is contayned, not onely the high Enterprise and Valiauntness of th'emperour Charles the V. and his army (in his Voyage made to the Towne of Argier in Affrique, agaynst the Turckes) but also the myserable Chaunces of Wynde and Wether. 1542; rptd Harleian Misc. vol. IV. [From Caroli V. Imperatoris Expeditio in Africam ad Argieriam, Paris, 1542, etc.]
John Leland. The laboriouse Journey & serche of Johan Leylande, for Englandes Antiquitees, geven of him as a newe yeares gyfte [1546] to Kynge Henry, with declaracyons enlarged by Johan Bale. 1549; 1596; 1722; 1772; 1895; 1906 (with next item, vol. I).
—— [The Itinerary of John Leland c. 1540.] Ed. Thomas Hearne, 9 vols. Oxford, 1710–17, 1745–4 and 1768–9; ed. L. Toulmin Smith, 5 vols. 1906–10.
Sir Thomas Hoby. A Booke of the Travaile and Lief of Me Thomas Hoby. Ed. Edgar Powell, Camden Misc. vol. X, 1902. [Travels on the Continent, 1547–1555, written by 1564. BM. Egerton MS 2148.]
An excellent Discourse of Jhon Fox an inglishman who Delivered 266 Christians [from the galleys]. 1579; 1589 and 1599 (in Hakluyt); rptd Arber. [1579 edn not apparently

extant; formerly ascribed to Anthony Munday, or Mundy, as well as the following item, an elaboration.]

The Admirable Deliverance of 266. Christians by John Reynard Englishman from the captivitie of the Turkes. 1608; rptd Harleian Misc. vol. I.

Anthony Mundy. The English Romayne Life. Discovering: The lives of the Englishmen at Roome. 1582; 1590; rptd Harleian Misc. vol. VII; ed. G. B. Harrison, 1925.

Giraldus Cambrensis. Itinerarium Cambriae: Seu Laboriosae Baldvini Cantuar. Archiepiscopi per Walliam legationis descriptio. In Pontici Virunnii Britannicae Historiae Libri sex, per Davidum Povelum. 1585. [Also in Gulielmi Camdeni, Anglica, Hibernica, Normannica, Cambrica a veteribus scripta, Frankfort, 1602 and 1603.]

—— Cambriae Descriptio. 1585 (as above); 1602 and 1603 (as above).

—— Topographia Hiberniae, sive de Mirabilibus Hiberniae. [In Camden, as above, 1602 and 1603.]

[All in Opera, 7 vols. 1861–77; tr. Eng. 1806 and 1863.]

Humphrey Mote. The Primrose of London with her valiant adventure on the Spanish coast. Truely published by Humphrey Mote. 1585; 1871; tr. Dutch, Leyden, 1585.

Nicolas de Nicolay, Seigneur d'Arfeuille. The Navigations, peregrinations and voyages, made into Turkie. Translated out of the French by T. Washington the younger. 1585; rptd Harleian Voyages, vol. I. [From Les quatre premiers livres des navigations et peregrinations orientales, Lyon, 1568, etc.]

Marc-Antonio Pigafetta. Itinerario Di Marc' Antonio Pigafetta gentil'huomo Vicentino [from Vienna to Constantinople and return 1567–1568]. 1585. [Edn and trn in preparation by the Hakluyt Soc.]

Henry Haslop. Newes Out of the Coast of Spaine. The true Report of the honourable service for England, perfourmed by Sir Frauncis Drake upon Cales; and also since that in the Cape S. Vincent and Cape Saker. 1587.

Robert Leng. The true Discripcion of the last voiage [1587] of that worthy Captayne, Sir Frauncis Drake, Knight, with his service done against the Spanyardes. Ed. (from MS) Clarence Hopper, Camden Misc. vol. V, 1863.

Thomas Saunders. A true Discription and breefe Discourse, Of a most lamentable Voiage, made laterie [1584–1585] to Tripolie in Barbarie, in a Ship named the Jesus. Set foorth by Thomas Saunders, one of those Captives. 1587; 1589 and 1599 (in Hakluyt); rptd Arber.

[Anthony Wingfield.] A True Coppie of a Discourse written by a Gentleman, employed in the late Voyage of Spain and Portingale. 1589; 1599 (in Hakluyt); 1625 (in Purchas); ed. J. P. Collier, 1870. Tr. Latin, 1589 (as Ephemeris expeditionis Norreysii & Draki in Lusitaniam), Frankfort, 1590 (as Brevis et fida narratio), Nuremberg, 1590 (in Narrationes duae (with account of West Indies voyage, 1585)); German, Munich, [1590].

Richard Ferris. The most dangerous and memorable adventure of Richard Ferris to rowe by sea to the citie of Bristowe. 1590; ed. J. P. Collier (in Illustrations of Early English Popular Literature, vol. II, 1863); rptd E. Arber (English Garner, vol. VI, 1883).

Petruccio Ubaldini. A Discourse concerninge the Spanish fleete invadinge Englande in the yeare 1588 and overthrowne by her Maties: Navie. Written in Italian by Petruccio Ubaldini and translated for A. Ryther. 1590; 1740; rptd in Harleian Misc. vol. I. [Pbd with a vol. of drawings: Expeditionis Hispanorum In Angliam vera descriptio, by Robert Adams. The narrative and drawings rptd Roxburghe Club, 1919. Ubaldini's MS is BM. Royal 14 A x; its original English form, written by or for Lord Howard, is Cott. Julius F x, fols. 111–7, ed. Sir J. K. Laughton, Navy Records Soc. 1894.]

Edward Webbe. The Rare and most wonderful thinges which Edward Webbe an Englishman borne, hath seen and passed in his troublesome travaile, in the Landes of Jewrie, Egipt, Gtecia, Russia, and in the Land of Prester John. [1590?]; [1590]; 1590; [1600]; ed. E. Arber, 1868; ed. facs. E. W. Arber, 1889; ed. E. Goldsmid, Edinburgh, 1885.

Sir Jerome Horsey. A Relacion or Memoriall abstracted owt of Sir Jerom Horsey his Travells, Imploiments, Services and Negociacions [in Russia, 1573–91]; ed. E. A. Bond, Hakluyt Soc. 1856. [From BM. Harleian MS 1813.]

[Sir Walter Ralegh.] A Report of the Truth of the fight about the Iles of Açores this last Sommer. Betwixt The Revenge, one of her Majesties Shippes, And an Armada of the King of Spaine. 1591; 1599 (in Hakluyt, vol. II); rptd Harleian Misc. vol. X; Somers Tracts, vol. I, 1751 and 1809; Astley, vol. I; Schwabe, vol. I; Prévost, vol. I; Pinkerton, vol. I; ed. E. Arber, 1871 and 1895, rptd Boston, 1902; 1908; facs. 1915.

Francis Seall. A Treatise of my Lord of Comberlans Shippes Voyage (in anno 1592) and of theyr takynge of the greate Carracte.

Ed. C. L. Kingsford, Navy Records Soc. 1912 (in Naval Miscellany, vol. II). [BM. Harleian MS 540, fols. 111–4.]

The Sea-Mans Triumph. Declaring the honorable actions of such gentlemen Captaines and Sailers, as were at the taking of the great Carrick. 1592; part rptd Arber.

H. R. Newes from the Levane Seas. Discribing the many perrilous events of Edward Glenham, Esquire [in a privateering voyage]. 1594.

Richard Hasleton. Strange and Wonderfull Things happened to Richard Hasleton in his Ten yeares Travailes in many forraine countries [1582–1593, in slavery to the Moors]. 1595; rptd Arber.

Gervase Markham. The Most Honorable Tragedie of Sir Richard Grinvile, Knight. 1595; ed. E. Arber, 1871, 1895; ed. E. Goldsmid, Edinburgh, 1883. [Verse.]

William Spelman. A Dialoge or Confabulation Betwen two travellers, which treateth of ther hard adventures in the tyme of ther travell through Dyvers Kingdomes & Contries [in Europe]. Ed. J. E. L. Pickering, Roxburghe Club, 1896. [Written c. 1595?]

William Warner. Albions England: A Continued Historie of the same Kingdome, from the Originals of the first Inhabitants thereof. 1596; 1597; 1602; 1612; rptd A. Chalmers (The Works of the English Poets, vol. IV, 1810). [The first three edns, 1586, 1589, 1592, do not include the eleventh and twelfth bks, which contain the Russia voyage narratives as derived from Hakluyt.]

Sir William Slingsby. The voyadge to Calis in Andaluzia, faithfully related by Sr W. Slyngisbye employed in that service, A.D. 1596. Ed. J. S. Corbett, Navy Records Soc. 1902. [From Alnwick MSS.]

Edward Wright. The Voyage of the right Ho. George Earle of Cumberland to the Azores. 1599 (in his Certaine Errors in Navigation); 1599 (in Hakluyt, vol. II); rptd Harleian Voyages, vol. II; Pinkerton, vol. I; Arber.

A true Report and description of the taking of the Iland of St. Maries 1599. 1600. [Tr. from Dutch.]

A true report of a great Fight at sea between certaine Ships belonging to sundrye merchants of England and five well approoved ships of warre of the King of Spaines. [1600.]

Thomas Dallam. [The Diary of Master Thomas Dallam, 1599–1600, of a voyage to Constantinople.] Ed. J. T. Bent, Hakluyt Soc. 1893.

William Kemp. Kemps nine daies Wonder, performed in a daunce from London to Norwich. 1600; rptd Camden Soc. 1840; ed. facs. 1876; rptd E. Arber (English Garner, vol. VII, 1883); ed. (from MS) E. Goldsmid, Edinburgh, 1884.

A Brief Discourse of the Memorable Voyage to Portugall, Anno 1589, by Sir John Norice and Sir Francis Drake. [In A True Discourse Historicall, of the Succeeding Governours in the Netherlands. 1602. Tr. T. Churchyard and R. Robinson from E. van Meteren's Historiae Belgicae.]

[Henry Timberlake.] A True and strange discourse of the travailes of two English Pilgrimes: what admirable accidents befell them in their journey to Jerusalem, Gaza, Grand Cayro, Alexandria, and other places. 1603; 1608; 1609; 1611; 1612; 1616; 1620; 1631; 1683, 1685 and 1759 (in R. B., Two Journeys to Jerusalem); 1786 (in R. B., Memorable Remarks); Bristol, 1796 (in Richard Burton, Judaeorum memorabilia); rptd Harleian Misc. vol. I,

John Sanderson. [The Travels of John Sanderson in the Levant, 1584–1602]. Part in Purchas; ed. Sir William Foster, Hakluyt Soc. 1931. [Written by 1604. BM. Lansdowne MS. 241.]

Sir Thomas Smithes Voiage and Entertainment in Rushia. With the tragicall ends of two Emperors, and one Empresse. 1605.

Robert Tresswell. A Relation of such things as were observed to happen in the Journey of Charles Earle of Nottingham Ambassadour to the King of Spaine. 1605; rptd Somers Tracts, vol. II, 1809; Harleian Misc. vol. II.

A. N. A true Relation of the Travels of M. Bush, a Gentleman: who made a Pynace, in which hee past by Ayre, Land, and Water: From Lamborne to London. 1608.

Andrew Barker. A True and Certaine Report of the Beginning, Proceedings, Overthrowes, and now present Estate of Captaine Ward and Danseker, the two late famous Pirates. 1609.

[William Biddulph.] The Travels of certaine Englishmen into Africa, Asia, Troy, Bythinia, Thracia, and to the Blacke Sea, [and Palestine, 1600–1608]. 1609; 1612; rptd Purchas; Harleian Voyages, vol. I.

[Gerrit de Veer.] The True and perfect Description of three Voyages by the Ships of Holland and Zeland, on the North sides of Norway, Muscovia, and Tartaria. 1609; rptd Purchas; Harris, vol. I; Harleian Voyages, vol. II; 1812 (in A Selection, etc.); ed. C. T. Beke, Hakluyt Soc. 1853; ed. K. Beynen, Hakluyt Soc. 1876; [Tr. William Phillip from the Waerachtige Beschrijvinghe van drie seylagien, Amsterdam, 1598.]

Thomas Coryat. Coryats crudities, hastily gobled up in five moneths travells. 1611; 3 vols. 1776; 2 vols. Glasgow, 1905. [See also Voyages to Asia.]

49

[Robert Fotherbie.] A Short Discourse of a Voyage made 1613 to the late discovered countrye of Greenland [= Spitsbergen]; and a breife discription of the same countrie. Archaeologia Americana, vol. IV, Boston, 1860. [From MS in Library of American Antiquarian Soc. Worcester, Mass.]

William Davies. A true Relation of the Travailes and most miserable Captivitie of William Davies, Barber-Surgion of London, under the Duke of Florence. 1614; rptd Harleian Voyages, vol. I.

George Sandys. A Relation of a Journey begun An. Dom. 1610. Foure Bookes, Containing a description of the Turkish Empire, of Aegypt, of the Holy Land, of the remote parts of Italy, and Ilands adjoyning. 1615; 1621; 1627; 1632; 1637; 1652 (as Sandys Travailes); 1658; 1673; 1864. Tr. Dutch, Amsterdam, 1653 and 1654, Utrecht, 1654, Amsterdam, 1659 and 1665; German, Frankfort, 1669. [Extracts in Purchas and Harris.]

H. R. A True Relation of a most worthy and notable fight [June, 1616], by two small shippes of the Citie of London: the Vineyard and the Unicorne, against six great Gallies of Tunes in the Straights. [1616.]

Fynes Moryson. An Itinerary written by Fynes Moryson, Gent. (Containing his ten yeers travell through the twelve dominions of Germany, Bohmerland, Switzerland, Netherland, Denmarke, Poland, Italy, Turky, France, England, Scotland, and Ireland). 1617. [Pt IV, ed. from MS Charles Hughes as Shakespeare's Europe, 1903; complete edn, 4 vols. Glasgow, 1907–8.]

John Taylor. Three Weekes, three daies, and three houres Observation And Travel, From London to Hamburgh. 1617; 1630 (in Workes); rptd Manchester, 1869 (in Spenser Soc. edn of Workes); ed. Charles Hindley, 1872 (in Works); 1888 (in Early Prose and Poetical Works).

—— A Fight at Sea famously fought by the Dolphin of London, against five of the Turkes Men of Warre and a Satty, 1616. 1617; 1630 (in Workes); rptd Manchester, 1869 (in Spenser Soc. edn of Workes); Arber.

—— The Pennyles Pilgrimage, Or the Moneylesse perambulation, of John Taylor, On Foot from London to Edenborough. 1618; 1630 (in Workes); rptd Manchester, 1869 (in Spenser Soc. edn of Workes); 1888 (in Early Works).

—— Taylor his Travels: from the Citty of London in England to the Citty of Prague in Bohemia. 1620; 1630 (in Workes); rptd Manchester, 1869 (in Spenser Soc. edn of Workes).

John Taylor. The Voyage of Mr. Roger Bird and the Writer hereof, in a Boat of browne-Paper, from London to Quinborough in Kent. 1620 (in The Praise of Hemp-Seed); 1630 (in Workes); rptd Manchester, 1869 (in Spenser Soc. edn of Workes).

—— A Verry Merry Wherry-Ferry-Voyage: Or Yorke for my Money. 1622; 1630 (in Workes); Manchester, 1869 (as above); ed. C. Hindley 1872 (in Works); 1888 (in Early Prose and Poetical Works).

—— Prince Charles his Welcome from Spaine: And the Relation of such Townes as are scituate in the wayes to take post-horse at, from London to Dover: and from Callice to Madrid. 1623; 1630 (in Workes); Manchester, 1869 (as above).

—— A New Discovery By Sea, With a Wherry from London to Salisbury. 1623; 1630 (in Workes); Manchester, 1869 (as above); 1872 (as above); 1888 (as above).

—— A Famous Fight at Sea. 1627; 1630 (in Workes); 1869 (as above). [See Voyages to Asia, p. 784 below.]

—— Taylor on Thame Isis: Or The Description of the Two Famous Rivers of Thame and Isis. 1632; Manchester, 1870 (in Works Not Included in the Folio Volume, vol. I, Spenser Soc.).

—— A brave and memorable and dangerous Sea Fight foughten neere the road of Tittawan in Barbary. [1636.]

—— Taylors Travels and Circular Perambulation, of the Famous Cities of London and Westminster. 1636; Manchester, 1873 (as above, vol. II).

—— The Honorable, and Memorable Foundations, Erections, Raisings, and Ruines, of divers Cities within ten Shires. Also, a Relation of the Wine Tavernes. 1636 (bis); Manchester, 1877 (as above, vol. IV).

—— The Carriers Cosmographie. or A Briefe Relation, of the Innes, in, and neere London, where the Carriers doe usually come. 1637; Manchester, 1873 (as above, vol. II); rptd Arber.

—— Part of this Summers Travels. Or News from Hell, Hull, and Hallifax. [1639]; Manchester, 1870 (as above, vol. I); ed. C. Hindley, 1872 (in Works); 1888 (in Early Prose and Poetical Works).

—— A Valorous and Perillous Sea-fight. Fought with three Turkish ships, Pirats or men of Warre, on the coast of Cornewall by the good Ship named the Elizabeth of Plimmouth. 1640; 1640 (as A brave and valiant Sea Fight); Manchester, 1877 (as above, vol. IV).

—— John Taylors last Voyage and Adventure, Performed with a Scullers Boate, from London to Oxford, Gloucester, and Hereford. 1641; Manchester, 1873 (as above, vol. II).

John Taylor. Tailors Travels, from London, to the Isle of Wight. 1648; ed. J. O. Halliwell [-Phillipps] (Literature of the Sixteenth and Seventeenth Centuries Illustrated, 1851); Manchester, 1877 (as above, vol. IV).

—— John Taylors Wandering, to see the Wonders of the West. How he travelled from London to the Lands end, and home againe. 1649; Manchester, 1870 (as above, vol. I); ed. C. Hindley, 1872 (in Works).

—— A Late Weary Merry Voyage, from London to Gravesend, to Cambridge. 1650.

—— A Short Relation of a Long Journey Made Round or Ovall By encompassing the Principalitie of Wales. [1653]; Manchester, 1870 (as above, vol. I); ed. C. Hindley, 1872 (in Works).

—— The Certain Travailes of an uncertain Journey [in Sussex and Kent]. 1653; ed. C. Hindley, 1872 (in Works); Manchester, 1873 (as above, vol. II).

Richard Bernard. The Fabulous Foundation of the Popedome. Whereunto Is Added a Chronographicall Description of Pauls peregrination with Peters travells, and the reasons why he could not be at Rome. Oxford, 1619.

Heinrich Buenting. Itinerarium Totius Sacrae Scripturae, or, The Travels of the Holy Patriarchs, Prophets, Judges, Kings, our Saviour Christ, and his Apostles. Done into English by R. B. 1619; 1636. [From the German original, Helmstädt, 1581, etc.]

J. B[utton]. Algiers Voyage in A Journall or Briefe Reportory of all occurrents hapning in the fleet of ships sent out against the Pirates of Algiers. 1621; rptd Purchas; ed. E. P. Statham (in History of the Family of Maunsell, vol. I, 1917). [From State Papers Domestic, James I, 122, 106.]

John Rawlins. The famous and wonderfull recoverie of a ship of Bristoll called the Exchange from the Turkish pirates of Argier. 1622; rptd Purchas; Arber.

Sir Richard Wynne. [Relation of the Journey of Prince Charles to Madrid, 1623.] Ed. Thomas Hearne (in Historia Ricardi II, 1729); ed. J. O. Halliwell[-Phillipps] (in Autobiography of Sir Simonds D'Ewes, vol II, 1845).

Sir William Monson. [The Naval Tracts, in six books. Books I and II relating to naval voyages to date of first writing, 1624, pbd in part in Megalopsychy, 1682 (as A true and exact Account of the Wars with Spain in the reign of Queen Elizabeth).] 1704 (in Churchill, vol. III, first complete edn); ed. (from MS) M. Oppenheim, Navy Records Soc. 1902–14.

Sir John Glanville. A relation touching the Fleete and Armie of King Charles, sett forth in the first year of his hignes Raigne [to Cadiz]. Ed. A. B. Grosart, Camden Soc. 1883. [From Eliot MS, written 1625.]

Edward Cecil, Viscount Wimbledon. A Journall, and Relation of the action, which Edward Lord Cecyl did undertake upon the Coast of Spaine. 1626; 1627; tr. German, 1628 (in De Bry, Indiae Orientalis Appendix).

—— [A defence of his action against the charge by the Earl of Essex and others.] 1724 (in Sir Richard Granville, Two Original Journals).

A true Relation of a brave English Stratagem, practised lately upon a Sea-Towne in Galizia by an English Ship alone of 30. Tonne. 1626; rptd E. Arber (English Garner, vol. I, 1877).

Sir Richard Granville. Journal of the expedition to the Isle of Rhee in France, Anno 1627. 1724 (in Two Original Journals).

A Relation of a brave and resolute Sea-fight, made by Sir Kenelam Digby on the Bay of Scandarone, with certaine Galegasses and Galeasses, belonging to the States of Venice. 1628 (in Articles of Agreement Made Betweene the French King and those of Rochell).

Sir Kenelm Digby. [Journal of a voyage into the Mediterranean, 1628.] Ed. (from MS) John Bruce, Camden Soc. 1868.

Charles Robson. Newes from Aleppo. A Letter [concerning his voyage] by Charles Robson, Preacher to the Company of our English Merchants at Aleppo. 1628.

James Wadsworth. The English Spanish Pilgrime. Or, A New Discoverie of Spanish Popery, and Jesuiticall Stratagems. 1629; 1630 (bis). [Travels in Spain, France, and Flanders.]

—— Further Observations of the English Spanish Pilgrime, Concerning Spaine. 1630 (bis).

—— The Present Estate of Spayne, Or A true relation of some remarkable things touching the Court, and Government of Spayne. 1630 (bis).

Edward Pellham. Gods Power and Providence, Shewed, in the Miraculous Preservation and Deliverance of eight Englishmen, left by mischance in Green-land [= Spitsbergen], Anno 1630. 1631; rptd Churchill, vol. IV; ed. A. White, Hakluyt Soc. 1855.

Peter Mundy. [The travels of Peter Mundy to Spain and Turkey, 1617–1628; in Southern England, 1635; in England and Wales, 1639; to Danzig and Archangel, 1639–1647. Being Relations I–III, XX, XXXI, XXXI–XXXV respectively of the Itinerarium Mundii, the first draft completed 1634.] Ed. Sir R. C. Temple, Hakluyt Soc. 1907–24. [BM. Harleian MS 2286, dated 1634, copied and continued in Bodleian MS Rawl. A 315. See also Voyages to Asia, p. 781 below.]

A Relation of a Short Survey of 26 Counties [north from Norwich], observed in a seven weeks journey begun 1634, by a Captain, a Lieutenant, and an Ancient. Ed. L. G. Wickham Legg, 1904. [BM. Lansdowne MS 213.]

Sir William Brereton. The Journal of Sir William Brereton, 1634 [to Holland]. [In Chetham Soc. Remains, vol. I, 1844.]

—— The Journal of Sir William Brereton, 1635 [to northern England, Scotland, northern Ireland]. [In Chetham Soc. Remains, vol. I, 1844.]

Henry Blount. A Voyage into the Levant. A Breife Relation of a Journey, lately performed [1634–1636] from England by the way of Venice, into Dalmatia, Sclavonia, Bosnah, Hangary, Macedonia, Thessaly, Thrace, Rhodes and Egypt. 1636; 1637; 1638; 1650; 1664; 1669; 1671; rptd Harleian Voyages, vol. I; Pinkerton, vol. x. Tr. Dutch, Van der Aa; German, Helmstädt, 1687.

Sydnam Poyntz. A True Relation of these German warres from Mansfield's going out of England which was in the yeare (1624) untill this last yeare 1636. Ed. A. T. S. Goodrick, Camden Soc. 1908. [Bibliothèque Nationale MS, Fonds anglais 55.]

William Crowne. A True Relation of All the Remarkable Places and Passages Observed in the Travels of Thomas Lord Howard, Ambassadour Extraordinary to his sacred Majesty Ferdinand the Emperour of Germanie, Anno Domini 1636. 1637.

Robert Monro. Monro His Expedition with the worthy Scots Regiment levied in August 1626 for his Majesties Service of Denmark. 1637.

John Dunton. A True Journall of the Sally Fleet, with the Proceedings of the Voyage. Whereunto is annexed a List of Sally Captives names, and the places where they dwell. 1637; rptd Harleian Voyages, vol. II; Churchill, vol. VIII, 1752.

Randulph Mayeres. Mayeres His Travels: containing a true Recapitulation of all the remarkable passages which befell in the Authors Peregrinations and Voyages [military and naval, partly in verse] [1638.]

John Aston. [The Journal of John Aston to Scotland, 1639.] Surtees Soc. 1910.

Two famous Sea-fights. Lately made, Betwixt the Fleetes of the King of Spaine, and the Fleetes of the Hollanders. The one, in the West-Indyes: The Other, betwixt Callis and Gravelin. 1639.

Thomas Carve. Itinerarium R. D. Thomae Carve Tipperariensis; Sacellani maioris In Legione strenuissimi Domini Colonelli D. Walteri Deveroux. Mainz, 1639, 1640 and 1641; Spire, 1646; 1859; tr. German, Mainz, 1640. [In Latin.]

Francis Knight. A Relation of Seaven Yeares Slaverie under the Turkes of Argeire, suffered by an English Captive Merchant. 1640 (bis); rptd Harleian Voyages, vol. II.

Sad News from the Seas. Being a relation of the losse of that good ship the Merchant Royall, which was cast away ten leagues from the Lands end. 1641.

Joyfull Newes from Sea: Or good tidings from my Lord of Warwicke, of his encounter with some Spanish Ships [off Ireland], with the happy successe he obtained thereby. 1642.

Newes from Sally: Of a Strange Delivery Of Foure English captives [taken on a return voyage from La Rochelle] from the slavery of the Turkes. 1642.

Edward, Baron Herbert of Cherbury. The Life of Edward, Lord Herbert of Cherbury [including his continental travels 1608–24, written c. 1643]. Strawberry-Hill, 1764; 1770; Dublin, 1771; 1792; 1824; 1826; 1853; Boston, 1877; 1877; ed. Sir Sidney Lee, 1886 and 1904; 1888; 1904; 1912; Newtown, Montgomeryshire, 1928.

—— Expeditio in Ream insulam, Anno 1630. 1656 (ed. Timothy Baldwin); rptd (from MS) Philobiblon Soc. 1860 (as The Expedition to the Isle of Rhe).

John Evelyn. Memoirs illustrative of the Life and Writings of John Evelyn comprising his Diary [with the account of his travels in the Low Countries 1641 and in France, Italy, and Switzerland, 1643–47]. Ed. W. Bray, 2 vols. 1818, etc.

John Raymond. An Itinerary, contayning a voyage made through Italy in the years 1646 and 1647. Illustrated with divers figures of antiquities. 1648.

The Common-Wealths Great Ship Commonly called the Soveraigne of the Seas, built in the yeare, 1637. With all the Fights we have had with the Hollander, since the Engagement of Lieutenant-Admirall Trompe neer Dover, against the English Fleet under the Command of Generall Blake. 1653.

Richard Fleckno. A Relation Of ten Years Travells in Europe, Asia, Affrique, and America [1652–1654]. All by way of Letters occasionally written to divers noble Personages. [1654?]; 1665.

Joachim Hane. A short Relacion of the severall wonderfull passages which I did meete withall in my jorney into France [1653–4]. Ed. (from the Clarke Papers) Sir

C. H. Firth, Oxford, 1896 (as The Journal of Joachim Hane).

Bulstrode Whitelocke. [A Journal of the Swedish Embassy in the years 1653 and 1654.] Ed. Charles Morton, 2 vols. 1772; ed. Henry Reeve, 2 vols. 1855.

Samuel Brett. A Narrative Of the Proceedings Of a great Councel of Jews, Assembled in the Plain of Ageda in Hungaria. Also, A Relation Of some other Observations in his Travels beyond the Seas. 1655; 1683 (in T. H., Two Journeys to Jerusalem); 1759 (in R. B., Two Journeys); 1786 (in R. B., Memorable Remarks upon the Jewish Nation); 1796 (in Richard Burton, Judaeorum Memorabilia); 1876; rptd Harleian Misc. vol. I.

Sir William Penn. [Journals of various naval services, 1644–1655 and later.] Ptd Granville Penn (in Memorials of Sir William Penn, 2 vols. 1833).

A brief Relation or Remonstrance of the Injurious proceedings and Inhumane cruelties of the Turks [of Alexandria], perpetrated on the commander and company of the Ship Lewis of London. [1657.]

Thomas Bispham. Iter Australe, A Reginensibus Oxon. Anno 1658. Expeditum. [Oxford? 1658?] [Latin verse, on a journey in southern England.]

Sir John Reresby, Bart. [Travels to Italy, 1654–1658.] 1813 and 1904 (in The Travels and Memoirs).

Francis Mortoft. Francis Mortoft: His Book, Being his Travels through France and Italy, 1658–1659. Ed. Malcolm Lettes, Hakluyt Soc. 1925. [BM. Sloane MS 2142.]

Iter Carolinum, Being A Succinct Relation of the Necessitated Marches, Retreats, and Sufferings Of His Majesty Charles the I [1641–1648]. Collected by a daily attendant. 1660; rptd Somers Tracts, vol. v, 1809.

Ogier Ghiselin de Busbecq. Omnia quae extant. Oxford, 1660; 1660 (with Georgievitz, see 2(c), p. 777 below, 1570); tr. Eng. (in part) 1694, 1744, Glasgow, 1761, Oxford, 1927; tr. (complete) C. E. Forster, 2 vols. 1881.

(b) Descriptions of the British Isles

Bede. Historiae Ecclesiasticae Gentis Anglorum Libri V. [Strasburg, 1475?], etc.; rptd in Opera Omnia, Basle, 8 vols. 1563, etc.; ed. A. Wheelock, Cambridge, 1643, 2 vols. 1644, 1722, etc.

—— History of the Church of Englande [translated by T. Stapleton]. Antwerp, 1565; St Omer, 1622 and 1626, etc.

Ranulf Higden. Therfor I entende to sette in this booke the discripcion of this said Ile of Britayne. 1480; 1498. [Also in Bk I of the Polychronicon, 1482, 1495, 1527. Also appended to This present cronycle of Englonde, 1497, 1502, 1504, 1510, 1515 (bis); 1520; 1528.] [Tr. John of Trevisa, 1377.]

John Major. De Britanniae descriptione. [In Bk I of the Historia Majoris Britanniae, tam Angliae quam Scotiae, Paris, [1521], Edinburgh, 1740.] Tr. A. Constable, Scottish Hist. Soc. 1892.

Hector Boethius. Scotorum regni descriptio. [In his Scotorum Historiae a prima gentis origine, [Paris, 1526], Paris, 1575; tr. John Bellenden, Heir beginnis the hystory and croniklis of Scotland. Edinburgh, [c. 1536]; ed. Thomas Maitland, The Works of John Bellenden, vols. I, II, Edinburgh, 1822; tr. 'out of the Scotish' William Harrison, The Description of Scotlande, in Raphael Holinshed, The firste Volume of the Chronicles of England, 1577, 1587, 1805, 1807. Tr. Italian Petruccio Ubaldini, Descrittione del Regno di Scotia, Antwerp [or London], 1588.]

John Ben. Descriptio Insularum Orchadiarum, Anno 1529, per me Joannem Ben ibidem Colentem. [In George Barry, History of the Orkney Islands, Edinburgh, 1805 and 1808, Kirkwall, 1867.] Scottish Hist. Soc. 1908.

Caius Julius Caesar. Julius Caesars commentaryes. Newly translated owte of laten in to Englyshe [by John Tiptoft], as much as concernyth thys realm of England. 1530.

—— The eyght bookes of C. Julius Caesar conteyning his martiall exploytes in the Realme of Gallia. 1565; 1578; 1590. [Tr. Arthur Golding.]

—— C. Julii Caesaris Commentarii. 1585; 1590; 1601.

—— Observations upon Caesars Comentaries. 1609; [1609?]. [Ed. and tr. C. Edmundes.]

—— The Commentaries of C. Julius Caesar. 1655; 1677; 1695; 1719. [Tr. C. Edmundes.]

Polydore Virgil. De divisione Britanniae. [In the Anglicae Historiae Libri XXVI, Basle, 1534 and 1546; 2 vols. Ghent 1556–7; (Libri XXVII) Basle, 1555, 1556, 1557 and 1570, 2 vols. Douay, 1603, Leyden, 1651; tr. Camden Soc. 1846 (The First Eight Books).]

Andrew Boorde. The Peregrination of Doctor Boarde. Ed. Thomas Hearne (in De Vita et Gestis Henrici II, vol. II, 1735). [Written c. 1542.]

[Alexander Lindsay?] La Navigation du Roy d'Escosse Jaques cinquiesme autour de son Royaume [1546]. Paris, 1583. [A routier, tr. Nicolas de Nicolay. Retranslated in Miscellanea Antiqua, London, 1710 and in Miscellanea Scotica, vol. III, Glasgow, 1819].

Donald Monro. A Description of the Westerne Isles of Scotland by Mr Donald Monro, quho travelled through maney of them in Anno 1549. Edinburgh, 1774; 1818 (in Scottish Tracts, vol. II); 1884; Scottish Hist. Soc. 1908.

John Bale. Descriptiones Angliae, Scotiae, Hyberniae. [In his Scriptorum illustrium majoris Brytanniae Catalogus, Basle, 1557-9.] [Compiled from Paulus Jovius, George Lily, John Leland, and Polydore Virgil.]

Robert Talbot. Annotationes in eam partem itinerarii Antonini quae ad Britanniam pertinet. Ed.Thomas Hearne(with Leland's Itinerary, Oxford, 1712, etc.) [Written c. 1558.]

J. B., Gentleman. A Letter sent by J. B. Gentleman unto his very frende Mayster R. C. Esquire, wherin is contained a large discourse of the peopling & inhabiting the Cuntrie called the Ardes, and other adjacent in the North of Ireland. [1572.]

Humphrey Llwyd. Commentarioli Britannicae Descriptionis Fragmentum. Cologne, 1572; ed. Moses Williams, 1731; tr. Eng. Thomas Twyne, 1573 (as The Breviary of Britayne); 1729 (in John Lewis, The History of Great Britain).

—— De Mona Druidum Insula. [In Sir John Pryce,Historiae Brytanniae Defensio, 1573; in Abraham Ortelius, Parergon, Antwerp, 1579, etc.; 1731, with preceding item. Tr. in Abraham Ortelius, Theatre of the Whole World, 1606.]

—— A description of Cambria. [In The History of Cambria, now called Wales, 1584, 1697, 1774, 1811, Merthyr, 1812, Shrewsbury, 1832.]

John Hooker. The Discription of the Cittie of Excester, Collected and gathered by John Vowel alias Hooker. [1576]; Exeter, 1775.

William Lambard. A Perambulation of Kent: Conteining the description, Hystorie, and Customes of that Shyre. 1576; 1596; [1636]; rptd Chatham, 1826.

—— Dictionarium Angliae Topographicum et Historicum. 1730. [Compiled c. 1577.]

William Harrison. An historicall description of the Islande of Britayne. [In Raphael Holinshed, The firste Volume of the Chronicles of England, 1577, 1587, 1805, 1807.]

—— The Description of Scotlande, from Hector Boethius. Ibid. [See above, 1526.]

Richard Stanihurst. A Treatise Conteining a plaine and perfect description of Ireland. Compiled by Richard Stanihurst. [In Raphael Holinshed, The second volume of Chronicles, 1577, 1586, 1805, 1807.]

Richard Stanihurst. De Rebus in Hibernia Gestis, Libri Quattuor. Antwerp, 1584. [Bk I descriptive.]

John Leslie. Regionum et Insularum Scotiae Descriptio. [In De Origine, Moribus, et Rebus Gestis Scotorum.] Rome, 1578; Amsterdam, 1675; 1725 (in S. Jebb, De Vita Mariae Reginae, vol. I); tr. (in James Dalrymple, The Historie of Scotland, 1596, STS. 1888).

Rice Merrick. Morganiae Archaiographia [c. 1578]. Ed. Sir Thomas Phillipps (as A Book of Glamorganshire Antiquities), Middle Hill, 1825. [From MS at Queen's College,Oxford.]

John Derricke. The Image of Irelande, with a discourse of Woodkarne, wherin is most lively expressed, the Nature, and qualitie of the saied wilde Irish Woodkarne. 1581; rptd Somers Tracts, vol. I, 1809; ed. John Small, Edinburgh, 1883.

George Buchanan. [A description of Scotland.] [In Rerum Scoticarum Historia, Edinburgh, 1582 and 1583, Frankfort, 1584, 1594 and 1624, Utrecht, 1668 and 1697, Edinburgh, 1700 and 1727, Aberdeen, 1762. Also in Elzevir Respublica Scotiae, Leyden, 1627. Tr. Eng. The History of Scotland, 1690, etc.; Spanish, in J. Blaeu,Atlas major, vol. IV, Amsterdam, 1659; French, in J. Blaeu, Le Grand Atlas, vol. VI, Amsterdam, 1667.]

Sir Thomas Smith. De Republica Anglorum. The maner of Government or policie of the Realme of England. 1583; 1584; 1589, 1594, 1601, 1609, 1612, 1621, 1633, 1635, 1640 (as The Common-Welth of England); 1691; ed. L. Alston and F. W. Maitland, Cambridge, 1906. Tr. Latin [1610?], Leyden, 1625, 1630, and 1641; Dutch, Amsterdam, 1673 (in part); German, Hamburg, 1688.

William Smith. The Vale-Royall of England, or, The County Palatine of Chester [written 1585]. 1656; ed. and expanded by George Ormerod (History of the County Palatine, vol. I, 1819 and 1882).

—— The Particuler Description of England, With the Portratures of Certaine of the Cheiffest Citties and Townes. Ed. H. B. Wheatley and E. W. Ashbee, 1879. [Written 1588. BM. Sloane MS 2596.]

Giraldus Cambrensis. [See p. 768 above, Voyages in Europe, 1585.]

William Camden. Britannia: sive florentissimorum regnorum Angliae, Scotiae, Hiberniae chorographica descriptio. 2 pts, 1586; 1587; Frankfort, 1590; 1590; 1594; 1600; 1607; Frankfort, 1616; Amsterdam, 1617 and 1639 (in Epitomen contracta a R. Vitellio). Tr. Eng. Philemon Holland (as Britain, or a Chorographicall Description), 1610; 1637; 1695; 2 vols. 1722; 2 vols. 1753;

2 vols. 1772; ed. R. Gough, 3 vols. 1789, 1806; abridged (as The Abridgment of Camdens Britannia) 1626; 2 vols. 1701.

William Camden. Remaines of a greater Worke concerning Britaine: But especially England, and the Inhabitants thereof. 1605; 1614; 1623; 1629; 1636; 1637; 1657; 1674;.1856.

Thomas Churchyard. The Worthines of Wales: Wherein are more than a thousand severall things rehearsed. 1587; 1776.

Robert Payne. A Briefe description of Ireland: made in this year. 1589. by Robert Payne unto xxv of his partners. 1589; 1590; Irish Archaeological Soc. 1841.

John Norden. Speculum Britanniae. The first parte An historicall, chorographicall discription of Middlesex. 1593; 1637; 1723.

—— Essex Discribed by Jo. Norden [1594]. Ed. Sir Henry Ellis, Camden Soc. 1840. [Hatfield MS.]

—— Nordens Preparative to his Speculum Britanniae. Intended A reconciliation of sundrie propositions by divers persons tended. 1596; 1723 (with the Middlesex and the Hartfordshire).

—— Speculi Britanniae Pars. The description of Hartfordshire. 1598; 1723 (with the preceding); Ware, 1903.

—— Speculi Britanniae pars altera; or a delineation of Northamptonshire [1610]. 1720.

—— England. An intended Guyde for English Travailers. Shewing in generall, how far one Citie, & many Shire-Townes in England, are distant from other. 1625; 1635; 1643; [1677?]; [1680?].

—— Speculi Britanniae Pars; a topographical and chorographical description of Cornwall. 1728.

[John Monipennie.] Description of whole Scotland, with all the Iles, and names thereof. [In his Certaine matters Composed together.] Edinburgh, [1594?]; [1597]; 1603; rptd Somers Tracts, vol. III, 1809.

—— A true description and division of the whole Realme of Scotland. [In The abridgment or Summarie of the Scots Chronicles.] 1612 (bis); Edinburgh, 1633, 1650, 1662, 1818 (in Miscellanea Scotica, vol. I); Glasgow, 1820.

John Stow. A Survay of London, contayning the Originall, Antiquity, Increase, modern Estate, and description of that Citie. 1598; 1599; 1603; 1618; 1633; 2 vols. 1720; 2 vols. 1734–5; 2 vols. 1753; 2 vols. 1754–5; ed. W.J. Thoms, 1842 and 1876; ed. Henry Morley, 1890, 1893 and [1908]; ed. C. L. Kingsford, 3 vols. Oxford, 1908–27; ed. H.B. Wheatley, [1912].

John Dymmok. A Treatice of Ireland. Ed. Richard Butler, Irish Archaeological Soc. 1842. [c. 1600. BM. Harl. MS 1291.]

[George Coryat.] Descriptio Angliae, et Descriptio Londini: Two Poems in Latin Verse. 1763. [Written c. 1600?]

Richard Carew. The Survey of Cornwall. 1602; ed. H. C. (i.e. P. des Maizeaux), 1723, 1769; ed. T. Tonkin and F., Baron de Dunstanville, 1811.

Sampson Erdeswicke. A Survey of Staffordshire. Containing, The Antiquities of that County. 1717; 1723; 1798 (in S. Shaw, The History of Staffordshire); ed. Thomas Horwood, 1820, 1844. [Written 1591–1603; entered Stationers' Register, 1656–7.]

Barnabe Rich. A New Description of Ireland: Wherein is described the disposition of the Irish whereunto they are inclined. 1610.

John Speed. The Theatre of the Empire of Great Britain: Presenting An Exact Geography of the Kingdomes of England, Scotland, Ireland, and the Iles adjoyning. 1611; 1627; 1631; 1676 (with A Prospect of the Most Famous Parts of the World, see above); tr. Latin Philemon Holland, 1616 (as Theatrum Imperii Magnae Britanniae).

—— [A description of England and Wales. Bound sheets as taken from The Theatre, each county dated 1615.]

—— England Wales Scotland and Ireland Described and Abridged from a farr Larger Voulume. [1620?]; 1627; 1666.

Michael Drayton. Poly-Olbion. [1612]; 1613 (as Poly-Olbion. Or A Chorographicall Description of this renowmed Isle of Great Britaine); 1622; 1748 (in Works); 1753 (in Works); 1793 (in R. Anderson, Poets of Great Britain, vol. III); 1810 (in A. Chalmers, English Poets, vol. IV); Roxburghe Club, 1856; 1876 (in Works); Spenser Soc. 1889.

Edward Thornes. Encomium Salopiae, Or The Description of the Pleasant Situation of the ancient and famous Towne of Shrowesbury. 1615. [Verse.]

Thomas Gainesford. The glory of England, or A True Description of many excellent prerogatives and remarkable blessings, whereby she triumpheth over all the Nations of the World. 1618; 1619; 1620.

Henry Manship. [The History of Great Yarmouth, written 1619.] Ed. (from MS) Charles John Palmer, Great Yarmouth, 1854.

William Burton. The Description of Leicester Shire; Containing Matters of Antiquitye, Historye, Armorye and Genealogy. [1622]; Lynn, 1777; 1795 (in John Nichols, The History of the County of Leicester).

Joannes de Laet. Respublica sive Status Regni Scotiae et Hiberniae. Leyden, 1627. [Taken from Buchanan, Camden, Boethius, Morrison, Giraldus, Stanihurst.]

Joannes de Laet. Angliae chorographica descriptio. [In Thomae Smithi Angli De Republica Anglorum, Leyden, 1630. Taken from Camden, Speed, Barclay, Lambard.]

Ane Description of certaine Pairts of the Highlands of Scotland [c. 1630?]. Ed. (from MS) Sir Arthur Mitchell, Scottish Hist. Soc. Edinburgh, 1906.

Sir John Dodridge. The History of the Ancient and moderne Estate of the Principality of Wales, Dutchy of Cornewall, and Earledome of Chester. 1630; 1714.

Wilhelm Bedwell. A Briefe Description of the towne of Tottenham High-Crosse in Middlesex. 1631; 1718.

Edmund Campion. [A description of Ireland: 7 chapters of] The Historie of Ireland. Ed. Sir James Ware, Dublin, 1633; Dublin, 1809 (in Ancient Irish Histories).

Edmund Spenser. A View of the State of Ireland. Ed. Sir James Ware (in The Historie of Ireland, Dublin, 1633); Dublin, 1809 (in Ancient Irish Histories). [For other edns, see under Spenser, p. 418 above.]

Sir Thomas Stafford. Pacata Hibernia. Ireland Appeased And Reduced Or, An Historie Of The Late Warres of Ireland, especially within the Province of Mounster, under the Government of Sir George Carew [1599–1602]. 1633; ·2 vols. Dublin, 1810; ed. Standish O'Grady, 2 vols. 1896.

A Direction for the English Traviller, by which he shal be inabled to Coast about all England and Wales. 1635; 1636; 1643; 1657 (as A Book of the names of all parishes, market towns, etc. in England and Wales); 1662; 1668; 1677.

William Somner. The Antiquities of Canterbury; or, A Survey of that Ancient Citie, with the suburbs and Cathedrall. 1640; 1703.

G. N. A Geographicall Description of the Kingdom of Ireland. According to the 5 Provinces, and 32 Counties. 1642.

[Timothy Pont?] Noates and Observations of dyvers Parts of the Hielands and Isles of Scotland. Ed. Sir A. Mitchell, Scottish Hist. Soc. Edinburgh, 1907. [Written c. 1644.]

Richard Butcher. The Survey and Antiquities of the Towne of Stamford In the County of Lincolne. 1646; 1717; 1727 (in F. Peck, Academia Tertia Anglicana).

Ireland Or a Booke: Together with an Exact Mappe of the most principall Townes great and small, in the said Kingdome. 1647.

David Buchanan. Provinciae Edinburgenae Descriptio. Ed. Sir A. Mitchell, Scottish Hist. Soc. 1907. [Written c. 1647.]

James Gordon. Abredoniae utriusque descriptio. Spalding Club, Aberdeen, 1842; ed. Sir A. Mitchell, Scottish Hist. Soc. 1907. [Written c. 1647.]

[Sir Anthony Weldon.] Terrible Newes from Scotland. 1647; 1649 (as A Perfect Description of the People and Country of Scotland); 1659; 1837 (in Abbotsford Club Misc. vol. I). [Written 1617, BM. Lansdowne MS 973; wrongly ascribed to James Howell.]

John Woodhouse. A Guide for Strangers in the Kingdome of Ireland. Wherein the High-Wayes and Roads from all the Sea-Townes, Market Parishes, great or small is truely set down. 1647.

—— The Map of Ireland, with the exact Dimensions of the Provinces. With the names of all the Townes and places great and small alphabetically set downe. 1653.

W. G[ray]. Chorographia, Or A Survey of Newcastle Upon Tine. As Also, A Relation of the County of Northumberland. 1649; rptd Harleian Misc. vol. III; Newcastle Soc. Antiquaries, 1813 and 1819.

Gerard Boate. Irelands Naturall History. Being a true and ample Description of its Situation, Greatness, Shape, and Nature. Published by Samuell Hartlib. 1652; 1657; Dublin, 1726; 1755; 1860 (in A Collection of Tracts Illustrative of the Natural History of Ireland, vol. I); tr. French, Paris, 1666.

Sir James Ware. De Hibernia & Antiquitatibus ejus Disquisitiones. 1654; 1658; tr. Eng. 1704 (in The Antiquities and History of Ireland), with separate title-page dated Dublin, 1705); Dublin, 1764 (in The Whole Works of Sir James Ware, vol. II); Dublin, 1860 (in A Collection of Tracts, vol. I).

Thomas Porter. A New Booke of Mapps, Being A ready Guide or Direction for any Stranger, or other, who is to Travel in England, Scotland, & Ireland. 1655.

Villare Anglicum: or A View of the Townes of England. Collected by the appointment of Sir Henry Spelman Knight. 1656; 1678; 1698, 1727 (in Works). [A gazetteer.]

Sir William Dugdale. Antiquities Of Warwickshire Illustrated: Beautified With Maps, Prospects and Portraictures. 1656; 2 vols. 1730; Coventry, 1765; Warwick, 1786.

Thomas Tucker. Report on the Settlement of the Revenue of Excise and Customs in Scotland, 1656. Ed. J. A. Murray, Bannatyne Club, Edinburgh, 1825.

James Howell. Londinopolis; An Historicall Discourse or Perlustration Of the City of London. 1657; [1660?].

Richard Kilburne. A brief Survey Of The County Of Kent. Viz. The Names of the Parishes in the same. 1657. [An epitome of the next item.]

—— A Topographie, Or, Survey Of The County of Kent. With some Chronological, Historicall, and other matters touching the same. 1659.

Richard Franck. Northern Memoirs, calculated for the Meridian of Scotland. Wherein most of the Cities, Citadels, Sea-ports, are described. Writ in the year 1658. 1694; ed. Sir Walter Scott, Edinburgh, 1821.

William Burton. A Commentary On Antoninus His Itinerary, or Journies Of the Romane Empire, so far as it concerneth Britain. 1658.

Richard Hawkins. A Discourse of the Nationall Excellencies of England. 1658.

[John Evelyn.] A Character of England. As it was lately presented in a Letter, to a Noble Man of France. 1659 (bis); rptd Harleian Misc. vol. x; Somers Tracts. vol. vii, 1812; 1825 (in Miscellaneous Writings).

Edward Leigh. England Described: Or the several Counties & Shires thereof briefly handled, to set forth the Glory of this Nation. 1659.

Thomas Philipott. Villare Cantianum: or Kent Surveyed and Illustrated. Being an exact Description of all the Parishes, Burroughs, Villages, and Mannors. 1659; Lynn, 1776.

J. Childrey. Britannia Baconica: Or, The Natural Rarities of England, Scotland, & Wales. According as they are to be found in every Shire. 1660; 1661; 1662; tr. French, Paris, 1667 (bis).

(c) Descriptions of Europe and the Mediterranean Countries

Gulielmus Caorsin. The siege of the noble and invyncyble cytee of Rhodes [in 1480]. [1490?]; ed. H. W. Fincham, 1926. [Tr. John Kay from the Obsidionis Rhodie urbis descriptio, Rome, [1480?].]

The Copy of a Carete, cumposynge the Circuet of the Worlde, and the Compace of every Yland. [In The Customs of London, otherwise called Arnold's Chronicle.] [1503?]; [1521?]; rptd 1811. [Ptd separately as Mappa Mundi. Otherwyse called the Compasse and Cyrcuet of the worlde, [1536?]. Partly ptd in The Compost of Ptholomeus, 2nd edn, as The Rutter, of the dystaunces from one Porte or Countree to another, [1535?].]

Pierre Garcie. The Rutter of the Sea with the Havens, Rodes, Soundings, Kennings, Windes, Floods, and Ebbes. [1528?]; [1550?], [1553?], and [1587?] (adding A newe Rutter of the Sea, for the North parties). [Tr. Robert Copland from the Routier, Rouen, n.d.]

Benedetto Ramberti. The order of the Greate Turckes courte, of his menne of warre, and of all hys conquestes, with the summe of Mahumetes doctryne. Translated oute of French. 1524 (for 1542). [From the Libri tre delle Cose de Turchi, Venice, 1539, etc.]

Paulus Jovius. A shorte treatise upon the Turkes Chronicles, compyled by Paulus Jovius. Drawen oute of the Italyen tong in to Latyne, and translated out of Latyne into englysh by Peter Ashton. 1546. [From the Commentarii delle cose de Turchi, Venice, [1531?], etc., Latin edn, Wittenberg, 1537, etc.]

Andrew Boorde. The fyrst boke of the Introduction of Knowledge. The whych dothe teache a man to know the usage and fashion of all maner of countreys. [1548]; 1555; [1562?]; ed. F. J. Furnivall, EETS. Ex. Ser. 1870.

William Thomas. The historie of Italie, a boke excedyng profitable to be redde. 1549; 1561.

Sebastian Münster. The Description of Swedland, Gotland, and Finland, the auncient estate of theyr kynges, the most horrible and incredible tiranny of the second Christiern, Kyng of Denmarke. Collected and gathered chieflye out of Sebastian Mounster. By George North. 1561. [From the Cosmographia, Basle, 1550, etc. See also p. 765 above, General Descriptions, 1553.]

Andrea Cambini. Two very notable Commentaries, The One Of The Originall of the Turcks and Empire of the house of Ottomanno, written by Andrewe Cambini, and thother of the warres of the Turcke against George Scanderbeg. Translated oute of Italian into Englishe by John Shute. 1562. [From the Libro della origine de Turchi, Florence, 1529, etc., and Francesco Sansovino, Dell' Historia Universale Dell' Origine Et Imperio De Turchi, Venice, 1560–1.]

Polybius. The Hystories of the most famous and worthy Cronographer Polybius. Englished by C. W[atson]. 1568.

—— The History of Polybius the Megalopolitan. Translated into English by Edward Grimeston. 1633; 1634 (bis).

Bartholomaeus Georgievitz. The ofspring of the house of Ottomanno, and officers pertaining to the greate Turkes Court. Whereunto is added Bartholomeus Georgieviz Epitome, of the Customes, Rytes, Ceremonies, and Religion of the Turkes. Englished by Hugh Gough. [1570?] [From the De Origine Imperii Turcorum, Wittenberg, 1562, including the De Moribus, condictionibus et nequicia Turcorum, Rome, 1480?], etc.]

—— De Turcorum Moribus Epitome. [In A. Gislenii Busbequii Quae Extant omnia, 1660.]

Nestore Martinengo. The true Report of all the successe of Famagosta, a Citie in Cyprus. Englished out of Italian by William Malim. 1572; 1599 (in Hakluyt); rptd 1810. [From L'Assedio e presa di Famagosta, Verona, 1572.]

Hieronymus Turlerus. The Traveiler of Jerome Turler, devided into two Bookes. The first of the maner, and order of traveiling oversea. The second comprehending an excellent description of the most delicious Realme of Naples in Italy. 1575. [From the De Peregrinatione, et Agro Neapolitano, Strasburg, 1574.]

Richard Rowlands. The Post of the World. Wherein is contayned the antiquities and originall of the most famous Cities in Europe. With their trade and traficke. With their wayes and distance of myles. 1576. [From an unidentified German source.]

Herodotus. The Famous Hystory of Herodotus. Conteyning the Discourse of dyvers Countreys. 1584; ed. Leonard Whibley, 1924 (Tudor Translations). [Bks I–II, tr. B. R.]

—— Herodoti historiarum liber primus. Oxford, 1591.

Caius Julius Caesar. [See Descriptions of the British Isles, p. 773 above, 1530.]

The Safegard of Sailers and great Rutter. Contayning the Courses, Dystances, Deapths, Soundings, Flouds and Ebbes, with the marks for the entring of sundry Harboroughs. Translated out of Dutch into English, by Robert Norman Hydrographer. 1584; 1587; 1590; 1600; augmented by E. Wright, 1605, 1612, 1640, and 1671.

Lucas Wagenaer. The Mariners Mirrour wherin may playnly be seen the courses, heights, distances, depths, soundings, flouds and ebs, set fourth in divers exact Sea-charts. And now fitted with necessarie additions for the use of Englishmen by Anthony Ashley. [1588.] [From the Spieghel der Zeevaert, Amsterdam, 1584, etc.]

Giles Fletcher. Of the Russe Common Wealth. or Maner of Government by the Russe Emperour, with the manners and fashions of the people of that Countrey. 1591; 1598 (part in Hakluyt, vol. I); 1625 (in Purchas); 1643 and 1656 (as The History of Russia); abridged Harris, vol. I; ed. E. A. Bond, Hakluyt Soc. 1856; tr. Russian, 1867 and 1891.

[John Eliot.] The Survay or Topographical Description of France: With a new Mappe, helping greatly for the Surveying of every particular Country, Cittye, Fortresse, River, Mountaine, and Forrest. 1592; 1593.

Lodovico Guicciardini. The Description of the Low countreys and of the Provinces thereof, gathered into an Epitome out of the Historie of Guicchardini. 1593. [Tr. Thomas Danett from the Descrittione di tutti i Paesi Bassi, Antwerp, 1567, etc.]

Christian van Adrichom. A briefe Description of Hierusalem and of the Suburbs therof. 1595; 1654; York, 1666. [Tr. Thomas Tymme from the Jerusalem et suburbarum descriptio, Cologne, 1584, etc.]

Philippus Lonicerus. The Policy of the Turkish Empire. The first Booke. Containing the State and summe of the Turkes Religion. 1597. [Adapted by an anonymous translator from the Chronicorum Turcicorum Tomus Primus, Frankfort, 1578.]

Publius Cornelius Tacitus. The Description of Germanie. [In The Annales of Cornelius Tacitus, 1598, 1604, 1612, 1622, and 1640. Tr. R. Grenewey.]

Gasparo Contarini. The Common-wealth and Government of Venice, translated out of Italian by Lewes Lewknor Esquire. 1599. [From the Italian version, Venice, 1544, etc., of the De Magistratibus et Republica Venetorum, Paris, 1543, etc.]

The Mahumetane or Turkish Historie, containing three Bookes: translated by Raffe Carr. 1600. [From various sources.]

Girolamo Conestaggio. The Historie of the Uniting of the Kingdom of Portugall to the Crowne of Castill: Containing the last warres of the Portugals. The description of Portugall. Of the East Indies, the Isles of Terceres, and other dependences. 1600. [Tr. for Edward Blunt from the Dell' Unione del Regno di Portogallo, Genoa, 1585, etc.]

Joannes Bartholomaeus Marlianus. A Summarie Collected by John Bartholmew Marlianus, Touching the Topographie of Rome in ancient time. [In The Romane Historie written by T. Livius, tr. Philemon Holland, 1600 and 1659. From the Epitome, 1552, etc. of the Antiquae Romae Topographia, Rome, 1534.]

Flavius Josephus. The Famous and Memorable Works of Josephus, a man of much Honour and Learning among the Jewes. Faithfully translated out of the Latin, and French, by Tho[mas] Lodge. 1602; 1609; 1620; 1632 (bis); 1640; 1655–6.

Richard Knolles. The Generall Historie of the Turkes, from The first beginning of that Nation. Faithfully collected out of the best Histories. 1603; 1610; 1621; 1631; 1638; 3 vols. 1687–1700; 2 vols. 1701.

Lazzaro Soranzo. The Ottoman of Lazaro Soranzo. Wherein is delivered aswell a report of the might and power of Mahamet the third as also a true Description of divers peoples, Countries, Citties, and Voyages. Translated out of Italian into English, by Abraham Hartwell. 1603. [From L'Ottomano, Ferrara, 1599, etc.]

Sir Robert Dallington. The View of Fraunce. 1604 (unauthorized edn).

—— A Method for Travell. Shewed by Taking the view of France, As it stoode in the Yeare of our Lord 1598. [1605?]

Sir Robert Dallington. A Survey of the Great Dukes State of Tuscany. In the yeare of our Lord 1596. 1605 (bis).

[Sir Edwin Sandys]. A Relation of the State of Religion: and with what hopes and policies it hath beene framed, and is maintained in the severall states of these westerne parts of the world. 1605 (3 edns, all unauthorized).

—— Europae Speculum. Or, A View or Survey of the State of Religion. Hague, 1629; 1632 (bis); 1637; 1638; 1673; 1687. Tr. Italian, [Geneva?], 1625; French, Geneva, 1626; Dutch, Haarlingen, 1675. [Written 1599.]

J. B., Merchant. The Merchants Avizo. Verie Necessarie For their Sons and Servants, when they first send them beyond the Seas, as to Spaine and Portingale, or other Countries. 1607; 1616; 1640. [Licensed 1589, and probably pbd then.]

Ammianus Marcellinus. The Roman Historie, containing such Acts and occurrents as passed under Constantius, Julianus, and Valens. Done by Philemon Holland. 1609.

Ro. C. A True Historicall discourse of Muley Hamets rising to the three Kingdomes of Moruccoes with a view of Moorish customs. 1609; rptd Purchas (in part); ed. H. de Castries, Les Sources Inédites de l'Histoire du Maroc, Archives de l'Angleterre, vol. II, 1925.

Sir George Carew. A Relation of the State of France, with the Characters of Henry IV and the Principal Persons of that Court. Drawn up by Sir George Carew, upon his Return from his Embassy there in 1609. Ed. Thomas Birch (in An Historical View of the Negotiations Between the Courts of England, France, and Brussels, pp. 415–528, 1749).

Jean François Le Petit. The Low-Country Common Wealth Contayninge An exact discription of the Eight United Provinces now made free. Translated out of french by Ed. Grimeston. 1609. [From La grande chronique ancienne et moderne, de Hollande, etc., Dordrecht, 1601.]

A True Description and Direction of what is most worthy to be seen in all Italy. Harleian Misc. vol. v. [From MS, written 1610?]

Willem Janszoon Blaeu. The Light of Navigation. Wherein are declared and pourtrayed, all the Coasts and Havens of the West, North and East Seas. Amsterdam, 1612, 1620 and 1622. [From Het Licht der Zeevaert, Amsterdam, 1608, etc.]

—— The Sea-Mirrour. Containing A Briefe Instruction in the Art of Navigation: And A Description of the Easterne, Northerne and Westerne Navigation. Amsterdam, 1625. [From the Zeespiegel, Amsterdam, 1623, etc.]

Thomas de Fougasses. The Generall Historie of the Magnificent State of Venice. From the First Foundation Thereof untill this Present. Englished by W. Shute. 2 vols. 1612. [From the Histoire Generale de Venise, Paris, 1608.]

John Barclay. Icon Animorum. 1614; Paris, 1614 and 1617; Strasburg, 1623 (with the Euphormion); Frankfort, 1625; Leyden, 1625; Milan, 1664; Frankfort, 1668 and 1675; Dresden, 1680; Leipzig, 1733; Augsburg, 1774. Tr. Eng. T[homas] M[ay], 1631 and 1633 (as The Mirrour of Mindes, Or; Barclay's Icon animorum); French, Reims, 1623, Paris, 1625 (bis); German, Bremen, 1649, Frankfort, 1660, Pest, 1784, Münster, 1821; Heidelberg, 1902.

Thomas Godwyn. Romanae Historiae Anthologia. An English Exposition of the Romane Antiquities. Oxford, 1614, 1616, 1620, 1623, 1625, 1628, 1631, 1633, 1638, 1642; 1648; 1655; 1658; 1661; 1668; 1674; 1680; 1685; 1689; 1696.

—— Synopsis Antiquitatum Hebraicarum, ad explicationem utriusque Testamenti valde necessaria. Oxford, 1616. Tr. Eng. 1625, 1626, 1628, 1631, 1634, 1641, 1655, 1667, 1671, 1678, and 1685 (expanded as Moses and Aaron. Civil and Ecclesiastical Rites, Used By The ancient Hebrewes); Latin (from English version), Utrecht, 1698, Bremen, 1710, Frankfort, 1710, 2 vols. Leyden, 1723–4, Venice, 1744 (in B. Ugolinus, Thesaurus Antiquitatum, vol. III).

[Ottaviano Bon.] A Description of the Grand Signors Seraglio, or Turkish Emperours Court. 1625 (in Purchas); ed. John Greaves, 1650, 1653; 1737 (in Miscellaneous Works of John Greaves, vol. II). [Pbd as by Robert Withers, actually tr. by him from Italian MS, ed. Guglielmo Burchet, Venice, 1865.]

Sir Thomas Overbury. His Observations in his Travailes upon the State of the XVII Provinces as they Stood 1609. 1626; 1651 (as Observations Upon the Provinces United. And On the State of France); rptd 1856 (in Miscellaneous Works); Harleian Misc. vol. VIII; Harleian Voyages, vol. I; rptd E. Arber (English Garner, vol. IV, 1882); tr. French, Ghent, 1853.

Gabriel Richardson. Of the State of Europe XIIII Bookes. Containing The Historie, and Relation of the Many Provinces Hereof. Oxford, 1627.

A Short Survey Of The Kingdome of Sweden Containing a Briefe Description of all the Provinces of this whole Dominion. 1632. [From the Dutch.]

Francis Rous. Archaeologiae Atticae Libri Tres. Three Bookes of the Atticke Antiquities. Containing The description of the Citties glory, government, division of the People and Townes. Oxford, 1637; 1643; Oxford, 1649, 1654 (enlarged to 7 bks); ed. [Zachariah Bogan], Oxford, 1662, 1667, 1675, London, 1685.

Jacob Colom. The first Part. The first Book of the fierie Sea-Columne, wherein The Description of the Whole North-Sea. Amsterdam, 1639; Amsterdam, 1649 (as The New Fierie Sea-Colomne). [From De Vyerighe Colom, Amsterdam, 1632, etc.]

Thomas Fuller. The Historie of the Holy Warre [1095–1294]. Cambridge, 1639, 1640, 1647, 1651; rptd 1840.

—— A Pisgah-Sight of Palestine and the Confines Thereof, with The History of the Old and New Testament acted thereon. 1650; 1662; 1689; rptd 1869.

The European Mercury. Describing the Highwayes and Stages from place to place, through the most remarkable parts of Christendome. 1641. [Tr. from the Italian by James Wadsworth.]

James Ussher. A Geographicall and Historicall disquisition, touching the Lydian or Proconsular Asia; and the seven Metropoliticall Churches contained therein. Oxford, 1641 (in Certaine Briefe Treatises. Written By Divine Learned Men, concerning the ancient and Moderne government of the Church); Oxford, 1643; rptd Harleian Voyages, vol. i; Dublin, 1847–64 (in Works); tr. Latin, 1687, 1688 (in Opuscula duo), Bremen, 1701.

James Howell. Instructions For Forreine Travell. Showing by what cours, and in what compasse of time, one may take an exact Survey of the Kingdomes and States of christendome. 1642; 1650; ed. Edward Arber, 1869.

—— Epistolae Ho-Elianae. Familiar Letters Domestic and Forren. 1645; 1650; 1655; 1673; 1678; 1688; 1705; 1713; 1726; 1737; Aberdeen, 1753; 1754; ed. Joseph Jacobs, 1890 and 2 vols. 1892; ed. W. H. Bennett, 2 vols. 1890; ed. O. Smeaton, 3 vols. 1903 (Temple Classics); ed. Agnes Repplier, Boston, 1907.

—— S. P. Q. V. A Survay of the Signorie of Venice, Of Her admired policy, and method of Government. 1651.

—— Brief description of Asia and the Holy Land. [In his trn of Josephus, The Wonderful and Most Deplorable History of the latter Times of the Jews, 1652, 1653, 1662, 1669, 1684, 1699.]

—— A German Diet: Or, The Ballance of Europe Wherein The Power and Weakness

of all the kingdoms and States of Christendom are impartially poizd. 1653.

James Howell. Parthenopoeia. [See p. 781 below, 1654.]

—— Londinopolis. [See p. 776 above, British Isles, 1657.]

[Owen Felltham.] Three Moneths Observations of the Low-Countries, Especially Holland. Containing A brief Description of the Country, Customes, Religion, Manners, and Dispositions of the People. 1648; 1652. [Pirated edns of the next item.]

—— A brief Character of the Low-Countries under the States. Being three weeks observation of the Vices and Vertues of the Inhabitants. 1652; 1660; 1661 (in his Resolves); 1662; 1770.

The Alcoran of Mahomet, translated out of Arabique into French by the Sieur Du Ryer, And newly Englished. 1649; 1649; 1688; 1719 (in A Complete History of the Turks).

Hugo Grotius. A Treatise Of The Antiquity of the Common-wealth of the Battavers whichis now the Hollanders. Translated out of both the Latin and Dutch into English, By Tho. Woods. 1649. [From the Liber de antiquitate Reipublicae Batavicae, Leyden, 1610, etc.; Dutch version Haarlem, 1641.]

A Book and Map of all Europe, With the names of all the Towns of note in that known quarter of the World. 1650.

John Milton. A Brief History of Moscovia, And of Other Less-Known Countries Lying Eastward of Russia as far as Cathay. 1682, etc. [See under Milton, p. 468 above. Written c. 1650?]

Leon Modena. The History of the Rites, Customs, and Manner of Life, of the Present Jews, throughout the World. Translated by Edmund Chilmead. 1650; 1707 (as The History of the Present Jews). [From the Historia de gli riti hebraici, Paris, 1637, etc.]

The Land of Canaan As it was possessed by the twelve Tribes, the promised Land or whole Palestina. 1652.

Guido Bentivoglio. Historicall Relations Of The United Provinces Of Flanders, Written Originally in Italian By Cardinall Bentivoglio: And now Rendred into English By Henry Earle of Monmouth. 1652. [From the Relationi fatte in tempo delle sue nuntiature di Fiandra, Cologne, 1629, etc.]

J[ohn] E[velyn]. The State of France, as it stood in the IXth yeer of this present Monarch, Lewis XIIII. Written to a Friend by J. E. 1652; rptd 1825 (in Miscellaneous Writings).

Khojah Effendi (Sa'd al-Dîn Ibn Hasanjan). The Reign of Sultan Orchan Second King of the Turks [1325–1359]. Translated out of Hojah Effendi, an eminent Turkish Historian. By William Seaman. 1652. [From the Latin version, Annales Sultanorum, of J. Leunclavius, Frankfort, 1588.]

Petrus Cunaeus. Of The Common-Wealth Of The Hebrews. Translated by C. B. 1653. [From the de Republica Hebraeorum libri III, Leyden, 1631, etc.]

Procopius. The History Of The Warres Of the Emperour Justinian In Eight Books. Englished by Henry Holcroft, Knight. 1653.

A Description & Plat of the Sea-Coasts of England, from London, all along the Coasts to the Orchades. As Also: All those parts over against us. 1653. [A routier.]

Girolamo Lunadoro and Fioravante Martinelli. The Court of Rome. Wherein is sett forth the whole government thereof. And a Direction for such as shall Travell to Rome. Translated out of Italian into English by H[enry] C[ogan]. 1654. [From the Relatione della Corte di Roma, Rome, 1635, etc. and the Roma ricercata nel suo Sito, Rome, 1644, etc., respectively.]

Scipione Mazzella. Parthenopoeia, Or The History Of The Most Noble and Renowned Kingdom Of Naples. The first Part By Scipio Mazzella, Made English By Mr. Samson Lennard. The Second Part Compil'd By James Howell. 1654. [From the Descrittione Del Regno Di Napoli, Naples 1586, etc.]

Peter Heylyn. France Painted to the Life. By a Learned and Impartial Hand. 1656; 1657; 1673; 1679. [Unauthorized edns of the next item.]

—— A Full Relation Of two Journeys: The One [1625] Into the Main-Land of France. The Other [1629], Into some of the adjacent Ilands. 1656. [Written as observations rather than as narrative.]

[Francis Osborne.] Political Reflections Upon The Government Of The Turks, etc. By the Author of the late Advice to a Son. Oxford, 1656; 1673, etc. (in Works).

Donald Lupton. Flanders. Or, An Exact and Compendious Description of that fair, great, and fat Countrey of Flanders. 1658.

Olaus Magnus. A Compendious History of the Goths, Swedes, and Vandals, and other northern nations. 1658. [From the Historia de gentibus septentrionalibus, Rome, 1555, etc.]

Samuel Morland. The History Of The Evangelical Churches of the Valleys of Piemont. Containing A most exact Geographical Description of the Place. 1658.

A Character of France. To which is added, Gallus Castratus, or an Answer to a late Slanderous Pamphlet, called The Character of England. 1659.

The Character Of Italy: Or, The Italian Anatomiz'd By An English Chyrurgion. 1660.

The Character Of Spain: Or, An Epitome Of Their Virtues and Vices. 1660.

Andrew Moore. A Compendious History of the Turks: Containing An Exact Account of the Originall of that People; the Rise of the Othoman Family. 1660 (for 1659?).

Franciscus Schottus. Italy. In Its Original Glory, Ruine and Revival, Being an Exact Survey Of the Whole Geography, and History, Of That Famous Country. 1660. [Tr. Edmund Warcupp from the Itinerari Italiae Rerumq. Romanarum Libri Tres, Antwerp, 1600, etc., and the Itinerario, Padua, 1629, etc.]

(3) AFRICA AND ASIA

(a) Voyages to Farther Africa and Asia

'Sir John Mandeville.' Here endeth the boke of John Maundvyle, Knight of wayes to Jerusalem & of marveylys of ynde. 1496; 1499; [1500?]; [1501?]; 1503; 1568; [1583?]; 1618; 1625 (in Purchas); 1632; [1640?]; 1657; [1660?]; 1670; 1677; 1684; 1696; 1705; [1710]; [1715?]; [1720?]; 1725; 1839; 1848 (in T. Wright, Early Travels in Palestine); 1866; 1875 (bis); 1887; 1895; 1928; ed. (with 2 French versions, from MSS) G. F. Warner, Roxburghe Club, 1889; ed. (from MS) A. W. Pollard, 1900; ed. Paul Hamelius, EETS. 1919–23. [Latin version in Hakluyt, 1589 only.]

Balthasar Springer. Of the newe landes and of ye people founde by the messengers of the Kynge of portyngale named Emanuel. [Antwerp? 1509?]; ed. E. Arber (in The First Three English Books on America, Birmingham, 1885). [The first part of a pamphlet printed by John of Doesborowe, also containing: Of the X. Dyvers nacyons crystened: Of Pope Johnn and his landes. Springer's narrative in German, Augsburg, [1508?]; in Flemish, Antwerp, 1508. The pamphlet is listed in the Short-Title Catalogue under Emmanuel.]

Damianus de Goes. The legacye or embassate of prester John unto Emanuell, Kynge of Portyngale. 1533. [Tr. John More from the Legatio, Antwerp, 1532.]

Giosafatte Barbaro. [Travels to Tana and Persia, 1436–1452 and 1471.] Ed. Lord Stanley of Alderley, Hakluyt Soc. 1873. [Tr. c. 1550, William Thomas, from the Viaggi fatti da Venezia, Venice, 1543, etc. BM. Royal MS 17 C x.]

Bernardino de Escalante. A discourse of the navigation which the Portugales doe make to the Realmes and Provinces of the East partes of the world. Translated out of Spanish by John Frampton. 1579; rptd Harleian Voyages, vol. II. [From the Discurso de la navigacion, Seville, 1577.]

Marco Polo. The most noble and famous travels of Marcus Paulus, one of the nobilitie of the State of Venice, into the East partes of the world, as Armenia, Persia, Arabia, Tartary, with many other Kingdoms and Provinces. 1579; ed. N. M. Penzer, 1929. [From the Spanish version, Cosmographia breve, Seville, 1503, etc. Other English versions in Purchas; in Harris, vol. I; in Pinkerton, vol. VII; by William Marsden, 1818, etc.; by Hugh Murray, Edinburgh, 1844, etc.; by Henry Yule, 1871, etc.; by Aldo Ricci, 1931.]

Fernão Lopes de Castanheda. The first Booke of the Historie of the Discoverie and Conquest of the East Indias, enterprised by the Portingales, in their daungerous Navigations. 1582. [Tr. Nicholas Lichfeild from the Historia do descobrimento, bk. I, Coimbra, 1551.]

Juan González de Mendoza. L' Historia Del Gran Regno Della China, Composta primieramente in ispagnuolo, E poi fatta vulgare da Francesco Avanzi. Vinegia [i.e. London], 1587.

—— The Historie of the great and mightie kingdome of China, and the Situation therof: Togither with the great riches, huge Citties, politike governement, and rare inventions in the same. Translated out of Spanish by R[obert] Parke. 1588; ed. Sir G. T. Staunton, Hakluyt Soc. 1853–4. [From the Historia del gran Reyno de la China, Rome, 1585, etc.]

Cesare Federici. The Voyage and Travaile [1563–1581]: of M. Caesar Frederick, Merchant of Venice, into the East India, the Indies, and beyond the Indies. 1588; 1599 (in Hakluyt); 1625 (in Purchas). [Tr. Thomas Hickok from the Viaggio nell' India Orientale, Venice, 1587.]

Filippo Pigafetta. A Report of the Kingdome of Congo, a Region of Africa. And of the Countries that border rounde about the same. Translated out of Italian by Abraham Hartwell. 1597; rptd Purchas; Harleian Voyages, vol. II. [Retranslated by Margarete Hutchinson, 1881. From the Relatione del Reame di Congo, Rome, 1591.]

Jan Huighen van Linschoten. John Huighen van Linschoten his Discours of Voyages into ye Easte and West Indies. 1598; part rptd Purchas; ed. A. C. Burnell and P. A. Tiele, Hakluyt Soc. 1885. [Tr. William

Phillip from the Itinerario, Amsterdam, 1596.]

The Description of a voyage made by certaine Ships of Holland [1595–1597] into the East Indies. Translated out of Dutch into English by W[illiam] P[hillip]. 1598; rptd Harleian Voyages, vol. II; 1812 (in A Selection, etc.). [From the Verhael vande Reyse, Middelburg, 1597.]

Cornelis Geritszoon. An Addition to the Sea Journal Or navigation of the Hollanders unto Java. Compiled by Cornelius Geraldson. 1598; rptd Harleian Voyages, vol. II. [From the Appendix ofte By-voechsel achter tJournael vande Reyse, Middelburg, 1598.]

A True Report of the gainefull, prosperous and speedy voiage [1598–1599] to Java in the East Indies, performed by a fleete of eight ships of Amsterdam. [1599?]; rptd 1812 (in A Selection, etc.) [From an unidentified Dutch original.]

The Conquest of the Grand Canaries, made this last Summer by threescore and thirteene saile of [Dutch] shippes: with the taking of a towne in the Isle of Gomera. 1599.

Ellert de Jonghe. The True and perfect declaration of the mighty army by sea under the conduct of Peter Vander Does. 1600; rptd 1812 (in A Selection, etc.). [From the Waerachtigh verhael vande machtighe Scheeps-Armade, Amsterdam, 1600, relating to the same expedition as the preceding item.]

A True Report of Sir Anthony Shierlies Journey overland to Venice, from thence by sea to Antioch, Aleppo, and Babilon, and soe to Casbine in Persia: Reported by two gentlemen, who have followed him in the same. 1600.

The Journall, or Dayly Register, Contayning a True manifestation, and Historicall declaration of the voyage, accomplished by eight shippes of Amsterdam [to the East Indies, 1598–1600]. 1601. [Tr. William Walker from the Journael ofte Dagh-register, Amsterdam, 1600.]

William Parry. A new and large discourse of the Travels of sir Anthony Sherley Knight, by Sea and over Land, to the Persian Empire. Written by William Parry, Gentleman, who accompanied Sir Anthony. 1601; rptd Purchas (in part); ed. J. P. Collier (Illustrations of Early English Popular Literature, vol. II, 1864).

A True and Large Discourse of the Voyage of the Whole Fleete of Ships Set forth the 20. of April 1601. by the Governours and Assistants of the East Indian Marchants in London, to the East Indies. 1603.

BOOKS OF TRAVEL

A True and perfect Relation of the Newes sent from Amsterdam Concerning the fight of five Dutch shippes in the East Indies, against the Portugall Fleete. 1603.

The Last East-Indian Voyage. Containing Much varietie of the State of the severall kingdomes where they have traded. Begun by one of the Voyage. 1606; ed. J. B. Corney, Hakluyt Soc. 1855; tr. Dutch, Van der Aa.

Edmund Scott. An Exact Discourse Of the Subtilties, Fashions, Pollicies, Religion, and Ceremonies of the East Indians as well Chyneses as Javans. Whereunto is added a briefe Description of Java Major. 1606; rptd Purchas; Harris, vol. i; Harleian Voyages, vol. i.

[Anthony Nixon.] The Three English Brothers. Sir Thomas Sherley his Travels. Sir Anthony Sherley his Embassage to the Christian Princes. Master Robert Sherley his wars against the Turkes, with his marriage to the Emperour of Persia his Neece. 1607.

George Manwaring. A true discourse of Sir Anthony Sherley's Travels into Persia, what accidents did happen in the waye, with the businesse he was employed in from the Sophi. 1825 (in The Three Brothers). [From MS, written c. 1607.]

An historicall and true discourse of a voyage made by the admiral Cornelis Mateleif into the East Indies [1605–1608]. 1608. [From the Breeder Verhael van tghene den Admirael Cornelis Matelief, Rotterdam, 1608.]

[Thomas Middleton]. Sir Robert Sherley, Sent Ambassadour, in the Name of the King Of Persia, to Sigismond the third, King of Poland and Swecia. 1609; rptd Harleian Misc. vol. v.

John Cartwright. The Preachers Travels: wherein is set down a true journall to the confines of the East Indies, through the great countryes of Syria, Mesopotamia, Armenia, Media, Hircania, and Parthia. 1611; 1647; part rptd Purchas; Harleian Voyages, vol. i; tr. Dutch, Van der Aa.

Peter Floris, his Voyage to the East Indies in the Globe, 1611–15. The Contemporary Translation of his Journal. Ed. W. H. Moreland, Hakluyt Soc. 1934.

Thomas Best. The Voyage of Thomas Best to the East Indies, 1612–14. Ed. Sir W. Foster, Hakluyt Soc. 1934.

Robert Coverte. A true and almost incredible report of an Englishman that (being cast away in the good ship called the Assention in Cambaya) travelled by land throw many unknowne Kingdomes and Cities. 1612; 1614; 1631; rptd Harleian Voyages, vol. ii. Tr. German, Hulsius, pt 15, 1617 and 1648; De Bry, Eastern Voyages, pt 11, 1618 and

1628; Schwabe, vol. i; Latin, De Bry, Eastern Voyages, pt 11, 1619; Dutch, Van der Aa.

Sir Anthony Sherley. Sir Antony Sherley His Relation of his Travels into Persia. The Dangers, and Distresses, which befell him in his passage, both by sea and land, and his strange and unexpected deliverances. 1613; rptd Purchas (abridged); Harleian Misc. vol. x; tr. Dutch, Van der Aa.

The great Victory which God hath given unto eight Holland shippes, in their passage toward the East Indies: Against 17. great Spanish shippes. Translated out of the dutch Copie. Middelburg, 1613.

John Saris. The Voyage of Captain John Saris from Java to Japan 1613. Ed. Sir E. M. Satow, Hakluyt Soc. 1900. [From India Office MSS, Marine Records xiv.]

William Lithgow. A most delectable and true discourse of an admired and painefull peregrination from Scotland to the most famous Kingdomes in Europe, Asia, and Affricke. 1614; 1616; 1623; rptd Purchas (in part); 1632 (as The Totall Discourse, of the Rare Adventures, and painefull Peregrinations of long nineteene years travayles); 1640; 1682; 1692; Edinburgh, 1770; Leith, 1814; Glasgow, 1906; 1928, abridged; tr. Dutch, Amsterdam, 1652, 1656, 1659.

Henri de Feynes de Monfart. An Exact and Curious Survey of all the East Indies, even to Canton the chiefe Cittie of China: All duly performed [1608–1612] by land. Newly translated out of the Travailers Manuscript. 1615; rptd Somers Tracts, vol. i, 1751, and vol. iii, 1809; tr. French, 1630, etc.

Thomas Coryat. Thomas Coriate Traveller for the English Wits: Greeting, from the Court of the Great Mogul. 1616 (bis). [Later edns with the next item.]

—— Mr Thomas Coriat to his friends in England sendeth greeting: from Agra 1616. 1618; 1630 (in The Workes of John Taylor); 1776 (in Works, vol. iii); 1926 (in W. Foster, Early Travels in India).

Nicholas Withington. A Briefe Discoverye of some Things best worth noteinge in the Travells [1612–1616] of Nicholas Withington, a Factor in the East Indiase. 1735 (in A Journey by John Cockburn); 1926 (in W. Foster, Early Travels in India). [Abridged in Purchas.]

John Jourdain. A Journall kept by John Jourdain in a voiage for the East Indies sett fourth by the Honourable Companie [1608–1617]. Ed. W. Foster, Hakluyt Soc. 1905. [From BM. Sloane MS 858.]

Letters Received by the East India Company from its Servants in the East 1602–1617. Ed. F. C. Danvers and W. Foster, 6 vols.

1896–1902. [Including many accounts of voyages; letters after 1617 ptd in calendar form.]

William Adams. Letters from Japan 1611–1617. Ed. Thomas Rundall, Hakluyt Soc. 1850. [From India Office MSS.]

—— The Log-Book of William Adams 1614–1619. Ed. C. J. Purnell, Trans. Japan Soc. London, 1916.

Sir Thomas Roe. The Embassy of Sir Thomas Roe to India 1615–1619. Ed. W. Foster, Hakluyt Soc. 2 pts, 1899; ed. W. Foster, Oxford, 1926 (revised and abridged). [MS diary and letters, BM. Add. MSS 6115, 19277. Abridgements in Purchas, Churchill, Harris, Pinkerton; in Dutch, Amsterdam, 1656; in French, in M. Thevenot, Divers Voyages, vol. I, 1663, and in Prévost, vol. XIII; in German, Schwabe, vol. XI.]

Edward Saris. Journals of Edward Saris, Japan to Cochin-China, 1617–1618. Ed. C. J. Purnell, Trans. Japan Soc. of London, XIII, 1916. [From India Office, Marine Records, XXVI.]

Richard Cocks. The Diary of Richard Cocks, Cape-Merchant in the English Factory in Japan, 1615–1622. Ed. E. M. Thompson, Hakluyt Soc. 1883; 2 vols. Tokyo, 1899. [BM. Add. MSS 31300 and 31301.]

A True Relation Without all exception, of strange and Admirable Accidents which lately happened in the Kingdome of the great Magor, or Magull. Written and certified by eye-witnesses. 1622; rptd Harleian Misc. vol. I. [Relating to the voyage of 1618.]

The True Relation of that worthy Sea Fight which two of the East India Shipps had with 4 Portugals in the Persian Gulph; with the lamentable death of Captaine Andrew Shilling. 1622.

Richard Jobson. The Golden Trade: Or, A discovery of the River Gambra, and the Golden Trade of the Aethiopians. 1623; rptd Purchas (abridged); Astley, vol. II; Harleian Voyages, vol. II; ed. C. G. Kingsley, Teignmouth, 1904.

Xenophon. The Historie of Xenophon: containing The Ascent of Cyrus into the higher countries. Wherein is described the admirable journey of ten thousand Grecians from Asia the Lesse into the territories of Babylon, and their retrait from thence into Greece. Translated by Joh. Bingham. 1623.

John Taylor. A Famous Fight at Sea. Where foure English Ships under Captain John Weddell, and foure Dutch Ships, fought three dayes in the Gulph of Persia against 8. Portugall Gallions, and 32. Frigots [in

1625]. 1627; 1630 (in Workes); rptd Manchester, 1869 (in Spenser Soc. edn of Workes).

C[hristopher] F[arewell]. An East-India Colation; Or, A Discourse of Travels Collected by the Author in a Voyage he made unto the East-Indies. 1633. [Voyage of 1613–1615.]

Sir T[homas] H[erbert]. A Relation of Some Yeares Travaile [1627–1630], Into Afrique and the greater Asia, especially the Territories of the Persian Monarchie. 1634; 1638; 1639; 1665; 1677; rptd Harris, vol. I, abridged; abridged and ed. Sir W. Foster, 1928. Tr. Flemish, Dordrecht, 1658; French, Paris, 1663.

Peter Mundy. A Breife Relation of Certaine Journeies and Voyages into Fraunce, Spaine, Turkey and East India. [Relations IV–XIX, of Indian voyages 1628–1634.] Ed. Sir R. C. Temple, Hakluyt Soc. 1914. [Written by 1634, BM. Harl. MS 2286; copied 1639 and later in Bodl. Rawl. MS A 315.]

—— Itinerarium Mundii. That is A Memoriall or Sundry Relations of certaine Voiages Journeies ettc. [Relations XXI–XXX, of Indian voyage 1636–1638.] Ed. Sir R. C. Temple, Hakluyt Soc. 2 pts, 1919. [From Rawl. A 315, copied 1639 and continued later. Relations of voyages in Europe are listed p. 771 above, under Europe. Relation of last Indian voyage, 1655–1656, still unpbd.]

William Bruton. Newes from the East-Indies: Or, A Voyage [1633] to Bengalla one of the greatest Kingdomes under the Great Mogull. 1638; rptd Harleian Voyages, vol. II; 1812 (in A Selection, etc.).

A Most Execrable and Barbarous Murder done by an East-Indian Devil, or a Native of Java-Major, in the Road of Bantam, Aboard an English Ship [in 1641]. 1642.

Fernão Mendes Pinto. The Voyages and Adventures of Fernand Mendez Pinto, A Portugall: during his travels for the space of one and twenty years in the kingdoms of Ethiopia, China, Tartaria, Conchinchina, Calaminham, Siam, Pegu, Japan, and a great part of the East Indies. Done into English by H[enry] C[ogan]. 1653; 1663; 1692. [From the Peregrinação, Madrid, 1614, etc. Portion earlier in Purchas.]

Luis de Camoens. The Lusiad, Or, Portugals Historicall Poem: Written In the Portingall Language by Luis de Camoens; And Now newly put into English by Richard Fanshaw. 1655. [From Os Lusiadas, Lisbon, 1572, etc.]

Edward Terry. A Voyage to East-India [1615–1619], within that rich and most spacious Empire of the Great Mogol. Observed by Edward Terry, then Chaplain to the Right Honorable Sr. Thomas Row Knight. 1655; 1665 (in The Travels of Pietro della Valle); 1777; ed. W. Foster, 1921 (in Early Travels in India).

Sir Richard Stayner. A true relation of the destroying the Spanish shipps at the Isle of Tenariff, the 20th Aprill, 1657, from the first Intelligence we had of them as we lay before Cales. Ed. C. H. Firth, Navy Records Soc. 1912. [BM. Add. MS 32093, fol. 372.]

Vincent Le Blanc. The World Surveyed: Or, The Famous Voyages & Travailes of Vincent le Blanc, or White of Marseilles: Who from the Age of Fourteen years, to Threescore and Eighteen, Travelled through most parts of the World. Rendred into English by F[rancis] B[rooke]. 1660. [From Les voyages fameux, Paris, 1648, etc.]

(b) Descriptions of Farther Africa and Asia

Haiton of Armenia. Here begynneth a lytell Cronycle [of Asia]. [1530?] [From Les fleurs des hystoyres de la terre dorient, Paris, [1515?], etc. Part in Purchas, retranslated from Ramusio's Viaggi.]

The strange and marveilous newes lately come from the great Kingdome of Chyna. Translated out of the Castlyn tongue by T. N[icholas?]. [1577?]

[Thomas Nichols]. A Pleasant description of the fortunate Ilandes, called the Ilands of Canaria, with their straunge fruits and commodities. 1583; rptd Hakluyt, vol. II, 1599; Astley, vol. II; tr. German, in Schwabe, vol. II.

Giovanni Tommaso Minadoi. The History of the Warres betweene the Turkes and the Persians. 1595. [Tr. Abraham Hartwell from the Historia della guerra fra Turchi e Persiani, Venice, 1588, etc.]

Agatharchides. Excerpta Quaedam ex Agatharchide de rubro Mari. [In Agatharchidis et Memnonis Historicorum, quae supersunt, omnia, è Graeco iam recèns in Latinum traducta: per Rich. Brettum, Oxford, 1597. Greek and Latin.]

Memnon de Statu Heracl. Ponticae (excerpta quaedam). *Ibid.*

Jean Du Bec-Crispin. The Historie of the Great Emperour Tamerlan. Drawen from the auncient Monuments of the Arabians. Newly translated out of Franch by H. M. 1597; part rptd Purchas. [From the Histoire du grand Empereur Tamerlanes, Rouen, 1595.]

Johannes Leo Africanus. A geographical Historie of Africa, Written in Arabicke and Italian by John Leo a More. Before which is prefixed a generall description of Africa. Translated and collected by John Pory. 1600; part rptd Purchas; Harris, vol. I; ed. R. Brown, Hakluyt Soc. 3 vols. 1896. [From the Descrittione dell' Africa, in Ramusio, vol. I, 1550, etc.]

Frederik de Houtman. Dialogues In the English And Malaiane Languages: Or, Certain Common Formes of Speech, First Written in Latin, Malaian and Madagascar tongues, by Gotardus Arthusius, translated into the English tongue by Augustine Spalding. 1614. [Ultimately from the Spraecke ende Woord-Boeck, Amsterdam, 1603, etc.]

W[illiam] B[edwell]. The Arabian Trudgman, That is, Certaine Arabicke Termes, as Names of Places, titles of honour, dignitie, &c, oft used by writers. 1615.

Henry Lord. A Display of two forraigne sects in the East Indies vizt: The sect of the Banians the Ancient Natives of India And the sect of the Persees. 1630; rptd Churchill, vol. VI; Pinkerton, vol. VIII; tr. French, 1667 and 1723.

Cristoforo Borri. Cochin-China: Containing many admirable Rarities and Singularities of that Countrey. Extracted out of an Italian Relation And published by Robert Ashley. 1633; retranslated Churchill, vol. II; Pinkerton, vol. IX. [From the first part of the Relatione della Nuova Missione, Rome, 1631.]

Michel Baudier. The History of the Imperiall Estate of the Grand Seigneurs: Their Habitations, Lives, Titles, Qualities, Exercises, Workes. Translated out of French by E[dward] G[rimeston]. 1635. [From the Histoire generale du Serrail et de la Cour du grand Seigneur; ensemble l'histoire de la cour du Roy de la Chine, Paris, 1624, etc.]

—— The History of the Court of the King of China. Translated by A. G. 1682; rptd Harleian Voyages, vol. II. [A portion of the above.]

Wa[lter] Hamond. A Paradox. Prooving, That the Inhabitants of the Isle called Madagascar, or St. Laurence, (In Temporall things) are the happiest People in the World. 1640; part rptd Harleian Misc. vol. I.

——. Madagascar, The Richest And most Fruitfull Island In the World. Wherein The Temperature of the Clymate, the Nature of the Inhabitants, and the facility and benefit of a Plantation by our people there, are compendiously described. 1643.

50

The East-India Trade. A true Narration of divers Ports in East-India; of the Commodities, and Trade one Kingdome holdeth with another; whereby it appeareth, how much profit this Nation is deprived by restraint of Trade to those parts. [1641?]

Richard Boothby. A Breife Discovery or Description Of the most Famous Island of Madagascar or St. Laurence in Asia neare unto East-India. 1646; rptd Harleian Voyages, vol. II.

John Greaves. Pyramidographia: Or A Description Of The Pyramids in Aegypt. 1646; rptd Churchill, vol. II; tr. French, in M. Thevenot, Relations, 1663.

—— A Description of the Grand Signors Seraglio. 1650; 1653. [Ed. John Greaves, as by Robert Withers: see Europe, 1625, p. 767 above.]

—— Chorasmiae, et Mawaralnahrae, Hoc Est, Regionum extra fluvium Oxum descriptio, Ex Tabulis Abulfedae Ismaelis. 1650; 1698 (with further material, in J. Hudson, Geographiae Veteris Scriptores Graeci Minores, vol. III); 1711. [Persian text, with Latin version.]

—— Binae Tabulae Geographicae, Una Nassir Eddini Persae, Altera Ulug Beigi Tatari. 1652. [Persian texts, with Latin version.]

Powle Waldegrave. An Answer to Mr. Boothbies Book, Of The Description Of the Island of Madagascar. In Vindication Of the Honorable Society of merchants trading to East-India. 1649.

Robert Hunt. The Island of Assada, Neere Madagascar Impartially defined, being a Discription of the Situation, Fertility and People therein Inhabiting. 1650.

Edward Pocock. Specimen Historiae Arabum, sive Gregorii Abul Farajii De Origine & Moribus Arabum succincta Narratio. 1650. [Brief text, Arabic and Latin, with lengthy notes.]

—— The Nature of the Drink Kauhi, or Coffe, and the Berry of which it is made. Described by an Arabian Phisitian. 1659. [Arabic and English text, 4 pp.]

J[ohn] D[arell]. Strange News from th' Indies: or, East-India Passages further discovered. 1652.

[Samuel Clarke.] The Life of Tamerlane the Great, With His Wars against the Great Duke of Moso, the King of China, Bajazet the Great Turk. 1653.

Martinus Martini. Bellum Tartaricum, or the Conquest of The Empire of China, By the Invasion of the Tartars, who in these last seven years, have wholly subdued that vast Empire. 1654; 1655 (with the next item). [From the De bello Tartarico, Antwerp, 1654.]

Alvaro Semmedo. The History of That Great and Renowned Monarchy of China. Wherein all the particular Provinces are accurately described. Now put into English by a Person of Quality. 1655. [From the Imperio de la China, in Portuguese, Madrid, 1642, via the Italian, Rome, 1643.]

(4) AMERICA

(a) Voyages to America

The Voyage of the Barbara to Brazil, Anno 1540. Ed. R. G. Marsden, Navy Records Soc. 1912 (in Naval Miscellany, vol. II). [From High Court of Admiralty Oyer et Terminer 34, The examinacyon of George Mone, etc.]

Jean Ribaut. The Whole and true discovery of Terra Florida (englished the Florishing lande). Never founde out before the last yere 1562. 1563; 1582 (in Hakluyt's Divers Voyages); rptd New York, 1875 (in Historical Collections of Louisiana and Florida, New York); ed. H. P. Biggar, EHR. XXXII, 1917 (from Sloane MS 3644); ed. facs. Jeannette Thurber, Publications Florida State Historical Soc. VII, 1927; tr. Dutch Van der Aa.

[Nicholas Le Challeux.] A true and perfect description of the last voyage or Navigation, attempted by Capitaine John Rybaut into Terra Florida, this yeare past, 1565. [1566]; rptd Americana Ser. 1920. [From the Discours de l'histoire de la Floride, Dieppe, 1566.]

André Thevet. The New found worlde, or Antarctike, wherein is contained wonderful and strange things, as well of humaine creatures, as Beastes. 1568. [Tr. from Les Singularitez de la France Antarctique, Paris, 1558, etc.]

Sir John Hawkins. A true Declaration of the troublesome voyadge of M. John Hauikins to the parties of Guynea and the West Indies. 1569; 1589, 1600 (in Hakluyt); rptd Arber; ed. C. R. Markham, Hakluyt Soc. 1878; rptd Payne; ed. H. S. Burrage (in Original Narratives, 1906); Americana Ser. 1921; ed. facs. G. R. G. Conway, Mexico, 1926.

An Account of Hawkins' Third Slaving Voyage, 1569. Ed. J. A. Williamson (in Sir John Hawkins, 1927). [BM. Cotton MS Otho E VIII, fols. 17–41.]

An account of Frobisher's First Voyage, 1576. Ed. R. Collinson, Hakluyt Soc. 1867. [BM. Cotton MS Otho E VIII, fol. 47.]

Dionyse Settle. A true reporte of the laste voyage into the West and Northwest regions &c. 1577, worthily atchieved by Capteine Frobisher. 1577; 1589, 1600 (in Hakluyt); rptd Pinkerton, vol. XII; facs. Providence, Rhode Island, 1868; Americana Ser. 1925. Tr. French, [Geneva], 1578; German, Nuremberg, 1580; Latin, Nuremberg, 1580, Hamburg, 1675; Italian, Naples, 1582; Dutch, Van der Aa.

[George Best]. A true Discourse of the late voyages of discoverie, for the finding of a passage to Cathaya, by the Northweast, under the conduct of Martin Frobisher Generall. 1578; 1600 (in Hakluyt); rptd Pinkerton, vol. XII; ed. R. Collinson, Hakluyt Soc. 1867; rptd Payne, 1886 (Cassell's National Lib.). Tr. Dutch, [Amsterdam, 1640?], Amsterdam, 1678, and in Van der Aa; German, Nuremberg, 1679; French, in J. F. Bernard, Recueil de voiages au Nord, Amsterdam, 1715, 1720 and 1731.

Thomas Churchyarde. A Prayse, and Reporte of Maister Martyne Forboishers [second] Voyage to Meta Incognita. 1578; rptd Americana Ser. 1921.

Thomas Ellis. A true report of the third and last voyage into Meta incognita: atchieved by the worthie Capteine, M. Martine Frobisher Esquire. Anno. 1578. Written by Thomas Ellis Sailer and one of the companie. [1578]; 1589, 1600 (in Hakluyt); rptd Pinkerton, vol. XII; Americana Ser. 1922; tr. Dutch, Van der Aa.

Edward Sellman. An Account of Frobisher's Third Voyage, 1578. Ed. (from MS) R. Collinson, Hakluyt Soc. 1867.

Francisco López de Gómara. The Pleasant Historie of the Conquest of the Weast India, now called new Spayne, atchieved by the worthy Prince Hernando Cortes. Translated out of the Spanish tongue, by T[homas] N[icholas]. 1578; 1596; part rptd Purchas. [From La Istoria de las Indias, y Conquista de Mexico, Saragossa, 1552, etc.]

Jacques Cartier. A Shorte and briefe narration of the two Navigations and Discoveries [1534–1535] to the Northweast partes called Newe France, turned into English by John Florio. 1580; 1600 (in Hakluyt); rptd Churchill, vol. IV; Pinkerton, vol. XII; ed. H. S. Burrage (in Original Narratives, 1906). Retranslation by H. P. Biggar, Ottawa, 1924. [Florio's trn from Ramusio's Viaggi, vol. III, 1556, etc.]

John Cooke. For fraunses Drake, Knight, sone to Sir [Edmund] Drake, vickar of Upchurche, in Kent. Anno dñi 1577. [A MS account of part of the voyage of circumnavigation, Harleian 540, fol. 93.] Ed. W. S. W. Vaux, Hakluyt Soc. 1854; ed. Sir

R. C. Temple (The World Encompassed, Argonaut Ser. 1926).

Francis Fletcher. The First Part of the second voiage about the world attempted continued and happily accomplished with the tyme of 3 years by Mr Ffrancis Drake. Written & Faithfully Layed downe by Ffrancis Fletcher. Ed. Sir R. C. Temple (The World Encompassed, Argonaut Ser. 1926). [BM. Sloane MS 61. This is the basis of the younger Drake's narrative, The World Encompassed, 1628, see below. Other narratives in Hakluyt.]

Agustín de Zárate. The strange and delectable History of the discoverie and Conquest of the Provinces of Peru, in the South Sea. Translated out of the Spanish tongue, by T[homas] Nicholas. 1581. [From the Historia del descubrimiento y conquista del Peru, Antwerp, 1555, etc.]

R[ichard] H[akluyt]. Divers voyages, touching the discoverie of America, and the Ilands adjacent unto the same, made first of all by our Englishmen, and afterward by the Frenchmen and Britons. 1582; ed. J. W. Jones, Hakluyt Soc. 1850. [Most of the items rptd in the Voyages, vol. III, 1600.]

Captain [Christopher] Carleill. A discourse upon the entended Voyage to the hethermost partes of America. [1583]; 1589, 1600 (in Hakluyt); rptd Americana Ser. 1923.

[Sir] G[eorge] P[eckham]. A true Reporte, Of the late discoveries, and possession, taken in the right of the Crowne of England, of the New-found Landes: By Sir Humfrey Gilbert. 1583; 1589, 1600 (in Hakluyt); rptd Mag. American Hist. LXVIII, Tarrytown, New York, 1920; Americana Ser. 1927.

The discourse and description of the voyage of Sir Frawncis Drake and Mr. Captaine Frobisher, set forward 1585 [to the West Indies]. Ed. J. S. Corbett, Navy Records Soc. 1898. [BM. Royal MS 7 C XVI, art. 36.]

Antonio de Espejo. El Viaje Que Hizo Antonio de Espejo [1583] en nuevo Mexico. Impressa en Madrid, anno de 1586. Y de nuevo en Paris en mesmo anno, a la costa de Richardo Hakluyt. Paris, 1586. [Extracted from Mendoza's China, Madrid, 1586. Hakluyt was probably responsible also for the French version by Martin Basanier, Paris, 1586.] Tr. A. F., 1587 (as New Mexico, otherwise the voiage of Anthony of Espeio); rptd Americana Ser. 1921; ed. F. W. Hodge, New York, 1928. [The narrative was also included in Parke's English version of Mendoza's China, 1588 (see voyages to Asia, p. 782 above), though not in the Italian version, 1587. Another version, presumably by Hakluyt, in the Voyages, vol. III, 1600. Retranslated from MS by H. E. Bolton, Original Narratives, 1916.]

788   RENAISSANCE TO RESTORATION

René de Laudonnière. L'Histoire notable de la Floride situee es Indes Occidentales, contenant les trois voyages faits en icelle par certains Capitaines & Pilotes François [1562–1565]. Paris, 1586; rptd Paris, 1853. [Discovered and pbd by Hakluyt, ed. Martin Basanier.] Tr. Eng. (as A Notable Historie Containing foure voyages made by Certayne French Captaynes unto Florida. Newly translated, by R[ichard] H[akluyt]), 1587, 1600 (in the Voyages); German, De Bry, pt 14, 1631; Dutch, Van der Aa.

Thomas Greepe. The true and perfecte Newes of the woorthy and valiaunt exploytes, performed and doone by that valiant Knight Syr Frauncis Drake: Not onely at Sancto Domingo, and Carthagena, but also now at Cales. [1587]; rptd Americana Ser. 1924. [Verse.]

Thomas Cates. A Summarie and True Discourse of Sir Frances Drakes West Indian Voyage. 1589 (bis); 1600 (in Hakluyt); 1653 (in Sir Francis Drake Revived, see 1626 below); 1812 (in A Selection, etc.); rptd Payne. Tr. Latin, Leyden, 1588, Nuremberg, 1590 (in Narrationes duae (with account of the Portugal voyage)); French, Leyden, 1588; German, Nuremberg, 1589. [Begun by Walter Biggs, carried on by Lieutenant Cripps, 'published' by Thomas Cates.]

Job Hortop. The Rare Travailes of Job Hortop, an Englishman. Wherin is declared the dangers he escaped in his voiage to Gynnie [and Mexico, with Hawkins, 1569]. 1591 (bis); 1600 (in Hakluyt); rptd Arber; Americana Ser. 1925; ed. facs. G. R. G. Conway, Mexico City, 1928.

H[enry] R[oberts]. Our Ladys Retorne to England, accompanied with saint Frances and the good Jesus of Viona in Portugal, who, comming from Brasell, arrived at Clovelly. 1592.

—— Lancaster his Allarums, honorable Assaultes, and supprising of block-houses in Brasill. [1595.]

Captain Wyatt. An Account of Robert Dudley's Voyage to the West Indies, 1594. Ed. G. F. Warner, Hakluyt Soc. 1899. [From BM. Sloane MS 858.]

Abram Kendall. [An Account of the same.] Ed. G. F. Warner, Hakluyt Soc. 1899. [First ptd in Italian in Robert Dudley, Arcano del Mare, Florence, 1646 and 1661; retranslated for the English edn.]

[Sir Richard Hawkins.] Treslado de una carta de R. Hauquines, escrita en el puerto de Perico 1594 para embiar a su padre. [Seville? 1595?] [Retranslated by J. A. Williamson in the following item.]

—— The Observations of Sir Richard Hawkins Knight, in his Voaige into the South Sea.

Anno Domini 1593. 1622; rptd Purchas; Harris, vol. I; ed. C. R. D. Bethune, Hakluyt Soc. 1847; ed. C. R. Markham, Hakluyt Soc. 1878; ed. J. A. Williamson, 1934.

Thomas Maynarde. Sir Francis Drake his Voyage, 1595. 1653 (in Sir Francis Drake Revived; see 1626, below); ed. W. D. Cooley, Hakluyt Soc. 1849. [BM. Add. MS 5209.]

Henry Savile. A Libell Of Spanish Lies: Found At The Sacke of Cales, discoursing the fight in the West Indies, and of the death of Sir Francis Drake. With an answere briefely confuting the Spanish lies, and a short Relation of the fight according to truth. 1596; 1600 (in Hakluyt, vol. III).

Sir Walter Ralegh. The Discoverie of the Large Rich, and Bewtifull Empyre of Guiana, with a relation of the great and Golden Citie of Manoa (which the Spanyards call El Dorado). 1596 (4 edns); 1600 (in Hakluyt); 1751 (in T. Birch, Works of Sir Walter Raleigh, vol. II); 1805 (in Arthur Cayley, Life of Sir Walter Raleigh, vol. I); Edinburgh, 1820 (in The History of the World); Oxford, 1829 (in Works, vol. VIII); ed. Sir R. H. Schomburgk, Hakluyt Soc. 1848; rptd Payne; ed. H. Morley, 1887; ed. W. H. D. Rouse, 1905 and 1913; ed. V. T. Harlow, Argonaut Ser. 1928. Tr. German, in Hulsius, pt 5, 1598, 1599, 1601, 1603, 1612, in Schwaben, 1747; Dutch, Amsterdam, 1598, 1605, 1617, 1644, and in Van der Aa; Latin, in Hulsius, pt 5, 1599, De Bry, pt 8, 1599 and 1625; French, 1722 (in Voyages de F. Coréal), Amsterdam, 1738 (in Recueil de voyages dans l'Amérique méridionale, vol. I).

—— Of the Voyage for Guiana. 1820 (in The History of the World); ed. Schomburgk, as above, 1848; ed. Harlow, as above, 1928. [c. 1596. BM. Sloane MS 1133.] [For the Guiana voyage, 1618, see below.]

Lawrence Keymis. A Relation of the second Voyage to Guiana; performed and written in the yeare 1596. 1596; 1600 (in Hakluyt). Tr. Latin, in De Bry, pt 8, 1599 and 1625; Dutch, Amsterdam, 1605 and 1619; German, in Schwabe, vol. XVI; French, 1722 (with Ralegh), 1738 (ibid.).

John Brierton. A Briefe and true Relation of the Discoverie of the North part of Virginia: Made this present yeare 1602, by Captaine Bartholowmew Gilbert. Written by M. John Brereton one of the voyage. 1602; 1602 (augmented). First issue: ed. facs. L. S. Livingston, New York, 1903; ed. H. S. Burrage (in Original Narratives 1906). Second issue: rptd 3 Collections Massachusetts Hist. Soc. vol. VIII, 1843; ed. G. P. Winship (in Sailors' Narratives of Voyages, along the New England Coast, Boston 1905).

James Rosier. A True Relation of the most prosperous Voyage made this present yeere 1605, by Captaine George Waymouth, in the Discovery of the land of Virginia. 1605; part rptd Purchas; ed. G. Prince, Bath, Maine, 1860; ed. H. S. Burrage, Gorges Soc. Portland, Maine, 1887; ed. G. P. Winship (in Sailors' Narratives, Boston, 1905); ed. H. S. Burrage (in Original Narratives, 1906).

James Hall. A Report to King Christian IV on the Danish Expedition to Greenland under Captain John Cunningham, 1605. Ed. C. C. A. Gosch, Hakluyt Soc. 1897. [BM. Royal MS 17 A xlviii.]

A Relatyon of the Discovery of our river, from James Forte into the Maine: made by Capt. Christofer Newport [May and June 1607]. Ed. E. E. Hale, Archaeologia Americana, vol. iv, Boston, 1860; ed. E. Arber (in Works of Captain John Smith, Introduction, 1884, etc.). [State Papers Colonial, America, i, 15.]

[James Davies.] The Relation of a Voyage unto New-England Began from the Lizard, ye First of June 1607. By Captn. Popham & Captn Gilbert. Ed. B. F. De Costa, Boston, 1880; ed. H. O. Thayer, Gorges Soc. Portland, Maine, 1892; ed. G. P. Winship (in Sailors' Narratives, Boston, 1905); ed. H. S. Burrage (in Original Narratives, 1906). [Lambeth MS.]

John Nicholl. An Houre Glasse of Indian Newes. Or A true and tragicall discourse, shewing the most lamentable miseries indured by 67 Englishmen, which were sent for a supply to the planting in Guiana in the yeare 1605. 1607; rptd Purchas (abridged); Americana Ser. 1925.

Captain John Smith. A True Relation of such occurrences and accidents of noate as hath hapned in Virginia since the first planting of that Collony. 1608; Richmond, Virginia, 1845; ed. Charles Deane, Boston, 1866; ed. E. Arber (in Works of Captain John Smith, Birmingham, 1884; 2 vols. 1895; 2 vols. Edinburgh, 1910); ed. L. G. Tyler (in Original Narratives, 1907).

—— A Map of Virginia. With a Description of the Countrey, the Commodities, People, Government and Religion. Oxford, 1612; 1624 (in Smith's Generall History); rptd Purchas (abridged); ed. E. Arber, op. cit.; ed. L. G. Tyler, op. cit.

—— A Description of New England: or the Observations, and discoveries, of Captain John Smith in the North of America 1614: with the successe of sixe Ships, that went 1615. 1616; 1837 (3 Collections Massachusetts Hist. Soc. vol. vi; Force, Tracts, vol. ii; ed. Charles Deane, Boston, 1865; ed. E. Arber, op. cit.; ed. G. P. Winship (in Sailors'

Narratives, 1905). Tr. Latin, De Bry, pt 10, 1619; German, Hulsius, pt 14, 1617 and 1628, De Bry, pt 10, 1618.

Captain John Smith. New Englands Trials. Declaring the successe of 26. Ships employed thether within these sixe yeares: with the benefit of that Countrey by sea and land. 1620; 1622. The first edn: ed. Charles Deane, Cambridge, U.S.A. 1873; ed. E. Arber, op. cit. The second edn: Force, Tracts, vol. ii; ed. Charles Deane, Cambridge, U.S.A. 1867; ed. E. Arber, op. cit.

—— The Generall Historie of Virginia, New-England, and the Summer Isles. 1624;1625; 1626; 1627; 1631; 1632; rptd Pinkerton, vol. xiii; ed. E. Arber, op. cit.;rptd Glasgow, 1907 (with The True Travels).

—— The True Travels, Adventures, and Observations of Captaine John Smith, in Europe, Asia, Affrica, and America, from Anno Domini 1593 to 1629. Together with a continuation of his generall History. 1630; rptd Churchill, vol. ii; ed. J. H. Rice, Richmond, Virginia, 1819; ed. E. Arber, op. cit., 1884, etc.; 2 vols. Glasgow, 1907 (with the Generall History); tr. Dutch, Van der Aa.

—— Advertisements For the unexperienced Planters of New-England, or any where. With the yearely proceedings of this Country in Fishing and Planting, since the yeare 1614. 1631; 1833 (in 3 Collections Massachusetts Hist. Soc. vol. iii); ed. Charles Deane, Boston, 1865; ed. E. Arber, op. cit.

[Edward-Maria Wingfield.] Here followeth what happened in Jatnes Towne, in Virginia, after Captayne Newports departure for Engliund [in 1607]. Ed. Charles Deane, Archaeologia Americana, vol. iv, Boston, 1860; ed. E. Arber (Works of John Smith, 1884, 1895, 1910).

Henry Spelman. Henry Spelmans Relation of Virginea, 1609. Ed. James F. Hunnewell, 1872; ed. E. Arber (Works of John Smith, 1884, 1895, 1910).

R[obert] J[ohnson]. Nova Britannia. Offring Most excellent fruites by planting in Virginia. 1609; rptd Force, Tracts, vol. i; ed. Joseph Sabin, New York, 1867.

—— The new Life of Virginea: declaring the former Successe and present estate of that plantation, being the second part of Nova Britannia. 1612; rptd Force, Tracts, vol. i.

A Gentleman of Elvas. Virginia richly valued, By the description of the maine land of Florida, her next neighbour: out of the foure yeers discoverie of Don Ferdinando de Soto, translated out of Portuguese by Richard Hakluyt. 1609; 1611 (as The Worthye and Famous History, of the Conquest of Terra Florida); rptd Purchas, abridged; 1812 (in A Selection, etc.); Force, Tracts, vol. iv; ed. W. B. Rye, Hakluyt Soc. 1851. [From the Relaçam verdadeira dos trabalhos, Evora, 1557. Another trn, from the French, 1686, rptd Harris, vol. i; another by Buckingham Smith, New York, 1866, rptd E. G. Bourne, Narratives of De Soto, New York, 1904 and 1922, and T. H. Lewis, Original Narratives, 1907.]

Thomas West, Lord De la Warr. [A Letter to the Patentees in England relative to the voyage of 1610.] Ed. R. H. Major, Hakluyt Soc. 1849. [BM. Harl. MS 7009, fol. 58.]

—— The Relation of the Right Honourable the Lord De-la-Warre, Lord Governour and Captaine Generall of the Colonie, planted in Virginea. 1611; rptd Purchas; facs. New York, 1867; ed. Alexander Brown (in Genesis of the United States, vol. i, Boston, 1890); ed. L. G. Lyon (in Original Narratives, 1907).

[Silvester Jourdan.] A Discovery of the Barmudas, Otherwise called the Ile of Divels: By Sir Thomas Gates, Sir George Sommers, and Captayne Newport. 1610; 1613 (as A plaine Description of the Barmudas); rptd 1812 (in A Selection, etc.); Force, Tracts, vol. iii.

R[ichard] Rich. Newes from Virginia. The Lost Flocke Triumphant; With the happy arrival of Sr Thomas Gates into Virginia. With the maner of their distresse in the Iland of Devils (otherwise called Bermoothawes). 1610; ed. J. O. Halliwell[-Phillipps], 1865 and 1874; ed. E. D. Neill (in Early Settlement of Virginia, Minneapolis, 1878); rptd Mag. of American Hist. New York, 1883; Boston, 1890 (in A. Brown, Genesis of the United States, vol. i). [Verse.]

A True And Sincere declaration of the purpose and ends of the Plantation begun in Virginia, of the degrees which it hath received; and meanes by which it hath been advanced: and the resolution and conclusion of his Majestie's Councel of that Colony. Set forth by the authority of the Governors and Councellors. 1610; ed. A. Brown (in Genesis of the United States, vol. i, Boston, 1890).

A True Declaration of the estate of the Colonie in Virginia, With a confutation of such scandalous reports as have tended to the disgrace of so worthy an enterprise. Published by advise and direction of the Councell of Virginia. 1610; rptd Force, Tracts, vol. iii.

Sir Thomas Dale. [A Report on Virginia, in a letter to Lord Salisbury, August 17, 1611.] Ed. A. Brown (in Genesis of the United States, vol. i, Boston, 1890). [S.P. Col. America, i, 26.]

John Gatonbe. A Voyage into the North-West Passage, undertaken in the year 1612, by Captain James Hall. Churchill, vol. vi, 1732, etc.; ed. C. C. A. Gosch, Hakluyt Soc. 1897.

William Strachey. The Historie of Travaile into Virginia Britannia, expressing the Cosmographie and Comodities of The Country. 1625 (in Purchas, part); ed. R. H. Major, Hakluyt Soc. 1849. [c. 1612. BM. Sloane MS 1622; collated with Bodleian MS Ashmole 1758 by A. Brown, in Genesis of the United States, vol. ii, Boston, 1890.]

Robert Harcourt. A Relation of a Voyage to Guiana. Describing the Climat, Scituation, fertilitie, provisions and commodities of that Country. 1613; 1626; abridged in Purchas; ed. C. A. Harris, Hakluyt Soc. 1928. [First edn rptd Harleian Misc. vol. vi.]

Alexander Whitaker. Good Newes from Virginia. Wherein Also is a Narration of the present State of that country, and of our Colonies there. 1613; rptd Purchas; photo. facs. New York, 1936.

William Baffin. A True Relation of such thinges as happened during the voyage of 1615. Ed. Thomas Rundall, Hakluyt Soc. 1849. [BM. Add. MS 12206.]

Ralph Hamor. A true Discourse of the present Estate of Virginia, and the successe of the affaires there till the 18. of June 1614. 1615; Albany, New York, 1860. Tr. German, Hulsius, pt 13, 1617, De Bry, pt 10, 1618; Latin, De Bry, pt 10, 1619.

Lewis Hughes. A Letter sent into England from the Summer Ilands. 1615; rptd Americana Series, 1926.

—— A Plaine and true relation of the Goodnes of God towards the Sommer Ilandes. 1621; rptd Americana Ser. 1926.

John Rolf. A true relation of the state of Virginia 1616. Virginia Hist. Register, i, Richmond, Virginia, 1848. [BM. Royal MS 18 A xi.]

Pedro Fernández de Quirós. Terra Australis incognita, or A new Southerne Discoverie, Containing A fifth part of the World. Latcly found out By Ferdinand De Quir. 1617; rptd Purchas. [1723]; retranslation, Hakluyt Soc. 1904. [From the Spanish, Petition of 1610, Seville.]

R. M. Newes of Sr Walter Rauleigh. With The true Description of Guiana. Sent from a Gentleman of his Fleet 1617. 1618; rptd Force, Tracts, vol. iii.

Sir Walter Ralegh. [Journal of his Second Voyage to Guiana, 1618.] Ed. Sir R. H. Schomburgk, Hakluyt Soc. 1848; ed. H. Morley, 1887; ed. V. T. Harlow, Argonaut Ser. 1932. [BM. Cotton MS Titus B viii, fols. 162–75.]

Sir Walter Ralegh. Sir Walter Rawleigh His Apologie For his voyage to Guiana. 1650 and 1667 (in his Judicious and Select Essayes and Observations); 1700 and 1702 (in An Abridgment of Sir Walter Raleigh's History of the World); 1751 (in T. Birch, Works of Sir Walter Raleigh, vol. II); 1805 and 1806 (in T. Cayley, Life of Sir Walter Raleigh, vol. II); 1820 (in Raleigh's History of the World, vol. VI); 1829 (in Works, Oxford, vol. VIII); ed. V. T. Harlow, Argonaut Ser. 1932.

The Relation of a Wonderfull Voiage made by William Cornelison Schouten of Horne. Shewing how South from the Straights of Magelan, he sayled round about the world. 1619; rptd Purchas; 1766 (in John Callander, Terra Australis Cognita, vol. II); 1770 (in A. Dalrymple, An Historicall Collection, vol. II); [1778?] (in J. H. Moore, A New Collection of Voyages, vol. I). [Tr. William Phillip from the Journael ofte Beschryvinge, Amsterdam, 1618.]

Richard Whitbourne. A Discourse and Discovery of New-Found-Land, with many reasons to proove how worthy and beneficiall a Plantation may there be made. 1620; 1622; 1623; part rptd Purchas. Tr. German, De Bry, pt 13, 1628; Hulsius, pt 20, 1629; Latin, Hulsius, pt 20, 1629.

—— A Discourse containing A Loving Invitation for the advancement of his Majesties most hopefull Plantation in the New-Found Land. 1622 (bis); 1622 (included with the preceding item); 1623 (with the preceding); ed. Michael Carroll (The Seal and Herring Fisheries of Newfoundland, Montreal, 1873).

Edward Winne. A Letter to Sir George Calvert, from Feryland in Newfounland. 1621; 1622; 1622 (included with Whitbourne's Loving Invitation, second issue); 1622 (included with Whitbourne's Discourse and Discovery); 1623 (with Whitbourne's Discourse and Discovery).

M. C. A true Relation of a wonderfull Sea-Fight betweene two great and well appointed Spanish Ships, and a small English ship [off Guadeloupe]. 1621; Amsterdam, 1621 (abridged as A Notable and Wonderfull Sea-Fight).

A briefe Relation of the Discovery and Plantation of New England: and of sundry accidents therein occurring, from [1607 to 1622]. 1622; rptd Purchas; 2 Collections Massachusetts Hist. Soc. vol. VIII, 1819 and 1826; ed. J. P. Baxter, Prince Soc. Boston, 1890. [Written for the President and Councell.]

[William Bradford and Edward Winslow.] A Relation or Journal of the beginning and proceedings of the English Plantation setled at Plimouth in New England. [Ed. G. Mourt], 1622; abridged in Purchas; ed. A. Young (in Memorials of the Pilgrim Fathers, Boston, 1841); ed. H. M. Dexter, Boston, 1865; ed. E. Arber (in The Story of the Pilgrim Fathers, 1897).

Nathaniel Butler. The Historye of the Bermudaes or Summer Islands [1609–1622]. Ed. J. H. Lefroy, Hakluyt Soc. 1882. [BM. Sloane MS 750.]

Sir Richard Hawkins. The Observations, etc. [See above, 1595.]

Richard Norwood. Insularum de la Bermuda detectio. Ed. Champlin Burrage (with the next item), Boston, 1918. [Written c. 1622.]

John Pory. John Pory's Lost Description of Plymouth Colony in the Earliest Days. Ed. Champlin Burrage, Boston, 1918. [From MS in Carter Brown Lib.; two letters, c. 1622.]

A True Relation Of That Which Lately Hapned To the great Spanish Fleet, and Galeons of Terra Firma in America. With many strange Deliveries of Captaines, and Souldiers in the tempest. Faithfully translated out of the Spanish Originall. 1623; rptd Americana Ser. 1923.

E[dward] W[inslow]. Good Newes from New England: or A true Relation of things very remarkable at the Plantation of Plimouth in New England [1621–1623]. 1624 (bis); abridged in Purchas; ed. A. Young (in Memorials of the Pilgrim Fathers, Boston, 1841); ed. E. Arber (in The Story of the Pilgrim Fathers, 1897); rptd [1910] (in Chronicles of the Pilgrim Fathers (Everyman's Lib.)).

A True Relation of the Fleete which went under the Admirall Jaquis Le Hermite [1623–1626] through the Straights of Magellane towards the Coasts of Peru, and the Towne of Lima in the West-Indies. 1625. [From the Waerachtigh Verhael Van het succes van de Vlote, Amsterdam. 1625: news-letter preliminary to the full report of the voyage.]

J[an] B[aers?]. A Plaine And True Relation, Of The going forth of a Holland Fleete 1623, to the Coast of Brasile. With The taking in of Salvedoe, and also, The base delivery up of the said Towne. By I. B. that hath ben an eye and eare-witnesse. Rotterdam, 1626.

Sir Francis Drake reviv'd; calling upon this dull or effeminate Age to follow his noble steps for gold and silver. 1626; 1628; 1653 (see below); rptd Arber. [An account, by Philip Nichols and others, of the Panama voyage 1572, revised and ed. by Drake himself with dedication to Queen Elizabeth of 1592–3.]

Sir Francis Drake. The World Encompassed by Sir Francis Drake, being his next voyage to that to Nombre de Dios. 1628; 1635; 1653 (see next item); rptd Harleian Voyages, vol. II; ed. W. S. W. Vaux, Hakluyt Soc. 1854; ed. Sir R. C. Temple, Argonaut Ser. 1926.

—— Sir Francis Drake Revived. Being a Summary and true Relation of foure severall Voyages. 1653. [Including: Sir Francis Drake Reviv'd, as of 1626; The World Encompassed, as of 1628; (Thomas Cates) A Summarie and True Discourse, as of 1589; (T. Maynarde) A Full Relation of another Voyadge into the West-Indies, 1595. Abridged 1682 as The Voyages of The Ever Renowned Sr. Francis Drake Into the West Indies. Condensed [1690?] as a chap-book of 24 pp., entitled The Voyages and Travels of that Renowned Captain, etc.]

Christopher Levett. A Voyage into New England Begun in 1623 and ended in 1624. 1628; rptd 1843 (in 3 Collections Massachusetts Hist. Soc. vol. VIII); 1847 (in Collections Maine Hist. Soc. vol. II, Portland, Maine); ed. J. P. Baxter, Gorges Soc. Portland, Maine, 1893; ed. G. P. Winship (in Sailors' Narratives, 1905).

A true Relation Of the vanquishing Of the Towne Olinda, Cituated in the Capitania of Phernambuco. Through the Renowned and Valiant Sea-Man Henry C. Lonck, for the Licensed West-India Company. Amsterdam, 1630.

[Francis Higginson.] New-Englands Plantation. Or, a short and true Description of the Commodities and Discommodities of that Countrey. 1630 (3 edns); part rptd Force, Tracts, vol. I; Essex Book and Print Club, vol. I, Salem, Mass. 1908.

—— A True Relacion of ye last voyage to new England, declaring all circumstances with ye manner of ye passage we had by sea. Ed. Thomas Hutchinson, Boston, 1769; rptd Prince Soc. Boston, 1865; rptd Essex Book and Print Club, vol. I, Salem, Mass. 1908; ed. Edward L. Smith (in Rev. Ralph Smith, Boston, 1921).

Thomas Dudley. [Letter to the Countess of Lincoln, 28 March 1631, giving an account of his voyage.] Boston, 1696 (in Massachusetts, or The First Planters); rptd from MS Collections New Hampshire Hist. Soc. vol. IV, 1834; rptd Force, Tracts, vol. II; rptd A. Young (in Chronicles of Massachusetts Bay, Boston, 1846).

Sir Henry Colt. The Voyage of Sr Henrye Colt Knight to ye Ilands of ye Antilleas in

ye Shipp called ye Alexander. Ed. V. T. Harlow, Hakluyt Soc. 1925. [A letter from St Christophers; 1631: MS in Cambridge University Lib.]

Father Andrew White. Declaratio Coloniae— A Declaration of the Colony of the Lord Baltamore in Maryland, 1632. Tr. N. C. Brooks, Force, Tracts, vol. IV; Latin text ed. and tr. J. H. Converse, Maryland Hist. Soc. 1874; rptd C. C. Hall (in Original Narratives, 1910). [MS in Archives of the Society of Jesus, Rome.]

—— A Relation of The successefull beginnings of the Lord Baltemores Plantation in Mary-Land; Being an extract of certaine Letters written from thence. 1634; ed. J. G. Shea, Baltimore, 1865; ptd from MS Maryland Hist. Soc. 1899; 1910 (in C. C. Hall, Original Narratives). [English version of the next item.]

—— Relatio Itineris in Marylandiam, 1634. Tr. N. C. Brooks, Force, Tracts, vol. IV; Latin text ed. and tr. J. H. Converse, Maryland Hist. Soc. 1874-5. [MS in Archives of the Society of Jesus, Rome.]

Thomas James. The strange and dangerous voyage of Captaine Thomas James, in his intended discovery of the Northwest Passage. With An Appendix concerning Longitude, by Master Henry Gellibrand. 1633; 1740; rptd Churchill, vol. II; Harris, vol. I; and other abridgements; ed. R. M. Christy, Hakluyt Soc. 1894.

Captain Thomas Yong. A briefe Relation of a voyage lately made by me since my departure from Virginia, upon a discovery [up the Delaware River]. Ed. P. C. J. Weston (Documents Connected with the History of South Carolina, 1856); rptd 1871 (in 4 Collections Massachusetts Hist. Soc. vol. IX); Maryland Hist. Soc. 1876; 1912 (in A. C. Myers, Original Narratives). [MS in Virginia State Lib., a letter to Sir Francis Windebanke, Secretary of State, from Jamestown, 1634.]

A Relation of Maryland; Together, With a Map of the Countrey, The Conditions of Plantation. 1635; ed. Joseph Sabin, New York, 1865; ed. C. C. Hall (in Original Narratives, 1910).

Luke Fox. North-West Fox, Or, Fox from the North-west passage. Beginning With King Arthur. 1635; ed. R. M. Christy, Hakluyt Soc. 2 pts, 1894.

Richard Mather. A Voyage to New England, 1635. Ed. A. Young (in Chronicles of Massachusetts Bay, Boston, 1846).

Anthony Thacher. A Relation of a Shipwreck on the New England Coast, 1635. Ed. A. Young (in Chronicles of Massachusetts Bay, Boston, 1846).

William Jackson. A Briefe Journall or a Succinct and true relation of the most remarkable passages observed in that voyage undertaken by Captaine William Jackson to the Westerne Indies or Continent of America [1642–1645]. Ed. V. T. Harlow, Camden Misc. vol. XIII, 1924.

William Bradford. [History of Plymouth Plantation, 1606–1646.] Ptd 1856 (in 4 Collections Massachusetts Hist. Soc. vol. III); ed. J. A. Doyle, 1896; ed. facs. Boston, 1898; ed. W. T. Davis (Original Narratives, 1908); ed. W. C. Ford, Boston, 1912. [MS formerly at Fulham Palace, now in Massachusetts State Lib.]

The Case of Mainwaring, Hawes, Payne and others, Concerning a Depredation made [in 1637] by the Spanish-West-India Fleete, upon the Ship Elizabeth. Restitution sought in Spayne, Justice denied, and Justice Petitioned of Parliament. 1646.

Thomas Gage. The English-American his Travail by Sea and Land [1625–1637]: Or, A New Survey of the West India's. 1648; 1655; 1677; 1699; 1702; 1711; ed. A. P. Newton, 1928. Tr. French, Paris, 1663, 1672, 1677, 1680, 1691, Amsterdam, 1695, 1699, 1720, Paris, 1721, 1722; Dutch, Utrecht, 1682, Amsterdam, 1700; German, Leipzig, 1693.

John Winthrop. A Journal of the Transactions and Occurrences in Massachusetts, 1630–1649. Ed. James Savage, 2 vols. Boston, 1825–6, and 1853; rptd J. K. Hosmer (Original Narratives, 2 vols. 1908).

Colonel Norwood. A Voyage to Virginia, 1649. Ptd Churchill, vol. VI, 1732; Force, Tracts, vol. III.

Edward Bland. The Discovery of New Brittaine. Begun 1650. From Fort Henry to the Fals of Blandina, first River in New Brittaine. 1651; ed. Joseph Sabin, New York, 1873; ed. A. S. Salley (in Original Narratives, 1911); Americana Ser. 1923.

Edward Johnson. A History of New-England. From the English planting in the Yeere 1628. until the yeere 1652. 1654 (bis); 1659 (in Gorges, America Painted to the Life, see below); rptd 2 Collections Massachusetts Hist. Soc. 1814–1819; ed. W. F. Poole, Andover, Mass. 1867; ed. J. F. Jameson (as The Wonder-working Providence, Original Narratives, 2 vols. 1910).

Francis Yeardley. A Letter to John Farrar, Esq., of Excursions into Carolina, 1654. Thurloe State Papers, vol. II, 1742; ed. A. S. Salley (in Original Narratives, 1911).

A great and wonderful Victory obtained by the English Forces under General Pen and General Venables against the French and others in the West Indies. 1655 (3 April).

Three Great and Bloody Fights between the English and the French: the first by Gen. Pen and Gen. Venables against St. Christophers. The second neer St. Mallows. The third neer the Isle of Majorica, by Gen. Blake. 1655 (10 April).

J. Daniell. [A letter from Jamaica, 3 June 1655.] Thurloe State Papers, vol. III, 1742. [An account of the West Indies naval voyage.]

A Dialogue containing a Compendious Discourse concerning the Present Designe in the West Indies. 1655 (20 Sept.).

I. S. A Brief and perfect Journal of the late Proceedings and Successe of the English Army in the West-Indies, Continued until June the 24th. 1655. By I. S. an Eyewitnesse. 1655 (19 Dec.); rptd Harleian Misc. vol. III.

Sir William Penn. [Journals relating to the West Indies expedition, 1654–1655]. Ptd Granville Penn (Memorials of Sir William Penn, 2 vols. 1833).

General Robert Venables. [A Narrative by General Venables of his expedition to the island of Jamaica and the conquest thereof.] St Jago de la Vega, 1800 (in Interesting Tracts, Relating to the Island of Jamaica); ed. C. H. Firth, Camden Soc. 1900. [From BM. Add. MSS 11410 and 12429.]

A True Narrative of the late success of the fleet of this Commonwealth against the King of Spains West-India Fleet. 1656.

An Attempt on the Island of Jamaica, and taking the Town of St. Jago de la viga 1655. With a true Narrative of the late Successe against the King of Spains West India Fleet. 1657 (in A Book of the Continuation of Forreign Passages).

[Edward Doyley.] A Narrative of the Great Success God hath been pleased to give His Highness Forces in Jamaica. As it was Communicated in a Letter from the Governour of Jamaica. 1658.

[Sir] Ferdinando Gorges. America Painted to the Life. The True History of the Spaniards Proceedings, As also, Of the Original Undertakings of the Advancement of Plantations into those parts. 1659. [Pt II, A Brief Narration of the Originall Undertakings, by Sir Ferdinando Gorges, rptd in 3 Collections Massachusetts Hist. Soc. vol. VI, 1837; in Collections Maine Hist. Soc. 1847; ed. J. P. Baxter, Prince Soc. Boston, 1890. Pt III, America Painted to the Life, is Edward Johnson, The History of New England, 1654, see above.]

Marcellus Rivers and Oxenbridge Foyle. Englands Slavery, or Barbados Merchandize: Represented in a Petition to the High and Honourable Court of Parliament. 1659. [Concerning a voyage of 1656.]

(b) Descriptions of America

Sir Humfrey Gilbert. A Discourse of a Discoverie for a new Passage to Cataia. 1576; 1589 and 1600 (in Hakluyt); rptd 1886 (Cassell's National Lib.); ed. C. Slafter, Prince Soc. Boston, 1903.

Nicolás Monardes. Joyfull Newes out of the newe founde worlde, wherein is declared the rare and singular vertues of diverse and sundrie Hearbes, Trees, Oyles, Plantes, and Stones. Englished by John Frampton. 1577 (part); 1580; 1596 (complete); ed. S. Gaselee, 2 vols. 1925 (Tudor Translations). [From the Historia Medicinal de las Cosas de nuestras Indias Occidentales, Seville, 1574, etc.]

Martín Fernández de Enciso. A Briefe Description of the Portes, Creekes, Bayes and Havens, of the Weast India: translated out of the Castill tongue by John Frampton. 1578. [From the Suma de geographia, Seville, 1519, etc.; see Roger Barlow, 1541, above, p. 765.]

Bartolomé de las Casas. The Spanish Colonie, or Briefe Chronicle of the Acts and gestes of the Spaniardes in the West Indies translated into English by M. M. S. 1583; rptd Purchas (abridged). [From the French version, Antwerp, 1579, etc. of the Brevissima relacion de la destruycion de las Indias, Seville, 1552, etc.]

—— The Tears of the Indians. 1656. [Another trn by John Phillips.]

Richard Hakluyt. A Particuler Discourse concerning the great necessitie and manifolde comodyties that are like to growe to this Realme of Englande by the Westerne discoveries lately attempted, written 1584. Ed. Leonard Woods and Charles Deane, 2 Collections Maine Hist. Soc. Cambridge, U.S.A. 1877 (as The Discourse on the Western Planting). [MS in New York Public Lib.; less complete copy in State Papers Domestic, Elizabeth 195, 127.]

Thomas Hariot. A briefe and true Report of the new found Land of Virginia. Discovered by the English Colony there seated. 1588; 1589, 1600 (in Hakluyt); rptd Pinkerton, vol. xii; ed. I. N. Tarbox, Prince Soc. Boston, 1884; rptd facs. Manchester, 1888; ed. Henry Stevens, 1900; ed. L. S. Livingston, New York, 1903; ed. R. G. Adams, Ann Arbor, 1931. Tr. Latin, De Bry, pt 1, 1590, 1608, 1634; French, De Bry, pt 1, 1590; German, De Bry, pt 1, 1590, 1600, 1620; in M. Dresser, Historien und Bericht von dem Königreich China, 1597.

John Davis. The Worldes Hydrographical Discription. Whereby appeares that from England there is a short and speedie passage into the South Seas. 1595; rptd 1812 (in A Selection, etc.); ed. A. H. Markham, Hakluyt Soc. 1880; Americana Ser. 1925.

José de Acosta. The Naturall and Morall Historie of the East and West Indies. 1604; part rptd Purchas; Harris, vol. i; ed. C. R. Markham, Hakluyt Soc. 2 pts, 1880. [Tr. Edward Grimstone from the Historia natural y moral de las Indias, Seville, 1590, etc.]

Marc Lescarbot. Nova Francia: Or the Description of that part of New France, which is one continent with Virginia. Described in the three late Voyages and Plantation made by Monsieur de Monts. Translated out of French into English by P[ierre] E[rondelle]. 1609; [1624]; rptd Harleian Voyages, vol. ii; ed. H. P. Biggar, 1928. [The descriptive portions of the Histoire de la Nouvelle-France, Paris, 1609. Complete re-translation by W. L. Grant, Champlain Soc. 3 pts, Toronto, 1907–14.]

[Sir Dudley Digges.] Fata mihi totum mea sunt agitanda per orbem. 1611; 1612 (as Of the Circumference of the Earth: Or, A Treatise of the North-east [= west] passage).

John Mason. A briefe Discourse of the Newfound-land, with the Situation, Temperature, and Commodities thereof. 1620; ed. D. Laing, Bannatyne Club, 1867; ed. J. W. Dean, Prince Soc. Boston, 1887.

More Excellent Observations of the Estate and Affaires Of Holland. In a discourse, shewing how necessarie it is to Trade into the West Indies. Faithfully translated out of the Dutch. 1622.

Edward Waterhouse. A Declaration of the State of the Colony and Affaires in Virginia. With a Relation of the Barbarous Massacre. And, a Treatise annexed, Written by Henry Briggs, of the Northwest passage to the South Sea through the Continent of Virginia, and by Fretum Hudson. 1622. [The Briggs treatise rptd in Purchas.]

T. C. A short Discourse of the New-Found-Land: Contaynig diverse Reasons and inducements, for the planting of that Countrey. Dublin, 1623.

Sir William Alexander. An Encouragement to Colonies. 1624; 1625; 1630 (as The Mapp And Description of New-England); rptd Bannatyne Club, 1867; ed. E. F. Slafter, Prince Soc. Boston, 1873.

Richard Eburne. A plaine Path-Way to Plantations: With certaine Motives for a present Plantation in New-found land above the rest. 1624.

[Sir Robert Gordon.] Encouragements. For such as shall intention to bee Under-takers in the new plantation of Cape Briton, now New Galloway in America, By Mee Lochinvar. Edinburgh, 1625; rptd Bannatyne Club, 1867.

John Hagthorpe. Englands-Exchequer. Or A Discourse of the Sea and Navigation with some things concerning Plantations. 1625.

William Morrell. New England. Or A Briefe Enarration of the Ayre, Earth, Water, Fish, and Fowles of that country: in Latine and English Verse. 1625; rptd Collections Massachusetts Hist. Soc. vol. I, 1792, 1806, and 1859; ed. J. F. Hunnewell, Boston, 1895.

[William Vaughan.] Cambrensium Caroleia. Quibus Precepta necessaria ad Rempublicam intexuntur: ex Australissima Novae Terrae Plaga. 1625. [Verse.]

—— The Golden Fleece, Under which are discouvered the wayes to get wealth. Transported from Cambrioll Colchos. 1626.

Breefe Notes of the River Amazones and of the Coast of Guiana. 1627; rptd Americana Ser. 1920. [3 copies in State Papers Colonial, America and West Indies, C. O. 1/4, nos. 5, 6, 7. Based on MS by Roger North (?), ibid. no. 4.]

R[obert] H[ayman]. Quodlibets, lately come over from New Britaniola, Old-Newfound-Land. Epigrams and other small Parcels. 1628. [Verse.]

[John White.] The Planters plea. Or The grounds of Plantations Examined. Together with a manifestation of the causes mooving such as have lately undertaken a Plantation in New-England. 1630; rptd Force, Tracts, vol. II.

I. D. A Publication of Guianas Plantation Newly undertaken by the Earle of Barkshire and Company for that most famous River of the Amazones in America. 1632; rptd Harleian Misc. vol. X.

William Wood. New Englands Prospect. A true, lively, and experimentall description of that part of America, commonly called New England. 1634; 1635; 1639; ed. Charles Deane, Prince Soc. Boston, 1865; ed. H. W. Boynton, Boston, 1898.

Thomas Morton. New English Canaan or New Canaan. Containing an Abstract of New England. Amsterdam, 1637; rptd Force, Tracts, vol. II; ed. C. F. Adams, Boston, 1883.

Philip Vincent. A True Relation of the Late Battell fought in New England, between the English and the Salvages. With the present state of things there. 1637; 1638 (bis); rptd 1837 (in 3 Collections Massachusetts Hist. Soc. vol. VI); ed. C. Orr (History of the Pequot War, Cleveland, 1897).

John Underhill. Newes from America; or, a new and experimentall Discoverie of New-England. Also a discovery of Queenapoick, Agu-wom, Hudsons River, Long Island. 1638; rptd 1837 (in 3 Collections Massachusetts Hist. Soc. vol. VI); ed. C. Orr (History of the Pequot War, Cleveland, 1897); ed. D. H. Underhill [Brooklyn?], 1902.

Antonio Colmenero de Ledesma. A Curious Treatise Of The Nature and Quality of Chocolate. 1640; [1652?]; 1685. [From the Curioso tratado del Chocolate, Madrid, 1631, etc.: tr. Don Diego de Vades-forte, or James Wadsworth.]

Robert Evelin. A Direction for Adventurers, and the true description of the healthiest, pleasantest, and richest Plantation of new Albion, in North Virginia, with a letter from Mayster Robert Evelin. 1641; 1648 (in Beauchamp Plantagenet, see below); rptd Americana Ser. 1922.

Thomas Lechford. Plain Dealing: or, Newes from New-England. A short view of New-Englands present Government, both Ecclesiasticall and Civill. 1642; 1644 (as New-Englands Advice to Old-England); rptd 1833 (in 3 Collections Massachusetts Hist. Soc. vol. III); ed. J. H. Trumbull. Boston, 1867.

Certain Inducements to Well Minded People to transport Themselves, or some Servants, or Agents for them into the West Indies, for the Propagating of the Gospel and Increase of Trade. [1643?]; ed. Joseph Sabin, New York, 1865.

Roger Williams. A Key into the Language of America: or an Help to the Language of the Natives, in that part of America, called New England. Together with brief Observations of the Customs, Manners, and Worship. [1643]; rptd Collections Massachusetts Hist. Soc. vol. III, 1794, 1810, vol. V, 1798, 1816, 1835; Collections Rhode Island Hist. Soc. 1827 (from Bodleian MS); ed. J. H. Trumbull, Boston, 1866.

William Castell. A Short Discoverie of the Coasts and Continent of America, From the Equinoctiall Northward, and of the adjacent Isles. 1644 (bis); rptd Harleian Voyages, vol. II.

Good news from New England: with An exact relation of the first planting that Countrey: With The names of the severall Towns, and who be Preachers to them. 1648; rptd 1852 (in 4 Collections Massachusetts Hist. Soc. vol. I). [Mainly verse.]

A Perfect Description of Virginia: being, A full and true Relation of the present State of the Plantation sent from Virginia. 1649; rptd Force, Tracts, vol. II.

[Beauchamp Plantagenet.] A Description of the Province of New Albion. And a Direction for Adventurers with small stock to get two for one. 1648; rptd Force, Tracts, vol. II; rptd G. D. Scull (in The Evelyns in America, Oxford, 1881). [The Direction taken from Evelin, 1641, above.]

William Bullock. Virginia Impartially examined, and left to publick view. 1649; rptd Force, Tracts, vol. III.

E[dward] W[illiams]. Virgo triumphans: or, Virginia richly and truly valued; more especially the South part thereof: viz. The fertile Carolana. 1650 (bis); rptd Force, Tracts, vol. III.

—— Virginias Discovery of Silke-Wormes, with their benefit. And the implanting of Mulberry Trees. Also The dressing and keeping of Vines, for the rich Trade of making Wines there. 1650 (with previous item).

Tho[mas] Thorowgood. Jewes in America, or, Probabilities that the Americans are of that Race. With earnest desires for effectuall endeavors to make them Christian. 1650; 1652 (as Digitus Dei).

—— Jews in America, or probabilities that those Indians are Judaical, made more probable. 1660.

George Gardyner. A Description of the New World. Or, America Islands and Continent: and by what people those Regions are now inhabited. And what places are there desolate. 1651.

Arthur Woodnoth. A short Collection of the Most Remarkable Passages from the originall to the dissolution of the Virginia Company. 1651.

Sir Hamon L'Estrange. Americans no Jewes, or Improbabilities that the Americans are of that race. 1652.

[Thomas Peake?] America: or An exact Description of the West-Indies: More especially of those Provinces which are under the Dominion of the King of Spain. Faithfully represented by N. N. Gent. 1655.

John Hammond. Leah and Rachel, or, the Two Fruitfull Sisters Virginia, and Mary-Land: Their Present Condition, Impartially stated and related. 1656; rptd Force, Tracts, vol. III; ed. C. C. Hall (in Original Narratives, 1910).

Richard Ligon. A true & exact History of the Island of Barbados. Illustrated with a Mapp of the Island. 1657; 1673; tr. French, 1674 (in Recueil de divers Voyages fait en Afrique et en l'Amérique).

A True Description of Jamaica, With the Fertility, Commodities, and Healthfulness of the place. As also the Towns, Havens, Creeks, Promontories, and the Circuit of the whole Island. 1657.

Lion Gardener. [A Relation of the Pequot Warres, written 1660.] Ptd 3 Collections Massachusetts Hist. Soc. vol. III, 1833.

Sir Balthazar Gerbier. A Sommary Description, Manifesting that greater Profits are to bee done in the hott then in the could parts off the Coast off America. Amsterdam, 1660.

—— Advertysement For men inclyned to Plantacions in America. Rotterdam, 1660; Amsterdam, 1660 (with the preceding item).

Samuel Maverick. A briefe discription of New England [1660] and the severall townes therein, together with the present government thereof. Ed. J. W. Dean, Boston, 1885.

(5) CRITICAL AND HISTORICAL WORKS

[The most important secondary material is to be found in the recent edns of individual narratives and authors as given above. The following additional lists include: (a) some secondary works on the voyage literature and the historical background; (b) some studies of the contemporary literary influence of the voyages; (c) some special bibliographies.]

(a) Surveys and Special Studies

Peschel, O. F. Geschichte des Zeitalters der Entdeckungen. Stuttgart, 1858, 1877.

Ruge, Sophus. Geschichte des Zeitalters der Entdeckungen. Berlin, 1881.

Winsor, Justin. Narrative and Critical History of America. 8 vols. Boston, 1886–9.

—— Cartier to Frontenac. Geographical Discovery in the Interior of North America. Boston, 1894.

Gravière, Jurien de la. Les Anglais et les Hollandais dans les Mers Polaires et dans la Mer des Indes. 2 vols. Paris, 1890.

Social England. Ed. H. D. Traill, 6 vols. 1893–7, 1894–7, 1901–4. [Vol. II, ch. 8, C. R. Beazley, The Cabots; vol. III, ch. 10, W. L. Clowes, Maritime Warfare and Commerce; vol. III, ch. 11, C. R. Beazley, Travel and Exploration, 1512–1558; vol. III, ch. 12, C. R. Beazley, Exploration under Elizabeth (also in Trans. Royal Hist. Soc. N.S. IX, 1895); vol. IV, ch. 13, C. R. Beazley, Exploration and Colonisation, 1603–1642.]

Froude, J. A. English Seamen in the Sixteenth Century. 1895 (bis); 1901; 1923; 1925.

The Royal Navy. A History. Ed. Sir W. L. Clowes, 7 vols. 1897–1903. [Vol. I, ch. 12, H. W. Wilson, Voyages and Discoveries, 1399–1485; vol. I, ch. 16, Sir Clements Markham, Voyages and Discoveries, 1485–1603; vol. II, ch. 19, Sir Clements Markham, Voyages and Discoveries, 1603–1649.]

Corbett, Sir J. S. Drake and the Tudor Navy. 2 vols. 1898, 1899.

—— The Successors of Drake. 1900.

—— England in the Mediterranean, 1603–1713. 2 vols. 1904.

Hunter, Sir W. W. A History of British India. 2 vols. 1899–1900.

Underhill, J. G. Spanish Literature in the England of the Tudors. New York, 1899. [Ch. 5, The Historians of the Indies.]

Einstein, Lewis. The Italian Renaissance in England. New York, 1902. [Ch. 3, The Traveller.]

Errera, Carlo. L' Epoca delle Grandi Scoperte Geografiche [to 1522]. Milan. 1902, 1910, 1926.

Günther, Siegmund. Das Zeitalter der Entdeckungen. Leipzig, 1902, 1905.

The Cambridge Modern History. Ed. Sir A. W. Ward et al., 13 vols. 1902–11. [Vol. I, ch. 1, E. J. Payne, The Age of Discovery; vol. I, ch. 2, E. J. Payne, The New World; vol. IV, ch. 25, H. E. Egerton, The Transference of Colonial Power to the United Provinces and England.]

Hugues, L. Cronologia delle Scoperte e delle Esplorazioni Geografiche Dall' Anno 1492 a tutto il Secolo XIX. Milan, 1903.

Böhme, Max. Die grossen Reisesammlungen des 16. Jahrhunderts und ihre Bedeutung. Strasburg, 1904.

Hume, Martin. Spanish Influence on English Literature. 1905. [Ch. vii: The Literature of Travel and of War.]

Raleigh, Sir Walter. The English Voyages of the Sixteenth Century. Glasgow, 1906, 1910, 1923. [Also in vol. XII of Hakluyt's Voyages, Hakluyt Soc. Glasgow, 1905.]

Ker, W. P. The Elizabethan Voyagers. TLS. 12 July 1907. [Rptd in Collected Essays, vol. I, 1925.]

Robinson, C. N. and Leyland, John. The Literature of the Sea, From the Origins to Hakluyt. CHEL. vol. IV, 1909.

—— Seafaring and Travel. CHEL. vol. IV, 1909.

Scott, W. R. The Constitution and Finance of English, Scottish and Irish Joint-Stock Companies to 1720. 3 vols. Cambridge, 1910–2.

Bates, E. S. Touring in 1600. 1911.

Heawood, Edward. A History of Geographical Discovery in the Seventeenth and Eighteenth Centuries. Cambridge, 1912.

Williamson, J. A. Maritime Enterprise, 1485–1558. Oxford, 1913.

Howard, Clare. English Travellers of the Renaissance. 1914.

Shakespeare's England. Vol. I, Oxford, 1916. [Ch. 5, L. G. Carr Laughton, The Navy:

Ships and Sailors; ch. 6, J. D. Rogers, Voyages and Exploration: Geography: Maps; ch. 7, Charles Hughes, Land Travel.]

Cambridge History of American Literature. Ed. W. P. Trent et al., vol. I, 1918. [Ch. 1, G. P. Winship, Travellers and Explorers, 1583–1763; ch. 2, J. S. Bassett, The Historians, 1607–1783.]

Gillespie, J. E. The Influence of Oversea Expansion on England to 1700. New York, 1920.

Markham, Sir C. R. The Lands of Silence. A History of Arctic and Antarctic Exploration. Cambridge, 1921. [See also The Royal Navy, above, 1897.]

Mutschmann, H. Studies concerning the Origin of Paradise Lost [in Hakluyt]. Acta et Commentationes Universitatis Dorpatensis, v, 1924.

Parkes, Joan. Travel in England in the Seventeenth Century. 1925.

Parks, G. B. Richard Hakluyt and the English Voyages. American Geographical Soc. New York, 1928.

—— Frobisher's Third Voyage, 1578. Huntington Lib. Bulletin, April 1935.

The Cambridge History of the British Empire. Ed. J. Holland Rose et al., vol. I, 1929. [Ch. 2, J. A. Williamson, England and the Opening of the Atlantic; ch. 3, A. P. Newton, The Beginnings of English Colonisation, 1569–1618; ch. 4, J. H. Rose, Sea Power, 1580–1660; ch. 5, A. P. Newton, The Great Emigration, 1618–1648.]

Taylor, E. G. R. Tudor Geography, 1485–1583. 1930.

—— Samuel Purchas. Geographical Journ. LXXV, 1930.

—— Late Tudor and Early Stuart Geography, 1583–1650. 1934.

—— The Original Writings and Correspondence of the Two Richard Hakluyts. 2 vols. 1936.

Baker, J. N. L. A History of Geographical Exploration and Discovery. 1931.

The Great Age of Discovery. Ed. A. P. Newton, 1932.

Rice, W. G. Early English Travellers to Greece and the Levant. [In Essays and Studies by Members of the English Department, Ann Arbor, 1933.]

(b) Literary Influences

Lee, Vernon. The Italy of the Elizabethan Dramatists. [In Euphorion, 1885.]

Elze, Theodor. Venezianische Skizzen zu Shakespeare. Munich, 1899.

Naval Songs and Ballads. Ed. Sir C. H. Firth, Navy Records Soc. 1908.

Robinson, C. N. and Leyland, John. The British Tar in Fact and Fiction. 1909.

Whall, W. B. Shakespeare's Sea Terms Explained. Bristol, 1910.

Eckhardt, Eduard. Die Dialekt- und Ausländertypen des älteren Englischen Dramas. Teil 2: Die Ausländertypen. Louvain, 1911. (Bang's Materialien, vol. XXXII.)

Wann, Louis. The Oriental in Elizabethan Drama. MP. XII, 1914.

Brie, Friedrich. Imperialistische Strömungen in der englischen Literatur. Halle, 1916, 1928. [Also Ang. XL, 1916.]

Gilbert, A. H. A Geographical Dictionary of Milton. New Haven, 1919.

—— Pierre Davity: His Geography and Its Use by Milton. Geographical Rev. VII, 1919.

Thompson, E. N. S. Milton's Knowledge of Geography. Stud. Phil. XVI, 1919.

Grossmann, Rudolf. Spanien und das Elisabethanische Drama. Hamburg, 1920.

Whitney, Lois. Spenser's Use of the Literature of Travel in The Faerie Queene. MP. XIX, 1921.

—— Did Shakespeare Know Leo Africanus? PMLA. XXXVII, 1922.

Cawley, R. R. Warner and the Voyagers. MP. XX, 1922.

—— Drayton and the Voyagers. PMLA. XXXVIII, 1923.

—— Shakespeare's Use of the Voyagers in The Tempest. PMLA. XLI, 1926.

—— George Gascoigne and the Siege of Famagusta. MLN. XLIII, 1928.

Atkinson, Geoffroy. Les Relations de Voyages du Dix-Septième Siècle et l'Evolution des Idées. Paris, [1924].

Hughes, W. J. Wales and the Welsh in English Literature from Shakespeare to Scott. 1924.

Seaton, Ethel. Marlowe's Map. E. & S. x, 1924.

—— Fresh Sources for Marlowe. RES. v, 1929.

Sugden, E. H. A Topographical Dictionary to the Works of Shakespeare and his Fellow Dramatists. Manchester, 1925.

Sencourt, Robert. India in English Literature. 1926.

Treneer, Anne. The Sea in English Literature. From Beowulf to Donne. 1926.

Hull, V. E. N. The English and Welsh Topographical Sources of Polyolbion. Abstract in Harvard Summaries of Theses, vol. II, pp. 177–9, Cambridge, U.S.A. 1930.

Watson, H. F. The Sailor in English Fiction and Drama, 1550–1800. New York, 1931.

(c) Special Bibliographies

Catalogue of Books of Voyages and Travels. [In John Pinkerton, A Collection of Voyages and Travels, vol. XVII, 1814.]

Tiele, P. A. Mémoire Bibliographique sur les Journaux des Navigateurs Néerlandais et sur les Anciennes Éditions Hollandaises des Journaux de Navigateurs Étrangers. Amsterdam, 1867.

Sabin, Joseph. Bibliotheca Americana. A Dictionary of Books Relating to America. New York, 1872–.

Amat di San Filippo, Pietro. Bibliografia dei Viaggiatori Italiani. Rome, 1874.

—— Biografia dei Viaggiatori Italiani colla Bibliografia delle loro opere. [Vol. I of Studi bibliografici e biografici sulla Storia della Geografia in Italia, Rome, 1875 and 1882.]

Anderson, J. P. The Book of British Topography. 1881.

Roehricht, Reinhold. Bibliotheca Geographica Palaestinae. Berlin, 1890.

Scott, M. A. Elizabethan Translations from the Italian. PMLA. XIV, 1899. [§ iv a, Voyages and Discovery; b, History and Politics. Rptd Boston, 1916 (§§ ix, x).]

A Catalogue of Books Relating to the Discovery and Early History of North and South America Forming a Part of the Library of E. D. Church. Ed. G. W. Cole, 5 vols. New York, 1907.

Bourgeois, Émile and André, Louis. Les Sources de l'Histoire de France. IIIe Partie, tome I, ch. 1: Voyages. Paris, 1913.

Mitchell, Sir Arthur and Cash, C. G. A Contribution to the Bibliography of Scottish Topography. 2 vols. Scottish History Soc. Edinburgh, 1917.

Forster, Sir William. A Guide to the India Office Records, 1600–1858. 1919.

Atkinson, Geoffrey. La Littérature géographique française de la Renaissance [to 1610]. Paris, 1927.

Bibliography of British History. Stuart Period. Ed. Godfrey Davies, Oxford, 1928. [Ch. vi, pt 2, Descriptions of England, Travel, &c.; ch. xv, Voyages and Travels.]

Manwaring, G. E. Bibliography of British Naval History. 1930.

Bibliography of British History. Tudor Period, 1485–1603. Ed. C. Read, Oxford, 1933. [Ch. on Discovery, Exploration and Colonization.]

G. B. P.

VII. TRANSLATIONS INTO ENGLISH

Translations from the Greek and Latin Classics. Translations from Medieval and Contemporary Authors. Bibliographies, Summaries and Critical Estimates.

[In the following lists translations of poetry are in verse and of prose in prose unless otherwise stated. With the exception of versions of short poems and occasional passages they are as complete as it has been possible to make them for the authors selected, though there may well be omissions for the years 1640–60. The basis of selection has been the literary merit or status of the originals, and for a full view of the subject the following sections should also be consulted: Literary Relations with the Continent (pp. 325–45 above); Education (pp. 364–80 above); The English Bible (pp. 672–6 above); Versions of the Psalms (pp. 677–9 above); Prose Fiction (pp. 732–6 above); Books of Travel (pp. 763–98 above); Historians, Biographers and Antiquaries (pp. 823–43 below); Scholars and Scholarship (pp. 852–63 below); Science and Pseudo-Science (pp. 879–94 below). Phrases in foreign languages have sometimes been omitted from titles, even when standing first.]

A. TRANSLATIONS FROM THE GREEK AND LATIN CLASSICS

ACHILLES TATIUS

B[urton], W[illiam]. The most delectable and pleasaunt History of Clitophon and Leucippe. 1597; Oxford, 1638; ed. S. Gaselee and H. F. B. Brett-Smith, Oxford, 1923.

H[odges], A[nthony]. The loves of Clitophon and Leucippe. A most elegant history. Oxford, 1638.

AELIAN

Fleming, Abraham. Claudius. A Registre of Hystories, delivered in Englyshe (as well according to the Greeke text as Latine). 1576.

B[ingham], J[ohn]. Aelianus Tacticus. The Tactiks of Aelian. [1616.] [Pt 2,] 1629; 1631.

AESOP

Bullokar, William. Æsopź Fablz in tru Ortŏgraphy with Grammar-nŏtz. 1585; ed. M. Plessow, Berlin, 1906.

Sturtevant, Simon. The Etymologist of Æsops Fables, containing the construing of his Latine fables into English: Also the Etymologist of Phaedrus fables, containing the construing of Phaedrus into English, verbatim. Both very necessarie helps for young schollers. 1602.

[Brinsley, J.] Esops fables translated for the grammar-schoole. 1624. [First ptd with Pueriles Confabulatiunculae, 1617.]

A., R. The Fabulist Metamorphosed, And Mythologized. Or The Fables Of Esop, Translated into English verse, and moralized. 1634.

B[arret], W. The Fables of Aesop. With his whole life: Translated into English Verse and Moralliz'd. As also Emblematically Illustrated with Pictures. 1639.

Aesop's Fables [45] with the Fables of Phaedrus [31, *i.e.* Bk I] moralized, translated verbatim [from G. H. Goudanus]. Published by H. P. 1646.

Willan, Leonard. The Phrygian Fabulist; or the Fables of Aesop [231]; moraliz'd. 1650. [Verse.]

Ogilby, J[ohn]. The Fables of Aesop paraphras'd in verse. 1651.

Aesops Fables [213] with their moralls, in prose and verse grammatically translated. 1651.

[Shirley, James.] Introductorium Anglo-Latino-Graecum: complectens Colloquia familiaria, Aesopi fabulas, et Luciani selectiores Mortuorum Dialogos. 1656.

ANACREON

Stanley, Thomas. Anacreon, Bion, Moschus. Kisses by Secundus. Cupid Crucified by Ausonius. Venus Vigils. 1651; rptd Sir S. E. Brydges, 1815. [Anacreon only rptd A. H. Bullen, 1893.]

APPIAN

B., W. An Auncient Historie and exquisite Chronicle of the Romanes warres. With a continuation from the death of Sextus Pompeius till the overthrow of Antonie and Cleopatra. 2 pts, 1578. [Pt 2 only by W. B.]

APULEIUS

Adlington, William. The XI Bookes of The Golden Asse, conteininge Metamorphosie of Lucius Apuleius with the Mariage of Cupide and Psiches. 1566; 1571; 1582; 1596; 1639; ed. A. Lang, 1887; ed. C. Whibley, 1893 (Tudor Translations); ed. T. Seccombe, 1913; ed. E. B. Osborn, 1923; ed. F. J. H. Darton, 1924; ed. W. H. D. Rouse, 1929 (selections).

ARISTOPHANES

B., H. B. The World's Idol, or Plutus the God of Wealth. 1659.

ARISTOTLE

[Wilkinson, John.] The Ethiques. 1547. [From the Italian compendium of B. Latini.]

The Problemes of Aristotle, with other Philosophers and Physitions. Wherein are contayned divers questions, with their answers, touching the estate of mans bodie. 1595; Edinburgh, 1595; 1597; 1607.

D., I. Aristotle's Politiques, or discourses of government. 1598. [From the French of Loys le Roy, called Regius.]

[Hobbes, Thomas.] A Briefe of the Art of Rhetorique. [1637?]; [1655?].

[H. R. Palmer, List of English Editions and Translations of Greek and Latin Classics printed before 1641, 1911, includes as trns, besides a medical appendix by Thomas Hyll, [1550?], Thomas Wilson's Arte of Rhetorique, 1553, and various books on logic by Rollo MacIlmaine, 1574, M. [Thomas] Blundevile, 1599, Anthony Wotton, 1626, R. F[age], 1632. P. Ramus's name appears on all the title-pages in the second group except Blundevile's.]

MARCUS AURELIUS

Casaubon, M[eric]. Marcus Aurelius Antoninus The Roman Emperor, His Meditations Concerning Himselfe: with Notes. 1634; 1635; ed. W. H. D. Rouse, 1898 (as The Golden Book of Marcus Aurelius), 1900, 1906 (Everyman's Lib.).

AUSONIUS

Kendall, Timothy. [Epigrams. In Flowers of Epigrammes, 1577.]

Beaumont, Sir John. [The sixteenth Idyll. In Bosworth-Field, 1629.]

Stanley, Thomas. Europa [by Moschus]. Cupid Crucified [by Ausonius, Latin and English]. Venus Vigils. 1649; 1651; rptd Sir S. E. Brydges, 1815.

[See also Turbervile under Greek Anthology and Fanshawe under Horace.]

BION

[See under Anacreon.]

CAESAR

[Tiptoft, John (Earl of Worcester).] Julius Cesars commentaryes as much as concernyth thys realm of England. 1530. [English and Latin in parallel columns. Printer W. Rastell?]

Golding, Arthur. The eyght bookes of Caius Julius Caesar conteyning his martiall exploytes in Gallia and the Countries bordering. 1565; 1578; 1590.

Edmondes, Sir Clement. [Commentaries. In Observations upon the five first bookes of Cæsars Commentaries, 1600, 1604 (adds sixth and seventh bks), 1609 (adds Civil Wars, bks I–III), 1655.]

C[ruso], T. The Complete Captain, or, An Abbridgement of Cesars warres, With observations. Written by the Duke of Rohan. Cambridge, 1640. [Appendix.]

DIONYSIUS CATO

Taverner, Richard. Catonis Disticha Moralia Ex Castigatione D. Erasmi una cum annotationibus & scholiis Richardi Taverneri anglico idiomate conscriptis. 1540; 1553; 1562; 1572; 1580; 1592; 1620. [Latin and English.]

[Burrant, Robert.] Preceptes of Cato the Sage. With annotacions of D. Erasmus. 1545 (no copy extant?); 1553; 1560.

Cato construed. First doen in Laten and Frenche by Maturinus Corderius and now englished to the comforte of all young Schollers. 1577 (no copy extant?); 1584.

Bullokar, William. The short sentencez of the wýz Cato. [Pt 2 of Aeşopź fablź in tru Ortŏgraphy, 1585. Separate title-page.]

[Brinsley, John.] Cato (concerning the precepts of common life) translated Grammatically. 1612; 1622.

P[enkethman], J[ohn]. A Handful of Honesty or, Cato in English Verse. 1623; 1624.

Baker, Sir Richard. Cato Variegatus, or Catoes Morall Distichs: Translated and Paraphras'd with variations of Expressing, in English verse. 1636.

Hoole, Charles. 1. Catonis disticha de moribus; 2. Dicta insignia septem Sapientium Graeciae; 3. Mimi Publiani, sive Senecae proverbia, Anglo-Latina. 1659.

CEBES

[Poyntz, Sir Francis.] The Tables of Cebes the philosopher. [c. 1530]; 1560.

[See also under Epictetus.]

CICERO

Whittington, Robert. The thre bookes of Tullyes Offyces bothe in latyne tonge and in englysshe. 1534; 1540.

—— Tullius de senectute, Bothe in latyn and Englysshe tonge. [1535?]

—— The Paradox of Marcus Tullius Cicero. 1540.

Harington, John. The Booke of freendeship. 1550; 1562; rptd 1904; ed. W. H. D. Rouse, 1907.

Grimald, Nicolas. M. Tullius Ciceroe's thre boks of dueties, to Marcus his sonne. 1553; 1556; 1558; 1568; 1574; 1583; 1588; 1590; 1596; [1600?]; 1610. [Latin and English.]

Sherry, Richard. The oration which Cicero made to Cesar of Marcus Marcellus. [In Treatise of the Figures of Grammer and Rhetorike, 1555.]

G[ylby], G[oddred]. An Epistle, or letter of exhortation to Quintus. 1561.

Dolman, John. Those fyve questions which Marke Tullye Cicero, disputed in his Manor of Tusculanum. 1561.

[Newton, Thomas.] The Booke of M. T. Cicero entituled Paradoxa Stoicorum. Wherunto is annexed Scipio hys Dreame. 1569. [Scipio's Dream, ed. W. H. D. Rouse, 1907.]

[——] The Worthye Booke of old age. 1569; ed. W. H. D. Rouse, 1907.

—— Fowre several Treatises of M. Tullius Cicero. Conteyninge Discourses of Frendshippe; Old age: Paradoxes: and Scipio his Dreame. 1577.

W., T. A certaine draught taken out of Ciceroes Epistles for the exercise of children in the Latin speache. 1575. [Latin and English.]

Fleming, Abraham. [Select Epistles. In Panoplie of Epistles, 1576.]

The Latine Grammar [of Ramus] Whereunto is joyned a Grammatical Analysis uppon an Epistle of Tullie. Cambridge, 1585.

[Haine, William?] Certain Epistles of Tully verbally translated. 1611.

[Brinsley, John.] The firste Booke of Tullies Offices translated Grammatically. 1616; 1631.

[Webbe, Joseph.] The Familiar Epistles of M. T. Cicero Englished and Conferred with the French, Italian and other translations. [1620.]

S., E. G. Scipio's Dreame, or the Statesman's Extasie. 1627.

Austin, William. Cato Major: or the Book of Old Age. 1648.

[See also under P. de Mornay, p. 817 below.]

CLAUDIAN

Digges, Leonard. The Rape of Proserpine. Translated into English verse. 1617; 1628.

Beaumont, Sir John. [Epigrams, in Bosworth-Field, 1629.]

QUINTUS CURTIUS

Brende, John. The Historie of Quintus Curtius, conteyning the Actes of the greate Alexander. 1553; 1561; 1570; 1584; 1592; 1602; 1614.

DARES PHRYGIUS

Paynell, Thomas. The faythfull and true storye of the distruction of Troye. 1553.

DEMOSTHENES

Wilson, Thomas. The three Orations of Demosthenes in favour of the Olynthians, with those his fower Orations against King Philip of Macedonie. Demosthenes's lyfe is set foorth and gathered out of Plutarch, Lucian, Suidas and others. 1570.

G[okin], T[homas]. The first oration against Philip of Macedon. 1623.

DIODORUS SICULUS

Stocker, Thomas. A righte noble History of the Successors of Alexander, taken out of Diodorus Siculus [Bk 18] and Plutarch. 1569. [From French.]

C[ogan]. H[enry]. The History of Diodorus Siculus. 1653.

DIONYSIUS PERIEGETES

Twyne, Thomas. The Surveye of the World, or Situation of the Earth. 1572.

EPICTETUS

Sandford, James. The Manuell of Epictetus, translated out of Greeke into French, and now into English. Hereunto are annexed the apothegs. 1567.

Healey, John. Epictetus his Manuall. And Cebes his Table. 1610; 1616 (adds Theophrastus his Morall Characters); 1636. [Theophrastus, ed. W. H. D. Rouse, 1899 (Temple Classics).]

EUCLID

Billingsley, Sir Henry. The Elements of Geometrie of Euclide. With a very fruitfull Preface made by M[aster] J[ohn] Dee. 1570.

EUNAPIUS SARDIANUS

The Lyves, of Phylosophers and Oratours. [1579.] [From the Latin of H. Junius Hornamus.]

EURIPIDES

Gascoigne, George and Kinwelmersh, Francis. Jocasta: a Tragedie written in Greke by Euripides; translated and digested into Acte by George Gascoygne and Francis Kinwelmershe, of Grayes Inne, and there by them presented, 1566. [From the Italian adaptation of the Phoenissae by Lodovico Dolce. For edns see under Gascoigne, p. 414 above.]

Lumley, Jane, Lady. Iphigenia at Aulis. Ed. (from MS c. 1555) H. Child, Malone Soc. 1909.

EUTROPIUS

Haward, Nicholas. A briefe Chronicle, where in are described shortlye the Originall and successive estate of the Romaine weale publique. 1564.

FLORUS

[Bolton, Edmund.] The Roman Histories of Lucius Julius Florus. [1618 or 1619]; [1621?]; 1636; 1658 (corrected, amended, and with annotations by M. Casaubon).

[See also Holland under Livy.]

FRONTINUS

Morison, [Sir] Richard. The Strategemes, sleyghtes, and policies of warre. 1539.

GALEN

Gale, Thomas. Certain Workes of Galens called Methodus medendi. 1586.
[Other translators cited by H. R. Palmer are R. Copland, [1541], W. Turner, [1568], G. Baker, 1574, J. Jones, 1574, P. English, 1656.]

Greek Anthology

Turbervile, George. Epitaphes, Epigrams, Songs and Sonets. 1567; 1570; rptd J. P. Collier, [1867]. [See H. B. Lathrop, MLN. XLIII, 1928, pp. 223–9, for pieces from the Anthology.]

Kendall, Timothy. Out of Greek Epigrammes. [61 trns; in Flowers of Epigrammes, 1577.]

HELIODORUS

Underdowne, Thomas. An Æthiopian Historie. [1569?]; 1587; 1606; 1622 (rev. W. Barrett); ed. C. Whibley, 1895 (Tudor Translations); rev. F. A. Wright, 1923; ed. G. Saintsbury, 1924. [From the Latin of S. Warszewicki.]

Fraunce, Abraham. The Beginning of Heliodorus his Æthiopicall History in English Hexameters. [From Underdown. In The Countesse of Pembrokes Yvychurch, 1591.]

Lisle, William. The Faire Æthiopian. 1631; 1638. [Verse.]

[See also Sandford under Plutarch.]

HERODIAN

Smyth, Nicholas. The History of Herodian Translated into Latin by Angelus Politianus and into Englyshe, by Nicholas Smyth. [1550?]

M[axwell], J[ames]. Herodian of Alexandria his History of twenty Roman Caesars and Emperors. 1629; 1635.

Stapylton, C. B. Herodian of Alexandria his imperiall history of twenty Roman Caesars and Empcrours of his timc. Converted into an heroick Poem. 1652.

[Pts of Herodian and Suetonius were adapted in the Mirror for Magistrates. See D. Bush, Stud. Phil. XXII, 1925, pp. 256–66.]

HERODOTUS

R[ich?], B[arnabe?]. The Famous Hystory of Herodotus, Conteyning the Discourse of dyvers Countreys, the succession of theyr Kyngs. Devided into nine Bookes, entituled with the names of the nine Muses. 1584; A. Lang, 1888 (bk II only); ed. L. Whibley,

1925 (Tudor Translations, ser. 2). [Bks I and II only.]

HESIOD

Chapman, George. The Georgicks of Hesiod; Translated Elaborately out of the Greek. 1618; ed. R. H. Shepherd (The Works of Chapman, vol. III, 1875).

HIPPOCRATES

Llwyd, Humphrey. The Aphorismes of Hypocrates redacted to a certayne order. [In trn of Petrus Hispanus (Pope John XXI), The Treasury of Healthe, [1550?] (bis), 1558, 1585.]

H., S. The whole Aphorismes of Hippocrates. 1610.

Lowe, Peter. The Presages of Divine Hippocrates. 1612; 1634.

[Other trns, [1530?], 1599.]

HOMER

Hall, Arthur. Ten books of Homers Iliades, translated out of French. 1581.

Fraunce, Abraham. [Selected passages. In Arcadian Rhetorike, 1588.]

Colse, Peter. Penelopes Complaint: Or A Mirrovr for Wanton Minions. Written in English Verse. 1596; ed. A. B. Grosart, Manchester, 1880. [A free adaptation and paraphrase of some passages.]

Chapman, George. Seaven Bookes of the Iliades of Homere, Prince of Poets. Translated according to the Greke in judgement of his best Commentaries. 1598. [The bks are 1, 2, 7–11.]

—— Achilles Shield. Translated as the other seven Bookes of Homer, out of his eighteenth booke of Iliades. 1598.

—— Homer, Prince of Poets, translated according to the Greeke in twelve Bookes of his Iliads. [1610?] (re-issued 1611); ed. W. C. Taylor, 2 vols. 1843; ed. H. Morley, 1884.

—— The Iliads of Homer, Prince of Poets. Never before in any languag truely translated. With a Comment uppon some of his chiefe places. [1611]; 1612. [The first complete edn of Chapman's Iliad.]

—— The Whole Works of Homer; Prince of Poetts, in his Iliads, and Odysses. [c. 1612]; [1616?]; ed. R. Hooper, 4 vols. 1857; ed. R. H. Shepherd, 1871; rptd 2 vols. Oxford, 1931.

—— Homers Odysses [bks I–XII]. [1614?]

—— Homers Odysses [bks I–XXIV]. [1615?]

—— The Crowne of all Homers Workes, Batrachomyomachia Or the Battaile of Frogs and Mise. His Hymn's and Epigrams. [1624?]; ed. S. W. Singer, 1818; ed. R. Hooper, 1858; rptd 1904.

F[owldes], W[illiam]. The Strange, wonderfull and bloudy Battell betweene Frogs and Mise; paraphrastically done into English Heroycall Verse. 1603; 1634; ed. F. Wild, Vienna, 1918. [A freely expanded paraphrase.]

Grantham, Thomas. The First [part of the second and the third] Booke of Homer's Iliads. 1660.

Ogilby, John. Homer his Iliads. 1660.

HORACE

Evans, Lewis. The Fyrste twoo Satars or poyses of Horace. [1565.]

—— The Second Poesye of Horace. [1565.]

Drant, Thomas. A Medicinable Morall, that is, the two Bookes of Horace his Satyres, Englyshed accordyng to the prescription of Saint Hierome. 1566. [On priority of Drant's or Evans's trn see O. L. Jiriczek, Sh. Jb. LV, 1919, p. 129.]

—— Horace his Art of Poetrie, pistles and Satyrs, Englished. 1567. [Drant's prefaces and portions of text rptd by O. L. Jiriczek, in Sh. Jb. XLVII, 1911, pp. 42–68, 1919, p. 129.]

Webbe, William. [Passages from the Epistles. In A Discourse of English Poetrie, 1586, ed. J. Haslewood, Ancient Critical Essays upon English Poets and Poësy, vol. II, 1815.]

[Ashmore, John.] Certain selected Odes of Horace. 1621.

H[awkins], Sir T[homas]. Odes [and four epodes] Contayning much Morallity and sweetnesse. Selected and Translated. 1625; 1631; 1635 (Latin and English); 1638 (Latin and English); 1652.

Beaumont, Sir John. [Sixth satire of the second book, 29th Ode of the third book and second epode. In Bosworth-Field, 1629.]

Rider, Henry. All the Odes and Epodes. Translated into English verse. 1638.

Jonson, Ben. Q. Horatius Flaccus: His Art of Poetry Englished. 1640; ed. E. H. Blakeney (in Horace on the Art of Poetry, 1928).

S[mith], J[ohn]. The Lyrick Poet. Odes and Satyres. 1649. [Selections.]

[Fanshawe, Sir Richard.] Selected Parts of Horace, Prince of Lyricks. Concluding With a Piece out of Ausonius and another out of Virgil [part of Georgics, bk III]. 1652. [Latin and English.]

[Holyday, Barten.] All Horace his Lyrics or his four books of Odes and his book of Epodes. 1653. [Based on Hawkins's version.]

ISOCRATES

Elyot, Sir Thomas. The Doctrinall of Princes. [1534] (bis); [1548?]. [The Ad Nicoclem.]

[Bury, John.] Paranesis or admonytion to Demonicus, whereto is annexed [Benedict Burgh's trn, 1484, of] Cato in olde Englysh meter. 1557 (colophon 1558).

Fleming, Abraham. The Extract of Epistles out of Isocrates. [In Panoplie of Epistles, 1576.]

Forrest, Thomas. A perfite Looking Glasse of all Estates: in three Orations of Morall instructions. Translated into Lataine by Hieronimus Wulfius. 1580.

[Brinsley, John.] Admonition to Demonicus. [In Cato translated Grammatically, 1622.]

Barnes, Thomas. Archidamus, or the Councell of Warre. 1624.

JOSEPHUS

Lodge, Tho[mas]. The Famous and Memorable Workes of Josephus. Faithfully translated out of the Latin, and French. 1602; 1609; 1620; 1632 (bis); 1640; 1655–6.

Markham, Gervase and Sampson, William. The true Tragedie of Herod and Antipas. 1622 (bis). [Based on Josephus, bks XIV and XV.]

JUVENAL

B[arksted?], W. That which seemes best is worst. Exprest in a paraphrastical transcript of Juvenals tenth Satyre. With Virginias death. 1617.

Beaumont, Sir John. [Satire X. In Bosworth-Field, 1629.]

Chapman, George. A Justification Of A Strange Action of Nero; [etc.]: Also a just reproofe of a Romane smell-Feast, being the fifth Satyre of Juvenall. 1629; ed. R. H. Shepherd (The Works of Chapman, vol. III, 1875).

Biddle, John. The Two first Satyrs of Juvenal. [In Virgil's Bucolicks Englished, 1634.]

[Stapleton, Sir Robert.] The first six bookes of Juvenal. Oxford, 1644.

—— Juvenal's Sixteen Satyrs, or, A Survey of the Manners and Actions of Mankind. With Arguments, Marginall Notes, and Annotations. 1647; 1660 (as Mores Hominum).

LIVY

Bellenden, John. The First Five Books of the Roman History. Ed. (from MS c. 1533) [T. Maitland], Edinburgh, 1822; ed. W. A. Craigie, STS. 1901.

Cope, Sir Anthony. The Historie of two the most noble Captaines of the worlde, Anniball and Scipio, translated into Englishe out of Titus Livius and other authores. 1544; 1548; 1561; 1590.

Wilson, Thomas. The Hystorie of P. Sulpitius Consull. [2 pp. prefixed to his trn of Demosthenes, The Three Orations, 1570.]

P[iot], L[azarus]. [Selections. In The Orator [tr. from A. Sylvain (*i.e.* A. Van Den Busche)]: Handling a hundred severall Discourses: Some of the Arguments drawne from Titus Livius, 1596.]

Holland, Philemon. The Romane Historie written by Titus Livius of Padua. Also, the Breviaries of L. Florus. 1600; 1659.

LONGINUS

H[all], J[ohn]. ΠΕΡΙ ΥΨΟΥΣ. Or, Dionysius Longinus of the Height of Eloquence. 1652.

LONGUS

Day, Angel. Daphnis and Chloe Excellently describing the weight of affection, [etc.], finished in a Pastorall termed The Shepheards Holidaie. 1587; ed. J. Jacobs, 1890. [From the French of J. Amyot.]

Thornley, George. Daphnis and Chloe. A sweet and pleasant pastorall romance for young ladies. 1657; rptd 1893; ed. G. Saintsbury, 1923.

LUCAN

Marlowe, Christopher. Lucans first Booke, translated line for line. 1600; ed. C. F. T. Brooke (in Works of Marlowe, Oxford, 1910).

Gorges, Sir Arthur. Lucans Pharsalia. Translated into English. Whereunto is annexed the life of the Authour. 1614.

M[ay], T[homas]. Lucan's Pharsalia. 1626 (bks I–III); 1627 (complete); 1631; 1635; 1650; 1659.

Beaumont, Sir John. [Selections. In Bosworth-Field, 1629.]

LUCIAN

A dialog of the poet Lucyan, fer his fantesye faynyd for a mery pastyme. Interlocutores Menippus and Philonides. [1530?] ['Johannes Rastell me fieri fecit.' The Necromantia.]

[Elyot, Sir Thomas.] A Dialogue betwene Lucian and Diogenes of the life harde and sharpe and of the lyfe tendre and delicate. N.d.

Fletcher, Giles. Doris and Galatea. [In Licia, 1593.]

Hickes, Francis. Certaine select dialogues of Lucian, together with his true historie. Oxford, 1634; rptd 1925. [The True Historie, ed. C. Whibley, 1894; ed. J. S. Phillimore, 1927.]

Heywood, T[homas]. Pleasant Dialogues and Dramma's selected out of Lucian, Erasmus,

Textor, Ovid, etc. 1637; ed. W. Bang, Louvain, 1903 (Materialien, vol. III).

[See also Shirley under Æsop.]

LUCRETIUS

Evelyn, J[ohn]. An Essay on the first book of T. Lucretius Carus De Rerum Natura. Interpreted and Made English Verse. 1656.

AMMIANUS MARCELLINUS

Holland, Philemon. The Romane Historie. 1609.

MARTIAL

Martial to Himselfe, treating of Worldly Blessedness, in Latin, English, and Walsch. 1571. [Bk x.]

Kendall, Timothy. Epigrammes out of Martial. [In Flowers of Epigrammes, 1577.]

May, Thomas. Selected Epigrams of Martial. 1629.

Fletcher, R. Ex otio Negotium. Or, Martial his Epigrams. 1656. [Selection.]

Pecke, Thomas. Libellus de Spectaculis: Or, an Account of the Most memorable Monuments of the Romane Glory. 1659. [General title-page, Parnassi Puerperium, [etc.].]

[Pts of Martial, bk I were tr. by Sir Edward Sherburne in his Salmacis, 1651. The Earl of Surrey translated Epigram 47 (see H. H. Hudson, MLN. XXXVIII, 1923, pp. 481–3).]

POMPONIUS MELA

Golding, Arthur. The worke of Pomponius Mela. The Cosmographer, concerninge the Situation of the world. 1585; 1590 ('whereunto is added that learned worke of Julius Solinus Polyhistor').

MOSCHUS

[See under Ausonius.]

MUSÆUS

Marlowe, Christopher and Chapman, George. Hero and Leander. 1598 (*bis*); 1600; 1606; 1629; 1637. [First two sestiads by Marlowe, continuation by Chapman.]

Chapman, George. The Divine Poem of Musaeus. 1616.

Stapleton, Sir Robert. Ερωτοπαιγνιον. The Loves of Hero and Leander, Written By Musaeus. Oxford, 1645; 1647 (rev. text, with Annotations, as Musaeus on the loves of Hero and Leander; includes Leander's letter to Hero, and her answer, taken out of Ovid).

ONOSANDER

Whitehorne, Peter. Onosandro Platonico, of the Generall Captaine, and of his office. 1563. [From the Italian of Fabio Cotta.]

OVID

The flores of Ovide de arte amandi with theyr englysshe afore them: and two alphabete tablys. 1513. [Latin and English.]

H[owell?], T[homas?]. The fable of Ovid treting of Narcissus, translated into Englysh Mytre. 1560.

Peend, Thomas. The pleasant fable of Hermaphroditus and Salmacis. 1565.

Golding, Arthur. The Fyrst Fower Bookes of P. Ovidius Nasos worke, intitled Metamorphosis, translated into Englishe meter. 1565.

—— The xv Bookes of P. Ovidius Naso, entytuled Metamorphosis, translated into English meeter. 1567; 1575; 1584; 1587; 1593; 1603; 1612; ed. W. H. D. Rouse, 1904.

Turbervile, George. The Heroycall Epistles of the Learned Poet Publius Ovidius Naso, In Englishe Verse; with Aulus [Angelus] Sabinus Aunsweres to certaine of the same. 1567; [1569]; [1570?]; [1580?]; 1600; [1605]; ed. F. S. Boas, 1928.
[Helen's epistle to Paris is in John Lyly's Euphues; see M. P. Tilley, MLN. xlv, 1930, pp. 301–8.]

[Underdown, Thomas.] Ovid his Invective against Ibis. Translated into English Meeter. 1569; 1577.

[Churchyard, Thomas.] The Thre first bookes of Ovids De Tristibus. [1572]; 1578; 1580; rptd Roxburghe Club, 1816.

Marlow[e], C[hristopher]. Certaine of Ovids Elegies. Middelburg, [1590?].

—— All Ovids Elegies: 3. Bookes. Epigrams by [Sir] J[ohn] D[avies]. Middelburg, [c. 1597]; [1600?]; [1635?]; [1640?]; rptd 1925.

L., F. Ovid His Remedie of Love. Translated and Intituled to the Youth of England. 1600.

[Beaumont, Francis.] Salmacis and Hermaphroditus. 1602; rptd Shakespeare Soc. 1847.

Heywood, Thomas. Troia Britanica: or, Great Britaines Troy. 1609. [Passages from Heroides, De Arte Amandi, De Remedio Amoris.]

—— Publii Ovidii Nasonis de Arte Amandi or, The Art of Love. [1612]; Amsterdam, [1635?]; [1640?] (Heywood's trn appropriated by H. Austin). [See A. M. Clark, Library, Dec. 1922.]

—— Two Dramas: Jupiter and Io, and Apollo and Daphne. [Tr. from or founded on the two stories in the Metamorphosis. In Pleasant Dialogues and Dramma's, 1637, ed. W. Bang, Louvain, 1903 (Materialien, vol. iii).]

A[ustin], H. The Scourge of Venus: or, The wanton Lady, With the rare birth of Adonis. 1613; 1614 (bis); 1620; ed. A. B. Grosart, 1876. [Myrrha and Cinyras, Metamorphoses, bk x.]

B[rinsley], J[ohn]. Ovid's Metamorphosis Translated grammatically and also according to the propriety of our English tongue, as farre as Grammar and the verse will well beare. 1618; 1656. [Bk I, fables 1–9.]

Overbury, Sir Thomas. The first and second part of The Remedy of Love. 1620.

S[andys], G[eorge]. Ovid's Metamorphosis Englished. 1626; 1628; 1638; 1656.

—— Ovid's Metamorphosis Englished, mythologiz'd, and Represented in Figures. An essay to the Translation of Virgil's Aeneis. Oxford, 1632; 1640.

Gresham, James. The Picture of Incest. Lively portraicted in the Historie of Cinyras and Myrrha. 1626; ed. A. B. Grosart, Manchester, 1876.

Hatton, Richard. Ovid's Walnuttree transplanted. 1627.

R[eynolds], H[enry]. The Tale of Narcissus briefly Mythologised. [In Mythomystes, 1632.]

S[altonstall], W[ye]. Ovids Tristia Containinge five Bookes of mournfull Elegies. 1633; 1637.

—— Ovids Heroicall Epistles. 1636; 1639.

—— Ovid de Ponto. Containing foure books of Elegies. 1639; 1640.

[Carpenter, John.] Ovids Remedy of Love. Directing Lovers how they may by Reason suppresse the passion of Love. 1636.

Sherburne, John. Ovids Heroicall Epistles. 1639.

Catlin, Zachary. Publ. Ovid. De Tristibus: or Mournefull Elegies, in five bookes. 1639.

Gower, John. Ovids Festivalls, or Romane Calendar. Translated into English verse equinumerally. 1640.

[Hall, Thomas.] Wisdom's Conquest, Or, an explanation and grammaticall translation of the thirteenth book of Ovid's Metamorphoses. 1651.

[——] Phaetons Folly; or, the dounfal of Pride: a translation of the second book of Ovid's Metamorphosis, paraphrastically and grammatically; as a supplement to Mr. Brinslyes translation of the first book. An Essay on the first elegy of Ovid's De Tristibus. 1655.

Jones, John. Ovid's Invective or Curse against Ibis. Oxford, 1658.

[See also Stapleton under Musaeus.]

PERSIUS

Holyday, Barten. Aulus Persius Flaccus his Satires. Oxford, 1616; Oxford, 1617; 1617; 1635; 1650.

Beaumont, Sir John. The second satire of Persius. [In Bosworth-Field, 1629.]

Pervigilium Veneris
[See under Ausonius.]

PLATO

Spenser, Edw. [Edmund?] Axiochus. A most excellent Dialogue by Plato the Phylosopher: concerning the shortnesse and uncertainty of this life, with the contrary ends of the good and wicked. 1592; ed. F. M. Padelford, Baltimore, 1934.
[See also under Philippe de Mornay, p. 817 below.]

PLAUTUS

A New Enterlued for Chyldren to playe, named Jacke Jugeler. [An imitation of the Amphitruo. For edns see p. 521 above.]
W[arner], W[illiam]. Menæcmi. A pleasant comœdie. 1595; ed. W. C. H[azlitt], 1875 (in Shakespeare's Library, vol. v); ed. W. H. D. Rouse, 1911.

PLINY, THE ELDER

A[lday?], J[ohn?] A Summarie of the Antiquities, and wonders of the worlde, abstracted out of the sixtene first bookes of Plinie, translated oute of French. [1566]; 1585, 1587 (as The Secrets and wonders of the world). [From the French version of P. de Changy.]
Holland, Philemon. The Historie of the World. Commonly called, The Naturall Historie. 2 vols. 1601; 2 vols. 1634 (re-issued 1635).

PLINY, THE YOUNGER

Fleming, Abraham. Extract of Epistles out of C. Plinius and others. [In Panoplie of Epistles, 1576.]
Stapleton, Sir Robert. Pliny's Panegyricke: publike thankes to the Emperour Trajan. Oxford, 1644.

PLUTARCH

Wyatt, Sir Thomas. Tho. wyatis translatyon of Plutarches boke of the Quyete of mynde. [1528]; ed. facs. C. R. Baskervill, Cambridge, U.S.A. 1931
The governaunce of good helthe, Erasmus beynge interpretoure. [1530?]
Practica Plutarche the excellent Phylosopher. [1530?] [Extracts; medical prescriptions.]
[Elyot, Sir Thomas?] Howe one may take profite of his enmyes. [1533?]; [1550?] (with the Tables of Cebes).
Elyot, Sir Thomas. The Education or bringinge up of children. [1535?]

[Hales, John.] The preceptes of the excellent clerke & grave philosopher Plutarche for the preservation of good Healthe. 1543.
Sandford, James. The Amorous and Tragicall Tales of Plutarch. Whereunto is annexed the Hystorie of Cariclea and Theagenes and the Sayings of the Greeke Philosophers. 1567.
Grant, Edward. A President for Parentes translated and partly augmented by Ed. Grant. 1571; Cambridge, 1595.
North, Sir Thomas. The Lives of the noble Grecians and Romanes; translated into French by J. Amyot. 1579; 1595; 1603; 1612; 1631; 1657; Shakespeare's Plutarch, ed. W. W. Skeat, Oxford, 1875; ed. G. Wyndham, 6 vols. 1895 (Tudor Translations); ed. C. F. T. Brooke, 2 vols. 1909; rptd 8 vols. Oxford, 1928; 5 vols. 1929–30. [Lives of Epaminodas and Philip of Macedon, etc. 1602, incorporated in 1603 and subsequent edns, which contain also more lives from Æmylius Probus.]
Blundeville, Thomas. Three Morall Treatises. The Learned Prince: The Fruites of Foes: The Port of Rest. 1580.
Clapham, John. A Philosophical Treatise concerning the quietness of the mind. 1589. [From the French of Amyot.]
Inimicus amicus; an excellent treatise shewing how a man may reape profit by his enemy. 1601.
Holland, Philemon. The Philosophie, commonlie called, the Morals. 1603; 1657; ed. J. Jacobs, 1888; ed. F. B. Jevons, 1892; ed. (in part) E. H. Blakeney, [1911] (Everyman's Lib.)

[See also under Cebes and Diodorus Siculus, and Queen Elizabeth's Englishings of Boethius, Plutarch, etc., ed. C. Pemberton, 1899.]

POLYBIUS

W[atson], C[hristopher]. The Hystories of the most famous and worthy Cronographer Polybius. 1568. [Bk I only.]
Grimstone, Edward. The History of Polybius the Megalopolitan according to the Greeke Originall. 1633; 1634 (bis).
[Raleigh, Sir Walter.] A Notable and Memorable Story of the cruel war between the Carthaginians and their own Mercenaries. Gathered out of Polybius and other authors. 1647. [From The History of the World, bk v, ch. 2.]

PROCLUS

Salesbury, William. The Descripcion of the Sphere or Frame of the worlde. [1550.] [From the Latin version of Thomas Linacre.]

SALLUST

Barclay, Alexander. Here begynneth the famous cronycle of the warre against Jugurth. [1520?] (*bis*). [Rptd with Thomas Paynell's trn of C. Felicius, The Conspiracie of Catiline, 2 vols. 1557.]

[Heywood, Thomas.] The Two most worthy and Notable Histories, viz. The Conspiracie of Cateline and The Warre which Jugurth for many yeares maintained. 1608; ed. C. Whibley, 1924 (Tudor Translations, ser. 2.).

[Crosse, William.] The Workes of Caius Crispus Salustius. 1629.

SENECA

Whittington, Robert. L. A. Senecae ad Gallionem de Remediis Fortuitorum. The remedyes agaynst all casuall chaunces. Dialogus inter sensum et rationem. A Dialogue between Sensualyte and Reason. 1547. [Latin and English.]

Heywood, Jasper. The Sixt Tragedie of the most grave and prudent author, Lucius, Anneus, Seneca, entituled Troas. 1559 (*bis*); [1560?].

—— The Seconde Tragedie of Seneca entituled Thyestes. 1560.

—— Lucii Annei Senecæ Tragedia prima qui inscribitur Hercules Furens. The first Tragedie of Lucius Anneus Seneca, intituled Hercules Furens. 1561. [Latin and English.]

[Heywood's 3 trns were ed. H. de Vocht, Louvain, 1913 (W. Bang's Materialen zur Kunde des älteren englischen Dramas, vol. XLI). On Troas see W. W. Greg, Library, XI, 1930, pp. 162–70.]

Neville, Alexander. The Lamentable Tragedie of Œdipus the Sonne of Laius. 1563.

Studley, John. The Eyght Tragedie of Seneca, entituled Agamemnon. 1566.

—— The seventh Tragedie of Seneca, Entitled Medea. 1566. [Studley's Agamemnon and Medea were ed. E. M. Spearing, Louvain, 1913 (W. Bang's Materialen zur Kunde des älteren englischen Dramas, vol. XXXVIII).]

N[uce], T[homas]. The ninth Tragedie of Lucius Anneus Seneca, called Octavia. [1566.]

A[ggas?], E[dward?]. [Selections from the philosophical works. No title-page. 1577? Bound with P. de Mornay. Excellent Discours de la Vie et de la Mort, 1581. See M. St C. Byrne, Library, IV, 1924, pp. 277–85.]

Golding, Arthur. The woorke of the excellent Philosopher Lucius Annæus Seneca concerning Benefyting. 1578.

Newton, Thomas *et al.* Seneca his tenne Tragedies, translated [by J. Heywood, A. Neville, J. Studley, T. Nuce and T. Nenton]. 1581; ed. T. S. Eliot, 2 vols. 1927 (Tudor Translations, ser. 2).

Lodge, Thomas. The Workes of Lucius Annæus Seneca, Both Morrall and Naturall. 1614; 1620; 1632. [With a life of Seneca by J. Lipsius. On Benefits, rptd W. H. D. Rouse, 1899 (Temple Classics).]

'Philophrastes' (Sir Ralph Freeman). Lucius Annæus Seneca, the Philosopher, his booke of Consolation to Marcia. Translated into an English poem. 1635.

[Freeman, Sir Ralph.] Lucius Annæus Seneca, the Philosopher: his Booke of the Shortnesse of Life. Translated into an English poem. 1636; 1663.

S[herburne], [Sir] E[dward]. Medea: a Tragedie. 1648.

—— Seneca's Answer to Lucilius his Quære; why Good Men suffer misfortunes, seeing there is a Divine Providence. Translated into English verse. 1648.

Prestwich, Edmund. Hippolitus. Translated out of Seneca. With other Poems of the same Author. 1651.

P[ordage], S[amuel]. Troades Englished (with comments annexed). 1660.

[See also under P. de Mornay, p. 817 below.]

SOPHOCLES

W[ase], C[hristopher]. Electra. 2 pts, Hague, 1649.

STATIUS

S[tephens], T[homas]. An Essay upon Statius; or, the five first books of P. Papinius Statius, his Thebais. 1648. [See J. M., GM. XXXIII, 1850, pp. 35–40, and A. Sparke, N. & Q. 23 April 1927, p. 302.]

Howard, Sir Robert. Achilleis. [In Poems, 1660.]

SUETONIUS

Holland, Philemon. The Historie of twelve Caesars. 1606; ed. C. Whibley, 1899 (Tudor Translations); ed. J. H. Freese, [1923]. [See also under Herodian.]

TACITUS

[Savile, Sir Henry.] The Ende of Nero and Beginning of Galba. Fower bookes of the Histories of Cornelius Tacitus. The Life of Agricola. Oxford, 1591; 1598; 1604; 1612; 1622; 1640.

[Grenewey, Richard.] The Annales of Cornelius Tacitus. The Description of Germanie. 1598; 1604; 1612; 1622; 1640. [Pbd as pt 2 of Savile's trn.]

TERENCE

Terens in englysh. Andria. [1520?] [English with Latin in margin.]

Udall, Nicholas. Floures for Latine Spekynge selected and gathered out of Terence. 1533; 1538; 1560.

Udall, Nicholas and Higgins, J[ohn]. Flowers or eloquent phrases of the Latine speach gathered out of al the sixe Comœdies of Terence wherof those of the first thre were selected by Nicolas Udall. And those of the latter three by J. Higgins. 1575; 1581.

Kyffin, Maurice. Andria, the first Comœdie of Terence. 1588.

B[ernard], R[ichard]. Terence in English. Cambridge, 1598, 1607; 1614; 1629; 1641. [Latin and English. Each edn 'much amended.']

Newman, Thomas. The two first comedies of Terence called Andria and the Eunuch Fitted for schollers Private action in their Schooles. 1627.

Webbe, [George]. The first comedy of Pub. Terentius called Andria, or the Woman of Andros. English and Latine. Claused for such as would write or speake the pure Language of this Author, especially after the Method of Dr. Webbe. 1629.

—— The Second Comedie of Pub. Terentius called Eunuchus, English and Latine. The uses whereof the Reader may finde in the Epistle before the first Comedie. 1629.

THEOCRITUS

Sixe Idillia; that is, sixe small, or petty poems. Oxford, 1588; rptd 1922. [Rptd E. Arber, English Garner, vol. VIII, 1896, and in A. H. Bullen's Some Longer Elizabethan Poems, 1903. See O. L. Jiriczek, Sh. Jb. LV, 1919, pp. 30–4.]

Bradshaw, Thomas. The Shepherds Starre, Now of late merveilous orient in the East. 1591. [A paraphrase on the third idyll of Theocritus, in dialogue form.]

Sherburne, Sir Edward. The Penitent Murderer; The Shepherd. [Idylls 31 and 21, in Salmacis, 1651.]

THEOPHRASTUS

[See under Epictetus.]

THUCYDIDES

Nicolls, Thomas. The hystory writtone by Thucidides the Athenyan. 1550. [From the French of C. de Seyssel.]

History. Translated into Englishe. 1607.

Hobbes, Thomas. Eight Bookes of the Peloponnesian Warre. 1629; 1634; ed. Sir W. Molesworth and W. B. Whittaker, 1845. [The Funeral Oration rptd 1929.]

TROGUS POMPEIUS

[Norton, Thomas.] Orations, of Arsanes agaynst Philip the trecherous kyng of Macedone. [1560?] [First and third oration from Justin's Epitome.]

Golding, Arthur. Thabridgment of the Histories of Trogus Pompeius, collected and wrytten by Justine. 1564; 1570 ('corrected'); 1578.

W[ilkins], G[eorge]. The Historie of Justine. Whereunto is added a briefe collection of the lives and manners of all the Emperours unto Rudulphus now raigning. 1606.

Codrington, Robert. The History of Justine, taken out of the four and forty books of Trogus Pompeius. 1654.

VEGETIUS

Sadler, John. The Four bookes of Flavius Vegetius Renatus of Martiall policye. 1572.

VIRGIL

Howard, Henry (Earl of Surrey). Certain bokes [i.e. II and IV] of Virgiles Æneis turned into English meter. 1557; rptd Roxburghe Club, 1814; ed. F. M. Padelford (Poems of Surrey, Seattle, 1920); ed. H. Hartman, Oxford, 1933 (bk IV only).

Phaer, Thomas. The seven first bookes of the Eneidos of Virgill, converted in Englishe meter. 1558.

—— The nyne fyrst Bookes of the Eneidos with so much of the tenthe Booke as coulde be founde. 1562.

Phaer, Thomas and Twyne, Thomas. The whole XII. Bookes of the Æneidos of Virgill. Whereof the first IX. and part of the tenth were converted into English meeter by Thomas Phaer, and the residue supplied by Thomas Twyne. There is added Virgils life out of Donatus. 1573; 1584 (adds as 13th bk the supplement by Twyne of Maphaeus Vegius); 1596; 1600; 1607; 1620.

Fleming, Abraham. The Bucolikes drawne into Englishe verse for verse. 1575.

F[leming], A[braham]. The Bucoliks of Publius Virgilius Maro. Together with his Georgiks conteyning foure bookes. 1589.

Stanyhurst, Richard. The first foure bookes of Virgil his Aeneis translated intoo English heroicall Verse. Leyden, 1582; 1583; 1600; rptd E. Arber, 1880.

[Fraunce, Abraham?] The Lamentation of Corydon, for the love of Alexis, verse for verse out of Latine. [In The Lawiers Logike, 1588, and in The Countesse of Pembrokes Yvychurch, 1591.]

Spenser, Edmund. Virgils Gnat. [In Complaints, 1591.]

[Brinsley, John.] Virgils Eclogues, with his Booke De Apibus. 1620; 1633.

Wroth, Sir Thomas. The Destruction of Troy, or the Acts of Aeneas. Translated out of the second booke of the Æneads, Latine and English. Also a centurie of Epigrams and a Motto upon the Creede. 1620.

Didos death [Æneid, bk IV]. Translated By one that hath no name. 1622.

P[enkethman], J[ohn]. The Epigrams of P. Virgilius Maro, and others. 1624.

L[isle], W[illiam]. Virgils Eclogues translated into English. 1628.

May, Tho[mas]. Virgil's Georgicks Englished. 1628.

Beaumont, Sir John. [Translations from Virgil's fourth Eclogue. In Bosworth-Field, 1629.]

Vicars, John. The XII Aeneids of Virgil Translated into English deca-syllables. 1632.

Sandys, George. The first Booke of Virgils Æneis. [In Ovid's Metamorphosis, Oxford, 1632, London, 1640.]

Biddle, John. Virgil's Bucolicks Englished Whereunto is added the Translation of the two first Satyrs of Juvenal. 1634.

Stapleton, Sir Robert. Dido and Aeneas. The Fourth Booke of Virgils Aeneis now Englished. [1634.]

[Denham, Sir John.] The Destruction of Troy, an essay upon the second book of Virgils Æneis. Written 1636. 1656. [Rptd in Denham's Works, 1668, etc.; ed. T. H. Banks, New Haven, 1928.]

Ogilby, John. The Works of Publius Virgilius Maro. 1649; 1650; 1654.

Fanshawe, Sir Richard. The Fourth Book of the Aeneid on the loves of Dido and Aeneas done into English. 1652; ed. A. L. Irvine, Oxford, 1924. [Spenserian stanzas.]

Harrington, Sir John. An essay upon two of Virgil's Eclogues and two books of his Aeneis. 1658. [Eclogues 1 and 9, Aeneid bks 1 and 2.]

—— Virgil's Aeneis. 1659. [Bks 3–6.]

[Howard, Sir Robert.] The fourth book of Virgill: of the loves of Dido and Aeneas. [In Poems, 1660.]

[See also Fanshawe under Horace. For Gavin Douglas's version of the Aeneid see pp. 259–60 above.]

XENOPHON

Hervet, Gentian [and Lupset, Thomas]. Xenophons Treatise of Householde. 1532; 1537; 1544; [after 1547]; 1557; 1573.

Barker, William. The Bookes of Xenophon, contayning the discipline, schole, and education of Cyrus. [1560?] (6 bks); 1567 ('the VIII bookes').

Bingham, John. The Historie of Xenophon: containing The Ascent of Cyrus into the higher countries and retrait from thence. 1623.

Holland, Philemon. Cyrupaedia. The Institution and Life of Cyrus. 1632; rptd 1936.

[See also under Grisone, p. 814 below.]

B. TRANSLATIONS FROM MEDIAEVAL AND CONTEMPORARY AUTHORS

ÆNEAS SILVIUS

[See E. S. Piccolomini.]

CORNELIUS AGRIPPA

Clapham, David. The Commendation of Matrimony. 1540; 1545.

—— A Treatise of the Nobilitie of Woman Kynde. 1542.

Barker, William. The Nobility of Women. Ed. (from MS dated 1559) R. W. Bond, 2 vols. Roxburghe Club, 1904–5. [From Lodovico Domenichi, but based on Agrippa.]

San[ford], Ja[mes]. Henrie Cornelius Agrippa, of the Vanitie and uncertaintie of Artes and Sciences. 1569; 1575.

F[reake?], J. Three books of occult philosophy. 1651; ed. W. F. Whitehead, Chicago, 1898.

C., H. [Henry Care or Hugh Crompton?]. The Glory of Women. Translated into prose but now turned into English heroicall verse. 1652.

Fleetwood, Edward. The Glory of Women. 1652.

Turner, Robert. Henry Cornelius Agrippa His Fourth Book Of Occult Philosophy. 1655. [With several other works on magic.]

LEON BATTISTA ALBERTI

Hecatonphila. The Art of Love or Love discovered in an hundred severall kinds. 1598.

MATEO ALEMÁN

[Mabbe, James.] The Rogue: or the Life of Guzman de Alfarache. 1622 (re-issued 1623); 2 pts, Oxford, 1630; 3 pts, 1634; 2 pts, 1656; ed. J. Fitzmaurice-Kelly, 4 vols. 1924 (Tudor Translations, ser. 2).

ALESSIO (*i.e.* GIROLAMO RUSCELLI?)

Ward, William. The Secretes of the reverende Mayster Alexis of Piemount, Conteinyng Remedies agaynst diseases. Pt 1: 1558; 1559; 1562; 1568; 1580; 1615. Pt 2: 1560; 1563; [1568?]; [1580]; 1614. Pt 3: 1562; 1566; 1578; 1614. [From French.]

Androse, Richard. A verye excellent Booke. The fourth and finall booke of secretes. 1569; 1578; 1614.

Amadis of Gaul

Paynell, Thomas. The Treasurie of Amadis of Fraunce. [1567 or 1573?] [On identity of the translator, see H. Salter and A. F. Pollard, TLS. 12, 26 Feb., 12 March 1931.]

[Munday, Anthony.] The First Book of Amadis of Gaule. [1590–2?] The Second Booke of Amadis de Gaula. 1595. 4 pts, 1619–8. [Bk II of this trn is by Lazarus Piot, but it is uncertain whether Lazarus Piot, or Pyott, was merely a pseudonym of Munday's. On this see M. St C. Byrne, Anthony Munday and his Books, Library, I, 1921.]

Kirkman, Francis. The famous and renowned history of Amadis de Gaula. Being the sixt Part never before Published. [1652.]

ARETINO

[See L. Bruni.]

ARIOSTO

Gascoigne, George. Supposes: a comedie. [1573] (in A Hundreth sundrie Flowres); [1575] (in The posies of George Gascoygne); 1587 (in The whole workes of George Gascoygne); ed. J. W. Cunliffe, Boston, 1906, Cambridge, U.S.A. 1907; ed. R. W. Bond (in Early Plays from the Italian, Oxford, 1911). [Performed at Gray's Inn, 1566.]

Harington, Sir John. Orlando Furioso in English Heroical Verse. 1591; 1607; 1634 (with Harington's Epigrams).

T[ofte], R[obert]. Two tales translated out of Ariosto. 1597.

[——] Ariosto's Satyres, in seven famous discourses. By Gervis Markham [really Tofte]. 1608; 1611.

[5 nos. of Musica Transalpina, 1588, are trns of stanzas in Orlando Furioso. See E. G. Ainsworth, RES. VII, 1931, pp. 327–30.]

SAINT AUGUSTINE

Paynell, Thomas. Twelve sermons. N.d.

Lesse, Nicholas. A Worke of the Predestination of Saints. Item, Of the vertue of perseveraunce to thend. 1550.

Scory, John. Two bokes of the noble doctor and B. S. Augustine of the Predestinacion of saintes, thother perseveraunce unto thende. [Emden, 1556?]

Certaine select Prayers, gathered out of S. Augustines Meditations. Also his manuell or booke of the Contemplation of Christ. 1574; 1575; 1577; 1585; 1586.

Rogers, Thomas. A Pretious Booke of Heavenlie Meditations. Whereunto is annexed Saint Augustines Psalter. 1581; 1600; 1612; 1616; 1629; 1640.

—— A right Christian treatise entituled S. Augustines praiers. 1581; 1591; 1600; 1604.

H[ealey], J[ohn]. St. Augustine, Of the Citie of God. 1610; 1620.

[Matthew, Sir Tobie.] The Confessions of the incomparable doctour S. Augustine. [St Omer,] 1620; 1638.

Batt, Antony. A Heavenly Treasure of Comfortable Meditations and Prayers. 1624.

[Floyd, John.] The Meditations. Paris, 1631.

Watts, William. Saint Augustines Confessions. 1631; Paris, 1638.

The Kernell or Extract of the historicall part of S. Augustins Confessions. Paris, 1638.

[Woodhead, Abraham.] The Life of S. Augustine. The first part. Written by himself in the first ten books of his Confessions. 1660.

LUIS DE ÁVILA Y ZÚÑIGA

[Wilkinson, John.] The Comentaries of Don Lewes de Avela and Suniga which treateth of the great wars in Germany, made by Charles the fifth. 1555.

FRANCIS BACON

[See p. 869 below.]

JEAN LOUIS GUEZ DE BALZAC

T[irwhyt], W[illiam]. The Letters of Monsieur De Balzac. 1634; 1638.

Baker, Sir Richard. New Epistles of Monsieur De Balzac, being the second and third volumes. 2 vols. 1638.

—— Letters of Mounseur de Balzac. 1, 2, 3, and 4th parts. Now collected into One Volume. 1654 (engraved title, 1655). [Includes the 2 previous items.]

G., H. The Prince. 1648.

Balzac's remaines; or, his last letters. 1658.

W., R. Aristippus; or, M. de Balsac's Masterpiece; being a discourse concerning the Court. 1659.

BANDELLO

Br[oke], Ar[thur]. The Tragicall Historye of Romeus and Juliet, written in Italian by Bandell. 1562; ed. J. J. Munro, 1908. [A poem, through the French version of Boiastuau, 1559.]

Fenton, Sir Geoffrey. Certaine Tragicall Discourses written oute of Frenche and Latin. 1567; 1579; ed. R. L. Douglas, 1898 (Tudor Translations); ed. R. L. Douglas and H. Harris, 1924. [From Belleforest's and Boiastuau's French version.]

[Achelly], T[homas]. Violenta and Didaco. Translated into English Meter. 1576.

[See also under Boccaccio.]

JOHN BARCLAY

Long, Kingsmill. Barclay his Argenis translated out of Latine. 1625; 1636. [The verses tr. by Thomas May.]

Le Grys, Sir Robert and May, Thomas. John Barclay his Argenis translated, the prose by Sir Robert Le Grys and the verses by Thomas May. 1629.

M[ay], Th[omas]. The Mirrour of Mindes. 2 pts, 1631; 1633.

[Man, Judith.] An Epitome of the history of faire Argenis and Polyarchus put into French by N. Coeffeteau. 1640.

BEDE

Stapleton, Thomas. The History of the Church of Englande. Translated out of Latin. Antwerp, 1565; St Omer, 1622, 1626; ed. P. Hereford, Oxford, 1930.

BEZA

G[olding], A[rthur]. A Tragedie Of Abrahams Sacrifice. 1577; ed. M. W. Wallace, Toronto, 1906.

[Among the translators of various others of Beza's works were R[obert] F[yll], T. W[ilcox], I. S., J. Fielde, T. S[tocker], A. Gilbie, A. Golding, J. Stockwood, [J. Penry].]

BIDPAI

North, Sir Thomas. The Moral Philosophie of Doni: drawne out of the auncient writers. First compiled in the Indian tongue, and now Englished out of the Italian. 1570; 1601; ed. J. Jacobs, 1888.

BOCCACCIO

Elyot, Sir Thomas. The boke named the Governour. 1531. [For rpts see p. 670 above. Bk II, ch. xii is a trn of Boccaccio's Titus and Gisippus.]

C., T. A pleasant and delightful history of Galesus, Cymon and Iphigenia. [1560?]

G[rantham], H. A pleasaunt disport of divers noble personages entitled Philocopo. [1566?]; 1571; 1587; ed. E. Hutton, 1927.

T., C. A notable historye of Nastagio and Traversari. 1569. [In verse.]

[Young, Bartholomew.] Amorous Fiammetta. Done into English by B. Giovano del M. Temp. 1587; ed. E. Hutton, 1926; ed. K. H. Josling, 1929.

The Decameron, containing an hundred pleasant novels. 2 vols. 1620; 1625 (vol. I only, as The Modell of Wit Preserved to posterity by John Boccaccio); 1634; 2 pts, 1657–5; ed. E. Hutton, 4 vols. 1909 (Tudor Translations). [The first complete trn.]

BOCCACCIO AND BANDELLO

Turbervile, George. Tragical Tales, translated by Turbervile, in time of his troubles. 1576; rptd Edinburgh, 1837. [7 by Boccaccio; 2 by Bandello.]

[Versions of Boccaccio's tales may be found in other collections, such as Painter's Palace of Pleasure and H. C.'s Forest of Fancy, [1579].]

BOCCALINI

[Florio, John and Vaughan, William.] The New-Found Politicke. 1626. [See M. W. Croll, MLN. XXXIV, 1919.]

[Carey], Henry (Earl of Monmouth). I Ragguagli di Parnasso, or Advertisements from Parnassus, in two centuries, with the Politick Touch-Stone. 1656.

JACOB BOEHME

[For trns of Boehme's writings, 1645–50, see p. 336 above.]

BOETHIUS

Colvile, George. Boetius de Consolationae Philosophiae. The boke of Boecius, called the comforte of philosophye. 1556; ed. E. B. Bax, 1897. [Latin and English.]

T., J. Five Bookes, of philosophicall comfort. 1609; ed. H. F. Stewart and E. K. Rand, 1918 (Loeb Classical Lib.) [On J. T., see C. B. Dolson and W. E. Houghton, AJ. Phil. XLII, 1921, p. 266, LI, 1930, pp. 243–50.]

M., S. E. Boethius de Consolatione Anglo-Latine expressus per S. M. E. [for S. E. M.]. 1654. [Contains the life of Boethius from P. Bertius and J. M. Rota. On the identity of the translator (probably Edward Spencer) see W. E. Houghton, RES. VII, 1931, pp. 160–7.]

[See also Queen Elizabeth's Englishings of Boethius, Plutarch, etc. ed. C. Pemberton, 1899.]

BOIARDO

T[ofte], R[obert]. Orlando Innamorato. The three first Bookes done into English heroicall Verse. 1598.

SEBASTIAN BRANT

[See p. 336 above.]

LEONARDO BRUNI (ARETINO)

Golding, A[rthur]. The Historie of Leonard Aretino, concerning the Warres betwene the Imperialles and Gothes for the possession of Italy. 1563.

JOHN CAIUS

Fleming, Abraham. Of Englishe Dogges. 1576; rptd E. Arber (in An English Garner, pt III, 1880); ed. E. S. Roberts, Cambridge, 1912 (in Works of Caius).

CALVIN

[Coverdale, Miles]. A faythful and moste Godly Treatyse concernynge the Sacrament. [1549?] [2 edns, n.d.]

N[orton], T[homas]. The Institution of Christian Religion. 1561; 1562; 1574; 1578; 1580; 1582; 1587; 1599; 1611; 1634.

Fetherstone, Christopher. An abridgement of
the Institution of Christian religion. By
W. Lawne. Edinburgh, 1585; [Edinburgh?]
1586; [Edinburgh?] 1587.

[Among the translators of various others of
Calvin's works were: G. G[ylby], H. Holland,
T. Tymme, [W. Fulke?], C. Cotton, E. P[aget],
C. Rosdell, R. V[aux], N. B., W. H., T. Stocker,
A. Golding, [R. G.], T. Broke, J. Fielde, L.
T[homson], [A. L.], J. H[armer], W. Warde,
A. M[unday], S. Wythers.]

CAMDEN

[See p. 827 below.]

CAMOENS

Fanshawe, Sir Richard. The Lusiad, Or,
Portugals Historicall Poem. 1655.

GIROLAMO CARDANO

Bedingfield, Thomas. Cardanus Comforte.
1573; 1576 ('corrected and augmented').

GIOVANNI DELLA CASA

Peterson, Robert. Galateo of Maister John
Della Casa. 1576; ed. H. J. Reid, 1892; ed.
J. E. Spingarn, Boston, 1914.

H[awkins], F[rancis]. Youth's Behavior or
Decency in Conversation among men.
1646 (4th edn); 1651; 1654. [An epitome of
the Galateo. See M. P. Tilley, Romanic
Rev. IX, 1918, pp. 309–12.]

MATHIAS CASIMIR

[See p. 328 above.]

CASTIGLIONE

Hoby, [Sir] Thomas. The Courtyer. 1561;
1577; 1588; 1603; ed. Sir W. Raleigh, 1900
(Tudor Translations); ed. W. H. D. Rouse,
[1928] (Everyman's Lib.).

GIROLAMO CATANEO

G[rantham?], H[enry?] Most Briefe Tables to
knowe redily how many ranckes of foote-
men armed with Corslettes, as unarmed, go
to the making of a just battayle. 1574;
[1588]. [Ptd with Macchiavelli's Arte of
Warre.]

Celestina

[Rastell, John.] A new comodye in englysh
in maner Of an enterlude [of Calisto and
Melebea]. [c. 1527]; rptd Malone Soc. 1908;
ed. H. W. Allen (with Mabbe's trn of
Celestina, 1923). [An adaptation of a section
of Celestina.]

[Mabbe, James.] The Spanish Bawd, represented in Celestina, or the tragicke-comedy
of Calisto and Melibea. 1631; ed. J. Fitzmaurice-Kelly, 1894 (Tudor Translations);
ed. H. W. Allen, 1923.

CERVANTES

[Shelton, Thomas.] The History of the
Valorous and Wittie Knight-Errant Don
Quixote of the Mancha. Pt 1 : 1612; [1620?].
Pt 2: 1620; 1652. Both pts: ed. J. Fitz-
maurice-Kelly, 4 vols. 1896 (Tudor Trans-
lations); ed. F. J. H. Darton, 2 vols. 1923.

The Travels of Persiles and Sigismunda. 1619.
[Dedication signed M. L.]

[Mabbe, James.] Exemplarie novells. 1640;
1654 (as Delight in Severall Shapes); rptd
1928 (The Spanish Ladie and Two Other
Stories).

ALAIN CHARTIER

Delectable demaundes and pleasaunt Questions, with their several aunswers in matters
of Love. [1566]; 1596.

CINTHIO

[See G. B. Giraldi.]

MATTHIEU COIGNET

Hoby, Sir Edward. Politique discourses
upon trueth and lying. 1586.

GUIDO DELLE COLONNE

Paynell, Thomas. The faythfull and true
Storye of the destruction of Troye. 1553.

PHILIPPE DE COMINES

[Danett, Thomas.] The Historie of Philip de
Commines. 1596; 1601; 1614; ed. C.
Whibley, 2 vols. 1897 (Tudor Translations).

B., R. An Epitome of all the lives of the kings
of France. 1639.

GIROLAMO CONESTAGGIO

[Blount, Edward.] The Historie of the
Uniting of the Kingdom of Portugall to the
Crowne of Castill. 1600.

GASPARO CONTARINI

Lewkenor, Sir Lewis. The Common-wealth
and Government of Venice. 1599.

PIERRE CORNEILLE

Rutter, Joseph. The Cid, a tragicomedy.
1637.

Lower, Sir William. Polyeuctes, or The
Martyr. 1655.

—— Horatius: a Roman Tragedie. 1656.

CLAUDIO CORTE

[Bedingfield, Thomas.] The Art of Riding.
1584.

MARTÍN CORTÉS

Eden, Richard. The Arte of Navigation.
1561; 1572; 1579; 1584; 1589; 1596 (corrected and augmented by John Tapp),
1609, 1615.

CYRANO DE BERGERAC

Satyrical Characters and handsome Descriptions in letters written to severall persons of quality. 1658.
St Serf, Sir Thomas. Σεληναρχια, or the Government of the World in the Moon. 1659; ed. C. H. Page, New York, 1899.

FRIEDRICH DEDEKIND

F., R. The Schoole of Slovenrie: or Cato turned wrong side outward. 1605; rptd Berlin, 1904.

DESCARTES

A Discourse of a method for the well guiding of reason. 1649.
The Passions of the Soule. In three Books. 1650.
[Brouncker, William, Viscount.] Renatus Des-Cartes Excellent Compendium of Musick. 1653.

PHILIPPE DESPORTES

M[arkham], G[ervase]. Rodomonths Infernall, or the Divell conquered. Ariostos conclusions Paraphrastically translated. [1607.]

DU BARTAS

[See G. de Saluste du Bartas.]

GUILLAUME DU BELLAY

Ive, Paul. Instructions for the Warres. 1580.

JOACHIM DU BELLAY

[Trns from Du Bellay by Edmund Spenser appear in van der Noodt's Theatre, 1569, and in his own Complaints, 1591, as Visions of Bellay and Ruines of Rome.]

ERASMUS

[For the English trns from Erasmus see p. 665 above.]

HENRI ESTIENNE

A mervaylous Discourse upon the Lyfe, deedes, and behaviour of Katherine de Medicis. Heydelberge [London?], 1575; Cracow, 1576.
N[orth], G[eorge]. The Stage of Popish Toyes. Compiled by G. N. 1581.
C[arew?], R. A World of Wonders. 1607 (re-issued Edinburgh, 1608).

FROISSART

Bourchier, John (Baron Berners). The first [second] volume of sir Johan Froyssart: of the cronycles of England, Fraunce, Spayne. 2 vols. 1523–5; [1545]; ed. W. P. Ker, 6 vols. 1901–3 (Tudor Translations); rptd 8 vols. Oxford, 1927–8. [See G. Schleich, Archiv, CLXVI, 1934, pp. 18–25.]

Golding, Pe[te]r. An Epitome of Frossard, compiled by J. Sleydane. 1608; 1611.

FEDERICO FURIO CERIOL

Blundeville, Thomas. A very briefe and profitable Treatise declaring howe many counsells a prince ought to have. [1570.]

ROBERT GARNIER

[See p. 333 above.]

GIOVANNI BATTISTA GELLI

Iden, Henry. Circes. 1557; [1558–9].
Barker, William. The Fearful Fancies of the Florentine Cooper. 1568; 1599.

INNOCENT GENTILLET

Bowes, Sir Jerome. An Apology or defence for Christians of Fraunce which are of the Evangelicall religion. 1579.
Patrick, Simon. A discourse upon the meanes of wel governing a Kingdome against Nicholas Machiavell. 1602; 1608.

CONRAD GESNER

Morwyng, Peter. The Treasure of Evonymus: conteyninge the wonderfull hid secretes of nature. [1559]; 1565.
Baker, George. The newe Jewell of Health. 1576.
—— The practise of the new and old phisicke. 1599.
Topsell, Edward. The Historie of the Foure-Footid Beastes. 1607; 1658.

GIOVANNI BATTISTA GIRALDI (CINTHIO)

[Bryskett, Lodowick.] A Discourse of Civill Life. 1606. [Adaptation.]
[Trns and adaptations of various tales from Gli Hecatommithi of Cinthio appear in the Elizabethan story books by Barnabe Rich, George Whetstone, Brian Melbancke, and others.]

REGINALDUS GONSALVIUS MONTANUS

[Skinner, Vincent.] A Discovery and playne declaration of sundry subtill practices of the Holy Inquisition of Spayne. 1568; 1569; 1625.

POPE GREGORY I

Lyfe of S. Gregorys mother. 1515; [Canterbury, 1549?].
W[oodewarde], P[hilippe]. The Dialogues of S. Gregorie. Paris, 1608; ed. E. G. Gardner, 1911.
The second booke of the dialogues. 1638.

PIERRE GRINGOIRE (VAUDEMONT)

Barclay, Alexander. The Castell of Labour. Paris, [1503?]; [1505?]; 1506 (bis); ed. A. W. Pollard, Roxburghe Club, 1905.

FEDERICO GRISONE

[Blundeville, Thomas.] A newe booke containing the arte of ryding and breakinge greate Horses. [1560?] [Adapted and abridged.]

Astley, John. The Art of Riding out of Xenophon and Gryson Verie expert and excellent horssemen. 1584.

HUGO GROTIUS

[See p. 327 above.]

GIOVANNI BATTISTA GUARINI

[Dymock, Edward.] Il Pastor Fido or the faithfull Shepheard. 1602; 1633.

Sidnam, Jonathan. The Faithfull Sheapheard. [Written 1630. BM. Add. MS 29493.]

Fanshawe, Sir Richard. Il Pastor Fido, the faithfull Shepheard. With an addition of divers other Poems. 1648. [Separate title-page of Pastor Fido dated 1647.]

STEFANO GUAZZO

Pettie, George. The Civile Conversation of M. Steeven Guazzo. 1581 (3 bks, from the French of G. Chapping); 1586 (adds bk iv, tr. from the Italian by Bartholomew Young); ed. Sir E. Sullivan, 2 vols. 1925 (Tudor Translations, ser. 2).

T., W. Civill considerations upon many and sundrie histories. 1601. [From the French version of G. Chappuys.]

ANTONIO DE GUEVARA

Bourchier, John (Baron Berners). The Golden Boke of Marcus Aurelius. 1534 (12 more edns between 1535 and 1586); ed. J. M. G. Olivares, Berlin, 1916. [From the French version of René Bertaut.]

Briant, Sir Francis. A Dispraise of the life of a Courtier. 1548; 1575 (as A Looking-Glasse for the Courte).

North, Sir Thomas. The Diall of princes. 1557; 2 pts, 1568 (rev. and adds as bk 4 The favoured Courtier); 1582; 1619; ed. (selections, with introduction and bibliography) K. N. Colville, 1919. [From the French of Bertaut.]

Hellowes, Edward. Familiar Epistles of Sir Antonie Guevara. 1574; 1577; 1584.

—— A Chronicle, conteyning the lives of tenne Emperours of Rome. 1577.

—— A Booke of the invention of the arte of navigation. 1578.

Fenton, Sir Geoffrey. Golden Epistles, gathered, as wel out of the remaynder of Guevaraes woorkes, as other Authours Latin French and Italian. 1575; 1577; 1582. [Supplement to Hellowes. All but 2 from Guevara through the French.]

The Mount of Calvarie. 1595; 1618. [Pt 2, 1597.]

Vaughan, Henry. The Praise and Happiness of the Countrie-Life. [In Olor Iscanus, 1651, abridged.]

[Painter's Palace of Pleasure, tome II, novels 12–14 correspond to Guevara's Letters, Bk II, 30–4, I, 63, II, 26.]

FRANCESCO GUICCIARDINI

Fenton, Sir Geoffrey. The Historie of Guicciardin, conteining the Warres of Italie. 1579; 1599; 1618.

A briefe collection of all the notable things in the hystorie of Guicchiardine. 1591.

I., W. Two discourses which are wanting in the thirde and fourth Bookes of his Historie. 1595. [Italian, French and English.]

[Dallington, Sir Robert.] Aphorismes Civill and Militarie exemplified out of the first Quarterne of F. Guicciardini. 1613; 1629.

P., P. Choice Proverbs and Dialogues in Italian and English. Also delightfull Stories and Apothegms taken out of Guicciardine. 1660.

LODOVICO GUICCIARDINI

Sanford, John. The Garden of pleasure. 1573; 1576.

[Danett, Thomas.] The Description of the Low countreys, gathered into an Epitome out of the Historie of Guicchardini. 1593.

DIEGO HERNANDEZ DE SAN PEDRO

Bourchier, John (Baron Berners). The castell of love. [1540?] (fragment); [1549?]; [1560?]. [From a French version. See W. G. Crane, PMLA. XLIX, 1934, pp. 1032–5.]

'Hollyband, Claudius' (i.e. Claude Desainliens). The Pretie and wittie Historie of Arnalt & Lucenda. 1575; 1597; 1608. [From the Italian version of Bartolomeo Miraffi.]

L[awrence], L[eonard]. A small Treatise betwixt Arnalte and Lucenda. Turn'd into English verse. 1639.

JUAN DE DIOS HUARTE NAVARRO

C[arew], R[ichard]. Examen de Ingenios. The Examination of mens Wits. 1594; 1596; 1604; 1616.

Huon of Bordeaux

Bourchier, John (Baron Berners). The Boke of Huon of Burdeux. [1534?]; 1601 (3rd edn); ed. Sir S. Lee, 3 pts, EETS. 1882–7.

JAQUES HURAULT

Golding, Arthur. Politicke, Moral and Martial Discourses. 1595.

JOANNES DE MEDIOLANO

Paynell, Thomas. Regimen Sanitatis Salerni. 1528; 1530; 1535; 1541; 1557; 1575; 1597; 1617; 1634.

Harington, Sir John. The Englishmans doctor, Or, the Schoole of Salerne. 1607; 1608; 1609; 1617; 1624; ed. F. R. Packard and F. H. Garrison, 1922.

POPE JOHN XXI (PETRUS HISPANUS)

Llwyd, Humphrey. The Treasuri of Helth, contaynynge many profytable Medicines. [1550?]; 1558; 1585.

GAUTIER DE COSTES DE LA CALPRENÈDE

[Digby, George (Earl of Bristol).] Cassandra. The Fam'd Romance rendered into English by an Honorable Person. 1652. [Bks I–III.]

Loveday, R[obert] et al. Hymen's Praeludia: or, Love's Master-Piece. Being the first Part of Cleopatra. [Cléopâtre, pts 1–3 tr. R. Loveday, 1652–5; pts 4–7 tr. J[ohn] C[oles], 1656–8; pt 8 tr. J[ames] W[ebb], 1658; pts 11–12 tr. J[ohn] D[avies], 1659.]

Cleopatra A New Romance. Now Englished by a Gent. of the Inner Temple. 1652.

Cotterell, Sir Charles. Cassandra: the fam'd. Now Rendred into English. 1667. [1st edn c. 1653?]

FRANÇOIS DE LA NOUE

A[ggas], E[dward]. The Politicke and militarie discourses of the Lord de la Noue. 1587.

[Munday, Anthony.] The Declaration of the Lord de la Noue, upon his taking arms for the defence of Sedan and Jametz. 1589.

A discourse upon the declaration published by the lord de Noue. 1589. [English and French.]

PIERRE DE LA PRIMAUDAYE

B[owes], T[homas]. The French Academie, wherin is discoursed the institution of Manners. 1586; 1589; 1594; 1602; 1614. [Pt 2, 1594, 1605.]

Dolman, Richard. The third volume of the French Academy. 1601. [The whole in 4 bks, 1618 (bk IV tr. W. P.).]

Lazarillo de Tormes

Rowland, David. The pleasant history of Lazarillo de Tormes. 1586; 1596; 1624; 1639; ed. J. E. V. Crofts, Oxford, 1924. [Entered Stationers' Register 1569.]

P., W. [William Phiston or Fiston?]. The most pleasaunt and delectable histoire of Lazarillo de Tormes. The second parte. 1596.

[J. de Luna's Pursuit of the historie of Lazarillo de Tormes was tr. by T. W. Calkley, 1622, 1631.]

JOHN LELAND

Robinson, Richard. A Learned and True Assertion of the Life, Actes, and death of Prince Arthure, King of great Brittaine. 1582; ed. W. E. Mead, EETS. 1925.

GIOVANNI PAOLO LOMAZZO

H[aydocke], R[ichard]. A Tracte Containing the Artes of Curious Paintinge, Carvinge, Buildinge. Oxford, 1598.

LUIS DE GRANADA

[Hopkins, Richard.] Of Prayer and meditation. Paris, 1582; Rouen, 1584; 1592; 1599; 1602; Douai, 1612; 1623; 1633.

[——]. A Memoriall of a Christian Life. Rouen, 1586, 1599; Douai, 1612; St Omer, 1625.

Meres, Francis. Grenadas Devotion. 1598 (anon.).

—— Granadas Spirituall and heavenlie exercises. 1598; Edinburgh, 1600.

—— The sinners guyde. 1598; 1614.

[Gibbons, Richard.] Of prayer and meditation, abridged and translated. Louvain, 1599.

[——] A Spirituall Doctrine conteining a rule to live wel. Louvain, 1599; St Omer, 1630.

An excellent treatise of consideration and prayer. 1601. [Also issued with some edns of Of Prayer and meditation.]

L[odge], T[homas]. The Flowers of Lodowicke of Granado. The first part. 1601. [From Michael ab Isselt's Flores Lodovici Granatensis.]

A paradise of prayers. 1633 (4th edn).

LUTHER

The chiefe and pryncypall Articles of the Christen faythe with other thre very profitable bokes. 1548.

A commentarie of M. doctor martin luther upon Galathians, translated for the unlearned. 1575; 1577; 1580; 1588; 1603; 1615; 1616; 1635; 1644.

Bull, Henry. A commentarie upon the fiftene psalmes, called Psalmi gradum. 1577; 1615; 1637.

G[ace], W[illiam]. Special and chosen sermons. 1578; 1581.

Bell, James. A Treatise Touching the Libertie of a Christian. 1579; 1636.

[Other translators of Luther's writings were: T. Newton, 'Eusebius Pamphilus', W. Lynne, J. Fox, W. W., R. Argentine, M. Coverdale, E. Ferrers, H. Bell. Many trns unsigned.]

MACCHIAVELLI

Whitehorne, Peter. The Arte of Warre, set forthe in Englishe. 2 pts, 1560–2; 3 pts, 1574; 3 pts, 1588; ed. (with Bedingfield's trn of The Florentine Historie and Dacres's trn of The Prince) H. Cust, 2 vols. 1905 (Tudor Translations).

B[edingfield], Thomas. The Florentine Historie. 1595.

D[acres], E[dward]. Machiavels discourses upon the first decade of T. Livius. 1636.

—— Nicholas Machiavel's Prince, also the Life of Castruccio Castracani of Lucca. And the meanes Duke Valentine us'd to put to death Vitellozzo Vitelli. 1640.

The Divell a married man; or the Divell hath met with his match. [1647.]

MANTUAN

[See B. Spagnuoli.]

PEDRO DE MEDINA

Frampton, John. The Arte of navigation. 1581; 1595.

MELANCHTHON

Beauchamp, Lewis. A very godly defense defending the mariage of Preistes sent unto the Kyng of England Henry the aight. [Ipswich, 1541.]

A newe work concerning both partes of the sacrament to be receyved of the lay peple. 1543; [1546?] (3 edns).

C., J. The epistle of P. Melancton made unto Kynge Henry the eyght for the revokinge of the six artycles. 1547.

Lesse, Nicholas. The Justification of man by faith only. 1548.

Rogers, John. A waying and considering of the Interim. 1548.

G[oodale], J[ohn]. A civile nosegay wherein is contayned not onylye the offyce and dewty of all magistrates and judges but of all subjectes. [1550?]

Bradford, John. A Godly treatyse of Prayer. [1553?]

Brooke, John. Of two wonderful popish monsters. 1579.

R[obinson], R[ichard]. A godly and learned assertion in defence of the true church. 1580.

[Other translators from Melanchthon include John Bale and J. Bradforde. For some other anon. versions see p. 327 above.]

BERNARDINO DE MENDOZA

Hoby, Sir Edward. Theorique and practise of warre. 1597.

PEDRO MEXÍA

Fortescue, Thomas. The Foreste, or Collection of Histories. 1571; [1576]. [From the French version of Claude Gruget.]

N[ewton?], T[homas?]. A Delectable Dialogue concerning phisicke and phisitions. 1580.

T[raheron], W[illiam]. The Historie of all the Romane Emperors. 1604; 1623 (as The Imperial Historie, with continuation by E. Grimeston).

[Milles, Thomas.] The Treasurie of auncient and moderne Times containing the Learned Collections, Judicious Readings, and memorable Observations, translated out of Pedro Mexia and M. Francesco Sansovino, etc. 1613.

—— 'Αρχαιο-πλοῦτος, containing ten following bookes to the former Treasurie. 1619.

B[aildon], J[ohn?]. The Rarities of the World, touching the beginning of Kingdomes and Common-Wealths. 1651. [Selected from Silva de varia lecio, 1540.]

GIOVANNI TOMMASO MINADOI

Hartwell, Abraham. The History of the Warres betweene the Turkes and the Persians. 1595.

MONTAIGNE

Florio, John. The Essayes or Morall, Politike and Militarie Discourses of Lo: Michaell de Montaigne. 1603; 1613; 1632 (adds Index); ed. G. Saintsbury, 6 vols. 1892–3 (Tudor Translations); ed. A. R. Waller, 6 vols. 1897; ed. D. MacCarthy, 3 vols. 1928; ed. J. I. M. Stewart, 2 vols. 1931.

JORGE DE MONTEMAYOR

Googe, Barnabe. Eglogs, epytaphes, and Sonettes. 1563. [Fifth and sixth eclogues borrowed from the Diana. See T. P. Harrison, Texas University Bulletin (Studies in English), no. 5, 1921, pp. 68–78.]

Young, Bartholomew. Diana. 1598. [Also trn by Sir Thomas Wilson (1560?–1629) in BM. Add. MS 18638.]

SIR THOMAS MORE

[See p. 666 above.]

PHILIPPE DE MORNAY

A[ggas], E[dward]. The Defense of Death. 1576; 1577.

—— On the truth of the christian religion. 1576.

F[ield], J[ohn]. A Notable Treatise of the Church. 1579; 1580; 1581; 1606.

Sidney, Sir Philip and Golding, Arthur. A Woorke Concerning the trewnesse of the Christian Religion. 1587; 1592; 1604; 1617.

Sidney, later Herbert, Mary (Countess of Pembroke). Discourse of Life and Death. Antonius a Tragedie written also in French by R. Garnier. Both done in English by the Countesse of Pembroke. 1592; 1600; 1606; 1607.

Six excellent treatises of life and death. 1607. [Contains also Plato's supposititious work, Axiochus, and selections from Cicero and Seneca.]

[Other translators of Mornay's writings were: R. S., I. V(erneuil?), S. Lennard, J. Healey, J. Bulteel, A. M(unday).]

REMIGIO NANNINI

T., W. Civil Considerations upon Many and Sundry Histories containing rules and precepts for Princes, Commonwealths. 1601. [From the French of Gabriel Chappuys.]

FRANCESCO NEGRI DE BASSANO

Cheeke, Henry. A certayne tragedie entituled Freewyl. [1589.]

BERNARDINO OCHINO

[Argentine, Richard.] Sermons. Ipswich, 1548.

Ponet, John. A tragoedie or Dialogue of the unjuste usurped primacie of the Bishop of Rome. 1549; ed. C. E. Plumptre, 1899.

[Argentine, Richard and Cooke, Anne (Lady Bacon).] Certayne sermons. [1550?] [25; 6 tr. by Argentine and 14 (also pbd separately) by Anne Cooke.]

C[ooke], A[nne] (Lady Bacon). Sermons (to the number of 25) concerning the predestination and election of God. [1570?] [Anne Cooke, Lady Bacon, was also the translator of Bishop Jewel's Apologie, 1562–4.]

Phiston, William [i.e. Fiston]. Certain godly and very profitable Sermons of Faith, Hope, and Charity. 1580.

A Dialogue of Polygamy rendered into English by a Person of Quality. 1657.

DIEGO ORTÚÑEZ DE CALAHORRA

T[yler], M[argaret]. The Mirrour of princely deedes and knighthood. [1578]; [1580?]; [1599?].

P., R. The second part of the first booke of the myrrour of knighthood. 1585; 1599. The third part of the first booke. [1586?]; [1598 or 1599?].

[Bks 4–9 of the Mirrour, not by Ortúñez, were tr. by R. P., 1583, 1598, and by L. A., 1598–1601.]

JERONIMO OSORIO DA FONSECA

Shacklock, Richard. An epistle to Elizabeth, Quene of England. Antwerp, 1565.

Fenn, John. A learned treatis wherein he confuteth a certayne aunswere made by M. W. Haddon. Louvain, 1568.

Blandie, William. The five Bookes of Hieronimus Osorius contayning a discussion of civill and Christian nobilitie. 1576.

JOHN OWEN

[See p. 859 below.]

ANTONIO DALLA PAGLIA

G[olding?], A[rthur?]. The benefite that Christians receive by Jesus Christ crucified. 1573; [1575?]; 1580; 1633; 1638.

Courtenay, Edward (Earl of Devonshire). The Benefite of Christ's Death. Ed. (from MS dated 1548) C. Babington, 1855.

MARCELLUS PALINGENIUS
(i.e. P. A. MANZOLLI)

Googe, Barnabe. The Zodiake of Life. 1565; 1576 (rev.); 1588. [Bks 1–3, 1560; bks 1–6, 1561.]

PARACELSUS

[See p. 327 above.]

PASCAL

Les Provinciales: or, the Mysteries of Jesuitisme discover'd in certain Letters. 1657; 1658.

PETRARCH

Parker, Henry (Baron Morley). The Tryumphes of Fraunces Petrarcke. [1565?]; rptd Roxburghe Club, 1887.

Twyne, Thomas. Phisicke against Fortune, as well prosperous as adverse. 1579.

Spenser, Edmund. Petrarches Visions [standomi un giorno solo, alla fenestra]. [In Complaints, 1591. See also sonnets in Van der Noodt's Theatre, 1569.]

Chapman, George. Petrarch's seven penetentiall psalmes. 1612.

Hume, Anna. The Triumphs of Love, Chastitie, Death. Edinburgh, 1644.

PHILIBERT DE VIENNE

North, George. The Philosopher of the Court. 1575.

JOANNES PHILIPPSON (SLEIDANUS)

Daus, John. A famouse Cronicle of oure Time. 1560.

Wythers, Stephen. A briefe Chronicle of the foure principall empyres. 1563.

The key of historie: abridgement of the foure chief monarchies. 1627; 1631; 1635.

Mock Majesty: or the Siege of Munster: a true story of King John Becock and his companions the anabaptists. 1644. [A trn of part of Sleidan's Commentaries.]

H[ughes], W[illiam]. Munster and Abingdon, or the open rebellion there and unhappy tumult here. Sleidans. Comm. L. 10. Oxford, 1657.
[See also under Froissart.]

ENEA SILVIO PICCOLOMINI (*i.e.* POPE PIUS II, KNOWN AS ÆNEAS SILVIUS)

The goodlie history of the Ladye Lucres of Scene in Tuskane. [1550?]; 1560; 1567.
Braunche, William. The most excellent historie of Euryalus and Lucresia. 1596.
Aleyn, Charles. The Historie of Eurialus and Lucretia. 1639; rptd Roxburghe Club, 1875.

E. S. PICCOLOMINI AND BAPTISTA SPAGNUOLI (MANTUAN)

Barclay, Alexander. The Eglogs of Alexander Barclay, the first thre out of Miserie curialium. [*c.* 1515] (3 edns); [1521?] (*bis*); rptd Spenser Soc. 1870. [Much adaptation. The first three, from Æneas Silvius, rptd in De Curialium Miseriis Epistola, ed. W. P. Mustard, Baltimore, 1928; ed. B. White, EETS. CLXXV, 1928. For Barclay's use of Mantuan's Eclogues see Mantuanus, ed. W. P. Mustard, Baltimore, 1911.]

GIOVANNI PICO DELLA MIRANDOLA
[See p. 327 above.]

MARCO POLO

[Frampton, John.] The most noble and famous travels of Marcus Paulus into the East partes of the world. 1579; ed. N. M. Penzer, 1929. [From the Spanish version. Anther trn is included in Samuel Purchas's Hakluytus Posthumus, 1625, rptd Hakluyt Soc. Glasgow, 1905–7.]

Primaleon

[Munday, Anthony.] Primaleon of Greece. First booke: 1595. Second booke: 1596. 3 pts, 1619.

FRANCISCO DE QUEVEDO VILLEGAS
[See p. 734 above.]

Les Quinze Joyes de Mariage

[Tofte, Robert.] The Batchelars Banquet. 1603; 1604; 1626; 1631; ed. F. P. Wilson, Oxford, 1929.

RABELAIS

Urquhart, Sir Thomas. The First [Second] Book of the works of Mr. Francis Rabelais. 2 vols. 1653; ed. J. L. May, 2 vols. 1927. [Completed by Peter Motteux, 1708.]
[John Eliot's Ortho-Epia Gallica, 1593, contains translated extracts from Rabelais. For

list see H. Brown, Rabelais in English Literature, Cambridge, U.S.A., 1933, pp. 216–20.]

PIERRE DE LA RAMÉE (RAMUS)
[See under Aristotle and p. 327 above.]

ANNIBALE ROMEI

K[epers], J[ohn]. The Courtiers Academie. [1598.]

GUILLAUME DE SALUSTE DU BARTAS

James I, King. Uranie. [In Essays of a Prentise in the Divine Art of Poesie, Edinburgh, 1584, 1585.]
——— The Furies. [Part of Semaine 2, jour 1, in His Majesties Poeticall Exercises at vacant houres, 1591.]
Hudson, Thomas. The historie of Judith. 1584. [Rptd in 1608 edn of Sylvester's trn.]
Sylvester, Joshua. A canticle of the victorie obteined by Henrie the Fourth, at Ivry. 1590; 1615.
——— Bartas his Devine Weekes and Workes. 1605; 1608; 1611; 1613; 1621; 1633; 1641. [Pts appeared 1592, 1595, 1598, 1606, 1607.]
Winter, Thomas. The Second Day of the First Weeke. 1603 (anon.).
——— The third dayes creation Done verse for verse. 1604.
L[odge], T[homas]. A learned summary upon the famous poeme of William of Salust. 1621; 1637; 1638
Lisle, William. Foure Bookes of Dubartas in French and English. 1637. [Pts appeared 1595, 1598, 1625.]

[For a list of trns from Du Bartas from 1584 to 1641 see A. H. Upham, French Influence in English Literature, New York, 1909, pp. 152–3.]

FRANCESCO SANSOVINO

Hichcock, Robert. The Quintesence of Wit. 1590.
[See also under Mexía.]

PAOLO SARPI

A full and satisfactorie answer to the late unadvised Bull against Venice. 1606.
An apology or apologiticall answere made unto Cardinall Bellarmine. 1607.
Brent, [Sir] N[athaniel]. The Historie of the Councel of Trent. 1620; 1629; 1640.
B[edell], W[illiam]. The free [true] schoole of warre. 1625.
P[otter], C[hristopher]. The history of the quarrels of Pope Paul V with the state of Venice. 1626.
Gentilis, Robert. The history of the Inquisition. 1639.
[Roe, Sir Thomas.] A discourse upon the reasons of the resolution taken in the Valteline. [1650?]

MADELEINE DE SCUDÉRY

Cogan, Henry. Ibrahim. Or the Illustrious Bassa. 1652. [The whole work.]

G., F. Artamenes or the Grand Cyrus. 5 vols. 1653–5.

[Wolley, Edward.] Curia Politiae, or the Apologies of Severall Princes. 1654.

B., T. A Triumphant Arch erected and consecrated to the Glory of the Feminine Sex. 1654; 1656.

[Davies, John and Havers, George.] Clelia. 5 vols. 1656–61. [Pts 1–3 tr. Davies, pts 4–5 tr. Havers.]

JOHANNES SECUNDUS

[See under Anacreon, p. 799 above.]

JEAN DE SERRES

Timms, Thomas. The Thre Parts of Commentaries of the Civill Warres of Fraunce. 1574. [The fourth Parte, 1576.]

Golding, Arthur. The Lyfe of the most godly capteine Jasper Colignie Shatilion. 1576.

Stockwood, John. A godlie and learned commentarie upon Ecclesiastes. 1585.

Grimeston, Edward. A general Inventorie of the History of France unto 1598. 1607; 1611 ('continued unto this present'); 1624 ('continued unto 1622'). [See F. S. Boas, MP. III, 1906.]

SLEIDANUS

[See J. Philippson.]

BAPTISTA SPAGNUOLI (MANTUAN)

Bale, John. A lamentable complaynte of Baptista Mantuanus. [1560?]

Turbervile, George. The Eglogs of the poet B. Mantuan. 1567; 1572.

Harvey, Tho[mas]. The Bucolicks of Baptist Mantuan in ten Eclogues. 1656.

[See also under Piccolomini.]

NICCOLÓ TARTAGLIA

Lucar, Cyprian. Three Books of Colloquies concerning the Arte of Shooting in great and small peeces of Artillerie. 1588.

TASSO

K[yd], T[homas]. The householders philosophie. 1588.

Fraunce, Abraham. The affectionate life and unfortunate death of Phillis and Amyntas. [In The Countesse of Pembrokes Yvychurch, 1591.]

C[arew], R[ichard]. Godfrey of Bulloigne or the Recouverie of Hierusalem. An Heroicall poeme. 1594; ed. A. B. Grosart, Manchester, 1881. [5 cantos, Italian and English.]

Fairfax, Edward. Godfrey of Bulloigne or the Recoverie of Jerusalem. 1600; 1624.

[Reynolds, Henry.] Torquato Tassos Aminta Englisht. 1628.

Dancer, John. Aminta: the famous pastoral. Translated in English verse. 1660.

[T. Watson's Amyntas, the indebtedness of which to Tasso has been exaggerated, was tr. by Abraham Fraunce, 1587, 1588, 1589, 1596. For Thomas Stanley's trns from Tasso see Thomas Stanley, 1647–1657, ed. L. I. Guiney, Hull, 1907.]

Till Eulenspiegel

[Andrewe, Lawrence?] Tyll Howleglas. Antwerp, [c. 1510] (fragment).

[Copland, William?] A merye jest of a man called Howleglas, and of many marvelous thinges and jestes that he did in his lyffe. [1528?]; [1530?]; [c. 1559–1563]. [See F. W. D. Brie, Eulenspiegel in England, Berlin, 1903.]

ANTONIO DE TORQUEMADA

[Walker, Ferdinand.] The Spanish Mandevile of miracles. 1600; 1618.

HONORÉ D'URFÉ

The History of Astrea. The First Part. 1620.

D[avies], J[ohn]. Astrea. A Romance, translated by a Person of Quality. 3 vols. 1657–8.

FRANCISCO DE VALDÉS

Thorius, John. The Serjeant major. 1590.

CRISPIN VAN DE PASS

Hortus Floridus. The First Book Contayning a very lively and true description of the Flowers. [1615]; ed. E. S. Rohde, 1928.

PIERRE VIRET

Scoloker, Anthony. A notable collection of places of the Sacred Scriptures. 1548.

[Viret's other translators included T. Stocker, J. Brooke, J. Shute, T. S(hute), F. H.]

JUAN LUIS VIVES

Hyrde, Richard. The instruction of a Christen woman. [1529?]; [1540?]; 1541; 1547 [1541]; 1557; 1585; 1592.

Morrison, [Sir] Richard. An introduction to wysedome. 1540; 1544; 1550; [1550?]; 1564.

Paynell, Thomas. The office and duetie of an husband. [1553?]

VINCENT VOITURE

D[avies], J[ohn]. Letters of Affaires, Love and Courtship. Written to Several Persons of Honour and Quality. 2 pts, 1657.

ULRICH ZWINGLI

The rekening and declaration of the faith of Huldrik Zwingly. Zurich, 1543; 1548.

Argentine, Richard. Certeyne Preceptes. 1548; 1550.

[Véron, Jean.] A short pathwaye to the ryghte and true understanding of the holye Scriptures. Worcester, 1550.

—— The ymage of both pastoures. 1550.

Cotsforde, Thomas. The accompt rekenynge and confession of the faith of Huldrik Zwinglius. Geneva, 1555.

A briefe rehersal of the death of Christ. [1560?]

C. BIBLIOGRAPHIES, SUMMARIES AND CRITICAL ESTIMATES

Farmer, Richard. An Essay on the Learning of Shakespeare. 1767.

Warton, T. History of English Poetry. Vol. III, 1781; ed. W. C. Hazlitt, vol. IV, 1871.

Ancient Translations from Classic Authors. [Drawn up by G. Steevens and ptd in E. Malone's Prolegomena to Shakespeare, 1790.]

Moss, J. W. A Manual of Classical Bibliography. 2 vols. 1825; 2 vols. 1837 (rev.).

Herford, C. H. Studies in the Literary Relations of England and Germany in the Sixteenth Century. Cambridge, 1886.

Schmidt, H. Richard Stanyhurst's Übersetzung von Vergils Aeneide I–IV. Ihr Verhältnis zum Original. Breslau, [1887].

Jusserand, J. J. The English Novel in the Time of Shakespeare. Tr. Eng. 1890.

Koeppel, E. Studien zur Geschichte der italienischen Novelle in der englischen Litteratur des sechzehnten Jahrhunderts. QF. LXX, 1892.

Cunliffe, J. W. The Influence of Seneca on Elizabethan Tragedy. 1893.

Chandler, F. W. Romances of Roguery. Pt I, New York, 1899.

Underhill, J. G. Spanish Literature in the England of the Tudors. New York, 1899.

Einstein, Lewis. The Italian Renaissance in England. New York, 1902.

Voyages and Travels. Ed. C. R. Beazley, 2 vols. 1903. (Arber's English Garner.)

Bolle, W. Die gedruckten englischen Liederbücher bis 1600. Berlin, 1903.

Brie, F. W. D. Eulenspiegel in England. Berlin, 1903.

—— Die erste Übersetzung einer italienischen Novelle ins Englische durch Henry Parker, Lord Morley. Archiv, CXXIV, 1907. [Masuccio, Novellino 49, trn rptd from BM. MS Royal 18 A LXII.]

Carpenter, F. I. Thomas Watson's Italian Madrigals Englished. 1590. JEGP. II, 1903.

Elizabethan Sonnets, with an Introduction by Sidney Lee. 1904.

Fest, O. Über Surrey's Virgilübersetzung. Berlin, 1904.

The Works of Thomas Nashe. Ed. R. B. McKerrow, 5 vols. 1904–10.

Elizabethan Critical Essays. Ed. G. Gregory Smith, 2 vols. Oxford, 1904.

Kastner, L. E., Berdan, J. M., Ruutz-Rees, C., Moore, C. J. Athenaeum, 22, 29 Oct. 1904; MLN. XXIII–V, 1908–10; MLR. III–VII, 1908–12, XVIII, 1923. [Articles relative to borrowings by sonneteers.]

Whibley, C. Literary Portraits. 1904. [Montaigne, etc.]

—— Translators. CHEL. vol. IV, 1909.

Imelmann, R. Surreys Aeneis IV in ursprünglicher Gestalt. Sh. Jb. XLI, 1905.

Snell, F. J. The Age of Transition. Vol. II, 1905.

Minor Poets of the Caroline Period. Ed. G. Saintsbury, 3 vols. Oxford, 1905–21.

Greg, W. W. Pastoral Romances and Pastoral Poetry. 1906.

Thomas Stanley: his Original Lyrics, Complete, in their collected readings of 1647, 1651, 1657. With an Introduction, Textual Notes, a List of Editions, an Appendix of Translations and a Portrait. Ed. L. I. Guiney, Hull, 1907.

Schelling, F. E. Elizabethan Drama, 1558–1642. 2 vols. Boston, 1908.

—— English Literature During the Lifetime of Shakespeare. New York, 1910.

Upham, A. H. The French Influence in English Literature from the Accession of Elizabeth to the Restoration. New York, 1908.

de Vocht, H. De Invloed van Erasmus op de Engelsche Tooneelliteratuur der XVIe en XVIIe Eeuwen. Ghent, 1908.

—— The Earliest English Translations of Erasmus' Colloquies, 1536–1566. Louvain, 1928. [R. Pruvost, RES. V, 1929, pp. 306–7, cites an English verse abridgment of De Pueris Instituendis.]

Fehlauer, F. Die englischen Übersetzungen von Boethius De Consolatione Philosophiae. Berlin, 1909. [See also Boethius, ed. H. F. Stewart and E. K. Rand, Loeb Lib. 1918.]

Harris, W. J. The First Printed Translations into English of the Great Foreign Classics. [1909.]

Jockers, E. Die englischen Seneca-Übersetzer des 16. Jahrhunderts. Strasburg, 1909.

Fitzmaurice-Kelly, J. The Relations between Spanish and English Literature. Liverpool, 1910.

Hatcher, O. L. Aims and Methods of Elizabethan Translators. E. Studien, XLIV, 1910.

Kerlin, R. T. Theocritus in English Literature. Lynchburg, 1910.

Lee, Sir S. The French Renaissance in England. 19̃).

Schulze, K. Die Satiren Halls, ihre Abhängigkeit von den altrömischen Satirikern und ihre Realbeziehungen auf die Shakespearezeit. Berlin, 1910.

Morgan, C. E. The Rise of the Novel of Manners. New York, 1911. [Supplemented by A. H. Upham, MLN. xxvii, 1912, pp. 220–4; xxviii, 1913, p. 94.]

Palmer, H. R. List of English Editions and Translations of Greek and Latin Classics Printed before 1641. With an Introduction by V. Scholderer. Bibliog. Soc. 1911.

Brenner, J. W. Phaer's Virgilübersetzung in ihrem Verhältnis zum Original. Heidelberg, 1912.

Esdaile, A. A List of English Tales and Prose Romances Printed before 1740. Bibliog. Soc. 1912.

Spearing, E. M. The Elizabethan Translations of Seneca's Tragedies. Cambridge, 1912. [Also in MLR. iv, 1909, pp. 437–61, xv, 1920, pp. 359–63.]

Wolff, S. L. The Greek Romances in Elizabethan Prose Fiction. New York, 1912.

Bailey, M. L. Milton and Jakob Boehme. New York, 1914. [Especially ch. iii, Boehme in England.]

Cooper, C. B. Some Elizabethan Opinions of the Poetry and Character of Ovid. Chicago, 1915.

Koch, A. Die schottische Liviusübersetzung des John Bellenden. Königsberg, 1915.

Scott, M. A. Elizabethan Translations from the Italian. New York, 1916. [Supplemented by C. R. Baskervill, MP. xvi, 1919, pp. 213–8; J. de Perott, Romanic Rev. ix, 1918, pp. 304–8.]

Foster, F. M. K. English Translations from the Greek. New York, 1918. [Addns and corrections for Homer by D. Bush, PMLA. xli, 1926, pp. 335–41.]

Willcock, G. D. A Hitherto Uncollated Version of Surrey's Translation of the Fourth Book of the Aeneid. MLR. xiv, 1919, xv, 1920, xvii, 1922.

Wright, H. G. Life and Works of Arthur Hall of Grantham. Manchester, 1919.

Amos, F. R. Early Theories of Translation. New York, 1920.

Berdan, J. M. Early Tudor Poetry. New York, 1920.

Padelford, F. M. The Poems of Henry Howard, Earl of Surrey. Seattle, 1920.

Thomas, H. Spanish and Portuguese Romances of Chivalry. Cambridge, 1920.

Thomas, H. Three Translators of Gongora and other Spanish Poets during the Seventeenth Century. Revue Hispanique, xlviii, 1920. [Thomas Stanley, Sir Richard Fanshawe, Philip Ayres; English and Spanish texts.]

—— English Translations of Portuguese Books before 1640. Library, iv, 1923.

—— The English Translations of Guevara's Works. [In Estudios in Memoriam de Adolfo Bonilla, vol. ii, Madrid, 1930.]

Chambrun, C. (Longworth). Giovanni Florio: Un Apôtre de la Renaissance en Angleterre. Paris, 1921.

Harrison, T. P. Googe's Eglogs and Montemayor's Diana. University of Texas Bulletin, Studies in English No. 5, 1921.

—— Bartholomew Yong, Translator. MLR. xxi, 1926.

Morgan, B. Q. Bibliography of German Literature in English Translation. Madison, 1922.

Colville, K. N. Fame's Twilight. 1923. [Thomas North and John Barclay.]

Harrington, K. P. Catullus and his Influence. Boston, 1923.

Modersohn, A. B. Cicero im englischen Geistesleben des 16. Jahrhunderts. Archiv, cxlix, 1923.

Specimens of Tudor Translations from the Classics. Ed. O. L. Jiriczek, Heidelberg, 1923.

Bush, D. The Classical Tales in Painter's Palace of Pleasure. JEGP. xxiii, 1924.

—— Musaeus in English Verse. MLN. xliii, 1928, xlv, 1930.

—— Mythology and the Renaissance Tradition in English Poetry. Minneapolis, 1932.

Duckett, E. S. Catullus in English Poetry. Northampton, Mass. 1925.

Hayes, G. R. Anthony Munday's Romances of Chivalry. Library, vi, 1925, vii, 1926.

Merrill, L. R. Life and Poems of Nicholas Grimald. New Haven, 1925. [See also H. H. Hudson, Grimald's Translations from Beza, MLN. xxxix, 1924.]

Pompen, A. The English Versions of the Ship of Fools. 1925.

Praz, M. Stanley, Sherburne, and Ayres as Translators and Imitators of Italian, Spanish, and French Poets. MLR. xx, 1925.

Whipple, T. K. Martial and the English Epigram from Sir Thomas Wyatt to Ben Jonson. Berkeley, 1925. [Supplemented by H. B. Lathrop, MLN. xliii, 1928, pp. 223–9.]

Pollard, A. W. and Redgrave, G. R. A Short-Title Catalogue of Books printed in England, Scotland and Ireland and of English Books printed abroad, 1475–1640. Bibliog. Soc. 1926.

Schoell, F. Études sur l'Humanisme continental en Angleterre à la Fin de la Renaissance. Paris, 1926.

Wilder, M. L. Jonson's Indebtedness to Latin Authors, shown chiefly in his Non-Dramatic Poems. Ithaca, 1926.

Conley, C. H. The First English Translators of the Classics. New Haven, 1927.

Hasselkuss, H. K. Der Petrarkismus in der Sprache der englischen Sonettdichter der Renaissance. Münster, 1927.

Nixon, P. Martial and the Modern Epigram. New York, 1927.

Prothero, R. E. (Baron Ernle). The Light Reading of Our Ancestors. 1927.

Emperor, J. B. The Catullian Influence in English Lyric Poetry, *circa* 1600–1650. Columbia, Missouri, 1928.

Turner, C. Anthony Munday: An Elizabethan Man of Letters. Berkeley, 1928.

Spanish Short Stories of the Sixteenth Century in Contemporary Translations. Ed. J. B. Trend, 1928. (World's Classics.)

Baker, E. A. History of the English Novel. Vol. II, 1929.

Dodge, R. E. N. The Text of the Gerusalemme Liberata in the Versions of Carew and Fairfax. PMLA. XLIV, 1929. [See also W. L. Bullock, PMLA. XLV, 1930, pp. 330–5.]

Scott, J. G. Les Sonnets élisabéthains: les Sources et l'Apport personnel. Paris, 1929.

McClure, N. E. The Letters and Epigrams of Sir John Harington. Philadelphia, 1930. [Martial.]

Smith, F. S. The Classics in Translation. 1930.

Matthiessen, F. O. Translation: An Elizabethan Art. Cambridge, U.S.A. 1931.

Chester, A. G. Thomas May: Man of Letters, 1595–1650. Philadelphia, 1932.

Gates, W. B. The Dramatic Works and Translations of Sir William Lower. Philadelphia, 1932.

Koszul, A. L'Offrande d'un Traducteur. Notes sur l'Anglais de John Florio. Revue Anglo-Américaine, IX, 1932.

Wright, L. B. Translations for the English Middle Class. Library, XIII, 1932.

Brown, Huntington. Rabelais in English Literature. Cambridge, U.S.A. 1933.

Lathrop, H. B. Translations from the Classics into English, 1477–1620. Madison, 1933.

Pruvost, R. Le Daphnis et Chloe d'Angel Day, 1587. Revue Anglo-Américaine, X, 1933.

Van der Haar, D. Richard Stonyhurst's Aeneis. Amsterdam, 1933.

Yates, F. A. John Florio. Cambridge, 1934.

C. H. C.

6. HISTORY, PHILOSOPHY, SCIENCE AND OTHER FORMS OF LEARNING

I. HISTORIANS, BIOGRAPHERS AND ANTIQUARIES

I. 1500–1558

A. HALL AND LELAND

EDWARD HALL (d. 1547)

The union of the two noble and illustre famelies of Lancastre and York. 1548; 1550; [c. 1560]; [ed. Sir Henry Ellis], 1809.

Authorities

Tanner, T. Bibliotheca Britannico-Hibernica. 1748.
Gairdner, J. England. 1879. (Early Chronicles of Europe Ser.). [Pp. 300–4.]
Brewer, J. S. The Reign of Henry VIII. Ed. J. Gairdner, 2 vols. 1884.
Ward, Sir A. W. Henry VI. University Press Shakespeare. New York, 1907. [Introduction.]
Pollard, A. F. Edward Hall's Will and Chronicle. Bulletin Inst. Hist. Research, IX, 1931–2.
Pollard, G. The Bibliographical History of Hall's Chronicle. Bulletin Inst. Hist. Research, X, 1932–3.

JOHN LELAND (1506–1552)

Assertio inclytissimi Arturii Regis Britanniae. 1544; tr. Eng. R. Robinson, 1582 (as A Learned and True Assertion of the Life of Prince Arthure); ed. (with Robinson's trn) W. E. Mead (appended to C. Middleton, The Famous Historie of Chinon of England, 2 pts, EETS. 1925).
The laboryouse journey & serche of Johan Leylande, geven of hym as a newe yeares gyfte to Kynge Henry the viii. 1549; rptd 1596 (in R. Brooke, Discoverie of Certaine Errours); 1631 (in J. Weever, Funerall Monuments); 1710 (in Itinerary, ed. T. Hearne, vol. I); [Oxford, 1722]; Oxford, 1772 (in W. Huddesford, Lives of Leland, etc.); ed. W. A. Copinger, 1895.
The Itinerary of John Leland the Antiquary. Ed. T. Hearne, 9 vols. Oxford, 1710–12, 1745–4, 1770; ed. L. Toulmin Smith, 11 pts in 5 vols. 1906–10.

Authorities

Bale, J. [Preface to] The laboryouse journey. 1549.
Burton, Edward (attrib.). Life of Leland, with Notes and Bibliography. 1896.
Huddesford, W. Lives of Leland, Hearne and Wood. 2 vols. Oxford, 1772.
Smith, L. Toulmin. [Introduction to] The Itinerary. Vol. I, 1907.

B. MINOR HISTORIANS

ROBERT FABYAN (d. 1513)

[Begin] 'Prima Pars Cronecarum. For that in the accomptynge.' 2 vols. 1516; 2 vols. 1533; 1542 (expurgated); 1559 (with continuation by another hand to 8 Jan. 1559; another issue is continued to 8 May 1559); ed. Sir Henry Ellis, 1811 (as The new chronicles of England and France).

RICHARD ARNOLD (d. 1521?)

Chronicle. [Begin] 'In this booke is Conteyned the names of the baylifs Custos mairs and sherefs of the cite of london.' [Antwerp, 1503?]; [Southwark, 1521]; ed. [F. Douce], 1811 (as The Customs of London, otherwise called Arnold's Chronicle).

POLYDORE VERGIL (1470?–1555?)

Polydori Vergilii Urbinatis Anglicae Historiae Libri xxvi. Basle, 1534, 1546, 1555 (continued to 1538), and 1556; 2 vols. Ghent, 1556–7; Basle, 1570; Leyden, 1651; tr. Eng. as Three Books of Polydore Vergil's English History, comprising the reigns of Henry VI, Edward IV, and Richard III. From an early translation, among the MSS. of the old Royal Library in the BM. Ed. Sir Henry Ellis, Camden Soc. 1844; Polydore Vergil's English History, from an early translation. Vol. I, containing the first eight books, comprising the period prior to the Norman conquest. Ed. Sir Henry Ellis, Camden Soc. 1846.

CHARLES WRIOTHESLEY (1508?–1562)

A Chronicle of England during the Reigns of the Tudors. Ed. W. D. Hamilton, 2 vols. Camden Soc. 1875–7.

NICHOLAS HARPSFIELD (1519?–1575)

A Treatise on the Pretended Divorce between Henry VIII and Catharine of Aragon. Ed. N. Pocock, Camden Soc. 1878. [Only the last part is historical.]

Life of Sir Thomas More. Ed. in part Lord Acton, together with historical portion of the Treatise, [Philobiblon Soc.?] 1877; ed. R. W. Chambers and E. V. Hitchcock (The Tudor Lives of Sir Thomas More, EETS. 1932.).

THOMAS LANQUET (or LANKET) (1521–1545)

An Epitome of Cronicles continued to the reigne of Edwarde the sixt by T. Cooper. 1569 (for 1549); 1559 (by R. Crowley); 1560 (Coopers Chronicle unto the late death of Queene Marie); 1565 (bis).

JOHN PROCTOR (1521?–1584)

The historie of Wyates rebellion. 1554; 1555.

WILLIAM PATTEN (fl. 1548–1580)

The expedicion into Scotlande of the most woorthely fortunate prince Edward, Duke of Soomerset. 30 June, 2 Ed. VI. 1548; rptd Sir J. G. Dalyell (Fragments of Scotish history, Edinburgh, 1798); rptd E. Arber (English Garner, vol. III, pp. 51–155, 1880).

LONDON AND OTHER TOWN CHRONICLES

Chronicles of London. Ed., with Introduction and Notes, C. L. Kingsford, Oxford, 1905.

Six Town Chronicles of England. Ed. R. Flenley, Oxford, 1911. [Valuable introduction on town chronicles, and bibliography of London chronicles, pp. 96–8.]

The Chronicle of Calais. Ed. J. G. Nichols, Camden Soc. 1846.

A London Chronicle during the reigns of Henry VII and Henry VIII. Ed. C. Hopper, Camden Misc. vol. IV, 1859.

Chronicle of the Grey Friars of London. Ed. J. G. Nichols, Camden Soc. 1852.

ANONYMOUS AND MISCELLANEOUS

The Chronicle of Queen Jane, and of two years of Queen Mary. Written by a resident in the Tower of London. Ed. J. G. Nichols, Camden Soc. 1850.

Narratives of the Days of the Reformation, chiefly from the MSS. of John Foxe the Martyrologist; with two contemporary biographies of archbishop Cranmer. Ed. J. G. Nichols, Camden Soc. 1859.

C. MINOR BIOGRAPHERS

WILLIAM ROPER (1496–1578)

The Mirrour of Vertue in Worldly Greatnes. Or The Life of Syr T. More. Paris [St Omer], 1626; rptd T. Hearne, [Oxford], 1716, 1879

(Pitt Press Ser.); ed. from better MS J. Lewis, 1729, 1731, and Dublin, 1765, 1835; ed. S. W. Singer. 1817; 1822; ed. E. Rhys, [1890]; ed. Sir I. Gollancz, 1902, 1903; rptd 1910 (Bohn's Standard Lib.).

GEORGE CAVENDISH (1500–1561?)

Life of Cardinal Wolsey. 1641 (as The negotiations of Thomas Woolsey); 1667; 1706; 1742 (in J. Grove, History of Cardinal Wolsey); 1745 (Harleian Misc. vol. v); ed. J. Grove, 1761 (more accurate version); 1810 (Harleian Misc. rev. T. Park, vol. v); ed. from MSS C. Wordsworth (Ecclesiastical Biography, vol. I, 1810, 1818, 1837, 1853); ed. S. W. Singer, 2 vols. 1825, 1827, 1885 (Morley's Universal Lib.) and [1907] (New Universal Lib.); ed. J. Holmes, 1852; ed. E. H., 1855; ed. F. S. Ellis, 1893 (Kelmscott Press) and 1899 (Temple Classics); Chipping Campden, 1930.

Metrical Visions. [Included in Life, ed. S. W. Singer, 1825, etc.]

G. P.

II. 1558–1603

A. FOXE, PARKER, HOLINSHED AND STOW

JOHN FOXE (1516–1587)

Commentarii Rerum in Ecclesia Gestarum. Liber primus. Strasburg, 1554; 1564 (?1554, as Chronicon Ecclesiae, Continens Historiam Rerum).

Rerum in Ecclesia Gestarum commentarii. 2 pts, Basle, 1559–63.

Actes and Monuments. 1563; 2 vols. 1570, 1576 and 1583; 1596; 1610; 3 vols. 1632–1, 1641 and 1684; ed. S. R. Cattley, with a dissertation by G. Townsend, 8 vols. 1837–41; rev. M. H. Seymour, 1838; rev. G. Townsend, 8 vols. 1843–9; rev. J. Pratt, with introduction by J. Stoughton, 8 vols. [1877].

Authorities

Day, R. [Preface to trn of Foxe's Christus Triumphans, 1579.]

Life. [Attrib. to Foxe's son Samuel, prefixed to vol. II of 1641 edn of Actes and Monuments.]

Maitland, S. R. A review of Foxe's History of the Waldenses. 1837.

—— Six Letters on Foxe's Acts and Monuments. 1837.

—— Twelve Letters on Foxe's Acts and Monuments. 1841.

—— Notes on the contributions of G. Townsend to the new edition of Fox's Martyrology. 3 pts. 1841–2.

Maitland, S. R. Remarks on Cattley's defence of his edition of Foxe's Martyrology. 1842.
Winter, W. Biographical Notes on John Foxe. 1876.

MATTHEW PARKER (1504–1575)

De Antiquitate Britannicae Ecclesiae et Privilegiis Ecclesiae Cantuariensis, cum Archiepiscopis ejusdem 70. [Lambeth], 1572; Hanover, 1605 (imperfect); ed. S. Drake, 1729.
[Parker also edited:
Elegans, illustris, et facilis rerum, praesertim Britannicarum, narratio, quam Matthaeus Westmonasteriensis Flores Historiarum scripsit. 2 pts, [London], 1567; 1570 (Flores Historiarum per Matthaeum Westmonasteriensem collecti).
Matthaei Paris historia major. 1571.
Ælfredi Regis Res Gestae ab Asserio conscriptae. 1574.
Historia brevis Thomæ Walsingham et Ypodigma Neustriæ. 1574.
See J. Strype, The Life and Acts of Matthew Parker, 1711 and 3 vols. Oxford, 1821.
See also p. 671 above.]

RAPHAEL HOLINSHED (d. 1580?)

The Firste (Laste) volume of the Chronicles of England, Scotlande, and Irelande, etc. 4 pts, 1577; 3 vols. 1587. [Certain portions of vols. II and III were ordered to be excised, and 4 new leaves were printed to fill the gaps in vol. III. The missing pages were rptd 1722–3, and on two other occasions before the end of 1728; rptd 6 vols. 1807–8; ed. R. S. Wallace, 1923 (Richard II, Henry IV and Henry V only).]

Authorities

Courtenay, T. P. Commentaries on the Historical Plays of Shakspeare. 2 vols. 1840.
Furnivall, F. J. Harrison's Description of England in Shakspere's Youth. The II and III Books. New Shakspere Soc. 1877–1909.
Boswell-Stone, W. G. Shakspere's Holinshed: the Chronicle and the Historical Plays compared. 1896; 1907.

JOHN STOW (1525?–1605)

The workes of Geffrey Chaucer, with divers addicions, whiche were never in printe before. 1561. [Notes on Chaucer and list of Lydgate's works ptd in T. Speght's edn of Chaucer. 1598 and 1602.]
A Summarie of Englyshe Chronicles. 1565; 1566; 1570; 1574; [1575]; 1590; continued by E. H[owes], 1607, 1611 and 1618.

The Summarie of Englyshe Chronicles abridged. 1566; 1567; 1573; 1584; [1587]; 1598; 1604.
The Chronicles of England. [1580]; 1592 (as The Annales of England); 1601; 1605; ed. E. Howes, 1615 and 1631.
A Survay of London. 1598; 1603; rev. A. M[unday], 1618; rev. A. M[unday], H. D[yson] et al., 1633; rev. J. Strype, 2 vols. 1720 and 1754–5; rev. R. Seymour (i.e. John Mottley), 2 vols. 1734–5; rev. a Gentleman of the Inner Temple, 2 vols. 1753; rev. W. J. Thoms, 1842 and 1876; ed. H. Morley. 1889 and 1893; ed. C. L. Kingsford, 2 vols. Oxford, 1908–27 (best edn, from text of 1603).
[See C. L. Kingsford, Introduction to his edn of Survey, 1908.]

B. MINOR HISTORIANS
RICHARD GRAFTON (d. 1572?)

An abridgement of the Chronicles of England. 1562; 1563, 1564; 1570; 1572.
A Manuell of the Chronicles of Englande. 1565.
[Begin] 'This Chronicle [of Briteyn], beginning at William the Conquerour, endeth wyth Queene Elizabeth.' 1568; 1569 (A chronicle at large); ed. [Sir Henry Ellis], 2 vols. 1809.

HUMPHREY LLWYD (1527–1568)

Commentarioli Britannicae Descriptionis Fragmentum. Cologne, 1572; ed. Moses Williams, 1731 (with De Mona); tr. Eng. T. Twyne, The Breviary of Britayn, 1573; rptd J. Lewis, The History of Great Britain, 1729.
De Mona Druidum Insula. 1573 (in Sir John Price, Historiae Brytannicae Defensio); Antwerp, 1579, etc. (in Abraham Ortelius Theatrum Orbis Terrarum, Parergon); ed. Moses Williams, 1723 and 1731 (with Commentariolum); tr. Eng. 1606 (in Abraham Ortelius, Theatre of the Whole World).
The historie of Cambria, now called Wales. 1584; ed. W. Wynne, 1697, 1702, 1774, 1811 and Merthyr, 1812; ed R. Lloyd, Shrewsbury, 1832. [Eng. trn of a version of Brut y Tywysogion, to which is prefixed Sir John Price's Description of Cambria, enlarged by Llwyd.]

WILLIAM LAMBARD (1536–1601)

APXAIONOMIA, Sive de priscis anglorum legibus libri. 1568; ed. A. Whelock (with Bede's Historia Ecclesiastica, 2 vols. Cambridge, 1644).
A Perambulation of Kent. 1576; 1596; [1636]; 1656; Chatham, 1826 (from 1596 edn, with life of Lambard).

Eirenarcha: or of The Office of the Justices of Peace. 1581; 1582 (bis); 1588 (bis); 1591; 1592; 1594; 1599, etc.

The duties of constables, borsholders, tything-men. 1583; 1584; 1587; 1591; 1594; 1599, etc.

Archion, or, a Comentary upon the High Courts of Justice in England. 1635 (bis).

Dictionarium Angliae Topographicum et Historicum. 1730. [Written c. 1577.]

SIR THOMAS SMITH (1513–1577)

De Republica Anglorum. The maner of governement of England. 1583; 1584; 1589 (as The Common-Welth of England); 1594; 1601; 1609; 1612; 1621; 1633; 1635; 1640; 1691; ed. L. Alston and F. W. Maitland, Cambridge, 1906. Tr. Latin [1610?], Leyden, 1625, 1630 and 1641; Dutch (partial), Amsterdam, 1673; German, Hamburg, 1688.

NICHOLAS SANDERS (1530?–1581)

De Origine ac Progressu Schismatis Anglicani. Editus et auctus per Edouardum Rishtonum. Cologne, 1585; Rome, 1586; Ingoldstadt, 1588; Cologne, 1610, 1628. Tr. French, 1587, Paris, 1676, 1678, Hague, 1715; German, Salzburg, 1594; Eng., with introduction and notes, D. Lewis, 1877.

DAVID POWELL (1552?–1598)

The historie of Cambria. 1584. [See above under Llwyd. Powell's corrections, etc. made the book a new work.]

Pontici Virunnii Britannicae Historiae Libri Sex [with the 'Itinerarium' and 'Descriptio' of Giraldus Cambrensis, and De Britannica Historia Recte Intelligenda Epistola]. 1585.

RICHARD CAREW (1555–1620)*

Godfrey of Bulloigne or the Recouverie of Hierusalem. An Heroicall poeme written in Italian by Seig. Torquato Tasso and translated into English by R. C. Esquire: and now the first part containing five Cantos Imprinted in both Languages. 1594; ed. A. B. Grosart, Manchester, 1881.

Examen de Ingenios. The Examination of mens Wits. By John Huarte. Translated out of the Spanish tongue by M. Camillo Camilli. Englished out of his Italian by R. C. Esquire. 1594; 1596; 1604; 1616.

A Herrings Tayle: Contayning a Poeticall fiction of divers matters worthie the reading. 1598 (anon.). [Attributable to Carew chiefly on the evidence of the West Country words, many of which only appear elsewhere in the Survey.]

The Survey of Cornwall. 1602; ed. H. C. [i.e. P. des Maizeaux], 1723 and 1769 (with Excellencie of the English Tongue); ed. T. Tonkin and Francis Baron de Dunstanville, 1811.

The Excellencie of the English Tongue, by R. C. of Anthony Esquire to W. C. [In 2nd edn of Camden's Remaines, 1614, and subsequent edns, 1623, 1629, 1636, 1657, 1674 and 1870; rptd P. des Maizeaux with Survey, 1723 and 1769; ed. G. Gregory Smith from BM. MS (Cotton F. xi, fol. 265) in Elizabethan Critical Essays, vol. ii, Oxford, 1904.]

SAMPSON ERDESWICKE (d. 1603)

A Survey of Staffordshire. 1717 (inaccurate text); 1723; 1798–1801 (with S. Shaw's History of Staffordshire); ed. T. Harwood, Westminster, 1820 and 1844.

The True Use of Armorie. By William Wyrley 1592; 1853. [Attrib. to Erdeswicke.]

EDMUND SPENSER (1552?–1599)

[See pp. 417–9 above.]

JOHN NORDEN (1548–1625?)

Speculum Britanniae. The first parte, discription of Middlesex. 1593; 1637; 1723.

Nordens Preparative to his Speculum Britanniae. 1596; 1723 (with the Middlesex and the Hartfordshire).

Speculi Britanniae pars; the description of Hartfordshire. 1598; 1723 (with the above); Ware, 1903 (with biography).

Speculi Britanniae Pars Altera: or, a Delineation of Northamptonshire. 1720.

Speculi Britanniae Pars: a description of Cornwall. 1728.

Speculi Britanniae Pars: An historical and chorographical description of Essex, 1594. Ed. Sir H. Ellis, Camden Soc. 1840.

The Surveyors Dialogue. 1607; 1610; 1618; 1738; ed. J. W. Papworth. Architectural Publication Soc. Detached Essays, vi, 1853.

A description of the honor of Winsor. [Maps and abstracts of portions of MS in R. R. Tighe and J. E. Davis, Annals of Windsor, 2 vols. 1858.]

England, An Intended Guyde, for English Travailers. 1625; 1635, 1636 and 1643 (as A Direction for the English Traviller).

C. MINOR BIOGRAPHIES AND AUTOBIOGRAPHIES

Life of Fisher

The life of Fisher, once attributed to R. Hall. Ed. F. van Ortroy, Analecta Bollandiana, x, xii, 1891, 1893; ed. R. Bayne, EETS. 1921.

---

* The bibliography of Carew has been contributed by Mr A. K. Hamilton Jenkin.

THOMAS STAPLETON (1535–1598)

The History of the Church of Englande. Compiled by Venerable Bede, Englishman. Translated out of Latin. Antwerp, 1565; St Omer, 1622; 1626; rptd Oxford, 1930.

Tres Thomae. [St T. the Apostle, St T. of Canterbury, and T. More]. Douay, 1588; Cologne, 1612. [The life of More was in 1689 rptd both separately (Gratz, [1689]) and as preface to More's collected Latin works. Tr. P. E. Hallett, 1928.]

DAVID MOYSIE (fl. 1590)

Memoirs of the Affairs of Scotland, 1577–1603. Edinburgh, 1755; rptd Bannatyne Club, Edinburgh, 1830.

SIR FRANCIS VERE (1560–1609)

The Commentaries, Being Diverse pieces of service, wherein he had command. Ed. W. Dillingham, Cambridge, 1657; rptd E. Arber, English Garner, vol. VII, 1883.

G. P.

III. 1603–1660

A. CAMDEN, RALEGH, BURTON, WALTON, PRYNNE, HOWELL, WHITELOCKE, SIR THOMAS BROWNE, FULLER, AND URQUHART

WILLIAM CAMDEN (1551–1623)

Britannia sive florentissimorum regnorum, Angliae, Scotiae, Hiberniae Chorographica descriptio. 1586; 1587; Frankfort, 1590; 1590; 1594; 1600; 1607; Frankfort, 1617, etc.; tr. P. Holland, 2 pts 1610 and 1637; E. Gibson, 1695, 2 vols. 1722, 1753, and with corrections by G. Scott, 1772; R. Gough, 3 vols. 1789 and 4 vols. 1806.

Remaines of a Greater Worke, Concerning Britaine. 2 pts, 1605; 1614; 1623; 1629; 1636; 1637, etc.; rptd 1870.

Annales Rerum Anglicarum, et Hibernicarum Regnante Elizabetha. Pt 1, 1615; pts 1 and 2, Leyden, 1625; pt 2, 1627; Leyden, 1639; Amsterdam, 1677; ed. T. Hearne, 3 vols. [Oxford], 1717. Tr. French P. de Bellegent, pt 1, 1624, pts 1 and 2, Paris, 1627; Eng. pt 1, A. Darcie, 1625 [from French], pt 2, T. Browne, 1629; pts 1 and 2, R. N[orton], 1630; 1635. [Later Eng. edns 1675, 1688, and in White Kennett's Complete History, vol. II, 1706.]

Regni Regis Jacobi I Annalium Apparatus. Memorabilia de seipso.

[Both in T. Smith, V. Cl. Gulielmi Camdeni Epistolae, 1691. Eng. trn (with omissions) of first ptd by White Kennett, Complete History, vol. II, 1706.]

Authorities

Brooke, R. A Discoverie of Certaine Errours in Britannia. [1596.]

Bolton, E. Hypercritica. 1722. [See below, Minor Historians, p. 837.]

Wheare, D. Parentatio Historica. [In Camdeni Insignia, Oxford, 1624.]

Fuller, T. Holy and Profane State. Cambridge, 1642.

Smith, T. Camdeni Epistolae. 1691.

G. P.

SIR WALTER RALEGH (1552?–1618)

(a) Bibliography

[There are bibliographies of Ralegh by T. N. Brushfield, Plymouth, 1886 (rev. Exeter, 1908), and by W. Eames, New York, 1886.]

(b) Collected Works

Judicious and Select Essayes and Observations upon The first Invention of Shipping. The Misery of Invasive Warre. The Navy Royall and Sea-Service. With his Apologie for his voyage to Guiana. 1650 (re-issued 1667).

Remains of Sir Walter Raleigh. [1.] Maxims of State. [2.] Advice to his Son: his Son's advice to his Father. [3.] The Sceptick. [4.] Observations concerning the Magnificency of Cities. [5.] Seat of Government. [6.] Observations touching Trade with the Hollander. [7.] Letters. [8.] Poems. [9.] Speech before he was Beheaded. [10.] The Prerogative of Parliaments. 1651 (as the Sceptick, containing 3, 4, 5, 7, 8, 9); 1651 (as Maxims of State, containing 1 and 2); 1656 (all but 10); 1657 (all but 6 and 10); 1657 (as Remains, all but 10); 1661 (complete); 1664; 1669; 1675; 1681; 1702 (with additional letters).

Three Discourses. I. Of a War with Spain. II. Of the Original Cause of War. III. Of Ecclesiastical Power. Published by Phillip Ralegh, Esq. his only Grandson. 1702. [The chapter 'On Unnatural War' is ptd for the first time.]

The Works of Sir Walter Ralegh. Ed. T. Birch, 2 vols. 1751. [Omits several minor pieces and the History of the World.]

The Works of Sir Walter Ralegh. 8 vols. Oxford, 1829.

Selections from Historie of the World, Letters, etc. Ed. G. E. Hadow, Oxford, 1917.

(c) Separate Works

(i) Historical

The History of the World. 1614 (*bis*); 1617 (*bis*); 1621; 1628; 1630; 1634; 1652; 1666; 1671; 1677; 1687; 1736; rptd Edinburgh, 1820 (with the Discovery of Guiana, Considerations for a Voyage to Guiana, Orders to the Fleet and Apology for Guiana). [Until 1652 the engraved title-page keeps the first date, 1614.]

An Abridgment of Sir Walter Raleigh's History of the World. To which is Added, His Premonition to Princes. [Ed. L. Echard], 1698.

An Abridgment [etc.] Second edition, with some Genuine Remains. I. Of the first Invention of Shipping. II. A Relation of the Action at Cadiz. III. A Dialogue between a Jesuite and a Recusant. IV. An Apology for his Voyage to Guiana. Publish'd by Phillip Raleigh. 1700; 1702.

Tubus Historicus: An Historicall Perspective. 1636.

A Discourse of Tenures which were before the Conquest. Ed. J. Gutch, Collectanea Curiosa, vol. I, 1761.

(ii) Naval and Military

A Report of the fight about the Iles of Açores. 1591. [Rptd in Hakluyt's Voyages, vol. II, 1598, Somers Tracts, vol. I, 1751 and 1809, Arber's Reprints, 1895, Boston, 1902, London, 1908.]

The Discoverie of Guiana. 1596 (3 edns); 1598 (in Hakluyt's Voyages, vol. III); Nuremberg, 1599, 1601 and 1603; Frankfort, 1612 and 1663; Amsterdam, 1598, 1605 and 1644; Leyden, 1706; ed. R. H. Schomburgk, Hakluyt Soc. 1848 (with some unpbd documents including the Journal of the last voyage); ed. V. T. Harlow, 1928 (with Spanish documents).

Opinions on the Alarm of an Invasion. 1596. [By Ralegh and others.]

Orders to the Fleet, 1617. [Licensed 17 March 1618. No ptd copy extant. See Newes of Sir Walter Rauleigh, 1618. Rptd from MS in Works, 1751, 1829, in A. Cayley's Life, vol. II, 1805, appended to The History of the World, 1820, and separately by Navy Records Soc. 1905.]

Apologie for his voyage to Guiana. 1650.

A Discourse of the Originall Cause of Naturall Warre with the Mysery of Invasive Warre. 1650.

A Military Discourse. 1734.

Arguments to manifest the Advantages of a good Fleet. Added to Sir Clement Edmonds' Observations on landing forces for invasion. 1759.

(iii) Political and Philosophical

The Prerogative of Parliaments. Middelburg, 1628 (*bis*); Hamburg, 1628; [London], 1640; rptd Somers Tracts, vol. IV, 1750 and vol. III, 1809, Harleian Misc. vol. v, 1744 and 1808.

Instructions to his Sonne. 1632 (*bis*); 1633 (*bis*); Edinburgh, 1634; 1636; rptd 1728.

The Prince or Maxims of State. 1642; rptd Somers Tracts, vol. III, 1809.

The Cabinet-Council. Published by John Milton. 1658; 1661 (as Aphorisms of State); 1692 (as The Arts of Empire Discabineted); 1697 (as The Secrets of Government).

The Interest of England with Regard to Foreign Alliances Explained in Two Discourses. 1. Concerning a Match between the Lady Elizabeth and the Prince of Piemont. 2. Touching a Marriage between prince Henry of England and a Daughter of Savoy. 1750.

A Treatise of the Soule. [In Works, 1829.]

(iv) Poetical

The Poems of Sir Walter Raleigh. Ed. Sir S. E. Brydges, Lee Priory Press, 1813 and London, 1814.

Poems by Sir Henry Wotton, Sir Walter Raleigh and others. Ed. J. Hannah, 1845.

The Poems of Sir Walter Raleigh and other Courtly Poets. Ed. J. Hannah, 1870, 1910.

The Poems of Sir Walter Ralegh. Ed. A. M. C. Latham, 1929.

(v) Doubtful Works

The life and death of Mahomet. 1637.

Observations concerning the royall navy. 1650. [Attrib. by H. E. Sandison (Arthur Gorges, 1928) to Gorges.]

Observations touching Trade with the Hollander. 1653. [Several variants pbd.]

An Introduction to a Breviary of the History of England. 1693.

A Discourse of Sea-Ports. 1700 (re-issued 1701 as An Essay on Ways to Maintain the Honour of England).

(vi) Lost Works

Treatise of the West Indies. [See Dedication to Discovery of Guiana.]

Discourse how war may be made against Spain and the Indies. [See Three Discourses, vol. I.]

Treatise on the Art of War by Sea. [See the History of the World, bk 5, pt 2.]

Of Mines and Trials of Minerals. [See à Wood, Athenae Oxonienses, vol. II, 1692, p. 243.]

Of the Present State of Spain. [See à Wood, Athenae Oxonienses, vol. II, 1692, p. 243.]

(d) Biography and Criticism

(i) Biography

Naunton, R. Fragmenta Regalia. 1641; ed. E. Arber, 1895.

Winstanley, W. England's Worthies. 1660.

Shirley, J. Life of Sir Walter Raleigh. 1677.

à Wood, A. Athenae Oxonienses. 2 vols. 1691–2; ed. P. Bliss, 6 vols. 1813–20.

Prince, J. Worthies of Devon. 1701.

Aubrey, J. Brief Lives. 1813; ed. A. Clark, 2 vols. Oxford, 1898.

Oldys, W. Life. [Prefixed to History of the World, 1736, and Works, 1829.]

Birch, T. Life. [Prefixed to Works, 1751 and 1829.]

Cayley, A. Life of Sir Walter Raleigh. 2 vols. 1805.

Edwards, E. Life of Sir Walter Raleigh. Together with his Letters. 2 vols. 1868.

St John, J. A. Life of Sir Walter Raleigh. 1868. [Spanish documents.]

Creighton, L. Life of Sir Walter Raleigh. 1877.

Gosse, Sir E. Raleigh. 1886.

Stebbing, W. Sir Walter Raleigh. 1891; 1899 (adds bibliography).

Hume, M. A. S. Sir Walter Raleigh. 1897. [Spanish documents.]

Rodd, R. Sir Walter Raleigh. 1904. [Naval.]

Waldman, M. Sir Walter Raleigh. 1928.

Harlow, V. T. Sir Walter Raleigh's Last Voyage. 1932.

Anthony, I. Ralegh and his World. New York, 1934.

Thompson, Edward. Sir Walter Ralegh. 1935.

(ii) Criticism

Gosse, Sir E. Sir Walter Raleigh's Cynthia. Athenaeum, 2, 9 Jan. 1886.

Firth, Sir C. H. Sir Walter Raleigh's History of the World. Proc. British Academy, VIII, 1918.

Harrison, G. B. Willobie his Avisa. 1926. [An account of the enquiry into Ralegh's atheism held in 1594. See also Loves Labours Lost, ed. Sir A. Quiller-Couch and J. D. Wilson, Cambridge, 1923.]

Kempner, N. Ralegh's Staatstheoretische Schriften. Leipzig, 1928.

Beau, J. La Religion de Sir Walter Raleigh. Revue anglo-américaine, June 1934.

A. M. C. L.

ROBERT BURTON (1577–1640]

(a) The Anatomy of Melancholy

The Anatomy of Melancholy, What it is. With all the Kindes, Causes, Symptomes, Prognostickes, and Several Cures of it. In Three Maine Partitions with their several Sections, Members and Subsections. Philosophically, Medicinally, Historically, Opened and Cut up. By Democritus Junior. Oxford, 1621; Oxford, 1624; Oxford, 1628 (with the engraved title-page, the Latin elegiacs, Democritus Junior ad Librum suum, and the Authors Abstract of Melancholy, Διαλογικῶς); Oxford, 1632 (adds The Argument of the Frontispiece); Edinburgh, Oxford and London, 1638; Oxford and London, 1651 or 1652; 1660; 1676; rptd [Stephen Jones], 2 vols. 1800, etc.; 2 vols. Philadelphia, 1836; 1845 (with trns of many Latin quotations); ed. A. R. Shilleto (with introduction by A. H. Bullen), 3 vols. 1893, 1896, 1904 and 1923; 2 vols. 1925 (omits marginal notes); ed. Floyd Dell and Paul Jordan-Smith, 2 vols. New York, 1927 and 1 vol. 1930 (omits marginal notes and translates all Latin); ed. H. Jackson, 3 vols. 1932 (Everyman's Lib.). [For other rpts see the tentative list by G. H. Doane, American Collector, v, 1928.]

Melancholy; drawn chiefly from Burton's Anatomy. 1801; 1824; 1827; 1865; 1881.

Burton the Anatomist, being Extracts from the Anatomy of Melancholy. Ed. G. C. F. Mead and R. C. Clift (with preface by W. H. D. Rouse), 1925.

(b) Other Writings

Philosophaster, Comoedia; Poemata adhuc sparsim edita, nunc in unum collecta. Ed. W. E. Buckley, Roxburghe Club, Hertford, 1862. [The poems had appeared in: Academiae Oxoniensis Pietas erga Jacobum Regem, Oxford, 1603; Musa Hospitalis, Ecclesiae Christi, Oxon., Oxford, 1605; Justa Oxoniensium [to the memory of Prince Henry], 1612; Death Repealed, Verses on Lord Bayning, Oxford, 1638; and similar collections. Buckley omits the Latin elegiacs to Francis Holyoake in his edn of Rider's Dictionarie, 1617.]

Philosophaster. With an English Translation [and] Burton's Minor Writings in Prose and Verse. Ed. P. Jordan-Smith, Palo Alto, 1931.

(c) Biography and Criticism

(i) Biography

Burton, W. A Description of Leicestershire. 1622. [Pp. 176–9.]

Lluelyn, Martin. Elegie: On the Death of Master R. B. [In Men-Miracles, with other Poems, Oxford, 1646.]

à Wood, A. Athenae Oxonienses. 2 vols. 1691–2; ed. P. Bliss, 6 vols. 1813–20. [Ed. Bliss, vol. I, p. 28, note, vol. II, p. 652.]

Hearne, T. Remarks and Collections. Oxford Hist. Soc. 1885–. [21 May 1711, 2 Aug. 1713, 23 and 28 Jan. 1734.]

Kennett, White. A Register and Chronicle. Vol. I, 1728, p. 320.

Nichols, J. The History and Antiquities of the County of Leicester. 8 vols. 1795–1815. [Vol. III, pp. 415–9, 557–9, 1137, vol. IV, pp. 635, 668.]

(ii) Comment and Criticism

Fuller, Thomas. The Worthies of England. 1662. [Pt II, p. 134.]

Herring, Thomas. Letters to William Duncombe. 1777. [Pp. 148–50.]

Warton, Thomas. Poems upon several occasions by John Milton. 1791 (2nd edn). [Especially pp. 94–6.]

Boswell, James. Life of Johnson. Ed. G. Birkbeck Hill, 6 vols. Oxford, 1887. [Vol. II, pp. 121, 440. vol. III, p. 415.]

Ferriar, John. Illustrations of Sterne. 2 vols. 1812 (2nd edn). [Vol. I, pp. 82–120, vol. II, pp. 9–63.]

Jusserand, J. J. Histoire littéraire du Peuple anglais. 2 vols. Paris, 1894–1904; tr. Eng. 3 vols. 1895–1909.

Bensly, Edward. Burton's Anatomy of Melancholy. N. & Q. Ser. 9, XI, XII, Ser. 10, I, II, III, IV, V, VI, VII, X, 1897–1908. [Passages from earlier authors identified.]

—— Burton and Fletcher. N. & Q. 15 Dec. 1906.

—— A Hitherto Unknown Source of Montaigne and Burton. Athenaeum, 5 Sept. 1908. [See also 6 and 13 June.]

—— Burton and Jacques Ferrand. N. & Q. 10 April 1909.

—— Theodorus Prodromus, John Barclay and Robert Burton. N. & Q. 6 Feb. 1909.

—— Robert Burton, John Barclay and John Owen. CHEL. vol. IV, ch. 13, 1909.

Dieckow, Fritz. John Florios englische Übersetzung der Essais Montaignes und Lord Bacons, Ben Jonsons und Robert Burtons Verhältnis zu Montaigne. Strasburg, 1903.

Lake, Bernard. A General Introduction to Charles Lamb, together with a Special Study of his Relation to Robert Burton. Leipzig, 1903.

Whibley, Charles. Literary Portraits. 1904.

Osler, Sir William. Burton's Anatomy of Melancholy. Yale Rev. 1914. [Expanded in Proc. Oxford Bibliog. Soc. I, 1925.]

Lowes, J. L. The Loveres Maladye of Hereos. MP. XI, 1914.

Duff, E. Gordon. The Fifth Edition of Burton's Anatomy of Melancholy. Library, IV, 1923.

Madan, Falconer, et al. Oxford Bibliog. Soc. I, pt 3, 1925. [Contributions by F. Madan,

Sir W. Osler, E. Gordon Duff, E. Bensly, S. Gibson, and F. R. D. Needham, all on Burton.]

Hughes, M. Y. Burton on Spenser. PMLA. XLI, 1926.

Jordan-Smith, P. Bibliographia Burtoniana. A Study of The Anatomy of Melancholy, with a Bibliography of Burton's Writings. Palo Alto, 1931.

Boddy, M. P. Burton in the XVIII Century. N. & Q. 22 Sept. 1934.

(d) Burton's Library

Macray, W. D. Annals of the Bodleian Library. 1890.

Aitken, P. H. The Cypher of Burton's Signature Solved. Athenaeum, 24 Aug. 1912. [Two lists of Burton's books received by the Bodleian and Christ Church Lib., ed. S. Gibson and F. R. D. Needham, are in Proc. Oxford Bibliog. Soc. I, 1925.]

(e) Imitations and Borrowings

Greenwood, William. Ἀπογραφὴ στοργῆς. Or, A Description of the Passion of Love. 1657. ΠΕΡΙΑΜΜΑ 'ΕΠΙΔΗΜΙΟΝ: Or, Vulgar Errours in Practice Censured. 1659.   E. B.

IZAAK WALTON (1593–1683)

(a) Bibliography

Westwood, T. The Chronicle of 'The Compleat Angler'. 1864. [Rptd with addns in Marston's edn of The Compleat Angler, 1888.]

Wood, A. A Bibliography of 'The Complete Angler.' New York, 1900.

Butt, J. E. A Bibliography of Izaak Walton's Lives. Proc. Oxford Bibliog. Soc. II, 1930. [See also the bibliographical notes in The Compleat Walton, ed. G. L. Keynes, 1929.]

(b) Collected Works

The Compleat Walton. Ed. G. L. Keynes, 1929.

(c) The Compleat Angler

The Compleat Angler or the Contemplative Man's Recreation. 1653; 1655 ('much enlarged'); 1661 (a few alterations, re-issued 1664); 1668.

The Universal Angler, Made so, by Three Books of Fishing. The First Written by Mr. Izaak Walton. 1676 (adds Cotton's Instructions, etc.).

The Compleat Angler. Ed. Moses Browne, 1750; ed. Sir John Hawkins, 1760; ed. Sir H. Nicolas, 2 vols. 1836; ed. [G. W. Bethune], New York, 1847; ed. R. B. Marston, 2 vols. 1888.

(d) The Lives

The Life and Death of Dr. Donne. 1640 (in LXXX Sermons. By John Donne); 1658 (much enlarged, as The Life of John Donne); ed. [T. E. Tomlins], 1852 and 1865.

The Life of Sir Henry Wotton. 1651 (in Reliquiae Wottonianae); 1654 (in Reliquiae Wottonianae, with addns and alterations); 1672 (in Reliquiae Wottonianae, with slight addns and alterations; rptd 1685).

The Life of Mr. Rich. Hooker. 1665; 1666 (with some addns and alterations, in The Works of Mr. Richard Hooker; rptd 1676, 1682, 1705, 1723); ed. J. Keble, Oxford, 1836 (in The Works of Hooker, vol. i).

The Life of Mr. George Herbert. 1670; 1674 (with slight alterations, in The Temple. By Mr. George Herbert; rptd 1679).

The Life of Dr. Sanderson. 1678; 1681 (with numerous small addns and alterations, in XXXV Sermons by Robert Sanderson; rptd 1686 and re-issued 1689); ed. W. Jacobson, Oxford, 1854 (in The Works of Sanderson, vol. vi).

The Lives of Dr. John Donne, Sir Henry Wotton, Mr. Richard Hooker, Mr. George Herbert. 1670 (alterations and addns in the first three Lives; second appearance of Herbert's); 1675 (addns to Donne, alterations in Hooker and Herbert); ed., with Life, T. Zouch, York, 1796 (adds Sanderson).

(e) Miscellaneous Works

Songs and other poems. By Alex. Brome. 1661. [Contains Walton's Daman and Dorus.]

Love and Truth. 1680 (anon.). [Archbishop Sancroft's attribution to Walton is confirmed by stylistic evidence.]

Waltoniana. Ed. R. H. Shepherd, 1878. [Contains all Walton's prose and verse remains, except two pieces to be found in The Compleat Walton, ed. G. L. Keynes, 1929.]

(f) Biography and Criticism

[Nicolas's introduction to his edn of The Compleat Angler is the most authoritative life of Walton; his few errors have been corrected by Marston in the introduction to his edn of The Compleat Angler. Criticism of Walton is apt to deal in wordy rapture, from which the subjoined list is comparatively free: to these books should be added the following introductions to reprints of The Compleat Angler: A. Lang, [1896], R. Le Gallienne, [1896]; and G. Saintsbury's Introduction to the World's Classics rpt of The Lives, 1927.]

Franck, R. Northern Memoirs. 1694.

Lamb, C. Letters. Ed. T. N. Talfourd, 1837. [Refers to The Compleat Angler in a letter to Coleridge, 1796.]

Hazlitt, W. The Round Table. Vol. i, no. 18, 1815. [Rev. for his Lectures on the English Poets, 1818: lecture on Thomson and Cowper.]

Irving, Washington. The Sketch Book of Geoffrey Crayon, Gent. Vol. ii, 1820.

Wordsworth, W. Poems. Vol. iii, 1820.

—— Ecclesiastical Sketches. 1822.

Landor, W. S. Imaginary Conversations. Vol. v, no. 12, 1829.

Lowell, J. R. Latest Literary Essays and Addresses. 1891.

Marston, R. B. Walton and Some Earlier Writers on Fish and Fishing. 1894.

Beeching, H. C. Religio Laici. 1902.

Stauffer, D. A. English Biography before 1700. Cambridge, U.S.A. 1930.

Butt, J. E. Izaak Walton's Methods in Biography. E. & S. xix, 1934.

—— Izaak Walton's Collections for Fulman's Life of John Hales. MLR. xxix, 1934.

J. E. B.

WILLIAM PRYNNE (1600–1669)

Histrio-Mastix: The Players Scourge, or, Actors tragædie. 1633; tr. Dutch, Leyden, 1639.

The Antipathie of the English Lordly Prelacie both to regall monarchy, and civill unity. 2 pts, 1641.

The Soveraigne Power of Parliaments & Kingdomes. 4 pts, 1643. [Title of pt 1, The Treachery and Disloyalty of Papists to their Soveraignes.]

The Opening of The Great Seale of England. 1643; rptd Somers Tracts, ed. Sir W. Scott, vol. iv, 1810.

A Breviate of the Life of William Laud. 1644.

Hidden Workes of Darkenes Brought to Publike Light, or, A Necessary Introduction to the History of the Archbishop of Canterburie's Triall. 1645.

Canterburie's Doome. Or The First Part of a Compleat History of the Tryall of William Laud. 1646.

Irenarches Redivivus. Or, A briefe Collection of Statutes concerning Justices Of Peace. 1648.

A Plea for the Lords: or, A Vindication of the Power of the House of Peeres. 1648.

The First Part of an Historical Collection of the ancient Parliaments of England. 1649.

A legal vindication of the liberties of England against Illegal Taxes. 1649.

A Seasonable, Legall, and Historicall Vindication of the Good, Old, Fundamental
Liberties of all English Freemen. 3 pts,
1654–7; 1655 (pts 1, 2).

A Short Demurrer To the Jewes Long discontinued Remitter into England. 1656.

An Exact Abridgement of the Records in the
Tower of London, collected By Sir Robert
Cotton. 1657. [Revised by Prynne.]

A Plea for the Lords, and House of Peers. 1658.
[Expansion of A Plea for the Lords, 1648.]

A Brief Register of the several Kinds of
Parliamentary Writs. 4 pts, 1659–64.

The Signal Loyalty and Devotion of Gods
true Saints towards their Kings. 2 pts,
1660; ed. in part C. Wordsworth, Henry
Bradshaw Soc. 1892.

An Exact Chronological Vindication and Historical Demonstration of our British,
Roman [etc.] Kings Supreme Ecclesiastical
Jurisdiction. 3 vols. 1666. [Vol. III rptd as
The History of King John, King Henry III.
And King Edward the I, 1670; rptd 1672
(as Antiquae Constitutiones Regni Angliae
circa Juris dictionem Ecclesiasticam; Index,
1775). A fourth volume was left half ptd:
there is a copy at Lincoln's Inn.]

Aurum Reginae, or A Compendious Tractate
Concerning Queen-Gold. 1668.

Brief Animadversions on the Fourth Part of
the Institutes of the Lawes of England,
Compiled by Sir Edward Cooke. 1669.

Authorities

Documents relating to the proceedings against
William Prynne, in 1634 and 1637. Ed. J.
Bruce and S. R. Gardiner, Camden Soc.
1877.

à Wood, A. Athenae Oxonienses. Ed. P. Bliss,
1813–20, vol. III, p. 844, [Gives full list of
Prynne's works.]

Kirby, E. W. William Prynne: a Study in
Puritanism. Cambridge, U.S.A. 1931.
[With bibliography of Prynne's writings.]

G. P.

JAMES HOWELL (1594?–1666)

ΔΕΝΔΡΟΛΟΓΙΑ: Dodona's Grove, or, The
Vocall Forrest. 1640; 1644 (with Parables,
reflecting upon the Times, and England's
Teares, for the present Warres); (with
England s Tears, and The Pre-eminence of
Parliament) 1645 and 1649; second part,
1650. Tr. Latin, 1646; French, Paris, 1641;
1648.

The Vote, or a Poeme Royall, presented to His
Majestie for a New-Yeares-Gift. 1642; 1647,
etc. (in Epistolae, vol. II); 1654 (in Minor
Works).

Instructions for forreine Travell. 1642; 1650;
rptd E. Arber, 1869, etc.

The True Informer, Who Discovereth the sad
Distempers in Great Brittany. Oxford, 1643;
1661 (in Divers Discourses, as Casual Discourses and Interlocutions betwixt Patricius
and Peregrin Touching the Distractions of
the Times).

A Discourse, or Parly, continued betwixt
Partricius and Peregrine (upon their landing
in France) touching the civill Wars of
England and Ireland. 1643; 1661 (in Divers
Discourses).

Parables, reflecting Upon the Times. Paris,
1643; 1644 (with Dodona's Grove); 1661
(in Divers Discourses, as Apologs, or Fables
Mythologiz'd).

Mercurius Hibernicus: Or, A Discourse of the
late Insurrection in Ireland. Bristol, 1644;
1661 (in Divers Discourses, as Of The Land
of Ire).

The Preheminence and Pedigree of Parlement.
1644; 1644 (with England's Teares); 1645;
1645 and 1649 (with Dodona's Grove); 1661
(in Divers Discourses as A Vindication of
His Majesty); 1677; rptd Harleian Misc., ed.
T. Park, vols. I, VI, 1808–10, and Somers
Tracts, vol. V, 1809.

England's Teares, for the present Wars. 1644;
1644 (with The Preheminence of Parliament); 1644, 1645, and 1649 (with Dodona's
Grove); rptd Harleian Misc. vol. VIII, 1811,
and Somers Tracts, vol. V, 1811. Tr. Latin,
1646; Dutch, 1649.

Epistolae Ho-Elianae. Familiar Letters Domestic and Forren. Vol. I, 1645; vol. II, 1647;
vols. I, II and III, 1650; collected edn with
vol. IV, 1655. Later edns, 1673, 1678, 4 vols,
1688, 1705, 1713, 1726, 1737, 1754; ed. J.
Jacobs, 2 vols. 1890–2; ed. O. Smeaton,
3 vols. 1903 (Temple Classics).

Lustra Ludovici, or the Life of Lewis XIII. 1646.

A Letter To the Earle of Pembrooke Concerning
the Times. 1647; 1654 (in Minor Works);
1661 (in Divers Discourses).

A defence of the treaty of Newport. 1648
(anon.) [Attrib. to Howell.]

Bella Scot-Anglica. A Brief of all the Battels
'twixt England and Scotland. 1648 (anon.);
1654 (in Minor Works).

The Instruments of a King: The Sword. The
Sceptre. The Crowne. 1648; 1654 (in Minor
Works); 1661 (in Divers Discourses, as The
Sway of the Sword).

A Venice Looking-Glasse: Or, A Letter Written
from London to Rome, touching these
present distempers. 1648; 1654 (in Minor
Works); 1661 (in Divers Discourses, as
An Italian Prospective).

A Winter Dreame. 1649; 1654 (in Minor
Works); 1661 (in Divers Discourses, as A
Nocturnal Progres); rptd Harleian Misc.
vol. VII, 1811.

A Trance. Or Newes from Hell. 1649; 1654 (in Minor Works, as Mercurius Acheronticus).

An Inquisition after Blood. To the Parliament and To the Army. 1649 (anon.); 1654 (in Minor Works); 1661 (in Divers Discourses, as A Glance upon the Ile of Wight).

S.PQ.V. A Survay of the Signorie of Venice. 1651.

The Vision: or A Dialog between the Soul and the Bodie. 1651.

Ah, Ha; Tumulus, Thalamus: Two counter-poems. 1653.

A German Diet: or, The Ballance of Europe. 1653.

Some of Mr Howell's Minor Works. 1654. [Reprints.]

An Admonition to My Lord Protector and his Council Of their present Danger. 1654. [Attrib.]

Some Sober Inspections Made into the Cariage and Consults of the Late-long parlement. 1655; 1656; 1658; 1660.

Londinopolis; An Historicall Discourse or Perlustration Of the City of London [and] Westminster. 1657. [Includes a bibliography of Howell's writings.]

A Discours of the Empire, and of The Election of A King of the Romans. 1658; 1659.

ΠΑΡΟΙΜΙΟΓΡΑΦΙΑ. Proverbs, Or, Old Sayed Sawes & Adages, in English, Italian, French and Spanish whereunto the British [Welsh] are added. 1659.

A Particular vocabulary, or Nomenclature In English, Italian, French, and Spanish [of technical terms]. 1659.

Lexicon Tetraglotton, An English-French-Italian-Spanish Dictionary. 1660–59. [With the two preceding books.]

England's Joy, Expressed to Monck. 1660. [Attrib.]

Θηρολογια. The Parly of Beasts. 1660.

A late Letter From Florence Touching these present Distempers of England. 1660; 1661 (in Divers Discourses, as Advice Sent from the Prime Statesman of Florence).

Divers Historicall Discourses Of the late Popular Insurrections. 1661; 1661 (Twelve Several Treatises, of the late Revolutions). [Reprints.]

A Cordial for the Cavaliers. 1661.

Som Sober Inspections Made Into those Ingredients That went to the Composition of A late cordial. 1661.

A Brief Account of the Royal Matches since the year 800. 1662. [Attrib.]

A New English Grammar, for Forreners to learn English. 1662. [With a Spanish grammar, etc. and notes on travel in Spain and Portugal.]

Poems On several Choice and Various Subjects. Ed. Payne Fisher, 1663; 1664

(as Poems Upon divers Emergent Occasions).

ΠΡΟΕΔΡΙΑ-ΒΑΣΙΛΙΚΗ. A Discourse Concerning the Precedency of Kings. [With] A distinct Treatise of Ambassadors. 1664; tr. Latin, 1664.

A Discours of Dunkirk. 1664.

[Howell also pbd a number of trns, including:

St Paul's Late Progres Upon Earth, About a Divorce 'twixt Christ and the Church of Rome. 1644. [From the Italian of Ferrante Pallavicino.]

An Exact Historie of The late Revolutions in Naples. 2 pts, 1650–2 (pt 2, The Second Part of Massaniello); 1663–4; 1679–63. [From the Italian of Alessandro Giraffi.]

The Process and Pleadings In the Court of Spain upon the death of Antonie Ascham. 1651; rptd Harleian Misc. vol. IV, 1809.

The Wonderful, and most deplorable History of the Latter Times of the Jews. Written first in Hebrew. 1652; 1653; 1662; 1669; 1684; 1699.

The Nuptialls of Peleus and Thetis. 1654.

Howell edited the following:

Cotgrave's French and English Dictionary. 1650; 1660; 1673.

Cottoni posthuma. 1651; 1672; 1679; ed. E. Goldsmid, Edinburgh, 1884–7.

Parthenopoeia, or the History of Naples. 1654. [Pt I tr. from Italian of S. Mazzella by S. Lennard: pt II compiled by Howell from various Italian writers.]

Finetti Philoxenis. 1656.]

Authorities

Bensly, E. James Howell. Aberystwyth Stud. III–VI, 1922–4, VIII, IX, 1926–7.

Vann, W. H. Notes on the Writings of James Howell. Waco, 1924. [Full bibliography.]

G. P.

BULSTRODE WHITELOCKE (1605–1675)

Memorials of the English affairs: from the beginning of the reign of King Charles the First, to King Charles the Second his happy restauration. 1682; 1732; rptd 4 vols. Oxford, 1853.

Essays ecclesiastical & civil. To which is subjoined a Treatise of the work of the sessions of the peace. 1706.

Memorials of English affairs, from the suppos'd expedition of Brute to the end of the reign of James the First. With some account of his [Whitelocke's] life and writings by W. Penn, and a preface by J. Welwood. 1709.

Notes uppon the Kings writt for choosing members of Parlement XIII Car. II being disquisitions on the government of England by King Lords and Commons. Ed. C. Morton, 2 vols. 1766.

A Journal of the Swedish Ambassy, in the years 1653 and 1654. Ed. C. Morton, 2 vols. 1772; ed. H. Reeve, 2 vols. 1855; tr. Swedish, Upsala, 1777.

Annals of his life. [Extracts only ptd in R. H. Whitelocke's life, 1860.]

Authorities

Oldmixon, J. Clarendon and Whitlock compar'd. 1727.

Clarendon and Whitlock Farther Compar'd. Or, A Discovery Of Mistakes by Oldmixon. 1739.

Norton, C. [Preface to his edn of Swedish Ambassy, 1772; rptd in Reeve's edn, 1855.]

Whitelocke, R. H. Memoirs, biographical and historical, of Bulstrode Whitelocke. 1860.

G. P.

SIR THOMAS BROWNE (1605–1682)

(a) Bibliography

Keynes, Geoffrey. A Bibliography of Sir Thomas Browne. Cambridge, 1924.

Leroy, O. A French Bibliography of Sir Thomas Browne. 1931.

(b) Collected Works

The Works of the Learned Sr Thomas Brown. Containing I. Enquiries into Vulgar and Common Errors. II. Religio Medici: with Annotations and Observations upon it. III. Hydriotaphia; or, Urn-Burial: Together with The Garden of Cyrus. IV. Certain Miscellany Tracts. 1686; tr. Dutch, Amsterdam, 1688.

Posthumous Works of the Learned Sir Thomas Browne. Printed from his Original Manuscripts, viz. I. Repertorium: Or, The Antiquities of the Cathedral Church of Norwich. II. An Account of some Urnes; etc. found at Brampton in Norfolk, Anno 1667. III. Letters between Sir William Dugdale and Sir Tho. Browne. IV. Miscellanies. To which is prefix'd his Life [containing John Whitefoot's Minutes]. 1712.

Works including his Life and Correspondence. Ed. Simon Wilkin, 4 vols. 1835–6, 1852. [Regarded as one of the best edited books in the English language, and still of the greatest value.]

Works. Ed. C. Sayle, 3 vols. 1904–7, etc. [Omits correspondence.]

Works. Ed. Geoffrey Keynes, 6 vols. 1928–31. [The whole text newly edited, with a fresh transcript of the letters, etc.]

(c) Single Works

Religio Medici. 1642 (2 unauthorized edns); 1643 (authorized edn); 1645 (bis); 1656; 1659; 1659 (with other works); 1669; 1672 (with other works); 1678; 1682; 1685 (with other works); 1736 (bis); 1738; 1754; ed. J. A. St John, 1838; ed. H. Gardiner, 1845; ed. Willis Bund, 1869; ed. W. A. Greenhill, 1881, etc. (best separate edn); ed. J. A. Symonds, 1886; ed. W. Murison, Cambridge, 1922. Tr. Latin, Leyden, 1644 (bis), Paris, 1644, 1650, 1652, 1665, 1677, 1692 and 1743; Dutch, Leyden, 1665 and 1683; French, 1668; German, Preuzlau, 1746. [See also C. Williams, A Bibliography of the Religio Medici, 1905 and 1907.]

Pseudodoxia Epidemica; or, Enquiries into Very many received Tenents, and commonly presumed Truths. 1646; 1650 (with alterations and addns)· 1658 (bis); 1669; 1672. Tr. Dutch, Amsterdam, 1668; German, Frankfort, 1680; French, 2 vols. Paris, 1733 (bis); Italian, 2 vols. Venice, 1737 and 1743.

Hydriotaphia, Urne-buriall, or, A Discourse of the Sepulchrall Urnes lately found in Norfolk. Together with The Garden of Cyrus, or the Quincunciall Lozenge, or Net-work Plantations of the Ancients. 1658; 1658, 1659 and 1669 (with other works); 1736; ed. Sir J. Evans, 1893; ed. W. A. Greenhill, 1896; ed. W. Murison, Cambridge, 1922; rptd facs. 1927; ed. J. Carter, 1932. [Frequently rptd with Religio Medici.]

Certain Miscellany Tracts. 1683 (re-issued 1684).

A Letter to a Friend Upon occasion of the Death of his Intimate Friend. 1690. [Frequently rptd with Religio Medici.]

Christian Morals. Published from the original manuscript. Ed. J. Jeffrey, Cambridge, 1716, Halle, 1723; ed. Samuel Johnson, 1756; ed. S. C. Roberts, Cambridge, 1927. [Frequently rptd with Religio Medici.]

(d) Biography and Criticism

Digby, Sir Kenelm. Observations upon Religio Medici. 1643.

Ross, Alexander. Medicus Medicatus. 1645.

Hale, Sir Matthew. A Trial of Witches. 1682.

Whitefoot, John. Minutes for the Life. 1712 (in Posthumous Works).

Heister, E. F. Apologia pro Medicis. Amsterdam, 1736.

Johnson, Samuel. Life. 1756 (with Christian Morals).

Hazlitt, William. Lectures on the Age of Elizabeth. 1820.

Coleridge, S. T. Literary Remains. 2 vols. 1836.

Wilkin, Simon. Memoir. 1836 (in Works, vol. I).

Milsand, J. Thomas Browne, le Médecin de Norwich. Revue des deux Mondes, 1 April 1858.

Stephen, Sir Leslie. Hours in a Library. Ser. 2. 1876.

Pater, Walter. Appreciations. 1889.

Dowden, E. Puritan and Anglican. 1900.

Williams, C. The Pedigree of Sir Thomas Browne. 1902.

—— A Souvenir of Sir Thomas Browne. 1905.

—— A Bibliography of the Religio Medici. 1905; 1907.

Gosse, Sir Edmund. Sir Thomas Browne. 1905. (English Men of Letters Ser.)

Osler, Sir William. The Religio Medici. Library, VII, 1906.

—— An Alabama Student. 1908.

Schonack, W. Sir Thomas Browne's Religio Medici. 1911.

Saintsbury, George. Antiquaries. CHEL. vol. VII, ch. 10, 1911.

Keith, Sir Arthur. The Skull of Sir Thomas Browne. TLS. 11 May 1922.

Strachey, Lytton. Books and Characters. 1922.

Tildesley, M. L. Sir Thomas Browne, His Skull, Portraits, and Ancestry. 1923.

Howell, A. C. Sir Thomas Browne and Seventeenth-Century Scientific Thought. Stud. Phil. XXII, 1925.

Ashton, A. J. Sir Thomas Browne en famille. English Rev. XLIII, XLIV, 1926-7.

Sir Thomas Browne. TLS. 24 May 1928.

Tyler, D. Sir Thomas Browne's Part in a Witch Trial in 1664. Ang. LIV, 1930.

Leroy, O. Le Chevalier Thomas Browne. Paris, 1931.

Thaler, A. Sir Thomas Browne and the Elizabethans. Stud. Phil. XXVIII, 1931.

Carter, J. The Iniquity of Oblivion Foil'd. Colophon, pt 13, 1933.

Cawley, R. R. Sir Thomas Browne and his Reading. PMLA. XLVIII, 1933.

Kane, R. J. James Crossley, Sir Thomas Browne and the Fragment on Mummies. RES. IX, 1933.

Loiseau, J. Sir Thomas Browne Écrivain 'métaphysique.' Revue anglo-américaine, X, 1933.

G. L. K.

THOMAS FULLER (1608–1661)

[A bibliography of Fuller's works is contained in J. E. Bailey's Life, 1874. This has been superseded by S. Gibson, A Bibliography of the Works of Thomas Fuller, Proc. Oxford Bibliog. Soc. IV, 1936.]

(a) Poetical Works

David's Hainous Sin, Heartie Repentance, Heavie Punishment. 1631; rptd 1869.

A Panegyrick to His Majesty on his Happy Return. 1660.

Poems and Translations in Verse. Ed. A. B. Grosart, Edinburgh, 1868.

(b) Principal Writings

The Historie of the Holy Warre. Cambridge, 1639, 1640, 1647, 1651; rptd 1840.

The Holy State. The Profane State. Cambridge, 1642, 1648, 1652 and 1663; rptd 1840; ed. J. Nichols, 1841.

Good Thoughts in Bad Times. Exeter, 1645; 1645; 1646.

Andronicus, or the Unfortunate Politician. 1646 (3 edns); 1649; 1659. [Also in The Profane State, 1648, etc.]

Good Thoughts in Worse Times. 1647.

Good Thoughts in Bad Times, together with Good Thoughts in Worse Times. 1649; 1652; 1657; 1659; 1665; 1669; 1680; rptd 1830 (with Mixt Contemplations).

A Pisgah-Sight of Palestine. 1650; 1662; rptd 1869.

The Church-History of Britain. With the History of the University of Cambridge, and The History of Waltham Abbey in Essex. 1655; ed. J. Nichols, 3 vols. 1837, etc.; ed. J. S. Brewer, 6 vols. 1845.

Mixt Contemplations in Better Times. 1660; rptd 1830 (with Bad Times and Worse Times).

The History of the Worthies of England. 1662; 1684 (abridged as Anglorum Speculum); ed. J. Nichols, 2 vols. 1811; ed. P. A. Nuttall, 3 vols. 1840. [Index ptd in the 18th century or by Pickering, c. 1825, added to some copies of first edn.]

Thomas Fuller: Selections, with Essays by Charles Lamb, Leslie Stephen, etc. Ed. E. K. Broadus, Oxford, 1929.

(c) Sermons

Joseph's Party-coloured Coat. 1640; rptd 1867.

Fast Sermon preached on Innocent's Day. 1642.

Sermon on the day of His Majesty's Inauguration. 1643.

Sermon of Reformation. 1643.

Jacob's Vow. 1644.

Fear of Losing the Old Light. 1646.

Cause and Cure of a Wounded Conscience. 1647; 1649; rptd 1810.

Sermon of Assurance. 1647.
Sermon of Contentment. 1648.
The Just Man's Funeral. 1649.
Comment on the 4th Chapter of St Matthew. 1652.
Perfection and Peace. 1653.
Comment on Ruth. 1654; rptd 1868.
A Triple Reconciler. 1654.
Life out of Death. 1655.
Collection of Four Sermons with Notes upon Jonah. 1656.
The Best Name on Earth. 1657; 1659.
Sermon Preached at St Clemens Danes. 1657.
Collected Sermons. Ed. J. E. Bailey and W. E. Axon, 2 vols. 1891.

(d) Controversial Works

Truth Maintained. 1643.
The Infant's Advocate. 1653.
The Appeal of Injured Innocence. 1659.
An Alarum to the Counties of England. 1660.

(e) Contributions

Abel Redivivus, or, the Dead yet Speaking. 1651; 1652. [A few of the lives by Fuller.]
Ephemeris Parliamentaria. 1654; 1658; 1660. [Preface by Fuller.]
Sermons of Mr Henry Smith. 1657. [Life of Smith by Fuller.]

(f) Biography and Criticism

The Life of that Reverend Divine and Learned Historian, Dr Thomas Fuller. 1661; 1662.
Coleridge, S. T. Literary Remains. 2 vols. 1836.
Russell, A. T. Memorials of the Life and Works of Thomas Fuller. 1844.
Rogers, Henry. An Essay on the Life and Genius of Thomas Fuller. 1856.
Grosart, A. B. The Poems and Translations in Verse. Edinburgh, 1868. [Introduction and notes.]
Bailey, J. E. The Life of Thomas Fuller, with Notices of his Books, his Kinsmen, and his Friends. 1874. [The standard authority.]
Fuller, M. Life, Times and Writings of Thomas Fuller. 2 vols. 1884.
Thompson, E. N. S. Literary Bypaths of the Renaissance. New Haven, 1924.
Kellett, E. E. Thomas Fuller. London Quart. Rev. cxlv, 1926.
Lyman, D. B. The Great Tom Fuller. Berkeley, 1935.

G. L. K.

Sir Thomas Urquhart (1611–1660)

(a) Collected Works

Tracts of the Learned and Celebrated Antiquarian Sir Thomas Urquhart. [Ed. D. Herd], Edinburgh, 1774 (re-issued 1782).

[Contains: Ekskubalauron, Pantochronochanon, Logopandecteision.]
The Works of Sir Thomas Urquhart. Ed. [G. Maitland], Maitland Club, Edinburgh, 1834. [Omits the Rabelais.]

(b) Separate Works

Epigrams: Divine and Moral. 1641; 1646.
The Trissotetras: or, A Most Exquisite Table For Resolving all manner of Triangles. 1645 (re-issued 1650).
ΕΚΣΚΥΒΑΛΑΥΡΟΝ: or, The Discovery of A most exquisite Jewel, found in the kennel of Worcester-streets, anno 1651. Serving To frontal a Vindication of the honour of Scotland. 1652.
ΠΑΝΤΟΧΡΟΝΟΧΑΝΟΝ: Wherein is displayed A most exact Directory for all particular Chronologies, in what Family soever: And that by deducing the true Pedigree of the Urquharts, in the house of Cromartie, since the Creation of the world, until 1652. 1652.
Logopandecteision, or an Introduction to the Universal Language. 1653.
The First Book of the Works of Mr. Francis Rabelais, now faithfully translated into English. 1653; 1664. The Second Book. By S. T. U. C. 1653; 1664. The Third Book. 1693.
The Works of F. Rabelais, M.D. Done out of French by Sir Tho. Urchard Kt and others. 2 vols. 1694. [Bks i and ii rptd with new introductory matter.]
The Whole Works of F. Rabelais, M.D. Done out of French, by Sir Thomas Urchard, Knight, Mr. Motteux, and Others. 2 vols. 1708; ed. J. Ozell, 5 vols. 1737; ed. T. Martin, Edinburgh, 1838; ed. A. Wallis, 5 vols. 1897; ed. C. Whibley, 3 vols. 1900 (Tudor Translations).
The History of the Admirable Crichton. Retrospective Rev. vi, 1822; ed. H. Miles, 1927 (as Life and Death of Admirable Crichton). [From Ekskubalauron.]

(c) Biography and Criticism

Irving, D. Lives of Scotish Writers. 2 vols. Edinburgh, 1839.
Miller, H. Scenes and Legends of the North of Scotland. 1850.
Whibley, C. Sir Thomas Urquhart. New Rev. xvii, 1897. [Rptd in Studies in Frankness, 1910.]
Willcock, J. Sir Thomas Urquhart of Cromartie Knight. 1899.
Brown, Huntington. Rabelais in English Literature. Cambridge, U.S.A. 1933.

J. E. B.

B. MINOR HISTORIANS

FRANCIS BACON, VISCOUNT ST ALBANS (1561–1626)

[See pp. 868–71 below.]

SAMUEL DANIEL (1562–1619)

The civile wars between the two houses of Lancaster and Yorke. Bks 1–4, 1595; bk 5, 1595; bks 1–5 rptd 1599 (in The Poeticall Essayes); bks 1–6, 1601 (in Works); complete edn with bks 7–8, 1609. [Verse.]

The Collection of the Historie of England. Part ɪ [to end of Stephen], 1612, 1613; complete edn [to end of Edward III], [1618]; 1621; 1626; 1634; 2 pts, 1650 (with continuation by J. Trussell) 1685; rptd. 1706 (in White Kennett, Complete History, vol. ɪ).

[See also H. Sellers, A Bibliography of the Works of Samuel Daniel, Proc. Oxford Bibliog. Soc. ɪɪ, 1927–30, and pp. 422–3 above.]

SIR GEORGE CAREW (d. 1612)

A Relation of the State of France, 1609. Ed. T. Birch (in An Historical View of the Negotiations Between the Courts of England, France, and Brussels, 1749).

SIR JOHN DAVIES (1569–1626)

A Discoverie of the True Causes why Ireland was never entirely Subdued untill his Majesties Raigne. 1612; 1613; Dublin, 1644; 1704 (in J. Ware, Antiquities of Ireland, 1705); 1747; Dublin, 1761; ed. G. Chalmers (in Historical tracts, 1786 and Dublin, 1787); rptd A. B. Grosart (Works, 3 vols. 1869–76); ed. H. Morley (in Ireland under Elizabeth and James I, 1890).

Le Primer Report des cases Resolues en les Courts del Roy. Dublin, 1615; 1628; 1674; Dublin, 1762 (tr. Eng.); Edinburgh, 1907 (English Reports, vol. LXXX).

[For Davies's poems see pp. 426–7 above.]

SIR JOHN HAYWARD (1564?–1627)

The First Part of the Life and Raigne of King Henrie the IIII. 1599; 1642 (with Sir R. Cotton's Short view of the raign of Henry III).

An answer to the first part of a certaine conference, concerning succession. 1603; 1683 (as The Right of Succession asserted).

A treatise of union of England and Scotland. 1604.

A report of a discourse concerning supreme power in affaires of religion. 1606 (anon.); 1607; 1624 (as Of Supremacie in Affaires of Religion).

The lives of the III Normans, Kings of England. 1613; rptd Harleian Misc. ed. T. Park, vols. ɪɪ, ɪx, 1809–12.

The life and raigne of King Edward the sixt. 1630; 1636 (with appendix The Beginning of the Reigne of Queene Elizabeth); rptd 1706 (in White Kennett, Complete History, vol. ɪɪ).

Annals of the first four years of the reign of Queen Elizabeth [of which The Beginning is a part]. Ed. J. Bruce, Camden Soc. 1840.

WILLIAM FARMER (fl. 1614)

Certaine Chroniculary Discourses, for the Years of our Lord, 1612–15. Dublin, 1772 (in J. Lodge, Desiderata Curiosa Hibernica).

Annals of Ireland from the Year 1594 to 1613. Ed. C. L. Falkiner, EIIR. xxɪɪ, 1907.

JOHN SPEED (1552?–1629)

The Theatre of the Empire of Great Britain. 1611; 1627 (re-issued 1631); 2 pts, 1676; tr. Latin P. Holland, 1616.

The History of Great Britaine. 1611; 1614; 1623; 1627; 1632; 1650. [Continuation of Theatre.]

SIR WILLIAM MONSON (1569–1643)

Naval tracts. 1704 (in A. and J. Churchill's Collection of Voyages, vol. ɪɪɪ); ed. M. Oppenheim, 5 vols. Navy Records Soc. 1902–14. [Excerpt ptd as A true and exact account of the Wars with Spain in the reign of Queen Elizabeth, 1682.]

EDMUND BOLTON (1575?–1633?)

The Elements of Armories. 1610 (signed E. B.).

The Roman histories of Lucius Julius Florus. Tr. E. M. B. [1619]; [1621?]; 1636 (dedication signed Philanactophil).

Nero Caesar, or Monarchie Depraved. 1624 (dedication signed Philanactophil); 1627.

The Cities Advocate, in this case or question of Honor and Armes; Whether Apprentiship extinguisheth Gentry. 1629 (anon.); 1674 (as The Cities great Concern, In this Case).

Hypercritica; or A Rule of Judgment for writing, or reading our History's. Ptd Anthony Hall (in Nicolai Triveti Annalium Continuatio, Oxford, 1722); rptd J. Haslewood (Ancient Critical Essays upon English Poets and Poësy, vol. ɪɪ, 1815).

FRANCIS GODWIN, BISHOP OF HEREFORD
(1562–1633)

A Catalogue of the Bishops of England. 1601; 1615 (with additions and A Discourse concerning the first conversion of Britaine, and A Discourse concerning such Englishmen as have beene Cardinals); [1625] (as The Succession of the bishops of England); tr. Latin by Godwin, 2 pts, 1616 (as De Praesulibus Angliae Commentarius); ed. and continued by W. Richardson, Cambridge, 1743.

Rerum Anglicarum Henrico VIII, Edwardo VI, et Maria regnantibus, Annales. 1616 (anon.); 1628; 1653. Tr. Eng. M. Godwin, 1630 and 1676 (with Bacon's History of Henry VII); J. H[ughes], 1706 (in White Kennett, Complete History, vol. II); French, Paris, 1647.

Ad commentarium de praesulibus Angliae appendix. [1621?]

Catalogus Episcoporum Bathoniensium Et Wellensium. [Partly ptd T. Hearne in John de Trokelowe, Annales Edwardi II, 1729, and John de Whethamstede, Chronicon, 2 vols. Oxford, 1732.]

SIR GEORGE BUC (d. 1623)

The Third Universitie of England. Or A Treatise of the Foundations of all the Colledges, Auncient Schooles of Priviledge, and of Houses of Learning, and Liberall Arts, within and about the most famous Cittie of London. [Appended to J. Stow's Annales, ed. E. Howes, 1615.]

The History of the Life and Reigne of Richard The Third. 1646 (re-issued 1647); rptd 1706 (in White Kennett, Complete History, vol. I).

GEORGE, BARON CAREW AND EARL OF TOTNES (1555–1629)

[Tr. The History of Ireland by Maurice Regan, and a contemporary French account of Richard II's visit to Ireland in 1399. Both ptd in W. Harris, Hibernica, 1747.]

Letters from George Lord Carew to Sir Thomas Roe. Ed. Sir J. Maclean, Camden Soc. 1860.

[See also Sir Thomas Stafford below.]

FYNES MORYSON (1566–1630)

An Itinerary Written By Fynes Moryson Containing His Ten Yeeres Travell Through the Twelve Dominions of Germany, Bohmenland, Sweitzerland, Netherland, Denmarke, Poland, Italy, Turky, France, England, Scotland, and Ireland. Divided into III Parts. 1617; rptd 4 vols. Glasgow, 1907–8. [Part of a 4th pt, ed C. Hughes,

1903 (as Shakespeare's Europe); 2nd pt, with ch. v of bk iii of 3rd pt rptd 2 vols. Dublin, 1735 (as An History of Ireland, From 1599 to 1603); The Description of Ireland, ed. H. Morley, Carisbrooke Lib. vol. x, 1890.]

GEORGE CARLETON, BISHOP OF CHICHESTER (1559–1628)

A Thankfull Remembrance of Gods Mercy. In an Historicall Collection of the Deliverances of the Church and State of England, from the beginning of Queene Elizabeth. 1624; 1625; 1627; 1630.

Vita Bernardi Gilpini. 1628; tr. Eng. [W. Freake], 1629; 1636 (4th edn); rptd 1752, 1810, etc. (in C. Wordsworth, Ecclesiastical Biography, vol. IV).

JOHN SPOTTISWOODE, ARCHBISHOP OF ST ANDREWS (1565–1639)

The History of the Church of Scotland, Beginning the Year of our Lord 203, and continued to the end of the Reign of James VI. 1655; 1677; ed. M. Russell and M. Napier, 3 vols. Spottiswoode Soc. and Bannatyne Club, Edinburgh, 1847–51.

SIR ROBERT NAUNTON (1563–1635)

Fragmenta Regalia, or observations on the late Q. Elizabeth, her times and favorites. 1641, 1642 (both inaccurate text); 1653 (rev. edn); rptd E. Arber, 1870, and frequently before. Tr. French, Amsterdam, 1703 (in Gregorio Leti, La Vie d'Elizabeth, vol. II); by J. le Pelletier, 1745; Italian, Amsterdam, 1693 (in G. Leti, Historia overo vita di Elisabetta).

SIR THOMAS STAFFORD (fl. 1633)

Pacata Hibernia. Or, an Historie of the Late Warres of Ireland, especially within the Province of Mounster, under the Government of Sir George Carew. 1633; rptd 2 vols. Dublin, 1810; ed. S. O'Grady, 2 vols. 1896. [Inspired by the papers of Lord Carew.]

THOMAS HOBBES (1588–1679)

[See pp. 871–3 below.]

ARTHUR WILSON (1595–1652)

The History of Great Britain, being the life and reign of King James I. 1653; 1706 (in White Kennett, Complete History, vol. II).

Observations of God's Providence, in the Tract of my Life. Ed. F. Peck (in Desiderata Curiosa, vol. II, 1735); ed. P. Bliss (as appendix to Wilson's play The Inconstant Lady, Oxford, 1814).

[See also p. 651 above.]

DAVID CALDERWOOD (1575–1650)

The True History of the Church of Scotland, From the beginning of the Reformation, unto the end of the Reigne of King James VI. [Rotterdam], 1678 (re-issued 1680); ed. T. Thomson, 8 vols. Wodrow Soc. Edinburgh, 1842–9. [These are from different summaries of the principal work.]

JOHN TRUSSELL (*fl.* 1636–1642)

A Continuation of the Collection of the History of England, beginning where S. Daniell ended. 1636.

WALTER BALCANQUHALL (1586?–1645)

A Large Declaration concerning The Late Tumults in Scotland. By the King. 1639. [Attrib.]

PETER HEYLYN (1600–1662)

Microcosmus, or A Little Description of the Great World. By P. H. Oxford, 1621; Oxford, 1625; Oxford, 1627; Oxford, 1629; Oxford, 1633 (6th edn); Oxford, 1636; Oxford, 1639; 1652 (as Cosmographie), etc.

The History of That most famous Saynt and Souldier St George of Cappadocia. 1631; 1633.

The History of the Sabbath. 2 pts, 1636; 1681 (in Historical and Miscellaneous Tracts).

ΗΡΩΟΛΟΓΙΑ Anglorum. Or, An help to English History. By Robert Hall. 1641; 1642; 1652; 1671; 1675; 1680; rptd 1773, 1786.

The Historie of Episcopacie. By Theophilus Churchman. 2 pts, 1642; 1657 (with Ecclesia vindicata); 1681 (in Historical and Miscellaneous Tracts).

France Painted to the Life, By a Learned and Impartial hand. 1656; 1657. [Pirated edns of following.]

A Full Relation Of two Journeys: The One Into the Main-Land of France. The Other, Into some of the adjacent Ilands. 1656.

Observations on The Historie of King Charles: by H. L. 1656.

Extraneus Vapulans. 1656.

Ecclesia vindicata: or, the Church of England Justified. 1657. [Includes The Historie of Episcopacy, first ptd 1642; rptd in Historical and Miscellaneous Tracts, 1681.]

Respondet Petrus [reply to Nicholas Bernard, with] An Appendix In Answer to Mr Sandersons History of K. Charles. 1658.

A Short View of the Life and Reign of King Charles. 1658 (anon.).

Examen Historicum. 2 pts, 1659.

Ecclesia Restaurata; or, the History of the Reformation. 2 pts, 1661–0; 1670; 1674; ed. J. C. Robertson, 2 vols. Ecclesiastical Hist. Soc. 1849.

Cyprianus Anglicus: or, the History of William [Laud] Archbishop of Canterbury. Ed. H. Heylyn, 1668; 1671; 2 pts, Dublin, 1719.

Aerius Redivivus: or, the History of the Presbyterians. Oxford, 1670; 1672.

ΚΕΙΜΗΛΙΑ ᾽ΕΚΚΛΗΣΙΑΣΤΙΚΑ. Historical and Miscellaneous Tracts. 1681. [Reprints.]

[For a fuller bibliography see A. à Wood, Athenae Oxonienses, ed. P. Bliss, 1813–20, vol. III, pp. 557–67.]

SIR RICHARD BAKER (1568–1645)

A Chronicle of the Kings of England From the Time of the Romans Goverment unto the Raigne of King Charles. 1643; 1653; 1660 (continued), etc.; tr. Dutch, Amsterdam, 1649.

Theatrum Redivivum, or the Theatre Vindicated in Answer to Mr Pryn's Histrio-Mastix. 1662; 1670 (as Theatrum Triumphans).

THOMAS MAY (1595–1650)

A Discourse concerning the Successe of Former Parliaments. 1642 (anon.); 1644.

The Character of a Right Malignant. [1644] (anon.). [Attribution doubtful.]

The Lord George Digby's Cabinet And Dr Gaff's Negotiations. 1646 (anon.).

The History of the Parliament Of England: Which began November the third, M.DC.XL. With a short and necessary view of some precedent yeares. 1647; ed. F. Maseres, 1812; rptd Oxford, 1854.

Historiae Parliamenti Angliae Breviarium Tribus partibus explicitum. [1650]; 1651; tr. Eng. (as A Breviary of the History Of the Parliament of England). 1650, 1655, ed. F. Maseres, Select Tracts, 1815.

The Changeable Covenant. 1650 (anon.). [Attribution doubtful.]

[For May's plays and trns see A. G. Chester, Thomas May, Philadelphia, 1932, and pp. 648, 804, 811 above.]

JOSHUA SPRIGGE (1618–1684)

Anglia Rediviva; Englands Recovery: being the History of the Army under Sr. Thomas Fairfax. 1647; rptd Oxford, 1854. [Sprigge is said to have been helped by Nathaniel Fiennes.]

NEHEMIAH WALLINGTON (1598–1658)

Historical notes and meditations, 1583–1649. Ed. R. Webb (in Historical Notices of events occurring chiefly in the Reign of Charles I. 2 vols. 1869).

SIR EDWARD WALKER (1612–1677)

The Order of the Ceremonies used at the Celebration of St George's Feast at Windsor. 1671; 1674 (anon.).

Historical Discourses, upon Several Occasions. 1705; 1707 (as Historical Collections).

A Circumstantial Account of the Preparations for the Coronation of Charles II, and a minute detail of that splendid ceremony. 1820.

HENRY GUTHRY, BISHOP OF DUNKELD (1600?–1676)

Memoirs: Wherein the Conspiracies and Rebellion against King Charles I are briefly and faithfully related. 1702; Glasgow, 1747, and [with life by G. Crawfurd] 1748.

SIR HAMON L'ESTRANGE (1605–1660)

The Reign of King Charles, by H. L. 1655; 1656.

The Alliance of Divine Offices Exhibiting all the Liturgies of the Church of England Since the Reformation. 1659; 1690; 1699; rptd Library of Anglo-Catholic Theology, Oxford, 1846.

WILLIAM LILLY (1602–1681)

Monarchy or no Monarchy in England. 1651; ed. F. Maseres, Select Tracts, 1815. [Includes Several Observations upon the Life and Death of Charles late King of England; rptd, with addns, as True History of King James the First, and King Charles the First, 1715; ed. C. Burman in The Lives of Elias Ashmole and William Lilly, 1774.]

History of His Life and Times. 1715; ed. C. Burman, 1774 (with Ashmole's life); 1822 and 1826.

RICHARD BELLINGS (d. 1677)

History of the Irish Confederation and the War in Ireland. [Bks II and III only inaccurately ptd in Desiderata Curiosa Hibernica (by J. Lodge), vol. II, 1772.] Ed. Sir J. T. Gilbert, 7 vols. Dublin, 1882–91.

GODFREY GOODMAN (1583–1656)

The Court of King James the First. Ed. J. S. Brewer, 2 vols. 1839.

SIR WILLIAM SANDERSON (1586?–1676)

Aulicus Coquinariæ: or a Vindication in, Answer to a Pamphlet, entituled The Court and Character of King James [by Sir A. Weldon]. 1650 (anon.); rptd Sir W. Scott (in Secret History of the Court of James I, 2 vols. Edinburgh, 1811).

A Compleat History of The Lives and Reigns of Mary Queen of Scotland, And of Her Son James. 2 pts, 1656, 5.

An Answer to a Scurrilous Pamphlet, intituled, Observations upon a Compleat History of Mary Queen of Scotland, and her Son James. 1656.

A Compleat History of the Life and Raigne of King Charles from His Cradle to his Grave. 1658.

Post Haste, a reply to Dr Peter Heylyn's appendix. 1658.

Peter pursued. 1658.

FRANCIS OSBORNE (1593–1659)

A seasonable expostulation with the Netherlands, declaring their ingratitude to and the necessity of their agreement with the commonwealth of England. Oxford, 1652 (anon.).

A Perswasive to a Mutuall Compliance under the Present Government. [and] A Plea for A Free State compared with Monarchy. Oxford, 1652.

Politicall Reflections upon The Government of the Turks. 1656 (anon.).

Advice to a Son. Pt I, Oxford, 1656 (anon.); pt II, 1658, etc.; ed. E. A. Parry, 1896.

Historical memoires on the reigns of Queen Elizabeth, and King James. 1658 (anon.); rptd Sir W. Scott (in Secret History of the Court of James the First, 2 vols. Edinburgh, 1811).

A Miscellany Of Sundry Essayes, Paradoxes [etc.], 1659.

Collected Works. 1673, etc. [Best edn, 2 vols. 1722.]

ANONYMOUS

The Secret History of the reign of James I. [In The Autobiography and Correspondence of Sir Simonds D'Ewes, ed. J. O. Halliwell [-Phillipps], 2 vols. 1845.]

The reign of Charles I. 1656.   G. P.

C. BIOGRAPHIES AND AUTO-BIOGRAPHIES

JOHN GERARD (1564–1637)

Narratio P. Johannis Gerardi de rebus a se in Anglia gestis. Tr. and ed. G. R. Kingdon (as During the Persecution), 1886.

A narrative of the gunpowder plot. Ed. J. Morris (in The Condition of Catholics under James I, 1871, 1872, and as The Life of Father John Gerard, 1881).

CRESACRE MORE (1572–1649)

The Life and Death of Sir Thomas Moore. By M. T. M[ore, or rather C. More]. [St Omer or Douai, 1631]; 1726; ed. J. Hunter, 1828.

ROBERT CAREY, EARL OF MONMOUTH (1560?–1639)

Memoirs Of the Life of Robert Cary. Written by Himself. Ed. John Earl of Corke and Orrery, 1759; ed. Sir W. Scott, Edinburgh, 1808; ed. G. H. Powell, 1905.

SYDNAM POYNTZ (*fl.* 1624–50)

The Vindication of Colonel General Poyntz, against The false and malicious Slanders secretly cast forth against him. 1645.
The Vindication Of Collonell Generall Points Against The Slanders cast forth against him by the Army. [n.p.] 1648.
A true relation of these German warres (1624 to 1636). Ed. A. T. S. Goodrick, Royal Hist. Soc. 1908.

PHINEAS PETT (1570–1647)

Autobiography. Ed. W. G. Perrin, Navy Records Soc. 1918.

SIR SIMONDS D'EWES (1602–1650)

The Journals of all the Parliaments During the Reign of Queen Elizabeth. Ed. P. Bowes, 1682; 1693.
The Autobiography and Correspondence. Ed. J. O. Halliwell[-Phillipps], 2 vols. 1845. [Contains also The Secret History of the Reign of King James I; and An Account of the Journey of the Prince's Servants into Spain, 1623, by Sir Richard Wynne.]
College Life in the Time of James [the First]. Ed. J. H. Marsden, 1851. [Compiled from D'Ewes's diary.]
The Journal of Sir Simonds D'Ewes. Ed. W. Notestein, New Haven, 1923.

ROBERT BLAIR (1593–1666)

The Life of Mr Robert Blair, Minister of St Andrews, containing his autobiography, 1593–1636, with supplement to 1680, by Mr W. Row. Ed. T. M'Crie, Wodrow Soc. Edinburgh, 1848.

ROBERT MONROE, MAJOR-GENERAL (d. 1680)

Monro His Expedition with the Worthy Scots Regiment. 2 pts, 1637.
A True Relation Of the proceedings of the Scottish Armie now in Ireland, By three Letters. The First Sent from Monroe. 1642.
A Letter Of great Consequence; Sent by Monro, out of the Kingdom of Ireland, Concerning the state of the Rebellion there [etc.]. Ordered by the Commons [to] be printed. 1643.
A Full Relation of the Expedition Of Monroe in the Province of Vulster. By Authority. 1644.

WILLIAM LAUD, ARCHBISHOP OF CANTERBURY (1573–1645)

Diary. [First ptd in garbled form by W. Prynne in a Breviate of the Life of W. Laud, 1644.]
The History of the Troubles and Tryal of William Laud. Wrote by himself. To which is prefixed The Diary of his Own Life. Ed. H. Wharton, 1695.
An Historical Account of all Material Transactions Relating to the University of Oxford [during Laud's chancellorship]. [In The Second Volume of the Remains, ed. H. Wharton, 1700.]

[All rptd in The Works of William Laud, ed. W. Scott and J. Bliss, Library of Anglo-Catholic Theology, 7 vols. in 9, Oxford, 1847–60. See also p. 698 above.]

EDWARD WALSINGHAM (*fl.* 1643–1654)

Britannicæ Virtutis Imago. Or, the life of Major Generall Smith. Oxford, 1644.
Alter Britanniæ Heros: or the Life of Sir Henry Gage. Oxford, 1645.
Life of Sir John Digby. Ed. G. Bernard, Camden Misc. vol. XII, 1910.

JOSEPH HALL, BISHOP OF EXETER AND NORWICH (1574–1656)

An Humble Remonstrance to the High Court of Parliament, by A dutifull Sonne of the Church. 1640. [Began pamphlet war with 'Smectymnuus' and Milton.]
Hard Measure. 1647; 1660 (in The Shaking of the Olive-Tree); 1710.
Observations Of some Specialties of Divine Providence In the Life of Joseph Hall. 1660 (with Hard Measure in The Shaking of the Olive Tree).
The Works of Joseph Hall. Ed. J. Pratt, 10 vols. 1808; ed. P. Hall, 12 vols. Oxford, 1837–9; ed. P. Wynter, 10 vols. Oxford, 1863.
Complete Poems. Ed. A. B. Grosart, Manchester, 1879.

[For Hall's other writings see p. 697 above.]

— ROE

Memoirs of some Actions in which Collonel John Birch was engaged [1642–1646]. [By his secretary, Roe.] Ed. J. and T. W. Webb, Military Memoir of Colonel John Birch, Camden Soc. 1873.

EDWARD HERBERT, BARON HERBERT OF CHERBURY (1583–1648)

The Life and Raigne of King Henry the eighth. 1649; 1672; 1682; 1706 (in White Kennett, Complete History, vol. II).

The Expedition to the Isle of Rhe. [Tr. Latin by T. Baldwin, 1656. Original ed. Earl of Powis, Philobiblon Soc. 1860.]

The Life of Edward Lord Herbert Of Cherbury, Written by himself. Strawberry-Hill, 1764; 1770; 1771; 1792; 1809; 1824; 1826; ed. Sir S. Lee, 1886 and [1906].

[For Herbert's poems see p. 476 above, and for his philosophical writings p. 875 below.]

Sir Anthony Weldon (d. 1649?)

The court and character of King James. 1650; 1651 (whereto is added The court of King Charles); rptd Sir W. Scott (in Secret History of the Court of James I, 2 vols. Edinburgh, 1811).

Ralph, Baron Hopton (1598–1652)

Narrative of his campaign in the West (1642–44). Ed. C. E. H. Chadwyck Healey (as Bellum Civile), Somerset Record Soc. 1902.

Sir Kenelm Digby (1603–1665)

Private Memoirs of Sir Kenelm Digby. Written by himself. [Ed. Sir N. H. Nicolas], 1827. [The castrations are ptd in E. W. Bligh, Sir K. Digby and his Venetia, 1932.]

Journal of a Voyage into the Mediterranean, 1628. Ed. J. Bruce, Camden Soc. 1868.

Sir Thomas Herbert (1606–1682)

A Relation of Some Yeares Travaile, begunne Anno 1626. Into Afrique and the greater Asia. [With 2nd title-page A Discription of the Persian Monarchy Now beinge.] 1634; 1638; 1639; 1665; 1677; ed. J. Harris, Navigantium atque Itinerantium Bibliotheca, vol. I, 1705; ed. J. H. Moore, New and Complete Collection of Voyages and Travels, vol. II, [1780?]; abridged and ed. Sir W. Foster, 1928. Tr. Dutch, Dordrecht, 1658; French, Paris, 1663.

Threnodia Carolina. 1678; 1702, 1711, and ed. G. Nicol, 1813 (in Memoirs of the Two last Years of Charles I).

Sir Hugh Cholmley (1600–1657)

Memoirs. 1787; rptd 1870.

Some Observations touching the Hothams. [In State Papers collected by Edward, Earl of Clarendon, ed. R. Scrope vol. II, Oxford, 1773.]

Memorials touching the Battle of York. Ed. Sir C. H. Firth (in Two Accounts of the Battle of Marston Moor, EHR. v, 1890).

Memorialls tuching Scarbrough. Ed. Sir C. H. Firth, Sir Hugh Cholmley's Narrative of

the Siege of Scarborough, 1644–5, EHR. xxxii, 1917.

Sir Henry Slingsby (1602–1658)

The Diary of Sir Henry Slingsby. Ed. D. Parsons, 1836. [First pbd in abridged version with the autobiography of Captain John Hodgson as Original Memoirs, written during the great civil war, ed. [Sir Walter Scott], Edinburgh, 1806.]

John Ashburnham (1603–1671)

A Narrative of his Attendance on King Charles the First. 2 vols. 1830.

John, Baron Berkeley (d. 1678)

Memoirs. 1699; 1702; rptd Harleian Misc. ed. T. Park, vol. IX, 1812; ed. F. Maseres, Select Tracts, 1815. [Included as appendix to John Ashburnham's Narrative, 1830.]

Henry Townshend (fl. 1640–1663)

Diary of Henry Townshend of Elmley Lovett 1640–1663. Ed. J. W. Willis Bund, 4 pts, Worcestershire Hist. Soc. 1915–20.

Sir Philip Monckton (1620?–1679)

The Monckton Papers. Ed. E. Peacock, Philobiblon Soc. Misc. vol. xv, 1877–84.

Anne, Lady Halkett (1622–1699)

Autobiography. Ed. J. G. Nichols, Camden Soc. 1875.

Margaret Cavendish, Duchess of Newcastle (1624?–1674)

Poems, and fancies. 1653; 1664.

A true Relation of my Birth, Breeding, and Life. [In Natures Pictures drawn by Fancies Pencil, 1656.] Rptd Lee Priory Press, 1814; ed. [with life of the Duke] M. A. Lower, 1872; ed. [with a selection from her works as The Cavalier and his Lady] E. Jenkins, 1872; ed. [with life of Duke] Sir C. H. Firth, 1886 and 1906.

Playes. 1662.

Plays, Never before Printed. 1668.

The Life of William Cavendishe, Duke of Newcastle. 1667; 1675; ed. [with life of Duchess] M. A. Lower, 1872; ed. Sir C. H. Firth, 1886 and 1906.

[See also p. 642 above.]

Memoirs of Charles I

Memoirs of the Two last Years of King Charles I. By Sir Tho. Herbert, Major Huntington, Col. Edw. Coke, and Mr Hen. Firebrace [etc.]. 1702; 1711; ed. G. Nicol, 1813.

D. ANTIQUARIES

SIR HENRY SPELMAN (1564?–1641)

De non temerandis ecclesiis. A Tracte Of the Rights and Respect due unto Churches. 1613; Edinburgh, 1616; 1616; Oxford, 1646.

Archæologus. In modum Glossarii. Pt 1, 1626; pts 1 and 2, Glossarium Archaiologicum, ed. C. Spelman, 1664.

Concilia, Decreta, Leges, Constitutiones, in Re Ecclesiarum orbis Britannici. Vol. I, 1639; vol. II, ed. C. Spelman, 1664.

The growth, propagation, and condition of tenures by knight service. 1641.

De Sepultura. 1641.

Tithes too hot to be Touched. Ed. J. Stephens, 1646 (re-issued as The Larger Treatise concerning Tithes, 1647).

An Apology of the Treatise De non temerandis Ecclesiis. Also his Epistle to Richard Carew concerning tithes. Ed. J. Stephens, 1647.

Aspilogia. Ed. E. Biss, 1654.

Villare Anglicum: or a View of the Townes of England. 1656. [By Spelman and R. Dodsworth.]

Of the Law Terms. 1684.

The History and Fate of Sacrilege. 1698; rptd 1846 and 1853; ed. C. F. S. Warren, 1895. Tr. French (abridged), 1698, Brussels, 1787; German, Regensburg, 1878.

Reliquiæ Spelmannianæ. The Posthumous Works of Sir H. Spelman Relating to the Laws and Antiquities of England. With the Life of the Author. Ed. E. Gibson, Oxford, 1698.

The English Works of Sir Henry Spelman, Together with his Posthumous Works, Relating to the Laws and Antiquities of England; [and] the Life of the Author. Ed. E. Gibson, 1723; 2 pts, 1727.

THOMAS HABINGTON (1560–1647)

The Epistle of Gildas. Tr. [T. Habington], 1638.

The Antiquities of the Cathedral Church of Worcester; to which are added Antiquities of Chichester and Lichfield. [Ed. R. Rawlinson], 1717; 1723.

A Survey of Worcestershire. Ed. J. Amphlett, 7 pts, Worcestershire Hist. Soc. 1893–9.

WILLIAM SOMNER (1598–1669)

The Antiquities of Canterbury. 1640; ed. N. Battely, 1703.

Dictionarium Saxonico-Latino-Anglicum. 2 pts, Oxford, 1659; Oxford, 1701 (with addns by T. Benson).

A Treatise of Gavelkind, Both Name and Thing. 1660; 1726 (with life by White Kennett, rev. and much enlarged).

Chartham News: or a Brief Relation of some Strange Bones there lately digged up. Ed. J. Sumner, 1669; 1703 (in Antiquities of Canterbury).

A Treatise Of the Roman Ports and Forts in Kent. Ed. J. Brome, with notes by E. Gibson, and a life of Somner by White Kennett, Oxford, 1693.

SIR ROGER TWYSDEN (1597–1672)

The Commoners Liberty: or, the English-Mans Birth-Right. 1648 (anon.).

Historiæ Anglicanæ Scriptores x. 1652. Ed. by Twysden.

An Historicall Vindication of the Church of England In point of Schism, As it stands separated from the Roman. 1657; 1675; rptd Cambridge, 1847.

Certaine Considerations upon the Government of England. Ed. J. M. Kemble, Camden Soc. 1849.

An Historicall Narrative of the two howses of Parliament and either of them, their committees and Agents violent proceedings against Sr. Roger Twysden. Ed. (as Journal) L. B. L[arking] (in Archaeologia Cantiana, I–IV, Kent Archaeological Soc. 1858–61).

MATTHEW CARTER (fl. 1660)

A Most True Relation of That as Honourable as unfortunate Expedition of Kent, Essex, and Colchester. [n.p.], 1650; [ed. P. Morant and T. Luffkin, Colchester, n.d. Several rpts.]

Honor redivivus or An analysis of Honor and Armory. 1655; 1660; 1669; 1673.

G. P.

II. ECONOMISTS AND POLITICAL THEORISTS

(1) MODERN AUTHORITIES

(a) Bibliographies

Dictionnaire de l'Économie Politique. Ed. C. Coquelin and C. Guillaumin, 3 vols. Paris, 1873.

Handwörterbuch der Staatswissenschaften. Ed. L. Elster, A. Weber and F. Wieser, 8 vols. and Supplement, Jena, 1923–9 (4th edn).

Palgrave's Dictionary of Political Economy. Ed. H. Higgs, 3 vols. 1926.

A London Bibliography of the Social Sciences. 3 vols. 1931.

(b) General Works

Sinclair, Sir J. The History of the Public Revenue of the British Empire. 3 vols. 1803–4 (3rd edn). [With bibliography.]

McCulloch, J. R. The Literature of Political Economy. 1845.

Roscher, W. Zur Geschichte der Englischen Volkswirthschaftlehre. Abhandlungen der philologische-historische Classe der königlichen sächsischen Gesellschaft der Wissenschaft, vol. II, Leipzig, 1857.

Ingram, J. K. A History of Political Economy. Edinburgh, 1888.

Dowell, S. History of Taxation and Taxes in England. 4 vols. 1888 (2nd edn).

Hall, Hubert. A History of the Custom Revenue of England. 1892.

Cossa, L. Introduction to the Study of Political Economy. Tr. Eng. 1892.

Cunningham, W. Growth of English Industry and Commerce. 3 vols. Cambridge, 1905–7.

Haney, L. H. History of Economic Thought. New York, 1922.

Ashley, W. J. An Introduction to English Economic History and Theory. 2 vols. 1923–5.

(c) Select Documents

Shaw, W. A. Select Tracts and Documents Illustrative of English Monetary History. 1896.

Bland, A. E., Brown, P. A. and Tawney, R. H. English Economic History. Select Documents. 1914.

Tawney, R. H. and Power, E. Tudor Economic Documents. 3 vols. 1924.

University of London. Catalogue of the Collection of English, Scottish and Irish Proclamations in the Goldsmiths' Library. 1928.

—— Catalogue of the Collection of Broadsides in the Goldsmiths' Library. 1930.

(2) CONTEMPORARY WRITINGS

(a) Politics

Dudley, E. The Tree of the Common Wealth. Written by him while a prisoner in the Tower in the years 1509 and 1510, and under sentence of death for High Treason. Manchester, 1859.

Coke, J. The Debate betweene the Heraldes of Englande and Fraunce. 1550.

Goodman, C. How Superior Powers ought to be obeyed of their Subjects: and wherein they may lawfully by Gods worde be disobeyed and resisted. Wherein also is declared the cause of all this present miserie in England, and the oneley way to remedy the same. Geneva, 1558.

Buchanan, G. Ane admonition direct to the trew Lordis mantenaris of justice and obedience to the Kingis graces authorite. Stirling, 1571.

Buchanan, G. De Jure Regni apud Scotos, Dialogus. [Edinburgh,] 1579.

Smith, Sir T. De Republica Anglorum. 1583; ed. L. Alston and F. W. Maitland, Cambridge, 1906.

Parsons, R. A Conference about the next Succession to the Crowne of Ingland. 1594.

Knyveth, Sir H. Defence of the Realme. 1596; ed. C. Hughes, Oxford, 1906.

Spenser, E. A View of the State of Ireland. Dublin, 1633. [Written 1596; rptd in Globe edn of Works, 1869, etc.]

James I. The true Lawe of Free Monarchies; or the reciprocle and mutuall dutie betwixt a free king and his naturall subjects. 1598.

—— Works. 1616.

Bacon, F. (Viscount St Albans). Works. Ed. J. Spedding, R. L. Ellis, and D. D. Heath, 7 vols. 1857–9.

Bodin, J. Consilia de Principe recte instituendo. Cum praeceptis cujusdam principis politicis. Erfurt, 1603.

—— The six bookes of a Commonweale. 1606.

Hayward, Sir J. An Answer to the first Part of a certain conference concerning Succession. 1603. [See Parsons above.]

Cowell, J. The Interpreter: or Booke containing the signification of Words and Termes mentioned in the Lawe-Writers, or Statutes requiring any Exposition. Cambridge, 1607.

Davies, Sir John. A discoverie of the true causes why Ireland was never entirely subdued untill the beginning of his Majesties happie raigne. 1612.

Camden, W. Annales Rerum Anglicarum et Hibernicarum, regnante Elizabetha. 2 pts, 1615–27.

Fortescue, Sir J. De Laudibus Legum Angliae. Ed. J. Selden, 1616. [Latin and English.]

Grotius, Hugo. De Jure Belli et Pacis. Paris, 1625; tr. Eng. C. Barksdale, 1654; tr. and ed. W. Whewell, 3 vols. Cambridge, 1853.

Selden, J. Mare Clausum. 1635.

Prynne, W. The Antipathie of the English Prelacie, both to Regall Monarchy, and Civill Unity. 2 pts, 1641.

—— A legal vindication of the liberties of England against Illegal Taxes. 1649.

Hobbes, T. De Cive. Paris, 1642. [Rptd in English Works, ed. Sir W. Molesworth, 1839.]

—— Leviathan. Or the Matter, Form and Power of a Commonwealth, Ecclesiastical and Civil. 1652; ed. H. Morley, 1885; ed. A. R. Waller, Cambridge, 1904; ed. W. G. Pogson-Smith, Oxford, 1909.

Machiavelli, N. Il Principe. [Written 1513.] Tr. Eng. 1640; ed. H. Morley, 1883.

(b) Usury

Sanders, N. A brief Treatise of Usurie. Louvain, 1568.

Porder, R. A Sermon with a Treatise against Usurie. 1570.

Wilson, T. A Discourse uppon usurye. 1572; ed. R. H. Tawney, 1925.

Caesar, M. P. A general discourse against the damnable sect of Usurers. Tr. Eng. T. Rogers, 1578.

Hemmingsen, N. A Godlie treatise concernyng the Lawful use of Riches. Tr. Eng. T. Rogers, 1578.

Lodge, T. An Alarum against Usurers. 1584.

Smith, H. Examination of Usury, in two sermons. 1591.

Andrewes, L. De usuris, theologica determinatio, habita in publica schola theologica Cantabrigiae. 1593.

The Death of Usury, or, the Disgrace of usurers. 1594.

Mosse, M. The Arraignment and Conviction of Usurie. 1595.

Bell, T. The Speculation of Usurie. 1596. [A copy of this tract, believed to be unique, is in the Cambridge University Lib.]

Fenton, R. A treatise of Usurie. 1612.

Culpepper, Sir T. A Tract against Usurie. 1621.

Blaxton, John. Usury arraigned and condemned. 1625.

—— The English usurer. 1634.

Bagshawe, E. A Short and private discourse betweene Mr Bolton and one M. S. concerning usury. Published by E. B. 1637.

Holmes, N. Usury is injury. 1640.

Filmer, Sir R. Quaestio quodlibetica or a discourse whether it be lawfull to take use for money. 1653.

(c) Colonies

Hariot, T. A briefe and true report of the new-found land of Virginia. 1588; ed. R. G. Adams, Ann Arbor, 1931.

Symonds, W. Virginia; a sermon preached in the presence of the Adventurers and Planters for Virginia. 1609.

J[ohnson?], R. Nova Britannia. Offring most excellent fruites by Planting in Virginia. 1609.

Alexander, Sir W. An Encouragement to Colonies. 1624; rptd Bannatyne Club, 1867.

Smith, Capt. J. The generall Historie of Virginia, New England, and the Summer Isles. 1624. [Rptd in Works, ed. E. Arber, 1884.]

—— Advertisements for the un-experienced Planters of New-England, or any where. Or the Path-way to experience to erect a Plantation. 1631.

Vaughan, William. The Golden Fleece. 1626. [Newfoundland.]

Wood, William. New England's Prospect. 1634.

Bullock, W. Virginia impartially examined. 1649.

Ll., O. A despised Virgin Beautified, or Virginia benefited. 1653.

Phillips, Sir T. A letter to King Charles i concerning the Plantations of the Londoners. Ed. W. Harris (in Hibernica, 1757).

(d) Pauperism

Fish, S. A Supplicacyon for the Beggars. [1529?]; ed. F. J. Furnivall, EETS. Ex. Ser. 1871.

Awdeley, J. Fraternity of Vacabones. 1561; ed. E. Viles and F. J. Furnivall, 1907.

Harman, T. A Caveat or Warening for common cursetores Vulgarly called Vagabones. 1567; ed. E. Viles and F. J. Furnivall, 1907 (with above).

S., M. Greevous Grones for the Poore done by a Well-willer who wisheth that the Poore of England might be so provided for as none should neade to go a begging. 1622.

Stanleye's remedy or, the way to reform wandring beggers, thieves, highway-robbers and pickpockets. 1646.

Cooke, Sir J. Unum Necessarium, or the Poore Man's Case. 1648.

Chamberlen, P. The Poore Man's Advocate. 1649.

Moore, J. The Crying Sin of England of not caring for the poor wherein Inclosure being such as doth unpeople Towns and uncorn fields is arraigned. 1653.

(e) Agriculture and Fisheries

[See also Agriculture and Gardening, pp. 391–2 above.]

Walter of Henley's Husbandry, together with an anonymous Husbandry, Seneschausie and Robert Grosseteste's Rules. The transcripts, translation and glossary by E. Lamond. 1890.

Fitzherbert. [The Book of Surveying.] Here begynneth a ryght frutefull mater; and hath to name the boke of surveying and improuvementes. 1523.

—— The boke of husbandrie. 1523.

[These books have been generally supposed to be by Sir Anthony Fitzherbert. They are attrib. to his brother John Fitzherbert of Norbury, in EHR. xii, 1897, p. 225. See also Cunningham's Growth of English Industry and Commerce, vol. i, 1905. In his edn of the Boke of Husbandrie W. W. Skeat upholds the claims of Sir Anthony. See also s.v. 'Fitzherbert', Palgrave's Dictionary of Political Economy.]

Markham, Gervase. [See pp. 704–6 above.]

Tusser, T. A hundreth good pointes of husbandrie. 1557.

—— Five hundreth pointes of good husbandrie. 1573; ed. W. Payne and S. J. Herrtage, 1878.

—— Foure bookes of husbandry. 1577.

Hitchcock, R. A Pollitique Platt for the honour of the Prince, the greate profite of the publique state, relief of the poore, preservation of the riche, reformation of Roges and Idle persones, and the wealthe of thousands that knowes not how to live. 1580.

Hill, T. The Profitable Art of Gardening. 1599.

Keymor, J. J. Keymor's observation made upon the Dutch fishing, about the year 1601. Demonstrating that there is more wealth raised out of herrings and other fish in his Majestie's Seas by the neighbouring nations in one year, than the King of Spain hath from the Indies in four. 1664.

Norden, J. The surveyors dialogue. 1607.

Vaughan, R. Most approved and long experienced Water-Workes containing the manner of Winter and Summer drowning of Medow and Pasture thereby to make those grounds more fertile, ten for one. 1610.

Gentleman, Tobias. England's way to win wealth, and to employ ships and mariners. 1614; rptd E. Arber (English Garner, vol. IV, 1882).

Britain's Buss, or A computation as well of the Charge of a Buss or Herring Fishing Ship. 1615; rptd E. Arber (English Garner, vol. II, 1880).

Burroughes, Sir J. An historical account of the Royal Fishery of Great Britain. 1630.

S., E. England's Royal Fishery Revived. 1630.

Best, H. Rural Economy in Yorkshire in 1641. Ed. C. B. Robinson, Surtees Soc. 1857.

The Anti-Projector, or the history of the Fenproject. [1646 or 1650?]

Blith, W. The English improver, or a new survey of Husbandry. 1649.

Hartlib, Samuel. A discourse of Husbandry used in Brabant and Flanders. 1650. [Really written by Sir R. Weston. See DNB. s.v. 'Hartlib.']

—— Samuel Hartlib his Legacie; or an enlargement of the Discourse of Husbandry used in Brabant and Flanders. 1651.

—— The Compleat Husband-Man. 2 pts, 1659–2.

Petty, Sir W. The History of the Survey of Ireland, commonly called the Down Survey. Ed. T. A. Larcom, Irish Archaeological Soc. 1851.

Dugdale, Sir W. The History of Imbanking and drayning of divers Fens and Marshes, both in forein parts and in this Kingdom; and of the improvements thereby. 1662.

(f) Other Works

Armstrong, C. Treatise concerning the Staple and the Commodities of the Realm. 1519.

Fitzherbert, Sir A. The new booke of Justyces of Peas. 1541.

More, Sir T. A fruteful and pleasaunt worke of the beste state of a publyque weale, and of the new yle called Utopia translated by Raphe Robynson. 1551; ed J. R. Lumby, Cambridge, 1879.

Respublica [1553]. A Play on the Social Condition of England at the Accession of Queen Mary. Ed. L. A. Magnus, EETS. 1905.

Davanzati, Sir B. A Discourse upon Coins. 1558.

Harrison, W. An historicall description of the Islande of Britayne. 1577.

[Hales, J.]. A Discourse of the Common Weal of this realm of England. 1591; ed. E. Lamond, Cambridge, 1893.

Jeninges, E. A brief Discovery of the damages that happen to this realm by disordered and unlawfull diet. The benefites and commodities that otherwise might ensue. With a perswasion of the people, for a better maintenance to the Navie. 1593.

Malynes, G. de. St George for England, allegorically described. 1601.

—— A Treatise of the Canker of England's Commonwealth. 1601.

—— England's View in the unmasking of two Paradoxes. 1602.

—— Consuetudo vel Lex Mercatoria, or, the Ancient Law Merchant. 1622.

—— The Maintenance of Free Trade, according to the three essentiall parts of traffique, or, an answer to a treatise of Free Trade [by E. Misselden] lately published. 1622.

—— The Centre of the Circle of Commerce. Or, a refutation of a Treatise intituled The Circle of Commerce, or the Ballance of Trade, lately published by E. M[isselden]. 1623.

[The original MS notes embodied in a portion of the above works are to be found in BM. Cott. MS Otho, E x, 65 ff.]

Wheeler, J. A treatise of commerce, wherein are shewed the commodities arising by a wel ordered Trade such as that of Merchantes Adventurers is proved to be. 1601.

—— The Lawes, Customes, and Ordinances of the Fellowshippe of Merchantes Adventurers of the Realme of England. 1608; ed. W. E. Lingelbach, Philadelphia, 1902.

Milles, T. The Replie, Or Second Apologie. That is to say, an Answer to a confused Treatise of Publicke Commerce. 1604.

—— The Custumer's Alphabet and Primer. Conteining their creed, their Ten Commandments and Forme of Prayers. 1608.

—— The Customer's Apologie. [1609?]

[Hall, Joseph]. Mundus alter et idem. Frankfort (really London?), [1605]; tr. Eng. J. H[ealey], [1609?] (ed. H. Brown, Cambridge, U.S.A. 1937).

Botero, G. The Causes of the Greatness of Cities. 1606.

Forset, Edwin. A Comparative Discourse of the Bodies Natural and Politique. 1606.

Standish, A. The Commons complaint. 1611.

May, J. A Declaration of the Estate of Clothing now used within this realme of England with an Apologie for the Alneger, shewing the necessarie use of his Office. 1613.

Cotton, Sir R. A Discourse of Foreign War. Account of all the Taxation from the Conquest. 1614.

—— A Discourse touching alteration of Coyne. 1626.

Digges, Sir D. The Defence of Trade, in a letter to Sir T. Smith. 1615.

—— The Trades Increase. 1615.

Selden, J. The History of Tithes. 1618.

Tillesley, R. Animadversions upon M. Selden's History of Tithes. 1619.

Montagu, R. Diatribae upon the first part of the late History of Tithes. 1621.

Mun, T. A Discourse of Trade from England into the East Indies. 1621.

—— England's Treasure by forraign trade; or, the ballance of our forraign trade is the rule of our treasure. 1664. [Posthumous. Mun died in 1641.]

Heath, Sir R. Propositions showing the great utility of a bank, and recommendation for erecting one in London. [1622. In State Papers, Domestic, James I, vol. cxxx, p. 30.]

Misselden, E. Free Trade; or, the Means to make trade flourish. 1622.

—— The Circle of Commerce. Or the Ballance of Trade, in defence of Free Trade: opposed to Malynes Little fish and his Great Whale, and poized against them in the Scale. 1623.

Roberts, Lewis. The Merchant's Mappe of Commerce; wherein the Universal Manner and Matter of Trade, is compendiously handled. 1638.

—— The Treasure of Traffike; or, a Discourse of Forraigne Trade. 1641.

Parker, H. The case of ship-money. 1640.

—— Of a Free Trade. 1648.

Roe, Sir T. Speech in Parliament, wherein he sheweth the causes of the Decay of Coin and Trade in this Land. 1641.

Milton, John. Prose Works. 5 vols. 1877–8. (Bohn's Standard Lib.)

Battie, J. The Merchants Remonstrance. 1648.

Violet, T. A true Discovery to the Commons of England how they have been cheated of almost all the gold and silver coin of this realme. 1650.

—— The Advancement of Merchandize; or certain Propositions for the improvement of Trade and against the transportation of gold and silver. 1651.

Harrington, J. The Commonwealth of Oceana [1656], and other Works. Ed. J. Toland, 1737.

H. H.

III. LEGAL WRITERS

(1) GENERAL AUTHORITIES FOR THE HISTORY OF ENGLISH LAW

Ames, J. B. Lectures on Legal History and Miscellaneous Legal Essays. Cambridge, U.S.A. 1913.

Brunner, H. Überblick über die Geschichte der französischen, normannischen und englischen Rechtsquellen. [In F. von Holtzendorff's Encyclopädie der Rechtswissenschaft, Leipzig, 1880; tr. Eng. W. Hastie, as Essay on the Sources of the Law of England, 1888.]

—— Deutsche Rechtsgeschichte. 2 vols. Leipzig, 1887–92.

Crabb, G. History of the English Law. 1829.

Dugdale, Sir W. Origines juridiciales. 1666; 1671; 1680.

Glasson, E. Histoire du Droit et des Institutions politiques, civiles et judiciaires de l'Angleterre. 6 vols. Paris, 1882–3.

Holdsworth, Sir W. S. A History of English Law. 3 vols. 1903–9; 3 vols. 1914; 9 vols. 1922–6.

—— Sources and Literature of English Law. 1925.

Jenks, Edward. Short History of English Law. 1912; 1920; 1924; 1928.

Kent, J. Commentaries on American Law. 4 vols. New York, 1826–30; rev. O. W. Holmes, Boston, 1873.

Pollock, Sir F. and Maitland, F. W. History of English Law before the Time of Edward I. 2 vols. 1898 (2nd edn).

Putnam, B. H. Early Treatises on the Practice of the Justices of the Peace in the Fifteenth and Sixteenth Centuries. Oxford, 1924.

Reeves, John. History of English Law, to the Death of Elizabeth. 5 vols. 1814–29 (3rd edn); rev. F. W. Finlason, 3 vols. 1869.

Select Essays in Anglo-American Legal History. 3 vols. Cambridge, U.S.A. 1908–10.

Winfield, P. H. Chief Sources of English Legal History. 1926.

(2) BIBLIOGRAPHIES OF ENGLISH LEGAL HISTORY

Advocates, Faculty of. Catalogue of Printed Books in the Library. 7 vols. Edinburgh, 1873–9.

Arber, Edward. The Term Catalogues 1668–1709. 3 vols. 1903–6.

Basset, Thomas. Catalogue of Common and Statute Law Books. 1673; 1682; 1684; 1694; 1699; 1700.

Beale, J. H. The Ames Foundation. A Bibliography of Early English Law Books. Cambridge, U.S.A. 1926.

Bridgman, R. W. A Short View of Legal Bibliography, containing some Critical Observations on the Authority of the Reporters and Other Law Writers. 1807.

Chipman, F. E. An Index to Legal Periodical Literature, 1898–1922. 2 vols. Boston, 1919–24. [Continuation of L. A. Jones.]

Clarke, John. Bibliotheca Legum; or, Complete Catalogue of the Common and Statute Law Books of the United Kingdom. 1819.

College of Advocates. Catalogue of the Books in the Library in Doctors Commons. 1818; 1848.

Cowley, J. D. A Bibliography of Abridgments, Digests, Dictionaries and Indexes of English Law to the Year 1800. Selden Soc. 1932.

Encyclopaedia of the Laws of England. 15 vols. 1906–9 (2nd edn). Supplement, 2 vols. 1914–9.

Foreign Office. Catalogue of Printed Books in the Library. 1926.

Fox, J. C. Handbook of English Law Reports, from the Last Quarter of the Eighteenth Century to the Year 1865. 1913.

Fulbecke, W. A Direction or Preparative to the Study of Law. 1600. [Contains a chapter on standard authors.]

Gray's Inn. Catalogue of Books in the Library of the Honourable Society. 1872–7; 1888; 1906.

Harvard University. Catalogue of the Library of the Law School. 2 vols. Cambridge, U.S.A. 1909.

Hicks, F. C. Materials and Methods of Legal Research, with Bibliographical Manual. Rochester, N.Y. 1923.

Index to Legal Periodicals. [Pbd by the] American Ass. of Law Libraries. 1908–. Chicago, 1909–.

Jelf, E. A. Where to find your Law, being a Discursive Bibliographical Essay upon the Various Divisions and Sub-divisions of the Law of England, and the Statutes, Reports of Cases and Text Books containing such Law. 1897; 1907.

Jones, L. A. An Index to Legal Periodical Literature [tc 1899]. 2 vols. Boston, 1888–99. [Continued by F. E. Chipman.]

Law Society. Catalogue of the Library. 1851; 1869; 1891. Supplement, 1906.

Lincoln's Inn. Catalogue of Printed Books in the Library. 1835; 1859. Supplement, 1890.

London, W. A Catalogue of the most Vendible Books in England. 1658. Supplement, 1660. [Contains a section on books of the Common and Civil law.]

Maitland, F. W. English Law and the Renaissance. 1901. [Contains, among the notes pp. 90–4, lists of law books available 1550 and 1600.]

Maxwell, W. H. and L. F. A Bibliography of English Law to 1932. 3 vols. 1925–33.

Middle Temple. Bibliotheca Societatis in Ordinem juxta Rerum Naturam Redacta ac digesta: V Iduum Sept. MDCC. Auspicio et Sumptu Barth. Shower, Militis. 1700.

—— Catalogus Librorum Bibliothecae Ordine Dictionarii dispositus [et] Appendix. 1734.

—— Catalogus continens Libros qui additi fuerunt, ab Anno 1734 ad hoc Tempus. 1766.

—— A Catalogue of the Printed Books in the Library of the Honourable Society. Ed. C. E. A. Bedwell, 3 vols. 1914. Supplement, ed. H. A. C. Sturgess, 1925.

Procurators, Faculty of. Catalogue of the Books in the Library. Glasgow, 1903. Supplement, Glasgow, 1923.

Reed, W. Bibliotheca nova Legum Angliae; or a Complete Catalogue of Law Books. 1809.

Soule, C. C. The Lawyer's Reference Manual of Law Books and Citations. Boston, 1883.

—— Legal Abbreviations. Being Citations of American, English, Colonial and Foreign Law Text-books and Reports. [Rptd from The Lawyer's Manual, 1883], with Additions to date by W. T. Rogers. 1911.

—— Year Book Bibliography. Harvard Law Rev. XIV, Cambridge, U.S.A. 1901.

Steele, Robert. What Fifteenth Century Books are about.—Law. Library, VI, 1905.

Wallace, J. W. The Reporters. Boston, 1882 (4th edn).

Worrall, John, Bibliotheca Legum: or a New and Complete List of all the Common and Statute Law Books. 1749; 1763; 1765; 1768.

Worrall, John and Brooke, Edward. Biblio-theca Legum Angliae. Pt I, A Catalogue of the Common and Statute Law Books of this Realm. Pt II, containing a General Account of the Laws and Law-writers of England. 2 vols. 1788.

(3) THE CHIEF WORKS IN ENGLISH LEGAL LITERATURE, 1500–1660

Articuli ad narrationes novas. 1525; 1547.

Ashe, Thomas. Le promptuarie, ou repertory generall de les annales, et plusors autres livres del common ley d'Engleterre. 2 vols. 1614.

Aucthoritie of al Justices of Peace, with divers warrants, presentments and indictments thereunto annexed. 1580; 1589.

Bacon, Sir Francis (Viscount St Albans). Works, collected and edited by James Spedding, R. L. Ellis and D. D. Heath. 7 vols. 1857–9; 7 vols. 1870.

—— Ordinances for the better administration of justice in the Chancery. 1623; 1640; 1642; 1656.

—— The use of the law. 1629; 1630; 1636; 1639. [Not by Bacon?]

—— The elements of the common lawes of England. 1630.

—— Collection of some principall rules and maxims of the Common Lawes of England. 1630.

—— The learned reading of Sir Francis Bacon upon the statute of uses. 1642; rptd 1785; rptd 1806.

Bacon, Nathaniel. An historical discourse of the uniformity of the Government of England. 2 pts, 1647–51; 1689; 1739; 1760. [This work was ptd secretly in 1672 and 1682. The publishers were prosecuted.]

Bekinson, J. (de). De supremo et absoluto regis imperio. 1546.

Brooke, Sir Robert. Le graunde abridgement. 1568; 1586.

—— A reading upon the Statute of Magna Carta cap. 16. 1641.

—— A reading upon the Statute of Limitations. 1647.

Brownlow, R. Brevia judicialia: or, an exact collection of approved forms of all sorts of judiciall writs in the Common Bench. 1662.

—— Declarations and pleadings in English: the forme of proceeding in Courts of Law. 1652; 1693.

—— Writs judiciall, shewing the formes, nature, and entries of all manner of execu-tions, in reall, personall and mixt actions, as they are now used in the Court of Common Pleas. 1653.

Callis, Robert. The reading upon the statute of 23 H. VIII, cap. 5, of sewers, delivered at Grays Inn, 1622. 1647; 1685; 1686; rptd 1810; rptd 1824.

Calthrope, Charles. The relation betweene the lord of a mannor and the coppyholder, his tenant. 1635; 1650. [The edn pbd in 1650 was included in The compleat copy-holder by Sir Edward Coke.]

Clayton, J. Topicks in the laws of England. 1646; 1647.

Coke, Sir Edward. A booke of entries. 1614; 1671.

—— First part of the Institutes of the Lawes of England: or commentarie upon Littleton. 1628. [The first edn of this work was very incorrect. The second edn, rev. and cor-rected by the author, was pbd in 1629. There are in all nineteen edns, of which the eighteenth (1823) and nineteenth (1832) are rpts of the seventeenth (1817). These three are much preferred to the earlier edns. The first American edn, in 3 vols., by Thomas Day, was pbd in Philadelphia in 1812.]

—— A little treatise of bail and mainprize. 1635; 1637. [Also included in the first part of his Institutes, 1684, 1703, 1719 and 1735, and in his Three Law Tracts, 1764.]

—— The compleat copyholder wherein is con-tained a learned discourse of the antiquity and nature of mannors and copy-holds. 1650.

—— Declarations and other pleadings, in the eleven parts of [his] Reports. 1659.

—— Reading on the Statute 27 Edward I. 1662.

Cowell, John. Institutiones juris Anglicani ad methodum et seriem institutionum im-perialium compositae et digestae. Cam-bridge, 1605 and 1630.

—— The interpreter; or Booke containing the signification of words and termes men-tioned in the lawe writers, or statutes. Cambridge, 1607; 1637; 1658; 1672; 1684; 1701; 1708; 1727.

Crompton, Richard. Office et auctoritie de justices de Peace. 1583; 1617.

—— L'authoritie et jurisdiction des Courts de la Majestie de la Roygne. 1594; 1637.

Dalton, Michael. The countrey justice. 1618. [Various subsequent edns down to 1746.]

—— Officium Vicecomitum, or the office and authoritie of sherifs. 1623; 1662; 1670; 1682; 1700. [Also abridged edns of 1638 and 1651.]

Diversite des Courtes. [See Fitzherbert, Sir Anthony.]

Doddridge, Sir John. The Lawyers light, or a true direction for the study of the law. 1629.

—— A compleat parson: or a description of advowsons, or church-living. 1630; 1641.

—— The English lawyer. Describing a method for the managing of the lawes of this land. 1631.

Duck, Sir Arthur. De usu et authoritate juris civilis Romanorum. 1653; tr. Eng. (with Ferriere's History of the Roman or Civil Law), 1724.

Finch, Sir Henry. Law: or discourse thereof. 1613; 1627; 1636; 1661; 1678; 1759. [Until the publication of Blackstone's Commentaries this was regarded as the great elementary text book for law students.]

—— Nomotechnia, c'est a scavoir un description del common leys d'Angleterre. 1613; tr. Eng. 1759. [This is not the same as Finch's Law above. There are many very material differences.]

Fitzherbert, Sir Anthony. Le graunde abridgement. 1516.

—— Diversite des courts et lour jurisdiccions. 1523; 1525; 1526; 1528; 1530; 1533; [1534–5]; 1543; 1561.

—— La nouvelle Natura brevium. 1534. [Several edns to 1635. Trns appeared from 1652 to 1793.]

—— L'Office et auctoritie de justices de peace. 1538. Tr. with commentary Sir M. Hale, 1635.

—— L'Office de Viconts Bailiffes, Escheators, Constables, Coroners. 1538.

Fulbecke, William. A direction or preparitive to the study of the lawe. 1600; 1620; 1829.

—— A parallele or conference of the civil law, the canon law, and the common law of the Realme of England. 1601; 1618.

Gentilis, Albericus. De legationibus. 1583; ed. facs. and tr. G. J. Laing, 2 vols. New York, 1924.

—— De jure belli libri tres. Oxford, 1588; Hanover, 1598; 1612; ed. T. E. Holland, Oxford, 1877; ed. facs. and tr. J. C. Rolfe, 2 vols. Oxford, 1933.

—— Hispanicae advocationis libri duo. 1613; 1661; ed. facs. (from 1661 edn) and tr. F. F. Abbott, 2 vols. 1921. [For an estimate and the scheme of these three works, see Walker's History of the Law of Nations, vol. I, pp. 249–74. The DNB. contains a complete list of Gentilis' writings, published and unpublished.]

Hawke, Michael. The groundes of the laws of England. 1657.

Herne, John. The pleader: containing perfect presidents and formes of declarations, pleadings, issues, judgments, and proceedings, in all kinds of actions, reall, personall, and mixt. 1657.

Hobbes, Thomas. De Corpore politico, or the elements of law, moral and politick. 1650; 1652.

Intrationum liber omnibus legum Angliae studiosis apprime necessarius in se complectens diversas formas placitorum. 1546.

Jones, John. The works in reference to the putting all the law into English, and reforming the abuses thereof: discovering a readie waie how men may recover their debts with little trouble and less charges 1651.

Kitchin, John. Le Courte Leete, et Court Baron. Et les cases et matters necessarie pur Seneschals de ceux courts a scier, pur les Students de les measons de Chauncerie. [1579] (in Aucthoritie of al Justices of Peace, 1580); 1580; 1581; 1585; 1587; 1598; 1602; 1613; 1623.

—— Jurisdictions; or, the lawful authority of Courts Leet, Courts Baron, Court of Marshalseyes, Court of Pypowder, and Ancient Demesne. 1651; 1653; 1656; 1663; 1675.

Lambard, William. ΑΡΧΑΙΟΝΟΜΙΑ, sive de priscis Anglorum Legibus libri. 1568; 1644 (with Bede's Historia Ecclesiastica).

—— Eirenarcha, or the Office of Justices of the Peace. 1581; 1602.

—— The duty of Constables. 1582; 1602.

—— Archion, or a commentary upon the High Courts of Justice. 1635.

Malynes, Gerard. Consuetudo vel Lex mercatoria: or ancient law merchant. 1622; 1629; 1636; 1656; 1686.

Manwood, John. A Brefe Collection of the Lawes of the Forest. 1592; 1615; 1665; 1718 (re-issued 1744).

Meriton, George. Landlord's law. 1655; 1681.

Novae Narrationes. 1515; 1561.

Perkins, John. The Profitable Booke [perutilis tractatus magistri Jo. Parkins]. 1532; 1567; 1827.

Plowden, Edmund. Les comentaries ou les Reportes. 1571; 1578; 1588; 1816.

—— Les Quaeres. [Included in some edns of the Reports. Tr. Eng. [1620?], 1662, 1761, 1779, 1816.]

Prynne, William. The soveraigne power of parliaments and kingdomes. 1643.

—— A Seasonable, Legall, and Historicall Vindication and chronologicall collection of the good old fundamentall liberties [and] laws of all English freemen. 3 pts, 1654–7.

—— A brief register, kalendar and survey of the several kinds, forms, of all parliamentary writs. 4 pts, 1659–64.

Pulton, Ferdinando. An abstract of all the Penal Statutes. 1560; 1577; 1579; 1586; 1600.

—— Collection of Statutes. [Pbd in several edns between 1606 and 1670.]

—— De Pace Regis et Regni, viz. A treatise declaring which be the great and generall offences of the realme. 1609; 1610; 1615; 1623.

Rastell, John. Exposiciones Terminorum Legum Anglorum. 1527. [Sometimes attrib. to his son William who pbd an English trn, 1563 and 1567. Rptd several times and known in the 17th cent. as Les Termes de la Ley. There have been many other edns down to 1812.]

Rastell, William. A collection of all the Statutes from the beginning of Magna Carta until the yere of our Lord 1557. 1559; 1618. [Continued by Pulton (q.v.).]

—— A colleccion of Entrees, of Declaracions, Barres, Replicacions and divers other matters. 1566; 1574; 1596; 1670.

Registrum Omnium Brevium, tam Originalium, quam Judicialium. 1531; 1553, etc.

Returna Brevium. 1516; 1519, etc. to 1547.

St German, Christopher. Doctor and Student. [First pbd as Dialogus de Fundamentis Legum Angliae et de Conscientia, 1523. Many later edns to 1886.]

Scobell, Henry. A collection of acts and ordinances, 1640 to 1656. 1658. [Continuation of Pulton's (q.v.) collection.]

Selden, John. Opera omnia. Ed. D. Wilkins, 3 vols. 1726. [Standard edn.]

—— Jani Anglorum facies altera. 1610; 2 vols. 1673; 1681. [Another edn in Tracts, 1683.]

—— De Laudibus Legum Angliae. 1616. [By Sir John Fortescue. Edited by Selden with the Summae attrib. to Ralph de Hengham.]

—— Brief discourse concerning the power of peers and commons of Parliament in point of judicature. Written by a learned antiquerie. 1619; 1640; 1680.

—— The History of tythes; the practice of payment of them, the positive laws made for them, the opinions touching the right of them. 1618. [This book was suppressed by order of the Court of High Commission.]

—— Mare clausum. 1635; 1636; Hague, 1636; Leyden, 1636; 1652; 1663.

—— De jure naturali et gentium, juxta disciplinam Ebroeorum. 1640; Strasburg, 1665; Leipzig, 1665.

—— Ad Fletam dissertatio [with introductory dissertation]. 1647; tr. 'with notes by the editor of Britton,' 1771; tr. and ed. D. Ogg, Cambridge, 1925.

—— Brief discourse touching the office of Lord Chancellor. Ed. W. Dugdale. 1671; 1677.

—— England's Epinomis. [In Tracts, 1683.]

Sheppard, William. Cabinet of the clerk of the justice of the peace. 1641.

—— Sure guide for His Majesty's Justices of the peace. 1649; 1652; 1663; 1669.

—— Whole office of the country justice of peace. 2 pts in 1 vol. 1650; 1655–6.

Sheppard, William. The precedent of precedents. 1655; ed. T. W. Williams, 1825.

—— Epitome of all the common and statute laws of this nation in force. 1656; 1658. [Several other works were written by Sheppard. The Touchstone of Common Assurances, 1641, is also known by his name, but there is some doubt as to whether he was the author.]

Smith, Sir Thomas. De Republica Anglorum. 1583, etc.; ed. F. W. Maitland and L. Alston, Cambridge, 1906.

Somner, William. Treatise of gavelkind both name and thing. 1660; 1663; 1726.

Spelman, Sir Henry. Archaeologus. In modum glossarii. Vol. I, 1626; vol. II, ed. W. Dugdale, 1664; 1687.

—— Concilia, decreta, leges, constitutiones, in re Ecclesiarum orbis Britannici. Vol. I, 1639; vol. II, ed. W. Dugdale, 1664.

—— Reliquiae Spelmannianae. Ed. E. Gibson, 1698; 1723.

Staundford, Sir W. Les plees del Coron. 1557; 1560; 1567; 1574; 1583; 1607.

—— An exposicion of the King's prerogative. 1567; 1568; 1577; 1590; 1607.

Style, William. The practical register consisting of rules, orders and observations concerning the practice of the common laws at Westminster. 1657; 1694; 1707 (4th edn). [Continuation by John Lilly, 2 vols. 1710.]

Swinburne, Henry. A briefe treatise of Testaments and Last Willes. 1590; 1611; 1635; 1640; 1677; 1728; 1734; 1793; 1803.

—— A treatise of Spousals or Matrimonial Contracts. 1686; 1711.

Terms de la Ley. [See Rastell (John).]

Theloall, Simon. La digest des briefes originals et des choses concernant eux. 1579; 1687.

Wentworth, Thomas. The office and duty of Executors. 1641, etc. (to 1829). [This work has been ascribed to Sir John Doddridge. The first two edns were anonymous. An edn was pbd in Philadelphia in 1832.]

West, W. Symboleographie. 1590, etc. (to 1647).

Wilkinson, John. A treatise collected out of the statutes of this kingdom, and according to common experience of the lawes, concerning the office and authoritie of coroners and sherifs: together with an easie and plain method for the keeping of a Court Leet, Court Baron and Hundred Court, etc. 1618.

Wingate, Edmund. Statuta pacis: or, perfect table of all the statutes which concerne the office of a justice of the peace. 1641; 1644.

—— Justice revived. The office of justice. 1644; 1661.

—— An exact abridgment of all the statutes from Magna Charta to 1641. 1655; 1675; 1681; 1689.

Wingate, Edmund. The body of the common law of England. 1655; 1658; 1662; 1678.
—— Maxims of reason, or the reason of the common law of England. 1658.
—— The exact constable. 1660.
Zouche, Richard. Elementa jurisprudentiae. 1629; 1665.
—— Descriptio juris et judicii feudalis. 1634.
—— Descriptio juris et judicii temporalis. 1636. [Also with R. Mocket's Tractatus de Politia Ecclesiae Anglicanae, 1683, 1705.]
—— Descriptio juris et judicii ecclesiastici. 1636. [Also in Mocket's Tractatus de Politia Ecclesiae Anglicanae, 1683, 1705.]
—— Descriptio juris et judicii sacri. 1640.
—— Descriptio juris et judicii militaris. 1640; 1652; 1665.
—— Descriptio juris et judicii maritimi. 1640.
—— Descriptio juris et judicii fecialis. 1650; ed. T. E. Holland, with trn by J. L. Brierly, 2 vols. Washington, 1911.
—— Cases and questions resolved in the civil law. 1652.
—— Specimen questionum juris civilis. 1653.

H. A. C. S.

IV. SCHOLARS AND SCHOLARSHIP

General Authorities. Works of General Learning. Biblical Scholarship. The Early Fathers and Schoolmen. Disputational Learning. Ecclesiastical and Theological Learning. Latin. Greek.

[This section is mainly concerned with the period 1590–1660. For the earlier years the section on Education, pp. 364–80 above, should be consulted. Reference should also be made to the section Translations into English, pp. 799–822 above.]

(1) GENERAL AUTHORITIES

Aubrey, John. Brief Lives, chiefly of Contemporaries. Ed. Andrew Clark, 2 vols. Oxford, 1898.
Baillet, A. Jugemens des Savans. 8 vols. Paris, 1722–30; Amsterdam, 1725.
Basire, Isaac. Correspondence in the Reigns of Charles I and Charles II and Memoir. Ed. W. N. Darnell, 1831.
Beard, C. The Reformation of the 16th Century in its Relation to Modern Thought and Knowledge. 1883. (Hibbert Lectures.) [See especially lectures on Reformation in Switzerland, Rise of Protestant Scholasticism, the Reformation in England, Growth of the Critical Spirit, and the Development of Philosophical Method and Scientific Investigation.]
Begley, Walter. Nova Solyma: the Ideal City, an Anonymous Romance in Latin, 1648,

with Introduction, Translation, Literary Essays and a Bibliography. 2 vols. 1902.
Birch, U. Anna van Schurman. Artist, Scholar, Saint. 1909.
Bowes, R. Catalogue of Books printed at or relating to Cambridge. 1894.
Brüggemann, L. W. View of the English Editions, Translations and Illustrations of the Ancient Greek and Latin Authors. Stettin, 1797.
Burnet, Gilbert. Life of Sir Matthew Hale. 1682.
Calamy, Edmund. The Nonconformists' Memorial. Ed. Samuel Palmer, 3 vols. 1802–3.
Casaubon, Meric. Vindicatio Patris. 1624; tr. Eng. 1624 (as The vindication or defence of Isaac Casaubon).
Cattermole, R. Literature of the Church of England. 2 vols. 1844.
Child, Gilbert W. Church and State under the Tudors. 1890. [Shows the influence of Geneva on English church doctrine and constitution.]
Christie, R. C. The Old Church and School Libraries of Lancashire. Chetham Soc. 1885.
Cox, Robert. The Literature of the Sabbath Question. 2 vols. 1865. [Full bibliography of works on the Sabbath, one of the controversial subjects of learned discourse of the puritan times.]
Dexter, H. M. and Morton. The England and Holland of the Pilgrims. Boston, 1905. [With an index of publications of Separatist literature and controversy.]
Dibdin, T.F. An Introduction to the Knowledge of Rare and Valuable Editions of the Greek and Latin Classics. 2 vols. 1827 (4th edn).
Dircks, Henry. A Biographical Memoir of Samuel Hartlib with Bibliographical Notices. 1865. [For a number of letters between Hartlib and Dr Worthington see Worthington's Diary, ed. J. Crossley and R. C. Christie, 3 pts, Chetham Soc. 1847–86.]
Fell, John. Life of Sir Matthew Hale [with catalogue of his printed books and MSS, pp. 95–8] and Life of Henry Hammond. Oxford, 1856.
Growoll, A. and Eames, W. Three Centuries of English Book Trade Bibliography. New York, 1903.
Hacket, John. Scrinia Reserata: A Memorial offered to the great Deservings of John Williams (Archbishop of York). 2 vols. 1693.
Hamilton, Sir William. Discussions on Philosophy and Literature, Education and University Reform. 1853 (2nd edn). [Contains important matter on the History of Logic, pp. 118–76; and an account of the History of the University of Leyden, pp. 373–9.]

Hathaway, C. M. The Alchemist by Ben Jonson. New York, 1903. [With an introduction giving an account of alchemical learning of the time.]

Heywood, J. and Wright, T. Cambridge University Transactions during the Puritan Controversies of the 16th and 17th Centuries. 2 vols. 1854.

Laurie, S. S. Studies in the History of Educational Opinion. Cambridge, 1903.

Madan, Falconer. The Early Oxford Press, '1468'–1640. Oxford, 1895.

Mayor, J. E. B. Autobiography of Matthew Robinson. 1856. [Contains Matthew Poole's Model for the maintaining of students of choice abilities at the University and principally in order to the Ministry, 1648.]

—— Spain, Portugal, the Bible. Cambridge, 1892. [Valuable details as to the relation of English and foreign reformers.]

Middleton, Erasmus. Biographia Evangelica: or an Historical Account of the Lives and Deaths of the most eminent and evangelical Authors or Preachers both British and Foreign, in the several Denominations of Protestants from the Beginning of the Reformation to the present Time. 4 vols. 1779–86.

Mitchell, A. F. The Westminster Assembly: its History and Standards. 1883. (Baird Lectures.)

Moore, Norman. The History of the Study of Medicine in the British Isles. Oxford, 1908. (Fitzpatrick Lectures.)

Morhof, D. G. Polyhistor Literarius, Philosophicus et Practicus. Lübeck, 1714.

Mullinger, J. Bass. Cambridge Characteristics in the 17th Century. Cambridge, 1867.

—— The University of Cambridge from the Royal Injunctions of 1535 to the Accession of Charles I. Cambridge, 1884.

Parkinson, R. Life of Adam Martindale, written by Himself. Chetham Soc. 1845. [Contains many educational references.]

Parr, Richard. Life of James Usher, late Lord Archbishop of Armagh. 1686. [Valuable for accounts of learning of the times. Contains 323 letters to or from Ussher.]

Pattison, Mark. Isaac Casaubon. Oxford, 1892 (2nd edn). [Contains valuable sketches of the scholarship of the times in England and abroad.]

—— Essays. 2 sers. Oxford, 1889. [Including in Ser. I The Stephenses, Joseph Scaliger, Calvin at Geneva; in Ser. II Learning in the Church of England.]

Payne, J. F. Thomas Sydenham. 1900. (Masters of Medicine Ser.)

Power, Sir D'Arcy. William Harvey. 1897. (Masters of Medicine Ser.)

Quick, R. H. Essays on Educational Reformers. 1868.

St John, Wallace. Contest for Liberty of Conscience in England. Chicago, 1900. [With bibliography.]

Sandys, Sir J. E. A History of Classical Scholarship. From the Revival of Learning to the End of the 18th Century in Italy, France, England and Netherlands. 3 vols. Cambridge, 1903–8. [Vol. II, 1921 (3rd edn).]

Schickler, Baron F. de. Les Églises du Refuge en Angleterre. 3 vols. Paris, 1892.

Shaw, W. A. History of the English Church during the Civil Wars and under the Commonwealth, 1640–1660. 2 vols. 1900.

Smith, P. A. History of Education for the English Bar. 1860.

Todd, H. J. The Polyglot Bible. Memoirs and Writings of the Rt Rev. Brian Walton, Lord Bishop of Chester. With Notices of his Coadjutors in that Illustrious Work; of the Cultivation of Oriental Learning in this Country, preceding and during their Time; and of the Authorised English Version of the Bible. 2 vols. 1821.

Underhill, J. G. Spanish Literature in the England of the Tudors. New York, 1899.

Walker, John. Sufferings of the Clergy in the late Times of the Grand Rebellion. 1714.

Walton, Joseph. Early History of Legal Studies in England. 1900.

Ward, John. Lives of the Professors of Gresham College. 1740.

Wase, Christopher. Considerations concerning Free Schools, as settled in England. 1678. [Important account of secondary schools in England from the reformation onwards.]

Watson, Foster. Scholars and Scholarship, 1600–60. CHEL. vol. VII, 1911.

Weld, C. R. History of the Royal Society. 2 vols. 1848.

à Wood, Anthony. Athenae Oxonienses. Ed. P. Bliss, 4 vols. 1813–20.

Wordsworth, Christopher. Scholae Academicae: some Account of the Studies at the English Universities in the Eighteenth Century. 1877.

Worthington, John. Diary and Correspondence. Ed. J. Crossley and R. C. Christie, 3 pts, Chetham Soc. 1847–86. [Worthington edited Joseph Mead's works and his Correspondence affords a mirror of the learned life of the times.]

Young, Sir George. History of Greek Literature in England from the Earliest Times to the End of the Reign of James I. Cambridge, 1862.

[For English dictionaries see J. A. H. Murray, The Evolution of English Lexicography, Oxford, 1900, and M. M. Mathews, A Survey of English Dictionaries, 1933. For contemporary books in Divinity, History, Physic and Chirurgery, Mathematics, Common

854 RENAISSANCE TO RESTORATION

and Civil Law, Hebrew, Latin and Greek, see William London's Catalogue (see below, p. 855). For the school text-books of the period see John Brinsley, Ludus Literarius, 1612; and his Consolation for our Grammar Schools, 1622; and Charles Hoole, New Discovery of the Old Art of Teaching School, 1660, which gives a list of 300 school books, arranged for use in each of the six forms of a school. William London, Catalogue of the most Vendible Books, 1660, includes section on books useful for schools and scholars. For books used in grammar school teaching in all subjects see Foster Watson's English Grammar Schools to 1660: their Curriculum and Practice, Cambridge, 1908. For books of instruction, other than those used in the grammar school, see Foster Watson, The Beginnings of the Teaching of Modern Subjects, 1909. For biographies of scholars see General Dictionary: Historical and Critical, founded on Bayle, by J. P. Bernard, Thomas Birch. etc., 10 vols. 1735. For an account of rhetoric study see G. H. Mair, Introduction to reprint of Wilson's Art of Rhetoric, Oxford, 1909.]

(2) CONTEMPORARY WORKS OF GENERAL LEARNING

Brerewood, Edward. Enquiries touching the Diversity of Languages and Religion through the chiefe Parts of the World. 1614; 1622; 1674.

Brinsley, John. Ludus Literarius, or the Grammar Schoole; shewing how to proceed from the first entrance into learning, to the highest perfection required in the Grammar Schooles with ease, certainty and delight, both to Masters and Schollers; onely according to our common Grammar, and ordinary Classical authours, etc. 1612; 1627; ed. E. T. Campagnac, Liverpool, 1917.

Clarke, John (headmaster of Lincoln Grammar School). Paroemiologia anglo-latina or Proverbs English and Latin; methodically disposed according to the commonplace heads in Erasmus his Adages. 1639. [Clarke says, in his preface, he has gathered from Erasmus, scholars and friends, 'over and besides my own observation of many golden proverbs dropping from vulgar mouths *ima de plebe*.' The most complete collection of English proverbs was that of John Ray, the naturalist, A Collection of English Proverbs with short Annotations, 1670, the preface to which gives an account of the previous English collections.]

Clarke, Samuel. The Marrow of Ecclesiastical History with Lives of 148 Fathers, School-

men, and modern Divines. 1649; 1654 (enlarged); 1675.

Crow, William. An exact Collection or Catalogue of our English Writers on the Old and New Testament. 1663. [This consists of 270 pages of close type, giving references to English commentators on every book of the Bible, and almost to every chapter, and often to nearly every verse of a chapter. Crow's book was followed by Bishop Wilkins's Catalogue in 1668.]

Dury, John. The Reformed School. [1649?]

Estienne, Henri. The Art of Making Devises. Treating of Hieroglyphicks, Symboles, Emblemes, Aenigmas, Sentences, Parables, Reverses of Medalls, Arms, Blazons, Cimiers, Cyphres and Rebus. Translated into English by Thomas Blount. 1650. [The making of 'devices' involved some pictorial representation together with a symbolic meaning. When this is expressed in words it becomes an emblem. In the 16th and 17th cents., emblem-books were a recognised recreation to the scholar. We learn from Farnaby and Hoole that they were used in schools as helps in phrase-making in both Latin and Greek prose and verse composition. Amongst the English emblem-writers were Geoffrey Whitney, Choice of Emblems, 1586; Andrew Willet, 1598; Peacham's Minerva Britannia, 1612; Francis Quarles, 1635; George Wither, 1635. The foreign emblem-writers, Alciat, Bocchius, Jovius, Maccius, quickened language study, especially Latin (by presenting the foreign languages along with pictures of what was described in words) as well as serving for scholarly recreation. On emblem literature see H. Green, Shakespere and the Emblem-writers, 1870, and pp. 478–9 above.]

Habington, Thomas. The Epistle of Gildas, entitled De Excidio et Conquestu Britanniae, translated into English. 1638.

Hales, John. Golden Remains. 1659.

Harvey, William. Exercitatio Anatomica de Motu Cordis et Sanguinis in Animalibus. 1628.

Heylyn, Peter. Cosmographie in four bookes, containing the horographie and historie of the whole world. 1652.

Hoole, Charles. A New Discovery of the Old Art of Teaching School. 1660; ed. E. T. Campagnac, Liverpool, 1913. [This work, which contains the most complete school text-book bibliography, is extremely rare. There is a rpt in Henry Barnard's English Pedagogy, ser. 2, Hartford, U.S.A. 1876. The summarised list of about 300 school text books is given in A. F. Leach's Yorkshire Schools, vol. II of the Yorkshire Archaeological Soc. Record Ser. (vol. XXXIII), 1903.]

Horne, Thomas. Manuductio in aedem Palladis, quâ Utilissima Methodus Authores bonos legendi indigitatur. 1641. [Perhaps the best book on the method of classical study in the earlier stages, in the period.]

Howell, James. Lexicon Tetraglotton [English, French, Italian, Spanish]. 1660. [Howell pays great attention to the collection of proverbs in all these languages 'to take off the reproach which useth to be cast' upon the subject. Leigh, in his Foelix Consortium, 1663, gives a list of collections in various languages. See also John Clarke above.]

Junius, Franciscus [i.e. François Du Jon]. The Painting of the Ancients, in three Bookes: Declaring by Historicall observations and examples, the Beginning, Progresse, and Consummation of that most Noble Art. And how those ancient Artificers attained to their still so much admired Excellencie. 1638. [Written first in Latin, Amsterdam, 1637.]

—— Caedmonis monachi paraphrasis poetica Genesios. Amsterdam, 1655. [Gothicum Glossarium, quo Argentii Codicis Vocabula explicantur, 1664, and in 1665, an edn of the Moeso-Gothic text of Ulphilas; Quatuor D.N.I.C. Evangeliorum Versiones perantiquae duae, Gothica scilicet [by Junius] et Anglo-Saxonica [by T. Marshall], Dordrecht, 1665.]

Leigh, Edward. Foelix Consortium, or a fit Conjunction of Religion and Learning. Of Learning the Excellency and Usefulness of it, the Liberal Arts, the chiefest Languages, the Universities and Publick Schools of several Nations. Particularising the Men eminent for Religion and Learning divine or humane, among the Jews, Christian, Ancient or Modern Writers, Protestants or Papists, Characterising their Persons, and giving Judgment of their Works. 1663.

London, William. A Catalogue of The Most vendible Books in England, Orderly and Alphabetically Digested; Under the Heads of Divinity, History, Physick, and Chyrurgery, Law, Arithmetick, Geometry, Astrologie, Dialling, Measuring Land and Timber, Gageing, Navigation, Architecture, Horsemanship, Faulconry, Merchandize, Limning, Military Discipline, Heraldry, Fortification and Fireworks, Husbandry, Gardening, Romances, Poems, Playes, &c. With Hebrew, Greek and Latin Books, for Schools and Scholars. The like Work never yet performed by any. Varietas Delectat. 1658. Supplementary list, 1660. [This book contains an Epistle Dedicatory to the Gentry, Ministers of the Gospel and others. Of a Peculiar Choice to the Wise, Learned and Studious in the Northern Counties of Northumberland, Bhpk (Bishopric) of Durham, Westmoreland and Cumberland.]

Minsheu, John. 'Ηγεμὼν εἰς τὰς Γλώσσας, id est Ductor in Linguas. The Guide into Tongues. Cum illarum harmonia, et etymologiis, Originationibus, Rationibus, et Derivationibus, in omnibus his undecim linguis, viz. 1 Anglica, 2 Cambro-Britanica, 3 Belgica, 4 Germanica, 5 Gallica, 6 Italica, 7 Hispanica, 8 Lusitanica seu Portugallica, 9 Latina, 10 Graeca, 11 Hebrea. 1617. [The enterprise was approved by the University of Oxford and by the 'learned men,' Wm. Bedwell, And. Downes and A. Cappel, pastor of the French Church, London.]

Somner, William. Dictionarium Saxonico-Latino-Anglicum cum Grammatica et Glossario Aelfrici. Oxford, 1659.

Spelman, Sir John. Psalterium Davidis Latino-Saxonicum Vetus. 1640.

—— The Life of King Alfred the Great. Ed. T. Hearne, Oxford, 1709. [A Latin version by Christopher Wase, with a commentary by Obadiah Walker, was pbd at Oxford, 1678.]

Ware, Sir James. De Scriptoribus Hiberniae. Dublin, 1639.

(3) BIBLICAL SCHOLARSHIP

Walton, Brian (bishop of Chester). Biblia Sacra Polyglotta, complectentia Textus Originales, Hebraicum, cum Pentateucho Samaritano, Chaldaicum, Graecum. Versionumque Antiquarum, Samaritanae, Graecae LXXII. Interp., Chaldaicae, Syriacae, Arabicae, Aethiopicae, Persicae, Vulg. Lat. quicquid comparari poterat. Cum Textuum & Versionum Orientalium Translationibus Latinis ex vetustissimis MSS. undique conquisitis, optimisque exemplaribus impressis, summa fide collatis. Cum Apparatu, Appendicibus, Tabulis, Variis Lectionibus, etc. 6 vols. 1657. [The great triumph in oriental studies by English scholars of the period. The following scholars appear to have assisted Brian Walton in the undertaking: Edmund Castell, Archbishop Ussher, Herbert Thorndike, Edward Pococke, John Lightfoot, Thomas Greaves, Abraham Whelock, Samuel Clarke (architypographus of the University of Oxford), Dudley Loftus, John Vicars, David Stokes, Thomas Smith, Thomas Hyde, Richard Heath, Alexander Huish, Thomas Pierce, Henry Hammond, Patrick Young, Archbishop Sheldon, Archbishop Sterne, Bishop Sanderson, Bishop Ferne, William Fuller, Bruno Ryves, Samuel Baker, Richard Drake, John Johnson, Meric Casaubon, John Selden, William Norris, Claude Hardie.]

Pearson, John (bishop of Chester) *et al.*
Critici Sacri: sive doctissimorum virorum in
SS. Biblia Annotationes et Tractatus. Ed.
John Pearson, A. Scattergood, F. Gouldman
and R. Pearson, 9 vols. 1660; 13 vols.
Amsterdam, 1698–1732.

Poole, Matthew. Synopsis Criticorum Aliorumque S. Scripturae Interpretum Opera
Matthaei Poli. 5 vols. 1669–76. [The two
works above named, the Critici Sacri and
the Synopsis, are the most learned collections of annotations and treatises on the
Bible of the period. They include the work
of both foreign and English scholars.]

Commentaries in English on the whole Bible

The Douay Commentary. 1609.
Commentaries. Ed. John Mayer, 7 vols. 1653.
The Annotations of John Diodati. 1656.
The Dutch Annotations. Tr. Theodore Haak,
2 vols. 1657.
The English Annotations. 2 vols. 1657.

[For commentaries on the separate books of
the Bible, see W. Crow, in general list. In no
direction were the energies of learned men more
concentrated than on scriptural commentaries
in this period. Amongst the most elaborate
and best known were Caryl on Job; Greenhill
on Ezekiel; Burroughs on Hosea; Gouge and
also Owen, on the Hebrews; Manton on James;
Jenkins on Jude; Wilkins on Ecclesiastes;
Francis Taylor on Proverbs; Gataker on
Isaiah, Jeremiah and Lamentations; Meric
Casaubon on the Psalms; Ley on the Four
Evangelists and on the Pentateuch; Mede on
the Apocalypse.]

Ainsworth, Henry. The Booke of Psalmes,
Englished both in Prose and Metre. Amster-
dam, 1612.
—— Solomon's Song of Songs in English
Metre. 1623.

Bois, John. Veteris Interpretis cum Beza
aliisque recentioribus Collatio in quatuor
Evangeliis et Apostolorum Actis. Opus
auspiciis Lanceloti [Andrewes] Wintoniensis
Episcopi coeptum et profectum. 1655.

Burgess, Anthony. 145 Expository Sermons
on the whole 17th chapter according to
John. 1656.

Cosin, John (bishop of Durham). A Scholastical
History of the Canon of the Holy Scripture.
1657.

Diodati, Giovanni. Pious Annotations upon
the Holy Bible. 1643.

Ferrar, Nicholas [of Little Gidding]. The
Actions and Doctrine and other Passages concerning our Lord Jesus Christ, as they are related by the Foure Evangelists, reduced into
one complete body of Historie. 1635. [Com-
piled by Nicholas Ferrar and his family.]

Fuller, Nicholas. Miscellaneorum Theologi-
corum, quibus non modo Scripturae Divinae, sed et aliorum classicorum Auctorum
plurima monumenta explicantur atque
illustrantur. Oxford, 1616.

Hildesham, Arthur. Lectures upon the Fourth
of John. 1629; 1632.
—— CLII Lectures upon Psalm LI. 1635.

Leigh, Edward. Critica Sacra in two parts;
the first containing Observations on all the
Radices or Primitive Hebrew Words of the
Old Testament; the second, Philologicall
and Theological Observations upon all
the Greek Words of the New Testament.
1650.

Lightfoot, John. On the Canon of Scripture.
1652.

Mede (or Mead), Joseph. Clavis Apocalyptica
ex innatis et insitis Visionum characteribus
eruta et demonstrata. Cambridge, 1627.
—— The Key of the Revelation searched and
demonstrated out of the naturall and proper
characters of the visions. Translated by
Richard More, with a Preface written by
Dr Twisse. 1643.

Smith, Miles. [Said to have written the Preface to the Authorised Version of the Bible,
1611.]

[For names of further books on the Bible
and Bible scholarship see W. Crow in general
list and section on divinity books in William
London's Catalogue (1660).]

(4) THE EARLY FATHERS AND SCHOOLMEN

Burton, William. Annotations to the first
Epistle of Clement the Apostle to the
Corinthians. 1647. [Set forth in Latin by
Patrick Young, 1633, from which this English trn was made 'to cure the many distract-
ing schisms of the time.']
—— Clement the blessed Paul's fellow labourer
in the Gospel, his first Epistle to the Corinthians. 1650.

Bustus, Matthaeus. Joannis Metropolitani
Euchaitensis Versus Iambici In princi-
palium festorum pictas in tabulis historias
atque alia varia compositi; Nunc primum
in lucem edita. Eton, 1610.

Evelyn, John. The Golden Book of St Chrysostom, concerning the Education of children
translated into English by J[ohn] E[velyn]
Esq. 1659.

Harmar, John. Eclogae Sententiarum et
Similitudinum e D. Chrysostomo decerptae,
Graec. et Lat. cum Annot. 1622.
—— Lexicon, Etymologicon Graecum, junc-
tim cum Scapula. 1637.

Healey, John. Of the Citie of God with the learned comments of Jo. Ludovicius Vives. Englished first by J. H. and now in this second edition compared with the Latin Original, and in very many places corrected and amended. 1620. [1st edn, 1610.]

Humphrey, R. Christian Offices Cristall glass, written by S. Ambrose. 1637.

Montagu, Richard (bishop of Norwich). Sancti Gregorii Nazianzeni in Julianum Invectivae duae. Cum Scholiis graecis nunc primum editis et eiusdem Authoris nonnullis aliis. Omnia ex Bibliotheca clarissimi viri D. Henrici Savilii edidit R. M[ontagu]. Eton, 1610.

—— Nonni Panopolitani collectio et expositio historiarum fabularumque in Gregorii Nazianzeni Orationes, sive Steleleuticas duas adversus Julianum Augustum. Graece, ex codice Bibl. Vindobonensis edidit R. Montagu, cum Gregorii Nazianzeni utraque in Julianum invectiva. Eton, 1610.

—— Eusebii de Demonstratione Evangelica libri decem, omnia studio R. M. Latine facta, notis illustrata. 1628.

—— Φωτιου 'Επιστολαι. Photii sanctissimi Patriarchae Constantinopolitani Epistolae Latine redditae et Notis subinde illustratae. 1651.

—— Sancti Justini Apologia prima pro Christianis; cum Tryphone Judaeo Dialogus; subjunctis emendationibus et notis Montacutii. 1700.

Rutherford, Samuel (1600–1661). [Mentioned in Milton's poem On the new forcers of Conscience. For his works, see DNB.]

Savile, Sir Henry. S. Joannis Chrysostomi Opera Graece. 8 vols. Eton, 1610–3.

Spencer, William. Origenis contra Celsum libri octo. Eiusdem Philocalia. Gulielmus Spencerus utriusque operis versionem recognovit, et annotationes adjecit. Cambridge, 1658.

Ussher (or Usher), James. Polycarpi et Ignatii Epistolae. Graec. Lat. cum de eorum dissertatione Scriptis, deque Apostolicis Canonibus et Constitutionibus Clementi tributis. Oxford, 1644. [Text (with Latin trn)—ex trium manuscriptorum codicum collatione, integritati suae restitutae. The Barnabae Epistola was to have been included but the copy of the MS was burnt by fire whilst with the printers.]

—— Historia dogmatica controversiae inter orthodoxos et pontificios de scripturis et sacris vernaculis nunc primum edita. Accesserunt ejusdem dissertationes duae de Pseudo-Dionysii scriptis et de epistola ad Laodicenos, ante hac ineditae. Ed. Henry Wharton, 1690.

Whelock, Abraham. Quatuor Evangeliorum Domini Nostri Jesu Christi versio Persica Syriacam et Arabicam suavissime redolens: Ad verba et mentem Graeci Textus fideliter et venuste concinnata. Codicibus tribus Manuscriptis ex Oriente in Academias utrasque Anglorum perlatis, operose invicem diligenterque collatis. 1657.

Young, Patrick (Patricius Junius). Clementis ad Corinthios Epistola prior. Ex laceris reliquiis vetustissimi Exemplaris Bibliothecae regiae, eruit, lacunas explevit, Latinè vertit et notis brevioribus illustravit Patricius Junius. Oxford, 1633.

—— Catena Graecorum Patrum in beatum Job collectore Niceta, Heracleae Metropolita, ex duobus MSS. Bibliothecae Bodleianae codicibus, graece nunc primum in lucem edita, et latine versa. Accessit ad calcem textus Jobi ζιχηρως, juxta veram et germanam Septuaginta Seniorum interpretationem, ex venerando Bibliothecae Regiae MS. codice, et totius orbis antiquissimo ac praestantissimo. 1637.

(5) DISPUTATIONAL LEARNING

Chillingworth, William. The Religion of Protestants a safe way to Salvation; or an answer to a booke entituled, Mercy and Truth; or, charity maintained by Catholiques, which pretends to prove the contrary. Oxford, 1638. [Chillingworth makes much use of John Daillé, a learned French divine, 'at about the same time lord Falkland did in his writings; who was wont to say it was worth a voyage to Paris to be acquainted with him.']

Crakanthorp, Richard. Justinian the Emperor defended against Cardinal Baronius. 1616.

—— Defensio Ecclesiae Anglicanae contra M. Anton. de Dominis Archiep. Spalatensis Injurias. 1625. ['Which book was held to be the most exact piece for controversy since the time of the reformation,' Wood.]

—— Vigilius Dormitans. Rome's Seer Overseen. Wherein the exceeding frauds of Cardinall Baronius and Bineus are clearly discovered. Opus posthumum. 1631.

Featley, Daniel. [Author of nearly 40 different works, chiefly controversial.] Roma Ruens. 1644. [Against Rome.]

—— The Dippers Dipt. 1644. [Against the baptists.]

Montagu, Richard (bishop of Norwich). Appello Caesarem. 1625.

Rainolds, John. De Romanae ecclesiae idololatria. Oxford, 1596. [Rainolds was 'placed by Colomies as amongst the first six in copiousness of erudition whom Protestantism had produced,' Hallam.]

Sutcliffe, Matthew. De Missa Papistica variisque synagogae Rom. circa Eucharistiae Sacramentum erroribus et corruptelis, adversus R. Bellarminum [etc.] 1603.

Twisse, William. Vindiciae Gratiae, Potestatis ac Providentiae Dei. Amsterdam, 1632. [686 close printed double columns, folio pages.]

[For further contemporary books of disputational literature see section on Divinity in William London's Catalogue (1660) in the Contemporary list above, p. 855.]

(6) Ecclesiastical and Theological Learning

Baronius, Caesar, Cardinal. Annales Ecclesiastici. 12 vols. Rome, 1588–1609.

Bilson, Thomas (bishop of Winchester). De Perpetua Ecclesiae Christi Gubernatione. 1611.

Birckbek, Simon. The Protestant's Evidence taken out of good records, showing that for 1500 years next after Christ, divers worthy guides of God's Church have taught as the Church of England now doth. 1635. ['Valued by Selden and other learned men,' Wood.]

Casaubon, Isaac. De rebus sacris et ecclesiasticis exercitationes XVI ad Baronii Prolegomena in Annales. 1614.

Casaubon, Meric. On Credulity and Incredulity in things natural, civil and divine. 1668. [Further part of work issued in 1670.]

Clarke, Samuel (minister of St Benetfink). The Marrow of Ecclesiastical Historie, conteined in the Lives of the Fathers and other Learned Men. 1650; 1675 (3rd edn).

Crakanthorp, Richard. De Providentia Dei Tractatus. Cambridge, 1623.

Field, Richard. Of the Church. 4 books, 1606. 5th book, 1610.

Hall, Joseph (bishop of Norwich). Polemices Sacrae pars prior. Roma Irreconciliabilis. 1611.

Leigh, Edward. Treatise of Divinity. In Three Books. 1646.

—— System or Body of Divinity. In 10 Books. 1654.

Mason, Francis. Vindiciae Ecclesiae Anglicanae: sive de legitimo ejusdem ministerio, id est, de Episcoporum Successione, Consecratione, Electione, et Confirmatione Libri v. Ed. Sir N. Brent, 1625.

Montagu, Richard (bishop of Norwich). Diatribae upon the first part of the late History of Tithes. 1621. [An attack on Selden's History of Tithes, in which Montagu argues that tithes are due by divine right, and have prevailed in all religions, heathen as well as Jewish and Christian.]

—— Analecta Ecclesiasticarum Exercitationum. 1622. [In answer to the Annales Ecclesiastici of Baronius.]

Montagu, Richard. Apparatus ad Origines Ecclesiasticas, collectore R. Montacutio. Oxford, 1635.

—— R. Montacutii de Originibus Ecclesiasticis Commentationum tomus primus. 1636.

—— ΘΕΑΝΘΡΩΠΙΚΟΝ: seu, de Vita Jesu Christi Originum Ecclesiasticarum libri duo. Accedit Graecorum versio et Index utriusque Partis. 1640[–36]. [Bk II not published.]

—— The Acts and Monuments of the Church before Christ Incarnate. 1642.

Pearson, John (bishop of Chester). Exposition of the Creed. 1659.

Rainolds, William. Calvino-Turcismus. Antwerp, 1597. ['Work of recondite learning,' Casaubon.]

Saltonstall, Wye. Ecclesiastical Histories of Eusebius. 1650. [5th edn of Meredith Hanmer's trn (1577) to which were now added: Eusebius's Four Books concerning the life of the Emperor Constantine and two Orations by W. S.]

Savile, Sir Henry. Thomae Bradwardini, archiepiscopi olim Cantuariensis, de causa Dei contra Pelagium et de virtute causarum. 1618.

Simson, Archibald. Hieroglyphica animalium terrestrium, volatilium, natatilium, reptilium, insectorum, vegetivorum, metallorum, lapidum, etc., quae in Scripturis Sacris inveniuntur et plurimorum aliorum, cum eorum interpretationibus, etc. 2 vols. Edinburgh, 1622–4.

Ussher (or Usher), James. De Ecclesiarum Christianarum Successione et Statu. 1613.

—— Britannicarum Ecclesiarum Antiquitates. Dublin, 1639.

—— Cronologia Sacra. Oxford, 1660. [This was completed at Ussher's request by Gerard Langbaine 'as the only man on whose learning he could rely.']

—— De Romanae Ecclesiae symbolo apostolico vetere aliisque Fidei formulis diatriba. 1647.

—— Annales Veteris et Novi Testamenti. 2 vols. 1650–4.

—— De Graeca Septuaginta. Interpretum versione syntagma. 1655.

[For list of MS works not ptd, see R. Parr's Life of Ussher, 1686, pp. 106–8.]

Whelock, Abraham. Bedae Historia Ecclesiastica Gentis Anglorum v libris Latine, cum Saxonica Versione Alfredi Regis cumque Notis Abr. Wheloci: adiecta etiam Chronologia Saxonica, Sax. Lat. Cambridge, 1643; Cambridge, 1644 ('Additis insuper Legibus Anglo-Saxonicis Sax. Lat. et Legibus Edwardi et Gulielmi Bastardi, latine, et Wilhelmi Conquestoris gallice et latine et Henrici I, latine tantum').

Young, Patrick (Patricius Junius). Gilberti
Foliot Episcopi Londiniensis Expositio in
Canticum Canticorum, una cum compendio
Alcuini. Nunc primum è Bibliotheca Regia
in lucem prodiit, Opera & Studio Patricii
Junii. 1638.

[For further contemporary books on ecclesiastical and theological subjects, see sections
on divinity in William London's Catalogue
(1660) in the Contemporary list, above,
p. 855. For books on Cases of Conscience, see
under Conscience in Robert Watt, Bibliotheca
Britannica, 4 vols. Edinburgh, 1824.]

(7) Latin Learning

John Owen (1564?–1622)*

(a) Works

Epigrammatum Joannis Owen Cambro-Bri-
tanni Libri Tres. Ad Illustrissimam D.
Mariam Neville. 1606 (bis); 1607; 1612.
Epigrammatum Joannis Owen Cambro-Bri-
tanni Ad Excellentissimam D. Arbellam
Stuart Liber Singularis. 1607.
Epigrammatum Joannis Owen Oxoniensis,
Cambro-Britanni, Libri Tres. Ad Henricum
Principem Cambriae Duo. Ad Carolum
Eboracensem unus. 1612.
Epigrammatum Joannis Owen Cambro-Bri-
tanni Oxoniensis. Ad Tres Mecaenates,
Libri Tres. Ad Edwardum Noel equitem &
Baronetum, unus. Ad Gulielmum Sidley
equitem & Baronetum, alter. Ad Rogerum
Owen equitem auratum, Tertius. 1612.
Epigrammatum Joannis Owen Libri Decem.
Leipzig, 1615; Leyden, 1628, etc.; ed. A. A.
Renouard, Paris, 1794; ed. F. A. Ebert,
Leipzig, 1824.

(b) Translations into English

Vicars, John. Epigrams Of That most wittie
and worthie Epigrammatist Mr John Owen.
1619.
H[ayman], R[obert]. Quodlibets, Lately
Come Over From New Britaniola, Old
Newfound-land. The first foure Bookes being
the Authors owne: the rest translated out of
Mr John Owen, and other rare Authors.
1628.
Harflete, Henry. A Banquet of Essays, Fetcht
out of Famous Owen's Confectionary. 1653.
[Essays on Ep. 1, 2, with a trn.]
Pecke, Thomas. Parnasi Puerperium: or,
Some Wellwishes to Ingenuity, in the
Translation of Six Hundred, of Owens
Epigrams. 1659.

Harvey, Thomas. John Owen's Latin Epigrams, Englished. 1677.
[Translations of isolated epigrams are
frequent. See, e.g., William Cowper, Poetical
Works, ed. H. S. Milford, p. 563, 1926.]

(c) Criticism

Urban, Erich. Owenus und die deutschen
Epigrammatiker des XVII. Jahrhunderts.
Berlin, 1890.
Bensly, Edward. Robert Burton, John Bar-
clay and John Owen. CHEL. vol. iv, ch. 13,
1909.
—— John Owen the Epigrammatist. N. & Q.
9 Jan. 1909.

John Barclay (1582–1621)

(a) Bibliography

Dukas, Jules. Étude bibliographique et littéraire sur le Satyricon de Jean Barclay.
Paris, 1880.
Collignon, Albert. Notes historiques, littéraires et bibliographiques sur l'Argenis de
Jean Barclay. Paris, 1902.
—— Le Portrait des Esprits (Icon Animorum)
de Jean Barclay. Nancy, 1906.
Becker, P. A. Johann Barclay, 1582–1621.
Zeitschrift für vergleichende Litteraturgeschichte, xv, 1903.
Schmid, K. F. John Barclays Argenis. Eine
literarhistorische Untersuchung. i. Ausgaben der Argenis, ihrer Forsetzungen
und Übersetzungen. Berlin, 1904.

(b) Works

In P. Statii Papinii Thebaidos libros iiii commentarii. Pont-à-Mousson, 1601.
Euphormionis Lusinini Satyricon. 1603 (no
copies extant); Paris, 1605 ('emendatum et
auctum'). Euphormionis Lusinini Satyricon Pars Secunda. Paris, 1607. Euphormionis Satyrici Apologia pro se. Paris,
1610. Joannis Barclaii Icon Animorum.
1614. [Both pts of Euphormio were rptd
together with Apologia, with separate titles
and pagination, n.p. 1610–1. These three,
with Icon Animorum, were rptd in the same
way, n.p. 1616, also Strasburg, 1623 (with
key), London, 1624, Rouen, 1628, Amsterdam, 1628, etc. and ed. L. G. Bugnot,
Leyden, 1674.]
Ad Jacobum I, carmen gratulatorium. Paris,
1603.
Sylvae. 1606. [Latin verses.]
Johannis Barclaii Pietas. Paris, 1612. [A defence of his father against Cardinal Bellar-
min.]

* The bibliographies of Owen and Barclay are by Professor Edward Bensly.

Poemata. 1615.

Paraenesis ad Sectarios. Rome, 1617.

Joannis Barclaii Argenis. Paris, 1621, 1622, 1623, 1624 and 1625; Frankfort, 1626 (adds Explicatio nominum); Leyden, 1627 (adds Discursus in Argeniden and an Elenchus nominum̂); Leyden, 1630 (adds further Discursus), etc.; ed. L. G. Bugnot, Leyden, 1659.

Carminum libri II cum lib. III ex Argenide. Cologne, 1626.

Series Patefacti Divinitus Parricidii in Regem Britanniae cogitate: Nonis ixbribus MDCV. Amsterdam, 1628 (appended to Euphormio), etc.

In Phaethonta Gallicium [i.e. Mancini]. Paris, [?] (signed I. B.).

Poematum Libri duo. Oxford, 1636.

Delitiae Poetarum Scotorum. 1637. [Pt I, pp. 76–136.]

[There are also verses by Barclay in W. Barclay's edn of Tacitus, Paris, 1599, and a preface in W. Barclay's De Potestate Papae, 1609.]

(c) Translations into English

[For the trns into languages other than English see the bibliographies of Dukas and Schmid.]

Long, Kingsmill. Barclay His Argenis, or, the Loves of Poliarchus and Argenis. 1625; 1636. [The verses by Thomas May.]

Le Grys, Sir Robert and May, Thomas. John Barclay His Argenis, the Prose upon His Majesties Command: By Sir Robert Le Grys, Knight: And the Verses by Thomas May, Esquire. 1629.

M[ay], Th[omas]. The Mirrour of Mindes. 1631; 1633.

John Barclay his Vindication of the Intercession of Saints. By a Person of Quality. 1688. [Paraenesis ad Haereticos, bk II, ch. 7.]

John Barclay his defence of the Eucharist. By a Person of Quality. 1688. [Paraenesis ad Haereticos, bk II, ch. 11.]

Jacob, John. The Adventures of Poliarchus and Argenis. Dublin, 1734. [An abridgement: see E. Bensly, MLR. IV, 1909.]

[Reeve, Clara.] The Phoenix; or, the History of Polyarchus and Argenis. 4 vols. 1772.

[A trn of Argenis by Ben Jonson was entered at Stationers' Hall, 2 Oct. 1623.]

(d) Biography and Criticism

[For a summary of the original sources for Barclay's life and a list of later biographical studies, see P. A. Becker, Zeitschrift für vergleichende Litteraturgeschichte, xv, 1903.]

Dalrymple, Sir David (Lord Hailes). Sketch of the Life of John Barclay. 1786.

Coleridge, S. T. Literary Remains, 2 vols. 1836. [Vol. I, pp. 255–8.]

Dukas, Jules. Étude bibliographique et littéraire sur le Satyricon de Jean Barclay. Paris, 1880.

Körting, Heinrich. Geschichte des französischen Romans im XVII. Jahrhundert. 2 vols. Leipzig, 1885–7.

Urbain, Charles. Apropos de Jean de Barclay. Bulletin du Bibliophile, 1891. [Unpbd letters.]

Collignon, Albert. Notes sur l'Euphormion de Jean Barclay. Nancy, 1901.

—— Notes historiques, littéraires et bibliographiques sur l'Argenis de Jean Barclay. Paris, 1902.

—— Le Portrait des Esprits (Icon Animorum) de Jean Barclay. Nancy, 1906. [Appendix C: Note complémentaire sur l'Argenis.]

Becker, P. A. Johann Barclay, 1582–1621. Zeitschrift für vergleichende Litteraturgeschichte, xv, 1903.

Schmid, K. F. John Barclays Argenis. Eine literarhistorische Untersuchung. I. Ausgaben der Argenis, ihrer Fortsetzungen und Übersetzungen. Berlin, 1904. [Pp. 167–74, 17th and 18th century works on Argenis.]

Bensly, Edward. Robert Burton, John Barclay and John Owen. CHEL. vol. IV, ch. 13, 1909.

Bond, J. A. Quinti Horatii Flacci Poemata, cum Notis. 1606.

—— Persii Flacci Satyrae. 1614. [With notes.]

Brinsley, John. [For list of his school textbooks of classical authors, see his Ludus Literarius (1612), above, p. 365.]

Busby, Richard. Juvenalis et Persii Satirae in usum Scholae Westmonasteriensis. 1656.

—— Martialis Epigrammata in usum Scholae Westmonasteriensis. 1661.

Casaubon, Isaac. Persii Flacci Satirarum Liber. 1647 (3rd edn with addns by Meric Casaubon).

Cogan, Thomas. Epistolarum familiarium Ciceronis Epitome. Cambridge, 1602.

Dempster, Thomas. Antiquitatum Romanarum corpus absolutissimum, in quo praeter ea, quae Joannes Rosinus delineaverat, infinita supplentur, mutantur, adduntur. 1613.

—— Nomenclatura Scriptorum Scotorum. Bologna, 1619.

—— Apparatus ad Historiam Scoticam Scriptorum Scotorum Nomenclatura. Bologna, 1622.

Edmundson, Henry (d. 1659). Lingua linguarum. The natural language of languages; wherein it is desired and endeavoured that Tongues may be brought to teach themselves and Words may be best fancied, understood and remembered. 1658. [In a vocabulary contrived and built upon analogy.]
—— Homonyma et Synonyma Linguae Latinae conjuncta et distincta. Oxford, 1661.
Evelyn, John. Essay on First Book of Lucretius de rerum natura with a metrical Version and Notes. 1656.
Farnaby, T. J. Juvenalis et A. Persii Flacci Satyrae; cum annotationibus marginalibus. 1612.
—— Senecae Tragoediae. 1613. [Ed. with notes.]
—— Martialis Epigrammaton libri. 1615. [Ed. with notes.]
—— Lucani Pharsalia. 1618. [With notes.]
—— P. Virgilii Maronis Opera notis admarginalibus illustrata a T. F. 1634.
Farnaby, Thomas and Casaubon, Meric. P. Terentii Afri Comoediae sex; ex recensione Heinsiana, cum adnotationibus T. F. in quatuor priores & Merici Casauboni Is. filii, in duas posteriores. 1651.
[Gott, Samuel.] Novae Solymae libri sex. 1648 (re-issued 1649 as Nova Solyma); ed. and tr. W. Begley, 2 vols. 1902.
Gouldman, Francis. Dictionarium. 1664. [A 'comprisal' of the Latin Dictionaries of Thomas Thomas, John Rider (1589), Thomas and P. Holland (1615). In his preface, Gouldman gives a history of the origins and sources of the whole range of Latin Dictionaries in England from Elyot's Dictionary (1538) to his own (1664).]
[Hall, Joseph.] Mundus alter et idem. Anth. Mercurio Britannico. Frankfort (really London?), [1605]; tr. Eng. J. H[ealey], [1609?] (ed. H. Brown, Cambridge, U.S.A. 1937).
Heath, John. Two Centuries of Epigrammes. 1610.
Holyoke, Francis. Dictionarium Etymologicum Latinum. 1633. [In the final form, 1677–6, there are three parts, English-Latin, Latin-English, and a Dictionary of Names. This was ed. and enlarged by the compiler's son Thomas Holyoke, who claims that in the English-Latin part there are 10,000 more words than in any previous Dictionary.]
Jackson, Henry. [Added marginal notes and copious Index to the de Tradendis Disciplinis of J. L. Vives, part of the de Disciplinis Libri xii, pbd at Leyden, 1612.]
James, William. ['Had a chief hand' (Anthony à Wood) in The English Introduction to the

Latin Tongue for the use of the Lower Forms in Westminster School, 1659.]
Jones, Basset. Hermaelogium; or an essay at the rationality of the Art of Speaking as a Supplement to Lilye's Grammar, philosophically, mythologically and emblematically offered. 1659.
Kynaston (or Kinaston), Sir Francis. [Trn of first and second books of Chaucer's Troilus and Criseyde into Latin, Oxford, 1635. Prefaced by fifteen short Latin poems.]
Leech, John. Epigrammatum Libri quatuor. 1622.
Ogilby, John. P. Virgilii Maronis Opera per J. Ogilvium edita. 1658. [With illustrations by Hollar, Faithorne, Lombart and others.]
Pengry, Moses. Cooper's Hill [by John Denham] latine redditum. 1676.
Savile, Sir Henry. The Ende of Nero and Beginning of Galba, Four books of the Histories of Tacitus. The Life of Agricola. Oxford, 1591; 1612 (4th edn). [Notes put into Latin by Is. Gruter and ptd at Amsterdam, 1649.]
—— A view of certain militar matters. 1591. [In his trn of Tacitus.]
Stapylton, Sir Robert. Juvenal's Sixteen Satyrs. With Arguments, Marginal Notes and Annotations clearing the obscure places out of the History, Lawes, and Ceremonies of the Romans. 1647.
Stephens, Thomas. An Essay upon Statius; or five Books of his Thebais translated into English verse by T[homas] S[tephens]. 1648.
—— Publii Papinii Statii Sylvarum libri v et duo Achilleidos, cum notis marginalibus. Cambridge, 1651.
Stradling, Sir John. Epigrammatum Libri quatuor. 1607.
Thomas, Thomas [and Holland, Philemon]. Dictionarium. 1615.
Weston, Elizabeth Jane. Parthenicon Elizabethae Joannae Westoniae Virginis nobilissimae, poetriae florentissimae, linguarum plurimarum peritissimae. Lib. i, ii, iii. Prague, [c. 1606]. [With a list of learned women beginning with Deborah and ending with Elizabeth Weston.]
[For Latin academic plays see pp. 654–63 above.]

(8) GREEK LEARNING

Barrow, Isaac. Euclidis Elementorum libri xv breviter demonstrati. Cambridge, 1655; tr. Eng. 1660.
Burton, William. A Commentary on Antoninus his Itinerary or Journies of the Romane Empire so far as it concerneth Britain. 1658.
Busby, Richard (headmaster of Westminster School). Graecae Grammatices Rudimenta. [c. 1660.]

Camden, William. Institutio Graecae Grammatices Compendiaria in usum Regiae Scholae Westmonasteriensis. 1597. [The standard Greek Grammar for the 17th cent. as Lily's Grammar was for Latin.]

Casaubon, Isaac. [For the works of Casaubon, see list in Mark Pattison's Life of Casaubon, 1892, pp. 475 ff.]

Casaubon, Meric. Marci Antonini Imperatoris de Seipso et ad Seipsum libri XII; nunc Xylandri versionem locis plurimis emendavit, et novam fecit; in Antonini libros Notas et Emendationes adjecit Mericus Casaubonus. 1632.

—— Marcus Aurelius Antoninus the Roman Emperour, his Meditations concerning Himself [in English]. 1634.

—— De verborum usu et accuratae eorum cognitionis utilitate diatriba. 1647.

—— De quatuor Linguis commentationis pars prior quae, de Lingua Hebraica: et de Lingua Saxonica. 1650. [Casaubon did not finish the Latin and Greek.]

—— Cebetis Tabula Gr. et Lat. cum notis M. C. cum Epicteto. Cambridge, 1659.

—— Notae et Emendationes in Optatum Afrum Milevitani episcopum de Schismate Donatistarum. 1631.

—— De nupera Homeri editione Lugduno-Batavica Hackiana; cum Latina versione et Didymi scholiis; sed et Eustathio et locis aliquot insignioribus ad Odysseam pertinentibus [etc.]. 1659.

Chilmead, Edmund. De Musica antiquâ Graecâ. [At end of Oxford edn of Aratus, ed. J. Fell, bishop of Oxford, 1672.]

Donne, John. The auncient History of the Septuagint. Written in Greeke by Aristeus 1900 years since. Concerning the first translation of the holy Bible by the 72 Interpreters. 1633.

Downes, Andrew. Eratosthenes, hoc est, brevis et luculenta Defensio Lysiae pro caede Eratosthenis, praelectionibus illustrata. Cambridge, 1593.

—— [Notes in Sir Henry Savile's edn of St Chrysostom, vol. VIII, 1613.]

—— Praelectiones in Philippicam de Pace Demosthenis. 1621.

—— [Letters in Greek to Casaubon. (Epistolae.)]

—— [Greek verses on death of Dr Whittaker (St John's College).]

—— [Greek and Latin verses on death of Prince Henry, 1612.]

Duport, James (regius professor of Greek, Cambridge). Θρηνοθριαμβος, sive Liber Job Graeco carmine redditus autore J[acobo] D[uport]. Cambridge, 1637.

—— Σολομων 'Εμμετρος, sive tres libri Solomonis scilicet, Proverbia, Ecclesiastes,

Cantica, Graeco carmine donati per J. D. 1646.

—— Homeri Poetarum omnium saeculorum facile Principis Gnomologia duplici Parallelismo illustrata: Uno ex locis S. Scripturae, quibus Gnomae Homericae aut prope affines aut non prorsus absimiles. Altero ex Gentium Scriptoribus; ubi Citationes, Parodiae, Allusiones et denique loci Paralleli, etc. Cambridge, 1660.

—— Βιβλος της Δημοσιας Ευχης. 1665. [The Book of Common Prayer in ancient Greek.]

—— Δαβιδης 'Εμμετρος, sive metaphrasis libri Psalmorum. 1666.

Everard, Dr John. Divine Pymander of Hermes Trismegistus translated into English. 1650.

Farnaby, Thomas. Tabulae Graecae Linguae. [n.d.]

Gataker, Thomas. Marci Antonini Imperatoris de rebus suis, sive de eis quae ad se pertinere censebat, Libri XII, Locis haud paucis repurgati, suppleti, restituti: Versione insuper Latina nova; Lectionibus item variis, Locisque parallelis, ad marginem adjectis; Ac Commentario perpetuo, explicati atque illustrati. Cambridge, 1652. [For other contributions to classical learning by Gataker, see his Cinnus, sive adversaria miscellanea, 1651, and his Posthuma, 1659.]

Goulston, Theodore. Aristotelis de Poetica Liber, Latine conversus, et analytica methodo illustratus. 1623.

Greaves, John and Foster, Samuel. Lemmata Archimedis, apud Graecos et Latinos jam pridem desiderata, e vetusto codice manuscripto Arabico a J. G. traducta, et cum Arabum scholiis publicata, edidit et suis animadversionibus illustravit S. F. 1659. [For edns of other writings on Greek mathematicians by Englishmen of the period, see John Wallis, Opera mathematica, vol. III, Oxford, 1699–3.]

Grimeston (or Grimston), Edward. The History of Polybius. Translated into English by E. G. 1633.

H., S. The whole Aphorisms of Hippocrates translated into English. 1610.

Hall, John (of Gray's Inn). Hierocles upon the Golden Verses of Pythagoras Englished by J. H. 1657.

Healey, John. Epictetus his Manuall. And Cebes his Table. Out of the Greek originall. 1610.

Hodges, Anthony. Achilles Tatius. The Loves of Clitophon and Leucippe Englished by A. H. Oxford, 1638.

Langbaine, Gerard. Dionysii Longini Rhetoris de grandi Loquentia. 1636. [Ed. and tr. into Latin with notes by Langbaine. Longinus of the Height of Eloquence was tr. into English by John Hall in 1652.]

Price, John. Commentarii in varios Novi Testamenti libros. Annotationes in Psalmorum librum [etc.]. 1660. [A learned work in its grasp of Greek and especially in its illustrative passages from church doctors as well as from classical sources.]

Rainolds, John. Plutarchi Chaeronensis I de utilitate ex hostibus capienda. II de morbis animi et corporis. D. Johanne Rainoldo Interprete. Oxford, 1614.

Selden, John. Marmora Arundelliana, sive Saxa graece incisa, ex venerandis priscae Orientis gloriae ruderibus, auspiciis et impensis Ill. Thomae, Comitis Arundelliae etc. vindicata et in aedibus ejus hortisque disposita. Accedunt Inscriptiones aliquot veteris Latii, ex ejusdem vetustatis Thesauro selectae. Publicavit et Commentariolos adjecit Joh. Seldenus. 1628. [Selden was assisted by Richard James and Patrick Young.]

Shirley, James. Εἰσαγωγή, sive Introductorium Anglo-Latino-Graecum. Complectens Colloquia familiaria, Aesopi Fabulas, et Luciani Selectiores Mortuorum Dialogos. In usum scholarum. 1656. [The dialogues of Lucian occupy 64 pp. The book is a Greek reading-book; there is no grammar.]

Stanley, Thomas. Anacreon; Bion; Moschus; Kisses by Secundus; Cupid crucified by Ausonius: Venus Vigills. Translated into English with Notes. 1651.

Stapylton, C. B. Herodian of Alexandria his Imperiall History converted into an heroick poem. 1652.

Stapylton (or Stapleton), Sir Robert. Musaeus, on the loves of Hero and Leander [with annotations by Stapleton]. 1647.

Stubbe, Henry. Otium Literarum. Sive Miscellanea quaedam Poemata. Oxford, 1656. [Includes Deliciae Poetarum Anglicanorum in Graecum translatae, 1656 (and 1658). Stubbe tr. into Greek from Randolph and Crashaw in Horae Subsecivae, 1651.]

Thornley (or Thorneley), George. Longus. Daphnis and Cloe. Translated into English. 1657.

Ussher (or Usher), James. De Graeca Septuaginta Interpretum versione syntagma: cum Libri Estherae editione Origenicâ, & vetere Graecâ alterâ, ex Arundelliana Bibliotheca nunc primum in lucem producta. 1655.

Wallis, John (Savilian professor of Geometry at Oxford). Claudii Ptolemaei harmonicorum libri tres. Ex codd. MSS. undecim, nunc primum graece editi. J. Wallis recensuit, edidit, versione et notis illustravit et auctarium adjecit. Oxford, 1682. [First Greek text of the work (with Latin trn) and contains an account of Greek music, also a collection of passages from ancient authors bearing on musical theory, some from MSS copies. A work of considerable research and scholarship.]

W[ase], C[hristopher]. Electra of Sophocles. Hague, 1649.

Winterton, Ralph. Poetae Minores Graeci. Hesiodus, Theocritus, Moschus, Bion Smyrn., Simmias Rhod., Musaeus, Theognis, Phocylides, Pythagoras, Solon, Tyrtaeus, Simonides, Rhianus, Linus, Callimachus, Evenus Par., Eratosthenes, Menecrates, Posidippus, Metrodorus, Fragmenta quaedam Philemonis, etc. Cambridge, 1635.

F. W. rev. J. K. H. T.

V. LITERARY CRITICISM

[The following list should be supplemented by the section The Puritan Attack on the Stage, pp. 507–13 above, which deals fully with the various attacks upon the stage and the apologies they provoked. A useful list of contemporary foreign critics, by J. E. Spingarn, will be found in CHEL. vol. vii, ch. 11.]

A. SELECTIONS

[For anthologies of Shakespearian criticism see p. 590 above.]

Haslewood, Joseph. Ancient Critical Essays upon English Poets and Poësy. 2 vols. 1811–5. (Haslewood.)

Vaughan, C. E. English Literary Criticism. 1896.

Collins, J. C. Critical Essays and Literary Fragments. 1903. (Arber's English Garner.)

Saintsbury, George. Loci Critici. Boston, 1903.

Gregory Smith, G. Elizabethan Critical Essays. 2 vols. Oxford, 1904. [A full and representative collection with a detailed introduction. The standard work.] (Gregory Smith.)

Spingarn, J. E. Critical Essays of the Seventeenth Century. 3 vols. Oxford, 1908–9. [A sequel to Gregory Smith's collection with an important introduction.] (Spingarn.)

Klein, David. Literary Criticism from the Elizabethan Dramatists. New York, 1910.

Cowl, R. P. The Theory of Poetry in England. 1914.

Jones, E. D. English Critical Essays. (Sixteenth, Seventeenth and Eighteenth Centuries.) 1922. (World's Classics.)

Bradley, J. F. and Adams, J. Q. The Jonson Allusion-Book, 1597–1700. New Haven, 1923.

Chambers, Sir E. K. The Elizabethan Stage. 4 vols. Oxford, 1923. [Appendix C, vol. iv, prints extracts from documents of literary criticism.] (Chambers.)

Chambers, Sir E. K. William Shakespeare. 2 vols. Oxford, 1930. [Vol. II, Appendix C, The Shakespeare-Mythos.]

Spurgeon, C. F. E. Five Hundred Years of Chaucer Criticism and Allusion. 3 vols. Cambridge, 1925.

Gebert, Clara. An Anthology of Elizabethan Dedications and Prefaces. Philadelphia, 1933.

B. INDIVIDUAL CRITICS

[Full bibliographies of many of the writers included here will be found elsewhere in the Bibliography. These should be referred to for further details about modern rpts and collected edns, as also for general biographical and critical studies.]

LEONARD COX

The Arte or Crafte of Rhetoryke. [1524]; 1532; ed. F. I. Carpenter, Chicago, 1899.

ROGER ASCHAM (1515–1568)

Toxophilus, the schole of shootinge. 1545; 1571 ('newlye perused'); 1589; ed. E. Arber, Birmingham, 1868. Selections in Gregory Smith.

The scholemaster, or plain and perfite way of teachyng children the Latin tong. 1570; 1571(bis); 1571(for 1573); 1589; ed. J.E.B. Mayor, 1863; ed. E. Arber, Birmingham, 1869; ed. J. Holzamer, Vienna, 1881. Selections in Gregory Smith.

English Works. Ed. W. Aldis Wright, Cambridge, 1904.

[See also p. 671 above.]

THOMAS WILSON (1525?–1581)

The Arte of Rhetorique. 1553 (for 1554); 1560 ('Newlie sette forth again'); 1562; 1563; 1567; 1580; 1584; 1585; ed. G. H. Mair, Oxford, 1909.

[See also pp. 671–2 above.]

RICHARD EDWARDS (1523?–1566)

The excellent Comedie of Damon and Pythias. 1571. [Prologue.] Rptd Chambers.

[See also pp. 519–20 above.]

GEORGE GASCOIGNE (1525?–1577)

Certayne notes of Instruction concerning the making of verse or ryme in English. 1575 (in The Posies); rptd G. Saintsbury (in Loci Critici, Boston, 1903) and Gregory Smith.

[See also pp. 414–5 above.]

GEORGE WHETSTONE (1544?–1587?)

The Right Excellent And Famous Historye Of Promos and Cassandra. 1578. [Epistle to William Fleetwood rptd Gregory Smith; extracts in Chambers.]

A Touchstone for the Time. 1584 (as an 'Addition' to A Mirour for Magistrates of Cyties); rptd Gregory Smith.

[See also p. 440 above.]

STEPHEN GOSSON (1555–1624)

The Schoole of Abuse. 1579; 1586; rptd Somers Tracts, ed. Sir W. Scott, vol. III, 1810; ed. J. P. Collier, Shakespeare Soc. 1841; ed. E. Arber, Birmingham, 1868. Summarised in Chambers.

THOMAS LODGE (1558?–1625)

[A Defence of Poetry, Music, and Stage Plays.] [1579?]; ed. D. Laing, Shakespeare Soc. 1853; rptd in part Gregory Smith.

[See also pp. 527–9 above.]

E[DWARD] K[IRKE] (1553–1613)

Spenser, Edmund. The Shepheardes Calender. 1579, etc. [Epistle dedicatory and notes by Kirke.] Rptd Gregory Smith.

[See also under Spenser, pp. 417–9 above.]

GABRIEL HARVEY (1545?–1630)

Three Proper, and wittie, familiar Letters [to and from Spenser]. 1580; ed. E. de Selincourt (in Complete Poetical Works of Edmund Spenser, Oxford, 1912). Extracts in Gregory Smith.

Two Other, very commendable Letters, of the same mens writing. 1580; ed. E. de Selincourt (as above); rptd in part Gregory Smith.

Foure letters, and certaine sonnets: especially touching Robert Greene. 1592; ed. G. B. Harrison, 1922. Extracts in Gregory Smith.

Pierces supererogation. 1593. Extracts in Gregory Smith.

A new letter of notable contents. 1593. Extracts in Gregory Smith.

[See also pp. 704–5 above.]

RICHARD STANYHURST (1547–1618)

The first foure bookes of Virgil his Aeneis. Leyden, 1582; ed. E. Arber, 1880. [Dedication and Preface rptd in part Gregory Smith.]

WILLIAM WEBBE (b. 1552?)

A Discourse of English Poetrie. 1586; rptd Haslewood and Gregory Smith; ed. E. Arber, 1870.

ABRAHAM FRAUNCE (fl. 1587–1633)

The Arcadian Rhetoricke. 1588; summarised in Gregory Smith.

[See also p. 436 above.]

THOMAS NASHE (1567–1601)

To the Gentlemen Students of Both Universities. [Epistle prefixed to Greene's Menaphon, 1589.] Rptd Gregory Smith; summarised in Chambers.

Sidney, Sir Philip. Astrophel and Stella. 1591, etc. [Preface.] Rptd *Gregory Smith.*
Strange News. 1592; rptd *Gregory Smith.*
[See also p. 533 above.]

[GEORGE PUTTENHAM] (d. 1590)

The Arte of English Poesie. 1589; rptd *Haslewood* and *Gregory Smith*; ed. E. Arber, Birmingham, 1869; ed. G. D. Willcock and A. Walker, Cambridge, 1936.
[See W. L. Rushton, Shakespeare and 'The Arte of English Poesie,' Liverpool, 1909; B. M. Ward, The Authorship of 'The Arte of English Poesie,' RES. I, 1925.]

SIR JOHN HARINGTON (1561–1612)

A Preface, or rather a Briefe Apologie of Poetrie, and of the Author and Translator. [Prefixed to his trn of Orlando Furioso, 1591.] Rptd *Gregory Smith* and in part *Chambers.*
[See also p. 705 above.]

SIR PHILIP SIDNEY (1554–1586)

The Defence of Poesie. 1595; 1595 (as An Apologie for Poetrie); 1598 (appended to Arcadia); ed. E. Arber, Birmingham, 1868; ed. E. Shuckburgh, Cambridge, 1891; ed. A. S. Cook, Boston, 1901; rptd *Gregory Smith*; ed. J. C. Collins, Oxford, 1907; rptd facs. 1927.
[See also pp. 419–21 above.]

FRANCIS BACON (1561–1626)

Essayes. 1597; 1612 (enlarged); 1625 (enlarged again); ed. E. Arber, 1871.
The Twoo Bookes of the Proficience and Advancement of Learning. 1605; ed. W. A. Wright, Oxford, 1869; ed. T. Case, 1906.
De Sapientia Veterum. 1609.
[See E. Flügel, Bacon's Historia Literaria, Ang. XXII, 1899. See also pp. 868–71 below.]

GEORGE CHAPMAN (1559?–1634)

Seaven bookes of the Iliades of Homer prince of Poets. 1598. [Dedication, rptd *Gregory Smith.*]
Achilles Shield. 1598. [Dedication, rptd *Gregory Smith.*]
The Iliads of Homer, Prince of Poets. [1611.] [Prefaces.]
[See also pp. 609–11 above.]

FRANCIS MERES (1565–1647)

Palladis Tamia: With Treasury. 1598; rptd in part J. C. Collins (in Critical Essays, 1903) and *Gregory Smith*; ed. D. C. Allen, Urbana, 1933 ('Poetrie' section only).

WILLIAM VAUGHAN (1577–1641)

The Golden Grove. 1600. Summarised in *Gregory Smith.*

THOMAS CAMPION (1567–1620)

Observations in the Art of English Poesie. 1602; rptd *Gregory Smith*; ed. G. B. Harrison, 1925.
[See also pp. 425–6 above.]

SAMUEL DANIEL (1562–1619)

A Defence of Ryme. 1602, etc. (in The Works of Samuel Daniel); rptd *Haslewood* and *Gregory Smith*; ed. G. B. Harrison, 1925; ed. A. C. Sprague, Cambridge, U.S.A. 1930.
[See also pp. 422–3 above.]

MICHAEL DRAYTON (1563–1631)

To the Reader. 1603 (in The Barrons Wars).
Epistle to Henry Reynolds, Esquire, of Poets and Poesie. 1627 (in The Battaile of Agincourt); rptd *Spingarn.*
[See also pp. 423–5 above.]

JOHN HOSKINS (1566–1638)

Directions for Speech and Style. Ed. H. H. Hudson, Princeton, 1936.

THOMAS HEYWOOD (d. 1650?)

An Apology for Actors. 1612; 1658 (as Actors Vindication); rptd Shakespeare Soc. 1841.
[See A. M. Clark, Thomas Heywood as a Critic, MLN. XXXVII, 1922. See also pp. 622–7 above.]

JOHN WEBSTER (1580?–1625?)

The White Divel. 1612, etc. [Preface, rptd *Spingarn.*]
[See also pp. 629–30 above.]

RICHARD CAREW (1555–1620)

The Excellencie of the English Tongue. 1614 (in 2nd edn of Camden's Remains); ed. *Gregory Smith* (from BM. MS Cotton F XI, fol. 265).
[See also p. 826 above.]

EDMUND BOLTON (1575?–1633?)

Hypercritica: or a Rule of Judgement for writing or reading our History's. [Written c. 1618; first ptd by Anthony Hall at end of his Nicolai Triveti Annalium Continuatio, Oxford, 1722.] Rptd *Haslewood* and *Spingarn.* [See R. C. Steele, Edmund Bolton, Cambridge Rev. 24 Feb. 1923.]

HENRY PEACHAM (1576?–1643?)

The Compleat Gentleman. 1622; 1634; 1661; ed. G. S. Gordon, Oxford, 1906. Extracts in *Spingarn.*

GEORGE HAKEWILL (1578–1649)

An Apologie or Declaration of the Power and Providence of God in the Government of the World. 1627; 1630; 1635.
[See A. H. Bullen, Hakewill's Apologie, in Elizabethans, 1924.]

HENRY REYNOLDS

Mythomystes, wherein a short Survay is taken of the Nature and Value of true Poesy and Depth of the Ancients above our Moderne Poets. [1632?]; rptd *Spingarn*.

SIR WILLIAM ALEXANDER (1567?–1640)

Anacrisis: or a Censure of some Poets Ancient and Modern. [Written c. 1634; first ptd in Works of William Drummond of Hawthornden, Edinburgh, 1711.] Rptd *Spingarn*.
[See also p. 432 above.]

BEN JONSON (1573?–1637)

Timber: or, Discoveries; made upon Men and Matter. 1641 (at end of Workes, vol. II); ed. F. E. Schelling, Boston, 1892; ed. M. Castelain, Paris, [1906]; ed. G. B. Harrison, 1923. Critical sections rptd *Spingarn*.
Conversations with Drummond. Edinburgh, 1711 (in Drummond's Works); ed. from MS D. Laing, Shakespeare Soc. 1842; ed. R. F. Patterson, 1924. Critical sections rptd *Spingarn*.

[Many of the prefaces, epistles dedicatory, prologues and epilogues of Jonson's plays, as well as some of his poems, epigrams and passages in the plays themselves, contain critical material. For these see pp. 613–9 above.]

JOHN MILTON (1608–1674)

The Reason of Church-governement. 1641. Critical sections rptd *Spingarn*.
An Apology [for] Smectymnuus. 1642. Critical sections rptd *Spingarn*.
Areopagitica. 1644; ed. J. W. Hales, Oxford, 1866; ed. E. Arber, 1868.
Of Education. [1644], etc.; ed. O. Browning, Cambridge, 1883. Critical sections rptd *Spingarn*.
The Verse. [Prefixed in 1668 to copies then remaining of the first edn (1667) of Paradise Lost.] Rptd *Spingarn*.
Of that sort of Dramatic Poem which is call'd Tragedy. [Prefixed to Samson Agonistes, 1671.] Rptd *Spingarn*.
[See Ida Langdon, Milton's Theory of Poetry, New Haven, 1924. See also pp. 463–73 above.]

ALEXANDER ROSS (1590–1654)

Mel Heliconium, or Poeticall Honey gathered out of the weeds of Parnassus. 1642.
Gnomologicon Poëticum, hoc est, sententiae veterum Poëtarum insigniores. 1647.
Mystagogus Poeticus, or the Muses Interpreter, explaining the historicall Mysteries and mystical Histories of the ancient Greek and Latine Poets. 1647; 1648; 1653; 1664; 1675.

SIR KENELM DIGBY (1603–1665)

Observations on the 22. Stanza in the 9th. Canto of the 2d. Book of Spencers Faery Queen. 1643. [Written 1628.]
Concerning Spencer. Ed. (from BM. Add MS 41846) E. W. Bligh (in Sir Kenelm Digby and his Venetia, 1932).

JAMES HOWELL (1594?–1666)

Epistolae Ho-Elianae: Familiar Letters Domestick and Foreign. 4 vols. 1645–55, etc.; ed. Joseph Jacobs, 2 vols. 1890–2; ed. O. Smeaton, 3 vols. 1903 (Temple Classics).
[See also pp. 832–3 above.]

[GEORGE WITHER?] (1588–1667)

The Great Assises holden in Parnassus by Apollo and his Assessours. 1645; rptd Spenser Soc. 1885.

SIR JOHN SUCKLING (1609–1642)

A Session of the Poets. 1646 (in Fragmenta Aurea); rptd *Spingarn*.
[See also p. 456 above.]

JOHN WILKINS (1614–1672)

Ecclesiastes, or a Discourse concerning the Gift of Preaching as it fals under the Rules of Art. 1646; 1647; 1651; 1653; 1659; 1679; 1695.

SIR JOHN DENHAM (1615–1669)

To Sir Richard Fanshawe upon his translation of Pastor Fido. [In Fanshawe's Il Pastor Fido, 1648.]
[See also pp. 457–8 above.]

SAMUEL GOTT

Novae Solymae libri sex. 1648; tr. Eng. and ed. W. Begley, 2 vols. 1902. [Numerous critical passages.]

SIR WILLIAM DAVENANT (1606–1668)

A Discourse upon Gondibert, an heroick poem written by Sir W. D'Avenant, with an answer to it by Mr Hobbs. Paris, 1650; 1651 (in Gondibert); rptd *Spingarn*.
[See also pp. 453–5 above.]

THOMAS HOBBES (1588–1679)

Answer of Mr. Hobbes to Sr Will. D'Avenant's Preface before Gondibert. Paris, 1650 (with Davenant's preface); 1651 (with Gondibert); rptd *Spingarn*.

To the Honourable Edward Howard, Esq., on his intended impression of his Poem of the British Princes. 1669 (prefixed to Howard's British Princes).

To the Reader concerning the Vertues of an Heroique Poem. 1675 (prefixed to Hobbes's trn of the Odyssey); rptd *Spingarn*.
[See also pp. 871–3 below.]

SAMUEL SHEPPARD

The Socratick Session: or the Arraignment and Conviction of Julius Scaliger. [In Epigrams. 1651.]
[See H. E. Rollins, Stud. Phil. XXIV, 1927. See also p. 477 above.]

JOHN COLLOP

Poesis Rediviva: or Poesie Reviv'd. 1656.
[Epistle Dedicatory and various poems. See J. Drinkwater, A Book for Bookmen, 1926.]

ABRAHAM COWLEY (1618–1667)

Poems. 4 parts, viz. I, Miscellanies; II, The Mistress; III, Pindarique Odes; IV, Davideis. 1656. [Preface, rptd *Spingarn*, and notes to Odes and Davideis.]
[On the lost Discourse concerning Style see A. H. Nethercot, RES. II, 1926. See also pp. 458–9 above.]

JOSHUA POOLE

The English Parnassus, or a Helpe to English Poesie. 1656; 1677. [The preface, 'being a Short Illustration of English Poesy,' is signed J. D. See Bodleian Quart. Record, IV, 1923.]

JOHN SMITH

The Mysterie of Rhetorique Unvail'd. 1657; 1665; 1673; 1688.

JOHN HALES (1584–1656)

The Method of reading profane History. [In Golden Remaines, 1659, 1673 and 1688.]

R[ICHARD] B[RATHWAITE] (1588?–1673)

A comment upon the two tales of Sir Jeffray Chaucer, Knight [the Miller's Tale and the Wife of Bath's]. 1665; ed. C. F. E. Spurgeon, Chaucer Soc. 1901 and Cambridge, 1925 (in Five Hundred Years of Chaucer Criticism). [Written c. 1615.]
[See also pp. 711–2 above.]

(C) GENERAL HISTORY AND CRITICISM

[The following brief list may be supplemented by the general Introduction to the period (pp. 319–25 above), the introductions to the different forms—Poetry (pp. 406–8 above), Drama (pp. 492–6 above), Fiction (pp. 726–8 above)—and by the critical material on various individual writers, especially Spenser (pp. 418–9 above), Shakespeare (pp. 590–8 above), Jonson (pp. 617–9 above) and Milton (pp. 468–73 above). The best general surveys of the subject are by G. Gregory Smith, in the introduction to his Elizabethan Critical Essays, vol. I, Oxford, 1904, and by J. E. Spingarn, in the introduction to his Critical Essays of the Seventeenth Century, vol. I, Oxford, 1908.]

Schelling, F. E. Poetic and Verse Criticism of the Reign of Elizabeth. Philadelphia, 1891.
Wylie, L. J. Studies in the Evolution of English Criticism. Boston, 1894.
Hamelius, Paul. Die Kritik in der englischen Literatur des 17. and 18. Jahrhunderts. Leipzig, 1897.
Gayley, C. M. and Scott, F. N. An Introduction to the Methods and Materials of Literary Criticism. Boston, 1899.
Spingarn, J. E. A History of Literary Criticism in the Renaissance. New York, 1899.
—— Jacobean and Caroline Criticism. CHEL. vol. VII, ch. 11, 1911.
Saintsbury, George. History of Criticism and Literary Taste in Europe. 3 vols. Edinburgh, 1900–4.
—— Elizabethan Criticism. CHEL. vol. III, ch. 14, 1909.
—— A History of English Criticism. Edinburgh, 1911.
Brotanek, R. Trajano Boccalinis Einfluss auf die englische Literatur. Archiv, CXI, 1903.
Symmes, H. S. Les Débuts de la Critique dramatique en Angleterre jusqu'à la Mort de Shakespeare. Paris, 1903.
Upham, A. H. The French Influence in English Literature from the Accession of Elizabeth to the Restoration. New York, 1908.
Diede, Otto. Der Streit der Alten und der Modernen in der englischen Literaturgeschichte des 16. und 17. Jahrhunderts. Greifswald, 1912.
Miller, G. M. The Historical Point of View in English Criticism from 1550–1770. Heidelberg, 1913.
Borinski, Karl. Die Antike in Poetik und Kunsttheorie. Leipzig, 1914.
Routh, James. The Rise of Classical English Criticism to the Death of Dryden. New Orleans, 1915.
Croll, M. W. Attic Prose in the Seventeenth Century. Stud. Phil. XVIII, 1921.

Croll, M. W. Attic Prose: Lipsius, Montaigne, Bacon. [In Schelling Aniversary Papers. New York, 1923.]

Clark, D. L. Rhetoric and Poetry in the Renaissance. New York, 1922.

Willey, Basil. Tendencies in Renaissance Literary Theory. 1922.

—— The Seventeenth-Century Background. 1934.

Bullock, W. L. Spenser and Renaissance Criticism. PMLA. xLVI, 1931.

Thüme, Hans. Beiträge zur Geschichte des Geniebegriffs in England. Halle, 1927.

Vines, Sherard. The Course of English Classicism. 1930.

Bateson, F. W. English Poetry and the English Language. Oxford, 1934.

White, Harold O. Plagiarism and Imitation during the English Renaissance. Cambridge, U.S.A. 1935.

Williamson, G. Senecan Style in the Seventeenth Century. PQ. xiv, 1936.　W. P. B.

VI. BACON, HOBBES AND OTHER PHILOSOPHICAL WRITERS

Modern Studies

Tulloch, J. English Puritanism and its Leaders. 1861.

—— Rational Theology and Christian Philosophy in England in the Seventeenth Century. 2 vols. Edinburgh, 1872–4.

de Rémusat, C. Histoire de la Philosophie en Angleterre depuis Bacon jusqu'à Locke. Paris, 1875.

Freudenthal, J. Beiträge zur Geschichte der englischen Philosophie. Archiv für Geschichte der Philosophie, iv, 1891.

Graham, W. English Political Philosophy from Hobbes to Maine. 1899.

Sorley, W. R. A History of English Philosophy. 1921. [Relevant chs. based on CHEL. vol. iv, ch. xiv, vol. vii, ch. xii, 1909–11.]

Mullinger, J. B. Platonists and Latitudinarians. CHEL. vol. viii, 1912.

Taylor, H. O. Thought and Expression in the Sixteenth Century. 2 vols. New York, 1921.

Inge, W. R. The Platonic Tradition in English Religious Thought. 1926.

Powicke, F. J. The Cambridge Platonists. 1926.

Saurat, D. Milton et le Matérialisme chrétien en Angleterre. Paris, 1928.

Nicolson, M. H. Christ's College and the Latitude-Men. MP. xxvii, 1929.

—— The Early Stage of Cartesianism in England. Stud. Phil. xxvi, 1929.

Smith, Preserved. A History of Modern Culture. Vol. i, New York, 1930.

Muirhead, J. H. The Platonic Tradition in Anglo-Saxon Philosophy. 1931.

Cassirer, E. Die Platonische Renaissance in England und die Schule von Cambridge. Leipzig, 1932.

Willey, B. The Seventeenth-Century Background. 1934.

Wolf, A. A History of Science, Technology and Philosophy in the Sixteenth and Seventeenth Centuries. 1935. [See also pp. 321–5 above.]

FRANCIS BACON (1561–1626)

(1) Collected Works

(a) Collections chiefly of works unpublished in his life-time:

(i) Collected by W. Rawley: Certaine Miscellany works. 1629. Operum moralium et civilium tomus primus. 1638. Resuscitatio. 1657, 1661, 1671. Opuscula varia posthuma. 1658, Amsterdam, 1663.

(ii) Collected by I. Gruter: Scripta in naturali et universali philosophia. Amsterdam, 1653.

(iii) Collected by R. Stephens: Letters written during the reign of King James. 1702. Letters and Remains. 1734.

(iv) Other collections: The Remaines being Essays and Letters and other pieces. 1648 (re-issued 1656 as The Mirrour of State and Eloquence). Baconiana. Or Certain Genuine Remains. Ed. T. T[enison], 1679 (re-issued 1684).

(b) Editions of collected works: by J. B. Schönwetter and I. Gruter, Frankfort,1665; J. Blackbourne, 4 vols. 1730; D. Mallet, 4 vols. 1740; R. Stephens, R. Locker and T. Birch, 5 vols. 1765; A. Lasalle, French trn, 15 vols. Dijon, 1801–4; B. Montagu, 16 vols. 1825–36; J. Spedding, R. L. Ellis and D. D. Heath, 14 vols. 1857–74. [In the last-named edn, vols. i–iii contain the Philosophical Works, vols. iv–v trns of the same, vols. vi–vii Literary and Professional Works, vols. viii–xiv the Letters and the Life. The Philosophical Works were ed. in 1 vol. J. M. Robertson, 1905.]

(2) Philosophical Works
(Spedding's arrangement)

(a) Parts of the 'Instauratio Magna'

[Writings pbd for the first time in posthumous collections have the date of the collection given in round brackets.]

Francisci de Verulamio Summi Angliae Cancellarii Instauratio Magna. 1620; Leyden, 1645,1650; Amsterdam,1660; ed.T.Fowler,

1878,1889. [After two pages beginning 'Franciscus de Verulamio sic cogitavit,' an epistle dedicatory to the king, preface, distributio operis and a page announcing 'deest pars prima instaurationis, quae complectitur partitiones scientiarum,' there follows a second title-page: Pars Secunda Operis, quae dicitur Novum Organum, sive Indicia Vera de interpretatione naturae. The same vol. also contains: Parasceve ad Historiam Naturalem et Experimentalem.]

Opera. Tomus primus. Qui continet De Augmentis Scientiarum libros IX. 1623 (the second title is: de Dignitate et Augmentis Scientiarum libri IX); ed. W. Rawley, 1635; Leyden, 1645, 1652; Amsterdam, 1662; tr. Eng. G. Wats, Oxford, 1640.

Historia Naturalis et Experimentalis ad condendam philosophiam: sive Phaenomena Universi: quae est Instaurationis Magnae pars tertia. 1622. [This vol. contains Historia Ventorum (rptd separately Leyden, 1638, 1648 (bis), Amsterdam, 1662, and tr. Eng. R. G., 1653), also titles and 'aditus' to five other Historiae, namely, Densi et Rari, Gravis et Levis, Sympathiae et Antipathiae Rerum, Sulphuris Mercurii et Salis, Vitae et Mortis.]

Historia Vitae et Mortis. Sive Titulus Secundus in Historia Naturali et Experimentali ad condendam philosophiam: quae est Instaurationis Magnae pars tertia. 1623; Dillingen, 1645; Amsterdam, 1663. Tr. Eng. 1638 (2 versions, by W. Rawley and anon.); French, Paris, 1647.

Historia Densi et Rari (1658).

Sylva Sylvarum: or A Natural History. In ten centuries. Written by the Right Honourable Francis Lord Verulam, Viscount St Alban. Published after the author's death by William Rawley. 1627; 1628; 1631; 1635; 1639; Leyden, 1648; 1651; 1658; Amsterdam, 1661; 1664; 1670; 1676, etc.; tr. French, Paris, 1631.

Scala intellectus, sive Filum Labyrinthi (1653). [A preface intended for the fourth part of the Instauratio.]

Prodromi, sive Anticipationes Philosophiae Secundae (1653). [A preface intended for the fifth part of the Instauratio.]

(b) Works connected with the 'Instauratio,' but not intended to be included in it

Cogitationes de natura rerum (1653).

De Fluxu et Refluxu Maris (1653).

De Principiis atque Originibus secundum Fabulas Cupidinis et Coeli (1653).

New Atlantis: a work unfinished. [First pbd by Rawley at the end of the vol. containing Sylva Sylvarum in 1627. Ed. G. C. Moore Smith, Cambridge, 1900.]

(c) Works originally designed for parts of the 'Instauratio' but superseded or abandoned

Cogitationes de Scientia Humana. [A series of fragments of uncertain date, first pbd by Spedding (Bacon's Works, vol. III), who supplied the title.]

Valerius Terminus of the Interpretation of Nature; with the annotations of Hermes Stella (1734).

The Twoo Bookes of Francis Bacon of the Proficience and Advancement of Learning Divine and Humane. 1605; 1629; Oxford, 1633; ed. W. A. Wright, 1869, 1900; ed. T. Case, 1906.

Filum Labyrinthi, sive Formula Inquisitionis (1734). [Little else than an English version of the Cogitata et Visa.]

De Interpretatione Naturae Prooemium (1653).

Temporis Partus Masculus sive Instauratio Magna Imperii Humani in Universum (1653).

Partis Instaurationis Secundae Delineatio et Argumentum, et Redargutio philosophiarum (1653, in part).

Cogitata et Visa: de Interpretatione Naturae, sive Scientia Operativa (1653).

Filum Labyrinthi; sive Inquisitio Legitima de Motu (1653).

Sequela Cartarum; sive Inquisitio Legitima de Calore et Frigore (1734).

Historia et Inquisitio Prima de Sono et Auditu, et de Forma Soni et Latente Processu Soni; sive Sylva Soni et Auditus (1658).

Phaenomena Universi; sive Historia Naturalis ad Condendam Philosophiam (1653).

Descriptio Globi Intellectualis et Thema Coeli (1653).

De Interpretatione Naturae Sententiae XII (1653).

Aphorismi et Consilia (1653).

(3) LITERARY WORKS

Essayes. Religious Meditations. Places of perswasion and disswasion. Seene and allowed. 1597; 1598; 1606. [There are 10 essays in this vol. The Religious Meditations are in Latin and are entitled Meditationes Sacrae; the Places of perswasion and disswasion are in English and are entitled Coulers of Good and Evill; a fragment.]

The Essaies of Sir Francis Bacon Knight the kings solliciter generall. 1612 (bis); 1613 (3 edns); Edinburgh, 1614; 1624. [This vol. contains essays only—38 in number, 29 of them new, and the rest corrected and enlarged.]

The Essayes or Counsels, Civill and Morall, of
Francis Lo. Verulam, Viscount St Alban.
1625; 1629; 1632; 1639; 1664; 1668, etc.;
ed. R. Whateley, 1856; ed. W. A. Wright,
Cambridge, 1862; ed. E. Arber, 1869; ed.
E. A. Abbott, 2 vols. 1879. Tr. Italian,
1617 (by Sir T. Matthew); French, 1619 (by
Sir A. Gorges) and Paris, 1621 (by J.
Baudouin); Latin, 1638 (by Ben Jonson and
others, in Opera Moralia); German, Nurem-
berg, 1654. [This vol. contains 58 essays,
20 of them being new and most of the rest
altered and enlarged.]
Francisci Baconi De Sapientia Veterum Liber,
ad inclytam academiam Cantabrigiensem.
1609; 1617; Leyden, 1633 (bis); 1634. Tr.
Eng. Sir A. Gorges, 1619; French, Paris,
1619; Italian, 1618 (by Sir T. Matthew).
The Historie of the Raigne of King Henry the
Seventh. 1622; 1629; 1641, etc.; ed. J. R.
Lumby, Cambridge, 1876. Tr. French,
Paris, 1627; Latin, Leyden, 1642.
Advertisement touching an Holy Warre.
Written in the year 1622. 1629.
Of the True Greatness of the Kingdom of
Britain (1734).
Apophthagmes new and old. 1625; 1626;
1658.
Promus of Formularies and Elegancies. [Be-
gun 1594, pbd 1883, and in part by Sped-
ing, vol. VII.]
The Translation of Certaine Psalmes into
English Verse. 1625.
The Poems of Francis Bacon. Ed. A. B.
Grosart, Fuller Worthies' Misc. vol. I, 1870.

(4) PROFESSIONAL WORKS

The Charge of Sir Francis Bacon touching
Duells. 1614.
Ordinances for the better administration of
justice in the Chancery. 1623; 1640; 1642;
1656.
The Elements of the Common Lawes of Eng-
land. 2 pts, 1630; 1636–5; 1639. [Pt 1,
A Collection of some principal Rules and
Maximes of the Common Lawes of England
(written c. 1597); pt 2, The Use of the Law,
first ptd anon. 1629 appended to Sir J.
Doddridge, The Lawyers Light, is probably
not by Bacon.]
Cases of Treason. 1641; rptd Harleian Misc.
vol. v, 1744, 1808.
Three Speeches of Sir Francis Bacon. 1641.
[2nd speech on the 'Naturalization of the
Scotch in England' also pbd separately
1641.]
The Argument of Sir Francis Bacon, Knight,
His Majesty's Solicitor-general, in the Case
of the Post-Nati of Scotland. [Delivered
before Easter Term, 1608; first ptd in Three
Speeches, 1641.]

The Learned Reading of Sir Francis Bacon
upon the Statute of Uses. 1642. [Read at
Gray's Inn in the Lent vacation, 1600.]
A Charge Given by Sr. Francis Bacon. 1662.
The Arguments of Law of Sir Francis Bacon,
Knight, The King's Solicitor-General, in
certain great and difficult cases. [Rev.
Bacon in 1616, but not pbd by him; first
ptd by Blackbourne in 1730.]
The Argument of Sir Francis Bacon, Knight,
Attorney-General in the King's Bench, in
the Case De Rege Inconsulto. [Delivered
25 Jan. 1616; first ptd in Collectanea
Juridica, vol. I, 1791.]
Argument in Chudleigh's Case. [Easter Term,
1594; tr. from Law French and ptd in
Spedding's edn, vol. VII.]
Reports on Cases decided by Bacon in the
Court of Chancery (1617–1621). Ed. J.
Ritchie, 1932.

(5) OCCASIONAL WRITINGS

A Declaration of the Practices and Treasons
attempted and committed by Robert, late
Earle of Essex. 1601 (anon).
A Brief Discourse touching the Happy Union
of the Kingdoms of England and Scotland.
1603 (anon.).
Certain Considerations touching the better
Pacification and Edification of the Church
of England. 1604 (anon.) (3 edns); 1640
(bis). [Written 1603.]
Sir Francis Bacon his Apologie, in certaine
imputations concerning the late Earle of
Essex. 1604 (bis); 1605; 1642; tr. Dutch,
1603.
Considerations touching a Warre with Spaine.
1629; rptd Harleian Misc. vol. v, 1744,
1808; tr. French, Paris, 1634.
The Confession of Faith. 1641. [Written
1603.]
A wise and moderate Discourse concerning
church-affaires. 1641; 1663 (as True peace).
An Essay of a King. 1642; 1647 (as XVI.
Propositions concerning a King). [Not by
Bacon?]
The Felicity of Queen Elizabeth: And Her
Times, With other Things. 1651. [Written
1608.]
A Letter of Advice written by Sr. Francis
Bacon to the Duke of Buckingham. 1661.
A Conference of Pleasure, composed for some
Festive Occasion about 1592. Ed. J.
Spedding, 1870.

(6) BIOGRAPHY AND CRITICISM

Memoriae Francisci Baconis de Verulamio
Sacrum. Ed. W. Rawley, 1626; ed. and tr.
E. K. Rand, Boston, 1904.

Clerke, G. De plenitudine mundi brevis et philosophica dissertatio in qua defenditur Cartesiana philosophia contra sententias Francisci Baconi. 1660.

de Maistre, J. M. Examen de la Philosophie de Bacon. Paris, 1836.

Hallam, H. Introduction to the Literature of Europe. 4 vols. 1837–9. [Ch. xx.]

Macaulay, T. B. Edinburgh Rev. July 1837.

Craik, G. L. Bacon, his Writings and his Philosophy. 1846.

Spedding, J. Evenings with a Reviewer. 2 vols. 1848.

Ellis, R. L. General Preface to the Philosophical Works. [Bacon's Works, vol. i. 1857.]

de Rémusat, C. Bacon: sa Vie, son Temps, sa Philosophie, et son Influence jusqu'à nos Jours. Paris, 1857.

Whewell, W. The Philosophy of Discovery. 1860. [Chs. xv, xvi.]

Manning, H. E. Flaws in the Philosophy of Francis Bacon. [In Essays on Religion and Literature, ser. 3, 1874.]

Fischer, Kuno. Franz Bacon und seine Nachfolger. Leipzig, 1875.

—— Francis Bacon und seine Schule. Entwicklungsgeschichte der Erfahrungsphilosophie. [Geschichte der neueren Philosophie, vol. x, Heidelberg, 1904.]

Abbott, E. A. Bacon and Essex. 1877.

—— Bacon: an Account of his Life and Works. 1885.

Church, R. W. Bacon. 1884.

Nichol, J. Bacon. 2 pts, Edinburgh, 1888–9.

Janet, P. Baco Verulamius alchemicis philosophis quid debuerit. Angers, 1889.

Lalande, A. Quid de Mathematica senserit Baconus Verulamius. Paris, 1899.

—— Les Théories de l'Induction. Paris, 1929. [Pp. 40–82.]

Lee, Sir Sidney. Great Englishmen of the Sixteenth Century. 1904.

Colville, J. Francis Bacon as an Educational Theorist. [In Some Old-fashioned Educationists, 1907.]

Steeves, G. W. Francis Bacon. A Sketch of his Life, Works and Literary Friends. 1910. [Bibliographical.]

Villey, P. Montaigne et François Bacon. Paris, 1913.

Allbutt, Sir T. C. Palissy, Bacon and the Revival of Natural Science. 1914.

Crane, R. S. The Relation of Bacon's Essays to his Program for the Advancement of Learning. [In Schelling Aniversary Papers, New York, 1923.]

Croll, M. Attic Prose: Lipsius, Montaigne, Bacon. [In Schelling Aniversary Papers, New York, 1923.]

Levi, A. Il Pensiero di Francesco Bacone considerato in Relazione con le Filosofie della Natura del Rinascimento e col Razionalismo cartesiano. Turin, 1925.

Brochard, V. Études de Philosophie ancienne et de Philosophie moderne. Paris, 1925. [Pp. 303–19.]

Broad, C. D. The Philosophy of Francis Bacon. Cambridge, 1926.

Taylor, A. E. Francis Bacon. Proc. British Academy, 1926.

White, Sir W. H. Bacon, Gilbert and Harvey. 1927.

Zeitlin, J. The Development of Bacon's Essays. JEGP. xxvii, 1928.

Bundy, M. W. Bacon's True Opinion of Poetry. Stud. Phil. xxvii, 1930.

Sturt, M. Francis Bacon. A Biography. 1932.

Lemmi, C. W. The Classic Deities in Bacon. A Study in Mythological Symbolism. Baltimore, 1933.

Williams, Charles. Bacon. 1933.

THOMAS HOBBES (1588–1679)

(1) Collected Works

Thomae Hobbes Malmesburiensis Opera Philosophica, quae Latine scripsit, Omnia accuratius edita. Amsterdam, 1668. [Pt i, De Corpore, De Homine, and De Cive; pt. ii, other mathematical and physical pieces; pt iii, a Latin trn of Leviathan, with a new appendix instead of the Review and Conclusion.]

Hobbes's Tripos in Three Discourses. 1684 (3rd edn).

The Moral and Political Works of Thomas Hobbes of Malmesbury. Never before collected together. 1750.

Thomae Hobbes Malmesburiensis Opera philosophica quae Latine scripsit. 5 vols. The English Works. 11 vols. Ed. Sir W. Molesworth, 1839–45. [The only complete edn.]

(2) Single Works

Eight Books of the Peloponnesian Warre written by Thucydides the son of Olorus interpreted with faith and diligence immediately out of the Greek. 1629; 1634; 1676; rptd 1822.

De Mirabilibus Pecci Carmen. 1636; [1666]; 1678 (with Eng. trn 'by a person of quality'); 1683 (5th edn).

A briefe of the art of rhetorique; [1637?]; [1655?]; 1681 (as The Whole Art of Rhetoric).

The Elements of Law Natural and Politic. [Circulated in MS 1640, first pbd as a whole and under this title by F. Tönnies, 1889.]

Objectiones ad Cartesii Meditationes de prima philosophia vulgo dictae Objectiones Tertiae. [In R. Descartes's Meditationes, Amsterdam, 1641.]

Tractatus Opticus. [In M. Mersenne's Cogitata Physico-Mathematica, Paris, 1644.]

Elementorum Philosophiae Sectio tertia, De Cive. Paris, 1642; Amsterdam, 1647 (bis; with new notes and preface, as Elementa Philosophica De Cive); Amsterdam, 1669; tr. French, Amsterdam, 1649.

Humane Nature; or the Fundamental Elements of Policie. 1650; 1651. [Consists of chs. i–xiii of The Elements of Law.]

De Corpore Politico; or the Elements of Law, Moral and Politick. 1650; 1652; tr. French, Leyden, 1652. [Consists of chs. xiv–end of The Elements of Law.]

Epistolica dissertatio de principiis justi et decori; continens apologiam pro tractatu de cive. Amsterdam, 1651.

Philosophicall Rudiments concerning Government and Society. 1651. [An English version of De Cive.]

Leviathan Or the Matter, Forme, and Power of A Commonwealth Ecclesiasticall and Civil. 1651; 1651 (3rd edn; for 1672?); ed. A. R. Waller, Cambridge, 1904; ed. W. G. Pogson Smith, 1909. Tr. Dutch, Amsterdam, 1667; Latin, Amsterdam, 1670.

Of Libertie and Necessitie. 1654; rptd 1839. [A publication, not authorized by Hobbes, of a reply by him to the arguments of bishop Bramhall, written for the marquis of Newcastle in 1646.]

The Questions concerning Liberty, Necessity, and Chance. 1656.

Elementorum Philosophiae Sectio prima, De Corpore. 1655; tr. Eng. 1656 (with an appendix entitled 'Six Lessons to the Professors of Mathematics').

Elementorum Philosophiae Sectio secunda, De Homine. 1658.

Στιγμαι Αγεωμετρίας, Αγροικίας Αντιπολιτείας, Αμαθείας, or Marks of the Absurd Geometry, Rural Language, Scottish Church Politics, and Barbarisms of John Wallis. 1657.

Examinatio et Emendatio Mathematicae hodiernae qualis explicatur in libris Johannis Wallisii. 1660.

Dialogus Physicus, sive de Natura Aeris. Item de duplicatione cubi. 1661.

Seven Philosophical Problems and Two Propositions of Geometry with an Apology for Himself and his Writings. 1662.

Problemata Physica. 1662.

Mr Hobbes considered in his loyalty, religion, reputation and manners. 1662; 1680 (as Considerations upon the Reputation, etc.).

De Principiis et Ratiocinatione Geometrarum. 1666.

Quadratura Circuli. Cubatio Sphaerae. Duplicatio Cubi. 1669.

Rosetum Geometricum cum censura brevi doctrinae Wallisianae de motu. 1671.

Three Papers presented to the Royal Society against Dr Wallis. 1671.

Lux Mathematica excussa collisionibus Johannis Wallisii et Thomae Hobbesii. 1672.

The Travels of Ulysses, as they were related by himself in Homer's 9th, 10th, 11th, and 12th books of his Odysses. 1673.

Principia et Problemata aliquot geometrica antehac desperata nunc breviter explicata et demonstrata. 1674.

The Iliads and Odysses of Homer. Translated out of Greek into English. 1676; 1677; 1686. [Homer's Odysses, 1675.]

Decameron Physiologicum; or Ten Dialogues of Natural Philosophy. 1678.

The History of the Civil Wars of England. 1679 (imperfect); 1680 (as Behemoth); ed. from MS F. Tönnies, 1889.

Thomae Hobbesii Malmesburiensis Vita carmine expressa. 1679; 1681 (with biographical addns by Richard Blackbourne, Thomas Rymer and John Aubrey); tr. Eng. 1680.

An Historical Narration concerning Heresie and the punishment thereof. 1680.

A Dialogue between a Philosopher and a Student of the Common Laws of England. 1681.

Tracts of Mr Thomas Hobbs of Malmesbury. 1682. [Behemoth; An answer to a Book published by Dr Bramhall; Narration of Heresie; Philosophical Problems.]

Historia Ecclesiastica carmine elegiaco concinnata. 1688; tr. Eng. 1722.

(3) BIOGRAPHY AND CRITICISM

[For contemporary English criticism of Hobbes see under Boyle, Bramhall, Dowel, Eachard, Hyde, Lawson, Lucy, Pierce, Ross, Stubbe, Tenison, Tyrrell, Wallis, Ward and Whitehall, in the following section.]

Moramus, G. Animadversiones in Elementa Philosophica, sect. 1, de corp. 1665.

Cocquius, G. Hobbes ἐλεγχομενος, sive Vindiciae contra tractatus T. Hobbesii. Utrecht, 1668.

Cumberland, R. De Legibus Naturae disquisitio in qua Elementa Philosophiae Hobbianae refutantur. 1672.

Kortholt, C. De tribus impostoribus magnis [Cherbury, Hobbes and Spinoza]. Kiel, 1680; Hamburg, 1700.

Berns, M. Altar der Atheïsten. Hamburg, 1692.

Hampton, B. The Existence of the Human Soul after death proved. 1711.

von Leibniz, G. W. Essais de Théodicée. Amsterdam, 1712.

Innes, A. 'Αρετη-λογια, or an inquiry into the origin of moral virtue. 1728.

von Feuerbach, J. P. A. Anti-Hobbes. Erfurt, 1798.

von Sigwart, H. C. W. Vergleichung der Rechts- und Staats-Theorieen des Spinoza und Hobbes. Tübingen, 1842.

Whedon, D. Freedom of Will. 1864.

Nuescheler, H. Die Staatstheorie des Thomas Hobbes. Zurich, 1865.

Baumann, J. J. Die Lehren von Raum, Zeit und Mathematik in der neueren Philosophie. Vol. I, Berlin, 1868.

Dessauer, M. Spinoza und Hobbes. Begründung ihrer Staats- und Religionstheorieen, durch ihre philosophischen Systeme. Breslau, 1868.

Tönnies, F. Anmerkungen über die Philosophie des Hobbes. Vierteljahresschrift für wissenschaftliche Philosophie, 1879–81.

—— Hobbes Leben und Lehre. Stuttgart, 1896; Osterwieck, 1912 (enlarged as Hobbes, der Mann und der Denker).

Robertson, G. C. Hobbes. Edinburgh, 1886.

Larsen, E. Thomas Hobbes. Filosofi. Copenhagen, 1891.

Chevrillon, A. Qui fuerint saeculo XVII im primis apud Hobbesium Anglicae solutae orationis progressus. Lille, 1893.

Lyon, G. La Philosophie de Hobbes. Paris, 1893.

Brandt, G. Thomas Hobbes. Grundlinien seiner Philosophie, insbesondere seine Lehre von Erkennen. Kiel, 1895.

Tarantino, G. Saggio sulle Idee morali e politiche di T. Hobbes. Naples, 1900.

Iodice, A. Le Teorie di Hobbes e Spinoza nella Società moderna. Naples, 1901.

Romano, M. Hobbes e Spencer. Avola, 1902.

Stephen, Sir L. Hobbes. 1904. (English Men of Letters Ser.)

Rickaby, J. Free Will and Four English Philosophers. 1906.

Loveday, T. An Early Criticism of Hobbes. Mind, xvii, 1908.

Taylor, A. E. Thomas Hobbes. 1908.

Balz, A. G. A. Idea and Essence in the Philosophies of Hobbes and Spinoza. 1918.

—— The Psychology of Ideas in Hobbes. [In Studies in the History of Ideas, vol. I, New York, 1918.]

Dewey, J. The Motivation of Hobbes's political Philosophy. [In Studies in the History of Ideas, vol. I, New York, 1918.]

Lord, H. G. The Attempt of Hobbes to base Ethics on Psychology. [In Studies in the History of Ideas, vol. I, New York, 1918.]

von Brockdorff, C. L. G. C. Hobbes im Lichte seiner didaktischen und pädagogischen Bedeutung. Kiel, 1919.

Smyrniadis, B. Les Doctrines de Hobbes, Locke et Kant, sur le Droit de l'Insurrection. Paris, 1921.

Catlin, G. Thomas Hobbes as Philosopher, Publicist and Man of Letters. 1922.

Moser, H. Thomas Hobbes, seine logische Problematik und ihre erkenntnistheorischen Voraussetzungen. Berlin, 1923.

Nicolson, M. H. Milton and Hobbes. Stud. Phil. xxiii, 1926.

Brandt, F. Thomas Hobbes's Mechanical Conception of Nature. Paris, 1928.

Bredvold, L. I. Dryden, Hobbes and the Royal Society. MP. xxv, 1928.

Landry, B. Hobbes. Paris, 1930.

Laird, J. Hobbes. 1934.

OTHER PHILOSOPHICAL WRITERS

[Cross references have not generally been included in this section to the theologians (see pp. 694–703 above) and scientists (see pp. 879–94 below) of the period.]

SIR THOMAS MORE (1478–1535)

Libellus vere aureus nec minus salutaris quam festivus, de optimo reip. statu, deque nova Insula Utopiæ. [Louvain, 1516], etc.; tr. Eng. Raphe Robynson, 1551, etc.

[See also pp. 666–8 above.]

WILLIAM BALDWIN

Treatise of moral Phylosophie, contayning the Sayinges of the Wyse. 1547. [Rptd at least 17 times by 1640.]

THOMAS WILSON (1525?–1581)

The Rule of Reason, conteining the arte of logique. 1551, etc.

The Arte of Rhetorique. 1553, etc.

[See also p. 671 above.]

RALPH LEVER (d. 1585)

Arte of Reason rightly termed Witcraft. 1573.

EVERARD DIGBY

Theoria analytica, Viam ad Monarchiam Scientiarum demonstrans, totius Philosophiae et reliquarum Scientiarum, necnon primorum postremorumque Philosophorum mysteria arcanaque dogmata enucleans. 1579.

De duplici methodo libri duo, unicam P. Rami methodum refutantes. 1580.

Everardi Digbei Cantabrigiensis admonitioni Francisci Mildapetti responsio. 1580.

De Arte Natandi. 1587; tr. Eng. C. Middleton, 1595.

[For Digby see J. Freudenthal, Beiträge zur Geschichte der englischen Philosophie, Archiv für Geschichte der Philosophie, IV, 1891.]

SIR WILLIAM TEMPLE (1555–1623)

Francisci Mildapetti Navarreni ad Everardum Digbeium Anglum Admonitio de unica P. Rami Methodo rejectis ceteris retinenda. 1580.

Pro Mildapetti de unica methodo defensione contra Diplodophilum, commentatio Gulielmi Tempelli, e Regio Collegio Cantabrigiensis. Huc accessit nonnullarum e physicis et ethicis quaestionum explicatio, una cum epistola de Rami dialectica ad Joannem Piscatorem Argentinensem. 1581; Frankfort, 1584.

P. Rami Dialecticae libri duo, scholiis G. Tempelli Cantabrigiensis illustrati. Cambridge, 1584; Frankfort, 1591, 1595.

Jacobi Martini Scoti Dunkeldensis philosophiae professoris publici, in Academia Taurinensi, de prima simplicium et concretorum corporum generatione disputatio. Cambridge, 1584; Frankfort, 1591, 1595. [Martin's book was first pbd at Turin, 1577.]

[For Temple see J. Freudenthal, Beiträge zur Geschichte der englischen Philosophie, Archiv für Geschichte der Philosophie, v, 1892.]

JOHN CASE (d. 1600)

Summa veterum interpretum in universam Dialecticam Aristotelis. 1584; Oxford, 1592; Frankfort, 1593; Oxford, 1598.

Speculum moralium questionum in universam ethicen Aristotelis. Oxford, 1585; Frankfort, 1589; Oxford, 1596.

Sphaera civitatis. Oxford, 1588.

Reflexus speculi moralis. Oxford, 1596.

Thesaurus Oeconomiae. Oxford, 1597.

Lapis philosophicus. Oxford, 1599; 1612.

Ancilla philosophiae. Oxford, 1599.

JOHN SANDERSON (d. 1602)

Institutionum dialecticarum libri quatuor. Antwerp, 1589; Oxford, 1594, 1602, 1609.

WILLIAM PERKINS (1558–1602)

Armilla aurea. Cambridge, 1590, [1591?], [1592].

The Whole Treatise of the Cases of Conscience. 1608.

[See also p. 683 above.]

SIR RICHARD BARCKLEY

A Discourse of the Felicitie of Man: or his Summum bonum. 1598; 1603, ed. T. Heywood, 1631.

SIR JOHN DAVIES (1569–1626)

Nosce Teipsum. This Oracle expounded in two Elegies. 1. Of Humane knowledge. 2. Of the Soule of Man, and the immortalitie thereof. 1599.

The Complete Poems. Ed. A. B. Grosart, 1869, 1876.

[See also pp. 426–7 above.]

JOSEPH HALL (1574–1656)

Characters of Vertues and Vices. 1608.

Resolutions and Decisions of Diverse practi call cases of Conscience. 1649.

[See also p. 697 and p. 841 above.]

JOHN SELDEN (1584–1654)

The Duello or Single Combat. 1610.

Joannis Seldeni De Dis Syris Syntagmata II. 1617.

The Historie of Tithes. 1618 (bis).

Joannis Seldeni De Successionibus ad leges Ebraeorum. 1631; 1636.

Joannis Seldeni Mare Clausum seu De Dominio Maris. 1635; 1636; Hague, 1636; Leyden, 1636; Amsterdam, 1636.

Joannis Seldeni De jure Naturali & Gentium Juxta Disciplinam Ebraeorum, 1640; Leipzig, 1665; Strasburg, 1665.

A Brief Discourse of the Powers of the Peers and Commons. 1640 (anon., bis).

Table-Talk. Ed. R. Milward, 1689; ed. S. H. Reynolds, Oxford, 1892.

Opera Omnia. Ed. D. Wilkins, 3 vols. 1726.

[For Selden's legal works see p. 851 above.]

ROBERT SANDERSON (1587–1663)

Logicae artis compendium. Oxford, 1615 (anon.), 1618, 1631, 1664 (6th edn).

De juramenti promissorii obligatione praelectiones septem. Habitae A.D. MDCXLVI. 1647; 1670; 1686; tr. Eng. ('by his Majesties speciall command'), 1655.

De obligatione conscientiae praelectiones decem habitae A.D. MDCXLVII. 1660; 1661; 1686; 1696; ed. W. Whewell, Cambridge, 1851; ed. and tr. Eng. C. Wordsworth, Lincoln, 1877.

The Works. Ed. W. Jacobson. 6 vols. Oxford, 1854.

[See also p. 700 above.]

ROBERT FLUDD (1574–1637)

Utriusque Cosmi majoris scilicet et minoris, Metaphysica, physica atque technica Historia. 2 vols. Frankfort, 1617–21.

Medicina Catholica, seu mysticum artis medicandi sacrarum (Integrum Morborum mysterium). 5 pts. Frankfort, 1629–30.

Clavis Philosophiae et Alchymiae. Frankfort, 1633.

Philosophia Moysaica. Gouda, 1638; tr. Eng. 1659.

RICHARD CRAKANTHORP (1567–1624)

Introductio in metaphysicam. Oxford, 1619.

Logicae libri quinque de praedicabilibus. 1622; Oxford, 1677–6 (4th edn and including other works).

De Providentia Dei tractatus. Cambridge, 1623.

[See also p. 857 above.]

NATHANAEL CARPENTER (1589–1628?)

Philosophia libera, triplici exercitationum Decade proposita, in qua adversus hujus temporis Philosophos dogmata quaedam nova discutiuntur. Frankfort, 1621; Oxford, 1622, 1636.

MARTIN FOTHERBY (1549?–1619)

Atheomastix: clearing foure truthes, against atheists and infidels. 1622.

EDWARD HERBERT (BARON HERBERT OF CHERBURY) (1581–1648)

(a) Works

De Veritate, prout distinguitur a Revelatione, a Verisimili, a Possibili, et a Falso. Paris, 1624; 1633; Paris, 1636; 1659; tr. French, Paris, 1639.

De Causis Errorum: una cum tractatu de Religione Laici. 1645; 1656.

De Religione Gentilium, errorumque apud eos causis. Amsterdam, 1663, 1700; tr. Eng. 1709.

Religio Laici. Ed. H. G. Wright, MLR. XXVIII, 1933. [A different work from that above.]

[For the non-philosophical works, see pp. 476 and 842 above.]

(b) Biography and Criticism

Lechler, G. V. Geschichte des englischen Deismus. Stuttgart, 1841.

de Rémusat, C. Lord Herbert de Cherbury. Paris, 1874.

Sorley, W. R. The Philosophy of Lord Herbert of Cherbury. Mind, III, 1894.

Güttler, C. Eduard Lord Herbert von Cherbury. Munich, 1897.

GEORGE HAKEWILL (1578–1649)

An Apologie or Declaration of the Power and Providence of God. Oxford, 1627, 1630, 1635.

[For Hakewill see A. H. Bullen, Elizabethans, 1924.]

WILLIAM AMES (1576–1633)

Guilielmi Amesii, de conscientia et ejus jure vel casibus. Amsterdam, 1630, 1631, 1634, 1635, 1654; Oxford, 1659; Amsterdam, 1670; tr. Eng. 1639.

ROBERT GREVILLE, BARON BROOKE (1608–1643)

A Discourse opening the nature of that Episcopacie which is exercised in England. 1641; 1642 ('enlarged').

The Nature of Truth, its union and unity with the Soule. 1640 (re-issued 1641).

[For Greville see J. Freudenthal, Beiträge zur Geschichte der englischen Philosophie, Archiv für Geschichte der Philosophie, VI, 1893.]

SAMUEL HARTLIB (d. 1670?)

A Description of the famous Kingdom of Macaria. 1641; rptd Harleian Misc. vol I, 1744, 1808.

[See also p. 846 above.]

HENRY MORE (1614–1687)

(a) Bibliography

Landes, M. W. Philosophical Writings of Henry More. Ed. F. I. Mackinnon, New York, 1925, pp. 233–45.

(b) Collected and Selected Works

Philosophical Poems. Cambridge, 1647 (bis); ed. A. B. Grosart, 1876, 1878 (as The Complete Poems of Dr Henry More) (Chertsey Worthies' Lib.). [Rpt of ΨΥΧΩΔΙΑ Platonica and Democritus Platonissans with 'An addition of some few smaller poems.']

A Collection of several Philosophical Writings. 1662; 1712. [Conjectura Cabbalistica, Enthusiasmus Triumphatus, Immortality of the Soule, Antidote against Atheism, and correspondence with and concerning Descartes.]

Henrici Mori Cantabrigiensis Opera. 3 vols. 1675–9. [Latin versions by More himself of his principal works with autobiographical Praefatio Generalissima.]

The Theological Works. According to the author's improvements in his Latin edition. 1708. [Explanation of Godliness, Enquiry into Iniquity, Exposition of Epistles to Seven Churches, Discourse of Grounds of Faith, Antidote against Idolatry, Divine Hymns.]

Philosophical Writings of Henry More. Ed. F. I. Mackinnon, New York, 1925. [Selections from Antidote against Atheism, Enchiridion Ethicum and Immortality of the Soule, with a summary of More's philosophy.]

Philosophical Poems of Henry More. Comprising 'Psychozoia' and Minor Poems. Ed. G. Bullough, Manchester, 1931. [Selections, with detailed introduction and summaries of poems omitted.]

(c) Separate Works

ΨΥΧΩΔΙΑ Platonica: or a Platonicall Song of the Soul, consisting of foure severall Poems. By H. M. Cambridge, 1642.

Democritus Platonissans, or an Essay upon the Infinity of Worlds out of Platonick Principles. Cambridge, 1646. [In verse.]

Observations upon [Thomas Vaughan's] Anthroposophia Theomagica and Anima Magica abscondita. By Alazonomastix Philalethes. 1650.

The Second Lash of Alazonomastix. Cambridge, 1651. [Rptd with the preceding item in Enthusiasmus Triumphatus, 1656.]

An Antidote against Atheism: or, An Appeal to the Natural Faculties of the Mind of Man, whether there be not a God. 1652; 1653; 1655 ('corrected and enlarged; with an appendix').

Conjectura Cabbalistica, or a Conjectural Essay of interpreting the Mind of Moses, in the first three chapters of Genesis, according to a threefold Cabbala, viz. Literal, Philosophical, Mystical. 1653.

Enthusiasmus Triumphatus, or a Discourse of the Nature, Causes, Kinds, and Cure of Enthusiasme: written by Philosophilus Parresiastes and prefixed to Alazonomastix his Observations and Reply. 1656.

The Immortality of the Soule, so farre forth as it is demonstrable from the Knowledge of Nature and the Light of Reason. 1659.

An Explanation of the Grand Mystery of Godliness: or a True and Faithful Representation of the Everlasting Gospel of our Lord and Saviour Jesus Christ. 1660. [4 chs. rptd 1681 as Tetractys Anti-Astrologica.]

Free-Parliament proposed to tender consciences; and published for the use of the members now elected. By Alazonomastix Philalethes. 1660.

A modest Enquiry into the Mystery of Iniquity. 1664. [Appended is The Apology of Dr Henry More.]

Enchiridion Ethicum, praecipua Moralis Philosophiae Rudimenta complectens, illustrata ut plurimum Veterum Monumentis, et ad Probitatem Vitae perpetuo accommodata. 1667; 1668; 1669; Amsterdam, 1679, 1695; 1695; 1696; 1711. [Partial English version by More himself in Joseph Glanvill's Saducismus Triumphatus, 1681; rptd separately 1690 (facs. New York, 1930).]

Divine Dialogues, containing sundry Disquisitions & Instructions concerning the Attributes of God and His Providence in the World. Collected and compiled by Franciscus Palaeopolitanus. 1668; 1713; 3 vols. Glasgow, 1743. [Appended is A brief discourse of the true grounds of the certainty of faith.]

Philosophiae Teutonicae Censura. 1670. [Criticism of Boehme.]

Enchiridion Metaphysicum, sive de rebus incorporeis succincta & luculenta Dissertatio. 1671 (signed H. M.). [Attack on Descartes.]

A brief Reply to a late Answer to Dr Henry More his Antidote against Idolatry. 1672. [Includes rpt of An Antidote against Atheism.]

Remarks upon two late ingenious Discourses [by Sir Matthew Hale]. 1676.

Apocalypsis Apocalypseos, or the Revelation of St John the Divine unveiled. Containing a brief Exposition of the whole Book of the Apocalypse. 1680.

A plain and continued Exposition of the several Prophecies or Divine Visions of the Prophet Daniel. 1681.

An Answer to several Remarks upon Dr Henry More his Expositions of the Apocalypse and Daniel by S. E. 1684.

A briefe Discourse of the Real Presence of the Body and Blood of Christ in the Celebration of the Holy Eucharist. 1686 (bis).

Discourses on several texts of Scripture. Ed. J. Worthington, 1692.

Letters on several subjects. Ed. E. Elys, 1694.

A Collection of Aphorisms. In two parts. 1704.

Divine Hymns. 1706.

[More also contributed to Kabbala denudata, ed. C. K. de Rosenroth, vol. I, 1677 (tr. Eng. 1677), and Joseph Glanvill's Saducismus Triumphatus, 1681, as well as providing elaborate notes to Glanvill's and George Rust's Two choice and useful treatises, 1682. His letters to John Norris are in Norris's The Theory and Regulation of Love, Oxford, 1688, and The Diary and Correspondence of Dr John Worthington, ed. J. Crossley, Chetham Soc. 1847–86, includes his letters to Worthington. Other letters will be found in Ward's Life and Conway Letters, ed. M. H. Nicolson, New Haven, 1930.]

(d) Biography and Criticism

'Eugenius Philalethes' (Thomas Vaughan). The Man-mouse taken in a Trape. 1650.

Ward, Richard. The Life of the Learned and Pious Dr Henry More. 1710; ed. M. F. Howard, 1711.

Benson, A. C. Essays. 1896.

Powicke, F. J. The Cambridge Platonists. 1926. [Ch. vi.]

Lamprecht, S. P. Innate Ideas in the Cambridge Platonists. Philosophical Rev. xxxv, 1926.

Anderson, Paul R. Science in Defence of Liberal Religion: a Study of Henry More's Attempt to link Religion with Science. New York, 1933.

RALPH CUDWORTH (1617–1688)

(a) Works

A Discourse concerning the True Notion of the Lords Supper. By R. C. 1642; 1670 (adds the 2 sermons); 1676.

The Union of Christ and The Church; In a Shadow. By R. C. 1642.

A Sermon Preached Before the Honourable House of Commons, March 31. 1647. Cambridge, 1647; rptd facs. New York, 1930.

Dantur rationes boni et mali aeternae et indispensabiles. Cambridge, 1651. [In verse.]

A Sermon Preached to the Honourable Society of Lincolnes-Inne. 1664.

The True Intellectual System of the Universe: The first part; wherein all the Reason and Philosophy of Atheism is confuted. 1678; ed. T. Birch, 2 vols. 1743, 4 vols. 1829; ed. J. Harrison, 3 vols. 1845; tr. Latin, J. L. von Mosheim, 2 vols. Jena, 1733 (with elaborate biographical and critical notes, tr. Eng. in Harrison's edn). [Abridged by Thomas Wise, 2 vols. 1706.]

A Treatise concerning Eternal and Immutable Morality. Ed. E. Chandler, 1731.

A Treatise on Freewill. Ed. J. Allen, 1838.

(b) Criticism

Janet, P. Essai sur le Médiateur plastique de Cudworth. Paris, 1860.

Lowrey, C. E. The Philosophy of Cudworth. 1884.

Scott, W. R. An Introduction to Cudworth's Treatise concerning Eternal and Immutable Morality. 1891.

Schmitz, K. J. Cudworth und der Platonismus. Bonn, 1919.

Powicke, F. J. The Cambridge Platonists. 1926. [Ch. iv.]

JOHN WALLIS (1616–1703)

Truth tried, or Animadversions on a Treatise published by Robert lord Brook. 1643.

Johannis Wallisii Elenchus geometriae Hobbianae. Oxford, 1655.

Due correction for Mr Hobbes; or schoole discipline, for not saying his lessons right. Oxford, 1656.

Hobbiani puncti dispunctio in answer to M. Hobs's Στιγμαί. Oxford, 1657.

Hobbius heauton-timorumenos. Oxford, 1662.

Thomae Hobbes quadratura circuli confutata. Oxford, 1669.

[See also p. 702 above.]

JOHN BRAMHALL (1594–1663)

The Serpent Salve; or, A Remedy for the biting of an Aspe. 1644. [A defence of monarchy, and criticism of the view that all power is derived from the people.]

A Defence of the True Liberty of Human Actions from Antecedent and Extrinsicall Necessity. 1655.

Castigations of Mr Hobbes his last Animadversions in the case concerning Liberty and Universal Necessity. With an appendix concerning the catching of Leviathan or the great Whale. 1658.

Works. 4 vols. Dublin, 1674–7; 5 vols. Oxford, 1842.

[See J. H. Loewe, John Bramhall und sein Verhältniss zu Thomas Hobbes, Prague, 1887; W. J. Sparrow-Simpson, Archbishop Bramhall, 1927; T. S. Eliot, For Lancelot Andrewes, 1928.]

SIR KENELM DIGBY (1603–1665)

Two Treatises. In the one of which, the Nature of Bodies; in the other, the Nature of Mans soule; is looked into: in way of Discovery of the Immortality of reasonable soules. Paris, 1644; 1645; 1658; 1665.

Of bodies, and of man's soul. To discover the immortality of reasonable souls. With two discourses of the powder of sympathy and of the vegetation of plants. 1669.

[For Digby's other writings see E. W. Bligh, Sir Kenelm Digby and his Venetia, 1932, pp. 307–12.]

ALEXANDER ROSS (1591–1654)

The Philosophicall Touch-Stone; or Observations upon Sir K. Digbie's Discourses. 1645.

Arcana Microcosmi. 1651; 1652.

Πανσέβεια: or, a View of all Religions in the World. 1653; 1655; 1658; 1664; 1696 (6th edn).

Leviathan drawn out with a hook; or Animadversions on Mr Hobbes his Leviathan. 1653.

[For Ross's poems see p. 477 above; his astronomical writings are listed p. 883 below.]

THOMAS WHITE (1593–1676)

Institutionum Peripateticarum ad mentem K. Digbaei pars theorica. Leyden. 1646, 1647; tr. Eng. 1656.

The Grounds of Obedience and Government. 1655 (bis).

Scirri, sive sceptices et scepticorum à jure disputationis exclusio. 1663.

SIR ROBERT FILMER (d. 1653)

The Free-holders Grand Inquest, Touching our Sovereign Lord the King And His Parliament. 1647.

The Anarchy of a Limited or Mixed Monarchy. 1648.

The Necessity of the Absolute Power of all Kings. 1648.

Observations concerning the Originall of Government. 1652. [Criticism of Hobbes.]
Patriarcha: or the Natural Power of Kings. 1680.

NATHANAEL CULVERWEL (d. 1651?)

Spiritual Optciks; or a glasse discovering the imperfection of a Christians knowledge in this life. Ed. W. Dillingham, 1651.
An Elegant and Learned Discourse of the Light of Nature; with several other treatises. Ed. W. Dillingham, 1652; 1654; 1661; Oxford, 1669; ed. J. Brown and J. Cairns, 1857.
[Selections in The Cambridge Platonists, ed. E. T. Campagnac, Oxford, 1901, pp. 213–321. For criticism see F. J. Powicke, The Cambridge Platonists, 1926, ch. v.]

SETH WARD (1617–1689)

A philosophicall essay towards an eviction of the being and attributes of God. 1652.
Vindiciae academiarum, with an appendix concerning what M. Hobbs and M. Dell have published on this argument. 1654.
In Thomae Hobbii philosophiam exercitatio epistolica. Oxford, 1656.
[See also p. 702 above.]

JOHN PORDAGE (1607–1681)

Truth appearing. 1655.
Theologia mystica. 1683.

THOMAS STANLEY (1625–1678)

The History of Philosophy: containing The Lives, Opinions, Actions and Discourses of the Philosophers of every Sect. 4 vols. 1655–62; 1687; 1701; tr. Latin, Amsterdam, 1690.
[For Stanley's poems see p. 478 above.]

JAMES HARRINGTON (1611–1677)

The Common-wealth of Oceana. 1656; 1658; ed. H. Morley, 1887; ed. S. B. Liljegren, Lund, 1924.
The Prerogative of Popular Government. 2 pts, 1658–7.
A Discourse shewing that the spirit of Parliaments with a Council in the interval, is not to be trusted for a Settlement. 1659.
A Discourse upon this saying 'the Spirit of the nation is not yet to be trusted with Liberty.' [1659.]
The Art of Law-giving: in III books. 1659.
Aphorisms political. [1659.]
Political Discourses: tending to the introduction of a free Commonwealth in England. 1660.
The Oceana and other Works collected by John Toland. 1700; 1737 (fuller collection).
[See R. Koebner, Oceana, E. Studien, LXVIII, 1934.]

GEORGE LAWSON (d. 1678).

An Examination of the Political part of Mr Hobbs his Leviathan. 1657; 1663.

MATTHEW WREN (1585–1665)

Considerations on Mr Harrington's Oceana. 1657.
Monarchy asserted in vindication of the Considerations upon Mr Harrington's Oceana. Oxford, 1659, 1660.

THOMAS PIERCE (1622–1691)

Αυτοκατακρισις with occasional reflexions on Master Hobbs. 1658.

HENRY STUBBE (1632–1676)

Clamor Rixa. 1657. [An attack on Hobbes.]
The Commonwealth of Oceana put into the Ballance. 1660.
Campanella revived, or an inquiry into the history of the Royal Society. 1670.

JOHN SMITH (1618–1652)

Select Discourses. As also a sermon preached by Simon Patrick at the author's funeral. With a brief account of his life and death. Ed. J. Worthington, 1660; Cambridge, 1673; ed. Sir D. Dalrymple (Lord Hailes), Edinburgh, 1756. [Selections in The Cambridge Platonists, ed. E. T. Campagnac, Oxford, 1901, pp. 79–209. For criticism see F. J. Powicke, The Cambridge Platonists, 1926, ch. iii.]

ROBERT BOYLE (1627–1691)

An Examen of Mr T. Hobbes his Dialogus physicus de natura aeris. 1662. [Appended to New Experiments Physico-Mechanical, Touching the Air, Oxford, 1662 (2nd edn).]
New Experiments and Observations touching Cold. To which are added an Examen of antiperistasis, and an examen of Mr Hobs's doctrine about cold. 1665; 1683.
Tracts, containing Animadversions upon Mr Hobbes's problemata de vacuo. 1674; tr. Latin, 1676.
[For Boyle's other writings see J. F. Fulton, A Bibliography of Robert Boyle, Oxford, 1932.]

WILLIAM LUCY (1594–1677)

Observations and Confutations of errours in Mr Hobbs his Leviathan. 1663.

THEOPHILUS GALE (1628–1678)

The Court of the Gentiles. 4 pts, Oxford 1669–77.
Idea Theologiae. 1673.
Philosophia Generalis. 1676.

SAMUEL PARKER (1640–1688)

Tentamina physico-theologica de Deo. 1665.
A free and impartial Censure of the Platonick
    Philosophie. Oxford, 1666, 1667.
Disputationes de Deo et divina providentia.
    1678.

THOMAS TENISON (1636–1715)

The Creed of Mr Hobbes examined. 1670.

ANTOINE LEGRAND (d. 1699)

Philosophia veterum e mente Renati Des-
    cartes more scholastico breviter digesta.
    1671.
Institutio philosophiae secundum principia
    Renati Descartes. 1672; 1675 (3rd edn);
    1680; tr. Eng. R. Blome, 1694. [An ex-
    pansion of Philosophia veterum.]
Apologia pro R. Des-Cartes contra Samuelum
    Parkerum. 1670; Nuremberg, 1081.

JOHN EACHARD (1636?–1697)

Mr Hobbs's State of Nature Considered, In a
    Dialogue between Philautus and Timothy.
    1672.
Some Opinions of Mr Hobbs considered in a
    second dialogue between Philautus and
    Timothy. 1673.

JOHN MILTON (1608–1674)

Artis logicae plenior institutio. 1672.
[See also pp. 463–73 above.]

EDWARD HYDE, EARL OF CLARENDON
(1609–1674)

A brief view of the dangerous errors in Hobbes's
    Leviathan. 1676.

JOHN WHITEHALL

The Leviathan found out: or the Answer to
    Mr Hobbes's Leviathan. 1679.

JAMES TYRRELL (1642–1718)

Patriarcha non Monarcha. 1681.
A Brief Disquisition of the Law of Nature as
    also confutations of Mr Hobbs's principles.
    1692; 1701 (enlarged).

JOHN DOWEL

The Leviathan heretical: or refutation of a
    book of [Hobbes'], entituled The Historical
    Narration of Heresie. Oxford, 1683.

BENJAMIN WHICHCOTE (1609–1683)

(a) Works

Θεοφορουμενα Δογματα, or, some select Notions
    of the Learned Benj. Whichcote, D.D.,
    faithfully collected from him by a Pupil
    and Particular Friend. 1685.
Select Sermons. 1698 (with preface by Shaftes-
    bury); ed. W. Wishart, Edinburgh, 1742.
Several Discourses, examined and corrected by
    his own Notes. Ed. J. Jeffery, 4 vols. 1701–7;
    4 vols. Aberdeen, 1751 (as The Works).
The True Notion of Peace in the Kingdom or
    Church of Christ, stated in a Sermon on the
    malignity of Popery. Ed. J. Jeffery, 1717.
Moral and Religious Aphorisms: published by
    Dr Jeffery. Now republished with very large
    additions. Ed. S. Salter, 1753; ed. W. R.
    Inge, 1931.
The Cambridge Platonists. Ed. E. T. Cam-
    pagnac, Oxford, 1901, pp. 1–75. [Selections
    from Sermons and Aphorisms.]

(b) Biography and Criticism

Tillotson, J. Sermon preached at the Funeral
    of the Reverend Benj. Whichcote. 1683.
Westcott, B. F. Benjamin Whichcote. [In
    Masters in English Theology, ed. A. Barry,
    1877.]
Powicke, F. J. The Cambridge Platonists.
    1926. [Ch. ii.]

W. R. S., rev. S. V. K.

VII. SCIENCE AND PSEUDO-
SCIENCE

General Authorities. Encyclopedias of Know-
ledge. Mathematics. Astronomy. Astrology.
Geography and Navigation. Alchemy and
Chemistry. Medicine. Anatomy and Surgery.
Herbals. Zoology. Witchcraft and Magic.

(1) GENERAL AUTHORITIES

Traill, H. D. et al. Social England. 6 vols.
    1894–1905. [Has the following sections:
    C. Creighton, Public Health, vols. III, IV;
    R. R. Steele, Occult Sciences, vol. III;
    R. R. Steele, Witchcraft and Alchemy, vol.
    IV; T. Whittaker, Natural Science, vols.
    III, IV.]
Seager, H. W. Natural History in Shake-
    speare's Time. 1896.
Robin, P. A. The Old Physiology in English
    Literature. 1911.
Shakespeare's England. 2 vols. Oxford, 1916.
    [Ch. xiv, A. H. G. Doran, Medicine. Ch. xv,
    The Sciences: (1) E. B. Knobel, Astronomy;
    (2) R. R. Steele, Alchemy; (3) Natural
    History: C. T. Onions, Animals; Sir W.
    T. Thiselton-Dyer, Plants.]

Zeitlinger, H. and Sotheran, H. C. Bibliotheca Chemico-mathematica: Catalogue of Works in many Tongues on Exact and Applied Science. 2 vols. 1921.

Taylor, H. O. Thought and Expression in the Sixteenth Century. 2 vols. New York, 1921.

Gunther, R. T. Early Science in Oxford. 4 vols. Oxford, 1923–5.

Smith, Preserved. A History of Modern Culture. The Great Renewal, 1543–1687. New York, 1930.

Wolf, A. A History of Science, Technology and Philosophy in the Sixteenth and Seventeenth Centuries. 1935.

(2) ENCYCLOPEDIAS OF KNOWLEDGE

Woodville (or Wydeville), Anthony, Earl Rivers (1442?–1483). The dictes or sayengis of the philosophres. Westminster, 1477; [1480?]; [1489]; 1528; ed. facs. W. Blades, 1877. [From the French.]

Caxton, William (1422?–1491). The Myrrour of the worlde. [1481]; [1490]; [1529?]; ed. O. H. Prior, EETS. Ex. Ser. 1913. [From the French.]

Trevisa, John de (1326–1412). Bartholomeus de proprietatibus rerum. [1495?]; 1535; ed. Stephan Batman, 1582 (as Batman uppon Bartolome his Booke De Proprietatibus Rerum). [From Bartholomaeus Anglicus. Extracts from 1535 edn in Medieval Lore from Bartholomew Anglicus, ed. R. R. Steele, 1905.]

A[lday?], J[ohn?]. A Summarie of the Antiquities and wonders of the worlde, abstracted out of Plinie. [1566]; 1585 (as The Secrets and wonders of the world]; 1587. [From the French version of P. de Changy.]

San[ford], Ja[mes]. Henrie Cornelius Agrippa, of the Vanitie and uncertaintie of Artes and Sciences. 1569; 1575.

Blundeville, Thomas. M. Blundeville His Exercises, containing Sixe Treatises, Cosmographie, Astronomie, as also in the Arte of Navigation. 1594; 1597; [1606–5]; 1613; [1622–1]; 1636 (re-issued 1638).

Holland, Philemon (1552–1637). The Historie of the World, commonly called the Naturall Historie of C. Plinius Secundus. 2 vols. 1601; 2 vols. 1634 (re-issued 1635). [Extracts in The Elizabethan Zoo, ed. M. St Clare Byrne, 1926.]

Bacon, Francis. [See special bibliography, pp. 868–71 above.]

(3) MATHEMATICS

(a) Modern Authorities

de Morgan, A. Arithmetical Books. 1847.

Cantor, M. Vorlesungen über Geschichte der Mathematik. 3 vols. Leipzig, 1880–1900, 1922.

Ball, W. W. R. History of the Study of Mathematics at Cambridge. Cambridge, 1889.

Smith, D. E. History of Mathematics. Boston, 1923–.

Yeldham, F. A. The Story of Reckoning in the Middle Ages. 1926.

Cajori, F. History of Mathematical Notations. Chicago, 1928.

(b) Contemporary Treatises

Tunstall, Cuthbert (1474–1559). De Arte Supputandi libri quattuor. 1522; Paris, 1529; 1538; Strasburg, 1551.

Recorde, Robert (1510?–1588). The grounde of artes, teachynge the worke and practise of Arithmetike. 1542; 1543; 1561; 1575; 1582; 1590, etc. Augmented by John Dee, 1618, etc. [Part ('Accomptynge by Counters') in R. R. Steele, The Earliest Arithmetics in English, EETS. Ex. Ser. 1922. See F. P. Barnard, The Casting Counter and the Casting Board, Oxford, 1916.]

—— The pathway to Knowledg, containing the first principles of Geometrie. 1551; 1574; 1602.

—— The whetstone of witte, whiche is the seconde parte of Arithmetike. 1557. [See L. C. Karpinski, Bibliotheca Mathematica, XIII, Leipzig, 1913.]

—— Record's arithmeticke. Also the art of decimall arithmeticke by R. N[orton]. 1615.

Buckley, William (d. 1570?). Arithmetica memorativa nunc primum in lucem edita. 1567; 1567 (with John Seton's Dialectica); 1572; 1574; 1577; 1584; 1611; 1617; Cambridge, 1631.

Baker, Humphrey (fl. 1562–1587). The Well Spryng of Sciences, whiche teacheth the perfecte woork and practise of Arithmeticke. 1568; 1574; 1580; 1583; 1591; 1598; 1602, etc.

Digges, Leonard (d. 1559?). A Book named Tectonicon briefly shewynge the exacte measurynge all maner lande. 1562; 1592; 1605; 1614, etc.

—— A Geometricall Practise, named Pantometria. 1571; 1591. [Part of the first book of this, The Theodelitus, ed. R. T. Gunther, Oxford, 1927.]

—— An Arithmeticall Militare Treatise, named Stratioticos. 1579; 1590.

Billingsley, Sir Henry (d. 1606). The Elements of Geometrie of the most auncient Philosopher Euclide of Megara. 1570. [Preface by John Dee.]

Digges, Thomas (1545–1595). Alae seu Scalae Mathematicae, quibus visibilium remotissima Coelorum Theatra conscendi possit. 1573. [Also edited works of his father, Leonard Digges (q.v.).]

Blagrave, John (d. 1611). The Mathematicall Jewell. 1585.
—— Baculum Familiare, a Booke of the making and use of a Staffe. 1590.
—— The Art of Dyalling in two parts. 1609.
Hood, Thomas. A Copie of the Speache made by the Mathematicall Lecturer. 1588.
—— The elementes of geometrie. 1590. [From La Ramée.]
—— The Use of the Jacobs Staff. 1590.
—— The use of the two Mathematicall Instruments, the Crosse-Staffe and the Jacobs Staffe. 1590; 1596.
—— The use of the Celestial Globe in plane. 1590.
—— The Use of both the Globes. 1592.
—— The Marriners guide. [With W. Bourne, The Regiment for the Sea, 1596.]
—— The elements of arithmeticke. 1596. [From Urstitius.]
—— The making and use of a Sector. 1598.
Fale, Thomas. Horologiographia; The Art of Dialling. 1593; 1626 (re-issued 1627); 1633; 1652.
Norton, Robert (d. 1635). A Mathematicall Appendix for Mariners at Sea. 1604.
—— Disme: the Art of Tenths, or decimall arithmeticke. 1608; 1614; ed. Henry Lyte, 1619. [From Stevin.]
Handson, Raphe. Trigonometry: or the Doctrine of Triangles. 1614; 1630; 1631. [From Pitiscus.]
Napier (or Neper), John (1550–1617). Mirifici Logarithmorum Canonis descriptio. Edinburgh, 1614; rptd F. Masere (Scriptores Logarithmici, 1807); tr. Eng. Edward Wright (q.v.), 1616, 1618, and H. Filipowski, Edinburgh, 1857.
—— Rabdologiae, seu numerationis per virgulas libri duo. Edinburgh, 1615; 1617; Berlin, 1623; Verona, 1623.
—— Mirifici Logarithmorum Canonis Constructio. Edinburgh, 1619; tr. Eng. Edinburgh, 1889.
—— De Arte Logistica. Ed. Mark Napier, Edinburgh, 1839.
[See E. W. Hobson, John Napier and the Invention of Logarithms, 1914; Napier Tercentenary Memorial Volume, Royal Soc. Edinburgh, 1915; Mark Napier, Memoirs of John Napier of Merchiston, Edinburgh, 1834; see also Briggs and Speidell below.]
Wright, Edward (1558?–1615). A Description of the admirable Table of Logarithmes. 1616; 1618. [From Napier.]
Speidell, John. A Geometricall Extraction, Or a Compendious Collection of the Chiefe and choyse Problemes. 1616; 1617.
—— New Logarithmes. The First invention whereof was, by the Honourable Lo. John Nepair Baron of Marchiston. 1619; 1624.

Speidell, John. A briefe treatise of sphaericall triangles, whereunto is annexed a geometricall extraction. 1627.
—— An arithmeticall extraction. 1628.
Briggs, Henry (1561–1630). Logarithmorum Chilias Prima. 1617.
—— Arithmetica Logarithmica sive Logarithmorum Chiliadis Triginta. 1624.
—— The first chiliad of logarithmes. [1630?]
—— Logarithmicall arithmeticke, first invented by J. Neper, Baron of Merchistoun. 1631.
—— Trigonometria Britannica. Ed. H. Gellibrand, 1633; tr. Eng. 1658.
Gunter, Edmund (1581–1626). Canon triangulorum sive tabulae sinuum et tangentium artificialium. 1620; 1623; tr. Eng. (as A Canon of triangles) 1620, 1623.
—— De Sectore et radio. 1623; tr. Eng. (as The description and use of the sector) 1623, 1624, 1636.
—— The description and use of his Majesties dials in White-Hall Garden. 1624.
—— Collected Works. 1624; ed. Samuel Foster, 1636; ed. William Leybourn, 1673.
[See F. Cajori, On the History of Gunter's Scale and Slide Rule during the XVII Century, University of California Publications in Mathematics, vol. i, no. 9, Berkeley, 1920.]
Wingate, Edmund (1596–1656). La usage de la regle de proportion en arithmetique. Paris, 1624; tr. Eng. 1626, 1645.
—— The Construction and use of the line of proportion. 1628.
—— Arithmetique made easie. 1630; 1650; 1568; 1678, etc.
—— Λογαριθμοτεχνια or the construction of the logarithmeticall tables. 2 pts, 1635 (2nd edn).
—— Ludus mathematicus or the mathematical Game. 1681.
Foster, Samuel (d. 1652). The Use of the Quadrant. 1624; 1652; 1653; 1662; 1673 (with Gunter).
—— The Art of Dialling. 1638; 1675.
—— Posthuma Forster, the description of a ruler. Ed. E. Wingate, 1652.
—— Elliptical or Azimuthal Horologiography. 1654.
Harriot, Thomas (1560–1621). Artis Analyticae Praxis ad Aequationes Algebraicas nova methodo resolvendas. 1631.
Norwood, Richard (1590?–1675). Trigonometrie. Or The Doctrine of Triangles. 1631; 1634.
—— The Seamans practice. 1637.
Oughtred, William (1575–1660). Clavis Mathematicae. 1631; 1648; 1652 (with Wren); 1667, etc.; tr. Eng. 1647, and E. Halley, 1694.

Oughtred, William. Arithmeticae in numeris et speciebus institutio, quasi clavis Mathematicae est. 1631.

—— The circles of proportion and the horizontall instrument. 1632 (bis); 1633; 1660.

—— The just Apologie against the slaunderous insimulations of Richard Delamaine. [1633?]

—— Mathematicall Recreations. 1633; 1653; 1674.

—— The new artificial gauging line or rod. 1633.

—— The description and use of the double horizontall dyall. 1636; 1652.

—— The Solution of all Sphaerical triangles by the Planisphaere. 1651.

—— Trigonometria. [Ed. R. Stokes and A. Haughton,] 1657; tr. Eng. R. Stokes (as Trigonometrie), 1657.

—— Opuscula mathematica hactenus inedita. Ed. Sir Charles Scarborough, 1677. [See F. Cajori, William Oughtred, a Great Seventeenth Century Teacher of Mathematics, Chicago, 1916; F. Cajori, A List of Oughtred's Mathematical Symbols, University of California Publications in Mathematics, vol. I, no. 8, Berkeley, 1920.]

Delamaine, Richard. Grammelogia Or The Mathematicall Ring. 1631.

Gellibrand, Henry (1597–1636). Trigonometria Britannica. 1633; tr. Eng. 1658. [From Briggs.]

—— An Institution Trigonometricall. 1635; 1652.

Wren, Sir Christopher (1632–1723). Horologiorum sciotericorum in plano, geometrice solum, sine calculo trigonometrico. 1652. [Contains also Oughtred, Clavis mathematicae.]

—— [4 tracts on cycloids in John Wallis (q.v.), Mathematical Works, 1658.]

Ward, Seth (1617–1689). Vindiciae Academiarum. 1654.

—— Idea trigonometriae demonstratae. Oxford, 1654–3.

—— Astronomia geometrica. 1656.

—— In Thomae Hobbii Philosophiam Exercitatio Epistolica. Oxford, 1656.

Hobbes, Thomas (1588–1679). Elementorum Philosophiae; sectio prima de corpore. 1655; tr. Eng. 1656.

—— Examinatio et emendatio Mathematicae hodiernae qualis explicatur in libris Johannis Wallisii. 1660.

Wallis, John (1616–1703). Arithmetica Infinitorum. Oxford, 1655.

—— Elenchus geometriae Hobbianae. Oxford, 1655.

—— Due Correction for Mr. Hobbes, or school discipline for not saying his lessons right. Oxford, 1656.

Wallis, John. Hobbiani Puncti Dispunctio, or the undoing of Mr. Hobs's points. Oxford, 1657.

—— Opera mathematicorum. Oxford, 1657.

—— Mathesis Universalis. Oxford, 1657.

—— Mathematical Works. 1658.

—— Tractatus duo, prior de Cycloide. Oxford, 1659.

(4) Astronomy*

(a) Modern Authorities

Grant, R. History of Physical Astronomy. 1852.

Houzeau, J. C. and Lancaster, A. Bibliographie générale de l'Astronomie. 2 vols. Brussels, 1887–9.

Galle, J. G. Cometenbahnen. Leipzig, 1894.

Dreyer, J. L. E. History of Planetary Systems. Cambridge, 1906.

Orchard, T. N. Milton's Astronomy. 1913.

Schroeter, J. F. Sonnenfinsternisse von 600 bis 1800. Oslo, 1923.

Johnson, F. R. Astronomical Thought in Renaissance England, 1500–1645. Baltimore, 1937.

(b) Contemporary Treatises

Linacre, Thomas (1460?–1524). De Sphaera. Venice, 1499; 1547; 1549, etc.; tr. Eng. (as The descripicion of the sphere) William Salesbury, [1550?]. [From Proclus.]

—— Scriptores Astronomici Veteres. Venice, 1499. [Text of one treatise by Linacre.]

Askham (or Ascham), Anthony. A Lytel treatyse of Astronomy, declaryng the leape yere, and what is the cause thereof. 1552.

Digges, Leonard. A prognostication of right good effect. 1555 (re-issued 1556); 1564; 1567; 1576 (enlarged by Thomas Digges); 1578; 1583; 1592; 1596; 1605; ed. R. T. Gunther, Oxford, 1927. [Thomas Digges's addn is largely a trn of Copernicus, bk I. See F. R. Johnson and S. V. Larkey, Thomas Digges, the Copernican System, and the Idea of the Infinity of the Universe in 1576, Huntington Lib. Bulletin, April 1934.]

Recorde, Robert. The Castle of Knowledge (Containing the Explication of the sphere, bothe celestiall and materiall). 1556; 1596.

Field, John. Ephemeris anni 1557 currentis juxta Copernici et Reinhaldi canones. 1556.

Fulke, William (1538–1589). A Goodly Gallerye to behold the naturall causes of all kynde of meteors. 1563; 1571; 1601; 1602; 1634; 1635 (re-issued 1640); 1655.

Hill, Thomas. A contemplation of mysteries containing the rare effectes and significations of certayne Cometes. 1571; [1590?].

—— The schoole of skil. 1599.

---

* The Astronomy and Astrology sections have been revised by Mr D. C. Collins.

Dee, John (1527–1608). Parallaticae Commentationis Praxeosque Nucleus quidam. Ed. T. Digges, 1573.

Cheyne, James (d. 1602). De Priore Astronomiae Parte, seu de Sphaëra. Douay, 1575.

—— De Sphaera seu Globi Coelestis Fabrica, Brevis Praeceptio. Douay, 1575.

—— Jacobi Cheynii Ab Arnage I.V.L. De Geographia Libri Duo. Douay, 1576.

Fleming, Abraham (1552?–1607). Of all blasing starres in generale. 1577; 1618 (as A Treatise of blazing starres). [A trn.]

Bruno, Giordano (1548–1600). La cena de le ceneri. 1584 (anon.).

—— Della causa, principio et una. Venice [for London], 1584.

—— Del' infinito universo et mondi. Venice [for London], 1584.

Hartgill, George. Calendaria, sive tabulae astronomicae universales. 1594; tr. Eng. (as Generall Calendars, or Most Easie Astronomicall Tables) 1594.

Blagrave, John (d. 1611). Astrolabium uranicum generale. 1596.

Norden, John (1548–1625?). Vicissitudo Rerum. 1600 (re-issued 1601); ed. facs. D. C. Collins, Shakespeare Ass. 1932.

Blundeville, Thomas. The Theoriques of the seven planets, shewing all their diverse motions. 1602.

Lydiat, Thomas (1572–1646). Solis et lunae periodus. 1620.

Brerewood (or Bryerwood), Edward (1565?–1613). Tractatus duo quorum primus de Meteoris, secundus de oculo. Oxford, 1631, 1637, 1659.

Learned Tico Brahae, his astronomicall Conjectur, of the new and much Admired * which appeared in the year 1572. 1632. [Has eulogy of Brahe by James I.]

Ross, Alexander (1591–1654). Commentum de terræ motu circulari. 1634.

—— The New Planet no Planet: Or, the Earth no wandring Star. 1646.

Wilkins, John (1614–1672). The Discovery of a World in the Moone. 1638 (anon.); 1684.

—— A Discourse tending to prove that 'tis probable our Earth is one of the Planets. 1640.

—— Mathematicall Magick. 1648.

Ward, Seth (1617–1689). De Cometis, ubi de Cometarum Natura disseritur. Oxford, 1653.

—— In Ismaelis Bullialdi Astronomiae Philolaicae Fundamenta Inquisitio Brevis. Oxford, 1653.

—— Astronomia geometrica. 1656.

Horrocks, Jeremiah (1617–1641). Venus in sole visa. Danzig, 1662 (in J. Hevelius' Mercurius in Sole visus); tr. Eng. A. P. Whatton, 1859. [Written 1639.]

Horrocks, Jeremiah. Opera Posthuma. Ed. John Wallis, 1672. [See S. B. Gaythorpe, Jeremiah Horrocks: 'The Pride and Boast of British Astronomy,' 1909.]

[The mathematical works listed above, pp. 880–2, of Leonard and Thomas Digges, Thomas Hood, Thomas Fale, Samuel Foster and Seth Ward should also be consulted.]

(5) Astrology
(a) Modern Authorities

Whewell, W. History of the Inductive Sciences 3 vols. 1857 (rev. edn).

Wilson, J. A Dictionary of Astrology. 1885.

Proctor, R. A. Myths and Marvels of Astronomy. 1893.

Saxl, F. Verzeichnis astrologischer und mythologischer illustrierter Handschriften des Mittelalters. 2 pts, Heidelberg, 1915–27.

Bosanquet, E. F. English Printed Almanacks and Prognostications, a Bibliographical History to the year 1600. Bibliog. Soc. 1917. [Corrigenda and Addenda, 1928.]

—— Seventeenth Century Almanacks. Library, x, 1930.

Boll, Franz. Sternglaube und Sterndeutung, die Geschichte und das Wesen der Astrologie. Leipzig, 1926.

[See also under Astronomy above.]

(b) Contemporary Treatises

The boke of Knowledge of Thynges unknowen apperteyninge to astronomye. 1530; 1585; 1616; 1637; 1697. [From Godfridus.]

The compost of Ptholomeus. [1532?]; [1535?]; [1540?]; [1635?]. [From the French.]

Boorde, Andrew (1490?–1549). The pryncyples of Astronomye in maner a pronosticacyon. [c. 1550.]

Withers, Fabian. Briefe Introductions unto the arte of chiromancy; whereunto is also annexed as well the artificiall, as naturall astrologie. 1558; 1576; 1598; 1615. [From Indagine.]

—— A Briefe and most easie introduction to the Astrologicall Judgement of the starres. 1583; 1598. [From Dariot.]

Fulke, William. Antiprognosticon contra inutiles astrologorum praedictiones. 1560; tr. Eng. W. Painter, 1560.

G., G. An admonicion against Astrology Judicialle and other curiosities that raigne now in the world. 1561. [From Calvin.]

Coxe, Francis. A short treatise declaringe the detestable wickednesse of magicall sciences. [1561.]

'Arcandam.' The most excellent Profitable, and pleasaunt Booke to finde the fatall destiny of everyman. 1562; 1578; 1592; 1626; 1630; 1634; 1637

Maplet, John (d. 1592). The diall of destiny. 1581.

Harvey, Richard (d. 1623?). An astrological discourse. Upon the conjunction of Saturne and Jupiter. 1583 (bis). [Parodied by Nash (q.v.).]

Harvey, John (1563?–1592). An astrologicall addition to the late discourse upon the conjunction of Saturne and Jupiter. 1583. [See Richard Harvey.]

—— A Discoursive probleme concerning Prophesies. 1588.

P., W. Foure Great Lyers. [c. 1585.]

Nash, Thomas (1567–1601). A wonderful strange and miraculous Astrologicall Prognostication. 1591.

Kelway, Thomas. A learned Astronomical discourse of the judgement of Nativities. 1593. [From Auger Ferrier.]

Baker, Humphrey. The rules and right Documents touchinge the use and practise of the common almanackes, which are named Ephemerides. [Before 1595.] [A trn.]

Covell, William (d. 1614?). Polimanteia, or, The meanes lawfull and unlawfull to Judge of the fall of a commonwealth. 1595.

Chamber, John (1546–1604). A Treatise Against Judiciall Astrologie. 1601.

Heydon, Sir Christopher (d. 1623). A Defence of Judiciall Astrologie, In Answer to A Treatise by M. John Chamber. Cambridge, 1603.

—— An Astrological discourse. 1650.

Wright, Thomas. A Succinct Philosophicall declaration of the nature of Clymactericall yeeres. 1604.

Lydiat, Thomas. Praelectio astronomica de natura coeli. 1605.

Melton, Sir John (d. 1640). Astrologaster, Or the Figure-Caster. Rather the Arraignment of Artless Astrologers. 1620.

Carleton, George (1559–1628). Αστρολογο-μανια. The madnesse of astrologers; or, an examination of Sir C. Heydon's booke. 1624; 1651.

Geree, John (1601?–1649). Astrologo-Mastix, or a discovery of the vanity and iniquity of Judicial Astrology. 1646.

Lilly, William (1602–1681). Christian Astrology Modestly Treated in three books. 1647; ed. 'Zadkiel' (J. M. Morrison), 1835.

—— Monarchy Or No Monarchy in England. 1651.

—— An Easie Method Whereby to Judge the Effects depending on Eclipses. 1652.

—— Anima Astrologiae or a Guide for Astrologers. 1676.

Holmes, Nathaniel (1599–1678). Daemonologie and Theologie. 1650.

Raunce, John. A brief Declaration against Judicial Astrologie. 1650.

Ramesey, William. A Reply to a Scandalous Pamphlet by John Raunce. 1650.

—— Lux Veritatis; or Christian Judicial Astrology vindicated, in answer to N. Holmes. 1651.

—— Vox Stellarum; or the voice of the starres. 1652.

—— A Short Discourse of the Eclipse of the Sunne. 1652.

Warren, Hardick. Magick and Astrology vindicated from false aspersions. 1651.

Rowland, William. Judiciall Astrologie, judicially condemned, upon an examination of Sir Christopher Heydons Apology and of Will. Ramsey's Morologie. 1652.

'Philastrogus'. Lillies Ape Whipt. 1652.

Vicars, John (1580?–1652). Against William Li-Lie. 1652.

Brayne, J. Astrology proved to be the Doctrine of Daemons. [1653?]

Swadlin, Thomas. Divinity no Enemy to Astrology. 1653.

(6) Geography and Navigation

(a) Modern Authorities

Heawood, E. History of Geographical Discovery in the Seventeenth and Eighteenth Centuries. 1912. (Cambridge Geographical Ser.)

Taylor, E. G. R. Tudor Geography. 1930.

—— Late Tudor and Early Stuart Geography, 1583–1650. 1934.

(b) Contemporary Treatises

[Rastell, John (1470–1536).] A New interlude and a mery of the nature of the iiij elements. [1519.] [For rpts see p. 514 above.]

Copland, Robert. The Rutter of the Sea. 1528. [From Garcie.]

Eden, Richard (1521?–1576). A Treatyse of the newe India, after the description of Sebastian Munster. 1553.

—— The Decades of the Newe worlde of West India. 1555; rptd E. Arber (First Three English Books on America, 1885). [From Pietro Martire d'Anghiera.]

—— The Arte of Navigation. 1561; 1572; 1584; 1596; 1609. [From Cortes.]

—— A briefe collection gathered oute of the cosmographye of Sebastian Munster. 1572; 1574.

—— A Very Necessarie and Profitable Booke concerning Navigation. [1579?] [From Taisnier.]

Cuningham, William. The Cosmographical Glasse: Conteinyng the Pleasant principles of Cosmographie, Geographie, Navigation. 1559.

Twyne, Thomas (1543–1613). The Surveye of the World. 1572. [From Dionysius Periegetes.]
—— A short and pithy discourse, concerning earthquakes. 1580; ed. R. E. Ockenden, Oxford, 1936.
Bourne, William (d. 1583). A regiment for the Sea. 1576; 1596 (with Hood's The Marriners Guide); 1620.
Dee, John. General and rare Memorials pertaining to the perfecte arte of Navigation. 1577.
Hellowes, Edward (*fl.* 1574–1600). A Booke of the Invention of the Art of Navigation. 1578. [From Guevara.]
Golding, Arthur (1536?–1605?). A discourse upon the earthquake. 1580.
Ashley, Sir Anthony (1551–1627). The Mariners Mirrour together with the rules and instruments of navigation. [Holland?], 1588.
Abbot, George (1502–1633). A briefe description of the whole worlde. 1599; 1600; 1605; 1608; 1617; 1620; 1623; 1634; 1636.
Wright, Edward. The Haven-finding Art by the Latitude and variation. 1599. [From Stevin.]
—— Certaine Errors in Navigation. 1599; 1610.
—— The Description and use of the Sphaere. 1613; 1627.
—— A Short Treatise of Dialling. 1614.
Norden, John. The Surveyors Dialogue. 1607; 1610 (*bis*); 1618; ed. J. W. Papworth, Architectural Publication Soc. Detached Essays, VI, 1853.
[See A. W. Pollard, The Unity of John Norden: Surveyor and Religious Writer, Library, VII, 1926. See also p. 826 above.]
Aspley, John. Speculum Nauticum; a looking glasse for sea-men. 1624; 1647; 1662.
Pemble, William (1592?–1623). A briefe introduction to Geography. Oxford, 1630; 1635; 1658; 1675, etc. [Also in The Workes of W. Pemble, 1635, etc.]
S[altonstall], W[ye]. Historia mundi, or Mercators atlas. 1635; 1637; [1639?].
Saltonstall, Charles. The Navigator, shewing and Explaining all the Chiefe principles and parts in the famous Art of Navigation. 1636; 1642; [1660?].
Hexham, Henry (1585?–1650?) Atlas, or a geographicke description of the world. 2 vols. Amsterdam, 1636, 1638, 1641. [From Mercator.]

The Magnet and Compass.

Hellmann, G. Neudrucke von Schriften und Karten über Meteorologie und Erdmagnetismus. Berlin, 1893–8. [Has facs. edns of Norman, Borough and Gellibrand.]

Norman, Robert. The new Attractive: Containing a short Discourse of the Magnes or Lodestone. Hereunto are annexed Certaine Necessarie rules for the art of Navigation. 1581; 1585; 1596; 1614; ed. G. Hellmann, Berlin, 1898.
—— The Safeguard of Sailers: or Great Rutter, Containing the Courses, Distances, Depthes, Soundings. 1584; 1587; 1590; 1600; 1605; 1612; 1640.
Borough, William (1536–1599). A discours of the Variation of the Cumpas, or Magneticall Needle. 1581; 1585; 1596; 1611; ed. G. Hellmann, Berlin, 1893.
Barlow, William (d. 1625). The Navigators Supply. 1597.
—— Magneticall Advertisements: or observations, and experiments concerning the nature and properties of the Loadstone. 1616; 1618.
—— A briefe discovery of the idle Animadversions of M. Ridley. 1618.
Gilbert, William (1540–1603). Guilielmi Gilberti Colcestrenris, medici londinensis, de Magnete, Magneticisque Corporibus, et de Magno Magnete tellure. 1600; tr. Eng. P. Fleury Mottelay, 1893, and Gilbert Club, 1900 (notes by S. P. Thompson).
—— Tractatus, sive Physiologia nova de Magnete. Sedan, 1628 and 1633.
—— De Mundo nostro sublunari philosophia nova. Amsterdam, 1651. [Ed. by his brother, William Gilbert.]
[See S. P. Thompson, William Gilbert and Terrestrial Magnetism, 1903.]
Blundeville, Thomas. The Theoriques of the seven planets, shewing all their diverse motions. 1602. [Has description of Gilbert's Magnet.]
Ridley, Mark (1560–1624). A Short Treatise of Magneticall Bodies, and Motions. 1613.
—— Magneticall Animadversions upon certaine Magneticall Advertisements from W. Barlow. 1617.
Gellibrand, Henry. A Discourse Mathematical of the Variation of the Magneticall Needle. 1635; ed. G. Hellmann, Berlin, 1897.

(7) ALCHEMY AND CHEMISTRY

(a) Modern Authorities

Thomson, Thomas. The History of Chemistry. 2 vols. 1830.
Kopp, H. Die Alchemie in älterer und neuerer Zeit. 2 vols. Heidelberg, 1886.
Berthelot, M. La Chimie au Moyen Age. 3 vols. Paris, 1893.
Ferguson, John. Bibliotheca Chemica. Glasgow, 1906.
Mercer, J. E. Alchemy: its Science and Romance. 1921. [Popular introduction.]

(b) Contemporary Treatises

Norton, Thomas (*fl.* 1477). The Ordinall of Alchemy. 1652 (in E. Ashmole's Theatrum Chemicum); ed. J. Holmyard, 1928.

Kelley, Edward (1555–1595). [Works in Ashmole's Theatrum Chemicum, 1652; ed. E. A. Waite, 1893.]

Dee, John. Monas Hieroglyphica. Antwerp, 1564; Frankfort, 1591; tr. French G. de Givry, Paris, 1925.

—— Rogeri Baconis Angli Epistola de Secretis Operibus Artis et Naturae. Ed. John Dee, Hamburg, 1618; tr. Eng. T. M. (as Frier Bacon his discovery of the Miracles of Art, Nature, and Magick), 1659.

—— A True and Faithful Relation of What passed for many Years Between Dr. John Dee and Some Spirits. 1659.

—— The Compendious Rehearsal of John Dee. Ed. T. Hearne (in Johannis Glastoniensis Chronicon, 1726); ed. J. Crossley, Chetham Misc. vol. xxiv, 1851.

[See C. F. Smith, John Dee, 1909; G. M. Hort, Dr John Dee: Elizabethan Mystic and Astrologer, 1922.]

Ripley, George (d. 1490?). The Compound of Alchemy. 1591. [Rptd in E. Ashmole, Theatrum Chemicum, 1652.]

—— Opera Omnia Chemica. Cassel, 1649.

Bacon, Roger (1214?–1294). The Mirror of Alchemy. 1597.

[See R. R. Steele, The History and Method of Science, ed. C. Singer, vol. ii, 1917; D. W. Singer, Alchemical Treatises ascribed to Roger Bacon, Speculum, vii, 1932.]

Russel, Thomas. Diacatholicon aureum, or a general powder of gold, purging all offensive humours in mans bodie. 1602.

Tymme, Thomas (d. 1620). The Practise of Chymicall and Hermeticall Physicke. 1605. [From Duchesne.]

—— A Dialogue Philosophicall. Wherein Natures Secret Closet is Opened. 1612.

Anthonie, Francis. Medicinae, chymicae, et veri potabilis auri assertio. Cambridge, 1610.

—— Apologia veritatis illucescentis pro auro potabili. 1616.

—— The apologie; or defence of a verity concerning Aurum Potabile. 1616; 1684 (in Collectanea Chymica); rptd 1893.

Rawlin, Thomas. Admonitio pseudo-chymicis, in quo D. D. Antonii aurum potabile obiter refutatur. [After 1610.]

Gwinne, Mathew (1558?–1627). In assertorem chymicae Fran. Antonium adversaria. 1611.

Sturtevant, Simon. Metallica, or the Treatise of Metallica. 1612; ed. J. N. Bagnall (with Rovenzon and Dud Dudley's Mettallum Martis), 1855 and 1858.

Rovenzon, John. A Treatise of Metallica, but not that which was published by Mr. Simon Sturtevant. 1613; ed. J. N. Bagnall (with Sturtevant and Dud Dudley's Mettallum Martis), 1855 and 1858.

Gedde, Walter. A booke of sundry draughts principally for the glaziers; whereunto is annexed how to anniel glas. 1615–6; rptd facs. 1898.

Cotta, John (1575?–1650?). Cotta contra Antonium, manifesting Doctor Antony his Apologie for Aurum potabile to be false. Oxford, 1623.

Foster, William (1591–1643). Hoplo-crisma-Spongus, or a Sponge to wipe away the Weapon-Salve. 1629; 1641.

Malthus, Francis. A treatise of artificial fireworks. 1629.

Fludd, Robert (1574–1637). Doctor Fludds answer unto M. Foster. 1631; 1638.

—— Philosophia Moysaica. Gouda, 1638; tr. Eng. 1659.

[Published many works in Latin abroad.]

Babington, John. Pyrotechnia Or, A Discourse of Artificiall Fireworks. 1635.

Plattes, Gabriel. A discovery of infinite treasure, hidden since the worlds beginning. 1638; 1639.

—— A discovery of subterraneall treasure, viz. of all manner of mines and mineralls. 1639; 1653; 1679, etc.

Ashmole, Elias (1617–1692) [used anagram, 'James Hasolle']. Fasciculus Chemicus: Or Chymical Collections. 1650.

—— Theatrum Chemicum Britannicum. 1652.

—— The Way to Bliss. 1658.

Vaughan, Thomas (1622–1666) [pseudonym 'Eugenius Philalethes']. Anthroposophia Theomagica; or a Discourse of the Nature of Man. 1650.

—— Anima Magica Abscondita: Or a Discourse of the Universall Spirit of Nature. 1650.

—— Magia Adamica: Or the Antiquitie of Magic. 1650.

—— The Man-Mouse taken in a trap. 1650.

—— Lumen de Lumine. 1651; ed. E. A. Waite, 1910.

—— The Fame and Confession of the Fraternity, of the Rosie Cross. 1652; ed. F. N. Pryce, 1923.

—— Euphrates, Or the Waters of the East. 1655.

—— The Chymists Key; or the True Doctrine of Corruption and Generation. 1657.

[See E. A. Waite, The Magical Writings of T. Vaughan, 1888, and The Works of Thomas Vaughan, 1919. See also under Henry Vaughan, p. 462 above.]

F[reake?], J. A Description of New Philo-
sophical Furnaces, Or A new Art of Distilling.
1651. [From Glauber.]
—— Three books of occult philosophy. 1651;
ed. W. F. Whitehead, Chicago, 1898. [From
Agrippa.]
Parkhurst, Ferdinand. Medicina Diastatica
Or Sympatheticall Mumie. 1653. [From
Paracelsus.]
'Eireneus, Philalethes' (b. 1622) [often attrib.
to George Starkey (d. 1655)]. The Marrow
of Alchemy. 1654; 1709 (in A True Light
of Alchymy).
Turner, Robert. Henry Cornelius Agrippa's
fourth Book of Occult Philosophy. 1655.
—— Paracelsus of the Supreme Mysteries of
Nature. 1656.
—— Of the Chymical Transmutation, Gene-
alogy, and Generation of Metals. 1657.
[From Paracelsus.]
'Rosicrucian.' Themis Aurea: The Laws of
the Fraternity of the Rosie Crosse. 1656.
[See H. Jennings, The Rosicrucians, 1887;
E. A. Waite, The Real History of the
Rosicrucians, 1887.]
Digby, Sir Kenelm (1603–1665). A Late Dis-
course Touching the Cure of Wounds by the
Powder of Sympathy. Tr. (from French)
R. White, 1658 (bis); 1660; 1664.
—— Two Treatises: in the one of which the
Nature of Bodies; in the other the Nature of
Mans Soule; is looked into. Paris, 1644;
1645; 1658; 1665; 1669.
H., J. Aurora, and Treasure of the philosophers.
1659. [Attrib. erroneously to James Howell;
possibly is Elias Ashmole, who used anagram
'James Hasolle.' Also attrib. to John
Hardinge, and J. Hall. From Paracelsus.]
—— The Triumphant Chariot of Antimony.
1660; 1661; ed. E. A. Waite, 1893. [From
Basil Valentine.]
—— Paracelsus his Archidoxes in ten Books.
1661.
[See also the works of John Hester, under
Medicine, and Anatomy and Surgery, below.]

(8) Medicine

(a) Modern Authorities

Bucknill, J. C. The Medical Knowledge of
Shakespeare. 1860.
Creighton, C. A History of Epidemics in
Britain. 2 vols. Cambridge, 1891–4.
Moyes, John. Medicine and Kindred Arts in
the Plays of Shakespeare. Glasgow, 1896.
Crawfurd, Raymond. The King's Evil. Ox-
ford, 1911.
Wilson, F. P. The Plague in Shakespeare's
London. Oxford, 1927.

Power, Sir D'Arcy. Medicine in the British
Isles. New York, 1930.
Comrie, J. D. History of Scottish Medicine.
2 vols. 1932.

(b) Contemporary Treatises

A litil boke the which traytied many gode
thinges for the Pestilence. [1486?]; [1488?];
[1490?]; [1510?]; [1520?]. [Extracts in
D. W. Singer, Some Plague Tractates, Proc.
Royal Soc. Medicine, IX, 1916. Tr. Eng. from
Canutus. See A. C. Klebs and E. Droz,
Remèdes contre la Peste, Paris, 1925.]
Caxton, William (1422?–1491). In this tretyse
that is cleped Governayle of helthe. 1489; [?]
(W. de Worde); rptd W. Blades, 1858.
Linacre, Thomas. De Sanitate tuenda. Paris,
1517 and 1538; Venice, 1523; Cologne, 1526;
Tübingen, 1541; Lyons, 1548 and 1549.
[From Galen.]
—— Methodus Medendi. Paris, 1519 and
1538; Venice, 1527. [From Galen.]
—— Galeni Pergamensis de temperamentis et
de inequali intemperie libri tres. Cambridge,
1521; ed. facs. J. F. Payne, 1881.
—— Galeni Pergameni de Pulsuum usu. 1522.
—— Galeni Pergameni de Naturalibus Facul-
tatibus libri tres. 1523; Lyons, 1548.
—— Galeni Pergameni de symptomatum
differentiis liber unus. Ejusdem de sympto-
matum causis libri tres. 1524.
[See J. N. Johnson, The Life of Thomas
Linacre. 2 vols. 1835; Sir W. Osler, Thomas
Linacre, Cambridge, 1908.]
The seynge of Uryns. 1525; 1526; [1530?];
[1540?]; [1541?]; 1544; 1548; [1550?] (bis);
1555; 1562.
A newe boke of medecynes intytulyed the
Treasure of pore men. [1526?]; 1539 (bis);
1540; 1544; 1551; 1556; [1560?].
The Judycyall of Uryns. [1527?]
Copland, Robert (fl. 1508–1547). Secreta
Secretorum. The secrete of secretes of
Arystotle. 1528. [Spurious.]
—— The Hye Way to the Spyttel Hous.
[1536?] [Rptd A. V. Judges, The Eliza-
bethan Underworld, 1930.]
Paynell, Thomas (fl. 1528–1568). Schola
Salernitana. Regimen sanitatis Salerni.
1528; 1530; 1535; 1541; 1557; 1575, etc.
—— De Morbo Gallico. 1533; 1536; 1539;
1540. [From Ulrich von Hutten.]
—— A moche profitable Treatise against the
Pestilence. 1534.
The Antidotharius, in the which thou mayest
lerne how thou shalt make playsters, salves,
[etc.]. [1530?]; [1538?] (bis); [1542?];
[1545?].
Prognosticacion drawn out of Ipocras.
[1530?]

Moulton, Thomas. This is the Myrrour or Glasse of Helth. [1539?] (*bis*); [1540?] (3 edns); [1541?] (*bis*); [1545?]; [1546?]; [1550?] (*bis*); [1565?]; [1580?].

Elyot, Sir Thomas (1499?–1546). The Castel of helth. 1539; 1541; 1547; [1559?]; [1560?]; 1561; 1572; 1580; 1587, etc.; rptd photo. facs. New York. 1936.

Boorde, Andrew. The book for to lerne a man to be wyse in buylding of his house for the helth of body. [1540?]

—— A compendyous Regyment or a dyetary of Helth. [1542?]; [1547?]; 1562, etc.; ed. F. J. Furnivall, EETS. Ex. Ser. 1870.

—— The Breviary of Healthe. 1552; 1557; 1575; 1587; 1598. [Extracts in Furnivall.]

Phaer (or Phayer), Thomas (1510?–1560). The Regiment of Lyfe, whereunto is added a treatise of the pestilence with the booke of speciall remedies for all diseases in young children. 1544; 1546; 1550; 1553; 1560; [1565?]; 1567; [1578?], 1596; [?]. [From Goeurot.]

[See John Rühra, Annals of Medical History, vol. ii, New York, 1919.]

Caius, John (1510–1573). De Medendi Methodo libri duo, ex Cl. Galeni & Jo. Baptistæ Montani. Basle, 1544 and 1558.

——De tuenda Valetudine. Basle, 1549. [Galen.]

—— A Boke, or Counseill against the disease commonly called the sweate, or sweatyng sicknesse. 1552; rptd J. C. F. Hecker (in The Epidemics of the Middle Ages, 1844).

—— Opera aliquot et versiones. Louvain, 1556; 1721.

—— Works. Ed. E. S. Roberts [with Life of Caius by John Venn], Cambridge, 1912.

Recorde, Robert. The Urinal of Physicke. 1547; 1548; 1567; 1599.

Llwyd, Humphrey (1527–1568). The treasuri of helth. [1550?] (*bis*); 1558; 1585. [From Petrus Hispanus, Pope John XXI.]

—— A litel treatise conteyninge the jugement of urynes. 1553. [From Vasseus.]

Ward, William (1534–1604?). The Secretes of Alexis of Piemount, conteinyng remedies agaynst diseases. 1558; 1559; 1562; 1568; 1580; 1615.

—— The Seconde Parte of the Secretes. 1560; 1563; [1568?]; [1580]; 1614.

—— The Thyrde and Last Parte of the Secretes. 1562; 1566; 1578; 1614.

Bullein, William (d. 1576). Bulleins Bulwarke of defence againste all Sicknes, Sornes, and Woundes. 1562; 1579.

—— A comfortable Regiment against Pleurisi. 1562.

—— A dialogue bothe pleasaunt and pietifull, against the fever Pestilence. 1564; 1573; 1578; ed. M. W. and A. H. Bullen, EETS. Ex. Ser. 1888.

Bullein, William. A newe Boke entituled the Governement of Healthe. 1558 (*bis*); 1559; 1595.

[See A. H. Bullen, Elizabethans, 1924.]

Newton, Thomas (1542?–1607). The Touchstone of Complexions. 1565; 1576; 1581; 1633. [From Lemnius.]

—— A Delectable Dialogue concerning Phisick and Phisitions. 1580. [From Mexia.]

—— Approved Medicines and Cordial Receiptes. 1580.

—— The Olde mans Dietarie. 1586. [Contains first ptd English version of the Hippocratic Oath.]

—— An Herbal for the Bible. 1587. [From Lemnius.]

Skeyne, Gilbert (1522?–1599). Ane Breve Description of the Pest. Edinburgh, 1568; ed. W. F. Skene, Bannatyne Club, 1860.

Androse, Richard. A very excellent booke. The fourth and finall booke of secretes. 1569; 1578; 1614. [From Alexis of Piedmont.]

Baker, George (1540–1600). The Composition or making of the Oil called Oleum Magistrale. 1574.

—— The Newe Jewell of Health. 1576. [From Gesner.]

—— The practise of the new and old phisicke. 1599. [From Gesner.]

Bright, Timothy (1551?–1615). [The inventor of modern shorthand in Characterie; an art of short, swift, and secret writing, 1588.] A Treatise wherein is declared the sufficiencie of English Medicines. 1580 (*bis*); 1615.

—— Hygiena, id est de Sanitate tuenda medicinae. 1582.

—— Medicinae therapeuticae. 1583.

—— In physicam G. A. Scribonii animadversiones. 1584; Frankfort, 1593. [Dedicated to Sir Philip Sidney.]

—— A Treatise of Melancholy, Containing the causes thereof. 1586 (*bis*); 1613.

[See M. Levy, William Shakespeare and Timothy Bright, 1910; W. J. Carlton, Timothe Bright, 1911; M. I. O'Sullivan, Hamlet and Dr Timothy Bright, PMLA. xli, 1926.]

Hester, John (d. 1593). A Compendium of the rationall secretes of Phiorvanti. 1582.

—— These Oiles, waters, and other Compositions; made to be solde. [1585?]

—— An excellent Treatise teaching howe to cure the French-pockes, drawne out of Paracelsus. 1590. [From Hermanni.]

—— The Pearle of Practise, for Phisicke and Chirurgerie. 1594.

—— A hundred and foureteene experiments and cures. 1596; [1596?]; 1633. [From Paracelsus.]

—— The first part of the Key of Philosophie. 1596.

Aristotle. Problemata. 1583; tr. Eng. 1595; Edinburgh, 1595; 1597; 1607, etc. [See Sir D'Arcy Power, The Foundations of Medical History, Baltimore, 1931.]

Barrough, Philip. The Method of Phisicke. 1583; 1590; 1596; 1601; 1610; 1617; 1624; 1634.

Cogan, Thomas (1545?–1607). The Haven of Health. 1584; 1588; 1589; 1596; 1605; 1612; 1636.

Kellwaye, Simon. A defensative against the Plague. 1593.

Present Remedies against the plague. 1594; 1603; ed. facs. (from 1603 edn) W. P. Barrett, Shakespeare Ass. 1933.

Harington, Sir John (1561–1612). The Metamorphosis of Ajax. 1596; ed. P. Warlock and J. Lindsay, 1928.

—— The Englishmans Doctor. Or the Schoole of Salerne. 1607; 1608; 1609; Edinburgh, 1613 (in Conservandae bonae valetudinis praecepta); 1617; 1624; ed. F. R. Packard and F. H. Garrison, 1922.

Wateson, George. A Rich Storehouse or Treasury for the Diseased. 1596; 1607 (corrected and enlarged by A. T.); 1612; 1616; 1630; 1631.

—— The Cures of the Diseased in remote regions. 1598; ed. Charles Singer, Oxford, 1915.

Tooker, William (1558?–1621). Charisma: Sive Donum Sanationis. 1597. [On the King's evil.]

Mosan, J. Praxis medicinae universalis, or a general practise of physicke, 1598; 1605; 1611. [From Wirsung.]

Lodge, Thomas (1558?–1625). A Treatise of the Plague. 1603.

—— The Poore mans Talent. Ed. Sir E. Gosse (in The Complete Works of Thomas Lodge, vol. IV, Hunterian Club, 1883).

Dekker, Thomas (1570?–1641?). The Wonderfull Yeare. [1603?]; rptd 1924.

—— The Ravens Almanacke, foretelling of a plague, famine and civile warre. 1609.

—— A rod for run-awayes. 1625.

[See F. P. Wilson, The Plague Pamphlets of Thomas Dekker, Oxford, 1926.]

Jorden, Edward (1569–1632). A briefe discourse of a disease called the Suffocation of the Mother. 1603.

—— A Discourse of naturall Bathes and minerall Waters. 1631; 1632; 1633; ed. Thomas Guidott, 1669 and 1673.

Grahame, Simion (1570?–1614). The Anatomie of humors. Edinburgh, 1609; rptd Bannatyne Club, 1830.

H., S. The whole Aphorismes of Hippocrates. 1610.

Cotta, John (1575?–1650?). A short Discoverie of the Dangers of ignorant Practisers of Physicke. 1612; 1617; 1619.

College of Physicians, London. Pharmacopoea Londinensis. 1618 (bis); 1627; 1632; 1638.

Burton, Robert (1577–1640). The anatomy of melancholy. 1621; 1624; 1628; 1632; 1638, etc. [See also pp. 829–30 above.]

Hart. James (b. 1580–1590). The Arraignment of Urines. 2 pts, 1623–5. [From Forestus.]

—— The Anatomie of Urines, or the second part of our discourse. 1625; 1652.

—— κλινική or the Diet of the Diseased. 1633.

Taylor, John (1580–1653). The Fearefull Summer: or Londons Calamitie. Oxford, 1625; 1636. [Also in collected Workes, 1630; rptd Spenser Soc. 1868–9.]

Harvey, William (1578–1657). Exercitatio Anatomica de Motu Cordis et Sanguinis in Animalibus. Frankfort, 1628; Venice, 1635; Leyden, 1639; Padua, 1643; Amsterdam, 1645; Rotterdam, 1654 and 1660; London, 1660; Rotterdam, 1671, etc.; rptd collotype facs. Royal College of Physicians, 1928. Tr. Eng. (as The Anatomical Exercises of Dr William Harvey, concerning the motion of the Heart and Blood) 1653, 1673 (ed. Geoffrey Keynes, 1928); M. Ryan, 1832; R. Willis (in edn of Works, Sydenham Soc.), 1847, 1889, and 1907, 1923 (Everyman's Lib.); G. Moreton, Canterbury, 1894 (with facs. of Latin original); C. D. Leake, Springfield, 1928 and 1930 (with facs. of original). [See Charles Singer, The Discovery of the Circulation of the Blood, 1922.]

—— Exercitatio Anatomica De Circulatione sanguinis. Ad Joannem Riolanum. Cambridge, 1649; Rotterdam, 1649; Paris, 1650. [Later included with edns of De Motu Cordis.]

—— Exercitationes de Generatione Animalium. 1651; Amsterdam, 1651 (3 edns) and 1662; Padua, 1666; Amsterdam, 1674; Hague, 1680; tr. Eng. (as Anatomical Exercitations, concerning the Generation of Living Creatures) 1653, and R. Willis (in Works, 1847).

—— Bibliotheca Anatomica. Ed. D. Le Clerc and J. J. Mangetus, Geneva, 1685 and 1699.

—— Opera Omnia. Leyden, 1737; 1766; tr. Eng. (as The Works of William Harvey) Robert Willis, Sydenham Soc. 1847.

—— Prelectiones Anatomiae Universalis. 1886. [Autotype reproduction of MS in BM. dated 1616.]

[See Sir D'Arcy Power, William Harvey, 1897; Geoffrey Keynes, A Bibliography of the Writings of William Harvey, 1928; Archibald Malloch, William Harvey, New York, 1929; Sir Wilmot Herringham, The Life and Times of William Harvey, Oxford, 1930.]

Primerose, James (d. 1659). Exercitationes in librum de motu cordis. Adversus G. Harveum. 1630.
—— Academia Monspeliensis descripta. 1631.
—— De vulgi in medicina erroribus. 1638; tr. Eng. R. Wittie, 1651.
—— The Antimoniall Cup twice Cast. Tr. Eng. R. Wittie, 1640.
Brian, Thomas. The Pisse-prophet or Certaine Pisse-pot Lectures. 1637.
W., T. The Charitable Physitian, shewing the manner to make and prepare all remedies. 1639. [Gives prices of drugs, etc. From Philibert Guibert.]
Browne, Sir Thomas (1605–1682). Religio Medici. 1642 (*bis*); 1643 (first authorised edn); 1645, etc.
—— Pseudodoxia Epidemica; or Enquiries into very many received Tenents. 1646; 1650; 1658; 1659; 1669; 1672; 1686, etc. [See Geoffrey Keynes, A Bibliography of Sir Thomas Browne, 1924. See also pp. 834–5 above.]
Ross, Alexander. Medicus Medicatus: or the physicians religion cured. 1645.
—— Arcana Microcosmi: or the hid secrets of man's body disclosed. 1651; 1652 ('with a refutation of Doctor Brown's Vulgar Errors, the Lord Bacon's Natural History, and Doctor Harvey's Book de Generatione').
Whistler, Daniel (1619–1684). De Morbo puerili Anglorum quem vocant 'The Rickets.' Leyden, 1645; 1684.
Culpeper, Nicholas (1616–1654). Pharmacopoeia Londinensis: Or the London Dispensatory. 1649; 1653; 1661; 1667; 1683.
—— Semeiotica Uranica or an Astrological judgment of Diseases. 1651; 1655; 1658.
—— A Directory for Midwives. 1651; 1656; 1693.
—— The English Physitian: or an Astrologo-Physical Discourse of the Vulgar Herbs of this Nation. 1652; 1653; 1661; 1695, etc.; ed. (as Culpeper's Complete Herbal), 1923. [See Selections from the English Physician, ed. O. W. Hunt, 1929.]
—— The Anatomy of the body of Man. 1653. [From Veslingius.]
—— Culpepers School of Physick. 1659; 1678.
Charleton, Walter (1619–1707). A Ternary of Paradoxes. The Magnetic Cure of Wounds. Nativity of Tartar in Wine. Image of God in Man. 1650. [From van Helmont.]
—— Natural History of Nutrition, Life and Voluntary Motion. 1659.
Glisson, Francis (1597–1677). Tractatus de Rachitide. 1650; tr. Eng. 1668.
Andrews, William. The Astrological Physitian, shewing how to find out the cause and nature of a disease. 1656.

Hall, John (1575–1635) [married Shakespeare's eldest daughter]. Select Observations on English Bodies, and Cures both Empiricall and Historicall. Tr. Eng. J. C[ook], 1657, 1679, 1683.
Thompson, J. Helmont Disguised; or The vulgar Errors of Impericall and unskilfull Practisers of Physick confuted. 1657.

(9) ANATOMY AND SURGERY

(a) *Modern Authorities*

South, J. F. Memorials of the Craft of Surgery in England. Ed. Sir D'Arcy Power, 1886.
Young, Sidney. Annals of the Barber-Surgeons of London. 1890.
Power, Sir D'Arcy. The Elizabethan Revival of Surgery. 1902.
—— The Place of the Tudor Surgeons in English Literature. Proc. Royal Soc. Medicine, 1927.
—— Epoch-making Books in British Surgery. British Journ. of Surgery, 1927–30. [John of Arderne, Gale, Clowes, Lowe, Woodall, Johnson's Parey.]
—— Selected Writings. Oxford, 1931.

(b) *Contemporary Treatises*

The noble experyence of the vertuous handywarke of surgeri. 1525. [From Hieronymus von Braunschweig.]
Jonas. The byrth of Mankynde. 1540. [For later edns see Raynalde. From Rösslin.]
Copland, Robert. The questyonary of Cyurgyens. 1542; 1579 (and Guydos questions, newly corrected, by George Baker). [From Guy de Chauliac.]
Traheron, Bartholomew (1510?–1558). The most excellent workes of Chirurgerye, made by John Vigon. 1543; 1550; 1571; 1586.
Raynalde, Thomas (*fl.* 1540–1551). The byrth of mankynde, otherwyse named the Womans booke. 1545; 1552; 1560; 1565 (*bis*); [1585?]; 1598, etc. [See Sir D'Arcy Power, The Birth of Mankind. A Bibliographical Study, Library, VIII, 1927.]
Geminus, Thomas (1500?–1570). Compendiosa totius anatomie delineatio. 1545. [From Vesalius. Part tr. Eng. Nicholas Udall (*q.v.*) 1553 and 1559.]
Udall, Nicholas (1505–1556). Compendiosa totius anatomie delineatio. 1553; 1559. [Geminus edn of Vesalius, tr. into English. Does not contain trn of Vesalius Epitome, but instead adds a treatise almost identical with Vicary's The Anatomy of Man's body. See S. V. Larkey, Library, XIII, 1933, pp. 367–94.]

Vicary, Thomas (1490?–1561). A profitable treatise of the Anatomie of mans body. 1548 (no copy extant); 1577; rptd F. J. Furnivall, EETS. Ex. Ser. 1887.

—— The Englishmans treasure. With the true anatomye of mans body. 1585; 1586; 1587; 1596; 1613; 1626; 1633, etc. [See Sir D'Arcy Power, Notes on the Bibliography of three Sixteenth Century English Books, Library, II, 1922; and The Education of a Surgeon under Thomas Vicary, British Journ. Surgery, 1921.]

Gale, Thomas (1507–1587). Certaine Workes of Chirurgerie. 1563; 1586.

—— Certaine workes of Galens called Methodus Medendi. 1586.

Halle, John (1529?–1566?). A most excellent and learned woorke called Chirurgia parva Lanfranci. 1565. [Contains an Historicall expostulation against the beastly abuses of Chyrurgerie and Physicke. Rptd Percy Soc. 1842. See Sir D'Arcy Power, John Halle and Sixteenth Century Consultations, Proc. Royal Soc. Medicine, 1918.]

Banister, John (1540–1610). A needefull, new and necessarie treatise of chyrurgerie. 1575; 1633.

—— The Historie of Man, sucked from the sappe of the most approved Anathomistes. 1578.

—— A compendious chyrurgerie. 1585. [From Wecker.]

—— An antidotarie Chyrurgicall. 1589.

—— The Works of John Banister. 1633.

Clowes, William (1540?–1604). A treatise touching the cure of the Morbus Gallicus by Unctions. 1579; 1585. [Rptd in the following two books.]

—— A proved practise for all young Chirurgians, concerning burnings with gunpowder, and woundes made with gunshot, etc. 1588; 1591.

—— A profitable and necessarie booke of observations for all those that are burned with the flame of gunpowder. 1596; 1637.

—— A right fruitefull Treatise for the artificiall cure of Struma, the Evill cured by Kinges. 1602.

Hester, John (d. 1593). A short Discours upon Chirurgerie. 1580; 1626. [From Fiorvanti.]

—— The Sclopotarie of Quercetanus, or his booke containing the cure of wounds received by shot of gunne. 1590.

Read, John (fl. 1587–1588). A most excellent Method of curing woundes. 1588. [From Arcaeus. Contains first ptd edn of John of Arderne's treatise on fistulo in ano, and one of the earliest English versions of the Hippocratic Oath.]

Lowe, Peter (1550?–1612?). An Easie certaine and perfect method to cure the Spanish sicknes. 1596.

—— A Discourse of the whole Art of Chyrurgerie. With the Presages of Hyppocrates. 1597; 1612–11; 1634; 1654–5. [From Canape.] [See James Finlayson, Account of the Life and Works of Maister Peter Lowe, Glasgow, 1889.]

Crooke, Helkiah (1576–1635). Μικροκοσμογραφία. A description of the body of man. 1615; 1631.

—— An explanation of the fashion and use of instruments of chirurgery. 1634. [From Paré.]

Read, Alexander (1586?–1641). Σωματογραφία 'Ανθρωπίνα or a Description of the Body of Man. 1616; 1634. [From Crooke.]

—— The Chirurgicall Lectures of tumors and ulcers. 1632.

—— A Treatise of all the Muscles of the whole Bodie. 1637; 1650; 1659.

—— A Treatise of the first part of Chirurgerie. 1638; 1650; 1687.

—— The Manuall of the Anatomy or Dissection of the Body of Man. 1638; 1642; 1650; 1653. [See Walter Menzies, Alexander Read, Physician and Surgeon, Library, XII, 1931.]

Woodall, John (1556?–1643). The Surgeons mate. 1617; 1639 ('with a treatise of the cure of the plague'); 1655.

—— Woodalls Viaticum; the path-way to the Surgions Chest. 1628; 1639.

—— The Cure of the Plague, by an antidote called Aurum Vitae. 1640 (bis).

Johnson, Thomas (d. 1644). The Workes of Ambrose Parey. 1634; 1649; 1665; 1678.

Cooke, James. Mellificium Chirurgiae; or the marrow of many good authors. [Before 1655?]; 1662; 1676.

—— Supplementum Chirurgiae; or the supplement to the Marrow of Chyrurgerie. 1655. [See H. E. Clark, A Rare Medical Work and its Author, 1899.]

Glisson, Francis. De Hepatis. 1654; Amsterdam, 1659.

Wharton, Thomas (1614–1673). Adenographia. 1656; Amsterdam, 1659.

Jackson, Henry. Μικροκοσμογραφία. 1660; 1664. [From Berengarius of Carpi.]

(10) HERBALS

(a) Modern Authorites

Grindon, L. H. Shakspere Flora. Manchester, 1883.

Ellacombe, H. N. Plant-lore of Shakespeare. 1884.

Arber, Agnes. Herbals. Cambridge, 1912.
Rohde, E. S. The Old English Herbals. 1922.
Gunther, R. T. Early British Botanists and their Gardens. Oxford, 1922.
Savage, F. G. The Flora and Folk-Lore of Shakespeare. 1923.

(b) Contemporary Treatises

A newe mater: the which is called an Herball. 1525; 1526; [1530?] (as Macers herbal practysed by Doctor Lynacro); [1530?] (as A newe herball of Macer); [1535?] (as A boke of the propertyes of herbes); [1535?]; [1541?]; 1541; 1546; ed. Anthony Askham, 1550 (as A little herball); 1561; ed. Walter Cary, 1552; [1553?]; [1560?]. [From Latin.]
The Grete Herball. 1526; 1529; 1539; 1561.
Andrewe, Laurence (fl. 1510–1537). The vertuose boke of dystyllatyon. 1527; [1528?]; [1530?]. [From Hieronymus von Braunschweig.]
Turner, William (d. 1568). Libellus de re herbaria novus. 1538; rptd (with life) B. D. Jackson, 1877.
—— Historia de Naturis Herbarum. Cologne, 1544.
—— The Names of herbes in Greke, Latin, Englishe, Duche and Frenche. 1548; ed. J. Britten, English Dialect Soc. 1881.
—— A newe herball. 1551 (and second part 'With the Booke of the natures of the bathes in England'); Cologne, 1562, 1568 (First and seconde partes with the thirde parte).
—— A newe boke of the natures of all wines. 1568.
Secretes of the Vertues of Herbes. [N.d.]; [1560?]; [1570?]; 1595; 1599, etc. [Erroneously attrib. to Albertus Magnus.]
Frampton, John (fl. 1577–1596). The three bookes written in the Spanishe tonge. 1577 (also issued as Joyfull newes out of the newe founde worlde); 1580 (Whereunto are added three other bookes of the Bezoar stone); 1596; ed. S. Gaselee, 1925. [From Monardes.]
Lyte, Henry (1529?–1607). A niewe herball or historie of plantes. 1578; 1586; 1595; 1619; 1606 (as Rams little Dodeon. A briefe epitome of the new Herbal abridged by W. Ram). [From Dodoens.]
Gerard, John (1545–1612). Catalogus arborum. 1596; 1599; ed. B. D. Jackson, 1876.
—— The herball, or generall historie of Plantes. 1597; 1633 (very much enlarged by T. Johnson, q.v.); 1634; 1636.
[See M. Woodward, Gerard's Herball. The Essence thereof distilled, from the Edition of Thomas Johnson, 1636, 1927; Alice M. Tudor, A Little Book of Healing Herbs, gathered from an Old Herball, 1927.]

Langham, William. The Garden of Health, conteyning the vertues and properties of Simples and Plants. 1579 (for 1597); 1633.
Johnson, Thomas (d. 1644). Iter plantarum investigationis in agrum Cantianum. 1629.
—— Descriptio itineris plantarum suscepti in agrum Cantianum. 1632.
—— Mercurius botanicus sive plantarum gratia suscepti itineris anno 1634 descriptio. 3 pts [1634–41]; tr. Eng. W. Jenkyn Thomas, Bangor, 1908.
—— Opuscula Omnia Botanica. Ed. T. S. Ralph, 1847.
Parkinson, John (1567–1650). Paradisi in sole, or a garden of flowers. 1629 (re-issued 1635).
—— Theatrum botanicum; the theater of plants, or an herball of a large extent. 1640.
How, William (1620–1656). Phytologia Britannica. 1650.
Culpeper, Nicholas. The English Physitian: or an Astrologo-physical Discourse of the vulgar Herbs of this Nation, 1652; 1653; 1661; 1695; ed. (as Culpeper's Complete Herbal) 1923. [Selections, ed. O. W. Hunt, 1929.]
Coles, W. Adam in Eden: or Nature's Paradise. The history of plants, fruits, herbs, and flowers. 1657.

(11) ZOOLOGY

[See also the sections on Horsemanship and Farriery, and Hunting, Coursing, Hawking, Fowling, Angling, pp. 393–4 above.]

(a) Modern Authorities

Shipley, A. E. Zoology in the Time of Shakespeare. Edinburgh Rev. July 1912.

(b) Contemporary Treatises

Turner, William. Avium praecipuarum, quarum apud Plinium et Aristotelem mentio est, brevis & succincta historia. Cologne, 1544; ed. A. H. Evans (Turner on Birds), 1913.
—— Dialogus de avibus et earum nominibus. Cologne, 1544.
Wotton, Edward. De Differentiis Animalium. Paris, 1552.
Maplet, John (d. 1592). A Greene Forest, or a naturall historie. 1567; rptd 1930.
Caius, John (1510–1573). De Canibus Britannicis. 1570; tr. Eng. A. Fleming, 1576 ('Of English Dogs', rptd in E. Arber, An English Garner, vol. III, 1880.)
Moffett, Thomas (1553–1604). The silkewormes and their flies. 1599.

Moffett, Thomas. Insectorum sive minimorum animalium theatrum. 1634; tr. Eng. J. Rowland (appended to 1658 edn of Topsell.)

Topsell, Edward (d. 1638?). The historie of fourefootid beastes collected out of all the volumes of Conrad Gesner. 1607; ed. J. R[owland], 1658 (with Moffett's Theatre of Insects).

—— The historie of serpents; or the second booke of living creatures. 1608. [Extracts in The Elizabethan Zoo, ed. M. St Clare Byrne, 1926.]

Geffe, N. The perfect use of silkwormes. 1607. [From Olivier de Serres.]

Stallenge, William. Instructions for the increasing of mulberie trees and breeding of silke-wormes. 1609 (bis).

Butler, Charles (d. 1647). The Feminine Monarchie, or a Treatise concerning Bees. 1609; 1623; 1634 (as The Feminin' Monarchi', or the Histori of Bee's [in phonetic spelling]).

Morrell, William. New England. Or a briefe enarration of the ayre, earth, water, fish and fowles of that country. 1625.

Animalium quadrupedum, avium delineationes: A Booke of beast birds, etc. [1628?]; 1630.

Levett, John. The ordering of bees. 1634.

(12) WITCHCRAFT AND MAGIC

(a) Modern Authorities

Sharpe, C. K. Historical Account of the Belief in Witchcraft in Scotland. 1884.

Lea, C. H. A History of the Inquisition of the Middle Ages. 3 vols. 1888.

Moore, G. H. Bibliographical Notes on Witchcraft. 1888.

Winsor. J. The Literature of Witchcraft in New England. Proc. American Antiquarian Soc. 1895.

Jaggard, W. Folklore, Superstition and Witchcraft in Shakespeare. A Bibliography. 1896.

Ferguson, John. Bibliographical Notes on the Witchcraft Literature of Scotland. Edinburgh, 1897.

Notestein, W. A History of Witchcraft in England from 1558 to 1781. American Hist. Ass. 1911.

Murray, M. A. The Witch-Cult in Western Europe. Oxford, 1921.

Summers, M. The History of Witchcraft and Demonology. 1926.

—— The Geography of Witchcraft. 1927.

Ewen, C. L'E. Witch-Hunting and Witch-Trials. 1929.

Kittredge, G. L. Witchcraft in Old and New England. Cambridge, U.S.A. 1929.

(b) Contemporary Treatises

[Fuller bibliographies will be found in the works of Notestein and Murray listed above.]

H[arrison], R[obert] (d. 1585?). Of ghostes and spirites walking by night. 1572; 1596; ed. J. Dover Wilson and M. Yardley, Shakespeare Ass. 1929. [From Lavater.]

Brigges, Agnes. The disclosing of a late counterfeyted possesion by the devyl in two maydens. [1574.]

'Cooper, Margaret.' A true and most dreadfull discourse of a Woman possessed with the Devill. 1584; rptd Weston, 1886.

Scot, Reginald (1538?–1599). The discoverie of Witchcraft. 1584; 1651; 1665; rptd 1886; ed. M. Summers, 1930.

Gifford, George (d. 1620). A discourse of the subtill practises of Devilles. 1587.

—— A Dialogue concerning Witches And Witchcrafts. 1593; 1603; rptd Percy Soc. 1842.

Holland, Henry (d. 1604). A Treatise against Witchcraft. 1590.

—— Spirituall preservatives against the Pestilence. 1593.

The most strange discoverie of the three witches of Warboys. 1593.

Nash, Thomas (1567–1601). The Terrors of the Night, Or a Discourse of Apparitions. 1594.

—— Works. Ed. R. B. McKerrow, 5 vols. 1904–10.

Darrell, John. A brief narration of the possession of W. Sommers. 1598.

James I (1566–1625). Daemonologie, in forme of a dialogue. Edinburgh, 1598; 1603; rptd 1924.

Harsnet, Samuel (1561–1631). A discovery of the fraudulent practises of J. Darrell. 1599.

—— A declaration of egregious popish impostors. 1603 (re-issued 1604, 1605).

Jorden, Edward (1569–1632). A briefe discourse of a disease called the suffocation of the Mother. 1603.

Perkins, William (1558–1602). A Discourse of the Damned Art of Witchcraft. 1608; 1610; 1629.

Mason, James. The Anatomie of Sorcerie. 1612.

Potts, Thomas. The Wonderfull Discoverie of Witches in the Countie of Lancaster. 1613–12; rptd 1838 and Chetham Soc. 1845; ed. G. B. Harrison, 1929.

Cotta, John. The Triall of Witchcraft shewing the true methode of the discovery. 1616; 1624; 1625.

Roberts, Alexander. A Treatise of Witchcraft. With a true Narration of the Witchcrafts which Mary Smith did practise. 1616.

Cooper, Thomas. The Mystery of Witch-Craft. 1617.

Bernard, Richard (1568–1641). A Guide to Grand Jury Men. 1627; 1629; 1630.

Fairfax, Edward (d. 1635). A Discourse of Witchcraft. Philobiblon Soc. Misc. vol. v, 1858–9; rptd Harrogate, 1882.

Davenport, John (1597–1670). The Witches of Huntingdon. 1646.

Gaule, John. Select cases of Conscience touching Witches and Witchcrafts. 1646.

Gaule, John. Occult Philosophie. [N.d.]

Hopkins, Mathew (d. 1647). The Discovery of Witches. 1647; ed. M. Summers, 1928.

Stearne, J. A confirmation and Discovery of Witchcraft. 1648.

Filmer, Sir Robert (d. 1653). An advertisement to the Jurymen of England touching Witches. 1653.

Gardiner, R. Englands Grievance Discovered. 1655.

S. V. L.

7. SCOTTISH LITERATURE

I. GENERAL INTRODUCTION

[In addition to the bibliographies listed below, the following sources of information should be borne in mind: the county histories of Scotland; the publications of the Abbotsford, Bannatyne, Hunterian, Maitland and Spalding (3 sers.) Clubs, and the Scottish Text Society (STS.); the Scottish Historical Review, Glasgow, 1903–28; and Scottish Notes and Queries, Aberdeen, 1888– . The Mitchell Library, Glasgow, has a unique collection of books relating to Scotland.]

(1) BIBLIOGRAPHIES

Aldis, H. G. A List of Books printed in Scotland before 1700. Edinburgh Bibliog. Soc. 1904.

Terry, C. S. A Catalogue of the Publications of Scottish Historical and Kindred Clubs and Societies. Glasgow, 1909.

Geddie, W. A Bibliography of Middle-Scots Poets. STS. 1912.

Cowan, W. A Bibliography of the Book of Common Order and Psalm Book of the Church of Scotland, 1556–1644. Edinburgh, 1913.

Maclean, D. Typographia Scoto-Gadelica, Books in the Gaelic of Scotland, 1567 to 1914. Edinburgh, 1915. [Based on J. Reid, Bibliotheca Scoto-Celtica, Glasgow, 1832.]

Fasti Ecclesiae Scoticanae. 7 vols. Edinburgh, 1915–28. [Contains bibliographies of church and parish histories.]

Black, G. F. A List of Works relating to Scotland. New York, 1916.

Anderson, A. K. A Short Bibliography on Scottish History and Literature. Glasgow, 1922.

Bibliography of Scottish History. National Book Council, 1926; Stirling Lib. Glasgow, 1927.

Pollard, A. W. and Redgrave, G. R. A Short-title catalogue of Books printed in England, Scotland and Ireland, 1475–1640. Bibliog. Soc. 1926.

Johnstone, J. F. K. and Robertson, A. W. Bibliographia Aberdoniensis. Vol. I, 1472–1640; vol. II, 1640–1700. Third Spalding Club, Aberdeen, 1929–30.

Stuart, M. Guide to Works of Reference on the History and Genealogy of Scottish Families. Edinburgh, 1930.

(2) LITERARY HISTORIES

Irving, D. The Lives of the Scottish Poets, with Dissertations on the Literary History of Scotland. 2 vols. Edinburgh, 1804.
—— Lives of Scotish Writers. 2 vols. Edinburgh, 1839.
—— The History of Scotish Poetry. Ed. J. A. Carlyle, Edinburgh, 1861.

Ross, J. M. Scottish History and Literature to the Period of the Reformation. Ed. J. Brown, Glasgow, 1884.

Walker, H. Three Centuries of Scottish Literature. 2 vols. Glasgow, 1893.

Henderson, T. F. Scottish Vernacular Literature. 1898; 1910. Sir David Lyndsay and the Later Scottish 'Makaris'. CHEL. vol. III, ch. 6, 1909.
—— Scottish Popular Poetry before Burns. CHEL. vol. IX, ch. 14, 1912.

Millar, J. H. A Literary History of Scotland. 1903.
—— Scottish Prose of the 17th and 18th Centuries. Glasgow, 1912.

Brown, P. H. Reformation and Renascence in Scotland. CHEL. vol. III, ch. 7, 1909.

Gregory Smith, G. Scottish Literature. 1919.

Mill, A. J. Medieval Plays in Scotland. 1928.

Mackenzie, A. M. An Historical Survey of Scottish Literature to 1714. 1933.

(3) THE CULTURAL AND SOCIAL BACKGROUND

(a) The Universities

[The following university histories are especially useful for the information, biographical and bibliographical, they provide about their members.]

Studies in the History and Development of the University of Aberdeen. Ed. P. J. Anderson, 1906. [With excellent bibliography, including university theses and disputations.]

McCulloch, W. E. Viri illustres Universitatum Aberdoniensium. Aberdeen, 1923.

Votiva Tabella: a Memorial Volume of St Andrews University. Glasgow, 1911.

Broer, A. History of the University of Edinburgh. 3 vols. Edinburgh, 1830.

Glasgow Quatercentenary Studies. Ed. G. Neilson, Glasgow, 1907.

Coutts, J. History of the University of Glasgow. Glasgow, 1909.

(b) Miscellaneous Aspects

Williams, A. M. The Scottish School of Rhetoric. Glasgow, 1897.

Leith, W. F. Pre-Reformation Scholars in Scotland in the XVIth Century. Glasgow, 1915. [With bibliography.]

Fleming, J. A. Flemish Influence in Britain. 2 vols. Glasgow, 1930.

Grant, I. F. The Social and Economic Development of Scotland before 1603. Edinburgh, 1930.

Murray, D. Chapters in the History of Book-keeping, Accountancy and Commercial Arithmetic. Glasgow, 1930.

II. POETRY AND DRAMA

A. GENERAL COLLECTIONS AND ANTHOLOGIES

Delitiae Poetarum Scotorum. Ed. [A. Johnston], 2 vols. Amsterdam, 1637.

Poetarum Scotorum Musae sacrae. Ed. W. Lauder, Edinburgh, 1739.

Ancient Scotish Poems. Ed. J. Pinkerton, 2 vols. Edinburgh, 1786. (*Pinkerton*.)

Chronicle of Scottish Poetry. Ed. J. Sibbald, 4 vols. Edinburgh, 1802. (*Sibbald*.)

Various Pieces of Fugitive Scotish Poetry; principally of the Seventeenth Century. Ed. [D. Laing], 2 sers. 1825–53.

Scotish Elegiac Verses, 1629–1729. Ed. [J. Maidment], Edinburgh, 1842.

A Book of Scotish Pasquils, 1568–1715. Ed. [J. Maidment], Edinburgh, 1868.

The Sempill Ballads. Ed. T. G. Stevenson, 1872.

Satirical Poems of the Time of the Reformation. Ed. J. Cranstoun, 3 vols. STS. 1884–93. [See F. Wollmann, Über politisch-satirische Gedichte aus der Schott-Reformationzeit, Vienna, 1898.]

Musa Latina Aberdonensis. Ed. Sir W. D. Geddes and W. K. Leask, 3 vols. New Spalding Club, 1892–1910.

Scottish Poetry of the Sixteenth Century. Ed. G. Eyre-Todd. Glasgow, 1892.

Scottish Poetry of the Seventeenth Century. Ed. G. Eyre-Todd, Glasgow, 1895.

News out of Scotland. Ed. E. M. Brougham, 1926.

A Century of Broadside Elegies. Ed. J. W. Draper, 1928.

Scottish Poetry from Barbour to James VI. Ed. M. M. Gray, 1936.

B. THE LATER SCOTTISH 'MAKARIS'

A. ARBUTHNOT (1538–1593)

[See *Pinkerton*, and The Maitland Quarto Manuscript, ed. W. A. Craigie, STS. 1920.]

JOHN BUREL

[Poems.] Edinburgh, [1595?]. [Unique copy in BM., title wanting. Contents: verse dedication To the Richt High, Lodwik, Duke of Lenox: verse preface: Pamphilus speakand of Lufe [colophon, Heir endis the Historie of Pamphilus], and The Adition of the Translater: An Application concerning our Kings Majesties Persoun: The discriptioun of the Queens Majesties Maist Honorable Entry into Edinburgh, 19 May 1590: The Passage of the Pilgremer, devidit into twa pairts. The Discriptioun of the Queens Majesties Maist Honorable Entry, and The Passage of the Pilgremer rptd in J. Watson, Choice Collection of Comic and Serious Scots Poems, Edinburgh, 1706–1711, and Glasgow, 1869. The Discriptioun rptd in *Sibbald*, vol. III.]

WILLIAM FOWLER OF HAWICK

An Answer to the Calumnious Letter and Erroneous propositiouns of an Apostate named M. Jo. Hammiltoun. Edinburgh, 1581. [Prose.]

An Epitaph Upon the Death of the Right Honorable M. Robert Bowes Esquire, Thesaurer of Barwick: who ended this Life, the sixteenth of November, 1596. Edinburgh, 1597.

A Funeral Sonet, Written vpon the death of the Honorable, and maist verteous Gentlewoman, Elizabeth Dowglas, spouse to M. Samuell Coburne Laird of Temple-Hall. Edinburgh, [1597?].

The Works of William Fowler. Ed. H. W. Meikle, STS. 1914–. [The Drummond MS and Hawthornden MSS contain other poems. Extracts from The Triumphs of Petrarch ptd J. Leyden, Scottish Descriptive Poems, Edinburgh, 1803. See also under the Elizabethan Sonneteers, p. 432 above.]

ALEXANDER HUME (1560?–1609)

Ane Treatise of Conscience. Edinburgh, 1594.

A Treatise of the Felicitie, of the life to come. Edinburgh, 1594.

Hymnes, or Sacred Songs, wherein the right use of Poesie may be espied. Wherein are added the experience of the Author's youth, and certaine precepts serving the practise of Sanctification. Edinburgh, 1594; rptd Bannatyne Club, 1832.

Of the Day Estival; a Poem. [See J. Leyden, Scotish Descriptive Poems, 1803.]

The Practise of Sanctification. Ed. R. M. Fergusson, Paisley, 1901.

The Poems of Alexander Hume. Ed. A. Lawson, STS. 1902.

SIR PATRICK HUME OF POLWART

The Promine, Contemning the maner, place, and time of the maist Illuster King James the sext, his first passing to the feildis. Edinburgh, 1580; rptd D. Laing, Select Remains of the Ancient Scottish Poetry of Scotland, Edinburgh, 1822. [See also Alexander Montgomerie, below p. 898.]

JAMES VI OF SCOTLAND (1566–1625)

The Essayes of a Prentise in the Divine Art of Poesie. Edinburgh, 1584; 1585; ed. R. P. Gillies, 1814; ed. E. Arber, 1869.
His Majesties Poetical Exercises at vacant houres. Edinburgh, 1591; rptd 1818; tr. Dutch, Middelburg, 1593.
New Poems by James I of England, from a hitherto Unpublished Manuscript [BM. Add. MS 24195]. Ed. A. F. Westcott, New York, 1911.
[See also p. 911 below.]

WILLIAM LAUDER (1520?–1573)

Ane Compendious and breve Tractate, Concernyng ye Office and dewtie of Kyngis, Spiritual Pastoris, and temporall Jugis Laitlie Compylit be William Lauder. For the faithfull Instructioun of Kyngis and Prencis. [St. Andrews?], 1556; rptd P. Hall, The Crypt, 1827.
Ane Godlie Tractate or Mirrour. Quhairintill may be easilie perceauit quho Thay are that ar Ingraftit in to Christ. Maid upone this pairt of Text. Written in the Fyftene Chaptour of the Evangell of Iohne. [1568]. [Includes The Lamentatioun of the Pure Twiching the Miserabill Estait of the Present Warld. At Perth. Primo Februarie 1568 [1569], [Edinburgh, 1570?].]
Ane Prettie Mirrour or Conference, betuix the Faithfull Protestant and the Dissemblit false Hypocreit. [Edinburgh, 1570?] [Includes Ane trew and breve Sentencious Descriptioun of the Nature of Scotland, and Ane Gude Exempill be the Butterflie, instructing Men to hait all Harlottrie.]
The Extant Poetical Works of William Lauder. EETS. 2 pts. Pt i, ed. F. Hall, 1864; pt ii, ed. F. J. Furnivall, 1870.

SIR DAVID LINDSAY (1490?–1555)

(a) Bibliography

Poetical Works. Ed. D. Laing, 3 vols. 1879. [Includes bibliography.]
Hamer, Douglas. The Bibliography of Sir David Lindsay. Library, x, 1929.
Poetical Works. Ed. D. Hamer, STS. 1931– . [Includes bibliography.]

(b) Collected Poems

Poetical Works. Ed. G. Chalmers, 3 vols. 1806.
Sir David Lyndesay's Works. Ed. F. Hall, J. Small, and J. A. H. Murray, 5 pts, EETS. 1865–71. [Pt i rev. 1883.]
Poetical Works. Ed. D. Laing, 2 vols. 1871; 3 vols. 1879.
Poetical Works. Ed. D. Hamer, STS. 1931– .

(c) Separate Poems

[For discussions of lost early Scottish-printed quartos of seven poems see Douglas Hamer's bibliographies.]

The complaynte and testament of a Popinjay which lyeth sore wounded and maye not dye, tyll every man hathe herd what he sayth. 1538. [English trn.]
The Tragedy of the late most reverende father David, by the mercie of God Cardinall and archbishoppe of sainct Andrewes. And of the whole realme of Scotland primate, Legate and Chaunceler. And Administrator of the bishoprich of Merapois in Fraunce. And Commendator perpetuall of the Abay of Aberbrothok. [English trn. Item 2 in The Tragical death of David Beaton (by Robert Burrant?), [1548?].]
Ane Dialog betuix Experience and ane Courteour, Off the Miserabyll Estait of the Warld. And is Devidit in Foure Partis. As efter Followis. [St Andrews? 1554?] (John Scot); Rouen, 1558 (bis, quarto and octavo). [To both French edns are added rpts of lost quartos of The Testament and Complaynt of our Soverane Lordis Papyngo, The Dreme of Sir David Lindsay, The Deploratioun of the Deith of Quene Magdalene, and The Tragedy of the Maister [sic] Reverende Fader David [Beaton]. The Dialog was separately rptd by John Scot, c. 1559–60. To unsold copies of the 1st edn, and to all copies of the 2nd edn, of the Dialog, were appended rpts, by Scot, of The Testament and Complaynt of the Papyngo, The Dreme, The Deploratioun of the Deith of Quene Magdalene, and The Complaynt of Sir David Lindsay.]
Ane Dialogue betweene Experience and a Courtier, first compiled in the Schottische tongue, nowe newly corrected and made perfit Englishe [i.e. translated]. 1566 (contains trns of The Tragedie of the Late Cardinal Beaton, The Testament and Complaynt of a Papyngo, The Dreame of Sir David Lindsay, and The Deploratioun of the Deith of Queene Magdalene); 1575 (with 120 lines of The Complaynt and Confession of Bagsche); 1581.

Dialogus Eller En Samtale Imellon For-
farenhed oc en Hofftienere om Verdens
elendige væsen oc begribis udi fire Bøger
om Monarchier. Copenhagen, 1591.
[Danish trn of Ane Dialog, together with
The Dreme, The Complaynt, The Testament and Complaynt of the Papyngo, The
Tragedy of the Late Cardinal Beaton, and
The Deploratioun.]
The Warkis of the famous and vorthie Knicht
Schir David Lyndesay of the Mont, Alias,
Lyoun King of Armes. Newly correctit, and
vindicate from the former errouris quhair-
with thay war befoir corruptit: and aug-
mentit with sindrie warkis quhilk was not
befoir Imprentit. Edinburgh, 1568 (re-
issued 1569, 1571), 1574, [1579?] (re-
issued 1582), 1592, 1597 (preliminaries
dated 1597 covering two edns), 1610, 1614,
1617, 1619, 1628, 1630, 1634, [1645?],
1648, 1665, 1670, 1672, 1683, 1696, 1709,
1712, 1714, 1716, 1720, 1754, 2 vols.
1776–7.
The Historie of Ane Nobil and Wailzeand
Squyer William Meldrum, umquhyle Laird
of Cleische and Bynnis. Edinburgh, 1594
(rptd from a lost edn c. 1579), 1610, 1634,
1669, 1683, 1696, 1711.
Ane Satyre of the Thrie Estaits, in commendation of vertew and vituperation of vyce.
Edinburgh, 1602; ed. J. Sibbald, Edinburgh, 1802.
A Supplication in contemplation [sic] of Side
Tailes and Muzzled Faces. Edinburgh,
[1690?]. [A broadside.]

(d) Biography and Criticism

Tytler, P. F. Lives of the Scottish Worthies.
3 vols. 1831–43. [Vol. III.]
Lindsay, A. W. C. (Earl of Crawford and
Balcarres). Lives of the Lindsays. 3 vols.
1840 and 1858.
Murray, Sir J. A. H. Hawick Archaeological
Society. Annual Report, 1871.
Knauff, G. Studien über Sir David Lyndsay.
Berlin, 1885.
Aschenberg, H. Sir David Lyndsay's Leben
und Werke. I. Sein Leben [II not pbd].
Gladbach, 1891.
Koeppel, E. Sir David Lyndsay's Anspiel-
ungen auf mittelenglische Dichtungen.
Archiv, CVII, 1902.
Lange, A. Lyndesay's Monarche und die
Chronica Carionis. Giessen, 1904.
Mill, A. J. The Influence of Continental
Drama on Lyndsay's Satyre of the Thrie
Estaitis. MLR. xxv, 1930.
—— Representations of Lyndsay's Satyre of
the Thrie Estaitis. PMLA. XLVII, 1932.
[Corrections, PMLA. XLVIII, 1933, pp. 315–
6.]

SIR RICHARD MAITLAND
(1496–1586)

[See Pinkerton, Sibbald, vol. III, and The
Maitland Quarto Manuscript, ed. W. A. Craigie,
STS. 1920.]

ELIZABETH MELVILL, LADY CULROSS
THE YOUNGER

Ane Godlie Dreame, Compylit in Scottish
Meter, be M.M. Gentelwoman in Culros, at
the requeist of her Freindes. Edinburgh,
1603, [1604?], 1606, 1620, 1644, 1692, 1718.
[A rpt of the 1692 edn appeared at Glasgow,
1889.]

ALEXANDER MONTGOMERIE
(1556?–1610?)

(a) Works

The Cherrie and the Slaye. Composed into
Scottis Meeter. Edinburgh, 1597, 1597
('Prented according to a Copie corrected be
the Author himselfe'), 1636, 1645, 1668,
1682, 1726, 1746, 1751, 1754, 1805; rptd
J. Watson (Choice Collection of Serious and
Comic Scots Poems, 1709–11, rptd 1869);
rptd facs. 1885 (priv. ptd).
  The Cherry and the Sloe, corrected and
  modernized. By J. D. Edinburgh, 1779;
  Aberdeen, 1792; Kilmarnock, 1817.
  Cerasum et Sylvestre Prunum. Opus
  poematicum. Authore primo A. Mont-
  gomrio. Nunc rursus auctum & in latinos
  versus translatum, per T. D. S. P. M. B. P. P.
  [i.e. Thomas Dempsterus, Scotus, etc.]
  Ortenburg, 1631; rptd Edinburgh, 1796.
The Mindes Melodie. Contayning certayne
Psalmes of the Kinglie Prophete David,
applyed to a new pleasant tune. Edinburgh, 1605.
The Flytting betwixt Montgomerie and [Sir
Patrick Hume of] Polwart. Newlie corrected and ammended. Edinburgh, 1629,
1688.
Poems. Ed. D. Irving. 1821.
Poems. Ed. J. Cranstoun, STS. 1887. [Sup-
plementary vol. ed. G. Stevenson, STS.
1910.]

(b) Criticism

Hoffman, O. Studien zu Alexander Mont-
gomerie. Altenburg, 1894.
Brotanek, R. Untersuchungen über das
Leben und die Dichtungen Alexander
Montgomeries. Vienna, 1896.
Maclean, Catherine M. Alexander Scott,
Montgomerie, and Drummond of Haw-
thornden as Lyric Poets. 1915.

JOHN ROLLAND OF DALKEITH

Ane Treatise callit the Court of Venus, devidit into four Buikis. Newlie Compylit be Johne Rolland in Dalkeith. Edinburgh, 1575; ed. W. Gregor, STS. 1884.

The sevin Seages Translatit out of prois in Scottis meter be Johne Rolland in Dalkeith, with ane Moralitie efter everie Doctouris Tale, and siclike efter the Emprice Tale. Edinburgh, 1578, 1592–5, 1620, 1631; rptd *Sibbald*, vol. III; D. Laing, Bannatyne Club, 1837; ed. G. F. Black, STS. 1932.

[See G. Buchner, Die Historia Septem Sapientum. Nebst einer Untersuchung über die Quelle der Sevin Seages des Johne Rolland, Erlangen, 1890.]

ALEXANDER SCOTT (1525?–1584)

(a) Collected Poems

Poems from a Manuscript written in the year 1568 [the Bannatyne]. Ed. D. Laing, 1821.

The Poems of Alexander Scott. Glasgow, 1882.

The Poems of Alexander Scott. Ed. J. Cranstoun, STS. 1896.

The Poems of Alexander Scott, edited from the Bannatyne MS. and the Maitland MS. by A. K. Donald. EETS. 1902.

(b) Selections

Ramsay, A. The Evergreen. 1724. [7 poems.]

Dalrymple, D. (Lord Hailes). Ancient Scotish Poems. 1770. [7 poems.]

Sibbald, vol. III. [15 poems.]

[A modernised version of some poems was pbd by W. Mackean, Paisley, 1887.]

(c) Criticism

Maclean, Catherine M. Alexander Scott, Montgomerie, and Drummond of Hawthornden as Lyric Poets. 1915.

D. H.

C. THE LATER POETS, 1603–1660

HENRY ADAMSON (d. 1639)

The muses threnodie containing varietie of pleasant poeticall descriptions with the most remarkable antiquities of Scotland. Edinburgh, 1638.

An antient poem concerning Perth and its environs. Ed. J. Cant, Perth [1774]. [See T. H. Marshall, History of Perth, Perth, 1849.]

JOHN ADAMSON (d. 1653)

The muses welcome to the high and mightie Prince James at his Majesties happie return to Scotland. Edinburgh, 1618. [A collection of complimentary poems ed. by Adamson addressed to James I, on the occasion of his revisiting Scotland in 1617.]

SIR WILLIAM ALEXANDER, EARL OF STIRLING (1567?–1640)

[See p. 432 above.]

SIR ROBERT AYTON (1570–1638)

[See p. 474 above.]

JOHN BARCLAY (1582–1621)

[See pp. 859–60 above.]

ALEXANDER CRAIG OF ROSECRAIG (1567?–1627)

Poetical essayes. 1604.

Amorose songes. 1606.

Poetical recreations. Edinburgh, 1609.

The pilgrime and the heremite. Aberdeen, 1631.

Poetical Works. Now first collected. Hunterian Club, Glasgow, 1873.

WILLIAM DRUMMOND OF HAWTHORNDEN (1585–1649)

[See pp. 444–5 above.]

ALEXANDER GARDYNE (1585?–1634?)

A garden of grave and godlie flowres. Edinburgh, 1609; rptd Abbotsford Club, 1845.

The theatre of Scottish kings. Edinburgh, 1709; rptd Abbotsford Club, 1845.

A Theatre of Scottish worthies. Hunterian Club, Glasgow, 1878.

PATRICK GORDON (*fl.* 1614–1650)

Neptunus Britannicus. 1614. [On the death of Prince Henry, etc.]

The famous historye of Penardo and Laissa in heroik verse. Dordrecht, 1615.

The famous historie of the renouned and valiant Prince Robert, surnamed the Bruce, king of Scotlande, in heroik verse. Dordrecht, 1615.

[Gordon may be author of A Short Abridgement of Britane's Distemper, ed. J. Dunn, Spalding Club, Aberdeen, 1844. See Scottish Hist. Rev. Oct. 1904.]

SIMION GRAHAME (1570?–1614)

The passionate sparke of a relenting minde. 1604; rptd Bannatyne Club, 1830.

The anatomie of humors. Edinburgh, 1609; rptd Bannatyne Club, 1830.

ANNA HUME

The triumphs of love, chastitie, death; translated out of Petrarch. Edinburgh, 1644.

[Anna Hume also superintended the publication of her father's (David Hume) History of Douglas and Angus.]

ARTHUR JOHNSTON (1587–1641)

Epigrammata. Aberdeen, 1632.
Parerga. Aberdeen, 1632.
Poemata omnia. Middelburg, 1642.

[Vols. I and II of Musa Latina Aberdonensis, New Spalding Club, 1892–5, contain all Johnston's secular poems. Johnston also edited the well-known collection Delitiae Poetarum Scotorum, 2 vols. Amsterdam, 1637. See T. D. Robb, Scottish Hist. Rev. April 1913.]

GEORGE LAUDER

The Scottish souldier. Edinburgh, 1629.
Wight. Edinburgh, 1629.

[Both rptd A. Boswell, Frondes Caducae, Auchinleck, 1818. See also other pieces in Laing's Fugitive Scotish Poetry, 1853.]

WILLIAM LITHGOW (1582–1645?)

The totall discourse of the rare adventures and painfull peregrinations of long nineteene yeares. 1614; Edinburgh, [1770] (11th edn).
The pilgrimes farewell to his native countrey of Scotland. Edinburgh, 1618.
Scotlands welcome to her native sonne and sovereigne lord, King Charles. Edinburgh, [1633].
A true and experimentall discourse, upon the last siege of Breda. 1637.
The gushing teares of godly sorrow; containing the causes, conditions, and remedies of sinne. Edinburgh, 1640.
A true experimentall and exact relation [of the] siege of Newcastle. Edinburgh, 1645; rptd Somers Tracts, vol. V, 1810.
The Poetical Remains of William Lithgow now first collected. Ed. J. Maidment, Edinburgh, 1863, Glasgow, 1906.

ANDREW MELVILLE (1545–1622)

Poemata. [In Delitiae Poetarum Scotorum, ed. A. Johnston, Amsterdam, 1637.]

JAMES GRAHAM, MARQUIS OF MONTROSE (1612–1650)

Poems. [In J. Watson's Choice Collection of Scots Poems, 1711, and Mark Napier's Montrose and the Covenanters, 1838. See J. Buchan's Life, 1913.]

SIR WILLIAM MURE OF ROWALLAN (1594–1657)

A spirituall hymne. Edinburgh, 1628.
The true crucifixe for true catholickes. Edinburgh, 1629.
The Joy of Tears or cordials of comfort, springing up in the region of sorrow. [Edinburgh?] 1635 (anon.); ed. C. Davis (in Miscellany Volume, STS. 1933).

The cry of blood and of a broken covenant. Edinburgh, 1650. [On the execution of Charles I.]
The History and Descent of the House of Rowallane. Glasgow, 1825.
Works. Ed. W. Tough, 2 vols. STS. 1898. [Mure's Dido and Aeneas is ptd for the first time in this edn. Omits The Joy of Tears.]

SIR DAVID MURRAY OF GORTHY (1567–1629)

The tragicall death of Sophonisba. 1611.
Poems. Ed. T. Kinnear, Bannatyne Club, 1823.

Philotus

Philotus: quhair in we may persave the greit inconveniences that fallis out in the mariage betweene age and youth. Edinburgh, 1603, 1612; ed. J. W. Mackenzie, Bannatyne Club, 1835; ed. A. J. Mill (in Miscellany Volume, STS. 1933). [Rptd in Pinkerton's Scottish Poems, vol. III, 1792. An anonymous comedy, the plot of which is taken from a tale by Barnabe Rich.]

ANDREW RAMSAY (1574–1659)

Miscellanea et epigrammata sacra. Edinburgh, 1633.
Poemata sacra. Edinburgh, 1633.
A warning to come out of Babylon, in a sermon. Edinburgh, 1638.

THE SEMPILLS

The Poems of the Sempills of Beltrees, now first collected, with Biographical Notices by James Paterson. Edinburgh, 1849.

H. G. A. rev. A. M. W.

III. PROSE

A. REFORMATION AND RENAISSANCE

[The chapter on the Anglican settlement and the Scottish reformation in vol. II of the Cambridge Modern History, by F. W. Maitland, and the bibliography attached to that chapter should be consulted. Useful bibliographies will also be found in P. Hume Brown's History of Scotland, vols. I and II, Cambridge, 1902, 1905.]

ALEXANDER ALANE (ALESIUS) (1500–1565)

(a) Works

Alexandri Alesii Epistola contra decretum quoddam Episcoporum in Scotia, quod prohibet legere Novi Testamenti libros lingua vernacula. [No place or date on title-page, but at the end of the book the date MD.XXXIII is given. In C. H. and T. Cooper's Athenae Cantabrigienses, vol. I, 1858, p. 239, 1542 and 1543 are given as the dates of other edns.]

De restituendis scholis, oratio habita ab Alexandro Alesio in Academia Francofordiana ad Oderam. Frankfort, 1540.

De authoritate verbi Dei liber contra Episcopum Lundensem. Strasburg, 1542.

Cohortatio ad concordiam pietatis ac doctrinae christianae defensionem. Leipzig, 1544.

De Argumento Epistolae ad Romanos. Leipzig, 1547.

In caput VIII Epistolae Pauli ad Romanos disputatio. Leipzig, 1548.

Edinburgi Regiae Scotorum Urbis Descriptio. [Contributed to Sebastian Münster's Cosmographia, Basle, 1550.]

Alexandri Alesii Scoti Responsio ad Cochleae Calumnias. [Leipzig, 1551.]

Commentarius in Evangelium Joannis. Basle, 1553.

[The extant works of Alane number about thirty, mostly controversial. See DNB. and Hay Fleming, in A. F. Mitchell, The Scottish Reformation, its Epochs, Episodes, Leaders, and Distinctive Characteristics, 1900.]

(b) Later Authorities

M'Crie, T. Life of John Knox. Edinburgh, 1812. [Note 1.]

Lorimer, P. Precursors of Knox, or Memoirs of Patrick Hamilton, Alexander Alane or Alesius, and Sir David Lindsay of the Mount. 1857. [Also embodied in J. A. Wylie's Ter-Centenary of the Scottish Reformation, Edinburgh, 1860.]

—— The Scottish Reformation. A Historical Sketch. 1860.

RICHARD BANNATYNE (d. 1635)

Journal of the Transactions in Scotland 1570–1573. [In Sir J. G. Dalyell, Illustrations of Scottish History, Edinburgh, 1806.]

Memorials of Transactions in Scotland, M.D. LXIX–M.D. LXXIII. Ed. E. R. Pitcairn, Bannatyne Club, Edinburgh, 1836.

The Last Days of John Knox, with Notes by D. H. Fleming. Knox Club, Edinburgh, 1913.

JOHN BELLENDEN (fl. 1533–1587)

Croniklis of Scotland with the cosmography and dyscription thairof. Compilit by the noble clerk maister Hector Boece, channoune of Aberdene. Translatit laitly in our vulgar and common language be maister John Bellenden. Edinburgh, [1535]; rptd 2 vols. Bannatyne Club, Edinburgh, 1821.

The First Five Books of the Roman History. Ed. [T. Maitland], Edinburgh, 1822; ed. W. A. Craigie, STS. 1901.

[See R. W. Chambers and W. W. Seton, Bellenden's Translation of Boece, Scottish Hist. Rev. XVII, XIX, 1921–3.

ROBERT BIRRELL

The Diary of Robert Birrell containing divers passages ' of staite and others memorable accidents. From the 1532 zeir of our redemption till ye beginning of the zeir 1605. [Contained in Sir J. G. Dalyell, Fragments of Scottish History, Edinburgh, 1798. Extracts, Edinburgh, 1820.]

HECTOR BOETHIUS (BOECE) (1465?–1536)

Episcoporum Murthlacensium et Aberdonensium Vitae. Paris, 1522; rptd Bannatyne Club, Edinburgh, 1825; ed. and tr. J. Moir, New Spalding Club, Aberdeen, 1894.

Scotorum Historiae. Paris, 1526, [1547?]. [Bellenden's trn is noted above.]

The Buik of the Croniclis of Scotland. Ed. W. B. D. Turnbull, 3 vols. Rolls Ser. 1858. [A metrical trn of Boece's history by William Stewart (1481?–1550?), apparently undertaken by royal command and completed c. 1535.]

GEORGE BUCHANAN (1506–1582)

[George Buchanan, Glasgow Quatercentenary Studies, 1907, contains a complete bibliography by D. Murray. See also The Writings of Buchanan in George Buchanan, a Memorial, St Andrews [1907].]

(a) Collected Works

Opera Omnia, ad optimorum codicum fidem summo studio recognita et castigata curante Thoma Rudimanno. Edinburgh, 1715.

Opera Omnia cum indicibus memorabilium, et prefatione Petri Burmanni. Leyden, 1725. [This is a rev. edn of Ruddiman.]

The Works of Mr George Buchanan in the Scottish Language. Edinburgh, 1823.

Vernacular Writings of George Buchanan. Ed. P. H. Brown, STS. 1892.

(b) Separate Works

Rudimenta grammatices Thomae Linacri ex Anglico sermone in Latinum versa, interprete Georgio Buchanano. Paris, 1533, 1537, etc.

Medea Euripidis poetae tragici Georgio Buchanano Scoto interprete. Paris, 1544.

Jephthes, sive Votum, tragoedia. Auctore Georgio Buchanano Scoto. Paris, 1554, 1557, 1575. Tr. French, Paris, 1573, etc.; Polish, Cracow, 1587; Italian, Venice, 1600; German, Brunswick, 1604; Eng. W. Tait, Edinburgh, 1750, C. C. Truro, 1853, A. G. Mitchell, Paisley, [1903].

Euripidis poetae tragici Alcestis Georgio Buchanano Scoto interprete. Paris, 1556, 1557; Wittemberg, 1581.

De Caleto nuper ab Henrico II. Francorum Rege invictiss. recepta, Georgii Buchanani carmen. Paris, 1558.

Psalmorum Davidis paraphrasis poetica, nunc primum edita, authore Georgio Buchanano, Scoto, poetarum nostri saeculi facile principe. [Paris?], 1566, etc.

Georgii Buchanani Scoti, Franciscanus. Varia eiusdem authoris poemata. [Paris?] 1566.

Georgii Buchanani Scoti, poetarum nostri saeculi facile principis. Elegiarum Liber I, Sylvarum Liber I, Endecasyllabon Lib. I. Paris, 1567, 1579.

Georgii Buchanani Scoti poetae eximij Franciscanus & fratres, quibus accessere varia eiusdem & aliorum poemata. Basle, [1568]; tr.(as The Franciscan Friar, a Satire) G. Provand, Glasgow, 1809, and (as The Franciscan; a Poem) A. Gibb, Edinburgh, [1871].

The Chamaeleon: Or, The Crafty Statesman: describ'd in the character of Mr Maitland of Lethington, Secretary of Scotland. 1710; ed. (from MS) Glasgow, 1818. [The original MS in the Cotton Lib. bears the date 1570.]

Ane admonitioun direct to the trew Lordis, maintenaris of justice, and obedience to the Kingis grace. M. G. B. Stirling, 1571; 1571.

De Maria Scotorum regina, totaque ejus contra Regem conjuratione, foedo cum Bothuelio adulterio, nefaria in maritum crudelitate et rabie, horrendo insuper et deterrimo ejusdem parricidio: plena et tragica planè historia. [No date or place, but probably ptd by John Day, before November, 1571. The title was subsequently changed to Detectio Mariae Reginae, etc.]

Ane detectioun of the duinges of Marie Quene of Scottes, touchand the murder of hir husband, and hir conspiracie, adulterie and pretensed mariage with the Erle Bothwell: and ane Defence of the trew Lordis, mainteineris of the Kingis Graces actioun and authoritie. Translated out of the Latine. [Probably ptd by John Day, November 1571. Contains more than the original Latin, and now not generally held to be the work of Buchanan. Also 1571; St Andrews, 1572; tr French, 'Edinburgh,' 1572 (Irving suggests that it was ptd at La Rochelle by the Huguenots).]

Baptistes, sive Calumnia, tragoedia, auctore Georgio Buchanano Scoto. 1578; Frankfort, 1579; tr. Eng. A. Gibb, Edinburgh, 1870; A. G. Mitchell, Paisley, 1904; A. Brown, Edinburgh, 1906.

De Jure Regni apud Scotos, dialogus, authore Georgio Buchanano Scoto. Edinburgh, 1579.

Rerum Scoticarum Historia auctore Georgio Buchanano Scoto. Edinburgh, 1582; [Oberwesel], 1583; Frankfort, 1584; Frankfort, 1594.

Georgii Buchanani Scoti Franciscanus et Fratres. Elegiarum liber I, Silvarum Liber I, Hendecasyllabon liber I, Epigrammaton liber III, De Sphaera fragmentum. G[eneva], 1584.

De Prosodia Libellus. Edinburgh, [1595], etc.

(c) Biography and Criticism

Irving, D. Memoirs of the Life and Writings of George Buchanan. Edinburgh, 1805, 1817 (rev. edn).

Brown, P. H. George Buchanan, Humanist and Reformer. Edinburgh, 1890.

Henriquez, J. C. George Buchanan in the Lisbon Inquisition: the Records of his Trial with a Translation of Some of the Papers, and an Introduction. Lisbon, 1906.

Macmillan, D. George Buchanan, a Biography. Edinburgh, 1906.

George Buchanan, Glasgow Quatercentenary Studies. Glasgow, 1907.

George Buchanan, a Memorial, 1506–1906. Contributions by Various Writers, compiled and edited by D. A. Millar. St Andrews, [1907].

Photographs of Five Documents connected with the Imprisonment, Trial, Sentence, and Release of George Buchanan by the Inquisition in Portugal, with Descriptive Letterpress by J. C. Guthrie. Edinburgh, 1907.

Lebègue, R. George Buchanan: son Influence en France et en Portugal. Coimbra, 1931.

The Complaynt of Scotland

The Complaynt of Scotland, vyth ane exortatione to the three Estaits, to be vigilante on the Diffens of their Public Veil. [Paris, 1549]; ed. (with preliminary dissertation and Glossary) J. Leyden, Edinburgh, 1801; ed. J. A. H. Murray, EETS. 1872. [See Critiques by D. Herd and Others upon the New Edition of 'The Complaint of Scotland,' with Observations in Answer by the Editor, Dr J. C. Leyden, Edinburgh, 1829. For the dependence of the author of The Complaynt on Alain Chartier, see W. A. Neilson, J[E]GP. I, 1897; and for his plagiarism from St Gelais see W. A. Craigie, Mod. Quart. Lang. and Lit. I, 1898.]

JOHN CRAIG (1512?–1600)

Short Summe of the Whole Catechisme. Edinburgh, 1581, 1632; ed. T. G. Law, Edinburgh, 1883.

Ane Forme of Examination before Communion. Edinburgh, 1592; rptd Edinburgh, 1739, and n.p. 1764.

JOHN DAVIDSON (1549?–1604,
Minister at Prestonpans)

Ane dialog betwixt a clerk and a courteour. Edinburgh, 1573.
Ane brief commendatioun of Uprichtness. St Andrews, 1573.
D. Bancroft's rashnes. Edinburgh, 1595.
Memorial of two worthye christians. Edinburgh, 1595.
Some helps for young schollers in Christ. Edinburgh, 1602.
Mr John Davidson's Catechism, with preliminary discourse by W. Jameson. Edinburgh, 1708.
Poetical Remains: with a Biographical Account of the Author and various Illustrative Papers. Ed. J. Maidment, Edinburgh, 1829.
Ane dialog betwixt a clerk and a courteour. Ed. J. Maidment, Edinburgh, 1829. [A different pbn from the foregoing.]
Rogers, C. Three Scottish Reformers with their Poetical Remains and Mr Davidson's 'Helps for young scholars in Christ.' 1874.

Diurnal of Remarkable Occurrents

Diurnal of Remarkable Occurrents that have passed within the Country of Scotland since the Death of King James the Fourth till the year M.D.LXXV. from a Manuscript in the Possession of Sir John Maxwell of Pollock, Baronet. Maitland Club, Edinburgh, 1833; ed. J. Thomson, Bannatyne Club, 1833.

Gude and Godlie Ballatis

Gude and Godlie Ballatis. The haill hundreth and Fiftie Psalmes of David, in Inglis meter, be Thomas Sternholde. Wyth utheris diveris Poyetis, quhilk completis the haill Psalmes. As efter followis of the best Interpretouris. Edinburgh, 1567, 1576, 1600, and 1601; ed. D. Laing, Edinburgh, 1868.
A Compendious Book of Godly and Spiritual Songs commonly known as 'The Gude and Godlie Ballatis' reprinted from the Edition of 1567. Ed. A. F. Mitchell, STS. 1897. [This edn contains a bibliography of the Ballads. Regarding the indebtedness of the authors of the Ballads to German sources see C. H. Herford, Studies on the Literary Relations of England and Germany in the Sixteenth Century, Cambridge, 1886, and Mitchell's comments on the book, pp. cxiv ff. of his edn of the Ballads. See also W. B. Warfield, Mitchell's Gude and Godlie Ballads, Presbyterian and Reformed Rev. New York, x, 1899, p. 160.]

JOHN HAMILTON (1511?–1571,
Archbishop of St Andrews)

The Catechism of John Hamilton, archbishop of St Andrews. St Andrews, 1552; Edinburgh, 1580; rptd facs. Edinburgh, 1882; ed. (with Introduction and Glossary, and a Preface by W. E. Gladstone) T. G. Law, Oxford, 1884.
Ane godlie exhortation maid and sett forth be Johane, Archbishop of Sanctandrois. St Andrews, 1559. [This tract is known as the 'Twopenny Faith.' Rptd Bannatyne Misc. vol. III, Edinburgh, 1855. Also rptd with the 1882 edn of the Catechism.]

PATRICK HAMILTON (1504?–1528)

A most excelent treatise called Patericks Places. 1598. [The treatise appears in D. Laing's edn of John Knox's works, vol. I, pp. 19–35. See John Foxe, Actes and Monumentis of matters most speciall and memorable, happening in the Church, vol. II, pp. 887–95, 1610. See also the following biographies: Anon. Dundee, 1792; J. P. Lawson, Edinburgh, 1828; P. Lorimer, 1857; T. P. Johnston, Edinburgh, 1882.]
Historie and Life of King James the Sext; being the Account of the Affairs of Scotland from the Year 1566 to the Year 1596, with a Continuation to the Year 1617. Bannatyne Club, Edinburgh, 1825.

QUINTIN KENNEDY (1520–1564,
Abbot of Crossraguel)

Ane Oratione Set furth be Maister Quintin Kennedy. Ed. [Sir] A. B[oswell], Edinburgh, 1812.
Heir followeth the coppie of the reasoning which was betwix the Abbote of Crossraguell and John Knox in Mayboill, concerning the mass. Edinburgh, 1563; ed. A. Boswell, Edinburgh, 1812. [An account of Kennedy, with the titles of his works (too voluminous to be given here) will be found in D. Laing's edn of John Knox's works, vol. VI, pp. 149–220. Laing has there printed the Reasonyng between Knox and Kennedy. See also Charters of the Abbey of Crossraguel, 2 vols. Ayrshire and Galloway Archaeological Ass. Edinburgh, 1886.]

SIR WILLIAM KIRKCALDY OF GRANGE (d. 1573)

[Poems attrib. to Kirkcaldy will be found in Sir J. G. Dalyell's Scottish Poems of the 16th Century, 2 vols. Edinburgh, 1801; and in Satirical Poems of the Time of the Reformation, ed. J. Cranstoun, 3 vols. STS. 1884–93. See also J. Grant, Memoirs and Adventures of Sir William Kirkcaldy of Grange, Edinburgh, 1849; and L. Barbé, Kirkcaldy of Grange, Edinburgh, 1897.]

JOHN KNOX (1505–1572)

(a) Works

A Confessioun and declaration of praiers added therunto by Jhon Knox, minister of Christes most sacred Evangely, upon the death of that most verteous and moste famous King Edward the VI kynge of Englande. Rome, 1554.

A faythfull admonitioun made by John Knox, unto the professors of God's truth in England. Zurich, 1554.

A godly letter sent to the fayethfull in London, Newcastell, Barwyke; and to all other within the realme of Englande that love the cominge of oure Lorde Jesus. Rome, 1554; Wittenberg, 1554 (as An admonition or warning).

The Copie of a letter sent to the ladye Mary dowagire, Regent of Scotland by John Knox in the yeare 1556. There is also a notable sermon, made by the sayde John Knox, wherin is evydentlye proved that the masse is and alwayes hath ben abhominable before God and Idolatrye. Scrutamini Scripturas. [Geneva? 1556.]

The first blast of the trumpet against the monstruous regiment of women. 1558; rptd E. Arber, 1878.

The appellation of John Knox from the cruelle sentence pronounced against him by the false bishoppes and clergie of Scotland. Geneva, 1558.

An answer to a great nomber of blasphemous cavillations written by an Anabaptist, and adversarie to Gods eternal Predestination and confuted by John Knox, minister of Gods Worde in Scotland. [Geneva], 1560; 1591.

John Knox to his loving brethren whome God ones gloriously gathered in the church of Edinburgh, and now ar dispersed for tryall of our faith. Stirling, 1571.

An answer to a letter of Tyrie. St. Andrews, 1572. [For Tyrie's side in the controversy, see Catholic Tractates, ed. T. G. Law, STS. 1901.]

A brieff discours off the troubles begonne at Franckford in Germany Anno Domini 1554 Abowte the Booke of common praier and ceremonies. 1575.

The Expositioun uppon the syxt Psalme of David, wherein is declared hys cross, complaintes, and praiers. [?]; 1580 (under different title).

Sermon upon the tentations of Christ. 1583.

A Comfortable Epistell sente to the afflicted church of Christ, exhortyng them to beare his crosse wyth patience. Wrytten by the man of God. J. K. [?]

A moste wholsome talke and communication betwixt the prentyse and the pryest touching the matter of auricular confessioun. [?]

A confutation of all such arguments as the Popes catholykes doe bring for to prove the mutilate receauyng of the sacrament under one kynde. [?]

The Historie of the reformatioun of religioun within the realm of Scotland. 1586 (imperfect); ed. David Buchanan, 1644; Edinburgh, 1644; ed. M. Crawford, Edinburgh, 1732; rev. and ed. C. Lennox, Edinburgh, 1906.

The Liturgy of the Church of Scotland, or John Knox's Book of Common Order. Ed. and rev. G. Cumming, 1840. [See also G. W. Sprott and T. Leishman, Edinburgh, 1868; and G. W. Sprott, Edinburgh, 1871.]

[The only complete edn of Knox's works is that of D. Laing, 6 vols. Bannatyne Club, Edinburgh, 1846–64, rptd Edinburgh, 1895. A bibliography is attached to each separate work.]

(b) Biographical Studies

Smeton, T. Ad virulentum A. Hamiltonii dialogum responsio. Adjecta est vera historia extremae vitae et obitus J. Knoxii. Edinburgh, 1579.

M'Crie, T. Life of John Knox. Edinburgh, 1812.

Lorimer, P. John Knox and the Church of England. 1875.

Brown, P. H. John Knox, a Biography. 2 vols. 1895.

M'Cunn, Florence. John Knox. 1895.

Innes, Taylor. John Knox. Edinburgh, 1905.

Lang, Andrew. John Knox and the Reformation. 1905.

Hewat, K. Makers of the Scottish Church. Edinburgh, 1920. [Contains a full treatment of Knox and Craig with bibliographies.]

Muir, Edwin. John Knox. 1929.

[See also under Richard Bannatyne, above.]

(c) Articles in Periodicals

Lang, Andrew. Knox as Historian. Scottish Hist. Rev. II, 1905.

Fleming, J. H. Influence of John Knox. Scottish Hist. Rev. II, 1905.

Raitt, R. S. John Knox. Fortnightly Rev. LXXVIII, 1905.

—— John Knox. Quarterly Rev. CCV, 1906.

FRIAR KYLLOUR

[The only mention of Kyllour is to be found in Knox's Historie of the Reformatioun, ed. D. Laing, vol. I, p. 62. Knox ascribes to him a Historye of Christis Passioun in forme of a play.]

JOHN LESLIE, BISHOP OF ROSS
(1527–1596)

A treatise concerning the defence of the
honour of Marie, Queene of Scotland made
by Morgan Philippes, Bachelar of Divinitie,
[pseud.]. Liège, 1571.
Libri duo, quorum unus: piae afflicti animi
consolationes. Ad D. Mariam Scotorum
Reginam. Paris, 1574.
De Origine, Moribus, et Rebus Gestis Sco-
torum. Libri decem. Authore Joanne
Leslaeo Scoto, Episcopo Rossensi. Rome,
1578, and 1675.
De titulo et jure Mariae Scotorum Reginae.
Rheims, 1580.
De illustrium foeminarum in repub. admini-
stranda authoritate libellus. Rheims, 1580.
A treatise towching the right, title, and
interest of Marie Queene of Scotland.
Rheims, 1584.
The History of Scotland from the Death of
King James I in the Year M.CCCC.XXXVI to
the Year M.D.LXI by John Lesley, Bishop of
Ross. Bannatyne Club, Edinburgh, 1830.
The Historie of Scotland wrytten first in Latin
by the most Reverend and Worthy Jhone
Leslie Bishop of Rosse and translated by
Father James Dalrymple. Ed. E. G. Cody,
2 vols. STS. 1888–95.

[See The Case of the Bishop of Ross,
Resident to the Queen of Scots, Somers
Tracts, ed. Sir Walter Scott, vol. I, 1809.]

ROBERT LINDSAY OF PITSCOTTIE
(1500?–1565?)

The History of Scotland from 21 February,
1436, to March, 1565. In which are contained Accounts of many remarkable passages altogether from our other Historians.
Done from the most authentick and most
correct manuscripts. Edinburgh, 1728
(modernised); Glasgow, 1749.
The Historie and Cronicles of Scotland from
the Slaughter of King James the First to
the one thousunde fyve hundreith thrie
scoir fyftein zeir. Written and collected by
Robert Lindesay of Pitscottie. Ed. A. J. G.
Mackay, 3 vols. STS. 1899–1911.

SIR JOHN MAITLAND OF THIRLSTANE
(1545?–1595)

[Poems attrib. to Maitland will be found
in the following collections: Sir Richard Maitland of Lethingtoun's Manuscript Collection
of Poems, 1555–86, in the Pepysian Lib.
Magdalene College, Cambridge, Fol. MS,
p. 357; Ancient Scottish Poems never before
in Print, but now published from the MS.
Collections of Sir Richard Maitland, ed. John
Pinkerton, 2 vols. 1786; The Poems of Sir

Richard Maitland, Knight, with an Appendix
of Selections from the Poems of Sir John
Maitland, Lord Thirlstane and of Thomas
Maitland, edited from the Drummond MS in
the Library of the University of Edinburgh,
Maitland Club, Glasgow, 1830; The Sempill
Ballatis, ed. and pbd by Thomas George
Stevenson, Edinburgh, 1872; Satirical Poems
of the Time of the Reformation, ed. J. Cran-
stoun, STS. 3 vols. 1884–93; isolated poems
also occur in The Maitland Quarto Manuscript,
ed. W. A. Craigie, STS. 1920, and The Maitland
Folio Manuscript, ed. W. A. Craigie, 2 vols.
STS. 1919–27.]

JOHN MAJOR (1469–1550)

Historia Majoris Britanniae. Paris, 1521;
rptd Edinburgh, 1740; tr. Eng. A. Constable,
with a bibliography by T. G. Law, STS.
1891.

SIR JAMES MELVILLE, OF HALHILL
(1535–1617)

Memoirs containing an account of affairs of
state relating to the kingdoms of England and
Scotland under the reigns of Queen Elizabeth, Mary, Queen of Scots, and King
James. 1683; ed. (from original MS) T. Thomson, Bannatyne Club, Edinburgh, 1827;
rptd 1922 (Abbey Classics); tr. French,
Hague, 1694, Lyons, 1695, Amsterdam,
1704, and 'Edimbourg' (place unknown),
1745; Edinburgh, 1735; Glasgow, 1751.

JAMES MELVILLE, MINISTER OF KILRENNY
(1556–1614)

Fruitfull and comfortable exhortatioun anent
Death. Edinburgh, 1597.
A Spiritual Propine of a Pastour to his people.
Edinburgh, 1598. [A catechism.]
Diary, 1556–1601. Bannatyne Club, Edin-
burgh, 1829.
Autobiography and Diary. Ed. R. Pitcairn,
Wodrow Soc. Edinburgh, 1842.

DAVID MOYSIE (fl. 1582–1603)

Memoirs of the Affairs of Scotland; containing
an account of the most remarkable transactions in that kingdom, 1577–1603 together
with a discourse of the conspiracy of the
Earl of Gowrie. Edinburgh, 1755; rptd
Bannatyne Club, Edinburgh, 1830.

ROBERT SEMPILL (1595?–1665?)

The Evergreen: A Collection of Scots Poems
wrote by the Ingenious before 1600. By
Allan Ramsay. 2 vols. Edinburgh, 1724;
rptd 1876. [Ramsay gives three poems by
Sempill from the Bannatyne MS.]

The Sempill Ballates. Ed. T. G. Stevenson, Edinburgh, 1872. [This collection contains all Sempill's pieces which appear in the Bannatyne MS, but many are erroneously assigned to him.]
Satirical Poems of the Time of the Reformation. Ed. J. Cranstoun, 3 vols. STS. 1884–93. [Twelve poems in this collection are assigned to Sempill.]

[Many of Sempill's poems were ptd as single sheets. For the titles of these see H. G. Aldis, Books printed in Scotland before 1700, Edinburgh, 1904.]

NINIAN WINZET (1518–1592)

Certane tractatis for Reformatioun of Doctryne and maneris, set furth at the desyre, and in ye name of ye afflictit Catholikis, of inferiour ordour of Clergie, and layit men in Scotland, be Niniane Winzet, ane Catholike Preist borne in Renfrew. Edinburgh, 1562; ed. D. Laing, Maitland Club, Edinburgh, 1835.
The last blast of the trompet of Godes Worde aganis the usurpit auctoritie of Johne Knox and his Calviniane brether intrudit precheouris. Edinburgh, 1562.
Flagellum sectariorum qui religionis pretextu seditiones excitare student. Ingolstadt, 1562.
The buke of four-scoir three questions proponit to ye precheouris of ye Protestants in Scotland by ye Catholicks. Antwerp, 1563; 1580.
Certane Tractates together with the Book of Fourscore Three Questions and a Translation of Vincentius Lerinensis by Ninian Winzet. Ed. J. K. Hewison, 2 vols. STS. 1888. [This edn contains a full bibliography of Winzet in vol. I, pp. lxxix ff.]

P. H. B., rev. W. F.

B. THEOLOGY AND RELIGIOUS CONTROVERSY, 1603–1660

JOHN ADAMSON (d. 1653)

The Muses welcome to the High and Mightie Prince James. [And] Planctus et vota musarum in augustissimi monarchae Jacobi recessu è Scotia in Angliam, Augusti 4 anno 1617. Edinburgh, 1618.
Στοιχείωσις eloquiorum Dei, sive methodus religionis christianae catechetica. Edinburgh, 1637 (2nd edn).
Dioptra gloriae divinae: seu enarratio Psalmi xix, et in eundem meditationes. Edinburgh, 1637.

WALTER BALCANQUHALL (1586?–1645)

[See p. 839 above.]

ROBERT BARON (1593?–1639)

Philosophia theologiae ancillans. St Andrews, 1621; Amsterdam, 1649.
Disputatio theologica, de formali objecto fidei. Aberdeen, 1627.
Ad Georgii Turnebulli Tetragonismum pseudographum apodixis catholica, sive apologia pro Disputatione de formali objecto fidei. Aberdeen, 1631. [Like Baron, Turnbull was a professor in Marischal College, Aberdeen; he wrote Principles of Moral Philosophy.]
Disputatio theologica, de vero discrimine peccati mortalis et venialis. Aberdeen, 1633; Amsterdam, [1649].
Metaphysica generalis opus postumum. Leyden, 1657.

[See Studies in the History and Development of the University of Aberdeen, ed. P. J. Anderson, 1906; D. Macmillan's Aberdeen Doctors, 1909; W. E. McCulloch, Viri Illustres Universitatum Abredonensium, 1923.]

HUGH BINNING (1627–1653)

The common principles of Christian religion clearly proved. Glasgow, 1659; Edinburgh, 1672; Glasgow, 1728.
The sinner's sanctuary, being XL Sermons. Edinburgh, 1670.
Heart-humiliation. Edinburgh, [1676]; Glasgow, 1725.
Several sermons. To which is subjoined an essay upon Christian Love. Glasgow, 1760.
Works. Edinburgh, 1735; Glasgow, 1768 (with Life); ed. J. Cochrane, 3 vols. Edinburgh, 1839–40; ed. M. Leishman, Edinburgh, 1851.

ROBERT BOYD (1578–1627)

Hecatombe Christiana, hymnus ἑκατόνστροφος ad Christum servatorem. Edinburgh, 1627; Edinburgh, 1825; tr. Sir W. Mure (as A Spirituall Hymne), Edinburgh, 1628.
In Epistolam Pauli Apostoli ad Ephesios praelectiones supra cc. 1652.

[Poems by Boyd are included in Delitiae Poetarum Scotorum, 1637, and Poetarum Scotorum musæ sacræ, 1739.]

ZACHARY BOYD (1585?–1653)

The last battell of the soule in death, carefulle digested for the comfort of the sicke. Edinburgh, 1628; ed. (with an Account of the Author and his Works) G. Neil, Glasgow, 1831.
The balme of Gilead prepared for the sicke. Edinburgh, 1629.
Rex pater patriae instar pelicani liberos suos fovere debet. Edinburgh, 1633.
A clear form of catechising. Glasgow, 1639.

Four letters of comforts for the deaths of the Earle of Haddingtoun and of the Lord Boyd. Glasgow, 1640; ed. J. S[mall], Edinburgh, [1878].

1. Crosses, 2. Comforts, 3. Counsels, needfull to bee considered, and carefully to be laid up in the hearts of the godly, in these boysterous broiles and bloody times. Glasgow, 1643.

The garden of Zion: wherein the life and death of godly and wicked men in scriptures are to be seene. 2 vols. Glasgow, 1644. [In verse.]

The psalmes of David in meeter. Glasgow, 1646 (3rd edn).

Spiritual songs or, holy poems. Edinburgh, 1686.

Two oriental pearls, grace and glory. Edinburgh, 1718.

Four Poems from Zion's Flowers. Ed. G. Neil, Glasgow, 1855.

ROBERT BRUCE (1559–1631)

Sermons preached in the kirk of Edinburgh. Edinburgh, 1591.

The way to true peace and rest; delivered at Edinborough in xvi sermons. 1617.

Narrative concerning his Troubles in the Year 1600. Bannatyne Club, Edinburgh, 1827.

Sermons. Ed. W. Cunningham, Wodrow Soc. 1843.

[See D. C. Macnicol, Robert Bruce, with 3 Portraits, 5 Plates, and 2 Facsimiles, Edinburgh, 1907: an uncritical panegyric.]

JOHN CAMERON (1579–1625)

[See Scottish Hist. Rev. July 1910 and DNB.]

JOHN CORBET (1603–1641)

The ungirding of the Scottish armour: or an answer to the informations for defensive arms against the Kings Majestie drawn up at Edinburgh. Dublin, 1639.

The Covenant

[For the history of the famous General Demands, Replyes and Duplyes made by the Aberdeen Doctors to the Commissioners of the General Assembly who, in 1638, visited Aberdeen on behalf of the Covenant, see Studies in the History and Development of the University of Aberdeen, ed. P. J. Anderson, 1906, pp. 400–1; W. E. McCullough, Viri Illustres Universitatum Abredonensium, pp. 53–5; J. M. Bulloch's A History of the University of Aberdeen, 1895, and D. Macmillan's Aberdeen Doctors, 1909.]

DAVID DICKSON (1583–1663)

True Christian love. To be sung with any of the common tunes of the Psalms. Edinburgh, 1634; Glasgow, 1772 (contains fragments of edns of 1634 and 1700).

A short explanation of the Epistle of Paul to the Hebrewes. Aberdeen, 1635.

Expositio analytica omnium apostolicarum epistolarum. Glasgow, 1645; tr. W. Petchford, 1659.

A brief exposition of the evangel of Jesus Christ according to Matthew. Glasgow, 1647.

A brief explication of the Psalms. 3 pts, 1653–5.

Therapeutica sacra: seu de curandis casibus conscientiae circa regenerationem per foederum divinorum prudentem applicationem libri tres. 1656; tr. (by Dickson), Edinburgh, 1695 (2nd edn).

Truth's victory over error, with Life by R. Wodrow, Glasgow, 1772; Kilmarnock, 1787.

Select Practical Writings. Edinburgh, 1845.

WILLIAM DOUGLAS

Academiarum vindiciae, in quibus novantium praejudicia contra academias etiam reformatas averruncantur, eorundemque institutio recta proponitur. Aberdeen, 1659.

The stable trueths of the kirk require a sutable behaviour. Holden forth by way of a sermon. Aberdeen, 1660.

JAMES DURHAM (1622–1658)

A commentarie upon the Book of the Revelation. Edinburgh, 1658.

The dying man's testament to the Church of Scotland; or, a treatise concerning scandal. Edinburgh, 1659.

Clavis Cantici; or, an exposition of the Song of Solomon. Edinburgh, 1668.

The law unsealed: or a practical exposition of the ten commandments. Glasgow, 1676 (2nd edn).

The blessednesse of the death of those that die in the Lord discoursed in seven very searching, but very sweet sermons. 1681.

The great corruption of subtile self; discovered, and driven from its lurking holes. In seven sermons. Edinburgh, 1686.

Christ crucified: or the marrow of the Gospel evidently holden forth in lxxii sermons on the whole 53 chapter of Isaiah. Edinburgh, 1700 (3rd edn).

An exposition of the whole Book of Job. With short Life. Glasgow, 1759.

JAMES FERGUSSON (1621–1667)

A brief exposition of the Epistles of Paul to the Philippians and Colossians. Edinburgh, 1656.

A brief exposition of the Epistles of Paul to the Galatians and Ephesians. Edinburgh, 1659.

A brief exposition of the Epistles of Paul to the Thessalonians. Glasgow, 1675.

A brief relation of the errors of toleration, Erastianism, independency and separation. Edinburgh, 1692.

A Brief Refutation of the Doctrine of Erastianism, with Prefatory Note by R. S. Candlish. Cupar, 1843.

JOHN FORBES (1593–1648)

Irenicum amatoribus veritatis et pacis in ecclesia Scoticana. Aberdeen, 1629.

Gemitus ecclesiae Scoticanae, sive tractatus de sacrilegio'. Aberdeen, 1631.

Libri octavi theologiæ moralis. Aberdeen,1632.

A peaceable warning to the subjects in Scotland. Aberdeen, 1638.

Instructiones historico-theologicae. Amsterdam, 1645.

Opera omnia. 2 vols. Amsterdam, 1702–3.

[See note on Robert Baron for biographical matter. See also Arnoldus Montanus, Forbesius contractus, Amsterdam, 1663, and G. D. Henderson, John Forbes of Corse in Exile, Aberdeen University Rev. Nov. 1929.]

PATRICK FORBES (1564–1635)

An exquisite commentarie upon the Revelation of Saint John. 1613.

Eubulus; or a dialogue, wherein a rugged Romish ryme (inscrybed Catholicke questions to the protestant) is confuted and the Questions thereof answered. Aberdeen, 1627.

[See Funerals of a Right Reverend Father in God, Patrick Forbes of Corse, Bishop of Aberdeen, Aberdeen, 1635. Contains Latin verses by the chief Scottish scholars of the day; ed. C. F. Shand, Spottiswoode Soc. Edinburgh, 1845.]

GEORGE GILLESPIE (1613–1648)

A dispute against the English-Popish ceremonies, obtruded upon the Church of Scotland. 1637.

Certaine brief observations and antiquaeries: on Master Prin his Twelve questions about church-government. 1644.

Wholsome severity reconciled with Christian liberty. Or, the true resolution of a present controversie concerning liberty of conscience. 1645.

Aaron's rod blossoming, or the divine ordinance of church government vindicated. 1646.

An usefull case of conscience discussed and resolved, concerning associations and confederacies with idolaters, infidels, hereticks, or any other known enemies of truth and godlinesse. Edinburgh, 1649.

A treatise of miscellany questions: wherein many usefull questions and cases of conscience are discussed and resolved. Edinburgh, 1649.

Notes of Debates and Proceedings of the Assembly of Divines and other Commissioners at Westminster. Ed. D. Meek, Edinburgh, 1846.

Works, now first collected. With Memoir of his Life and Writings, by W. M. Hetherington. 2 vols. Edinburgh, 1846.

[Gillespie also engaged in a pamphleteering controversy with Thomas Coleman, an opponent in the Westminster Assembly. See Scottish Hist. Rev. Oct. 1907, p. 73, Oct. 1910, p. 50.]

ANDREW GRAY (1633–1656)

The mystery of faith opened up. Glasgow, 1659.

Directions and instigations to the duty of prayer. Glasgow, 1669.

Great and precious promises. Edinburgh, 1669.

The spiritual warfare; or, some sermons concerning the nature of mortification. Edinburgh, 1671.

Whole works. Glasgow, 1762.

WILLIAM GUILD (1586–1657)

Levi his complaint: or, the moane of the poor ministrie. Edinburgh, 1617.

Moses unvailed; or, those figures which served unto the patterne and shaddow of heavenly things, pointing out the Messiah Christ Jesus, briefly explained. 1620.

Issachars asse braying under a double burden; or, the uniting of churches. Aberdeen, 1622.

The old Roman Catholik, as at first he was taught by Paul; in opposition to the new Roman Catholik, as of latter he is taught by the pope. Aberdeen, 1649.

Isagoge Catechetica. Aberdeen. [1649.]

[See J. Shirrefs, An enquiry into the life, writings and character of William Guild, Aberdeen, 1799 (2nd edn).]

ALEXANDER HENDERSON (1583?–1646)

The government and order of the Church of Scotland. Edinburgh, 1641.

Sermons, Prayers, and Pulpit Addresses. Ed. R. T. Martin, 1867.

[See J. Aiton, The Life and Times of Alexander Henderson, Edinburgh, 1836, and T. M'Crie, Life of Alexander Henderson, Edinburgh, 1846.]

WILLIAM LESLIE (d. 1654?)

Vindiciæ theologicæ pro perseverantia sanctorum in gratia salvifica. Aberdeen, 1627.

[One of the Aberdeen Doctors.]

JOHN MAXWELL (1590?–1647)

Sacro-sancta regum majestas: or, the sacred and royall prerogative of Christian kings. Oxford, 1644. [This was answered by Samuel Rutherford in Lex, Rex, 1644.]
The burthen of Issachar: or, the tyrannicall power and practises of the presbyteriall government in Scotland. 1646.

ALEXANDER ROSS (1591–1654)

[See pp. 477, 877 and 883 above.]

SAMUEL RUTHERFORD (1600–1661)

Exercitationes apologeticae pro divina gratia adversus Jacobum Arminianum ejusque asseclas. Amsterdam, 1636.
A peaceable and temperate plea for Paul's presbytery in Scotland. 1642.
Lex, Rex; the law and the prince. A dispute for the just prerogative of king and people. 1644. [Written chiefly as a reply to Maxwell's Sacro-sancta regum majestas, Oxford, 1644; it was burned by the common hangman at the Restoration.]
The due right of presbyteries. 1644.
The divine right of church government and excommunication. 1646.
A survey of the spirituall Antichrist. 1648.
Disputatio scholastica de divina providentia. Edinburgh, 1649.
A free disputation against pretended liberty of conscience. 1649.
The covenant of life opened; or a treatise of the covenant of grace. Edinburgh, 1655.
Influences of the life of grace. 1659.
Joshua redivivus, or Mr Rutherfoord's letters; now published for the use of all the people of God. 1664; ed. A. A. Bonar, 2 vols. Edinburgh, 1863.
Examen Arminianismi. Utrecht, 1668.
Quaint Sermons. Ed. A. A. Bonar, 1885.
Religious Letters, written to eminent individuals during the persecution in Scotland. Aberdeen, n.d.
[See T. Murray, Life of Samuel Rutherford, Edinburgh, 1828.]

SIR JAMES SEMPILL (1566–1625)

Sacrilege sacredly handled, that is according to Scripture onely; for the use of all churches in generall, but more especially for those of North Britaine. 1619.
A picktooth for the Pope, or the packman's paternoster, set down in a dialogue betwixt a packman and a priest. Edinburgh, [1630?], etc.

JAMES SIBBALD (1590?–1650?)

[See p. 911 below.]

ANDREW STRACHAN

Vindiciæ cultus divini. Aberdeen, 1634.

WILLIAM STRUTHER

Christian observations and resolutions; or, the daylie practise of the renewed man. 2 pts, Edinburgh, 1628–9.
A looking glasse for princes and people. Edinburgh, 1632.
A looking glasse for princes and popes; or, a vindication of the sacred authoritie of princes from the anti-Christian usurpation of the popes. Edinburgh, 1632.
True happines, or King Davids choice. Edinburgh, 1633.

ARCHIBALD SYMSON (1564?–1628)

Christes testament unfolded: or, seaven godlie and learned sermons on our Lords seaven last words. Edinburgh, 1620.
Heptameron, the seven dayes: that is, meditations and prayers, upon the worke of the Lords creation. St Andrews, 1621.
Samsons seaven lockes of haire: allegorically expounded, and compared to the seaven spirituall vertues. St Andrews, 1621.
Hieroglyphica animalium quae in scripturis sacris inveniuntur. 4 pts, Edinburgh, 1622–4.
A sacred septenarie, or, a godly and fruitful exposition of the seven psalmes of repentance. 1623.

H. G. A., rev. A. M. W.

C. HISTORIANS AND ANTIQUARIANS, 1603–1660

[See also C. S. Terry, An Index to the Papers relating to Scotland in the Historical MSS. Commission Reports, Glasgow, 1908.]

ROBERT BAILLIE (1599–1662)

The Letters and Journals. Ed. D. Laing, 3 vols. Bannatyne Club, Edinburgh, 1841–2.

SIR WILLIAM BAILLIE OF LAMINGTON (fl. 1648)

Vindication for his own Part of Kilsyth and Preston. [Ptd with the above, vol. II.]

WILLIAM BARCLAY (1546–1608)

De Regno et Regali Potestate. Paris, 1600.
De Rebus Creditis et de Jurejurando. Paris, 1605.
De Potestate Papae. 1609.
[See Scottish Hist. Rev. Jan. 1914, Oct. 1914.]

ROBERT BLAIR (1593–1666)
[See p. 841 above.]

DAVID CALDERWOOD (1575–1650)
[See p. 839 above.]

SIR THOMAS CRAIG (1538–1608)

Jus feudale. 1655.
Scotland's sovereignty asserted against those
who maintain that Scotland is a feu, or fee-
liege of England. Translated from the
Latin by G. Ridpath. 1695.
The right of succession to the kingdom of
England. Tr. Eng. J. Gatherer, 1703.
De Unione Regnorum Britanniae Tractatus.
Ed. and tr. C. S. Terry, Scottish Hist. Soc.
Edinburgh, 1909.
[See P. F. Tytler, Life of Sir Thomas Craig,
Edinburgh, 1823. Sir Thomas Craig also
wrote various complimentary Latin poems
addressed to royal personages. See Delitiæ
Poetarum Scotorum, 1637, and Scottish
Hist. Rev. April 1915.]

THOMAS CRAWFURD (d. 1662)

History of the University of Edinburgh from
1580 to 1646. Edinburgh, 1808.

JAMES GORDON (1615?–1686)

History of Scots Affairs, from 1637 to 1641.
Ed. J. Robertson and G. Grub, 3 vols.
Spalding Club, 1841. [See appendix to the
preface for a portion of memoirs of Scottish
Affairs by James Man, or Main (1700?–
1761).]
Abredoniæ utriusque descriptio. Ed. Cosmo
Innes, Spalding Club, Edinburgh, 1842. [An
inaccurate trn of the Latin MS, which is in
the National Lib. Edinburgh.]

DAVID HUME OF GODSCROFT
(1560?–1630)

Poemata omnia. Paris, 1639.
The history of the houses of Douglas and
Angus. Edinburgh, 1644 (re-issued 1648 as,
A generall history of Scotland). [An earlier
edn was ptd, but apparently not pbd, about
1630.]
De familia Humia Wedderburnensi liber. Ed.
J. Miller, Abbotsford Club, 1839.

ROBERT JOHNSTON (1567–1639)

The history of Scotland during the minority
of King James VI. Done into English by
T. M. 1648.
Historia rerum Britannicarum, ut et multa-
rum Gallicarum, Belgicarum et Germanicarum, ab anno 1572–1628. Amsterdam,
1655.

SIR JAMES MELVILLE OF HALHILL
(1535–1617)
[See p. 905 above.]

JAMES MELVILLE (1556–1614)
[See p. 905 above.]

ROBERT MONTEITH (fl. 1621–1660)

Histoire des troubles de la Grand Bretagne
(1633–1649). Paris, 1661.
The history of the troubles of Great Britain,
containing a particular account of the most
remarkable passages in Scotland from 1633
to 1650. Tr. James Ogilvie, 1735.

JOHN ROW (1586–1646)

The History of the Kirk in Scotland, from the
Year 1558 to August 1637. With a Continuation to July 1639, by his Son John Row.
Ed. D. Laing, Wodrow Society, 1842, and
Maitland Club, 1842. [This history, though
ptd for the first time in 1842, circulated
widely in MS in the 17th cent.]

SIR JOHN SCOT OF SCOTSTARVET
(1585–1670)

The staggering state of the Scots statesmen,
for one hundred years, viz. from 1550 to
1650. Edinburgh, 1754.
[For his Trew Relation, see G. Neilson,
Scottish Hist. Rev. 1914, Jan. and July 1915,
July and Oct. 1916. Delitiæ Poetarum
Scotorum (1637), ed. A. Johnston, was pbd
under the auspices of Sir John Scot, who was
a liberal patron of letters.]

PATRICK SIMSON (1556–1618)

A short compend of the historie of the first
ten persecutions moved against Christians.
5 pts, Edinburgh, 1613–6.

JOHN SPALDING (fl. 1650)

History of the troubles and memorable transactions in Scotland from the year 1625 to
1645. 2 vols. Aberdeen, 1792; Bannatyne
Club, 1828–9; Spalding Club, 1850–1.

JOHN SPOTTISWODE (1565–1639)
[See p. 838 above.]

GEORGE WISHART (1599–1671)

De rebus auspiciis serenissimi et potentissimi
Caroli sub imperio illustrissimi Jacobi
Montisrosarum Marchionis anno 1644 et
duobus sequentibus praeclare gestis, commentarius. 1647.

REF
Z
2011
B28
15,676

CAMROSE LUTHERAN COLLEGE
LIBRARY

The history of the King's Majesties affairs in Scotland, under the conduct of James Marques of Montrose, 1644–46. 1648. [A trn of the preceding. It was rptd, with a continuation, in 1652, under the title of Montrose redivivus. A 2nd trn, with the title A complete history of the wars in Scotland; under Montrose, was pbd in 1720; and a 3rd, entitled Memoirs of the Marquis of Montrose, in 1756. An excellent critical edn of the complete Latin text, with a new trn, was brought out by A. D. Murdoch and H. F. M. Simpson in 1893. For a rare pamphlet, A true relation, etc. on Montrose's campaigns, see Scottish Hist. Rev. Oct. 1904, p. 49; the National Lib. Edinburgh and the Bodleian possess copies.]

H. G. A., *rev.* A. M. W.

D. MISCELLANEOUS WRITERS, 1603–1660

WILLIAM BARCLAY (1570?–1630?)

Nepenthes; or the vertues of tabacco. Edinburgh, 1614.
Callirhoe, the nymph of Aberdene. Edinburgh, 1615.
The nature of the new found well at Kinghorne. Edinburgh, 1618.
Sylvae tres. Edinburgh, 1619.

THOMAS DEMPSTER (1579?–1625)

[See p. 860 above.]

PATRICK GORDON (1635–1699)

Passages from the Diary of. Ed. J. Robertson, Spalding Club, Aberdeen, 1859.

GILBERT GRAY (d. 1616)

Oratio funebris. Edinburgh, 1614.
Oratio de illustribus Scotiae Scriptoribus. Aberdeen, 1623 (no copy known); rptd 1708 (in George Mackenzie's Lives of Writers of the Scots Nation, vol. i).

ALEXANDER HUME

A diduction of the true and catholik meaning of our Saviour his words, This is my bodie, in the institution of his laste supper. Edinburgh, 1602.
Grammatica nova. Edinburgh, 1612.
Prima elementa grammatica. Edinburgh, 1612.
Of the Orthographie and Congruitie of the Britan Tongue. Ed. H. B. Wheatley, EETS. 1865.

JAMES VI, KING OF SCOTLAND (1566–1625)

The essayes of a prentise in the divine art of poesie. Edinburgh, 1584.

His Majesties poeticall exercises at vacant houres. Edinburgh, 1591.
Daemonologie. Edinburgh, 1597; ed. G. B. Harrison, 1924.
The true lawe of free monarchies. Edinburgh, 1598.
Βασιλικὸν Δῶρον. Edinburgh, 1599.
A counter blaste to tobacco. 1604.
Workes. 1616.
New Poems. Ed. A. F. Westcott, New York, 1911.
Political Works. Ed. C. H. McIlwain, 1918.

[See H. M. Chew in Social and Political Ideas of some Great Thinkers of the 16th and 17th Centuries, ed. F. J. Hearnshaw, 1926. See also p. 897 above.]

Lachrymae Academiae

Lachrymæ academiæ Marischallanæ. Aberdeen, 1623. [Greek, Latin, and English verses on the death of the founder of Marischal College, Aberdeen.]

DAVID LEECH (*fl.* 1628–1653)

Philosophia Illachrymans. Aberdeen, 1637.

JOHN MAKLUIRE

The buckler of bodilie health, whereby health may be defended, and sicknesse repelled. Edinburgh, 1630.
Sanitatis semita. Edinburgh, 1630.

JOHN NAPIER OF MERCHISTON (1550–1617)

[See p. 881 above.]

WILLIAM OGSTON (d. 1667)

Oratio funebris. Aberdeen, [1623.] [On the death of the founder of Marischal College.]

JOHN ROW (1598?–1672?)

Hebraeae linguae institutiones. Χιλιάς Hebraica: seu, vocabularium continens praecipuas radices linguae Hebraeae, numero 1000. 2 pts, Glasgow, 1644. [In 1646 the General Assembly of the Church of Scotland recommended to general use this work, which was the first of its kind ptd in Scotland.]
Εὐχαριστία Βασιλική. Ad illustrissimum monarchum Carolum II carmen. Aberdeen, 1660.

JAMES SIBBALD (1590?–1650?)

Assertiones Philosophicae. Aberdeen, 1623.
Theses Philosophicae. Aberdeen, 1625, 1626.
Theses Theologicae de primatu B. Petri. Aberdeen, 1627.

[One of the Aberdeen Doctors.]

SIR THOMAS URQUHART (1611–1660)

[See p. 836 above.]

DAVID WEDDERBURN (1580–1646)

In obitu summae spei Principis Henrici. Edinburgh, 1612.

A short introduction to grammar. Aberdeen, [1632].

Institutiones grammaticae. Editio secunda. Aberdeen, 1633.

Meditationum campestrium, seu epigrammaton moralium centuriae duae. Aberdeen, 1643. Centuria tertia. Aberdeen, 1644.

Persius enucleatus, sive commentarius in Persium. Amsterdam, 1664.

H. G. A., *rev.* A. M. W.